P9-CCO-053

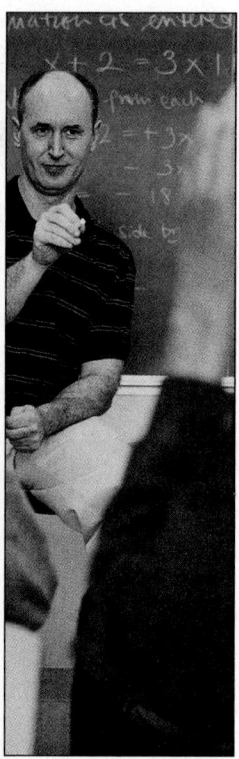

Success in Accounting is just a click away...

With *WileyPLUS*, students and instructors will experience success in the classroom.

When students succeed—when they stay on-task and make the breakthrough that turns confusion into confidence—they are empowered to realize the possibilities for greatness that lies within each of them. Our goal is to create an environment where students reach their full potential and experience the exhilaration of academic success that will last them a lifetime. *WileyPLUS* can help you reach that goal.

Wiley**PLUS** is an online suite of resources—including the complete text—that will help any student:

- come to class better prepared for lectures
- get immediate feedback and context-sensitive help on assignments and quizzes
- track progress throughout the course

"I just wanted to say how much this program helped me in studying... I was able to actually see my mistakes and correct them. ... I really think that other students should have the chance to use *WileyPLUS*."

Ashlee Krisko, *Oakland University*

www.wiley.com/college/wileyplus

80% of students surveyed said it improved their understanding of the material.*

*Based on a spring 2005 survey of 972 student users of *WileyPLUS*

TO THE INSTRUCTOR

WileyPLUS is built around the activities you perform

Prepare & Present

Create outstanding class presentations using a wealth of resources, such as PowerPoint™ slides, interactive simulations, and more. Plus you can easily upload any materials you have created into your course, and combine them with the resources Wiley provides you with.

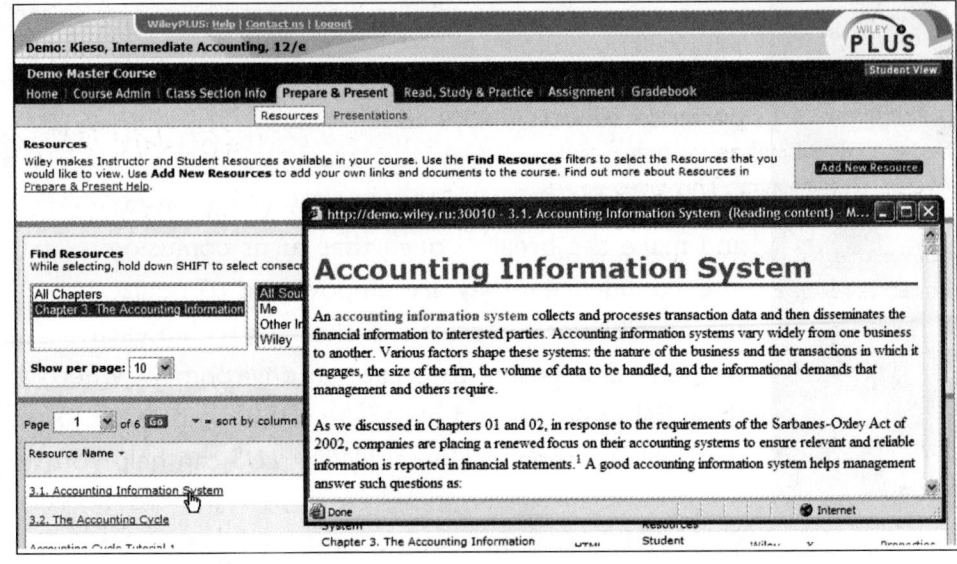

Create Assignments

Automate the assigning and grading of homework or quizzes by using the provided question banks, or by writing your own. Student results will be automatically graded and recorded in your gradebook. *WileyPLUS* also links homework problems to relevant sections of the online text, hints, or solutions—context-sensitive help where students need it most!

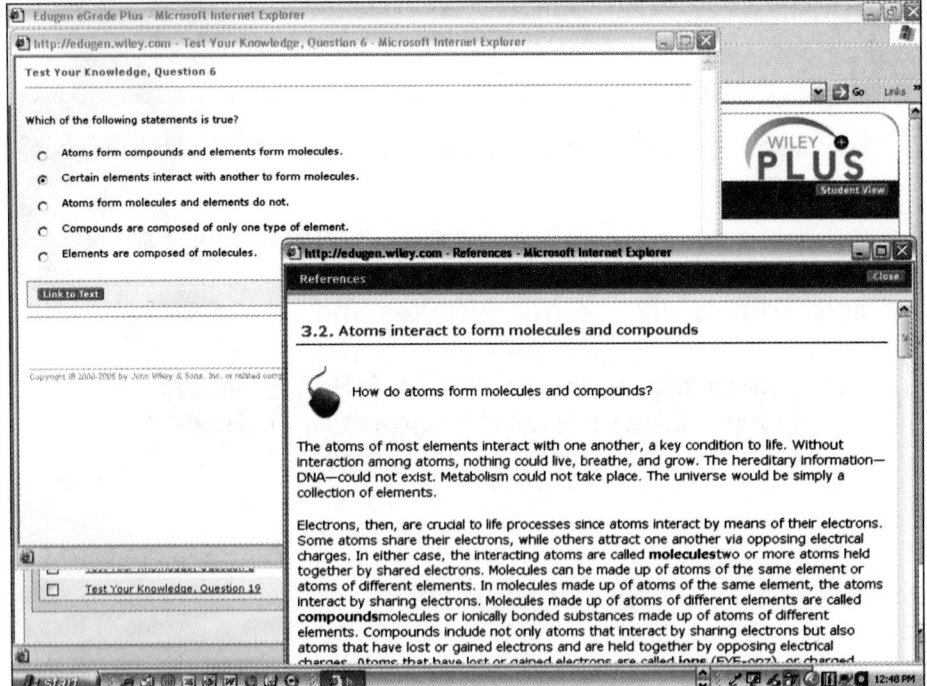

in your class each day. With Wiley**PLUS** you can:

Track Student Progress

Keep track of your students' progress via an instructor's gradebook, which allows you to analyze individual and overall class results. This gives you an accurate and realistic assessment of your students' progress and level of understanding.

Now Available with WebCT and Blackboard!

Now you can seamlessly integrate all of the rich content and resources available with *WileyPLUS* with the power and convenience of your WebCT or BlackBoard course. You and your students get the best of both worlds with single sign-on, an integrated gradebook, list of assignments and roster, and more. If your campus is using another course management system, contact your local Wiley Representative.

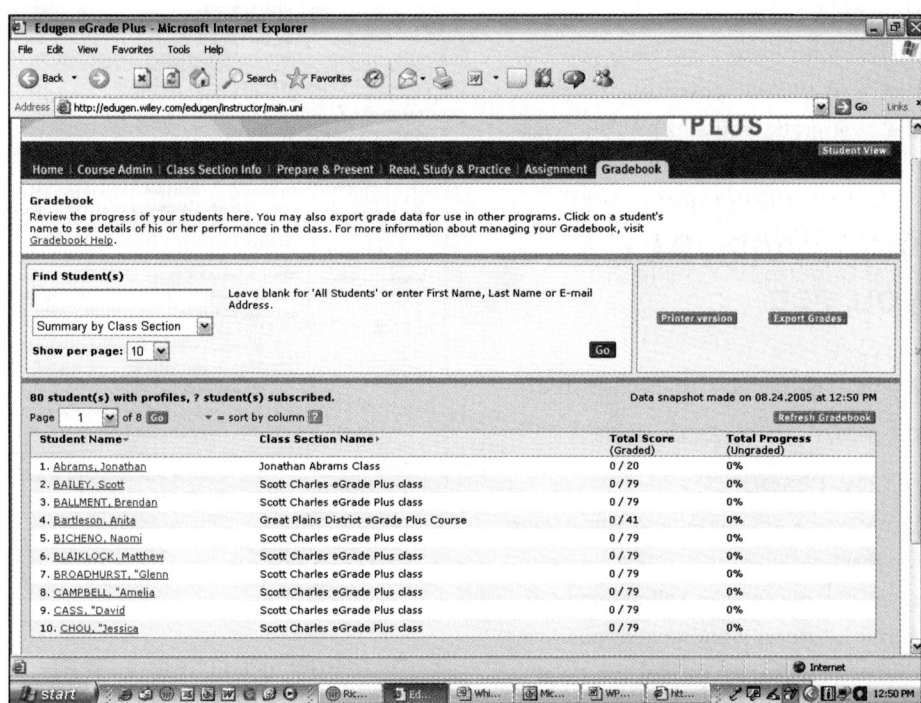

"I studied more for this class than I would have without *WileyPLUS*."

Melissa Lawler, *Western Washington Univ.*

For more information on what *WileyPLUS* can do to help your students reach their potential, please visit

www.wiley.com/college/wileyplus

76% of students surveyed said it made them better prepared for tests.*

*Based on a spring 2005 survey of 972 student users of *WileyPLUS*

TO THE STUDENT

You have the potential to make a difference!

WileyPLUS is a powerful online system packed with features to help you make the most of your potential, and get the best grade you can!

With Wiley**PLUS** you get:

A complete online version of your text and other study resources

Study more effectively and get instant feedback when you practice on your own. Resources like self-assessment quizzes, tutorials, and animations bring the subject matter to life, and help you master the material.

Problem-solving help, instant grading, and feedback on your homework and quizzes

You can keep all of your assigned work in one location, making it easy for you to stay on task. Plus, many homework problems contain direct links to the relevant portion of your text to help you deal with problem-solving obstacles at the moment they come up.

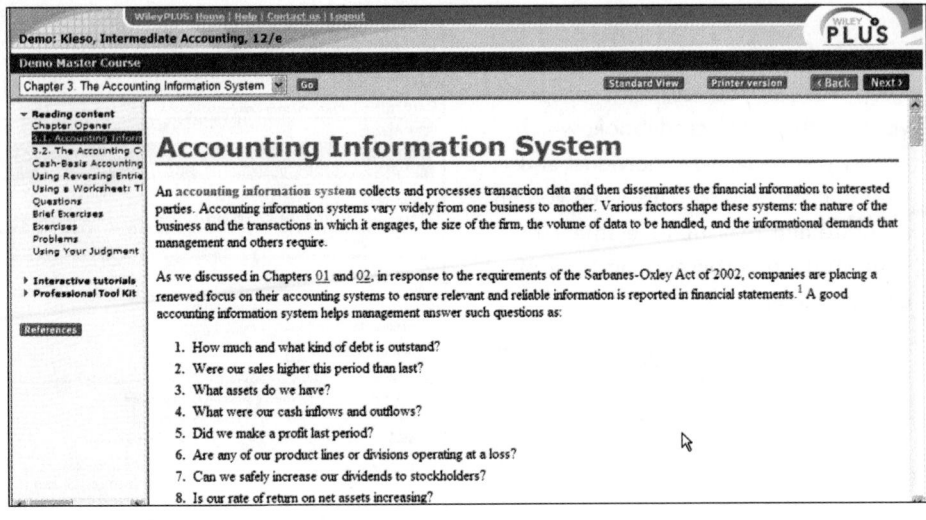

The ability to track your progress and grades throughout the term.

A personal gradebook allows you to monitor your results from past assignments at any time. You'll always know exactly where you stand.

If your instructor uses *WileyPLUS*, you will receive a URL for your class. If not, your instructor can get more information about *WileyPLUS* by visiting www.wiley.com/college/wileyplus

---

"It has been a great help, and I believe it has helped me to achieve a better grade."

Michael Morris, *Columbia Basin College*

69% of students surveyed said it helped them get a better grade.*

*Based on a spring 2005 survey of 972 student users of *WileyPLUS*

TWELFTH EDITION — 2007 FASB UPDATE

INTERMEDIATE ACCOUNTING

DONALD E. KIESO PH.D., C.P.A.

KPMG Peat Marwick Emeritus Professor of Accounting

Northern Illinois University

DeKalb, Illinois

JERRY J. WEYGANDT PH.D., C.P.A.

Arthur Andersen Alumni Professor of Accounting

University of Wisconsin

Madison, Wisconsin

TERRY D. WARFIELD PH.D.

Associate Professor

University of Wisconsin

Madison, Wisconsin

WILEY

John Wiley & Sons

Dedicated to our wives, Donna, Enid, and Mary, for their love, support, and encouragement

VICE PRESIDENT & EXECUTIVE PUBLISHER	Donald Fowley
ASSOCIATE PUBLISHER	Christopher DeJohn
ASSOCIATE EDITOR	Brian Kamins
DEVELOPMENT EDITOR	Ann Torbert
SENIOR PRODUCTION EDITOR	Valerie Vargas
SENIOR MARKETING MANAGER	Julia Flohr
CREATIVE DIRECTOR	Harry Nolan
TEXT DESIGNER	Nancy Fields
PRODUCTION SERVICES MANAGEMENT	Suzanne Ingrao/Ingrao Associates
SENIOR ILLUSTRATION EDITOR	Anna Melhorn
SENIOR MEDIA EDITOR	Allie Morris
PROJECT EDITOR	Ed Brislin
EDITORIAL ASSISTANT	Kathryn Fraser
MARKETING ASSISTANT	Carly DeCandia
PRODUCTION ASSISTANT	Matt Winslow
COVER PHOTO	© Jan Stromme/Lonely Planet Images/Getty Images, Inc.
COVER DESIGN	Howard Grossman

This book was set in Palatino by Aptara, Inc. and printed and bound by R.R. Donnelley & Sons, Inc.—Jefferson City. The cover was printed by Lehigh Press.

This book is printed on acid free paper. ∞

Copyright © 2008 John Wiley & Sons, Inc. All rights reserved. No part of this publication may be reproduced, stored in a retrieval system or transmitted in any form or by any means, electronic, mechanical, photocopying, recording, scanning or otherwise, except as permitted under Sections 107 or 108 of the 1976 United States Copyright Act, without either the prior written permission of the Publisher, or authorization through payment of the appropriate per-copy fee to the Copyright Clearance Center, Inc. 222 Rosewood Drive, Danvers, MA 01923, website www.copyright.com. Requests to the Publisher for permission should be addressed to the Permissions Department, John Wiley & Sons, Inc., 111 River Street, Hoboken, NJ 07030-5774, (201)748-6011, fax (201)748-6008, website http://www.wiley.com/go/permissions.

To order books or for customer service, please call 1-800-CALL WILEY (225-5945).

Material from the Uniform CPA Examinations and Unofficial Answers, copyright © 1965, 1966, 1967, 1968, 1969, 1970, 1971, 1972, 1973, 1974, 1975, 1976, 1977, 1978, 1979, 1980, 1981, 1982, 1983, 1984, 1985, 1986, 1987, 1988, 1990, 1991, 1992, and 1993 by the American Institute of Certified Public Accountants, Inc., is adapted with permission.

This book contains quotations from *Accounting Research Bulletins, Accounting Principles Board Opinions, Accounting Principles Board Statements, Accounting Interpretations,* and *Accounting Terminology Bulletins,* copyright © 1953, 1956, 1966, 1968, 1969, 1970, 1971, 1972, 1973, 1974, 1975, 1976, 1977, 1978, 1979, 1980, 1981, 1982 by the American Institute of Certified Public Accountants, Inc., 1211 Avenue of the Americas, New York, NY 10036.

This book contains citations from various FASB pronouncements. Copyright © by Financial Accounting Standards Board, 401 Merritt 7, P.O. Box 5116, Norwalk, CT 06856 U.S.A. Reprinted with permission. Copies of complete documents are available from Financial Accounting Standards Board.

Material from the Certificate in Management Accounting Examinations, copyright © 1975, 1976, 1977, 1978, 1979, 1980, 1981, 1982, 1983, 1984, 1985, 1986, 1987, 1988, 1989, 1990, 1991, 1992, and 1993 by the Institute of Certified Management Accountants, 10 Paragon Drive, Montvale, NJ 07645, is adapted with permission.

Material from the Certified Internal Auditor Examinations, copyright © May 1984, November 1984, May 1986 by The Institute of Internal Auditors, 249 Maitland Ave., Altemonte Springs, FL 32701, is adapted with permission.

The financial statements and accompanying notes reprinted from the 2004 Annual Report of The Procter & Gamble Company are courtesy of P&G, copyright © 2004, all rights reserved.

ISBN-13 978-0-470-12874-9
ISBN-10 0-470-128747

Printed in the United States of America

10 9 8 7 6 5 4 3 2 1

ABOUT THE AUTHORS

Donald E. Kieso, Ph.D., C.P.A., received his bachelor's degree from Aurora University and his doctorate in accounting from the University of Illinois. He has served as chairman of the Department of Accountancy and is currently the KPMG Peat Marwick Emeritus Professor of Accounting at Northern Illinois University. He has public accounting experience with Price Waterhouse & Co. (San Francisco and Chicago) and Arthur Andersen & Co. (Chicago) and research experience with the Research Division of the American Institute of Certified Public Accountants (New York). He has done postdoctorate work as a Visiting Scholar at the University of California at Berkeley and is a recipient of NIU's Teaching Excellence Award and four Golden Apple Teaching Awards. Professor Kieso is the author of other accounting and business books and is a member of the American Accounting Association, the American Institute of Certified Public Accountants, and the Illinois CPA Society. He has served as a member of the Board of Directors of the Illinois CPA Society, the AACSB's Accounting Accreditation Committees, the State of Illinois Comptroller's Commission, as Secretary-Treasurer of the Federation of Schools of Accountancy, and as Secretary-Treasurer of the American Accounting Association. Professor Kieso served as a charter member of the national Accounting Education Change Commission. He is the recipient of the Outstanding Accounting Educator Award from the Illinois CPA Society, the FSA's Joseph A. Silvoso Award of Merit, and the NIU Foundation's Humanitarian Award for Service to Higher Education.

Jerry J. Weygandt, Ph.D., C.P.A., is Arthur Andersen Alumni Professor of Accounting at the University of Wisconsin—Madison. He Holds a Ph.D. in accounting from the University of Illinois. Articles by Professor Weygandt have appeared in the *Accounting Review, Journal of Accounting Research, Accounting Horizons, Journal of Accountancy,* and other academic and professional journals. These articles have examined such financial reporting issues as accounting for price-level adjustments, pensions, convertible securities, stock option contracts, and interim reports. Professor Weygandt is author of other accounting and financial reporting books and is a member of the American Accounting Association, the American Institute of Certified Public Accountants, and the Wisconsin Society of Certified Public Accountants. He has served on numerous committees of the American Accounting Association and as a member of the editorial board of the *Accounting Review;* he also has served as President and Secretary-Treasurer of the American Accounting Association. In addition, he has been actively involved with the American Institute of Certified Public Accountants and has been a member of the Accounting Standards Executive Committee (AcSEC) of that organization. He has served on the FASB task force that examined the reporting issues related to accounting for income taxes and as a trustee of the Financial Accounting Foundation. Professor Weygandt has received the Chancellor's Award for Excellence in Teaching and the Beta Gamma Sigma Dean's Teaching Award. He is on the board of directors of M & I Bank of Southern Wisconsin. He is the recipient of the Wisconsin Institute of CPA's Outstanding Educator's Award and the Lifetime Achievement Award. In 2001 he received the American Accounting Association's Outstanding Accounting Educator Award.

Terry D. Warfield, Ph.D., is associate professor of accounting at the University of Wisconsin—Madison. He received a B.S. and M.B.A. from Indiana University and a Ph.D. in accounting from the University of Iowa. Professor Warfield's area of expertise is financial reporting, and prior to his academic career, he worked for five years in the banking industry. He served as the Academic Accounting Fellow in the Office of the Chief Accountant at the U.S. Securities and Exchange Commission in Washington, D.C. from 1995–1996. Professor Warfield's primary research interests concern financial accounting standards and disclosure policies. He has published scholarly articles in *The*

Accounting Review, Journal of Accounting and Economics, Research in Accounting Regulation, and *Accounting Horizons,* and he has served on the editorial boards of *The Accounting Review, Accounting Horizons,* and *Issues in Accounting Education.* He has served as president of the Financial Accounting and Reporting Section, the Financial Accounting Standards Committee of the American Accounting Association (Chair 1995–1996), and on the AAA-FASB Research Conference Committee. Professor Warfield has received teaching awards at both the University of Iowa and the University of Wisconsin, and he was named to the Teaching Academy at the University of Wisconsin in 1995. Professor Warfield has developed and published several case studies based on his research for use in accounting classes. These cases have been selected for the AICPA Professor-Practitioner Case Development Program and have been published in *Issues in Accounting Education.*

PREFACE

THE ACCOUNTING ENVIRONMENT

Since the 11th Edition of *Intermediate Accounting*, much has happened in the financial reporting arena. Given the series of accounting scandals and eroding public confidence in auditing and financial reporting, Congress passed the most important legislation since the Securities Act of 1934, the Sarbanes-Oxley Act of 2002. That legislation and the resulting Public Accounting Oversight Board established as a result of it now compel the profession to reexamine its most fundamental concepts and principles.

With this reexamination come many questions related to financial reporting: How, for example, should we value assets and liabilities? What should be the proper reporting for off-balance-sheet financing transactions? How should we account for the complex hybrid and derivative securities that are increasing in use? What should be the proper reporting for the many restatements that are taking place in corporate America? How quickly should we converge international and U.S. GAAP? What is the proper reporting for defined-benefit pension plans? These are difficult questions, but ones that need serious study and action.

Some judge these questions mundane compared to larger questions faced by society, such as what we should do with Social Security, health-care reform, or international relationships. Yet, the accounting scandals have focused attention on the importance of proper accounting to all of us. Consider, for example, the over 90 million Americans who have investments in stocks either directly, through mutual funds, or through employer-sponsored retirement funds. Consider the numerous retirees who are now suffering hardship because the companies they worked for reported incorrect information in attempts to hype stock prices or compensation. Or think of the many Americans who trusted corporate financial reports and invested in companies like **WorldCom**, **Enron**, and **Fannie Mae**, only to find that the numbers were wrong. What these events tell us is that accounting is essential for our economy to function effectively. Without high-quality accounting standards, capital markets cannot efficiently allocate capital to its best use in building and maintaining our economy and way of life. Thus, we must get the accounting right!

We believe that recent legislation will be helpful, because it puts increased emphasis on proper and high-quality reporting. Companies, and the individuals who run these companies, must adhere to sound reporting practices or face severe sanctions. It is an exciting time for those involved in financial reporting. Interest has never been higher in developing and reporting information that will be useful to interested parties. We therefore believe it imperative that *every student of business understands the fundamentals of accounting and financial reporting to ensure that the system will be continually developed and improved.*

LINKING THE ACCOUNTING ENVIRONMENT WITH ACCOUNTING EDUCATION

In this edition of *Intermediate Accounting*, we continue a tradition, begun over 30 years ago, of helping students understand, prepare, and use financial information by linking accounting education with the "real-world" accounting environment. As indicated above, the importance of students understanding the role of financial information in capital markets has never been more important.

An important feature of *Intermediate Accounting,* therefore, is an enhanced effort to provide more perspective on the information provided by financial reporting. As a result, special boxed insights titled "What Do the Numbers Mean?" illustrate how reporting methods affect the decisions of financial statement users. By means of these boxes, originally introduced in the 11th Edition, we hope to convey the excitement and ever-changing nature of accounting, illuminating its significance and highlighting its importance.

In addition, for the 12th Edition, we have added at the *Gateway to the Profession* portal (the book's companion website) a "B set" of additional exercises online, as well as information about access to additional versions of the Professional Simulations and a new "Accounting in Action" continuing problem. The continuing problem provides students a real-world context in which to apply the concepts they are learning in the textbook. The *Gateway to the Profession* also provides students and instructors access to all the material previously delivered on the *Take Action! CD.*

The 12th Edition of *Intermediate Accounting* introduces a revised element to the "Using Your Judgment" section of the end-of-chapter material. A "Professional Simulation" in each chapter provides students with a new and integrative context for applying the concepts introduced in the chapter. To complement the Professional Simulation, in the 12th Edition we have introduced in each chapter a "Professional Research" case. These cases give students an opportunity to conduct authoritative research using the Financial Accounting Research System (FARS). These new and enhanced elements are patterned after the computerized CPA exam. They expand the focus of many of the elements of the *Gateway to the Professional* portal (writing, working in teams, using the analyst's toolkit) to help students learn how to use accounting facts and procedures in various business contexts.

Another key feature of this edition is the introduction of **WileyPLUS**, an online suite of resources, including access to an online version of the complete text. Within WileyPLUS, the online version of the text will be integrated with the Accounting Research database (FARS). Students will be able to conduct authoritative research in a seamless environment. In addition, WileyPLUS contains all of the elements of the *Gateway to the Profession* portal, plus a homework management system and resources for creating class presentations. (See page xvi for a complete description of this content-rich resource.)

Throughout the book, we continue to strive for a balanced discussion of conceptual and procedural presentations so that these elements are mutually reinforcing. In addition, text discussions explain the rationale behind business transactions before addressing the accounting and reporting for those transactions. As in prior editions, we have thoroughly revised and updated the text to include all the latest developments in the accounting profession and practice. For example, we have completely revised the chapter on accounting changes and error corrections to reflect new accounting standards for accounting changes. Benefiting from the comments and recommendations of adopters of the 11th Edition, we have made significant revisions: We have expanded explanations where necessary; simplified complicated discussions and illustrations; integrated realism to heighten interest and relevancy; and added new topics and coverage to maintain currency. Finally, to provide the instructor with flexibility of use and no loss in topic coverage, we have moved discussions of less commonly used methods and more complex or specialized topics to the *Gateway to the Profession* portal.

NEW FEATURES

Based on extensive reviews, focus groups, and interactions with other intermediate accounting instructors and students, we have developed a number of new pedagogical features and content changes, designed both to help students learn more effectively and to answer the changing needs of the course.

Editorial Review

The 12th Edition of *Intermediate Accounting* has undergone an editorial review and line-by-line editing process to improve the readability of the text. The goals of this process were to retain the book's numerous examples and analogies that set the standard in the intermediate accounting course, but to simplify words and reduce sentence and paragraph length wherever possible without sacrificing precision. This review placed emphasis on introducing an active voice and conversational style in the presentation.

Major Chapter Revisions

In response to new FASB standards, we have significantly revised several chapters:

- Chapters 4 and 22 have been revised in response to the new standard on *accounting changes*. They now include comprehensive illustrations with a focus on the presentation of comparative statements when reporting accounting changes and errors.
- Chapter 10 presents a revised section on exchanges of nonmonetary assets and introduces the concept of commercial substance in accounting for exchanges.
- Chapter 16 has been revised in light of the new standard on stock-based compensation, which requires recognition of compensation expense using the fair-value model. A revised chapter-end appendix covers the accounting for restricted stock and stock appreciation rights.
- The 2007 FASB Update edition includes a completely revised Chapter 20, reflecting new *SFAS No. 158*.

New Appendixes

In addition to the revised appendix for Chapter 16 (see above), we also developed two new appendixes: on the accounting for variable-interest entities (Chapter 17), and on international accounting (Chapter 24). We added Appendix 24B in order to provide additional insight into the issue of convergence of U.S. and international accounting standards. For more on convergence issues, also see the front and back endpapers. We believe that convergence will continue to gain momentum and that students should be aware of this issue as their careers develop.

FARS Cases

In response to increased demand for accounting research skills and the requirements of the computerized CPA exam, each chapter now has a Professional Research case. These new cases give students an opportunity to conduct authoritative research, using either the Financial Accounting Research System (FARS) CD-ROM or FARS Online. Both of these products are available through John Wiley & Sons Higher Education Division.

Updated Supplements

All supplements are updated. In particular, the Solutions Manual questions are newly classified by textbook learning objective, the PowerPoint presentations are newly designed, and there are more review questions and over 400 new Test bank questions.

Gateway to the Profession Portal

The book companion *website at www.wiley.com/college/kieso* (with separate areas for instructors and for students) has been completely revamped. At this website, now titled *Gateway to the Profession*, students can access the following resources:

- A "B set" of additional exercises, providing additional practice opportunities for students (solutions available to instructors).
- For each chapter, a new "Accounting in Action" continuing problem, which follows the evolution of CM² Corporation from a start-up to an initial public

offering (IPO). The continuing problem provides students with a real-world context in which to apply the concepts they are learning in the textbook. Instructors can use the continuing problem in its entirety or in parts, as desired.

- Information about access to online and additional versions of the Professional Simulations, which are found in each chapter of the text.

- Financial statements for **The Procter & Gamble Company**, **The Coca-Cola Company**, and **PepsiCo**.

- Access to the Student, Analyst, and Professional Toolkits previously delivered on the *Take Action! CD*. We describe the content of these three toolkits later in the preface (see pages xvii–xx).

ENHANCED FEATURES OF THE 12TH EDITION

We have continued and enhanced many of the features of the 11th Edition of *Intermediate Accounting*, including the following.

Real-World Emphasis

Johnson&Johnson

*WHAT DO THE
NUMBERS MEAN?*

P&G

PEPSICO

One of the goals of the intermediate accounting course is to orient students to the application of accounting principles and techniques in practice. Accordingly, we have continued our practice of using numerous examples from real companies throughout the text. The names of these real companies are highlighted in red. Illustration and exhibits marked by the icon shown here in the margin, or by company logos, are excerpts from actual financial statements of real firms.

At the start of each chapter, we have updated and introduced new chapter-opening vignettes to provide an even better real-world context that helps motivate student interest in the chapter topic. Also, throughout the chapters, the "What Do the Numbers Mean?" boxed inserts also provide real-world extensions of the material presented in the text.

In addition, Appendix 5B contains the 2004 annual report of **The Procter & Gamble Company (P&G)**. The book's website contains the 2004 annual reports of **The Coca-Cola Company** and of **PepsiCo, Inc.** Problems in the *Using Your Judgment* section (see description below) involve study of the P&G annual report or comparison of the annual reports of The Coca-Cola Company and PepsiCo. Also, links to many real-company financial reports appear in the company database at the *Gateway to the Profession* portal.

Currency and Accuracy

Accounting continually changes as its environment changes; an up-to-date book is therefore a necessity. As in past editions, we have strived to make this edition the most up-to-date and accurate textbook available.

International Coverage

**INTERNATIONAL
INSIGHT**

Having a basic understanding of international accounting is becoming ever more important as the profession moves toward convergence of GAAP and international standards. Thus, we continue to include marginal *International Insights*, marked with the icon shown here, which we updated throughout to reflect changes in international accounting. These paragraphs compare IASB standards and accounting practices with U.S. GAAP. This feature helps students understand that other countries sometimes use different recognition and measurement principles to report financial information. In addition, a *new* appendix on international accounting follows Chapter 24.

Streamlined Presentation

We also have continued our efforts to keep the topic coverage of *Intermediate Accounting* in line with the way instructors are *currently* teaching the course. Accordingly, we have moved some optional topics into chapter-end appendixes, and we have omitted altogether some topics that formerly were covered in appendixes. Often, these omitted topics have been moved to the *Gateway to the Profession* portal. Details are listed in the specific content changes below and in the portal content on pages xvii–xx.

Additional Exercises

Our study of the intermediate accounting course indicates the importance of the end-of-chapter Exercises for teaching and practicing important accounting concepts. In the 12th Edition, therefore, we have prepared an additional set of exercises. These new exercises are available at the *Gateway to the Profession* portal. (Solutions are available at the instructor's portion of the website.)

Using Your Judgment Section

We have revised and updated the *Using Your Judgment* section at the end of each chapter. Elements included in this section include the following:

- A Financial Reporting Problem, featuring **The Procter & Gamble Company**.
- A Financial Statement Analysis Case that asks students to use the information in published accounting reports to conduct financial analysis.
- A Comparative Analysis Case, featuring **The Coca-Cola Company** and **PepsiCo, Inc.**, that asks students to compare and contrast the financial reporting for these two companies.
- A Research Case, that asks students to read articles from the popular financial press and apply them to the chapter topic.
- An International Reporting Case that explores differences in reporting by international companies.
- A Professional Research: Financial Accounting and Reporting case that gives students practice conducting authoritative research using the Financial Accounting Research System (FARS).
- A Professional Simulation, newly revised for this edition, which models the computerized CPA exam.

The *Using Your Judgment* assignments are designed to help develop students' critical thinking, analytical, and research skills.

CONTENT CHANGES

The following list outlines the content revisions and improvements made in chapters of the 12th Edition.

Chapter 1
- Enhanced discussion of the GAAP hierarchy.
- Reduced emphasis on AICPA.
- Updated international discussion.
- Enhanced discussion of the Sarbanes-Oxley Act of 2002.

Chapter 2
- Enhanced discussion of fair values and their use in financial accounting.

Chapter 3
- Enhanced coverage of the accounting cycle, with complete discussion and comprehensive example of Pioneer Advertising from inception to preparation of the financial statements.

- Improved discussion of financial statements in the chapter with illustration of the use of a worksheet in an appendix.

Chapter 4

- Updated illustration in the chapter-opening vignette.
- New chart on irregular items.
- New discussion of income statement reporting of a change in accounting principle.

Chapter 5

- Updated chapter-opening vignette on balance sheet and cash flow quality.
- New "What Do the Numbers Mean?" box on contractual commitments.
- Incorporated "significant non-cash financing and investing activities" into the statement of cash flows.

Chapter 7

- New chapter-opening vignette on abuse of allowance accounts.
- New illustration of the role of credit card operations and bad debts at major retailers.

Chapter 8

- Updated chapter-opening vignette on the importance of inventory information.

Chapter 9

- New "What Do the Numbers Mean?" box on the deficient reporting of lower-of-cost-or-market recoveries.

Chapter 10

- Updated chapter-opening vignette on variation in fixed assets across companies.
- Major rewrite of the discussion of nonmonetary exchanges in response to the recent FASB standard.

Chapter 11

- Updated chapter-opening vignette on recent changes in international accounting for impairments.

Chapter 12

- New "What Do the Numbers Mean?" box on impairment issues at **Krispy Kreme**.
- Rewrite of negative goodwill discussion.

Chapter 13

- New chapter-opening vignette related to international differences in the definition of a liability.
- Enhanced introduction to the discussion of contingencies.

Chapter 14

- New "What Do the Numbers Mean?" box on the economics of bonds.
- Enhanced "What Do the Numbers Mean?" box on bond ratings and default risk.
- Expanded discussion of required disclosures of long-term liabilities, including the recent SEC rule on contractual obligations.

Chapter 15

- New chapter-opening vignette on the importance of dividends in stock yields.
- New illustration on the prevalence of stock buy-backs.
- Updated discussion on responses to the new standard on redeemable preferred stock.

Chapter 16

- New chapter-opening vignette on stock options.
- Enhanced discussion of the distinctions between debt and equity and its relationship to hybrid or dilutive securities.
- Major rewrite of the discussion of stock-based compensation in response to the recent standard, including new illustrations and exhibits.
- New "What Do the Numbers Mean?" box on contingently convertible bonds (CoCos).
- New appendix on restricted stock and stock appreciation rights, based on the accounting guidance in the recent standard.

Chapter 17

- Updated chapter-opening vignette on international accounting for equity investments.
- New "What Do the Numbers Mean?" box on fair value accounting at **Morgan Stanley**.
- New "What Do the Numbers Mean?" box on off-balance-sheet transactions.
- New "What Do the Numbers Mean?" box on impairments.
- Reorganized discussion of fair value hedges in Appendix 17A.
- New appendix (Appendix 17B) on variable-interest entities.

Chapter 18

- New chapter-opening vignette on revenue recognition.
- New "What Do the Numbers Mean?" box on the revenue recognition challenges of gift cards.

Chapter 19

- New chapter-opening vignette on uncertain tax provisions.
- Enhanced discussion of net operating losses (NOLs) and when they can be used.
- New "What Do the Numbers Mean?" box on NOLs.

Chapter 20

- Completely updated and revised chapter; includes discussion of the new postretirement benefit standard, *SFAS No. 158*.
- New chapter-opening vignette on changes in pension plan use.
- New "What Do the Numbers Mean?" box on mix of defined-benefit and defined-contribution plans.
- New "What Do the Numbers Mean?" box on pension underfunding.
- New illustration of pension worksheet in Excel format.
- Updated discussion on the **Pension Benefit Guarantee Corporation**.
- New examples of real-world disclosures under *SAFS No. 158*.
- New "What Do the Numbers Mean?" box on GASB.
- Three new Exercises and four new Problems on pension and postretirement benefits.
- Eliminated discussion in appendix of OPEB transition adjustment, given its limited applicability.

Chapter 21

- New discussion of the leasing market, with special emphasis on lessors.
- New chart on equipment leasing growth.
- New "What Do the Numbers Mean?" box on recognition problems related to operating leases.

Chapter 22

- Complete rewrite of first section concerning accounting changes and errors, incorporating the guidance in the recent FASB standard.
- New emphasis on preparation of comparative statements.

Chapter 23

- Updated the treatment of stock options in response to the recent standard.
- Updated "What Do the Numbers Mean?" box on manipulation of operating cash flow.

Chapter 24

- New discussion of expanded disclosure requirements in the wake of the Sarbanes-Oxley Act of 2002.
- New "What Do the Numbers Mean?" box on the importance of disclosure for efficient securities markets.
- New discussion of managements' reporting on and auditor attestation on the effectiveness of internal controls.
- Enhanced discussion of Internet reporting with emphasis on "XBRL."
- New appendix (Appendix 24B) on international accounting.

END-OF-CHAPTER ASSIGNMENT MATERIAL

At the end of each chapter, we have provided a comprehensive set of review and homework material. This section consists of Questions, Brief Exercises, Exercises, Problems, and short Concepts for Analysis exercises. These materials are followed by the Using Your Judgment section, described earlier (see page xiii). For this edition, we have updated many of these end-of-chapter materials. All of the assignment materials have been class-tested and/or double-checked for accuracy and clarity.

The Questions are designed primarily for review, self-testing, and classroom discussion purposes, as well as for homework assignments. Typically a Brief Exercise covers one topic, and an Exercise covers one or two topics. The Problems are designed to develop a professional level of achievement and are more challenging and time-consuming to solve than the Exercises. In the 12th Edition, the Brief Exercises, Exercises, and Problems now are classified by learning objective number. All Brief Exercises and Exercises and selected Problems are available in WileyPLUS with automatic grading capability.

The Concepts for Analysis (formerly called Conceptual Cases) generally require discussion, as opposed to quantitative solutions. They are intended to confront the student with situations calling for conceptual analysis and the exercise of judgment in identifying issues and problems and in evaluating alternatives.

Separate icons next to Exercises, Problems, and Concepts for Analysis indicate homework materials that offer more than just a quantitative challenge. Homework materials that are especially suited for group assignments, for example, are identified by the red icon shown here in the margin. Homework materials suitable as writing assignments are marked with the pencil icon shown here in the margin. Items that address ethics issues are identified by the scale (balance) icon. Homework materials that can be solved using the Excel Problems supplement are identified by the spreadsheet icon shown at left.

Probably no more than one-fourth of the total exercise, problem, and concepts for analysis material must be used to cover the subject matter adequately. Consequently, problem assignments may be varied from year to year without repetition. As noted earlier, a *new* additional set of Exercises is available at the book's website, to provide an even wider assortment of exercises from which to choose.

WileyPLUS

As described earlier, **WileyPLUS** is a suite of resources that contains online homework, with access to an online version of the text. WileyPLUS gives you the technology to create an environment where students reach their full potential and experience academic success. Instructor resources include a wealth of presentation and preparation tools, easy-to-navigate assignment and assessment tools, and a complete system to administer and manage your course exactly as you wish.

WileyPLUS is built around the activities you regularly perform:

- **Prepare and present class presentations** using relevant Wiley resources such as PowerPoint™ slides, image galleries, animations, and other WileyPLUS materials. You can also upload your own resources or web pages to use in conjunction with Wiley materials.

- **Create assignments** by choosing from end-of-chapter exercises, selected problems, and test bank questions organized by chapter, study objective, level of difficulty, and source—or add your own questions. WileyPLUS automatically grades students' homework and quizzes and records the results in your gradebook.

- **Offer context-sensitive help to students, 24/7.** When you assign homework or quizzes, you decide if and when students get access to hints, solutions, or answers where appropriate. Or they can be linked to relevant sections of their complete, online text for additional help whenever and wherever they need it most.

- **Track student progress.** You can analyze students' results and assess their level of understanding on an individual and class level using the WileyPLUS gradebook, and you can export data to your own personal gradebook.

- Seamlessly integrate all of the rich WileyPLUS content and resources with the power and convenience of your **WebCT** course—with a single sign-on.

In addition to the classroom presentation tools, the homework management system, and the online version of the text, **WileyPLUS** offers rich content in the *Gateway to the Profession* portal.

Content of the *Gateway to the Profession* Portal

As noted earlier, the *Gateway to the Profession* portal includes the Analyst's Toolkit, the Professional Toolkit, and the Student Toolkit, whose content is described below.

Analyst's Toolkit

Tools in the Analyst's Toolkit consist of the following items.

Database of Real Companies. Links to more than 20 annual reports of well-known companies, including three international companies, are provided at the *Gateway to the Profession* portal. Classes can use these annual reports in a variety of ways. For example, they can use them to illustrate different presentations of financial information or to compare note disclosures across companies. In addition, classes can use these reports to analyze a company's financial condition and compare its prospects with those of other companies in the same industry. Assignment material provides some examples of different types of analysis that students can perform. Each of the companies in the database of real companies is identified by a Web address to facilitate the gathering of additional information, if desired.

Additional Enrichment Material. An online chapter on Financial Statement Analysis is provided at the portal, along with related assignment material. This chapter can also be used in conjunction with the database of annual reports of real companies.

Spreadsheet Tools. Present value templates are provided. These templates can be used to solve time value of money problems.

Additional Internet Links. A number of useful links related to financial analysis are provided to expand expertise in analyzing real-world reporting.

Professional Toolkit

Consistent with expanding beyond technical accounting knowledge, the *Gateway to the Profession* materials emphasize certain skills necessary to become a successful accountant or financial manager. The following materials will help students develop needed professional skills.

Writing Materials. A primer on professional communications gives students a framework for writing professional materials. This primer discusses issues such as the top-ten writing problems, strategies for rewriting, how to do revisions, and tips on clarity. This primer has been class-tested and is effective in helping students enhance their writing skills.

Group-Work Materials. Recent evaluations of accounting education have identified the need to develop more skills in group problem solving. The *Gateway to the Profession* portal provides a second primer dealing with the role that work-groups play in organizations. Information is included on what makes a successful group, how you can participate effectively in the group, and do's and don'ts of group formation.

Ethics. The Professional Toolkit contains expanded materials on the role of ethics in the profession, including references to speeches and articles on ethics in accounting; codes of ethics for major professional bodies; and examples and additional case studies on ethics.

Career Professional Spotlights. Every student should have a good understanding of the profession he or she is entering. Career vignettes on the *Gateway to the Profession* portal indicate the types of work that accountants do. Other aspects of the spotlights on careers are included at the *Gateway to the Profession* to help students make successful career choices. These include important links to websites that can provide useful career information to facilitate the student's efforts in this area.

Student Toolkit

Also included at the *Gateway to the Profession* are features that help students process and understand the course materials. They are:

Interactive Tutorials. To help students better understand some of the more difficult topics in intermediate accounting, we have developed a number of interactive tutorials that provide expanded discussion and explanation in a visual and narrative context. Topics addressed are:

- the accounting cycle
- accounting for bad debts (recording uncollectible accounts)
- disposition (transfer) of receivables
- inventory methods
- dollar-value LIFO
- interest capitalization
- depreciation methods

These tutorials are for the benefit of the student and should require no use of class time on the part of instructors.

Expanded Discussion and Illustrations. The Expanded Discussion section provides additional topics not covered in depth in the textbook. *The Gateway to the Profession* gives the flexibility to enrich or expand the course by discussion of additional topics such as those listed below. Topics included, with appropriate chapter linkage, are as follows.

Gateway to the Profession Topics

Chapter 1

- Expanded discussion of ethical issues in financial accounting.

Chapter 2

- Discussion of accounting for changing prices.

Chapter 3
- Presentation of worksheet using the periodic inventory method.
- Specialized journals and methods of processing accounting data.
- Tutorial on the accounting cycle.

Chapter 6
- Present-value–based measurements, including an expanded discussion of spreadsheet tools for solving present-value problems.

Chapter 7
- Discussion of how a four-column bank reconciliation (the proof of cash) can be used for control purposes.
- Expanded example, with accounting entries, of transfers of receivables without recourse.
- Tutorial on the accounting for bad debts.
- Tutorial on transfer of receivables.

Chapter 8
- Tutorial on inventory methods (cost flow assumptions).
- Tutorial on LIFO issues, including dollar-value LIFO.

Chapter 10
- Tutorial on interest capitalization.

Chapter 11
- Discussion of lesser-used depreciation methods, such as the retirement and replacement methods.
- Tutorial on depreciation methods.

Chapter 12
- Expanded discussion on valuing goodwill.

Chapter 13
- Expanded discussion on property taxes.

Chapter 15
- Expanded discussion on the par value method for treasury stock.
- Expanded discussion on quasi-reorganizations.

Chapter 16
- Comprehensive earnings per share illustration.

Chapter 17
- Illustration of accounting entries for transfers of investment securities.
- Expanded discussion of special issues related to investments.

Chapter 19
- Discussion of the conceptual aspects of interperiod tax allocation, including the deferred and net of tax methods.
- Discussion, with examples, of accounting for intraperiod tax allocations.

Chapter 21
- Discussion of real estate leases and leveraged leases.

Chapter 23
- Discussion, with a detailed example, of the T-account method for preparing a statement of cash flows.

Chapter 24

- Discussion of accounting for changing prices, both for general and specific price-level changes.
- Financial analysis primer.

In addition to these materials, illustrative disclosures of financial reporting practices are provided.

Self-Study Tests and Additional Self-Tests. Each chapter on the *Gateway to the Profession* portal includes two sets of self-tests, to allow students to check their understanding of key concepts from the chapter. The software automatically grades the tests and points students to material they need to study further.

Glossary. A complete glossary of all the key terms used in the text is provided, in alphabetical order as well as via Wiley's Flash card technology for drill and practice. Page numbers show where these key terms appear in the text.

Learning-Style Survey. Research on left brain/right brain differences and also on learning and personality differences suggests that each person has preferred ways to receive and communicate information. After taking this learning-style quiz, students will be able to identify their particular learning styles and pinpoint the study aids in the textbook that will help them learn the material.

In summary, the *Gateway to the Profession* portal is a comprehensive complement to the 12th Edition of *Intermediate Accounting*, providing new materials as well as a new way to communicate those materials.

SUPPLEMENTARY MATERIALS

Accompanying this textbook is an improved and expanded package of student learning aids and instructor teaching aids. The *Intermediate Accounting*, 12th Edition, *Gateway to the Profession* portal at *www.wiley.com/college/kieso* provides various tools for students and instructors. This portal offers expanded materials in the three toolkits previously described. In addition, as described earlier, WileyPLUS offers resources to help you prepare class presentations, create assignments, offer help to students, and track student progress.

Other teaching and learning aids to supplement the textbook are described below.

Instructor Teaching Aids

The following teaching aids are available to support instructors using the 12th Edition.

Instructor's Resource CD. The *Instructor's Resource CD* contains electronic versions of the Instructor's Manual, Solutions Manual, Test Bank, computerized Test Bank, PowerPoint™ presentations, and other instructor resources.

Solutions Manual, Vols. 1 and 2. The *Solutions Manual* provides answers to all end-of-chapter questions, brief exercises, exercises, problems, and case materials. Classification tables categorize solutions by topic, and the new solutions manual also categorizes solutions by textbook learning objective. The estimated time to complete exercises, problems, and cases is provided.

Test Bank: Vols. 1 and 2. The 12th Edition Test Bank contains *over 400 new testing questions*. Exercises, problems, true/false, multiple choice, and conceptual short-answer questions help instructors test students' knowledge and communication skills.

Computerized Test Bank. This easy-to-use program allows instructors to create multiple versions of the same test. This computerized test bank also has authoring capabilities and randomizing functions.

Instructor's Manual, Vols. 1 and 2. The *Instructor's Manual* contains lecture outlines, chapter reviews, sample syllabi, printed teaching transparency masters, and much more.

Solutions Transparencies, Vols. 1 and 2. These acetate transparencies contain solutions to textbook end-of-chapter material. The transparencies contain large, bold type for classroom presentation.

PowerPoint™ Presentations. The PowerPoint™ presentations are designed to enhance classroom presentation of chapter topics and examples. The 12th Edition templates now have a new design with review questions and many examples illustrating textbook content.

Teaching Transparencies. These four-color acetates provide illustrations of key concepts for classroom viewing.

Solutions to Rockford Practice Set. This supplement provides solutions to the *Rockford Practice Set*, which is available in print form or electronically through the premium version of WileyPLUS.

Solutions to Excel Workbook Templates. Available for download from the KWW website, these are solutions to the *Solving Problems Using Excel Workbook* templates.

Course Management Resources. Course content cartridges are available from both WebCT and Blackboard.

Periodic Newsletters. The textbook is supplemented by the publication of periodic newsletters. These faculty-oriented supplements include the following sections:

- "Update"—Provides the latest information about new accounting standards promulgated since the text was published.

- "Financial Reporting Challenges"—Addresses a contemporary issue being debated by accounting professionals and standard setters, which may result in a new accounting standard.

- "By the Way. . ."—Provides a "heads up" to instructors on topics addressed in the text (usually the subject of a recent change in accounting standards), to increase instructors' awareness of its implications for their courses.

- "CPA Exam Update"—Offers the latest information about the CPA exam. This item is prepared by Debra R. Hopkins (CPA, CIA), CPA Review Director, Northern Illinois University, DeKalb, Illinois.

Student Learning Aids

Student Study Guide, Vols. 1 and 2. Each chapter of the Study Guide contains a chapter review, chapter outline, and a glossary of key terms. Demonstration problems, multiple-choice, true/false, matching, and other exercises are included.

Problem-Solving Survival Guide, Vols. 1 and 2. This study guide contains exercises and problems that help students develop their intermediate accounting problem-solving skills. Explanations assist in the approach, set-up, and completion of accounting problems. Tips alert students to common pitfalls and misconceptions.

Working Papers, Vols. 1 and 2. The working papers are printed templates that can help students correctly format their textbook accounting solutions. Working paper templates are available for all end-of-chapter brief exercises, exercises, problems, and cases.

Excel Working Papers, Vols. 1 and 2. The *Excel Working Papers* are Excel templates that students can use to correctly format their textbook accounting solutions. Working paper templates are available for all end-of-chapter brief exercises, exercises, problems, and cases.

Solving Problems Using Excel Workbook. A useful introduction to Excel, this workbook helps students work with preprogrammed spreadsheets, and it explains how students can design their own spreadsheet. This workbook is packaged with a CD containing Excel templates that allow students to complete the selected end-of-chapter exercises and problems identified by a spreadsheet icon in the margin of the main textbook.

Rockford Corporation: An Accounting Practice Set. This practice set helps students review the accounting cycle and the preparation of financial statements.

Rockford Corporation: A Computerized Accounting Practice Set. The computerized Rockford practice set is a general ledger software version of the printed practice set. Available on CD-ROM.

ACKNOWLEDGMENTS

We thank the many users of our 11th Edition who contributed to the revision through their comments and instructive criticism. Special thanks are extended to the focus group participants and the primary reviewers of and contributors to our 12th Edition manuscript.

Lisa Bostick
University of Tampa

Greg Brookins
Santa Monica College

Laura Delaune
Louisiana State University

Lynda Dennis
University of Central Florida

Claire Eckstein
CUNY—Baruch

Dave Farber
Michigan State University

Clyde Galbraith
West Chester University

Ellen Goldberg
Northern Virginia Community College

Marty Gosman
Quinnipiac College

Julia Higgs
Florida Atlantic University

Geoffrey Horlick
St. Francis College

Marilyn Hunt
University of Central Florida

Cynthia Jeffrey
Iowa State University

Mary Jo Jones
Eastern University

Art Joy
University of South Florida

Celina Jozci
University of South Florida

Lisa Koonce
University of Texas at Austin

Timothy Lindquist
University of Northern Iowa

Barbara Lippincott
University of Tampa

Gary Luoma
University of Southern California

Daphne Main
University of New Orleans

Ed Nathan
University of Houston

Hugo Nurnberg
CUNY – Baruch

Ann O'Brien
University of Wisconsin—Madison

Anne Oppegard
Augustana College, SD

Alee Phillips
University of Kansas

Marlene Plumlee
University of Utah

Wing Poon
Montclair State University

Jay Price
Utah State University

Paul (Jep) Robertson
Henderson State University

Larry Roman
Cuyahoga Community College

Bob Rouse
College of Charleston

Tim Shea
University of Wisconsin – Madison

Jerry Siebel
University of South Florida

Karen Squires
University of Tampa

Douglas Smith
Samford University

Gary Taylor
University of Alabama

Lynn Thomas
Kansas State University

Tom Tierney
University of Wisconsin—Madison

David Weiner
University of San Francisco

Steve Zeff
Rice University

We also thank other colleagues who provided helpful criticism and made valuable suggestions as members of focus groups, survey participants, or as adopters and reviewers of previous editions.

Diana Adcox
University of North Florida

Noel Addy
Mississippi State University

Roberta Allen
Texas Tech University

James Bannister
University of Hartford

Charles Baril
James Madison University

Kathleen Buaer
Midwestern State University

Janice Bell
California State University at Northridge

Larry Bergin
Winona State University

Lynn Bible
University of Nevada, Reno

John C. Borke
University of Wisconsin—Platteville

Tiffany Bortz
University of Texas, Dallas

Phillip Buchanan
George Mason University

Tom Buchman
University of Colorado, Boulder

Suzanne M. Busch
California State University—Hayward

Eric Carlsen
Kean College of New Jersey

Tom Carment
Northeastern State University

Tommy Carnes
Western Carolina University

Robert Cluskey
Tennessee State University

Edwin Cohen
DePaul University

W. Terry Dancer
Arkansas State University

Lee Dexter
Moorhead State University

Judith Doing
University of Arizona

Joanne Duke
San Francisco State University

Richard Dumont
Teikyo Post University

William Dwyer
DeSales University

Dean S. Eiteman
Indiana University—Pennsylvania

Larry R. Falcetto
Emporia State University

Richard Fern
Eastern Kentucky University

Richard Fleischman
John Carroll University

Stephen L. Fogg
Temple University

William Foster
New Mexico State University

Clyde Galbraith
West Chester University

Marshall Geiger
University of Richmond

Susan Gill
Washington State University

Harold Goedde
State University of New York at Oneonta

Lynford E. Graham
Rutgers University

Donald J. Griffin
Cayuga Community College

Marcia I. Halvorsen
University of Cincinnati

Garry Heesacker
Central Washington University

Kenneth Henry
Florida International University

Wayne M. Higley
Buena Vista University

Judy Hora
University of San Diego

Geoffrey R. Horlick
St. Francis College

Kathy Hsu
University of Louisiana, Layfayette

M. Zarar Iqbal
California Polytechnic State University—San Luis Obispo

Daniel Ivancevich
University of North Carolina at Wilmington

Susan Ivancevich
University of North Carolina at Wilmington

Cynthia Jeffrey
Iowa State University

Scott Jeris
San Francisco State University

James Johnston
Louisiana Tech University

Jeff Jones
University of Texas—San Antonio

Celina Jozsi
University of South Florida

Douglas W. Kieso
Aurora University

Paul D. Kimmel
University of Wisconsin—Milwaukee

Martha King
Emporia State University

Florence Kirk
State University of New York at Oswego

Mark Kohlbeck
Florida Atlantic University

Lisa Koonce
University of Texas—Austin

Steve Lafave
Augsburg College

Ellen Landgraf
Loyola University, Chicago

Tom Largay
Thomas College

David B. Law
Youngstown State University

Henry LeClerc
Suffolk Community College—Selden Campus

Patsy Lee
University of Texas—Arlington

Lydia Leporte
Tidewater Community College

Timothy Lindquist
University of Northern Iowa

Tom Linsmeier
Michigan State University

Ellen Lippman
University of Portland

Daphne Main
University of New Orleans

Mostafa Maksy
Northeastern Illinois University

Danny Matthews
Midwestern State University

Noel McKeon
Florida Community College

Robert J. Matthews
New Jersey City University

Robert Milbrath
University of Houston

James Miller
Gannon University

John Mills
University of Nevada—Reno

Joan Monnin-Callahan
University of Cincinnati

Mohamed E. Moustafa
California State University—Long Beach

Siva Nathan
Georgia State University

Kermit Natho
Georgia State University

Joseph Nicassio
Westmoreland County Community College

Patricia Parker
Columbus State Community College

Richard Parker
Olivet College

Obeau S. Persons
Rider University

Ray Pfeiffer
University of Massachusetts—Amherst

Robert Rambo
University of New Orleans

Debbie Rankin
Lincoln University

MaryAnn Reynolds
Western Washington University

Vernon Richardson
University of Arkansas

Richard Riley
West Virginia University

Jeffrey D. Ritter
St. Norbert College

Paul (Jep) Robertson
Henderson State University

Steven Rock
University of Colorado

John Rossi
Moravian College

Tim Ryan
Southern Illinois University

Victoria Rymer
University of Maryland

James Sander
Butler University

John Sander
University of Southern Maine

George Sanders
Western Washington University

Howard Shapiro
Eastern Washington University

Douglas Sharp
Wichita State University

Phil Siegel
Florida Atlantic University

John R. Simon
Northern Illinois University

Keith Smith
George Washington University

Pam Smith
Northern Illinois University

Billy S. Soo
Boston College

Carlton D. Stolle
Texas A&M University

William Stout
University of Louisville

Pamela Stuerke
Case Western Reserve University

Ron Stunda
Birmingham Southern College

Eric Sussman
University of California. Los Angeles

Diane L. Tanner
University of North Florida

Gary Testa
Brooklyn College

Paula B. Thomas
Middle Tennessee State University

Elizabeth Venuti
Hofstra University

James D. Waddington, Jr.,
Hawaii Pacific University

Dick Wasson
Southwestern College

Frank F. Weinberg
Golden Gate University

Jeannie Welsh
LaSalle University

Shari H. Wescott
Houston Baptist University

Michael Willenborg
University of Connecticut

William H. Wilson
Oregon Health University

Kenneth Wooling
Hampton University

Joni Young
University of New Mexico

Paul Zarowin
New York University

Stephen A. Zeff
Rice University

In addition, we thank the following colleagues who contributed to several of the unique features of this edition.

Gateway to the Profession Portal and FARS Cases

Jack Cathey
University of North Carolina—Charlotte

Michelle Ephraim
Worcester Polytechnic Institute

Erik Frederickson
Madison, Wisconsin

Jason Hart
Deloitte & Touche, Milwaukee

Kelly Krieg
E & Y, Milwaukee

Jeremy Kunicki
Walgreens

Andrew Prewitt
KPMG, Chicago

Jeff Seymour
KPMG, Minneapolis

Matt Sullivan
Deloitte & Touche, Milwaukee

Jen Vaughn
PricewaterhouseCoopers, Chicago

Erin Viel
PricewaterhouseCoopers, Milwaukee

Edward Wertheim
Northeastern University

Ancillary Authors, Contributors, Proofers, and Accuracy Checkers

Mary Ann Benson

John C. Borke
University of Wisconsin—Platteville

Jack Cathey
University of North Carolina—Charlotte

Betty Connor
University of Colorado at Denver

Robert Derstine
Villanova University

Gregory Dold
Southwestern College

Jan Duffy
Iowa State University

Jim Emig
Villanova University

Larry Falcetto
Emporia State University

Tom Forehand
State University of New York—New Paltz

Rosemary Fullerton
Utah State University

Clyde Galbraith
West Chester University

Alicia Gmeiner
Elm Street Publishing Services

Edwin Hackleman
Delta Software

Coby Harmon
University of California, Santa Barbara

Wayne Higley
Buena Vista University

Debra R. Hopkins
Northern Illinois University

Judi Hora
University of San Diego

Marilyn F. Hunt

Douglas W. Kieso
Aurora University

Mark Kohlbeck
Florida Atlantic University

Jennifer Laudermilch
PricewaterhouseCoopers

Ann Martin
University of Colorado at Denver

Barbara Muller
Arizona State University

Don Newell
Delta Software

Tom Noland
University of Houston

Paul (Jep) Robertson
Henderson State University

Rex A. Schildhouse
University of Phoenix—San Diego

Alice Sineath
Forsyth Technical Community College

Dick D. Wasson
Southwestern College, San Diego University

WileyPLUS Developers and Reviewers

James Mraz

Jan Mardon

Melanie Yon

Perspectives and "From Classroom to Career" Interviews

Stuart Weiss, *Stuart Weiss Business Writing, Inc., Portland, Oregon*

Practicing Accountants and Business Executives

From the fields of corporate and public accounting, we owe thanks to the following practitioners for their technical advance and for consenting to interviews.

Ron Bernard
NFL Enterprises

Mike Crooch
FASB

Tracy Golden
Deloitte & Touche

John Gribble
PricewaterhouseCoopers

Darien Griffin
S.C. Johnson & Son Wax

Michael Lehman
Sun Microsystems, Inc.

Michele Lippert
Evoke.com

Sue McGrath
Vision Capital Management

David Miniken
Sweeney Conrad

Robert Sack
University of Virginia

Clare Schulte
Deloitte & Touche

Willie Sutton
Mutual Community Savings Bank, Durham, NC

Lynn Turner
Glass, Lewis, LLP

Gary Valenzuela
Yahoo!

Rachel Woods
PricewaterhouseCoopers

Arthur Wyatt
Arthur Anderson & Co., and the University of Illinois—Urbana

In addition, we appreciate the exemplary support and professional commitment given us by the development, marketing, production, and editorial staffs of John Wiley & Sons, including the following: Susan Elbe, Chris DeJohn, Mark Bonadeo, Amy Scholz, Alison Stanley, Ed Brislin, Allie Morris, Vanessa Ahrens, Jeanine Furino, Harry Nolan, Anna Melhorn, and Lenore Belton. Thanks to Terry Ann Kremer for her careful line edit of the book and to Ann Torbert for her editorial assistance in pulling together the various pieces of the manuscript. Thanks, too, to Suzanne Ingrao for her production work, to the management and staff at TechBooks for their work on the textbook, and to Alicia Gmeiner and the management and staff at Elm Street Publishing Services for their work on the solutions manual.

We also appreciate the cooperation of the American Institute of Certified Public Accountants and the Financial Accounting Standards Board in permitting us to quote from their pronouncements. We thank The Procter & Gamble Company for permitting us to use its 2004 annual report for our specimen financial statements. We also acknowledge permission from the American Institute of Certified Public Accountants, the Institute of Management Accountants, and the Institute of Internal Auditors to adapt and use material from the Uniform CPA Examinations, the CMA Examinations, and the CIA Examination, respectively.

If this book helps teachers instill in their students an appreciation for the challenges, worth, and limitations of accounting, if it encourages students to evaluate critically and understand financial accounting theory and practice, and if it prepares students for advanced study, professional examinations, and the successful and ethical pursuit of their careers in accounting or business, then we will have attained our objectives.

Suggestions and comments from users of this book will be appreciated.

Donald E. Kieso
Somonauk, Illinois

Jerry J. Weygandt
Madison, Wisconsin

Terry D. Warfield
Madison, Wisconsin

BRIEF CONTENTS

CONTENTS

FINANCIAL ACCOUNTING AND ACCOUNTING STANDARDS

The Size of the New York Phone Book, If Necessary

Enron, Global Crossing, Kmart, WorldCom, Williams Cos., and **Xerox** are all companies that the Securities and Exchange Commission (SEC) recently scrutinized because of accounting issues. Share prices of all these companies have declined substantially. Investors punish any company whose quality of earnings is in doubt.

The unfortunate part of accounting scandals is that we all pay. For example, Enron's market capitalization totaled $80 billion before disclosure of its accounting irregularities. Today, it is bankrupt. Employees lost their pension money and investors their savings. Further, the entire stock market caught "Enronitis," a distrust of accounting that has led to substantial declines in the overall stock market. At one point, at least 10 congressional committees were inquiring into corporate governance issues, and Congress introduced over 30 Enron-related bills that addressed matters such as regulation of derivative securities, auditor–client conflicts, and development of an oversight body to regulate the accounting profession.

Companies have also taken steps to respond to the many investor concerns about the completeness and reliability of the accounting numbers. Many companies now expand the financial disclosures in their annual reports. For example, **General Electric**'s CEO Jeffrey Immelt stated, "I want people to think about GE as we think of GE—as a transparent company." He noted that GE's annual report will be "the size of New York City's phone book, if necessary" to provide the information needed to help investors and creditors make the proper investing decisions.

We believe that meaningful reform will come out of these recent investigations into sloppy or fraudulent accounting. Although many consider the United States to have the finest financial reporting system in the world, we must do better. As former chair of the FASB Ed Jenkins remarked recently, "If anything positive results . . . it may be that [these accounting issues] serve as an indelible reminder to all that transparent financial reporting does matter and that lack of transparency imposes significant costs on all who participate [in our markets]."

Learning Objectives

After studying this chapter, you should be able to:

1 Identify the major financial statements and other means of financial reporting.

2 Explain how accounting assists in the efficient use of scarce resources.

3 Describe some of the challenges facing accounting.

4 Identify the objectives of financial reporting.

5 Explain the need for accounting standards.

6 Identify the major policy-setting bodies and their role in the standard-setting process.

7 Explain the meaning of generally accepted accounting principles.

8 Describe the impact of user groups on the standard-setting process.

9 Understand issues related to ethics and financial accounting.

As our opening story indicates, companies must provide relevant and reliable information so that our capital markets work efficiently. This chapter explains the environment of financial reporting and the many factors affecting it, as follows.

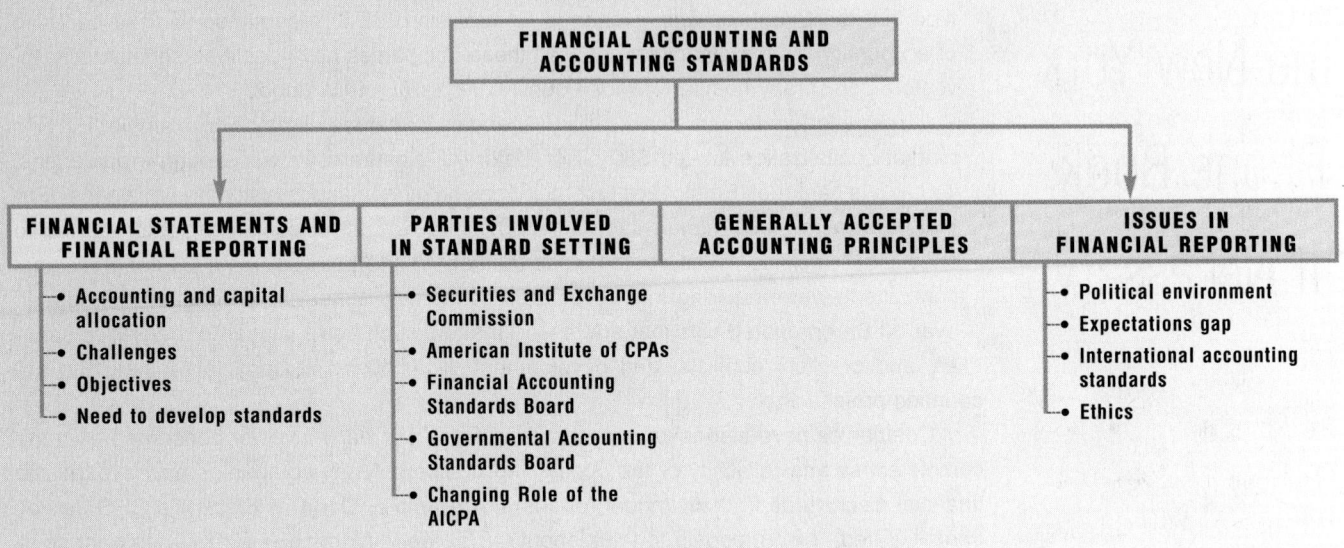

FINANCIAL STATEMENTS AND FINANCIAL REPORTING

The essential characteristics of accounting are: (1) the identification, measurement, and communication of financial information about (2) economic entities to (3) interested parties. **Financial accounting** is the process that culminates in the preparation of financial reports on the enterprise for use by both internal and external parties. Users of these financial reports include investors, creditors, managers, unions, and government agencies. In contrast, **managerial accounting** is the process of identifying, measuring, analyzing, and communicating financial information needed by management to plan, control, and evaluate a company's operations.

Financial statements are the principal means through which a company communicates its financial information to those outside it. These statements provide a company's history quantified in money terms. The **financial statements** most frequently provided are (1) the balance sheet, (2) the income statement, (3) the statement of cash flows, and (4) the statement of owners' or stockholders' equity. Note disclosures are an integral part of each financial statement.

Some financial information is better provided, or can be provided only, by means of **financial reporting** other than formal financial statements. Examples include the president's letter or supplementary schedules in the corporate annual report, prospectuses, reports filed with government agencies, news releases, management's forecasts, and social or environmental impact statements. Companies may need to provide such information because of authoritative pronouncement, regulatory rule, or custom. Or they may supply it because management wishes to disclose it voluntarily.

OBJECTIVE 1
Identify the major financial statements and other means of financial reporting.

In this textbook, we focus on the development of two types of financial information: (1) the basic financial statements and (2) related disclosures.

Accounting and Capital Allocation

Resources are limited. As a result, people try to conserve them and ensure that they are used effectively. Efficient use of resources often determines whether a business thrives. This fact places a substantial burden on the accounting profession.

OBJECTIVE 2
Explain how accounting assists in the efficient use of scarce resources.

Accountants must measure performance accurately and fairly on a timely basis, so that the right managers and companies are able to attract investment capital. For example, relevant and reliable financial information allows investors and creditors to compare the income and assets employed by such companies as **IBM, McDonald's, Microsoft**, and **Ford**. Because these users can assess the relative return and risks associated with investment opportunities, they channel resources more effectively. Illustration 1-1 shows how this process of capital allocation works.

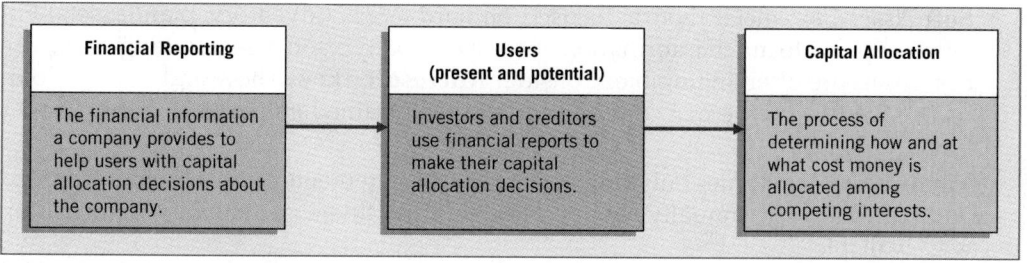

ILLUSTRATION 1-1
Capital Allocation Process

An effective process of capital allocation is critical to a healthy economy. It promotes productivity, encourages innovation, and provides an efficient and liquid market for buying and selling securities and obtaining and granting credit.[1] As we indicated in our opening story, unreliable and irrelevant information leads to poor capital allocation, which adversely affects the securities markets.

IT'S NOT THE ECONOMY, ANYMORE, STUPID

It's not the economy anymore. It's the accounting. That's what many investors seem to be saying these days. As indicated in our opening story, even the slightest hint of any accounting irregularity at a company leads to a subsequent pounding of the company's stock price. For example, recent editions of the *Wall Street Journal* had the following headlines related to accounting and its effects on the economy.

WHAT DO THE NUMBERS MEAN?

- Stocks take a beating as accounting woes spread beyond **Enron**.
- Once hot **Krispy Kreme** ousts its CEO amid accounting woes.
- **Nortel** unveils new accounting flubs.
- Accounting woes at **AIG** take their toll on insurers' shares.
- Bank stocks fall as investors take issue with **PNC**'s accounting.

It now has become clear that investors must trust the accounting numbers or they will abandon the market and put their resources elsewhere. With investor uncertainty, the cost of capital increases for companies who need additional resources. In short, relevant and reliable financial information is necessary for markets to be efficient.

---

[1]AICPA Special Committee on Financial Reporting, "Improving Business Reporting—A Customer Focus," *Journal of Accountancy*, Supplement (October 1994).

The Challenges Facing Financial Accounting

OBJECTIVE 3
Describe some of the challenges facing accounting.

Much is right about financial reporting in the United States. We presently have the most liquid, deep, secure, and efficient public capital markets of any country at any time in history. One reason for this success is that our financial statements and related disclosures capture and organize financial information in a useful and reliable fashion. However, much still needs to be done. For example, if we move to the year 2020 and look back at financial reporting today, we might read the following:

- **Nonfinancial Measurements.** Financial reports failed to provide some key performance measures widely used by management, such as customer satisfaction indexes, backlog information, and reject rates on goods purchased.
- **Forward-looking Information.** Financial reports failed to provide forward-looking information needed by present and potential investors and creditors. One individual noted that financial statements in 2005 should have started with the phrase, "Once upon a time," to signify their use of historical cost and accumulation of past events.
- **Soft Assets.** Financial reports focused on hard assets (inventory, plant assets) but failed to provide much information about a company's soft assets (intangibles). The best assets are often intangible. Consider **Microsoft**'s know-how and market dominance, **Dell**'s unique marketing setup and well-trained employees, and **J. Crew**'s brand image.
- **Timeliness.** Companies only prepared financial statements quarterly, and provided audited financials annually. Little to no real-time financial statement information was available.

We believe each of these challenges must be met for the accounting profession to provide the type of information needed for an efficient capital allocation process. We are confident that changes will occur, based on these positive signs:

- Already some companies voluntarily disclose information deemed relevant to investors. Often such information is nonfinancial. For example, regional banking companies, such as **BankOne Corp., Fifth Third Bancorp**, and **Sun Trust Banks**, now include data on loan growth, credit quality, fee income, operating efficiency, capital management, and management strategy.
- Initially, companies used the World Wide Web to provide limited financial data. Now most companies publish their annual reports in several formats on the Web. The most innovative companies offer sections of their annual reports in a format that the user can readily manipulate, such as in an Excel spreadsheet format. Companies also format their financial reports using extensible business reporting language (XBRL), which permits quicker and lower cost access to companies' financial information.
- More accounting standards now require the recording or disclosing of fair value information. For example, companies either record investments in stocks and bonds, debt obligations, and derivatives at fair value or companies show information related to fair values in the notes to the financial statements.

Changes in these directions will enhance the relevance of financial reporting and provide useful information to financial statement readers.

INTERNATIONAL INSIGHT

The objectives of financial reporting differ across nations. Traditionally, the primary objective of accounting in many continental European nations and in Japan was conformity with the law. In contrast, Canada, the U.K., the Netherlands, and many other nations share the U.S. view that the primary objective is to provide information for investors.

Objectives of Financial Reporting

OBJECTIVE 4
Identify the objectives of financial reporting.

To establish a foundation for financial accounting and reporting, the accounting profession identified a set of objectives of financial reporting by business enterprises. Financial reporting should provide information that:

1 Is useful to present and potential investors and creditors and other users **in making rational investment, credit, and similar decisions**. The information should be comprehensible to those who have a **reasonable understanding** of business and economic activities and are willing to study the information with reasonable diligence.

2 Helps present and potential investors, creditors, and other users **assess the amounts, timing, and uncertainty of prospective cash receipts** from dividends or interest and the proceeds from the sale, redemption, or maturity of securities or loans. Since investors' and creditors' cash flows are related to enterprise cash flows, financial reporting should provide information to help investors, creditors, and others assess the amounts, timing, and uncertainty of prospective net cash inflows to the related enterprise.

3 **Clearly portrays the economic resources of an enterprise, the claims to those resources** (obligations of the enterprise to transfer resources to other entities and owners' equity), and the effects of transactions, events, and circumstances that change its resources and claims to those resources.[2]

In brief, the objectives of financial reporting are to provide information that is (1) useful in investment and credit decisions, (2) useful in assessing cash flow prospects, and (3) about company resources, claims to those resources, and changes in them.

The emphasis on "assessing cash flow prospects" does not mean that the cash basis is preferred over the accrual basis of accounting. That is not the case. Information based on **accrual accounting generally better indicates a company's present and continuing ability to generate favorable cash flows** than does information limited to the financial effects of cash receipts and payments.[3]

Recall from your first accounting course the objective of **accrual-basis accounting**: It ensures that a company records events that change its financial statements in the periods in which the events occur, rather than only in the periods in which it receives or pays cash. Using the accrual basis to determine net income means that a company recognizes revenues when it earns them rather than when it receives cash. Similarly, it recognizes expenses when it incurs them rather than when it pays them. Under accrual accounting, a company generally recognizes revenues when it makes sales. The company can then relate the revenues to the economic environment of the period in which they occurred. Over the long run, trends in revenues and expenses are generally more meaningful than trends in cash receipts and disbursements.

The Need to Develop Standards

The main controversy in setting accounting standards is, "Whose rules should we play by, and what should they be?" The answer is not immediately clear. Users of financial accounting statements have both coinciding and conflicting needs for information of various types. To meet these needs, and to satisfy the fiduciary[4] reporting responsibility of management, companies prepare a single set of **general-purpose financial statements**. Users expect these statements to present fairly, clearly, and completely the company's financial operations.

The accounting profession has attempted to develop a set of standards that are generally accepted and universally practiced. Otherwise, each enterprise would have to develop its own standards. Further, readers of financial statements would have to familiarize themselves with every company's peculiar accounting and

> **OBJECTIVE 5**
> Explain the need for accounting standards.

---

[2]"Objectives of Financial Reporting by Business Enterprises," *Statement of Financial Accounting Concepts No. 1* (Stamford, Conn.: FASB, November 1978), pars. 5–8.

[3]*SFAC No. 1*, p. iv. As used here, *cash flow* means "cash generated and used in operations." The term *cash flows* also frequently means cash obtained by borrowing and used to repay borrowing, cash used for investments in resources and obtained from the disposal of investments, and cash contributed by or distributed to owners.

[4]Management's fiduciary responsibility is to manage assets with care and trust.

reporting practices. It would be almost impossible to prepare statements that could be compared.

This common set of standards and procedures is called **generally accepted accounting principles (GAAP)**. The term "generally accepted" means either that an authoritative accounting rule-making body has established a principle of reporting in a given area or that over time a given practice has been accepted as appropriate because of its universal application.[5] Although principles and practices continue to provoke both debate and criticism, most members of the financial community recognize them as the standards that over time have proven to be most useful. We present a more extensive discussion of what constitutes GAAP later in this chapter.

PARTIES INVOLVED IN STANDARD SETTING

OBJECTIVE 6
Identify the major policy-setting bodies and their role in the standard-setting process.

INTERNATIONAL INSIGHT

The International Organization of Securities Commissions (IOSCO), established in 1987, consists of more than 100 securities regulatory agencies or securities exchanges from all over the world. Collectively, its members represent a substantial proportion of the world's capital markets. The SEC is a member of IOSCO.

Four organizations are instrumental in the development of financial accounting standards (GAAP) in the United States:

1. Securities and Exchange Commission (SEC)
2. American Institute of Certified Public Accountants (AICPA)
3. Financial Accounting Standards Board (FASB)
4. Government Accounting Standards Board (GASB)

Securities and Exchange Commission (SEC)

External financial reporting and auditing developed in tandem with the growth of the industrial economy and its capital markets. However, when the stock market crashed in 1929 and the nation's economy plunged into the Great Depression, there were calls for increased government regulation of business generally, and especially financial institutions and the stock market.

As a result of these events, the federal government established the **Securities and Exchange Commission (SEC)** to help develop and standardize financial information presented to stockholders. The SEC is a federal agency. It administers the Securities Exchange Act of 1934 and several other acts. Most companies that issue securities to the public or are listed on a stock exchange are required to file audited financial statements with the SEC. In addition, the SEC has broad powers to prescribe, in whatever detail it desires, the accounting practices and standards to be employed by companies that fall within its jurisdiction. The SEC currently exercises oversight over 12,000 companies that are listed on the major exchanges (e.g., the New York Stock Exchange and the Nasdaq).

Public/Private Partnership

At the time the SEC was created, no group—public or private—issued accounting standards. The SEC encouraged the creation of a private standard-setting body because it believed that the private sector had the appropriate resources and talent to achieve this daunting task. As a result, accounting standards have developed in the private sector either through the American Institute of Certified Public Accountants (AICPA) or the Financial Accounting Standards Board (FASB).

The SEC has affirmed its support for the FASB by indicating that financial statements conforming to standards set by the FASB are presumed to have substantial authoritative support. In short, the **SEC requires registrants to adhere to GAAP**. In addition, the SEC indicated in its reports to Congress that "it continues to believe that the initiative for establishing and improving accounting standards should remain in the private sector, subject to Commission oversight."

---

[5]The terms *principles* and *standards* are used interchangeably in practice and throughout this textbook.

SEC Oversight

The SEC's partnership with the private sector works well. The SEC acts with remarkable restraint in the area of developing accounting standards. Generally, **the SEC relies on the FASB to develop accounting standards**.

The SEC's involvement in the development of accounting standards varies. In some cases, the SEC rejects a standard proposed by the private sector. In other cases, the SEC prods the private sector into taking quicker action on certain reporting problems, such as accounting for investments in debt and equity securities and the reporting of derivative instruments. In still other situations, the SEC communicates problems to the FASB, responds to FASB exposure drafts, and provides the FASB with counsel and advice upon request.

The SEC's mandate is to establish accounting principles. The private sector, therefore, must listen carefully to the views of the SEC. In some sense the private sector is the formulator and the implementor of the standards.[6] However, when the private sector fails to address accounting problems as quickly as the SEC would like, the partnership between the SEC and the private sector can be strained. This occurred in the recent deliberations on the accounting for business combinations and intangible assets, and concerns over the accounting for off-balance sheet special-purpose entities, highlighted in the failure of **Enron**.

Enforcement

As we indicated earlier, companies listed on a stock exchange must submit their financial statements to the SEC. If the SEC believes that an accounting or disclosure irregularity exists regarding the form or content of the financial statements, it sends a deficiency letter to the company. Companies usually resolve these deficiency letters quickly. However, if disagreement continues, the SEC may issue a "stop order," which prevents the registrant from issuing or trading securities on the exchanges. The Department of Justice may also file criminal charges for violations of certain laws. The SEC process, private sector initiatives, and civil and criminal litigation help to ensure the integrity of financial reporting for public companies.

American Institute of Certified Public Accountants (AICPA)

The **American Institute of Certified Public Accountants (AICPA)**, which is the national professional organization of practicing Certified Public Accountants (CPAs), has been an important contributor to the development of GAAP. Various committees and boards established since the founding of the AICPA have contributed to this effort.

Committee on Accounting Procedure

At the urging of the SEC, the AICPA appointed the Committee on Accounting Procedure in 1939. The **Committee on Accounting Procedure (CAP)**, composed of practicing CPAs, issued 51 **Accounting Research Bulletins** during the years 1939 to 1959. These bulletins dealt with a variety of accounting problems. But this problem-by-problem approach failed to provide the needed structured body of accounting principles. In response, in 1959 the AICPA created the Accounting Principles Board.

INTERNATIONAL INSIGHT

Nations also differ in the degree to which they developed national standards and consistent accounting practices. One indicator of the level of a nation's accounting is the nature of the accounting profession within the country. For example, the Netherlands, the U.K., Canada, and the U.S. established professional accounting bodies in the nineteenth century. In contrast, Hong Kong, Singapore, and Korea established similar bodies only in the last half century.

---

[6]One writer described the relationship of the FASB and SEC and the development of financial reporting standards using the analogy of a pearl. The pearl (a financial reporting standard) "is formed by the reaction of certain oysters (FASB) to an irritant (the SEC)—usually a grain of sand—that becomes embedded inside the shell. The oyster coats this grain with layers of nacre, and ultimately a pearl is formed. The pearl is a joint result of the irritant (SEC) and oyster (FASB); without both, it cannot be created." John C. Burton, "Government Regulation of Accounting and Information," *Journal of Accountancy* (June 1982).

Accounting Principles Board

The major purposes of the **Accounting Principles Board (APB)** were to (1) advance the written expression of accounting principles, (2) determine appropriate practices, and (3) narrow the areas of difference and inconsistency in practice. To achieve these objectives, the APB's mission was twofold: to develop an overall conceptual framework to assist in the resolution of problems as they become evident and to substantively research individual issues before the AICPA issued pronouncements. The Board's 18 to 21 members, selected primarily from public accounting, also included representatives from industry and academia. The Board's official pronouncements, called **APB Opinions**, were intended to be based mainly on research studies and be supported by reasons and analysis. Between its inception in 1959 and its dissolution in 1973, the APB issued 31 opinions.

Unfortunately, the APB came under fire early, charged with lack of productivity and failing to act promptly to correct alleged accounting abuses. Later the APB tackled numerous thorny accounting issues, only to meet a buzz saw of opposition from industry and CPA firms. It also ran into occasional governmental interference. In 1971 the accounting profession's leaders, anxious to avoid governmental rule-making, appointed a Study Group on Establishment of Accounting Principles. Commonly known as the **Wheat Committee** for its chair Francis Wheat, this group examined the organization and operation of the APB and determined the necessary changes to attain better results. The Study Group submitted its recommendations to the AICPA Council in the spring of 1972. The AICPA Council adopted the recommendations in total, and implemented them by early 1973.

Financial Accounting Standards Board (FASB)

The Wheat Committee's recommendations resulted in the demise of the APB and the creation of a new standard-setting structure composed of three organizations—the Financial Accounting Foundation (FAF), the Financial Accounting Standards Board (FASB), and the Financial Accounting Standards Advisory Council (FASAC). The **Financial Accounting Foundation** selects the members of the FASB and the Advisory Council, funds their activities, and generally oversees the FASB's activities.

The major operating organization in this three-part structure is the **Financial Accounting Standards Board (FASB)**. Its mission is to establish and improve standards of financial accounting and reporting for the guidance and education of the public, which includes issuers, auditors, and users of financial information. The expectations of success and support for the new FASB relied on several significant differences between it and its predecessor, the APB:

INTERNATIONAL INSIGHT

The U.S. legal system is based on English common law, whereby the government generally allows professionals to make the rules. The private sector, therefore, develops these rules (standards). Conversely, some countries follow codified law, which leads to government-run accounting systems.

1 **Smaller Membership.** The FASB consists of seven members, replacing the relatively large 18-member APB.

2 **Full-time, Remunerated Membership.** FASB members are well-paid, full-time members appointed for renewable 5-year terms. The APB members volunteered their part-time work.

3 **Greater Autonomy.** The APB was a senior committee of the AICPA. The FASB is not part of any single professional organization. It is appointed by and answerable only to the Financial Accounting Foundation.

4 **Increased Independence.** APB members retained their private positions with firms, companies, or institutions. FASB members must sever all such ties.

5 **Broader Representation.** All APB members were required to be CPAs and members of the AICPA. Currently, it is not necessary to be a CPA to be a member of the FASB.

In addition to research help from its own staff, the FASB relies on the expertise of various task force groups formed for various projects and on the **Financial Accounting Standards Advisory Council (FASAC)**. FASAC consults with the FASB on major policy and technical issues and also helps select task force members.

Due Process

In establishing financial accounting standards, the FASB relies on two basic premises: (1) The FASB should be responsive to the needs and viewpoints of the entire economic community, not just the public accounting profession. (2) It should operate in full view of the public through a "due process" system that gives interested persons ample opportunity to make their views known. To ensure the achievement of these goals, the FASB follows specific steps to develop a typical FASB Statement of Financial Accounting Standards, as Illustration 1-2 shows.

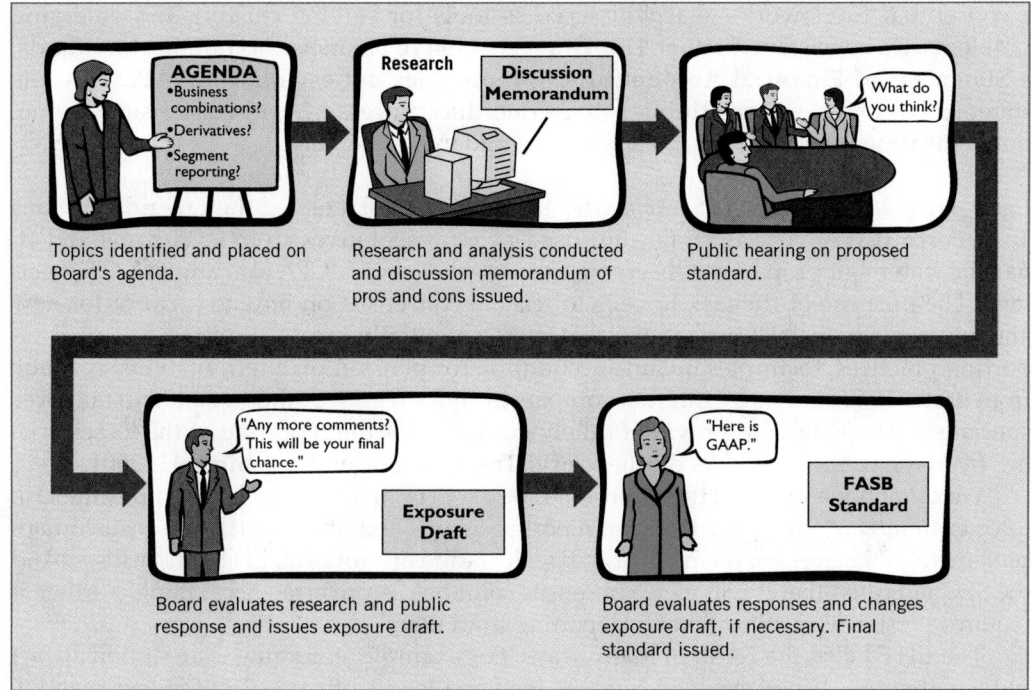

ILLUSTRATION 1-2
The Due Process System of the FASB

The passage of a new FASB **Standards Statement** requires the support of four of the seven Board members. FASB Statements are considered GAAP and thereby binding in practice. All ARBs and APB Opinions implemented by 1973 (when the FASB formed) continue to be effective until amended or superseded by FASB pronouncements. In recognition of possible misconceptions of the term "principles," the FASB uses the term **financial accounting standards** in its pronouncements.

Types of Pronouncements

The FASB issues three major types of pronouncements:

1 Standards, Interpretations, and Staff Positions.

2 Financial Accounting Concepts.

3 Emerging Issues Task Force Statements.

Standards, Interpretation, and Staff Positions. Financial accounting **standards** issued by the FASB are considered generally accepted accounting principles. In addition, the FASB also issues **interpretations** that modify or extend existing standards. Interpretations have the same authority, and require the same votes for passage, as standards. The APB also issued interpretations of APB Opinions. Both types of interpretations are now considered authoritative for purposes of determining GAAP. Finally, the FASB issues staff positions, which provide interpretive guidance and also minor amendments to standards and interpretations. These staff positions have the same authority as standards and interpretations. The Board also has issued FASB Technical Bulletins, which

provide timely guidance on selected issues; staff positions are now used in lieu of technical bulletins. Since replacing the APB, the FASB has issued 154 standards, 47 interpretations, and over 30 staff positions. (See list at the back of the book.)

Financial Accounting Concepts. As part of a long-range effort to move away from the problem-by-problem approach, the FASB in November 1978 issued the first in a series of **Statements of Financial Accounting Concepts** as part of its conceptual framework project. (See list at the back of the book.) The series sets forth fundamental objectives and concepts that the Board uses in developing future standards of financial accounting and reporting. The Board intends to form a cohesive set of interrelated concepts—a conceptual framework—that will serve as tools for solving existing and emerging problems in a consistent manner. Unlike a Statement of Financial Accounting Standards, **a Statement of Financial Accounting Concepts does not establish GAAP.** Concepts statements, however, pass through the same due process system (discussion memo, public hearing, exposure draft, etc.) as do standards statements.

Emerging Issues Task Force Statements. In 1984 the FASB created the **Emerging Issues Task Force (EITF).** The EITF is comprised of representatives from CPA firms and financial statement preparers. Observers from the SEC and AICPA also attend EITF meetings. The purpose of the task force is to reach a consensus on how to account for new and unusual financial transactions that may potentially create differing financial reporting practices. Examples include accounting for pension plan terminations, revenue from barter transactions by Internet companies, and excessive amounts paid to takeover specialists. The EITF also provided timely guidance for the reporting of the losses arising from the terrorist attacks on the World Trade Center on September 11, 2001.

We cannot overestimate the importance of the EITF. In one year, for example, the task force examined 61 emerging financial reporting issues and arrived at a consensus on approximately 75 percent of them. The FASB reviews and approves all EITF consensuses. And the SEC indicated that it will view consensus solutions as preferred accounting. Further, it requires persuasive justification for departing from them.

The EITF helps the FASB in many ways. For example, emerging issues often attract public attention. If not resolved quickly, they can lead to financial crises and scandal. They can also undercut public confidence in current reporting practices. The next step, possible governmental intervention, would threaten the continuance of standard setting in the private sector. The EITF identifies controversial accounting problems as they arise. The EITF determines whether it can quickly resolve them, or whether to involve the FASB in solving them. In essence, it becomes a "problem filter" for the FASB. Thus, the FASB will hopefully work on more pervasive long-term problems, while the EITF deals with short-term emerging issues.

Governmental Accounting Standards Board (GASB)

Financial statements prepared by state and local governments are not comparable with financial reports prepared by private business organizations. The lack of comparability was highlighted in the 1970s when a number of large cities such as New York and Cleveland faced potential bankruptcy. As result, the **Governmental Accounting Standards Board (GASB)** came into being.

The operational structure of the GASB is similar to that of the FASB. That is, it has an advisory council called the Governmental Accounting Standards Advisory Council (GASAC), and has its own technical staff and task forces to assist its work.

The creation of the GASB was controversial. Many believe that there should be only one standard-setting body—the FASB. It was hoped that dividing standard-setting between the GASB, which deals with state and local government reporting, and the FASB, which addresses reporting for all other entities, would not lead to conflict. Since we are primarily concerned with financial reports prepared by profit-seeking organizations, this textbook focuses on standards issued by the FASB. Illustration 1-3 shows the current formal organizational structure for the development of financial reporting standards.

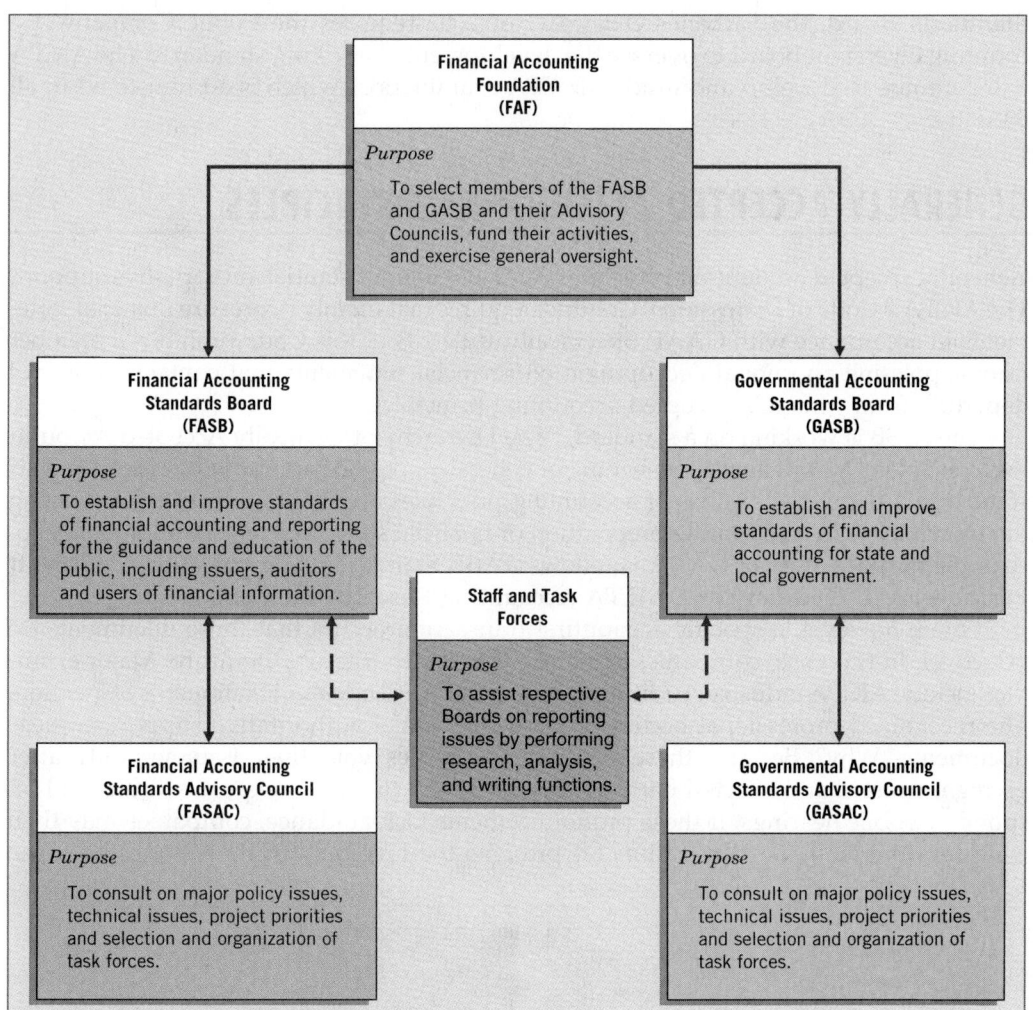

ILLUSTRATION 1-3
Organizational Structure
for Setting Accounting
Standards

Changing Role of the AICPA

For several decades the AICPA provided leadership in developing accounting principles and rules. More than any other organization, it regulated the accounting profession, and developed and enforced accounting practice. When the FASB replaced the Accounting Principles Board, the AICPA established the **Accounting Standards Executive Committee (AcSEC)** as the committee authorized to speak for the AICPA in the area of financial accounting and reporting. It does so through various written communications:

Audit and Accounting Guides summarize the accounting practices of specific industries and provide specific guidance on matters not addressed by the FASB. Examples are accounting for casinos, airlines, colleges and universities, banks, insurance companies, and many others.

Statements of Position (SOP) provide guidance on financial reporting topics until the FASB sets standards on the issue in question. SOPs may update, revise, and clarify audit and accounting guides or provide free-standing guidance.

Practice Bulletins indicate AcSEC's views on narrow financial reporting issues not considered by the FASB.

Recently, the role of the AICPA in standard-setting has diminished. The FASB and the AICPA agree that, after a transition period, the AICPA and AcSEC no longer will issue authoritative accounting guidance for public companies. Furthermore, while the AICPA has been the leader in developing auditing standards through its **Auditing**

Standards Board, the Sarbanes-Oxley Act of 2002 requires the Public Company Accounting Oversight Board to oversee the development of auditing standards. The AICPA will continue to develop and grade the CPA examination, which is administered in all 50 states.

GENERALLY ACCEPTED ACCOUNTING PRINCIPLES

OBJECTIVE 7
Explain the meaning of generally accepted accounting principles.

Generally accepted accounting principles (GAAP) have substantial authoritative support. The AICPA's Code of Professional Conduct requires that members prepare financial statements in accordance with GAAP. Specifically, Rule 203 of this Code prohibits a member from expressing an unqualified opinion on financial statements that contain a material departure from generally accepted accounting principles.

The FASB is working on a standard, "The Hierarchy of Generally Accepted Accounting Principles," that defines the meaning of generally accepted accounting principles. This standard identifies the sources of accounting principles and the framework for selecting the principles to be used in the preparation of financial statements. The standard categorizes the major sources of GAAP as follows: **FASB Standards, Interpretations, and Staff Positions; APB Opinions**; and **AICPA Accounting Research Bulletins**.[7]

Often, however, a specific accounting transaction occurs that these documents do not cover. In this case, companies must use other authoritative literature. Major examples include AICPA Industry Auditing and Accounting Guides and Statements of Position. The recognized professional bodies provide substantial authoritative support to these documents. Why? Because these professional bodies vote their issuance only after giving interested and affected parties the opportunity to react to exposure drafts and respond at public hearings. If these pronouncements lack guidance, companies may then consider other sources. Illustration 1-4 presents the hierarchy of these sources.[8] If the

ILLUSTRATION 1-4
The House of GAAP

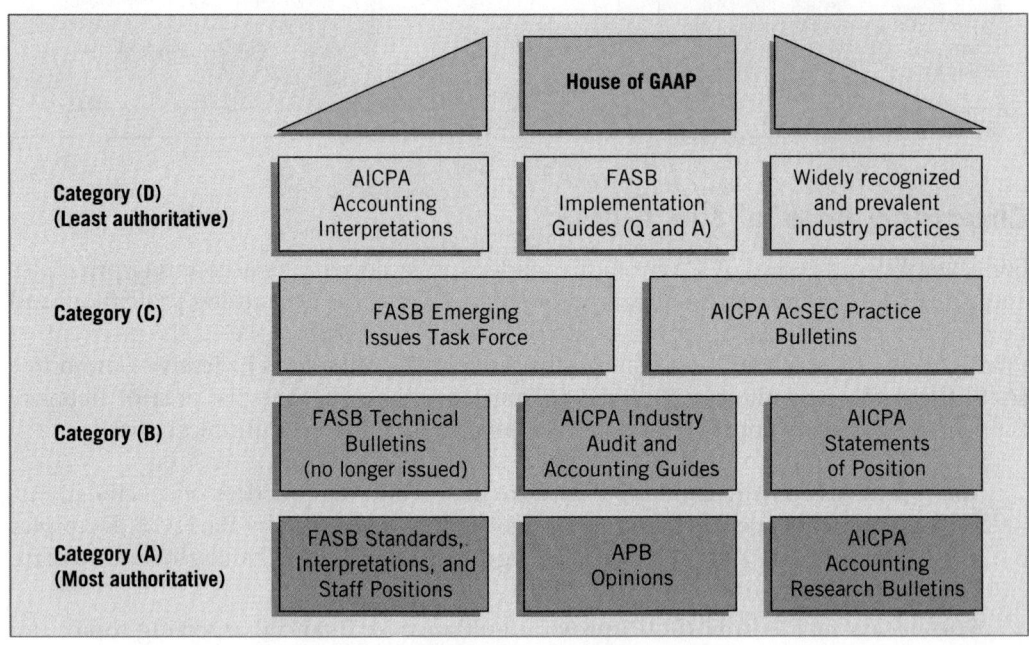

---

[7]The auditing literature presented the GAAP hierarchy prior to the issuance of this standard. The FASB decided that the GAAP hierarchy should be directed specifically to the company because it is the company (not the auditor) that is responsible for selecting the accounting principles for financial statements. As a result, the GAAP hierarchy should reside in the accounting literature, not the auditing literature. "The Hierarchy of Generally Accepted Accounting Principles," *Proposed Statement of Financial Accounting Standards* (Norwalk, Conn.: FASB, April 28, 2005.)

[8]See for example, Douglas Sauter, "Remodeling the House of GAAP," *Journal of Accountancy* (July 1991), pp. 30–37.

accounting treatment of an event is not specified by a Category A pronouncement, then Categories B through D should be investigated. If there is a conflict between pronouncements in B through D, companies should follow the higher category. For example, B is higher than C.

If none of these pronouncements addresses the event, companies seek support from other accounting literature. Examples include FASB Concepts Statements, International Accounting Standards, and accounting articles.[9]

YOU HAVE TO STEP BACK

WHAT DO THE NUMBERS MEAN?

Should the accounting profession have principles-based standards or rules-based standards? Critics of the profession today say that over the past three decades, standard-setters have moved away from broad accounting principles aimed at ensuring that companies' financial statements are fairly presented.

Instead, these critics say, standard-setters have moved toward drafting voluminous rules that, if technically followed in "check-box" fashion, may shield auditors and companies from legal liability. That has resulted in companies creating complex capital structures that comply with GAAP but hide billions of dollars of debt and other obligations. To add fuel to the fire, the chief accountant of the enforcement division of the SEC recently noted, "One can violate SEC laws and still comply with GAAP."

In short, what he is saying is that it is not enough just to check the boxes. You then have to step back and determine whether the *overall impression* created by GAAP financial statements fairly portrays the underlying economics of the company. It is a tough standard, but one that auditors and corporate management should strive to achieve.

Sources: Adapted from S. Liesman, "SEC Accounting Cop's Warning: Playing by the Rules May Not Head Off Fraud Issues," *Wall Street Journal* (February 12, 2002), p. C7. See also "Study Pursuant to Section 108(d) of the Sarbanes-Oxley Act of 2002 on the Adoption by the United States Financial Reporting System of a Principles-Based Accounting System," *SEC* (July 25, 2003).

ISSUES IN FINANCIAL REPORTING

Since the implementation of an accounting standard may affect many interests, much discussion often occurs about who should develop these standards and to whom they should apply. We discuss some of the major issues below.

Standard Setting in a Political Environment

User groups are possibly the most powerful force influencing the development of accounting standards. User groups consist of those most interested in or affected by accounting standards, rules, and procedures. Like lobbyists in our state and national capitals, user groups play a significant role. **Accounting standards are as much a product**

---

[9]A reasonable question to ask is, "Why is one set of documents more authoritative than others?" There are two explanations. First, at the time the AICPA or FASB developed a standard, the SEC recognized these organizations as the appropriate body to establish accounting principles. Second, in most cases, a document is more authoritative if, before the document is issued, its contents are (a) debated in a public forum, (b) exposed in writing to the public for comment, and (c) approved by the Board.

Existing GAAP comprises over 2,000 pronouncements. Recently the FASB has started a project to codify all these pronouncements into one major document. Everything in this document will be considered authoritative. Any material excluded would be considered non-authoritative.

of political action as they are of careful logic or empirical findings. User groups may want particular economic events accounted for or reported in a particular way, and they fight hard to get what they want. They know that the most effective way to influence the standards is to participate in the formulation of these standards or to try to influence or persuade the formulator of them.

OBJECTIVE 8
Describe the impact of user groups on the standard-setting process.

These user groups often target the FASB, to pressure it to influence changes in the existing standards and the development of new ones.[10] In fact, these pressures have been multiplying. Some influential groups demand that the accounting profession act more quickly and decisively to solve its problems. Other groups resist such action, preferring to implement change more slowly, if at all. Illustration 1-5 shows the various user groups that apply pressure.

ILLUSTRATION 1-5
User Groups that Influence the Formulation of Accounting Standards

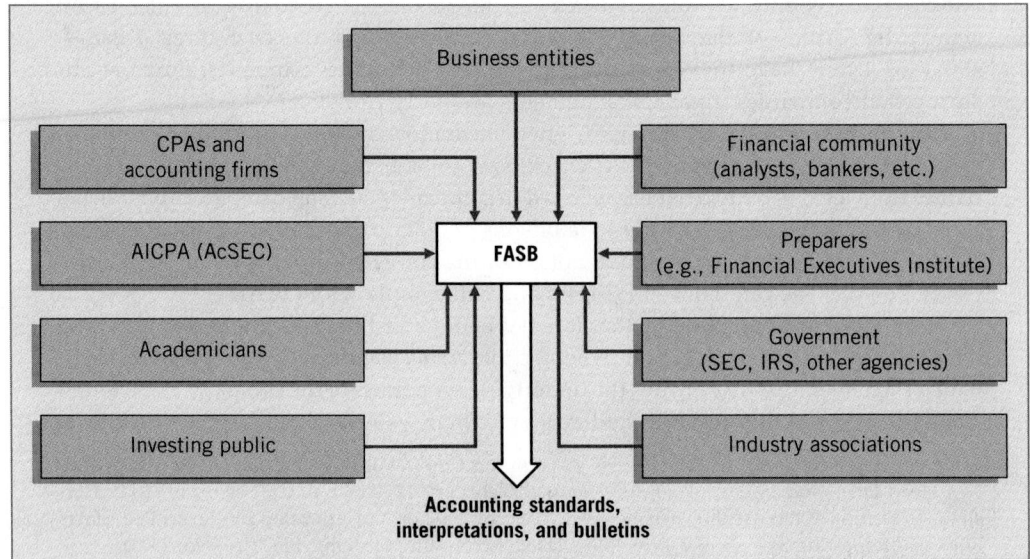

Should there be politics in setting standards for financial accounting and reporting? Why not? We have politics at home; at school; at the fraternity, sorority, and dormitory; at the office; at church, temple, and mosque. Politics is everywhere. Standard setting is part of the real world, and it cannot escape politics and political pressures.

WHAT DO THE NUMBERS MEAN?

THE ECONOMIC CONSEQUENCES OF GOODWILL

Investors generally ignore an accounting change, except when it substantially affects net income. Recently issued goodwill rules are one such change. Under previous GAAP, companies with goodwill charged it to revenues over time. Under new rules, companies no longer have to write off this cost. The effect on the bottom line for some companies is substantial. For example, assuming no goodwill amortization, **International Paper** estimates an income increase of 21 percent, **Johnson Controls** 16 percent, and **Pepsi Bottling Group** 30 percent.

Some believe this change will increase their stock's attractiveness. Others argue that it should have no effect because the write-off is a mere bookkeeping charge. Still others argue that the change has no effect on cash flows, but that investors will perceive the company to be more profitable, and therefore a good buy in the marketplace. In short, the numbers have consequences. What do you think?

---

[10]FASB board members acknowledged that they undertook many of the Board's projects, such as "Accounting for Contingencies," "Accounting for Pensions," "Statement of Cash Flows," and "Accounting for Derivatives," due to political pressure.

That is not to say that politics in standard setting is a negative force. Considering the **economic consequences**[11] of many accounting standards, special interest groups should vocalize their reactions to proposed standards. What the Board should *not* do is issue pronouncements that are primarily politically motivated. While paying attention to its constituencies, the Board should base its standards on sound research and a conceptual framework that has its foundation in economic reality.

The Expectations Gap

Accounting scandals at companies like **Enron, Cendant, Sunbeam, Rite-Aid, Xerox,** and **WorldCom** have attracted the attention of Congress. In 2002, it enacted legislation—the **Sarbanes-Oxley Act**. The new law increases the resources for the SEC to combat fraud and curb poor reporting practices.[12] And the SEC has increased its policing efforts, approving new auditor independence rules and materiality guidelines for financial reporting. In addition, the Sarbanes-Oxley Act introduces sweeping changes to the institutional structure of the accounting profession. The following are some of the key provisions of the legislation.

- Establishes an oversight board, the **Public Company Accounting Oversight Board (PCAOB)**, for accounting practices. The PCAOB has oversight and enforcement authority and establishes auditing, quality control, and independence standards and rules.
- Implements stronger independence rules for auditors. Audit partners, for example, are required to rotate every five years and auditors are prohibited from offering certain types of consulting services to corporate clients.
- Requires CEOs and CFOs to personally certify that financial statements and disclosures are accurate and complete and requires CEOs and CFOs to forfeit bonuses and profits when there is an accounting restatement.
- Requires audit committees to be comprised of independent members and members with financial expertise.
- Requires codes of ethics for senior financial officers.

In addition, Section 404 of the Sarbanes-Oxley Act requires public companies to attest to the effectiveness of their internal controls over financial reporting. **Internal controls** are a system of checks and balances designed to prevent and detect fraud and errors. Most companies have these systems in place, but many have never completely documented them. Companies are finding that it is a costly process but perhaps badly needed. Already intense examination of internal controls has found lingering problems in the way companies operate. Recently, 424 companies reported deficiencies in internal control.[13] Many problems involved closing the books, revenue recognition deficiencies, reconciling accounts, or dealing with inventory. **SunTrust Bank**, for example, fired three officers after discovering errors in how the company calculates its allowance for bad debts. And **Visteon**, a car parts supplier, said it found problems recording and managing receivables from its largest customer, **Ford Motor**.

Will these changes be enough? The **expectations gap**—what the public thinks accountants *should* do and what accountants think they *can* do—is difficult to close. Due

---

[11]*Economic consequences* means the impact of accounting reports on the wealth positions of issuers and users of financial information, and the decision-making behavior resulting from that impact. The resulting behavior of these individuals and groups could have detrimental financial effects on the providers of the financial information. See Stephen A. Zeff, "The Rise of 'Economic Consequences'," *Journal of Accountancy* (December 1978), pp. 56–63. We extend appreciation to Professor Zeff for his insights on this chapter.

[12]*Sarbanes-Oxley Act of 2002*, H. R. Rep. No. 107-610 (2002).

[13]Leah Townsend, "Internal Control Deficiency Disclosures—Interim Alert," *Yellow Card— Interim Trend Alert* (April 12, 2005), Glass, Lewis & Co., LLC.

to the number of fraudulent reporting cases, some question whether the profession is doing enough. Although the profession can argue rightfully that accounting cannot be responsible for every financial catastrophe, it must continue to strive to meet the needs of society. However, efforts to meet these needs will become more costly to society. The development of a highly transparent, clear, and reliable system will require considerable resources.

International Accounting Standards

INTERNATIONAL INSIGHT

Foreign accounting firms that provide an audit report for a U.S.-listed company are subject to the authority of the accounting oversight board (mandated by the Sarbanes-Oxley Act).

Former Secretary of the Treasury Lawrence Summers indicated that the single most important innovation shaping the capital markets was the idea of generally accepted accounting principles. He went on to say that we need something similar internationally.

We believe that the Secretary is right. Relevant and reliable financial information is a necessity for viable capital markets. Unfortunately, companies outside the United States often prepare financial statements using standards different from U.S. GAAP. As a result, international companies such as **Coca-Cola, Microsoft**, and **IBM** have to develop financial information in different ways. Beyond the additional costs these companies incur, users of the financial statements often must understand at least two sets of GAAP. (Understanding one set is hard enough!) It is not surprising therefore that there is a growing demand for one set of high-quality international standards.

Presently, there are two sets of standards accepted for international use—U.S. GAAP and the International Financial Reporting Standards (IFRS) issued by the London-based **International Accounting Standards Board (IASB)**. As you will learn, there are many similarities between U.S. and IASB standards.

U.S. companies that list overseas are still permitted to use U.S. GAAP. Conversely foreign companies listed on our exchanges are required to reconcile their financial information to U.S. GAAP. The reason for the reconciliation is that U.S. GAAP is more extensive and detailed than the IASB standards.

Already 90 countries use IFRS, and the European Union now requires all listed companies in Europe (over 7,000 companies) to use it. The FASB and the IASB are now working hard to find common ground related to existing and proposed standards. Both parties recognize that global markets will best be served if only one set of GAAP is used. The task will not be easy, but the environment is conducive to convergence of the two systems. As Mary Barth, a member of the IASB noted, "There is still a lot to do, but I would never have dreamed we would be working as closely with the FASB as we do today."

Throughout the textbook, we provide in the margins international insights to help you understand the international reporting environment. In addition, Appendix 24B has an expanded discussion of international accounting.

Ethics in the Environment of Financial Accounting

OBJECTIVE 9
Understand issues related to ethics and financial accounting.

Robert Sack, a noted commentator on the subject of accounting ethics, observed, "Based on my experience, new graduates tend to be idealistic . . . thank goodness for that! Still it is very dangerous to think that your armor is all in place and say to yourself, 'I would have never given in to that.' The pressures don't explode on us; they build, and we often don't recognize them until they have us."

These observations are particularly appropriate for anyone entering the business world. In accounting, as in other areas of business, we frequently encounter ethical dilemmas. Some of these dilemmas are simple and easy to resolve. However, many are not, requiring difficult choices among allowable alternatives.

Companies that concentrate on "maximizing the bottom line," "facing the challenges of competition," and "stressing short-term results" place accountants in an environment of conflict and pressure. Basic questions such as, "Is this way of communicating financial information good or bad?" "Is it right or wrong?" "What should I do in the circumstance?" cannot always be answered by simply adhering to GAAP or following the rules of the profession. Technical competence is not enough when encountering ethical decisions.

Doing the right thing is not always easy or obvious. The pressures "to bend the rules," "to play the game," "to just ignore it" can be considerable. For example, "Will my decision affect my job performance negatively?", "Will my superiors be upset?", "Will my colleagues be unhappy with me?" are often questions business people face in making a tough ethical decision. The decision is more difficult because there is no comprehensive ethical system to provide guidelines.

Time, job, client, personal, and peer pressures can complicate the process of ethical sensitivity and selection among alternatives. Throughout this textbook, **we present ethical considerations to help sensitize you** to the type of situations you may encounter in the performance of your professional responsibility.

Expanded Discussion of Ethical Issues in Financial Reporting

HERE COME THE POLITICS

Given the many recent accounting scandals mentioned so far in the text, it is not surprising that both political parties are working to ensure that corporate management be ethical. President Bush, for example, announced a set of proposals to crack down on unethical behavior by corporate officials, expanding the offenses subject to criminal and civil penalties. And both the SEC and the Justice Department are to get more funding to combat financial fraud. At the same time, Democrats in Congress have pushed for more corporate-reform initiatives. So it is not surprising that both houses in Congress passed the Sarbanes-Oxley Act of 2002 with almost unanimous support and the president quickly signed it into law.

One thing is certain: Recent financial reporting undermined consumer confidence in corporate America and the capital markets. Because these issues hurt the U.S. economy, we can expect politicians to continue to seek solutions.

WHAT DO THE NUMBERS MEAN?

Conclusion

Bob Herz, FASB chairman, believes that there are three fundamental considerations the FASB must keep in mind in its standard-setting activities: (1) improvement in financial reporting, (2) simplification of the accounting literature and the standard-setting process, and (3) international convergence. These are notable objectives, and the Board is making good progress on all three dimensions. Issues such as off-balance-sheet financing, measurement of fair values, enhanced criteria for revenue recognition, and stock option accounting are examples of where the Board has exerted leadership. Improvements in financial reporting should follow.

Also, the Board is making it easier to understand what GAAP is. Presently GAAP is contained in a number of different documents. The lack of a single source makes it difficult to access and understand generally accepted principles. The Board is embarked on a long-term project ("the codification") that will compile GAAP in one document. This codification will organize existing GAAP by accounting topic regardless of its source (FASB Statements, APB Opinions, and so on). The codified standards will then be considered to be GAAP and to be authoritative, and all other literature will be considered non-authoritative.

Finally, international convergence is underway. Some projects already are completed and differences eliminated. Many more are on the drawing board. The crisis caused in the capital markets due to accounting irregularities of companies like **Enron, Krispy Kreme, Fannie Mae, Xerox**, and a host of others has caused the profession to reexamine its processes and standards. At present, we believe that the profession is reacting responsibly to remedy identified shortcomings.

SUMMARY OF LEARNING OBJECTIVES

1. Identify the major financial statements and other means of financial reporting. Companies most frequently provide (1) the balance sheet, (2) the income statement, (3) the statement of cash flows, and (4) the statement of owners' or stockholders' equity. Financial reporting other than financial statements may take various forms. Examples include the president's letter and supplementary schedules in the corporate annual report, prospectuses, reports filed with government agencies, news releases, management's forecasts, and descriptions of a company's social or environmental impact.

2. Explain how accounting assists in the efficient use of scarce resources. Accounting provides reliable, relevant, and timely information to managers, investors, and creditors to allow resource allocation to the most efficient enterprises. Accounting also provides measurements of efficiency (profitability) and financial soundness.

3. Describe some of the challenges facing accounting. Financial reports fail to provide (1) some key performance measures widely used by management, (2) forward-looking information needed by investors and creditors, (3) sufficient information on a company's soft assets (intangibles), and (4) real-time financial information.

4. Identify the objectives of financial reporting. The objectives of financial reporting are to provide information that is (1) useful in investment and credit decisions, (2) useful in assessing cash flow prospects, and (3) about enterprise resources, claims to those resources, and changes in them.

5. Explain the need for accounting standards. The accounting profession has attempted to develop a set of standards that is generally accepted and universally practiced. Without this set of standards, each company would have to develop its own standards. Readers of financial statements would have to familiarize themselves with every company's peculiar accounting and reporting practices. As a result, it would be almost impossible to prepare statements that could be compared.

6. Identify the major policy-setting bodies and their role in the standard-setting process. The *Securities and Exchange Commission (SEC)* is a federal agency that has the broad powers to prescribe, in whatever detail it desires, the accounting standards to be employed by companies that fall within its jurisdiction. The *American Institute of Certified Public Accountants (AICPA)* issued standards through its Committee on Accounting Procedure and Accounting Principles Board. The *Financial Accounting Standards Board (FASB)* establishes and improves standards of financial accounting and reporting for the guidance and education of the public.

7. Explain the meaning of generally accepted accounting principles. Generally accepted accounting principles (GAAP) are those principles that have substantial authoritative support, such as FASB Standards, Interpretations, and Staff Positions, APB Opinions and Interpretations, AICPA Accounting Research Bulletins, and other authoritative pronouncements.

8. Describe the impact of user groups on the standard-setting process. User groups may want particular economic events accounted for or reported in a particular way, and they fight hard to get what they want. They especially target the FASB to influence changes in the existing standards and the development of new ones. Because of the accelerated rate of change and the increased complexity of our economy, these pressures have been multiplying. Accounting standards are as much a product of political action as they are of careful logic or empirical findings. The IASB is working with U.S. standard setters toward international convergence of standards.

9. **Understand issues related to ethics and financial accounting.** Financial accountants are called on for moral discernment and ethical decision making. Decisions sometimes are difficult because a public consensus has not emerged to formulate a comprehensive ethical system that provides guidelines in making ethical judgments.

QUESTIONS

1. Differentiate broadly between financial accounting and managerial accounting.

2. Differentiate between "financial statements" and "financial reporting."

3. How does accounting help the capital allocation process?

4. What are some of the major challenges facing the accounting profession?

5. What are the major objectives of financial reporting?

6. Of what value is a common set of standards in financial accounting and reporting?

7. What is the likely limitation of "general-purpose financial statements"?

8. In what way is the Securities and Exchange Commission concerned about and supportive of accounting principles and standards?

9. What was the Committee on Accounting Procedure, and what were its accomplishments and failings?

10. For what purposes did the AICPA in 1959 create the Accounting Principles Board?

11. Distinguish among Accounting Research Bulletins, Opinions of the Accounting Principles Board, and Statements of the Financial Accounting Standards Board.

12. If you had to explain or define "generally accepted accounting principles or standards," what essential characteristics would you include in your explanation?

13. In what ways was it felt that the statements issued by the Financial Accounting Standards Board would carry greater weight than the opinions issued by the Accounting Principles Board?

14. How are FASB discussion memoranda and FASB exposure drafts related to FASB "statements"?

15. Distinguish between FASB "statements of financial accounting standards" and FASB "statements of financial accounting concepts."

16. What is Rule 203 of the Code of Professional Conduct?

17. Rank from the most authoritative to the least authoritative, the following three items: FASB Technical Bulletins, AICPA Practice Bulletins, and FASB Standards.

18. The chairman of the FASB at one time noted that "the flow of standards can only be slowed if (1) producers focus less on quarterly earnings per share and tax benefits and more on quality products, and (2) accountants and lawyers rely less on rules and law and more on professional judgment and conduct." Explain his comment.

19. What is the purpose of FASB Staff Positions?

20. Explain the role of the Emerging Issues Task Force in establishing generally accepted accounting principles.

21. What is the purpose of the Governmental Accounting Standards Board?

22. What are some possible reasons why another organization, such as the Governmental Accounting Standards Board, should not issue financial reporting standards?

23. What are the sources of pressure that change and influence the development of accounting principles and standards?

24. Some individuals have indicated that the FASB must be cognizant of the economic consequences of its pronouncements. What is meant by "economic consequences"? What dangers exist if politics play too much of a role in the development of financial reporting standards?

25. If you were given complete authority in the matter, how would you propose that accounting principles or standards should be developed and enforced?

26. One writer recently noted that 99.4 percent of all companies prepare statements that are in accordance with GAAP. Why then is there such concern about fraudulent financial reporting?

27. What is the "expectations gap"? What is the profession doing to try to close this gap?

28. The Sarbanes-Oxley Act was enacted to combat fraud and curb poor reporting practices. What are some key provisions of this legislation?

29. A number of foreign countries have reporting standards that differ from those in the United States. What are some of the main reasons why reporting standards are often different among countries?

30. Why would it be advantageous for U.S. GAAP and International GAAP to be the same?

31. How are financial accountants challenged in their work to make ethical decisions? Is technical mastery of GAAP not sufficient to the practice of financial accounting?

CONCEPTS FOR ANALYSIS

CA1-1 (Financial Accounting) Alan Rodriquez has recently completed his first year of studying accounting. His instructor for next semester has indicated that the primary focus will be the area of financial accounting.

Instructions
   (a) Differentiate between financial accounting and managerial accounting.
   (b) One part of financial accounting involves the preparation of financial statements. What are the financial statements most frequently provided?
   (c) What is the difference between financial statements and financial reporting?

CA1-2 (Objectives of Financial Reporting) Celia Cruz, a recent graduate of the local state university, is presently employed by a large manufacturing company. She has been asked by Angeles Ochoa, controller, to prepare the company's response to a current Discussion Memorandum published by the Financial Accounting Standards Board (FASB). Cruz knows that the FASB has issued seven *Statements of Financial Accounting Concepts,* and she believes that these concept statements could be used to support the company's response to the Discussion Memorandum. She has prepared a rough draft of the response citing *Statement of Financial Accounting Concepts No. 1,* "Objectives of Financial Reporting by Business Enterprises."

Instructions
   (a) Identify the three objectives of financial reporting as presented in *Statement of Financial Accounting Concepts No. 1 (SFAC No. 1).*
   (b) Describe the level of sophistication expected of the users of financial information by *SFAC No. 1.*
(CMA adapted)

CA1-3 (Accounting Numbers and the Environment) Hardly a day goes by without an article appearing on the crises affecting many of our financial institutions in the United States. It is estimated that the savings and loan (S&L) debacle of the 1980s, for example, ended up costing $500 billion ($2,000 for every man, woman, and child in the United States). Some argue that if the S&Ls had been required to report their investments at market value instead of cost, large losses would have been reported earlier, which would have signaled regulators to close those S&Ls and, therefore, minimize the losses to U.S. taxpayers.

Instructions
Explain how reported accounting numbers might affect an individual's perceptions and actions. Cite two examples.

CA1-4 (Need for Accounting Standards) Some argue that having various organizations establish accounting principles is wasteful and inefficient. Rather than mandating accounting standards, each company could voluntarily disclose the type of information it considered important. In addition, if an investor wants additional information, the investor could contact the company and pay to receive the additional information desired.

Instructions
Comment on the appropriateness of this viewpoint.

CA1-5 (AICPA's Role in Standard Setting) One of the major groups involved in the standard-setting process is the American Institute of Certified Public Accountants. Initially it was the primary organization that established accounting principles in the United States. Subsequently it relinquished most of its power to the FASB.

Instructions
   (a) Identify the two committees of the AICPA that established accounting principles prior to the establishment of the FASB.
   (b) Speculate as to why these two organizations failed. In your answer, identify steps the FASB has taken to avoid failure.
   (c) What is the present role of the AICPA in the standard-setting environment?

CA1-6 (FASB Role in Standard Setting) A press release announcing the appointment of the trustees of the new Financial Accounting Foundation stated that the Financial Accounting Standards Board (to be appointed by the trustees) ". . . will become the established authority for setting accounting principles under which corporations report to the shareholders and others" (AICPA news release July 20, 1972).

Instructions
   (a) Identify the sponsoring organization of the FASB and the process by which the FASB arrives at a decision and issues an accounting standard.

(b) Indicate the major types of pronouncements issued by the FASB and the purposes of each of these pronouncements.

CA1-7 (Government Role in Standard Setting) Recently an article stated "the setting of accounting standards in the United States is now about 70 years old. It is a unique process in our society, one that has undergone numerous changes over the years. The standards are established by a private sector entity that has no dominant sponsor and is not part of any professional organization or trade association. The governmental entity that provides oversight, on the other hand, is far more a friend than a competitor or an antagonist."

Instructions

Identify the governmental entity that provides oversight and indicate its role in the standard-setting process.

 CA1-8 (Politicization of Standard Setting) Some accountants have said that politicization in the development and acceptance of generally accepted accounting principles (i.e., standard setting) is taking place. Some use the term "politicization" in a narrow sense to mean the influence by governmental agencies, particularly the Securities and Exchange Commission, on the development of generally accepted accounting principles. Others use it more broadly to mean the compromise that results when the bodies responsible for developing generally accepted accounting principles are pressured by interest groups (SEC, American Accounting Association, businesses through their various organizations, Institute of Management Accountants, financial analysts, bankers, lawyers, and so on).

Instructions

(a) The Committee on Accounting Procedure of the AICPA was established in the mid- to late 1930s and functioned until 1959, at which time the Accounting Principles Board came into existence. In 1973, the Financial Accounting Standards Board was formed and the APB went out of existence. Do the reasons these groups were formed, their methods of operation while in existence, and the reasons for the demise of the first two indicate an increasing politicization (as the term is used in the broad sense) of accounting standard setting? Explain your answer by indicating how the CAP, the APB, and the FASB operated or operate. Cite specific developments that tend to support your answer.

(b) What arguments can be raised to support the "politicization" of accounting standard setting?

(c) What arguments can be raised against the "politicization" of accounting standard setting?

(CMA adapted)

CA1-9 (Models for Setting Accounting Standards) Presented below are three models for setting accounting standards.

1. The purely political approach, where national legislative action decrees accounting standards.
2. The private, professional approach, where financial accounting standards are set and enforced by private professional actions only.
3. The public/private mixed approach, where standards are basically set by private-sector bodies that behave as though they were public agencies and whose standards to a great extent are enforced through governmental agencies.

Instructions

(a) Which of these three models best describes standard setting in the United States? Comment on your answer.

(b) Why do companies, financial analysts, labor unions, industry trade associations, and others take such an active interest in standard setting?

(c) Cite an example of a group other than the FASB that attempts to establish accounting standards. Speculate as to why another group might wish to set its own standards.

CA1-10 (Standard-Setting Terminology) Andrew Wyeth, an administrator at a major university, recently said, "I've got some CDs in my IRA, which I set up to beat the IRS." As elsewhere, in the world of accounting and finance, it often helps to be fluent in abbreviations and acronyms.

Instructions

Presented below is a list of common accounting acronyms. Identify the term for which each acronym stands, and provide a brief definition of each term.

(a)	AICPA	**(e)**	FAF	**(i)**	CPA	**(m)**	GASB
(b)	CAP	**(f)**	FASAC	**(j)**	FASB		
(c)	ARB	**(g)**	SOP	**(k)**	SEC		
(d)	APB	**(h)**	GAAP	**(l)**	IASB		

CA1-11 (Accounting Organizations and Documents Issued) Presented below are a number of accounting organizations and types of documents they have issued.

Instructions

Match the appropriate document to the organization involved. Note that more than one document may be issued by the same organization. If no document is provided for an organization, write in "0."

Organization

1. _____ Accounting Standards Executive Committee
2. _____ Accounting Principles Board
3. _____ Committee on Accounting Procedure
4. _____ Financial Accounting Standards Board

Document

(a) Opinions
(b) Practice Bulletins
(c) Accounting Research Bulletins
(d) Financial Accounting Standards
(e) Statements of Position

CA1-12 (Accounting Pronouncements) Standard setting bodies have issued a number of authoritative pronouncements. A list is provided on the left, below, with a description of these pronouncements on the right.

Instructions

Match the description to the pronouncements.

1. _____ Staff Positions
2. _____ Interpretations (of the Financial Accounting Standards Board)
3. _____ Statement of Financial Accounting Standards
4. _____ EITF Statements
5. _____ Opinions
6. _____ Statement of Financial Accounting Concepts

(a) Official pronouncements of the APB.
(b) Sets forth fundamental objectives and concepts that will be used in developing future standards.
(c) Primary document of the FASB that establishes GAAP.
(d) Provides additional guidance on implementing or applying FASB Standards or Interpretations.
(e) Provides guidance on how to account for new and unusual financial transactions that have the potential for creating diversity in financial reporting practices.
(f) Represent extensions or modifications of existing standards.

CA1-13 (Issues Involving Standard Setting) When the FASB issues new standards, the implementation date is usually 12 months from date of issuance, with early implementation encouraged. Paula Popovich, controller, discusses with her financial vice president the need for early implementation of a standard that would result in a fairer presentation of the company's financial condition and earnings. When the financial vice president determines that early implementation of the standard will adversely affect the reported net income for the year, he discourages Popovich from implementing the standard until it is required.

Instructions

Answer the following questions.
(a) What, if any, is the ethical issue involved in this case?
(b) Is the financial vice president acting improperly or immorally?
(c) What does Popovich have to gain by advocacy of early implementation?
(d) Which stakeholders might be affected by the decision against early implementation?

(CMA adapted)

CA1-14 (Securities and Exchange Commission) The U.S. Securities and Exchange Commission (SEC) was created in 1934 and consists of five commissioners and a large professional staff. The SEC professional staff is organized into five divisions and several principal offices. The primary objective of the SEC is to support fair securities markets. The SEC also strives to foster enlightened stockholder participation in corporate decisions of publicly traded companies. The SEC has a significant presence in financial markets, the development of accounting practices, and corporation-shareholder relations, and has the power to exert influence on entities whose actions lie within the scope of its authority.

Instructions

(a) Explain from where the Securities and Exchange Commission receives its authority.
(b) Describe the official role of the Securities and Exchange Commission in the development of financial accounting theory and practices.

(c) Discuss the interrelationship between the Securities and Exchange Commission and the Financial Accounting Standards Board with respect to the development and establishment of financial accounting theory and practices.

(CMA adapted)

CA1-15 (Standard-Setting Process) In 1973, the responsibility for developing and issuing rules on accounting practices was given to the Financial Accounting Foundation and, in particular, to an arm of the foundation called the Financial Accounting Standards Board (FASB). The generally accepted accounting principles established by the FASB are enunciated through a publication series entitled *Statements of Financial Accounting Standards.* These statements are issued periodically, and over 150 have been issued. The statements have a significant influence on the way in which financial statements are prepared by U.S. corporations.

Instructions
(a) Describe the process by which a topic is selected or identified as appropriate for study by the Financial Accounting Standards Board (FASB).
(b) Once a topic is considered appropriate for consideration by the FASB, a series of steps is followed before a *Statement of Financial Accounting Standards* is issued. Describe the major steps in the process leading to the issuance of a standard.
(c) Identify at least three other organizations that influence the setting of generally accepted accounting principles (GAAP).

(CMA adapted)

CA1-16 (Financial Reporting Pressures) Presented below is abbreviated testimony from Troy Normand in the **WorldCom** case. He was a manager in the corporate reporting department and is one of five individuals who pleaded guilty. He is testifying in hopes of receiving no prison time when he is ultimately sentenced.

Q. Mr. Normand, if you could just describe for the jury how the meeting started and what was said during the meeting?

A. I can't recall exactly who initiated the discussion, but right away Scott Sullivan acknowledged that he was aware we had problems with the entries, David Myers had informed him, and we were considering resigning.

He said that he respected our concerns but that we weren't being asked to do anything that he believed was wrong. He mentioned that he acknowledged that the company had lost focus quite a bit due to the preparations for the Sprint merger, and that he was putting plans in place and projects in place to try to determine where the problems were, why the costs were so high.

He did say he believed that the initial statements that we produced, that the line costs in those statements could not have been as high as they were, that he believes something was wrong and there was no way that the costs were that high.

I informed him that I didn't believe the entry we were being asked to do was right, that I was scared, and I didn't want to put myself in a position of going to jail for him or the company. He responded that he didn't believe anything was wrong, nobody was going to be going to jail, but that if it later was found to be wrong, that he would be the person going to jail, not me.

He asked that I stay, don't jump off the plane, let him land it softly, that's basically how he put it. And he mentioned that he had a discussion with Bernie Ebbers asking Bernie to reduce projections going forward and that Bernie had refused.

Q. Mr. Normand, you said that Mr. Sullivan said something about don't jump out of the plane. What did you understand him to mean when he said that?

A. Not to quit.

Q. During this meeting, did Mr. Sullivan say anything about whether you would be asked to make entries like this in the future?

A. Yes, he made a comment that from that point going forward we wouldn't be asked to record any entries, high-level late adjustments, that the numbers would be the numbers.

Q. What did you understand that to be mean, the numbers would be the numbers?

A. That after the preliminary statements were issued, with the exception of any normal transaction, valid transaction, we wouldn't be asked to be recording any more late entries.

Q. I believe you testified that Mr. Sullivan said something about the line cost numbers not being accurate. Did he ask you to conduct any analysis to determine whether the line cost numbers were accurate?

A. No, he did not.

Q. Did anyone ever ask you to do that?

A. No.

Q. Did you ever conduct any such analysis?

A. No, I didn't.

Q. During this meeting, did Mr. Sullivan ever provide any accounting justification for the entry you were asked to make?
A. No, he did not.
Q. Did anything else happen during the meeting?
A. I don't recall anything else.
Q. How did you feel after this meeting?
A. Not much better actually. I left his office not convinced in any way that what we were asked to do was right. However, I did question myself to some degree after talking with him wondering whether I was making something more out of what was really there.

Instructions
Answer the following questions.
  (a) What appears to be the ethical issue involved in this case?
  (b) Is Troy Normand acting improperly or immorally?
  (c) What would you do if you were Troy Normand?
  (d) Who are the major stakeholders in this case?

CA1-17 **(Economic Consequences)** Presented below are comments made in the financial press.

Instructions
Prepare responses to the requirements in each item.
  (a) Rep. John Dingell, the ranking Democrat on the House Commerce Committee, threw his support behind the FASB's controversial derivatives accounting standard and encouraged the FASB to adopt the rule promptly. Indicate why a member of Congress might feel obligated to comment on this proposed FASB standard.
  (b) In a strongly worded letter to Senator Lauch Faircloth (R-NC) and House Banking Committee Chairman Jim Leach (R-IA), the American Institute of Certified Public Accountants (AICPA) cautioned against government intervention in the accounting standard-setting process, warning that it had the potential of jeopardizing U.S. capital markets. Explain how government intervention could possibly affect capital markets adversely.

 CA1-18 **(Standard-Setting Process, Economic Consequences)** The following letter was sent to the SEC and the FASB by leaders of the business community.

Dear Sirs:

The FASB has been struggling with accounting for derivatives and hedging for many years. The FASB has now developed, over the last few weeks, a new approach that it proposes to adopt as a final standard. We understand that the Board intends to adopt this new approach as a final standard without exposing it for public comment and debate, despite the evident complexity of the new approach, the speed with which it has been developed and the significant changes to the exposure draft since it was released more than one year ago. Instead, the Board plans to allow only a brief review by selected parties, limited to issues of operationality and clarity, and would exclude questions as to the merits of the proposed approach.

As the FASB itself has said throughout this process, its mission does not permit it to consider matters that go beyond accounting and reporting considerations. Accordingly, the FASB may not have adequately considered the wide range of concerns that have been expressed about the derivatives and hedging proposal, including concerns related to the potential impact on the capital markets, the weakening of companies' ability to manage risk, and the adverse control implications of implementing costly and complex new rules imposed at the same time as other major initiatives, including the Year 2000 issues and a single European currency. We believe that these crucial issues must be considered, if not by the FASB, then by the Securities and Exchange Commission, other regulatory agencies, or Congress.

We believe it is essential that the FASB solicit all comments in order to identify and address all material issues that may exist before issuing a final standard. We understand the desire to bring this process to a prompt conclusion, but the underlying issues are so important to this nation's businesses, the customers they serve and the economy as a whole that expediency cannot be the dominant consideration. As a result, we urge the FASB to expose its new proposal for public comment, following the established due process procedures that are essential to acceptance of its standards, and providing sufficient time to affected parties to understand and assess the new approach.

We also urge the SEC to study the comments received in order to assess the impact that these proposed rules may have on the capital markets, on companies' risk management practices, and on management and financial controls. These vital public policy matters deserve consideration as part of the Commission's oversight responsibilities.

We believe that these steps are essential if the FASB is to produce the best possible accounting standard while minimizing adverse economic effects and maintaining the competitiveness of U.S. businesses in the international marketplace.

Very truly yours,

(This letter was signed by the chairs of 22 of the largest U.S. companies.)

Instructions
Answer the following questions.

- **(a)** Explain the "due process" procedures followed by the FASB in developing a financial reporting standard.
- **(b)** What is meant by the term "economic consequences" in accounting standard setting?
- **(c)** What economic consequences arguments are used in this letter?
- **(d)** What do you believe is the main point of the letter?
- **(e)** Why do you believe a copy of this letter was sent by the business community to influential members of the United States Congress?

USING YOUR JUDGMENT

Financial Reporting Problem

Kate Jackson, a new staff accountant, is confused because of the complexities involving accounting standard setting. Specifically, she is confused by the number of bodies issuing financial reporting standards of one kind or another and the level of authoritative support that can be attached to these reporting standards. Kate decides that she must review the environment in which accounting standards are set, if she is to increase her understanding of the accounting profession.

Kate recalls that during her accounting education there was a chapter or two regarding the environment of financial accounting and the development of accounting standards. However, she remembers that her instructor placed little emphasis on these chapters.

Instructions
(a) Help Kate by identifying key organizations involved in accounting standard setting.

(b) Kate asks for guidance regarding authoritative support. Please assist her by explaining what is meant by authoritative support.

(c) Give Kate a historical overview of how standard setting has evolved so that she will not feel that she is the only one to be confused.

(d) What authority for compliance with GAAP has existed throughout the period of standard setting?

International Reporting Case

Michael Sharpe, former Deputy Chairman of the International Accounting Standards Committee (IASC), made the following comments to the 63rd Annual Conference of the Financial Executives Institute (FEI).

There is an irreversible movement towards the harmonization of financial reporting throughout the world. The international capital markets require an end to:

1   The confusion caused by international companies announcing different results depending on the set of accounting standards applied. Recent announcements by **Daimler-Benz** [now **DaimlerChrysler**] highlight the confusion that this causes.

2   Companies in some countries obtaining unfair commercial advantages from the use of particular national accounting standards.

3   The complications in negotiating commercial arrangements for international joint ventures caused by different accounting requirements.

4   The inefficiency of international companies having to understand and use a myriad of different accounting standards depending on the countries in which they operate and the countries in which they raise capital and debt. Executive talent is wasted on keeping up to date with numerous sets of accounting standards and the never-ending changes to them.

5   The inefficiency of investment managers, bankers, and financial analysts as they seek to compare financial reporting drawn up in accordance with different sets of accounting standards.

6 Failure of many stock exchanges and regulators to require companies subject to their jurisdiction to provide comparable, comprehensive, and transparent financial reporting frameworks giving international comparability.

Instructions

(a) What is the International Accounting Standards Board?

(b) What stakeholders might benefit from the use of International Accounting Standards?

(c) What do you believe are some of the major obstacles to harmonization?

Professional Research: Financial Accounting and Reporting

As a newly enrolled accounting major, you are anxious to better understand accounting institutions and sources of accounting literature. As a first step, you decide to explore the FASB's Statement of Financial Accounting Concepts No. 1 (CON 1).

Instructions

Using the **Financial Accounting Research System (FARS)**, respond to the following items. (Provide text strings used in your search.)

(a) Find *Statement of Financial Accounting Concepts No. 1*. List three ways to access it on FARS.

(b) According to CON 1, "…financial reporting includes not only financial statements but also other means of communicating information." What other means are there of communicating information?

(c) According to CON 1, "…many people base economic decisions on their relationships to and knowledge about business enterprises and thus are potentially interested in the information provided by financial reporting." Indicate some of the users and the information they are most directly concerned with in economic decision making.

Professional Simulation

In this simulation you are asked questions regarding accounting principles. Prepare response to all parts.

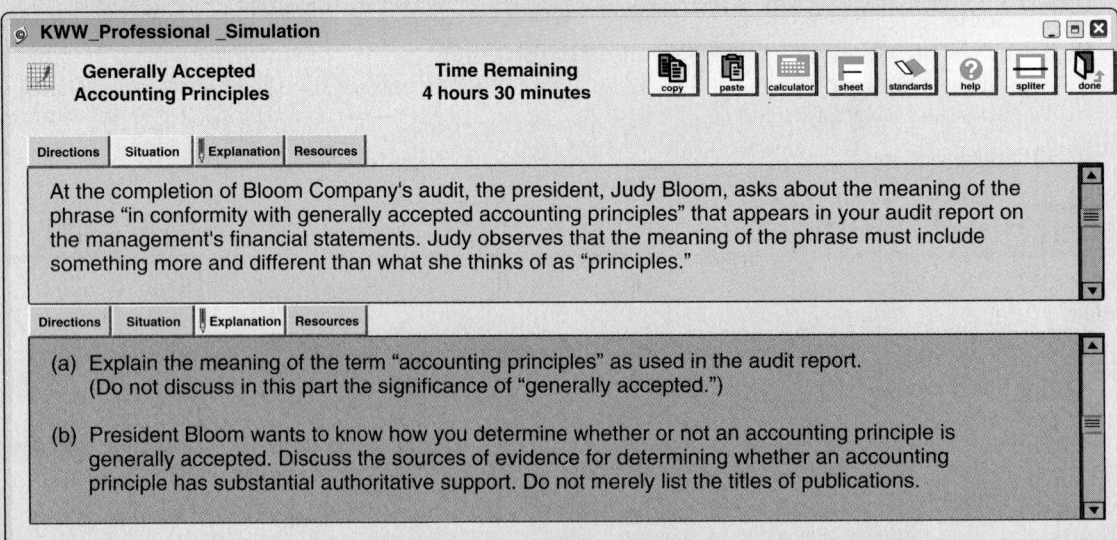

Remember to check the book's companion website to find additional resources for this chapter.

CONCEPTUAL FRAMEWORK UNDERLYING FINANCIAL ACCOUNTING

Show Me the Earnings!

The growth of new-economy business on the Internet has led to the development of new measures of performance. When **Priceline.com** splashed on the dot-com scene, it touted steady growth in a measure called "unique offers by users" to explain its heady stock price. To draw investors to its stock, **Drugstore.com** focused on the number of "unique customers" at its website. After all, new businesses call for new performance measures, right?

Not necessarily. In fact, these indicators failed to show any consistent relationship between profits and website visits. Eventually, as the graphs below show, the profits never materialized, and stock prices fell. The lesson here: Although the new economy may require some new measures, investors need to be careful not to forget the reliable traditional ones.[1]

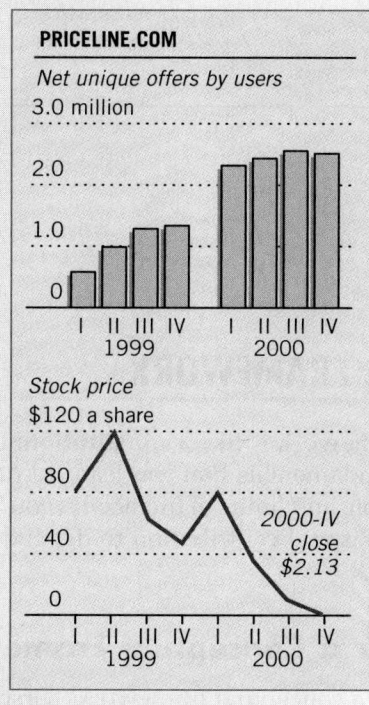

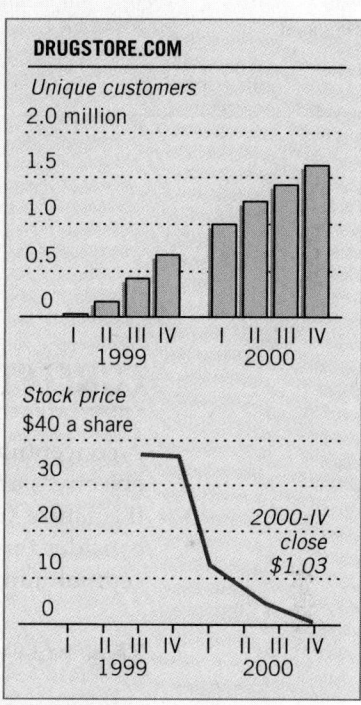

[1]Story and graphs adapted from Gretchen Morgenson, "How Did They Value Stocks? Count the Absurd Ways," *New York Times* (March 18, 2001), section 3, p. 1.

Learning Objectives

After studying this chapter, you should be able to:

1 Describe the usefulness of a conceptual framework.

2 Describe the FASB's efforts to construct a conceptual framework.

3 Understand the objectives of financial reporting.

4 Identify the qualitative characteristics of accounting information.

5 Define the basic elements of financial statements.

6 Describe the basic assumptions of accounting.

7 Explain the application of the basic principles of accounting.

8 Describe the impact that constraints have on reporting accounting information.

As our opening story indicates, users of financial statements need relevant and reliable information. To help develop this type of financial information, financial accounting and reporting relies on a conceptual framework. In this chapter, we discuss the basic concepts underlying the conceptual framework, as follows.

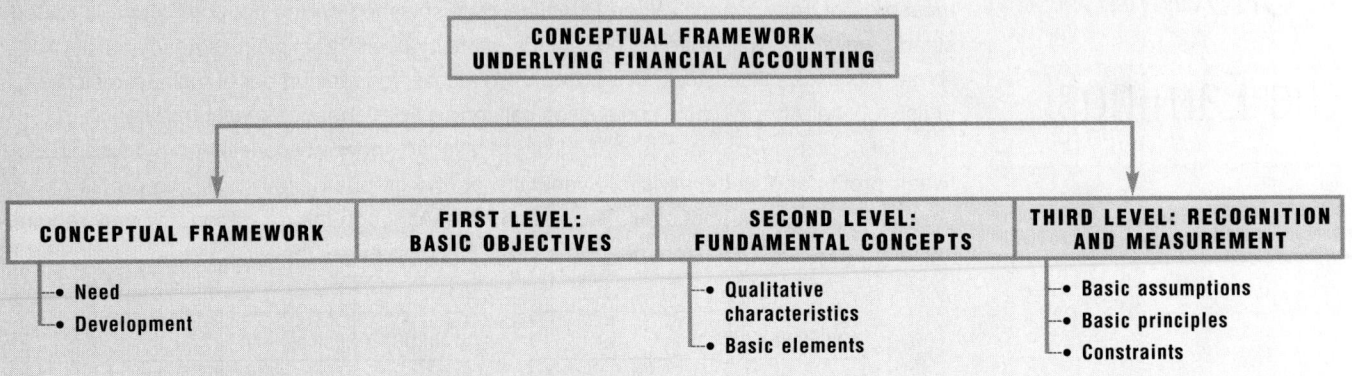

```
                    CONCEPTUAL FRAMEWORK
                 UNDERLYING FINANCIAL ACCOUNTING

CONCEPTUAL FRAMEWORK   FIRST LEVEL:      SECOND LEVEL:        THIRD LEVEL: RECOGNITION
                       BASIC OBJECTIVES  FUNDAMENTAL CONCEPTS AND MEASUREMENT

• Need                                   • Qualitative        • Basic assumptions
• Development                              characteristics    • Basic principles
                                         • Basic elements     • Constraints
```

CONCEPTUAL FRAMEWORK

A **conceptual framework** is like a **constitution**: It is "a coherent system of interrelated objectives and fundamentals that can lead to consistent standards and that prescribes the nature, function, and limits of financial accounting and financial statements."[2] Many consider the FASB's real contribution to depend on the quality and utility of the conceptual framework.

The Need for a Conceptual Framework

OBJECTIVE 1

Describe the usefulness of a conceptual framework.

Why do we need a conceptual framework? First, to be useful, standard setting should build on and relate to an established body of concepts and objectives. A soundly developed conceptual framework thus enables the FASB to issue more useful and consistent standards over time. **A coherent set of standards and rules should result.** The framework should increase financial statement users' understanding of and confidence in financial reporting. It should enhance comparability among companies' financial statements.

Second, the profession should be able to more quickly solve new and emerging **practical problems by referring to an existing framework of basic theory.** For example, **Sunshine Mining** (a silver-mining company) sold two issues of bonds. It can redeem them either with $1,000 in cash or with 50 ounces of silver, whichever is worth

---

[2] "Conceptual Framework for Financial Accounting and Reporting: Elements of Financial Statements and Their Measurement," *FASB Discussion Memorandum* (Stamford, Conn.: FASB, 1976), page 1 of the "Scope and Implications of the Conceptual Framework Project" section. For an excellent discussion of the functions of the conceptual framework, see Reed K. Storey and Sylvia Storey, Special Report, "The Framework of Financial Accounting and Concepts" (Norwalk, Conn.: FASB, 1998), pp. 85–88.

more at maturity. Both bond issues have a stated interest rate of 8.5 percent. At what amounts should Sunshine or the buyers of the bonds record them? What is the amount of the premium or discount on the bonds? And how should Sunshine amortize this amount, if the bond redemption payments are to be made in silver (the future value of which is unknown at the date of issuance?) Consider that Sunshine cannot know, at the date of issuance, the value of future silver bond redemption payments.

It is difficult, if not impossible, for the FASB to prescribe the proper accounting treatment quickly for situations like this. Practicing accountants, however, must resolve such problems on a daily basis. How? Though good judgment and with the help of a universally accepted conceptual framework, practitioners can quickly focus on an acceptable treatment.

WHAT'S YOUR PRINCIPLE?

WHAT DO THE NUMBERS MEAN?

The need for a conceptual framework is highlighted by recent accounting scandals such as those at **Enron, Healthsouth,** and other companies. To restore public confidence in the financial reporting process, Congress passed the Sarbanes-Oxley Act of 2002 ("SOX"). One of the provisions of SOX is a requirement for the Securities and Exchange Commission (SEC) to evaluate the usefulness of "principles-based" accounting standards relative to the current set of accounting standards (which many argue are too "rules-based").

Some have suggested a move toward principles-based standards because they believe that companies exploited the detailed provisions in rules-based standards to manage accounting reports, rather than report the economic substance of transactions. For example, many of the off-balance-sheet arrangements of Enron avoided transparent reporting by barely achieving 3 percent outside equity ownership, a requirement in an obscure accounting standard interpretation. Enron's financial engineers were able to structure transactions to achieve a desired accounting treatment, even if that accounting treatment did not reflect the transaction's true nature.

In 2003 the SEC issued a report recommending that accounting standard setters move away from a rules-based approach toward a more principles-based approach ("Study Pursuant to Section 108(d) . . ."). If the profession adopts this approach, accounting standards will be more conceptual in nature, and the financial reporting objective of each standard will be more clearly stated. Top management's financial reporting responsibility will shift from demonstrating compliance with rules to demonstrating that a company has attained financial reporting objectives.

Source: "Study Pursuant to Section 108(d) of the Sarbanes-Oxley Act of 2002 on the Adoption by the United States Financial Reporting System of a Principles-Based Accounting System," *www.sec.gov/news/studies/principlesbasedstand.htm.*

Development of a Conceptual Framework

Over the years, numerous organizations developed and published their own conceptual frameworks, but no single framework was universally accepted and relied on in practice. In 1976 the FASB began to develop a conceptual framework that would be a basis for setting accounting standards and for resolving financial reporting controversies. The FASB has since issued six Statements of Financial Accounting Concepts that relate to financial reporting for business exterprises.[3] They are as follows.

> **OBJECTIVE 2**
> Describe the FASB's efforts to construct a conceptual framework.

---

[3]The FASB also issued a Statement of Financial Accounting Concepts that relates to non-business organizations: "Objectives of Financial Reporting by Nonbusiness Organizations," *Statement of Financial Accounting Concepts No. 4* (December 1980).

INTERNATIONAL INSIGHT

The IASB has also issued a conceptual framework. The FASB and the IASB have agreed on a joint project to develop a common conceptual framework–one that converges and improves upon the existing frameworks of the two boards.

1 *SFAC No. 1*, "Objectives of Financial Reporting by Business Enterprises," presents the goals and purposes of accounting.

2 *SFAC No. 2*, "Qualitative Characteristics of Accounting Information," examines the characteristics that make accounting information useful.

3 *SFAC No. 3*, "Elements of Financial Statements of Business Enterprises," provides definitions of items in financial statements, such as assets, liabilities, revenues, and expenses.

4 *SFAC No. 5*, "Recognition and Measurement in Financial Statements of Business Enterprises," sets forth fundamental recognition and measurement criteria and guidance on what information should be formally incorporated into financial statements and when.

5 *SFAC No. 6*, "Elements of Financial Statements," replaces *SFAC No. 3* and expands its scope to include not-for-profit organizations.

6 *SFAC No. 7*, "Using Cash Flow Information and Present Value in Accounting Measurements," provides a framework for using expected future cash flows and present values as a basis for measurement.

Illustration 2-1 provides an overview of the conceptual framework.[4] The first level lists the **objectives**—that is, the goals and purposes of accounting. Ideally, accounting standards developed according to a conceptual framework will result in more useful accounting reports.

ILLUSTRATION 2-1
Conceptual Framework for Financial Reporting

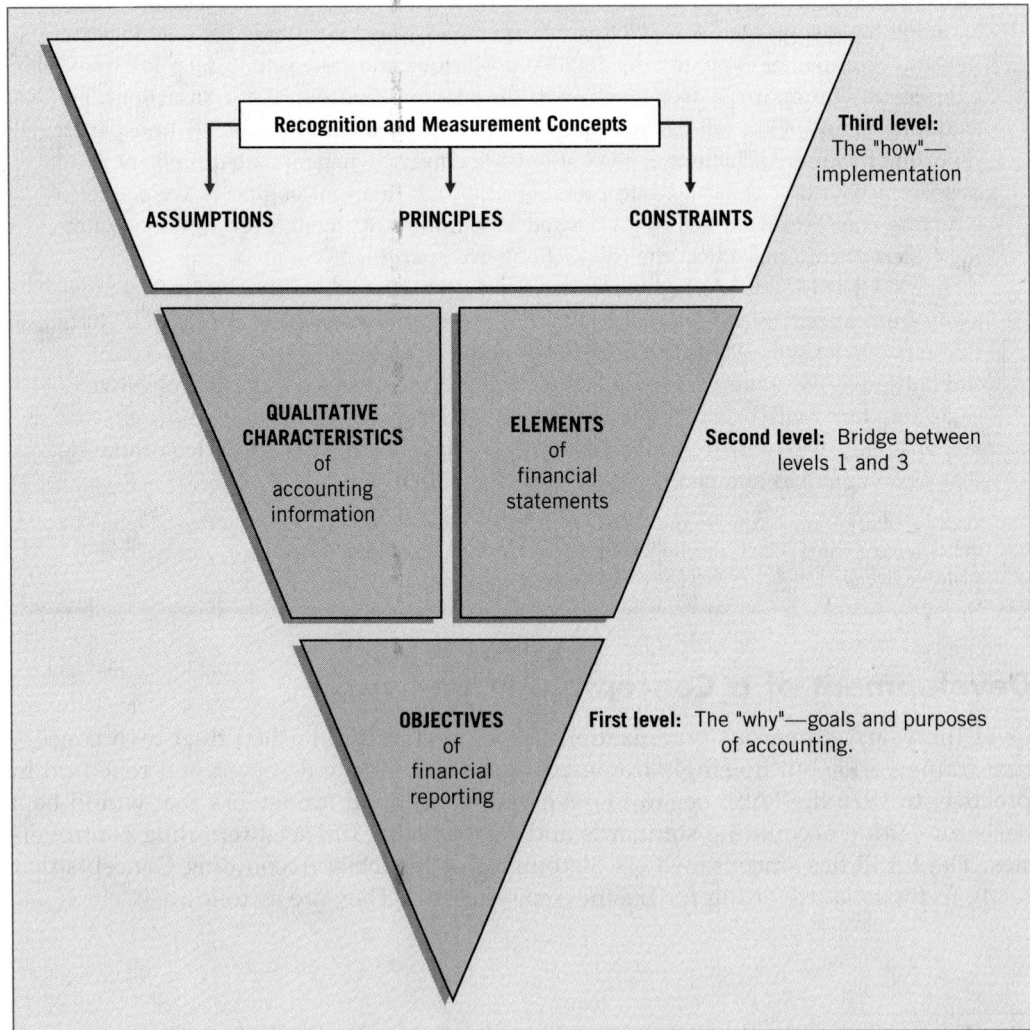

[4]Adapted from William C. Norby, *The Financial Analysts Journal* (March–April 1982), p. 22.

The second level provides the **qualitative characteristics** that make accounting information useful and the **elements** of financial statements (assets, liabilities, and so on). The third level identifies the **recognition and measurement concepts** used in establishing and applying accounting standards. These concepts include assumptions, principles, and constraints that describe the present reporting environment. We examine these three levels of the conceptual framework next.

FIRST LEVEL: BASIC OBJECTIVES

As we discussed in Chapter 1, the **objectives of financial reporting** are to provide information that is: (1) useful to those making investment and credit decisions, who have a reasonable understanding of business and economic activities; (2) helpful to present and potential investors, creditors, and other users in assessing the amounts, timing, and uncertainty of future cash flows; and (3) about economic resources, the claims to those resources, and the changes in them.

The objectives, therefore, broadly concern information that is useful to investor and creditor decisions. That concern narrows to the investors' and creditors' interest in receiving cash from their investments in, or loans to, business enterprises. Finally, the objectives focus on the financial statements, which provide information useful in assessing future cash flows. This approach is referred to as **decision usefulness**.

To provide information to decision makers, companies prepare general-purpose financial statements. These statements provide the most useful information possible at the least cost. However, users do need reasonable knowledge of business and financial accounting matters to understand the information contained in financial statements. This point is important. It means that financial statement preparers assume a level of competence on the part of users. This assumption impacts the way and the extent to which companies report information.

OBJECTIVE 3
Understand the objectives of financial reporting.

INTERNATIONAL INSIGHT

In Switzerland, Germany, Korea, and other nations, the primary providers of capital to companies are large banks. Creditors maintain very close ties to companies and can obtain information directly from them. Creditors do not need to rely on publicly available information, and financial information focuses on creditor protection. This process of capital allocation, however, is changing. It is likely that the need for publicly available information will change as well.

SECOND LEVEL: FUNDAMENTAL CONCEPTS

The objectives (first level) focus on the goals and purposes of accounting. Later, we will discuss the ways these goals and purposes are implemented (third level). What, then, is the purpose of the second level? The second level provides conceptual building blocks that explain the qualitative characteristics of accounting information and define the elements of financial statements. That is, the second level forms a bridge between the **why** of accounting (the objectives) and the **how** of accounting (recognition and measurement).

Qualitative Characteristics of Accounting Information

Should companies like **Walt Disney** or **Kellogg's** provide information in their financial statements on how much it costs them to acquire their assets (historical cost basis) or how much the assets are currently worth (fair-value basis)? Should **PepsiCo** combine and show as one company the four main segments of its business, or should it report PepsiCo Beverages, Frito Lay, Quaker Foods, and PepsiCo International as four separate segments?

How does a company choose an acceptable accounting method, the amount and types of information to disclose, and the format in which to present it? The answer: By determining **which alternative provides the most useful information for decision-making purposes (decision usefulness)**. The FASB identified the **qualitative characteristics** of accounting information that distinguish better (more useful) information from inferior (less useful) information for decision-making purposes.[5] In addition, the

OBJECTIVE 4
Identify the qualitative characteristics of accounting information.

---

[5]"Qualitative Characteristics of Accounting Information," *Statement of Financial Accounting Concepts No. 2* (Stamford, Conn.: FASB, May 1980).

FASB identified certain constraints (cost-benefit and materiality) as part of the conceptual framework (discussed later in the chapter). As Illustration 2-2 shows, the characteristics may be viewed as a hierarchy.

ILLUSTRATION 2-2
Hierarchy of Accounting
Qualities

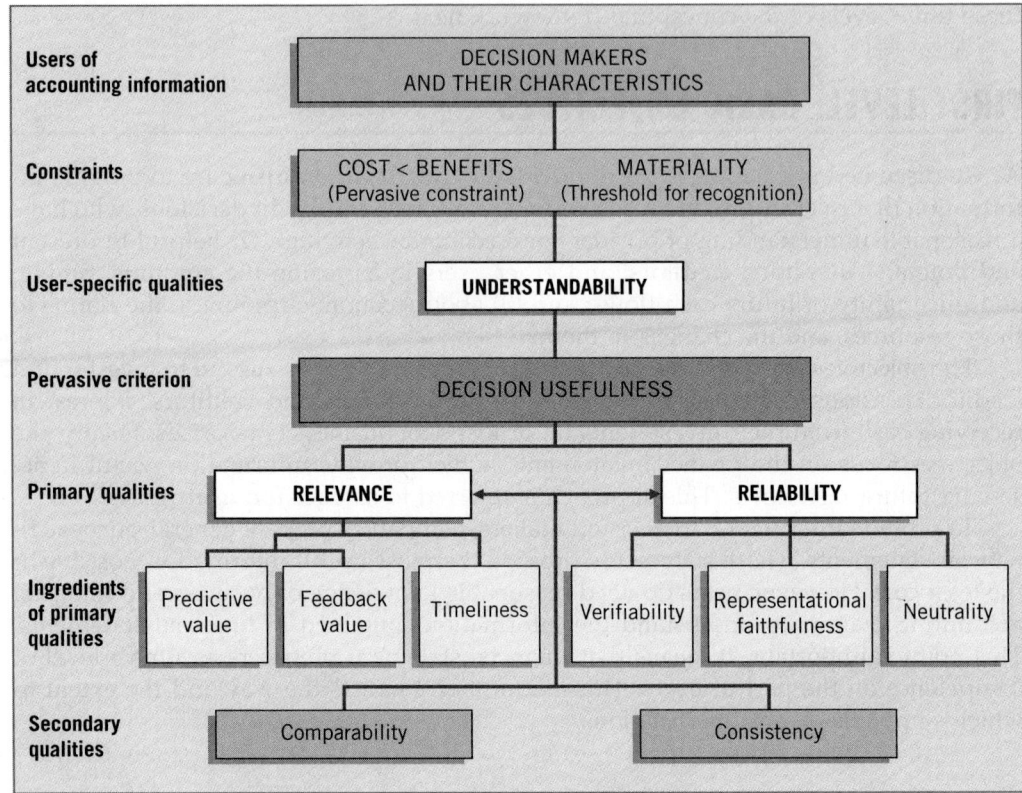

Decision Makers (Users) and Understandability

Decision makers vary widely in the types of decisions they make, how they make decisions, the information they already possess or can obtain from other sources, and their ability to process the information. For information to be useful, there must be a connection (linkage) between these users and the decisions they make. This link, **understandability**, is the quality of information that lets reasonably informed users see its significance.

For example, assume that **IBM Corp.** issues a three-months' report that shows interim earnings way down. This interim report provides relevant and reliable information for decision-making purposes. Now say that some users, upon reading the report, decide to sell their stock. Other users, however, do not understand the report's content and significance. They are surprised when IBM declares a smaller year-end dividend and the value of the stock declines. Thus, although IBM presented highly relevant and reliable information, it was useless to those who did not understand it.

Primary Qualities: Relevance and Reliability

Relevance and reliability are the two primary qualities that make accounting information useful for decision making. As stated in FASB *Concepts Statement No. 2*, "the qualities that distinguish 'better' (more useful) information from 'inferior' (less useful) information are primarily the qualities of relevance and reliability, with some other characteristics that those qualities imply."[6]

---

[6]Ibid., par. 15.

Relevance. To be relevant, accounting information must be capable of making a difference in a decision.[7] Information with no bearing on a decision is irrelevant. Relevant information helps users predict the ultimate outcome of past, present, and future events. That is, it has **predictive value**. Relevant information also helps users confirm or correct prior expectations; it has **feedback value**. For example, when **UPS (United Parcel Service)** issues an interim report, the information in it is relevant because it provides both a basis for forecasting annual earnings and feedback on past performance.

Finally, relevant information is available to decision makers before it loses its capacity to influence their decisions. It has **timeliness**. If UPS waited to report its interim results until six months after the end of the period, the information would be much less useful for decision-making purposes. **For information to be relevant, it needs predictive or feedback value, presented on a timely basis.**

Reliability. Accounting information is reliable to the extent that **it is verifiable, is a faithful representation, and is reasonably free of error and bias**. Reliability is a necessity, because most users have neither the time nor the expertise to evaluate the factual content of the information.

Verifiability occurs when independent measurers, using the same methods, obtain similar results. For example, would several independent auditors reach the same conclusion about a set of financial statements? If not, then the statements are not verifiable. Auditors could not render an opinion on such statements.

Representational faithfulness means that the numbers and descriptions match what really existed or happened. If **General Motors'** income statement reports sales of $225 billion when it had sales of $193.5 billion, then the statement fails to faithfully represent the proper sales amount.

Neutrality means that a company cannot select information to favor one set of interested parties over another. Unbiased information must be the overriding consideration. For example, in the notes to financial statements, tobacco companies such as **R. J. Reynolds** should not suppress information about the numerous lawsuits that have been filed because of tobacco-related health concerns—even though such disclosure is damaging to the company.

Neutrality in standard setting has come under increasing attack. Some argue that the FASB should not issue standards that cause undesirable economic effects on an industry or company. We disagree. Standards must be free from bias, or we will no longer have credible financial statements. Without credible financial statements, individuals will no longer use this information. An analogy demonstrates the point: In the United States, many individuals bet on boxing matches because such contests are assumed not to be fixed. But nobody bets on wrestling matches. Why? Because the public assumes that wrestling matches are rigged. If financial information is biased (rigged), the public will lose confidence and no longer use it.

Secondary Qualities: Comparability and Consistency

Information about a company is more useful if decision makers can compare it with similar information about another company and with similar information about the same company at other points in time. The first of these qualities is **comparability**, and the second is **consistency**.

Comparability. Information that is measured and reported in a similar manner for different companies is considered comparable. Comparability enables users to identify the real similarities and differences in economic events between companies.

For example, the accounting for pensions in the United States differs from that in Japan. In the United States, companies record pension cost as incurred. In Japan, companies record little or no charge to income for these costs. As a result, it is difficult to compare and evaluate the financial results of **General Motors** or **Ford** to Japanese competitors.

---

[7]Ibid., par. 47.

Also, resource allocation decisions involve evaluating alternatives. A valid evaluation can be made only if comparable information is available.

Consistency. When a company applies the same accounting treatment to similar events, from period to period, the company shows consistent use of accounting standards. The idea of consistency does not mean, however, that companies cannot switch from one accounting method to another. A company *can* change methods, but it must first demonstrate that the newly adopted method is preferable to the old. If approved, the company must then disclose the nature and effect of the accounting change, as well as the justification for it, in the financial statements for the period in which it made the change.[8] When a change in accounting principles occurs, the auditor refers to it in an explanatory paragraph of the audit report. This paragraph identifies the nature of the change and refers the reader to the note in the financial statements that discusses the change in detail.[9]

<table>
<tr><td align="right">**YOU MAY NEED A MAP**</td></tr>
</table>

WHAT DO THE NUMBERS MEAN?

Beyond touting nonfinancial measures to investors (see opening story), many companies increasingly promote the performance of their companies through the reporting of various "pro-forma" earnings measures. A recent survey of newswire reports found 36 instances of the reporting of pro-forma measures in just a three-day period.

Pro-forma measures are standard measures (such as earnings) that companies adjust, usually for one-time or nonrecurring items. For example, companies usually adjust earnings for the effects of an extraordinary item. Such adjustments make the numbers more comparable to numbers reported in periods without the unusual item.

However, rather than increasing comparability, it appears that some companies use pro-forma reporting to accentuate the positive in their results. Examples include **Yahoo Inc.** and **Cisco**, which define pro-forma income after adding back payroll tax expense. **Level 8 Systems** transformed an operating loss into a pro-forma profit by adding back expenses for depreciation and amortization of intangible assets.

Lynn Turner, former Chief Accountant at the SEC, calls such earnings measures EBS— "Everything but Bad Stuff." To provide investors a more complete picture of company profitability, not the story preferred by management, the SEC issued Regulation G (REG G). REG G requires companies to reconcile non-GAAP financial measures to GAAP, thereby giving investors a roadmap to analyze adjustments companies make to their GAAP numbers to arrive at pro-forma results.

Sources: Adapted from Gretchen Morgenson, "How Did They Value Stocks? Count the Absurd Ways," *New York Times* (March 18, 2001), section 3, p. 1; and Gretchen Morgenson, "Expert Advice: Focus on Profit," *New York Times* (March 18, 2001), section 3, p. 14. See also SEC Regulation G, "Conditions for Use of Non-GAAP Financial Measures, "Release No. 33–8176 (March 28, 2003).

Basic Elements

OBJECTIVE 5
Define the basic elements of financial statements.

An important aspect of developing any theoretical structure is the body of **basic elements** or definitions to be included in it. Accounting uses many terms with distinctive and specific meanings. These terms constitute the language of business or the jargon of accounting.

---

[8]Surveys indicate that users highly value consistency. They note that a change tends to destroy the comparability of data before and after the change. Some companies assist users to understand the pre- and post-change data. Generally, however, users say they lose the ability to analyze over time. It is hoped that the new standard on accounting changes will improve the comparability of the data before and after the change.

[9]"Reports on Audited Financial Statements," *Statement on Auditing Standards No. 58* (New York: AICPA, April 1988), par. 34.

One such term is **asset**. Is it merely something we own? Or is an asset something we have the right to use, as in the case of leased equipment? Or is it anything of value used by a company to generate revenues—in which case, should we also consider the managers of a company as an asset?

As this example illustrates, it seems necessary, therefore, to develop basic definitions for the elements of financial statements. *Concepts Statement No. 6* defines the ten interrelated elements that most directly relate to measuring the performance and financial status of a business enterprise. We list them here for review and information purposes; you need not memorize these definitions at this point. We will explain and examine each of these elements in more detail in subsequent chapters.

ELEMENTS OF FINANCIAL STATEMENTS

ASSETS. Probable future economic benefits obtained or controlled by a particular entity as a result of past transactions or events.

LIABILITIES. Probable future sacrifices of economic benefits arising from present obligations of a particular entity to transfer assets or provide services to other entities in the future as a result of past transactions or events.

EQUITY. Residual interest in the assets of an entity that remains after deducting its liabilities. In a business enterprise, the equity is the ownership interest.

INVESTMENTS BY OWNERS. Increases in net assets of a particular enterprise resulting from transfers to it from other entities of something of value to obtain or increase ownership interests (or equity) in it. Assets are most commonly received as investments by owners, but that which is received may also include services or satisfaction or conversion of liabilities of the enterprise.

DISTRIBUTIONS TO OWNERS. Decreases in net assets of a particular enterprise resulting from transferring assets, rendering services, or incurring liabilities by the enterprise to owners. Distributions to owners decrease ownership interests (or equity) in an enterprise.

COMPREHENSIVE INCOME. Change in equity (net assets) of an entity during a period from transactions and other events and circumstances from nonowner sources. It includes all changes in equity during a period except those resulting from investments by owners and distributions to owners.

REVENUES. Inflows or other enhancements of assets of an entity or settlement of its liabilities (or a combination of both) during a period from delivering or producing goods, rendering services, or other activities that constitute the entity's ongoing major or central operations.

EXPENSES. Outflows or other using up of assets or incurrences of liabilities (or a combination of both) during a period from delivering or producing goods, rendering services, or carrying out other activities that constitute the entity's ongoing major or central operations.

GAINS. Increases in equity (net assets) from peripheral or incidental transactions of an entity and from all other transactions and other events and circumstances affecting the entity during a period except those that result from revenues or investments by owners.

LOSSES. Decreases in equity (net assets) from peripheral or incidental transactions of an entity and from all other transactions and other events and circumstances affecting the entity during a period except those that result from expenses or distributions to owners.[10]

---

[10]"Elements of Financial Statements," *Statement of Financial Accounting Concepts No. 6* (Stamford, Conn.: FASB, December 1985), pp. ix and x.

The FASB classifies the elements into two distinct groups. The first group of three elements—assets, liabilities, and equity—describes amounts of resources and claims to resources at a **moment in time**. The other seven elements describe transactions, events, and circumstances that affect a company during a **period of time**. The first class, affected by elements of the second class, provides at any time the cumulative result of all changes. This interaction is referred to as "articulation." That is, key figures in one financial statement correspond to balances in another.

THIRD LEVEL: RECOGNITION AND MEASUREMENT CONCEPTS

The third level of the framework consists of concepts that implement the basic objectives of level one. These concepts explain how companies should recognize, measure, and report financial elements and events. The FASB sets forth most of these in its *Statement of Financial Accounting Concepts No. 5*, "Recognition and Measurement in Financial Statements of Business Enterprises." According to *SFAC No. 5*, to be recognized, an item (event or transaction) must meet the definition of an "element of financial statements" as defined in *SFAC No. 6* and must be measurable. Most aspects of current practice follow these recognition and measurement concepts.

The accounting profession continues to use the concepts in *SFAC No. 5* as operational guidelines. Here, we identify the concepts as basic assumptions, principles, and constraints. Not everyone uses this classification system, so focus your attention more on **understanding the concepts** than on how we classify and organize them. These concepts serve as guidelines in responding to controversial financial reporting issues.

Basic Assumptions

> **OBJECTIVE 6**
> **Describe the basic assumptions of accounting.**

Four basic assumptions underlie the financial accounting structure: (1) **economic entity**, (2) **going concern**, (3) **monetary unit**, and (4) **periodicity**. We'll look at each in turn.

Economic Entity Assumption

The economic entity assumption **means that economic activity can be identified with a particular unit of accountability.** In other words, a company keeps its activity separate and distinct from its owners and any other business unit. At the most basic level, the economic entity assumption dictates that **Panera Bread Company** record the company's financial activities separate from those of its owners and managers. Equally important, financial statement users need to be able to distinguish the activities and elements of different companies, such as **General Motors, Ford,** and **DaimlerChrysler.** If users could not distinguish the activities of different companies, how would they know which company financially outperformed the other?

The entity concept does not apply solely to the segregation of activities among competing companies, such as **Best Buy** and **Circuit City.** An individual, department, division, or an entire industry could be considered a separate entity if we choose to define it in this manner. Thus, **the entity concept does not necessarily refer to a legal entity.** A parent and its subsidiaries are separate **legal** entities, but merging their activities for accounting and reporting purposes does not violate the **economic entity** assumption.[11]

---

[11]The concept of the entity is changing. For example, defining the "outer edges" of companies is now harder. Public companies often consist of multiple public subsidiaries, each with joint ventures, licensing arrangements, and other affiliations. Increasingly, companies form and dissolve joint ventures or customer-supplier relationships in a matter of months or weeks. These "virtual companies" raise accounting issues about how to account for the entity. See Steven H. Wallman, "The Future of Accounting and Disclosure in an Evolving World: The Need for Dramatic Change," *Accounting Horizons* (September 1995).

WHOSE COMPANY IS IT?

The importance of the entity assumption is illustrated by scandals involving **W. R. Grace** and, more recently, **Adelphia**. In both cases, senior company employees entered into transactions that blurred the line between the employee's financial interests and those of the company. At Adelphia, among many other self-dealings, the company guaranteed over $2 billion of loans to the founding family. W. R. Grace used company funds to pay for an apartment and chef for the company chairman. As a result of these transactions, these insiders benefitted at the expense of shareholders. Additionally, the financial statements failed to disclose the transactions. Such disclosure would have allowed shareholders to sort out the impact of the employee transactions on company results.

WHAT DO THE NUMBERS MEAN?

Going Concern Assumption

Most accounting methods rely on the **going concern assumption—that the company will have a long life**. Despite numerous business failures, most companies have a fairly high continuance rate. As a rule, we expect companies to last long enough to fulfill their objectives and commitments.

This assumption has significant implications. The historical cost principle would be of limited usefulness if we assume eventual liquidation. Under a liquidation approach, for example, a company would better state asset values at net realizable value (sales price less costs of disposal) than at acquisition cost. **Depreciation and amortization policies are justifiable and appropriate only if we assume some permanence to the company.** If a company adopts the liquidation approach, the current/non-current classification of assets and liabilities loses much of its significance. Labeling anything a fixed or long-term asset would be difficult to justify. Indeed, listing liabilities on the basis of priority in liquidation would be more reasonable.

The going concern assumption applies in most business situations. **Only where liquidation appears imminent is the assumption inapplicable.** In these cases a total revaluation of assets and liabilities can provide information that closely approximates the company's net realizable value. You will learn more about accounting problems related to a company in liquidation in advanced accounting courses.

Monetary Unit Assumption

The **monetary unit assumption** means that money is the common denominator of economic activity and provides an appropriate basis for accounting measurement and analysis. That is, the monetary unit is the most effective means of expressing to interested parties changes in capital and exchanges of goods and services. **The monetary unit is relevant, simple, universally available, understandable, and useful.** Application of this assumption depends on the even more basic assumption that quantitative data are useful in communicating economic information and in making rational economic decisions.

In the United States, accounting ignores price-level changes (inflation and deflation) and assumes that the unit of measure—the dollar—remains reasonably stable. We therefore use the monetary unit assumption to justify adding 1980 dollars to 2007 dollars without any adjustment. The FASB in *SFAC No. 5* indicated that it expects the dollar, unadjusted for inflation or deflation, to continue to be used to measure items recognized in financial statements. Only if circumstances change dramatically (such as if the United States experiences high inflation similar to that in many South American countries) will the FASB again consider "inflation accounting."

INTERNATIONAL INSIGHT

Due to their experiences with persistent inflation, several South American countries produce "constant-currency" financial reports. Typically, companies in these countries use a general price-level index to adjust for the effects of inflation.

Accounting for Changing Prices

Periodicity Assumption

To measure the results of a company's activity accurately, we would need to wait until it liquidates. Decision makers, however, cannot wait that long for such information.

Users need to know a company's performance and economic status on a timely basis so that they can evaluate and compare firms, and take appropriate actions. Therefore, companies must report information periodically.

The **periodicity** (or **time period**) **assumption** implies that a company can divide its economic activities into artificial time periods. These time periods vary, but the most common are monthly, quarterly, and yearly.

The shorter the time period, the more difficult it is to determine the proper net income for the period. A month's results usually prove less reliable than a quarter's results, and a quarter's results are likely to be less reliable than a year's results. Investors desire and demand that a company quickly process and disseminate information. Yet the quicker a company releases the information, the more likely the information will include errors. **This phenomenon provides an interesting example of the trade-off between relevance and reliability in preparing financial data.**

The problem of defining the time period becomes more serious as product cycles shorten and products become obsolete more quickly. Many believe that, given technology advances, companies need to provide more online, real-time financial information to ensure the availability of relevant information.

Basic Principles of Accounting

OBJECTIVE 7
Explain the application of the basic principles of accounting.

We generally use four basic **principles of accounting** to record transactions: (1) historical cost, (2) revenue recognition, (3) matching, and (4) full disclosure. Again, we look at each in turn.

Historical Cost Principle

GAAP requires that companies account for and report most assets and liabilities on the basis of acquisition price. This is often referred to as the **historical cost principle**. Cost has an important advantage over other valuations: **it is reliable**. To illustrate this advantage, consider the problems if companies select current selling price instead. Companies might have difficulty establishing a value for unsold items. Every member of the accounting department might value the assets differently. Further, how often would it be necessary to establish sales value? All companies close their accounts at least annually. Some compute their net income every month. These companies would have to place a sales value on every asset each time they wished to determine income. Critics raise similar objections against current cost (replacement cost, present value of future cash flows) and any other basis of valuation **except historical cost**.

What about liabilities? Do companies account for them on a cost basis? Yes, they do. Companies issue liabilities, such as bonds, notes, and accounts payable, in exchange for assets, or perhaps services, for an agreed-upon price. **This price, established by the exchange transaction, is the "cost" of the liability.** A company uses this amount to record the liability in the accounts and report it in financial statements.

In general, users prefer historical cost because it provides them with a reliable benchmark for measuring historical trends. However, **fair value information** may be more useful for certain types of assets and liabilities and in certain industries. For example, companies report many financial instruments, including derivatives, at fair value, and inventories at lower of cost or market. Certain industries, such as brokerage houses and mutual funds, prepare their basic financial statements on a fair value basis.

At initial acquisition, historical cost equals fair value. In subsequent periods, as market and economic conditions change, historical cost and fair value often diverge. As a result, fair value measures or estimates often provide more relevant information about the expected future cash flows related to the asset or liability. For example, when long-lived assets decline in value, a fair value measure determines any impairment loss.

The FASB now appears to support greater use of fair value measurements in the financial statements. The Board believes that fair value information is more relevant to users than historical cost. Fair value measurement, it is argued, provides better insight into the value of a company's asset and liabilities (its financial position) and provides a better basis for assessing future cash flow prospects.

The FASB is developing a standard on "Fair Value Measurements," which provides guidance on how to measure fair value. This standard applies to both financial and nonfinancial assets that are measured at fair value. As a result, we should now have increased consistency and comparability when fair value measurements are used in the financial statements and related notes. Such consistency and comparability is very much needed in light of controversies using fair values at companies like **Enron** (valuation of energy contracts) and **J. P. Morgan** (valuation of its bond portfolio). In addition, this new standard clarifies and incorporates the guidance in *Concepts Statement 7*, "Using Cash Flow Information and Present Value in Accounting Measurements," for using present value techniques to estimate future cash flows, and it provides enhanced disclosure of fair value information.[12]

As we indicated above, we presently have a "mixed-attribute" system that permits the use of historical cost, fair value, and other valuation bases. Although the historical cost principle continues to be the primary basis for valuation, recording and reporting of fair value information is increasing.

Revenue Recognition Principle

A crucial question for many companies is when to recognize revenue. Revenue recognition generally occurs (1) when **realized** or **realizable** and (2) when **earned**. This approach has often been referred to as the **revenue recognition principle**.

A company **realizes** revenues when it exchanges products (goods or services), merchandise, or other assets for cash or claims to cash. Revenues are realizable when assets received or held are readily convertible into cash or claims to cash. Assets are readily convertible when they are salable or interchangeable in an active market at readily determinable prices without significant additional cost.

In addition to the first test (realized or realizable), a company delays recognition of revenues until earned. Revenues are considered **earned** when the company substantially accomplishes what it must do to be entitled to the benefits represented by the revenues.[13] Generally, an objective test, such as a sale, indicates the point at which a company recognizes revenue. The sale provides an objective and verifiable measure of revenue—the sales price. Any basis for revenue recognition short of actual sale opens the door to wide variations in practice. **Recognition at the time of sale provides a uniform and reasonable test.**

However, as Illustration 2-3 (page 40) shows, exceptions to the rule exist. We discuss these exceptions in the following sections.

During Production. A company can recognize revenue **before** it completes the job in certain long-term construction contracts. In this method, a company recognizes revenue periodically, based on the percentage of the job it has completed. Although technically a transfer of ownership has not occurred, the earning process is considered substantially completed at various stages of construction. If it is not possible to obtain dependable estimates of cost and progress, then a company delays revenue recognition until it completes the job.

At End of Production. At times, a company may recognize revenue **after completion of the production cycle but before the sale takes place**. This occurs if products or other assets are salable in an active market at readily determinable prices without significant

---

[12]"Fair Value Measurement," *Proposed Statement of Financial Accounting Standards* (Norwalk, Conn.: FASB, October 21, 2005).

[13]"Recognition and Measurement in Financial Statements of Business Enterprises," *Statement of Financial Accounting Concepts No. 5* (Stamford, Conn.: FASB, December 1984), par. 83(a) and (b).

ILLUSTRATION 2-3
Timing of Revenue
Recognition

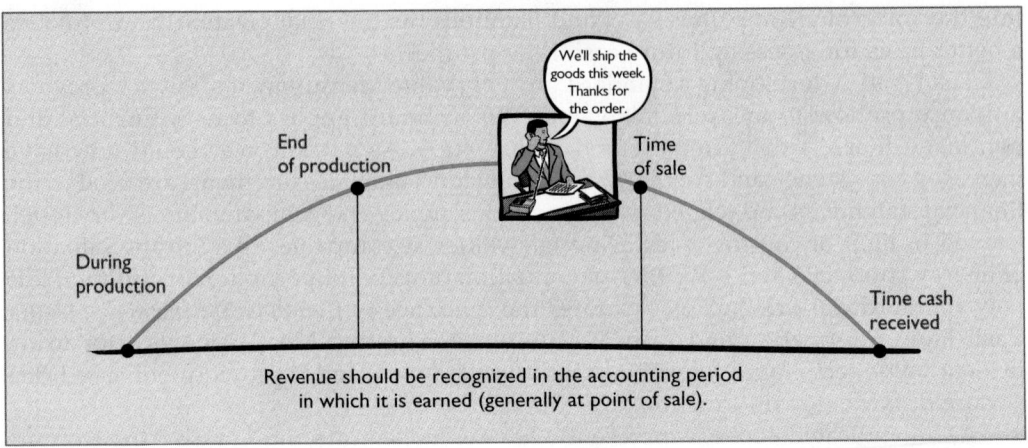

Revenue should be recognized in the accounting period
in which it is earned (generally at point of sale).

additional cost. An example is the mining of certain minerals. Once a company mines the mineral, a ready market at a quoted price exists. The same holds true for some agricultural products.

Upon Receipt of Cash. **Receipt of cash is another basis for revenue recognition.** Companies use the cash-basis approach only when collection is uncertain at the time of sale.

One form of the cash basis is the **installment-sales method**. Here, a company requires payment in periodic installments over a long period of time. Its most common use is in retail, such as for farm and home equipment and furnishings. Companies frequently justify the installment-sales method based on the high risk of not collecting an account receivable. In some instances, this reasoning may be valid. Generally, though, if a sale has been completed, the company should recognize the sale; if bad debts are expected, the company should record them as separate estimates.

To summarize, a company records revenue in the period when realized or realizable and when earned. Normally, this is the date of sale. But circumstances may dictate application of the percentage-of-completion approach, the end-of-production approach, or the receipt-of-cash approach.

---

*WHAT DO THE
NUMBERS MEAN?*

NO TAKE-BACKS!

Investors in **Lucent Technologies** got an unpleasant surprise when the SEC forced the company to restate its financial results. What happened? Lucent violated one of the fundamental criteria for revenue recognition—the "no take-back" rule. This rule holds that a company should not book revenue on inventory that it shipped if the customer can return it at some point in the future. In this particular case, Lucent agreed to take back shipped inventory from its distributors if they could not sell the items to their customers.

Lucent recorded the sales on the shipped goods, which helped it report continued sales growth. However, Lucent's distributors did indeed return many of those shipped goods. The restatement erased $679 million in revenues, turning an operating profit into a loss. In response, Lucent's stock price declined $1.31 per share or 8.5 percent. Lucent has since changed its policy. It now records inventory as sold only when the final customer buys the equipment, not when Lucent ships the inventory to the distributor.

The lesson for investors: Review a company's revenue recognition policy for indications that revenues may be overstated due to generous return provisions for inventory. And remember, no take-backs!

Source: Adapted from S. Young, "Lucent Slashes First Quarter Outlook, Erases Revenue from Latest Quarter," *Wall Street Journal Online Edition* (December 22, 2000).

Matching Principle

In recognizing expenses, the approach is "Let the expense follow the revenues." Companies recognize expenses not when they pay wages or make a product, but when the work (service) or the product actually contributes to revenue. Thus, companies tie expense recognition to revenue recognition. This practice is referred to as the **matching principle**, because it dictates that **efforts (expenses) be matched with accomplishment (revenues) whenever it is reasonable and practicable to do so**.

Some costs, however, are difficult to associate with revenue. As a result, some other approach must be developed. Often, companies use a "rational and systematic" allocation policy that will approximate the matching principle. This type of expense recognition involves assumptions about the benefits that a company receives as well as the cost associated with those benefits. For example, a company like **Intel** or **Motorola** allocates the cost of a long-lived asset over all of the accounting periods during which it uses the asset because the asset contributes to the generation of revenue throughout its useful life.

HOLLYWOOD ACCOUNTING

WHAT DO THE NUMBERS MEAN?

Hollywood accounting illustrates that the problem of expense recognition is as complex as that of revenue recognition. Following then-existing GAAP standards, major motion picture studios capitalized advertising and marketing costs, and then amortized these costs against revenues over the life of the film. As a result, many investors suggested that the studios overstated their profit numbers. Under a new GAAP standard, the studios must now amortize these costs over no more than three months. In many cases, the studios have to expense them immediately.

Similarly, the studios often allocated the costs related to abandoned projects to overhead, thus spreading them out over the lives of the successful projects. Not anymore. The studios must now expense these costs as incurred.

Here is a rough estimate of the amounts of capitalized advertising costs some major studios charged off in response to the change in GAAP.

Studio (Parent Company)	Capitalized Advertising (in millions)
Columbia Tri-Star (Sony)	$200
Paramount (Viacom)	200
20th Century Fox (News Corp)	150

The more conservative approach results from a stricter application of the definitions of assets and expenses. While many argue that advertising and marketing costs have future service potential, difficulty in reliably measuring these benefits suggests they are not assets. Therefore, a very short amortization period or immediate write-off is justified. Under these new guidelines, investors will have more reliable measures for assessing the performance of companies in this industry.

Companies charge some costs to the current period as expenses (or losses) simply because they cannot determine a connection with revenue. Examples of these types of costs are officers' salaries and other administrative expenses.

Costs are generally classified into two groups: **product costs** and **period costs**. **Product costs**, such as material, labor, and overhead, attach to the product. Companies carry these costs into future periods if they recognize the revenue from the product in subsequent periods. **Period costs**, such as officers' salaries and other administrative expenses, attach to the period. Companies charge off such costs in the immediate period, even though benefits associated with these costs may occur in the future. Why? Because companies cannot determine a direct relationship between period costs and revenue. Illustration 2-4 (page 42) summarizes these expense recognition procedures.

ILLUSTRATION 2-4
Expense Recognition

Type of Cost	Relationship	Recognition
Product costs: • Material • Labor • Overhead	Direct relationship between cost and revenue.	Recognize in period of revenue (matching).
Period costs: • Salaries • Administrative costs	No direct relationship between cost and revenue.	Expense as incurred.

As indicated in the discussion of Hollywood accounting, there is some debate about the conceptual validity of the matching principle. A major concern is that matching permits companies to defer certain costs and treat them as assets on the balance sheet. In fact, these costs may not have future benefits. If abused, this principle permits the balance sheet to become a "dumping ground" for unmatched costs. In addition, there appears to be no objective definition of "systematic and rational."

Full Disclosure Principle

In deciding what information to report, companies follow the general practice of providing information that is of sufficient importance to influence the judgment and decisions of an informed user. Often referred to as the **full disclosure principle**, it recognizes that the nature and amount of information included in financial reports reflects a series of judgmental trade-offs. These trade-offs strive for (1) sufficient detail to disclose matters that **make a difference** to users, yet (2) sufficient condensation to make the **information understandable**, keeping in mind costs of preparing and using it.

Users find information about financial position, income, cash flows, and investments in one of three places: (1) within the main body of financial statements, (2) in the notes to those statements, or (3) as supplementary information.

As discussed in Chapter 1, the **financial statements** are the balance sheet, income statement, statement of cash flows, and statement of owners' equity. They are a structured means of communicating financial information. To be recognized in the main body of financial statements, **an item should meet the definition of a basic element, be measurable with sufficient certainty, and be relevant and reliable.**[14]

Disclosure is not a substitute for proper accounting. As a former chief accountant of the SEC noted, "Good disclosure does not cure bad accounting any more than an adjective or adverb can be used without, or in place of, a noun or verb." Thus, for example, cash-basis accounting for cost of goods sold is misleading, even if a company discloses accrual-basis amounts in the notes to the financial statements.

The **notes to financial statements** generally amplify or explain the items presented in the main body of the statements. If the main body of the financial statements gives an incomplete picture of the performance and position of the company, the notes should provide the additional information needed. Information in the notes does not have to be quantifiable, nor does it need to qualify as an element. Notes can be partially or totally narrative. Examples of notes include descriptions of the accounting policies and methods used in measuring the elements reported in the statements, explanations of uncertainties and contingencies, and statistics and details too voluminous for inclusion in the statements. The notes can be essential to understanding the company's performance and position.

Supplementary information may include details or amounts that present a different perspective from that adopted in the financial statements. It may be quantifiable information that is high in relevance but low in reliability. For example, oil and gas companies typically provide information on proven reserves as well as the related discounted cash flows.

---

[14]*SFAC No. 5*, par. 63.

Supplementary information may also include management's explanation of the financial information and its discussion of the significance of that information. For example, many business combinations have produced financing arrangements that demand new accounting and reporting practices and principles. In each of these situations, the same problem must be faced: making sure the company presents enough information to ensure that the **reasonably prudent investor** will not be misled.

We discuss the content, arrangement, and display of financial statements, along with other facets of full disclosure, in Chapters 4, 5, and 24.

Constraints

In providing information with the qualitative characteristics that make it useful, companies must consider two overriding factors that limit (constrain) the reporting. These constraints are: (1) the **cost-benefit relationship** and (2) **materiality**. We also review two other less-dominant yet important constraints that are part of the reporting environment: **industry practices** and **conservatism**.

OBJECTIVE 8
Describe the impact that constraints have on reporting accounting information.

Cost-Benefit Relationship

Too often, users assume that information is free. But preparers and providers of accounting information know that it is not. Therefore, companies must consider the **cost-benefit relationship**: They must weigh the costs of providing the information against the benefits that can be derived from using it. Standard-setting bodies and governmental agencies use cost-benefit analysis before making final their informational requirements. In order to justify requiring a particular measurement or disclosure, the benefits perceived to be derived from it must exceed the costs perceived to be associated with it.

A corporate executive made the following remark to the FASB about a proposed standard: "In all my years in the financial arena, I have never seen such an absolutely ridiculous proposal. . . . To dignify these 'actuarial' estimates by recording them as assets and liabilities would be virtually unthinkable except for the fact that the FASB has done equally stupid things in the past. . . . For God's sake, use common sense just this once."[15] Although extreme, this remark indicates the frustration expressed by members of the business community about standard setting, and whether the benefits of a given standard exceed the costs.

The difficulty in cost-benefit analysis is that the costs and especially the benefits are not always evident or measurable. The costs are of several kinds: costs of collecting and processing, of disseminating, of auditing, of potential litigation, of disclosure to competitors, and of analysis and interpretation. Benefits to preparers may include greater management control and access to capital at a lower cost. Users may receive better information for allocation of resources, tax assessment, and rate regulation. As noted earlier, benefits are generally more difficult to quantify than are costs.

The recent implementation of the provisions of the Sarbanes-Oxley Act of 2002 illustrates the challenges in assessing costs and benefits of standards. One study estimated the increased costs of complying with the new internal-control standards related to the financial reporting process to be an average of $7.8 million per company. However, the study concluded that ". . .quantifying the benefits of improved more reliable financial reporting is not fully possible."[16]

Despite the difficulty in assessing the costs and benefits of its standards, the FASB attempts to determine that each proposed standard will fill a significant need and that the costs imposed to meet the standard are justified in relation to overall benefits of

---

[15]"Decision-Usefulness: The Overriding Objective," *FASB Viewpoints* (October 19, 1983), p. 4.

[16]Charles Rivers and Associates, "Sarbanes-Oxley Section 404: Costs and Remediation of Deficiencies" letter from Deloitte and Touche, Ernst and Young, KPMG, and Pricewaterhouse-Coopers to the SEC (April 11, 2005).

the resulting information. In addition, the Board seeks input on costs and benefits as part of its due process.[17]

Materiality

The materiality constraint concerns an item's impact on a company's overall financial operations. An item is *material* if its inclusion or omission would influence or change the judgment of a reasonable person.[18] It is *immaterial*, and therefore irrelevant, if it would have no impact on a decision maker. In short, **it must make a difference** or a company need not disclose it.

The point involved here is of **relative size and importance**. If the amount involved is significant when compared with the other revenues and expenses, assets and liabilities, or net income of the company, sound and acceptable standards should be followed in reporting it. If the amount is so small that it is unimportant when compared with other items, applying a particular standard may be considered of less importance.

It is difficult to provide firm guidelines in judging when a given item is or is not material. Materiality varies both with relative amount and with relative importance. For example, the two sets of numbers presented below illustrate relative size.

ILLUSTRATION 2-5
Materiality Comparison

	Company A	Company B
Sales	$10,000,000	$100,000
Costs and expenses	9,000,000	90,000
Income from operations	$ 1,000,000	$ 10,000
Unusual gain	$ 20,000	$ 5,000

During the period in question, the revenues and expenses, and therefore the net incomes of Company A and Company B, are proportional. Each reported an unusual gain. In looking at the abbreviated income figures for Company A, it appears insignificant whether the amount of the unusual gain is set out separately or merged with the regular operating income. The gain is only 2 percent of the net income. If merged, it would not seriously distort the net income figure. Company B has had an unusual gain of only $5,000. However, it is relatively much more significant than the larger gain realized by A. For Company B, an item of $5,000 amounts to 50 percent of its income from operations. Obviously, the inclusion of such an item in ordinary operating income would affect the amount of that income materially. Thus we see the importance of the **relative size** of an item in determining its materiality.

Companies and their auditors generally adopt the rule of thumb that anything under 5 percent of net income is considered immaterial. However, the SEC indicates that a company may use this percentage for an initial assessment of materiality, but it must also consider other factors.[19] For example, companies can no longer fail to record items in order to meet consensus analysts' earnings numbers, preserve a positive earnings trend, convert a loss to a profit or vice versa, increase management compensation, or hide an illegal transaction like a bribe. In other words, **companies must consider both quantitative and qualitative factors in determining whether an item is material.**

---

[17]For example, as part of its project on "Share-Based Payment," *SFAS No. 123R*, the Board conducted a field study and surveyed commercial software providers to collect information on the costs of measuring the fair values of share-based compensation arrangements.

[18]*SFAC No. 2*, par. 132, sets forth the essence of materiality: "The omission or misstatement of an item in a financial report is material if, in the light of surrounding circumstances, the magnitude of the item is such that it is probable that the judgment of a reasonable person relying upon the report would have been changed or influenced by the inclusion or correction of the item." The auditing profession also adopted this same concept of materiality. See "Audit Risk and Materiality in Conducting an Audit," *Statement on Auditing Standards No. 47* (New York: AICPA, 1983), par. 6.

[19]"Materiality," *SEC Staff Accounting Bulletin No. 99* (Washington, D.C.: SEC, 1999).

The SEC also indicated that in determining materiality, companies must consider each misstatement separately and the aggregate effect of all misstatements. For example, at one time, **General Dynamics** disclosed that its Resources Group improved its earnings by $5.8 million. At the same time, it disclosed that one of its other subsidiaries had taken write-offs of $6.7 million. Although both numbers exceeded the $2.5 million that General Dynamics as a whole earned for the year, the company disclosed neither as unusual because it considered the net effect on earnings as immaterial. **This practice is prohibited** because each item must be considered separately. In addition, even though an individual item may be immaterial, it may be considered material when added to other immaterial items. Companies must disclose such items.

Materiality factors in a great many internal accounting decisions, too. Examples of such judgments that companies must make include: the amount of classification required in a subsidiary expense ledger, the degree of accuracy required in prorating expenses among the departments of a company, and the extent to which adjustments should be made for accrued and deferred items. Only by **the exercise of good judgment and professional expertise** can reasonable and appropriate answers be found, which is the materiality constraint sensibly applied.

LIVING IN A MATERIAL WORLD

WHAT DO THE NUMBERS MEAN?

The first line of defense for many companies caught "cooking the books" had been to argue that a questionable accounting item is immaterial. That defense has not been working so well lately, in the wake of recent accounting meltdowns at **Enron** and **Global Crossing** and the tougher rules on materiality issued by the SEC (*SAB 99*).

For example, the SEC alleged in a case against **Sunbeam** that the company racked up so many immaterial adjustments that they added up to a material misstatement that misled investors about the company's financial position. More recently, the SEC called for a number of companies, such as **Jack in the Box, McDonalds**, and **AIG**, to restate prior financial statements for the effects of incorrect accounting. In some cases, the restatements did not meet traditional materiality thresholds. Don Nicholaisen, SEC Chief Accountant, observed that whether the amount is material or not-material, some transactions appear to be "flat out intended to mislead investors." In essence he is saying that any wrong accounting for a transaction can represent important information to the users of financial statements.

Responding to new concerns about materiality, blue-chip companies such as **IBM** and **General Electric** are providing expanded disclosures of transactions that used to fall below the materiality radar. As a result, some good may yet come from the recent accounting failures.

Source: Adapted from K. Brown and J. Weil, "A Lot More Information Is 'Material' After Enron," *Wall Street Journal Online Edition* (February 22, 2002); S. D. Jones and R. Gibson, "Restaurants Serve Up Restatements," *Wall Street Journal* (January 26, 2005), p. C3; and R. McTauge, "Nicholaisen Says Restatement Needed When Deal Lacks Business Purpose," *Securities Regulation & Law Reporter* (May 9, 2005).

Industry Practices

Another practical consideration is **industry practices**. **The peculiar nature of some industries and business concerns** sometimes requires departure from basic theory. For example, public-utility companies report noncurrent assets first on the balance sheet to highlight the industry's capital-intensive nature. Agricultural companies often report crops at market value because it is costly to develop accurate cost figures on individual crops.

Such variations from basic theory are infrequent, yet they do exist. Whenever we find what appears to be a violation of basic accounting theory, we should determine whether some peculiarity of the industry explains the violation before we criticize the procedures followed.

Conservatism

Few conventions in accounting are as misunderstood as the constraint of conservatism. Conservatism means **when in doubt, choose the solution that will be least likely to overstate assets and income**. Note that the conservatism convention does not urge that net assets or net income be *understated*. Unfortunately, some interpret conservatism to mean just that.

All that conservatism does, properly applied, is provide a reasonable guide in difficult situations: Refrain from overstatement of net income and net assets. Examples of conservatism in accounting are the use of the lower-of-cost-or-market approach in valuing inventories, and the rule that companies recognize accrued net losses on firm purchase commitments for goods for inventory. When in doubt, it is better to understate than overstate net income and net assets. Of course, if no doubt exists, there is no need to apply this constraint.

Summary of the Structure

Illustration 2-6 presents the conceptual framework discussed in this chapter. It is similar to Illustration 2-1, except that it provides additional information for each level. We cannot overemphasize the usefulness of this conceptual framework in helping to understand many of the problem areas that we examine in later chapters.

ILLUSTRATION 2-6
Conceptual Framework
for Financial Reporting

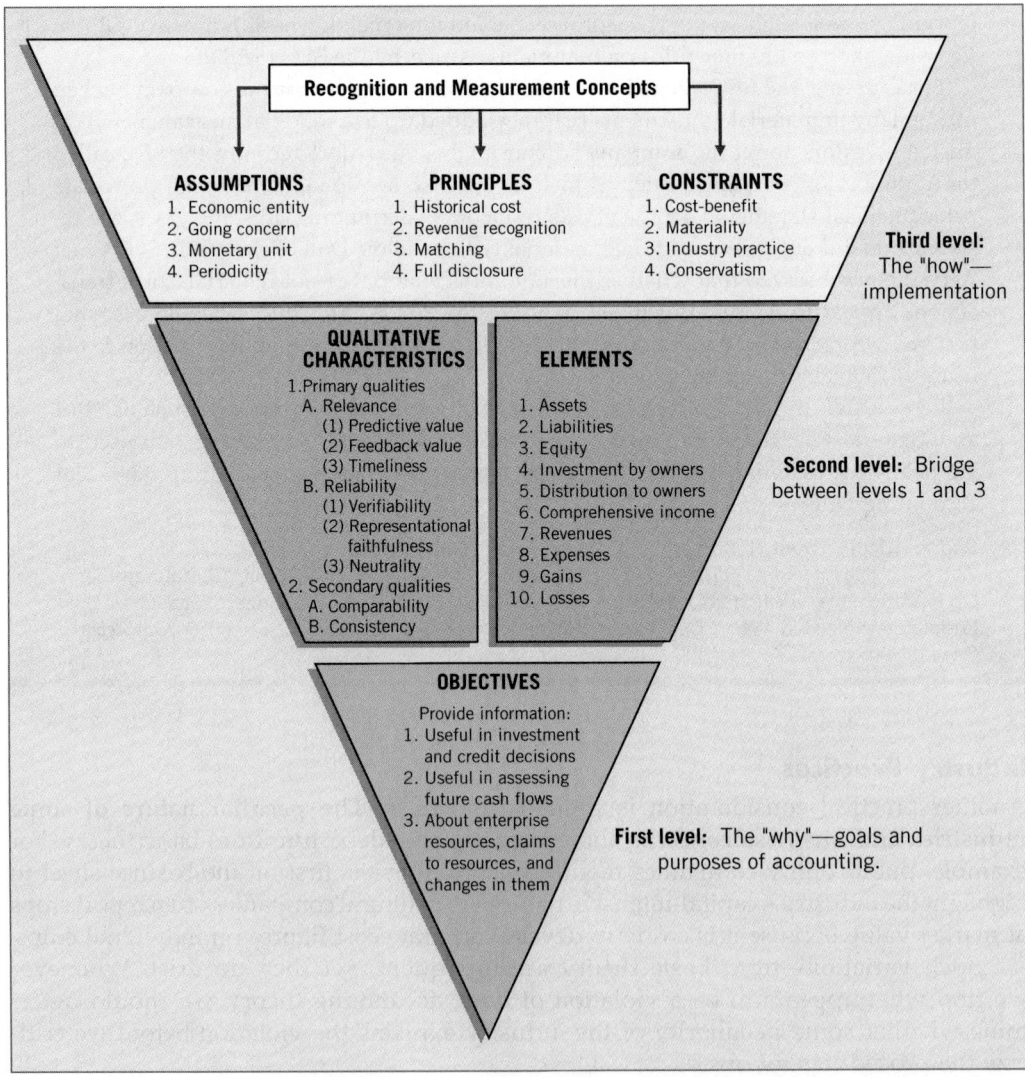

SUMMARY OF LEARNING OBJECTIVES

1. Describe the usefulness of a conceptual framework. The accounting profession needs a conceptual framework to: (1) build on and relate to an established body of concepts and objectives, (2) provide a framework for solving new and emerging practical problems, (3) increase financial statement users' understanding of and confidence in financial reporting, and (4) enhance comparability among companies' financial statements.

2. Describe the FASB's efforts to construct a conceptual framework. The FASB issued six Statements of Financial Accounting Concepts that relate to financial reporting for business enterprises. These concept statements provide the basis for the conceptual framework. They include objectives, qualitative characteristics, and elements. In addition, measurement and recognition concepts are developed.

3. Understand the objectives of financial reporting. Financial reporting should provide information that is: (1) useful to those making investment and credit decisions who have a reasonable understanding of business activities; (2) helpful to present and potential investors, creditors, and others in assessing future cash flows; and (3) about economic resources and the claims to and changes in them.

4. Identify the qualitative characteristics of accounting information. The overriding criterion by which accounting choices can be judged is decision usefulness—that is, providing information that is most useful for decision making. Relevance and reliability are the two primary qualities. Comparability and consistency are the secondary qualities, that make accounting information useful for decision making.

5. Define the basic elements of financial statements. The basic elements of financial statements are: (1) assets, (2) liabilities, (3) equity, (4) investments by owners, (5) distributions to owners, (6) comprehensive income, (7) revenues, (8) expenses, (9) gains, and (10) losses. We define these ten elements on page 35.

6. Describe the basic assumptions of accounting. Four basic assumptions underlying financial accounting are: (1) *Economic entity:* The activity of a company can be kept separate and distinct from its owners and any other business unit. (2) *Going concern:* The company will have a long life. (3) *Monetary unit:* Money is the common denominator by which economic activity is conducted, and the monetary unit provides an appropriate basis for measurement and analysis. (4) *Periodicity:* The economic activities of a company can be divided into artificial time periods.

7. Explain the application of the basic principles of accounting. (1) *Historical cost principle:* Existing GAAP requires that companies account for and report most assets and liabilities on the basis of acquisition price. (2) *Revenue recognition:* A company generally recognizes revenue when (a) realized or realizable and (b) earned. (3) *Matching principle:* A company recognizes expenses when the work (service) or the product actually makes its contribution to revenue. (4) *Full disclosure principle:* Companies generally provide information that is of sufficient importance to influence the judgment and decisions of an informed user.

8. Describe the impact that constraints have on reporting accounting information. The constraints and their impact are: (1) *Cost-benefit relationship:* The cost of providing the information must be weighed against the benefits that can be derived from using the information. (2) *Materiality:* Sound and acceptable standards should be followed if the amount involved is significant when compared with the other revenues and expenses, assets and liabilities, or net income of the company. (3) *Industry practices:* Follow the general practices in the company's industry, which sometimes requires departure from basic theory. (4) *Conservatism:* When in doubt, choose the solution that will be least likely to overstate net assets and net income.

KEY TERMS

assumption, *36*
comparability, *33*
conceptual framework, *28*
conservatism, *46*
consistency, *33*
constraints, *43*
cost-benefit relationship, *43*
decision usefulness, *31*
earned (revenue), *39*
economic entity assumption, *36*
elements, basic, *34*
feedback value, *33*
full disclosure principle, *42*
going concern assumption, *37*
historical cost principle, *38*
industry practices, *45*
matching principle, *41*
materiality, *44*
monetary unit assumption, *37*
neutrality, *33*
notes to financial statements, *42*
objectives of financial reporting, *31*
period costs, *41*
periodicity (time period) assumption, *38*
predictive value, *33*
principles of accounting, *38*
product costs, *41*
qualitative characteristics, *31*
realizable (revenue), *39*
realized (revenue), *39*
relevance, *32*
reliability, *32*
representational faithfulness, *33*
revenue recognition principle, *39*
supplementary information, *42*
timeliness, *33*
understandability, *32*
verifiability, *33*

QUESTIONS

1. What is a conceptual framework? Why is a conceptual framework necessary in financial accounting?

2. What are the primary objectives of financial reporting as indicated in *Statement of Financial Accounting Concepts No. 1?*

3. What is meant by the term "qualitative characteristics of accounting information"?

4. Briefly describe the two primary qualities of useful accounting information.

5. According to the FASB conceptual framework, the objectives of financial reporting for business enterprises are based on the needs of the users of financial statements. Explain the level of sophistication that the Board assumes about the users of financial statements.

6. What is the distinction between comparability and consistency?

7. Why is it necessary to develop a definitional framework for the basic elements of accounting?

8. Expenses, losses, and distributions to owners are all decreases in net assets. What are the distinctions among them?

9. Revenues, gains, and investments by owners are all increases in net assets. What are the distinctions among them?

10. What are the four basic assumptions that underlie the financial accounting structure?

11. The life of a business is divided into specific time periods, usually a year, to measure results of operations for each such time period and to portray financial conditions at the end of each period.

    (a) This practice is based on the accounting assumption that the life of the business consists of a series of time periods and that it is possible to measure accurately the results of operations for each period. Comment on the validity and necessity of this assumption.

    (b) What has been the effect of this practice on accounting? What is its relation to the accrual system? What influence has it had on accounting entries and methodology?

12. What is the basic accounting problem created by the monetary unit assumption when there is significant inflation? What appears to be the FASB position on a stable monetary unit?

13. The chairman of the board of directors of the company for which you are chief accountant has told you that he has little use for accounting figures based on cost. He believes that replacement values are of far more significance to the board of directors than "out-of-date costs." Present some arguments to convince him that accounting data should still be based on cost.

14. When is revenue generally recognized? Why has that date been chosen as the point at which to recognize the revenue resulting from the entire producing and selling process?

15. Magnus Eatery operates a catering service specializing in business luncheons for large corporations. Magnus requires customers to place their orders 2 weeks in advance of the scheduled events. Magnus bills its customers on the tenth day of the month following the date of service and requires that payment be made within 30 days of the billing date. Conceptually, when should Magnus recognize revenue related to its catering service?

16. What is the difference between realized and realizable? Give an example of where the concept of realizable is used to recognize revenue.

17. What is the justification for the following deviations from recognizing revenue at the time of sale?

    (a) Installment sales method of recognizing revenue.

    (b) Recognition of revenue at completion of production for certain agricultural products.

    (c) The percentage-of-completion basis in long-term construction contracts.

18. Jane Hull Company paid $135,000 for a machine in 2007. The Accumulated Depreciation account has a balance of $46,500 at the present time. The company could sell the machine today for $150,000. The company president believes that the company has a "right to this gain." What does the president mean by this statement? Do you agree?

19. Three expense recognition methods (associating cause and effect, systematic and rational allocation, and immediate recognition) were discussed in the text under the matching principle. Indicate the basic nature of each of these types of expenses and give two examples of each.

20. *Statement of Financial Accounting Concepts No. 5* identifies four characteristics that an item must have before it is recognized in the financial statements. What are these four characteristics?

21. Briefly describe the types of information concerning financial position, income, and cash flows that might be provided: (a) within the main body of the financial statements, (b) in the notes to the financial statements, or (c) as supplementary information.

22. In January 2008, Alan Jackson Inc. doubled the amount of its outstanding stock by selling on the market an additional 10,000 shares to finance an expansion of the business. You propose that this information be shown by a footnote on the balance sheet as of December 31, 2007. The president objects, claiming that this sale took place after December 31, 2007, and, therefore, should not be shown. Explain your position.

23. Describe the two major constraints inherent in the presentation of accounting information.

24. What are some of the costs of providing accounting information? What are some of the benefits of accounting information? Describe the cost-benefit factors that should be considered when new accounting standards are being proposed.

25. How are materiality (and immateriality) related to the proper presentation of financial statements? What factors and measures should be considered in assessing the materiality of a misstatement in the presentation of a financial statement?

26. The treasurer of Joan Osborne Co. has heard that conservatism is a doctrine that is followed in accounting and, therefore, proposes that several policies be followed that are conservative in nature. State your opinion with respect to each of the policies listed below.

(a) The company gives a 2-year warranty to its customers on all products sold. The estimated warranty costs incurred from this year's sales should be entered as an expense this year instead of an expense in the period in the future when the warranty is made good.

(b) When sales are made on account, there is always uncertainty about whether the accounts are collectible. Therefore, the treasurer recommends recording the sale when the cash is received from the customers.

(c) A personal liability lawsuit is pending against the company. The treasurer believes there is an even chance that the company will lose the suit and have to pay damages of $200,000 to $300,000. The treasurer recommends that a loss be recorded and a liability created in the amount of $300,000.

(d) The inventory should be valued at "cost or market, whichever is lower" because the losses from price declines should be recognized in the accounts in the period in which the price decline takes place.

BRIEF EXERCISES

(LO 4) **BE2-1** Discuss whether the changes described in each of the cases below require recognition in the CPA's audit report as to consistency. (Assume that the amounts are material.)

(a) The company changed its inventory method to FIFO from weighted-average, which had been used in prior years.

(b) The company disposed of one of the two subsidiaries that had been included in its consolidated statements for prior years.

(c) The estimated remaining useful life of plant property was reduced because of obsolescence.

(d) The company is using an inventory valuation method that is different from those used by all other companies in its industry.

(LO 4) **BE2-2** Identify which qualitative characteristic of accounting information is best described in each item below. (Do not use relevance and reliability.)

(a) The annual reports of **Best Buy Co.** are audited by certified public accountants.

(b) **Black & Decker** and **Cannondale Corporation** both use the FIFO cost flow assumption.

(c) **Starbucks Corporation** has used straight-line depreciation since it began operations.

(d) **Motorola** issues its quarterly reports immediately after each quarter ends.

(LO 5) **BE2-3** For each item below, indicate to which category of elements of financial statements it belongs.

(a) Retained earnings   **(e)** Depreciation   **(h)** Dividends

(b) Sales   **(f)** Loss on sale of equipment   **(i)** Gain on sale of investment

(c) Additional paid-in capital   **(g)** Interest payable   **(j)** Issuance of common stock

(d) Inventory

(LO 6) **BE2-4** Identify which basic assumption of accounting is best described in each item below.

(a) The economic activities of **FedEx Corporation** are divided into 12-month periods for the purpose of issuing annual reports.

(b) **Solectron Corporation, Inc.** does not adjust amounts in its financial statements for the effects of inflation.

(c) **Walgreen Co.** reports current and noncurrent classifications in its balance sheet.

(d) The economic activities of **General Electric** and its subsidiaries are merged for accounting and reporting purposes.

(LO 7) **BE2-5** Identify which basic principle of accounting is best described in each item below.

    (a) **Norfolk Southern Corporation** reports revenue in its income statement when it is earned instead of when the cash is collected.

    (b) **Yahoo, Inc.** recognizes depreciation expense for a machine over the 2-year period during which that machine helps the company earn revenue.

    (c) **Oracle Corporation** reports information about pending lawsuits in the notes to its financial statements.

    (d) **Eastman Kodak Company** reports land on its balance sheet at the amount paid to acquire it, even though the estimated fair market value is greater.

(LO 8) **BE2-6** What accounting constraints are illustrated by the items below?

    (a) Zip's Farms, Inc. reports agricultural crops on its balance sheet at market value.

    (b) Crimson Tide Corporation does not accrue a contingent lawsuit gain of $650,000.

    (c) Wildcat Company does not disclose any information in the notes to the financial statements unless the value of the information to financial statement users exceeds the expense of gathering it.

    (d) Sun Devil Corporation expenses the cost of wastebaskets in the year they are acquired.

(LO 8) **BE2-7** Presented below are three different transactions related to materiality. Explain whether you would classify these transactions as material.

    (a) Marcus Co. has reported a positive trend in earnings over the last 3 years. In the current year, it reduces its bad debt allowance to ensure another positive earnings year. The impact of this adjustment is equal to 3% of net income.

    (b) Sosa Co. has an extraordinary gain of $3.1 million on the sale of plant assets and a $3.3 million loss on the sale of investments. It decides to net the gain and loss because the net effect is considered immaterial. Sosa Co.'s income for the current year was $10 million.

    (c) Seliz Co. expenses all capital equipment under $25,000 on the basis that it is immaterial. The company has followed this practice for a number of years.

(LO 6) **BE2-8** If the going concern assumption is not made in accounting, discuss the differences in the amounts shown in the financial statements for the following items.

    (a) Land.

    (b) Unamortized bond premium.

    (c) Depreciation expense on equipment.

    (d) Merchandise inventory.

    (e) Prepaid insurance.

(LO 6, 7, 8) **BE2-9** What accounting assumption, principle, or modifying convention does **Target Corporation** use in each of the situations below?

    (a) Target uses the lower of cost or market basis to value inventories.

    (b) Target was involved in litigation over the last year. This litigation is disclosed in the financial statements.

    (c) Target allocates the cost of its depreciable assets over the life it expects to receive revenue from these assets.

    (d) Target records the purchase of a new **Dell** PC at its cash equivalent price.

(LO 5) **BE2-10** Explain how you would decide whether to record each of the following expenditures as an asset or an expense. Assume all items are material.

    (a) Legal fees paid in connection with the purchase of land are $1,500.

    (b) Benjamin Bratt, Inc. paves the driveway leading to the office building at a cost of $21,000.

    (c) A meat market purchases a meat-grinding machine at a cost of $3,500.

    (d) On June 30, Alan and Alda, medical doctors, pay 6 months' office rent to cover the month of July and the next 5 months.

    (e) Tim Taylor's Hardware Company pays $9,000 in wages to laborers for construction on a building to be used in the business.

    (f) Nancy Kwan's Florists pays wages of $2,100 for November to an employee who serves as driver of their delivery truck.

EXERCISES

(LO 4, 8) **E2-1** **(Qualitative Characteristics)** *SFAC No. 2* identifies the qualitative characteristics that make accounting information useful. Presented below are a number of questions related to these qualitative characteristics and underlying constraints.

(a) What is the quality of information that enables users to confirm or correct prior expectations?

(b) Identify the two overall or pervasive constraints developed in *SFAC No. 2.*

(c) The chairman of the SEC at one time noted, "If it becomes accepted or expected that accounting principles are determined or modified in order to secure purposes other than economic measurement, we assume a grave risk that confidence in the credibility of our financial information system will be undermined." Which qualitative characteristic of accounting information should ensure that such a situation will not occur? (Do not use reliability.)

(d) Billy Owens Corp. switches from FIFO to average cost to FIFO over a 2-year period. Which qualitative characteristic of accounting information is not followed?

(e) Assume that the profession permits the savings and loan industry to defer losses on investments it sells, because immediate recognition of the loss may have adverse economic consequences on the industry. Which qualitative characteristic of accounting information is not followed? (Do not use relevance or reliability.)

(f) What are the two primary qualities that make accounting information useful for decision making?

(g) Rex Chapman, Inc. does not issue its first-quarter report until after the second quarter's results are reported. Which qualitative characteristic of accounting is not followed? (Do not use relevance.)

(h) Predictive value is an ingredient of which of the two primary qualities that make accounting information useful for decision-making purposes?

(i) Ronald Coles, Inc. is the only company in its industry to depreciate its plant assets on a straight-line basis. Which qualitative characteristic of accounting information may not be followed? (Do not use industry practices.)

(j) Jeff Malone Company has attempted to determine the replacement cost of its inventory. Three different appraisers arrive at substantially different amounts for this value. The president, nevertheless, decides to report the middle value for external reporting purposes. Which qualitative characteristic of information is lacking in these data? (Do not use reliability or representational faithfulness.)

(LO 4) **E2-2** **(Qualitative Characteristics)** The qualitative characteristics that make accounting information useful for decision-making purposes are as follows.

Relevance	Timeliness	Representational faithfulness
Reliability	Verifiability	Comparability
Predictive value	Neutrality	Consistency
Feedback value		

Instructions

Identify the appropriate qualitative characteristic(s) to be used given the information provided below.

(a) Qualitative characteristic being employed when companies in the same industry are using the same accounting principles.

(b) Quality of information that confirms users' earlier expectations.

(c) Imperative for providing comparisons of a company from period to period.

(d) Ignores the economic consequences of a standard or rule.

(e) Requires a high degree of consensus among individuals on a given measurement.

(f) Predictive value is an ingredient of this primary quality of information.

(g) Two qualitative characteristics that are related to both relevance and reliability.

(h) Neutrality is an ingredient of this primary quality of accounting information.

(i) Two primary qualities that make accounting information useful for decision-making purposes.

(j) Issuance of interim reports is an example of what primary ingredient of relevance?

(LO 5) **E2-3** **(Elements of Financial Statements)** Ten interrelated elements that are most directly related to measuring the performance and financial status of an enterprise are provided below.

Assets	Distributions to owners	Expenses
Liabilities	Comprehensive income	Gains
Equity	Revenues	Losses
Investments by owners		

Instructions

Identify the element or elements from page 51 associated with the 12 items below.

(a) Arises from peripheral or incidental transactions.

(b) Obligation to transfer resources arising from a past transaction.

(c) Increases ownership interest.

(d) Declares and pays cash dividends to owners.

(e) Increases in net assets in a period from nonowner sources.

(f) Items characterized by service potential or future economic benefit.

(g) Equals increase in assets less liabilities during the year, after adding distributions to owners and subtracting investments by owners.

(h) Arises from income statement activities that constitute the entity's ongoing major or central operations.

(i) Residual interest in the assets of the enterprise after deducting its liabilities.

(j) Increases assets during a period through sale of product.

(k) Decreases assets during the period by purchasing the company's own stock.

(l) Includes all changes in equity during the period, except those resulting from investments by owners and distributions to owners.

(LO 6, 7, 8) **E2-4** **(Assumptions, Principles, and Constraints)** Presented below are the assumptions, principles, and constraints used in this chapter.

1. Economic entity assumption	**5.** Historical cost principle	**9.** Materiality
2. Going concern assumption	**6.** Matching principle	**10.** Industry practices
3. Monetary unit assumption	**7.** Full disclosure principle	**11.** Conservatism
4. Periodicity assumption	**8.** Cost-benefit relationship	

Instructions

Identify by number the accounting assumption, principle, or constraint that describes each situation below. Do not use a letter more than once.

(a) Allocates expenses to revenues in the proper period.

(b) Indicates that market value changes subsequent to purchase are not recorded in the accounts. (Do not use revenue recognition principle.)

(c) Ensures that all relevant financial information is reported.

(d) Rationale why plant assets are not reported at liquidation value. (Do not use historical cost principle.)

(e) Anticipates all losses, but reports no gains.

(f) Indicates that personal and business record keeping should be separately maintained.

(g) Separates financial information into time periods for reporting purposes.

(h) Permits the use of market value valuation in certain specific situations.

(i) Requires that information significant enough to affect the decision of reasonably informed users should be disclosed. (Do not use full disclosure principle.)

(j) Assumes that the dollar is the "measuring stick" used to report on financial performance.

(LO 6, 7, 8) **E2-5** **(Assumptions, Principles, and Constraints)** Presented below are a number of operational guidelines and practices that have developed over time.

Instructions

Select the assumption, principle, or constraint that most appropriately justifies these procedures and practices. (Do not use qualitative characteristics.)

(a) Market value changes are not recognized in the accounting records.

(b) Lower of cost or market is used to value inventories.

(c) Financial information is presented so that investors will not be misled.

(d) Intangible assets are capitalized and amortized over periods benefited.

(e) Repair tools are expensed when purchased.

(f) Agricultural companies use market value for purposes of valuing crops.

(g) Each enterprise is kept as a unit distinct from its owner or owners.

(h) All significant postbalance sheet events are reported.

(i) Revenue is recorded at point of sale.

(j) All important aspects of bond indentures are presented in financial statements.

(k) Rationale for accrual accounting.

(l) The use of consolidated statements is justified.

(m) Reporting must be done at defined time intervals.

(n) An allowance for doubtful accounts is established.

(o) All payments out of petty cash are charged to Miscellaneous Expense. (Do not use conservatism.)

    (p)   Goodwill is recorded only at time of purchase.

    (q)   No profits are anticipated and all possible losses are recognized.

    (r)   A company charges its sales commission costs to expense.

(LO 7)   **E2-6**   **(Full Disclosure Principle)**   Presented below are a number of facts related to R. Kelly, Inc. Assume that no mention of these facts was made in the financial statements and the related notes.

Instructions

Assume that you are the auditor of R. Kelly, Inc. and that you have been asked to explain the appropriate accounting and related disclosure necessary for each of these items.

    (a)   The company decided that, for the sake of conciseness, only net income should be reported on the income statement. Details as to revenues, cost of goods sold, and expenses were omitted.

    (b)   Equipment purchases of $170,000 were partly financed during the year through the issuance of a $110,000 notes payable. The company offset the equipment against the notes payable and reported plant assets at $60,000.

    (c)   R. Kelly has reported its ending inventory at $2,100,000 in the financial statements. No other information related to inventories is presented in the financial statements and related notes.

    (d)   The company changed its method of valuing inventories from weighted-average to FIFO. No mention of this change was made in the financial statements.

(LO 7)   **E2-7**   **(Accounting Principles—Comprehensive)**   Presented below are a number of business transactions that occurred during the current year for Fresh Horses, Inc.

Instructions

In each of the situations, discuss the appropriateness of the journal entries in terms of generally accepted accounting principles.

    (a)   The president of Fresh Horses, Inc. used his expense account to purchase a new Suburban solely for personal use. The following journal entry was made.

Miscellaneous Expense	29,000	
Cash		29,000

    (b)   Merchandise inventory that cost $620,000 is reported on the balance sheet at $690,000, the expected selling price less estimated selling costs. The following entry was made to record this increase in value.

Merchandise Inventory	70,000	
Revenue		70,000

    (c)   The company is being sued for $500,000 by a customer who claims damages for personal injury apparently caused by a defective product. Company attorneys feel extremely confident that the company will have no liability for damages resulting from the situation. Nevertheless, the company decides to make the following entry.

Loss from Lawsuit	500,000	
Liability for Lawsuit		500,000

    (d)   Because the general level of prices increased during the current year, Fresh Horses, Inc. determined that there was a $16,000 understatement of depreciation expense on its equipment and decided to record it in its accounts. The following entry was made.

Depreciation Expense	16,000	
Accumulated Depreciation		16,000

    (e)   Fresh Horses, Inc. has been concerned about whether intangible assets could generate cash in case of liquidation. As a consequence, goodwill arising from a purchase transaction during the current year and recorded at $800,000 was written off as follows.

Retained Earnings	800,000	
Goodwill		800,000

    (f)   Because of a "fire sale," equipment obviously worth $200,000 was acquired at a cost of $155,000. The following entry was made.

Equipment	200,000	
Cash		155,000
Revenue		45,000

(LO 7)   **E2-8**   **(Accounting Principles—Comprehensive)**   Presented on page 54 is information related to Garth Brooks, Inc.

Instructions

Comment on the appropriateness of the accounting procedures followed by Garth Brooks, Inc.

(a) Depreciation expense on the building for the year was $60,000. Because the building was increasing in value during the year, the controller decided to charge the depreciation expense to retained earnings instead of to net income. The following entry is recorded.

Retained Earnings	60,000	
Accumulated Depreciation — Buildings		60,000

(b) Materials were purchased on January 1, 2006, for $120,000 and this amount was entered in the Materials account. On December 31, 2006, the materials would have cost $141,000, so the following entry is made.

Inventory	21,000	
Gain on Inventories		21,000

(c) During the year, the company purchased equipment through the issuance of common stock. The stock had a par value of $135,000 and a fair market value of $450,000. The fair market value of the equipment was not easily determinable. The company recorded this transaction as follows.

Equipment	135,000	
Common Stock		135,000

(d) During the year, the company sold certain equipment for $285,000, recognizing a gain of $69,000. Because the controller believed that new equipment would be needed in the near future, she decided to defer the gain and amortize it over the life of any new equipment purchased.

(e) An order for $61,500 has been received from a customer for products on hand. This order was shipped on January 9, 2007. The company made the following entry in 2006.

Accounts Receivable	61,500	
Sales		61,500

See the book's website, www.wiley.com/college/kieso, for Additional Exercises.

CONCEPTS FOR ANALYSIS

CA2-1 (Conceptual Framework—General) Roger Morgan has some questions regarding the theoretical framework in which standards are set. He knows that the FASB and other predecessor organizations have attempted to develop a conceptual framework for accounting theory formulation. Yet, Roger's supervisors have indicated that these theoretical frameworks have little value in the practical sense (i.e., in the real world). Roger did notice that accounting standards seem to be established after the fact rather than before. He thought this indicated a lack of theory structure but never really questioned the process at school because he was too busy doing the homework.

Roger feels that some of his anxiety about accounting theory and accounting semantics could be alleviated by identifying the basic concepts and definitions accepted by the profession and considering them in light of his current work. By doing this, he hopes to develop an appropriate connection between theory and practice.

Instructions

(a) Help Roger recognize the purpose of and benefit of a conceptual framework.

(b) Identify any *Statements of Financial Accounting Concepts* issued by FASB that may be helpful to Roger in developing his theoretical background.

CA2-2 (Conceptual Framework—General) The Financial Accounting Standards Board (FASB) has developed a conceptual framework for financial accounting and reporting. The FASB has issued seven *Statements of Financial Accounting Concepts.* These statements are intended to set forth objectives and fundamentals that will be the basis for developing financial accounting and reporting standards. The objectives identify the goals and purposes of financial reporting. The fundamentals are the underlying concepts of financial accounting that guide the selection of transactions, events, and circumstances to be accounted for; their recognition and measurement; and the means of summarizing and communicating them to interested parties.

The purpose of *Statement of Financial Accounting Concepts No. 2,* "Qualitative Characteristics of Accounting Information," is to examine the characteristics that make accounting information useful. The characteristics or qualities of information discussed in SFAC No. 2 are the ingredients that make information useful and the qualities to be sought when accounting choices are made.

Instructions

(a) Identify and discuss the benefits that can be expected to be derived from the FASB's conceptual framework study.

(b) What is the most important quality for accounting information as identified in *Statement of Financial Accounting Concepts No. 2*? Explain why it is the most important.

(c) *Statement of Financial Accounting Concepts No. 2* describes a number of key characteristics or qualities for accounting information. Briefly discuss the importance of any three of these qualities for financial reporting purposes.

(CMA adapted)

CA2-3 **(Objectives of Financial Reporting)** Regis Gordon and Kathy Medford are discussing various aspects of the FASB's pronouncement *Statement of Financial Accounting Concepts No. 1*, "Objectives of Financial Reporting by Business Enterprises." Regis indicates that this pronouncement provides little, if any, guidance to the practicing professional in resolving accounting controversies. He believes that the statement provides such broad guidelines that it would be impossible to apply the objectives to present-day reporting problems. Kathy concedes this point but indicates that objectives are still needed to provide a starting point for the FASB in helping to improve financial reporting.

Instructions

(a) Indicate the basic objectives established in *Statement of Financial Accounting Concepts No. 1*.

(b) What do you think is the meaning of Kathy's statement that the FASB needs a starting point to resolve accounting controversies?

 CA2-4 **(Qualitative Characteristics)** Accounting information provides useful information about business transactions and events. Those who provide and use financial reports must often select and evaluate accounting alternatives. FASB *Statement of Financial Accounting Concepts No. 2*, "Qualitative Characteristics of Accounting Information," examines the characteristics of accounting information that make it useful for decision making. It also points out that various limitations inherent in the measurement and reporting process may necessitate trade-offs or sacrifices among the characteristics of useful information.

Instructions

(a) Describe briefly the following characteristics of useful accounting information.

(1) Relevance   (4) Comparability
(2) Reliability   (5) Consistency
(3) Understandability

(b) For each of the following pairs of information characteristics, give an example of a situation in which one of the characteristics may be sacrificed in return for a gain in the other.

(1) Relevance and reliability.   (3) Comparability and consistency.
(2) Relevance and consistency.   (4) Relevance and understandability.

(c) What criterion should be used to evaluate trade-offs between information characteristics?

CA2-5 **(Revenue Recognition and Matching Principle)** After the presentation of your report on the examination of the financial statements to the board of directors of Bones Publishing Company, one of the new directors expresses surprise that the income statement assumes that an equal proportion of the revenue is earned with the publication of every issue of the company's magazine. She feels that the "crucial event" in the process of earning revenue in the magazine business is the cash sale of the subscription. She says that she does not understand why most of the revenue cannot be "recognized" in the period of the sale.

Instructions

(a) List the various accepted times for recognizing revenue in the accounts and explain when the methods are appropriate.

(b) Discuss the propriety of timing the recognition of revenue in Bones Publishing Company's accounts with:

(1) The cash sale of the magazine subscription.

(2) The publication of the magazine every month.

(3) Both events, by recognizing a portion of the revenue with the cash sale of the magazine subscription and a portion of the revenue with the publication of the magazine every month.

CA2-6 **(Revenue Recognition and Matching Principle)** On June 5, 2006, McCoy Corporation signed a contract with Sulu Associates under which Sulu agreed (1) to construct an office building on land owned by Mc-Coy, (2) to accept responsibility for procuring financing for the project and finding tenants, and (3) to manage the property for 35 years. The annual net income from the project, after debt service, was to be divided equally between McCoy Corporation and Sulu Associates. Sulu was to accept its share of future net income as full payment for its services in construction, obtaining finances and tenants, and management of the project.

By May 31, 2007, the project was nearly completed, and tenants had signed leases to occupy 90% of the available space at annual rentals totaling $4,000,000. It is estimated that, after operating expenses and debt service, the annual net income will amount to $1,500,000.

The management of Sulu Associates believed that (a) the economic benefit derived from the contract with McCoy should be reflected on its financial statements for the fiscal year ended May 31, 2007, and directed that revenue be accrued in an amount equal to the commercial value of the services Sulu had rendered during the year, (b) this amount should be carried in contracts receivable, and (c) all related expenditures should be charged against the revenue.

Instructions

(a) Explain the main difference between the economic concept of business income as reflected by Sulu's management and the measurement of income under generally accepted accounting principles.

(b) Discuss the factors to be considered in determining when revenue should be recognized for the purpose of accounting measurement of periodic income.

(c) Is the belief of Sulu's management in accordance with generally accepted accounting principles for the measurement of revenue and expense for the year ended May 31, 2007? Support your opinion by discussing the application to this case of the factors to be considered for asset measurement and revenue and expense recognition.

(AICPA adapted)

CA2-7 (Matching Principle) An accountant must be familiar with the concepts involved in determining earnings of a business entity. The amount of earnings reported for a business entity is dependent on the proper recognition, in general, of revenue and expense for a given time period. In some situations, costs are recognized as expenses at the time of product sale. In other situations, guidelines have been developed for recognizing costs as expenses or losses by other criteria.

Instructions

(a) Explain the rationale for recognizing costs as expenses at the time of product sale.

(b) What is the rationale underlying the appropriateness of treating costs as expenses of a period instead of assigning the costs to an asset? Explain.

(c) In what general circumstances would it be appropriate to treat a cost as an asset instead of as an expense? Explain.

(d) Some expenses are assigned to specific accounting periods on the basis of systematic and rational allocation of asset cost. Explain the underlying rationale for recognizing expenses on the basis of systematic and rational allocation of asset cost.

(e) Identify the conditions under which it would be appropriate to treat a cost as a loss.

(AICPA adapted)

CA2-8 (Matching Principle) Accountants try to prepare income statements that are as accurate as possible. A basic requirement in preparing accurate income statements is to match costs against revenues properly. Proper matching of costs against revenues requires that costs resulting from typical business operations be recognized in the period in which they expired.

Instructions

(a) List three criteria that can be used to determine whether such costs should appear as charges in the income statement for the current period.

(b) As generally presented in financial statements, the following items or procedures have been criticized as improperly matching costs with revenues. Briefly discuss each item from the viewpoint of matching costs with revenues and suggest corrective or alternative means of presenting the financial information.

(1) Receiving and handling costs.

(2) Valuation of inventories at the lower of cost or market.

(3) Cash discounts on purchases.

CA2-9 (Matching Principle) Carlos Rodriguez sells and erects shell houses, that is, frame structures that are completely finished on the outside but are unfinished on the inside except for flooring, partition studding, and ceiling joists. Shell houses are sold chiefly to customers who are handy with tools and who have time to do the interior wiring, plumbing, wall completion and finishing, and other work necessary to make the shell houses livable dwellings.

Rodriguez buys shell houses from a manufacturer in unassembled packages consisting of all lumber, roofing, doors, windows, and similar materials necessary to complete a shell house. Upon commencing operations in a new area, Rodriguez buys or leases land as a site for its local warehouse, field office, and display houses. Sample display houses are erected at a total cost of $30,000 to $44,000 including the cost of the unassembled packages. The chief element of cost of the display houses is the unassembled packages, inasmuch as erection is a short, low-cost operation. Old sample models are torn down or altered into new models every 3 to 7 years. Sample display houses have little salvage value because dismantling and moving costs amount to nearly as much as the cost of an unassembled package.

Instructions

(a) A choice must be made between (1) expensing the costs of sample display houses in the periods in which the expenditure is made and (2) spreading the costs over more than one period. Discuss the advantages of each method.

(b) Would it be preferable to amortize the cost of display houses on the basis of (1) the passage of time or (2) the number of shell houses sold? Explain.

(AICPA adapted)

CA2-10 (Qualitative Characteristics) Recently, your Uncle Waldo Ralph, who knows that you always have your eye out for a profitable investment, has discussed the possibility of your purchasing some corporate bonds. He suggests that you may wish to get in on the "ground floor" of this deal. The bonds being issued by Cricket Corp. are 10-year debentures which promise a 40% rate of return. Cricket manufactures novelty/party items.

You have told Waldo that, unless you can take a look at Cricket's financial statements, you would not feel comfortable about such an investment. Believing that this is the chance of a lifetime, Uncle Waldo has procured a copy of Cricket's most recent, unaudited financial statements which are a year old. These statements were prepared by Mrs. John Cricket. You peruse these statements, and they are quite impressive. The balance sheet showed a debt-to-equity ratio of 0.10 and, for the year shown, the company reported net income of $2,424,240.

The financial statements are not shown in comparison with amounts from other years. In addition, no significant note disclosures about inventory valuation, depreciation methods, loan agreements, etc. are available.

Instructions

Write a letter to Uncle Waldo explaining why it would be unwise to base an investment decision on the financial statements that he has provided to you. Be sure to explain why these financial statements are neither relevant nor reliable.

CA2-11 (Matching) Hinckley Nuclear Power Plant will be "mothballed" at the end of its useful life (approximately 20 years) at great expense. The matching principle requires that expenses be matched to revenue. Accountants Jana Kingston and Pete Henning argue whether it is better to allocate the expense of mothballing over the next 20 years or ignore it until mothballing occurs.

Instructions

Answer the following questions.

(a) What stakeholders should be considered?
(b) What ethical issue, if any, underlies the dispute?
(c) What alternatives should be considered?
(d) Assess the consequences of the alternatives.
(e) What decision would you recommend?

CA2-12 (Cost-Benefit) The AICPA Special Committee on Financial Reporting proposed the following constraints related to financial reporting.

1. Business reporting should exclude information outside of management's expertise or for which management is not the best source, such as information about competitors.
2. Management should not be required to report information that would significantly harm the company's competitive position.
3. Management should not be required to provide forecasted financial statements. Rather, management should provide information that helps users forecast for themselves the company's financial future.
4. Other than for financial statements, management need report only the information it knows. That is, management should be under no obligation to gather information it does not have, or does not need, to manage the business.
5. Companies should present certain elements of business reporting only if users and management agree they should be reported—a concept of flexible reporting.
6. Companies should not have to report forward-looking information unless there are effective deterrents to unwarranted litigation that discourages companies from doing so.

Instructions

For each item, briefly discuss how the proposed constraint addresses concerns about the costs and benefits of financial reporting.

USING YOUR JUDGMENT

Financial Reporting Problem

P&G The Procter & Gamble Company (P&G)

The financial statements of P&G are presented in Appendix 5B or can be accessed on the KWW website.

Instructions

Refer to P&G's financial statements and the accompanying notes to answer the following questions.

(a) Using the notes to the consolidated financial statements, determine P&G's revenue recognition policies. Discuss the impact of trade promotions on P&G's financial statements.

(b) Give two examples of where historical cost information is reported in P&G's financial statements and related notes. Give two examples of the use of fair value information reported in either the financial statements or related notes.

(c) How can we determine that the accounting principles used by P&G are prepared on a basis consistent with those of last year?

(d) What is P&G's accounting policy related to advertising? What accounting principle does P&G follow regarding accounting for advertising? Where are advertising expenses reported in the financial statements?

Financial Statement Analysis Case

Wal-Mart

Wal-Mart Stores provided the following disclosure in a recent annual report.

> *New accounting pronouncement (partial)* ... the Securities and Exchange Commission issued Staff Accounting Bulletin No. 101—"Revenue Recognition in Financial Statements" (*SAB 101*). This SAB deals with various revenue recognition issues, several of which are common within the retail industry. As a result of the issuance of this SAB ... the Company is currently evaluating the effects of the SAB on its method of recognizing revenues related to layaway sales and will make any accounting method changes necessary during the first quarter of [next year].

In response to *SAB 101* Wal-Mart changed its revenue recognition policy for layaway transactions, in which Wal-Mart sets aside merchandise for customers who make partial payment. Before the change, Wal-Mart recognized all revenue on the sale at the time of the layaway. After the change, Wal-Mart does not recognize revenue until customers satisfy all payment obligations and take possession of the merchandise.

Instructions

(a) Discuss the expected effect on income (1) in the year that Wal-Mart makes the changes in its revenue recognition policy, and (2) in the years following the change.

(b) Evaluate the extent to which Wal-Mart's previous revenue policy was consistent with the revenue recognition principle.

(c) If all retailers had used a revenue recognition policy similar to Wal-Mart's before the change, are there any concerns with respect to the qualitative characteristic of comparability? Explain.

Comparative Analysis Case

The Coca-Cola Company

 **PEPSICO**

The Coca-Cola Company and PepsiCo, Inc.

Instructions

Go to the KWW website, and use information found there to answer the following questions related to **The Coca-Cola Company** and **PepsiCo, Inc.**

(a) What are the primary lines of business of these two companies as shown in their notes to the financial statements?

(b) Which company has the dominant position in beverage sales?

(c) How are inventories for these two companies valued? What cost allocation method is used to report inventory? How does their accounting for inventories affect comparability between the two companies?

(d) Which company changed its accounting policies during 2004 which affected the consistency of the financial results from the previous year? What were these changes?

Research Case

Retrieval of Information on Public Company

There are several commonly available indexes that enable individuals to locate articles previously included in numerous business publications and periodicals. Articles can generally be searched by company or by subject matter. Four common indexes are the *Wall Street Journal Index*, *Business Abstracts* (formerly the *Business Periodical Index*), *Predicasts F&S Index*, and *ABI/Inform*.

Instructions

Use one of these resources to find an article about a company in which you are interested. Read the article and answer the following questions. (*Note:* Your library may have CD-ROM versions of these indexes.)

(a) What is the article about?

(b) What company-specific information is included in the article?

(c) Identify any accounting-related issues discussed in the article.

International Reporting Case

As discussed in Chapter 1, the **International Accounting Standards Board (IASB)** develops accounting standards for many international companies. The IASB also has developed a conceptual framework to help guide the setting of accounting standards. Following is an Overview of the IASB Framework.

Objective of Financial Statements
> To provide information about the financial position, performance, and changes in financial position of an enterprise that is useful to a wide range of users in making economic decisions.

Underlying Assumptions
Accrual basis
Going concern

Qualitative Characteristics of Financial Statements
Understandability	Reliability (continued)
Relevance	Neutrality
Materiality	Prudence
Reliability	Completeness
Faithful representation	Comparability
Substance over form	

Constraints on Relevant and Reliable Information
Timeliness
Balance between benefit and cost
Balance between qualitative characteristics

True and Fair Presentation

Elements of Financial Statements

Asset: A resource controlled by the enterprise as a result of past events and from which future economic benefits are expected to flow to the enterprise.

Liability: A present obligation of the enterprise arising from past events, the settlement of which is expected to result in an outflow from the enterprise of resources embodying economic benefits.

Equity: The residual interest in the assets of the enterprise after deducting all its liabilities.

Income: Increases in economic benefits during the accounting period in the form of inflows or enhancements of assets or decreases of liabilities that result in increases in equity, other than those relating to contributions from equity participants.

Expenses: Decreases in economic benefits during the accounting period in the form of outflows or depletions of assets or incurrences of liabilities that result in decreases in equity, other than those relating to distributions to equity participants.

Instructions

Identify at least three similarities and at least three differences between the FASB and IASB conceptual frameworks as revealed in the above Overview.

Professional Research: Financial Accounting and Reporting

Your aunt recently received the annual report for a company in which she has invested. The report notes that the statements have been prepared in accordance with "generally accepted accounting principles." She has also heard that certain terms have special meanings in accounting relative to everyday use. She would like you to explain the meaning of terms she has come across related to accounting.

Instructions

Using the **Financial Accounting Research System (FARS)**, respond to the following items. (Provide text strings used in your search.)

(a) How is "materiality" defined in the conceptual framework?

(b) The concepts statements provide several examples in which specific quantitative materiality guidelines are provided to firms. Identity at least two of these examples. Do you think the materiality guidelines should be quantified? Why or why not?

(c) The concepts statements discuss the concept of "articulation" between financial statement elements. Briefly summarize the meaning of this term and how it relates to an entity's financial statements.

Professional Simulation

In this simulation you are asked to address questions regarding the FASB's conceptual framework. Prepare responses to all parts.

KWW_Professional _Simulation

| Conceptual Framework | Time Remaining 4 hours 10 minutes | copy | paste | calculator | sheet | standards | help | splitter | done |

Directions | **Situation** | **Explanation** | **Research** | **Resources**

A friend of yours is one of seven shareholders in a small start-up company. He is evaluating information about the company that was discussed at a recent shareholders' meeting. No mention of these facts was made in the financial statements or the related notes. Given your accounting background, he thought you would know the appropriate treatment of these items.

1. The company is concerned that one of its patents will be worthless in the event of liquidation. As a result, this intangible asset was written off through the following entry.

Retained Earnings	7,000	
Patent		7,000

2. The company is being sued for $15,000 by a customer claiming damages caused by a defective product. The attorney for the company is confident that the company will have no liability for damages. To be safe, the company made the following entry.

Loss from Lawsuit	15,000	
Lawsuit Liability		15,000

3. The company president used her expense account to purchase a new Hummer solely for her personal use. The following entry was made.

Miscellaneous Expense	55,000	
Cash		55,000

Directions | **Situation** | **Explanation** | **Research** | **Resources**

For each situation, prepare a brief explanation for the appropriate accounting and related disclosure required for each of the items.

Directions | **Situation** | **Explanation** | **Research** | **Resources**

Your friend had an extensive discussion with other shareholders on the subject of materiality. He argues for a strict quantitative definition of materiality, while the other shareholders believe that both quantitative and qualitative indicators should be considered in evaluating whether an item is material. Using the Financial Accounting Research System (FARS) database, discuss how the Conceptual Framework defines and operationalizes materiality.

Remember to check the book's companion website to find additional resources for this chapter.

wiley.com/college/kieso

CHAPTER THREE

THE ACCOUNTING INFORMATION SYSTEM

Needed: A Reliable Information System

Maintaining a set of accounting records is not optional. The **Internal Revenue Service (IRS)** requires that businesses prepare and retain a set of records and documents that can be audited. The Foreign Corrupt Practices Act (federal legislation) requires public companies to ". . . make and keep books, records, and accounts, which, in reasonable detail, accurately and fairly reflect the transactions and dispositions of the assets. . . ." But beyond these two reasons, a company that fails to keep an accurate record of its business transactions may lose revenue and is more likely to operate inefficiently.

Consider, for example, the **Long Island Railroad (LIRR)**, once one of the nation's busiest commuter lines. The LIRR lost money because of poor recordkeeping. It forgot to bill some customers, mistakenly paid some payables twice, and neglected to record redemptions of bonds. **FFP Marketing**, which operates convenience stores in 11 states, provides another example. The SEC forced it to restate earnings when an audit uncovered faulty bookkeeping for its credit card accounts and fuel payables.

Inefficient accounting also cost the **City of Cleveland**, Ohio. An audit discovered over 313 examples of dysfunctional accounting, costing taxpayers over $1.3 million. Its poor accounting system resulted in the Cleveland treasurer's ignorance of available cash, which led to missed investment opportunities. Further, delayed recording of pension payments created the false impression of $13 million in the city coffers.

Even the use of computers is no assurance of accuracy and efficiency. "The conversion to a new system called MasterNet fouled up data processing records to the extent that **Bank of America** was frequently unable to produce or deliver customer statements on a timely basis," said an executive at one of the country's largest banks.

Although these situations may occur only rarely in large organizations, they illustrate the point: Companies must properly maintain accounts and detailed records or face unnecessary costs. The SEC suspended trading in FFP Marketing's stock until it corrected the errors and re-issued financial statements. The City of Cleveland's municipal bond rating took a hit because of its poor accounting practices.

Learning Objectives

After studying this chapter, you should be able to:

1 Understand basic accounting terminology.

2 Explain double-entry rules.

3 Identify steps in the accounting cycle.

4 Record transactions in journals, post to ledger accounts, and prepare a trial balance.

5 Explain the reasons for preparing adjusting entries.

6 Prepare financial statements from the adjusted trial balance.

7 Prepare closing entries.

8 Explain how to adjust inventory accounts at year-end.

As the opening story indicates, a reliable information system is a necessity for all companies. The purpose of this chapter is to explain and illustrate the features of an accounting information system. The content and organization of this chapter are as follows.

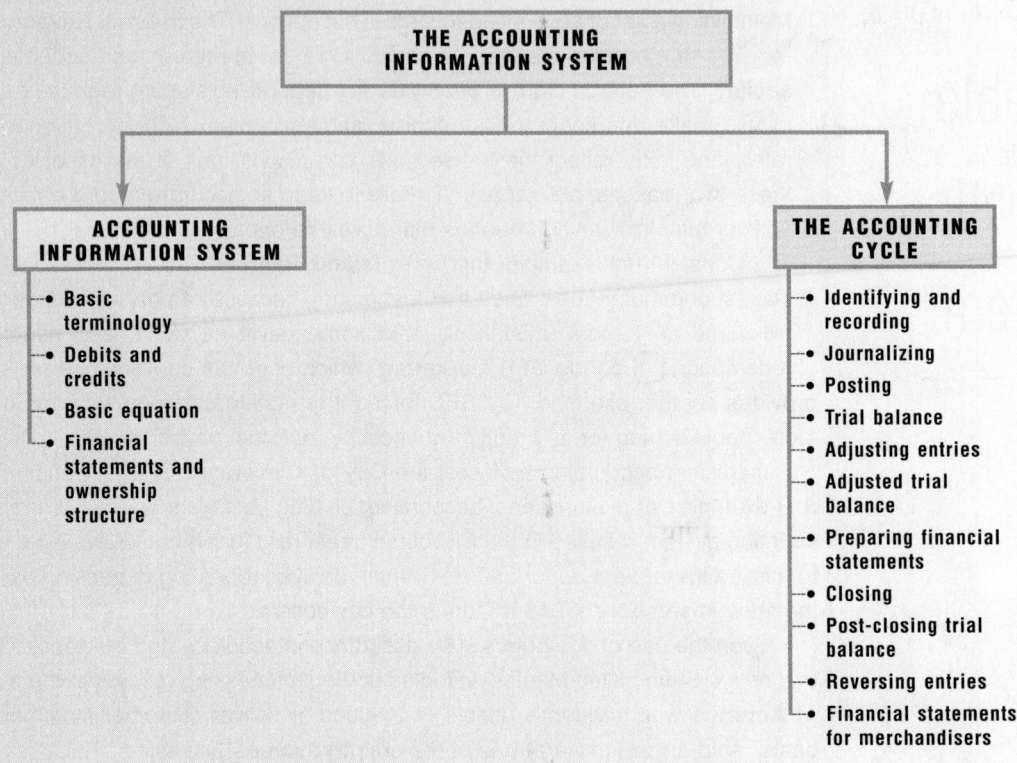

THE ACCOUNTING INFORMATION SYSTEM

ACCOUNTING INFORMATION SYSTEM
- Basic terminology
- Debits and credits
- Basic equation
- Financial statements and ownership structure

THE ACCOUNTING CYCLE
- Identifying and recording
- Journalizing
- Posting
- Trial balance
- Adjusting entries
- Adjusted trial balance
- Preparing financial statements
- Closing
- Post-closing trial balance
- Reversing entries
- Financial statements for merchandisers

ACCOUNTING INFORMATION SYSTEM

An **accounting information system** collects and processes transaction data and then disseminates the financial information to interested parties. Accounting information systems vary widely from one business to another. Various factors shape these systems: the nature of the business and the transactions in which it engages, the size of the firm, the volume of data to be handled, and the informational demands that management and others require.

As we discussed in Chapters 1 and 2, in response to the requirements of the Sarbanes-Oxley Act of 2002, companies are placing a renewed focus on their accounting systems to ensure relevant and reliable information is reported in financial statements.[1] A good accounting information system helps management answer such questions as:

How much and what kind of debt is outstanding?

Were our sales higher this period than last?

What assets do we have?

What were our cash inflows and outflows?

---

[1]One study of first compliance with the internal-control testing provisions of the Sarbanes-Oxley Act documented material weaknesses for about 13 percent of companies reporting in 2004 and 2005. L. Townsend, "Internal Control Deficiency Disclosures–Interim Alert," *Yellow Card–Interim Trend Alert* (April 12, 2005) Glass, Lewis & Co., LLC.

Did we make a profit last period?

Are any of our product lines or divisions operating at a loss?

Can we safely increase our dividends to stockholders?

Is our rate of return on net assets increasing?

Management can answer many other questions with the data provided by an efficient accounting system. A well-devised accounting information system benefits every type of company.

Basic Terminology

Financial accounting rests on a set of concepts (discussed in Chapters 1 and 2) for identifying, recording, classifying, and interpreting transactions and other events relating to enterprises. You therefore need to understand the **basic terminology employed in collecting accounting data**.

BASIC TERMINOLOGY

> **OBJECTIVE 1**
> Understand basic accounting terminology.

EVENT. A happening of consequence. An event generally is the source or cause of changes in assets, liabilities, and equity. Events may be external or internal.

TRANSACTION. An **external event** involving a transfer or exchange between two or more entities.

ACCOUNT. A systematic arrangement that shows the effect of transactions and other events on a specific element (asset, liability, and so on). Companies keep a separate account for each asset, liability, revenue, and expense, and for capital (owners' equity).

REAL AND NOMINAL ACCOUNTS. Real (permanent) **accounts** are asset, liability, and equity accounts; they appear on the balance sheet. **Nominal** (temporary) **accounts** are revenue, expense, and dividend accounts; except for dividends, they appear on the income statement. Companies periodically close nominal accounts; they do not close real accounts.

LEDGER. The book (or computer printouts) containing the accounts. A **general ledger** is a collection of all the asset, liability, owners' equity, revenue, and expense accounts. A **subsidiary ledger** contains the details related to a given general ledger account.

JOURNAL. The "book of original entry" where the company initially records transactions and selected other events. Various amounts are transferred from the book of original entry, the journal, to the ledger.

POSTING. The process of transferring the essential facts and figures from the book of original entry to the ledger accounts.

TRIAL BALANCE. The list of all open accounts in the ledger and their balances. The trial balance taken immediately after all adjustments have been posted is called an **adjusted trial balance**. A trial balance taken immediately after closing entries have been posted is called a **post-closing** or **after-closing trial balance**. Companies may prepare a trial balance at any time.

ADJUSTING ENTRIES. Entries made at the end of an accounting period to bring all accounts up to date on an accrual basis, so that the company can prepare correct financial statements.

FINANCIAL STATEMENTS. Statements that reflect the collection, tabulation, and final summarization of the accounting data. Four statements are involved: (1) The balance sheet shows the financial condition of the enterprise at the end of a period.

(2) The **income statement** measures the results of operations during the period. (3) The **statement of cash flows** reports the cash provided and used by operating, investing, and financing activities during the period. (4) The **statement of retained earnings** reconciles the balance of the retained earnings account from the beginning to the end of the period.

CLOSING ENTRIES. The formal process by which the enterprise reduces all nominal accounts to zero and determines and transfers the net income or net loss to an owners' equity account. Also known as "closing the ledger," "closing the books," or merely "closing."

OBJECTIVE 2
Explain double-entry rules.

Debits and Credits

The terms **debit** (Dr.) and **credit** (Cr.) mean left and right, respectively. These terms do not mean increase or decrease, but instead describe *where* a company makes entries in the recording process. That is, when a company enters an amount on the left side of an account, it **debits** the account. When it makes an entry on the right side, it **credits** the account. When comparing the totals of the two sides, an account shows a **debit balance** if the total of the debit amounts exceeds the credits. An account shows a **credit balance** if the credit amounts exceed the debits.

The positioning of debits on the left and credits on the right is simply an accounting custom. We could function just as well if we reversed the sides. However, the United States adopted the custom, now the rule, of having debits on the left side of an account and credits on the right side, similar to the custom of driving on the right-hand side of the road. This rule applies to all accounts.

The equality of debits and credits provides the basis for the double-entry system of recording transactions (sometimes referred to as double-entry bookkeeping). Under the universally used **double-entry accounting** system, a company records the dual (two-sided) effect of each transaction in appropriate accounts. This system provides a logical method for recording transactions. It also offers a means of proving the accuracy of the recorded amounts. If a company records every transaction with equal debits and credits, then the sum of all the debits to the accounts must equal the sum of all the credits.

Illustration 3-1 presents the basic guidelines for an accounting system. Increases to all asset and expense accounts occur on the left (or debit side) and decreases on the

ILLUSTRATION 3-1
Double-entry (Debit and Credit) Accounting System

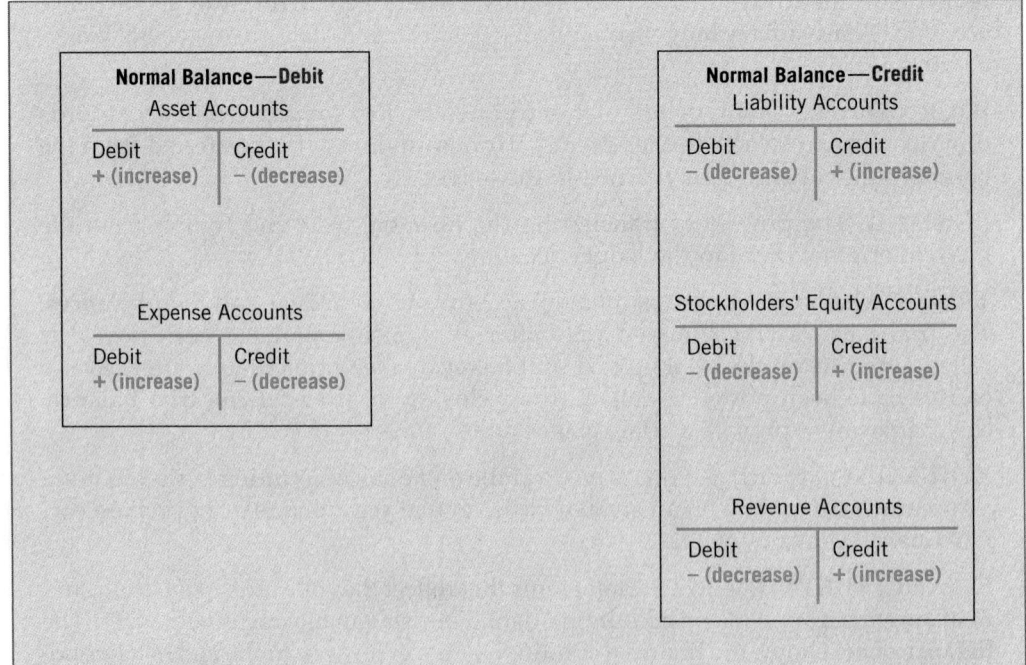

right (or credit side). Conversely, increases to all liability and revenue accounts occur on the right (or credit side) and decreases on the left (or debit side). A company increases stockholders' equity accounts, such as Common Stock and Retained Earnings, on the credit side, but increases Dividends on the debit side.

Basic Equation

In a double-entry system, for every debit there must be a credit, and vice versa. This leads us, then, to the basic equation in accounting (Illustration 3-2).

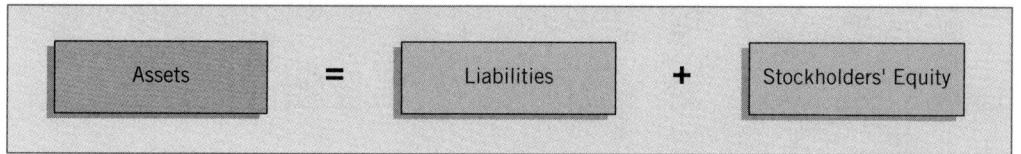

ILLUSTRATION 3-2
The Basic Accounting Equation

Illustration 3-3 expands this equation to show the accounts that make up stockholders' equity. The figure also shows the debit/credit rules and effects on each type of account. Study this diagram carefully. It will help you understand the fundamentals of the double-entry system. Like the basic equation, the expanded basic equation must also balance (total debits equal total credits).

ILLUSTRATION 3-3
Expanded Basic Equation and Debit/Credit Rules and Effects

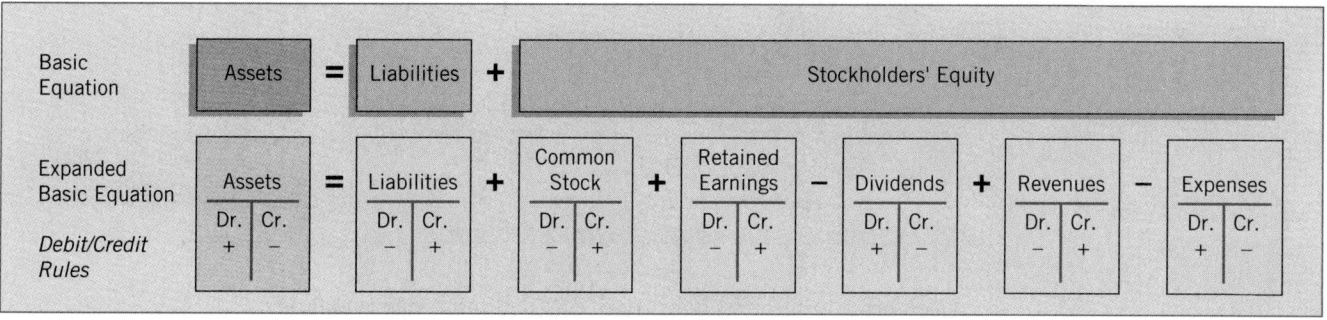

Every time a transaction occurs, the elements of the equation change. However, the basic equality remains. To illustrate, consider the following eight different transactions for Perez Inc.

1 Owners invest $40,000 in exchange for common stock.

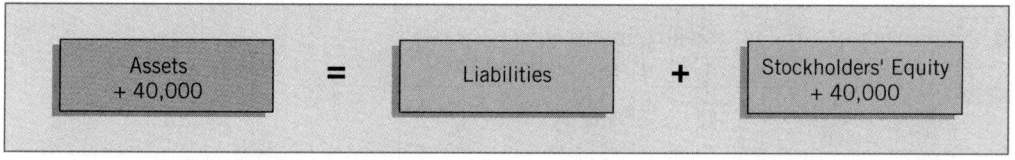

2 Disburse $600 cash for secretarial wages.

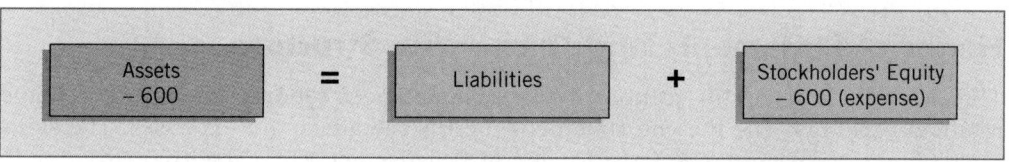

3 Purchase office equipment priced at $5,200, giving a 10 percent promissory note in exchange.

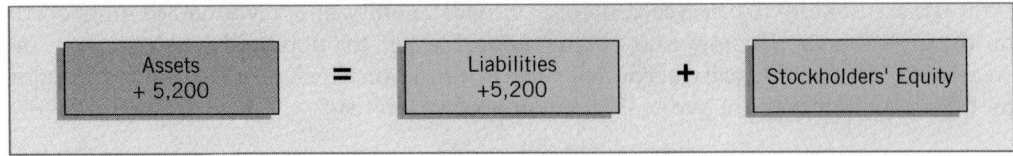

4 Receive $4,000 cash for services rendered.

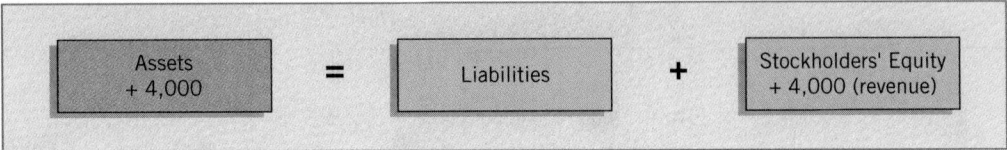

5 Pay off a short-term liability of $7,000.

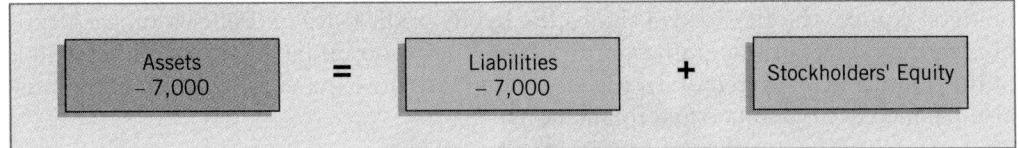

6 Declare a cash dividend of $5,000.

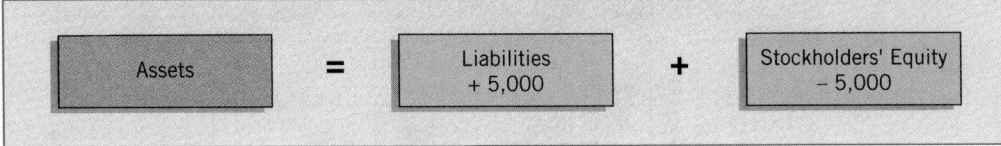

7 Convert a long-term liability of $80,000 into common stock.

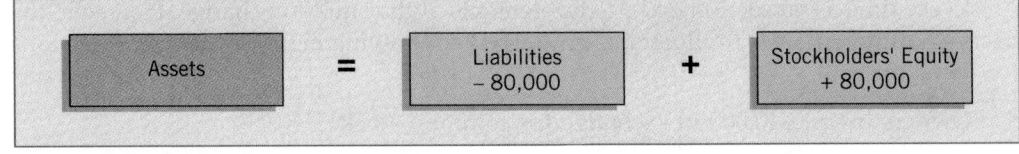

8 Pay cash of $16,000 for a delivery van.

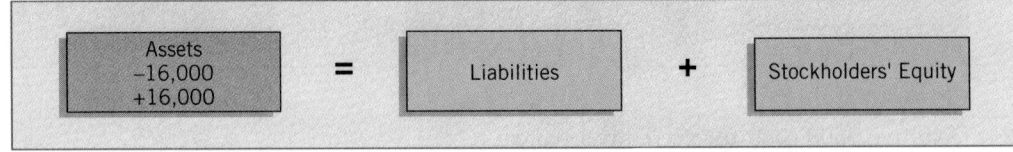

Financial Statements and Ownership Structure

The stockholders' equity section of the balance sheet reports common stock and retained earnings. The income statement reports revenues and expenses. The statement of retained earnings reports dividends. Because a company transfers dividends, revenues, and expenses to retained earnings at the end of the period, a change in any one of these three items affects stockholders' equity. Illustration 3-4 shows the stockholders' equity relationships.

ILLUSTRATION 3-4
Financial Statements and
Ownership Structure

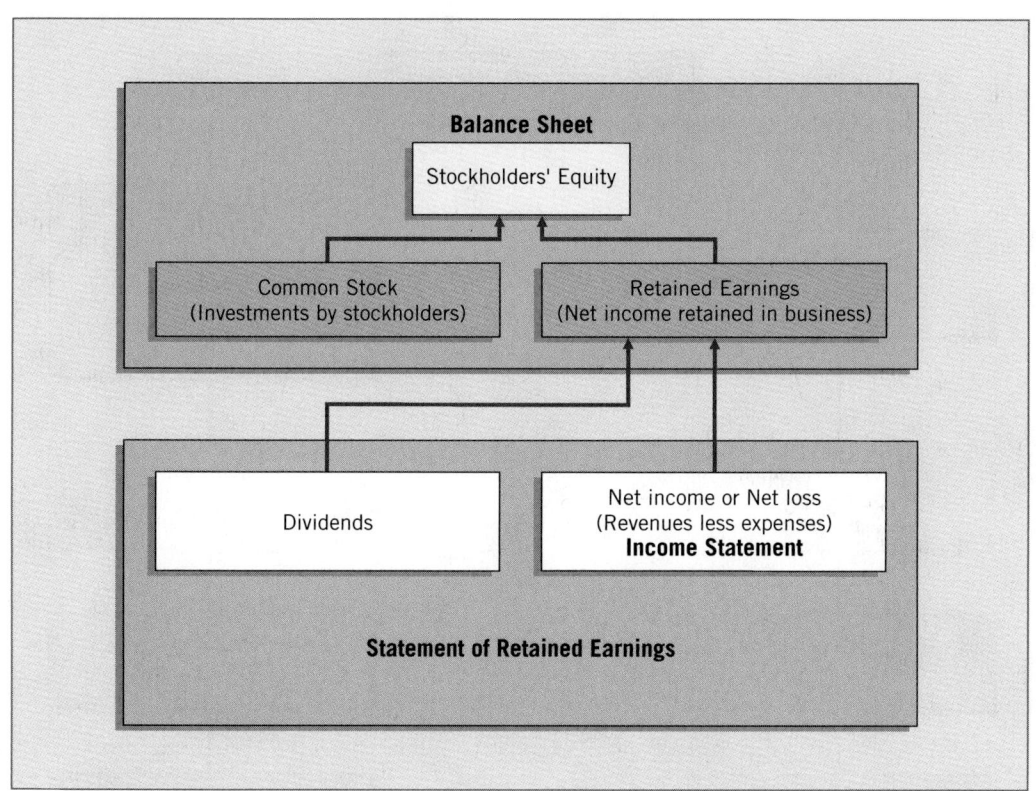

The enterprise's ownership structure dictates the types of accounts that are part of or affect the equity section. A corporation commonly uses Common Stock, Additional Paid-in Capital, Dividends, and Retained Earnings accounts. A proprietorship or a partnership uses a Capital account and a Drawing account: A Capital account indicates the owner's or owners' investment in the company. A Drawing account tracks withdrawals by the owner(s).

Illustration 3-5 summarizes and relates the transactions affecting owners' equity to the nominal (temporary) and real (permanent) classifications and to the types of business ownership.

ILLUSTRATION 3-5
Effects of Transactions on
Owners' Equity Accounts

| | | Ownership Structure | | | |
| | | Proprietorships and Partnerships | | Corporations | |
Transactions Affecting Owners' Equity	Impact on Owners' Equity	Nominal (Temporary) Accounts	Real (Permanent) Accounts	Nominal (Temporary) Accounts	Real (Permanent) Accounts
Investment by owner(s)	Increase		Capital		Common Stock and related accounts
Revenues earned	Increase	Revenue ⎫		Revenue ⎫	
Expenses incurred	Decrease	Expense ⎬ Capital	Capital	Expense ⎬	Retained Earnings
Withdrawal by owner(s)	Decrease	Drawing ⎭		Dividends ⎭	

THE ACCOUNTING CYCLE

Illustration 3-6 shows the steps in the **accounting cycle**. An enterprise normally uses these accounting procedures to record transactions and prepare financial statements.

OBJECTIVE 3
Identify steps in the accounting cycle.

ILLUSTRATION 3-6
The Accounting Cycle

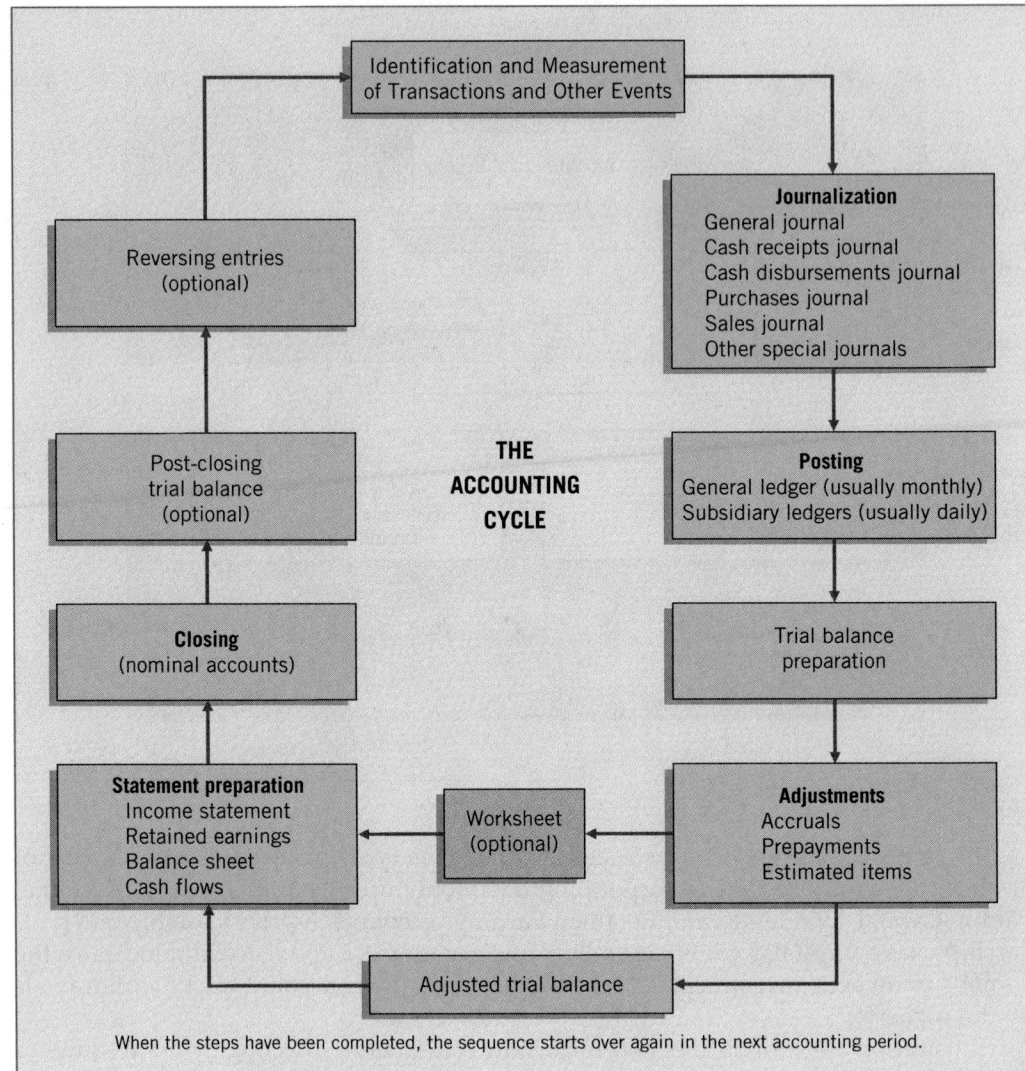

Accounting Cycle Tutorial

Identifying and Recording Transactions and Other Events

The first step in the accounting cycle is analysis of transactions and selected other events. The first problem is to determine what to record. Although GAAP provides guidelines, no simple rules exist that state which events a company should record. Although changes in a company's personnel or managerial policies may be important, the company should not record these items in the accounts. On the other hand, a company should record all cash sales or purchases—no matter how small.

The concepts we presented in Chapter 2 determine what to recognize in the accounts. An item should be recognized in the financial statements if it is an element, is measurable, and is relevant and reliable. Consider human resources. **R. G. Barry & Co.** at one time reported as supplemental data total assets of $14,055,926, including $986,094 for "Net investments in human resources." **AT&T** and **ExxonMobil Company** also experimented with human resource accounting. Should we value employees for balance sheet and income statement purposes? Certainly skilled employees are an important asset (highly relevant), but the problems of determining their value and measuring it reliably have not yet been solved. Consequently, human resources are not recorded. Perhaps when measurement techniques become more sophisticated and accepted, such information will be presented, if only in supplemental form.

The FASB uses the phrase "transactions and other events and circumstances that affect a business enterprise" to describe the sources or causes of changes in an entity's

UNDERLYING CONCEPTS

Assets are probable economic benefits controlled by a particular entity as a result of a past transaction or event. Do human resources of a company meet this definition?

assets, liabilities, and equity.[2] Events are of two types: (1) **External events** involve interaction between an entity and its environment, such as a transaction with another entity, a change in the price of a good or service that an entity buys or sells, a flood or earthquake, or an improvement in technology by a competitor. (2) **Internal events** occur within an entity, such as using buildings and machinery in operations, or transferring or consuming raw materials in production processes.

Many events have both external and internal elements. For example, hiring an employee, which involves an exchange of salary for labor, is an external event. Using the services of labor is part of production, an internal event. Further, an entity may initiate and control events, such as the purchase of merchandise or use of a machine. Or, events may be beyond its control, such as an interest rate change, theft, or a tax hike.

Transactions are types of external events. They may be an exchange between two entities where each receives and sacrifices value, such as purchases and sales of goods or services. Or, transactions may be transfers in one direction only. For example, an entity may incur a liability without directly receiving value in exchange, such as charitable contributions. Other examples include investments by owners, distributions to owners, payment of taxes, gifts, casualty losses, and thefts.

In short, an enterprise records as many events as possible that affect its financial position. As discussed earlier in the case of human resources, it omits some events because of tradition and others because of complicated measurement problems. Recently, however, the accounting profession shows more receptiveness to accepting the challenge of measuring and reporting events previously viewed as too complex and immeasurable.

Journalizing

A company records in **accounts** those transactions and events that affect its assets, liabilities, and equities. The **general ledger** contains all the asset, liability, stockholders' equity, revenue, and expense accounts. A **T-account** (see Illustration 3-3, page 65) shows the effect of transactions on particular asset, liability, equity, revenue, and expense accounts.

In practice, companies do not record transactions and selected other events originally in the ledger. A transaction affects two or more accounts, each of which is on a different page in the ledger. Therefore, in order to have a complete record of each transaction or other event in one place, a company uses a **journal** (also called "the book of original entry"). In its simplest form, a **general journal** chronologically lists transactions and other events, expressed in terms of debits and credits to accounts.

Illustration 3-7 depicts the technique of journalizing, using the first two transactions for Softbyte, Inc. These transactions were:

> September 1   Stockholders invested $15,000 cash in the corporation in exchange for shares of stock.
>
> Purchased computer equipment for $7,000 cash.

The J1 indicates these two entries are on the first page of the general journal.

> **OBJECTIVE 4**
> Record transactions in journals, post to ledger accounts, and prepare a trial balance.

GENERAL JOURNAL J1

Date	Account Titles and Explanation	Ref.	Debit	Credit
2007 Sept. 1	Cash		15,000	
	Common Stock			15,000
	(Issued shares of stock for cash)			
1	Computer Equipment		7,000	
	Cash			7,000
	(Purchased equipment for cash)			

ILLUSTRATION 3-7
Technique of Journalizing

---

[2]"Elements of Financial Statements of Business Enterprises," *Statement of Financial Accounting Concepts No. 6* (Stamford, Conn.: FASB, 1985), pp. 259–260.

Expanded Discussion of Special Journals

Each **general journal entry** consists of four parts: (1) the accounts and amounts to be debited (Dr.), (2) the accounts and amounts to be credited (Cr.), (3) a date, and (4) an explanation. A company enters debits first, followed by the credits (slightly indented). The explanation begins below the name of the last account to be credited and may take one or more lines. A company completes the "Ref." column at the time it posts the accounts.

In some cases, a company uses **special journals** in addition to the general journal. Special journals summarize transactions possessing a common characteristic (e.g., cash receipts, sales, purchases, cash payments). As a result, using them reduces bookkeeping time.

Posting

The procedure of transferring journal entries to the ledger accounts is called **posting**. Posting involves the following steps.

1 In the ledger, enter in the appropriate columns of the debited account(s) the date, journal page, and debit amount shown in the journal.

2 In the reference column of the journal, write the account number to which the debit amount was posted.

3 In the ledger, enter in the appropriate columns of the credited account(s) the date, journal page, and credit amount shown in the journal.

4 In the reference column of the journal, write the account number to which the credit amount was posted.

Illustration 3-8 diagrams these four steps, using the first journal entry of Softbyte, Inc. The illustration shows the general ledger accounts in **standard account form**. Some

ILLUSTRATION 3-8
Posting a Journal Entry

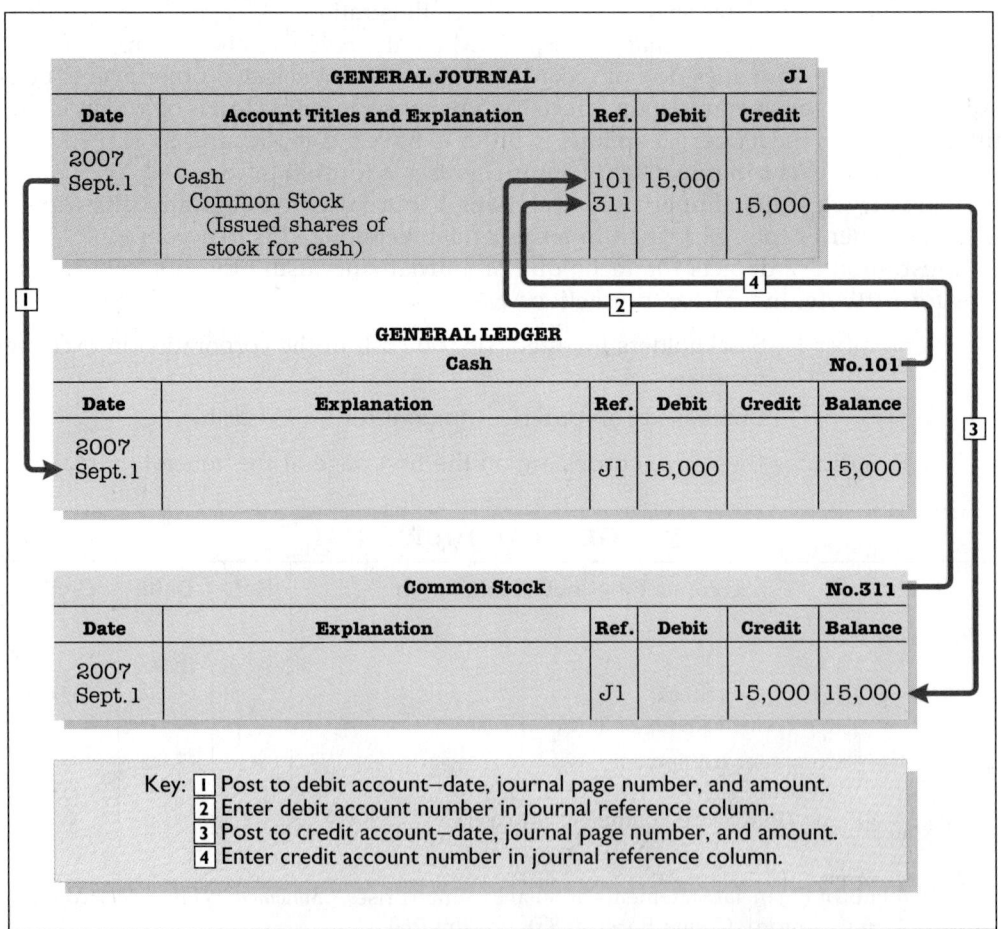

companies call this form the **three-column form of account** because it has three money columns—debit, credit, and balance. The balance in the account is determined after each transaction. The explanation space and reference columns provide special information about the transaction. The boxed numbers indicate the sequence of the steps.

The numbers in the "Ref." column of the general journal refer to the ledger accounts to which a company posts the respective items. For example, the "101" placed in the column to the right of "Cash" indicates that the company posted this $15,000 item to Account No. 101 in the ledger.

The posting of the general journal is completed when a company records all of the posting reference numbers opposite the account titles in the journal. Thus the number in the posting reference column serves two purposes: (1) It indicates the ledger account number of the account involved. (2) It indicates the completion of posting for the particular item. Each company selects its own numbering system for its ledger accounts. Many begin numbering with asset accounts and then follow with liabilities, owners' equity, revenue, and expense accounts, in that order.

The ledger accounts in Illustration 3-8 show the accounts after completion of the posting process. The reference J1 (General Journal, page 1) indicates the source of the data transferred to the ledger account.

Expanded Example. To show an expanded example of the basic steps in the recording process, we use the October transactions of Pioneer Advertising Agency Inc. Pioneer's accounting period is a month. Illustrations 3-9 through 3-18 show the journal entry and posting of each transaction. For simplicity, we use a T-account form instead of the standard account form. Study the transaction analyses carefully.

The purpose of transaction analysis is (1) to identify the type of account involved, and (2) to determine whether a debit or a credit is required. You should always perform this type of analysis before preparing a journal entry. Doing so will help you understand the journal entries discussed in this chapter as well as more complex journal entries in later chapters. Keep in mind that every journal entry affects one or more of the following items: assets, liabilities, stockholders' equity, revenues, or expenses.

1 October 1: Stockholders invest $100,000 cash in an advertising venture to be known as Pioneer Advertising Agency Inc.

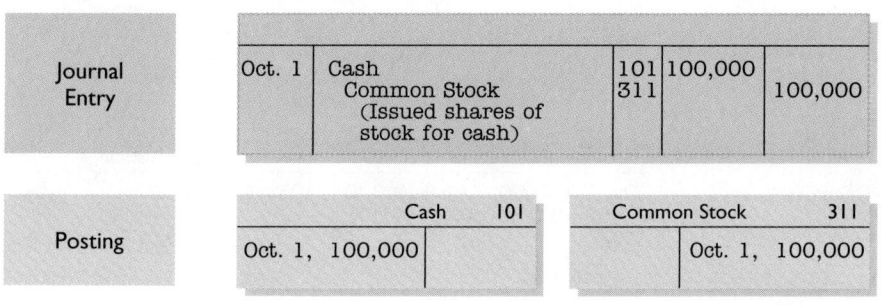

ILLUSTRATION 3-9
Investment of Cash by Stockholders

2 October 1: Pioneer Advertising purchases office equipment costing $50,000 by signing a 3-month, 12%, $50,000 note payable.

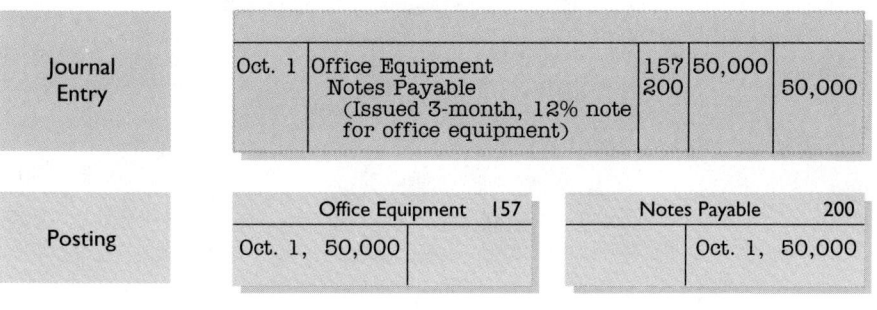

ILLUSTRATION 3-10
Purchase of Office Equipment

3 October 2: Pioneer Advertising receives a $12,000 cash advance from R. Knox, a client, for advertising services that are expected to be completed by December 31.

ILLUSTRATION 3-11
Receipt of Cash for
Future Service

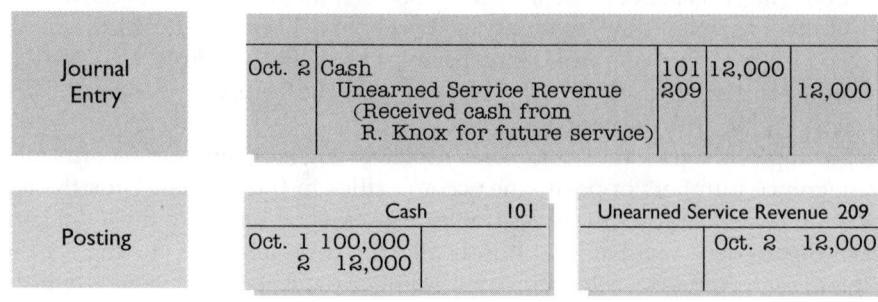

4 October 3: Pioneer Advertising pays $9,000 office rent, in cash, for October.

ILLUSTRATION 3-12
Payment of Monthly Rent

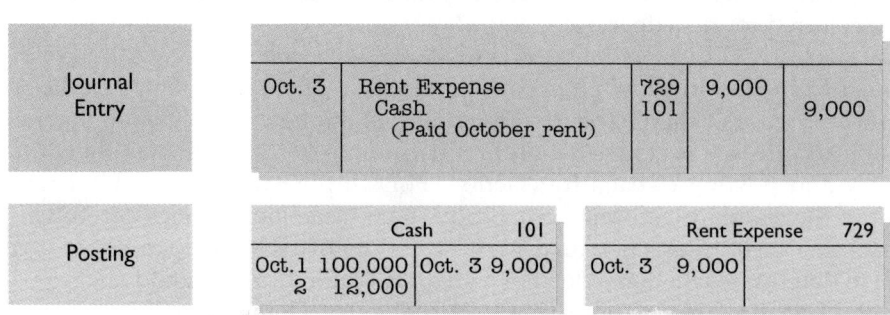

5 October 4: Pioneer Advertising pays $6,000 for a one-year insurance policy that will expire next year on September 30.

ILLUSTRATION 3-13
Payment for Insurance

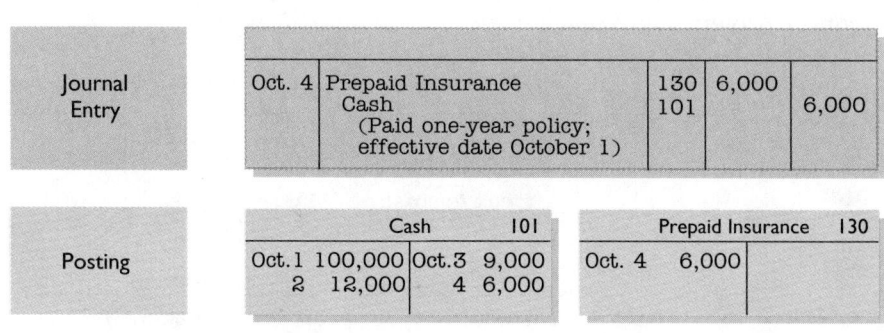

6 October 5: Pioneer Advertising purchases, for $25,000 on account, an estimated 3-month supply of advertising materials from Aero Supply.

ILLUSTRATION 3-14
Purchase of Supplies on
Account

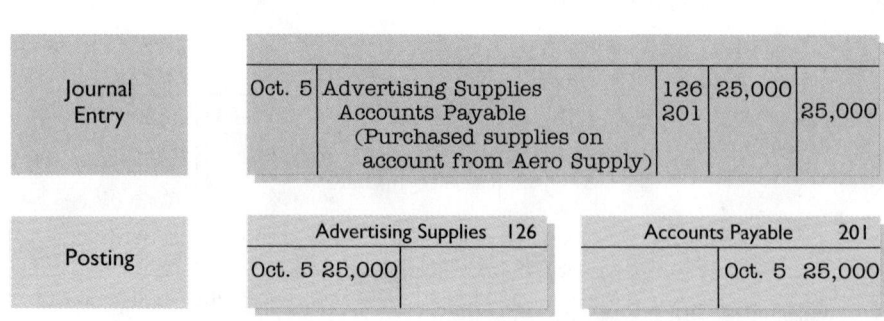

7 October 9: Pioneer Advertising signs a contract with a local newspaper for advertising inserts (flyers) to be distributed starting the last Sunday in November. Pioneer will start work on the content of the flyers in November. Payment of $7,000 is due following delivery of the Sunday papers containing the flyers.

> A business transaction has not occurred. There is only an agreement between Pioneer Advertising and the newspaper for the services to be provided in November. Therefore, no journal entry is necessary in October.

ILLUSTRATION 3-15
Signing a Contract

8 October 20: Pioneer Advertising's board of directors declares and pays a $5,000 cash dividend to stockholders.

ILLUSTRATION 3-16
Declaration and Payment of Dividend by Corporation

Journal Entry	Oct. 20	Dividends	332	5,000	
		Cash	101		5,000
		(Declared and paid a cash dividend)			

Posting		Cash	101			Dividends	332
	Oct.1 100,000	Oct. 3 9,000			Oct. 20 5,000		
	2 12,000	4 6,000					
		20 5,000					

9 October 26: Pioneer Advertising pays employee salaries in cash. Employees are paid once a month, every four weeks. The total payroll is $10,000 per week, or $2,000 per day. In October, the pay period began on Monday, October 1. As a result, the pay period ended on Friday, October 26, with salaries of $40,000 being paid.

ILLUSTRATION 3-17
Payment of Salaries

Journal Entry	Oct. 26	Salaries Expense	726	40,000	
		Cash	101		40,000
		(Paid salaries to date)			

Posting		Cash	101			Salaries Expense	726
	Oct.1 100,000	Oct.3 9,000			Oct.26 40,000		
	2 12,000	4 6,000					
		20 5,000					
		26 40,000					

10 October 31: Pioneer Advertising receives $28,000 in cash and bills Copa Company $72,000 for advertising services of $100,000 provided in October. (See Illustration 3-18 on the following page.)

Journal Entry	Oct. 31	Cash	101	28,000
		Accounts Receivable	112	72,000
		Service Revenue	400		100,000
		(Recognize revenue for services provided)		

Posting

Cash		101			Accounts Receivable	112		Service Revenue	400
Oct.1	100,000	Oct.3	9,000	Oct. 31	72,000			Oct. 31	100,000
2	12,000	4	6,000						
31	28,000	20	5,000						
		26	40,000						

ILLUSTRATION 3-18
Recognize Revenue for
Services Provided

Trial Balance

A **trial balance** lists accounts and their balances at a given time. A company usually prepares a trial balance at the end of an accounting period. The trial balance lists the accounts in the order in which they appear in the ledger, with debit balances listed in the left column and credit balances in the right column. The totals of the two columns must agree.

The trial balance proves the mathematical equality of debits and credits after posting. Under the double-entry system this equality occurs when the sum of the debit account balances equals the sum of the credit account balances. A trial balance also uncovers errors in journalizing and posting. In addition, it is useful in the preparation of financial statements. The procedures for preparing a trial balance consist of:

1 Listing the account titles and their balances.
2 Totaling the debit and credit columns.
3 Proving the equality of the two columns.

For example, Illustration 3-19 presents the trial balance prepared from the ledger of Pioneer Advertising Agency Inc. Note that the total debits ($287,000) equal the total credits ($287,000). A trial balance also often shows account numbers to the left of the account titles.

ILLUSTRATION 3-19
Trial Balance
(Unadjusted)

PIONEER ADVERTISING AGENCY INC.
TRIAL BALANCE
OCTOBER 31, 2007

	Debit	Credit
Cash	$ 80,000	
Accounts Receivable	72,000	
Advertising Supplies	25,000	
Prepaid Insurance	6,000	
Office Equipment	50,000	
Notes Payable		$ 50,000
Accounts Payable		25,000
Unearned Service Revenue		12,000
Common Stock		100,000
Dividends	5,000	
Service Revenue		100,000
Salaries Expense	40,000	
Rent Expense	9,000	
	$287,000	$287,000

A trial balance does not prove that a company recorded all transactions or that the ledger is correct. Numerous errors may exist even though the trial balance columns agree. For example, the trial balance may balance even when a company (1) fails to journalize a transaction, (2) omits posting a correct journal entry, (3) posts a journal entry twice, (4) uses incorrect accounts in journalizing or posting, or (5) makes offsetting errors in recording the amount of a transaction. In other words, as long as a company posts equal debits and credits, even to the wrong account or in the wrong amount, the total debits will equal the total credits.

Adjusting Entries

In order for a company, like **McDonald's**, to record revenues in the period in which it earns them, and to recognize expenses in the period in which it incurs them, McDonald's makes **adjusting entries** at the end of the accounting period. In short, adjustments ensure that McDonald's follows the revenue recognition and matching principles.

The use of adjusting entries makes it possible to report on the balance sheet the appropriate assets, liabilities, and owners' equity at the statement date. Adjusting entries also make it possible to report on the income statement the proper revenues and expenses for the period. However, the trial balance—the first pulling together of the transaction data—may not contain up-to-date and complete data. This occurs for the following reasons.

> **OBJECTIVE 5**
> Explain the reasons for preparing adjusting entries.

1 Some events are not journalized daily because it is not expedient. Examples are the consumption of supplies and the earning of wages by employees.

2 Some costs are not journalized during the accounting period because these costs expire with the passage of time rather than as a result of recurring daily transactions. Examples of such costs are building and equipment deterioration and rent and insurance.

3 Some items may be unrecorded. An example is a utility service bill that will not be received until the next accounting period.

Adjusting entries are required every time a company, such as **Coca-Cola**, prepares financial statements. At that time, Coca-Cola must analyze each account in the trial balance to determine whether it is complete and up-to-date for financial statement purposes. The analysis requires a thorough understanding of Coca-Cola's operations and the interrelationship of accounts. Because of this involved process, usually a skilled accountant prepares the adjusting entries. In gathering the adjustment data, Coca-Cola may need to make inventory counts of supplies and repair parts. Further, it may prepare supporting schedules of insurance policies, rental agreements, and other contractual commitments. Companies often prepare adjustments after the balance sheet date. However, they date the entries as of the balance sheet date.

Types of Adjusting Entries

Adjusting entries are classified as either prepayments or accruals. Each of these classes has two subcategories, as Illustration 3-20 shows.

Prepayments	Accruals
1. **Prepaid Expenses.** Expenses paid in cash and recorded as assets before they are used or consumed.	3. **Accrued Revenues.** Revenues earned but not yet received in cash or recorded.
2. **Unearned Revenues.** Revenues received in cash and recorded as liabilities before they are earned.	4. **Accrued Expenses.** Expenses incurred but not yet paid in cash or recorded.

ILLUSTRATION 3-20
Classes of Adjusting Entries

We review specific examples and explanations of each type of adjustment in subsequent sections. We base each example on the October 31 trial balance of Pioneer Advertising Agency Inc. (Illustration 3-19). We assume that Pioneer uses an accounting period of one month. Thus, Pioneer will make monthly adjusting entries, dated October 31.

Adjusting Entries for Prepayments

As we indicated earlier, prepayments are either prepaid expenses or unearned revenues. Adjusting entries for prepayments, required at the statement date, record the portion of the prepayment that represents the **expense incurred or the revenue earned** in the current accounting period.

If a company does not make an adjustment for these prepayments, the asset and liability are overstated, and the related expense and revenue are understated. For example, in Pioneer's trial balance (Illustration 3-19), the balance in the asset Advertising Supplies shows only supplies purchased. This balance is overstated; the related expense account, Supplies Expense, is understated because the cost of supplies used has not been recognized. Thus the adjusting entry for prepayments will decrease a balance sheet account and increase an income statement account. Illustration 3-21 shows the effects of adjusting entries for prepayments.

ILLUSTRATION 3-21
Adjusting Entries for Prepayments

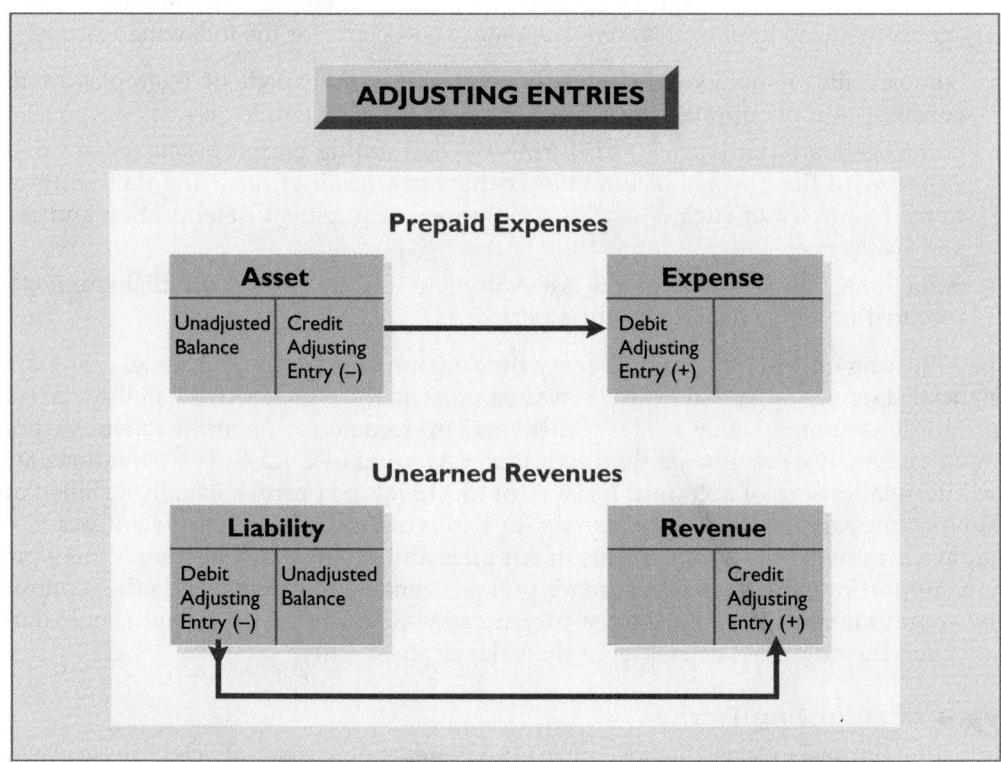

Prepaid Expenses. Assets paid for and recorded before a company, uses them are called **prepaid expenses.** When a company incurs a cost, it debits an asset account to show the service or benefit it will receive in the future. Prepayments often occur in regard to insurance, supplies, advertising, and rent. In addition, companies make prepayments when purchasing buildings and equipment.

Prepaid expenses expire either with the passage of time (e.g., rent and insurance) or **through use and consumption** (e.g., supplies). The expiration of these costs does not require daily recurring entries, an unnecessary and impractical task. Accordingly, a company, like **Walgreens,** usually postpones the recognition of such cost expirations until it prepares financial statements. At each statement date, Walgreens makes adjusting entries to record the expenses that apply to the current accounting period and to show the unexpired costs in the asset accounts.

As was shown above, prior to adjustment, assets are overstated and expenses are understated. Thus, the prepaid expense adjusting entry results in a debit to an expense account and a credit to an asset account.

Supplies. A business enterprise may use several different types of supplies. For example, a CPA firm will use office supplies such as stationery, envelopes, and accounting paper. An advertising firm will stock advertising supplies such as graph paper, video film, and poster paper. Supplies are generally debited to an asset account when they are acquired. Recognition of supplies used is generally deferred until the adjustment process. At that time, a physical inventory (count) of supplies is taken. The difference between the balance in the Supplies (asset) account and the cost of supplies on hand represents the supplies used (expense) for the period.

For example, Pioneer (see Illustration 3-19) purchased advertising supplies costing $25,000 on October 5. Pioneer therefore debited the asset Advertising Supplies. This account shows a balance of $25,000 in the October 31 trial balance. An inventory count at the close of business on October 31 reveals that $10,000 of supplies are still on hand. Thus, the cost of supplies used is $15,000 ($25,000 − $10,000). Pioneer makes the following adjusting entry.

Oct. 31

Advertising Supplies Expense	15,000	
Advertising Supplies		15,000
(To record supplies used)		

After Pioneer posts the adjusting entry, the two supplies accounts in T-account form show the following.

Advertising Supplies				Advertising Supplies Expense		
10/ 5	25,000	10/31	Adj. 15,000	10/31	Adj. 15,000	
10/31	Bal. 10,000					

The asset account Advertising Supplies now shows a balance of $10,000, which equals the cost of supplies on hand at the statement date. In addition, Advertising Supplies Expense shows a balance of $15,000, which equals the cost of supplies used in October. **Without an adjusting entry, October expenses are understated and net income overstated by $15,000. Moreover, both assets and owners' equity are overstated by $15,000 on the October 31 balance sheet.**

Insurance. Most companies maintain fire and theft insurance on merchandise and equipment, personal liability insurance for accidents suffered by customers, and automobile insurance on company cars and trucks. The extent of protection against loss determines the cost of the insurance (the amount of the premium to be paid.) The insurance policy specifies the term and coverage. The minimum term usually covers one year, but three- to five-year terms are available and may offer lower annual premiums. A company usually debits insurance premiums to the asset account Prepaid Insurance when paid. At the financial statement date, it then debits Insurance Expense and credits Prepaid Insurance for the cost that expired during the period.

For example, on October 4, Pioneer paid $6,000 for a one-year fire insurance policy, beginning October 1. Pioneer debited the cost of the premium to Prepaid Insurance at that time. This account still shows a balance of $6,000 in the October 31 trial balance. An analysis of the policy reveals that $500 ($6,000 ÷ 12) of insurance expires each month. Thus, Pioneer makes the following adjusting entry.

Oct. 31

Insurance Expense	500	
Prepaid Insurance		500
(To record insurance expired)		

Sidebar

Supplies

Oct. 5

Supplies purchased; record asset

Oct. 31

Supplies used; record supplies expense

A	=	L	+	SE
				−15,000
−15,000				

Cash Flows
no effect

ILLUSTRATION 3-22
Supplies Accounts after Adjustment

Insurance

Oct. 4

Insurance purchased; record asset

Insurance Policy			
Oct	Nov	Dec	Jan
$500	$500	$500	$500
Feb	March	April	May
$500	$500	$500	$500
June	July	Aug	Sept
$500	$500	$500	$500
1 YEAR $6,000			

Oct. 31

Insurance expired; record insurance expense

A	=	L	+	SE
				−500
−500				

Cash Flows
no effect

After Pioneer posts the adjusting entry, the insurance-related accounts show:

ILLUSTRATION 3-23
Insurance Accounts after
Adjustment

Prepaid Insurance					Insurance Expense			
10/ 4	6,000	10/31	Adj.	500	10/31	Adj.	500	
10/31	Bal. 5,500							

The asset Prepaid Insurance shows a balance of $5,500, which represents the unexpired cost for the remaining 11 months of coverage. At the same time, the balance in Insurance Expense equals the insurance cost that expired in October. **Without an adjusting entry, October expenses are understated by $500 and net income overstated by $500. Moreover, both assets and owners' equity also are overstated by $500 on the October 31 balance sheet.**

Depreciation. Companies, like **Caterpillar** or **Boeing**, typically own various productive facilities, such as buildings, equipment, and motor vehicles. These assets provide a service for a number of years. The term of service is commonly referred to as the **useful life** of the asset. Because Caterpillar, for example, expects an asset such as a building to provide service for many years, Caterpillar records the building as an asset, rather than an expense, in the year the building is acquired. Caterpillar records such assets at cost, as required by the historical cost principle.

According to the matching principle, Caterpillar should report a portion of the cost of a long-lived asset as an expense during each period of the asset's useful life. The process of **depreciation** allocates the cost of an asset to expense over its useful life in a rational and systematic manner.

Need for depreciation adjustment. Generally accepted accounting principles (GAAP) view the acquisition of productive facilities as a long-term prepayment for services. The need for making periodic adjusting entries for depreciation is, therefore, the same as we described for other prepaid expenses. That is, a company recognizes the expired cost (expense) during the period and reports the unexpired cost (asset) at the end of the period. The primary causes of depreciation of a productive facility are actual use, deterioration due to the elements, and obsolescence. For example, at the time Caterpillar acquires an asset, the effects of these factors cannot be known with certainty. Therefore, Caterpillar must estimate them. **Thus, depreciation is an estimate rather than a factual measurement of the expired cost.**

To estimate depreciation expense, Caterpillar often divides the cost of the asset by its useful life. For example, if Caterpillar purchases equipment for $10,000 and expects its useful life to be 10 years, Caterpillar records annual depreciation of $1,000.

In the case of Pioneer Advertising, it estimates depreciation on its office equipment to be $4,800 a year (cost $50,000 less salvage value $2,000 divided by useful life of 10 years), or $400 per month. Accordingly, Pioneer recognizes depreciation for October by the following adjusting entry.

Depreciation

Oct. 1

Office equipment purchased; record asset ($50,000)

Office Equipment			
Oct	Nov	Dec	Jan
$400	$400	$400	$400
Feb	March	April	May
$400	$400	$400	$400
June	July	Aug	Sept
$400	$400	$400	$400
Depreciation = $4,800/year			

Oct. 31
  Depreciation recognized;
  record depreciation expense

A	=	L	+	SE
				−400
−400				

Cash Flows
no effect

ILLUSTRATION 3-24
Accounts after
Adjustment for
Depreciation

	Oct. 31		
Depreciation Expense		400	
Accumulated Depreciation—Office Equipment			400
(To record monthly depreciation)			

After Pioneer posts the adjusting entry, the accounts show the following.

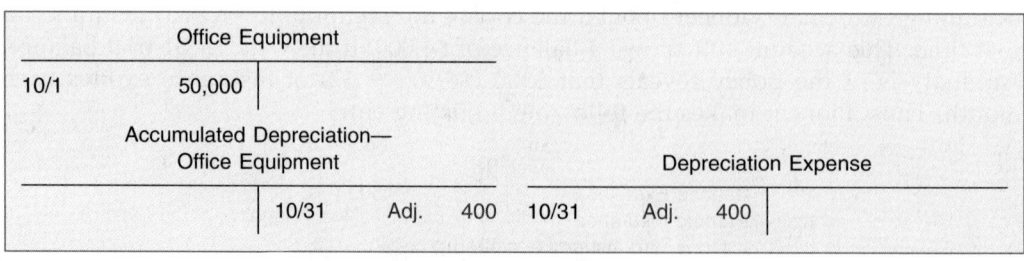

Office Equipment								
10/1	50,000							

Accumulated Depreciation— Office Equipment					Depreciation Expense			
		10/31	Adj.	400	10/31	Adj.	400	

The balance in the accumulated depreciation account will increase $400 each month. Therefore, after journalizing and posting the adjusting entry at November 30, the balance will be $800.

Statement presentation. Accumulated Depreciation—Office Equipment is a contra asset account. A **contra asset account** offsets an asset account on the balance sheet. This means that the accumulated depreciation account offsets the Office Equipment account on the balance sheet. Its normal balance is a credit. Pioneer uses this account instead of crediting Office Equipment in order to disclose both the original cost of the equipment and the total expired cost to date. In the balance sheet, Pioneer deducts Accumulated Depreciation—Office Equipment from the related asset account as follows.

Office equipment	$50,000	
Less: Accumulated depreciation—office equipment	400	$49,600

ILLUSTRATION 3-25
Balance Sheet Presentation of Accumulated Depreciation

The **book value** of any depreciable asset is the difference between its cost and its related accumulated depreciation. In Illustration 3-25, the book value of the equipment at the balance sheet date is $49,600. Note that the asset's book value generally differs from its market value because depreciation is not a matter of valuation but rather a means of cost allocation.

Note also that depreciation expense identifies that portion of the asset's cost that expired in October. As in the case of other prepaid adjustments, without this adjusting entry, total assets, total owners' equity, and net income are overstated, and depreciation expense is understated.

A company records depreciation expense for each piece of equipment, such as delivery or store equipment, and for all buildings. A company also establishes related accumulated depreciation accounts for the above, such as Accumulated Depreciation—Delivery Equipment; Accumulated Depreciation—Store Equipment; and Accumulated Depreciation—Buildings.

Unearned Revenues. Revenues received in cash and recorded as liabilities before a company earns them are called **unearned revenues**. Such items as rent, magazine subscriptions, and customer deposits for future service may result in unearned revenues. Airlines, such as **Northwest**, **American**, and **Southwest**, treat receipts from the sale of tickets as unearned revenue until they provide the flight service. Tuition received prior to the start of a semester is another example of unearned revenue. Unearned revenues are the opposite of prepaid expenses. Indeed, unearned revenue on the books of one company is likely to be a prepayment on the books of the company that made the advance payment. For example, if we assume identical accounting periods, a landlord will have unearned rent revenue when a tenant has prepaid rent.

When a company, such as **Intel**, receives payment for services to be provided in a future accounting period, it credits an unearned revenue (a liability) account to recognize the obligation that exists. It subsequently earns the revenues through rendering service to a customer. However, making daily recurring entries to record this revenue is impractical. Therefore, Intel delays recognition of earned revenue until the adjustment process. Then Intel makes an adjusting entry to record the revenue that it earned and to show the liability that remains. In the typical case, liabilities are overstated and revenues are understated prior to adjustment. **Thus, the adjusting entry for unearned revenues results in a debit (decrease) to a liability account and a credit (increase) to a revenue account.**

For example, Pioneer Advertising received $12,000 on October 2 from R. Knox for advertising services expected to be completed by December 31. Pioneer credited the payment to Unearned Service Revenue. This account shows a balance of $12,000 in the October 31 trial balance. Analysis reveals that Pioneer earned $4,000 of these services in October. Thus, Pioneer makes the following adjusting entry.

Unearned Revenues

Oct. 2

Thank you in advance for your work

I will finish by Dec. 31

~$12,000

Cash is received in advance; liability is recorded

Oct. 31

Service is provided; revenue is recorded

A	=	L	+	SE
−4,000				
				+4,000

Cash Flows
no effect

ILLUSTRATION 3-26
Service Revenue
Accounts after
Prepayments Adjustment

Oct. 31

Unearned Service Revenue	4,000	
Service Revenue		4,000
(To record revenue for services provided)		

After Pioneer posts the adjusting entry, the accounts show the following.

Unearned Service Revenue						Service Revenue			
10/31	Adj.	4,000	10/ 2		12,000		10/31	Bal.	100,000
			10/31	Bal.	8,000		31	Adj.	4,000

The liability Unearned Service Revenue now shows a balance of $8,000, which represents the remaining advertising services expected to be performed in the future. At the same time, Service Revenue shows total revenue earned in October of $104,000. **Without this adjustment, revenues and net income are understated by $4,000 in the income statement. Moreover, liabilities are overstated and owners' equity are understated by $4,000 on the October 31 balance sheet.**

Adjusting Entries for Accruals

The second category of adjusting entries is accruals. Companies make adjusting entries for accruals to record unrecognized revenues earned and expenses incurred in the current accounting period. Without an accrual adjustment, the revenue account (and the related asset account) or the expense account (and the related liability account) are understated. Thus, the adjusting entry for accruals **will increase both a balance sheet and an income statement account**. Illustration 3-27 shows adjusting entries for accruals.

ILLUSTRATION 3-27
Adjusting Entries for
Accruals

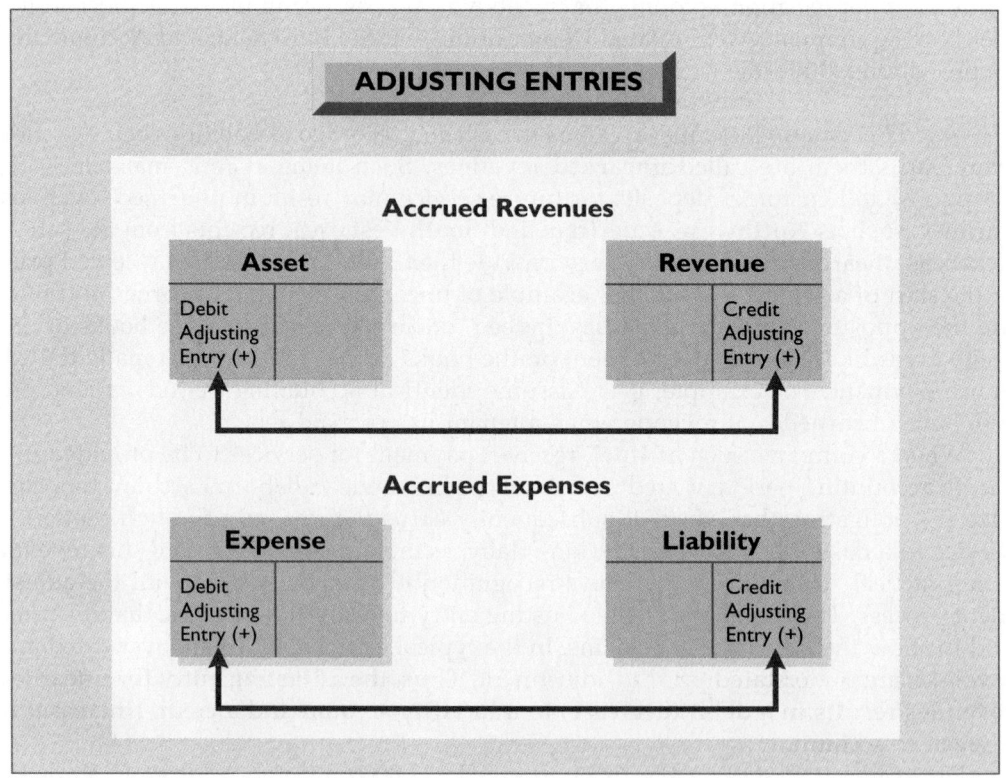

Accrued Revenues. Revenues earned but not yet received in cash or recorded at the statement date are **accrued revenues**. A company accrues revenues with the passing of time, as in the case of interest revenue and rent revenue. Because interest and rent do not involve daily transactions, these items are often unrecorded at the statement date. Or accrued revenues may result from unbilled or uncollected services that a company performed, as in the case of commissions and fees. A company does not record commissions or fees daily, because only a portion of the total service has been provided.

An adjusting entry shows the receivable that exists at the balance sheet date and records the revenue that a company earned during the period. Prior to adjustment both assets and revenues are understated. Accordingly, **an adjusting entry** for accrued revenues results in a debit (increase) to an asset account and a credit (increase) to a revenue account.

In October Pioneer earned $2,000 for advertising services that it did not bill to clients before October 31. Pioneer therefore did not yet record these services. Thus, Pioneer makes the following adjusting entry.

	Oct. 31		
Accounts Receivable		2,000	
Service Revenue			2,000
(To record revenue for services provided)			

A	=	L	+	SE
+2,000				
				+2,000

Cash Flows
no effect

After Pioneer posts the adjusting entry, the accounts show the following.

Accounts Receivable			Service Revenue		
10/31	72,000		10/31		100,000
31	Adj. 2,000		31		4,000
			31	Adj.	2,000
10/31	Bal. 74,000		10/31		Bal. 106,000

ILLUSTRATION 3-28
Receivable and Revenue Accounts after Accrual Adjustment

The asset Accounts Receivable shows that clients owe $74,000 at the balance sheet date. The balance of $106,000 in Service Revenue represents the total revenue earned during the month ($100,000 + $4,000 + $2,000). **Without an adjusting entry, assets and owners' equity on the balance sheet, and revenues and net income on the income statement, are understated.**

Accrued Expenses. Expenses incurred but not yet paid or recorded at the statement date are called **accrued expenses**, such as interest, rent, taxes, and salaries. Accrued expenses result from the same causes as accrued revenues. In fact, an accrued expense on the books of one company is an accrued revenue to another company. For example, the $2,000 accrual of service revenue by Pioneer is an accrued expense to the client that received the service.

Adjustments for accrued expenses record the obligations that exist at the balance sheet date and recognize the expenses that apply to the current accounting period. Prior to adjustment, both liabilities and expenses are understated. Therefore, the adjusting entry for accrued expenses results in a debit (increase) to an expense account and a credit (increase) to a liability account.

Accrued Interest. Pioneer signed a three-month note payable in the amount of $50,000 on October 1. The note requires interest at an annual rate of 12 percent. Three factors determine the amount of the interest accumulation: (1) the face value of the note; (2) the interest rate, which is always expressed as an annual rate; and (3) the length of time the note is outstanding. The total interest due on Pioneer's $50,000 note at its due date three months hence is $1,500 ($50,000 × 12% × 3/12), or $500 for one month. Illustration 3-29 shows the formula for computing interest and its application to Pioneer. Note that the formula expresses the time period as a fraction of a year.

ILLUSTRATION 3-29
Formula for Computing
Interest

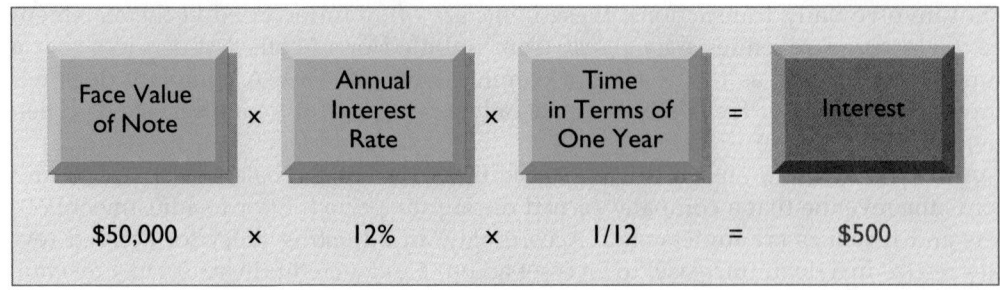

Pioneer makes the accrued expense adjusting entry at October 31 as follows.

A	=	L	+	SE
				−500
+500				

Cash Flows
no effect

	Oct. 31		
Interest Expense		500	
Interest Payable			500
(To record interest on notes payable)			

After Pioneer posts this adjusting entry, the accounts show the following.

ILLUSTRATION 3-30
Interest Accounts after
Adjustment

Interest Expense				Interest Payable		
10/31	500				10/31	500

Interest Expense shows the interest charges applicable to the month of October. Interest Payable shows the amount of interest owed at the statement date. Pioneer will not pay this amount until the note comes due at the end of three months. Why does Pioneer use the Interest Payable account instead of crediting Notes Payable? By recording interest payable separately, Pioneer discloses the two types of obligations (interest and principal) in the accounts and statements. **Without this adjusting entry, both liabilities and interest expense are understated, and both net income and owners' equity are overstated.**

Accrued Salaries. Companies pay for some types of expenses, such as employee salaries and commissions, after the services have been performed. For example, Pioneer last paid salaries on October 26. It will not pay salaries again until November 23. However, as shown in the calendar below, three working days remain in October (October 29–31).

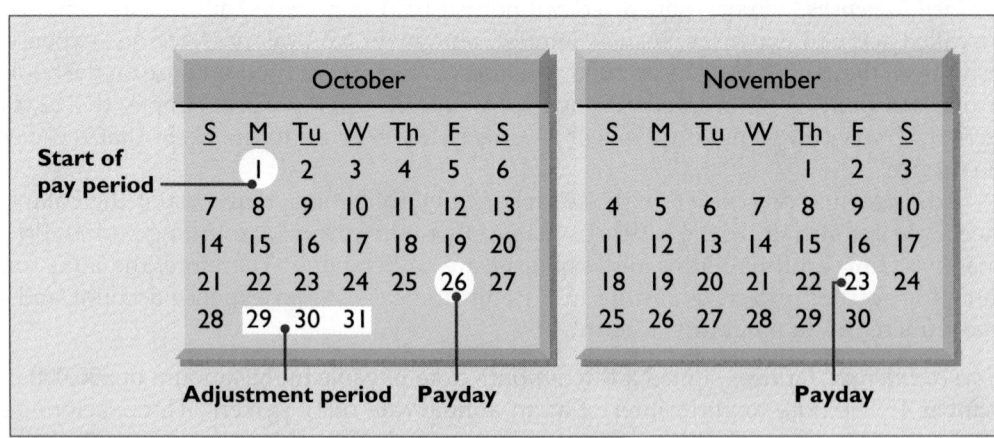

At October 31, the salaries for these days represent an accrued expense and a related liability to Pioneer. The employees receive total salaries of $10,000 for a five-day work week, or $2,000 per day. Thus, accrued salaries at October 31 are $6,000 ($2,000 × 3). Pioneers makes the adjusting entry as follows.

Oct. 31

Salaries Expense	6,000	
Salaries Payable		6,000
(To record accrued salaries)		

A	=	L	+	SE
				−6,000
		+6,000		

Cash Flows
no effect

After Pioneer posts this adjusting entry, the accounts show the following.

ILLUSTRATION 3-31
Salary Accounts after
Adjustment

Salaries Expense		Salaries Payable	
10/26 40,000			10/31 Adj. 6,000
31 Adj. 6,000			
10/31 Bal. 46,000			

After this adjustment, the balance in Salaries Expense of $46,000 (23 days × $2,000) is the actual salary expense for October. The balance in Salaries Payable of $6,000 is the amount of the liability for salaries owed as of October 31. **Without the $6,000 adjustment for salaries, both Pioneer's expenses and liabilities are understated by $6,000.**

Pioneer pays salaries every four weeks. Consequently, the next payday is November 23, when it will again pay total salaries of $40,000. The payment consists of $6,000 of salaries payable at October 31 plus $34,000 of salaries expense for November (17 working days as shown in the November calendar × $2,000). Therefore, Pioneer makes the following entry on November 23.

Nov. 23

Salaries Payable	6,000	
Salaries Expense	34,000	
Cash		40,000
(To record November 23 payroll)		

A	=	L	+	SE
		−6,000		
				−34,000
−40,000				

Cash Flows
−40,000

This entry eliminates the liability for Salaries Payable that Pioneer recorded in the October 31 adjusting entry. This entry also records the proper amount of Salaries Expense for the period between November 1 and November 23.

AM I COVERED?

Rather than purchasing insurance to cover casualty losses and other obligations, some companies "self-insure." That is, a company decides to pay for any possible claims, as they arise, out of its own resources. The company also purchases an insurance policy to cover losses that exceed certain amounts.

For example, **Almost Family, Inc.**, a healthcare services company, has a self-insured employee health-benefit program. However, Almost Family ran into accounting problems when it failed to record an accrual of the liability for benefits not covered by its back-up insurance policy. This led to restatement of Almost Family's fiscal results for the accrual of the benefit expense.

*WHAT DO THE
NUMBERS MEAN?*

Bad Debts

Bad Debts. Proper matching of revenues and expenses dictates recording bad debts as an expense of the period in which a company earned revenue instead of the period in which the company writes off the accounts or notes. The proper valuation of the receivable balance also requires recognition of uncollectible receivables. Proper matching and valuation require an adjusting entry.

At the end of each period, a company, such as **General Mills**, estimates the amount of receivables that will later prove to be uncollectible. General Mills bases the estimate on various factors: the amount of bad debts it experienced in past years, general economic conditions, how long the receivables are past due, and other factors that indicate

Oct. 31
Uncollectible accounts;
record bad debt expense

the extent of uncollectibility. To illustrate, assume that, based on past experience, Pioneer reasonably estimates a bad debt expense for the month of $1,600. It makes the adjusting entry for bad debts as follows.

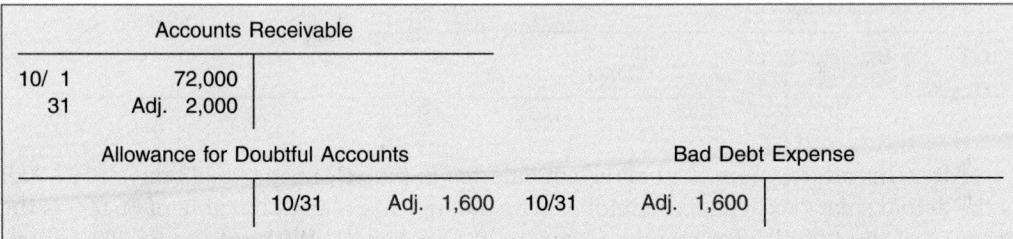

	A	= L	+	SE
	−1,600			−1,600

Oct. 31		
Bad Debt Expense	1,600	
Allowance for Doubtful Accounts		1,600
(To record monthly bad debt expense)		

After Pioneer posts the adjusting entry, the accounts show the following.

ILLUSTRATION 3-32
Accounts after
Adjustment for Bad
Debt Expense

Accounts Receivable		
10/ 1	72,000	
31	Adj. 2,000	

Allowance for Doubtful Accounts			Bad Debt Expense	
	10/31	Adj. 1,600	10/31 Adj. 1,600	

A company often expresses bad debts as a percentage of the revenue on account for the period. Or a company may compute bad debts by adjusting the Allowance for Doubtful Accounts to a certain percentage of the trade accounts receivable and trade notes receivable at the end of the period.

Adjusted Trial Balance

After journalizing and posting all adjusting entries, Pioneer prepares another trial balance from its ledger accounts. This trial balance is called an **adjusted trial balance**. It shows the balance of all accounts, including those adjusted, at the end of the accounting period. The adjusted trial balance thus shows the effects of all financial events that occurred during the accounting period.

ILLUSTRATION 3-33
Adjusted Trial Balance

PIONEER ADVERTISING AGENCY INC.
ADJUSTED TRIAL BALANCE
OCTOBER 31, 2007

	Debit	Credit
Cash	$ 80,000	
Accounts Receivable	74,000	
Allowance for Doubtful Accounts		$ 1,600
Advertising Supplies	10,000	
Prepaid Insurance	5,500	
Office Equipment	50,000	
Accumulated Depreciation—		
Office Equipment		400
Notes Payable		50,000
Accounts Payable		25,000
Interest Payable		500
Unearned Service Revenue		8,000
Salaries Payable		6,000
Common Stock		100,000
Dividends	5,000	
Service Revenue		106,000
Salaries Expense	46,000	
Advertising Supplies Expense	15,000	
Rent Expense	9,000	
Insurance Expense	500	
Interest Expense	500	
Depreciation Expense	400	
Bad Debt Expense	1,600	
	$297,500	$297,500

Preparing Financial Statements

Pioneer can prepare financial statements directly from the adjusted trial balance. Illustrations 3-34 and 3-35 show the interrelationships of data in the adjusted trial balance and the financial statements.

OBJECTIVE 6
Prepare financial statements from the adjusted trial balance.

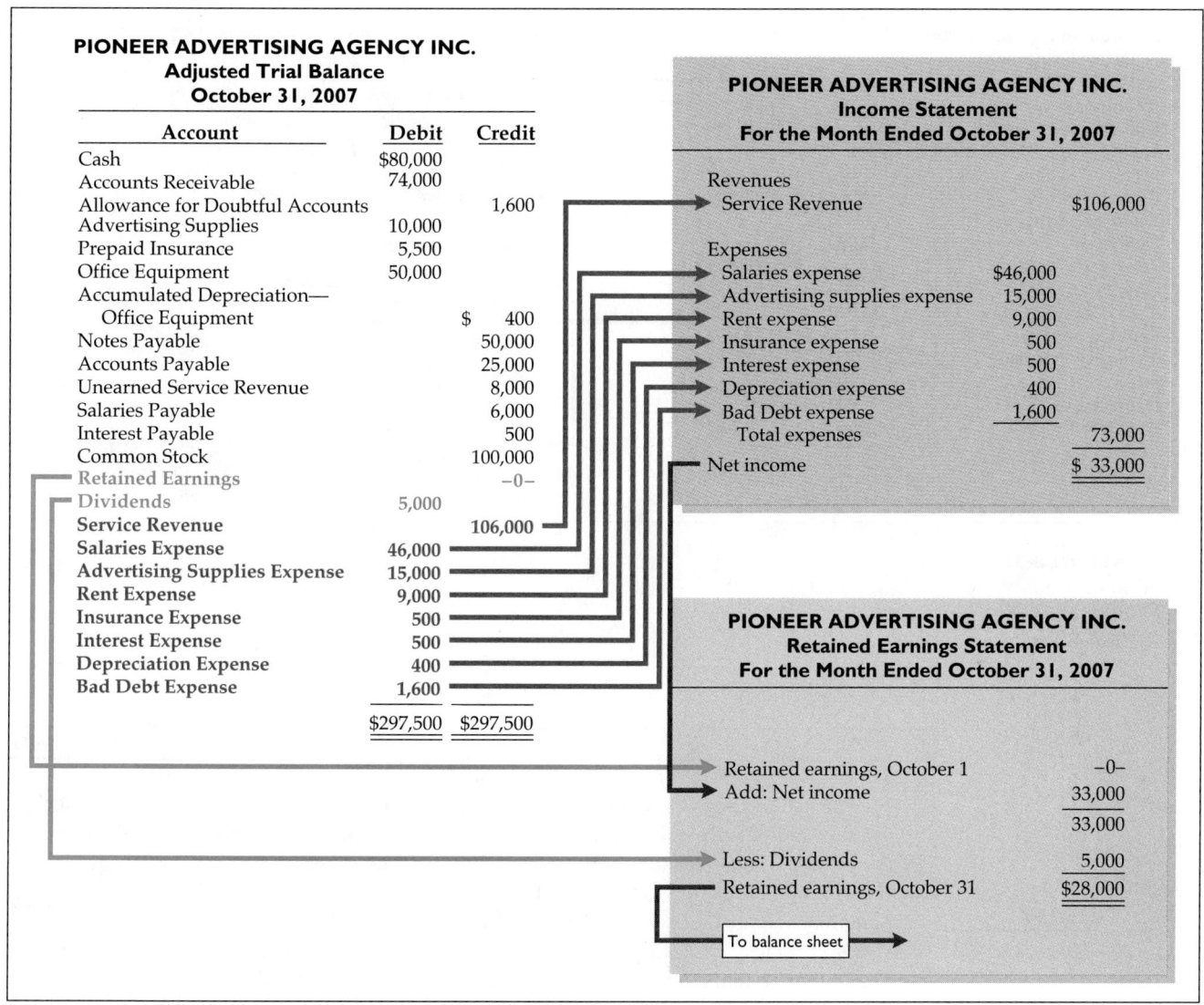

ILLUSTRATION 3-34
Preparation of the Income Statement and Retained Earnings Statement from the Adjusted Trial Balance

As Illustration 3-34 shows, Pioneer begins preparation of the income statement from the revenue and expense accounts. It derives the retained earnings statement from the retained earnings and dividends accounts and the net income (or net loss) shown in the income statement. As Illustration 3-35 shows, Pioneer then prepares the balance sheet from the asset and liability accounts, the common stock account, and the ending retained earnings balance as reported in the retained earnings statement.

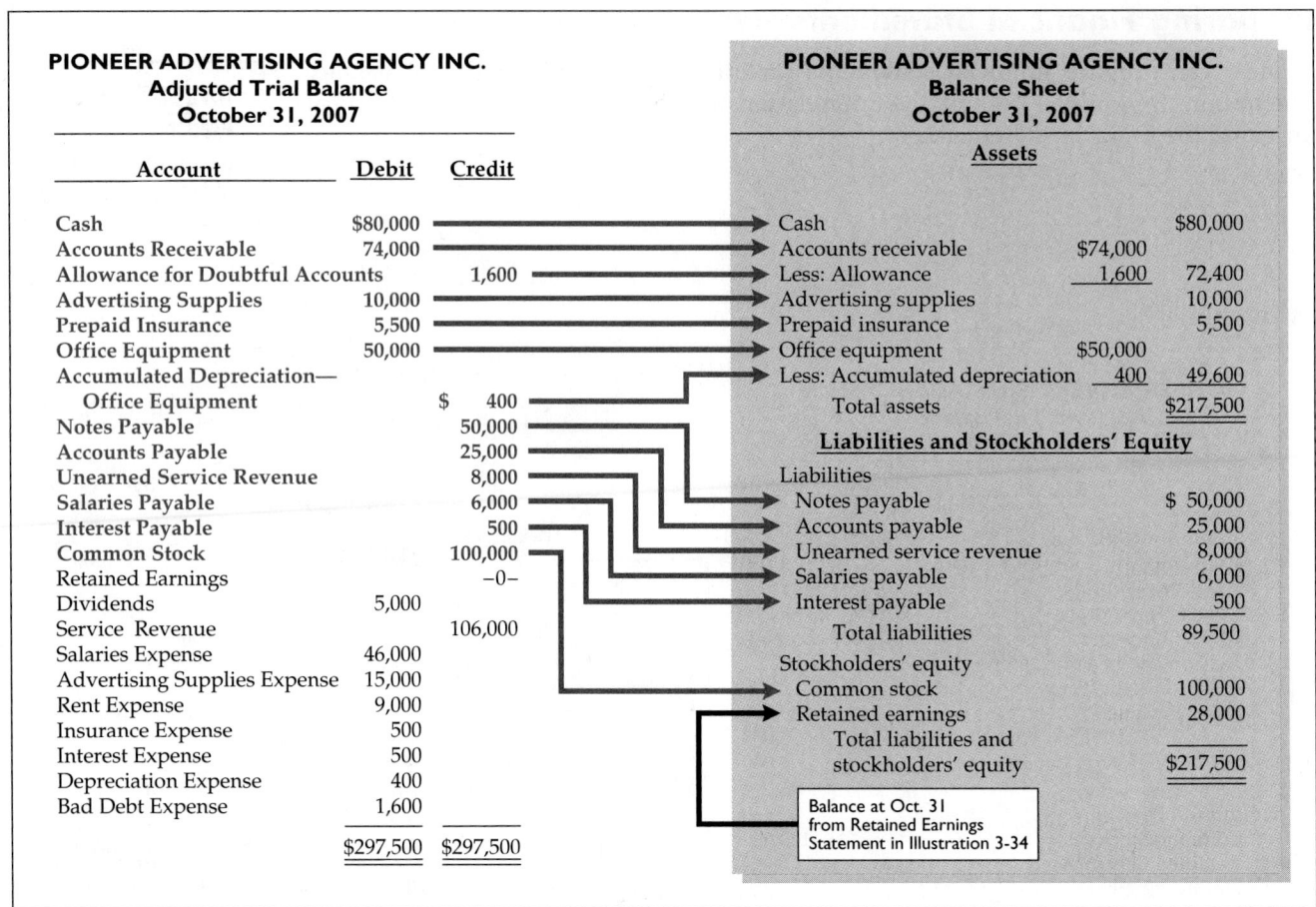

ILLUSTRATION 3-35
Preparation of the
Balance Sheet from the
Adjusted Trial Balance

24/7 ACCOUNTING

WHAT DO THE NUMBERS MEAN?

To achieve the vision of "24/7 accounting," a company must be able to update revenue, income, and balance sheet numbers every day within the quarter and publish them on the Internet. Such real-time reporting responds to the demand for more timely financial information made available to all investors—not just to analysts with access to company management.

Two obstacles typically stand in the way of 24/7 accounting: having the necessary accounting systems to close the books on a daily basis, and reliability concerns associated with unaudited real-time data. Only a few companies have the necessary accounting capabilties. **Cisco Systems**, which pioneered the concept of the 24-hour close, is one such company.

Closing

OBJECTIVE 7
Prepare closing entries.

Basic Process

The **closing process** reduces the balance of nominal (temporary) accounts to zero in order to prepare the accounts for the next period's transactions. In the closing process Pioneer transfers all of the revenue and expense account balances (income statement items) to a clearing or suspense account called Income Summary. The Income Summary account matches revenues and expenses.

Pioneer uses this clearing account only at the end of each accounting period. The account represents the net income or net loss for the period. It then transfers the net result of this matching (the net income or net loss) to an owners' equity account. (For a corporation, the owners' equity account is retained earnings; for proprietorships and partnerships, it is a capital account.) Companies post all such **closing entries** to the appropriate general ledger accounts.

Closing Entries

In practice, companies generally prepare closing entries only at the end of a company's annual accounting period. However, to illustrate the journalizing and posting of closing entries, we will assume that Pioneer Advertising Agency Inc. closes its books monthly. Illustration 3-36 shows the closing entries at October 31.

ILLUSTRATION 3-36
Closing Entries Journalized

	GENERAL JOURNAL		J3
Date	**Account Titles and Explanation**	**Debit**	**Credit**
	Closing Entries		
	(1)		
Oct. 31	Service Revenue	106,000	
	Income Summary		106,000
	(To close revenue account)		
	(2)		
31	Income Summary	73,000	
	Advertising Supplies Expense		15,000
	Depreciation Expense		400
	Insurance Expense		500
	Salaries Expense		46,000
	Rent Expense		9,000
	Interest Expense		500
	Bad Debt Expense		1,600
	(To close expense accounts)		
	(3)		
31	Income Summary	33,000	
	Retained Earnings		33,000
	(To close net income to retained earnings)		
	(4)		
31	Retained Earnings	5,000	
	Dividends		5,000
	(To close dividends to retained earnings)		

A couple of cautions about preparing closing entries: (1) Avoid unintentionally doubling the revenue and expense balances rather than zeroing them. (2) Do not close Dividends through the Income Summary account. **Dividends are not expenses, and they are not a factor in determining net income.**

Posting Closing Entries

Illustration 3-37 shows the posting of closing entries and the ruling of accounts. All temporary accounts have zero balances after posting the closing entries. In addition, note that the balance in Retained Earnings represents the accumulated undistributed earnings of Pioneer at the end of the accounting period. Pioneer reports this amount in the balance sheet as the ending amount reported on the retained earnings statement. As noted above, **Pioneer uses the Income Summary account only in closing.** It does not journalize and post entries to this account during the year.

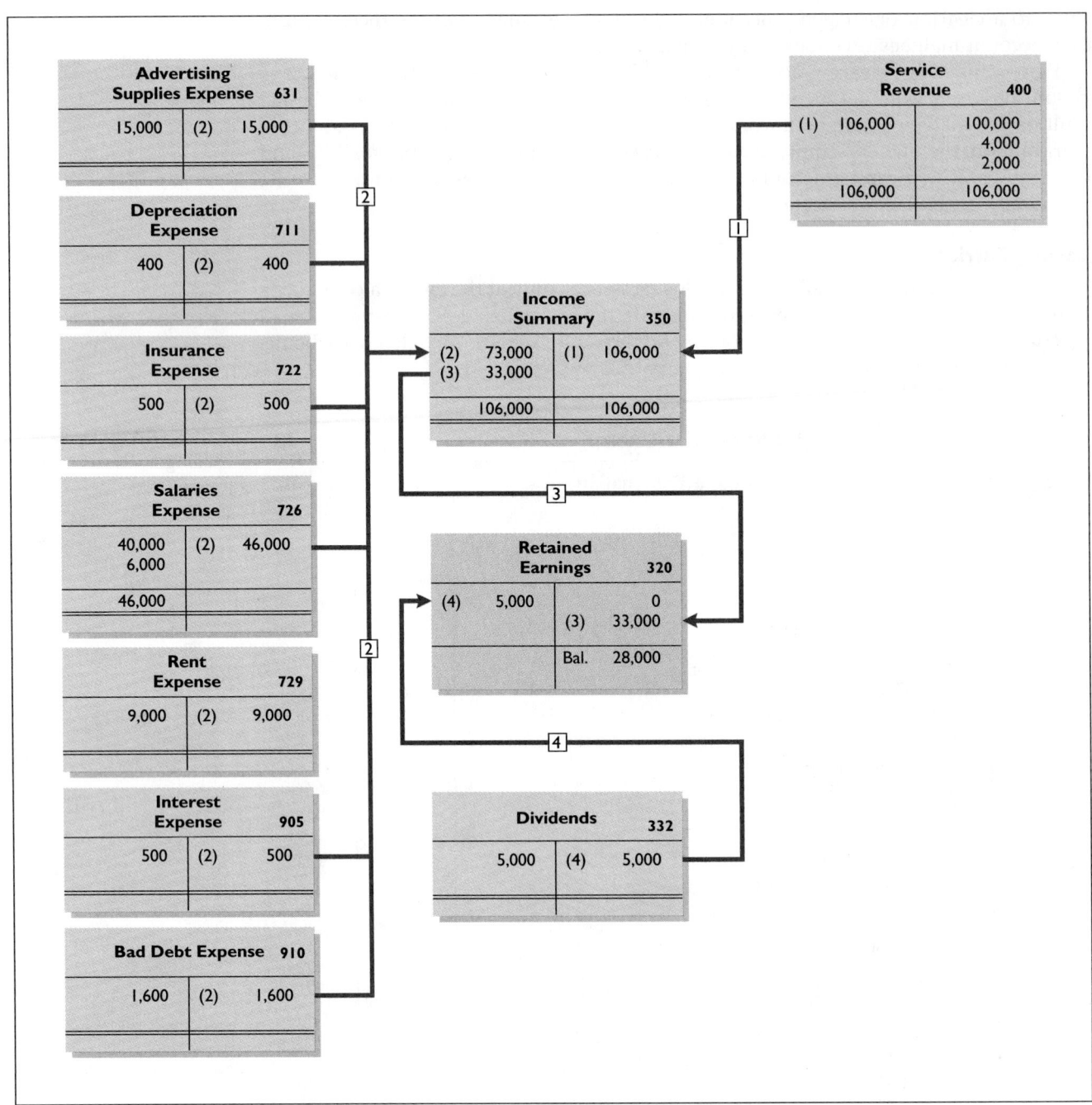

ILLUSTRATION 3-37
Posting of Closing Entries

As part of the closing process, Pioneer totals, balances, and double-rules the **temporary accounts**—revenues, expenses, and dividends—as shown in T-account form in Illustration 3-37. It does not close the **permanent accounts**—assets, liabilities, and stockholders' equity (Common Stock and Retained Earnings). Instead, the preparer draws a single rule beneath the current-period entries, and enters beneath the single rules the account balance to be carried forward to the next period. (For example, see Retained Earnings.)

After the closing process, each income statement account and the dividend account are balanced out to zero and are ready for use in the next accounting period.

Post-Closing Trial Balance

Recall that a trial balance is prepared after entering the regular transactions of the period, and that a second trial balance (the adjusted trial balance) occurs after posting the adjusting entries. A company may take a third trial balance after posting the closing entries.

The trial balance after closing, called the **post-closing trial balance**, consists only of asset, liability, and owners' equity accounts—the real accounts.

Reversing Entries

After preparing the financial statements and closing the books, a company may reverse some of the adjusting entries before recording the regular transactions of the next period. Such entries are called **reversing entries**. A company makes a reversing entry at the beginning of the next accounting period; this entry is the exact opposite of the related adjusting entry made in the previous period. Making reversing entries is an optional step in the accounting cycle that a company may perform at the beginning of the next accounting period. Appendix 3B discusses reversing entries in more detail.

The Accounting Cycle Summarized

A summary of the steps in the accounting cycle shows a logical sequence of the accounting procedures used during a fiscal period:

1 Enter the transactions of the period in appropriate journals.
2 Post from the journals to the ledger (or ledgers).
3 Take an unadjusted trial balance (trial balance).
4 Prepare adjusting journal entries and post to the ledger(s).
5 Take a trial balance after adjusting (adjusted trial balance).
6 Prepare the financial statements from the second trial balance.
7 Prepare closing journal entries and post to the ledger(s).
8 Take a trial balance after closing (post-closing trial balance).
9 Prepare reversing entries (optional) and post to the ledger(s).

A company normally completes all of these steps in every fiscal period.

STATEMENTS, PLEASE

WHAT DO THE NUMBERS MEAN?

The use of a worksheet at the end of each month or quarter enables a company to prepare interim financial statements even though it closes the books only at the end of each year. For example, assume that **Google** closes its books on December 31, but it wants monthly financial statements. To do this, at the end of January, Google prepares an adjusted trial balance (using a worksheet as illustrated in Appendix 3C) to supply the information needed for statements for January.

At the end of February, it uses a worksheet again. Note that because Google did not close the accounts at the end of January, the income statement taken from the adjusted trial balance on February 28 will present the net income for two months. If Google wants an income statement for only the month of February, the company obtains it by subtracting the items in the January income statement from the corresponding items in the income statement for the two months of January and February.

If Google executes such a process daily, it can realize "24/7 accounting" (see box on page 86).

Financial Statements for a Merchandising Company

Pioneer Advertising Agency Inc. is a service company. A detailed set of financial statements is now shown for a merchandising company, Uptown Cabinet Corp. The financial statements on pages 90 and 91 are prepared from the adjusted trial balance.

Income Statement

The income statement for Uptown is self-explanatory. The income statement classifies amounts into such categories as gross profit on sales, income from operations, income before taxes, and net income. Although earnings per share information is required to be shown on the face of the income statement for a corporation, we omit this item here; it will be discussed more fully later in the text. *(For homework problems, do not present earnings per share information unless required to do so).*

ILLUSTRATION 3-38
An Income Statement

UPTOWN CABINET CORP. INCOME STATEMENT FOR THE YEAR ENDED DECEMBER 31, 2007			
Net sales			$400,000
Cost of goods sold			316,000
Gross profit on sales			84,000
Selling expenses			
Sales salaries expense		$20,000	
Traveling expense		8,000	
Advertising expense		2,200	
Total selling expenses		30,200	
Administrative expenses			
Salaries, office and general	$19,000		
Depreciation expense—furniture and equipment	6,700		
Property tax expense	5,300		
Rent expense	4,300		
Bad debt expense	1,000		
Telephone and Internet expense	600		
Insurance expense	360		
Total administrative expenses		37,260	
Total selling and administrative expenses			67,460
Income from operations			16,540
Other revenues and gains			
Interest revenue			800
			17,340
Other expenses and losses			
Interest expense			1,700
Income before income taxes			15,640
Income taxes			3,440
Net income			$ 12,200

Statement of Retained Earnings

A corporation may retain the net income earned in the business, or it may distribute it to stockholders by payment of dividends. In the illustration, Uptown added the net income earned during the year to the balance of retained earnings on January 1, thereby increasing the balance of retained earnings. Deducting dividends of $2,000 results in the ending retained earnings balance of $26,400 on December 31.

ILLUSTRATION 3-39
A Statement of Retained Earnings

UPTOWN CABINET CORP. STATEMENT OF RETAINED EARNINGS FOR THE YEAR ENDED DECEMBER 31, 2007	
Retained earnings, January 1	$16,200
Add: Net income	12,200
	28,400
Less: Dividends	2,000
Retained earnings, December 31	$26,400

Balance Sheet

The balance sheet for Uptown is a classified balance sheet. Interest receivable, prepaid insurance, and prepaid rent expense are included as current assets. Uptown considers these assets current because they will be converted into cash or used by the business within a relatively short period of time. Uptown deducts the amount of Allowance for Doubtful Accounts from the total of accounts, notes, and interest receivable because it estimates that only $54,800 of $57,800 will be collected in cash.

In the property, plant, and equipment section, Uptown deducts the accumulated depreciation from the cost of the furniture and equipment. The difference represents the book or carrying value of the furniture and equipment.

The balance sheet shows property tax payable as a current liability because it is an obligation that is payable within a year. The balance sheet also shows other short-term liabilities such as accounts payable.

The bonds payable, due in 2015, are long-term liabilities. As a result, the balance sheet shows the account in a separate section. (The company paid interest on the bonds on December 31.)

Because Uptown is a corporation, the capital section of the balance sheet, called the stockholders' equity section in the illustration, differs somewhat from the capital section for a proprietorship. Total stockholders' equity consists of the common stock, which is the original investment by stockholders, and the earnings retained in the business. *For homework purposes, unless instructed otherwise, prepare an unclassified balance sheet.*

ILLUSTRATION 3-40
A Balance Sheet

UPTOWN CABINET CORP. BALANCE SHEET AS OF DECEMBER 31, 2007			
Assets			
Current assets			
Cash			$ 1,200
Notes receivable	$16,000		
Accounts receivable	41,000		
Interest receivable	800	$57,800	
Less: Allowance for doubtful accounts		3,000	54,800
Merchandise inventory			40,000
Prepaid insurance			540
Prepaid rent expense			500
Total current assets			97,040
Property, plant, and equipment			
Furniture and equipment		67,000	
Less: Accumulated depreciation		18,700	
Total property, plant, and equipment			48,300
Total assets			$145,340
Liabilities and Stockholders' Equity			
Current liabilities			
Notes payable			$ 20,000
Accounts payable			13,500
Property tax payable			2,000
Income tax payable			3,440
Total current liabilities			38,940
Long-term liabilities			
Bonds payable, due June 30, 2015			30,000
Total liabilities			68,940
Stockholders' equity			
Common stock, $5.00 par value, issued and outstanding, 10,000 shares		$50,000	
Retained earnings		26,400	
Total stockholders' equity			76,400
Total liabilities and stockholders' equity			$145,340

Closing Entries

Uptown makes closing entries as follows.

General Journal
December 31, 2007

Interest Revenue	800	
Sales	400,000	
Income Summary		400,800
(To close revenues to Income Summary)		
Income Summary	388,600	
Cost of Goods Sold		316,000
Sales Salaries Expense		20,000
Traveling Expense		8,000
Advertising Expense		2,200
Salaries, Office and General		19,000
Depreciation Expense—Furniture and Equipment		6,700
Rent Expense		4,300
Property Tax Expense		5,300
Bad Debt Expense		1,000
Telephone and Internet Expense		600
Insurance Expense		360
Interest Expense		1,700
Income Tax Expense		3,440
(To close expenses to Income Summary)		
Income Summary	12,200	
Retained Earnings		12,200
(To close Income Summary to Retained Earnings)		
Retained Earnings	2,000	
Dividends		2,000
(To close Dividends to Retained Earnings)		

Inventory and Cost of Goods Sold

OBJECTIVE 8
Explain how to adjust inventory accounts at year-end.

Because Uptown is a merchandising company, it has inventory. Companies with inventory generally use a **perpetual inventory system**. With such a system, a company records the cost of the inventory purchased and sold directly in the Inventory account as the purchases and sales occur. Therefore, the balance in the Inventory account should represent the ending inventory amount, and no adjusting entries are needed. To ensure this accuracy, a physical count of the items in inventory is performed on an annual basis.

With the perpetual inventory system, because the company debits purchases directly to the Inventory account, it does not use a Purchases account. However, the company does use a Cost of Goods Sold account to accumulate the issuances from inventory. That is, when inventory is sold, the company credits the cost of the sold goods to Inventory and debits Cost of Goods Sold. In closing the accounts, the company credits Cost of Goods Sold and debits Income Summary.

With a **periodic inventory system**, a company uses a Purchases account to record purchases of inventory during the period. Here, the Inventory account remains **unchanged** during the period. The Inventory account represents the beginning inventory amount throughout the period. Then, at the end of the accounting period the company must adjust the inventory account by **closing out the beginning inventory amount** and **recording the ending inventory amount**. A company determines the ending inventory by physically counting the items on hand and valuing them at cost or at the lower-of-cost-or-market. Under the periodic inventory system, a company therefore determines the cost of goods sold by adding the beginning inventory together with net purchases and deducting the ending inventory.

To illustrate how to compute cost of goods sold with a periodic inventory system, assume that Collegiate Apparel Shop begins with an inventory of $30,000. It records purchases of $200,000, transportation-in of $6,000, purchase returns and allowances of $1,000, and purchase discounts of $3,000. The ending inventory is $26,000. Collegiate computes cost of goods sold as shown in Illustration 3-41.

Beginning inventory		$ 30,000
Purchases	$200,000	
Less: Purchase returns and allowances	$1,000	
Purchase discounts	3,000	4,000
Net purchases	196,000	
Plus: Transportation-in	6,000	
Cost of goods purchased		202,000
Cost of goods available for sale		232,000
Less: Ending inventory		26,000
Cost of goods sold		$206,000

ILLUSTRATION 3-41
Computation of Cost of Goods Sold under Periodic Inventory System

Cost of goods sold will be the same amount whether a company uses the perpetual or periodic method.

SUMMARY OF LEARNING OBJECTIVES

1. Understand basic accounting terminology. Understanding the following eleven terms helps in understanding key accounting concepts: (1) Event. (2) Transaction. (3) Account. (4) Real and nominal accounts. (5) Ledger. (6) Journal. (7) Posting. (8) Trial balance. (9) Adjusting entries. (10) Financial statements. (11) Closing entries.

2. Explain double-entry rules. The left side of any account is the debit side; the right side is the credit side. All asset and expense accounts are increased on the left or debit side and decreased on the right or credit side. Conversely, all liability and revenue accounts are increased on the right or credit side and decreased on the left or debit side. Stockholders' equity accounts, Common Stock and Retained Earnings, are increased on the credit side. Dividends is increased on the debit side.

3. Identify steps in the accounting cycle. The basic steps in the accounting cycle are (1) identifying and measuring transactions and other events; (2) journalizing; (3) posting; (4) preparing an unadjusted trial balance; (5) making adjusting entries; (6) preparing an adjusted trial balance; (7) preparing financial statements; and (8) closing.

4. Record transactions in journals, post to ledger accounts, and prepare a trial balance. The simplest journal form chronologically lists transactions and events expressed in terms of debits and credits to particular accounts. The items entered in a general journal must be transferred (posted) to the general ledger. Companies should prepare an unadjusted trial balance at the end of a given period after they have recorded the entries in the journal and posted them to the ledger.

5. Explain the reasons for preparing adjusting entries. Adjustments achieve a proper matching of revenues and expenses, so as to determine net income for the current period and to achieve an accurate statement of end-of-the-period balances in assets, liabilities, and owners' equity accounts.

6. Prepare financial statements from the adjusted trial balance. Companies can prepare financial statements directly from the adjusted trial balance. The income statement is prepared from the revenue and expense accounts. The statement of retained earnings is prepared from the retained earnings account, dividends, and net income (or net loss). The balance sheet is prepared from the asset, liability, and equity accounts.

7. Prepare closing entries. In the closing process, the company transfers all of the revenue and expense account balances (income statement items) to a clearing account called Income Summary, which is used only at the end of the fiscal year. Revenues

KEY TERMS

account, *63*
accounting cycle, *67*
accounting information system, *62*
accrued expenses, *81*
accrued revenues, *80*
adjusted trial balance, *84*
adjusting entry, *63, 75*
balance sheet, *63*
book value, *79*
closing entries, *64, 87*
closing process, *86*
contra asset account, *79*
credit, *64*
debit, *64*
depreciation, *78*
double-entry accounting, *64*
event, *63*
financial statements, *63*
general journal, *69*
general ledger, *69*
income statement, *64*
journal, *63*
ledger, *63*
nominal accounts, *63*
periodic inventory system, *92*
perpetual inventory system, *92*
post-closing trial balance, *89*
posting, *63, 70*
prepaid expenses, *76*

and expenses are matched in the Income Summary account. The net result of this matching represents the net income or net loss for the period. That amount is then transferred to an owners' equity account (Retained Earnings for a corporation and capital accounts for proprietorships and partnerships).

8. **Explain how to adjust inventory accounts at year-end.** Under a perpetual inventory system the balance in the Inventory account represents the ending inventory amount. When companies maintain the inventory records in a periodic inventory system, they use a Purchases account; the Inventory account is unchanged during the period. The Inventory account represents the beginning inventory amount throughout the period. At the end of the accounting period the company must adjust the Inventory account by closing out the beginning inventory amount and recording the ending inventory amount.

APPENDIX

3A Cash-Basis Accounting versus Accrual-Basis Accounting

OBJECTIVE 9
Differentiate the cash basis of accounting from the accrual basis of accounting.

Most companies use **accrual-basis accounting**: They recognize revenue when it is earned and expenses in the period incurred, without regard to the time of receipt or payment of cash.

Some small enterprises and the average individual taxpayer, however, use a strict or modified cash-basis approach. Under the **strict cash basis**, companies record revenue only when they receive cash, and they record expenses only when they disperse cash. Determining income on the cash basis rests upon collecting revenue and paying expenses. The cash basis ignores two principles: the revenue recognition principle and the matching principle. Consequently, cash-basis financial statements are not in conformity with GAAP.

An illustration will help clarify the differences between accrual-basis and cash-basis accounting. Assume that Quality Contractor signs an agreement to construct a garage for $22,000. In January, Quality begins construction, incurs costs of $18,000 on credit, and by the end of January delivers a finished garage to the buyer. In February, Quality collects $22,000 cash from the customer. In March, Quality pays the $18,000 due the creditors. Illustrations 3A-1 and 3A-2 show the net incomes for each month under cash-basis accounting and accrual-basis accounting.

ILLUSTRATION 3A-1
Income Statement—Cash
Basis

QUALITY CONTRACTOR INCOME STATEMENT—CASH BASIS For the Month of				
	January	February	March	Total
Cash receipts	$-0-	$22,000	$ -0-	$22,000
Cash payments	-0-	-0-	18,000	18,000
Net income (loss)	$-0-	$22,000	$(18,000)	$ 4,000

QUALITY CONTRACTOR
INCOME STATEMENT—ACCRUAL BASIS
For the Month of

	January	February	March	Total
Revenues	$22,000	$–0–	$–0–	$22,000
Expenses	18,000	–0–	–0–	18,000
Net income (loss)	$ 4,000	$–0–	$–0–	$ 4,000

ILLUSTRATION 3A-2
Income Statement—
Accrual Basis

For the three months combined, total net income is the same under both cash-basis accounting and accrual-basis accounting. The difference is in the **timing** of revenues and expenses. The basis of accounting also affects the balance sheet. Illustrations 3A-3 and 3A-4 show Quality Contractor's balance sheets at each month-end under the cash basis and the accrual basis.

QUALITY CONTRACTOR
BALANCE SHEETS—CASH BASIS
As of

	January 31	February 28	March 31
Assets			
Cash	$–0–	$22,000	$4,000
Total assets	$–0–	$22,000	$4,000
Liabilities and Owners' Equity			
Owners' equity	$–0–	$22,000	$4,000
Total liabilities and owners' equity	$–0–	$22,000	$4,000

ILLUSTRATION 3A-3
Balance Sheets—Cash
Basis

QUALITY CONTRACTOR
BALANCE SHEETS—ACCRUAL BASIS
As of

	January 31	February 28	March 31
Assets			
Cash	$ –0–	$22,000	$4,000
Accounts receivable	22,000	–0–	–0–
Total assets	$22,000	$22,000	$4,000
Liabilities and Owners' Equity			
Accounts payable	$18,000	$18,000	$ –0–
Owners' equity	4,000	4,000	4,000
Total liabilities and owners' equity	$22,000	$22,000	$4,000

ILLUSTRATION 3A-4
Balance Sheets—Accrual
Basis

Analysis of Quality's income statements and balance sheets shows the ways in which cash-basis accounting is inconsistent with basic accounting theory:

1 The cash basis understates revenues and assets from the construction and delivery of the garage in January. It ignores the $22,000 of accounts receivable, representing a near-term future cash inflow.

2 The cash basis understates expenses incurred with the construction of the garage and the liability outstanding at the end of January. It ignores the $18,000 of accounts payable, representing a near-term future cash outflow.

3 The cash basis understates owners' equity in January by not recognizing the revenues and the asset until February. It also overstates owners' equity in February by not recognizing the expenses and the liability until March.

In short, cash-basis accounting violates the accrual concept underlying financial reporting.

The **modified cash basis** is a mixture of the cash basis and the accrual basis. It is based on the pure cash basis but with modifications that have substantial support, such as capitalizing and depreciating plant assets or recording inventory. This method is often followed by professional services firms (doctors, lawyers, accountants, consultants) and by retail, real estate, and agricultural operations.[1]

CONVERSION FROM CASH BASIS TO ACCRUAL BASIS

Not infrequently companies want to convert a cash basis or a modified cash basis set of financial statements to the accrual basis for presentation to investors and creditors. To illustrate this conversion, assume that Dr. Diane Windsor, like many small business owners, keeps her accounting records on a cash basis. In the year 2007, Dr. Windsor received $300,000 from her patients and paid $170,000 for operating expenses, resulting in an excess of cash receipts over disbursements of $130,000 ($300,000 − $170,000). At January 1 and December 31, 2007, she has accounts receivable, unearned service revenue, accrued liabilities, and prepaid expenses as shown in Illustration 3A-5.

ILLUSTRATION 3A-5
Financial Information
Related to Dr. Diane
Windsor

	January 1, 2007	December 31, 2007
Accounts receivable	$12,000	$9,000
Unearned service revenue	–0–	4,000
Accrued liabilities	2,000	5,500
Prepaid expenses	1,800	2,700

Service Revenue Computation

To convert the amount of cash received from patients to service revenue on an accrual basis, we must consider changes in accounts receivable and unearned service revenue during the year. Accounts receivable at the beginning of the year represents revenues earned last year that are collected this year. Ending accounts receivable indicates revenues earned this year that are not yet collected. Therefore, to compute revenue on an accrual basis, we subtract beginning accounts receivable and add ending accounts receivable, as the formula in Illustration 3A-6 shows.

ILLUSTRATION 3A-6
Conversion of Cash
Receipts to Revenue—
Accounts Receivable

Similarly, beginning unearned service revenue represents cash received last year for revenues earned this year. Ending unearned service revenue results from collections this year that will be recognized as revenue next year. Therefore, to compute revenue

---

[1] Companies in the following situations might use a cash or modified cash basis.

(1) A company that is primarily interested in cash flows (for example, a group of physicians that distributes cash-basis earnings for salaries and bonuses).

(2) A company that has a limited number of financial statement users (small, closely held company with little or no debt).

(3) A company that has operations that are relatively straightforward (small amounts of inventory, long-term assets, or long-term debt).

on an accrual basis, we add beginning unearned service revenue and subtract ending unearned service revenue, as the formula in Illustration 3A-7 shows.

ILLUSTRATION 3A-7
Conversion of Cash Receipts to Revenue—Unearned Service Revenue

Therefore, for Dr. Windsor's dental practice, to convert cash collected from customers to service revenue on an accrual basis, we would make the computations shown in Illustration 3A-8.

Cash receipts from customers		$300,000
− Beginning accounts receivable	$(12,000)	
+ Ending accounts receivable	9,000	
+ Beginning unearned service revenue	−0−	
− Ending unearned service revenue	(4,000)	(7,000)
Service revenue (accrual)		$293,000

ILLUSTRATION 3A-8
Conversion of Cash Receipts to Service Revenue

Operating Expense Computation

To convert cash paid for operating expenses during the year to operating expenses on an accrual basis, we must consider changes in prepaid expenses and accrued liabilities. First, we need to recognize as this year's expenses the amount of beginning prepaid expenses. (The cash payment for these occurred last year.) Therefore, to arrive at operating expense on an accrual basis, we add the beginning prepaid expenses balance to cash paid for operating expenses.

Conversely, ending prepaid expenses result from cash payments made this year for expenses to be reported next year. (Under the accrual basis, Dr. Windsor would have deferred recognizing these payments as expenses until a future period.) To convert these cash payments to operating expenses on an accrual basis, we deduct ending prepaid expenses from cash paid for expenses, as the formula in Illustration 3A-9 shows.

ILLUSTRATION 3A-9
Conversion of Cash Payments to Expenses—Prepaid Expenses

Similarly, beginning accrued liabilities result from expenses recognized last year that require cash payments this year. Ending accrued liabilities relate to expenses recognized this year that have not been paid. To arrive at expense on an accrual basis, we deduct beginning accrued liabilities and add ending accrued liabilities to cash paid for expenses, as the formula in Illustration 3A-10 shows.

ILLUSTRATION 3A-10
Conversion of Cash Payments to Expenses—Accrued Liabilities

Therefore, for Dr. Windsor's dental practice, to convert cash paid for operating expenses to operating expenses on an accrual basis, we would make the computations shown in Illustration 3A-11.

Cash paid for operating expenses		$170,000
+ Beginning prepaid expense	$1,800	
– Ending prepaid expense	(2,700)	
– Beginning accrued liabilities	(2,000)	
+ Ending accrued liabilities	5,500	2,600
Operating expenses (accrual)		$172,600

This entire conversion can be completed in worksheet form as shown in Illustration 3A-12.

ILLUSTRATION 3A-12
Conversion of Statement
of Cash Receipts and
Disbursements to Income
Statement

DIANE WINDSOR, D.D.S.
Conversion of Income Statement Data from Cash Basis to Accrual Basis
For the Year 2007

	A	B	C	D	E
		Cash Basis	Adjustments Add	Adjustments Deduct	Accrual Basis
1					
2	Collections from customers	$300,000			
3	– Accounts receivable, Jan. 1			$12,000	
4	+ Accounts receivable, Dec. 31		$9,000		
5	+ Unearned service revenue, Jan. 1		—	—	
6	– Unearned service revenue, Dec. 31			4,000	
7	Service revenue				$293,000
8	Disbursement for expenses	170,000			
9	+ Prepaid expenses, Jan. 1		1,800		
10	– Prepaid expenses, Dec. 31			2,700	
11	– Accrued liabilities, Jan. 1			2,000	
12	+ Accrued liabilities, Dec. 31		5,500		
13	Operating expenses				172,600
14	Excess of cash collections over disbursements—cash basis	$130,000			
15	Net income—accrual basis				$120,400

Sheet1 / Sheet2 / Sheet3

Using this approach, we adjust collections and disbursements on a cash basis to revenue and expense on an accrual basis, to arrive at accrual net income. In any conversion from the cash basis to the accrual basis, depreciation or amortization is an additional expense in arriving at net income on an accrual basis.

THEORETICAL WEAKNESSES OF THE CASH BASIS

The cash basis reports exactly when cash is received and when cash is disbursed. To many people that information represents something concrete. Isn't cash what it is all about? Does it make sense to invent something, design it, produce it, market and sell it, if you aren't going to get cash for it in the end? Many frequently say, "Cash is the real bottom line," and also, "Cash is the oil that lubricates the economy." If so, then what is the merit of accrual accounting?

Today's economy is considerably more lubricated by credit than by cash. The accrual basis, not the cash basis, recognizes all aspects of the credit phenomenon. Investors, creditors, and other decision makers seek timely information about an enterprise's *future* cash flows. Accrual-basis accounting provides this information by reporting the cash inflows and outflows associated with earnings activities as soon as these companies can estimate these cash flows with an acceptable degree of certainty. Receivables and payables are forecasters of future cash inflows and outflows. In other words, accrual-basis accounting aids in predicting future cash flows by reporting transactions and other events with cash consequences at the time the transactions and events occur, rather than when the cash is received and paid.

> **SUMMARY OF LEARNING OBJECTIVE FOR APPENDIX 3A**

9. Differentiate the cash basis of accounting from the accrual basis of accounting. The cash basis of accounting records revenues when cash is received and expenses when cash is paid. The accrual basis recognizes revenue when earned and expenses in the period incurred, without regard to the time of the receipt or payment of cash. Accrual-basis accounting is theoretically preferable because it provides information about future cash inflows and outflows associated with earnings activities as soon as companies can estimate these cash flows with an acceptable degree of certainty. Cash-basis accounting is not in conformity with GAAP.

APPENDIX 3B

Using Reversing Entries

Use of reversing entries simplifies the recording of transactions in the next accounting period. The use of reversing entries, however, does not change the amounts reported in the financial statements for the previous period.

ILLUSTRATION OF REVERSING ENTRIES—ACCRUALS

A company most often uses reversing entries to reverse two types of adjusting entries: accrued revenues and accrued expenses. To illustrate the optional use of reversing entries for accrued expenses, we use the following transaction and adjustment data.

> **OBJECTIVE 10**
> Identify adjusting entries that may be reversed.

1 October 24 (initial salary entry): Paid $4,000 of salaries incurred between October 10 and October 24.

2 October 31 (adjusting entry): Incurred salaries between October 25 and October 31 of $1,200, to be paid in the November 8 payroll.

3 November 8 (subsequent salary entry): Paid salaries of $2,500. Of this amount, $1,200 applied to accrued wages payable at October 31 and $1,300 to wages payable for November 1 through November 8.

Illustration 3B-1 (page 100) shows the comparative entries.

The comparative entries show that the first three entries are the same whether or not the company uses reversing entries. The last two entries differ. The November 1 reversing entry eliminates the $1,200 balance in Salaries Payable, created by the October 31 adjusting entry. The reversing entry also creates a $1,200 credit balance in the Salaries Expense account. As you know, it is unusual for an expense account to have a credit balance. However, the balance is correct in this instance. Why? Because the company will debit the entire amount of the first salary payment in the new accounting period to Salaries Expense. This debit eliminates the credit balance. The resulting debit balance in the expense account will equal the salaries expense incurred in the new accounting period ($1,300 in this example).

When a company makes reversing entries, it debits all cash payments of expenses to the related expense account. This means that on November 8 (and every payday) the company debits Salaries Expense for the amount paid without regard to the existence of any accrued salaries payable. Repeating the same entry simplifies the recording process in an accounting system.

REVERSING ENTRIES NOT USED			REVERSING ENTRIES USED		
Initial Salary Entry					
Oct. 24	Salaries Expense	4,000	Oct. 24	Salaries Expense	4,000
	Cash	4,000		Cash	4,000
Adjusting Entry					
Oct. 31	Salaries Expense	1,200	Oct. 31	Salaries Expense	1,200
	Salaries Payable	1,200		Salaries Payable	1,200
Closing Entry					
Oct. 31	Income Summary	5,200	Oct. 31	Income Summary	5,200
	Salaries Expense	5,200		Salaries Expense	5,200
Reversing Entry					
Nov. 1	No entry is made.		Nov. 1	Salaries Payable	1,200
				Salaries Expense	1,200
Subsequent Salary Entry					
Nov. 8	Salaries Payable	1,200	Nov. 8	Salaries Expense	2,500
	Salaries Expense	1,300		Cash	2,500
	Cash	2,500			

ILLUSTRATION 3B-1
Comparison of Entries for Accruals, with and without Reversing Entries

ILLUSTRATION OF REVERSING ENTRIES—PREPAYMENTS

Up to this point, we assumed the recording of all prepayments as prepaid expense or unearned revenue. In some cases, though, a company records prepayments directly in expense or revenue accounts. When this occurs, a company may also reverse prepayments.

To illustrate the use of reversing entries for prepaid expenses, we use the following transaction and adjustment data.

1 December 10 (initial entry): Purchased $20,000 of office supplies with cash.

2 December 31 (adjusting entry): Determined that $5,000 of office supplies are on hand.

Illustration 3B-2 shows the comparative entries.

ILLUSTRATION 3B-2
Comparison of Entries for Prepayments, with and without Reversing Entries

REVERSING ENTRIES NOT USED			REVERSING ENTRIES USED		
Initial Purchase of Supplies Entry					
Dec. 10	Office Supplies	20,000	Dec. 10	Office Supplies Expense	20,000
	Cash	20,000		Cash	20,000
Adjusting Entry					
Dec. 31	Office Supplies Expense	15,000	Dec. 31	Office Supplies	5,000
	Office Supplies	15,000		Office Supplies Expense	5,000
Closing Entry					
Dec. 31	Income Summary	15,000	Dec. 31	Income Summary	15,000
	Office Supplies Expense	15,000		Office Supplies Expense	15,000
Reversing Entry					
Jan. 1	No entry		Jan. 1	Office Supplies Expense	5,000
				Office Supplies	5,000

After the adjusting entry on December 31 (regardless of whether using reversing entries), the asset account Office Supplies shows a balance of $5,000, and Office Supplies Expense shows a balance of $15,000. If the company initially debits Office Supplies Expense when it purchases the supplies, it then makes a reversing entry to return to the expense account the cost of unconsumed supplies. The company then continues to debit Office Supplies Expense for additional purchases of office supplies during the next period.

Prepaid items are generally entered in real accounts (assets and liabilities), thus making reversing entries unnecessary. This approach is used because it is advantageous for items that a company needs to apportion over several periods (e.g., supplies and parts inventories). However, for other items that do not follow this regular pattern and that may or may not involve two or more periods, a company ordinarily enters them initially in revenue or expense accounts. The revenue and expense accounts may not require adjusting, and the company thus systematically closes them to Income Summary.

Using the nominal accounts adds consistency to the accounting system. It also makes the recording more efficient, particularly when a large number of such transactions occur during the year. For example, the bookkeeper knows to expense invoice items (except for capital asset acquisitions). He or she need not worry whether an item will result in a prepaid expense at the end of the period, because the company will make adjustments at the end of the period.

Summary of Reversing Entries

We summarize guidelines for reversing entries as follows.

1 All accrued items should be reversed.

2 All prepaid items for which a company debited or credited the original cash transaction to an expense or revenue account should be reversed.

3 Adjusting entries for depreciation and bad debts are not reversed.

Recognize that reversing entries do not have to be used. Therefore, some accountants avoid them entirely.

SUMMARY OF LEARNING OBJECTIVE FOR APPENDIX 3B

---

10. Identify adjusting entries that may be reversed. Reversing entries are most often used to reverse two types of adjusting entries: accrued revenues and accrued expenses. Prepayments may also be reversed if the initial entry to record the transaction is made to an expense or revenue account.

APPENDIX

3C

Using a Worksheet: The Accounting Cycle Revisited

In this appendix we provide an additional illustration of the end-of-period steps in the accounting cycle and illustrate the use of a worksheet in this process. Using a **worksheet** often facilitates the end-of-period (monthly, quarterly, or annually) accounting and reporting process. Use of a worksheet helps a company prepare the financial statements on a more timely basis. How? With a worksheet, a company need not wait until it journalizes and posts the adjusting and closing entries.

A company prepares a worksheet either on columnar paper or within an electronic spreadsheet. In either form, a company uses the worksheet to adjust account balances and to prepare financial statements.

The worksheet does not replace the financial statements. Instead, it is an informal device for accumulating and sorting information needed for the financial statements. Completing the worksheet provides considerable assurance that a company properly handled all of the details related to the end-of-period accounting and statement

> **OBJECTIVE 11**
> Prepare a 10-column worksheet.

preparation. The 10-column worksheet in Illustration 3C-1 (page 103) provides columns for the first trial balance, adjustments, adjusted trial balance, income statement, and balance sheet.

Worksheet Columns

Trial Balance Columns

Uptown Cabinet Corp., shown in Illustration 3C-1, obtains data for the trial balance from its ledger balances at December 31. The amount for Merchandise Inventory, $40,000, is the year-end inventory amount, which results from the application of a perpetual inventory system.

Adjustments Columns

After Uptown enters all adjustment data on the worksheet, it establishes the equality of the adjustment columns. It then extends the balances in all accounts to the adjusted trial balance columns.

Adjustments Entered on the Worksheet

Items (a) through (g) below serve as the basis for the adjusting entries made in the worksheet for Uptown shown in Illustration 3C-1.

(a) Depreciation of furniture and equipment at the rate of 10% per year based on original cost of $67,000.

(b) Estimated bad debts of one-quarter of 1 percent of sales ($400,000).

(c) Insurance expired during the year $360.

(d) Interest accrued on notes receivable as of December 31, $800.

(e) The Rent Expense account contains $500 rent paid in advance, which is applicable to next year.

(f) Property taxes accrued December 31, $2,000.

(g) Income tax payable estimated $3,440.

The adjusting entries shown on the December 31, 2007, worksheet are as follows.

(a)		
Depreciation Expense—Furniture and Equipment	6,700	
Accumulated Depreciation—Furniture and Equipment		6,700
(b)		
Bad Debt Expense	1,000	
Allowance for Doubtful Accounts		1,000
(c)		
Insurance Expense	360	
Prepaid Insurance		360
(d)		
Interest Receivable	800	
Interest Revenue		800
(e)		
Prepaid Rent Expense	500	
Rent Expense		500
(f)		
Property Tax Expense	2,000	
Property Tax Payable		2,000
(g)		
Income Tax Expense	3,440	
Income Tax Payable		3,440

Uptown Cabinet transfers the adjusting entries to the Adjustments columns of the worksheet, often designating each by letter. The trial balance lists any new accounts resulting from the adjusting entries, as illustrated on the worksheet. (For example, see the accounts listed in rows 27 through 35 in Illustration 3C-1.) Uptown then totals and balances the Adjustments columns.

Adjusted Trial Balance

The adjusted trial balance shows the balance of all accounts after adjustment at the end of the accounting period. For example, Uptown adds the $2,000 shown opposite the Allowance for Doubtful Accounts in the Trial Balance Cr. column to the $1,000 in the Adjustments Cr. column. The company then extends the $3,000 total to the Adjusted Trial Balance Cr. column. Similarly, Uptown reduces the $900 debit opposite Prepaid Insurance by the $360 credit in the Adjustments column. The result, $540, is shown in the Adjusted Trial Balance Dr. column.

Income Statement and Balance Sheet Columns

Uptown extends all the debit items in the Adjusted Trial Balance columns into the Income Statement or Balance Sheet columns to the right. It similarly extends all the credit items.

The next step is to total the Income Statement columns. Uptown needs the amount of net income or loss for the period to balance the debit and credit columns. The net income of $12,200 is shown in the Income Statement Dr. column because revenues exceeded expenses by that amount.

UPTOWN CABINET CORP.
Ten-Column Worksheet for The Year Ended December 31, 2007

	Accounts	Trial Balance Dr.	Trial Balance Cr.	Adjustments Dr.	Adjustments Cr.	Adjusted Trial Balance Dr.	Adjusted Trial Balance Cr.	Income Statement Dr.	Income Statement Cr.	Balance Sheet Dr.	Balance Sheet Cr.
2	Cash	1,200				1,200				1,200	
3	Notes receivable	16,000				16,000				16,000	
4	Accounts receivable	41,000				41,000				41,000	
5	Allowance for doubtful accounts		2,000		(b) 1,000		3,000				3,000
6	Merchandise inventory	40,000				40,000				40,000	
7	Prepaid insurance	900			(c) 360	540				540	
8	Furniture and equipment	67,000				67,000				67,000	
9	Accumulated depreciation–furniture and equipment		12,000		(a) 6,700		18,700				18,700
10	Notes payable		20,000				20,000				20,000
11	Accounts payable		13,500				13,500				13,500
12	Bonds payable		30,000				30,000				30,000
13	Common stock		50,000				50,000				50,000
14	Retained earnings, Jan. 1, 2007		16,200				16,200				16,200
15	Dividends	2,000				2,000				2,000	
16	Sales		400,000				400,000		400,000		
17	Cost of goods sold	316,000				316,000		316,000			
18	Sales salaries expense	20,000				20,000		20,000			
19	Advertising expense	2,200				2,200		2,200			
20	Traveling expense	8,000				8,000		8,000			
21	Salaries, office and general	19,000				19,000		19,000			
22	Telephone and Internet expense	600				600		600			
23	Rent expense	4,800			(e) 500	4,300		4,300			
24	Property tax expense	3,300		(f) 2,000		5,300		5,300			
25	Interest expense	1,700				1,700		1,700			
26	**Totals**	543,700	543,700								
27	Depreciation expense–furniture and equipment			(a) 6,700		6,700		6,700			
28	Bad debt expense			(b) 1,000		1,000		1,000			
29	Insurance expense			(c) 360		360		360			
30	Interest receivable			(d) 800		800				800	
31	Interest revenue				(d) 800		800		800		
32	Prepaid rent expense			(e) 500		500				500	
33	Property tax payable				(f) 2,000		2,000				2,000
34	Income tax expense			(g) 3,440				3,440			
35	Income tax payable				(g) 3,440						3,440
36	**Totals**			14,800	14,800	554,200	554,200	388,600	400,800		
37	Net income							12,200			12,200
38	**Totals**							400,800	400,800	169,040	169,040

Sheet1 / Sheet2 / Sheet3

ILLUSTRATION 3C-1
Use of a Worksheet

Uptown then balances the Income Statement columns. The company also enters the net income of $12,200 in the Balance Sheet Cr. column as an increase in retained earnings.

Preparing Financial Statements from a Worksheet

The worksheet provides the information needed for preparation of the financial statements without reference to the ledger or other records. In addition, the worksheet sorts the data into appropriate columns, which facilitates the preparation of the statements. The financial statements for Uptown Cabinet are shown in Chapter 3, pages 90–91.

SUMMARY OF LEARNING OBJECTIVE FOR APPENDIX 3C

KEY TERM

worksheet, *101*

11. Prepare a 10-column worksheet. The 10-column worksheet provides columns for the first trial balance, adjustments, adjusted trial balance, income statement, and balance sheet. The worksheet does not replace the financial statements. Instead, it is an informal device for accumulating and sorting information needed for the financial statements.

Note: All asterisked Questions, Exercises, Problems, and Cases relate to material contained in the appendixes to the chapter.

QUESTIONS

1. Give an example of a transaction that results in:

(a) A decrease in an asset and a decrease in a liability.

(b) A decrease in one asset and an increase in another asset.

(c) A decrease in one liability and an increase in another liability.

2. Do the following events represent business transactions? Explain your answer in each case.

(a) A computer is purchased on account.

(b) A customer returns merchandise and is given credit on account.

(c) A prospective employee is interviewed.

(d) The owner of the business withdraws cash from the business for personal use.

(e) Merchandise is ordered for delivery next month.

3. Name the accounts debited and credited for each of the following transactions.

(a) Billing a customer for work done.

(b) Receipt of cash from customer on account.

(c) Purchase of office supplies on account.

(d) Purchase of 15 gallons of gasoline for the delivery truck.

4. Why are revenue and expense accounts called temporary or nominal accounts?

5. Omar Morena, a fellow student, contends that the double-entry system means that each transaction must be recorded twice. Is Omar correct? Explain.

6. Is it necessary that a trial balance be taken periodically? What purpose does it serve?

7. Indicate whether each of the items below is a real or nominal account and whether it appears in the balance sheet or the income statement.

(a) Prepaid Rent.

(b) Salaries and Wages Payable.

(c) Merchandise Inventory.

(d) Accumulated Depreciation.

(e) Office Equipment.

(f) Service Revenue.

(g) Office Salaries Expense.

(h) Supplies on Hand.

8. Employees are paid every Saturday for the preceding work week. If a balance sheet is prepared on Wednesday, December 31, what does the amount of wages earned during the first three days of the week (12/29, 12/30, 12/31) represent? Explain.

9. (a) How do the components of revenues and expenses differ between a merchandising company and a service enterprise? (b) Explain the income measurement process of a merchandising company.

10. What is the purpose of the Cost of Goods Sold account? (Assume a periodic inventory system.)

11. Under a perpetual system, what is the purpose of the Cost of Goods Sold account?

12. If the $3,900 cost of a new microcomputer and printer purchased for office use were recorded as a debit to Purchases, what would be the effect of the error on the balance sheet and income statement in the period in which the error was made?

13. What differences are there between the trial balance before closing and the trial balance after closing with respect to the following accounts?

(a) Accounts Payable.

(b) Expense accounts.

(c) Revenue accounts.

(d) Retained Earnings account.

(e) Cash.

14. What are adjusting entries and why are they necessary?

15. What are closing entries and why are they necessary?

16. John Damon, maintenance supervisor for Red Sox Insurance Co., has purchased a riding lawnmower and accessories to be used in maintaining the grounds around corporate headquarters. He has sent the following information to the accounting department.

Cost of mower and accessories	$3,000	Date purchased	7/1/07
Estimated useful life	5 yrs	Monthly salary of groundskeeper	$1,100
		Estimated annual fuel cost	$150

Compute the amount of depreciation expense (related to the mower and accessories) that should be reported on Red Sox's December 31, 2007, income statement. Assume straight-line depreciation.

17. Selanne Enterprises made the following entry on December 31, 2007.

Interest Expense	10,000	
Interest Payable		10,000
(To record interest expense due on loan from Anaheim National Bank.)		

What entry would Anaheim National Bank make regarding its outstanding loan to Selanne Enterprises? Explain why this must be the case.

18. Distinguish between cash-basis accounting and accrual-basis accounting. Why is accrual-basis accounting acceptable for most business enterprises and the cash-basis unacceptable in the preparation of an income statement and a balance sheet?

19. When wages expense for the year is computed, why are beginning accrued wages subtracted from, and ending accrued wages added to, wages paid during the year?

20. List two types of transactions that would receive different accounting treatment using (a) strict cash-basis accounting, and (b) a modified cash basis.

21. What are reversing entries, and why are they used?

22. "A worksheet is a permanent accounting record, and its use is required in the accounting cycle." Do you agree? Explain.

BRIEF EXERCISES

(LO 4) **BE3-1** Transactions for Argot Company for the month of May are presented below. Prepare journal entries for each of these transactions. (You may omit explanations.)

May 1 B.D. Argot invests $3,000 cash in exchange for common stock in a small welding corporation.
     3 Buys equipment on account for $1,100.
   13 Pays $400 to landlord for May rent.
   21 Bills Noble Corp. $500 for welding work done.

(LO 4) **BE3-2** Brett Favre Repair Shop had the following transactions during the first month of business. Journalize the transactions. (Omit explanations.)

Aug. 2 Invested $12,000 cash and $2,500 of equipment in the business.
    7 Purchased supplies on account for $400. (Debit asset account.)
  12 Performed services for clients, for which $1,300 was collected in cash and $670 was billed to the clients.
  15 Paid August rent $600.
  19 Counted supplies and determined that only $270 of the supplies purchased on August 7 are still on hand.

(LO 4, 5) **BE3-3** On July 1, 2007, Blair Co. pays $18,000 to Hindi Insurance Co. for a 3-year insurance contract. Both companies have fiscal years ending December 31. For Blair Co. journalize the entry on July 1 and the adjusting entry on December 31.

(LO 4, 5) **BE3-4** Using the data in BE3-3, journalize the entry on July 1 and the adjusting entry on December 31 for Hindi Insurance Co. Hindi uses the accounts Unearned Insurance Revenue and Insurance Revenue.

(LO 4, 5) **BE3-5** Assume that on February 1, **Procter & Gamble (P&G)** paid $840,000 in advance for 2 years' insurance coverage. Prepare P&G's February 1 journal entry and the annual adjusting entry on June 30.

(LO 4, 5) **BE3-6** Mogilny Corporation owns a warehouse. On November 1, it rented storage space to a lessee (tenant) for 3 months for a total cash payment of $2,700 received in advance. Prepare Mogilny's November 1 journal entry and the December 31 annual adjusting entry.

(LO 4, 5) **BE3-7** Catherine Janeway Company's weekly payroll, paid on Fridays, totals $6,000. Employees work a 5-day week. Prepare Janeway's adjusting entry on Wednesday, December 31, and the journal entry to record the $6,000 cash payment on Friday, January 2.

(LO 5) **BE3-8** Included in Martinez Company's December 31 trial balance is a note receivable of $10,000. The note is a 4-month, 12% note dated October 1. Prepare Martinez's December 31 adjusting entry to record $300 of accrued interest, and the February 1 journal entry to record receipt of $10,400 from the borrower.

(LO 5) **BE3-9** Prepare the following adjusting entries at August 31 for **Walgreens**.

    (a) Interest on notes payable of $400 is accrued.
    (b) Fees earned but unbilled total $1,400.
    (c) Salaries earned by employees of $700 have not been recorded.
    (d) Bad debt expense for year is $900.

Use the following account titles: Service Revenue, Accounts Receivable, Interest Expense, Interest Payable, Salaries Expense, Salaries Payable, Allowance for Doubtful Accounts, and Bad Debt Expense.

(LO 5) **BE3-10** At the end of its first year of operations, the trial balance of Rafael Company shows Equipment $30,000 and zero balances in Accumulated Depreciation—Equipment and Depreciation Expense. Depreciation for the year is estimated to be $3,000. Prepare the adjusting entry for depreciation at December 31, and indicate the balance sheet presentation for the equipment at December 31.

(LO 8) **BE3-11** Willis Corporation has beginning inventory $81,000; Purchases $540,000; Freight-in $16,200; Purchase Returns $5,800; Purchase Discounts $5,000; and ending inventory $70,200. Compute cost of goods sold.

(LO 7) **BE3-12** Karen Sepaniak has year-end account balances of Sales $828,900; Interest Revenue $13,500; Cost of Goods Sold $556,200; Operating Expenses $189,000; Income Tax Expense $35,100; and Dividends $18,900. Prepare the year-end closing entries.

(LO 9) ***BE3-13** Smith Company had cash receipts from customers in 2007 of $152,000. Cash payments for operating expenses were $97,000. Smith has determined that at January 1, accounts receivable was $13,000, and prepaid expenses were $17,500. At December 31, accounts receivable was $18,600, and prepaid expenses were $23,200. Compute (a) service revenue and (b) operating expenses.

(LO 10) ***BE3-14** Assume that **Best Buy** made a December 31 adjusting entry to debit Salaries Expense and credit Salaries Payable for $3,600 for one of its departments. On January 2, Best Buy paid the weekly payroll of $6,000. Prepare Best Buy's (a) January 1 reversing entry; (b) January 2 entry (assuming the reversing entry was prepared); and (c) January 2 entry (assuming the reversing entry was not prepared).

EXERCISES

(LO 4) **E3-1 (Transaction Analysis—Service Company)** Beverly Crusher is a licensed CPA. During the first month of operations of her business (a sole proprietorship), the following events and transactions occurred.

April	2	Invested $32,000 cash and equipment valued at $14,000 in the business.
	2	Hired a secretary-receptionist at a salary of $290 per week payable monthly.
	3	Purchased supplies on account $700. (Debit an asset account.)
	7	Paid office rent of $600 for the month.
	11	Completed a tax assignment and billed client $1,100 for services rendered. (Use Service Revenue account.)
	12	Received $3,200 advance on a management consulting engagement.
	17	Received cash of $2,300 for services completed for Ferengi Co.
	21	Paid insurance expense $110.
	30	Paid secretary-receptionist $1,160 for the month.
	30	A count of supplies indicated that $120 of supplies had been used.
	30	Purchased a new computer for $6,100 with personal funds. (The computer will be used exclusively for business purposes.)

Instructions
Journalize the transactions in the general journal. (Omit explanations.)

(LO 4) **E3-2 (Corrected Trial Balance)** The trial balance of Wanda Landowska Company (shown on the next page) does not balance. Your review of the ledger reveals the following: (a) Each account had a normal balance. (b) The debit footings in Prepaid Insurance, Accounts Payable, and Property Tax Expense were each understated $100. (c) A transposition error was made in Accounts Receivable and Service Revenue; the correct balances for Accounts Receivable and Service Revenue are $2,750 and $6,690, respectively. (d) A debit posting to Advertising Expense of $300 was omitted. (e) A $1,500 cash drawing by the owner was debited to Wanda Landowska, Capital, and credited to Cash.

WANDA LANDOWSKA COMPANY
TRIAL BALANCE
APRIL 30, 2007

	Debit	Credit
Cash	$ 4,800	
Accounts Receivable	2,570	
Prepaid Insurance	700	
Equipment		$ 8,000
Accounts Payable		4,500
Property Tax Payable	560	
Wanda Landowska, Capital		11,200
Service Revenue	6,960	
Salaries Expense	4,200	
Advertising Expense	1,100	
Property Tax Expense		800
	$20,890	$24,500

Instructions
Prepare a correct trial balance.

(LO 4)   **E3-3   (Corrected Trial Balance)**   The trial balance of Blues Traveler Corporation does not balance.

BLUES TRAVELER CORPORATION
TRIAL BALANCE
APRIL 30, 2007

	Debit	Credit
Cash	$ 5,912	
Accounts Receivable	5,240	
Supplies on Hand	2,967	
Furniture and Equipment	6,100	
Accounts Payable		$ 7,044
Common Stock		8,000
Retained Earnings		2,000
Service Revenue		5,200
Office Expense	4,320	
	$24,539	$22,244

An examination of the ledger shows these errors.

1. Cash received from a customer on account was recorded (both debit and credit) as $1,380 instead of $1,830.
2. The purchase on account of a computer costing $3,200 was recorded as a debit to Office Expense and a credit to Accounts Payable.
3. Services were performed on account for a client, $2,250, for which Accounts Receivable was debited $2,250 and Service Revenue was credited $225.
4. A payment of $95 for telephone charges was entered as a debit to Office Expenses and a debit to Cash.
5. The Service Revenue account was totaled at $5,200 instead of $5,280.

Instructions
From this information prepare a corrected trial balance.

(LO 4)   **E3-4   (Corrected Trial Balance)**   The trial balance of Watteau Co. (shown on the next page) does not balance.

WATTEAU CO.
TRIAL BALANCE
JUNE 30, 2007

	Debit	Credit
Cash		$ 2,870
Accounts Receivable	$ 3,231	
Supplies	800	
Equipment	3,800	
Accounts Payable		2,666
Unearned Service Revenue	1,200	
Common Stock		6,000
Retained Earnings		3,000
Service Revenue		2,380
Wages Expense	3,400	
Office Expense	940	
	$13,371	$16,916

Each of the listed accounts should have a normal balance per the general ledger. An examination of the ledger and journal reveals the following errors.

1. Cash received from a customer on account was debited for $570, and Accounts Receivable was credited for the same amount. The actual collection was for $750.
2. The purchase of a computer printer on account for $500 was recorded as a debit to Supplies for $500 and a credit to Accounts Payable for $500.
3. Services were performed on account for a client for $890. Accounts Receivable was debited for $890 and Service Revenue was credited for $89.
4. A payment of $65 for telephone charges was recorded as a debit to Office Expense for $65 and a debit to Cash for $65.
5. When the Unearned Service Revenue account was reviewed, it was found that $325 of the balance was earned prior to June 30.
6. A debit posting to Wages Expense of $670 was omitted.
7. A payment on account for $206 was credited to Cash for $206 and credited to Accounts Payable for $260.
8. A dividend of $575 was debited to Wages Expense for $575 and credited to Cash for $575.

Instructions
Prepare a correct trial balance. (*Note:* It may be necessary to add one or more accounts to the trial balance.)

(LO 5) **E3-5** **(Adjusting Entries)** The ledger of Duggan Rental Agency on March 31 of the current year includes the following selected accounts before adjusting entries have been prepared.

	Debit	Credit
Prepaid Insurance	$ 3,600	
Supplies	2,800	
Equipment	25,000	
Accumulated Depreciation—Equipment		$ 8,400
Notes Payable		20,000
Unearned Rent Revenue		9,300
Rent Revenue		60,000
Interest Expense	–0–	
Wage Expense	14,000	

An analysis of the accounts shows the following.

1. The equipment depreciates $250 per month.
2. One-third of the unearned rent was earned during the quarter.
3. Interest of $500 is accrued on the notes payable.
4. Supplies on hand total $850.
5. Insurance expires at the rate of $300 per month.

Instructions
Prepare the adjusting entries at March 31, assuming that adjusting entries are made quarterly. Additional accounts are: Depreciation Expense; Insurance Expense; Interest Payable; and Supplies Expense. (Omit explanations.)

(LO 5) **E3-6** **(Adjusting Entries)** Karen Weller, D.D.S., opened a dental practice on January 1, 2007. During the first month of operations the following transactions occurred.

1. Performed services for patients who had dental plan insurance. At January 31, $750 of such services was earned but not yet billed to the insurance companies.
2. Utility expenses incurred but not paid prior to January 31 totaled $520.
3. Purchased dental equipment on January 1 for $80,000, paying $20,000 in cash and signing a $60,000, 3-year note payable. The equipment depreciates $400 per month. Interest is $500 per month.
4. Purchased a one-year malpractice insurance policy on January 1 for $12,000.
5. Purchased $1,600 of dental supplies. On January 31, determined that $500 of supplies were on hand.

Instructions
Prepare the adjusting entries on January 31. (Omit explanations.) Account titles are: Accumulated Depreciation—Dental Equipment; Depreciation Expense; Service Revenue; Accounts Receivable; Insurance Expense; Interest Expense; Interest Payable; Prepaid Insurance; Supplies; Supplies Expense; Utilities Expense; and Utilities Payable.

(LO 5) **E3-7** **(Analyze Adjusted Data)** A partial adjusted trial balance of Piper Company at January 31, 2007, shows the following.

PIPER COMPANY ADJUSTED TRIAL BALANCE JANUARY 31, 2007		
	Debit	Credit
Supplies	$ 700	
Prepaid Insurance	2,400	
Salaries Payable		$ 800
Unearned Revenue		750
Supplies Expense	950	
Insurance Expense	400	
Salaries Expense	1,800	
Service Revenue		2,000

Instructions
Answer the following questions, assuming the year begins January 1.

(a) If the amount in Supplies Expense is the January 31 adjusting entry, and $850 of supplies was purchased in January, what was the balance in Supplies on January 1?
(b) If the amount in Insurance Expense is the January 31 adjusting entry, and the original insurance premium was for one year, what was the total premium and when was the policy purchased?
(c) If $2,500 of salaries was paid in January, what was the balance in Salaries Payable at December 31, 2006?
(d) If $1,600 was received in January for services performed in January, what was the balance in Unearned Revenue at December 31, 2006?

(LO 5) **E3-8** **(Adjusting Entries)** Andy Roddick is the new owner of Ace Computer Services. At the end of August 2007, his first month of ownership, Roddick is trying to prepare monthly financial statements. Below is some information related to unrecorded expenses that the business incurred during August.

1. At August 31, Roddick owed his employees $1,900 in wages that will be paid on September 1.
2. At the end of the month he had not yet received the month's utility bill. Based on past experience, he estimated the bill would be approximately $600.
3. On August 1, Roddick borrowed $30,000 from a local bank on a 15-year mortgage. The annual interest rate is 8%.
4. A telephone bill in the amount of $117 covering August charges is unpaid at August 31.

Instructions
Prepare the adjusting journal entries as of August 31, 2007, suggested by the information above.

(LO 5) **E3-9** **(Adjusting Entries)** Selected accounts of Urdu Company are shown below.

Supplies				Accounts Receivable			
Beg. Bal.	800	10/31	470	10/17	2,400		
				10/31	1,650		

Salaries Expense				Salaries Payable			
10/15	800					10/31	600
10/31	600						

Unearned Service Revenue				Supplies Expense			
10/31	400	10/20	650	10/31	470		

Service Revenue			
		10/17	2,400
		10/31	1,650
		10/31	400

Instructions

From an analysis of the T-accounts, reconstruct (a) the October transaction entries, and (b) the adjusting journal entries that were made on October 31, 2007. Prepare explanations for each journal entry.

(LO 5) **E3-10** **(Adjusting Entries)** Greco Resort opened for business on June 1 with eight air-conditioned units. Its trial balance on August 31 is as follows.

GRECO RESORT
TRIAL BALANCE
AUGUST 31, 2007

	Debit	Credit
Cash	$ 19,600	
Prepaid Insurance	4,500	
Supplies	2,600	
Land	20,000	
Cottages	120,000	
Furniture	16,000	
Accounts Payable		$ 4,500
Unearned Rent Revenue		4,600
Mortgage Payable		60,000
Common Stock		91,000
Retained Earnings		9,000
Dividends	5,000	
Rent Revenue		76,200
Salaries Expense	44,800	
Utilities Expense	9,200	
Repair Expense	3,600	
	$245,300	$245,300

Other data:

1. The balance in prepaid insurance is a one-year premium paid on June 1, 2007.
2. An inventory count on August 31 shows $450 of supplies on hand.
3. Annual depreciation rates are cottages (4%) and furniture (10%). Salvage value is estimated to be 10% of cost.
4. Unearned Rent Revenue of $3,800 was earned prior to August 31.
5. Salaries of $375 were unpaid at August 31.
6. Rentals of $800 were due from tenants at August 31.
7. The mortgage interest rate is 8% per year.

Instructions

(a) Journalize the adjusting entries on August 31 for the 3-month period June 1–August 31. (Omit explanations.)

(b) Prepare an adjusted trial balance on August 31.

(LO 6) **E3-11** **(Prepare Financial Statements)** The adjusted trial balance of Anderson Cooper Co. as of December 31, 2007, contains the following.

ANDERSON COOPER CO.
ADJUSTED TRIAL BALANCE
DECEMBER 31, 2007

Account Titles	Dr.	Cr.
Cash	$19,472	
Accounts Receivable	6,920	
Prepaid Rent	2,280	
Equipment	18,050	
Accumulated Depreciation		$ 4,895
Notes Payable		5,700
Accounts Payable		5,472
Common Stock		20,000
Retained Earnings		11,310
Dividends	3,000	
Service Revenue		11,590
Salaries Expense	6,840	
Rent Expense	2,260	
Depreciation Expense	145	
Interest Expense	83	
Interest Payable		83
	$59,050	$59,050

Instructions

(a) Prepare an income statement.

(b) Prepare a statement of retained earnings.

(c) Prepare a classified balance sheet.

(LO 6) **E3-12** **(Prepare Financial Statements)** Santo Design Agency was founded by Thomas Grant in January 2003. Presented below is the adjusted trial balance as of December 31, 2007.

SANTO DESIGN AGENCY
ADJUSTED TRIAL BALANCE
DECEMBER 31, 2007

	Dr.	Cr.
Cash	$ 11,000	
Accounts Receivable	21,500	
Art Supplies	5,000	
Prepaid Insurance	2,500	
Printing Equipment	60,000	
Accumulated Depreciation		$ 35,000
Accounts Payable		5,000
Interest Payable		150
Notes Payable		5,000
Unearned Advertising Revenue		5,600
Salaries Payable		1,300
Common Stock		10,000
Retained Earnings		3,500
Advertising Revenue		61,500
Salaries Expense	11,300	
Insurance Expense	850	
Interest Expense	500	
Depreciation Expense	7,000	
Art Supplies Expense	3,400	
Rent Expense	4,000	
	$127,050	$127,050

Instructions

   (a) Prepare an income statement and a statement of retained earnings for the year ending December 31, 2007, and an unclassified balance sheet at December 31.
   (b) Answer the following questions.
       (1) If the note has been outstanding 6 months, what is the annual interest rate on that note?
       (2) If the company paid $17,500 in salaries in 2007, what was the balance in Salaries Payable on December 31, 2006?

(LO 7) **E3-13** **(Closing Entries)** The adjusted trial balance of Lopez Company shows the following data pertaining to sales at the end of its fiscal year, October 31, 2007: Sales $800,000, Freight-out $12,000, Sales Returns and Allowances $24,000, and Sales Discounts $15,000.

Instructions

   (a) Prepare the sales revenue section of the income statement.
   (b) Prepare separate closing entries for (1) sales and (2) the contra accounts to sales.

(LO 7) **E3-14** **(Closing Entries)** Presented below is information related to Gonzales Corporation for the month of January 2007.

Cost of goods sold	$208,000	Salary expense	$ 61,000
Freight-out	7,000	Sales discounts	8,000
Insurance expense	12,000	Sales returns and allowances	13,000
Rent expense	20,000	Sales	350,000

Instructions

Prepare the necessary closing entries.

(LO 8) **E3-15** **(Missing Amounts)** Presented below is financial information for two different companies.

	Alatorre Company	Eduardo Company
Sales	$90,000	(d)
Sales returns	(a)	$ 5,000
Net sales	81,000	95,000
Cost of goods sold	56,000	(e)
Gross profit	(b)	38,000
Operating expenses	15,000	23,000
Net income	(c)	15,000

Instructions

Compute the missing amounts.

(LO 8) **E3-16** **(Find Missing Amounts—Periodic Inventory)** Financial information is presented below for four different companies.

	Pamela's Cosmetics	Dean's Grocery	Anderson Wholesalers	Baywatch Supply Co.
Sales	$78,000	(c)	$144,000	$100,000
Sales returns	(a)	$ 5,000	12,000	9,000
Net sales	74,000	94,000	132,000	(g)
Beginning inventory	16,000	(d)	44,000	24,000
Purchases	88,000	100,000	(e)	85,000
Purchase returns	6,000	10,000	8,000	(h)
Ending inventory	(b)	48,000	30,000	28,000
Cost of goods sold	64,000	72,000	(f)	72,000
Gross profit	10,000	22,000	18,000	(i)

Instructions

Determine the missing amounts (a–i). Show all computations.

(LO 8) **E3-17** **(Cost of Goods Sold Section—Periodic Inventory)** The trial balance of the Neville Mariner Company at the end of its fiscal year, August 31, 2007, includes the following accounts: Merchandise Inventory $17,500; Purchases $149,400; Sales $200,000; Freight-in $4,000; Sales Returns and Allowances $4,000; Freight-out $1,000; and Purchase Returns and Allowances $2,000. The ending merchandise inventory is $25,000.

Instructions

Prepare a cost of goods sold section for the year ending August 31.

(LO 7) **E3-18** **(Closing Entries for a Corporation)** Presented on the next page are selected account balances for Homer Winslow Co. as of December 31, 2007.

Merchandise Inventory 12/31/07	$ 60,000	Cost of Goods Sold	$225,700
Common Stock	75,000	Selling Expenses	16,000
Retained Earnings	45,000	Administrative Expenses	38,000
Dividends	18,000	Income Tax Expense	30,000
Sales Returns and Allowances	12,000		
Sales Discounts	15,000		
Sales	410,000		

Instructions

Prepare closing entries for Homer Winslow Co. on December 31, 2007. (Omit explanations.)

(LO 4) **E3-19** **(Transactions of a Corporation, Including Investment and Dividend)** Scratch Miniature Golf and Driving Range Inc. was opened on March 1 by Scott Verplank. The following selected events and transactions occurred during March.

Mar. 1 Invested $50,000 cash in the business in exchange for common stock.
  3 Purchased Michelle Wie's Golf Land for $38,000 cash. The price consists of land $10,000; building $22,000; and equipment $6,000. (Make one compound entry.)
  5 Advertised the opening of the driving range and miniature golf course, paying advertising expenses of $1,600.
  6 Paid cash $1,480 for a one-year insurance policy.
  10 Purchased golf equipment for $2,500 from Singh Company, payable in 30 days.
  18 Received golf fees of $1,200 in cash.
  25 Declared and paid a $500 cash dividend.
  30 Paid wages of $900.
  30 Paid Singh Company in full.
  31 Received $750 of fees in cash.

Scratch uses the following accounts: Cash; Prepaid Insurance; Land; Buildings; Equipment; Accounts Payable; Common Stock; Dividends; Service Revenue; Advertising Expense; and Wages Expense.

Instructions

Journalize the March transactions. (Provide explanations for the journal entries.)

(LO 9) *E3-20 **(Cash to Accrual Basis)** Jill Accardo, M.D., maintains the accounting records of Accardo Clinic on a cash basis. During 2007, Dr. Accardo collected $142,600 from her patients and paid $55,470 in expenses. At January 1, 2007, and December 31, 2007, she had accounts receivable, unearned service revenue, accrued expenses, and prepaid expenses as follows. (All long-lived assets are rented.)

	January 1, 2007	December 31, 2007
Accounts receivable	$9,250	$15,927
Unearned service revenue	2,840	4,111
Accrued expenses	3,435	2,108
Prepaid expenses	1,917	3,232

Instructions

Prepare a schedule that converts Dr. Accardo's "excess of cash collected over cash disbursed" for the year 2007 to net income on an accrual basis for the year 2007.

(LO 9) *E3-21 **(Cash and Accrual Basis)** Wayne Rogers Corp. maintains its financial records on the cash basis of accounting. Interested in securing a long-term loan from its regular bank, Wayne Rogers Corp. requests you as its independent CPA to convert its cash-basis income statement data to the accrual basis. You are provided with the following summarized data covering 2006, 2007, and 2008.

	2006	2007	2008
Cash receipts from sales:			
On 2006 sales	$295,000	$160,000	$30,000
On 2007 sales	–0–	355,000	90,000
On 2008 sales			408,000
Cash payments for expenses:			
On 2006 expenses	185,000	67,000	25,000
On 2007 expenses	40,000[a]	160,000	55,000
On 2008 expenses		45,000[b]	218,000

[a]Prepayments of 2007 expenses.
[b]Prepayments of 2008 expenses.

Instructions

(a) Using the data above, prepare abbreviated income statements for the years 2006 and 2007 on the cash basis.

(b) Using the data above, prepare abbreviated income statements for the years 2006 and 2007 on the accrual basis.

(LO 5, 10) ***E3-22 (Adjusting and Reversing Entries)** When the accounts of Daniel Barenboim Inc. are examined, the adjusting data listed below are uncovered on December 31, the end of an annual fiscal period.

1. The prepaid insurance account shows a debit of $5,280, representing the cost of a 2-year fire insurance policy dated August 1 of the current year.
2. On November 1, Rental Revenue was credited for $1,800, representing revenue from a subrental for a 3-month period beginning on that date.
3. Purchase of advertising materials for $800 during the year was recorded in the Advertising Expense account. On December 31, advertising materials of $290 are on hand.
4. Interest of $770 has accrued on notes payable.

Instructions
Prepare the following in general journal form.
(a) The adjusting entry for each item.
(b) The reversing entry for each item where appropriate.

(LO 11) ***E3-23 (Worksheet)** Presented below are selected accounts for Alvarez Company as reported in the worksheet at the end of May 2007.

Accounts	Adjusted Trial Balance		Income Statement		Balance Sheet	
	Dr.	Cr.	Dr.	Cr.	Dr.	Cr.
Cash	9,000					
Merchandise Inventory	80,000					
Sales		450,000				
Sales Returns and Allowances	10,000					
Sales Discounts	5,000					
Cost of Goods Sold	250,000					

Instructions
Complete the worksheet by extending amounts reported in the adjusted trial balance to the appropriate columns in the worksheet. Do not total individual columns.

(LO 11) ***E3-24 (Worksheet and Balance Sheet Presentation)** The adjusted trial balance for Ed Bradley Co. is presented in the following worksheet for the month ended April 30, 2007.

ED BRADLEY CO.
WORKSHEET (PARTIAL)
FOR THE MONTH ENDED APRIL 30, 2007

Account Titles	Adjusted Trial Balance		Income Statement		Balance Sheet	
	Dr.	Cr.	Dr.	Cr.	Dr.	Cr.
Cash	$19,472					
Accounts Receivable	6,920					
Prepaid Rent	2,280					
Equipment	18,050					
Accumulated Depreciation		$ 4,895				
Notes Payable		5,700				
Accounts Payable		5,472				
Bradley, Capital		34,960				
Bradley, Drawing	6,650					
Service Revenue		11,590				
Salaries Expense	6,840					
Rent Expense	2,260					
Depreciation Expense	145					
Interest Expense	83					
Interest Payable		83				

Instructions
Complete the worksheet and prepare a classified balance sheet.

(LO 11) *E3-25 (Partial Worksheet Preparation) Jurassic Park Co. prepares monthly financial statements from a worksheet. Selected portions of the January worksheet showed the following data.

JURASSIC PARK CO.
WORKSHEET (PARTIAL)
FOR THE MONTH ENDED JANUARY 31, 2007

Account Title	Trial Balance Dr.	Trial Balance Cr.	Adjustments Dr.	Adjustments Cr.	Adjusted Trial Balance Dr.	Adjusted Trial Balance Cr.
Supplies	3,256			(a) 1,500	1,756	
Accumulated Depreciation		6,682		(b) 257		6,939
Interest Payable		100		(c) 50		150
Supplies Expense			(a) 1,500		1,500	
Depreciation Expense			(b) 257		257	
Interest Expense			(c) 50		50	

During February no events occurred that affected these accounts, but at the end of February the following information was available.

(a) Supplies on hand	$715
(b) Monthly depreciation	$257
(c) Accrued interest	$ 50

Instructions
Reproduce the data that would appear in the February worksheet, and indicate the amounts that would be shown in the February income statement.

See the book's website, www.wiley.com/college/kieso, for Additional Exercises.

PROBLEMS

(LO 4, 6, 7) **P3-1 (Transactions, Financial Statements—Service Company)** Listed below are the transactions of Shigeki Muruyama, D.D.S., for the month of September.

Sept. 1 Muruyama begins practice as a dentist and invests $20,000 cash.
2 Purchases furniture and dental equipment on account from Green Jacket Co. for $17,280.
4 Pays rent for office space, $680 for the month.
4 Employs a receptionist, Michael Bradley.
5 Purchases dental supplies for cash, $942.
8 Receives cash of $1,690 from patients for services performed.
10 Pays miscellaneous office expenses, $430.
14 Bills patients $5,120 for services performed.
18 Pays Green Jacket Co. on account, $3,600.
19 Withdraws $3,000 cash from the business for personal use.
20 Receives $980 from patients on account.
25 Bills patients $2,110 for services performed.
30 Pays the following expenses in cash: office salaries $1,400; miscellaneous office expenses $85.
30 Dental supplies used during September, $330.

Instructions
(a) Enter the transactions shown above in appropriate general ledger accounts. Use the following ledger accounts: Cash; Accounts Receivable; Supplies on Hand; Furniture and Equipment; Accumulated Depreciation; Accounts Payable; Shigeki Muruyama, Capital; Service Revenue; Rent Expense; Miscellaneous Office Expense; Office Salaries Expense; Supplies Expense; Depreciation Expense; and Income Summary. Allow 10 lines for the Cash and Income Summary accounts, and 5 lines for each of the other accounts needed. Record depreciation using a 5-year life on the furniture and equipment, the straight-line method, and no salvage value. Do not use a drawing account.

(b) Prepare a trial balance.
(c) Prepare an income statement, an unclassified balance sheet, and a statement of owner's equity.
(d) Close the ledger.
(e) Prepare a post-closing trial balance.

(LO 5, 6) **P3-2** **(Adjusting Entries and Financial Statements)** Yount Advertising Agency was founded in January 2003. Presented below are adjusted and unadjusted trial balances as of December 31, 2007.

	Unadjusted		Adjusted	
	Dr.	Cr.	Dr.	Cr.
	YOUNT ADVERTISING AGENCY			
	TRIAL BALANCE			
	DECEMBER 31, 2007			
Cash	$ 11,000		$ 11,000	
Accounts Receivable	20,000		21,500	
Art Supplies	8,400		5,000	
Prepaid Insurance	3,350		2,500	
Printing Equipment	60,000		60,000	
Accumulated Depreciation		$ 28,000		$ 35,000
Accounts Payable		5,000		5,000
Interest Payable		–0–		150
Notes Payable		5,000		5,000
Unearned Advertising Revenue		7,000		5,600
Salaries Payable		–0–		1,300
Common Stock		10,000		10,000
Retained Earnings		3,500		3,500
Advertising Revenue		58,600		61,500
Salaries Expense	10,000		11,300	
Insurance Expense			850	
Interest Expense	350		500	
Depreciation Expense			7,000	
Art Supplies Expense			3,400	
Rent Expense	4,000		4,000	
	$117,100	$117,100	$127,050	$127,050

Instructions
(a) Journalize the annual adjusting entries that were made. (Omit explanations.)
(b) Prepare an income statement and a statement of retained earnings for the year ending December 31, 2007, and an unclassified balance sheet at December 31.
(c) Answer the following questions.
  (1) If the note has been outstanding 3 months, what is the annual interest rate on that note?
  (2) If the company paid $13,500 in salaries in 2007, what was the balance in Salaries Payable on December 31, 2006?

(LO 5) **P3-3** **(Adjusting Entries)** A review of the ledger of Oklahoma Company at December 31, 2007, produces the following data pertaining to the preparation of annual adjusting entries.

1. Salaries Payable $0. There are eight salaried employees. Salaries are paid every Friday for the current week. Five employees receive a salary of $700 each per week, and three employees earn $500 each per week. December 31 is a Tuesday. Employees do not work weekends. All employees worked the last 2 days of December.
2. Unearned Rent Revenue $369,000. The company began subleasing office space in its new building on November 1. Each tenant is required to make a $5,000 security deposit that is not refundable until occupancy is terminated. At December 31, the company had the following rental contracts that are paid in full for the entire term of the lease.

Date	Term (in months)	Monthly Rent	Number of Leases
Nov. 1	6	$4,000	5
Dec. 1	6	$8,500	4

3. Prepaid Advertising $13,200. This balance consists of payments on two advertising contracts. The contracts provide for monthly advertising in two trade magazines. The terms of the contracts are as shown at the top of page 117.

Contract	Date	Amount	Number of Magazine Issues
A650	May 1	$6,000	12
B974	Oct. 1	7,200	24

The first advertisement runs in the month in which the contract is signed.

4. Notes Payable $80,000. This balance consists of a note for one year at an annual interest rate of 12%, dated June 1.

Instructions

Prepare the adjusting entries at December 31, 2007. (Show all computations).

(LO 4, 5, 6, 7) **P3-4 (Financial Statements, Adjusting and Closing Entries)** The trial balance of Daphne Main Fashion Center contained the following accounts at November 30, the end of the company's fiscal year.

DAPHNE MAIN FASHION CENTER
TRIAL BALANCE
NOVEMBER 30, 2007

	Debit	Credit
Cash	$ 26,700	
Accounts Receivable	33,700	
Merchandise Inventory	45,000	
Store Supplies	5,500	
Store Equipment	85,000	
Accumulated Depreciation—Store Equipment		$ 18,000
Delivery Equipment	48,000	
Accumulated Depreciation—Delivery Equipment		6,000
Notes Payable		51,000
Accounts Payable		48,500
Common Stock		90,000
Retained Earnings		8,000
Sales		757,200
Sales Returns and Allowances	4,200	
Cost of Goods Sold	497,400	
Salaries Expense	140,000	
Advertising Expense	26,400	
Utilities Expense	14,000	
Repair Expense	12,100	
Delivery Expense	16,700	
Rent Expense	24,000	
	$978,700	$978,700

Adjustment data:

1. Store supplies on hand totaled $3,500.
2. Depreciation is $9,000 on the store equipment and $7,000 on the delivery equipment.
3. Interest of $11,000 is accrued on notes payable at November 30.

Other data:

1. Salaries expense is 70% selling and 30% administrative.
2. Rent expense and utilities expense are 80% selling and 20% administrative.
3. $30,000 of notes payable are due for payment next year.
4. Repair expense is 100% administrative.

Instructions

(a) Journalize the adjusting entries.
(b) Prepare an adjusted trial balance.
(c) Prepare a multiple-step income statement and retained earnings statement for the year and a classified balance sheet as of November 30, 2007.
(d) Journalize the closing entries.
(e) Prepare a post-closing trial balance.

(LO 5) **P3-5 (Adjusting Entries)** The accounts listed on the next page appeared in the December 31 trial balance of the Jane Alexander Theater.

	Debit	Credit
Equipment	$192,000	
Accumulated Depreciation—Equipment		$ 60,000
Notes Payable		90,000
Admissions Revenue		380,000
Advertising Expense	13,680	
Salaries Expense	57,600	
Interest Expense	1,400	

Instructions

(a) From the account balances listed above and the information given below, prepare the annual adjusting entries necessary on December 31. (Omit explanations.)

(1) The equipment has an estimated life of 16 years and a salvage value of $40,000 at the end of that time. (Use straight-line method.)

(2) The note payable is a 90-day note given to the bank October 20 and bearing interest at 10%. (Use 360 days for denominator.)

(3) In December 2,000 coupon admission books were sold at $25 each. They could be used for admission any time after January 1.

(4) Advertising expense paid in advance and included in Advertising Expense $1,100.

(5) Salaries accrued but unpaid $4,700.

(b) What amounts should be shown for each of the following on the income statement for the year?

(1) Interest expense.	(3) Advertising expense.
(2) Admissions revenue.	(4) Salaries expense.

(LO 5, 6) **P3-6** **(Adjusting Entries and Financial Statements)** Presented below are the trial balance and the other information related to Carlos Beltran, a consulting engineer.

CARLOS BELTRAN, CONSULTING ENGINEER
TRIAL BALANCE
DECEMBER 31, 2007

	Debit	Credit
Cash	$ 31,500	
Accounts Receivable	49,600	
Allowance for Doubtful Accounts		$ 750
Engineering Supplies Inventory	1,960	
Unexpired Insurance	1,100	
Furniture and Equipment	25,000	
Accumulated Depreciation—Furniture and Equipment		6,250
Notes Payable		7,200
Carlos Beltran, Capital		35,010
Service Revenue		100,000
Rent Expense	9,750	
Office Salaries Expense	28,500	
Heat, Light, and Water Expense	1,080	
Miscellaneous Office Expense	720	
	$149,210	$149,210

1. Fees received in advance from clients $6,900.
2. Services performed for clients that were not recorded by December 31, $4,900.
3. Bad debt expense for the year is $1,430.
4. Insurance expired during the year $480.
5. Furniture and equipment is being depreciated at $12\frac{1}{2}$% per year.
6. Carlos Beltran gave the bank a 90-day, 10% note for $7,200 on December 1, 2007.
7. Rent of the building is $750 per month. The rent for 2007 has been paid, as has that for January 2008.
8. Office salaries earned but unpaid December 31, 2007, $2,510.

Instructions

(a) From the trial balance and other information given, prepare annual adjusting entries as of December 31, 2007. (Omit explanations.)

(b) Prepare an income statement for 2007, a classified balance sheet, and a statement of owner's equity. Carlos Beltran withdrew $17,000 cash for personal use during the year.

(LO 5, 6) **P3-7** **(Adjusting Entries and Financial Statements)** Ana Alicia Advertising Corp. was founded in January 2003. Presented on the next page are the adjusted and unadjusted trial balances as of December 31, 2007.

ANA ALICIA ADVERTISING CORP.
TRIAL BALANCE
DECEMBER 31, 2007

	Unadjusted Dr.	Unadjusted Cr.	Adjusted Dr.	Adjusted Cr.
Cash	$ 7,000		$ 7,000	
Accounts Receivable	19,000		22,000	
Art Supplies	8,500		5,500	
Prepaid Insurance	3,250		2,500	
Printing Equipment	60,000		60,000	
Accumulated Depreciation		$ 27,000		$ 33,750
Accounts Payable		5,000		5,000
Interest Payable				150
Notes Payable		5,000		5,000
Unearned Service Revenue		7,000		5,600
Salaries Payable				1,500
Common Stock		10,000		10,000
Retained Earnings		4,500		4,500
Service Revenue		58,600		63,000
Salaries Expense	10,000		11,500	
Insurance Expense			750	
Interest Expense	350		500	
Depreciation Expense			6,750	
Art Supplies Expense	5,000		8,000	
Rent Expense	4,000		4,000	
	$117,100	$117,100	$128,500	$128,500

Instructions

(a) Journalize the annual adjusting entries that were made. (Omit explanations.)

(b) Prepare an income statement and a statement of retained earnings for the year ending December 31, 2007, and an unclassified balance sheet at December 31, 2007.

(c) Answer the following questions.

(1) If the useful life of equipment is 8 years, what is the expected salvage value?

(2) If the note has been outstanding 3 months, what is the annual interest rate on that note?

(3) If the company paid $12,500 in salaries in 2007, what was the balance in Salaries Payable on December 31, 2006?

(LO 4, 5, 6, 7) *P3-8 **(Adjusting and Closing)** Following is the trial balance of the Platteville Golf Club, Inc. as of December 31. The books are closed annually on December 31.

PLATTEVILLE GOLF CLUB, INC.
TRIAL BALANCE
DECEMBER 31

	Debit	Credit
Cash	$ 15,000	
Accounts Receivable	13,000	
Allowance for Doubtful Accounts		$ 1,100
Prepaid Insurance	9,000	
Land	350,000	
Buildings	120,000	
Accumulated Depreciation of Buildings		38,400
Equipment	150,000	
Accumulated Depreciation of Equipment		70,000
Common Stock		400,000
Retained Earnings		82,000
Dues Revenue		200,000
Greens Fee Revenue		8,100
Rental Revenue		15,400
Utilities Expense	54,000	
Salaries Expense	80,000	
Maintenance Expense	24,000	
	$815,000	$815,000

Instructions

(a) Enter the balances in ledger accounts. Allow five lines for each account.

(b) From the trial balance and the information given, prepare annual adjusting entries and post to the ledger accounts. (Omit explanations.)
   (1) The buildings have an estimated life of 25 years with no salvage value (straight-line method).
   (2) The equipment is depreciated at 10% per year.
   (3) Insurance expired during the year $3,500.
   (4) The rental revenue represents the amount received for 11 months for dining facilities. The December rent has not yet been received.
   (5) It is estimated that 15% of the accounts receivable will be uncollectible.
   (6) Salaries earned but not paid by December 31, $3,600.
   (7) Dues paid in advance by members $8,900.

(c) Prepare an adjusted trial balance.

(d) Prepare closing entries and post.

(LO 4, 5, 6, 7) ***P3-9 (Adjusting and Closing)** Presented below is the December 31 trial balance of Nancy Drew Boutique.

NANCY DREW BOUTIQUE TRIAL BALANCE DECEMBER 31		
	Debit	Credit
Cash	$ 18,500	
Accounts Receivable	42,000	
Allowance for Doubtful Accounts		$ 700
Inventory, December 31	80,000	
Prepaid Insurance	5,100	
Furniture and Equipment	84,000	
Accumulated Depreciation—Furniture and Equipment		35,000
Notes Payable		28,000
Common Stock		80,600
Retained Earnings		10,000
Sales		600,000
Cost of Goods Sold	398,000	
Sales Salaries Expense	50,000	
Advertising Expense	6,700	
Administrative Salaries Expense	65,000	
Office Expense	5,000	
	$754,300	$754,300

Instructions

(a) Construct T-accounts and enter the balances shown.

(b) Prepare adjusting journal entries for the following and post to the T-accounts. (Omit explanations.) Open additional T-accounts as necessary. (The books are closed yearly on December 31.)
   (1) Bad debts are estimated to be $1,400.
   (2) Furniture and equipment is depreciated based on a 6-year life (no salvage value).
   (3) Insurance expired during the year $2,550.
   (4) Interest accrued on notes payable $3,360.
   (5) Sales salaries earned but not paid $2,400.
   (6) Advertising paid in advance $700.
   (7) Office supplies on hand $1,500, charged to Office Expense when purchased.

(c) Prepare closing entries and post to the accounts.

(LO 9) ***P3-10 (Cash and Accrual Basis)** On January 1, 2007, Jill Monroe and Jenni Meno formed a computer sales and service enterprise in Soapsville, Arkansas, by investing $90,000 cash. The new company, Razorback Sales and Service, has the following transactions during January.

1. Pays $6,000 in advance for 3 months' rent of office, showroom, and repair space.

2. Purchases 40 personal computers at a cost of $1,500 each, 6 graphics computers at a cost of $3,000 each, and 25 printers at a cost of $450 each, paying cash upon delivery.

3. Sales, repair, and office employees earn $12,600 in salaries during January, of which $3,000 was still payable at the end of January.
4. Sells 30 personal computers at $2,550 each, 4 graphics computers for $4,500 each, and 15 printers for $750 each; $75,000 is received in cash in January, and $30,750 is sold on a deferred payment basis.
5. Other operating expenses of $8,400 are incurred and paid for during January; $2,000 of incurred expenses are payable at January 31.

Instructions

(a) Using the transaction data above, prepare (1) a cash-basis income statement, and (2) an accrual-basis income statement for the month of January.

(b) Using the transaction data above, prepare (1) a cash-basis balance sheet and (2) an accrual-basis balance sheet as of January 31, 2007.

(c) Identify the items in the cash basis financial statements that make cash-basis accounting inconsistent with the theory underlying the elements of financial statements.

(LO 5, 6, 7, 11) ***P3-11 (Worksheet, Balance Sheet, Adjusting and Closing Entries)** Noah's Ark has a fiscal year ending on September 30. Selected data from the September 30 work sheet are presented below.

NOAH'S ARK
WORKSHEET
FOR THE YEAR ENDED SEPTEMBER 30, 2007

	Trial Balance		Adjusted Trial Balance	
	Dr.	Cr.	Dr.	Cr.
Cash	37,400		37,400	
Supplies	18,600		1,200	
Prepaid Insurance	31,900		3,900	
Land	80,000		80,000	
Equipment	120,000		120,000	
Accumulated Depreciation		36,200		43,000
Accounts Payable		14,600		14,600
Unearned Admissions Revenue		2,700		1,700
Mortgage Payable		50,000		50,000
N. Y. Berge, Capital		109,700		109,700
N. Y. Berge, Drawing	14,000		14,000	
Admissions Revenue		278,500		279,500
Salaries Expense	109,000		109,000	
Repair Expense	30,500		30,500	
Advertising Expense	9,400		9,400	
Utilities Expense	16,900		16,900	
Property Taxes Expense	18,000		21,000	
Interest Expense	6,000		12,000	
Totals	491,700	491,700		
Insurance Expense			28,000	
Supplies Expense			17,400	
Interest Payable				6,000
Depreciation Expense			6,800	
Property Taxes Payable				3,000
Totals			507,500	507,500

Instructions

(a) Prepare a complete worksheet.

(b) Prepare a classified balance sheet. (*Note:* $10,000 of the mortgage payable is due for payment in the next fiscal year.)

(c) Journalize the adjusting entries using the worksheet as a basis.

(d) Journalize the closing entries using the worksheet as a basis.

(e) Prepare a post-closing trial balance.

USING YOUR JUDGMENT

Financial Reporting Problem

P&G **The Procter & Gamble Company (P&G)**

The financial statements of P&G are presented in Appendix 5B or can be accessed on the KWW website.

Instructions

Refer to these financial statements and the accompanying notes to answer the following questions.

(a) What were P&G's total assets at June 30, 2004? At June 30, 2003?

(b) How much cash (and cash equivalents) did P&G have on June 30, 2004?

(c) What were P&G's research and development costs in 2002? In 2004?

(d) What were P&G's revenues in 2002? In 2004?

(e) Using P&G's financial statements and related notes, identify items that may result in adjusting entries for prepayments and accruals.

(f) What were the amounts of P&G's depreciation and amortization expense in 2002, 2003, and 2004?

Financial Statement Analysis Case

Kellogg's **Kellogg Company**

Kellogg Company has its headquarters in Battle Creek, Michigan. The company manufactures and sells ready-to-eat breakfast cereals and convenience foods including cookies, toaster pastries, and cereal bars. Selected data from Kellogg Company's 2003 annual report follows (dollar amounts in millions).

	2003	2002	2001
Sales	$8,811.50	$8,304.10	$7,548.40
Gross profit %	44.40	45.50	44.20
Operating profit	$1,544.10	$1,508.1	$1,167.9
Net cash flow less capital expenditures	$923.8	$746.4	$855.5
Net earnings	$787.1	$720.9	$473.6

In its 2003 annual report, Kellogg Company disclosed that its financial model is designed to achieve sustainable financial performance. To measure financial performance, Kellogg focuses on realistic targets related to sales, gross profit margin, earnings growth, and cash flow.

Instructions

(a) Compute the percentage change in sales, operating profit, net cash flow, and net earnings from year to year for the years presented.

(b) Evaluate Kellogg's performance. Which trend seems most favorable? Which trend seems least favorable? What are the implications of these trends for Kellogg's sustainable performance objectives? Explain.

Comparative Analysis Case

The Coca-Cola Company

🌐 **PEPSICO**

The Coca-Cola Company and PepsiCo, Inc.

Instructions

Go to the KWW website and use information found there to answer the following questions related to The Coca-Cola Company and PepsiCo, Inc.

(a) Which company had the greater percentage increase in total assets from 2003 to 2004?

(b) Using the Selected Financial Data section of these two companies, determine their 5-year compound growth rates related to net sales and income from continuing operations.

(c) Which company had more depreciation and amortization expense for 2004? Provide a rationale as to why there is a difference in these amounts between the two companies.

Research Case

The Enterprise Standard Industrial Classification (SIC) coding scheme, a published classification of firms into separate industries, is commonly used in practice. SIC codes permit identification of company activities on three levels of detail. Two-digit codes designate a "major group," three-digit codes designate an "industry group," and four-digit codes identify a specific "industry."

Instructions

Use the *Standard Industrial Classification Manual* (published by the U.S. Government's Office of Management and Budget in 1987) to answer the following questions.

(a) On what basis are SIC codes assigned to companies?

(b) Identify the major group/industry group/industry represented by the following codes.

12	3571	75
271	7033	872

(c) Identify the SIC code for the following industries.

   (1) Golfing equipment—manufacturing.
   (2) Worm farms.
   (3) Felt tip markers—manufacturing.
   (4) Household appliance stores, electric or gas—retail.
   (5) Advertising agencies.

(d) You are interested in examining several companies in the passenger airline industry. Determine the appropriate two-, three-, and four-digit SIC codes. Use *Wards Business Directory of U.S. Private and Public Companies (Vol. 5)* to compile a list of the five largest parent companies (by total sales) in the industry. *Note:* If Wards is not available, alternative sources include *Standard & Poor's Register of Corporations, Directors, and Executives, Standard & Poor's Industry Surveys,* and the Dun & Bradstreet *Million Dollar Directory.*

Professional Research: Financial Accounting and Reporting

Recording transactions in the accounting system requires knowledge of the important characteristics of the elements of financial statements, such as assets and liabilities. In addition, accountants must understand the inherent uncertainty in accounting measures and distinctions between related accounting concepts that are important in evaluating the effects of transactions on the financial statements.

Instructions

Using the **Financial Accounting Research System (FARS)**, provide explanations for the following items. (Provide text strings used in your search.)

(a) The three essential characteristics of assets.

(b) The three essential characteristics of liabilities.

(c) Uncertainty and its effect on financial statements.

(d) The difference between realization and recognition.

Professional Simulation

In this simulation you are asked to address questions regarding the accounting information system. Prepare responses to all parts.

KWW_Professional_Simulation

| Accounting Information System | Time Remaining 3 hours 50 minutes | copy | paste | calculator | sheet | standard | help | splitter | done |

Directions | **Situation** | **Journal Entries** | **Financial Statements** | **Explanation** | **Resources**

Nalezny Advertising Agency was founded by Casey Hayward in January 2004. Presented below are both the adjusted and unadjusted trial balances as of December 31, 2007.

Nalezny Advertising Agency
Trial Balance
December 31, 2007

	Unadjusted Dr.	Unadjusted Cr.	Adjusted Dr.	Adjusted Cr.
Cash	$11,000		$11,000	
Accounts Receivable	20,000		21,500	
Art Supplies	8,400		5,000	
Printing Equipment	60,000		60,000	
Accumulated Depreciation		$28,000		$35,000
Accounts Payable		5,000		5,000
Unearned Advertising Revenue		7,000		5,600
Salaries Payable		–0–		1,300
Common Stock		10,000		10,000
Retained Earnings		4,800		4,800
Advertising Revenue		58,600		61,500
Salaries Expense	10,000		11,300	
Depreciation Expense			7,000	
Art Supplies Expense			3,400	
Rent Expense	4,000		4,000	
	$113,400	$113,400	$123,200	$123,200

Directions | **Situation** | **Journal Entries** | **Financial Statements** | **Explanation** | **Resources**

Journalize the annual adjusting entries that were made. (Omit explanations.)

Directions | **Situation** | **Journal Entries** | **Financial Statements** | **Explanation** | **Resources**

Prepare an income statement for the year ending December 31, 2007, and an unclassified balance sheet at December 31.

Directions | **Situation** | **Journal Entries** | **Financial Statements** | **Explanation** | **Resources**

Describe the remaining steps in the accounting cycle to be completed by Nalezny for 2007.

Remember to check the book's companion website to find additional resources for this chapter.

INCOME STATEMENT AND RELATED INFORMATION

Which Income Number?

Recently, 40 percent of the companies in the Standards and Poor's 500 provided investors a choice in reported income numbers. In addition to income measured according to generally accepted accounting principles (GAAP), companies also reported an income measure that they adjusted for certain items. Companies make these adjustments because they believe the items are not representative of operating results. In some cases these adjustments are quite large. As we show in the following table, in a recent quarter the reporting of such "pro forma" income measures put a very different spin on operating results. In some cases (**JDS-Uniphase**, **PMC-Sierra**, and **Yahoo**), a loss under GAAP measurement rules became an operating profit after pro forma adjustments.

Company	Earnings Per Share Pro Forma	GAAP		Company	Earnings Per Share Pro Forma	GAAP
JDS-Uniphase	$0.14	−$1.13		**PMC-Sierra**	0.02	−0.38
Checkfree	0.04	−1.17		**Qualcomm**	0.29	0.18
Amazon.com	−0.22	−0.66		**Yahoo**	0.01	−0.02

Characteristic of pro forma reporting practices is Amazon.com. It adjusted for items such as stock-based compensation, amortization of goodwill and intangibles, impairment charges, and equity in losses of investees. All of these adjustments make pro forma earnings higher than GAAP income. In its earnings announcement, Amazon defended its pro forma reporting, saying that it gives better insight into the fundamental operations of the business.

So what's wrong with focusing investors on the fundamentals of the business? According to Ed Jenkins, former chair of the FASB, one problem is that there are no standards for the reporting of pro forma numbers. As a result, investors will have a hard time comparing Amazon's pro forma measure with that reported by another company, which has a different idea of what is fundamental to its business. Also, there is concern that companies may use pro forma reporting to deflect investor attention from bad news. In response, the SEC issued Regulation G, which requires companies to reconcile non-GAAP financial measures to GAAP. This regulation provides investors with a roadmap to analyze adjustments companies make to their GAAP numbers to arrive at pro forma results.[1]

---

[1]Story adapted from David Henry, "The Numbers Game," *Business Week* (May 14, 2001), pp. 100–110. See also SEC Regulation G, "Conditions for Use of Non-GAAP Financial Measures," *Release No. 33-8176* (March 28, 2003).

Learning Objectives

After studying this chapter, you should be able to:

1 Understand the uses and limitations of an income statement.

2 Prepare a single-step income statement.

3 Prepare a multiple-step income statement.

4 Explain how to report irregular items.

5 Explain intraperiod tax allocation.

6 Identify where to report earnings per share information.

7 Prepare a retained earnings statement.

8 Explain how to report other comprehensive income.

As we indicate in the opening story, investors need complete and comparable information on income and its components to assess company profitability correctly. In this chapter we examine the many different types of revenues, expenses, gains, and losses that affect the income statement and related information, as follows.

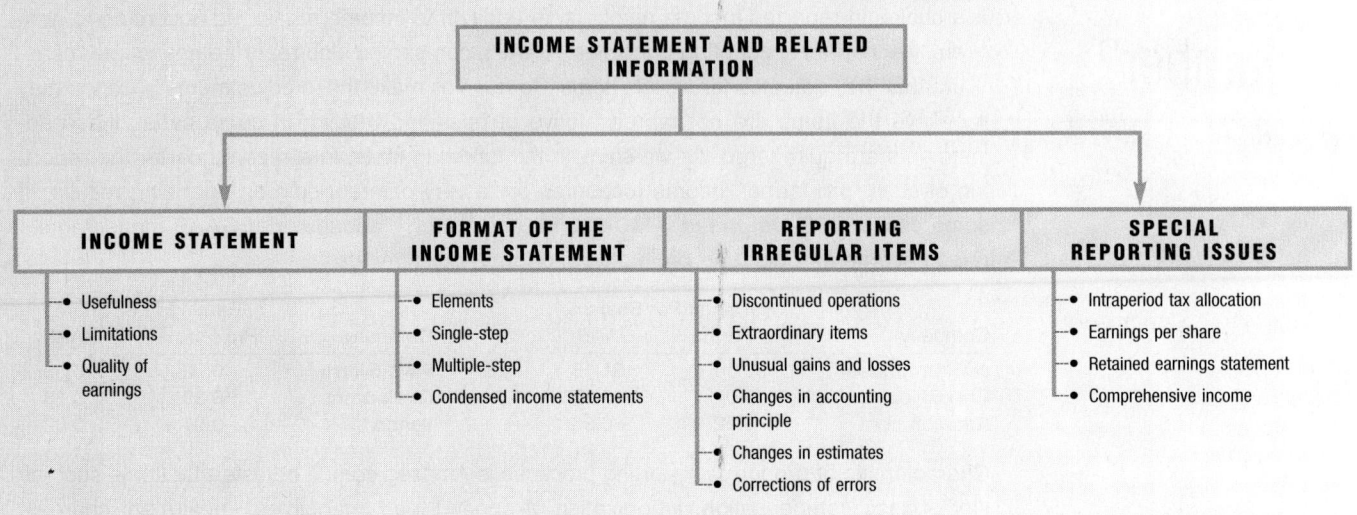

INCOME STATEMENT

OBJECTIVE 1
Understand the uses and limitations of an income statement.

The **income statement** is the report that measures the success of company operations for a given period of time. (It is also often called the statement of income or statement of earnings.[2]) The business and investment community uses the income statement to determine profitability, investment value, and creditworthiness. It provides investors and creditors with information that helps them predict the **amounts, timing, and uncertainty of future cash flows**.

Usefulness of the Income Statement

The income statement helps users of financial statements predict future cash flows in a number of ways. For example, investors and creditors use the income statement information to:

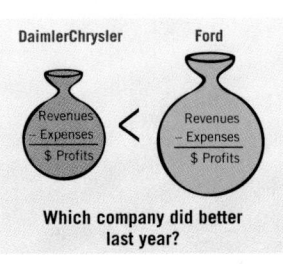

DaimlerChrysler   Ford

Which company did better last year?

1   **Evaluate the past performance of the company.** Examining revenues and expenses indicates how the company performed and allows comparison of its performance to its competitors. For example, analysts use the income data provided by **Daimler-Chrysler** to compare its performance to that of **Ford**.

2   **Provide a basis for predicting future performance.** Information about past performance helps to determine important trends that, if continued, provide

---

[2]*Accounting Trends and Techniques—2004* (New York: AICPA) indicates that out of 600 companies surveyed, 242 used the term *income* in the title of income statements, 261 used *operations* (many companies had net losses), and 90 used *earnings*.

information about future performance. For example, **General Electric** at one time reported consistent increases in revenues. Obviously past success does not necessarily translate into future success. However, analysts can better predict future revenues, and hence earnings and cash flows, if a reasonable correlation exists between past and future performance.

3 **Help assess the risk or uncertainty of achieving future cash flows.** Information on the various components of income—revenues, expenses, gains, and losses—highlights the relationships among them. It also helps to assess the risk of not achieving a particular level of cash flows in the future. For example, investors and creditors often segregate **IBM**'s operating performance from other nonrecurring sources of income because IBM primarily generates revenues and cash through its operations. Thus, results from continuing operations usually have greater significance for predicting future performance than do results from nonrecurring activities and events.

In summary, information in the income statement—revenues, expenses, gains, and losses—helps users evaluate past performance. It also provides insights into the likelihood of achieving a particular level of cash flows in the future.

Limitations of the Income Statement

Because net income is an estimate and reflects a number of assumptions, income statement users need to be aware of certain limitations associated with its information. Some of these limitations include:

1 **Companies omit items from the income statement that they cannot measure reliably.** Current practice prohibits recognition of certain items from the determination of income even though the effects of these items can arguably affect the company's performance. For example, a company may not record unrealized gains and losses on certain investment securities in income when there is uncertainty that it will ever realize the changes in value. In addition, more and more companies, like **Cisco Systems** and **Microsoft**, experience increases in value due to brand recognition, customer service, and product quality. A common framework for identifying and reporting these types of values is still lacking.

2 **Income numbers are affected by the accounting methods employed.** One company may depreciate its plant assets on an accelerated basis; another chooses straight-line depreciation. Assuming all other factors are equal, the first company will report lower income. In effect, we are comparing apples to oranges.

3 **Income measurement involves judgment.** For example, one company in good faith may estimate the useful life of an asset to be 20 years while another company uses a 15-year estimate for the same type of asset. Similarly, some companies may make optimistic estimates of future warranty returns and bad debt write-offs, which results in lower expense and higher income.

In summary, several limitations of the income statement reduce the usefulness of its information for predicting the amounts, timing, and uncertainty of future cash flows.

Quality of Earnings

So far, our discussion has highlighted the importance of information in the income statement for investment and credit decisions, including the evaluation of the company and its managers.[3] Companies try to meet or beat Wall Street expectations so that the

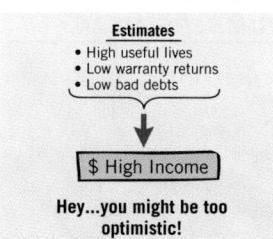

---

[3]In support of the usefulness of income information, accounting researchers have documented an association between the market prices of companies and reported income. See W. H. Beaver, "Perspectives on Recent Capital Markets Research," *The Accounting Review* (April 2002), pp. 453–474.

market price of their stock and the value of management's stock options increase. As a result, companies have incentives to manage income to meet earnings targets or to make earnings look less risky.

Recently, the SEC has expressed concern that the motivations to meet earnings targets may override good business practices. This erodes the quality of earnings and the quality of financial reporting. As indicated by one SEC chairman, "Managing may be giving way to manipulation; integrity may be losing out to illusion."[4] As a result, the SEC has started to take decisive action to prevent the practice of earnings management.

What is **earnings management**? It is often defined as the planned timing of revenues, expenses, gains, and losses to smooth out bumps in earnings. In most cases, companies use earnings management to increase income in the current year at the expense of income in future years. For example, they prematurely recognize sales (i.e., before earned) in order to boost earnings. As one commentator noted, ". . . it's like popping a cork in [opening] a bottle of wine before it is ready."

Companies also use earnings management to decrease current earnings in order to increase income in the future. The classic case is the use of "cookie jar" reserves. Companies establish these reserves by using unrealistic assumptions to estimate liabilities for such items as loan losses, restructuring charges, and warranty returns. The companies then reduce these reserves in the future to increase reported income in the future.

Such earnings management negatively affects the **quality of earnings** if it distorts the information in a way that is less useful for predicting future earnings and cash flows. Markets rely on trust. The bond between shareholders and the company must remain strong. Investors or others losing faith in the numbers reported in the financial statements will damage U.S. capital markets. As we mentioned in the opening story, we need heightened scrutiny of income measurement and reporting to ensure the quality of earnings and investors' confidence in the income statement.

WHAT DO THE NUMBERS MEAN?

MANAGE UP, MANAGE DOWN

Managing earnings up or down adversely affects the quality of earnings. For example, **W. R. Grace** managed earnings down by taking excess "cookie jar" reserves in good earnings years. During the early 1990s, Grace was growing fast, with profits increasing 30 percent annually. Analysts' targets had Grace growing 24 percent each year. Worried about meeting these growth expectations, Grace began stashing away excess profits in an all-purpose reserve (a "cookie jar"). In 1995, when profits fell below expectations, Grace wanted to reduce this reserve and so increase income. The SEC objected, noting this violated generally accepted accounting principles.

More recently, **MicroStrategy** managed earnings up by booking revenue for future software upgrades, even though it had not yet delivered them. And **Rent-Way, Inc.** managed its earnings up by understating some $65 million in expenses relating to such items as automobile maintenance and insurance payments.

Does the market value accounting quality? Apparently so: The stock of each of these companies took a beating in the marketplace when the earnings management practices came to light. For example, Rent-Way's stock price plummeted from above $25 per share to below $10 per share when it announced restatements for its improper expense accounting. So, whether managing earnings up or down, companies had better be prepared to pay the price for poor accounting quality.

---

[4]A. Levitt, "The Numbers Game." Remarks to NYU Center for Law and Business, September 28, 1998 (Securities and Exchange Commission, 1998).

FORMAT OF THE INCOME STATEMENT

Elements of the Income Statement

Net income results from revenue, expense, gain, and loss transactions. The income statement summarizes these transactions. This method of income measurement, the **transaction approach**, focuses on the income-related activities that have occurred during the period.[5] The statement can further classify income by customer, product line, or function or by operating and nonoperating, continuing and discontinued, and regular and irregular categories.[6] The following lists more formal definitions of income-related items, referred to as the major elements of the income statement.

ELEMENTS OF FINANCIAL STATEMENTS

REVENUES. Inflows or other enhancements of assets of an entity or settlements of its liabilities during a period from delivering or producing goods, rendering services, or other activities that constitute the entity's ongoing major or central operations.

EXPENSES. Outflows or other using-up of assets or incurrences of liabilities during a period from delivering or producing goods, rendering services, or carrying out other activities that constitute the entity's ongoing major or central operations.

GAINS. Increases in equity (net assets) from peripheral or incidental transactions of an entity except those that result from revenues or investments by owners.

LOSSES. Decreases in equity (net assets) from peripheral or incidental transactions of an entity except those that result from expenses or distributions to owners.[7]

Revenues take many forms, such as sales, fees, interest, dividends, and rents. Expenses also take many forms, such as cost of goods sold, depreciation, interest, rent, salaries and wages, and taxes. Gains and losses also are of many types, resulting from the sale of investments or plant assets, settlement of liabilities, write-offs of assets due to impairments or casualty.

The distinction between revenues and gains, and between expenses and losses, depend to a great extent on the typical activities of the company. For example, when **McDonald's** sells a hamburger, it records the selling price as revenue. However, when McDonald's sells land, it records any excess of the selling price over the book value as a gain. This difference in treatment results because the sale of the hamburger is part of McDonald's regular operations. The sale of land is not.

INTERNATIONAL INSIGHT

Companies in some nations prepare financial reporting on the same basis as tax returns. In such cases, companies have incentives to *minimize* reported income.

---

[5]The most common alternative to the transaction approach is the **capital maintenance approach** to income measurement. Under this approach, a company determines income for the period based on the change in equity, after adjusting for capital contributions (e.g., investments by owners) or distributions (e.g., dividends). The main drawback associated with the capital maintenance approach is that the components of income are not evident in its measurement. The Internal Revenue Service uses the capital maintenance approach to identify unreported income and refers to this approach as the "net worth check."

[6]The term "irregular" encompasses transactions and other events that are derived from developments outside the normal operations of the business.

[7]"Elements of Financial Statements," *Statement of Financial Accounting Concepts No. 6* (Stamford, Conn.: FASB, 1985), pars. 78–89.

We cannot overemphasize the importance of reporting these elements. Most decision makers find the *parts* of a financial statement to be more useful than the whole. As we indicated earlier, investors and creditors are interested in predicting the amounts, timing, and uncertainty of future income and cash flows. Having income statement elements shown in some detail and in comparison with prior years' data allows decision makers to better assess future income and cash flows.

Single-Step Income Statements

OBJECTIVE 2
Prepare a single-step income statement.

In reporting revenues, gains, expenses, and losses, companies often use a format known as the **single-step income statement**. The single-step statement consists of just two groupings: revenues and expenses. Expenses are deducted from revenues to arrive at net income or loss, hence the expression "single-step." Frequently companies report income tax separately as the last item before net income to indicate its relationship to income before income tax. Illustration 4-1 shows the single-step income statement of Dan Deines Company.

ILLUSTRATION 4-1
Single-Step Income
Statement

DAN DEINES COMPANY		
INCOME STATEMENT		
FOR THE YEAR ENDED DECEMBER 31, 2007		
Revenues		
Net sales	$2,972,413	
Dividend revenue	98,500	
Rental revenue	72,910	
Total revenues	3,143,823	
Expenses		
Cost of goods sold	1,982,541	
Selling expenses	453,028	
Administrative expenses	350,771	
Interest expense	126,060	
Income tax expense	66,934	
Total expenses	2,979,334	
Net income	$ 164,489	
Earnings per common share	$1.74	

Companies that use the single-step income statement in financial reporting typically do so because of its simplicity. In recent years, though, the multiple-step form has gained popularity.[8]

The primary advantage of the single-step format lies in its simple presentation and the absence of any implication that one type of revenue or expense item has priority over another. This format thus eliminates potential classification problems.

Multiple-Step Income Statements

OBJECTIVE 3
Prepare a
multiple-step
income statement.

Some contend that including other important revenue and expense classifications makes the income statement more useful. These further classifications include:

1 A separation of operating and nonoperating activities of the company. For example, companies often present income from operations followed by sections entitled "Other revenues and gains" and "Other expenses and losses." These other categories include such transactions as interest revenue and expense, gains or losses from sales of long-term assets, and dividends received.

---

[8]*Accounting Trends and Techniques—2004* (New York: AICPA). Of the 600 companies surveyed by the AICPA, 467 employed the multiple-step form, and 133 employed the single-step income statement format. This is a reversal from 1983, when 314 used the single-step form and 286 used the multiple-step form.

2 A classification of expenses by functions, such as merchandising (cost of goods sold), selling, and administration. This permits immediate comparison with costs of previous years and with other departments in the same year.

Companies use a **multiple-step income statement** to recognize these additional relationships. This statement separates operating transactions from nonoperating transactions, and matches costs and expenses with related revenues. It highlights certain intermediate components of income that analysts use to compute ratios for assessing the performance of the company.

Intermediate Components of the Income Statement

When a company uses a multiple-step income statement, it may prepare some or all of the following sections or subsections.

INCOME STATEMENT SECTIONS

1 OPERATING SECTION. A report of the revenues and expenses of the company's principal operations.
  (a) **Sales or Revenue Section.** A subsection presenting sales, discounts, allowances, returns, and other related information. Its purpose is to arrive at the net amount of sales revenue.
  (b) **Cost of Goods Sold Section.** A subsection that shows the cost of goods that were sold to produce the sales.
  (c) **Selling Expenses.** A subsection that lists expenses resulting from the company's efforts to make sales.
  (d) **Administrative or General Expenses.** A subsection reporting expenses of general administration.

2 NONOPERATING SECTION. A report of revenues and expenses resulting from secondary or auxiliary activities of the company. In addition, special gains and losses that are infrequent or unusual, but not both, are normally reported in this section. Generally these items break down into two main subsections:
  (a) **Other Revenues and Gains.** A list of the revenues earned or gains incurred, generally net of related expenses, from nonoperating transactions.
  (b) **Other Expenses and Losses.** A list of the expenses or losses incurred, generally net of any related incomes, from nonoperating transactions.

3 INCOME TAX. A short section reporting federal and state taxes levied on income from continuing operations.

4 DISCONTINUED OPERATIONS. Material gains or losses resulting from the disposition of a segment of the business.

5 EXTRAORDINARY ITEMS. Unusual and infrequent material gains and losses.

6 EARNINGS PER SHARE.

Although the content of the operating section is always the same, the organization of the material can differ. The breakdown above uses a **natural expense classification**. Manufacturing concerns and merchandising companies in the wholesale trade commonly use this. Another classification of operating expenses, recommended for retail stores, uses a **functional expense classification** of administrative, occupancy, publicity, buying, and selling expenses.

Usually, financial statements provided to external users have less detail than internal management reports. Internal reports include more expense categories—usually grouped along lines of responsibility. This detail allows top management to judge staff performance. Irregular transactions such as discontinued operations and extraordinary items are reported separately, following income from continuing operations.

Dan Deines Company's statement of income illustrates the multiple-step income statement. This statement, shown in Illustration 4-2, includes items 1, 2, 3, and 6

ILLUSTRATION 4-2
Multiple-Step Income
Statement

*Income Statements
for Real Companies*

DAN DEINES COMPANY			
INCOME STATEMENT			
FOR THE YEAR ENDED DECEMBER 31, 2007			
Sales Revenue			
Sales			$3,053,081
Less: Sales discounts		$ 24,241	
Sales returns and allowances		56,427	80,668
Net sales revenue			2,972,413
Cost of Goods Sold			
Merchandise inventory, Jan. 1, 2007		461,219	
Purchases	$1,989,693		
Less: Purchase discounts	19,270		
Net purchases	1,970,423		
Freight and transportation-in	40,612	2,011,035	
Total merchandise available for sale		2,472,254	
Less: Merchandise inventory, Dec. 31, 2007		489,713	
Cost of goods sold			1,982,541
Gross profit on sales			989,872
Operating Expenses			
Selling expenses			
Sales salaries and commissions	202,644		
Sales office salaries	59,200		
Travel and entertainment	48,940		
Advertising expense	38,315		
Freight and transportation-out	41,209		
Shipping supplies and expense	24,712		
Postage and stationery	16,788		
Depreciation of sales equipment	9,005		
Telephone and Internet expense	12,215	453,028	
Administrative expenses			
Officers' salaries	186,000		
Office salaries	61,200		
Legal and professional services	23,721		
Utilities expense	23,275		
Insurance expense	17,029		
Depreciation of building	18,059		
Depreciation of office equipment	16,000		
Stationery, supplies, and postage	2,875		
Miscellaneous office expenses	2,612	350,771	803,799
Income from operations			186,073
Other Revenues and Gains			
Dividend revenue		98,500	
Rental revenue		72,910	171,410
			357,483
Other Expenses and Losses			
Interest on bonds and notes			126,060
Income before income tax			231,423
Income tax			66,934
Net income for the year			$ 164,489
Earnings per common share			$1.74

from the list on page 131.[9] Note that in arriving at net income, the statement presents three subtotals of note:

1 Net sales revenue

2 Gross profit on sales

3 Income from operations

The disclosure of net sales revenue is useful because Deines reports regular revenues as a separate item. It discloses irregular or incidental revenues elsewhere in the income statement. As a result, analysts can more easily understand and assess trends in revenue from continuing operations.

Similarly, the reporting of gross profit provides a useful number for evaluating performance and predicting future earnings. Statement readers may study the trend in gross profits to determine how successfully a company uses its resources. They also may use that information to understand how competitive pressure affected profit margins.

Finally, disclosing income from operations highlights the difference between regular and irregular or incidental activities. This disclosure helps users recognize that incidental or irregular activities are unlikely to continue at the same level. Furthermore, disclosure of operating earnings may assist in comparing different companies and assessing operating efficiencies.

Condensed Income Statements

In some cases a single income statement cannot possibly present all the desired expense detail. To solve this problem, a company includes only the totals of expense groups in the statement of income. It then also prepares supplementary schedules to support the totals. This format may thus reduce the income statement itself to a few lines on a single sheet. For this reason, readers who wish to study all the reported data on operations must give their attention to the supporting schedules. For example, consider the income statement shown in Illustration 4-3 for Dan Deines Company. This statement is a condensed version of the more detailed multiple-step statement presented earlier. It is more representative of the type found in practice.

DAN DEINES COMPANY INCOME STATEMENT FOR THE YEAR ENDED DECEMBER 31, 2007		
Net sales		$2,972,413
Cost of goods sold		1,982,541
Gross profit		989,872
Selling expenses (see Note D)	$453,028	
Administrative expenses	350,771	803,799
Income from operations		186,073
Other revenues and gains		171,410
		357,483
Other expenses and losses		126,060
Income before income tax		231,423
Income tax		66,934
Net income for the year		$ 164,489
Earnings per share		$1.74

ILLUSTRATION 4-3
Condensed Income Statement

Illustration 4-4 shows an example of a supporting schedule, cross-referenced as Note D and detailing the selling expenses.

---

[9]Companies must include *earnings per share* or *net loss per share* on the face of the income statement.

ILLUSTRATION 4-4
Sample Supporting
Schedule

Note D: Selling expenses	
Sales salaries and commissions	$202,644
Sales office salaries	59,200
Travel and entertainment	48,940
Advertising expense	38,315
Freight and transportation-out	41,209
Shipping supplies and expense	24,712
Postage and stationery	16,788
Depreciation of sales equipment	9,005
Telephone and Internet expense	12,215
Total selling expenses	$453,028

How much detail should a company include in the income statement? On the one hand, a company wants to present a simple, summarized statement so that readers can readily discover important factors. On the other hand, it wants to disclose the results of all activities and to provide more than just a skeleton report. As we showed above, the income statement always includes certain basic elements, but companies can present them in various formats.

REPORTING IRREGULAR ITEMS

OBJECTIVE 4
Explain how to report irregular items.

As the use of a multiple-step or condensed income statement illustrates, GAAP allows flexibility in the presentation of the components of income. However, the FASB developed specific guidelines in two important areas: what to include in income and how to report certain unusual or irregular items.

What should be included in net income has been a controversy for many years. For example, should companies report irregular gains and losses, and corrections of revenues and expenses of prior years, as part of retained earnings? Or should companies first present them in the income statement and then carry them to retained earnings?

This issue is extremely important because the number and magnitude of irregular items are substantial. For example, Illustration 4-5 identifies the most common types and number of irregular items reported in a survey of 600 large companies. Notice that more than one-third of the surveyed firms reported restructuring charges, which often contain write-offs and other one-time items. About 20 percent of the surveyed firms reported either an extraordinary item or a discontinued operation charge. And many companies had two or more accounting changes in 2003.[10]

ILLUSTRATION 4-5
Number of Irregular
Items Reported in a
Recent Year by 600
Large Companies

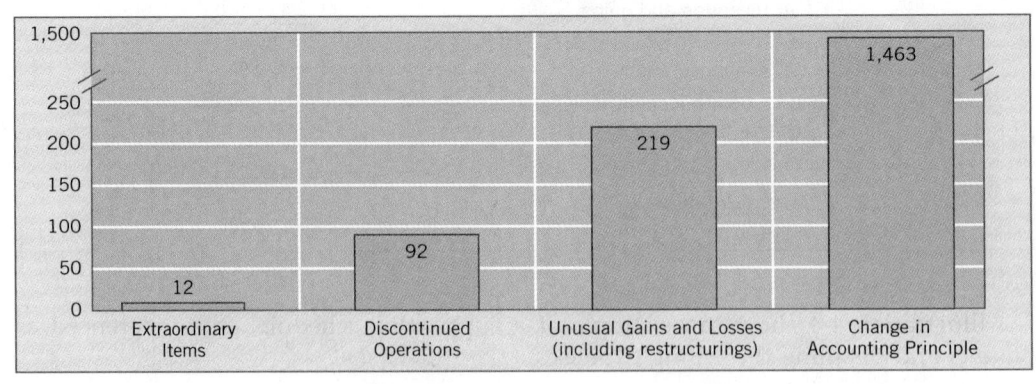

---

[10]*Accounting Trends and Techniques—2004* (New York: AICPA).

As our opening story discusses, we need consistent and comparable income reporting practices to avoid "promotional" information reported by companies. Developing a framework for reporting irregular items is important to ensure reliable income information.[11]

Some users advocate a **current operating performance approach** to income reporting. These analysts argue that the most useful income measure reflects only regular and recurring revenue and expense elements. Irregular items do not reflect a company's future earning power.

In contrast, others warn that a focus on operating income potentially misses important information about a company's performance. Any gain or loss experienced by the company, whether directly or indirectly related to operations, contributes to its long-run profitability. As one analyst notes, "write-offs matter. . . . They speak to the volatility of (past) earnings."[12] As a result, analysts can use some nonoperating items to assess the riskiness of future earnings. Furthermore, determining which items are operating and which are irregular requires judgment. This might lead to differences in the treatment of irregular items and to possible manipulation of income measures.

ARE ONE-TIME CHARGES BUGGING YOU?

Which number—net income or income from operations—should an analyst use in evaluating companies that have unusual items? Some argue that operating income better represents what will happen in the future. Others note that special items are often no longer special. For example, one study noted that in 2001, companies in the Standard & Poor's 500 index wrote off items totaling $165 billion—more than in the prior five years combined.

A study by Multex.com and the *Wall Street Journal* indicated that analysts should not ignore these charges. Based on data for companies taking unusual charges from 1996–2001, the study documented that companies reporting the largest unusual charges had more negative stock price performance following the charge, compared to companies with smaller charges. Thus, rather than signaling the end of bad times, these unusual charges indicated poorer future earnings.

In fact, some analysts use these charges to weed out stocks that may be headed for a fall. Following the "cockroach theory," any charge indicating a problem raises the probability of more problems. Thus, investors should be wary of the increasing use of restructuring and other one-time charges, which may bury expenses that signal future performance declines.

Source: Adapted from J. Weil and S. Liesman, "Stock Gurus Disregard Most Big Write-offs, But They Often Hold Vital Clues to Outlook," *Wall Street Journal Online* (December 31, 2001).

WHAT DO THE NUMBERS MEAN?

So, what to do? The accounting profession has **adopted a modified all-inclusive concept and requires application of this approach in practice**. This approach indicates that companies record most items, including irregular ones, as part of net income.[13] In addition, companies are required to highlight irregular items in the financial statements so that users can better determine the long-run earning power of the company.

INTERNATIONAL INSIGHT

In many countries the "modified all-inclusive" income statement approach does not parallel that of the U.S. For example, companies in these countries take some gains and losses directly to owners' equity accounts instead of reporting them on the income statement.

---

[11]The FASB and other international accounting standard setters continue to study the best way to report income. See *Reporting Financial Performance: A Proposed Approach* (Norwalk, Conn.: FASB, September 1999).

[12]D. McDermott, "Latest Profit Data Stir Old Debate Between Net and Operating Income," *Wall Street Journal* (May 3, 1999).

[13]The FASB issued a statement of concepts that offers some guidance on this topic—"Recognition and Measurement in Financial Statements of Business Enterprises," *Statement of Financial Accounting Concepts No. 5* (Stamford, Conn.: FASB, 1984).

Irregular items fall into six general categories, which we discuss in the following sections:

1 Discontinued operations.

2 Extraordinary items.

3 Unusual gains and losses.

4 Changes in accounting principle.

5 Changes in estimates.

6 Corrections of errors.

Discontinued Operations

As Illustration 4-5 shows, one of **the most common types of irregular items is discontinued operations.** A **discontinued operation** occurs when two things happen: (a) a company eliminates the results of operations and cash flows of a *component* from its ongoing operations, and (b) there is no significant continuing involvement in that component after the disposal transaction.

To illustrate a **component,** S. C. Johnson manufactures and sells consumer products. It has several product groups, each with different product lines and brands. For S. C. Johnson, a product group is the lowest level at which it can clearly distinguish the operations and cash flows from the rest of the company's operations. Therefore each product group is a component of the company. If a component were disposed of, S. C. Johnson would classify it as a discontinued operation.

Here is another example. Assume that Softso Inc. has experienced losses with certain brands in its beauty-care products group. As a result, Softso decides to sell that part of its business. It will discontinue any continuing involvement in the product group after the sale. In this case, Softso eliminates the operations and the cash flows of the product group from its ongoing operations, and reports it as a discontinued operation.

On the other hand, assume Softso decides to remain in the beauty-care business but will discontinue the brands that experienced losses. Because Softso cannot differentiate the cash flows from the brands from the cash flows of the product group as a whole, it cannot consider the brands a component. Softso does not classify any gain or loss on the sale of the brands as a discontinued operation.

Companies report as discontinued operations (in a separate income statement category) the gain or loss from **disposal of a component of a business.** In addition, companies report the **results of operations of a component that has been or will be disposed of** separately from continuing operations. Companies show the effects of discontinued operations net of tax as a separate category, after continuing operations but before extraordinary items.[14]

To illustrate, Multiplex Products, Inc., a highly diversified company, decides to discontinue its electronics division. During the current year, the electronics division lost $300,000 (net of tax). Multiplex sold the division at the end of the year at a loss of $500,000 (net of tax). Multiplex shows the information on the current year's income statement as follows.

ILLUSTRATION 4-6
Income Statement
Presentation of
Discontinued Operations

Income from continuing operations		$20,000,000
Discontinued operations		
Loss from operation of discontinued electronics division (net of tax)	$300,000	
Loss from disposal of electronics division (net of tax)	500,000	800,000
Net income		$19,200,000

[14]"Accounting for the Impairment or Disposal of Long-Lived Assets," *Statement of Financial Accounting Standards No. 144* (Norwalk, Conn.: FASB, 2001), par. 4. This standard requires discontinued-operation reporting, even though the assets disposed of (i.e., component of the business) do not meet the definition of a business segment.

Companies use the phrase **"Income from continuing operations"** only when gains or losses on discontinued operations occur.

Extraordinary Items

Extraordinary items are nonrecurring **material** items that differ significantly from a company's typical business activities. The criteria for extraordinary items are as follows.

> Extraordinary items are events and transactions that are distinguished by their unusual nature **and** by the infrequency of their occurrence. Classifying an event or transaction as an extraordinary item requires meeting **both** of the following criteria:
>
> **(a) Unusual Nature.** The underlying event or transaction should possess a high degree of abnormality and be of a type clearly unrelated to, or only incidentally related to, the ordinary and typical activities of the company, taking into account the environment in which it operates.
>
> **(b) Infrequency of Occurrence.** The underlying event or transaction should be of a type that the company does not reasonably expect to recur in the foreseeable future, taking into account the environment in which the company operates.[15]

For further clarification, the following gains and losses are **not extraordinary items**.

> **(a)** Write-down or write-off of receivables, inventories, equipment leased to others, deferred research and development costs, or other intangible assets.
>
> **(b)** Gains or losses from exchange or translation of foreign currencies, including those relating to major devaluations and revaluations.
>
> **(c)** Gains or losses on disposal of a component of an entity (reported as a discontinued operation).
>
> **(d)** Other gains or losses from sale or abandonment of property, plant, or equipment used in the business.
>
> **(e)** Effects of a strike, including those against competitors and major suppliers.
>
> **(f)** Adjustment of accruals on long-term contracts.[16]

The above items are not considered extraordinary "because they are usual in nature and may be expected to recur as a consequence of customary and continuing business activities."

Only rarely does an event or transaction clearly meet the criteria for an extraordinary item.[17] For example, a company classifies gains or losses such as (a) and (d) above as extraordinary if they **resulted directly from a major casualty** (such as an earthquake), **an expropriation**, or a **prohibition under a newly enacted law or regulation**. Such circumstances clearly meet the criteria of unusual and infrequent. For example, **Weyerhaeuser Company** (forest and lumber) incurred an extraordinary item (an approximate $36 million loss) as a result of volcanic activity at Mount St. Helens. The eruption destroyed standing timber, logs, buildings, equipment, and transportation systems covering 68,000 acres.

In determining whether an item is extraordinary, **a company must consider the environment in which it operates.** The environment includes such factors as industry characteristics, geographic location, and the nature and extent of governmental regulations. Thus, the FASB accords extraordinary item treatment to the loss from hail damages to a tobacco grower's crops if hailstorm damage in its locality is rare. On the other hand, frost damage to a citrus grower's crop in Florida does not qualify as extraordinary because frost damage normally occurs there every three or four years.

INTERNATIONAL INSIGHT

Classification of items as extraordinary differs across nations. Even in countries with similar criteria for identifying extraordinary items, they are not interpreted identically. Thus, what is extraordinary in the U.S. is not necessarily extraordinary elsewhere.

---

[15]"Reporting the Results of Operations," *Opinions of the Accounting Principles Board No. 30* (New York: AICPA, 1973), par. 20.

[16]Ibid., par. 23, as amended by "Accounting for the Impairment or Disposal of Long-lived Assets," *Statement of Financial Accounting Standards No. 144* (Norwalk, Conn.: FASB, 2001).

[17]*Accounting Trends and Techniques—2004* (New York: AICPA) indicates that just 12 of the 600 companies surveyed reported an extraordinary item.

Similarly, when a company sells the only significant security investment it has ever owned, the gain or loss meets the criteria of an extraordinary item. Another company, however, that has a portfolio of securities acquired for investment purposes would not report such a sales as an extraordinary item. Sale of such securities is part of its ordinary and typical activities.[18]

In addition, considerable judgment must be exercised in determining whether to report an item as extraordinary. For example, the government condemned the forestlands of some paper companies to preserve state or national parks or forests. Is such an event extraordinary, or is it part of a paper company's normal operations? Such determination is not easy. Much depends on the frequency of previous condemnations, the expectation of future condemnations, materiality, and the like.[19]

WHAT DO THE NUMBERS MEAN?

EXTRAORDINARY TIMES

No recent event better illustrates the difficulties of determining whether a transaction meets the definition of extraordinary than the financial impacts of the terrorist attack on the World Trade Center on September 11, 2001.

To many, this event, which resulted in the tragic loss of lives, jobs, and in some cases, entire businesses, clearly meets the criteria for unusual and infrequent. For example, in the wake of the terrorist attack that destroyed the World Trade Center and turned much of lower Manhattan including Wall Street into a war zone, airlines, insurance companies, and other businesses recorded major losses due to property damage, business disruption, and suspension of airline travel and of securities trading.

But, to the surprise of many, the FASB did not permit extraordinary item reporting for losses arising from the terrorist attacks. The reason? After much deliberation, the Emerging Issues Task Force (EITF) of the FASB decided that measurement of the possible loss was too difficult. Take the airline industry as an example: What portion of the airlines' losses after September 11 was related to the terrorist attack, and what portion was due to the ongoing recession? Also, the FASB did not want companies to use the attack as a reason for reporting as extraordinary some losses that had little direct relationship to the attack. Indeed, energy company **AES** and shoe retailer **Footstar**, who both were experiencing profit pressure before 9/11, put some of the blame for their poor performance on the attack.

Source: Julie Creswell, "Bad News Bearers Shift the Blame," *Fortune* (October 15, 2001), p. 44.

Companies must show extraordinary items net of taxes in a separate section in the income statement, usually just before net income. After listing the usual revenues, expenses, and income taxes, the remainder of the statement shows the following.

ILLUSTRATION 4-7
Income Statement Placement of Extraordinary Items

Income before extraordinary items
Extraordinary items (less applicable income tax of $_____)
Net income

---

[18]Debt extinguishments had been the most common reason for companies reporting extraordinary items. The FASB has now eliminated extraordinary item treatment for these gains and losses, unless they are both unusual and infrequent in nature ("Rescission of FASB Statements No. 4, 44, and 64 and Technical Corrections," *Statement of Financial Accounting Standards No. 145* (Norwalk, Conn.: FASB, 2002). Thus, reporting an extraordinary item is likely to become a rare event in the future.

[19]Because assessing the materiality of individual items requires judgment, determining what is extraordinary is difficult. However, in making materiality judgments, companies should consider extraordinary items individually, and not in the aggregate. "Reporting the Results of Operations," op. cit., par. 24.

For example, Illustration 4-8 shows how **Keystone Consolidated Industries** reported an extraordinary loss.

Keystone Consolidated Industries, Inc.

Income before extraordinary item	$11,638,000
Extraordinary item—flood loss (Note E)	1,216,000
Net income	$10,422,000

Note E: Extraordinary Item. The Keystone Steel and Wire Division's Steel Works experienced a flash flood on June 22. The extraordinary item represents the estimated cost, net of related income taxes of $1,279,000, to restore the steel works to full operation.

ILLUSTRATION 4-8
Income Statement Presentation of Extraordinary Items

Unusual Gains and Losses

Because of the restrictive criteria for extraordinary items, financial statement users must carefully examine the financial statements for items that are **unusual or infrequent but not both**. Recall that companies cannot consider items such as write-downs of inventories and transaction gains and losses from fluctuation of foreign exchange as extraordinary items. Thus, companies sometimes show these items with their normal recurring revenues and expenses. If not material in amount, companies combine these with other items in the income statement. If material, companies must disclose them separately, and report them **above** "Income (loss) before extraordinary items."

For example, **PepsiCo, Inc.** presented an unusual charge in its income statement, as Illustration 4-9 shows.

PEPSICO

PepsiCo, Inc.
(in millions)

Net sales	$20,917
Costs and expenses, net	
Cost of sales	8,525
Selling, general, and administrative expenses	9,241
Amortization of intangible assets	199
Unusual items (Note 2)	290
Operating income	$ 2,662

Note 2 (Restructuring Charge)

Dispose and write down assets	$183
Improve productivity	94
Strengthen the international bottler structure	13
Net loss	$290

The net charge to strengthen the international bottler structure includes proceeds of $87 million associated with a settlement related to a previous Venezuelan bottler agreement, which were partially offset by related costs.

ILLUSTRATION 4-9
Income Statement Presentation of Unusual Charges

Restructuring charges, like the one PepsiCo reported, have been common in recent years (see also Illustration 4-5). A **restructuring charge** relates to a major reorganization of company affairs, such as costs associated with employee layoffs, plant closing costs, write-offs of assets, and so on. A company should not report a restructuring charge as an extraordinary item, because these write-offs are part of a company's ordinary and typical activities.

Companies tend to **report unusual items in a separate section just above "Income from operations before income taxes"** and "Extraordinary items," especially when there are multiple unusual items. For example, when **General Electric Company** experienced multiple unusual items in one year, it reported them in a separate "Unusual items" section of the income statement below "Income before unusual items and income taxes." When preparing a multiple-step income statement for homework purposes, you should report unusual gains and losses in the "Other revenues and gains" or "Other expenses and losses" section unless you are instructed to prepare a separate unusual items section.[20]

In dealing with events that are either unusual or nonrecurring but not both, the profession attempted to prevent a practice that many believed was misleading. Companies often reported such transactions on a net-of-tax basis and prominently displayed the earnings per share effect of these items. Although not captioned "Extraordinary items," companies presented them in the same manner. Some had referred to these as "first cousins" to extraordinary items.

As a consequence, the Board specifically **prohibited a net-of-tax treatment for such items**, to ensure that users of financial statements can easily differentiate extraordinary items—reported net of tax—from material items that are unusual or infrequent, but not both.

Changes in Accounting Principle

UNDERLYING CONCEPTS

Companies can change principles, but they must demonstrate that the newly adopted principle is preferable to the old one. Such changes result in lost consistency from period to period.

Changes in accounting occur frequently in practice, because important events or conditions may be in dispute or uncertain at the statement date. One type of accounting change results when a company adopts a different accounting principle. Changes in accounting principle include a change in the method of inventory pricing from FIFO to average cost, or a change in accounting for construction contracts from the percentage-of-completion to the completed-contract method.[21]

A company recognizes a change in accounting principle by making a **retrospective adjustment** to the financial statements. Such an adjustment recasts the prior years' statements on a basis consistent with the newly adopted principle. The company records the cumulative effect of the change for prior periods as an adjustment to beginning retained earnings of the earliest year presented.

To illustrate, Gaubert Inc. decided in March 2007 to change from FIFO to weighted-average inventory pricing. Gaubert's income before taxes, using the new weighted-average method in 2007, is $30,000. Illustration 4-10 presents the pretax income data for 2005 and 2006 for this example.

ILLUSTRATION 4-10
Calculation of a Change in Accounting Principle

Year	FIFO	Weighted-Average Method	Excess of FIFO over Weighted-Average Method
2005	$40,000	$35,000	$5,000
2006	30,000	27,000	3,000
Total			$8,000

---

[20]Many companies report "one-time items." However, some companies take restructuring charges practically every year. **Citicorp** (now **Citigroup**) took restructuring charges six years in a row, between 1988 and 1993; **Eastman Kodak Co.** did so five out of six years in 1989 to 1994. Research indicates that the market discounts the earnings of companies that report a series of "nonrecurring" items. Such evidence supports the contention that these elements reduce the quality of earnings. J. Elliott and D. Hanna, "Repeated Accounting Write-offs and the Information Content of Earnings," *Journal of Accounting Research* (Supplement, 1996).

[21]"Accounting Changes and Error Corrections," *Statement of Financial Accounting Standards No. 154* (Norwalk, Conn.: FASB, 2005). In Chapter 22, we examine in greater detail the problems related to accounting changes.

Illustration 4-11 shows the information Gaubert presented in its comparative income statements, based on a 30 percent tax rate.

	2007	2006	2005
Income before taxes	$30,000	$27,000	$35,000
Income tax	9,000	8,100	10,500
Net income	$21,000	$18,900	$24,500

ILLUSTRATION 4-11
Income Statement
Presentation of a Change
in Accounting Principle

Thus, under the retrospective approach, the company recasts the prior years' income numbers under the newly adopted method. This approach thus preserves comparability across years.

Changes in Estimates

Estimates are inherent in the accounting process. For example, companies estimate useful lives and salvage values of depreciable assets, uncollectible receivables, inventory obsolescence, and the number of periods expected to benefit from a particular expenditure. Not infrequently, due to time, circumstances, or new information, even estimates originally made in good faith must be changed. A company accounts for such **changes in estimates** in the period of change if they affect only that period, or in the period of change and future periods if the change affects both.

To illustrate a change in estimate that affects only the period of change, assume that DuPage Materials Corp. consistently estimated its bad debt expense at 1 percent of credit sales. In 2006 however, DuPage determines that it must revise upward the estimate of bad debts for the current year's credit sales to 2 percent, or double the prior years' percentage. The 2 percent rate is necessary to reduce accounts receivable to net realizable value. Using 2 percent results in a bad debt charge of $240,000, or double the amount using the 1 percent estimate for prior years, DuPage records the provision at December 31, 2006, as follows.

Bad Debt Expense	240,000	
Allowance for Doubtful Accounts		240,000

DuPage includes the entire change in estimate in 2006 income because the change does not affect future periods. **Companies do not handle changes in estimate retrospectively.** That is, such changes are not carried back to adjust prior years. (We examine changes in estimate that affect both the current and future periods in greater detail in Chapter 22.) **Changes in estimate are not considered errors or extraordinary items.**

Corrections of Errors

Errors occur as a result of mathematical mistakes, mistakes in the application of accounting principles, or oversight or misuse of facts that existed at the time financial statements were prepared. In recent years, many companies have corrected for errors in their financial statements. For example, one consulting group noted that error-driven restatements were up 28 percent (to 414 restatements) in 2004.[22] The most common errors involved improper reporting of revenue, accounting for stock options, allowances for receivables, inventories, restructurings, and loss contingencies.

Companies must correct errors by making proper entries in the accounts and reporting the corrections in the financial statements. Corrections of errors are treated as **prior period adjustments**, similar to changes in accounting principles. Companies record a correction of an error in the year in which it is discovered. They report the

---

[22]Carrie Johnson, "Restatements Up 28% in 2004," *Washingtonpost.com* (January 20, 2005), p. E 04.

error in the financial statements as an adjustment to the beginning balance of retained earnings. If a company prepares comparative financial statements, it should restate the prior statements for the effects of the error.

To illustrate, in 2008, Hillsboro Co. determined that it incorrectly overstated its accounts receivable and sales revenue by $100,000 in 2007. In 2008, Hillboro makes the following entry to correct for this error (ignore income taxes).

Retained Earnings	100,000	
Accounts Receivable		100,000

UNDERLYING CONCEPTS

The AICPA Special Committee on Financial Reporting indicates a company's core activities—usual and recurring events—provide the best historical data from which users determine trends and relationships and make their predictions about the future. Therefore, companies should separately display the effects of core and non-core activities.

Retained Earnings is debited because sales revenue, and therefore net income, was overstated in a prior period. Accounts Receivable is credited to reduce this overstated balance to the correct amount.

Summary of Irregular Items

The public accounting profession now tends to accept a modified all-inclusive income concept instead of the current operating performance concept. Except for changes in accounting principle and error corrections, which are charged or credited directly to retained earnings, companies close all other irregular gains or losses or nonrecurring items to Income Summary and include them in the income statement.

Of these irregular items, companies classify **discontinued operations of a component** of a business as a separate item in the income statement, after "Income from continuing operations." Companies show the **unusual**, **material**, **nonrecurring items** that significantly differ from the typical or customary business activities in a separate

ILLUSTRATION 4-12
Summary of Irregular Items in the Income Statement

Type of Situation[a]	Criteria	Examples	Placement on Income Statement
Discontinued operations	Disposal of a component of a business for which the company can clearly distinguish operations and cash flows from the rest of the company's operations.	Sale by diversified company of major division that represents only activities in electronics industry. Food distributor that sells wholesale to supermarket chains and through fast-food restaurants decides to discontinue the division that sells to one of two classes of customers.	Show in separate section after continuing operations but before extraordinary items. (Shown net of tax.)
Extraordinary items	Material, and both unusual and infrequent (nonrecurring).	Gains or losses resulting from casualties, an expropriation, or a prohibition under a new law.	Show in separate section entitled "Extraordinary items." (Shown net of tax.)
Unusual gains or losses, not considered extraordinary	Material; character typical of the customary business activities; unusual or infrequent but not both.	Write-downs of receivables, inventories; adjustments of accrued contract prices; gains or losses from fluctuations of foreign exchange; gains or losses from sales of assets used in business.	Show in separate section above income before extraordinary items. Often reported in "Other revenues and gains" or "Other expenses and losses" section. (Not shown net of tax.)
Changes in principle	Change from one generally accepted principle to another.	Change in the basis of inventory pricing from FIFO to average cost.	Recast prior years' income statements on the same basis as the newly adopted principle.
Changes in estimates	Normal, recurring corrections and adjustments.	Changes in the realizability of receivables and inventories; changes in estimated lives of equipment, intangible assets; changes in estimated liability for warranty costs, income taxes, and salary payments.	Show change only in the affected accounts. (Not shown net of tax.)
Corrections of errors	Mistake, misuse of facts.	Error in reporting revenue.	Restate prior years' income statements to correct for error.

[a]This summary provides only the general rules to be followed in accounting for the various situations described above. Exceptions do exist in some of these situations.

"Extraordinary items" section below "Discontinued operations." They separately disclose other items of a material amount that are of an **unusual or nonrecurring** nature and are **not considered extraordinary**.

Because of the numerous intermediate income figures created by the reporting of these irregular items, readers must carefully evaluate earnings information reported by the financial press. Illustration 4-12 (page 142) summarizes the basic concepts that we previously discussed. Although simplified, the chart provides a useful framework for determining the treatment of special items affecting the income statement.

SPECIAL REPORTING ISSUES

Intraperiod Tax Allocation

Companies report irregular items (except for unusual gains and losses) on the income statement or statement of retained earnings net of tax. This procedure is called **intraperiod tax allocation**, that is, allocation within a period. It relates the income tax expense (sometimes referred to as the income tax provision) of the fiscal period to the **specific items** that give rise to the amount of the tax provision.

> **OBJECTIVE 5**
> Explain intraperiod tax allocation.

Intraperiod tax allocation helps financial statement users better understand the impact of income taxes on the various components of net income. For example, readers of financial statements will understand how much income tax expense relates to "income from continuing operations" and how much relates to certain irregular transactions and events. This approach should help users to better predict the amount, timing, and uncertainty of future cash flows. In addition, intraperiod tax allocation discourages statement readers from using pretax measures of performance when evaluating financial results, and thereby recognizes that income tax expense is a real cost.

Companies use intraperiod tax allocation on the income statement for the following items: (1) income from continuing operations, (2) discontinued operations, and (3) extraordinary items. The general concept is "**let the tax follow the income**."

To compute the income tax expense attributable to "Income from continuing operations," a company would find the income tax expense related to both the revenue and expense transactions used in determining this income. (In this computation, the company does not consider the tax consequences of items excluded from the determination of "Income from continuing operations.") Companies then associate a separate tax effect with each irregular item (e.g., discontinued operations and extraordinary items). Here we look in more detail at calculation of intraperiod tax allocation for extraordinary gains and losses.

Extraordinary Gains

In applying the concept of intraperiod tax allocation, assume that Schindler Co. has income before income tax and extraordinary item of $250,000. It has an extraordinary gain of $100,000 from a condemnation settlement received on one its properties. Assuming a 30 percent income tax rate, Schindler presents the following information on the income statement.

Income before income tax and extraordinary item		$250,000
Income tax		75,000
Income before extraordinary item		175,000
Extraordinary gain—condemnation settlement	$100,000	
Less: Applicable income tax	30,000	70,000
Net income		$245,000

ILLUSTRATION 4-13
Intraperiod Tax Allocation, Extraordinary Gain

Schindler determines the income tax of $75,000 ($250,000 × 30%) attributable to "Income before income tax and extraordinary item" from revenue and expense transactions related to this income. Schindler omits the tax consequences of items excluded from the determination of "Income before income tax and extraordinary item." The company shows a separate tax effect of $30,000 as "Extraordinary gain—condemnation settlement."

Extraordinary Losses

To illustrate the reporting of an extraordinary loss, assume that Schindler Co. has income before income tax and extraordinary item of $250,000. It suffers an extraordinary loss from a major casualty of $100,000. Assuming a 30 percent tax rate, Schindler presents the income tax on the income statement as shown in Illustration 4-14. In this case, the loss provides a positive tax benefit of $30,000. Schindler, therefore, subtracts it from the $100,000 loss.

ILLUSTRATION 4-14
Intraperiod Tax Allocation, Extraordinary Loss

Income before income tax and extraordinary item		$250,000
Income tax		75,000
Income before extraordinary item		175,000
Extraordinary item—loss from casualty	$100,000	
Less: Applicable income tax reduction	30,000	70,000
Net income		$105,000

Companies may also report the tax effect of an extraordinary item by means of a note disclosure, as illustrated below.

ILLUSTRATION 4-15
Note Disclosure of Intraperiod Tax Allocation

Income before income tax and extraordinary item	$250,000
Income tax	75,000
Income before extraordinary item	175,000
Extraordinary item, less applicable income tax reduction (Note 1)	70,000
Net income	$105,000

Note 1: During the year the Company suffered a major casualty loss of $70,000, net of applicable income tax reduction of $30,000.

Earnings per Share

OBJECTIVE 6
Identify where to report earnings per share information.

A company customarily sums up the results of its operations in one important figure: net income. However, the financial world has widely accepted an even more distilled and compact figure as the most significant business indicator—**earnings per share** (EPS).

The computation of earnings per share is usually straightforward. **Earnings per share is net income minus preferred dividends (income available to common stockholders), divided by the weighted average of common shares outstanding.**[23]

To illustrate, assume that Lancer, Inc. reports net income of $350,000. It declares and pays preferred dividends of $50,000 for the year. The weighted average number of common shares outstanding during the year is 100,000 shares. Lancer computes earnings per share of $3, as shown in Illustration 4-16.

ILLUSTRATION 4-16
Equation Illustrating Computation of Earnings per Share

$$\frac{\text{Net Income} - \text{Preferred Dividends}}{\text{Weighted Average of Common Shares Outstanding}} = \text{Earnings per Share}$$

$$\frac{\$350,000 - \$50,000}{100,000} = \$3$$

---

[23]In calculating earnings per share, companies deduct preferred dividends from net income if the dividends are declared or if they are cumulative though not declared.

Note that EPS measures the number of dollars earned by each share of common stock. It does not represent the dollar amount paid to stockholders in the form of dividends.

Prospectuses, proxy material, and annual reports to stockholders commonly use the "net income per share" or "earnings per share" ratio. The financial press, statistical services like Standard & Poor's, and Wall Street securities analysts also highlight EPS. Because of its importance, **companies must disclose earnings per share on the face of the income statement**. A company that reports a discontinued operation or an extraordinary item must report per share amounts for these line items either on the face of the income statement or in the notes to the financial statements.[24]

To illustrate, consider the income statement for Poquito Industries Inc. shown in Illustration 4-17. Notice the order in which Poquito shows the data, with per share information at the bottom. Assume that the company had 100,000 shares outstanding for the entire year. The Poquito income statement, as Illustration 4-17 shows, is highly condensed. Poquito would need to describe items such as "Unusual charge," "Discontinued operations," and "Extraordinary item" fully and appropriately in the statement or related notes.

ILLUSTRATION 4-17
Income Statement

POQUITO INDUSTRIES INC. INCOME STATEMENT FOR THE YEAR ENDED DECEMBER 31, 2007		
Sales revenue		$1,420,000
Cost of goods sold		600,000
Gross profit		820,000
Selling and administrative expenses		320,000
Income from operations		500,000
Other revenues and gains		
Interest revenue		10,000
Other expenses and losses		
Loss on disposal of part of Textile Division	$ (5,000)	
Unusual charge—loss on sale of investments	(45,000)	(50,000)
Income from continuing operations before income tax		460,000
Income tax		184,000
Income from continuing operations		276,000
Discontinued operations		
Income from operations of Pizza Division, less applicable income tax of $24,800	54,000	
Loss on disposal of Pizza Division, less applicable income tax of $41,000	(90,000)	(36,000)
Income before extraordinary item		240,000
Extraordinary item—loss from earthquake, less applicable income tax of $23,000		(45,000)
Net income		$ 195,000
Per share of common stock		
Income from continuing operations		$2.76
Income from operations of discontinued division, net of tax		0.54
Loss on disposal of discontinued operation, net of tax		(0.90)
Income before extraordinary item		2.40
Extraordinary loss, net of tax		(0.45)
Net income		$1.95

Many corporations have simple capital structures that include only common stock. For these companies, a presentation such as "Earnings per common share" is appropriate on the income statement. In many instances, however, companies' earnings per

---

[24]"Earnings Per Share," *Statement of Financial Accounting Standards No. 128* (Norwalk, Conn.: FASB, 1996).

share are subject to dilution (reduction) in the future because existing contingencies permit the issuance of additional common shares.[25]

In summary, the simplicity and availability of EPS figures lead to their widespread use. Because of the importance that the public, even the well-informed public, attaches to earnings per share, companies must make the EPS figure as meaningful as possible.

Retained Earnings Statement

OBJECTIVE 7
Prepare a retained earnings statement.

Net income increases retained earnings. A net loss decreases retained earnings. Both cash and stock dividends decrease retained earnings. Changes in accounting principles (generally) and prior period adjustments may increase or decrease retained earnings. Companies charge or credit these adjustments (net of tax) to the opening balance of retained earnings. This excludes the adjustments from the determination of net income for the current period.

Companies may show retained earnings information in different ways. For example, some companies prepare a separate retained earnings statement, as Illustration 4-18 shows.

ILLUSTRATION 4-18
Retained Earnings
Statement

TIGER WOODS INC.		
RETAINED EARNINGS STATEMENT		
FOR THE YEAR ENDED DECEMBER 31, 2007		
Retained earnings, January 1, as reported		$1,050,000
Correction for understatement of net income in prior period (inventory error)		50,000
Retained earnings, January 1, as adjusted		1,100,000
Add: Net income		360,000
		1,460,000
Less: Cash dividends	$100,000	
Stock dividends	200,000	300,000
Retained earnings, December 31		$1,160,000

The reconciliation of the beginning to the ending balance in retained earnings provides information about why net assets increased or decreased during the year. The association of dividend distributions with net income for the period indicates what management is doing with earnings: It may be "plowing back" into the business part or all of the earnings, distributing all current income, or distributing current income plus the accumulated earnings of prior years.[26]

Restrictions of Retained Earnings

Companies often restrict retained earnings to comply with contractual requirements, board of directors' policy, or current necessity. Generally, companies disclose in the notes to the financial statements the amounts of restricted retained earnings. In some cases, companies transfer the amount of retained earnings restricted to an account titled **Appropriated Retained Earnings**. The retained earnings section may therefore report two separate amounts—(1) retained earnings free (unrestricted) and (2) retained earnings appropriated (restricted). The total of these two amounts equals the total retained earnings.

---

[25]Ibid. We discuss the computational problems involved in accounting for these dilutive securities in earnings per share computations in Chapter 16.

[26]*Accounting Trends and Techniques—2004* (New York: AICPA) indicates that most companies (593 of 600 surveyed) present changes in retained earnings either within the statement of stockholders' equity (586 firms) or in a separate statement of retained earnings. Only 2 of the 600 companies prepare a combined statement of income and retained earnings.

Comprehensive Income

Companies generally include in income all revenues, expenses, and gains and losses recognized during the period. These items are classified within the income statement so that financial statement readers can better understand the significance of various components of net income. Changes in accounting principles and corrections of errors are excluded from the calculation of net income because their effects relate to prior periods.

In recent years, there is increased use of fair values for measuring assets and liabilities. Furthermore, possible reporting of gains and losses related to changes in fair value have placed a strain on income reporting. Because fair values are continually changing, some argue that recognizing these gains and losses in net income is misleading. The FASB agrees and has identified a limited number of transactions that should be recorded directly to stockholders equity. One example is unrealized gains and losses on available-for-sale securities.[27] These gains and losses are excluded from net income, thereby reducing volatility in net income due to fluctuations in fair value. At the same time disclosure of the potential gain or loss is provided.

Companies include these items that bypass the income statement in a measure called comprehensive income. **Comprehensive income** includes all changes in equity during a period *except* those resulting from investments by owners and distributions to owners. Comprehensive income, therefore, includes the following: all revenues and gains, expenses and losses reported in net income, and all gains and losses that bypass net income but affect stockholders' equity. These items—non-owner changes in equity that bypass the income statement—are referred to as **other comprehensive income**.

The FASB decided that companies must display the components of other comprehensive income in one of three ways: **(1) a second income statement; (2) a combined statement of comprehensive income; or (3) as a part of the statement of stockholders' equity.** [28] Regardless of the format used, companies must add net income to other comprehensive income to arrive at comprehensive income. Companies are not required to report earnings per share information related to comprehensive income.[29]

To illustrate, assume that V. Gill Inc. reports the following information for 2007: sales revenue $800,000; cost of goods sold $600,000; operating expenses $90,000; and an unrealized holding gain on available-for-sale securities of $30,000, net of tax.

> **OBJECTIVE 8**
> Explain how to report other comprehensive income.

Second Income Statement

Illustration 4-19 (page 148) shows the two-income statement format based on the above information for V. Gill. Reporting comprehensive income in a separate statement indicates that the gains and losses identified as other comprehensive income have the same status as traditional gains and losses. Placing net income as the starting point in the comprehensive income statement highlights the relationship of the statement to the traditional income statement.

---

[27]We further discuss available-for-sale securities in Chapter 17. Additional examples of other comprehensive items are translation gains and losses on foreign currency, excess of additional pension liability over unrecognized prior service cost, and unrealized gains and losses on certain hedging transactions.

[28]"Reporting Comprehensive Income," *Statement of Financial Accounting Standards No. 130* (Norwalk, Conn.: FASB, June 1997). *Accounting Trends and Techniques—2004* (New York: AICPA) indicates that for the 600 companies surveyed, 580 report comprehensive income. Most companies (488 of 580) include comprehensive income as part of the statement of stockholders' equity.

[29]A company must display the components of other comprehensive income either (1) net of related tax effects, or (2) before related tax effects, with one amount shown for the aggregate amount of tax related to the total amount of other comprehensive income. Both alternatives must show each component of other comprehensive income, net of related taxes either in the face of the statement or in the notes.

ILLUSTRATION 4-19
Two-Statement Format:
Comprehensive Income

V. GILL INC.
INCOME STATEMENT
FOR THE YEAR ENDED DECEMBER 31, 2007

Sales revenue	$800,000
Cost of goods sold	600,000
Gross profit	200,000
Operating expenses	90,000
Net income	$110,000

V. GILL INC.
COMPREHENSIVE INCOME STATEMENT
FOR THE YEAR ENDED DECEMBER 31, 2007

Net income	$110,000
Other comprehensive income	
Unrealized holding gain, net of tax	30,000
Comprehensive income	$140,000

Combined Statement of Comprehensive Income

The second approach to reporting other comprehensive income provides a **combined statement** of comprehensive income. In this approach, the traditional net income is a subtotal, with total comprehensive income shown as a final total. The combined statement has the advantage of not requiring the creation of a new financial statement. However, burying net income as a subtotal on the statement is a disadvantage.

Statement of Stockholders' Equity

A third approach reports other comprehensive income items in a **statement of stockholders' equity** (often referred to as statement of changes in stockholders' equity). This statement reports the changes in each stockholder's equity account and in total stockholders' equity during the year. Companies often prepare **in columnar form** the statement of stockholders' equity. In this format, they use columns for each account and for total stockholders' equity.

To illustrate, assume the same information for V. Gill. The company had the following stockholder equity account balances at the beginning of 2007: Common Stock $300,000; Retained Earnings $50,000; and Accumulated Other Comprehensive Income $60,000. No changes in the Common Stock account occurred during the year. Illustration 4-20 shows a statement of stockholders' equity for V. Gill.

V. GILL INC.
STATEMENT OF STOCKHOLDERS' EQUITY
FOR THE YEAR ENDED DECEMBER 31, 2007

	Total	Comprehensive Income	Retained Earnings	Accumulated Other Comprehensive Income	Common Stock
Beginning balance	$410,000		$ 50,000	$60,000	$300,000
Comprehensive income					
Net income	110,000	$110,000	110,000		
Other comprehensive income					
Unrealized holding gain, net of tax	30,000	30,000		30,000	
Comprehensive income		$140,000			
Ending balance	$550,000		$160,000	$90,000	$300,000

Most companies use the statement of stockholders' equity approach to provide information related to other comprehensive income. Because many companies already provide a statement of stockholders' equity, adding additional columns to display information related to comprehensive income is not costly.

*Examples of
Comprehensive Income
Reporting*

Balance Sheet Presentation

Regardless of the display format used, V. Gill reports the **accumulated other comprehensive income** of $90,000 in the stockholders' equity section of the balance sheet as follows.

V. GILL INC. BALANCE SHEET AS OF DECEMBER 31, 2007 (STOCKHOLDERS' EQUITY SECTION)	
Stockholders' equity	
Common stock	$300,000
Retained earnings	160,000
Accumulated other comprehensive income	90,000
Total stockholders' equity	$550,000

ILLUSTRATION 4-21
Presentation of
Accumulated Other
Comprehensive Income
in the Balance Sheet

By providing information on the components of comprehensive income, as well as accumulated other comprehensive income, the company communicates information about all changes in net assets.[30] With this information, users will better understand the quality of the company's earnings.

SUMMARY OF LEARNING OBJECTIVES

1. Understand the uses and limitations of an income statement. The income statement provides investors and creditors with information that helps them predict the amounts, timing, and uncertainty of future cash flows. Also, the income statement helps users determine the risk (level of uncertainty) of not achieving particular cash flows. The limitations of an income statement are: (1) The statement does not include many items that contribute to general growth and well-being of a company. (2) Income numbers are often affected by the accounting methods used. (3) Income measures are subject to estimates.

The *transaction approach* focuses on the activities that occurred during a given period. Instead of presenting only a net change in net assets, it discloses the components of the change. The transaction approach to income measurement requires the use of revenue, expense, loss, and gain accounts.

2. Prepare a single-step income statement. In a single-step income statement, just two groupings exist: revenues and expenses. Expenses are deducted from revenues to arrive at net income or loss—a single subtraction. Frequently, companies report income tax separately as the last item before net income.

3. Prepare a multiple-step income statement. A multiple-step income statement shows two further classifications: (1) a separation of operating results from those obtained through the subordinate or nonoperating activities of the company; and (2) a classification of expenses by functions, such as merchandising or manufacturing, selling, and administration.

KEY TERMS

accumulated other
   comprehensive
   income, *149*

appropriated retained
   earnings, *146*

capital maintenance
   approach, *129 (ftn)*

changes in estimates, *141*

comprehensive income,
   147

current operating
   performance
   approach, *135*

discontinued operation,
   136

earnings management,
   128

earnings per share, *144*

extraordinary items, *137*

income statement, *126*

intraperiod tax allocation,
   143

irregular items, *136*

---

[30]Corrections of errors and changes in accounting principles are not considered other comprehensive income items.

4. Explain how to report irregular items. Companies generally close irregular gains or losses or nonrecurring items to Income Summary and include them in the income statement as follows: (1) Discontinued operations of a component of a business are classified as a separate item, after continuing operations. (2) The unusual, material, nonrecurring items that are significantly different from the customary business activities are shown in a separate section for extraordinary items, below discontinued operations. (3) Other items of a material amount that are of an unusual or nonrecurring nature and are not considered extraordinary are separately disclosed as a component of continuing operations. Changes in accounting principle and corrections of errors are adjusted through retained earnings.

5. Explain intraperiod tax allocation. Companies should relate the tax expense for the year to specific items on the income statement to provide a more informative disclosure to statement users. This procedure, intraperiod tax allocation, relates the income tax expense for the fiscal period to the following items that affect the amount of the tax provisions: (1) income from continuing operations, (2) discontinued operations, and (3) extraordinary items.

6. Identify where to report earnings per share information. Because of the inherent dangers of focusing attention solely on earnings per share, the profession concluded that companies must disclose earnings per share on the face of the income statement. A company that reports a discontinued operation or an extraordinary item must report per share amounts for these line items either on the face of the income statement or in the notes to the financial statements.

7. Prepare a retained earnings statement. The retained earnings statement should disclose net income (loss), dividends, adjustments due to changes in accounting principles, error corrections, and restrictions of retained earnings.

8. Explain how to report other comprehensive income. Companies report the components of other comprehensive income in a second statement, a combined statement of comprehensive income, or in a statement of stockholders' equity.

QUESTIONS

1. What kinds of questions about future cash flows do investors and creditors attempt to answer with information in the income statement?

2. How can information based on past transactions be used to predict future cash flows?

3. Identify at least two situations in which important changes in value are not reported in the income statement.

4. Identify at least two situations in which application of different accounting methods or accounting estimates results in difficulties in comparing companies.

5. Explain the transaction approach to measuring income. Why is the transaction approach to income measurement preferable to other ways of measuring income?

6. What is earnings management?

7. How can earnings management affect the quality of earnings?

8. Why should caution be exercised in the use of the income figure derived in an income statement? What are the objectives of generally accepted accounting principles in their application to the income statement?

9. A *Wall Street Journal* article noted that **MicroStrategy** reported higher income than its competitors by using a more aggressive policy for recognizing revenue on future upgrades to its products. Some contend that MicroStrategy's quality of earnings is low. What does the term "quality of earnings" mean?

10. What is the major distinction (a) between revenues and gains and (b) between expenses and losses?

11. What are the advantages and disadvantages of the single-step income statement?

12. What is the basis for distinguishing between operating and nonoperating items?

13. Distinguish between the modified all-inclusive income statement and the current operating performance income statement. According to present generally accepted accounting principles, which is recommended? Explain.

14. How should correction of errors be reported in the financial statements?

15. Discuss the appropriate treatment in the financial statements of each of the following.

(a) An amount of $113,000 realized in excess of the cash surrender value of an insurance policy on the life of one of the founders of the company who died during the year.

(b) A profit-sharing bonus to employees computed as a percentage of net income.

(c) Additional depreciation on factory machinery because of an error in computing depreciation for the previous year.

(d) Rent received from subletting a portion of the office space.

(e) A patent infringement suit, brought 2 years ago against the company by another company, was settled this year by a cash payment of $725,000.

(f) A reduction in the Allowance for Doubtful Accounts balance, because the account appears to be considerably in excess of the probable loss from uncollectible receivables.

16. Indicate where the following items would ordinarily appear on the financial statements of Allepo, Inc. for the year 2007.

(a) The service life of certain equipment was changed from 8 to 5 years. If a 5-year life had been used previously, additional depreciation of $425,000 would have been charged.

(b) In 2007 a flood destroyed a warehouse that had a book value of $1,600,000. Floods are rare in this locality.

(c) In 2007 the company wrote off $1,000,000 of inventory that was considered obsolete.

(d) An income tax refund related to the 2004 tax year was received.

(e) In 2004, a supply warehouse with an expected useful life of 7 years was erroneously expensed.

(f) Allepo, Inc. changed from weighted-average to FIFO inventory pricing.

17. Give the section of a multiple-step income statement in which each of the following is shown.

(a) Loss on inventory write-down.

(b) Loss from strike.

(c) Bad debt expense.

(d) Loss on disposal of a component of the business.

(e) Gain on sale of machinery.

(f) Interest revenue.

(g) Depreciation expense.

(h) Material write-offs of notes receivable.

18. Barry Bonds Land Development, Inc. purchased land for $70,000 and spent $30,000 developing it. It then sold the land for $160,000. Tom Glavine Manufacturing purchased land for a future plant site for $100,000. Due to a change in plans, Glavine later sold the land for $160,000. Should these two companies report the land sales, both at gains of $60,000, in a similar manner?

19. You run into Rex Grossman at a party and begin discussing financial statements. Rex says, "I prefer the single-step income statement because the multiple-step format generally overstates income." How should you respond to Rex?

20. Federov Corporation has eight expense accounts in its general ledger which could be classified as selling expenses. Should Federov report these eight expenses separately in its income statement or simply report one total amount for selling expenses?

21. Jose DeLeon Investments reported an unusual gain from the sale of certain assets in its 2007 income statement. How does intraperiod tax allocation affect the reporting of this unusual gain?

22. What effect does intraperiod tax allocation have on reported net income?

23. Letterman Company computed earnings per share as follows.

$$\frac{\text{Net income}}{\text{Common shares outstanding at year-end}}$$

Letterman has a simple capital structure. What possible errors might the company have made in the computation? Explain.

24. Maria Shriver Corporation reported 2007 earnings per share of $7.21. In 2008, Maria Shriver reported earnings per share as follows.

On income before extraordinary item	$6.40
On extraordinary item	1.88
On net income	$8.28

Is the increase in earnings per share from $7.21 to $8.28 a favorable trend?

25. What is meant by "tax allocation within a period"? What is the justification for such practice?

26. When does tax allocation within a period become necessary? How should this allocation be handled?

27. During 2007, Natsume Sozeki Company earned income of $1,000,000 before income taxes and realized a gain of $450,000 on a government-forced condemnation sale of a division plant facility. The income is subject to income taxation at the rate of 34%. The gain on the sale of the plant is taxed at 30%. Proper accounting suggests that the unusual gain be reported as an extraordinary item. Illustrate an appropriate presentation of these items in the income statement.

28. On January 30, 2006, a suit was filed against Pierogi Corporation under the Environmental Protection Act. On August 6, 2007, Pierogi Corporation agreed to settle the action and pay $920,000 in damages to certain current and former employees. How should this settlement be reported in the 2007 financial statements? Discuss.

29. Tiger Paper Company decided to close two small pulp mills in Conway, New Hampshire, and Corvallis, Oregon. Would these closings be reported in a separate section entitled "Discontinued operations after income from continuing operations"? Discuss.

30. What major types of items are reported in the retained earnings statement?

31. Generally accepted accounting principles usually require the use of accrual accounting to "fairly present" income. If the cash receipts and disbursements method of accounting will "clearly reflect" taxable income, why does this method not usually also "fairly present" income?

32. State some of the more serious problems encountered in seeking to achieve the ideal measurement of periodic net income. Explain what accountants do as a practical alternative.

33. What is meant by the terms *elements* and *items* as they relate to the income statement? Why might items have to be disclosed in the income statement?

34. What are the three ways that other comprehensive income may be displayed (reported)?

35. How should the disposal of a component of a business be disclosed in the income statement?

BRIEF EXERCISES

(LO 2) **BE4-1** Tim Allen Co. had sales revenue of $540,000 in 2007. Other items recorded during the year were:

Cost of goods sold	$320,000
Wage expense	120,000
Income tax expense	25,000
Increase in value of company reputation	15,000
Other operating expenses	10,000
Unrealized gain on value of patents	20,000

Prepare a single-step income statement for Allen for 2007. Allen has 100,000 shares of stock outstanding.

(LO 2) **BE4-2** Turner Corporation had net sales of $2,400,000 and interest revenue of $31,000 during 2007. Expenses for 2007 were: cost of goods sold $1,250,000; administrative expenses $212,000; selling expenses $280,000; interest expense $45,000. Turner's tax rate is 30%. The corporation had 100,000 shares of common stock authorized and 70,000 shares issued and outstanding during 2007. Prepare a single-step income statement for the year ended December 31, 2007.

(LO 3) **BE4-3** Using the information provided in BE4-2, prepare a condensed multiple-step income statement for Turner Corporation.

(LO 3, 4) **BE4-4** Green Day Corporation had income from continuing operations of $12,600,000 in 2007. During 2007, it disposed of its restaurant division at an after-tax loss of $189,000. Prior to disposal, the division operated at a loss of $315,000 (net of tax) in 2007. Green Day had 10,000,000 shares of common stock outstanding during 2007. Prepare a partial income statement for Green Day beginning with income from continuing operations.

(LO 4, 5) **BE4-5** J. Depp Corporation had income before income taxes for 2007 of $7,300,000. In addition, it suffered an unusual and infrequent pretax loss of $770,000 from a volcano eruption. The corporation's tax rate is 30%. Prepare a partial income statement for J. Depp beginning with income before income taxes. The corporation had 5,000,000 shares of common stock outstanding during 2007.

(LO 4) **BE4-6** During 2007 Lebron James Company changed from FIFO to weighted-average inventory pricing. Pretax income in 2006 and 2005 (James's first year of operations) under FIFO was $160,000 and $180,000, respectively. Pretax income using weighted-average pricing in the prior years would have been $145,000 in 2006 and $170,000 in 2005. In 2007, Lebron James Company reported pretax income (using weighted-average pricing) of $190,000. Show comparative income statements for Lebron James Company, beginning with "Income before income tax," as presented on the 2007 income statement. (The tax rate in all years is 30%.)

(LO 4) **BE4-7** Jana Kingston Company has recorded bad debt expense in the past at a rate of 1½% of net sales. In 2007, Kingston decides to increase its estimate to 2%. If the new rate had been used in prior years, cumulative bad debt expense would have been $380,000 instead of $285,000. In 2007, bad debt expense will be $120,000 instead of $90,000. If Kingston's tax rate is 30%, what amount should it report as the cumulative effect of changing the estimated bad debt rate?

(LO 6) **BE4-8** In 2007, Kirby Puckett Corporation reported net income of $1,200,000. It declared and paid preferred stock dividends of $250,000. During 2007, Puckett had a weighted average of 190,000 common shares outstanding. Compute Puckett's 2007 earnings per share.

(LO 7) **BE4-9** Lincoln Corporation has retained earnings of $675,000 at January 1, 2007. Net income during 2007 was $2,400,000, and cash dividends declared and paid during 2007 totaled $75,000. Prepare a retained earnings statement for the year ended December 31, 2007.

(LO 4, 7) **BE4-10** Using the information from BE4-9, prepare a retained earnings statement for the year ended December 31, 2007. Assume an error was discovered: land costing $80,000 (net of tax) was charged to repairs expense in 2004.

(LO 8) **BE4-11** On January 1, 2007, Creative Works Inc. had cash and common stock of $60,000. At that date the company had no other asset, liability or equity balances. On January 2, 2007, it purchased for cash $20,000 of equity securities that it classified as available-for-sale. It received cash dividends of $3,000 during the year on these securities. In addition, it has an unrealized holding gain on these securities of $5,000 net of tax. Determine the following amounts for 2007: (a) net income; (b) comprehensive income; (c) other comprehensive income; and (d) accumulated other comprehensive income (end of 2007).

EXERCISES

(LO 2) **E4-1** **(Computation of Net Income)** Presented below are changes in all the account balances of Fritz Reiner Furniture Co. during the current year, except for retained earnings.

	Increase (Decrease)		Increase (Decrease)
Cash	$ 79,000	Accounts Payable	$(51,000)
Accounts Receivable (net)	45,000	Bonds Payable	82,000
Inventory	127,000	Common Stock	125,000
Investments	(47,000)	Additional Paid-in Capital	13,000

Instructions

Compute the net income for the current year, assuming that there were no entries in the Retained Earnings account except for net income and a dividend declaration of $19,000 which was paid in the current year.

(LO 2) **E4-2** **(Income Statement Items)** Presented below are certain account balances of Paczki Products Co.

Rental revenue	$ 6,500	Sales discounts	$ 7,800
Interest expense	12,700	Selling expenses	99,400
Beginning retained earnings	114,400	Sales	390,000
Ending retained earnings	134,000	Income tax	31,000
Dividend revenue	71,000	Cost of goods sold	184,400
Sales returns	12,400	Administrative expenses	82,500

Instructions

From the foregoing, compute the following: (a) total net revenue, (b) net income, (c) dividends declared during the current year.

(LO 2) **E4-3** **(Single-step Income Statement)** The financial records of LeRoi Jones Inc. were destroyed by fire at the end of 2007. Fortunately the controller had kept certain statistical data related to the income statement as presented below.

1. The beginning merchandise inventory was $92,000 and decreased 20% during the current year.
2. Sales discounts amount to $17,000.
3. 20,000 shares of common stock were outstanding for the entire year.
4. Interest expense was $20,000.
5. The income tax rate is 30%.
6. Cost of goods sold amounts to $500,000.

7. Administrative expenses are 20% of cost of goods sold but only 8% of gross sales.
8. Four-fifths of the operating expenses relate to sales activities.

Instructions

From the foregoing information prepare an income statement for the year 2007 in single-step form.

(LO 2, 3) **E4-4** **(Multiple-step and Single-step)** Two accountants for the firm of Elwes and Wright are arguing about the merits of presenting an income statement in a multiple-step versus a single-step format. The discussion involves the following 2007 information related to P. Bride Company ($000 omitted).

Administrative expense	
Officers' salaries	$ 4,900
Depreciation of office furniture and equipment	3,960
Cost of goods sold	60,570
Rental revenue	17,230
Selling expense	
Transportation-out	2,690
Sales commissions	7,980
Depreciation of sales equipment	6,480
Sales	96,500
Income tax	9,070
Interest expense	1,860

Instructions

(a) Prepare an income statement for the year 2007 using the multiple-step form. Common shares outstanding for 2007 total 40,550 (000 omitted).

(b) Prepare an income statement for the year 2007 using the single-step form.

(c) Which one do you prefer? Discuss.

(LO 3, 4) **E4-5** **(Multiple-step and Extraordinary Items)** The following balances were taken from the books of Maria Conchita Alonzo Corp. on December 31, 2007.

Interest revenue	$ 86,000	Accumulated depreciation—equipment	$ 40,000
Cash	51,000	Accumulated depreciation—building	28,000
Sales	1,380,000	Notes receivable	155,000
Accounts receivable	150,000	Selling expenses	194,000
Prepaid insurance	20,000	Accounts payable	170,000
Sales returns and allowances	150,000	Bonds payable	100,000
Allowance for doubtful		Administrative and general	
accounts	7,000	expenses	97,000
Sales discounts	45,000	Accrued liabilities	32,000
Land	100,000	Interest expense	60,000
Equipment	200,000	Notes payable	100,000
Building	140,000	Loss from earthquake damage	
Cost of goods sold	621,000	(extraordinary item)	150,000
		Common stock	500,000
		Retained earnings	21,000

Assume the total effective tax rate on all items is 34%.

Instructions

Prepare a multiple-step income statement; 100,000 shares of common stock were outstanding during the year.

(LO 2, 3) **E4-6** **(Multiple-step and Single-step)** The accountant of Whitney Houston Shoe Co. has compiled the following information from the company's records as a basis for an income statement for the year ended December 31, 2007.

Rental revenue	$ 29,000
Interest on notes payable	18,000
Market appreciation on land above cost	31,000
Wages and salaries—sales	114,800
Materials and supplies—sales	17,600
Income tax	37,400
Wages and salaries—administrative	135,900
Other administrative expenses	51,700
Cost of goods sold	496,000
Net sales	980,000
Depreciation on plant assets (70% selling, 30% administrative)	65,000
Cash dividends declared	16,000

There were 20,000 shares of common stock outstanding during the year.

Instructions

(a) Prepare a multiple-step income statement.

(b) Prepare a single-step income statement.

(c) Which format do you prefer? Discuss.

(LO 2, 4, 6) **E4-7 (Income Statement, EPS)** Presented below are selected ledger accounts of Tucker Corporation as of December 31, 2007.

Cash	$ 50,000
Administrative expenses	100,000
Selling expenses	80,000
Net sales	540,000
Cost of goods sold	210,000
Cash dividends declared (2007)	20,000
Cash dividends paid (2007)	15,000
Discontinued operations (loss before income taxes)	40,000
Depreciation expense, not recorded in 2006	30,000
Retained earnings, December 31, 2006	90,000
Effective tax rate 30%	

Instructions

(a) Compute net income for 2007.

(b) Prepare a partial income statement beginning with income from continuing operations before income tax, and including appropriate earnings per share information. Assume 10,000 shares of common stock were outstanding during 2007.

(LO 3, 4, 5, 6, 7) **E4-8 (Multiple-step Statement with Retained Earnings)** Presented below is information related to Ivan Calderon Corp. for the year 2007.

Net sales	$1,300,000	Write-off of inventory due to obsolescence	$ 80,000
Cost of goods sold	780,000	Depreciation expense omitted by accident in 2006	55,000
Selling expenses	65,000	Casualty loss (extraordinary item) before taxes	50,000
Administrative expenses	48,000	Cash dividends declared	45,000
Dividend revenue	20,000	Retained earnings at December 31, 2006	980,000
Interest revenue	7,000	Effective tax rate of 34% on all items	

Instructions

(a) Prepare a multiple-step income statement for 2007. Assume that 60,000 shares of common stock are outstanding.

(b) Prepare a separate retained earnings statement for 2007.

(LO 6) **E4-9 (Earnings Per Share)** The stockholders' equity section of Tkachuk Corporation appears below as of December 31, 2007.

8% preferred stock, $50 par value, authorized		
100,000 shares, outstanding 90,000 shares		$ 4,500,000
Common stock, $1.00 par, authorized and issued 10 million shares		10,000,000
Additional paid-in capital		20,500,000
Retained earnings	$134,000,000	
Net income	33,000,000	167,000,000
		$202,000,000

Net income for 2007 reflects a total effective tax rate of 34%. Included in the net income figure is a loss of $18,000,000 (before tax) as a result of a major casualty, which should be classified as an extraordinary item. Preferred stock dividends of $360,000 were declared and paid in 2007. Dividends of $1,000,000 were declared and paid to common stockholders in 2007.

Instructions

Compute earnings per share data as it should appear on the income statement of Tkachuk Corporation.

(LO 3, 4, 5, 6) **E4-10 (Condensed Income Statement—Periodic Inventory Method)** Presented below are selected ledger accounts of Spock Corporation at December 31, 2007.

Cash	$ 185,000	Sales salaries	$284,000
Merchandise inventory	535,000	Office salaries	346,000
Sales	4,275,000	Purchase returns	15,000
Advances from customers	117,000	Sales returns	79,000
Purchases	2,786,000	Transportation-in	72,000
Sales discounts	34,000	Accounts receivable	142,500
Purchase discounts	27,000	Sales commissions	83,000

Travel and entertainment—sales	$ 69,000	Telephone—sales	$ 17,000
Accounting and legal services	33,000	Utilities—office	32,000
Insurance expense—office	24,000	Miscellaneous office expenses	8,000
Advertising	54,000	Rental revenue	240,000
Transportation-out	93,000	Extraordinary loss (before tax)	70,000
Depreciation of office equipment	48,000	Interest expense	176,000
Depreciation of sales equipment	36,000	Common stock ($10 par)	900,000

Spock's effective tax rate on all items is 34%. A physical inventory indicates that the ending inventory is $686,000.

Instructions

Prepare a condensed 2007 income statement for Spock Corporation.

(LO 7) **E4-11** **(Retained Earnings Statement)** Eddie Zambrano Corporation began operations on January 1, 2004. During its first 3 years of operations, Zambrano reported net income and declared dividends as follows.

	Net income	Dividends declared
2004	$ 40,000	$ –0–
2005	125,000	50,000
2006	160,000	50,000

The following information relates to 2007.

Income before income tax	$240,000
Prior period adjustment: understatement of 2005 depreciation expense (before taxes)	$ 25,000
Cumulative decrease in income from change in inventory methods (before taxes)	$ 35,000
Dividends declared (of this amount, $25,000 will be paid on Jan. 15, 2008)	$100,000
Effective tax rate	40%

Instructions

(a) Prepare a 2007 retained earnings statement for Eddie Zambrano Corporation.

(b) Assume Eddie Zambrano Corp. restricted retained earnings in the amount of $70,000 on December 31, 2007. After this action, what would Zambrano report as total retained earnings in its December 31, 2007, balance sheet?

(LO 4, 5, 6) **E4-12** **(Earnings per Share)** At December 31, 2006, Shiga Naoya Corporation had the following stock outstanding.

10% cumulative preferred stock, $100 par, 107,500 shares	$10,750,000
Common stock, $5 par, 4,000,000 shares	20,000,000

During 2007, Shiga Naoya did not issue any additional common stock. The following also occurred during 2007.

Income from continuing operations before taxes	$23,650,000
Discontinued operations (loss before taxes)	$ 3,225,000
Preferred dividends declared	$ 1,075,000
Common dividends declared	$ 2,200,000
Effective tax rate	35%

Instructions

Compute earnings per share data as it should appear in the 2007 income statement of Shiga Naoya Corporation. (Round to two decimal places.)

(LO 4, 5, 6) **E4-13** **(Change in Accounting Principle)** Tim Mattke Company began operations in 2005 and for simplicity reasons, adopted weighted-average pricing for inventory. In 2007, in accordance with other companies in its industry, Mattke changed its inventory pricing to FIFO. The pretax income data is reported below.

Year	Weighted-Average	FIFO
2005	$370,000	$395,000
2006	390,000	430,000
2007	410,000	450,000

Instructions

(a) What is Mattke's net income in 2007? Assume a 35% tax rate in all years.

(b) Compute the cumulative effect of the change in accounting principle from weighted-average to FIFO inventory pricing.

(c) Show comparative income statements for Tim Mattke Company, beginning with income before income tax, as presented on the 2007 income statement.

(LO 3, 8) **E4-14 (Comprehensive Income)**   Roxanne Carter Corporation reported the following for 2007: net sales $1,200,000; cost of goods sold $750,000; selling and administrative expenses $320,000; and an unrealized holding gain on available-for-sale securities $18,000.

Instructions

Prepare a statement of comprehensive income, using the two-income statement format. Ignore income taxes and earnings per share.

(LO 7, 8) **E4-15 (Comprehensive Income)**   C. Reither Co. reports the following information for 2007: sales revenue $700,000; cost of goods sold $500,000; operating expenses $80,000; and an unrealized holding loss on available-for-sale securities for 2007 of $60,000. It declared and paid a cash dividend of $10,000 in 2007.

   C. Reither Co. has January 1, 2007, balances in common stock $350,000; accumulated other comprehensive income $80,000; and retained earnings $90,000. It issued no stock during 2007.

Instructions

Prepare a statement of stockholders' equity.

(LO 2, 4, 5, 6, 7, 8) **E4-16 (Various Reporting Formats)**   The following information was taken from the records of Roland Carlson Inc. for the year 2007. Income tax applicable to income from continuing operations $187,000; income tax applicable to loss on discontinued operations $25,500; income tax applicable to extraordinary gain $32,300; income tax applicable to extraordinary loss $20,400; and unrealized holding gain on available-for-sale securities $15,000.

Extraordinary gain	$ 95,000	Cash dividends declared	$ 150,000
Loss on discontinued operations	75,000	Retained earnings January 1, 2007	600,000
Administrative expenses	240,000	Cost of goods sold	850,000
Rent revenue	40,000	Selling expenses	300,000
Extraordinary loss	60,000	Sales	1,900,000

Shares outstanding during 2007 were 100,000.

Instructions

(a) Prepare a single-step income statement for 2007.
(b) Prepare a retained earnings statement for 2007.
(c) Show how comprehensive income is reported using the second income statement format.

See the book's website, www.wiley.com/college/kieso, for Additional Exercises.

PROBLEMS

(LO 3, 4, 5, 6, 7) **P4-1 (Multiple-step Income, Retained Earnings)**   Presented below is information related to American Horse Company for 2007.

Retained earnings balance, January 1, 2007	$ 980,000
Sales for the year	25,000,000
Cost of goods sold	17,000,000
Interest revenue	70,000
Selling and administrative expenses	4,700,000
Write-off of goodwill (not tax deductible)	820,000
Income taxes for 2007	905,000
Gain on the sale of investments (normal recurring)	110,000
Loss due to flood damage—extraordinary item (net of tax)	390,000
Loss on the disposition of the wholesale division (net of tax)	440,000
Loss on operations of the wholesale division (net of tax)	90,000
Dividends declared on common stock	250,000
Dividends declared on preferred stock	70,000

Instructions

Prepare a multiple-step income statement and a retained earnings statement. American Horse Company decided to discontinue its entire wholesale operations and to retain its manufacturing operations. On September 15, American Horse sold the wholesale operations to Rogers Company. During 2007, there were 300,000 shares of common stock outstanding all year.

(LO 2, 6, 7) **P4-2 (Single-step Income, Retained Earnings, Periodic Inventory)**   Presented on page 158 is the trial balance of Mary J. Blige Corporation at December 31, 2007.

MARY J. BLIGE CORPORATION
TRIAL BALANCE
YEAR ENDED DECEMBER 31, 2007

	Debits	Credits
Purchase Discounts		$ 10,000
Cash	$ 205,100	
Accounts Receivable	105,000	
Rent Revenue		18,000
Retained Earnings		260,000
Salaries Payable		18,000
Sales		1,000,000
Notes Receivable	110,000	
Accounts Payable		49,000
Accumulated Depreciation—Equipment		28,000
Sales Discounts	14,500	
Sales Returns	17,500	
Notes Payable		70,000
Selling Expenses	232,000	
Administrative Expenses	99,000	
Common Stock		300,000
Income Tax Expense	38,500	
Cash Dividends	45,000	
Allowance for Doubtful Accounts		5,000
Supplies	14,000	
Freight-in	20,000	
Land	70,000	
Equipment	140,000	
Bonds Payable		100,000
Gain on Sale of Land		30,000
Accumulated Depreciation—Building		19,600
Merchandise Inventory	89,000	
Building	98,000	
Purchases	610,000	
Totals	$1,907,600	$1,907,600

A physical count of inventory on December 31 resulted in an inventory amount of $124,000.

Instructions
Prepare a single-step income statement and a retained earnings statement. Assume that the only changes in retained earnings during the current year were from net income and dividends. Thirty thousand shares of common stock were outstanding the entire year.

(LO 4, 5, 6)

P4-3 (Irregular Items) Tony Rich Inc. reported income from continuing operations before taxes during 2007 of $790,000. Additional transactions occurring in 2007 but not considered in the $790,000 are as follows.

1. The corporation experienced an uninsured flood loss (extraordinary) in the amount of $80,000 during the year. The tax rate on this item is 46%.
2. At the beginning of 2005, the corporation purchased a machine for $54,000 (salvage value of $9,000) that had a useful life of 6 years. The bookkeeper used straight-line depreciation for 2005, 2006, and 2007 but failed to deduct the salvage value in computing the depreciation base.
3. Sale of securities held as a part of its portfolio resulted in a loss of $57,000 (pretax).
4. When its president died, the corporation realized $110,000 from an insurance policy. The cash surrender value of this policy had been carried on the books as an investment in the amount of $46,000 (the gain is nontaxable).
5. The corporation disposed of its recreational division at a loss of $115,000 before taxes. Assume that this transaction meets the criteria for discontinued operations.
6. The corporation decided to change its method of inventory pricing from average cost to the FIFO method. The effect of this change on prior years is to increase 2005 income by $60,000 and decrease 2006 income by $20,000 before taxes. The FIFO method has been used for 2007. The tax rate on these items is 40%.

Instructions

Prepare an income statement for the year 2007 starting with income from continuing operations before taxes. Compute earnings per share as it should be shown on the face of the income statement. Common shares outstanding for the year are 80,000 shares. (Assume a tax rate of 30% on all items, unless indicated otherwise.)

(LO 3, 4, 6, 7) **P4-4 (Multiple- and Single-step Income, Retained Earnings)** The following account balances were included in the trial balance of J.R. Reid Corporation at June 30, 2007.

Sales	$1,678,500	Depreciation of office furniture	
Sales discounts	31,150	and equipment	$ 7,250
Cost of goods sold	896,770	Real estate and other local taxes	7,320
Sales salaries	56,260	Bad debt expense—selling	4,850
Sales commissions	97,600	Building expense—prorated	
Travel expense—salespersons	28,930	to administration	9,130
Freight-out	21,400	Miscellaneous office expenses	6,000
Entertainment expense	14,820	Sales returns	62,300
Telephone and Internet expense—sales	9,030	Dividends received	38,000
Depreciation of sales equipment	4,980	Bond interest expense	18,000
Building expense—prorated to sales	6,200	Income taxes	133,000
Miscellaneous selling expenses	4,715	Depreciation understatement due	
Office supplies used	3,450	to error—2004 (net of tax)	17,700
Telephone and Internet expense—		Dividends declared on	
administration	2,820	preferred stock	9,000
		Dividends declared on common	
		stock	32,000

The Retained Earnings account had a balance of $337,000 at July 1, 2006. There are 80,000 shares of common stock outstanding.

Instructions

(a) Using the multiple-step form, prepare an income statement and a retained earnings statement for the year ended June 30, 2007.

(b) Using the single-step form, prepare an income statement and a retained earnings statement for the year ended June 30, 2007.

(LO 4, 5, 6, 7) **P4-5 (Irregular Items)** Presented below is a combined single-step income and retained earnings statement for Sandy Freewalt Company for 2007.

		(000 omitted)
Net sales		$640,000
Costs and expenses		
Cost of goods sold		500,000
Selling, general, and administrative expenses		66,000
Other, net		17,000
		583,000
Income before income tax		57,000
Income tax		19,400
Net income		37,600
Retained earnings at beginning of period, as previously reported	$141,000	
Adjustment required for correction of error	(7,000)	
Retained earnings at beginning of period, as restated		134,000
Dividends on common stock		(12,200)
Retained earnings at end of period		$159,400

Additional facts are as follows.

1. "Selling, general, and administrative expenses" for 2007 included a usual but infrequently occurring charge of $10,500,000.

2. "Other, net" for 2007 included an extraordinary item (charge) of $9,000,000. If the extraordinary item (charge) had not occurred, income taxes for 2007 would have been $22,400,000 instead of $19,400,000.

3. "Adjustment required for correction of an error" was a result of a change in estimate (useful life of certain assets reduced to 8 years and a catch-up adjustment made).

4. Sandy Freewalt Company disclosed earnings per common share for net income in the notes to the financial statements.

Instructions

Determine from these additional facts whether the presentation of the facts in the Sandy Freewalt Company income and retained earnings statement is appropriate. If the presentation is not appropriate, describe the appropriate presentation and discuss its theoretical rationale. (Do not prepare a revised statement.)

(LO 4, 5, 7) **P4-6** **(Retained Earnings Statement, Prior Period Adjustment)** Below is the retained earnings account for the year 2007 for LeClair Corp.

Retained earnings, January 1, 2007		$257,600
Add:		
Gain on sale of investments (net of tax)	$41,200	
Net income	84,500	
Refund on litigation with government, related to the year 2004 (net of tax)	21,600	
Recognition of income earned in 2006, but omitted from income statement in that year (net of tax)	25,400	172,700
		430,300
Deduct:		
Loss on discontinued operations (net of tax)	25,000	
Write-off of goodwill (net of tax)	60,000	
Cumulative effect on income of prior years in changing from LIFO to FIFO inventory valuation in 2007 (net of tax)	18,200	
Cash dividends declared	32,000	135,200
Retained earnings, December 31, 2007		$295,100

Instructions

(a) Prepare a corrected retained earnings statement. LeClair Corp. normally sells investments of the type mentioned above. FIFO inventory was used in 2007 to compute net income.

(b) State where the items that do not appear in the corrected retained earnings statement should be shown.

(LO 4, 5, 6) **P4-7** **(Income Statement, Irregular Items)** Rap Corp. has 100,000 shares of common stock outstanding. In 2007, the company reports income from continuing operations before income tax of $1,210,000. Additional transactions not considered in the $1,210,000 are as follows.

1. In 2007, Rap Corp. sold equipment for $40,000. The machine had originally cost $80,000 and had accumulated depreciation of $36,000. The gain or loss is considered ordinary.
2. The company discontinued operations of one of its subsidiaries during the current year at a loss of $190,000 before taxes. Assume that this transaction meets the criteria for discontinued operations. The loss on operations of the discontinued subsidiary was $90,000 before taxes; the loss from disposal of the subsidiary was $100,000 before taxes.
3. An internal audit discovered that amortization of intangible assets was understated by $35,000 (net of tax) in a prior period. The amount was charged against retained earnings.
4. The company had a gain of $145,000 on the condemnation of much of its property. The gain is taxed at a total effective rate of 40%. Assume that the transaction meets the requirements of an extraordinary item.

Instructions

Analyze the above information and prepare an income statement for the year 2007, starting with income from continuing operations before income tax. Compute earnings per share as it should be shown on the face of the income statement. (Assume a total effective tax rate of 38% on all items, unless otherwise indicated.)

CONCEPTS FOR ANALYSIS

CA4-1 **(Identification of Income Statement Deficiencies)** John Amos Corporation was incorporated and began business on January 1, 2007. It has been successful and now requires a bank loan for additional working capital to finance expansion. The bank has requested an audited income statement for the year 2007. The accountant for John Amos Corporation provides you with the following income statement (page 161) which John Amos plans to submit to the bank.

JOHN AMOS CORPORATION
INCOME STATEMENT

Sales		$850,000
Dividends		32,300
Gain on recovery of insurance proceeds from		
earthquake loss (extraordinary)		38,500
		920,800
Less:		
Selling expenses	$101,100	
Cost of goods sold	510,000	
Advertising expense	13,700	
Loss on obsolescence of inventories	34,000	
Loss on discontinued operations	48,600	
Administrative expense	73,400	780,800
Income before income tax		140,000
Income tax		56,000
Net income		$ 84,000

Instructions
Indicate the deficiencies in the income statement presented above. Assume that the corporation desires a single-step income statement.

 CA4-2 (Income Reporting Deficiencies) The following represents a recent income statement for **Boeing Company**.

	($ in millions)
Sales	$21,924
Costs and expenses	20,773
Income from operations	1,151
Other income	122
Interest and debt expense	(130)
Earnings before income taxes	1,143
Income taxes	(287)
Net income	$ 856

It includes only *five* separate numbers (two of which are in billions of dollars), *two* subtotals, and the net earnings figure.

Instructions
(a) Indicate the deficiencies in the income statement.
(b) What recommendations would you make to Boeing to improve the usefulness of its income statement?

 **CA4-3 (Extraordinary Items)** Jeff Foxworthy, vice-president of finance for Red Neck Company, has recently been asked to discuss with the company's division controllers the proper accounting for extraordinary items. Jeff Foxworthy prepared the factual situations presented below as a basis for discussion.

1. An earthquake destroys one of the oil refineries owned by a large multinational oil company. Earthquakes are rare in this geographical location.
2. A publicly held company has incurred a substantial loss in the unsuccessful registration of a bond issue.
3. A large portion of a cigarette manufacturer's tobacco crops are destroyed by a hailstorm. Severe damage from hailstorms is rare in this locality.
4. A large diversified company sells a block of shares from its portfolio of securities acquired for investment purposes.
5. A company that operates a chain of warehouses sells the excess land surrounding one of its warehouses. When the company buys property to establish a new warehouse, it usually buys more land than it expects to use for the warehouse with the expectation that the land will appreciate in value. Twice during the past 5 years the company sold excess land.
6. A company experiences a material loss in the repurchase of a large bond issue that has been outstanding for 3 years. The company regularly repurchases bonds of this nature.
7. A railroad experiences an unusual flood loss to part of its track system. Flood losses normally occur every 3 or 4 years.

8. A machine tool company sells the only land it owns. The land was acquired 10 years ago for future expansion, but shortly thereafter the company abandoned all plans for expansion but decided to hold the land for appreciation.

Instructions

Determine whether the foregoing items should be classified as extraordinary items. Present a rationale for your position.

 CA4-4 (Earnings Management) Grace Inc. has recently reported steadily increasing income. The company reported income of $20,000 in 2004, $25,000 in 2005, and $30,000 in 2006. A number of market analysts have recommended that investors buy the stock because they expect the steady growth in income to continue. Grace is approaching the end of its fiscal year in 2007, and it again appears to be a good year. However, it has not yet recorded warranty expense.

Based on prior experience, this year's warranty expense should be around $5,000, but some managers have approached the controller to suggest a larger, more conservative warranty expense should be recorded this year. Income before warranty expense is $43,000. Specifically, by recording an $8,000 warranty accrual this year, Grace could report an increase in income for this year and still be in a position to cover its warranty costs in future years.

Instructions

(a) What is earnings management?
(b) Assume income before warranty expense is $43,000 for both 2007 and 2008 and that total warranty expense over the 2-year period is $10,000. What is the effect of the proposed accounting in 2007? In 2008?
(c) What is the appropriate accounting in this situation?

 CA4-5 (Earnings Management) Arthur Miller, controller for the Salem Corporation, is preparing the company's income statement at year-end. He notes that the company lost a considerable sum on the sale of some equipment it had decided to replace. Since the company has sold equipment routinely in the past, Miller knows the losses cannot be reported as extraordinary. He also does not want to highlight it as a material loss since he feels that will reflect poorly on him and the company. He reasons that if the company had recorded more depreciation during the assets' lives, the losses would not be so great. Since depreciation is included among the company's operating expenses, he wants to report the losses along with the company's expenses, where he hopes it will not be noticed.

Instructions

(a) What are the ethical issues involved?
(b) What should Miller do?

CA4-6 (Income Reporting Items) Woody Allen Corp. is an entertainment firm that derives approximately 30% of its income from the Casino Royale Division, which manages gambling facilities. As auditor for Woody Allen Corp., you have recently overheard the following discussion between the controller and financial vice-president.

VICE-PRESIDENT: If we sell the Casino Royale Division, it seems ridiculous to segregate the results of the sale in the income statement. Separate categories tend to be absurd and confusing to the stockholders. I believe that we should simply report the gain on the sale as other income or expense without detail.

CONTROLLER: Professional pronouncements would require that we disclose this information separately in the income statement. If a sale of this type is considered unusual and infrequent, it must be reported as an extraordinary item.

VICE-PRESIDENT: What about the walkout we had last month when employees were upset about their commission income? Would this situation not also be an extraordinary item?

CONTROLLER: I am not sure whether this item would be reported as extraordinary or not.

VICE-PRESIDENT: Oh well, it doesn't make any difference because the net effect of all these items is immaterial, so no disclosure is necessary.

Instructions

(a) On the basis of the foregoing discussion, answer the following questions: Who is correct about handling the sale? What would be the correct income statement presentation for the sale of the Casino Royale Division?
(b) How should the walkout by the employees be reported?
(c) What do you think about the vice-president's observation on materiality?
(d) What are the earnings per share implications of these topics?

CA4-7 (Identification of Income Statement Weaknesses) The following financial statement was prepared by employees of Cynthia Taylor Corporation.

CYNTHIA TAYLOR CORPORATION
INCOME STATEMENT
YEAR ENDED DECEMBER 31, 2007

Revenues	
Gross sales, including sales taxes	$1,044,300
Less: Returns, allowances, and cash discounts	56,200
Net sales	988,100
Dividends, interest, and purchase discounts	30,250
Recoveries of accounts written off in prior years	13,850
Total revenues	1,032,200
Costs and expenses	
Cost of goods sold, including sales taxes	465,900
Salaries and related payroll expenses	60,500
Rent	19,100
Freight-in and freight-out	3,400
Bad debt expense	27,800
Total costs and expenses	576,700
Income before extraordinary items	455,500
Extraordinary items	
Loss on discontinued styles (Note 1)	71,500
Loss on sale of marketable securities (Note 2)	39,050
Loss on sale of warehouse (Note 3)	86,350
Total extraordinary items	196,900
Net income	$ 258,600
Net income per share of common stock	$2.30

Note 1: New styles and rapidly changing consumer preferences resulted in a $71,500 loss on the disposal of discontinued styles and related accessories.

Note 2: The corporation sold an investment in marketable securities at a loss of $39,050. The corporation normally sells securities of this nature.

Note 3: The corporation sold one of its warehouses at an $86,350 loss.

Instructions

Identify and discuss the weaknesses in classification and disclosure in the single-step income statement above. You should explain why these treatments are weaknesses and what the proper presentation of the items would be in accordance with GAAP.

 CA4-8 (Classification of Income Statement Items) As audit partner for Noriyuki and Morita, you are in charge of reviewing the classification of unusual items that have occurred during the current year. The following material items have come to your attention.

1. A merchandising company incorrectly overstated its ending inventory 2 years ago. Inventory for all other periods is correctly computed.
2. An automobile dealer sells for $137,000 an extremely rare 1930 S type Invicta which it purchased for $21,000 10 years ago. The Invicta is the only such display item the dealer owns.
3. A drilling company during the current year extended the estimated useful life of certain drilling equipment from 9 to 15 years. As a result, depreciation for the current year was materially lowered.
4. A retail outlet changed its computation for bad debt expense from 1% to ½ of 1% of sales because of changes in its customer clientele.
5. A mining concern sells a foreign subsidiary engaged in uranium mining, although it (the seller) continues to engage in uranium mining in other countries.
6. A steel company changes from the average-cost method to the FIFO method for inventory costing purposes.
7. A construction company, at great expense, prepared a major proposal for a government loan. The loan is not approved.
8. A water pump manufacturer has had large losses resulting from a strike by its employees early in the year.

9. Depreciation for a prior period was incorrectly understated by $950,000. The error was discovered in the current year.
10. A large sheep rancher suffered a major loss because the state required that all sheep in the state be killed to halt the spread of a rare disease. Such a situation has not occurred in the state for 20 years.
11. A food distributor that sells wholesale to supermarket chains and to fast-food restaurants (two distinguishable classes of customers) decides to discontinue the division that sells to one of the two classes of customers.

Instructions
From the foregoing information, indicate in what section of the income statement or retained earnings statement these items should be classified. Provide a brief rationale for your position.

CA4-9 (Comprehensive Income) Ferguson Arthur, Jr., controller for Jenkins Corporation, is preparing the company's financial statements at year-end. Currently, he is focusing on the income statement and determining the format for reporting comprehensive income. During the year, the company earned net income of $400,000 and had unrealized gains on available-for-sale securities of $20,000. In the previous year net income was $410,000, and the company had no unrealized gains or losses.

Instructions
(a) Show how income and comprehensive income will be reported on a comparative basis for the current and prior years, using the separate income statement format.
(b) Show how income and comprehensive income will be reported on a comparative basis for the current and prior years, using the combined income statement format.
(c) Which format should Arthur recommend?

USING YOUR JUDGMENT

Financial Reporting Problem

 The Procter & Gamble Company (P&G)
The financial statements of P&G are presented in Appendix 5B or can be accessed on the KWW website.

Instructions
Refer to P&G's financial statements and the accompanying notes to answer the following questions.
(a) What type of income statement format does P&G use? Indicate why this format might be used to present income statement information.
(b) What are P&G's primary revenue sources?
(c) Compute P&G's gross profit for each of the years 2002–2004. Explain why gross profit increased in 2004.
(d) Why does P&G make a distinction between operating and nonoperating revenue?
(e) What financial ratios did P&G choose to report in its "Financial Summary" section covering the years 1994–2004?

Financial Statement Analysis Cases

Case 1 Bankruptcy Prediction
The Z-score bankruptcy prediction model uses balance sheet and income information to arrive at a Z-Score, which can be used to predict financial distress:

$$Z = \frac{\text{Working capital}}{\text{Total assets}} \times 1.2 + \frac{\text{Retained earnings}}{\text{Total assets}} \times 1.4 + \frac{\text{EBIT}}{\text{Total assets}} \times 3.3 + \frac{\text{Sales}}{\text{Total assets}} \times .99$$

$$+ \frac{\text{MV equity}}{\text{Total liabilities}} \times 0.6$$

EBIT is earnings before interest and taxes. MV Equity is the market value of common equity, which can be determined by multiplying stock price by shares outstanding.

Following extensive testing, it has been shown that companies with Z-scores above 3.0 are unlikely to fail; those with Z-scores below 1.81 are very likely to fail. While the original model was developed for publicly held manufacturing companies, the model has been modified to apply to companies in various industries, emerging companies, and companies not traded in public markets.

Instructions

(a) Use information in the financial statements of a company like **Walgreens** or **Deere & Co.** to compute the Z-score for the past 2 years.

(b) Interpret your result. Where does the company fall in the financial distress range?

(c) The Z-score uses EBIT as one of its elements. Why do you think this income measure is used?

Case 2 Dresser Industries

Dresser Industries provides products and services to oil and natural gas exploration, production, transmission and processing companies. A recent income statement is reproduced below. Dollar amounts are in millions.

Sales	$2,697.0
Service revenues	1,933.9
Share of earnings of unconsolidated affiliates	92.4
Total revenues	4,723.3
Cost of sales	1,722.7
Cost of services	1,799.9
Total costs of sales and services	3,522.6
Gross earnings	1,200.7
Selling, engineering, administrative and general expenses	(919.8)
Special charges	(70.0)
Other income (deductions)	
Interest expense	(47.4)
Interest earned	19.1
Other, net	4.8
Earnings before income taxes and other items below	187.4
Income taxes	(79.4)
Minority interest	(10.3)
Earnings from continuing operations	97.7
Discontinued operations	(35.3)
Earnings before extraordinary items	62.4
Extraordinary items	(6.3)
Net earnings	$56.1

Instructions

Assume that 177,636,000 shares of stock were issued and outstanding. Prepare the per-share portion of the income statement. Remember to begin with "Income from continuing operations."

Case 3 P/E Ratios

One of the more closely watched ratios by investors is the price/earnings or P/E ratio. By dividing price per share by earnings per share, analysts get insight into the value the market attaches to a company's earnings. More specifically, a high P/E ratio (in comparison to companies in the same industry) may suggest the stock is overpriced. Also, there is some evidence that companies with low P/E ratios are underpriced and tend to outperform the market. However, the ratio can be misleading.

P/E ratios are sometime misleading because the E (earnings) is subject to a number of assumptions and estimates that could result in overstated earnings and a lower P/E. Some analysts conduct "revenue analysis" to evaluate the quality of an earnings number. Revenues are less subject to management estimates and all earnings must begin with revenues. These analysts also compute the price-to-sales ratio (PSR = price per share ÷ sales per share) to assess whether a company is performing well compared to similar companies. If a company has a price-to-sales ratio significantly higher than its competitors, investors may be betting on a stock that has yet to prove itself. [*Source*: Janice Revell, "Beyond P/E," *Fortune* (May 28, 2001), p. 174.]

Instructions

(a) Identify some of the estimates or assumptions that could result in overstated earnings.

(b) Compute the P/E ratio and the PSR for **Tootsie Roll** and **Hershey's** for 2004.

(c) Use these data to compare the quality of each company's earnings.

Comparative Analysis Case

The Coca-Cola Company

PEPSICO

The Coca-Cola Company and PepsiCo, Inc.

Instructions

Go to the KWW website and use information found there to answer the following questions related to The Coca-Cola Company and PepsiCo, Inc.

(a) What type of income format(s) is used by these two companies? Identify any differences in income statement format between these two companies.

(b) What are the gross profits, operating profits, and net incomes for these two companies over the 3-year period 2002–2004? Which company has had better financial results over this period of time?

(c) Identify the irregular items reported by these two companies in their income statements over the 3-year period 2002–2004. Do these irregular items appear to be significant?

(d) Refer to Coca-Cola's Management Analysis section under "Reconciliation of Non-GAAP Financial Measures". What adjustments does Coca-Cola make to arrive at "adjusted net income"? Why does Coca-Cola make these adjustments?

Research Cases

Case 1

Most libraries maintain the annual reports of large companies on file or on microfiche.

Instructions

Obtain the 2004 annual reports for **Goodyear Tire and Rubber Co.** and **Northrop Grumman Corp.**, and answer the following questions concerning their income statements. (*Note:* Larger libraries may have CD-ROM products such as *Laser Disclosure* or *Compact Disclosure*. Goodyear Tire and Rubber Co. and Northrop Grumman Corp. can be found online in the SEC EDGAR database.)

(a) Describe the major differences between the income statement formats.

(b) Identify any irregular items on either of the income statements.

(c) Neither company includes a separate line for depreciation expense. Does depreciation expense appear on another financial statement?

(d) Northrop Grumman's income statement includes significantly more detail than Goodyear's. Which presentation do you prefer? Why?

Case 2

The April 1996 issue of the *Journal of Accountancy* includes an article by Dennis R. Beresford, L. Todd Johnson, and Cheri L. Reither, entitled "Is a Second Income Statement Needed?"

Instructions

Read the article and answer the following questions.

(a) On what basis would the "second income statement" be prepared? Briefly describe this basis.

(b) Why is there a perceived need for a second income statement?

(c) Identify three alternatives for reporting the proposed measure of income.

International Reporting Case

Presented below is the income statement for a British company, **Avon Rubber PLC.**

Avon Rubber PLC

Consolidated Profit and Loss Account
for the year ended 30 September

	Before exceptional items £'000	Exceptional items £'000	Total £'000
Turnover	250,509	–	250,509
Cost of sales	(209,739)	–	(209,739)
Gross profit	40,770	–	40,770
Net operating expenses (including £681,000 (2002; £626,000) goodwill amortisation)	(30,349)	(6,701)	(37,050)
Operating profit	10,421	(6,701)	3,720
Share of profits of joint venture and associate	21	–	21
Total operating profit including joint venture and associate	10,442	(6,701)	3,741
Loss on disposal of fixed assets	–	(1,205)	(1,205)
Loss on disposal of operations	–	(568)	(568)
Profit on ordinary activities before interest	10,442	(8,474)	1,968
Interest receivable	609	–	609
Interest payable	(4,032)	–	(4,032)
Profit/(loss) on ordinary activities before taxation	7,019	(8,474)	(1,455)
Taxation	(2,810)	2,500	(310)
Profit/(loss) on ordinary activities after taxation	4,209	(5,974)	(1,765)
Minority interests	194	–	194
Profit/(loss) for the financial year	4,403	(5,974)	(1,571)
Dividends	(2,031)	–	(2,031)
Retained profit/(loss) for the financial year	2,372	(5,974)	(3,602)
Earnings/(loss) per ordinary share			
Basic			(5.7)p

Instructions

(a) Review the Avon Rubber income statement and identify at least three differences between the British income statement and an income statement of a U.S. company as presented in the chapter.

(b) Identify any irregular items reported by Avon Rubber. Is the reporting of these irregular items in Avon's income statement similar to reporting of these items in U.S. companies' income statements? Explain.

Professional Research: Financial Accounting and Reporting

Your client took accounting a number of years ago and was unaware of comprehensive income reporting. He is not convinced that any accounting standards exist for comprehensive income.

Instructions

Using the **Financial Accounting Research System (FARS)**, respond to the following items. (Provide text strings used in your search.)

(a) What statement addresses comprehensive income directly? When was it issued?
(b) Provide the definition of comprehensive income.
(c) Define classifications within net income; give examples.
(d) Define classifications within other comprehensive income; give examples.
(e) What are reclassification adjustments?

Professional Simulation

In this simulation you are asked to compute various income amounts. Assume a tax rate of 30% and 100,000 shares of common stock outstanding during the year. Prepare responses to all parts.

KWW_Professional _Simulation

Income Statement | **Time Remaining** 3 hours 30 minutes | copy paste calculator sheet standards help splitter done

Directions | Situation | Explanation | Measurement | Resources

Jude Law Corporation provides you with the following pre-tax information for the period.

Sales	$3,200,000
Cost of goods sold	1,650,000
Interest revenue	10,000
Loss from abandonment of plant assets	40,000
Selling expenses	340,000
Administrative expenses	280,000
Cumulative effect on prior years of change from FIFO to average cost for inventory costing purposes	50,000
Loss from earthquake (unusual and infrequent)	40,000
Gain on disposal of a component of Jude Law Corporation's business	90,000

Directions | Situation | Explanation | Measurement | Resources

Explain the proper accounting treatment for loss on abandonment of plant assets, gain on disposal of a component of a business, and change in inventory costing methods.

Directions | Situation | Explanation | Measurement | Resources

Compute the following five items.
(a) Gross profit.
(b) Income from operations.
(c) Income from continuing operations before income taxes.
(d) Net income.
(e) Earnings per share.

Remember to check the book's companion website to find additional resources for this chapter.

CHAPTER FIVE

BALANCE SHEET AND STATEMENT OF CASH FLOWS

"There Ought to Be a Law"

As one manager noted, "There ought to be a law that before you can buy a stock, you must be able to read a balance sheet." We agree, and the same can be said for a statement of cash flows.

Krispy Kreme Doughnuts provides an example of how stunning earnings growth can hide real problems. Not long ago the doughnut maker was a glamour stock with a 60 percent earnings per share growth rate and a price-earnings ratio around 70. Seven months later its stock price had dropped 72 percent. What happened? Stockholders alleged that Krispy Kreme may have been inflating its revenues and not taking enough bad debt expense (which inflated both assets and income). In addition, Krispy Kreme's operating cash flow was negative. Most financially sound companies throw off positive cash flow.

Here are additional examples of how one rating agency rated the earnings quality of some companies, using some key balance sheet and statement of cash flow measurements.

Earnings-Quality Winners

Company	Earnings-Quality Indicators
Avon Products	Strong cash flow
Capital One Financial	Conservatively capitalized
Ecolab	Good management of working capital
Timberland	Minimal off-balance-sheet commitments

Earnings-Quality Losers

Company	Earnings-Quality Indicators
Ford Motor	High debt and underfunded pension plan
Kroger	High goodwill and debt
Ryder System	Negative free cash flow
Teco Energy	Selling assets to meet liquidity needs

Just as a deteriorating balance sheet and statement of cash flows warn of earnings declines (and falling stock prices), improving balance sheet and cash flow information is a leading indicator of improved earnings.[1]

---

[1]Adapted from Gretchen Morgenson, "How Did They Value Stocks? Count the Absurd Ways," *New York Times on the Web* (March 18, 2001), and from K. Badanhausen, J. Gage, C. Hall, and M. Ozanian, "Beyond Balance Sheet: Earnings Quality," *Forbes.com* (January 28, 2005).

Learning Objectives

After studying this chapter, you should be able to:

1 Explain the uses and limitations of a balance sheet.

2 Identify the major classifications of the balance sheet.

3 Prepare a classified balance sheet using the report and account formats.

4 Determine which balance sheet information requires supplemental disclosure.

5 Describe the major disclosure techniques for the balance sheet.

6 Indicate the purpose of the statement of cash flows.

7 Identify the content of the statement of cash flows.

8 Prepare a statement of cash flows.

9 Understand the usefulness of the statement of cash flows.

Readers of the financial statements sometimes ignore important information in the balance sheet and statement of cash flows. As our opening story shows, analyzing these financial statements helps investors avoid surprises in earnings. In this chapter we examine the many different types of assets, liabilities, and stockholders' equity items that affect the balance sheet and the statement of cash flows. The content and organization of the chapter are as follows.

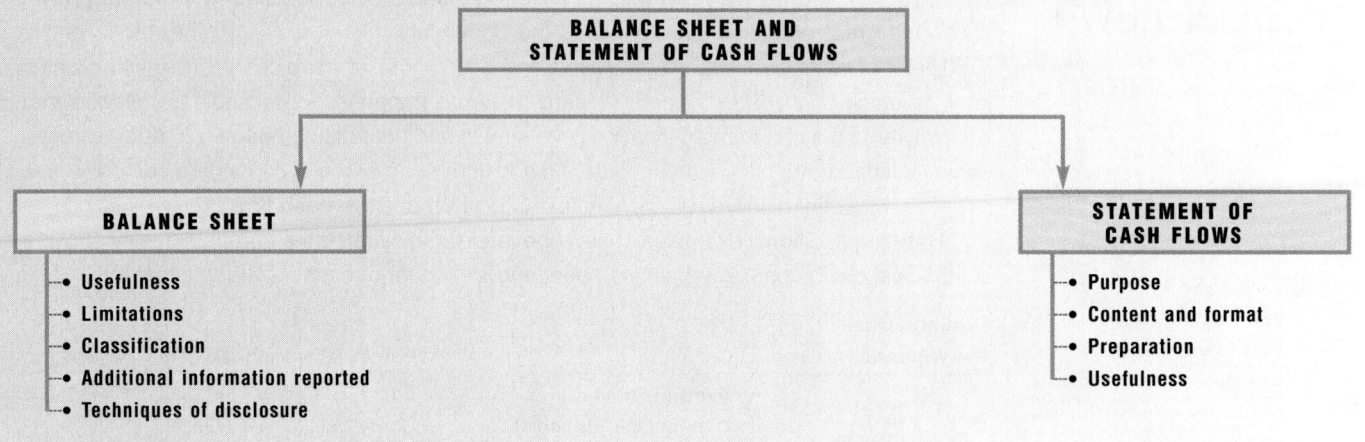

| SECTION 1 | *BALANCE SHEET* |

OBJECTIVE 1
Explain the uses and limitations of a balance sheet.

The **balance sheet**, sometimes referred to as the **statement of financial position**, reports the assets, liabilities, and stockholders' equity of a business enterprise at a specific date. This financial statement provides information about the nature and amounts of investments in enterprise resources, obligations to creditors, and the owners' equity in net resources.[2] It therefore helps in predicting the amounts, timing, and uncertainty of future cash flows.

USEFULNESS OF THE BALANCE SHEET

By providing information on assets, liabilities, and stockholders' equity, the balance sheet provides a basis for computing rates of return and evaluating the capital structure of the enterprise. As our opening story indicates, analysts also use information in the balance sheet to assess a company's risk[3] and future cash flows. In this regard,

---

[2]*Accounting Trends and Techniques—2004* (New York: AICPA) indicates that approximately 96 percent of the companies surveyed used the term "balance sheet." The term "statement of financial position" is used infrequently, although it is conceptually appealing.

[3]Risk conveys the unpredictability of future events, transactions, circumstances, and results of the company.

analysts use the balance sheet to assess a company's liquidity, solvency, and financial flexibility.

Liquidity describes "the amount of time that is expected to elapse until an asset is realized or otherwise converted into cash or until a liability has to be paid."[4] Creditors are interested in short-term liquidity ratios, such as the ratio of cash (or near cash) to short-term liabilities. These ratios indicate whether a company, like **Amazon**, will have the resources to pay its current and maturing obligations. Similarly, stockholders assess liquidity to evaluate the possibility of future cash dividends or the buyback of shares. In general, the greater Amazon's liquidity, the lower its risk of failure.

Solvency refers to the ability of a company to pay its debts as they mature. For example, when a company carries a high level of long-term debt relative to assets, it has lower solvency than a similar company with a low level of long-term debt. Companies with higher debt are relatively more risky because they will need more of their assets to meet their fixed obligations (interest and principal payments).

Liquidity and solvency affect a company's **financial flexibility**, which measures the "ability of an enterprise to take effective actions to alter the amounts and timing of cash flows so it can respond to unexpected needs and opportunities."[5] For example, a company may become so loaded with debt—so financially inflexible—that it has little or no sources of cash to finance expansion or to pay off maturing debt. A company with a high degree of financial flexibility is better able to survive bad times, to recover from unexpected setbacks, and to take advantage of profitable and unexpected investment opportunities. Generally, the greater an enterprise's financial flexibility, the lower its risk of failure.

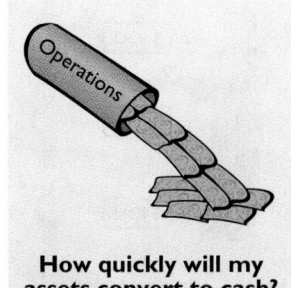

How quickly will my assets convert to cash?

Obligation Ocean

We are drowning in a sea of debt!

GROUNDED

WHAT DO THE NUMBERS MEAN?

The terrorist attacks of September 11, 2001, showed how vulnerable the major airlines are to falling demand for their services. Since that infamous date, major airlines have reduced capacity and slashed jobs to avoid bankruptcy. **United Airlines**, the second largest U.S. air carrier, **Northwest Airlines**, the fourth largest U.S. carrier, **US Airways**, the seventh largest U.S. carrier, and several smaller competitors have filed for bankruptcy.

Here are some statements made in a recent annual report of **Delta Airlines**, whose auditors have noted that there is substantial doubt about the company's ability to continue as a going concern.

> "If we are unsuccessful in further reducing our operating costs...we will need to restructure our costs under Chapter 11 of the U.S. Bankruptcy Code.... We have substantial liquidity needs and there is no assurance that we will be able to obtain the necessary financing to meet those needs on acceptable terms, if at all."

The financial distress related to the airline industry was not an insider's secret. The airlines' balance sheets clearly revealed their financial inflexibility and low liquidity even before September 11. For example, major airlines such as **Braniff**, **Continental**, **Eastern**, **Midway**, and **America West** declared bankruptcy before September 11.

Conversely, some airlines have done well. In 2004, **Southwest Airlines** recorded its 32nd consecutive year of profitability.

---

[4]"Reporting Income, Cash Flows, and Financial Position of Business Enterprises," *Proposed Statement of Financial Accounting Concepts* (Stamford, Conn.: FASB, 1981), par. 29.

[5]"Reporting Income, Cash Flows, and Financial Position of Business Enterprises," *Proposed Statement of Financial Accounting Concepts* (Stamford, Conn.: FASB, 1981), par. 25.

Hmm... I wonder if they will pay me back?

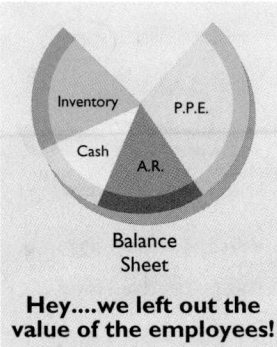

Hey....we left out the value of the employees!

LIMITATIONS OF THE BALANCE SHEET

Some of the major limitations of the balance sheet are:

1 Most assets and liabilities are reported at **historical cost**. As a result, the information provided in the balance sheet has high reliability. But it is often criticized for not reporting a more relevant fair value. For example, **Georgia-Pacific** owns timber and other assets that may appreciate in value after purchase. Yet, Georgia-Pacific reports any increase only if and when it sells the assets.

2 Companies use **judgments and estimates** to determine many of the items reported in the balance sheet. For example, in its balance sheet, **Dell** estimates the amount of receivables that it will collect, the useful life of its warehouses, and the number of computers that will be returned under warranty.

3 The balance sheet necessarily **omits many items that are of financial value** but that a company cannot record objectively. For example, the knowledge and skill of **Intel** employees in developing new computer chips are arguably the company's most significant asset. However, because Intel cannot reliably measure the value of its employees and other intangible assets (such as customer base, research superiority, and reputation), it does not recognize these items in the balance sheet. Similarly, many other liabilities are reported in an "off-balance-sheet" manner, if at all.

The recent bankruptcy of the seventh-largest U.S. company, **Enron**, highlights the omission of important items in the balance sheet. In Enron's case, it failed to disclose certain off-balance-sheet financing obligations in its main financial statements.[6]

CLASSIFICATION IN THE BALANCE SHEET

OBJECTIVE 2
Identify the major classifications of the balance sheet.

Balance sheet accounts are **classified**. That is, balance sheets group together similar items to arrive at significant subtotals. Furthermore, the material is arranged so that important relationships are shown.

The FASB has often noted that the parts and subsections of financial statements can be more informative than the whole. Therefore, the FASB discourages the reporting of summary accounts alone (total assets, net assets, total liabilities, etc.). Instead, companies should report and classify individual items in sufficient detail to permit users to assess the amounts, timing, and uncertainty of future cash flows. Such classification also makes it easier for users to evaluate the company's liquidity and financial flexibility, profitability, and risk.

To classify items in financial statements, companies group those items with similar characteristics and separate items with different characteristics.[7] For example, companies should report separately:

1 Assets that differ in their **type or expected function** in the company's central operations or other activities. For example, **IBM** reports merchandise inventories separately from property, plant, and equipment.

2 Assets and liabilities with **different implications for the company's financial flexibility**. For example, a company that uses assets in its operations, like **Walgreens**, should report those assets separately from assets held for investment and assets subject to restrictions, such as leased equipment.

3 Assets and liabilities with **different general liquidity characteristics**. For example, **Boeing Company** reports cash separately from inventories.

---

[6]We discuss several of these omitted items (such as leases and other off-balance-sheet arrangements) in later chapters. See Wayne Upton, Jr., Special Report: *Business and Financial Reporting, Challenges from the New Economy* (Norwalk, Conn.: FASB, 2001).

[7]"Reporting Income, Cash Flows, and Financial Positions of Business Enterprises," *Proposed Statement of Financial Accounting Concepts* (Stamford, Conn.: FASB, 1981), par. 51.

The three general classes of items included in the balance sheet are assets, liabilities, and equity. We defined them in Chapter 2 as follows.

ELEMENTS OF THE BALANCE SHEET

1 *ASSETS.* Probable future economic benefits obtained or controlled by a particular entity as a result of past transactions or events.

2 *LIABILITIES.* Probable future sacrifices of economic benefits arising from present obligations of a particular entity to transfer assets or provide services to other entities in the future as a result of past transactions or events.

3 *EQUITY.* Residual interest in the assets of an entity that remains after deducting its liabilities. In a business enterprise, the equity is the ownership interest.[8]

Companies then further divide these items into several subclassifications. Illustration 5-1 indicates the general format of balance sheet presentation.

Assets	Liabilities and Owners' Equity
Current assets	Current liabilities
Long-term investments	Long-term debt
Property, plant, and equipment	Owners' equity
Intangible assets	Capital stock
Other assets	Additional paid-in capital
	Retained earnings

ILLUSTRATION 5-1
Balance Sheet Classifications

A company may classify the balance sheet in some other manner, but you usually see little departure from these major subdivisions in practice. A proprietorship or partnership does present the classifications within the owners' equity section a little differently, as we will show later in the chapter.

Current Assets

Current assets are cash and other assets a company expects to convert into cash, sell, or consume either in one year or in the operating cycle, whichever is longer. The operating cycle is the average time between when a company acquires materials and supplies and when it receives cash for sales of the product (for which it acquired the materials and supplies). The cycle operates from cash through inventory, production, receivables, and back to cash. When several operating cycles occur within one year, a company uses the one-year period. If the operating cycle is more than one year, a company uses the longer period.

Current assets are presented in the balance sheet in order of liquidity. The five major items found in the current assets section, and their bases of valuation, are shown in Illustration 5-2.

Item	Basis of Valuation
Cash and cash equivalents	Fair value
Short-term investments	Generally, fair value
Receivables	Estimated amount collectible
Inventories	Lower of cost or market
Prepaid expenses	Cost

ILLUSTRATION 5-2
Current Assets and Basis of Valuation

---

[8]"Elements of Financial Statements of Business Enterprises," *Statement of Financial Accounting Concepts No. 6* (Stamford, Conn.: FASB, 1985), paras. 25, 35 and 49.

A company does not report these five items as current assets if it does not expect to realize them in one year or in the operating cycle, whichever is longer. For example, a company excludes cash restricted for purposes other than payment of current obligations or for use in current operations from the current assets section. **Generally, if a company expects to convert an asset into cash or to use it to pay a current liability within a year or the operating cycle, whichever is longer, it classifies the asset as current.**

This rule, however, is subject to interpretation. A company classifies an investment in common stock as either a current asset or a noncurrent asset depending on management's intent. When it has small holdings of common stocks or bonds that it will hold long-term, it should not classify them as current.

Although a current asset is well defined, certain theoretical problems also develop. For example, how is including prepaid expenses in the current assets section justified? The rationale is that if a company did not pay these items in advance, it would instead need to use other current assets during the operating cycle. If we follow this logic to its ultimate conclusion, however, any asset previously purchased saves the use of current assets during the operating cycle and would be considered current.

Another problem occurs in the current-asset definition when a company consumes plant assets during the operating cycle. Conceptually, it seems that a company should place an amount equal to the current depreciation charge on the plant assets in the current assets section, because it will consume them in the next operating cycle. However, this conceptual problem is ignored. This example illustrates that the formal distinction made between some current and noncurrent assets is somewhat arbitrary.

Cash

Cash is generally considered to consist of currency and demand deposits (monies available on demand at a financial institution.) **Cash equivalents** are short-term highly liquid investments that will mature within three months or less. Most companies use the caption "Cash and cash equivalents," and they indicate that this amount approximates fair value.

A company must disclose any restrictions or commitments related to the availability of cash. As an example, see the excerpt from the annual report of **Alterra Healthcare Corp.** in Illustration 5-3.

ILLUSTRATION 5-3
Balance Sheet
Presentation of
Restricted Cash

Alterra
AGING WITH CHOICE

Alterra Healthcare Corp.

Current assets

Cash	$18,728,000
Restricted cash and investments (Note 7)	7,191,000

Note 7: Restricted Cash and Investments. Restricted cash and investments consist of certificates of deposit restricted as collateral for lease arrangements and debt service with interest rates ranging from 4.0% to 5.5%.

Alterra Healthcare restricted cash to meet an obligation due currently. Therefore, Alterra included this restricted cash under current assets.

If a company restricts cash for purposes other than current obligations, it excludes the cash from current assets. Illustration 5-4 shows an example of this, excerpted from the annual report of **Owens Corning, Inc.**

Owens Corning, Inc.
(in millions)

Current assets

Cash and cash equivalents	$ 70
Restricted securities—Fibreboard—current portion (Note 23)	900

Other assets

Restricted securities—Fibreboard (Note 23)	938

Note 23 (in part). The Insurance Settlement funds are held in and invested by the Fibreboard Settlement Trust (the "Trust") and are available to satisfy Fibreboard's pending and future asbestos related liabilities. . . . The assets of the Trust are comprised of cash and marketable securities (collectively, the "Trust Assets") and are reflected on Owens Corning's consolidated balance sheet as restricted assets. These assets are reflected as current assets or other assets, with each category denoted "Restricted securities—Fibreboard."

ILLUSTRATION 5-4
Balance Sheet
Presentation of Current
and Noncurrent
Restricted Cash

Short-Term Investments

Companies group investments in debt and equity securities into three separate portfolios for valuation and reporting purposes:

Held-to-maturity: Debt securities that a company has the positive intent and ability to hold to maturity.

Trading: Debt and equity securities bought and held primarily for sale in the near term to generate income on short-term price differences.

Available-for-sale: Debt and equity securities not classified as held-to-maturity or trading securities.

A company should report trading securities (whether debt or equity) as current assets. It classifies individual held-to-maturity and available-for-sale securities as current or noncurrent depending on the circumstances. It should report held-to-maturity securities at amortized cost. All trading and available-for-sale securities are reported at fair value.[9]

For example, see Illustration 5-5, which is an excerpt from the annual report of **Intuit Inc.** with respect to its available-for-sale investments.

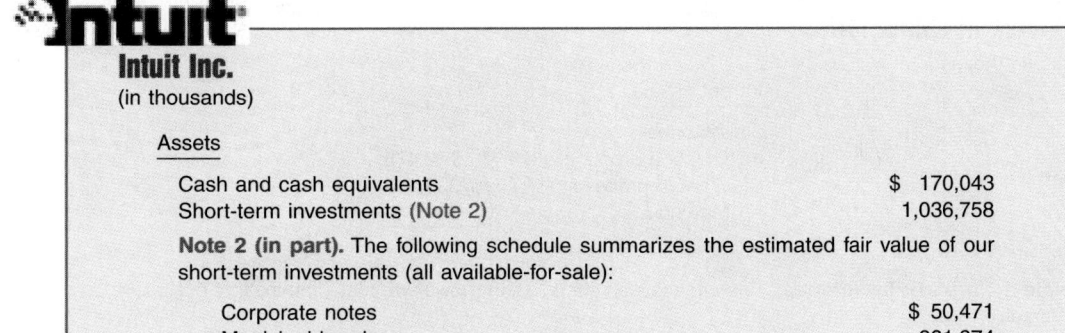

Intuit Inc.
(in thousands)

Assets

Cash and cash equivalents	$ 170,043
Short-term investments (Note 2)	1,036,758

Note 2 (in part). The following schedule summarizes the estimated fair value of our short-term investments (all available-for-sale):

Corporate notes	$ 50,471
Municipal bonds	931,374
U.S. government securities	54,913

ILLUSTRATION 5-5
Balance Sheet
Presentation of
Investments in
Securities

---

[9]"Accounting for Certain Investments in Debt and Equity Securities," *Statement of Financial Accounting Standards No. 115* (Norwalk, Conn.: FASB, 1993).

Receivables

A company should clearly identify any anticipated loss due to uncollectibles, the amount and nature of any nontrade receivables, and any receivables used as collateral. Major categories of receivables should be shown in the balance sheet or the related notes. For receivables arising from unusual transactions (such as sale of property, or a loan to affiliates or employees), companies should separately classify these as long-term, unless collection is expected within one year. **Mack Trucks, Inc.** reported its receivables as shown in Illustration 5-6.

ILLUSTRATION 5-6
Balance Sheet
Presentation of
Receivables

Mack Trucks, Inc.

Current assets	
Trade receivables	
Accounts receivable	$102,212,000
Affiliated companies	1,157,000
Installment notes and contracts	625,000
Total	103,994,000
Less: Allowance for uncollectible accounts	8,194,000
Trade receivables—net	95,800,000
Receivables from unconsolidated financial subsidiaries	22,106,000

UNDERLYING CONCEPTS

The lower-of-cost-or-market valuation reflects the use of *conservatism* in accounting.

Inventories

To present inventories properly, a company discloses the basis of valuation (e.g., lower-of-cost-or-market) and the method of pricing (e.g., FIFO or LIFO). A manufacturing concern (like **Abbott Laboratories**, shown in Illustration 5-7) also indicates the stage of completion of the inventories.

ILLUSTRATION 5-7
Balance Sheet
Presentation of
Inventories, Showing
Stage of Completion

Abbott Laboratories
(in thousands)

Current assets	
Inventories	
Finished products	$ 772,478
Work in process	338,818
Materials	384,148
Total inventories	1,495,444

Note 1 (in part): Inventories. Inventories are stated at the lower of cost (first-in, first-out basis) or market.

Weyerhaeuser Company, a forestry company and lumber manufacturer with several finished-goods product lines, reported its inventory as shown in Illustration 5-8.

Weyerhaeuser Company

Current assets

Inventories—at FIFO lower of cost or market

Logs and chips	$ 68,471,000
Lumber, plywood and panels	86,741,000
Pulp, newsprint and paper	47,377,000
Containerboard, paperboard, containers and cartons	59,682,000
Other products	161,717,000
Total product inventories	423,988,000
Materials and supplies	175,540,000

ILLUSTRATION 5-8
Balance Sheet Presentation of Inventories, Showing Product Lines

Prepaid Expenses

A company includes prepaid expenses in current assets if it will receive benefits (usually services) within one year or the operating cycle, whichever is longer.[10] As we discussed earlier, these items are current assets because if they had not already been paid, they would require the use of cash during the next year or the operating cycle. A company reports prepaid expenses at the amount of the unexpired or unconsumed cost.

A common example is the prepayment for an insurance policy. A company classifies it as a prepaid expense because the payment precedes the receipt of the benefit of coverage. Other common prepaid expenses include prepaid rent, advertising, taxes, and office or operating supplies. **Knight Ridder, Inc.**, for example, listed its prepaid expenses in current assets as shown in Illustration 5-9.

Knight Ridder, Inc.

(in thousands)

Current assets

Cash, including short-term cash investments of $7,001	$ 41,661
Accounts receivable, net of allowances of $20,238	416,498
Inventories	52,786
Prepaids	30,767
Other current assets	34,382

ILLUSTRATION 5-9
Balance Sheet Presentation of Prepaid Expenses

Noncurrent Assets

Noncurrent assets are those not meeting the definition of current assets. They include a variety of items, as we discuss in the following sections.

Long-Term Investments

Long-term investments, often referred to simply as investments, normally consist of one of four types:

1 Investments in securities, such as bonds, common stock, or long-term notes.

2 Investments in tangible fixed assets not currently used in operations, such as land held for speculation.

---

[10]*Accounting Trends and Techniques—2004* (New York: AICPA) in its survey of 600 annual reports identified 351 companies that reported prepaid expenses.

3 Investments set aside in special funds such as a sinking fund, pension fund, or plant expansion fund. This includes the cash surrender value of life insurance.

4 Investments in nonconsolidated subsidiaries or affiliated companies.

Companies expect to hold long-term investments for many years. They usually present them on the balance sheet just below "Current assets," in a separate section called "Investments." Realize that many securities classified as long-term investments are, in fact, readily marketable. But a company does not include them as current assets unless it intends to convert them to cash in the short-term—that is, within a year or in the operating cycle, whichever is longer. As indicated earlier, securities classified as available-for-sale are reported at fair value, and held-to-maturity securities are reported at amortized cost.

Motorola, Inc. reported its investments section, located between "Property, plant, and equipment" and "Other assets," as shown in Illustration 5-10.

ILLUSTRATION 5-10
Balance Sheet
Presentation of Long-
Term Investments

Motorola, Inc.
(in millions)

Investments	
Equity investments	$ 872
Other investments	2,567
Fair value adjustment to available-for-sale securities	2,487
Total	$5,926

Property, Plant, and Equipment

Property, plant, and equipment are tangible long-lived assets used in the regular operations of the business. These assets consist of physical property such as land, buildings, machinery, furniture, tools, and wasting resources (timberland, minerals). With the exception of land, a company either depreciates (e.g., buildings) or depletes (e.g., timberlands or oil reserves) these assets.

Mattel, Inc. presented its property, plant, and equipment in its balance sheet as shown in Illustration 5-11.

ILLUSTRATION 5-11
Balance Sheet
Presentation of
Property, Plant, and
Equipment

Mattel, Inc.

Property, plant, and equipment	
Land	$ 32,793,000
Buildings	257,430,000
Machinery and equipment	564,244,000
Capitalized leases	23,271,000
Leasehold improvements	74,988,000
	952,726,000
Less: Accumulated depreciation	472,986,000
	479,740,000
Tools, dies and molds, net	168,092,000
Property, plant, and equipment, net	647,832,000

A company discloses the basis it uses to value property, plant, and equipment; any liens against the properties; and accumulated depreciation–usually in the notes to the statements.

Intangible Assets

Intangible assets lack physical substance and are not financial instruments (see definition on page 186). They include patents, copyrights, franchises, goodwill, trademarks, trade names, and customer lists. A company writes off (amortizes) limited-life intangible assets over their useful lives. It periodically assesses indefinite-life intangibles (such as goodwill) for impairment. Intangibles can represent significant economic resources, yet financial analysts often ignore them, because valuation is difficult.

PepsiCo, Inc. reported intangible assets in its balance sheet as shown in Illustration 5-12.

PEPSICO

PepsiCo, Inc.
(in millions)

Intangible assets	
Goodwill	$3,374
Trademarks	1,320
Other identifiable intangibles	147
Total intangibles	$4,841

ILLUSTRATION 5-12
Balance Sheet
Presentation of Intangible
Assets

Other Assets

The items included in the section "Other assets" vary widely in practice. Some include items such as long-term prepaid expenses, prepaid pension cost, and noncurrent receivables. Other items that might be included are assets in special funds, deferred income taxes, property held for sale, and restricted cash or securities. A company should limit this section to include only unusual items sufficiently different from assets included in specific categories.

Liabilities

Similar to assets, companies classify liabilities as current or long-term.

Current Liabilities

Current liabilities are the obligations that a company reasonably expects to liquidate either through the use of current assets or the creation of other current liabilities. This concept includes:

1 Payables resulting from the acquisition of goods and services: accounts payable, wages payable, taxes payable, and so on.

2 Collections received in advance for the delivery of goods or performance of services, such as unearned rent revenue or unearned subscriptions revenue.

3 Other liabilities whose liquidation will take place within the operating cycle, such as the portion of long-term bonds to be paid in the current period or short-term obligations arising from purchase of equipment.

At times, a liability that is payable within the next year is not included in the current liabilities section. This occurs either when the company expects to refinance the debt through another long-term issue[11] or to retire the debt out of noncurrent assets. This approach is used because liquidation does not result from the use of current assets or the creation of other current liabilities.

Companies do not report current liabilities in any consistent order. In general, though, companies most commonly list notes payable, accounts payable, or short-term

---

[11]"Classification of Short-term Obligations Expected to Be Refinanced," *Statement of Financial Accounting Standards No. 6* (Stamford, Conn.: FASB, 1975).

debt as the first item. Income taxes payable, current maturities of long-term debt, or other current liabilities are commonly listed last. For example, see **Halliburton Company**'s current liabilities section in Illustration 5-13.

ILLUSTRATION 5-13
Balance Sheet
Presentation of
Current Liabilities

Halliburton Company
(in millions)

Current liabilities	
Short-term notes payable	$1,570
Accounts payable	782
Accrued employee compensation and benefits	267
Unearned revenues	386
Income taxes payable	113
Accrued special charges	6
Current maturities of long-term debt	8
Other current liabilities	694
Total current liabilities	3,826

Current liabilities include such items as trade and nontrade notes and accounts payable, advances received from customers, and current maturities of long-term debt. If the amounts are material, companies classify income taxes and other accrued items separately. A company should fully describe in the notes any information about a secured liability—for example, stock held as collateral on notes payable—to identify the assets providing the security.

The excess of total current assets over total current liabilities is referred to as **working capital** (sometimes called **net working capital**). Working capital represents the net amount of a company's relatively liquid resources. That is, it is the liquidity buffer available to meet the financial demands of the operating cycle.

Companies seldom disclose an amount for working capital on the balance sheet. But bankers and other creditors compute it as an indicator of the short-run liquidity of a company. To determine the actual liquidity and availability of working capital to meet current obligations, however, requires analysis of the composition of the current assets and their nearness to cash.

**WHAT DO THE
NUMBERS MEAN?**

"SHOW ME THE ASSETS!"

Recently, concerned about the liquidity and solvency of many dot-com companies, creditors have demanded more assurance that these companies can pay their bills when due. A key indicator for creditors is the amount of working capital. For example, when a report predicted that **Amazon.com**'s working capital would turn negative, the company's vendors began to explore steps that would ensure that Amazon would pay them.

Some vendors have demanded that their dot-com customers sign notes stating that the goods shipped to them serve as collateral for the transaction. Other vendors began shipping goods on consignment—an arrangement whereby the vendor retains ownership of the goods until a third party buys and pays for them.

Such creditor protection measures arise from creditors' concerns about dot-coms' lack of tangible assets that they can convert to cash to meet short-term obligations. For example, the primary asset for many dot-coms is its customer list. However, these lists have little resale value because privacy agreements prohibit sharing the customer information.

With fewer hard assets that they can convert to cash, a dot-com can experience a severe credit squeeze as vendors curtail shipments or take other measures to limit their financial risk. Such actions can further erode the company's liquidity and financial flexibility.

Long-Term Liabilities

Long-term liabilities are obligations that a company does not reasonably expect to liquidate within the normal operating cycle. Instead, it expects to pay them at some date beyond that time. Bonds payable, notes payable, some deferred income tax amounts, lease obligations, and pension obligations are the most common examples. **Companies classify long-term liabilities that mature within the current operating cycle as current liabilities if payment of the obligation requires the use of current assets.**

Generally, long-term liabilities are of three types:

1 Obligations arising from specific financing situations, such as the issuance of bonds, long-term lease obligations, and long-term notes payable.

2 Obligations arising from the ordinary operations of the company, such as pension obligations and deferred income tax liabilities.

3 Obligations that depend on the occurrence or non-occurrence of one or more future events to confirm the amount payable, or the payee, or the date payable, such as service or product warranties and other contingencies.

Companies generally provide a great deal of supplementary disclosure for long-term liabilities, because most long-term debt is subject to various covenants and restrictions for the protection of lenders.[12]

It is desirable to report any premium or discount separately as an addition to or subtraction from the bonds payable. Companies frequently describe the terms of all long-term liability agreements (including maturity date or dates, rates of interest, nature of obligation, and any security pledged to support the debt) in notes to the financial statements. Illustration 5-14 provides an example of this, taken from an excerpt from **The Great Atlantic & Pacific Tea Company**'s financials.

The Great Atlantic & Pacific Tea Company, Inc.

Total current liabilities	$978,109,000
Long-term debt (See note)	254,312,000
Obligations under capital leases	252,618,000
Deferred income taxes	57,167,000
Other non-current liabilities	127,321,000

Note: Indebtedness. Debt consists of:

9.5% senior notes, due in annual installments of $10,000,000	$ 40,000,000
Mortgages and other notes due through 2011 (average interest rate of 9.9%)	107,604,000
Bank borrowings at 9.7%	67,225,000
Commercial paper at 9.4%	100,102,000
	314,931,000
Less: Current portion	(60,619,000)
Total long-term debt	$254,312,000

ILLUSTRATION 5-14
Balance Sheet Presentation of Long-Term Debt

---

[12]Companies usually explain the pertinent rights and privileges of the various securities (both debt and equity) outstanding in the notes to the financial statements. Examples of information that companies should disclose are dividend and liquidation preferences, participation rights, call prices and dates, conversion or exercise prices or rates and pertinent dates, sinking fund requirements, unusual voting rights, and significant terms of contracts to issue additional shares. "Disclosure of Information about Capital Structure," *Statement of Financial Accounting Standards No. 129* (Norwalk: FASB, 1997), par. 4.

Owners' Equity

The **owners' equity** (**stockholders' equity**) section is one of the most difficult sections to prepare and understand. This is due to the complexity of capital stock agreements and the various restrictions on stockholders' equity imposed by state corporation laws, liability agreements, and boards of directors. Companies usually divide the section into three parts:

STOCKHOLDERS' EQUITY SECTION

1 *CAPITAL STOCK.* The par or stated value of the shares issued.
2 *ADDITIONAL PAID-IN CAPITAL.* The excess of amounts paid in over the par or stated value.
3 *RETAINED EARNINGS.* The corporation's undistributed earnings.

For capital stock, companies must disclose the par value and the authorized, issued, and outstanding share amounts. A company usually presents the additional paid-in capital in one amount, although subtotals are informative if the sources of additional capital are varied and material. The retained earnings amount may be divided between the **unappropriated** (the amount that is usually available for dividend distribution) and **restricted** (e.g., by bond indentures or other loan agreements) amounts. In addition, companies show any capital stock reacquired (treasury stock) as a reduction of stockholders' equity.

Illustration 5-15 presents an example of the stockholders' equity section from **Quanex Corporation**.

ILLUSTRATION 5-15
Balance Sheet
Presentation of
Stockholders' Equity

Quanex Corporation
(in thousands)

Stockholders' equity (Note 12):	
Preferred stock, no par value, 1,000,000 shares authorized;	
345,000 issued and outstanding	$ 86,250
Common stock, $0.50 par value, 25,000,000 shares authorized;	
13,638,005 shares issued and outstanding	6,819
Additional paid-in capital	87,260
Retained earnings	57,263
	$237,592

The ownership or stockholders' equity accounts in a corporation differ considerably from those in a partnership or proprietorship. Partners show separately their permanent capital accounts and the balance in their temporary accounts (drawing accounts). Proprietorships ordinarily use a single capital account that handles all of the owner's equity transactions.

Balance Sheet Format

OBJECTIVE 3
Prepare a classified balance sheet using the report and account formats.

One common arrangement that companies use in presenting a classified balance sheet is the **account form**. It lists assets, by sections, on the left side, and liabilities and stockholders' equity, by sections, on the right side. The main disadvantage is the need for a sufficiently wide space in which to present the items side by side. Often, the account form requires two facing pages.

To avoid this disadvantage, the **report form** lists the sections one above the other, on the same page. See, for example, Illustration 5-16, which lists assets, followed by liabilities and stockholders' equity directly below, on the same page.[13]

ILLUSTRATION 5-16
Classified Report Form
Balance Sheet

SCIENTIFIC PRODUCTS, INC.
BALANCE SHEET
DECEMBER 31, 2006

Assets

Current assets

Cash		$ 42,485	
Available-for-sale securities—at fair value		28,250	
Accounts receivable	$165,824		
Less: Allowance for doubtful accounts	1,850	163,974	
Notes receivable		23,000	
Inventories—at average cost		489,713	
Supplies on hand		9,780	
Prepaid expenses		16,252	
Total current assets			$ 773,454

Long-term investments

Investments in Warren Co.			87,500

Property, plant, and equipment

Land—at cost		125,000	
Buildings—at cost	975,800		
Less: Accumulated depreciation	341,200	634,600	
Total property, plant, and equipment			759,600

Intangible assets

Goodwill			100,000
Total assets			$1,720,554

Liabilities and Stockholders' Equity

Current liabilities

Notes payable to banks		$ 50,000	
Accounts payable		197,532	
Accrued interest on notes payable		500	
Income taxes payable		62,520	
Accrued salaries, wages, and other liabilities		9,500	
Deposits received from customers		420	
Total current liabilities			$ 320,472

Long-term debt

Twenty-year 12% debentures, due January 1, 2016			500,000
Total liabilities			820,472

Stockholders' equity

Paid in on capital stock			
Preferred, 7%, cumulative			
Authorized, issued, and outstanding,			
30,000 shares of $10 par value	$300,000		
Common—			
Authorized, 500,000 shares of			
$1 par value; issued and			
outstanding, 400,000 shares	400,000		
Additional paid-in capital	37,500	737,500	
Retained earnings		162,582	
Total stockholders' equity			900,082
Total liabilities and stockholders' equity			$1,720,554

UNDERLYING CONCEPTS

The presentation of balance sheet information meets one of the objectives of financial reporting—to provide information about enterprise resources, claims to resources, and changes in them.

[13]*Accounting Trends and Techniques—2004* (New York: AICPA) indicates that all of the 600 companies surveyed use either the "report form" (506) or the "account form" (94), sometimes collectively referred to as the "customary form."

Infrequently, companies use other balance sheet formats. For example, companies sometimes deduct current liabilities from current assets to arrive at working capital. Or, they deduct all liabilities from all assets.

WHAT DO THE NUMBERS MEAN?

Presentation of Balance Sheet Formats for Various Real Companies

---

WARNING SIGNALS

Analysts use balance sheet information in models designed to predict financial distress. Researcher E. I. Altman pioneered a bankruptcy-prediction model that derives a "Z-score" by combining balance sheet and income measures in the following equation.

$$Z = \frac{\text{Working capital}}{\text{Total assets}} \times 1.2 + \frac{\text{Retained earnings}}{\text{Total assets}} \times 1.4 + \frac{\text{EBIT}}{\text{Total assets}} \times 3.3$$
$$+ \frac{\text{Sales}}{\text{Total assets}} \times 0.99 + \frac{\text{MV equity}}{\text{Total liabilities}} \times 0.6$$

Following extensive testing, Altman found that companies with Z-scores above 3.0 are unlikely to fail. Those with Z-scores below 1.81 are very likely to fail.

Altman developed the original model for publicly held manufacturing companies. He and others have modified the model to apply to companies in various industries, emerging companies, and companies not traded in public markets.

At one time, the use of Z-scores was virtually unheard of among practicing accountants. Today, auditors, management consultants, and courts of law use this measure to help evaluate the overall financial position and trends of a firm. In addition, banks use Z-scores for loan evaluation. While a low score does not guarantee bankruptcy, the model has been proven accurate in many situations.

Source: Adapted from E. I. Altman and E. Hotchkiss, *Corporate Financial Distress and Bankruptcy*, 3rd edition (New York: John Wiley and Sons, 2005).

ADDITIONAL INFORMATION REPORTED

OBJECTIVE 4
Determine which balance sheet information requires supplemental disclosure.

The balance sheet is not complete if a company simply lists the assets, liabilities, and owners' equity accounts. It still needs to provide important supplemental information. This may be information not presented elsewhere in the statement, or it may elaborate on items in the balance sheet. There are normally four types of information that are supplemental to account titles and amounts presented in the balance sheet. They are listed below.

SUPPLEMENTAL BALANCE SHEET INFORMATION

1 *CONTINGENCIES.* Material events that have an uncertain outcome.
2 *ACCOUNTING POLICIES.* Explanations of the valuation methods used or the basic assumptions made concerning inventory valuations, depreciation methods, investments in subsidiaries, etc.
3 *CONTRACTUAL SITUATIONS.* Explanations of certain restrictions or covenants attached to specific assets or, more likely, to liabilities.
4 *FAIR VALUES.* Disclosures of fair values, particularly for financial instruments.

Contingencies

A **contingency** is an existing situation involving uncertainty as to possible gain (gain contingency) or loss (loss contingency) that will ultimately be resolved when one or more future events occur or fail to occur. In short, contingencies are material events with an uncertain future. Examples of gain contingencies are tax operating-loss carry-forwards or company litigation against another party. Typical loss contingencies relate to litigation, environmental issues, possible tax assessments, or government investigations. We examine the accounting and reporting requirements involving contingencies more fully in Chapter 13.

UNDERLYING CONCEPTS

The basis for including additional information should meet the *full disclosure* principle. That is, the information should be of sufficient importance to influence the judgment of an informed user.

Accounting Policies

APB Opinion No. 22 recommends disclosure for all significant accounting principles and methods that involve selection from among alternatives or those that are peculiar to a given industry.[14] For instance, companies can compute inventories under several cost flow assumptions (e.g., LIFO and FIFO), depreciate plant and equipment under several accepted methods (e.g., double-declining balance and straight-line), and carry investments at different valuations (e.g., cost, equity, and fair value). Sophisticated users of financial statements know of these possibilities and examine the statements closely to determine the methods used.

Companies must also disclose information about the nature of their operations, the use of estimates in preparing financial statements, certain significant estimates, and vulnerabilities due to certain concentrations.[15] Illustration 5-17 shows an example of such a disclosure.

Chesapeake Corporation

Risks and Uncertainties. Chesapeake operates in three business segments which offer a diversity of products over a broad geographic base. The Company is not dependent on any single customer, group of customers, market, geographic area or supplier of materials, labor or services. Financial statements include, where necessary, amounts based on the judgments and estimates of management. These estimates include allowances for bad debts, accruals for landfill closing costs, environmental remediation costs, loss contingencies for litigation, self-insured medical and workers' compensation insurance and determinations of discount and other rate assumptions for pensions and postretirement benefit expenses.

ILLUSTRATION 5-17
Balance Sheet Disclosure of Significant Risks and Uncertainties

Disclosure of significant accounting principles and methods and of risks and uncertainties is particularly useful if given in a separate **Summary of Significant Accounting Policies** preceding the notes to the financial statements or as the initial note.

Contractual Situations

Companies should disclose contractual situations, if significant, in the notes to the financial statements. For example, they must clearly state the essential provisions of lease contracts, pension obligations, and stock option plans in the notes. Analysts want to know not only the amount of the liabilities, but also how the different contractual provisions affect the company at present and in the future.

---

[14]"Disclosure of Accounting Policies," *Opinions of the Accounting Principles Board No. 22* (New York: AICPA, 1972).

[15]"Disclosure of Certain Significant Risks and Uncertainties," *Statement of Position 94-6* (New York: AICPA, 1994).

Companies must disclose the following commitments if the amounts are material: commitments related to obligations to maintain working capital, to limit the payment of dividends, to restrict the use of assets, and to require the maintenance of certain financial ratios. Management must exercise considerable judgment to determine whether omission of such information is misleading. The rule in this situation is, "When in doubt, disclose." It is better to disclose a little too much information than not enough.

WHAT DO THE NUMBERS MEAN?

WHAT ABOUT YOUR COMMITMENTS?

Many of the recent accounting scandals related to the nondisclosure of significant contractual obligations. In response, the SEC has mandated that companies disclose contractual obligations in a tabular summary in the management discussion and analysis section of the company's annual report.

Presented below, as an example, is a disclosure from **The Procter & Gamble Company**.

Contractual Commitments, as of June 30, 2004 ($ in millions)

	Total	Less Than 1 Year	1–3 Years	3–5 Years	After 5 Years
Recorded liabilities					
Total debt	$20,399	$ 8,229	$3,954	$1,935	$ 6,281
Capital leases	252	30	46	169	7
Wella domination and profit transfer agreement	1,106	1,106	–	–	–
Other					
Interest payments relating to long-term debt	7,587	715	1,202	874	4,796
Operating leases	920	186	284	185	265
Minimum pension funding[1]	702	237	465	–	–
Purchase obligations[2]	5,471	1,640	1,334	955	1,542
Total contractual commitments	$36,437	$12,143	$7,285	$4,118	$12,891

[1]Represents future pension payments to comply with local funding requirements. The projected payments beyond fiscal year 2007 are not currently determinable.

[2]The amounts indicated in this line primarily reflect future contractual payments under various take-or-pay arrangements entered into as part of the normal course of business.

Fair Values

As we discussed in Chapter 2, companies use historical cost as the primary valuation basis in financial statements. However, fair value information may be more useful for certain types of assets and liabilities. This is particularly so in the case of financial instruments.

Financial instruments are defined as cash, an ownership interest, or a contractual right to receive or obligation to deliver cash or another financial instrument. Such contractual rights to receive cash or other financial instruments are assets. Contractual obligations to pay are liabilities. Cash, investments, accounts receivable, and payables are examples of financial instruments.

Financial instruments are increasing both in use and variety. As a consequence of the increasing use, companies must disclose both the carrying value and the estimated fair values of their financial instruments. For example, **YUM! Brands Inc.**, a franchiser of restaurants such as Pizza Hut and Taco Bell, provides extensive disclosures of the fair value of its financial instrument assets and liabilities, as shown in Illustration 5-18. We provide more extensive discussion of financial instrument accounting and reporting in Chapters 7, 14, 16, and 17.

YUM! Brands Inc.

The carrying amounts and fair values of our other financial instruments subject to fair value disclosures are as follows:

	Carrying Amount	Fair Value
Debt		
Short-term borrowings and long-term debt, excluding capital leases and the derivative instrument adjustments	$ 1,925	$ 2,181
Debt-related derivative instruments		
Open contracts in a net asset position	31	31
Lease guarantees	8	37
Guarantees of supporting financial arrangements of certain franchisees, unconsolidated affiliates and other third parties	8	10
Letters of credit	–	3

We estimated the fair value of debt, debt-related derivative instruments, foreign currency-related derivative instruments, guarantees and letters of credit using market quotes and calculations based on market rates.

ILLUSTRATION 5-18
Disclosure of Financial Instrument Fair Values

TECHNIQUES OF DISCLOSURE

Companies should disclose as completely as possible the effect of various contingencies on financial condition, the methods of valuing assets and liabilities, and the company's contracts and agreements. To disclose this pertinent information, companies may use parenthetical explanations, notes, cross reference and contra items, and supporting schedules.

OBJECTIVE 5
Describe the major disclosure techniques for the balance sheet.

Parenthetical Explanations

Companies often provide additional information by parenthetical explanations following the item. For example, Illustration 5-19 shows a parenthetical explanation of the number of shares issued by **Ford Motor Company** on the balance sheet under Stockholders' Equity.

Ford Motor Company

Stockholders' Equity (in millions)

Common stock, par value $0.01 per share (1,837 million shares issued)	$18

ILLUSTRATION 5-19
Parenthetical Disclosure of Shares Issued—Ford Motor Company

This additional pertinent balance sheet information adds clarity and completeness. It has an advantage over a note because it brings the additional information into the body of the statement where readers will less likely overlook it. Companies, however, should avoid lengthy parenthetical explanations, which might be distracting.

UNDERLYING CONCEPTS

The user-specific quality of *understandability* requires accountants to be careful in describing transactions and events.

Notes

Companies use notes if they cannot conveniently show additional explanations as parenthetical explanations. Illustration 5-20 (page 188) shows how **International Paper Company** reported its inventory costing methods in its accompanying notes.

ILLUSTRATION 5-20
Note Disclosure

International Paper Company

(Note 11)

Inventories by major category were (millions):

Raw materials	$ 371
Finished pulp, paper and packaging products	1,796
Finished lumber and panel products	184
Operating supplies	351
Other	16
Total inventories	$2,718

The last-in, first-out inventory method is used to value most of International Paper's U.S. inventories. Approximately 70% of total raw materials and finished products inventories were valued using this method. If the first-in, first-out method had been used, it would have increased total inventories balances by approximately $170 million.

Companies commonly use notes to disclose the following: the existence and amount of any preferred stock dividends in arrears, the terms of or obligations imposed by purchase commitments, special financial arrangements and instruments, depreciation policies, any changes in the application of accounting principles, and the existence of contingencies.

Notes therefore must present all essential facts as completely and succinctly as possible. Careless wording may mislead rather than aid readers. Notes should add to the total information made available in the financial statements, not raise unanswered questions or contradict other portions of the statements. The following notes illustrate the presentation of such information.

ILLUSTRATION 5-21
More Note
Disclosures

Alberto-Culver Company

Note 3: Long-Term Debt. Various borrowing arrangements impose restrictions on such items as total debt, working capital, dividend payments, treasury stock purchases and interest expense. The company was in compliance with these arrangements and $68 million of consolidated retained earnings was not restricted as to the payment of dividends and purchases of treasury stock.

Consolidated Papers, Inc.

Note 7: Commitments. The company had capital expenditure purchase commitments outstanding of approximately $17 million.

Willamette Industries, Inc.

Note 4: Property, Plant, and Equipment (partial): The company changed its accounting estimates relating to depreciation. The estimated service lives for most machinery and equipment were extended five years. The change was based upon a study performed by the company's engineering department, comparisons to typical industry practices, and the effect of the company's extensive capital investments which have resulted in a mix of assets with longer productive lives due to technological advances. As a result of the change, net income was increased $51,900, or $0.46 per diluted share.

Cross-Reference and Contra Items

Companies "cross-reference" a direct relationship between an asset and a liability on the balance sheet. For example, as shown in Illustration 5-22, on December 31, 2006, a company might show the following entries—one listed among the current assets, and the other listed among the current liabilities.

Current Assets (in part)	
Cash on deposit with sinking fund trustee for redemption of bonds payable—see Current liabilities	$800,000

Current Liabilities (in part)	
Bonds payable to be redeemed in 2007—see Current assets	$2,300,000

ILLUSTRATION 5-22
Cross-Referencing and Contra Items

This cross-reference points out that the company will redeem $2,300,000 of bonds payable currently, for which it has only set aside $800,000. Therefore, it needs additional cash from unrestricted cash, from sales of investments, from profits, or from some other source. Alternatively, the company can show the same information parenthetically.

Another common procedure is to establish contra or adjunct accounts. A **contra account** on a balance sheet reduces either an asset, liability, or owners' equity account. Examples include Accumulated Depreciation and Discount on Bonds Payable. Contra accounts provide some flexibility in presenting the financial information. With the use of the Accumulated Depreciation account, for example, a reader of the statement can see the original cost of the asset as well as the depreciation to date.

An **adjunct account**, on the other hand, increases either an asset, liability, or owners' equity account. An example is Premium on Bonds Payable, which, when added to the Bonds Payable account, describes the total bond liability of the company.

Supporting Schedules

Often a company needs a separate schedule to present more detailed information about certain assets or liabilities, as follows.

Property, plant, and equipment	
Land, buildings, equipment, and other fixed assets—net (see Schedule 3)	$643,300

ILLUSTRATION 5-23
Disclosure through Use of Supporting Schedules

SCHEDULE 3
LAND, BUILDINGS, EQUIPMENT, AND OTHER FIXED ASSETS

	Total	Land	Buildings	Equip.	Other Fixed Assets
Balance January 1, 2007	$740,000	$46,000	$358,000	$260,000	$76,000
Additions in 2007	161,200		120,000	38,000	3,200
	901,200	46,000	478,000	298,000	79,200
Assets retired or sold in 2007	31,700			27,000	4,700
Balance December 31, 2007	869,500	46,000	478,000	271,000	74,500
Depreciation taken to January 1, 2007	196,000		102,000	78,000	16,000
Depreciation taken in 2007	56,000		28,000	24,000	4,000
	252,000		130,000	102,000	20,000
Depreciation on assets retired in 2007	25,800			22,000	3,800
Depreciation accumulated December 31, 2007	226,200		130,000	80,000	16,200
Book value of assets	$643,300	$46,000	$348,000	$191,000	$58,300

INTERNATIONAL INSIGHT

Internationally, accounting terminology is a problem. Confusion arises even between nations that share a language. For example, U.S. investors normally think of "stock" as "equity" or "ownership"; to the British, "stocks" means inventory. In the United States "fixed assets" generally refers to "property, plant, and equipment"; in Britain the category includes more items.

Terminology

The account titles in the general ledger do not necessarily represent the best terminology for balance sheet purposes. Companies often use brief account titles and include technical terms that only accountants understand. But many persons unacquainted with accounting terminology examine balance sheets. Thus, balance sheets should contain descriptions that readers will generally understand and clearly interpret.

For example, companies have used the term "reserve" in differing ways: to describe amounts deducted from assets (contra accounts such as accumulated depreciation and allowance for doubtful accounts), as a part of the title of contingent or estimated liabilities, and to describe an appropriation of retained earnings. Because of the different meanings attached to this term, misinterpretation often resulted from its use. Therefore, the profession has recommended that companies use the word **reserve** only to describe an appropriation of retained earnings. The use of the term in this narrower sense—to describe appropriated retained earnings—has resulted in a better understanding of its significance when it appears in a balance sheet. However, the term "appropriated" appears more logical, and we encourage its use.

For years the profession has recommended that the use of the word **surplus** be discontinued in balance sheet presentations of owners' equity. The use of the terms *capital surplus*, *paid-in surplus*, and *earned surplus* is confusing. Although condemned by the profession, these terms appear all too frequently in current financial statements.

SECTION 2	*STATEMENT OF CASH FLOWS*

Chapter 2 indicated that one of the three basic objectives of financial reporting is "assessing the amounts, timing, and uncertainty of cash flows." The three financial statements we have looked at so far—the income statement, the statement of stockholders' equity, and the balance sheet—each present some information about the cash flows of an enterprise during a period. But they do so to a limited extent. For instance, the income statement provides information about resources provided by operations, but not exactly cash. The statement of stockholders' equity shows the amount of cash used to pay dividends or purchase treasury stock. Comparative balance sheets might show what assets the company has acquired or disposed of and what liabilities it has incurred or liquidated.

UNDERLYING CONCEPTS

The statement of cash flows meets one of the objectives of financial reporting—to help assess the amounts, timing, and uncertainty of future cash flows.

However, none of these statements presents a detailed summary of all the cash inflows and outflows, or the sources and uses of cash during the period. To fill this need, the FASB requires the **statement of cash flows** (also called the **cash flow statement**).[16]

PURPOSE OF THE STATEMENT OF CASH FLOWS

OBJECTIVE 6

Indicate the purpose of the statement of cash flows.

The primary purpose of a statement of cash flows is to provide relevant information about the cash receipts and cash payments of an enterprise during a period. To achieve this purpose, the statement of cash flows reports the following: (1) the cash effects of operations during a period, (2) investing transactions, (3) financing transactions, and (4) the net increase or decrease in cash during the period.[17]

Reporting the sources, uses, and net increase or decrease in cash helps investors, creditors, and others know what is happening to a company's most liquid resource. Be-

---

[16]"Statement of Cash Flows," *Statement of Financial Accounting Standards No. 95* (Stamford, Conn.: FASB, 1987).

[17]The FASB recommends the basis as "cash and cash equivalents." **Cash equivalents** are liquid investments that mature within three months or less.

cause most individuals maintain a checkbook and prepare a tax return on a cash basis, they can comprehend the information reported in the statement of cash flows, such as causes and effects of cash inflows and outflows and the net change in cash.

The statement of cash flows provides answers to the following simple but important questions:

1 Where did the cash come from during the period?

2 What was the cash used for during the period?

3 What was the change in the cash balance during the period?

WATCH THAT CASH FLOW

Investors usually focus on net income measured on an accrual basis. However, information on cash flows can be important for assessing a company's liquidity, financial flexibility, and overall financial performance. The graph below shows **W. T. Grant's** financial performance over 7 years.

WHAT DO THE NUMBERS MEAN?

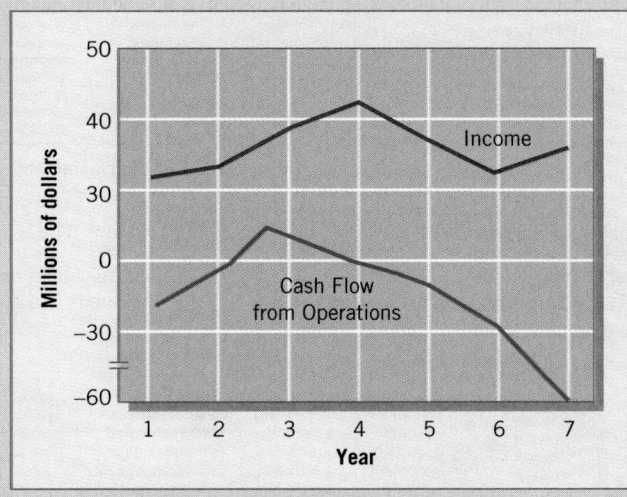

Although W. T. Grant showed consistent profits and even some periods of earnings growth, its cash flow began to "go south" starting in about year 3. The company filed for bankruptcy shortly after year 7. Financial statement readers who studied the company's cash flows would have found an early-warning signal of W. T. Grant's problems.

CONTENT AND FORMAT OF THE STATEMENT OF CASH FLOWS

Companies classify cash receipts and cash payments during a period into three different activities in the statement of cash flows—operating, investing, and financing activities, defined as follows.

OBJECTIVE 7
Identify the content of the statement of cash flows.

1 **Operating activities** involve the cash effects of transactions that enter into the determination of net income.

2 **Investing activities** include making and collecting loans and acquiring and disposing of investments (both debt and equity) and property, plant, and equipment.

3 **Financing activities** involve liability and owners' equity items. They include (a) obtaining resources from owners and providing them with a return on their investment, and (b) borrowing money from creditors and repaying the amounts borrowed.

Illustration 5-24 shows the basic format of the statement of cash flows.

ILLUSTRATION 5-24
Basic Format of Cash
Flow Statement

Statement of Cash Flows	
Cash flows from operating activities	$XXX
Cash flows from investing activities	XXX
Cash flows from financing activities	XXX
Net increase (decrease) in cash	XXX
Cash at beginning of year	XXX
Cash at end of year	$XXX

Illustration 5-25 graphs the inflows and outflows of cash classified by activity.

ILLUSTRATION 5-25 Cash Inflows and Outflows

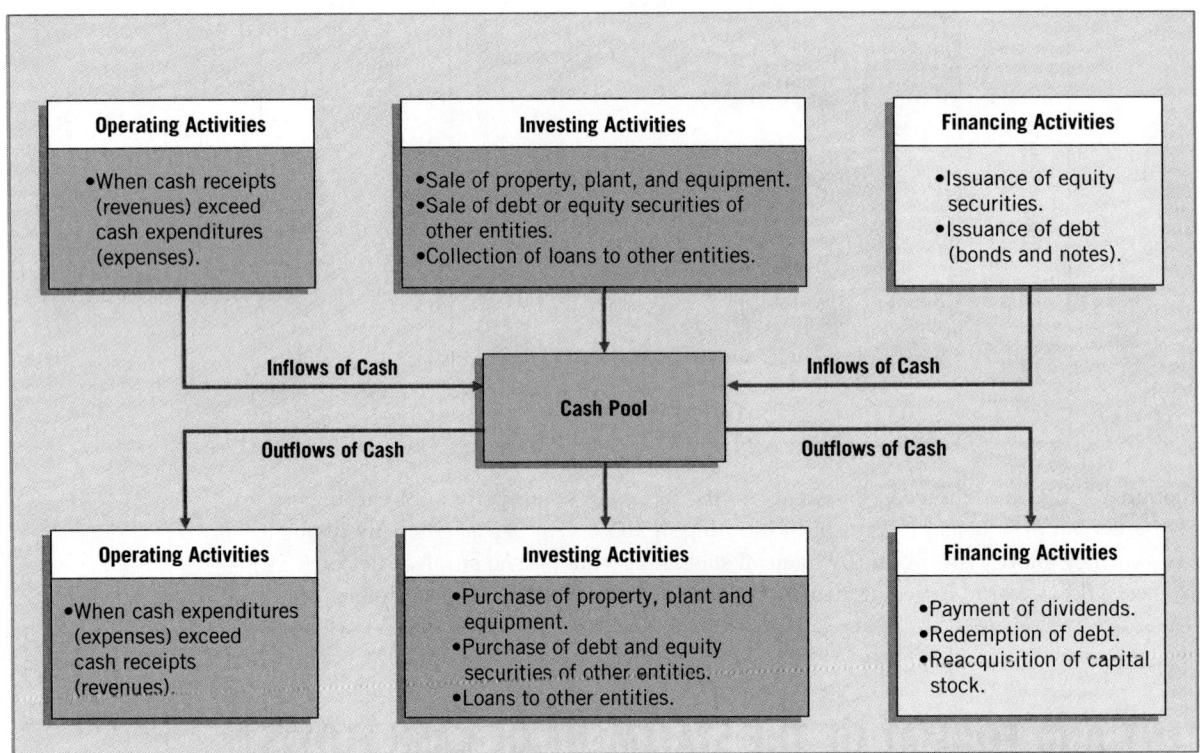

The statement's value is that it helps users evaluate liquidity, solvency, and financial flexibility. As we indicated earlier in the chapter, **liquidity** refers to the "nearness to cash" of assets and liabilities. **Solvency** is the firm's ability to pay its debts as they mature. **Financial flexibility** is a company's ability to respond and adapt to financial adversity and unexpected needs and opportunities.

We have devoted Chapter 23 entirely to the preparation and content of the statement of cash flows. The intervening chapters will cover several elements and complex topics that affect the content of a typical statement of cash flows. The presentation in this chapter is introductory—a reminder of the existence of the statement of cash flows and its usefulness.

PREPARATION OF THE STATEMENT OF CASH FLOWS

Companies obtain the information to prepare the statement of cash flows from several sources: (1) comparative balance sheets, (2) the current income statement, and (3) selected transaction data. Preparing the statement of cash flows from these sources involves four steps:

1 Determine the cash provided by or used in operating activities.
2 Determine the cash provided by or used in investing and financing activities.
3 Determine the change (increase or decrease) in cash during the period.
4 Reconcile the change in cash with the beginning and the ending cash balances.

The following simple example demonstrates how companies apply these steps in preparing a statement of cash flows.

On January 1, 2007, in its first year of operations, Telemarketing Inc. issued 50,000 shares of $1 par value common stock for $50,000 cash. The company rented its office space, furniture, and telecommunications equipment and performed marketing services throughout the first year. In June 2007 the company purchased land for $15,000. Illustration 5-26 shows the company's comparative balance sheets at the beginning and end of 2007.

OBJECTIVE 8
Prepare a statement of cash flows.

INTERNATIONAL INSIGHT

Not all countries require statements of cash flows. Some countries require a statement reporting sources and applications of "funds" (often defined as working capital). Others have no requirement for either cash or funds flow statements.

ILLUSTRATION 5-26   Comparative Balance Sheets

	TELEMARKETING INC. BALANCE SHEETS		
Assets	Dec. 31, 2007	Jan. 1, 2007	Increase/Decrease
Cash	$31,000	$–0–	$31,000 Increase
Accounts receivable	41,000	–0–	41,000 Increase
Land	15,000	–0–	15,000 Increase
Total	$87,000	$–0–	
Liabilities and Stockholders' Equity			
Accounts payable	$12,000	$–0–	12,000 Increase
Common stock	50,000	–0–	50,000 Increase
Retained earnings	25,000	–0–	25,000 Increase
Total	$87,000	$–0–	

Illustration 5-27 presents the income statement and additional information.

ILLUSTRATION 5-27
Income Statement Data

	TELEMARKETING INC. INCOME STATEMENT FOR THE YEAR ENDED DECEMBER 31, 2007	
Revenues		$172,000
Operating expenses		120,000
Income before income tax		52,000
Income tax		13,000
Net income		$ 39,000

Additional information:
Dividends of $14,000 were paid during the year.

Cash provided by operating activities is the excess of cash receipts over cash payments from operating activities. Companies determine this amount by converting net income on an accrual basis to a cash basis. To do so, they add to or deduct from net income those items in the income statement that do not affect cash. This procedure requires that a company analyze not only the current year's income statement but also the comparative balance sheets and selected transaction data.

Analysis of Telemarketing's comparative balance sheets reveals two items that will affect the computation of net cash provided by operating activities:

1 The increase in accounts receivable reflects a noncash increase of $41,000 in revenues.

2 The increase in accounts payable reflects a noncash increase of $12,000 in expenses.

Therefore, to arrive at cash provided by operations, Telemarketing Inc. deducts from net income the increase in accounts receivable ($41,000), and it adds back to net income the increase in accounts payable ($12,000). As a result of these adjustments, the company determines cash provided by operations to be $10,000, computed as shown in Illustration 5-28.

ILLUSTRATION 5-28
Computation of Net Cash
Provided by Operations

Net income		$39,000
Adjustments to reconcile net income		
to net cash provided by operating activities:		
Increase in accounts receivable	$(41,000)	
Increase in accounts payable	12,000	(29,000)
Net cash provided by operating activities		$10,000

Telemarketing Inc.'s only investing activity was the land purchase. It had two financing activities: (1) the increase of $50,000 in common stock resulting from the issuance of 50,000 shares for cash, and (2) the payment of $14,000 cash in dividends. Illustration 5-29 presents Telemarketing Inc.'s statement of cash flows for 2007.

INTERNATIONAL INSIGHT

International Accounting Standard 7 requires a statement of cash flows. Both international standards and U.S. GAAP specify that the cash flows must be classified as operating, investing, or financing.

ILLUSTRATION 5-29   Statement of Cash Flows

TELEMARKETING INC. STATEMENT OF CASH FLOWS FOR THE YEAR ENDED DECEMBER 31, 2007		
Cash flows from operating activities		
Net income		$39,000
Adjustments to reconcile net income to		
net cash provided by operating activities:		
Increase in accounts receivable	$(41,000)	
Increase in accounts payable	12,000	(29,000)
Net cash provided by operating activities		10,000
Cash flows from investing activities		
Purchase of land	(15,000)	
Net cash used by investing activities		(15,000)
Cash flows from financing activities		
Issuance of common stock	50,000	
Payment of cash dividends	(14,000)	
Net cash provided by financing activities		36,000
Net increase in cash		31,000
Cash at beginning of year		–0–
Cash at end of year		$31,000

The increase in cash of $31,000 reported in the statement of cash flows agrees with the increase of $31,000 in cash calculated from the comparative balance sheets.

Not all of a company's significant activities involve cash. Examples of significant noncash activities are:

1 Issuance of common stock to purchase assets.

2 Conversion of bonds into common stock.

3 Issuance of debt to purchase assets.

4 Exchanges of long-lived assets.

Significant financing and investing activities that do not affect cash are not reported in the body of the statement of cash flows. Rather, these activities are reported in either a separate schedule at the bottom of the statement of cash flows or in separate notes to the financial statements. Such reporting of these noncash activities satisfies the full disclosure principle. *In solving homework assignments, you should present significant noncash activities in a separate schedule at the bottom of the statement of cash flows.*

Illustration 5-30 shows an example of a comprehensive statement of cash flows. Note that the company purchased equipment through the issuance of $50,000 of bonds, which is a significant noncash transaction.

ILLUSTRATION 5-30
Comprehensive Statement of Cash Flows

NESTOR COMPANY
STATEMENT OF CASH FLOWS
FOR THE YEAR ENDED DECEMBER 31, 2007

Cash flows from operating activities		
Net income		$320,750
Adjustments to reconcile net income to net cash provided by operating activities:		
Depreciation expense	$88,400	
Amortization of intangibles	16,300	
Gain on sale of plant assets	(8,700)	
Increase in accounts receivable (net)	(11,000)	
Decrease in inventory	15,500	
Decrease in accounts payable	(9,500)	91,000
Net cash provided by operating activities		411,750
Cash flows from investing activities		
Sale of plant assets	90,500	
Purchase of equipment	(182,500)	
Purchase of land	(70,000)	
Net cash used by investing activities		(162,000)
Cash flows from financing activities		
Payment of cash dividend	(19,800)	
Issuance of common stock	100,000	
Redemption of bonds	(50,000)	
Net cash provided by financing activities		30,200
Net increase in cash		279,950
Cash at beginning of year		135,000
Cash at end of year		$414,950
Noncash investing and financing activities		
Purchase of equipment through issuance of $50,000 of bonds		

Additional Disclosures of Cash Flow Reporting

USEFULNESS OF THE STATEMENT OF CASH FLOWS

OBJECTIVE 9
Understand the usefulness of the statement of cash flows.

"Happiness is a positive cash flow" is certainly true. Although net income provides a long-term measure of a company's success or failure, cash is the lifeblood of a company. Without cash, a company will not survive. For small and newly developing companies, cash flow is the single most important element for survival. Even medium and large companies must control cash flow.

Creditors examine the cash flow statement carefully because they are concerned about being paid. They begin their examination by finding net cash provided by operating activities. A high amount indicates that a company is able to generate sufficient cash from operations to pay its bills without further borrowing. Conversely, a low or negative amount of net cash provided by operating activities indicates that a company may have to borrow or issue equity securities to acquire sufficient cash to pay its bills. Consequently, creditors look for answers to the following questions in the company's cash flow statements.

1 How successful is the company in generating net cash provided by operating activities?

2 What are the trends in net cash flow provided by operating activities over time?

3 What are the major reasons for the positive or negative net cash provided by operating activities?

You should recognize that companies can fail even though they report net income. The difference between net income and net cash provided by operating activities can be substantial. Companies such as **W. T. Grant Company** and **Prime Motor Inn**, for example, reported high net income numbers but negative net cash provided by operating activities. Eventually both companies filed for bankruptcy.

In addition, substantial increases in receivables and/or inventory can explain the difference between positive net income and negative net cash provided by operating activities. For example, in its first year of operations Hu Inc. reported a net income of $80,000. Its net cash provided by operating activities, however, was a negative $95,000, as shown in Illustration 5-31.

ILLUSTRATION 5-31
Negative Net Cash Provided by Operating Activities

HU INC.		
NET CASH FLOW FROM OPERATING ACTIVITIES		
Cash flows from operating activities		
Net income		$ 80,000
Adjustments to reconcile net income to net cash provided by operating activities:		
Increase in receivables	$ (75,000)	
Increase in inventories	(100,000)	(175,000)
Net cash provided by operating activities		$(95,000)

Hu could easily experience a "cash crunch" because it has its cash tied up in receivables and inventory. If Hu encounters problems in collecting receivables, or if inventory moves slowly or becomes obsolete, its creditors may have difficulty collecting on their loans.

CASH IS KING?

WHAT DO THE NUMBERS MEAN?

Analysts increasingly use cash-flow-based measures of income, such as cash flow provided by operations, instead of or in addition to net income. The reason for the change is that they have been losing faith in accrual-accounting-based net income numbers.

Sadly, these days even cash flow from operations isn't always what it seems to be. For example, in 2002 **WorldCom, Inc.** disclosed that it had improperly capitalized expenses: It moved $3.8 billion of cash outflows from the "Cash from operating activities" section of the cash flow statement to the "Investing activities" section, thereby greatly enhancing cash provided by operating activities.

Similarly, in 2002 **Dynegy, Inc.** restated its cash flow statement for 2001. In doing so, the company removed $300 million tied to its complex natural gas trading operation from operating cash flow and instead put that amount into the financing section—a drop of 37 percent in cash flow from operations.

Source: Henny Sender, "Sadly, These Days Even Cash Flow Isn't Always What It Seems To Be," *Wall Street Journal Online* (May 8, 2002).

Financial Liquidity

Readers of financial statements often assess liquidity by using the **current cash debt coverage ratio**. It indicates whether the company can pay off its current liabilities from its operations in a given year. Illustration 5-32 shows the formula for this ratio.

$$\frac{\text{Net Cash Provided by Operating Activities}}{\text{Average Current Liabilities}} = \frac{\text{Current Cash}}{\text{Debt Coverage Ratio}}$$

ILLUSTRATION 5-32
Formula for Current Cash Debt Coverage Ratio

The higher the current cash debt coverage ratio, the less likely a company will have liquidity problems. For example, a ratio near 1:1 is good: It indicates that the company can meet all of its current obligations from internally generated cash flow.

Financial Flexibility

The **cash debt coverage ratio** provides information on financial flexibility. It indicates a company's ability to repay its liabilities from net cash provided by operating activities, without having to liquidate the assets employed in its operations. Illustration 5-33 shows the formula for this ratio. (Notice its similarity to the current cash debt coverage ratio. However, because it uses average total liabilities in place of average current liabilities, it takes a somewhat longer-range view.)

$$\frac{\text{Net Cash Provided by Operating Activities}}{\text{Average Total Liabilities}} = \frac{\text{Cash Debt}}{\text{Coverage Ratio}}$$

ILLUSTRATION 5-33
Formula for Cash Debt Coverage Ratio

The higher this ratio, the less likely the company will experience difficulty in meeting its obligations as they come due. It signals whether the company can pay its debts and survive if external sources of funds become limited or too expensive.

Free Cash Flow

A more sophisticated way to examine a company's financial flexibility is to develop a free cash flow analysis. **Free cash flow** is the amount of discretionary cash flow a company has for purchasing additional investments, retiring its debt, purchasing treasury stock, or simply adding to its liquidity. Financial statement users calculate free cash flow as net cash provided by operating activities less capital expenditures and dividends. Obviously, the greater the amount of free cash flow, the greater the company's amount of financial flexibility.

Questions that a free cash flow analysis answers are:

1 Is the company able to pay its dividends without resorting to external financing?

2 If business operations decline, will the company be able to maintain its needed capital investment?

3 What is the amount of discretionary cash flow that can be used for additional investment, retirement of debt, purchase of treasury stock, or addition to liquidity?

Illustration 5-34 (on page 198) is a free cash flow analysis using the cash flow statement for Nestor Company (shown in Illustration 5-30).

ILLUSTRATION 5-34
Free Cash Flow
Computation

NESTOR COMPANY FREE CASH FLOW ANALYSIS	
Net cash provided by operating activities	$411,750
Less: Capital expenditures	(252,500)
Dividends	(19,800)
Free cash flow	$139,450

This analysis shows that Nestor has a positive, and substantial, net cash provided by operating activities of $411,750. Nestor's statement of cash flows reports that the company purchased equipment of $182,500 and land of $70,000 for total capital spending of $252,500.

In a free cash flow analysis, we first deduct capital spending, to indicate it is the least discretionary expenditure a company generally makes. (Without continued efforts to maintain and expand facilities, it is unlikely that Nestor can continue to maintain its competitive position.) We then deduct dividends. Although a company *can* cut its dividend, it usually will do so only in **a financial emergency**. The amount resulting after these deductions is the company's free cash flow. Nestor has more than sufficient cash flow to meet its dividend payment and therefore has satisfactory financial flexibility.

As you can see from looking back at Illustration 5-30, Nestor used its free cash flow to redeem bonds and add to its liquidity. If it finds additional investments that are profitable, it can increase its spending without putting its dividend or basic capital spending in jeopardy. Companies that have strong financial flexibility can take advantage of profitable investments even in tough times. In addition, strong financial flexibility frees companies from worry about survival in poor economic times. In fact, those with strong financial flexibility often fare better in a poor economy because they can take advantage of opportunities that other companies cannot.

KEY TERMS

account form, *182*

adjunct account, *189*

available-for-sale securities, *175*

balance sheet, *170*

cash debt coverage ratio, *197*

contingency, *185*

contra account, *189*

current assets, *173*

current cash debt coverage ratio, *197*

current liabilities, *179*

financial flexibility, *171*

financial instruments, *186*

financing activities, *191*

free cash flow, *197*

held-to-maturity securities, *175*

intangible assets, *179*

SUMMARY OF LEARNING OBJECTIVES

1. Explain the uses and limitations of a balance sheet. The balance sheet provides information about the nature and amounts of investments in enterprise resources, obligations to creditors, and the owners' equity. The balance sheet contributes to financial reporting by providing a basis for (1) computing rates of return, (2) evaluating the capital structure of the enterprise, and (3) assessing the liquidity, solvency, and financial flexibility of the enterprise.

Three limitations of a balance sheet are: (1) The balance sheet does not reflect fair value because accountants use a historical cost basis in valuing and reporting most assets and liabilities. (2) Companies must use judgments and estimates to determine certain amounts, such as the collectibility of receivables and the useful life of long-term tangible and intangible assets. (3) The balance sheet omits many items that are of financial value to the business but cannot be recorded objectively, such as human resources, customer base, and reputation.

2. Identify the major classifications of the balance sheet. The general elements of the balance sheet are assets, liabilities, and equity. The major classifications of assets are current assets; long-term investments; property, plant, and equipment; intangible assets; and other assets. The major classifications of liabilities are current and long-term liabilities. The balance sheet of a corporation generally classifies owners' equity as capital stock, additional paid-in capital, and retained earnings.

3. Prepare a classified balance sheet using the report and account formats. The report form lists liabilities and stockholders' equity directly below assets on the same page. The account form lists assets, by sections, on the left side, and liabilities and stockholders' equity, by sections, on the right side.

4. Determine which balance sheet information requires supplemental disclosure. Four types of information normally are supplemental to account titles and amounts presented in the balance sheet: (1) *Contingencies:* Material events that have an uncertain outcome. (2) *Accounting policies:* Explanations of the valuation methods used or the basic assumptions made concerning inventory valuation, depreciation methods, investments in subsidiaries, etc. (3) *Contractual situations:* Explanations of certain restrictions or covenants attached to specific assets or, more likely, to liabilities. (4) *Fair values:* Disclosures related to fair values, particularly related to financial instruments.

5. Describe the major disclosure techniques for the balance sheet. Companies use four methods to disclose pertinent information in the balance sheet: (1) *Parenthetical explanations:* Parenthetical information provides additional information or description following the item. (2) *Notes:* A company uses notes if it cannot conveniently show additional explanations or descriptions as parenthetical explanations. (3) *Cross-reference and contra items:* Companies "cross-reference" a direct relationship between an asset and a liability on the balance sheet. (4) *Supporting schedules:* Often a company needs a separate schedule to present more detailed information about certain assets or liabilities, because the balance sheet provides just a single summary item.

6. Indicate the purpose of the statement of cash flows. The primary purpose of a statement of cash flows is to provide relevant information about the cash receipts and cash payments of an enterprise during a period. Reporting the sources, uses, and net change in cash enables financial statement readers to know what is happening to a company's most liquid resource.

7. Identify the content of the statement of cash flows. In the statement of cash flows, companies classify their cash receipts and cash payments during a period into three different activities: (1) *Operating activities:* Involve the cash effects of transactions that enter into the determination of net income. (2) *Investing activities:* Include making and collecting loans, and acquiring and disposing of investments (both debt and equity) and of property, plant, and equipment. (3) *Financing activities:* Involve liability and owners' equity items. Financing activities include (a) obtaining capital from owners and providing them with a return on their investment, and (b) borrowing money from creditors and repaying the amounts borrowed.

8. Prepare a statement of cash flows. The information to prepare the statement of cash flows usually comes from (1) comparative balance sheets, (2) the current income statement, and (3) selected transaction data. Companies follow these steps to prepare the statement of cash flows from these sources: (1) Determine the cash provided by operating activities. (2) Determine the cash provided by or used in investing and financing activities. (3) Determine the change (increase or decrease) in cash during the period. (4) Reconcile the change in cash with the beginning and ending cash balances.

9. Understand the usefulness of the statement of cash flows. Creditors examine the cash flow statement carefully because they are concerned about being paid. The net cash flow provided by operating activities in relation to the company's liabilities is helpful in making this assessment. Two ratios used in this regard are the current cash debt ratio and the cash debt ratio. In addition, the amount of free cash flow provides creditors and stockholders with a picture of the company's financial flexibility.

investing activities, *191*
liquidity, *171*
long-term investments, *177*
long-term liabilities, *181*
operating activities, *191*
owners' (stockholders') equity, *182*
property, plant, and equipment, *178*
report form, *183*
reserve, *190*
solvency, *171*
statement of cash flows, *190*
trading securities, *175*
working capital, *180*

APPENDIX

5A

Ratio Analysis—A Reference

USING RATIOS TO ANALYZE PERFORMANCE

OBJECTIVE 10
Identify the major types of financial ratios and what they measure.

Analysts and other interested parties can gather qualitative information from financial statements by examining relationships between items on the statements and identifying trends in these relationships. A useful starting point in developing this information is ratio analysis.

A **ratio** expresses the mathematical relationship between one quantity and another. Ratio analysis expresses the relationship among pieces of selected financial statement data, in a **percentage**, a **rate**, or a simple **proportion**.

To illustrate, **IBM Corporation** recently had current assets of $46,970 million and current liabilities of $39,798 million. We find the ratio between these two amounts by dividing current assets by current liabilities. The alternative means of expression are:

Percentage: Current assets are 118% of current liabilities.

Rate: Current assets are 1.18 times as great as current liabilities.

Proportion: The relationship of current assets to current liabilities is 1.18:1.

To analyze financial statements, we classify ratios into four types, as follows:

Expanded Discussion of Financial Statement Analysis

MAJOR TYPES OF RATIOS

LIQUIDITY RATIOS. Measures of the company's short-term ability to pay its maturing obligations.

ACTIVITY RATIOS. Measures of how effectively the company uses its assets.

PROFITABILITY RATIOS. Measures of the degree of success or failure of a given company or division for a given period of time.

COVERAGE RATIOS. Measures of the degree of protection for long-term creditors and investors.

In Chapter 5 we discussed two ratios related to the statement of cash flows (current cash debt coverage and cash debt coverage). Throughout the remainder of the textbook, we provide ratios to help you understand and interpret the information presented in financial statements. Illustration 5A-1 presents the ratios that we will use throughout the text. You should find this chart helpful as you examine these ratios in more detail in the following chapters. An appendix to Chapter 24 further discusses financial statement analysis.

ILLUSTRATION 5A-1 A Summary of Financial Ratios

Ratio	Formula	Purpose or Use
I. Liquidity		
1. Current ratio	$\dfrac{\text{Current assets}}{\text{Current liabilities}}$	Measures short-term debt-paying ability
2. Quick or acid-test ratio	$\dfrac{\text{Cash, marketable securities, and receivables (net)}}{\text{Current liabilities}}$	Measures immediate short-term liquidity
3. Current cash debt coverage ratio	$\dfrac{\text{Net cash provided by operating activities}}{\text{Average current liabilities}}$	Measures a company's ability to pay off its current liabilities in a given year from its operations
II. Activity		
4. Receivables turnover	$\dfrac{\text{Net sales}}{\text{Average trade receivables (net)}}$	Measures liquidity of receivables
5. Inventory turnover	$\dfrac{\text{Cost of goods sold}}{\text{Average inventory}}$	Measures liquidity of inventory
6. Asset turnover	$\dfrac{\text{Net sales}}{\text{Average total assets}}$	Measures how efficiently assets are used to generate sales
III. Profitability		
7. Profit margin on sales	$\dfrac{\text{Net income}}{\text{Net sales}}$	Measures net income generated by each dollar of sales
8. Rate of return on assets	$\dfrac{\text{Net income}}{\text{Average total assets}}$	Measures overall profitability of assets
9. Rate of return on common stock equity	$\dfrac{\text{Net income minus preferred dividends}}{\text{Average common stockholders' equity}}$	Measures profitability of owners' investment
10. Earnings per share	$\dfrac{\text{Net income minus preferred dividends}}{\text{Weighted shares outstanding}}$	Measures net income earned on each share of common stock
11. Price-earnings ratio	$\dfrac{\text{Market price of stock}}{\text{Earnings per share}}$	Measures the ratio of the market price per share to earnings per share
12. Payout ratio	$\dfrac{\text{Cash dividends}}{\text{Net income}}$	Measures percentage of earnings distributed in the form of cash dividends
IV. Coverage		
13. Debt to total assets	$\dfrac{\text{Total debt}}{\text{Total assets}}$	Measures the percentage of total assets provided by creditors
14. Times interest earned	$\dfrac{\text{Income before interest expense and taxes}}{\text{Interest expense}}$	Measures ability to meet interest payments as they come due
15. Cash debt coverage ratio	$\dfrac{\text{Net cash provided by operating activities}}{\text{Average total liabilities}}$	Measures a company's ability to repay its total liabilities in a given year from its operations
16. Book value per share	$\dfrac{\text{Common stockholders' equity}}{\text{Outstanding shares}}$	Measures the amount each share would receive if the company were liquidated at the amounts reported on the balance sheet

SUMMARY OF LEARNING OBJECTIVE FOR APPENDIX 5A

10. Identify the major types of financial ratios and what they measure. Ratios express the mathematical relationship between one quantity and another, expressed as a percentage, a rate, or a proportion. *Liquidity* ratios measure the short-term ability to pay maturing obligations. *Activity* ratios measure the effectiveness of asset usage. *Profitability* ratios measure the success or failure of an enterprise. *Coverage* ratios measure the degree of protection for long-term creditors and investors.

KEY TERMS

activity ratios, *200*
coverage ratios, *200*
liquidity ratios, *200*
profitability ratios, *200*
ratio analysis, *200*

APPENDIX

5B

Specimen Financial Statements: The Procter & Gamble Company

The following pages contain the financial statements, accompanying notes, and other information from the 2004 annual report of **The Procter & Gamble Company (P&G)**. The Procter & Gamble Company manufactures and markets a range of consumer products in various countries throughout the world. The Company markets over 300 branded products in more than 160 countries. It manages its business in five product segments: Fabric and Home Care, Baby and Family Care, Beauty Care, Health Care, and Snacks and Beverages.

We do not expect that you will comprehend P&G's financial statements and the accompanying notes in their entirety at your first reading. But we expect that by the time you complete the material in this textbook, your level of understanding and interpretive ability will have grown enormously.

At this point we recommend that you take 20 to 30 minutes to scan the following statements and notes. Your goal should be to familiarize yourself with the contents and accounting elements. Throughout the following 19 chapters, when you are asked to refer to specific parts of P&G's financial statements, do so! Then, when you have completed reading this book, we challenge you to reread P&G's financials to see how much greater and more sophisticated your understanding of them has become.

P&G

Consumers around the world trust P&G brands – such as Pampers, Tide, Ariel, Pantene, Wella, Always, Crest, Bounty, Charmin, Olay, Pringles, Iams, Downy, Actonel, Folgers and Head & Shoulders – to make everyday life a little bit better. Almost 110,000 P&G people in over 80 countries worldwide work hard to earn that trust.

Touching lives, improving life. P&G.

Financial Highlights

Amounts in millions except per share amounts	Years Ended June 30		
	2004	2003	% Change
Net Sales	**$51,407**	$43,377	19%
Operating Income	**9,827**	7,853	25%
Net Earnings	**6,481**	5,186	25%
Per Common Share[1]			
Diluted Net Earnings	**2.32**	1.85	25%
Dividends	**0.93**	0.82	13%

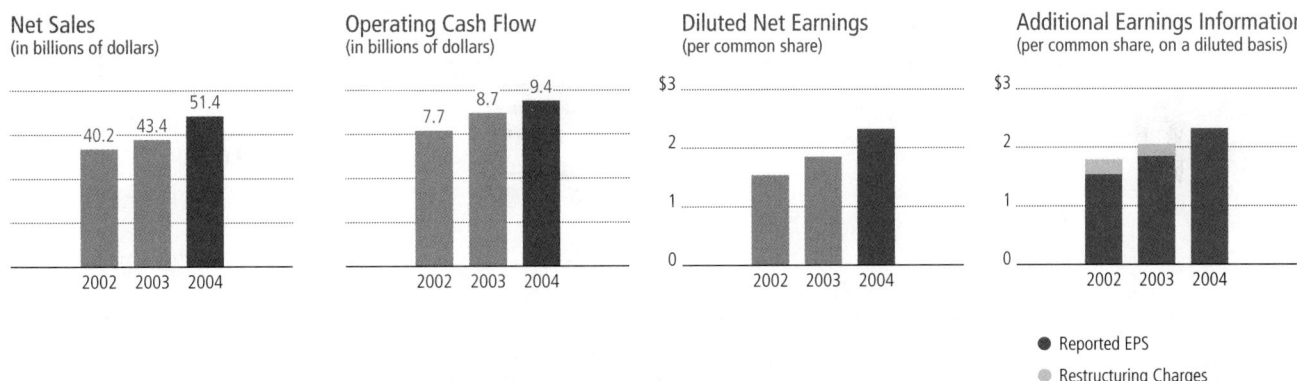

Net Sales (in billions of dollars): 2002 40.2, 2003 43.4, 2004 51.4

Operating Cash Flow (in billions of dollars): 2002 7.7, 2003 8.7, 2004 9.4

Diluted Net Earnings (per common share): 2002, 2003, 2004

Additional Earnings Information (per common share, on a diluted basis): 2002, 2003, 2004
● Reported EPS
● Restructuring Charges

Fellow Shareholders,

P&G is delivering broad-based, organic growth driven by clear strategies and a unique combination of P&G strengths. P&G's performance has accelerated over the past three years, and we are confident double-digit earnings-per-share growth is sustainable for the foreseeable future.

Sustaining P&G's Growth

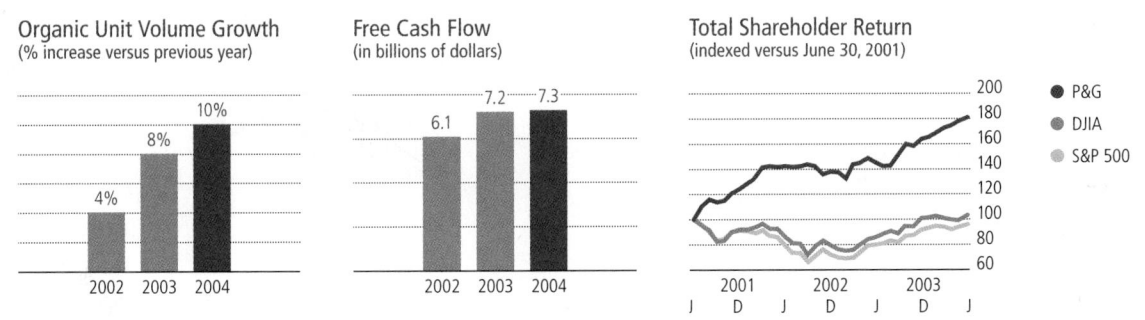

Organic Unit Volume Growth (% increase versus previous year): 2002 4%, 2003 8%, 2004 10%

Free Cash Flow (in billions of dollars): 2002 6.1, 2003 7.2, 2004 7.3

Total Shareholder Return (indexed versus June 30, 2001):
● P&G
● DJIA
● S&P 500

Three years of strong performance is a good start, but it's long-term performance that counts. Consistent performance is not easy. Growing P&G sales 4%–6% per year is roughly the equivalent of adding a brand the size of Tide – every year.

We're confident P&G can reliably deliver the future growth to which we've committed. Our strategies are working. There still is room to grow. Our strengths enable us to respond to external trends and challenges. Major changes are improving the consistency of P&G performance.

Build existing core businesses into strong global leaders.

Grow leading brands in big countries with winning customers. Accelerate growth in Western Europe.

Accelerate faster-growing, higher-margin health and beauty businesses.

Accelerate growth in developing markets and with lower-income consumers.

P&G strategies, strengths, and the systemic and structural changes we've made to improve the reliability of our performance should give shareholders confidence that P&G can sustain double-digit earnings-per-share growth for the foreseeable future.

A.G. Lafley
Chairman of the Board,   August 6, 2004
President and Chief Executive

Management's Responsibility for Financial Reporting

Procter & Gamble has been built through the generations by the character of its people. That character is reflected in our Purpose, Values and Principles and in how well we live them as individuals and as a Company. High quality financial reporting is one of our responsibilities – one that we execute with integrity.

High quality financial reporting is characterized by accuracy, objectivity and transparency. Management is responsible for maintaining an effective system of internal controls over financial reporting to deliver those characteristics in all material respects. The Board of Directors, through its Audit Committee, provides oversight. They have engaged Deloitte & Touche LLP to audit our consolidated financial statements, on which they have issued an unqualified opinion.

Our commitment to providing timely, accurate and understandable information to investors encompasses:

Communicating expectations to employees. Key employee responsibilities are reinforced through the Company's "Worldwide Business Conduct Manual," which sets forth the Company's commitment to conduct its business affairs with high ethical standards. Every one of P&G's employees – from senior management on down – is held personally accountable for compliance. The Worldwide Business Conduct Manual is available on our website at www.pg.com.

Maintaining a strong internal control environment. Our system of internal controls includes written policies and procedures, segregation of duties and the careful selection and development of employees. The system is designed to provide reasonable assurance that transactions are executed as authorized and appropriately recorded, that assets are safeguarded and that accounting records are sufficiently reliable to permit the preparation of financial statements that conform in all material respects with accounting principles generally accepted in the United States of America. We monitor these internal controls through control self-assessments by business unit management and an ongoing program of internal audits around the world.

Executing financial stewardship. We maintain specific programs and activities to ensure that employees understand their fiduciary responsibilities to shareholders. This ongoing effort encompasses financial discipline in our strategic and daily business decisions and brings particular focus to maintaining accurate financial reporting and effective controls through process improvement, skill development and oversight.

Exerting rigorous oversight of the business. We continuously review our business results and strategic choices. Our Global Leadership Council is actively involved – from understanding strategies to reviewing key initiatives, financial performance and control assessments. The intent is to ensure we remain objective in our assessments, constructively challenge the approach to business opportunities, identify potential issues and ensure reward and recognition systems are appropriately aligned with results.

Engaging our Disclosure Committee. We maintain disclosure controls and procedures designed to ensure that information required to be disclosed is recorded, processed, summarized and reported timely and accurately. Our Disclosure Committee is a group of senior-level executives responsible for evaluating disclosure implications of significant business activities and events. The Committee reports its findings to the CEO and CFO, providing an effective process to evaluate our external disclosure obligations.

Encouraging strong and effective corporate governance from our Board of Directors. We have an active, capable and diligent Board that meets the required standards for independence, and we welcome the Board's oversight as a representative of the shareholders. Our Audit Committee comprises independent directors with the financial knowledge and experience to provide appropriate oversight. We review significant accounting policies, financial reporting and internal control matters with them and encourage their independent discussions with our external auditors. Our corporate governance guidelines, as well as the charter of the Audit Committee and certain other committees of our Board, are available on our website at www.pg.com.

P&G has a strong history of doing what's right. We know great companies are built on strong ethical standards and principles. Our financial results are delivered from that culture of accountability, and we take responsibility for the quality and accuracy of our financial reporting. We present this information proudly, with the expectation that those who use it will understand our Company, recognize our commitment to performance with integrity and share our confidence in P&G's future.

A. G. Lafley

Chairman of the Board,
President and Chief Executive

Clayton C. Daley, Jr.

Chief Financial Officer

Report of Independent Registered Public Accounting Firm

Deloitte.

To the Board of Directors and Shareholders of
The Procter & Gamble Company:

We have audited the accompanying consolidated balance sheets of The Procter & Gamble Company and subsidiaries (the "Company") as of June 30, 2004 and 2003 and the related consolidated statements of earnings, shareholders' equity and cash flows for each of the three years in the period ended June 30, 2004. These financial statements are the responsibility of the Company's management. Our responsibility is to express an opinion on these financial statements based on our audits.

We conducted our audits in accordance with standards of the Public Company Accounting Oversight Board (United States). Those standards require that we plan and perform the audits to obtain reasonable assurance about whether the financial statements are free of material misstatement. An audit includes examining, on a test basis, evidence supporting the amounts and disclosures in the nancial statements. An audit also includes assessing the accounting principles used and signi cant estimates made by management, as well as evaluating the overall financial statement presentation. We believe that our audits provide a reasonable basis for our opinion.

In our opinion, such consolidated financial statements present fairly, in all material respects, the nancial position of the Company at June 30, 2004 and 2003 and the results of its operations and cash flows for each of the three years in the period ended June 30, 2004, in conformity with accounting principles generally accepted in the United States of America.

Deloitte + Touche LLP

Deloitte & Touche LLP   August 6, 2004
Cincinnati, Ohio

Consolidated Statements of Earnings

	Years Ended June 30		
Amounts in millions except per share amounts	**2004**	2003	2002
Net Sales	**$51,407**	$43,377	$40,238
Cost of products sold	**25,076**	22,141	20,989
Selling, general and administrative expense	**16,504**	13,383	12,571
Operating Income	**9,827**	7,853	6,678
Interest expense	**629**	561	603
Other non-operating income, net	**152**	238	308
Earnings Before Income Taxes	**9,350**	7,530	6,383
Income taxes	**2,869**	2,344	2,031
Net Earnings	**$6,481**	$5,186	$4,352
Basic Net Earnings Per Common Share[1]	**$2.46**	$1.95	$1.63
Diluted Net Earnings Per Common Share[1]	**$2.32**	$1.85	$1.54
Dividends Per Common Share[1]	**$0.93**	$0.82	$0.76

[1] Restated for two-for-one stock split effective May 21, 2004.

See accompanying Notes to Consolidated Financial Statements

Consolidated Statements of Cash Flows

Amounts in millions	2004	2003	2002
	Years ended June 30		
Cash and Cash Equivalents, Beginning of Year	**$5,912**	$3,427	$2,306
Operating Activities			
Net earnings	6,481	5,186	4,352
Depreciation and amortization	1,733	1,703	1,693
Deferred income taxes	415	63	389
Change in accounts receivable	(159)	163	96
Change in inventories	56	(56)	159
Change in accounts payable, accrued and other liabilities	625	936	684
Change in other operating assets and liabilities	(88)	178	(98)
Other	299	527	467
Total Operating Activities	**9,362**	8,700	7,742
Investing Activities			
Capital expenditures	(2,024)	(1,482)	(1,679)
Proceeds from asset sales	230	143	227
Acquisitions	(7,476)	(61)	(5,471)
Change in investment securities	(121)	(107)	88
Total Investing Activities	**(9,391)**	(1,507)	(6,835)
Financing Activities			
Dividends to shareholders	(2,539)	(2,246)	(2,095)
Change in short-term debt	4,911	(2,052)	1,394
Additions to long-term debt	1,963	1,230	1,690
Reductions of long-term debt	(1,188)	(1,060)	(461)
Proceeds from the exercise of stock options	555	269	237
Treasury purchases	(4,070)	(1,236)	(568)
Total Financing Activities	**(368)**	(5,095)	197
Effect of Exchange Rate Changes on Cash and Cash Equivalents	(46)	387	17
Change in Cash and Cash Equivalents	**(443)**	2,485	1,121
Cash and Cash Equivalents, End of Year	**$5,469**	$5,912	$3,427
Supplemental Disclosure			
Cash payments for:			
Interest	$630	$538	$629
Income taxes	1,634	1,703	941
Non-cash spin-off of Jif and Crisco businesses	-	-	150
Acquisition of Businesses			
Fair value of assets acquired, excluding cash	$11,954	$61	$6,042
Fair value of liabilities assumed	(4,478)	-	(571)
Acquisitions	**7,476**	61	5,471

See accompanying Notes to Consolidated Financial Statements

Consolidated Balance Sheets
Assets

Amounts in millions	June 30 2004	2003
Current Assets		
Cash and cash equivalents	$5,469	$5,912
Investment securities	423	300
Accounts receivable	4,062	3,038
Inventories		
Materials and supplies	1,191	1,095
Work in process	340	291
Finished goods	2,869	2,254
Total Inventories	4,400	3,640
Deferred income taxes	958	843
Prepaid expenses and other receivables	1,803	1,487
Total Current Assets	**17,115**	15,220
Property, Plant and Equipment		
Buildings	5,206	4,729
Machinery and equipment	19,456	18,222
Land	642	591
	25,304	23,542
Accumulated depreciation	(11,196)	(10,438)
Net Property, Plant and Equipment	**14,108**	13,104
Goodwill and Other Intangible Assets		
Goodwill	19,610	11,132
Trademarks and other intangible assets, net	4,290	2,375
Net Goodwill and Other Intangible Assets	**23,900**	13,507
Other Non-Current Assets	1,925	1,875
Total Assets	**$57,048**	$43,706

Consolidated Balance Sheets
Liabilities and Shareholders' Equity

Amounts in millions	June 30 2004	2003
Current Liabilities		
Accounts payable	$3,617	$2,795
Accrued and other liabilities	7,689	5,512
Taxes payable	2,554	1,879
Debt due within one year	8,287	2,172
Total Current Liabilities	22,147	12,358
Long-Term Debt	12,554	11,475
Deferred Income Taxes	2,261	1,396
Other Non-Current Liabilities	2,808	2,291
Total Liabilities	39,770	27,520
Shareholders' Equity[1]		
Convertible Class A preferred stock, stated value $1 per share (600 shares authorized)	1,526	1,580
Non-Voting Class B preferred stock, stated value $1 per share (200 shares authorized)	-	-
Common stock, stated value $1 per share (5,000 shares authorized; shares outstanding: 2004 - 2,543.8, 2003 - 2,594.4)	2,544	2,594
Additional paid-in capital	2,425	1,634
Reserve for ESOP debt retirement	(1,283)	(1,308)
Accumulated other comprehensive income	(1,545)	(2,006)
Retained earnings	13,611	13,692
Total Shareholders' Equity	17,278	16,186
Total Liabilities and Shareholders' Equity	$57,048	$43,706

[1] Restated for two-for-one stock split effective May 21, 2004.

Consolidated Statements of Shareholders' Equity

(Restated for two-for-one stock split effective May 21, 2004)

Dollars in millions/ Shares in thousands	Common Shares Outstanding	Common Stock	Preferred Stock	Additional Paid-In Capital	Reserve for ESOP Debt Retirement	Accumulated Other Comprehensive Income	Retained Earnings	Total	Total Comprehensive Income
Balance June 30, 2001	2,591,476	$2,591	$1,701	$762	$(1,375)	$(2,120)	$10,451	$12,010	
Net earnings							4,352	4,352	$4,352
Other comprehensive income:									
Financial statement translation						263		263	263
Net investment hedges, net of $238 tax						(397)		(397)	(397)
Other, net of tax benefits						(106)		(106)	(106)
Total comprehensive income									$4,112
Dividends to shareholders:									
Common							(1,971)	(1,971)	
Preferred, net of tax benefits							(124)	(124)	
Spin-off of Jif and Crisco							(150)	(150)	
Treasury purchases	(15,363)	(15)		25[1,2]			(578)	(568)	
Employee plan issuances	16,646	17		344				361	
Preferred stock conversions	8,781	9	(67)	58				-	
ESOP debt guarantee reduction					36			36	
Balance June 30, 2002	2,601,540	2,602	1,634	1,189	(1,339)	(2,360)	11,980	13,706	
Net earnings							5,186	5,186	$5,186
Other comprehensive income:									
Financial statement translation						804		804	804
Net investment hedges, net of $251 tax						(418)		(418)	(418)
Other, net of tax benefits						(32)		(32)	(32)
Total comprehensive income									$5,540
Dividends to shareholders:									
Common							(2,121)	(2,121)	
Preferred, net of tax benefits							(125)	(125)	
Treasury purchases	(28,276)	(28)		20[1,2]			(1,228)	(1,236)	
Employee plan issuances	14,312	14		377				391	
Preferred stock conversions	6,819	6	(54)	48				-	
ESOP debt guarantee reduction					31			31	
Balance June 30, 2003	2,594,395	2,594	1,580	1,634	(1,308)	(2,006)	13,692	16,186	
Net earnings							6,481	6,481	$6,481
Other comprehensive income:									
Financial statement translation						750		750	750
Net investment hedges, net of $207 tax						(348)		(348)	(348)
Other, net of tax benefits						59		59	59
Total comprehensive income									$6,942
Dividends to shareholders:									
Common							(2,408)	(2,408)	
Preferred, net of tax benefits							(131)	(131)	
Treasury purchases	(79,893)	(80)		33[2]			(4,023)	(4,070)	
Employee plan issuances	22,678	23		711				734	
Preferred stock conversions	6,658	7	(54)	47				-	
ESOP debt guarantee reduction					25			25	
Balance June 30, 2004	2,543,838	$2,544	$1,526	$2,425	$(1,283)	$(1,545)	$13,611	$17,278	

[1] Premium on equity put options totaled $6 and $18 for 2003 and 2002, respectively.
[2] Includes impacts arising from stock split.

See accompanying Notes to Consolidated Financial Statements

Notes to Consolidated Financial Statements

Note 1 Summary of Significant Accounting Policies

Nature of Operations

The Procter & Gamble Company's (the Company) business is focused on providing consumer branded products of superior quality and value. The Company markets approximately 300 consumer products in more than 160 countries around the world. Our products are sold primarily through retail operations including mass merchandisers, grocery stores, membership club stores and drug stores.

Basis of Presentation

The Consolidated Financial Statements include The Procter & Gamble Company and its controlled subsidiaries. Intercompany transactions are eliminated in consolidation. Investments in certain companies over which the Company exerts significant influence, but does not control the financial and operating decisions, are accounted for as equity method investments.

Use of Estimates

Preparation of financial statements in conformity with accounting principles generally accepted in the United States of America (U.S. GAAP) requires management to make estimates and assumptions that affect the amounts reported in the Consolidated Financial Statements and accompanying disclosures. These estimates are based on management's best knowledge of current events and actions the Company may undertake in the future. Estimates are used in accounting for, among other items, consumer and trade promotion accruals, pensions, post-employment benefits, stock options, useful lives for depreciation and amortization, future cash flows associated with impairment testing for goodwill and long-lived assets, deferred tax assets, potential income tax assessments and contingencies. Actual results may ultimately differ from estimates, although management does not believe such changes would materially affect the financial statements in any individual year.

Revenue Recognition

Sales are recognized when revenue is realized or realizable and has been earned. Most revenue transactions represent sales of inventory, and the revenue recorded includes shipping and handling costs, which generally are included in the list price to the customer. The Company's policy is to recognize revenue when title to the product, ownership and risk of loss transfer to the customer, which generally is on the date of shipment. A provision for payment discounts and product return allowances is recorded as a reduction of sales in the same period that the revenue is recognized.

Trade promotions, consisting primarily of customer pricing allowances, merchandising funds and consumer coupons, are offered through various programs to customers and consumers. Sales are recorded net of trade promotion spending, which is recognized as incurred, generally at the time of the sale. Most of these arrangements have terms of approximately one year. Accruals for expected payouts under these programs are included as accrued marketing and promotion in the accrued and other current liabilities line in the Consolidated Balance Sheets.

Cost of Products Sold

Cost of products sold primarily comprises direct materials and supplies consumed in the manufacture of product, as well as manufacturing labor and direct overhead expense necessary to acquire and convert the purchased materials and supplies into finished product. Cost of products sold also includes the cost to distribute products to customers, inbound freight costs, internal transfer costs, warehousing costs and other shipping and handling activity. Shipping and handling costs invoiced to customers are included in net sales.

Selling, General and Administrative

Selling, general and administrative expense primarily includes marketing expenses, including the cost of media, advertising and related costs; selling expenses; research and development costs; administrative and other indirect overhead costs; and other miscellaneous operating items.

Other Non-Operating Income, Net

Other non-operating income, net primarily includes interest and investment income and gains and losses from divestitures.

Currency Translation

Financial statements of operating subsidiaries outside the United States of America (U.S.) generally are measured using the local currency as the functional currency. Adjustments to translate those statements into U.S. dollars are recorded in other comprehensive income (OCI). For subsidiaries operating in highly inflationary economies, the U.S. dollar is the functional currency. Remeasurement adjustments for financial statements in highly inflationary economies and other transactional exchange gains and losses are reflected in earnings.

Cash Flow Presentation

The Statement of Cash Flows is prepared using the indirect method, which reconciles net earnings to cash flow from operating activities. These adjustments include the removal of timing differences between the occurrence of operating receipts and payments and their recognition in net earnings. The adjustments also remove from operating activities cash flows arising from investing and financing activities, which are

Millions of dollars except per share amounts

presented separately from operating activities. Cash flows from foreign currency transactions and operations are translated at an average exchange rate for the period. Cash flows from hedging activities are included in the same category as the items being hedged. Cash flows from derivative instruments designated as net investment hedges are classified as financing activities. Cash flows from other derivative instruments used to manage interest, commodity or currency exposures are classified as operating activities. Cash paid for acquisitions is classified as investing activities.

Cash Equivalents

Highly liquid investments with maturities of three months or less when purchased are considered cash equivalents and recorded at cost.

Investments

Investment securities consist of readily-marketable debt and equity securities. These securities are reported at fair value. Unrealized gains or losses on securities classified as trading are charged to earnings. Unrealized gains or losses on securities classified as available for sale are recorded net of tax in OCI.

Other investments that are not controlled and over which the Company does not have the ability to exercise significant influence are accounted under the cost method.

Inventory Valuation

Inventories are valued at cost, which is not in excess of current market prices. Product-related inventories are primarily maintained on the first-in, first-out method. Minor amounts of product inventories, including certain cosmetics and commodities are maintained on the last-in, first-out method. The cost of spare part inventories is maintained using the average cost method.

Goodwill and Other Intangible Assets

The cost of intangible assets with determinable useful lives is amortized to reflect the pattern of economic benefits consumed, principally on a straight-line basis over the estimated periods benefited. Goodwill and indefinite-lived intangibles are not amortized, but are evaluated annually for impairment. The Company evaluates a number of factors to determine whether an indefinite life is appropriate, including the competitive environment, market share, brand history, operating plan and the macroeconomic environment of the country in which the brand is sold. Due to the nature of the Company's business, there are a number of brand intangibles that have been determined to have

indefinite lives. If it is determined that a brand intangible does not have an indefinite life, the Company's policy is to amortize such assets over the expected useful life, which generally ranges from 5 to 20 years. Patents, technology and other intangibles with contractual terms are amortized over their respective contractual lives. Other non-contractual intangible assets with determinable lives are amortized over periods ranging from 5 to 20 years.

Where certain events or changes in operating conditions occur, lives on intangible assets with determinable lives may be adjusted and an impairment assessment may be performed on the recoverability of the carrying amounts. The annual evaluation for impairment of goodwill and indefinite-lived intangibles is based on valuation models that incorporate internal projections of expected future cash flows and operating plans.

Property, Plant and Equipment

Property, plant and equipment are recorded at cost reduced by accumulated depreciation. Depreciation expense is recognized over the assets' estimated useful lives using the straight-line method. Machinery and equipment includes office furniture and equipment (15-year life), computer equipment and capitalized software (3 to 5-year lives) and manufacturing equipment (3 to 20-year lives). Buildings are depreciated over an estimated useful life of 40 years. Estimated useful lives are periodically reviewed and, where appropriate, changes are made prospectively. Where certain events or changes in operating conditions occur, asset lives may be adjusted and an impairment assessment may be performed on the recoverability of the carrying amounts.

Fair Values of Financial Instruments

Certain financial instruments are required to be recorded at fair value. The estimated fair values of such financial instruments, including certain debt instruments, investment securities and derivatives, have been determined using market information and valuation methodologies, primarily discounted cash flow analysis. These estimates require considerable judgment in interpreting market data and changes in assumptions or estimation methods could significantly affect the fair value estimates. However, the Company does not believe any such changes would have a material impact on its financial condition or results of operations. Other financial instruments, including cash equivalents, other investments and short-term debt, are recorded at cost, which approximates fair value. The fair valve of long-term debt is disclosed in Note 6.

Stock-Based Compensation

The Company has employee stock option plans, which are described more fully in Note 8. The Company accounts for its employee stock option plans under the intrinsic value recognition and measurement provisions of Accounting Principles Board (APB) Opinion No. 25, "Accounting for Stock Issued to Employees," and related interpretations. As stock options have been issued with exercise prices equal to the market value of the underlying shares on the grant date, no compensation expense has resulted.

Had compensation expense for the plans been determined based on the fair value of the options on the grant date, consistent with SFAS No. 123, "Accounting for Stock-Based Compensation," the Company's net earnings and earnings per common share would have been as follows:

| | Years ended June 30 | | |
	2004[1]	2003	2002
Net Earnings			
As reported	**$6,481**	$5,186	$4,352
Pro forma adjustments	**(325)**	(398)	(442)
Pro forma	**6,156**	4,788	3,910
Net Earnings Per Common Share			
Basic			
As reported	**$2.46**	$1.95	$1.63
Pro forma adjustments	**(0.12)**	(0.15)	(0.17)
Pro forma	**2.34**	1.80	1.46
Diluted			
As reported	**2.32**	1.85	1.54
Pro forma adjustments	**(0.12)**	(0.15)	(0.15)
Pro forma	**2.20**	1.70	1.39

[1] During the current year, the timing of the annual grant was moved from September to February resulting in lower expense, as the associated pro forma expense is amortized over the three-year vesting period.

Stock Split

In March 2004, the Company's Board of Directors approved a two-for-one stock split effective for common and preferred shareholders of record as of May 21, 2004. The financial statements, notes and other references to share and per share data have been restated to reflect the stock split for all periods presented.

New Pronouncements and Reclassifications

No new accounting pronouncements issued or effective during the fiscal year have had or are expected to have a material impact on the financial statements. Certain reclassifications of prior years' amounts have been made to conform to the current year presentation.

Note 2 Restructuring Program

In 1999, concurrent with a reorganization of its operations into product-based Global Business Units, the Company initiated a multi-year restructuring program. Costs included enrollment reductions, manufacturing consolidations and portfolio choices to scale back or discontinue under-performing businesses and initiatives. Total restructuring program charges were $751 in 2003, including $351 in separations related to approximately 5,000 people, $190 in asset write-downs and $87 in accelerated depreciation related to long-lived assets that were taken out of service prior to the end of their normal service period. Total restructuring program charges were $958 in 2002, including $393 in separations related to approximately 7,400 people, $208 in asset write-downs and $135 in accelerated depreciation.

At June 30, 2003, the program was substantially complete with a re-maining reserve of $335. Substantially all of this liability was settled through cash payments by the end of 2004.

The Company continues to undertake projects to maintain a competitive cost structure, including manufacturing streamlining and work force rationalization, as part of its normal operations.

Note 3 Acquisitions and Spin-Off

Wella Acquisition

On September 2, 2003, the Company acquired a controlling interest in Wella AG (Wella). Through a stock purchase agreement with the majority shareholders of Wella and a tender offer made on the remaining shares, the Company acquired a total of 81% of Wella's outstanding shares, including 99% of Wella's outstanding voting class shares. In June 2004, the Company and Wella entered into a Domination and Profit Transfer Agreement (the Domination Agreement) pursuant to which the Company is entitled to exercise full operating control and receive 100% of the future earnings of Wella. As consideration for the Domination Agreement, the Company will pay the holders of the remaining outstanding shares of Wella a guaranteed perpetual annual dividend payment. Alternatively, the remaining Wella shareholders may elect to tender their shares to the Company for an agreed price. The fair value of the total guaranteed annual dividend payments is $1.11 billion, which approximates the cost if all remaining shares were tendered. Because the Domination Agreement transfers operational and economic control of the remaining outstanding shares to the Company, it has been accounted for as an acquisition of the remaining shares, with a liability recorded equal to the fair value of the guaranteed payments. Because of the tender feature, the liability is recorded as a current liability in the accrued and other liabilities line of the Consolidated Balance Sheets. Payments made under the guaranteed annual dividend provisions will be allocated between interest expense and a reduction of the liability, as appropriate. The total purchase price for Wella, including acquisition costs, was $6.27 billion based on exchange rates at the acquisition dates. It was funded with a combination of cash, debt and the liability recorded under the Domination Agreement

The acquisition of Wella, with over $3 billion in annual net sales, gives the Company access to the professional hair care category plus greater scale and scope in hair care, hair colorants, cosmetics and fragrance products, while providing potential for significant synergies. The operating results of the Wella business are reported in the Company's Beauty Care business segment beginning September 2, 2003.

The following table provides pro forma results of operations for the years ended June 30, 2004, 2003 and 2002, as if Wella had been acquired as of the beginning of each fiscal year presented. The pro forma results include certain adjustments, including adjustments to convert Wella's historical financial information from International Accounting Standards (IAS) into U.S. GAAP, estimated interest impacts from funding of the acquisition and estimated amortization of definite-lived intangible assets. However, pro forma results do not include any anticipated cost savings or other effects of the integration of Wella. Accordingly, such amounts are not necessarily indicative of the results that would have occurred if the acquisition had occurred on the dates indicated or that may result in the future.

Pro forma results	Years ended June 30		
	2004	2003	2002
Net Sales	**$51,958**	$46,751	$43,070
Net Earnings	**6,402**	5,222	4,345
Diluted Net Earnings per Common Share	**$2.29**	$1.86	$1.54

The Company is in the process of finalizing independent appraisals for certain assets to assist management in allocating the purchase price to the individual assets acquired and liabilities assumed. This may result in adjustments to the carrying values of Wella's recorded assets and liabilities, including the amount of any residual value allocated to goodwill. The Company is also completing its analysis of collaboration plans that may result in additional purchase price allocation adjustments. The preliminary allocation of the purchase price included in the current period balance sheet is based on the current best estimates of man-

agement and is subject to revision based on final determination of fair values and collaboration plans. The Company anticipates the valuations and other studies will be completed prior to the anniversary date of the acquisition. The preliminary allocation of the total purchase price of Wella resulted in the following condensed balance sheet of assets acquired and liabilities assumed.

Current assets	$1,825
Property, plant and equipment	443
Goodwill	5,864
Intangible assets	1,709
Other non-current assets	225
Total assets acquired	10,066
Current liabilities	2,114
Non-current liabilities	1,679
Total liabilities assumed	3,793
Net assets acquired	6,273

The Wella acquisition resulted in $5.86 billion in goodwill, all of which was allocated to the Beauty Care segment, and $1.71 billion in total intangible assets acquired with $1.15 billion allocated to trademarks with indefinite lives. The remaining $556 of acquired intangibles have determinable useful lives and were assigned to trademarks of $267, patents and technology of $10, professional customer relationships of $214 and license and other intangible assets of $65. Total intangible assets acquired with determinable lives have a weighted-average life of 11 years (8 years for trademarks, 5 years for patents and technology, 15 years for professional customer relationships and 23 years for license and other intangible assets).

China Venture
On June 18, 2004, the Company purchased the remaining 20% stake in its China venture from its partner, Hutchison Whampoa China Ltd. (Hutchison), giving the Company full ownership in its operations in China. The net purchase price was $1.85 billion, which is the purchase price of $2.00 billion net of minority interest and related obligations that were eliminated as a result of the transaction. The acquisition was funded by debt. The fair value of the incremental individual assets and liabilities acquired approximates current book value. Accordingly, the purchase price was recorded as goodwill, which was allocated to multiple business segments.

Millions of dollars except per share amounts

Clairol Acquisition

On November 16, 2001, the Company completed the acquisition of the Clairol business from The Bristol-Myers Squibb Company for approximately $5.03 billion in cash, financed primarily with debt. The operating results of the Clairol business are reported in the Company's Beauty Care segment beginning November 16, 2001.

The following table provides pro forma results of operations for the year ended June 30, 2002 as if Clairol had been acquired as of the beginning of the fiscal year. Pro forma information for 2004 and 2003 is not presented as the results of Clairol are included with those of the Company for the entire year. The pro forma results include adjustments for estimated interest expense on acquisition funding and amortization of definite-lived intangible assets. However, pro forma results do not include any anticipated cost savings or other effects of the integration of Clairol. Accordingly, such amounts are not necessarily indicative of the results that would have occurred if the acquisition had closed on the dates indicated or that may result in the future.

	Year ended June 30
Pro forma results	2002
Net Sales	$40,780
Net Earnings	4,406
Diluted Net Earnings per Common Share	$1.56

Jif and Crisco Spin-off

On May 31, 2002, the Jif peanut butter and Crisco shortening brands were spun off to the Company's shareholders and subsequently merged into The J.M. Smucker Company (Smucker). The Company's shareholders received one new common Smucker share for every 50 shares held in the Company, totaling 26 million shares, or approximately $900 in market value. This transaction was not included in the results of operations, since a spin-off to the Company's shareholders is recorded at net book value, or $150, in a manner similar to dividends.

Other minor business purchases and intangible asset acquisitions totaled $384, $61 and $446 in 2004, 2003 and 2002, respectively.

Note 4 Goodwill and Intangible Assets

The change in net carrying amount of goodwill for the years ended June 30, 2004 and 2003 was allocated by reportable business segment as follows:

	2004	2003
Fabric and Home Care, beginning of year	$460	$451
Acquisitions	148	-
Translation and other	6	9
End of year	**614**	460
Baby and Family Care, beginning of year	884	830
Acquisitions	19	-
Translation and other	38	54
End of year	**941**	884
Beauty Care, beginning of year	6,600	6,542
Acquisitions	7,277	-
Translation and other	580	58
End of year	**14,457**	6,600
Health Care, beginning of year	2,908	2,866
Acquisitions	386	-
Translation and other	21	42
End of year	**3,315**	2,908
Snacks and Beverages, beginning of year	280	277
Translation and other	3	3
End of year	**283**	280
Goodwill, Net, beginning of year	11,132	10,966
Acquisitions	7,830	-
Translation and other	648	166
End of year	**19,610**	11,132

For the year ended June 30, 2004, goodwill increased primarily due to the acquisition of Wella and the purchase of the remaining stake in the China venture.

Identifiable intangible assets as of June 30, 2004 and 2003 were comprised of:

	June 30, 2004		June 30, 2003	
	Gross Carrying Amount	Accumulated Amortization	Gross Carrying Amount	Accumulated Amortization
Intangible Assets with Determinable Lives				
Trademarks	$1,012	$155	$499	$85
Patents and technology	518	250	492	204
Other	554	165	316	140
	2,084	570	1,307	429
Trademarks with Indefinite Lives	2,945	169	1,666	169
	5,029	739	2,973	598

Millions of dollars except per share amounts

The amortization of intangible assets for the years ended June 30, 2004, 2003 and 2002 was $165, $100 and $97, respectively. Estimated amortization expense over the next five years is as follows: 2005 - $171; 2006 - $169; 2007 - $119; 2008 - $106; and 2009 - $104. Such estimates do not reflect the impact of future foreign exchange rate changes.

Note 5 Supplemental Financial Information

Selected components of current and non-current liabilities were as follows:

	June 30	
	2004	2003
Accrued and Other Current Liabilities		
Marketing and promotion	**$1,876**	$1,802
Liability under Wella		
Domination Agreement	**1,106**	-
Compensation expenses	**1,049**	804
Other	**3,658**	2,906
	7,689	5,512
Other Non-Current Liabilities		
Pension benefits	**$1,798**	$1,301
Other postretirement benefits	**142**	181
Other	**868**	809
	2,808	2,291

Selected Operating Expenses

Research and development costs are charged to earnings as incurred and were $1,802 in 2004, $1,665 in 2003 and $1,601 in 2002. Advertising costs are charged to earnings as incurred and were $5,504 in 2004, $4,373 in 2003 and $3,773 in 2002. Both of these are components of selling, general and administrative expense.

Note 6 Short-Term and Long-Term Debt

	June 30	
	2004	2003
Short-Term Debt		
USD commercial paper	**$6,059**	$717
Non-USD commercial paper	**149**	147
Current portion of long-term debt	**1,518**	1,093
Other	**561**	215
	8,287	2,172

The weighted average short-term interest rates were 1.5% and 3.6% as of June 30, 2004 and 2003, respectively. The rate decrease reflected an increase in commercial paper within short-term debt.

	June 30	
	2004	2003
Long-Term Debt		
6.60% USD note due December, 2004	**$1,000**	$1,000
4.00% USD note due April, 2005	**400**	400
5.75% EUR note due September, 2005	**1,827**	1,725
1.50% JPY note due December, 2005	**503**	459
3.50% CHF note due February, 2006	**240**	222
5.40% EUR note due August, 2006	**365**	-
4.75% USD note due June, 2007	**1,000**	1,000
6.13% USD note due May, 2008	**500**	500
4.30% USD note due August, 2008	**500**	500
3.50% USD note due December, 2008	**650**	-
6.88% USD note due September, 2009	**1,000**	1,000
2.00% JPY note due June, 2010	**458**	417
9.36% ESOP debentures due 2007-2021[1]	**1,000**	1,000
4.85% USD note due December, 2015	**700**	-
8.00% USD note due September, 2024	**200**	200
6.45% USD note due January, 2026	**300**	300
6.25% GBP note due January, 2030	**906**	827
5.25% GBP note due January, 2033	**363**	331
5.50% USD note due February, 2034	**500**	-
Debt assumed by acquiring non-cash capital leases	**252**	146
All other long-term debt	**1,408**	2,541
Current portion of long-term debt	**(1,518)**	(1,093)
	12,554	11,475

[1] Debt issued by the ESOP is guaranteed by the Company and must be recorded as debt of the Company as discussed in Note 9.

Long-term weighted average interest rates were 4.0% and 3.7% as of June 30, 2004 and 2003, respectively, and included the effects of related interest rate swaps discussed in Note 7.

The fair value of the long-term debt was $13,168 and $12,396 at June 30, 2004 and 2003, respectively. Long-term debt maturities during the next five fiscal years are as follows: 2005 - $1,518; 2006 - $2,625; 2007 - $1,433; 2008 - $972; and 2009 - $1,150. The Company has no material obligations that are secured.

Millions of dollars except per share amounts

Note 7 Risk Management Activities

As a multinational company with diverse product offerings, the Company is exposed to market risks, such as changes in interest rates, currency exchange rates and commodity pricing. To manage the volatility related to these exposures, the Company evaluates exposures on a consolidated basis to take advantage of logical exposure netting. For the remaining exposures, the Company enters into various derivative transactions. Such derivative transactions, which are executed in accordance with the Company's policies in areas such as counterparty exposure and hedging practices, are accounted for under SFAS No. 133, "Accounting for Derivative Instruments and Hedging Activities," as amended and interpreted. The Company does not hold or issue derivative financial instruments for speculative trading purposes.

At inception, the Company formally designates and documents the financial instrument as a hedge of a specific underlying exposure. The Company formally assesses, both at inception and at least quarterly on an ongoing basis, whether the financial instruments used in hedging transactions are effective at offsetting changes in either the fair value or cash flows of the related underlying exposure. Fluctuations in the derivative value generally are offset by changes in the fair value or cash flows of the exposures being hedged. This offset is driven by the high degree of effectiveness between the exposure being hedged and the hedging instrument. Any ineffective portion of an instrument's change in fair value is immediately recognized in earnings.

Credit Risk
The Company has established strict counterparty credit guidelines and normally enters into transactions with investment grade financial institutions. Counterparty exposures are monitored daily and downgrades in credit rating are reviewed on a timely basis. Credit risk arising from the inability of a counterparty to meet the terms of the Company's financial instrument contracts generally is limited to the amounts, if any, by which the counterparty's obligations exceed the obligations of the Company. The Company does not expect to incur material credit losses on its risk management or other financial instruments.

Interest Rate Management
The Company's policy is to manage interest cost using a mixture of fixed-rate and variable-rate debt. To manage this risk in a cost efficient manner, the Company enters into interest rate swaps in which the Company agrees to exchange, at specified intervals, the difference between fixed and variable interest amounts calculated by reference to an agreed-upon notional principal amount.

Interest rate swaps that meet specific conditions under SFAS No. 133 are accounted for as fair value hedges. Changes in the fair value of both the hedging instruments and the underlying debt obligations are immediately recognized in earnings as equal and offsetting gains and losses in the interest expense component of the income statement. The fair value of the Company's interest rate swap agreements was a net asset of $45 and $322 at June 30, 2004 and 2003, respectively. All existing fair value hedges are 100% effective. As a result, there is no impact to earnings due to hedge ineffectiveness.

Foreign Currency Management
The Company manufactures and sells its products in a number of countries throughout the world and, as a result, is exposed to movements in foreign currency exchange rates. The purpose of the Company's foreign currency hedging program is to reduce the risk caused by short-term changes in exchange rates.

The Company primarily utilizes forward exchange contracts and purchased options with maturities of less than 18 months and currency swaps with maturities up to 5 years. These instruments are intended to offset the effect of exchange rate fluctuations on forecasted sales, inventory purchases, intercompany royalties and intercompany loans denominated in foreign currencies and are therefore accounted for as cash flow hedges. The fair value of these instruments at June 30, 2004 and June 30, 2003 was $47 and $27 in assets and $140 and $92 in liabilities, respectively. The effective portion of the changes in fair value for these instruments are reported in OCI and reclassified into earnings in the same financial statement line item and in the same period or periods during which the hedged transactions affect earnings. The ineffective portion, which is not material for any year presented, is immediately recognized in earnings.

Certain instruments used by the Company for foreign exchange risk do not meet the requirements for hedge accounting treatment. In these cases, the change in value of the instruments is designed to offset the foreign currency impact of intercompany financing transactions, income from international operations and other balance sheet revaluations. The fair value of these instruments at June 30, 2004 and 2003 was $71 and $113 in assets and $26 and $26 in liabilities, respectively. The gain or loss on these instruments is immediately recognized in earnings. The net impact of such instruments, included in selling, general and administrative expense, was $80, $264 and $50 of gains in 2004, 2003 and 2002, respectively, which substantially offset foreign currency transaction losses of the items being hedged.

Millions of dollars except per share amounts

Net Investment Hedging

The Company hedges certain net investment positions in major currencies. To accomplish this, the Company borrows directly in foreign currency and designates a portion of foreign currency debt as a hedge of net investments in foreign subsidiaries. In addition, certain foreign currency swaps are designated as hedges of the Company's related foreign net investments. Under SFAS No. 133, changes in the fair value of these instruments are immediately recognized in OCI, to offset the change in the value of the net investment being hedged. Currency effects of these hedges reflected in OCI were a $348 and $418 after-tax loss in 2004 and 2003, respectively. Accumulated net balances were a $586 after-tax loss in 2004 and a $238 after-tax loss in 2003.

Commodity Price Management

Raw materials used by the Company are subject to price volatility caused by weather, supply conditions, political and economic variables and other unpredictable factors. To manage the volatility related to certain anticipated inventory purchases, the Company uses futures and options with maturities generally less than one year and swap contracts with maturities up to five years. These market instruments are designated as cash flow hedges under SFAS No. 133. Accordingly, the mark-to-market gain or loss on qualifying hedges is reported in OCI and reclassified into cost of products sold in the same period or periods during which the hedged transaction affects earnings. Qualifying cash flow hedges currently recorded in OCI are not considered material. The mark-to-market gain or loss on non-qualifying, excluded and ineffective portions of hedges is immediately recognized in cost of products sold. Commodity hedging activity was not material to the Company's financial statements for any of the years presented.

Note 8 Earnings Per Share and Stock Options

Net Earnings Per Common Share

Net earnings less preferred dividends (net of related tax benefits) are divided by the weighted average number of common shares outstanding during the year to calculate basic net earnings per common share. Diluted net earnings per common share are calculated to give effect to stock options and assuming conversion of preferred stock (see Note 9).

Net earnings and common share balances used to calculate basic and diluted net earnings per share were as follows:

	Years ended June 30		
	2004	2003	2002
Net Earnings	**$6,481**	$5,186	$4,352
Preferred dividends, net of tax benefit	**(131)**	(125)	(124)
Net earnings available to common shareholders	**6,350**	5,061	4,228
Preferred dividends, net of tax benefit	**131**	125	124
Preferred dividend impact on funding of ESOP	**(4)**	(9)	(12)
Diluted net earnings	**6,477**	5,177	4,340

	Years ended June 30		
Shares in millions	**2004**	2003	2002
Basic weighted average common shares outstanding	**2,580.1**	2,593.2	2,594.8
Effect of dilutive securities			
Conversion of preferred shares[1]	**164.0**	170.2	177.6
Exercise of stock options[2]	**46.0**	39.2	37.5
Diluted weighted average common shares outstanding	**2,790.1**	2,802.6	2,809.9

[1] Despite being included currently in diluted net earnings per common share, the actual conversion to common stock occurs pursuant to the repayment of the ESOP debt through 2021.

[2] Approximately 38 million in 2004, 66 million in 2003 and 72 million in 2002 of the Company's outstanding stock options were not included in the diluted net earnings per share calculation because to do so would have been antidilutive (i.e., the exercise price exceeded market value).

Stock-Based Compensation

The Company has a primary stock-based compensation plan under which stock options are granted annually to key managers and directors with exercise prices equal to the market price of the underlying shares on the date of grant. Grants were made under plans approved by shareholders in 1992, 2001 and 2003. Grants issued since September 2002 are vested after three years and have a ten-year life. Grants issued from July 1998 through August 2002 are vested after three years and have a fifteen-year life, while grants issued prior to July 1998 are vested after one year and have a ten-year life. The Company also makes other minor grants to employees, for which vesting terms and option lives are not substantially different.

Millions of dollars except per share amounts

Had the provision of SFAS No. 123 expensing been applied, the Company's net earnings and earnings per common share would have been impacted as summarized in the discussion of the Company's stock-based compensation accounting policy in Note 1. In calculating the impact for options granted, the Company has estimated the fair value of each grant using the Black-Scholes option-pricing model. Assumptions are evaluated and revised, as necessary, to reflect market conditions and experience. The following assumptions were used:

Options Granted	Years ended June 30		
	2004	2003	2002
Interest rate	**3.8%**	3.9%	5.4%
Dividend yield	**1.8%**	1.8%	2.2%
Expected volatility	**20%**	20%	20%
Expected life in years	**8**	8	12

The following table summarizes stock option activity during 2004, 2003 and 2002:

Options in Thousands	June 30		
	2004	2003	2002
Outstanding, beginning of year	**259,598**	240,326	208,392
Granted	**40,866**	35,759	50,080
Jif and Crisco spin-off adjustment	**-**	-	1,622
Exercised	**(22,307)**	(13,904)	(16,297)
Canceled	**(1,864)**	(2,583)	(3,471)
Outstanding, end of year	**276,293**	259,598	240,326
Exercisable	**151,828**	118,202	92,664
Available for grant	**165,399**	203,593	229,071
Average price			
Outstanding, beginning of year	**$35.75**	$33.34	$31.82
Granted	**51.06**	45.68	35.09
Exercised	**24.88**	19.35	14.53
Outstanding, end of year	**38.85**	35.75	33.34
Exercisable, end of year	**35.39**	35.44	28.50
Weighted average fair value of options granted during the year	**12.50**	10.99	10.57

Stock options outstanding at June 30, 2004 were in the following exercise price ranges:

	Outstanding Options		
Range of Prices	Number Outstanding (Thousands)	Weighted Avg. Exercise Price	Weighted Avg. Remaining Contractual Life in Years
$16.43 to 30.11	**36,863**	**$24.07**	**2.6**
31.01 to 34.84	**95,260**	**32.72**	**11.5**
35.10 to 46.24	**82,825**	**43.70**	**6.9**
48.73 to 52.98	**61,345**	**50.69**	**9.9**

Stock options exercisable at June 30, 2004 were in the following exercise price ranges:

	Exercisable Options	
Range of Prices	Number Exercisable (Thousands)	Weighted Average Exercise Price
$16.43 to 30.11	**36,863**	**$24.07**
31.01 to 34.84	**48,426**	**31.06**
35.10 to 46.24	**43,624**	**42.36**
48.73 to 52.98	**22,915**	**49.49**

The Company repurchases common shares to mitigate the dilutive impact of options. Beyond that, the Company may make additional discretionary purchases based on cash availability, market trends and other factors.

In limited cases, the Company also issues stock appreciation rights, generally in countries where stock options are not permitted by local governments. The obligations and associated compensation expense are adjusted for changes in intrinsic value. The impact of these adjustments is not material.

Note 9 Postretirement Benefits and Employee Stock Ownership Plan

The Company offers various postretirement benefits to its employees.

Defined Contribution Retirement Plans
The most prevalent employee benefit plans offered are defined contribution plans, which cover substantially all employees in the U.S., as well as employees in certain other countries. These plans are fully funded.

Millions of dollars except per share amounts

Under the defined contribution plans, the Company generally makes contributions to participants based on individual base salaries and years of service. In the U.S., the contribution is set annually. Historically, the Company has contributed approximately 15% of total participants' annual wages and salaries.

The Company maintains The Procter & Gamble Profit Sharing Trust (Trust) and Employee Stock Ownership Plan (ESOP) to provide a portion of the funding for the U.S. defined contribution plan, as well as other retiree benefits. Operating details of the ESOP are provided at the end of this Note. The fair value of the ESOP Series A shares reduces the Company's cash contribution required to fund the U.S. defined contribution plan. Defined contribution expense, which approximates the Company's cash contribution to the plan that is funded in the subsequent year, was $274, $286 and $279 in 2004, 2003 and 2002, respectively.

Defined Benefit Retirement Plans and Other Retiree Benefits
Certain other employees, primarily outside the U.S., are covered by local defined benefit pension plans as well as other retiree benefit plans.

The Company also provides certain other retiree benefits, primarily health care and life insurance, for substantially all U.S. employees who become eligible for these benefits when they meet minimum age and service requirements. Generally, the health care plans require cost sharing with retirees and pay a stated percentage of expenses, reduced by deductibles and other coverages. These benefits primarily are funded by ESOP Series B shares, as well as certain other assets contributed by the Company.

The Medicare Prescription Drug, Improvement and Modernization Act of 2003 was signed into law on December 8, 2003. This Act introduces a Medicare prescription-drug benefit beginning in 2006 as well as a federal subsidy to sponsors of retiree health care plans that provide a benefit at least "actuarially equivalent" to the Medicare benefit. Management has concluded that the Company's plans are at least "actuarially equivalent" to the Medicare benefit and, accordingly, has included the federal subsidy from the Act in the normal year-end measurement process for other retiree benefit plans. The impact is a reduction to the benefit obligation of $195 as of June 30, 2004. The impact to net periodic pension cost and to benefits paid in future years is not expected to be material.

Obligation and Funded Status. The Company uses a June 30 measurement date for its defined benefit retirement plans and other retiree benefit plans. The following provides a reconciliation of benefit obligations, plan assets and funded status of these plans:

	Pension Benefits		Other Retiree Benefits	
Years ended June 30	**2004**	2003	**2004**	2003
Change in benefit obligation				
Benefit obligation at beginning of year[1]	**$3,543**	$2,970	**$2,914**	$2,135
Service cost	**157**	124	**89**	62
Interest cost	**204**	173	**172**	150
Participants' contributions	**14**	7	**31**	27
Amendments	**50**	(33)	**(258)**	(2)
Actuarial loss (gain)	**5**	138	**(460)**	645
Acquisitions	**590**	42	**7**	-
Curtailments and settlements	**(39)**	(29)	**(8)**	-
Special termination benefits	**12**	1	**41**	7
Currency translation	**288**	305	**5**	13
Benefit payments	**(208)**	(155)	**(133)**	(123)
Benefit obligation at end of year[1]	**4,616**	3,543	**2,400**	2,914
Change in plan assets				
Fair value of plan assets at beginning of year	**$1,558**	$1,332	**$2,277**	$2,347
Actual return on plan assets	**194**	(36)	**651**	1
Acquisitions	**185**	1	**-**	-
Employer contributions	**412**	337	**18**	25
Participants' contributions	**14**	7	**31**	27
Settlements	**(21)**	(27)	**-**	-
Currency translation	**129**	99	**(1)**	-
Benefit payments	**(208)**	(155)	**(133)**	(123)
Fair value of plan assets at end of year	**2,263**	1,558	**2,843**	2,277
Funded status	**(2,353)**	(1,985)	**443**	(637)

[1] For the pension benefit plans, the benefit obligation is the projected benefit obligation. For other retiree benefit plans, the benefit obligation is the accumulated postretirement benefit obligation.

Millions of dollars except per share amounts

| | Years ended June 30 | | | |
| | Pension Benefits | | Other Retiree Benefits | |
	2004	2003	**2004**	2003
Calculation of net amount recognized				
Funded status at end of year	**$(2,353)**	$(1,985)	**$443**	$(637)
Unrecognized net actuarial loss (gain)	**902**	930	**(344)**	435
Unrecognized transition amount	**12**	13	**-**	-
Unrecognized prior service cost	**38**	(9)	**(259)**	(2)
Net amount recognized	**(1,401)**	(1,051)	**(160)**	(204)
Classification of net amount recognized				
Prepaid benefit cost	**$253**	$173	**$1**	$2
Accrued benefit cost	**(1,872)**	(1,407)	**(161)**	(206)
Intangible asset	**75**	31	**-**	-
Accumulated other comprehensive income	**143**	152	**-**	-
Net amount recognized	**(1,401)**	(1,051)	**(160)**	(204)

The underfunding of pension benefits is primarily a function of the different funding incentives that exist outside of the U.S. In certain countries where the Company has major operations, there are no legal requirements or financial incentives provided to companies to pre-fund pension obligations. In these instances, benefit payments are typically paid directly from the Company's cash as they become due, rather than through the creation of a separate pension fund.

The accumulated benefit obligation for all defined benefit retirement plans was $3,822 and $2,850 at June 30, 2004 and June 30, 2003, respectively. Plans with accumulated benefit obligations in excess of plan assets and plans with projected benefit obligations in excess of plan assets as of June 30, consist of the following:

| | Years ended June 30 | | | |
| | Accumulated Benefit Obligation Exceeds Fair Value of Plan Assets | | Projected Benefit Obligation Exceeds Fair Value of Plan Assets | |
	2004	2003	**2004**	2003
Projected benefit obligation	**$2,809**	$2,945	**$4,059**	$3,179
Accumulated benefit obligation	**2,396**	2,310	**3,320**	2,492
Fair value of plan assets	**638**	979	**1,676**	1,186

Net Periodic Benefit Cost. Components of the net periodic benefit cost were as follows:

| | Years ended June 30 | | | | | |
| | Pension Benefits | | | Other Retiree Benefits | | |
	2004	2003	2002	**2004**	2003	2002
Service cost	**$157**	$124	$114	**$89**	$62	$49
Interest cost	**204**	173	153	**172**	150	116
Expected return on plan assets	**(153)**	(127)	(133)	**(329)**	(333)	(320)
Amortization of deferred amounts	**3**	4	7	**(1)**	(1)	(1)
Curtailment and settlement loss (gain)	**-**	5	1	**-**	-	(1)
Recognized net actuarial loss (gain)	**28**	13	9	**1**	(27)	(64)
Gross benefit cost	**239**	192	151	**(68)**	(149)	(221)
Dividends on ESOP preferred stock	**-**	-	-	**(73)**	(74)	(76)
Net periodic benefit cost	**239**	192	151	**(141)**	(223)	(297)

Millions of dollars except per share amounts

Assumptions. The Company determines its actuarial assumptions on an annual basis. These assumptions are weighted to reflect each country that may have an impact on the cost of providing retirement benefits. The weighted-average assumptions for the defined benefit and other retiree benefit calculations, as well as assumed health care cost trend rates, for the years ended June 30, are as follows:

	Years ended June 30			
	Pension Benefits		Other Retiree Benefits	
Actuarial assumptions	**2004**	2003	**2004**	2003
Assumptions used to determine benefit obligations[1]				
Discount rate	**5.2%**	5.1%	**6.1%**	5.8%
Rate of compensation increase	**3.1%**	3.1%	-	-
Assumptions used to determine net periodic pension cost[2]				
Discount rate	**5.1%**	5.6%	**5.8%**	7.0%
Expected return on plan assets	**7.4%**	7.7%	**9.5%**	9.5%
Rate of compensation increase	**3.0%**	3.5%	-	-
Assumed health care cost trend rates				
Health care cost trend rates assumed for next year[3]	-	-	**9.7%**	11.4%
Rate that the health care cost trend rate is assumed to decline to (ultimate trend rate)	-	-	**5.1%**	5.0%
Year that the rate reaches the ultimate trend rate	-	-	**2010**	2010

[1] Determined as of end of year.
[2] Determined as of beginning of year.
[3] Rate is applied to current plan costs net of Medicare; estimated initial rate for "gross eligible charges" (charges inclusive of Medicare) is 7.7% for 2004 and 8.8% for 2003.

Several factors are considered in developing the estimate for the long-term expected rate of return on plan assets. For the defined benefit plans, these include historical rates of return of broad equity and bond indices and projected long-term rates of return from pension investment consultants. The expected long-term rates of return for plan assets are 8%-9% for equities and 5%-6% bonds. The rate of return on other retiree benefit plan assets, comprised primarily of Company stock, is based on the long-term projected return of 9.5% and reflects the historical pattern of favorable returns on the Company's stock relative to broader market indices (e.g., S&P 500).

Assumed health care cost trend rates could have a significant effect on the amounts reported for the other retiree benefit plans. A one-percentage point change in assumed health care cost trend rates would have the following effects:

	One-Percentage Point Increase	One-Percentage Point Decrease
Effect on total service and interest cost components	**$51**	**$(46)**
Effect on postretirement benefit obligation	**323**	**(268)**

Plan Assets. The Company's target asset allocation for the year ending June 30, 2005 and actual asset allocation by asset category as of June 30, 2004, and 2003, are as follows:

	Target Allocation	
	Pension Benefits	Other Retiree Benefits
Asset Category	2005	2005
Equity securities[1]	64%	99%
Debt securities	32%	1%
Real estate	4%	-%
Total	**100%**	**100%**

	Plan Asset Allocation at June 30			
	Pension Benefits		Other Retiree Benefits	
Asset Category	**2004**	2003	**2004**	2003
Equity securities[1]	**64%**	62%	**99%**	99%
Debt securities	**32%**	35%	**1%**	1%
Real estate	**4%**	3%	**-%**	-%
Total	**100%**	**100%**	**100%**	**100%**

[1] Equity securities for other retiree plan assets include Company stock, net of Series B ESOP debt (see Note 6), of $2,744 and $2,182, as of June 30, 2004 and 2003, respectively.

Millions of dollars except per share amounts

The Company's investment objective for defined benefit plan assets is to meet the plans' benefit obligations, while minimizing the potential for future required Company plan contributions. The investment strategies focus on asset class diversification, liquidity to meet benefit payments and an appropriate balance of long-term investment return and risk. Target ranges for asset allocations are determined by matching the actuarial projections of the plans' future liabilities and benefit payments with expected long-term rates of return on the assets, taking into account investment return volatility and correlations across asset classes. Plan assets are diversified across several investment managers and are generally invested in liquid funds that are selected to track broad market equity and bond indices. Investment risk is carefully controlled with plan assets rebalanced to target allocations on a periodic basis and continual monitoring of investment managers performance relative to the investment guidelines established with each investment manager.

Cash Flows. Management's best estimate of its cash requirements for the defined benefit plans and other retiree benefit plans for the year ending June 30, 2005 is $237 and $20, respectively. For the defined benefit plans, this is comprised of expected benefit payments of $71, which are paid directly to participants of unfunded plans from employer assets, as well as expected contributions to funded plans of $166. For other retiree benefit plans, this is comprised of expected contributions that will be used directly for benefit payments. Expected contributions are dependent on many variables, including the variability of the market value of the assets as compared to the obligation and other market or regulatory conditions. In addition, the Company takes into consideration its business investment opportunities and resulting cash requirements. Accordingly, actual funding may differ greatly from current estimates.

Total benefit payments expected to be paid to participants, which include payments funded from the Company's assets, as discussed above, as well as payments paid from the plans are as follows:

	Years ended June 30	
	Pension Benefits	Other Retiree Benefits
Expected benefit payments		
2005	$191	$144
2006	177	152
2007	193	166
2008	207	176
2009	207	185
2010 – 2014	1,180	1,058

Employee Stock Ownership Plan

The Company maintains the ESOP to provide funding for certain employee benefits discussed in the preceding paragraphs.

The ESOP borrowed $1.00 billion in 1989 and the proceeds were used to purchase Series A ESOP Convertible Class A Preferred Stock to fund a portion of the defined contribution retirement plan in the U.S. Principal and interest requirements were paid by the Trust from dividends on the preferred shares and from advances from the Company. The final payment for the original borrowing of $1.00 billion was made in 2004 and the remaining debt of the ESOP consists of amounts owed to the Company. Each share is convertible at the option of the holder into one share of the Company's common stock. The dividend for the current year was $0.93 per share. The liquidation value is $6.82 per share.

In 1991, the ESOP borrowed an additional $1.00 billion. The proceeds were used to purchase Series B ESOP Convertible Class A Preferred Stock to fund a portion of retiree health care benefits. These shares are considered plan assets, net of the associated debt, of the Other Retiree Benefits plan discussed above. Debt service requirements are funded by preferred stock dividends and cash contributions from the Company. Each share is convertible at the option of the holder into one share of the Company's common stock. The dividend for the current year was $1.02 per share. The liquidation value is $12.96 per share.

As permitted by Statement of Position (SOP) 93-6, "Employers Accounting for Employee Stock Ownership Plans," the Company has elected, where applicable, to continue its practices, which are based on SOP 76-3, "Accounting Practices for Certain Employee Stock Ownership Plans." ESOP debt, which is guaranteed by the Company, is recorded as debt (see Note 6). Preferred shares issued to the ESOP are offset by the reserve for ESOP debt retirement in the Consolidated Balance Sheets and the Consolidated Statements of Shareholders' Equity. Interest incurred on the ESOP debt is recorded as interest expense. Dividends on all preferred shares, net of related tax benefits, are charged to retained earnings.

Millions of dollars except per share amounts

As required by SOP 76-3, the preferred shares of the ESOP are allocated based on debt service requirements, net of advances made by the Company to the Trust. The number of preferred shares outstanding at June 30, was as follows:

Shares in Thousands	June 30		
	2004	2003	2002
Allocated	**62,511**	64,492	66,191
Unallocated	**28,296**	31,534	35,374
Total Series A	**90,807**	96,026	101,565
Allocated	**21,399**	20,648	19,738
Unallocated	**48,528**	50,718	52,908
Total Series B	**69,927**	71,366	72,646

For purposes of calculating diluted net earnings per common share, the preferred shares held by the ESOP are considered converted from inception. Diluted net earnings are calculated assuming that all preferred shares are converted to common, and therefore are adjusted to reflect the incremental ESOP funding that would be required due to the difference in dividend rate between preferred and common shares (see Note 8).

Note 10 Income Taxes

Under SFAS No. 109, "Accounting for Income Taxes," income taxes are recognized for the amount of taxes payable for the current year and for the impact of deferred tax liabilities and assets, which represent future tax consequences of events that have been recognized differently in the financial statements than for tax purposes. Deferred tax assets and liabilities are established using the enacted statutory tax rates and are adjusted for changes in such rates in the period of change. Earnings before income taxes consisted of the following:

	Years ended June 30		
	2004	2003	2002
United States	**$6,023**	$4,920	$4,411
International	**3,327**	2,610	1,972
	9,350	7,530	6,383

The income tax provision consisted of the following:

	Years ended June 30		
	2004	2003	2002
Current Tax Expense			
U.S. Federal	**$1,508**	$1,595	$975
International	**830**	588	551
U.S. State and Local	**116**	98	116
	2,454	2,281	1,642
Deferred Tax Expense			
U.S. Federal	**348**	125	571
International and other	**67**	(62)	(182)
	415	63	389
	2,869	2,344	2,031

The Company's effective income tax rate was 30.7%, 31.1% and 31.8% in 2004, 2003 and 2002, respectively, compared to the U.S. statutory rate of 35.0%. The country mix impacts of foreign operations reduced the Company's effective tax rate to a larger degree in 2004 than the previous fiscal years: 4.1% in 2004, 3.8% in 2003 and 3.1% in 2002. The Company's higher effective tax rate in 2002 also reflected the impact of restructuring costs. Taxes impacted shareholders' equity with credits of $351 and $361 for the years ended June 30, 2004 and 2003, respectively. These primarily relate to the tax effects of net investment hedges and tax benefits from the exercise of stock options.

The Company has undistributed earnings of foreign subsidiaries of $16.75 billion at June 30, 2004, for which deferred taxes have not been provided. Such earnings are considered indefinitely invested in the foreign subsidiaries. If such earnings were repatriated, additional tax expense may result, although the calculation of such additional taxes is not practicable.

Millions of dollars except per share amounts

Deferred income tax assets and liabilities were comprised of the following:

	June 30	
	2004	2003
Deferred Tax Assets		
Unrealized loss on financial instruments	**$381**	$287
Loss and other carryforwards	**365**	311
Advance payments	**226**	182
Other postretirement benefits	**95**	93
Other	**1,169**	820
Valuation allowances	**(342)**	(158)
	1,894	1,535
Deferred Tax Liabilities		
Fixed assets	**(1,350)**	(1,175)
Goodwill and other intangible assets	**(1,281)**	(410)
Other	**(352)**	(287)
	(2,983)	(1,872)

Net operating loss carryforwards were $1,398 and $1,222 at June 30, 2004 and June 30, 2003, respectively. If unused, $299 will expire between 2005 and 2014. The remainder, totaling $1,099 at June 30, 2004, may be carried forward indefinitely.

Note 11 Commitments and Contingencies

Guarantees

In conjunction with certain transactions, primarily divestitures, the Company may provide routine indemnifications (e.g., retention of previously existing environmental, tax and employee liabilities) whose terms range in duration and often are not explicitly defined. Generally, the maximum obligation under such indemnifications is not explicitly stated and, as a result, the overall amount of these obligations cannot be reasonably estimated. Other than obligations recorded as liabilities at the time of divestiture, historically the Company has not made significant payments for these indemnifications. The Company believes that if it were to incur a loss in any of these matters, the loss would not have a material effect on the Company's financial condition or results of operations.

In certain situations, the Company guarantees loans for suppliers and customers. The total amount of guarantees issued under such arrangements is not material.

Off-Balance Sheet Arrangements

The Company does not have off-balance sheet financing arrangements, including variable interest entities, under FASB Interpretation No. 46, "Consolidation of Variable Interest Entities," that have a material impact on the financial statements.

Purchase Commitments

The Company has purchase commitments for materials, supplies, services and property, plant and equipment as part of the normal course of business. Due to the proprietary nature of many of the Company's materials and processes, certain supply contracts contain penalty provisions for early termination. The Company does not expect potential payments under these provisions to materially affect results of operations or its financial condition in any individual year.

Operating Leases

The Company leases certain property and equipment for varying periods under operating leases. Future minimum rental commitments under noncancellable operating leases are as follows: 2005 - $186; 2006 - $150; 2007 - $134; 2008 - $99; 2009 - $86; and $265 thereafter.

Litigation

The Company is subject to various lawsuits and claims with respect to matters such as governmental regulations, income taxes and other actions arising out of the normal course of business. The Company is also subject to contingencies pursuant to environmental laws and regulations that in the future may require the Company to take action to correct the effects on the environment of prior manufacturing and waste disposal practices. Accrued environmental liabilities for remediation and closure costs were $36 and $34 at June 30, 2004 and 2003, respectively. Current year expenditures were not material.

While considerable uncertainty exists, in the opinion of management and Company counsel, the ultimate liabilities resulting from such lawsuits and claims will not materially affect the Company's financial condition.

Millions of dollars except per share amounts

Note 12 Segment Information

The Company is organized into five product-based Global Business Units. The segments, which are generally determined by the product type and end-point user benefits offered, manufacture and market products as follows:

- Fabric and Home Care includes laundry detergents, dish care, fabric enhancers and surface cleaners.
- Beauty Care includes retail and professional hair care, skin care, feminine care, cosmetics, fine fragrances and personal cleansing.
- Baby and Family Care includes diapers, baby wipes, bath tissue and kitchen towels.
- Health Care includes oral care, personal health care, pharmaceuticals and pet health and nutrition.
- Snacks and Beverages includes coffee, snacks, commercial services and juice. In August 2004, the Company divested the juice business.

Effective July 1, 2004, the Company realigned its businesses and associated management responsibilities to three business units: Beauty Care; Health, Baby and Family Care; and Household Care, which will include the current Fabric and Home Care business as well as the Snacks and Beverages business.

The accounting policies of the operating segments are generally the same as those described in Note 1, Summary of Significant Accounting Policies. Differences from these policies and U.S. GAAP primarily reflect: income taxes, which are reflected in the business segments using estimated local statutory rates; the recording of fixed assets at historical exchange rates in certain high inflation economies; and the treatment of unconsolidated investees. Unconsolidated investees are managed as integral parts of the Company's business units for management and segment reporting purposes. Accordingly, these partially owned operations are reflected as consolidated subsidiaries in segment results, with 100% recognition of the individual income statement line items through before-tax earnings, while after-tax earnings are adjusted to reflect only the Company's ownership percentage. Entries to eliminate the individual revenues and expenses, adjusting the method of accounting to the equity method as required by U.S. GAAP, are included in Corporate.

Corporate includes certain operating and non-operating activities that are not reflected in the operating results used internally to measure and evaluate the operating segments, as well as eliminations to adjust management reporting principles to U.S. GAAP. Operating activities in Corporate include the results of incidental businesses managed at the corporate level along with the elimination of individual revenues and expenses generated by companies over which the Company exerts significant influence, but does not control. Operating elements also comprise intangible asset amortization, certain employee benefit costs and other general corporate items. The non-operating elements include financing and investing activities. In addition, Corporate includes the historical results of certain divested businesses of the former Food and Beverage segment. Corporate assets primarily include cash, investment securities, goodwill and other non-current intangible assets.

The Company had net sales in the U.S. of $23,688, $21,853 and $21,198 for the years ended June 30, 2004, 2003 and 2002, respectively. Assets in the U.S. totaled $23,687 and $23,424 as of June 30, 2004 and 2003, respectively.

The Company's largest customer, Wal-Mart Stores, Inc. and its affiliates, accounted for 17%, 18% and 17% of consolidated net sales in 2004, 2003 and 2002, respectively. These sales occurred primarily in the U.S.

Millions of dollars except per share amounts

		Fabric and Home Care	Beauty Care	Baby and Family Care	Health Care	Snacks and Beverages	Corporate	Total
Net Sales	**2004**	**$13,868**	**$17,122**	**$10,718**	**$6,991**	**$3,482**	**$(774)**	**$51,407**
	2003	12,560	12,221	9,933	5,796	3,238	(371)	43,377
	2002	11,618	10,723	9,233	4,979	3,249	436	40,238
Before-Tax Earnings	**2004**	**3,287**	**3,662**	**1,623**	**1,448**	**557**	**(1,227)**	**9,350**
	2003	3,080	2,899	1,448	1,034	460	(1,391)	7,530
	2002	2,728	2,354	1,272	795	476	(1,242)	6,383
Net Earnings	**2004**	**2,203**	**2,422**	**996**	**962**	**363**	**(465)**	**6,481**
	2003	2,059	1,984	882	706	306	(751)	5,186
	2002	1,831	1,610	738	521	303	(651)	4,352
Depreciation and Amortization	**2004**	**331**	**393**	**550**	**153**	**119**	**187**	**1,733**
	2003	332	345	558	156	125	187	1,703
	2002	326	339	503	163	121	241	1,693
Total Assets	**2004**	**5,512**	**7,869**	**7,229**	**2,639**	**1,831**	**31,968**	**57,048**
	2003	5,174	5,389	6,974	2,642	2,040	21,487	43,706
Capital Expenditures	**2004**	**538**	**433**	**714**	**164**	**134**	**41**	**2,024**
	2003	357	343	548	144	125	(35)	1,482
	2002	368	354	702	158	125	(28)	1,679

Note 13 Quarterly Results (Unaudited)

		Quarters Ended				
		Sept 30	Dec 31	Mar 31	Jun 30	Total Year
Net Sales	**2003–2004**	**$12,195**	**$13,221**	**$13,029**	**$12,962**	**$51,407**
	2002–2003	10,796	11,005	10,656	10,920	43,377
Operating Income	**2003–2004**	**2,643**	**2,742**	**2,303**	**2,139**	**9,827**
	2002–2003	2,179	2,248	1,957	1,469	7,853
Net Earnings	**2003–2004**	**1,761**	**1,818**	**1,528**	**1,374**	**6,481**
	2002–2003	1,464	1,494	1,273	955	5,186
Diluted Net Earnings Per Common Share[1]	**2003–2004**	**$0.63**	**$0.65**	**$0.55**	**$0.50**	**$2.32**
	2002–2003	0.52	0.53	0.46	0.34	1.85

[1] Restated for two-for-one stock split effective May 21, 2004.

Millions of dollars except per share amounts

Financial Summary (Unaudited)

	2004	2003	2002	2001	2000	1999	1998	1997	1996
Net Sales	$51,407	$43,377	$40,238	$ 39,244	$39,951	$38,125	$37,154	$35,764	$35,284
Operating Income	9,827	7,853	6,678	4,736	5,954	6,253	6,055	5,488	4,815
Net Earnings	6,481	5,186	4,352	2,922	3,542	3,763	3,780	3,415	3,046
Net Earnings Margin	12.6%	12.0%	10.8%	7.4%	8.9%	9.9%	10.2%	9.5%	8.6%
Basic Net Earnings Per									
Common Share[1]	$2.46	$1.95	$1.63	$1.08	$1.30	$1.38	$1.37	$1.22	$1.07
Diluted Net Earnings									
Per Common Share[1]	2.32	1.85	1.54	1.03	1.23	1.29	1.28	1.14	1.00
Dividends Per									
Common Share[1]	0.93	0.82	0.76	0.70	0.64	0.57	0.51	0.45	0.40
Restructuring									
Program Charges[2]	$-	$751	$958	$1,850	$814	$481	$-	$-	$-
Research and									
Development Expense	1,802	1,665	1,601	1,769	1,899	1,726	1,546	1,469	1,399
Advertising Expense	5,504	4,373	3,773	3,612	3,793	3,639	3,801	3,574	3,374
Total Assets	57,048	43,706	40,776	34,387	34,366	32,192	31,042	27,598	27,762
Capital Expenditures	2,024	1,482	1,679	2,486	3,018	2,828	2,559	2,129	2,179
Long-Term Debt	12,554	11,475	11,201	9,792	9,012	6,265	5,774	4,159	4,678
Shareholders' Equity	17,278	16,186	13,706	12,010	12,287	12,058	12,236	12,046	11,722

[1] Restated for two-for-one stock split effective May 21, 2004.
[2] Restructuring program charges, on an after-tax basis, totaled $538, $706, $1,475, $688 and $385 for 2003, 2002, 2001, 2000 and 1999 respectively.

QUESTIONS

1. How does information from the balance sheet help users of the financial statements?

2. What is meant by solvency? What information in the balance sheet can be used to assess a company's solvency?

3. A recent financial magazine indicated that the airline industry has poor financial flexibility. What is meant by financial flexibility, and why is it important?

4. Discuss at least two situations in which estimates could affect the usefulness of information in the balance sheet.

5. Safin Company reported an increase in inventories in the past year. Discuss the effect of this change on the current ratio (current assets ÷ current liabilities). What does this tell a statement user about Safin Company's liquidity?

6. What is meant by liquidity? Rank the following assets from one to five in order of liquidity.

(a) Goodwill.

(b) Inventories.

(c) Buildings.

(d) Short-term investments.

(e) Accounts receivable.

7. What are the major limitations of the balance sheet as a source of information?

8. Discuss at least two items that are important to the value of companies like **Intel** or **IBM** but that are not recorded in their balance sheets. What are some reasons why these items are not recorded in the balance sheet?

9. How does separating current assets from property, plant, and equipment in the balance sheet help analysts?

10. In its December 31, 2007, balance sheet Oakley Corporation reported as an asset, "Net notes and accounts receivable, $7,100,000." What other disclosures are necessary?

11. Should available-for-sale securities always be reported as a current asset? Explain.

12. What is the relationship between current assets and current liabilities?

13. The New York Knicks, Inc. sold 10,000 season tickets at $2,000 each. By December 31, 2007, 18 of the 40 home games had been played. What amount should be reported as a current liability at December 31, 2007?

14. What is working capital? How does working capital relate to the operating cycle?

15. In what section of the balance sheet should the following items appear, and what balance sheet terminology would you use?

(a) Treasury stock (recorded at cost).

(b) Checking account at bank.

(c) Land (held as an investment).

(d) Sinking fund.

(e) Unamortized premium on bonds payable.

(f) Copyrights.

(g) Pension fund assets.

(h) Premium on capital stock.

(i) Long-term investments (pledged against bank loans payable).

16. Where should the following items be shown on the balance sheet, if shown at all?

(a) Allowance for doubtful accounts receivable.

(b) Merchandise held on consignment.

(c) Advances received on sales contract.

(d) Cash surrender value of life insurance.

(e) Land.

(f) Merchandise out on consignment.

(g) Franchises.

(h) Accumulated depreciation of plant and equipment.

(i) Materials in transit—purchased f.o.b. destination.

17. State the generally accepted accounting principle applicable to the balance sheet valuation of each of the following assets.

(a) Trade accounts receivable.

(b) Land.

(c) Inventories.

(d) Trading securities (common stock of other companies).

(e) Prepaid expenses.

18. Refer to the definition of assets on page 173. Discuss how a leased building might qualify as an asset of the lessee (tenant) under this definition.

19. Christine Agazzi says, "Retained earnings should be reported as an asset, since it is earnings which are reinvested in the business." How would you respond to Agazzi?

20. The creditors of Nick Anderson Company agree to accept promissory notes for the amount of its indebtedness with a proviso that two-thirds of the annual profits must be applied to their liquidation. How should these notes be reported on the balance sheet of the issuing company? Give a reason for your answer.

21. What are some of the techniques of disclosure for the balance sheet?

22. What is a "Summary of Significant Accounting Policies"?

23. What types of contractual obligations must be disclosed in great detail in the notes to the balance sheet? Why do you think these detailed provisions should be disclosed?

24. What is the profession's recommendation in regard to the use of the term "surplus"? Explain.

25. What is the purpose of a statement of cash flows? How does it differ from a balance sheet and an income statement?

26. The net income for the year for Won Long, Inc. is $750,000, but the statement of cash flows reports that the cash provided by operating activities is $640,000. What might account for the difference?

27. Net income for the year for Jenkins, Inc. was $750,000, but the statement of cash flows reports that cash provided by operating activities was $860,000. What might account for the difference?

28. Differentiate between operating activities, investing activities, and financing activities.

29. Each of the following items must be considered in preparing a statement of cash flows. Indicate where each item is to be reported in the statement, if at all. Assume that net income is reported as $90,000.

(a) Accounts receivable increased from $32,000 to $39,000 from the beginning to the end of the year.

(b) During the year, 10,000 shares of preferred stock with a par value of $100 a share were issued at $115 per share.

(c) Depreciation expense amounted to $14,000, and bond premium amortization amounted to $5,000.

(d) Land increased from $10,000 to $30,000.

30. Marker Co. has net cash provided by operating activities of $900,000. Its average current liabilities for the period are $1,000,000, and its average total liabilities are $1,500,000. Comment on the company's liquidity and financial flexibility, given this information.

31. Net income for the year for Hatfield, Inc. was $750,000, but the statement of cash flows reports that cash provided by operating activities was $860,000. Hatfield also reported capital expenditures of $75,000 and paid dividends in the amount of $20,000. Compute Hatfield's free cash flow.

32. What is the purpose of a free cash flow analysis?

BRIEF EXERCISES

(LO 3) **BE5-1** La Bouche Corporation has the following accounts included in its December 31, 2007, trial balance: Accounts Receivable $110,000; Inventories $290,000; Allowance for Doubtful Accounts $8,000; Patents $72,000; Prepaid Insurance $9,500; Accounts Payable $77,000; Cash $27,000. Prepare the current assets section of the balance sheet listing the accounts in proper sequence.

(LO 3) **BE5-2** Jodi Corporation's adjusted trial balance contained the following asset accounts at December 31, 2007: Cash $7,000; Land $40,000; Patents $12,500; Accounts Receivable $90,000; Prepaid Insurance $5,200; Inventory $34,000; Allowance for Doubtful Accounts $4,000; Trading Securities $11,000. Prepare the current assets section of the balance sheet, listing the accounts in proper sequence.

(LO 3) **BE5-3** Included in Goo Goo Dolls Company's December 31, 2007, trial balance are the following accounts: Prepaid Rent $5,200; Held-to-Maturity Securities $61,000; Unearned Fees $17,000; Land Held for Investment $39,000; Long-term Receivables $42,000. Prepare the long-term investments section of the balance sheet.

(LO 3) **BE5-4** Adam Ant Company's December 31, 2007, trial balance includes the following accounts: Inventories $120,000; Buildings $207,000; Accumulated Depreciation–Equipment $19,000; Equipment $190,000; Land Held for Investment $46,000; Accumulated Depreciation–Buildings $45,000; Land $61,000; Timberland $70,000. Prepare the property, plant, and equipment section of the balance sheet.

(LO 3) **BE5-5** Mason Corporation has the following accounts included in its December 31, 2007, trial balance: Trading Securities $21,000; Goodwill $150,000; Prepaid Insurance $12,000; Patents $220,000; Franchises $110,000. Prepare the intangible assets section of the balance sheet.

(LO 3) **BE5-6** Mickey Snyder Corporation's adjusted trial balance contained the following asset accounts at December 31, 2007: Prepaid Rent $12,000; Goodwill $40,000; Franchise Fees Receivable $2,000; Franchises $47,000; Patents $33,000; Trademarks $10,000. Prepare the intangible assets section of the balance sheet.

(LO 3) **BE5-7** John Hawk Corporation's adjusted trial balance contained the following liability accounts at December 31, 2007. Bonds Payable (due in 3 years) $100,000; Accounts Payable $72,000; Notes Payable (due in 90 days) $12,500; Accrued Salaries $4,000; Income Taxes Payable $7,000. Prepare the current liabilities section of the balance sheet.

(LO 3) **BE5-8** Included in Ewing Company's December 31, 2007, trial balance are the following accounts: Accounts Payable $240,000; Pension Liability $375,000; Discount on Bonds Payable $24,000; Advances from Customers $41,000; Bonds Payable $400,000; Wages Payable $27,000; Interest Payable $12,000; Income Taxes Payable $29,000. Prepare the current liabilities section of the balance sheet.

(LO 3) **BE5-9** Use the information presented in BE5–8 for Ewing Company to prepare the long-term liabilities section of the balance sheet.

(LO 3) **BE5-10** Kevin Flynn Corporation's adjusted trial balance contained the following accounts at December 31, 2007: Retained Earnings $120,000; Common Stock $700,000; Bonds Payable $100,000; Additional Paid-in Capital $200,000; Goodwill $55,000; Accumulated Other Comprehensive Loss $150,000. Prepare the stockholders' equity section of the balance sheet.

(LO 3) **BE5-11** Young Company's December 31, 2007, trial balance includes the following accounts: Investment in Common Stock $70,000; Retained Earnings $114,000; Trademarks $31,000; Preferred Stock $172,000; Common Stock $55,000; Deferred Income Taxes $88,000; Additional Paid-in Capital $174,000. Prepare the stockholders' equity section of the balance sheet.

(LO 8) **BE5-12** Midwest Beverage Company reported the following items in the most recent year.

Net income	$40,000
Dividends paid	5,000
Increase in accounts receivable	10,000
Increase in accounts payable	5,000
Purchase of equipment (capital expenditure)	8,000
Depreciation expense	4,000
Issue of notes payable	20,000

Compute net cash provided by operating activities, the net change in cash during the year, and free cash flow.

(LO 8) **BE5-13** Kes Company reported 2007 net income of $151,000. During 2007, accounts receivable increased by $13,000 and accounts payable increased by $9,500. Depreciation expense was $39,000. Prepare the cash flows from operating activities section of the statement of cash flows.

(LO 8) **BE5-14** Yorkis Perez Corporation engaged in the following cash transactions during 2007.

Sale of land and building	$181,000
Purchase of treasury stock	40,000
Purchase of land	37,000
Payment of cash dividend	85,000
Purchase of equipment	53,000
Issuance of common stock	147,000
Retirement of bonds	100,000

Compute the net cash provided (used) by investing activities.

(LO 8) **BE5-15** Use the information presented in BE5-14 for Yorkis Perez Corporation to compute the net cash used (provided) by financing activities.

(LO 9) **BE5-16** Using the information in BE5-14, determine Yorkis Perez's free cash flow, assuming that it reported net cash provided by operating activities of $400,000.

EXERCISES

(LO 2, 3) **E5-1** **(Balance Sheet Classifications)** Presented below are a number of balance sheet accounts of Deep Blue Something, Inc.

    (a) Investment in Preferred Stock.
    (b) Treasury Stock.
    (c) Common Stock.
    (d) Cash Dividends Payable.
    (e) Accumulated Depreciation.
    (f) Warehouse in Process of Construction.
    (g) Petty Cash.

    (h) Accrued Interest on Notes Payable.
    (i) Deficit.
    (j) Trading Securities.
    (k) Income Taxes Payable.
    (l) Unearned Subscription Revenue.
    (m) Work in Process.
    (n) Accrued Vacation Pay.

Instructions
For each of the accounts above, indicate the proper balance sheet classification. In the case of borderline items, indicate the additional information that would be required to determine the proper classification.

(LO 2, 3) **E5-2** **(Classification of Balance Sheet Accounts)** Presented on the next page are the captions of Faulk Company's balance sheet.

(a)	Current assets.	**(f)**	Current liabilities.
(b)	Investments.	**(g)**	Non-current liabilities.
(c)	Property, plant, and equipment.	**(h)**	Capital stock.
(d)	Intangible assets.	**(i)**	Additional paid-in capital.
(e)	Other assets.	**(j)**	Retained earnings.

Instructions

Indicate by letter where each of the following items would be classified.

1.	Preferred stock.	**11.**	Cash surrender value of life insurance.
2.	Goodwill.	**12.**	Notes payable (due next year).
3.	Wages payable.	**13.**	Office supplies.
4.	Trade accounts payable.	**14.**	Common stock.
5.	Buildings.	**15.**	Land.
6.	Trading securities.	**16.**	Bond sinking fund.
7.	Current portion of long-term debt.	**17.**	Merchandise inventory.
8.	Premium on bonds payable.	**18.**	Prepaid insurance.
9.	Allowance for doubtful accounts.	**19.**	Bonds payable.
10.	Accounts receivable.	**20.**	Taxes payable.

(LO 2, 3) **E5-3 (Classification of Balance Sheet Accounts)** Assume that Fielder Enterprises uses the following headings on its balance sheet.

(a)	Current assets.	**(f)**	Current liabilities.
(b)	Investments.	**(g)**	Long-term liabilities.
(c)	Property, plant, and equipment.	**(h)**	Capital stock.
(d)	Intangible assets.	**(i)**	Paid-in capital in excess of par.
(e)	Other assets.	**(j)**	Retained earnings.

Instructions

Indicate by letter how each of the following usually should be classified. If an item should appear in a note to the financial statements, use the letter "N" to indicate this fact. If an item need not be reported at all on the balance sheet, use the letter "X."

1.	Unexpired insurance.	**12.**	Twenty-year issue of bonds payable that will mature within the next year. (No sinking fund exists, and refunding is not planned.)
2.	Stock owned in affiliated companies.		
3.	Unearned subscriptions revenue.		
4.	Advances to suppliers.	**13.**	Machinery retired from use and held for sale.
5.	Unearned rent revenue.	**14.**	Fully depreciated machine still in use.
6.	Preferred stock.	**15.**	Accrued interest on bonds payable.
7.	Premium on preferred stock.	**16.**	Salaries that company budget shows will be paid to employees within the next year.
8.	Copyrights.		
9.	Petty cash fund.	**17.**	Discount on bonds payable. (Assume related to bonds payable in No. 12.)
10.	Sales tax payable.		
11.	Accrued interest on notes receivable.	**18.**	Accumulated depreciation.

(LO 2, 3) **E5-4 (Preparation of a Classified Balance Sheet)** Assume that Denis Savard Inc. has the following accounts at the end of the current year.

1.	Common Stock.	**14.**	Accumulated Depreciation—Buildings.
2.	Discount on Bonds Payable.	**15.**	Cash Restricted for Plant Expansion.
3.	Treasury Stock (at cost).	**16.**	Land Held for Future Plant Site.
4.	Note Payable, short-term.	**17.**	Allowance for Doubtful Accounts— Accounts Receivable.
5.	Raw Materials.		
6.	Preferred Stock Investments—Long-term.	**18.**	Retained Earnings.
7.	Unearned Rent Revenue.	**19.**	Premium on Common Stock.
8.	Work in Process.	**20.**	Unearned Subscriptions Revenue.
9.	Copyrights.	**21.**	Receivables—Officers (due in one year).
10.	Buildings.	**22.**	Finished Goods.
11.	Notes Receivable (short-term).	**23.**	Accounts Receivable.
12.	Cash.	**24.**	Bonds Payable (due in 4 years).
13.	Accrued Salaries Payable.		

Instructions

Prepare a classified balance sheet in good form. (No monetary amounts are necessary.)

(LO 3) **E5-5** **(Preparation of a Corrected Balance Sheet)** Uhura Company has decided to expand its operations. The bookkeeper recently completed the balance sheet presented below in order to obtain additional funds for expansion.

UHURA COMPANY
BALANCE SHEET
FOR THE YEAR ENDED 2007

Current assets	
Cash	$230,000
Accounts receivable (net)	340,000
Inventories at lower of average cost or market	401,000
Trading securities—at cost (fair value $120,000)	140,000
Property, plant, and equipment	
Building (net)	570,000
Office equipment (net)	160,000
Land held for future use	175,000
Intangible assets	
Goodwill	80,000
Cash surrender value of life insurance	90,000
Prepaid expenses	12,000
Current liabilities	
Accounts payable	135,000
Notes payable (due next year)	125,000
Pension obligation	82,000
Rent payable	49,000
Premium on bonds payable	53,000
Long-term liabilities	
Bonds payable	500,000
Stockholders' equity	
Common stock, $1.00 par, authorized	
400,000 shares, issued 290,000	290,000
Additional paid-in capital	160,000
Retained earnings	?

Instructions

Prepare a revised balance sheet given the available information. Assume that the accumulated depreciation balance for the buildings is $160,000 and for the office equipment, $105,000. The allowance for doubtful accounts has a balance of $17,000. The pension obligation is considered a long-term liability.

(LO 2, 3) **E5-6** **(Corrections of a Balance Sheet)** The bookkeeper for Geronimo Company has prepared the following balance sheet as of July 31, 2007.

GERONIMO COMPANY
BALANCE SHEET
AS OF JULY 31, 2007

Cash	$ 69,000	Notes and accounts payable	$ 44,000
Accounts receivable (net)	40,500	Long-term liabilities	75,000
Inventories	60,000	Stockholders' equity	155,500
Equipment (net)	84,000		$274,500
Patents	21,000		
	$274,500		

The following additional information is provided.

1. Cash includes $1,200 in a petty cash fund and $15,000 in a bond sinking fund.
2. The net accounts receivable balance is comprised of the following three items: (a) accounts receivable—debit balances $52,000; (b) accounts receivable—credit balances $8,000; (c) allowance for doubtful accounts $3,500.
3. Merchandise inventory costing $5,300 was shipped out on consignment on July 31, 2007. The ending inventory balance does not include the consigned goods. Receivables in the amount of $5,300 were recognized on these consigned goods.

4. Equipment had a cost of $112,000 and an accumulated depreciation balance of $28,000.
5. Taxes payable of $6,000 were accrued on July 31. Geronimo Company, however, had set up a cash fund to meet this obligation. This cash fund was not included in the cash balance, but was offset against the taxes payable amount.

Instructions

Prepare a corrected classified balance sheet as of July 31, 2007, from the available information, adjusting the account balances using the additional information.

(LO 3) **E5-7 (Current Assets Section of the Balance Sheet)** Presented below are selected accounts of Yasunari Kawabata Company at December 31, 2007.

Finished Goods	$ 52,000	Cost of Goods Sold	$2,100,000
Revenue Received in Advance	90,000	Notes Receivable	40,000
Equipment	253,000	Accounts Receivable	161,000
Work-in-Process	34,000	Raw Materials	207,000
Cash	37,000	Supplies Expense	60,000
Short-term Investments in Stock	31,000	Allowance for Doubtful Accounts	12,000
Customer Advances	36,000	Licenses	18,000
Cash Restricted for Plant Expansion	50,000	Additional Paid-in Capital	88,000
		Treasury Stock	22,000

The following additional information is available.

1. Inventories are valued at lower of cost or market using LIFO.
2. Equipment is recorded at cost. Accumulated depreciation, computed on a straight-line basis, is $50,600.
3. The short-term investments have a fair value of $29,000. (Assume they are trading securities.)
4. The notes receivable are due April 30, 2009, with interest receivable every April 30. The notes bear interest at 6%. (*Hint:* Accrue interest due on December 31, 2007.)
5. The allowance for doubtful accounts applies to the accounts receivable. Accounts receivable of $50,000 are pledged as collateral on a bank loan.
6. Licenses are recorded net of accumulated amortization of $14,000.
7. Treasury stock is recorded at cost.

Instructions

Prepare the current assets section of Yasunari Kawabata Company's December 31, 2007, balance sheet, with appropriate disclosures.

(LO 2) **E5-8 (Current vs. Long-term Liabilities)** Frederic Chopin Corporation is preparing its December 31, 2007, balance sheet. The following items may be reported as either a current or long-term liability.

1. On December 15, 2007, Chopin declared a cash dividend of $2.50 per share to stockholders of record on December 31. The dividend is payable on January 15, 2008. Chopin has issued 1,000,000 shares of common stock, of which 50,000 shares are held in treasury.
2. At December 31, bonds payable of $100,000,000 are outstanding. The bonds pay 12% interest every September 30 and mature in installments of $25,000,000 every September 30, beginning September 30, 2008.
3. At December 31, 2006, customer advances were $12,000,000. During 2007, Chopin collected $30,000,000 of customer advances, and advances of $25,000,000 were earned.

Instructions

For each item above indicate the dollar amounts to be reported as a current liability and as a long-term liability, if any.

(LO 2, 3) **E5-9 (Current Assets and Current Liabilities)** The current assets and current liabilities sections of the balance sheet of Allessandro Scarlatti Company appear as follows.

ALLESSANDRO SCARLATTI COMPANY
BALANCE SHEET (PARTIAL)
DECEMBER 31, 2007

Cash		$ 40,000	Accounts payable	$ 61,000
Accounts receivable	$89,000		Notes payable	67,000
Less: Allowance for				$128,000
doubtful accounts	7,000	82,000		
Inventories		171,000		
Prepaid expenses		9,000		
		$302,000		

The following errors in the corporation's accounting have been discovered:

1. January 2008 cash disbursements entered as of December 2007 included payments of accounts payable in the amount of $39,000, on which a cash discount of 2% was taken.
2. The inventory included $27,000 of merchandise that had been received at December 31 but for which no purchase invoices had been received or entered. Of this amount, $12,000 had been received on consignment; the remainder was purchased f.o.b. destination, terms 2/10, n/30.
3. Sales for the first four days in January 2008 in the amount of $30,000 were entered in the sales book as of December 31, 2007. Of these, $21,500 were sales on account and the remainder were cash sales.
4. Cash, not including cash sales, collected in January 2008 and entered as of December 31, 2007, totaled $35,324. Of this amount, $23,324 was received on account after cash discounts of 2% had been deducted; the remainder represented the proceeds of a bank loan.

Instructions

(a) Restate the current assets and current liabilities sections of the balance sheet in accordance with good accounting practice. (Assume that both accounts receivable and accounts payable are recorded gross.)

(b) State the net effect of your adjustments on Allesandro Scarlatti Company's retained earnings balance.

(LO 3, 4) **E5-10** **(Current Liabilities)** Norma Smith is the controller of Baylor Corporation and is responsible for the preparation of the year-end financial statements. The following transactions occurred during the year.

(a) On December 20, 2007, an employee filed a legal action against Baylor for $100,000 for wrongful dismissal. Management believes the action to be frivolous and without merit. The likelihood of payment to the employee is remote.

(b) Bonuses to key employees based on net income for 2007 are estimated to be $150,000.

(c) On December 1, 2007, the company borrowed $600,000 at 8% per year. Interest is paid quarterly.

(d) Credit sales for the year amounted to $10,000,000. Baylor's expense provision for doubtful accounts is estimated to be 3% of credit sales.

(e) On December 15, 2007, the company declared a $2.00 per share dividend on the 40,000 shares of common stock outstanding, to be paid on January 5, 2008.

(f) During the year, customer advances of $160,000 were received; $50,000 of this amount was earned by December 31, 2007.

Instructions

For each item above, indicate the dollar amount to be reported as a current liability. If a liability is not reported, explain why.

(LO 3) **E5-11** **(Balance Sheet Preparation)** Presented below is the adjusted trial balance of Kelly Corporation at December 31, 2007.

	Debits	Credits
Cash	$?	
Office Supplies	1,200	
Prepaid Insurance	1,000	
Equipment	48,000	
Accumulated Depreciation—Equipment		$ 4,000
Trademarks	950	
Accounts Payable		10,000
Wages Payable		500
Unearned Service Revenue		2,000
Bonds Payable, due 2014		9,000
Common Stock		10,000
Retained Earnings		25,000
Service Revenue		10,000
Wages Expense	9,000	
Insurance Expense	1,400	
Rent Expense	1,200	
Interest Expense	900	
Total	$?	$?

Additional information:

1. Net loss for the year was $2,500.
2. No dividends were declared during 2007.

Instructions
Prepare a classified balance sheet as of December 31, 2007.

(LO 3) **E5-12** **(Preparation of a Balance Sheet)** Presented below is the trial balance of John Nalezny Corporation at December 31, 2007.

	Debits	Credits
Cash	$ 197,000	
Sales		$ 8,100,000
Trading Securities (at cost, $145,000)	153,000	
Cost of Goods Sold	4,800,000	
Long-term Investments in Bonds	299,000	
Long-term Investments in Stocks	277,000	
Short-term Notes Payable		90,000
Accounts Payable		455,000
Selling Expenses	2,000,000	
Investment Revenue		63,000
Land	260,000	
Buildings	1,040,000	
Dividends Payable		136,000
Accrued Liabilities		96,000
Accounts Receivable	435,000	
Accumulated Depreciation—Buildings		152,000
Allowance for Doubtful Accounts		25,000
Administrative Expenses	900,000	
Interest Expense	211,000	
Inventories	597,000	
Extraordinary Gain		80,000
Long-term Notes Payable		900,000
Equipment	600,000	
Bonds Payable		1,000,000
Accumulated Depreciation—Equipment		60,000
Franchise	160,000	
Common Stock ($5 par)		1,000,000
Treasury Stock	191,000	
Patent	195,000	
Retained Earnings		78,000
Additional Paid-in Capital		80,000
Totals	$12,315,000	$12,315,000

Instructions
Prepare a balance sheet at December 31, 2007, for John Nalezny Corporation. Ignore income taxes.

(LO 7) **E5-13** **(Statement of Cash Flows—Classifications)** The major classifications of activities reported in the statement of cash flows are operating, investing, and financing. Classify each of the transactions listed below as:

1. Operating activity—add to net income.
2. Operating activity—deduct from net income.
3. Investing activity.
4. Financing activity.
5. Reported as significant noncash activity.

The transactions are as follows.

(a) Issuance of capital stock.
(b) Purchase of land and building.
(c) Redemption of bonds.
(d) Sale of equipment.
(e) Depreciation of machinery.
(f) Amortization of patent.
(g) Issuance of bonds for plant assets.
(h) Payment of cash dividends.
(i) Exchange of furniture for office equipment.
(j) Purchase of treasury stock.
(k) Loss on sale of equipment.
(l) Increase in accounts receivable during the year.
(m) Decrease in accounts payable during the year.

(LO 8) **E5-14** **(Preparation of a Statement of Cash Flows)** The comparative balance sheets of Constantine Cavamanlis Inc. at the beginning and the end of the year 2007 appear on the next page.

CONSTANTINE CAVAMANLIS INC.			
BALANCE SHEETS			
Assets	Dec. 31, 2007	Jan. 1, 2007	Inc./Dec.
Cash	$ 45,000	$ 13,000	$32,000 Inc.
Accounts receivable	91,000	88,000	3,000 Inc.
Equipment	39,000	22,000	17,000 Inc.
Less: Accumulated depreciation	(17,000)	(11,000)	6,000 Inc.
Total	$158,000	$112,000	
Liabilities and Stockholders' Equity			
Accounts payable	$ 20,000	$ 15,000	5,000 Inc.
Common stock	100,000	80,000	20,000 Inc.
Retained earnings	38,000	17,000	21,000 Inc.
Total	$158,000	$112,000	

Net income of $44,000 was reported, and dividends of $23,000 were paid in 2007. New equipment was purchased and none was sold.

Instructions
Prepare a statement of cash flows for the year 2007.

(LO 8, 9) **E5-15 (Preparation of a Statement of Cash Flows)** Presented below is a condensed version of the comparative balance sheets for Zubin Mehta Corporation for the last two years at December 31.

	2007	2006
Cash	$177,000	$ 78,000
Accounts receivable	180,000	185,000
Investments	52,000	74,000
Equipment	298,000	240,000
Less: Accumulated depreciation	(106,000)	(89,000)
Current liabilities	134,000	151,000
Capital stock	160,000	160,000
Retained earnings	307,000	177,000

Additional information:
Investments were sold at a loss (not extraordinary) of $10,000; no equipment was sold; cash dividends paid were $30,000; and net income was $160,000.

Instructions
(a) Prepare a statement of cash flows for 2007 for Zubin Mehta Corporation.
(b) Determine Zubin Mehta Corporation's free cash flow.

(LO 8, 9) **E5-16 (Preparation of a Statement of Cash Flows)** A comparative balance sheet for Shabbona Corporation is presented below.

	December 31	
Assets	2007	2006
Cash	$ 73,000	$ 22,000
Accounts receivable	82,000	66,000
Inventories	180,000	189,000
Land	71,000	110,000
Equipment	260,000	200,000
Accumulated depreciation—equipment	(69,000)	(42,000)
Total	$597,000	$545,000
Liabilities and Stockholders' Equity		
Accounts payable	$ 34,000	$ 47,000
Bonds payable	150,000	200,000
Common stock ($1 par)	214,000	164,000
Retained earnings	199,000	134,000
Total	$597,000	$545,000

Additional information:

1. Net income for 2007 was $125,000.
2. Cash dividends of $60,000 were declared and paid.
3. Bonds payable amounting to $50,000 were retired through issuance of common stock.

Instructions

(a) Prepare a statement of cash flows for 2007 for Shabbona Corporation.
(b) Determine Shabbona Corporation's current cash debt coverage ratio, cash debt coverage ratio, and free cash flow. Comment on its liquidity and financial flexibility.

(LO 3, 8)   **E5-17** **(Preparation of a Statement of Cash Flows and a Balance Sheet)** Grant Wood Corporation's balance sheet at the end of 2006 included the following items.

Current assets	$235,000	Current liabilities	$150,000
Land	30,000	Bonds payable	100,000
Building	120,000	Common stock	180,000
Equipment	90,000	Retained earnings	44,000
Accum. depr.—building	(30,000)	Total	$474,000
Accum. depr.—equipment	(11,000)		
Patents	40,000		
Total	$474,000		

The following information is available for 2007.

1. Net income was $55,000.
2. Equipment (cost $20,000 and accumulated depreciation $8,000) was sold for $10,000.
3. Depreciation expense was $4,000 on the building and $9,000 on equipment.
4. Patent amortization was $2,500.
5. Current assets other than cash increased by $29,000. Current liabilities increased by $13,000.
6. An addition to the building was completed at a cost of $27,000.
7. A long-term investment in stock was purchased for $16,000.
8. Bonds payable of $50,000 were issued.
9. Cash dividends of $30,000 were declared and paid.
10. Treasury stock was purchased at a cost of $11,000.

Instructions

(Show only totals for current assets and current liabilities.)
(a) Prepare a statement of cash flows for 2007.
(b) Prepare a balance sheet at December 31, 2007.

(LO 8, 9)   **E5-18** **(Preparation of a Statement of Cash Flows, Analysis)** The comparative balance sheets of Madrasah Corporation at the beginning and end of the year 2007 appear below.

MADRASAH CORPORATION			
BALANCE SHEETS			
Assets	Dec. 31, 2007	Jan. 1, 2007	Inc./Dec.
Cash	$ 20,000	$ 13,000	$ 7,000 Inc.
Accounts receivable	106,000	88,000	18,000 Inc.
Equipment	39,000	22,000	17,000 Inc.
Less: Accumulated depreciation	(17,000)	(11,000)	6,000 Inc.
Total	$148,000	$112,000	
Liabilities and Stockholders' Equity			
Accounts payable	$ 20,000	$ 15,000	5,000 Inc.
Common stock	100,000	80,000	20,000 Inc.
Retained earnings	28,000	17,000	11,000 Inc.
Total	$148,000	$112,000	

Net income of $44,000 was reported, and dividends of $33,000 were paid in 2007. New equipment was purchased and none was sold.

Instructions

(a) Prepare a statement of cash flows for the year 2007.

(b) Compute the current ratio (current assets ÷ current liabilities) as of January 1, 2007, and December 31, 2007, and compute free cash flow for the year 2007.

(c) In light of the analysis in (b), comment on Madrasah's liquidity and financial flexibility.

See the book's website, www.wiley.com/college/kieso, for Additional Exercises.

PROBLEMS

(LO 3) **P5-1** **(Preparation of a Classified Balance Sheet, Periodic Inventory)** Presented below is a list of accounts in alphabetical order.

Accounts Receivable	Land
Accrued Wages	Land for Future Plant Site
Accumulated Depreciation—Buildings	Loss from Flood
Accumulated Depreciation—Equipment	Notes Payable (due next year)
Advances to Employees	Patent
Advertising Expense	Payroll Taxes Payable
Allowance for Doubtful Accounts	Pension Obligations
Bond Sinking Fund	Petty Cash
Bonds Payable	Preferred Stock
Building	Premium on Bonds Payable
Cash in Bank	Premium on Preferred Stock
Cash on Hand	Prepaid Rent
Cash Surrender Value of Life Insurance	Purchases
Commission Expense	Purchase Returns and Allowances
Common Stock	Retained Earnings
Copyright	Sales
Dividends Payable	Sales Discounts
Equipment	Sales Salaries
Gain on Sale of Equipment	Trading Securities
Interest Receivable	Transportation-in
Inventory—Beginning	Treasury Stock (at cost)
Inventory—Ending	Unearned Subscriptions Revenue

Instructions

Prepare a classified balance sheet in good form. (No monetary amounts are to be shown.)

(LO 3) **P5-2** **(Balance Sheet Preparation)** Presented below are a number of balance sheet items for Letterman, Inc., for the current year, 2007.

Goodwill	$ 125,000	Accumulated depreciation—	
Payroll taxes payable	177,591	equipment	$ 292,000
Bonds payable	300,000	Inventories	239,800
Discount on bonds payable	15,000	Rent payable—short-term	45,000
Cash	360,000	Taxes payable	98,362
Land	480,000	Long-term rental obligations	480,000
Notes receivable	545,700	Common stock, $1 par value	200,000
Notes payable to banks	265,000	Preferred stock, $10 par value	150,000
Accounts payable	590,000	Prepaid expenses	87,920
Retained earnings	?	Equipment	1,470,000
Income taxes receivable	97,630	Trading securities	121,000
Unsecured notes payable		Accumulated depreciation—	
(long-term)	1,600,000	building	170,200
		Building	1,640,000

Instructions

Prepare a classified balance sheet in good form. Common stock authorized was 400,000 shares, and preferred stock authorized was 20,000 shares. Assume that notes receivable and notes payable are short-term, unless stated otherwise. Cost and fair value of trading securities are the same.

(LO 3) **P5–3** **(Balance Sheet Adjustment and Preparation)** The adjusted trial balance of Side Kicks Company and other related information for the year 2007 are presented on the next page.

SIDE KICKS COMPANY
ADJUSTED TRIAL BALANCE
DECEMBER 31, 2007

	Debits	Credits
Cash	$ 41,000	
Accounts Receivable	163,500	
Allowance for Doubtful Accounts		$ 8,700
Prepaid Insurance	5,900	
Inventory	308,500	
Long-term Investments	339,000	
Land	85,000	
Construction Work in Progress	124,000	
Patents	36,000	
Equipment	400,000	
Accumulated Depreciation of Equipment		140,000
Unamortized Discount on Bonds Payable	20,000	
Accounts Payable		148,000
Accrued Expenses		49,200
Notes Payable		94,000
Bonds Payable		400,000
Common Stock		500,000
Premium on Common Stock		45,000
Retained Earnings		138,000
	$1,522,900	$1,522,900

Additional information:

1. The LIFO method of inventory value is used.
2. The cost and fair value of the long-term investments that consist of stocks and bonds is the same.
3. The amount of the Construction Work in Progress account represents the costs expended to date on a building in the process of construction. (The company rents factory space at the present time.) The land on which the building is being constructed cost $85,000, as shown in the trial balance.
4. The patents were purchased by the company at a cost of $40,000 and are being amortized on a straight-line basis.
5. Of the unamortized discount on bonds payable, $2,000 will be amortized in 2008.
6. The notes payable represent bank loans that are secured by long-term investments carried at $120,000. These bank loans are due in 2008.
7. The bonds payable bear interest at 8% payable every December 31, and are due January 1, 2018.
8. 600,000 shares of common stock of a par value of $1 were authorized, of which 500,000 shares were issued and outstanding.

Instructions
Prepare a balance sheet as of December 31, 2007, so that all important information is fully disclosed.

(LO 3, 4) **P5-4 (Preparation of a Corrected Balance Sheet)** Presented below and on the next page is the balance sheet of Russell Crowe Corporation as of December 31, 2007.

RUSSELL CROWE CORPORATION
BALANCE SHEET
DECEMBER 31, 2007

Assets	
Goodwill (Note 2)	$ 120,000
Buildings (Note 1)	1,640,000
Inventories	312,100
Land	750,000
Accounts receivable	170,000
Treasury stock (50,000 shares)	87,000
Cash on hand	175,900
Assets allocated to trustee for plant expansion	
Cash in bank	70,000
U.S. Treasury notes, at cost and fair value	138,000
	$3,463,000

Equities

Notes payable (Note 3)	$ 600,000
Common stock, authorized and issued, 1,000,000 shares, no par	1,150,000
Retained earnings	658,000
Appreciation capital (Note 1)	570,000
Federal income taxes payable	75,000
Reserve for depreciation recorded to date on the building	410,000
	$3,463,000

Note 1: Buildings are stated at cost, except for one building that was recorded at appraised value. The excess of appraisal value over cost was $570,000. Depreciation has been recorded based on cost.

Note 2: Goodwill in the amount of $120,000 was recognized because the company believed that book value was not an accurate representation of the fair market value of the company. The gain of $120,000 was credited to Retained Earnings.

Note 3: Notes payable are long-term except for the current installment due of $100,000.

Instructions

Prepare a corrected classified balance sheet in good form. The notes above are for information only.

(LO 3) P5-5 (Balance Sheet Adjustment and Preparation) Presented below is the balance sheet of Stephen King Corporation for the current year, 2007.

STEPHEN KING CORPORATION				
BALANCE SHEET				
DECEMBER 31, 2007				
Current assets	$ 449,000	Current liabilities	$ 344,000
Investments	640,000	Long-term liabilities	1,000,000
Property, plant, and equipment	1,720,000	Stockholders' equity	1,770,000
Intangible assets	305,000		$3,114,000
	$3,114,000		

The following information is presented.

1. The current assets section includes: cash $114,000, accounts receivable $170,000 less $10,000 for allowance for doubtful accounts, inventories $180,000, and unearned revenue $5,000. Inventories are stated on the lower of FIFO cost or market.
2. The investments section includes: the cash surrender value of a life insurance contract $40,000; investments in common stock, short-term (trading) $80,000 and long-term (available-for-sale) $270,000, and bond sinking fund $250,000. The cost and fair value of investments in common stock are the same.
3. Property, plant, and equipment includes: buildings $1,040,000 less accumulated depreciation $360,000; equipment $450,000 less accumulated depreciation $180,000; land $500,000; and land held for future use $270,000.
4. Intangible assets include: a franchise $165,000; goodwill $100,000; and discount on bonds payable $40,000.
5. Current liabilities include: accounts payable $104,000; notes payable—short-term $80,000 and long-term $120,000; and taxes payable $40,000.
6. Long-term liabilities are composed solely of 7% bonds payable due 2015.
7. Stockholders' equity has: preferred stock, no par value, authorized 200,000 shares, issued 70,000 shares for $450,000; and common stock, $1.00 par value, authorized 400,000 shares, issued 100,000 shares at an average price of $10. In addition, the corporation has retained earnings of $320,000.

Instructions

Prepare a balance sheet in good form, adjusting the amounts in each balance sheet classification as affected by the information given above.

(LO 3, 8, 9) P5-6 (Preparation of a Statement of Cash Flows and a Balance Sheet) Alistair Cooke Inc. had the balance sheet shown on the following page at December 31, 2006.

ALISTAIR COOKE INC.
BALANCE SHEET
DECEMBER 31, 2006

Cash	$ 20,000	Accounts payable	$ 30,000
Accounts receivable	21,200	Long-term notes payable	41,000
Investments	32,000	Common stock	100,000
Plant assets (net)	81,000	Retained earnings	23,200
Land	40,000		
			$194,200
	$194,200		

During 2007 the following occurred.

1. Alistair Cooke Inc. sold part of its investment portfolio for $17,000. This transaction resulted in a gain of $3,400 for the firm. The company classifies its investments as available-for-sale.
2. A tract of land was purchased for $18,000 cash.
3. Long-term notes payable in the amount of $16,000 were retired before maturity by paying $16,000 cash.
4. An additional $24,000 in common stock was issued at par.
5. Dividends totalling $8,200 were declared and paid to stockholders.
6. Net income for 2007 was $32,000 after allowing for depreciation of $12,000.
7. Land was purchased through the issuance of $30,000 in bonds.
8. At December 31, 2007, Cash was $39,000, Accounts Receivable was $41,600, and Accounts Payable remained at $30,000.

Instructions

(a) Prepare a statement of cash flows for 2007.
(b) Prepare an unclassified balance sheet as it would appear at December 31, 2007.
(c) How might the statement of cash flows help the user of the financial statements? Compute two cash flow ratios.

(LO 1, 3, 8, 9) **P5-7 (Preparation of a Statement of Cash Flows and Balance Sheet)** Jay Leno Inc. had the following balance sheet at December 31, 2006.

JAY LENO INC.
BALANCE SHEET
DECEMBER 31, 2006

Cash	$ 20,000	Accounts payable	$ 30,000
Accounts receivable	21,200	Bonds payable	41,000
Investments	32,000	Common stock	100,000
Plant assets (net)	81,000	Retained earnings	23,200
Land	40,000		
			$194,200
	$194,200		

During 2007 the following occurred.

1. Leno liquidated its available-for-sale investment portfolio at a loss of $3,000.
2. A tract of land was purchased for $38,000.
3. An additional $26,000 in common stock was issued at par.
4. Dividends totaling $10,000 were declared and paid to stockholders.
5. Net income for 2007 was $35,000, including $12,000 in depreciation expense.
6. Land was purchased through the issuance of $30,000 in additional bonds.
7. At December 31, 2007, Cash was $66,200, Accounts Receivable was $42,000, and Accounts Payable was $40,000.

Instructions

(a) Prepare a statement of cash flows for the year 2007 for Leno.
(b) Prepare the balance sheet as it would appear at December 31, 2007.
(c) Compute Leno's free cash flow and the current cash debt coverage ratio for 2007.
(d) Use the analysis of Leno to illustrate how information in the balance sheet and statement of cash flows helps the user of the financial statements.

CONCEPTS FOR ANALYSIS

CA5-1 **(Reporting the Financial Effects of Varied Transactions)** In an examination of Juan Acevedo Corporation as of December 31, 2007, you have learned that the following situations exist. No entries have been made in the accounting records for these items.

1. The corporation erected its present factory building in 1992. Depreciation was calculated by the straight-line method, using an estimated life of 35 years. Early in 2007, the board of directors conducted a careful survey and estimated that the factory building had a remaining useful life of 25 years as of January 1, 2007.
2. An additional assessment of 2006 income taxes was levied and paid in 2007.
3. When calculating the accrual for officers' salaries at December 31, 2007, it was discovered that the accrual for officers' salaries for December 31, 2006, had been overstated.
4. On December 15, 2007, Acevedo Corporation declared a cash dividend on its common stock outstanding, payable February 1, 2008, to the common stockholders of record December 31, 2007.

Instructions
Describe fully how each of the items above should be reported in the financial statements of Acevedo Corporation for the year 2007.

CA5-2 **(Current Asset and Liability Classification)** Below are the titles of a number of debit and credit accounts as they might appear on the balance sheet of Ethan Allen Corporation as of October 31, 2007.

Debits	Credits
Interest Accrued on U.S. Government Securities	Capital Stock—Preferred
Notes Receivable	11% First Mortgage Bonds, due in 2014
Petty Cash Fund	Preferred Cash Dividend, payable Nov. 1, 2007
U.S. Government Securities	Allowance for Doubtful Accounts Receivable
Treasury Stock	Federal Income Taxes Payable
Unamortized Bond Discount	Customers' Advances (on contracts to be completed next year)
Cash in Bank	Premium on Bonds Redeemable in 2007
Land	Officers' 2007 Bonus Accrued
Inventory of Operating Parts and Supplies	Accrued Payroll
Inventory of Raw Materials	Notes Payable
Patents	Accrued Interest on Bonds
Cash and U.S. Government Bonds Set Aside for Property Additions	Accumulated Depreciation
Investment in Subsidiary	Accounts Payable
Accounts Receivable:	Capital in Excess of Par
U.S. Government Contracts	Accrued Interest on Notes Payable
Regular	8% First Mortgage Bonds, to be redeemed in 2007 out of current assets
Installments—Due Next Year	
Installments—Due After Next year	
Goodwill	
Inventory of Finished Goods	
Inventory of Work in Process	
Deficit	

Instructions
Select the current asset and current liability items from among these debits and credits. If there appear to be certain borderline cases that you are unable to classify without further information, mention them and explain your difficulty, or give your reasons for making questionable classifications, if any.

(AICPA adapted)

CA5-3 **(Identifying Balance Sheet Deficiencies)** The assets of Annika Sorenstam Corporation are presented on the next page (000s omitted).

ANNIKA SORENSTAM CORPORATION
BALANCE SHEET (PARTIAL)
DECEMBER 31, 2007

Assets

Current assets		
Cash		$ 100,000
Unclaimed payroll checks		27,500
Trading securities (fair value $30,000) at cost		37,000
Accounts receivable (less bad debt reserve)		75,000
Inventories—at lower of cost (determined by the next-in, first-out method) or market		240,000
Total current assets		479,500
Tangible assets		
Land (less accumulated depreciation)		80,000
Buildings and equipment	$800,000	
Less: Accumulated depreciation	250,000	550,000
Net tangible assets		630,000
Long-term investments		
Stocks and bonds		100,000
Treasury stock		70,000
Total long-term investments		170,000
Other assets		
Discount on bonds payable		19,400
Sinking fund		975,000
Total other assets		994,400
Total assets		$2,273,900

Instructions

Indicate the deficiencies, if any, in the foregoing presentation of Annika Sorenstam Corporation's assets.

CA5-4 (Critique of Balance Sheet Format and Content) Presented below and on the next page is the balance sheet of Bellemy Brothers Corporation (000s omitted).

BELLEMY BROTHERS CORPORATION
BALANCE SHEET
DECEMBER 31, 2007

Assets

Current assets		
Cash	$26,000	
Marketable securities	18,000	
Accounts receivable	25,000	
Merchandise inventory	20,000	
Supplies inventory	4,000	
Stock investment in Subsidiary Company	20,000	$113,000
Investments		
Treasury stock		25,000
Property, plant, and equipment		
Buildings and land	91,000	
Less: Reserve for depreciation	31,000	60,000
Other assets		
Cash surrender value of life insurance		19,000
Total assets		$217,000

Liabilities and Stockholders' Equity

Current liabilities		
Accounts payable	$22,000	
Reserve for income taxes	15,000	
Customers' accounts with credit balances	1	$ 37,001
Deferred credits		
Unamortized premium on bonds payable		2,000
Long-term liabilities		
Bonds payable		60,000
Total liabilities		99,001

Common stock		
Common stock, par $5	85,000	
Earned surplus	24,999	
Cash dividends declared	8,000	117,999
Total liabilities and stockholders' equity		$217,000

Instructions
Evaluate the balance sheet presented. State briefly the proper treatment of any item criticized.

CA5-5 (Presentation of Property, Plant, and Equipment) Andrea Pafko, corporate comptroller for Nicholson Industries, is trying to decide how to present "Property, plant, and equipment" in the balance sheet. She realizes that the statement of cash flows will show that the company made a significant investment in purchasing new equipment this year, but overall she knows the company's plant assets are rather old. She feels that she can disclose one figure titled "Property, plant, and equipment, net of depreciation," and the result will be a low figure. However, it will not disclose the age of the assets. If she chooses to show the cost less accumulated depreciation, the age of the assets will be apparent. She proposes the following.

Property, plant, and equipment, net of depreciation	$10,000,000

rather than	
Property, plant, and equipment	$50,000,000
Less: Accumulated depreciation	(40,000,000)
Net book value	$10,000,000

Instructions
Answer the following questions.

(a) What are the ethical issues involved?

(b) What should Pafko do?

CA5-6 (Cash Flow Analysis) The partner in charge of the James Spencer Corporation audit comes by your desk and leaves a letter he has started to the CEO and a copy of the cash flow statement for the year ended December 31, 2007. Because he must leave on an emergency, he asks you to finish the letter by explaining: (1) the disparity between net income and cash flow; (2) the importance of operating cash flow; (3) the renewable source(s) of cash flow; and (4) possible suggestions to improve the cash position.

JAMES SPENCER CORPORATION
STATEMENT OF CASH FLOWS
FOR THE YEAR ENDED DECEMBER 31, 2007

Cash flows from operating activities		
Net income		$100,000
Adjustments to reconcile net income to net cash provided by operating activities:		
Depreciation expense	$ 10,000	
Amortization expense	1,000	
Loss on sale of fixed assets	5,000	
Increase in accounts receivable (net)	(40,000)	
Increase in inventory	(35,000)	
Decrease in accounts payable	(41,000)	(100,000)
Net cash provided by operating activities		–0–
Cash flows from investing activities		
Sale of plant assets	25,000	
Purchase of equipment	(100,000)	
Purchase of land	(200,000)	
Net cash used by investing activities		(275,000)
Cash flows from financing activities		
Payment of dividends	(10,000)	
Redemption of bonds	(100,000)	
Net cash used by financing activities		(110,000)
Net decrease in cash		(385,000)
Cash balance, January 1, 2007		400,000
Cash balance, December 31, 2007		$ 15,000

Date

James Spencer, III, CEO
James Spencer Corporation
125 Wall Street
Middleton, Kansas 67458

Dear Mr. Spencer:

I have good news and bad news about the financial statements for the year ended December 31, 2007. The good news is that net income of $100,000 is close to what we predicted in the strategic plan last year, indicating strong performance this year. The bad news is that the cash balance is seriously low. Enclosed is the Statement of Cash Flows, which best illustrates how both of these situations occurred simultaneously . . .

Instructions
Complete the letter to the CEO, including the four components requested by your boss.

USING YOUR JUDGMENT

Financial Reporting Problem

The Procter & Gamble Company (P&G)

The financial statements of **P&G** are presented in Appendix 5B or can be accessed on the KWW website.

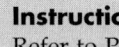

Instructions
Refer to P&G's financial statements and the accompanying notes to answer the following questions.

(a) What alternative formats could P&G have adopted for its balance sheet? Which format did it adopt?

(b) Identify the various techniques of disclosure P&G might have used to disclose additional pertinent financial information. Which technique does it use in its financials?

(c) In what classifications are P&G's investments reported? What valuation basis does P&G use to report its investments? How much working capital did P&G have on June 30, 2004? On June 30, 2003?

(d) What were P&G's cash flows from its operating, investing, and financing activities for 2004? What were its trends in net cash provided by operating activities over the period 2002 to 2004? Explain why the change in accounts payable and in accrued and other liabilities is added to net income to arrive at net cash provided by operating activities.

(e) Compute P&G's (1) current cash debt coverage ratio, (2) cash debt coverage ratio, and (3) free cash flow for 2004. What do these ratios indicate about P&G's financial condition?

Financial Statement Analysis Cases

Case 1 Uniroyal Technology Corporation

Uniroyal Technology Corporation (UTC), with corporate offices in Sarasota, Florida, is organized into three operating segments. The high-performance plastics segment is responsible for research, development, and manufacture of a wide variety of products, including orthopedic braces, graffiti-resistant seats for buses and airplanes, and a static-resistant plastic used in the central processing units of microcomputers. The coated fabrics segment manufactures products such as automobile seating, door and instrument panels, and specialty items such as waterproof seats for personal watercraft and stain-resistant, easy-cleaning upholstery fabrics. The foams and adhesives segment develops and manufactures products used in commercial roofing applications.

The following items relate to operations in a recent year.

1 Serious pressure was placed on profitability by sharply increasing raw material prices. Some raw materials increased in price 50% during the past year. Cost containment programs were instituted and product prices were increased whenever possible, which resulted in profit margins actually improving over the course of the year.

2 The company entered into a revolving credit agreement, under which UTC may borrow the lesser of $15,000,000 or 80% of eligible accounts receivable. At the end of the year, approximately $4,000,000 was outstanding under this agreement. The company plans to use this line of credit in the upcoming year to finance operations and expansion.

Instructions

(a) Should investors be informed of raw materials price increases, such as described in item 1? Does the fact that the company successfully met the challenge of higher prices affect the answer? Explain.

(b) How should the information in item 2 be presented in the financial statements of UTC?

Case 2 Sherwin-Williams Company

Sherwin-Williams, based in Cleveland, Ohio, manufactures a wide variety of paint and other coatings, which are marketed through its specialty stores and in other retail outlets. The company also manufactures paint for automobiles. The Automotive Division has had financial difficulty. During a recent year, five branch locations of the Automotive Division were closed, and new management was put in place for the branches remaining. The following titles were shown on Sherwin-Williams's balance sheet for that year.

Accounts payable	Machinery and equipment
Accounts receivable, less allowance	Other accruals
Accrued taxes	Other capital
Buildings	Other current assets
Cash and cash equivalents	Other long-term liabilities
Common stock	Postretirement obligations other than pensions
Employee compensation payable	Retained earnings
Finished goods inventories	Short-term investments
Intangibles and other assets	Taxes payable
Land	Work in process and raw materials inventories
Long-term debt	

Instructions

(a) Organize the accounts in the general order in which they would have been presented in a classified balance sheet.

(b) When several of the branch locations of the Automotive Division were closed, what balance sheet accounts were most likely affected? Did the balance in those accounts decrease or increase?

Case 3 Deere and Company

Below is the SEC-mandated disclosure of contractual obligations provided by **Deere & Company** in its 2004 annual report. Deere & Company reported current assets of $17,855 and total current liabilities of $7,888 at October 31, 2004. All dollars are in millions.

Aggregate Contractual Obligations

Most of the company's contractual obligations to make payments to third parties are debt obligations. In addition, the company has off-balance sheet obligations for the purchases of raw materials and services along with agreements for future lease payments. The payment schedule for these contractual obligations in millions of dollars is as follows:

	Total	Less than 1 year	1–3 years	3–5 years	More than 5 years
Total debt					
Equipment Operations	$ 2,958	$ 312	$ 281	$ 8	$2,357
Financial Services	11,265	3,146	4,393	1,541	2,185
Total	14,223	3,458	4,674	1,549	4,542
Purchase obligations	2,306	2,274	32		
Operating leases	367	75	130	59	103
Capital leases	12	2	3	2	5
Contractual obligations	$16,908	$5,809	$4,839	$1,610	$4,650

Instructions

(a) Compute Deere & Company's working capital and current ratio (current assets ÷ current liabilities) with and without the contractual obligations reported in the schedule.

(b) Briefly discuss how the information provided in the contractual obligation disclosure would be useful in evaluating Deere & Company for loans: (1) due in one year, (2) due in five years.

Case 4 Amazon.com

The incredible growth of **Amazon.com** has put fear into the hearts of traditional retailers. Amazon's stock price has soared to amazing levels. However, it is often pointed out in the financial press that the company did not report its first profit until 2003. The following financial information is taken from Amazon's 2003 financial statements.

($ in millions)	2003	2002
Current assets	$1,821	$1,616
Total assets	2,162	1,990
Current liabilities	1,253	1,066
Total liabilities	3,198	3,343
Cash provided by operations	392	174
Capital expenditures	46	39
Dividends paid	0	0
Net income(loss)	35	(149)
Sales	5,264	3,933

Instructions

(a) Calculate free cash flow for Amazon for 2003 and 2002 and discuss its ability to finance expansion from internally generated cash. Thus far Amazon has avoided purchasing large warehouses. Instead, it has used those of others. It is possible, however, that in order to increase customer satisfaction the company may have to build its own warehouses. If this happens, how might your impression of its ability to finance expansion change?

(b) Discuss any potential implications of the change in Amazon's cash provided by operations from 2002 to 2003.

(c) Based on your findings in parts (a) and (b), can you conclude whether or not Amazon's amazing stock price is justified?

Comparative Analysis Case

The Coca-Cola Company and PepsiCo, Inc.

Instructions

Go to the KWW website and use information found there to answer the following questions related to **The Coca-Cola Company** and **PepsiCo, Inc.**

(a) What format(s) did these companies use to present their balance sheets?

(b) How much working capital did each of these companies have at the end of 2004? Speculate as to their rationale for the amount of working capital they maintain.

(c) What is the most significant difference in the asset structure of the two companies? What causes this difference?

(d) What are the companies' annual and 4-year (2000–2004) growth rates in total assets and long-term debt?

(e) What were these two companies' trends in net cash provided by operating activities over the period 2002 to 2004?

(f) Compute both companies' (1) current cash debt coverage ratio, (2) cash debt coverage ratio, and (3) free cash flow. What do these ratios indicate about the financial condition of the two companies?

(g) What ratios do each of these companies use in the Management's Discussion and Analysis section of the annual report to explain their financial condition related to debt financing?

Research Case

Publicly-owned companies registered with the Securities and Exchange Commission electronically file required reports via the EDGAR (Electronic Data Gathering, Analysis, and Retrieval) system.

EDGAR can easily be accessed via the Internet (**www.sec.gov**) using the following steps.

1 Select "Filings and Forms (EDGAR)" from the home page.

2 Select "Search for company filings."

3 Select "CIK Lookup" and enter the name(s) of the company(ies) you are investigating. Write down the CIK number(s) and return to the previous page.

4 To examine filings, click on "Historical EDGAR Archives" and enter the appropriate CIK number (including all zeroes). When the list of filings appears, click on the desired filing under the "Company name" column.

Instructions

(a) Determine the CIK numbers for the following companies: **Ford Motor Co.** and **Wisconsin Electric**.

(b) Examine the balance sheet formats included in the following filings.
   (1) Ford Motor Co. Form 10-K (html version) filed March 10, 2005.
   (2) Wisconsin Electric annual report to shareholders (10-K, html version) filed March 11, 2005.

Do you notice anything "unusual" about the balance sheet formats? Why do you think the balance sheets are presented in this manner?

International Reporting Case

Presented below is the balance sheet for **Tomkins PLC**, a British company.

Instructions
(a) Identify at least three differences in balance sheet reporting between British and U.S. firms, as shown in Tomkins's balance sheet.
(b) Review Tomkins's balance sheet and identify how the format of this financial statement provides useful information, as illustrated in the chapter.

ᏘOMKINS

TOMKINS PLC
Consolidated Balance Sheet
at January 3, 2004

CAPITAL EMPLOYED		
Fixed assets		
Intangible assets		216.7
Tangible assets		793.7
Investments		7.4
		1,017.8
Current assets		
Stock		373.9
Debtors		624.2
Cash		175.6
		1,173.7
Current liabilities		
Creditors: amounts falling due within one year		(502.3)
Net current assets		671.4
Total assets less current liabilities		1,689.2
Creditors: amounts falling due after more than one year		(488.4)
Provisions for liabilities and charges		(423.5)
Net assets		777.3
CAPITAL AND RESERVES		
Called up share capital		
Ordinary shares		38.7
Convertible cumulative preference shares		337.2
Redeemable convertible cumulative preference shares		—
		375.9
Share premium account		92.8
Capital redemption reserve		461.9
Own shares		(6.4)
Profit and loss account		(180.2)
Shareholders' funds		
Equity shareholders' funds	406.8	
Non-equity shareholders' funds	337.2	744.0
Equity minority interest		33.3
		777.3

Professional Research: Financial Accounting and Reporting

In light of the full disclosure principle, investors and creditors need to know the balances for assets, liabilities, and equity as well as the accounting policies adopted by management to measure the items reported in the balance sheet.

Instructions

Using the **Financial Accounting Research System (FARS)**, respond to the following items. (Provide text strings used in your search.)

(a) Identify the statement that addresses the disclosure of accounting policies.

(b) How are "Accounting Policies" defined in the standard?

(c) What are the three scenarios that would result in detailed disclosure of the accounting methods used?

(d) What are some examples of common disclosures that are required under this statement?

Professional Simulation

In this simulation you are asked to address questions related to the balance sheet. Prepare responses to all parts.

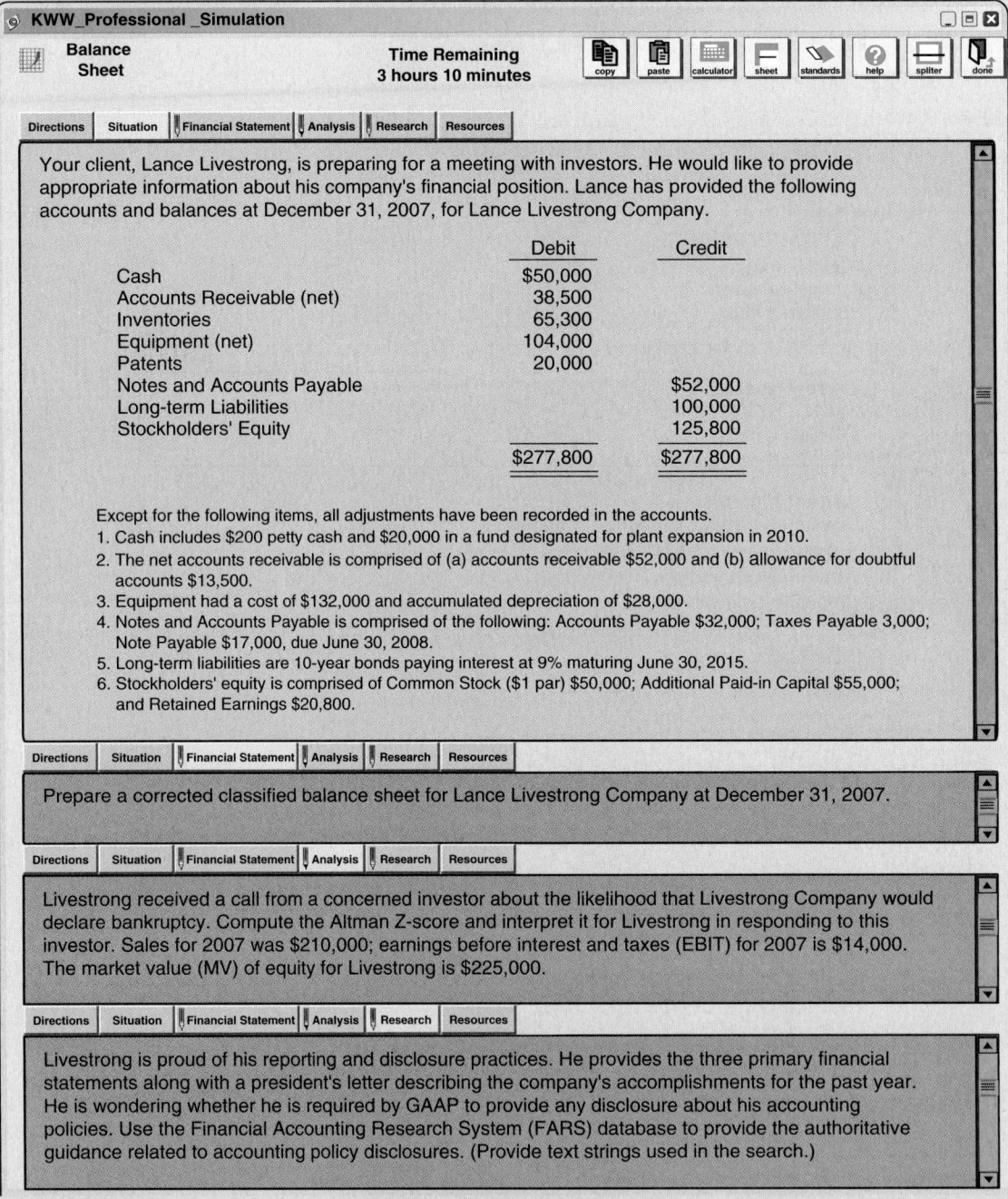

KWW_Professional _Simulation

Balance Sheet — Time Remaining 3 hours 10 minutes

copy | paste | calculator | sheet | standards | help | splitter | done

Directions | Situation | Financial Statement | Analysis | Research | Resources

Your client, Lance Livestrong, is preparing for a meeting with investors. He would like to provide appropriate information about his company's financial position. Lance has provided the following accounts and balances at December 31, 2007, for Lance Livestrong Company.

	Debit	Credit
Cash	$50,000	
Accounts Receivable (net)	38,500	
Inventories	65,300	
Equipment (net)	104,000	
Patents	20,000	
Notes and Accounts Payable		$52,000
Long-term Liabilities		100,000
Stockholders' Equity		125,800
	$277,800	$277,800

Except for the following items, all adjustments have been recorded in the accounts.
1. Cash includes $200 petty cash and $20,000 in a fund designated for plant expansion in 2010.
2. The net accounts receivable is comprised of (a) accounts receivable $52,000 and (b) allowance for doubtful accounts $13,500.
3. Equipment had a cost of $132,000 and accumulated depreciation of $28,000.
4. Notes and Accounts Payable is comprised of the following: Accounts Payable $32,000; Taxes Payable 3,000; Note Payable $17,000, due June 30, 2008.
5. Long-term liabilities are 10-year bonds paying interest at 9% maturing June 30, 2015.
6. Stockholders' equity is comprised of Common Stock ($1 par) $50,000; Additional Paid-in Capital $55,000; and Retained Earnings $20,800.

Directions | Situation | Financial Statement | Analysis | Research | Resources

Prepare a corrected classified balance sheet for Lance Livestrong Company at December 31, 2007.

Directions | Situation | Financial Statement | Analysis | Research | Resources

Livestrong received a call from a concerned investor about the likelihood that Livestrong Company would declare bankruptcy. Compute the Altman Z-score and interpret it for Livestrong in responding to this investor. Sales for 2007 was $210,000; earnings before interest and taxes (EBIT) for 2007 is $14,000. The market value (MV) of equity for Livestrong is $225,000.

Directions | Situation | Financial Statement | Analysis | Research | Resources

Livestrong is proud of his reporting and disclosure practices. He provides the three primary financial statements along with a president's letter describing the company's accomplishments for the past year. He is wondering whether he is required by GAAP to provide any disclosure about his accounting policies. Use the Financial Accounting Research System (FARS) database to provide the authoritative guidance related to accounting policy disclosures. (Provide text strings used in the search.)

Remember to check the book's companion website to find additional resources for this chapter.

wiley.com/college/kieso

ACCOUNTING AND THE TIME VALUE OF MONEY

The Magic of Interest

Sidney Homer, author of *A History of Interest Rates*, wrote, "$1,000 invested at a mere 8 percent for 400 years would grow to $23 quadrillion—$5 million for every human on earth. But the first 100 years are the hardest." This startling quote highlights the power of time and compounding interest on money. Equally significant, although Homer did not mention it, is the fact that a small difference in the interest rate makes a big difference in the amount of monies accumulated over time.

Taking an example more realistic than Homer's 400-year investment, assume that you had $20,000 in a tax-free retirement account. Half the money is in stocks returning 12 percent, and the other half is in bonds earning 8 percent. Assuming reinvested profits and quarterly compounding, your bonds would be worth $22,080 after 10 years, a doubling of their value. But your stocks, returning 4 percent more, would be worth $32,620, or triple your initial value. The following chart shows this impact.

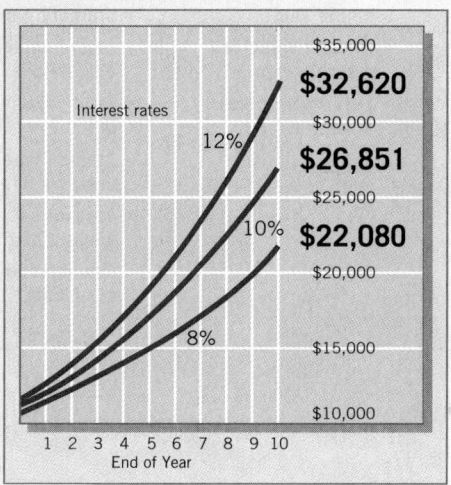

Because of interest paid on investments, money received a week from today is not the same as money received today. Business people are acutely aware of this timing factor, and they invest and borrow only after carefully analyzing the relative amounts of cash flows over time.

Learning Objectives

After studying this chapter, you should be able to:

1 Identify accounting topics where the time value of money is relevant.

2 Distinguish between simple and compound interest.

3 Use appropriate compound interest tables.

4 Identify variables fundamental to solving interest problems.

5 Solve future and present value of 1 problems.

6 Solve future value of ordinary and annuity due problems.

7 Solve present value of ordinary and annuity due problems.

8 Solve present value problems related to deferred annuities and bonds.

9 Apply expected cash flows to present value measurement.

As we indicated in the opening story, the timing of the returns on an investment has an important effect on the worth of the investment (asset). Similarly, the timing of debt repayment has an important effect on the value of the debt commitment (liability). As a financial expert, you will be expected to make present and future value measurements and to understand their implications. The purpose of this chapter is to present the tools and techniques that will help you measure the present value of future cash inflows and outflows. The content and organization of the chapter are as follows.

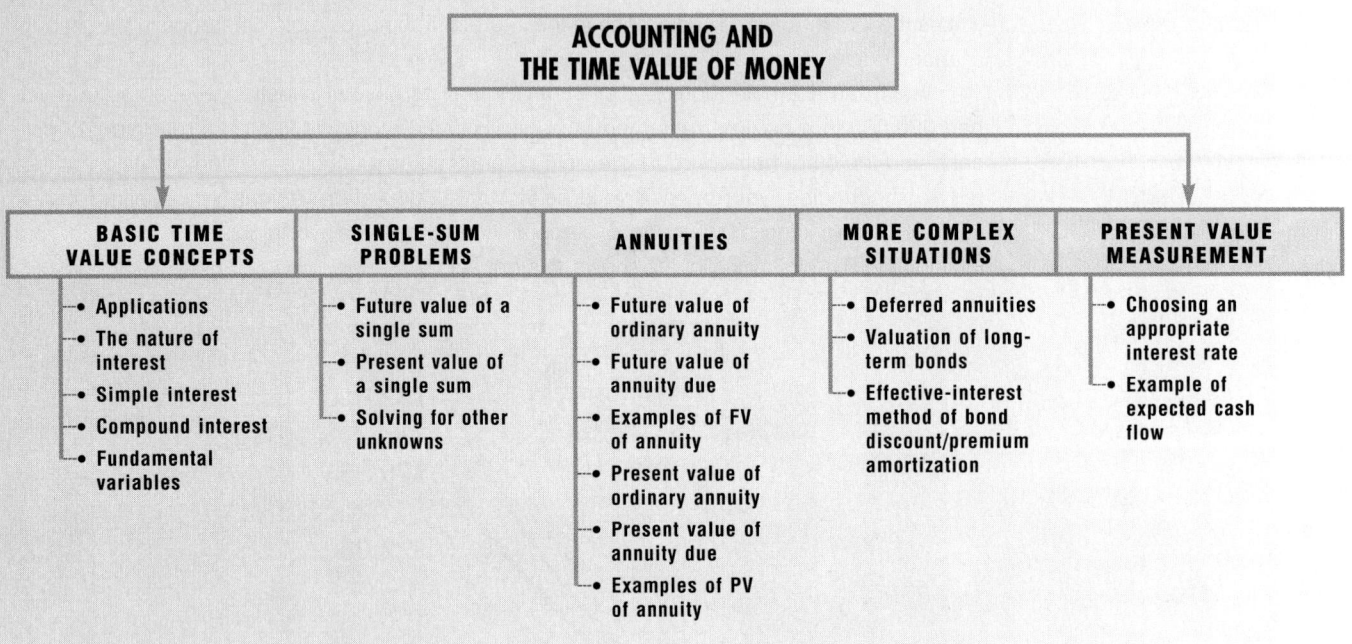

BASIC TIME VALUE CONCEPTS

OBJECTIVE 1
Identify accounting topics where the time value of money is relevant.

In accounting (and finance), the phrase **time value of money** indicates a relationship between time and money—that a dollar received today is worth more than a dollar promised at some time in the future. Why? Because of the opportunity to invest today's dollar and receive interest on the investment. Yet, when deciding among investment or borrowing alternatives, it is essential to be able to compare today's dollar and tomorrow's dollar on the same footing—to "compare apples to apples." Investors do that by using the concept of **present value**, which has many applications in accounting.

Applications of Time Value Concepts

Financial reporting uses different measurements in different situations—historical cost for equipment, net realizable value for some inventories, fair value for investments. As we discussed in Chapter 2, the FASB increasingly is requiring the use of fair values in the measurement of assets and liabilities. According to the FASB's recent standard on fair value measurements, the most useful fair value measures are based on prices established in active markets. However, for many assets and liabilities, market-based fair value information is not readily available. In these cases, fair value can be estimated based on the expected future cash flows related to the asset or liability.

Using present value techniques, these future cash flows then can be converted into present values.[1]

Because of the increased use of present values in this and other contexts, it is important to understand present value techniques.[2] We list some of the applications of present value-based measurements to accounting topics below; we discuss many of these in the following chapters.

PRESENT VALUE-BASED ACCOUNTING MEASUREMENTS

1 *NOTES.* Valuing noncurrent receivables and payables that carry no stated interest rate or a lower than market interest rate.

2 *LEASES.* Valuing assets and obligations to be capitalized under long-term leases and measuring the amount of the lease payments and annual leasehold amortization.

3 *PENSIONS AND OTHER POSTRETIREMENT BENEFITS.* Measuring service cost components of employers' postretirement benefits expense and postretirement benefits obligation.

4 *LONG-TERM ASSETS.* Evaluating alternative long-term investments by discounting future cash flows. Determining the value of assets acquired under deferred payment contracts. Measuring impairments of assets.

5 *SINKING FUNDS.* Determining the contributions necessary to accumulate a fund for debt retirements.

6 *BUSINESS COMBINATIONS.* Determining the value of receivables, payables, liabilities, accruals, and commitments acquired or assumed in a "purchase."

7 *DISCLOSURES.* Measuring the value of future cash flows from oil and gas reserves for disclosure in supplementary information.

8 *INSTALLMENT CONTRACTS.* Measuring periodic payments on long-term purchase contracts.

In addition to accounting and business applications, compound interest, annuity, and present value concepts apply to personal finance and investment decisions. In purchasing a home or car, planning for retirement, and evaluating alternative investments, you will need to understand time value of money concepts.

The Nature of Interest

Interest is payment for the use of money. It is the excess cash received or repaid over and above the amount lent or borrowed (**principal**). For example, Corner Bank lends Hillfarm Company $10,000 with the understanding that it will repay $11,500. The excess over $10,000, or $1,500, represents interest expense.

The lender generally states the amount of interest as a rate over a specific period of time. For example, if Hillfarm borrowed $10,000 for one year before repaying $11,500, the rate of interest is 15 percent per year ($1,500 ÷ $10,000). The custom of

---

[1]"Fair Value Measurement," Proposed *Statement of Financial Accounting Standards* (Norwalk, Conn.: FASB, October 21, 2005).

[2]Many recent standards, such as *FASB Statements No. 106, 107, 109, 113, 114, 116, 141, 142,* and *144,* have addressed the issue of present value in the pronouncement or related basis for conclusions.

expressing interest as a percentage rate is an established business practice.[3] In fact, business managers make investing and borrowing decisions on the basis of the rate of interest involved, rather than on the actual dollar amount of interest to be received or paid.

How is the interest rate determined? One important factor is the level of credit risk (risk of nonpayment) involved. Other factors being equal, the higher the credit risk, the higher the interest rate. Low-risk borrowers like **Microsoft** or **Intel** can probably obtain a loan at or slightly below the going market rate of interest. However, a bank would probably charge the neighborhood delicatessen several percentage points above the market rate, if granting the loan at all.

The amount of interest involved in any financing transaction is a function of three variables:

VARIABLES IN INTEREST COMPUTATION

1 *PRINCIPAL.* The amount borrowed or invested.
2 *INTEREST RATE.* A percentage of the outstanding principal.
3 *TIME.* The number of years or fractional portion of a year that the principal is outstanding.

Thus, the following three relationships apply:

- The larger the principal amount, the larger the dollar amount of interest.
- The higher the interest rate, the larger the dollar amount of interest.
- The longer the time period, the larger the dollar amount of interest.

Simple Interest

OBJECTIVE 2
Distinguish between simple and compound interest.

Companies compute **simple interest** on the amount of the principal only. It is the return on (or growth of) the principal for one time period. The following equation expresses simple interest.[4]

$$\text{Interest} = p \times i \times n$$

where

p = principal
i = rate of interest for a single period
n = number of periods

To illustrate, Barstow Electric Inc. borrows $10,000 for 3 years with a simple interest rate of 8% per year. It computes the total interest it will pay as follows.

$$
\begin{aligned}
\text{Interest} &= p \times i \times n \\
&= \$10{,}000 \times .08 \times 3 \\
&= \$2{,}400
\end{aligned}
$$

---

[3]Federal law requires the disclosure of interest rates on an **annual basis** in all contracts. That is, instead of stating the rate as "1% per month," contracts must state the rate as "12% per year" if it is simple interest or "12.68% per year" if it is compounded monthly.

[4]Business mathematics and business finance textbooks traditionally state simple interest as: $I(\text{interest}) = P(\text{principal}) \times R(\text{rate}) \times T(\text{time})$.

If Barstow borrows $10,000 for 3 months at 8%, the interest is $200, computed as follows.

$$\text{Interest} = \$10,000 \times .08 \times 3/12$$
$$= \$200$$

Compound Interest

John Maynard Keynes, the legendary English economist, supposedly called it magic. Mayer Rothschild, the founder of the famous European banking firm, proclaimed it the eighth wonder of the world. Today, people continue to extol its wonder and its power. The object of their affection? Compound interest.

We compute **compound interest** on principal **and** on any interest earned that has not been paid or withdrawn. It is the return on (or growth of) the principal for two or more time periods. Compounding computes interest not only on the principal but also on the interest earned to date on that principal, assuming the interest is left on deposit.

To illustrate the difference between simple and compound interest, assume that Vasquez Company deposits $10,000 in the Last National Bank, where it will earn simple interest of 9% per year. It deposits another $10,000 in the First State Bank, where it will earn compound interest of 9% per year compounded annually. In both cases, Vasquez will not withdraw any interest until 3 years from the date of deposit. Illustration 6-1 shows the computation of interest Vasquez will receive, as well as its accumulated year-end balance.

ILLUSTRATION 6-1
Simple vs. Compound Interest

Last National Bank				First State Bank		
Simple Interest Calculation	Simple Interest	Accumulated Year-end Balance		Compound Interest Calculation	Compound Interest	Accumulated Year-end Balance
Year 1 $10,000.00 × 9%	$ 900.00	$10,900.00		Year 1 $10,000.00 × 9%	$ 900.00	$10,900.00
Year 2 $10,000.00 × 9%	900.00	$11,800.00		Year 2 $10,900.00 × 9%	981.00	$11,881.00
Year 3 $10,000.00 × 9%	900.00	$12,700.00		Year 3 $11,881.00 × 9%	1,069.29	$12,950.29
	$2,700		$250.29 Difference		$2,950.29	

Note in the illustration above that simple interest uses the initial principal of $10,000 to compute the interest in all 3 years. **Compound interest uses the accumulated balance (principal plus interest to date) at each year-end to compute interest in the succeeding year.** This explains the larger balance in the compound interest account.

Obviously, any rational investor would choose compound interest, if available, over simple interest. In the example above, compounding provides $250.29 of additional interest revenue. For practical purposes, compounding assumes that unpaid interest earned becomes a part of the principal. Furthermore, the accumulated balance at the end of each year becomes the new principal sum on which interest is earned during the next year.

Compound interest is the typical interest computation applied in business situations. This occurs particularly in our economy, where companies use and finance large amounts of long-lived assets over long periods of time. Financial managers view and evaluate their investment opportunities in terms of a series of periodic returns, each of which they can reinvest to yield additional returns. Simple interest usually applies only to short-term investments and debts that involve a time span of one year or less.

WHAT DO THE
NUMBERS MEAN?

| **A PRETTY GOOD START** |

The current debate on Social Security reform provides a great context to illustrate the power of compounding. One proposed idea is for the government to give $1,000 to every citizen at birth. This gift would be deposited in an account that would earn interest tax-free until the citizen retires. Assuming the account earns a modest 5% annual return until retirement at age 65, the $1,000 would grow to $23,839. With monthly compounding, the $1,000 deposited at birth would grow to $25,617.

Why start so early? If the government waited until age 18 to deposit the money, it would grow to only $9,906 with annual compounding. That is, reducing the time invested by a third results in more than a 50% reduction in retirement money. The example illustrates the importance of starting early when the power of compounding is involved.

Compound Interest Tables (see pages 302–311)

OBJECTIVE 3
Use appropriate compound interest tables.

We present five different types of compound interest tables at the end of this chapter. These tables should help you study this chapter as well as solve other problems involving interest.

| **INTEREST TABLES AND THEIR CONTENTS** |

1 *FUTURE VALUE OF 1* TABLE. Contains the amounts to which 1 will accumulate if deposited now at a specified rate and left for a specified number of periods. (Table 1)

2 *PRESENT VALUE OF 1* TABLE. Contains the amounts that must be deposited now at a specified rate of interest to equal 1 at the end of a specified number of periods. (Table 2)

3 *FUTURE VALUE OF AN ORDINARY ANNUITY OF 1* TABLE. Contains the amounts to which periodic rents of 1 will accumulate if the payments (rents) are invested at the **end** of each period at a specified rate of interest for a specified number of periods. (Table 3)

4 *PRESENT VALUE OF AN ORDINARY ANNUITY OF 1* TABLE. Contains the amounts that must be deposited now at a specified rate of interest to permit withdrawals of 1 at the **end** of regular periodic intervals for the specified number of periods. (Table 4)

5 *PRESENT VALUE OF AN ANNUITY DUE OF 1* TABLE. Contains the amounts that must be deposited now at a specified rate of interest to permit withdrawals of 1 at the **beginning** of regular periodic intervals for the specified number of periods. (Table 5)

Illustration 6-2 lists the general format and content of these tables. It shows how much principal plus interest a dollar accumulates to at the end of each of five periods, at three different rates of compound interest.

ILLUSTRATION 6-2
Excerpt from Table 6-1

FUTURE VALUE OF 1 AT COMPOUND INTEREST (EXCERPT FROM TABLE 6-1, PAGE 303)			
Period	9%	10%	11%
1	1.09000	1.10000	1.11000
2	1.18810	1.21000	1.23210
3	1.29503	1.33100	1.36763
4	1.41158	1.46410	1.51807
5	1.53862	1.61051	1.68506

The compound tables rely on basic formulas. For example, the formula to determine the future value factor (*FVF*) for 1 is:

$$FVF_{n,i} = (1 + i)^n$$

where

$FVF_{n,i}$ = future value factor for *n* periods at *i* interest

n = number of periods

i = rate of interest for a single period

Financial calculators include preprogrammed $FVF_{n,i}$ and other time value of money formulas. We illustrate the use of these tools to solve time value of money problems in Appendix 6A.

To illustrate the use of interest tables to calculate compound amounts, assume an interest rate of 9%. Illustration 6-3 shows the future value to which 1 accumulates (the future value factor).

Period	Beginning-of-Period Amount	Multiplier × (1 + i)	=	End-of-Period Amount*	Formula (1 + i)ⁿ
1	1.00000	1.09		1.09000	$(1.09)^1$
2	1.09000	1.09		1.18810	$(1.09)^2$
3	1.18810	1.09		1.29503	$(1.09)^3$

*Note that these amounts appear in Table 6-1 in the 9% column.

ILLUSTRATION 6-3
Accumulation of Compound Amounts

Throughout our discussion of compound interest tables, note the intentional use of the term **periods** instead of **years**. Interest is generally expressed in terms of an annual rate. However, many business circumstances dictate a compounding period of less than one year. In such circumstances, a company must convert the annual interest rate to correspond to the length of the period. To convert the "annual interest rate" into the "compounding period interest rate," a company **divides the annual rate by the number of compounding periods per year**.

In addition, companies determine the number of periods by **multiplying the number of years involved by the number of compounding periods per year**. To illustrate, assume an investment of $1 for 6 years at 8% annual interest compounded **quarterly**. Using Table 6-1, page 302, read the factor that appears in the 2% column on the 24th row—6 years × 4 compounding periods per year, namely 1.60844, or approximately $1.61. Thus, all compound interest tables use the term **periods**, not **years**, to express the quantity of *n*. Illustration 6-4 shows how to determine (1) the interest rate per compounding period and (2) the number of compounding periods in four situations of differing compounding frequency.[5]

12% Annual Interest Rate over 5 Years Compounded	Interest Rate per Compounding Period	Number of Compounding Periods
Annually (1)	.12 ÷ 1 = .12	5 years × 1 compounding per year = 5 periods
Semiannually (2)	.12 ÷ 2 = .06	5 years × 2 compoundings per year = 10 periods
Quarterly (4)	.12 ÷ 4 = .03	5 years × 4 compoundings per year = 20 periods
Monthly (12)	.12 ÷ 12 = .01	5 years × 12 compoundings per year = 60 periods

ILLUSTRATION 6-4
Frequency of Compounding

[5]Because interest is theoretically earned (accruing) every second of every day, it is possible to calculate interest that is **compounded continuously**. Using the natural, or Napierian, system of logarithms facilitates computations involving continuous compounding. As a practical matter, however, most business transactions assume interest to be compounded no more frequently than daily.

How often interest is compounded can substantially affect the rate of return. For example, a 9% annual interest compounded **daily** provides a 9.42% yield, or a difference of 0.42%. The 9.42% is the **effective yield**.[6] The annual interest rate (9%) is the **stated, nominal,** or **face rate.** When the compounding frequency is greater than once a year, the effective interest rate will always exceed the stated rate.

Illustration 6-5 shows how compounding for five different time periods affects the effective yield and the amount earned by an investment of $10,000 for one year.

ILLUSTRATION 6-5
Comparison of Different
Compounding Periods

Interest Rate	Compounding Periods				
	Annually	Semiannually	Quarterly	Monthly	Daily
8%	8.00% $800	8.16% $816	8.24% $824	8.30% $830	8.33% $833
9%	9.00% $900	9.20% $920	9.31% $931	9.38% $938	9.42% $942
10%	10.00% $1,000	10.25% $1,025	10.38% $1,038	10.47% $1,047	10.52% $1,052

Fundamental Variables

OBJECTIVE 4
Identify variables fundamental to solving interest problems.

The following four variables are fundamental to all compound interest problems.

FUNDAMENTAL VARIABLES

1 *RATE OF INTEREST.* This rate, unless otherwise stated, is an annual rate that must be adjusted to reflect the length of the compounding period if less than a year.

2 *NUMBER OF TIME PERIODS.* This is the number of compounding periods. (A period may be equal to or less than a year.)

3 *FUTURE VALUE.* The value at a future date of a given sum or sums invested assuming compound interest.

4 *PRESENT VALUE.* The value now (present time) of a future sum or sums discounted assuming compound interest.

Illustration 6-6 depicts the relationship of these four fundamental variables in a **time diagram.**

---

[6]The formula for calculating the **effective rate**, in situations where the compounding frequency (*n*) is greater than once a year, is as follows.

$$\text{Effective rate} = (1 + i)^n - 1$$

To illustrate, if the stated annual rate is 8% compounded quarterly (or 2% per quarter), the effective annual rate is:

$$
\begin{aligned}
\text{Effective rate} &= (1 + .02)^4 - 1 \\
&= (1.02)^4 - 1 \\
&= 1.0824 - 1 \\
&= .0824 \\
&= 8.24\%
\end{aligned}
$$

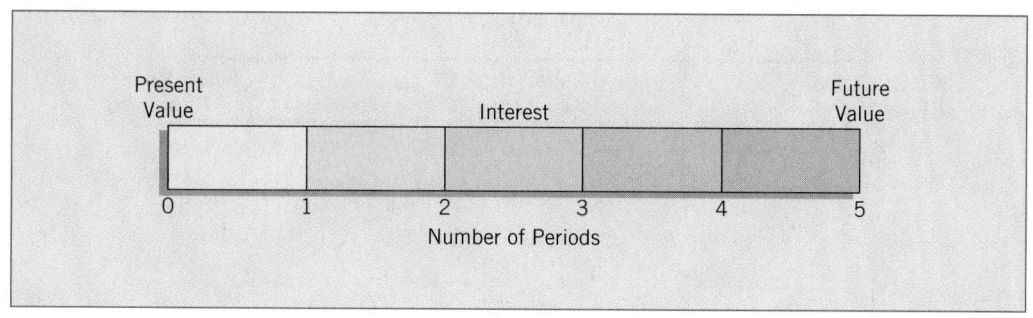

ILLUSTRATION 6-6
Basic Time Diagram

In some cases, all four of these variables are known. However, at least one variable is unknown in many business situations. To better understand and solve the problems in this chapter, we encourage you to sketch compound interest problems in the form of the preceding time diagram.

SINGLE-SUM PROBLEMS

Many business and investment decisions involve a single amount of money that either exists now or will in the future. Single-sum problems are generally classified into one of the following two categories.

OBJECTIVE 5
Solve future and present value of 1 problems.

1 Computing the **unknown** future value of a known single sum of money that is invested now for a certain number of periods at a certain interest rate.

2 Computing the **unknown** present value of a known single sum of money in the future that is discounted for a certain number of periods at a certain interest rate.

When analyzing the information provided, determine first whether the problem involves a future value or a present value. Then apply the following general rules, depending on the situation:

- **If solving for a future value**, *accumulate* all cash flows to a future point. In this instance, interest increases the amounts or values over time so that the future value exceeds the present value.

- **If solving for a present value**, *discount* all cash flows from the future to the present. In this case, **discounting** reduces the amounts or values, so that the present value is less than the future amount.

Preparation of time diagrams aids in identifying the unknown as an item in the future or the present. Sometimes the problem involves neither a future value nor a present value. Instead, the unknown is the interest or discount rate, or the number of compounding or discounting periods.

Future Value of a Single Sum

To determine the **future value** of a single sum, multiply the future value factor by its present value (principal), as follows.

$$FV = PV \ (FVF_{n,i})$$

where

$$FV = \text{future value}$$
$$PV = \text{present value (principal or single sum)}$$
$$FVF_{n,i} = \text{future value factor for } n \text{ periods at } i \text{ interest}$$

To illustrate, Bruegger Co. wants to determine the future value of $50,000 invested for 5 years compounded annually at an interest rate of 11%. Illustration 6-7 (on page 260) shows this investment situation in time-diagram form.

ILLUSTRATION 6-7
Future Value
Time Diagram
($n = 5, i = 11\%$)

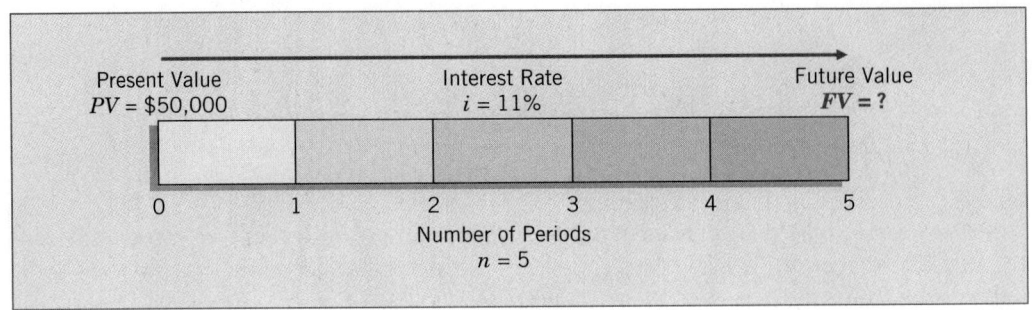

Using the future value formula, Bruegger solves this investment problem as follows.

$$\text{Future value} = PV \, (FVF_{n,i})$$
$$= \$50{,}000 \, (FVF_{5,11\%})$$
$$= \$50{,}000 \, (1 + .11)^5$$
$$= \$50{,}000 \, (1.68506)$$
$$= \$84{,}253$$

To determine the future value factor of 1.68506 in the formula above, Bruegger uses a financial calculator or reads the appropriate table, in this case Table 6-1 (11% column and the 5-period row).

Companies can apply this time diagram and formula approach to routine business situations. To illustrate, assume that **Commonwealth Edison Company** deposited $250 million in an escrow account with **Northern Trust Company** at the beginning of 2007 as a commitment toward a power plant to be completed December 31, 2010. How much will the company have on deposit at the end of 4 years if interest is 10%, compounded semiannually?

With a known present value of $250 million, a total of 8 compounding periods (4 × 2), and an interest rate of 5% per compounding period (.10 ÷ 2), the company can time-diagram this problem and determine the future value as shown in Illustration 6-8.

ILLUSTRATION 6-8
Future Value
Time Diagram
($n = 8, i = 5\%$)

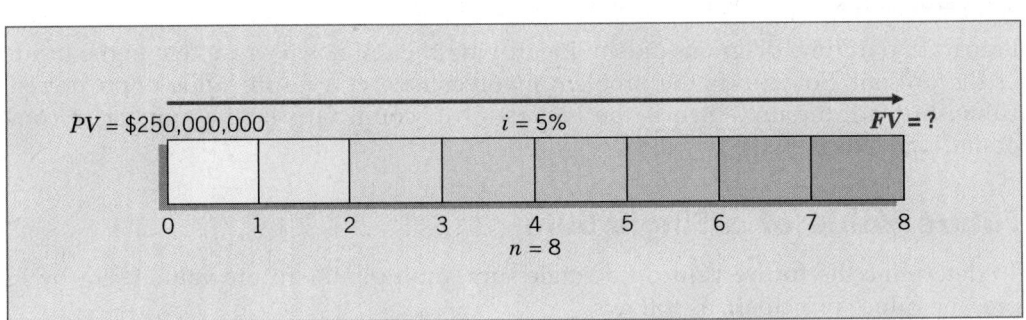

$$\text{Future value} = \$250{,}000{,}000 \, (FVF_{8,5\%})$$
$$= \$250{,}000{,}000 \, (1 + .05)^8$$
$$= \$250{,}000{,}000 \, (1.47746)$$
$$= \$369{,}365{,}000$$

Using a future value factor found in Table 1 (5% column, 8-period row), we find that the deposit of $250 million will accumulate to $369,365,000 by December 31, 2010.

Present Value of a Single Sum

The Bruegger example on page 260 showed that $50,000 invested at an annually compounded interest rate of 11% will equal $84,253 at the end of 5 years. It follows, then, that $84,253, 5 years in the future, is worth $50,000 now. That is, $50,000 is the present value of $84,253. The **present value** is the amount needed to invest now, to produce a known future value.

The present value is always a smaller amount than the known future value, due to earned and accumulated interest. In determining the future value, a company moves forward in time using a process of **accumulation**. In determining present value, it moves backward in time using a process of **discounting**.

As indicated earlier, a "present value of 1 table" appears at the end of this chapter as Table 6-2. Illustration 6-9 demonstrates the nature of such a table. It shows the present value of 1 for five different periods at three different rates of interest.

PRESENT VALUE OF 1 AT COMPOUND INTEREST
(EXCERPT FROM TABLE 6-2, PAGE 305)

Period	9%	10%	11%
1	0.91743	0.90909	0.90090
2	0.84168	0.82645	0.81162
3	0.77218	0.75132	0.73119
4	0.70843	0.68301	0.65873
5	0.64993	0.62092	0.59345

ILLUSTRATION 6-9
Excerpt from Table 6-2

The following formula is used to determine the present value of 1 (present value factor):

$$PVF_{n,i} = \frac{1}{(1 + i)^n}$$

where

$$PVF_{n,i} = \text{present value factor for } n \text{ periods at } i \text{ interest}$$

To illustrate, assuming an interest rate of 9%, the present value of 1 discounted for three different periods is as shown in Illustration 6-10.

Discount Periods	1	$\div$ $(1 + i)^n$	= Present Value*	Formula $1/(1 + i)^n$
1	1.00000	1.09	.91743	$1/(1.09)^1$
2	1.00000	$(1.09)^2$	.84168	$1/(1.09)^2$
3	1.00000	$(1.09)^3$	.77218	$1/(1.09)^3$

*Note that these amounts appear in Table 6-2 in the 9% column.

ILLUSTRATION 6-10
Present Value of $1
Discounted at 9% for
Three Periods

The present value of any single sum (future value), then, is as follows.

$$PV = FV \ (PVF_{n,i})$$

where

$$PV = \text{present value}$$
$$FV = \text{future value}$$
$$PVF_{n,i} = \text{present value factor for } n \text{ periods at } i \text{ interest}$$

To illustrate, what is the present value of $84,253 to be received or paid in 5 years discounted at 11% compounded annually? Illustration 6-11 (on page 262) shows this problem as a time diagram.

ILLUSTRATION 6-11
Present Value
Time Diagram
($n = 5$, $i = 11\%$)

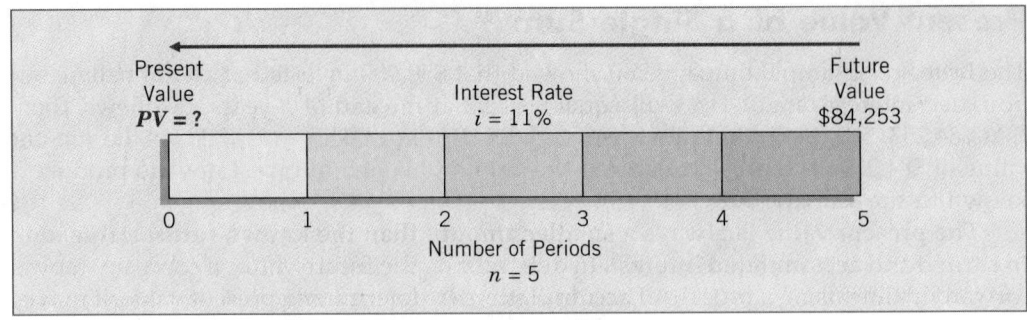

Using the formula, we solve this problem as follows.

$$\text{Present value} = FV\ (PVF_{n,i})$$

$$= \$84{,}253\ (PVF_{5,11\%})$$

$$= \$84{,}253\left(\frac{1}{(1 + .11)^5}\right)$$

$$= \$84{,}253\ (.59345)$$

$$= \$50{,}000$$

To determine the present value factor of 0.59345, use a financial calculator or read the present value of a single sum in Table 6-2 (11% column, 5-period row).

The time diagram and formula approach can be applied in a variety of situations. For example, assume that your rich uncle decides to give you $2,000 for a trip to Europe when you graduate from college 3 years from now. He proposes to finance the trip by investing a sum of money now at 8% compound interest that will provide you with $2,000 upon your graduation. The only conditions are that you graduate and that you tell him how much to invest now.

To impress your uncle, you set up the time diagram in Illustration 6-12 and solve this problem as follows.

ILLUSTRATION 6-12
Present Value
Time Diagram
($n = 3$, $i = 8\%$)

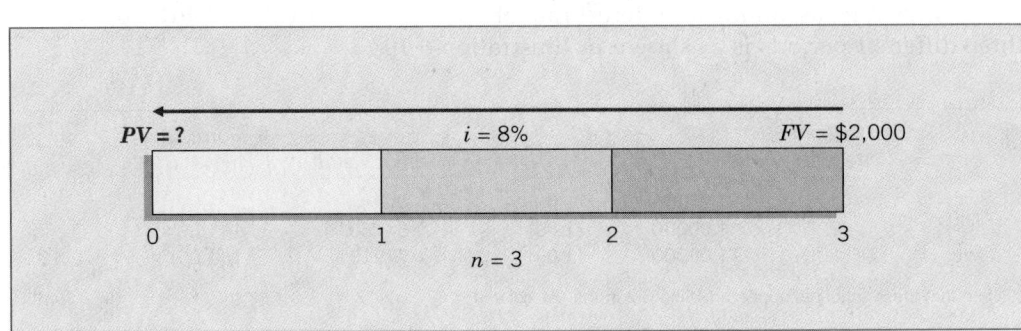

$$\text{Present value} = \$2{,}000\ (PVF_{3,8\%})$$

$$= \$2{,}000\left(\frac{1}{(1 + .08)^3}\right)$$

$$= \$2{,}000\ (.79383)$$

$$= \$1{,}587.66$$

Advise your uncle to invest $1,587.66 now to provide you with $2,000 upon graduation. To satisfy your uncle's other condition, you must pass this course (and many more).

Solving for Other Unknowns in Single-Sum Problems

In computing either the future value or the present value in the previous single-sum illustrations, both the number of periods and the interest rate were known. In many business situations, both the future value and the present value are known, but the number of periods or the interest rate is unknown. The following two examples are single-sum problems (future value and present value) with either an unknown number of periods (n) or an unknown interest rate (i). These examples, and the accompanying solutions, demonstrate that knowing any three of the four values (future value, FV; present value, PV; number of periods, n; interest rate, i) allows you to derive the remaining unknown variable.

Example—Computation of the Number of Periods

The Village of Somonauk wants to accumulate $70,000 for the construction of a veterans monument in the town square. At the beginning of the current year, the Village deposited $47,811 in a memorial fund that earns 10% interest compounded annually. How many years will it take to accumulate $70,000 in the memorial fund?

In this illustration, the Village knows both the present value ($47,811) and the future value ($70,000), along with the interest rate of 10%. Illustration 6-13 depicts this investment problem as a time diagram.

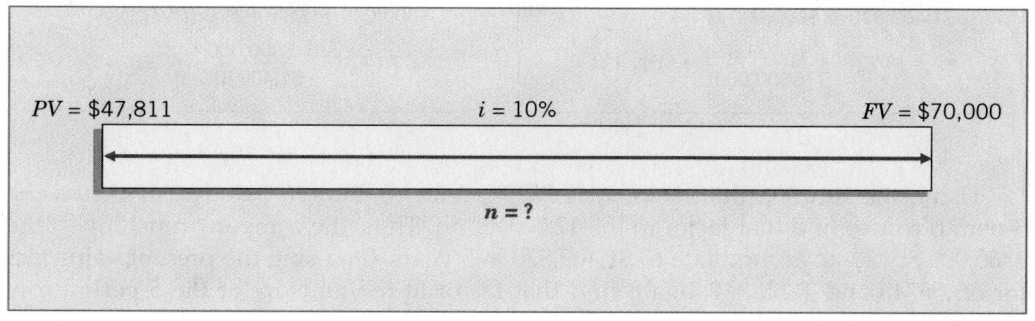

$PV = \$47,811$ $i = 10\%$ $FV = \$70,000$

$n = ?$

ILLUSTRATION 6-13
Time Diagram to Solve for Unknown Number of Periods

Knowing both the present value and the future value allows the Village to solve for the unknown number of periods. It may use either the future value or the present value formulas, as shown in Illustration 6-14.

Future Value Approach	Present Value Approach
$FV = PV\,(FVF_{n,10\%})$	$PV = FV\,(PVF_{n,10\%})$
$\$70,000 = \$47,811\,(FVF_{n,10\%})$	$\$47,811 = \$70,000\,(PVF_{n,10\%})$
$FVF_{n,10\%} = \dfrac{\$70,000}{\$47,811} = 1.46410$	$PVF_{n,10\%} = \dfrac{\$47,811}{\$70,000} = .68301$

ILLUSTRATION 6-14
Solving for Unknown Number of Periods

Using the future value factor of 1.46410, refer to Table 6-1 and read down the 10% column to find that factor in the 4-period row. Thus, it will take 4 years for the $47,811 to accumulate to $70,000 if invested at 10% interest compounded annually. Or, using the present value factor of 0.68301, refer to Table 6-2 and read down the 10% column to find that factor in the 4-period row.

Example—Computation of the Interest Rate

Advanced Design, Inc. needs $1,409,870 for basic research 5 years from now. The company currently has $800,000 to invest for that purpose. At what rate of interest must it invest the $800,000 to fund basic research projects of $1,409,870, 5 years from now?

The time diagram in Illustration 6-15 depicts this investment situation.

ILLUSTRATION 6-15
Time Diagram to Solve
for Unknown Interest
Rate

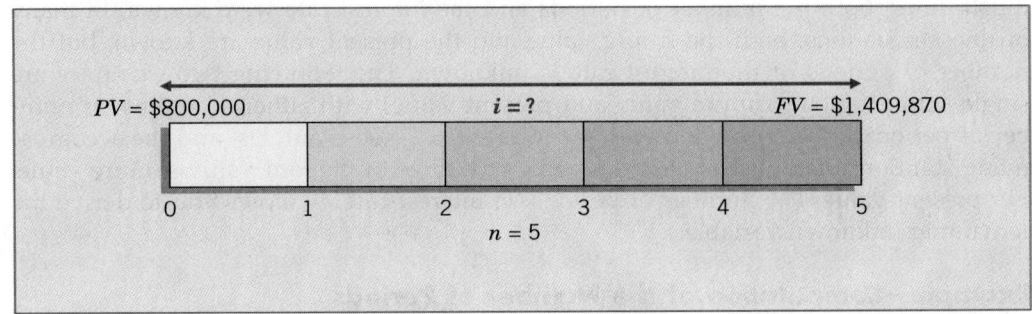

Advanced Design may determine the unknown interest rate from either the future value approach or the present value approach, as Illustration 6-16 shows.

ILLUSTRATION 6-16
Solving for Unknown
Interest Rate

Future Value Approach	Present Value Approach
$FV = PV\,(FVF_{5,i})$	$PV = FV\,(PVF_{5,i})$
$\$1,409,870 = \$800,000\,(FVF_{5,i})$	$\$800,000 = \$1,409,870\,(PVF_{5,i})$
$FVF_{5,i} = \dfrac{\$1,409,870}{\$800,000} = 1.76234$	$PVF_{5,i} = \dfrac{\$800,000}{\$1,409,870} = .56743$

Using the future value factor of 1.76234, refer to Table 6-1 and read across the 5-period row to find that factor in the 12% column. Thus, the company must invest the $800,000 at 12% to accumulate to $1,409,870 in 5 years. Or, using the present value factor of .56743 and Table 6-2, again find that factor at the juncture of the 5-period row and the 12% column.

ANNUITIES

The preceding discussion involved only the accumulation or discounting of a single principal sum. However, many situations arise in which a series of dollar amounts are paid or received periodically, such as installment loans or sales; regular, partially recovered invested funds; or a series of realized cost savings.

For example, a life insurance contract involves a series of equal payments made at equal intervals of time. Such a process of periodic payment represents the accumulation of a sum of money through an annuity. An **annuity**, by definition, requires the following: (1) periodic payments or receipts (called **rents**) of the same amount, (2) the same-length interval between such rents, and (3) compounding of **interest** once each interval. The **future value of an annuity** is the sum of all the rents plus the accumulated compound interest on them.

Note that the rents may occur at either the beginning or the end of the periods. If the rents occur at the end of each period, an annuity is classified as an **ordinary annuity**. If the rents occur at the beginning of each period, an annuity is classified as an **annuity due**.

OBJECTIVE 6
Solve future value of
ordinary and annuity
due problems.

Future Value of an Ordinary Annuity

One approach to determining the future value of an annuity computes the value to which **each** of the rents in the series will accumulate, and then totals their individual future values.

For example, assume that $1 is deposited at the **end** of each of 5 years (an ordinary annuity) and earns 12% interest compounded annually. Illustration 6-17 shows the computation of the future value, using the "future value of 1" table (Table 6-1) for each of the five $1 rents.

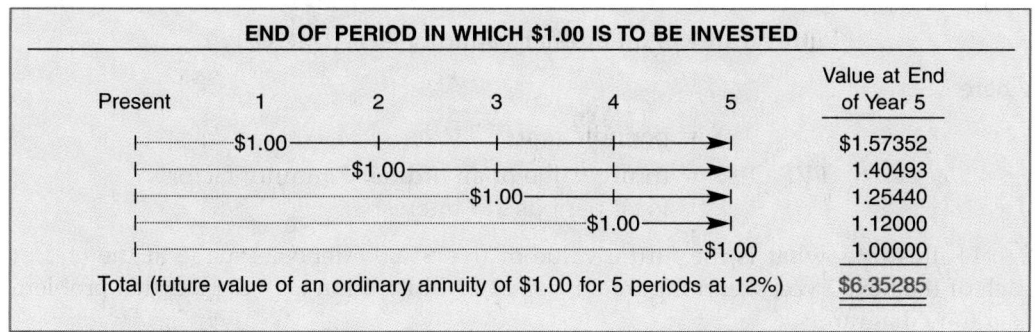

ILLUSTRATION 6-17
Solving for the Future
Value of an Ordinary
Annuity

Because an ordinary annuity consists of rents deposited at the end of the period, those rents earn no interest during the period. For example, the third rent earns interest for only two periods (periods four and five). It earns no interest for the third period since it is not deposited until the end of the third period. When computing the future value of an ordinary annuity, the number of compounding periods will always be **one less than the number of rents**.

The foregoing procedure for computing the future value of an ordinary annuity always produces the correct answer. However, it can become cumbersome if the number of rents is large. A formula provides a more efficient way of expressing the future value of an ordinary annuity of 1. This formula sums the individual rents plus the compound interest, as follows:

$$FVF\text{-}OA_{n,i} = \frac{(1 + i)^n - 1}{i}$$

where

$$FVF\text{-}OA_{n,i} = \text{future value factor of an ordinary annuity}$$
$$i = \text{rate of interest per period}$$
$$n = \text{number of compounding periods}$$

For example, $FVF\text{-}OA_{5,12\%}$ refers to the value to which an ordinary annuity of 1 will accumulate in 5 periods at 12% interest.

Using the formula above has resulted in the development of tables, similar to those used for the "future value of 1" and the "present value of 1" for both an ordinary annuity and an annuity due. Illustration 6-18 provides an excerpt from the "future value of an ordinary annuity of 1" table.

	FUTURE VALUE OF AN ORDINARY ANNUITY OF 1 (EXCERPT FROM TABLE 6-3, PAGE 307)			
	Period	10%	11%	12%
	1	1.00000	1.00000	1.00000
	2	2.10000	2.11000	2.12000
	3	3.31000	3.34210	3.37440
	4	4.64100	4.70973	4.77933
	5	6.10510	6.22780	6.35285*

*Note that this annuity table factor is the same as the sum of the future values of 1 factors shown in Illustration 6-17.

ILLUSTRATION 6-18
Excerpt from Table 6-3

Interpreting the table, if $1 is invested at the end of each year for 4 years at 11% interest compounded annually, the value of the annuity at the end of the fourth year is $4.71 (4.70973 × $1.00). Now, multiply the factor from the appropriate line and column of the table by the dollar amount of **one rent** involved in an ordinary annuity. The result: the accumulated sum of the rents and the compound interest to the date of the last rent.

The following formula computes the future value of an ordinary annuity.

$$\text{Future value of an ordinary annuity} = R \ (FVF\text{-}OA_{n,i})$$

where

$$R = \text{periodic rent}$$
$$FVF\text{-}OA_{n,i} = \text{future value of an ordinary annuity factor}$$
$$\text{for } n \text{ periods at } i \text{ interest}$$

To illustrate, what is the future value of five $5,000 deposits made at the end of each of the next 5 years, earning interest of 12%? Illustration 6-19 depicts this problem as a time diagram.

ILLUSTRATION 6-19
Time Diagram for Future
Value of Ordinary
Annuity ($n = 5, i = 12\%$)

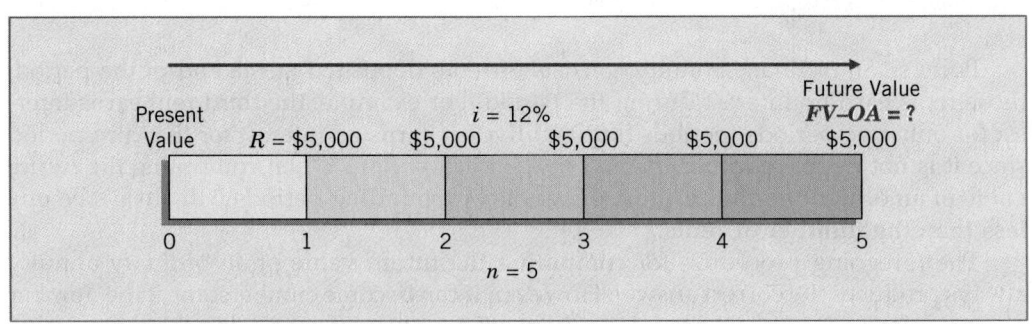

Use of the formula solves this investment problem as follows.

$$\text{Future value of an ordinary annuity} = R \ (FVF\text{-}OA_{n,i})$$
$$= \$5,000 \ (FVF\text{-}OA_{5,12\%})$$
$$= \$5,000 \left(\frac{(1 + .12)^5 - 1}{.12} \right)$$
$$= \$5,000 \ (6.35285)$$
$$= \$31,764.25$$

To determine the future value of an ordinary annuity factor of 6.35285 in the formula above, use a financial calculator or read the appropriate table, in this case, Table 6-3 (12% column and the 5-period row).

To illustrate these computations in a business situation, assume that Hightown Electronics deposits $75,000 at the end of each 6-month period for the next 3 years, to accumulate enough money to meet debts that mature in 3 years. What is the future value that the company will have on deposit at the end of 3 years if the annual interest rate is 10%? The time diagram in Illustration 6-20 depicts this situation.

ILLUSTRATION 6-20
Time Diagram for Future
Value of Ordinary
Annuity ($n = 6, i = 5\%$)

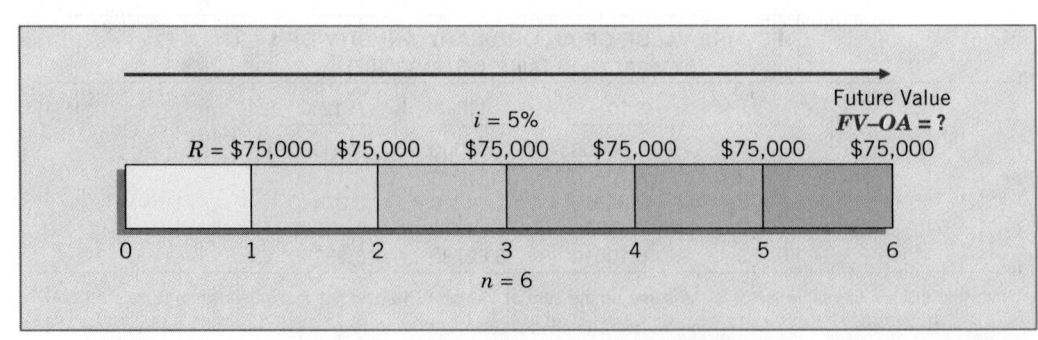

The formula solution for the Hightown Electronics situation is as follows.

$$\text{Future value of an ordinary annuity} = R\ (FVF\text{-}OA_{n,i})$$
$$= \$75,000\ (FVF\text{-}OA_{6,5\%})$$
$$= \$75,000\left(\frac{(1+.05)^6 - 1}{.05}\right)$$
$$= \$75,000\ (6.80191)$$
$$= \$510,143.25$$

Thus, six 6-month deposits of $75,000 earning 5% per period will grow to $510,143.25.

Future Value of an Annuity Due

The preceding analysis of an ordinary annuity assumed that the periodic rents occur at the **end** of each period. Recall that an **annuity due** assumes periodic rents occur at the **beginning** of each period. This means an annuity due will accumulate interest during the first period (in contrast to an ordinary annuity rent, which will not). In other words, the two types of annuities differ in the number of interest accumulation periods involved.

If rents occur at the end of a period (ordinary annuity), in determining the **future value of an annuity** there will be one less interest period than if the rents occur at the beginning of the period (annuity due). Illustration 6-21 shows this distinction.

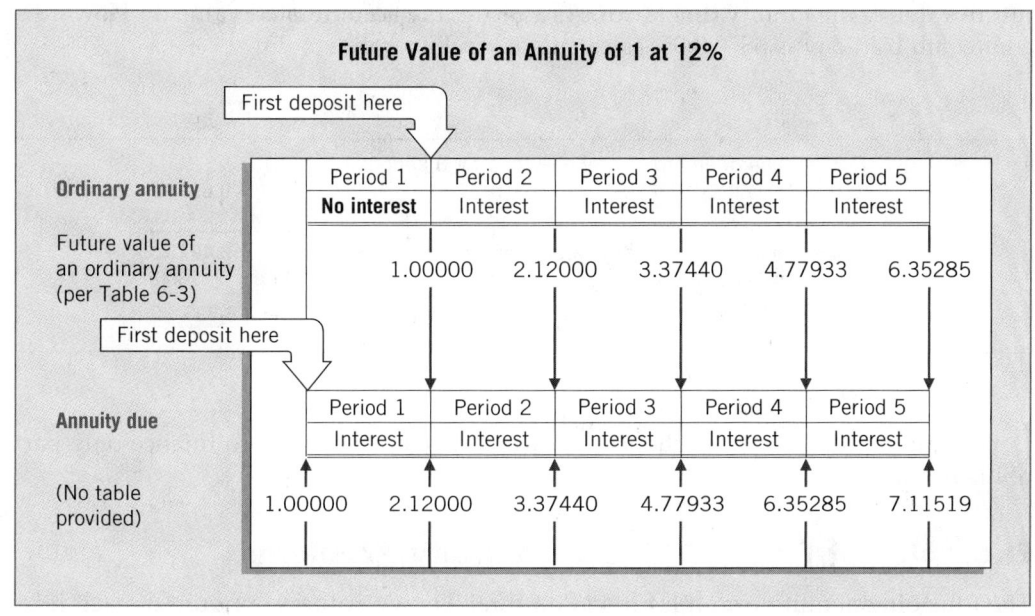

ILLUSTRATION 6-21
Comparison of the Future Value of an Ordinary Annuity with an Annuity Due

In this example, the cash flows from the annuity due come exactly one period earlier than for an ordinary annuity. As a result, the future value of the annuity due factor is exactly 12% higher than the ordinary annuity factor. For example, the value of an ordinary annuity factor at the end of period one at 12% is 1.00000, whereas for an annuity due it is 1.12000.

To find the future value of an annuity due factor, multiply the future value of an ordinary annuity factor by 1 plus the interest rate. For example, to determine the future value of an annuity due interest factor for 5 periods at 12% compound interest, simply multiply the future value of an ordinary annuity interest factor for 5 periods (6.35285), by one plus the interest rate (1 + .12), to arrive at 7.11519 (6.35285 × 1.12).

To illustrate the use of the ordinary annuity tables in converting to an annuity due, assume that Sue Lotadough plans to deposit $800 a year on each birthday of her son

Howard. She makes the first deposit on his tenth birthday, at 6% interest compounded annually. Sue wants to know the amount she will have accumulated for college expenses by her son's eighteenth birthday.

If the first deposit occurs on Howard's tenth birthday, Sue will make a total of 8 deposits over the life of the annuity (assume no deposit on the eighteenth birthday), as shown in Illustration 6-22. Because all the deposits are made at the beginning of the periods, they represent an annuity due.

ILLUSTRATION 6-22
Annuity Due
Time Diagram

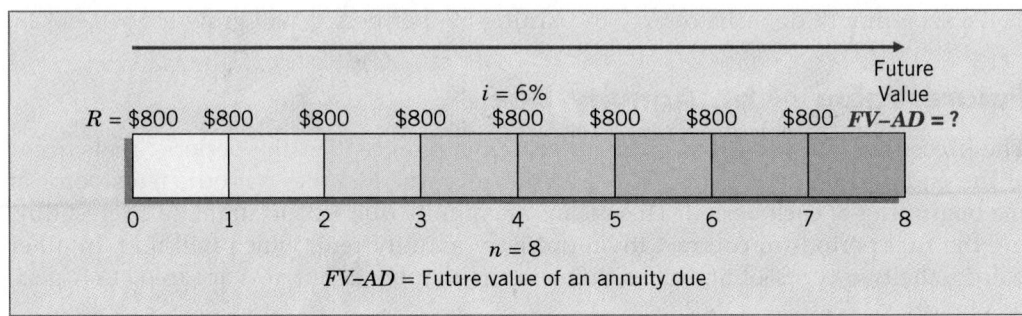

FV–AD = Future value of an annuity due

Referring to the "future value of an ordinary annuity of 1" table for 8 periods at 6%, Sue finds a factor of 9.89747. She then multiplies this factor by (1 + .06) to arrive at the future value of an annuity due factor. As a result, the accumulated value on Howard's eighteenth birthday is $8,393.05, as calculated in Illustration 6-23.

ILLUSTRATION 6-23
Computation of
Accumulated Value of
Annuity Due

1. Future value of an ordinary annuity of 1 for 8 periods at 6% (Table 6-3)	9.89747
2. Factor (1 + .06)	× 1.06
3. Future value of an annuity due of 1 for 8 periods at 6%	10.49132
4. Periodic deposit (rent)	× $800
5. Accumulated value on son's eighteenth birthday	$8,393.05

Depending on the college he chooses, Howard may have enough to finance only part of his first year of school.

Examples of Future Value of Annuity Problems

The foregoing annuity examples relied on three known values—amount of each rent, interest rate, and number of periods. Using these values enables us to determine the unknown fourth value, future value.

The first two future value problems we present illustrate the computations of (1) the amount of the rents and (2) the number of rents. The third problem illustrates the computation of the future value of an annuity due.

Computation of Rent

Assume that you plan to accumulate $14,000 for a down payment on a condominium apartment 5 years from now. For the next 5 years, you earn an annual return of 8% compounded semiannually. How much should you deposit at the end of each 6-month period?

The $14,000 is the future value of 10 (5 × 2) semiannual end-of-period payments of an unknown amount, at an interest rate of 4% (8% ÷ 2). Illustration 6-24 depicts this problem as a time diagram.

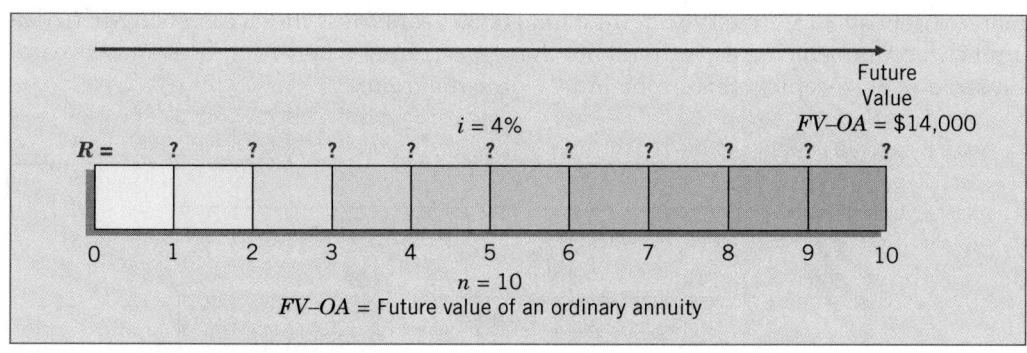

Using the formula for the future value of an ordinary annuity, you determine the amount of each rent as follows.

$$\text{Future value of an ordinary annuity} = R \ (FVF\text{-}OA_{n,i})$$

$$\$14,000 = R \ (FVF\text{-}OA_{10,4\%})$$

$$\$14,000 = R(12.00611)$$

$$R = \$1,166.07$$

Thus, you must make 10 semiannual deposits of $1,166.07 each in order to accumulate $14,000 for your down payment.

Computation of the Number of Periodic Rents

Suppose that a company's goal is to accumulate $117,332 by making periodic deposits of $20,000 at the end of each year, which will earn 8% compounded annually while accumulating. How many deposits must it make?

The $117,332 represents the future value of $n(?)$ $20,000 deposits, at an 8% annual rate of interest. Illustration 6-25 depicts this problem in a time diagram.

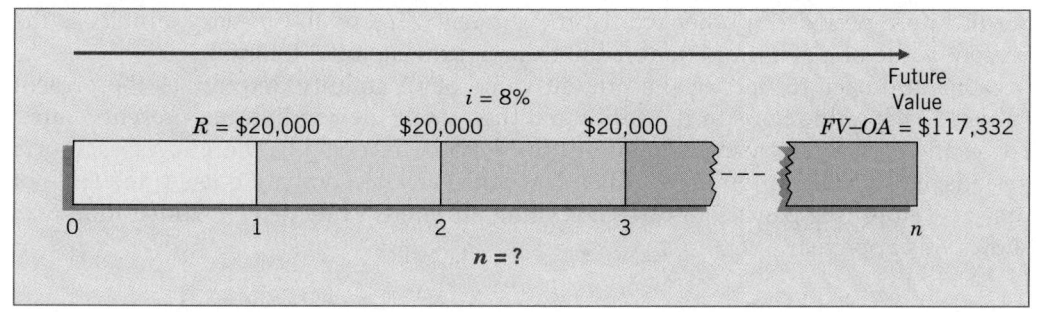

ILLUSTRATION 6-25
Future Value of Ordinary
Annuity Time Diagram,
to Solve for Unknown
Number of Periods

Using the future value of an ordinary annuity formula, the company obtains the following factor.

$$\text{Future value of an ordinary annuity} = R \ (FVF\text{-}OA_{n,i})$$

$$\$117,332 = \$20,000 \ (FVF\text{-}OA_{n,8\%})$$

$$FVF\text{-}OA_{n,8\%} = \frac{\$117,332}{\$20,000} = 5.86660$$

Use Table 6-3 and read down the 8% column to find 5.86660 in the 5-period row. Thus, the company must make five deposits of $20,000 each.

Computation of the Future Value

To create his retirement fund, Walter Goodwrench, a mechanic, now works weekends. Mr. Goodwrench deposits $2,500 today in a savings account that earns 9% interest. He plans to deposit $2,500 every year for a total of 30 years. How much cash will Mr. Good-wrench accumulate in his retirement savings account, when he retires in 30 years? Illustration 6-26 depicts this problem in a time diagram.

ILLUSTRATION 6-26
Future Value
Annuity Due
Time Diagram
($n = 30$, $i = 9\%$)

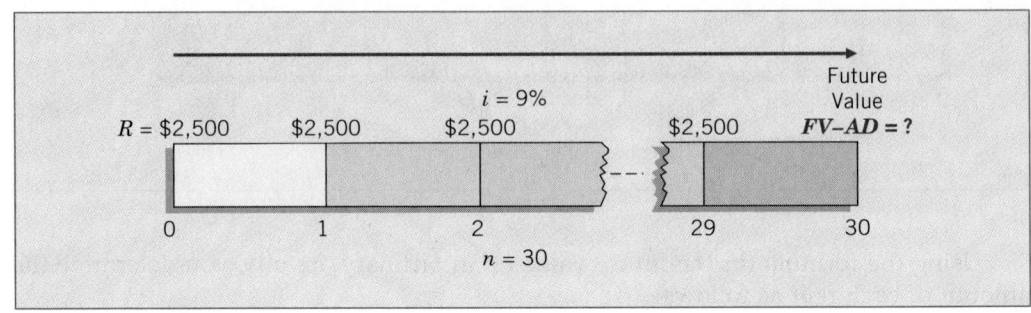

Using the "future value of an ordinary annuity of 1" table, Mr. Goodwrench computes the solution as shown in Illustration 6-27.

ILLUSTRATION 6-27
Computation of
Accumulated Value of an
Annuity Due

1. Future value of an ordinary annuity of 1 for 30 periods at 9%	136.30754
2. Factor (1 + .09)	× 1.09
3. Future value of an annuity due of 1 for 30 periods at 9%	148.57522
4. Periodic rent	× $2,500
5. Accumulated value at end of 30 years	$371,438

Present Value of an Ordinary Annuity

OBJECTIVE 7
Solve present value of
ordinary and annuity
due problems.

The present value of an annuity is **the single sum** that, if invested at compound interest now, would provide for an annuity (a series of withdrawals) for a certain number of future periods. In other words, the present value of an ordinary annuity is the present value of a series of equal rents, to withdraw at equal intervals.

One approach to finding the present value of an annuity determines the present value of each of the rents in the series and then totals their individual present values. For example, we may view an annuity of $1, to be received at the **end** of each of 5 periods, as separate amounts. We then compute each present value using the table of present values (see pages 303–304), assuming an interest rate of 12%. Illustration 6-28 shows this approach.

ILLUSTRATION 6-28
Solving for the Present
Value of an Ordinary
Annuity

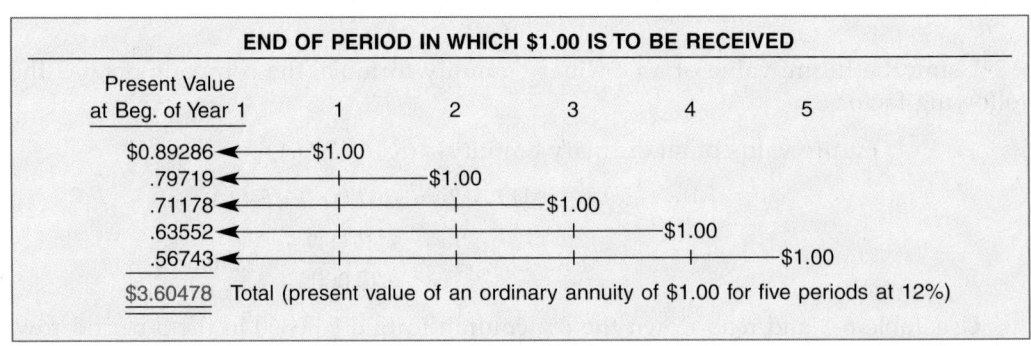

This computation tells us that if we invest the single sum of $3.60 today at 12% interest for 5 periods, we will be able to withdraw $1 at the end of each period for 5 periods. We can summarize this cumbersome procedure by the following formula.

$$PVF\text{-}OA_{n,i} = \frac{1 - \dfrac{1}{(1 + i)^n}}{i}$$

The expression $PVF\text{-}OA_{n,i}$ refers to the present value of an ordinary annuity of 1 factor for n periods at i interest. Ordinary annuity tables base present values on this formula. Illustration 6-29 shows an excerpt from such a table.

ILLUSTRATION 6-29
Excerpt from Table 6-4

PRESENT VALUE OF AN ORDINARY ANNUITY OF 1
(EXCERPT FROM TABLE 6-4, PAGE 309)

Period	10%	11%	12%
1	0.90909	0.90090	0.89286
2	1.73554	1.71252	1.69005
3	2.48685	2.44371	2.40183
4	3.16986	3.10245	3.03735
5	3.79079	3.69590	3.60478*

*Note that this annuity table factor is equal to the sum of the present value of 1 factors shown in Illustration 6-28.

The general formula for the present value of any ordinary annuity is as follows.

Present value of an ordinary annuity = $R\ (PVF\text{-}OA_{n,i})$

where

R = periodic rent (ordinary annuity)

$PVF\text{-}OA_{n,i}$ = present value of an ordinary annuity of 1 for n periods at i interest

To illustrate with an example, what is the present value of rental receipts of $6,000 each, to be received at the end of each of the next 5 years when discounted at 12%? This problem may be time-diagrammed and solved as shown in Illustration 6-30.

ILLUSTRATION 6-30
Present Value of Ordinary
Annuity Time Diagram

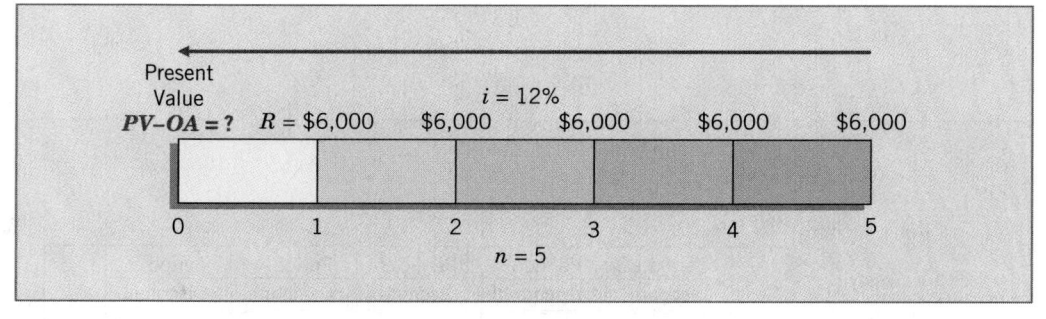

The formula for this calculation is as shown below.

Present value of an ordinary annuity = $R\ (PVF\text{-}OA_{n,i})$

= $6,000 $(PVF\text{-}OA_{5,12\%})$

= $6,000 (3.60478)

= $21,628.68

The present value of the 5 ordinary annuity rental receipts of $6,000 each is $21,628.68. To determine the present value of the ordinary annuity factor 3.60478, use a financial calculator or read the appropriate table, in this case Table 6-4 (12% column and 5-period row).

WHAT DO THE NUMBERS MEAN?

Time value of money concepts also can be relevant to public policy debates. For example, several states had to determine how to receive the payments from tobacco companies as settlement for a national lawsuit against the companies for the healthcare costs of smoking.

The **State of Wisconsin** was due to collect 25 years of payments totaling $5.6 billion. The state could wait to collect the payments, or it could sell the payments to an investment bank (a process called *securitization*). If it were to sell the payments, it would receive a lump-sum payment today of $1.26 billion. Is this a good deal for the state? Assuming a discount rate of 8% and that the payments will be received in equal amounts (e.g., an annuity), the present value of the tobacco payment is:

$$\$5.6 \text{ billion} \div 25 = \$224 \text{ million} \times 10.67478^* = \$2.39 \text{ billion}$$

$$*PV\text{-}OA(i = 8\%, n = 25)$$

Why would some in the state be willing to take just $1.26 billion today for an annuity whose present value is almost twice that amount? One reason is that Wisconsin was facing a hole in its budget that could be plugged in part by the lump-sum payment. Also, some believed that the risk of not getting paid by the tobacco companies in the future makes it prudent to get the money earlier.

If this latter reason has merit, then the present value computation above should have been based on a higher interest rate. Assuming a discount rate of 15%, the present value of the annuity is $1.448 billion ($5.6 billion ÷ 25 = $224 million; $224 million × 6.46415), which is much closer to the lump-sum payment offered to the State of Wisconsin.

Present Value of an Annuity Due

In our discussion of the present value of an ordinary annuity, we discounted the final rent based on the number of rent periods. In determining the present value of an annuity due, there is always one fewer discount period. Illustration 6-31 shows this distinction.

ILLUSTRATION 6-31
Comparison of Present Value of an Ordinary Annuity with an Annuity Due

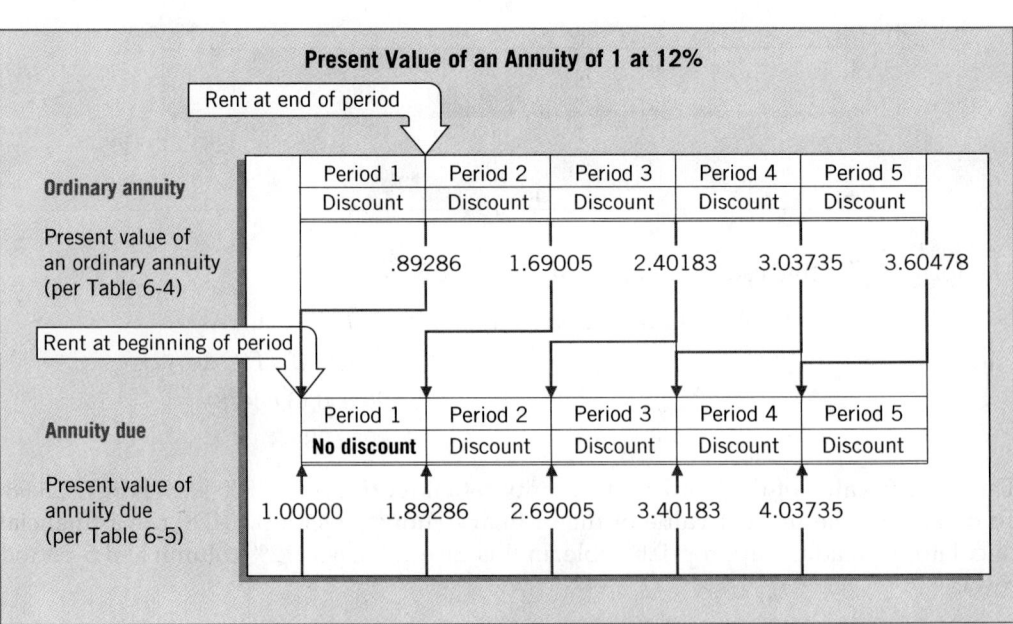

Because each cash flow comes exactly one period sooner in the present value of the annuity due, the present value of the cash flows is exactly 12% higher than the present value of an ordinary annuity. Thus, **to find the present value of an annuity due factor, multiply the present value of an ordinary annuity factor by 1 plus the interest rate** (that is, $1 + i$).

To determine the present value of an annuity due interest factor for 5 periods at 12% interest, take the present value of an ordinary annuity for 5 periods at 12% interest (3.60478) and multiply it by 1.12 to arrive at the present value of an annuity due, 4.03735 (3.60478 × 1.12). We provide present value of annuity due factors in Table 6-5.

To illustrate, Space Odyssey, Inc., rents a communications satellite for 4 years with annual rental payments of $4.8 million to be made at the beginning of each year. If the relevant annual interest rate is 11%, what is the present value of the rental obligations? Illustration 6-32 shows the company's time diagram for this problem.

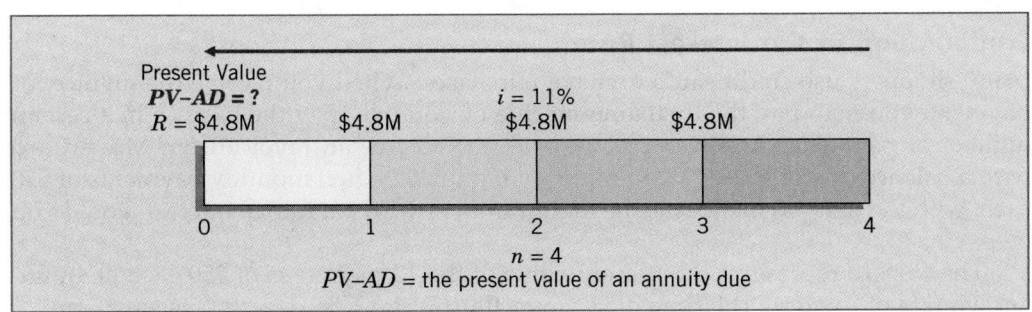

ILLUSTRATION 6-32
Present Value of Annuity Due Time Diagram ($n = 4$, $i = 11\%$)

Illustration 6-33 shows the computations to solve this problem.

1. Present value of an ordinary annuity of 1 for 4 periods at 11% (Table 6-4)	3.10245
2. Factor (1 + .11)	× 1.11
3. Present value of an annuity due of 1 for 4 periods at 11%	3.44372
4. Periodic deposit (rent)	× $4,800,000
5. Present value of payments	$16,529,856

ILLUSTRATION 6-33
Computation of Present Value of an Annuity Due

Using Table 6-5 also locates the desired factor 3.44371 and computes the present value of the lease payments to be $16,529,808. (The difference in computations is due to rounding.)

Examples of Present Value of Annuity Problems

In the following three examples, we demonstrate the computation of (1) the present value, (2) the interest rate, and (3) the amount of each rent.

Computation of the Present Value of an Ordinary Annuity

You have just won a lottery totaling $4,000,000. You learn that you will receive a check in the amount of $200,000 at the end of each of the next 20 years. What amount have you really won? That is, what is the present value of the $200,000 checks you will receive over the next 20 years? Illustration 6-34 (on page 274) shows a time diagram of this enviable situation (assuming an appropriate interest rate of 10%).

You calculate the present value as follows:

$$\text{Present value of an ordinary annuity} = R\,(PVF\text{-}OA_{n,i})$$
$$= \$200{,}000\,(PVF\text{-}OA_{20,10\%})$$
$$= \$200{,}000\,(8.51356)$$
$$= \$1{,}702{,}712$$

ILLUSTRATION 6-34
Time Diagram to Solve
for Present Value of
Lottery Payments

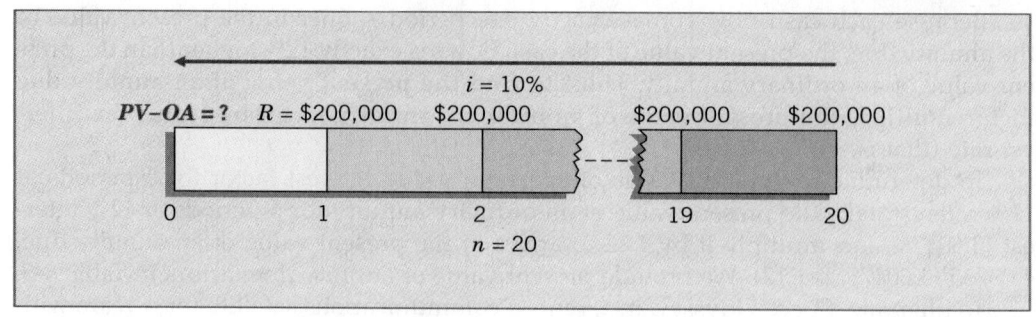

As a result, if the state deposits $1,702,712 now and earns 10% interest, it can withdraw $200,000 a year for 20 years to pay you the $4,000,000.

Computation of the Interest Rate

Many shoppers use credit cards to make purchases. When you receive the invoice for payment, you may pay the total amount due or you may pay the balance in a certain number of payments. For example, assume you receive an invoice from MasterCard with a balance due of $528.77. You may pay it off in 12 equal monthly payments of $50 each, with the first payment due one month from now. What rate of interest would you be paying?

The $528.77 represents the present value of the 12 payments of $50 each at an unknown rate of interest. The time diagram in Illustration 6-35 depicts this situation.

ILLUSTRATION 6-35
Time Diagram to Solve
for Effective Interest Rate
on Loan

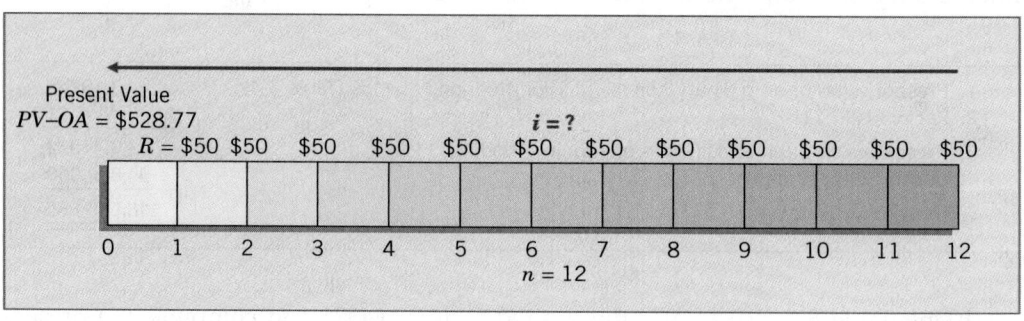

You calculate the rate as follows.

$$\text{Present value of an ordinary annuity} = R \; (PVF\text{-}OA_{n,i})$$

$$\$528.77 = \$50 \; (PVF\text{-}OA_{12,i})$$

$$(PVF\text{-}OA_{12,i}) = \frac{\$528.77}{\$50} = 10.57540$$

Referring to Table 6-4 and reading across the 12-period row, you find 10.57534 in the 2% column. Since 2% is a monthly rate, the nominal annual rate of interest is 24% (12 × 2%). The effective annual rate is 26.82413% $[(1 + .02)^{12} - 1]$. Obviously, you are better off paying the entire bill now if possible.

Computation of a Periodic Rent

Norm and Jackie Remmers have saved $36,000 to finance their daughter Dawna's college education. They deposited the money in the Bloomington Savings and Loan Association, where it earns 4% interest compounded semiannually. What equal amounts can their daughter withdraw at the end of every 6 months during her 4 college years, without exhausting the fund? Illustration 6-36 shows a time diagram of this situation.

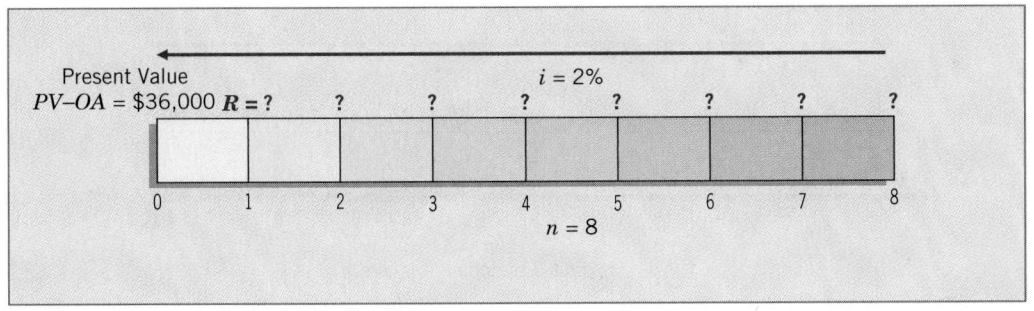

ILLUSTRATION 6-36
Time Diagram for
Ordinary Annuity for a
College Fund

Determining the answer by simply dividing $36,000 by 8 withdrawals is wrong. Why? Because that ignores the interest earned on the money remaining on deposit. Dawna must consider that interest is compounded semiannually at 2% (4% ÷ 2) for 8 periods (4 years × 2). Thus, using the same present value of an ordinary annuity formula, she determines the amount of each withdrawal that she can make as follows.

$$\text{Present value of an ordinary annuity} = R\,(PVF\text{-}OA_{n,i})$$

$$\$36,000 = R\,(PVF\text{-}OA_{8,2\%})$$

$$\$36,000 = R\,(7.32548)$$

$$R = \$4,914.35$$

MORE COMPLEX SITUATIONS

Solving time value problems often requires using more than one table. For example, a business problem may need computations of both present value of a single sum and present value of an annuity. Two such common situations are:

1 Deferred annuities.
2 Bond problems.

> **OBJECTIVE 8**
> Solve present value problems related to deferred annuities and bonds.

Deferred Annuities

A **deferred annuity** is an annuity in which the rents begin after a specified number of periods. A deferred annuity does not begin to produce rents until two or more periods have expired. For example, "an **ordinary annuity** of six annual rents deferred 4 years" means that no rents will occur during the first 4 years, and that the first of the six rents will occur at the end of the fifth year. "An **annuity due** of six annual rents deferred 4 years" means that no rents will occur during the first 4 years, and that the first of six rents will occur at the beginning of the fifth year.

Future Value of a Deferred Annuity

Computing the future value of a deferred annuity is relatively straightforward. Because there is no accumulation or investment on which interest may accrue, the future value of a deferred annuity is the same as the future value of an annuity not deferred. That is, computing the future value simply ignores the deferred period.

To illustrate, assume that Sutton Corporation plans to purchase a land site in 6 years for the construction of its new corporate headquarters. Because of cash flow problems, Sutton budgets deposits of $80,000, on which it expects to earn 5% annually, only at the end of the fourth, fifth, and sixth periods. What future value will Sutton have accumulated at the end of the sixth year? Illustration 6-37 shows a time diagram of this situation.

ILLUSTRATION 6-37
Time Diagram for Future
Value of Deferred
Annuity

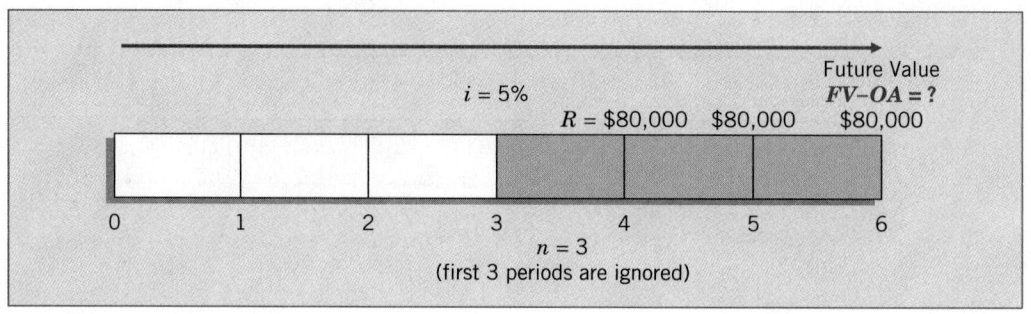

Sutton determines the value accumulated by using the standard formula for the future value of an ordinary annuity:

$$\text{Future value of an ordinary annuity} = R\ (FVF\text{-}OA_{n,i})$$
$$= \$80,000\ (FVF\text{-}OA_{3,5\%})$$
$$= \$80,000\ (3.15250)$$
$$= \$252,200$$

Present Value of a Deferred Annuity

Computing the present value of a deferred annuity must recognize the interest that accrues on the original investment during the deferral period.

To compute the present value of a deferred annuity, we compute the present value of an ordinary annuity of 1 as if the rents had occurred for the entire period. We then subtract the present value of rents that were not received during the deferral period. We are left with the present value of the rents actually received subsequent to the deferral period.

To illustrate, Tom Bytehead has developed and copyrighted tutorial software for students in advanced accounting. He agrees to sell the copyright to Campus Micro Systems for six annual payments of $5,000 each. The payments will begin 5 years from today. Given an annual interest rate of 8%, what is the present value of the six payments?

This situation is an ordinary annuity of 6 payments deferred 4 periods. The time diagram in Illustration 6-38 depicts this sales agreement.

ILLUSTRATION 6-38
Time Diagram for Present
Value of Deferred
Annuity

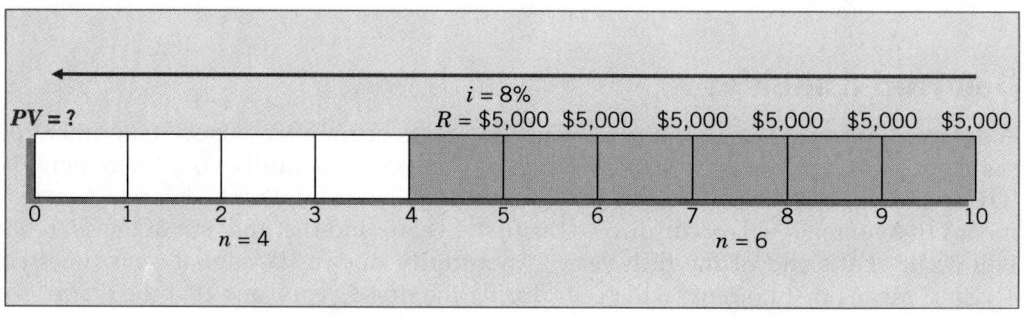

Two options are available to solve this problem. The first is to use only Table 6-4, as shown in Illustration 6-39.

ILLUSTRATION 6-39
Computation of the
Present Value of a
Deferred Annuity

1. Each periodic rent		$5,000
2. Present value of an ordinary annuity of 1 for total periods (10) [number of rents (6) plus number of deferred periods (4)] at 8%	6.71008	
3. Less: Present value of an ordinary annuity of 1 for the number of deferred periods (4) at 8%	−3.31213	
4. Difference		× 3.39795
5. Present value of six rents of $5,000 deferred 4 periods		$16,989.75

The subtraction of the present value of an annuity of 1 for the deferred periods eliminates the nonexistent rents during the deferral period. It converts the present value of an ordinary annuity of $1.00 for 10 periods to the present value of 6 rents of $1.00, deferred 4 periods.

Alternatively, Bytehead can use both Table 6-2 and Table 6-4 to compute the present value of the 6 rents. He can first discount the annuity 6 periods. However, because the annuity is deferred 4 periods, he must treat the present value of the annuity as a future amount to be discounted another 4 periods. The time diagram in Illustration 6-40 depicts this two-step process.

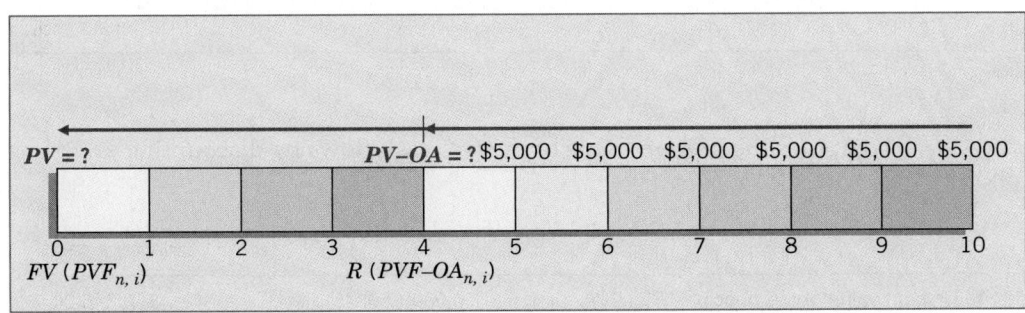

ILLUSTRATION 6-40
Time Diagram for Present Value of Deferred Annuity (2-Step Process)

Calculation using formulas would be done in two steps, as follows.

Step 1: Present value of
an ordinary annuity $= R \, (PVF\text{-}OA_{n,i})$
$= \$5,000 \, (PVF\text{-}OA_{6,8\%})$
$= \$5,000 \, (4.62288)$
(Table 6-4, Present value of an ordinary annuity)
$= \$23,114.40$

Step 2: Present value of
a single sum $= FV \, (PVF_{n,i})$
$= \$23,114.40 \, (PVF_{4,8\%})$
$= \$23,114.40 \, (.73503)$
(Table 6-2, Present value of a single sum)
$= \$16,989.78$

The present value of $16,989.78 computed above is the same as in Illustration 6-39, although computed differently. (The $0.03 difference is due to rounding.)

Valuation of Long-Term Bonds

A long-term bond produces two cash flows: (1) periodic interest payments during the life of the bond, and (2) the principal (face value) paid at maturity. At the date of issue, bond buyers determine the present value of these two cash flows using the market rate of interest.

The periodic interest payments represent an annuity. The principal represents a single-sum problem. The current market value of the bonds is the combined present values of the interest annuity and the principal amount.

To illustrate, Alltech Corporation on January 1, 2007 issues $100,000 of 9% bonds due in 5 years with interest payable annually at year-end. The current market rate of interest for bonds of similar risk is 11%. What will the buyers pay for this bond issue?

The time diagram in Illustration 6-41 depicts both cash flows.

ILLUSTRATION 6-41
Time Diagram to Solve
for Bond Valuation

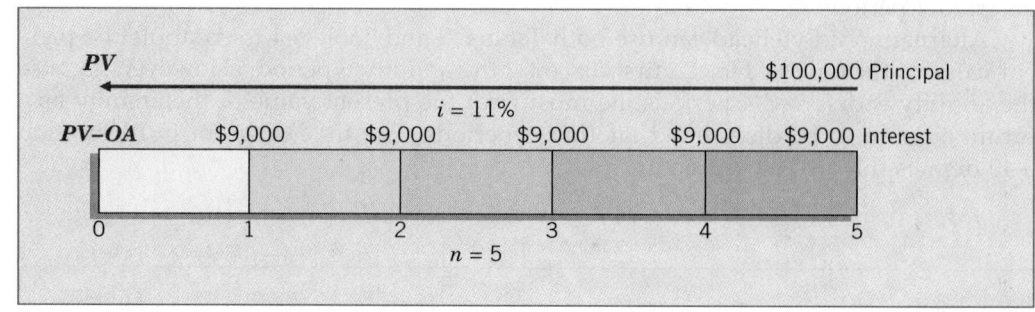

Alltech computes the present value of the two cash flows by discounting at 11% as follows.

ILLUSTRATION 6-42
Computation of the
Present Value of an
Interest-Bearing Bond

1. Present value of the principal: FV ($PVF_{5,11\%}$) = $100,000 (.59345)	$59,345.00
2. Present value of the interest payments: R ($PVF\text{-}OA_{5,11\%}$) = $9,000 (3.69590)	33,263.10
3. Combined present value (market price)—carrying value of bonds	$92,608.10

By paying $92,608.10 at date of issue, the buyers of the bonds will realize an effective yield of 11% over the 5-year term of the bonds. This is true because Alltech discounted the cash flows at 11%.

Effective-Interest Method of Amortization of Bond Discount or Premium

In the previous example (Illustration 6-42), Alltech Corporation issued bonds at a discount, computed as follows.

ILLUSTRATION 6-43
Computation of Bond
Discount

Maturity value (face amount) of bonds		$100,000.00
Present value of the principal	$59,345.00	
Present value of the interest	33,263.10	
Proceeds (present value and cash received)		92,608.10
Discount on bonds issued		$ 7,391.90

Alltech amortizes (writes off to interest expense) the amount of this discount over the life of the bond issue.

The preferred procedure for amortization of a discount or premium is the **effective-interest method**. Under the effective-interest method:

1 The company issuing the bond first computes bond interest expense by multiplying the carrying value of the bonds at the beginning of the period by the effective interest rate.

2 The company then determines the bond discount or premium amortization by comparing the bond interest expense with the interest to be paid.

Illustration 6-44 depicts the computation of bond amortization.

*Use of Spreadsheets
to Calculate Bond
Amortization*

ILLUSTRATION 6-44
Amortization
Computation

The effective-interest method produces a periodic interest expense equal to **a constant percentage of the carrying value of the bonds**. Since the percentage used is the effective rate of interest incurred by the borrower at the time of issuance, the effective-interest method results in matching expenses with revenues.

We can use the data from the Alltech Corporation example to illustrate the effective-interest method of amortization. Alltech issued $100,000 face value of bonds at a discount of $7,391.90, resulting in a carrying value of $92,608.10. Illustration 6-45 shows the effective-interest amortization schedule for Alltech's bonds.

ILLUSTRATION 6-45
Effective-Interest
Amortization Schedule

SCHEDULE OF BOND DISCOUNT AMORTIZATION
5-YEAR, 9% BONDS SOLD TO YIELD 11%

Date	Cash Interest Paid	Interest Expense	Bond Discount Amortization	Carrying Value of Bonds
1/1/07				$92,608.10
12/31/07	$9,000[a]	$10,186.89[b]	$1,186.89[c]	93,794.99[d]
12/31/08	9,000	10,317.45	1,317.45	95,112.44
12/31/09	9,000	10,462.37	1,462.37	96,574.81
12/31/10	9,000	10,623.23	1,623.23	98,198.04
12/31/11	9,000	10,801.96	1,801.96	100,000.00
	$45,000	$52,391.90	$7,391.90	

[a]$100,000 ×.09 = $9,000 [c]$10,186.89 − $9,000 = $1,186.89
[b]$92,608.10 ×.11 = $10,186.89 [d]$92,608.10 + $1,186.89 = $93,794.99

We use the amortization schedule illustrated above for note and bond transactions in Chapters 7 and 14.

PRESENT VALUE MEASUREMENT

OBJECTIVE 9
Apply expected cash flows to present value measurement.

In the past, most accounting calculations of present value relied on the most likely cash flow amount. *Concepts Statement No. 7* introduces an **expected cash flow approach**.[7] It uses a range of cash flows and incorporates the probabilities of those cash flows to provide a more relevant measurement of present value.

To illustrate the expected cash flow model, assume that there is a 30% probability that future cash flows will be $100, a 50% probability that they will be $200, and a 20% probability that they will be $300. In this case, the expected cash flow would be $190 [($100 × 0.3) + ($200 × 0.5) + ($300 × 0.2)]. Traditional present value approaches would use the most likely estimate ($200). However, that estimate fails to consider the different probabilities of the possible cash flows.

---

[7]"Using Cash Flow Information and Present Value in Accounting Measurements," *Statement of Financial Accounting Concepts No. 7* (Norwalk, Conn.: FASB, 2000).

FED WATCHING

A popular pastime in today's financial markets is "Fed watching." Why is the practice of following the policy decisions of the Federal Reserve Bank and its chair, Alan Greenspan (now Ben Bernanke), of interest? Through a number of policy options, the Fed has the ability to move interest rates up or down—and these rate changes can affect the wealth of all market participants. For example, if the Fed wants to raise rates (because the overall economy is getting overheated), it can raise the discount rate, which is the rate banks pay to borrow money from the Fed. This rate increase will factor into the rates banks and other creditors use to lend money. As a result, companies will think twice about borrowing money to expand their businesses. The result will be a slowing economy. A rate cut does just the opposite: It makes borrowing cheaper, and can help the economy expand as more companies borrow to expand their operations.

But what is good for the borrowers may not be so good for lenders. Banks earn interest on loans and investments and pay interest to depositors, and recently, with long-term rates remaining at nearly all-time lows, some banks are now at risk if interest rates rise. This is because the banks get squeezed when they make long-term loans at fixed rates (e.g., 30-year mortgage loans) but pay depositors variable rates on shorter-term deposits (e.g., 6-month certificates of deposit). The banks lose if the Fed raises rates because they will continue to earn lower returns on their long-term loans but pay higher interest on deposits.

Some banks–**Fifth-Third Bank** and **New York Community Bancorp**—recently incurred significant charges to change the balance of their assets and liabilities to guard against higher interest rates. So it is not surprising that all companies, whether borrowers or lenders, are Fed watchers.

Source: Adapted from David Franecki, "Thanks, Alan: These Stock Groups Stand to Gain from Fed Rate Cuts," *Barrons Online* (January 22, 2001); and A. C. Puwaslki; "Banks Exposed to a Flattening Yield Curve and Rising Interest Rates," *Industry Analysis: Regional Banks and Thrifts*, Center for Financial Research and Analysis (February 23, 2005).

Choosing an Appropriate Interest Rate

After determining expected cash flows, a company must then use the proper interest rate to discount the cash flows. The interest rate used for this purpose has three components:

THREE COMPONENTS OF INTEREST

1 *PURE RATE OF INTEREST (2%–4%).* This would be the amount a lender would charge if there were no possibilities of default and no expectation of inflation.

2 *EXPECTED INFLATION RATE OF INTEREST (0%–?).* Lenders recognize that in an inflationary economy, they are being paid back with less valuable dollars. As a result, they increase their interest rate to compensate for this loss in purchasing power. When inflationary expectations are high, interest rates are high.

3 *CREDIT RISK RATE OF INTEREST (0%–5%).* The government has little or no credit risk (i.e., risk of nonpayment) when it issues bonds. A business enterprise, however, depending upon its financial stability, profitability, etc., can have a low or a high credit risk.

The FASB takes the position that after computing the expected cash flows, a company should discount those cash flows by the **risk-free rate of return**. That rate is defined as **the pure rate of return plus the expected inflation rate**. The Board notes that the expected cash flow framework adjusts for credit risk because it incorporates the probability of receipt or payment into the computation of expected cash flows. Therefore, the rate used to discount the expected cash flows should consider only the pure rate of interest and the inflation rate.

Example of Expected Cash Flow

To illustrate, assume that Al's Appliance Outlet offers a 2-year warranty on all products sold. In 2007 Al's Appliance sold $250,000 of a particular type of clothes dryer. Al's Appliance entered into an agreement with Ralph's Repair to provide all warranty service on the dryers sold in 2007. To determine the warranty expense to record in 2007 and the amount of warranty liability to record on the December 31, 2007, balance sheet, Al's Appliance must measure the fair value of the agreement. Since there is not a ready market for these warranty contracts, Al's Appliance uses expected cash flow techniques to value the warranty obligation.

Based on prior warranty experience, Al's Appliance estimates the expected cash outflows associated with the dryers sold in 2007, as shown in Illustration 6-46.

	Cash Flow Estimate	×	Probability Assessment	=	Expected Cash Flow
2007	$3,800		20%		$ 760
	6,300		50%		3,150
	7,500		30%		2,250
			Total		$6,160
2008	$5,400		30%		$1,620
	7,200		50%		3,600
	8,400		20%		1,680
			Total		$6,900

ILLUSTRATION 6-46
Expected Cash Outflows—Warranties

Applying expected cash flow concepts to these data, Al's Appliance estimates warranty cash outflows of $6,160 in 2008 and $6,900 in 2009.

Illustration 6-47 shows the present value of these cash flows, assuming a risk-free rate of 5 percent and cash flows occurring at the end of the year.

Year	Expected Cash Flow	×	PV Factor, $i = 5\%$	=	Present Value
2007	$6,160		0.95238		$ 5,866.66
2008	6,900		0.90703		6,258.51
			Total		$12,125.17

ILLUSTRATION 6-47
Present Value of Cash Flows

SUMMARY OF LEARNING OBJECTIVES

1. Identify accounting topics where the time value of money is relevant. Some of the applications of present value–based measurements to accounting topics are: (1) notes, (2) leases, (3) pensions and other postretirement benefits, (4) long-term assets, (5) sinking funds, (6) business combinations, (7) disclosures, and (8) installment contracts.

2. Distinguish between simple and compound interest. See items 1 and 2 in the Fundamental Concepts on page 283.

3. Use appropriate compound interest tables. In order to identify which of the five compound interest tables to use, determine whether you are solving for (1) the future value of a single sum, (2) the present value of a single sum, (3) the future value of a series of sums (an annuity), or (4) the present value of a series of sums (an annuity). In addition, when a series of sums (an annuity) is involved, identify whether these sums are received or paid (1) at the beginning of each period (annuity due) or (2) at the end of each period (ordinary annuity).

4. Identify variables fundamental to solving interest problems. The following four variables are fundamental to all compound interest problems: (1) *Rate of interest:* unless otherwise stated, an annual rate, adjusted to reflect the length of the compounding period if less than a year. (2) *Number of time periods:* the number of compounding periods (a period may be equal to or less than a year). (3) *Future value:* the value at a future date of a given sum or sums invested assuming compound interest. (4) *Present value:* the value now (present time) of a future sum or sums discounted assuming compound interest.

5. Solve future and present value of 1 problems. See items 5(a) and 6(a) in the Fundamental Concepts on page 283.

6. Solve future value of ordinary and annuity due problems. See item 5(b) in the Fundamental Concepts on page 283.

7. Solve present value of ordinary and annuity due problems. See item 6(b) in the Fundamental Concepts on page 283.

8. Solve present value problems related to deferred annuities and bonds. Deferred annuities are annuities in which rents begin after a specified number of periods. The future value of a deferred annuity is computed the same as the future value of an annuity not deferred. To find the present value of a deferred annuity, compute the present value of an ordinary annuity of 1 as if the rents had occurred for the entire period, and then subtract the present value of rents not received during the deferral period. The current market value of bonds combines the present values of the interest annuity and the principal amount.

9. Apply expected cash flows to present value measurement. The expected cash flow approach uses a range of cash flows and the probabilities of those cash flows to provide the most likely estimate of expected cash flows. The proper interest rate used to discount the cash flows is the risk-free rate of return.

FUNDAMENTAL CONCEPTS

1 *SIMPLE INTEREST*. Interest on principal only, regardless of interest that may have accrued in the past.

2 *COMPOUND INTEREST*. Interest accrues on the unpaid interest of past periods as well as on the principal.

3 *RATE OF INTEREST*. Interest is usually expressed as an annual rate, but when the compounding period is shorter than one year, the interest rate for the shorter period must be determined.

4 *ANNUITY*. A series of payments or receipts (called rents) that occur at equal intervals of time. Types of annuities:
   (a) *Ordinary Annuity*. Each rent is payable (receivable) at the end of the period.
   (b) *Annuity Due*. Each rent is payable (receivable) at the beginning of the period.

5 *FUTURE VALUE*. Value at a later date of a single sum that is invested at compound interest.
   (a) *Future Value of 1* (or value of a single sum). The future value of $1 (or a single given sum), *FV*, at the end of *n* periods at *i* compound interest rate (Table 6-1).
   (b) *Future Value of an Annuity*. The future value of a series of rents invested at compound interest. In other words, the accumulated total that results from a series of equal deposits at regular intervals invested at compound interest. Both deposits and interest increase the accumulation.
     (1) *Future Value of an Ordinary Annuity*. The future value on the date of the last rent (Table 6-3).
     (2) *Future Value of an Annuity Due*. The future value one period after the date of the last rent. When an annuity due table is not available, use Table 6-3 with the following formula.

$$\text{Value of annuity due of 1 for } n \text{ rents} = \text{(Value of ordinary annuity for } n \text{ rents)} \times (1 + \text{interest rate})$$

6 *PRESENT VALUE*. The value at an earlier date (usually now) of a given future sum discounted at compound interest.
   (a) *Present Value of 1* (or present value of a single sum). The present value (worth) of $1 (or a given sum), due *n* periods hence, discounted at *i* compound interest (Table 6-2).
   (b) *Present Value of an Annuity*. The present value (worth) of a series of rents discounted at compound interest. In other words, it is the sum when invested at compound interest that will permit a series of equal withdrawals at regular intervals.
     (1) *Present Value of an Ordinary Annuity*. The value now of $1 to be received or paid at the end of each period (rents) for *n* periods, discounted at *i* compound interest (Table 6-4).
     (2) *Present Value of an Annuity Due*. The value now of $1 to be received or paid at the beginning of each period (rents) for *n* periods, discounted at *i* compound interest (Table 6-5). To use Table 4 for an annuity due, apply this formula.

$$\text{Present value of annuity due of 1 for } n \text{ rents} = \text{(Present value of an ordinary annuity of } n \text{ rents)} \times (1 + \text{interest rate})$$

6A Using Financial Calculators

OBJECTIVE 10
Use a financial calculator to solve time value of money problems.

Business professionals, once they have mastered the underlying concepts in Chapter 6, will often use a financial (business) calculator to solve time value of money problems. In many cases, they must use calculators if interest rates or time periods do not correspond with the information provided in the compound interest tables.

To use financial calculators, you enter the time value of money variables into the calculator. Illustration 6A-1 shows the five most common keys used to solve time value of money problems.[1]

ILLUSTRATION 6A-1
Financial Calculator Keys

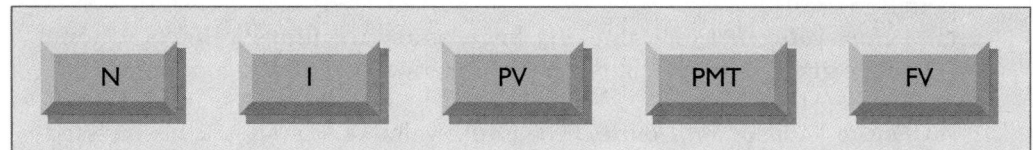

where

$$N \quad = \text{number of periods}$$
$$I \quad = \text{interest rate per period (some calculators use I/YR or i)}$$
$$PV \quad = \text{present value (occurs at the beginning of the first period)}$$
$$PMT = \text{payment (all payments are equal, and none are skipped)}$$
$$FV \quad = \text{future value (occurs at the end of the last period)}$$

Use of Spreadsheets to Solve Time Value of Money Problems

In solving time value of money problems in this appendix, you will generally be given three of four variables and will have to solve for the remaining variable. The fifth key (the key not used) is given a value of zero to ensure that this variable is not used in the computation.

FUTURE VALUE OF A SINGLE SUM

To illustrate the use of a financial calculator, let's assume that you want to know the future value of $50,000 invested to earn 11%, compounded annually for 5 years, as pictured in Illustration 6A-2.

ILLUSTRATION 6A-2
Calculator Solution for
Future Value of a Single
Sum

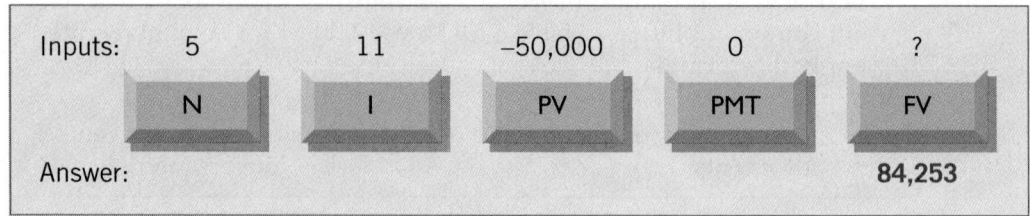

---

[1]On many calculators, these keys are actual buttons on the face of the calculator; on others, they appear on the display after the user accesses a present value menu.

The diagram shows you the information (inputs) to enter into the calculator: N = 5, I = 11, PV = −50,000, and PMT = 0. You then press FV for the answer: $84,253. This is the same answer as shown on page 260, when we used compound interest tables to compute the future value of a single sum. As indicated, the PMT key was given a value of zero because a series of payments did not occur in this problem.

Plus and Minus

The use of plus and minus signs in time value of money problems with a financial calculator can be confusing. Most financial calculators are programmed so that the positive and negative cash flows in any problem offset each other. In the future value problem above, we identified the 50,000 initial investment as a negative (outflow); the answer 84,253 was shown as a positive, reflecting a cash inflow. If the 50,000 were entered as a positive, then the final answer would have been reported as a negative (−84,253).

Hopefully, the sign convention will not cause confusion. If you understand what is required in a problem, you should be able to interpret a positive or negative amount in determining the solution to a problem.

Compounding Periods

In the problem above, we assumed that compounding occurs once a year. Some financial calculators have a default setting, which assumes that compounding occurs 12 times a year. You must determine what default period has been programmed into your calculator and change it as necessary to arrive at the proper compounding period.

Rounding

Most financial calculators store and calculate using 12 decimal places. As a result, because compound interest tables generally have factors only up to 5 decimal places, a slight difference in the final answer can result. In most time value of money problems, the final answer will not include more than two decimal points.

PRESENT VALUE OF A SINGLE SUM

To illustrate how a present value problem is solved using a financial calculator, assume that you want to know the present value of $84,253 to be received in 5 years, discounted at 11% compounded annually. Illustration 6A-3 pictures this problem.

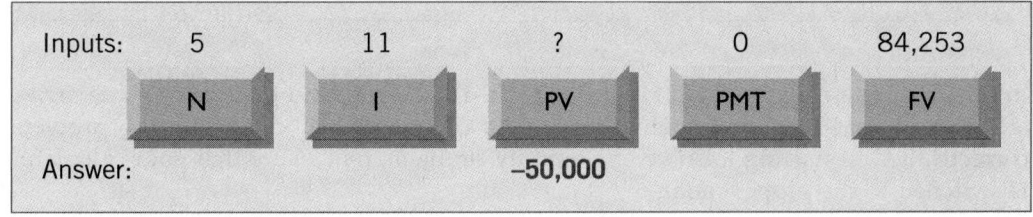

ILLUSTRATION 6A-3
Calculator Solution for Present Value of a Single Sum

In this case, you enter N = 5, I = 11, PMT = 0, FV = 84,253, and then press the PV key to find the present value of $50,000.

FUTURE VALUE OF AN ORDINARY ANNUITY

To illustrate the future value of an ordinary annuity, assume that you are asked to determine the future value of five $5,000 deposits made at the end of each of the next 5 years, each of which earns interest at 12%, compounded annually, as pictured in Illustration 6A-4 (on page 286).

ILLUSTRATION 6A-4
Calculator Solution for
Future Value of an
Ordinary Annuity

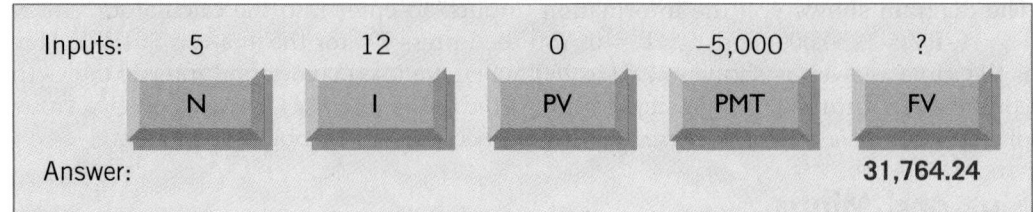

ILLUSTRATION 6A-4
Calculator Solution for
Future Value of an
Ordinary Annuity

In this case, you enter N = 5, I = 12, PV = 0, PMT = −5,000, and then press FV to arrive at the answer $31,764.24.[2] The $5,000 payments are shown as negatives because the deposits represent cash outflows that will accumulate with interest to the amount to be received (cash inflow) at the end of 5 years.

FUTURE VALUE OF AN ANNUITY DUE

Recall from the discussion in Chapter 6 that in any annuity problem you must determine whether the periodic payments occur at the *beginning* or the *end* of the period. If the first payment occurs at the beginning of the period, most financial calculators have a key marked "Begin" (or "Due") that you press to switch from the end-of-period payment mode (for an ordinary annuity) to beginning-of-period payment mode (for an annuity due). For most calculators, the word BEGIN is displayed to indicate that the calculator is set for an annuity due problem. (Some calculators use DUE.)

To illustrate a future value of an annuity due problem, let's revisit a problem from Chapter 6: Sue Lotadough plans to deposit $800 per year in a fund on each of her son's birthdays, starting today (his tenth birthday). All amounts on deposit in the fund will earn 6% compounded annually. Sue wants to know the amount she will have accumulated for college expenses on her son's eighteenth birthday. She will make 8 deposits into the fund. (Assume no deposit will be made on the eighteenth birthday.) This problem is pictured in Illustration 6A-5.

ILLUSTRATION 6A-5
Calculator Solution for
Future Value of an
Annuity Due

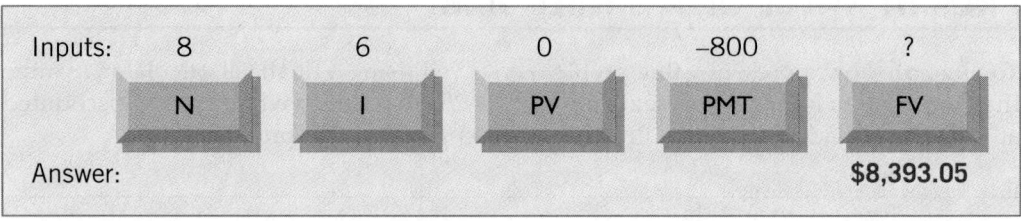

In this case, you enter N = 8, I = 6, PV = 0, PMT = −800, and then press FV to arrive at the answer of $8,393.05. You must be in the BEGIN or DUE mode to solve this problem correctly. Before starting to solve any annuity problem, make sure that your calculator is switched to the proper mode.

PRESENT VALUE OF AN ORDINARY ANNUITY

To illustrate how to solve a present value of an ordinary annuity problem using a financial calculator, assume that you are asked to determine the present value of rental receipts of $6,000 each to be received at the end of each of the next 5 years, when discounted at 12%, as pictured in Illustration 6A-6.

---

[2]Note that on page 266 the answer using the compound interest tables is $31,764.25—a difference of 1 cent due to rounding.

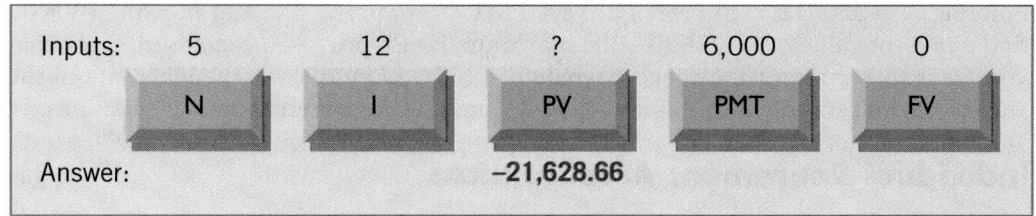

ILLUSTRATION 6A-6
Calculator Solution for
Present Value of an
Ordinary Annuity

In this case, you enter N = 5, I = 12, PMT = 6,000, FV = 0, and then press PV to arrive at the answer of $21,628.66.[3]

USEFUL APPLICATIONS OF THE FINANCIAL CALCULATOR

With a financial calculator you can solve for any interest rate or for any number of periods in a time value of money problem. Here are some examples of these applications.

Auto Loan

Assume you are financing a car with a 3-year loan. The loan has a 9.5% nominal annual interest rate, compounded monthly. The price of the car is $6,000, and you want to determine the monthly payments, assuming that the payments start one month after the purchase. This problem is pictured in Illustration 6A-7.

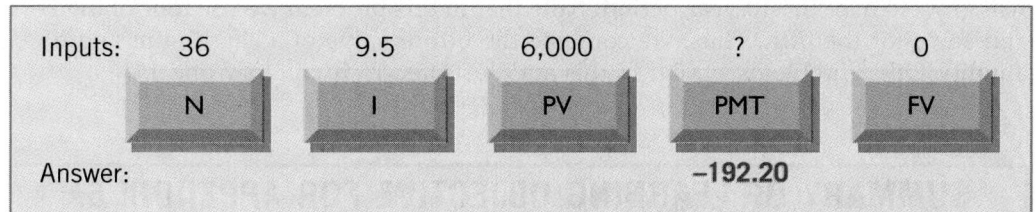

ILLUSTRATION 6A-7
Calculator Solution for
Auto Loan Payments

By entering N = 36 (12 × 3), I = 9.5, PV = 6,000, FV = 0, and then pressing PMT, you can determine that the monthly payments will be $192.20. Note that the payment key is usually programmed for 12 payments per year. Thus, you must change the default (compounding period) if the payments are different than monthly.

Mortgage Loan Amount

Let's say you are evaluating financing options for a loan on your house. You decide that the maximum mortgage payment you can afford is $700 per month. The annual interest rate is 8.4%. If you get a mortgage that requires you to make monthly payments over a 15-year period, what is the maximum purchase price you can afford? Illustration 6A-8 depicts this problem.

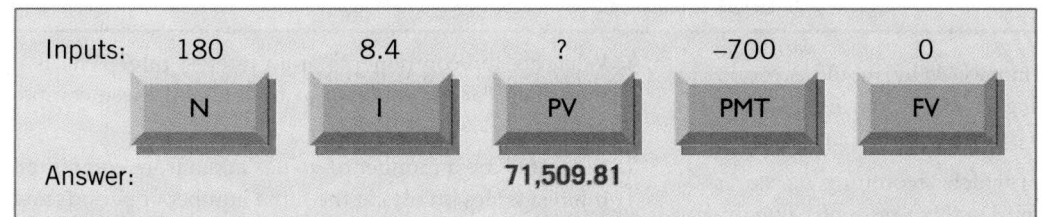

ILLUSTRATION 6A-8
Calculator Solution for
Mortgage Amount

---

[3]If the rental payments were received at the beginning of the year, then it would be necessary to switch to the BEGIN or DUE mode. In this case, the present value of the payments would be $24,224.10.

Entering N = 180 (12 × 15 years), I = 8.4, PMT = −700, FV = 0, and pressing PV, you find a present value of $71,509.81—the maximum house price you can afford, given that you want to keep your mortgage payments at $700. Note that by changing any of the variables, you can quickly conduct "what-if" analyses for different factual situations.

Individual Retirement Account (IRA)

Assume you opened an IRA on April 15, 1997, with a deposit of $2,000. Since then you have deposited $100 in the account every 2 weeks (26 deposits per year, with the first $100 deposit made on April 29, 1997). The account pays 7.6% annual interest compounded semi-monthly (with each deposit). How much will be in the account on April 15, 2007? Illustration 6A-9 depicts this problem.

ILLUSTRATION 6A-9
Calculator Solution for
IRA Balance

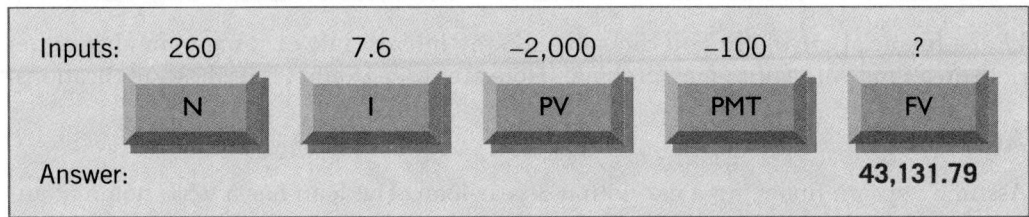

By entering N = 260 (26 × 10 years), I = 7.6, PV = −2,000, PMT = −100, and pressing FV, you determine the future value of $43,131.79. This is the amount that the IRA will grow to over the 10-year period. Note that in this problem we use four of the keys and solve for the fifth. Thus, we combine the future value of a single sum and of an annuity. Other problems similar to this are illustrated in Chapters 7 and 14.

SUMMARY OF LEARNING OBJECTIVE FOR APPENDIX 6A

10. Use a financial calculator to solve time value of money problems. Financial calculators can be used to solve the same and additional problems as those solved with time value of money tables. One enters into the financial calculator the amounts for all but one of the unknown elements of a time value of money problem (periods, interest rate, payments, future or present value). Particularly useful situations involve interest rates and compounding periods not presented in the tables.

Note: All **asterisked** Exercises and Problems relate to material contained in the chapter appendix. You will need a calculator for these assignments.

QUESTIONS

1. What is the time value of money? Why should accountants have an understanding of compound interest, annuities, and present value concepts?

2. Identify three situations in which accounting measures are based on present values. Do these present value applications involve single sums or annuities, or both single sums and annuities? Explain.

3. What is the nature of interest? Distinguish between "simple interest" and "compound interest."

4. What are the components of an interest rate? Why is it important for accountants to understand these components?

5. Presented are a number of values taken from compound interest tables involving the same number of periods and the same rate of interest. Indicate what each of these four values represents.

(a) 6.71008   (c) .46319

(b) 2.15892   (d) 14.48656

6. Bill Jones is considering two investment options for a $1,000 gift he received for graduation. Both investments have 8% annual interest rates. One offers quarterly compounding; the other compounds on a semiannual basis. Which investment should he choose? Why?

7. Brenda Starr deposited $18,000 in a money market certificate that provides interest of 10% compounded quarterly if the amount is maintained for 3 years. How much will Brenda Starr have at the end of 3 years?

8. Charlie Brown will receive $50,000 on December 31, 2012 (5 years from now) from a trust fund established by his father. Assuming the appropriate interest rate for discounting is 12% (compounded semiannually), what is the present value of this amount today?

9. What are the primary characteristics of an annuity? Differentiate between an "ordinary annuity" and an "annuity due."

10. Linus, Inc. owes $30,000 to Peanuts Company. How much would Linus have to pay each year if the debt is retired through four equal payments (made at the end of the year), given an interest rate on the debt of 12%? (Round to two decimal places.)

11. The Forths are planning for a retirement home. They estimate they will need $160,000, 4 years from now to purchase this home. Assuming an interest rate of 10%, what amount must be deposited at the end of each of the 4 years to fund the home price? (Round to two decimal places.)

12. Assume the same situation as in Question 11, except that the four equal amounts are deposited at the beginning of the period rather than at the end. In this case, what amount must be deposited at the beginning of each period? (Round to two decimals.)

13. Explain how the future value of an ordinary annuity interest table is converted to the future value of an annuity due interest table.

14. Explain how the present value of an ordinary annuity interest table is converted to the present value of an annuity due interest table.

15. In a book named *Treasure,* the reader has to figure out where a 2.2 pound, 24 kt gold horse has been buried. If the horse is found, a prize of $25,000 a year for 20 years is provided. The actual cost of the publisher to purchase an annuity to pay for the prize is $210,000. What

interest rate (to the nearest percent) was used to determine the amount of the annuity? (Assume end-of-year payments.)

16. Greg Norman Enterprises leases property to Tiger Woods, Inc. Because Tiger Woods, Inc. is experiencing financial difficulty, Norman agrees to receive five rents of $10,000 at the end of each year, with the rents deferred 3 years. What is the present value of the five rents discounted at 12%?

17. Answer the following questions.

(a) On May 1, 2007, Liselotte Neumann Company sold some machinery to Tee-off Company on an installment contract basis. The contract required five equal annual payments, with the first payment due on May 1, 2007. What present value concept is appropriate for this situation?

(b) On June 1, 2007, Mike Brisky Inc. purchased a new machine that it does not have to pay for until May 1, 2009. The total payment on May 1, 2009, will include both principal and interest. Assuming interest at a 12% rate, the cost of the machine would be the total payment multiplied by what time value of money concept?

(c) Kelly Gibson Inc. wishes to know how much money it will have available in 5 years if five equal amounts of $35,000 are invested, with the first amount invested immediately. What interest table is appropriate for this situation?

(d) Patty Sheehan invests in a "jumbo" $200,000, 3-year certificate of deposit at First Wisconsin Bank. What table would be used to determine the amount accumulated at the end of 3 years?

18. Recently Vickie Maher was interested in purchasing a Honda Acura. The salesperson indicated that the price of the car was either $27,000 cash or $6,900 at the end of each of 5 years. Compute the effective interest rate to the nearest percent that Vickie would pay if she chooses to make the five annual payments.

19. Recently, property/casualty insurance companies have been criticized because they reserve for the total loss as much as 5 years before it may happen. The IRS has joined the debate because they say the full reserve is unfair from a taxation viewpoint. What do you believe is the IRS position?

BRIEF EXERCISES

(LO 5) **BE6-1** Steve Allen invested $10,000 today in a fund that earns 8% compounded annually. To what amount will the investment grow in 3 years? To what amount would the investment grow in 3 years if the fund earns 8% annual interest compounded semiannually?

(LO 5) **BE6-2** Itzak Perlman needs $20,000 in 4 years. What amount must he invest today if his investment earns 12% compounded annually? What amount must he invest if his investment earns 12% annual interest compounded quarterly?

(LO 5) **BE6-3** Natalie Portman will invest $30,000 today. She needs $222,000 in 21 years. What annual interest rate must she earn?

(LO 5) **BE6-4** Dan Webster will invest $10,000 today in a fund that earns 5% annual interest. How many years will it take for the fund to grow to $13,400?

(LO 6) **BE6-5** Anne Boleyn will invest $5,000 a year for 20 years in a fund that will earn 12% annual interest. If the first payment into the fund occurs today, what amount will be in the fund in 20 years? If the first payment occurs at year-end, what amount will be in the fund in 20 years?

(LO 6) **BE6-6** William Cullen Bryant needs $200,000 in 10 years. How much must he invest at the end of each year, at 11% interest, to meet his needs?

(LO 5) **BE6-7** Jack Thompson's lifelong dream is to own his own fishing boat to use in his retirement. Jack has recently come into an inheritance of $400,000. He estimates that the boat he wants will cost $350,000 when he retires in 5 years. How much of his inheritance must he invest at an annual rate of 12% (compounded annually) to buy the boat at retirement?

(LO 5) **BE6-8** Refer to the data in BE6-7. Assuming quarterly compounding of amounts invested at 12%, how much of Jack Thompson's inheritance must be invested to have enough at retirement to buy the boat?

(LO 6) **BE6-9** Luther Vandross is investing $12,961 at the end of each year in a fund that earns 10% interest. In how many years will the fund be at $100,000?

(LO 7) **BE6-10** Grupo Rana wants to withdraw $20,000 each year for 10 years from a fund that earns 8% interest. How much must he invest today if the first withdrawal is at year-end? How much must he invest today if the first withdrawal takes place immediately?

(LO 7) **BE6-11** Mark Twain's VISA balance is $1,124.40. He may pay it off in 18 equal end-of-month payments of $75 each. What interest rate is Mark paying?

(LO 7) **BE6-12** Corinne Dunbar is investing $200,000 in a fund that earns 8% interest compounded annually. What equal amounts can Corinne withdraw at the end of each of the next 20 years?

(LO 6) **BE6-13** Bayou Inc. will deposit $20,000 in a 12% fund at the end of each year for 8 years beginning December 31, 2007. What amount will be in the fund immediately after the last deposit?

(LO 7) **BE6-14** Hollis Stacy wants to create a fund today that will enable her to withdraw $20,000 per year for 8 years, with the first withdrawal to take place 5 years from today. If the fund earns 8% interest, how much must Hollis invest today?

(LO 8) **BE6-15** Acadian Inc. issues $1,000,000 of 7% bonds due in 10 years with interest payable at year-end. The current market rate of interest for bonds of similar risk is 8%. What amount will Acadian receive when it issues the bonds?

(LO 7) **BE6-16** Walt Frazier is settling a $20,000 loan due today by making 6 equal annual payments of $4,864.51. Determine the interest rate on this loan, if the payments begin one year after the loan is signed.

(LO 7) **BE6-17** Consider the loan in BE6-16. What payments must Walt Frazier make to settle the loan at the same interest rate but with the 6 payments beginning on the day the loan is signed?

EXERCISES

(Interest rates are per annum unless otherwise indicated.)

(LO 3) **E6-1** **(Using Interest Tables)** For each of the following cases, indicate (a) to what rate columns, and (b) to what number of periods you would refer in looking up the interest factor.

1. In a future value of 1 table

Annual Rate	Number of Years Invested	Compounded
a. 9%	9	Annually
b. 12%	5	Quarterly
c. 10%	15	Semiannually

2. In a present value of an annuity of 1 table

Annual Rate	Number of Years Involved	Number of Rents Involved	Frequency of Rents
a. 9%	25	25	Annually
b. 10%	15	30	Semiannually
c. 12%	7	28	Quarterly

(LO 2, 5) **E6-2 (Simple and Compound Interest Computations)** Alan Jackson invests $20,000 at 8% annual interest, leaving the money invested without withdrawing any of the interest for 8 years. At the end of the 8 years, Alan withdrew the accumulated amount of money.

Instructions

(a) Compute the amount Alan would withdraw assuming the investment earns simple interest.

(b) Compute the amount Alan would withdraw assuming the investment earns interest compounded annually.

(c) Compute the amount Alan would withdraw assuming the investment earns interest compounded semiannually.

(LO 5, 6, 7) **E6-3 (Computation of Future Values and Present Values)** Using the appropriate interest table, answer each of the following questions. (Each case is independent of the others.)

(a) What is the future value of $7,000 at the end of 5 periods at 8% compounded interest?

(b) What is the present value of $7,000 due 8 periods hence, discounted at 11%?

(c) What is the future value of 15 periodic payments of $7,000 each made at the end of each period and compounded at 10%?

(d) What is the present value of $7,000 to be received at the end of each of 20 periods, discounted at 5% compound interest?

(LO 6, 7) **E6-4 (Computation of Future Values and Present Values)** Using the appropriate interest table, answer the following questions. (Each case is independent of the others).

(a) What is the future value of 20 periodic payments of $4,000 each made at the beginning of each period and compounded at 8%?

(b) What is the present value of $2,500 to be received at the beginning of each of 30 periods, discounted at 10% compound interest?

(c) What is the future value of 15 deposits of $2,000 each made at the beginning of each period and compounded at 10%? (Future value as of the end of the fifteenth period.)

(d) What is the present value of six receipts of $1,000 each received at the beginning of each period, discounted at 9% compounded interest?

(LO 6, 7) **E6-5 (Computation of Present Value)** Using the appropriate interest table, compute the present values of the following periodic amounts due at the end of the designated periods.

(a) $30,000 receivable at the end of each period for 8 periods compounded at 12%.

(b) $30,000 payments to be made at the end of each period for 16 periods at 9%.

(c) $30,000 payable at the end of the seventh, eighth, ninth, and tenth periods at 12%.

(LO 5, 6, 7) **E6-6 (Future Value and Present Value Problems)** Presented below are three unrelated situations.

(a) Dwayne Wade Company recently signed a lease for a new office building, for a lease period of 10 years. Under the lease agreement, a security deposit of $12,000 is made, with the deposit to be returned at the expiration of the lease, with interest compounded at 10% per year. What amount will the company receive at the time the lease expires?

(b) Serena Williams Corporation, having recently issued a $20 million, 15-year bond issue, is committed to make annual sinking fund deposits of $600,000. The deposits are made on the last day of each year and yield a return of 10%. Will the fund at the end of 15 years be sufficient to retire the bonds? If not, what will the deficiency be?

(c) Under the terms of his salary agreement, president Rex Walters has an option of receiving either an immediate bonus of $40,000, or a deferred bonus of $70,000 payable in 10 years. Ignoring tax considerations, and assuming a relevant interest rate of 8%, which form of settlement should Walters accept?

(LO 8) **E6-7 (Computation of Bond Prices)** What would you pay for a $50,000 debenture bond that matures in 15 years and pays $5,000 a year in interest if you wanted to earn a yield of:

(a) 8%? **(b)** 10%? **(c)** 12%?

(LO 8) **E6-8 (Computations for a Retirement Fund)** Clarence Weatherspoon, a super salesman contemplating retirement on his fifty-fifth birthday, decides to create a fund on an 8% basis that will enable him to withdraw $20,000 per year on June 30, beginning in 2014 and continuing through 2017. To develop this fund, Clarence intends to make equal contributions on June 30 of each of the years 2010–2013.

Instructions

(a) How much must the balance of the fund equal on June 30, 2013, in order for Clarence Weatherspoon to satisfy his objective?

(b) What are each of Clarence's contributions to the fund?

(LO 5) **E6-9** **(Unknown Rate)** LEW Company purchased a machine at a price of $100,000 by signing a note payable, which requires a single payment of $123,210 in 2 years. Assuming annual compounding of interest, what rate of interest is being paid on the loan?

(LO 5) **E6-10** **(Unknown Periods and Unknown Interest Rate)** Consider the following independent situations.

(a) Mike Finley wishes to become a millionaire. His money market fund has a balance of $92,296 and has a guaranteed interest rate of 10%. How many years must Mike leave that balance in the fund in order to get his desired $1,000,000?

(b) Assume that Serena Williams desires to accumulate $1 million in 15 years using her money market fund balance of $182,696. At what interest rate must Serena's investment compound annually?

(LO 7) **E6-11** **(Evaluation of Purchase Options)** Sosa Excavating Inc. is purchasing a bulldozer. The equipment has a price of $100,000. The manufacturer has offered a payment plan that would allow Sosa to make 10 equal annual payments of $16,274.53, with the first payment due one year after the purchase.

Instructions

(a) How much total interest will Sosa pay on this payment plan?

(b) Sosa could borrow $100,000 from its bank to finance the purchase at an annual rate of 9%. Should Sosa borrow from the bank or use the manufacturer's payment plan to pay for the equipment?

(LO 5, **E6-12** **(Analysis of Alternatives)** The Black Knights Inc., a manufacturer of high-sugar, low-sodium, **6, 7)** low-cholesterol TV dinners, would like to increase its market share in the Sunbelt. In order to do so, Black Knights has decided to locate a new factory in the Panama City area. Black Knights will either buy or lease a site depending upon which is more advantageous. The site location committee has narrowed down the available sites to the following three buildings.

Building A: Purchase for a cash price of $600,000, useful life 25 years.

Building B: Lease for 25 years with annual lease payments of $69,000 being made at the beginning of the year.

Building C: Purchase for $650,000 cash. This building is larger than needed; however, the excess space can be sublet for 25 years at a net annual rental of $7,000. Rental payments will be received at the end of each year. The Black Knights Inc. has no aversion to being a landlord.

Instructions

In which building would you recommend that The Black Knights Inc. locate, assuming a 12% cost of funds?

(LO 8) **E6-13** **(Computation of Bond Liability)** Lance Armstrong Inc. manufactures cycling equipment. Recently the vice president of operations of the company has requested construction of a new plant to meet the increasing demand for the company's bikes. After a careful evaluation of the request, the board of directors has decided to raise funds for the new plant by issuing $2,000,000 of 11% term corporate bonds on March 1, 2007, due on March 1, 2022, with interest payable each March 1 and September 1. At the time of issuance, the market interest rate for similar financial instruments is 10%.

Instructions

As the controller of the company, determine the selling price of the bonds.

(LO 8) **E6-14** **(Computation of Pension Liability)** Nerwin, Inc. is a furniture manufacturing company with 50 employees. Recently, after a long negotiation with the local labor union, the company decided to initiate a pension plan as a part of its compensation plan. The plan will start on January 1, 2007. Each employee covered by the plan is entitled to a pension payment each year after retirement. As required by accounting standards, the controller of the company needs to report the pension obligation (liability). On the basis of a discussion with the supervisor of the Personnel Department and an actuary from an insurance company, the controller develops the following information related to the pension plan.

Average length of time to retirement	15 years
Expected life duration after retirement	10 years
Total pension payment expected each year after retirement for all employees. Payment made at the end of the year.	$700,000 per year

The interest rate to be used is 8%.

Instructions

On the basis of the information above, determine the present value of the pension obligation (liability).

(LO 5, 6) **E6-15 (Investment Decision)** Andrew Bogut just received a signing bonus of $1,000,000. His plan is to invest this payment in a fund that will earn 8%, compounded annually.

Instructions

(a) If Bogut plans to establish the AB Foundation once the fund grows to $1,999,000, how many years until he can establish the foundation?

(b) Instead of investing the entire $1,000,000, Bogut invests $300,000 today and plans to make 9 equal annual investments into the fund beginning one year from today. What amount should the payments be if Bogut plans to establish the $1,999,000 foundation at the end of 9 years?

(LO 6, 7) **E6-16 (Retirement of Debt)** Jesper Parnevik borrowed $70,000 on March 1, 2005. This amount plus accrued interest at 12% compounded semiannually is to be repaid March 1, 2015. To retire this debt, Jesper plans to contribute to a debt retirement fund five equal amounts starting on March 1, 2010, and for the next 4 years. The fund is expected to earn 10% per annum.

Instructions

How much must be contributed each year by Jesper Parnevik to provide a fund sufficient to retire the debt on March 1, 2015?

(LO 7) **E6-17 (Computation of Amount of Rentals)** Your client, Ron Santo Leasing Company, is preparing a contract to lease a machine to Souvenirs Corporation for a period of 25 years. Santo has an investment cost of $365,755 in the machine, which has a useful life of 25 years and no salvage value at the end of that time. Your client is interested in earning an 11% return on its investment and has agreed to accept 25 equal rental payments at the end of each of the next 25 years.

Instructions

You are requested to provide Santo with the amount of each of the 25 rental payments that will yield an 11% return on investment.

(LO 5, 7) **E6-18 (Least Costly Payoff)** Assume that **Sonic Foundry Corporation** has a contractual debt outstanding. Sonic has available two means of settlement: It can either make immediate payment of $2,600,000, or it can make annual payments of $300,000 for 15 years, each payment due on the last day of the year.

Instructions

Which method of payment do you recommend, assuming an expected effective interest rate of 8% during the future period?

(LO 5, 7) **E6-19 (Least Costly Payoff)** Assuming the same facts as those in E6-18 except that the payments must begin now and be made on the first day of each of the 15 years, what payment method would you recommend?

(LO 9) **E6-20 (Expected Cash Flows)** For each of the following, determine the expected cash flows.

	Cash Flow Estimate	Probability Assessment
(a)	$ 3,800	20%
	6,300	50%
	7,500	30%
(b)	$ 5,400	30%
	7,200	50%
	8,400	20%
(c)	$(1,000)	10%
	2,000	80%
	5,000	10%

(LO 9) **E6-21 (Expected Cash Flows and Present Value)** Andrew Kelly is trying to determine the amount to set aside so that he will have enough money on hand in 2 years to overhaul the engine on his vintage used car. While there is some uncertainty about the cost of engine overhauls in 2 years, by conducting some research online, Andrew has developed the following estimates.

Engine Overhaul Estimated Cash Outflow	Probability Assessment
$200	10%
450	30%
550	50%
750	10%

Instructions
How much should Andrew Kelly deposit today in an account earning 6%, compounded annually, so that he will have enough money on hand in 2 years to pay for the overhaul?

(LO 10) *E6-22 **(Determine Interest Rate)** Reba McEntire wishes to invest $19,000 on July 1, 2007, and have it accumulate to $49,000 by July 1, 2017.

Instructions
Use a financial calculator to determine at what exact annual rate of interest Reba must invest the $19,000.

(LO 10) *E6-23 **(Determine Interest Rate)** On July 17, 2006, Tim McGraw borrowed $42,000 from his grandfather to open a clothing store. Starting July 17, 2007, Tim has to make ten equal annual payments of $6,500 each to repay the loan.

Instructions
Use a financial calculator to determine what interest rate Tim is paying.

(LO 10) *E6-24 **(Determine Interest Rate)** As the purchaser of a new house, Patty Loveless has signed a mortgage note to pay the Memphis National Bank and Trust Co. $14,000 every 6 months for 20 years, at the end of which time she will own the house. At the date the mortgage is signed the purchase price was $198,000, and a down payment of $20,000 was made. The first payment will be made 6 months after the date the mortgage is signed.

Instructions
Using a financial calculator, compute the exact rate of interest earned on the mortgage by the bank.

See the book's website, www.wiley.com/college/kieso, for Additional Exercises.

PROBLEMS

(Interest rates are per annum unless otherwise indicated.)

(LO 5, 6, 7) **P6-1 (Various Time Value Situations)** Answer each of these unrelated questions.

(a) On January 1, 2007, Aaron Brown Corporation sold a building that cost $250,000 and that had accumulated depreciation of $100,000 on the date of sale. Brown received as consideration a $275,000 noninterest-bearing note due on January 1, 2010. There was no established exchange price for the building, and the note had no ready market. The prevailing rate of interest for a note of this type on January 1, 2007, was 9%. At what amount should the gain from the sale of the building be reported?

(b) On January 1, 2007, Aaron Brown Corporation purchased 200 of the $1,000 face value, 9%, 10-year bonds of Walters Inc. The bonds mature on January 1, 2017, and pay interest annually beginning January 1, 2008. Brown purchased the bonds to yield 11%. How much did Brown pay for the bonds?

(c) Aaron Brown Corporation bought a new machine and agreed to pay for it in equal annual installments of $4,000 at the end of each of the next 10 years. Assuming that a prevailing interest rate of 8% applies to this contract, how much should Brown record as the cost of the machine?

(d) Aaron Brown Corporation purchased a special tractor on December 31, 2007. The purchase agreement stipulated that Brown should pay $20,000 at the time of purchase and $5,000 at the end of each of the next 8 years. The tractor should be recorded on December 31, 2007, at what amount, assuming an appropriate interest rate of 12%?

(e) Aaron Brown Corporation wants to withdraw $100,000 (including principal) from an investment fund at the end of each year for 9 years. What should be the required initial investment at the beginning of the first year if the fund earns 11%?

(LO 5, 6, 7) **P6-2 (Various Time Value Situations)** Using the appropriate interest table, provide the solution to each of the following four questions by computing the unknowns.

(a) What is the amount of the payments that Tom Brokaw must make at the end of each of 8 years to accumulate a fund of $70,000 by the end of the eighth year, if the fund earns 8% interest, compounded annually?

(b) Anderson Cooper is 40 years old today and he wishes to accumulate $500,000 by his sixty-fifth birthday so he can retire to his summer place on Lake Hopatcong. He wishes to accumulate this amount by making equal deposits on his fortieth through his sixty-fourth birthdays. What annual deposit must Anderson make if the fund will earn 12% interest compounded annually?

(c) Jane Pauley has $20,000 to invest today at 9% to pay a debt of $56,253. How many years will it take her to accumulate enough to liquidate the debt?

(d) Maria Shriver has a $27,600 debt that she wishes to repay 4 years from today; she has $18,181 that she intends to invest for the 4 years. What rate of interest will she need to earn annually in order to accumulate enough to pay the debt?

(LO 5, 6, 7) **P6-3 (Analysis of Alternatives)** Assume that **Wal-Mart, Inc.** has decided to surface and maintain for 10 years a vacant lot next to one of its discount-retail outlets to serve as a parking lot for customers. Management is considering the following bids involving two different qualities of surfacing for a parking area of 12,000 square yards.

Bid A: A surface that costs $5.25 per square yard to install. This surface will have to be replaced at the end of 5 years. The annual maintenance cost on this surface is estimated at 20 cents per square yard for each year except the last year of its service. The replacement surface will be similar to the initial surface.

Bid B: A surface that costs $9.50 per square yard to install. This surface has a probable useful life of 10 years and will require annual maintenance in each year except the last year, at an estimated cost of 9 cents per square yard.

Instructions

Prepare computations showing which bid should be accepted by Wal-Mart, Inc. You may assume that the cost of capital is 9%, that the annual maintenance expenditures are incurred at the end of each year, and that prices are not expected to change during the next 10 years.

(LO 6, 7) **P6-4 (Evaluating Payment Alternatives)** Terry O'Malley has just learned he has won a $900,000 prize in the lottery. The lottery has given him two options for receiving the payments: (1) If Terry takes all the money today, the state and federal governments will deduct taxes at a rate of 46% immediately. (2) Alternatively, the lottery offers Terry a payout of 20 equal payments of $62,000 with the first payment occurring when Terry turns in the winning ticket. Terry will be taxed on each of these payments at a rate of 25%.

Instructions

Assuming Terry can earn an 8% rate of return (compounded annually) on any money invested during this period, which pay-out option should he choose?

(LO 5, 6, 7) **P6-5 (Analysis of Alternatives)** Sally Brown died, leaving to her husband Linus an insurance policy contract that provides that the beneficiary (Linus) can choose any one of the following four options.

(a) $55,000 immediate cash.

(b) $3,700 every 3 months payable at the end of each quarter for 5 years.

(c) $18,000 immediate cash and $1,600 every 3 months for 10 years, payable at the beginning of each 3-month period.

(d) $4,000 every 3 months for 3 years and $1,200 each quarter for the following 25 quarters, all payments payable at the end of each quarter.

Instructions

If money is worth 2½% per quarter, compounded quarterly, which option would you recommend that Linus exercise?

(LO 8) **P6-6 (Purchase Price of a Business)** During the past year, Nicole Bobek planted a new vineyard on 150 acres of land that she leases for $27,000 a year. She has asked you as her accountant to assist her in determining the value of her vineyard operation.

The vineyard will bear no grapes for the first 5 years (1–5). In the next 5 years (6–10), Nicole estimates that the vines will bear grapes that can be sold for $60,000 each year. For the next 20 years (11–30) she expects the harvest will provide annual revenues of $100,000. But during the last 10 years (31–40) of the vineyard's life, she estimates that revenues will decline to $80,000 per year.

During the first 5 years the annual cost of pruning, fertilizing, and caring for the vineyard is estimated at $9,000; during the years of production, 6–40, these costs will rise to $10,000 per year. The relevant market rate of interest for the entire period is 12%. Assume that all receipts and payments are made at the end of each year.

Instructions

Dick Button has offered to buy Nicole's vineyard business by assuming the 40-year lease. On the basis of the current value of the business, what is the minimum price Nicole should accept?

(LO 5, 6, 7) **P6-7 (Time Value Concepts Applied to Solve Business Problems)** Answer the following questions related to Derek Lee Inc.

(a) Derek Lee Inc. has $572,000 to invest. The company is trying to decide between two alternative uses of the funds. One alternative provides $80,000 at the end of each year for 12 years, and the other is to receive a single lump sum payment of $1,900,000 at the end of the 12 years. Which alternative should Lee select? Assume the interest rate is constant over the entire investment.

(b) Derek Lee Inc. has completed the purchase of new Dell computers. The fair market value of the equipment is $824,150. The purchase agreement specifies an immediate down payment of $200,000 and semiannual payments of $76,952 beginning at the end of 6 months for 5 years. What is the interest rate, to the nearest percent, used in discounting this purchase transaction?

(c) Derek Lee Inc. loans money to John Kruk Corporation in the amount of $600,000. Lee accepts an 8% note due in 7 years with interest payable semiannually. After 2 years (and receipt of interest for 2 years), Lee needs money and therefore sells the note to Chicago National Bank, which demands interest on the note of 10% compounded semiannually. What is the amount Lee will receive on the sale of the note?

(d) Derek Lee Inc. wishes to accumulate $1,300,000 by December 31, 2017, to retire bonds outstanding. The company deposits $300,000 on December 31, 2007, which will earn interest at 10% compounded quarterly, to help in the retirement of this debt. In addition, the company wants to know how much should be deposited at the end of each quarter for 10 years to ensure that $1,300,000 is available at the end of 2017. (The quarterly deposits will also earn at a rate of 10%, compounded quarterly.) (Round to even dollars.)

(LO 6, 7) **P6-8 (Analysis of Alternatives)** Homer Simpson Inc., a manufacturer of steel school lockers, plans to purchase a new punch press for use in its manufacturing process. After contacting the appropriate vendors, the purchasing department received differing terms and options from each vendor. The Engineering Department has determined that each vendor's punch press is substantially identical and each has a useful life of 20 years. In addition, Engineering has estimated that required year-end maintenance costs will be $1,000 per year for the first 5 years, $2,000 per year for the next 10 years, and $3,000 per year for the last 5 years. Following is each vendor's sale package.

Vendor A: $45,000 cash at time of delivery and 10 year-end payments of $15,000 each. Vendor A offers all its customers the right to purchase at the time of sale a separate 20-year maintenance service contract, under which Vendor A will perform all year-end maintenance at a one-time initial cost of $10,000.

Vendor B: Forty seminannual payments of $8,000 each, with the first installment due upon delivery. Vendor B will perform all year-end maintenance for the next 20 years at no extra charge.

Vendor C: Full cash price of $125,000 will be due upon delivery.

Instructions
Assuming that both Vendor A and B will be able to perform the required year-end maintenance, that Simpson's cost of funds is 10%, and the machine will be purchased on January 1, from which vendor should the press be purchased?

(LO 5, 6, 7) **P6-9 (Analysis of Business Problems)** Jean-Luc is a financial executive with Starship Enterprises. Although Jean-Luc has not had any formal training in finance or accounting, he has a "good sense" for numbers and has helped the company grow from a very small company ($500,000 sales) to a large operation ($45 million in sales). With the business growing steadily, however, the company needs to make a number of difficult financial decisions in which Jean-Luc feels a little "over his head." He therefore has decided to hire a new employee with "numbers" expertise to help him. As a basis for determining whom to employ, he has decided to ask each prospective employee to prepare answers to questions relating to the following situations he has encountered recently. Here are the questions.

(a) In 2005, Starship Enterprises negotiated and closed a long-term lease contract for newly constructed truck terminals and freight storage facilities. The buildings were constructed on land owned by the company. On January 1, 2006, Starship took possession of the leased property. The 20-year lease is effective for the period January 1, 2006, through December 31, 2025. Advance rental payments of $800,000 are payable to the lessor (owner of facilities) on January 1 of each of the first 10 years of the lease term. Advance payments of $300,000 are due on January 1 for each of the last 10 years of the lease term. Starship has an option to purchase all the leased facilities for $1 on December 31, 2025. At the time the lease was negotiated, the fair market value of the truck terminals and freight storage facilities was approximately $7,200,000. If the company had borrowed the money to purchase the facilities, it would have had to pay 10% interest. Should the company have purchased rather than leased the facilities?

(b) Last year the company exchanged a piece of land for a non-interest-bearing note. The note is to be paid at the rate of $12,000 per year for 9 years, beginning one year from the date of disposal of the land. An appropriate rate of interest for the note was 11%. At the time the land was originally purchased, it cost $90,000. What is the fair value of the note?

(c) The company has always followed the policy to take any cash discounts on goods purchased. Recently the company purchased a large amount of raw materials at a price of $800,000 with terms 2/10, n/30 on which it took the discount. Starship has recently estimated its cost of funds at 10%. Should Starship continue this policy of always taking the cash discount?

(LO 5, 6, 7) **P6-10** **(Analysis of Lease vs. Purchase)** Jose Rijo Inc. owns and operates a number of hardware stores in the New England region. Recently the company has decided to locate another store in a rapidly growing area of Maryland. The company is trying to decide whether to purchase or lease the building and related facilities.

Purchase: The company can purchase the site, construct the building, and purchase all store fixtures. The cost would be $1,650,000. An immediate down payment of $400,000 is required, and the remaining $1,250,000 would be paid off over 5 years at $300,000 per year (including interest). The property is expected to have a useful life of 12 years, and then it will be sold for $500,000. As the owner of the property, the company will have the following out-of-pocket expenses each period.

Property taxes (to be paid at the end of each year)	$40,000
Insurance (to be paid at the beginning of each year)	27,000
Other (primarily maintenance which occurs at the end of each year)	16,000
	$83,000

Lease: First National Bank has agreed to purchase the site, construct the building, and install the appropriate fixtures for Rijo Inc. if Rijo will lease the completed facility for 12 years. The annual costs for the lease would be $240,000. Rijo would have no responsibility related to the facility over the 12 years. The terms of the lease are that Rijo would be required to make 12 annual payments (the first payment to be made at the time the store opens and then each following year). In addition, a deposit of $100,000 is required when the store is opened. This deposit will be returned at the end of the twelfth year, assuming no unusual damage to the building structure or fixtures.

Currently the cost of funds for Rijo Inc. is 10%.

Instructions
Which of the two approaches should Rijo Inc. follow?

(LO 8) **P6-11** **(Pension Funding)** You have been hired as a benefit consultant by Maugarite Alomar, the owner of Attic Angels. She wants to establish a retirement plan for herself and her three employees. Maugarite has provided the following information: The retirement plan is to be based upon annual salary for the last year before retirement and is to provide 50% of Maugarite's last-year annual salary and 40% of the last-year annual salary for each employee. The plan will make annual payments at the beginning of each year for 20 years from the date of retirement. Maugarite wishes to fund the plan by making 15 annual deposits beginning January 1, 2007. Invested funds will earn 12% compounded annually. Information about plan participants as of January 1, 2007, is as follows.

Maugarite Alomar, owner: Current annual salary of $40,000; estimated retirement date January 1, 2032.

Kenny Rogers, flower arranger: Current annual salary of $30,000; estimated retirement date January 1, 2037.

Anita Baker, sales clerk: Current annual salary of $15,000; estimated retirement date January 1, 2027.

Willie Nelson, part-time bookkeeper: Current annual salary of $15,000; estimated retirement date January 1, 2022.

In the past, Maugarite has given herself and each employee a year-end salary increase of 4%. Maugarite plans to continue this policy in the future.

Instructions
(a) Based upon the above information, what will be the annual retirement benefit for each plan participant? (Round to the nearest dollar.) (*Hint:* Maugarite will receive raises for 24 years.)
(b) What amount must be on deposit at the end of 15 years to ensure that all benefits will be paid? (Round to the nearest dollar.)
(c) What is the amount of each annual deposit Maugarite must make to the retirement plan?

(LO 8) **P6-12** **(Pension Funding)** James Qualls, newly appointed controller of KBS, is considering ways to reduce his company's expenditures on annual pension costs. One way to do this is to switch KBS's pension fund assets from First Security to NET Life. KBS is a very well-respected computer manufacturer that recently has experienced a sharp decline in its financial performance for the first time in its 25-year history. Despite financial problems, KBS still is committed to providing its employees with good pension and postretirement health benefits.

Under its present plan with First Security, KBS is obligated to pay $43 million to meet the expected value of future pension benefits that are payable to employees as an annuity upon their retirement from the company. On the other hand, NET Life requires KBS to pay only $35 million for identical future pension benefits. First Security is one of the oldest and most reputable insurance companies in North America. NET Life has a much weaker reputation in the insurance industry. In pondering the significant difference in annual pension costs, Qualls asks himself, "Is this too good to be true?"

Instructions

Answer the following questions.

(a) Why might NET Life's pension cost requirement be $8 million less than First Security's requirement for the same future value?

(b) What ethical issues should James Qualls consider before switching KBS's pension fund assets?

(c) Who are the stakeholders that could be affected by Qualls's decision?

(LO 7, 9) **P6-13 (Expected Cash Flows and Present Value)** Larry's Lawn Equipment sells high-quality lawn mowers and offers a 3-year warranty on all new lawn mowers sold. In 2007, Larry sold $300,000 of new specialty mowers for golf greens for which Larry's service department does not have the equipment to do the service. Larry has entered into an agreement with Mower Mavens to provide all warranty service on the special mowers sold in 2007. Larry wishes to measure the fair value of the agreement to determine the warranty liability for sales made in 2007. The controller for Larry's Lawn Equipment estimates the following expected warranty cash outflows associated with the mowers sold in 2007.

Year	Cash Flow Estimate	Probability Assessment
2008	$2,000	20%
	4,000	60%
	5,000	20%
2009	$2,500	30%
	5,000	50%
	6,000	20%
2010	$3,000	30%
	6,000	40%
	7,000	30%

Instructions

Using expected cash flow and present value techniques, determine the value of the warranty liability for the 2007 sales. Use an annual discount rate of 5%. Assume all cash flows occur at the end of the year.

(LO 7, 9) **P6-14 (Expected Cash Flows and Present Value)** At the end of 2007, Richards Company is conducting an impairment test and needs to develop a fair value estimate for machinery used in its manufacturing operations. Given the nature of Richard's production process, the equipment is for special use. (No second-hand market values are available.) The equipment will be obsolete in 2 years, and Richard's accountants have developed the following cash flow information for the equipment.

Year	Net Cash Flow Estimate	Probability Assessment
2008	$6,000	40%
	8,000	60%
2009	$ (500)	20%
	2,000	60%
	3,000	20%
	Scrap value	
2009	$ 500	50%
	700	50%

Instructions

Using expected cash flow and present value techniques, determine the fair value of the machinery at the end of 2007. Use a 6% discount rate. Assume all cash flows occur at the end of the year.

(LO 10) ***P6-15 (Various Time Value of Money Situations)** Using a financial calculator, provide a solution to each of the following questions.

(a) What is the amount of the payments that Karla Zehms must make at the end of each of 8 years to accumulate a fund of $70,000 by the end of the eighth year, if the fund earns 7.25% interest, compounded annually?

(b) Bill Yawn is 40 years old today, and he wishes to accumulate $500,000 by his sixty-fifth birthday so he can retire to his summer place on Lake Winnebago. He wishes to accumulate this amount by making equal deposits on his fortieth through sixty-fourth birthdays. What annual deposit must Bill make if the fund will earn 9.65% interest compounded annually?

(c) Jane Mayer has a $26,000 debt that she wishes to repay 4 years from today. She has $17,000 that she intends to invest for the 4 years. What rate of interest will she need to earn annually in order to accumulate enough to pay the debt?

(LO 10) ***P6-16** **(Various Time Value of Money Situations)** Using a financial calculator, solve for the unknowns in each of the following situations.

(a) Wayne Eski wishes to invest $150,000 today to ensure payments of $20,000 to his son at the end of each year for the next 15 years. At what interest rate must the $150,000 be invested? (Round the answer to two decimal points.)

(b) On June 1, 2007, Shelley Long purchases lakefront property from her neighbor, Joey Brenner, and agrees to pay the purchase price in seven payments of $16,000 each, the first payment to be payable June 1, 2008. (Assume that interest compounded at an annual rate of 7.35% is implicit in the payments.) What is the purchase price of the property?

(c) On January 1, 2007, Cooke Corporation purchased 200 of the $1,000 face value, 8% coupon, 10-year bonds of Howe Inc. The bonds mature on January 1, 2017, and pay interest annually beginning January 1, 2008. Cooke purchased the bonds to yield 10.65%. How much did Cooke pay for the bonds?

(LO 10) ***P6-17** **(Various Time Value of Money Situations)** Using a financial calculator, provide a solution to each of the following situations.

(a) On March 12, 2007, William Scott invests in a $180,000 insurance policy that earns 5.25% compounded annually. The annuity policy allows William to receive annual payments, the first of which is payable to William on March 12, 2008. What will be the amount of each of the 20 equal annual receipts?

(b) Bill Schroeder owes a debt of $35,000 from the purchase of his new sport utility vehicle. The debt bears annual interest of 9.1% compounded monthly. Bill wishes to pay the debt and interest in equal monthly payments over 8 years, beginning one month hence. What equal monthly payments will pay off the debt and interest?

(c) On January 1, 2007, Sammy Sosa offers to buy Mark Grace's used snowmobile for $8,000, payable in five equal installments, which are to include 8.25% interest on the unpaid balance and a portion of the principal. If the first payment is to be made on January 1, 2007, how much will each payment be?

(d) Repeat the requirements in part (c), assuming Sosa makes the first payment on December 31, 2007.

USING YOUR JUDGMENT

Financial Reporting Problem

 The Procter & Gamble Company (P&G)

The financial statements and accompanying notes of **P&G** are presented in Appendix 5B or can be accessed on the KWW website.

 **Instructions**

(a) Examining each item in P&G's balance sheet, identify those items that require present value, discounting, or interest computations in establishing the amount reported. (The accompanying notes are an additional source for this information.)

(b) (1) What interest rates are disclosed by P&G as being used to compute interest and present values?
(2) Why are there so many different interest rates applied to P&G's financial statement elements (assets, liabilities, revenues, and expenses)?

Financial Statement Analysis Case

Consolidated Natural Gas Company

Consolidated Natural Gas Company (CNG), with corporate headquarters in Pittsburgh, Pennsylvania, is one of the largest producers, transporters, distributors, and marketers of natural gas in North America.

Periodically, the company experiences a decrease in the value of its gas and oil producing properties, and a special charge to income was recorded in order to reduce the carrying value of those assets.

Assume the following information: In 2005, CNG estimated the cash inflows from its oil and gas producing properties to be $350,000 per year. During 2006, the write-downs described above caused the estimate to be decreased to $275,000 per year. Production costs (cash outflows) associated with all these properties were estimated to be $125,000 per year in 2005, but this amount was revised to $175,000 per year in 2006.

Instructions

(Assume that all cash flows occur at the end of the year.)

(a) Calculate the present value of net cash flows for 2005–2007 (three years), using the 2005 estimates and a 10% discount factor.

(b) Calculate the present value of net cash flows for 2006–2008 (three years), using the 2006 estimates and a 10% discount factor.

(c) Compare the results using the two estimates. Is information on future cash flows from oil and gas producing properties useful, considering that the estimates must be revised each year? Explain.

Research Cases

Case 1

To access the Internet and EDGAR, follow the steps outlined in the Research Case on page 248.

Firms registered with the U.S. Securities and Exchange Commission (SEC) are required to file an annual report on Form 10-K within 60 days of their fiscal year end. The Form 10-K includes certain information not provided in a firm's annual report to shareholders.

Instructions

Examine the most recent Form 10-K of a company of your choice and answer the following questions.

(a) Each 10-K is required to include information regarding several aspects of a firm, referenced by item numbers. Identify the 14 items included in the 10-K.

(b) Each 10-K must include the firm's financial statements. Does the 10-K you examined include the firm's financial statements? If not, how did the firm comply with the financial statement requirement?

(c) What financial statement schedules are included with the 10-K you examined?

Case 2

In May 2001 the FASB published the first of a series of articles entitled *Understanding the Issues*, which are designed to enhance FASB constituents' understanding of various accounting issues. In the first installment, "Expected Cash Flows," Ed Trott and Wayne Upton explained issues related to *FASB Concepts Statement No. 7.*

Instructions

The article can be accessed at the FASB website (**www.fasb.org**). Read the article and answer the following questions.

(a) What are the three areas in which the FASB received objections to its exposure draft for *Concepts Statement No. 7*?

(b) What has been the traditional approach to estimating cash flows and present values? What were some of the problems with the "traditional approach to present value"?

(c) What are the principles the Board identified in application of present value to accounting measurements?

(d) How do present values computed using the model in *Concepts Statement No. 7* include the effects of inflation?

Professional Research: Financial Accounting and Reporting

At a recent meeting of the accounting staff in your company, the controller raised the issue of using present value techniques to conduct impairment tests for some of the company's fixed assets. Some of the more senior members of the staff admitted having little knowledge of present value concepts in this context, but they had heard about a recent FASB Concepts Statement that may be relevant. As the junior staff in the department, you have been asked to conduct some research of the authoritative literature on this topic and report back at the staff meeting next week.

Instructions

Using the **Financial Accounting Research System (FARS)**, respond to the following items. (Provide text strings used in your search.)

(a) Identify the recent concept statement that addresses present value measurement in accounting.

(b) What are some of the contexts in which present value concepts are applied in accounting measurement?

(c) Provide definitions for the following terms:
- **(1)** Best estimate.
- **(2)** Estimated cash flow (contrasted to expected cash flow).
- **(3)** Fresh-start measurement.
- **(4)** Interest methods of allocation.

Professional Simulation

In this simulation you are asked to address questions concerning the application of time value of money concepts to accounting problems. Prepare responses to all parts.

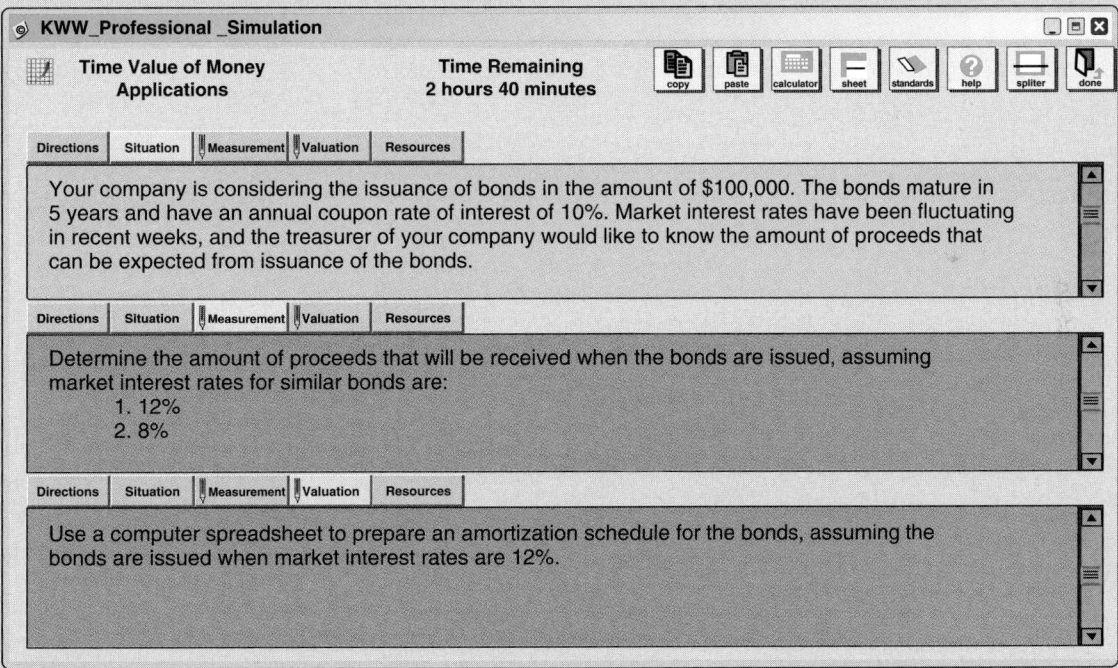

KWW_Professional _Simulation

Time Value of Money Applications   **Time Remaining 2 hours 40 minutes**   copy | paste | calculator | sheet | standards | help | spliter | done

Directions | Situation | Measurement | Valuation | Resources

Your company is considering the issuance of bonds in the amount of $100,000. The bonds mature in 5 years and have an annual coupon rate of interest of 10%. Market interest rates have been fluctuating in recent weeks, and the treasurer of your company would like to know the amount of proceeds that can be expected from issuance of the bonds.

Directions | Situation | Measurement | Valuation | Resources

Determine the amount of proceeds that will be received when the bonds are issued, assuming market interest rates for similar bonds are:
1. 12%
2. 8%

Directions | Situation | Measurement | Valuation | Resources

Use a computer spreadsheet to prepare an amortization schedule for the bonds, assuming the bonds are issued when market interest rates are 12%.

Remember to check the book's companion website to find additional resources for this chapter.

TABLE 6-1 FUTURE VALUE OF 1 (FUTURE VALUE OF A SINGLE SUM)

$$FVF_{n,i} = (1 + i)^n$$

(n) Periods	2%	2½%	3%	4%	5%	6%
1	1.02000	1.02500	1.03000	1.04000	1.05000	1.06000
2	1.04040	1.05063	1.06090	1.08160	1.10250	1.12360
3	1.06121	1.07689	1.09273	1.12486	1.15763	1.19102
4	1.08243	1.10381	1.12551	1.16986	1.21551	1.26248
5	1.10408	1.13141	1.15927	1.21665	1.27628	1.33823
6	1.12616	1.15969	1.19405	1.26532	1.34010	1.41852
7	1.14869	1.18869	1.22987	1.31593	1.40710	1.50363
8	1.17166	1.21840	1.26677	1.36857	1.47746	1.59385
9	1.19509	1.24886	1.30477	1.42331	1.55133	1.68948
10	1.21899	1.28008	1.34392	1.48024	1.62889	1.79085
11	1.24337	1.31209	1.38423	1.53945	1.71034	1.89830
12	1.26824	1.34489	1.42576	1.60103	1.79586	2.01220
13	1.29361	1.37851	1.46853	1.66507	1.88565	2.13293
14	1.31948	1.41297	1.51259	1.73168	1.97993	2.26090
15	1.34587	1.44830	1.55797	1.80094	2.07893	2.39656
16	1.37279	1.48451	1.60471	1.87298	2.18287	2.54035
17	1.40024	1.52162	1.65285	1.94790	2.29202	2.69277
18	1.42825	1.55966	1.70243	2.02582	2.40662	2.85434
19	1.45681	1.59865	1.75351	2.10685	2.52695	3.02560
20	1.48595	1.63862	1.80611	2.19112	2.65330	3.20714
21	1.51567	1.67958	1.86029	2.27877	2.78596	3.39956
22	1.54598	1.72157	1.91610	2.36992	2.92526	3.60354
23	1.57690	1.76461	1.97359	2.46472	3.07152	3.81975
24	1.60844	1.80873	2.03279	2.56330	3.22510	4.04893
25	1.64061	1.85394	2.09378	2.66584	3.38635	4.29187
26	1.67342	1.90029	2.15659	2.77247	3.55567	4.54938
27	1.70689	1.94780	2.22129	2.88337	3.73346	4.82235
28	1.74102	1.99650	2.28793	2.99870	3.92013	5.11169
29	1.77584	2.04641	2.35657	3.11865	4.11614	5.41839
30	1.81136	2.09757	2.42726	3.24340	4.32194	5.74349
31	1.84759	2.15001	2.50008	3.37313	4.53804	6.08810
32	1.88454	2.20376	2.57508	3.50806	4.76494	6.45339
33	1.92223	2.25885	2.65234	3.64838	5.00319	6.84059
34	1.96068	2.31532	2.73191	3.79432	5.25335	7.25103
35	1.99989	2.37321	2.81386	3.94609	5.51602	7.68609
36	2.03989	2.43254	2.89828	4.10393	5.79182	8.14725
37	2.08069	2.49335	2.98523	4.26809	6.08141	8.63609
38	2.12230	2.55568	3.07478	4.43881	6.38548	9.15425
39	2.16474	2.61957	3.16703	4.61637	6.70475	9.70351
40	2.20804	2.68506	3.26204	4.80102	7.03999	10.28572

TABLE 6-1   FUTURE VALUE OF 1

8%	9%	10%	11%	12%	15%	(n) Periods
1.08000	1.09000	1.10000	1.11000	1.12000	1.15000	1
1.16640	1.18810	1.21000	1.23210	1.25440	1.32250	2
1.25971	1.29503	1.33100	1.36763	1.40493	1.52088	3
1.36049	1.41158	1.46410	1.51807	1.57352	1.74901	4
1.46933	1.53862	1.61051	1.68506	1.76234	2.01136	5
1.58687	1.67710	1.77156	1.87041	1.97382	2.31306	6
1.71382	1.82804	1.94872	2.07616	2.21068	2.66002	7
1.85093	1.99256	2.14359	2.30454	2.47596	3.05902	8
1.99900	2.17189	2.35795	2.55803	2.77308	3.51788	9
2.15892	2.36736	2.59374	2.83942	3.10585	4.04556	10
2.33164	2.58043	2.85312	3.15176	3.47855	4.65239	11
2.51817	2.81267	3.13843	3.49845	3.89598	5.35025	12
2.71962	3.06581	3.45227	3.88328	4.36349	6.15279	13
2.93719	3.34173	3.79750	4.31044	4.88711	7.07571	14
3.17217	3.64248	4.17725	4.78459	5.47357	8.13706	15
3.42594	3.97031	4.59497	5.31089	6.13039	9.35762	16
3.70002	4.32763	5.05447	5.89509	6.86604	10.76126	17
3.99602	4.71712	5.55992	6.54355	7.68997	12.37545	18
4.31570	5.14166	6.11591	7.26334	8.61276	14.23177	19
4.66096	5.60441	6.72750	8.06231	9.64629	16.36654	20
5.03383	6.10881	7.40025	8.94917	10.80385	18.82152	21
5.43654	6.65860	8.14028	9.93357	12.10031	21.64475	22
5.87146	7.25787	8.95430	11.02627	13.55235	24.89146	23
6.34118	7.91108	9.84973	12.23916	15.17863	28.62518	24
6.84847	8.62308	10.83471	13.58546	17.00000	32.91895	25
7.39635	9.39916	11.91818	15.07986	19.04007	37.85680	26
7.98806	10.24508	13.10999	16.73865	21.32488	43.53532	27
8.62711	11.16714	14.42099	18.57990	23.88387	50.06561	28
9.31727	12.17218	15.86309	20.62369	26.74993	57.57545	29
10.06266	13.26768	17.44940	22.89230	29.95992	66.21177	30
10.86767	14.46177	19.19434	25.41045	33.55511	76.14354	31
11.73708	15.76333	21.11378	28.20560	37.58173	87.56507	32
12.67605	17.18203	23.22515	31.30821	42.09153	100.69983	33
13.69013	18.72841	25.54767	34.75212	47.14252	115.80480	34
14.78534	20.41397	28.10244	38.57485	52.79962	133.17552	35
15.96817	22.25123	30.91268	42.81808	59.13557	153.15185	36
17.24563	24.25384	34.00395	47.52807	66.23184	176.12463	37
18.62528	26.43668	37.40434	52.75616	74.17966	202.54332	38
20.11530	28.81598	41.14479	58.55934	83.08122	232.92482	39
21.72452	31.40942	45.25926	65.00087	93.05097	267.86355	40

TABLE 6-2   PRESENT VALUE OF 1 (PRESENT VALUE OF A SINGLE SUM)

$$PVF_{n,i} = \frac{1}{(1+i)^n} = (1+i)^{-n}$$

(n) Periods	2%	2½%	3%	4%	5%	6%
1	.98039	.97561	.97087	.96154	.95238	.94340
2	.96117	.95181	.94260	.92456	.90703	.89000
3	.94232	.92860	.91514	.88900	.86384	.83962
4	.92385	.90595	.88849	.85480	.82270	.79209
5	.90573	.88385	.86261	.82193	.78353	.74726
6	.88797	.86230	.83748	.79031	.74622	.70496
7	.87056	.84127	.81309	.75992	.71068	.66506
8	.85349	.82075	.78941	.73069	.67684	.62741
9	.83676	.80073	.76642	.70259	.64461	.59190
10	.82035	.78120	.74409	.67556	.61391	.55839
11	.80426	.76214	.72242	.64958	.58468	.52679
12	.78849	.74356	.70138	.62460	.55684	.49697
13	.77303	.72542	.68095	.60057	.53032	.46884
14	.75788	.70773	.66112	.57748	.50507	.44230
15	.74301	.69047	.64186	.55526	.48102	.41727
16	.72845	.67362	.62317	.53391	.45811	.39365
17	.71416	.65720	.60502	.51337	.43630	.37136
18	.70016	.64117	.58739	.49363	.41552	.35034
19	.68643	.62553	.57029	.47464	.39573	.33051
20	.67297	.61027	.55368	.45639	.37689	.31180
21	.65978	.59539	.53755	.43883	.35894	.29416
22	.64684	.58086	.52189	.42196	.34185	.22751
23	.63416	.56670	.50669	.40573	.32557	.26180
24	.62172	.55288	.49193	.39012	.31007	.24698
25	.60953	.53939	.47761	.37512	.29530	.23300
26	.59758	.52623	.46369	.36069	.28124	.21981
27	.58586	.51340	.45019	.34682	.26785	.20737
28	.57437	.50088	.43708	.33348	.25509	.19563
29	.56311	.48866	.42435	.32065	.24295	.18456
30	.55207	.47674	.41199	.30832	.23138	.17411
31	.54125	.46511	.39999	.29646	.22036	.16425
32	.53063	.45377	.38834	.28506	.20987	.15496
33	.52023	.44270	.37703	.27409	.19987	.14619
34	.51003	.43191	.36604	.26355	.19035	.13791
35	.50003	.42137	.35538	.25342	.18129	.13011
36	.49022	.41109	.34503	.24367	.17266	.12274
37	.48061	.40107	.33498	.23430	.16444	.11579
38	.47119	.39128	.32523	.22529	.15661	.10924
39	.46195	.38174	.31575	.21662	.14915	.10306
40	.45289	.37243	.30656	.20829	.14205	.09722

TABLE 6-2   PRESENT VALUE OF 1

8%	9%	10%	11%	12%	15%	(n) Periods
.92593	.91743	.90909	.90090	.89286	.86957	1
.85734	.84168	.82645	.81162	.79719	.75614	2
.79383	.77218	.75132	.73119	.71178	.65752	3
.73503	.70843	.68301	.65873	.63552	.57175	4
.68058	.64993	.62092	.59345	.56743	.49718	5
.63017	.59627	.56447	.53464	.50663	.43233	6
.58349	.54703	.51316	.48166	.45235	.37594	7
.54027	.50187	.46651	.43393	.40388	.32690	8
.50025	.46043	.42410	.39092	.36061	.28426	9
.46319	.42241	.38554	.35218	.32197	.24719	10
.42888	.38753	.35049	.31728	.28748	.21494	11
.39711	.35554	.31863	.28584	.25668	.18691	12
.36770	.32618	.28966	.25751	.22917	.16253	13
.34046	.29925	.26333	.23199	.20462	.14133	14
.31524	.27454	.23939	.20900	.18270	.12289	15
.29189	.25187	.21763	.18829	.16312	.10687	16
.27027	.23107	.19785	.16963	.14564	.09293	17
.25025	.21199	.17986	.15282	.13004	.08081	18
.23171	.19449	.16351	.13768	.11611	.07027	19
.21455	.17843	.14864	.12403	.10367	.06110	20
.19866	.16370	.13513	.11174	.09256	.05313	21
.18394	.15018	.12285	.10067	.08264	.04620	22
.17032	.13778	.11168	.09069	.07379	.04017	23
.15770	.12641	.10153	.08170	.06588	.03493	24
.14602	.11597	.09230	.07361	.05882	.03038	25
.13520	.10639	.08391	.06631	.05252	.02642	26
.12519	.09761	.07628	.05974	.04689	.02297	27
.11591	.08955	.06934	.05382	.04187	.01997	28
.10733	.08216	.06304	.04849	.03738	.01737	29
.09938	.07537	.05731	.04368	.03338	.01510	30
.09202	.06915	.05210	.03935	.02980	.01313	31
.08520	.06344	.04736	.03545	.02661	.01142	32
.07889	.05820	.04306	.03194	.02376	.00993	33
.07305	.05340	.03914	.02878	.02121	.00864	34
.06763	.04899	.03558	.02592	.01894	.00751	35
.06262	.04494	.03235	.02335	.01691	.00653	36
.05799	.04123	.02941	.02104	.01510	.00568	37
.05369	.03783	.02674	.01896	.01348	.00494	38
.04971	.03470	.02430	.01708	.01204	.00429	39
.04603	.03184	.02210	.01538	.01075	.00373	40

TABLE 6-3 FUTURE VALUE OF AN ORDINARY ANNUITY OF 1

$$\text{FVF-OA}_{n,i} = \frac{(1 + i)^n - 1}{i}$$

(n) Periods	2%	2½%	3%	4%	5%	6%
1	1.00000	1.00000	1.00000	1.00000	1.00000	1.00000
2	2.02000	2.02500	2.03000	2.04000	2.05000	2.06000
3	3.06040	3.07563	3.09090	3.12160	3.15250	3.18360
4	4.12161	4.15252	4.18363	4.24646	4.31013	4.37462
5	5.20404	5.25633	5.30914	5.41632	5.52563	5.63709
6	6.30812	6.38774	6.46841	6.63298	6.80191	6.97532
7	7.43428	7.54743	7.66246	7.89829	8.14201	8.39384
8	8.58297	8.73612	8.89234	9.21423	9.54911	9.89747
9	9.75463	9.95452	10.15911	10.58280	11.02656	11.49132
10	10.94972	11.20338	11.46338	12.00611	12.57789	13.18079
11	12.16872	12.48347	12.80780	13.48635	14.20679	14.97164
12	13.41209	13.79555	14.19203	15.02581	15.91713	16.86994
13	14.68033	15.14044	15.61779	16.62684	17.71298	18.88214
14	15.97394	16.51895	17.08632	18.29191	19.59863	21.01507
15	17.29342	17.93193	18.59891	20.02359	21.57856	23.27597
16	18.63929	19.38022	20.15688	21.82453	23.65749	25.67253
17	20.01207	20.86473	21.76159	23.69751	25.84037	28.21288
18	21.41231	22.38635	23.41444	25.64541	28.13238	30.90565
19	22.84056	23.94601	25.11687	27.67123	30.53900	33.75999
20	24.29737	25.54466	26.87037	29.77808	33.06595	36.78559
21	25.78332	27.18327	28.67649	31.96920	35.71925	39.99273
22	27.29898	28.86286	30.53678	34.24797	38.50521	43.39229
23	28.84496	30.58443	32.45288	36.61789	41.43048	46.99583
24	30.42186	32.34904	34.42647	39.08260	44.50200	50.81558
25	32.03030	34.15776	36.45926	41.64591	47.72710	54.86451
26	33.67091	36.01171	38.55304	44.31174	51.11345	59.15638
27	35.34432	37.91200	40.70963	47.08421	54.66913	63.70577
28	37.05121	39.85980	42.93092	49.96758	58.40258	68.52811
29	38.79223	41.85630	45.21885	52.96629	62.32271	73.63980
30	40.56808	43.90270	47.57542	56.08494	66.43885	79.05819
31	42.37944	46.00027	50.00268	59.32834	70.76079	84.80168
32	44.22703	48.15028	52.50276	62.70147	75.29883	90.88978
33	46.11157	50.35403	55.07784	66.20953	80.06377	97.34316
34	48.03380	52.61289	57.73018	69.85791	85.06696	104.18376
35	49.99448	54.92821	60.46208	73.65222	90.32031	111.43478
36	51.99437	57.30141	63.27594	77.59831	95.83632	119.12087
37	54.03425	59.73395	66.17422	81.70225	101.62814	127.26812
38	56.11494	62.22730	69.15945	85.97034	107.70955	135.90421
39	58.23724	64.78298	72.23423	90.40915	114.09502	145.05846
40	60.40198	67.40255	75.40126	95.02552	120.79977	154.76197

TABLE 6-3   FUTURE VALUE OF AN ORDINARY ANNUITY OF 1

8%	9%	10%	11%	12%	15%	(n) Periods
1.00000	1.00000	1.00000	1.00000	1.00000	1.00000	1
2.08000	2.09000	2.10000	2.11000	2.12000	2.15000	2
3.24640	3.27810	3.31000	3.34210	3.37440	3.47250	3
4.50611	4.57313	4.64100	4.70973	4.77933	4.99338	4
5.86660	5.98471	6.10510	6.22780	6.35285	6.74238	5
7.33592	7.52334	7.71561	7.91286	8.11519	8.75374	6
8.92280	9.20044	9.48717	9.78327	10.08901	11.06680	7
10.63663	11.02847	11.43589	11.85943	12.29969	13.72682	8
12.48756	13.02104	13.57948	14.16397	14.77566	16.78584	9
14.48656	15.19293	15.93743	16.72201	17.54874	20.30372	10
16.64549	17.56029	18.53117	19.56143	20.65458	24.34928	11
18.97713	20.14072	21.38428	22.71319	24.13313	29.00167	12
21.49530	22.95339	24.52271	26.21164	28.02911	34.35192	13
24.21492	26.01919	27.97498	30.09492	32.39260	40.50471	14
27.15211	29.36092	31.77248	34.40536	37.27972	47.58041	15
30.32428	33.00340	35.94973	39.18995	42.75328	55.71747	16
33.75023	36.97371	40.54470	44.50084	48.88367	65.07509	17
37.45024	41.30134	45.59917	50.39593	55.74972	75.83636	18
41.44626	46.01846	51.15909	56.93949	63.43968	88.21181	19
45.76196	51.16012	57.27500	64.20283	72.05244	102.44358	20
50.42292	56.76453	64.00250	72.26514	81.69874	118.81012	21
55.45676	62.87334	71.40275	81.21431	92.50258	137.63164	22
60.89330	69.53194	79.54302	91.14788	104.60289	159.27638	23
66.76476	76.78981	88.49733	102.17415	118.15524	184.16784	24
73.10594	84.70090	98.34706	114.41331	133.33387	212.79302	25
79.95442	93.32398	109.18177	127.99877	150.33393	245.71197	26
87.35077	102.72314	121.09994	143.07864	169.37401	283.56877	27
95.33883	112.96822	134.20994	159.81729	190.69889	327.10408	28
103.96594	124.13536	148.63093	178.39719	214.58275	377.16969	29
113.28321	136.30754	164.49402	199.02088	241.33268	434.74515	30
123.34587	149.57522	181.94343	221.91317	271.29261	500.95692	31
134.21354	164.03699	201.13777	247.32362	304.84772	577.10046	32
145.95062	179.80032	222.25154	275.52922	342.42945	644.66553	33
158.62667	196.98234	245.47670	306.83744	384.52098	765.36535	34
172.31680	215.71076	271.02437	341.58955	431.66350	881.17016	35
187.10215	236.12472	299.12681	380.16441	484.46312	1014.34568	36
203.07032	258.37595	330.03949	422.98249	543.59869	1167.49753	37
220.31595	282.62978	364.04343	470.51056	609.83053	1343.62216	38
238.94122	309.06646	401.44778	523.26673	684.01020	1546.16549	39
259.05652	337.88245	442.59256	581.82607	767.09142	1779.09031	40

TABLE 6-4 PRESENT VALUE OF AN ORDINARY ANNUITY OF 1

$$PVF\text{-}OA_{n,i} = \frac{1 - \dfrac{1}{(1+i)^n}}{i}$$

(n) Periods	2%	2½%	3%	4%	5%	6%
1	.98039	.97561	.97087	.96154	.95238	.94340
2	1.94156	1.92742	1.91347	1.88609	1.85941	1.83339
3	2.88388	2.85602	2.82861	2.77509	2.72325	2.67301
4	3.80773	3.76197	3.71710	3.62990	3.54595	3.46511
5	4.71346	4.64583	4.57971	4.45182	4.32948	4.21236
6	5.60143	5.50813	5.41719	5.24214	5.07569	4.91732
7	6.47199	6.34939	6.23028	6.00205	5.78637	5.58238
8	7.32548	7.17014	7.01969	6.73274	6.46321	6.20979
9	8.16224	7.97087	7.78611	7.43533	7.10782	6.80169
10	8.98259	8.75206	8.53020	8.11090	7.72173	7.36009
11	9.78685	9.51421	9.25262	8.76048	8.30641	7.88687
12	10.57534	10.25776	9.95400	9.38507	8.86325	8.38384
13	11.34837	10.98319	10.63496	9.98565	9.39357	8.85268
14	12.10625	11.69091	11.29607	10.56312	9.89864	9.29498
15	12.84926	12.38138	11.93794	11.11839	10.37966	9.71225
16	13.57771	13.05500	12.56110	11.65230	10.83777	10.10590
17	14.29187	13.71220	13.16612	12.16567	11.27407	10.47726
18	14.99203	14.35336	13.75351	12.65930	11.68959	10.82760
19	15.67846	14.97889	14.32380	13.13394	12.08532	11.15812
20	16.35143	15.58916	14.87747	13.59033	12.46221	11.46992
21	17.01121	16.18455	15.41502	14.02916	12.82115	11.76408
22	17.65805	16.76541	15.93692	14.45112	13.16300	12.04158
23	18.29220	17.33211	16.44361	14.85684	13.48857	12.30338
24	18.91393	17.88499	16.93554	15.24696	13.79864	12.55036
25	19.52346	18.42438	17.41315	15.62208	14.09394	12.78336
26	20.12104	18.95061	17.87684	15.98277	14.37519	13.00317
27	20.70690	19.46401	18.32703	16.32959	14.64303	13.21053
28	21.28127	19.96489	18.76411	16.66306	14.89813	13.40616
29	21.84438	20.45355	19.18845	16.98371	15.14107	13.59072
30	22.39646	20.93029	19.60044	17.29203	15.37245	13.76483
31	22.93770	21.39541	20.00043	17.58849	15.59281	13.92909
32	23.46833	21.84918	20.38877	17.87355	15.80268	14.08404
33	23.98856	22.29188	20.76579	18.14765	16.00255	14.23023
34	24.49859	22.72379	21.13184	18.41120	16.19290	14.36814
35	24.99862	23.14516	21.48722	18.66461	16.37419	14.49825
36	25.48884	23.55625	21.83225	18.90828	16.54685	14.62099
37	25.96945	23.95732	22.16724	19.14258	16.71129	14.73678
38	26.44064	24.34860	22.49246	19.36786	16.86789	14.84602
39	26.90259	24.73034	22.80822	19.58448	17.01704	14.94907
40	27.35548	25.10278	23.11477	19.79277	17.15909	15.04630

TABLE 6-4   PRESENT VALUE OF AN ORDINARY ANNUITY OF 1

8%	9%	10%	11%	12%	15%	(n) Periods
.92593	.91743	.90909	.90090	.89286	.86957	1
1.78326	1.75911	1.73554	1.71252	1.69005	1.62571	2
2.57710	2.53130	2.48685	2.44371	2.40183	2.28323	3
3.31213	3.23972	3.16986	3.10245	3.03735	2.85498	4
3.99271	3.88965	3.79079	3.69590	3.60478	3.35216	5
4.62288	4.48592	4.35526	4.23054	4.11141	3.78448	6
5.20637	5.03295	4.86842	4.71220	4.56376	4.16042	7
5.74664	5.53482	5.33493	5.14612	4.96764	4.48732	8
6.24689	5.99525	5.75902	5.53705	5.32825	4.77158	9
6.71008	6.41766	6.14457	5.88923	5.65022	5.01877	10
7.13896	6.80519	6.49506	6.20652	5.93770	5.23371	11
7.53608	7.16073	6.81369	6.49236	6.19437	5.42062	12
7.90378	7.48690	7.10336	6.74987	6.42355	5.58315	13
8.24424	7.78615	7.36669	6.98187	6.62817	5.72448	14
8.55948	8.06069	7.60608	7.19087	6.81086	5.84737	15
8.85137	8.31256	7.82371	7.37916	6.97399	5.95424	16
9.12164	8.54363	8.02155	7.54879	7.11963	6.04716	17
9.37189	8.75563	8.20141	7.70162	7.24967	6.12797	18
9.60360	8.95012	8.36492	7.83929	7.36578	6.19823	19
9.81815	9.12855	8.51356	7.96333	7.46944	6.25933	20
10.01680	9.29224	8.64869	8.07507	7.56200	6.31246	21
10.20074	9.44243	8.77154	8.17574	7.64465	6.35866	22
10.37106	9.58021	8.88322	8.26643	7.71843	6.39884	23
10.52876	9.70661	8.98474	8.34814	7.78432	6.43377	24
10.67478	9.82258	9.07704	8.42174	7.84314	6.46415	25
10.80998	9.92897	9.16095	8.48806	7.89566	6.49056	26
10.93516	10.02658	9.23722	8.54780	7.94255	6.51353	27
11.05108	10.11613	9.30657	8.60162	7.98442	6.53351	28
11.15841	10.19828	9.36961	8.65011	8.02181	6.55088	29
11.25778	10.27365	9.42691	8.69379	8.05518	6.56598	30
11.34980	10.34280	9.47901	8.73315	8.08499	6.57911	31
11.43500	10.40624	9.52638	8.76860	8.11159	6.59053	32
11.51389	10.46444	9.56943	8.80054	8.13535	6.60046	33
11.58693	10.51784	9.60858	8.82932	8.15656	6.60910	34
11.65457	10.56682	9.64416	8.85524	8.17550	6.61661	35
11.71719	10.61176	9.67651	8.87859	8.19241	6.62314	36
11.77518	10.65299	9.70592	8.89963	8.20751	6.62882	37
11.82887	10.69082	9.73265	8.91859	8.22099	6.63375	38
11.87858	10.72552	9.75697	8.93567	8.23303	6.63805	39
11.92461	10.75736	9.77905	8.95105	8.24378	6.64178	40

TABLE 6-5 PRESENT VALUE OF AN ANNUITY DUE OF 1

$$\text{PVF-AD}_{n,i} = 1 + \frac{1 - \dfrac{1}{(1+i)^{n-1}}}{i}$$

(n) Periods	2%	2½%	3%	4%	5%	6%
1	1.00000	1.00000	1.00000	1.00000	1.00000	1.00000
2	1.98039	1.97561	1.97087	1.96154	1.95238	1.94340
3	2.94156	2.92742	2.91347	2.88609	2.85941	2.83339
4	3.88388	3.85602	3.82861	3.77509	3.72325	3.67301
5	4.80773	4.76197	4.71710	4.62990	4.54595	4.46511
6	5.71346	5.64583	5.57971	5.45182	5.32948	5.21236
7	6.60143	6.50813	6.41719	6.24214	6.07569	5.91732
8	7.47199	7.34939	7.23028	7.00205	6.78637	6.58238
9	8.32548	8.17014	8.01969	7.73274	7.46321	7.20979
10	9.16224	8.97087	8.78611	8.43533	8.10782	7.80169
11	9.98259	9.75206	9.53020	9.11090	8.72173	8.36009
12	10.78685	10.51421	10.25262	9.76048	9.30641	8.88687
13	11.57534	11.25776	10.95400	10.38507	9.86325	9.38384
14	12.34837	11.98319	11.63496	10.98565	10.39357	9.85268
15	13.10625	12.69091	12.29607	11.56312	10.89864	10.29498
16	13.84926	13.38138	12.93794	12.11839	11.37966	10.71225
17	14.57771	14.05500	13.56110	12.65230	11.83777	11.10590
18	15.29187	14.71220	14.16612	13.16567	12.27407	11.47726
19	15.99203	15.35336	14.75351	13.65930	12.68959	11.82760
20	16.67846	15.97889	15.32380	14.13394	13.08532	12.15812
21	17.35143	16.58916	15.87747	14.59033	13.46221	12.46992
22	18.01121	17.18455	16.41502	15.02916	13.82115	12.76408
23	18.65805	17.76541	16.93692	15.45112	14.16300	13.04158
24	19.29220	18.33211	17.44361	15.85684	14.48857	13.30338
25	19.91393	18.88499	17.93554	16.24696	14.79864	13.55036
26	20.52346	19.42438	18.41315	16.62208	15.09394	13.78336
27	21.12104	19.95061	18.87684	16.98277	15.37519	14.00317
28	21.70690	20.46401	19.32703	17.32959	15.64303	14.21053
29	22.28127	20.96489	19.76411	17.66306	15.89813	14.40616
30	22.84438	21.45355	20.18845	17.98371	16.14107	14.59072
31	23.39646	21.93029	20.60044	18.29203	16.37245	14.76483
32	23.93770	22.39541	21.00043	18.58849	16.59281	14.92909
33	24.46833	22.84918	21.38877	18.87355	16.80268	15.08404
34	24.98856	23.29188	21.76579	19.14765	17.00255	15.23023
35	25.49859	23.72379	22.13184	19.41120	17.19290	15.36814
36	25.99862	24.14516	22.48722	19.66461	17.37419	15.49825
37	26.48884	24.55625	22.83225	19.90828	17.54685	15.62099
38	26.96945	24.95732	23.16724	20.14258	17.71129	15.73678
39	27.44064	25.34860	23.49246	20.36786	17.86789	15.84602
40	27.90259	25.73034	23.80822	20.58448	18.01704	15.94907

TABLE 6-5   PRESENT VALUE OF AN ANNUITY DUE OF 1

8%	9%	10%	11%	12%	15%	(n) Periods
1.00000	1.00000	1.00000	1.00000	1.00000	1.00000	1
1.92593	1.91743	1.90909	1.90090	1.89286	1.86957	2
2.78326	2.75911	2.73554	2.71252	2.69005	2.62571	3
3.57710	3.53130	3.48685	3.44371	3.40183	3.28323	4
4.31213	4.23972	4.16986	4.10245	4.03735	3.85498	5
4.99271	4.88965	4.79079	4.69590	4.60478	4.35216	6
5.62288	5.48592	5.35526	5.23054	5.11141	4.78448	7
6.20637	6.03295	5.86842	5.71220	5.56376	5.16042	8
6.74664	6.53482	6.33493	6.14612	5.96764	5.48732	9
7.24689	6.99525	6.75902	6.53705	6.32825	5.77158	10
7.71008	7.41766	7.14457	6.88923	6.65022	6.01877	11
8.13896	7.80519	7.49506	7.20652	6.93770	6.23371	12
8.53608	8.16073	7.81369	7.49236	7.19437	6.42062	13
8.90378	8.48690	8.10336	7.74987	7.42355	6.58315	14
9.24424	8.78615	8.36669	7.98187	7.62817	6.72448	15
9.55948	9.06069	8.60608	8.19087	7.81086	6.84737	16
9.85137	9.31256	8.82371	8.37916	7.97399	6.95424	17
10.12164	9.54363	9.02155	8.54879	8.11963	7.04716	18
10.37189	9.75563	9.20141	8.70162	8.24967	7.12797	19
10.60360	9.95012	9.36492	8.83929	8.36578	7.19823	20
10.81815	10.12855	9.51356	8.96333	8.46944	7.25933	21
11.01680	10.29224	9.64869	9.07507	8.56200	7.31246	22
11.20074	10.44243	9.77154	9.17574	8.64465	7.35866	23
11.37106.	10.58021	9.88322	9.26643	8.71843	7.39884	24
11.52876	10.70661	9.98474	9.34814	8.78432	7.43377	25
11.67478	10.82258	10.07704	9.42174	8.84314	7.46415	26
11.80998	10.92897	10.16095	9.48806	8.89566	7.49056	27
11.93518	11.02658	10.23722	9.54780	8.94255	7.51353	28
12.05108	11.11613	10.30657	9.60162	8.98442	7.53351	29
12.15841	11.19828	10.36961	9.65011	9.02181	7.55088	30
12.25778	11.27365	10.42691	9.69379	9.05518	7.56598	31
12.34980	11.34280	10.47901	9.73315	9.08499	7.57911	32
12.43500	11.40624	10.52638	9.76860	9.11159	7.59053	33
12.51389	11.46444	10.56943	9.80054	9.13535	7.60046	34
12.58693	11.51784	10.60858	9.82932	9.15656	7.60910	35
12.65457	11.56682	10.64416	9.85524	9.17550	7.61661	36
12.71719	11.61176	10.67651	9.87859	9.19241	7.62314	37
12.77518	11.65299	10.70592	9.89963	9.20751	7.62882	38
12.82887	11.69082	10.73265	9.91859	9.22099	7.63375	39
12.87858	11.72552	10.75697	9.93567	9.23303	7.63805	40

CASH AND RECEIVABLES

No-Tell Nortel

Recently, **Nortel** announced that its net income for 2003 was really half what it originally reported. In addition, the company had understated net income for 2002. How could this happen? One reason: It appears that Nortel set up "cookie jar" reserves, using the allowance for doubtful accounts as the cookie jar. As the following chart shows, in 2002 Nortel overestimated the amount of bad debt expense (with a sizable allowance for doubtful accounts). Then, in 2003 Nortel slashed the amount of bad debt expense, even though the total money owed by customers remained nearly unchanged. In 2002, its allowance was 19 percent of receivables compared to 10 percent in 2003—quite a difference.

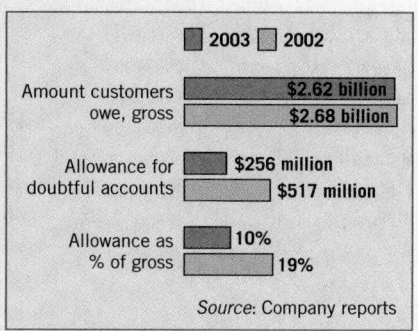

	2003	2002
Amount customers owe, gross	$2.62 billion	$2.68 billion
Allowance for doubtful accounts	$256 million	$517 million
Allowance as % of gross	10%	19%

Source: Company reports

It is difficult to determine if the allowance was too high in 2002 or too low in 2003, or both. Whatever the case, the use of the allowance cookie jar permitted Nortel to report higher operating margins and net income in 2003.

This analysis suggests the importance of looking carefully at the amount of bad debt expense reported in annual reports. Sometimes companies use it to artificially *decrease* income. Others understate bad debt expense to *increase* income. For example, analysts have noted that many large hospitals, such as **Tenet Healthcare** and **HCA**, may be facing increasing uncollectible accounts that are presently not fully reflected in their balance sheets.

Adapted from J. Weil, "At Nortel, Warning Signs Existed Months Ago, *Wall Street Journal* (May 18, 2004), p. C3; and B. McLean, "Reality Checkup," *Fortune* (January 12, 2004), p. 140.

Learning Objectives

After studying this chapter, you should be able to:

1 Identify items considered as cash.

2 Indicate how to report cash and related items.

3 Define receivables and identify the different types of receivables.

4 Explain accounting issues related to recognition of accounts receivable.

5 Explain accounting issues related to valuation of accounts receivable.

6 Explain accounting issues related to recognition of notes receivable.

7 Explain accounting issues related to valuation of notes receivable.

8 Explain accounting issues related to disposition of accounts and notes receivable.

9 Describe how to report and analyze receivables.

As our opening story indicates, estimating the collectibility of accounts receivable has important implications for accurate reporting of operating profits, net income, and assets. In this chapter we discuss cash and receivables—two assets that are important to companies as diverse as **Nortel** and **Tenet Healthcare**. The content and organization of the chapter are as follows.

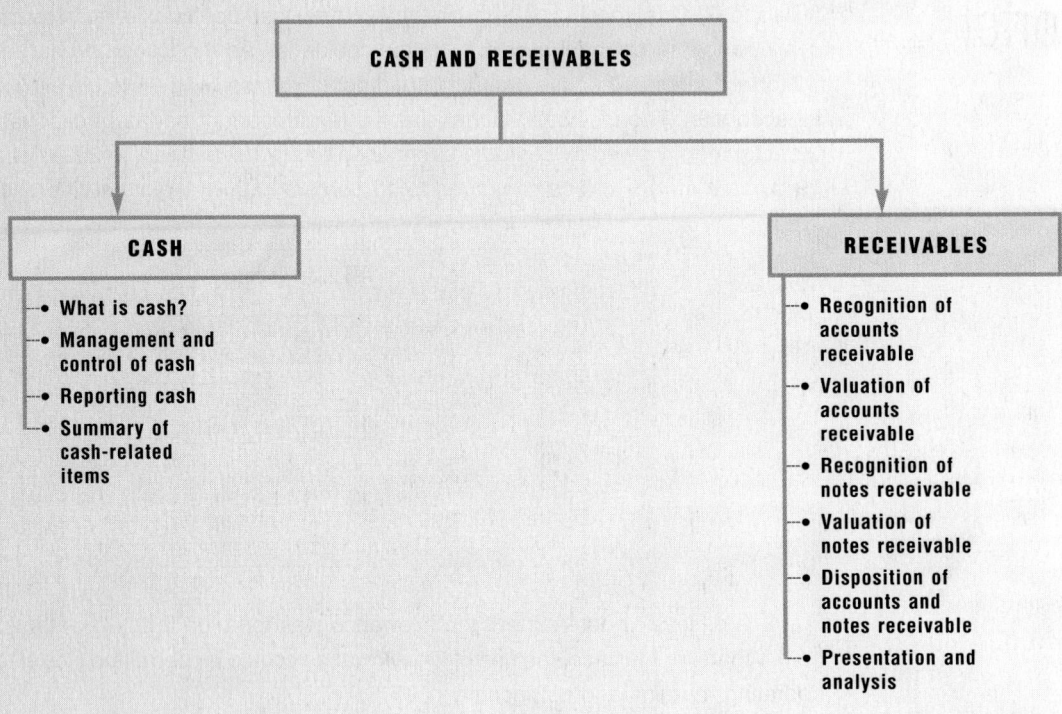

SECTION 1	*CASH*

WHAT IS CASH?

OBJECTIVE 1
Identify items considered cash.

Cash, the most liquid of assets, is the standard medium of exchange and the basis for measuring and accounting for all other items. Companies generally classify cash as a current asset. Cash consists of coin, currency, and available funds on deposit at the bank. Negotiable instruments such as money orders, certified checks, cashier's checks, personal checks, and bank drafts are also viewed as cash. What about savings accounts? Banks do have the legal right to demand notice before withdrawal. But, because banks rarely demand prior notice, savings accounts nevertheless are considered cash.

Some negotiable instruments provide small investors with an opportunity to earn interest. These items, more appropriately classified as temporary investments than as cash, include money market funds, money market savings certificates, certificates of deposit (CDs), and similar types of deposits and "short-term paper."[1] These securities usually contain restrictions or penalties on their conversion to cash. Money market funds that provide checking account privileges, however, are usually classified as cash.

Certain items present classification problems: Companies treat **postdated checks and I.O.U.s** as receivables. They also treat **travel advances** as receivables if collected from employees or deducted from their salaries. Otherwise, companies classify the travel advance as a prepaid expense. **Postage stamps on hand** are classified as part of office supplies inventory or as a prepaid expense. Because **petty cash funds and change funds are used** to meet current operating expenses and liquidate current liabilities, companies include these funds in current assets as cash.

MANAGEMENT AND CONTROL OF CASH

Cash is the asset most susceptible to improper diversion and use. Management faces two problems in accounting for cash transactions: (1) to establish proper controls to prevent any unauthorized transactions by officers or employees, and (2) to provide information necessary to properly manage cash on hand and cash transactions. Yet even with sophisticated control devices, errors can and do happen. For example, the *Wall Street Journal* ran a story entitled "A $7.8 Million Error Has a Happy Ending for a Horrified Bank." The story described how **Manufacturers Hanover Trust Co.** mistakenly overpaid about $7.8 million in cash dividends to its stockholders. (As implied in the headline, most stockholders returned the monies.)

To safeguard cash and to ensure the accuracy of the accounting records for cash, companies need effective **internal control** over cash. Provisions of the Sarbanes-Oxley Act of 2002 call for enhanced efforts to increase the quality of internal control (for cash and other assets). Such efforts are expected to result in improved financial reporting.

However, the increasing volume of transactions conducted with the swipe of a debit or credit card presents new challenges to the effort to maintain control over liquid assets. As one writer noted, "In 5,000 years there have been only four times that we have changed the way we pay—there was barter to coinage; coins to paper; paper to checks; and then cards. Just since 1995, the amount of stuff that American consumers buy using plastic has increased 430 percent."[2] In 2003, for the first time, Americans bought more using cards than cash.[3] In addition, electronic commerce conducted over the Internet continues to grow.

---

[1]A variety of "short-term paper" is available for investment. For example, **certificates of deposit** (CDs) represent formal evidence of indebtedness, issued by a bank, subject to withdrawal under the specific terms of the instrument. Issued in $1,000 to $100,000 denominations, they have maturities anywhere from 7 days to 10 years and generally pay interest at the short-term interest rate in effect at the date of issuance.

Banks and savings and loan associations issue **money-market savings certificates** in denominations of $10,000 or more for 6-month periods (6 to 48 months). The interest rate is tied to the 26-week Treasury bill rate.

In **money-market funds**, a variation of the mutual fund, the mix of Treasury bills and commercial paper making up the fund's portfolio determines the yield. Most money-market funds require an initial minimum investment of $1,000; many allow withdrawal by check or wire transfer.

Treasury bills are U.S. government obligations generally issued with 4-, 13-, and 26-week maturities; they are sold in $10,000 denominations at weekly government auctions.

Commercial paper is a short-term note issued by corporations with good credit ratings. Often issued in $5,000 and $10,000 denominations, these notes generally yield a higher rate than Treasury bills.

[2]K. Brooker, "Just One Word: Plastic," *Fortune* (February 23, 2004), p. 130.

[3]Ibid, p. 132. Non-U.S. consumers are even bigger users of digital cash than U.S. consumers. For example, non-check payments in Japan and Europe comprise over 70 percent of all payment transactions. U.S. consumers' continued use of checks and cash for payment raises fraud concerns, though, as duplication technology makes it easier to forge checks and currency.

Each of these trends contributes to the shift from cold cash to digital cash, and poses new challenges for the control of cash. In the appendix to this chapter, we discuss some of the basic control procedures used to ensure the correct reporting of cash.

REPORTING CASH

OBJECTIVE 2
Indicate how to report cash and related items.

Although the reporting of cash is relatively straightforward, a number of issues merit special attention. These issues relate to the reporting of:

1 Restricted cash.
2 Bank overdrafts.
3 Cash equivalents.

Restricted Cash

Petty cash, payroll, and dividend funds are examples of cash set aside for a particular purpose. In most situations, these fund balances are not material. Therefore, companies do not segregate them from cash in the financial statements. When material in amount, companies segregate **restricted cash** from "regular" cash for reporting purposes. Companies classify restricted cash either in the current assets or in the long-term assets section, depending on the date of availability or disbursement. Classification in the current section is appropriate if using the cash for payment of existing or maturing obligations (within a year or the operating cycle, whichever is longer). On the other hand, companies show the restricted cash in the long-term section of the balance sheet if holding the cash for a longer period of time.

Cash classified in the long-term section is frequently set aside for plant expansion, retirement of long-term debt or, in the case of **International Thoroughbred Breeders**, for entry fee deposits.

ILLUSTRATION 7-1
Disclosure of
Restricted Cash

International Thoroughbred Breeders

Restricted cash and investments (See Note) $3,730,000

Note: Restricted Cash. At year-end, the Company had approximately $3,730,000, which was classified as restricted cash and investments. These funds are primarily cash received from horsemen for nomination and entry fees to be applied to upcoming racing meets, purse winnings held in trust for horsemen, and amounts held for unclaimed ticketholder winnings.

Banks and other lending institutions often require customers to maintain minimum cash balances in checking or savings accounts. The SEC defines these minimum balances, called **compensating balances**, as "that portion of any demand deposit (or any time deposit or certificate of deposit) maintained by a corporation which constitutes support for existing borrowing arrangements of the corporation with a lending institution. Such arrangements would include both outstanding borrowings and the assurance of future credit availability."[4]

---

[4]*Accounting Series Release No. 148*, "Amendments to Regulations S-X and Related Interpretations and Guidelines Regarding the Disclosure of Compensating Balances and Short-Term Borrowing Arrangements," Securities and Exchange Commission (November 13, 1973). The SEC defines 15 percent of liquid assets (current cash balances, whether restricted or not, plus marketable securities) as being material, thereby requiring additional reporting.

To avoid misleading investors about the amount of cash available to meet recurring obligations, the SEC recommends that companies state separately **legally restricted deposits** held as compensating balances against **short-term** borrowing arrangements among the "Cash and cash equivalent items" in current assets. Companies should classify separately restricted deposits held as compensating balances against **long-term** borrowing arrangements as noncurrent assets in either the investments or other assets sections, using a caption such as "Cash on deposit maintained as compensating balance." In cases where compensating balance arrangements exist without agreements that restrict the use of cash amounts shown on the balance sheet, companies should describe the arrangements and the amounts involved in the notes.

INTERNATIONAL INSIGHT

Among other potential restrictions, companies need to determine whether any of the cash in accounts outside the U.S. is restricted by regulations against exportation of currency.

Bank Overdrafts

Bank overdrafts occur when a company writes a check for more than the amount in its cash account. Companies should report bank overdrafts in the current liabilities section, adding them to the amount reported as accounts payable. If material, companies should disclose these items separately, either on the face of the balance sheet or in the related notes.[5]

Bank overdrafts are generally not offset against the cash account. A major exception is when available cash is present in another account in the same bank on which the overdraft occurred. Offsetting in this case is required.

Cash Equivalents

A current classification that has become popular is "Cash and cash equivalents."[6] **Cash equivalents** are short-term, highly liquid investments that are both (a) readily convertible to known amounts of cash, and (b) so near their maturity that they present insignificant risk of changes in interest rates. Generally, only investments with original maturities of three months or less qualify under these definitions. Examples of cash equivalents are Treasury bills, commercial paper, and money market funds. Some companies combine cash with temporary investments on the balance sheet. In these cases, they describe the amount of the temporary investments either parenthetically or in the notes.

Additional Disclosures of Restricted Cash

SUMMARY OF CASH-RELATED ITEMS

Cash and cash equivalents include the medium of exchange and most negotiable instruments. If the item cannot be quickly converted to coin or currency, a company separately classifies it as an investment, receivable, or prepaid expense. Companies segregate and classify cash that is unavailable for payment of currently maturing liabilities in the long-term assets section. Illustration 7-2 (page 318) summarizes the classification of cash-related items.

---

[5]Bank overdrafts usually occur because of a simple oversight by the company writing the check. Banks often expect companies to have overdrafts from time to time and therefore negotiate a fee as payment for this possible occurrence. However, at one time, **E. F. Hutton** (a large brokerage firm) began intentionally overdrawing its accounts by astronomical amounts—on some days exceeding $1 billion—thus obtaining interest-free loans that it could invest. Because the amounts were so large and fees were not negotiated in advance, E. F. Hutton came under criminal investigation for its actions.

[6]*Accounting Trends and Techniques—2004*, indicates that approximately 6 percent of the companies surveyed use the caption "Cash," 83 percent use "Cash and cash equivalents," and 4 percent use a caption such as "Cash and marketable securities" or similar terminology.

ILLUSTRATION 7-2
Classification of Cash-
Related Items

Classification of Cash, Cash Equivalents, and Noncash Items		
Item	Classification	Comment
Cash	Cash	If unrestricted, report as cash. If restricted, identify and classify as current and noncurrent assets.
Petty cash and change funds	Cash	Report as cash.
Short-term paper	Cash equivalents	Investments with maturity of less than 3 months, often combined with cash.
Short-term paper	Temporary investments	Investments with maturity of 3 to 12 months.
Postdated checks and IOU's	Receivables	Assumed to be collectible.
Travel advances	Receivables	Assumed to be collected from employees or deducted from their salaries.
Postage on hand (as stamps or in postage meters)	Prepaid expenses	May also be classified as office supplies inventory.
Bank overdrafts	Current liability	If right of offset exists, reduce cash.
Compensating balances	Cash separately classified as a deposit maintained as compensating balance	Classify as current or noncurrent in the balance sheet. Disclose separately in notes details of the arrangement.

WHAT DO THE
NUMBERS MEAN?

TOO MUCH OF A GOOD THING?

Can it ever be a bad thing to have too much cash on hand? Maybe so. As the data in the following table indicate, **General Motors** and some other major companies have been stockpiling cash at levels not recently seen.

Company	Total Cash (in billions)
General Motors	$54.8
Berkshire Hathaway	$36.0
Ford Motor Company	$33.6
Hewlett-Packard	$13.9
Intel	$13.5

Given the low returns on cash, investors may ask why companies maintain such large cash balances. Some companies with good growth prospects plan to use these resources to fuel growth. They intend to step up spending on property, plant, and equipment or on research and development. Or they may hold cash in order to acquire other companies that have growth prospects. However, without good use for stockpiled cash, stockholders would be better served by a payout in the form of a cash dividend.

SECTION 2	*RECEIVABLES*

Receivables are claims held against customers and others for money, goods, or services. For financial statement purposes, companies classify receivables as either **current** (short-term) or **noncurrent** (long-term). Companies expect to collect **current receivables** within a year or during the current operating cycle, whichever is longer. They classify all other receivables as **noncurrent**. Receivables are further classified in the balance sheet as either trade or nontrade receivables.

Customers often owe a company amounts for goods bought or services rendered. A company may subclassify these **trade receivables**, usually the most significant item it possesses, into accounts receivable and notes receivable. **Accounts receivable** are oral promises of the purchaser to pay for goods and services sold. They represent "open accounts" resulting from short-term extensions of credit. A company normally collects them within 30 to 60 days. **Notes receivable** are written promises to pay a certain sum of money on a specified future date. They may arise from sales, financing, or other transactions. Notes may be short-term or long-term.

Nontrade receivables arise from a variety of transactions. Some examples of nontrade receivables are:

1 Advances to officers and employees.
2 Advances to subsidiaries.
3 Deposits paid to cover potential damages or losses.
4 Deposits paid as a guarantee of performance or payment.
5 Dividends and interest receivable.
6 Claims against:
   (a) Insurance companies for casualties sustained.
   (b) Defendants under suit.
   (c) Governmental bodies for tax refunds.
   (d) Common carriers for damaged or lost goods.
   (e) Creditors for returned, damaged, or lost goods.
   (f) Customers for returnable items (crates, containers, etc.).

Because of the peculiar nature of nontrade receivables, companies generally report them as separate items in the balance sheet. Illustration 7-3 shows the reporting of trade and non-trade receivables in the balance sheets of **Adolph Coors Company** and **Seaboard Corporation**.

OBJECTIVE 3
Define receivables and identify the different types of receivables.

ILLUSTRATION 7-3
Receivables Balance Sheet Presentations

Adolph Coors Company
(in thousands)

Current assets	
Cash and cash equivalents	$160,038
Short-term investments	96,190
Accounts and notes receivable	
Trade, less allowance for doubtful accounts of $299	106,962
Subsidiaries	11,896
Other, less allowance for certain claims of $584	7,751
Inventories	102,660
Other supplies, less allowance for obsolete supplies of $3,968	27,729
Prepaid expenses and other assets	12,848
Deferred tax asset	22,917
Total current assets	$548,991

Seaboard Corporation
(in thousands)

Current assets		
Cash and cash equivalents		$ 19,760
Short-term investments		91,375
Receivables		
Trade	$194,966	
Due from foreign affiliates	36,662	
Other	41,816	
		273,444
Allowance for doubtful receivables		(29,801)
Net receivables		243,643
Inventories		218,030
Deferred income taxes		14,132
Prepaid expenses and deposits		23,760
Total current assets		$610,700

The basic issues in accounting for accounts and notes receivable are the same: **recognition**, **valuation**, and **disposition**. We discuss these basic issues for accounts and notes receivable next.

RECOGNITION OF ACCOUNTS RECEIVABLE

OBJECTIVE 4
Explain accounting issues related to recognition of accounts receivable.

In most receivables transactions, the amount to be recognized is the exchange price between the two parties. **The exchange price is the amount due from the debtor** (a customer or a borrower). Some type of business document, often an invoice, serves as evidence of the exchange price. Two factors may complicate the measurement of the exchange price: (1) the availability of discounts (trade and cash discounts), and (2) the length of time between the sale and the due date of payments (the interest element).

Trade Discounts

Prices may be subject to a trade or quantity discount. Companies use such **trade discounts** to avoid frequent changes in catalogs, to alter prices for different quantities purchased, or to hide the true invoice price from competitors.

Trade discounts are commonly quoted in percentages. For example, say your textbook has a list price of $90, and the publisher sells it to college bookstores for list less a 30 percent trade discount. The publisher then records the receivable at $63 per textbook. The publisher, per normal practice, simply deducts the trade discount from the list price and bills the customer net.

As another example, **Maxwell House** at one time sold a 10-ounce jar of its instant coffee listing at $5.85 to supermarkets for $5.05, a trade discount of approximately 14 percent. The supermarkets in turn sold the instant coffee for $5.20 per jar. Maxwell House records the receivable and related sales revenue at $5.05 per jar, not $5.85.

Cash Discounts (Sales Discounts)

Companies offer **cash discounts** (**sales discounts**) to induce prompt payment. Cash discounts generally read in terms such as 2/10, n/30 (2 percent if paid within 10 days, gross amount due in 30 days), or 2/10, E.O.M., net 30, E.O.M. (2 percent if paid any time before the tenth day of the following month, with full payment received by the thirtieth of the following month).

Companies usually take sales discounts unless their cash is severely limited. Why? A company that receives a 1 percent reduction in the sales price for payment within 10 days, total payment due within 30 days, effectively earns 18.25 percent (.01 ÷ [20/365]), or at least avoids that rate of interest cost.

Companies usually record sales and related sales discount transactions by entering the receivable and sale at the gross amount. Under this method, companies recognize sales discounts only when they receive payment within the discount period. The income statement shows sales discounts as a deduction from sales to arrive at net sales.

Some contend that sales discounts not taken reflect penalties added to an established price to encourage prompt payment. That is, the seller offers sales on account at a slightly higher price than if selling for cash. The cash discount offered offsets the increase. Thus, customers who pay within the discount period actually purchase at the cash price. Those who pay after expiration of the discount period pay a penalty for the delay—an amount in excess of the cash price. Per this reasoning, companies record sales and receivables net. They subsequently debit any discounts not taken to Accounts Receivable and credit to Sales Discounts Forfeited. The entries in Illustration 7-4 show the difference between the gross and net methods.

Gross Method			Net Method		
Sales of $10,000, terms 2/10, n/30					
Accounts Receivable	10,000		Accounts Receivable	9,800	
Sales		10,000	Sales		9,800
Payment of $4,000 received within discount period					
Cash	3,920		Cash	3,920	
Sales Discounts	80		Accounts Receivable		3,920
Accounts Receivable		4,000			
Payment of $6,000 received after discount period					
Cash	6,000		Accounts Receivable	120	
Accounts Receivable		6,000	Sales Discounts		
			Forfeited		120
			Cash	6,000	
			Accounts Receivable		6,000

If using the gross method, a company reports sales discounts as a deduction from sales in the income statement. Proper matching dictates that the company also reasonably estimates the expected discounts to be taken and charge that amount against sales. If using the net method, a company considers Sales Discounts Forfeited as an "Other revenue" item.[7]

Theoretically, the recognition of Sales Discounts Forfeited is correct. The receivable is stated closer to its realizable value, and the net sales figure measures the revenue earned from the sale. As a practical matter, however, companies seldom use the net method because it requires additional analysis and bookkeeping. For example, the net method requires adjusting entries to record sales discounts forfeited on accounts receivable that have passed the discount period.

Nonrecognition of Interest Element

Ideally, a company should measure receivables in terms of their present value, that is, the discounted value of the cash to be received in the future. When expected cash receipts require a waiting period, the receivable face amount is not worth the amount that the company ultimately receives.

To illustrate, assume that **Best Buy** makes a sale on account for $1,000 with payment due in four months. The applicable annual rate of interest is 12 percent, and payment is made at the end of four months. The present value of that receivable is not $1,000 but $961.54 ($1,000 × .96154). In other words, the $1,000 Best Buy receives four months from now is not the same as the $1,000 received today.

Theoretically, any revenue after the period of sale is interest revenue. In practice, companies ignore interest revenue related to accounts receivable because the amount of the discount is not usually material in relation to the net income for the period. The profession specifically excludes from present value considerations "receivables arising from transactions with customers in the normal course of business which are due in customary trade terms not exceeding approximately one year."[8]

UNDERLYING CONCEPTS

Materiality means it must make a difference to a decision maker. The FASB believes that present value concepts can be ignored for short-term receivables.

VALUATION OF ACCOUNTS RECEIVABLE

Reporting of receivables involves (1) classification and (2) valuation on the balance sheet. Classification involves determining the length of time each receivable will be outstanding. Companies classify receivables intended to be collected within a year or the operating cycle, whichever is longer, as current. All other receivables are classified as long-term.

---

[7]To the extent that discounts not taken reflect a short-term financing, some argue that companies could use an interest revenue account to record these amounts.

[8]"Interest on Receivables and Payables," *Opinions of the Accounting Principles Board No. 21* (New York: AICPA, 1971), par. 3(a).

OBJECTIVE 5
Explain accounting
issues related to
valuation of accounts
receivable.

Companies value and report short-term receivables at net realizable value—the net amount they expect to receive in cash. Determining net realizable value requires estimating both uncollectible receivables and any returns or allowances to be granted.

Uncollectible Accounts Receivable

As one revered accountant aptly noted, the credit manager's idea of heaven probably would be a place where everyone (eventually) paid his or her debts.[9] The recent experiences of **Circuit City, Sears** (now **Sears Holdings**), **Target**, and **Kohls**, as shown in Illustration 7-5, indicate the importance of credit sales for many companies. Note that for Sears, increased bad debt expense led to a lower stock price, which prompted Sears to sell its credit card portfolio to **Citigroup** in 2003.

ILLUSTRATION 7-5
Credit and Its Costs

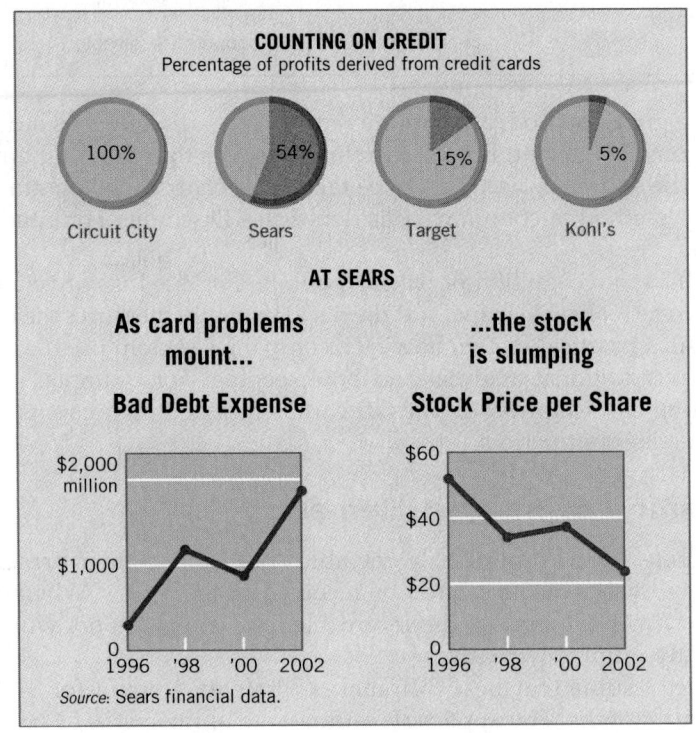

Sales on any basis other than cash make uncertain the possibility of collecting the account. An uncollectible account receivable is a loss of revenue that requires, through proper entry in the accounts, a decrease in the asset accounts receivable and a related decrease in income and stockholders' equity. Companies recognize the loss in revenue and the decrease in income by recording bad debt expense.

Companies use two procedures to record uncollectible accounts:

METHODS FOR RECORDING UNCOLLECTIBLES

1 *DIRECT WRITE-OFF METHOD.* No entry is made until a specific account has definitely been established as uncollectible. Then the loss is recorded by crediting Accounts Receivable and debiting Bad Debt Expense.

2 *ALLOWANCE METHOD.* An estimate is made of the expected uncollectible accounts from all sales made on account or from the total of outstanding receivables. This estimate is entered as an expense and an indirect reduction in accounts receivable (via an increase in the allowance account) in the period in which the sale is recorded.

---

[9]William J. Vatter, *Managerial Accounting* (Englewood Cliffs, N.J.: Prentice-Hall, 1950), p. 60.

The **direct write-off method** records the bad debt in the period in which a company determines that it cannot collect a specific receivable. In contrast, the **allowance method** enters the expense on an estimated basis in the accounting period in which the sales on account occur.

Supporters of the **direct write-off method** (which is used for tax purposes) contend that it records facts, not estimates. It assumes that a good account receivable resulted from each sale, and that later events revealed certain accounts to be uncollectible and worthless. From a practical standpoint this method is simple and convenient to apply. But the direct write-off method is theoretically deficient: It usually fails to match costs with revenues of the period. Nor does it result in receivables being stated at estimated realizable value on the balance sheet. **As a result, using the direct write-off method is not considered appropriate, except when the amount uncollectible is immaterial.**

Advocates of the **allowance method** believe that companies should record bad debt expense in the same period as the sale, to properly match expenses and revenues and to achieve a proper carrying value for accounts receivable. They contend that although estimates are involved, companies can predict the percentage of uncollectible receivables from past experiences, present market conditions, and an analysis of the outstanding balances. Many companies set their credit policies to provide for a certain percentage of uncollectible accounts. (In fact, many feel that failure to reach that percentage means that they are losing sales due to overly restrictive credit policies.)

The FASB considers the collectibility of receivables a loss contingency. Thus, the allowance method is appropriate in situations where it is probable that an asset has been impaired and that the amount of the loss can be reasonably estimated.[10]

A receivable is a prospective cash inflow. The probability of its collection must be considered in valuing cash flows. These estimates normally are based either on (1) percentage of sales or (2) outstanding receivables.

Percentage-of-Sales (Income Statement) Approach

If there is a fairly stable relationship between previous years' credit sales and bad debts, then a company can convert that relationship into a percentage and use it to determine this year's bad debt expense.

The **percentage-of-sales approach** matches costs with revenues because it relates the charge to the period in which a company records the sale. To illustrate, assume that Chad Shumway Corp. estimates from past experience that about 2 percent of credit sales become uncollectible. If Chad Shumway has credit sales of $400,000 in 2007, it records bad debt expense using the percentage-of-sales method as follows.

Bad Debt Expense	8,000	
Allowance for Doubtful Accounts		8,000

The Allowance for Doubtful Accounts is a valuation account (i.e., a contra asset), subtracted from trade receivables on the balance sheet.[11] The amount of bad debt expense and the related credit to the allowance account are unaffected by any balance currently existing in the allowance account. Because the bad debt expense estimate is related to a nominal account (Sales), any balance in the allowance is ignored. Therefore, the percentage of sales method achieves a proper matching of cost and revenues. This method is frequently referred to as the **income statement approach**.

Percentage-of-Receivables (Balance Sheet) Approach

Using past experience, a company can estimate the percentage of its outstanding receivables that will become uncollectible, without identifying specific accounts. This procedure provides a reasonably accurate estimate of the receivables' realizable value. But,

UNDERLYING CONCEPTS

The percentage-of-sales method illustrates the matching principle, which relates expenses to revenues earned.

---

[10]"Accounting for Contingencies," *Statement of Financial Accounting Standards No. 5* (Stamford, Conn.: FASB, 1975), par. 8.

[11]The account description employed for the allowance account is usually Allowance for Doubtful Accounts or simply Allowance. *Accounting Trends and Techniques—2004*, for example, indicates that approximately 86 percent of the companies surveyed used "allowance" in their description.

it does not fit the concept of matching cost and revenues. Rather, it simply reports receivables in the balance sheet at net realizable value. Hence it is referred to as the **percentage-of-receivables** (or **balance sheet**) **approach.**

Companies may apply this method using one **composite rate** that reflects an estimate of the uncollectible receivables. Or, companies may set up an **aging schedule** of accounts receivable, which applies a different percentage based on past experience to the various age categories. An aging schedule also identifies which accounts require special attention by indicating the extent to which certain accounts are past due. The following schedule of Wilson & Co. is an example.

ILLUSTRATION 7-6
Accounts Receivable
Aging Schedule

WILSON & CO.
AGING SCHEDULE

Name of Customer	Balance Dec. 31	Under 60 days	61–90 days	91–120 days	Over 120 days
Western Stainless Steel Corp.	$ 98,000	$ 80,000	$18,000		
Brockway Steel Company	320,000	320,000			
Freeport Sheet & Tube Co.	55,000				$55,000
Allegheny Iron Works	74,000	60,000		$14,000	
	$547,000	$460,000	$18,000	$14,000	$55,000

Summary

Age	Amount	Percentage Estimated to be Uncollectible	Required Balance in Allowance
Under 60 days old	$460,000	4%	$18,400
61–90 days old	18,000	15%	2,700
91–120 days old	14,000	20%	2,800
Over 120 days	55,000	25%	13,750
Year-end balance of allowance for doubtful accounts			$37,650

Wilson reports bad debt expense of $37,650 for this year, assuming that no balance existed in the allowance account.

To change the illustration slightly, **assume that the allowance account had a credit balance of $800 before adjustment.** In this case, Wilson adds $36,850 ($37,650 – $800) to the allowance account, and makes the following entry.

Bad Debt Expense	36,850	
Allowance for Doubtful Accounts		36,850

Wilson therefore states the balance in the Allowance account at $37,650. **If the Allowance balance before adjustment had a debit balance of $200,** then Wilson records bad debt expense of $37,850 ($37,650 desired balance + $200 debit balance). In the percentage-of-receivables method, Wilson **cannot ignore** the balance in the allowance account, because the percentage is related to a real account (Accounts Receivable).

Companies usually do not prepare an aging schedule to determine bad debt expense. Rather, they prepare it as a control device to determine the composition of receivables and to identify delinquent accounts. Companies base the estimated loss percentage developed for each category on previous loss experience and the advice of credit department personnel.

Tutorial on Recording Uncollectible Accounts

Whether using a composite rate or an aging schedule, the primary objective of the percentage of outstanding receivables method for financial statement purposes is to report receivables in the balance sheet at net realizable value. However, it is deficient in that it may not match the bad debt expense to the period in which the sale takes place.

The allowance for doubtful accounts as a percentage of receivables will vary, depending on the industry and the economic climate. Companies such as **Eastman Kodak, General Electric,** and **Monsanto** have recorded allowances ranging from $3 to $6 per

$100 of accounts receivable. Other large companies, such as **CPC International** ($1.48), **Texaco** ($1.23), and **USX Corp.** ($0.78), have had bad debt allowances of less than $1.50 per $100. At the other extreme are hospitals that allow for $15 to $20 per $100 of accounts receivable.[12]

GOING FOR BROKE

The start of the new millennium has been a tough one for companies and their investors, creditors, and employees. **Enron, Kmart,** and **WorldCom** all declared bankruptcy—with WorldCom representing the largest bankruptcy ever. The trend seems to be continuing.

It is not surprising that banks and other creditors are raising their lending standards to guard against future loan defaults. Even so, some question whether creditors have set up reasonable bad debt allowances to ensure that financial performance is reported accurately. Indeed, one recent analysis for hospitals (mentioned in our opening story) indicates that additional bad debt expense needed to properly reflect future write-offs could result in an earnings hit of as much as 18 percent for some hospitals. That will be tough medicine for these companies to swallow.

Source: Adapted from: Julie Creswell, "First Going for Broke," *Fortune* (February 18, 2002), pp. 24–25; Bethany McLean, "Reality Check-up," *Fortune* (January 12, 2004), pp. 140.

WHAT DO THE NUMBERS MEAN?

In summary, the percentage-of-receivables method results in a more accurate valuation of receivables on the balance sheet. From a matching viewpoint, the percentage-of-sales approach provides the better results. Illustration 7-7 relates these methods to the basic theory.

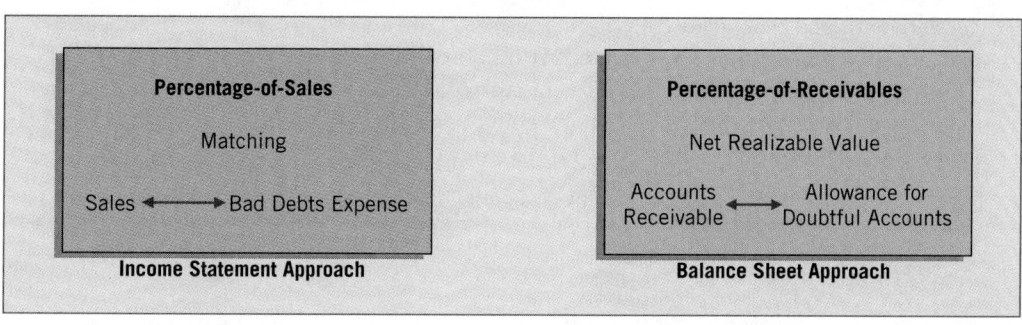

ILLUSTRATION 7-7
Comparison of Methods for Estimating Uncollectibles

The account title employed for the allowance account is usually Allowance for Doubtful Accounts or simply Allowance.

---

[12]A U.S. Department of Commerce study indicated, as a general rule, the following relationships between the age of accounts receivable and their uncollectibility.

30 days or less	4% uncollectible
31–60 days	10% uncollectible
61–90 days	17% uncollectible
91–120 days	26% uncollectible

After 120 days, an approximate 3–4 percent increase in uncollectibles for every 30 days outstanding occurs for the remainder of the first year.

INTERNATIONAL INSIGHT

The U.S. has criticized some countries' use of excess reserves to manage income. These same countries would argue that **Suntrust Banks'** accounting for loan losses is a similar practice.

Regardless of the method chosen, determining the expense associated with uncollectible accounts requires a large degree of judgment. Recent concern exists that, similar to **Nortel** in our opening story, some banks use this judgment to manage earnings. By overestimating the amounts of uncollectible loans in a good earnings year, the bank can "save for a rainy day" in a future period. In future (less-profitable) periods, banks can reduce the overly conservative allowance for loan loss account to increase earnings. In this regard, the SEC brought action against **Suntrust Banks**, requiring a reversal of $100 million of bad debt expense. This reversal increased aftertax profit by $61 million.[13]

Collection of Accounts Receivable Written Off

When a company determines a particular account receivable to be uncollectible, it removes the balance from the books by debiting Allowance for Doubtful Accounts and crediting Accounts Receivable. If it eventually collects on a receivable that it previously wrote off, it first reestablishes the receivable by debiting Accounts Receivable and crediting Allowance for Doubtful Accounts. The company then debits Cash and credits the customer's account for the amount received.

If using the direct write-off approach, the company debits the amount collected to Cash and credits a revenue account entitled Uncollectible Amounts Recovered, with proper notation in the customer's account.

WHAT DO THE NUMBERS MEAN?

> ### COLLECTION IS A CLICK AWAY
>
> What do lenders do with uncollectible receivables? After they record bad debts on their books, they next to try to collect what they can from the deadbeat customers. Some lenders auction their bad loans in the market for distressed debt, usually paying a fee of 5–15 percent to a distressed debt broker, who arranges the sale.
>
> Recently, several Web sites have sprung up to provide a meeting place between lenders with bad loans and collectors. These sites are sort of an "eBay of deadbeats." For example, **Bank One Corp.** listed $211 million of unpaid credit card receivables on **DebtforSale.com**. While the lendors generally recover less than 10 percent of the face value of the receivables in an auction, by going online they can reduce the costs of their bad debts. Online services charge just 0.5–1 percent for their auction services.
>
> *Source:* Adapted from P. Gogoi, "An eBay of Deadbeats," *Business Week* (September 18, 2000), p. 124.

RECOGNITION OF NOTES RECEIVABLE

A note receivable is supported by a formal **promissory note**, a written promise to pay a certain sum of money at a specific future date. Such a note is a negotiable instrument that a **maker** signs in favor of a designated **payee** who may legally and readily sell or otherwise transfer the note to others. Although notes contain an interest element because of the time value of money, companies classify them as interest-bearing or noninterest-bearing. **Interest-bearing notes** have a stated rate of interest. **Zero-interest-bearing notes** (noninterest-bearing) include interest as part of their face amount. Notes receivable are considered fairly liquid, even if long-term, because companies may easily convert them to cash (although they might pay a fee to do so).

---

[13]Recall from our earnings management discussion in Chapter 4 that increasing or decreasing income through management manipulation can reduce the quality of financial reports.

Companies frequently accept notes receivable from customers who need to extend the payment period of an outstanding receivable. Or they require notes from high-risk or new customers. In addition, companies often use notes in loans to employees and subsidiaries, and in the sales of property, plant, and equipment. In some industries (e.g., the pleasure and sport boat industry) notes support all credit sales. The majority of notes, however, originate from lending transactions. The basic issues in accounting for notes receivable are the same as those for accounts receivable: **recognition, valuation, and disposition**.

Companies generally record short-term notes at face value (less allowances) because the interest implicit in the maturity value is immaterial. A general rule is that notes treated as cash equivalents (maturities of three months or less and easily converted to cash) are not subject to premium or discount amortization.

However, companies should record and report long-term notes receivable at the **present value of the cash they expect to collect**. When the interest stated on an interest-bearing note equals the effective (market) rate of interest, the note sells at face value.[14] When the stated rate differs from the market rate, the cash exchanged (present value) differs from the face value of the note. Companies then record this difference, either a discount or a premium, and amortize it over the life of a note to approximate the effective (market) interest rate. This illustrates one of the many situations in which time value of money concepts are applied to accounting measurement.

> **OBJECTIVE 6**
> Explain accounting issues related to recognition of notes receivable.

Note Issued at Face Value

To illustrate the discounting of a note issued at face value, assume that Bigelow Corp. lends Scandinavian Imports $10,000 in exchange for a $10,000, three-year note bearing interest at 10 percent annually. The market rate of interest for a note of similar risk is also 10 percent. We show the time diagram depicting both cash flows in Illustration 7-8.

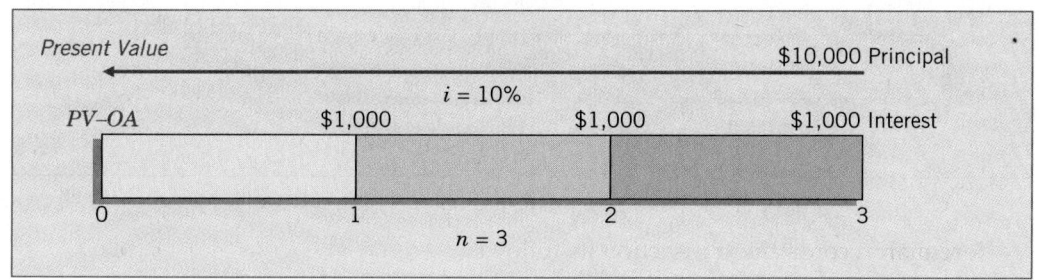

ILLUSTRATION 7-8
Time Diagram for Note Issued at Face Value

Bigelow computes the present value or exchange price of the note as follows.

Face value of the note		$10,000
Present value of the principal:		
$10,000 ($PVF_{3,10\%}$) = $10,000 × .75132	$7,513	
Present value of the interest:		
$1,000 ($PVF\text{-}OA_{3,10\%}$) = $1,000 × 2.48685	2,487	
Present value of the note		10,000
Difference		$ –0–

ILLUSTRATION 7-9
Present Value of Note—Stated and Market Rates the Same

---

[14]The **stated interest rate**, also referred to as the face rate or the coupon rate, is the rate contracted as part of the note. The **effective-interest rate**, also referred to as the *market rate* or the *effective yield*, is the rate used in the market to determine the value of the note —that is, the discount rate used to determine present value.

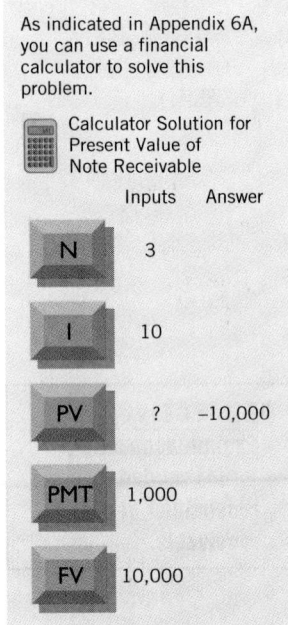

As indicated in Appendix 6A, you can use a financial calculator to solve this problem.

Calculator Solution for Present Value of Note Receivable

Inputs	Answer
N	3
I	10
PV	? −10,000
PMT	1,000
FV	10,000

In this case, the present value of the note equals its face value, because the effective and stated rates of interest are also the same. Bigelow records the receipt of the note as follows.

Notes Receivable	10,000	
Cash		10,000

Bigelow recognizes the interest earned each year as follows.

Cash	1,000	
Interest Revenue		1,000

Note Not Issued at Face Value

Zero-Interest-Bearing Notes

If a company receives a zero-interest-bearing note, its present value is the cash paid to the issuer. Because the company knows both the future amount and the present value of the note, it can compute the interest rate. This rate is often referred to as the **implicit interest rate**. Companies record the difference between the future (face) amount and the present value (cash paid) as a discount and amortize it to interest revenue over the life of the note.

To illustrate, Jeremiah Company receives a three-year, $10,000 zero-interest-bearing note, the present value of which is $7,721.80. The implicit rate that equates the total cash to be received ($10,000 at maturity) to the present value of the future cash flows ($7,721.80) is 9 percent (the present value of 1 for three periods at 9 percent is .77218). We show the time diagram depicting the one cash flow in Illustration 7-10.

ILLUSTRATION 7-10
Time Diagram for Zero-Interest-Bearing Note

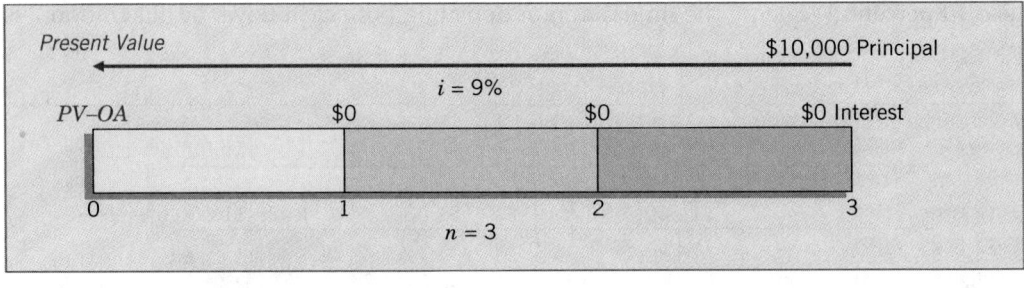

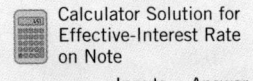

Calculator Solution for Effective-Interest Rate on Note

Inputs	Answer
N	3
I	? 9
PV	−7,721.80
PMT	0
FV	10,000

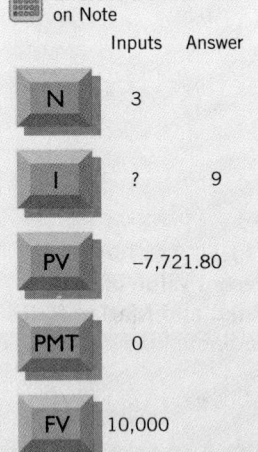

Jeremiah records the transaction as follows:

Notes Receivable	10,000.00	
Discount on Notes Receivable ($10,000 − $7,721.80)		2,278.20
Cash		7,721.80

The Discount on Notes Receivable is a valuation account. Companies report it on the balance sheet as a contra-asset account to notes receivable. They then amortize the discount, and recognize interest revenue annually using the **effective-interest method**. Illustration 7-11 (page 329) shows the three-year discount amortization and interest revenue schedule.

Jeremiah records interest revenue at the end of the first year using the effective-interest method as follows.

Discount on Notes Receivable	694.96	
Interest Revenue ($7,721.80 × 9%)		694.96

The amount of the discount, $2,278.20 in this case, represents the interest revenue Jeremiah will receive from the note over the three years.

Interest-Bearing Notes

Often the stated rate and the effective rate differ. The zero-interest-bearing note is one example.

SCHEDULE OF NOTE DISCOUNT AMORTIZATION EFFECTIVE-INTEREST METHOD 0% NOTE DISCOUNTED AT 9%			
	Cash Received	Interest Revenue	Discount Amortized	Carrying Amount of Note
Date of issue				$7,721.80
End of year 1	$ –0–	$ 694.96[a]	$ 694.96[b]	8,416.76[c]
End of year 2	–0–	757.51	757.51	9,174.27
End of year 3	–0–	825.73[d]	825.73	10,000.00
	$ –0–	$2,278.20	$2,278.20	

[a]$7,721.80 × .09 = $694.96 [c]$7,721.80 + $694.96 = $8,416.76
[b]$694.96 – 0 = $694.96 [d]5¢ adjustment to compensate for rounding

ILLUSTRATION 7-11
Discount Amortization
Schedule—Effective-
Interest Method

To illustrate a more common situation, assume that Morgan Corp. makes a loan to Marie Co. and receives in exchange a three-year, $10,000 note bearing interest at 10 percent annually. The market rate of interest for a note of similar risk is 12 percent. We show the time diagram depicting both cash flows in Illustration 7-12.

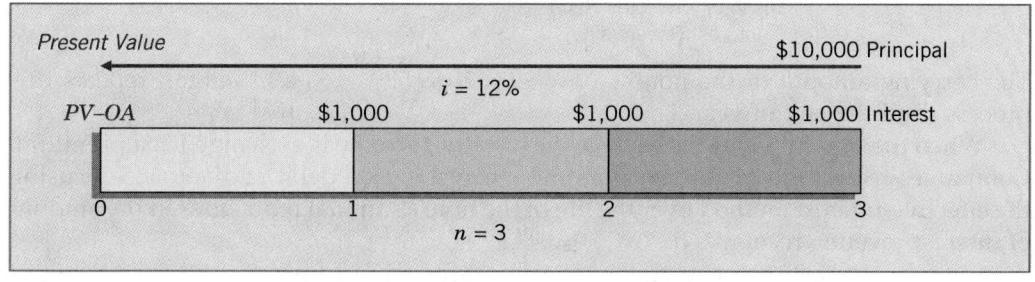

ILLUSTRATION 7-12
Time Diagram for
Interest-Bearing Note

Morgan computes the present value of the two cash flows as follows.

Face value of the note		$10,000
Present value of the principal:		
$10,000 ($PVF_{3,12\%}$) = $10,000 × .71178	$7,118	
Present value of the interest:		
$1,000 ($PVF\text{-}OA_{3,12\%}$) = $1,000 × 2.40183	2,402	
Present value of the note		9,520
Difference (Discount)		$ 480

ILLUSTRATION 7-13
Computation of Present
Value—Effective Rate
Different from Stated
Rate

In this case, because the effective rate of interest (12 percent) exceeds the stated rate (10 percent), the present value of the note is less than the face value. That is, Morgan exchanged the note at a **discount**. Morgan records the receipt of the note at a discount as follows.

Notes Receivable	10,000	
Discount on Notes Receivable		480
Cash		9,520

Morgan then amortizes the discount and recognizes interest revenue annually using the **effective-interest method**. Illustration 7-14 (page 330) shows the three-year discount amortization and interest revenue schedule.

ILLUSTRATION 7-14
Discount Amortization
Schedule—Effective-
Interest Method

	Cash Received	Interest Revenue	Discount Amortized	Carrying Amount of Note
SCHEDULE OF NOTE DISCOUNT AMORTIZATION				
EFFECTIVE-INTEREST METHOD				
10% NOTE DISCOUNTED AT 12%				
Date of issue				$ 9,520
End of year 1	$1,000[a]	$1,142[b]	$142[c]	9,662[d]
End of year 2	1,000	1,159	159	9,821
End of year 3	1,000	1,179	179	10,000
	$3,000	$3,480	$480	

[a]$10,000 × 10% = $1,000   [c]$1,142 − $1,000 = $142
[b]$9,520 × 12% = $1,142   [d]$9,520 + $142 = $9,662

On the date of issue, the note has a present value of $9,520. Its unamortized discount—additional interest revenue spread over the three-year life of the note—is $480.

At the end of year 1, Morgan receives $1,000 in cash. But its interest revenue is $1,142 ($9,520 × 12%). The difference between $1,000 and $1,142 is the amortized discount, $142. Morgan records receipt of the annual interest and amortization of the discount for the first year as follows (amounts per amortization schedule).

Cash	1,000	
Discount on Notes Receivable	142	
Interest Revenue		1,142

The carrying amount of the note is now $9,662 ($9,520 + $142). Morgan repeats this process until the end of year 3.

When the present value exceeds the face value, the note is exchanged at a premium. Companies record the premium on a note receivable as a debit and amortize it using the effective-interest method over the life of the note as annual reductions in the amount of interest revenue recognized.

Notes Received for Property, Goods, or Services

When a **note is received in exchange for property, goods, or services** in a bargained transaction entered into at arm's length, the stated interest rate is presumed to be fair unless:

1 No interest rate is stated, or

2 The stated interest rate is unreasonable, or

3 The face amount of the note is materially different from the current cash sales price for the same or similar items or from the current market value of the debt instrument.[15]

In these circumstances, the company measures the present value of the note by the fair value of the property, goods, or services or by an amount that reasonably approximates the market value of the note.

To illustrate, Oasis Development Co. sold a corner lot to Rusty Pelican as a restaurant site. Oasis accepted in exchange a five-year note having a maturity value of $35,247 and no stated interest rate. The land originally cost Oasis $14,000. At the date of sale the land had a fair market value of $20,000. Given the criterion above, Oasis uses the fair market value of the land, $20,000, as the present value of the note. Oasis therefore records the sale as:

Notes Receivable	35,247	
Discount on Notes Receivable ($35,247 − $20,000)		15,247
Land		14,000
Gain on Sale of Land ($20,000 − $14,000)		6,000

Calculator Solution for Effective-Interest Rate on Note

	Inputs	Answer
N	5	
I	?	12
PV	−20,000	
PMT	0	
FV	35,247	

---

[15]"Interest on Receivables and Payables," *Opinions of the Accounting Principles Board No. 21* (New York: AICPA, 1971), par. 12.

Oasis amortizes the discount to interest revenue over the five-year life of the note using the effective-interest method.

Choice of Interest Rate

In note transactions, other factors involved in the exchange, such as the fair market value of the property, goods, or services, determine the effective or real interest rate. But, if a company cannot determine that fair value, and if the note has no ready market, determining the present value of the note is more difficult. To estimate the present value of a note under such circumstances, the company must approximate an applicable interest rate that may differ from the stated interest rate. This process of interest-rate approximation is called **imputation**. The resulting interest rate is called an **imputed interest rate**.

The prevailing rates for similar instruments, from issuers with similar credit ratings, affect the choice of a rate. Restrictive covenants, collateral, payment schedule, and the existing prime interest rate also impact the choice. A company determines the imputed interest rate when it receives the note. It ignores any subsequent changes in prevailing interest rates.

VALUATION OF NOTES RECEIVABLE

Like accounts receivable, companies record and report short-term notes receivable at their net realizable value—that is, at their face amount less all necessary allowances. The primary notes receivable allowance account is Allowance for Doubtful Accounts. The computations and estimations involved in valuing short-term notes receivable and in recording bad debt expense and the related allowance **exactly parallel that for trade accounts receivable**. Companies estimate the amount of uncollectibles by using either a percentage of sales revenue or an analysis of the receivables.

OBJECTIVE 7
Explain accounting issues related to valuation of notes receivable.

Long-term notes receivable, however, pose additional estimation problems. For evidence, we need only look at the problems that financial institutions, most notably money-center banks, have had in collecting receivables from energy loans, real estate loans, and loans to less-developed countries.[16]

A company considers a note receivable **impaired** when collecting all amounts due (both principal and interest) will likely not occur. We discuss impairments, as well as restructurings, of receivables and debts in detail in Appendix 14A.

PUTTING THE SQUEEZE ON

When the economy slows, lenders such as **J.P. Morgan** and **First Chicago** get stingier in granting new loans or renewing loans to existing customers. This tightening of loans is referred to as a "credit squeeze."

However, it is sometimes difficult for banks to cut back on lending when the economy goes from good times to bad. When times are good and banks are competing for lending business, lenders often grant business customers "lines of credit" as a sweetener to close a loan. In contrast to a term loan that is supported by a note, a line of credit allows borrowing on a day-to-day basis.

When times turn bad, the bank can cut back on loans via notes receivable, but it still must honor the lines of credit, even to weak customers. For example, **Xerox Inc.** got a $7 billion line of credit before it hit the skids. Although denied by the traditional loan markets, Xerox has been able to draw on its line of credit to make ends meet. Thus, what seemed like of good competitive tool in good times has put the squeeze on *lenders* when times have turned bad.

Source: Adapted from H. Timmons and D. Sparks, "Feeling a Credit Squeeze," *Business Week* (December 4, 2000), pp. 148–149.

WHAT DO THE NUMBERS MEAN?

---

[16]A wise person once said that a bank lending money to a Third World country is like lending money to one's children: You should never expect to get the interest, let alone the principal.

DISPOSITION OF ACCOUNTS AND NOTES RECEIVABLE

OBJECTIVE 8
Explain accounting
issues related to
disposition of accounts
and notes receivable.

In the normal course of events, companies collect accounts and notes receivable when due and then remove them from the books. However, the growing size and significance of credit sales and receivables has led to changes in this "normal course of events." **In order to accelerate the receipt of cash from receivables, the owner may transfer accounts or notes receivables to another company for cash.**

There are various reasons for this early transfer. First, for competitive reasons, providing sales financing for customers is virtually mandatory in many industries. In the sale of durable goods, such as automobiles, trucks, industrial and farm equipment, computers, and appliances, most sales are on an installment contract basis. Many major companies in these industries have created wholly-owned subsidiaries specializing in receivables financing. For example, **General Motors Corp.** has **General Motors Acceptance Corp. (GMAC)**, and **John Deere** has **John Deere Credit**.

Second, the **holder** may sell receivables because money is tight and access to normal credit is unavailable or too expensive. Also, a firm may sell its receivables, instead of borrowing, to avoid violating existing lending agreements.

Finally, billing and collection of receivables are often time-consuming and costly. Credit card companies such as **MasterCard, VISA, American Express, Diners Club, Discover**, and others take over the collection process and provide merchants with immediate cash.

Conversely, some **purchasers** of receivables buy them to obtain the legal protection of ownership rights afforded a purchaser of assets versus the lesser rights afforded a secured creditor. In addition, banks and other lending institutions may need to purchase receivables because of legal lending limits. That is, they cannot make any additional loans but they can buy receivables and charge a fee for this service.

The transfer of receivables to a third party for cash happens in one of two ways:

1 Secured borrowing.
2 Sales of receivables.

Secured Borrowing

A company often uses receivables as collateral in a borrowing transaction. In fact, a creditor often requires that the debtor designate (assign) or pledge[17] receivables as security for the loan. If the loan is not paid when due, the creditor can convert the collateral to cash —that is, to collect the receivables.

To illustrate, on March 1, 2007, Howat Mills, Inc. provides (assigns) $700,000 of its accounts receivable to Citizens Bank as collateral for a $500,000 note. Howat Mills continues to collect the accounts receivable; the account debtors are not notified of the arrangement. Citizens Bank assesses a finance charge of 1 percent of the accounts receivable and interest on the note of 12 percent. Howat Mills makes monthly payments to the bank for all cash it collects on the receivables. Illustration 7-15 (page 333) shows the entries for the secured borrowing for Howatt Mills and Citizens Bank.

In addition to recording the collection of receivables, Howat Mills must recognize all discounts, returns and allowances, and bad debts. Each month Howat Mills uses the proceeds from the collection of the accounts receivable to retire the note obligation. In addition, it pays interest on the note.[18]

---

[17]If a company transfers the receivables for custodial purposes, the custodial arrangement is often referred to as a **pledge**.

[18]What happens if Citizens Bank collected the transferred accounts receivable rather than Howat Mills? Citizens Bank would simply remit the cash proceeds to Howat Mills, and Howat Mills would make the same entries shown in Illustration 7-15. As a result, Howat Mills reports these "collaterized" receivables as an asset on the balance sheet.

Howat Mills, Inc.			Citizens Bank		
Transfer of accounts receivable and issuance of note on March 1, 2007					
Cash	493,000		Notes Receivable	500,000	
Finance Charge	7,000*		Finance Revenue		7,000*
Notes Payable		500,000	Cash		493,000
*(1% × $700,000)					
Collection in March of $440,000 of accounts less cash discounts of $6,000 plus receipt of $14,000 sales returns					
Cash	434,000				
Sales Discounts	6,000				
Sales Returns	14,000		(No entry)		
Accounts Receivable		454,000			
($440,000 + $14,000 = $454,000)					
Remitted March collections plus accrued interest to the bank on April 1					
Interest Expense	5,000*		Cash	439,000	
Notes Payable	434,000		Interest Revenue		5,000*
Cash		439,000	Notes Receivable		434,000
*($500,000 × .12 × 1/12)					
Collection in April of the balance of accounts less $2,000 written off as uncollectible					
Cash	244,000				
Allowance for Doubtful Accounts	2,000		(No entry)		
Accounts Receivable		246,000*			
*($700,000 − $454,000)					
Remitted the balance due of $66,000 ($500,000 − $434,000) on the note plus interest on May 1					
Interest Expense	660*		Cash	66,660	
Notes Payable	66,000		Interest Revenue		660*
Cash		66,660	Notes Receivable		66,000
*($66,000 × .12 × 1/12)					

ILLUSTRATION 7-15
Entries for Transfer of Receivables—Secured Borrowing

Sales of Receivables

Sales of receivables have increased substantially in recent years. A common type is a sale to a factor. **Factors** are finance companies or banks that buy receivables from businesses for a fee and then collect the remittances directly from the customers. **Factoring receivables** is traditionally associated with the textile, apparel, footwear, furniture, and home furnishing industries.[19] Illustration 7-16 shows a typical factoring arrangement.

ILLUSTRATION 7-16
Basic Procedures in Factoring

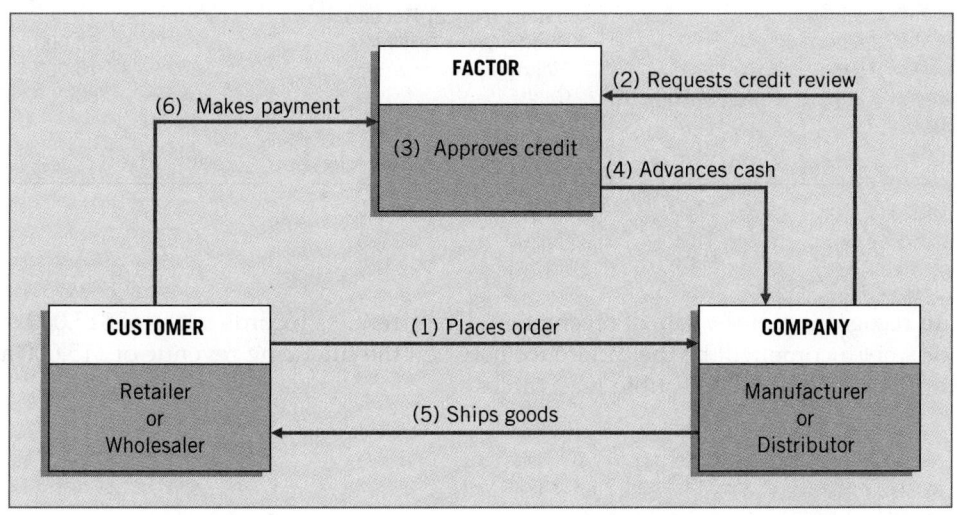

[19]Credit cards like **MasterCard** and **VISA** are a type of factoring arrangement. Typically the purchaser of the receivable charges a ¾–1½ percent commission of the receivables purchased (the commission is 4–5 percent for credit card factoring).

A recent phenomenon in the sale (transfer) of receivables is securitization. **Securitization** takes a pool of assets such as credit card receivables, mortgage receivables, or car loan receivables, and sells shares in these pools of interest and principal payments. This, in effect, creates securities backed by these pools of assets. Virtually every asset with a payment stream and a long-term payment history is a candidate for securitization.

What are the differences between factoring and securitization? Factoring usually involves sale to only one company, fees are high, the quality of the receivables is low, and the seller afterward does not service the receivables. In a securitization, many investors are involved, margins are tight, the receivables are of higher quality, and the seller usually continues to service the receivables.

In either a factoring or a securitization transaction, a company sells receivables on either a **without recourse** or a **with recourse** basis.[20]

Sale without Recourse

When buying receivables **without recourse**, the purchaser assumes the risk of collectibility and absorbs any credit losses. The transfer of accounts receivable in a nonrecourse transaction is an outright sale of the receivables both in form (transfer of title) and substance (transfer of control). In nonrecourse transactions, as in any sale of assets, the seller debits Cash for the proceeds and credits Accounts Receivable for the face value of the receivables. The seller recognizes the difference, reduced by any provision for probable adjustments (discounts, returns, allowances, etc.), as a Loss on the Sale of Receivables. The seller uses a Due from Factor account (reported as a receivable) to account for the proceeds retained by the factor to cover probable sales discounts, sales returns, and sales allowances.

Comprehensive Illustration of Sale Without Recourse

To illustrate, Crest Textiles, Inc. factors $500,000 of accounts receivable with Commercial Factors, Inc., on a **without recourse** basis. Crest Textiles transfers the receivable records to Commercial Factors, which will receive the collections. Commercial Factors assesses a finance charge of 3 percent of the amount of accounts receivable and retains an amount equal to 5 percent of the accounts receivable (for probable adjustments). Crest Textiles and Commercial Factors make the following journal entries for the receivables transferred without recourse.

ILLUSTRATION 7-17
Entries for Sale of Receivables Without Recourse

Crest Textiles, Inc.			Commercial Factors, Inc.		
Cash	460,000		Accounts (Notes) Receivable	500,000	
Due from Factor	25,000*		Due to Crest Textiles		25,000
Loss on Sale of Receivables	15,000**		Financing Revenue		15,000
Accounts (Notes) Receivable		500,000	Cash		460,000
*(5% × $500,000)					
**(3% × $500,000)					

In recognition of the sale of receivables, Crest Textiles records a loss of $15,000. The factor's net income will be the difference between the financing revenue of $15,000 and the amount of any uncollectible receivables.

---

[20]**Recourse** is the right of a transferee of receivables to receive payment from the transferor of those receivables for (1) failure of the debtors to pay when due, (2) the effects of prepayments, or (3) adjustments resulting from defects in the eligibility of the transferred receivables. See "Accounting for Transfers and Servicing of Financial Assets and Extinguishments of Liabilities," *Statement of Financial Accounting Standards No. 140* (Stamford, Conn.: FASB, 2000), p. 155.

Sale with Recourse

For receivables sold **with recourse**, the seller guarantees payment to the purchaser in the event the debtor fails to pay. To record this type of transaction, the seller uses a **financial components approach**, because the seller has a continuing involvement with the receivable.[21] In this approach, each party to the sale only recognizes the assets and liabilities that it controls after the sale.

To illustrate, assume the same information as in Illustration 7-17 for Crest Textiles and for Commercial Factors, except that Crest Textiles sold the receivables on a with-recourse basis. Crest Textiles determines that this recourse obligation has a fair value of $6,000. To determine the loss on the sale of the receivables, Crest Textiles computes the net proceeds from the sale as follows.

Cash received	$460,000	
Due from factor	25,000	$485,000
Less: Recourse obligation		6,000
Net proceeds		$479,000

ILLUSTRATION 7-18
Net Proceeds Computation

Net proceeds are cash or other assets received in a sale less any liabilities incurred. Crest Textiles then computes the loss as follows.

Carrying (book) value	$500,000
Net proceeds	479,000
Loss on sale of receivables	$ 21,000

ILLUSTRATION 7-19
Loss on Sale Computation

Illustration 7-20 shows the journal entries for both Crest Textiles and Commercial Factors for the receivables sold with recourse.

Crest Textiles, Inc.			Commercial Factors, Inc.		
Cash	460,000		Accounts Receivable	500,000	
Due from Factor	25,000		Due to Crest Textiles		25,000
Loss on Sale of			Financing Revenue		15,000
Receivables	21,000		Cash		460,000
Accounts (Notes)					
Receivable		500,000			
Recourse Liability		6,000			

ILLUSTRATION 7-20
Entries for Sale of Receivables with Recourse

---

[21]Accounting standards before *SFAS No. 140* generally required that the transferor account for financial assets transferred as an inseparable unit that had been entirely sold or entirely retained. Those standards were difficult to apply and produced inconsistent and arbitrary results. Values are now assigned to such components as the recourse provision, servicing rights, and agreement to reacquire.

Tutorial on the Disposition of Receivables

In this case, Crest Textiles recognizes a loss of $21,000. In addition, it records a liability of $6,000 to indicate the probable payment to Commercial Factors for uncollectible receivables. If Commercial Factors collects all the receivables, Crest Textiles eliminates its recourse liability and increases income. Commercial Factors' net income is the financing revenue of $15,000. It will have no bad debts related to these receivables.

WHAT DO THE NUMBERS MEAN?

> ## UGLY DUCKLINGS
>
> **Ugly Duckling** is a used-car dealer that has carved out a niche by selling cars to customers with questionable credit histories. Ugly Duckling and other "sub-prime lenders" earn a profit by loaning money to riskier borrowers so they can purchase automobiles or homes. To compensate for the higher probability of default of these customers, sub-prime lenders charge higher rates of interest on these high-risk loans. In many instances these companies package their sub-prime loans and sell them as securities. However, recognition of gains on these transfers of receivables is appropriate only if Ugly Duckling can reasonably estimate the proportion of the loans that borrowers will not repay (the receivables are sold with recourse).
>
> However, estimating loan defaults is difficult. If sub-prime lenders fail to set rates high enough to cover unexpected higher rates of default, a severe cash squeeze will result. In addition, if too many of the loans that it sells then default, Ugly Duckling will have to take them back, thereby eliminating any gain it recorded on the original sale. Indeed, in one year alone, **ContiFinancial** had to write off over $654 million in sub-prime loans. Similarly, bank regulators had to step in and take over **Superior Bank FSB**, which specialized in sub-prime loans, because it overestimated the value of its sub-prime loans.
>
> Thus, the sub-prime lending business is a risky one. Depending on default and interest rate assumptions on these receivables, companies like Ugly Duckling may not survive to grow into lending swans.

INTERNATIONAL INSIGHT

The IASB has a similar conceptual approach to the sale of receivables, although it provides more flexibility in implementation.

Secured Borrowing versus Sale

The FASB concluded that a sale occurs only if the seller surrenders control of the receivables to the buyer. The following three conditions must be met before a company can record a sale:

1 The transferred asset has been isolated from the transferor (put beyond reach of the transferor and its creditors).

2 The transferees have obtained the right to pledge or exchange either the transferred assets or beneficial interests in the transferred assets.

3 The transferor does not maintain effective control over the transferred assets through an agreement to repurchase or redeem them before their maturity.

If the three conditions are met, a sale occurs. Otherwise, the transferor should record the transfer as a secured borrowing. If sale accounting is appropriate, a company must still consider assets obtained and liabilities incurred in the transaction. Illustration 7-21 (page 337) shows the rules of accounting for transfers of receivables. As it shows, if there is continuing involvement in a sale transaction, a company must record the assets obtained and liabilities incurred.

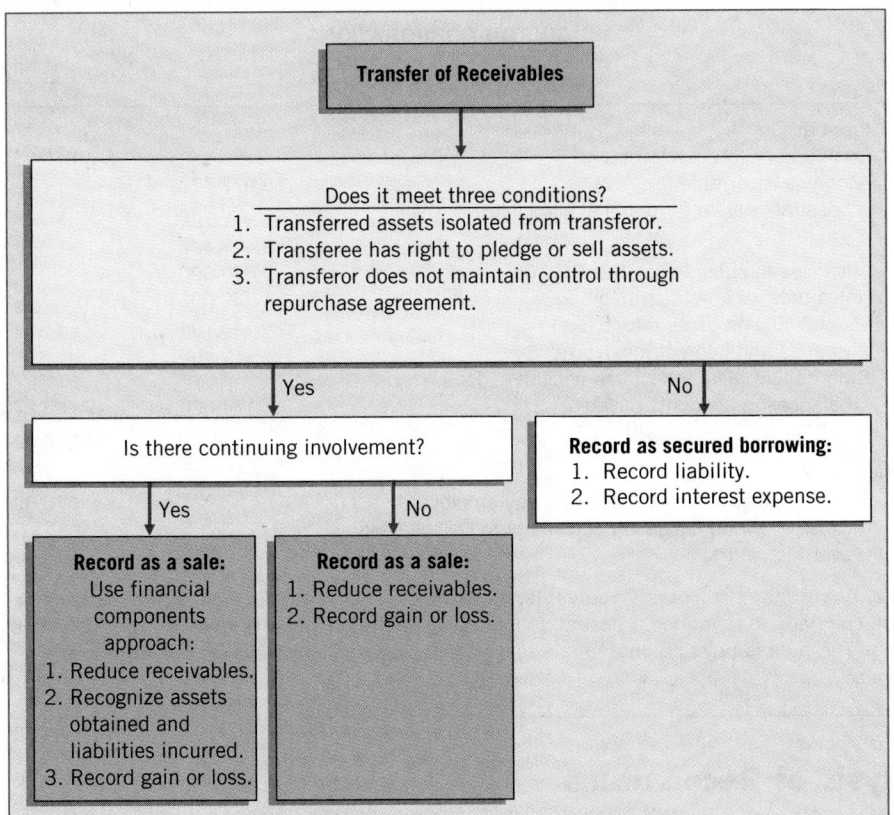

ILLUSTRATION 7-21
Accounting for Transfers
of Receivables

PRESENTATION AND ANALYSIS

Presentation of Receivables

The general rules in classifying receivables are:

1 Segregate the different types of receivables that a company possesses, if material.

2 Appropriately offset the valuation accounts against the proper receivable accounts.

3 Determine that receivables classified in the current assets section will be converted into cash within the year or the operating cycle, whichever is longer.

4 Disclose any loss contingencies that exist on the receivables.

5 Disclose any receivables designated or pledged as collateral.

6 Disclose all significant concentrations of credit risk arising from receivables.[22]

The assets sections of Colton Corporation's balance sheet in Illustration 7-22 (page 338) show many of the disclosures required for receivables.

> **OBJECTIVE 9**
> **Describe how to report and analyze receivables.**

---

[22]Concentrations of credit risk exist when receivables have common characteristics that may affect their collection. These common characteristics might be companies in the same industry or same region of the country. For example, **Quantum Corporation** reported that sales of its disk drives to its top five customers (including **Hewlett-Packard**) represented nearly 40 percent of its revenues in 2003. Financial statements users want to know if a substantial amount of receivables from such sales are to customers facing uncertain economic conditions. No numerical guidelines are provided as to what is meant by a "concentration of credit risk."

Three items should be disclosed with an identified concentration: (1) information on the characteristic that determines the concentration, (2) the amount of loss that could occur upon nonperformance, and (3) information on any collateral related to the receivable. "Disclosures about Fair Value of Financial Instruments," *Statement of Financial Accounting Standards No. 107* (Norwalk, Conn.: FASB, 1991), par. 15.

ILLUSTRATION 7-22
Disclosure of Receivables

*Additional Disclosures
of Receivables*

**INTERNATIONAL
INSIGHT**

Holding receivables that it will
pay in a foreign currency represents risk that the exchange
rate may move against the
company. This results in a decrease in the amount collected
in terms of U.S. dollars.
Companies engaged in cross-
border transactions often
"hedge" these receivables by
buying contracts to exchange
currencies at specified amounts
at future dates.

COLTON CORPORATION
BALANCE SHEET (PARTIAL)
AS OF DECEMBER 31, 2007

Current assets		
Cash and cash equivalents		$ 1,870,250
Accounts receivable (Note 2)	$8,977,673	
Less: Allowance for doubtful accounts	500,226	
	8,477,447	
Advances to subsidiaries due 9/30/08	2,090,000	
Notes receivable—trade (Note 2)	1,532,000	
Federal income taxes refundable	146,704	
Dividends and interest receivable	75,500	
Other receivables and claims (including debit		
balances in accounts payable)	174,620	12,496,271
Total current assets		14,366,521
Noncurrent receivables		
Notes receivable from officers and key employees		376,090
Claims receivable (litigation settlement to be collected		
over four years)		585,000

Note 2: Accounts and Notes Receivable. In November 2007, the Company arranged with a
finance company to refinance a part of its indebtedness. The loan is evidenced by a 12% note
payable. The note is payable on demand and is secured by substantially all the accounts
receivable.

Analysis of Receivables

Receivables Turnover Ratio

Analysts frequently compute financial ratios to evaluate the liquidity of a company's accounts receivable. To assess the liquidity of the receivables, they use the **receivables
turnover ratio**. This ratio measures the number of times, on average, a company collects
receivables during the period. The ratio is computed by dividing net sales by average (net)
receivables outstanding during the year. Theoretically, the numerator should include only
net credit sales, but this information is frequently unavailable. However, if the relative
amounts of credit and cash sales remain fairly constant, the trend indicated by the ratio
will still be valid. Barring significant seasonal factors, average receivables outstanding can
be computed from the beginning and ending balances of net trade receivables.

To illustrate, **Circuit City** reported 2004 net sales of $9,745 million, its beginning and
ending accounts receivable balances were $380 million and $580 million, respectively.
Illustration 7-23 shows the computation of its accounts receivables turnover ratio.

ILLUSTRATION 7-23
Computation of Accounts
Receivable Turnover

$$\frac{\text{Net Sales}}{\text{Average Trade Receivables (net)}} = \frac{\text{Accounts Receivable}}{\text{Turnover}}$$

$$\frac{\$9,745}{(\$580 + \$380)/2} = 20.3 \text{ times, or every 18 days } (365 \div 20.3)$$

UNDERLYING CONCEPTS

Providing information that will
help users assess a company's
current liquidity and prospective cash flows is a primary
objective of accounting.

This information[23] shows how successful the company is in collecting its outstanding receivables. If possible, an aging schedule should also be prepared to help determine
how long receivables have been outstanding. A satisfactory receivables turnover may
have resulted because certain receivables were collected quickly though others have been
outstanding for a relatively long period. An aging schedule would reveal such patterns.

---

[23]Often the receivables turnover is transformed to **days to collect accounts receivable** or **days
outstanding**—an average collection period. In this case, 20.3 is divided into 365 days, resulting in
18 days. Several figures other than 365 could be used. A common alternative is 360 days because
it is divisible by 30 (days) and 12 (months). *Use 365 days in any homework computations.*

SUMMARY OF LEARNING OBJECTIVES

1. Identify items considered cash. To be reported as "cash," an asset must be readily available for the payment of current obligations and free from contractual restrictions that limit its use in satisfying debts. Cash consists of coin, currency, and available funds on deposit at the bank. Negotiable instruments such as money orders, certified checks, cashier's checks, personal checks, and bank drafts are also viewed as cash. Savings accounts are usually classified as cash.

2. Indicate how to report cash and related items. Companies report cash as a current asset in the balance sheet. The reporting of other related items are: (1) *Restricted cash:* The SEC recommends that companies state separately legally restricted deposits held as compensating balances against short-term borrowing among the "Cash and cash equivalent items" in current assets. Restricted deposits held against long-term borrowing arrangements should be separately classified as noncurrent assets in either the investments or other assets sections. (2) *Bank overdrafts:* Companies should report overdrafts in the current liabilities section and usually add them to the amount reported as accounts payable. If material, these items should be separately disclosed either on the face of the balance sheet or in the related notes. (3) *Cash equivalents:* Companies often report this item together with cash as "Cash and cash equivalents."

3. Define receivables and identify the different types of receivables. Receivables are claims held against customers and others for money, goods, or services. The receivables are classified into three types: (1) current or noncurrent, (2) trade or nontrade, (3) accounts receivable or notes receivable.

4. Explain accounting issues related to recognition of accounts receivable. Two issues that may complicate the measurement of accounts receivable are: (1) The availability of discounts (trade and cash discounts), and (2) the length of time between the sale and the payment due dates (the interest element).

Ideally, companies should measure receivables in terms of their present value—that is, the discounted value of the cash to be received in the future. The profession specifically excludes from the present-value considerations receivables arising from normal business transactions that are due in customary trade terms within approximately one year.

5. Explain accounting issues related to valuation of accounts receivable. Companies value and report short-term receivables at net realizable value—the net amount expected to be received in cash, which is not necessarily the amount legally receivable. Determining net realizable value requires estimating uncollectible receivables.

6. Explain accounting issues related to recognition of notes receivable. Companies record short-term notes at face value and long-term notes receivable at the present value of the cash they expect to collect. When the interest stated on an interest-bearing note equals the effective (market) rate of interest, the note sells at face value. When the stated rate differs from the effective rate, a company records either a discount or premium.

7. Explain accounting issues related to valuation of notes receivable. Like accounts receivable, companies record and report short-term notes receivable at their net realizable value. The same is also true of long-term receivables. Special issues relate to uncollectibles and impairments.

8. Explain accounting issues related to disposition of accounts and notes receivable. To accelerate the receipt of cash from receivables, the owner may transfer the receivables to another company for cash in one of two ways: (1) *Secured borrowing:* A creditor often requires that the debtor designate or pledge receivables as security for the loan. (2) *Sales (factoring) of receivables:* Factors are finance companies or banks that buy receivables from businesses and then collect the remittances directly from the customers. In many cases, transferors may have some continuing involvement with the receivable sold. Companies use a financial components approach to record this type of transaction.

KEY TERMS

accounts receivable, *319*
aging schedule, *324*
allowance method, *323*
bank overdrafts, *317*
cash, *314*
cash discounts, *320*
cash equivalents, *317*
compensating balances, *316*
direct write-off method, *323*
factoring receivables, *333*
financial components approach, *335*
imputed interest rate, *331*
net realizable value, *322*
nontrade receivables, *319*
notes receivable, *319*
percentage-of-receivables approach, *324*
percentage-of-sales approach, *323*
promissory note, *326*
receivables, *318*
receivables turnover ratio, *338*
restricted cash, *316*
sales discounts, *320*
securitization, *334*
trade discounts, *320*
trade receivables, *319*
with recourse, *335*
without recourse, *334*
zero-interest-bearing notes, *326*

9. **Describe how to report and analyze receivables.** Companies should report receivables with appropriate offset of valuation accounts against receivables, classify receivables as current or noncurrent, identify pledged or designated receivables, and identify concentrations of risks arising from receivables. Analysts assess receivables based on turnover and the days outstanding.

APPENDIX
7A

Cash Controls

As we indicated in Chapter 7, cash creates many management and control problems. In this appendix, we discuss some of the basic control issues related to cash.

USING BANK ACCOUNTS

OBJECTIVE 10
Explain common techniques employed to control cash.

INTERNATIONAL INSIGHT

Multinational corporations often have cash accounts in more than one currency. For financial statement purposes, these corporations typically translate these currencies into U.S. dollars, using the exchange rate in effect at the balance sheet date.

To obtain desired control objectives, a company can vary the number and location of banks and the types of bank accounts. For large companies operating in multiple locations, the location of bank accounts can be important. Establishing collection accounts in strategic locations can accelerate the flow of cash into the company by shortening the time between a customer's mailing of a payment and the company's use of the cash. Multiple collection centers generally reduce the size of a company's **collection float**. This is the difference between the amount on deposit according to the company's records and the amount of collected cash according to the bank record.

Large, multilocation companies frequently use **lockbox accounts** to collect in cities with heavy customer billing. The company rents a local post office box and authorizes a local bank to pick up the remittances mailed to that box number. The bank empties the box at least once a day and immediately credits the company's account for collections. The greatest advantage of a lockbox is that it accelerates the availability of collected cash. Generally, in a lockbox arrangement the bank microfilms the checks for record purposes and provides the company with a deposit slip, a list of collections, and any customer correspondence. Thus, a lockbox system improves the control over cash and accelerates collection of cash. If the income generated from accelerating the receipt of funds exceeds the cost of the lockbox system, then it is a worthwhile undertaking.

The **general checking account** is the principal bank account in most companies and frequently the only bank account in small businesses. A company deposits in and disburses cash from this account. A company cycles all transactions through it. For example, a company deposits from and disburses to all other bank accounts through the general checking account.

Companies use **imprest bank accounts** to make a specific amount of cash available for a limited purpose. The account acts as a clearing account for a large volume of checks or for a specific type of check. To clear a specific and intended amount through the imprest account, a company transfers that amount from the general checking account or other source. Companies often use imprest bank accounts for disbursing payroll checks, dividends, commissions, bonuses, confidential expenses (e.g., officers' salaries), and travel expenses.

THE IMPREST PETTY CASH SYSTEM

Almost every company finds it necessary to pay small amounts for miscellaneous expenses such as taxi fares, minor office supplies, and employee's lunches. Disbursements by check for such items is often impractical, yet some control over them is important.

A simple method of obtaining reasonable control, while adhering to the rule of disbursement by check, is the **imprest system for petty cash** disbursements. This is how the system works:

1 The company designates a petty cash custodian, and gives the custodian a small amount of currency from which to make payments. It records transfer of funds to petty cash as:

Petty Cash	300	
Cash		300

2 The petty cash custodian obtains signed receipts from each individual to whom he or she pays cash, attaching evidence of the disbursement to the petty cash receipt. Petty cash transactions are not recorded until the fund is reimbursed; someone other than the petty cash custodian records those entries.

3 When the supply of cash runs low, the custodian presents to the general cashier a request for reimbursement supported by the petty cash receipts and other disbursement evidence. The custodian receives a company check to replenish the fund. At this point, the company records transactions based on petty cash receipts.

Office Supplies Expense	42	
Postage Expense	53	
Entertainment Expense	76	
Cash Over and Short	2	
Cash		173

4 If the company decides that the amount of cash in the petty cash fund is excessive, it lowers the fund balance as follows.

Cash	50	
Petty Cash		50

A company makes entries to the Petty Cash account only to increase or decrease the size of the fund.

A company uses a **Cash Over and Short** account when the petty cash fund fails to prove out. That is, an error occurs such as incorrect change, overpayment of expense, or lost receipt. If cash proves out **short** (i.e., the sum of the receipts and cash in the fund is less than the imprest amount), the company debits the shortage to the Cash Over and Short account. If cash proves out **over**, it credits the overage to Cash Over and Short. The company closes Cash Over and Short only at the end of the year. It generally shows Cash Over and Short on the income statement as an "Other expense or revenue."

There are usually expense items in the fund except immediately after reimbursement. Therefore, to maintain accurate financial statements, a company must reimburse the funds at the end of each accounting period and also when nearly depleted.

Under the imprest system the petty cash custodian is responsible at all times for the amount of the fund on hand either as cash or in the form of signed receipts. These receipts provide the evidence required by the disbursing officer to issue a reimbursement check. Further, a company follows two additional procedures to obtain more complete control over the petty cash fund:

1 A superior of the petty cash custodian makes surprise counts of the fund from time to time to determine that a satisfactory accounting of the fund has occurred.

2 The company cancels or mutilates petty cash receipts after they have been submitted for reimbursement, so that they cannot be used to secure a second reimbursement.

PHYSICAL PROTECTION OF CASH BALANCES

Not only must a company safeguard cash receipts and cash disbursements through internal control measures, but it must also protect the cash on hand and in banks. Because receipts become cash on hand and disbursements are made from cash in banks, adequate control of receipts and disbursements is part of the protection of cash balances, along with certain other procedures.

Physical protection of cash is so elementary a necessity that it requires little discussion. A company should make every effort to minimize the cash on hand in the office. It should only have on hand a petty cash fund, the current day's receipts, and perhaps funds for making change. Insofar as possible, it should keep these funds in a vault, safe, or locked cash drawer. The company should transmit intact each day's receipts to the bank as soon as practicable. Accurately stating the amount of available cash both in internal management reports and in external financial statements is also extremely important.

Every company has a record of cash received, disbursed, and the balance. Because of the many cash transactions, however, errors or omissions may occur in keeping this record. Therefore, a company must periodically prove the balance shown in the general ledger. It can count cash actually present in the office—petty cash, change funds, and undeposited receipts—for comparison with the company records. For cash on deposit, a company prepares a bank reconciliation—a reconciliation of the company's record and the bank's record of the company's cash.

RECONCILIATION OF BANK BALANCES

At the end of each calendar month the bank supplies each customer with a **bank statement** (a copy of the bank's account with the customer) together with the customer's checks that the bank paid during the month.[1] If neither the bank nor the customer made any errors, if all deposits made and all checks drawn by the customer reached the bank within the same month, and if no unusual transactions occurred that affected either the company's or the bank's record of cash, the balance of cash reported by the bank to the customer equals that shown in the customer's own records. This condition seldom occurs for one or more of the reconciling items presented below. Hence, a company expects differences between its record of cash and the bank's record. Therefore, it must reconcile the two to determine the nature of the differences between the two amounts.

RECONCILING ITEMS

1 *DEPOSITS IN TRANSIT.* End-of-month deposits of cash recorded on the depositor's books in one month are received and recorded by the bank in the following month.

2 *OUTSTANDING CHECKS.* Checks written by the depositor are recorded when written but may not be recorded by (may not "clear") the bank until the next month.

3 *BANK CHARGES.* Charges recorded by the bank against the depositor's balance for such items as bank services, printing checks, **not-sufficient-funds (NSF) checks**, and safe-deposit box rentals. The depositor may not be aware of these charges until the receipt of the bank statement.

4 *BANK CREDITS.* Collections or deposits by the bank for the benefit of the depositor that may be unknown to the depositor until receipt of the bank statement. Examples are note collection for the depositor and interest earned on interest-bearing checking accounts.

5 *BANK OR DEPOSITOR ERRORS.* Errors on either the part of the bank or the part of the depositor cause the bank balance to disagree with the depositor's book balance.

---

[1] As we mentioned in Chapter 7, paper checks continue to be used as a means of payment. However, ready availability of desktop publishing software and hardware has created new opportunities for check fraud in the form of duplicate, altered, and forged checks. At the same time, new fraud-fighting technologies, such as ultraviolet imaging, high-capacity barcodes, and biometrics, are being developed. These technologies convert paper documents into electronically processed document files, thereby reducing the risk of fraud.

A **bank reconciliation** is a schedule explaining any differences between the bank's and the company's records of cash. If the difference results only from transactions not yet recorded by the bank, the company's record of cash is considered correct. But, if some part of the difference arises from other items, either the bank or the company must adjust its records.

A company may prepare two forms of a bank reconciliation. One form reconciles from the bank statement balance to the book balance or vice versa. The other form reconciles both the bank balance and the book balance to a correct cash balance. Most companies use this latter form. Illustration 7A-1 shows a sample of that form and its common reconciling items.

Balance per bank statement (end of period)		$$$
Add: Deposits in transit	$$	
Undeposited receipts (cash on hand)	$$	
Bank errors that understate the bank statement balance	$$	$$
		$$$
Deduct: Outstanding checks	$$	
Bank errors that overstate the bank statement balance	$$	$$
Correct cash balance		$$$
Balance per depositor's books		$$$
Add: Bank credits and collections not yet recorded in the books	$$	
Book errors that understate the book balance	$$	$$
		$$$
Deduct: Bank charges not yet recorded in the books	$$	
Book errors that overstate the book balance	$$	$$
Correct cash balance		$$$

ILLUSTRATION 7A-1
Bank Reconciliation Form and Content

This form of reconciliation consists of two sections: (1) "Balance per bank statement" and (2) "Balance per depositor's books." Both sections end with the same "Correct cash balance." The correct cash balance is the amount to which the books must be adjusted and is the amount reported on the balance sheet. **Companies prepare adjusting journal entries for all the addition and deduction items appearing in the "Balance per depositor's books" section.** Companies should immediately call to the bank's attention any errors attributable to it.

To illustrate, Nugget Mining Company's books show a cash balance at the Denver National Bank on November 30, 2007, of $20,502. The bank statement covering the month of November shows an ending balance of $22,190. An examination of Nugget's accounting records and November bank statement identified the following reconciling items.

1   A deposit of $3,680 that Nugget mailed November 30 does not appear on the bank statement.

2   Checks written in November but not charged to the November bank statement are:

Check #7327	$ 150
#7348	4,820
#7349	31

3   Nugget has not yet recorded the $600 of interest collected by the bank November 20 on Sequoia Co. bonds held by the bank for Nugget.

4   Bank service charges of $18 are not yet recorded on Nugget's books.

5   The bank returned one of Nugget's customer's checks for $220 with the bank statement, marked "NSF." The bank treated this bad check as a disbursement.

6   Nugget discovered that it incorrectly recorded check #7322, written in November for $131 in payment of an account payable, as $311.

7   A check for Nugent Oil Co. in the amount of $175 that the bank incorrectly charged to Nugget accompanied the statement.

Nugget reconciled the bank and book balances to the correct cash balance of $21,044 as shown in Illustration 7A-2 (page 344).

ILLUSTRATION 7A-2
Sample Bank
Reconciliation

NUGGET MINING COMPANY			
BANK RECONCILIATION			
DENVER NATIONAL BANK, NOVEMBER 30, 2007			
Balance per bank statement (end of period)			$22,190
Add: Deposit in transit	(1)	$3,680	
Bank error—incorrect check charged to account by bank	(7)	175	3,855
			26,045
Deduct: Outstanding checks	(2)		5,001
Correct cash balance			$21,044
Balance per books			$20,502
Add: Interest collected by the bank	(3)	$ 600	
Error in recording check #7322	(6)	180	780
			21,282
Deduct: Bank service charges	(4)	18	
NSF check returned	(5)	220	238
Correct cash balance			$21,044

The journal entries required to adjust and correct Nugget's books in early December 2007 are taken from the items in the "Balance per books" section and are as follows.

Expanded Discussion of a Four-Column Bank Reconciliation

Cash	600	
Interest Revenue		600
(To record interest on Sequoia Co. bonds, collected by bank)		
Cash	180	
Accounts Payable		180
(To correct error in recording amount of check #7322)		
Office Expense—Bank Charges	18	
Cash		18
(To record bank service charges for November)		
Accounts Receivable	220	
Cash		220
(To record customer's check returned NSF)		

After posting the entries, Nugget's cash account will have a balance of $21,044. Nugget should return the Nugent Oil Co. check to Denver National Bank, informing the bank of the error.

WHAT DO THE NUMBERS MEAN?

BOUNCE A CHECK, GET BANNED

Rebecca Cobos overdrew her checking account at a **Bank of America** branch in Los Angeles. When she could not immediately repay the bank, it not only closed her account but also had her, in effect, banned for five years from opening a checking account at most other banks.

Bank of America did so by reporting the 23-year-old university secretary to **Chex-Systems**, a national database to which 80 percent of banks in the country subscribe. Once lodged in ChexSystems, your name automatically stays there for five years, whether your offense was bouncing a check or two or committing serious fraud. The large majority of banks using ChexSystems reject any checking-account applicant they find in the database.

Maintained by a unit of the check-printing company **Deluxe Corp.**, ChexSystems currently has about seven million names on file. Bank officials and executives of the unit, called eFund, defend the database as a valuable weapon in the battle against fraud and high-risk customers. And there is no denying that many of those who end up in the database have been financially careless, or worse.

Source: Paul Beckett, "It's Not in the Mail," *Wall Street Journal* (August 1, 2000), p. A1.

SUMMARY OF LEARNING OBJECTIVE FOR APPENDIX 7A

KEY TERMS

bank reconciliation, *343*

imprest system for petty cash, *341*

not-sufficient-funds (NSF) checks, *342*

10. Explain common techniques employed to control cash. The common techniques employed to control cash are: (1) *Using bank accounts:* A company can vary the number and location of banks and the types of accounts to obtain desired control objectives. (2) *The imprest petty cash system:* It may be impractical to require small amounts of various expenses be paid by check, yet some control over them is important. (3) *Physical protection of cash balances:* Adequate control of receipts and disbursements is a part of the protection of cash balances. Every effort should be made to minimize the cash on hand in the office. (4) *Reconciliation of bank balances:* Cash on deposit is not available for count and is proved by preparing a bank reconciliation.

Note: All **asterisked** Questions, Brief Exercises, Exercises, Problems, and Concepts for Analysis relate to material covered in the appendix to the chapter.

QUESTIONS

1. What may be included under the heading of "cash"?

2. In what accounts should the following items be classified?

(a) Coins and currency.

(b) U.S. Treasury (government) bonds.

(c) Certificate of deposit.

(d) Cash in a bank that is in receivership.

(e) NSF check (returned with bank statement).

(f) Deposit in foreign bank (exchangeability limited).

(g) Postdated checks.

(h) Cash to be used for retirement of long-term bonds.

(i) Deposits in transit.

(j) 100 shares of **Dell** stock (intention is to sell in one year or less).

(k) Savings and checking accounts.

(l) Petty cash.

(m) Stamps.

(n) Travel advances.

3. Define a "compensating balance." How should a compensating balance be reported?

4. Michael Tilsen Thomas Inc. reported in a recent annual report "Restricted cash for debt redemption." What section of the balance sheet would report this item?

5. What are the reasons that a company gives trade discounts? Why are trade discounts not recorded in the accounts like cash discounts?

6. What are two methods of recording accounts receivable transactions when a cash discount situation is involved? Which is more theoretically correct? Which is used in practice more of the time? Why?

7. What are the basic problems that occur in the valuation of accounts receivable?

8. What is the theoretical justification of the allowance method as contrasted with the direct write-off method of accounting for bad debts?

9. Indicate how well the percentage-of-sales method and the aging method accomplish the objectives of the allowance method of accounting for bad debts.

10. Of what merit is the contention that the allowance method lacks the objectivity of the direct write-off method? Discuss in terms of accounting's measurement function.

11. Explain how the accounting for bad debts can be used for earnings management.

12. Because of calamitous earthquake losses, Kishwaukee Company, one of your client's oldest and largest customers, suddenly and unexpectedly became bankrupt. Approximately 30% of your client's total sales have been made to Kishwaukee Company during each of the past several years. The amount due from Kishwaukee Company—none of which is collectible—equals 22% of total accounts receivable, an amount that is considerably in excess of what was determined to be an adequate provision for doubtful accounts at the close of the preceding year. How would your client record the write-off of the Kishwaukee Company receivable if it is using the allowance method of accounting for bad debts? Justify your suggested treatment.

13. What is the normal procedure for handling the collection of accounts receivable previously written off using the direct write-off method? The allowance method?

14. On January 1, 2007, John Singer Co. sells property for which it had paid $690,000 to Sargent Company, receiving in return Sargent's zero-interest-bearing note for $1,000,000 payable in 5 years. What entry would John Singer make to record the sale, assuming that John Singer frequently sells similar items of property for a cash sales price of $620,000?

15. What is "imputed interest"? In what situations is it necessary to impute an interest rate for notes receivable? What are the considerations in imputing an appropriate interest rate?

16. Indicate three reasons why a company might sell its receivables to another company.

17. When is the financial components approach to recording the transfers of receivables used? When should a transfer of receivables be recorded as a sale?

18. Hale Hardware is planning to factor some of its receivables. The cash received will be used to pay for inventory purchases. The factor has indicated that it will require "recourse" on the sold receivables. Explain to the controller of Hale Hardware what "recourse" is and how the recourse will be reflected in Hale's financial statements after the sale of the receivables.

19. Outkast Outfitters Company includes in its trial balance for December 31 an item for Accounts Receivable $769,000. This balance consists of the following items:

Due from regular customers	$523,000
Refund receivable on prior year's income taxes (an established claim)	15,500
Travel advance to employees	22,000
Loan to wholly owned subsidiary	45,500
Advances to creditors for goods ordered	61,000
Accounts receivable assigned as security for loans payable	75,000
Notes receivable past due plus interest on these notes	27,000
Total	$769,000

Illustrate how these items should be shown in the balance sheet as of December 31.

20. What is the accounts receivable turnover ratio, and what type of information does it provide?

21. You are evaluating Hawthorn Downs Racetrack for a potential loan. An examination of the notes to the financial statements indicates restricted cash at year-end amounts to $100,000. Explain how you would use this information in evaluating Hawthorn's liquidity.

*22. Distinguish among the following: (1) a general checking account, (2) an imprest bank account, and (3) a lockbox account.

BRIEF EXERCISES

(LO 1) **BE7-1** Stowe Enterprises owns the following assets at December 31, 2007.

Cash in bank—savings account	63,000	Checking account balance	17,000
Cash on hand	9,300	Postdated checks	750
Cash refund due from IRS	31,400	Certificates of deposit (180-day)	90,000

What amount should be reported as cash?

(LO 4) **BE7-2** Montoya Co. uses the gross method to record sales made on credit. On June 1, 2007, it made sales of $40,000 with terms 3/15, n/45. On June 12, 2007, Montoya received full payment for the June 1 sale. Prepare the required journal entries for Montoya Co.

(LO 4) **BE7-3** Use the information from BE7-2, assuming Montoya Co. uses the net method to account for cash discounts. Prepare the required journal entries for Montoya Co.

(LO 5) **BE7-4** Battle Tank, Inc. had net sales in 2007 of $1,200,000. At December 31, 2007, before adjusting entries, the balances in selected accounts were: Accounts Receivable $250,000 debit, and Allowance for Doubtful Accounts $2,100 credit. If Battle Tank estimates that 2% of its net sales will prove to be uncollectible, prepare the December 31, 2007, journal entry to record bad debt expense.

(LO 5) **BE7-5** Use the information presented in BE7-4 for Battle Tank, Inc.

(a) Instead of estimating the uncollectibles at 2% of net sales, assume that 10% of accounts receivable will prove to be uncollectible. Prepare the entry to record bad debts expense.

(b) Instead of estimating uncollectibles at 2% of net sales, assume Battle Tank prepares an aging schedule that estimates total uncollectible accounts at $24,600. Prepare the entry to record bad debts expense.

(LO 6) **BE7-6** Addams Family Importers sold goods to Acme Decorators for $20,000 on November 1, 2007, accepting Acme's $20,000, 6-month, 6% note. Prepare Addams's November 1 entry, December 31 annual adjusting entry, and May 1 entry for the collection of the note and interest.

(LO 6) **BE7-7** Aero Acrobats lent $15,944 to Afterburner, Inc., accepting Afterburner's 2-year, $20,000, zero-interest-bearing note. The implied interest rate is 12%. Prepare Aero's journal entries for the initial transaction, recognition of interest each year, and the collection of $20,000 at maturity.

(LO 8) **BE7-8** On October 1, 2007, Akira, Inc. assigns $1,000,000 of its accounts receivable to Alisia National Bank as collateral for a $700,000 note. The bank assesses a finance charge of 2% of the receivables assigned and interest on the note of 9%. Prepare the October 1 journal entries for both Akira and Alisia.

(LO 8) **BE7-9** CRC Incorporated factored $100,000 of accounts receivable with Fredrick Factors Inc. on a without recourse basis. Fredrick assesses a 2% finance charge of the amount of accounts receivable and retains an amount equal to 6% of accounts receivable for possible adjustments. Prepare the journal entry for CRC Incorporated and Fredrick Factors to record the factoring of the accounts receivable to Fredrick.

(LO 8) **BE7-10** Use the information in BE7-9 for CRC. Assume that the receivables are sold with recourse. Prepare the journal entry for CRC to record the sale, assuming that the recourse obligation has a fair value of $7,500.

(LO 8) **BE7-11** Keyser Woodcrafters sells $200,000 of receivables to Commercial Factors, Inc. on a with recourse basis. Commercial assesses a finance charge of 5% and retains an amount equal to 4% of accounts receivable. Keyser estimates the fair value of the recourse obligation to be $8,000. Prepare the journal entry for Keyser to record the sale.

(LO 8) **BE7-12** Use the information presented in BE7-11 for Keyser Woodcrafters but assume that the recourse obligation has a fair value of $4,000, instead of $8,000. Prepare the journal entry and discuss the effects of this change in the value of the recourse obligation on Keyser's financial statements.

(LO 9) **BE7-13** The financial statements of **General Mills, Inc.** report net sales of $5,416,000,000. Accounts receivable are $277,300,000 at the beginning of the year and $337,800,000 at the end of the year. Compute General Mills's accounts receivable turnover ratio. Compute General Mills's average collection period for accounts receivable in days.

(LO 10) *****BE7-14** Genesis Company designated Alex Kidd as petty cash custodian and established a petty cash fund of $200. The fund is reimbursed when the cash in the fund is at $17. Petty cash receipts indicate funds were disbursed for office supplies $94 and miscellaneous expense $87. Prepare journal entries for the establishment of the fund and the reimbursement.

(LO 10) *****BE7-15** Jaguar Corporation is preparing a bank reconciliation and has identified the following potential reconciling items. For each item, indicate if it is (1) added to balance per bank statement, (2) deducted from balance per bank statement, (3) added to balance per books, or (4) deducted from balance per books.

    (a) Deposit in transit $5,500.   **(d)** Outstanding checks $7,422.
    (b) Interest credited to Jaguar's account $31.   **(e)** NSF check returned $377.
    (c) Bank service charges $25.

(LO 10) *****BE7-16** Use the information presented in BE7-15 for Jaguar Corporation. Prepare any entries necessary to make Jaguar's accounting records correct and complete.

EXERCISES

(LO 1) **E7-1** **(Determining Cash Balance)** The controller for Clint Eastwood Co. is attempting to determine the amount of cash to be reported on its December 31, 2007, balance sheet. The following information is provided.

  1. Commercial savings account of $600,000 and a commercial checking account balance of $900,000 are held at First National Bank of Yojimbo.
  2. Money market fund account held at Volonte Co. (a mutual fund organization) permits Eastwood to write checks on this balance, $5,000,000.
  3. Travel advances of $180,000 for executive travel for the first quarter of next year (employee to reimburse through salary reduction).
  4. A separate cash fund in the amount of $1,500,000 is restricted for the retirement of long-term debt.
  5. Petty cash fund of $1,000.
  6. An I.O.U. from Marianne Koch, a company customer, in the amount of $190,000.
  7. A bank overdraft of $110,000 has occurred at one of the banks the company uses to deposit its cash receipts. At the present time, the company has no deposits at this bank.
  8. The company has two certificates of deposit, each totaling $500,000. These CDs have a maturity of 120 days.
  9. Eastwood has received a check that is dated January 12, 2008, in the amount of $125,000.
  10. Eastwood has agreed to maintain a cash balance of $500,000 at all times at First National Bank of Yojimbo to ensure future credit availability.
  11. Eastwood has purchased $2,100,000 of commercial paper of Sergio Leone Co. which is due in 60 days.
  12. Currency and coin on hand amounted to $7,700.

Instructions

   (a) Compute the amount of cash to be reported on Eastwood Co.'s balance sheet at December 31, 2007.

   (b) Indicate the proper reporting for items that are not reported as cash on the December 31, 2007, balance sheet.

(LO 1)   **E7-2**   **(Determine Cash Balance)**   Presented below are a number of independent situations.

Instructions

For each individual situation, determine the amount that should be reported as cash. If the item(s) is not reported as cash, explain the rationale.

    1. Checking account balance $925,000; certificate of deposit $1,400,000; cash advance to subsidiary of $980,000; utility deposit paid to gas company $180.

    2. Checking account balance $600,000; an overdraft in special checking account at same bank as normal checking account of $17,000; cash held in a bond sinking fund $200,000; petty cash fund $300; coins and currency on hand $1,350.

    3. Checking account balance $590,000; postdated check from customer $11,000; cash restricted due to maintaining compensating balance requirement of $100,000; certified check from customer $9,800; postage stamps on hand $620.

    4. Checking account balance at bank $37,000; money market balance at mutual fund (has checking privileges) $48,000; NSF check received from customer $800.

    5. Checking account balance $700,000; cash restricted for future plant expansion $500,000; short-term Treasury bills $180,000; cash advance received from customer $900 (not included in checking account balance); cash advance of $7,000 to company executive, payable on demand; refundable deposit of $26,000 paid to federal government to guarantee performance on construction contract.

(LO 3, 4)   **E7-3**   **(Financial Statement Presentation of Receivables)**   Jim Carrie Company shows a balance of $181,140 in the Accounts Receivable account on December 31, 2006. The balance consists of the following.

Installment accounts due in 2007	$23,000
Installment accounts due after 2007	34,000
Overpayments to creditors	2,640
Due from regular customers, of which $40,000 represents	
accounts pledged as security for a bank loan	79,000
Advances to employees	1,500
Advance to subsidiary company (made in 2002)	81,000

Instructions

Illustrate how the information above should be shown on the balance sheet of Jim Carrie Company on December 31, 2006.

(LO 3, 4)   **E7-4**   **(Determine Ending Accounts Receivable)**   Your accounts receivable clerk, Mitra Adams, to whom you pay a salary of $1,500 per month, has just purchased a new Buick. You decided to test the accuracy of the accounts receivable balance of $82,000 as shown in the ledger.

   The following information is available for your *first year* in business.

(1) Collections from customers	$198,000
(2) Merchandise purchased	320,000
(3) Ending merchandise inventory	90,000
(4) Goods are marked to sell at 40% above cost	

Instructions

Compute an estimate of the ending balance of accounts receivable from customers that should appear in the ledger and any apparent shortages. Assume that all sales are made on account.

(LO 4)   **E7-5**   **(Record Sales Gross and Net)**   On June 3, Arnold Company sold to Chester Company merchandise having a sale price of $3,000 with terms of 2/10, n/60, f.o.b. shipping point. An invoice totaling $90, terms n/30, was received by Chester on June 8 from John Booth Transport Service for the freight cost. On June 12, the company received a check for the balance due from Chester Company.

Instructions

   (a) Prepare journal entries on the Arnold Company books to record all the events noted above under each of the following bases.

      (1) Sales and receivables are entered at gross selling price.

      (2) Sales and receivables are entered at net of cash discounts.

   (b) Prepare the journal entry under basis 2, assuming that Chester Company did not remit payment until July 29.

(LO 4) **E7-6** **(Recording Sales Transactions)** Presented below is information from Perez Computers Incorporated.

July 1 Sold $20,000 of computers to Robertson Company with terms 3/15, n/60. Perez uses the gross method to record cash discounts.

10 Perez received payment from Robertson for the full amount owed from the July transactions.

17 Sold $200,000 in computers and peripherals to The Clark Store with terms of 2/10, n/30.

30 The Clark Store paid Perez for its purchase of July 17.

Instructions
Prepare the necessary journal entries for Perez Computers.

(LO 5) **E7-7** **(Recording Bad Debts)** Duncan Company reports the following financial information before adjustments.

	Dr.	Cr.
Accounts Receivable	$100,000	
Allowance for Doubtful Accounts		$ 2,000
Sales (all on credit)		900,000
Sales Returns and Allowances	50,000	

Instructions
Prepare the journal entry to record Bad Debt Expense assuming Duncan Company estimates bad debts at (a) 1% of net sales and (b) 5% of accounts receivable.

(LO 5) **E7-8** **(Recording Bad Debts)** At the end of 2007 Aramis Company has accounts receivable of $800,000 and an allowance for doubtful accounts of $40,000. On January 16, 2008, Aramis Company determined that its receivable from Ramirez Company of $6,000 will not be collected, and management authorized its write-off.

Instructions
(a) Prepare the journal entry for Aramis Company to write off the Ramirez receivable.
(b) What is the net realizable value of Aramis Company's accounts receivable before the write-off of the Ramirez receivable?
(c) What is the net realizable value of Aramis Company's accounts receivable after the write-off of the Ramirez receivable?

(LO 5) **E7-9** **(Computing Bad Debts and Preparing Journal Entries)** The trial balance before adjustment of Reba McIntyre Inc. shows the following balances.

	Dr.	Cr.
Accounts Receivable	$90,000	
Allowance for Doubtful Accounts	1,750	
Sales (all on credit)		$680,000

Instructions
Give the entry for estimated bad debts assuming that the allowance is to provide for doubtful accounts on the basis of (a) 4% of gross accounts receivable and (b) 1% of net sales.

(LO 5) **E7-10** **(Bad-Debt Reporting)** The chief accountant for Emily Dickinson Corporation provides you with the following list of accounts receivable written off in the current year.

Date	Customer	Amount
March 31	E. L. Masters Company	$7,800
June 30	Stephen Crane Associates	6,700
September 30	Amy Lowell's Dress Shop	7,000
December 31	R. Frost, Inc.	9,830

Emily Dickinson Corporation follows the policy of debiting Bad Debt Expense as accounts are written off. The chief accountant maintains that this procedure is appropriate for financial statement purposes because the Internal Revenue Service will not accept other methods for recognizing bad debts.

All of Emily Dickinson Corporation's sales are on a 30-day credit basis. Sales for the current year total $2,200,000, and research has determined that bad debt losses approximate 2% of sales.

Instructions
(a) Do you agree or disagree with Dickinson's policy concerning recognition of bad debt expense? Why or why not?
(b) By what amount would net income differ if bad debt expense was computed using the percentage-of-sales approach?

(LO 5) **E7-11** **(Bad Debts—Aging)** Danica Patrick, Inc. includes the following account among its trade receivables.

Hopkins Co.

1/1	Balance forward	700	1/28	Cash (#1710)	1,100
1/20	Invoice #1710	1,100	4/2	Cash (#2116)	1,350
3/14	Invoice #2116	1,350	4/10	Cash (1/1 Balance)	155
4/12	Invoice #2412	1,710	4/30	Cash (#2412)	1,000
9/5	Invoice #3614	490	9/20	Cash (#3614 and	
10/17	Invoice #4912	860		part of #2412)	790
11/18	Invoice #5681	2,000	10/31	Cash (#4912)	860
12/20	Invoice #6347	800	12/1	Cash (#5681)	1,250
			12/29	Cash (#6347)	800

Instructions

Age the balance and specify any items that apparently require particular attention at year-end.

(LO 4, 5, 8) **E7-12** **(Journalizing Various Receivable Transactions)** Presented below is information related to James Garfield Corp.

July 1 James Garfield Corp. sold to Warren Harding Co. merchandise having a sales price of $8,000 with terms 2/10, net/60. Garfield records its sales and receivables net.

5 Accounts receivable of $9,000 (gross) are factored with Andrew Jackson Credit Corp. without recourse at a financing charge of 9%. Cash is received for the proceeds; collections are handled by the finance company. (These accounts were all past the discount period.)

9 Specific accounts receivable of $9,000 (gross) are pledged to Alf Landon Credit Corp. as security for a loan of $6,000 at a finance charge of 6% of the amount of the loan. The finance company will make the collections. (All the accounts receivable are past the discount period.)

Dec. 29 Warren Harding Co. notifies Garfield that it is bankrupt and will pay only 10% of its account. Give the entry to write off the uncollectible balance using the allowance method. (*Note:* First record the increase in the receivable on July 11 when the discount period passed.)

Instructions

Prepare all necessary entries in general journal form for Garfield Corp.

(LO 8) **E7-13** **(Assigning Accounts Receivable)** On April 1, 2007, Rasheed Company assigns $400,000 of its accounts receivable to the Third National Bank as collateral for a $200,000 loan due July 1, 2007. The assignment agreement calls for Rasheed Company to continue to collect the receivables. Third National Bank assesses a finance charge of 2% of the accounts receivable, and interest on the loan is 10% (a realistic rate of interest for a note of this type).

Instructions

(a) Prepare the April 1, 2007, journal entry for Rasheed Company.

(b) Prepare the journal entry for Rasheed's collection of $350,000 of the accounts receivable during the period from April 1, 2007, through June 30, 2007.

(c) On July 1, 2007, Rasheed paid Third National all that was due from the loan it secured on April 1, 2007. Prepare the journal entry to record this payment.

(LO 5, 8) **E7-14** **(Journalizing Various Receivable Transactions)** The trial balance before adjustment for Phil Collins Company shows the following balances.

	Dr.	Cr.
Accounts Receivable	$82,000	
Allowance for Doubtful Accounts	2,120	
Sales		$430,000

Instructions

Using the data above, give the journal entries required to record each of the following cases. (Each situation is independent.)

1. To obtain additional cash, Collins factors without recourse $25,000 of accounts receivable with Stills Finance. The finance charge is 10% of the amount factored.
2. To obtain a one-year loan of $55,000, Collins assigns $65,000 of specific receivable accounts to Crosby Financial. The finance charge is 8% of the loan; the cash is received and the accounts turned over to Crosby Financial.
3. The company wants to maintain the Allowance for Doubtful Accounts at 5% of gross accounts receivable.
4. The company wishes to increase the allowance account by 1½% of net sales.

(LO 8) **E7-15** **(Transfer of Receivables with Recourse)** Ames Quartet Inc. factors receivables with a carrying amount of $200,000 to Joffrey Company for $160,000 on a with recourse basis.

Instructions

The recourse provision has a fair value of $1,000. This transaction should be recorded as a sale. Prepare the appropriate journal entry to record this transaction on the books of Ames Quartet Inc.

(LO 8) **E7-16 (Transfer of Receivables with Recourse)** Beyoncé Corporation factors $175,000 of accounts receivable with Kathleen Battle Financing, Inc. on a with recourse basis. Kathleen Battle Financing will collect the receivables. The receivables records are transferred to Kathleen Battle Financing on August 15, 2007. Kathleen Battle Financing assesses a finance charge of 2% of the amount of accounts receivable and also reserves an amount equal to 4% of accounts receivable to cover probable adjustments.

Instructions

(a) What conditions must be met for a transfer of receivables with recourse to be accounted for as a sale?

(b) Assume the conditions from part (a) are met. Prepare the journal entry on August 15, 2007, for Beyoncé to record the sale of receivables, assuming the recourse obligation has a fair value of $2,000.

(LO 8) **E7-17 (Transfer of Receivables without Recourse)** JFK Corp. factors $300,000 of accounts receivable with LBJ Finance Corporation on a without recourse basis on July 1, 2007. The receivables records are transferred to LBJ Finance, which will receive the collections. LBJ Finance assesses a finance charge of 1½% of the amount of accounts receivable and retains an amount equal to 4% of accounts receivable to cover sales discounts, returns, and allowances. The transaction is to be recorded as a sale.

Instructions

(a) Prepare the journal entry on July 1, 2007, for JFK Corp. to record the sale of receivables without recourse.

(b) Prepare the journal entry on July 1, 2007, for LBJ Finance Corporation to record the purchase of receivables without recourse.

(LO 6, 7) **E7-18 (Note Transactions at Unrealistic Interest Rates)** On July 1, 2007, Agincourt Inc. made two sales.

1. It sold land having a fair market value of $700,000 in exchange for a 4-year zero-interest-bearing promissory note in the face amount of $1,101,460. The land is carried on Agincourt's books at a cost of $590,000.

2. It rendered services in exchange for a 3%, 8-year promissory note having a face value of $400,000 (interest payable annually).

Agincourt Inc. recently had to pay 8% interest for money that it borrowed from British National Bank. The customers in these two transactions have credit ratings that require them to borrow money at 12% interest.

Instructions

Record the two journal entries that should be recorded by Agincourt Inc. for the sales transactions above that took place on July 1, 2007.

(LO 6, 7) **E7-19 (Notes Receivable with Unrealistic Interest Rate)** On December 31, 2005, Ed Abbey Co. performed environmental consulting services for Hayduke Co. Hayduke was short of cash, and Abbey Co. agreed to accept a $200,000 zero-interest-bearing note due December 31, 2007, as payment in full. Hayduke is somewhat of a credit risk and typically borrows funds at a rate of 10%. Abbey is much more creditworthy and has various lines of credit at 6%.

Instructions

(a) Prepare the journal entry to record the transaction of December 31, 2005, for the Ed Abbey Co.

(b) Assuming Ed Abbey Co.'s fiscal year-end is December 31, prepare the journal entry for December 31, 2006.

(c) Assuming Ed Abbey Co.'s fiscal year-end is December 31, prepare the journal entry for December 31, 2007.

(LO 9) **E7-20 (Analysis of Receivables)** Presented below is information for Jones Company.

1. Beginning-of-the-year Accounts Receivable balance was $15,000.

2. Net sales (all on account) for the year were $100,000. Jones does not offer cash discounts.

3. Collections on accounts receivable during the year were $70,000.

Instructions

(a) Prepare (summary) journal entries to record the items noted above.

(b) Compute Jones's accounts receivable turnover ratio for the year. The company does not believe it will have any bad debts.

(c) Use the turnover ratio computed in (b) to analyze Jones's liquidity. The turnover ratio last year was 6.0.

(LO 8)   **E7-21   (Transfer of Receivables)**   Use the information for Jones Company as presented in E7-20. Jones is planning to factor some accounts receivable at the end of the year. Accounts totaling $25,000 will be transferred to Credit Factors, Inc. with recourse. Credit Factors will retain 5% of the balances for probable adjustments and assesses a finance charge of 4%. The fair value of the recourse obligation is $1,200.

Instructions

(a)   Prepare the journal entry to record the sale of the receivables.

(b)   Compute Jones's accounts receivables turnover ratio for the year, assuming the receivables are sold, and discuss how factoring of receivables affects the turnover ratio.

(LO 10)   *__E7-22__   (Petty Cash)**   Carolyn Keene, Inc. decided to establish a petty cash fund to help ensure internal control over its small cash expenditures. The following information is available for the month of April.

1.   On April 1, it established a petty cash fund in the amount of $200.
2.   A summary of the petty cash expenditures made by the petty cash custodian as of April 10 is as follows.

Delivery charges paid on merchandise purchased	$60.00
Supplies purchased and used	25.00
Postage expense	33.00
I.O.U. from employees	17.00
Miscellaneous expense	36.00

The petty cash fund was replenished on April 10. The balance in the fund was $27.

3.   The petty cash fund balance was increased $100 to $300 on April 20.

Instructions

Prepare the journal entries to record transactions related to petty cash for the month of April.

(LO 10)   *__E7-23__   (Petty Cash)**   The petty cash fund of Fonzarelli's Auto Repair Service, a sole proprietorship, contains the following.

1. Coins and currency		$ 15.20
2. Postage stamps		2.90
3. An I.O.U. from Richie Cunningham, an		
employee, for cash advance		40.00
4. Check payable to Fonzarelli's Auto Repair from		
Pottsie Weber, an employee, marked NSF		34.00
5. Vouchers for the following:		
Stamps	$ 20.00	
Two Rose Bowl tickets for Nick Fonzarelli	170.00	
Printer cartridge	14.35	204.35
		$296.45

The general ledger account Petty Cash has a balance of $300.

Instructions

Prepare the journal entry to record the reimbursement of the petty cash fund.

(LO 10)   *__E7-24__   (Bank Reconciliation and Adjusting Entries)**   Angela Lansbury Company deposits all receipts and makes all payments by check. The following information is available from the cash records.

June 30 Bank Reconciliation

Balance per bank	$ 7,000
Add: Deposits in transit	1,540
Deduct: Outstanding checks	(2,000)
Balance per books	$ 6,540

Month of July Results

	Per Bank	Per Books
Balance July 31	$8,650	$9,250
July deposits	5,000	5,810
July checks	4,000	3,100
July note collected (not included in July deposits)	1,000	—
July bank service charge	15	—
July NSF check from a customer, returned by the bank	335	—
(recorded by bank as a charge)		

Instructions

(a) Prepare a bank reconciliation going from balance per bank and balance per book to correct cash balance.

(b) Prepare the general journal entry or entries to correct the Cash account.

(LO 10) *****E7-25** **(Bank Reconciliation and Adjusting Entries)** Logan Bruno Company has just received the August 31, 2007, bank statement, which is summarized below.

County National Bank	Disbursements	Receipts	Balance
Balance, August 1			$ 9,369
Deposits during August		$32,200	41,569
Note collected for depositor, including $40 interest		1,040	42,609
Checks cleared during August	$34,500		8,109
Bank service charges	20		8,089
Balance, August 31			8,089

The general ledger Cash account contained the following entries for the month of August.

Cash			
Balance, August 1	10,050	Disbursements in August	34,903
Receipts during August	35,000		

Deposits in transit at August 31 are $3,800, and checks outstanding at August 31 total $1,050. Cash on hand at August 31 is $310. The bookkeeper improperly entered one check in the books at $146.50 which was written for $164.50 for supplies (expense); it cleared the bank during the month of August.

Instructions

(a) Prepare a bank reconciliation dated August 31, 2007, proceeding to a correct balance.

(b) Prepare any entries necessary to make the books correct and complete.

(c) What amount of cash should be reported in the August 31 balance sheet?

> **See the book's website, www.wiley.com/college/kieso, for Additional Exercises.**

PROBLEMS

(LO 2) **P7-1** **(Determine Proper Cash Balance)** Dumaine Equipment Co. closes its books regularly on December 31, but at the end of 2007 it held its cash book open so that a more favorable balance sheet could be prepared for credit purposes. Cash receipts and disbursements for the first 10 days of January were recorded as December transactions. The following information is given.

1. January cash receipts recorded in the December cash book totaled $39,640, of which $22,000 represents cash sales, and $17,640 represents collections on account for which cash discounts of $360 were given.

2. January cash disbursements recorded in the December check register liquidated accounts payable of $26,450 on which discounts of $250 were taken.

3. The ledger has not been closed for 2007.

4. The amount shown as inventory was determined by physical count on December 31, 2007.

The company uses the periodic method of inventory.

Instructions

(a) Prepare any entries you consider necessary to correct Dumaine's accounts at December 31.

(b) To what extent was Dumaine Equipment Co. able to show a more favorable balance sheet at December 31 by holding its cash book open? (Compute working capital and the current ratio.) Assume that the balance sheet that was prepared by the company showed the following amounts:

	Dr.	Cr.
Cash	$39,000	
Receivables	42,000	
Inventories	67,000	
Accounts payable		$45,000
Other current liabilities		14,200

(LO 5) **P7-2** **(Bad-Debt Reporting)** Presented below are a series of unrelated situations.

1. Spock Company's unadjusted trial balance at December 31, 2007, included the following accounts.

	Debit	Credit
Allowance for doubtful accounts	$4,000	
Net sales		$1,500,000

Spock Company estimates its bad debt expense to be $1\frac{1}{2}$% of net sales. Determine its bad debt expense for 2007.

2. An analysis and aging of Scotty Corp. accounts receivable at December 31, 2007, disclosed the following.

Amounts estimated to be uncollectible	$ 180,000
Accounts receivable	1,750,000
Allowance for doubtful accounts (per books)	125,000

What is the net realizable value of Scotty's receivables at December 31, 2007?

3. Uhura Co. provides for doubtful accounts based on 3% of credit sales. The following data are available for 2007.

Credit sales during 2007	$2,100,000
Allowance for doubtful accounts 1/1/07	17,000
Collection of accounts written off in prior years	
(customer credit was reestablished)	8,000
Customer accounts written off as uncollectible during 2007	30,000

What is the balance in the Allowance for Doubtful Accounts at December 31, 2007?

4. At the end of its first year of operations, December 31, 2007, Chekov Inc. reported the following information.

Accounts receivable, net of allowance for doubtful accounts	$950,000
Customer accounts written off as uncollectible during 2007	24,000
Bad debt expense for 2007	84,000

What should be the balance in accounts receivable at December 31, 2007, before subtracting the allowance for doubtful accounts?

5. The following accounts were taken from Chappel Inc.'s trial balance at December 31, 2007.

	Debit	Credit
Net credit sales		$750,000
Allowance for doubtful accounts	$ 14,000	
Accounts receivable	410,000	

If doubtful accounts are 3% of accounts receivable, determine the bad debt expense to be reported for 2007.

Instructions
Answer the questions relating to each of the five independent situations as requested.

(LO 5) **P7-3** **(Bad-Debt Reporting—Aging)** Mary Pierce Corporation operates in an industry that has a high rate of bad debts. Before any year-end adjustments, the balance in Pierce's Accounts Receivable account was $555,000 and the Allowance for Doubtful Accounts had a credit balance of $35,000. The year-end balance reported in the balance sheet for the Allowance for Doubtful Accounts will be based on the aging schedule shown below.

Days Account Outstanding	Amount	Probability of Collection
Less than 16 days	$300,000	.98
Between 16 and 30 days	100,000	.90
Between 31 and 45 days	80,000	.85
Between 46 and 60 days	40,000	.75
Between 61 and 75 days	20,000	.40
Over 75 days	15,000	.00

Instructions
(a) What is the appropriate balance for the Allowance for Doubtful Accounts at year-end?
(b) Show how accounts receivable would be presented on the balance sheet.
(c) What is the dollar effect of the year-end bad debt adjustment on the before-tax income?

(CMA adapted)

(LO 5) **P7-4** **(Bad-Debt Reporting)** From inception of operations to December 31, 2007, Blaise Pascal Corporation provided for uncollectible accounts receivable under the allowance method: provisions were made monthly at 2% of credit sales; bad debts written off were charged to the allowance account; recoveries of bad debts previously written off were credited to the allowance account; and no year-end adjustments to the allowance account were made. Pascal's usual credit terms are net 30 days.

The balance in the Allowance for Doubtful Accounts was $154,000 at January 1, 2007. During 2007 credit sales totaled $9,000,000, interim provisions for doubtful accounts were made at 2% of credit sales, $95,000 of bad debts were written off, and recoveries of accounts previously written off amounted to $15,000. Pascal installed a computer facility in November 2007, and an aging of accounts receivable was prepared for the first time as of December 31, 2007. A summary of the aging is as follows.

Classification by Month of Sale	Balance in Each Category	Estimated % Uncollectible
November–December 2007	$1,080,000	2%
July–October	650,000	10%
January–June	420,000	25%
Prior to 1/1/07	150,000	70%
	$2,300,000	

Based on the review of collectibility of the account balances in the "prior to 1/1/07" aging category, additional receivables totaling $60,000 were written off as of December 31, 2007. The 70% uncollectible estimate applies to the remaining $90,000 in the category. Effective with the year ended December 31, 2007, Pascal adopted a new accounting method for estimating the allowance for doubtful accounts at the amount indicated by the year-end aging analysis of accounts receivable.

Instructions

(a) Prepare a schedule analyzing the changes in the Allowance for Doubtful Accounts for the year ended December 31, 2007. Show supporting computations in good form. (*Hint*: In computing the 12/31/07 allowance, subtract the $60,000 write-off).

(b) Prepare the journal entry for the year-end adjustment to the Allowance for Doubtful Accounts balance as of December 31, 2007.

(AICPA adapted)

(LO 5) **P7-5 (Bad-Debt Reporting)** Presented below is information related to the Accounts Receivable accounts of Gulistan Inc. during the current year 2007.

1. An aging schedule of the accounts receivable as of December 31, 2007, is as follows.

Age	Net Debit Balance	% to Be Applied after Correction Is Made
Under 60 days	$172,342	1%
61–90 days	136,490	3%
91–120 days	39,924*	6%
Over 120 days	23,644	$4,200 definitely
	$372,400	uncollectible; estimated remainder uncollectible is 25%

*The $2,740 write-off of receivables is related to the 91-to-120 day category.

2. The Accounts Receivable control account has a debit balance of $372,400 on December 31, 2007.
3. Two entries were made in the Bad Debt Expense account during the year: (1) a debit on December 31 for the amount credited to Allowance for Doubtful Accounts, and (2) a credit for $2,740 on November 3, 2007, and a debit to Allowance for Doubtful Accounts because of a bankruptcy.
4. The Allowance for Doubtful Accounts is as follows for 2007.

	Allowance for Doubtful Accounts			
Nov. 3	Uncollectible accounts written off	2,740	Jan. 1	Beginning balance	8,750
			Dec. 31	5% of $372,400	18,620

5. A credit balance exists in the Accounts Receivable (61–90 days) of $4,840, which represents an advance on a sales contract.

Instructions

Assuming that the books have not been closed for 2007, make the necessary correcting entries.

(LO 3, 4, 5) **P7-6 (Journalize Various Accounts Receivable Transactions)** The balance sheet of Antonio Vivaldi Company at December 31, 2007, includes the following.

Notes receivable	$ 36,000	
Accounts receivable	182,100	
Less: Allowance for doubtful accounts	17,300	200,800

Transactions in 2007 include the following.

1. Accounts receivable of $138,000 were collected including accounts of $40,000 on which 2% sales discounts were allowed.
2. $6,300 was received in payment of an account which was written off the books as worthless in 2007. (*Hint:* Reestablish the receivable account.)
3. Customer accounts of $17,500 were written off during the year.
4. At year-end the Allowance for Doubtful Accounts was estimated to need a balance of $20,000. This estimate is based on an analysis of aged accounts receivable.

Instructions

Prepare all journal entries necessary to reflect the transactions above.

(LO 8) **P7-7** **(Assigned Accounts Receivable—Journal Entries)** Nikos Company finances some of its current operations by assigning accounts receivable to a finance company. On July 1, 2007, it assigned, under guarantee, specific accounts amounting to $100,000. The finance company advanced to Nikos 80% of the accounts assigned (20% of the total to be withheld until the finance company has made its full recovery), less a finance charge of ½% of the total accounts assigned.

On July 31 Nikos Company received a statement that the finance company had collected $55,000 of these accounts and had made an additional charge of ½% of the total accounts outstanding as of July 31. This charge is to be deducted at the time of the first remittance due Nikos Company from the finance company. (*Hint:* Make entries at this time.) On August 31, 2007, Nikos Company received a second statement from the finance company, together with a check for the amount due. The statement indicated that the finance company had collected an additional $30,000 and had made a further charge of ½% of the balance outstanding as of August 31.

Instructions

Make all entries on the books of Nikos Company that are involved in the transactions above.

(AICPA adapted)

(LO 6) **P7-8** **(Notes Receivable with Realistic Interest Rate)** On October 1, 2007, Jeppo Farm Equipment Company sold a pecan-harvesting machine to Lujan Brothers Farm, Inc. In lieu of a cash payment Lujan Brothers Farm gave Jeppo a 2-year, $100,000, 8% note (a realistic rate of interest for a note of this type). The note required interest to be paid annually on October 1. Jeppo's financial statements are prepared on a calendar-year basis.

Instructions

Assuming Lujan Brothers Farm fulfills all the terms of the note, prepare the necessary journal entries for Jeppo Farm Equipment Company for the entire term of the note.

(LO 6) **P7-9** **(Notes Receivable Journal Entries)** On December 31, 2007, Menachem Inc. rendered services to Begin Corporation at an agreed price of $91,844.10, accepting $36,000 down and agreeing to accept the balance in four equal installments of $18,000 receivable each December 31. An assumed interest rate of 11% is imputed.

Instructions

Prepare the entries that would be recorded by Menachem Inc. for the sale and for the receipts and interest on the following dates. (Assume that the effective interest method is used for amortization purposes.)

(a) December 31, 2007. **(c)** December 31, 2009. **(e)** December 31, 2011.
(b) December 31, 2008. **(d)** December 31, 2010.

(LO 6, 7) **P7-10** **(Comprehensive Receivables Problem)** Connecticut Inc. had the following long-term receivable account balances at December 31, 2006.

Note receivable from sale of division	$1,800,000
Note receivable from officer	400,000

Transactions during 2007 and other information relating to Connecticut's long-term receivables were as follows.

1. The $1,800,000 note receivable is dated May 1, 2006, bears interest at 9%, and represents the balance of the consideration received from the sale of Connecticut's electronics division to New York Company. Principal payments of $600,000 plus appropriate interest are due on May 1, 2007, 2008, and 2009. The first principal and interest payment was made on May 1, 2007. Collection of the note installments is reasonably assured.

2. The $400,000 note receivable is dated December 31, 2006, bears interest at 8%, and is due on December 31, 2009. The note is due from Sean May, president of Connecticut Inc. and is collateralized by 10,000 shares of Connecticut's common stock. Interest is payable annually on December 31, and all interest payments were paid on their due dates through December 31, 2007. The quoted market price of Connecticut's common stock was $45 per share on December 31, 2007.

3. On April 1, 2007, Connecticut sold a patent to Pennsylvania Company in exchange for a $200,000 zero-interest-bearing note due on April 1, 2009. There was no established exchange price for the patent, and the note had no ready market. The prevailing rate of interest for a note of this type at April 1, 2007, was 12%. The present value of $1 for two periods at 12% is 0.797 (use this factor). The patent had a carrying value of $40,000 at January 1, 2007, and the amortization for the year ended December 31, 2007, would have been $8,000. The collection of the note receivable from Pennsylvania is reasonably assured.

4. On July 1, 2007, Connecticut sold a parcel of land to Harrisburg Company for $200,000 under an installment sale contract. Harrisburg made a $60,000 cash down payment on July 1, 2007, and signed a 4-year 11% note for the $140,000 balance. The equal annual payments of principal and interest on the note will be $45,125 payable on July 1, 2008, through July 1, 2011. The land could have been sold at an established cash price of $200,000. The cost of the land to Connecticut was $150,000. Circumstances are such that the collection of the installments on the note is reasonably assured.

Instructions

(a) Prepare the long-term receivables section of Connecticut's balance sheet at December 31, 2007.

(b) Prepare a schedule showing the current portion of the long-term receivables and accrued interest receivable that would appear in Connecticut's balance sheet at December 31, 2007.

(c) Prepare a schedule showing interest revenue from the long-term receivables that would appear on Connecticut's income statement for the year ended December 31, 2007.

(LO 8, 9) **P7-11 (Income Effects of Receivables Transactions)** Radisson Company requires additional cash for its business. Radisson has decided to use its accounts receivable to raise the additional cash and has asked you to determine the income statement effects of the following contemplated transactions.

1. On July 1, 2007, Radisson assigned $400,000 of accounts receivable to Stickum Finance Company. Radisson received an advance from Stickum of 85% of the assigned accounts receivable less a commission of 3% on the advance. Prior to December 31, 2007, Radisson collected $220,000 on the assigned accounts receivable, and remitted $232,720 to Stickum, $12,720 of which represented interest on the advance from Stickum.

2. On December 1, 2007, Radisson sold $300,000 of net accounts receivable to Wunsch Company for $250,000. The receivables were sold outright on a without recourse basis.

3. On December 31, 2007, an advance of $120,000 was received from First Bank by pledging $160,000 of Radisson's accounts receivable. Radisson's first payment to First Bank is due on January 30, 2008.

Instructions

Prepare a schedule showing the income statement effects for the year ended December 31, 2007, as a result of the above facts.

(LO 10) ***P7-12 (Petty Cash, Bank Reconciliation)** Bill Howe is reviewing the cash accounting for Kappeler, Inc., a local mailing service. Howe's review will focus on the petty cash account and the bank reconciliation for the month ended May 31, 2007. He has collected the following information from Kappeler's bookkeeper for this task.

Petty Cash

1. The petty cash fund was established on May 10, 2007, in the amount of $250.
2. Expenditures from the fund by the custodian as of May 31, 2007, were evidenced by approved receipts for the following.

Postage expense	$33.00
Mailing labels and other supplies	75.00
I.O.U. from employees	30.00
Shipping charges	57.45
Newspaper advertising	22.80
Miscellaneous expense	15.35

On May 31, 2007, the petty cash fund was replenished and increased to $300; currency and coin in the fund at that time totaled $16.40.

Bank Reconciliation

<table>
<thead>
<tr><th colspan="4" align="center">THIRD NATIONAL BANK
BANK STATEMENT</th></tr>
<tr><th></th><th>Disbursements</th><th>Receipts</th><th>Balance</th></tr>
</thead>
<tbody>
<tr><td>Balance, May 1, 2007</td><td></td><td></td><td>$8,769</td></tr>
<tr><td>Deposits</td><td></td><td>$28,000</td><td></td></tr>
<tr><td>Note payment direct from customer (interest of $30)</td><td></td><td>930</td><td></td></tr>
<tr><td>Checks cleared during May</td><td>$31,150</td><td></td><td></td></tr>
<tr><td>Bank service charges</td><td>27</td><td></td><td></td></tr>
<tr><td>Balance, May 31, 2007</td><td></td><td></td><td>6,522</td></tr>
</tbody>
</table>

Kappeler's Cash Account

Balance, May 1, 2007	$ 9,150
Deposits during May 2007	31,000
Checks written during May 2007	(31,835)

Deposits in transit are determined to be $3,000, and checks outstanding at May 31 total $550. Cash on hand (besides petty cash) at May 31, 2007, is $246.

Instructions

(a) Prepare the journal entries to record the transactions related to the petty cash fund for May.

(b) Prepare a bank reconciliation dated May 31, 2007, proceeding to a correct cash balance, and prepare the journal entries necessary to make the books correct and complete.

(c) What amount of cash should be reported in the May 31, 2007, balance sheet?

(LO 10) *P7-13 **(Bank Reconciliation and Adjusting Entries)** The cash account of Jose Orozco Co. showed a ledger balance of $3,969.85 on June 30, 2007. The bank statement as of that date showed a balance of $4,150. Upon comparing the statement with the cash records, the following facts were determined.

1. There were bank service charges for June of $25.
2. A bank memo stated that Bao Dai's note for $900 and interest of $36 had been collected on June 29, and the bank had made a charge of $5.50 on the collection. (No entry had been made on Orozco's books when Bao Dai's note was sent to the bank for collection.)
3. Receipts for June 30 for $2,890 were not deposited until July 2.
4. Checks outstanding on June 30 totaled $2,136.05.
5. The bank had charged the Orozco Co.'s account for a customer's uncollectible check amounting to $453.20 on June 29.
6. A customer's check for $90 had been entered as $60 in the cash receipts journal by Orozco on June 15.
7. Check no. 742 in the amount of $491 had been entered in the cash journal as $419, and check no. 747 in the amount of $58.20 had been entered as $582. Both checks had been issued to pay for purchases of equipment.

Instructions

(a) Prepare a bank reconciliation dated June 30, 2007, proceeding to a correct cash balance.

(b) Prepare any entries necessary to make the books correct and complete.

(LO 10) *P7-14 **(Bank Reconciliation and Adjusting Entries)** Presented below is information related to Tanizaki Inc.

Balance per books at October 31, $41,847.85; receipts $173,523.91; disbursements $166,193.54. Balance per bank statement November 30, $56,274.20.

The following checks were outstanding at November 30.

1224	$1,635.29
1230	2,468.30
1232	3,625.15
1233	482.17

Included with the November bank statement and not recorded by the company were a bank debit memo for $27.40 covering bank charges for the month, a debit memo for $572.13 for a customer's check returned and marked NSF, and a credit memo for $1,400 representing bond interest collected by the bank in the name of Tanizaki Inc. Cash on hand at November 30 recorded and awaiting deposit amounted to $1,915.40.

Instructions

(a) Prepare a bank reconciliation (to the correct balance) at November 30, for Tanizaki Inc. from the information above.

(b) Prepare any journal entries required to adjust the cash account at November 30.

CONCEPTS FOR ANALYSIS

CA7-1 (Bad-Debt Accounting) Ariel Company has significant amounts of trade accounts receivable. Ariel uses the allowance method to estimate bad debts instead of the direct write-off method. During the year, some specific accounts were written off as uncollectible, and some that were previously written off as uncollectible were collected.

Instructions

(a) What are the deficiencies of the direct write-off method?

(b) What are the two basic allowance methods used to estimate bad debts, and what is the theoretical justification for each?

(c) How should Ariel account for the collection of the specific accounts previously written off as uncollectible?

CA7-2 (Various Receivable Accounting Issues) Anne Archer Company uses the net method of accounting for sales discounts. Anne Archer also offers trade discounts to various groups of buyers.

On August 1, 2007, Archer sold some accounts receivable on a without recourse basis. Archer incurred a finance charge.

Archer also has some notes receivable bearing an appropriate rate of interest. The principal and total interest are due at maturity. The notes were received on October 1, 2007, and mature on September 30, 2009. Archer's operating cycle is less than one year.

Instructions

(a) **(1)** Using the net method, how should Archer account for the sales discounts at the date of sale? What is the rationale for the amount recorded as sales under the net method?

   (2) Using the net method, what is the effect on Archer's sales revenues and net income when customers do not take the sales discounts?

(b) What is the effect of trade discounts on sales revenues and accounts receivable? Why?

(c) How should Archer account for the accounts receivable factored on August 1, 2007? Why?

(d) How should Archer account for the note receivable and the related interest on December 31, 2007? Why?

CA7-3 (Bad-Debt Reporting Issues) Orlando Bloom conducts a wholesale merchandising business that sells approximately 5,000 items per month with a total monthly average sales value of $250,000. Its annual bad debt ratio has been approximately $1\frac{1}{2}\%$ of sales. In recent discussions with his bookkeeper, Mr. Bloom has become confused by all the alternatives apparently available in handling the Allowance for Doubtful Accounts balance. The following information has been shown.

1. An allowance can be set up (a) on the basis of a percentage of sales or (b) on the basis of a valuation of all past due or otherwise questionable accounts receivable. Those considered uncollectible can be charged to such allowance at the close of the accounting period, or specific items can be charged off directly against (1) Gross Sales or to (2) Bad Debt Expense in the year in which they are determined to be uncollectible.

2. Collection agency and legal fees, and so on, incurred in connection with the attempted recovery of bad debts can be charged to (a) Bad Debt Expense, (b) Allowance for Doubtful Accounts, (c) Legal Expense, or (d) General Expense.

3. Debts previously written off in whole or in part but currently recovered can be credited to (a) Other Revenue, (b) Bad Debt Expense, or (c) Allowance for Doubtful Accounts.

Instructions

Which of the foregoing methods would you recommend to Mr. Bloom in regard to (1) allowances and charge-offs, (2) collection expenses, and (3) recoveries? State briefly and clearly the reasons supporting your recommendations.

CA7-4 (Basic Note and Accounts Receivable Transactions)

Part 1

On July 1, 2007, John Depp Company, a calendar-year company, sold special-order merchandise on credit and received in return an interest-bearing note receivable from the customer. John Depp Company will receive interest at the prevailing rate for a note of this type. Both the principal and interest are due in one lump sum on June 30, 2008.

Instructions

When should John Depp Company report interest revenue from the note receivable? Discuss the rationale for your answer.

Part 2

On December 31, 2007, John Depp Company had significant amounts of accounts receivable as a result of credit sales to its customers. Depp uses the allowance method based on credit sales to estimate bad debts. Past experience indicates that 2% of credit sales normally will not be collected. This pattern is expected to continue.

Instructions

(a) Discuss the rationale for using the allowance method based on credit sales to estimate bad debts. Contrast this method with the allowance method based on the balance in the trade receivables accounts.

(b) How should John Depp Company report the allowance for doubtful accounts on its balance sheet at December 31, 2007? Also, describe the alternatives, if any, for presentation of bad debt expense in John Depp Company's 2007 income statement.

(AICPA adapted)

CA7-5 (Bad-Debt Reporting Issues) Rosita Arenas Company sells office equipment and supplies to many organizations in the city and surrounding area on contract terms of 2/10, n/30. In the past, over 75% of the credit customers have taken advantage of the discount by paying within 10 days of the invoice date.

The number of customers taking the full 30 days to pay has increased within the last year. Current indications are that less than 60% of the customers are now taking the discount. Bad debts as a percentage of gross credit sales have risen from the 1.5% provided in past years to about 4% in the current year.

The controller has responded to a request for more information on the deterioration in collections of accounts receivable with the report reproduced below.

ROSITA ARENAS COMPANY
FINANCE COMMITTEE REPORT—ACCOUNTS RECEIVABLE COLLECTIONS
MAY 31, 2007

The fact that some credit accounts will prove uncollectible is normal. Annual bad debt write-offs have been 1.5% of gross credit sales over the past five years. During the last fiscal year, this percentage increased to slightly less than 4%. The current Accounts Receivable balance is $1,600,000. The condition of this balance in terms of age and probability of collection is as follows.

Proportion of Total	Age Categories	Probability of Collection
68%	not yet due	99%
15%	less than 30 days past due	96½%
8%	30 to 60 days past due	95%
5%	61 to 120 days past due	91%
2½%	121 to 180 days past due	70%
1½%	over 180 days past due	20%

The Allowance for Doubtful Accounts had a credit balance of $43,300 on June 1, 2006. Rosita Arenas Company has provided for a monthly bad debts expense accrual during the current fiscal year based on the assumption that 4% of gross credit sales will be uncollectible. Total gross credit sales for the 2006–2007 fiscal year amounted to $4,000,000. Write-offs of bad accounts during the year totaled $145,000.

Instructions

(a) Prepare an accounts receivable aging schedule for Rosita Arenas Company using the age categories identified in the controller's report to the finance committee showing:
  (1) The amount of accounts receivable outstanding for each age category and in total.
  (2) The estimated amount that is uncollectible for each category and in total.

(b) Compute the amount of the year-end adjustment necessary to bring Allowance for Doubtful Accounts to the balance indicated by the age analysis. Then prepare the necessary journal entry to adjust the accounting records.

(c) In a recessionary environment with tight credit and high interest rates:
  (1) Identify steps Rosita Arenas Company might consider to improve the accounts receivable situation.
  (2) Then evaluate each step identified in terms of the risks and costs involved.

(CMA adapted)

CA7-6 (Sale of Notes Receivable) Sergey Luzov Wholesalers Co. sells industrial equipment for a standard 3-year note receivable. Revenue is recognized at time of sale. Each note is secured by a lien on the equipment and has a face amount equal to the equipment's list price. Each note's stated interest rate is below the customer's market rate at date of sale. All notes are to be collected in three equal annual installments beginning one year after sale. Some of the notes are subsequently sold to a bank with recourse, some are subsequently sold without recourse, and some are retained by Luzov. At year end, Luzov evaluates all outstanding notes receivable and provides for estimated losses arising from defaults.

Instructions

(a) What is the appropriate valuation basis for Luzov's notes receivable at the date it sells equipment?

(b) How should Luzov account for the sale, without recourse, of a February 1, 2007, note receivable sold on May 1, 2007? Why is it appropriate to account for it in this way?

(c) At December 31, 2007, how should Luzov measure and account for the impact of estimated losses resulting from notes receivable that it
    (1) Retained and did **not** sell?
    (2) Sold to bank with recourse?

(AICPA adapted)

CA7-7 (Zero-Interest-Bearing Note Receivable) On September 30, 2006, Tiger Machinery Co. sold a machine and accepted the customer's zero-interest-bearing note. Tiger normally makes sales on a cash basis. Since the machine was unique, its sales price was not determinable using Tiger's normal pricing practices.

After receiving the first of two equal annual installments on September 30, 2007, Tiger immediately sold the note with recourse. On October 9, 2008, Tiger received notice that the note was dishonored, and it paid all amounts due. At all times prior to default, the note was reasonably expected to be paid in full.

Instructions

(a) (1) How should Tiger determine the sales price of the machine?
    (2) How should Tiger report the effects of the zero-interest-bearing note on its income statement for the year ended December 31, 2006? Why is this accounting presentation appropriate?

(b) What are the effects of the sale of the note receivable with recourse on Tiger's income statement for the year ended December 31, 2007, and its balance sheet at December 31, 2007?

(c) How should Tiger account for the effects of the note being dishonored?

CA7-8 (Reporting of Notes Receivable, Interest, and Sale of Receivables) On July 1, 2007, Gale Sondergaard Company sold special-order merchandise on credit and received in return an interest-bearing note receivable from the customer. Sondergaard will receive interest at the prevailing rate for a note of this type. Both the principal and interest are due in one lump sum on June 30, 2008.

On September 1, 2007, Sondergaard sold special-order merchandise on credit and received in return a zero-interest-bearing note receivable from the customer. The prevailing rate of interest for a note of this type is determinable. The note receivable is due in one lump sum on August 31, 2009.

Sondergaard also has significant amounts of trade accounts receivable as a result of credit sales to its customers. On October 1, 2007, some trade accounts receivable were assigned to Irene Dunne Finance Company on a non-notification (Sondergaard handles collections) basis for an advance of 75% of their amount at an interest charge of 8% on the balance outstanding.

On November 1, 2007, other trade accounts receivable were sold on a without recourse basis. The factor withheld 5% of the trade accounts receivable factored as protection against sales returns and allowances and charged a finance charge of 3%.

Instructions

(a) How should Sondergaard determine the interest revenue for 2007 on the:
    (1) Interest-bearing note receivable? Why?
    (2) Zero-interest-bearing note receivable? Why?

(b) How should Sondergaard report the interest-bearing note receivable and the zero-interest-bearing note receivable on its balance sheet at December 31, 2007?

(c) How should Sondergaard account for subsequent collections on the trade accounts receivable assigned on October 1, 2007, and the payments to Irene Dunne Finance? Why?

(d) How should Sondergaard account for the trade accounts receivable factored on November 1, 2007? Why?

(AICPA adapted)

CA7-9 **(Accounting for Zero-Interest-Bearing Note)** Soon after beginning the year-end audit work on March 10 at Engone Company, the auditor has the following conversation with the controller.

CONTROLLER: The year ended March 31st should be our most profitable in history and, as a consequence, the board of directors has just awarded the officers generous bonuses.

AUDITOR: I thought profits were down this year in the industry, according to your latest interim report.

CONTROLLER: Well, they were down, but 10 days ago we closed a deal that will give us a substantial increase for the year.

AUDITOR: Oh, what was it?

CONTROLLER: Well, you remember a few years ago our former president bought stock in Rocketeer Enterprises because he had those grandiose ideas about becoming a conglomerate. For 6 years we have not been able to sell this stock, which cost us $3,000,000 and has not paid a nickel in dividends. Thursday we sold this stock to Campbell Inc. for $4,000,000. So, we will have a gain of $700,000 ($1,000,000 pretax) which will increase our net income for the year to $4,000,000, compared with last year's $3,800,000. As far as I know, we'll be the only company in the industry to register an increase in net income this year. That should help the market value of the stock!

AUDITOR: Do you expect to receive the $4,000,000 in cash by March 31st, your fiscal year-end?

CONTROLLER: No. Although Campbell Inc. is an excellent company, they are a little tight for cash because of their rapid growth. Consequently, they are going to give us a $4,000,000 zero-interest-bearing note with payments of $400,000 per year for the next 10 years. The first payment is due on March 31 of next year.

AUDITOR: Why is the note zero-interest-bearing?

CONTROLLER: Because that's what everybody agreed to. Since we don't have any interest-bearing debt, the funds invested in the note do not cost us anything and besides, we were not getting any dividends on the Rocketeer Enterprises stock.

Instructions

Do you agree with the way the controller has accounted for the transaction? If not, how should the transaction be accounted for?

 CA7-10 **(Receivables Management)** As the manager of the accounts receivable department for Vicki Maher Leather Goods, Ltd., you recently noticed that Percy Shelley, your accounts receivable clerk who is paid $1,200 per month, has been wearing unusually tasteful and expensive clothing. (This is Vicki Maher's first year in business.) This morning, Shelley drove up to work in a brand new Lexus.

Naturally suspicious by nature, you decide to test the accuracy of the accounts receivable balance of $132,000 as shown in the ledger. The following information is available for your first year (precisely 9 months ended September 30, 2007) in business.

(1) Collections from customers	$198,000
(2) Merchandise purchased	360,000
(3) Ending merchandise inventory	90,000
(4) Goods are marked to sell at 40% above cost.	

Instructions

Assuming all sales were made on account, compute the ending accounts receivable balance that should appear in the ledger, noting any apparent shortage. Then, draft a memo dated October 3, 2007, to John Castle, the branch manager, explaining the facts in this situation. Remember that this problem is serious, and you do not want to make hasty accusations.

 CA7-11 **(Bad-Debt Reporting)** Santo Company is a subsidiary of Hughes Corp. The controller believes that the yearly allowance for doubtful accounts for Santo should be 2% of net credit sales. The president, nervous that the parent company might expect the subsidiary to sustain its 10% growth rate, suggests that the controller increase the allowance for doubtful accounts to 3% yearly. The supervisor thinks that the lower net income, which reflects a 6% growth rate, will be a more sustainable rate for Santo Company.

Instructions

(a) Should the controller be concerned with Santo Company's growth rate in estimating the allowance? Explain your answer.

(b) Does the president's request pose an ethical dilemma for the controller? Give your reasons.

USING YOUR JUDGMENT

Financial Reporting Problem

 **The Procter & Gamble Company (P&G)**

The financial statements of **P&G** are presented in Appendix 5B or can be accessed on the KWW website.

Instructions

Refer to P&G's financial statements and the accompanying notes to answer the following questions.

(a) What criteria does P&G use to classify "Cash and cash equivalents" as reported in its balance sheet?

(b) As of June 30, 2004, what balances did P&G have in cash and cash equivalents? What were the major uses of cash during the year?

(c) P&G reports no allowance for doubtful accounts, suggesting that bad debt expense is not material for this company. Is it reasonable that a company like P&G would not have material bad debt expense? Explain.

Financial Statement Analysis Cases

Case 1 Occidental Petroleum Corporation

Occidental Petroleum Corporation reported the following information in its 2003 Annual Report.

Occidental Petroleum Corporation
Consolidated Balance Sheets
(in millions)

Assets at December 31,	2003	2002
Current assets		
Cash and cash equivalents	$ 683	$ 146
Trade receivables, net of allowances	804	608
Receivables from joint ventures, partnerships, and other	330	321
Inventories	510	491
Prepaid expenses and other	147	307
Total current assets	2,474	1,873
Long-term receivables, net	264	275

Notes to Consolidated Financial Statements

Cash and Cash Equivalents. Cash equivalents consist of highly liquid investments. Cash equivalents totaled approximately $661 million and $116 million at December 31, 2003 and 2002, respectively.

Trade Receivables. Occidental has agreement to sell, under a revolving sale program, an undivided percentage ownership interest in a designated pool of non-interest-bearing receivables. Under this program, Occidental serves as the collection agent with respect to the receivables sold. An interest in new receivables is sold as collections are made from customers. The balance sold at December 31, 2003, was $360 million.

Instructions

(a) What items other than coin and currency may be included in "cash"?

(b) What items may be included in "cash equivalents"?

(c) What are compensating balance arrangements, and how should they be reported in financial statements?

(d) What are the possible differences between cash equivalents and short-term (temporary) investments?

(e) Assuming that the sale agreement meets the criteria for sale accounting, cash proceeds were $345 million, the carrying value of the receivables sold was $360 million, and the fair value of the recourse obligation was $15 million, what was the effect on income from the sale of receivables?

(f) Briefly discuss the impact of the transaction in (e) on Occidental's liquidity.

Case 2 Microsoft Corporation

Microsoft is the leading developer of software in the world. To continue to be successful Microsoft must generate new products, which requires significant amounts of cash. Shown on page 364 is the current asset and current liability information from Microsoft's June 30, 2004, balance sheet (in millions). Following the Microsoft data is the current asset and current liability information for **Oracle** (in millions), another major software developer.

MICROSOFT CORPORATION
BALANCE SHEETS (PARTIAL)
As of June 30
(in millions)

Current assets	2004	2003
Cash and equivalents	$15,982	$ 6,438
Short-term investments	44,610	42,610
Accounts receivable	5,890	5,196
Other	4,084	4,729
Total current assets	$70,566	$58,973
Total current liabilities	$14,969	$13,974

ORACLE
BALANCE SHEETS (PARTIAL)
As of May 31
(in millions)

Current assets	2004	2003
Cash and equivalents	$ 4,138	$ 4,737
Short-term investments	4,449	1,782
Receivables	2,012	1,920
Other current assets	737	788
Total current assets	$11,336	$9,227
Current liabilities	$ 4,272	$4,158

Part 1 (Cash and Cash Equivalents)

Instructions

(a) What is the definition of a cash equivalent? Give some examples of cash equivalents. How do cash equivalents differ from other types of short-term investments?

(b) Calculate (1) the current ratio and (2) working capital for each company for 2004 and discuss your results.

(c) Is it possible to have too many liquid assets?

Part 2 (Accounts Receivables)

Microsoft provided the following disclosure related to its accounts receivable.

Allowance for Doubtful Accounts. The allowance for doubtful accounts reflects our best estimate of probable losses inherent in the accounts receivable balance. We determine the allowance based on known troubled accounts, historical experience, and other currently available evidence. Activity in the allowance for doubtful accounts is as follows:

(in millions)

Year Ended June 30	Balance at beginning of period	Charged to costs and expenses	Write-offs and other	Balance at end of period
2002	$174	$192	$(157)	$209
2003	209	118	(85)	242
2004	242	44	(120)	166

Instructions

(a) Compute Microsoft's receivables turnover ratio for 2004 and discuss your results. Microsoft had sales revenue of $36,835 million in 2004.

(b) Reconstruct the summary journal entries for 2004 based on the information in the disclosure.

(c) Briefly discuss how the accounting for bad debts affects the analysis in Part 2 (a).

Comparative Analysis Case

The Coca-Cola Company and PepsiCo, Inc.

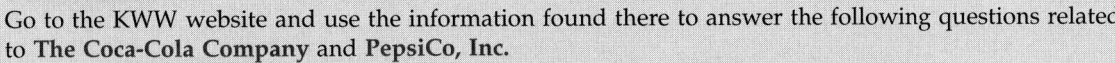

Instructions

Go to the KWW website and use the information found there to answer the following questions related to **The Coca-Cola Company** and **PepsiCo, Inc.**

(a) What were the cash and cash equivalents reported by Coca-Cola and PepsiCo at the end of 2004? What does each company classify as cash equivalents?

(b) What were the accounts receivable (net) for Coca-Cola and PepsiCo at the end of 2004? Which company reports the greater allowance for doubtful accounts receivable (amount and percentage of gross receivable) at the end of 2004?

(c) Assuming that all "net operating revenues" (Coca-Cola) and all "net sales" (PepsiCo) were net *credit* sales, compute the receivables turnover ratio for 2004 for Coca-Cola and PepsiCo; also compute the days outstanding for receivables. What is your evaluation of the difference?

Research Cases

Case 1

Accounting Trends and Techniques, published annually by the American Institute of Certified Public Accountants, is a survey of 600 annual reports to stockholders. The survey covers selected industrial, merchandising, and service companies.

Instructions

Examine the section regarding the use of receivables for financing and answer the following questions.

(a) For the most recent year, how many of the companies surveyed disclosed (1) receivables sold, and (2) receivables used as collateral?

(b) Examine the disclosure provided by a company that sold receivables and a company that used its receivables as collateral. Summarize the major terms of the transactions.

Case 2

The January 20, 1999, edition of the *Wall Street Journal* contained an article by Jonathan Weil titled "**Americredit** Accounting Practices Are Criticized by Research Firm."

Instructions

Read the article and answer the following questions.

(a) Why is Americredit's accounting for receivables criticized?

(b) How does the "cash-out" method of accounting for loan sales respond to the criticisms from part (a)?

(c) What are warning signs that investors can use to identify problems at sub-prime lenders?

Professional Research: Financial Accounting and Reporting

As the new staff person in your company's treasury department, you have been asked to conduct research related to a proposed transfer of receivables. Your supervisor wants the authoritative sources for the following items that are discussed in the securitization agreement.

Instructions

Using the **Financial Accounting Research System (FARS)**, respond to the following items. (Provide text strings used in your search.)

(a) List the current statement and the previous statement that addressed transfers of receivables.

(b) Provide definitions for the following:

  (1) Transfer.

  (2) Recourse.

  (3) Collateral.

(c) Provide other examples (besides recourse and collateral) that qualify as continuing involvement.

Professional Simulation

In this simulation you are asked to address various requirements regarding the accounting for receivables. Prepare responses to all parts.

KWW_Professional_Simulation

| Accounting Receivables | Time Remaining 2 hours 20 minutes | copy | paste | calculator | sheet | standards | help | spliter | done |

| Directions | Situation | Measurement | Financial Statement | Analysis | Explanation | Resources |

Mike Horn Corporation manufactures sweatshirts for sale to athletic-wear retailers. The following information was available for Horn for the years ended December 31, 2006 and 2007.

	December 31, 2006	December 31, 2007
Cash	$ 20,000	$ 15,000
Trade accounts receivable	40,000	?
Allowance for doubtful accounts	5,500	?
Inventories	85,000	80,000
Current liabilities	80,000	86,000
Total credit sales	480,000	550,000
Collections on trade accounts receivable	440,000	500,000

During 2007, Horn had the following transactions.

1. On June 30, sales of $50,000 to a major customer were settled, with Horn accepting a 1-year $50,000 note bearing 11% interest, payable at maturity.

2. Horn factors some accounts receivable at the end of the year. Accounts totaling $40,000 are transferred to First Factors, Inc. with recourse. First Factors will receive the collections from Horn's customers and retain 6% of the balances. Horn is assessed a finance charge of 4% on this transfer. The fair value of the recourse obligation is $4,000.

3. On the basis of the latest available information, the 2007 provision for bad debts is estimated to be 0.8% of credit sales. Horn charged off as uncollectible, accounts with balances of $2,300.

| Directions | Situation | Measurement | Financial Statement | Analysis | Explanation | Resources |

Based on the above transactions, determine the balance for Trade Accounts Receivable and the Allowance for Doubtful Accounts at December 31, 2007.

| Directions | Situation | Measurement | Financial Statement | Analysis | Explanation | Resources |

Prepare the current assets section of Horn's balance sheet at December 31, 2007. The cash balance at December 31, 2007, reflects the following items: checking account $9,600; postage stamps $100; petty cash $300; currency $3,000; customers' checks (post-dated) $2,000.

| Directions | Situation | Measurement | Financial Statement | Analysis | Explanation | Resources |

Compute the current ratio and the receivables turnover ratio for Horn at December 31, 2007. Use these measures to analyze Horn's liquidity. The receivables turnover ratio in 2006 was 10.37.

| Directions | Situation | Measurement | Financial Statement | Analysis | Explanation | Resources |

Discuss how the Analysis above would be affected if Horn had transferred the receivables in a secured borrowing transaction.

Remember to check the book's companion website to find additional resources for this chapter.

wiley.com/college/kieso

VALUATION OF INVENTORIES: A COST-BASIS APPROACH

Inventories in the Crystal Ball

A substantial increase in inventory may be a leading indicator of an upcoming decline in profit margins. Take the auto industry as an example. Detroit's inventories have been growing for several years because the domestic manufacturers like to run the factories at full capacity, even if they are not selling cars as fast as they can make them. The current arrangement is particularly tough for **General Motors**. It overproduces and then tries to push the sales with incentives and month-long "blow-out" sales. GM is hoping that the ever-growing market will cover the problem until customer demand grows to the point where the cars are purchased without so many incentives.

But recently, all that was growing was GM inventories. Not too long ago, the average sticker on a Cadillac DeVille was $54,193, but the net price after incentives was $42,211. This meant that the factory was giving up a substantial amount of profit through rebates, dealer cash, or lease or interest rate subsidies. A similar deal could be had at **Ford**, which was selling Explorers for $25,745 net, a 24 percent reduction for various factory incentives. But inventories at GM and Ford continued to grow, even with these significant incentives.[1]

These data concern investors. As one analyst remarked, "When inventory grows faster than sales, profits drop." That is, when companies face slowing sales and growing inventory, then markdowns in prices usually result. These markdowns, in turn, lead to lower sales revenue and income, thereby squeezing profit margins on sales.[2]

Research supporting these observations indicates that increases in retailers' inventory translate into lower prices and lower net income.[3] Interestingly, the same research found that for manufacturers, only increases in finished goods inventory lead to future profit declines. Increases in raw materials and work-in-process inventories signal that the company is building its inventory to meet increased demand. Therefore, future sales and income will be higher. These research results reinforce the usefulness of the GAAP requirement for manufacturers to disclose their inventory components on the balance sheet or in related notes.

---

[1]J. Flint, "Inventories: Too Much of a Good Thing," *Forbes.com* (September 21, 2004).

[2]S. Pulliam, "Heard on the Street," *Wall Street Journal* (May 21, 1997), p. C1.

[3]Victor Bernard and J. Noel, "Do Inventory Disclosures Predict Sales and Earnings?" *Journal of Accounting, Auditing, and Finance* (March 1991), pp. 145–182.

Learning Objectives

After studying this chapter, you should be able to:

1 Identify major classifications of inventory.

2 Distinguish between perpetual and periodic inventory systems.

3 Identify the effects of inventory errors on the financial statements.

4 Understand the items to include as inventory cost.

5 Describe and compare the cost flow assumptions used to account for inventories.

6 Explain the significance and use of a LIFO reserve.

7 Understand the effect of LIFO liquidations.

8 Explain the dollar-value LIFO method.

9 Identify the major advantages and disadvantages of LIFO.

10 Understand why companies select given inventory methods.

As our opening story indicates, information on inventories and changes in inventory helps to predict financial performance. In this chapter we discuss the basic issues related to accounting and reporting for inventory. The content and organization of the chapter are as follows.

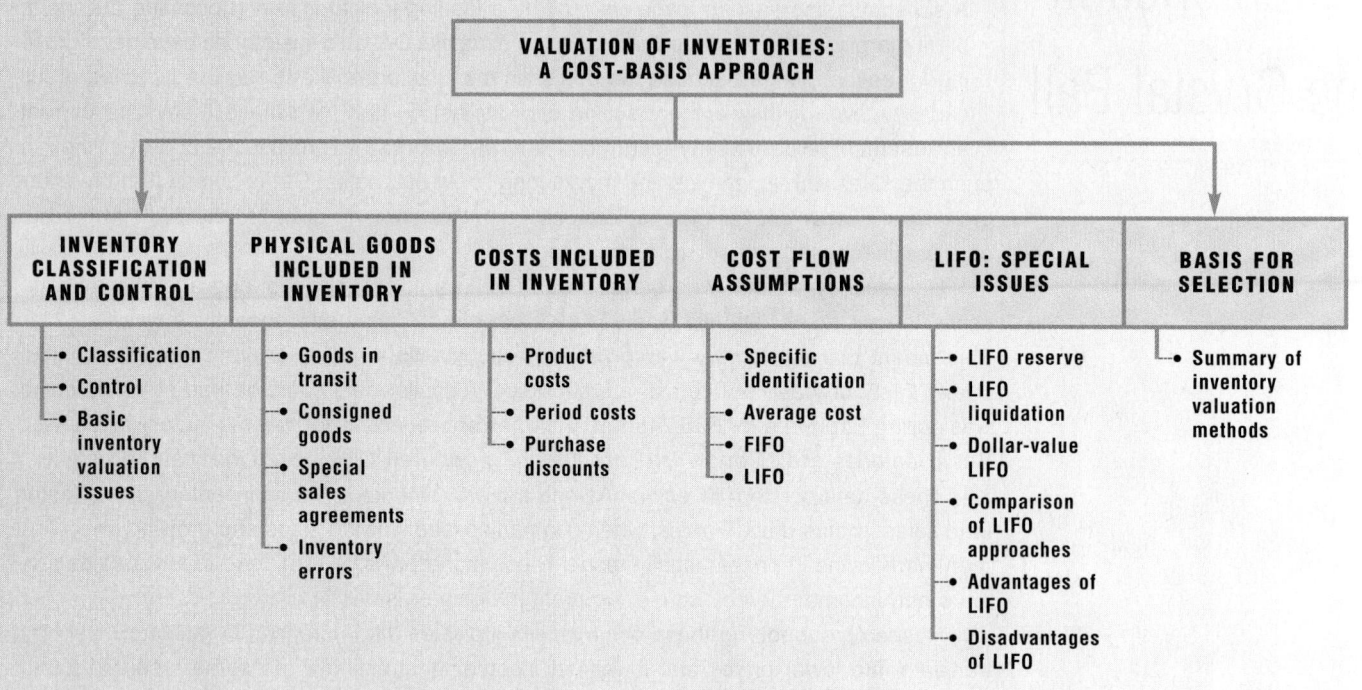

INVENTORY CLASSIFICATION AND CONTROL

Classification

OBJECTIVE 1
Identify major classifications of inventory.

Inventories are asset items that a company holds for sale in the ordinary course of business, or goods that it will use or consume in the production of goods to be sold. The description and measurement of inventory require careful attention. The investment in inventories is frequently the largest current asset of merchandising (retail) and manufacturing businesses.

A **merchandising concern,** such as **Wal-Mart**, usually purchases its merchandise in a form ready for sale. It reports the cost assigned to unsold units left on hand as **merchandise inventory.** Only one inventory account, Merchandise Inventory, appears in the financial statements.

Manufacturing concerns, on the other hand, produce goods to sell to merchandising firms. Many of the largest U.S. businesses are manufacturers, such as **Boeing, IBM, ExxonMobil, Procter & Gamble, Ford,** and **Motorola.** Although the products they produce may differ, manufacturers normally have three inventory accounts—Raw Materials, Work in Process, and Finished Goods.

A company reports the cost assigned to goods and materials on hand but not yet placed into production as **raw materials inventory.** Raw materials include the wood to make a baseball bat or the steel to make a car. These materials can be traced directly to the end product.

At any point in a continuous production process some units are only partially processed. The cost of the raw material for these unfinished units, plus the direct labor

UNDERLYING CONCEPTS

Because inventory provides future economic benefits to the company (revenue from sales), it meets the definition of an asset. Inventory costs will be matched against revenue in the period that sales occur.

cost applied specifically to this material and a ratable share of manufacturing overhead costs, constitute the **work in process inventory**.

Companies report the costs identified with the completed but unsold units on hand at the end of the fiscal period as **finished goods inventory**. Illustration 8-1 contrasts the financial statement presentation of inventories of **Wal-Mart** (a merchandising company) with those of **Caterpillar** (a manufacturing company.) The remainder of the balance sheet is essentially similar for the two types of companies.

ILLUSTRATION 8-1
Comparison of Presentation of Current Assets for Merchandising and Manufacturing Companies

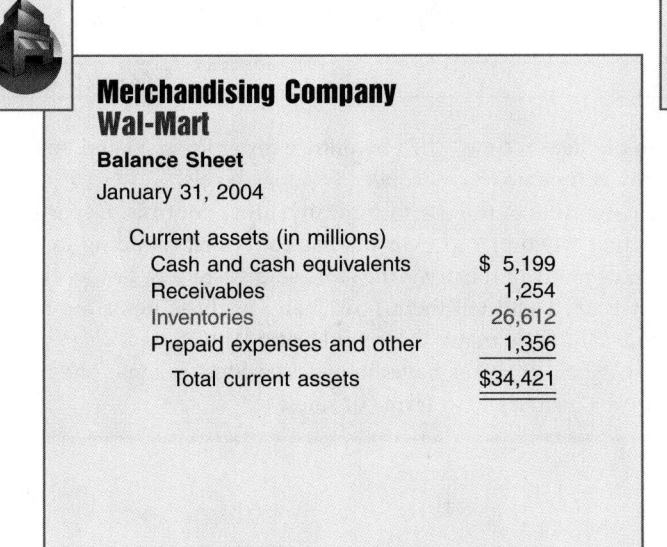

Merchandising Company
Wal-Mart

Balance Sheet
January 31, 2004

Current assets (in millions)	
Cash and cash equivalents	$ 5,199
Receivables	1,254
Inventories	26,612
Prepaid expenses and other	1,356
Total current assets	$34,421

Manufacturing Company
Caterpillar

Balance Sheet
December 31, 2004

Current assets (in millions)		
Cash		$ 445
Accounts receivable		13,969
Inventories		
Raw materials	$1,592	
Work in process	664	
Finished goods	2,209	
Supplies	210	
Total inventories		4,675
Other current assets		1,767
Total current assets		$20,856

As indicated above, a manufacturing company, like **Caterpillar**, also might include a Manufacturing or Factory **Supplies Inventory** account. In it, Caterpillar would include such items as machine oils, nails, cleaning material, and the like—supplies that are used in production but are not the primary materials being processed.

Illustration 8-2 shows the differences in the flow of costs through a merchandising company and a manufacturing company.

Additional Inventory Disclosures

ILLUSTRATION 8-2
Flow of Costs through Manufacturing and Merchandising Companies

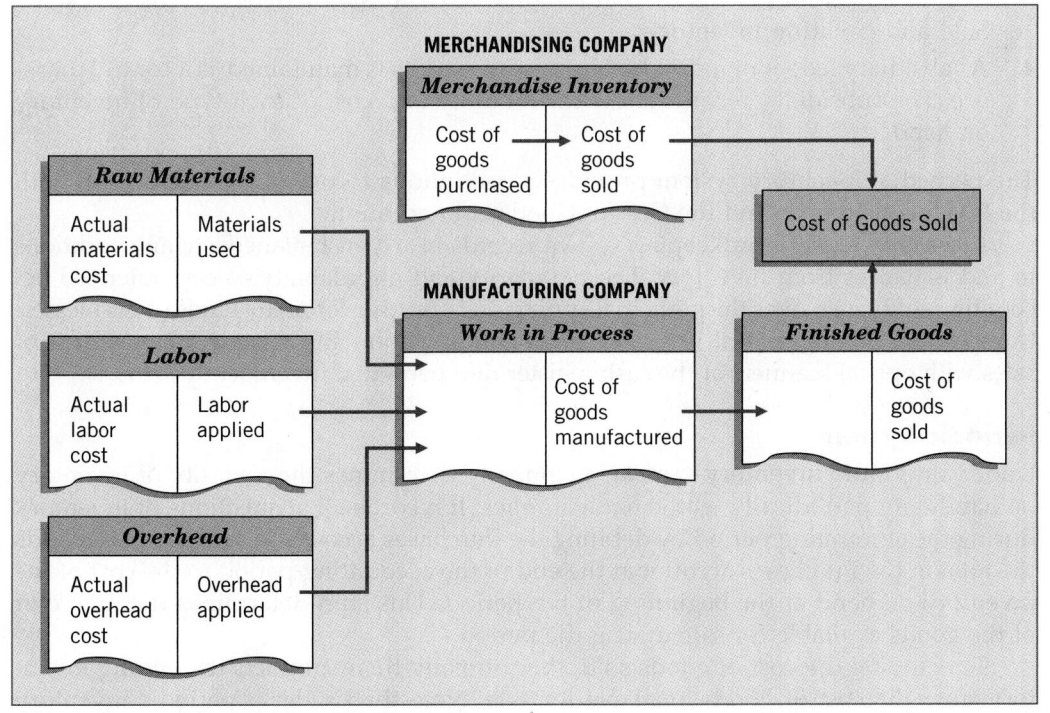

Control

For various reasons, management is vitally interested in inventory planning and control. Whether a company manufactures or merchandises goods, it needs an accurate accounting system with up-to-date records. It may lose sales and customers if it does not stock products in the desired style, quality, and quantity. Further, companies must monitor inventory levels carefully to limit the financing costs of carrying large amounts of inventory.

Companies use one of two types of systems for maintaining accurate inventory records—the perpetual system or the periodic system.

WHAT DO THE
NUMBERS MEAN?

STAYING LEAN

With the introduction and use of "just-in-time" (JIT) inventory order systems and better supplier relationships, many companies have leaner inventory levels.

Wal-Mart provides a classic example of the use of tight inventory controls. Department managers use a scanner that when placed over the bar code corresponding to a particular item, will tell them how many of the items the store sold yesterday, last week, and over the same period last year. It will tell them how many of those items are in stock, how many are on the way, and how many the neighboring Wal-Marts are carrying (in case one store runs out). Such practices have helped Wal-Mart become one of the top-ranked companies on the Fortune 500 in terms of sales.

Perpetual System

OBJECTIVE 2
Distinguish between perpetual and periodic inventory systems.

A **perpetual inventory system** continuously tracks changes in the Inventory account. That is, a company records all purchases and sales (issues) of goods directly in the Inventory account **as they occur.** The accounting features of a perpetual inventory system are as follows.

1 Purchases of merchandise for resale or raw materials for production are debited to Inventory rather than to Purchases.

2 Freight-in, purchase returns and allowances, and purchase discounts are debited to Inventory rather than in separate accounts.

3 Cost of goods sold is recorded at the time of each sale by debiting Cost of Goods Sold and crediting Inventory.

4 A subsidiary ledger of individual inventory records is maintained as a control measure. The subsidiary records show the quantity and cost of each type of inventory on hand.

The perpetual inventory system provides a continuous record of the balances in both the Inventory account and the Cost of Goods Sold account.

A computerized recordkeeping system records nearly instantaneously any additions to and issuances from inventory. The popularity and affordability of computerized accounting software makes the perpetual system cost-effective for many kinds of businesses. Companies like **Target, Best Buy,** and **Sears Holdings** now incorporate the recording of sales with optical scanners at the cash register into perpetual inventory systems.

Periodic System

Under a **periodic inventory system**, a company determines the quantity of inventory on hand only periodically, as the name implies. It records all acquisitions of inventory during the accounting period by debiting the Purchases account. A company then adds the total in the Purchases account at the end of the accounting period to the cost of the inventory on hand at the beginning of the period. This sum determines the total cost of the goods available for sale during the period.

To compute the cost of goods sold, the company then subtracts the ending inventory from the cost of goods available for sale. Note that under a periodic inventory system, the cost of goods sold is a residual amount that depends on a physically counted ending inventory.

Once a year, companies take the **physical inventory count** required by a periodic system.[4] However, most companies need more current information regarding their inventory levels to protect against stockouts or overpurchasing and to aid in preparation of monthly or quarterly financial data. As a consequence, many companies use a **modified perpetual inventory system**. This system provides detailed inventory records of increases and decreases in quantities only—not dollar amounts. It is merely a memorandum device outside the double-entry system, which helps in determining the level of inventory at any point in time.

Whether a company maintains a perpetual inventory in quantities and dollars or in quantities only, or has no perpetual inventory record at all, it probably takes a physical inventory once a year. No matter what type of inventory records companies use, they all face the danger of loss and error. Waste, breakage, theft, improper entry, failure to prepare or record requisitions, and other similar possibilities may cause the inventory records to differ from the actual inventory on hand. Thus all companies need periodic verification of the inventory records by actual count, weight, or measurement, with the counts compared with the detailed inventory records. A company corrects the records to agree with the quantities actually on hand.

Insofar as possible, companies should take the physical inventory near the end of their fiscal year, to properly report inventory quantities in their annual accounting reports. Because this is not always possible, however, physical inventories taken within two or three months of the year's end are satisfactory, if a company maintains detailed inventory records with a fair degree of accuracy.

To illustrate the difference between a perpetual and a periodic system, assume that Fesmire Company had the following transactions during the current year.

Beginning inventory	100 units at $ 6 =	$ 600
Purchases	900 units at $ 6 =	$5,400
Sales	600 units at $12 =	$7,200
Ending inventory	400 units at $ 6 =	$2,400

Fesmire records these transactions during the current year as shown in Illustration 8-3.

Perpetual Inventory System		Periodic Inventory System	
1. Beginning inventory, 100 units at $6:			
The inventory account shows the inventory on hand at $600.		The inventory account shows the inventory on hand at $600.	
2. Purchase 900 units at $6:			
Inventory 5,400		Purchases 5,400	
Accounts Payable 5,400		Accounts Payable 5,400	
3. Sale of 600 units at $12:			
Accounts Receivable 7,200		Accounts Receivable 7,200	
Sales 7,200		Sales 7,200	
Cost of Goods Sold 3,600		(No entry)	
(600 at $6)			
Inventory 3,600			
4. End-of-period entries for inventory accounts, 400 units at $6:			
No entry necessary.		Inventory (ending, by count) 2,400	
The account, Inventory, shows the ending		Cost of Goods Sold 3,600	
balance of $2,400		Purchases 5,400	
($600 + $5,400 − $3,600).		Inventory (beginning) 600	

ILLUSTRATION 8-3
Comparative Entries—
Perpetual vs. Periodic

---

[4]In recent years, some companies have developed methods of determining inventories, including statistical sampling, that are sufficiently reliable to make unnecessary an annual physical count of each item of inventory.

When a company uses a perpetual inventory system and a difference exists between the perpetual inventory balance and the physical inventory count, it needs a separate entry to adjust the perpetual inventory account. To illustrate, assume that at the end of the reporting period, the perpetual inventory account reported an inventory balance of $4,000. However, a physical count indicates $3,800 is actually on hand. The entry to record the necessary write-down is as follows.

Inventory Over and Short	200	
Inventory		200

Perpetual inventory overages and shortages generally represent a misstatement of cost of goods sold. The difference results from normal and expected shrinkage, breakage, shoplifting, incorrect recordkeeping, and the like. Inventory Over and Short therefore adjusts Cost of Goods Sold. In practice, companies sometimes report Inventory Over and Short in the "Other revenues and gains" or "Other expenses and losses" section of the income statement, depending on its balance. Note that a company using the periodic inventory system does not report the account Inventory Over and Short. The reason: The periodic method does not have accounting records against which to compare the physical count. Instead, a company buries inventory overages and shortages in cost of goods sold.

BASIC ISSUES IN INVENTORY VALUATION

Goods sold (or used) during an accounting period seldom correspond exactly to the goods bought (or produced) during that period. As a result, inventories either increase or decrease during the period. Companies must then allocate the cost of all the goods available for sale (or use) between the goods that were sold or used and those that are still on hand. The **cost of goods available for sale or use** is the *sum* of (1) the cost of the goods on hand at the beginning of the period, and (2) the cost of the goods acquired or produced during the period. The **cost of goods sold** is the *difference* between (1) the cost of goods available for sale during the period and (2) the cost of goods on hand at the end of the period. Illustration 8-4 shows these calculations.

ILLUSTRATION 8-4
Computation of Cost of Goods Sold

Beginning inventory, Jan. 1	$100,000
Cost of goods acquired or produced during the year	800,000
Total cost of goods available for sale	900,000
Ending inventory, Dec. 31	200,000
Cost of goods sold during the year	$700,000

Valuing inventories can be complex. It requires determining the following.

1 **The physical goods to include in inventory** (who owns the goods?—goods in transit, consigned goods, special sales agreements).

2 **The costs to include in inventory** (product vs. period costs).

3 **The cost flow assumption to adopt** (specific identification, average cost, FIFO, LIFO, retail, etc.).

We explore these basic issues in the next three sections.

PHYSICAL GOODS INCLUDED IN INVENTORY

Technically, a company should record purchases when it obtains legal title to the goods. In practice, however, a company records acquisitions when it receives the goods. Why? Because it is difficult to determine the exact time of legal passage of title for every purchase. In addition, no material error likely results from such a practice if consistently applied. Illustration 8-5 indicates the general guidelines companies use in evaluating whether the seller or buyer reports an item as inventory. Exceptions to the general guidelines can arise for goods in transit and consigned goods.

ILLUSTRATION 8-5
Guidelines for
Determining Ownership

Goods in Transit

Sometimes purchased merchandise remains in transit—not yet received—at the end of a fiscal period. The accounting for these shipped goods depends on who owns them. For example, a company like **Walgreens** determines ownership by applying the "passage of title" rule. If a supplier ships goods to Walgreens **f.o.b. shipping point**, title passes to Walgreens when the supplier delivers the goods to the common carrier, who acts as an agent for Walgreens. (The abbreviation f.o.b. stands for free on board.) If the supplier ships the goods **f.o.b. destination**, title passes to Walgreens only when it receives the goods from the common carrier. "Shipping point" and "destination" are often designated by a particular location, for example, f.o.b. Denver.

When Walgreens obtains legal title to goods, it must record them as purchases in that fiscal period, assuming a periodic inventory system. Thus, goods shipped to Walgreens f.o.b. shipping point, but in transit at the end of the period, belong to Walgreens. It should show the purchase in its records, because legal title to these goods passed to Walgreens upon shipment of the goods. To disregard such purchases results in understating inventories and accounts payable in the balance sheet, and understating purchases and ending inventories in the income statement.

Consigned Goods

Companies market certain products through a **consignment** shipment. Under this arrangement, a company like Williams' Art Gallery (the consignor) ships various art merchandise to **Sotheby's Holdings** (the consignee), who acts as Williams' agent in selling the **consigned goods**. Sotheby's agrees to accept the goods without any liability, except to exercise due care and reasonable protection from loss or damage, until it sells the goods to a third party. When Sotheby's sells the goods, it remits the revenue, less a selling commission and expenses incurred in accomplishing the sale, to Williams.

Goods out on consignment remain the property of the consignor (Williams in the example above). Williams thus includes the goods in its inventory at purchase price or production cost. Occasionally, and only for a significant amount, the consignor shows the inventory out on consignment as a separate item. Sometimes a consignor reports the inventory on consignment in the notes to the financial statements. For example, **Eagle Clothes, Inc.** reported the following related to consigned goods: "Inventories consist of finished goods shipped on consignment to customers of the Company's subsidiary **April-Marcus, Inc.**"

The consignee makes no entry to the inventory account for goods received. Remember, these goods remain the property of the consignor until sold. In fact, the consignee should be extremely careful *not* to include any of the goods consigned as a part of inventory.

Special Sales Agreements

As we indicated earlier, transfer of legal title is the general guideline used to determine whether a company should include an item in inventory. Unfortunately, transfer of legal title and the underlying substance of the transaction often do not match. For example, legal title may have passed to the purchaser, but the seller of the goods retains the risks of ownership. Conversely, transfer of legal title may not occur, but the economic substance of the transaction is such that the seller no longer retains the risks of ownership.

Three special sales situations are illustrated here to indicate the types of problems companies encounter in practice. These are:

1 Sales with buyback agreement.
2 Sales with high rates of return.
3 Sales on installment.

Sales with Buyback Agreement

Sometimes an enterprise finances its inventory without reporting either the liability or the inventory on its balance sheet. This approach, often referred to as a **product financing arrangement**, usually involves a "sale" with either an implicit or explicit "buyback" agreement.

To illustrate, Hill Enterprises transfers ("sells") inventory to Chase, Inc. and simultaneously agrees to repurchase this merchandise at a specified price over a specified period of time. Chase then uses the inventory as collateral and borrows against it. Chase uses the loan proceeds to pay Hill, which repurchases the inventory in the future. Chase employs the proceeds from repayment to meet its loan obligation.

The essence of this transaction is that Hill Enterprises is financing its inventory—and retaining risk of ownership—even though it transferred to Chase technical legal title to the merchandise. By structuring a transaction in this manner, Hill avoids personal property taxes in certain states. Other advantages of this transaction for Hill are the removal of the current liability from its balance sheet and the ability to manipulate income. For Chase, the purchase of the goods may solve a LIFO liquidation problem (discussed later), or Chase may enter into a similar reciprocal agreement at a later date.

These arrangements are often described in practice as **"parking transactions."** In this situation, Hill simply parks the inventory on Chase's balance sheet for a short period of time. When a repurchase agreement exists at a set price and this price covers all costs of the inventory plus related holding costs, Hill should report the inventory and related liability on its books.[5]

Sales with High Rates of Return

In industries such as publishing, music, toys, and sporting goods, formal or informal agreements often exist that permit purchasers to return inventory for a full or partial refund.

To illustrate, Quality Publishing Company sells textbooks to Campus Bookstores with an agreement that Campus may return for full credit any books not sold. Historically, Campus Bookstores returned approximately 25 percent of the textbooks from Quality Publishing. How should Quality Publishing report its sales transactions?

One alternative is to record the sale at the full amount and establish an estimated sales returns and allowances account. A second possibility is to not record any sale until circumstances indicate the amount of inventory the buyer will return. The key question

UNDERLYING CONCEPTS

Recognizing revenue at the time the inventory is "parked" violates the revenue recognition principle. This principle requires that the earning process be substantially completed. In this case, the economic benefits remain under the control of the seller.

---

[5]"Accounting for Product Financing Arrangements," *Statement of Financial Accounting Standards No. 49* (Stamford, Conn.: FASB, 1981).

is: Under what circumstances should Quality Publishing consider the inventory sold? The answer is that **when Quality Publishing can reasonably estimate the amount of returns**, it should consider the goods sold. Conversely, if returns are unpredictable, Quality Publishing should not consider the goods sold and it should not remove the goods from its inventory.[6]

Sales on Installment

"Goods sold on installment" describes any type of sale in which the sale agreement requires payment in periodic installments over an extended period of time. Because the risk of loss from uncollectibles is higher in installment-sale situations than in other sales transactions, the seller sometimes withholds legal title to the merchandise until the buyer has made all the payments.

The question is whether the seller should consider the inventory sold, even though legal title has not passed. The answer is that **the seller should exclude the goods from its inventory if it can reasonably estimate the percentage of bad debts**.

UNDERLYING CONCEPTS

For goods sold on installment, companies should recognize revenues because they have been substantially earned and are reasonably estimable. Collection is not the most critical event if bad debts can be reasonably estimated.

NO PARKING!

In one of the more elaborate accounting frauds, employees at **Kurzweil Applied Intelligence Inc.** booked millions of dollars in phony inventory sales during a two-year period that straddled two audits and an initial public stock offering. They dummied up phony shipping documents and logbooks to support bogus sales transactions. Then they shipped high-tech equipment, not to customers, but to a public warehouse for "temporary" storage, where some of it sat for 17 months. (Kurzweil still had ownership.)

To foil auditors' attempts to verify the existence of the inventory, Kurzweil employees moved the goods from warehouse to warehouse. To cover the fraudulently recorded sales transactions as auditors closed in, the employees brought back the still-hidden goods, under the pretense that the goods were returned by customers. When auditors uncovered the fraud, the bottom dropped out of Kurzweil's stock.

Source: Adapted from "Anatomy of a Fraud," *Business Week* (September 16, 1996), pp. 90–94.

WHAT DO THE NUMBERS MEAN?

Effect of Inventory Errors

Items incorrectly included or excluded in determining cost of goods sold through inventory misstatements will result in errors in the financial statements. Let's look at two cases, assuming a periodic inventory system.

Ending Inventory Misstated

What would happen if **IBM** correctly records its beginning inventory and purchases, but fails to include some items in ending inventory? In this situation, we would have the following effects on the financial statements at the end of the period.

OBJECTIVE 3
Identify the effects of inventory errors on the financial statements.

Balance Sheet		Income Statement	
Inventory	Understated	Cost of goods sold	Overstated
Retained earnings	Understated		
Working capital	Understated	Net income	Understated
(current assets less current liabilities)			
Current ratio	Understated		
(current assets divided by current liabilities)			

ILLUSTRATION 8-6
Financial Statement Effects of Misstated Ending Inventory

---

[6]"Revenue Recognition When Right of Return Exists," *Statement of Financial Accounting Standards No. 48* (Stamford, Conn.: FASB, 1981).

UNDERLYING CONCEPTS

When inventory is misstated, its presentation lacks representational usefulness.

If ending inventory is understated, working capital and the current ratio are understated. If cost of goods sold is overstated, then net income is understated.

To illustrate the effect on net income over a two-year period (2006–2007), assume that Jay Weiseman Corp. understates its ending inventory by $10,000 in 2006; all other items are correctly stated. The effect of this error is to decrease net income in 2006 and to increase net income in 2007. The error is counterbalanced (offset) in 2007 because beginning inventory is understated and net income is overstated. As Illustration 8-7 shows, the income statement misstates the net income figures for both 2006 and 2007, although the *total* for the two years is correct.

ILLUSTRATION 8-7
Effect of Ending
Inventory Error on Two
Periods

JAY WEISEMAN CORP.
(All figures assumed)

	Incorrect Recording		Correct Recording	
	2006	2007	2006	2007
Revenues	$100,000	$100,000	$100,000	$100,000
Cost of goods sold				
Beginning inventory	25,000	→20,000	25,000	→30,000
Purchased or produced	45,000	60,000	45,000	60,000
Goods available for sale	70,000	80,000	70,000	90,000
Less: Ending inventory	20,000* ←	40,000	30,000 ←	40,000
Cost of goods sold	50,000	40,000	40,000	50,000
Gross profit	50,000	60,000	60,000	50,000
Administrative and selling expenses	40,000	40,000	40,000	40,000
Net income	$ 10,000	$ 20,000	$ 20,000	$ 10,000

Total income
for two years = $30,000

Total income
for two years = $30,000

*Ending inventory understated by $10,000 in 2006.

If Weiseman *overstates* ending inventory in 2006, the reverse effect occurs: Inventory, working capital, current ratio, and net income are overstated and cost of goods sold is understated. The effect of the error on net income will be counterbalanced in 2007, but the income statement misstates both years' net income figures.

Purchases and Inventory Misstated

Suppose that Bishop Company does not record as a purchase certain goods that it owns and does not count them in ending inventory. The effect on the financial statements (assuming this is a purchase on account) is as follows.

ILLUSTRATION 8-8
Financial Statement
Effects of Misstated
Purchases and Inventory

Balance Sheet		Income Statement	
Inventory	Understated	Purchases	Understated
Retained earnings	No effect	Cost of goods sold	No effect
Accounts payable	Understated	Net income	No effect
Working capital	No effect	Inventory (ending)	Understated
Current ratio	Overstated		

Omission of goods from purchases and inventory results in an understatement of inventory and accounts payable in the balance sheet; it also results in an understatement of purchases and ending inventory in the income statement. However, the omission of such goods does not affect net income for the period. Why not? Because Bishop understates both purchases and ending inventory by the same amount—the error is thereby offset in cost of goods sold. Total working capital is unchanged, but the current ratio is overstated because of the omission of equal amounts from inventory and accounts payable.

To illustrate the effect on the current ratio, assume that Bishop *understated* accounts payable and ending inventory by $40,000. Illustration 8-9 shows the understated and correct data.

Purchases and Ending Inventory Understated		Purchases and Ending Inventory Correct	
Current assets	$120,000	Current assets	$160,000
Current liabilities	$ 40,000	Current liabilities	$ 80,000
Current ratio	3 to 1	Current ratio	2 to 1

ILLUSTRATION 8-9
Effects of Purchases and Ending Inventory Errors

The understated data indicate a current ratio of 3 to 1, whereas the correct ratio is 2 to 1. Thus, understatement of accounts payable and ending inventory can lead to a "window dressing" of the current ratio. That is, Bishop can make the current ratio appear better than it is.

If Bishop *overstates* both purchases (on account) and ending inventory, then the effects on the balance sheet are exactly the reverse: The financial statements overstate inventory and accounts payable, and understate the current ratio. The overstatement does not affect cost of goods sold and net income because the errors offset one another. Similarly, working capital is not affected.

We cannot overemphasize the importance of proper inventory measurement in presenting accurate financial statements. For example, **Leslie Fay**, a women's apparel maker, had accounting irregularities that wiped out one year's net income and caused a restatement of the prior year's earnings. One reason: It inflated inventory and deflated cost of goods sold. **Anixter Bros. Inc.** had to restate its income by $1.7 million because an accountant in the antenna manufacturing division overstated the ending inventory, thereby reducing its cost of sales. Similarly, **AM International** allegedly recorded as sold products that were only being rented. As a result, inaccurate inventory and sales figures inappropriately added $7.9 million to pretax income.

COSTS INCLUDED IN INVENTORY

One of the most important problems in dealing with inventories concerns the dollar amount at which to carry the inventory in the accounts. **Companies generally account for the acquisition of inventories, like other assets, on a cost basis.**

OBJECTIVE 4
Understand the items to include as inventory cost.

Product Costs

Product costs are those costs that "attach" to the inventory. As a result, a company records product costs in the inventory account. These costs are directly connected with bringing the goods to the buyer's place of business and converting such goods to a salable condition. Such charges include freight charges on goods purchased, other direct costs of acquisition, and labor and other production costs incurred in processing the goods up to the time of sale.

It seems proper also to allocate to inventories a share of any buying costs or expenses of a purchasing department, storage costs, and other costs incurred in storing or handling the goods before their sale. However, because of the practical difficulties involved in allocating such costs and expenses, companies usually exclude these items in valuing inventories.

A manufacturing company's costs include direct materials, direct labor, and manufacturing overhead costs. Manufacturing overhead costs include indirect materials, indirect labor, and various costs, such as depreciation, taxes, insurance, and heat and electricity.

WHAT DO THE NUMBERS MEAN?

| *IT WAS THE WILD WEST* |

The practice of promotional payments, also known as vendor allowances, is widespread in the retail world. Eager to meet sales targets or promote their products through shelf placements and in store advertisements, vendors have been happy to grease the palms of retailers with rebates, allowances, and price breaks.

The question is, "How should retailers account for these payments?" Until recently some retailers recorded the payments as a reduction of selling expense. Unfortunately, in some of these cases the retailers had not actually sold the goods. Others accounted for them as a reduction of cost of goods sold.

Recently the SEC sued three executives of **Kmart Holding** and some Kmart vendors for their role in a $24 million accounting fraud that booked vendor allowances early. The scheme apparently allowed some Kmart managers to meet internal profit-margin targets. Similarly, **Royal Ahold** (a large Dutch supermarket operator) discovered that its U.S. Foodservice unit had improperly accounted for vendor payments, resulting in overstated earnings of at least $500 million. In addition, it found inflated profits at two of its other subsidiaries, also caused by improper accounting for vendor payments.

One analyst noted that it was like "the Wild West out there" because the lack of rules about when to recognize these payments and how to classify them allowed a certain amount of lawlessness. As a result, the FASB recently ruled that unless certain conditions are met, these payments must reduce cost of goods sold on the income statement. The accounting now appears right, but it took some frauds to close the accounting gap in this area.

Source: C. Schneider, "Retailers and Vendor Allowances," *CFO.com* (August 13, 2003).

Period Costs

Period costs are those costs that are indirectly related to the acquisition or production of goods. Period costs such as selling expenses and, under ordinary circumstances, general and administrative expenses are therefore not included as part as part of inventory cost.

UNDERLYING CONCEPTS

In capitalizing interest, companies apply both constraints—materiality and cost/benefit.

Yet, conceptually, these expenses are as much a cost of the product as the initial purchase price and related freight charges attached to the product. Why then do companies exclude these costs from inventoriable items? Because companies generally consider selling expenses as more directly related to the cost of goods sold than to the unsold inventory. In addition, period costs, especially administrative expenses, are so unrelated or indirectly related to the immediate production process that any allocation is purely arbitrary.[7]

Interest is another period cost. Companies usually expense **interest costs** associated with getting inventories ready for sale. Supporters of this approach argue that interest costs are really a **cost of financing**. Others contend that interest costs incurred to finance activities associated with readying inventories for sale are as much a **cost**

---

[7]Companies should not record abnormal freight, handling costs, and amounts of wasted materials (spoilage) as inventory costs. If the costs associated with the actual level of spoilage or product defects are greater than the costs associated with normal spoilage or defects, the company should charge the excess as an expense in the current period. "Inventory Costs: An Amendment of ARB No. 43, Chapter 4," *Statement of Financial Accounting Standards No. 151* (Norwalk, Conn.: FASB 2004.)

of the asset as materials, labor, and overhead. Therefore, they reason, companies should capitalize interest costs.

The FASB ruled that companies should capitalize interest costs related to assets constructed for internal use or assets produced as discrete projects (such as ships or real estate projects) for sale or lease.[8] The FASB emphasized that these discrete projects should take considerable time, entail substantial expenditures, and be likely to involve significant amounts of interest cost. A company should not capitalize interest costs for inventories that it routinely manufactures or otherwise produces in large quantities on a repetitive basis. In this case, the informational benefit does not justify the cost.

Treatment of Purchase Discounts

The use of a **Purchase Discounts** account in a periodic inventory system indicates that the company is reporting its purchases and accounts payable at the gross amount. If a company uses this **gross method**, it reports purchase discounts as a deduction from purchases on the income statement.

Another approach is to record the purchases and accounts payable at an amount **net of the cash discounts**. In this approach, the company records failure to take a purchase discount within the discount period in a Purchase Discounts Lost account. If a company uses this **net method**, it considers purchase discounts lost as a financial expense and reports it in the "Other expenses and losses" section of the income statement. This treatment is considered better for two reasons: (1) It provides a correct reporting of the cost of the asset and related liability. (2) It can measure management inefficiency by holding management responsible for discounts not taken.

To illustrate the difference between the gross and net methods, assume the following transactions.

ILLUSTRATION 8-10
Entries under Gross and Net Methods

Gross Method			Net Method		
Purchase cost $10,000, terms 2/10, net 30:					
Purchases	10,000		Purchases	9,800	
Accounts Payable		10,000	Accounts Payable		9,800
Invoices of $4,000 are paid within discount period:					
Accounts Payable	4,000		Accounts Payable	3,920	
Purchase Discounts		80	Cash		3,920
Cash		3,920			
Invoices of $6,000 are paid after discount period:					
Accounts Payable	6,000		Accounts Payable	5,880	
Cash		6,000	Purchase Discounts Lost	120	
			Cash		6,000

UNDERLYING CONCEPTS

Not using the net method because of resultant difficulties is an example of the application of the cost/benefit constraint.

Many believe that the somewhat more complicated net method is not justified by the resulting benefits. This could account for the widespread use of the less logical but simpler gross method. In addition, some contend that management is reluctant to report in the financial statements the amount of purchase discounts lost.

---

[8]"Capitalization of Interest Cost," *Statement of Financial Accounting Standards No. 34* (Stamford, Conn.: FASB, 1979). The reporting rules related to interest cost capitalization have their greatest impact in accounting for long-term assets. We therefore discuss them in Chapter 10.

WHAT DO THE NUMBERS MEAN?

Does it really matter *where* a company reports certain costs in its income statement, as long as it includes them all as expenses in computing income?

For e-tailers, such as **Amazon.com** or **Drugstore.com**, *where* they report certain selling costs does appear to be important. Contrary to well-established retailer practices, these companies insist on reporting some selling costs—fulfillment costs related to inventory shipping and warehousing—as part of administrative expenses, instead of as cost of goods sold. This practice is allowable within GAAP, *if* applied consistently and adequately disclosed. Although the practice doesn't affect the bottom line, it does make the e-tailers' gross margins look better. For example, at one time Amazon.com reported $265 million of these costs in one quarter. Some experts thought Amazon.com should include those charges in costs of goods sold, which would substantially lower its gross profit, as shown below.

(in millions)

	E-tailer Reporting	Traditional Reporting
Sales	$2,795	$2,795
Cost of goods sold	2,132	2,397
Gross profit	$ 663	$ 398
Gross margin %	24%	14%

Similarly, if **Drugstore.com** and **eToys.com** made similar adjustments, their gross margins would go from positive to negative.

Thus, if you want to be able to compare the operating results of e-tailers to other traditional retailers, it might be a good idea to have a good accounting map in order to navigate their income statements and how they report certain selling costs.

Source: Adapted from P. Elstrom, "The End of Fuzzy Math?" *Business Week*, e.Biz—Net Worth (December 11, 2000). See also *EITF No. 00–10*, "Accounting for Shipping and Handling Fees and Costs." Under this standard, companies must disclose the accounting policy for classifying these selling costs in income.

WHICH COST FLOW ASSUMPTION TO ADOPT?

OBJECTIVE 5
Describe and compare the cost flow assumptions used to account for inventories.

During any given fiscal period, companies typically purchase merchandise at several different prices. If a company prices inventories at cost and it made numerous purchases at different unit costs, which cost price should it use? Conceptually, a specific identification of the given items sold and unsold seems optimal. But this measure often proves both expensive and impossible to achieve. Consequently, companies use one of several systematic inventory **cost flow assumptions**.

Indeed, the actual physical flow of goods and the cost flow assumption often greatly differ. **There is no requirement that the cost flow assumption adopted be consistent with the physical movement of goods.** A company's major objective in selecting a method should be to choose the one that, under the circumstances, most clearly reflects periodic income.[9]

To illustrate, assume that Call-Mart Inc. had the following transactions in its first month of operations.

Date	Purchases	Sold or Issued	Balance
March 2	2,000 @ $4.00		2,000 units
March 15	6,000 @ $4.40		8,000 units
March 19		4,000 units	4,000 units
March 30	2,000 @ $4.75		6,000 units

---

[9]"Restatement and Revision of Accounting Research Bulletins," *Accounting Research Bulletin No. 43* (New York: AICPA, 1953), Ch. 4, Statement 4.

From this information, Call-Mart computes the ending inventory of 6,000 units and the cost of goods available for sale (beginning inventory + purchases) of $43,900 [(2,000 @ $4.00) + (6,000 @ $4.40) + (2,000 @ $4.75)]. The question is, which price or prices should it assign to the 6,000 units of ending inventory? The answer depends on which cost flow assumption it uses.

Specific Identification

Specific identification calls for identifying each item sold and each item in inventory. A company includes in cost of goods sold the costs of the specific items sold. It includes in inventory the costs of the specific items on hand. This method may be used only in instances where it is practical to separate physically the different purchases made. As a result, most companies only use this method when handling a relatively small number of costly, easily distinguishable items. In the retail trade this includes some types of jewelry, fur coats, automobiles, and some furniture. In manufacturing it includes special orders and many products manufactured under a job cost system.

To illustrate, assume that Call-Mart Inc.'s 6,000 units of inventory consists of 1,000 units from the March 2 purchase, 3,000 from the March 15 purchase, and 2,000 from the March 30 purchase. Illustration 8-11 shows how Call-Mart computes the ending inventory and cost of goods sold.

Date	No. of Units	Unit Cost	Total Cost
March 2	1,000	$4.00	$ 4,000
March 15	3,000	4.40	13,200
March 30	2,000	4.75	9,500
Ending inventory	6,000		$26,700
Cost of goods available for sale (computed in previous section)		$43,900	
Deduct: Ending inventory		26,700	
Cost of goods sold		$17,200	

ILLUSTRATION 8-11
Specific Identification Method

This method appears ideal. Specific identification matches actual costs against actual revenue. Thus, a company reports ending inventory at actual cost. In other words, **under specific identification the cost flow matches the physical flow of the goods.** On closer observation, however, this method has certain deficiencies.

Some argue that specific identification allows a company to manipulate net income. For example, assume that a wholesaler purchases identical plywood early in the year at three different prices. When it sells the plywood, the wholesaler can select either the lowest or the highest price to charge to expense. It simply selects the plywood from a specific lot for delivery to the customer. A business manager, therefore, can manipulate net income by delivering to the customer the higher- or lower-priced item, depending on whether the company seeks lower or higher reported earnings for the period.

Another problem relates to the arbitrary allocation of costs that sometimes occurs with specific inventory items. For example, a company often faces difficulty in relating shipping charges, storage costs, and discounts directly to a given inventory item. This results in allocating these costs somewhat arbitrarily, leading to a "breakdown" in the precision of the specific identification method.[10]

---

[10]The motion picture industry provides a good illustration of the cost allocation problem. Often actors receive a percentage of net income for a given movie or television program. Some actors, however, have alleged that their programs have been extremely profitable to the motion picture studios but they have received little in the way of profit sharing. Actors contend that the studios allocate additional costs to successful projects to avoid sharing profits.

Average Cost

As the name implies, the **average cost method** prices items in the inventory on the basis of the average cost of all similar goods available during the period. To illustrate use of the periodic inventory method (amount of inventory computed at the end of the period), Call-Mart computes the ending inventory and cost of goods sold using a **weighted-average method** as follows.

ILLUSTRATION 8-12
Weighted-Average
Method—Periodic
Inventory

Date of Invoice	No. Units	Unit Cost	Total Cost
March 2	2,000	$4.00	$ 8,000
March 15	6,000	4.40	26,400
March 30	2,000	4.75	9,500
Total goods available	10,000		$43,900

Weighted-average cost per unit $\dfrac{\$43,900}{10,000} = \$4.39$

Inventory in units 6,000 units
Ending inventory 6,000 × $4.39 = $26,340

Cost of goods available for sale	$43,900
Deduct: Ending inventory	26,340
Cost of goods sold	$17,560

In computing the average cost per unit, Call-Mart includes the beginning inventory, if any, both in the total units available and in the total cost of goods available.

Companies use the **moving-average method** with perpetual inventory records. Illustration 8-13 shows the application of the average cost method for perpetual records.

ILLUSTRATION 8-13
Moving-Average
Method—Perpetual
Inventory

Date	Purchased		Sold or Issued	Balance	
March 2	(2,000 @ $4.00)	$ 8,000		(2,000 @ $4.00)	$ 8,000
March 15	(6,000 @ 4.40)	26,400		(8,000 @ 4.30)	34,400
March 19			(4,000 @ $4.30)		
			$17,200	(4,000 @ 4.30)	17,200
March 30	(2,000 @ 4.75)	9,500		(6,000 @ 4.45)	26,700

In this method, Call-Mart computes a **new average unit cost** each time it makes a purchase. For example, on March 15, after purchasing 6,000 units for $26,400, Call-Mart has 8,000 units costing $34,400 ($8,000 plus $26,400) on hand. The average unit cost is $34,400 divided by 8,000, or $4.30. Call-Mart uses this unit cost in costing withdrawals until it makes another purchase. At that point, Call-Mart computes a new average unit cost. Accordingly, the company shows the cost of the 4,000 units withdrawn on March 19 at $4.30, for a total cost of goods sold of $17,200. On March 30, following the purchase of 2,000 units for $9,500, Call-Mart determines a new unit cost of $4.45, for an ending inventory of $26,700.

Companies often use average cost methods for practical rather than conceptual reasons. These methods are simple to apply and objective. They are not as subject to income manipulation as some of the other inventory pricing methods. In addition, proponents of the average cost methods reason that measuring a specific physical flow of inventory is often impossible. Therefore, it is better to cost items on an average-price basis. This argument is particularly persuasive when dealing with similar inventory items.

First-In, First-Out (FIFO)

The **FIFO (first-in, first-out) method** assumes that a company uses goods in the order in which it purchases them. In other words, the FIFO method assumes that **the first goods purchased are the first used** (in a manufacturing concern) **or the first sold** (in a merchandising concern). The inventory remaining must therefore represent the most recent purchases.

To illustrate, assume that Call-Mart uses the periodic inventory system. It determines its cost of the ending inventory by taking the cost of the most recent purchase and working back until it accounts for all units in the inventory. Call-Mart determines its ending inventory and cost of goods sold as shown in Illustration 8-14.

Date	No. Units	Unit Cost	Total Cost
March 30	2,000	$4.75	$ 9,500
March 15	4,000	4.40	17,600
Ending inventory	6,000		$27,100

Cost of goods available for sale		$43,900
Deduct: Ending inventory		27,100
Cost of goods sold		$16,800

ILLUSTRATION 8-14
FIFO Method—Periodic Inventory

If Call-Mart instead uses a perpetual inventory system in quantities and dollars, it attaches a cost figure to each withdrawal. Then the cost of the 4,000 units removed on March 19 consists of the cost of the items purchased on March 2 and March 15. Illustration 8-15 shows the inventory on a FIFO basis perpetual system for Call-Mart.

Date	Purchased		Sold or Issued	Balance	
March 2	(2,000 @ $4.00)	$ 8,000		2,000 @ $4.00	$ 8,000
March 15	(6,000 @ 4.40)	26,400		2,000 @ 4.00 } 6,000 @ 4.40 }	34,400
March 19			2,000 @ $4.00 } 2,000 @ 4.40 } ($16,800)	4,000 @ 4.40	17,600
March 30	(2,000 @ 4.75)	9,500		4,000 @ 4.40 } 2,000 @ 4.75 }	27,100

ILLUSTRATION 8-15
FIFO Method—Perpetual Inventory

Here, the ending inventory is $27,100, and the cost of goods sold is $16,800 [(2,000 @ 4.00) + (2,000 @ $4.40)].

Notice that in these two FIFO examples, the cost of goods sold ($16,800) and ending inventory ($27,100) are the same. **In all cases where FIFO is used, the inventory and cost of goods sold would be the same at the end of the month whether a perpetual or periodic system is used.** Why? Because the same costs will always be first in and, therefore, first out. This is true whether a company computes cost of goods sold as it sells goods throughout the accounting period (the perpetual system) or as a residual at the end of the accounting period (the periodic system).

One objective of FIFO is to approximate the physical flow of goods. When the physical flow of goods is actually first-in, first-out, the FIFO method closely approximates specific identification. At the same time, it prevents manipulation of income. With FIFO, a company cannot pick a certain cost item to charge to expense.

Another advantage of the FIFO method is that the ending inventory is close to current cost. Because the first goods in are the first goods out, the ending inventory amount consists of the most recent purchases. This is particularly true with rapid inventory turnover. This approach generally approximates replacement cost on the balance sheet when price changes have not occurred since the most recent purchases.

However, the FIFO method fails to match current costs against current revenues on the income statement. A company charges the oldest costs against the more current revenue, possibly distorting gross profit and net income.

INTERNATIONAL INSIGHT

International accounting standards do not permit LIFO.

Last-In, First-Out (LIFO)

The **LIFO (last-in, first-out) method** matches the cost of the last goods purchased against revenue. If Call-Mart Inc. uses a periodic inventory system, it assumes that **the cost of the total quantity sold or issued during the month comes from the most recent purchases**. Call Mart prices the ending inventory by using the total units as a basis of computation and disregards the exact dates of sales or issuances. For example, assume that the cost of the 4,000 units withdrawn absorbed the 2,000 units purchased on March 30 and 2,000 of the 6,000 units purchased on March 15. Illustration 8-16 shows how Call-Mart computes the inventory and related cost of goods sold, using the periodic inventory method.

ILLUSTRATION 8-16
LIFO Method—Periodic
Inventory

Date of Invoice	No. Units	Unit Cost	Total Cost
March 2	2,000	$4.00	$ 8,000
March 15	4,000	4.40	17,600
Ending inventory	6,000		$25,600
Goods available for sale		$43,900	
Deduct: Ending inventory		25,600	
Cost of goods sold		$18,300	

If Call-Mart keeps a perpetual inventory record in quantities and dollars, use of the LIFO method results in **different ending inventory and cost of goods sold amounts than the amounts calculated under the periodic method**. Illustration 8-17 shows these differences under the perpetual method.

ILLUSTRATION 8-17
LIFO Method—Perpetual
Inventory

Date	Purchased		Sold or Issued		Balance	
March 2	(2,000 @ $4.00)	$ 8,000			2,000 @ $4.00	$ 8,000
March 15	(6,000 @ 4.40)	26,400			2,000 @ 4.00 } 6,000 @ 4.40 }	34,400
March 19			(4,000 @ $4.40) $17,600		2,000 @ 4.00 } 2,000 @ 4.40 }	16,800
March 30	(2,000 @ 4.75)	9,500			2,000 @ 4.00 } 2,000 @ 4.40 } 2,000 @ 4.75 }	26,300

Tutorial on Inventory Methods

The month-end periodic inventory computation presented in Illustration 8-16 (inventory $25,600 and cost of goods sold $18,300) shows a different amount from the perpetual inventory computation (inventory $26,300 and cost of goods sold $17,600). The periodic system matches the total withdrawals for the month with the total purchases for the month in applying the last-in, first-out method. In contrast, the perpetual system matches each withdrawal with the immediately preceding purchases. In effect, the periodic computation assumed that Call Mart included the cost of the goods that it purchased on March 30 in the sale or issue on March 19.

SPECIAL ISSUES RELATED TO LIFO

LIFO Reserve

OBJECTIVE 6
Explain the significance and use of a LIFO reserve.

Many companies use LIFO for tax and external reporting purposes. However, they maintain a FIFO, average cost, or standard cost system for internal reporting purposes. There are several reasons to do so: (1) Companies often base their pricing decisions on a FIFO, average, or standard cost assumption, rather than on a LIFO basis. (2) Record-keeping on some other basis is easier because the LIFO assumption usually does not approximate the physical flow of the product. (3) Profit-sharing and other bonus arrangements often depend on a non-LIFO inventory assumption. Finally, (4) the use of a pure LIFO system is troublesome for interim periods, which require estimates of year-end quantities and prices.

The difference between the inventory method used for internal reporting purposes and LIFO is the Allowance to Reduce Inventory to LIFO or the **LIFO reserve**. The change in the allowance balance from one period to the next is the **LIFO effect**. The LIFO effect is the adjustment that companies must make to the accounting records in a given year.

To illustrate, assume that Acme Boot Company uses the FIFO method for internal reporting purposes and LIFO for external reporting purposes. At January 1, 2007, the Allowance to Reduce Inventory to LIFO balance is $20,000. At December 31, 2007, the balance should be $50,000. As a result, Acme Boot realizes a LIFO effect of $30,000 and makes the following entry at year-end.

Cost of Goods Sold	30,000	
Allowance to Reduce Inventory to LIFO		30,000

Acme Boot deducts the Allowance to Reduce Inventory to LIFO from inventory to ensure that it states the inventory on a LIFO basis at year-end.

Companies should disclose either the LIFO reserve or the replacement cost of the inventory, as shown in Illustration 8-18.[11]

American Maize-Products Company

Inventories (Note 3)	$80,320,000

Note 3: Inventories. At December 31, $31,516,000 of inventories were valued using the LIFO method. This amount is less than the corresponding replacement value by $3,765,000.

ILLUSTRATION 8-18
Note Disclosures of
LIFO Reserve

Brown Shoe Company, Inc.
(in thousands)

	Current Year	Previous Year
Inventories, (Note 1)	$365,989	$362,274

Note 1 (partial): Inventories. Inventories are valued at the lower of cost or market determined principally by the last-in, first-out (LIFO) method. If the first-in, first-out (FIFO) cost method had been used, inventories would have been $11,709 higher in the current year and $13,424 higher in the previous year.

*Additional LIFO Reserve
Disclosures*

LIFO Liquidation

Up to this point, we have emphasized a **specific-goods approach** to costing LIFO inventories (also called **traditional LIFO** or **unit LIFO**). This approach is often unrealistic for two reasons:

OBJECTIVE 7
**Understand the effect
of LIFO liquidations.**

1 When a company has many different inventory items, the accounting cost of tracking each inventory item is expensive.

2 Erosion of the LIFO inventory can easily occur. Referred to as **LIFO liquidation**, this often distorts net income and leads to substantial tax payments.

---

[11]The AICPA Task Force on LIFO Inventory Problems, *Issues Paper* (New York: AICPA, November 30, 1984), pars. 2–24. The SEC has endorsed this issues paper, and therefore the paper has authoritative status for GAAP purposes.

**WHAT DO THE
NUMBERS MEAN?**

COMPARING APPLES TO APPLES

Investors commonly use the current ratio to evaluate a company's liquidity. They compute the current ratio as current assets divided by current liabilities. A higher current ratio indicates that a company is better able to meet its current obligations when they come due. However, it is not meaningful to compare the current ratio for a company using LIFO to one for a company using FIFO. It would be like comparing apples to oranges, since the two companies measure inventory (and cost of goods sold) differently.

To make the current ratio comparable on an apples-to-apples basis, analysts use the LIFO reserve. The following adjustments should do the trick:

Inventory Adjustment: LIFO inventory + LIFO reserve = FIFO inventory

(For cost of goods sold, add the *change* in the LIFO reserve to LIFO cost of goods sold to yield the comparable FIFO amount.)

For **Brown Shoe, Inc.** (see Illustration 8-18), with current assets of $487.8 million and current liabilities of $217.8 million, the current ratio using LIFO is: $487.8 ÷ $217.8 = 2.2. After adjusting for the LIFO effect, Brown's current ratio under FIFO would be: ($487.8 + $11.7) ÷ $217.8 = 2.3.

Thus, without the LIFO adjustment, the Brown Shoe current ratio is understated.

To understand the LIFO liquidation problem, assume that Basler Co. has 30,000 pounds of steel in its inventory on December 31, 2007, with cost determined on a specific-goods LIFO approach.

		Ending Inventory (2007)	
	Pounds	Unit Cost	LIFO Cost
2004	8,000	$ 4	$ 32,000
2005	10,000	6	60,000
2006	7,000	9	63,000
2007	5,000	10	50,000
	30,000		$205,000

As indicated, the ending 2007 inventory for Basler comprises costs from past periods. These costs are called **layers** (increases from period to period). The first layer is identified as the base layer. Illustration 8-19 shows the layers for Basler.

ILLUSTRATION 8-19
Layers of LIFO Inventory

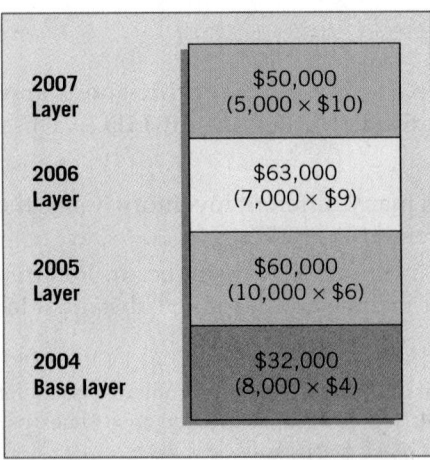

Note the increased price of steel over the 4-year period. In 2008, due to metal short-ages, Basler had to liquidate much of its inventory (a LIFO liquidation). At the end of 2008, only 6,000 pounds of steel remained in inventory. Because the company uses LIFO, Basler liquidates the most recent layer, 2007, first, followed by the 2006 layer, and so on. The result: Basler matches costs from preceding periods against sales revenues re-ported in current dollars. As Illustration 8-20 shows, this leads to a distortion in net in-come and increased taxable income in the current period. Unfortunately **LIFO liqui-dations can occur frequently when using a specific-goods LIFO approach**.

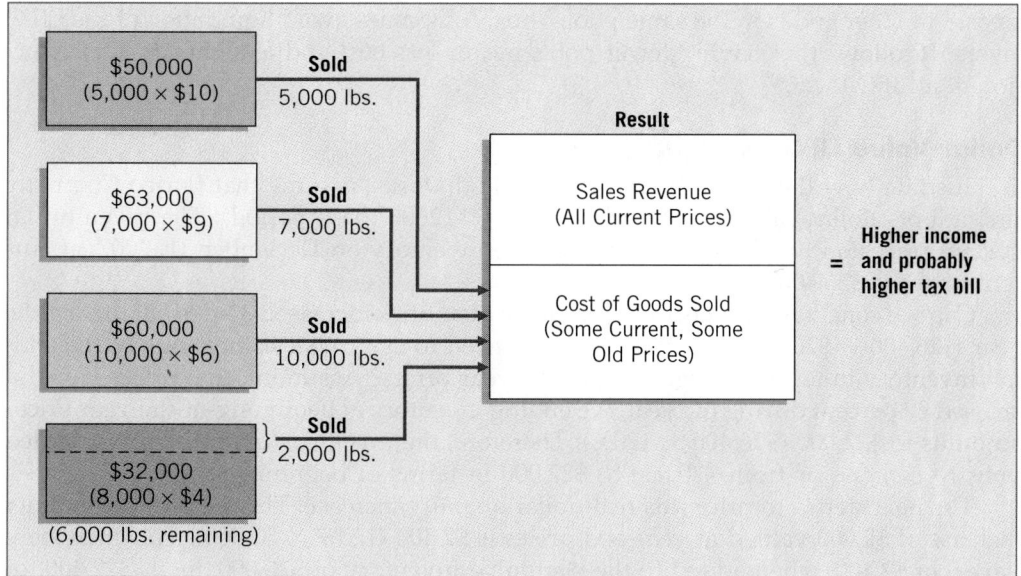

ILLUSTRATION 8-20
LIFO Liquidation

To alleviate the LIFO liquidation problems and to simplify the accounting, com-panies can combine goods into pools. A **pool** groups items of a similar nature. Thus, instead of only identical units, a company combines, and counts as a group, a number of similar units or products. This method, the **specific-goods pooled LIFO approach**, usually results in fewer LIFO liquidations. Why? Because the reduction of one quan-tity in the pool may be offset by an increase in another.

The specific-goods pooled LIFO approach eliminates some of the disadvantages of the specific-goods (traditional) accounting for LIFO inventories. This pooled approach, using quantities as its measurement basis, however, creates other problems.

First, most companies continually change the mix of their products, materials, and production methods. As a result, in employing a pooled approach using quantities, companies must continually redefine the pools. This can be time consuming and costly. Second, even when practical, the approach often results in an erosion ("LIFO liquida-tion") of the layers, thereby losing much of the LIFO costing benefit. An erosion of the layers results due to replacement of a specific good or material in the pool with an-other good or material. The new item may not be similar enough to be treated as part of the old pool. Therefore a company may need to recognize any inflationary profit de-ferred on the old goods as it replaces them.

Dollar-Value LIFO

The dollar-value LIFO method overcomes the problems of redefining pools and erod-ing layers. **The dollar-value LIFO method determines and measures any increases and decreases in a pool in terms of total dollar value, not the physical quantity of the goods in the inventory pool.**

Such an approach has two important advantages over the specific-goods pooled approach. First, companies may include a broader range of goods in a dollar-value

OBJECTIVE 8
Explain the dollar-value LIFO method.

Tutorial on Dollar-Value LIFO

LIFO pool. Second, a dollar-value LIFO pool permits replacement of goods that are similar items, similar in use, or interchangeable. (In contrast, a specific-goods LIFO pool only allows replacement of items that are substantially identical.)

Thus, dollar-value LIFO techniques help protect LIFO layers from erosion. Because of this advantage, companies frequently use the dollar-value LIFO method in practice.[12] Companies use the more traditional LIFO approaches only when dealing with few goods and expecting little change in product mix.

Under the dollar-value LIFO method, one pool may contain the entire inventory. However, companies generally use several pools.[13] In general, the more goods included in a pool, the more likely that increases in the quantities of some goods will offset decreases in other goods in the same pool. Thus, companies avoid liquidation of the LIFO layers. It follows that having fewer pools means less cost and less chance of a reduction of a LIFO layer.[14]

Dollar-Value LIFO Example

To illustrate how the dollar-value LIFO method works, assume that Enrico Company first adopts dollar-value LIFO on December 31, 2006 (base period). The inventory at current prices on that date was $20,000. The inventory on December 31, 2007, at current prices is $26,400.

Can we conclude that Enrico's inventory quantities increased 32 percent during the year ($26,400 ÷ $20,000 = 132%)? First, we need to ask: What is the value of the ending inventory in terms of beginning-of-the-year prices? Assuming that prices have increased 20 percent during the year, the ending inventory at beginning-of-the-year prices amounts to $22,000 ($26,400 ÷ 120%). Therefore, the inventory quantity has increased only 10 percent, or from $20,000 to $22,000 in terms of beginning-of-the-year prices.

The next step is to price this real-dollar quantity increase. This real-dollar quantity increase of $2,000 valued at year-end prices is $2,400 (120% × $2,000). This increment (layer) of $2,400, when added to the beginning inventory of $20,000, totals $22,400 for the December 31, 2007, inventory, as shown below.

First layer—(beginning inventory) in terms of 100	$20,000
Second layer—(2007 increase) in terms of 120	2,400
Dollar-value LIFO inventory, December 31, 2007	$22,400

Note that a layer forms only when the ending inventory at base-year prices exceeds the beginning inventory at base-year prices. And only when a new layer forms must Enrico compute a new index.

---

[12]A study by James M. Reeve and Keith G. Stanga disclosed that the vast majority of respondent companies applying LIFO use the dollar-value method or the dollar-value retail method to apply LIFO. Only a small minority of companies use the specific-goods (unit LIFO) approach or the specific-goods pooling approach. See J.M. Reeve and K.G. Stanga, "The LIFO Pooling Decision," *Accounting Horizons* (June 1987), p. 27.

[13]The Reeve and Stanga study (ibid.) reports that most companies have only a few pools—the median is six for retailers and three for nonretailers. But the distributions are highly skewed; some companies have 100 or more pools. Retailers that use LIFO have significantly more pools than nonretailers. About a third of the nonretailers (mostly manufacturers) use a single pool for their entire LIFO inventory.

[14]A later study shows that when quantities are increasing, multiple pools over a period of time may produce (under rather general conditions) significantly higher cost of goods sold deductions than a single-pool approach. When a stock-out occurs, a single-pool approach may lessen the layer liquidation for that year, but it may not erase the cumulative cost of goods sold advantage accruing to the use of multiple pools built up over the preceding years. See William R. Coon and Randall B. Hayes, "The Dollar Value LIFO Pooling Decision: The Conventional Wisdom Is Too General," *Accounting Horizons* (December 1989), pp. 57–70.

Comprehensive Dollar-Value LIFO Example

To illustrate the use of the dollar-value LIFO method in a more complex situation, assume that Bismark Company develops the following information.

December 31	Inventory at End-of-Year Prices	÷ Price Index (percentage)	= End-of-Year Inventory at Base-Year Prices
(Base year) 2004	$200,000	100	$200,000
2005	299,000	115	260,000
2006	300,000	120	250,000
2007	351,000	130	270,000

At December 31, 2004, Bismark computes the ending inventory under dollar-value LIFO as $200,000, as Illustration 8-21 shows.

Ending Inventory at Base-Year Prices	Layer at Base-Year Prices	Price Index (percentage)	Ending Inventory at LIFO Cost
$200,000	$200,000 ×	100 =	$200,000

ILLUSTRATION 8-21
Computation of 2004
Inventory at LIFO Cost

At December 31, 2005, a comparison of the ending inventory at base-year prices ($260,000) with the beginning inventory at base-year prices ($200,000) indicates that the quantity of goods (in base-year prices) increased $60,000 ($260,000 − $200,000). Bismark prices this increment (layer) at the 2005 index of 115 percent to arrive at a new layer of $69,000. Ending inventory for 2005 is $269,000, composed of the beginning inventory of $200,000 and the new layer of $69,000. Illustration 8-22 shows the computations.

Ending Inventory at Base-Year Prices	Layers at Base-Year Prices	Price Index (percentage)	Ending Inventory at LIFO Cost
$260,000	→2004 $200,000 ×	100 =	$200,000
	→2005 60,000 ×	115 =	69,000
	$260,000		$269,000

ILLUSTRATION 8-22
Computation of 2005
Inventory at LIFO Cost

At December 31, 2006, a comparison of the ending inventory at base-year prices ($250,000) with the beginning inventory at base-year prices ($260,000) indicates a decrease in the quantity of goods of $10,000 ($250,000 − $260,000). If the ending inventory at base-year prices is less than the beginning inventory at base-year prices, **a company must subtract the decrease from the most recently added layer. When a decrease occurs, the company "peels off" previous layers at the prices in existence when it added the layers.** In Bismark's situation, this means that it removes $10,000 in base-year prices from the 2005 layer of $60,000 at base-year prices. It values the balance of $50,000 ($60,000 − $10,000) at base-year prices at the 2005 price index of 115 percent. As a result, it now values this 2005 layer at $57,500 ($50,000 × 115%). Therefore, Bismark computes the ending inventory at $257,500, consisting of the beginning inventory of $200,000 and the second layer of $57,500. Illustration 8-23 (on page 390) shows the computations for 2006.

ILLUSTRATION 8-23
Computation of 2006
Inventory at LIFO Cost

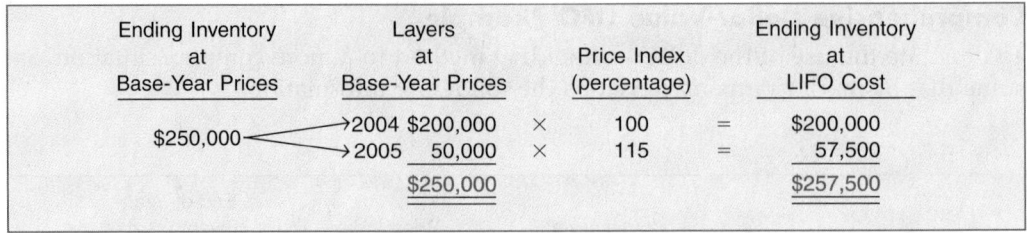

Note that if Bismark eliminates a layer or base (or portion thereof), it cannot rebuild it in future periods. That is, the layer is gone forever.

At December 31, 2007, a comparison of the ending inventory at base-year prices ($270,000) with the beginning inventory at base-year prices ($250,000) indicates an increase in the quantity of goods (in base-year prices) of $20,000 ($270,000 − $250,000). After converting the $20,000 increase to the 2007 price index, the ending inventory is $283,500, composed of the beginning layer of $200,000, a 2005 layer of $57,500, and a 2007 layer of $26,000 ($20,000 × 130%). Illustration 8-24 shows this computation.

ILLUSTRATION 8-24
Computation of 2007
Inventory at LIFO Cost

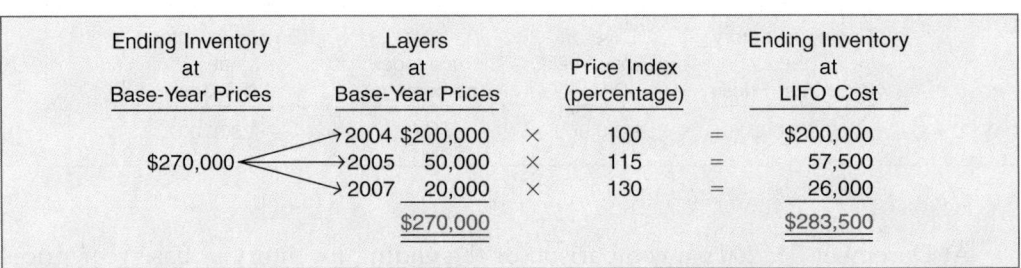

The ending inventory at base-year prices must always equal the total of the layers at base-year prices. Checking that this situation exists will help to ensure correct dollar-value computations.

Selecting a Price Index

Obviously, price changes are critical in dollar-value LIFO. How do companies determine the price indexes? Many companies use the general price-level index that the federal government prepares and publishes each month. The most popular general external price-level index is the **Consumer Price Index for Urban Consumers** (CPI-U).[15] Companies also use more-specific external price indexes. For instance, various organizations compute and publish daily indexes for most commodities (gold, silver, other metals, corn, wheat, and other farm products). Many trade associations prepare indexes for specific product lines or industries. Any of these indexes may be used for dollar-value LIFO purposes.

When a relevant specific external price index is not readily available, a company may compute its own specific internal price index. The desired approach is to price ending inventory at the most current cost. Therefore, a company that chose to compute its own specific internal price index would ordinarily determine current cost by referring to the actual cost of the goods it most recently had purchased. The price index provides a measure of the change in price or cost levels between the base year and the current year. The company then computes the index for each year after the base year. The general formula for computing the index is as follows.

---

[15]Indexes may be **general** (composed of several commodities, goods, or services) or **specific** (for one commodity, good, or service). Additionally, they may be **external** (computed by an outside party, such as the government, commodity exchange, or trade association) or **internal** (computed by the enterprise for its own product or service).

ILLUSTRATION 8-25
Formula for Computing a
Price Index

$$\frac{\text{Ending Inventory for the Period at Current Cost}}{\text{Ending Inventory for the Period at Base-Year Cost}} = \text{Price Index for Current Year}$$

This approach is generally referred to as the **double-extension method**. As its name implies, the value of the units in inventory is extended at *both* base-year prices and current-year prices.

To illustrate this computation, assume that Toledo Company's base-year inventory (January 1, 2007) consisted of the following.

Items	Quantity	Cost per Unit	Total Cost
A	1,000	$ 6	$ 6,000
B	2,000	20	40,000
January 1, 2007, inventory at base-year costs			$46,000

Examination of the ending inventory indicates that the company holds 3,000 units of Item A and 6,000 units of Item B on December 31, 2007. The most recent actual purchases related to these items were as follows.

Items	Purchase Date	Quantity Purchased	Cost per Unit
A	December 1, 2007	4,000	$ 7
B	December 15, 2007	5,000	25
B	November 16, 2007	1,000	22

Toledo double-extends the inventory as shown in Illustration 8-26.

ILLUSTRATION 8-26
Double-Extension
Method of Determining a
Price Index

	12/31/07 Inventory at Base-Year Costs			12/31/07 Inventory at Current-Year Costs		
Items	Units	Base-Year Cost per Unit	Total	Units	Current-Year Cost per Unit	Total
A	3,000	$ 6	$ 18,000	3,000	$ 7	$ 21,000
B	6,000	20	120,000	5,000	25	125,000
B				1,000	22	22,000
			$138,000			$168,000

After the inventories are double-extended, Toledo uses the formula in Illustration 8-25 to develop the index for the current year (2007), as follows.

ILLUSTRATION 8-27
Computation of 2007
Index

$$\frac{\text{Ending Inventory for the Period at Current Cost}}{\text{Ending Inventory for the Period at Base-Year Cost}} = \frac{\$168,000}{\$138,000} = 121.74\%$$

Toledo then applies this index (121.74%) to the layer added in 2007. Note in this illustration that Toledo used the most recent actual purchases to determine current cost; alternatively, it could have used other approaches such as FIFO and average cost. Whichever flow assumption is adopted, a company must use it consistently from one period to another.

Use of the double-extension method is time consuming and difficult where substantial technological change has occurred or where many items are involved. That is, as time passes, the company must determine a new base-year cost for new products, and must keep a base-year cost for each inventory item.[16]

Comparison of LIFO Approaches

We present three different approaches to computing LIFO inventories in this chapter—specific-goods LIFO, specific-goods pooled LIFO, and dollar-value LIFO. As we indicated earlier, the use of the specific-goods LIFO is unrealistic. Most companies have numerous goods in inventory at the end of a period. Costing (pricing) them on a unit basis is extremely expensive and time consuming.

The specific-goods pooled LIFO approach reduces recordkeeping and clerical costs. In addition, it is more difficult to erode the layers because the reduction of one quantity in the pool may be offset by an increase in another. Nonetheless, the pooled approach using quantities as its measurement basis can lead to untimely LIFO liquidations.

As a result, **most companies using a LIFO system employ dollar-value LIFO.** Although the approach appears complex, the logic and the computations are actually quite simple, after determining an appropriate index.

However, problems do exist with the dollar-value LIFO method. The selection of the items to be put in a pool can be subjective.[17] Such a determination, however, is extremely important because manipulation of the items in a pool without conceptual justification can affect reported net income. For example, the SEC noted that some companies have set up pools that are easy to liquidate. As a result, to increase income, a company simply decreases inventory, thereby matching low-cost inventory items to current revenues.

To curb this practice, the SEC has taken a much harder line on the number of pools that companies may establish. In a well-publicized case, **Stauffer Chemical Company** increased the number of LIFO pools from 8 to 280, boosting its net income by $16,515,000 or approximately 13 percent.[18] Stauffer justified the change in its Annual Report on the basis of "achieving a better matching of cost and revenue." The SEC required Stauffer to reduce the number of its inventory pools, contending that some pools were inappropriate and alleging income manipulation.

Major Advantages of LIFO

OBJECTIVE 9
Explain the major advantages and disadvantages of LIFO.

One obvious advantage of LIFO approaches is that the LIFO cost flow often approximates the physical flow of the goods in and out of inventory. For instance, in a coal pile, the last coal in is the first coal out because it is on the top of the pile. The coal remover is not going to take the coal from the bottom of the pile! The coal taken first is the coal placed on the pile last.

However, this is one of only a few situations where the actual physical flow corresponds to LIFO. Therefore most adherents of LIFO use other arguments for its widespread use, as follows.

---

[16]To simplify the analysis, companies may use another approach, initially sanctioned by the Internal Revenue Service for tax purposes. Under this method, a company obtains an index from an outside source or by double-extending only a sample portion of the inventory. For example, the IRS allows all companies to use as their inflation rate for a LIFO pool 80% of the inflation rate reported by the appropriate consumer or producer price indexes prepared by the Bureau of Labor Statistics (BLS). Once the company obtains the index, it divides the ending inventory at current cost by the index to find the base-year cost. Using generally available external indexes greatly simplifies LIFO computations, and frees companies from having to compute internal indexes.

[17]It is suggested that companies analyze how inventory purchases are affected by price changes, how goods are stocked, how goods are used, and if future liquidations are likely. See William R. Cron and Randall Hayes, ibid., p. 57.

[18]Commerce Clearing House, *SEC Accounting Rules* (Chicago: CCH, 1983), par. 4035.

Matching

LIFO matches the more recent costs against current revenues to provide a better measure of current earnings. During periods of inflation, many challenge the quality of non-LIFO earnings, noting that failing to match current costs against current revenues **creates transitory or "paper" profits ("inventory profits")**. Inventory profits occur when the inventory costs matched against sales are less than the inventory replacement cost. This results in understating the cost of goods sold and overstating profit. Using LIFO (rather than a method such as FIFO) matches current costs against revenues, thereby reducing inventory profits.

Tax Benefits/Improved Cash Flow

LIFO's popularity mainly stems from its tax benefits. As long as the price level increases and inventory quantities do not decrease, a deferral of income tax occurs. Why? Because a company matches the items it most recently purchased (at the higher price level) against revenues. For example, when **Fuqua Industries** switched to LIFO, it realized a tax savings of about $4 million. Even if the price level decreases later, the company still temporarily deferred its income taxes. Thus, use of LIFO in such situations improves a company's cash flow.[19]

The tax law requires that if a company uses LIFO for tax purposes, it must also use LIFO for financial accounting purposes[20] (although neither tax law nor GAAP requires a company to pool its inventories in the same manner for book and tax purposes). This requirement is often referred to as the **LIFO conformity rule**. Other inventory valuation methods do not have this requirement.

Future Earnings Hedge

With LIFO, future price declines will not substantially affect a company's future reported earnings. The reason: Since the company records the most recent inventory as sold first, there is not much ending inventory at high prices vulnerable to a price decline. Thus LIFO eliminates or substantially minimizes write-downs to market as a result of price decreases. In contrast, inventory costed under FIFO is more vulnerable to price declines, which can reduce net income substantially.

Major Disadvantages of LIFO

Despite its advantages, LIFO has the following drawbacks.

Reduced Earnings

Many corporate managers view the lower profits reported under the LIFO method in inflationary times as a distinct disadvantage. They would rather have higher reported profits than lower taxes. Some fear that investors may misunderstand an accounting change to LIFO, and that the lower profits may cause the price of the company's stock to fall.

Inventory Understated

LIFO may have a distorting effect on a company's balance sheet. The inventory valuation is normally outdated because the oldest costs remain in inventory. This understatement makes the working capital position of the company appear worse than it

---

[19]In periods of rising prices, the use of fewer pools will translate into greater income tax benefits through the use of LIFO. The use of fewer pools allows companies to offer inventory reductions on some items and inventory increases in others. In contrast, the use of more pools increases the likelihood of liquidating old, low-cost inventory layers and incurring negative tax consequences. See Reeve and Stanga, ibid., pp. 28–29.

[20]Management often selects an accounting procedure because a lower tax results from its use, instead of an accounting method that is conceptually more appealing. Throughout this textbook, we identify accounting procedures that provide income tax benefits to the user.

really is. A good example is **Caterpillar**, which uses LIFO costing for most of its inventory, valued at $4.7 billion at year-end 2004. Under FIFO costing, Caterpillar's inventories have a value of $6.8 billion—almost 50 percent higher than the LIFO amount.

The magnitude and direction of this variation between the carrying amount of inventory and its current price depend on the degree and direction of the price changes and the amount of inventory turnover. The combined effect of rising product prices and avoidance of inventory liquidations increases the difference between the inventory carrying value at LIFO and current prices of that inventory. This magnifies the balance sheet distortion attributed to the use of LIFO.

Physical Flow

LIFO does not approximate the physical flow of the items except in specific situations (such as the coal pile discussed earlier). Originally companies could use LIFO only in certain circumstances. This situation has changed over the years. Now, physical flow characteristics no longer determine whether a company may employ LIFO.

Involuntary Liquidation/Poor Buying Habits

If a company eliminates the base or layers of old costs, it may match old, irrelevant costs against current revenues. A distortion in reported income for a given period may result, as well as detrimental income tax consequences.[21]

Because of the liquidation problem, LIFO may cause poor buying habits. A company may simply purchase more goods and match these goods against revenue to avoid charging the old costs to expense. Furthermore, recall that with LIFO, a company may attempt to manipulate its net income at the end of the year simply by altering its pattern of purchases.[22]

One survey uncovered the following reasons why companies reject LIFO.[23]

ILLUSTRATION 8-28
Why Do Companies
Reject LIFO? Summary of
Responses

Reasons to Reject LIFO	Number	% of Total*
No expected tax benefits		
No required tax payment	34	16%
Declining prices	31	15
Rapid inventory turnover	30	14
Immaterial inventory	26	12
Miscellaneous tax related	38	17
	159	74%
Regulatory or other restrictions	26	12%
Excessive cost		
High administrative costs	29	14%
LIFO liquidation–related costs	12	6
	41	20%
Other adverse consequences		
Lower reported earnings	18	8%
Bad accounting	7	3
	25	11%

*Percentage totals more than 100% as some companies offered more than one explanation.

[21]The AICPA Task Force on LIFO Inventory Problems recommends that companies disclose the effects on income of LIFO inventory liquidations in the notes to the financial statements, but that they do not afford special treatment to the effects in the income statement. *Issues Paper* (New York: AICPA, 1984), pp. 36–37.

[22]For example, **General Tire and Rubber** accelerated raw material purchases at the end of the year to minimize the book profit from a liquidation of LIFO inventories and to minimize income taxes for the year.

[23]Michael H. Granof and Daniel Short, "Why Do Companies Reject LIFO?" *Journal of Accounting, Auditing, and Finance* (Summer 1984), pp. 323–333, Table 1, p. 327.

BASIS FOR SELECTION OF INVENTORY METHOD

How does a company choose among the various inventory methods? Although no absolute rules can be stated, preferability for LIFO usually occurs in either of the following circumstances: (1) if selling prices and revenues have been increasing faster than costs, thereby distorting income, and (2) in situations where LIFO has been traditional, such as department stores and industries where a fairly constant "base stock" is present (such as refining, chemicals, and glass).[24]

Conversely, LIFO is probably inappropriate in the following circumstances: (1) where prices tend to lag behind costs; (2) in situations where specific identification is traditional, such as in the sale of automobiles, farm equipment, art, and antique jewelry; or (3) where unit costs tend to decrease as production increases, thereby nullifying the tax benefit that LIFO might provide.[25]

Tax consequences are another consideration. Switching from FIFO to LIFO usually results in an immediate tax benefit. However, switching from LIFO to FIFO can result in a substantial tax burden. For example, when **Chrysler** (now **DaimlerChrysler**) changed from LIFO to FIFO, it became responsible for an additional $53 million in taxes that the company had deferred over 14 years of LIFO inventory valuation. Why, then, would Chrysler, and other companies, change to FIFO? The major reason was the profit crunch of that era. Although Chrysler showed a loss of $7.6 million after the switch, the loss would have been $20 million *more* if the company had not changed its inventory valuation from LIFO to FIFO.

It is questionable whether companies should switch from LIFO to FIFO for the sole purpose of increasing reported earnings. Intuitively one would assume that companies with higher reported earnings would have a higher share valuation (common stock price). However, some studies have indicated that the users of financial data exhibit a much higher sophistication than might be expected. Share prices are the same and, in some cases, even higher under LIFO in spite of lower reported earnings.[26]

The concern about reduced income resulting from adoption of LIFO has even less substance now because the IRS has relaxed the LIFO conformity rule which requires a company employing LIFO for tax purposes to use it for book purposes as well. The IRS has relaxed restrictions against providing non-LIFO income numbers as supplementary information. As a result, companies now provide supplemental non-LIFO disclosures. While not intended to override the basic LIFO method adopted for financial reporting, these disclosures may be useful in comparing operating income and working capital with companies not on LIFO.

For example, **JCPenney, Inc.** a LIFO user, presented the information in its annual report as shown in Illustration 8-29 (on page 396).

---

[24]*Accounting Trends and Techniques—2004* reports that of 833 inventory method disclosures, 251 used LIFO, 384 used FIFO, 167 used average cost, and 31 used other methods. Because of steady or falling raw materials costs and costs savings from electronic data interchange and just-in-time technologies in recent years, many businesses using LIFO no longer experience substantial tax benefits. Even some companies for which LIFO is creating a benefit are finding that the administrative costs associated with LIFO are higher than the LIFO benefit obtained. As a result, some companies are moving to FIFO or average cost.

[25]See Barry E. Cushing and Marc J. LeClere, "Evidence on the Determinants of Inventory Accounting Policy Choice," *The Accounting Review* (April 1992), pp. 355–366, Table 4, p. 363, for a list of factors hypothesized to affect FIFO–LIFO choices.

[26]See, for example, Shyam Sunder, "Relationship Between Accounting Changes and Stock Prices: Problems of Measurement and Some Empirical Evidence," *Empirical Research in Accounting: Selected Studies, 1973* (Chicago: University of Chicago), pp. 1–40. But see Robert Moren Brown, "Short-Range Market Reaction to Changes to LIFO Accounting Using Preliminary Earnings Announcement Dates," *The Journal of Accounting Research* (Spring 1980), which found that companies that do change to LIFO suffer a short-run decline in the price of their stock.

ILLUSTRATION 8-29
Supplemental
Non-LIFO Disclosure

INTERNATIONAL INSIGHT

Many U.S. companies that have international operations use LIFO for U.S. purposes but use FIFO for their foreign subsidiaries.

JCPenney, Inc.

Some companies in the retail industry use the FIFO method in valuing part or all of their inventories. Had JCPenney used the FIFO method and made no other assumptions with respect to changes in income resulting therefrom, income and income per share from continuing operations would have been:

Income from continuing operations (in millions)	$325
Income from continuing operations per share	$4.63

Relaxation of the LIFO conformity rule has led some companies to select LIFO as their inventory valuation method because they will be able to disclose FIFO income numbers in the financial reports if they so desire.[27]

Companies often combine inventory methods. For example, **John Deere** uses LIFO for most of its inventories, and prices the remainder using FIFO. **Hershey Foods** follows the same practice. One reason for these practices is that certain product lines can be highly susceptible to deflation instead of inflation. In addition, if the level of inventory is unstable, unwanted involuntary liquidations may result in certain product lines if using LIFO. Finally, for high inventory turnover in certain product lines, a company cannot justify LIFO's additional recordkeeping and expense. In such cases, a company often uses average cost because it is easy to compute.[28]

Although a company may use a variety of inventory methods to assist in accurate computation of net income, once it selects a pricing method, it must apply it consistently thereafter. If conditions indicate that the inventory pricing method in use is unsuitable, the company must seriously consider all other possibilities before selecting another method. It should clearly explain any change and disclose its effect in the financial statements.

Inventory Valuation Methods—Summary Analysis

The preceding sections of this chapter described a number of inventory valuation methods. Here we present a brief summary of the three major inventory methods to show the effects these valuation methods have on the financial statements. This comparison assumes periodic inventory procedures and the following selected data.

Selected Data		
Beginning cash balance		$ 7,000
Beginning retained earnings		$10,000
Beginning inventory:	4,000 units @ $3	$12,000
Purchases:	6,000 units @ $4	$24,000
Sales:	5,000 units @ $12	$60,000
Operating expenses		$10,000
Income tax rate		40%

---

[27]Note that a company can use one variation of LIFO for financial reporting purposes and another for tax without violating the LIFO conformity rule. Such a relaxation has caused many problems because the general approach to accounting for LIFO has been "whatever is good for tax is good for financial reporting."

[28]For an interesting discussion of the reasons for and against the use of FIFO and average cost, see Michael H. Granof and Daniel G. Short "For Some Companies, FIFO Accounting Makes Sense," *Wall Street Journal* (August 30, 1982), and the subsequent rebuttal by Gary C. Biddle "Taking Stock of Inventory Accounting Choices," *Wall Street Journal* (September 15, 1982).

Illustration 8-30 shows the comparative results on net income of the use of average cost, FIFO, and LIFO.

	Average Cost	FIFO	LIFO
Sales	$60,000	$60,000	$60,000
Cost of goods sold	18,000[a]	16,000[b]	20,000[c]
Gross profit	42,000	44,000	40,000
Operating expenses	10,000	10,000	10,000
Income before taxes	32,000	34,000	30,000
Income taxes (40%)	12,800	13,600	12,000
Net income	$19,200	$20,400	$18,000

[a]4,000 @ $3 = $12,000
6,000 @ $4 = 24,000
$36,000

$36,000 ÷ 10,000 = $3.60
$3.60 × 5,000 = $18,000

[b]4,000 @ $3 = $12,000
1,000 @ $4 = 4,000
$16,000

[c]5,000 @ $4 = $20,000

ILLUSTRATION 8-30
Comparative Results of Average Cost, FIFO, and LIFO Methods

Notice that gross profit and net income are lowest under LIFO, highest under FIFO, and somewhere in the middle under average cost.

Illustration 8-31 shows the final balances of selected items at the end of the period.

	Inventory	Gross Profit	Taxes	Net Income	Retained Earnings	Cash
Average Cost	$18,000 (5,000 × $3.60)	$42,000	$12,800	$19,200	$29,200 ($10,000 + $19,200)	$20,200[a]
FIFO	$20,000 (5,000 × $4)	$44,000	$13,600	$20,400	$30,400 ($10,000 + $20,400)	$19,400[a]
LIFO	$16,000 (4,000 × $3) (1,000 × $4)	$40,000	$12,000	$18,000	$28,000 ($10,000 + $18,000)	$21,000[a]

[a]Cash at year-end	=	Beg. Balance	+	Sales	−	Purchases	−	Operating expenses	−	Taxes
Average cost—$20,200	=	$7,000	+	$60,000	−	$24,000	−	$10,000	−	$12,800
FIFO—$19,400	=	$7,000	+	$60,000	−	$24,000	−	$10,000	−	$13,600
LIFO—$21,000	=	$7,000	+	$60,000	−	$24,000	−	$10,000	−	$12,000

ILLUSTRATION 8-31
Balances of Selected Items Under Alternative Inventory Valuation Methods

LIFO results in the highest cash balance at year-end (because taxes are lower). This example assumes that prices are rising. The opposite result occurs if prices are declining.

SUMMARY OF LEARNING OBJECTIVES

1. **Identify major classifications of inventory.** Only one inventory account, Merchandise Inventory, appears in the financial statements of a merchandising concern. A manufacturer normally has three inventory accounts: Raw Materials, Work in Process, and Finished Goods. Companies report the cost assigned to goods and materials on hand but not yet placed into production as raw materials inventory. They report the cost of the raw materials on which production has been started but not completed, plus the direct labor cost applied specifically to this material and a ratable share of manufacturing overhead costs, as work in process inventory. Finally, they report the costs

identified with the completed but unsold units on hand at the end of the fiscal period as finished goods inventory.

2. Distinguish between perpetual and periodic inventory systems. A perpetual inventory system maintains a continuous record of inventory changes in the Inventory account. That is, a company records all purchases and sales (issues) of goods directly in the Inventory account as they occur. Under a periodic inventory system, companies determine the quantity of inventory on hand only periodically. A company debits a Purchases account, but the Inventory account remains the same. It determines cost of goods sold at the end of the period by subtracting ending inventory from cost of goods available for sale. A company ascertains ending inventory by physical count.

3. Identify the effects of inventory errors on the financial statements. *If the company misstates ending inventory:* (1) In the balance sheet, the inventory and retained earnings will be misstated, which will lead to miscalculation of the working capital and current ratio, and (2) in the income statement the cost of goods sold and net income will be misstated. If the company misstates purchases (and related accounts payable) and inventory: (1) In the balance sheet, the inventory and accounts payable will be misstated, which will lead to miscalculation of the current ratio, and (2) in the income statement, purchases and ending inventory will be misstated.

4. Understand the items to include as inventory cost. Product costs are those costs that attach to the inventory and are recorded in the inventory account. Such charges include freight charges on goods purchased, other direct costs of acquisition, and labor and other production costs incurred in processing the goods up to the time of sale. Period costs are those costs that are indirectly related the acquisition or production of the goods. These changes, such as selling expense and general and administrative expenses, are therefore not included as part of inventory cost.

5. Describe and compare the cost flow assumptions used to account for inventories. (1) *Average cost* prices items in the inventory on the basis of the average cost of all similar goods available during the period. (2) *First-in, first-out (FIFO)* assumes that a company uses goods in the order in which it purchases them. The inventory remaining must therefore represent the most recent purchases. (3) *Last-in, first-out (LIFO)* matches the cost of the last goods purchased against revenue.

6. Explain the significance and use of a LIFO reserve. The difference between the inventory method used for internal reporting purposes and LIFO is referred to as the Allowance to Reduce Inventory to LIFO, or the LIFO reserve. The change in LIFO reserve is referred to as the LIFO effect. Companies should disclose either the LIFO reserve or the replacement cost of the inventory in the financial statements.

7. Understand the effect of LIFO liquidations. LIFO liquidations match costs from preceding periods against sales revenues reported in current dollars. This distorts net income and results in increased taxable income in the current period. LIFO liquidations can occur frequently when using a specific-goods LIFO approach.

8. Explain the dollar-value LIFO method. For the dollar-value LIFO method, companies determine and measure increases and decreases in a pool in terms of total dollar value, not the physical quantity of the goods in the inventory pool.

9. Identify the major advantages and disadvantages of LIFO. The major advantages of LIFO are the following: (1) It matches recent costs against current revenues to provide a better measure of current earnings. (2) As long as the price level increases and inventory quantities do not decrease, a deferral of income tax occurs in LIFO. (3) Because of the deferral of income tax, cash flow improves. Major disadvantages are: (1) reduced earnings, (2) understated inventory, (3) does not approximate physical flow of the items except in peculiar situations, and (4) involuntary liquidation issues.

10. **Understand why companies select given inventory methods.** Companies ordinarily prefer LIFO in the following circumstances: (1) if selling prices and revenues have been increasing faster than costs and (2) if a company has a fairly constant "base stock." Conversely, LIFO would probably not be appropriate in the following circumstances: (1) if sale prices tend to lag behind costs, (2) if specific identification is traditional, and (3) when unit costs tend to decrease as production increases, thereby nullifying the tax benefit that LIFO might provide.

QUESTIONS

1. In what ways are the inventory accounts of a retailing company different from those of a manufacturing company?

2. Why should inventories be included in (a) a statement of financial position and (b) the computation of net income?

3. What is the difference between a perpetual inventory and a physical inventory? If a company maintains a perpetual inventory, should its physical inventory at any date be equal to the amount indicated by the perpetual inventory records? Why?

4. Mariah Carey, Inc. indicated in a recent annual report that approximately $19 million of merchandise was received on consignment. Should Mariah Carey, Inc. report this amount on its balance sheet? Explain.

5. What is a product financing arrangement? How should product financing arrangements be reported in the financial statements?

6. Where, if at all, should the following items be classified on a balance sheet?

(a) Goods out on approval to customers.

(b) Goods in transit that were recently purchased f.o.b. destination.

(c) Land held by a realty firm for sale.

(d) Raw materials.

(e) Goods received on consignment.

(f) Manufacturing supplies.

7. At the balance sheet date Paula Abdul Company held title to goods in transit amounting to $214,000. This amount was omitted from the purchases figure for the year and also from the ending inventory. What is the effect of this omission on the net income for the year as calculated when the books are closed? What is the effect on the company's financial position as shown in its balance sheet? Is materiality a factor in determining whether an adjustment for this item should be made?

8. Define "cost" as applied to the valuation of inventories.

9. Distinguish between product costs and period costs as they relate to inventory.

10. **Ford Motor Co.** is considering alternate methods of accounting for the cash discounts it takes when paying suppliers promptly. One method suggested was to report these discounts as financial income when payments are made. Comment on the propriety of this approach.

11. Konerko Inc. purchases 300 units of an item at an invoice cost of $30,000. What is the cost per unit? If the goods are shipped f.o.b. shipping point and the freight bill was $1,500, what is the cost per unit if Konerko Inc. pays the freight charges? If these items were bought on 2/10, n/30 terms and the invoice and the freight bill were paid within the 10-day period, what would be the cost per unit?

12. Specific identification is sometimes said to be the ideal method of assigning cost to inventory and to cost of goods sold. Briefly indicate the arguments for and against this method of inventory valuation.

13. FIFO, weighted average, and LIFO methods are often used instead of specific identification for inventory valuation purposes. Compare these methods with the specific identification method, discussing the theoretical propriety of each method in the determination of income and asset valuation.

14. How might a company obtain a price index in order to apply dollar-value LIFO?

15. Describe the LIFO double-extension method. Using the following information, compute the index at December 31, 2007, applying the double-extension method to a LIFO pool consisting of 25,500 units of product A and 10,350 units of product B. The base-year cost of product A is $10.20 and of product B is $37.00. The price at December 31, 2007, for product A is $19.00 and for product B is $45.60.

16. As compared with the FIFO method of costing inventories, does the LIFO method result in a larger or smaller net income in a period of rising prices? What is the comparative effect on net income in a period of falling prices?

17. What is the dollar-value method of LIFO inventory valuation? What advantage does the dollar-value method have over the specific goods approach of LIFO inventory valuation? Why will the traditional LIFO inventory costing method and the dollar-value LIFO inventory costing method produce different inventory valuations if the composition of the inventory base changes?

18. Explain the following terms.

(a) LIFO layer. (b) LIFO reserve. (c) LIFO effect.

19. On December 31, 2006, the inventory of Mario Lemieux Company amounts to $800,000. During 2007, the company decides to use the dollar-value LIFO method of costing inventories. On December 31, 2007, the inventory is $1,026,000 at December 31, 2007, prices. Using the De-

cember 31, 2006, price level of 100 and the December 31, 2007, price level of 108, compute the inventory value at December 31, 2007, under the dollar-value LIFO method.

20. In an article that appeared in the *Wall Street Journal*, the phrases "phantom (paper) profits" and "high LIFO profits" through involuntary liquidation were used. Explain these phrases.

WILEY PLUS

BRIEF EXERCISES

(LO 1) BE8-1 Included in the December 31 trial balance of Billie Joel Company are the following assets.

Cash	$ 190,000	Work in process	$200,000
Equipment (net)	1,100,000	Receivables (net)	400,000
Prepaid insurance	41,000	Patents	110,000
Raw materials	335,000	Finished goods	150,000

Prepare the current assets section of the December 31 balance sheet.

(LO 2) BE8-2 Alanis Morrissette Company uses a perpetual inventory system. Its beginning inventory consists of 50 units that cost $30 each. During June, the company purchased 150 units at $30 each, returned 6 units for credit, and sold 125 units at $50 each. Journalize the June transactions.

(LO 4) BE8-3 Mayberry Company took a physical inventory on December 31 and determined that goods costing $200,000 were on hand. Not included in the physical count were $15,000 of goods purchased from Taylor Corporation, f.o.b. shipping point, and $22,000 of goods sold to Mount Pilot Company for $30,000, f.o.b. destination. Both the Taylor purchase and the Mount Pilot sale were in transit at year-end. What amount should Mayberry report as its December 31 inventory?

(LO 3) BE8-4 Gavin Bryars Enterprises reported cost of goods sold for 2007 of $1,400,000 and retained earnings of $5,200,000 at December 31, 2007. Gavin Bryars later discovered that its ending inventories at December 31, 2006 and 2007, were overstated by $110,000 and $45,000, respectively. Determine the corrected amounts for 2007 cost of goods sold and December 31, 2007, retained earnings.

(LO 5) BE8-5 Jose Zorilla Company uses a periodic inventory system. For April, when the company sold 700 units, the following information is available.

	Units	Unit Cost	Total Cost
April 1 inventory	250	$10	$ 2,500
April 15 purchase	400	12	4,800
April 23 purchase	350	13	4,550
	1,000		$11,850

Compute the April 30 inventory and the April cost of goods sold using the average cost method.

(LO 5) BE8-6 Data for Jose Zorilla Company are presented in BE8-5. Compute the April 30 inventory and the April cost of goods sold using the FIFO method.

(LO 5) BE8-7 Data for Jose Zorilla Company are presented in BE8-5. Compute the April 30 inventory and the April cost of goods sold using the LIFO method.

(LO 8) BE8-8 Easy-E Company had ending inventory at end-of-year prices of $100,000 at December 31, 2005; $123,200 at December 31, 2006; and $134,560 at December 31, 2007. The year-end price indexes were 100 at 12/31/05, 110 at 12/31/06, and 116 at 12/31/07. Compute the ending inventory for Easy-E Company for 2005 through 2007 using the dollar-value LIFO method.

(LO 8) BE8-9 Wingers uses the dollar-value LIFO method of computing its inventory. Data for the past 3 years follow.

Year Ended December 31	Inventory at Current-year Cost	Price Index
2005	$19,750	100
2006	21,708	108
2007	25,935	114

Instructions

Compute the value of the 2006 and 2007 inventories using the dollar-value LIFO method.

EXERCISES

(LO 4) **E8-1 (Inventoriable Costs)** Presented below is a list of items that may or may not be reported as inventory in a company's December 31 balance sheet.

  1. Goods out on consignment at another company's store.
  2. Goods sold on an installment basis (bad debts can be reasonably estimated).
  3. Goods purchased f.o.b. shipping point that are in transit at December 31.
  4. Goods purchased f.o.b. destination that are in transit at December 31.
  5. Goods sold to another company, for which our company has signed an agreement to repurchase at a set price that covers all costs related to the inventory.
  6. Goods sold where large returns are predictable.
  7. Goods sold f.o.b. shipping point that are in transit at December 31.
  8. Freight charges on goods purchased.
  9. Interest costs incurred for inventories that are routinely manufactured.
 10. Costs incurred to advertise goods held for resale.
 11. Materials on hand not yet placed into production by a manufacturing firm.
 12. Office supplies.
 13. Raw materials on which a manufacturing firm has started production, but which are not completely processed.
 14. Factory supplies.
 15. Goods held on consignment from another company.
 16. Costs identified with units completed by a manufacturing firm, but not yet sold.
 17. Goods sold f.o.b. destination that are in transit at December 31.
 18. Short-term investments in stocks and bonds that will be resold in the near future.

Instructions
Indicate which of these items would typically be reported as inventory in the financial statements. If an item should **not** be reported as inventory, indicate how it should be reported in the financial statements.

(LO 4) **E8-2 (Inventoriable Costs)** In your audit of Jose Oliva Company, you find that a physical inventory on December 31, 2007, showed merchandise with a cost of $441,000 was on hand at that date. You also discover the following items were all excluded from the $441,000.

  1. Merchandise of $61,000 which is held by Oliva on consignment. The consignor is the Max Suzuki Company.
  2. Merchandise costing $38,000 which was shipped by Oliva f.o.b. destination to a customer on December 31, 2007. The customer was expected to receive the merchandise on January 6, 2008.
  3. Merchandise costing $46,000 which was shipped by Oliva f.o.b. shipping point to a customer on December 29, 2007. The customer was scheduled to receive the merchandise on January 2, 2008.
  4. Merchandise costing $83,000 shipped by a vendor f.o.b. destination on December 30, 2007, and received by Oliva on January 4, 2008.
  5. Merchandise costing $51,000 shipped by a vendor f.o.b. seller on December 31, 2007, and received by Oliva on January 5, 2008.

Instructions
Based on the above information, calculate the amount that should appear on Oliva's balance sheet at December 31, 2007, for inventory.

(LO 4) **E8-3 (Inventoriable Costs)** Assume that in an annual audit of **Harlowe Inc.** at December 31, 2007, you find the following transactions near the closing date.

  1. A special machine, fabricated to order for a customer, was finished and specifically segregated in the back part of the shipping room on December 31, 2007. The customer was billed on that date and the machine excluded from inventory although it was shipped on January 4, 2008.
  2. Merchandise costing $2,800 was received on January 3, 2008, and the related purchase invoice recorded January 5. The invoice showed the shipment was made on December 29, 2007, f.o.b. destination.
  3. A packing case containing a product costing $3,400 was standing in the shipping room when the physical inventory was taken. It was not included in the inventory because it was marked "Hold for shipping instructions." Your investigation revealed that the customer's order was dated December 18, 2007, but that the case was shipped and the customer billed on January 10, 2008. The product was a stock item of your client.

4. Merchandise received on January 6, 2008, costing $680 was entered in the purchase journal on January 7, 2008. The invoice showed shipment was made f.o.b. supplier's warehouse on December 31, 2007. Because it was not on hand at December 31, it was not included in inventory.
5. Merchandise costing $720 was received on December 28, 2007, and the invoice was not recorded. You located it in the hands of the purchasing agent; it was marked "on consignment."

Instructions

Assuming that each of the amounts is material, state whether the merchandise should be included in the client's inventory, and give your reason for your decision on each item.

(LO 2, 4) **E8-4 (Inventoriable Costs—Perpetual)** Colin Davis Machine Company maintains a general ledger account for each class of inventory, debiting such accounts for increases during the period and crediting them for decreases. The transactions below relate to the Raw Materials inventory account, which is debited for materials purchased and credited for materials requisitioned for use.

1. An invoice for $8,100, terms f.o.b. destination, was received and entered January 2, 2007. The receiving report shows that the materials were received December 28, 2006.
2. Materials costing $28,000, shipped f.o.b. destination, were not entered by December 31, 2006, "because they were in a railroad car on the company's siding on that date and had not been unloaded."
3. Materials costing $7,300 were returned to the supplier on December 29, 2006, and were shipped f.o.b. shipping point. The return was entered on that date, even though the materials are not expected to reach the supplier's place of business until January 6, 2007.
4. An invoice for $7,500, terms f.o.b. shipping point, was received and entered December 30, 2006. The receiving report shows that the materials were received January 4, 2007, and the bill of lading shows that they were shipped January 2, 2007.
5. Materials costing $19,800 were received December 30, 2006, but no entry was made for them because "they were ordered with a specified delivery of no earlier than January 10, 2007."

Instructions

Prepare correcting general journal entries required at December 31, 2006, assuming that the books have not been closed.

(LO 3, 4) **E8-5 (Inventoriable Costs—Error Adjustments)** Craig Company asks you to review its December 31, 2007, inventory values and prepare the necessary adjustments to the books. The following information is given to you.

1. Craig uses the periodic method of recording inventory. A physical count reveals $234,890 of inventory on hand at December 31, 2007.
2. Not included in the physical count of inventory is $13,420 of merchandise purchased on December 15 from Browser. This merchandise was shipped f.o.b. shipping point on December 29 and arrived in January. The invoice arrived and was recorded on December 31.
3. Included in inventory is merchandise sold to Champy on December 30, f.o.b. destination. This merchandise was shipped after it was counted. The invoice was prepared and recorded as a sale on account for $12,800 on December 31. The merchandise cost $7,350, and Champy received it on January 3.
4. Included in inventory was merchandise received from Dudley on December 31 with an invoice price of $15,630. The merchandise was shipped f.o.b. destination. The invoice, which has not yet arrived, has not been recorded.
5. Not included in inventory is $8,540 of merchandise purchased from Glowser Industries. This merchandise was received on December 31 after the inventory had been counted. The invoice was received and recorded on December 30.
6. Included in inventory was $10,438 of inventory held by Craig on consignment from Jackel Industries.
7. Included in inventory is merchandise sold to Kemp f.o.b. shipping point. This merchandise was shipped after it was counted. The invoice was prepared and recorded as a sale for $18,900 on December 31. The cost of this merchandise was $10,520, and Kemp received the merchandise on January 5.
8. Excluded from inventory was a carton labeled "Please accept for credit." This carton contains merchandise costing $1,500 which had been sold to a customer for $2,600. No entry had been made to the books to reflect the return, but none of the returned merchandise seemed damaged.

Instructions

(a) Determine the proper inventory balance for Craig Company at December 31, 2007.
(b) Prepare any correcting entries to adjust inventory to its proper amount at December 31, 2007. Assume the books have not been closed.

(LO 4) **E8-6 (Determining Merchandise Amounts—Periodic)** Two or more items are omitted in each of the following tabulations of income statement data. Fill in the amounts that are missing.

	2005	2006	2007
Sales	$290,000	$?	$410,000
Sales returns	11,000	13,000	?
Net sales	?	347,000	?
Beginning inventory	20,000	32,000	?
Ending inventory	?	?	?
Purchases	?	260,000	298,000
Purchase returns and allowances	5,000	8,000	10,000
Transportation-in	8,000	9,000	12,000
Cost of goods sold	233,000	?	293,000
Gross profit on sales	46,000	91,000	97,000

(LO 4) **E8-7 (Purchases Recorded Net)** Presented below are transactions related to Tom Brokaw, Inc.

May 10 Purchased goods billed at $15,000 subject to cash discount terms of 2/10, n/60.
  11 Purchased goods billed at $13,200 subject to terms of 1/15, n/30.
  19 Paid invoice of May 10.
  24 Purchased goods billed at $11,500 subject to cash discount terms of 2/10, n/30.

Instructions

(a) Prepare general journal entries for the transactions above under the assumption that purchases are to be recorded at net amounts after cash discounts and that discounts lost are to be treated as financial expense.

(b) Assuming no purchase or payment transactions other than those given above, prepare the adjusting entry required on May 31 if financial statements are to be prepared as of that date.

(LO 4) **E8-8 (Purchases Recorded, Gross Method)** Cruise Industries purchased $10,800 of merchandise on February 1, 2007, subject to a trade discount of 10% and with credit terms of 3/15, n/60. It returned $2,500 (gross price before trade or cash discount) on February 4. The invoice was paid on February 13.

Instructions

(a) Assuming that Cruise uses the perpetual method for recording merchandise transactions, record the purchase, return, and payment using the gross method.

(b) Assuming that Cruise uses the periodic method for recording merchandise transactions, record the purchase, return, and payment using the gross method.

(c) At what amount would the purchase on February 1 be recorded if the net method were used?

(LO 2) **E8-9 (Periodic versus Perpetual Entries)** Fong Sai-Yuk Company sells one product. Presented below is information for January for Fong Sai-Yuk Company.

Jan. 1	Inventory	100 units at $5 each 500	410
4	Sale	80 units at $8 each 640	
11	Purchase	150 units at $6 each 900	300
13	Sale	120 units at $8.75 each 1050	
20	Purchase	160 units at $7 each 1120	110
27	Sale	100 units at $9 each 900	

Fong Sai-Yuk uses the FIFO cost flow assumption. All purchases and sales are on account.

Instructions

(a) Assume Fong Sai-Yuk uses a periodic system. Prepare all necessary journal entries, including the end-of-month closing entry to record cost of goods sold. A physical count indicates that the ending inventory for January is 110 units.

(b) Compute gross profit using the periodic system.

(c) Assume Fong Sai-Yuk uses a perpetual system. Prepare all necessary journal entries.

(d) Compute gross profit using the perpetual system.

(LO 3) **E8-10 (Inventory Errors—Periodic)** Ann M. Martin Company makes the following errors during the current year. (In all cases, assume ending inventory in the following year is correctly stated.)

1. Ending inventory is overstated, but purchases and related accounts payable are recorded correctly.
2. Both ending inventory and purchases and related accounts payable are understated. (Assume this purchase was recorded and paid for in the following year.)
3. Ending inventory is correct, but a purchase on account was not recorded. (Assume this purchase was recorded and paid for in the following year.)

Instructions
Indicate the effect of each of these errors on working capital, current ratio (assume that the current ratio is greater than 1), retained earnings, and net income for the current year and the subsequent year.

(LO 3) **E8-11** **(Inventory Errors)** At December 31, 2006, Stacy McGill Corporation reported current assets of $370,000 and current liabilities of $200,000. The following items may have been recorded incorrectly.

1. Goods purchased costing $22,000 were shipped f.o.b. shipping point by a supplier on December 28. McGill received and recorded the invoice on December 29, 2006, but the goods were not included in McGill's physical count of inventory because they were not received until January 4, 2004.
2. Goods purchased costing $15,000 were shipped f.o.b. destination by a supplier on December 26. McGill received and recorded the invoice on December 31, but the goods were not included in McGill's 2006 physical count of inventory because they were not received until January 2, 2007.
3. Goods held on consignment from Claudia Kishi Company were included in McGill's December 31, 2006, physical count of inventory at $13,000.
4. Freight-in of $3,000 was debited to advertising expense on December 28, 2006.

Instructions
(a) Compute the current ratio based on McGill's balance sheet.
(b) Recompute the current ratio after corrections are made.
(c) By what amount will income (before taxes) be adjusted up or down as a result of the corrections?

(LO 3) **E8-12** **(Inventory Errors)** The net income per books of Linda Patrick Company was determined without knowledge of the errors indicated.

Year	Net Income per Books	Error in Ending Inventory	
2002	$50,000	Overstated	$ 3,000
2003	52,000	Overstated	9,000
2004	54,000	Understated	11,000
2005	56,000	No error	
2006	58,000	Understated	2,000
2007	60,000	Overstated	8,000

Instructions
Prepare a work sheet to show the adjusted net income figure for each of the 6 years after taking into account the inventory errors.

(LO 2, 5) **E8-13** **(FIFO and LIFO—Periodic and Perpetual)** Inventory information for Part 311 of Monique Aaron Corp. discloses the following information for the month of June.

June 1	Balance	300 units @ $10	June 10	Sold	200 units @ $24
11	Purchased	800 units @ $12	15	Sold	500 units @ $25
20	Purchased	500 units @ $13	27	Sold	300 units @ $27

Instructions
(a) Assuming that the periodic inventory method is used, compute the cost of goods sold and ending inventory under (1) LIFO and (2) FIFO.
(b) Assuming that the perpetual inventory method is used and costs are computed at the time of each withdrawal, what is the value of the ending inventory at LIFO?
(c) Assuming that the perpetual inventory method is used and costs are computed at the time of each withdrawal, what is the gross profit if the inventory is valued at FIFO?
(d) Why is it stated that LIFO usually produces a lower gross profit than FIFO?

(LO 5) **E8-14** **(FIFO, LIFO and Average Cost Determination)** John Adams Company's record of transactions for the month of April was as follows.

Purchases			Sales		
April 1 (balance on hand)	600 @	$6.00	April 3	500 @	$10.00
4	1,500 @	6.08	9	1,400 @	10.00
8	800 @	6.40	11	600 @	11.00
13	1,200 @	6.50	23	1,200 @	11.00
21	700 @	6.60	27	900 @	12.00
29	500 @	6.79		4,600	
	5,300				

Instructions

(a) Assuming that periodic inventory records are kept in units only, compute the inventory at April 30 using (1) LIFO and (2) average cost.

(b) Assuming that perpetual inventory records are kept in dollars, determine the inventory using (1) FIFO and (2) LIFO.

(c) Compute cost of goods sold assuming periodic inventory procedures and inventory priced at FIFO.

(d) In an inflationary period, which inventory method—FIFO, LIFO, average cost—will show the highest net income?

(LO 5) **E8-15** **(FIFO, LIFO, Average Cost Inventory)** Shania Twain Company was formed on December 1, 2006. The following information is available from Twain's inventory records for Product BAP.

	Units	Unit Cost
January 1, 2007 (beginning inventory)	600	$ 8.00
Purchases:		
January 5, 2007	1,200	9.00
January 25, 2007	1,300	10.00
February 16, 2007	800	11.00
March 26, 2007	600	12.00

A physical inventory on March 31, 2007, shows 1,600 units on hand.

Instructions

Prepare schedules to compute the ending inventory at March 31, 2007, under each of the following inventory methods.

(a) FIFO. (b) LIFO. (c) Weighted average.

(LO 2, 5) **E8-16** **(Compute FIFO, LIFO, Average Cost—Periodic)** Presented below is information related to Blowfish radios for the Hootie Company for the month of July.

Date	Transaction	Units In	Unit Cost	Total	Units Sold	Selling Price	Total
July 1	Balance	100	$4.10	$ 410			
6	Purchase	800	4.20	3,360			
7	Sale				300	$7.00	$ 2,100
10	Sale				300	7.30	2,190
12	Purchase	400	4.50	1,800			
15	Sale				200	7.40	1,480
18	Purchase	300	4.60	1,380			
22	Sale				400	7.40	2,960
25	Purchase	500	4.58	2,290			
30	Sale				200	7.50	1,500
	Totals	2,100		$9,240	1,400		$10,230

Instructions

(a) Assuming that the periodic inventory method is used, compute the inventory cost at July 31 under each of the following cost flow assumptions.

(1) FIFO.
(2) LIFO.
(3) Weighted-average.

(b) Answer the following questions.

(1) Which of the methods used above will yield the lowest figure for gross profit for the income statement? Explain why.

(2) Which of the methods used above will yield the lowest figure for ending inventory for the balance sheet? Explain why.

(LO 2, 5) **E8-17** **(FIFO and LIFO—Periodic and Perpetual)** The following is a record of Pervis Ellison Company's transactions for Boston Teapots for the month of May 2007.

May 1	Balance 400 units @ $20	May 10	Sale 300 units @ $38
12	Purchase 600 units @ $25	20	Sale 540 units @ $38
28	Purchase 400 units @ $30		

Instructions

(a) Assuming that perpetual inventories are **not** maintained and that a physical count at the end of the month shows 560 units on hand, what is the cost of the ending inventory using (1) FIFO and (2) LIFO?

(b) Assuming that perpetual records are maintained and they tie into the general ledger, calculate the ending inventory using (1) FIFO and (2) LIFO.

(LO 2, 5) **E8-18 (FIFO and LIFO; Income Statement Presentation)** The board of directors of Ichiro Corporation is considering whether or not it should instruct the accounting department to shift from a first-in, first-out (FIFO) basis of pricing inventories to a last-in, first-out (LIFO) basis. The following information is available.

Sales	21,000 units @ $50
Inventory, January 1	6,000 units @ 20
Purchases	6,000 units @ 22
	10,000 units @ 25
	7,000 units @ 30
Inventory, December 31	8,000 units @ ?
Operating expenses	$200,000

Instructions

Prepare a condensed income statement for the year on both bases for comparative purposes.

(LO 5) **E8-19 (FIFO and LIFO Effects)** You are the vice-president of finance of Sandy Alomar Corporation, a retail company that prepared two different schedules of gross margin for the first quarter ended March 31, 2007. These schedules appear below.

	Sales ($5 per unit)	Cost of Goods Sold	Gross Margin
Schedule 1	$150,000	$124,900	$25,100
Schedule 2	150,000	129,400	20,600

The computation of cost of goods sold in each schedule is based on the following data.

	Units	Cost per Unit	Total Cost
Beginning inventory, January 1	10,000	$4.00	$40,000
Purchase, January 10	8,000	4.20	33,600
Purchase, January 30	6,000	4.25	25,500
Purchase, February 11	9,000	4.30	38,700
Purchase, March 17	11,000	4.40	48,400

Jane Torville, the president of the corporation, cannot understand how two different gross margins can be computed from the same set of data. As the vice-president of finance you have explained to Ms. Torville that the two schedules are based on different assumptions concerning the flow of inventory costs, i.e., FIFO and LIFO. Schedules 1 and 2 were not necessarily prepared in this sequence of cost flow assumptions.

Instructions

Prepare two separate schedules computing cost of goods sold and supporting schedules showing the composition of the ending inventory under both cost flow assumptions.

(LO 2, 5) **E8-20 (FIFO and LIFO—Periodic)** Howie Long Shop began operations on January 2, 2007. The following stock record card for footballs was taken from the records at the end of the year.

Date	Voucher	Terms	Units Received	Unit Invoice Cost	Gross Invoice Amount
1/15	10624	Net 30	50	$20	$1,000
3/15	11437	1/5, net 30	65	16	1,040
6/20	21332	1/10, net 30	90	15	1,350
9/12	27644	1/10, net 30	84	12	1,008
11/24	31269	1/10, net 30	76	11	836
	Totals		365		$5,234

A physical inventory on December 31, 2007, reveals that 100 footballs were in stock. The bookkeeper informs you that all the discounts were taken. Assume that Howie Long Shop uses the invoice price less discount for recording purchases.

Instructions

(a) Compute the December 31, 2007, inventory using the FIFO method.

(b) Compute the 2007 cost of goods sold using the LIFO method.

(c) What method would you recommend to the owner to minimize income taxes in 2007, using the inventory information for footballs as a guide?

(LO 6) **E8-21** **(LIFO Effect)** The following example was provided to encourage the use of the LIFO method.

In a nutshell, LIFO subtracts inflation from inventory costs, deducts it from taxable income, and records it in a LIFO reserve account on the books. The LIFO benefit grows as inflation widens the gap between current-year and past-year (minus inflation) inventory costs. This gap is:

	With LIFO	Without LIFO
Revenues	$3,200,000	$3,200,000
Cost of goods sold	2,800,000	2,800,000
Operating expenses	150,000	150,000
Operating income	250,000	250,000
LIFO adjustment	40,000	0
Taxable income	$210,000	$250,000
Income taxes @ 36%	$ 75,600	$ 90,000
Cash flow	$174,400	$160,000
Extra cash	$14,400	0
Increased cash flow	9%	0%

Instructions

(a) Explain what is meant by the LIFO reserve account.

(b) How does LIFO subtract inflation from inventory costs?

(c) Explain how the cash flow of $174,400 in this example was computed. Explain why this amount may not be correct.

(d) Why does a company that uses LIFO have extra cash? Explain whether this situation will always exist.

(LO 5, 8) **E8-22** **(Alternative Inventory Methods—Comprehensive)** Tori Amos Corporation began operations on December 1, 2006. The only inventory transaction in 2006 was the purchase of inventory on December 10, 2006, at a cost of $20 per unit. None of this inventory was sold in 2006. Relevant information is as follows.

Ending inventory units		
December 31, 2006		100
December 31, 2007, by purchase date		
December 2, 2007	100	
July 20, 2007	50	150

During the year the following purchases and sales were made.

Purchases		Sales	
March 15	300 units at $24	April 10	200
July 20	300 units at 25	August 20	300
September 4	200 units at 28	November 18	150
December 2	100 units at 30	December 12	200

The company uses the periodic inventory method.

Instructions

(a) Determine ending inventory under (1) specific identification, (2) FIFO, (3) LIFO and (4) average cost.

(b) Determine ending inventory using dollar-value LIFO. Assume that the December 2, 2007, purchase cost is the current cost of inventory. (*Hint:* The beginning inventory is the base layer priced at $20 per unit.)

(LO 8) **E8-23** **(Dollar-Value LIFO)** Oasis Company has used the dollar-value LIFO method for inventory cost determination for many years. The following data were extracted from Oasis' records.

Date	Price Index	Ending Inventory at Base Prices	Ending Inventory at Dollar-Value LIFO
December 31, 2005	105	$92,000	$92,600
December 31, 2006	?	97,000	98,350

Instructions
Calculate the index used for 2006 that yielded the above results.

(LO 8) **E8-24 (Dollar-Value LIFO)**   The dollar-value LIFO method was adopted by Enya Corp. on January 1, 2007. Its inventory on that date was $160,000. On December 31, 2007, the inventory at prices existing on that date amounted to $140,000. The price level at January 1, 2007, was 100, and the price level at December 31, 2007, was 112.

Instructions
- **(a)** Compute the amount of the inventory at December 31, 2007, under the dollar-value LIFO method.
- **(b)** On December 31, 2008, the inventory at prices existing on that date was $172,500, and the price level was 115. Compute the inventory on that date under the dollar-value LIFO method.

(LO 8) **E8-25 (Dollar-Value LIFO)**   Presented below is information related to Dino Radja Company.

Date	Ending Inventory (End-of-Year Prices)	Price Index
December 31, 2004	$ 80,000	100
December 31, 2005	115,500	105
December 31, 2006	108,000	120
December 31, 2007	122,200	130
December 31, 2008	154,000	140
December 31, 2009	176,900	145

Instructions
Compute the ending inventory for Dino Radja Company for 2004 through 2009 using the dollar-value LIFO method.

(LO 8) **E8-26 (Dollar-Value LIFO)**   The following information relates to the Jimmy Johnson Company.

Date	Ending Inventory (End-of-Year Prices)	Price Index
December 31, 2003	$ 70,000	100
December 31, 2004	90,300	105
December 31, 2005	95,120	116
December 31, 2006	105,600	120
December 31, 2007	100,000	125

Instructions
Use the dollar-value LIFO method to compute the ending inventory for Johnson Company for 2003 through 2007.

See the book's website, www.wiley.com/college/kieso, for Additional Exercises.

PROBLEMS

(LO 4, 5, 8) **P8-1 (Various Inventory Issues)**   The following independent situations relate to inventory accounting.

1. Jag Co. purchased goods with a list price of $150,000, subject to trade discounts of 20% and 10%, with no cash discounts allowable. How much should Jag Co. record as the cost of these goods?

2. Francis Company's inventory of $1,100,000 at December 31, 2006, was based on a physical count of goods priced at cost and before any year-end adjustments relating to the following items.
   - **a.** Goods shipped from a vendor f.o.b. shipping point on December 24, 2006, at an invoice cost of $69,000 to Francis Company were received on January 4, 2007.
   - **b.** The physical count included $29,000 of goods billed to Sakic Corp. f.o.b. shipping point on December 31, 2006. The carrier picked up these goods on January 3, 2007.

   What amount should Francis report as inventory on its balance sheet?

3. Mark Messier Corp. had 1,500 units of part M.O. on hand May 1, 2006, costing $21 each. Purchases of part M.O. during May were as follows.

	Units	Unit Cost
May 9	2,000	$22.00
17	3,500	23.00
26	1,000	24.00

A physical count on May 31, 2006, shows 2,100 units of part M.O. on hand. Using the FIFO method, what is the cost of part M.O. inventory at May 31, 2006? Using the LIFO method, what is the inventory cost? Using the average cost method, what is the inventory cost?

4. Forsberg Company adopted the dollar-value LIFO method on January 1, 2006 (using internal price indexes and multiple pools). The following data are available for inventory pool A for the 2 years following adoption of LIFO.

Inventory	At Base-Year Cost	At Current-Year Cost
1/1/06	$200,000	$200,000
12/31/06	240,000	252,000
12/31/07	256,000	286,720

Computing an internal price index and using the dollar-value LIFO method, at what amount should the inventory be reported at December 31, 2007?

5. Eric Lindros Inc., a retail store chain, had the following information in its general ledger for the year 2007.

Merchandise purchased for resale	$909,400
Interest on notes payable to vendors	8,700
Purchase returns	16,500
Freight-in	22,000
Freight-out	17,100
Cash discounts on purchases	6,800

What is Lindros' inventoriable cost for 2007?

Instructions

Answer each of the preceding questions about inventories, and explain your answers.

(LO 4) **P8-2** **(Inventory Adjustments)** James T. Kirk Company, a manufacturer of small tools, provided the following information from its accounting records for the year ended December 31, 2007.

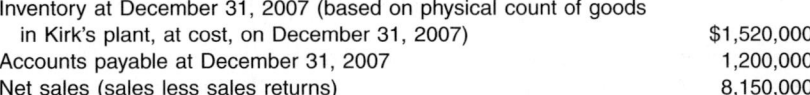

Inventory at December 31, 2007 (based on physical count of goods in Kirk's plant, at cost, on December 31, 2007)	$1,520,000
Accounts payable at December 31, 2007	1,200,000
Net sales (sales less sales returns)	8,150,000

Additional information is as follows.

1. Included in the physical count were tools billed to a customer f.o.b. shipping point on December 31, 2007. These tools had a cost of $31,000 and were billed at $40,000. The shipment was on Kirk's loading dock waiting to be picked up by the common carrier.

2. Goods were in transit from a vendor to Kirk on December 31, 2007. The invoice cost was $71,000, and the goods were shipped f.o.b. shipping point on December 29, 2007.

3. Work in process inventory costing $30,000 was sent to an outside processor for plating on December 30, 2007.

4. Tools returned by customers and held pending inspection in the returned goods area on December 31, 2007, were not included in the physical count. On January 8, 2008, the tools costing $32,000 were inspected and returned to inventory. Credit memos totaling $47,000 were issued to the customers on the same date.

5. Tools shipped to a customer f.o.b. destination on December 26, 2007, were in transit at December 31, 2007, and had a cost of $21,000. Upon notification of receipt by the customer on January 2, 2008, Kirk issued a sales invoice for $42,000.

6. Goods, with an invoice cost of $27,000, received from a vendor at 5:00 p.m. on December 31, 2007, were recorded on a receiving report dated January 2, 2008. The goods were not included in the physical count, but the invoice was included in accounts payable at December 31, 2007.

7. Goods received from a vendor on December 26, 2007, were included in the physical count. However, the related $56,000 vendor invoice was not included in accounts payable at December 31, 2007, because the accounts payable copy of the receiving report was lost.

8. On January 3, 2008, a monthly freight bill in the amount of $6,000 was received. The bill specifically related to merchandise purchased in December 2007, one-half of which was still in the inventory at December 31, 2007. The freight charges were not included in either the inventory or in accounts payable at December 31, 2007.

Instructions

Using the format shown below, prepare a schedule of adjustments as of December 31, 2007, to the initial amounts per Kirk's accounting records. Show separately the effect, if any, of each of the eight transactions on the December 31, 2007, amounts. If the transactions would have no effect on the initial amount shown, enter NONE.

	Inventory	Accounts Payable	Net Sales
Initial amounts	$1,520,000	$1,200,000	$8,150,000
Adjustments—increase (decrease)			
1			
2			
3			
4			
5			
6			
7			
8			
Total adjustments			
Adjusted amounts	$	$	$

(AICPA adapted)

(LO 4) **P8-3** **(Purchases Recorded Gross and Net)** Some of the transactions of William Dubois Company during August are listed below. Dubois uses the periodic inventory method.

August 10 Purchased merchandise on account, $9,000, terms 2/10, n/30.
13 Returned part of the purchase of August 10, $1,200, and received credit on account.
15 Purchased merchandise on account, $12,000, terms 1/10, n/60.
25 Purchased merchandise on account, $15,000, terms 2/10, n/30.
28 Paid invoice of August 15 in full.

Instructions
(a) Assuming that purchases are recorded at gross amounts and that discounts are to be recorded when taken:
 (1) Prepare general journal entries to record the transactions.
 (2) Describe how the various items would be shown in the financial statements.
(b) Assuming that purchases are recorded at net amounts and that discounts lost are treated as financial expenses:
 (1) Prepare general journal entries to enter the transactions.
 (2) Prepare the adjusting entry necessary on August 31 if financial statements are to be prepared at that time.
 (3) Describe how the various items would be shown in the financial statements.
(c) Which of the two methods do you prefer and why?

(LO 2, 5) **P8-4** **(Compute FIFO, LIFO, and Average Cost—Periodic and Perpetual)** Taos Company's record of transactions concerning part X for the month of April was as follows.

Purchases		Sales	
April 1 (balance on hand)	100 @ $5.00	April 5	300
4	400 @ 5.10	12	200
11	300 @ 5.30	27	800
18	200 @ 5.35	28	100
26	500 @ 5.60		1400
30	200 @ 5.80		
	1700		

Instructions
(a) Compute the inventory at April 30 on each of the following bases. Assume that perpetual inventory records are kept in units only. Carry unit costs to the nearest cent.
 (1) First-in, first-out (FIFO).

(2) Last-in, first-out (LIFO).

(3) Average cost.

(b) If the perpetual inventory record is kept in dollars, and costs are computed at the time of each withdrawal, what amount would be shown as ending inventory in 1, 2, and 3 above? Carry average unit costs to four decimal places.

(LO 2, 5) **P8-5 (Compute FIFO, LIFO and Average Cost—Periodic and Perpetual)** Some of the information found on a detail inventory card for David Letterman Inc. for the first month of operations is as follows.

Date	Received No. of Units	Received Unit Cost	Issued, No. of Units	Balance, No. of Units
January 2	1,200	$3.00		1,200
7			700	500
10	600	3.20		1,100
13			500	600
18	1,000	3.30	300	1,300
20			1,100	200
23	1,300	3.40		1,500
26			800	700
28	1,500	3.60		2,200
31			1,300	900

Instructions

(a) From these data compute the ending inventory on each of the following bases. Assume that perpetual inventory records are kept in units only. Carry unit costs to the nearest cent and ending inventory to the nearest dollar.

(1) First-in, first-out (FIFO).

(2) Last-in, first-out (LIFO).

(3) Average cost.

(b) If the perpetual inventory record is kept in dollars, and costs are computed at the time of each withdrawal, would the amounts shown as ending inventory in 1, 2, and 3 above be the same? Explain and compute.

(LO 2, 5) **P8-6 (Compute FIFO, LIFO, Average Cost—Periodic and Perpetual)** Iowa Company is a multiproduct firm. Presented below is information concerning one of its products, the Hawkeye.

Date	Transaction	Quantity	Price/Cost
1/1	Beginning inventory	1,000	$12
2/4	Purchase	2,000	18
2/20	Sale	2,500	30
4/2	Purchase	3,000	23
11/4	Sale	2,000	33

Instructions

Compute cost of goods sold, assuming Iowa uses:

(a) Periodic system, FIFO cost flow.

(b) Perpetual system, FIFO cost flow.

(c) Periodic system, LIFO cost flow.

(d) Perpetual system, LIFO cost flow.

(e) Periodic system, weighted-average cost flow.

(f) Perpetual system, moving-average cost flow.

(LO 5) **P8-7 (Financial Statement Effects of FIFO and LIFO)** The management of Maine Company has asked its accounting department to describe the effect upon the company's financial position and its income statements of accounting for inventories on the LIFO rather than the FIFO basis during 2007 and 2008. The accounting department is to assume that the change to LIFO would have been effective on January 1, 2007, and that the initial LIFO base would have been the inventory value on December 31, 2006. Presented below are the company's financial statements and other data for the years 2007 and 2008 when the FIFO method was employed.

	Financial Position as of 12/31/06	Financial Position as of 12/31/07	Financial Position as of 12/31/08
Cash	$ 90,000	$130,000	$ 141,600
Accounts receivable	80,000	100,000	120,000
Inventory	120,000	140,000	180,000
Other assets	160,000	170,000	200,000
Total assets	$450,000	$540,000	$ 641,600

Accounts payable	$ 40,000	$ 60,000	$ 80,000
Other liabilities	70,000	80,000	110,000
Common stock	200,000	200,000	200,000
Retained earnings	140,000	200,000	251,600
Total liabilities and equity	$450,000	$540,000	$ 641,600

	Income for Years Ended	
	12/31/07	12/31/08
Sales	$900,000	$1,350,000
Less: Cost of goods sold	505,000	770,000
Other expenses	205,000	304,000
	710,000	1,074,000
Income before income taxes	190,000	276,000
Income taxes (40%)	76,000	110,400
Net income	$114,000	$ 165,600

Other data:

1. Inventory on hand at December 31, 2006, consisted of 40,000 units valued at $3.00 each.
2. Sales (all units sold at the same price in a given year):

    2007—150,000 units @ $6.00 each   2008—180,000 units @ $7.50 each

3. Purchases (all units purchased at the same price in given year):

    2007—150,000 units @ $3.50 each   2008—180,000 units @ $4.50 each

4. Income taxes at the effective rate of 40% are paid on December 31 each year.

Instructions
Name the account(s) presented in the financial statements that would have different amounts for 2008 if LIFO rather than FIFO had been used, and state the new amount for each account that is named. Show computations.

(CMA adapted)

(LO 8) **P8-8** **(Dollar-Value LIFO)** Falcon's Televisions produces television sets in three categories: portable, midsize, and flat-screen. On January 1, 2006, Falcon adopted dollar-value LIFO and decided to use a single inventory pool. The company's January 1 inventory consists of:

Category	Quantity	Cost per Unit	Total Cost
Portable	6,000	$100	$ 600,000
Midsize	8,000	250	2,000,000
Flat-screen	3,000	400	1,200,000
	17,000		$3,800,000

During 2006, the company had the following purchases and sales.

Category	Quantity Purchased	Cost per Unit	Quantity Sold	Selling Price per Unit
Portable	15,000	$120	14,000	$150
Midsize	20,000	300	24,000	405
Flat-screen	10,000	460	6,000	600
	45,000		44,000	

Instructions
(Round to four decimals.)

(a) Compute ending inventory, cost of goods sold, and gross profit.
(b) Assume the company uses three inventory pools instead of one. Repeat instruction (a).

(LO 8) **P8-9** **(Internal Indexes—Dollar-Value LIFO)** On January 1, 2006, Adis Abeba Wholesalers Inc. adopted the dollar-value LIFO inventory method for income tax and external financial reporting purposes. However, Abeba continued to use the FIFO inventory method for internal accounting and management purposes. In applying the LIFO method, Abeba uses internal conversion price indexes and the multiple pools approach under which substantially identical inventory items are grouped into LIFO inventory pools. The following data were available for inventory pool no. 1, which comprises products A and B, for the 2 years following the adoption of LIFO.

| | **FIFO Basis per Records** | | |
	Units	Unit Cost	Total Cost
Inventory, 1/1/06			
Product A	10,000	$30	$300,000
Product B	9,000	25	225,000
			$525,000
Inventory, 12/31/06			
Product A	17,000	35	$595,000
Product B	9,000	26	234,000
			$829,000
Inventory, 12/31/07			
Product A	13,000	40	$520,000
Product B	10,000	32	320,000
			$840,000

Instructions

(a) Prepare a schedule to compute the internal conversion price indexes for 2006 and 2007. Round indexes to two decimal places.

(b) Prepare a schedule to compute the inventory amounts at December 31, 2006 and 2007, using the dollar-value LIFO inventory method.

(AICPA adapted)

(LO 8) **P8-10 (Internal Indexes—Dollar-Value LIFO)** Presented below is information related to Mellon Collie Corporation for the last 3 years.

Item	Quantities in Ending Inventories	**Base-Year Cost**		**Current-Year Cost**	
		Unit Cost	Amount	Unit Cost	Amount
December 31, 2005					
A	9,000	$2.00	$18,000	$2.40	$21,600
B	6,000	3.00	18,000	3.55	21,300
C	4,000	5.00	20,000	5.40	21,600
		Totals	$56,000		$64,500
December 31, 2006					
A	9,000	$2.00	$18,000	$2.60	$23,400
B	6,800	3.00	20,400	3.75	25,500
C	6,000	5.00	30,000	6.40	38,400
		Totals	$68,400		$87,300
December 31, 2007					
A	8,000	$2.00	$16,000	$2.70	$21,600
B	8,000	3.00	24,000	4.00	32,000
C	6,000	5.00	30,000	6.20	37,200
		Totals	$70,000		$90,800

Instructions

Compute the ending inventories under the dollar-value LIFO method for 2005, 2006, and 2007. The base period is January 1, 2005, and the beginning inventory cost at that date was $45,000. Compute indexes to two decimal places.

(LO 8) **P8-11 (Dollar-Value LIFO)** Warren Dunn Company cans a variety of vegetable-type soups. Recently, the company decided to value its inventories using dollar-value LIFO pools. The clerk who accounts for inventories does not understand how to value the inventory pools using this new method, so, as a private consultant, you have been asked to teach him how this new method works.

He has provided you with the following information about purchases made over a 6-year period.

Date	Ending Inventory (End-of-Year Prices)	Price Index
Dec. 31, 2003	$ 80,000	100
Dec. 31, 2004	115,500	105
Dec. 31, 2005	108,000	120
Dec. 31, 2006	131,300	130
Dec. 31, 2007	154,000	140
Dec. 31, 2008	174,000	145

You have already explained to him how this inventory method is maintained, but he would feel better about it if you were to leave him detailed instructions explaining how these calculations are done and why he needs to put all inventories at a base-year value.

Instructions

(a) Compute the ending inventory for Warren Dunn Company for 2003 through 2008 using dollar-value LIFO.

(b) Using your computation schedules as your illustration, write a step-by-step set of instructions explaining how the calculations are done. Begin your explanation by briefly explaining the theory behind this inventory method, including the purpose of putting all amounts into base-year price levels.

CONCEPTS FOR ANALYSIS

CA8-1 **(Inventoriable Costs)** You are asked to travel to Milwaukee to observe and verify the inventory of the Milwaukee branch of one of your clients. You arrive on Thursday, December 30, and find that the inventory procedures have just been started. You spot a railway car on the sidetrack at the unloading door and ask the warehouse superintendent, Predrag Danilovic, how he plans to inventory the contents of the car. He responds, "We are not going to include the contents in the inventory."

Later in the day, you ask the bookkeeper for the invoice on the carload and the related freight bill. The invoice lists the various items, prices, and extensions of the goods in the car. You note that the carload was shipped December 24 from Albuquerque, f.o.b. Albuquerque, and that the total invoice price of the goods in the car was $35,300. The freight bill called for a payment of $1,500. Terms were net 30 days. The bookkeeper affirms the fact that this invoice is to be held for recording in January.

Instructions

(a) Does your client have a liability that should be recorded at December 31? Discuss.

(b) Prepare a journal entry(ies), if required, to reflect any accounting adjustment required. Assume a perpetual inventory system is used by your client.

(c) For what possible reason(s) might your client wish to postpone recording the transaction?

CA8-2 **(Inventoriable Costs)** Brian Erlacher, an inventory control specialist, is interested in better understanding the accounting for inventories. Although Brian understands the more sophisticated computer inventory control systems, he has little knowledge of how inventory cost is determined. In studying the records of Sherman Enterprises, which sells normal brand-name goods from its own store and on consignment through Lovey Smith Inc., he asks you to answer the following questions.

Instructions

(a) Should Sherman Enterprises include in its inventory normal brand-name goods purchased from its suppliers but not yet received if the terms of purchase are f.o.b. shipping point (manufacturer's plant)? Why?

(b) Should Sherman Enterprises include freight-in expenditures as an inventory cost? Why?

(c) If Sherman Enterprises purchases its goods on terms 2/10, net 30, should the purchases be recorded gross or net? Why?

(d) What are products on consignment? How should they be reported in the financial statements?

(AICPA adapted)

CA8-3 **(Inventoriable Costs)** Jack McDowell, the controller for McDowell Lumber Company, has recently hired you as assistant controller. He wishes to determine your expertise in the area of inventory accounting and therefore asks you to answer the following unrelated questions.

(a) A company is involved in the wholesaling and retailing of automobile tires for foreign cars. Most of the inventory is imported, and it is valued on the company's records at the actual inventory cost plus freight-in. At year-end, the warehousing costs are prorated over cost of goods sold and ending inventory. Are warehousing costs considered a product cost or a period cost?

(b) A certain portion of a company's "inventory" is composed of obsolete items. Should obsolete items that are not currently consumed in the production of "goods or services to be available for sale" be classified as part of inventory?

(c) A company purchases airplanes for sale to others. However, until they are sold, the company charters and services the planes. What is the proper way to report these airplanes in the company's financial statements?

(d) A company wants to buy coal deposits but does not want the financing for the purchase to be reported on its financial statements. The company therefore establishes a trust to acquire the coal deposits. The company agrees to buy the coal over a certain period of time at specified prices. The trust is able to finance the coal purchase and pay off the loan as it is paid by the company for the minerals. How should this transaction be reported?

CA8-4 (Accounting Treatment of Purchase Discounts) Wayne Gretzky Corp., a household appliances dealer, purchases its inventories from various suppliers. Gretzky has consistently stated its inventories at the lower of cost (FIFO) or market.

Instructions
Gretzky is considering alternate methods of accounting for the cash discounts it takes when paying its suppliers promptly. From a theoretical standpoint, discuss the acceptability of each of the following methods.

(a) Financial income when payments are made.
(b) Reduction of cost of goods sold for the period when payments are made.
(c) Direct reduction of purchase cost.

(AICPA adapted)

CA8-5 (General Inventory Issues) In January 2007, Wesley Crusher Inc. requested and secured permission from the commissioner of the Internal Revenue Service to compute inventories under the last-in, first-out (LIFO) method and elected to determine inventory cost under the dollar-value LIFO method. Crusher Inc. satisfied the commissioner that cost could be accurately determined by use of an index number computed from a representative sample selected from the company's single inventory pool.

Instructions
(a) Why should inventories be included in (1) a balance sheet and (2) the computation of net income?
(b) The Internal Revenue Code allows some accountable events to be considered differently for income tax reporting purposes and financial accounting purposes, while other accountable events must be reported the same for both purposes. Discuss why it might be desirable to report some accountable events differently for financial accounting purposes than for income tax reporting purposes.
(c) Discuss the ways and conditions under which the FIFO and LIFO inventory costing methods produce different inventory valuations. Do not discuss procedures for computing inventory cost.

(AICPA adapted)

CA8-6 (LIFO Inventory Advantages) Jean Honore, president of Fragonard Co., recently read an article that claimed that at least 100 of the country's largest 500 companies were either adopting or considering adopting the last-in, first-out (LIFO) method for valuing inventories. The article stated that the firms were switching to LIFO to (1) neutralize the effect of inflation in their financial statements, (2) eliminate inventory profits, and (3) reduce income taxes. Ms. Honore wonders if the switch would benefit her company.

Fragonard currently uses the first-in, first-out (FIFO) method of inventory valuation in its periodic inventory system. The company has a high inventory turnover rate, and inventories represent a significant proportion of the assets.

Ms. Honore has been told that the LIFO system is more costly to operate and will provide little benefit to companies with high turnover. She intends to use the inventory method that is best for the company in the long run rather than selecting a method just because it is the current fad.

Instructions
(a) Explain to Ms. Honore what "inventory profits" are and how the LIFO method of inventory valuation could reduce them.
(b) Explain to Ms. Honore the conditions that must exist for Fragonard Co. to receive tax benefits from a switch to the LIFO method.

CA8-7 (Average Cost, FIFO, and LIFO) Prepare a memorandum containing responses to the following items.

(a) Describe the cost flow assumptions used in average cost, FIFO, and LIFO methods of inventory valuation.
(b) Distinguish between weighted-average cost and moving-average cost for inventory costing purposes.
(c) Identify the effects on both the balance sheet and the income statement of using the LIFO method instead of the FIFO method for inventory costing purposes over a substantial time period when purchase prices of inventoriable items are rising. State why these effects take place.

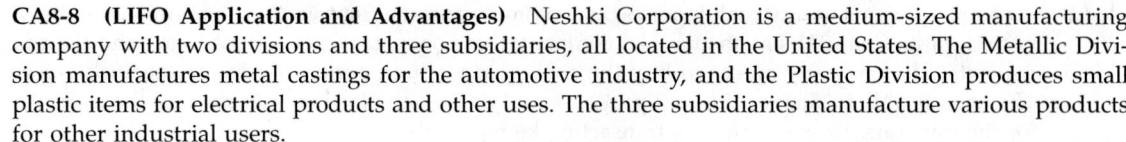

CA8-8 (LIFO Application and Advantages) Neshki Corporation is a medium-sized manufacturing company with two divisions and three subsidiaries, all located in the United States. The Metallic Division manufactures metal castings for the automotive industry, and the Plastic Division produces small plastic items for electrical products and other uses. The three subsidiaries manufacture various products for other industrial users.

Neshki Corporation plans to change from the lower of first-in, first-out (FIFO) cost or market method of inventory valuation to the last-in, first-out (LIFO) method of inventory valuation to obtain tax benefits. To make the method acceptable for tax purposes, the change also will be made for its annual financial statements.

Instructions
   (a) Describe the establishment of and subsequent pricing procedures for each of the following LIFO inventory methods.
   (1) LIFO applied to units of product when the periodic inventory system is used.
   (2) Application of the dollar-value method to LIFO units of product.
   (b) Discuss the specific advantages and disadvantages of using the dollar-value LIFO application as compared to specific goods LIFO (unit LIFO). Ignore income tax considerations.
   (c) Discuss the general advantages and disadvantages claimed for LIFO methods.

CA8-9 (Dollar-Value LIFO Issues) Maria Callas Co. is considering switching from the specific goods LIFO approach to the dollar-value LIFO approach. Because the financial personnel at Callas know very little about dollar-value LIFO, they ask you to answer the following questions.

   (a) What is a LIFO pool?
   (b) Is it possible to use a LIFO pool concept and not use dollar-value LIFO? Explain.
   (c) What is a LIFO liquidation?
   (d) How are price indexes used in the dollar-value LIFO method?
   (e) What are the advantages of dollar-value LIFO over specific goods LIFO?

CA8-10 (FIFO and LIFO) Günter Grass Company is considering changing its inventory valuation method from FIFO to LIFO because of the potential tax savings. However, the management wishes to consider all of the effects on the company, including its reported performance, before making the final decision.

The inventory account, currently valued on the FIFO basis, consists of 1,000,000 units at $7 per unit on January 1, 2007. There are 1,000,000 shares of common stock outstanding as of January 1, 2007, and the cash balance is $400,000.

The company has made the following forecasts for the period 2007–2009.

	2007	2008	2009
Unit sales (in millions of units)	1.1	1.0	1.3
Sales price per unit	$10	$10	$12
Unit purchases (in millions of units)	1.0	1.1	1.2
Purchase price per unit	$7	$8	$9
Annual depreciation (in thousands of dollars)	$300	$300	$300
Cash dividends per share	$0.15	$0.15	$0.15
Cash payments for additions to and replacement of plant and equipment (in thousands of dollars)	$350	$350	$350
Income tax rate	40%	40%	40%
Operating expenses (exclusive of depreciation) as a percent of sales	15%	15%	15%
Common shares outstanding (in millions)	1	1	1

Instructions
   (a) Prepare a schedule that illustrates and compares the following data for Günter Grass Company under the FIFO and the LIFO inventory method for 2007–2009. Assume the company would begin LIFO at the beginning of 2007.
   (1) Year-end inventory balances.   **(3)** Earnings per share.
   (2) Annual net income after taxes.   **(4)** Cash balance.
   Assume all sales are collected in the year of sale and all purchases, operating expenses, and taxes are paid during the year incurred.
   (b) Using the data above, your answer to (a), and any additional issues you believe need to be considered, prepare a report that recommends whether or not Günter Grass Company should change to the LIFO inventory method. Support your conclusions with appropriate arguments.

(CMA adapted)

CA8-11 **(LIFO Choices)** Gamble Company uses the LIFO method for inventory costing. In an effort to lower net income, company president Oscar Gamble tells the plant accountant to take the unusual step of recommending to the purchasing department a large purchase of inventory at year-end. The price of the item to be purchased has nearly doubled during the year, and the item represents a major portion of inventory value.

Instructions

Answer the following questions.

(a) Identify the major stakeholders. If the plant accountant recommends the purchase, what are the consequences?

(b) If Gamble Company were using the FIFO method of inventory costing, would Oscar Gamble give the same order? Why or why not?

USING YOUR JUDGMENT

Financial Statement Analysis Cases

Case 1 T J International

T J International was founded in 1969 as Trus Joist International. The firm, a manufacturer of specialty building products, has its headquarters in Boise, Idaho. The company, through its partnership in the Trus Joist MacMillan joint venture, develops and manufactures engineered lumber. This product is a high-quality substitute for structural lumber, and uses lower-grade wood and materials formerly considered waste. The company also is majority owner of the Outlook Window Partnership, which is a consortium of three wood and vinyl window manufacturers.

Following is T J International's adapted income statement and information concerning inventories from its annual report.

T J International

Sales	$618,876,000
Cost of goods sold	475,476,000
Gross profit	143,400,000
Selling and administrative expenses	102,112,000
Income from operations	41,288,000
Other expense	24,712,000
Income before income tax	16,576,000
Income taxes	7,728,000
Net income	$ 8,848,000

Inventories. Inventories are valued at the lower of cost or market and include material, labor, and production overhead costs. Inventories consisted of the following:

	Current Year	Prior Year
Finished goods	$27,512,000	$23,830,000
Raw materials and work-in-progress	34,363,000	33,244,000
	61,875,000	57,074,000
Reduction to LIFO cost	(5,263,000)	(3,993,000)
	$56,612,000	$53,081,000

The last-in, first-out (LIFO) method is used for determining the cost of lumber, veneer, Microllam lumber, TJI joists, and open web joists. Approximately 35 percent of total inventories at the end of the current year were valued using the LIFO method. The first-in, first-out (FIFO) method is used to determine the cost of all other inventories.

Instructions

(a) How much would income before taxes have been if FIFO costing had been used to value all inventories?

(b) If the income tax rate is 46.6%, what would income tax have been if FIFO costing had been used to value all inventories? In your opinion, is this difference in net income between the two methods material? Explain.

(c) Does the use of a different costing system for different types of inventory mean that there is a different physical flow of goods among the different types of inventory? Explain.

Case 2 Noven Pharmaceuticals, Inc.

Noven Pharmaceuticals, Inc., headquartered in Miami, Florida, describes itself in a recent annual report as follows.

Noven Pharmaceuticals, Inc.

Noven is a place of ideas—a company where scientific excellence and state-of-the-art manufacturing combine to create new answers to human needs. Our transdermal delivery systems speed drugs painlessly and effortlessly into the bloodstream by means of a simple skin patch. This technology has proven applications in estrogen replacement, but at Noven we are developing a variety of systems incorporating bestselling drugs that fight everything from asthma, anxiety and dental pain to cancer, heart disease and neurological illness. Our research portfolio also includes new technologies, such as iontophoresis, in which drugs are delivered through the skin by means of electrical currents, as well as products that could satisfy broad consumer needs, such as our anti-microbial mouthrinse.

Noven also reported in its annual report that its activities to date have consisted of product development efforts, some of which have been independent and some of which have been completed in conjunction with **Rhone-Poulenc Rorer (RPR)** and **Ciba-Geigy**. The revenues so far have consisted of money received from licensing fees, "milestone" payments (payments made under licensing agreements when certain stages of the development of a certain product have been completed), and interest on its investments. The company expects that it will have significant revenue in the upcoming fiscal year from the launch of its first product, a transdermal estrogen delivery system.

The current assets portion of Noven's balance sheet follows.

Cash and cash equivalents	$12,070,272
Securities held to maturity	23,445,070
Inventory of supplies	1,264,553
Prepaid and other current assets	825,159
Total current assets	$37,605,054

Inventory of supplies is recorded at the lower of cost (first-in, first-out) or net realizable value and consists mainly of supplies for research and development.

Instructions

(a) What would you expect the physical flow of goods for a pharmaceutical manufacturer to be most like: FIFO, LIFO, or random (flow of goods does not follow a set pattern)? Explain.

(b) What are some of the factors that Noven should consider as it selects an inventory measurement method?

(c) Suppose that Noven had $49,000 in an inventory of transdermal estrogen delivery patches. These patches are from an initial production run, and will be sold during the coming year. Why do you think that this amount is not shown in a separate inventory account? In which of the accounts shown is the inventory likely to be? At what point will the inventory be transferred to a separate inventory account?

Case 3 Albertson's

Albertson's reported that its inventory turnover ratio increased from 8.2 times in 2003 to 8.4 times in 2004. The following data appear in Albertson's annual report.

	Jan. 31, 2002	Jan. 30, 2003	Jan. 29, 2004
Total revenues	$36,605	$35,626	$35,436
Cost of sales	26,179	25,248	25,306
Year-end inventories of FIFO	3,793	3,256	3,611
Year-end inventories of LIFO	3,196	2,973	3,035

(a) Compute Albertson's inventory turnover ratios for 2003 and 2004, using:
  (1) Cost of sales and LIFO inventory.
  (2) Cost of sales and FIFO inventory.
(b) Some firms calculate inventory turnover using sales rather than cost of goods sold in the numerator. Calculate Albertson's 2003 and 2004 turnover, using:
  (1) Sales and LIFO inventory.
  (2) Sales and FIFO inventory.
(c) Describe the method that Albertson's appears to use.
(d) State which method you would choose to evaluate Albertson's performance. Justify your choice.

Research Cases

Case 1

As indicated in the chapter, the FIFO and LIFO inventory methods can result in significantly different income statement and balance sheet figures. However, it is possible to convert income for a LIFO firm to its FIFO-based equivalent. To assist financial statement users in this task, firms using LIFO are required to disclose in their footnotes the "LIFO reserve" (LR)—i.e., the difference between the inventory balance shown on the balance sheet and the amount that would have been reported had the firm used current cost (or FIFO), as illustrated for **Brown Shoe Company** on page 385.

The following equation can be used to convert LIFO cost of goods sold (COGS) to FIFO COGS.

$$COGS_{FIFO} = COGS_{LIFO} - LIFO \text{ effect}$$

where

$$LIFO \text{ effect} = [LR_{ending} - LR_{beginning}]$$

The following equation can be used to convert LIFO net income (NI) to FIFO net income.

$$NI_{FIFO} = NI_{LIFO} + (LIFO \text{ effect}) (1 - \text{tax rate})$$

Instructions
Obtain the annual report of a firm that reports a LIFO reserve in its footnotes.
(a) Identify the LIFO reserve at the two most recent balance sheet dates.
(b) Determine the LIFO effect during the most recent year.
(c) By how much would cost of goods sold during the most recent year change if the firm used FIFO?
(d) By how much would net income during the most recent year change if the firm used FIFO? (*Hint:* To estimate the tax rate, divide income tax expense by income before taxes.)

Case 2

The "Fortune 500" issue of *Fortune* magazine can serve as a useful reference. This annual issue, generally appearing in late April or early May, contains a great deal of information regarding the largest U.S. industrial and service companies.

Instructions
Examine the most recent edition and answer the following questions.
(a) Identify the three largest U.S. corporations in terms of revenue, profit, assets, market value, and employees.
(b) Identify the largest corporation in your state (by total revenue).

Professional Research: Financial Accounting and Reporting

In conducting year-end inventory counts, your audit team is debating the impact of the client's right of return policy both on inventory valuation and revenue recognition. The assistant controller argues that there is no need to worry about the return policies since they have not changed in a while. The audit senior wants a more authoritative answer and has asked you to conduct some research of the authoritative literature, before she presses the point with the client.

Instructions
Using the **Financial Accounting Research System (FARS),** respond to the following items. (Provide text strings used in your search.)
(a) Which statement addresses revenue recognition when right of return exists?
(b) When is this statement important for a company?

(c) Sales with high rates of return can ultimately cause inventory to be misstated. Why are returns allowed? Should different industries be able to make different types of return policies?

(d) In what situations would a reasonable estimate of returns be difficult to make?

Professional Simulation

In this simulation you are asked to address questions regarding inventory valuation and measurement. Prepare responses to all parts.

KWW_Professional _Simulation

| Inventory Valuation | Time Remaining 2 hours 0 minutes | copy | paste | calculator | sheet | standards | help | spliter | done |

Directions | **Situation** | **Measurement** | **Analysis** | **Explanation** | **Resources**

Norwel Company makes miniature circuit boards that are components of wireless phones and personal organizers. The company has experienced strong growth, and you are especially interested in how well Norwel is managing its inventory balances. You have collected the following information for the current year.

Inventory at the beginning of year	$125.5 million
Inventory at the end of year, before any adjustments	$116.7 million
Total cost of goods sold, before any adjustments	$1,776.4 million

The company values inventory at lower of cost (using LIFO cost flow assumption) or market.

Directions | **Situation** | **Measurement** | **Analysis** | **Explanation** | **Resources**

Compute Norwel's inventory turnover ratio for the current year.

Directions | **Situation** | **Measurement** | **Analysis** | **Explanation** | **Resources**

Use a computer spreadsheet to prepare a schedule showing the impact of the following items on Norwel's inventory turnover ratio.

(a) During the year, Norwel recorded sales and costs of goods sold on $2 million of units shipped to various wholesalers on consignment. At year-end, none of these units have been sold by wholesalers.

(b) Shipping contracts changed 2 months ago from f.o.b. shipping point to f.o.b. destination. At the end of the year, $5 million of products are en route to China (and will not arrive until after financial statements are released). Current inventory balances do not reflect this change in policy.

(c) To be more consistent with industry inventory valuation practices, Norwel changed from LIFO to FIFO for its inventory of high-speed circuit boards. This inventory is currently carried at $724 million (cost of goods sold, $941 million). Data for this item of inventory for the year are as follows.

Month	Units purchased	Inventory sold	Price per unit	Units balance
January 1	100		$3.10	100
April 10	150		3.20	250
October 20		130		120
November 20	250		3.50	370
December 15		150		220

Directions | **Situation** | **Measurement** | **Analysis** | **Explanation** | **Resources**

Prepare a brief memorandum to Norwel's management discussing the advantages of adopting the LIFO cost flow assumption.

Remember to check the book's companion website to find additional resources for this chapter.

www.wiley.com/college/kieso

INVENTORIES: ADDITIONAL VALUATION ISSUES

What Do Inventory Changes Tell Us?

Department stores face an ongoing challenge: They need to keep enough inventory to meet customer demand, but not to accumulate too much inventory. If demand falls short of expectations, the department store may be forced to reduce prices on its existing inventory, thus losing sales revenue.

For example, the following table shows recent annual sales and inventory trends for major retailers, compared to the prior year.

Company	Sales	Inventory
Nordstrom	+10.59%	+ 1.73%
Federated Department Stores	+ 2.40%	− 2.95%
JCPenney	+ 3.59%	+ 0.41%
Wal-Mart	+11.63%	+ 9.06%
May Department Stores	+ 8.23%	+13.34%
Target	+11.62%	+18.83%
Best Buy	+17.21%	+25.52%
Circuit City	− 1.97%	+ 7.63%
Sears	−12.22%	+ 4.01%

Source: Company reports, fiscal years 2003 and 2004.

For over half of these retailers, inventories grew faster than sales from one year to the next—a trend that should raise warning flags for investors. Rising levels of inventories indicate that fewer shoppers are turning out to buy merchandise compared to activity in the prior period. As one analyst remarked, ". . . when inventory grows faster than sales, profits drop." That is, when retailers face slower sales and growing inventory, markdowns in prices are usually not far behind. These markdowns, in turn, lead to lower sales revenue and income.

Bankruptcies of retailers like **Ames Department Stores**, **Montgomery Ward**, and **Bradlees Stores** indicate the consequences of poor inventory management. And more recently, **Kmart**, which filed for bankruptcy in January 2002 and has since been acquired by **Sears Holdings**, was in an inventory "Catch-22." In order to work out of bankruptcy, Kmart needed to keep its shelves stocked so that customers would continue to shop in its remaining stores. However, vendors who were worried about Kmart's ability to manage its inventory were reluctant to ship goods without assurances that they would get paid. Thus, investors, creditors, and vendors keep an eye on information about inventories in the retail industry.

Learning Objectives

After studying this chapter, you should be able to:

1 Describe and apply the lower-of-cost-or-market rule.

2 Explain when companies value inventories at net realizable value.

3 Explain when companies use the relative sales value method to value inventories.

4 Discuss accounting issues related to purchase commitments.

5 Determine ending inventory by applying the gross profit method.

6 Determine ending inventory by applying the retail inventory method.

7 Explain how to report and analyze inventory.

As our opening story indicates, information on inventories and changes in inventory helps to predict financial performance—in particular, profits. In this chapter we discuss some of the valuation and estimation concepts that companies use to develop relevant inventory information. The content and organization of the chapter are as follows.

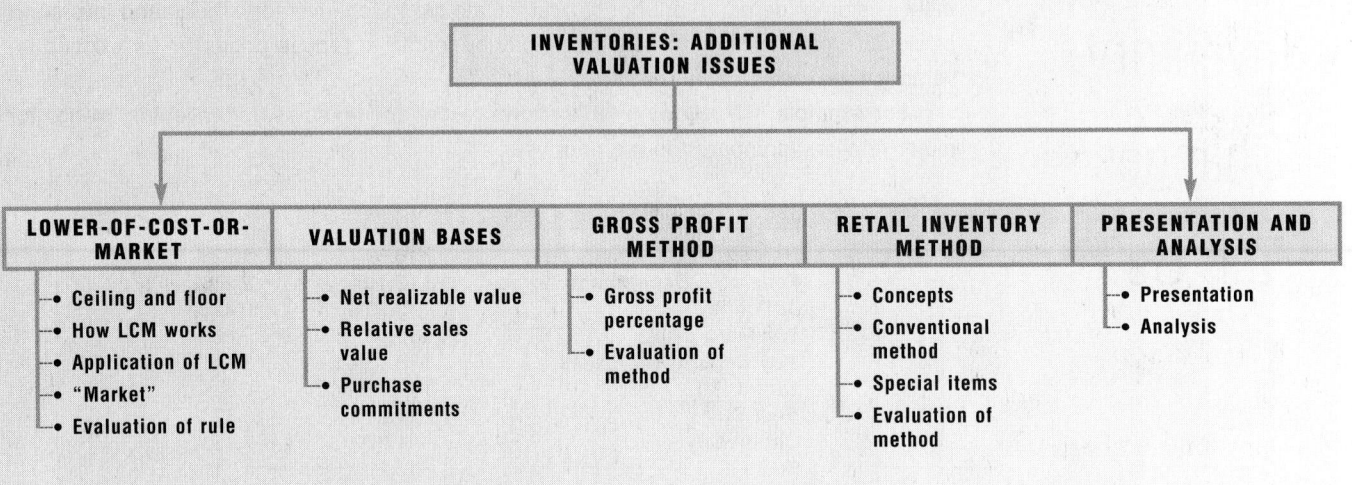

INVENTORIES: ADDITIONAL VALUATION ISSUES

LOWER-OF-COST-OR-MARKET	VALUATION BASES	GROSS PROFIT METHOD	RETAIL INVENTORY METHOD	PRESENTATION AND ANALYSIS
• Ceiling and floor • How LCM works • Application of LCM • "Market" • Evaluation of rule	• Net realizable value • Relative sales value • Purchase commitments	• Gross profit percentage • Evaluation of method	• Concepts • Conventional method • Special items • Evaluation of method	• Presentation • Analysis

LOWER-OF-COST-OR-MARKET

<table>
<tr><td>

OBJECTIVE 1
Describe and apply the lower-of-cost-or-market rule.

</td><td>

Inventories are recorded at their cost. However, if inventory declines in value below its original cost, a major departure from the historical cost principle occurs. Whatever the reason for a decline—obsolescence, price-level changes, or damaged goods—a company should write down the inventory to market to report this loss. **A company abandons the historical cost principle when the future utility (revenue-producing ability) of the asset drops below its original cost.** Companies therefore **report inventories at the lower-of-cost-or-market** at each reporting period.

</td></tr>
</table>

Illustration 9-1 shows how **Eastman Kodak** and **Best Buy** reported this information.

ILLUSTRATION 9-1
Lower-of-Cost-or-
Market Disclosures

EASTMAN KODAK

Notes to Financial Statements

The company reduces the carrying value to a lower-of-cost-or-market basis for those items that are excess, obsolete, or slow moving based on management's analysis of inventory levels and future sales forecasts.

BEST BUY

Notes to Financial Statements

Merchandise inventories are recorded at the lower of average cost or market.

Recall that **cost** is the acquisition price of inventory computed using one of the historical cost-based methods—specific identification, average cost, FIFO, or LIFO. The term **market** in the phrase "the lower-of-cost-or-market" (LCM) generally means the cost to replace the item by purchase or reproduction. For a retailer like **Nordstrom**, the term "market" refers to the market in which it purchases goods, not the market in which it sells them. For a manufacturer like **William Wrigley Jr.**, the term "market" refers to the cost to reproduce. Thus the rule really means that **companies value goods at cost or cost to replace, whichever is lower**.

For example, say **Target** purchased a **Timex** calculator wristwatch for $30 for resale. Target can sell the wristwatch for $48.95 and replace it for $25. It should therefore value the wristwatch at $25 for inventory purposes under the lower-of-cost-or-market rule. Target can use the lower-of-cost-or-market rule of valuation after applying any of the cost flow methods discussed above to determine the inventory cost.

A departure from cost is justified because **a company should charge a loss of utility against revenues in the period in which the loss occurs**, not in the period of sale. Note also that the lower-of-cost-or-market method is **a conservative approach to inventory valuation**. That is, when doubt exists about the value of an asset, a company should use the lower value for the asset, which also reduces net income.

UNDERLYING CONCEPTS

The use of the lower-of-cost-or-market rule is an excellent example of the conservatism constraint.

Lower-of-Cost-or-Market—Ceiling and Floor

Why use replacement cost to represent market value? Because a decline in the replacement cost of an item usually reflects or predicts a decline in selling price. Using replacement cost allows a company to maintain a consistent rate of gross profit on sales (normal profit margin). Sometimes, however, a reduction in the replacement cost of an item fails to indicate a corresponding reduction in its utility. This requires using two additional valuation limitations to value ending inventory—net realizable value and net realizable value less a normal profit margin.

Net realizable value (NRV) is the estimated selling price in the ordinary course of business, less reasonably predictable costs of completion and disposal (often referred to as net selling price). A normal profit margin is subtracted from that amount to arrive at **net realizable value less a normal profit margin**.

To illustrate, assume that Jerry Mander Corp. has unfinished inventory with a sales value of $1,000, estimated cost of completion of $300, and a normal profit margin of 10 percent of sales. Jerry Mander determines the following net realizable value.

Inventory—sales value	$1,000
Less: Estimated cost of completion and disposal	300
Net realizable value	700
Less: Allowance for normal profit margin (10% of sales)	100
Net realizable value less a normal profit margin	$ 600

ILLUSTRATION 9-2
Computation of Net Realizable Value

The general **lower-of-cost-or-market** rule is: **A company values inventory at the lower-of-cost-or-market, with market limited to an amount that is not more than net realizable value or less than net realizable value less a normal profit margin.**[1]

The **upper (ceiling)** is the net realizable value of inventory. The **lower (floor)** is the the net realizable value less a normal profit margin. What is the rationale for these two limitations? Establishing these limits for the value of the inventory prevents companies from over- or understating inventory.

---

[1]"Restatement and Revision of Accounting Research Bulletins," *Accounting Research Bulletin No. 43* (New York: AICPA, 1953), Ch. 4, par. 8.

The maximum limitation, **not to exceed the net realizable value (ceiling),** prevents overstatement of the value of obsolete, damaged, or shopworn inventories. That is, if the replacement cost of an item exceeds its net realizable value, a company should not report inventory at replacement cost. The company can receive only the selling price less cost of disposal. To report the inventory at replacement cost would result in an overstatement of inventory and understatement of the loss in the current period.

To illustrate, assume that **Staples** paid $1,000 for a color laser printer that it can now replace for $900. The printer's net realizable value is $700. At what amount should Staples report the laser printer in the financial statements? To report the replacement cost of $900 overstates the ending inventory and understates the loss for the period. Therefore, Staples should report the printer at $700.

The minimum limitation (floor) is **not to be less than net realizable value reduced by an allowance for an approximately normal profit margin.** The floor establishes a value below which a company should not price inventory, regardless of replacement cost. It makes no sense to price inventory below net realizable value less a normal margin. This minimum amount (floor) measures what the company can receive for the inventory and still earn a normal profit. Use of a floor deters understatement of inventory and overstatement of the loss in the current period.

Illustration 9-3 graphically presents the guidelines for valuing inventory at the lower-of-cost-or-market.

UNDERLYING CONCEPTS

Setting a floor and a ceiling increases the relevancy of the inventory presentation. The inventory figure provides a better understanding of how much revenue the inventory will generate.

ILLUSTRATION 9-3
Inventory Valuation—
Lower of Cost or Market

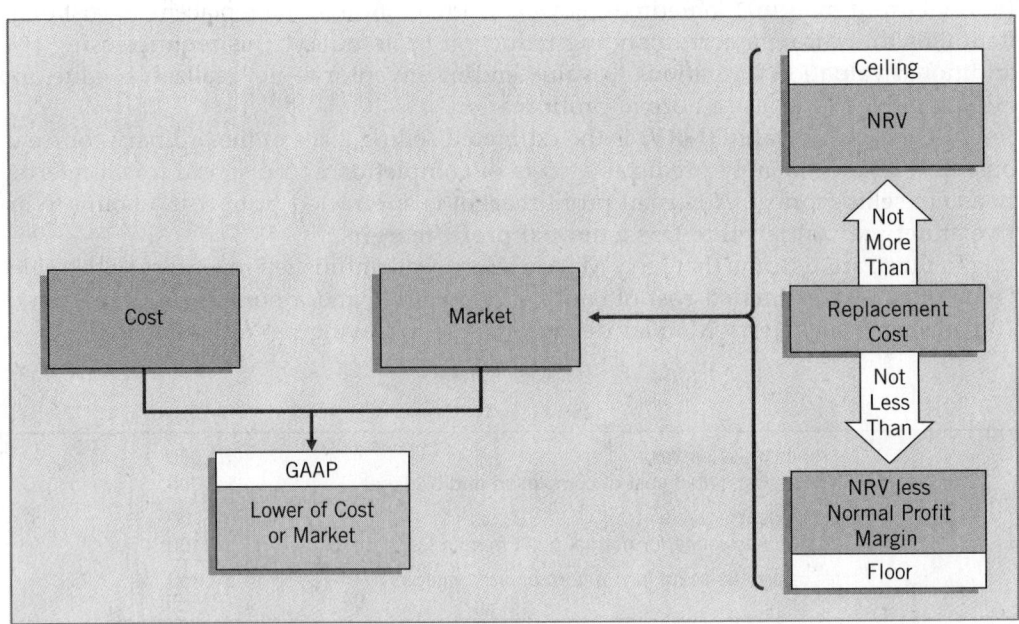

How Lower-of-Cost-or-Market Works

The **designated market value** is the amount that a company compares to cost. It is **always the middle value of three amounts**: replacement cost, net realizable value, and net realizable value less a normal profit margin. To illustrate how to compute designated market value, assume the information relative to the inventory of Regner Foods, Inc., as shown in Illustration 9-4 (on page 425).

Regner Foods then compares designated market value to cost to determine the lower-of-cost-or-market. It determines the final inventory value as shown in Illustration 9-5 (on page 425).

ILLUSTRATION 9-4
Computation of
Designated Market Value

Food	Replacement Cost	Net Realizable Value (Ceiling)	Net Realizable Value Less a Normal Profit Margin (Floor)	Designated Market Value
Spinach	$ 88,000	$120,000	$104,000	$104,000
Carrots	90,000	100,000	70,000	90,000
Cut beans	45,000	40,000	27,500	40,000
Peas	36,000	72,000	48,000	48,000
Mixed vegetables	105,000	92,000	80,000	92,000

Designated Market Value Decision:

Spinach	Net realizable value less a normal profit margin is selected because it is the middle value.
Carrots	Replacement cost is selected because it is the middle value.
Cut beans	Net realizable value is selected because it is the middle value.
Peas	Net realizable value less a normal profit margin is selected because it is the middle value.
Mixed vegetables	Net realizable value is selected because it is the middle value.

ILLUSTRATION 9-5
Determining Final
Inventory Value

Food	Cost	Replacement Cost	Net Realizable Value (Ceiling)	Net Realizable Value Less a Normal Profit Margin (Floor)	Designated Market Value	Final Inventory Value
Spinach	$ 80,000	$ 88,000	$120,000	$104,000	$104,000	$ 80,000
Carrots	100,000	90,000	100,000	70,000	90,000	90,000
Cut beans	50,000	45,000	40,000	27,500	40,000	40,000
Peas	90,000	36,000	72,000	48,000	48,000	48,000
Mixed vegetables	95,000	105,000	92,000	80,000	92,000	92,000
						$350,000

Final Inventory Value:

Spinach	Cost ($80,000) is selected because it is lower than designated market value (net realizable value less a normal profit margin).
Carrots	Designated market value (replacement cost, $90,000) is selected because it is lower than cost.
Cut beans	Designated market value (net realizable value, $40,000) is selected because it is lower than cost.
Peas	Designated market value (net realizable value less a normal profit margin, $48,000) is selected because it is lower than cost.
Mixed vegetables	Designated market value (net realizable value, $92,000) is selected because it is lower than cost.

The application of the lower-of-cost-or-market rule incorporates only losses in value that occur in the normal course of business from such causes as style changes, shift in demand, or regular shop wear. A company reduces damaged or deteriorated goods to net realizable value. When material, it may carry such goods in separate inventory accounts.

Methods of Applying Lower-of-Cost-or-Market

In the Regner Foods illustration, we assumed that the company applied the lower-of-cost-or-market rule to each individual type of food. However, companies may apply the lower-of-cost-or-market rule either directly to each item, to each category, or to the total of the inventory. If a company follows a major category or total inventory approach in applying the lower-of-cost-or-market rule, increases in market prices tend to offset decreases in market prices. To illustrate, assume that Regner Foods separates its food products into two major categories, frozen and canned, as shown in Illustration 9-6.

ILLUSTRATION 9-6
Alternative Applications of Lower-of-Cost-or-Market

| | | | Lower-of-Cost-or-Market By: | | |
	Cost	Designated Market	Individual Items	Major Categories	Total Inventory
Frozen					
Spinach	$ 80,000	$104,000	$ 80,000		
Carrots	100,000	90,000	90,000		
Cut beans	50,000	40,000	40,000		
Total frozen	230,000	234,000		$230,000	
Canned					
Peas	90,000	48,000	48,000		
Mixed vegetables	95,000	92,000	92,000		
Total canned	185,000	140,000		140,000	
Total	$415,000	$374,000	$350,000	$370,000	$374,000

If Regner Foods applied the lower-of-cost-or-market rule to individual items, the amount of inventory is $350,000. If applying the rule to major categories, it jumps to $370,000. If applying LCM to the total inventory, it totals $374,000. Why this difference? When a company uses a major categories or total inventory approach, market values higher than cost offset market values lower than cost. For Regner Foods, using the major categories approach partially offsets the high market value for spinach. Using the total inventory approach totally offsets it.

Companies usually price inventory on an item-by-item basis. In fact, tax rules require that companies use an individual-item basis barring practical difficulties. In addition, the individual-item approach gives the most conservative valuation for balance sheet purposes.[2] Often, a company prices inventory on a total-inventory basis when it offers only one end product (comprised of many different raw materials). If it produces several end products, a company might use a category approach instead. The method selected should be the one that most clearly reflects income. **Whichever method a company selects, it should apply the method consistently from one period to another.**[3]

Recording "Market" Instead of Cost

One of two methods is used for recording inventory at market. One method, referred to as the **direct method**, substitutes the (lower) market value figure for cost when valuing the inventory. As a result, the company does not report a loss in the income statement because the cost of goods sold already includes the amount of the loss. The second method, referred to as the **indirect method** or **allowance method**, does not change the cost amount. Rather, it establishes a separate contra asset account and a loss account to record the write-off.

We use the following inventory data to illustrate entries under both methods.

Cost of goods sold (before adjustment to market)	$108,000
Ending inventory (cost)	82,000
Ending inventory (at market)	70,000

---

[2]If a company uses dollar-value LIFO, determining the LIFO cost of an individual item may be more difficult. The company might decide that it is more appropriate to apply the lower-of-cost-or-market rule to the total amount of each pool. The AICPA Task Force on LIFO Inventory Problems concluded that the most reasonable approach to applying the lower-of-cost-or-market provisions to LIFO inventories is to base the determination on reasonable groupings of items. A pool constitutes a reasonable grouping.

[3]Inventory accounting for financial statement purposes can be different from income tax purposes. For example, companies cannot use the lower-of-cost-or-market rule with LIFO for tax purposes. However, companies may use the lower-of-cost-or-market and LIFO for financial accounting purposes.

Illustration 9-7 shows the entries for both the direct and indirect methods, assuming the use of a **perpetual** inventory system.

Direct Method		Indirect or Allowance Method	
To reduce inventory from cost to market:			
Cost of Goods Sold	12,000	Loss Due to Market	
Inventory	12,000	Decline of Inventory	12,000
		Allowance to Reduce	
		Inventory to Market	12,000

ILLUSTRATION 9-7
Accounting for the Reduction of Inventory to Market—Perpetual Inventory System

Identifying the loss due to market decline shows the loss separate from cost of goods sold in the income statement (but not as an extraordinary item). The advantage of this approach is that it does not distort the cost of goods sold.

Illustration 9-8 contrasts the differing amounts reported in the income statements under the two methods, using data from the preceding illustration.

Direct Method	
Revenue from sales	$200,000
Cost of goods sold (after adjustment to market*)	120,000
Gross profit on sales	$ 80,000

Indirect or Allowance Method	
Revenue from sales	$200,000
Cost of goods sold	108,000
Gross profit on sales	92,000
Loss due to market decline of inventory	12,000
	$ 80,000

*Cost of goods sold (before adjustment to market)	$ 108,000
Difference between inventory at cost and market ($82,000–$70,000)	12,000
Cost of goods sold (after adjustment to market)	$ 120,000

ILLUSTRATION 9-8
Income Statement Presentation—Direct and Indirect Methods of Reducing Inventory to Market

The direct-method presentation buries the loss in the cost of goods sold. The indirect-method presentation is preferable, because it clearly discloses the loss resulting from the market decline of inventory prices.

Using the indirect method, the company would report the Allowance to Reduce Inventory to Market on the balance sheet as a $12,000 deduction from the inventory. This deduction permits both the income statement and the balance sheet to show the ending inventory of $82,000, although the balance sheet shows a net amount of $70,000. It also keeps subsidiary inventory ledgers and records in correspondence with the control account without changing unit prices.

Use of an allowance account permits balance sheet disclosure of the inventory at cost and at the lower of cost or market. However, it raises the problem of how to dispose of the balance of the allowance account in the following period. If the company still has on hand the merchandise in question, it should retain the allowance account. If it does not keep that account, the company will overstate beginning inventory and cost of goods. However, **if the company has sold the goods**, then it should close the account. It then establishes a "new allowance account" for any decline in inventory value that takes place in the current year.[4]

UNDERLYING CONCEPTS

The income statement under the direct method presentation lacks *representational faithfulness.* The cost of goods sold does not represent what it purports to represent. However, allowing this presentation illustrates the concept of materiality. That is, the presentation does not affect net income and would not "change the judgment of a reasonable person."

---

[4]The AICPA Task Force on LIFO Inventory Problems concluded that for LIFO inventories, companies should close the allowance from the prior year and should base the allowance at the end of the year on a new lower-of-cost-or-market computation. *Issues Paper* (New York: AICPA, November 30, 1984), pp. 50–55.

Some accountants leave the allowance account on the books. They merely adjust the balance at the next year-end to agree with the discrepancy between cost and the lower-of-cost-or-market at that balance sheet date. Thus, if prices are falling, the company records a loss. If prices are rising, the company recovers a loss recorded in prior years, and it records a "gain," as shown in Illustration 9-9. Note that this "gain" is not really a gain, but a recovery of a previously recognized loss.

ILLUSTRATION 9-9
Effect on Net Income of Reducing Inventory to Market

Date	Inventory at Cost	Inventory at Market	Amount Required in Valuation Account	Adjustment of Valuation Account Balance	Effect on Net Income
Dec. 31, 2006	$188,000	$176,000	$12,000	$12,000 inc.	Loss
Dec. 31, 2007	194,000	187,000	7,000	5,000 dec.	Gain
Dec. 31, 2008	173,000	174,000	0	7,000 dec.	Gain
Dec. 31, 2009	182,000	180,000	2,000	2,000 inc.	Loss

UNDERLYING CONCEPTS

The inconsistency in the presentation of inventory is an example of the trade-off between *relevancy and reliability*. Market is more relevant than cost, and cost is more reliable than market. Apparently, relevance takes precedence in a down market, and reliability is more important in an up market.

We can think of this net "gain" under the indirect method as the excess of the credit effect of closing the beginning allowance balance over the debit effect of setting up the current year-end allowance account. Recognizing a gain or loss has the same effect on net income as closing the allowance balance to beginning inventory or to cost of goods sold.

WHAT DO THE NUMBERS MEAN?

"PUT IT IN REVERSE"

The lower-of-cost-or-market rule is designed to provide timely information about the decline in the value of inventory. When the value of inventory declines, income takes a hit in the period of the write-down.

What happens in the periods after the write-down? For some companies, gross margins and bottom lines get a boost when they sell inventory that had been written down in a previous period. For example, as the following table shows, **Vishay Technologies, Transwitch,** and **Cisco Systems** reported gains from selling inventory that had previously been written down. The table also evaluates how clearly these companies disclosed the effects of the reversal of inventory write-downs.

Company	Gain from reversal	Disclosure
Vishay Inter-Technology	Not available	Poor—The semi-conductor company did not mention the gain in its earnings announcement. Two weeks later in an SEC filing, Vishay disclosed the gain on the inventory that it had written down.
Transwitch	$600,000	Poor—The company did not mention the gain in its earnings announcement. Three weeks later in an SEC filing, the company disclosed the gain on the inventory that it had written down.
Cisco Systems	$525 million	Full—The networking giant detailed in its earnings release and in SEC filings the gains from selling inventory it had previously written off.

For Transwitch, the reversal of fortunes amounted to 23 percent of net income. The problem is that the $600,000 credit had little to do with the company's ongoing operations, and the company did not do a good job disclosing the effect of the reversal on current-year profitability.

Even when companies do disclose a reversal, it is sometimes hard to determine the impact on income. For example, **Intel** disclosed that is had sold inventory that had been written down in prior periods but did not specify how much reserved inventory was sold.

After the recent accounting scandals, transparency of financial reporting has become a top priority. With better disclosure of the reversals that boost profits in the current period, financial transparency would also get a boost.

Source: S. E. Ante, "The Secret Behind Those Profit Jumps," *Business Week Online* (December 8, 2003).

Evaluation of the Lower-of-Cost-or-Market Rule

The lower-of-cost-or-market rule suffers some conceptual deficiencies:

1 A company recognizes decreases in the value of the the asset and the charge to expense in the period in which the loss in utility occurs—not in the period of sale. On the other hand, it recognizes increases in the value of the asset only at the point of sale. This inconsistent treatment can distort income data.

2 Application of the rule results in inconsistency because a company may value the inventory at cost in one year and at market in the next year.

3 Lower-of-cost-or-market values the inventory in the balance sheet conservatively, but its effect on the income statement may or may not be conservative. Net income for the year in which a company takes the loss is definitely lower. Net income of the subsequent period may be higher than normal if the expected reductions in sales price do not materialize.

4 Application of the lower-of-cost-or-market rule uses a "normal profit" in determining inventory values. Since companies estimate "normal profit" based on past experience (which they may not attain in the future), this subjective measure presents an opportunity for income manipulation.

Many financial statement users appreciate the lower-of-cost-or-market rule because they at least know that it prevents overstatement of inventory. In addition, recognizing all losses but anticipating no gains generally results in lower income.

VALUATION BASES

Valuation at Net Realizable Value

For the most part, companies record inventory at cost or at the lower-of-cost-or-market.[5] However, many believe that for purposes of applying the lower-of-cost-or-market rule, companies should define "market" as **net realizable value** (selling price less estimated costs to complete and sell), rather than as replacement cost. This argument is based on the fact that the amount that companies will collect from this inventory in the future is the net realizable value.[6]

Under limited circumstances, support exists for **recording inventory at net realizable value**, even if that amount is above cost. GAAP permits this exception to the normal recognition rule under the following conditions: (1) when there is a controlled market with a quoted price applicable to all quantities, and (2) when no significant costs of disposal

> **OBJECTIVE 2**
> Explain when companies value inventories at net realizable value.

---

[5]Manufacturing companies frequently employ a **standardized cost system** that predetermines the unit costs for material, labor, and manufacturing overhead and that values raw materials, work in process, and finished goods inventories at their standard costs. For financial reporting purposes, it is acceptable to price inventories at standard costs if there is no significant difference between the actual costs and standard costs. If there is a significant difference, companies should adjust the inventory amounts to actual cost. In *Accounting Research and Terminology Bulletin, Final Edition,* the profession notes that "**standard costs are acceptable if adjusted at reasonable intervals to reflect current conditions.**" **Burlington Industries** and **Hewlett-Packard** use standard costs for valuing at least a portion of their inventories.

[6]"The Accounting Basis of Inventories," *Acconting Research Study No. 13* (New York: AICPA, 1973) recommends that companies adopt net realizable value. We also should note that companies frequently fail to apply the rules of lower-of-cost-or-market in practice. For example, companies rarely compute and apply the lower limit—net realizable value less a normal markup—because it is a fairly subjective computation. In addition, companies often do not reduce inventory to market unless its disposition is expected to result in a loss. Furthermore, if the net realizable value of finished goods exceeds cost, companies usually assume that both work in process and raw materials do also. In practice, therefore, *ARB No. 43* is considered a guide, and accountants often exercise professional judgment in lieu of following this pronouncement literally.

INTERNATIONAL INSIGHT

The U.S. is the only country that defines *market* as something other than net realizable value.

are involved. For example, mining companies ordinarily report inventories of certain minerals (rare metals, especially) at selling prices because there is often a controlled market without significant costs of disposal. Similar treatment is given agricultural products that are immediately marketable at quoted prices.

A third reason for allowing valuation at net realizable value is that sometimes it is too difficult to obtain the cost figures. Cost figures are not difficult to determine in, say, a manufacturing plant, where the company combines various raw materials and purchased parts to create a finished product. The manufacturer can use the cost basis to account for various items in inventory, because it knows the cost of each individual component part. The situation is different in a meat-packing plant, however. The "raw material" consists of, say, cattle, each unit of which the company purchases as a whole and then divides into parts that are the products. Instead of one product out of many raw materials or parts, the meat-packing company makes many products from one "unit" of raw material. To allocate the cost of the animal "on the hoof" into the cost of, say, ribs, chuck, and shoulders, is a practical impossibility. It is much easier and more useful for the company to determine the market price of the various products and value them in the inventory at selling price less the various costs necessary to get them to market (costs such as shipping and handling). Hence, because of a peculiarity of the industry, meat-packing companies sometimes carry **inventories at sales price less distribution costs**.

Valuation Using Relative Sales Value

OBJECTIVE 3
Explain when companies use the relative sales value method to value inventories.

A special problem arises when a company buys a group of varying units in a single **lump-sum purchase**, also called a **basket purchase**.

To illustrate, assume that Woodland Developers purchases land for $1 million that it will subdivide into 400 lots. These lots are of different sizes and shapes but can be roughly sorted into three groups graded A, B, and C. As woodland sells the lots, it apportions the purchase cost of $1 million among the lots sold and the lots remaining on hand.

You might wonder why Woodland would not simply divide the total cost of $1 million by 400 lots, to get a cost of $2,500 for each lot. This approach would not recognize that the lots vary in size, shape, and attractiveness. Therefore, to accurately value each unit, the common and most logical practice is to allocate the total among the various units on the basis of their **relative sales value**.

Illustration 9-10 shows the allocation of relative sales value for the Woodland Developers example.

ILLUSTRATION 9-10
Allocation of Costs, Using Relative Sales Value

Lots	Number of Lots	Sales Price Per Lot	Total Sales Price	Relative Sales Price	Total Cost	Cost Allocated to Lots	Cost Per Lot
A	100	$10,000	$1,000,000	100/250	$1,000,000	$ 400,000	$4,000
B	100	6,000	600,000	60/250	1,000,000	240,000	2,400
C	200	4,500	900,000	90/250	1,000,000	360,000	1,800
			$2,500,000			$1,000,000	

Using the amounts given in the "Cost Per Lot" column, Woodland can determine the cost of lots sold and the gross profit as follows.

ILLUSTRATION 9-11
Determination of Gross Profit, Using Relative Sales Value

Lots	Number of Lots Sold	Cost Per Lot	Cost of Lots Sold	Sales	Gross Profit
A	77	$4,000	$308,000	$ 770,000	$ 462,000
B	80	2,400	192,000	480,000	288,000
C	100	1,800	180,000	450,000	270,000
			$680,000	$1,700,000	$1,020,000

The ending inventory is therefore $320,000 ($1,000,000 − $680,000).

Woodland also can compute this inventory amount another way. The ratio of cost to selling price for all the lots is $1 million divided by $2,500,000, or 40 percent. Accordingly, if the total sales price of lots sold is, say $1,700,000, then the cost of the lots sold is 40 percent of $1,700,000, or $680,000. The inventory of lots on hand is then $1 million less $680,000, or $320,000.

The petroleum industry widely uses the relative sales value method to value (at cost) the many products and by-products obtained from a barrel of crude oil.

Purchase Commitments—A Special Problem

In many lines of business, a company's survival and continued profitability depends on its having a sufficient stock of merchandise to meet customer demand. Consequently, it is quite common for a company to make **purchase commitments**, which are agreements to buy inventory weeks, months, or even years in advance. Generally, the seller retains title to the merchandise or materials covered in the purchase commitments. Indeed, the goods may exist only as natural resources as unplanted seed (in the case of agricultural commodities), or as work in process (in the case of a product).[7]

Usually it is neither necessary nor proper for the buyer to make any entries to reflect commitments for purchases of goods that the seller has not shipped. Ordinary orders, for which the buyer and seller will determine prices at the time of shipment and **which are subject to cancellation**, do not represent either an asset or a liability to the buyer. Therefore the buyer need not record such purchase commitments or report them in the financial statements.

What happens, though, if a buyer enters into a formal, noncancelable purchase contract? Even then, the buyer recognizes no asset or liability at the date of inception, **because the contract is "executory" in nature**: Neither party has fulfilled its part of the contract. However, if material, the buyer should disclose such contract details in a note to its financial statements. Illustration 9-12 shows an example of a purchase commitment disclosure.

> **Note 1**: Contracts for the purchase of raw materials in 2007 have been executed in the amount of $600,000. The market price of such raw materials on December 31, 2006, is $640,000.

OBJECTIVE 4
Discuss accounting issues related to purchase commitments.

ILLUSTRATION 9-12
Disclosure of Purchase Commitment

In the disclosure in Illustration 9-12, the contract price was less than the market price at the balance sheet date. **If the contract price is greater than the market price, and the buyer expects that losses will occur when the purchase is effected, the buyer should recognize losses in the period during which such declines in market prices take place.**[8]

As an example, in the early 1980s many Northwest forest-product companies such as **Boise Cascade**, **Georgia-Pacific**, and **Weyerhaeuser** signed long-term timber-cutting contracts with the **U.S. Forest Service**. These contracts required that the companies pay $310 per thousand board feet for timber-cutting rights. Unfortunately, the market price for timber-cutting rights in late 1984 dropped to $80 per thousand board feet. As a result, a number of these companies had long-term contracts that, if fulfilled, would result in substantial future losses.

---

[7]A recent study noted that about 30 percent of public companies have purchase commitments outstanding, with an estimated value of $725 billion ("SEC Staff Report on Off-Balance Sheet Arrangements, Special Purpose Entities, and Related Issues,") http://www.sec.gov/news/studies/soxoffbalancerpt.pdf, June 2005). Purchase commitments are popular because the buyer can secure a supply of inventory at a known price. The seller also benefits in these arrangements by knowing how much to produce.

[8]*Accounting Research Bulletin No. 43*, op. cit., par. 16.

Reporting the loss is *conservative*. However, reporting the decline in market price is debatable because no asset is recorded. This area demonstrates the need for good definitions of assets and liabilities.

To illustrate the accounting problem, assume that St. Regis Paper Co. signed timber-cutting contracts to be executed in 2007 at a price of $10,000,000. Assume further that the market price of the timber cutting rights on December 31, 2008, dropped to $7,000,000. St. Regis would make the following entry on December 31, 2008.

Unrealized Holding Gain or Loss—Income		
(Purchase Commitments)	3,000,000	
Estimated Liability on Purchase Commitments		3,000,000

St. Regis would report this unrealized holding loss in the income statement under "Other expenses and losses." And because the contract is to be executed within the next fiscal year, St. Regis would report the Estimated Liability on Purchase Commitments in the current liabilities section on the balance sheet. When St. Regis cuts the timber at a cost of $10 million, it would make the following entry.

Purchases (Inventory)	7,000,000	
Estimated Liability on Purchase Commitments	3,000,000	
Cash		10,000,000

The result of the purchase commitment was that St. Regis paid $10 million for a contract worth only $7 million. It recorded the loss in the previous period—when the price actually declined.

If St. Regis can partially or fully recover the contract price before it cuts the timber, it reduces the Estimated Liability on Purchase Commitments. In that case, it then reports in the period of the price increase a resulting gain for the amount of the partial or full recovery. For example, Congress permitted some of the forest-products companies to buy out of their contracts at reduced prices in order to avoid potential bankruptcies. To illustrate, assume that Congress permitted St. Regis to reduce its contract price and therefore its commitment by $1,000,000. The entry to record this transaction is as follows.

Estimated Liability on Purchase Commitments	1,000,000	
Unrealized Holding Gain or Loss—Income		
(Purchase Commitments)		1,000,000

If the market price at the time St. Regis cuts the timber is more than $2,000,000 below the contract price, St. Regis will have to recognize an additional loss in the period of cutting and record the purchase at the lower-of-cost-or-market.

Are purchasers at the mercy of market price declines? Not totally. Purchasers can protect themselves against the possibility of market price declines of goods under contract by hedging. In **hedging**, the purchaser in the purchase commitment simultaneously enters into a contract in which it agrees to sell in the future the same quantity of the same (or similar) goods at a fixed price. Thus the company holds a *buy position* in a purchase commitment and a *sell position* in a futures contract in the same commodity. The purpose of the hedge is to offset the price risk of the buy and sell positions: The company will be better off under one contract by approximately (maybe exactly) the same amount by which it is worse off under the other contract.

For example, St. Regis Paper Co. could have hedged its purchase commitment contract with a futures contract for timber rights of the same amount. In that case, its loss of $3,000,000 on the purchase commitment could have been offset by a $3,000,000 gain on the futures contract.[9]

As easy as this makes it sound, accounting for purchase commitments is still unsettled and controversial. Some argue that companies should report purchase commitments

---

[9]Appendix 17A provides a complete discussion of hedging and the use of derivatives such as futures.

as assets and liabilities at the time they sign the contract.[10] Others believe that the present recognition at the delivery date is more appropriate. *FASB Concepts Statement No. 6* states, "a purchase commitment involves both an item that might be recorded as an asset and an item that might be recorded as a liability. That is, it involves both a right to receive assets and an obligation to pay. . . . If both the right to receive assets and the obligation to pay were recorded at the time of the purchase commitment, the nature of the loss and the valuation account that records it when the price falls would be clearly seen." Although the discussion in *Concepts Statement No. 6* does not exclude the possibility of recording assets and liabilities for purchase commitments, it contains no conclusions or implications about whether companies should record them.[11]

THE GROSS PROFIT METHOD OF ESTIMATING INVENTORY

OBJECTIVE 5
Determine ending inventory by applying the gross profit method.

Companies take a physical inventory to verify the accuracy of the perpetual inventory records or, if no records exist, to arrive at an inventory amount. Sometimes, however, taking a physical inventory is impractical. In such cases, companies use substitute measures to approximate inventory on hand.

One substitute method of verifying or determining the inventory amount is the **gross profit method** (also called the **gross margin method**). Auditors widely use this method in situations where they need only an estimate of the company's inventory (e.g., interim reports). Companies also use this method when fire or other catastrophe destroys either inventory or inventory records. The gross profit method relies on three assumptions:

1 The beginning inventory plus purchases equal total goods to be accounted for.

2 Goods not sold must be on hand.

3 The sales, reduced to cost, deducted from the sum of the opening inventory plus purchases, equal ending inventory.

To illustrate, assume that Cetus Corp. has a beginning inventory of $60,000 and purchases of $200,000, both at cost. Sales at selling price amount to $280,000. The gross profit on selling price is 30 percent. Cetus applies the gross margin method as follows.

Beginning inventory (at cost)		$ 60,000
Purchases (at cost)		200,000
Goods available (at cost)		260,000
Sales (at selling price)	$280,000	
Less: Gross profit (30% of $280,000)	84,000	
Sales (at cost)		196,000
Approximate inventory (at cost)		$ 64,000

ILLUSTRATION 9-13
Application of Gross Profit Method

[10]See, for example, Yuji Ijiri, *Recognition of Contractual Rights and Obligations, Research Report* (Stamford, Conn.: FASB, 1980), who argues that companies should capitalize firm purchase commitments. "Firm" means that it is unlikely that companies can avoid performance under the contract without a severe penalty.

Also, see Mahendra R. Gujarathi and Stanley F. Biggs, "Accounting for Purchase Commitments: Some Issues and Recommendations," *Accounting Horizons* (September 1988), pp. 75–78. They conclude, "Recording an asset and liability on the date of inception for the noncancelable purchase commitments is suggested as the first significant step towards alleviating the accounting problems associated with the issue. At year-end, the potential gains and losses should be treated as contingencies under *FASB 5* which provides a coherent structure for the accounting and informative disclosure for such gains and losses."

[11]"Elements of Financial Statements," *Statement of Financial Accounting Concepts No. 6* (Stamford, Conn.: FASB, 1985), pars. 251–253.

The current period's records contain all the information Cetus needs to compute inventory at cost, except for the gross profit percentage. Cetus determines the gross profit percentage by reviewing company policies or prior period records. In some cases, companies must adjust this percentage if they consider prior periods unrepresentative of the current period.[12]

Computation of Gross Profit Percentage

In most situations, the **gross profit percentage** is stated as a percentage of selling price. The previous illustration, for example, used a 30 percent gross profit on sales. Gross profit on selling price is the common method for quoting the profit for several reasons: (1) Most companies state goods on a retail basis, not a cost basis. (2) A profit quoted on selling price is lower than one based on cost. This lower rate gives a favorable impression to the consumer. (3) The gross profit based on selling price can never exceed 100 percent.[13]

In Illustration 9-13, the gross profit was a given. But how did Cetus derive that figure? To see how to compute a gross profit percentage, assume that an article cost $15 and sells for $20, a gross profit of $5. As shown in the computations in Illustration 9-14, this markup is ¼ or 25 percent of retail, and ⅓ or, 33⅓ percent of cost.

ILLUSTRATION 9-14
Computation of Gross Profit Percentage

$$\frac{\text{Markup}}{\text{Retail}} = \frac{\$5}{\$20} = 25\% \text{ at retail} \qquad \frac{\text{Markup}}{\text{Cost}} = \frac{\$5}{\$15} = 33\frac{1}{3}\% \text{ on cost}$$

Although companies normally compute the gross profit on the basis of selling price, you should understand the basic relationship between markup on cost and markup on selling price. For example, assume that a company marks up a given item by 25 percent. What, then, is the **gross profit on selling price**? To find the answer, assume that the item sells for $1. In this case, the following formula applies.

$$\text{Cost} + \text{Gross profit} = \text{Selling price}$$

$$C + .25C = SP$$

$$(1 + .25)C = SP$$

$$1.25C = \$1.00$$

$$C = \$0.80$$

---

[12]An alternative method of estimating inventory using the gross profit percentage is considered by some to be less complicated than the traditional method. This alternative method uses the standard income statement format as follows. (Assume the same data as in the Cetus example above.)

Sales		$280,000		$280,000
Cost of sales				
Beginning inventory	$ 60,000		$ 60,000	
Purchases	200,000		200,000	
Goods available for sale	260,000		260,000	
Ending inventory	(3) ?		(3) 64,000 Est.	
Cost of goods sold		(2) ?		(2)196,000 Est.
Gross profit on sales (30%)		(1) ?		(1) 84,000 Est.

Compute the unknowns as follows: first the gross profit amount, then cost of goods sold, and finally the ending inventory, as shown below.
  (1) $280,000 × 30% = $84,000 (gross profit on sales).
  (2) $280,000 − $84,000 = $196,000 (cost of goods sold).
  (3) $260,000 − $196,000 = $64,000 (ending inventory).

[13]The terms *gross margin percentage, rate of gross profit,* and *percentage markup* are synonymous, although companies more commonly use *markup* in reference to cost and *gross profit* in reference to sales.

The gross profit equals $0.20 ($1.00 − $0.80). The rate of gross profit on selling price is therefore 20 percent ($0.20/$1.00).

Conversely, assume that the gross profit on selling price is 20 percent. What is the **markup on cost**? To find the answer, again assume that the item sells for $1. Again, the same formula holds:

$$\text{Cost} + \text{Gross profit} = \text{Selling price}$$

$$C + .20SP = SP$$

$$C = (1 - .20)SP$$

$$C = .80SP$$

$$C = .80(\$1.00)$$

$$C = \$0.80$$

As in the previous example, the markup equals $0.20 ($1.00 − $0.80). The markup on cost is 25 percent ($0.20/$0.80).

Retailers use the following formulas to express these relationships:

ILLUSTRATION 9-15
Formulas Relating to
Gross Profit

1. Gross profit on selling price $= \dfrac{\text{Percentage markup on cost}}{100\% + \text{Percentage markup on cost}}$

2. Percentage markup on cost $= \dfrac{\text{Gross profit on selling price}}{100\% - \text{Gross profit on selling price}}$

To understand how to use these formulas, consider their application in the following calculations.

ILLUSTRATION 9-16
Application of Gross
Profit Formulas

Gross Profit on Selling Price	Percentage Markup on Cost
Given: 20% $\longrightarrow$	$\dfrac{.20}{1.00 - .20} = 25\%$
Given: 25% $\longrightarrow$	$\dfrac{.25}{1.00 - .25} = 33\frac{1}{3}\%$
$\dfrac{.25}{1.00 + .25} = 20\% \longleftarrow$	Given: 25%
$\dfrac{.50}{1.00 + .50} = 33\frac{1}{3}\% \longleftarrow$	Given: 50%

Because selling price exceeds cost, and with the gross profit amount the same for both, **gross profit on selling price will always be less than the related percentage based on cost**. Note that companies do not multiply sales by a cost-based markup percentage. Instead, they must convert the gross profit percentage to a percentage based on selling price.

Evaluation of Gross Profit Method

What are the major disadvantages of the gross profit method? One disadvantage is that **it provides an estimate**. As a result, companies must take a physical inventory once a year to verify the inventory. Second, the gross profit method **uses past percentages** in determining the markup. Although the past often provides answers to the future, a current rate is more appropriate. Note that whenever significant fluctuations occur, companies should adjust the percentage as appropriate. Third, companies must be **careful in applying a blanket gross profit rate**. Frequently, a store or department handles merchandise with widely varying rates of gross profit. In these situations, the company may need to apply the gross profit method by subsections, lines of merchandise, or a similar basis that classifies merchandise according to their respective rates of gross profit. The gross profit method is normally unacceptable for financial reporting purposes because it provides only an estimate. GAAP requires a physical inventory as additional verification of the inventory indicated in the records. Nevertheless, GAAP permits the gross profit method to determine ending inventory for interim (generally quarterly) reporting purposes, provided a company discloses the use of this method. Note that the gross profit method will follow closely the inventory method used (FIFO, LIFO, average cost) because it relies on historical records.

WHAT DO THE NUMBERS MEAN?

THE SQUEEZE

Managers and analysts closely follow gross profits. A small change in the gross profit rate can significantly affect the bottom line. In 1993, **Apple Computer** suffered a textbook case of shrinking gross profits. In response to pricing wars in the personal computer market, Apple had to quickly reduce the price of its signature Macintosh computers—reducing prices more quickly than it could reduce its costs. As a result its gross profit rate fell from 44 percent in 1992 to 40 percent in 1993. Though the drop of 4 percent seems small, its impact on the bottom line caused Apple's stock price to drop from $57 per share on June 1, 1993, to $27.50 by mid-July 1993.

As another example, **Debenham**, the second largest department store in the United Kingdom, experienced a 14 percentage share price decline. The cause? Mark-downs on slow moving inventory reduced its gross margin.

Source: Alison Smith, "Debenham's Shares Hit by Warning," *Financial Times* (July 24, 2002), p. 21.

RETAIL INVENTORY METHOD

OBJECTIVE 6
Determine ending inventory by applying the retail inventory method.

Accounting for inventory in a retail operation presents several challenges. Retailers with certain types of inventory may use the specific identification method to value their inventories. Such an approach makes sense when a retailer holds significant individual inventory units, such as automobiles, pianos, or fur coats. However, imagine attempting to use such an approach at **Target**, **True-Value Hardware**, **Sears Holdings**, or **Bloomingdale's**—high-volume retailers that have many different types of merchandise. It would be extremely difficult to determine the cost of each sale, to enter cost codes on the tickets, to change the codes to reflect declines in value of the merchandise, to allocate costs such as transportation, and so on.

An alternative is to compile the inventories at retail prices. For most retailers, an observable pattern between cost and price exists. The retailer can then use a formula to convert retail prices to cost. This method is called the retail inventory method. **It requires that the retailer keep a record of (1) the total cost and retail value of goods purchased, (2) the total cost and retail value of the goods available for sale, and (3) the sales for the period.** Use of the retail inventory method is very common. For example, **Safeway** supermarkets uses the retail inventory method, as does **Target Corp.**, **Wal-Mart**, and **Best Buy**.

Here is how it works at a company like **Best Buy**: Beginning with the retail value of the goods available for sale, Best Buy deducts the sales for the period. This calculation determines an estimated inventory (goods on hand) at retail. It next computes the cost-to-retail ratio for all goods. The formula for this computation is to divide the cost of total goods available for sale at cost by the total goods available at retail price. Finally, to obtain ending inventory at cost, Best Buy applies the cost-to-retail ratio to the ending inventory valued at retail. Illustration 9-17 shows the retail inventory method calculations for Best Buy (assumed data).

ILLUSTRATION 9-17
Retail Inventory Method

BEST BUY (current period)	Cost	Retail
Beginning inventory	$14,000	$ 20,000
Purchases	63,000	90,000
Goods available for sale	$77,000	110,000
Deduct: Sales		85,000
Ending inventory, at retail		$ 25,000

Ratio of cost to retail ($77,000 ÷ $110,000) = 70%
Ending inventory at cost (70% of $25,000) = $ 17,500

There are different versions of the retail inventory method. These include the **conventional** method (based on lower-of-average-cost-or-market), the **cost** method, the **LIFO retail** method, and the **dollar-value LIFO** retail method. Regardless of which version a company uses, the IRS, various retail associations, and the accounting profession all sanction use of the retail inventory method. One of its advantages is that a company like **Target** can approximate the inventory balance **without a physical count**. However, to avoid a potential overstatement of the inventory, Target makes periodic inventory counts. Such counts are especially important in retail operations where loss due to shoplifting or breakage is common.

The retail inventory method is particularly useful for any type of interim report, because such reports usually need a fairly quick and reliable measure of the inventory. Also, insurance adjusters often use this method to estimate losses from fire, flood, or other type of casualty. This method also acts as a **control device** because a company will have to explain any deviations from a physical count at the end of the year. Finally, the retail method **expedites the physical inventory count** at the end of the year. The crew taking the physical inventory need record only the retail price of each item. The crew does not need to look up each item's invoice cost, thereby saving time and expense.

Retail-Method Concepts

The amounts shown in the "Retail" column of Illustration 9-17 represent the original retail prices, assuming no price changes. In practice, though, retailers frequently mark up or mark down the prices they charge buyers.

For retailers, the term **markup** means an additional markup of the original retail price. (In another context, such as the gross profit discussion on page 435, we often think of markup on the basis of cost.) **Markup cancellations** are decreases in prices of merchandise that the retailer had marked up above the original retail price.

In a competitive market, retailers often need to use **markdowns**, which are decreases in the original sales prices. Such cuts in sales prices may be necessary because of a decrease in the general level of prices, special sales, soiled or damaged goods, overstocking, and market competition. Markdowns are common in retailing these days. **Markdown cancellations** occur when the markdowns are later offset by increases in the prices of goods that the retailer had marked down—such as after a one-day sale, for example. Neither a markup cancellation nor a markdown cancellation can exceed the original markup or markdown.

To illustrate these concepts, assume that Designer Clothing Store recently purchased 100 dress shirts from Marroway, Inc. The cost for these shirts was $1,500, or $15 a shirt. Designer Clothing established the selling price on these shirts at $30 a shirt. The shirts were selling quickly in anticipation of Father's Day, so the manager added a markup of $5 per shirt. This markup made the price too high for customers, and sales slowed. The manager then reduced the price to $32. At this point we would say that the shirts at Designer Clothing have had a markup of $5 and a markup cancellation of $3.

Right after Father's Day, the manager marked down the remaining shirts to a sale price of $23. At this point, an additional markup cancellation of $2 has taken place, and a $7 markdown has occurred. If the manager later increases the price of the shirts to $24, a markdown cancellation of $1 would occur.

Retail Inventory Method with Markups and Markdowns— Conventional Method

Retailers use markup and markdown concepts in developing the proper inventory valuation at the end of the accounting period. To obtain the appropriate inventory figures, companies must give proper treatment to markups, markup cancellations, markdowns, and markdown cancellations.

To illustrate the different possibilities, consider the data for In-Fusion Inc., shown in Illustration 9-18. In-Fusion can calculate its ending inventory at cost under two assumptions, A and B. (We'll explain the reasons for the two later.)

Assumption A: Computes a cost ratio after markups (and markup cancellations) but before markdowns.

Assumption B: Computes a cost ratio after both markups and markdowns (and cancellations).

ILLUSTRATION 9-18
Retail Inventory Method with Markups and Markdowns

	Cost	Retail
Beginning inventory	$ 500	$ 1,000
Purchases (net)	20,000	35,000
Markups		3,000
Markup cancellations		1,000
Markdowns		2,500
Markdown cancellations		2,000
Sales (net)		25,000

IN-FUSION INC.

	Cost		Retail
Beginning inventory	$ 500		$ 1,000
Purchases (net)	20,000		35,000
Merchandise available for sale	20,500		36,000
Add: Markups		$3,000	
Less: Markup cancellations		(1,000)	
Net markups			2,000
	20,500		38,000
(A) Cost-to-retail ratio $\dfrac{\$20,500}{\$38,000} = 53.9\%$			
Deduct:			
Markdowns		2,500	
Less: Markdown cancellations		(2,000)	
Net markdowns			500
	$20,500		37,500
(B) Cost-to-retail ratio $\dfrac{\$20,500}{\$37,500} = 54.7\%$			
Deduct: Sales (net)			25,000
Ending inventory at retail			$12,500

The computations for In-Fusion are:

Ending inventory at retail × Cost ratio = Value of ending inventory
Assumption A: $12,500 × 53.9% = $6,737.50
Assumption B: $12,500 × 54.7% = $6,837.50

The question becomes: Which assumption and which percentage should In-Fusion use to compute the ending inventory valuation? The answer depends on which retail inventory method In-Fusion chooses.

One approach uses only assumption A (a cost ratio using markups but not markdowns). It approximates the lower-of-average-cost-or-market. We will refer to this approach as the **conventional retail inventory method** or the **lower-of-cost-or-market approach**.

To understand why this method considers only the markups, not the markdowns, in the cost percentage, you must understand how a retail business operates. A markup normally indicates an increase in the market value of the item. On the other hand, a markdown means a decline in the utility of that item. Therefore, to approximate the lower-of-cost-or-market, we would consider markdowns a current loss and so would not include them in calculating the cost-to-retail ratio. Omitting the markdowns would make the cost-to-retail ratio lower, which leads to an approximate lower-of-cost-or-market.

An example will make the distinction between the two methods clear: In-Fusion purchased two items for $5 apiece; the original sales price was $10 each. One item was subsequently written down to $2. Assuming no sales for the period, **if markdowns are considered** in the cost-to-retail ratio (assumption B—the **cost method**), we compute the ending inventory in the following way.

Markdowns Included in Cost-to-Retail Ratio		
	Cost	Retail
Purchases	$10	$20
Deduct: Markdowns		8
Ending inventory, at retail		$12

Cost-to-retail ratio $\dfrac{\$10}{\$12} = 83.3\%$

Ending inventory at cost ($12 × .833) = $10

ILLUSTRATION 9-19
Retail Inventory Method Including Markdowns— Cost Method

This approach (the cost method) reflects an **average cost** of the two items of the commodity without considering the loss on the one item. It values ending inventory at $10.

If markdowns are not considered in the cost-to-retail ratio (assumption A—the **conventional retail method**), we compute the ending inventory as follows.

Markdowns Not Included in Cost-to-Retail Ratio		
	Cost	Retail
Purchases	$10	$20

Cost-to-retail ratio $\dfrac{\$10}{\$20} = 50\%$

Deduct: Markdowns		8
Ending inventory, at retail		$12

Ending inventory, at cost ($12 × .50) = $6

ILLUSTRATION 9-20
Retail Inventory Method Excluding Markdowns— Conventional Method (LCM)

Under this approach (the conventional retail method, in which markdowns are **not considered**), ending inventory would be $6. The inventory valuation of $6 reflects two inventory items, one inventoried at $5 and the other at $1. It reflects the fact that In-Fusion reduced the sales price from $10 to $2, and reduced the cost from $5 to $1.[14]

---

[14]This figure is not really market (replacement cost), but it is net realizable value less the normal margin that is allowed. In other words, the sale price of the goods written down is $2, but subtracting a normal margin of 50 percent ($5 cost, $10 price), the figure becomes $1.

To approximate the lower-of-cost-or-market, In-Fusion must establish the **cost-to-retail ratio**. It does this by dividing the cost of goods available for sale by the sum of the original retail price of these goods plus the net markups. This calculation excludes markdowns and markdown cancellations. Illustration 9-21 shows the basic format for the retail inventory method using the lower-of-cost-or-market approach along with the In-Fusion Inc. information.

ILLUSTRATION 9-21
Comprehensive
Conventional Retail
Inventory Method Format

	Cost		Retail
	IN-FUSION INC.		
Beginning inventory	$ 500.00		$ 1,000.00
Purchases (net)	20,000.00		35,000.00
Totals	20,500.00		36,000.00
Add: Net markups			
Markups		$3,000.00	
Markup cancellations		1,000.00	2,000.00
Totals	$20,500.00 ←		→ 38,000.00
Deduct: Net markdowns			
Markdowns		2,500.00	
Markdown cancellations		2,000.00	500.00
Sales price of goods available			37,500.00
Deduct: Sales (net)			25,000.00
Ending inventory, at retail			$12,500.00

$$\text{Cost-to-retail ratio} = \frac{\text{Cost of goods available}}{\text{Original retail price of goods available, plus net markups}}$$

$$= \frac{\$20,500}{\$38,000} = 53.9\%$$

Ending inventory at lower of cost or market (53.9% × $12,500.00) = $ 6,737.50

Because an averaging effect occurs, an exact lower-of-cost-or-market inventory valuation is ordinarily not obtained, but an adequate approximation can be achieved. In contrast, adding net markups **and** deducting net markdowns yields **approximate cost**.

Special Items Relating to Retail Method

The retail inventory method becomes more complicated when we consider such items as freight-in, purchase returns and allowances, and purchase discounts. In the retail method, we treat such items as follows.

- **Freight costs** are part of the purchase cost.
- **Purchase returns** are ordinarily considered as a reduction of the price at both cost and retail.
- **Purchase discounts and allowances** usually are considered as a reduction of the cost of purchases.

In short, the treatment for the items affecting the cost column of the retail inventory approach follows the computation for cost of goods available for sale.[15]

Note also that **sales returns and allowances** are considered as proper adjustments to gross sales. However, when sales are recorded gross, companies do not recognize **sales discounts**. To adjust for the sales discount account in such a situation would provide an ending inventory figure at retail that would be overvalued.

---

[15]When the purchase allowance is not reflected by a reduction in the selling price, no adjustment is made to the retail column.

In addition, a number of special items require careful analysis:

- **Transfers-in** from another department are reported in the same way as purchases from an outside enterprise.
- **Normal shortages** (breakage, damage, theft, shrinkage) should reduce the retail column because these goods are no longer available for sale. Such costs are reflected in the selling price because a certain amount of shortage is considered normal in a retail enterprise. As a result, companies do not consider this amount in computing the cost-to-retail percentage. Rather, to arrive at ending inventory at retail, they show normal shortages as a deduction similar to sales.
- **Abnormal shortages**, on the other hand, are deducted from both the cost and retail columns and reported as a special inventory amount or as a loss. To do otherwise distorts the cost-to-retail ratio and overstates ending inventory.
- **Employee discounts** (given to employees to encourage loyalty, better performance, and so on) are deducted from the retail column in the same way as sales. These discounts should not be considered in the cost-to-retail percentage because they do not reflect an overall change in the selling price.

Illustration 9-22 shows some of these concepts. The company, Extreme Sport Apparel, determines its inventory using the conventional retail inventory method.

EXTREME SPORT APPAREL			
	Cost		**Retail**
Beginning inventory	$ 1,000		$ 1,800
Purchases	30,000		60,000
Freight-in	600		—
Purchase returns	(1,500)		(3,000)
Totals	30,100		58,800
Net markups			9,000
Abnormal shortage	(1,200)		(2,000)
Totals	$28,900 ⟵⟶		65,800
Deduct:			
Net markdowns			1,400
Sales		$36,000	
Sales returns		(900)	35,100
Employee discounts			800
Normal shortage			1,300
			$27,200

Cost-to-retail ratio = $\dfrac{\$28,900}{\$65,800}$ = 43.9%

Ending inventory at lower of cost or market (43.9% × $27,200) = **$11,940.80**

ILLUSTRATION 9-22
Conventional Retail Inventory Method— Special Items Included

Evaluation of Retail Inventory Method

Companies like **Gap Inc., Circuit City**, or your local department store use the retail inventory method of computing inventory for the following reasons: (1) to permit the computation of net income without a physical count of inventory, (2) as a control measure in determining inventory shortages, (3) in regulating quantities of merchandise on hand, and (4) for insurance information.

One characteristic of the retail inventory method is that it **has an averaging effect on varying rates of gross profit**. This can be problematic when companies apply the method to an entire business, where rates of gross profit vary among departments. There is no allowance for possible distortion of results because of such differences.

Companies refine the retail method under such conditions by computing inventory separately by departments or by classes of merchandise with similar gross profits. In addition, the reliability of this method assumes that the distribution of items in inventory is similar to the "mix" in the total goods available for sale.

PRESENTATION AND ANALYSIS

Presentation of Inventories

OBJECTIVE 7
Explain how to report and analyze inventory.

Additional Inventory Disclosures

Accounting standards require financial statement disclosure of the composition of the inventory, inventory financing arrangements, and the inventory costing methods employed. The standards also require the consistent application of costing methods from one period to another.

Manufacturers should report the inventory composition either in the balance sheet or in a separate schedule in the notes. The relative mix of raw materials, work in process, and finished goods helps in assessing liquidity and in computing the stage of inventory completion.

Significant or unusual financing arrangements relating to inventories may require note disclosure. Examples include transactions with related parties, product financing arrangements, firm purchase commitments, involuntary liquidation of LIFO inventories, and pledging of inventories as collateral. Companies should present inventories pledged as collateral for a loan in the current assets section rather than as an offset to the liability.

A company should also report the basis on which it states inventory amounts (lower-of-cost-or-market) and the method used in determining cost (LIFO, FIFO, average cost, etc.). For example, the annual report of **Mumford of Wyoming** contains the following disclosures.

ILLUSTRATION 9-23
Disclosure of
Inventory Methods

Mumford of Wyoming

Note A: Significant Accounting Policies

Live feeder cattle and feed—last-in, first-out (LIFO) cost, which is below approximate market	$854,800
Live range cattle—lower of principally identified cost or market	$1,240,500
Live sheep and supplies—lower of first-in, first-out (FIFO) cost or market	$674,000
Dressed meat and by-products—principally at market less allowances for distribution and selling expenses	$362,630

The preceding illustration shows that a company can use different pricing methods for different elements of its inventory. If Mumford changes the method of pricing any of its inventory elements, it must report a change in accounting principle. For example, if Mumford changes its method of accounting for live sheep from FIFO to average cost, it should separately report this change, along with the effect on income, in the current and prior periods. Changes in accounting principle require an explanatory paragraph in the auditor's report describing the change in method.

Fortune Brands, Inc. reported its inventories in its annual report as follows (note the "trade practice" followed in classifying inventories among the current assets).

Fortune Brands, Inc.

Current assets

Inventories (Note 2)

Leaf tobacco	$ 563,424,000
Bulk whiskey	232,759,000
Other raw materials, supplies and work in process	238,906,000
Finished products	658,326,000
	$1,693,415,000

Note 2: Inventories

Inventories are priced at the lower of cost (average; first-in, first-out; and minor amounts at last-in, first-out) or market. In accordance with generally recognized trade practice, the leaf tobacco and bulk whiskey inventories are classified as current assets, although part of such inventories due to the duration of the aging process, ordinarily will not be sold within one year.

ILLUSTRATION 9-24
Disclosure of Trade Practice in Valuing Inventories

The following inventory disclosures by **Newmont Gold Company** reveal the use of different bases of valuation, including market value, for different classifications of inventory.

Newmont Gold Company

Current assets	
Inventories (Note 2)	$44,303,000
Noncurrent assets	
Inventories—ore in stockpiles (Note 2)	$5,250,000

Note 2: Inventories

Inventories included in current assets at December 31 were:

Ore and in-process inventory	$11,303,000
Gold bullion and gold precipitates	24,209,000
Materials and supplies	8,791,000
	$44,303,000

Ore and in-process inventory and materials and supplies are stated at the lower of average cost or net realizable value. Gold bullion and gold precipitates are stated at market value, less a provision for estimated refining and delivery charges. Expenditures capitalized as ore and in-process inventory include labor, material and other production costs.

Noncurrent inventories are stated at the lower of average cost or net realizable value and represent ore in stockpiles anticipated to be processed in future years.

ILLUSTRATION 9-25
Disclosure of Different Bases of Valuation

Analysis of Inventories

As our opening story illustrates, the amount of inventory that a company carries can have significant economic consequences. As a result, companies must manage inventories. But, inventory management is a double-edged sword. It requires constant attention. On the one hand, management wants to stock a great variety and quantity of items. Doing so will provide customers with the greatest selection. However, such an inventory policy may incur excessive carrying costs (e.g., investment, storage, insurance, taxes, obsolescence, and damage). On the other hand, low inventory levels lead to stockouts, lost sales, and disgruntled customers.

Using financial ratios helps companies to chart a middle course between these two dangers. Common ratios used in the management and evaluation of inventory levels are inventory turnover and a related measure, average days to sell the inventory.

Inventory Turnover Ratio

The **inventory turnover ratio** measures the number of times on average a company sells the inventory during the period. It measures the liquidity of the inventory. To compute inventory turnover, divide the cost of goods sold by the average inventory on hand during the period.

Barring seasonal factors, analysts compute average inventory from beginning and ending inventory balances. For example, in its 2004 annual report **Kellogg Company** reported a beginning inventory of $649.8 million, an ending inventory of $681 million, and cost of goods sold of $5,299 million for the year. Illustration 9-26 shows the inventory turnover formula and Kellogg Company's 2004 ratio computation below.

ILLUSTRATION 9-26
Inventory Turnover Ratio

$$\text{Inventory Turnover} = \frac{\text{Cost of Goods Sold}}{\text{Average Inventory}}$$

$$= \frac{\$5,299}{(\$681 + \$649.8)/2} = 8 \text{ times}$$

Average Days to Sell Inventory

A variant of the inventory turnover ratio is the **average days to sell inventory**. This measure represents the average number of days' sales for which a company has inventory on hand. For example, the inventory turnover for Kellogg Company of 8 times divided into 365 is approximately 45.6 days.

There are typical levels of inventory in every industry. However, companies that keep their inventory at lower levels with higher turnovers than those of their competitors, and that still can satisfy customer needs, are the most successful.

SUMMARY OF LEARNING OBJECTIVES

KEY TERMS

average days to sell inventory, 444

conventional retail inventory method, 439

cost-to-retail ratio, 436

designated market value, 424

gross profit method, 433

gross profit percentage, 434

hedging, 432

inventory turnover ratio, 444

lower limit (floor), 423

lower-of-cost-or-market (LCM), 423

lump-sum (basket) purchase, 430

markdown, 437

markdown cancellations, 437

market (for LCM), 423

markup, 437

markup cancellations, 437

1. Describe and apply the lower-of-cost-or-market rule. If inventory declines in value below its original cost, for whatever reason, a company should write down the inventory to reflect this loss. The general rule is to abandon the historical cost principle when the future utility (revenue-producing ability) of the asset drops below its original cost.

2. Explain when companies value inventories at net realizable value. Companies value inventory at net realizable value when: (1) there is a controlled market with a quoted price applicable to all quantities, (2) no significant costs of disposal are involved, and (3) the cost figures are too difficult to obtain.

3. Explain when companies use the relative sales value method to value inventories. When a company purchases a group of varying units at a single lump-sum price—a so-called basket purchase—the company may allocate the total purchase price to the individual items on the basis of relative sales value.

4. Discuss accounting issues related to purchase commitments. Accounting for purchase commitments is controversial. Some argue that companies should report purchase commitment contracts as assets and liabilities at the time the contract is signed. Others believe that recognition at the delivery date is most appropriate. The FASB neither excludes nor recommends the recording of assets and liabilities for purchase commitments, but it notes that if companies recorded such contracts at the time of commitment, the nature of the loss and the valuation account should be reported when the price falls.

5. Determine ending inventory by applying the gross profit method. Companies follow these steps to determine ending inventory by the gross profit method: (1) Compute the gross profit percentage on selling price. (2) Compute gross profit by multiplying net sales by the gross profit percentage. (3) Compute cost of goods sold by subtracting gross profit from net sales. (4) Compute ending inventory by subtracting cost of goods sold from total goods available for sale.

6. **Determine ending inventory by applying the retail inventory method.** Companies follow these steps to determine ending inventory by the conventional retail method: (1) To estimate inventory at retail, deduct the sales for the period from the retail value of the goods available for sale. (2) To find the cost-to-retail ratio for all goods passing through a department or firm, divide the total goods available for sale at cost by the total goods available at retail. (3) Convert the inventory valued at retail to approximate cost by applying the cost-to-retail ratio.

7. **Explain how to report and analyze inventory.** Accounting standards require financial statement disclosure of: (1) the composition of the inventory (in the balance sheet or a separate schedule in the notes); (2) significant or unusual inventory financing arrangements; and (3) inventory costing methods employed (which may differ for different elements of inventory). Accounting standards also require the consistent application of costing methods from one period to another. Common ratios used in the management and evaluation of inventory levels are inventory turnover and average days to sell the inventory.

APPENDIX 9A

LIFO Retail Methods

> **OBJECTIVE 8**
> Determine ending inventory by applying the LIFO retail methods.

A number of retail establishments have changed from the more conventional treatment to a **LIFO retail method**. For example, the world's largest retailer, **Wal-Mart** uses the LIFO retail method. The primary reason to do so is for the tax advantages associated with valuing inventories on a LIFO basis. In addition, adoption of LIFO results in a better matching of costs and revenues.

The use of LIFO retail is made under two assumptions: (1) stable prices and (2) fluctuating prices.

STABLE PRICES—LIFO RETAIL METHOD

It is much more complex to compute the final inventory balance using a LIFO flow than using the conventional retail method. Under the LIFO retail method, companies like **Wal-Mart** or **Target** consider **both markups and markdowns** in obtaining the proper cost-to-retail percentage. Furthermore, since the LIFO method is concerned only with the additional layer, or the amount that should be subtracted from the previous layer, the beginning inventory is excluded from the cost-to-retail percentage.

A major assumption of the LIFO retail method is that the markups and markdowns apply only to the goods purchased during the current period and not to the beginning inventory. This assumption is debatable and may explain why some companies do not adopt this method.

Illustration 9A-1 (page 446) presents the major concepts involved in the LIFO retail method applied to the Hernandez Company. Note that, to simplify the accounting, we have assumed that the price level has remained unchanged.

ILLUSTRATION 9A-1
LIFO Retail Method—
Stable Prices

	Cost	Retail
Beginning inventory—2007	$ 27,000	$ 45,000
Net purchases during the period	346,500	480,000
Net markups		20,000
Net markdowns		(5,000)
Total (excluding beginning inventory)	346,500 ⟷ 495,000	
Total (including beginning inventory)	$373,500	540,000
Net sales during the period		(484,000)
Ending inventory at retail		$ 56,000

Establishment of cost-to-retail percentage under
assumptions of LIFO retail ($346,500 ÷ $495,000) = 70%

Illustration 9A-2 indicates that the inventory is composed of two layers: the beginning inventory and the additional increase that occurred in the inventory this period (2007). When we start the next period (2008), the beginning inventory will be composed of those two layers. If an increase in inventory occurs again, an additional layer will be added.

ILLUSTRATION 9A-2
Ending Inventory at LIFO
Cost, 2007—Stable Prices

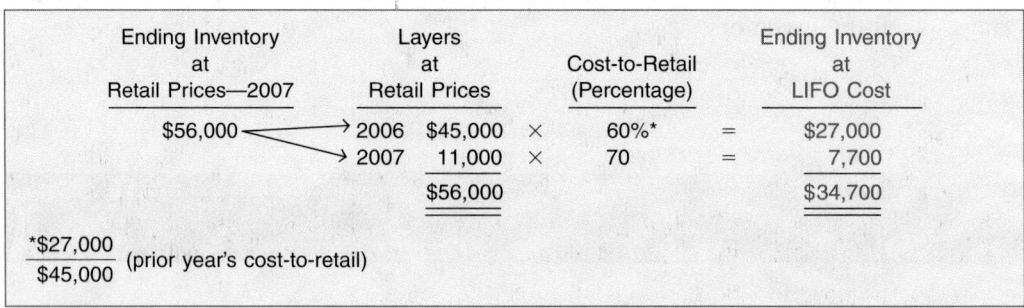

Ending Inventory at Retail Prices—2007	Layers at Retail Prices		Cost-to-Retail (Percentage)		Ending Inventory at LIFO Cost
$56,000	2006	$45,000 ×	60%*	=	$27,000
	2007	11,000 ×	70	=	7,700
		$56,000			$34,700

*$27,000 / $45,000 (prior year's cost-to-retail)

However, if the final inventory figure is below the beginning inventory, Hernandez must reduce the beginning inventory starting with the most recent layer. For example, assume that the ending inventory for 2008 at retail is $50,000. Illustration 9A-3 shows the computation of the ending inventory at cost. Notice that the 2007 layer is reduced from $11,000 to $5,000.

ILLUSTRATION 9A-3
Ending Inventory at LIFO
Cost, 2008—Stable Prices

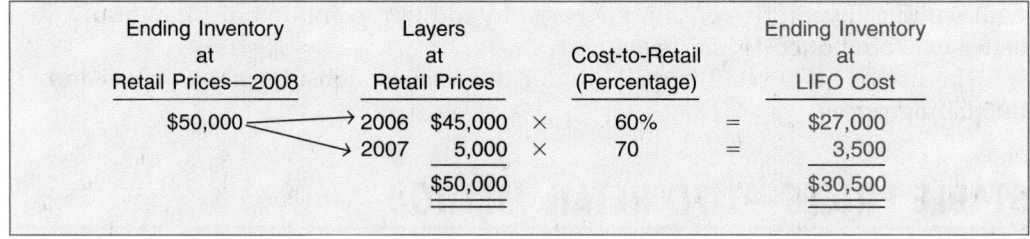

Ending Inventory at Retail Prices—2008	Layers at Retail Prices		Cost-to-Retail (Percentage)		Ending Inventory at LIFO Cost
$50,000	2006	$45,000 ×	60%	=	$27,000
	2007	5,000 ×	70	=	3,500
		$50,000			$30,500

FLUCTUATING PRICES—DOLLAR-VALUE LIFO RETAIL METHOD

The previous example simplified the LIFO retail method by ignoring changes in the selling price of the inventory. Let us now assume that a change in the price level of the inventories occurs (as is usual). If the price level does change, the company must **eliminate the price change** so as to measure the real increase in inventory, not the dollar increase. This approach is referred to as the **dollar-value LIFO retail method**.

To illustrate, assume that the beginning inventory had a retail market value of $10,000 and the ending inventory had a retail market value of $15,000. Assume further that the price level has risen from 100 to 125. It is inappropriate to suggest that a real increase in inventory of $5,000 has occurred. Instead, the company must deflate the ending inventory at retail, as the computation in Illustration 9A-4 shows.

Ending inventory at retail (deflated) $15,000 ÷ 1.25*	$12,000	
Beginning inventory at retail	10,000	
Real increase in inventory at retail	$ 2,000	
Ending inventory at retail on LIFO basis:		
First layer	$10,000	
Second layer ($2,000 × 1.25)	2,500	$12,500

*1.25 = 125 ÷ 100

ILLUSTRATION 9A-4
Ending Inventory at Retail—Deflated and Restated

This approach is essentially the dollar-value LIFO method discussed in Chapter 8. In computing the LIFO inventory under a dollar-value LIFO approach, the company finds the dollar increase in inventory and deflates it to beginning-of-the-year prices. This indicates whether actual increases or decreases in quantity have occurred. If an increase in quantities occurs, the company prices this increase at the new index, in order to compute the value of the new layer. If a decrease in quantities happens, the company subtracts the increase from the most recent layers to the extent necessary.

The following computations, based on those in Illustration 9A-1 for Hernandez Company, illustrate the differences between the dollar-value LIFO retail method and the regular LIFO retail approach. Assume that the current 2007 price index is 112 (prior year = 100) and that the inventory ($56,000) has remained unchanged. In comparing Illustrations 9A-1 and 9A-5, note that the computations involved in finding the cost-to-retail percentage are exactly the same. However, the dollar-value method determines the increase that has occurred in the inventory in terms of base-year prices.

	Cost	Retail
Beginning inventory—2007	$ 27,000	$ 45,000
Net purchases during the period	346,500	480,000
Net markups		20,000
Net markdowns		(5,000)
Total (excluding beginning inventory)	346,500 ⟷	495,000
Total (including beginning inventory)	$373,500	540,000
Net sales during the period at retail		(484,000)
Ending inventory at retail		$ 56,000

Establishment of cost-to-retail percentage under
assumptions of LIFO retail ($346,500 ÷ $495,000) = **70%**

A. Ending inventory at retail prices deflated to base-year prices	
$56,000 ÷ 112 =	$50,000
B. Beginning inventory (retail) at base-year prices	45,000
C. Inventory increase (retail) from beginning of period	$ 5,000

ILLUSTRATION 9A-5
Dollar-Value LIFO Retail Method—Fluctuating Prices

From this information, we compute the inventory amount at cost:

Ending Inventory at Base-Year Retail Prices—2007	Layers at Base-Year Retail Prices		Price Index (percentage)		Cost-to-Retail (percentage)		Ending Inventory at LIFO Cost
$50,000 ⟶	2006	$45,000 ×	100%	×	60%	=	$27,000
⟶	2007	5,000 ×	112	×	70	=	3,920
		$50,000					$30,920

ILLUSTRATION 9A-6
Ending Inventory at LIFO Cost, 2007—Fluctuating Prices

As Illustration 9A-6 shows, before the conversion to cost takes place, Hernandez must restate layers of a particular year to the prices in effect in the year when the layer was added.

Note the difference between the LIFO approach (stable prices) and the dollar-value LIFO method as indicated below.

ILLUSTRATION 9A-7
Comparison of Effect of Price Assumptions

	LIFO (stable prices)	LIFO (fluctuating prices)
Beginning inventory	$27,000	$27,000
Increment	7,700	3,920
Ending inventory	$34,700	$30,920

The difference of $3,780 ($34,700 − $30,920) results from an increase in the **price** of goods, not from an increase in the **quantity** of goods.

Subsequent Adjustments under Dollar-Value LIFO Retail

The dollar-value LIFO retail method follows the same procedures in subsequent periods as the traditional dollar-value method discussed in Chapter 8. That is, when a real increase in inventory occurs, Hernandez adds a new layer.

To illustrate, using the data from the previous example, assume that the retail value of the 2008 ending inventory at current prices is $64,800, the 2008 price index is 120 percent of base-year, and the cost-to-retail percentage is 75 percent. In base-year dollars, the ending inventory is therefore $54,000 ($64,800/120%). Illustration 9A-8 shows the computation of the ending inventory at LIFO cost.

ILLUSTRATION 9A-8
Ending Inventory at LIFO Cost, 2008—Fluctuating Prices

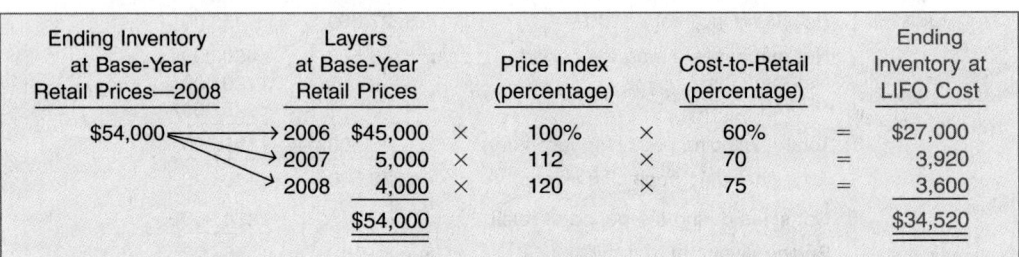

Ending Inventory at Base-Year Retail Prices—2008	Layers at Base-Year Retail Prices		Price Index (percentage)		Cost-to-Retail (percentage)		Ending Inventory at LIFO Cost
$54,000	2006	$45,000	× 100%	×	60%	=	$27,000
	2007	5,000	× 112	×	70	=	3,920
	2008	4,000	× 120	×	75	=	3,600
		$54,000					$34,520

Conversely, when a real decrease in inventory develops, Hernandez "peels off" previous layers at prices in existence when the layers were added. To illustrate, assume that in 2008 the ending inventory in base-year prices is $48,000. The computation of the LIFO inventory is as follows.

ILLUSTRATION 9A-9
Ending Inventory at LIFO Cost, 2008—Fluctuating Prices

Ending Inventory at Base-Year Retail Prices—2008	Layers at Base-Year Retail Prices		Price Index (percentage)		Cost-to-Retail (percentage)		Ending Inventory at LIFO Cost
$48,000	2006	$45,000	× 100%	×	60%	=	$27,000
	2007	3,000	× 112	×	70	=	2,352
		$48,000					$29,352

The advantages and disadvantages of the lower-of-cost-or-market method (conventional retail) versus LIFO retail are the same for retail operations as for non-retail operations. As a practical matter, a company's selection of which retail inventory method to use often involves determining which method provides a lower taxable income. It might appear that retail LIFO will provide the lower taxable income in a period of rising prices. But this is not always the case. LIFO will provide an approximate current cost matching, but it states ending inventory at cost. The conventional retail method may have a large write-off because of the use of the lower-of-cost-or-market approach, which may offset the LIFO current cost matching.

CHANGING FROM CONVENTIONAL RETAIL TO LIFO

Because conventional retail is a lower-of-cost-or-market approach, the company must restate beginning inventory to a cost basis when changing from the conventional retail to the LIFO method.[1] The usual approach is to compute the cost basis from the purchases of the prior year, adjusted for both markups and markdowns.[2]

To illustrate, assume that Clark Clothing Store employs the conventional retail method but wishes to change to the LIFO retail method beginning in 2007. The amounts shown by the firm's books are as follows.

	At Cost	At Retail
Inventory, January 1, 2007	$ 5,120	$ 15,000
Net purchases in 2007	47,250	100,000
Net markups in 2007		7,000
Net markdowns in 2007		2,000
Sales in 2007		95,000

Illustration 9A-10 shows computation of ending inventory under the **conventional retail method** for 2007.

	Cost	Retail
Inventory January 1, 2007	$ 5,210	$ 15,000
Net purchases	47,250	100,000
Net additional markups		7,000
	$52,460	122,000
Net markdowns		(2,000)
Sales		(95,000)
Ending inventory at retail		$ 25,000
Establishment of cost-to-retail percentage ($52,460 ÷ $122,000) =		43%
December 31, 2007, inventory at cost		
Inventory at retail		$ 25,000
Cost-to-retail ratio		× 43%
Inventory at cost under conventional retail		$ 10,750

ILLUSTRATION 9A-10
Conventional Retail
Inventory Method

Clark Clothing can then quickly approximate the ending inventory for 2007 under the **LIFO retail method** as shown in Illustration 9A-11 (page 450).

---

[1]Changing from the conventional retail method to LIFO retail represents a change in accounting principle. We provide an expanded discussion of accounting principle changes in Chapter 22.

[2]A logical question to ask is, "Why are only the purchases from the prior period considered and not also the beginning inventory?" Apparently the IRS believes that "the purchases-only approach" provides a more reasonable cost basis. The IRS position is debatable. However, for our purposes, it seems appropriate to use the purchases-only approach.

ILLUSTRATION 9A-11
Conversion to LIFO
Retail Inventory Method

December 31, 2007, Inventory at LIFO Cost

$$\text{Ending inventory} \quad \frac{\text{Retail}}{\$25,000} \times \frac{\text{Ratio}}{45\%^*} = \frac{\text{LIFO}}{\$11,250}$$

*The cost-to-retail ratio was computed as follows:

$$\frac{\text{Net purchases at cost}}{\substack{\text{Net purchases at retail plus} \\ \text{markups less markdowns}}} = \frac{\$47,250}{\$100,000 + \$7,000 - \$2,000} = 45\%$$

The difference of $500 ($11,250 − $10,750) between the LIFO retail method and the conventional retail method in the ending inventory for 2007 is the amount by which the company must adjust beginning inventory for 2008. The entry to adjust the inventory to a cost basis is as follows.

Inventory	500	
Adjustment to Record Inventory at Cost		500

SUMMARY OF LEARNING OBJECTIVE FOR APPENDIX 9A

8. Determine ending inventory by applying the LIFO retail methods. The application of LIFO retail is made under two assumptions: stable prices and fluctuating prices.

Procedures under stable prices: (a) Because the LIFO method is a cost method, both markups and markdowns must be considered in obtaining the proper cost-to-retail percentage. (b) Since the LIFO method is concerned only with the additional layer, or the amount that should be subtracted from the previous layer, the beginning inventory is excluded from the cost-to-retail percentage. (c) The markups and markdowns apply only to the goods purchased during the current period and not to the beginning inventory.

Procedures under fluctuating prices: The steps are the same as for stable prices except that in computing the LIFO inventory under a dollar-value LIFO approach, the dollar increase in inventory is found and deflated to beginning-of-the-year prices. Doing so will determine whether actual increases or decreases in quantity have occurred. If quantities increase, this increase is priced at the new index to compute the new layer. If quantities decrease, the decrease is subtracted from the most recent layers to the extent necessary.

Note: All **asterisked** Questions, Brief Exercises, Exercises, Problems, and Concepts for Analysis relate to material contained in the appendix to the chapter.

QUESTIONS

1. Where there is evidence that the utility of inventory goods, as part of their disposal in the ordinary course of business, will be less than cost, what is the proper accounting treatment?

2. Explain the rationale for the ceiling and floor in the lower-of-cost-or-market method of valuing inventories.

3. Why are inventories valued at the lower-of-cost-or-market? What are the arguments against the use of the LCM method of valuing inventories?

4. What approaches may be employed in applying the lower-of-cost-or-market procedure? Which approach is normally used and why?

5. In some instances accounting principles require a departure from valuing inventories at cost alone. Determine the proper unit inventory price in the following cases.

	Cases				
	1	2	3	4	5
Cost	$15.90	$16.10	$15.90	$15.90	$15.90
Net realizable value	14.30	19.20	15.20	10.40	16.40
Net realizable value less normal profit	12.80	17.60	13.75	8.80	14.80
Market (replacement cost)	14.80	17.20	12.80	9.70	16.80

6. What method(s) might be used in the accounts to record a loss due to a price decline in the inventories? Discuss.

7. What factors might call for inventory valuation at sales prices (net realizable value or market price)?

8. Under what circumstances is relative sales value an appropriate basis for determining the price assigned to inventory?

9. At December 31, 2008, Kidman Co. has outstanding purchase commitments for purchase of 150,000 gallons, at $6.40 per gallon, of a raw material to be used in its manufacturing process. The company prices its raw material inventory at cost or market, whichever is lower. Assuming that the market price as of December 31, 2008, is $5.90, how would you treat this situation in the accounts?

10. What are the major uses of the gross profit method?

11. Distinguish between gross profit as a percentage of cost and gross profit as a percentage of sales price. Convert the following gross profit percentages based on cost to gross profit percentages based on sales price: 20% and 33⅓%. Convert the following gross profit percentages based on sales price to gross profit percentages based on cost: 33⅓% and 60%.

12. Carole Lombard Co. with annual net sales of $6 million maintains a markup of 25% based on cost. Lombard's expenses average 15% of net sales. What is Lombard's gross profit and net profit in dollars?

13. A fire destroys all of the merchandise of Rosanna Arquette Company on February 10, 2008. Presented below is information compiled up to the date of the fire.

Inventory, January 1, 2008	$ 400,000
Sales to February 10, 2008	1,750,000
Purchases to February 10, 2008	1,140,000
Freight-in to February 10, 2008	60,000
Rate of gross profit on selling price	40%

What is the approximate inventory on February 10, 2008?

14. What conditions must exist for the retail inventory method to provide valid results?

15. The conventional retail inventory method yields results that are essentially the same as those yielded by the lower-of-cost-or-market method. Explain. Prepare an illustration of how the retail inventory method reduces inventory to market.

16. **(a)** Determine the ending inventory under the conventional retail method for the furniture department of Gin Blossoms Department Stores from the following data.

	Cost	Retail
Inventory, Jan. 1	$ 149,000	$ 283,500
Purchases	1,400,000	2,160,000
Freight-in	70,000	
Markups, net		92,000
Markdowns, net		48,000
Sales		2,235,000

(b) If the results of a physical inventory indicated an inventory at retail of $240,000, what inferences would you draw?

17. **Deere and Company** reported inventory in its balance sheet as follows:

Inventories $1,999,100,000

What additional disclosures might be necessary to present the inventory fairly?

18. Of what significance is inventory turnover to a retail store?

*19. What modifications to the conventional retail method are necessary to approximate a LIFO retail flow?

BRIEF EXERCISES

(LO 1, 2) **BE9-1** Presented below is information related to Alstott Inc.'s inventory.

(per unit)	Skis	Boots	Parkas
Historical cost	$190.00	$106.00	$53.00
Selling price	217.00	145.00	73.75
Cost to distribute	19.00	8.00	2.50
Current replacement cost	203.00	105.00	51.00
Normal profit margin	32.00	29.00	21.25

Determine the following: (a) the two limits to market value (i.e., the ceiling and the floor) that should be used in the lower-of-cost-or-market computation for skis; (b) the cost amount that should be used in the lower-of-cost-or-market comparison of boots; and (c) the market amount that should be used to value parkas on the basis of the lower-of-cost-or-market.

(LO 1, 2)   **BE9-2**   Robin Corporation has the following four items in its ending inventory.

Item	Cost	Replacement Cost	Net Realizable Value (NRV)	NRV Less Normal Profit Margin
Jokers	$2,000	$1,900	$2,100	$1,600
Penguins	5,000	5,100	4,950	4,100
Riddlers	4,400	4,550	4,625	3,700
Scarecrows	3,200	2,990	3,830	3,070

Determine the final lower-of-cost-or-market inventory value for each item.

(LO 1, 2)   **BE9-3**   Battletoads Inc. uses a perpetual inventory system. At January 1, 2008, inventory was $214,000 at both cost and market value. At December 31, 2008, the inventory was $286,000 at cost and $269,000 at market value. Prepare the necessary December 31 entry under (a) the direct method and (b) the indirect method.

(LO 3)   **BE9-4**   PC Plus buys 1,000 computer game CDs from a distributor who is discontinuing those games. The purchase price for the lot is $6,000. PC Plus will group the CDs into three price categories for resale, as indicated below.

Group	No. of CDs	Price per CD
1	100	$ 5.00
2	800	10.00
3	100	15.00

Determine the cost per CD for each group, using the relative sales value method.

(LO 4)   **BE9-5**   Beavis Company signed a long-term noncancelable purchase commitment with a major supplier to purchase raw materials in 2008 at a cost of $1,000,000. At December 31, 2007, the raw materials to be purchased have a market value of $930,000. Prepare any necessary December 31 entry.

(LO 4)   **BE9-6**   Use the information for Beavis Company from BE9-5. In 2008, Beavis paid $1,000,000 to obtain the raw materials which were worth $930,000. Prepare the entry to record the purchase.

(LO 5)   **BE9-7**   Big Hurt Corporation's April 30 inventory was destroyed by fire. January 1 inventory was $150,000, and purchases for January through April totaled $500,000. Sales for the same period were $700,000. Big Hurt's normal gross profit percentage is 31% on sales. Using the gross profit method, estimate Big Hurt's April 30 inventory that was destroyed by fire.

(LO 6)   **BE9-8**   Bimini Inc. had beginning inventory of $12,000 at cost and $20,000 at retail. Net purchases were $120,000 at cost and $170,000 at retail. Net markups were $10,000; net markdowns were $7,000; and sales were $157,000. Compute ending inventory at cost using the conventional retail method.

(LO 7)   **BE9-9**   In its 2004 annual report, **Wal-Mart** reported inventory of $26,612 million on January 31, 2004, and $24,401 million on January 31, 2003, cost of sales of $198,747 million for fiscal year 2004, and net sales of $256,329 million. Compute Wal-Mart's inventory turnover and the average days to sell inventory for the fiscal year 2004.

(LO 8)   ***BE9-10**   Use the information for Bimini Inc. from BE9-8. Compute ending inventory at cost using the LIFO retail method.

(LO 8)   ***BE9-11**   Use the information for Bimini Inc. from BE9-8, and assume the price level increased from 100 at the beginning of the year to 120 at year-end. Compute ending inventory at cost using the dollar-value LIFO retail method.

EXERCISES

(LO 1, 2)   **E9-1**   **(Lower-of-Cost-or-Market)**   The inventory of 3T Company on December 31, 2008, consists of the following items.

Part No.	Quantity	Cost per Unit	Cost to Replace per Unit
110	600	$90	$100
111	1,000	60	52
112	500	80	76
113	200	170	180
120	400	205	208
121[a]	1,600	16	14
122	300	240	235

ªPart No. 121 is obsolete and has a realizable value of $0.20 each as scrap.

Instructions

(a) Determine the inventory as of December 31, 2008, by the lower-of-cost-or-market method, applying this method directly to each item.

(b) Determine the inventory by the lower-of-cost-or-market method, applying the method to the total of the inventory.

(LO 1, 2) **E9-2 (Lower-of-Cost-or-Market)** Smashing Pumpkins Company uses the lower-of-cost-or-market method, on an individual-item basis, in pricing its inventory items. The inventory at December 31, 2008, consists of products D, E, F, G, H, and I. Relevant per-unit data for these products appear below.

	Item D	Item E	Item F	Item G	Item H	Item I
Estimated selling price	$120	$110	$95	$90	$110	$90
Cost	75	80	80	80	50	36
Replacement cost	120	72	70	30	70	30
Estimated selling expense	30	30	30	25	30	30
Normal profit	20	20	20	20	20	20

Handwritten: ΛRU 90 80 65 65 50 60
Handwritten: ΛRUm 70 60 45 45 60 40

Instructions

Using the lower-of-cost-or-market rule, determine the proper unit value for balance sheet reporting purposes at December 31, 2008, for each of the inventory items above.

(LO 1, 2) **E9-3 (Lower-of-Cost-or-Market)** Michael Bolton Company follows the practice of pricing its inventory at the lower-of-cost-or-market, on an individual-item basis.

Item No.	Quantity	Cost per Unit	Cost to Replace	Estimated Selling Price	Cost of Completion and Disposal	Normal Profit
1320	1,200	$3.20	$3.00	$4.50	$0.35	$1.25
1333	900	2.70	2.30	3.50	0.50	0.50
1426	800	4.50	3.70	5.00	0.40	1.00
1437	1,000	3.60	3.10	3.20	0.25	0.90
1510	700	2.25	2.00	3.25	0.80	0.60
1522	500	3.00	2.70	3.80	0.40	0.50
1573	3,000	1.80	1.60	2.50	0.75	0.50
1626	1,000	4.70	5.20	6.00	0.50	1.00

Instructions

From the information above, determine the amount of Bolton Company inventory.

(LO 1, 2) **E9-4 (Lower-of-Cost-or-Market—Journal Entries)** Corrs Company began operations in 2007 and determined its ending inventory at cost and at lower-of-cost-or-market at December 31, 2007, and December 31, 2008. This information is presented below.

	Cost	Lower-of-Cost-or-Market
12/31/07	$346,000	$327,000
12/31/08	410,000	395,000

Instructions

(a) Prepare the journal entries required at December 31, 2007, and December 31, 2008, assuming that the inventory is recorded at market, and a perpetual inventory system (direct method) is used.

(b) Prepare journal entries required at December 31, 2007, and December 31, 2008, assuming that the inventory is recorded at cost and an allowance account is adjusted at each year-end under a perpetual system.

(c) Which of the two methods above provides the higher net income in each year?

(LO 1, 2) **E9-5 (Lower-of-Cost-or-Market—Valuation Account)** Presented below is information related to Candlebox Enterprises.

	Jan. 31	Feb. 28	Mar. 31	Apr. 30
Inventory at cost	$15,000	$15,100	$17,000	$13,000
Inventory at the lower-of-cost-or-market	14,500	12,600	15,600	12,300
Purchases for the month		20,000	24,000	26,500
Sales for the month		29,000	35,000	40,000

Instructions

(a) From the information, prepare (as far as the data permit) monthly income statements in columnar form for February, March, and April. The inventory is to be shown in the statement at cost, the gain or loss due to market fluctuations is to be shown separately, and a valuation account is to be set up for the difference between cost and the lower of cost or market.

(b) Prepare the journal entry required to establish the valuation account at January 31 and entries to adjust it monthly thereafter.

(LO 1, 2) **E9-6** **(Lower-of-Cost-or-Market—Error Effect)** Winans Company uses the lower-of-cost-or-market method, on an individual-item basis, in pricing its inventory items. The inventory at December 31, 2007, included product X. Relevant per-unit data for product X appear below.

Estimated selling price	$45
Cost	40
Replacement cost	35
Estimated selling expense	14
Normal profit	9

There were 1,000 units of product X on hand at December 31, 2007. Product X was incorrectly valued at $35 per unit for reporting purposes. All 1,000 units were sold in 2008.

Instructions

Compute the effect of this error on net income for 2007 and the effect on net income for 2008, and indicate the direction of the misstatement for each year.

(LO 3) **E9-7** **(Relative Sales Value Method)** Phil Collins Realty Corporation purchased a tract of unimproved land for $55,000. This land was improved and subdivided into building lots at an additional cost of $34,460. These building lots were all of the same size but owing to differences in location were offered for sale at different prices as follows.

Group	No. of Lots	Price per Lot
1	9	$3,000
2	15	4,000
3	17	2,400

Operating expenses for the year allocated to this project total $18,200. Lots unsold at the year-end were as follows.

Group 1	5 lots
Group 2	7 lots
Group 3	2 lots

Instructions

At the end of the fiscal year Phil Collins Realty Corporation instructs you to arrive at the net income realized on this operation to date.

(LO 3) **E9-8** **(Relative Sales Value Method)** During 2008, Pretenders Furniture Company purchases a carload of wicker chairs. The manufacturer sells the chairs to Pretenders for a lump sum of $59,850, because it is discontinuing manufacturing operations and wishes to dispose of its entire stock. Three types of chairs are included in the carload. The three types and the estimated selling price for each are listed below.

Type	No. of Chairs	Estimated Selling Price Each
Lounge chairs	400	$90
Armchairs	300	80
Straight chairs	700	50

During 2008, Pretenders sells 200 lounge chairs, 100 armchairs, and 120 straight chairs.

Instructions

What is the amount of gross profit realized during 2008? What is the amount of inventory of unsold straight chairs on December 31, 2008?

(LO 4) **E9-9** **(Purchase Commitments)** Marvin Gaye Company has been having difficulty obtaining key raw materials for its manufacturing process. The company therefore signed a long-term noncancelable purchase commitment with its largest supplier of this raw material on November 30, 2008, at an agreed price of $400,000. At December 31, 2008, the raw material had declined in price to $365,000.

Instructions

What entry would you make on December 31, 2008, to recognize these facts?

(LO 4) **E9-10** **(Purchase Commitments)** At December 31, 2008, Indigo Girls Company has outstanding noncancelable purchase commitments for 36,000 gallons, at $3.00 per gallon, of raw material to be used in its manufacturing process. The company prices its raw material inventory at cost or market, whichever is lower.

Instructions

(a) Assuming that the market price as of December 31, 2008, is $3.30, how would this matter be treated in the accounts and statements? Explain.

(b) Assuming that the market price as of December 31, 2008, is $2.70, instead of $3.30, how would you treat this situation in the accounts and statements?

(c) Give the entry in January 2009, when the 36,000-gallon shipment is received, assuming that the situation given in (b) above existed at December 31, 2008, and that the market price in January 2009 was $2.70 per gallon. Give an explanation of your treatment.

(LO 5) **E9-11 (Gross Profit Method)** Each of the following gross profit percentages is expressed in terms of cost.

1. 20%.   3. 33⅓%.
2. 25%.   4. 50%.

Instructions

Indicate the gross profit percentage in terms of sales for each of the above.

(LO 5) **E9-12 (Gross Profit Method)** Mark Price Company uses the gross profit method to estimate inventory for monthly reporting purposes. Presented below is information for the month of May.

Inventory, May 1	$ 160,000
Purchases (gross)	640,000
Freight-in	30,000
Sales	1,000,000
Sales returns	70,000
Purchase discounts	12,000

Instructions

(a) Compute the estimated inventory at May 31, assuming that the gross profit is 30% of sales.

(b) Compute the estimated inventory at May 31, assuming that the gross profit is 30% of cost.

(LO 5) **E9-13 (Gross Profit Method)** Tim Legler requires an estimate of the cost of goods lost by fire on March 9. Merchandise on hand on January 1 was $38,000. Purchases since January 1 were $72,000; freight-in, $3,400; purchase returns and allowances, $2,400. Sales are made at 33⅓% above cost and totaled $100,000 to March 9. Goods costing $10,900 were left undamaged by the fire; remaining goods were destroyed.

Instructions

(a) Compute the cost of goods destroyed.

(b) Compute the cost of goods destroyed, assuming that the gross profit is 33⅓% of sales.

(LO 5) **E9-14 (Gross Profit Method)** Rasheed Wallace Company lost most of its inventory in a fire in December just before the year-end physical inventory was taken. The corporation's books disclosed the following.

Beginning inventory	$170,000	Sales	$650,000
Purchases for the year	390,000	Sales returns	24,000
Purchase returns	30,000	Rate of gross margin on net sales	40%

Merchandise with a selling price of $21,000 remained undamaged after the fire. Damaged merchandise with an original selling price of $15,000 had a net realizable value of $5,300.

Instructions

Compute the amount of the loss as a result of the fire, assuming that the corporation had no insurance coverage.

(LO 5) **E9-15 (Gross Profit Method)** You are called by Tim Duncan of Spurs Co. on July 16 and asked to prepare a claim for insurance as a result of a theft that took place the night before. You suggest that an inventory be taken immediately. The following data are available.

Inventory, July 1	$ 38,000
Purchases—goods placed in stock July 1–15	85,000
Sales—goods delivered to customers (gross)	116,000
Sales returns—goods returned to stock	4,000

Your client reports that the goods on hand on July 16 cost $30,500, but you determine that this figure includes goods of $6,000 received on a consignment basis. Your past records show that sales are made at approximately 40% over cost. Duncan's insurance covers only goods owned.

Instructions

Compute the claim against the insurance company.

(LO 5) **E9-16** **(Gross Profit Method)** Gheorghe Moresan Lumber Company handles three principal lines of merchandise with these varying rates of gross profit on cost.

Lumber	25%
Millwork	30%
Hardware and fittings	40%

On August 18, a fire destroyed the office, lumber shed, and a considerable portion of the lumber stacked in the yard. To file a report of loss for insurance purposes, the company must know what the inventories were immediately preceding the fire. No detail or perpetual inventory records of any kind were maintained. The only pertinent information you are able to obtain are the following facts from the general ledger, which was kept in a fireproof vault and thus escaped destruction.

	Lumber	Millwork	Hardware
Inventory, Jan. 1, 2008	$ 250,000	$ 90,000	$ 45,000
Purchases to Aug. 18, 2008	1,500,000	375,000	160,000
Sales to Aug. 18, 2008	2,080,000	533,000	210,000

Instructions

Submit your estimate of the inventory amounts immediately preceding the fire.

(LO 5) **E9-17** **(Gross Profit Method)** Presented below is information related to Warren Moon Corporation for the current year.

Beginning inventory	$ 600,000	
Purchases	1,500,000	
Total goods available for sale		$2,100,000
Sales		2,500,000

Instructions

Compute the ending inventory, assuming that **(a)** gross profit is 45% of sales; **(b)** gross profit is 60% of cost; **(c)** gross profit is 35% of sales; and **(d)** gross profit is 25% of cost.

(LO 6) **E9-18** **(Retail Inventory Method)** Presented below is information related to Bobby Engram Company.

	Cost	Retail
Beginning inventory	$ 58,000	$100,000
Purchases (net)	122,000	200,000
Net markups		10,345
Net markdowns		26,135
Sales		186,000

Instructions

(a) Compute the ending inventory at retail.
(b) Compute a cost-to-retail percentage (round to two decimals) under the following conditions.
   (1) Excluding both markups and markdowns.
   (2) Excluding markups but including markdowns.
   (3) Excluding markdowns but including markups.
   (4) Including both markdowns and markups.
(c) Which of the methods in (b) above (1, 2, 3, or 4) does the following?
   (1) Provides the most conservative estimate of ending inventory.
   (2) Provides an approximation of lower-of-cost-or-market.
   (3) Is used in the conventional retail method.
(d) Compute ending inventory at lower-of-cost-or-market (round to nearest dollar).
(e) Compute cost of goods sold based on (d).
(f) Compute gross margin based on (d).

(LO 6) **E9-19** **(Retail Inventory Method)** Presented below is information related to Ricky Henderson Company.

	Cost	Retail
Beginning inventory	$ 200,000	$ 280,000
Purchases	1,375,000	2,140,000
Markups		95,000
Markup cancellations		15,000
Markdowns		35,000
Markdown cancellations		5,000
Sales		2,200,000

Instructions
Compute the inventory by the conventional retail inventory method.

(LO 6) **E9-20** **(Retail Inventory Method)** The records of Ellen's Boutique report the following data for the month of April.

Sales	$99,000	Purchases (at cost)	$48,000
Sales returns	2,000	Purchases (at sales price)	88,000
Markups	10,000	Purchase returns (at cost)	2,000
Markup cancellations	1,500	Purchase returns (at sales price)	3,000
Markdowns	9,300	Beginning inventory (at cost)	30,000
Markdown cancellations	2,800	Beginning inventory (at sales price)	46,500
Freight on purchases	2,400		

Instructions
Compute the ending inventory by the conventional retail inventory method.

(LO 7) **E9-21** **(Analysis of Inventories)** The financial statements of **General Mills, Inc**'s. 2004 annual report disclose the following information.

(in millions)	May 30, 2004	May 25, 2003	May 26, 2002
Inventories	$1,063	$1,082	$1,055

	Fiscal Year	
	2004	2003
Sales	$11,070	$10,506
Cost of goods sold	6,584	6,109
Net income	1,055	917

Instructions
Compute General Mills's **(a)** inventory turnover and **(b)** the average days to sell inventory for 2004 and 2003.

(LO 8) ***E9-22** **(Retail Inventory Method—Conventional and LIFO)** Helen Keller Company began operations on January 1, 2006, adopting the conventional retail inventory system. None of the company's merchandise was marked down in 2006 and, because there was no beginning inventory, its ending inventory for 2006 of $38,100 would have been the same under either the conventional retail system or the LIFO retail system.

On December 31, 2007, the store management considers adopting the LIFO retail system and desires to know how the December 31, 2007, inventory would appear under both systems. All pertinent data regarding purchases, sales, markups, and markdowns are shown below. There has been no change in the price level.

	Cost	Retail
Inventory, Jan. 1, 2007	$ 38,100	$ 60,000
Markdowns (net)		13,000
Markups (net)		22,000
Purchases (net)	130,900	178,000
Sales (net)		167,000

Instructions
Determine the cost of the 2007 ending inventory under both **(a)** the conventional retail method and **(b)** the LIFO retail method.

(LO 8) ***E9-23** **(Retail Inventory Method—Conventional and LIFO)** Leonard Bernstein Company began operations late in 2006 and adopted the conventional retail inventory method. Because there was no beginning inventory for 2006 and no markdowns during 2006, the ending inventory for 2006 was $14,000 under both the conventional retail method and the LIFO retail method. At the end of 2007, management wants to compare the results of applying the conventional and LIFO retail methods. There was no change in the price level during 2007. The following data are available for computations.

	Cost	Retail
Inventory, January 1, 2007	$14,000	$20,000
Sales		80,000
Net markups		9,000
Net markdowns		1,600
Purchases	58,800	81,000
Freight-in	7,500	
Estimated theft		2,000

Instructions
Compute the cost of the 2007 ending inventory under both **(a)** the conventional retail method and **(b)** the LIFO retail method.

(LO 8) ***E9-24 (Dollar-Value LIFO Retail)** You assemble the following information for Seneca Department Store, which computes its inventory under the dollar-value LIFO method.

	Cost	Retail
Inventory on January 1, 2007	$216,000	$300,000
Purchases	364,800	480,000
Increase in price level for year		9%

Instructions
Compute the cost of the inventory on December 31, 2007, assuming that the inventory at retail is **(a)** $294,300 and **(b)** $365,150.

(LO 8) ***E9-25 (Dollar-Value LIFO Retail)** Presented below is information related to Langston Hughes Corporation.

	Price Index	LIFO Cost	Retail
Inventory on December 31, 2008, when dollar-value LIFO is adopted	100	$36,000	$ 74,500
Inventory, December 31, 2009	110	?	100,100

Instructions
Compute the ending inventory under the dollar-value LIFO method at December 31, 2009. The cost-to-retail ratio for 2009 was 60%.

(LO 8) ***E9-26 (Conventional Retail and Dollar-Value LIFO Retail)** Amiras Corporation began operations on January 1, 2007, with a beginning inventory of $30,100 at cost and $50,000 at retail. The following information relates to 2007.

	Retail
Net purchases ($108,500 at cost)	$150,000
Net markups	10,000
Net markdowns	5,000
Sales	126,900

Instructions
  (a) Assume Amiras decided to adopt the conventional retail method. Compute the ending inventory to be reported in the balance sheet.
  (b) Assume instead that Amiras decides to adopt the dollar-value LIFO retail method. The appropriate price indexes are 100 at January 1 and 110 at December 31. Compute the ending inventory to be reported in the balance sheet.
  (c) On the basis of the information in part (b), compute cost of goods sold.

(LO 8) ***E9-27 (Dollar-Value LIFO Retail)** Connie Chung Corporation adopted the dollar-value LIFO retail inventory method on January 1, 2006. At that time the inventory had a cost of $54,000 and a retail price of $100,000. The following information is available.

	Year-End Inventory at Retail	Current Year Cost—Retail %	Year-End Price Index
2006	$118,720	57%	106
2007	138,750	60%	111
2008	125,350	61%	115
2009	162,500	58%	125

The price index at January 1, 2006, is 100.

Instructions
Compute the ending inventory at December 31 of the years 2006–2009. Round to the nearest dollar.

(LO 8) ***E9-28 (Change to LIFO Retail)** John Olerud Ltd., a local retailing concern in the Bronx, N.Y., has decided to change from the conventional retail inventory method to the LIFO retail method starting on January 1, 2008. The company recomputed its ending inventory for 2007 in accordance with the procedures necessary to switch to LIFO retail. The inventory computed was $212,600.

Instructions

Assuming that John Olerud Ltd.'s ending inventory for 2007 under the conventional retail inventory method was $205,000, prepare the appropriate journal entry on January 1, 2008.

See the book's website, www.wiley.com/college/kieso, for Additional Exercises.

PROBLEMS

(LO 1, 2) **P9-1** **(Lower-of-Cost-or-Market)** Grant Wood Company manufactures desks. Most of the company's desks are standard models and are sold on the basis of catalog prices. At December 31, 2008, the following finished desks appear in the company's inventory.

Finished Desks	A	B	C	D
2008 catalog selling price	$450	$480	$900	$1,050
FIFO cost per inventory list 12/31/08	470	450	830	960
Estimated current cost to manufacture (at December 31, 2008, and early 2009)	460	440	610	1,000
Sales commissions and estimated other costs of disposal	45	60	90	130
2009 catalog selling price	500	540	900	1,200

The 2008 catalog was in effect through November 2008 and the 2009 catalog is effective as of December 1, 2008. All catalog prices are net of the usual discounts. Generally, the company attempts to obtain a 20% gross margin on selling price and has usually been successful in doing so.

Instructions

At what amount should each of the four desks appear in the company's December 31, 2008, inventory, assuming that the company has adopted a lower-of-FIFO-cost-or-market approach for valuation of inventories on an individual-item basis?

(LO 1, 2) **P9-2** **(Lower-of-Cost-or-Market)** T. Allen Home Improvement Company installs replacement siding, windows, and louvered glass doors for single family homes and condominium complexes in northern New Jersey and southern New York. The company is in the process of preparing its annual financial statements for the fiscal year ended May 31, 2007, and Tim Taylor, controller for T. Allen, has gathered the following data concerning inventory.

At May 31, 2007, the balance in T. Allen's Raw Material Inventory account was $408,000, and the Allowance to Reduce Inventory to Market had a credit balance of $29,500. Taylor summarized the relevant inventory cost and market data at May 31, 2007, in the schedule below.

Taylor assigned Patricia Richardson, an intern from a local college, the task of calculating the amount that should appear on T. Allen's May 31, 2007, financial statements for inventory under the lower-of-cost-or-market rule as applied to each item in inventory. Richardson expressed concern over departing from the cost principle.

	Cost	Replacement Cost	Sales Price	Net Realizable Value	Normal Profit
Aluminum siding	$ 70,000	$ 62,500	$ 64,000	$ 56,000	$ 5,100
Cedar shake siding	86,000	79,400	94,000	84,800	7,400
Louvered glass doors	112,000	124,000	186,400	168,300	18,500
Thermal windows	140,000	122,000	154,800	140,000	15,400
Total	$408,000	$387,900	$499,200	$449,100	$46,400

Instructions

(a) **(1)** Determine the proper balance in the Allowance to Reduce Inventory to Market at May 31, 2007.

  (2) For the fiscal year ended May 31, 2007, determine the amount of the gain or loss that would be recorded due to the change in the Allowance to Reduce Inventory to Market.

(b) Explain the rationale for the use of the lower-of-cost-or-market rule as it applies to inventories.

(CMA adapted)

(LO 1, 2) **P9-3** **(Entries for Lower-of-Cost-or-Market—Direct and Allowance)** Mary Stuart Company determined its ending inventory at cost and at lower of cost or market at December 31, 2006, December 31, 2007, and December 31, 2008, as shown on page 460.

	Cost	Lower-of-Cost-or-Market
12/31/06	$650,000	$650,000
12/31/07	780,000	722,000
12/31/08	900,000	830,000

Instructions

(a) Prepare the journal entries required at December 31, 2007, and at December 31, 2008, assuming that a perpetual inventory system and the direct method of adjusting to market is used.

(b) Prepare the journal entries required at December 31, 2007, and at December 31, 2008, assuming that a perpetual inventory is recorded at cost and reduced to market through the use of an allowance account (indirect method).

(LO 5) **P9-4** **(Gross Profit Method)** David Hasselholf Company lost most of its inventory in a fire in December just before the year-end physical inventory was taken. Corporate records disclose the following.

Inventory (beginning)	$ 80,000	Sales	$415,000
Purchases	280,000	Sales returns	21,000
Purchase returns	28,000	Gross profit % based on net selling price	34%

Merchandise with a selling price of $30,000 remained undamaged after the fire, and damaged merchandise has a salvage value of $7,150. The company does not carry fire insurance on its inventory.

Instructions

Prepare a formal labeled schedule computing the fire loss incurred. (Do not use the retail inventory method.)

(LO 5) **P9-5** **(Gross Profit Method)** On April 15, 2008, fire damaged the office and warehouse of John Kimmel Corporation. The only accounting record saved was the general ledger, from which the trial balance below was prepared.

JOHN KIMMEL CORPORATION
Trial Balance
March 31, 2008

Cash	$ 20,000	
Accounts receivable	40,000	
Inventory, December 31, 2007	75,000	
Land	35,000	
Building and equipment	110,000	
Accumulated depreciation		$ 41,300
Other assets	3,600	
Accounts payable		23,700
Other expense accruals		10,200
Capital stock		100,000
Retained earnings		52,000
Sales		135,000
Purchases	52,000	
Other expenses	26,600	
	$362,200	$362,200

The following data and information have been gathered.

1. The fiscal year of the corporation ends on December 31.
2. An examination of the April bank statement and canceled checks revealed that checks written during the period April 1–15 totaled $13,000: $5,700 paid to accounts payable as of March 31, $3,400 for April merchandise shipments, and $3,900 paid for other expenses. Deposits during the same period amounted to $12,950, which consisted of receipts on account from customers with the exception of a $950 refund from a vendor for merchandise returned in April.
3. Correspondence with suppliers revealed unrecorded obligations at April 15 of $10,600 for April merchandise shipments, including $2,300 for shipments in transit (f.o.b. shipping point) on that date.
4. Customers acknowledged indebtedness of $36,000 at April 15, 2008. It was also estimated that customers owed another $8,000 that will never be acknowledged or recovered. Of the acknowledged indebtedness, $600 will probably be uncollectible.

5. The companies insuring the inventory agreed that the corporation's fire-loss claim should be based on the assumption that the overall gross profit ratio for the past 2 years was in effect during the current year. The corporation's audited financial statements disclosed this information:

| | Year Ended December 31 | |
	2007	2006
Net sales	$530,000	$390,000
Net purchases	280,000	235,000
Beginning inventory	50,000	75,200
Ending inventory	75,000	50,000

6. Inventory with a cost of $7,000 was salvaged and sold for $3,500. The balance of the inventory was a total loss.

Instructions
Prepare a schedule computing the amount of inventory fire loss. The supporting schedule of the computation of the gross profit should be in good form.

(AICPA adapted)

(LO 6) 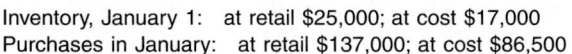 **P9-6 (Retail Inventory Method)** The records for the Clothing Department of Magdalena Aguilar's Discount Store are summarized below for the month of January.

Inventory, January 1:   at retail $25,000; at cost $17,000
Purchases in January: at retail $137,000; at cost $86,500
Freight-in: $7,000
Purchase returns: at retail $3,000; at cost $2,300
Transfers in from suburban branch: at retail $13,000; at cost $9,200
Net markups: $8,000
Net markdowns: $4,000
Inventory losses due to normal breakage, etc.:   at retail $400
Sales at retail: $85,000
Sales returns: $2,400

Instructions
(a) Compute the inventory for this department as of January 31, at retail prices.
(b) Compute the ending inventory using lower-of-average-cost-or-market.

(LO 6) **P9-7 (Retail Inventory Method)** Presented below is information related to Edward Braddock Inc.

	Cost	Retail
Inventory, 12/31/07	$250,000	$ 390,000
Purchases	914,500	1,460,000
Purchase returns	60,000	80,000
Purchase discounts	18,000	—
Gross sales (after employee discounts)	—	1,460,000
Sales returns	—	97,500
Markups	—	120,000
Markup cancellations	—	40,000
Markdowns	—	45,000
Markdown cancellations	—	20,000
Freight-in	79,000	—
Employee discounts granted	—	8,000
Loss from breakage (normal)	—	2,500

Instructions
Assuming that Edward Braddock Inc. uses the conventional retail inventory method, compute the cost of its ending inventory at December 31, 2008.

(LO 6) **P9-8 (Retail Inventory Method)** Jared Jones Inc. uses the retail inventory method to estimate ending inventory for its monthly financial statements. The following data pertain to a single department for the month of October 2008.

Inventory, October 1, 2008	
At cost	$ 52,000
At retail	78,000
Purchases (exclusive of freight and returns)	
At cost	262,000
At retail	423,000
Freight-in	16,600
Purchase returns	
At cost	5,600
At retail	8,000
Additional markups	9,000
Markup cancellations	2,000
Markdowns (net)	3,600
Normal spoilage and breakage	10,000
Sales	380,000

Instructions

(a) Using the conventional retail method, prepare a schedule computing estimated lower-of-cost-or-market inventory for October 31, 2008.

(b) A department store using the conventional retail inventory method estimates the cost of its ending inventory as $60,000. An accurate physical count reveals only $47,000 of inventory at lower-of-cost-or-market. List the factors that may have caused the difference between the computed inventory and the physical count.

(LO 1, 2, 4, 7) **P9-9 (Statement and Note Disclosure, LCM, and Purchase Commitment)** Garth Brooks Specialty Company, a division of Fresh Horses Inc., manufactures three models of gear shift components for bicycles that are sold to bicycle manufacturers, retailers, and catalog outlets. Since beginning operations in 1975, Brooks has used normal absorption costing and has assumed a first-in, first-out cost flow in its perpetual inventory system. The balances of the inventory accounts at the end of Brooks's fiscal year, November 30, 2007, are shown below. The inventories are stated at cost before any year-end adjustments.

Finished goods	$647,000
Work-in-process	112,500
Raw materials	240,000
Factory supplies	69,000

The following information relates to Brooks's inventory and operations.

1. The finished goods inventory consists of the items analyzed below.

	Cost	Market
Down tube shifter		
Standard model	$ 67,500	$ 67,000
Click adjustment model	94,500	87,000
Deluxe model	108,000	110,000
Total down tube shifters	270,000	264,000
Bar end shifter		
Standard model	83,000	90,050
Click adjustment model	99,000	97,550
Total bar end shifters	182,000	187,600
Head tube shifter		
Standard model	78,000	77,650
Click adjustment model	117,000	119,300
Total head tube shifters	195,000	196,950
Total finished goods	$647,000	$648,550

2. One-half of the head tube shifter finished goods inventory is held by catalog outlets on consignment.
3. Three-quarters of the bar end shifter finished goods inventory has been pledged as collateral for a bank loan.
4. One-half of the raw materials balance represents derailleurs acquired at a contracted price 20 percent above the current market price. The market value of the rest of the raw materials is $127,400.
5. The total market value of the work-in-process inventory is $108,700.
6. Included in the cost of factory supplies are obsolete items with an historical cost of $4,200. The market value of the remaining factory supplies is $65,900.

7. Brooks applies the lower-of-cost-or-market method to each of the three types of shifters in finished goods inventory. For each of the other three inventory accounts, Brooks applies the lower-of-cost-or-market method to the total of each inventory account.

8. Consider all amounts presented above to be material in relation to Brooks' financial statements taken as a whole.

Instructions

(a) Prepare the inventory section of Brooks's balance sheet as of November 30, 2007, including any required note(s).

(b) Without prejudice to your answer to (a), assume that the market value of Brooks' inventories is less than cost. Explain how this decline would be presented in Brooks' income statement for the fiscal year ended November 30, 2007.

(c) Assume that Brooks has a firm purchase commitment for the same type of derailleur included in the raw materials inventory as of November 30, 2007, and that the purchase commitment is at a contracted price 15% greater than the current market price. These derailleurs are to be delivered to Brooks after November 30, 2007. Discuss the impact, if any, that this purchase commitment would have on Brooks's financial statements prepared for the fiscal year ended November 30, 2007.

(CMA adapted)

(LO 1, 2) **P9-10 (Lower-of-Cost-or-Market)** Fortner Co. follows the practice of valuing its inventory at the lower-of-cost-or-market. The following information is available from the company's inventory records as of December 31, 2006.

Item	Quantity	Unit Cost	Replacement Cost/Unit	Estimated Selling Price/Unit	Completion & Disposal Cost/Unit	Normal Profit Margin/Unit
A	1,100	$7.50	$8.40	$10.50	$1.50	$1.80
B	800	8.20	8.00	9.40	0.90	1.20
C	1,000	5.60	5.40	7.20	1.10	0.60
D	1,000	3.80	4.20	6.30	0.80	1.50
E	1,400	6.40	6.30	6.80	0.70	1.00

Instructions

Finn Berge is an accounting clerk in the accounting department of Fortner Co., and he cannot understand why the market value keeps changing from replacement cost to net realizable value to something that he cannot even figure out. Finn is very confused, and he is the one who records inventory purchases and calculates ending inventory. You are the manager of the department and an accountant.

(a) Calculate the lower-of-cost-or-market using the "individual item" approach.

(b) Show the journal entry he will need to make in order to write down the ending inventory from cost to market.

(c) Then write a memo to Finn explaining what designated market value is as well as how it is computed. Use your calculations to aid in your explanation.

(LO 8) ***P9-11 (Conventional and Dollar-Value LIFO Retail)** As of January 1, 2008, Carl Sandburg Inc. installed the retail method of accounting for its merchandise inventory.

To prepare the store's financial statements at June 30, 2008, you obtain the following data.

	Cost	Selling Price
Inventory, January 1	$ 30,000	$ 43,000
Markdowns		10,500
Markups		9,200
Markdown cancellations		6,500
Markup cancellations		3,200
Purchases	108,800	155,000
Sales		159,000
Purchase returns	2,800	4,000
Sales returns and allowances		8,000

Instructions

(a) Prepare a schedule to compute Sandburg's June 30, 2008, inventory under the conventional retail method of accounting for inventories.

(b) Without prejudice to your solution to part (a), assume that you computed the June 30, 2008, inventory to be $54,000 at retail and the ratio of cost to retail to be 70%. The general price level has increased from 100 at January 1, 2008, to 108 at June 30, 2008. Prepare a schedule to compute the June 30, 2008, inventory at the June 30 price level under the dollar-value LIFO retail method.

(AICPA adapted)

(LO 8) *P9-12 (Retail, LIFO Retail, and Inventory Shortage)** Late in 2004, Sara Teasdale and four other investors took the chain of Sprint Department Stores private, and the company has just completed its third year of operations under the ownership of the investment group. Elinor Wylie, controller of Sprint Department Stores, is in the process of preparing the year-end financial statements. Based on the preliminary financial statements, Teasdale has expressed concern over inventory shortages, and she has asked Wylie to determine whether an abnormal amount of theft and breakage has occurred. The accounting records of Sprint Department Stores contain the following amounts on November 30, 2007, the end of the fiscal year.

	Cost	Retail
Beginning inventory	$ 68,000	$100,000
Purchases	248,200	400,000
Net markups		50,000
Net markdowns		110,000
Sales		330,000

According to the November 30, 2007, physical inventory, the actual inventory at retail is $107,000.

Instructions
   (a) Describe the circumstances under which the retail inventory method would be applied and the advantages of using the retail inventory method.
   (b) Assuming that prices have been stable, calculate the value, at cost, of Sprint Department Stores' ending inventory using the last-in, first-out (LIFO) retail method. Be sure to furnish supporting calculations.
   (c) Estimate the amount of shortage, at retail, that has occurred at Sprint Department Stores during the year ended November 30, 2007.
   (d) Complications in the retail method can be caused by such items as (1) freight-in costs, (2) purchase returns and allowances, (3) sales returns and allowances, and (4) employee discounts. Explain how each of these four special items is handled in the retail inventory method.

(CMA adapted)

(LO 8) *P9-13 (Change to LIFO Retail)** Ulysses Grant Stores Inc., which uses the conventional retail inventory method, wishes to change to the LIFO retail method beginning with the accounting year ending December 31, 2007.

   Amounts as shown below appear on the store's books before adjustment.

	At Cost	At Retail
Inventory, January 1, 2007	$ 13,600	$ 24,000
Purchases in 2007	116,200	184,000
Markups in 2007		12,000
Markdowns in 2007		5,500
Sales in 2007		170,000

You are to assume that all markups and markdowns apply to 2007 purchases, and that it is appropriate to treat the entire inventory as a single department.

Instructions
Compute the inventory at December 31, 2007, under the following methods.

   (a) The conventional retail method.
   (b) The last-in, first-out retail method, effecting the change in method as of January 1, 2007. Assume that the cost-to-retail percentage for 2006 was recomputed correctly in accordance with procedures necessary to change to LIFO. This ratio was 57%.

(AICPA adapted)

(LO 8) *P9-14 (Change to LIFO Retail; Dollar-Value LIFO Retail)** Rudyard Kipling Department Store converted from the conventional retail method to the LIFO retail method on January 1, 2006, and is now considering converting to the dollar-value LIFO inventory method. During your examination of the financial statements for the year ended December 31, 2007, management requested that you furnish a summary showing certain computations of inventory cost for the past 3 years.

   Here is the available information.

   1. The inventory at January 1, 2005, had a retail value of $56,000 and cost of $26,700 based on the conventional retail method.

2. Transactions during 2005 were as follows.

	Cost	Retail
Gross purchases	$311,000	$554,000
Purchase returns	5,200	10,000
Purchase discounts	6,000	
Gross sales (after employee discounts)		551,000
Sales returns		9,000
Employee discounts		3,000
Freight-in	17,600	
Net markups		20,000
Net markdowns		12,000

3. The retail value of the December 31, 2006, inventory was $73,500, the cost ratio for 2006 under the LIFO retail method was 61%, and the regional price index was 105% of the January 1, 2006, price level.

4. The retail value of the December 31, 2007, inventory was $65,880, the cost ratio for 2007 under the LIFO retail method was 60%, and the regional price index was 108% of the January 1, 2006, price level.

Instructions

(a) Prepare a schedule showing the computation of the cost of inventory on hand at December 31, 2005, based on the conventional retail method.

(b) Prepare a schedule showing the recomputation of the inventory to be reported on December 31, 2005, in accordance with procedures necessary to convert from the conventional retail method to the LIFO retail method beginning January 1, 2006. Assume that the retail value of the December 31, 2005, inventory was $63,000.

(c) Without prejudice to your solution to part (b), assume that you computed the December 31, 2005, inventory (retail value $63,000) under the LIFO retail method at a cost of $34,965. Prepare a schedule showing the computations of the cost of the store's 2006 and 2007 year-end inventories under the dollar-value LIFO method.

(AICPA adapted)

CONCEPTS FOR ANALYSIS

CA9-1 (Lower-of-Cost-or-Market) You have been asked by the financial vice-president to develop a short presentation on the lower-of-cost-or-market method for inventory purposes. The financial VP needs to explain this method to the president, because it appears that a portion of the company's inventory has declined in value.

Instructions

The financial VP asks you to answer the following questions.

(a) What is the purpose of the lower-of-cost-or-market method?

(b) What is meant by "market"? (*Hint:* Discuss the ceiling and floor constraints.)

(c) Do you apply the lower-of-cost-or-market method to each individual item, to a category, or to the total of the inventory? Explain.

(d) What are the potential disadvantages of the lower-of-cost-or-market method?

CA9-2 (Lower-of-Cost-or-Market) The market value of Lake Corporation's inventory has declined below its cost. Vickie Maher, the controller, wants to use the allowance method to write down inventory because it more clearly discloses the decline in market value and does not distort the cost of goods sold. Her supervisor, financial vice-president Doug Brucki, prefers the direct method to write down inventory because it does not call attention to the decline in market value.

Instructions

Answer the following questions.

(a) What, if any, is the ethical issue involved?

(b) Is any stakeholder harmed if Brucki's preference is used?

(c) What should Vickie Maher do?

CA9-3 (Lower-of-Cost-or-Market) Lena Horne Corporation purchased a significant amount of raw materials inventory for a new product that it is manufacturing.

Horne uses the lower-of-cost-or-market rule for these raw materials. The replacement cost of the raw materials is above the net realizable value, and both are below the original cost.

Horne uses the average cost inventory method for these raw materials. In the last 2 years, each purchase has been at a lower price than the previous purchase, and the ending inventory quantity for each period has been higher than the beginning inventory quantity for that period.

Instructions
    (a) **(1)** At which amount should Horne's raw materials inventory be reported on the balance sheet? Why?
         (2) In general, why is the lower-of-cost-or-market rule used to report inventory?
    (b) What would have been the effect on ending inventory and cost of goods sold had Horne used the LIFO inventory method instead of the average-cost inventory method for the raw materials? Why?

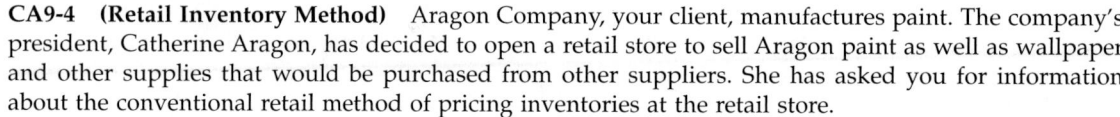 **CA9-4 (Retail Inventory Method)** Aragon Company, your client, manufactures paint. The company's president, Catherine Aragon, has decided to open a retail store to sell Aragon paint as well as wallpaper and other supplies that would be purchased from other suppliers. She has asked you for information about the conventional retail method of pricing inventories at the retail store.

Instructions
Prepare a report to the president explaining the retail method of pricing inventories. Your report should include the following points.
    (a) Description and accounting features of the method.
    (b) The conditions that may distort the results under the method.
    (c) A comparison of the advantages of using the retail method with those of using cost methods of inventory pricing.
    (d) The accounting theory underlying the treatment of net markdowns and net markups under the method.

                                                      (AICPA adapted)

CA9-5 (Cost Determination, LCM, Retail Method) E. A. Poe Corporation, a retailer and wholesaler of national brand-name household lighting fixtures, purchases its inventories from various suppliers.

Instructions
    (a) **(1)** What criteria should be used to determine which of Poe's costs are inventoriable?
         (2) Are Poe's administrative costs inventoriable? Defend your answer.
    (b) **(1)** Poe uses the lower-of-cost-or-market rule for its wholesale inventories. What are the theoretical arguments for that rule?
         (2) The replacement cost of the inventories is below the net realizable value less a normal profit margin, which, in turn, is below the original cost. What amount should be used to value the inventories? Why?
    (c) Poe calculates the estimated cost of its ending inventories held for sale at retail using the conventional retail inventory method. How would Poe treat the beginning inventories and net markdowns in calculating the cost ratio used to determine its ending inventories? Why?

                                                      (AICPA adapted)

 CA9-6 (Purchase Commitments) Vineland Company signed a long-term purchase contract to buy timber from the U.S. Forest Service at $300 per thousand board feet. Under these terms, Vineland must cut and pay $6,000,000 for this timber during the next year. Currently the market value is $250 per thousand board feet. At this rate, the market price is $5,000,000. Ruben Walker, the controller, wants to recognize the loss in value on the year-end financial statements, but the financial vice-president, Billie Hands, argues that the loss is temporary and should be ignored. Walker notes that market value has remained near $250 for many months, and he sees no sign of significant change.

Instructions
    (a) What are the ethical issues, if any?
    (b) Is any particular stakeholder harmed by the financial vice-president's decision?
    (c) What should the controller do?

*CA9-7 (Retail Inventory Method and LIFO Retail) Presented below are a number of items that may be encountered in computing the cost to retail percentage when using the conventional retail method or the LIFO retail method.

    1. Markdowns.
    2. Markdown cancellations.

    3. Cost of items transferred in from other departments.

4. Retail value of items transferred in from other departments.
5. Sales discounts.
6. Purchases discounts (purchases recorded gross).
7. Estimated retail value of goods broken or stolen.
8. Cost of beginning inventory.
9. Retail value of beginning inventory.
10. Cost of purchases.
11. Retail value of purchases.
12. Markups.
13. Markup cancellations.
14. Employee discounts (sales recorded net).

Instructions

For each of the items listed above, indicate whether this item would be considered in the cost to retail percentage under **(a)** conventional retail and **(b)** LIFO retail.

USING YOUR JUDGMENT

Financial Reporting Problem

 The Procter & Gamble Company (P&G)

The financial statements of **P&G** are presented in Appendix 5B or can be accessed at the book's website.

Instructions

Refer to P&G's financial statements and the accompanying notes to answer the following questions.

(a) How does P&G value its inventories? Which inventory costing method does P&G use as a basis for reporting its inventories?

(b) How does P&G report its inventories in the balance sheet? In the notes to its financial statements, what three descriptions are used to classify its inventories?

(c) What costs does P&G include in inventory?

(d) What was P&G's inventory turnover ratio in 2004? What is its gross profit percentage? Evaluate P&G's inventory turnover ratio and its gross profit percentage.

Financial Statement Analysis Cases

Case 1 Sonic, Inc.

Sonic, Inc., reported the following information regarding 2006–2007 inventory.

Sonic, Inc.		
	2007	2006
Current assets		
Cash	$ 153,010	$ 538,489
Accounts receivable, net of allowance for doubtful accounts of $46,000 in 2007 and $160,000 in 2006	1,627,980	2,596,291
Inventories (Note 2)	1,340,494	1,734,873
Other current assets	123,388	90,592
Assets of discontinued operations	—	32,815
Total current assets	3,244,872	4,993,060

Notes to Consolidated Financial Statements

Note 1 (in part): Nature of Business and Significant Accounting Policies

Inventories—Inventories are stated at the lower-of-cost-or-market. Cost is determined by the last-in, first-out (LIFO) method by the parent company and by the first-in, first-out (FIFO) method by its subsidiaries.

Note 2: Inventories

Inventories consist of the following.

	2007	2006
Raw materials	$1,264,646	$2,321,178
Work in process	240,988	171,222
Finished goods and display units	129,406	711,252
Total inventories	1,635,040	3,203,652
Less: Amount classified as long-term	294,546	1,468,779
Current portion	$1,340,494	$1,734,873

Inventories are stated at the lower of cost determined by the LIFO method or market for Sonic, Inc. Inventories for the two wholly-owned subsidiaries, Sonic Command, Inc. (U.S.) and Sonic Limited (U.K.) are stated on the FIFO method which amounted to $566,000 at October 31, 2006. No inventory is stated on the FIFO method at October 31, 2007. Included in inventory stated at FIFO cost was $32,815 at October 31, 2006, of Sonic Command inventory classified as an asset from discontinued operations (see Note 14). If the FIFO method had been used for the entire consolidated group, inventories after an adjustment to the lower-of-cost-or-market, would have been approximately $2,000,000 and $3,800,000 at October 31, 2007 and 2006, respectively.

Inventory has been written down to estimated net realizable value, and results of operations for 2007, 2006, and 2005 include a corresponding charge of approximately $868,000, $960,000, and $273,000, respectively, which represents the excess of LIFO cost over market.

Inventory of $294,546 and $1,468,779 at October 31, 2007 and 2006, respectively, shown on the balance sheet as a noncurrent asset represents that portion of the inventory that is not expected to be sold currently.

Reduction in inventory quantities during the years ended October 31, 2007, 2006, and 2005 resulted in liquidation of LIFO inventory quantities carried at a lower cost prevailing in prior years as compared with the cost of fiscal 2004 purchases. The effect of these reductions was to decrease the net loss by approximately $24,000, $157,000 and $90,000 at October 31, 2007, 2006, and 2005, respectively.

Instructions

(a) Why might Sonic, Inc., use two different methods for valuing inventory?

(b) Comment on why Sonic, Inc. might disclose how its LIFO inventories would be valued under FIFO.

(c) Why does the LIFO liquidation reduce operating costs?

(d) Comment on whether Sonic would report more or less income if it had been on a FIFO basis for all its inventory.

Case 2 Barrick Gold Corporation

Barrick Gold Corporation, with headquarters in Toronto, Canada, is the world's most profitable and largest gold mining company outside South Africa. Part of the key to Barrick's success has been due to its ability to maintain cash flow while improving production and increasing its reserves of gold-containing property. During 2004, Barrick achieved record growth in cash flow, production, and reserves.

The company maintains an aggressive policy of developing previously identified target areas that have the possibility of a large amount of gold ore, and that have not been previously developed. Barrick limits the riskiness of this development by choosing only properties that are located in politically stable regions, and by the company's use of internally generated funds, rather than debt, to finance growth.

Barrick's inventories are as follows:

Inventories (in millions, US dollars)

Current	
Gold in process	$133
Mine operating supplies	82
	$215
Non-current (included in Other assets)	
Ore in stockpiles	$65

Instructions

(a) Why do you think that there are no finished goods inventories? Why do you think the raw material, ore in stockpiles, is considered to be a non-current asset?

(b) Consider that Barrick has no finished goods inventories. What journal entries are made to record a sale?

(c) Suppose that gold bullion that cost $1.8 million to produce was sold for $2.4 million. The journal entry was made to record the sale, but no entry was made to remove the gold from the gold in process inventory. How would this error affect the following?

Balance Sheet		Income Statement	
Inventory	?	Cost of goods sold	?
Retained earnings	?	Net income	?
Accounts payable	?		
Working capital	?		
Current ratio	?		

Comparative Analysis Case

The Coca-Cola Company and PepsiCo, Inc.

Instructions

Go to the book's website and use information found there to answer the following questions related to **The Coca-Cola Company** and **PepsiCo, Inc.**

(a) What is the amount of inventory reported by Coca-Cola at December 31, 2004, and by PepsiCo at December 25, 2004? What percent of total assets is invested in inventory by each company?

(b) What inventory costing methods are used by Coca-Cola and PepsiCo? How does each company value its inventories?

(c) In the notes, what classifications (description) are used by Coca-Cola and PepsiCo to categorize their inventories?

(d) Compute and compare the inventory turnover ratios and days to sell inventory for Coca-Cola and PepsiCo for 2004. Indicate why there might be a significant difference between the two companies.

Research Cases

Case 1

Numerous companies have established home pages on the Internet, for example, **Boston Beer Company** (www.samadams.com), **Ford Motor Company** (www.ford.com), and **Kodak** (www.kodak.com). You undoubtedly have noticed company Internet addresses in television commercials or magazine advertisements.

Instructions

Examine the home pages of any two companies and answer the following questions.

(a) What type of information is available?

(b) Is any accounting-related information presented?

(c) Would you describe the home page as informative, promotional, or both? Why?

Case 2

The September 23, 1994, edition of the *Wall Street Journal* includes an article titled "**CompUSA** Auctions Notebook Computers Through Bulk Sale."

Instructions

Read the article and answer the following questions.

(a) At what amount did CompUSA estimate the retail value of the computers? What was the estimate made by one of the bidders?

(b) What was wrong with the computers?

(c) What were the rules of the auction as specified by CompUSA?

(d) CompUSA had just recorded a $3 million inventory write-down in the preceding quarter. Based on the information in the article, does it appear that additional write-downs were called for?

Professional Research: Financial Accounting and Reporting

Jones Co. is in a technology-intensive industry. Recently, one of its competitors introduced a new product with technology that might render obsolete some of Jones's inventory. The accounting staff wants to follow the appropriate authoritative literature in determining the accounting for this significant market event.

Instructions

Using the **Financial Accounting Research System (FARS)**, respond to the following items. (Provide text strings used in your search.)

(a) Identify the authoritative literature addressing inventory pricing. (*Hint:* Do not ignore the literature issued by predecessors to the FASB.)

(b) List three types of goods that are classified as inventory. What characteristic will automatically exclude an item from being classified as inventory?

(c) Define "market" as used in the phrase "lower-of-cost-or-market."

(d) Explain when it is acceptable to state inventory above cost and which industries allow this practice.

Professional Simulation

In this simulation you are asked to address questions relating to inventory valuation and measurement. Prepare responses to all parts.

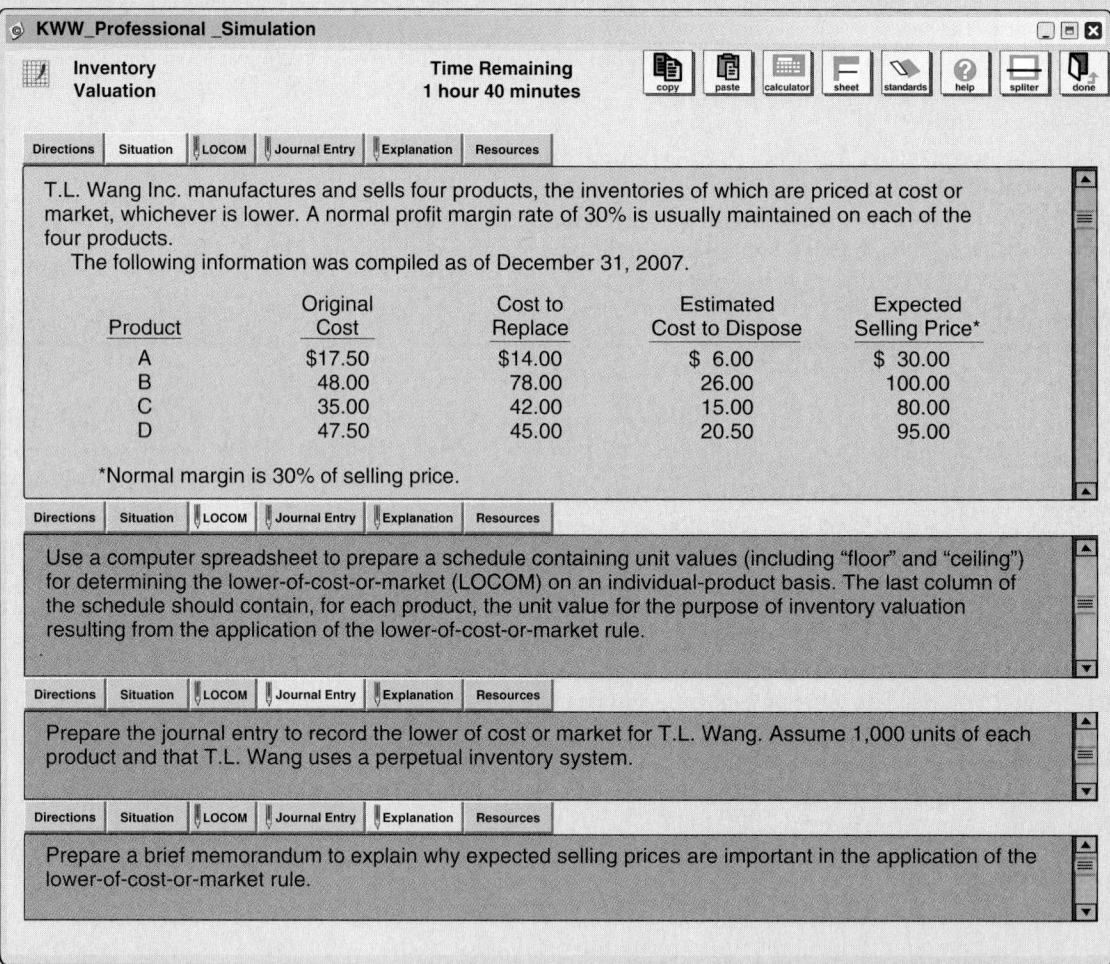

KWW_Professional _Simulation

Inventory Valuation

Time Remaining 1 hour 40 minutes

Directions | Situation | LOCOM | Journal Entry | Explanation | Resources

T.L. Wang Inc. manufactures and sells four products, the inventories of which are priced at cost or market, whichever is lower. A normal profit margin rate of 30% is usually maintained on each of the four products.

The following information was compiled as of December 31, 2007.

Product	Original Cost	Cost to Replace	Estimated Cost to Dispose	Expected Selling Price*
A	$17.50	$14.00	$ 6.00	$ 30.00
B	48.00	78.00	26.00	100.00
C	35.00	42.00	15.00	80.00
D	47.50	45.00	20.50	95.00

*Normal margin is 30% of selling price.

Directions | Situation | LOCOM | Journal Entry | Explanation | Resources

Use a computer spreadsheet to prepare a schedule containing unit values (including "floor" and "ceiling") for determining the lower-of-cost-or-market (LOCOM) on an individual-product basis. The last column of the schedule should contain, for each product, the unit value for the purpose of inventory valuation resulting from the application of the lower-of-cost-or-market rule.

Directions | Situation | LOCOM | Journal Entry | Explanation | Resources

Prepare the journal entry to record the lower of cost or market for T.L. Wang. Assume 1,000 units of each product and that T.L. Wang uses a perpetual inventory system.

Directions | Situation | LOCOM | Journal Entry | Explanation | Resources

Prepare a brief memorandum to explain why expected selling prices are important in the application of the lower-of-cost-or-market rule.

Remember to check the book's companion website to find additional resources for this chapter.

ACQUISITION AND DISPOSITION OF PROPERTY, PLANT, AND EQUIPMENT

Where Have All the Assets Gone?

Investments in long-lived assets, such as property, plant, and equipment, are important elements in many companies' balance sheets. As the chart below indicates, major companies, such as **Southwest Airlines** and **Wal-Mart**, recently reported property, plant, and equipment (PP&E) as a percent of total assets ranging from 54 percent up to nearly 77 percent.

However, for various strategic reasons, many companies are now shedding property, plant, and equipment. Instead, they are paying others to manufacture and assemble products—functions they previously performed in their own facilities. Companies are also reducing fixed assets by outsourcing warehousing and distribution. Such logistics outsourcing can cut companies' own costs for keeping and managing inventories, and spare them the need to invest in advanced tracking technologies increasingly required by retailers. In a recent year more than 80 percent of the country's 100 biggest companies used third-party logistics providers.[1] As a result, some companies such as **Nortel** and **Lucent** are decreasing their investment in long-lived assets, as the following chart shows.

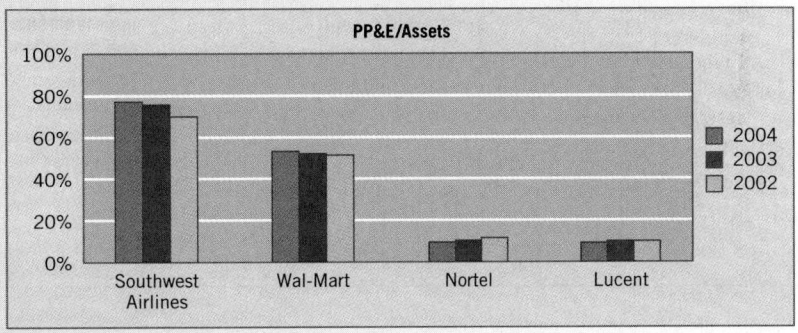

Nortel is a good example of these strategies. It has sold and outsourced certain facilities in order to reduce its direct manufacturing activities and costs. Nortel also sold its training and headset businesses. Further, it has aggressively outsourced other operations to reduce costs. Reductions in these areas will enable Nortel and other outsourcing companies to concentrate on their core operations and better manage investments in property, plant and equipment.

---

[1]Adapted from Chapter 1 in Grady Means and David Schneider, *MetaCapitalism: The e-Business Revolution and the Design of 21ˢᵗ-Century Companies and Markets* (New York: John Wiley and Sons, 2000); and Kris Maher, "Global Goods Jugglers," *Wall Street Journal Online* (July 5, 2005).

Learning Objectives

After studying this chapter, you should be able to:

1 Describe property, plant, and equipment.

2 Identify the costs to include in initial valuation of property, plant, and equipment.

3 Describe the accounting problems associated with self-constructed assets.

4 Describe the accounting problems associated with interest capitalization.

5 Understand accounting issues related to acquiring and valuing plant assets.

6 Describe the accounting treatment for costs subsequent to acquisition.

7 Describe the accounting treatment for the disposal of property, plant, and equipment.

As we indicate in the opening story, a company like **Southwest Airlines** has a substantial investment in property, plant, and equipment. Conversely, other companies, such as **Nortel**, have a minor investment in these types of assets. In this chapter, we discuss the proper accounting for the acquisition, use, and disposition of property, plant, and equipment. The content and organization of the chapter are as follows.

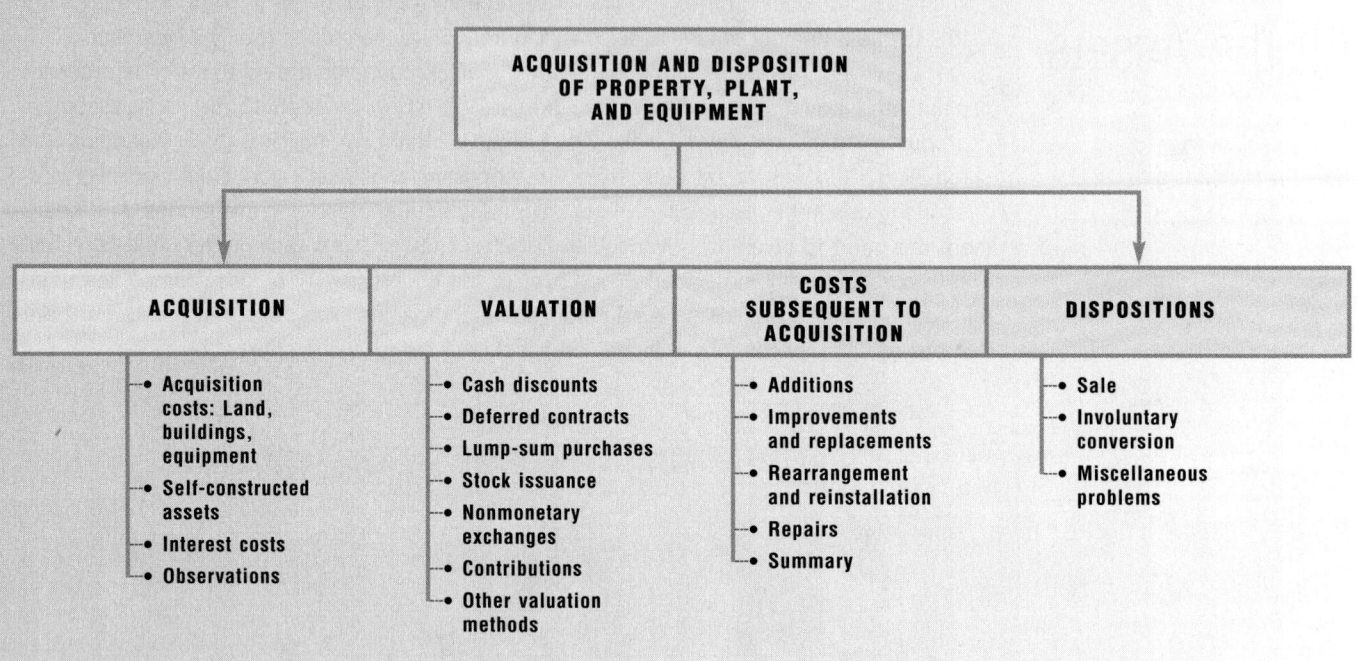

ACQUISITION AND DISPOSITION OF PROPERTY, PLANT, AND EQUIPMENT

ACQUISITION
- Acquisition costs: Land, buildings, equipment
- Self-constructed assets
- Interest costs
- Observations

VALUATION
- Cash discounts
- Deferred contracts
- Lump-sum purchases
- Stock issuance
- Nonmonetary exchanges
- Contributions
- Other valuation methods

COSTS SUBSEQUENT TO ACQUISITION
- Additions
- Improvements and replacements
- Rearrangement and reinstallation
- Repairs
- Summary

DISPOSITIONS
- Sale
- Involuntary conversion
- Miscellaneous problems

OBJECTIVE 1
Describe property, plant, and equipment.

Companies like **Boeing, Target,** and **Starbucks** use assets of a durable nature. Such assets are called **property, plant, and equipment.** Other terms commonly used are **plant assets** and **fixed assets.** We use these terms interchangeably throughout this textbook.

Property, plant, and equipment include land, building structures (offices, factories, warehouses), and equipment (machinery, furniture, tools). The major characteristics of property, plant, and equipment are as follows.

1 They are acquired for use in operations and not for resale. Only assets used in normal business operations are classified as property, plant, and equipment. For example, an idle building is more appropriately classified separately as an investment. Land developers or subdividers classify land as inventory.

2 They are long-term in nature and usually depreciated. Property, plant, and equipment yield services over a number of years. Companies allocate the cost of the investment in these assets to future periods through periodic depreciation charges. The exception is land, which is depreciated only if a material decrease in value occurs, such as a loss in fertility of agricultural land because of poor crop rotation, drought, or soil erosion.

3 They possess physical substance. Property, plant, and equipment are tangible assets characterized by physical existence or substance. This differentiates them from intangible assets, such as patents or goodwill. Unlike raw material, however, property, plant, and equipment do not physically become part of a product held for resale.

UNDERLYING CONCEPTS

Market value is relevant to inventory but less so for property, plant, and equipment which, consistent with the going concern assumption, are held for use in the business, not for sale like inventory.

ACQUISITION AND VALUATION OF PROPERTY, PLANT, AND EQUIPMENT

OBJECTIVE 2
Identify the costs to include in initial valuation of property, plant, and equipment.

Most companies use historical cost as the basis for valuing property, plant, and equipment. **Historical cost measures the cash or cash equivalent price of obtaining the asset and bringing it to the location and condition necessary for its intended use.** For example, companies like **Kellogg Co.** consider the purchase price, freight costs, sales taxes, and installation costs of a productive asset as part of the asset's cost. It then allocates these costs to future periods through depreciation. Further, Kellogg **adds to the asset's cost** any related costs incurred **after the asset's acquisition,** such as additions, improvements, or replacements, **if they provide future service potential.** Otherwise, Kellogg expenses these costs immediately.

Disagreement does exist concerning differences between historical cost and other valuation methods (such as replacement cost or fair market value) **arising after acquisition.** *APB Opinion No. 6* states, "property, plant, and equipment should not be written up to reflect appraisal, market, or current values which are above cost." Although the opinion notes minor exceptions, current standards indicate that departures from historical cost are rare. The main reasons for this position are as follows:

1 At the date of acquisition, cost reflects fair value.

2 Historical cost involves actual, not hypothetical, transactions and so is the most reliable.

3 Companies should not anticipate gains and losses but should recognize gains and losses only when the asset is sold.

INTERNATIONAL INSIGHT

In many nations, such as Great Britain and Brazil, companies may revalue their fixed assets at amounts above historical cost. These revaluations may be at appraisal values or at amounts linked to a specified index.

Cost of Land

All expenditures made to acquire land and ready it for use are considered part of the land cost. Thus, when **Wal-Mart** or **Home Depot** purchases land on which to build a new store, its land costs typically include (1) the purchase price; (2) closing costs, such as title to the land, attorney's fees, and recording fees; (3) costs incurred in getting the land in condition for its intended use, such as grading, filling, draining, and clearing; (4) assumption of any liens, mortgages, or encumbrances on the property; and (5) any additional land improvements that have an indefinite life.

Expanded Discussion of Alternative Valuation Methods

For example, when Home Depot purchases land for the purpose of constructing a building, it considers all costs incurred up to the excavation for the new building as land costs. **Removal of old buildings—clearing, grading, and filling—is a land cost because this activity is necessary to get the land in condition for its intended purpose.** Home Depot treats any proceeds from getting the land ready for its intended use, such as salvage receipts on the demolition of an old building or the sale of cleared timber, as **reductions in the price of the land.**

In some cases, when Home Depot purchases land, it may assume certain obligations on the land such as back taxes or liens. In such situations, the cost of the land is the cash paid for it, plus the encumbrances. In other words, if the purchase price of the land is $50,000 cash, but Home Depot assumes accrued property taxes of $5,000 and liens of $10,000, its land cost is $65,000.

Home Depot also might incur **special assessments** for local improvements, such as pavements, street lights, sewers, and drainage systems. It should charge these costs to the Land account because they are relatively permanent in nature. That is, after installation, they are maintained by the local government. In addition, Home Depot should charge any permanent improvements it makes, such as landscaping, to the Land account. It records separately any **improvements with limited lives,** such as private driveways, walks, fences, and parking lots, as Land Improvements. These costs are depreciated over their estimated lives.

Generally, land is part of property, plant, and equipment. However, if the major purpose of acquiring and holding land is speculative, a company more appropriately classifies the land as an **investment**. If a real estate concern holds the land for resale, it should classify the land as **inventory**.

In cases where land is held as an investment, what accounting treatment should be given for taxes, insurance, and other direct costs incurred while holding the land? Many believe these costs should be capitalized. The reason: They are not generating revenue from the investment at this time. Companies generally use this approach except when the asset is currently producing revenue (such as rental property).

Cost of Buildings

The cost of buildings should include all expenditures related directly to their acquisition or construction. These costs include (1) materials, labor, and overhead costs incurred during construction and (2) professional fees and building permits. Generally, companies contract others to construct their buildings. Companies consider all costs incurred, from excavation to completion, as part of the building costs.

But how should companies account for an old building that is on the site of a newly proposed building? Is the cost of removal of the old building a cost of the land or a cost of the new building? Recall that **if a company purchases land with an old building on it, then the cost of demolition less its salvage value is a cost of getting the land ready for its intended use and relates to the land rather than to the new building**. In other words, all costs of getting an asset ready for its intended use are costs of that asset.

Cost of Equipment

The term "equipment" in accounting includes delivery equipment, office equipment, machinery, furniture and fixtures, furnishings, factory equipment, and similar fixed assets. The cost of such assets includes the purchase price, freight and handling charges incurred, insurance on the equipment while in transit, cost of special foundations if required, assembling and installation costs, and costs of conducting trial runs. Costs thus include all expenditures incurred in acquiring the equipment and preparing it for use.

Self-Constructed Assets

OBJECTIVE 3
Describe the accounting problems associated with self-constructed assets.

Occasionally companies construct their own assets. Determining the cost of such machinery and other fixed assets can be a problem. Without a purchase price or contract price, the company must allocate costs and expenses to arrive at the cost of the **self-constructed asset**. Materials and direct labor used in construction pose no problem. A company can trace these costs directly to work and material orders related to the fixed assets constructed.

However, the assignment of indirect costs of manufacturing creates special problems. These indirect costs, called **overhead** or burden, include power, heat, light, insurance, property taxes on factory buildings and equipment, factory supervisory labor, depreciation of fixed assets, and supplies.

Companies can handle indirect costs in one of two ways:

1 *Assign no fixed overhead to the cost of the constructed asset.* The major argument for this treatment is that indirect overhead is generally fixed in nature; it does not increase as a result of constructing one's own plant or equipment. This approach assumes that the company will have the same costs regardless of whether it constructs the asset or not. Therefore, to charge a portion of the overhead costs to the equipment will normally reduce current expenses and consequently overstate income of the current period. However, the company would assign to the cost of the constructed asset variable overhead costs that increase as a result of the construction.

INTERNATIONAL INSIGHT

Under international accounting standards, historical cost is the benchmark (preferred) treatment for property, plant, and equipment. However, companies may also use revalued amounts. If using revaluation, companies must revalue the class of assets regularly.

2 *Assign a portion of all overhead to the construction process.* This approach, called a **full-costing approach**, is appropriate if one believes that costs attach to all products and assets manufactured or constructed. Under this approach, a company assigns a portion of all overhead to the construction process, as it would to normal production. Advocates say that failure to allocate overhead costs understates the initial cost of the asset and results in an inaccurate future allocation.

Companies should assign to the asset **a pro rata portion** of the fixed overhead to determine its cost. Companies use this treatment extensively because many believe that it results in a better matching of costs with revenues.

If the allocated overhead results in recording construction costs in excess of the costs that an outside independent producer would charge, the company should record the excess overhead as a period loss rather than capitalize it. This avoids capitalizing the asset at more than its probable market value.[2]

Interest Costs During Construction

The proper accounting for interest costs has been a long-standing controversy. Three approaches have been suggested to account for the interest incurred in financing the construction of property, plant, and equipment:

> **OBJECTIVE 4**
> Describe the accounting problems associated with interest capitalization.

1 *Capitalize no interest charges during construction.* Under this approach, interest is considered a cost of financing and not a cost of construction. Some contend that if a company had used stock (equity) financing rather than debt, it would not incur this cost. The major argument against this approach is that the use of cash, whatever its source, has an associated implicit interest cost, which should not be ignored.

2 *Charge construction with all costs of funds employed, whether identifiable or not.* This method maintains that the cost of construction should include the cost of financing, whether by cash, debt, or stock. Its advocates say that all costs necessary to get an asset ready for its intended use, including interest, are part of the asset's cost. Interest, whether actual or imputed, is a cost, just as are labor and materials. A major criticism of this approach is that imputing the cost of equity capital (stock) is subjective and outside the framework of a historical cost system.

3 *Capitalize only the actual interest costs incurred during construction.* This approach agrees in part with the logic of the second approach—that interest is just as much a cost as are labor and materials. But this approach capitalizes only interest costs incurred through debt financing. (That is, it does not try to determine the cost of equity financing.) Under this approach, a company that uses debt financing will have an asset of higher cost than a company that uses stock financing. Some consider this approach unsatisfactory because they believe the cost of an asset should be the same whether it is financed with cash, debt, or equity.

Illustration 10-1 (page 476) shows how a company might add interest costs (if any) to the cost of the asset under the three capitalization approaches.

---

[2] The Accounting Standards Executive Committee (AcSEC) of the AICPA has issued an exposure draft related to property, plant, and equipment. In this exposure draft, AcSEC argues against allocation of overhead. Instead, it basically supports capitalization of only direct costs (costs directly related to the specific activities involved in the construction process). AcSEC was concerned that the allocation of overhead costs may lead to overly aggressive allocations and therefore misstatements of income. In addition, not reporting these costs as period costs during the construction period may affect comparisons of period costs and resulting net income from one period to the next. See Accounting Standards Executive Committee, "Accounting for Certain Costs and Activities Related to Property, Plant, and Equipment," Exposure Draft (New York: AICPA, June 29, 2001).

ILLUSTRATION 10-1
Capitalization of Interest
Costs

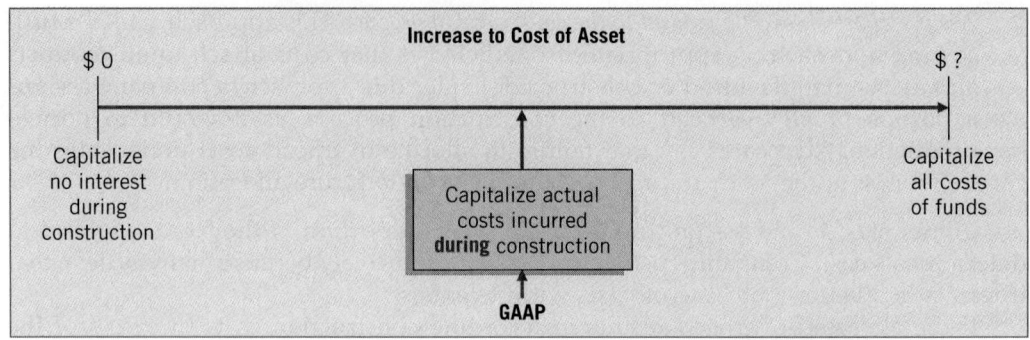

GAAP requires the third approach—capitalizing actual interest (with modification). This method follows the concept that the **historical cost of acquiring an asset includes all costs (including interest) incurred to bring the asset to the condition and location necessary for its intended use.** The rationale for this approach is that during construction, the asset is not generating revenues. Therefore, a company should defer (capitalize) interest costs.[3] Once construction is complete, the asset is ready for its intended use and a company can earn revenues. At this point the company should report interest as an expense and match it to these revenues. It follows that the company should expense any interest cost incurred in purchasing an asset that is ready for its intended use.

To implement this general approach, companies consider three items:

1 Qualifying assets.
2 Capitalization period.
3 Amount to capitalize.

Qualifying Assets

To qualify for interest capitalization, assets must require a period of time to get them ready for their intended use. A company capitalizes interest costs starting with the first expenditure related to the asset. Capitalization continues until the company substantially readies the asset for its intended use.

Assets that qualify for interest cost capitalization include assets under construction for a company's own use (including buildings, plants, and large machinery) and assets intended for sale or lease that are constructed or otherwise produced as discrete projects (e.g., ships or real estate developments).

Examples of assets that do not qualify for interest capitalization are (1) assets that are in use or ready for their intended use, and (2) assets that the company does not use in its earnings activities and that are not undergoing the activities necessary to get them ready for use. Examples of this second type include land remaining undeveloped and assets not used because of obsolescence, excess capacity, or need for repair.

Capitalization Period

The **capitalization period** is the period of time during which a company must capitalize interest. It begins with the presence of three conditions:

1 Expenditures for the asset have been made.
2 Activities that are necessary to get the asset ready for its intended use are in progress.
3 Interest cost is being incurred.

Interest capitalization **continues as long as these three conditions are present.** The capitalization period ends when the asset is substantially complete and ready for its intended use.

INTERNATIONAL INSIGHT

Under international accounting standards, companies may capitalize interest, but it is not the preferred treatment. The benchmark treatment is to expense interest in the period incurred.

---

[3]"Capitalization of Interest Cost," *Statement of Financial Accounting Standards No. 34* (Stamford, Conn.: FASB, 1979).

Amount to Capitalize

The amount of interest to capitalize is limited to the lower of actual interest cost incurred during the period or avoidable interest. **Avoidable interest** is the amount of interest cost during the period that a company could theoretically avoid if it had not made expenditures for the asset. If the actual interest cost for the period is $90,000 and the avoidable interest is $80,000, the company capitalizes only $80,000. Or, if the actual interest cost is $80,000 and the avoidable interest is $90,000, it still capitalizes only $80,000. In no situation should interest cost include a cost of capital charge for stockholders' equity. Furthermore, GAAP requires interest capitalization for a qualifying asset only if its effect, compared with the effect of expensing interest, is material.[4]

To apply the avoidable interest concept, a company determines the potential amount of interest that it may capitalize during an accounting period by multiplying the interest rate(s) by the **weighted-average accumulated expenditures** for qualifying assets during the period.

Weighted-Average Accumulated Expenditures. In computing the weighted-average accumulated expenditures, a company weights the construction expenditures by the amount of time (fraction of a year or accounting period) that it can incur interest cost on the expenditure.

To illustrate, assume a 17-month bridge construction project with current-year payments to the contractor of $240,000 on March 1, $480,000 on July 1, and $360,000 on November 1. The company computes the weighted-average accumulated expenditures for the year ended December 31 as follows.

Expenditures			Capitalization		Weighted-Average
Date	Amount	×	Period*	=	Accumulated Expenditures
March 1	$ 240,000		10/12		$200,000
July 1	480,000		6/12		240,000
November 1	360,000		2/12		60,000
	$1,080,000				$500,000

*Months between date of expenditure and date interest capitalization stops or end of year, whichever comes first (in this case December 31).

ILLUSTRATION 10-2
Computation of Weighted-Average Accumulated Expenditures

To compute the weighted-average accumulated expenditures, a company weights the expenditures by the amount of time that it can incur interest cost on each one. For the March 1 expenditure, the company associates 10 months' interest cost with the expenditure. For the expenditure on July 1, it incurs only 6 months' interest costs. For the expenditure made on November 1, the company incurs only 2 months of interest cost.

Interest Rates. Companies follow these principles in selecting the appropriate interest rates to be applied to the weighted-average accumulated expenditures:

1 For the portion of weighted-average accumulated expenditures that is less than or equal to any amounts borrowed specifically to finance construction of the assets, **use the interest rate incurred on the specific borrowings.**

[4]Ibid., summary paragraph.

2 For the portion of weighted-average accumulated expenditures that is greater than any debt incurred specifically to finance construction of the assets, **use a weighted average of interest rates incurred on all other outstanding debt during the period.**[5]

Illustration 10-3 shows the computation of a weighted-average interest rate for debt greater than the amount incurred specifically to finance construction of the assets.

ILLUSTRATION 10-3
Computation of
Weighted-Average
Interest Rate

	Principal	Interest
12%, 2-year note	$ 600,000	$ 72,000
9%, 10-year bonds	2,000,000	180,000
7.5%, 20-year bonds	5,000,000	375,000
	$7,600,000	$627,000

$$\text{Weighted-average interest rate} = \frac{\text{Total interest}}{\text{Total principal}} = \frac{\$627,000}{\$7,600,000} = 8.25\%$$

Comprehensive Example of Interest Capitalization

To illustrate the issues related to interest capitalization, assume that on November 1, 2006, Shalla Company contracted Pfeifer Construction Co. to construct a building for $1,400,000 on land costing $100,000 (purchased from the contractor and included in the first payment). Shalla made the following payments to the construction company during 2007.

January 1	March 1	May 1	December 31	Total
$210,000	$300,000	$540,000	$450,000	$1,500,000

Pfeifer Construction completed the building, ready for occupancy, on December 31, 2007. Shalla had the following debt outstanding at December 31, 2007.

Specific Construction Debt

1. 15%, 3-year note to finance purchase of land and construction of the building, dated December 31, 2006, with interest payable annually on December 31 .... $750,000

Other Debt

2. 10%, 5-year note payable, dated December 31, 2003, with interest payable annually on December 31 .... $550,000
3. 12%, 10-year bonds issued December 31, 2002, with interest payable annually on December 31 .... $600,000

Shalla computed the weighted-average accumulated expenditures during 2003 as shown in Illustration 10-4.

ILLUSTRATION 10-4
Computation of
Weighted-Average
Accumulated
Expenditures

Expenditures			Current Year Capitalization		Weighted-Average
Date	Amount	×	Period	=	Accumulated Expenditures
January 1	$ 210,000		12/12		$210,000
March 1	300,000		10/12		250,000
May 1	540,000		8/12		360,000
December 31	450,000		0		0
	$1,500,000				$820,000

[5]The interest rate to be used may rely exclusively on an average rate of all the borrowings, if desired. For our purposes, we use the specific borrowing rate followed by the average interest rate because we believe it to be more conceptually consistent. Either method can be used; *FASB Statement No. 34* does not provide explicit guidance on this measurement. For a discussion of this issue and others related to interest capitalization, see Kathryn M. Means and Paul M. Kazenski, "SFAS 34: Recipe for Diversity," *Accounting Horizons* (September 1988); and Wendy A. Duffy, "A Graphical Analysis of Interest Capitalization," *Journal of Accounting Education* (Fall 1990).

Note that the expenditure made on December 31, the last day of the year, does not have any interest cost.

Shalla computes the avoidable interest as shown in Illustration 10-5.

ILLUSTRATION 10-5
Computation of
Avoidable Interest

Weighted-Average Accumulated Expenditures	×	Interest Rate	=	Avoidable Interest
$750,000		.15 (construction note)		$112,500
70,000ᵃ		.1104 (weighted average of other debt)ᵇ		7,728
$820,000				$120,228

ᵃThe amount by which the weighted-average accumulated expenditures exceeds the specific construction loan.

ᵇWeighted-average interest rate computation:

	Principal	Interest
10%, 5-year note	$ 550,000	$ 55,000
12%, 10-year bonds	600,000	72,000
	$1,150,000	$127,000

$$\text{Weighted-average interest rate} = \frac{\text{Total interest}}{\text{Total principal}} = \frac{\$127,000}{\$1,150,000} = 11.04\%$$

The company determines the actual interest cost, which represents the maximum amount of interest that it may capitalize during 2007, as shown in Illustration 10-6.

ILLUSTRATION 10-6
Computation of Actual
Interest Cost

Construction note	$750,000 ×.15	=	$112,500
5-year note	$550,000 ×.10	=	55,000
10-year bonds	$600,000 ×.12	=	72,000
Actual interest			$239,500

The interest cost that Shalla capitalizes is the lesser of $120,228 (avoidable interest) and $239,500 (actual interest), or $120,228.

Shalla records the following journal entries during 2007:

January 1

Land	100,000	
Building (or Construction in Process)	110,000	
Cash		210,000

March 1

Building	300,000	
Cash		300,000

May 1

Building	540,000	
Cash		540,000

December 31

Building	450,000	
Cash		450,000
Building (Capitalized Interest)	120,228	
Interest Expense ($239,500 − $120,228)	119,272	
Cash ($112,500 + $55,000 + $72,000)		239,500

Tutorial on Interest Capitalization

Shalla should write off capitalized interest cost as part of depreciation over the useful life of the assets involved and not over the term of the debt. It should disclose the total interest cost incurred during the period, with the portion charged to expense and the portion capitalized indicated.

At December 31, 2007, Shalla discloses the amount of interest capitalized either as part of the nonoperating section of the income statement or in the notes accompanying the financial statements. We illustrate both forms of disclosure, in Illustrations 10-7 and 10-8.

ILLUSTRATION 10-7
Capitalized Interest Reported in the Income Statement

Income from operations		XXXX
Other expenses and losses:		
Interest expense	$239,500	
Less: Capitalized interest	120,228	119,272
Income before taxes on income		XXXX
Income taxes		XXX
Net income		XXXX

ILLUSTRATION 10-8
Capitalized Interest Disclosed in a Note

Note 1: Accounting Policies. *Capitalized Interest.* During 2007 total interest cost was $239,500, of which $120,228 was capitalized and $119,272 was charged to expense.

Special Issues Related to Interest Capitalization

Two issues related to interest capitalization merit special attention:

1 Expenditures for land.
2 Interest revenue.

Expenditures for Land. When a company purchases land with the intention of developing it for a particular use, interest costs associated with those expenditures qualify for interest capitalization. If it purchases land as a site for a structure (such as a plant site), **interest costs capitalized during the period of construction are part of the cost of the plant, not the land**. Conversely, if the company develops land for lot sales, it includes any capitalized interest cost as part of the acquisition cost of the developed land. However, it should **not** capitalize interest costs involved in purchasing land held **for speculation** because the asset is ready for its intended use.

Interest Revenue. Companies frequently borrow money to finance construction of assets. They temporarily invest the excess borrowed funds in interest-bearing securities until they need the funds to pay for construction. During the early stages of construction, interest revenue earned may exceed the interest cost incurred on the borrowed funds.

Should companies offset interest revenue against interest cost when determining the amount of interest to capitalize as part of the construction cost of assets? In general, **companies should not net or offset interest revenue against interest cost**. Temporary or short-term investment decisions are not related to the interest incurred as part of the acquisition cost of assets. Therefore, companies should capitalize the interest incurred on qualifying assets whether or not they temporarily invest excess funds in short-term securities. Some criticize this approach because a company can defer the interest cost but report the interest revenue in the current period.

INTERNATIONAL INSIGHT

Under international accounting standards *(IAS No. 23)*, companies may capitalize interest, but it is not the preferred treatment. Thus, the financial statements of U.S. and IAS companies may not be comparable if capitalized interest costs are significant and the IAS company uses the preferred treatment. However, an analyst can convert the U.S. GAAP numbers to be comparable to the IAS company.

Observations

The interest capitalization requirement, while now universally adopted, is still debated. From a conceptual viewpoint, many believe that, for the reasons mentioned earlier, companies should either capitalize **no interest cost** or **all interest costs**, actual or imputed.

WHAT'S IN YOUR INTEREST?

The requirement to capitalize interest can significantly impact financial statements. For example, when earnings of building manufacturer **Jim Walter's Corporation** dropped from $1.51 to $1.17 per share, the company offset 11 cents per share of the decline by capitalizing the interest on coal mining projects and several plants under construction.

How do statement users determine the impact of interest capitalization on a company's bottom line? They examine the notes to the financial statements. Companies with material interest capitalization must disclose the amounts of capitalized interest relative to total interest costs. For example, **Anadarko Petroleum Corporation** capitalized nearly 30 percent of its total interest costs in a recent year and provided the following footnote related to capitalized interest.

Financial Footnotes

Total interest costs incurred during the year were $82,415,000. Of this amount, the Company capitalized $24,716,000. Capitalized interest is included as part of the cost of oil and gas properties. The capitalization rates are based on the Company's weighted-average cost of borrowings used to finance the expenditures.

WHAT DO THE NUMBERS MEAN?

VALUATION

Like other assets, **companies should record property, plant, and equipment at the fair market value of what they give up or at the fair value of the asset received, whichever is more clearly evident.** However, the process of asset acquisition sometimes obscures fair market value. For example, if a company buys land and buildings together for one price, how does it determine separate values for the land and buildings? We examine these types of accounting problems in the following sections.

Cash Discounts

When a company purchases plant assets subject to cash discounts for prompt payment, how should it report the discount? If it takes the discount, the company should consider the discount as a reduction in the purchase price of the asset. But should the company reduce the asset cost even if it does not take the discount?

Two points of view exist on this question. One approach considers the discount—whether taken or not—as a reduction in the cost of the asset. The rationale for this approach is that the real cost of the asset is the cash or cash equivalent price of the asset. In addition, some argue that the terms of cash discounts are so attractive that failure to take them indicates management error or inefficiency.

Proponents of the other approach argue that failure to take the discount should not always be considered a loss. The terms may be unfavorable, or it might not be prudent for the company to take the discount. At present, companies use both methods, though most prefer the former method.

OBJECTIVE 5
Understand accounting issues related to acquiring and valuing plant assets.

Deferred-Payment Contracts

Companies frequently purchase plant assets on long-term credit contracts, using notes, mortgages, bonds, or equipment obligations. **To properly reflect cost, companies account for assets purchased on long-term credit contracts at the present value of the consideration exchanged between the contracting parties at the date of the transaction.**

For example, Greathouse Company purchases an asset today in exchange for a $10,000 zero-interest-bearing note payable four years from now. The company would not record the asset at $10,000. Instead, the present value of the $10,000 note establishes the exchange price of the transaction (the purchase price of the asset). Assuming an appropriate interest rate of 9 percent at which to discount this single payment of $10,000 due four years from now, Greathouse records this asset at $7,084.30 ($10,000 × .70843). [See Table 6-2 for the present value of a single sum, $PV = \$10,000 \ (PVF_{4,9\%})$.]

When no interest rate is stated, or if the specified rate is unreasonable, the company imputes an appropriate interest rate. The objective is to approximate the interest rate that the buyer and seller would negotiate at arm's length in a similar borrowing transaction. In imputing an interest rate, companies consider such factors as the borrower's credit rating, the amount and maturity date of the note, and prevailing interest rates. **The company uses the cash exchange price of the asset acquired (if determinable) as the basis for recording the asset and measuring the interest element.**

To illustrate, Sutter Company purchases a specially built robot spray painter for its production line. The company issues a $100,000, five-year, zero-interest-bearing note to Wrigley Robotics, Inc. for the new equipment. The prevailing market rate of interest for obligations of this nature is 10 percent. Sutter is to pay off the note in five $20,000 installments, made at the end of each year. Sutter cannot readily determine the fair market value of this specially built robot. Therefore Sutter approximates the robot's value by establishing the market value (present value) of the note. Entries for the date of purchase and dates of payments, plus computation of the present value of the note, are as follows.

Date of Purchase

Equipment	75,816*	
Discount on Notes Payable	24,184	
Notes Payable		100,000

*Present value of note = $20,000 ($PVF\text{-}OA_{5,10\%}$)
            = $20,000 (3.79079); Table 6-4
            = $75,816

End of First Year

Interest Expense	7,582	
Notes Payable	20,000	
Cash		20,000
Discount on Notes Payable		7,582

Interest expense in the first year under the effective-interest approach is $7,582 [($100,000 − $24,184) × 10%]. The entry at the end of the second year to record interest and principal payment is as follows.

End of Second Year

Interest Expense	6,340	
Notes Payable	20,000	
Cash		20,000
Discount on Notes Payable		6,340

Interest expense in the second year under the effective-interest approach is $6,340 [($100,000 − $24,184) − ($20,000 − $7,582)] × 10%.

If Sutter did not impute an interest rate for deferred-payment contracts, it would record the asset at an amount greater than its fair value. In addition, Sutter would understate interest expense in the income statement for all periods involved.

Lump-Sum Purchases

A special problem of pricing fixed assets arises when a company purchases a group of plant assets at a single **lump-sum price**. When this common situation occurs, the company allocates the total cost among the various assets on the basis of their relative fair market values. The assumption is that costs will vary in direct proportion to fair value. This is the same principle that companies apply to allocate a lump-sum cost among different inventory items.

To determine fair market value, a company should use valuation techniques that are appropriate in the circumstances. In some cases, a single valuation technique will be appropriate. In other cases, multiple valuation approaches might have to be used.

To illustrate, Norduct Homes, Inc. decides to purchase several assets of a small heating concern, Comfort Heating, for $80,000. Comfort Heating is in the process of liquidation. Its assets sold are:

	Book Value	Fair Market Value
Inventory	$30,000	$ 25,000
Land	20,000	25,000
Building	35,000	50,000
	$85,000	$100,000

Norduct Homes allocates the $80,000 purchase price on the basis of the relative fair market values (assuming specific identification of costs is impracticable) in the following manner.

Inventory $\dfrac{\$25,000}{\$100,000} \times \$80,000 = \$20,000$

Land $\dfrac{\$25,000}{\$100,000} \times \$80,000 = \$20,000$

Building $\dfrac{\$50,000}{\$100,000} \times \$80,000 = \$40,000$

ILLUSTRATION 10-9
Allocation of Purchase Price—Relative Fair Market Value Basis

Issuance of Stock

When companies acquire property by issuing securities, such as common stock, the par or stated value of such stock fails to properly measure the property cost. If trading of the stock is active, **the market value of the stock issued is a fair indication of the cost of the property acquired. The stock is a good measure of the current cash equivalent price.**

For example, Upgrade Living Co. decides to purchase some adjacent land for expansion of its carpeting and cabinet operation. In lieu of paying cash for the land, the company issues to Deedland Company 5,000 shares of common stock (par value $10) that have a fair market value of $12 per share. Upgrade Living Co. records the following entry.

Land (5,000 × $12)	60,000	
Common Stock		50,000
Additional Paid-In Capital		10,000

If the company cannot determine the market value of the common stock exchanged, it establishes the market value of the property. It then uses the value of the property as the basis for recording the asset and issuance of the common stock.[6]

---

[6]The valuation approaches that should be used are the market, income, or cost approach, or a combination of these approaches. The *market approach* uses observable prices and other relevant information generated by market transactions involving comparable assets. The *income approach* uses valuation techniques to convert future amounts (for example, cash flows or earnings) to a single present value amount (discounted). The *cost approach* is based on the amount that currently would be required to replace the service capacity of an asset (often referred to as current replacement cost). In determining the fair value, the company should assume the highest and best use of the asset ("Fair Value Measurement," Proposed *Statement of Financial Accounting Standard* (Norwalk, Conn.: FASB, October 21, 2005).

Exchanges of Nonmonetary Assets

The proper accounting for exchanges of nonmonetary assets, such as property, plant, and equipment, is controversial.[7] Some argue that companies should account for these types of exchanges based on the fair value of the asset given up or the fair value of the asset received, with a gain or loss recognized. Others believe that they should account for exchanges based on the recorded amount (book value) of the asset given up, with no gain or loss recognized. Still others favor an approach that recognizes losses in all cases, but defers gains in special situations.

Ordinarily companies account for the exchange of nonmonetary assets on the basis of **the fair value of the asset given up or the fair value of the asset received, whichever is clearly more evident.**[8] Thus, companies **should recognize immediately** any gains or losses on the exchange. The rationale for immediate recognition is that most transactions have **commercial substance**, and therefore gains and losses should be recognized.

Meaning of Commercial Substance

As indicated above, fair value is the basis for measuring an asset acquired in a nonmonetary exchange if the transaction has commercial substance. An exchange has commercial substance if the future cash flows change as a result of the transaction. That is, if the two parties' economic positions change, the transaction has commercial substance.

For example, Andrew Co. exchanges some if its equipment for land held by Roddick Inc. It is likely that the timing and amount of the cash flows arising for the land will differ significantly from the cash flows arising from the equipment. As a result, both Andrew Co. and Roddick Inc. are in different economic positions. Therefore, the exchange has commercial substance, and the companies recognize a gain or loss on the exchange.

What if companies exchange similar assets, such as one truck for another truck?[9] Even in an exchange of similar assets, a change in the economic position of the company can result. For example, let's say the useful life of the truck received is significantly longer than that of the truck given up. The cash flows for the trucks can differ significantly. As a result, the transaction has commercial substance, and the company should use fair value as a basis for measuring the asset received in the exchange.

However, it is possible to exchange similar assets but not have a significant difference in cash flows. That is, the company is in the same economic position as before the exchange. In that case, the company recognizes a loss but generally defers a gain.

As we will see in the examples below, use of fair value generally results in recognizing a gain or loss at the time of the exchange. Consequently companies must

---

[7]Nonmonetary assets are items whose price in terms of the monetary unit may change over time. Monetary assets—cash and short- or long-term accounts and notes receivable—are fixed in terms of units of currency by contract or otherwise.

[8]"Accounting for Nonmonetary Transactions," *Opinions of the Accounting Principles Board No. 29* (New York: AICPA, 1973), par 18, and "Exchanges of Nonmonetary Assets, an Amendment of *APB Opinion No. 29*," *Statement of Financial Accounting Standards No. 153* (Norwalk, Conn: FASB, 2004).

[9]In previous accounting standards, the primary factor in determining whether to recognize gains on exchanges was whether the assets were "similar" in nature. This approach was problematic due to the subjectivity of determining similarity in the assets being exchanged. The new commercial-substance condition addresses this concern and contributes to international accounting convergence. The FASB and the IASB have agreed to resolve differences between the U.S. GAAP and International Financial Reporting Standards (IFRS). With the commercial-substance approach, U.S. GAAP and IFRS are now in agreement.

determine if the transaction has commercial substance. To make this determination, they must carefully evaluate the cash flow characteristics of the assets exchanged.[10]

Illustration 10-10 summarizes asset exchange situations and the related accounting.

Type of Exchange	Accounting Guidance
Exchange has commercial substance.	Recognize gains and losses immediately.
Exchange lacks commercial substance—no cash received.	Defer gains; recognize losses immediately.
Exchange lacks commercial substance—cash received.	Recognize partial gain; recognize losses immediately.*

*If cash is 25% or more of the fair value of the exchange, recognize entire gain because earnings process is complete.

ILLUSTRATION 10-10
Accounting for Exchanges

As Illustration 10-10 indicates, companies immediately recognize losses they incur on all exchanges. The accounting for gains depends on whether the exchange has commercial substance. If the exchange has commercial substance, the company recognizes the gain immediately. However, the profession modifies the rule for immediate recognition of a gain when an exchange lacks commercial substance: If the company receives no cash in such an exchange, it defers recognition of a gain. If the company receives cash in such an exchange, it recognizes part of the gain immediately.

To illustrate the accounting for these different types of transactions, we examine various loss and gain exchange situations.

Exchanges—Loss Situation

When a company exchanges nonmonetary assets and a loss results, the company recognizes the loss immediately. The rationale: Companies should not value assets at more than their cash equivalent price; if the loss were deferred, assets would be overstated. Therefore, companies recognize a loss immediately whether the exchange has commercial substance or not.

For example, Information Processing, Inc. trades its used machine for a new model at Jerrod Business Solutions Inc. The exchange has commercial substance. The used machine has a book value of $8,000 (original cost $12,000 less $4,000 accumulated depreciation) and a fair value of $6,000. The new model lists for $16,000. Jerrod gives Information Processing a trade-in allowance of $9,000 for the used machine. Information Processing computes the cost of the new asset as follows.

List price of new machine	$16,000
Less: Trade-in allowance for used machine	9,000
Cash payment due	7,000
Fair value of used machine	6,000
Cost of new machine	$13,000

ILLUSTRATION 10-11
Computation of Cost of New Machine

[10]The determination of the commercial substance of a transaction requires significant judgment. In determining whether future cash flows change, it is necessary to do one of two things: (1) Determine whether the risk, timing, and amount of cash flows arising for the asset received differ from the cash flows associated with the outbound asset. Or, (2) evaluate whether cash flows are affected with the exchange versus without the exchange. Also note that if companies cannot determine fair values of the assets exchanged, then they should use recorded book values in accounting for the exchange.

Information Processing records this transaction as follows:

Equipment	13,000	
Accumulated Depreciation—Equipment	4,000	
Loss on Disposal of Equipment	2,000	
Equipment		12,000
Cash		7,000

We verify the loss on the disposal of the used machine as follows:

ILLUSTRATION 10-12
Computation of Loss on
Disposal of Used
Machine

Fair value of used machine	$6,000
Book value of used machine	8,000
Loss on disposal of used machine	$2,000

Why did Information Processing not use the trade-in allowance or the book value of the old asset as a basis for the new equipment? The company did not use the trade-in allowance because it included a price concession (similar to a price discount). Few individuals pay list price for a new car. Dealers such as Jerrod often inflate trade-in allowances on the used car so that actual selling prices fall below list prices. To record the car at list price would state it at an amount in excess of its cash equivalent price because of the new car's inflated list price. Similarly, use of book value in this situation would overstate the value of the new machine by $2,000.[11]

Exchanges—Gain Situation

Has Commercial Substance. Now let's consider the situation in which a nonmonetary exchange has commercial substance and a gain is realized. In such a case, a company usually records the cost of a nonmonetary asset acquired in exchange for another nonmonetary asset at the **fair value of the asset given up**, and immediately recognizes a gain. The company should use the **fair value of the asset received** only if it is more clearly evident than the fair value of the asset given up.

To illustrate, Interstate Transportation Company exchanged a number of used trucks plus cash for a semi-truck. The used trucks have a combined book value of $42,000 (cost $64,000 less $22,000 accumulated depreciation). Interstate's purchasing agent, experienced in the second-hand market, indicates that the used trucks have a fair market value of $49,000. In addition to the trucks, Interstate must pay $11,000 cash for the semi-truck. Interstate computes the cost of the semi-truck as follows.

ILLUSTRATION 10-13
Computation of Semi-
Truck Cost

Fair value of trucks exchanged	$49,000
Cash paid	11,000
Cost of semi-truck	$60,000

Interstate records the exchange transaction as follows:

Semi-truck	60,000	
Accumulated Depreciation—Trucks	22,000	
Trucks		64,000
Gain on Disposal of Used Trucks		7,000
Cash		11,000

The gain is the difference between the fair value of the used trucks and their book value. We verify the computation as follows.

---

[11]Recognize that for Jerrod (the dealer), the asset given up in the exchange is considered inventory. As a result, Jerrod records a sale and related cost of goods sold. The used machine received by Jerrod is recorded at fair value.

ILLUSTRATION 10-14
Computation of Gain on
Disposal of Used Trucks

Fair value of used trucks		$49,000
Cost of used trucks	$64,000	
Less: Accumulated depreciation	22,000	
Book value of used trucks		42,000
Gain on disposal of used trucks		$ 7,000

In this case, Interstate is in a different economic position, and therefore the transaction has commercial substance. Thus, it **recognizes a gain**.

Lacks Commercial Substance—No Cash Received. We now assume that the Interstate Transportation Company exchange lacks commercial substance. That is, the economic position of Interstate did not change significantly as a result of this exchange. In this case, Interstate defers the gain of $7,000 and reduces the basis of the semi-truck. Illustration 10-15 shows two different but acceptable computations to illustrate this reduction.

ILLUSTRATION 10-15
Basis of Semi-Truck—Fair
Value vs. Book Value

Fair value of semi-truck	$60,000		Book value of used trucks	$42,000
Less: Gain deferred	7,000	OR	Plus: Cash paid	11,000
Basis of semi-truck	$53,000		Basis of semi-truck	$53,000

Interstate records this transaction as follows:

Semi-truck	53,000	
Accumulated Depreciation—Trucks	22,000	
Trucks		64,000
Cash		11,000

If the exchange lacks commercial substance, the company recognizes the gain (reflected in the basis of the semi-truck) when it later sells the semi-truck, not at the time of the exchange.

Lacks Commercial Substance—Some Cash Received. When a company receives cash (sometimes referred to as "boot") in an exchange that lacks commercial substance, it may immediately recognize a portion of the gain.[12] Illustration 10-16 shows the general formula for gain recognition when an exchange includes some cash.

ILLUSTRATION 10-16
Formula for Gain
Recognition, Some Cash
Received

$$\frac{\text{Cash Received (Boot)}}{\text{Cash Received (Boot)} + \text{Fair Value of Other Assets Received}} \times \text{Total Gain} = \begin{array}{c}\text{Recognized} \\ \text{Gain}\end{array}$$

To illustrate, assume that Queenan Corporation traded in used machinery with a book value of $60,000 (cost $110,000 less accumulated depreciation $50,000) and a fair value of $100,000. It receives in exchange a machine with a fair value of $90,000 plus cash of $10,000. Illustration 10-17 shows calculation of the total gain on the exchange.

ILLUSTRATION 10-17
Computation of Total
Gain

Fair value of machine exchanged	$100,000
Book value of machine exchanged	60,000
Total gain	$ 40,000

---

[12]When the monetary consideration is significant, i.e., **25 percent or more** of the fair value of the exchange, both parties consider the transaction a **monetary exchange**. Such "monetary" exchanges rely on the fair values to measure the gains or losses that are recognized in their entirety. *EITF Issue No. 86-29*, "Nonmonetary Transactions: Magnitude of Boot and the Exception to the Use of Fair Value," *Emerging Issues Task Force Abstracts* (October 1, 1987).

Generally, when a transaction lacks commercial substance, a company defers any gain. But because Queenan received $10,000 in cash, it recognizes a partial gain. The portion of the gain a company recognizes is the ratio of monetary assets (cash in this case) to the total consideration received. Queenan computes the partial gain as follows:

ILLUSTRATION 10-18
Computation of Gain Based on Ratio of Cash Received

$$\frac{\$10,000}{\$10,000 + \$90,000} \times \$40,000 = \$4,000$$

Because Queenan recognizes only a gain of $4,000 on this transaction, it defers the remaining $36,000 ($40,000 − $4,000) and reduces the basis (recorded cost) of the new machine. Illustration 10-19 shows the computation of the basis.

ILLUSTRATION 10-19
Computation of Gain Based on Ratio of Cost Received

Fair value of new machine	$90,000		Book value of old machine	$60,000
Less: Gain deferred	36,000	OR	Portion of book value presumed sold	6,000*
Basis of new machine	$54,000		Basis of new machine	$54,000

$$^*\frac{\$10,000}{\$100,000} \times \$60,000 = \$6,000$$

Queenan records the transaction with the following entry.

Cash	10,000	
Machine	54,000	
Accumulated Depreciation—Machine	50,000	
Machine		110,000
Gain on Disposal of Machine		4,000

The rationale for the treatment of a partial gain is as follows: Before a nonmonetary exchange that includes some cash, a company has an unrecognized gain, which is the difference between the book value and the fair value of the old asset. When the exchange occurs, a portion of the fair value is converted to a more liquid asset. The ratio of this liquid asset to the total consideration received is the portion of the total gain that the company realizes. Thus, the company recognizes and records that amount.

Illustration 10-20 presents in summary form the accounting requirements for recognizing gains and losses on exchanges of nonmonetary assets.[13]

ILLUSTRATION 10-20
Summary of Gain and Loss Recognition on Exchanges of Nonmonetary Assets

1. Compute the total gain or loss on the transaction. This amount is equal to the difference between the fair value of the asset given up and the book value of the asset given up.
2. If a loss is computed in step 1, always recognize the entire loss.
3. If a gain is computed in step 1,
   (a) and the exchange has commercial substance, recognize the entire gain.
   (b) and the exchange lacks commercial substance,
      (1) and no cash is involved, no gain is recognized.
      (2) and some cash is given, no gain is recognized.
      (3) and some cash is received, the following portion of the gain is recognized:

$$\frac{\text{Cash Received (Boot)}}{\text{Cash Received (Boot)} + \text{Fair Value of Other Assets Received}} \times \text{Total Gain}^*$$

*If the amount of cash exchanged is 25% or more, recognize entire gain.

---

[13]Adapted from an article by Robert Capettini and Thomas E. King, "Exchanges of Nonmonetary Assets: Some Changes," *The Accounting Review* (January 1976).

Companies disclose in their financial statements nonmonetary exchanges during a period. Such disclosure indicates the nature of the transaction(s), the method of accounting for the assets exchanged, and gains or losses recognized on the exchanges.[14]

ABOUT THOSE SWAPS

WHAT DO THE NUMBERS MEAN?

In a press release, Roy Olofson, former vice president of finance for Global Crossing, accused company executives of improperly describing the company's revenue to the public. He said the company had improperly recorded long-term sales immediately rather than over the term of the contract, had improperly booked as cash transactions swaps of capacity with other carriers, and had fired him when he blew the whistle.

The accounting for the swaps involves exchanges of similar network capacity. Companies have said they engage in such deals because swapping is quicker and less costly than building segments of their own networks, or because such pacts provide redundancies to make their own networks more reliable. In one expert's view, an exchange of similar network capacity is the equivalent of trading a blue truck for a red truck—it shouldn't boost a company's revenue.

But Global Crossing and Qwest, among others, counted as revenue the money received from the other company in the swap. (In general, in transactions involving leased capacity, the companies booked the revenue over the life of the contract.) Some of these companies then treated their own purchases as capital expenditures, which were not run through the income statement. Instead, the spending led to the addition of assets on the balance sheet (and an inflated bottom line.)

The SEC questioned some of these capacity exchanges, because it appeared they were a device to pad revenue. This reaction was not surprising, since revenue growth was a key factor in the valuation of companies such as Global Crossing and Qwest during the craze for tech stocks in the late 1990s and 2000.

Source: Adapted from Henny Sender, "Telecoms Draw Focus for Moves in Accounting," *Wall Street Journal* (March 26, 2002), p. C7.

Accounting for Contributions

Companies sometimes receive or make contributions (donations or gifts). Such contributions, nonreciprocal transfers, transfer assets in one direction. A contribution is often some type of asset (such as cash, securities, land, buildings, or use of facilities), but it also could be the forgiveness of a debt.

When companies acquire assets as donations, a strict cost concept dictates that the valuation of the asset should be zero. However, a departure from the cost principle seems justified; the only costs incurred (legal fees and other relatively minor expenditures) are not a reasonable basis of accounting for the assets acquired. To record nothing is to ignore the economic realities of an increase in wealth and assets. Therefore, companies use the **fair value of the asset** to establish its value on the books.

What then is the proper accounting for the credit in this transaction? Some believe the credit should be made to Donated Capital (an additional paid-in capital account). This approach views the increase in assets from a donation as contributed capital, rather than as earned revenue.

Others argue that companies should report donations as revenues from contributions. Their reasoning is that only the owners of a business contribute capital. At issue in this approach is whether the company should report revenue immediately or over the period that the asset is employed. For example, to attract new industry a city may

---

[14]"Accounting for Nonmonetary Transactions," op. cit., par. 28.

offer land, but the receiving enterprise may incur additional costs in the future (e.g., transportation or higher state income taxes) because the location is not the most desirable. As a consequence, some argue that company should defer the revenue and recognize it as the costs are incurred.

The FASB's position is that **in general, companies should recognize contributions received as revenues in the period received.**[15] Companies measure contributions at the fair value of the assets received.[16] To illustrate, Max Wayer Meat Packing, Inc. has recently accepted a donation of land with a fair value of $150,000 from the Memphis Industrial Development Corp. In return Max Wayer Meat Packing promises to build a packing plant in Memphis. Max Wayer's entry is:

Land	150,000	
Contribution Revenue		150,000

When a company contributes a nonmonetary asset, it should record the amount of the donation as an expense at the fair value of the donated asset. If a difference exists between the fair value of the asset and its book value, the company should recognize a gain or loss. To illustrate, Kline Industries donates land to the city of Los Angeles for a city park. The land cost $80,000 and has a fair market value of $110,000. Kline Industries records this donation as follows:

Contribution Expense	110,000	
Land		80,000
Gain on Disposal of Land		30,000

In some cases, companies promise to give (pledge) some type of asset in the future. Should companies record this promise immediately or when they give the assets? If the promise is **unconditional** (depends only on the passage of time or on demand by the recipient for performance), the company should report the contribution expense and related payable immediately. If the promise is **conditional**, the company recognizes expense in the period benefited by the contribution, generally when it transfers the asset.

Other Asset Valuation Methods

The exception to the historical cost principle for assets acquired through donation is based on fair value. Another exception is the **prudent cost** concept. This concept states that if for some reason a company ignorantly paid too much for an asset originally, it is theoretically preferable to charge a loss immediately.

For example, assume that a company constructs an asset at a cost much greater than its present economic usefulness. It would be appropriate to charge these excess costs as a loss to the current period, rather than capitalize them as part of the cost of the asset. In practice, the need to use the prudent cost approach seldom develops. Companies typically either use good reasoning in paying a given price or fail to recognize that they have overpaid.

What happens, on the other hand, if a company makes a bargain purchase or internally constructs a piece of equipment at a cost savings? Such savings should not result in immediate recognition of a gain under any circumstances.

---

[15]"Accounting for Contributions Received and Contributions Made," *Statement of Financial Accounting Standards No. 116* (Norwalk, Conn.: FASB, 1993). The scope of this standard excludes transfers of assets from governmental units to business enterprises. However, we believe that the basic requirements should hold also for these types of contributions. Therefore, companies should record all assets at fair value and all credits as revenue.

[16]"Accounting for Nonmonetary Transactions," op. cit., par. 18. Also, *FASB No. 116* indicates that companies should record expenses on contributions made at the fair value of the assets given up.

COSTS SUBSEQUENT TO ACQUISITION

After installing plant assets and readying them for use, a company incurs additional costs that range from ordinary repairs to significant additions. The major problem is allocating these costs to the proper time periods. **In general, costs incurred to achieve greater future benefits should be capitalized, whereas expenditures that simply maintain a given level of services should be expensed.** In order to capitalize costs, one of three conditions must be present:

1 The useful life of the asset must be increased.
2 The quantity of units produced from the asset must be increased.
3 The quality of the units produced must be enhanced.

For example, a company like **Boeing** should expense expenditures that do not increase an asset's future benefits. That is, it expenses immediately ordinary repairs that maintain the existing condition of the asset or restore it to normal operating efficiency.

Companies expense most expenditures below an established arbitrary minimum amount, say, $100 or $500. Although conceptually this treatment may be incorrect, expediency demands it. Otherwise, companies would set up depreciation schedules for such items as wastepaper baskets and ashtrays.

OBJECTIVE 6
Describe the accounting treatment for costs subsequent to acquisition.

UNDERLYING CONCEPTS

Expensing long-lived ashtrays and waste baskets is an application of the materiality constraint.

DISCONNECTED

It all started with a check of the books by an internal auditor for WorldCom Inc. The telecom giant's newly installed chief executive had asked for a financial review, and the auditor was spot-checking records of capital expenditures. She found the company was using an unorthodox technique to account for one of its biggest expenses: charges paid to local telephone networks to complete long-distance calls.

Instead of recording these charges as operating expenses, WorldCom recorded a significant portion as capital expenditures. The maneuver was worth hundreds of millions of dollars to WorldCom's bottom line. It effectively turned a loss for all of 2001 and the first quarter of 2002 into a profit. The graph below compares WorldCom's accounting to that under GAAP. Soon after this discovery, WorldCom filed for bankruptcy.

WHAT DO THE NUMBERS MEAN?

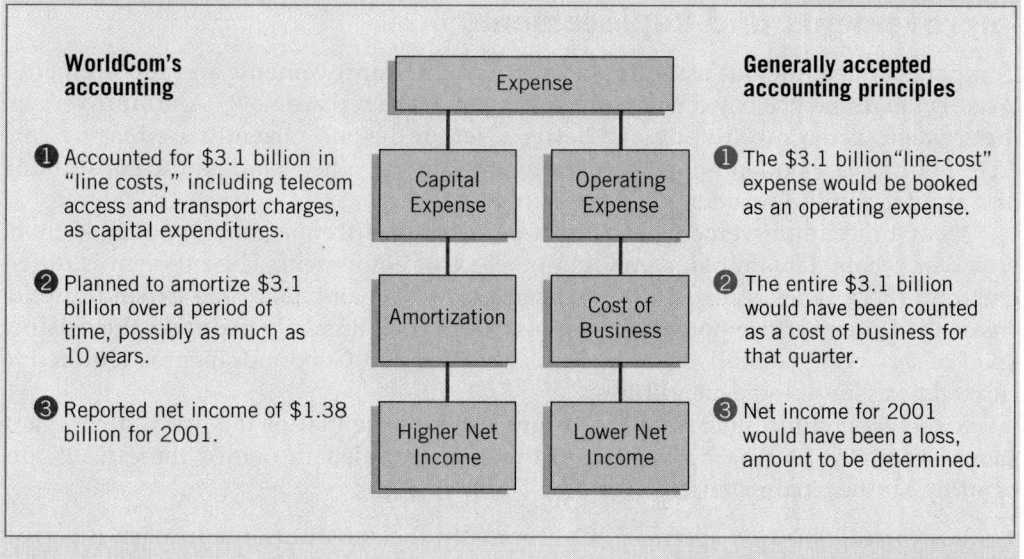

WorldCom's accounting

❶ Accounted for $3.1 billion in "line costs," including telecom access and transport charges, as capital expenditures.

❷ Planned to amortize $3.1 billion over a period of time, possibly as much as 10 years.

❸ Reported net income of $1.38 billion for 2001.

Expense → Capital Expense → Amortization → Higher Net Income

Expense → Operating Expense → Cost of Business → Lower Net Income

Generally accepted accounting principles

❶ The $3.1 billion "line-cost" expense would be booked as an operating expense.

❷ The entire $3.1 billion would have been counted as a cost of business for that quarter.

❸ Net income for 2001 would have been a loss, amount to be determined.

Source: Adapted from Jared Sandberg, Deborah Solomon, and Rebecca Blumenstein, "Inside World-Com's Unearthing of a Vast Accounting Scandal," *Wall Street Journal* (June 27, 2002,), p. A1.

The distinction between a **capital (asset) expenditure** and a **revenue (expense) expenditure** is not always clear-cut. Yet, in most cases, **consistent application of a capital/expense policy** is more important than attempting to provide general theoretical guidelines for each transaction. Generally, companies incur four major types of expenditures relative to existing assets.

MAJOR TYPES OF EXPENDITURES

ADDITIONS. Increase or extension of existing assets.

IMPROVEMENTS AND REPLACEMENTS. Substitution of an improved asset for an existing one.

REARRANGEMENT AND REINSTALLATION. Movement of assets from one location to another.

REPAIRS. Expenditures that maintain assets in condition for operation.

Additions

Additions should present no major accounting problems. By definition, **companies capitalize any addition to plant assets because a new asset is created**. For example, the addition of a wing to a hospital, or of an air conditioning system to an office, increases the service potential of that facility. Companies should capitalize such expenditures and match them against the revenues that will result in future periods.

One problem that arises in this area is the accounting for any changes related to the existing structure as a result of the addition. Is the cost incurred to tear down an old wall to make room for the addition, a cost of the addition or an expense or loss of the period? The answer is that it depends on the original intent. If the company had anticipated building an addition later, then this cost of removal is a proper cost of the addition. But if the company had not anticipated this development, it should properly report the removal as a loss in the current period on the basis of inefficient planning. Normally, the company retains the carrying amount of the old wall in the accounts, although theoretically the company should remove it.

Improvements and Replacements

Companies substitute one asset for another through **improvements** and **replacements**. What is the difference between an improvement and a replacement? An **improvement** (**betterment**) is the substitution of a **better asset** for the one currently used (say, a concrete floor for a wooden floor). A **replacement**, on the other hand, is the substitution of a **similar asset** (a wooden floor for a wooden floor).

Many times improvements and replacements result from a general policy to modernize or rehabilitate an older building or piece of equipment. The problem is differentiating these types of expenditures from normal repairs. Does the expenditure increase the **future service potential** of the asset? Or does it merely **maintain the existing level** of service? Frequently, the answer is not clear-cut. Good judgment is required to correctly classify these expenditures.

If the expenditure increases the future service potential of the asset, a company should capitalize it. The accounting is therefore handled in one of three ways, depending on the circumstances:

1 *Use the substitution approach.* Conceptually, the **substitution approach** is correct if the carrying amount of the old asset is available. It is then a simple matter to remove the cost of the old asset and replace it with the cost of the new asset.

To illustrate, Instinct Enterprises decides to replace the pipes in its plumbing system. A plumber suggests that the company use plastic tubing in place of the cast iron pipes and copper tubing. The old pipe and tubing have a book value of $15,000 (cost of $150,000 less accumulated depreciation of $135,000), and a scrap value of $1,000. The plastic tubing system costs $125,000. If Instinct pays $124,000 for the new tubing after exchanging the old tubing, it makes the following entry:

Plumbing System	125,000	
Accumulated Depreciation	135,000	
Loss on Disposal of Plant Assets	14,000	
Plumbing System		150,000
Cash ($125,000 − $1,000)		124,000

The problem is determining the book value of the old asset. Generally, the components of a given asset depreciate at different rates. However, generally no separate accounting is made. For example, the tires, motor, and body of a truck depreciate at different rates, but most companies use one rate for the entire truck. Companies can set separate depreciation rates, but it is often impractical. If a company cannot determine the carrying amount of the old asset, it adopts one of two other approaches.

2 *Capitalize the new cost.* Another approach capitalizes the improvement and keeps the carrying amount of the old asset on the books. The justification for this approach is that the item is sufficiently depreciated to reduce its carrying amount almost to zero. Although this assumption may not always be true, the differences are often insignificant. Companies usually handle improvements in this manner.

3 *Charge to accumulated depreciation.* In cases when a company does not improve the quantity or quality of the asset itself, but instead extends its useful life, the company debits the expenditure to Accumulated Depreciation rather than to an asset account. The theory behind this approach is that the replacement extends the useful life of the asset and thereby recaptures some or all of the past depreciation. The net carrying amount of the asset is the same whether debiting the asset or accumulated depreciation.

Rearrangement and Reinstallation

Companies incur **rearrangement and reinstallation costs** to benefit future periods. An example is the rearrangement and reinstallation of machines to facilitate future production.

If a company like **Eastman Kodak** can determine or estimate the original installation cost and the accumulated depreciation to date, it handles the rearrangement and reinstallation cost as a replacement. If not, which is generally the case, Eastman Kodak should capitalize the new costs (if material in amount) as an asset to be amortized over future periods expected to benefit. If these costs are immaterial, if they cannot be separated from other operating expenses, or if their future benefit is questionable, the company should immediately expense them.

Repairs

A company makes **ordinary repairs** to maintain plant assets in operating condition. It charges ordinary repairs to an expense account in the period incurred, on the basis that **it is the primary period benefited**. Maintenance charges that occur regularly include replacing minor parts, lubricating and adjusting equipment, repainting, and cleaning. A company treats these as ordinary operating expenses.

It is often difficult to distinguish a repair from an improvement or replacement. The major consideration is whether the expenditure benefits more than one year or one operating cycle, whichever is longer. If a **major repair** (such as an overhaul) occurs, several periods will benefit. A company should handle the cost as an addition, improvement, or replacement.[17]

If companies prepare income statements for short periods of time, say, monthly or quarterly, the same principles apply. Ordinary repairs and other regular maintenance charges for an annual period may benefit several quarters, and companies may need to allocate the cost among those periods. A company will often find it advantageous to concentrate its repair program at a certain time of the year, perhaps during the period of least activity or when the plant is shut down for vacation. Short-term comparative statements might be misleading if the company shows such expenditures as expenses of the quarter in which they were incurred. To give comparability to monthly or quarterly income statements, a company might use an account such as Allowance for Repairs so that it can better assign repair costs to the periods benefited.

To illustrate, Cricket Tractor Company estimated that its total repair expense for the year would be $720,000. It decided to charge each quarter for a portion of the repair cost even though the total cost for the year would occur in only two quarters.

End of First Quarter (zero repair costs incurred)

Repair Expense	180,000	
Allowance for Repairs (¼ × $720,000)		180,000

End of Second Quarter ($344,000 repair costs incurred)

Allowance for Repairs	344,000	
Cash, Wages Payable, Inventory, etc.		344,000
Repair Expense	180,000	
Allowance for Repairs (¼ × $720,000)		180,000

End of Third Quarter (zero repair costs incurred)

Repair Expense	180,000	
Allowance for Repairs (¼ × $720,000)		180,000

End of Fourth Quarter ($380,800 repair costs incurred)

Allowance for Repairs	380,800	
Cash, Wages Payable, Inventory, etc.		380,800
Repair Expense	184,800	
Allowance for Repairs		184,800
($344,000 + $380,800 − $180,000 − $180,000 − $180,000)		

Companies should not carry over a balance in the Allowance for Repairs account to the following year. The fourth quarter would normally absorb the variation from estimates. If a company prepares balance sheets during the year, it will add or subtract the Allowance account from the property, plant, and equipment section to determine a proper valuation.[18]

Summary of Costs Subsequent to Acquisition

Illustration 10-21 summarizes the accounting treatment for various costs incurred subsequent to the acquisition of capitalized assets.

---

[17]AcSEC has proposed (see footnote 2) that companies expense as incurred costs involved for planned major expenditures unless they represent an *additional* component or the *replacement* of an existing component. The "expense as incurred" approach is justified on the basis that these costs are relatively consistent from period to period, that they are not separately identifiable assets or property units in and of themselves, and that they serve only to restore assets to their original operating condition.

[18]Some might argue that the Allowance for Repairs account should be reported as a liability, because it has a credit balance. However, reporting a liability is inappropriate: To whom do you owe the amount? Placement in the stockholders' equity section is also illogical because no addition to the stockholders' investment has taken place.

Type of Expenditure	Normal Accounting Treatment
Additions	Capitalize cost of addition to asset account.
Improvements and replacements	(a) **Carrying value known:** Remove cost of and accumulated depreciation on old asset, recognizing any gain or loss. Capitalize cost of improvement/replacement. (b) **Carrying value unknown:** 　1. If the asset's useful life is extended, debit accumulated depreciation for cost of improvement/replacement. 　2. If the quantity or quality of the asset's productivity is increased, capitalize cost of improvement/replacement to asset account.
Rearrangement and reinstallation	(a) If original installation cost is **known**, account for cost of rearrangement/reinstallation as a replacement (carrying value known). (b) If original installation cost is **unknown** and rearrangement/reinstallation cost is **material** in amount and benefits future periods, capitalize as an asset. (c) If original installation cost is **unknown** and rearrangement/reinstallation cost is **not material or future benefit is questionable**, expense the cost when incurred.
Repairs	(a) **Ordinary:** Expense cost of repairs when incurred. (b) **Major:** As appropriate, treat as an addition, improvement, or replacement.

ILLUSTRATION 10-21
Summary of Costs
Subsequent to
Acquisition of Property,
Plant, and Equipment

DISPOSITIONS OF PLANT ASSETS

A company, like **Intel**, may retire plant assets voluntarily or dispose of them by sale, exchange, involuntary conversion, or abandonment. Regardless of the type of disposal, depreciation must be taken up to the date of disposition. Then, Intel should remove all accounts related to the retired asset. Generally, the book value of the specific plant asset does not equal its disposal value. As a result, a gain or loss develops. The reason: Depreciation is an estimate of cost allocation and not a process of valuation. **The gain or loss is really a correction of net income** for the years during which Intel used the fixed asset.

Intel should show gains or losses on the disposal of plant assets in the income statement along with other items from customary business activities. However, if it sold, abandoned, spun off, or otherwise disposed of the "operations of a component of a business," then it should report the results separately in the discontinued operations section of the income statement. That is, Intel should report any gain or loss from disposal of a business component with the related results of discontinued operations.

OBJECTIVE 7
Describe the
accounting treatment
for the disposal of
property, plant, and
equipment.

Sale of Plant Assets

Companies record depreciation for the period of time between the date of the last depreciation entry and the date of sale. To illustrate, assume that Barret Company recorded depreciation on a machine costing $18,000 for 9 years at the rate of $1,200 per year. If it sells the machine in the middle of the tenth year for $7,000, Barret records depreciation to the date of sale as:

Depreciation Expense	600	
Accumulated Depreciation—Machinery		600

The entry for the sale of the asset then is:

Cash	7,000	
Accumulated Depreciation—Machinery	11,400	
[($1,200 × 9)+ $600]		
Machinery		18,000
Gain on Disposal of Machinery		400

The book value of the machinery at the time of the sale is $6,600 ($18,000 − $11,400). Because the machinery sold for $7,000, the amount of the gain on the sale is $400.

Involuntary Conversion

Sometimes an asset's service is terminated through some type of **involuntary conversion** such as fire, flood, theft, or condemnation. Companies report the difference between the amount recovered (e.g., from a condemnation award or insurance recovery), if any, and the asset's book value as a gain or loss. They treat these gains or losses like any other type of disposition. In some cases, these gains or losses may be reported as extraordinary items in the income statement, **if the conditions of the disposition are unusual and infrequent in nature**.

To illustrate, Camel Transport Corp. had to sell a plant located on company property that stood directly in the path of an interstate highway. For a number of years the state had sought to purchase the land on which the plant stood, but the company resisted. The state ultimately exercised its right of eminent domain, which the courts upheld. In settlement, Camel received $500,000, which substantially exceeded the $200,000 book value of the plant and land (cost of $400,000 less accumulated depreciation of $200,000). Camel made the following entry.

Cash	500,000	
Accumulated Depreciation—Plant Assets	200,000	
Plant Assets		400,000
Gain on Disposal of Plant Assets		300,000

If the conditions surrounding the condemnation are judged to be unusual and infrequent, Camel's gain of $300,000 is reported as an extraordinary item.

Some object to the recognition of a gain or loss in certain *involuntary* conversions. For example, the federal government often condemns forests for national parks. The paper companies that owned these forests must report a gain or loss on the condemnation. However, companies such as **Georgia-Pacific** contend that no gain or loss should be reported because they must replace the condemned forest land immediately and so are in the same economic position as they were before. The issue is whether condemnation and subsequent purchase should be viewed as one or two transactions. *FASB Interpretation No. 30* rules against the companies by requiring "that gain or loss be recognized when a nonmonetary asset is involuntarily converted to monetary assets even though an enterprise reinvests or is obligated to reinvest the monetary assets in replacement nonmonetary assets."[19]

Miscellaneous Problems

If a company scraps or abandons an asset without any cash recovery, it recognizes a loss equal to the asset's book value. If scrap value exists, the gain or loss that occurs is the difference between the asset's scrap value and its book value. If an asset still can be used even though it is fully depreciated, it may be kept on the books at historical cost less depreciation.

Companies must disclose in notes to the financial statements the amount of fully depreciated assets in service. For example, **Petroleum Equipment Tools Inc.** in its annual report disclosed, "The amount of fully depreciated assets included in property, plant, and equipment at December 31 amounted to approximately $98,900,000."

---

[19]"Accounting for Involuntary Conversions of Nonmonetary Assets to Monetary Assets," *FASB Interpretation No. 30* (Stamford, Conn.: FASB, 1979), summary paragraph.

SUMMARY OF LEARNING OBJECTIVES

1. Describe property, plant, and equipment. The major characteristics of property, plant, and equipment are: (1) They are acquired for use in operations and not for resale. (2) They are long-term in nature and usually subject to depreciation. And (3) they possess physical substance.

2. Identify the costs to include in initial valuation of property, plant, and equipment. The costs included in initial valuation of property, plant, and equipment are as follows:

Cost of land: Includes all expenditures made to acquire land and to ready it for use. Land costs typically include (1) the purchase price; (2) closing costs, such as title to the land, attorney's fees, and recording fees; (3) costs incurred in getting the land in condition for its intended use, such as grading, filling, draining, and clearing; (4) assumption of any liens, mortgages, or encumbrances on the property; and (5) any additional land improvements that have an indefinite life.

Cost of buildings: Includes all expenditures related directly to their acquisition or construction. These costs include (1) materials, labor, and overhead costs incurred during construction, and (2) professional fees and building permits.

Cost of equipment: Includes the purchase price, freight and handling charges incurred, insurance on the equipment while in transit, cost of special foundations if required, assembling and installation costs, and costs of conducting trial runs.

3. Describe the accounting problems associated with self-constructed assets. Indirect costs of manufacturing create special problems because companies cannot easily trace these costs directly to work and material orders related to the constructed assets. Companies might handle these costs in one of two ways: (1) Assign no fixed overhead to the cost of the constructed asset. Or (2) assign a portion of all overhead to the construction process. Companies use the second method extensively.

4. Describe the accounting problems associated with interest capitalization. Only actual interest (with modifications) should be capitalized. The rationale for this approach is that during construction, the asset is not generating revenue and therefore companies should defer (capitalize) interest cost. Once construction is completed, the asset is ready for its intended use and revenues can be earned. Any interest cost incurred in purchasing an asset that is ready for its intended use should be expensed.

5. Understand accounting issues related to acquiring and valuing plant assets. The following issues relate to acquiring and valuing plant assets: (1) *Cash discounts:* Whether taken or not, they are generally considered a reduction in the cost of the asset; the real cost of the asset is the cash or cash equivalent price of the asset. (2) *Deferred-payment contracts:* Companies account for assets purchased on long-term credit contracts at the present value of the consideration exchanged between the contracting parties. (3) *Lump-sum purchase:* Allocate the total cost among the various assets on the basis of their relative fair market values. (4) *Issuance of stock:* If the stock is actively traded, the market value of the stock issued is a fair indication of the cost of the property acquired. If the market value of the common stock exchanged is not determinable, establish the value of the property and use it as the basis for recording the asset and issuance of the common stock. (5) *Exchanges of nonmonetary assets.* The accounting for exchanges of nonmonetary assets depends on whether the exchange has commercial substance. See Illustrations 10-10 (page 485) and 10-20 (page 488) for summaries of how to account for exchanges. (6) *Contributions:* Record at the fair value of the asset received, and credit revenue for the same amount.

6. Describe the accounting treatment for costs subsequent to acquisition. Illustration 10-21 (page 495) summarizes how to account for costs subsequent to acquisition.

KEY TERMS

additions, *492*

avoidable interest, *477*

capital expenditure, *492*

capitalization period, *476*

commercial substance, *484*

fixed assets, *472*

historical cost, *473*

improvements (betterments), *492*

involuntary conversion, *496*

lump-sum price, *482*

major repairs, *493*

nonmonetary assets, *484*

nonreciprocal transfers, *489*

ordinary repairs, *493*

plant assets, *472*

property, plant, and equipment, *472*

prudent cost, *490*

rearrangement and reinstallation costs, *493*

replacements, *492*

revenue expenditure, *492*

self-constructed asset, *474*

weighted-average accumulated expenditures, *477*

7. **Describe the accounting treatment for the disposal of property, plant, and equipment.** Regardless of the time of disposal, companies take depreciation up to the date of disposition, and then remove all accounts related to the retired asset. Gains or losses on the retirement of plant assets are shown in the income statement along with other items that arise from customary business activities. Gains or losses on involuntary conversions may be reported as extraordinary items.

QUESTIONS

1. What are the major characteristics of plant assets?

2. Esplanade Inc. owns land that it purchased on January 1, 2000, for $420,000. At December 31, 2007, its current value is $770,000 as determined by appraisal. At what amount should Esplanade report this asset on its December 31, 2007, balance sheet? Explain.

3. Name the items, in addition to the amount paid to the former owner or contractor, that may properly be included as part of the acquisition cost of the following plant assets.
   (a) Land.
   (b) Machinery and equipment.
   (c) Buildings.

4. Indicate where the following items would be shown on a balance sheet.
   (a) A lien that was attached to the land when purchased.
   (b) Landscaping costs.
   (c) Attorney's fees and recording fees related to purchasing land.
   (d) Variable overhead related to construction of machinery.
   (e) A parking lot servicing employees in the building.
   (f) Cost of temporary building for workers during construction of building.
   (g) Interest expense on bonds payable incurred during construction of a building.
   (h) Assessments for sidewalks that are maintained by the city.
   (i) The cost of demolishing an old building that was on the land when purchased.

5. Two positions have normally been taken with respect to the recording of fixed manufacturing overhead as an element of the cost of plant assets constructed by a company for its own use:
   (a) It should be excluded completely.
   (b) It should be included at the same rate as is charged to normal operations.

   What are the circumstances or rationale that support or deny the application of these methods?

6. The Buildings account of Diego Rivera Inc. includes the following items that were used in determining the basis for depreciating the cost of a building.
   (a) Organization and promotion expenses.

   (b) Architect's fees.
   (c) Interest and taxes during construction.
   (d) Interest revenue on investments held to fund construction of a building.

   Do you agree with these charges? If not, how would you deal with each of the items above in the corporation's books and in its annual financial statements?

7. Jones Company has purchased two tracts of land. One tract will be the site of its new manufacturing plant, while the other is being purchased with the hope that it will be sold in the next year at a profit. How should these two tracts of land be reported in the balance sheet?

8. One financial accounting issue encountered when a company constructs its own plant is whether the interest cost on funds borrowed to finance construction should be capitalized and then amortized over the life of the assets constructed. What is the justification for capitalizing such interest?

9. Provide examples of assets that do not qualify for interest capitalization.

10. What interest rates should be used in determining the amount of interest to be capitalized? How should the amount of interest to be capitalized be determined?

11. How should the amount of interest capitalized be disclosed in the notes to the financial statements? How should interest revenue from temporarily invested excess funds borrowed to finance the construction of assets be accounted for?

12. Discuss the basic accounting problem that arises in handling each of the following situations.
    (a) Assets purchased by issuance of capital stock.
    (b) Acquisition of plant assets by gift or donation.
    (c) Purchase of a plant asset subject to a cash discount.
    (d) Assets purchased on a long-term credit basis.
    (e) A group of assets acquired for a lump sum.
    (f) An asset traded in or exchanged for another asset.

13. Yukio Mishima Industries acquired equipment this year to be used in its operations. The equipment was delivered by the suppliers, installed by Mishima, and placed into operation. Some of it was purchased for cash with discounts available for prompt payment. Some of it was purchased under long-term payment plans for which the

interest charges approximated prevailing rates. What costs should Mishima capitalize for the new equipment purchased this year? Explain.

14. Adam Mickiewicz Co. purchased for $2,200,000 property that included both land and a building to be used in operations. The seller's book value was $300,000 for the land and $900,000 for the building. By appraisal, the fair market value was estimated to be $500,000 for the land and $2,000,000 for the building. At what amount should Mickiewicz report the land and the building at the end of the year?

15. Richardson Co. acquires machinery by paying $10,000 cash and signing a $5,000, 2-year, zero-interest-bearing note payable. The note has a present value of $4,058, and Richardson purchased a similar machine last month for $13,500. At what cost should the new equipment be recorded?

16. Sean May is evaluating two recent transactions involving exchanges of equipment. In one case, the exchange has commercial substance. In the second situation, the exchange lacks commercial substance. Explain to Sean the differences in accounting for these two situations.

17. Saadi Company purchased a heavy-duty truck on July 1, 2004, for $30,000. It was estimated that it would have a useful life of 10 years and then would have a trade-in value of $6,000. It was traded on August 1, 2008, for a similar truck costing $39,000; $13,000 was allowed as trade-in value (also fair value) on the old truck and $26,000 was paid in cash. A comparison of expected cash flows for the trucks indicates the exchange lacks commercial substance. What is the entry to record the trade-in? The company uses the straight-line method.

18. Once equipment has been installed and placed in operation, subsequent expenditures relating to this equipment are frequently thought of as repairs or general maintenance and, hence, chargeable to operations in the period in which the expenditure is made. Actually, determination of whether such an expenditure should be charged to operations or capitalized involves a much more careful analysis of the character of the expenditure.

What are the factors that should be considered in making such a decision? Discuss fully.

19. What accounting treatment is normally given to the following items in accounting for plant assets?

(a) Additions.

(b) Major repairs.

(c) Improvements and replacements.

20. New machinery, which replaced a number of employees, was installed and put in operation in the last month of the fiscal year. The employees had been dismissed after payment of an extra month's wages, and this amount was added to the cost of the machinery. Discuss the propriety of the charge. If it was improper, describe the proper treatment.

21. To what extent do you consider the following items to be proper costs of the fixed asset? Give reasons for your opinions.

(a) Overhead of a business that builds its own equipment.

(b) Cash discounts on purchases of equipment.

(c) Interest paid during construction of a building.

(d) Cost of a safety device installed on a machine.

(e) Freight on equipment returned before installation, for replacement by other equipment of greater capacity.

(f) Cost of moving machinery to a new location.

(g) Cost of plywood partitions erected as part of the remodeling of the office.

(h) Replastering of a section of the building.

(i) Cost of a new motor for one of the trucks.

22. Recently, Michelangelo Manufacturing Co. presented the account "Allowance for Repairs" in the long-term liabilities section. Evaluate this procedure.

23. Dimitri Enterprises has a number of fully depreciated assets that are still being used in the main operations of the business. Because the assets are fully depreciated, the president of the company decides not to show them on the balance sheet or disclose this information in the notes. Evaluate this procedure.

24. What are the general rules for how gains or losses on retirement of plant assets should be reported in income?

BRIEF EXERCISES

(LO 2) **BE10-1** Bonanza Brothers Inc. purchased land at a price of $27,000. Closing costs were $1,400. An old building was removed at a cost of $12,200. What amount should be recorded as the cost of the land?

(LO 4) **BE10-2** Brett Hull Company is constructing a building. Construction began on February 1 and was completed on December 31. Expenditures were $1,500,000 on March 1, $1,200,000 on June 1, and $3,000,000 on December 31. Compute Hull's weighted-average accumulated expenditures for interest capitalization purposes.

(LO 4) **BE10-3** Brett Hull Company (see BE10-2) borrowed $1,000,000 on March 1 on a 5-year, 12% note to help finance construction of the building. In addition, the company had outstanding all year a 13%, 5-year, $2,000,000 note payable and a 15%, 4-year, $3,500,000 note payable. Compute the weighted-average interest rate used for interest capitalization purposes.

(LO 4) **BE10-4** Use the information for Brett Hull Company from BE10-2 and BE10-3. Compute avoidable interest for Brett Hull Company.

(LO 5) **BE10-5** Chavez Corporation purchased a truck by issuing an $80,000, 4-year, zero-interest-bearing note to Equinox Inc. The market rate of interest for obligations of this nature is 12%. Prepare the journal entry to record the purchase of this truck.

(LO 5) **BE10-6** Cool Spot Inc. purchased land, building, and equipment from Pinball Wizard Corporation for a cash payment of $306,000. The estimated fair values of the assets are land $60,000, building $220,000, and equipment $80,000. At what amounts should each of the three assets be recorded?

(LO 5) **BE10-7** Dark Wizard Company obtained land by issuing 2,000 shares of its $10 par value common stock. The land was recently appraised at $85,000. The common stock is actively traded at $41 per share. Prepare the journal entry to record the acquisition of the land.

(LO 5) **BE10-8** Strider Corporation traded a used truck (cost $20,000, accumulated depreciation $18,000) for a small computer worth $3,700. Strider also paid $1,000 in the transaction. Prepare the journal entry to record the exchange. (The exchange has commercial substance.)

(LO 5) **BE10-9** Use the information for Strider Corporation from BE10-8. Prepare the journal entry to record the exchange, assuming the exchange lacks commercial substance.

(LO 5) **BE10-10** Sloan Company traded a used welding machine (cost $9,000, accumulated depreciation $3,000) for office equipment with an estimated fair value of $5,000. Sloan also paid $2,000 cash in the transaction. Prepare the journal entry to record the exchange. (The exchange has commercial substance.)

(LO 5) **BE10-11** Bubey Company traded a used truck for a new truck. The used truck cost $30,000 and has accumulated depreciation of $27,000. The new truck is worth $35,000. Bubey also made a cash payment of $33,000. Prepare Bubey's entry to record the exchange. (The exchange lacks commercial substance.)

(LO 5) **BE10-12** Buck Rogers Corporation traded a used truck for a new truck. The used truck cost $20,000 and has accumulated depreciation of $17,000. The new truck is worth $35,000. Rogers also made a cash payment of $33,000. Prepare Rogers' entry to record the exchange. (The exchange has commercial substance.)

(LO 6) **BE10-13** Indicate which of the following costs should be expensed when incurred.

   (a) $13,000 paid to rearrange and reinstall machinery.
   (b) $200 paid for tune-up and oil change on delivery truck.
   (c) $200,000 paid for addition to building.
   (d) $7,000 paid to replace a wooden floor with a concrete floor.
   (e) $2,000 paid for a major overhaul on a truck, which extends the useful life.

(LO 7) **BE10-14** Sim City Corporation owns machinery that cost $20,000 when purchased on January 1, 2004. Depreciation has been recorded at a rate of $3,000 per year, resulting in a balance in accumulated depreciation of $9,000 at December 31, 2006. The machinery is sold on September 1, 2007, for $10,500. Prepare journal entries to (a) update depreciation for 2007 and (b) record the sale.

(LO 7) **BE10-15** Use the information presented for Sim City Corporation in BE10-14, but assume the machinery is sold for $5,200 instead of $10,500. Prepare journal entries to (a) update depreciation for 2007 and (b) record the sale.

WILEY PLUS **EXERCISES**

(LO 2) **E10-1 (Acquisition Costs of Realty)** The following expenditures and receipts are related to land, land improvements, and buildings acquired for use in a business enterprise. The receipts are enclosed in parentheses.

(a)	Money borrowed to pay building contractor (signed a note) *other*	$(275,000)
(b)	Payment for construction from note proceeds *Buu*	275,000
(c)	Cost of land fill and clearing *land*	8,000
(d)	Delinquent real estate taxes on property assumed by purchaser *land*	7,000
(e)	Premium on 6-month insurance policy during construction *Buu*	6,000
(f)	Refund of 1-month insurance premium because construction completed early *Bul*	(1,000)
(g)	Architect's fee on building *Buil*	22,000
(h)	Cost of real estate purchased as a plant site (land $200,000 and building $50,000) *land*	250,000
(i)	Commission fee paid to real estate agency *land*	9,000
(j)	Installation of fences around property *land iml*	4,000

(k)	Cost of razing and removing building *land*	11,000
(l)	Proceeds from salvage of demolished building *land*	(5,000)
(m)	Interest paid during construction on money borrowed for construction *Build*	13,000
(n)	Cost of parking lots and driveways *impor*	19,000
(o)	Cost of trees and shrubbery planted (permanent in nature) *Land*	14,000
(p)	Excavation costs for new building *land Build*	3,000

Instructions

Identify each item by letter and list the items in columnar form, using the headings shown below. All receipt amounts should be reported in parentheses. For any amounts entered in the Other Accounts column also indicate the account title.

Item	Land	Land Improvements	Building	Other Accounts

(LO 2) E10-2 (Acquisition Costs of Realty) Martin Buber Co. purchased land as a factory site for $400,000. The process of tearing down two old buildings on the site and constructing the factory required 6 months.

The company paid $42,000 to raze the old buildings and sold salvaged lumber and brick for $6,300. Legal fees of $1,850 were paid for title investigation and drawing the purchase contract. Martin Buber paid $2,200 to an engineering firm for a land survey, and $68,000 for drawing the factory plans. The land survey had to be made before definitive plans could be drawn. Title insurance on the property cost $1,500, and a liability insurance premium paid during construction was $900. The contractor's charge for construction was $2,740,000. The company paid the contractor in two installments: $1,200,000 at the end of 3 months and $1,540,000 upon completion. Interest costs of $170,000 were incurred to finance the construction.

Instructions

Determine the cost of the land and the cost of the building as they should be recorded on the books of Martin Buber Co. Assume that the land survey was for the building.

(LO 2) E10-3   (Acquisition Costs of Trucks) Kelly Clarkson Corporation operates a retail computer store. To improve delivery services to customers, the company purchases four new trucks on April 1, 2007. The terms of acquisition for each truck are described below.

1. Truck #1 has a list price of $15,000 and is acquired for a cash payment of $13,900.
2. Truck #2 has a list price of $16,000 and is acquired for a down payment of $2,000 cash and a zero-interest-bearing note with a face amount of $14,000. The note is due April 1, 2008. Clarkson would normally have to pay interest at a rate of 10% for such a borrowing, and the dealership has an incremental borrowing rate of 8%.
3. Truck #3 has a list price of $16,000. It is acquired in exchange for a computer system that Clarkson carries in inventory. The computer system cost $12,000 and is normally sold by Clarkson for $15,200. Clarkson uses a perpetual inventory system.
4. Truck #4 has a list price of $14,000. It is acquired in exchange for 1,000 shares of common stock in Clarkson Corporation. The stock has a par value per share of $10 and a market value of $13 per share.

Instructions

Prepare the appropriate journal entries for the foregoing transactions for Clarkson Corporation.

(LO 2, 3) E10-4 (Purchase and Self-Constructed Cost of Assets) Worf Co. both purchases and constructs various equipment it uses in its operations. The following items for two different types of equipment were recorded in random order during the calendar year 2008.

Purchase

Cash paid for equipment, including sales tax of $5,000	$105,000
Freight and insurance cost while in transit	2,000
Cost of moving equipment into place at factory	3,100
Wage cost for technicians to test equipment	4,000
Insurance premium paid during first year of operation on this equipment	1,500
Special plumbing fixtures required for new equipment	8,000
Repair cost incurred in first year of operations related to this equipment	1,300

Construction

Material and purchased parts (gross cost $200,000; failed to take 2% cash discount)	$200,000
Imputed interest on funds used during construction (stock financing)	14,000
Labor costs	190,000
Allocated overhead costs (fixed—$20,000; variable—$30,000)	50,000
Profit on self-construction	30,000
Cost of installing equipment	4,400

Instructions

Compute the total cost for each of these two pieces of equipment. If an item is not capitalized as a cost of the equipment, indicate how it should be reported.

(LO 2, 3, 4) **E10-5 (Treatment of Various Costs)** Ben Sisko Supply Company, a newly formed corporation, incurred the following expenditures related to Land, to Buildings, and to Machinery and Equipment.

Abstract company's fee for title search		$ 520
Architect's fees		3,170
Cash paid for land and dilapidated building thereon		87,000
Removal of old building	$20,000	
Less: Salvage	5,500	14,500
Interest on short-term loans during construction		7,400
Excavation before construction for basement		19,000
Machinery purchased (subject to 2% cash discount, which was not taken)		55,000
Freight on machinery purchased		1,340
Storage charges on machinery, necessitated by noncompletion of building when machinery was delivered		2,180
New building constructed (building construction took 6 months from date of purchase of land and old building)		485,000
Assessment by city for drainage project		1,600
Hauling charges for delivery of machinery from storage to new building		620
Installation of machinery		2,000
Trees, shrubs, and other landscaping after completion of building (permanent in nature)		5,400

Instructions

Determine the amounts that should be debited to Land, to Buildings, and to Machinery and Equipment. Assume the benefits of capitalizing interest during construction exceed the cost of implementation. Indicate how any costs not debited to these accounts should be recorded.

(LO 3, 4) **E10-6 (Correction of Improper Cost Entries)** Plant acquisitions for selected companies are as follows.

1. Belanna Industries Inc. acquired land, buildings, and equipment from a bankrupt company, Torres Co., for a lump-sum price of $700,000. At the time of purchase, Torres's assets had the following book and appraisal values.

	Book Values	Appraisal Values
Land	$200,000	$150,000
Buildings	250,000	350,000
Equipment	300,000	300,000

To be conservative, the company decided to take the lower of the two values for each asset acquired. The following entry was made.

Land	150,000	
Buildings	250,000	
Equipment	300,000	
Cash		700,000

2. Harry Enterprises purchased store equipment by making a $2,000 cash down payment and signing a 1-year, $23,000, 10% note payable. The purchase was recorded as follows.

Store Equipment	27,300	
Cash		2,000
Note Payable		23,000
Interest Payable		2,300

3. Kim Company purchased office equipment for $20,000, terms 2/10, n/30. Because the company intended to take the discount, it made no entry until it paid for the acquisition. The entry was:

Office Equipment	20,000	
Cash		19,600
Purchase Discounts		400

4. Kaisson Inc. recently received at zero cost land from the Village of Cardassia as an inducement to locate its business in the Village. The appraised value of the land is $27,000. The company made no entry to record the land because it had no cost basis.

5. Zimmerman Company built a warehouse for $600,000. It could have purchased the building for $740,000. The controller made the following entry.

Warehouse	740,000	
Cash		600,000
Profit on Construction		140,000

Instructions

Prepare the entry that should have been made at the date of each acquisition.

(LO 4) **E10-7 (Capitalization of Interest)** Harrisburg Furniture Company started construction of a combination office and warehouse building for its own use at an estimated cost of $5,000,000 on January 1, 2007. Harrisburg expected to complete the building by December 31, 2007. Harrisburg has the following debt obligations outstanding during the construction period.

Construction loan—12% interest, payable semiannually, issued	
December 31, 2006	$2,000,000
Short-term loan—10% interest, payable monthly, and principal payable	
at maturity on May 30, 2008	1,400,000
Long-term loan—11% interest, payable on January 1 of each	
year. Principal payable on January 1, 2011	1,000,000

Instructions

(Carry all computations to two decimal places.)

   (a) Assume that Harrisburg completed the office and warehouse building on December 31, 2007, as planned at a total cost of $5,200,000, and the weighted average of accumulated expenditures was $3,600,000. Compute the avoidable interest on this project.

   (b) Compute the depreciation expense for the year ended December 31, 2008. Harrisburg elected to depreciate the building on a straight-line basis and determined that the asset has a useful life of 30 years and a salvage value of $300,000.

(LO 4) **E10-8 (Capitalization of Interest)** On December 31, 2006, Alma-Ata Inc. borrowed $3,000,000 at 12% payable annually to finance the construction of a new building. In 2007, the company made the following expenditures related to this building: March 1, $360,000; June 1, $600,000; July 1, $1,500,000; December 1, $1,500,000. Additional information is provided as follows.

   1. Other debt outstanding

10-year, 13% bond, December 31, 2000, interest payable annually	$4,000,000
6-year, 10% note, dated December 31, 2004, interest payable annually	$1,600,000

   2. March 1, 2007, expenditure included land costs of $150,000

   3. Interest revenue earned in 2007 $49,000

Instructions

   (a) Determine the amount of interest to be capitalized in 2007 in relation to the construction of the building.

   (b) Prepare the journal entry to record the capitalization of interest and the recognition of interest expense, if any, at December 31, 2007.

(LO 4) **E10-9 (Capitalization of Interest)** On July 31, 2007, Amsterdam Company engaged Minsk Tooling Company to construct a special-purpose piece of factory machinery. Construction was begun immediately and was completed on November 1, 2007. To help finance construction, on July 31 Amsterdam issued a $300,000, 3-year, 12% note payable at Netherlands National Bank, on which interest is payable each July 31. $200,000 of the proceeds of the note was paid to Minsk on July 31. The remainder of the proceeds was temporarily invested in short-term marketable securities (trading securities) at 10% until November 1. On November 1, Amsterdam made a final $100,000 payment to Minsk. Other than the note to Netherlands, Amsterdam's only outstanding liability at December 31, 2007, is a $30,000, 8%, 6-year note payable, dated January 1, 2004, on which interest is payable each December 31.

Instructions

   (a) Calculate the interest revenue, weighted-average accumulated expenditures, avoidable interest, and total interest cost to be capitalized during 2007. Round all computations to the nearest dollar.

   (b) Prepare the journal entries needed on the books of Amsterdam Company at each of the following dates.

      (1) July 31, 2007.

      (2) November 1, 2007.

      (3) December 31, 2007.

(LO 4)   **E10-10   (Capitalization of Interest)**   The following three situations involve the capitalization of interest.

Situation I

On January 1, 2007, Oksana Baiul, Inc. signed a fixed-price contract to have Builder Associates construct a major plant facility at a cost of $4,000,000. It was estimated that it would take 3 years to complete the project. Also on January 1, 2007, to finance the construction cost, Oksana Baiul borrowed $4,000,000 payable in 10 annual installments of $400,000, plus interest at the rate of 10%. During 2007, Oksana Baiul made deposit and progress payments totaling $1,500,000 under the contract; the weighted-average amount of accumulated expenditures was $800,000 for the year. The excess borrowed funds were invested in short-term securities, from which Oksana Baiul realized investment income of $250,000.

Instructions

What amount should Oksana Baiul report as capitalized interest at December 31, 2007?

Situation II

During 2007, Midori Ito Corporation constructed and manufactured certain assets and incurred the following interest costs in connection with those activities.

	Interest Costs Incurred
Warehouse constructed for Ito's own use	$30,000
Special-order machine for sale to unrelated customer, produced according to customer's specifications	9,000
Inventories routinely manufactured, produced on a repetitive basis	8,000

All of these assets required an extended period of time for completion.

Instructions

Assuming the effect of interest capitalization is material, what is the total amount of interest costs to be capitalized?

Situation III

Peggy Fleming, Inc. has a fiscal year ending April 30. On May 1, 2007, Peggy Fleming borrowed $10,000,000 at 11% to finance construction of its own building. Repayments of the loan are to commence the month following completion of the building. During the year ended April 30, 2008, expenditures for the partially completed structure totaled $7,000,000. These expenditures were incurred evenly throughout the year. Interest earned on the unexpended portion of the loan amounted to $650,000 for the year.

Instructions

How much should be shown as capitalized interest on Peggy Fleming's financial statements at April 30, 2008?

(CPA adapted)

(LO 2,   **E10-11   (Entries for Equipment Acquisitions)**   Jane Geddes Engineering Corporation purchased con-
3, 5)   veyor equipment with a list price of $10,000. Presented below are three independent cases related to the equipment. (Round to nearest dollar.)

   (a)   Geddes paid cash for the equipment 8 days after the purchase. The vendor's credit terms are 2/10, n/30. Assume that equipment purchases are recorded gross.

   (b)   Geddes traded in equipment with a book value of $2,000 (initial cost $8,000), and paid $9,500 in cash one month after the purchase. The old equipment could have been sold for $400 at the date of trade. (The exchange has commercial substance.)

   (c)   Geddes gave the vendor a $10,800 zero-interest-bearing note for the equipment on the date of purchase. The note was due in one year and was paid on time. Assume that the effective interest rate in the market was 9%.

Instructions

Prepare the general journal entries required to record the acquisition and payment in each of the independent cases above. Round to the nearest dollar.

(LO 2,   **E10-12   (Entries for Asset Acquisition, Including Self-Construction)**   Below are transactions related to
3, 5)   Fred Couples Company.

   (a)   The City of Pebble Beach gives the company 5 acres of land as a plant site. The market value of this land is determined to be $81,000.

   (b)   13,000 shares of common stock with a par value of $50 per share are issued in exchange for land and buildings. The property has been appraised at a fair market value of $810,000, of which $180,000 has been allocated to land and $630,000 to buildings. The stock of Fred Couples Company is not listed on any exchange, but a block of 100 shares was sold by a stockholder 12 months ago at $65 per share, and a block of 200 shares was sold by another stockholder 18 months ago at $58 per share.

(c) No entry has been made to remove from the accounts for Materials, Direct Labor, and Overhead the amounts properly chargeable to plant asset accounts for machinery constructed during the year. The following information is given relative to costs of the machinery constructed.

Materials used	$12,500
Factory supplies used	900
Direct labor incurred	15,000
Additional overhead (over regular) caused by construction of machinery, excluding factory supplies used	2,700
Fixed overhead rate applied to regular manufacturing operations	60% of direct labor cost
Cost of similar machinery if it had been purchased from outside suppliers	44,000

Instructions
Prepare journal entries on the books of Fred Couples Company to record these transactions.

(LO 2, 5) **E10-13 (Entries for Acquisition of Assets)** Presented below is information related to Zonker Company.

1. On July 6 Zonker Company acquired the plant assets of Doonesbury Company, which had discontinued operations. The appraised value of the property is:

Land	$ 400,000
Building	1,200,000
Machinery and equipment	800,000
Total	$2,400,000

Zonker Company gave 12,500 shares of its $100 par value common stock in exchange. The stock had a market value of $168 per share on the date of the purchase of the property.

2. Zonker Company expended the following amounts in cash between July 6 and December 15, the date when it first occupied the building.

Repairs to building	$105,000
Construction of bases for machinery to be installed later	135,000
Driveways and parking lots	122,000
Remodeling of office space in building, including new partitions and walls	161,000
Special assessment by city on land	18,000

3. On December 20, the company paid cash for machinery, $260,000, subject to a 2% cash discount, and freight on machinery of $10,500.

Instructions
Prepare entries on the books of Zonker Company for these transactions.

(LO 5) **E10-14 (Purchase of Equipment with Zero-Interest-Bearing Debt)** Chippewas Inc. has decided to purchase equipment from Central Michigan Industries on January 2, 2007, to expand its production capacity to meet customers' demand for its product. Chippewas issues an $800,000, 5-year, zero-interest-bearing note to Central Michigan for the new equipment when the prevailing market rate of interest for obligations of this nature is 12%. The company will pay off the note in five $160,000 installments due at the end of each year over the life of the note.

Instructions
(a) Prepare the journal entry(ies) at the date of purchase. (Round to nearest dollar in all computations.)
(b) Prepare the journal entry(ies) at the end of the first year to record the payment and interest, assuming that the company employs the effective-interest method.
(c) Prepare the journal entry(ies) at the end of the second year to record the payment and interest.
(d) Assuming that the equipment had a 10-year life and no salvage value, prepare the journal entry necessary to record depreciation in the first year. (Straight-line depreciation is employed.)

(LO 5) **E10-15 (Purchase of Computer with Zero-Interest-Bearing Debt)** Cardinals Corporation purchased a computer on December 31, 2006, for $105,000, paying $30,000 down and agreeing to pay the balance in five equal installments of $15,000 payable each December 31 beginning in 2007. An assumed interest rate of 10% is implicit in the purchase price.

Instructions

(a) Prepare the journal entry(ies) at the date of purchase. (Round to two decimal places.)

(b) Prepare the journal entry(ies) at December 31, 2007, to record the payment and interest (effective-interest method employed).

(c) Prepare the journal entry(ies) at December 31, 2008, to record the payment and interest (effective-interest method employed).

(LO 5) **E10-16** **(Asset Acquisition)** Hayes Industries purchased the following assets and constructed a building as well. All this was done during the current year.

Assets 1 and 2

These assets were purchased as a lump sum for $100,000 cash. The following information was gathered.

Description	Initial Cost on Seller's Books	Depreciation to Date on Seller's Books	Book Value on Seller's Books	Appraised Value
Machinery	$100,000	$50,000	$50,000	$90,000
Office equipment	60,000	10,000	50,000	30,000

Asset 3

This machine was acquired by making a $10,000 down payment and issuing a $30,000, 2-year, zero-interest-bearing note. The note is to be paid off in two $15,000 installments made at the end of the first and second years. It was estimated that the asset could have been purchased outright for $35,900.

Asset 4

This machinery was acquired by trading in used machinery. (The exchange lacks commercial substance.) Facts concerning the trade-in are as follows.

Cost of machinery traded	$100,000
Accumulated depreciation to date of sale	40,000
Fair market value of machinery traded	80,000
Cash received	10,000
Fair market value of machinery acquired	70,000

Asset 5

Office equipment was acquired by issuing 100 shares of $8 par value common stock. The stock had a market value of $11 per share.

Construction of Building

A building was constructed on land purchased last year at a cost of $150,000. Construction began on February 1 and was completed on November 1. The payments to the contractor were as follows.

Date	Payment
2/1	$120,000
6/1	360,000
9/1	480,000
11/1	100,000

To finance construction of the building, a $600,000, 12% construction loan was taken out on February 1. The loan was repaid on November 1. The firm had $200,000 of other outstanding debt during the year at a borrowing rate of 8%.

Instructions

Record the acquisition of each of these assets.

(LO 5) **E10-17** **(Nonmonetary Exchange)** Busytown Corporation, which manufactures shoes, hired a recent college graduate to work in its accounting department. On the first day of work, the accountant was assigned to total a batch of invoices with the use of an adding machine. Before long, the accountant, who had never before seen such a machine, managed to break the machine. Busytown Corporation gave the machine plus $340 to Dick Tracy Business Machine Company (dealer) in exchange for a new machine. Assume the following information about the machines.

	Busytown Corp. (Old Machine)	Dick Tracy Co. (New Machine)
Machine cost	$290	$270
Accumulated depreciation	140	–0–
Fair value	85	425

Instructions

For each company, prepare the necessary journal entry to record the exchange. (The exchange has commercial substance.)

(LO 5) **E10-18 (Nonmonetary Exchange)** Cannóndale Company purchased an electric wax melter on April 30, 2008, by trading in its old gas model and paying the balance in cash. The following data relate to the purchase.

List price of new melter	$15,800
Cash paid	10,000
Cost of old melter (5-year life, $700 residual value)	11,200
Accumulated depreciation—old melter (straight-line)	6,300
Second-hand market value of old melter	5,200

Instructions

Prepare the journal entry(ies) necessary to record this exchange, assuming that the exchange **(a)** has commercial substance, and **(b)** lacks commercial substance. Cannondale's fiscal year ends on December 31, and depreciation has been recorded through December 31, 2007.

(LO 5) **E10-19 (Nonmonetary Exchange)** Carlos Arruza Company exchanged equipment used in its manufacturing operations plus $3,000 in cash for similar equipment used in the operations of Tony LoBianco Company. The following information pertains to the exchange.

	Carlos Arruza Co.	Tony LoBianco Co.
Equipment (cost)	$28,000	$28,000
Accumulated depreciation	19,000	10,000
Fair value of equipment	12,500	15,500
Cash given up	3,000	

Instructions

(a) Prepare the journal entries to record the exchange on the books of both companies. Assume that the exchange lacks commercial substance.

(b) Prepare the journal entries to record the exchange on the books of both companies. Assume that the exchange has commercial substance.

(LO 5) **E10-20 (Nonmonetary Exchange)** Dana Ashbrook Inc. has negotiated the purchase of a new piece of automatic equipment at a price of $8,000 plus trade-in, f.o.b. factory. Dana Ashbrook Inc. paid $8,000 cash and traded in used equipment. The used equipment had originally cost $62,000; it had a book value of $42,000 and a secondhand market value of $47,800, as indicated by recent transactions involving similar equipment. Freight and installation charges for the new equipment required a cash payment of $1,100.

Instructions

(a) Prepare the general journal entry to record this transaction, assuming that the exchange has commercial substance.

(b) Assuming the same facts as in (a) except that fair value information for the assets exchanged is not determinable. Prepare the general journal entry to record this transaction.

(LO 6) **E10-21 (Analysis of Subsequent Expenditures)** King Donovan Resources Group has been in its plant facility for 15 years. Although the plant is quite functional, numerous repair costs are incurred to maintain it in sound working order. The company's plant asset book value is currently $800,000, as indicated below.

Original cost	$1,200,000
Accumulated depreciation	400,000
Book value	$ 800,000

During the current year, the following expenditures were made to the plant facility.

(a) Because of increased demands for its product, the company increased its plant capacity by building a new addition at a cost of $270,000.

(b) The entire plant was repainted at a cost of $23,000.

(c) The roof was an asbestos cement slate. For safety purposes it was removed and replaced with a wood shingle roof at a cost of $61,000. Book value of the old roof was $41,000.

(d) The electrical system was completely updated at a cost of $22,000. The cost of the old electrical system was not known. It is estimated that the useful life of the building will not change as a result of this updating.

(e) A series of major repairs were made at a cost of $47,000, because parts of the wood structure were rotting. The cost of the old wood structure was not known. These extensive repairs are estimated to increase the useful life of the building.

Instructions

Indicate how each of these transactions would be recorded in the accounting records.

(LO 6) **E10-22 (Analysis of Subsequent Expenditures)** The following transactions occurred during 2008. Assume that depreciation of 10% per year is charged on all machinery and 5% per year on buildings, on a straight-line basis, with no estimated salvage value. Depreciation is charged for a full year on all fixed assets acquired during the year, and no depreciation is charged on fixed assets disposed of during the year.

Jan. 30 A building that cost $132,000 in 1991 is torn down to make room for a new building. The wrecking contractor was paid $5,100 and was permitted to keep all materials salvaged.

Mar. 10 Machinery that was purchased in 2001 for $16,000 is sold for $2,900 cash, f.o.b. purchaser's plant. Freight of $300 is paid on the sale of this machinery.

Mar. 20 A gear breaks on a machine that cost $9,000 in 2003. The gear is replaced at a cost of $8,000. The replacement does not extend the useful life of the machine.

May 18 A special base installed for a machine in 2002 when the machine was purchased has to be replaced at a cost of $5,500 because of defective workmanship on the original base. The cost of the machinery was $14,200 in 2002. The cost of the base was $3,500, and this amount was charged to the Machinery account in 2002.

June 23 One of the buildings is repainted at a cost of $6,900. It had not been painted since it was constructed in 2004.

Instructions

Prepare general journal entries for the transactions. (Round to the nearest dollar.)

(LO 6) **E10-23 (Analysis of Subsequent Expenditures)** Plant assets often require expenditures subsequent to acquisition. It is important that they be accounted for properly. Any errors will affect both the balance sheets and income statements for a number of years.

Instructions

For each of the following items, indicate whether the expenditure should be capitalized (C) or expensed (E) in the period incurred.

(a) _____ Improvement.

(b) _____ Replacement of a minor broken part on a machine.

(c) _____ Expenditure that increases the useful life of an existing asset.

(d) _____ Expenditure that increases the efficiency and effectiveness of a productive asset but does not increase its salvage value.

(e) _____ Expenditure that increases the efficiency and effectiveness of a productive asset and increases the asset's salvage value.

(f) _____ Expenditure that increases the quality of the output of the productive asset.

(g) _____ Improvement to a machine that increased its fair market value and its production capacity by 30% without extending the machine's useful life.

(h) _____ Ordinary repairs.

(LO 6) **E10-24 (Entries for Disposition of Assets)** On December 31, 2007, Travis Tritt Inc. has a machine with a book value of $940,000. The original cost and related accumulated depreciation at this date are as follows.

Machine	$1,300,000
Accumulated depreciation	360,000
Book value	$ 940,000

Depreciation is computed at $60,000 per year on a straight-line basis.

Instructions

Presented below is a set of independent situations. For each independent situation, indicate the journal entry to be made to record the transaction. Make sure that depreciation entries are made to update the book value of the machine prior to its disposal.

(a) A fire completely destroys the machine on August 31, 2008. An insurance settlement of $430,000 was received for this casualty. Assume the settlement was received immediately.

(b) On April 1, 2008, Tritt sold the machine for $1,040,000 to Dwight Yoakam Company.

(c) On July 31, 2008, the company donated this machine to the Mountain King City Council. The fair market value of the machine at the time of the donation was estimated to be $1,100,000.

(LO 7) **E10-25 (Disposition of Assets)** On April 1, 2007, Gloria Estefan Company received a condemnation award of $430,000 cash as compensation for the forced sale of the company's land and building, which stood in the path of a new state highway. The land and building cost $60,000 and $280,000, respectively, when they were acquired. At April 1, 2007, the accumulated depreciation relating to the building amounted to $160,000. On August 1, 2007, Estafan purchased a piece of replacement property for cash. The new land cost $90,000, and the new building cost $400,000.

Instructions

Prepare the journal entries to record the transactions on April 1 and August 1, 2007.

See the book's website, www.wiley.com/college/kieso, for Additional Exercises.

PROBLEMS

(LO 2) **P10-1** **(Classification of Acquisition and Other Asset Costs)** At December 31, 2006, certain accounts included in the property, plant, and equipment section of Craig Ehlo Company's balance sheet had the following balances.

Land	$230,000
Buildings	890,000
Leasehold improvements	660,000
Machinery and equipment	875,000

During 2007 the following transactions occurred.

1. Land site number 621 was acquired for $850,000. In addition, to acquire the land Ehlo paid a $51,000 commission to a real estate agent. Costs of $35,000 were incurred to clear the land. During the course of clearing the land, timber and gravel were recovered and sold for $13,000.

2. A second tract of land (site number 622) with a building was acquired for $420,000. The closing statement indicated that the land value was $300,000 and the building value was $120,000. Shortly after acquisition, the building was demolished at a cost of $41,000. A new building was constructed for $330,000 plus the following costs.

Excavation fees	$38,000
Architectural design fees	11,000
Building permit fee	2,500
Imputed interest on funds used during construction (stock financing)	8,500

The building was completed and occupied on September 30, 2007.

3. A third tract of land (site number 623) was acquired for $650,000 and was put on the market for resale.

4. During December 2007 costs of $89,000 were incurred to improve leased office space. The related lease will terminate on December 31, 2009, and is not expected to be renewed. (*Hint:* Leasehold improvements should be handled in the same manner as land improvements.)

5. A group of new machines was purchased under a royalty agreement that provides for payment of royalties based on units of production for the machines. The invoice price of the machines was $87,000, freight costs were $3,300, installation costs were $2,400, and royalty payments for 2007 were $17,500.

Instructions

(a) Prepare a detailed analysis of the changes in each of the following balance sheet accounts for 2007.

Land	Leasehold improvements
Buildings	Machinery and equipment

Disregard the related accumulated depreciation accounts.

(b) List the items in the situation that were not used to determine the answer to (a) above, and indicate where, or if, these items should be included in Ehlo's financial statements.

(AICPA adapted)

(LO 2, 7) **P10-2** **(Classification of Acquisition Costs)** Selected accounts included in the property, plant, and equipment section of Spud Webb Corporation's balance sheet at December 31, 2006, had the following balances.

Land	$ 300,000
Land improvements	140,000
Buildings	1,100,000
Machinery and equipment	960,000

During 2007 the following transactions occurred.

1. A tract of land was acquired for $150,000 as a potential future building site.
2. A plant facility consisting of land and building was acquired from Ken Norman Company in exchange for 20,000 shares of Webb's common stock. On the acquisition date, Webb's stock had a closing market price of $37 per share on a national stock exchange. The plant facility was carried on Norman's books at $110,000 for land and $320,000 for the building at the exchange date. Current appraised values for the land and building, respectively, are $230,000 and $690,000.
3. Items of machinery and equipment were purchased at a total cost of $400,000. Additional costs were incurred as follows.

Freight and unloading	$13,000
Sales taxes	20,000
Installation	26,000

4. Expenditures totaling $95,000 were made for new parking lots, streets, and sidewalks at the corporation's various plant locations. These expenditures had an estimated useful life of 15 years.
5. A machine costing $80,000 on January 1, 1999, was scrapped on June 30, 2007. Double-declining-balance depreciation has been recorded on the basis of a 10-year life.
6. A machine was sold for $20,000 on July 1, 2007. Original cost of the machine was $44,000 on January 1, 2004, and it was depreciated on the straight-line basis over an estimated useful life of 7 years and a salvage value of $2,000.

Instructions

(a) Prepare a detailed analysis of the changes in each of the following balance sheet accounts for 2007.

　　　Land
　　　Land improvements
　　　Buildings
　　　Machinery and equipment

(*Hint:* Disregard the related accumulated depreciation accounts.)

(b) List the items in the fact situation that were not used to determine the answer to (a), showing the pertinent amounts and supporting computations in good form for each item. In addition, indicate where, or if, these items should be included in Spud Webb's financial statements.

(AICPA adapted)

(LO 2, 3, 5) **P10-3 (Classification of Land and Building Costs)** Lenny Wilkins Company was incorporated on January 2, 2008, but was unable to begin manufacturing activities until July 1, 2008, because new factory facilities were not completed until that date.

The Land and Building account reported the following items during 2008.

January 31	Land and building	$160,000
February 28	Cost of removal of building	9,800
May 1	Partial payment of new construction	60,000
May 1	Legal fees paid	3,770
June 1	Second payment on new construction	40,000
June 1	Insurance premium	2,280
June 1	Special tax assessment	4,000
June 30	General expenses	36,300
July 1	Final payment on new construction	40,000
December 31	Asset write-up	43,800
		399,950
December 31	Depreciation—2008 at 1%	4,000
December 31, 2008	Account balance	$395,950

The following additional information is to be considered.

1. To acquire land and building the company paid $80,000 cash and 800 shares of its 8% cumulative preferred stock, par value $100 per share. Fair market value of the stock is $107 per share.
2. Cost of removal of old buildings amounted to $9,800, and the demolition company retained all materials of the building.
3. Legal fees covered the following.

Cost of organization	$ 610
Examination of title covering purchase of land	1,300
Legal work in connection with construction contract	1,860
	$3,770

4. Insurance premium covered the building for a 2-year term beginning May 1, 2008.
5. The special tax assessment covered street improvements that are permanent in nature.
6. General expenses covered the following for the period from January 2, 2008, to June 30, 2008.

President's salary	$32,100
Plant superintendent covering supervision of new building	4,200
	$36,300

7. Because of a general increase in construction costs after entering into the building contract, the board of directors increased the value of the building $43,800, believing that such an increase was justified to reflect the current market at the time the building was completed. Retained earnings was credited for this amount.
8. Estimated life of building—50 years.
   Depreciation for 2008—1% of asset value (1% of $400,000, or $4,000).

Instructions

(a) Prepare entries to reflect correct land, building, and depreciation accounts at December 31, 2008.
(b) Show the proper presentation of land, building, and depreciation on the balance sheet at December 31, 2008.

(AICPA adapted)

(LO 2, 5, 7) **P10-4 (Dispositions, Including Condemnation, Demolition, and Trade-in)** Presented below is a schedule of property dispositions for Frank Thomas Co.

	Cost	Accumulated Depreciation	Cash Proceeds	Fair Market Value	Nature of Disposition
		Schedule of Property Dispositions			
Land	$40,000	—	$31,000	$31,000	Condemnation
Building	15,000	—	3,600	—	Demolition
Warehouse	70,000	$11,000	74,000	74,000	Destruction by fire
Machine	8,000	3,200	900	7,200	Trade-in
Furniture	10,000	7,850	—	3,100	Contribution
Automobile	8,000	3,460	2,960	2,960	Sale

The following additional information is available.

Land
On February 15, a condemnation award was received as consideration for unimproved land held primarily as an investment, and on March 31, another parcel of unimproved land to be held as an investment was purchased at a cost of $35,000.

Building
On April 2, land and building were purchased at a total cost of $75,000, of which 20% was allocated to the building on the corporate books. The real estate was acquired with the intention of demolishing the building, and this was accomplished during the month of November. Cash proceeds received in November represent the net proceeds from demolition of the building.

Warehouse
On June 30, the warehouse was destroyed by fire. The warehouse was purchased January 2, 2004, and had depreciated $11,000. On December 27, the insurance proceeds and other funds were used to purchase a replacement warehouse at a cost of $90,000.

Machine
On December 26, the machine was exchanged for another machine having a fair market value of $6,300 and cash of $900 was received. (The exchange lacks commercial substance.)

Furniture
On August 15, furniture was contributed to a qualified charitable organization. No other contributions were made or pledged during the year.

Automobile
On November 3, the automobile was sold to Ozzie Guillen, a stockholder.

Instructions
Indicate how these items would be reported on the income statement of Frank Thomas Co.

(AICPA adapted)

(LO 2,
4)

P10-5 (Classification of Costs and Interest Capitalization) On January 1, 2007, George Solti Corporation purchased for $600,000 a tract of land (site number 101) with a building. Solti paid a real estate broker's commission of $36,000, legal fees of $6,000, and title guarantee insurance of $18,000. The closing statement indicated that the land value was $500,000 and the building value was $100,000. Shortly after acquisition, the building was razed at a cost of $54,000.

Solti entered into a $3,000,000 fixed-price contract with Slatkin Builders, Inc. on March 1, 2007, for the construction of an office building on land site number 101. The building was completed and occupied on September 30, 2008. Additional construction costs were incurred as follows.

Plans, specifications, and blueprints	$21,000
Architects' fees for design and supervision	82,000

The building is estimated to have a 40-year life from date of completion and will be depreciated using the 150% declining balance method.

To finance construction costs, Solti borrowed $3,000,000 on March 1, 2007. The loan is payable in 10 annual installments of $300,000 plus interest at the rate of 10%. Solti's weighted-average amounts of accumulated building construction expenditures were as follows.

For the period March 1 to December 31, 2007	$1,200,000
For the period January 1 to September 30, 2008	1,900,000

Instructions

(a) Prepare a schedule that discloses the individual costs making up the balance in the land account in respect of land site number 101 as of September 30, 2008.

(b) Prepare a schedule that discloses the individual costs that should be capitalized in the office building account as of September 30, 2008. Show supporting computations in good form.

(AICPA adapted)

(LO 2,
4)

P10-6 (Interest During Construction) Jerry Landscaping began construction of a new plant on December 1, 2005. On this date the company purchased a parcel of land for $142,000 in cash. In addition, it paid $2,000 in surveying costs and $4,000 for a title insurance policy. An old dwelling on the premises was demolished at a cost of $3,000, with $1,000 being received from the sale of materials.

Architectural plans were also formalized on December 1, 2005, when the architect was paid $30,000. The necessary building permits costing $3,000 were obtained from the city and paid for on December 1 as well. The excavation work began during the first week in December with payments made to the contractor as follows.

Date of Payment	Amount of Payment
March 1	$240,000
May 1	360,000
July 1	60,000

The building was completed on July 1, 2006.

To finance construction of this plant, Jerry borrowed $600,000 from the bank on December 1, 2005. Jerry had no other borrowings. The $600,000 was a 10-year loan bearing interest at 8%.

Instructions

Compute the balance in each of the following accounts at December 31, 2005, and December 31, 2006.

(a) Land.
(b) Buildings.
(c) Interest Expense.

(LO 4)

P10-7 (Capitalization of Interest) Wordcrafters Inc. is a book distributor that had been operating in its original facility since 1982. The increase in certification programs and continuing education requirements in several professions has contributed to an annual growth rate of 15% for Wordcrafters since 2002. Wordcrafters' original facility became obsolete by early 2007 because of the increased sales volume and the fact that Wordcrafters now carries tapes and disks in addition to books.

On June 1, 2007, Wordcrafters contracted with Favre Construction to have a new building constructed for $4,000,000 on land owned by Wordcrafters. The payments made by Wordcrafters to Favre Construction are shown in the schedule below.

Date	Amount
July 30, 2007	$1,200,000
January 30, 2008	1,500,000
May 30, 2008	1,300,000
Total payments	$4,000,000

Construction was completed and the building was ready for occupancy on May 27, 2008. Wordcrafters had no new borrowings directly associated with the new building but had the following debt outstanding at May 31, 2008, the end of its fiscal year.

14½%, 5-year note payable of $2,000,000, dated April 1, 2004, with interest payable annually on April 1.

12%, 10-year bond issue of $3,000,000 sold at par on June 30, 2000, with interest payable annually on June 30.

The new building qualifies for interest capitalization. The effect of capitalizing the interest on the new building, compared with the effect of expensing the interest, is material.

Instructions

(a) Compute the weighted average accumulated expenditures on Wordcrafters' new building during the capitalization period.

(b) Compute the avoidable interest on Wordcrafters' new building.

(c) Some interest cost of Wordcrafters Inc. is capitalized for the year ended May 31, 2008.

(1) Identify the items relating to interest costs that must be disclosed in Wordcrafters' financial statements.

(2) Compute the amount of each of the items that must be disclosed.

(CMA adapted)

(LO 4) **P10-8** **(Nonmonetary Exchanges)** Susquehanna Corporation wishes to exchange a machine used in its operations. Susquehanna has received the following offers from other companies in the industry.

1. Choctaw Company offered to exchange a similar machine plus $23,000. (The exchange has commercial substance for both parties.)

2. Powhatan Company offered to exchange a similar machine. (The exchange lacks commercial substance for both parties.)

3. Shawnee Company offered to exchange a similar machine, but wanted $8,000 in addition to Susquehanna's machine. (The exchange has commercial substance for both parties.)

In addition, Susquehanna contacted Seminole Corporation, a dealer in machines. To obtain a new machine, Susquehanna must pay $93,000 in addition to trading in its old machine.

	Susquehanna	Choctaw	Powhatan	Shawnee	Seminole
Machine cost	$160,000	$120,000	$147,000	$160,000	$130,000
Accumulated depreciation	50,000	45,000	71,000	75,000	–0–
Fair value	92,000	69,000	92,000	100,000	185,000

Instructions

For each of the four independent situations, prepare the journal entries to record the exchange on the books of each company. (Round to nearest dollar.)

(LO 4) **P10-9** **(Nonmonetary Exchanges)** On August 1, Arna, Inc. exchanged productive assets with Bontemps, Inc. Arna's asset is referred to below as "Asset A," and Bontemps' is referred to as "Asset B." The following facts pertain to these assets.

	Asset A	Asset B
Original cost	$96,000	$110,000
Accumulated depreciation (to date of exchange)	45,000	52,000
Fair market value at date of exchange	60,000	75,000
Cash paid by Arna, Inc.	15,000	
Cash received by Bontemps, Inc.		15,000

Instructions

(a) Assuming that the exchange of Assets A and B has commercial substance, record the exchange for both Arna, Inc. and Bontemps, Inc. in accordance with generally accepted accounting principles.

(b) Assuming that the exchange of Assets A and B lacks commercial substance, record the exchange for both Arna, Inc. and Bontemps, Inc. in accordance with generally accepted accounting principles.

(LO 4) **P10-10** **(Nonmonetary Exchanges)** During the current year, Garrison Construction trades an old crane that has a book value of $80,000 (original cost $140,000 less accumulated depreciation $60,000) for a new crane from Keillor Manufacturing Co. The new crane cost Keillor $165,000 to manufacture and is classified as inventory. The following information is also available.

	Garrison Const.	Keillor Mfg. Co.
Fair market value of old crane	$ 72,000	
Fair market value of new crane		$190,000
Cash paid	118,000	
Cash received		118,000

Instructions

  (a) Assuming that this exchange is considered to have commercial substance, prepare the journal entries on the books of (1) Garrison Construction and (2) Keillor Manufacturing.

  (b) Assuming that this exchange lacks commercial substance for Garrison, prepare the journal entries on the books of Garrison Construction.

  (c) Assuming the same facts as those in (a), except that the fair market value of the old crane is $98,000 and the cash paid is $92,000, prepare the journal entries on the books of (1) Garrison Construction and (2) Keillor Manufacturing.

  (d) Assuming the same facts as those in (b), except that the fair market value of the old crane is $87,000 and the cash paid $103,000, prepare the journal entries on the books of (1) Garrison Construction and (2) Keillor Manufacturing.

(LO 2, 4, 7) **P10-11 (Purchases by Deferred Payment, Lump-sum, and Nonmonetary Exchanges)** Kent Adamson Company, a manufacturer of ballet shoes, is experiencing a period of sustained growth. In an effort to expand its production capacity to meet the increased demand for its product, the company recently made several acquisitions of plant and equipment. Tod Mullinger, newly hired in the position of fixed-asset accountant, requested that Watt Kaster, Adamson's controller, review the following transactions.

Transaction 1

On June 1, 2007, Adamson Company purchased equipment from Venghaus Corporation. Adamson issued a $20,000, 4-year, zero-interest-bearing note to Venghaus for the new equipment. Adamson will pay off the note in four equal installments due at the end of each of the next 4 years. At the date of the transaction, the prevailing market rate of interest for obligations of this nature was 10%. Freight costs of $425 and installation costs of $500 were incurred in completing this transaction. The appropriate factors for the time value of money at a 10% rate of interest are given below.

Future value of $1 for 4 periods	1.46
Future value of an ordinary annuity for 4 periods	4.64
Present value of $1 for 4 periods	0.68
Present value of an ordinary annuity for 4 periods	3.17

Transaction 2

On December 1, 2007, Adamson Company purchased several assets of Haukap Shoes Inc., a small shoe manufacturer whose owner was retiring. The purchase amounted to $210,000 and included the assets listed below. Adamson Company engaged the services of Tennyson Appraisal Inc., an independent appraiser, to determine the fair market values of the assets which are also presented below.

	Haukap Book Value	Fair Market Value
Inventory	$ 60,000	$ 50,000
Land	40,000	80,000
Building	70,000	120,000
	$170,000	$250,000

During its fiscal year ended May 31, 2008, Adamson incurred $8,000 for interest expense in connection with the financing of these assets.

Transaction 3

On March 1, 2005, Adamson Company exchanged a number of used trucks plus cash for vacant land adjacent to its plant site. (The exchange has commercial substance.) Adamson intends to use the land for a parking lot. The trucks had a combined book value of $35,000, as Adamson had recorded $20,000 of accumulated depreciation against these assets. Adamson's purchasing agent, who has had previous dealings in the second-hand market, indicated that the trucks had a fair market value of $46,000 at the time of the transaction. In addition to the trucks, Adamson Company paid $19,000 cash for the land.

Instructions

  (a) Plant assets such as land, buildings, and equipment receive special accounting treatment. Describe the major characteristics of these assets that differentiate them from other types of assets.

  (b) For each of the three transactions described above, determine the value at which Adamson Company should record the acquired assets. Support your calculations with an explanation of the underlying rationale.

  (c) The books of Adamson Company show the following additional transactions for the fiscal year ended May 31, 2008.

    (1) Acquisition of a building for speculative purposes.

    (2) Purchase of a 2-year insurance policy covering plant equipment.

    (3) Purchase of the rights for the exclusive use of a process used in the manufacture of ballet shoes.

For each of these transactions, indicate whether the asset should be classified as a plant asset. If it is a plant asset, explain why it is. If it is not a plant asset, explain why not, and identify the proper classification.

(CMA adapted)

CONCEPTS FOR ANALYSIS

CA10-1 (Acquisition, Improvements, and Sale of Realty) William Bradford Company purchased land for use as its corporate headquarters. A small factory that was on the land when it was purchased was torn down before construction of the office building began. Furthermore, a substantial amount of rock blasting and removal had to be done to the site before construction of the building foundation began. Because the office building was set back on the land far from the public road, Bradford Company had the contractor construct a paved road that led from the public road to the parking lot of the office building.

Three years after the office building was occupied, Bradford Company added four stories to the office building. The four stories had an estimated useful life of 5 years more than the remaining estimated useful life of the original office building.

Ten years later the land and building were sold at an amount more than their net book value, and Bradford Company had a new office building constructed in another state for use as its new corporate headquarters.

Instructions
  (a) Which of the expenditures above should be capitalized? How should each be depreciated or amortized? Discuss the rationale for your answers.
  (b) How would the sale of the land and building be accounted for? Include in your answer an explanation of how to determine the net book value at the date of sale. Discuss the rationale for your answer.

CA10-2 (Accounting for Self-Constructed Assets) Shanette Medical Labs, Inc., began operations 5 years ago producing stetrics, a new type of instrument it hoped to sell to doctors, dentists, and hospitals. The demand for stetrics far exceeded initial expectations, and the company was unable to produce enough stetrics to meet demand.

The company was manufacturing its product on equipment that it built at the start of its operations. To meet demand, more efficient equipment was needed. The company decided to design and build the equipment, because the equipment currently available on the market was unsuitable for producing stetrics.

In 2007, a section of the plant was devoted to development of the new equipment and a special staff was hired. Within 6 months a machine developed at a cost of $714,000 increased production dramatically and reduced labor costs substantially. Elated by the success of the new machine, the company built three more machines of the same type at a cost of $441,000 each.

Instructions
  (a) In general, what costs should be capitalized for self-constructed equipment?
  (b) Discuss the propriety of including in the capitalized cost of self-constructed assets:
    (1) The increase in overhead caused by the self-construction of fixed assets.
    (2) A proportionate share of overhead on the same basis as that applied to goods manufactured for sale.
  (c) Discuss the proper accounting treatment of the $273,000 ($714,000 − $441,000) by which the cost of the first machine exceeded the cost of the subsequent machines. This additional cost should not be considered research and development costs.

CA10-3 (Capitalization of Interest) Zucker Airline is converting from piston-type planes to jets. Delivery time for the jets is 3 years, during which substantial progress payments must be made. The multi-million-dollar cost of the planes cannot be financed from working capital; Zucker must borrow funds for the payments.

Because of high interest rates and the large sum to be borrowed, management estimates that interest costs in the second year of the period will be equal to one-third of income before interest and taxes, and one-half of such income in the third year.

After conversion, Zucker's passenger-carrying capacity will be doubled with no increase in the number of planes, although the investment in planes would be substantially increased. The jet planes have a 7-year service life.

Instructions

Give your recommendation concerning the proper accounting for interest during the conversion period. Support your recommendation with reasons and suggested accounting treatment. (Disregard income tax implications.)

(AICPA adapted)

 **CA10-4** **(Capitalization of Interest)** Petri Magazine Company started construction of a warehouse building for its own use at an estimated cost of $6,000,000 on January 1, 2005, and completed the building on December 31, 2005. During the construction period, Petri has the following debt obligations outstanding.

Construction loan—12% interest, payable semiannually, issued December 31, 2004	$2,000,000
Short-term loan—10% interest, payable monthly, and principal payable at maturity, on May 30, 2006	1,400,000
Long-term loan—11% interest, payable on January 1 of each year. Principal payable on January 1, 2008	2,000,000

Total cost amounted to $6,200,000, and the weighted average of accumulated expenditures was $4,000,000.

Dee Pettepiece, the president of the company, has been shown the costs associated with this construction project and capitalized on the balance sheet. She is bothered by the "avoidable interest" included in the cost. She argues that, first, all the interest is unavoidable—no one lends money without expecting to be compensated for it. Second, why can't the company use all the interest on all the loans when computing this avoidable interest? Finally, why can't her company capitalize all the annual interest that accrued over the period of construction?

Instructions

You are the manager of accounting for the company. In a memo, explain what avoidable interest is, how you computed it (being especially careful to explain why you used the interest rates that you did), and why the company cannot capitalize all its interest for the year. Attach a schedule supporting any computations that you use.

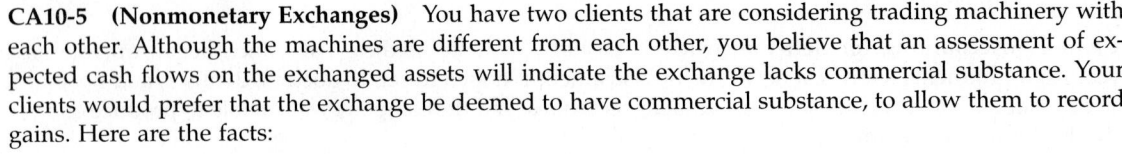 **CA10-5** **(Nonmonetary Exchanges)** You have two clients that are considering trading machinery with each other. Although the machines are different from each other, you believe that an assessment of expected cash flows on the exchanged assets will indicate the exchange lacks commercial substance. Your clients would prefer that the exchange be deemed to have commercial substance, to allow them to record gains. Here are the facts:

	Client A	Client B
Original cost	$100,000	$150,000
Accumulated depreciation	40,000	80,000
Market value	95,000	125,000
Cash received (paid)	(30,000)	30,000

Instructions

(a) Record the trade-in on Client A's books assuming the exchange has commercial substance.
(b) Record the trade-in on Client A's books assuming the exchange lacks commercial substance.
(c) Write a memo to the controller of Company A indicating and explaining the dollar impact on current and future statements of treating the exchange as having versus lacking commercial substance.
(d) Record the entry on Client B's books assuming the exchange has commercial substance.
(e) Record the entry on Client B's books assuming the exchange lacks commercial substance.
(f) Write a memo to the controller of Company B indicating and explaining the dollar impact on current and future statements of treating the exchange as having versus lacking commercial substance.

CA10-6 **(Costs of Acquisition)** The invoice price of a machine is $40,000. Various other costs relating to the acquisition and installation of the machine including transportation, electrical wiring, special base, and so on amount to $7,500. The machine has an estimated life of 10 years, with no residual value at the end of that period.

The owner of the business suggests that the incidental costs of $7,500 be charged to expense immediately for the following reasons.

1. If the machine should be sold, these costs cannot be recovered in the sales price.
2. The inclusion of the $7,500 in the machinery account on the books will not necessarily result in a closer approximation of the market price of this asset over the years, because of the possibility of changing demand and supply levels.
3. Charging the $7,500 to expense immediately will reduce federal income taxes.

Instructions

Discuss each of the points raised by the owner of the business.

(AICPA adapted)

CA10-7 (Cost of Land vs. Building) Field Company purchased a warehouse in a downtown district where land values are rapidly increasing. Adolph Phillips, controller, and Wilma Smith, financial vice-president, are trying to allocate the cost of the purchase between the land and the building. Noting that depreciation can be taken only on the building, Phillips favors placing a very high proportion of the cost on the warehouse itself, thus reducing taxable income and income taxes. Smith, his supervisor, argues that the allocation should recognize the increasing value of the land, regardless of the depreciation potential of the warehouse. Besides, she says, net income is negatively impacted by additional depreciation and will cause the company's stock price to go down.

Instructions

Answer the following questions.

(a) What stakeholder interests are in conflict?
(b) What ethical issues does Phillips face?
(c) How should these costs be allocated?

USING YOUR JUDGMENT

Financial Statement Analysis Case

Johnson & Johnson

Johnson & Johnson, the world's leading and most diversified health-care corporation, serves its customers through specialized worldwide franchises. Each of its franchises consists of a number of companies throughout the world that focus on a particular health care market, such as surgical sutures, consumer pharmaceuticals, or contact lenses. Information related to its property, plant, and equipment in its 2004 annual report is shown in the notes to the financial statements as follows.

Johnson & Johnson

Note 1: Property, Plant, and Equipment and Depreciation

Property, plant, and equipment are stated at cost. The Company utilizes the straight-line method of depreciation over the estimated useful lives of the assets:

Building and building equipment	20–40 years
Land and leasehold improvements	10–20 years
Machinery and equipment	2–13 years

Note 3: Property, Plant, and Equipment

At the end of 2004 and 2003, property, plant, and equipment at cost and accumulated depreciation were:

(dollars in millions)	2004	2003
Land and land improvements	$ 515	$ 491
Buildings and building equipment	5,907	5,242
Machinery and equipment	10,155	9,638
Construction in progress	1,787	1,681
	18,664	17,052
Less: Accumulated depreciation	8,228	7,206
	$10,436	$ 9,846

The Company capitalizes interest expense as part of the cost of construction of facilities and equipment. Interest expense capitalized in 2004, 2003, and 2002 was $136 million, $108 million, and $98 million, respectively.

Upon retirement or other disposal of fixed assets, the cost and related amount of accumulated depreciation or amortization are eliminated from the asset and accumulated depreciation accounts, respectively. The difference, if any, between the net asset value and the proceeds is recorded in earnings.

Johnson & Johnson's provided the following selected information in its 2004 cash flow statement.

Johnson&Johnson

Johnson & Johnson
2004 Annual Report
Consolidated Financial Statements (excerpts)

Net cash flows from operating activities	$11,131
Cash flows from investing activities	
Additions to property, plant and equipment	(2,175)
Proceeds from the disposal of assets	237
Acquisition of businesses, net of cash acquired (Note 17)	(580)
Purchases of investments	(11,617)
Sales of investments	12,061
Other	(273)
Net cash used by investing activities	(2,347)
Cash flows from financing activities	
Dividends to shareowners	(3,251)
Repurchase of common stock	(1,384)
Proceeds from short-term debt	514
Retirement of short-term debt	(1,291)
Proceeds from long-term debt	17
Retirement of long-term debt	(395)
Proceeds from the exercise of stock options	642
Net cash used by financing activities	(5,148)
Effect of exchange rate changes on cash and cash equivalents	190
(Decrease)/increase in cash and cash equivalents	3,826
Cash and cash equivalents, beginning of year (Note 1)	5,377
Cash and cash equivalents, end of year (Note 1)	$ 9,203
Supplemental cash flow data	
Cash paid during the year for:	
Interest	$ 222
Income taxes	3,880

Instructions

(a) What was the cost of buildings and building equipment at the end of 2004?

(b) Does Johnson & Johnson use a conservative or liberal method to depreciate its property, plant, and equipment?

(c) What was the actual interest expense incurred by the company in 2004?

(d) What is Johnson & Johnson's free cash flow? From the information provided, comment on Johnson & Johnson's financial flexibility.

Research Case

The March 26, 2002, *Wall Street Journal* includes an article by Henny Sender titled "Telecoms Draw Focus for Moves in Accounting."

Instructions

Read the article and answer the following questions.

(a) What is the EITF referred to in this article?

(b) Explain the accounting issue related to the exchange of similar network capacity.

(c) Why did the EITF not address the issues related to swaps that occurred at companies such as **Global Crossing** and **Qwest Communications**?

Professional Research: Financial Accounting and Reporting

Your client is in the planning phase for a major plant expansion, which will involve the construction of a new warehouse. The assistant controller does not believe that interest cost can be included in the cost of the warehouse, because it is a financing expense. Others on the planning team believe that some interest cost can be included in the cost of the warehouse, but no one could identify the specific authoritative guidance for this issue. Your supervisor asks you to research this issue.

Instructions

Using the **Financial Accounting Research System (FARS),** respond to the following items. (Provide text strings used in your search.)

(a) It is permissible to capitalize interest into the cost of assets? What standard addresses this issue?

(b) What are the objectives for capitalizing interest?

(c) Discuss which assets qualify for interest capitalization.

(d) Is there a limit to the amount of interest that may be capitalized in a period?

(e) What disclosures are required, if interest capitalization is allowed?

Professional Simulation

In this simulation you are asked to address questions regarding the accounting for property, plant, and equipment. Prepare responses to all parts.

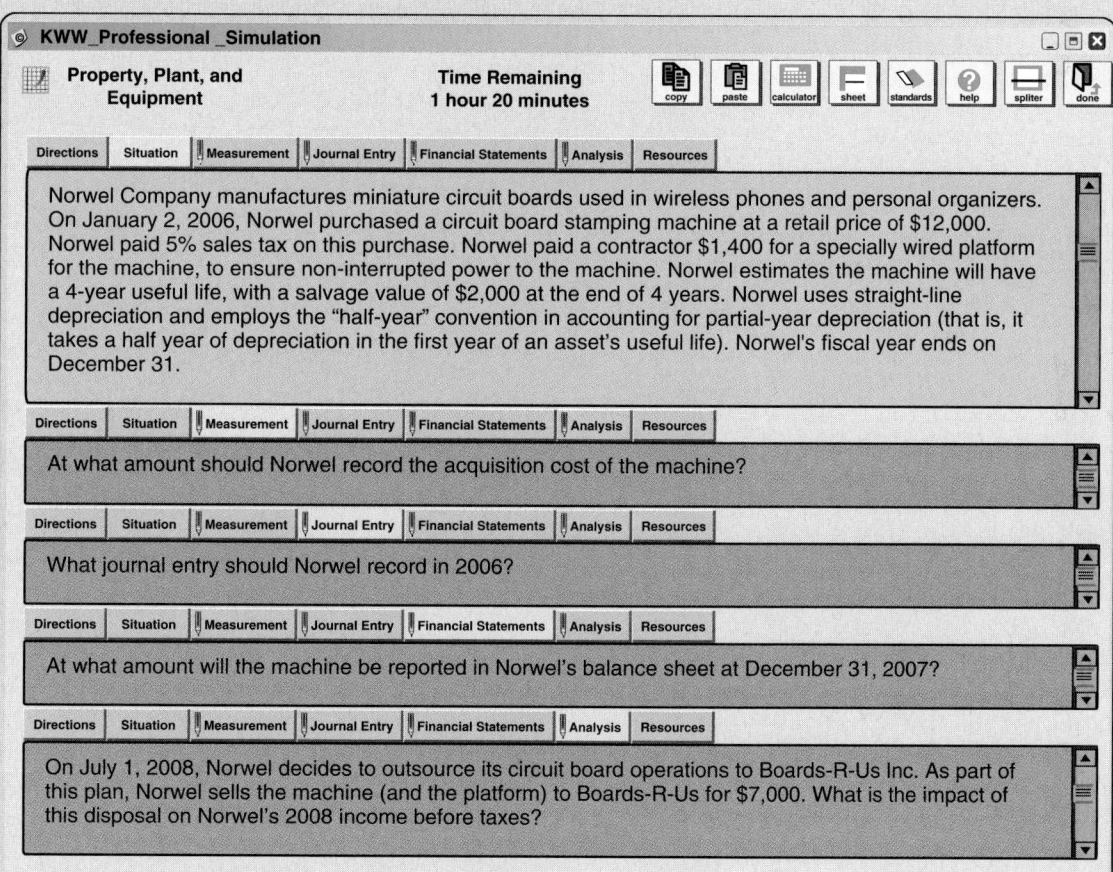

DEPRECIATION, IMPAIRMENTS, AND DEPLETION

Do They Matter?

The axiom on Wall Street has been that huge one-time charges don't really count. These highly unusual events don't truly reflect how a company is faring, so Wall Street ignores them. In the last few years write-offs have approached all-time highs. For example, over one-third of the companies surveyed by *Accounting Trends and Techniques* in 2004 reported asset impairments.

However, some companies have taken write-offs so regularly that they really are a reflection of ongoing business. When you adjust for the write-offs, earnings turn out to be far worse—and the companies' shares of stock turn out to be far more expensive. Presented below are data from three companies that recently had charges every year for five consecutive years.

Company	Net Income Before Write-Offs ($ mil)	Net Income After Write-Offs ($ mil)	Percentage Difference	EPS	EPS Adjusted	P/E	P/E Adjusted
International Paper	$591	$ 95	84%	$2.82	$0.46	15	90
Waste Management	755	130	83	1.43	0.25	18	102
Fortune Brands	322	61	81	3.30	0.63	13	67

For example, the data show that International Paper's adjusted earnings come in closer to $0.46 per share than $2.82. This means that its price-to-earnings ratio is closer to 90 than to 15. In short, these companies may be overpriced and are likely set for stock price declines.

One reason for more write-offs may be the tougher U.S. guidelines to determine when companies should consider property, plant, and equipment as impaired. These impairment rules are catching on internationally. Twenty-six Japanese companies adopted impairment standards similar to the U.S. standards, resulting in a combined loss of ¥814.1 billion (yen) in fiscal 2004. Adoption of the impairment standard both signals that the recent economic downturn was behind these companies and introduces more transparent accounting. Thus, while impairments are on the rise in the United States and elsewhere, investors are now receiving better information about fixed-asset values in financial statements.[1]

---

[1] Adapted from "Were Profits Inflated?" *Business Week* (March 4, 2002), p. 14, and from Michael K. Ozanian, "The Secret Charges, *Forbes* (March 4, 2002), p. 102. See also "Losses Pile Up under Stricter Accounting," *International Herald Tribune* (June 2, 2004).

Learning Objectives

After studying this chapter, you should be able to:

1 Explain the concept of depreciation.

2 Identify the factors involved in the depreciation process.

3 Compare activity, straight-line, and decreasing-charge methods of depreciation.

4 Explain special depreciation methods.

5 Explain the accounting issues related to asset impairment.

6 Explain the accounting procedures for depletion of natural resources.

7 Explain how to report and analyze property, plant, equipment, and natural resources.

As noted in the opening story, both U.S. and foreign companies are affected by impairment rules. These rules recognize that when economic conditions deteriorate, companies may need to write off an asset's cost to indicate the decline in its usefulness. The purpose of this chapter is to examine the depreciation process and the methods of writing off the cost of tangible assets and natural resources. The content and organization of the chapter are as follows.

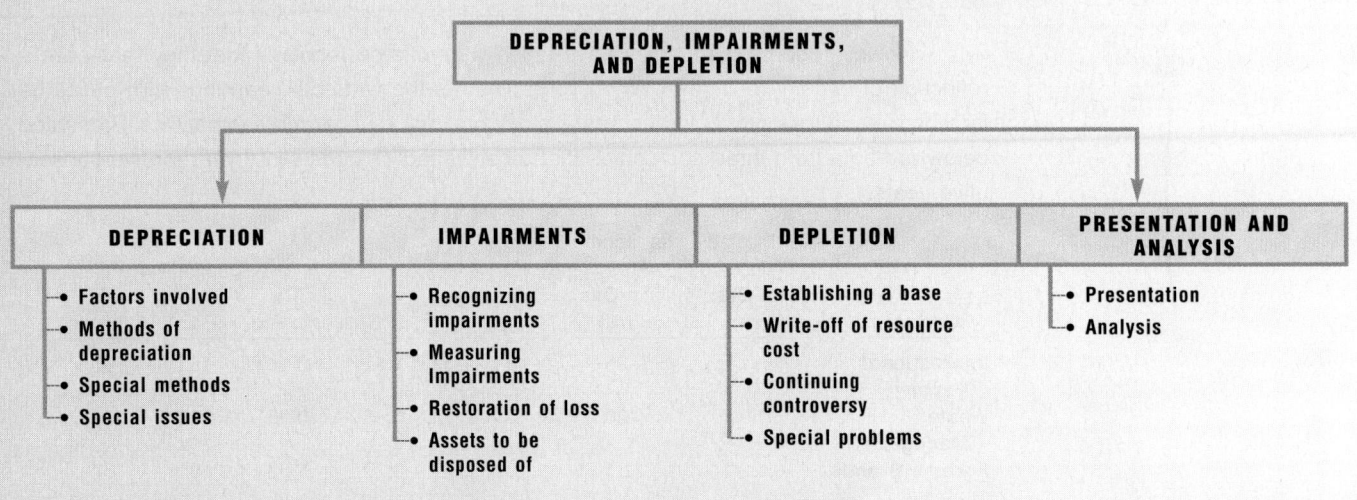

DEPRECIATION—A METHOD OF COST ALLOCATION

OBJECTIVE 1
Explain the concept of depreciation.

Most individuals at one time or another purchase and trade in an automobile. The automobile dealer and the buyer typically discuss what the trade-in value of the old car is. Also, they may talk about what the trade-in value of the new car will be in several years. In both cases a decline in value is considered to be an example of depreciation.

To accountants, however, depreciation is not a matter of valuation. Rather, **depreciation is a means of cost allocation.** Depreciation is the accounting process of allocating the cost of tangible assets to expense in a systematic and rational manner to those periods expected to benefit from the use of the asset. For example, a company like **Goodyear** (one of the world's largest tire manufacturers) does not depreciate assets on the basis of a decline in their fair market value. Instead, it depreciates through systematic charges to expense.

This approach is employed because the value of the asset may fluctuate between the time the asset is purchased and the time it is sold or junked. Attempts to measure these interim value changes have not been well received because values are difficult to measure objectively. Therefore, Goodyear charges the asset's cost to depreciation expense over its estimated life. It makes no attempt to value the asset at fair market value between acquisition and disposition. Companies use the cost allocation approach because it matches costs with revenues and because fluctuations in market value are uncertain and difficult to measure.

When companies write off the cost of long-lived assets over a number of periods, they typically use the term **depreciation**. They use the term **depletion** to describe the reduction in the cost of natural resources (such as timber, gravel, oil, and coal) over a period of time. The expiration of intangible assets, such as patents or copyrights, is called **amortization**.

Factors Involved in the Depreciation Process

Before establishing a pattern of charges to revenue, a company must answer three basic questions:

OBJECTIVE 2
Identify the factors involved in the depreciation process.

1 What depreciable base is to be used for the asset?
2 What is the asset's useful life?
3 What method of cost apportionment is best for this asset?

The answers to these questions involve combining several estimates into one single figure. Note the calculations assume perfect knowledge of the future, which is never attainable.

Depreciable Base for the Asset

The base established for depreciation is a function of two factors: the original cost, and salvage or disposal value. We discussed historical cost in Chapter 10. **Salvage value** is the estimated amount that a company will receive when it sells the asset or removes it from service. It is the amount to which a company writes down or depreciates the asset during its useful life. If an asset has a cost of $10,000 and a salvage value of $1,000, its **depreciation base** is $9,000.

Tutorial on Depreciation Methods

Original cost	$10,000
Less: Salvage value	1,000
Depreciation base	$ 9,000

ILLUSTRATION 11-1
Computation of Depreciation Base

From a practical standpoint, companies often assign a zero salvage value. Some long-lived assets, however, have substantial salvage values.

Estimation of Service Lives

The service life of an asset often differs from its physical life. A piece of machinery may be physically capable of producing a given product for many years beyond its service life. But a company may not use the equipment for all that time because the cost of producing the product in later years may be too high. For example, the old Slater cotton mill in Pawtucket, Rhode Island, is preserved in remarkable physical condition as an historic landmark in U.S. industrial development, although its service life was terminated many years ago.[2]

Companies retire assets for two reasons: **physical factors** (such as casualty or expiration of physical life) and **economic factors** (obsolescence). Physical factors are the wear and tear, decay, and casualties that make it difficult for the asset to perform indefinitely. These physical factors set the outside limit for the service life of an asset.

We can classify the economic or functional factors into three categories:

1 **Inadequacy** results when an asset ceases to be useful to a company because the demands of the firm have changed. An example would be the need for a larger building to handle increased production. Although the old building may still be sound, it may have become inadequate for the company's purpose.
2 **Supersession** is the replacement of one asset with another more efficient and economical asset. Examples would be the replacement of the mainframe computer with a PC network, or the replacement of the Boeing 767 with the Boeing 787.
3 **Obsolescence** is the catchall for situations not involving inadequacy and supersession.

---

[2]Taken from J. D. Coughlan and W. K. Strand, *Depreciation Accounting, Taxes and Business Decisions* (New York: The Ronald Press, 1969), pp. 10–12.

Because the distinction between these categories appears artificial, it is probably best to consider economic factors collectively instead of trying to make distinctions that are not clear-cut.

To illustrate the concepts of physical and economic factors, consider a new nuclear power plant. Which is more important in determining the useful life of a nuclear power plant—physical factors or economic factors? The limiting factors seem to be (1) ecological considerations, (2) competition from other power sources, and (3) safety concerns. Physical life does not appear to be the primary factor affecting useful life. Although the plant's physical life may be far from over, the plant may become obsolete in 10 years.

For a house, physical factors undoubtedly are more important than the economic or functional factors relative to useful life. Whenever the physical nature of the asset primarily determines useful life, maintenance plays an extremely vital role. The better the maintenance, the longer the life of the asset.[3]

In most cases, a company estimates the useful life of an asset based on its past experience with the same or similar assets. Others use sophisticated statistical methods to establish a useful life for accounting purposes. And in some cases, companies select arbitrary service lives. In a highly industrial economy such as that of the United States, where research and innovation are so prominent, technological factors have as much effect, if not more, on service lives of tangible plant assets as physical factors do.

WHAT DO THE
NUMBERS MEAN?

ALPHABET DUPE

Some companies try to imply that depreciation is not a cost. For example, in their press releases they will often make a bigger deal over earnings before interest, taxes, depreciation, and amortization (often referred to as EBITDA) than net income under GAAP. They like it because it "dresses up" their earnings numbers. Some on Wall Street buy this hype because they don't like the allocations that are required to determine net income. Some banks, without batting an eyelash, even let companies base their loan covenants on EBITDA.

For example, look at **Premier Parks**, which operates the Six Flags chain of amusement parks. Premier touts its EBITDA performance. But that number masks a big part of how the company operates—and how it spends its money. Premier argues that analysts should ignore depreciation for big-ticket items like roller coasters because the rides have a long life. Critics, however, say that the amusement industry has to spend as much as 50 percent of its EBITDA just to keep its rides and attractions current. Those expenses are not optional—let the rides get a little rusty, and ticket sales start to tail off. That means analysts really should view depreciation associated with the costs of maintaining the rides (or buying new ones) as an everyday expense. It also means investors in those companies should have strong stomachs.

What's the risk of trusting a fad accounting measure? Just look at a recent year's bankruptcy numbers. Of the 147 companies tracked by Moody's that defaulted on their debt, most borrowed money based on EBITDA performance. The bankers in those deals probably wish they had looked at a few other factors. Maybe it's time more investors did so too.

Source: Adapted from Herb Greenberg, Alphabet Dupe: Why EBITDA Falls Short," *Fortune* (July 10, 2000), p. 240.

---

[3]The airline industry also illustrates the type of problem involved in estimation. In the past, aircraft were assumed not to wear out—they just became obsolete. However, some jets have been in service as long as 20 years, and maintenance of these aircraft has become increasingly expensive. In addition, some recent air disasters have heightened the public's concern about worn-out aircraft. As a result, some airlines now replace aircraft not because of obsolescence but because of physical deterioration.

Methods of Depreciation

The third factor involved in the depreciation process is the **method** of cost apportionment. The profession requires that the depreciation method employed be "systematic and rational." Companies may use a number of depreciation methods, as follows.

1 Activity method (units of use or production).

2 Straight-line method.

3 Decreasing charge methods (accelerated):
   (a) Sum-of-the-years'-digits.
   (b) Declining-balance method.

4 Special depreciation methods:
   (a) Group and composite methods.
   (b) Hybrid or combination methods.[4]

UNDERLYING CONCEPTS

Depreciation attempts to match the cost of an asset to the periods that benefit from the use of that asset.

To illustrate these depreciation methods, assume that Stanley Coal Mines recently purchased an additional crane for digging purposes. Illustration 11-2 contains the pertinent data concerning this purchase.

Cost of crane	$500,000
Estimated useful life	5 years
Estimated salvage value	$ 50,000
Productive life in hours	30,000 hours

ILLUSTRATION 11-2
Data Used to Illustrate
Depreciation Methods

Activity Method

The **activity method** (also called the **variable-charge** or **units-of-production approach**) assumes that depreciation is **a function of use or productivity, instead of the passage of time**. A company considers the life of the asset in terms of either the **output** it provides (units it produces), or an **input** measure such as the number of hours it works. Conceptually, the proper cost association relies on output instead of hours used, but often the output is not easily measurable. In such cases, an input measure such as machine hours is a more appropriate method of measuring the dollar amount of depreciation charges for a given accounting period.

The crane poses no particular depreciation problem. Stanley can measure the usage (hours) relatively easily. If Stanley uses the crane for 4,000 hours the first year, the depreciation charge is:

OBJECTIVE 3
Compare activity, straight-line, and decreasing-charge methods of depreciation.

$$\frac{(\text{Cost less salvage}) \times \text{Hours this year}}{\text{Total estimated hours}} = \text{Depreciation charge}$$

$$\frac{(\$500,000 - \$50,000) \times 4,000}{30,000} = \$60,000$$

ILLUSTRATION 11-3
Depreciation Calculation,
Activity Method—Crane
Example

The major limitation of this method is that it is inappropriate in situations in which depreciation is a function of time instead of activity. For example, a building steadily deteriorates due to the elements (time) regardless of its use. In addition, where economic or functional factors affect an asset, independent of its use, the activity method loses much of its significance. For example, if a company is expanding rapidly, a particular building may soon become obsolete for its intended purposes. In both cases, activity is irrelevant. Another problem in using an activity method is the difficulty of estimating units of output or service hours received.

---

[4]*Accounting Trends and Techniques—2004* reports that of its 600 surveyed companies, for reporting purposes, 580 used straight-line, 22 used declining-balance, 5 used sum-of-the-years'-digits, 41 used an accelerated method (not specified), and 30 used units of production.

In cases where loss of services results from activity or productivity, the activity method matches costs and revenues the best. Companies that desire low depreciation during periods of low productivity, and high depreciation during high productivity, either adopt or switch to an activity method. In this way, a plant running at 40 percent of capacity generates 60 percent lower depreciation charges. **Inland Steel**, for example, switched to units-of-production depreciation at one time and reduced its losses by $43 million, or $1.20 per share.[5]

Straight-Line Method

UNDERLYING CONCEPTS

If benefits flow on a "straight-line" basis, then justification exists for matching the cost of the asset on a straight-line basis with these benefits.

The **straight-line method** considers depreciation a **function of time rather than a function of usage**. Companies widely use this method because of its simplicity. The straight-line procedure is often the most conceptually appropriate, too. When creeping obsolescence is the primary reason for a limited service life, the decline in usefulness may be constant from period to period. Stanley computes the depreciation charge for the crane as follows.

ILLUSTRATION 11-4
Depreciation Calculation, Straight-Line Method— Crane Example

$$\frac{\text{Cost less salvage}}{\text{Estimated service life}} = \text{Depreciation charge}$$

$$\frac{\$500,000 - \$50,000}{5} = \$90,000$$

The major objection to the straight-line method is that it rests on two tenuous assumptions: (1) The asset's economic usefulness is the same each year, and (2) the repair and maintenance expense is essentially the same each period.

One additional problem that occurs in using straight-line—as well as some others— is that distortions in the rate of return analysis (income/assets) develop. Illustration 11-5 indicates how the rate of return increases, given constant revenue flows, because the asset's book value decreases.

ILLUSTRATION 11-5
Depreciation and Rate of Return Analysis—Crane Example

Year	Depreciation Expense	Undepreciated Asset Balance (book value)	Income (after depreciation expense)	Rate of Return (Income ÷ Assets)
0		$500,000		
1	$90,000	410,000	$100,000	24.4%
2	90,000	320,000	100,000	31.2%
3	90,000	230,000	100,000	43.5%
4	90,000	140,000	100,000	71.4%
5	90,000	50,000	100,000	200.0%

Decreasing-Charge Methods

UNDERLYING CONCEPTS

The matching concept does not justify a constant charge to income. If the benefits from the asset decline as the asset ages, then a decreasing charge to income better matches cost to benefits.

The **decreasing-charge methods** provide for a higher depreciation cost in the earlier years and lower charges in later periods. Because these methods allow for higher early-year charges than in the straight-line method, they are often called **accelerated depreciation methods**.

What is the main justification for this approach? The rationale is that companies should charge more depreciation in earlier years because the asset is most productive in its earlier years. Furthermore, the accelerated methods provide a constant cost because the depreciation charge is lower in the later periods, at the time when the repair and maintenance costs are often higher. Generally, companies use one of two decreasing-charge methods: the sum-of-the-years'-digits method, or the declining-balance method.

---

[5]"Double Standard," *Forbes* (November 22, 1982), p. 178.

Sum-of-the-Years'-Digits. The **sum-of-the-years'-digits method** results in a decreasing depreciation charge based on a decreasing fraction of depreciable cost (original cost less salvage value). Each fraction uses the sum of the years as a denominator (5 + 4 + 3 + 2 + 1 = 15). The numerator is the number of years of estimated life remaining as of the beginning of the year. In this method, the numerator decreases year by year, and the denominator remains constant (5/15, 4/15, 3/15, 2/15, and 1/15). At the end of the asset's useful life, the balance remaining should equal the salvage value. Illustration 11-6 shows this method of computation.[6]

Year	Depreciation Base	Remaining Life in Years	Depreciation Fraction	Depreciation Expense	Book Value, End of Year
1	$450,000	5	5/15	$150,000	$350,000
2	450,000	4	4/15	120,000	230,000
3	450,000	3	3/15	90,000	140,000
4	450,000	2	2/15	60,000	80,000
5	450,000	1	1/15	30,000	50,000[a]
		15	15/15	$450,000	

[a]Salvage value.

ILLUSTRATION 11-6
Sum-of-the-Years'-Digits Depreciation Schedule— Crane Example

Declining-Balance Method. The **declining-balance method** utilizes a depreciation rate (expressed as a percentage) that is some multiple of the straight-line method. For example, the double-declining rate for a 10-year asset is 20 percent (double the straight-line rate, which is 1/10 or 10 percent). Companies apply the constant rate to the declining book value each year.

Unlike other methods, the declining-balance method **does not deduct the salvage value** in computing the depreciation base. The declining-balance rate is multiplied by the book value of the asset at the beginning of each period. Since the depreciation charge reduces the book value of the asset each period, applying the constant-declining-balance rate to a successively lower book value results in lower depreciation charges each year. This process continues until the book value of the asset equals its estimated salvage value. At that time the company discontinues depreciation.

Companies use various multiples in practice. For example, the **double-declining-balance method** depreciates assets at twice (200 percent) the straight-line rate. Illustration 11-7 shows Stanley's depreciation charges if using the double-declining approach.

Year	Book Value of Asset First of Year	Rate on Declining Balance[a]	Depreciation Expense	Balance Accumulated Depreciation	Book Value, End of Year
1	$500,000	40%	$200,000	$200,000	$300,000
2	300,000	40%	120,000	320,000	180,000
3	180,000	40%	72,000	392,000	108,000
4	108,000	40%	43,200	435,200	64,800
5	64,800	40%	14,800[b]	450,000	50,000

[a]Based on twice the straight-line rate of 20% ($90,000/$450,000 = 20%; 20% × 2 = 40%).
[b]Limited to $14,800 because book value should not be less than salvage value.

ILLUSTRATION 11-7
Double-Declining Depreciation Schedule— Crane Example

---

[6]What happens if the estimated service life of the asset is, let us say, 51 years? How would we calculate the sum-of-the-years'-digits? Fortunately mathematicians have developed the following formula that permits easy computation:

$$\frac{n(n+1)}{2} = \frac{51(51+1)}{2} = 1,326$$

Companies often switch from the declining-balance method to the straight-line method near the end of the asset's useful life to ensure that they depreciate the asset only to its salvage value.[7]

Special Depreciation Methods

OBJECTIVE 4
**Explain special
depreciation methods.**

Sometimes companies adopt special depreciation methods. Reasons for doing so might be that a company's assets have unique characteristics, or the nature of the industry. Two of these special methods are:

1 Group and composite methods.
2 Hybrid or combination methods.

Group and Composite Methods

Companies often depreciate multiple-asset accounts using one rate. For example, **AT&T** might depreciate telephone poles, microwave systems, or switchboards by groups.

Two methods of depreciating multiple-asset accounts exist: the group method and the composite method. The choice of method depends on the nature of the assets involved. Companies frequently use the **group method** when the assets are similar in nature and have approximately the same useful lives. They use the **composite approach** when the assets are dissimilar and have different lives. The group method more closely approximates a single-unit cost procedure because the dispersion from the average is not as great. The computation for group or composite methods is essentially the same: find an average and depreciate on that basis.

Companies determine the **composite depreciation rate** by dividing the depreciation per year by the total cost of the assets. To illustrate, Mooney Motors establishes the composite depreciation rate for its fleet of cars, trucks, and campers as shown in Illustration 11-8.

ILLUSTRATION 11-8
Depreciation Calculation,
Composite Basis

Asset	Original Cost	Residual Value	Depreciable Cost	Estimated Life (yrs.)	Depreciation per Year (straight-line)
Cars	$145,000	$25,000	$120,000	3	$40,000
Trucks	44,000	4,000	40,000	4	10,000
Campers	35,000	5,000	30,000	5	6,000
	$224,000	$34,000	$190,000		$56,000

Composite depreciation rate = $\frac{\$56,000}{\$224,000}$ = 25%

Composite life = 3.39 years ($190,000 ÷ $56,000)

If there are no changes in the asset account, Mooney will depreciate the group of assets to the residual or salvage value at the rate of $56,000 ($224,000 × 25%) a

[7]A pure form of the declining-balance method (sometimes appropriately called the "fixed percentage of book value method") has also been suggested as a possibility. This approach finds a rate that depreciates the asset exactly to salvage value at the end of its expected useful life. The formula for determination of this rate is as follows:

$$\text{Depreciation rate} = 1 - \sqrt[n]{\frac{\text{Salvage value}}{\text{Acquisition cost}}}$$

The life in years is n. After computing the depreciation rate, a company applies it on the declining book value of the asset from period to period, which means that depreciation expense will be successively lower. This method is not used extensively in practice due to cumbersome computations. Further, it is not permitted for tax purposes.

year. As a result, it will take Mooney 3.39 years to depreciate these assets. The length of time it takes a company to depreciate it assets on a composite basis is called the **composite life**.

We can highlight the differences between the group or composite method and the single-unit depreciation method by looking at asset retirements. If Mooney retires an asset before, or after, the average service life of the group is reached, it buries the resulting gain or loss in the Accumulated Depreciation account. This practice is justified because Mooney will retire some assets before the average service life and others after the average life. For this reason, the debit to Accumulated Depreciation is the difference between original cost and cash received. Mooney does not record a gain or loss on disposition.

To illustrate, suppose that Mooney Motors sold one of the campers with a cost of $5,000 for $2,600 at the end of the third year. The entry is:

Accumulated Depreciation	2,400	
Cash	2,600	
Cars, Trucks, and Campers		5,000

If Mooney purchases a new type of asset (mopeds, for example), it must compute a new depreciation rate and apply this rate in subsequent periods.

Illustration 11-9 presents a typical financial statement disclosure of the group depreciation method for **Ampco-Pittsburgh Corporation**.

Ampco-Pittsburgh Corporation

Depreciation rates are based on estimated useful lives of the asset groups. Gains or losses on normal retirements or replacements of depreciable assets, subject to composite depreciation methods, are not recognized; the difference between the cost of the assets retired or replaced and the related salvage value is charged or credited to the accumulated depreciation.

ILLUSTRATION 11-9
Disclosure of Group Depreciation Method

The group or composite method simplifies the bookkeeping process and tends to average out errors caused by over- or under-depreciation. As a result, gains or losses on disposals of assets do not distort periodic income.

On the other hand, the unit method has several advantages over the group or composite methods: (1) It simplifies the computation mathematically. (2) It identifies gains and losses on disposal. (3) It isolates depreciation on idle equipment. (4) It represents the best estimate of the depreciation of each asset, not the result of averaging the cost over a longer period of time. As a consequence, companies generally use the unit method. Unless stated otherwise, you should use the unit method in homework problems.[8]

Hybrid or Combination Methods

In addition to the depreciation methods already discussed, companies are free to develop their own special or tailor-made depreciation methods. GAAP requires only that the method result in the allocation of an asset's cost over the asset's life in a **systematic and rational manner**.

---

[8]AcSEC has indicated in an exposure draft that companies should use the unit approach whenever feasible. In fact, it indicates that an even better way to depreciate property, plant, and equipment is to use *component depreciation*. Under component depreciation, a company should depreciate over its expected useful life any part or portion of property, plant, and equipment that can be separately identified as an asset. For example, a company could separate the various components of a building (e.g., roof, heating and cooling system, elevator, leasehold improvements) and depreciate each component over its useful life.

For example, the steel industry widely uses a hybrid depreciation method, called the **production variable method** that is a combination straight-line/activity approach. The following note from **WHX Corporation**'s annual report explains one variation of this method.

ILLUSTRATION 11-10
Disclosure of Hybrid
Depreciation Method

*Expanded Discussion—
Special Depreciation
Methods*

WHX Corporation

The Company utilizes the modified units of production method of depreciation which recognizes that the depreciation of steelmaking machinery is related to the physical wear of the equipment as well as a time factor. The modified units of production method provides for straight-line depreciation charges modified (adjusted) by the level of raw steel production. In the prior year, depreciation under the modified units of production method was $21.6 million or 40% less than straight-line depreciation, and in the current year it was $1.1 million or 2% more than straight-line depreciation.

**WHAT DO THE
NUMBERS MEAN?**

DECELERATING DEPRECIATION

Which depreciation method should management select? Many believe that the method that best matches revenues with expenses should be used. For example, if revenues generated by the asset are constant over its useful life, select straight-line depreciation. On the other hand, if revenues are higher (or lower) at the beginning of the asset's life, then use a decreasing (or increasing) method. Thus, if a company can reliably estimate revenues from the asset, selecting a depreciation method that best matches costs with those revenues would seem to provide the most useful information to investors and creditors for assessing the future cash flows from the asset.

Managers in the real estate industry face a different challenge when considering depreciation choices. Real estate managers object to traditional depreciation methods because in their view, real estate often does not decline in value. In addition, because real estate is highly debt-financed, most real estate concerns report losses in earlier years of operations when the sum of depreciation and interest exceeds the revenue from the real estate project. As a result, real estate companies, like **Kimco Realty**, argue for some form of **increasing-charge** method of depreciation (lower depreciation at the beginning and higher depreciation at the end). With such a method, companies would report higher total assets and net income in the earlier years of the project.[9]

Special Depreciation Issues

We still need to discuss several special issues related to depreciation:

1 How should companies compute depreciation for partial periods?

2 Does depreciation provide for the replacement of assets?

3 How should companies handle revisions in depreciation rates?

---

[9]In this regard, real estate investment trusts (REITs) often report (in addition to net income) an earnings measure, funds from operations (FFO), that adjusts income for depreciation expense and other noncash expenses. This method is not GAAP. There is mixed empirical evidence about whether FFO or GAAP income is more useful to real estate investment trust investors. See, for example, Richard Gore and David Stott, "Toward a More Informative Measure of Operating Performance in the REIT Industry: Net Income vs. FFO," *Accounting Horizons* (December 1998); and Linda Vincent, "The Information Content of FFO for REITs," *Journal of Accounting and Economics* (January 1999).

Depreciation and Partial Periods

Companies seldom purchase plant assets on the first day of a fiscal period or dispose of them on the last day of a fiscal period. A practical question is: How much depreciation should a company charge for the partial periods involved?

In computing depreciation expense for partial periods, companies must determine the depreciation expense for the full year and then prorate this depreciation expense between the two periods involved. This process should continue throughout the useful life of the asset.

Assume, for example, that Steeltex Company purchases an automated drill machine with a 5-year life for $45,000 (no salvage value) on June 10, 2006. The company's fiscal year ends December 31. Steeltex therefore charges depreciation for only 6⅔ months during that year. The total depreciation for a full year (assuming straight-line depreciation) is $9,000 ($45,000/5). The depreciation for the first, partial year is therefore:

$$\frac{6\frac{2}{3}}{12} \times \$9,000 = \$5,000$$

The partial-period calculation is relatively simple when Steeltex uses straight-line depreciation. But how is partial-period depreciation handled when it uses an accelerated method such as sum-of-the-years'-digits or double-declining balance? As an illustration, assume that Steeltex purchased another machine for $10,000 on July 1, 2006, with an estimated useful life of five years and no salvage value. Illustration 11-11 shows the depreciation figures for 2006, 2007, and 2008.

	Sum-of-the-Years'-Digits	Double-Declining Balance
1st full year	(5/15 × $10,000) = $3,333.33	(40% × $10,000) = $4,000
2nd full year	(4/15 × 10,000) = 2,666.67	(40% × 6,000) = 2,400
3rd full year	(3/15 × 10,000) = 2,000.00	(40% × 3,600) = 1,440

Depreciation from July 1, 2006, to December 31, 2006

6/12 × $3,333.33 = $1,666.67	6/12 × $4,000 = $2,000

Depreciation for 2007

6/12 × $3,333.33 = $1,666.67	6/12 × $4,000 = $2,000
6/12 × 2,666.67 = 1,333.33	6/12 × 2,400 = 1,200
$3,000.00	$3,200

or ($10,000 − $2,000) × 40% = $3,200

Depreciation for 2008

6/12 × $2,666.67 = $1,333.33	6/12 × $2,400 = $1,200
6/12 × 2,000.00 = 1,000.00	6/12 × 1,440 = 720
$2,333.33	$1,920

or ($10,000 − $5,200) × 40% = $1,920

ILLUSTRATION 11-11
Calculation of Partial-Period Depreciation, Two Methods

Sometimes a company like Steeltex modifies the process of allocating costs to a partial period to handle acquisitions and disposals of plant assets more simply. It may compute depreciation for the full period on the opening balance in the asset account and not charge depreciation on acquisitions during the year. It then charges a full year of depreciation in the year of disposal. Other variations charge one-half year's depreciation both in the year of acquisition and in the year of disposal (referred to as the **half-year convention**), or charge a full year in the year of acquisition and none in the year of disposal.

In fact, Steeltex may adopt any one of these several fractional-year policies in allocating cost to the first and last years of an asset's life so long as it applies the method consistently. However, **unless otherwise stipulated, companies normally compute depreciation on the basis of the nearest full month.**

Illustration 11-12 shows depreciation allocated under five different fractional-year policies using the straight-line method on the $45,000 automated drill machine purchased by Steeltex Company on June 10, 2006, discussed earlier.

ILLUSTRATION 11-12
Fractional-Year
Depreciation Policies

Machine Cost = $45,000	Depreciation Allocated per Period Over 5-Year Life*					
Fractional-Year Policy	2006	2007	2008	2009	2010	2011
1. Nearest fraction of a year.	$5,000[a]	$9,000	$9,000	$9,000	$9,000	$4,000[b]
2. Nearest full month.	5,250[c]	9,000	9,000	9,000	9,000	3,750[d]
3. Half year in period of acquisition and disposal.	4,500	9,000	9,000	9,000	9,000	4,500
4. Full year in period of acquisition, none in period of disposal.	9,000	9,000	9,000	9,000	9,000	–0–
5. None in period of acquisition, full year in period of disposal.	–0–	9,000	9,000	9,000	9,000	9,000

[a]6.667/12 ($9,000)   [b]5.333/12 ($9,000)   [c]7/12 ($9,000)   [d]5/12 ($9,000)
*Rounded to nearest dollar.

Depreciation and Replacement of Fixed Assets

A common misconception about depreciation is that it provides funds for the replacement of fixed assets. Depreciation is like other expenses in that it reduces net income. It differs, though, in that **it does not involve a current cash outflow**.

To illustrate why depreciation does not provide funds for replacement of plant assets, assume that a business starts operating with plant assets of $500,000 that have a useful life of five years. The company's balance sheet at the beginning of the period is:

Plant assets	$500,000	Owners' equity	$500,000

If we assume that the company earns no revenue over the five years, the income statements are:

	Year 1	Year 2	Year 3	Year 4	Year 5
Revenue	$ –0–	$ –0–	$ –0–	$ –0–	$ –0–
Depreciation	(100,000)	(100,000)	(100,000)	(100,000)	(100,000)
Loss	$(100,000)	$(100,000)	$(100,000)	$(100,000)	$(100,000)

Total depreciation of the plant assets over the five years is $500,000. The balance sheet at the end of the five years therefore is:

Plant assets	–0–	Owners' equity	–0–

This extreme example illustrates that depreciation **in no way** provides funds for the replacement of assets. **The funds for the replacement of the assets come from the revenues** (generated through use of the asset). Without the revenues, no income materializes and no cash inflow results.

Revision of Depreciation Rates

When purchasing a plant asset, companies carefully determine depreciation rates based on past experience with similar assets and other pertinent information. The provisions for depreciation are only estimates, however. They may need to revise them during the life of the asset. Unexpected physical deterioration or unforeseen obsolescence may decrease the estimated useful life of the asset. Improved maintenance procedures, revision of operating procedures, or similar developments may prolong the life of the asset beyond the expected period.[10]

For example, assume that **International Paper Co.** purchased machinery with an original cost of $90,000. It estimates a 20-year life with no salvage value. However, during year 11, International Paper estimates that it will use the machine for an additional 20 years. Its total life, therefore, will be 30 years instead of 20. Depreciation has been recorded at the rate of 1/20 of $90,000, or $4,500 per year by the straight-line method. On the basis of a 30-year life, International Paper should have recorded depreciation as 1/30 of $90,000, or $3,000 per year. It has therefore overstated depreciation, and understated net income, by $1,500 for each of the past 10 years, or a total amount of $15,000. Illustration 11-13 shows this computation.

	Per Year	For 10 Years
Depreciation charged per books (1/20 × $90,000)	$4,500	$45,000
Depreciation based on a 30-year life (1/30 × $90,000)	3,000	30,000
Excess depreciation charged	$1,500	$15,000

ILLUSTRATION 11-13
Computation of Accumulated Difference Due to Revisions

International Paper should report this change in estimate in the current and prospective periods. It should not make any changes in previously reported results. And it does not adjust opening balances nor attempt to "catch up" for prior periods. The reason? Changes in estimates are a continual and inherent part of any estimation process. Continual restatement of prior periods would occur for revisions of estimates unless handled prospectively. Therefore, no entry is made at the time the change in estimate occurs. Charges for depreciation in subsequent periods (assuming use of the straight-line method) are determined by **dividing the remaining book value less any salvage value by the remaining estimated life**.

Machinery	$90,000
Less: Accumulated depreciation	45,000
Book value of machinery at end of 10th year	$45,000

Depreciation (future periods) = $45,000 book value ÷ 20 years remaining life = $2,250

ILLUSTRATION 11-14
Computing Depreciation after Revision of Estimated Life

The entry to record depreciation for each of the remaining 20 years is:

Depreciation Expense	2,250	
Accumulated Depreciation—Machinery		2,250

---

[10]As an example of a change in operating procedures, **General Motors** (GM) used to write off its tools—such as dies and equipment used to manufacture car bodies—over the life of the body type. Through this procedure, it expensed tools twice as fast as **Ford** and three times as fast as **DaimlerChrysler**. However, it slowed the depreciation process on these tools and lengthened the lives on its plant and equipment. These revisions reduced depreciation and amortization charges by approximately $1.23 billion, or $2.55 per share, in the year of the change. In Chapter 22, we provide a more complete discussion of changes in estimates.

**WHAT DO THE
NUMBERS MEAN?**

The amount of depreciation expense recorded depends on both the depreciation method used and estimates of service lives and salvage values of the assets. Differences in these choices and estimates can significantly impact a company's reported results and can make it difficult to compare the depreciation numbers of different companies.

For example, when **Willamette Industries** extended the estimated service lives of its machinery and equipment by five years, it increased income by nearly $54 million.

An analyst determines the impact of these management choices and judgments on the amount of depreciation expense by examining the notes to financial statements. For example, Willamette Industries provided the following note to its financial statements.

Note 4: Property, Plant, and Equipment (partial)	
	Range of Useful Lives
Land	—
Buildings	15–35
Machinery & equipment	5–25
Furniture & fixtures	3–15

During the year, the estimated service lives for most machinery and equipment were extended five years. The change was based upon a study performed by the company's engineering department, comparisons to typical industry practices, and the effect of the company's extensive capital investments which have resulted in a mix of assets with longer productive lives due to technological advances. As a result of the change, net income was increased by $54,000,000.

IMPAIRMENTS

OBJECTIVE 5
Explain the accounting issues related to asset impairment.

The general accounting standard of **lower-of-cost-or-market for inventories does not apply to property, plant, and equipment**. Even when property, plant, and equipment has suffered partial obsolescence, accountants have been reluctant to reduce the asset's carrying amount. Why? Because, unlike inventories, it is difficult to arrive at a fair value for property, plant, and equipment that is not subjective and arbitrary.

For example, **Falconbridge Ltd. Nickel Mines** had to decide whether to write off all or a part of its property, plant, and equipment in a nickel-mining operation in the Dominican Republic. The project had been incurring losses because nickel prices were low and operating costs were high. Only if nickel prices increased by approximately 33 percent would the project be reasonably profitable. Whether a write-off was appropriate depended on the future price of nickel. Even if the company decided to write off the asset, how much should be written off?

Recognizing Impairments

UNDERLYING CONCEPTS

The *going concern concept* assumes that the company can recover the investment in its assets. Under GAAP companies do not report the fair value of long-lived assets because a going concern does not plan to sell such assets. However, if the assumption of being able to recover the cost of the investment is not valid, then a company should report a reduction in value.

As discussed in the opening story, the FASB and international accounting standard-setters have developed rules for recognizing impairments on long-lived assets.[11] According to these standards, when the carrying amount of an asset is not recoverable, a company records a write-off. This write-off is referred to as an **impairment**.

---

[11]"Accounting for the Impairment or Disposal of Long-lived Assets," *Statement of Financial Accounting Standards No. 144* (Norwalk, Conn.: 2001).

Various events and changes in circumstances might lead to an impairment. Examples are:

a. A significant decrease in the market value of an asset.

b. A significant change in the extent or manner in which an asset is used.

c. A significant adverse change in legal factors or in the business climate that affects the value of an asset.

d. An accumulation of costs significantly in excess of the amount originally expected to acquire or construct an asset.

e. A projection or forecast that demonstrates continuing losses associated with an asset.

These events or changes in circumstances indicate that the company may not be able to recover the carrying amount of the asset. In that case, a **recoverability test** is used to determine whether an impairment has occurred.

To apply the first step of the recoverability test, a company like **UPS** estimates the future net cash flows expected from the **use of that asset and its eventual disposition**. If the sum of the expected future net cash flows (undiscounted) is **less than the carrying amount** of the asset, UPS considers the asset impaired. Conversely, if the sum of the expected future net cash flows (undiscounted) is **equal to or greater than the carrying amount** of the asset, no impairment has occurred.

The recoverability test therefore screens for asset impairment. For example, if the expected future net cash flows from an asset are $400,000 and its carrying amount is $350,000, no impairment has occurred. However, if the expected future net cash flows are $300,000, an impairment has occurred. The rationale for the recoverability test relies on a basic presumption: A balance sheet should report long-lived assets at no more than the carrying amounts that are recoverable.

Measuring Impairments

If the recoverability test indicates an impairment, UPS computes a loss. The **impairment loss** is the amount by which the carrying amount of the asset **exceeds its fair value**. How does UPS determine the fair value of an asset? It is measured based on the market value if an active market for the asset exists. If no active market exists, UPS uses the **present value of expected future net cash flows to determine fair value**.

To summarize, the process of determining an impairment loss is as follows.

1 Review events or changes in circumstances for possible impairment.

2 If the review indicates impairment, apply the recoverability test. If the sum of the expected future net cash flows from the long-lived asset is less than the carrying amount of the asset, an impairment has occurred.

3 Assuming an impairment, the impairment loss is the amount by which the carrying amount of the asset exceeds the fair value of the asset. The fair value is the market value or the present value of expected future net cash flows.

Impairment—Example 1

M. Alou Inc. has an asset that, due to changes in its use, it reviews for possible impairment. The asset's carrying amount is $600,000 ($800,000 cost less $200,000 accumulated depreciation). Alou determines the expected future net cash flows (undiscounted) from the use of the asset and its eventual disposal to be $650,000.

The recoverability test indicates that the $650,000 of expected future net cash flows from the asset's use exceed the carrying amount of $600,000. As a result, no impairment occurred. (Recall that the undiscounted future net cash flows must be less than the carrying amount for Alou to deem an asset to be impaired and to measure the impairment loss.) Therefore, M. Alou Inc. does not recognize an impairment loss in this case.

Impairment—Example 2

Assume the same facts as in Example 1, except that the expected future net cash flows from Alou's asset are $580,000 (instead of $650,000). The recoverability test indicates that the expected future net cash flows of $580,000 from the use of the asset are less than its carrying amount of $600,000. Therefore an impairment has occurred.

The difference between the carrying amount of Alou's asset and its fair value is the impairment loss. Assuming this asset has a market value of $525,000, Illustration 11-15 shows the loss computation.

ILLUSTRATION 11-15
Computation of
Impairment Loss

Carrying amount of the equipment	$600,000
Fair value of equipment (market value)	525,000
Loss on impairment	$ 75,000

M. Alou records the impairment loss as follows.

Loss on Impairment	75,000	
Accumulated Depreciation		75,000

M. Alou Inc. reports the impairment loss as part of income from continuing operations, in the "Other expenses and losses" section. Generally, Alou **should not report this loss as an extraordinary item**. Costs associated with an impairment loss are the same costs that would flow through operations and that it would report as part of continuing operations. Alou will continue to use these assets in operations. Therefore, it should not report the loss below "Income from continuing operations."

A company that recognizes an impairment loss should disclose the asset(s) impaired, the events leading to the impairment, the amount of the loss, and how it determined fair value (disclosing the interest rate used, if appropriate).

Restoration of Impairment Loss

After recording an impairment loss, the reduced carrying amount of an asset held for use becomes its new cost basis. A company does not change the new cost basis except for depreciation or amortization in future periods or for additional impairments.

To illustrate, assume that Damon Company at December 31, 2006, has equipment with a carrying amount of $500,000. Damon determines this asset is impaired and writes it down to its fair value of $400,000. At the end of 2007, Damon determines that the fair value of the asset is $480,000. The carrying amount of the equipment should not change in 2007 except for the depreciation taken in 2007. Damon **may not restore an impairment loss for an asset held for use**. The rationale for not writing the asset up in value is that the new cost basis puts the impaired asset on an equal basis with other assets that are unimpaired.

INTERNATIONAL INSIGHT

International accounting standards permit write-ups for subsequent recoveries of impairment. U.S. GAAP prohibits those write-ups, except for assets to be disposed of.

Impairment of Assets to Be Disposed of

What happens if a company intends to dispose of the impaired asset, instead of holding it for use? Recently **Kroger** recorded an impairment loss of $54 million on property, plant, and equipment it no longer needs due to store closures. In this case, Kroger reports the impaired asset at the lower of cost or net realizable value (fair value less cost to sell). Because Kroger intends to dispose of the assets in a short period of time, it uses net realizable value in order to provide a better measure of the net cash flows that it will receive from these assets.

Kroger does not depreciate or amortize assets held for disposal during the period it holds them. The rationale is that depreciation is inconsistent with the notion of assets to be disposed of and with the use of the lower of cost or net realizable value. In other words, **assets held for disposal are like inventory; companies should report them at the lower of cost or net realizable value.**

Because Kroger will recover assets held for disposal through sale rather than through operations, it continually revalues them. Each period, the assets are reported at the lower of cost or net realizable value. Thus **Kroger can write up or down an asset held for disposal in future periods, as long as the carrying value after the write-up never exceeds the carrying amount of the asset before the impairment.** Companies should report losses or gains related to these impaired assets as part of **income from continuing operations**.

Illustration 11-16 summarizes the key concepts in accounting for impairments.

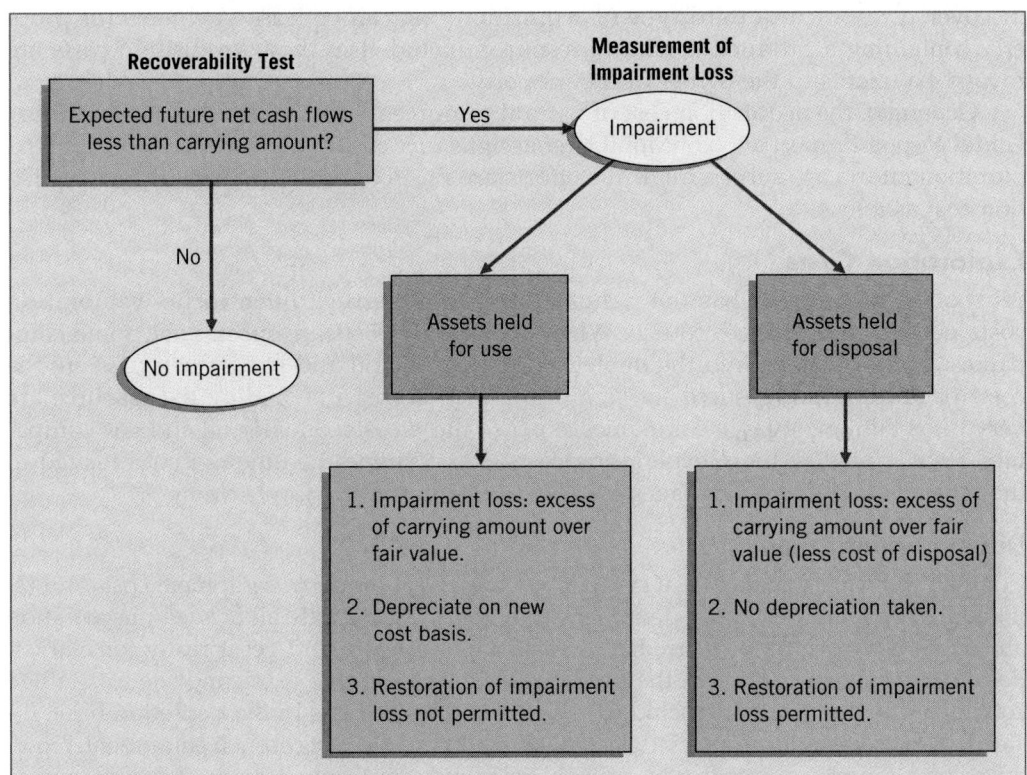

ILLUSTRATION 11-16
Graphic of Accounting
for Impairments

DEPLETION

Natural resources, often called wasting assets, include petroleum, minerals, and timber. They have two main features: (1) the complete removal (consumption) of the asset, and (2) replacement of the asset only by an act of nature. Unlike plant and equipment, natural resources are consumed physically over the period of use and do not maintain their physical characteristics. Still, the accounting problems associated with natural resources are similar to those encountered with fixed assets. The questions to be answered are:

OBJECTIVE 6
Explain the accounting procedures for depletion of natural resources.

1   How do companies establish the cost basis for write-off?
2   What pattern of allocation should companies employ?

Recall that the accounting profession uses the term **depletion** for the process of allocating the cost of natural resources.

Establishing a Depletion Base

How do we determine the depletion base for natural resources? For example, a company like **ExxonMobil** makes sizable expenditures to find natural resources, and for every successful discovery there are many failures. Furthermore, it encounters long delays between the time it incurs costs and the time it obtains the benefits from the extracted resources. As a result, a company in the extractive industries, like ExxonMobil, frequently adopts a conservative policy in accounting for the expenditures related to finding and extracting natural resources.

Computation of the depletion base involves four factors: (1) acquisition cost of the deposit, (2) exploration costs, (3) development costs, and (4) restoration costs.

Acquisition Costs

Acquisition cost is the price ExxonMobil pays to obtain the property right to search and find an undiscovered natural resource. It also can be the price paid for an already-discovered resource. A third type of acquisition cost can be lease payments for property containing a productive natural resource; included in these acquisition costs are royalty payments to the owner of the property.

Generally, the acquisition cost of natural resources is recorded in an account titled Undeveloped Property. ExxonMobil later assigns that cost to the natural resource if exploration efforts are successful. If the efforts are unsuccessful, it writes off the acquisition cost as a loss.

Exploration Costs

As soon as a company has the right to use the property, it often incurs **exploration costs** needed to find the resource. When exploration costs are substantial, some companies capitalize them into the depletion base. In the oil and gas industry, where the costs of finding the resource are significant and the risks of finding the resource are very uncertain, most large companies expense these costs. Smaller oil and gas companies often capitalize these exploration costs. We examine the unique issues related to the oil and gas industry on pages 539–541 (see "Continuing Controversy").

Development Costs

Companies divide **development costs** into two parts: (1) tangible equipment costs and (2) intangible development costs. Tangible equipment costs include all of the transportation and other heavy equipment needed to extract the resource and get it ready for market. Because companies can move the heavy equipment from one extracting site to another, companies do not normally include **tangible equipment costs in the depletion base.** Instead, they use separate depreciation charges to allocate the costs of such equipment. However, some tangible assets (e.g., a drilling rig foundation) cannot be moved. Companies depreciate these assets over their useful life or the life of the resource, whichever is shorter.

Intangible development costs, on the other hand, are such items as drilling costs, tunnels, shafts, and wells. These costs have no tangible characteristics but are needed for the production of the natural resource. **Intangible development costs are considered part of the depletion base.**

Restoration Costs

Companies sometimes incur substantial costs to restore property to its natural state after extraction has occurred. These are **restoration costs.** Companies consider **restoration costs part of the depletion base.** The amount included in the depletion base is the fair value of the obligation to restore the property after extraction. A more complete discussion of the accounting for restoration costs and related liabilities (sometimes referred to as asset retirement obligations) is provided in Chapter 13. Similar to other long-lived assets, companies deduct from the depletion base any salvage value to be received on the property.

Write-Off of Resource Cost

Once the company establishes the depletion base, the next problem is determining how to allocate the cost of the natural resource to accounting periods.

Normally, companies compute depletion on a **units-of-production method** (an activity approach). Thus, depletion is a function of the number of units extracted during the period. In this approach, the total cost of the natural resource less salvage value is divided by the number of units estimated to be in the resource deposit, to obtain a **cost**

per unit of product. To compute depletion, the cost per unit is then multiplied by the number of units extracted.

For example, MaClede Co. acquired the right to use 1,000 acres of land in Alaska to mine for gold. The lease cost is $50,000, and the related exploration costs on the property are $100,000. Intangible development costs incurred in opening the mine are $850,000. Total costs related to the mine before the first ounce of gold is extracted are, therefore, $1,000,000. MaClede estimates that the mine will provide approximately 100,000 ounces of gold. Illustration 11-17 shows computation of the depletion cost per unit (depletion rate).

$$\frac{\text{Total cost} - \text{Salvage value}}{\text{Total estimated units available}} = \text{Depletion cost per unit}$$

$$\frac{\$1,000,000}{100,000} = \$10 \text{ per ounce}$$

ILLUSTRATION 11-17
Computation of
Depletion Rate

If MaClede extracts 25,000 ounces in the first year, then the depletion for the year is $250,000 (25,000 ounces × $10). It records the depletion as follows:

Inventory	250,000	
Accumulated Depletion		250,000

MaClede debits Inventory for the total depletion for the year and credits Accumulated Depletion to reduce the carrying value of the natural resource. MaClede credits Inventory when it sells the inventory. The amount not sold remains in inventory and is reported in the current assets section of the balance sheet.

Sometimes companies do not use an Accumulated Depletion account. In that case, the credit goes directly to the natural resources asset account. MaClede's balance sheet would present the cost of the natural resource and the amount of accumulated depletion entered to date as follows:

Gold mine (at cost)	$1,000,000	
Less: Accumulated depletion	250,000	$750,000

ILLUSTRATION 11-18
Balance Sheet
Presentation of Natural
Resource

In the income statement, the depletion cost is part of the cost of goods sold.

MaClede may also depreciate on a units-of-production basis the tangible equipment used in extracting the gold. This approach is appropriate if it can directly assign the estimated lives of the equipment to one given resource deposit. If MaClede uses the equipment on more than one job, other cost allocation methods such as straight-line or accelerated depreciation methods would be more appropriate.

Continuing Controversy

A major controversy relates to the accounting for exploration costs in the oil and gas industry. Conceptually, the question is whether unsuccessful ventures are a cost of those that are successful. Those who hold the **full-cost concept** argue that the cost of drilling a dry hole is a cost needed to find the commercially profitable wells. Others believe that companies should capitalize only the costs of successful projects. This is the **successful-efforts concept**. Its proponents believe that the only relevant measure for a project is the cost directly related to that project, and that companies should report any remaining costs as period charges. In addition, they argue that an unsuccessful company will end up capitalizing many costs that will make it, over a short period of time, show no less income than does one that is successful.[12]

---

[12]Large international oil companies such as **ExxonMobil** use the successful-efforts approach. Most of the smaller, exploration-oriented companies use the full-cost approach. The differences in net income figures under the two methods can be staggering. Analysts estimated that the difference between full-cost and successful efforts for **ChevronTexaco** would be $500 million over a 10-year period (income lower under successful efforts).

The FASB has attempted to narrow the available alternatives, with little success. Here is a brief history of the debate.

1 **1977—The FASB issued *Statement No. 19*, which required oil and gas companies to follow successful efforts accounting.** Small oil and gas producers, voicing strong opposition, lobbied extensively in Congress. Governmental agencies assessed the implications of this standard from a public interest perspective and reacted contrary to the FASB's position.[13]

2 **1978—In response to criticisms of the FASB's actions, the SEC reexamined the issue and found both the successful-efforts and full-cost approaches inadequate. Neither method, said the SEC, reflects the economic substance of oil and gas exploration.** As a substitute, the SEC argued in favor of a yet-to-be developed method, **reserve recognition accounting (RRA)**, which it believed would provide more useful information. Under RRA, as soon as a company discovers oil, it reports the value of the oil on the balance sheet and in the income statement. Thus, RRA is a fair-value approach, in contrast to full-costing and successful-efforts, which are historical cost approaches.[14]

3 **1979–1981—As a result of the SEC's actions, the FASB issued another standard that suspended the requirement that companies follow successful-efforts accounting.** Therefore, full costing was again permissible. In attempting to implement RRA, however, the SEC encountered practical problems in estimating **(1) the amount of the reserves, (2) the future production costs, (3) the periods of expected disposal, (4) the discount rate, and (5) the selling price.** Companies needed an estimate for each of these to arrive at an accurate valuation of existing reserves. Estimating the future selling price, appropriate discount rate, and future extraction and delivery costs of reserves that are years away from realization can be a formidable task.

4 **1981—The SEC abandoned RRA in the primary financial statements of oil and gas producers.** The SEC decided that RRA did not possess the required degree of reliability for use as a primary method of financial reporting. However, it continued to stress the need for some form of fair-value–based disclosure for oil and gas reserves. As a result, the FASB issued *Statement No. 69*, "Disclosure about Oil and Gas Producing Activities," which requires current-value disclosures.

Currently, companies can use either the full-cost approach or the successful-efforts approach. It does seem ironic that Congress directed the FASB to develop one method of accounting for the oil and gas industry, and when the FASB did so, the government chose not to accept it. Subsequently, the SEC attempted to develop a new approach, failed, and then urged the FASB to develop the disclosure requirements in this area. After all these changes, the two alternatives still exist.[15]

---

[13]The Department of Energy indicated that companies using the full-cost method at that time would reduce their exploration activities because of the unfavorable earnings impact associated with successful-efforts accounting. The Justice Department asked the SEC to postpone adoption of one uniform method of accounting in the oil and gas industry until the SEC could determine whether the information reported to investors would be enhanced and competition constrained by adoption of the successful-efforts method.

[14]The use of RRA would make a substantial difference in the balance sheets and income statements of oil companies. For example, **Atlantic Richfield Co.** at one time reported net producing property of $2.6 billion. Under RRA, the same properties would be valued at $11.8 billion. Similarly, **Standard Oil of Ohio**, which reported net producing properties of $1.7 billion, would have reported approximately $10.7 billion in producing properties under RRA.

[15]One requirement of the full-cost approach is that companies can capitalize costs only up to a ceiling, which is the present value of company reserves. Companies must expense costs above that ceiling. When the price of oil fell in the mid-1980s, so did the present value of companies' reserves, thus forcing expensing of costs beyond the ceiling. Companies lobbied for leniency, but the SEC decided that the write-offs had to be taken. **Mesa Limited Partnerships** restated its $31 million profit to a $169 million loss, and **Pacific Lighting** restated its $44.5 million profit to a $70.5 million loss.

This controversy in the oil and gas industry provides a number of lessons. First, it demonstrates the strong influence that the federal government has in financial reporting matters. Second, the concern for economic consequences places pressure on the FASB to weigh the economic effects of any required standard. Third, the experience with RRA highlights the problems that accompany any proposed change from an historical-cost to a fair-value approach. Fourth, this controversy illustrates the difficulty of establishing standards when affected groups have differing viewpoints. Finally, it reinforces the need for a conceptual framework with carefully developed guidelines for recognition, measurement, and reporting, so that interested parties can more easily resolve issues of this nature in the future.

UNDERLYING CONCEPTS

Failure to consider the economic consequences of accounting principles is a frequent criticism of the profession. However, the neutrality concept requires that the statements be free from bias. Freedom from bias requires that the statements reflect economic reality, even if undesirable effects occur.

Special Problems in Depletion Accounting

Accounting for natural resources has some interesting problems that are not common to most other types of assets. Four categories of depletion accounting problems exist:

1 Difficulty of estimating recoverable reserves.

2 Problems of discovery value.

3 Tax aspects of natural resources.

4 Accounting for liquidating dividends.

Estimating Recoverable Reserves

Not infrequently companies need to change the estimate of recoverable reserves. They do so either because they have new information or because more sophisticated production processes are available. Natural resources such as oil and gas deposits and some rare metals have recently provided the greatest challenges. Estimates of these reserves are in large measure merely "knowledgeable guesses."

This problem is the **same as accounting for changes in estimates for the useful lives of plant and equipment**. The procedure is to **revise the depletion rate on a prospective basis**: A company divides the remaining cost by the new estimate of the recoverable reserves. This approach has much merit because the required estimates are so shaky.

RAH-RAH SURPRISE

Recent cuts in the estimates of oil and natural gas reserves at **Royal Dutch/Shell, El Paso Corporation**, and other energy companies highlight the importance of reserve disclosures. Investors appear to believe that these disclosures provide useful information for assessing the future cash flows from a company's oil and gas reserves. For example, when Shell's estimates turned out to be overly optimistic (to the tune of 3.9 billion barrels or 20 percent of reserves), Shell's stock price fell.

The experience at Shell and other companies has led the SEC to look at how companies are estimating their "proved" reserves. *Proved reserves* are quantities of oil and gas that can be shown ". . . with reasonable certainty to be recoverable in future years. . . ." The phrase "reasonable certainty" is crucial to this guidance, but differences in interpretation of what is reasonably certain can result in a wide range of estimates.

In one case, for example, **ExxonMobil**'s estimate was 29 percent higher than an estimate the SEC developed. ExxonMobil was more optimistic about the effects of new technology that enables the industry to retrieve more of the oil and gas it finds. Thus, to ensure the continued usefulness of RRA disclosures, the SEC may have to work on a measurement methodology that keeps up with technology changes in the oil and gas industry.

Source: S. Labaton and J. Gerth, "At Shell, New Accounting and Rosier Outlook," *New York Times* (nytimes.com) (March 12, 2004); and J. Ball, C. Cummins, and B. Bahree, "Big Oil Differs with SEC on Methods to Calculate the Industry's Reserves," *Wall Street Journal* (February 24, 2005), p. C1.

WHAT DO THE NUMBERS MEAN?

Discovery Value

Discovery value accounting is similar to reserve recognition accounting. RRA specifically relates to the oil and gas industry, whereas **discovery value** is a broader term associated with the entire natural resources area. As indicated earlier, current standards do not allow discovery values.

However, if the accounting standard were to change, to allow discovery value to be recorded, companies would debit an asset account and credit an Unrealized Appreciation account. Unrealized Appreciation is part of stockholders' equity. The company then would transfer Unrealized Appreciation to revenue as it sells the natural resources.

A similar issue arises with resources such as growing timber, aging liquor, and maturing livestock that increase in value over time. One method is to record the increase in value as the accretion occurs: to debit the asset account and credit revenue or an unrealized revenue account. These increases can be substantial. **Boise Cascade** at one time valued its timber resources at $1.7 billion, while their book value was approximately $289 million. Accountants have been hesitant to record these increases because of the uncertainty regarding the final sales price and the problem of estimating the costs involved in getting the resources ready for sale.

Tax Aspects of Natural Resources

Some of the most controversial provisions of the Internal Revenue Code relate to the tax aspects of accounting for natural resources. The tax law has long provided a deduction against revenue from oil, gas, and most minerals for the greater of **cost** or **percentage depletion**. The percentage (statutory) depletion allows some companies a write-off ranging from 5 percent to 22 percent (depending on the natural resource) of gross revenue received. As a result of this tax benefit, the amount of depletion may exceed the cost assigned to a given natural resource. An asset's carrying amount may be zero, but the company may take a depletion deduction if it has gross revenue.

The significance of the percentage depletion allowance is now greatly reduced, since Congress repealed it for most oil and gas companies.

Liquidating Dividends

A company often owns as its only major asset a property from which it intends to extract natural resources. If the company does not expect to purchase additional properties, it may gradually distribute to stockholders their capital investments by paying **liquidating dividends**, which are dividends greater than the amount of accumulated net income.

The major accounting problem is to distinguish between dividends that are a return of capital and those that are not. Because the dividend is a return of the investor's original contribution, the company issuing a liquidating dividend should debit Paid-in Capital in Excess of Par for that portion related to the original investment, instead of debiting Retained Earnings.

To illustrate, at year-end, Callahan Mining had a retained earnings balance of $1,650,000, accumulated depletion on mineral properties of $2,100,000, and paid-in capital in excess of par of $5,435,493. Callahan's board declared a dividend of $3 a share on the 1,000,000 shares outstanding. It records the $3,000,000 cash dividend as follows.

Retained Earnings	1,650,000	
Paid-in Capital in Excess of Par	1,350,000	
Cash		3,000,000

Callahan must inform stockholders that the $3 dividend per share represents a $1.65 ($1,650,000 ÷ 1,000,000 shares) per share return on investment and a $1.35 ($1,350,000 ÷ 1,000,000 shares) per share liquidating dividend.

PRESENTATION AND ANALYSIS

Presentation of Property, Plant, Equipment, and Natural Resources

A company should disclose the basis of valuation—usually historical cost—for property, plant, equipment, and natural resources along with pledges, liens, and other commitments related to these assets. It should not offset any liability secured by property, plant, equipment, and natural resources against these assets. Instead, this obligation should be reported in the liabilities section. The company should segregate property, plant, and equipment not currently employed as producing assets in the business (such as idle facilities or land held as an investment) from assets used in operations.

When depreciating assets, a company credits a valuation account normally called Accumulated Depreciation. Using an Accumulated Depreciation account permits the user of the financial statements to see the original cost of the asset and the amount of depreciation that the company charged to expense in past years.

When depleting natural resources, some companies use an Accumulated Depletion account. Many, however, simply credit the natural resource account directly. The rationale for this approach is that the natural resources are physically consumed, making direct reduction of the cost of the natural resources appropriate.

Because of the significant impact on the financial statements of the depreciation method(s) used, companies should disclose the following.

a. Depreciation expense for the period.

b. Balances of major classes of depreciable assets, by nature and function.

c. Accumulated depreciation, either by major classes of depreciable assets or in total.

d. A general description of the method or methods used in computing depreciation with respect to major classes of depreciable assets.[16]

Special disclosure requirements relate to the oil and gas industry. Companies engaged in these activities must disclose the following in their financial statements: (1) the basic method of accounting for those costs incurred in oil and gas producing activities (e.g., full-cost versus successful-efforts), and (2) how the company disposes of costs relating to extractive activities (e.g., dispensing immediately versus depreciation and depletion.)[17]

The 2004 annual report of **International Paper Company** in Illustration 11-19 (page 544) shows an acceptable disclosure. It uses condensed balance sheet data supplemented with details and policies in notes to the financial statements.

> **OBJECTIVE 7**
> Explain how to report and analyze property, plant, equipment, and natural resources.

---

[16]"Omnibus Opinion—1967," *Opinions of the Accounting Principles Board No. 12* (New York: AICPA, 1967), par. 5. Some believe that companies should disclose the average useful life of the assets or the range of years of asset life to help users understand the age and life of property, plant, and equipment.

[17]Public companies, in addition to these two required disclosures, must include as supplementary information numerous schedules reporting reserve quantities; capitalized costs; acquisition, exploration, and development activities; and a standardized measure of discounted future net cash flows related to proved oil and gas reserve quantities. See "Disclosures about Oil and Gas Producing Activities," *Statement of Financial Accounting Standards Board No. 69* (Stamford, Conn.: FASB, 1982).

ILLUSTRATION 11-19
Disclosures for
Property, Plant,
Equipment, and Natural
Resources

International Paper Company

Consolidated Balance Sheet (partial)

In millions at December 31	2004	2003
Assets		
Total current assets	$ 9,319	$11,096
Plants, properties and equipment, net	13,432	13,260
Forestlands	3,936	3,979
Investments	679	678
Goodwill	4,994	4,793
Deferred charges and other assets	1,857	1,719
Total assets	$34,217	$35,525

Note 1 (partial)

Plants, Properties and Equipment   Plants, properties and equipment are stated at cost, less accumulated depreciation. Expenditures for betterments are capitalized whereas normal repairs and maintenance are expensed as incurred. The units-of-production method of depreciation is used for major pulp and paper mills and certain wood products facilities and the straight-line method for other plants and equipment. Annual straight-line depreciation rates are, for buildings, 2 1/2% to 8 1/2%, and, for machinery and equipment, 5% to 33%.

Forestlands   At December 31, 2004, International Paper and its subsidiaries owned or controlled about 6.8 million acres of forestlands in the United States, 1.2 million acres in Brazil, 785,000 acres in New Zealand, and had, through licenses and forest management agreements, harvesting rights on government owned forestlands in Russia. Forestlands include owned property as well as certain timber harvesting rights with terms of one or more years, and are stated at cost, less cost of timber harvested (COTH). Costs attributable to timber are charged against income as trees are cut. The rate charged is determined annually based on the relationship of incurred costs to estimated current merchantable volume.

Effective January 1, 2002, International Paper prospectively changed its method of accounting for mid-rotation fertilization expenditures to include such expenditures in the capitalized cost of forestlands. Accordingly, these costs are included as part of the COTH as trees are sold.

Note 11 (partial)

Plants, properties and equipment by major classification were:

In millions at December 31	2004	2003
Pulp, paper and packaging facilities		
Mills	$22,165	$21,234
Packaging plants	5,874	5,826
Wood products facilities	1,411	1,232
Other plants, properties and equipment	1,925	2,091
Gross cost	31,375	30,383
Less: Accumulated depreciation	17,943	17,123
Plants, properties and equipment, net	$13,432	$13,260

Analysis of Property, Plant, Equipment

Analysts evaluate assets relative to activity (turnover) and profitability.

*Additional Property,
Plant, and Equipment
Disclosures*

Asset Turnover Ratio

How efficiently a company uses its assets to generate sales is measured by the **asset turnover ratio**. This ratio divides net sales by average total assets for the period. The resulting number is the dollars of sales produced by each dollar invested in assets. To illustrate, we use the following data from the **Tootsie Roll Industries** 2004 annual report. Illustration 11-20 shows computation of the asset turnover ratio.

Tootsie Roll Industries

	(in millions)
Net sales	$420.1
Total assets, 12/31/04	811.8
Total assets, 12/31/03	665.3
Net income	64.2

$$\text{Asset turnover} = \frac{\text{Net sales}}{\text{Average total assets}}$$
$$= \frac{\$420.1}{(\$811.8 + \$665.3)/2}$$
$$= .569$$

ILLUSTRATION 11-20
Asset Turnover Ratio

The asset turnover ratio shows that Tootsie Roll generated sales of $0.57 per dollar of assets in the year ended December 31, 2004.

Asset turnover ratios vary considerably among industries. For example, a large utility like **Ameren** has a ratio of 0.32 times. A large grocery chain like **Kroger** has a ratio of 2.73 times. Thus, in comparing performance among companies based on the asset turnover ratio, you need to consider the ratio within the context of the industry in which a company operates.

Profit Margin on Sales Ratio

Another measure for analyzing the use of property, plant, and equipment is the **profit margin on sales ratio** (rate of return on sales). Calculated as net income divided by net sales, this profitability ratio does not, by itself, answer the question of how profitably a company uses its assets. But by relating the profit margin on sales to the asset turnover during a period of time, we can ascertain how profitably the company used assets during that period of time in a measure of the rate of return on assets. Using the Tootsie Roll Industries data shown above, we compute the profit margin on sales ratio and the rate of return on assets as follows.

$$\text{Profit margin on sales} = \frac{\text{Net income}}{\text{Net sales}}$$
$$= \frac{\$64.2}{\$420.1}$$
$$= 15.28\%$$
$$\text{Rate of return on assets} = \text{Profit margin on sales} \times \text{Asset turnover}$$
$$= 15.28\% \times .569$$
$$= 8.7\%$$

ILLUSTRATION 11-21
Profit Margin on Sales

Rate of Return on Assets

The rate of return a company achieves through use of its assets is the **rate of return on assets (ROA)**. Rather than using the profit margin on sales, we can compute it directly by dividing net income by average total assets. Using Tootsie Roll's data, we compute the ratio as follows.

$$\text{Rate of return on assets} = \frac{\text{Net income}}{\text{Average total assets}}$$
$$= \frac{\$64.2}{(\$811.8 + \$665.3)/2}$$
$$= 8.7\%$$

ILLUSTRATION 11-22
Rate of Return on Assets

The 8.7 percent rate of return computed in this manner equals (with rounding) the 8.7 percent rate computed by multiplying the profit margin on sales by the asset turnover. The rate of return on assets measures profitability well because it combines the effects of profit margin and asset turnover.

SUMMARY OF LEARNING OBJECTIVES

1. **Explain the concept of depreciation.** Depreciation allocates the cost of tangible assets to expense in a systematic and rational manner to those periods expected to benefit from the use of the asset.

2. **Identify the factors involved in the depreciation process.** Three factors involved in the depreciation process are: (1) determining the depreciation base for the asset, (2) estimating service lives, and (3) selecting a method of cost apportionment (depreciation).

3. **Compare activity, straight-line, and decreasing-charge methods of depreciation.** (1) *Activity method:* Assumes that depreciation is a function of use or productivity instead of the passage of time. The life of the asset is considered in terms of either the output it provides, or an input measure such as the number of hours it works. (2) *Straight-line method:* Considers depreciation a function of time instead of a function of usage. The straight-line procedure is often the most conceptually appropriate when the decline in usefulness is constant from period to period. (3) *Decreasing-charge methods:* Provides for a higher depreciation cost in the earlier years and lower charges in later periods. The main justification for this approach is that the asset is the most productive in its early years.

4. **Explain special depreciation methods.** Two special depreciation methods are: (1) *Group and composite methods:* The group method is frequently used when the assets are fairly similar in nature and have approximately the same useful lives. The composite method may be used when the assets are dissimilar and have different lives. (2) *Hybrid or combination methods:* These methods may combine straight-line/activity approaches.

5. **Explain the accounting issues related to asset impairment.** The process to determine an impairment loss is as follows: (1) Review events and changes in circumstances for possible impairment. (2) If events or changes suggest impairment, determine if the sum of the expected future net cash flows from the long-lived asset is less than the carrying amount of the asset. If less, measure the impairment loss. (3) The impairment loss is the amount by which the carrying amount of the asset exceeds the fair value of the asset.

After a company records an impairment loss, the reduced carrying amount of the long-lived asset is its new cost basis. Impairment losses may not be restored for assets held for use. If the company expects to dispose of the asset, it should report the impaired asset at the lower of cost or net realizable value. It is not depreciated. It can be continuously revalued, as long as the write-up is never to an amount greater than the carrying amount before impairment.

6. **Explain the accounting procedures for depletion of natural resources.** To account for depletion of natural resources, companies (1) establish the depletion base and (2) write off resource cost. Four factors are part of establishing the depletion base: (a) acquisition costs, (b) exploration costs, (c) development costs, and (d) restoration costs. To write off resource cost, companies normally compute depletion on the units-of-production method. Thus, depletion is a function of the number of units withdrawn during the period. To obtain a cost per unit of product, the total cost of the natural resource less salvage value is divided by the number of units estimated to be in the resource deposit, to obtain a cost per unit of product. To compute depletion, this cost per unit is multiplied by the number of units withdrawn.

7. **Explain how to report and analyze property, plant, equipment, and natural resources.** The basis of valuation for property, plant, and equipment and for natural resources should be disclosed along with pledges, liens, and other commitments related to these

assets. Companies should not offset any liability secured by property, plant, and equipment or by natural resources against these assets, but should report it in the liabilities section. When depreciating assets, credit a valuation account normally called Accumulated Depreciation. When depleting assets, use an accumulated depletion account, or credit the depletion directly to the natural resource account. Companies engaged in significant oil and gas producing activities must provide additional disclosures about these activities. Analysis may be performed to evaluate the asset turnover ratio, profit margin on sales, and rate of return on assets.

APPENDIX

11A

Income Tax Depreciation

For the most part, a financial accounting course does not address issues related to the computation of income taxes. However, because the concepts of tax depreciation are similar to those of book depreciation, and because tax depreciation methods are sometimes adopted for book purposes, we present an overview of this subject.

> **OBJECTIVE 8**
> Describe income tax methods of depreciation.

Congress passed the Accelerated Cost Recovery System (ACRS) as part of the Economic Recovery Tax Act of 1981. The goal was to stimulate capital investment through faster write-offs and to bring more uniformity to the write-off period. For assets purchased in the years 1981 through 1986, companies use ACRS and its preestablished "cost recovery periods" for various classes of assets.

In the Tax Reform Act of 1986 Congress enacted a **Modified Accelerated Cost Recovery System**, known as **MACRS**. It applies to depreciable assets placed in service in 1987 and later. The following discussion is based on these MACRS rules. Realize that tax depreciation rules are subject to change annually.[1]

MODIFIED ACCELERATED COST RECOVERY SYSTEM

The computation of depreciation under MACRS differs from the computation under GAAP in three respects: (1) a mandated tax life, which is generally shorter than the economic life; (2) cost recovery on an accelerated basis; and (3) an assigned salvage value of zero.

---

[1]For example, in an effort to jump-start the economy following the September 11, 2001, terrorist attacks, Congress passed the Job Creation and Worker Assistance Act of 2002 (the Act). The Act allows a 30 percent first-year bonus depreciation for assets placed into service after September 11, 2001, but before September 11, 2004. A follow-up provision enacted in 2003 extended the tax savings to assets placed in service before January 1, 2005. The law encourages companies to invest in fixed assets because they can front-load depreciation expense, which lowers taxable income and amount of taxes companies pay in the early years of an asset's life. Although the Act may be a good thing for the economy, it can distort cash flow measures—making them look artificially strong when the allowances are in place but reversing once the bonus depreciation expires. See D. Zion and B. Carcache, "Bonus Depreciation Boomerang," *Credit Suisse First Boston Equity Research* (February 19, 2004).

Tax Lives (Recovery Periods)

Each item of depreciable property belongs to a property class. The recovery period (depreciable tax life) of an asset depends on its property class.[2] Illustration 11A-1 presents the MACRS property classes.

ILLUSTRATION 11A-1
MACRS Property Classes

> **3-year property**—includes small tools, horses, and assets used in research and development activities
> **5-year property**—includes automobiles, trucks, computers and peripheral equipment, and office machines
> **7-year property**—includes office furniture and fixtures, agriculture equipment, oil exploration and development equipment, railroad track, manufacturing equipment, and any property not designated by law as being in any other class
> **10-year property**—includes railroad tank cars, mobile homes, boilers, and certain public utility property
> **15-year property**—includes roads, shrubbery, and certain low-income housing
> **20-year property**—includes waste-water treatment plants and sewer systems
> **27.5-year property**—includes residential rental property
> **39-year property**—includes nonresidential real property

Tax Depreciation Methods

Companies compute depreciation expense using the tax basis—usually the cost—of the asset. The depreciation method depends on the MACRS property class, as shown below.

ILLUSTRATION 11A-2
Depreciation Method for Various MACRS Property Classes

MACRS Property Class	Depreciation Method
3-, 5-, 7-, and 10-year property	Double-declining-balance
15- and 20-year property	150% declining-balance
27.5- and 39-year property	Straight-line

Depreciation computations for income tax purposes are based on the **half-year convention**. That is, a half year of depreciation is allowable in the year of acquisition and in the year of disposition.[3] A company depreciates an asset to a zero value so that there is no salvage value at the end of its MACRS life.

Use of IRS-published tables, shown in Illustration 11A-3, simplifies application of these depreciation methods.

Example of MACRS System

To illustrate depreciation computations under both the MACRS system and GAAP straight-line accounting, assume the following facts for a computer and peripheral equipment purchased by Denise Rode Company on January 1, 2006.

Acquisition date	January 1, 2006
Cost	$100,000
Estimated useful life	7 years
Estimated salvage value	$16,000
MACRS class life	5 years
MACRS method	200% declining-balance
GAAP method	Straight-line
Disposal proceeds—January 2, 2013	$11,000

---

[2]Tax depreciation changed numerous times in the 1980s and 1990s. For example, since 1980, Congress has enacted six different depreciation requirements. The tax life of certain real property changed from 35 years in 1980 to 15 in 1981, 18 in 1982, 19 in 1984, 31.5 in 1986, and 39 in 1993. As one writer noted, "It appears that the useful life of a depreciation law is 2.2 years."

[3]The tax law requires mid-quarter and mid-month conventions for MACRS purposes in certain circumstances.

			MACRS Depreciation Rates by Class of Property			
Recovery Year	3-year (200% DB)	5-year (200% DB)	7-year (200% DB)	10-year (200% DB)	15-year (150% DB)	20-year (150% DB)
1	33.33	20.00	14.29	10.00	5.00	3.750
2	44.45	32.00	24.49	18.00	9.50	7.219
3	14.81*	19.20	17.49	14.40	8.55	6.677
4	7.41	11.52*	12.49	11.52	7.70	6.177
5		11.52	8.93*	9.22	6.93	5.713
6		5.76	8.92	7.37	6.23	5.285
7			8.93	6.55*	5.90*	4.888
8			4.46	6.55	5.90	4.522
9				6.56	5.91	4.462*
10				6.55	5.90	4.461
11				3.28	5.91	4.462
12					5.90	4.461
13					5.91	4.462
14					5.90	4.461
15					5.91	4.462
16					2.95	4.461
17						4.462
18						4.461
19						4.462
20						4.461
21						2.231

*Switchover to straight-line depreciation.

Using the rates from the MACRS depreciation rate schedule for a 5-year class of property, Rode computes depreciation as follows for tax purposes.

MACRS Depreciation

2006	$100,000 × .20	=	$ 20,000
2007	$100,000 × .32	=	32,000
2008	$100,000 × .192	=	19,200
2009	$100,000 × .1152	=	11,520
2010	$100,000 × .1152	=	11,520
2011	$100,000 × .0576	=	5,760
Total depreciation			$100,000

Rode computes the depreciation under GAAP straight-line method, with $16,000 of estimated salvage value and an estimated useful life of 7 years, as shown in Illustration 11A-5.

GAAP Depreciation

($100,000 − $16,000) ÷ 7 = $12,000 annual depreciation
× 7 years

1/1/06–1/2/13 $84,000 total depreciation

The MACRS depreciation recovers the total cost of the asset on an accelerated basis. But, a taxable gain of $11,000 results from the sale of the asset at January 2, 2013. Therefore, the net effect on taxable income for the years 2006 through 2013 is $89,000 ($100,000 depreciation − $11,000 gain).

Under GAAP, the company recognizes a loss on disposal of $5,000 ($16,000 book value − $11,000 disposal proceeds). The net effect on income before income taxes for the years 2006 through 2013 is $89,000 ($84,000 depreciation + $5,000 loss), the same as the net effect of MACRS on taxable income.

Even though the net effects are equal in amount, the deferral of income tax payments under MACRS from early in the life of the asset to later in life is desirable. The different amounts of depreciation for income tax reporting and financial GAAP reporting in each year are a matter of timing and result in temporary differences, which require **interperiod tax allocation**. (See Chapter 19 for an extended treatment of this topic.)

Optional Straight-Line Method

INTERNATIONAL INSIGHT

In Switzerland, depreciation in the financial statements conforms to that on the tax returns. As a consequence, companies may depreciate as much as 80% of the cost of assets in the first year.

An alternate MACRS method exists for determining depreciation deductions. Based on the straight-line method, it is referred to as the **optional** (elective) **straight-line method**. This method applies to the six classes of property described earlier. The alternate MACRS applies the straight-line method to the MACRS recovery periods. It ignores salvage value.

Under the optional straight-line method, in the first year in which the property is put in service, the company deducts half of the amount of depreciation that would be permitted for a full year (half-year convention). Use the half-year convention for homework problems.

Tax versus Book Depreciation

GAAP requires that companies allocate the cost of depreciable assets to expense over the expected useful life of the asset in a systematic and rational manner. Some argue that from a cost-benefit perspective it would be better for companies to adopt the MACRS approach in order to eliminate the necessity of maintaining two different sets of records.

However, the tax laws and financial reporting have different objectives: The purpose of taxation is to raise revenue from constituents in an equitable manner. The purpose of financial reporting is to reflect the economic substance of a transaction as closely as possible and to help predict the amounts, timing, and uncertainty of future cash flows. Because these objectives differ, the adoption of one method for both tax and book purposes in all cases would be unfortunate.

KEY TERM

Modified Accelerated Cost Recovery System (MACRS), *547*

SUMMARY OF LEARNING OBJECTIVE FOR APPENDIX 11A

8. Describe income tax methods of depreciation. Congress enacted a Modified Accelerated Cost Recovery System (MACRS) in the Tax Reform Act of 1986. It applies to depreciable assets placed in service in 1987 and later. The computation of depreciation under MACRS differs from the computation under GAAP in three respects: (1) a mandated tax life, which is generally shorter than the economic life; (2) cost recovery on an accelerated basis; and (3) an assigned salvage value of zero.

Note: All **asterisked** Questions, Exercises, Problems, and Concepts for Analysis relate to material contained in the appendix to the chapter.

QUESTIONS

1. Distinguish between depreciation, depletion, and amortization.

2. Identify the factors that are relevant in determining the annual depreciation charge, and explain whether these factors are determined objectively or whether they are based on judgment.

3. Some believe that accounting depreciation measures the decline in the value of fixed assets. Do you agree? Explain.

4. Explain how estimation of service lives can result in unrealistically high valuations of fixed assets.

5. The plant manager of a manufacturing firm suggested in a conference of the company's executives that accountants should speed up depreciation on the machinery in the finishing department because improvements were rapidly making those machines obsolete and a depreciation fund big enough to cover their replacement is needed. Discuss the accounting concept of depreciation and the effect on a business concern of the depreciation recorded for plant assets, paying particular attention to the issues raised by the plant manager.

6. For what reasons are plant assets retired? Define inadequacy, supersession, and obsolescence.

7. What basic questions must be answered before the amount of the depreciation charge can be computed?

8. Elizabeth Ashley Company purchased a machine on January 2, 2006, for $600,000. The machine has an estimated useful life of 5 years and a salvage value of $100,000. Depreciation was computed by the 150% declining-balance method. What is the amount of accumulated depreciation at the end of December 31, 2007?

9. Linda Blair Company purchased machinery for $120,000 on January 1, 2007. It is estimated that the machinery will have a useful life of 20 years, salvage value of $15,000, production of 84,000 units, and working hours of 42,000. During 2007 the company uses the machinery for 14,300 hours, and the machinery produces 20,000 units. Compute depreciation under the straight-line, units-of-output, working hours, sum-of-the-years'-digits, and declining-balance (use 10% as the annual rate) methods.

10. What are the major factors considered in determining what depreciation method to use?

11. Under what conditions is it appropriate for a business to use the composite method of depreciation for its plant assets? What are the advantages and disadvantages of this method?

12. If Brad Pitt, Inc. uses the composite method and its composite rate is 7.5% per year, what entry should it make when plant assets that originally cost $50,000 and have been used for 10 years are sold for $16,000?

13. A building that was purchased December 31, 1982, for $2,400,000 was originally estimated to have a life of 50 years with no salvage value at the end of that time. Depreciation has been recorded through 2006. During 2007 an examination of the building by an engineering firm discloses that its estimated useful life is 15 years after 2006. What should be the amount of depreciation for 2007?

14. Armand Assante, president of Flatbush Company, has recently noted that depreciation increases cash provided by operations and therefore depreciation is a good source of funds. Do you agree? Discuss.

15. Melanie Mayron purchased a computer for $6,000 on July 1, 2007. She intends to depreciate it over 4 years using the double-declining balance method. Salvage value is $1,000. Compute depreciation for 2008.

16. Astaire Inc. is considering the write-down of its long-term plant because of a lack of profitability. Explain to the management of Astaire how to determine whether a write-off is permitted.

17. Last year Wilde Company recorded an impairment on an asset held for use. Recent appraisals indicate that the asset has increased in value. Should Wilde record this recovery in value?

18. Kuga Co. has equipment with a carrying amount of $700,000. The expected future net cash flows from the equipment are $705,000, and its fair value is $590,000. The equipment is expected to be used in operations in the future. What amount (if any) should Kuga report as an impairment to its equipment?

19. Explain how gains or losses on impaired assets should be reported in income.

20. It has been suggested that plant and equipment could be replaced more quickly if depreciation rates for income tax and accounting purposes were substantially increased. As a result, business operations would receive the benefit of more modern and more efficient plant facilities. Discuss the merits of this proposition.

21. Neither depreciation on replacement cost nor depreciation adjusted for changes in the purchasing power of the dollar has been recognized as generally accepted accounting principles for inclusion in the primary financial statements. Briefly present the accounting treatment that might be used to assist in the maintenance of the ability of a company to replace its productive capacity.

22. List (a) the similarities and (b) the differences in the accounting treatments of depreciation and cost depletion.

23. Describe cost depletion and percentage depletion. Why is the percentage depletion method permitted?

24. In what way may the use of percentage depletion violate sound accounting theory?

25. In the extractive industries, businesses may pay dividends in excess of net income. What is the maximum permissible? How can this practice be justified?

26. The following statement appeared in a financial magazine: "RRA—or Rah-Rah, as it's sometimes dubbed—has kicked up quite a storm. Oil companies, for example, are convinced that the approach is misleading. Major accounting firms agree." What is RRA? Why might oil companies believe that this approach is misleading?

27. Adriana Oil uses successful efforts accounting and also provides full-cost results as well. Under full-cost, Adriana Oil would have reported retained earnings of $42 million and net income of $4 million. Under successful efforts, retained earnings were $29 million, and net income was $3 million. Explain the difference between full costing and successful efforts accounting.

28. **Target Corporation** in 2004 reported net income of $3.2 billion, net sales of $45.7 billion, and average total assets of $29.8 billion. What is Target's asset turnover ratio? What is Target's rate of return on assets?

*29. What is a modified accelerated cost recovery system (MACRS)? Speculate as to why this system is now required for tax purposes.

BRIEF EXERCISES

(LO 4) **BE11-1** Castlevania Corporation purchased a truck at the beginning of 2007 for $42,000. The truck is estimated to have a salvage value of $2,000 and a useful life of 160,000 miles. It was driven 23,000 miles in 2007 and 31,000 miles in 2008. Compute depreciation expense for 2007 and 2008.

(LO 2, 3) **BE11-2** Cheetah Company purchased machinery on January 1, 2007, for $60,000. The machinery is estimated to have a salvage value of $6,000 after a useful life of 8 years. (a) Compute 2007 depreciation expense using the straight-line method. (b) Compute 2007 depreciation expense using the straight-line method assuming the machinery was purchased on September 1, 2007.

(LO 2, 3) **BE11-3** Use the information for Cheetah Company given in BE11-2. (a) Compute 2007 depreciation expense using the sum-of-the-years'-digits method. (b) Compute 2007 depreciation expense using the sum-of-the-years'-digits method assuming the machinery was purchased on April 1, 2007.

(LO 2, 3) **BE11-4** Use the information for Cheetah Company given in BE11-2. (a) Compute 2007 depreciation expense using the double-declining balance method. (b) Compute 2007 depreciation expense using the double-declining balance method assuming the machinery was purchased on October 1, 2007.

(LO 2, 3) **BE11-5** Garfield Company purchased a machine on July 1, 2008, for $25,000. Garfield paid $200 in title fees and county property tax of $125 on the machine. In addition, Garfield paid $500 shipping charges for delivery, and $475 was paid to a local contractor to build and wire a platform for the machine on the plant floor. The machine has an estimated useful life of 6 years with a salvage value of $3,000. Determine the depreciation base of Garfield's new machine. Garfield uses straight-line depreciation.

(LO 4) **BE11-6** Battlesport Inc. owns the following assets.

Asset	Cost	Salvage	Estimated Useful Life
A	$70,000	$ 7,000	10 years
B	50,000	10,000	5 years
C	82,000	4,000	12 years

Compute the composite depreciation rate and the composite life of Battlesport's assets.

(LO 2) **BE11-7** Myst Company purchased a computer for $7,000 on January 1, 2006. Straight-line depreciation is used, based on a 5-year life and a $1,000 salvage value. In 2008, the estimates are revised. Myst now feels the computer will be used until December 31, 2009, when it can be sold for $500. Compute the 2008 depreciation.

(LO 5) **BE11-8** Dinoland Company owns machinery that cost $900,000 and has accumulated depreciation of $360,000. The expected future net cash flows from the use of the asset are expected to be $500,000. The fair value of the equipment is $400,000. Prepare the journal entry, if any, to record the impairment loss.

(LO 6) **BE11-9** Genghis Khan Corporation acquires a coal mine at a cost of $400,000. Intangible development costs total $100,000. After extraction has occurred, Khan must restore the property (estimated fair value of the obligation is $75,000), after which it can be sold for $160,000. Khan estimates that 4,000 tons of coal can be extracted. If 700 tons are extracted the first year, prepare the journal entry to record depletion.

(LO 7) **BE11-10** In its 2004 annual report **Campbell Soup Company** reports beginning-of-the-year total assets of $6,205 million, end-of-the-year total assets of $6,675 million, total sales of $7,109 million, and net income of $647 million. (a) Compute Campbell's asset turnover ratio. (b) Compute Campbell's profit margin on sales. (c) Compute Campbell's rate of return on assets (1) using asset turnover and profit margin and (2) using net income.

(LO 8) *****BE11-11** Timecap Corporation purchased an asset at a cost of $40,000 on March 1, 2008. The asset has a useful life of 8 years and a salvage value of $4,000. For tax purposes, the MACRS class life is 5 years. Compute tax depreciation for each year 2008–2013.

EXERCISES

(LO 2, 3) **E11-1 (Depreciation Computations—SL, SYD, DDB)** Deluxe Ezra Company purchases equipment on January 1, Year 1, at a cost of $469,000. The asset is expected to have a service life of 12 years and a salvage value of $40,000.

Instructions

(a) Compute the amount of depreciation for each of Years 1 through 3 using the straight-line depreciation method.

(b) Compute the amount of depreciation for each of Years 1 through 3 using the sum-of-the-years'-digits method.

(c) Compute the amount of depreciation for each of Years 1 through 3 using the double-declining balance method. (In performing your calculations, round constant percentage to the nearest one-hundredth of a point and round answers to the nearest dollar.)

(LO 2, 3) **E11-2 (Depreciation—Conceptual Understanding)** Rembrandt Company acquired a plant asset at the beginning of Year 1. The asset has an estimated service life of 5 years. An employee has prepared depreciation schedules for this asset using three different methods to compare the results of using one method with the results of using other methods. You are to assume that the following schedules have been correctly prepared for this asset using (1) the straight-line method, (2) the sum-of-the-years'-digits method, and (3) the double-declining balance method.

Year	Straight-Line	Sum-of-the-Years'-Digits	Double-Declining Balance
1	$ 9,000	$15,000	$20,000
2	9,000	12,000	12,000
3	9,000	9,000	7,200
4	9,000	6,000	4,320
5	9,000	3,000	1,480
Total	$45,000	$45,000	$45,000

Instructions
Answer the following questions.

(a) What is the cost of the asset being depreciated?
(b) What amount, if any, was used in the depreciation calculations for the salvage value for this asset?
(c) Which method will produce the highest charge to income in Year 1?
(d) Which method will produce the highest charge to income in Year 4?
(e) Which method will produce the highest book value for the asset at the end of Year 3?
(f) If the asset is sold at the end of Year 3, which method would yield the highest gain (or lowest loss) on disposal of the asset?

(LO 2, 3) **E11-3 (Depreciation Computations—SYD, DDB—Partial Periods)** Judds Company purchased a new plant asset on April 1, 2007, at a cost of $711,000. It was estimated to have a service life of 20 years and a salvage value of $60,000. Judds' accounting period is the calendar year.

Instructions
(a) Compute the depreciation for this asset for 2007 and 2008 using the sum-of-the-years'-digits method.
(b) Compute the depreciation for this asset for 2007 and 2008 using the double-declining balance method.

(LO 2, 3) **E11-4 (Depreciation Computations—Five Methods)** Jon Seceda Furnace Corp. purchased machinery for $315,000 on May 1, 2007. It is estimated that it will have a useful life of 10 years, salvage value of $15,000, production of 240,000 units, and working hours of 25,000. During 2008 Seceda Corp. uses the machinery for 2,650 hours, and the machinery produces 25,500 units.

Instructions
From the information given, compute the depreciation charge for 2008 under each of the following methods. (Round to the nearest dollar.)

(a) Straight-line.
(b) Units-of-output.
(c) Working hours.
(d) Sum-of-the-years'-digits.
(e) Declining-balance (use 20% as the annual rate).

(LO 2, 3) **E11-5 (Depreciation Computations—Four Methods)** Robert Parish Corporation purchased a new machine for its assembly process on August 1, 2007. The cost of this machine was $117,900. The company estimated that the machine would have a salvage value of $12,900 at the end of its service life. Its life is estimated at 5 years and its working hours are estimated at 21,000 hours. Year-end is December 31.

Instructions
Compute the depreciation expense under the following methods. Each of the following should be considered unrelated.

(a) Straight-line depreciation for 2007.
(b) Activity method for 2007, assuming that machine usage was 800 hours.

    (c) Sum-of-the-years'-digits for 2008.
    (d) Double-declining balance for 2008.

(LO 2, 3)   **E11-6** **(Depreciation Computations—Five Methods, Partial Periods)** Muggsy Bogues Company purchased equipment for $212,000 on October 1, 2006. It is estimated that the equipment will have a useful life of 8 years and a salvage value of $12,000. Estimated production is 40,000 units and estimated working hours are 20,000. During 2006, Bogues uses the equipment for 525 hours and the equipment produces 1,000 units.

Instructions

Compute depreciation expense under each of the following methods. Bogues is on a calendar-year basis ending December 31.

    (a) Straight-line method for 2006.
    (b) Activity method (units of output) for 2006.
    (c) Activity method (working hours) for 2006.
    (d) Sum-of-the-years'-digits method for 2008.
    (e) Double-declining balance method for 2007.

(LO 2, 3)   **E11-7** **(Different Methods of Depreciation)** Jackel Industries presents you with the following information.

Description	Date Purchased	Cost	Salvage Value	Life in Years	Depreciation Method	Accumulated Depreciation to 12/31/07	Depreciation for 2008
Machine A	2/12/06	$142,500	$16,000	10	**(a)**	$33,350	**(b)**
Machine B	8/15/05	**(c)**	21,000	5	SL	29,000	**(d)**
Machine C	7/21/04	75,400	23,500	8	DDB	**(e)**	**(f)**
Machine D	10/12/**(g)**	219,000	69,000	5	SYD	70,000	**(h)**

Instructions

Complete the table for the year ended December 31, 2008. The company depreciates all assets using the half-year convention.

(LO 2, 3)   **E11-8** **(Depreciation Computation—Replacement, Nonmonetary Exchange)** George Zidek Corporation bought a machine on June 1, 2005, for $31,000, f.o.b. the place of manufacture. Freight to the point where it was set up was $200, and $500 was expended to install it. The machine's useful life was estimated at 10 years, with a salvage value of $2,500. On June 1, 2006, an essential part of the machine is replaced, at a cost of $1,980, with one designed to reduce the cost of operating the machine. The cost of the old part and related depreciation cannot be determined with any accuracy.

    On June 1, 2009, the company buys a new machine of greater capacity for $35,000, delivered, trading in the old machine which has a fair market value and trade-in allowance of $20,000. To prepare the old machine for removal from the plant cost $75, and expenditures to install the new one were $1,500. It is estimated that the new machine has a useful life of 10 years, with a salvage value of $4,000 at the end of that time. (The exchange has commercial substance.)

Instructions

Assuming that depreciation is to be computed on the straight-line basis, compute the annual depreciation on the new equipment that should be provided for the fiscal year beginning June 1, 2009. (Round to the nearest dollar.)

(LO 2, 3)   **E11-9** **(Composite Depreciation)** Presented below is information related to LeBron James Manufacturing Corporation.

Asset	Cost	Estimated Salvage	Estimated Life (in years)
A	$40,500	$5,500	10
B	33,600	4,800	9
C	36,000	3,600	9
D	19,000	1,500	7
E	23,500	2,500	6

Instructions

    (a) Compute the rate of depreciation per year to be applied to the plant assets under the composite method.
    (b) Prepare the adjusting entry necessary at the end of the year to record depreciation for the year.
    (c) Prepare the entry to record the sale of asset D for cash of $4,800. It was used for 6 years, and depreciation was entered under the composite method.

(LO 2, 3)   **E11-10** **(Depreciation Computations, SYD)** Five Satins Company purchased a piece of equipment at the beginning of 2004. The equipment cost $430,000. It has an estimated service life of 8 years and an expected salvage value of $70,000. The sum-of-the-years'-digits method of depreciation is being used. Someone has already correctly prepared a depreciation schedule for this asset. This schedule shows that $60,000 will be depreciated for a particular calendar year.

Instructions
Show calculations to determine for what particular year the depreciation amount for this asset will be $60,000.

(LO 2, 3) **E11-11 (Depreciation—Change in Estimate)** Machinery purchased for $60,000 by Tom Brady Co. in 2003 was originally estimated to have a life of 8 years with a salvage value of $4,000 at the end of that time. Depreciation has been entered for 5 years on this basis. In 2008, it is determined that the total estimated life should be 10 years with a salvage value of $4,500 at the end of that time. Assume straight-line depreciation.

Instructions
(a) Prepare the entry to correct the prior years' depreciation, if necessary.
(b) Prepare the entry to record depreciation for 2008.

(LO 2, 3) **E11-12 (Depreciation Computation—Addition, Change in Estimate)** In 1980, Herman Moore Company completed the construction of a building at a cost of $2,000,000 and first occupied it in January 1981. It was estimated that the building will have a useful life of 40 years and a salvage value of $60,000 at the end of that time.

Early in 1991, an addition to the building was constructed at a cost of $500,000. At that time it was estimated that the remaining life of the building would be, as originally estimated, an additional 30 years, and that the addition would have a life of 30 years, and a salvage value of $20,000.

In 2009, it is determined that the probable life of the building and addition will extend to the end of 2040 or 20 years beyond the original estimate.

Instructions
(a) Using the straight-line method, compute the annual depreciation that would have been charged from 1981 through 1990.
(b) Compute the annual depreciation that would have been charged from 1991 through 2008.
(c) Prepare the entry, if necessary, to adjust the account balances because of the revision of the estimated life in 2009.
(d) Compute the annual depreciation to be charged beginning with 2009.

(LO 2, 3) **E11-13 (Depreciation—Replacement, Change in Estimate)** Greg Maddox Company constructed a building at a cost of $2,200,000 and occupied it beginning in January 1988. It was estimated at that time that its life would be 40 years, with no salvage value.

In January 2008, a new roof was installed at a cost of $300,000, and it was estimated then that the building would have a useful life of 25 years from that date. The cost of the old roof was $160,000.

Instructions
(a) What amount of depreciation should have been charged annually from the years 1988 to 2007? (Assume straight-line depreciation.)
(b) What entry should be made in 2008 to record the replacement of the roof?
(c) Prepare the entry in January 2008, to record the revision in the estimated life of the building, if necessary.
(d) What amount of depreciation should be charged for the year 2008?

(LO 2, 3) **E11-14 (Error Analysis and Depreciation, SL and SYD)** Mike Devereaux Company shows the following entries in its Equipment account for 2008. All amounts are based on historical cost.

Equipment				
2008			2008	
Jan. 1	Balance	134,750	June 30 Cost of equipment sold	
Aug. 10	Purchases	32,000	(purchased prior	
12	Freight on equipment		to 2008)	23,000
	purchased	700		
25	Installation costs	2,700		
Nov. 10	Repairs	500		

Instructions
(a) Prepare any correcting entries necessary.
(b) Assuming that depreciation is to be charged for a full year on the ending balance in the asset account, compute the proper depreciation charge for 2008 under each of the methods listed

below. Assume an estimated life of 10 years, with no salvage value. The machinery included in the January 1, 2008, balance was purchased in 2006.

(1) Straight-line.
(2) Sum-of-the-years'-digits.

(LO 2, 3) **E11-15 (Depreciation for Fractional Periods)** On March 10, 2009, Lost World Company sells equipment that it purchased for $192,000 on August 20, 2002. It was originally estimated that the equipment would have a life of 12 years and a salvage value of $16,800 at the end of that time, and depreciation has been computed on that basis. The company uses the straight-line method of depreciation.

Instructions

(a) Compute the depreciation charge on this equipment for 2002, for 2009, and the total charge for the period from 2003 to 2008, inclusive, under each of the six following assumptions with respect to partial periods.
   (1) Depreciation is computed for the exact period of time during which the asset is owned. (Use 365 days for base.)
   (2) Depreciation is computed for the full year on the January 1 balance in the asset account.
   (3) Depreciation is computed for the full year on the December 31 balance in the asset account.
   (4) Depreciation for one-half year is charged on plant assets acquired or disposed of during the year.
   (5) Depreciation is computed on additions from the beginning of the month following acquisition and on disposals to the beginning of the month following disposal.
   (6) Depreciation is computed for a full period on all assets in use for over one-half year, and no depreciation is charged on assets in use for less than one-half year. (Use 365 days for base.)
(b) Briefly evaluate the methods above, considering them from the point of view of basic accounting theory as well as simplicity of application.

(LO 5) **E11-16 (Impairment)** Presented below is information related to equipment owned by Suarez Company at December 31, 2007.

Cost	$9,000,000
Accumulated depreciation to date	1,000,000
Expected future net cash flows	7,000,000
Fair value	4,800,000

Assume that Suarez will continue to use this asset in the future. As of December 31, 2007, the equipment has a remaining useful life of 4 years.

Instructions

(a) Prepare the journal entry (if any) to record the impairment of the asset at December 31, 2007.
(b) Prepare the journal entry to record depreciation expense for 2008.
(c) The fair value of the equipment at December 31, 2008, is $5,100,000. Prepare the journal entry (if any) necessary to record this increase in fair value.

(LO 5) **E11-17 (Impairment)** Assume the same information as E11-16, except that Suarez intends to dispose of the equipment in the coming year. It is expected that the cost of disposal will be $20,000.

Instructions

(a) Prepare the journal entry (if any) to record the impairment of the asset at December 31, 2007.
(b) Prepare the journal entry (if any) to record depreciation expense for 2008.
(c) The asset was not sold by December 31, 2008. The fair value of the equipment on that date is $5,300,000. Prepare the journal entry (if any) necessary to record this increase in fair value. It is expected that the cost of disposal is still $20,000.

(LO 5) **E11-18 (Impairment)** The management of Petro Garcia Inc. was discussing whether certain equipment should be written off as a charge to current operations because of obsolescence. This equipment has a cost of $900,000 with depreciation to date of $400,000 as of December 31, 2007. On December 31, 2007, management projected its future net cash flows from this equipment to be $300,000 and its fair value to be $230,000. The company intends to use this equipment in the future.

Instructions

(a) Prepare the journal entry (if any) to record the impairment at December 31, 2007.
(b) Where should the gain or loss (if any) on the write-down be reported in the income statement?
(c) At December 31, 2008, the equipment's fair value increased to $260,000. Prepare the journal entry (if any) to record this increase in fair value.
(d) What accounting issues did management face in accounting for this impairment?

(LO 6) **E11-19 (Depletion Computations—Timber)** Stanislaw Timber Company owns 9,000 acres of timberland purchased in 1996 at a cost of $1,400 per acre. At the time of purchase the land without the timber was valued at $400 per acre. In 1997, Stanislaw built fire lanes and roads, with a life of 30 years, at a cost of $84,000. Every year Stanislaw sprays to prevent disease at a cost of $3,000 per year and spends $7,000 to maintain the fire lanes and roads. During 1998, Stanislaw selectively logged and sold 700,000 board feet of timber, of the estimated 3,500,000 board feet. In 1999, Stanislaw planted new seedlings to replace the trees cut at a cost of $100,000.

Instructions
 (a) Determine the depreciation expense and the cost of timber sold related to depletion for 1998.
 (b) Stanislaw has not logged since 1998. If Stanislaw logged and sold 900,000 board feet of timber in 2009, when the timber cruise (appraiser) estimated 5,000,000 board feet, determine the cost of timber sold related to depletion for 2009.

(LO 6) **E11-20 (Depletion Computations—Oil)** Diderot Drilling Company has leased property on which oil has been discovered. Wells on this property produced 18,000 barrels of oil during the past year that sold at an average sales price of $55 per barrel. Total oil resources of this property are estimated to be 250,000 barrels.

  The lease provided for an outright payment of $500,000 to the lessor (owner) before drilling could be commenced and an annual rental of $31,500. A premium of 5% of the sales price of every barrel of oil removed is to be paid annually to the lessor. In addition, Diderot (lessee) is to clean up all the waste and debris from drilling and to bear the costs of reconditioning the land for farming when the wells are abandoned. The estimated fair value, at the time of the lease, of this clean-up and reconditioning is $30,000.

Instructions
From the provisions of the lease agreement, you are to compute the cost per barrel for the past year, exclusive of operating costs, to Diderot Drilling Company.

(LO 6) **E11-21 (Depletion Computations—Timber)** Forda Lumber Company owns a 7,000-acre tract of timber purchased in 2000 at a cost of $1,300 per acre. At the time of purchase the land was estimated to have a value of $300 per acre without the timber. Forda Lumber Company has not logged this tract since it was purchased. In 2007, Forda had the timber cruised. The cruise (appraiser) estimated that each acre contained 8,000 board feet of timber. In 2007, Forda built 10 miles of roads at a cost of $7,840 per mile. After the roads were completed, Forda logged and sold 3,500 trees containing 850,000 board feet.

Instructions
 (a) Determine the cost of timber sold related to depletion for 2007.
 (b) If Forda depreciates the logging roads on the basis of timber cut, determine the depreciation expense for 2007.
 (c) If Forda plants five seedlings at a cost of $4 per seedling for each tree cut, how should Forda treat the reforestation?

(LO 6) **E11-22 (Depletion Computations—Mining)** Alcide Mining Company purchased land on February 1, 2007, at a cost of $1,190,000. It estimated that a total of 60,000 tons of mineral was available for mining. After it has removed all the natural resources, the company will be required to restore the property to its previous state because of strict environmental protection laws. It estimates the fair value of this restoration obligation at $90,000. It believes it will be able to sell the property afterwards for $100,000. It incurred developmental costs of $200,000 before it was able to do any mining. In 2007 resources removed totaled 30,000 tons. The company sold 22,000 tons.

Instructions
Compute the following information for 2007.

 (a) Per unit material cost.
 (b) Total material cost of December 31, 2007, inventory.
 (c) Total materials cost in cost of goods sold at December 31, 2007.

(LO 6) **E11-23 (Depletion Computations—Minerals)** At the beginning of 2007, Aristotle Company acquired a mine for $970,000. Of this amount, $100,000 was ascribed to the land value and the remaining portion to the minerals in the mine. Surveys conducted by geologists have indicated that approximately 12,000,000 units of the ore appear to be in the mine. Aristotle incurred $170,000 of development costs associated with this mine prior to any extraction of minerals. It also determined that the fair value of its obligation to prepare the land for an alternative use when all of the mineral has been removed was $40,000. During 2007, 2,500,000 units of ore were extracted and 2,100,000 of these units were sold.

Instructions

Compute the following.

(a) The total amount of depletion for 2007.

(b) The amount that is charged as an expense for 2007 for the cost of the minerals sold during 2007.

(LO 7) E11-24 **(Ratio Analysis)** The 2004 Annual Report of **Eastman Kodak** contains the following information.

(in millions)	December 31, 2004	December 31, 2003
Total assets	$14,737	$14,846
Total liabilities	10,926	11,601
Net sales	13,516	12,909
Net income	556	253

Instructions

Compute the following ratios for Eastman Kodak for 2004.

(a) Asset turnover ratio.

(b) Rate of return on assets.

(c) Profit margin on sales.

(d) How can the asset turnover ratio be used to compute the rate of return on assets?

(LO 8) *E11-25 **(Book vs. Tax (MACRS) Depreciation)** Futabatei Enterprises purchased a delivery truck on January 1, 2007, at a cost of $27,000. The truck has a useful life of 7 years with an estimated salvage value of $6,000. The straight-line method is used for book purposes. For tax purposes the truck, having an MACRS class life of 7 years, is classified as 5-year property; the optional MACRS tax rate tables are used to compute depreciation. In addition, assume that for 2007 and 2008 the company has revenues of $200,000 and operating expenses (excluding depreciation) of $130,000.

Instructions

(a) Prepare income statements for 2007 and 2008. (The final amount reported on the income statement should be income before income taxes.)

(b) Compute taxable income for 2007 and 2008.

(c) Determine the total depreciation to be taken over the useful life of the delivery truck for both book and tax purposes.

(d) Explain why depreciation for book and tax purposes will generally be different over the useful life of a depreciable asset.

(LO 8) *E11-26 **(Book vs. Tax (MACRS) Depreciation)** Shimei Inc. purchased computer equipment on March 1, 2007, for $31,000. The computer equipment has a useful life of 10 years and a salvage value of $1,000. For tax purposes, the MACRS class life is 5 years.

Instructions

(a) Assuming that the company uses the straight-line method for book and tax purposes, what is the depreciation expense reported in (1) the financial statements for 2007 and (2) the tax return for 2007?

(b) Assuming that the company uses the double-declining balance method for both book and tax purposes, what is the depreciation expense reported in (1) the financial statements for 2007 and (2) the tax return for 2007?

(c) Why is depreciation for tax purposes different from depreciation for book purposes even if the company uses the same depreciation method to compute them both?

See the book's website, www.wiley.com/college/kieso, for Additional Exercises.

PROBLEMS

(LO 2, 3) P11-1 **(Depreciation for Partial Period—SL, SYD, and DDB)** Onassis Company purchased Machine #201 on May 1, 2007. The following information relating to Machine #201 was gathered at the end of May.

Price	$73,500
Credit terms	2/10, n/30
Freight-in costs	$ 970
Preparation and installation costs	$ 3,800
Labor costs during regular production operations	$10,500

It was expected that the machine could be used for 10 years, after which the salvage value would be zero. Onassis intends to use the machine for only 8 years, however, after which it expects to be able to sell it for $1,200. The invoice for Machine #201 was paid May 5, 2007. Onassis uses the calendar year as the basis for the preparation of financial statements.

Instructions

(a) Compute the depreciation expense for the years indicated using the following methods. (Round to the nearest dollar.)

(1) Straight-line method for 2007.

(2) Sum-of-the-years'-digits method for 2008.

(3) Double-declining balance method for 2007.

(b) Suppose Jackie Ari, the president of Onassis, tells you that because the company is a new organization, she expects it will be several years before production and sales reach optimum levels. She asks you to recommend a depreciation method that will allocate less of the company's depreciation expense to the early years and more to later years of the assets' lives. What method would you recommend?

(LO 2, 3) **P11-2 (Depreciation for Partial Periods—SL, Act., SYD, and DDB)** The cost of equipment purchased by Boris Becker, Inc., on June 1, 2007 is $67,000. It is estimated that the machine will have a $4,000 salvage value at the end of its service life. Its service life is estimated at 7 years; its total working hours are estimated at 42,000 and its total production is estimated at 525,000 units. During 2007 the machine was operated 6,000 hours and produced 55,000 units. During 2008 the machine was operated 5,500 hours and produced 48,000 units.

Instructions

Compute depreciation expense on the machine for the year ending December 31, 2007, and the year ending December 31, 2008, using the following methods.

(a) Straight-line.

(b) Units-of-output.

(c) Working hours.

(d) Sum-of-the-years'-digits.

(e) Declining balance (twice the straight-line rate).

(LO 2, 3) **P11-3 (Depreciation—SYD, Act., SL, and DDB)** The following data relate to the Plant Assets account of Arthur Fiedler, Inc. at December 31, 2007.

Plant Assets

	A	B	C	D
Original cost	$35,000	$51,000	$80,000	$80,000
Year purchased	2002	2003	2004	2006
Useful life	10 years	15,000 hours	15 years	10 years
Salvage value	$ 3,100	$ 3,000	$ 5,000	$ 5,000
Depreciation method	Sum-of-the-years'-digits	Activity	Straight-line	Double-declining balance
Accum. Depr. through 2007*	$23,200	$35,200	$15,000	$16,000

*In the year an asset is purchased, Fiedler, Inc. does not record any depreciation expense on the asset. In the year an asset is retired or traded in, Fiedler, Inc. takes a full year's depreciation on the asset.

The following transactions occurred during 2008.

(a) On May 5, Asset A was sold for $13,000 cash. The company's bookkeeper recorded this retirement in the following manner in the cash receipts journal.

Cash	13,000	
Asset A		13,000

(b) On December 31, it was determined that Asset B had been used 2,100 hours during 2008.

(c) On December 31, before computing depreciation expense on Asset C, the management of Fiedler, Inc. decided the useful life remaining from January 1, 2008, was 10 years.

(d) On December 31, it was discovered that a plant asset purchased in 2007 had been expensed completely in that year. This asset cost $22,000 and has a useful life of 10 years and no salvage value. Management has decided to use the double-declining balance method for this asset, which can be referred to as "Asset E."

Instructions

Prepare the necessary correcting entries for the year 2008. Record the appropriate depreciation expense on the above-mentioned assets.

(LO 2, 3) **P11-4 (Depreciation and Error Analysis)** A depreciation schedule for semitrucks of Oglala Manufacturing Company was requested by your auditor soon after December 31, 2008, showing the additions, retirements, depreciation, and other data affecting the income of the company in the 4-year period 2005 to 2008, inclusive. The following data were ascertained.

Balance of Semitrucks account, Jan. 1, 2005	
Truck No. 1 purchased Jan. 1, 2002, cost	$18,000
Truck No. 2 purchased July 1, 2002, cost	22,000
Truck No. 3 purchased Jan. 1, 2004, cost	30,000
Truck No. 4 purchased July 1, 2004, cost	24,000
Balance, Jan. 1, 2005	$94,000

The Semitrucks—Accumulated Depreciation account previously adjusted to January 1, 2005, and duly entered in the ledger, had a balance on that date of $30,200 (depreciation on the four trucks from the respective dates of purchase, based on a 5-year life, no salvage value). No charges had been made against the account before January 1, 2005.

Transactions between January 1, 2005, and December 31, 2008, and their record in the ledger were as follows.

July 1, 2005 Truck No. 3 was traded for a larger one (No. 5), the agreed purchase price of which was $34,000. Oglala Mfg. Co. paid the automobile dealer $15,000 cash on the transaction. The entry was a debit to Semitrucks and a credit to Cash, $15,000. The transaction has commercial substance.

Jan. 1, 2006 Truck No. 1 was sold for $3,500 cash; entry debited Cash and credited Semitrucks, $3,500.

July 1, 2007 A new truck (No. 6) was acquired for $36,000 cash and was charged at that amount to the Semitrucks account. (Assume truck No. 2 was not retired.)

July 1, 2007 Truck No. 4 was damaged in a wreck to such an extent that it was sold as junk for $700 cash. Oglala Mfg. Co. received $2,500 from the insurance company. The entry made by the bookkeeper was a debit to Cash, $3,200, and credits to Miscellaneous Income, $700, and Semitrucks, $2,500.

Entries for depreciation had been made at the close of each year as follows: 2005, $20,300; 2006, $21,100; 2007, $24,450; 2008, $27,800.

Instructions

(a) For each of the 4 years compute separately the increase or decrease in net income arising from the company's errors in determining or entering depreciation or in recording transactions affecting trucks, ignoring income tax considerations.

(b) Prepare one compound journal entry as of December 31, 2008, for adjustment of the Semitrucks account to reflect the correct balances as revealed by your schedule, assuming that the books have not been closed for 2008.

(LO 3, 6) **P11-5 (Depletion and Depreciation—Mining)** Richard Wright Mining Company has purchased a tract of mineral land for $600,000. It is estimated that this tract will yield 120,000 tons of ore with sufficient mineral content to make mining and processing profitable. It is further estimated that 6,000 tons of ore will be mined the first and last year and 12,000 tons every year in between. The land will have a residual value of $30,000.

The company builds necessary structures and sheds on the site at a cost of $36,000. It is estimated that these structures can serve 15 years but, because they must be dismantled if they are to be moved, they have no salvage value. The company does not intend to use the buildings elsewhere. Mining machinery installed at the mine was purchased second-hand at a cost of $48,000. This machinery cost the former owner $100,000 and was 50% depreciated when purchased. Richard Wright Mining estimates that about half of this machinery will still be useful when the present mineral resources have been exhausted but that dismantling and removal costs will just about offset its value at that time. The company does not intend to use the machinery elsewhere. The remaining machinery will last until about one-half the present estimated mineral ore has been removed and will then be worthless. Cost is to be allocated equally between these two classes of machinery.

Instructions

(a) As chief accountant for the company, you are to prepare a schedule showing estimated depletion and depreciation costs for each year of the expected life of the mine.

(b) Also compute the depreciation and depletion for the first year assuming actual production of 7,000 tons. Nothing occurred during the year to cause the company engineers to change their estimates of either the mineral resources or the life of the structures and equipment.

(LO 6) **P11-6** **(Depletion, Timber, and Extraordinary Loss)** Conan O'Brien Logging and Lumber Company owns 3,000 acres of timberland on the north side of Mount St. Helens, which was purchased in 1968 at a cost of $550 per acre. In 1980, O'Brien began selectively logging this timber tract. In May of 1980, Mount St. Helens erupted, burying the timberland of O'Brien under a foot of ash. All of the timber on the O'Brien tract was downed. In addition, the logging roads, built at a cost of $150,000, were destroyed, as well as the logging equipment, with a net book value of $300,000.

At the time of the eruption, O'Brien had logged 20% of the estimated 500,000 board feet of timber. Prior to the eruption, O'Brien estimated the land to have a value of $200 per acre after the timber was harvested. O'Brien includes the logging roads in the depletion base.

O'Brien estimates it will take 3 years to salvage the downed timber at a cost of $700,000. The timber can be sold for pulp wood at an estimated price of $3 per board foot. The value of the land is unknown, but must be considered nominal due to future uncertainties.

Instructions
- **(a)** Determine the depletion cost per board foot for the timber harvested prior to the eruption of Mount St. Helens.
- **(b)** Prepare the journal entry to record the depletion prior to the eruption.
- **(c)** If this tract represents approximately half of the timber holdings of O'Brien, determine the amount of the estimated loss and show how the losses of roads, machinery, and timber and the salvage of the timber should be reported in the financial statements of O'Brien for the year ended December 31, 1980.

(LO 6) **P11-7** **(Natural Resources—Timber)** Western Paper Products purchased 10,000 acres of forested timberland in March 2008. The company paid $1,700 per acre for this land, which was above the $800 per acre most farmers were paying for cleared land. During April, May, June, and July 2008, Western cut enough timber to build roads using moveable equipment purchased on April 1, 2008. The cost of the roads was $195,000, and the cost of the equipment was $189,000; this equipment was expected to have a $9,000 salvage value and would be used for the next 15 years. Western selected the straight-line method of depreciation for the moveable equipment. Western began actively harvesting timber in August and by December had harvested and sold 472,500 board feet of timber of the estimated 6,750,000 board feet available for cutting.

In March 2009, Western planted new seedlings in the area harvested during the winter. Cost of planting these seedlings was $120,000. In addition, Western spent $8,000 in road maintenance and $6,000 for pest spraying during calendar-year 2009. The road maintenance and spraying are annual costs. During 2009 Western harvested and sold 774,000 board feet of timber of the estimated 6,450,000 board feet available for cutting.

In March 2010, Western again planted new seedlings at a cost of $150,000, and also spent $15,000 on road maintenance and pest spraying. During 2010, the company harvested and sold 650,000 board feet of timber of the estimated 6,500,000 board feet available for cutting.

Instructions
Compute the amount of depreciation and depletion expense for each of the 3 years (2008, 2009, 2010). Assume that the roads are usable only for logging and therefore are included in the depletion base.

(LO 2, 3) **P11-8** **(Comprehensive Fixed Asset Problem)** Selig Sporting Goods Inc. has been experiencing growth in the demand for its products over the last several years. The last two Olympic Games greatly increased the popularity of basketball around the world. As a result, a European sports retailing consortium entered into an agreement with Selig's Roundball Division to purchase basketballs and other accessories on an increasing basis over the next 5 years.

To be able to meet the quantity commitments of this agreement, Selig had to obtain additional manufacturing capacity. A real estate firm located an available factory in close proximity to Selig's Roundball manufacturing facility, and Selig agreed to purchase the factory and used machinery from Starks Athletic Equipment Company on October 1, 2005. Renovations were necessary to convert the factory for Selig's manufacturing use.

The terms of the agreement required Selig to pay Starks $50,000 when renovations started on January 1, 2006, with the balance to be paid as renovations were completed. The overall purchase price for the factory and machinery was $400,000. The building renovations were contracted to Malone Construction at $100,000. The payments made, as renovations progressed during 2006, are shown below. The factory was placed in service on January 1, 2007.

	1/1	4/1	10/1	12/31
Starks	$50,000	$100,000	$100,000	$150,000
Malone		30,000	30,000	40,000

On January 1, 2006, Selig secured a $500,000 line-of-credit with a 12% interest rate to finance the purchase cost of the factory and machinery, and the renovation costs. Selig drew down on the line-of-credit to meet the payment schedule shown above; this was Selig's only outstanding loan during 2006.

Rob Stewart, Selig's controller, will capitalize the maximum allowable interest costs for this project. Selig's policy regarding purchases of this nature is to use the appraisal value of the land for book purposes and prorate the balance of the purchase price over the remaining items. The building had originally cost Starks $300,000 and had a net book value of $50,000, while the machinery originally cost $125,000 and had a net book value of $40,000 on the date of sale. The land was recorded on Starks' books at $40,000. An appraisal, conducted by independent appraisers at the time of acquisition, valued the land at $280,000, the building at $105,000, and the machinery at $45,000.

Linda Safford, chief engineer, estimated that the renovated plant would be used for 15 years, with an estimated salvage value of $30,000. Safford estimated that the productive machinery would have a remaining useful life of 5 years and a salvage value of $3,000. Selig's depreciation policy specifies the 200% declining-balance method for machinery and the 150% declining-balance method for the plant. One-half year's depreciation is taken in the year the plant is placed in service and one-half year is allowed when the property is disposed of or retired. Selig uses a 360-day year for calculating interest costs.

Instructions

(a) Determine the amounts to be recorded on the books of Selig Sporting Goods Inc. as of December 31, 2006, for each of the following properties acquired from Starks Athletic Equipment Company.
  (1) Land.   (2) Building.   (3) Machinery.
(b) Calculate Selig Sporting Goods Inc.'s 2007 depreciation expense, for book purposes, for each of the properties acquired from Starks Athletic Equipment Company.
(c) Discuss the arguments for and against the capitalization of interest costs.

(CMA adapted)

(LO 5) **P11-9 (Impairment)** Olsson Company uses special strapping equipment in its packaging business. The equipment was purchased in January 2007 for $8,000,000 and had an estimated useful life of 8 years with no salvage value. At December 31, 2008, new technology was introduced that would accelerate the obsolescence of Olsson's equipment. Olsson's controller estimates that expected future net cash flows on the equipment will be $5,300,000 and that the fair value of the equipment is $4,400,000. Olsson intends to continue using the equipment, but it is estimated that the remaining useful life is 4 years. Olsson uses straight-line depreciation.

Instructions

(a) Prepare the journal entry (if any) to record the impairment at December 31, 2008.
(b) Prepare any journal entries for the equipment at December 31, 2009. The fair value of the equipment at December 31, 2009, is estimated to be $4,600,000.
(c) Repeat the requirements for (a) and (b), assuming that Olsson intends to dispose of the equipment and that it has not been disposed of as of December 31, 2009.

(LO 2, 3) **P11-10 (Comprehensive Depreciation Computations)** Sheryl Crow Corporation, a manufacturer of steel products, began operations on October 1, 2006. The accounting department of Crow has started the fixed-asset and depreciation schedule presented on page 563. You have been asked to assist in completing this schedule. In addition to ascertaining that the data already on the schedule are correct, you have obtained the following information from the company's records and personnel.

1. Depreciation is computed from the first of the month of acquisition to the first of the month of disposition.
2. Land A and Building A were acquired from a predecessor corporation. Crow paid $820,000 for the land and building together. At the time of acquisition, the land had an appraised value of $90,000, and the building had an appraised value of $810,000.
3. Land B was acquired on October 2, 2006, in exchange for 2,500 newly issued shares of Crow's common stock. At the date of acquisition, the stock had a par value of $5 per share and a fair value of $30 per share. During October 2006, Crow paid $16,000 to demolish an existing building on this land so it could construct a new building.
4. Construction of Building B on the newly acquired land began on October 1, 2007. By September 30, 2008, Crow had paid $320,000 of the estimated total construction costs of $450,000. It is estimated that the building will be completed and occupied by July 2009.
5. Certain equipment was donated to the corporation by a local university. An independent appraisal of the equipment when donated placed the fair market value at $30,000 and the salvage value at $3,000.

6. Machinery A's total cost of $164,900 includes installation expense of $600 and normal repairs and maintenance of $14,900. Salvage value is estimated at $6,000. Machinery A was sold on February 1, 2008.

7. On October 1, 2007, Machinery B was acquired with a down payment of $5,740 and the remaining payments to be made in 11 annual installments of $6,000 each beginning October 1, 2007. The prevailing interest rate was 8%. The following data were abstracted from present-value tables (rounded).

Present value of $1.00 at 8%			Present value of an ordinary annuity of $1.00 at 8%	
10 years	.463		10 years	6.710
11 years	.429		11 years	7.139
15 years	.315		15 years	8.559

SHERYL CROW CORPORATION
Fixed Asset and Depreciation Schedule
For Fiscal Years Ended September 30, 2007, and September 30, 2008

Assets	Acquisition Date	Cost	Salvage	Depreciation Method	Estimated Life in Years	Depreciation Expense Year Ended September 30 2007	2008
Land A	October 1, 2006	$ (1)	N/A	N/A	N/A	N/A	N/A
Building A	October 1, 2006	(2)	$40,000	Straight-line	(3)	$17,450	(4)
Land B	October 2, 2006	(5)	N/A	N/A	N/A	N/A	N/A
Building B	Under Construction	$320,000 to date	—	Straight-line	30	—	(6)
Donated Equipment	October 2, 2006	(7)	3,000	150% declining balance	10	(8)	(9)
Machinery A	October 2, 2006	(10)	6,000	Sum-of-the-years'-digits	8	(11)	(12)
Machinery B	October 1, 2007	(13)	—	Straight-line	20	—	(14)

N/A—Not applicable

Instructions

For each numbered item on the schedule above, supply the correct amount. Round each answer to the nearest dollar.

(LO 2, 3) **P11-11 (Depreciation for Partial Periods—SL, Act., SYD, and DDB)** On January 1, 2005, a machine was purchased for $77,000. The machine has an estimated salvage value of $5,000 and an estimated useful life of 5 years. The machine can operate for 100,000 hours before it needs to be replaced. The company closed its books on December 31 and operates the machine as follows: 2005, 20,000 hrs; 2006, 25,000 hrs; 2007, 15,000 hrs; 2008, 30,000 hrs; 2009, 10,000 hrs.

Instructions

(a) Compute the annual depreciation charges over the machine's life assuming a December 31 year-end for each of the following depreciation methods.
    (1) Straight-line method.   (3) Sum-of-the-years'-digits method.
    (2) Activity method.   (4) Double-declining balance method.
(b) Assume a fiscal year-end of September 30. Compute the annual depreciation charges over the asset's life applying each of the following methods.
    (1) Straight-line method.
    (2) Sum-of-the-years'-digits method.
    (3) Double-declining balance method.

(LO 2, 3, 8)  ***P11-12 (Depreciation—SL, DDB, SYD, Act., and MACRS)** On January 1, 2005, Begen Company, a small machine-tool manufacturer, acquired for $1,100,000 a piece of new industrial equipment. The new equipment had a useful life of 5 years, and the salvage value was estimated to be $50,000. Begen estimates that the new equipment can produce 12,000 machine tools in its first year. It estimates that production will decline by 1,000 units per year over the remaining useful life of the equipment.

The following depreciation methods may be used: (1) straight-line; (2) double-declining balance; (3) sum-of-the-years'-digits; and (4) units-of-output. For tax purposes, the class life is 7 years. Use the MACRS tables for computing depreciation.

Instructions

(a) Which depreciation method would maximize net income for financial statement reporting for the 3-year period ending December 31, 2007? Prepare a schedule showing the amount of accumulated depreciation at December 31, 2007, under the method selected. Ignore present value, income tax, and deferred income tax considerations.

(b) Which depreciation method (MACRS or optional straight-line) would minimize net income for income tax reporting for the 3-year period ending December 31, 2007? Determine the amount of accumulated depreciation at December 31, 2007. Ignore present value considerations.

(AICPA adapted)

CONCEPTS FOR ANALYSIS

CA11-1 (Depreciation Basic Concepts) Prophet Manufacturing Company was organized January 1, 2007. During 2007, it has used in its reports to management the straight-line method of depreciating its plant assets.

On November 8 you are having a conference with Prophet's officers to discuss the depreciation method to be used for income tax and stockholder reporting. Frank Peretti, president of Prophet, has suggested the use of a new method, which he feels is more suitable than the straight-line method for the needs of the company during the period of rapid expansion of production and capacity that he foresees. Following is an example in which the proposed method is applied to a fixed asset with an original cost of $248,000, an estimated useful life of 5 years, and a salvage value of approximately $8,000.

Year	Years of Life Used	Fraction Rate	Depreciation Expense	Accumulated Depreciation at End of Year	Book Value at End of Year
1	1	1/15	$16,000	$ 16,000	$232,000
2	2	2/15	32,000	48,000	200,000
3	3	3/15	48,000	96,000	152,000
4	4	4/15	64,000	160,000	88,000
5	5	5/15	80,000	240,000	8,000

The president favors the new method because he has heard that:

1. It will increase the funds recovered during the years near the end of the assets' useful lives when maintenance and replacement disbursements are high.
2. It will result in increased write-offs in later years and thereby will reduce taxes.

Instructions

(a) What is the purpose of accounting for depreciation?

(b) Is the president's proposal within the scope of generally accepted accounting principles? In making your decision discuss the circumstances, if any, under which use of the method would be reasonable and those, if any, under which it would not be reasonable.

(c) The president wants your advice on the following issues.

(1) Do depreciation charges recover or create funds? Explain.

(2) Assume that the Internal Revenue Service accepts the proposed depreciation method in this case. If the proposed method were used for stockholder and tax reporting purposes, how would it affect the availability of cash flows generated by operations?

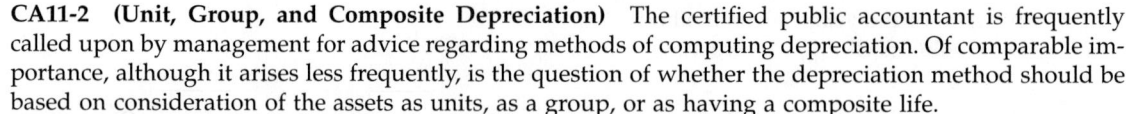 **CA11-2 (Unit, Group, and Composite Depreciation)** The certified public accountant is frequently called upon by management for advice regarding methods of computing depreciation. Of comparable importance, although it arises less frequently, is the question of whether the depreciation method should be based on consideration of the assets as units, as a group, or as having a composite life.

Instructions

(a) Briefly describe the depreciation methods based on treating assets as (1) units and (2) a group or as having a composite life.

(b) Present the arguments for and against the use of each of the two methods.

(c) Describe how retirements are recorded under each of the two methods.

(AICPA adapted)

CA11-3 **(Depreciation—Strike, Units-of-Production, Obsolescence)** Presented below are three different and unrelated situations involving depreciation accounting. Answer the question(s) at the end of each situation.

Situation I

Recently, Davenport Company experienced a strike that affected a number of its operating plants. The controller of this company indicated that it was not appropriate to report depreciation expense during this period because the equipment did not depreciate and an improper matching of costs and revenues would result. She based her position on the following points.

1. It is inappropriate to charge the period with costs for which there are no related revenues arising from production.
2. The basic factor of depreciation in this instance is wear and tear, and because equipment was idle, no wear and tear occurred.

Instructions
Comment on the appropriateness of the controller's comments.

Situation II

Sharapova Company manufactures electrical appliances, most of which are used in homes. Company engineers have designed a new type of blender which, through the use of a few attachments, will perform more functions than any blender currently on the market. Demand for the new blender can be projected with reasonable probability. In order to make the blenders, Sharapova needs a specialized machine that is not available from outside sources. It has been decided to make such a machine in Sharapova's own plant.

Instructions
(a) Discuss the effect of projected demand in units for the new blenders (which may be steady, decreasing, or increasing) on the determination of a depreciation method for the machine.
(b) What other matters should be considered in determining the depreciation method? Ignore income tax considerations.

Situation III

Venus Paper Company operates a 300-ton-per-day kraft pulp mill and four sawmills in Wisconsin. The company is in the process of expanding its pulp mill facilities to a capacity of 1,000 tons per day and plans to replace three of its older, less efficient sawmills with an expanded facility. One of the mills to be replaced did not operate for most of 2007 (current year), and there are no plans to reopen it before the new sawmill facility becomes operational.

In reviewing the depreciation rates and in discussing the residual values of the sawmills that were to be replaced, it was noted that if present depreciation rates were not adjusted, substantial amounts of plant costs on these three mills would not be depreciated by the time the new mill came on stream.

Instructions
What is the proper accounting for the four sawmills at the end of 2007?

CA11-4 **(Depreciation Concepts)** As a cost accountant for San Francisco Cannery, you have been approached by Merton Miller, canning room supervisor, about the 2006 costs charged to his department. In particular, he is concerned about the line item "depreciation." Miller is very proud of the excellent condition of his canning room equipment. He has always been vigilant about keeping all equipment serviced and well oiled. He is sure that the huge charge to depreciation is a mistake; it does not at all reflect the cost of minimal wear and tear that the machines have experienced over the last year. He believes that the charge should be considerably lower.

The machines being depreciated are six automatic canning machines. All were put into use on January 1, 2006. Each cost $469,000, having a salvage value of $40,000 and a useful life of 12 years. San Francisco depreciates this and similar assets using double-declining balance depreciation. Miller has also pointed out that if you used straight-line depreciation the charge to his department would not be so great.

Instructions
Write a memo to Merton Miller to clear up his misunderstanding of the term "depreciation." Also, calculate year-1 depreciation on all machines using both methods. Explain the theoretical justification for double-declining balance and why, in the long run, the aggregate charge to depreciation will be the same under both methods.

CA11-5   (Depreciation Choice)   Dusty Baker, Waveland Corporation's controller, is concerned that net income may be lower this year. He is afraid upper-level management might recommend cost reductions by laying off accounting staff, including him.

Baker knows that depreciation is a major expense for Waveland. The company currently uses the double-declining balance method for both financial reporting and tax purposes, and he's thinking of selling equipment that, given its age, is primarily used when there are periodic spikes in demand. The equipment has a carrying value of $2,000,000 and a market value of $2,180,000. The gain on the sale would be reported in the income statement. He doesn't want to highlight this method of increasing income. He thinks, "Why don't I increase the estimated useful lives and the salvage values? That will decrease depreciation expense and require less extensive disclosure, since the changes are accounted for prospectively. I may be able to save my job and those of my staff."

Instructions
Answer the following questions.
 (a)   Who are the stakeholders in this situation?
 (b)   What are the ethical issues involved?
 (c)   What should Baker do?

USING YOUR JUDGMENT

Financial Reporting Problem

P&G The Procter & Gamble Company (P&G)

The financial statements of **P&G** are presented in Appendix 5B or can be accessed on the KWW website .

Instructions
Refer to P&G's financial statements and the accompanying notes to answer the following questions.
 (a)   What descriptions are used by P&G in its balance sheet to classify its property, plant, and equipment?
 (b)   What method or methods of depreciation does P&G use to depreciate its property, plant, and equipment?
 (c)   Over what estimated useful lives does P&G depreciate its property, plant, and equipment?
 (d)   What amounts for depreciation and amortization expense did P&G charge to its income statement in 2004, 2003, and 2002?
 (e)   What were the capital expenditures for property, plant, and equipment made by P&G in 2004, 2003, and 2002?

Financial Statement Analysis Case

McDonald's Corporation

McDonald's is the largest and best-known global food service retailer, with more than 30,000 restaurants in 121 countries. On any day, McDonald's serves approximately 1 percent of the world's population. Presented on the next page is information related to McDonald's property and equipment.

Instructions
 (a)   What method of depreciation does McDonald's use?
 (b)   Does depreciation and amortization expense cause cash flow from operations to increase? Explain.
 (c)   What does the schedule of cash flow measures indicate?

McDonald's Corporation
Summary of Significant Accounting Policies Section

Property and Equipment. Property and equipment are stated at cost, with depreciation and amortization provided on the straight-line method over the following estimated useful lives: buildings—up to 40 years; leasehold improvements—lesser of useful lives of assets or lease terms including option periods; and equipment—3 to 12 years.

[In the notes to the financial statements:]

Property and Equipment
Net property and equipment consisted of:

(in millions)	December 31, 2004	2003
Land	$ 4,661.1	$ 4,483.0
Buildings and improvements on owned land	10,260.3	9,693.4
Buildings and improvements on leased land	10,520.7	9,792.1
Equipment, signs, and seating	4,426.1	4,090.5
Other	639.6	681.2
	30,507.8	28,740.2
Accumulated depreciation and amortization	(9,804.7)	(8,815.5)
Net property and equipment	$20,703.1	$19,924.7

Depreciation and amortization expense was (in millions):
2004–$1,138.3; 2003–$1,113.3; 2002–$971.1.

[In the management discussion and analysis section, McDonald's provides the following schedule.]

Cash Provided by Operations

(dollars in millions)	2004	2003	2002
Cash provided by operations	$3,904	$3,269	$2,890
Cash provided by operations as a percent of capital expenditures	275%	250%	144%

Comparative Analysis Case

The Coca-Cola Company and PepsiCo., Inc.

Instructions
Go to the book's website and use information found there to answer the following questions related to The Coca-Cola Company and PepsiCo, Inc.

(a) What amount is reported in the balance sheets as property, plant, and equipment (net) of Coca-Cola at December 31, 2004, and of PepsiCo at December 25, 2004? What percentage of total assets is invested in property, plant, and equipment by each company?

(b) What depreciation methods are used by Coca-Cola and PepsiCo for property, plant, and equipment? How much depreciation was reported by Coca-Cola and PepsiCo in 2004, 2003, and 2002?

(c) Compute and compare the following ratios for Coca-Cola and PepsiCo for 2004.

(1) Asset turnover.

(2) Profit margin on sales.

(3) Rate of return on assets.

(d) What amount was spent in 2004 for capital expenditures by Coca-Cola and PepsiCo? What amount of interest was capitalized in 2004?

Research Case

An article by Martin Peers and Robin Sidel, entitled "Days May Be Numbered for EBITDA's Role," appeared in the July 5, 2002, issue of the *Wall Street Journal*.

Instructions

Read the article and answer the following questions.

(a) Explain what is meant by EBITDA and why companies are reporting this number.

(b) Why has the WorldCom bankruptcy caused EBITDA to fall into disfavor as a performance metric?

(c) What is wrong with performance metrics such as EBITDA, cash earnings, or other pro-forma income measures?

International Reporting Case

Companies following international accounting standards are permitted to revalue fixed assets above the assets' historical costs. Such revaluations are allowed under various countries' standards and the standards issued by the International Accounting Standards Board (IASB). **Liberty International**, a real estate company, headquartered in United Kingdom (U.K.), follows U.K. standards. In a recent year, Liberty disclosed the following information on revaluations of its tangible fixed assets. The revaluation reserve measures the amount by which tangible fixed assets are recorded above historical cost and is reported in Liberty's stockholders' equity.

Liberty International

Completed Investment Properties

Completed investment properties are professionally valued on a market value basis by external valuers at the balance sheet date. Surpluses and deficits arising during the year are reflected in the revalution reserve.

Liberty reported the following additional data. Amounts for **Kimco Realty** (which follows U.S. GAAP) in the same year are provided for comparison.

	Liberty (pounds sterling, in thousands)	Kimco (dollars, in millions)
Total revenues	£ 741	$ 517
Average total assets	5,577	4,696
Net income	125	297

Instructions

(a) Compute the following ratios for Liberty and Kimco.

(1) Return on assets.

(2) Profit margin.

(3) Asset turnover.

How do these companies compare on these performance measures?

(b) Liberty reports a revaluation reserve of 1,952 pounds. Assume that 1,550 of this amount arose from an increase in the net replacement value of investment properties during the year. Prepare the journal entry to record this increase. (*Hint:* Credit the Revaluation Reserve account.)

(c) Under U.K. (and IASB) standards, are Liberty's assets and equity overstated? If so, why? When comparing Liberty to U.S. companies, like Kimco, what adjustments would you need to make in order to have valid comparisons of ratios such as those computed in (a) above?

Professional Research: Financial Accounting and Reporting

Nomar Garcia recently joined Hamm Company as a staff accountant in the controller's office. Hamm Company provides warehousing services for companies in several midwestern cities.

The location in Dubuque, Iowa, has not been performing well due to increased competition and the loss of several customers that have recently gone out of business. Nomar's department manager suspects that the plant and equipment may be impaired and wonders whether those assets should be written down. Given the company's prior success, this issue has never arisen in the past, and Nomar has been asked to conduct some research on this issue.

Instructions

Using the **Financial Accounting Research System (FARS)**, respond to the following items. (Provide text strings used in your search.)

(a) What accounting standard provides the authoritative guidance for asset impairments? Briefly discuss the scope of the standard (i.e., explain the types of transactions to which the standard applies).

(b) Give several examples of events that would cause an asset to be tested for impairment. Does it appear that Hamm should perform an impairment test? Explain.

(c) What is the best evidence of fair value? Describe alternate methods of estimating fair value.

Professional Simulation

In this simulation you are asked to address questions regarding the accounting for property, plant, and equipment. Prepare responses to all parts.

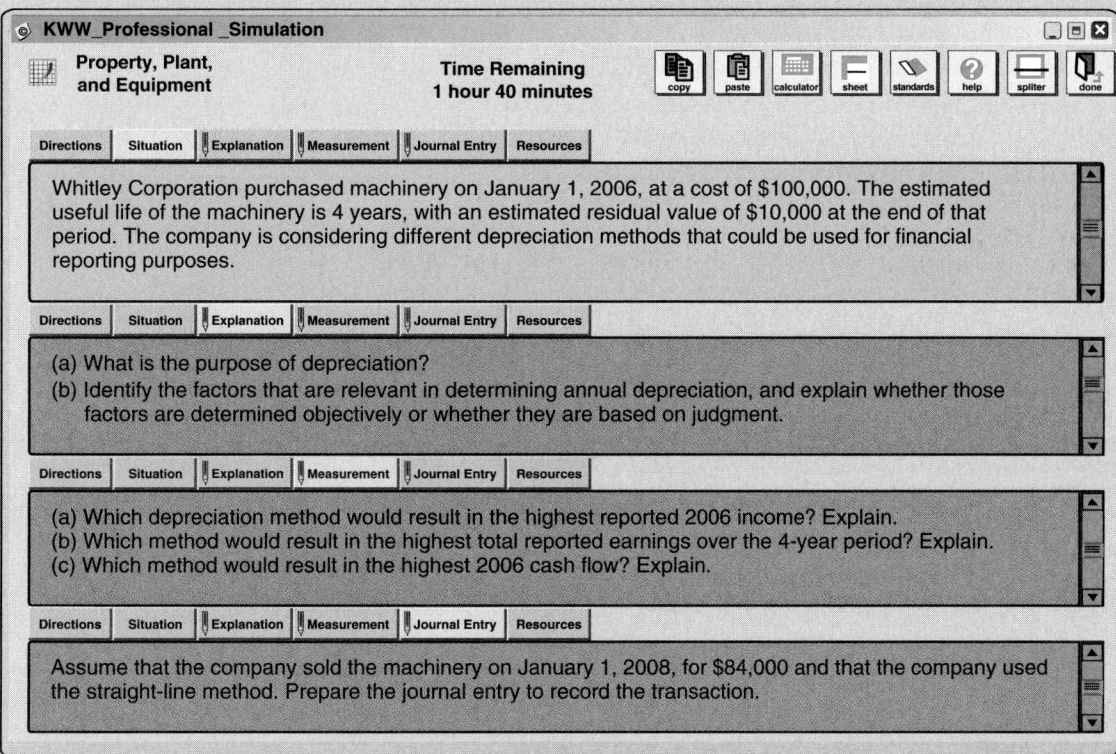

KWW_Professional _Simulation

Property, Plant, and Equipment

Time Remaining
1 hour 40 minutes

copy | paste | calculator | sheet | standards | help | splitter | done

Directions | Situation | Explanation | Measurement | Journal Entry | Resources

Whitley Corporation purchased machinery on January 1, 2006, at a cost of $100,000. The estimated useful life of the machinery is 4 years, with an estimated residual value of $10,000 at the end of that period. The company is considering different depreciation methods that could be used for financial reporting purposes.

Directions | Situation | Explanation | Measurement | Journal Entry | Resources

(a) What is the purpose of depreciation?
(b) Identify the factors that are relevant in determining annual depreciation, and explain whether those factors are determined objectively or whether they are based on judgment.

Directions | Situation | Explanation | Measurement | Journal Entry | Resources

(a) Which depreciation method would result in the highest reported 2006 income? Explain.
(b) Which method would result in the highest total reported earnings over the 4-year period? Explain.
(c) Which method would result in the highest 2006 cash flow? Explain.

Directions | Situation | Explanation | Measurement | Journal Entry | Resources

Assume that the company sold the machinery on January 1, 2008, for $84,000 and that the company used the straight-line method. Prepare the journal entry to record the transaction.

Remember to check the book's companion website to find additional resources for this chapter.

CHAPTER TWELVE

INTANGIBLE ASSETS

Untouchable

As shown in the graph below, tangible assets as a percent of all assets have declined dramatically in the last 50 years. Consequently, companies today increasingly derive value from intangible assets—intellectual property, technology, or reputation. Many well-known companies make most of their money from intangible assets: **Microsoft Corp.**'s software, **Pfizer Inc.**'s drug patents, and **Walt Disney Co.**'s film and television productions.

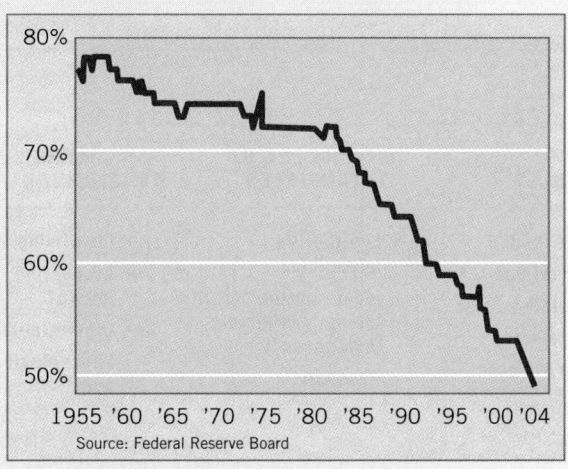

Tangible assets as a percentage of all assets of nonfinancial businesses

Source: Federal Reserve Board

However, the experience at **Winstar Communications** illustrates how quickly the value of intangible assets can erode. Just before Winstar filed for bankruptcy, it listed $5 billion in assets, a large share comprised of questionable intangible assets related to its customer base. Within just a few months, its assets fetched just $42 *million*. Winstar's investors and creditors learned the shocking speed at which the value of such assets can decline.

Perhaps Federal Reserve Chairman Alan Greenspan's remarks are relevant in these turbulent times: ". . . a firm is inherently fragile if its value-added emanates more from conceptual as distinct from physical assets. Trust and reputation can vanish overnight. A factory cannot."[1]

---

[1]Adapted from Greg Ip, "The Rise and Fall of Intangible Assets Leads to Shorter Company Life Spans, *Wall Street Journal Online* (April 4, 2002).

Learning Objectives

After studying this chapter, you should be able to:

1 Describe the characteristics of intangible assets.

2 Identify the costs to include in the initial valuation of intangible assets.

3 Explain the procedure for amortizing intangible assets.

4 Describe the types of intangible assets.

5 Explain the conceptual issues related to goodwill.

6 Describe the accounting procedures for recording goodwill.

7 Explain the accounting issues related to intangible-asset impairments.

8 Identify the conceptual issues related to research and development costs.

9 Describe the accounting for research and development and similar costs.

10 Indicate the presentation of intangible assets and related items.

As our opening story indicates, the accounting and reporting of intangibles is taking on increasing importance in this information age, especially for companies like **Microsoft Corp., Pfizer Inc.,** and **Walt Disney Co.** In this chapter we explain the basic conceptual and reporting issues related to intangible assets. The content and organization of the chapter are as follows.

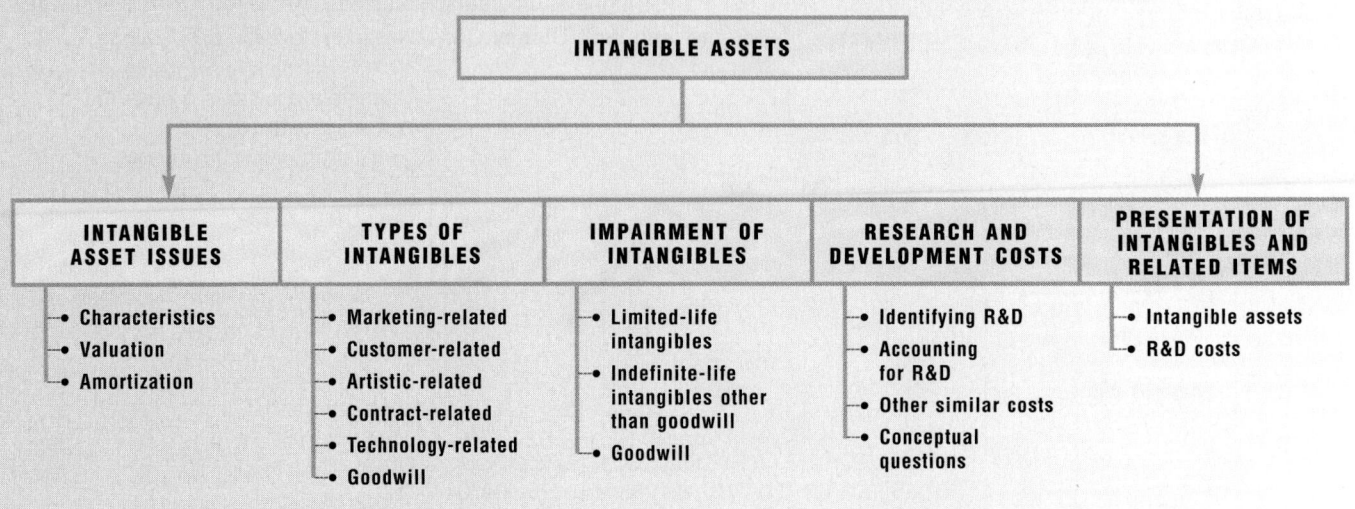

INTANGIBLE ASSET ISSUES

Characteristics

OBJECTIVE 1
Describe the characteristics of intangible assets.

Gap Inc.'s most important asset is its brand image, not its store fixtures. **Coca-Cola**'s success comes from its secret formula for making Coke, not its plant facilities. **America Online**'s subscriber base provides its most important asset, not its Internet connection equipment. As these examples show, we have an economy dominated today by information and service providers. For these companies, their major assets are often intangible in nature. Accounting for these intangibles is difficult.

What exactly are intangible assets? **Intangible assets** have two main characteristics.[2]

1 They lack physical existence. Unlike tangible assets such as property, plant, and equipment, intangible assets derive their value from the rights and privileges granted to the company using them.

2 They are not financial instruments. Assets such as bank deposits, accounts receivable, and long-term investments in bonds and stocks also lack physical substance. However, they are not classified as intangibles, because these assets are financial instruments. They derive their value from the right (claim) to receive cash or cash equivalents in the future.

In most cases, intangible assets provide benefits over a period of years. Therefore, companies normally classify them as long-term assets. We discuss the most common types

---

[2]"Goodwill and Other Intangible Assets," *Statement of Financial Accounting Standards No. 142* (Norwalk, Conn.: FASB, 2001).

of intangibles (patents, copyrights, franchises or licenses, trademarks or trade names, and goodwill) later in the chapter.

Valuation

Purchased Intangibles

Intangibles purchased from another party are **recorded at cost**. Cost includes all costs of acquisition and expenditures necessary to make the intangible asset ready for its intended use. Typical costs include purchase price, legal fees, and other incidental expenses.

If a company acquires intangibles for stock or in exchange for other assets, **the cost of the intangible is the fair value of the consideration given or the fair value of the intangible received, whichever is more clearly evident**. When a company buys several intangibles, or a combination of intangibles and tangibles, in a "basket purchase," it should allocate the cost on the basis of fair values. Essentially the accounting treatment for purchased intangibles closely parallels that for purchased tangible assets.

Internally Created Intangibles

Costs incurred internally to create intangibles are generally expensed. Thus, even though a company may incur substantial research and development costs to create an intangible, it expenses these costs.

How do companies justify this approach? Some argue that the costs incurred internally to create intangibles bear no relationship to their real value. Therefore, expensing these costs is appropriate. Others note that it is difficult to associate internal costs with a specific intangible. And others contend that due to the underlying subjectivity related to intangibles, companies should follow a conservative approach—that is, expense as incurred. As a result, **companies only capitalize direct costs** incurred in developing the intangible, such as legal costs.

> **OBJECTIVE 2**
> Identify the costs to include in the initial valuation of intangible assets.

> **UNDERLYING CONCEPTS**
>
> The basic attributes of intangibles, their uncertainty as to future benefits, and their uniqueness have discouraged valuation in excess of cost.

Amortization of Intangibles

Intangibles have either a limited (finite) useful life or an indefinite useful life. For example, a company like **Walt Disney** has both types of intangibles. Walt Disney **amortizes** its **limited life** intangible assets. It **does not amortize** intangible assets with an **indefinite life**.

> **OBJECTIVE 3**
> Explain the procedure for amortizing intangible assets.

Limited-Life Intangibles

The allocation of the cost of intangible assets in a systematic way is called **amortization**. Walt Disney amortizes its limited-life intangibles by systematic charges to expense over their useful life. The useful life should reflect the periods over which these assets will contribute to cash flows. Walt Disney considers these factors in determining useful life:

1. The expected use of the asset by the company.
2. The expected useful life of another asset or a group of assets to which the useful life of the intangible asset may relate (such as lease rights to a studio lot).
3. Any legal, regulatory, or contractual provisions that may limit the useful life.
4. Any legal, regulatory, or contractual provisions that enable renewal or extension of the asset's legal or contractual life without substantial cost. This factor assumes that there is evidence to support renewal or extension. Disney also must be able to accomplish renewal or extension without material modifications of the existing terms and conditions.

5 The effects of obsolescence, demand, competition, and other economic factors. Examples include the stability of the industry, known technological advances, legislative action that results in an uncertain or changing regulatory environment, and expected changes in distribution channels.

6 The level of maintenance expenditure required to obtain the expected future cash flows from the asset. For example, a material level of required maintenance in relation to the carrying amount of the asset may suggest a very limited useful life.[3]

The amount of amortization expense for a limited-life intangible asset should reflect the pattern in which the company consumes or uses up the asset, if the company can reliably determine that pattern. For example, assume that Second Wave, Inc. purchases a license to provide a limited quantity of a gene product, called Mega. Second Wave should amortize the cost of the license following the pattern of use of Mega. If it cannot determine the pattern of production or consumption, Second Wave should use the straight-line method of amortization. (*For homework problems, assume the use of the straight-line method unless stated otherwise.*)

When Second Wave amortizes these licenses, it should show the charges as expenses. It should credit either the appropriate asset accounts or separate accumulated amortization accounts.

The amount of an intangible asset to be amortized should be its cost less residual value. The residual value is assumed to be zero unless at the end of its useful life the intangible asset has value to another company. For example, if Hardy Co. commits to purchasing an intangible asset from U2D Co. at the end of the asset's useful life, U2D Co. should reduce the cost of its intangible asset by the residual value. Similarly, U2D Co. should consider market values, if reliably determined, for residual values.

What happens if the life of a limited-life intangible asset changes? In that case the remaining carrying amount should be amortized over the revised remaining useful life. Companies should, on a regular basis, evaluate the limited-life intangibles for impairment. Similar to property, plant, and equipment, an impairment loss should be recognized if the carrying amount of the intangible is not recoverable and its carrying amount exceeds its fair value.

Indefinite-Life Intangibles

If no legal, regulatory, contractual, competitive, or other factors limit the useful life of an intangible asset, a company considers its useful life indefinite. **Indefinite** means that there is no foreseeable limit on the period of time over which the intangible asset is expected to provide cash flows. A company does not amortize an intangible asset with an indefinite life.

To illustrate, assume that Double Clik, Inc. acquired a trademark that it uses to distinguish a leading consumer product. It renews the trademark every 10 years at minimal cost. All evidence indicates that this trademark product will generate cash flows for an indefinite period of time. In this case, the trademark has an indefinite life; Double Clik does not record any amortization.

Companies should test indefinite-life intangibles for impairment at least annually. The **impairment test** for indefinite-life intangibles differs from the one for limited-life intangibles in that only the fair value test is performed. There is no recoverability test related to indefinite-life intangibles. The reason: Indefinite-life intangible assets might never fail the undiscounted cash flows recoverability test because cash flows could extend indefinitely into the future.

Illustration 12-1 summarizes the accounting treatment for intangible assets.

---

[3]Ibid, par. 11.

	Manner Acquired			
Type of Intangible	Purchased	Internally Created	Amortization	Impairment Test
Limited-life intangibles	Capitalize	Expense*	Over useful life	Recoverability test and then fair value test
Indefinite-life intangibles	Capitalize	Expense*	Do not amortize	Fair value test

*Except for direct costs, such as legal costs.

ILLUSTRATION 12-1
Accounting Treatment for Intangibles

TYPES OF INTANGIBLE ASSETS

As indicated, the accounting for intangible assets depends on whether the intangible has a limited or an indefinite life. There are many different types of intangibles, often classified into the following six major categories.[4]

1 Marketing-related intangible assets.
2 Customer-related intangible assets.
3 Artistic-related intangible assets.
4 Contract-related intangible assets.
5 Technology-related intangible assets.
6 Goodwill.

OBJECTIVE 4
Describe the types of intangible assets.

Marketing-Related Intangible Assets

Companies primarily use **marketing-related intangible assets** in the marketing or promotion of products or services. Examples are trademarks or trade names, newspaper mastheads, Internet domain names, and noncompetition agreements.

A common form of a marketing-related intangible asset is a trademark or trade name. A trademark or trade name is a word, phrase, or symbol that distinguishes or identifies a particular company or product. Under common law, the right to use a trademark or trade name, whether registered or not, rests exclusively with the original user as long as the original user continues to use it. Registration with the U.S. Patent and Trademark Office provides legal protection for an **indefinite number of renewals for periods of 10 years each**. Therefore a company that uses an established trademark or trade name may properly consider it to have an indefinite life. Trade names like Kleenex, Pepsi-Cola, Buick, Excedrin, Wheaties, and Sunkist create immediate product identification in our minds, thereby enhancing marketability.

If a company acquires a trademark or trade name, it capitalizes the cost at the purchase price. If a company develops a trademark or trade name, it capitalizes costs related to securing it, such as attorney fees, registration fees, design costs, consulting fees, and successful legal defense costs. However, it excludes research and development costs. When the total cost of a trademark or trade name is insignificant, a company may simply expense it. In most cases, the life of a trademark or trade name is indefinite. Therefore companies do not amortize its cost.

The value of a marketing-related intangible can be substantial. Consider Internet domain names. The name **Drugs.com** recently sold for $800,000. The bidding for the name **Loans.com** approached $500,000.

---

[4]This classification framework is based on "Business Combinations," *Statement of Financial Accounting Standards No. 141* (Norwalk, Conn.: FASB, 2001).

Company names themselves identify qualities and characteristics that companies work hard and spend much to develop. In a recent year an estimated 1,230 companies took on new names in an attempt to forge new identities, and paid over $250 million to corporate-identity consultants. Among these were **Primerica** (formerly American Can), **Navistar** (formerly International Harvester), and **Nissan** (formerly Datsun).[5]

Customer-Related Intangible Assets

Customer-related intangible assets result from interactions with outside parties. Examples include customer lists, order or production backlogs, and both contractual and noncontractual customer relationships.

To illustrate, assume that We-Market Inc. acquires the customer list of a large newspaper for $6,000,000 on January 1, 2007. This customer database includes name, contact information, order history, and demographic information. We-Market expects to benefit evenly from the information over a three-year period. In this case, the customer list is a limited-life intangible that We-Market should amortize on a straight-line basis over the three-year period.

We-Market records the purchase of the customer list and the amortization of the customer list at the end of each year as follows.

January 1, 2007

Customer List	6,000,000	
Cash		6,000,000
(To record purchase of customer list)		

December 31, 2007, 2008, 2009

Customer List Amortization Expense	2,000,000	
Customer List (or Accumulated Customer List Amortization)		2,000,000
(To record amortization expense)		

The preceding example assumed no residual value for the customer list. But what if We-Market determines that it can sell the list for $60,000 to another company at the end of three years? In that case We-Market should subtract this residual value from the cost in order to determine the proper amortization expense for each year. Amortization expense would therefore be $1,980,000, as shown in Illustration 12-2.

ILLUSTRATION 12-2
Calculation of
Amortization Expense
with Residual Value

Cost	$6,000,000
Residual value	60,000
Amortization base	$5,940,000

Amortization expense per period: $1,980,000 ($5,940,000 ÷ 3)

Companies should assume a zero residual value unless the asset's useful life is less than the economic life and reliable evidence is available concerning the residual value.[6]

---

[5]To illustrate how various intangibles arise from a given product, consider how the creators of the highly successful game Trivial Pursuit protected their creation. First, they copyrighted the 6,000 questions that are at the heart of the game. Then they shielded the Trivial Pursuit name by applying for a registered trademark. As a third mode of protection, they obtained a design patent on the playing board's design as a unique graphic creation.

[6]"Goodwill and Other Intangible Assets," *Statement of Financial Accounting Standards No. 142* (Norwalk, Conn.: FASB, 2001), par. B55.

Artistic-Related Intangible Assets

Artistic-related intangible assets involve ownership rights to plays, literary works, musical works, pictures, photographs, and video and audiovisual material. Copyrights protect these ownership rights.

A **copyright** is a federally granted right that all authors, painters, musicians, sculptors, and other artists have in their creations and expressions. A copyright is granted for the **life of the creator plus 70 years**. It gives the owner, or heirs, the exclusive right to reproduce and sell an artistic or published work. Copyrights are not renewable. Companies may capitalize the costs of acquiring and defending a copyright. However, they must expense the research and development costs involved as incurred.

Copyrights can be valuable. For example, the **Walt Disney Company** faced the loss of its copyright on Mickey Mouse, which could have affected sales of billions of dollars of Mickey-related goods and services (including theme parks). This copyright was so valuable that Disney and many other big entertainment companies fought all the way to the Supreme Court (and won) an extension of copyright lives from 50 to 70 years. Another example of the value of these intangibles is **Really Useful Group**, which owns copyrights on the musicals of Andrew Lloyd Webber—*Cats, Phantom of the Opera, Jesus Christ-Superstar,* and others. It has little hard assets, yet analysts value it at over $300 million.

Generally, the useful life of the copyright is less than its legal life (life of the creator plus 70 years). Thus, Really Useful Group should allocate the costs of its copyrights to the years in which it expects to receive the benefits. The difficulty of determining the number of years over which it will receive benefits normally encourages a company like Really Useful Group to write off these costs over a fairly short period of time.

Contract-Related Intangible Assets

Contract-related intangible assets represent the value of rights that arise from contractual arrangements. Examples are franchise and licensing agreements, construction permits, broadcast rights, and service or supply contracts. A common form of contract-based intangible asset is a franchise.

A **franchise** is a contractual arrangement under which the franchisor grants the franchisee the right to sell certain products or services, to use certain trademarks or trade names, or to perform certain functions, usually within a designated geographical area. We deal with franchises everyday, from driving in an automobile purchased from a **Toyota** dealer, to eating lunch at **McDonald's**, to living in a home purchased through a **Century 21** real estate broker, or to vacationing at a **Marriott** resort.

The franchisor, having developed a unique concept or product, protects its concept or product through a patent, copyright, or trademark or trade name. The franchisee acquires the right to exploit the franchisor's idea or product by signing a franchise agreement.

A municipality (or other governmental body) and a company that uses public property often enter into another type of franchise arrangement. In such cases, a municipality allows a privately owned company to use public property in performing its services. Examples are the use of public waterways for a ferry service, the use of public land for telephone or electric lines, the use of phone lines for cable TV, the use of city streets for a bus line, or the use of the airwaves for radio or TV broadcasting. Such operating rights, obtained through agreements with governmental units or agencies, are frequently referred to as **licenses** or **permits**.

Franchises and licenses may be for a definite period of time, for an indefinite period of time, or perpetual. The company securing the franchise or license carries an intangible asset account entitled Franchise or License on its books, only when it can identify costs (such as a lump-sum payment in advance or legal fees and other expenditures) with the acquisition of the operating right. **A company should amortize the cost of a franchise (or license) with a limited life as operating expense over the life of the franchise.** It should not amortize a franchise with an indefinite life, or a perpetual franchise, but instead should carry it at cost.

Annual payments made under a franchise agreement should be entered as operating expenses in the period in which they are incurred. The payments do not represent an asset since they do not relate to future rights to use public property.

**WHAT DO THE
NUMBERS MEAN?**

SWEET TO SOUR

Krispy Kreme, the doughnut maker once dubbed the "hottest brand in the land," has taken a series of beatings. The latest: a formal inquiry by the Securities and Exchange Commission in October 2004 into its accounting. The problem seems to be with franchises Krispy Kreme reacquired a few years ago from owners who wanted to exit the business. Krispy Kreme decided to book most of the purchase price as an intangible asset called "reacquired franchise rights," which it does not amortize, or write-down, over time.

Management justified the accounting based on its belief that reacquired franchise rights have "indefinite lives." But critics charge that this artificially inflates profits and doesn't reflect the cost of the stores on its balance sheet. To compound its woes, some of the reacquired franchises were purchased from related parties, at prices some allege were too generous.

Accounting experts say it's unclear whether Krispy Kreme's method violates GAAP. One research firm found that all of the companies it follows with reacquired franchise rights amortize the costs over time. Krispy Kreme's methods are "definitely not conservative," according to one analyst.

The SEC probe couldn't have come at a worse time. Krispy Kreme's profits have plunged, and the stock lost about 75 percent of its value in the last year. Given the company's tumbling profits and hyper-aggressive accounting, investors should expect restatements and a big write-down when its auditor performs its annual impairment test. In other words, Krispy Kreme's outlook has gone from sweet to sour.

Source: Adapted from David Stires, "Accounting," *Fortune* (November 1, 2004), p. 42.

Technology-Related Intangible Assets

Technology-related intangible assets relate to innovations or technological advances. Examples are patented technology and trade secrets granted by the U.S. Patent and Trademark Office. A **patent** gives the holder exclusive right to use, manufacture, and sell a product or process **for a period of 20 years** without interference or infringement by others. With this exclusive right, fortunes can be made. For example, companies such as **Merck, Polaroid**, and **Xerox** were founded on patents.[7] The two principal kinds of patents are **product patents**, which cover actual physical products, and **process patents**, which govern the process of making products.

If a company like **Qualcomm** purchases a patent from an inventor (or other owner), the purchase price represents its cost. Qualcomm can capitalize other costs incurred in connection with securing a patent, as well as attorneys' fees and other unrecovered costs of a successful legal suit to protect the patent, as part of the patent cost. However, it **must expense as incurred** any research and development costs related to the **development** of the product, process, or idea that it subsequently patents. We discuss accounting for research and development costs in more detail on pages 587–590.

---

[7]Consider the opposite result: Sir Alexander Fleming, who discovered penicillin, decided not to use a patent to protect his discovery. He hoped that companies would produce it more quickly to help save sufferers. Companies, however, refused to develop it because they did not have the patent shield and, therefore, were afraid to make the investment.

Qualcomm should amortize the cost of a patent over its legal life or its useful life (the period benefits are received), whichever is **shorter**. If it owns a patent from the date it is granted, and Qualcomm expects the patent to be useful during its entire legal life, the company should amortize it over 20 years. If it appears that the patent will be useful for a shorter period of time, say, for five years, it should amortize its cost over five years.

Changing demand, new inventions superseding old ones, inadequacy, and other factors often limit the useful life of a patent to less than the legal life. For example, the useful life of patents in the pharmaceutical and drug industry is frequently less than the legal life because of the testing and approval period that follows their issuance. A typical drug patent has 5 to 11 years knocked off its 20-year legal life. Why? Because a drug-maker spends one to four years on animal tests, four to six years on human tests, and two to three years for the Food and Drug Administration to review the tests. All this time occurs after issuing the patent but before the product goes on a pharmacist's shelves.

PATENT BATTLES

WHAT DO THE NUMBERS MEAN?

From bioengineering to software design to the Internet, global competition is bringing battles over patents to the boiling point. For example, **Priceline.com** filed suit against **Microsoft** for launching Hotel Price Matcher, a service that operates much like the name-your-own-price-system Priceline pioneered.

Do you ever wonder who thought of the technology that saves your shipping and credit card information when you shop online? It was **Amazon.com**, which patented "one-click" shopping. To protect its technology, Amazon.com filed a complaint against **Barnesandnoble.com**, its rival in the Web-retailing wars, alleging infringement on its patent for one-click shopping. Even though Amazon.com and Barnesandnoble.com settled their dispute, patent battles continue between online retailers and independent software developers, claiming that companies like Amazon.com are unfairly undercutting its competition through these "business-method" patents.

Source: Adapted from "Battle over Patents Threatens to Damp Web's Innovative Spirit," *Wall Street Journal* (November 8, 1999); and L. Rohde, "Amazon, Barnes and Noble Settle Patent Dispute, *CNN.com* (March 8, 2002).

A company charges all legal fees and other costs incurred in successfully defending a patent suit to Patents, an asset account, because such a suit establishes the legal rights of the holder of the patent. Such costs should be amortized along with acquisition cost, over the remaining useful life of the patent.

Amortization expense should reflect the pattern, if reliably determined, in which a company uses up the patent.[8] A company may credit amortization of patents directly to the Patents account or to an Accumulated Patent Amortization account. To illustrate, assume that Harcott Co. incurs $180,000 in legal costs on January 1, 2007 to successfully defend a patent. The patent's useful life is 20 years, amortized on a straight-line basis. Harcott records the legal fees and the amortization at the end of 2007 as follows.

	January 1, 2007	
Patents	180,000	
Cash		180,000
(To record legal fees related to patent)		

	December 31, 2007	
Patent Amortization Expense	9,000	
Patents (or Accumulated Patent Amortization)		9,000
(To record amortization of patent)		

---

[8]Companies may compute amortization on a units-of-production basis in a manner similar to that described for depreciation on property, plant, and equipment. See Chapter 11, page 525.

We've said that a patent's useful life should not extend beyond its legal life of 20 years. However, companies often make small modifications or additions that lead to a new patent. For example, **Astra Zeneca Plc** filed for additional patents on minor modifications to its heartburn drug, Prilosec. The effect may be to extend the life of the old patent. In that case Astra Zeneca can apply the unamortized costs of the old patent to the new patent if the new patent provides essentially the same benefits.[9] Alternatively, if a patent becomes impaired because demand drops for the product, the asset should be written down or written off immediately to expense.

WHAT DO THE NUMBERS MEAN?

THE VALUE OF A SECRET FORMULA

The nuclear secrets contained within the Los Alamos nuclear lab seem easier to check out than a library book. But **The Coca-Cola Company** has managed to keep the recipe for the world's best-selling soft drink under wraps for more than 100 years. How has it done so?

Coca-Cola offers almost no information about its lifeblood. The only written copy of the formula resides in a bank vault in Atlanta. This handwritten sheet is available to no one except by vote of Coca-Cola's board of directors.

Can't science offer some clues? Coke purportedly contains 17 to 18 ingredients. That includes the usual caramel color and corn syrup, as well as a blend of oils known as 7X (rumored to be a mix of orange, lemon, cinnamon, and others). Distilling natural products like these is complicated, since they're made of thousands of compounds. One ingredient you will not find is cocaine. Although the original formula did contain trace amounts, today's Coke doesn't. When was it removed? That too is a secret.

Some experts indicate that the power of the Coca-Cola formula and related brand image account for almost 95 percent of Coke's $150 billion stock value.

Source: Adapted from Reed Tucker, "How Has Coke's Formula Stayed a Secret?" *Fortune* (July 24, 2000), p. 42.

Goodwill

OBJECTIVE 5
Explain the conceptual issues related to goodwill.

Although companies may capitalize certain costs to develop specifically identifiable assets such as patents and copyrights, the amounts capitalized are generally insignificant. But companies do record material amounts of intangible assets when purchasing intangible assets, particularly in situations involving the purchase of another business (often referred to as a business combination).

In a business combination, a company assigns the cost (purchase price), where possible, to the identifiable tangible and intangible net assets. It records the remainder in an intangible asset account called **Goodwill**. Goodwill is often referred to as the most intangible of intangible assets, because it is only identified with the business as a whole. The only way to sell it is to sell the business.

The problem of determining the proper cost to allocate to intangible assets in a business combination is complex. Many different types of intangibles may be considered, such as those we discussed earlier. It is extremely difficult not only to identify certain types of intangibles but also to assign a value to them in a business combination.

---

[9]Another example is **Eli Lilly**'s drug Prozac (prescribed to treat depression). In 1998 this product accounted for 43 percent of Eli Lilly's sales. The patent on Prozac expired in 2001, and the company was unable to extend its protection with a second-use patent for the use of Prozac to treat appetite disorders. Sales of the product slipped substantially as generic equivalents entered the market.

As a result, companies only record identifiable intangible assets that they can reliably measure. They record all other intangible assets, too difficult to identify or measure, as goodwill.[10]

Recording Goodwill

Internally Created Goodwill. **Goodwill generated internally should not be capitalized in the accounts.** The reason? Measuring the components of goodwill is simply too complex, and associating any costs with future benefits is too difficult. The future benefits of goodwill may have no relationship to the costs incurred in the development of that goodwill. To add to the mystery, goodwill may even exist in the absence of specific costs to develop it. Finally, because no objective transaction with outside parties takes place, a great deal of subjectivity—even misrepresentation—may occur.

OBJECTIVE 6
Describe the accounting procedures for recording goodwill.

Purchased Goodwill. Goodwill is recorded only when an entire business is purchased. Because goodwill is a "going concern" valuation, it cannot be separated from the business as a whole. To record goodwill, a company compares the fair market value of the net tangible and identifiable intangible assets with the purchase price of the acquired business. The difference is considered goodwill. This is why goodwill is sometimes referred to as a "plug," or "gap filler," or "**master valuation**" account. **Goodwill is the residual—the excess of cost over fair value of the identifiable net assets acquired.**

UNDERLYING CONCEPTS

Capitalizing goodwill only when it is purchased in an arm's-length transaction, and not capitalizing any goodwill generated internally, is another example of reliability winning out over relevance.

To illustrate, Multi-Diversified, Inc. decides that it needs a parts division to supplement its existing tractor distributorship. The president of Multi-Diversified is interested in buying a small concern in Chicago (Tractorling Company). Illustration 12-3 presents the balance sheet of Tractorling Company.

TRACTORLING CO.
BALANCE SHEET
AS OF DECEMBER 31, 2007

Assets		Equities	
Cash	$ 25,000	Current liabilities	$ 55,000
Receivables	35,000	Capital stock	100,000
Inventories	42,000	Retained earnings	100,000
Property, plant, and equipment, net	153,000		
Total assets	$255,000	Total equities	$255,000

ILLUSTRATION 12-3
Tractorling Balance Sheet

After considerable negotiation, Tractorling Company decides to accept Multi-Diversified's offer of $400,000. What, then, is the value of the goodwill, if any?

The answer is not obvious. Tractorling's historical cost-based balance sheet does not disclose the fair market values of its identifiable assets. Suppose, though, that as the negotiations progress, Multi-Diversified investigates Tractorling's underlying assets to determine their fair market values. Such an investigation may be accomplished

Expanded Discussion—
Valuing Goodwill

---

[10]*SFAS No. 141* provides detailed guidance regarding the recognition of identifiable intangible assets in a business combination. Using this guidance, it was expected that companies would recognize more identifiable intangible assets, and less goodwill, in the financial statements as a result of business combinations. According to *Accounting Trends and Techniques* (AICPA 2004), companies surveyed reported nearly twice as many identifiable intangible assets compared to the survey in 2001. There was little change in the number of survey companies reporting goodwill.

either through a purchase audit undertaken by Multi-Diversified's auditors or by an independent appraisal from some other source. The investigation determines the valuations shown in Illustration 12-4.

ILLUSTRATION 12-4
Fair Market Value of
Tractorling's Net Assets

Fair Market Values	
Cash	$ 25,000
Receivables	35,000
Inventories	122,000
Property, plant, and equipment, net	205,000
Patents	18,000
Liabilities	(55,000)
Fair market value of net assets	$350,000

Normally, differences between current fair market value and book value are more common among long-term assets than in the current assets category. Cash obviously poses no problems as to value. And receivables normally are fairly close to current valuation, although they may at times need certain adjustments due to inadequate bad debt provisions. Liabilities usually are stated at book value. However, if interest rates have changed since the company incurred the liabilities, a different valuation (such as present value based on expected cash flows) might be appropriate. Careful analysis must be made to determine that no unrecorded liabilities are present.

The $80,000 difference in Tractorling's inventories ($122,000 − $42,000) could result from a number of factors, the most likely being that the company uses LIFO. Recall that during periods of inflation, LIFO better matches expenses against revenues. However, it also creates a balance sheet distortion. Ending inventory consists of older layers costed at lower valuations.

In many cases, the values of long-term assets such as property, plant, and equipment, and intangibles may have increased substantially over the years. This difference could be due to inaccurate estimates of useful lives, continual expensing of small expenditures (say, less than $300), inaccurate estimates of salvage values, and the discovery of some unrecorded assets (as in Tractorling's case, where analysis determines Patents have a fair value of $18,000). Or, fair values may have substantially increased.

Since the investigation now determines the fair market value of net assets to be $350,000, why would Multi-Diversified pay $400,000? Undoubtedly, Tractorling points to its established reputation, good credit rating, top management team, well-trained employees, and so on. These factors make the value of the business greater than $350,000. At the same time, Multi-Diversified places a premium on the future earning power of these attributes as well as the basic asset structure of the company today. At this point in the negotiations, price can be a function of many factors. The most important is probably sheer skill at the bargaining table.

Multi-Diversified labels the difference between the purchase price of $400,000 and the fair market value of $350,000 as goodwill. Goodwill is viewed as one or a group of unidentifiable values (intangible assets), the cost of which "is measured by the difference between the cost of the group of assets or enterprise acquired and the sum of the assigned costs of individual tangible and identifiable intangible assets acquired less liabilities assumed."[11] This procedure for valuation, a **master valuation**

---

[11]The FASB expressed concern about measuring goodwill as a residual, but noted that there is no real measurement alternative since goodwill is not separable from the company as a whole. "Business Combinations," *Statement of Financial Accounting Standards No. 141* (Norwalk, Conn.: FASB, 2001), par. B145.

approach, assumes goodwill covers all the values that cannot be specifically identified with any identifiable tangible or intangible asset. Illustration 12-5 shows this approach.

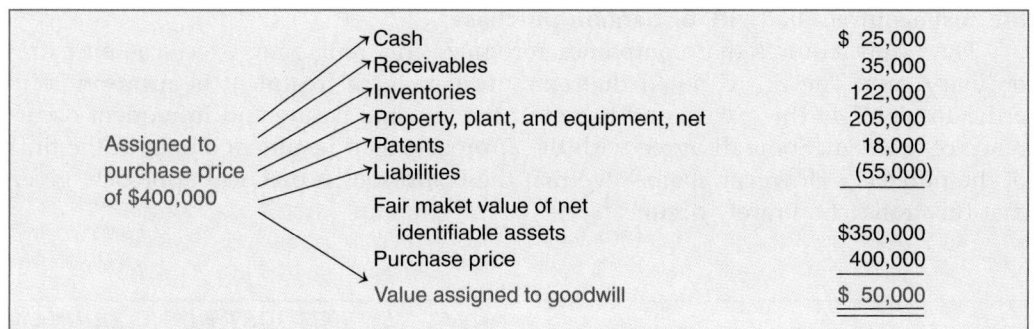

	Cash	$ 25,000
	Receivables	35,000
	Inventories	122,000
Assigned to	Property, plant, and equipment, net	205,000
purchase price	Patents	18,000
of $400,000	Liabilities	(55,000)
	Fair maket value of net	
	identifiable assets	$350,000
	Purchase price	400,000
	Value assigned to goodwill	$ 50,000

ILLUSTRATION 12-5
Determination of
Goodwill—Master
Valuation Approach

Multi-Diversified records this transaction as follows.

Cash	25,000	
Receivables	35,000	
Inventories	122,000	
Property, Plant, and Equipment	205,000	
Patents	18,000	
Goodwill	50,000	
Liabilities		55,000
Cash		400,000

Companies often identify goodwill on the balance sheet as the **excess of cost over the fair value** of the net assets acquired.

Goodwill Write-off

Companies that recognize goodwill in a business combination **consider it to have an indefinite life and therefore should not amortize it**. The reason: Investors find the amortization charge of little use in evaluating financial performance. In addition, although goodwill may decrease over time, predicting the actual life of goodwill and an appropriate pattern of amortization is extremely difficult.

Furthermore, goodwill often is the largest intangible asset on a company's balance sheet and the investment community wants to know the amount invested in goodwill. Therefore, **companies only adjust its carrying value when goodwill is impaired**. This approach significantly impacts the income statements of some companies. For example, **AOL Time Warner** (now **Time Warner**), **AT&T**, and other companies wrote off $750 billion of goodwill in a recent year. (See "What Do the Numbers Mean?" discussion on page 584.)

Some believe that goodwill's value eventually disappears. Therefore, they argue companies should charge goodwill to expense over the periods affected. Amortizing goodwill better matches expense with revenues. Others note that the accounting treatment for purchased goodwill and goodwill created internally should be consistent. They point out that companies immediately expense goodwill created internally and thus it does not appear as an asset. Companies should follow the same treatment, they argue, for purchased goodwill. Even though these arguments may have some merit, nonamortization of goodwill combined with an adequate impairment test should provide the most useful financial information to the investment community.

Negative Goodwill—Badwill

Negative goodwill (often referred to as a **bargain purchase** or **badwill**) arises when the fair value of the assets acquired exceeds the purchase price of the assets. This situation results from a market imperfection. In this case, the seller would have been better off to sell the assets individually than in total. However, situations do occur (e.g., a forced liquidation or distressed sale due to the death of a company founder), in which the purchase price is less than the value of the net identifiable assets. This results in a credit, which is referred to as **negative goodwill** or, alternatively, as **excess of fair value over the cost acquired**, **badwill**, or **bargain purchase**.

The FASB requires that companies recognize this remaining excess as an extra-ordinary gain. The Board noted that extraordinary gain treatment is appropriate in order to highlight the excess, and to reflect the unusual nature and infrequent occurrence of the item. Some disagree with the approach, as it results in a gain at the time of the purchase. However, we believe that the Board took a practical approach, given that this transaction rarely occurs.[12]

WHAT DO THE NUMBERS MEAN?

REAL NEWS OR JUST BOOKKEEPING?

Companies used 2002 to take massive write-offs. As Chief Investment Strategist Abby Joseph Cohen of **Goldman Sachs** noted, "Simply stated, many companies are writing off not only the kitchen sink but the bathtub as well." For instance, **AOL Time Warner Inc.** (now **Time Warner**) had a goodwill write-down in the first quarter of that year that—by itself—reduced S&P 500 earnings by $2 to $4 on an after-tax basis, Ms. Cohen said.

In her investment letter, Ms. Cohen attributed companies' massive write-downs to "the air"—that is, a confluence of the impacts from the September 11, 2001, terrorist attacks, the official announcement that the country is in a recession, and new rules for the write-down of goodwill.

Though earnings hits can be tough to swallow in the quarter in which they are taken, they often are not of lasting impact psychologically or operationally. "The quarter in which the write-offs are recorded typically bears the statistical brunt, but may not be reflective of performance in future quarters," according to Ms. Cohen.

Goodwill impairment issues continue to grab their share of business headlines. For example, **Hewlett-Packard** has received a fair amount of criticism for it failure to take goodwill impairment charges on goodwill arising from its merger with **Compaq**. HP's chief financial officer acknowledges the issue, but plays down its significance: "There's no question that if profitability doesn't improve, there will be an impairment charge." He makes the case that it wouldn't matter much, given that it would be just a book-keeping entry. What do you think? Is an impairment charge just an entry or can it provide some new information about the merits of the merger with Compaq?

Source: Carol J. Loomis, "Why Carly's Big Bet Is Failing," *Fortune* (February 7, 2005), p. 50.

IMPAIRMENT OF INTANGIBLE ASSETS

OBJECTIVE 7

Explain the accounting issues related to intangible-asset impairments.

In some cases, the carrying amount of a long-lived asset (property, plant, and equipment or intangible assets) is not recoverable. Therefore, a company needs a write-off. As discussed in Chapter 11, this write-off is referred to as an **impairment**.

Impairment of Limited-Life Intangibles

The rules that apply to **impairments of property, plant, and equipment also apply to limited-life intangibles**. As discussed in Chapter 11, a company should review property, plant, and equipment for impairment at certain points—whenever events or

---

[12]"Business Combinations," *Statement of Financial Accounting Standards No. 141* (Norwalk, Conn.: FASB, 2001), pars. B187–B192.

changes in circumstances indicate that the carrying amount of the assets may not be recoverable.

In performing this **recoverability test**, the company estimates the future cash flows expected from use of the assets and its eventual disposal. If the sum of the expected future net cash flows (undiscounted) is less than the carrying amount of the asset, the company would measure and recognize an impairment loss.[13] The company then uses the **fair value test**. This test measures the impairment loss by comparing the asset's fair value with its carrying amount. The impairment loss is the carrying amount of the asset less the fair value of the impaired asset. As with other impairments, the loss on the limited-life intangible is reported as part of income from continuing operations. The entry generally appears in the "Other expenses and losses" section.

To illustrate, assume that Lerch, Inc. has a patent on how to extract oil from shale rock. Unfortunately, reduced oil prices adversely affected the shale oil technology. Thus, the patent has provided little income to date. As a result, Lerch performs a **recoverability test**. It finds that the expected net future cash flows from this patent are $35 million, and Lerch's patent has a carrying amount of $60 million. Because the expected future net cash flows of $35 million are less than the carrying amount of $60 million, Lerch must determine an impairment loss.

Discounting the expected net future cash flows at its market rate of interest, Lerch determines the fair value of its patent to be $20 million. Illustration 12-6 shows the impairment loss computation (based on fair value).

Carrying amount of patent	$60,000,000
Fair value (based on present value computation)	20,000,000
Loss on impairment	$40,000,000

ILLUSTRATION 12-6
Computation of Loss on Impairment of Patent

Lerch records this loss as follows:

Loss on Impairment	40,000,000	
Patents		40,000,000

After recognizing the impairment, the reduced carrying amount of the patents is its new cost basis. Lerch should amortize the patent's new cost over its remaining useful life or legal life, whichever is shorter. Even if oil prices increase in subsequent periods, and the value of the patent increases, Lerch **may not recognize restoration of the previously recognized impairment loss**.

Impairment of Indefinite-Life Intangibles Other Than Goodwill

Indefinite-life intangibles (other than goodwill) should be tested for impairment at least annually. The impairment test for an indefinite-life asset other than goodwill is a **fair value test**. This test compares the fair value of the intangible asset with the asset's carrying amount. If the fair value of the intangible asset is less than the carrying amount, an impairment is recognized. Companies use this one-step test because many indefinite-life assets easily meet the recoverability test (because cash flows may extend many years into the future). **As a result, the recoverability test is not used.**

To illustrate, assume that Arcon Radio purchased a broadcast license for $2,000,000. The license is renewable every 10 years if the company provides appropriate service and does not violate Federal Communications Commission (FCC) rules and procedures. Arcon Radio has renewed the license with the FCC twice, at a minimal cost. Because

---

[13]"Accounting for the Impairment or Disposal of Long-lived Assets," *Statement of Financial Accounting Standards No. 144* (Norwalk, Conn.: 2001).

it expects cash flows to last indefinitely, Arcon Radio reports the license as an indefinite-life intangible asset. Recently the FCC decided to no longer renew broadcast licenses, but to auction these licenses to the highest bidder. Arcon Radio expects cash flows for the remaining two years of its existing license. Arcon Radio performs an impairment test and determines that the fair value of the intangible asset is $1,500,000. It therefore reports an impairment loss of $500,000, computed as follows.

ILLUSTRATION 12-7
Computation of Loss on Impairment of Broadcast License

Carrying amount of broadcast license	$2,000,000
Fair value of broadcast license	1,500,000
Loss on impairment	$ 500,000

Arcon Radio now reports the license at $1,500,000, its fair value. Even if the value of the license increases in the remaining two years, Arcon Radio may not restore the previously recognized impairment loss.

Impairment of Goodwill

The impairment rule for goodwill is a two-step process. First, a company should compare the fair value of the reporting unit to its carrying amount, including goodwill. If the fair value of the reporting unit exceeds the carrying amount, it does not consider goodwill impaired. The company does not have to do anything else.

To illustrate, assume that Kohlbuy Corporation has three divisions in its company. It purchased one division, Pritt Products, four years ago for $2 million. Unfortunately, Pritt experienced operating losses over the last three quarters. Kohlbuy management is now reviewing the division for purposes of recognizing an impairment. Illustration 12-8 lists the Pritt Division's net assets, including the associated goodwill of $900,000 from the purchase.

ILLUSTRATION 12-8
Net Assets of Pritt Division, Including Goodwill

Cash	$ 200,000
Receivables	300,000
Inventory	700,000
Property, plant, and equipment (net)	800,000
Goodwill	900,000
Less: Accounts and notes payable	(500,000)
Net assets	$2,400,000

Kohlbuy determines that the fair value of Pritt Division is $2,800,000. **As a result, it does not recognize any impairment, because the fair value of the division exceeds the carrying amount of the net assets.**

However, if the fair value of Pritt Division is less than the carrying amount of the net assets, then Kohlbuy performs a second step to determine possible impairment. In the second step, Kohlbuy determines the fair value of the goodwill (implied value of goodwill) and compares it to its carrying amount. To illustrate, assume that the fair value of the Pritt Division is $1,900,000 instead of $2,800,000. Illustration 12-9 computes the implied value of the goodwill in this case.[14]

---

[14]Illustration 12-9 assumes that the carrying amount equals the fair value of net identifiable assets (excluding goodwill). If different, companies use the fair value of the net identifiable assets (excluding goodwill) to determine the implied goodwill.

Fair value of Pritt Division		$1,900,000
Net identifiable assets (excluding goodwill) ($2,400,000 − $900,000)		1,500,000
Implied value of goodwill		$ 400,000

ILLUSTRATION 12-9
Determination of Implied
Value of Goodwill

Kohlbuy then compares the implied value of the goodwill to the recorded goodwill to determine impairment, as shown in Illustration 12-10.

Carrying amount of goodwill	$900,000
Implied value of goodwill	400,000
Loss on impairment	$500,000

ILLUSTRATION 12-10
Measurement of
Goodwill Impairment

Illustration 12-11 summarizes the impairment tests for various intangible assets.

Type of Intangible Asset	Impairment Test
Limited life	Recoverability test, then fair value test
Indefinite life other than goodwill	Fair value test
Goodwill	Fair value test on reporting unit, then fair value test on implied goodwill

ILLUSTRATION 12-11
Summary of Intangible
Asset Impairment Tests

RESEARCH AND DEVELOPMENT COSTS

Research and development (R&D) costs are not in themselves intangible assets. We present the accounting for R&D costs here, however, because research and development activities frequently result in the development of something that a company patents or copyrights (such as a new product, process, idea, formula, composition, or literary work).

Many companies spend considerable sums of money on research and development to create new products or processes, to improve present products, and to discover new knowledge that may be valuable at some future date. Illustration 12-12 shows the outlays for R&D made by selected U.S. companies.

OBJECTIVE 8
Identify the conceptual
issues related to
research and
development costs.

Company	R&D ($ million)	R&D/Sales	R&D/Net Income
Caterpillar	$ 928.0	3.07%	45.60%
Deere & Co.	611.6	3.06%	43.50%
Dell	463.0	0.94%	15.22%
General Mills	158.0	1.43%	14.98%
Hewlett-Packard	3,506.0	4.39%	100.26%
Johnson & Johnson	5,203.0	10.99%	61.15%
Kellogg	148.9	1.55%	16.72%
Merck	4,010.2	17.48%	68.98%

ILLUSTRATION 12-12
R&D Outlays, as a
Percentage of Sales and
Profits

INTERNATIONAL INSIGHT

International accounting standards require the capitalization of appropriate development expenditures. This conflicts with U.S. GAAP.

Two difficulties arise in accounting for these research and development (R&D) expenditures: (1) identifying the costs associated with particular activities, projects, or achievements, and (2) determining the magnitude of the future benefits and length of time over which such benefits may be realized. Because of these latter uncertainties, the accounting practice in this area has been simplified. **Companies must expense all research and development costs when incurred.**[15]

Identifying R&D Activities

Illustration 12-13 shows the definitions for **research activities** and **development activities**. These definitions differentiate research and development costs from similar costs.[16]

ILLUSTRATION 12-13
R&D Activities

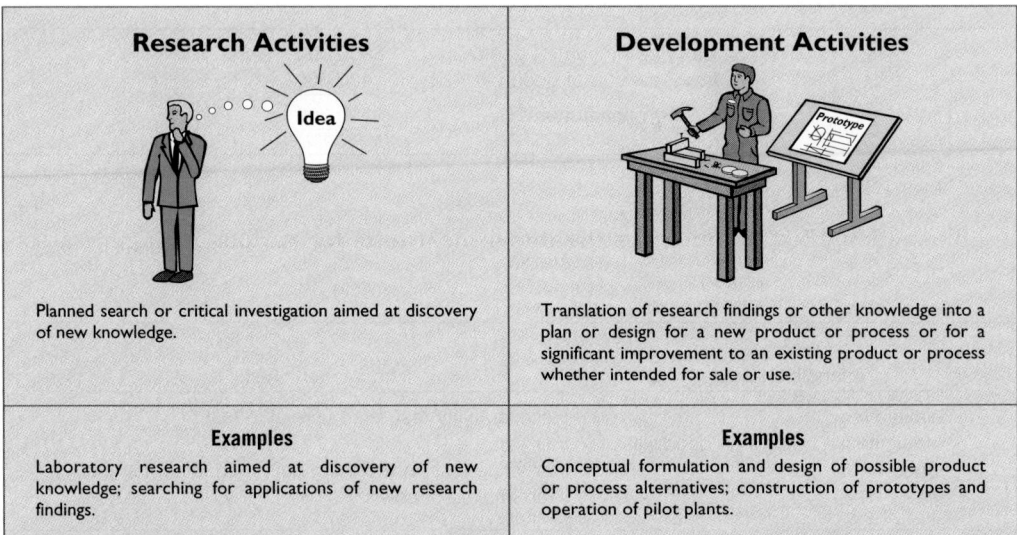

Research Activities	Development Activities
Planned search or critical investigation aimed at discovery of new knowledge.	Translation of research findings or other knowledge into a plan or design for a new product or process or for a significant improvement to an existing product or process whether intended for sale or use.
Examples	**Examples**
Laboratory research aimed at discovery of new knowledge; searching for applications of new research findings.	Conceptual formulation and design of possible product or process alternatives; construction of prototypes and operation of pilot plants.

Note that R&D activities do not include routine or periodic alterations to existing products, production lines, manufacturing processes, and other ongoing operations, even though these alterations may represent improvements. For example, routine ongoing efforts to refine, enrich, or improve the qualities of an existing product are not considered R&D activities.

Accounting for R&D Activities

OBJECTIVE 9
Describe the accounting for research and development and similar costs.

The costs associated with R&D activities and the accounting treatments accorded them are as follows.

1. *Materials, Equipment, and Facilities.* Expense the entire costs, **unless the items have alternative future uses** (in other R&D projects or otherwise), in which case carry as inventory and allocate as consumed; or capitalize and depreciate as used.

2. *Personnel.* Expense salaries, wages, and other related costs of personnel engaged in R&D as incurred.

3. *Purchased Intangibles.* Expense the entire cost, **unless the items have alternative future uses** (in other R&D projects or otherwise), in which case capitalize and amortize.

4. *Contract Services.* Expense the costs of services performed by others in connection with the R&D as incurred.

5. *Indirect Costs.* Include a reasonable allocation of indirect costs in R&D costs, except for general and administrative cost, which must be clearly related in order to be included in R&D.[17]

---

[15]"Accounting for Research and Development Costs," *Statement of Financial Accounting Standards No. 2* (Stamford, Conn.: FASB, 1974), par. 12.

[16]Ibid., par. 8.

[17]Ibid., par. 11.

Consistent with item 1 above, if a company owns a research facility consisting of buildings, laboratories, and equipment that conducts R&D activities and that has alternative future uses (in other R&D projects or otherwise), it should capitalize the facility as an operational asset. The company accounts for depreciation and other costs related to such research facilities as R&D expenses.[18]

To illustrate, assume that Next Century Incorporated develops, produces, and markets laser machines for medical, industrial, and defense uses.[19] Illustration 12-14 lists the types of expenditures related to its laser machine activities, along with the recommended accounting treatment.

ILLUSTRATION 12-14
Sample R&D
Expenditures and Their
Accounting Treatment

Next Century Incorporated

Type of Expenditure	Accounting Treatment
1. Construction of long-range research facility for use in current and future projects (three-story, 400,000-square-foot building).	Capitalize and depreciate as R&D expense.
2. Acquisition of R&D equipment for use on current project only.	Expense immediately as R&D.
3. Acquisition of machinery to be used on current and future R&D projects.	Capitalize and depreciate as R&D expense.
4. Purchase of materials to be used on current and future R&D projects.	Inventory and allocate to R&D projects; expense as consumed.
5. Salaries of research staff designing new laser bone scanner.	Expense immediately as R&D.
6. Research costs incurred under contract with New Horizon, Inc., and billable monthly.	Record as a receivable (reimbursable expenses).
7. Material, labor, and overhead costs of prototype laser scanner.	Expense immediately as R&D.
8. Costs of testing prototype and design modifications.	Expense immediately as R&D.
9. Legal fees to obtain patent on new laser scanner.	Capitalize as patent and amortize to overhead as part of cost of goods manufactured.
10. Executive salaries.	Expense as operating expense (general and administrative).
11. Cost of marketing research to promote new laser scanner.	Expense as operating expense (selling).
12. Engineering costs incurred to advance the laser scanner to full production stage.	Expense immediately as R&D.
13. Costs of successfully defending patent on laser scanner.	Capitalize as patent and amortize to overhead as part of cost of goods manufactured.
14. Commissions to sales staff marketing new laser scanner.	Expense as operating expense (selling).

[18]Companies in **the extractive industries** can use the following accounting treatment for the unique costs of research, exploration, and development activities and for those costs that are similar to but not classified as R&D costs: (1) expense as incurred, (2) capitalize and either depreciate or amortize over an appropriate period of time, or (3) accumulate as part of inventoriable costs. Choice of the appropriate accounting treatment for such costs is based on the degree of certainty of future benefits and the principle of matching revenues and expenses.

[19]Sometimes companies conduct R&D activities for other companies under a contractual arrangement. In this case, the contract usually specifies that the company performing the R&D work be reimbursed for all direct costs and certain specific indirect costs, plus a profit element. Because reimbursement is expected, the company doing the R&D work records the R&D costs as a receivable. The company for whom the work has been performed reports these costs as R&D and expenses them as incurred.

For a more complete discussion of how an enterprise should account for funding of its R&D by others, see "Research and Development Arrangements," *Statement of Financial Accounting Standards No. 68* (Stamford, Conn.: FASB, 1982).

Other Costs Similar to R&D Costs

Many costs have characteristics similar to research and development costs. Examples are:

1 Start-up costs for a new operation.

2 Initial operating losses.

3 Advertising costs.

4 Computer software costs.

For the most part, these costs are expensed as incurred, similar to the accounting for R&D costs. We briefly explain these costs in the following sections.

Start-Up Costs

Start-up costs are incurred for one-time activities to start a new operation. Examples include opening a new plant, introducing a new product or service, or conducting business in a new territory or with a new class of customers. Start-up costs include **organizational costs**, such as legal and state fees incurred to organize a new business entity.

The accounting for start-up costs is straightforward: **Expense start-up costs as incurred.** The profession recognizes that companies incur start-up costs with the expectation of future revenues or increased efficiencies. However, to determine the amount and timing of future benefits is so difficult that a conservative approach—expensing these costs as incurred—is required.[20]

To illustrate the type of costs that companies expense as start-up costs, assume that U.S.-based Hilo Beverage Company decides to construct a new plant in Brazil. This represents Hilo's first entry into the Brazilian market. As part of its overall strategy, Hilo plans to introduce the company's major U.S. brands into Brazil, on a locally produced basis. The following costs might be involved:

1 Travel-related costs; costs related to employee salaries; and costs related to feasibility studies, accounting, tax, and government affairs.

2 Training of local employees related to product, maintenance, computer systems, finance, and operations.

3 Recruiting, organizing, and training related to establishing a distribution network.

Hilo Beverage should expense all these start-up costs as incurred.

Start-up activities commonly occur at the same time as activities such as the acquisition of assets. For example, as it is incurring start-up costs for the new plant, Hilo also probably is buying or building property, plant, equipment, and inventory. Hilo should not immediately expense the costs of these assets. Instead, it should charge them to operations and report them on the balance sheet using appropriate GAAP reporting guidelines.

Initial Operating Losses

Some contend that companies should be allowed to capitalize initial operating losses incurred in the start-up of a business. They argue that such operating losses are a cost of starting a business and are unavoidable.

For example, assume that Hilo lost money in its first year of operations and wishes to capitalize this loss. Hilo's CEO argues that as the company becomes profitable, it will offset these losses in future periods. What do *you* think? We believe that this approach is unsound, since losses have no future service potential and therefore cannot be considered an asset.

---

[20]"Reporting on the Costs of Start-up Activities," *Statement of Position 98-5* (New York: AICPA, 1998).

GAAP requires that operating losses during the early years should not be capitalized. In short, **the accounting and reporting standards should be no different for an enterprise trying to establish a new business than they are for other enterprises.**[21]

Advertising Costs

Over the years, **PepsiCo** has hired various pop stars, such as Britney Spears and Beyoncé, to advertise its products. How should it report such advertising costs related to its star spokespeople? Pepsi could expense the costs in various ways:

1 When they have completed their singing assignments.

2 The first time the advertising runs.

3 Over the estimated useful life of the advertising.

4 In an appropriate fashion to each of the three periods identified above.

5 Over the period revenues are expected to result.

For the most part, Pepsi must expense advertising costs as incurred or the first time the advertising takes place. These two alternatives are permitted because whichever approach is followed, the results are essentially the same. On the other hand, companies record as assets any tangible assets used in advertising, such as billboards or blimps. The rationale is that such assets do have alternative future uses. Again the

---

BRANDED

WHAT DO THE NUMBERS MEAN?

For many companies, developing a strong brand image is as important as developing the products they sell. Now more than ever, companies see the power of a strong brand, enhanced by significant and effective advertising investments.

As the following chart indicates, the value of brand investments is substantial. **Coca-Cola** heads the list with an estimated brand value of nearly $70 billion.

The World's 10 Most Valuable Brands
(in billions)

1 **Coca-Cola**	$67.3	6 **Disney**	$27.1
2 **Microsoft**	61.3	7 **McDonald's**	25.0
3 **IBM**	53.8	8 **Nokia**	24.0
4 **GE**	44.1	9 **Toyota**	22.7
5 **Intel**	33.5	10 **Marlboro**	22.1

Source: 2004 data, from Interbrand Corp. and J. P. Morgan Chase.

Occasionally you may find the value of a brand included in a company's financial statements under goodwill. But generally you won't find the estimated values of brands recorded in companies' balance sheets. The reason? The subjectivity that goes into estimating a brand's value. In some cases, analysts base an estimate of brand value on opinion polls or on some multiple of ad spending. In estimating the brand values shown above, **Interbrand Corp.** estimates the percentage of the overall future revenues the brand will generate and then discounts the net cash flows, to arrive at a present value. Some analysts believe that information on brand values is relevant. Others voice valid concerns about the reliability of brand value estimates due to subjectivity in the estimates for revenues, costs, and the risk component of the discount rate.

Source: Adapted from Gerry Khermouch, "The Best Global Brands," *Businessweek* (August 5, 2002), pp. 93–95; and D. Brady, R. D. Hof, and A. Reinhardt, "Cult Brands," *Businessweek Online* (August 2, 2004).

---

[21]"Accounting and Reporting by Development Stage Enterprises," *Statement of Financial Accounting Standards No. 7* (Stamford, Conn.: FASB, 1975), par. 10. A company is considered to be in the developing stages when it is directing its efforts toward establishing a new business and either the company has not started the principal operations or it has earned no significant revenue.

profession has taken a conservative approach to recording advertising costs because defining and measuring the future benefits can be so difficult.[22]

Computer Software Costs

UNDERLYING CONCEPTS

The requirement that companies expense all R&D costs as incurred is an example of the conflict between relevance and reliability. Here, this requirement leans strongly in support of reliability, as well as conservatism, consistency, and comparability. No attempt is made to match costs and revenues.

A special problem arises in distinguishing R&D costs from selling and administrative activities. The FASB's intent was that companies exclude from the definition of R&D activities the acquisition, development, or improvement of a product or process **for use in their selling or administrative activities**. For example, the costs of software incurred by an airline in improving its computerized reservation system, or the costs incurred in developing a management information system **are not** research and development costs.

Accounting for computer software costs is a specialized and complicated accounting topic that we discuss and illustrate in Appendix 12A (pages 596–599).

Conceptual Questions

The requirement that companies expense immediately all R&D costs (as well as start-up costs) incurred internally is a conservative, practical solution. It ensures consistency in practice and uniformity among companies. But the practice of immediately writing off expenditures made in the expectation of benefiting future periods is conceptually incorrect.

Proponents of immediate expensing contend that from an income statement standpoint, long-run application of this standard frequently makes little difference. They argue that because of the ongoing nature of most companies' R&D activities, the amount of R&D cost charged to expense each accounting period is about the same, whether there is immediate expensing or capitalization and subsequent amortization. Others criticize this practice. They believe that the balance sheet should report an intangible asset related to expenditures that have future benefit. To preclude capitalization of all R&D expenditures removes from the balance sheet what may be a company's most valuable asset. This standard represents one of the many trade-offs made among relevance, reliability, and cost-benefit considerations.[23]

PRESENTATION OF INTANGIBLES AND RELATED ITEMS

Presentation of Intangible Assets

OBJECTIVE 10
Indicate the presentation of intangible assets and related items.

The reporting of intangible assets differs from the reporting of property, plant, and equipment in that contra accounts are not normally shown for intangibles. (See Illustration 12-15.) On the balance sheet, companies should report all intangible assets other than goodwill as a separate item. If goodwill is present, companies should report it separately. The FASB concluded that since goodwill and other intangible assets differ significantly from other types of assets, this disclosure benefits users of the balance sheet.

---

[22]"Reporting on Advertising Costs," *Statement of Position 93-7* (New York: AICPA, 1993). Note that there are some exceptions for immediate expensing of advertising costs when they relate to direct-response advertising, but this subject is beyond the scope of this book.

[23]Research findings indicate that capitalizing R&D costs may be helpful to investors. For example, one study showed a significant relationship between R&D outlays and subsequent benefits in the form of increased productivity, earnings, and shareholder value for R&D–intensive companies. Baruch Lev and Theodore Sougiannis, "The Capitalization, Amortization, and Value-Relevance of R&D," *Journal of Accounting and Economics* (February 1996).

Another study found that there was a significant decline in earnings usefulness for companies that were forced to switch from capitalizing to expensing R&D costs, and that the decline appears to persist over time. Martha L. Loudder and Bruce K. Behn, "Alternative Income Determination Rules and Earnings Usefulness: The Case of R&D Costs," *Contemporary Accounting Research* (Fall 1995).

On the income statement, companies should present amortization expense and impairment losses for intangible assets other than goodwill as part of continuing operations. Goodwill impairment losses should also be presented as a separate line item in the continuing operations section, unless the goodwill impairment is associated with a discontinued operation.

ILLUSTRATION 12-15
Intangible Asset
Disclosures

HARBAUGH COMPANY

Balance Sheet (partial)
(in thousands)

Intangible Assets (Note C)	$3,840
Goodwill (Note D)	2,575

Income Statement (partial)
(in thousands)

as part of Continuing operations

Amortization expense	$380
Impairment losses (goodwill)	46

Note C: Acquired Intangible Assets

	As of December 31, 2007	
	Gross Carrying Amount	Accumulated Amortization
Amortized intangible assets		
Trademark	$2,000	$(100)
Customer list	500	(310)
Other	60	(10)
Total	$2,560	$(420)
Unamortized intangible assets		
Licenses	$1,300	
Trademark	400	
Total	$1,700	

Aggregate Amortization Expense

For year ended 12/31/07	$380

Estimated Amortization Expense

For year ended 12/31/08	$200
For year ended 12/31/09	90
For year ended 12/31/10	70
For year ended 12/31/11	60
For year ended 12/31/12	50

Note D: Goodwill
The changes in the carrying amount of goodwill for the year ended December 31, 2007, are as follows:

($000s)	Technology Segment	Communications Segment	Total
Balance as of January 1, 2007	$1,413	$904	$2,317
Goodwill acquired during year	189	115	304
Impairment losses	—	(46)	(46)
Balance as of December 31, 2007	$1,602	$973	$2,575

The Communications segment is tested for impairment in the third quarter, after the annual forecasting process. Due to an increase in competition in the Texas and Louisiana cable industry, operating profits and cash flows were lower than expected in the fourth quarter of 2006 and the first and second quarters of 2007. Based on that trend, the earnings forecast for the next 5 years was revised. In September 2007, a goodwill impairment loss of $46 was recognized in the Communications reporting unit. The fair value of that reporting unit was estimated using the expected present value of future cash flows.

The notes to the financial statements should include information about acquired intangible assets, including the aggregate amortization expense for each of the succeeding 5 years. The notes should include information about changes in the carrying amount of goodwill during the period. As noted earlier, Illustration 12-15 shows the type of disclosure made related to intangible assets in the financial statements and related notes for Harbaugh Company.

Presentation of Research and Development Costs

Additional Disclosures of Intangibles and R&D Costs

Acceptable accounting practice requires that companies disclose in the financial statements (generally in the notes) the total R&D costs charged to expense each period for which they present an income statement. **Merck & Co., Inc.**, a global research pharmaceutical company, reported both internal and acquired research and development in its recent income statement, as shown in Illustration 12-16.

ILLUSTRATION 12-16
Income Statement
Disclosure of R&D Costs

Merck & Co., Inc.
(in millions)

	Years Ended December 31		
	2004	2003	2002
Sales	$22,938.6	$22,485.9	$21,445.8
Costs, expenses, and other			
Materials and production	4,959.8	4,436.9	4,004.9
Marketing and administrative	7,346.3	6,394.9	5,652.2
Research and development	4,010.2	3,279.9	2,677.2
Equity income from affiliates	(1,008.2)	(474.2)	(644.7)
Other (income) expense, net	(344.0)	(203.2)	104.5
	$14,964.1	$13,434.3	$11,794.1

In addition, Merck provides a discussion about R&D expenditures in its annual report, as shown in Illustration 12-17.

ILLUSTRATION 12-17
Merck's R&D
Disclosure

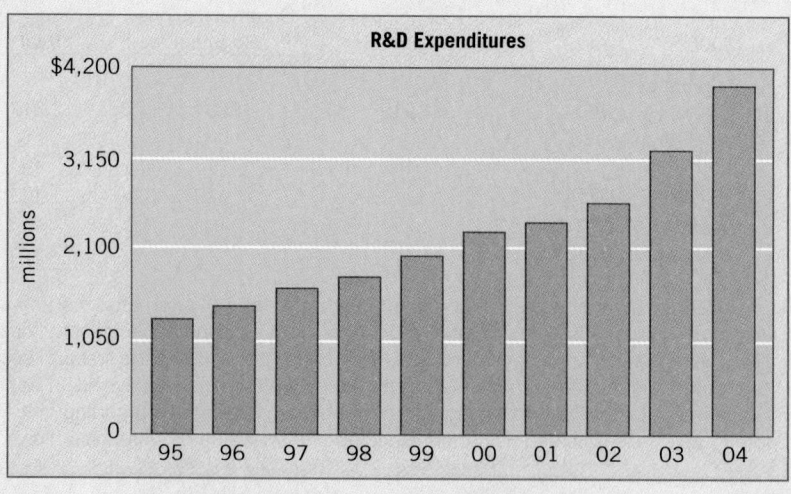

Merck & Co., Inc.

Research and development in the pharmaceutical industry is inherently a long-term process. The following data show an unbroken trend of year-to-year increases in the Company's research and development spending. For the period 1995 to 2004, the compounded annual growth rate in research and development was 13%.

SUMMARY OF LEARNING OBJECTIVES

1. Describe the characteristics of intangible assets. Intangible assets have two main characteristics: (1) They lack physical existence, and (2) they are not financial instruments. In most cases, intangible assets provide services over a period of years. As a result, they are normally classified as long-term assets.

2. Identify the costs to include in the initial valuation of intangible assets. Intangibles are recorded at cost. Cost includes all costs of acquisition and expenditures necessary to make the intangible asset ready for its intended use. If intangibles are acquired for stock or in exchange for other assets, the cost of the intangible is the fair value of the consideration given or the fair value of the intangible received, whichever is more clearly evident. When a company buys several intangibles, or a combination of intangibles and tangibles, in a "basket purchase," it should allocate the cost on the basis of fair values.

3. Explain the procedure for amortizing intangible assets. Intangibles have either a limited useful life or an indefinite useful life. Companies amortize intangible assets with a limited life. They do not amortize intangible assets with indefinite lives. Limited-life intangibles should be amortized by systematic charges to expense over their useful life. The useful life should reflect the period over which these assets will contribute to cash flows. The amount to report for amortization expense should reflect the pattern in which a company consumes or uses up the asset, if it can reliably determine that pattern. Otherwise the company should use a straight-line approach.

4. Describe the types of intangible assets. Major types of intangibles are: (1) *marketing-related intangibles*, used in the marketing or promotion of products or services; (2) *customer-related intangibles*, resulting from interactions with outside parties; (3) *artistic-related intangibles*, giving ownership rights to such items as plays and literary works; (4) *contract-related intangibles*, representing the value of rights that arise from contractual arrangements; (5) *technology-related intangibles*, relating to innovations or technological advances; and (6) *goodwill*, arising from business combinations.

5. Explain the conceptual issues related to goodwill. Goodwill is unique because unlike receivables, inventories, and patents that a company can sell or exchange individually in the marketplace, goodwill can be identified only with the company as a whole. Goodwill is a "going concern" valuation and is recorded only when an entire business is purchased. A company should not capitalize goodwill generated internally in the accounts, because measuring the components of goodwill is too complex and associating any costs with future benefits too difficult. The future benefits of goodwill may have no relationship to the costs incurred in the development of that goodwill. Goodwill may exist even in the absence of specific costs to develop it.

6. Describe the accounting procedures for recording goodwill. To record goodwill, a company compares the fair market value of the net tangible and identifiable intangible assets with the purchase price of the acquired business. The difference is considered goodwill. Goodwill is the residual—the excess of cost over fair value of the identifiable net assets acquired. Goodwill is often identified on the balance sheet as the excess of cost over the fair value of the net assets acquired.

7. Explain the accounting issues related to intangible-asset impairments. Impairment occurs when the carrying amount of the intangible asset is not recoverable. Companies use a recoverability test and a fair value test to determine impairments for limited-life intangibles. They use only a fair value test for indefinite-life intangibles. Goodwill impairments require a two-step process: First, test the fair value of the reporting unit, then do the fair value test on implied goodwill.

8. **Identify the conceptual issues related to research and development costs.** R&D costs are not in themselves intangible assets, but R&D activities frequently result in the development of something a company patents or copyrights. The difficulties in accounting for R&D expenditures are: (1) identifying the costs associated with particular activities, projects, or achievements, and (2) determining the magnitude of the future benefits and length of time over which a company may realize such benefits. Because of these latter uncertainties, companies are required to expense all research and development costs when incurred.

9. **Describe the accounting for research and development and similar costs.** Pages 587–589 show the costs associated with R&D activities and the accounting treatment accorded them. Many costs have characteristics similar to R&D costs. Examples are start-up costs, initial operating losses, and advertising costs. For the most part, these costs are expensed as incurred, similar to the accounting for R&D costs.

10. **Indicate the presentation of intangible assets and related items.** The reporting of intangibles differs from the reporting of property, plant, and equipment in that contra accounts are not normally shown. On the balance sheet, companies should report all intangible assets other than goodwill as a separate item. If goodwill is present, it too should be reported as a separate item. On the income statement, companies should report amortization expense and impairment losses in continuing operations. The notes to the financial statements have additional detailed information. Financial statements must disclose the total R&D costs charged to expense each period for which an income statement is presented.

APPENDIX
12A Accounting for Computer Software Costs

OBJECTIVE 11
Understand the accounting treatment for computer software costs.

Our economy is changing from a focus on manufacturing processes (tangible outputs) to a focus on information flow (intangible outputs).[1] As a result, the accounting for computer software products becomes increasingly important. This appendix discusses the basic issues involved in accounting for computer software.

DIVERSITY IN PRACTICE

Companies can either **purchase** computer software or **create** it. They may purchase or create software for **external use** (such as spreadsheet applications like Excel or Lotus 1-2-3) or for **internal use** (e.g., to establish a better internal accounting system).

---

[1]A major contributing factor was **IBM's** decision in 1969 to "unbundle" its hardware and software—to state the cost of the hardware and software separately. Previously, computer companies provided most application software free with the hardware. This unbundling led to the creation of a whole new industry, the software industry, whose members began selling software to hardware users.

How should companies account for the costs of developing software? Should they expense such costs immediately or capitalize and amortize them in the future? At one time, some companies expensed all software costs, and others capitalized such costs. Still others differentiated such costs on the basis of whether the software was purchased or created, or whether it was used for external or internal purposes.

Another major question is whether the costs involved in developing software are research and development costs. If they are actually R&D costs, then companies should expense them as incurred. If they are not R&D costs, then a strong case can be made for capitalization. As one financial executive of a software company, who argues for capitalization, noted, "The key distinction between our spending and R&D is recoverability. We know we are developing something we can sell."

THE PROFESSION'S POSITION

In an attempt to resolve the issue of how to account for software (at least for companies that sell computer software), the FASB issued *Statement of Financial Accounting Standards No. 86*, "Accounting for the Costs of Computer Software to Be Sold, Leased, or Otherwise Marketed."[2] The major recommendations of this pronouncement are:

1 Until a company has established **technological feasibility** for a software product, it should charge to R&D expense the costs incurred in creating the product.

2 Technological feasibility is established when the company has completed a detailed program design or a working model.

In short, the FASB has taken a conservative position in regard to computer software costs. For example, a company like **Microsoft** must expense all costs until it has completed the activities (planning, designing, coding, and testing) necessary to establish that it can produce the product to meet its design specifications. From that point on, Microsoft should capitalize subsequently incurred costs and amortize them to current and future periods.

Two additional points: First, **if Microsoft purchases software and it has alternative future uses, then it may be capitalized.** Second, **this standard applies only to the development of software that is to be sold, leased, or otherwise marketed to third parties** (i.e., for external use).

The profession has also indicated how to account for software to be used internally. Activities performed during the preliminary project stage of development (e.g., conceptual formulation and evaluation of alternatives) are similar to R&D costs. Companies should expense such costs immediately. Once the software is at the application development stage (e.g., at the coding or installation stages), its future economic benefits become probable. At that point, companies must capitalize the software costs. Finally, subsequent to the application development stage, costs related to training and application maintenance should be expensed as incurred.[3]

ACCOUNTING FOR CAPITALIZED SOFTWARE COSTS

If companies are to capitalize software costs, then they must establish a proper amortization pattern for such costs. As **a basis for amortization, one of two amounts is used: (1) the ratio of current revenues to current and anticipated revenues (the percent- of-revenue approach), or (2) the straight-line method over the remaining**

---

[2]"Accounting for the Cost of Computer Software to Be Sold, Leased, or Otherwise Marketed," *Statement of Financial Accounting Standards No. 86* (Stamford, Conn.: FASB, 1985). Also see Robert W. McGee, *Accounting for Software* (Homewood, Ill.: Dow Jones-Irwin, 1985).

[3]"Accounting for the Costs of Computer Software Developed or Obtained for Internal Use," *Statement of Position 98-1* (New York: AICPA, 1998).

useful life of the asset (straight-line approach). A company must use whichever of those amounts is greater. This rule can result in the use of the percent-of-revenue method one year and the straight-line method in another.[4]

To illustrate, assume that **AT&T** has capitalized software costs of $10 million, and current (first-year) revenues from sales of this product of $4 million. AT&T anticipates earning $16 million in additional future revenues from this product; it estimates that the product has an economic life of 4 years. Using the percent-of-revenue approach, AT&T's current (first) year's amortization is $2 million ($4,000,000/$20,000,000 times the capitalized software costs of $10,000,000). Using the straight-line approach, its amortization is $2.5 million ($10,000,000/4 years). Thus AT&T uses the straight-line approach because it results in the **greater amortization charge**.

REPORTING SOFTWARE COSTS

Much concern exists about the reliability of an asset such as software. Therefore, the FASB indicated that companies should value capitalized software costs at the **lower of unamortized cost (book value) or net realizable value**. If net realizable value is lower, then companies should write down the capitalized software costs to this value. Once companies have written down the costs, **they may not write them back up**.

In addition to the regular disclosures for R&D costs, companies should report in the financial statements the following information relating to software.

1 Unamortized software costs.

2 The total amount charged to expense and the amounts, if any, written down to net realizable value.

Again, these accounting and reporting requirements apply only to software **developed for external purposes**.

Illustration 12A-1 presents an example of software development cost disclosure, taken from the annual report of **Analogic Corporation**.

ILLUSTRATION 12A-1
Disclosure of Software
Development Costs

Analogic Corporation
(in thousands)

	2004	2003
Total current assets	$328,121	$335,903
Property, plant and equipment, net	91,077	83,926
Investments in and advances to affiliated companies	10,967	14,050
Capitalized software, net	9,502	6,339
Goodwill	1,565	2,306
Intangible assets, net	9,223	11,708
Other assets	1,616	3,185
Total assets	$452,071	$457,417

Significant Accounting Policies

Capitalized Software Costs: Software development costs incurred subsequent to establishing technological feasibility through general release of the software products are capitalized in accordance to SFAS No. 86 "Accounting for the Costs of Computer Software to be Sold, Leased, or Otherwise Marketed." Capitalized costs are amortized on a straight-line basis over the economic lives of the related products, generally three years. Amortization expense was $1,801, $1,813 and $1,772 in fiscal 2004, 2003, and 2002, respectively and is included in product cost of sales. The unamortized balance of capitalized software was $9,502 and $6,339 at July 31, 2004, and 2003, respectively.

---

[4]Because there are no revenues associated with software developed for internal use, amortization of these internal use capitalized costs is based on the straight-line approach.

SETTING STANDARDS FOR SOFTWARE ACCOUNTING

"It's unreasonable to expense all software costs, and it's unreasonable to capitalize all software costs," said **IBM**'s director of financial reporting. "If you subscribe to those two statements, then it follows that there is somewhere in between where development ends and capitalization begins. Now you have to define that point."[5] The FASB defined that point as **technological feasibility**, which is established upon completion of a detailed program design or a working model.

The difficulty of applying this criterion to software is that "there is no such thing as a real, specific, baseline design. But you could make it look like you have one as early or as late as you like," says Osman Erlop of **Hambrecht & Quist**.[6] That is, if a company wishes to capitalize, it draws up a detailed program design quickly. If it wants to expense lots of development costs, it simply holds off writing a detailed program design. And, once capitalized, the costs are amortized over the useful life specified by the developer. Because of either constant redesign or supersession, software's useful life is generally quite short (two to four years).

As another example, some companies "manage by the numbers." That is, they are very careful to identify projects that are worthwhile and capitalize the computer software costs associated with them. They believe that good projects must be capitalized and amortized in the future; otherwise, the concept of properly matching expense and revenues is abused. In contrast, other companies choose not to manage by the numbers. They simply expense all development costs. Companies that expense all these costs have no use for a standard that requires capitalization. In their view, it would mean only that they would need a more complex, more expensive cost accounting system, which would provide little if any benefit.

Financial analysts have reacted almost uniformly against any capitalization of software costs. They believe such costs should be expensed because of the rapid obsolescence of software and the potential for abuse that may result from capitalizing costs inappropriately. As Donald Kirk, a former chairman of the FASB, stated, "The Board is now faced with the problem of balancing what it thought was good theory with the costs for some companies of implementing a new accounting system with the concerns of users about the potential for abuse of the standard."[7]

Resolving the software accounting problem again demonstrates the difficulty of establishing reporting standards.

SUMMARY OF LEARNING OBJECTIVE FOR APPENDIX 12A

11. Understand the accounting treatment for computer software costs. Costs incurred in creating a software product should be charged to R&D expense when incurred until technological feasibility has been established for the product. Subsequent costs should be capitalized and amortized to current and future periods. Software that a company purchases for sale or lease to third parties and has alternative future uses may be capitalized and amortized using the greater of the percent-of-revenue approach or the straight-line approach.

Note: All **asterisked** Questions, Brief Exercises, Exercises, Problems, and Concepts for Analysis relate to material contained in the appendix to the chapter.

---

[5]"When Does Life Begin?" *Forbes* (June 16, 1986), pp. 72–74.

[6]Ibid.

[7]Donald J. Kirk, "Growing Temptation & Rising Expectation = Accelerating Regulation," *FASB Viewpoints* (June 12, 1985), p. 7.

QUESTIONS

1. What are the two main characteristics of intangible assets?

2. If intangibles are acquired for stock, how is the cost of the intangible determined?

3. Intangibles have either a limited useful life or an indefinite useful life. How should these two different types of intangibles be amortized?

4. Why does the accounting profession make a distinction between internally created intangibles and purchased intangibles?

5. In 2006 Sheila Wright Corp. spent $420,000 for "goodwill" visits by sales personnel to key customers. The purpose of these visits was to build a solid, friendly relationship for the future and to gain insight into the problems and needs of the companies served. How should this expenditure be reported?

6. What are factors to be considered in estimating the useful life of an intangible asset?

7. What should be the pattern of amortization for a limited-life intangible?

8. **Columbia Sportswear Company** acquired a trademark that is helpful in distinguishing one of its new products. The trademark is renewable every 10 years at minimal cost. All evidence indicates that this trademark product will generate cash flows for an indefinite period of time. How should this trademark be amortized?

9. Michael Redd Company spent $190,000 developing a new process, $45,000 in legal fees to obtain a patent, and $91,000 to market the process that was patented, all in the year 2006. How should these costs be accounted for in 2006?

10. Yellow 3 purchased a patent for $450,000 which has an estimated useful life of 10 years. Its pattern of use or consumption cannot be reliably determined. Prepare the entry to record the amortization of the patent in its first year of use.

11. Explain the difference between artistic-related intangible assets and contract-related intangible assets.

12. What is goodwill? What is negative goodwill?

13. Under what circumstances is it appropriate to record goodwill in the accounts? How should goodwill, properly recorded on the books, be written off in order to conform with generally accepted accounting principles?

14. In examining financial statements, financial analysts often write off goodwill immediately. Evaluate this procedure.

15. Astaire Inc. is considering the write-off of a limited life intangible because of its lack of profitability. Explain to the management of Astaire how to determine whether a write-off is permitted.

16. Last year Blair Company recorded an impairment on an intangible asset held for use. Recent appraisals indicate that the asset has increased in value. Should Blair record this recovery in value?

17. Explain how losses on impaired intangible assets should be reported in income.

18. Mills Company determines that its goodwill is impaired. It finds that its implied goodwill is $380,000 and its recorded goodwill is $400,000. The fair value of its identifiable assets is $1,450,000. What is the amount of goodwill impaired?

19. What is the nature of research and development costs?

20. Research and development activities may include (a) personnel costs, (b) materials and equipment costs, and (c) indirect costs. What is the recommended accounting treatment for these three types of R&D costs?

21. Which of the following activities should be expensed currently as R&D costs?

    (a) Testing in search for or evaluation of product or process alternatives.

    (b) Engineering follow-through in an early phase of commercial production.

    (c) Legal work in connection with patent applications or litigation, and the sale or licensing of patents.

22. Indicate the proper accounting for the following items.

    (a) Organization costs.

    (b) Advertising costs.

    (c) Operating losses.

23. In 2005, Cassie Logan Corporation developed a new product that will be marketed in 2006. In connection with the development of this product, the following costs were incurred in 2005: research and development costs $420,000; materials and supplies consumed $60,000; and compensation paid to research consultants $125,000. It is anticipated that these costs will be recovered in 2008. What is the amount of research and development costs that Cassie Logan should record in 2005 as a charge to expense?

24. Recently, a group of university students decided to incorporate for the purposes of selling a process to recycle the waste product from manufacturing cheese. Some of the initial costs involved were legal fees and office expenses incurred in starting the business, state incorporation fees, and stamp taxes. One student wishes to charge these costs against revenue in the current period. Another wishes to defer these costs and amortize them in the future. Which student is correct?

25. An intangible asset with an estimated useful life of 30 years was acquired on January 1, 1996, for $450,000. On January 1, 2006, a review was made of intangible assets and their expected service lives, and it was determined that this asset had an estimated useful life of 30 more years from the date of the review. What is the amount of amortization for this intangible in 2006?

*26. An article in the financial press stated, "More than half of software maker **Comserve**'s net worth is in a pile of tapes and ring-bound books. That raises some accountants' eyebrows." What is the profession's position regarding the incurrence of costs for computer software that will be sold?

*27. Matt Antonio, Inc. has incurred $6 million in developing a computer software product for sale to third parties. Of the $6 million costs incurred, $4 million is capitalized. The product produced from this development work has generated $2 million of revenue in 2007 and is anticipated to generate another $8 million in future years. The estimated useful life of the project is 4 years. How much of the capitalized costs should be amortized in 2007?

*28. In 2007, U-Learn Software developed a software package for assisting calculus instruction in business colleges, at a cost of $2,000,000. Although there are tens of thousands of calculus students in the market, college instructors seem to change their minds frequently on the use of teaching aids. Not one package has yet been ordered or delivered. Prepare an argument to advocate expensing the development cost in the current year. Offer an argument for capitalizing the development cost over its estimated useful life. Which stakeholders are harmed or benefited by either approach?

BRIEF EXERCISES

(LO 2, 3)   **BE12-1**   Doom Troopers Corporation purchases a patent from Judge Dredd Company on January 1, 2007, for $64,000. The patent has a remaining legal life of 16 years. Doom Troopers feels the patent will be useful for 10 years. Prepare Doom Troopers' journal entries to record the purchase of the patent and 2007 amortization.

(LO 2, 3)   **BE12-2**   Use the information provided in BE12-1. Assume that at January 1, 2009, the carrying amount of the patent on Doom Troopers' books is $51,200. In January, Doom Troopers spends $24,000 successfully defending a patent suit. Doom Troopers still feels the patent will be useful until the end of 2016. Prepare the journal entries to record the $24,000 expenditure and 2009 amortization.

(LO 2, 3)   **BE12-3**   Dr. Robotnik's, Inc., spent $60,000 in attorney fees while developing the trade name of its new product, the Mean Bean Machine. Prepare the journal entries to record the $60,000 expenditure and the first year's amortization, using an 8-year life.

(LO 9)   **BE12-4**   Incredible Hulk Corporation commenced operations in early 2007. The corporation incurred $70,000 of costs such as fees to underwriters, legal fees, state fees, and promotional expenditures during its formation. Prepare journal entries to record the $70,000 expenditure and 2007 amortization, if any.

(LO 2, 3)   **BE12-5**   Knuckles Corporation obtained a franchise from Sonic Hedgehog Inc. for a cash payment of $100,000 on April 1, 2007. The franchise grants Knuckles the right to sell certain products and services for a period of 8 years. Prepare Knuckles' April 1 journal entry and December 31 adjusting entry.

(LO 6)   **BE12-6**   On September 1, 2007, Dungeon Corporation acquired Dragon Enterprises for a cash payment of $750,000. At the time of purchase, Dragon's balance sheet showed assets of $620,000, liabilities of $200,000, and owners' equity of $420,000. The fair value of Dragon's assets is estimated to be $800,000. Compute the amount of goodwill acquired by Dungeon.

(LO 7)   **BE12-7**   Nobunaga Corporation owns a patent that has a carrying amount of $330,000. Nobunaga expects future net cash flows from this patent to total $190,000. The fair value of the patent is $110,000. Prepare Nobunaga's journal entry, if necessary, to record the loss on impairment.

(LO 7)   **BE12-8**   Evander Corporation purchased Holyfield Company 3 years ago and at that time recorded goodwill of $400,000. The Holyfield Division's net assets, including the goodwill, have a carrying amount of $800,000. The fair value of the division is estimated to be $1,000,000. Prepare Evander's journal entry, if necessary, to record impairment of the goodwill.

(LO 7)   **BE12-9**   Use the information provided in BE12-8. Assume that the fair value of the division is estimated to be $750,000 and the implied goodwill is $325,000. Prepare Evander's journal entry, if necessary, to record impairment of the goodwill.

(LO 9)   **BE12-10**   Dorsett Corporation incurred the following costs in 2007.

Cost of laboratory research aimed at discovery of new knowledge	$140,000
Cost of testing in search for product alternatives	100,000
Cost of engineering activity required to advance the design of a product to the manufacturing stage	210,000
	$450,000

Prepare the necessary 2007 journal entry or entries for Dorsett.

(LO 9)   **BE12-11**   Indicate whether the following items are capitalized or expensed in the current year.
(a)   Purchase cost of a patent from a competitor.
(b)   Research and development costs.
(c)   Organizational costs.
(d)   Costs incurred internally to create goodwill.

(LO 3, 9)   **BE12-12**   Langer Industries had one patent recorded on its books as of January 1, 2007. This patent had a book value of $240,000 and a remaining useful life of 8 years. During 2007, Langer incurred research and development costs of $96,000 and brought a patent infringement suit against a competitor. On December 1, 2007, Langer received the good news that its patent was valid and that its competitor could not use the process Langer had patented. The company incurred $85,000 to defend this patent. At what amount should patent(s) be reported on the December 31, 2007, balance sheet, assuming monthly amortization of patents?

(LO 3, 10)   **BE12-13**   Wiggens Industries acquired two copyrights during 2007. One copyright related to a textbook that was developed internally at a cost of $9,900. This textbook is estimated to have a useful life of 3 years from September 1, 2007, the date it was published. The second copyright (a history research textbook) was purchased from University Press on December 1, 2007, for $19,200. This textbook has an indefinite useful life. How should these two copyrights be reported on Wiggens' balance sheet as of December 31, 2007?

(LO 11)   *****BE12-14**   Earthworm Jim Corporation has capitalized software costs of $700,000, and sales of this product the first year totaled $420,000. Earthworm Jim anticipates earning $980,000 in additional future revenues from this product, which is estimated to have an economic life of 4 years. Compute the amount of software cost amortization for the first year.

EXERCISES

(LO 1, 4)   **E12-1   (Classification Issues—Intangibles)**   Presented below is a list of items that could be included in the intangible assets section of the balance sheet.

1.   Investment in a subsidiary company.
2.   Timberland.
3.   Cost of engineering activity required to advance the design of a product to the manufacturing stage.
4.   Lease prepayment (6 months' rent paid in advance).
5.   Cost of equipment obtained.
6.   Cost of searching for applications of new research findings.
7.   Costs incurred in the formation of a corporation.
8.   Operating losses incurred in the start-up of a business.
9.   Training costs incurred in start-up of new operation.
10.   Purchase cost of a franchise.
11.   Goodwill generated internally.
12.   Cost of testing in search for product alternatives.
13.   Goodwill acquired in the purchase of a business.
14.   Cost of developing a patent.
15.   Cost of purchasing a patent from an inventor.
16.   Legal costs incurred in securing a patent.
17.   Unrecovered costs of a successful legal suit to protect the patent.
18.   Cost of conceptual formulation of possible product alternatives.
19.   Cost of purchasing a copyright.
20.   Research and development costs.
21.   Long-term receivables.
22.   Cost of developing a trademark.
23.   Cost of purchasing a trademark.

Instructions
(a)   Indicate which items on the list above would generally be reported as intangible assets in the balance sheet.
(b)   Indicate how, if at all, the items not reportable as intangible assets would be reported in the financial statements.

(LO 1, 4) **E12-2** **(Classification Issues—Intangibles)** Presented below is selected account information related to Martin Burke Inc. as of December 21, 2007. All these accounts have debit balances.

Cable television franchises	Film contract rights
Music copyrights	Customer lists
Research and development costs	Prepaid expenses
Goodwill	Covenants not to compete
Cash	Brand names
Discount on notes payable	Notes receivable
Accounts receivable	Investments in affiliated companies
Property, plant, and equipment	Organization costs
Internet domain name	Land

Instructions

Identify which items should be classified as an intangible asset. For those items not classified as an intangible asset, indicate where they would be reported in the financial statements.

(LO 1, 4) **E12-3** **(Classification Issues—Intangible Asset)** Joni Hyde Inc. has the following amounts included in its general ledger at December 31, 2007.

Organization costs	$24,000
Trademarks	15,000
Discount on bonds payable	35,000
Deposits with advertising agency for ads to promote goodwill of company	10,000
Excess of cost over fair value of net identifiable assets of acquired subsidiary	75,000
Cost of equipment acquired for research and development projects; the equipment has an alternative future use	90,000
Costs of developing a secret formula for a product that is expected to be marketed for at least 20 years	80,000

Instructions

(a) On the basis of the information above, compute the total amount to be reported by Hyde for intangible assets on its balance sheet at December 31, 2007. Equipment has alternative future use.

(b) If an item is not to be included in intangible assets, explain its proper treatment for reporting purposes.

(LO 3, 9) **E12-4** **(Intangible Amortization)** Presented below is selected information for Alatorre Company.

1. Alatorre purchased a patent from Vania Co. for $1,000,000 on January 1, 2005. The patent is being amortized over its remaining legal life of 10 years, expiring on January 1, 2015. During 2007, Alatorre determined that the economic benefits of the patent would not last longer than 6 years from the date of acquisition. What amount should be reported in the balance sheet for the patent, net of accumulated amortization, at December 31, 2007?

2. Alatorre bought a franchise from Alexander Co. on January 1, 2006, for $400,000. The carrying amount of the franchise on Alexander's books on January 1, 2006, was $500,000. The franchise agreement had an estimated useful life of 30 years. Because Alatorre must enter a competitive bidding at the end of 2015, it is unlikely that the franchise will be retained beyond 2015. What amount should be amortized for the year ended December 31, 2007?

3. On January 1, 2007, Alatorre incurred organization costs of $275,000. What amount of organization expense should be reported in 2007?

4. Alatorre purchased the license for distribution of a popular consumer product on January 1, 2007, for $150,000. It is expected that this product will generate cash flows for an indefinite period of time. The license has an initial term of 5 years but by paying a nominal fee, Alatorre can renew the license indefinitely for successive 5-year terms. What amount should be amortized for the year ended December 31, 2007?

Instructions

Answer the questions asked about each of the factual situations.

(LO 2, 3, 8) **E12-5** **(Correct Intangible Asset Account)** As the recently appointed auditor for William J. Bryan Corporation, you have been asked to examine selected accounts before the 6-month financial statements of June 30, 2007, are prepared. The controller for William J. Bryan Corporation mentions that only one account is kept for Intangible Assets. The account is shown on the next page.

Intangible Assets

		Debit	Credit	Balance
Jan. 4	Research and development costs	940,000		940,000
Jan. 5	Legal costs to obtain patent	75,000		1,015,000
Jan. 31	Payment of 7 months' rent on property leased by Bryan	91,000		1,106,000
Feb. 11	Premium on common stock		250,000	856,000
March 31	Unamortized bond discount on bonds due March 31, 2027	84,000		940,000
April 30	Promotional expenses related to start-up of business	207,000		1,147,000
June 30	Operating losses for first 6 months	241,000		1,388,000

Instructions

Prepare the entry or entries necessary to correct this account. Assume that the patent has a useful life of 10 years.

(LO 3, 9) **E12-6** **(Recording and Amortization of Intangibles)** Rolanda Marshall Company, organized in 2006, has set up a single account for all intangible assets. The following summary discloses the debit entries that have been recorded during 2007.

1/2/07	Purchased patent (8-year life)	$ 350,000
4/1/07	Purchased goodwill (indefinite life)	360,000
7/1/07	Purchased franchise with 10-year life; expiration date 7/1/17	450,000
8/1/07	Payment of copyright (5-year life)	156,000
9/1/07	Research and development costs	215,000
		$1,531,000

Instructions

Prepare the necessary entries to clear the Intangible Assets account and to set up separate accounts for distinct types of intangibles. Make the entries as of December 31, 2007, recording any necessary amortization and reflecting all balances accurately as of that date. (Use straight-line amortization.)

(LO 2, 3) **E12-7** **(Accounting for Trade Name)** In early January 2006, Outkast Corporation applied for a trade name, incurring legal costs of $16,000. In January of 2007, Outkast incurred $7,800 of legal fees in a successful defense of its trade name.

Instructions

(a) Compute 2006 amortization, 12/31/06 book value, 2007 amortization, and 12/31/07 book value if the company amortizes the trade name over 10 years.

(b) Compute the 2007 amortization and the 12/31/07 book value, assuming that at the beginning of 2007, Outkast determines that the trade name will provide no future benefits beyond December 31, 2010.

(c) Ignoring the response for part (b), compute the 2008 amortization and the 12/31/08 book value, assuming that at the beginning of 2008, based on new market research, Outkast determines that the fair value of the trade name is $15,000. Estimated total future cash flows from the trade name is $16,000 on January 3, 2008.

(LO 9) **E12-8** **(Accounting for Organization Costs)** Horace Greeley Corporation was organized in 2006 and began operations at the beginning of 2007. The company is involved in interior design consulting services. The following costs were incurred prior to the start of operations.

Attorney's fees in connection with organization of the company	$15,000
Purchase of drafting and design equipment	10,000
Costs of meetings of incorporators to discuss organizational activities	7,000
State filing fees to incorporate	1,000
	$33,000

Instructions

(a) Compute the total amount of organization costs incurred by Greeley.

(b) Prepare the journal entry to record organization costs for 2007.

(LO 2, 3, 8) **E12-9** **(Accounting for Patents, Franchises, and R&D)** Jimmy Carter Company has provided information on intangible assets as follows.

A patent was purchased from Gerald Ford Company for $2,000,000 on January 1, 2006. Carter estimated the remaining useful life of the patent to be 10 years. The patent was carried in Ford's accounting records at a net book value of $2,000,000 when Ford sold it to Carter.

During 2007, a franchise was purchased from Ronald Reagan Company for $480,000. In addition, 5% of revenue from the franchise must be paid to Reagan. Revenue from the franchise for 2007 was $2,500,000. Carter estimates the useful life of the franchise to be 10 years and takes a full year's amortization in the year of purchase.

Carter incurred research and development costs in 2007 as follows.

Materials and equipment	$142,000
Personnel	189,000
Indirect costs	102,000
	$433,000

Carter estimates that these costs will be recouped by December 31, 2010. The materials and equipment purchased have no alternative uses.

On January 1, 2007, because of recent events in the field, Carter estimates that the remaining life of the patent purchased on January 1, 2006, is only 5 years from January 1, 2007.

Instructions

(a) Prepare a schedule showing the intangibles section of Carter's balance sheet at December 31, 2007. Show supporting computations in good form.

(b) Prepare a schedule showing the income statement effect for the year ended December 31, 2007, as a result of the facts above. Show supporting computations in good form.

(AICPA adapted)

(LO 2, 3) **E12-10 (Accounting for Patents)** During 2003, George Winston Corporation spent $170,000 in research and development costs. As a result, a new product called the New Age Piano was patented. The patent was obtained on October 1, 2003, and had a legal life of 20 years and a useful life of 10 years. Legal costs of $18,000 related to the patent were incurred as of October 1, 2003.

Instructions

(a) Prepare all journal entries required in 2003 and 2004 as a result of the transactions above.

(b) On June 1, 2005, Winston spent $9,480 to successfully prosecute a patent infringement suit. As a result, the estimate of useful life was extended to 12 years from June 1, 2005. Prepare all journal entries required in 2005 and 2006.

(c) In 2007, Winston determined that a competitor's product would make the New Age Piano obsolete and the patent worthless by December 31, 2008. Prepare all journal entries required in 2007 and 2008.

(LO 2, 3) **E12-11 (Accounting for Patents)** Tones Industries has the following patents on its December 31, 2006, balance sheet.

Patent Item	Initial Cost	Date Acquired	Useful Life at Date Acquired
Patent A	$30,600	3/1/03	17 years
Patent B	$15,000	7/1/04	10 years
Patent C	$14,400	9/1/05	4 years

The following events occurred during the year ended December 31, 2007.

1. Research and development costs of $245,700 were incurred during the year.
2. Patent D was purchased on July 1 for $36,480. This patent has a useful life of 9½ years.
3. As a result of reduced demands for certain products protected by Patent B, a possible impairment of Patent B's value may have occurred at December 31, 2007. The controller for Tones estimates the expected future cash flows from Patent B will be as follows.

Year	Expected Future Cash Flows
2008	$2,000
2009	2,000
2010	2,000

The proper discount rate to be used for these flows is 8%. (Assume that the cash flows occur at the end of the year.)

Instructions

(a) Compute the total carrying amount of Tones' patents on its December 31, 2006, balance sheet.

(b) Compute the total carrying amount of Tones' patents on its December 31, 2007, balance sheet.

(LO 5, 6) **E12-12** **(Accounting for Goodwill)** Fred Moss, owner of Moss Interiors, is negotiating for the purchase of Zweifel Galleries. The balance sheet of Zweifel is given in an abbreviated form below.

ZWEIFEL GALLERIES
BALANCE SHEET
AS OF DECEMBER 31, 2007

Assets		Liabilities and Stockholders' Equity		
Cash	$100,000	Accounts payable		$ 50,000
Land	70,000	Long-term notes payable		300,000
Building (net)	200,000	Total liabilities		350,000
Equipment (net)	175,000	Common stock	$200,000	
Copyright (net)	30,000	Retained earnings	25,000	225,000
Total assets	$575,000	Total liabilities and stockholders' equity		$575,000

Moss and Zweifel agree that:

1. Land is undervalued by $30,000.
2. Equipment is overvalued by $5,000.

Zweifel agrees to sell the gallery to Moss for $350,000.

Instructions
Prepare the entry to record the purchase of Zweifel Galleries on Moss's books.

(LO 3, 5, 6) **E12-13** **(Accounting for Goodwill)** On July 1, 2006, Brigham Corporation purchased Young Company by paying $250,000 cash and issuing a $100,000 note payable to Steve Young. At July 1, 2006, the balance sheet of Young Company was as follows.

Cash	$ 50,000	Accounts payable	$200,000
Receivables	90,000	Stockholders' equity	235,000
Inventory	100,000		$435,000
Land	40,000		
Buildings (net)	75,000		
Equipment (net)	70,000		
Trademarks	10,000		
	$435,000		

The recorded amounts all approximate current values except for land (fair value of $60,000), inventory (fair value of $125,000), and trademarks (fair value of $15,000).

Instructions
(a) Prepare the July 1 entry for Brigham Corporation to record the purchase.
(b) Prepare the December 31 entry for Brigham Corporation to record amortization of intangibles. The trademark has an estimated useful life of 4 years with a residual value of $3,000.

(LO 7) **E12-14** **(Copyright Impairment)** Presented below is information related to copyrights owned by Walter de la Mare Company at December 31, 2007.

Cost	$8,600,000
Carrying amount	4,300,000
Expected future net cash flows	4,000,000
Fair value	3,200,000

Assume that Walter de la Mare Company will continue to use this copyright in the future. As of December 31, 2007, the copyright is estimated to have a remaining useful life of 10 years.

Instructions
(a) Prepare the journal entry (if any) to record the impairment of the asset at December 31, 2007. The company does not use accumulated amortization accounts.
(b) Prepare the journal entry to record amortization expense for 2008 related to the copyrights.
(c) The fair value of the copyright at December 31, 2008, is $3,400,000. Prepare the journal entry (if any) necessary to record the increase in fair value.

(LO 6, 7) **E12-15 (Goodwill Impairment)** Presented below is net asset information related to the Carlos Division of Santana, Inc.

CARLOS DIVISION
NET ASSETS
AS OF DECEMBER 31, 2007
(IN MILLIONS)

Cash	$ 50
Receivables	200
Property, plant, and equipment (net)	2,600
Goodwill	200
Less: Notes payable	(2,700)
Net assets	$ 350

The purpose of the Carlos division is to develop a nuclear-powered aircraft. If successful, traveling delays associated with refueling could be substantially reduced. Many other benefits would also occur. To date, management has not had much success and is deciding whether a write-down at this time is appropriate. Management estimated its future net cash flows from the project to be $400 million. Management has also received an offer to purchase the division for $335 million. All identifiable assets' and liabilities' book and fair value amounts are the same.

Instructions
(a) Prepare the journal entry (if any) to record the impairment at December 31, 2007.
(b) At December 31, 2008, it is estimated that the division's fair value increased to $345 million. Prepare the journal entry (if any) to record this increase in fair value.

(LO 9) **E12-16 (Accounting for R&D Costs)** Leontyne Price Company from time to time embarks on a research program when a special project seems to offer possibilities. In 2006 the company expends $325,000 on a research project, but by the end of 2006 it is impossible to determine whether any benefit will be derived from it.

Instructions
(a) What account should be charged for the $325,000, and how should it be shown in the financial statements?
(b) The project is completed in 2007, and a successful patent is obtained. The R&D costs to complete the project are $110,000. The administrative and legal expenses incurred in obtaining patent number 472-1001-84 in 2007 total $16,000. The patent has an expected useful life of 5 years. Record these costs in journal entry form. Also, record patent amortization (full year) in 2007.
(c) In 2008, the company successfully defends the patent in extended litigation at a cost of $47,200, thereby extending the patent life to December 31, 2015. What is the proper way to account for this cost? Also, record patent amortization (full year) in 2008.
(d) Additional engineering and consulting costs incurred in 2008 required to advance the design of a product to the manufacturing stage total $60,000. These costs enhance the design of the product considerably. Discuss the proper accounting treatment for this cost.

(LO 9) **E12-17 (Accounting for R&D Costs)** Thomas More Company incurred the following costs during 2007 in connection with its research and development activities.

Cost of equipment acquired that will have alternative uses in future R&D projects over the next 5 years (uses straight-line depreciation)	$280,000
Materials consumed in R&D projects	59,000
Consulting fees paid to outsiders for R&D projects	100,000
Personnel costs of persons involved in R&D projects	128,000
Indirect costs reasonably allocable to R&D projects	50,000
Materials purchased for future R&D projects	34,000

Instructions
Compute the amount to be reported as research and development expense by More on its income statement for 2007. Assume equipment is purchased at the beginning of the year.

(LO 11) ***E12-18 (Accounting for Computer Software Costs)** New Jersey Inc. has capitalized computer software costs of $3,600,000 on its new "Trenton" software package. Revenues from 2007 (first year) sales are $2,000,000. Additional future revenues from "Trenton" for the remainder of its economic life, through 2011, are estimated to be $10,000,000.

Instructions

(a) What method or methods of amortization are to be applied in the write-off of capitalized computer software costs?

(b) Compute the amount of amortization for 2007 for "Trenton."

(LO 11) *E12-19 **(Accounting for Computer Software Costs)** During 2007, Delaware Enterprises Inc. spent $5,000,000 developing its new "Dover" software package. Of this amount, $2,200,000 was spent before technological feasibility was established for the product, which is to be marketed to third parties. The package was completed at December 31, 2007. Delaware expects a useful life of 8 years for this product with total revenues of $16,000,000. During the first year (2008), Delaware realizes revenues of $3,200,000.

Instructions

(a) Prepare journal entries required in 2007 for the foregoing facts.

(b) Prepare the entry to record amortization at December 31, 2008.

(c) At what amount should the computer software costs be reported in the December 31, 2007, balance sheet? Could the net realizable value of this asset affect your answer?

(d) What disclosures are required in the December 31, 2008, financial statements for the computer software costs?

(e) How would your answers for (a), (b), and (c) be different if the computer software was developed for internal use?

See the book's website, www.wiley.com/college/kieso, for Additional Exercises.

PROBLEMS

(LO 2, 3) **P12-1 (Correct Intangible Asset Account)** Esplanade Co., organized in 2006, has set up a single account for all intangible assets. The following summary discloses the debit entries that have been recorded during 2006 and 2007.

	Intangible Assets	
7/1/06	8-year franchise; expiration date 6/30/14	$ 42,000
10/1/06	Advance payment on laboratory space (2-year lease)	28,000
12/31/06	Net loss for 2006 including state incorporation fee, $1,000, and related legal fees of organizing, $5,000 (all fees incurred in 2006)	16,000
1/2/07	Patent purchased (10-year life)	74,000
3/1/07	Cost of developing a secret formula (indefinite life)	75,000
4/1/07	Goodwill purchased (indefinite life)	278,400
6/1/07	Legal fee for successful defense of patent purchased above	12,650
9/1/07	Research and development costs	160,000

Instructions

Prepare the necessary entries to clear the Intangible Assets account and to set up separate accounts for distinct types of intangibles. Make the entries as of December 31, 2007, recording any necessary amortization and reflecting all balances accurately as of that date. (Ignore income tax effects.)

(LO 2, 3)  **P12-2 (Accounting for Patents)** Ankara Laboratories holds a valuable patent (No. 758-6002-1A) on a precipitator that prevents certain types of air pollution. Ankara does not manufacture or sell the products and processes it develops. Instead, it conducts research and develops products and processes which it patents, and then assigns the patents to manufacturers on a royalty basis. Occasionally it sells a patent. The history of Ankara patent number 758-6002-1A is as follows.

Date	Activity	Cost
1997–1998	Research conducted to develop precipitator	$384,000
Jan. 1999	Design and construction of a prototype	87,600
March 1999	Testing of models	42,000
Jan. 2000	Fees paid engineers and lawyers to prepare patent application; patent granted June 30, 2000	62,050
Nov. 2001	Engineering activity necessary to advance the design of the precipitator to the manufacturing stage	81,500

Dec. 2002	Legal fees paid to successfully defend precipitator patent	35,700
April 2003	Research aimed at modifying the design of the patented precipitator	43,000
July 2007	Legal fees paid in unsuccessful patent infringement suit against a competitor	34,000

Ankara assumed a useful life of 17 years when it received the initial precipitator patent. On January 1, 2005, it revised its useful life estimate downward to 5 remaining years. Amortization is computed for a full year if the cost is incurred prior to July 1, and no amortization for the year if the cost is incurred after June 30. The company's year ends December 31.

Instructions
Compute the carrying value of patent No. 758-6002-1A on each of the following dates:

   (a) December 31, 2000.
   (b) December 31, 2004.
   (c) December 31, 2007.

(LO 2, 3)   **P12-3** **(Accounting for Franchise, Patents, and Trade Name)** Information concerning Haerhpin Corporation's intangible assets is as follows.

   1. On January 1, 2007, Haerhpin signed an agreement to operate as a franchisee of Hsian Copy Service, Inc. for an initial franchise fee of $75,000. Of this amount, $15,000 was paid when the agreement was signed, and the balance is payable in 4 annual payments of $15,000 each, beginning January 1, 2008. The agreement provides that the down payment is not refundable and no future services are required of the franchisor. The present value at January 1, 2007, of the 4 annual payments discounted at 14% (the implicit rate for a loan of this type) is $43,700. The agreement also provides that 5% of the revenue from the franchise must be paid to the franchisor annually. Haerhpin's revenue from the franchise for 2007 was $950,000. Haerhpin estimates the useful life of the franchise to be 10 years. (*Hint:* You may want to refer to Appendix 18A to determine the proper accounting treatment for the franchise fee and payments.)

   2. Haerhpin incurred $65,000 of experimental and development costs in its laboratory to develop a patent that was granted on January 2, 2007. Legal fees and other costs associated with registration of the patent totaled $13,600. Haerhpin estimates that the useful life of the patent will be 8 years.

   3. A trademark was purchased from Shanghai Company for $32,000 on July 1, 2004. Expenditures for successful litigation in defense of the trademark totaling $8,160 were paid on July 1, 2007. Haerhpin estimates that the useful life of the trademark will be 20 years from the date of acquisition.

Instructions
   (a) Prepare a schedule showing the intangible assets section of Haerhpin's balance sheet at December 31, 2007. Show supporting computations in good form.
   (b) Prepare a schedule showing all expenses resulting from the transactions that would appear on Haerhpin's income statement for the year ended December 31, 2007. Show supporting computations in good form.

(AICPA adapted)

(LO 9, 10)   **P12-4** **(Accounting for R&D Costs)** During 2005, Florence Nightingale Tool Company purchased a building site for its proposed research and development laboratory at a cost of $60,000. Construction of the building was started in 2005. The building was completed on December 31, 2006, at a cost of $280,000 and was placed in service on January 2, 2007. The estimated useful life of the building for depreciation purposes was 20 years. The straight-line method of depreciation was to be employed, and there was no estimated salvage value.

Management estimates that about 50% of the projects of the research and development group will result in long-term benefits (i.e., at least 10 years) to the corporation. The remaining projects either benefit the current period or are abandoned before completion. A summary of the number of projects and the direct costs incurred in conjunction with the research and development activities for 2007 appears below.

	Number of Projects	Salaries and Employee Benefits	Other Expenses (excluding Building Depreciation Charges)
Completed projects with long-term benefits	15	$ 90,000	$50,000
Abandoned projects or projects that benefit the current period	10	65,000	15,000
Projects in process—results indeterminate	5	40,000	12,000
Total	30	$195,000	$77,000

Upon recommendation of the research and development group, Florence Nightingale Tool Company acquired a patent for manufacturing rights at a cost of $80,000. The patent was acquired on April 1, 2006, and has an economic life of 10 years.

Instructions

If generally accepted accounting principles were followed, how would the items above relating to research and development activities be reported on the following financial statements?

(a) The company's income statement for 2007.

(b) The company's balance sheet as of December 31, 2007.

Be sure to give account titles and amounts, and briefly justify your presentation.

(CMA adapted)

(LO 5, 6) **P12-5 (Goodwill, Impairment)** On July 31, 2007, Postera Company paid $3,000,000 to acquire all of the common stock of Mendota Incorporated, which became a division of Postera. Mendota reported the following balance sheet at the time of the acquisition.

Current assets	$ 800,000	Current liabilities	$ 600,000
Noncurrent assets	2,700,000	Long-term liabilities	500,000
Total assets	$3,500,000	Stockholders' equity	2,400,000
		Total liabilities and	
		stockholders' equity	$3,500,000

It was determined at the date of the purchase that the fair value of the identifiable net assets of Mendota was $2,650,000. Over the next 6 months of operations, the newly purchased division experienced operating losses. In addition, it now appears that it will generate substantial losses for the foreseeable future. At December 31, 2007, Mendota reports the following balance sheet information.

Current assets	$ 450,000
Noncurrent assets (including goodwill recognized in purchase)	2,400,000
Current liabilities	(700,000)
Long-term liabilities	(500,000)
Net assets	$1,650,000

It is determined that the fair value of the Mendota Division is $1,850,000. The recorded amount for Mendota's net assets (excluding goodwill) is the same as fair value, except for property, plant, and equipment, which has a fair value $150,000 above the carrying value.

Instructions

(a) Compute the amount of goodwill recognized, if any, on July 31, 2007.

(b) Determine the impairment loss, if any, to be recorded on December 31, 2007.

(c) Assume that fair value of the Mendota Division is $1,500,000 instead of $1,850,000. Determine the impairment loss, if any, to be recorded on December 31, 2007.

(d) Prepare the journal entry to record the impairment loss, if any, and indicate where the loss would be reported in the income statement.

(LO 2, 3, 6, 7, 10) **P12-6 (Comprehensive Intangible Assets)** Montana Matt's Golf Inc. was formed on July 1, 2006, when Matt Magilke purchased the Old Master Golf Company. Old Master provides video golf instruction at kiosks in shopping malls. Magilke plans to integrate the instruction business into his golf equipment and accessory stores. Magilke paid $750,000 cash for Old Master. At the time Old Master's balance sheet reported assets of $650,000 and liabilities of $200,000 (thus owners' equity was $450,000). The fair value of Old Master's assets is estimated to be $800,000. Included in the assets is the Old Master trade name with a fair value of $10,000 and a copyright on some instructional books with a fair value of $20,000. The trade name has a remaining life of 5 years and can be renewed at nominal cost indefinitely. The copyright has a remaining life of 40 years.

Instructions

(a) Prepare the intangible assets section of Montana Matt's Golf Inc. at December 31, 2006. How much amortization expense is included in Montana Matt's income for the year ended December 31, 2006? Show all supporting computations.

(b) Prepare the journal entry to record amortization expense for 2007. Prepare the intangible assets section of Montana Matt's Golf Inc. at December 31, 2007. (No impairments are required to be recorded in 2007.)

(c) At the end of 2008, Magilke is evaluating the results of the instructional business. Due to fierce competition from online and television (e.g., the Golf Channel), the Old Master reporting unit has been losing money. Its book value is now $500,000. The fair value of the Old Master reporting unit is $430,000. The implied value of goodwill is $80,000. Magilke has collected the following information related to the company's intangible assets.

Intangible Asset	Expected Cash Flows (undiscounted)	Fair Values
Trade name	$ 9,000	$ 3,000
Copyright	30,000	25,000

Prepare the journal entries required, if any, to record impairments on Montana Matt's intangible assets. (Assume that any amortization for 2008 has been recorded.) Show supporting computations.

CONCEPTS FOR ANALYSIS

CA12-1 (Accounting for Pollution Expenditure) Phil Mickelson Company operates several plants at which limestone is processed into quicklime and hydrated lime. The Eagle Ridge plant, where most of the equipment was installed many years ago, continually deposits a dusty white substance over the surrounding countryside. Citing the unsanitary condition of the neighboring community of Scales Mound, the pollution of the Galena River, and the high incidence of lung disease among workers at Eagle Ridge, the state's Pollution Control Agency has ordered the installation of air pollution control equipment. Also, the Agency has assessed a substantial penalty, which will be used to clean up Scales Mound.

After considering the costs involved (which could not have been reasonably estimated prior to the Agency's action), Phil Mickelson Company decides to comply with the Agency's orders, the alternative being to cease operations at Eagle Ridge at the end of the current fiscal year. The officers of Mickelson agree that the air pollution control equipment should be capitalized and depreciated over its useful life, but they disagree over the period(s) to which the penalty should be charged.

Instructions
Discuss the conceptual merits and reporting requirements of accounting for the penalty in each of the following ways.

(a) As a charge to the current period.
(b) As a correction of prior periods.
(c) As a capitalizable item to be amortized over future periods.

(AICPA adapted)

CA12-2 (Accounting for Pre-Opening Costs) After securing lease commitments from several major stores, Lobo Shopping Center, Inc. was organized and built a shopping center in a growing suburb.

The shopping center would have opened on schedule on January 1, 2007, if it had not been struck by a severe tornado in December. Instead, it opened for business on October 1, 2007. All of the additional construction costs that were incurred as a result of the tornado were covered by insurance.

In July 2006, in anticipation of the scheduled January opening, a permanent staff had been hired to promote the shopping center, obtain tenants for the uncommitted space, and manage the property.

A summary of some of the costs incurred in 2006 and the first nine months of 2007 follows.

	2006	January 1, 2007 through September 30, 2007
Interest on mortgage bonds	$720,000	$540,000
Cost of obtaining tenants	300,000	360,000
Promotional advertising	540,000	557,000

The promotional advertising campaign was designed to familiarize shoppers with the center. Had it been known in time that the center would not open until October 2007, the 2006 expenditure for promotional advertising would not have been made. The advertising had to be repeated in 2007.

All of the tenants who had leased space in the shopping center at the time of the tornado accepted the October occupancy date on condition that the monthly rental charges for the first 9 months of 2007 be canceled.

Instructions
Explain how each of the costs for 2006 and the first 9 months of 2007 should be treated in the accounts of the shopping center corporation. Give the reasons for each treatment.

(AICPA adapted)

 **CA12-3** **(Accounting for Patents)** On June 30, 2007, your client, Bearcat Company, was granted two patents covering plastic cartons that it had been producing and marketing profitably for the past 3 years. One patent covers the manufacturing process, and the other covers the related products.

Bearcat executives tell you that these patents represent the most significant breakthrough in the industry in the past 30 years. The products have been marketed under the registered trademarks Evertight, Duratainer, and Sealrite. Licenses under the patents have already been granted by your client to other manufacturers in the United States and abroad and are producing substantial royalties.

On July 1, Bearcat commenced patent infringement actions against several companies whose names you recognize as those of substantial and prominent competitors. Bearcat's management is optimistic that these suits will result in a permanent injunction against the manufacture and sale of the infringing products as well as collection of damages for loss of profits caused by the alleged infringement.

The financial vice-president has suggested that the patents be recorded at the discounted value of expected net royalty receipts.

Instructions
- **(a)** What is the meaning of "discounted value of expected net receipts"? Explain.
- **(b)** How would such a value be calculated for net royalty receipts?
- **(c)** What basis of valuation for Bearcat's patents would be generally accepted in accounting? Give supporting reasons for this basis.
- **(d)** Assuming no practical problems of implementation, and ignoring generally accepted accounting principles, what is the preferable basis of valuation for patents? Explain.
- **(e)** What would be the preferable theoretical basis of amortization? Explain.
- **(f)** What recognition, if any, should be made of the infringement litigation in the financial statements for the year ending September 30, 2007? Discuss.

(AICPA adapted)

 **CA12-4** **(Accounting for Research and Development Costs)** Indiana Jones Co. is in the process of developing a revolutionary new product. A new division of the company was formed to develop, manufacture, and market this new product. As of year-end (December 31, 2007), the new product has not been manufactured for resale. However, a prototype unit was built and is in operation.

Throughout 2007 the new division incurred certain costs. These costs include design and engineering studies, prototype manufacturing costs, administrative expenses (including salaries of administrative personnel), and market research costs. In addition, approximately $900,000 in equipment (with an estimated useful life of 10 years) was purchased for use in developing and manufacturing the new product. Approximately $315,000 of this equipment was built specifically for the design development of the new product. The remaining $585,000 of equipment was used to manufacture the pre-production prototype and will be used to manufacture the new product once it is in commercial production.

Instructions
- **(a)** How are "research" and "development" defined in *Statement of Financial Accounting Standards No. 2*?
- **(b)** Briefly indicate the practical and conceptual reasons for the conclusion reached by the Financial Accounting Standards Board on accounting and reporting practices for research and development costs.
- **(c)** In accordance with *Statement of Financial Accounting Standards No. 2*, how should the various costs of Indiana Jones described above be recorded on the financial statements for the year ended December 31, 2007?

(AICPA adapted)

 CA12-5 **(Accounting for Research and Development Costs)** Waveland Corporation's research and development department has an idea for a project it believes will culminate in a new product that would be very profitable for the company. Because the project will be very expensive, the department requests approval from the company's controller, Ron Santo.

Santo recognizes that corporate profits have been down lately and is hesitant to approve a project that will incur significant expenses that cannot be capitalized due to the requirements of *FASB Statement No. 2*. He knows that if they hire an outside firm that does the work and obtains a patent for the process, Waveland Corporation can purchase the patent from the outside firm and record the expenditure as an asset. Santo knows that the company's own R&D department is first-rate, and he is confident they can do the work well.

Instructions
Answer the following questions.

- **(a)** Who are the stakeholders in this situation?
- **(b)** What are the ethical issues involved?
- **(c)** What should Santo do?

USING YOUR JUDGMENT

Financial Reporting Problem

P&G The Procter & Gamble Company (P&G)

The financial statements of **P&G** are presented in Appendix 5B or can be accessed on the KWW website.

Instructions

Refer to P&G's financial statements and the accompanying notes to answer the following questions.

(a) Does P&G report any intangible assets, especially goodwill, in its 2004 financial statements and accompanying notes?

(b) How much research and development (R&D) cost was expensed by P&G in 2004 and 2003? What percentage of sales revenue and net income did P&G spend on R&D in 2004 and 2003?

Financial Statement Analysis Case

Merck and Johnson & Johnson

Merck & Co., Inc. and **Johnson & Johnson** are two leading producers of health care products. Each has considerable assets, and each expends considerable funds each year toward the development of new products. The development of a new health care product is often very expensive, and risky. New products frequently must undergo considerable testing before approval for distribution to the public. For example, it took Johnson & Johnson 4 years and $200 million to develop its 1-DAY ACUVUE contact lenses. Below are some basic data compiled from the financial statements of these two companies.

(all dollars in millions)	Johnson & Johnson	Merck
Total assets	$53,317	$42,573
Total revenue	47,348	22,939
Net income	8,509	5,813
Research and development expense	5,203	4,010
Intangible assets	11,842	2,765

Instructions

(a) What kinds of intangible assets might a health care products company have? Does the composition of these intangibles matter to investors—that is, would it be perceived differently if all of Merck's intangibles were goodwill, than if all of its intangibles were patents?

(b) Suppose the president of Merck has come to you for advice. He has noted that by eliminating research and development expenditures the company could have reported $1.3 billion more in net income. He is frustrated because much of the research never results in a product, or the products take years to develop. He says shareholders are eager for higher returns, so he is considering eliminating research and development expenditures for at least a couple of years. What would you advise?

(c) The notes to Merck's financial statements note that Merck has goodwill of $1.1 billion. Where does recorded goodwill come from? Is it necessarily a good thing to have a lot of goodwill on your books?

Comparative Analysis Case

The Coca-Cola Company and PepsiCo, Inc.

The Coca-Cola Company

 **PEPSICO**

Instructions

Go to the book's website and use information found there to answer the following questions related to **The Coca-Cola Company** and **PepsiCo, Inc.**

(a) (1) What amounts for intangible assets were reported in their respective balance sheets by Coca-Cola and PepsiCo?

(2) What percentage of total assets is each of these reported amounts?

(3) What was the change in the amount of intangibles from 2003 to 2004 for Coca-Cola and PepsiCo?

(b) **(1)** On what basis and over what periods of time did Coca-Cola and PepsiCo amortize their intangible assets?

(2) What were the amounts of accumulated amortization reported by Coca-Cola and PepsiCo at the end of 2004 and 2003?

(3) What was the composition of the identifiable and unidentifiable intangible assets reported by Coca-Cola and PepsiCo at the end of 2004?

Research Case

The online edition of the March 5, 2002, *Wall Street Journal* includes an article by John Carreyrou titled "Vivendi May Reveal Write-Down of Up to $13 Billion for Goodwill."

Instructions
Read the story and answer the following questions.

(a) **Vivendi** currently prepares its financial statements using French GAAP. As revealed in the story, how do French and U.S. GAAP differ in the accounting for goodwill impairments? Does the story reveal other areas in which U.S. and French GAAP differ? Explain.

(b) Why are some analysts warning against reading too much negativity into Vivendi's expected goodwill write-down? Do you agree? Explain.

(c) What measure of profitability is used in the media business? Explain how, if at all, this measure of profitability might be affected by Vivendi's changes in accounting, as discussed in the story.

International Reporting Case

Bayer, Glaxo SmithKline, and Merck

Presented below are data and accounting policy notes for the goodwill of three international drug companies. **Bayer**, a German company, prepares its statements in accordance with International Financial Reporting Standards (IFRS); **Glaxo SmithKline** follows United Kingdom (U.K.) rules; and **Merck**, a U.S. company, prepares its financial statements in accordance with U.S. GAAP.

Related Information	Bayer (€ millions)	Glaxo SmithKline (£ millions)	Merck ($ millions)
Research and development expense	2,107	2,839	4,010
Amortization expense	0	12	0
Net income	603	4,302	5,813
Accumulated goodwill amortization	0	84	0
Stockholders' equity	12,268	10,091	17,288

Both U.S. GAAP and IFRS do not allow amortization of goodwill. Under U.K. standards, goodwill is amortized over useful lives not to exceed 20 years.

Instructions

(a) Compute the return on equity for each of these companies, and use this analysis to briefly discuss the relative profitability of the three companies.

(b) Assume that each of the companies uses the maximum allowable amortization period for goodwill (if any). Discuss how these companies' goodwill amortization policies affect your ability to compare their amortization expense and income.

(c) Some analysts believe that the only valid way to compare companies that follow different goodwill accounting practices is to treat all goodwill as an asset and record expense only if the goodwill is impaired.* Using the data above, make these adjustments as appropriate, and compare the profitability of the three drug companies, comparing this information to your analysis in (a).

(d) IFRS requires that development costs must be capitalized if technical and commercial feasibility of the resulting product has been established. Assume that Bayer recorded € 1 million of development costs in the year reported above. Discuss briefly how this accounting affects your ability to compare the financial results of Bayer and Merck.

---

*Trevor Harris, *Apples to Apples: Accounting for Value in World Markets* (New York: Morgan Stanley Dean Witter, February 1998).

Professional Research: Financial Accounting and Reporting

Mills Company is contemplating the purchase of a smaller company, which is a distributor of Mills's products. Top management of Mills is convinced that the acquisition will result in significant synergies in its selling and distribution functions. The financial management group (of which you are a part) has been asked to prepare some analysis of the effects of the acquisition on the combined company's financial statements. This is the first acquisition for Mills, and some of the senior staff insist that based on their recollection of goodwill accounting, any goodwill recorded on the acquisition will result in a "drag" on future earnings for goodwill amortization. Other younger members on the staff argue that goodwill accounting has changed. Your supervisor asks you to research this issue.

Instructions

Using the **Financial Accounting Research System (FARS)**, respond to the following items. (Provide text strings used in your search.)

(a) Identify the accounting standard that addresses goodwill and other intangible assets. When was it issued? Might this explain the disagreement among the accounting staff? Explain.

(b) Define goodwill.

(c) Is goodwill subject to amortization? Explain.

(d) When goodwill is recognized by a subsidiary, should it be tested for impairment at the consolidated level or the subsidiary level? Discuss.

Professional Simulation

In this simulation you are asked to address questions related to intangible assets and similar costs. Prepare responses to all parts.

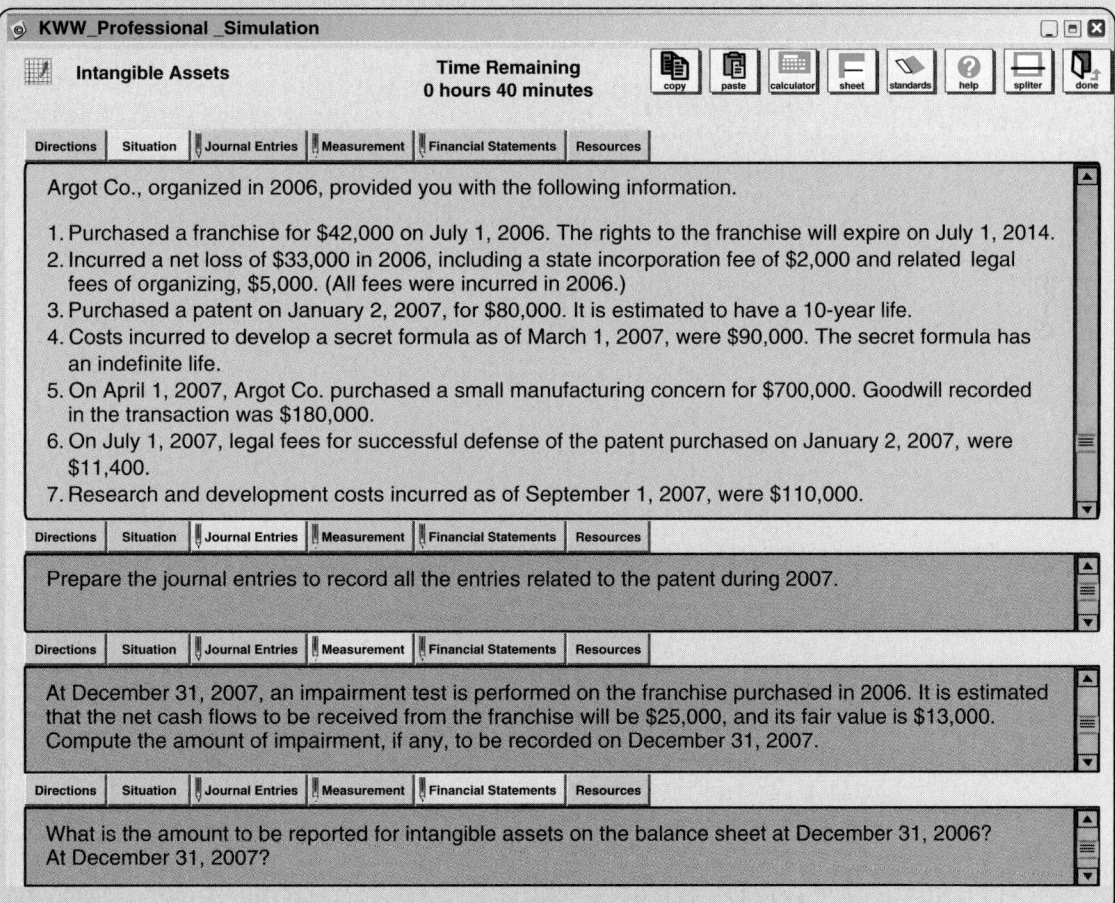

KWW_Professional _Simulation

Intangible Assets   Time Remaining 0 hours 40 minutes   copy | paste | calculator | sheet | standards | help | spliter | done

Directions | Situation | Journal Entries | Measurement | Financial Statements | Resources

Argot Co., organized in 2006, provided you with the following information.

1. Purchased a franchise for $42,000 on July 1, 2006. The rights to the franchise will expire on July 1, 2014.
2. Incurred a net loss of $33,000 in 2006, including a state incorporation fee of $2,000 and related legal fees of organizing, $5,000. (All fees were incurred in 2006.)
3. Purchased a patent on January 2, 2007, for $80,000. It is estimated to have a 10-year life.
4. Costs incurred to develop a secret formula as of March 1, 2007, were $90,000. The secret formula has an indefinite life.
5. On April 1, 2007, Argot Co. purchased a small manufacturing concern for $700,000. Goodwill recorded in the transaction was $180,000.
6. On July 1, 2007, legal fees for successful defense of the patent purchased on January 2, 2007, were $11,400.
7. Research and development costs incurred as of September 1, 2007, were $110,000.

Prepare the journal entries to record all the entries related to the patent during 2007.

At December 31, 2007, an impairment test is performed on the franchise purchased in 2006. It is estimated that the net cash flows to be received from the franchise will be $25,000, and its fair value is $13,000. Compute the amount of impairment, if any, to be recorded on December 31, 2007.

What is the amount to be reported for intangible assets on the balance sheet at December 31, 2006? At December 31, 2007?

Remember to check the book's companion website to find additional resources for this chapter.

wiley.com/college/kieso

CURRENT LIABILITIES AND CONTINGENCIES

Now You See It, Now You Don't

A look at the liabilities side of the balance sheet of the German company **Beru AG Corporation**, dated March 31, 2003, shows how international standards are changing the reporting of financial information. Here is how one liability was shown on this date:

> Anticipated losses arising from pending transactions 3,285,000 euros

Do you believe a liability should be reported for such transactions? *Anticipated losses* means the losses have not yet occurred; *pending transactions* mean that the condition that might cause the loss has also not occurred. So where is the liability? To whom does the company owe something? Where is the obligation?

U.S. GAAP provides guidance on this subject. A company can accrue a liability for a contingency only if an obligation has arisen from a past event, if payment is probable, and if the company can reasonably estimate the obligation. In short, under U.S. GAAP, companies cannot accrue anticipated future losses today.

German accounting rules are more permissive. They permit companies to report liabilities for possible future events. In essence, the establishment of this general-purpose "liability" provides a buffer for Beru if losses do materialize. If you take a more skeptical view, you might say the accounting rules let Beru smooth its income by charging expenses in good years and reducing expenses in bad years.

The story has a happy ending, from a U.S. accounting point of view. As we indicated earlier in the text, European companies switched to International Financial Reporting Standards (IFRS) in 2005. Because IFRS are similar to U.S. GAAP, liabilities like "Anticipated losses from pending transactions" disappear. So when we look at Beru's 2005 financial statements, we find a note stating that the company has reported as liabilities only obligations arising from past transactions that can be reasonably estimated.

Learning Objectives

After studying this chapter, you should be able to:

1 Describe the nature, type, and valuation of current liabilities.

2 Explain the classification issues of short-term debt expected to be refinanced.

3 Identify types of employee-related liabilities.

4 Identify the criteria used to account for and disclose gain and loss contingencies.

5 Explain the accounting for different types of loss contingencies.

6 Indicate how to present and analyze liabilities and contingencies.

As our opening story indicates, the convergence of U.S. GAAP with IFRS should lead to improved reporting of liabilities. In this chapter we explain the basic issues related to accounting and reporting for current and contingent liabilities. The content and organization of the chapter are as follows.

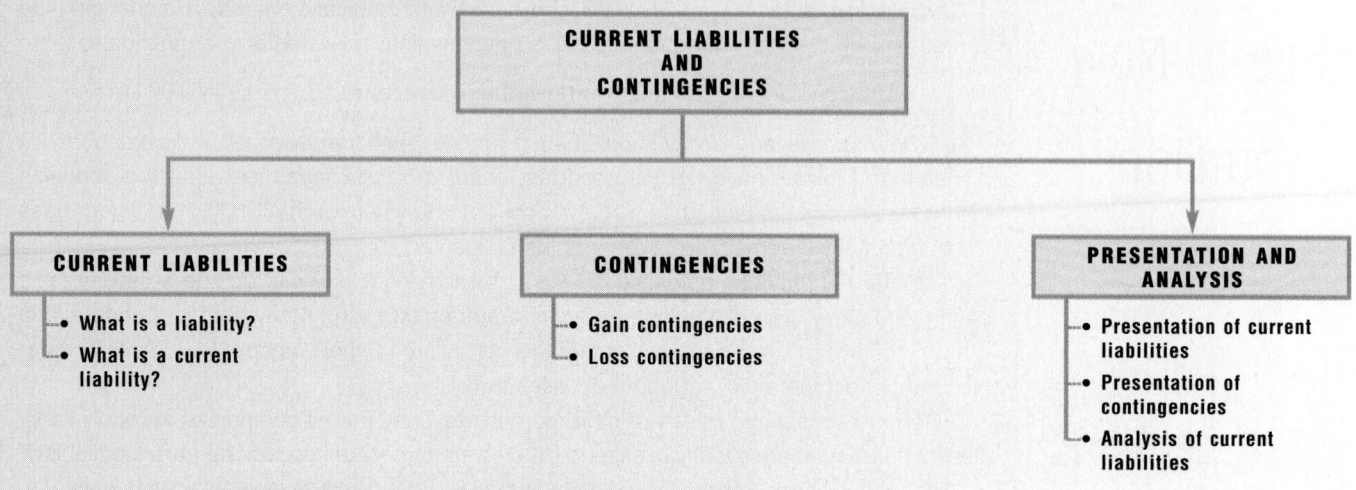

| SECTION 1 | *CURRENT LIABILITIES* |

WHAT IS A LIABILITY?

UNDERLYING CONCEPTS

To determine the appropriate classification of specific financial instruments, companies need proper definitions of assets, liabilities, and equities. They often use the conceptual framework definitions as the basis for resolving controversial classification issues.

The question, "What is a liability?" is not easy to answer. For example, is preferred stock a liability or an ownership claim? The first reaction is to say that preferred stock is in fact an ownership claim, and companies should report it as part of stockholders' equity. In fact, preferred stock has many elements of debt as well.[1] The issuer (and in some cases the holder) often has the right to call the stock within a specific period of time—making it similar to a repayment of principal. The dividend on the preferred stock is in many cases almost guaranteed (the cumulative provision)—making it look like interest. As a result, preferred stock is but one of many financial instruments that are difficult to classify.[2]

To help resolve some of these controversies, the FASB, as part of its conceptual framework study, defined liabilities as **"probable future sacrifices of economic benefits arising from present obligations of a particular entity to transfer assets**

---

[1]This illustration is not just a theoretical exercise. In practice, a number of preferred stock issues have all the characteristics of a debt instrument, except that they are called and legally classified as preferred stock. In some cases, the IRS has even permitted companies to treat the dividend payments as interest expense for tax purposes.

[2]The FASB has issued a new standard for addressing this issue: "Accounting for Certain Financial Instruments with Characteristics of Both Liabilities and Equity," *Statement of Financial Accounting Standards No. 150* (Norwalk, Conn.: FASB, 2003).

or provide services to other entities in the future as a result of past transactions or events."[3] In other words, a liability has three essential characteristics:

1 It is a present obligation that entails settlement by probable future transfer or use of cash, goods, or services.

2 It is an unavoidable obligation.

3 The transaction or other event creating the obligation has already occurred.

Because liabilities involve future disbursements of assets or services, one of their most important features is the date on which they are payable. A company must satisfy currently maturing obligations in the ordinary course of business to continue operating. Liabilities with a more distant due date do not, as a rule, represent a claim on the company's current resources. They are therefore in a slightly different category. This feature gives rise to the basic division of liabilities into (1) current liabilities and (2) long-term debt.

WHAT IS A CURRENT LIABILITY?

Recall that current assets are cash or other assets that companies reasonably expect to convert into cash, sell, or consume in operations within a single operating cycle or within a year (if completing more than one cycle each year). **Current liabilities** are **"obligations whose liquidation is reasonably expected to require use of existing resources properly classified as current assets, or the creation of other current liabilities."**[4] This definition has gained wide acceptance because it recognizes operating cycles of varying lengths in different industries. This definition also considers the important relationship between current assets and current liabilities.[5]

The **operating cycle** is the period of time elapsing between the acquisition of goods and services involved in the manufacturing process and the final cash realization resulting from sales and subsequent collections. Industries that manufacture products requiring an aging process, and certain capital-intensive industries, have an operating cycle of considerably more than one year. On the other hand, most retail and service establishments have several operating cycles within a year.

Here are some typical current liabilities:

1 Accounts payable.

2 Notes payable.

3 Current maturities of long-term debt.

4 Short-term obligations expected to be refinanced.

5 Dividends payable.

6 Customer advances and deposits.

7 Unearned revenues.

8 Sales taxes payable.

9 Income taxes payable.

10 Employee-related liabilities.

> **OBJECTIVE 1**
> Describe the nature, type, and valuation of current liabilities.

Accounts Payable

Accounts payable, or **trade accounts payable**, are balances owed to others for goods, supplies, or services purchased on open account. Accounts payable arise because of the time lag between the receipt of services or acquisition of title to assets and the payment

---

[3]"Elements of Financial Statements of Business Enterprises," *Statement of Financial Accounting Concepts No. 6* (Stamford, Conn.: FASB, 1980).

[4]Committee on Accounting Procedure, American Institute of Certified Public Accountants, "Accounting Research and Terminology Bulletins," Final Edition (New York: AICPA, 1961), p. 21.

[5]The FASB affirmed this concept of "maturity within one year or the operating cycle whichever is longer" in its definition of short-term obligations in *Statement No. 6*. "Classification of Short-term Obligations Expected to Be Refinanced," *Statement of Financial Accounting Standards No. 6* (Stamford, Conn.: FASB, 1975), par. 2.

for them. The terms of the sale (e.g., 2/10, n/30 or 1/10, E.O.M.) usually state this period of extended credit, commonly 30 to 60 days.

Most companies record liabilities for purchases of goods upon receipt of the goods. If title has passed to the purchaser before receipt of the goods, the company should record the transaction at the time of title passage. A company must pay special attention to transactions occurring near the end of one accounting period and at the beginning of the next. It needs to ascertain that the record of goods received (the inventory) agrees with the liability (accounts payable), and that it records both in the proper period.

Measuring the amount of an account payable poses no particular difficulty. The invoice received from the creditor specifies the due date and the exact outlay in money that is necessary to settle the account. The only calculation that may be necessary concerns the amount of cash discount. See Chapter 8 for illustrations of entries related to accounts payable and purchase discounts.

Notes Payable

Notes payable are written promises to pay a certain sum of money on a specified future date. They may arise from purchases, financing, or other transactions. Some industries require notes (often referred to as **trade notes payable**) as part of the sales/purchases transaction in lieu of the normal extension of open account credit. Notes payable to banks or loan companies generally arise from cash loans. Companies classify notes as short-term or long-term, depending on the payment due date. Notes may also be interest-bearing or zero-interest-bearing.

Interest-Bearing Note Issued

Assume that Castle National Bank agrees to lend $100,000 on March 1, 2007, to Landscape Co. if Landscape signs a $100,000, 6 percent, four-month note. Landscape records the cash received on March 1 as follows:

March 1

Cash	100,000	
Notes Payable		100,000
(To record issuance of 6%, 4-month note to Castle National Bank)		

If Landscape prepares financial statements semiannually, it makes the following adjusting entry to recognize interest expense and interest payable of $2,000 ($100,000 × 6% × 4/12) at June 30:

June 30

Interest Expense	2,000	
Interest Payable		2,000
(To accrue interest for 4 months on Castle National Bank note)		

If Landscape prepares financial statements monthly, its adjusting entry at the end of each month is $500 ($100,000 × 6% × 1/12).

At maturity (July 1), Landscape must pay the face value of the note ($100,000) plus $2,000 interest ($100,000 × 6% × 4/12). Landscape records payment of the note and accrued interest as follows.

July 1

Notes Payable	100,000	
Interest Payable	2,000	
Cash		102,000
(To record payment of Castle National Bank interest-bearing note and accrued interest at maturity)		

Zero-Interest-Bearing Note Issued

A company may issue a zero-interest-bearing note instead of an interest-bearing note. A zero-interest-bearing note does not explicitly state an interest rate on the face of the note. **Interest is still charged**, however. At maturity the borrower must pay back an amount greater than the cash received at the issuance date. In other words, the borrower receives in cash the present value of the note. The present value equals the face value of the note at maturity minus the interest or discount charged by the lender for the term of the note. In essence, the bank takes its fee "up front" rather than on the date the note matures.

To illustrate, assume that Landscape issues a $102,000, four-month, zero-interest-bearing note to Castle National Bank. The present value of the note is $100,000.[6] Landscape records this transaction as follows.

March 1

Cash	100,000	
Discount on Notes Payable	2,000	
Notes Payable		102,000
(To record issuance of 4-month, zero-interest-bearing note to Castle National Bank)		

Landscape credits the Notes Payable account for the face value of the note, which is $2,000 more than the actual cash received. It debits the difference between the cash received and the face value of the note to Discount on Notes Payable. **Discount on Notes Payable is a contra account to Notes Payable, and therefore is subtracted from Notes Payable on the balance sheet.** Illustration 13-1 shows the balance sheet presentation on March 1.

Current liabilities		
Notes payable	102,000	
Less: Discount on notes payable	2,000	100,000

ILLUSTRATION 13-1
Balance Sheet
Presentation of Discount

The amount of the discount, $2,000 in this case, represents the cost of borrowing $100,000 for 4 months. Accordingly, Landscape charges the discount to interest expense over the life of the note. That is, the Discount on Notes Payable balance **represents interest expense chargeable to future periods**. Thus, Landscape should not debit Interest Expense for $2,000 at the time of obtaining the loan. We discuss additional accounting issues related to notes payable in Chapter 14.

Current Maturities of Long-Term Debt

PepsiCo reports as part of its current liabilities the portion of bonds, mortgage notes, and other long-term indebtedness that matures within the next fiscal year. It categorizes this amount as **current maturities of long-term debt**. Companies, like PepsiCo, exclude long-term debts maturing currently as current liabilities if they are to be:

1 retired by assets accumulated for this purpose that properly have not been shown as current assets,

2 refinanced, or retired from the proceeds of a new debt issue, or

3 converted into capital stock.

In these situations, the use of current assets or the creation of other current liabilities does not occur. Therefore, classification as a current liability is inappropriate. A company should disclose the plan for liquidation of such a debt either parenthetically or by a note to the financial statements. When only a part of a long-term debt is to be

---

[6]The bank discount rate used in this example to find the present value is 5.96 percent.

paid within the next 12 months, as in the case of serial bonds that it retires through a series of annual installments, **the company reports the maturing portion of long-term debt as a current liability**, and the remaining portion as a long-term debt.

However, a company should classify as current any liability that is **due on demand** (callable by the creditor) or will be due on demand within a year (or operating cycle, if longer). Liabilities often become callable by the creditor when there is a violation of the debt agreement. For example, most debt agreements specify a given level of equity to debt be maintained, or specify that working capital be of a minimum amount. If the company violates an agreement, it must classify the debt as current because it is a reasonable expectation that existing working capital will be used to satisfy the debt. Only if a company can show that it is **probable** that it will cure (satisfy) the violation within the grace period specified in the agreements can it classify the debt as noncurrent.[7]

Short-Term Obligations Expected to Be Refinanced

OBJECTIVE 2
Explain the classification issues of short-term debt expected to be refinanced.

Short-term obligations are debts scheduled to mature within one year after the date of a company's balance sheet or within its operating cycle, whichever is longer. Some **short-term obligations** are **expected to be refinanced** on a long-term basis. These short-term obligations will not require the use of working capital during the next year (or operating cycle).[8]

At one time, the accounting profession generally supported the exclusion of short-term obligations from current liabilities if they were "expected to be refinanced." But the profession provided no specific guidelines, so companies determined whether a short-term obligation was "expected to be refinanced" based solely on management's **intent** to refinance on a long-term basis. Classification was not clear-cut. For example, a company might obtain a five-year bank loan but handle the actual financing with 90-day notes, which it must keep turning over (renewing). In this case, is the loan a long-term debt or a current liability? Another example was the **Penn Central Railroad** before it went bankrupt. The railroad was deep into short-term debt but classified it as long-term debt. Why? Because the railroad believed it had commitments from lenders to keep refinancing the short-term debt. When those commitments suddenly disappeared, it was "good-bye Pennsy." As the Greek philosopher Epictetus once said, "Some things in this world are not and yet appear to be."

Refinancing Criteria

To resolve these classification problems, the accounting profession has developed authoritative criteria for determining the circumstances under which short-term obligations may be properly excluded from current liabilities. A company is required to exclude a short-term obligation from current liabilities if **both** of the following conditions are met:

1 It must **intend to refinance** the obligation on a long-term basis.

2 It must **demonstrate an ability** to consummate the refinancing.[9]

Intention to refinance on a long-term basis means that the company intends to refinance the short-term obligation so that it will not require the use of working capital during the ensuing fiscal year (or operating cycle, if longer).

---

[7]"Classification of Obligations That Are Callable by the Creditor," *Statement of Financial Accounting Standards No. 78* (Stamford, Conn.: FASB, 1983).

[8]*Refinancing a short-term obligation on a long-term basis* means either replacing it with a long-term obligation or equity securities, or renewing, extending, or replacing it with short-term obligations for an uninterrupted period extending beyond one year (or the operating cycle, if longer) from the date of the enterprise's balance sheet.

[9]"Classification of Short-term Obligations Expected to Be Refinanced," *Statement of Financial Accounting Standards No. 6* (Stamford, Conn.: FASB, 1975), pars. 10 and 11.

The company demonstrates the **ability** to consummate the refinancing by:

(a) **Actually refinancing** the short-term obligation by issuing a long-term obligation or equity securities after the date of the balance sheet but before it is issued; or

(b) Entering into a **financing agreement** that clearly permits the company to refinance the debt on a long-term basis on terms that are readily determinable.

If an actual refinancing occurs, the portion of the short-term obligation to be excluded from current liabilities may not exceed the proceeds from the new obligation or equity securities used to retire the short-term obligation. For example, **Montavon Winery** had $3,000,000 of short-term debt. Subsequent to the balance sheet date, but before issuing the balance sheet, the company issued 100,000 shares of common stock, intending to use the proceeds to liquidate the short-term debt at its maturity. If Montavon's net proceeds from the sale of the 100,000 shares total $2,000,000, it can exclude from current liabilities only $2,000,000 of the short-term debt.

An additional question is whether a company should exclude from current liabilities a short-term obligation if it is paid off after the balance sheet date and replaced by long-term debt before the balance sheet is issued. To illustrate, Marquardt Company pays off short-term debt of $40,000 on January 17, 2008, and issues long-term debt of $100,000 on February 3, 2008. Marquardt's financial statements, dated December 31, 2007, are to be issued March 1, 2008. Should Marquardt exclude the $40,000 short-term debt from current liabilities? No—here's why: Repayment of the short-term obligation required the use of **existing** current assets **before** the company obtained funds through long-term financing. Therefore, Marquardt must include the short-term obligations in current liabilities at the balance sheet date (see graphical presentation below).

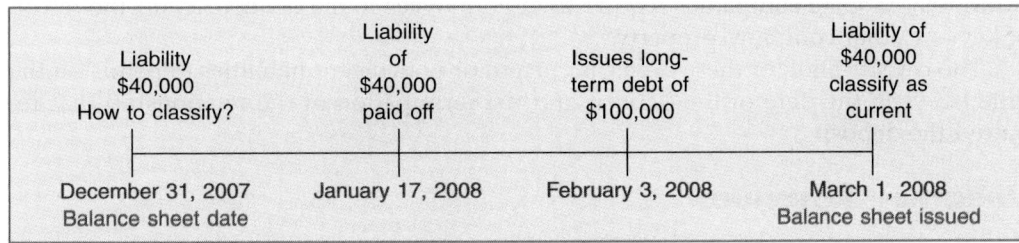

ILLUSTRATION 13-2
Short-Term Debt Paid Off after Balance Sheet Date and Later Replaced by Long-Term Debt

WHAT ABOUT THAT SHORT-TERM DEBT?

The evaluation of credit quality involves more than simply assessing a company's ability to repay loans. Credit analysts also evaluate debt management strategies. Analysts and investors will reward what they view as prudent management decisions with lower debt service costs and a higher stock price. The wrong decisions can bring higher debt costs and lower stock prices.

General Electric Capital Corp., a subsidiary of **General Electric**, recently experienced the negative effects of market scrutiny of its debt management policies. Analysts complained that GE had been slow to refinance its mountains of short-term debt. GE had issued these current obligations, with maturities of 270 days or less, when interest rates were low. However, in light of expectations that the Fed would raise interest rates, analysts began to worry about the higher interest costs GE would pay when it refinanced these loans. Some analysts recommended that it was time to reduce dependence on short-term credit. The reasoning goes that a shift to more dependable long-term debt, thereby locking in slightly higher rates for the long-term, is the better way to go.

Thus, scrutiny of GE debt strategies led to analysts' concerns about GE's earnings prospects. Investors took the analysis to heart, and GE experienced a 2-day 6 percent drop in its stock price.

Source: Adapted from Steven Vames, "Credit Quality, Stock Investing Seem to Go Hand in Hand," *Wall Street Journal* (April 1, 2002), p. R4.

WHAT DO THE NUMBERS MEAN?

Dividends Payable

UNDERLYING CONCEPTS

Preferred dividends in arrears do represent a probable future economic sacrifice, but the expected sacrifice does not result from a past transaction or past event. The sacrifice will result from a future event (declaration by the board of directors). Note disclosure improves the predictive value of the financial statements.

A **cash dividend payable** is an amount owed by a corporation to its stockholders as a result of board of directors' authorization. At the date of declaration the corporation assumes a liability that places the stockholders in the position of creditors in the amount of dividends declared. Because companies always pay cash dividends within one year of declaration (generally within three months), they classify them as current liabilities.

On the other hand, companies do not recognize accumulated but undeclared dividends on cumulative preferred stock as a liability. Why? Because **preferred dividends in arrears** are not an obligation until the board of directors authorizes the payment. Nevertheless, companies should disclose the amount of cumulative dividends unpaid in a note, or show it parenthetically in the capital stock section.

Dividends payable in the form of additional shares of stock are not recognized as a liability. Such **stock dividends** (as we discuss in Chapter 15) do not require future outlays of assets or services. Companies generally report such undistributed stock dividends in the stockholders' equity section because they represent retained earnings in the process of transfer to paid-in capital.

Customer Advances and Deposits

Current liabilities may include **returnable cash deposits** received from customers and employees. Companies may receive deposits from customers to guarantee performance of a contract or service or as guarantees to cover payment of expected future obligations. For example, a company like **Alltel Corp.** often requires a deposit on equipment that customers use to connect to the Internet or to access its other services. Alltel also may receive deposits from customers as guarantees for possible damage to property. Additionally, some companies require their employees to make deposits for the return of keys or other company property.

The classification of these items as current or noncurrent liabilities depends on the time between the date of the deposit and the termination of the relationship that required the deposit.

Unearned Revenues

A magazine publisher, such as **Golf Digest**, receives payment when a customer subscribes to its magazines. An airline company, such as **American Airlines**, sells tickets for future flights. And software companies, like **Microsoft**, issue coupons that allow customers to upgrade to the next version of their software. How do these companies account for **unearned revenues** that they receive before delivering goods or rendering services?

1 Upon receipt of the advance, debit Cash, and credit a current liability account identifying the source of the unearned revenue.

2 Upon earning the revenue, debit the unearned revenue account, and credit an earned revenue account.

To illustrate, assume that Allstate University sells 10,000 season football tickets at $50 each for its five-game home schedule. Allstate University records the sales of season tickets as follows:

August 6

Cash	500,000	
Unearned Football Ticket Revenue		500,000
(To record sale of 10,000 season tickets)		

After each game, Allstate University makes the following entry.

September 7

Unearned Football Ticket Revenue	100,000	
Football Ticket Revenue		100,000
(To record football ticket revenues earned)		

Unearned Football Ticket Revenue is, therefore, unearned revenue. Allstate University reports it as a current liability in the balance sheet. As revenue is earned, a transfer from unearned revenue to earned revenue occurs. Unearned revenue is material for some companies: In the airline industry, tickets sold for future flights represent almost 50 percent of total current liabilities.

Illustration 13-3 shows specific unearned and earned revenue accounts used in selected types of businesses.

Type of Business	Account Title	
	Unearned Revenue	Earned Revenue
Airline	Unearned Passenger Ticket Revenue	Passenger Revenue
Magazine publisher	Unearned Subscription Revenue	Subscription Revenue
Hotel	Unearned Rental Revenue	Rental Revenue
Auto dealer	Unearned Warranty Revenue	Warranty Revenue
Retailers	Unearned Gift Card Revenue	Sales Revenue

ILLUSTRATION 13-3
Unearned and Earned Revenue Accounts

The balance sheet should report obligations for any commitments that are redeemable in goods and services. The income statement should report revenues earned during the period.

MICROSOFT'S LIABILITIES—GOOD OR BAD?

Users of financial statements generally examine current liabilities to assess a company's liquidity and overall financial flexibility. Companies must pay many current liabilities, such as accounts payable, wages payable, and taxes payable, sooner rather than later. A substantial increase in these liabilities should raise a red flag about a company's financial position.

This is not the case for all current liabilities. For example, **Microsoft** has a current liability entitled "Unearned revenue" that has increased substantially year after year. Unearned revenue is a liability that arises from sales of Microsoft products such as *Windows* and *Office*. At the time of a sale, customers pay not only for the current version of the software but also for future upgrades. Microsoft recognizes sales revenue from the current version of the software and records as a liability (unearned revenue) the value of future upgrades to the software that it "owes" to customers.

Market analysts read such an increase in unearned revenue as a positive signal about Microsoft's sales and profitability. When Microsoft's sales are growing, its unearned revenue account increases. Thus, an *increase* in a liability is good news about Microsoft sales. At the same time, a decline in unearned revenue is bad news. As one analyst noted, a slowdown or reversal of the growth in Microsoft's unearned revenues indicates slowing sales, which is bad news for investors. Thus, increases in current liabilities can sometimes be viewed as good signs instead of bad.

Source: Adapted from David Bank, "Some Fans Cool to Microsoft, Citing Drop in Old Indicator," *Wall Street Journal* (October 28, 1999).

WHAT DO THE NUMBERS MEAN?

Sales Taxes Payable

Retailers like **Wal-Mart**, **Circuit City**, and **Gap** must collect sales taxes from customers on transfers of tangible personal property and on certain services and then must remit these taxes to the proper governmental authority. GAP, for example, sets up a liability to provide for taxes collected from customers but not yet remitted to the tax authority. The Sales Taxes Payable account should reflect the liability for sales taxes due various governments.

The entry below illustrates use of the Sales Taxes Payable account on a sale of $3,000 when a 4 percent sales tax is in effect.

Cash or Accounts Receivable	3,120	
Sales		3,000
Sales Taxes Payable		120

Sometimes the sales tax collections credited to the liability account are not equal to the liability as computed by the governmental formula. In such a case, GAP makes an adjustment of the liability account by recognizing a gain or a loss on sales tax collections.

Many companies do not segregate the sales tax and the amount of the sale at the time of sale. Instead, the company credits both amounts in total in the Sales account. Then, to reflect correctly the actual amount of sales and the liability for sales taxes, the company would debit the Sales account for the amount of the sales taxes due the government on these sales, and would credit the Sales Taxes Payable account for the same amount.

To illustrate, assume that the Sales account balance of $150,000 includes sales taxes of 4 percent. Thus, the amount recorded in the Sales account is comprised of the sales amount plus sales tax of 4 percent of the sales amount. Sales therefore are $144,230.77 ($150,000 ÷ 1.04) and the sales tax liability is $5,769.23 ($144,230.77 × 0.04; or $150,000 − $144,230.77). The following entry would record the amount due the taxing unit.

Sales	5,769.23	
Sales Taxes Payable		5,769.23

Income Taxes Payable

Any federal or state income tax varies in proportion to the amount of annual income. Using the best information and advice available, a business must prepare an income tax return and compute the income tax payable resulting from the operations of the current period. Corporations should classify as a current liability the taxes payable on net income, as computed per the tax return.[10] Unlike a corporation, proprietorships and partnerships are not taxable entities. Because the individual proprietor and the members of a partnership are subject to personal income taxes on their share of the business's taxable income, income tax liabilities do not appear on the financial statements of proprietorships and partnerships.

Most corporations must make periodic tax payments throughout the year in an authorized bank depository or a Federal Reserve Bank. These payments are based upon estimates of the total annual tax liability. As the estimated total tax liability changes, the periodic contributions also change. If in a later year the taxing authority assesses an additional tax on the income of an earlier year, the company should credit Income Taxes Payable and charge the related debit to current operations.

Differences between taxable income under the tax laws and accounting income under generally accepted accounting principles sometimes occur. Because of these differences, the amount of income tax payable to the government in any given year may differ substantially from income tax expense as reported on the financial statements. Chapter 19 is devoted solely to income tax matters and presents an extensive discussion of this complex topic.

Employee-Related Liabilities

Companies also report as a current liability amounts owed to employees for salaries or wages at the end of an accounting period. In addition, they often also report as current liabilities the following items related to employee compensation.

Expanded Discussion of Property Taxes Payable

OBJECTIVE 3
Identify types of employee-related liabilities.

---

[10]Corporate taxes are based on a progressive tax rate structure. Companies with taxable income of $50,000 or less are taxed at a 15 percent rate; higher levels of income are taxed at rates ranging up to 39 percent.

1 Payroll deductions.

2 Compensated absences.

3 Bonuses. (Accounting for bonuses is covered in Appendix 13A.)

Payroll Deductions

The most common types of payroll deductions are taxes, insurance premiums, employee savings, and union dues. **To the extent that a company has not remitted the amounts deducted to the proper authority at the end of the accounting period, it should recognize them as current liabilities.**

Social Security Taxes. Since January 1, 1937, Social Security legislation has provided federal old age, survivor, and disability insurance (O.A.S.D.I.) benefits for certain individuals and their families. Funds for these payments come from taxes levied on both the employer and the employee. Employers collect the employee's share of this tax by deducting it from the employee's gross pay, and remit it to the government along with their share. The government taxes both the employer and the employee at the same rate, currently 6.2 percent based on the employee's gross pay up to a $90,000 annual limit. The O.A.S.D.I. tax is usually referred to as F.I.C.A. (the Federal Insurance Contribution Act).

In 1965 Congress passed the first federal health insurance program for the aged—popularly known as **Medicare**. This two-part program alleviates the high cost of medical care for those over age 65. A separate Hospital Insurance tax, paid by both the employee and the employer at the rate of 1.45 percent on the employee's total compensation, finances the Basic Plan, which provides hospital and other institutional services. The Voluntary Plan covers the major part of doctors' bills and other medical and health services. Monthly payments from all who enroll, plus matching funds from the federal government, finance this plan.

The combination of the O.A.S.D.I. tax (F.I.C.A.) and the federal Hospital Insurance Tax is commonly referred to as the **Social Security tax**. The combined rate for these taxes, 7.65 percent on an employee's wages to $90,000 and 1.45 percent in excess of $90,000, changes intermittently by acts of Congress. **Companies should report the amount of unremitted employee and employer Social Security tax on gross wages paid as a current liability.**

Unemployment Taxes. Another payroll tax levied by the federal government in cooperation with state governments provides a system of unemployment insurance. All employers who meet the following criteria are subject to the Federal Unemployment Tax Act (F.U.T.A.): (1) those who paid wages of $1,500 or more during any calendar quarter in the year or preceding year, or (2) those who employed at least one individual on at least one day in each of 20 weeks during the current or preceding calendar year.

Only employers pay the unemployment tax. The rate of this tax is 6.2 percent on the first $7,000 of compensation paid to each employee during the calendar year. The employer receives a tax credit not to exceed 5.4 percent for contributions paid to a state plan for unemployment compensation. Thus, if an employer is subject to a state unemployment tax of 5.4 percent or more, it pays only 0.8 percent tax to the federal government.

State unemployment compensation laws differ both from the federal law and among various states. Therefore, employers must refer to the unemployment tax laws in each state in which they pay wages and salaries. The normal state tax may range from 3 percent to 7 percent or higher. However, all states provide for some form of **merit rating**, which reduces the state contribution rate. Employers who display by their benefit and contribution experience that they provide steady employment may receive this reduction—if the size of the state fund is adequate. In order not to penalize an employer who has earned a reduction in the state contribution rate, federal law allows a credit of 5.4 percent, even when the effective state contribution rate is less than 5.4 percent.

To illustrate, Appliance Repair Co. has a taxable payroll of $100,000. It is subject to a federal rate of 6.2 percent and a state contribution rate of 5.7 percent. However, its stable employment experience reduces the company's state rate to 1 percent. Appliance Repair computes its federal and state unemployment taxes as shown in Illustration 13-4.

ILLUSTRATION 13-4
Computation of
Unemployment Taxes

State unemployment tax payment (1% × $100,000)	$1,000
Federal unemployment tax [(6.2% − 5.4%) × $100,000]	800
Total federal and state unemployment tax	$1,800

Companies pay federal unemployment tax quarterly, and file a tax form annually. Companies also generally pay state contributions quarterly as well. Because both the federal and the state unemployment taxes accrue on earned compensation, companies should record the amount of accrued but unpaid employer contributions **as an operating expense and as a current liability when preparing financial statements at year-end**.

Income Tax Withholding. Federal and some state income tax laws require employers to withhold from each employee's pay the applicable income tax due on those wages. The employer computes the amount of income tax to withhold according to a government-prescribed formula or withholding tax table. That amount depends on the length of the pay period and each employee's taxable wages, marital status, and claimed dependents. If the income tax withheld plus the employee and the employer Social Security taxes exceeds specified amounts per month, the employer must make remittances to the government during the month. Illustration 13-5 summarizes payroll deductions and liabilities.

ILLUSTRATION 13-5
Summary of Payroll
Liabilities

Item	Who Pays	
Income tax withholding FICA taxes—employee share Union dues	Employee	Employer reports these amounts as liabilities until remitted.
FICA taxes—employer share Federal unemployment State unemployment	Employer	

Payroll Deductions Example. Assume a weekly payroll of $10,000 entirely subject to F.I.C.A. and Medicare (7.65%), federal (0.8%) and state (4%) unemployment taxes, with income tax withholding of $1,320 and union dues of $88 deducted. The company records the wages and salaries paid and the **employee payroll deductions** as follows:

Wages and Salaries Expense	10,000	
Withholding Taxes Payable		1,320
F.I.C.A. Taxes Payable		765
Union Dues Payable to Local No. 257		88
Cash		7,827

It records the **employer payroll taxes** as follows:

Payroll Tax Expense	1,245	
F.I.C.A. Taxes Payable		765
Federal Unemployment Tax Payable		80
State Unemployment Tax Payable		400

The employer must remit to the government its share of F.I.C.A. tax along with the amount of F.I.C.A. tax deducted from each employee's gross compensation. It should record all unremitted employer F.I.C.A. taxes as payroll tax expense and payroll tax payable.[11]

Compensated Absences

Compensated absences are paid absences from employment—such as vacation, illness, and holidays. Companies should accrue a liability for the cost of compensation for future absences if **all of the following conditions** exist.[12]

> **UNDERLYING CONCEPTS**
>
> When these four conditions exist, all elements in the definition of a liability exist. In addition, the matching concept requires that the company report the expense for the services in the same period as the revenue was generated.

(a) The employer's obligation relating to employees' rights to receive compensation for future absences is attributable to employees' services **already rendered**.

(b) The obligation relates to the rights that **vest or accumulate**.

(c) Payment of the compensation is **probable**.

(d) The amount can be **reasonably estimated**.[13]

Illustration 13-6 shows an example of an accrual for compensated absences, in an excerpt from the balance sheet of **Clarcor Inc.**

Clarcor Inc.

Current liabilities	
Accounts payable	$ 6,308
Accrued salaries, wages and commissions	2,278
Compensated absences	2,271
Accrued pension liabilities	1,023
Other accrued liabilities	4,572
	$16,452

ILLUSTRATION 13-6
Balance Sheet Presentation of Accrual for Compensated Absences

If an employer meets conditions (a), (b), and (c) but does not accrue a liability because of a failure to meet condition (d), it should disclose that fact. Illustration 13-7 (on page 630) shows an example of such a disclosure, in a note from the financial statements of **Gotham Utility Company**.

---

[11]A manufacturing company allocates all of the payroll costs (wages, payroll taxes, and fringe benefits) to appropriate cost accounts such as Direct Labor, Indirect Labor, Sales Salaries, Administrative Salaries, and the like. This abbreviated and somewhat simplified discussion of payroll costs and deductions is not indicative of the volume of records and clerical work that may be involved in maintaining a sound and accurate payroll system.

[12]"Accounting for Compensated Absences," *Statement of Financial Accounting Standards No. 43* (Stamford, Conn.: FASB, 1980), par. 6.

[13]*FASB Statement No. 112*, "Employers' Accounting for Postemployment Benefits," requires that companies apply these same four conditions to **postemployment benefits**. "Employers' Accounting for Postemployment Benefits," *Statement of Financial Accounting Standards No. 112* (Norwalk, Conn.: FASB, November 1992), par. 18. Companies provide **postemployment benefits** to past or inactive employees **after employment but prior to retirement**. Examples include salary continuation, supplemental unemployment benefits, severance pay, job training, and continuation of health and life insurance coverage.

ILLUSTRATION 13-7
Disclosure of Policy
for Compensated
Absences

Gotham Utility Company

Employees of the Company are entitled to paid vacation, personal, and sick days off, depending on job status, length of service, and other factors. Due to numerous differing union contracts and other agreements with nonunion employees, it is impractical to estimate the amount of compensation for future absences, and, accordingly, no liability has been reported in the accompanying financial statements. The Company's policy is to recognize the cost of compensated absences when actually paid to employees; compensated absence payments to employees totaled $2,786,000.

The following considerations are relevant to the accounting for compensated absences.

Vested rights exist when an employer has an obligation to make payment to an employee even after terminating his or her employment. Thus, vested rights are not contingent on an employee's future service. **Accumulated rights** are those that employees can carry forward to future periods if not used in the period in which earned. For example, assume that you earn four days of vacation pay as of December 31, the end of your employer's fiscal year. Company policy is that you will be paid for this vacation time even if you terminate employment. In this situation, your four days of vacation pay are vested, and your employer must accrue the amount.

Now assume that your vacation days are not vested, but that you can carry the four days over into later periods. Although the rights are not vested, they are accumulated rights for which the employer must make an accrual. However, the amount of the accrual is adjusted to allow for estimated forfeitures due to turnover.

A modification of the general rules relates to the issue of **sick pay**. If sick pay benefits vest, a company must accrue them. If sick pay benefits accumulate but do not vest, a company may choose whether to accrue them. Why this distinction? Companies may administer compensation designated as sick pay in one of two ways. In some companies, employees receive sick pay only if illness causes their absence. Therefore, these companies may or may not accrue a liability because its payment depends on future employee illness. Other companies allow employees to accumulate unused sick pay and take compensated time off from work even when not ill. For this type of sick pay, a company must accrue a liability because the company will pay it, regardless of whether employees become ill.

Companies should recognize the expense and related liability for compensated absences in the year earned by employees. For example, if new employees receive rights to two weeks' paid vacation at the beginning of their second year of employment, a company considers the vacation pay to be earned during the first year of employment.

What rate should a company use to accrue the compensated absence cost—the current rate or an estimated future rate? *FASB Statement No. 43* is silent on this subject. Therefore, companies will likely use the current rather than future rate. The future rate is less certain and raises time value of money issues. To illustrate, assume that Amutron Inc. began operations on January 1, 2006. The company employs 10 individuals and pays each $480 per week. Employees earned 20 unused vacation weeks in 2006. In 2007, the employees used the vacation weeks, but now they each earn $540 per week. Amutron accrues the accumulated vacation pay on December 31, 2006, as follows.

Wages Expense	9,600	
Vacation Wages Payable ($480 × 20)		9,600

At December 31, 2006, the company reports on its balance sheet a liability of $9,600. In 2007, it records the payment of vacation pay as follows.

Vacation Wages Payable	9,600	
Wages Expense	1,200	
Cash ($540 × 20)		10,800

In 2007 the use of the vacation weeks extinguishes the liability. Note that Amutron records the difference between the amount of cash paid and the reduction in the liability account as an adjustment to Wages Expense in the period when paid. This difference arises because it accrues the liability account at the rates of pay in effect during the period when employees *earned* the compensated time. The cash paid, however, depends on the rates in effect during the period when employees *used* the compensated time. If Amutron used the future rates of pay to compute the accrual in 2006, then the cash paid in 2007 would equal the liability.[14]

Bonus Agreements

Many companies give a **bonus** to certain or all employees in addition to their regular salaries or wages. Frequently the bonus amount depends on the company's yearly profit. For example, employees at **Ford Motor Company** share in the success of the company's operations on the basis of a complicated formula using net income as its primary basis for computation. A company may consider **bonus payments to employees** as additional wages and should include them as a deduction in determining the net income for the year.

To illustrate the entries for an employee bonus, assume that Palmer Inc. shows income for the year 2007 of $100,000. It will pay out bonuses of $10,700 in January 2008. Palmer makes an adjusting entry dated December 31, 2007, to record the bonuses as follows.

Employees' Bonus Expense	10,700	
Profit-Sharing Bonus Payable		10,700

In January 2008, when Palmer pays the bonus, it makes this journal entry:

Profit-Sharing Bonus Payable	10,700	
Cash		10,700

INTERNATIONAL INSIGHT

In Japan, companies do not treat bonuses to members of the board of directors and to the Commercial Code auditors as expenses. Instead, they consider such bonuses to be a distribution of profits and charge them against retained earnings.

Palmer should show the expense account in the income statement as an operating expense. **The liability, Profit-Sharing Bonus Payable, is usually payable within a short period of time. Companies should include it as a current liability in the balance sheet.** Similar to bonus agreements are contractual agreements for **conditional expenses**. Examples would be agreements covering rents or royalty payments conditional on the amount of revenues earned or the quantity of product produced or extracted. Conditional expenses based on revenues or units produced are usually less difficult to compute than bonus arrangements.

For example, assume that a lease calls for a fixed rent payment of $500 per month and 1 percent of all sales over $300,000 per year. The company's annual rent obligation would amount to $6,000 plus $0.01 of each dollar of revenue over $300,000. Or, a royalty agreement may give to a patent owner $1 for every ton of product resulting from the patented process, or give to a mineral rights owner $0.50 on every barrel of oil extracted. As the company produces or extracts each additional unit of product, it creates an additional obligation, usually a current liability.

## CONTINGENCIES	**SECTION 2**

Companies often are involved in situations where uncertainty exists about whether an obligation to transfer cash or other assets has arisen and/or the amount that will be required to settle the obligation. For example:

- **Merck** may be a defendant in a lawsuit, and any payment is contingent upon the outcome of a settlement or an administrative or court proceeding.

---

[14]Some companies have obligations for benefits paid to employees after they retire. The accounting and reporting standards for postretirement benefit payments are complex. These standards relate to two different types of **postretirement benefits**: (1) pensions, and (2) postretirement health care and life insurance benefits. We discuss these issues extensively in Chapter 20.

- **Ford Motor Co.** provides a warranty for a car it sells, and any payments are contingent on the number of cars that qualify for benefits under the warranty.
- **Briggs & Stratton** acts as a guarantor on a loan for another entity, and any payment is contingent on whether the other entity defaults.

Broadly, these situations are called contingencies. A **contingency** is "an existing condition, situation, or set of circumstances involving uncertainty as to possible gain **(gain contingency)** or loss **(loss contingency)** to an enterprise that will ultimately be resolved when one or more future events occur or fail to occur."[15]

GAIN CONTINGENCIES

OBJECTIVE 4
Identify the criteria used to account for and disclose gain and loss contingencies.

Gain contingencies are claims or rights to receive assets (or have a liability reduced) whose existence is uncertain but which may become valid eventually. The typical gain contingencies are:

1   Possible receipts of monies from gifts, donations, bonuses, and so on.
2   Possible refunds from the government in tax disputes.
3   Pending court cases with a probable favorable outcome.
4   Tax loss carryforwards (discussed in Chapter 19).

Companies follow a conservative policy in this area. Except for tax loss carryforwards, they do not record gain contingencies. A company discloses gain contingencies in the notes only when a high probability exists for realizing them. As a result, it is unusual to find information about contingent gains in the financial statements and the accompanying notes. Illustration 13-8 presents an example of a disclosure gain contingency.

ILLUSTRATION 13-8
Disclosure of Gain
Contingency

BMC Industries, Inc.

Note 13: Legal Matters. In the first quarter, a U.S. District Court in Miami, Florida, awarded the Company a $5.1 million judgment against **Barth Industries** (Barth) of Cleveland, Ohio and its parent, **Nesco Holdings, Inc.** (Nesco). The judgment relates to an agreement under which Barth and Nesco were to help automate the plastic lens production plant in Fort Lauderdale, Florida. The Company has not recorded any income relating to this judgment because Barth and Nesco have filed an appeal.

LOSS CONTINGENCIES

Loss contingencies involve possible losses. A liability incurred as a result of a loss contingency is by definition a contingent liability. **Contingent liabilities** depend on the occurrence of one or more future events to confirm either the amount payable, the payee, the date payable, or its existence. That is, these factors depend on a contingency.

When a loss contingency exists, the likelihood that the future event or events will confirm the incurrence of a liability can range from probable to remote. The FASB uses the terms **probable, reasonably possible**, and **remote** to identify three areas within that range and assigns the following meanings.

Probable. The future event or events are likely to occur.

Reasonably possible. The chance of the future event or events occurring is more than remote but less than likely.

Remote. The chance of the future event or events occurring is slight.

---

[15]"Accounting for Contingencies," *Statement of Financial Accounting Standards No. 5* (Stamford, Conn.: FASB, 1975), par. 1. According to *Accounting Trends and Techniques—2004*, the most common gain contingencies are related to operating loss carryforwards and other tax credits. The most common loss contingencies are related to litigation, environmental, and insurance losses.

Companies should accrue an estimated loss from a loss contingency by a charge to expense and a liability recorded only if **both** of the following conditions are met.[16]

1 Information available prior to the issuance of the financial statements indicates that it is **probable that a liability has been incurred** at the date of the financial statements.

2 The amount of the loss can be **reasonably estimated**.

To record a liability, a company does not need to know the exact payee nor the exact date payable. **What a company must know is whether it is probable that it incurred a liability.**

To meet the second criterion, a company needs to be able to reasonably determine an amount for the liability. To determine a reasonable estimate of the liability, a company may use its own experience, experience of other companies in the industry, engineering or research studies, legal advice, or educated guesses by qualified personnel. Illustration 13-9 shows an accrual recorded for a loss contingency, from the annual report of **Quaker State Oil Refining Company**.

Quaker State Oil Refining Company

Note 5: Contingencies. During the period from November 13 to December 23, a change in an additive component purchased from one of its suppliers caused certain oil refined and shipped to fail to meet the Company's low-temperature performance requirements. The Company has recalled this product and has arranged for reimbursement to its customers and the ultimate consumers of all costs associated with the product. Estimated cost of the recall program, net of estimated third party reimbursement, in the amount of $3,500,000 has been charged to current operations.

ILLUSTRATION 13-9
Disclosure of Accrual for Loss Contingency

Use of the terms probable, reasonably possible, and remote to classify contingencies involves judgment and subjectivity. Illustration 13-10 lists examples of loss contingencies and the general accounting treatment accorded them.

ILLUSTRATION 13-10
Accounting Treatment of Loss Contingencies

Usually Accrued

Loss Related to:

1. Collectibility of receivables
2. Obligations related to product warranties and product defects
3. Premiums offered to customers

Not Accrued

Loss Related to:

4. Risk of loss or damage of enterprise property by fire, explosion, or other hazards
5. General or unspecified business risks
6. Risk of loss from catastrophes assumed by property and casualty insurance companies, including reinsurance companies

May Be Accrued*

Loss Related to:

7. Threat of expropriation of assets
8. Pending or threatened litigation
9. Actual or possible claims and assessments**
10. Guarantees of indebtedness of others
11. Obligations of commercial banks under "standby letters of credit"
12. Agreements to repurchase receivables (or the related property) that have been sold

*Should be accrued when both criteria—probable and reasonably estimable—are met.
**Estimated amounts of losses incurred prior to the balance sheet date but settled subsequently should be accrued as of the balance sheet date.

---

[16]We discuss loss contingencies that result in the incurrence of a liability in this chapter. We discuss loss contingencies that result in the impairment of an asset (e.g., collectibility of receivables or threat of expropriation of assets) in other sections of this textbook.

Practicing accountants express concern over the diversity that now exists in the interpretation of "probable," "reasonably possible," and "remote." Current practice relies heavily on the exact language used in responses received from lawyers (such language is necessarily biased and protective rather than predictive). As a result, accruals and disclosures of contingencies vary considerably in practice. Some of the more common loss contingencies are:[17]

1 Litigation, claims, and assessments.
2 Guarantee and warranty costs.
3 Premiums and coupons.
4 Environmental liabilities.

As discussed in the opening story, companies do not record or report in the notes to the financial statements general risk contingencies inherent in business operations (e.g., the possibility of war, strike, uninsurable catastrophes, or a business recession).

Litigation, Claims, and Assessments

OBJECTIVE 5
Explain the accounting for different types of loss contingencies.

Companies must consider the following factors, among others, in determining whether to record a liability with respect to **pending or threatened** litigation and actual or possible **claims** and **assessments**.

1 The **time period** in which the underlying cause of action occurred.
2 The **probability** of an unfavorable outcome.
3 The ability to make a **reasonable estimate** of the amount of loss.

To report a loss and a liability in the financial statements, **the cause for litigation must have occurred on or before the date of the financial statements**. It does not matter that the company became aware of the existence or possibility of the lawsuit or claims after the date of the financial statements but before issuing them. To evaluate the probability of an unfavorable outcome, a company considers the following: the nature of the litigation; the progress of the case; the opinion of legal counsel; its own and others' experience in similar cases; and any management response to the lawsuit.

Companies can seldom predict the outcome of pending litigation, however, with any assurance. And, even if evidence available at the balance sheet date does not favor the company, it is hardly reasonable to expect the company to publish in its financial statements a dollar estimate of the probable negative outcome. Such specific disclosures might weaken the company's position in the dispute and encourage the plaintiff to intensify its efforts. A typical example of the wording of such a disclosure is the note to the financial statements of **Apple Computer, Inc.**, relating to its litigation concerning repetitive stress injuries, as shown in Illustration 13-11.

ILLUSTRATION 13-11
Disclosure of Litigation

Apple Computer, Inc.

"Repetitive Stress Injury" Litigation. The Company is named in numerous lawsuits (fewer than 100) alleging that the plaintiff incurred so-called "repetitive stress injury" to the upper extremities as a result of using keyboards and/or mouse input devices sold by the Company. On October 4, in a trial of one of these cases (*Dorsey v. Apple*) in the United States District Court for the Eastern District of New York, the jury rendered a verdict in favor of the Company, and final judgment in favor of the Company has been entered. The other cases are in various stages of pretrial activity. These suits are similar to those filed against other major suppliers of personal computers. Ultimate resolution of the litigation against the Company may depend on progress in resolving this type of litigation in the industry overall.

---

[17]*Accounting Trends and Techniques—2004* reports that of the 600 companies surveyed, companies report loss contingencies for the following: litigation, 506; environmental, 245; insurance, 122; governmental investigation, 94; possible tax assessments, 76; and others, 47.

With respect to **unfiled suits** and **unasserted claims and assessments**, a company must determine (1) the degree of **probability** that a suit may be filed or a claim or assessment may be asserted, and (2) the **probability** of an unfavorable outcome. For example, assume that the Federal Trade Commission investigates the Nawtee Company for restraint of trade, and institutes enforcement proceedings. Private claims of triple damages for redress often follow such proceedings. In this case, Nawtee must determine the probability of the claims being asserted **and** the probability of triple damages being awarded. If both are probable, if the loss is reasonably estimable, and if the cause for action is dated on or before the date of the financial statements, then Nawtee should accrue the liability.[18]

Guarantee and Warranty Costs

A **warranty (product guarantee)** is a promise made by a seller to a buyer to make good on a deficiency of quantity, quality, or performance in a product. Manufacturers commonly use it as a sales promotion technique. Automakers, for instance, "hyped" their sales by extending their new-car warranty to seven years or 100,000 miles. For a specified period of time following the date of sale to the consumer, the manufacturer may promise to bear all or part of the cost of replacing defective parts, to perform any necessary repairs or servicing without charge, to refund the purchase price, or even to "double your money back."

Warranties and guarantees entail future costs. These additional costs, sometimes called "after costs" or "post-sale costs," frequently are significant. Although the future cost is indefinite as to amount, due date, and even customer, a liability is probable in most cases. Companies should recognize this liability in the accounts if they can reasonably estimate it. The estimated amount of the liability includes all the costs that the company will incur after sale and delivery and that are incident to the correction of defects or deficiencies required under the warranty provisions. Warranty costs are a classic example of a loss contingency.

Companies use two basic methods of accounting for warranty costs: (1) the cash-basis method and (2) the accrual method.

Cash Basis

Under the **cash-basis method**, companies expense warranty costs as incurred. In other words, a **seller or manufacturer charges warranty costs to the period in which it complies with the warranty**. The company does not record a liability for future costs arising from warranties, nor does it charge the period of sale. Companies frequently justify use of this method, the only one recognized for income tax purposes, on the basis of expediency when warranty costs are immaterial or when the warranty period is relatively short. A company must use the cash-basis method when it does not accrue a warranty liability in the year of sale either because:

1 it is not probable that a liability has been incurred, or

2 it cannot reasonably estimate the amount of the liability.

Accrual Basis

If it is probable that customers will make warranty claims and a company can reasonably estimate the costs involved, the company must use the accrual method. Under the **accrual method**, companies charge warranty costs to operating expense **in the year of sale**. The accrual method is the generally accepted method. Companies should use it whenever the warranty is an integral and inseparable part of the sale and is viewed as a loss contingency. We refer to this approach as the **expense warranty approach**.

---

[18]Companies need not disclose contingencies involving an unasserted claim or assessment when no claimant has come forward unless (1) it is considered probable that a claim will be asserted, and (2) there is a reasonable possibility that the outcome will be unfavorable.

Example of Expense Warranty Approach. To illustrate the expense warranty method, assume that Denson Machinery Company begins production on a new machine in July 2006, and sells 100 units at $5,000 each by its year-end, December 31, 2006. Each machine is under warranty for one year. Denson estimates, based on past experience with a similar machine, that the warranty cost will average $200 per unit. Further, as a result of parts replacements and services rendered in compliance with machinery warranties, it incurs $4,000 in warranty costs in 2006 and $16,000 in 2007.

1 Sale of 100 machines at $5,000 each, July through December 2006:

Cash or Accounts Receivable	500,000	
Sales		500,000

2 Recognition of warranty expense, July through December 2006:

Warranty Expense	4,000	
Cash, Inventory, Accrued Payroll		4,000
(Warranty costs incurred)		
Warranty Expense	16,000	
Estimated Liability under Warranties		16,000
(To accrue estimated warranty costs)		

The December 31, 2006, balance sheet reports "Estimated liability under warranties" as a current liability of $16,000, and the income statement for 2006 reports "Warranty expense" of $20,000.

3 Recognition of warranty costs incurred in 2007 (on 2006 machinery sales):

Estimated Liability under Warranties	16,000	
Cash, Inventory, or Accrued Payroll		16,000
(Warranty costs incurred)		

If Denson Machinery applies the cash-basis method, it reports $4,000 as warranty expense in 2006 and $16,000 as warranty expense in 2007. It records all of the sale price as revenue in 2006. In many instances, application of the cash-basis method fails to match the warranty costs relating to the products sold during a given period with the revenues derived from such products. As such, **it violates the matching principle**. Where ongoing warranty policies exist year after year, the differences between the cash and the expense warranty bases probably would not be so great.

Sales-Warranty Approach. A warranty is sometimes **sold separately from the product**. For example, when you purchase a television set or DVD player, you are entitled to the manufacturer's warranty. You also will undoubtedly be offered an extended warranty on the product at an additional cost.[19]

In this case, the seller should recognize separately the sale of the television or DVD player, with the manufacturer's warranty and the sale of the extended warranty.[20] This approach is referred to as the **sales-warranty approach**. **Companies defer revenue on the sale of the extended warranty** and generally recognize it on a straight-line basis over the life of the contract. The seller of the warranty defers revenue because it has an obligation to perform services over the life of the contract. The seller should only defer and amortize costs that vary with and are directly related to the sale of the contracts (mainly commissions). It expenses those costs, such as employees' salaries, advertising, and general and administrative expenses that it would have incurred even if it did not sell a contract.

---

[19]A company separately prices a contract **if the customer has the option to purchase the services provided under the contract for an expressly stated amount separate from the price of the product. An extended warranty or product maintenance contract usually meets these conditions.

[20]"Accounting for Separately Extended Warranty and Product Maintenance Contracts," *FASB Technical Bulletin No. 90–1* (Stamford, Conn.: FASB, 1990).

To illustrate, assume you purchase a new automobile from Hanlin Auto for $20,000. In addition to the regular warranty on the auto (the manufacturer will pay for all repairs for the first 36,000 miles or three years, whichever comes first), you purchase at a cost of $600 an extended warranty that protects you for an additional three years or 36,000 miles. Hanlin Auto records the sale of the automobile (with the regular warranty) and the sale of the extended warranty on January 2, 2006, as follows:

Cash	20,600	
Sales		20,000
Unearned Warranty Revenue		600

It recognizes revenue at the end of the fourth year (using straight-line amortization) as follows.

Unearned Warranty Revenue	200	
Warranty Revenue		200

Because the extended warranty contract only starts after the regular warranty expires, Hanlin Auto defers revenue recognition until the fourth year. If it incurs the costs of performing services under the extended warranty contract on other than a straight-line basis (as historical evidence might indicate), Hanlin Auto should recognize revenue over the contract period in proportion to the costs it expected to incur in performing services under the contract.[21]

Premiums and Coupons

Numerous companies offer premiums (either on a limited or continuing basis) to customers in return for boxtops, certificates, coupons, labels, or wrappers. The **premium** may be silverware, dishes, a small appliance, a toy, or free transportation. Also, **printed coupons** that can be redeemed for a cash discount on items purchased are extremely popular.[22] A more recent marketing innovation is the **cash rebate**, which the buyer can obtain by returning the store receipt, a rebate coupon, and Universal Product Code (UPC label) or "bar code" to the manufacturer.

Companies offer premiums, coupon offers, and rebates to stimulate sales. Thus companies should charge the **costs of premiums and coupons to expense in the period of the sale** that benefits from the plan. The period that benefits is not necessarily the period in which the company offered the premium. At the end of the accounting period many premium offers may be outstanding and must be redeemed when presented in subsequent periods. In order to reflect the existing current liability and to match costs with revenues, the company estimates the number of outstanding premium offers that customers will present for redemption. The company then charges the cost of premium offers to Premium Expense. It credits the outstanding obligations to an account titled Estimated Liability for Premiums.

The following example illustrates the accounting treatment for a premium offer. Fluffy Cakemix Company offered its customers a large nonbreakable mixing bowl in exchange for 25 cents and 10 boxtops. The mixing bowl costs Fluffy Cakemix Company 75 cents, and the company estimates that customers will redeem 60 percent of

UNDERLYING CONCEPTS

Warranties and coupons are loss contingencies that satisfy the conditions necessary for a liability. Regarding the income statement, the *matching principle* requires that companies report the related expense in the period in which the sale occurs.

---

[21]Ibid, par. 3. The FASB recently issued additional disclosure requirements for warranties. A company must disclose its accounting policy and the method used to determine its warranty liability, and must present a tabular reconciliation of the changes in the product warranty liability. *FASB Interpretation No. 45*, "Guarantor's Accounting and Disclosure Requirements for Guarantees, Including Indirect Guarantees of Indebtedness of Others" (Norwalk, Conn.: FASB, 2002).

[22]Approximately 4 percent of coupons are redeemed. Redeemed coupons eventually make their way to the corporate headquarters of the stores that accept them. From there they are shipped to clearinghouses operated by **A. C. Nielsen Company** (of TV-rating fame) that count them and report back to the manufacturers who, in turn, reimburse the stores.

the boxtops. The premium offer began in June 2007 and resulted in the transactions journalized below. Fluffy Cakemix Company records purchase of 20,000 mixing bowls at 75 cents as follows.

Inventory of Premium Mixing Bowls	15,000	
Cash		15,000

The entry to record sales of 300,000 boxes of cake mix at 80 cents would be:

Cash	240,000	
Sales		240,000

Fluffy records the actual redemption of 60,000 boxtops, the receipt of 25 cents per 10 boxtops, and the delivery of the mixing bowls as follows.

Cash [(60,000 ÷ 10) × $0.25]	1,500	
Premium Expense	3,000	
Inventory of Premium Mixing Bowls		4,500
Computation: (60,000 ÷ 10) × $0.75 = $4,500		

Finally, Fluffy makes an end-of-period adjusting entry for estimated liability for outstanding premium offers (boxtops) as follows.

Premium Expense	6,000	
Estimated Liability for Premiums		6,000

Computation:

Total boxtops sold in 2007		300,000
Total estimated redemptions (60%)		180,000
Boxtops redeemed in 2007		60,000
Estimated future redemptions		120,000

Cost of estimated claims outstanding
(120,000 ÷ 10) × ($0.75 − $0.25) = $6,000

The December 31, 2007, balance sheet of Fluffy Cakemix Company reports an "Inventory of premium mixing bowls" of $10,500 as a current asset and "Estimated liability for premiums" of $6,000 as a current liability. The 2007 income statement reports a $9,000 "Premium expense" among the selling expenses.

FREQUENT FLYERS

WHAT DO THE NUMBERS MEAN?

Numerous companies offer premiums to customers in the form of a promise of future goods or services as an incentive for purchases today. Premium plans that have widespread adoption are the frequent-flyer programs used by all major airlines. On the basis of mileage accumulated, frequent-flyer members receive discounted or free airline tickets. Airline customers can earn miles toward free travel by making long-distance phone calls, staying in hotels, and charging gasoline and groceries on a credit card. Those free tickets represent an enormous potential liability because people using them may displace paying passengers.

When airlines first started offering frequent-flyer bonuses, everyone assumed that they could accommodate the free-ticket holders with otherwise-empty seats. That made the additional cost of the program so minimal that airlines didn't accrue it or report the small liability. But, as more and more paying passengers have been crowded off flights by frequent-flyer awardees, the loss of revenues has grown enormously. For example, **United Airlines** at one time reported a liability of $1.4 billion for advance ticket sales, some of which pertains to free frequent-flyer tickets.

Although the profession has studied the accounting for this transaction, no authoritative guidelines have been issued.

Environmental Liabilities

Estimates to clean up existing toxic waste sites total upward of $752 billion over a 30-year period. In addition, cost estimates of cleaning up our air and preventing future deterioration of the environment run even higher. The average environmental cost per company for various industries at one time was: high-tech companies, $2 million (6.1% of revenues); utilities, $340 million (6.1% of revenues); steel and metals, $50 million (2.9% of revenues), and oil companies, $430 million (1.9% of revenues).

These costs will only grow when considering "Superfund legislation." This federal legislation provides the Environmental Protection Agency (EPA) with the power to clean up waste sites and charge the clean-up costs to parties the EPA deems responsible for contaminating the site. These potentially responsible parties can have a significant liability.

In many industries, the construction and operation of long-lived assets involves obligations for the retirement of those assets. When a mining company opens up a strip mine, it may also commit to restore the land once it completes mining. Similarly, when an oil company erects an offshore drilling platform, it may be legally obligated to dismantle and remove the platform at the end of its useful life.

Accounting Recognition of Asset Retirement Obligations

A company must recognize an **asset retirement obligation (ARO)** when it has an existing legal obligation associated with the retirement of a long-lived asset and when it can reasonably estimate the amount of the liability. Companies should record the ARO at fair value.[23]

Obligating Events. Examples of existing legal obligations, which require recognition of a liability include, but are not limited to:

- decommissioning nuclear facilities,
- dismantling, restoring, and reclamation of oil and gas properties,
- certain closure, reclamation, and removal costs of mining facilities,
- closure and post-closure costs of landfills.

In order to capture the benefits of these long-lived assets, **the company is generally legally obligated for the costs associated with retirement of the asset, whether the company hires another party to perform the retirement activities or performs the activities with its own workforce and equipment**. AROs give rise to various recognition patterns. For example, the obligation may arise at the outset of the asset's use (e.g., erection of an oil-rig), or it may build over time (e.g., a landfill that expands over time).

Measurement. A company initially measures an ARO at fair value, which is defined as the amount that the company would pay in an active market to settle the ARO. While active markets do not exist for many AROs, companies should estimate fair value based on the best information available. Such information could include market prices of similar liabilities, if available. Alternatively, companies may use present value techniques to estimate fair value.

Recognition and Allocation. To record an ARO in the financial statements, a company includes the cost associated with the ARO in the carrying amount of the related long-lived asset, and records a liability for the same amount. It records an asset retirement cost as part of the related asset because these costs are tied to operating the asset and are necessary to prepare the asset for its intended use. Therefore, the specific asset (e.g., mine, drilling platform, nuclear power plant) should be increased because the future economic benefit comes from the use of this productive asset. **Companies should not**

---

[23]"Accounting for Asset Retirement Obligations," *Statement of Financial Accounting Standards No. 143* (Norwalk, Conn.: FASB, 2001).

record the capitalized asset retirement costs in a separate account because there is no future economic benefit that can be associated with these costs alone.

In subsequent periods, companies allocate the cost of the ARO to expense over the period of the related asset's useful life. Companies may use the straight-line method for this allocation, as well as other systematic and rational allocations.

Example of ARO Accounting Provisions. To illustrate the accounting for AROs, assume that on January 1, 2006, Wildcat Oil Company erected an oil platform in the Gulf of Mexico. Wildcat is legally required to dismantle and remove the platform at the end of its useful life, estimated to be five years. Wildcat estimates that dismantling and removal will cost $1,000,000. Based on a 10 percent discount rate, the present value of the asset retirement obligation is $620,920 ($1,000,000 × .62092). Wildcat records this ARO as follows.

January 1, 2006

Drilling Platform	620,920	
Asset Retirement Obligation		620,920

During the life of the asset, Wildcat allocates the asset retirement cost to expense. Using the straight-line method, Wildcat makes the following entries to record this expense.

December 31, 2006, 2007, 2008, 2009, 2010

Depreciation Expense ($620,920 ÷ 5)	124,184	
Accumulated Depreciation		124,184

In addition, Wildcat must accrue interest expense each period. Wildcat records interest expense and the related increase in the asset retirement obligation on December 31, 2006, as follows.

December 31, 2006

Interest Expense ($620,920 × 10%)	62,092	
Asset Retirement Obligation		62,092

On January 10, 2011, Wildcat contracts with Rig Reclaimers, Inc. to dismantle the platform at a contract price of $995,000. Wildcat makes the following journal entry to record settlement of the ARO.

January 10, 2011

Asset Retirement Obligation	1,000,000	
Gain on Settlement of ARO		5,000
Cash		995,000

Companies need to provide more extensive disclosure regarding environmental liabilities. In addition, companies should record more of these liabilities. The SEC believes that companies should not delay recognition of a liability due to significant uncertainty. The SEC argues that if the liability is within a range, and no amount within the range is the best estimate, then management should recognize the minimum amount of the range. That treatment is in accordance with *FASB Interpretation No. 14,* "Reasonable Estimation of the Amount of a Loss." The SEC also believes that companies should report environmental liabilities in the balance sheet independent of recoveries from third parties. Thus, companies may not net possible insurance recoveries against liabilities but must show them separately. Because there is much litigation regarding recovery of insurance proceeds, these "assets" appear to be gain contingencies. Therefore, companies should not be report these on the balance sheet.[24]

---

[24]As we indicated earlier, the FASB requires that, when some amount within the range appears at the time to be a better estimate than any other amount within the range, a company accrues that amount. When no amount within the range is a better estimate than any other amount, the company **accrues** the dollar amount at the low end of the range and **discloses** the dollar amount at the high end of the range. Unfortunately, in many cases, zero may arguably be the low point of the range, resulting in no liability being recognized. See *FASB Interpretation No. 14,* "Reasonable Estimation of the Amount of a Loss" (Stamford, Conn.: FASB, 1976), par. 3, and *FASB Statement No. 5,* "Accounting for Contingencies" (Stamford, Conn.: FASB, 1975).

MORE DISCLOSURE PLEASE

On November 19, 2001, Enron filed its third-quarter financial statements and reported on its balance sheet debt of approximately $13 billion. Yet on the same day, at a meeting to discuss its liquidity crisis, Enron informed its bankers that its debt was approximately $38 billion. Company officers described the difference of $25 billion as being either off-balance-sheet or on the balance sheet other than debt.

WHAT DO THE NUMBERS MEAN?

As a result of the Enron bankruptcy and other financial reporting scandals, Congress passed the Sarbanes-Oxley Act of 2002. One of its provisions mandates that the Securities and Exchange Commission conduct a study to determine the extent of off-balance-sheet transactions occurring in U.S. businesses.

Table 1 below indicates the extent of disclosure and recognition of contingent liabilities. The study classified contingent liabilities into three categories (1) litigation contingent liabilities, (2) environmental liabilities, and (3) guarantees. The statistics provided relate to reports filed by 10,100 companies listed on the U.S. stock exchanges in 2005.

Table 1

Type of Contingency	Companies Disclosing	Companies Recording
Litigation contingent liabilities	46.3%	5.1%
Environmental contingent liabilities	10.2%	5.1%
Guarantees	35.4%	10.2%

As Table 1 indicates, approximately 46 percent of companies disclosed litigation contingent liabilities, but only 5.1 percent recorded any liability related to these contingencies. On the other hand, 35 percent of the companies disclosed guarantees but a third of these companies (10.2 percent) recorded a liability for these contingencies.

Table 2 below shows the dollar amounts of the contingent liabilities companies disclosed and recorded.

Table 2

Type of Contingency	Companies Disclosing ($ millions)	Companies Recording ($ millions)
Litigation contingent liabilities	$52,354	$11,814
Environmental contingent liabilities	$23,414	$18,723
Guarantees	$46,535,399	$123,949

Table 2 indicates that companies disclosed litigation contingent liabilities of approximately $52 billion, but recorded only $11.8 billion as liabilities. Incredibly, companies disclosed more than $46 *trillion* of guarantees, a small fraction of which (just $124 billion) they recorded as liabilities.

The results of this study suggest that the FASB must continue to address the issue of contingencies to ensure that companies provide relevant and reliable information for these types of financial events.

Source: "Report and Recommendations Pursuant to Section 401(c) of the Sarbanes-Oxley Act of 2002 on Arrangements with Off-Balance Sheet Implications, Special Purpose Entities, and Transparency of Filings by Issuers," United States Securities and Exchange Commission, Office of Chief Accountant, Office of Economic Analyses, Division of Corporation Finance (June 2005).

Self-Insurance

As discussed earlier, contingencies are not recorded for general risks (e.g., losses that might arise due to poor expected economic conditions.) Similarly, companies do not record contingencies for more specific future risks such as allowances for repairs. The reason: These items do meet the definition of a liability because they do not arise from a past transaction but instead relate to future events.

Some companies take out insurance policies against the potential losses from fire, flood, storm, and accident. Other companies do not. The reasons: Some risks are not

UNDERLYING CONCEPTS

Even if companies can estimate the amount of losses with a high degree of certainty, the losses are not liabilities because they result from a future event and not from a past event.

insurable, the insurance rates are prohibitive (e.g., earthquakes and riots), or they make a business decision to self-insure. Self-insurance is another item that is not recognized as a contingency.

Despite its name, **self-insurance** is **not insurance**, **but risk assumption**. Any company that assumes its own risks puts itself in the position of incurring expenses or losses as they occur. There is little theoretical justification for the establishment of a liability based on a hypothetical charge to insurance expense. This is "as if" accounting. The conditions for accrual stated in *FASB Statement No. 5* are not satisfied prior to the occurrence of the event. Until that time there is no diminution in the value of the property. And unlike an insurance company, which has contractual obligations to reimburse policyholders for losses, a company can have no such obligation to itself and, hence, no liability either before or after the occurrence of damage.[25]

The note shown in Illustration 13-12 from the annual report of **Adolph Coors Company** is typical of the self-insurance disclosure.

ILLUSTRATION 13-12
Disclosure of Self-Insurance

Adolph Coors Company

Notes to Financial Statements

Note 4:   Commitments and Contingencies.   It is generally the policy of the Company to act as a self-insurer for certain insurable risks consisting primarily of physical loss to corporate property, business interruption resulting from such loss, employee health insurance programs, and workers' compensation. Losses and claims are accrued as incurred.

Exposure to **risks of loss resulting from uninsured past injury to others**, however, is an existing condition involving uncertainty about the amount and timing of losses that may develop. In such a case, a contingency exists. A company with a fleet of vehicles for example, would have to accrue uninsured losses resulting from injury to others or damage to the property of others that took place prior to the date of the financial statements (if the experience of the company or other information enables it to make a reasonable estimate of the liability). However, it should not establish a liability for **expected future injury** to others or damage to the property of others, even if it can reasonably estimate the amount of losses.

SECTION 3	*PRESENTATION AND ANALYSIS*

Presentation of Current Liabilities

OBJECTIVE 6
Indicate how to present and analyze liabilities and contingencies.

In practice, current liabilities are usually recorded and reported in financial statements at their full maturity value. Because of the short time periods involved, frequently less than one year, the difference between the present value of a current liability and the maturity value is usually not large. The profession accepts as immaterial any slight overstatement of liabilities that results from carrying current liabilities at maturity value.[26]

---

[25]"Accounting for Contingencies," *FASB Statement No. 5*, op. cit., par. 28. A commentary in *Forbes* (June 15, 1974), p. 42, stated its position on this matter quite succinctly: "The simple and unquestionable fact of life is this: Business is cyclical and full of unexpected surprises. Is it the role of accounting to disguise this unpleasant fact and create a fairyland of smoothly rising earnings? Or, should accounting reflect reality, warts and all—floods, expropriations and all manner of rude shocks?"

[26]"Interest on Receivables and Payables," *Opinions of the Accounting Principles Board No. 21* (New York: AICPA, 1971), par. 3. *APB Opinion No. 21* specifically exempts from present value measurements those payables arising from transactions with suppliers in the normal course of business that do not exceed approximately one year.

The current liabilities accounts are commonly presented as the first classification in the liabilities and stockholders' equity section of the balance sheet. Within the current liabilities section, companies may list the accounts in order of maturity, in descending order of amount, or in order of liquidation preference. Illustration 13-13 presents an excerpt of **Best Buy Company**'s financial statements that is representative of the reports of large corporations.

Best Buy Co. (dollars in thousands)	Feb. 26, 2005	Feb. 28, 2004
Current assets		
Cash and cash equivalents	$ 470	$ 245
Short-term investments	2,878	2,355
Receivables	375	343
Merchandise inventories	2,851	2,607
Other current assets	329	174
Total current assets	$6,903	$5,724
Current liabilities		
Accounts payable	$2,824	$2,460
Unredeemed gift card liabilities	410	300
Accrued compensation and related expenses	234	269
Accrued liabilities	844	724
Accrued income taxes	575	380
Current portion of long-term debt	72	368
Total current liabilities	$4,959	$4,501

ILLUSTRATION 13-13
Balance Sheet
Presentation of Current
Liabilities

*Additional Disclosures of
Current Liabilities*

Detail and supplemental information concerning current liabilities should be sufficient to meet the requirement of full disclosure. Companies should clearly identify secured liabilities, as well as indicate the related assets pledged as collateral. If the due date of any liability can be extended, a company should disclose the details. Companies should not offset current liabilities against assets that it will apply to their liquidation. Finally, current maturities of long-term debt are classified as current liabilities.

A major exception exists when a company will pay a currently maturing obligation from assets classified as long-term. For example, if a company will retire a bond payable using a bond sinking fund that is classified as a long-term asset, it should report the bonds payable in the long-term liabilities section. Presentation of this debt in the current liabilities section would distort the working capital position of the enterprise.

If a company excludes a short-term obligation from current liabilities because of refinancing, it should include the following in the note to the financial statements:

1 A general description of the financing agreement.
2 The terms of any new obligation incurred or to be incurred.
3 The terms of any equity security issued or to be issued.

When a company expects to refinance on a long-term basis by issuing equity securities, it is not appropriate to include the short-term obligation in stockholders' equity. At the date of the balance sheet, the obligation is a liability and not stockholders' equity. Illustration 13-14 (on page 644) shows the disclosure requirements for an actual refinancing situation.

ILLUSTRATION 13-14
Actual Refinancing of
Short-Term Debt

	December 31, 2006
Current liabilities	
Accounts payable	$ 3,600,000
Accrued payables	2,500,000
Income taxes payable	1,100,000
Current portion of long-term debt	1,000,000
Total current liabilities	$ 8,200,000
Long-term debt	
Notes payable refinanced in January 2007 (Note 1)	$ 2,000,000
11% bonds due serially through 2017	15,000,000
Total long-term debt	$17,000,000

Note 1: On January 19, 2007, the Company issued 50,000 shares of common stock and received proceeds totaling $2,385,000, of which $2,000,000 was used to liquidate notes payable that matured on February 1, 2007. Accordingly, such notes payable have been classified as long-term debt at December 31, 2006.

Presentation of Contingencies

Additional Disclosures of Contingencies

A company records a loss contingency and a liability if the loss is both probable and estimable. But, if the loss is **either probable or estimable but not both**, and if there is at least a **reasonable possibility** that a company may have incurred a liability, it must disclose the following in the notes.

1 The nature of the contingency.

2 An estimate of the possible loss or range of loss or a statement that an estimate cannot be made.

Illustration 13-15 presents an extensive litigation disclosure note from the financial statements of **Raymark Corporation**. The note indicates that Raymark charged actual losses to operations and that a further liability may exist, but that the company cannot currently estimate this liability.

ILLUSTRATION 13-15
Disclosure of Loss
Contingency through
Litigation

Raymark Corporation

Note I: Litigation.   Raymark is a defendant or co-defendant in a substantial number of lawsuits alleging wrongful injury and/or death from exposure to asbestos fibers in the air. The following table summarizes the activity in these lawsuits:

Claims	
Pending at beginning of year	8,719
Received during year	4,494
Settled or otherwise disposed of	(1,445)
Pending at end of year	11,768
Average indemnification cost	$3,364
Average cost per case, including defense costs	$6,499
Trial activity	
Verdicts for the Company	23
Total trials	36

The following table presents the cost of defending asbestos litigation, together with related insurance and workers' compensation expenses.

Included in operating profit	$ 1,872,000
Nonoperating expense	9,077,000
Total	$10,949,000

The Company is seeking to reasonably determine its liability. However, it is not possible to predict which theory of insurance will apply, the number of lawsuits still to be filed, the cost of settling and defending the existing and unfiled cases, or the ultimate impact of these lawsuits on the Company's consolidated financial statements.

Companies should disclose certain other contingent liabilities, even though the possibility of loss may be remote, as follows.

1 Guarantees of indebtedness of others.

2 Obligations of commercial banks under "stand-by letters of credit."

3 Guarantees to repurchase receivables (or any related property) that have been sold or assigned.

Disclosure should include the nature and amount of the guarantee and, if estimable, the amount that the company can recover from outside parties.[27] **Cities Service Company** disclosed its guarantees of others' indebtedness in the following note.

INTERNATIONAL INSIGHT

U.S. GAAP provides more guidance on the content of disclosures about contingencies than do IFRS.

Cities Service Company

Note 10: Contingent Liabilities. The Company and certain subsidiaries have guaranteed debt obligations of approximately $62 million of companies in which substantial stock investments are held. Also, under long-term agreements with certain pipeline companies in which stock interests are held, the Company and its subsidiaries have agreed to provide minimum revenue for product shipments. The Company has guaranteed mortgage debt ($80 million) incurred by a 50 percent owned tanker affiliate for construction of tankers which are under long-term charter contracts to the Company and others. It is not anticipated that any loss will result from any of the above described agreements.

ILLUSTRATION 13-16
Disclosure of Guarantees
of Indebtedness

Analysis of Current Liabilities

The distinction between current liabilities and long-term debt is important. It provides information about the liquidity of the company. Liquidity regarding a liability is the expected time to elapse before its payment. In other words, a liability soon to be paid is a current liability. A liquid company is better able to withstand a financial downturn. Also, it has a better chance of taking advantage of investment opportunities that develop.

Analysts use certain basic ratios such as net cash flow provided by operating activities to current liabilities, and the turnover ratios for receivables and inventory, to assess liquidity. Two other ratios used to examine liquidity are the current ratio and the acid-test ratio.

Current Ratio

The **current ratio** is the ratio of total current assets to total current liabilities. Illustration 13-17 shows its formula.

$$\text{Current ratio} = \frac{\text{Current assets}}{\text{Current liabilities}}$$

ILLUSTRATION 13-17
Formula for Current
Ratio

The ratio is frequently expressed as a coverage of so many times. Sometimes it is called the **working capital ratio** because working capital is the excess of current assets over current liabilities.

---

[27]As discussed earlier (footnote 21), the FASB recently issued additional disclosure and recognition requirements for guarantees. The interpretation responds to confusion about the application of *SFAS No. 5* to guarantees used in certain transactions. The new rules expand existing disclosure requirements for most guarantees, including loan guarantees such as standby letters of credit. It also will result in companies recognizing more liabilities at fair value for the obligations assumed under a guarantee (*FASB Interpretation No. 45*, op. cit.).

A satisfactory current ratio does not disclose that a portion of the current assets may be tied up in slow-moving inventories. With inventories, especially raw materials and work in process, there is a question of how long it will take to transform them into the finished product and what ultimately will be realized in the sale of the merchandise. Eliminating the inventories, along with any prepaid expenses, from the amount of current assets might provide better information for short-term creditors. Therefore, some analysts use the acid-test ratio in place of the current ratio.

Acid-Test Ratio

Many analysts favor an **acid-test** or **quick ratio** that relates total current liabilities to cash, marketable securities, and receivables. Illustration 13-18 shows the formula for this ratio. As you can see, the acid-test ratio does not include inventories.

ILLUSTRATION 13-18
Formula for Acid-Test Ratio

$$\text{Acid-test ratio} = \frac{\text{Cash} + \text{Short-term investments} + \text{Net receivables}}{\text{Current liabilities}}$$

To illustrate the computation of these two ratios, we use the information for **Best Buy Co.** in Illustration 13-13 (on page 643). Illustration 13-19 shows the computation of the current and acid-test ratios for Best Buy.

ILLUSTRATION 13-19
Computation of Current and Acid-Test Ratios for Best Buy Co.

$$\text{Current ratio} = \frac{\text{Current assets}}{\text{Current liabilities}} = \frac{\$6,903}{\$4,959} = 1.39 \text{ times}$$

$$\text{Acid-test ratio} = \frac{\text{Cash} + \text{Short-term investments} + \text{Net receivables}}{\text{Current liabilities}} = \frac{\$3,723}{\$4,959} = 0.75 \text{ times}$$

From this information, it appears that Best Buy's current position is adequate. However, the acid-test ratio is well below 1. A comparison to another retailer, **Circuit City**, whose current ratio is 2.13 and whose acid-test ratio is 0.75, indicates that Best Buy is carrying less inventory than its industry counterparts.

KEY TERMS

accumulated rights, *630*

acid-test (quick) ratio, *646*

assessments, *634*

asset retirement obligation, *639*

bonus, *631*

cash dividend payable, *624*

claims, *634*

compensated absences, *629*

contingency, *632*

contingent liabilities, *632*

current liabilities, *619*

current maturities of long-term debt, *621*

current ratio, *645*

SUMMARY OF LEARNING OBJECTIVES

1. **Describe the nature, type, and valuation of current liabilities.** Current liabilities are obligations whose liquidation a company reasonably expects to require the use of current assets or the creation of other current liabilities. Theoretically, liabilities should be measured by the present value of the future outlay of cash required to liquidate them. In practice, companies usually record and report current liabilities at their full maturity value.

There are several types of current liabilities, such as: (1) accounts payable, (2) notes payable, (3) current maturities of long-term debt, (4) dividends payable, (5) customer advances and deposits, (6) unearned revenues, (7) taxes payable, and (8) employee-related liabilities.

2. **Explain the classification issues of short-term debt expected to be refinanced.** A short-term obligation is excluded from current liabilities if both of the following conditions are met: (1) the company must intend to refinance the obligation on a long-term basis, *and* (2) it must demonstrate an ability to consummate the refinancing.

3. **Identify types of employee-related liabilities.** The employee-related liabilities are: (1) payroll deductions, (2) compensated absences, and (3) bonus agreements.

4. **Identify the criteria used to account for and disclose gain and loss contingencies.** Gain contingencies are not recorded. Instead, they are disclosed in the notes only when the probabilities are high that a gain contingency will occur. A company should accrue an estimated loss from a loss contingency by charging expense and recording a liability only if *both* of the following conditions are met: (1) Information available prior to the issuance of the financial statements indicates that it is probable that a liability has been incurred at the date of the financial statements, and (2) the amount of the loss can be reasonably estimated.

5. **Explain the accounting for different types of loss contingencies.** The following factors must be considered in determining whether to record a liability with respect to pending or threatened litigation and actual or possible claims and assessments: (1) the time period in which the underlying cause for action occurred; (2) the probability of an unfavorable outcome; and (3) the ability to reasonably estimate the amount of loss.

If it is probable that customers will make claims under warranties relating to goods or services that have been sold and it can reasonably estimate the costs involved, the company uses the accrual method. It charges warranty costs under the accrual basis to operating expense in the year of sale.

Premiums, coupon offers, and rebates are made to stimulate sales. Companies should charge their costs to expense in the period of the sale that benefits from the premium plan.

A company must recognize asset retirement obligations when it has an existing legal obligation related to the retirement of a long-lived asset and it can reasonably estimate the amount.

6. **Indicate how to present and analyze liabilities and contingencies.** The current liability accounts are usually presented as the first classification in the liabilities and stockholders' equity section of the balance sheet. Within the current liabilities section, companies may list the accounts in order of maturity, in descending order of amount, or in order of liquidation preference. Detail and supplemental information concerning current liabilities should be sufficient to meet the requirement of full disclosure. If the loss is either probable or estimable but not both, and if there is at least a reasonable possibility that a company may have incurred a liability, it should disclose in the notes both the nature of the contingency and an estimate of the possible loss. Two ratios used to analyze liquidity are the current and acid-test ratios.

APPENDIX 13A

Computation of Employees' Bonuses

Computing the amount of employee bonus based on income can be complex. For example, assume that Senbet Company has income of $100,000 before considering the bonus expense. According to the terms of the bonus agreement, Senbet is to set aside 20 percent of its income for distribution to employees. If the bonus were not itself an expense to be deducted in determining net income, the amount of the bonus could be computed very simply as 20 percent of the $100,000 income before bonus.

> **OBJECTIVE 7**
> Compute employee bonuses under differing arrangements.

However, the bonus itself is an expense that Senbet must deduct to determine the amount of income on which the bonus is to be based. Hence, the figure on which the bonus is to be computed is $100,000 reduced by the bonus. That is, the bonus is equal to 20 percent of $100,000 less the bonus. Stated algebraically:

$$B = 0.20\ (\$100,000 - B)$$
$$B = \$20,000 - 0.2B$$
$$1.2B = \$20,000$$
$$B = \$16,666.67$$

A similar problem results from the relationship of bonus payments to income taxes. Again, assume income of $100,000 computed without subtracting either the employees' bonus or income taxes. The bonus is to be based on income **after deducting income taxes but before deducting the bonus**. The rate of income tax is 40 percent, and the 20 percent bonus is a deductible expense for tax purposes. The bonus therefore equals 20 percent of $100,000 minus the tax; the tax equals 40 percent of $100,000 minus the bonus. Thus we have two simultaneous equations. By using B as the symbol for the bonus and T for the tax, we can state the equations algebraically as follows.

$$B = 0.20(\$100,000 - T)$$
$$T = 0.40\ (\$100,000 - B)$$

We can solve these equations by substituting the value of T as indicated in the second equation for T in the first equation:

$$B = 0.20[\$100,000 - 0.40(\$100,000 - B)]$$
$$B = 0.20(\$100,000 - \$40,000 + 0.4B)$$
$$B = 0.20(\$60,000 + 0.4B)$$
$$B = \$12,000 + 0.08B$$
$$0.92B = \$12,000$$
$$B = \$13,043.48$$

Substituting this value for B into the second equation allows us to solve for T:

$$T = 0.40\ (\$100,000 - \$13,043.48)$$
$$T = 0.40\ (\$86,956.52)$$
$$T = \$34,782.61$$

To prove these amounts, we work both back into the original equation:

$$B = 0.20\ (\$100,000 - T)$$
$$\$13,043.48 = 0.20\ (\$100,000 - \$34,782.61)$$
$$\$13,043.48 = 0.20\ (\$65,217.39)$$
$$\$13,043.48 = \$13,043.48$$

If the terms of the agreement provide for deducting both the tax and the bonus to arrive at the income figure on which to compute the bonus, the equations would be:

$$B = 0.20\ (\$100,000 - B - T)$$
$$T = 0.40\ (\$100,000 - B)$$

Substituting the value of T from the second equation into the first equation enables us to solve for B:

$$B = 0.20\ [\$100,000 - B - 0.40\ (\$100,000 - B)]$$
$$B = 0.20\ (\$100,000 - B - \$40,000 + 0.4B)$$
$$B = 0.20\ (\$60,000 - 0.6B)$$
$$B = \$12,000 - 0.12B$$
$$1.12B = \$12,000$$
$$B = \$10,714.29$$

We then substitute the value for B into the second equation above, and solve that equation for T:

$$T = 0.40\ (\$100,000 - \$10,714.29)$$
$$T = 0.40\ (\$89,285.71)$$
$$T = \$35,714.28$$

If we then substitute these values into the original bonus equation, we prove them as follows.

$$B = 0.20\ (\$100{,}000 - B - T)$$
$$\$10{,}714.29 = 0.20\ (\$100{,}000 - \$10{,}714.29 - \$35{,}714.28)$$
$$\$10{,}714.29 = 0.20\ (\$53{,}571.43)$$
$$\$10{,}714.29 = \$10{,}714.29$$

Drawing up a legal document such as a bonus agreement is a task for a lawyer, not an accountant. However, accountants are frequently called on to express an opinion on the agreement's feasibility. In this respect, one should always insist that the agreement state specifically whether income taxes and the bonus itself are expenses deductible in determining income for purposes of the bonus computation.

SUMMARY OF LEARNING OBJECTIVE FOR APPENDIX 13A

7. Compute employee bonuses under differing arrangements. If the bonus is based on net income and is deductible in determining net income, it may have to be determined algebraically. Its computation is made more difficult by the bonus being deductible for tax purposes and the taxes being deductible from the income on which the bonus is based.

Note: All **asterisked** Brief Exercises, Exercises, and Problems relate to material contained in the appendix to the chapter.

QUESTIONS

1. Distinguish between a current liability and a long-term debt.

2. Assume that your friend Greg Jonas, who is a music major, asks you to define and discuss the nature of a liability. Assist him by preparing a definition of a liability and by explaining to him what you believe are the elements or factors inherent in the concept of a liability.

3. Why is the liabilities section of the balance sheet of primary significance to bankers?

4. How are current liabilities related by definition to current assets? How are current liabilities related to a company's operating cycle?

5. Jon Bryant, a newly hired loan analyst, is examining the current liabilities of a corporate loan applicant. He observes that unearned revenues have declined in the current year compared to the prior year. Is this a positive indicator about the client's liquidity? Explain.

6. How is present value related to the concept of a liability?

7. What is the nature of a "discount" on notes payable?

8. How should a debt callable by the creditor be reported in the debtor's financial statements?

9. Under what conditions should a short-term obligation be excluded from current liabilities?

10. What evidence is necessary to demonstrate the ability to consummate the refinancing of short-term debt?

11. Discuss the accounting treatment or disclosure that should be accorded a declared but unpaid cash dividend; an accumulated but undeclared dividend on cumulative preferred stock; a stock dividend distributable.

12. How does unearned revenue arise? Why can it be classified properly as a current liability? Give several examples of business activities that result in unearned revenues.

13. What are compensated absences?

14. Under what conditions must an employer accrue a liability for the cost of compensated absences?

15. Under what conditions is an employer required to accrue a liability for sick pay? Under what conditions is an employer permitted but not required to accrue a liability for sick pay?

16. Caitlin Carter operates a health food store, and she has been the only employee. Her business is growing, and she is considering hiring some additional staff to help her in the store. Explain to her the various payroll deductions that she will have to account for, including their potential impact on her financial statements, if she hires additional staff.

17. Define (a) a contingency and (b) a contingent liability.

18. Under what conditions should a contingent liability be recorded?

19. Distinguish between a current liability and a contingent liability. Give two examples of each type.

20. How are the terms "probable," "reasonably possible," and "remote" related to contingent liabilities?

21. Contrast the cash basis method and the accrual method of accounting for warranty costs.

22. Kren Company has had a record-breaking year in terms of growth in sales and profitability. However, market research indicates that it will experience operating losses in two of its major businesses next year. The controller has proposed that the company record a provision for these future losses this year, since it can afford to take the charge and still show good results. Advise the controller on the appropriateness of this charge.

23. How does the expense warranty approach differ from the sales warranty approach?

24. Zucker-Abrahams Airlines Inc. awards members of its Flightline program a second ticket at half price, valid for 2 years anywhere on its flight system, when a full-price ticket is purchased. How would you account for the full-fare and half-fare tickets?

25. Northeast Airlines Co. awards members of its Frequent Fliers Club one free round-trip ticket, anywhere on its flight system, for every 50,000 miles flown on its planes. How would you account for the free ticket award?

26. When must a company recognize an asset retirement obligation?

27. Should a liability be recorded for risk of loss due to lack of insurance coverage? Discuss.

28. What factors must be considered in determining whether or not to record a liability for pending litigation? For threatened litigation?

29. Within the current liabilities section, how do you believe the accounts should be listed? Defend your position.

30. How does the acid-test ratio differ from the current ratio? How are they similar?

31. When should liabilities for each of the following items be recorded on the books of an ordinary business corporation?

(a) Acquisition of goods by purchase on credit.

(b) Officers' salaries.

(c) Special bonus to employees.

(d) Dividends.

(e) Purchase commitments.

BRIEF EXERCISES

(LO 1) **BE13-1** Congo Corporation uses a periodic inventory system and the gross method of accounting for purchase discounts. On July 1, Congo purchased $40,000 of inventory, terms 2/10, n/30, FOB shipping point. Congo paid freight costs of $1,200. On July 3, Congo returned damaged goods and received credit of $6,000. On July 10, Congo paid for the goods. Prepare all necessary journal entries for Congo.

(LO 1) **BE13-2** Peloton Company borrowed $50,000 on November 1, 2007, by signing a $50,000, 9%, 3-month note. Prepare Peloton's November 1, 2007, entry; the December 31, 2007, annual adjusting entry; and the February 1, 2008, entry.

(LO 1) **BE13-3** Kawasaki Corporation borrowed $50,000 on November 1, 2007, by signing a $51,125, 3-month, zero-interest-bearing note. Prepare Kawasaki's November 1, 2007, entry; the December 31, 2007, annual adjusting entry; and the February 1, 2008, entry.

(LO 1, 2) **BE13-4** At December 31, 2007, Fifa Corporation owes $500,000 on a note payable due February 15, 2008. (a) If Fifa refinances the obligation by issuing a long-term note on February 14 and using the proceeds to pay off the note due February 15, how much of the $500,000 should be reported as a current liability at December 31, 2007? (b) If Fifa pays off the note on February 15, 2008, and then borrows $1,000,000 on a long-term basis on March 1, how much of the $500,000 should be reported as a current liability at December 31, 2007?

(LO 1) **BE13-5** Game Pro Magazine sold 10,000 annual subscriptions on August 1, 2007, for $18 each. Prepare Game Pro's August 1, 2007, journal entry and the December 31, 2007, annual adjusting entry.

(LO 1) **BE13-6** Flintstones Corporation made credit sales of $30,000 which are subject to 6% sales tax. The corporation also made cash sales which totaled $19,610 including the 6% sales tax. (a) Prepare the entry to record Flintstones' credit sales. (b) Prepare the entry to record Flintstones' cash sales.

(LO 3) **BE13-7** Future Zone Corporation's weekly payroll of $23,000 included FICA taxes withheld of $1,426, federal taxes withheld of $2,990, state taxes withheld of $920, and insurance premiums withheld of $250. Prepare the journal entry to record Future Zone's payroll.

(LO 3) **BE13-8** Tale Spin Inc. provides paid vacations to its employees. At December 31, 2007, 30 employees have each earned 2 weeks of vacation time. The employees' average salary is $600 per week. Prepare Tale Spin's December 31, 2007, adjusting entry.

(LO 3) **BE13-9** Gargoyle Corporation provides its officers with bonuses based on income. For 2007, the bonuses total $450,000 and are paid on February 15, 2008. Prepare Gargoyle's December 31, 2007, adjusting entry and the February 15, 2008, entry.

(LO 4, 5) **BE13-10** Justice League Inc. is involved in a lawsuit at December 31, 2007. (a) Prepare the December 31 entry assuming it is probable that Justice League will be liable for $700,000 as a result of this suit. (b) Prepare the December 31 entry, if any, assuming it is *not* probable that Justice League will be liable for any payment as a result of this suit.

(LO 4, 5) **BE13-11** Kohlbeck Company recently was sued by a competitor for patent infringement. Attorneys have determined that it is probable that Kohlbeck will lose the case and that a reasonable estimate of damages to be paid by Kohlbeck is $200,000. In light of this case, Kohlbeck is considering establishing a $100,000 self-insurance allowance. What entry(ies), if any, should Kohlbeck record to recognize this loss contingency?

(LO 4, 5) **BE13-12** Darby's Drillers erects and places into service an off-shore oil platform on January 1, 2008, at a cost of $10,000,000. Darby is legally required to dismantle and remove the platform at the end of its useful life in 10 years. Darby estimates it will cost $1,000,000 to dismantle and remove the platform at the end of its useful life in 10 years. (The present value at January 1, 2008, of the dismantle and removal costs is $500,000.) Prepare the entry to record the asset retirement obligation.

(LO 4, 5) **BE13-13** Frantic Factory provides a 2-year warranty with one of its products which was first sold in 2007. In that year, Frantic spent $70,000 servicing warranty claims. At year-end, Frantic estimates that an additional $500,000 will be spent in the future to service warranty claims related to 2007 sales. Prepare Frantic's journal entry to record the $70,000 expenditure, and the December 31 adjusting entry.

(LO 4, 5) **BE13-14** LaRussa Corporation sells DVD players. The corporation also offers its customers a 2-year warranty contract. During 2007, LaRussa sold 15,000 warranty contracts at $99 each. The corporation spent $180,000 servicing warranties during 2007, and it estimates that an additional $900,000 will be spent in the future to service the warranties. Prepare LaRussa's journal entries for (a) the sale of contracts, (b) the cost of servicing the warranties, and (c) the recognition of warranty revenue.

(LO 4, 5) **BE13-15** Klax Company offers a set of building blocks to customers who send in 3 UPC codes from Klax cereal, along with 50¢. The blocks sets cost Klax $1.10 each to purchase and 60¢ each to mail to customers. During 2007, Klax sold 1,000,000 boxes of cereal. The company expects 30% of the UPC codes to be sent in. During 2007, 120,000 UPC codes were redeemed. Prepare Klax's December 31, 2007, adjusting entry.

(LO 7) ***BE13-16** Locke Company provides its president, Cyan Garamonde, with a bonus equal to 10% of income after deducting income tax and bonus. Income *before* deducting income tax and bonus is $265,000, and the tax rate is 40%. Compute the amount of Cyan Garamonde's bonus.

EXERCISES

(LO 1) **E13-1** **(Balance Sheet Classification of Various Liabilities)** How would each of the following items be reported on the balance sheet?

(a) Accrued vacation pay.
(b) Estimated taxes payable.
(c) Service warranties on appliance sales.
(d) Bank overdraft.
(e) Employee payroll deductions unremitted.
(f) Unpaid bonus to officers.
(g) Deposit received from customer to guarantee performance of a contract.
(h) Sales taxes payable.
(i) Gift certificates sold to customers but not yet redeemed.

(j) Premium offers outstanding.
(k) Discount on notes payable.
(l) Personal injury claim pending.
(m) Current maturities of long-term debts to be paid from current assets.
(n) Cash dividends declared but unpaid.
(o) Dividends in arrears on preferred stock.
(p) Loans from officers.

(LO 1) **E13-2** **(Accounts and Notes Payable)** The following are selected 2007 transactions of Sean Astin Corporation.

Sept. 1 Purchased inventory from Encino Company on account for $50,000. Astin records purchases gross and uses a periodic inventory system.

Oct. 1 Issued a $50,000, 12-month, 8% note to Encino in payment of account.

Oct. 1 Borrowed $50,000 from the Shore Bank by signing a 12-month, zero-interest-bearing $54,000 note.

Instructions

(a) Prepare journal entries for the selected transactions above.

(b) Prepare adjusting entries at December 31.

(c) Compute the total net liability to be reported on the December 31 balance sheet for:

(1) the interest-bearing note.

(2) the zero-interest-bearing note.

(LO 2) **E13-3 (Refinancing of Short-Term Debt)** On December 31, 2007, Hattie McDaniel Company had $1,200,000 of short-term debt in the form of notes payable due February 2, 2008. On January 21, 2008, the company issued 25,000 shares of its common stock for $38 per share, receiving $950,000 proceeds after brokerage fees and other costs of issuance. On February 2, 2008, the proceeds from the stock sale, supplemented by an additional $250,000 cash, are used to liquidate the $1,200,000 debt. The December 31, 2007, balance sheet is issued on February 23, 2008.

Instructions

Show how the $1,200,000 of short-term debt should be presented on the December 31, 2007, balance sheet, including note disclosure.

(LO 2) **E13-4 (Refinancing of Short-Term Debt)** On December 31, 2007, Kate Holmes Company has $7,000,000 of short-term debt in the form of notes payable to Gotham State Bank due in 2008. On January 28, 2008, Holmes enters into a refinancing agreement with Gotham that will permit it to borrow up to 60% of the gross amount of its accounts receivable. Receivables are expected to range between a low of $6,000,000 in May to a high of $8,000,000 in October during the year 2008. The interest cost of the maturing short-term debt is 15%, and the new agreement calls for a fluctuating interest at 1% above the prime rate on notes due in 2012. Holmes's December 31, 2007, balance sheet is issued on February 15, 2008.

Instructions

Prepare a partial balance sheet for Holmes at December 31, 2007, showing how its $7,000,000 of short-term debt should be presented, including footnote disclosure.

(LO 3) **E13-5 (Compensated Absences)** Matt Broderick Company began operations on January 2, 2006. It employs 9 individuals who work 8-hour days and are paid hourly. Each employee earns 10 paid vacation days and 6 paid sick days annually. Vacation days may be taken after January 15 of the year following the year in which they are earned. Sick days may be taken as soon as they are earned; unused sick days accumulate. Additional information is as follows.

Actual Hourly Wage Rate		Vacation Days Used by Each Employee		Sick Days Used by Each Employee	
2006	2007	2006	2007	2006	2007
$10	$11	0	9	4	5

Matt Broderick Company has chosen to accrue the cost of compensated absences at rates of pay in effect during the period when earned and to accrue sick pay when earned.

Instructions

(a) Prepare journal entries to record transactions related to compensated absences during 2006 and 2007.

(b) Compute the amounts of any liability for compensated absences that should be reported on the balance sheet at December 31, 2006 and 2007.

(LO 3) **E13-6 (Compensated Absences)** Assume the facts in the preceding exercise, except that Matt Broderick Company has chosen not to accrue paid sick leave until used, and has chosen to accrue vacation time at expected future rates of pay without discounting. The company used the following projected rates to accrue vacation time.

Year in Which Vacation Time Was Earned	Projected Future Pay Rates Used to Accrue Vacation Pay
2006	$10.75
2007	11.60

Instructions

(a) Prepare journal entries to record transactions related to compensated absences during 2006 and 2007.

(b) Compute the amounts of any liability for compensated absences that should be reported on the balance sheet at December 31, 2006, and 2007.

(LO 1) **E13-7** **(Adjusting Entry for Sales Tax)** During the month of June, Rowling Boutique had cash sales of $233,200 and credit sales of $153,700, both of which include the 6% sales tax that must be remitted to the state by July 15.

Instructions
Prepare the adjusting entry that should be recorded to fairly present the June 30 financial statements.

(LO 3) **E13-8** **(Payroll Tax Entries)** The payroll of YellowCard Company for September 2006 is as follows.
Total payroll was $480,000, of which $110,000 is exempt from Social Security tax because it represented amounts paid in excess of $90,000 to certain employees. The amount paid to employees in excess of $7,000 was $400,000. Income taxes in the amount of $80,000 were withheld, as was $9,000 in union dues. The state unemployment tax is 3.5%, but YellowCard Company is allowed a credit of 2.3% by the state for its unemployment experience. Also, assume that the current F.I.C.A. tax is 7.65% on an employee's wages to $90,000 and 1.45% in excess of $90,000. No employee for YellowCard makes more than $125,000. The federal unemployment tax rate is 0.8% after state credit.

Instructions
Prepare the necessary journal entries if the wages and salaries paid and the employer payroll taxes are recorded separately.

(LO 3) **E13-9** **(Payroll Tax Entries)** Green Day Hardware Company's payroll for November 2007 is summarized below.

| | | | Amount Subject to Payroll Taxes | |
| | | | Unemployment Tax | |
Payroll	Wages Due	F.I.C.A.	Federal	State
Factory	$120,000	$120,000	$40,000	$40,000
Sales	32,000	32,000	4,000	4,000
Administrative	36,000	36,000	—	—
Total	$188,000	$188,000	$44,000	$44,000

At this point in the year some employees have already received wages in excess of those to which payroll taxes apply. Assume that the state unemployment tax is 2.5%. The F.I.C.A. rate is 7.65% on an employee's wages to $90,000 and 1.45% in excess of $90,000. Of the $188,000 wages subject to F.I.C.A. tax, $20,000 of the sales wages is in excess of $90,000. Federal unemployment tax rate is 0.8% after credits. Income tax withheld amounts to $16,000 for factory, $7,000 for sales, and $6,000 for administrative.

Instructions
(a) Prepare a schedule showing the employer's total cost of wages for November by function. (Round all computations to nearest dollar.)
(b) Prepare the journal entries to record the factory, sales, and administrative payrolls including the employer's payroll taxes.

(LO 5) **E13-10** **(Warranties)** Soundgarden Company sold 200 color laser copiers in 2007 for $4,000 apiece, together with a one-year warranty. Maintenance on each copier during the warranty period averages $330.

Instructions
(a) Prepare entries to record the sale of the copiers and the related warranty costs, assuming that the accrual method is used. Actual warranty costs incurred in 2007 were $17,000.
(b) On the basis of the data above, prepare the appropriate entries, assuming that the cash basis method is used.

(LO 5) **E13-11** **(Warranties)** Sheryl Crow Equipment Company sold 500 Rollomatics during 2007 at $6,000 each. During 2007, Crow spent $20,000 servicing the 2-year warranties that accompany the Rollomatic. All applicable transactions are on a cash basis.

Instructions
(a) Prepare 2007 entries for Crow using the expense warranty approach. Assume that Crow estimates the total cost of servicing the warranties will be $120,000 for 2 years.
(b) Prepare 2007 entries for Crow assuming that the warranties are not an integral part of the sale. Assume that of the sales total, $150,000 relates to sales of warranty contracts. Crow estimates the total cost of servicing the warranties will be $120,000 for 2 years. Estimate revenues earned on the basis of costs incurred and estimated costs.

(LO 5) **E13-12** **(Premium Entries)** No Doubt Company includes 1 coupon in each box of soap powder that it packs, and 10 coupons are redeemable for a premium (a kitchen utensil). In 2007, No Doubt Company purchased 8,800 premiums at 80 cents each and sold 110,000 boxes of soap powder at $3.30 per box; 44,000 coupons were presented for redemption in 2007. It is estimated that 60% of the coupons will eventually be presented for redemption.

Instructions

Prepare all the entries that would be made relative to sales of soap powder and to the premium plan in 2007.

(LO 4, 5) **E13-13** **(Contingencies)** Presented below are three independent situations. Answer the question at the end of each situation.

1. During 2007, Salt-n-Pepa Inc. became involved in a tax dispute with the IRS. Salt-n-Pepa's attorneys have indicated that they believe it is probable that Salt-n-Pepa will lose this dispute. They also believe that Salt-n-Pepa will have to pay the IRS between $900,000 and $1,400,000. After the 2007 financial statements were issued, the case was settled with the IRS for $1,200,000. What amount, if any, should be reported as a liability for this contingency as of December 31, 2007?

2. On October 1, 2007, Alan Jackson Chemical was identified as a potentially responsible party by the Environmental Protection Agency. Jackson's management along with its counsel have concluded that it is probable that Jackson will be responsible for damages, and a reasonable estimate of these damages is $5,000,000. Jackson's insurance policy of $9,000,000 has a deductible clause of $500,000. How should Alan Jackson Chemical report this information in its financial statements at December 31, 2007?

3. Melissa Etheridge Inc. had a manufacturing plant in Bosnia, which was destroyed in the civil war. It is not certain who will compensate Etheridge for this destruction, but Etheridge has been assured by governmental officials that it will receive a definite amount for this plant. The amount of the compensation will be less than the fair value of the plant, but more than its book value. How should the contingency be reported in the financial statements of Etheridge Inc.?

(LO 5) **E13-14** **(Asset Retirement Obligation)** Oil Products Company purchases an oil tanker depot on January 1, 2007, at a cost of $600,000. Oil Products expects to operate the depot for 10 years, at which time it is legally required to dismantle the depot and remove the underground storage tanks. It is estimated that it will cost $75,000 to dismantle the depot and remove the tanks at the end of the depot's useful life.

Instructions

(a) Prepare the journal entries to record the depot and the asset retirement obligation for the depot on January 1, 2007. Based on an effective interest rate of 6%, the present value of the asset retirement obligation on January 1, 2007, is $41,879.

(b) Prepare any journal entries required for the depot and the asset retirement obligation at December 31, 2007. Oil Products uses straight-line depreciation; the estimated residual value for the depot is zero.

(c) On December 31, 2016, Oil Products pays a demolition firm to dismantle the depot and remove the tanks at a price of $80,000. Prepare the journal entry for the settlement of the asset retirement obligation.

(LO 5) **E13-15** **(Premiums)** Presented below are three independent situations.

1. Hairston Stamp Company records stamp service revenue and provides for the cost of redemptions in the year stamps are sold to licensees. Hairston's past experience indicates that only 80% of the stamps sold to licensees will be redeemed. Hairston's liability for stamp redemptions was $13,000,000 at December 31, 2006. Additional information for 2007 is as follows.

Stamp service revenue from stamps sold to licensees	$9,500,000
Cost of redemptions (stamps sold prior to 1/1/07)	6,000,000

If all the stamps sold in 2007 were presented for redemption in 2008, the redemption cost would be $5,200,000. What amount should Hairston report as a liability for stamp redemptions at December 31, 2007?

2. In packages of its products, Burnitz Inc. includes coupons that may be presented at retail stores to obtain discounts on other Burnitz products. Retailers are reimbursed for the face amount of coupons redeemed plus 10% of that amount for handling costs. Burnitz honors requests for coupon redemption by retailers up to 3 months after the consumer expiration date. Burnitz estimates that 60% of all coupons issued will ultimately be redeemed. Information relating to coupons issued by Burnitz during 2007 is as follows.

Consumer expiration date	12/31/07
Total face amount of coupons issued	$800,000
Total payments to retailers as of 12/31/07	330,000

What amount should Burnitz report as a liability for unredeemed coupons at December 31, 2007?

3. Roland Company sold 700,000 boxes of pie mix under a new sales promotional program. Each box contains one coupon, which submitted with $4.00, entitles the customer to a baking pan. Roland pays $6.00 per pan and $0.50 for handling and shipping. Roland estimates that 70% of the coupons will be redeemed, even though only 250,000 coupons had been processed during 2007. What amount should Roland report as a liability for unredeemed coupons at December 31, 2007?

(AICPA adapted)

(LO 6) **E13-16 (Financial Statement Impact of Liability Transactions)** Presented below is a list of possible transactions.

1. Purchased inventory for $80,000 on account (assume perpetual system is used).
2. Issued an $80,000 note payable in payment on account (see item 1 above).
3. Recorded accrued interest on the note from item 2 above.
4. Borrowed $100,000 from the bank by signing a 6-month, $112,000, zero-interest-bearing note.
5. Recognized 4 months' interest expense on the note from item 4 above.
6. Recorded cash sales of $75,260, which includes 6% sales tax.
7. Recorded wage expense of $35,000. The cash paid was $25,000; the difference was due to various amounts withheld.
8. Recorded employer's payroll taxes.
9. Accrued accumulated vacation pay.
10. Recorded an asset retirement obligation.
11. Recorded bonuses due to employees.
12. Recorded a contingent loss on a lawsuit that the company will probably lose.
13. Accrued warranty expense (assume expense warranty approach).
14. Paid warranty costs that were accrued in item 13 above.
15. Recorded sales of product and related warranties (assume sales warranty approach).
16. Paid warranty costs under contracts from item 15 above.
17. Recognized warranty revenue (see item 15 above).
18. Recorded estimated liability for premium claims outstanding.

Instructions
Set up a table using the format shown below and analyze the effect of the 18 transactions on the financial statement categories indicated.

#	Assets	Liabilities	Owners' Equity	Net Income
1				

Use the following code:
 I: Increase D: Decrease NE: No net effect

(LO 6) **E13-17 (Ratio Computations and Discussion)** Sprague Company has been operating for several years, and on December 31, 2007, presented the following balance sheet.

SPRAGUE COMPANY
BALANCE SHEET
DECEMBER 31, 2007

Cash	$ 40,000	Accounts payable	$ 80,000
Receivables	75,000	Mortgage payable	140,000
Inventories	95,000	Common stock ($1 par)	150,000
Plant assets (net)	220,000	Retained earnings	60,000
	$430,000		$430,000

The net income for 2007 was $25,000. Assume that total assets are the same in 2006 and 2007.

Instructions
Compute each of the following ratios. For each of the four indicate the manner in which it is computed and its significance as a tool in the analysis of the financial soundness of the company.

(a) Current ratio.   (c) Debt to total assets.
(b) Acid-test ratio.   (d) Rate of return on assets.

(LO 6) **E13-18** **(Ratio Computations and Analysis)** Prior Company's condensed financial statements provide the following information.

PRIOR COMPANY		
BALANCE SHEET		
	Dec. 31, 2007	Dec. 31, 2006
Cash	$ 52,000	$ 60,000
Accounts receivable (net)	198,000	80,000
Short-term investments	80,000	40,000
Inventories	440,000	360,000
Prepaid expenses	3,000	7,000
Total current assets	$ 773,000	$ 547,000
Property, plant, and equipment (net)	857,000	853,000
Total assets	$1,630,000	$1,400,000
Current liabilities	240,000	160,000
Bonds payable	400,000	400,000
Common stockholders' equity	990,000	840,000
Total liabilities and stockholders' equity	$1,630,000	$1,400,000

INCOME STATEMENT	
FOR THE YEAR ENDED 2007	
Sales	$1,640,000
Cost of goods sold	(800,000)
Gross profit	840,000
Selling and administrative expense	(440,000)
Interest expense	(40,000)
Net income	$ 360,000

Instructions

(a) Determine the following for 2007.
  (1) Current ratio at December 31.
  (2) Acid-test ratio at December 31.
  (3) Accounts receivable turnover.
  (4) Inventory turnover.
  (5) Rate of return on assets.
  (6) Profit margin on sales.
(b) Prepare a brief evaluation of the financial condition of Prior Company and of the adequacy of its profits.

(LO 6) **E13-19** **(Ratio Computations and Effect of Transactions)** Presented below and on page 637 is information related to Carver Inc.

CARVER INC.				
BALANCE SHEET				
DECEMBER 31, 2007				
Cash		$ 45,000	Notes payable (short-term)	$ 50,000
Receivables	$110,000		Accounts payable	32,000
Less: Allowance	15,000	95,000	Accrued liabilities	5,000
Inventories		170,000	Capital stock (par $5)	260,000
Prepaid insurance		8,000	Retained earnings	141,000
Land		20,000		
Equipment (net)		150,000		
		$488,000		$488,000

CARVER INC.
INCOME STATEMENT
FOR THE YEAR ENDED DECEMBER 31, 2007

Sales		$1,400,000
Cost of goods sold		
Inventory, Jan. 1, 2007	$200,000	
Purchases	790,000	
Cost of goods available for sale	990,000	
Inventory, Dec. 31, 2007	170,000	
Cost of goods sold		820,000
Gross profit on sales		580,000
Operating expenses		170,000
Net income		$ 410,000

Instructions

(a) Compute the following ratios or relationships of Carver Inc. Assume that the ending account balances are representative unless the information provided indicates differently.

   (1) Current ratio.
   (2) Inventory turnover.
   (3) Receivables turnover.
   (4) Earnings per share.
   (5) Profit margin on sales.
   (6) Rate of return on assets on December 31, 2007.

(b) Indicate for each of the following transactions whether the transaction would improve, weaken, or have no effect on the current ratio of Carver Inc. at December 31, 2007.

   (1) Write off an uncollectible account receivable, $2,200.
   (2) Purchase additional capital stock for cash.
   (3) Pay $40,000 on notes payable (short-term).
   (4) Collect $23,000 on accounts receivable.
   (5) Buy equipment on account.
   (6) Give an existing creditor a short-term note in settlement of account.

(LO 7) *E13-20 (Bonus Computation) Jud Buechler, president of the Supporting Cast Company, has a bonus arrangement with the company under which he receives 15% of the net income (after deducting taxes and bonuses) each year. For the current year, the net income before deducting either the provision for income taxes or the bonus is $299,750. The bonus is deductible for tax purposes, and the effective tax rate may be assumed to be 40%.

Instructions

(a) Compute the amount of Jud Buechler's bonus.
(b) Compute the appropriate provision for federal income taxes for the year.
(c) Prepare the December 31 entry to record the bonus (which will not be paid until next year).

(LO 7) *E13-21 (Bonus Computation and Income Statement Preparation) The incomplete income statement of Scottie Pippen Company follows.

SCOTTIE PIPPEN COMPANY
INCOME STATEMENT
FOR THE YEAR 2007

Revenue		$10,000,000
Cost of goods sold		7,000,000
Gross profit		3,000,000
Administrative and selling expenses	$1,000,000	
Profit-sharing bonus to employees	?	?
Income before income taxes		?
Income taxes		?
Net income		$?

The employee profit-sharing plan requires that 20% of all profits remaining after the deduction of the bonus and income taxes be distributed to the employees by the first day of the fourth month following each year-end. The federal income tax rate is 45%, and the bonus is tax-deductible.

Instructions
Complete the condensed income statement of Scottie Pippen Company for the year 2007.

(LO 7) *E13-22 **(Bonus Compensation)** Alan Iverson Company has a profit-sharing agreement with its employees that provides for deposit in a pension trust for the benefit of the employees of 25% of the net income after deducting (1) federal taxes on income, (2) the amount of the annual pension contribution, and (3) a return of 10% on the stockholders' equity as of the end of the year 2007.

Instructions
Compute the amount of the pension contribution under the assumption that the stockholders' equity at the end of 2007 before adding the net income for the year is $700,000; that net income for the year before either the pension contribution or tax is $300,000; and that the pension contribution is deductible for tax purposes. Use 40% as the applicable rate of tax.

See the book's website, **www.wiley.com/college/kieso**, for Additional Exercises.

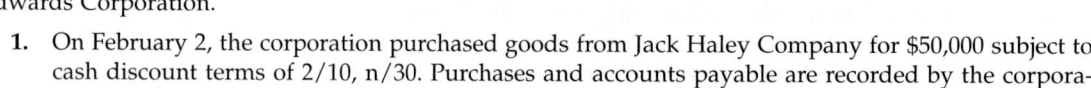

PROBLEMS

(LO 1) **P13-1** **(Current Liability Entries and Adjustments)** Described below are certain transactions of James Edwards Corporation.

1. On February 2, the corporation purchased goods from Jack Haley Company for $50,000 subject to cash discount terms of 2/10, n/30. Purchases and accounts payable are recorded by the corporation at net amounts after cash discounts. The invoice was paid on February 26.
2. On April 1, the corporation bought a truck for $40,000 from General Motors Company, paying $4,000 in cash and signing a one-year, 12% note for the balance of the purchase price.
3. On May 1, the corporation borrowed $86,000 from Chicago National Bank by signing a $92,000 zero-interest-bearing note due one year from May 1.
4. On August 1, the board of directors declared a $300,000 cash dividend that was payable on September 10 to stockholders of record on August 31.

Instructions
(a) Make all the journal entries necessary to record the transactions above using appropriate dates.
(b) James Edwards Corporation's year-end is December 31. Assuming that no adjusting entries relative to the transactions above have been recorded, prepare any adjusting journal entries concerning interest that are necessary to present fair financial statements at December 31. Assume straight-line amortization of discounts.

(LO 1, 5) **P13-2** **(Liability Entries and Adjustments)** Listed below are selected transactions of Kobe Bryant Department Store for the current year ending December 31.

1. On December 5, the store received $500 from the Phil Jackson Players as a deposit to be returned after certain furniture to be used in stage production was returned on January 15.
2. During December, cash sales totaled $834,750, which includes the 5% sales tax that must be remitted to the state by the fifteenth day of the following month.
3. On December 10, the store purchased for cash three delivery trucks for $99,000. The trucks were purchased in a state that applies a 5% sales tax.
4. The store determined it will cost $100,000 to restore the area surrounding one of its store parking lots, when the store is closed in 2 years. Bryant estimates the fair value of the obligation at December 31 is $84,000.

Instructions
Prepare all the journal entries necessary to record the transactions noted above as they occurred and any adjusting journal entries relative to the transactions that would be required to present fair financial statements at December 31. Date each entry. For simplicity, assume that adjusting entries are recorded only once a year on December 31.

(LO 3) **P13-3** **(Payroll Tax Entries)** Star Wars Company pays its office employee payroll weekly. Below is a partial list of employees and their payroll data for August. Because August is their vacation period, vacation pay is also listed.

Employee	Earnings to July 31	Weekly Pay	Vacation Pay to Be Received in August
Mark Hamill	$4,200	$180	—
Carrie Fisher	3,500	150	$300
Harrison Ford	2,700	110	220
Alec Guinness	7,400	250	—
Peter Cushing	8,000	290	580

Assume that the federal income tax withheld is 10% of wages. Union dues withheld are 2% of wages. Vacations are taken the second and third weeks of August by Fisher, Ford, and Cushing. The state unemployment tax rate is 2.5% and the federal is 0.8%, both on a $7,000 maximum. The F.I.C.A. rate is 7.65% on employee and employer on a maximum of $90,000 per employee. In addition, a 1.45% rate is charged both employer and employee for an employee's wage in excess of $90,000.

Instructions
Make the journal entries necessary for each of the four August payrolls. The entries for the payroll and for the company's liability are made separately. Also make the entry to record the monthly payment of accrued payroll liabilities.

(LO 3) **P13-4** **(Payroll Tax Entries)** Below is a payroll sheet for Jedi Import Company for the month of September 2007. The company is allowed a 1% unemployment compensation rate by the state; the federal unemployment tax rate is 0.8% and the maximum for both is $7,000. Assume a 10% federal income tax rate for all employees and a 7.65% F.I.C.A. tax on employee and employer on a maximum of $90,000. In addition, 1.45% is charged both employer and employee for an employee's wage in excess of $90,000 per employee.

Name	Earnings to Aug. 31	September Earnings	Income Tax Withholding	F.I.C.A.	State U.C.	Federal U.C.
B.D. Williams	$ 6,800	$ 800				
D. Prowse	6,300	700				
K. Baker	7,600	1,100				
F. Oz	13,600	1,900				
A. Daniels	105,000	15,000				
B. Mayhew	112,000	16,000				

Instructions
(a) Complete the payroll sheet and make the necessary entry to record the payment of the payroll.
(b) Make the entry to record the payroll tax expenses of Jedi Import Company.
(c) Make the entry to record the payment of the payroll liabilities created. Assume that the company pays all payroll liabilities at the end of each month.

(LO 5) **P13-5** **(Warranties, Accrual, and Cash Basis)** Jeeter Corporation sells computers under a 2-year warranty contract that requires the corporation to replace defective parts and to provide the necessary repair labor. During 2007 the corporation sells for cash 300 computers at a unit price of $3,500. On the basis of past experience, the 2-year warranty costs are estimated to be $155 for parts and $185 for labor per unit. (For simplicity, assume that all sales occurred on December 31, 2007.) The warranty is not sold separately from the computer.

Instructions
(a) Record any necessary journal entries in 2007, applying the cash basis method.
(b) Record any necessary journal entries in 2007, applying the expense warranty accrual method.
(c) What liability relative to these transactions would appear on the December 31, 2007, balance sheet and how would it be classified if the cash basis method is applied?
(d) What liability relative to these transactions would appear on the December 31, 2007, balance sheet and how would it be classified if the expense warranty accrual method is applied?

In 2008 the actual warranty costs to Jeeter Corporation were $21,400 for parts and $24,900 for labor.

(e) Record any necessary journal entries in 2008, applying the cash basis method.
(f) Record any necessary journal entries in 2008, applying the expense warranty accrual method.

(LO 5) **P13-6** **(Extended Warranties)** Brett Perriman Company sells televisions at an average price of $750 and also offers to each customer a separate 3-year warranty contract for $75 that requires the company to perform periodic services and to replace defective parts. During 2007, the company sold 300 televisions and 270 warranty contracts for cash. It estimates the 3-year warranty costs as $20 for parts and $40 for labor and accounts for warranties separately. Assume sales occurred on December 31, 2007, income is recognized on the warranties, and straight-line recognition of warranty revenues occurs.

Instructions

(a) Record any necessary journal entries in 2007.

(b) What liability relative to these transactions would appear on the December 31, 2007, balance sheet and how would it be classified?

In 2008, Brett Perriman Company incurred actual costs relative to 2007 television warranty sales of $2,000 for parts and $3,000 for labor.

(c) Record any necessary journal entries in 2008 relative to 2007 television warranties.

(d) What amounts relative to the 2007 television warranties would appear on the December 31, 2008, balance sheet and how would they be classified?

(LO 4, 5) **P13-7 (Warranties, Accrual, and Cash Basis)** Albert Pujols Company sells a machine for $7,400 under a 12-month warranty agreement that requires the company to replace all defective parts and to provide the repair labor at no cost to the customers. With sales being made evenly throughout the year, the company sells 650 machines in 2008 (warranty expense is incurred half in 2008 and half in 2009). As a result of product testing, the company estimates that the warranty cost is $370 per machine ($170 parts and $200 labor).

Instructions

Assuming that actual warranty costs are incurred exactly as estimated, what journal entries would be made relative to the following facts?

(a) Under application of the expense warranty accrual method for:
   (1) Sale of machinery in 2008.
   (2) Warranty costs incurred in 2008.
   (3) Warranty expense charged against 2008 revenues.
   (4) Warranty costs incurred in 2009.

(b) Under application of the cash basis method for:
   (1) Sale of machinery in 2008.
   (2) Warranty costs incurred in 2008.
   (3) Warranty expense charged against 2008 revenues.
   (4) Warranty costs incurred in 2009.

(c) What amount, if any, is disclosed in the balance sheet as a liability for future warranty costs as of December 31, 2008, under each method?

(d) Which method best reflects the income in 2008 and 2009 of Albert Pujols Company? Why?

(LO 5) **P13-8 (Premium Entries)** To stimulate the sales of its Alladin breakfast cereal, Khamsah Company places 1 coupon in each box. Five coupons are redeemable for a premium consisting of a children's hand puppet. In 2008, the company purchases 40,000 puppets at $1.50 each and sells 440,000 boxes of Alladin at $3.75 a box. From its experience with other similar premium offers, the company estimates that 40% of the coupons issued will be mailed back for redemption. During 2008, 105,000 coupons are presented for redemption.

Instructions

Prepare the journal entries that should be recorded in 2008 relative to the premium plan.

(LO 5, 6) **P13-9 (Premium Entries and Financial Statement Presentation)** Roberto Hernandez Candy Company offers a CD single as a premium for every five candy bar wrappers presented by customers together with $2.00. The candy bars are sold by the company to distributors for 30 cents each. The purchase price of each CD to the company is $1.80; in addition it costs 30 cents to mail each CD. The results of the premium plan for the years 2007 and 2008 are as follows. (All purchases and sales are for cash.)

	2007	2008
CDs purchased	250,000	330,000
Candy bars sold	2,895,400	2,743,600
Wrappers redeemed	1,200,000	1,500,000
2007 wrappers expected to be redeemed in 2008	290,000	
2008 wrappers expected to be redeemed in 2009		350,000

Instructions

(a) Prepare the journal entries that should be made in 2007 and 2008 to record the transactions related to the premium plan of the Roberto Hernandez Candy Company.

(b) Indicate the account names, amounts, and classifications of the items related to the premium plan that would appear on the balance sheet and the income statement at the end of 2007 and 2008.

(LO 4, 5) **P13-10** **(Loss Contingencies: Entries and Essay)** On November 24, 2007, 26 passengers on Branson Airlines Flight No. 901 were injured upon landing when the plane skidded off the runway. Personal injury suits for damages totaling $5,000,000 were filed on January 11, 2008, against the airline by 18 injured passengers. The airline carries no insurance. Legal counsel has studied each suit and advised Branson that it can reasonably expect to pay 60% of the damages claimed. The financial statements for the year ended December 31, 2007, were issued February 27, 2008.

Instructions

(a) Prepare any disclosures and journal entries required by the airline in preparation of the December 31, 2007, financial statements.

(b) Ignoring the Nov. 24, 2007, accident, what liability due to the risk of loss from lack of insurance coverage should Branson Airlines record or disclose? During the past decade the company has experienced at least one accident per year and incurred average damages of $3,200,000. Discuss fully.

(LO 4, 5) **P13-11** **(Loss Contingencies: Entries and Essays)** Ichiro Corporation, in preparation of its December 31, 2007, financial statements, is attempting to determine the proper accounting treatment for each of the following situations.

1. As a result of uninsured accidents during the year, personal injury suits for $350,000 and $60,000 have been filed against the company. It is the judgment of Ichiro's legal counsel that an unfavorable outcome is unlikely in the $60,000 case but that an unfavorable verdict approximating $225,000 will probably result in the $350,000 case.

2. Ichiro Corporation owns a subsidiary in a foreign country that has a book value of $5,725,000 and an estimated fair value of $8,700,000. The foreign government has communicated to Ichiro its intention to expropriate the assets and business of all foreign investors. On the basis of settlements other firms have received from this same country, Ichiro expects to receive 40% of the fair value of its properties as final settlement.

3. Ichiro's chemical product division consisting of five plants is uninsurable because of the special risk of injury to employees and losses due to fire and explosion. The year 2007 is considered one of the safest (luckiest) in the division's history because no loss due to injury or casualty was suffered. Having suffered an average of three casualties a year during the rest of the past decade (ranging from $60,000 to $700,000), management is certain that next year the company will probably not be so fortunate.

Instructions

(a) Prepare the journal entries that should be recorded as of December 31, 2007, to recognize each of the situations above.

(b) Indicate what should be reported relative to each situation in the financial statements and accompanying notes. Explain why.

(LO 5) **P13-12** **(Warranties and Premiums)** Ray Charles Music Emporium carries a wide variety of musical instruments, sound reproduction equipment, recorded music, and sheet music. Charles uses two sales promotion techniques—warranties and premiums—to attract customers.

Musical instruments and sound equipment are sold with a one-year warranty for replacement of parts and labor. The estimated warranty cost, based on past experience, is 2% of sales.

The premium is offered on the recorded and sheet music. Customers receive a coupon for each dollar spent on recorded music or sheet music. Customers may exchange 200 coupons and $20 for a CD player. Charles pays $34 for each CD player and estimates that 60% of the coupons given to customers will be redeemed.

Charles's total sales for 2007 were $7,200,000—$5,400,000 from musical instruments and sound reproduction equipment and $1,800,000 from recorded music and sheet music. Replacement parts and labor for warranty work totaled $164,000 during 2007. A total of 6,500 CD players used in the premium program were purchased during the year and there were 1,200,000 coupons redeemed in 2007.

The accrual method is used by Charles to account for the warranty and premium costs for financial reporting purposes. The balances in the accounts related to warranties and premiums on January 1, 2007, were as shown below.

Inventory of Premium CD Players	$39,950
Estimated Premium Claims Outstanding	44,800
Estimated Liability from Warranties	136,000

Instructions

Ray Charles Music Emporium is preparing its financial statements for the year ended December 31, 2007. Determine the amounts that will be shown on the 2007 financial statements for the following.

(1) Warranty Expense.
(2) Estimated Liability from Warranties.
(3) Premium Expense.

(4) Inventory of Premium CD Players.
(5) Estimated Premium Claims Outstanding.

(CMA adapted)

(LO 4, 5) **P13-13** **(Liability Errors)** You are the independent auditor engaged to audit Christine Agazzi Corporation's December 31, 2007, financial statements. Christine Agazzi manufactures household appliances. During the course of your audit, you discovered the following contingent liabilities.

1. Christine Agazzi began production of a new dishwasher in June 2007 and, by December 31, 2007, sold 100,000 to various retailers for $500 each. Each dishwasher is under a one-year warranty. The company estimates that its warranty expense per dishwasher will amount to $25. At year-end, the company had already paid out $1,000,000 in warranty expenses. Christine Agazzi's income statement shows warranty expenses of $1,000,000 for 2007. Agazzi accounts for warranty costs on the accrual basis.

2. In response to your attorney's letter, Robert Sklodowski, Esq., has informed you that Agazzi has been cited for dumping toxic waste into the Kishwaukee River. Clean-up costs and fines amount to $3,330,000. Although the case is still being contested, Sklodowski is certain that Agazzi will most probably have to pay the fine and clean-up costs. No disclosure of this situation was found in the financial statements.

3. Christine Agazzi is the defendant in a patent infringement lawsuit by Heidi Goldman over Agazzi's use of a hydraulic compressor in several of its products. Sklodowski claims that, if the suit goes against Agazzi, the loss may be as much as $5,000,000; however, Sklodowski believes the loss of this suit to be only reasonably possible. Again, no mention of this suit occurs in the financial statements.

As presented, these contingencies are not reported in accordance with GAAP, which may create problems in issuing a clean audit report. You feel the need to note these problems in the work papers.

Instructions

Heading each page with the name of the company, balance sheet date, and a brief description of the problem, write a brief narrative for each of the above issues in the form of **a memorandum** to be incorporated in the audit work papers. Explain what led to the discovery of each problem, what the problem really is, and what you advised your client to do (along with any appropriate journal entries) in order to bring these contingencies in accordance with GAAP.

(LO 7) ***P13-14** **(Bonus Computation)** Henryk Inc. has a contract with its president, Nathalie Sarraute, to pay her a bonus during each of the years 2006, 2007, 2008, and 2009. The federal income tax rate is 40% during the 4 years. The profit before deductions for bonus and federal income taxes was $250,000 in 2006, $308,000 in 2007, $350,000 in 2008, and $380,000 in 2009. The president's bonus of 12% is deductible for tax purposes in each year and is to be computed as follows.

(a) In 2006 the bonus is to be based on profit before deductions for bonus and income tax.
(b) In 2007 the bonus is to be based on profit after deduction of bonus but before deduction of income tax.
(c) In 2008 the bonus is to be based on profit before deduction of bonus but after deduction of income tax.
(d) In 2009 the bonus is to be based on profit after deductions for bonus and income tax.

Instructions

Compute the amounts of the bonus and the income tax for each of the 4 years.

(LO 5, 7) **P13-15** **(Warranty, Bonus, and Coupon Computation)** Hiaasen Company must make computations and adjusting entries for the following independent situations at December 31, 2007.

1. Its line of amplifiers carries a 3-year warranty against defects. On the basis of past experience the estimated warranty costs related to dollar sales are: first year after sale—2% of sales; second year after sale—3% of sales; and third year after sale—4% of sales. Sales and actual warranty expenditures for the first 3 years of business were:

	Sales	Warranty Expenditures
2005	$ 800,000	$ 6,500
2006	1,100,000	17,200
2007	1,200,000	62,000

Instructions

Compute the amount that Hiaasen Company should report as a liability in its December 31, 2007, balance sheet. Assume that all sales are made evenly throughout each year with warranty expenses also evenly spaced relative to the rates above.

*2. Hiaasen Company's profit-sharing plan provides that the company will contribute to a fund an amount equal to one-fourth of its net income each year. Income before deducting the profit-sharing contribution and taxes for 2007 is $1,035,000. The applicable income tax rate is 40%, and the profit-sharing contribution is deductible for tax purposes.

Instructions
Compute the amount to be contributed to the profit-sharing fund for 2007.

3. With some of its products, Hiaasen Company includes coupons that are redeemable in merchandise. The coupons have no expiration date and, in the company's experience, 40% of them are redeemed. The liability for unredeemed coupons at December 31, 2006, was $9,000. During 2007, coupons worth $25,000 were issued, and merchandise worth $8,000 was distributed in exchange for coupons redeemed.

Instructions
Compute the amount of the liability that should appear on the December 31, 2007, balance sheet.

(AICPA adapted)

CONCEPTS FOR ANALYSIS

CA13-1 **(Nature of Liabilities)** Presented below is the current liabilities section of Nomar Corporation.

	($000)	
	2007	2006
Current Liabilities		
Notes payable	$ 68,713	$ 7,700
Accounts payable	179,496	101,379
Compensation to employees	60,312	31,649
Accrued liabilities	158,198	77,621
Income taxes payable	10,486	26,491
Current maturities of long-term debt	16,592	6,649
Total current liabilities	$493,797	$251,489

Instructions
Answer the following questions.

(a) What are the essential characteristics that make an item a liability?
(b) How does one distinguish between a current liability and a long-term liability?
(c) What are accrued liabilities? Give three examples of accrued liabilities that Nomar might have.
(d) What is the theoretically correct way to value liabilities? How are current liabilities usually valued?
(e) Why are notes payable reported first in the current liabilities section?
(f) What might be the items that comprise Nomar's liability for "Compensation to employees"?

CA13-2 **(Current versus Noncurrent Classification)** D'Annunzio Corporation includes the following items in its liabilities at December 31, 2007.

1. Notes payable, $25,000,000, due June 30, 2008.
2. Deposits from customers on equipment ordered by them from D'Annunzio, $6,250,000.
3. Salaries payable, $3,750,000, due January 14, 2008.

Instructions
Indicate in what circumstances, if any, each of the three liabilities above would be excluded from current liabilities.

CA13-3 **(Refinancing of Short-Term Debt)** Levi Eshkol Corporation reports in the current liability section of its balance sheet at December 31, 2007 (its year-end), short-term obligations of $15,000,000, which includes the current portion of 12% long-term debt in the amount of $11,000,000 (matures in March 2008). Management has stated its intention to refinance the 12% debt whereby no portion of it will mature during 2008. The date of issuance of the financial statements is March 25, 2008.

Instructions
(a) Is management's intent enough to support long-term classification of the obligation in this situation?
(b) Assume that Eshkol Corporation issues $13,000,000 of 10-year debentures to the public in January 2008 and that management intends to use the proceeds to liquidate the $11,000,000 debt maturing in March 2008. Furthermore, assume that the debt maturing in March 2008 is paid from these proceeds prior to the issuance of the financial statements. Will this have any impact on the balance sheet classification at December 31, 2007? Explain your answer.
(c) Assume that Eshkol Corporation issues common stock to the public in January and that management intends to entirely liquidate the $11,000,000 debt maturing in March 2008 with the

proceeds of this equity securities issue. In light of these events, should the $11,000,000 debt maturing in March 2008 be included in current liabilities at December 31, 2007?

(d) Assume that Eshkol Corporation, on February 15, 2008, entered into a financing agreement with a commercial bank that permits Eshkol Corporation to borrow at any time through 2009 up to $15,000,000 at the bank's prime rate of interest. Borrowings under the financing agreement mature three years after the date of the loan. The agreement is not cancelable except for violation of a provision with which compliance is objectively determinable. No violation of any provision exists at the date of issuance of the financial statements. Assume further that the current portion of long-term debt does not mature until August 2008. In addition, management intends to refinance the $11,000,000 obligation under the terms of the financial agreement with the bank, which is expected to be financially capable of honoring the agreement.

(1) Given these facts, should the $11,000,000 be classified as current on the balance sheet at December 31, 2007?

(2) Is disclosure of the refinancing method required?

CA13-4 (Refinancing of Short-Term Debt) Medvedev Inc. issued $10,000,000 of short-term commercial paper during the year 2006 to finance construction of a plant. At December 31, 2006, the corporation's year-end, Medvedev intends to refinance the commercial paper by issuing long-term debt. However, because the corporation temporarily has excess cash, in January 2007 it liquidates $4,000,000 of the commercial paper as the paper matures. In February 2007, Medvedev completes an $18,000,000 long-term debt offering. Later during the month of February, it issues its December 31, 2006, financial statements. The proceeds of the long-term debt offering are to be used to replenish $4,000,000 in working capital, to pay $6,000,000 of commercial paper as it matures in March 2007, and to pay $8,000,000 of construction costs expected to be incurred later that year to complete the plant.

Instructions

(a) How should the $10,000,000 of commercial paper be classified on the December 31, 2006, January 31, 2007, and February 28, 2007, balance sheets? Give support for your answer and also consider the cash element.

(b) What would your answer be if, instead of a refinancing at the date of issuance of the financial statements, a financing agreement existed at that date?

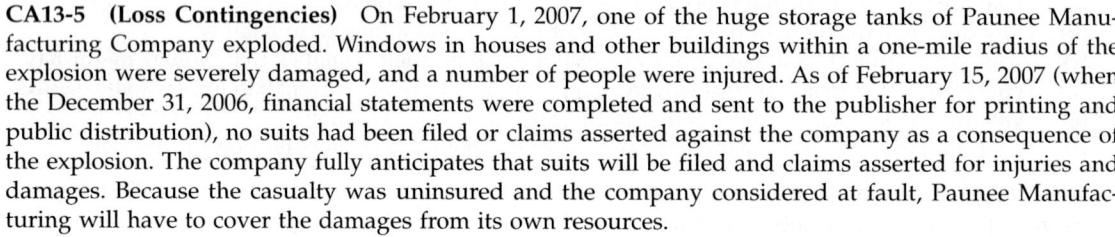 **CA13-5 (Loss Contingencies)** On February 1, 2007, one of the huge storage tanks of Paunee Manufacturing Company exploded. Windows in houses and other buildings within a one-mile radius of the explosion were severely damaged, and a number of people were injured. As of February 15, 2007 (when the December 31, 2006, financial statements were completed and sent to the publisher for printing and public distribution), no suits had been filed or claims asserted against the company as a consequence of the explosion. The company fully anticipates that suits will be filed and claims asserted for injuries and damages. Because the casualty was uninsured and the company considered at fault, Paunee Manufacturing will have to cover the damages from its own resources.

Instructions

Discuss fully the accounting treatment and disclosures that should be accorded the casualty and related contingent losses in the financial statements dated December 31, 2006.

CA13-6 (Loss Contingency) Presented below is a note disclosure for Federer Corporation.

Litigation and Environmental: The Company has been notified, or is a named or a potentially responsible party in a number of governmental (federal, state and local) and private actions associated with environmental matters, such as those relating to hazardous wastes, including certain sites which are on the United States EPA National Priorities List ("Superfund"). These actions seek cleanup costs, penalties and/or damages for personal injury or to property or natural resources.

In 2007, the Company recorded a pre-tax charge of $56,229,000, included in the "Other expense (income)—net" caption of the Company's consolidated statements of income, as an additional provision for environmental matters. These expenditures are expected to take place over the next several years and are indicative of the Company's commitment to improve and maintain the environment in which it operates. At December 31, 2007, environmental accruals amounted to $69,931,000, of which $61,535,000 are considered noncurrent and are included in the "Deferred credits and other liabilities" caption of the Company's consolidated balance sheets.

While it is impossible at this time to determine with certainty the ultimate outcome of environmental matters, it is management's opinion, based in part on the advice of independent counsel (after taking into account accruals and insurance coverage applicable to such actions) that when the costs are finally determined they will not have a material adverse effect on the financial position of the Company.

Instructions

Answer the following questions.

(a) What conditions must exist before a loss contingency can be recorded in the accounts?

(b) Suppose that Federer Corporation could not reasonably estimate the amount of the loss, although it could establish with a high degree of probability the minimum and maximum loss possible. How should this information be reported in the financial statements?

(c) If the amount of the loss is uncertain, how would the loss contingency be reported in the financial statements?

CA13-7 (Warranties and Loss Contingencies) The following two independent situations involve loss contingencies.

Part 1

Clarke Company sells two products, John and Henrick. Each carries a one-year warranty.

1. Product John—Product warranty costs, based on past experience, will normally be 1% of sales.
2. Product Henrick—Product warranty costs cannot be reasonably estimated because this is a new product line. However, the chief engineer believes that product warranty costs are likely to be incurred.

Instructions

How should Clarke report the estimated product warranty costs for each of the two types of merchandise above? Discuss the rationale for your answer. Do not discuss disclosures that should be made in Clarke's financial statements or notes.

Part 2

Toni Morrison Company is being sued for $4,000,000 for an injury caused to a child as a result of alleged negligence while the child was visiting the Toni Morrison Company plant in March 2007. The suit was filed in July 2007. Toni Morrison's lawyer states that it is probable that Toni Morrison will lose the suit and be found liable for a judgment costing anywhere from $400,000 to $2,000,000. However, the lawyer states that the most probable judgment is $800,000.

Instructions

How should Toni Morrison report the suit in its 2007 financial statements? Discuss the rationale for your answer. Include in your answer disclosures, if any, that should be made in Toni Morrison's financial statements or notes.

(AICPA adapted)

 CA13-8 (Warranties) The Elwood Company, owner of Bleacher Mall, charges Blue Clothing Store a rental fee of $600 per month plus 5% of yearly profits over $500,000. Jake Blue, the owner of the store, directs his accountant, Cab Callaway, to increase the estimate of bad debt expense and warranty costs in order to keep profits at $475,000.

Instructions

Answer the following questions.

(a) Should Callaway follow his boss's directive?

(b) Who is harmed if the estimates are increased?

(c) Is Jake Blue's directive ethical?

USING YOUR JUDGMENT

Financial Reporting Problem

 The Procter & Gamble Company (P&G)

The financial statements of **P&G** are presented in Appendix 5B or can be accessed on the KWW website.

 **Instructions**

Refer to these financial statements and the accompanying notes to answer the following questions.

(a) What was P&G's 2004 short-term debt and related weighted average interest rate on this debt?

(b) What was P&G's 2004 working capital, acid-test ratio, and current ratio? Comment on P&G's liquidity.

(c) What types of commitments and contingencies has P&G's reported in its financial statements? What is management's reaction to these contingencies?

Financial Statement Analysis Cases

Case 1 Northland Cranberries

Despite being a publicly traded company only since 1987, **Northland Cranberries** of Wisconsin Rapids, Wisconsin, is one of the world's largest cranberry growers. Despite its short life as a publicly traded corporation, it has engaged in an aggressive growth strategy. As a consequence, the company has taken on significant amounts of both short-term and long-term debt. The following information is taken from recent annual reports of the company.

Northland Cranberries	Current Year	Prior Year
Current assets	$ 6,745,759	$ 5,598,054
Total assets	107,744,751	83,074,339
Current liabilities	10,168,685	4,484,687
Total liabilities	73,118,204	49,948,787
Stockholders' equity	34,626,547	33,125,552
Net sales	21,783,966	18,051,355
Cost of goods sold	13,057,275	8,751,220
Interest expense	3,654,006	2,393,792
Income tax expense	1,051,000	1,917,000
Net income	1,581,707	2,942,954

Instructions

(a) Evaluate the company's liquidity by calculating and analyzing working capital and the current ratio.

(b) The following discussion of the company's liquidity was provided by the company in the Management Discussion and Analysis section of the company's annual report. Comment on whether you agree with management's statements, and what might be done to remedy the situation.

> The lower comparative current ratio in the current year was due to $3 million of short-term borrowing then outstanding which was incurred to fund the Yellow River Marsh acquisitions last year. As a result of the extreme seasonality of its business, the company does not believe that its current ratio or its underlying stated working capital at the current, fiscal year-end is a meaningful indication of the Company's liquidity. As of March 31 of each fiscal year, the Company has historically carried no significant amounts of inventories and by such date all of the Company's accounts receivable from its crop sold for processing under the supply agreements have been paid in cash, with the resulting cash received from such payments used to reduce indebtedness. The Company utilizes its revolving bank credit facility, together with cash generated from operations, to fund its working capital requirements throughout its growing season.

Case 2 Mohican Company

Presented below is the current liabilities section and related note of **Mohican Company**.

Mohican Company	(dollars in thousands)	
	Current Year	Prior Year
Current liabilities		
Current portion of long-term debt	$ 15,000	$ 10,000
Short-term debt	2,668	405
Accounts payable	29,495	42,427
Accrued warranty	16,843	16,741
Accrued marketing programs	17,512	16,585
Other accrued liabilities	35,653	33,290
Accrued and deferred income taxes	16,206	17,348
Total current liabilities	$133,377	$136,796

Notes to Consolidated Financial Statements

Note 1 (in part): Summary of Significant Accounting Policies and Related Data
Accrued Warranty The company provides an accrual for future warranty costs based upon the relationship of prior years' sales to actual warranty costs.

Instructions

Answer the following questions.

(a) What is the difference between the cash basis and the accrual basis of accounting for warranty costs?

(b) Under what circumstance, if any, would it be appropriate for Mohican Company to recognize deferred revenue on warranty contracts?

(c) If Mohican Company recognized deferred revenue on warranty contracts, how would it recognize this revenue in subsequent periods?

Comparative Analysis Case

The Coca-Cola Company and PepsiCo, Inc.

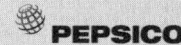

Instructions

Go to the book's website and use information found there to answer the following questions related to **The Coca-Cola Company** and **PepsiCo, Inc.**

(a) How much working capital do each of these companies have at the end of 2004?

(b) Compute both company's (a) current cash debt coverage ratio, (b) cash debt coverage ratio, (c) current ratio, (d) acid-test ratio, (e) receivable turnover ratio and (f) inventory turnover ratio for 2004. Comment on each company's overall liquidity.

(c) In PepsiCo's financial statements, it reports in the long-term debt section "short-term borrowings, reclassified." How can short-term borrowings be classified as long-term debt?

(d) What types of loss or gain contingencies do these two companies have at the end of 2004?

Research Cases

Case 1

Instructions

Obtain the most recent edition of *Accounting Trends and Techniques*. Examine the disclosures included under the section regarding gain contingencies, and answer the following questions.

(a) Determine the nature of each of the disclosed gain contingencies. Are there any common themes?

(b) How many of the footnotes include dollar amounts?

(c) What are the smallest and largest amounts disclosed?

Case 2

The January 25, 2002, edition of the *Wall Street Journal* contained an article by Schad Terhune titled "**Georgia Pacific** Says Asbestos Charge Will Result in Fourth Quarter Net Loss."

Instructions

Read the article and answer the following questions.

(a) Under what conditions does GAAP require firms to take charges for "anticipated claims"? Based on the information in the article, does it appear that Georgia-Pacific (GP) meets those conditions? Why or why not?

(b) Prepare the journal entry to record GP's $221 million charge. How would it be reported in the financial statements?

(c) Estimated losses must be based on a "reasonable" estimate. How did GP arrive at its estimate? Do you think this process would result in a reasonable estimate? Why or why not?

Case 3

As discussed in the chapter, an important consideration in evaluating current liabilities is a company's operating cycle. The operating cycle is the average time required to go from cash-to-cash in generating revenue. To determine the length of the operating cycle, two measures are used: the average days to sell inventory (inventory days) and the average days to collect receivables (receivable days). The inventory-days computation measures the average number of days it takes to move an item from raw materials or purchase to final sale (from the day it comes in the company's door to the point it is converted to cash or an account receivable). The receivable-days computation measures the average number of days it takes to collect an account.

Most businesses must then determine how to finance the period of time when the liquid assets are tied up in inventory and accounts receivable. To determine how much to finance, companies first determine how long it takes to pay their creditors, or *accounts payable days*. Accounts payable days measures the number of days it takes to pay a supplier invoice. Consider the following operating cycle worksheet for BOP Clothing Co. shown below.

	2006	2007
Cash	$ 45,000	$ 30,000
Accounts Receivable	250,000	325,000
Inventory	830,000	800,000
Accounts Payable	720,000	775,000
Purchases	1,100,000	1,425,000
Cost of Goods Sold	1,145,000	1,455,000
Sales	1,750,000	1,950,000
Operating Cycle		
Inventory days[1]	264.6	200.7
Receivable days[2]	52.1	60.8
Operating cycle	316.7	261.5
Less: Accounts payable days[3]	238.9	198.5
Days to be financed	77.8	63.0
Working capital	$405,000	$380,000
Current ratio	1.56	1.49
Acid-test ratio	0.41	0.46

[1]Inventory Days = (Inventory × 365)/Cost of Goods Sold
[2]Receivable Days = (Accounts Receivable × 365)/Sales
[3]Accounts Payable Days = (Accounts Payable × 365)/Purchases
 Purchases = Cost of Goods Sold + Ending Inventory − Beginning Inventory. The ratios above
 assume that other current assets and liabilities are negligible.

These data indicate that BOP has reduced its overall operating cycle (to 261.5 days) as well as the number of days to be financed with sources of funds other than accounts payable (from 78 to 63 days). Most businesses cannot finance the operating cycle with accounts payable financing alone, so working capital financing, usually short-term interest-bearing loans, is needed to cover the shortfall. In this case, BOP would need to borrow less money to finance its operating cycle in 2007 than in 2006.

Instructions

(a) Use the BOP analysis to briefly discuss how the operating cycle data relate to the amount of working capital and the current and acid-test ratios.

(b) Select two other real companies that are in the same industry and complete the operating cycle worksheet above, along with the working capital and ratio analysis. Briefly summarize and interpret the results. To simplify the analysis, you may use ending balances to compute turnover ratios.

[Adapted from Operating Cycle Worksheet at www.entrepreneur.com]

Professional Research: Financial Accounting and Reporting

Hincapie Co. manufactures specialty bike accessories. The company is known for product quality, and it has offered one of the best warranties in the industry on its higher-priced products—a lifetime guarantee, performing all the warranty work in its own shops. The warranty on these products is included in the sales price.

Due to the recent introduction and growth in sales of some products targeted to the low-price market, Hincapie is considering partnering with another company to do the warranty work on this line of products, if customers purchase a service contract at the time of original product purchase. Hincapie has called you to advise the company on the accounting for this new warranty arrangement.

Instructions

Using the **Financial Accounting Research System (FARS)**, respond to the following items. (Provide text strings used in your search.)

(a) Identify the accounting literature that addresses the accounting for the type of separately priced warranty that Hincapie is considering.

(b) When are warranty contracts considered separately priced?

(c) What are incremental direct acquisition costs and how should they be treated?

(d) How many letters of comment were received on this proposed Technical Bulletin? Why did some of the respondents feel that the effective date of this Technical Bulletin should be delayed?

Professional Simulation

In this simulation you are asked to address questions related to the accounting for current liabilities. Prepare responses to all parts.

KWW_Professional _Simulation

✐ Current Liabilities	Time Remaining 0 hours 20 minutes	copy · paste · calculator · sheet · standards · help · spliter · done

Directions | **Situation** | **Journal Entries** | **Explanation** | **Resources**

Alex Rodriguez Inc., a publishing company, is preparing its December 31, 2006, financial statements and must determine the proper accounting treatment for the following situations.

(a) Rodriguez sells subscriptions to several magazines for a 1-year, 2-year, or 3-year period. Cash receipts from subscribers are credited to magazine subscriptions collected in advance, and this account had a balance of $2,300,000 at December 31, 2006. Outstanding subscriptions at December 31, 2006, expire as follows.

During 2007—$600,000
During 2008— 500,000
During 2009— 800,000

(b) On January 2, 2006, Rodriguez discontinued collision, fire, and theft coverage on its delivery vehicles and became self-insured for these risks. Actual losses of $50,000 during 2006 were charged to delivery expense. The 2005 premium for the discontinued coverage amounted to $80,000, and the controller wants to set up a reserve for self-insurance by a debit to delivery expense of $30,000 and a credit to the reserve for self-insurance of $30,000.

(c) A suit for breach of contract seeking damages of $1,000,000 was filed by an author against Rodriguez on July 1, 2006. The company's legal counsel believes that an unfavorable outcome is probable. A reasonable estimate of the court's award to the plaintiff is in the range between $300,000 and $700,000. No amount within this range is a better estimate of potential damages than any other amount.

(d) The following items are listed as liabilities on the balance sheet on December 31, 2006.

Accounts payable	$ 420,000
Notes payable	750,000
Bonds payable	2,250,000

The accounts payable represent obligations to suppliers that were due in January 2007. The notes payable mature on various dates during 2007. The bonds payable mature on July 1, 2007.

Directions | **Situation** | **Journal Entries** | **Explanation** | **Resources**

For situations (a), (b), and (c), prepare the journal entry that should be recorded as of December 31, 2006.

Directions | **Situation** | **Journal Entries** | **Explanation** | **Resources**

Prepare a brief memorandum explaining the general rule for classifying a liability as current or non-current. Explain the conditions under which notes payable might be classified as current or non-current.

Remember to check the book's companion website to find additional resources for this chapter.

LONG-TERM LIABILITIES

Your Debt Is Killing My Stock

Traditionally, investors in the stock and bond markets operate in their own separate worlds. However, in recent volatile markets, even quiet murmurs in the bond market have been amplified into movements (usually negative) in stock prices. At one extreme, these gyrations heralded the demise of a company well before the investors could sniff out the problem.

The swift decline of **Enron** in late 2001 provided the ultimate lesson: A company with no credit is no company at all. As one analyst remarked, "You can no longer have an opinion on a company's stock without having an appreciation for its credit rating." Other energy companies, such as **Calpine**, **NRG Energy**, and **AES Corp.**, also felt the effect of Enron's troubles as lenders tightened or closed down the credit supply and raised interest rates on already-high levels of debt. The result? Stock prices took a hit.

Other industries are not immune from the negative stock price effects of credit problems. For example, analysts at **TheStreet.com** compiled a list of companies with high debt levels and low ability to cover interest costs. Among them is **Goodyear Tire and Rubber**, which reported debt six times greater than its equity. Goodyear is a classic example of how swift and crippling a heavy debt-load can be. Not too long ago, Goodyear had a high debt rating and was paying a good dividend. But with mounting operating losses, Goodyear's debt became a huge burden, its debt rating fell to junk-status, the company cut its dividend, and its stock price dropped 80%. This was yet another example of stock prices taking a hit due to concerns about credit quality. Thus, even if your investment tastes are in stocks, keep an eye on the liabilities.[1]

---

[1]Adapted from Steven Vames, "Credit Quality, Stock Investing Seem to Go Hand in Hand," *Wall Street Journal* (April 1, 2002), p. R4 and Herb Greenberg, "The Hidden Dangers of Debt," *Fortune* (July 21, 2003), p. 153.

Learning Objectives

After studying this chapter, you should be able to:

1 Describe the formal procedures associated with issuing long-term debt.

2 Identify various types of bond issues.

3 Describe the accounting valuation for bonds at date of issuance.

4 Apply the methods of bond discount and premium amortization.

5 Describe the accounting for the extinguishment of debt.

6 Explain the accounting for long-term notes payable.

7 Explain the reporting of off-balance-sheet financing arrangements.

8 Indicate how to present and analyze long-term debt.

As our opening story indicates, investors pay considerable attention to a company's liabilities. The stock market severely punishes companies with high debt levels and the related impact of higher interest costs on income performance. In this chapter we explain the accounting issues related to long-term debt. The content and organization of the chapter are as follows.

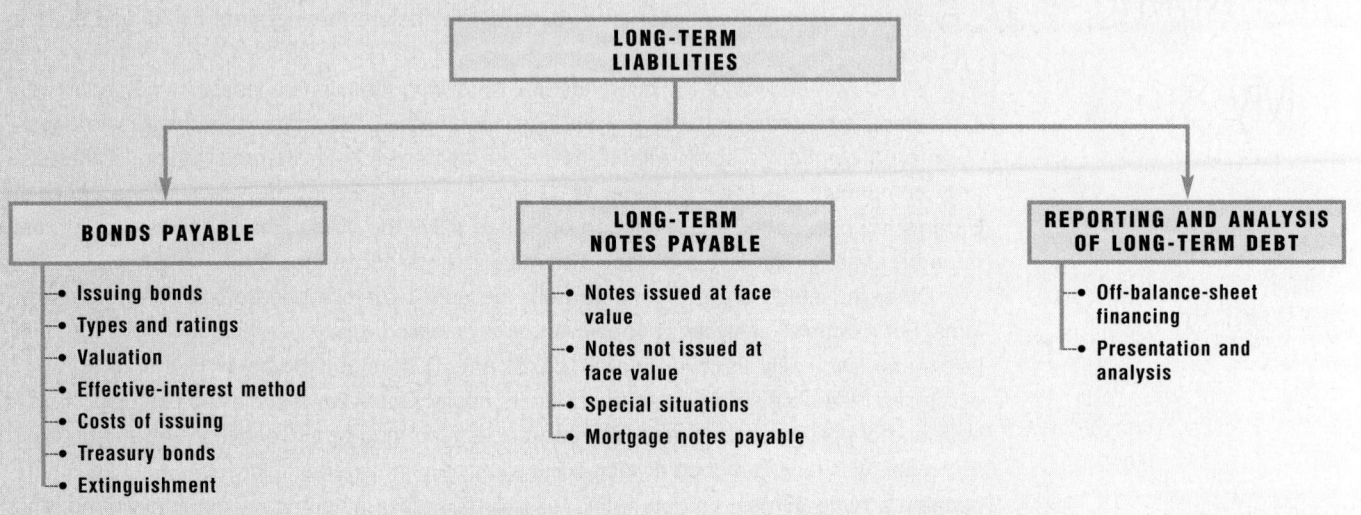

LONG-TERM LIABILITIES

BONDS PAYABLE
- Issuing bonds
- Types and ratings
- Valuation
- Effective-interest method
- Costs of issuing
- Treasury bonds
- Extinguishment

LONG-TERM NOTES PAYABLE
- Notes issued at face value
- Notes not issued at face value
- Special situations
- Mortgage notes payable

REPORTING AND ANALYSIS OF LONG-TERM DEBT
- Off-balance-sheet financing
- Presentation and analysis

SECTION 1	*BONDS PAYABLE*

Long-term debt consists of probable future sacrifices of economic benefits arising from present obligations that are not payable within a year or the operating cycle of the company, whichever is longer. Bonds payable, long-term notes payable, mortgages payable, pension liabilities, and lease liabilities are examples of long-term liabilities.

A corporation, per its bylaws, usually requires approval by the board of directors and the stockholders before bonds or notes can be issued. The same holds true for other types of long-term debt arrangements.

OBJECTIVE 1
Describe the formal procedures associated with issuing long-term debt.

Generally, long-term debt has various **covenants** or **restrictions** that protect both lenders and borrowers. The indenture or agreement often includes the amounts authorized to be issued, interest rate, due date(s), call provisions, property pledged as security, sinking fund requirements, working capital and dividend restrictions, and limitations concerning the assumption of additional debt. Companies should describe these features in the body of the financial statements or the notes if important for a complete understanding of the financial position and the results of operations.

Although it would seem that these covenants provide adequate protection to the long-term debtholder, many bondholders suffer considerable losses when companies add more debt to the capital structure. Consider what can happen to bondholders in leveraged buyouts (LBOs), which are usually led by management. In an LBO of **RJR Nabisco**, for example, solidly rated 9⅜ percent bonds due in 2016 plunged 20 percent in value when management announced the leveraged buyout. Such a loss in value occurs because the additional debt added to the capital structure increases the likelihood of default. Although covenants protect bondholders, they can still suffer losses when debt levels get too high.

ISSUING BONDS

A bond arises from a contract known as a **bond indenture**. A bond represents a promise to pay: (1) a sum of money at a designated maturity date, plus (2) periodic interest at a specified rate on the maturity amount (face value). Individual bonds are evidenced by a paper certificate and typically have a $1,000 face value. Companies usually make bond interest payments semiannually, although the interest rate is generally expressed as an annual rate. The main purpose of bonds is to borrow for the long term when the amount of capital needed is too large for one lender to supply. By issuing bonds in $100, $1,000, or $10,000 denominations, a company can divide a large amount of long-term indebtedness into many small investing units, thus enabling more than one lender to participate in the loan.

A company may sell an entire bond issue to an investment bank which acts as a selling agent in the process of marketing the bonds. In such arrangements, investment banks may either underwrite the entire issue by guaranteeing a certain sum to the company, thus taking the risk of selling the bonds for whatever price they can get (firm underwriting). Or they may sell the bond issue for a commission on the proceeds of the sale (best-efforts underwriting). Alternatively, the issuing company may sell the bonds directly to a large institution, financial or otherwise, without the aid of an underwriter (private placement).

TYPES AND RATINGS OF BONDS

Below, we define some of the more common types of bonds found in practice.

OBJECTIVE 2
Identify various types of bond issues.

> ## TYPES OF BONDS
>
> **SECURED AND UNSECURED BONDS. Secured bonds** are backed by a pledge of some sort of collateral. Mortgage bonds are secured by a claim on real estate. Collateral trust bonds are secured by stocks and bonds of other corporations. Bonds not backed by collateral are **unsecured**. A **debenture bond** is unsecured. A "junk bond" is unsecured and also very risky, and therefore pays a high interest rate. Companies often use these bonds to finance leveraged buyouts.
>
> **TERM, SERIAL BONDS, AND CALLABLE BONDS.** Bond issues that mature on a single date are called **term bonds**; issues that mature in installments are called **serial bonds**. Serially maturing bonds are frequently used by school or sanitary districts, municipalities, or other local taxing bodies that receive money through a special levy. **Callable bonds** give the issuer the right to call and retire the bonds prior to maturity.
>
> **CONVERTIBLE, COMMODITY-BACKED, AND DEEP-DISCOUNT BONDS.** If bonds are convertible into other securities of the corporation for a specified time after issuance, they are **convertible bonds**.
>
> Two types of bonds have been developed in an attempt to attract capital in a tight money market—commodity-backed bonds and deep-discount bonds. **Commodity-backed bonds** (also called **asset-linked bonds**) are redeemable in measures of a commodity, such as barrels of oil, tons of coal, or ounces of rare metal. To illustrate, **Sunshine Mining**, a silver-mining company, sold two issues of bonds redeemable with either $1,000 in cash or 50 ounces of silver, whichever is greater at maturity, and that have a stated interest rate of 8½ percent. The accounting problem is one of projecting the maturity value, especially since silver has fluctuated between $4 and $40 an ounce since issuance.
>
> **JCPenney Company** sold the first publicly marketed long-term debt securities in the United States that do not bear interest. These **deep-discount bonds**, also referred to as **zero-interest debenture bonds**, are sold at a discount that provides the buyer's total interest payoff at maturity.

REGISTERED AND BEARER (COUPON) BONDS. Bonds issued in the name of the owner are **registered bonds** and require surrender of the certificate and issuance of a new certificate to complete a sale. A **bearer** or **coupon bond**, however, is not recorded in the name of the owner and may be transferred from one owner to another by mere delivery.

INCOME AND REVENUE BONDS. Income bonds pay no interest unless the issuing company is profitable. **Revenue bonds**, so called because the interest on them is paid from specified revenue sources, are most frequently issued by airports, school districts, counties, toll-road authorities, and governmental bodies.

ALL ABOUT BONDS

WHAT DO THE NUMBERS MEAN?

How do investors monitor their bond investments? Typically, they review the bond listings found in the newspaper or online. Corporate bond listings in the financial press show the coupon or interest rate, maturity date, and last price. However, because corporate bonds are more actively traded by large institutional investors, the listings also indicate the current yield and include the volume traded. Corporate bond listings would look like those below.

Bonds	Cur. Yld.	Vol	Close	Net Chg.
BosCelts 6s38	9.2	22	65 3/8	+1/4
PacBell 6 5/8 34	6.7	5	99 1/8	−1/8

The companies issuing the bonds are listed in the first column—in this case, the professional basketball team the **Boston Celtics**, and the telecommunications company **Pacific Bell**. Immediately after the names, comes the interest rate paid by the bond as a percentage of its par value. The Celtics' bond pays 6 percent; PacBell's pays 6 5/8 percent. (The small "s" in the Celtics' listing simply separates the interest rate from the year the bond matures, 2038.) The PacBell bond matures in 2034.

Reading on, the basketball team's bond has a current yield of 9.2 percent based on its closing price of $653.75 per $1,000. The volume traded on the exchange the day before amounted to $22,000, and the price rose $2.50. Similarly, PacBell had a volume of $5,000 and closed nearer its par value, $991.25, down $1.25 for the day.

Also, as indicated in the chapter, interest rates and the bond's term to maturity have a real effect on bond prices. For example, an increase in interest rates will lead to a decline in bond values; a decrease in interest rates will lead to a rise in bond values. These effects are shown in the data reported below, based on three different bond funds.

Bond Price Changes in Response to Interest Rate Changes	1% Interest Rate Increase	1% Interest Rate Decrease
Short-term fund (2–5 years)	−2.5%	+2.5%
Intermediate-term fund (5 years)	−5%	+5%
Long-term fund (10 years)	−10%	+10%

Source: Data from The Vanguard Group.

Another factor that affects bond prices is the call feature, which decreases the value of the bond. Investors must be rewarded for the risk that the issuer will call the bond if interest rates decline, which forces the investor to reinvest at lower rates.

Source: The Bond Market Association (*www.investinginbonds.com*).

OBJECTIVE 3
Describe the accounting valuation for bonds at date of issuance.

VALUATION OF BONDS PAYABLE—DISCOUNT AND PREMIUM

The issuance and marketing of bonds to the public does not happen overnight. It usually takes weeks or even months. First, the issuing company must arrange for underwriters that will help market and sell the bonds. Then it must obtain the Securities and Exchange

Commission's approval of the bond issue, undergo audits, and issue a prospectus (a document which describes the features of the bond and related financial information). Finally, the company must generally have the bond certificates printed. Frequently the issuing company establishes the terms of a bond indenture well in advance of the sale of the bonds. Between the time the company sets these terms and the time it issues the bonds, the market conditions and the financial position of the issuing corporation may change significantly. Such changes affect the marketability of the bonds and thus their selling price.

The selling price of a bond issue is set by the supply and demand of buyers and sellers, relative risk, market conditions, and the state of the economy. The investment community values a bond at the **present value of its expected future cash flows**, which consist of (1) interest and (2) principal. The rate used to compute the present value of these cash flows is the interest rate that provides an acceptable return on an investment commensurate with the issuer's risk characteristics.

The interest rate written in the terms of the bond indenture (and often printed on the bond certificate) is known as the **stated, coupon,** or **nominal rate**. The issuer of the bonds sets this rate. The stated rate is expressed as a percentage of the **face value** of the bonds (also called the **par value, principal amount,** or **maturity value**).

If the rate employed by the investment community (buyers) differs from the stated rate, the present value of the bonds computed by the buyers (and the current purchase price) will differ from the face value of the bonds. The difference between the face value and the present value of the bonds determines the actual price that buyers pay for the bonds. This difference is either a discount or premium.[2] If the bonds sell for less than face value, they sell at a **discount**. If the bonds sell for more than face value, they sell at a **premium**.

The rate of interest actually earned by the bondholders is called the **effective yield** or **market rate**. If bonds sell at a discount, the effective yield exceeds the stated rate. Conversely, if bonds sell at a premium, the effective yield is lower than the stated rate. Several variables affect the bond's price while it is outstanding, most notably the market rate of interest. There is an inverse relationship between the market interest rate and the price of the bond.

Here we consider an example to illustrate the computation of the **present value of a bond issue**. Assume that ServiceMaster issues $100,000 in bonds, due in five years with 9 percent interest payable annually at year-end. At the time of issue, the market rate for such bonds is 11 percent. The time diagram in Illustration 14-1 depicts both the interest and the principal cash flows.

INTERNATIONAL INSIGHT

IFRS for long-term debt permit valuation of long-term debt and other liabilities at fair value with gains and losses on changes in fair value recorded in income (referred to as the "fair value option").

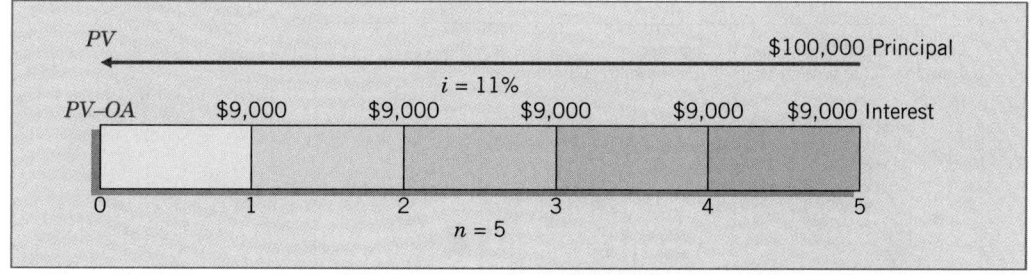

ILLUSTRATION 14-1
Time Diagram for Bond Cash Flows

---

[2]Until the 1950s, corporations commonly issued bonds with low, even-percentage coupons (such as 4 percent) to demonstrate their financial solidity. Frequently, large discounts resulted. More recently, it has become acceptable to set the stated rate of interest on bonds in rather precise fractions (such as 10 ⅝ percent). Companies usually attempt to align the stated rate as closely as possible with the market or effective rate at the time of issue.

Although discounts and premiums continue to occur, their absolute magnitude tends to be much smaller; many times it is immaterial. A study conducted in the mid-80's documented that of 685 new debt offerings, none were issued at a premium. Approximately 95 percent were issued either with no discount or at a price above 98. Now, however, zero-interest (deep discount) bonds are more popular, and they cause substantial discounts.

The actual principal and interest cash flows are discounted at an 11 percent rate for five periods as shown in Illustration 14-2.

ILLUSTRATION 14-2
Present Value
Computation of Bond
Selling at a Discount

Present value of the principal:	
$100,000 × .59345 (Table 6-2)	$59,345.00
Present value of the interest payments:	
$9,000 × 3.69590 (Table 6-4)	33,263.10
Present value (selling price) of the bonds	$92,608.10

By paying $92,608.10 at the date of issue, investors realize an effective rate or yield of 11 percent over the five-year term of the bonds. These bonds would sell at a discount of $7,391.90 ($100,000 − $92,608.10). The price at which the bonds sell is typically stated as a percentage of the face or par value of the bonds. For example, the ServiceMaster bonds sold for 92.6 (92.6% of par). If ServiceMaster had received $102,000, then the bonds sold for 102 (102% of par).

HOW'S MY RATING?

**WHAT DO THE
NUMBERS MEAN?**

Two major publication companies, **Moody's Investors Service** and **Standard & Poor's Corporation**, issue quality ratings on every public debt issue. The following table summarizes the ratings issued by Standard & Poor's, along with historical default rates on bonds with different ratings. As expected, bonds receiving the highest quality rating of AAA have the lowest historical default rates. Bonds rated below BBB, which are considered below investment grade ("junk bonds"), experience default rates ranging from 20 to 50 percent.

Original Rating	AAA	AA	A	BBB	BB	B	CCC
Default Rate*	0.52%	1.31	2.32	6.64	19.52	35.76	54.38

*Percentage of defaults by issuers recently rated by Standard & Poor's, based on rating they were initially assigned. *Source*: Data from Standard & Poor's Corp.

Debt ratings reflect credit quality. The market closely monitors these ratings when determining the required yield and pricing of bonds at issuance and in periods after issuance, especially if a bond's rating is upgraded or downgraded. Data on recent upgrades and downgrades suggest there are a lot more fallen angels (downgraded debt) than rising stars (upgraded debt).

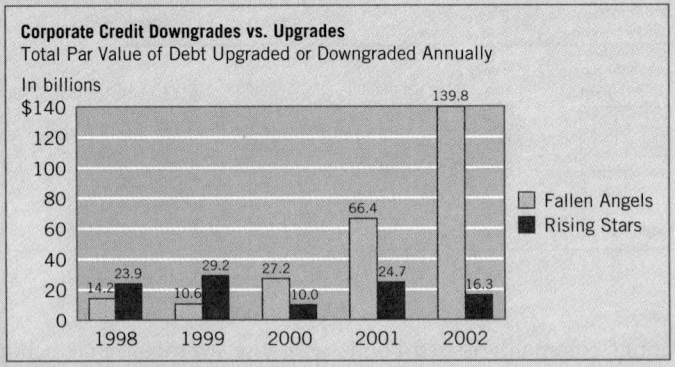

Corporate Credit Downgrades vs. Upgrades
Total Par Value of Debt Upgraded or Downgraded Annually

Source: J.P. Morgan Chase & Co.

Whereas the dollar amount of upgrades exceeded downgrades in 1999, the dollar amount of downgrades was more than seven times the rising-star amounts in 2002. It is not surprising, then, that bond investors and companies who issue bonds keep a close watch on debt ratings—both when bonds are issued and while the bonds are outstanding.

Source: A. Borrus, M. McNamee, and H. Timmons, "The Credit Raters: How They Work and How They Might Work Better," *Business Week* (April 8, 2002), pp. 38–40; and the T. Rowe Price Report (Winter 2003).

When bonds sell below face value, it means that investors demand a rate of interest **higher** than the stated rate. Usually this occurs because the investors can earn a greater rate on alternative investments of equal risk. They cannot change the stated rate, so they refuse to pay face value for the bonds. Thus, by changing the amount invested, they alter the effective rate of return. The investors receive interest at the stated rate computed on the face value, but they actually earn at **an effective rate that exceeds the stated rate because they paid less than face value for the bonds.** (Later in the chapter, in Illustrations 14-6 and 14-7, we show an illustration for a bond that sells at a premium.)

Bonds Issued at Par on Interest Date

When a company issues bonds on an interest payment date at par (face value), it accrues no interest. No premium or discount exists. The company simply records the cash proceeds and the face value of the bonds. To illustrate, if Buchanan Company issues at par 10-year term bonds with a par value of $800,000, dated January 1, 2007, and bearing interest at an annual rate of 10 percent payable semiannually on January 1 and July 1, it records the following entry:

Cash	800,000	
Bonds Payable		800,000

Buchanan records the first semiannual interest payment of $40,000 ($800,000 × .10 × 1/2) on July 1, 2007, as follows.

Bond Interest Expense	40,000	
Cash		40,000

It records accrued interest expense at December 31, 2007 (year-end) as follows.

Bond Interest Expense	40,000	
Bond Interest Payable		40,000

Bonds Issued at Discount or Premium on Interest Date

If Buchanan Company issues the $800,000 of bonds on January 1, 2007, at 97 (meaning 97 percent of par), it records the issuance as follows.

Cash ($800,000 × .97)	776,000	
Discount on Bonds Payable	24,000	
Bonds Payable		800,000

> **OBJECTIVE 4**
> Apply the methods of bond discount and premium amortization.

Recall from our earlier discussion that because of its relation to interest, **companies amortize the discount and charge it to interest expense over the period of time that the bonds are outstanding.**

The **straight-line method**[3] amortizes a constant amount each year. For example, using the bond discount of $24,000, Buchanan amortizes $2,400 to interest expense each year for 10 years ($24,000 ÷ 10 years). It records amortization annually as follows.

Bond Interest Expense	2,400	
Discount on Bonds Payable		2,400

At the end of the first year, 2007, following the amortization entry above, the unamortized balance in Discount on Bonds Payable is $21,600 ($24,000 − $2,400).

If Buchanan dates and sells the bonds on October 1, 2007, and if the fiscal year of the corporation ends on December 31, the discount amortized during 2007 would be only 3/12 of 1/10 of $24,000, or $600. Buchanan must also record three months of accrued interest on December 31.

---

[3]Although the effective-interest method is preferred for amortization of discount or premium, to keep these initial illustrations simple, we have chosen to use the straight-line method (which is acceptable if the results obtained are not materially different from those produced by the effective-interest method).

Premium on Bonds Payable is accounted for in a manner similar to that for Discount on Bonds Payable. If Buchanan dates and sells 10-year bonds with a par value of $800,000 on January 1, 2007, at 103, it records the issuance as follows.

Cash ($800,000 × 1.03)	824,000	
Premium on Bonds Payable		24,000
Bonds Payable		800,000

At the end of 2007 and for each year the bonds are outstanding, Buchanan amortizes the premium on a straight-line basis with the following entry.

Premium on Bonds Payable	2,400	
Bond Interest Expense		2,400

Amortization of a discount increases bond interest expense. Amortization of a premium decreases bond interest expense. Later in the chapter we discuss amortization of a discount or premium under the effective-interest method.

The issuer may call some bonds at a stated price after a certain date. This call feature gives the issuing corporation the opportunity to reduce its bonded indebtedness or take advantage of lower interest rates. **Whether callable or not, a company must amortize any premium or discount over the bond's life to maturity because early redemption (call of the bond) is not a certainty.**

Bonds Issued between Interest Dates

Companies usually make bond interest payments semiannually, on dates specified in the bond indenture. When companies issue bonds on other than the interest payment dates, **buyers of the bonds will pay the seller the interest accrued from the last interest payment date to the date of issue.** The purchasers of the bonds, in effect, pay the bond issuer in advance for that portion of the full six-months' interest payment to which they are not entitled because they have not held the bonds for that period. **Then, on the next semiannual interest payment date, purchasers will receive the full six-months' interest payment.**

To illustrate, assume that on March 1, 2007, Taft Corporation issues 10-year bonds, dated January 1, 2007, with a par value of $800,000. These bonds have an annual interest rate of 6 percent, payable semiannually on January 1 and July 1. Because Taft issues the bonds between interest dates, it records the bond issuance at **par plus accrued interest** as follows.

Cash	808,000	
Bonds Payable		800,000
Bond Interest Expense ($800,000 × .06 × 2/12)		8,000
(Interest Payable might be credited instead)		

The purchaser advances two months' interest. On July 1, 2007, four months after the date of purchase, Taft pays the purchaser six months' interest. Taft makes the following entry on July 1, 2007.

Bond Interest Expense	24,000	
Cash		24,000

The Bond Interest Expense account now contains a debit balance of $16,000, which represents the proper amount of interest expense—four months at 6 percent on $800,000.

The illustration above was simplified by having the January 1, 2007, bonds issued on March 1, 2007, **at par**. If, however, Taft issued the 6 percent bonds at 102, its March 1 entry would be:

Cash [($800,000 × 1.02) + ($800,000 × .06 × 2/12)]	824,000	
Bonds Payable		800,000
Premium on Bonds Payable ($800,000 × .02)		16,000
Bond Interest Expense		8,000

Taft would amortize the premium **from the date of sale** (March 1, 2007), not from the date of the bonds (January 1, 2007).

EFFECTIVE-INTEREST METHOD

The preferred procedure for amortization of a discount or premium is the **effective-interest method** (also called **present value amortization**). Under the effective-interest method, companies:

1 Compute bond interest expense first by multiplying the **carrying value** (book value) of the bonds at the beginning of the period by the effective interest rate.[4]

2 Determine the bond discount or premium amortization next by comparing the bond interest expense with the interest (cash) to be paid.

Illustration 14-3 depicts graphically the computation of the amortization.

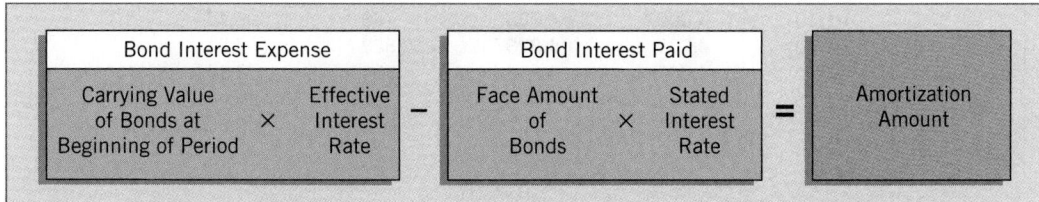

ILLUSTRATION 14-3
Bond Discount and
Premium Amortization
Computation

The effective-interest method produces a periodic interest expense equal to **a constant percentage of the carrying value of the bonds**. Since the percentage is the effective rate of interest incurred by the borrower at the time of issuance, the effective-interest method matches expenses with revenues better than the straight-line method.

Both the effective-interest and straight-line methods result in the **same total amount of interest expense over the term of the bonds**. However, when the annual amounts are materially different, generally accepted accounting principles require use of the effective-interest method.[5]

Bonds Issued at a Discount

To illustrate amortization of a discount under the effective-interest method, Evermaster Corporation issued $100,000 of 8 percent term bonds on January 1, 2007, due on January 1, 2012, with interest payable each July 1 and January 1. Because the investors required an effective-interest rate of 10 percent, they paid $92,278 for the $100,000 of bonds, creating a $7,722 discount. Evermaster computes the $7,722 discount as follows.[6]

Maturity value of bonds payable		$100,000
Present value of $100,000 due in 5 years at 10%, interest payable semiannually (Table 6-2); $FV(PVF_{10,5\%})$; ($100,000 × .61391)	$61,391	
Present value of $4,000 interest payable semiannually for 5 years at 10% annually (Table 6-4); $R(PVF\text{-}OA_{10,5\%})$; ($4,000 × 7.72173)	30,887	
Proceeds from sale of bonds		92,278
Discount on bonds payable		$ 7,722

ILLUSTRATION 14-4
Computation of Discount
on Bonds Payable

---

[4]The **carrying value** is the face amount minus any unamortized discount or plus any unamortized premium. The term *carrying value* is synonymous with *book value*.

[5]"Interest on Receivables and Payables," *Opinions of the Accounting Principles Board No. 21* (New York: AICPA, 1971), par. 16.

[6]Because companies pay interest semiannually, the interest rate used is 5% (10% × ½). The number of periods is 10 (5 years × 2).

The five-year amortization schedule appears in Illustration 14-5.

ILLUSTRATION 14-5
Bond Discount
Amortization Schedule

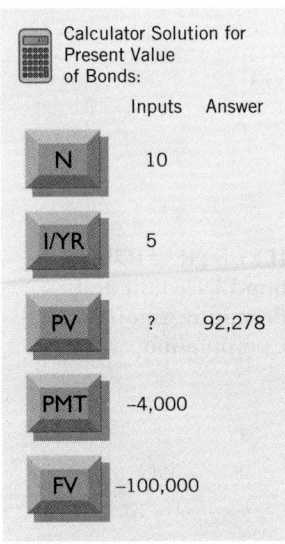

Calculator Solution for
Present Value
of Bonds:

	Inputs	Answer
N	10	
I/YR	5	
PV	?	92,278
PMT	–4,000	
FV	–100,000	

		SCHEDULE OF BOND DISCOUNT AMORTIZATION		
		EFFECTIVE-INTEREST METHOD—SEMIANNUAL INTEREST PAYMENTS		
		5-YEAR, 8% BONDS SOLD TO YIELD 10%		
Date	Cash Paid	Interest Expense	Discount Amortized	Carrying Amount of Bonds
1/1/07				$ 92,278
7/1/07	$ 4,000ª	$ 4,614ᵇ	$ 614ᶜ	92,892ᵈ
1/1/08	4,000	4,645	645	93,537
7/1/08	4,000	4,677	677	94,214
1/1/09	4,000	4,711	711	94,925
7/1/09	4,000	4,746	746	95,671
1/1/10	4,000	4,783	783	96,454
7/1/10	4,000	4,823	823	97,277
1/1/11	4,000	4,864	864	98,141
7/1/11	4,000	4,907	907	99,048
1/1/12	4,000	4,952	952	100,000
	$40,000	$47,722	$7,722	

ª$4,000 = $100,000 ×.08 × 6/12   ᶜ$614 = $4,614 − $4,000
ᵇ$4,614 = $92,278 ×.10 × 6/12   ᵈ$92,892 = $92,278 + $614

Evermaster records the issuance of its bonds at a discount on January 1, 2007, as follows:

Cash	92,278	
Discount on Bonds Payable	7,722	
Bonds Payable		100,000

It records the first interest payment on July 1, 2007, and amortization of the discount as follows:

Bond Interest Expense	4,614	
Discount on Bonds Payable		614
Cash		4,000

Evermaster records the interest expense accrued at December 31, 2007 (year-end) and amortization of the discount as follows:

Bond Interest Expense	4,645	
Bond Interest Payable		4,000
Discount on Bonds Payable		645

Bonds Issued at a Premium

Now assume that for the bond issue described above, investors are willing to accept an effective interest rate of 6 percent. In that case, they would pay $108,530 or a premium of $8,530, computed as follows.

ILLUSTRATION 14-6
Computation of Premium
on Bonds Payable

Maturity value of bonds payable		$100,000
Present value of $100,000 due in 5 years at 6%, interest payable semiannually (Table 6-2); $FV(PVF_{10,3\%})$; ($100,000 × .74409)	$74,409	
Present value of $4,000 interest payable semiannually for 5 years at 6% annually (Table 6-4); $R(PVF\text{-}OA_{10,3\%})$; ($4,000 × 8.53020)	34,121	
Proceeds from sale of bonds		108,530
Premium on bonds payable		$ 8,530

The five-year amortization schedule appears in Illustration 14-7.

<table>
<tr><td colspan="5">**SCHEDULE OF BOND PREMIUM AMORTIZATION**
EFFECTIVE-INTEREST METHOD—SEMIANNUAL INTEREST PAYMENTS
5-YEAR, 8% BONDS SOLD TO YIELD 6%</td></tr>
<tr><th>Date</th><th>Cash Paid</th><th>Interest Expense</th><th>Premium Amortized</th><th>Carrying Amount of Bonds</th></tr>
<tr><td>1/1/07</td><td></td><td></td><td></td><td>$108,530</td></tr>
<tr><td>7/1/07</td><td>$ 4,000^a</td><td>$ 3,256^b</td><td>$ 744^c</td><td>107,786^d</td></tr>
<tr><td>1/1/08</td><td>4,000</td><td>3,234</td><td>766</td><td>107,020</td></tr>
<tr><td>7/1/08</td><td>4,000</td><td>3,211</td><td>789</td><td>106,231</td></tr>
<tr><td>1/1/09</td><td>4,000</td><td>3,187</td><td>813</td><td>105,418</td></tr>
<tr><td>7/1/09</td><td>4,000</td><td>3,162</td><td>838</td><td>104,580</td></tr>
<tr><td>1/1/10</td><td>4,000</td><td>3,137</td><td>863</td><td>103,717</td></tr>
<tr><td>7/1/10</td><td>4,000</td><td>3,112</td><td>888</td><td>102,829</td></tr>
<tr><td>1/1/11</td><td>4,000</td><td>3,085</td><td>915</td><td>101,914</td></tr>
<tr><td>7/1/11</td><td>4,000</td><td>3,057</td><td>943</td><td>100,971</td></tr>
<tr><td>1/1/12</td><td>4,000</td><td>3,029</td><td>971</td><td>100,000</td></tr>
<tr><td></td><td>$40,000</td><td>$31,470</td><td>$8,530</td><td></td></tr>
</table>

^a$4,000 = $100,000 × .08 × 6/12
^b$3,256 = $108,530 × .06 × 6/12
^c$744 = $4,000 − $3,256
^d$107,786 = $108,530 − $744

ILLUSTRATION 14-7
Bond Premium
Amortization Schedule

Calculator Solution for
Present Value
of Bonds:

	Inputs	Answer
N	10	
I/YR	3	
PV	?	108,530
PMT	−4,000	
FV	−100,000	

Evermaster records the issuance of its bonds at a premium on January 1, 2007, as follows:

Cash	108,530	
Premium on Bonds Payable		8,530
Bonds Payable		100,000

Evermaster records the first interest payment on July 1, 2007, and amortization of the premium as follows:

Bond Interest Expense	3,256	
Premium on Bonds Payable	744	
Cash		4,000

Evermaster should amortize the discount or premium as an adjustment to interest expense over the life of the bond in such a way as to result in a **constant rate of interest** when applied to the carrying amount of debt outstanding at the beginning of any given period.

Accruing Interest

In our previous examples, the interest payment dates and the date the financial statements were issued were the same. For example, when Evermaster sold bonds at a premium (page 680), the two interest payment dates coincided with the financial reporting dates. However, what happens if Evermaster wishes to report financial statements at the end of February 2007? In this case, the company **prorates** the premium by the appropriate number of months, to arrive at the proper interest expense, as follows.

Interest accrual ($4,000 × 2/6)	$1,333.33
Premium amortized ($744 × 2/6)	(248.00)
Interest expense (Jan.–Feb.)	$1,085.33

ILLUSTRATION 14-8
Computation of Interest
Expense

Evermaster records this accrual as follows.

Bond Interest Expense	1,085.33	
Premium on Bonds Payable	248.00	
Bond Interest Payable		1,333.33

If the company prepares financial statements six months later, it follows the same procedure. That is, the premium amortized would be as follows.

ILLUSTRATION 14-9
Computation of Premium
Amortization

Premium amortized (March–June) ($744 × $^4/_6$)	$496.00
Premium amortized (July–August) ($766 × $^2/_6$)	255.33
Premium amortized (March–August 2004)	$751.33

The interest-accrual computation is much simpler if the company uses the straight-line method. For example, the total premium is $8,530, which Evermaster allocates evenly over the five-year period. Thus, premium amortization per month is $142.17 ($8,530 ÷ 60 months).

Classification of Discount and Premium

Discount on bonds payable is **not an asset**. It does not provide any future economic benefit. In return for the use of borrowed funds, a company must pay interest. A bond discount means that the company borrowed less than the face or maturity value of the bond. It therefore faces an actual (effective) interest rate higher than the stated (nominal) rate. Conceptually, discount on bonds payable is a liability valuation account. That is, it reduces the face or maturity amount of the related liability.[7] This account is referred to as a **contra account**.

Similarly, premium on bonds payable has no existence apart from the related debt. The lower interest cost results because the proceeds of borrowing exceed the face or maturity amount of the debt. Conceptually, premium on bonds payable is a *liability* valuation account. It adds to the face or maturity amount of the related liability.[8] This account is referred to as an **adjunct account**. As a result, **companies report bond discounts and bond premiums as a direct deduction from or addition to the face amount of the bond.**

COSTS OF ISSUING BONDS

The issuance of bonds involves engraving and printing costs, legal and accounting fees, commissions, promotion costs, and other similar charges. Companies are required to charge these costs to an asset account, often referred to as Unamortized Bond Issue Costs. Companies then allocate these Unamortized Bond Issue Costs over the life of the debt, in a manner similar to that used for discount on bonds.[9]

We disagree with this approach. Unamortized bond issue cost in our view is an expense (or a reduction of the related liability.)

Apparently the FASB also disagrees with the current GAAP treatment and notes in *Concepts Statement No. 6* that debt issue cost is not considered an asset because it provides no future economic benefit. The cost of issuing bonds, in effect, reduces the proceeds of the bonds issued and increases the effective interest rate. Companies may thus account for it the same as the unamortized discount.

---

[7]"Elements of Financial Statements of Business Enterprises," *Statement of Financial Accounting Concepts No. 6* (Stamford, Conn.: FASB, 1980).

[8]Ibid., par. 238.

[9]"Interest on Receivables and Payables," op. cit., par. 15.

There is an obvious difference between GAAP and *Concepts Statement No. 6*'s view of debt issue costs. However, until an issued standard supersedes existing GAAP, **unamortized bond issue costs are treated as a deferred charge and amortized over the life of the debt**.

To illustrate the accounting for costs of issuing bonds, assume that Microchip Corporation sold $20,000,000 of 10-year debenture bonds for $20,795,000 on January 1, 2007 (also the date of the bonds). Costs of issuing the bonds were $245,000. Microchip records the issuance of the bonds and amortization of the bond issue costs as follows.

January 1, 2007		
Cash	20,550,000	
Unamortized Bond Issue Costs	245,000	
Premium on Bonds Payable		795,000
Bonds Payable		20,000,000
(To record issuance of bonds)		
December 31, 2007		
Bond Issue Expense	24,500	
Unamortized Bond Issue Costs		24,500
(To amortize one year of bond issue		
costs—straight-line methods)		

Microchip continues to amortize the bond issue costs in the same way over the life of the bonds. Although the effective-interest method is preferred, in practice companies may use the straight-line method to amortize bond issue costs because it is easier and the results are not materially different.

TREASURY BONDS

Bonds payable that have been reacquired by the issuing corporation or its agent or trustee and have not been canceled are known as **treasury bonds**. Similar to treasury stock (discussed in Chapter 15), these bonds are reported on the balance sheet as a deduction from "Bonds payable." When the treasury bonds are later sold or canceled, the company credits the Treasury Bonds account.

EXTINGUISHMENT OF DEBT

How do companies record the payment of debt—often referred to as **extinguishment of debt**? If a company holds the bonds (or any other form of debt security) to maturity, the answer is straightforward: The company does not compute any gains or losses. It will have fully amortized any premium or discount and any issue costs at the date the bonds mature. As a result, the carrying amount will equal the maturity (face) value of the bond. As the maturity or face value will also equal the bond's market value at that time, no gain or loss exists.

In some cases, a company extinguishes debt before its maturity date.[10] The amount paid on extinguishment or redemption before maturity, including any call

> **OBJECTIVE 5**
> Describe the accounting for the extinguishment of debt.

---

[10]Some companies have attempted to extinguish debt through an in-substance defeasance. **In-substance defeasance** is an arrangement whereby a company provides for the future repayment of a long-term debt issue by placing purchased securities in an irrevocable trust. The company pledges the principal and interest of the securities in the trust to pay off the principal and interest of its own debt securities as they mature. However, it is not legally released from its primary obligation for the debt that is still outstanding. In some case, debt holders are not even aware of the transaction and continue to look to the company for repayment. This practice is not considered an extinguishment of debt, and therefore the company does not record a gain or loss.

premium and expense of reacquisition, is called the **reacquisition price**. On any specified date, the **net carrying amount** of the bonds is the amount payable at maturity, adjusted for unamortized premium or discount, and cost of issuance. Any excess of the net carrying amount over the reacquisition price is a **gain from extinguishment**. The excess of the reacquisition price over the net carrying amount is a **loss from extinguishment**. At the time of reacquisition, **the unamortized premium or discount, and any costs of issue applicable to the bonds, must be amortized up to the reacquisition date**.

To illustrate, assume that on January 1, 2000, General Bell Corp. issued at 97 bonds with a par value of $800,000, due in 20 years. It incurred bond issue costs totaling $16,000. Eight years after the issue date, General Bell calls the entire issue at 101 and cancels it.[11] At that time, the unamortized discount balance is $14,400, and the unamortized issue cost balance is $9,600. Illustration 14-10 indicates how General Bell computes the loss on redemption (extinguishment).

ILLUSTRATION 14-10
Computation of Loss on Redemption of Bonds

Reacquisition price ($800,000 × 1.01)		$808,000
Net carrying amount of bonds redeemed:		
Face value	$800,000	
Unamortized discount ($24,000* × 12/20)	(14,400)	
Unamortized issue costs ($16,000 × 12/20)		
(both amortized using straight-line basis)	(9,600)	776,000
Loss on redemption		$ 32,000

*[$800,000 × (1 − .97)]

General Bell records the reacquisition and cancellation of the bonds as follows:

Bonds Payable	800,000	
Loss on Redemption of Bonds	32,000	
Discount on Bonds Payable		14,400
Unamortized Bond Issue Costs		9,600
Cash		808,000

Note that it is often advantageous for the issuer to acquire the **entire** outstanding bond issue and replace it with a new bond issue bearing a lower rate of interest. The replacement of an existing issuance with a new one is called **refunding**. Whether the early redemption or other extinguishment of outstanding bonds is a nonrefunding or a refunding situation, a company should recognize the difference (gain or loss) between the reacquisition price and the net carrying amount of the redeemed bonds in income of the period of redemption.[12]

---

[11]The issuer of callable bonds must generally exercise the call on an interest date. Therefore, the amortization of any discount or premium will be up to date, and there will be no accrued interest. However, early extinguishments through purchases of bonds in the open market are more likely to be on other than an interest date. If the purchase is not made on an interest date, the discount or premium must be amortized, and the interest payable must be accrued from the last interest date to the date of purchase.

[12]Until recently, companies reported gains and losses on extinguishment of debt as extraordinary items. In response to concerns that such gains or losses are neither unusual nor infrequent, the FASB eliminated extraordinary item treatment for extinguishment of debt. "Recission of *FASB Statements No. 4, 44, and 64* and Technical Corrections," *Statement of Accounting Standards No. 145* (Norwalk, Conn.: FASB, 2002).

DEAD-WEIGHT DEBT

As the opening story in the chapter indicated, high debt levels translate into high interest costs, which are a drag on profitability. The chart below shows that the ratio of interest payments to earnings has been on an upward trend. This is bad news for companies that have a lot of debt on their balance sheet.

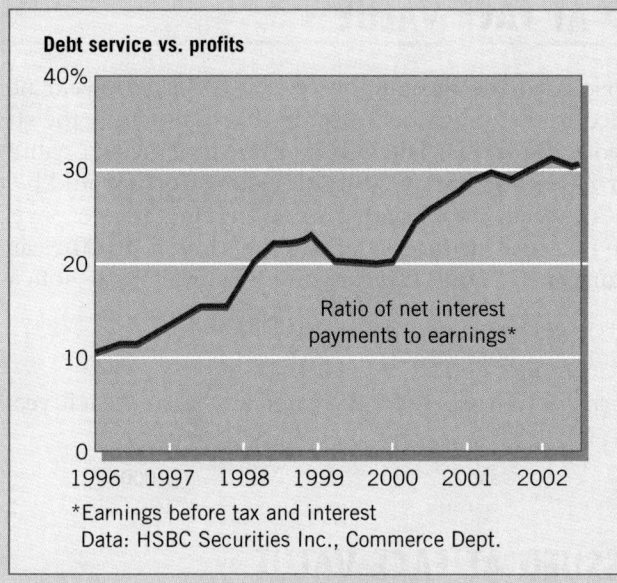

Debt service vs. profits

Ratio of net interest payments to earnings*

*Earnings before tax and interest
Data: HSBC Securities Inc., Commerce Dept.

However in a low interest rate environment, as experienced recently, companies with debt-laden balance sheets benefit when interest rates fall. **Exelon Corp.**, a Chicago-based energy company, is a good example. Exelon has been refinancing its long-term debt by retiring bonds with 6.5 percent rates in exchange for newly issued bonds with rates ranging from 3.7 percent to 5.9 percent. This refinancing saved Exelon approximately $30 million dollars in annual interest costs. Exelon was able to get out of its higher cost debt when the getting was good. Other debt-laden companies might not fare so well if interest rates rise before they can refinance.

Source: Adapted from Gregory Zuckerman, "Climb of Corporate Debt Trips Analysts' Alarm," *Wall Street Journal* (December 31, 2001), p. C1; and James Mehring, "The Dead Weight of Debt," *Business Week* (February 24, 2003), p. 60.

LONG-TERM NOTES PAYABLE	**SECTION 2**

The difference between current notes payable and long-term notes payable is the maturity date. As discussed in Chapter 13, short-term notes payable are those that companies expect to pay within a year or the operating cycle—whichever is longer. Long-term notes are similar in substance to bonds in that both have fixed maturity dates and carry either a stated or implicit interest rate. However, notes do not trade as readily as bonds in the organized public securities markets. Noncorporate and small corporate enterprises issue notes as their long-term instruments. Larger corporations issue both long-term notes and bonds.

Accounting for notes and bonds is quite similar. **Like a bond, a note is valued at the present value of its future interest and principal cash flows. The company amortizes any discount or premium over the life of the note**, just as it would the discount

> **OBJECTIVE 6**
> Explain the accounting for long-term notes payable.

or premium on a bond.[13] Companies compute the present value of an **interest-bearing note**, record its issuance, and amortize any discount or premium and accrual of interest in the same way that they do for bonds (as shown on pages 674–682 of this chapter).

As you might expect, accounting for long-term notes payable parallels accounting for long-term notes receivable as was presented in Chapter 7.

NOTES ISSUED AT FACE VALUE

In Chapter 7, we discussed the recognition of a $10,000, three-year note Scandinavian Imports issued at face value to Bigelow Corp. In this transaction, the stated rate and the effective rate were both 10 percent. The time diagram and present value computation on page 327 of Chapter 7 (see Illustration 7-9) for Bigelow Corp. would be the same for the issuer of the note, Scandinavian Imports, in recognizing a note payable. Because the present value of the note and its face value are the same, $10,000, Scandinavian would recognize no premium or discount. It records the issuance of the note as follows.

Cash	10,000	
Notes Payable		10,000

Scandinavian Imports would recognize the interest incurred each year as follows.

Interest Expense	1,000	
Cash		1,000

NOTES NOT ISSUED AT FACE VALUE

Zero-Interest-Bearing Notes

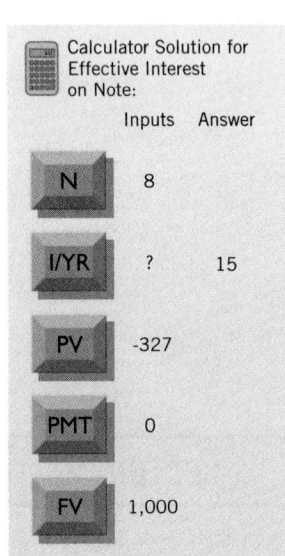

Calculator Solution for Effective Interest on Note:

	Inputs	Answer
N	8	
I/YR	?	15
PV	-327	
PMT	0	
FV	1,000	

If a company issues a zero-interest-bearing (non-interest-bearing) note[14] solely for cash, it measures the note's present value by the cash received. The implicit interest rate is the **rate that equates the cash received with the amounts to be paid in the future**. The issuing company records the difference between the face amount and the present value (cash received) as **a discount and amortizes that amount to interest expense over the life of the note**.

An example of such a transaction is Beneficial Corporation's offering of $150 million of zero-coupon notes (deep-discount bonds) having an eight-year life. With a face value of $1,000 each, these notes sold for $327—a deep discount of $673 each. The present value of each note is the cash proceeds of $327. We can calculate the interest rate by determining the rate that equates the amount the investor currently pays with the amount to be received in the future. Thus, Beneficial amortizes the discount over the eight-year life of the notes using an effective interest rate of 15 percent.[15]

---

[13]According to *APB Opinion No. 21*, all payables that represent commitments to pay money at a determinable future date are subject to present value measurement techniques, except for the following specifically excluded types:

1. Normal accounts payable due within one year.
2. Security deposits, retainages, advances, or progress payments.
3. Transactions between parent and subsidiary.
4. Obligations payable at some indeterminable future date.

[14]Although we use the term "note" throughout this discussion, the basic principles and methodology apply equally to other long-term debt instruments.

[15] $327 = $1,000(PVF_{8,i})$

$$PVF_{8,i} = \frac{\$327}{\$1,000} = .327$$

.327 = 15% (in Table 6-2 locate .32690).

To illustrate the entries and the amortization schedule, assume that Turtle Cove Company issued the three-year, $10,000, zero-interest-bearing note to Jeremiah Company illustrated on page 328 of Chapter 7 (notes receivable). The implicit rate that equated the total cash to be paid ($10,000 at maturity) to the present value of the future cash flows ($7,721.80 cash proceeds at date of issuance) was 9 percent. (The present value of $1 for 3 periods at 9 percent is $0.77218.) Illustration 14-11 shows the time diagram for the single cash flow.

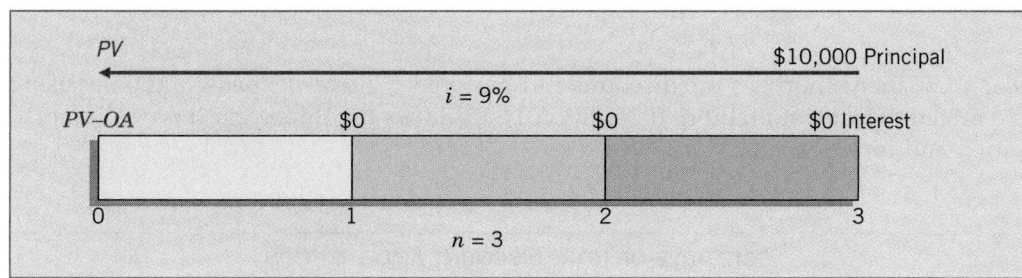

ILLUSTRATION 14-11
Time Diagram for Zero-Interest Note

Turtle Cove records issuance of the note as follows.

Cash	7,721.80	
Discount on Notes Payable	2,278.20	
Notes Payable		10,000.00

Turtle Cove amortizes the discount and recognizes interest expense annually using the **effective-interest method**. Illustration 14-12 shows the three-year discount amortization and interest expense schedule. (This schedule is similar to the note receivable schedule of Jeremiah Company in Illustration 7-11.)

ILLUSTRATION 14-12
Schedule of Note Discount Amortization

SCHEDULE OF NOTE DISCOUNT AMORTIZATION			
EFFECTIVE-INTEREST METHOD			
0% NOTE DISCOUNTED AT 9%			
	Cash Paid	Interest Expense	Discount Amortized	Carrying Amount of Note
Date of issue				$ 7,721.80
End of year 1	$–0–	$ 694.96[a]	$ 694.96[b]	8,416.76[c]
End of year 2	–0–	757.51	757.51	9,174.27
End of year 3	–0–	825.73[d]	825.73	10,000.00
	$–0–	$2,278.20	$2,278.20	

[a]$7,721.80 × .09 = $694.96
[b]$694.96 − 0 = $694.96
[c]$7,721.80 + $694.96 = $8,416.76
[d]5¢ adjustment to compensate for rounding

Turtle Cove records interest expense at the end of the first year using the effective-interest method as follows.

Interest Expense ($7,721.80 × 9%)	694.96	
Discount on Notes Payable		694.96

The total amount of the discount, $2,278.20 in this case, represents the expense that Turtle Cove Company will incur on the note over the three years.

Interest-Bearing Notes

The zero-interest-bearing note above is an example of the extreme difference between the stated rate and the effective rate. In many cases, the difference between these rates is not so great.

Consider the example from Chapter 7 where Marie Co. issued for cash a $10,000, three-year note bearing interest at 10 percent to Morgan Corp. The market rate of interest for a note of similar risk is 12 percent. Illustration 7-12 (page 329) shows the time diagram depicting the cash flows and the computation of the present value of this note. In this case, because the effective rate of interest (12%) is greater than the stated rate (10%), the present value of the note is less than the face value. That is, the note is exchanged at a **discount**. Marie Co. records the issuance of the note as follows.

Cash	9,520	
Discount on Notes Payable	480	
Notes Payable		10,000

Marie Co. then amortizes the discount and recognizes interest expense annually using the **effective-interest method**. Illustration 14-13 shows the three-year discount amortization and interest expense schedule.

ILLUSTRATION 14-13
Schedule of Note
Discount Amortization

	SCHEDULE OF NOTE DISCOUNT AMORTIZATION			
	EFFECTIVE-INTEREST METHOD			
	10% NOTE DISCOUNTED AT 12%			
	Cash Paid	Interest Expense	Discount Amortized	Carrying Amount of Note
Date of issue				$ 9,520
End of year 1	$1,000[a]	$1,142[b]	$142[c]	9,662[d]
End of year 2	1,000	1,159	159	9,821
End of year 3	1,000	1,179	179	10,000
	$3,000	$3,480	$480	

[a]$10,000 × 10% = $1,000   [c]$1,142 − $1,000 = $142
[b]$9,520 × 12% = $1,142   [d]$9,520 + $142 = $9,662

Marie Co. records payment of the annual interest and amortization of the discount for the first year as follows (amounts per amortization schedule).

Interest Expense	1,142	
Discount on Bonds Payable		142
Cash		1,000

When the present value exceeds the face value, Marie Co. exchanges the note at a premium. It does so by recording the premium as a credit and amortizing it using the effective-interest method over the life of the note as annual reductions in the amount of interest expense recognized.

SPECIAL NOTES PAYABLE SITUATIONS

Notes Issued for Property, Goods, and Services

Sometimes, companies may receive property, goods, or services in exchange for a note payable. When exchanging the debt instrument for property, goods, or services in a bargained transaction entered into at arm's length, the stated interest rate is presumed to be fair unless:

1 No interest rate is stated, or

2 The stated interest rate is unreasonable, or

3 The stated face amount of the debt instrument is materially different from the current cash sales price for the same or similar items or from the current market value of the debt instrument.

In these circumstances the company measures the present value of the debt instrument by the fair value of the property, goods, or services or by an amount that reasonably approximates the market value of the note.[16] If there is **no stated rate of interest, the amount of interest is the difference between the face amount of the note and the fair value of the property**.

For example, assume that Scenic Development Company sells land having a cash sale price of $200,000 to Health Spa, Inc. In exchange for the land, Health Spa gives a five-year, $293,866, zero-interest-bearing note. The $200,000 cash sale price represents the present value of the $293,866 note discounted at 8 percent for five years. Should both parties record the transaction on the sale date at the face amount of the note, which is $293,866? No—if they did, Health Spa's Land account and Scenic's sales would be overstated by $93,866 (the interest for five years at an effective rate of 8 percent). Similarly, interest revenue to Scenic and interest expense to Health Spa for the five-year period would be understated by $93,866.

Because the difference between the cash sale price of $200,000 and the $293,866 face amount of the note represents interest at an effective rate of 8 percent, the companies' transaction is recorded at the exchange date as follows.

Health Spa, Inc. (Buyer)			Scenic Development Company (Seller)		
Land	200,000		Notes Receivable	293,866	
Discount on Notes Payable	93,866		Discount on Notes Rec.		93,866
Notes Payable		293,866	Sales		200,000

ILLUSTRATION 14-14
Entries for Noncash Note Transactions

During the five-year life of the note, Health Spa amortizes annually a portion of the discount of $93,866 as a charge to interest expense. Scenic Development records interest revenue totaling $93,866 over the five-year period by also amortizing the discount. The effective-interest method is required, unless the results obtained from using another method are not materially different from those that result from the effective-interest method.

Choice of Interest Rate

In note transactions, the effective or market interest rate is either evident or determinable by other factors involved in the exchange, such as the fair market value of what is given or received. But, if a company cannot determine the fair value of the property, goods, services, or other rights, and if the note has no ready market, the problem of determining the present value of the note is more difficult. To estimate the present value of a note under such circumstances, a company must approximate an applicable interest rate that may differ from the stated interest rate. This process of interest-rate approximation is called **imputation**, and the resulting interest rate is called an **imputed interest rate**.

The prevailing rates for similar instruments of issuers with similar credit ratings affect the choice of a rate. Other factors such as restrictive covenants, collateral, payment schedule, and the existing prime interest rate also play a part. Companies determine the imputed interest rate when they issue a note; any subsequent changes in prevailing interest rates are ignored.

To illustrate, assume that on December 31, 2007, Wunderlich Company issued a promissory note to Brown Interiors Company for architectural services. The note has a face value of $550,000, a due date of December 31, 2012, and bears a stated interest rate of 2 percent, payable at the end of each year. Wunderlich cannot readily determine the fair value of the architectural services, nor is the note readily marketable. On the basis of Wunderlich's credit rating, the absence of collateral, the prime interest rate at that date, and the prevailing interest on Wunderlich's other outstanding debt, the

---

[16]"Interest on Receivables and Payables," op. cit., par. 12.

company imputes an 8 percent interest rate as appropriate in this circumstance. Illustration 14-15 shows the time diagram depicting both cash flows.

ILLUSTRATION 14-15
Time Diagram for
Interest-Bearing Note

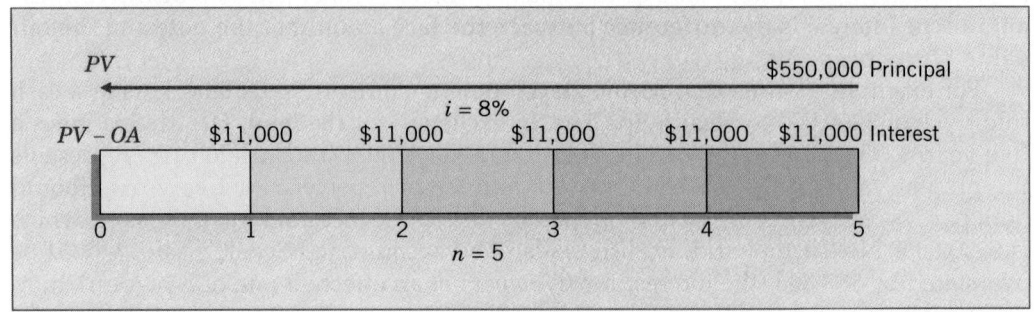

The present value of the note and the imputed fair value of the architectural services are determined as follows.

ILLUSTRATION 14-16
Computation of Imputed
Fair Value and Note
Discount

Face value of the note		$550,000
Present value of $550,000 due in 5 years at 8% interest payable annually (Table 6-2); $FV(PVF_{5,8\%})$; ($550,000 × .68058)	$374,319	
Present value of $11,000 interest payable annually for 5 years at 8%; $R(PVF\text{-}OA_{5,8\%})$; ($11,000 × 3.99271)	43,920	
Present value of the note		418,239
Discount on notes payable		$131,761

Wunderlich records issuance of the note in payment for the architectural services as follows.

December 31, 2007

Building (or Construction in Process)	418,239	
Discount on Notes Payable	131,761	
Notes Payable		550,000

The five-year amortization schedule appears below.

ILLUSTRATION 14-17
Schedule of Discount
Amortization Using
Imputed Interest Rate

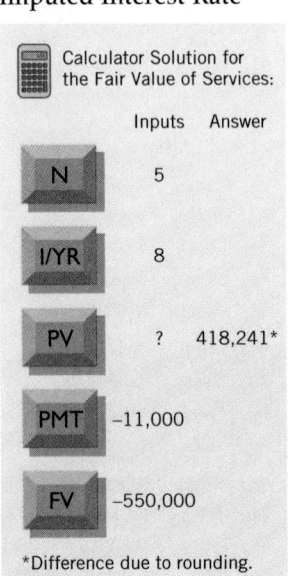

*Difference due to rounding.

SCHEDULE OF NOTE DISCOUNT AMORTIZATION
EFFECTIVE-INTEREST METHOD
2% NOTE DISCOUNTED AT 8% (IMPUTED)

Date	Cash Paid (2%)	Interest Expense (8%)	Discount Amortized	Carrying Amount of Note
12/31/07				$418,239
12/31/08	$11,000[a]	$ 33,459[b]	$ 22,459[c]	440,698[d]
12/31/09	11,000	35,256	24,256	464,954
12/31/10	11,000	37,196	26,196	491,150
12/31/11	11,000	39,292	28,292	519,442
12/31/12	11,000	41,558[e]	30,558	550,000
	$55,000	$186,761	$131,761	

[a]$550,000 × 2% = $11,000   [d]$418,239 + $22,459 = $440,698
[b]$418,239 × 8% = $33,459   [e]$3 adjustment to compensate for rounding.
[c]$33,459 − $11,000 = $22,459

Wunderlich records payment of the first year's interest and amortization of the discount as follows.

December 31, 2008

Interest Expense	33,459	
Discount on Notes Payable		22,459
Cash		11,000

MORTGAGE NOTES PAYABLE

The most common form of long-term notes payable is a mortgage note payable. A **mortgage note payable** is a promissory note secured by a document called a mortgage that pledges title to property as security for the loan. Individuals, proprietorships, and partnerships use mortgage notes payable more frequently than do corporations. (Corporations usually find that bond issues offer advantages in obtaining large loans.)

The borrower usually receives cash for the face amount of the mortgage note. In that case, the face amount of the note is the true liability, and no discount or premium is involved. When the lender assesses "points," however, the total amount received by the borrower is less than the face amount of the note.[17] Points raise the effective interest rate above the rate specified in the note. A **point** is 1 percent of the face of the note.

For example, assume that Harrick Co. borrows $1,000,000, signing a 20-year mortgage note with a stated interest rate of 10.75 percent as part of the financing for a new plant. If Associated Savings demands 4 points to close the financing, Harrick will receive 4 percent less than $1,000,000—or $960,000—but it will be obligated to repay the entire $1,000,000 at the rate of $10,150 per month. Because Harrick received only $960,000, and must repay $1,000,000, its effective interest rate is increased to approximately 11.3 percent on the money actually borrowed.

On the balance sheet, Harrick should report the mortgage note payable as a liability using a title such as "Mortgage Notes Payable" or "Notes Payable—Secured," with a brief disclosure of the property pledged in notes to the financial statements.

Mortgages may be payable in full at maturity or in installments over the life of the loan. If payable at maturity, Harrick classifies its mortgage payable as a long-term liability on the balance sheet until such time as the approaching maturity date warrants showing it as a current liability. If it is payable in installments, Harrick shows the current installments due as current liabilities, with the remainder as a long-term liability.

Lenders have partially replaced the traditional **fixed-rate mortgage** with alternative mortgage arrangements. Most lenders offer **variable-rate mortgages** (also called *floating-rate* or *adjustable-rate* mortgages) featuring interest rates tied to changes in the fluctuating market rate. Generally the variable-rate lenders adjust the interest rate at either one- or three-year intervals, pegging the adjustments to changes in the prime rate or the U.S. Treasury bond rate.

REPORTING AND ANALYSIS OF LONG-TERM DEBT	SECTION 3

Reporting of long-term debt is one of the most controversial areas in financial reporting. Because long-term debt has a significant impact on the cash flows of the company, reporting requirements must be substantive and informative. One problem is that the definition of a liability established in *Concepts Statement No. 6* and the recognition criteria established in *Concepts Statement No. 5* are sufficiently imprecise that some continue to argue that certain obligations need not be reported as debt.

OFF-BALANCE-SHEET FINANCING

What do **Krispy Kreme**, **Cisco**, **Enron**, and **Adelphia Communications** have in common? They all have been accused of using off-balance-sheet financing to minimize the reporting of debt on their balance sheets. **Off-balance-sheet financing** is an attempt to

OBJECTIVE 7
Explain the reporting of off-balance-sheet financing arrangements.

---

[17]Points, in mortgage financing, are analogous to the original issue discount of bonds.

borrow monies in such a way to prevent recording the obligations. It has become an issue of extreme importance. Many allege that Enron, in one of the largest corporate failures on record, hid a considerable amount of its debt off the balance sheet. As a result, any company that uses off-balance-sheet financing today risks investors dumping their stock. Consequently (as discussed in the opening story), their share price will suffer. Nevertheless, a considerable amount of off-balance-sheet financing continues to exist. As one writer noted, "The basic drives of humans are few: to get enough food, to find shelter, and to keep debt off the balance sheet."

Different Forms

Off-balance-sheet financing can take many different forms:

1 **Non-Consolidated Subsidiary:** Under GAAP, a parent company does not have to consolidate a subsidiary company that is less than 50 percent owned. In such cases, the parent therefore does not report the assets and liabilities of the subsidiary. All the parent reports on its balance sheet is the investment in the subsidiary. As a result, users of the financial statements may not understand that the subsidiary has considerable debt for which the parent may ultimately be liable if the subsidiary runs into financial difficulty.

2 **Special Purpose Entity (SPE):** A company creates a special purpose entity to perform a special project. To illustrate, assume that Clarke Company decides to build a new factory. However, management does not want to report the plant or the borrowing used to fund the construction on its balance sheet. It therefore creates an SPE, the purpose of which is to build the plant. (This arrangement is called a **project financing arrangement**.) The SPE finances and builds the plant. In return, Clarke guarantees that it or some outside party will purchase all the products produced by the plant. (Some refer to this as a **take-or-pay contract**). As a result, Clarke might not report the asset or liability on its books. The accounting rules in this area are complex; we discuss the accounting for SPE's in Appendix 17B.

3 **Operating Leases:** Another way that companies keep debt off the balance sheet is by leasing. Instead of owning the assets, companies lease them. Again, by meeting certain conditions, the company has to report only rent expense each period and to provide note disclosure of the transaction. Note that SPEs often use leases to accomplish off-balance-sheet treatment. We discuss accounting for lease transactions extensively in Chapter 21.

Rationale

Why do companies engage in off-balance-sheet financing? A major reason is that many believe that **removing debt enhances the quality of the balance sheet** and permits credit to be obtained more readily and at less cost.

Second, loan covenants often limit the amount of debt a company may have. As a result, the company uses off-balance-sheet financing, because **these types of commitments might not be considered in computing the debt limitation**.

Third, some argue that the asset side of the balance sheet is severely understated. For example, companies that use LIFO costing for inventories and depreciate assets on an accelerated basis will often have carrying amounts for inventories and property, plant, and equipment that are much lower than their current values. As an offset to these lower values, some believe that part of the debt does not have to be reported. In other words, **if companies report assets at current values**, less pressure would undoubtedly exist for off-balance-sheet financing arrangements.

Whether the arguments above have merit is debatable. The general idea of "out of sight, out of mind" may not be true in accounting. Many users of financial statements indicate that they factor these off-balance-sheet financing arrangements into their computations when assessing debt to equity relationships. Similarly, many loan covenants also attempt to account for these complex arrangements. Nevertheless, many companies still believe that benefits will accrue if they omit certain obligations from the balance sheet.

As a response to off-balance-sheet financing arrangements, the FASB has increased disclosure (note) requirements. This response is consistent with an "efficient markets" philosophy: the important question is not whether the presentation is off-balance-sheet or not, but whether the items are disclosed at all. In addition, the SEC, in response to the Sarbanes-Oxley Act of 2002, now requires companies to provide related information in their management discussion and analysis sections. Specifically, companies must disclose (1) all contractual obligations in a tabular format and (2) contingent liabilities and commitments in either a textual or tabular format.[18]

We believe that recording more obligations on the balance sheet will enhance financial reporting. Given the problems with companies such as **Enron, Dynergy, Williams Company, Adelphia Communications**, and **Calpine**, and the new Sarbanes-Oxley requirements, we expect that less off-balance-sheet financing will occur in the future.

OBLIGATED

The off-balance-sheet world is slowly but surely becoming more on-balance-sheet. New interpretations on guarantees (discussed in Chapter 13) and variable interest entities (discussed in Appendix 17B) are doing their part to increase the amount of debt reported on corporate balance sheets.

In addition, the SEC recently issued a rule that requires companies to disclose off-balance-sheet arrangements and contractual obligations that currently have, or are reasonably likely to have, a material future effect on the companies' financial condition. Companies now must include a tabular disclosure (following a prescribed format) in the management discussion and analysis section of the annual report. Presented below is **Best Buy**'s tabular disclosure of its contractual obligations.

WHAT DO THE NUMBERS MEAN?

Best Buy Co.
Contractual Obligations

The following table presents information regarding our contractual obligations by fiscal year ($ in millions):

Contractual Obligations	Total	Less than 1 year	1–3 years	3–5 years	More than 5 years
Long-term debt obligations	$ 425	$ 2	$ 408	$ 12	$ 3
Capital lease obligations	13	5	4	3	1
Master lease obligations	55	55	—	—	—
Financing lease obligations	107	10	17	19	61
Interest payments	218	23	37	32	126
Operating lease obligations	5,850	541	1,065	997	3,247
Purchase obligations	1,514	689	404	259	162
Total	$8,182	$1,325	$1,935	$1,322	$3,600

Note: For more information refer to Note 4, Debt; Note 7, Leases; and Note 11, Contingencies and Commitments, respectively, in the Notes to Consolidated Financial Statements.

INTERNATIONAL INSIGHT

There is no comparable institution to the SEC in international securities markets. As a result, many international companies (those not registered with the SEC) are not required to provide disclosures such as those related to contractual obligations.

Enron's abuse of off-balance-sheet financing to hide debt was shocking and inappropriate. One silver lining in the Enron debacle however is that the standard-setting bodies in the accounting profession are now providing increased guidance on companies' reporting of contractual obligations. We believe the new SEC rule which requires companies to report their obligations over a period of time will be extremely useful to the investment community.

---

[18]It is unlikely that the FASB will be able to stop all types of off-balance-sheet transactions. Financial engineering is the Holy Grail of Wall Street. Developing new financial instruments and arrangements to sell and market to customers is not only profitable, but also adds to the prestige of the investment firms that create them. Thus, new financial products will continue to appear that will test the ability of the FASB to develop appropriate accounting standards for them.

PRESENTATION AND ANALYSIS OF LONG-TERM DEBT

Presentation of Long-Term Debt

OBJECTIVE 8
Indicate how to present and analyze long-term debt.

Companies that have large amounts and numerous issues of long-term debt frequently report only one amount in the balance sheet, supported with comments and schedules in the accompanying notes. Long-term debt that **matures within one year** should be reported as a current liability, unless using noncurrent assets to accomplish retirement.

ILLUSTRATION 14-18
Long-Term Debt
Disclosure

Best Buy Co.
(dollars in millions)

	February 26, 2005	February 28, 2004
Total current assets	$6,903	$5,724
Current liabilities		
Accounts payable	$2,824	$2,460
Unredeemed gift card liabiliities	410	300
Accrued compensation and related expenses	234	269
Accrued liabilities	844	724
Accrued income taxes	575	380
Current portion of long-term debt	72	368
Total current liabilities	4,959	4,501
Long-term liabilities	358	247
Long-term debt	528	482

4. Debt (in part)	February 26, 2005	February 28, 2004
Convertible subordinated debentures, unsecured, due 2022, interest rate 2.25%	$402	$402
Convertible debentures, unsecured, due 2021, interest rate 2.75%	—	353
Master lease obligations, due 2006, interest rate 5.9%	55	58
Capital lease obligations, due 2005, interest rate ranging from 5.9% to 8.0%	13	16
Financing lease obligations, due 2008 to 2022, interest rates ranging from 5.6% to 6.0%	107	—
Mortgage and other debt, interest rates ranging from 1.8% to 8.9%	23	21
Total debt	600	850
Less: Current portion	(72)	(368)
Total long-term debt	$528	$482

The mortgage and other debt are secured by certain property and equipment with a net book value of $98 and $97 at February 26, 2005, and February 28, 2004, respectively.

The future maturities of long-term debt, including master and capitalized leases, consist of the following:

Fiscal Year	
2006	$ 72
2007	415
2008	14
2009	14
2010	20
Thereafter	65
	$600

The fair value of long-term debt approximated $603 and $902 as of February 26, 2005, and February 28, 2004, respectively, based on the ask prices quoted from external sources, compared with carrying values of $600 and $850, respectively.

If the company plans to refinance debt, convert it into stock, or retire it from a bond retirement fund, it should continue to report the debt as noncurrent. However, the company should disclose the method it will use in its liquidation.[19]

Note disclosures generally indicate the nature of the liabilities, maturity dates, interest rates, call provisions, conversion privileges, restrictions imposed by the creditors, and assets designated or pledged as security. Companies should show any assets pledged as security for the debt in the assets section of the balance sheet. The fair value of the long-term debt should also be disclosed if it is practical to estimate fair value. Finally, companies must disclose future payments for sinking fund requirements and maturity amounts of long-term debt during each of the next five years.[20] These disclosures aid financial statement users in evaluating the amounts and timing of future cash flows. Illustration 14-18 (on page 694) shows an example of the type of information provided for **Best Buy Co.** Note that if the company has any off-balance-sheet financing, it must provide extensive note disclosure.[21]

Analysis of Long-Term Debt

Long-term creditors and stockholders are interested in a company's long-run solvency, particularly its ability to pay interest as it comes due and to repay the face value of the debt at maturity. Debt to total assets and times interest earned are two ratios that provide information about debt-paying ability and long-run solvency.

Debt to Total Assets Ratio

The **debt to total assets ratio** measures the percentage of the total assets provided by creditors. To compute it, divide total debt (both current and long-term liabilities) by total assets, as Illustration 14-19 shows.

$$\text{Debt to total assets} = \frac{\text{Total debt}}{\text{Total assets}}$$

ILLUSTRATION 14-19
Computation of Debt to Total Assets Ratio

The higher the percentage of debt to total assets, the greater the risk that the company may be unable to meet its maturing obligations.

Times Interest Earned Ratio

The **times interest earned ratio** indicates the company's ability to meet interest payments as they come due. As shown in Illustration 14-20, it is computed by dividing income before interest expense and income taxes by interest expense.

$$\text{Times interest earned} = \frac{\text{Income before income taxes and interest expense}}{\text{Interest expense}}$$

ILLUSTRATION 14-20
Computation of Times Interest Earned Ratio

To illustrate these ratios, we use data from **Best Buy**'s 2005 annual report. Best Buy has total liabilities of $5,845 million, total assets of $10,294 million, interest expense of $44 million, income taxes of $509 million, and net income of $984 million. We

---

[19]"Balance Sheet Classification of Short-Term Obligations Expected to Be Refinanced," *FASB Statement of Financial Accounting Standards No. 6* (Stamford, Conn.: FASB, 1975), par. 15. Also see "Disclosure of Information about Capital Structure," *FASB Statement of Financial Accounting Standards No. 129* (Norwalk, Conn.: 1997), par. 4.

[20]"Disclosure of Long-Term Obligations," *FASB Statement of Financial Accounting Standards No. 47* (Stamford, Conn.: 1981), par. 10.

[21]Ibid.

compute Best Buy's debt to total assets and times interest earned ratios as shown in Illustration 14-21.

ILLUSTRATION 14-21
Computation of Long-Term Debt Ratios for Best Buy

$$\text{Debt to total assets} = \frac{\$5,845}{\$10,294} = 56.8\%$$

$$\text{Times interest earned} = \frac{(\$984 + \$44 + \$509)}{\$44} = 35 \text{ times}$$

Even though Best Buy has a relatively high debt to total assets percentage of 56.8 percent, its interest coverage of 35 times indicates it can easily meet its interest payments as they come due.

SUMMARY OF LEARNING OBJECTIVES

KEY TERMS

bearer (coupon) bonds, 674

bond discount, 675

bond indenture, 673

bond premium, 675

callable bonds, 673

carrying value, 679

commodity-backed bonds, 673

convertible bonds, 673

debenture bonds, 673

debt to total assets ratio, 695

deep-discount (zero-interest debenture) bonds, 673

effective-interest method, 679

effective yield, or market rate, 675

extinguishment of debt, 683

face, par, principal or maturity value, 675

imputation, 689

imputed interest rate, 689

income bonds, 674

long-term debt, 672

long-term notes payable, 685

mortgage notes payable, 691

off-balance-sheet financing, 691

refunding, 684

registered bonds, 674

1. Describe the formal procedures associated with issuing long-term debt. Incurring long-term debt is often a formal procedure. The bylaws of corporations usually require approval by the board of directors and the stockholders before corporations can issue bonds or can make other long-term debt arrangements. Generally, long-term debt has various covenants or restrictions. The covenants and other terms of the agreement between the borrower and the lender are stated in the bond indenture or note agreement.

2. Identify various types of bond issues. Various types of bond issues are: (1) Secured and unsecured bonds. (2) Term, serial, and callable bonds. (3) Convertible, commodity-backed, and deep-discount bonds. (4) Registered and bearer (coupon) bonds. (5) Income and revenue bonds. The variety in the types of bonds results from attempts to attract capital from different investors and risk takers and to satisfy the cash flow needs of the issuers.

3. Describe the accounting valuation for bonds at date of issuance. The investment community values a bond at the present value of its future cash flows, which consist of interest and principal. The rate used to compute the present value of these cash flows is the interest rate that provides an acceptable return on an investment commensurate with the issuer's risk characteristics. The interest rate written in the terms of the bond indenture and ordinarily appearing on the bond certificate is the stated, coupon, or nominal rate. The issuer of the bonds sets the rate and expresses it as a percentage of the face value (also called the par value, principal amount, or maturity value) of the bonds. If the rate employed by the buyers differs from the stated rate, the present value of the bonds computed by the buyers will differ from the face value of the bonds. The difference between the face value and the present value of the bonds is either a discount or premium.

4. Apply the methods of bond discount and premium amortization. The discount (premium) is amortized and charged (credited) to interest expense over the life of the bonds. Amortization of a discount increases bond interest expense, and amortization of a premium decreases bond interest expense. The profession's preferred procedure for amortization of a discount or premium is the effective-interest method. Under the effective-interest method, (1) bond interest expense is computed by multiplying the carrying value of the bonds at the beginning of the period by the effective-interest rate; then, (2) the bond discount or premium amortization is determined by comparing the bond interest expense with the interest to be paid.

5. Describe the accounting for the extinguishment of debt. At the time of reacquisition of long-term debt, the unamortized premium or discount and any costs of issue applicable to the debt must be amortized up to the reacquisition date. The reacquisition price is the amount paid on extinguishment or redemption before maturity, including any call premium and expense of reacquisition. On any specified date, the net carrying amount of the debt is the amount payable at maturity, adjusted for unamortized premium or discount and issue costs. Any excess of the net carrying amount over the reacquisition price is a gain from extinguishment. The excess of the reacquisition price over the net carrying amount is a loss from extinguishment. Gains and losses on extinguishments are recognized currently in income.

6. Explain the accounting for long-term notes payable.
Accounting procedures for notes and bonds are similar. Like a bond, a note is valued at the present value of its expected future interest and principal cash flows, with any discount or premium being similarly amortized over the life of the note. Whenever the face amount of the note does not reasonably represent the present value of the consideration in the exchange, a company must evaluate the entire arrangement in order to properly record the exchange and the subsequent interest.

7. Explain the reporting of off-balance-sheet financing arrangements.
Off-balance-sheet financing is an attempt to borrow funds in such a way to prevent recording obligations. Examples of off-balance-sheet arrangements are (1) non-consolidated subsidiaries, (2) special purpose entities, and (3) operating leases.

8. Indicate how to present and analyze long-term debt.
Companies that have large amounts and numerous issues of long-term debt frequently report only one amount in the balance sheet and support this with comments and schedules in the accompanying notes. Any assets pledged as security for the debt should be shown in the assets section of the balance sheet. Long-term debt that matures within one year should be reported as a current liability, unless retirement is to be accomplished with other than current assets. If a company plans to refinance the debt, convert it into stock, or retire it from a bond retirement fund, it should continue to report it as noncurrent, accompanied with a note explaining the method it will use in the debt's liquidation. Disclosure is required of future payments for sinking fund requirements and maturity amounts of long-term debt during each of the next five years. Debt to total assets and times interest earned are two ratios that provide information about debt-paying ability and long-run solvency.

APPENDIX 14A

Accounting for Troubled Debt

Practically every day the *Wall Street Journal* runs a story about some company in financial difficulty. For example, recently **Huffy Corp.**, a name that adorned the first bicycle of many American children, declared bankruptcy. Its creditors, Chinese suppliers, ended up taking a 30 percent equity stake in Huffy. Other examples are **Delphi**, **Northwest Airlines**, and **United Airlines**. The purpose of this appendix is to explain how creditors and debtors report information in financial statements related to these troubled debt situations. Two different types of situations result with troubled debt.

1 Impairments.
2 Restructurings:
  a. Settlements.
  b. Modification of terms.

For example, as in the case of Huffy's creditors, the creditor usually recognizes a loss on impairment. Subsequently, the creditor either modifies the terms of the loan, or settles it on terms unfavorable to the creditor. In unusual cases, the creditor forces the debtor into bankruptcy in order to ensure the highest possible collection on the loan.

IMPAIRMENTS

| **OBJECTIVE 9** |
| Describe the |
| accounting for a loan |
| impairment. |

A creditor considers a loan[1] impaired when it is probable,[2] based on current information and events, that it will not collect all amounts due (both principal and interest). Creditors should apply their normal review procedures in making the judgment as to the probability of collection.[3]

If considering a loan impaired, the creditor should measure the loss due to the **impairment** as the difference between the investment in the loan (generally the principal plus accrued interest) and the expected future cash flows discounted at the loan's historical effective interest rate.[4] When using the historical effective loan rate, the value of the investment will change only if some of the legally contracted cash flows are reduced. A company recognizes a loss in this case because the expected future cash flows have changed. The company ignores interest rate changes caused by current economic events that affect the fair value of the loan. In estimating future cash flows, the creditor should use reasonable and supportable assumptions and projections.[5]

Example of Loss on Impairment

On December 31, 2006, Prospect Inc. issued a $500,000, five-year, zero-interest-bearing note to Community Bank. Prospect issued the note to yield 10% annual interest. As a result, Prospect received, and Community Bank paid, $310,460 ($500,000 × .62092) on December 31, 2006.[6] The time diagram in Illustration 14A-1 depicts the factors involved.

ILLUSTRATION 14A-1
Time Diagram for Zero-Interest-Bearing Loan

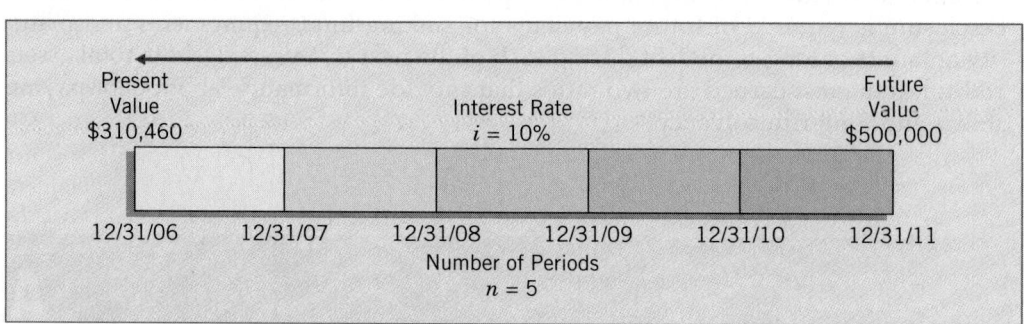

---

[1]*FASB Statement No. 114*, "Accounting by Creditors for Impairment of a Loan," (Norwalk, Conn.: FASB, May 1993), defines a loan as "a contractual right to receive money on demand or on fixed and determinable dates that is recognized as an asset in the creditor's statement of financial position." For example, accounts receivable with terms exceeding one year are considered loans.

[2]Recall the definitions of probable, reasonably possible, and remote with respect to contingencies, as defined in *FASB Statement No. 5*.

[3]Normal review procedures include examination of "watch lists," review of regulatory reports of examination, and examination of management reports of total loan amounts by borrower.

[4]The creditor may also, for the sake of expediency, use the market price of the loan (if such a price is available) or the fair value of collateral if it is a collateralized loan. *FASB Statement No. 114*, par. 13.

[5]*FASB Statement No. 114*, par. 15.

[6]Present value of $500,000 due in five years at 10%, annual compounding (Appendix 6-2) equals $500,000 × .62092.

Illustration 14A-2 shows how Community Bank (creditor) and Prospect (debtor) record these transactions.

December 31, 2006				
Community Bank (Creditor)			**Prospect Inc. (Debtor)**	
Notes Receivable	500,000		Cash	310,460
Discount on Notes			Discount on Notes	
Receivable		189,540	Payable	189,540
Cash		310,460	Notes Payable	500,000

Assuming that Community Bank and Prospect use the effective-interest method to amortize discounts, Illustration 14A-3 shows the amortization of the discount and the increase in the carrying amount of the note over the life of the note.

	COMMUNITY BANK			
Date	Cash Received (0%)	Interest Revenue (10%)	Discount Amortized	Carrying Amount of Note
12/31/06				$310,460
12/31/07	$0	$ 31,046[a]	$ 31,046	341,506[b]
12/31/08	0	34,151	34,151	375,657
12/31/09	0	37,566	37,566	413,223
12/31/10	0	41,322	41,322	454,545
12/31/11	0	45,455	45,455	500,000
Total	$0	$189,540	$189,540	

[a]$31,046 = $310,460 × .10
[b]$341,506 = $310,460 + $31,046

Unfortunately, during 2008 Prospect's business deteriorated due to increased competition and a faltering regional economy. After reviewing all available evidence at December 31, 2008, Community Bank determines that Prospect will probably pay back only $300,000 of the principal at maturity. As a result, Community Bank declares the loan impaired. It now needs to record a loss.

To determine the loss, Community Bank first computes the present value of the expected cash flows, discounted at the historical effective rate of interest (10%). This amount is $225,396. The time diagram in Illustration 14A-4 highlights the factors involved in this computation.

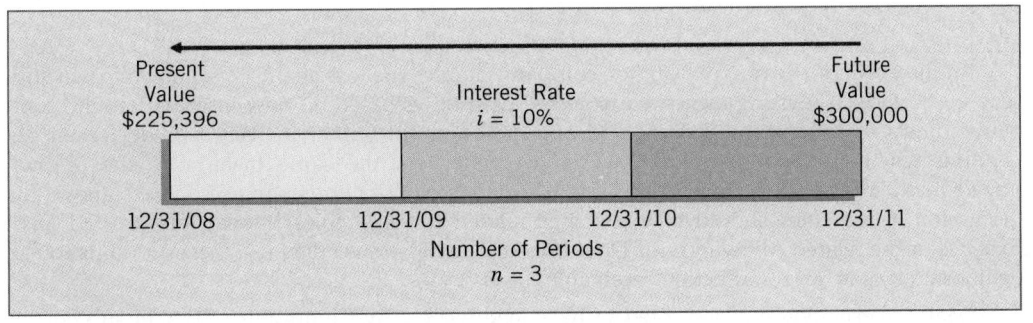

The loss due to impairment is the difference between the present value of the expected future cash flows and the recorded carrying amount of the investment in the loan. Illustration 14A-5 (on page 700) shows the calculation of the loss.

ILLUSTRATION 14A-5
Computation of Loss Due
to Impairment

Carrying amount of investment (12/31/08)—Illustration 14A-3	$375,657
Less: Present value of $300,000 due in 3 years at 10% interest compounded annually (Table 6-2); $FV(PVF_{3,10\%})$; ($300,000 × .75132)	225,396
Loss due to impairment	$150,261

The loss due to the impairment is $150,261, not $200,000 ($500,000 − $300,000). Why? Because Community Bank must measure the loss at a present-value amount, not an undiscounted amount, at the time it records the loss.

Community Bank records the loss as follows.

ILLUSTRATION 14A-6
Creditor and Debtor
Entries to Record Loss on
Note

December 31, 2008

Community Bank (Creditor)			Prospect Inc. (Debtor)
Bad Debt Expense	150,261		No entry
Allowance for Doubtful Accounts		150,261	

Community Bank (creditor) debits Bad Debt Expense for the expected loss. At the same time, it reduces the overall value of its loan receivable by crediting Allowance for Doubtful Accounts.[7] What entry does Prospect (the debtor) make? It makes no entry because it still legally owes $500,000.[8]

TROUBLED DEBT RESTRUCTURINGS

OBJECTIVE 10
Describe the
accounting for a debt
restructuring.

A **troubled debt restructuring** occurs when a creditor "for economic or legal reasons related to the debtor's financial difficulties grants a concession to the debtor that it would not otherwise consider."[9] Thus a troubled debt restructuring does not apply to modifications of a debt obligation that reflect general economic conditions leading to a reduced interest rate. Nor does it apply to the refunding of an old debt with new debt having an effective interest rate approximately equal to that of similar debt issued by nontroubled debtors.

A troubled debt restructuring involves one of two basic types of transactions:

1 Settlement of debt at less than its carrying amount.
2 Continuation of debt with a modification of terms.

---

[7]In the event of a loan write-off, the company charges the loss against the allowance. In subsequent periods, if revising estimated expected cash flows based on new information, the company adjusts the allowance account and bad debt account (either increased or decreased depending whether conditions improved or worsened) in the same fashion as the original impairment. We use the terms "loss" and "bad debt expense" interchangeably throughout this discussion. Companies should charge losses related to receivables transactions to Bad Debt Expense or the related Allowance for Doubtful Accounts, because they use these accounts to recognize changes in values affecting receivables.

[8]Many alternatives are permitted to recognize income by Community Bank in subsequent periods. See *FASB Statement No. 118*, "Accounting by Creditors for Impairment of a Loan—Income Recognition and Disclosures" (Norwalk, Conn.: FASB, October 1994) for appropriate methods.

[9]"Accounting by Debtors and Creditors for Troubled Debt Restructurings," *FASB Statement No. 15* (Norwalk, Conn.: FASB, June, 1977), par. 1.

Settlement of Debt

Settling a debt obligation can involve either a transfer of noncash assets (real estate, receivables, or other assets) or the issuance of the debtor's stock. In these situations, **the creditor should account for the noncash assets or equity interest received at their fair value**.

The debtor must determine the excess of the carrying amount of the payable over the fair value of the assets or equity transferred (gain). Likewise, the creditor must determine the excess of the receivable over the fair value of those same assets or equity interests transferred (loss). The debtor recognizes a gain equal to the amount of the excess. The creditor normally charges the excess (loss) against Allowance for Doubtful Accounts. In addition, the debtor recognizes a gain or loss on disposition of assets to the extent that the fair value of those assets differs from their carrying amount (book value).

Transfer of Assets

Assume that American City Bank loaned $20,000,000 to Union Mortgage Company. Union Mortgage, in turn, invested these monies in residential apartment buildings. However, because of low occupancy rates, it cannot meet its loan obligations. American City Bank agrees to accept from Union Mortgage real estate with a fair market value of $16,000,000 in full settlement of the $20,000,000 loan obligation. The real estate has a carrying value of $21,000,000 on the books of Union Mortgage. American City Bank (creditor) records this transaction as follows.

Real Estate	16,000,000	
Allowance for Doubtful Accounts	4,000,000	
Note Receivable from Union Mortgage		20,000,000

The bank records the real estate at fair market value. Further, it makes a charge to the Allowance for Doubtful Accounts to reflect the bad debt write-off.

Union Mortgage (debtor) records this transaction as follows.

Note Payable to American City Bank	20,000,000	
Loss on Disposition of Real Estate	5,000,000	
Real Estate		21,000,000
Gain on Restructuring of Debt		4,000,000

Union Mortgage has a loss on the disposition of real estate in the amount of $5,000,000 (the difference between the $21,000,000 book value and the $16,000,000 fair market value). It should show this as an ordinary loss on the income statement. In addition, it has a gain on restructuring of debt of $4,000,000 (the difference between the $20,000,000 carrying amount of the note payable and the $16,000,000 fair market value of the real estate).

Granting of Equity Interest

Assume that American City Bank agrees to accept from Union Mortgage 320,000 shares of common stock ($10 par) that has a fair market value of $16,000,000, in full settlement of the $20,000,000 loan obligation. American City Bank (creditor) records this transaction as follows.

Investment	16,000,000	
Allowance for Doubtful Accounts	4,000,000	
Note Receivable from Union Mortgage		20,000,000

It records the stock as an investment at the fair market value at the date of restructure.

Union Mortgage (debtor) records this transaction as follows.

Note Payable to American City Bank	20,000,000	
Common Stock		3,200,000
Additional Paid-in Capital		12,800,000
Gain on Restructuring of Debt		4,000,000

It records the stock issued in the normal manner. It records the difference between the par value and the fair value of the stock as additional paid-in capital.

Modification of Terms

In some cases, a debtor's serious short-run cash flow problems will lead it to request one or a combination of the following modifications:

1 Reduction of the stated interest rate.
2 Extension of the maturity date of the face amount of the debt.
3 Reduction of the face amount of the debt.
4 Reduction or deferral of any accrued interest.

The creditor's loss is based on expected cash flows discounted at the historical effective rate of the loan.[10] The debtor calculates its gain based on **undiscounted amounts**, as required by the previous standard. As a consequence, **the gain recorded by the debtor will not equal the loss recorded by the creditor under many circumstances.**[11]

Two examples demonstrate the accounting for a troubled debt restructuring by debtors and creditors:

1 The debtor does not record a gain.
2 The debtor does record a gain.

In both instances the creditor has a loss.

Example 1—No Gain for Debtor

This example demonstrates a restructuring in which the debtor records no gain.[12] On December 31, 2006, Morgan National Bank enters into a debt restructuring agreement with Resorts Development Company, which is experiencing financial difficulties. The bank restructures a $10,500,000 loan receivable issued at par (interest paid to date) by:

1 Reducing the principal obligation from $10,500,000 to $9,000,000;
2 Extending the maturity date from December 31, 2006, to December 31, 2010; and
3 Reducing the interest rate from 12% to 8%.

Debtor Calculations. The total future cash flow, after restructuring of $11,880,000 ($9,000,000 of principal plus $2,880,000 of interest payments[13]), exceeds the total pre-restructuring carrying amount of the debt of $10,500,000. Consequently, **the debtor**

---

[10]*FASB Statement No. 114*, par. 42.

[11]In response to concerns expressed about this nonsymmetric treatment, the FASB stated that *Statement No. 114* does not address debtor accounting because the FASB was concerned that expansion of the scope of the statement would delay its issuance. By basing the debtor calculation on undiscounted amounts, the amount of gain (if any) recognized by the debtor is reduced at the time the modification of terms occurs. If fair value were used, the gain recognized would be greater. The result of this approach is to spread the unrecognized gain over the life of the new agreement. We believe that this accounting is inappropriate and hopefully will change as more fair value measurements are introduced into the financial statements.

[12]Note that the examples given for restructuring assume the creditor made no previous entries for impairment. In actuality it is likely that, in accordance with *Statement No. 114*, the creditor would have already made an entry when the loan initially became impaired. Restructuring would, therefore, simply require an adjustment of the initial estimated bad debt by the creditor. Recall, however, that the debtor makes no entry upon impairment.

[13]Total interest payments are: $9,000,000 × .08 × 4 years = $2,880,000.

records no gain nor makes any adjustment to the carrying amount of the payable. As a result, Resorts Development (debtor) makes no entry at the date of restructuring.

The debtor must compute a new effective-interest rate in order to record interest expense in future periods. The new effective-interest rate equates the present value of the future cash flows specified by the new terms with the pre-restructuring carrying amount of the debt. In this case, Resorts Development computes the new rate by relating the pre-restructure carrying amount ($10,500,000) to the total future cash flow ($11,880,000). The rate necessary to discount the total future cash flow ($11,880,000), to a present value equal to the remaining balance ($10,500,000), is 3.46613%.[14]

On the basis of the effective rate of 3.46613%, the debtor prepares the schedule shown in Illustration 14A-7.

ILLUSTRATION 14A-7
Schedule Showing Reduction of Carrying Amount of Note

RESORTS DEVELOPMENT CO. (DEBTOR)

Date	Cash Paid (8%)	Interest Expense (3.46613%)	Reduction of Carrying Amount	Carrying Amount of Note
12/31/06				$10,500,000
12/31/07	$ 720,000ª	$ 363,944ᵇ	$ 356,056ᶜ	10,143,944
12/31/08	720,000	351,602	368,398	9,775,546
12/31/09	720,000	338,833	381,167	9,394,379
12/31/10	720,000	325,621	394,379	9,000,000
	$2,880,000	$1,380,000	$1,500,000	

ª$720,000 = $9,000,000 × .08
ᵇ$363,944 = $10,500,000 × 3.46613%
ᶜ$356,056 = $720,000 − $363,944

Calculator Solution for Interest Rate

	Inputs	Answer
N	4	
I/YR	?	3.466
PV	10,500,000	
PMT	−720,000	
FV	−9,000,000	

Thus, on December 31, 2007 (date of first interest payment after restructure), the debtor makes the following entry.

December 31, 2007

Notes Payable	356,056	
Interest Expense	363,944	
Cash		720,000

The debtor makes a similar entry (except for different amounts for debits to Notes Payable and Interest Expense) each year until maturity. At maturity, Resorts Development makes the following entry.

December 31, 2010

Notes Payable	9,000,000	
Cash		9,000,000

Creditor Calculations. Morgan National Bank (creditor) must calculate its loss based on the expected future cash flows discounted at the historical effective rate of the loan. It calculates this loss as shown in Illustration 14A-8 (on page 704).

---

[14]An accurate interest rate i can be found by using the formulas given at the tops of Tables 6-2 and 6-4 to set up the following equation.

$$\$10,500,000 = \frac{1}{(1 + i)^4} \times \$9,000,000 + \frac{1 - \dfrac{1}{(1 + i)^4}}{i} \times \$720,000$$

(from Table 6-2)   (from Table 6-4)

Solving algebraically for i, we find that $i = 3.46613\%$.

ILLUSTRATION 14A-8
Computation of Loss to
Creditor on Restructuring

Pre-restructure carrying amount		$10,500,000
Present value of restructured cash flows:		
Present value of $9,000,000 due in 4 years		
at 12%, interest payable annually (Table 6-2);		
$FV(PVF_{4,12\%})$; ($9,000,000 × .63552)	$5,719,680	
Present value of $720,000 interest payable annually for 4		
years at 12% (Table 6-4); $R(PVF\text{-}OA_{4,12\%})$;		
($720,000 × 3.03735)	2,186,892	
Present value of restructured cash flows		7,906,572
Loss on restructuring		$ 2,593,428

As a result, Morgan National Bank records bad debt expense as follows (assuming no establishment of an allowance balance from recognition of an impairment).

Bad Debt Expense	2,593,428	
Allowance for Doubtful Accounts		2,593,428

In subsequent periods, Morgan National Bank reports interest revenue based on the historical effective rate. Illustration 14A-9 provides the following interest and amortization information.

ILLUSTRATION 14A-9
Schedule of Interest and
Amortization after Debt
Restructuring

		MORGAN NATIONAL BANK (CREDITOR)		
Date	Cash Received (8%)	Interest Revenue (12%)	Increase of Carrying Amount	Carrying Amount of Note
12/31/06				$7,906,572
12/31/07	$ 720,000[a]	$ 948,789[b]	$ 228,789[c]	8,135,361
12/31/08	720,000	976,243	256,243	8,391,604
12/31/09	720,000	1,006,992	286,992	8,678,596
12/31/10	720,000	1,041,404[d]	321,404[d]	9,000,000
Total	$2,880,000	$3,973,428	$1,093,428	

[a]$720,000 = $9,000,000 × .08
[b]$948,789 = $7,906,572 × .12
[c]$228,789 = $948,789 − $720,000
[d]$28 adjustment to compensate for rounding.

On December 31, 2007, Morgan National Bank makes the following entry.

December 31, 2007

Cash	720,000	
Allowance for Doubtful Accounts	228,789	
Interest Revenue		948,789

The creditor makes a similar entry (except for different amounts debited to Allowance for Doubtful Accounts and credited to Interest Revenue) each year until maturity. At maturity, the company makes the following entry.

December 31, 2010

Cash	9,000,000	
Allowance for Doubtful Accounts	1,500,000	
Notes Receivable		10,500,000

Example 2—Gain for Debtor

If the pre-restructure carrying amount exceeds the total future cash flows as a result of a modification of the terms, the debtor records a gain. To illustrate, assume the facts in the previous example except that Morgan National Bank reduces the principal to $7,000,000 (and extends the maturity date to December 31, 2010, and reduces the interest from 12% to 8%). The total future cash flow is now $9,240,000 ($7,000,000 of principal plus $2,240,000 of interest[15]), which is $1,260,000 ($10,500,000 − $9,240,000) less than the pre-restructure carrying amount of $10,500,000.

Under these circumstances, Resorts Development (debtor) reduces the carrying amount of its payable $1,260,000 and records a gain of $1,260,000. On the other hand, Morgan National Bank (creditor) debits its Bad Debt Expense for $4,350,444. Illustration 14A-10 shows this computation.

Pre-restructure carrying amount		$10,500,000
Present value of restructured cash flows:		
Present value of $7,000,000 due in 4 years at 12%,		
interest payable annually (Table 6-2);		
$FV(PVF_{4,12\%})$; ($7,000,000 × .63552)	$4,448,640	
Present value of $560,000 interest payable annually		
for 4 years at 12% (Table 6-4);		
$R(PVF\text{-}OA_{4,12\%})$; ($560,000 × 3.03735)	1,700,916	6,149,556
Creditor's loss on restructuring		$ 4,350,444

ILLUSTRATION 14A-10
Computation of Loss to Creditor on Restructuring

Illustration 14A-11 shows the entries to record the gain and loss on the debtor's and creditor's books at the date of restructure, December 31, 2006.

ILLUSTRATION 14A-11
Debtor and Creditor Entries to Record Gain and Loss on Note

December 31, 2006 (date of restructure)			
Resorts Development Co. (Debtor)		**Morgan National Bank (Creditor)**	
Notes Payable	1,260,000	Bad Debt Expense	4,350,444
Gain on Restructuring of		Allowance for Doubtful Accounts	4,350,444
Debt	1,260,000		

For Resorts Development (debtor), because the new carrying value of the note ($10,500,000 − $1,260,000 = $9,240,000) equals the sum of the undiscounted cash flows ($9,240,000), the imputed interest rate is 0 percent. Consequently, all of the future cash flows reduce the principal balance, and the company recognizes no interest expense.

Morgan National reports the interest revenue in the same fashion as the previous example—that is, using the historical effective interest rate applied toward the newly discounted value of the note. Illustration 14A-12 shows interest computations.

ILLUSTRATION 14A-12
Schedule of Interest and Amortization after Debt Restructuring

MORGAN NATIONAL BANK (CREDITOR)				
Date	Cash Received (8%)	Interest Revenue (12%)	Increase in Carrying Amount	Carrying Amount of Note
12/31/06				$6,149,556
12/31/07	$ 560,000[a]	$ 737,947[b]	$177,947[c]	6,327,503
12/31/08	560,000	759,300	199,300	6,526,803
12/31/09	560,000	783,216	223,216	6,750,019
12/31/10	560,000	809,981[d]	249,981[d]	7,000,000
Total	$2,240,000	$3,090,444	$850,444	

[a]$560,000 = $7,000,000 × .08
[b]$737,947 = $6,149,556 × .12
[c]$177,947 = $737,947 − $560,000
[d]$21 adjustment to compensate for rounding.

---

[15]Total interest payments are: $7,000,000 × .08 × 4 years = $2,240,000.

The journal entries in Illustration 14A-13 demonstrate the accounting by debtor and creditor for periodic interest payments and final principal payment.

Resorts Development Co. (Debtor)			Morgan National Bank (Creditor)		
December 31, 2007 (date of first interest payment following restructure)					
Notes Payable	560,000		Cash	560,000	
Cash		560,000	Allowance for Doubtful Accounts	177,947	
			Interest Revenue		737,947
December 31, 2008, 2009, and 2010 (dates of 2nd, 3rd, and last interest payments)					
(Debit and credit same accounts as 12/31/07 using applicable amounts from appropriate amortization schedules.)					
December 31, 2010 (date of principal payment)					
Notes Payable	7,000,000		Cash	7,000,000	
Cash		7,000,000	Allowance for Doubtful Accounts	3,500,000	
			Notes Receivable		10,500,000

ILLUSTRATION 14A-13
Debtor and Creditor
Entries to Record Periodic
Interest and Final
Principal Payments

Concluding Remarks

The accounting for troubled debt is complex because the accounting standards allow for use of different measurement standards to determine the loss or gain reported. In addition, the assets and liabilities reported are sometimes not stated at cost or fair value, but at amounts adjusted for certain events but not others. This cumbersome accounting demonstrates the need for adoption of a comprehensive fair-value model for financial instruments that is consistent with finance concepts for pricing these financial instruments.

SUMMARY OF LEARNING OBJECTIVES

KEY TERMS

impairment, *698*
troubled debt
  restructuring, *700*

9. **Describe the accounting for a loan impairment.** A creditor bases an impairment loan loss on the difference between the present value of the future cash flows (using the historical effective interest rate) and the carrying amount of the note.

10. **Describe the accounting for a debt restructuring.** There are two types of debt settlements: (1) transfer of noncash assets, and (2) granting of equity interest. Creditors and debtors record losses and gains on settlements based on fair values. For accounting purposes there are also two types of restructurings with continuation of debt with modified terms: (1) the carrying amount of debt is less than the future cash flows, and (2) the carrying amount of debt exceeds the total future cash flows. Creditors record losses on these restructurings based on the expected future cash flows discounted at the historical effective interest rate. The debtor determines its gain based on undiscounted cash flows.

Note: All **asterisked** Questions, Brief Exercises, Exercises, and Problems relate to material contained in the appendix to the chapter.

QUESTIONS

1. (a) From what sources might a corporation obtain funds through long-term debt? (b) What is a bond indenture? What does it contain? (c) What is a mortgage?

2. Potlatch Corporation has issued various types of bonds such as term bonds, income bonds, and debentures. Differentiate between term bonds, mortgage bonds, collateral trust bonds, debenture bonds, income bonds, callable bonds, registered bonds, bearer or coupon bonds, convertible bonds, commodity-backed bonds, and deep discount bonds.

3. Distinguish between the following interest rates for bonds payable:

(a) yield rate   (d) market rate

(b) nominal rate   (e) effective rate

(c) stated rate

4. Distinguish between the following values relative to bonds payable:

(a) maturity value   (c) market value

(b) face value   (d) par value

5. Under what conditions of bond issuance does a discount on bonds payable arise? Under what conditions of bond issuance does a premium on bonds payable arise?

6. How should discount on bonds payable be reported on the financial statements? Premium on bonds payable?

7. What are the two methods of amortizing discount and premium on bonds payable? Explain each.

8. Zeno Company sells its bonds at a premium and applies the effective interest method in amortizing the premium. Will the annual interest expense increase or decrease over the life of the bonds? Explain.

9. Briggs and Stratton recently reported unamortized debt issue costs of $5.1 million. How should the costs of issuing these bonds be accounted for and classified in the financial statements?

10. Where should treasury bonds be shown on the balance sheet?

11. What is the "call" feature of a bond issue? How does the call feature affect the amortization of bond premium or discount?

12. Why would a company wish to reduce its bond indebtedness before its bonds reach maturity? Indicate how this can be done and the correct accounting treatment for such a transaction.

13. How are gains and losses from extinguishment of a debt classified in the income statement? What disclosures are required of such transactions?

14. What is done to record properly a transaction involving the issuance of a non-interest-bearing long-term note in exchange for property?

15. How is the present value of a non-interest-bearing note computed?

16. When is the stated interest rate of a debt instrument presumed to be fair?

17. What are the considerations in imputing an appropriate interest rate?

18. Differentiate between a fixed-rate mortgage and a variable-rate mortgage.

19. What disclosures are required relative to long-term debt and sinking fund requirements?

20. What is off-balance-sheet financing? Why might a company be interested in using off-balance-sheet financing?

21. What are some forms of off-balance-sheet financing?

22. What are take-or-pay contracts and through-put contracts?

*23. What are the types of situations that result in troubled debt?

*24. What are the general rules for measuring and recognizing gain or loss by both the debtor and the creditor in an impairment?

*25. What are the general rules for measuring gain or loss by both creditor and debtor in a troubled debt restructuring involving a settlement?

*26. (a) In a troubled debt situation, why might the creditor grant concessions to the debtor?

    (b) What type of concessions might a creditor grant the debtor in a troubled debt situation?

    (c) What is meant by "impairment" of a loan? Under what circumstances should a creditor or debtor recognize an impaired loan?

*27. What are the general rules for measuring and recognizing gain or loss by both the debtor and the creditor in a troubled debt restructuring involving a modification of terms?

*28. What is meant by "accounting symmetry" between the entries recorded by the debtor and creditor in a troubled debt restructuring involving a modification of terms? In what ways is the accounting for troubled debt restructurings and impairments non-symmetrical?

*29. Under what circumstances would a transaction be recorded as a troubled debt restructuring by only one of the two parties to the transaction?

BRIEF EXERCISES

(LO 3)   **BE14-1**   Ghostbusters Corporation issues $300,000 of 9% bonds, due in 10 years, with interest payable semiannually. At the time of issue, the market rate for such bonds is 10%. Compute the issue price of the bonds.

(LO 3, 4)   **BE14-2**   The Goofy Company issued $200,000 of 10% bonds on January 1, 2008. The bonds are due January 1, 2013, with interest payable each July 1 and January 1. The bonds are issued at face value. Prepare Goofy's journal entries for (a) the January issuance, (b) the July 1 interest payment, and (c) the December 31 adjusting entry.

(LO 3, 4)   **BE14-3**   Assume the bonds in BE14-2 were issued at 98. Prepare the journal entries for (a) January 1, (b) July 1, and (c) December 31. Assume The Goofy Company records straight-line amortization annually on December 31.

(LO 3, 4)   **BE14-4**   Assume the bonds in BE14-2 were issued at 103. Prepare the journal entries for (a) January 1, (b) July 1, and (c) December 31. Assume The Goofy Company records straight-line amortization annually on December 31.

(LO 3, 4)   **BE14-5**   Toy Story Corporation issued $500,000 of 6% bonds on May 1, 2008. The bonds were dated January 1, 2008, and mature January 1, 2013, with interest payable July 1 and January 1. The bonds were issued at face value plus accrued interest. Prepare Toy Story's journal entries for (a) the May 1 issuance, (b) the July 1 interest payment, and (c) the December 31 adjusting entry.

(LO 3, 4)   **BE14-6**   On January 1, 2008, Qix Corporation issued $400,000 of 7% bonds, due in 10 years. The bonds were issued for $372,816, and pay interest each July 1 and January 1. Qix uses the effective interest method. Prepare the company's journal entries for (a) the January 1 issuance, (b) the July 1 interest payment, and (c) the December 31 adjusting entry. Assume an effective interest rate of 8%.

(LO 3, 4)   **BE14-7**   Assume the bonds in BE14-6 were issued for $429,757 and the effective interest rate is 6%. Prepare the company's journal entries for (a) the January 1 issuance, (b) the July 1 interest payment, and (c) the December 31 adjusting entry.

(LO 3, 4)   **BE14-8**   Izzy Corporation issued $400,000 of 7% bonds on November 1, 2008, for $429,757. The bonds were dated November 1, 2008, and mature in 10 years, with interest payable each May 1 and November 1. Izzy uses the effective interest method with an effective rate of 6%. Prepare Izzy's December 31, 2008, adjusting entry.

(LO 8)   **BE14-9**   At December 31, 2008, Treasure Land Corporation has the following account balances:

Bonds payable, due January 1, 2016	$2,000,000
Discount on bonds payable	98,000
Bond interest payable	80,000

Show how the above accounts should be presented on the December 31, 2008, balance sheet, including the proper classifications.

(LO 4)   **BE14-10**   Austin Powers Corporation issued 10-year bonds on January 1, 2008. Costs associated with the bond issuance were $180,000. Powers uses the straight-line method to amortize bond issue costs. Prepare the December 31, 2008, entry to record 2008 bond issue cost amortization.

(LO 5)   **BE14-11**   On January 1, 2008, Uncharted Waters Corporation retired $600,000 of bonds at 99. At the time of retirement, the unamortized premium was $15,000 and unamortized bond issue costs were $5,250. Prepare the corporation's journal entry to record the reacquisition of the bonds.

(LO 6)   **BE14-12**   Jennifer Capriati, Inc. issued a $100,000, 4-year, 11% note at face value to Forest Hills Bank on January 1, 2008, and received $100,000 cash. The note requires annual interest payments each December 31. Prepare Capriati's journal entries to record (a) the issuance of the note and (b) the December 31 interest payment.

(LO 6)   **BE14-13**   McNabb Corporation issued a 4-year, $50,000, zero-interest-bearing note to Reid Company on January 1, 2008, and received cash of $31,776. The implicit interest rate is 12%. Prepare McNabb's journal entries for (a) the January 1 issuance and (b) the December 31 recognition of interest.

(LO 6)   **BE14-14**   Larry Byrd Corporation issued a 4-year, $50,000, 5% note to Magic Johnson Company on January 1, 2008, and received a computer that normally sells for $39,369. The note requires annual interest payments each December 31. The market rate of interest for a note of similar risk is 12%. Prepare Larry Byrd's journal entries for (a) the January 1 issuance and (b) the December 31 interest.

(LO 6)   **BE14-15**   King Corporation issued a 4-year, $50,000, zero-interest-bearing note to Salmon Company on January 1, 2008, and received cash of $50,000. In addition, King agreed to sell merchandise to Salmon at an amount less than regular selling price over the 4-year period. The market rate of interest for similar notes is 12%. Prepare King Corporation's January 1 journal entry.

(LO 9) ***BE14-16**   Assume that Toni Braxton Company has recently fallen into financial difficulties. By reviewing all available evidence on December 31, 2006, one creditor of Toni Braxton, the National American Bank, determined that Toni Braxton would pay back only 65% of the principal at maturity. As a result, the bank decided that the loan was impaired. If the loss is estimated to be $225,000, what entries should both Toni Braxton and National American Bank make to record this loss?

EXERCISES

(LO 2)   **E14-1**   **(Classification of Liabilities)**   Presented below are various account balances of K.D. Lang Inc.

    (a)   Unamortized premium on bonds payable, of which $3,000 will be amortized during the next year.
    (b)   Bank loans payable of a winery, due March 10, 2011. (The product requires aging for 5 years before sale.)
    (c)   Serial bonds payable, $1,000,000, of which $200,000 are due each July 31.
    (d)   Amounts withheld from employees' wages for income taxes.
    (e)   Notes payable due January 15, 2010.
    (f)   Credit balances in customers' accounts arising from returns and allowances after collection in full of account.
    (g)   Bonds payable of $2,000,000 maturing June 30, 2009.
    (h)   Overdraft of $1,000 in a bank account. (No other balances are carried at this bank.)
    (i)   Deposits made by customers who have ordered goods.

Instructions
Indicate whether each of the items above should be classified on December 31, 2008, as a current liability, a long-term liability, or under some other classification. Consider each one independently from all others; that is, do not assume that all of them relate to one particular business. If the classification of some of the items is doubtful, explain why in each case.

(LO 2)   **E14-2**   **(Classification)**   The following items are found in the financial statements.

    (a)   Discount on bonds payable
    (b)   Interest expense (credit balance)
    (c)   Unamortized bond issue costs
    (d)   Gain on repurchase of debt
    (e)   Mortgage payable (payable in equal amounts over next 3 years)
    (f)   Debenture bonds payable (maturing in 5 years)
    (g)   Notes payable (due in 4 years)
    (h)   Premium on bonds payable
    (i)   Treasury bonds
    (j)   Income bonds payable (due in 3 years)

Instructions
Indicate how each of these items should be classified in the financial statements.

(LO 3, 4)   **E14-3**   **(Entries for Bond Transactions)**   Presented below are two independent situations.

    1.   On January 1, 2007, Simon Company issued $200,000 of 9%, 10-year bonds at par. Interest is payable quarterly on April 1, July 1, October 1, and January 1.
    2.   On June 1, 2007, Garfunkel Company issued $100,000 of 12%, 10-year bonds dated January 1 at par plus accrued interest. Interest is payable semiannually on July 1 and January 1.

Instructions
For each of these two independent situations, prepare journal entries to record the following.

    (a)   The issuance of the bonds.
    (b)   The payment of interest on July 1.
    (c)   The accrual of interest on December 31.

(LO 3, 4)   **E14-4**   **(Entries for Bond Transactions—Straight-Line)**   Celine Dion Company issued $600,000 of 10%, 20-year bonds on January 1, 2008, at 102. Interest is payable semiannually on July 1 and January 1. Dion Company uses the straight-line method of amortization for bond premium or discount.

Instructions

Prepare the journal entries to record the following.

(a) The issuance of the bonds.

(b) The payment of interest and the related amortization on July 1, 2008.

(c) The accrual of interest and the related amortization on December 31, 2008.

(LO 3, 4)

E14-5 (Entries for Bond Transactions—Effective Interest) Assume the same information as in E14-4, except that Celine Dion Company uses the effective interest method of amortization for bond premium or discount. Assume an effective yield of 9.7705%.

Instructions

Prepare the journal entries to record the following. (Round to the nearest dollar.)

(a) The issuance of the bonds.

(b) The payment of interest and related amortization on July 1, 2008.

(c) The accrual of interest and the related amortization on December 31, 2008.

(LO 3, 4)

E14-6 (Amortization Schedules—Straight-line) Devon Harris Company sells 10% bonds having a maturity value of $2,000,000 for $1,855,816. The bonds are dated January 1, 2007, and mature January 1, 2012. Interest is payable annually on January 1.

Instructions

Set up a schedule of interest expense and discount amortization under the straight-line method.

(LO 3, 4)

E14-7 (Amortization Schedule—Effective Interest) Assume the same information as E14-6.

Instructions

Set up a schedule of interest expense and discount amortization under the effective interest method. (*Hint:* The effective interest rate must be computed.)

(LO 3, 4)

E14-8 (Determine Proper Amounts in Account Balances) Presented below are three independent situations.

(a) CeCe Winans Corporation incurred the following costs in connection with the issuance of bonds: (1) printing and engraving costs, $12,000; (2) legal fees, $49,000, and (3) commissions paid to underwriter, $60,000. What amount should be reported as Unamortized Bond Issue Costs, and where should this amount be reported on the balance sheet?

(b) George Gershwin Co. sold $2,000,000 of 10%, 10-year bonds at 104 on January 1, 2007. The bonds were dated January 1, 2007, and pay interest on July 1 and January 1. If Gershwin uses the straight-line method to amortize bond premium or discount, determine the amount of interest expense to be reported on July 1, 2007, and December 31, 2007.

(c) Ron Kenoly Inc. issued $600,000 of 9%, 10-year bonds on June 30, 2007, for $562,500. This price provided a yield of 10% on the bonds. Interest is payable semiannually on December 31 and June 30. If Kenoly uses the effective interest method, determine the amount of interest expense to record if financial statements are issued on October 31, 2007.

(LO 3, 4)

E14-9 (Entries and Questions for Bond Transactions) On June 30, 2008, Mischa Auer Company issued $4,000,000 face value of 13%, 20-year bonds at $4,300,920, a yield of 12%. Auer uses the effective interest method to amortize bond premium or discount. The bonds pay semiannual interest on June 30 and December 31.

Instructions

(a) Prepare the journal entries to record the following transactions.

    (1) The issuance of the bonds on June 30, 2008.

    (2) The payment of interest and the amortization of the premium on December 31, 2008.

    (3) The payment of interest and the amortization of the premium on June 30, 2009.

    (4) The payment of interest and the amortization of the premium on December 31, 2009.

(b) Show the proper balance sheet presentation for the liability for bonds payable on the December 31, 2009, balance sheet.

(c) Provide the answers to the following questions.

    (1) What amount of interest expense is reported for 2009?

    (2) Will the bond interest expense reported in 2009 be the same as, greater than, or less than the amount that would be reported if the straight-line method of amortization were used?

    (3) Determine the total cost of borrowing over the life of the bond.

    (4) Will the total bond interest expense for the life of the bond be greater than, the same as, or less than the total interest expense if the straight-line method of amortization were used?

(LO 3, 4) **E14-10 (Entries for Bond Transactions)** On January 1, 2007, Aumont Company sold 12% bonds having a maturity value of $500,000 for $537,907.37, which provides the bondholders with a 10% yield. The bonds are dated January 1, 2007, and mature January 1, 2012, with interest payable December 31 of each year. Aumont Company allocates interest and unamortized discount or premium on the effective interest basis.

Instructions
(a) Prepare the journal entry at the date of the bond issuance.
(b) Prepare a schedule of interest expense and bond amortization for 2007–2009.
(c) Prepare the journal entry to record the interest payment and the amortization for 2007.
(d) Prepare the journal entry to record the interest payment and the amortization for 2009.

(LO 3) **E14-11 (Information Related to Various Bond Issues)** Karen Austin Inc. has issued three types of debt on January 1, 2007, the start of the company's fiscal year.
(a) $10 million, 10-year, 15% unsecured bonds, interest payable quarterly. Bonds were priced to yield 12%.
(b) $25 million par of 10-year, zero-coupon bonds at a price to yield 12% per year.
(c) $20 million, 10-year, 10% mortgage bonds, interest payable annually to yield 12%.

Instructions
Prepare a schedule that identifies the following items for each bond: (1) maturity value, (2) number of interest periods over life of bond, (3) stated rate per each interest period, (4) effective interest rate per each interest period, (5) payment amount per period, and (6) present value of bonds at date of issue.

(LO 3, 4, 5) **E14-12 (Entry for Retirement of Bond; Bond Issue Costs)** On January 2, 2002, Banno Corporation issued $1,500,000 of 10% bonds at 97 due December 31, 2011. Legal and other costs of $24,000 were incurred in connection with the issue. Interest on the bonds is payable annually each December 31. The $24,000 issue costs are being deferred and amortized on a straight-line basis over the 10-year term of the bonds. The discount on the bonds is also being amortized on a straight-line basis over the 10 years. (Straight-line is not materially different in effect from the preferable "interest method".)

The bonds are callable at 101 (i.e., at 101% of face amount), and on January 2, 2007, Banno called $900,000 face amount of the bonds and retired them.

Instructions
Ignoring income taxes, compute the amount of loss, if any, to be recognized by Banno as a result of retiring the $900,000 of bonds in 2007 and prepare the journal entry to record the retirement.

(AICPA adapted)

(LO 3, 4, 5) **E14-13 (Entries for Retirement and Issuance of Bonds)** Matt Perry, Inc. had outstanding $6,000,000 of 11% bonds (interest payable July 31 and January 31) due in 10 years. On July 1, it issued $9,000,000 of 10%, 15-year bonds (interest payable July 1 and January 1) at 98. A portion of the proceeds was used to call the 11% bonds at 102 on August 1. Unamortized bond discount and issue cost applicable to the 11% bonds were $120,000 and $30,000, respectively.

Instructions
Prepare the journal entries necessary to record issue of the new bonds and the refunding of the bonds.

(LO 3, 4, 5) **E14-14 (Entries for Retirement and Issuance of Bonds)** On June 30, 1999, County Crows Company issued 12% bonds with a par value of $800,000 due in 20 years. They were issued at 98 and were callable at 104 at any date after June 30, 2007. Because of lower interest rates and a significant change in the company's credit rating, it was decided to call the entire issue on June 30, 2008, and to issue new bonds. New 10% bonds were sold in the amount of $1,000,000 at 102; they mature in 20 years. County Crows Company uses straight-line amortization. Interest payment dates are December 31 and June 30.

Instructions
(a) Prepare journal entries to record the retirement of the old issue and the sale of the new issue on June 30, 2008.
(b) Prepare the entry required on December 31, 2008, to record the payment of the first 6 months' interest and the amortization of premium on the bonds.

(LO 3, 4, 5) **E14-15 (Entries for Retirement and Issuance of Bonds)** Linda Day George Company had bonds outstanding with a maturity value of $300,000. On April 30, 2008, when these bonds had an unamortized discount of $10,000, they were called in at 104. To pay for these bonds, George had issued other bonds a month earlier bearing a lower interest rate. The newly issued bonds had a life of 10 years. The new bonds were issued at 103 (face value $300,000). Issue costs related to the new bonds were $3,000.

Instructions
Ignoring interest, compute the gain or loss and record this refunding transaction.

(AICPA adapted)

(LO 6) **E14-16** **(Entries for Zero-Interest-Bearing Notes)** On January 1, 2008, Ellen Greene Company makes the two following acquisitions.

1. Purchases land having a fair market value of $200,000 by issuing a 5-year, zero-interest-bearing promissory note in the face amount of $337,012.
2. Purchases equipment by issuing a 6%, 8-year promissory note having a maturity value of $250,000 (interest payable annually).

The company has to pay 11% interest for funds from its bank.

Instructions
(a) Record the two journal entries that should be recorded by Ellen Greene Company for the two purchases on January 1, 2008.
(b) Record the interest at the end of the first year on both notes using the effective interest method.

(LO 6) **E14-17** **(Imputation of Interest)** Presented below are two independent situations:

(a) On January 1, 2008, Robin Wright Inc. purchased land that had an assessed value of $350,000 at the time of purchase. A $550,000, zero-interest-bearing note due January 1, 2011, was given in exchange. There was no established exchange price for the land, nor a ready market value for the note. The interest rate charged on a note of this type is 12%. Determine at what amount the land should be recorded at January 1, 2008, and the interest expense to be reported in 2008 related to this transaction.
(b) On January 1, 2008, Sally Field Furniture Co. borrowed $5,000,000 (face value) from Gary Sinise Co., a major customer, through a zero-interest-bearing note due in 4 years. Because the note was zero-interest-bearing, Sally Field Furniture agreed to sell furniture to this customer at lower than market price. A 10% rate of interest is normally charged on this type of loan. Prepare the journal entry to record this transaction and determine the amount of interest expense to report for 2008.

(LO 6) **E14-18** **(Imputation of Interest with Right)** On January 1, 2006, Margaret Avery Co. borrowed and received $400,000 from a major customer evidenced by a zero-interest-bearing note due in 3 years. As consideration for the zero-interest-bearing feature, Avery agrees to supply the customer's inventory needs for the loan period at lower than the market price. The appropriate rate at which to impute interest is 8%.

Instructions
(a) Prepare the journal entry to record the initial transaction on January 1, 2006. (Round all computations to the nearest dollar.)
(b) Prepare the journal entry to record any adjusting entries needed at December 31, 2006. Assume that the sales of Avery's product to this customer occur evenly over the 3-year period.

(LO 8) **E14-19** **(Long-Term Debt Disclosure)** At December 31, 2006, Helen Reddy Company has outstanding three long-term debt issues. The first is a $2,000,000 note payable which matures June 30, 2009. The second is a $6,000,000 bond issue which matures September 30, 2010. The third is a $17,500,000 sinking fund debenture with annual sinking fund payments of $3,500,000 in each of the years 2008 through 2012.

Instructions
Prepare the note disclosure required by *FASB Statement No. 47*, "Disclosure of Long-term Obligations," for the long-term debt at December 31, 2006.

(LO 10) ***E14-20** **(Settlement of Debt)** Larisa Nieland Company owes $200,000 plus $18,000 of accrued interest to First State Bank. The debt is a 10-year, 10% note. During 2007, Larisa Nieland's business deteriorated due to a faltering regional economy. On December 31, 2007, First State Bank agrees to accept an old machine and cancel the entire debt. The machine has a cost of $390,000, accumulated depreciation of $221,000, and a fair market value of $190,000.

Instructions
(a) Prepare journal entries for Larisa Nieland Company and First State Bank to record this debt settlement.
(b) How should Larisa Nieland report the gain or loss on the disposition of machine and on restructuring of debt in its 2007 income statement?
(c) Assume that, instead of transferring the machine, Larisa Nieland decides to grant 15,000 shares of its common stock ($10 par) which has a fair market value of $190,000 in full settlement of the loan obligation. If First State Bank treats Larisa Nieland's stock as a trading investment, prepare the entries to record the transaction for both parties.

(LO 10) *E14-21** **(Term Modification without Gain—Debtor's Entries)** On December 31, 2007, the Firstar Bank enters into a debt restructuring agreement with Nicole Bradtke Company, which is now experiencing financial trouble. The bank agrees to restructure a 12%, issued at par, $2,000,000 note receivable by the following modifications:

1. Reducing the principal obligation from $2,000,000 to $1,600,000.
2. Extending the maturity date from December 31, 2007, to December 31, 2010.
3. Reducing the interest rate from 12% to 10%.

Bradtke pays interest at the end of each year. On January 1, 2011, Bradtke Company pays $1,600,000 in cash to Firstar Bank.

Instructions
(a) Based on *FASB Statement No. 114*, will the gain recorded by Bradtke be equal to the loss recorded by Firstar Bank under the debt restructuring?
(b) Can Bradtke Company record a gain under the term modification mentioned above? Explain.
(c) Assuming that the interest rate Bradtke should use to compute interest expense in future periods is 1.4276%, prepare the interest payment schedule of the note for Bradtke Company after the debt restructuring.
(d) Prepare the interest payment entry for Bradtke Company on December 31, 2009.
(e) What entry should Bradtke make on January 1, 2011?

(LO 10) *E14-22** **(Term Modification without Gain—Creditor's Entries)** Using the same information as in E14-21 above, answer the following questions related to Firstar Bank (creditor).

Instructions
(a) What interest rate should Firstar Bank use to calculate the loss on the debt restructuring?
(b) Compute the loss that Firstar Bank will suffer from the debt restructuring. Prepare the journal entry to record the loss.
(c) Prepare the interest receipt schedule for Firstar Bank after the debt restructuring.
(d) Prepare the interest receipt entry for Firstar Bank on December 31, 2009.
(e) What entry should Firstar Bank make on January 1, 2011?

(LO 10) *E14-23** **(Term Modification with Gain—Debtor's Entries)** Use the same information as in E14-21 above except that Firstar Bank reduced the principal to $1,300,000 rather than $1,600,000. On January 1, 2011, Bradtke pays $1,300,000 in cash to Firstar Bank for the principal.

Instructions
(a) Can Bradtke Company record a gain under this term modification? If yes, compute the gain for Bradtke Company.
(b) Prepare the journal entries to record the gain on Bradtke's books.
(c) What interest rate should Bradtke use to compute its interest expense in future periods? Will your answer be the same as in E14-21 above? Why or why not?
(d) Prepare the interest payment schedule of the note for Bradtke Company after the debt restructuring.
(e) Prepare the interest payment entries for Bradtke Company on December 31, of 2008, 2009, and 2010.
(f) What entry should Bradtke make on January 1, 2011?

(LO 10) *E14-24** **(Term Modification with Gain—Creditor's Entries)** Using the same information as in E14-21 and E14-23 above, answer the following questions related to Firstar Bank (creditor).

Instructions
(a) Compute the loss Firstar Bank will suffer under this new term modification. Prepare the journal entry to record the loss on Firstar's books.
(b) Prepare the interest receipt schedule for Firstar Bank after the debt restructuring.
(c) Prepare the interest receipt entry for Firstar Bank on December 31, 2008, 2009, and 2010.
(d) What entry should Firstar Bank make on January 1, 2011?

(LO 10) *E14-25** **(Debtor/Creditor Entries for Settlement of Troubled Debt)** Petra Langrova Co. owes $199,800 to Mary Joe Fernandez Inc. The debt is a 10-year, 11% note. Because Petra Langrova Co. is in financial trouble, Mary Joe Fernandez Inc. agrees to accept some property and cancel the entire debt. The property has a book value of $80,000 and a fair market value of $120,000.

Instructions
(a) Prepare the journal entry on Langrova's books for debt restructure.
(b) Prepare the journal entry on Fernandez's books for debt restructure.

(LO 10) *E14-26** **(Debtor/Creditor Entries for Modification of Troubled Debt)** Steffi Graf Corp. owes $225,000 to First Trust. The debt is a 10-year, 12% note due December 31, 2007. Because Graf Corp. is in financial trouble, First Trust agrees to extend the maturity date to December 31, 2009, reduce the principal to $200,000, and reduce the interest rate to 5%, payable annually on December 31.

Instructions

    (a) Prepare the journal entries on Graf's books on December 31, 2007, 2008, 2009.

    (b) Prepare the journal entries on First Trust's books on December 31, 2007, 2008, 2009.

(LO 9) **E14-27* **(Impairments)** On December 31, 2006, Iva Majoli Company borrowed $62,092 from Paris Bank, signing a 5-year, $100,000 zero-interest-bearing note. The note was issued to yield 10% interest. Unfortunately, during 2008, Majoli began to experience financial difficulty. As a result, at December 31, 2008, Paris Bank determined that it was probable that it would receive back only $75,000 at maturity. The market rate of interest on loans of this nature is now 11%.

Instructions

    (a) Prepare the entry to record the issuance of the loan by Paris Bank on December 31, 2006.

    (b) Prepare the entry (if any) to record the impairment of the loan on December 31, 2008, by Paris Bank.

    (c) Prepare the entry (if any) to record the impairment of the loan on December 31, 2008, by Majoli Company.

(LO 9) **E14-28* **(Impairments)** On December 31, 2006, Conchita Martinez Company signed a $1,000,000 note to Sauk City Bank. The market interest rate at that time was 12%. The stated interest rate on the note was 10%, payable annually. The note matures in 5 years. Unfortunately, because of lower sales, Conchita Martinez's financial situation worsened. On December 31, 2007, Sauk City Bank determined that it was probable that the company would pay back only $600,000 of the principal at maturity. However, it was considered likely that interest would continue to be paid, based on the $1,000,000 loan.

Instructions

    (a) Determine the amount of cash Conchita Martinez received from the loan on December 31, 2006.

    (b) Prepare a note amortization schedule for Sauk City Bank up to December 31, 2008.

    (c) Determine the loss on impairment that Sauk City Bank should recognize on December 31, 2008.

See the book's website, www.wiley.com/college/kieso, for Additional Exercises.

PROBLEMS

(LO 3, 4) **P14-1** **(Analysis of Amortization Schedule and Interest Entries)** The following amortization and interest schedule reflects the issuance of 10-year bonds by Terrel Brandon Corporation on January 1, 2000, and the subsequent interest payments and charges. The company's year-end is December 31, and financial statements are prepared once yearly.

		Amortization Schedule		
Year	Cash	Interest	Amount Unamortized	Book Value
1/1/2000			$5,651	$ 94,349
2000	$11,000	$11,322	5,329	94,671
2001	11,000	11,361	4,968	95,032
2002	11,000	11,404	4,564	95,436
2003	11,000	11,452	4,112	95,888
2004	11,000	11,507	3,605	96,395
2005	11,000	11,567	3,038	96,962
2006	11,000	11,635	2,403	97,597
2007	11,000	11,712	1,691	98,309
2008	11,000	11,797	894	99,106
2009	11,000	11,894		100,000

Instructions

    (a) Indicate whether the bonds were issued at a premium or a discount and how you can determine this fact from the schedule.

    (b) Indicate whether the amortization schedule is based on the straight-line method or the effective interest method and how you can determine which method is used.

(c) Determine the stated interest rate and the effective interest rate.

(d) On the basis of the schedule above, prepare the journal entry to record the issuance of the bonds on January 1, 2000.

(e) On the basis of the schedule above, prepare the journal entry or entries to reflect the bond transactions and accruals for 2000. (Interest is paid January 1.)

(f) On the basis of the schedule above, prepare the journal entry or entries to reflect the bond transactions and accruals for 2007. Brandon Corporation does not use reversing entries.

(LO 3, 4, 5)

P14-2 (Issuance and Retirement of Bonds) Palmiero Co. is building a new hockey arena at a cost of $2,000,000. It received a downpayment of $500,000 from local businesses to support the project, and now needs to borrow $1,500,000 to complete the project. It therefore decides to issue $1,500,000 of 10.5%, 10-year bonds. These bonds were issued on January 1, 2005, and pay interest annually on each January 1. The bonds yield 10%. Palmiero paid $50,000 in bond issue costs related to the bond sale.

Instructions

(a) Prepare the journal entry to record the issuance of the bonds and the related bond issue costs incurred on January 1, 2005.

(b) Prepare a bond amortization schedule up to and including January 1, 2009, using the effective interest method.

(c) Assume that on July 1, 2008, Palmiero Co. retires half of the bonds at a cost of $800,000 plus accrued interest. Prepare the journal entry to record this retirement.

(LO 3, 4)

P14-3 (Negative Amortization) Slippery Sales Inc. developed a new sales gimmick to help sell its inventory of new automobiles. Because many new car buyers need financing, Slippery offered a low downpayment and low car payments for the first year after purchase. It believes that this promotion will bring in some new buyers.

On January 1, 2007, a customer purchased a new $25,000 automobile, making a downpayment of $1,000. The customer signed a note indicating that the annual rate of interest would be 8% and that quarterly payments would be made over 3 years. For the first year, Slippery required a $300 quarterly payment to be made on April 1, July 1, October 1, and January 1, 2008. After this one-year period, the customer was required to make regular quarterly payments that would pay off the loan as of January 1, 2010.

Instructions

(a) Prepare a note amortization schedule for the first year.

(b) Indicate the amount the customer owes on the contract at the end of the first year.

(c) Compute the amount of the new quarterly payments.

(d) Prepare a note amortization schedule for these new payments for the next 2 years.

(e) What do you think of the new sales promotion used by Slippery?

(LO 3, 4, 5, 8)

P14-4 (Issuance and Retirement of Bonds; Income Statement Presentation) Chris Mills Company issued its 9%, 25-year mortgage bonds in the principal amount of $5,000,000 on January 2, 1993, at a discount of $250,000, which it proceeded to amortize by charges to expense over the life of the issue on a straight-line basis. The indenture securing the issue provided that the bonds could be called for redemption in total but not in part at any time before maturity at 104% of the principal amount, but it did not provide for any sinking fund.

On December 18, 2007, the company issued its 11%, 20-year debenture bonds in the principal amount of $6,000,000 at 102, and the proceeds were used to redeem the 9%, 25-year mortgage bonds on January 2, 2008. The indenture securing the new issue did not provide for any sinking fund or for retirement before maturity.

Instructions

(a) Prepare journal entries to record the issuance of the 11% bonds and the retirement of the 9% bonds.

(b) Indicate the income statement treatment of the gain or loss from retirement and the note disclosure required.

(LO 3, 4, 5)

P14-5 (Comprehensive Bond Problem) In each of the following independent cases the company closes its books on December 31.

1. Danny Ferry Co. sells $250,000 of 10% bonds on March 1, 2007. The bonds pay interest on September 1 and March 1. The due date of the bonds is September 1, 2010. The bonds yield 12%. Give entries through December 31, 2008.

2. Brad Dougherty Co. sells $600,000 of 12% bonds on June 1, 2007. The bonds pay interest on December 1 and June 1. The due date of the bonds is June 1, 2011. The bonds yield 10%. On October 1, 2008, Dougherty buys back $120,000 worth of bonds for $126,000 (includes accrued interest). Give entries through December 1, 2009.

Instructions

(Round to the nearest dollar.)

For the two cases prepare all of the relevant journal entries from the time of sale until the date indicated. Use the effective interest method for discount and premium amortization (construct amortization tables where applicable). Amortize premium or discount on interest dates and at year-end. (Assume that no reversing entries were made.)

(LO 3, 4, 5) **P14-6 (Issuance of Bonds between Interest Dates, Straight-line, Retirement)** Presented below are selected transactions on the books of Powerglide Corporation.

May 1, 2007	Bonds payable with a par value of $700,000, which are dated January 1, 2007, are sold at 106 plus accrued interest. They are coupon bonds, bear interest at 12% (payable annually at January 1), and mature January 1, 2017. (Use interest expense account for accrued interest.)
Dec. 31	Adjusting entries are made to record the accrued interest on the bonds, and the amortization of the proper amount of premium. (Use straight-line amortization.)
Jan. 1, 2008	Interest on the bonds is paid.
April 1	Bonds of par value of $420,000 are purchased at 102 plus accrued interest, and retired. (Bond premium is to be amortized only at the end of each year.)
Dec. 31	Adjusting entries are made to record the accrued interest on the bonds, and the proper amount of premium amortized.

Instructions

Prepare journal entries for the transactions above.

(LO 3, 4, 5) **P14-7 (Entries for Life Cycle of Bonds)** On April 1, 2007, Fontenot Company sold 12,000 of its 11%, 15-year, $1,000 face value bonds at 97. Interest payment dates are April 1 and October 1, and the company uses the straight-line method of bond discount amortization. On March 1, 2008, Fontenot took advantage of favorable prices of its stock to extinguish 3,000 of the bonds by issuing 100,000 shares of its $10 par value common stock. At this time, the accrued interest was paid in cash. The company's stock was selling for $31 per share on March 1, 2008.

Instructions

Prepare the journal entries needed on the books of Fontenot Company to record the following.

    (a) April 1, 2007: issuance of the bonds.
    (b) October 1, 2007: payment of semiannual interest.
    (c) December 31, 2007: accrual of interest expense.
    (d) March 1, 2008: extinguishment of 3,000 bonds. (No reversing entries made.)

(LO 6) **P14-8 (Entries for Zero-Interest-Bearing Note)** On December 31, 2007, Jose Luis Company acquired a computer from Cuevas Corporation by issuing a $400,000 zero-interest-bearing note, payable in full on December 31, 2011. Jose Luis Company's credit rating permits it to borrow funds from its several lines of credit at 10%. The computer is expected to have a 5-year life and a $50,000 salvage value.

Instructions

    (a) Prepare the journal entry for the purchase on December 31, 2007.
    (b) Prepare any necessary adjusting entries relative to depreciation (use straight-line) and amortization (use effective interest method) on December 31, 2008.
    (c) Prepare any necessary adjusting entries relative to depreciation and amortization on December 31, 2009.

(LO 6) **P14-9 (Entries for Zero-Interest-Bearing Note; Payable in Installments)** Sun Yat-sen Cosmetics Co. purchased machinery on December 31, 2006, paying $40,000 down and agreeing to pay the balance in four equal installments of $30,000 payable each December 31. An assumed interest of 8% is implicit in the purchase price.

Instructions

Prepare the journal entries that would be recorded for the purchase and for the payments and interest on the following dates.

    (a) December 31, 2006.   **(d)** December 31, 2009.
    (b) December 31, 2007.   **(e)** December 31, 2010.
    (c) December 31, 2008.

(LO 3, 4, 5, 8) **P14-10** **(Comprehensive Problem; Issuance, Classification, Reporting)** Presented below are four independent situations.

   (a) On March 1, 2008, Heide Co. issued at 103 plus accrued interest $3,000,000, 9% bonds. The bonds are dated January 1, 2008, and pay interest semiannually on July 1 and January 1. In addition, Heide Co. incurred $27,000 of bond issuance costs. Compute the net amount of cash received by Heide Co. as a result of the issuance of these bonds.

   (b) On January 1, 2007, Reymont Co. issued 9% bonds with a face value of $500,000 for $469,280 to yield 10%. The bonds are dated January 1, 2007, and pay interest annually. What amount is reported for interest expense in 2007 related to these bonds, assuming that Reymont used the effective interest method for amortizing bond premium and discount?

   (c) Czeslaw Building Co. has a number of long-term bonds outstanding at December 31, 2008. These long-term bonds have the following sinking fund requirements and maturities for the next 6 years.

	Sinking Fund	Maturities
2009	$300,000	$100,000
2010	100,000	250,000
2011	100,000	100,000
2012	200,000	—
2013	200,000	150,000
2014	200,000	100,000

   Indicate how this information should be reported in the financial statements at December 31, 2008.

   (d) In the long-term debt structure of Marie Curie Inc., the following three bonds were reported: mortgage bonds payable $10,000,000; collateral trust bonds $5,000,000; bonds maturing in installments, secured by plant equipment $4,000,000. Determine the total amount, if any, of debenture bonds outstanding.

(LO 4) **P14-11** **(Effective Interest Method)** Mathilda B. Reichenbacher, an intermediate accounting student, is having difficulty amortizing bond premiums and discounts using the effective interest method. Furthermore, she cannot understand why GAAP requires that this method be used instead of the straight-line method. She has come to you with the following problem, looking for help.

   On June 30, 2006, Joan Elbert Company issued $3,000,000 face value of 13%, 20-year bonds at $3,225,690, a yield of 12%. Elbert Company uses the effective interest method to amortize bond premiums or discounts. The bonds pay semiannual interest on June 30 and December 31. Compute the amortization schedule for four periods.

Instructions

Using the data above for illustrative purposes, write a short memo (1–1.5 pages double-spaced) to Mathilda, explaining what the effective interest method is, why it is preferable, and how it is computed. (Do not forget to include an amortization schedule, referring to it whenever necessary.)

(LO 9) ***P14-12** **(Loan Impairment Entries)** On January 1, 2007, Botosan Company issued a $1,200,000, 5-year, zero-interest-bearing note to National Organization Bank. The note was issued to yield 8% annual interest. Unfortunately, during 2008, Botosan fell into financial trouble due to increased competition. After reviewing all available evidence on December 31, 2008, National Organization Bank decided that the loan was impaired. Botosan will probably pay back only $800,000 of the principal at maturity.

Instructions

   (a) Prepare journal entries for both Botosan Company and National Organization Bank to record the issuance of the note on January 1, 2007. (Round to the nearest $10.)

   (b) Assuming that both Botosan Company and National Organization Bank use the effective interest method to amortize the discount, prepare the amortization schedule for the note.

   (c) Under what circumstances can National Organization Bank consider Botosan's note to be "impaired"?

   (d) Compute the loss National Organization Bank will suffer from Botosan's financial distress on December 31, 2008. What journal entries should be made to record this loss?

(LO 10) ***P14-13** **(Debtor/Creditor Entries for Continuation of Troubled Debt)** Jeremy Hillary is the sole shareholder of Hillary Inc., which is currently under protection of the U.S. bankruptcy court. As a "debtor in possession," he has negotiated the following revised loan agreement with Valley Bank. Hillary Inc.'s $400,000, 12%, 10-year note was refinanced with a $400,000, 5%, 10-year note.

Instructions

   (a) What is the accounting nature of this transaction?

   (b) Prepare the journal entry to record this refinancing:

      (1) On the books of Hillary Inc.

      (2) On the books of Valley Bank.

    (c) Discuss whether generally accepted accounting principles provide the proper information useful to managers and investors in this situation.

(LO 10) *P14-14 (Restructure of Note under Different Circumstances)** Sandro Corporation is having financial difficulty and therefore has asked Botticelli National Bank to restructure its $3 million note outstanding. The present note has 3 years remaining and pays a current rate of interest of 10%. The present market rate for a loan of this nature is 12%. The note was issued at its face value.

Instructions

Presented below are four independent situations. Prepare the journal entry that Sandro and Botticelli National Bank would make for each of these restructurings.

    (a) Botticelli National Bank agrees to take an equity interest in Sandro by accepting common stock valued at $2,200,000 in exchange for relinquishing its claim on this note. The common stock has a par value of $1,000,000.

    (b) Botticelli National Bank agrees to accept land in exchange for relinquishing its claim on this note. The land has a book value of $1,950,000 and a fair value of $2,400,000.

    (c) Botticelli National Bank agrees to modify the terms of the note, indicating that Sandro does not have to pay any interest on the note over the 3-year period.

    (d) Botticelli National Bank agrees to reduce the principal balance due to $2,500,000 and require interest only in the second and third year at a rate of 10%.

(LO 10) *P14-15 (Debtor/Creditor Entries for Continuation of Troubled Debt with New Effective Interest)** Mildred Corp. owes D. Taylor Corp. a 10-year, 10% note in the amount of $110,000 plus $11,000 of accrued interest. The note is due today, December 31, 2007. Because Mildred Corp. is in financial trouble, D. Taylor Corp. agrees to forgive the accrued interest, $10,000 of the principal, and to extend the maturity date to December 31, 2010. Interest at 10% of revised principal will continue to be due on 12/31 each year.

    Assume the following present value factors for 3 periods.

	$2\frac{1}{4}$%	$2\frac{3}{8}$%	$2\frac{1}{2}$%	$2\frac{5}{8}$%	$2\frac{3}{4}$%	3%
Single sum	.93543	.93201	.92859	.92521	.92184	.91514
Ordinary annuity of 1	2.86989	2.86295	2.85602	2.84913	2.84226	2.82861

Instructions

    (a) Compute the new effective interest rate for Mildred Corp. following restructure. (*Hint:* Find the interest rate that establishes approximately $121,000 as the present value of the total future cash flows.)

    (b) Prepare a schedule of debt reduction and interest expense for the years 2007 through 2010.

    (c) Compute the gain or loss for D. Taylor Corp. and prepare a schedule of receivable reduction and interest revenue for the years 2007 through 2010.

    (d) Prepare all the necessary journal entries on the books of Mildred Corp. for the years 2007, 2008, and 2009.

    (e) Prepare all the necessary journal entries on the books of D. Taylor Corp. for the years 2007, 2008, and 2009.

CONCEPTS FOR ANALYSIS

CA14-1 (Bond Theory: Balance Sheet Presentations, Interest Rate, Premium) On January 1, 2008, Branagh Company issued for $1,075,230 its 20-year, 13% bonds that have a maturity value of $1,000,000 and pay interest semiannually on January 1 and July 1. Bond issue costs were not material in amount. Below are three presentations of the long-term liability section of the balance sheet that might be used for these bonds at the issue date.

1. Bonds payable (maturing January 1, 2028)	$1,000,000
Unamortized premium on bonds payable	75,230
Total bond liability	$1,075,230
2. Bonds payable—principal (face value $1,000,000 maturing	
January 1, 2028)	$ 97,220[a]
Bonds payable—interest (semiannual payment $65,000)	978,010[b]
Total bond liability	$1,075,230

3. Bonds payable—principal (maturing January 1, 2028)	$1,000,000
Bonds payable—interest ($65,000 per period for 40 periods)	2,600,000
Total bond liability	$3,600,000

[a]The present value of $1,000,000 due at the end of 40 (6-month) periods at the yield rate of 6% per period.
[b]The present value of $65,000 per period for 40 (6-month) periods at the yield rate of 6% per period.

Instructions

(a) Discuss the conceptual merit(s) of each of the date-of-issue balance sheet presentations shown above for these bonds.

(b) Explain why investors would pay $1,075,230 for bonds that have a maturity value of only $1,000,000.

(c) Assuming that a discount rate is needed to compute the carrying value of the obligations arising from a bond issue at any date during the life of the bonds, discuss the conceptual merit(s) of using for this purpose:

(1) The coupon or nominal rate.

(2) The effective or yield rate at date of issue.

(d) If the obligations arising from these bonds are to be carried at their present value computed by means of the current market rate of interest, how would the bond valuation at dates subsequent to the date of issue be affected by an increase or a decrease in the market rate of interest?

(AICPA adapted)

CA14-2 (Various Long-Term Liability Conceptual Issues) Emma Thompson Company has completed a number of transactions during 2007. In January the company purchased under contract a machine at a total price of $1,200,000, payable over 5 years with installments of $240,000 per year. The seller has considered the transaction as an installment sale with the title transferring to Thompson at the time of the final payment.

On March 1, 2007, Thompson issued $10 million of general revenue bonds priced at 99 with a coupon of 10% payable July 1 and January 1 of each of the next 10 years. The July 1 interest was paid and on December 30 the company transferred $1,000,000 to the trustee, Branaugh Company, for payment of the January 1, 2008, interest.

Due to the depressed market for the company's stock, Thompson purchased $500,000 par value of their 6% convertible bonds for a price of $455,000. It expects to resell the bonds when the price of its stock has recovered.

As the accountant for Emma Thompson Company, you have prepared the balance sheet as of December 31, 2007, and have presented it to the president of the company. You are asked the following questions about it.

1. Why has depreciation been charged on equipment being purchased under contract? Title has not passed to the company as yet and, therefore, they are not our assets. Why should the company not show on the left side of the balance sheet only the amount paid to date instead of showing the full contract price on the left side and the unpaid portion on the right side? After all, the seller considers the transaction an installment sale.

2. What is bond discount? As a debit balance, why is it not classified among the assets?

3. Bond interest is shown as a current liability. Did we not pay our trustee, Branaugh Company, the full amount of interest due this period?

4. Treasury bonds are shown as a deduction from bonds payable issued. Why should they not be shown as an asset, since they can be sold again? Are they the same as bonds of other companies that we hold as investments?

Instructions

Outline your answers to these questions by writing a brief paragraph that will justify your treatment.

CA14-3 (Bond Theory: Price, Presentation, and Retirement) On March 1, 2008, Jackie Chan Company sold its 5-year, $1,000 face value, 9% bonds dated March 1, 2008, at an effective annual interest rate (yield) of 11%. Interest is payable semiannually, and the first interest payment date is September 1, 2008. Chan uses the effective interest method of amortization. Bond issue costs were incurred in preparing and selling the bond issue. The bonds can be called by Chan at 101 at any time on or after March 1, 2009.

Instructions

(a) (1) How would the selling price of the bond be determined?

(2) Specify how all items related to the bonds would be presented in a balance sheet prepared immediately after the bond issue was sold.

(b) What items related to the bond issue would be included in Chan's 2008 income statement, and how would each be determined?

(c) Would the amount of bond discount amortization using the effective interest method of amortization be lower in the second or third year of the life of the bond issue? Why?

(d) Assuming that the bonds were called in and retired on March 1, 2009, how should Norris report the retirement of the bonds on the 2009 income statement?

(AICPA adapted)

 **CA14-4 (Bond Theory: Amortization and Gain or Loss Recognition)**
Part I. The appropriate method of amortizing a premium or discount on issuance of bonds is the effective interest method.

Instructions
(a) What is the effective interest method of amortization and how is it different from and similar to the straight-line method of amortization?

(b) How is amortization computed using the effective interest method, and why and how do amounts obtained using the effective interest method differ from amounts computed under the straight-line method?

Part II. Gains or losses from the early extinguishment of debt that is refunded can theoretically be accounted for in three ways:

1. Amortized over remaining life of old debt.
2. Amortized over the life of the new debt issue.
3. Recognized in the period of extinguishment.

Instructions
(a) Develop supporting arguments for each of the three theoretical methods of accounting for gains and losses from the early extinguishment of debt.

(b) Which of the methods above is generally accepted and how should the appropriate amount of gain or loss be shown in a company's financial statements?

(AICPA adapted)

 CA14-5 (Off-Balance-Sheet Financing) Brad Pitt Corporation is interested in building its own soda can manufacturing plant adjacent to its existing plant in Partyville, Kansas. The objective would be to ensure a steady supply of cans at a stable price and to minimize transportation costs. However, the company has been experiencing some financial problems and has been reluctant to borrow any additional cash to fund the project. The company is not concerned with the cash flow problems of making payments, but rather with the impact of adding additional long-term debt to its balance sheet.

The president of Pitt, Aidan Quinn, approached the president of the Aluminum Can Company (ACC), their major supplier, to see if some agreement could be reached. ACC was anxious to work out an arrangement, since it seemed inevitable that Pitt would begin their own can production. The Aluminum Can Company could not afford to lose the account.

After some discussion a two part plan was worked out. First ACC was to construct the plant on Pitt's land adjacent to the existing plant. Second, Pitt would sign a 20-year purchase agreement. Under the purchase agreement, Pitt would express its intention to buy all of its cans from ACC, paying a unit price which at normal capacity would cover labor and material, an operating management fee, and the debt service requirements on the plant. The expected unit price, if transportation costs are taken into consideration, is lower than current market. If Pitt did not take enough production in any one year and if the excess cans could not be sold at a high enough price on the open market, Pitt agrees to make up any cash shortfall so that ACC could make the payments on its debt. The bank will be willing to make a 20-year loan for the plant, taking the plant and the purchase agreement as collateral. At the end of 20 years the plant is to become the property of Pitt.

Instructions
(a) What are project financing arrangements using special purpose entities?
(b) What are take-or-pay contracts?
(c) Should Pitt record the plant as an asset together with the related obligation?
(d) If not, should Pitt record an asset relating to the future commitment?
(e) What is meant by off-balance-sheet financing?

 CA14-6 (Bond Issue) Roland Carlson is the president, founder, and majority owner of Thebeau Medical Corporation, an emerging medical technology products company. Thebeau is in dire need of additional capital to keep operating and to bring several promising products to final development, testing, and production. Roland, as owner of 51% of the outstanding stock, manages the company's operations. He places heavy emphasis on research and development and long-term growth. The other principal stockholder is Jana Kingston who, as a nonemployee investor, owns 40% of the stock. Jana would like to

deemphasize the R & D functions and emphasize the marketing function to maximize short-run sales and profits from existing products. She believes this strategy would raise the market price of Thebeau's stock.

All of Roland's personal capital and borrowing power is tied up in his 51% stock ownership. He knows that any offering of additional shares of stock will dilute his controlling interest because he won't be able to participate in such an issuance. But, Jana has money and would likely buy enough shares to gain control of Thebeau. She then would dictate the company's future direction, even if it meant replacing Roland as president and CEO.

The company already has considerable debt. Raising additional debt will be costly, will adversely affect Thebeau's credit rating, and will increase the company's reported losses due to the growth in interest expense. Jana and the other minority stockholders express opposition to the assumption of additional debt, fearing the company will be pushed to the brink of bankruptcy. Wanting to maintain his control and to preserve the direction of "his" company, Roland is doing everything to avoid a stock issuance and is contemplating a large issuance of bonds, even if it means the bonds are issued with a high effective-interest rate.

Instructions

(a) Who are the stakeholders in this situation?

(b) What are the ethical issues in this case?

(c) What would you do if you were Roland?

USING YOUR JUDGMENT

Financial Reporting Problem

The Procter & Gamble Company (P&G)

The financial statements of P&G are presented in Appendix 5B or can be accessed on KWW website.

Instructions

Refer to P&G's financial statements and the accompanying notes to answer the following questions.

(a) What cash outflow obligations related to the repayment of long-term debt does P&G have over the next 5 years?

(b) P&G indicates that it believes that it has the ability to meet business requirements in the foreseeable future. Prepare an assessment of its solvency and financial flexibility using ratio analysis.

Financial Statement Analysis Cases

Case 1 Commonwealth Edison Co.

The following article appeared in the *Wall Street Journal*.

> **Bond Markets**
>
> *Giant Commonwealth Edison Issue Hits Resale Market With $70 Million Left Over*
>
> NEW YORK—**Commonwealth Edison Co.**'s slow-selling new 9¼% bonds were tossed onto the resale market at a reduced price with about $70 million still available from the $200 million offered Thursday, dealers said.
>
> The Chicago utility's bonds, rated double-A by Moody's and double-A-minus by Standard & Poor's, originally had been priced at 99.803, to yield 9.3% in 5 years. They were marked down yesterday the equivalent of about $5.50 for each $1,000 face amount, to about 99.25, where their yield jumped to 9.45%.

Instructions

(a) How will the development above affect the accounting for Commonwealth Edison's bond issue?

(b) Provide several possible explanations for the markdown and the slow sale of Commonwealth Edison's bonds.

Case 2 PepsiCo, Inc.

PepsiCo, Inc. based in Purchase, New York, is a leading company in the beverage industry.
Assume that the following events occurred relating to PepsiCo's long-term debt in a recent year.

1 The company decided on February 1 to refinance $500 million in short-term 7.4% debt to make it long-term 6%.

2 $780 million of long-term zero-coupon bonds with an effective interest rate of 10.1% matured July 1 and were paid.

3 On October 1, the company issued $200 million in Australian dollar 6.3% bonds at 102 and $95 million in Italian lira 11.4% bonds at 99.

4 The company holds $100 million in perpetual foreign interest payment bonds that were issued in 1989, and presently have a rate of interest of 5.3%. These bonds are called perpetual because they have no stated due date. Instead, at the end of every 10-year period after the bond's issuance, the bondholders and PepsiCo have the option of redeeming the bonds. If either party desires to redeem the bonds, the bonds must be redeemed. If the bonds are not redeemed, a new interest rate is set, based on the then-prevailing interest rate for 10-year bonds. The company does not intend to cause redemption of the bonds, but will reclassify this debt to current next year, since the bondholders could decide to redeem the bonds.

Instructions

(a) Consider event 1. What are some of the reasons the company may have decided to refinance this short-term debt, besides lowering the interest rate?

(b) What do you think are the benefits to the investor in purchasing zero-coupon bonds, such as those described in event 2? What journal entry would be required to record the payment of these bonds? If financial statements are prepared each December 31, in which year would the bonds have been included in short-term liabilities?

(c) Make the journal entry to record the bond issue described in event 3. Note that the bonds were issued on the same day, yet one was issued at a premium and the other at a discount. What are some of the reasons that this may have happened?

(d) What are the benefits to PepsiCo in having perpetual bonds as described in event 4? Suppose that in the current year the bonds are not redeemed and the interest rate is adjusted to 6% from 7.5%. Make all necessary journal entries to record the renewal of the bonds and the change in rate.

Comparative Analysis Case

The Coca-Cola Company

The Coca-Cola Company and PepsiCo, Inc.

Instructions

Go to the KWW website and use information found there to answer the following questions related to **The Coca-Cola Company** and **PepsiCo, Inc.**

(a) Compute the debt to total assets ratio and the times interest earned ratio for these two companies. Comment on the quality of these two ratios for both Coca-Cola and PepsiCo.

(b) What is the difference between the fair value and the historical cost (carrying amount) of each company's debt at year-end 2004? Why might a difference exist in these two amounts?

(c) Both companies have debt issued in foreign countries. Speculate as to why these companies may use foreign debt to finance their operations. What risks are involved in this strategy, and how might they adjust for this risk?

Research Cases

Case 1

Instructions

Use an appropriate source (such as those identified in Chapter 2 Research Case 1) to identify a firm that recently had its bond rating changed. Answer the following questions.

(a) Which rating agency(ies) changed the rating?

(b) What was the bond rating before and after the change?

(c) What reasons did the rating agency give in support of its action? What accounting data was used as support?

(d) Are additional changes possible?

Case 2

The February 2, 2002, edition of the *Wall Street Journal* includes an article by Mark Maremount entitled "Tyco May Alter Plan to Buy Back $11 Billion in Bonds with Tenders." (You can access the article at the KWW website.)

Instructions

Read the article and answer the following questions.

(a) Tyco had announced earlier that it intended to "tender" for $11 billion of its bonds. Now it says it may repurchase the bonds in the open market. What's the difference between a "tender" and an open-market purchase?

(b) How would the transaction (tender or repurchase) be reported in the income statement? That is, what amount would be reported, and where would it appear?

(c) Under U.S. GAAP, should Tyco write down its bonds to their current market value? What accounting principle would justify this treatment?

Professional Research: Financial Accounting and Reporting

Wie Company has been operating for just 2 years, producing specialty golf equipment for women golfers. To date, the company has been able to finance its successful operations with investments from its principal owner, Michelle Wie, and cash flows from operations. However, current expansion plans will require some borrowing to expand the company's production line.

As part of the expansion plan, Wie will acquire some used equipment by signing a zero-interest-bearing note. The note has a maturity value of $50,000 and matures in 5 years. A reliable fair value measure for the equipment is not available, given the age and specialty nature of the equipment. As a result, Wie's accounting staff is unable to determine an established exchange price for recording the equipment (nor the interest rate to be used to record interest expense on the long-term note). They have asked you to conduct some accounting research on this topic.

Instructions

Using the **Financial Accounting Research System (FARS)**, respond to the following items. (Provide text strings used in your search.)

(a) Identify the accounting standard that provides guidance on the zero-interest-bearing note. Use some of the examples to explain how the standard applies in this setting.

(b) How is present value determined when an established exchange price is not determinable and a note has no ready market? What is the resulting interest rate often called?

(c) Where should a discount or premium appear in the financial statements? What about issue costs?

Professional Simulation

In this simulation you are asked to address questions related to the accounting for long-term liabilities. Prepare responses to all parts.

KWW_Professional _Simulation

| Long-Term Liabilities | Time Remaining 4 hours 30 minutes | copy | paste | calculator | sheet | standards | help | splitter | done |

| Directions | Situation | Journal Entry | Analysis | Financial Statements | Resources |

Honoré de Balzac Inc. has been producing quality children's apparel for more than 25 years. The company's fiscal year runs from April 1 to March 31. The following information relates to the obligations of Balzac as of March 31, 2006.

Bonds Payable
Balzac issued $5,000,000 of 11% bonds on April 1, 2005. Market interest rates on that date for bonds of similar risk were 10%. Bonds mature on April 1, 2015; interest is paid annually on April 1.

Notes Payable
Balzac has signed several long-term notes with financial institutions and insurance companies. The maturities of these notes are given in the schedule below. The total unpaid interest for all of these notes amounts to $210,000 on March 31, 2006.

Due Date	Amount Due
April 1, 2006	$ 200,000
July 1, 2006	300,000
October 1, 2006	150,000
January 1, 2007	150,000
April 1, 2007–March 31, 2008	600,000
April 1, 2008–March 31, 2009	500,000
	$1,900,000

Asset Retirement Obligation
Balzac purchased a warehouse in 2001 for $300,000. In February 2006, due to the passage of a new wetlands restoration law, Balzac will be required to restore the wetlands surrounding the warehouse site when the warehouse is abandoned in 2010. Balzac has estimated that the present value of the cost to restore the site is $35,000.

| Directions | Situation | Journal Entry | Analysis | Financial Statements | Resources |

Prepare the journal entry for the issuance of the bonds and on the first interest payment date.

| Directions | Situation | Journal Entry | Analysis | Financial Statements | Resources |

Use a computer spreadsheet to prepare an amortization schedule for the bonds.

| Directions | Situation | Journal Entry | Analysis | Financial Statements | Resources |

Prepare the long-term liabilities section of the balance sheet and appropriate notes to the financial statements for Balzac Inc. as of March 31, 2006.

Remember to check the book's companion website to find additional resources for this chapter.

wiley.com/college/kieso

STOCKHOLDERS' EQUITY

Everything Else Equal?

Not all dividend payers are created equal. Some stocks provide a good dividend yield but also promise strong earnings growth. These stocks could provide a healthy one-two punch for investors. A good example is Seattle's **Plum Creek Timber**. It pays a dividend of close to 4.2 percent, and it also expects earnings to expand about 6 percent in the next year.

General Motors has a seemingly healthy dividend of 5.8 percent. But the big automaker had a loss of $1.1 billion in a recent quarter, and it is having trouble reducing its onerous health-care benefits. There is concern that GM may be forced to trim its dividend at some point to conserve cash. The following chart shows that dividends are an important part of total stock returns.

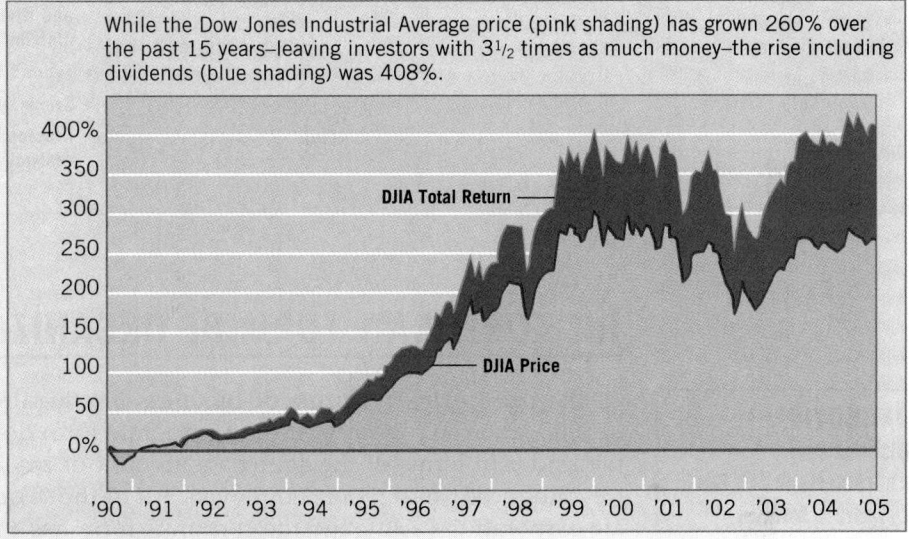

While the Dow Jones Industrial Average price (pink shading) has grown 260% over the past 15 years–leaving investors with 3½ times as much money–the rise including dividends (blue shading) was 408%.

Source: WSJ Marketing Data Group

As one analyst noted, "Investors have consistently underappreciated the value of compounding dividends in a portfolio. And dividends usually provide a strong degree of downside protection for a portfolio." But be wary when focusing on high-dividend stocks. Those with problems may find it difficult to keep their dividend payments going in the future.

Source: Adapted from Gary Zuckerman, "When Dividends Are Sweet, Be Choosy," *Wall Street Journal Online* (July 3, 2005).

Learning Objectives

After studying this chapter, you should be able to:

1 Discuss the characteristics of the corporate form of organization.

2 Identify the key components of stockholders' equity.

3 Explain the accounting procedures for issuing shares of stock.

4 Describe the accounting for treasury stock.

5 Explain the accounting for and reporting of preferred stock.

6 Describe the policies used in distributing dividends.

7 Identify the various forms of dividend distributions.

8 Explain the accounting for small and large stock dividends, and for stock splits.

9 Indicate how to present and analyze stockholders' equity.

As our opening story indicates, dividends combined with other information about a company can provide useful information to investors. In this chapter we explain the accounting issues for dividend transactions, as well as other transactions related to the stockholders' equity of a corporation. The content and organization of the chapter are as follows.

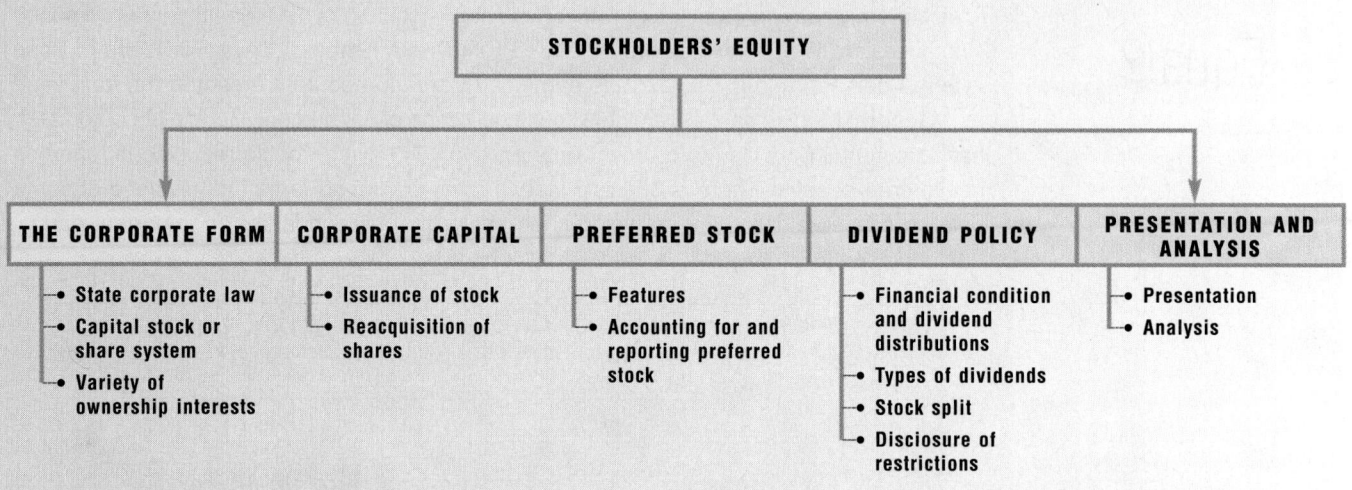

THE CORPORATE FORM OF ORGANIZATION

OBJECTIVE 1
Discuss the characteristics of the corporate form of organization.

Of the three **primary forms of business organization**—the proprietorship, the partnership, and the corporation—the corporate form dominates. The corporation is by far the leader in terms of the aggregate amount of resources controlled, goods and services produced, and people employed. All of the "Fortune 500" largest industrial firms are corporations. Although the corporate form has a number of advantages (as well as disadvantages) over the other two forms, its principal advantage is its facility for attracting and accumulating large amounts of capital.

The special characteristics of the corporate form that affect accounting include:

1 Influence of state corporate law.
2 Use of the capital stock or share system.
3 Development of a variety of ownership interests.

State Corporate Law

Anyone who wishes to establish a corporation must submit **articles of incorporation** to the state in which incorporation is desired. After fulfilling requirements, the state issues a corporation charter, thereby recognizing the company as a legal entity subject to state law. Regardless of the number of states in which a corporation has operating divisions, it is incorporated in only one state.

It is to the company's advantage to incorporate in a state whose laws favor the corporate form of business organization. **General Motors**, for example, is incorporated in Delaware; **U.S. Steel** is a New Jersey corporation. Some corporations have increasingly been incorporating in states with laws favorable to existing management. For example, to thwart possible unfriendly takeovers, at one time, **Gulf Oil** changed its state of incorporation to Delaware. There, the board of directors alone, without a vote of the shareholders, may approve certain tactics against takeovers.

Each state has its own business incorporation act. The accounting for stockholders' equity follows the provisions of these acts. In many cases states have adopted the principles contained in the Model Business Corporate Act prepared by the American Bar Association. State laws are complex and vary both in their provisions and in their definitions of certain terms. Some laws fail to define technical terms. As a result, terms often mean one thing in one state and another thing in a different state. These problems may be further compounded because legal authorities often interpret the effects and restrictions of the laws differently.

Capital Stock or Share System

Stockholders' equity in a corporation generally consists of a large number of units or shares. Within a given class of stock each share exactly equals every other share. The number of shares possessed determines each owner's interest. If a company has one class of stock divided into 1,000 shares, a person who owns 500 shares controls one-half of the ownership interest. One holding 10 shares has a one-hundredth interest.

Each share of stock has certain rights and privileges. Only by special contract can a company restrict these rights and privileges at the time it issues the shares. Owners must examine the articles of incorporation, stock certificates, and the provisions of the state law to ascertain such restrictions on or variations from the standard rights and privileges. In the absence of restrictive provisions, each share carries the following rights:

1 To share proportionately in profits and losses.

2 To share proportionately in management (the right to vote for directors).

3 To share proportionately in corporate assets upon liquidation.

4 To share proportionately in any new issues of stock of the same class—called the **preemptive right**.[1]

INTERNATIONAL INSIGHT

In the United States, stockholders are treated equally as far as access to financial information. That is not always the case in other countries. For example, in Mexico, foreign investors as well as minority investors often have difficulty obtaining financial data. These restrictions are rooted in the habits of companies that, for many years, were tightly controlled by a few stockholders and managers.

The first three rights are self-explanatory. The last right is used to protect each stockholder's proportional interest in the company. **The preemptive right protects an existing stockholder from involuntary dilution of ownership interest.** Without this right, stockholders might find their interest reduced by the issuance of additional stock without their knowledge, and at prices unfavorable to them. However, many corporations have eliminated the preemptive right. Why? Because this right makes it inconvenient for corporations to issue large amounts of additional stock, as they frequently do in acquiring other companies.

The share system easily allows one individual to transfer an interest in a company to another investor. For example, individuals owning shares in **Circuit City may sell them to others at any time and at any price without obtaining the consent of the company or other stockholders**. Each share is personal property of the owner, who may dispose of it at will. Circuit City simply maintains a list or subsidiary ledger of stockholders as a guide to dividend payments, issuance of stock rights, voting proxies, and the like. Because owners freely and frequently transfer shares, Circuit City must revise the subsidiary ledger of stockholders periodically, generally in advance of every dividend payment or stockholders' meeting.

In addition, the major stock exchanges require ownership controls that the typical corporation finds uneconomic to provide. Thus, corporations often use **registrars and transfer agents** who specialize in providing services for recording and transferring stock. The Uniform Stock Transfer Act and the Uniform Commercial Code govern the negotiability of stock certificates.

Variety of Ownership Interests

In every corporation one class of stock must represent the basic ownership interest. That class is called common stock. **Common stock** is the residual corporate interest that bears the ultimate risks of loss and receives the benefits of success. It is guaranteed

---

[1]This privilege is referred to as a **stock right** or **warrant**. The warrants issued in these situations are of short duration, unlike the warrants issued with other securities.

INTERNATIONAL INSIGHT

The U.S. and British systems of corporate governance and finance depend to a large extent on equity financing and the widely dispersed ownership of shares traded in highly liquid markets. The German and Japanese systems have relied more on debt financing, interlocking stock ownership, banker/directors, and worker/shareholder rights.

neither dividends nor assets upon dissolution. But common stockholders generally control the management of the corporation and tend to profit most if the company is successful. In the event that a corporation has only one authorized issue of capital stock, that issue is by definition common stock, whether so designated in the charter or not.

In an effort to broaden investor appeal, corporations may offer two or more classes of stock, each with different rights or privileges. In the preceding section we pointed out that each share of stock of a given issue has the same four inherent rights as other shares of the same issue. By special stock contracts between the corporation and its stockholders, however, the stockholder may sacrifice certain of these rights in return for other special rights or privileges. Thus special classes of stock, usually called **preferred stock**, are created. In return for any special preference, the preferred stockholder always sacrifices some of the inherent rights of common stock ownership.

A common type of preference is to give the preferred stockholders a prior claim on earnings. The corporation thus assures them a dividend, usually at a stated rate, before it distributes any amount to the common stockholders. In return for this preference the preferred stockholders may sacrifice their right to a voice in management or their right to share in profits beyond the stated rate.

What do the numbers mean?

CLASSY STOCK

Some companies grant preferences to different shareholders by issuing different classes of common stock. Blue-chip newspaper companies, such as **The New York Times, Dow Jones,** and **The Washington Post,** have two classes of stock. Also, **Ford** and **Comcast** are two-class companies.

Sometimes these different classes of shares trade at dramatically different prices. For example, **Molex** has issued both common shares and Class A common stock, with the common shares trading at up to a 15 percent premium over the Class A shares. Why the difference in price? The most common explanation is voting rights. In the Molex case, the common shareholders get one vote per share; Class A shares don't get to vote.

For most retail investors, voting rights are not that important. But for family-controlled companies, issuing newer classes of lower or non-voting stock effectively creates currency for acquisitions, increases liquidity, or puts a public value on the company without diluting the family's voting control. Thus, investors must carefully compare the apparent bargain prices for some classes of stock—they may end up as second-class citizens with no voting rights.

Source: Adapted from Lauren Rublin, "Separate but Equal," *Barons Online* (August 16, 1999); and Andy Serwer, "Dual-Listed Companies Aren't Fair or Balanced," *Fortune* (September 20, 2004), p. 83.

CORPORATE CAPITAL

OBJECTIVE 2
Identify the key components of stockholders' equity.

Owner's equity in a corporation is defined as stockholders' equity, shareholders' equity, or corporate capital. The following three categories normally appear as part of stockholders' equity:

1 Capital stock.
2 Additional paid-in capital.
3 Retained earnings.

The first two categories, capital stock and additional paid-in capital, constitute contributed (paid-in) capital. **Retained earnings** represents the earned capital of the company. **Contributed capital (paid-in capital)** is the total amount paid in on capital stock—the amount provided by stockholders to the corporation for use in the business. Contributed capital includes items such as the par value of all outstanding stock and premiums less discounts on issuance. **Earned capital** is the capital that develops from profitable operations. It consists of all undistributed income that remains invested in the company.

Stockholders' equity is the difference between the assets and the liabilities of the company. That is, the owners' or stockholders' interest in a company like **Walt Disney Co.** is a **residual interest.**[2] Stockholders' (owners') equity represents the cumulative net contributions by stockholders plus retained earnings. As a residual interest, stockholders' equity has no existence apart from the assets and liabilities of Disney—stockholders' equity equals net assets. Stockholders' equity is not a claim to specific assets but a claim against a portion of the total assets. Its amount is not specified or fixed; it depends on Disney's profitability. Stockholders' equity grows if it is profitable. It shrinks, or may disappear entirely, if Disney loses money.

Issuance of Stock

In issuing stock, companies follow these procedures: First, the state must authorize the stock, generally in a certificate of incorporation or charter. Next, the corporation offers shares for sale, entering into contracts to sell stock. Then, after receiving amounts for the stock, the corporation issues shares. The corporation generally makes no entry in the general ledger accounts when it receives its stock authorization from the state of incorporation.

> **OBJECTIVE 3**
> Explain the accounting procedures for issuing shares of stock.

We discuss the accounting problems involved in the issuance of stock under the following topics.

1 Accounting for par value stock.

2 Accounting for no-par stock.

3 Accounting for stock issued in combination with other securities (lump-sum sales).

4 Accounting for stock issued in noncash transactions.

5 Accounting for costs of issuing stock.

Par Value Stock

The par value of a stock has no relationship to its fair market value. At present, the par value associated with most capital stock issuances is very low. For example, **PepsiCo**'s par value is $0.01, **Kellogg**'s is $0.25, and **Hershey**'s is $1. Such values contrast dramatically with the situation in the early 1900s, when practically all stock issued had a par value of $100. Low par values help companies avoid the contingent liability associated with stock sold below par.[3]

To show the required information for issuance of par value stock, corporations maintain accounts for each class of stock as follows.

1 *Preferred Stock or Common Stock.* Together, these two stock accounts reflect the par value of the corporation's issued shares. The company credits these accounts

---

[2]"Elements of Financial Statements," *Statement of Financial Accounting Concepts No. 6* (Stamford, Conn.: FASB, 1985), par. 60.

[3]Companies rarely, if ever, issue stock at a value below par value. If issuing stock below par, the company records the discount as a debit to Additional Paid-in Capital. In addition, the corporation may call on the original purchaser or the current holder of the shares issued below par to pay in the amount of the discount to prevent creditors from sustaining a loss upon liquidation of the corporation.

when it originally issues the shares. It makes no additional entries in these accounts unless it issues additional shares or retires them.

2 *Additional Paid-in Capital (also called Paid-in Capital in Excess of Par).* The **Additional Paid-in Capital** account indicates any excess over par value paid in by stockholders in return for the shares issued to them. Once paid in, the excess over par becomes a part of the corporation's additional paid-in capital. The individual stockholder has no greater claim on the excess paid in than all other holders of the same class of shares.

No-Par Stock

Many states permit the issuance of capital stock without par value, called **no-par stock**. The reasons for issuance of no-par stock are twofold: First, issuance of no-par stock **avoids the contingent liability** (see footnote 3) that might occur if the corporation issued par value stock at a discount. Second, some confusion exists over the relationship (or rather the absence of a relationship) between the par value and fair market value. If shares have no par value, **the questionable treatment of using par value as a basis for fair value never arises**. This is particularly advantageous whenever issuing stock for property items such as tangible or intangible fixed assets.

A major disadvantage of no-par stock is that some states levy a high tax on these issues. In addition, in some states the total issue price for no-par stock may be considered legal capital, which could reduce the flexibility in paying dividends.

Corporations sell no-par shares, like par value shares, for whatever price they will bring. However, unlike par value shares, corporations issue them without a premium or a discount. The exact amount received represents the credit to common or preferred stock. For example, Video Electronics Corporation is organized with authorized common stock of 10,000 shares without par value. Video Electronics makes only a memorandum entry for the authorization, inasmuch as no amount is involved. If Video Electronics then issues 500 shares for cash at $10 per share, it makes the following entry:

Cash	5,000	
Common Stock—No-Par Value		5,000

If it issues another 500 shares for $11 per share, Video Electronics makes this entry:

Cash	5,500	
Common Stock—No-Par Value		5,500

True no-par stock should be carried in the accounts at issue price without any additional paid-in capital or discount reported. But some states require that no-par stock have a **stated value**. The stated value is a minimum value below which a company cannot issue it. Thus, instead of being no-par stock, such stated-value stock becomes, in effect, stock with a very low par value. It thus is open to all the criticism and abuses that first encouraged the development of no-par stock.[4]

If no-par stock has a stated value of $5 per share but sells for $11, all such amounts in excess of $5 are recorded as additional paid-in capital, which in many states is fully or partially available for dividends. Thus, no-par value stock, with a low stated value, permits a new corporation to commence its operations with additional paid-in capital that may exceed its stated capital. For example, if a company issued 1,000 of the shares with a $5 stated value at $15 per share for cash, it makes the following entry.

Cash	15,000	
Common Stock		5,000
Paid-in Capital in Excess of Stated Value		10,000

---

[4]*Accounting Trends and Techniques—2004* indicates that its 600 surveyed companies reported 655 issues of outstanding common stock, 570 par value issues, and 54 no-par issues; 6 of the no-par issues were shown at their stated (assigned) values.

Most corporations account for no-par stock with a stated value as if it were par value stock with par equal to the stated value.

Stock Issued with Other Securities (Lump-Sum Sales)

Generally, corporations sell classes of stock separately from one another. The reason to do so is to track the proceeds relative to each class, as well as relative to each lot. Occasionally, a corporation issues two or more classes of securities for a single payment or lump sum, in the acquisition of another company. The accounting problem in such **lump-sum sales** is how to allocate the proceeds among the several classes of securities. Companies use one of two methods of allocation: (1) the proportional method and (2) the incremental method.

Proportional Method. If the fair market value or other sound basis for determining relative value is available for each class of security, **the company allocates the lump sum received among the classes of securities on a proportional basis**. For instance, assume a company issues 1,000 shares of $10 stated value common stock having a market value of $20 a share, and 1,000 shares of $10 par value preferred stock having a market value of $12 a share, for a lump sum of $30,000. Illustration 15-1 shows how the company allocates the $30,000 to the two classes of stock.

Fair market value of common (1,000 × $20)   = $20,000
Fair market value of preferred (1,000 × $12) =   12,000

Aggregate fair market value $32,000

Allocated to common: $\frac{\$20,000}{\$32,000} \times \$30,000 = \$18,750$

Allocated to preferred: $\frac{\$12,000}{\$32,000} \times \$30,000 =$ 11,250

Total allocation $30,000

ILLUSTRATION 15-1
Allocation in Lump-Sum
Securities Issuance—
Proportional Method

Incremental Method. In instances where a company cannot determine the fair market value of all classes of securities, it may use the incremental method. It uses the market value of the securities as a basis for those classes that it knows, and allocates the remainder of the lump sum to the class for which it does not know the market value. For instance, if a company issues 1,000 shares of $10 stated value common stock having a market value of $20, and 1,000 shares of $10 par value preferred stock having no established market value, for a lump sum of $30,000, it allocates the $30,000 to the two classes as shown in Illustration 15-2.

Lump-sum receipt	$30,000
Allocated to common (1,000 × $20)	20,000
Balance allocated to preferred	$10,000

ILLUSTRATION 15-2
Allocation in Lump-Sum
Securities Issuance—
Incremental Method

If a company cannot determine fair value for any of the classes of stock involved in a lump-sum exchange, it may need to use other approaches. It may rely on an expert's appraisal. Or, if the company knows that one or more of the classes of securities issued will have a determinable market value in the near future, it may use a best estimate basis with the intent to adjust later, upon establishment of the future market value.

Stock Issued in Noncash Transactions

Accounting for the issuance of shares of stock for property or services involves an issue of valuation. **The general rule is: Companies should record stock issued for services or property other than cash at either the fair value of the stock issued or the fair value of the noncash consideration received, whichever is more clearly determinable.**

If a company can readily determine both, and the transaction results from an arm's-length exchange, there will probably be little difference in their fair values. In such cases the basis for valuing the exchange should not matter.

If a company cannot readily determine either the fair value of the stock it issues or the property or services it receives, it should employ an appropriate valuation technique. Depending on available data, the valuation may be based on market transactions involving comparable assets or the use of discounted expected future cash flows. Companies should avoid the use of the book, par, or stated values as a basis of valuation for these transactions.

A company may exchange unissued stock or treasury stock (issued shares that it has reacquired but not retired) for property or services. If it uses treasury shares, the cost of the treasury shares should not be considered the decisive factor in establishing the fair value of the property or services. Instead, it should use the fair value of the treasury stock, if known, to value the property or services. Otherwise, if it does not know the fair value of the treasury stock, it should use the fair value of the property or services received, if determinable.

The following series of transactions illustrates the procedure for recording the issuance of 10,000 shares of $10 par value common stock for a patent for Marlowe Company, in various circumstances.

1 Marlowe cannot readily determine the fair value of the patent, but it knows the fair value of the stock is $140,000.

Patent	140,000	
Common Stock (10,000 shares × $10 per share)		100,000
Paid-in Capital in Excess of Par		40,000

2 Marlowe cannot readily determine the fair value of the stock, but it determines the fair value of the patent is $150,000.

Patent	150,000	
Common Stock (10,000 shares × $10 per share)		100,000
Paid-in Capital in Excess of Par		50,000

3 Marlowe cannot readily determine the fair value of the stock nor the fair value of the patent. An independent consultant values the patent at $125,000 based on discounted expected cash flows.

Patent	125,000	
Common Stock (10,000 shares × $10 share)		100,000
Paid-in Capital in Excess of Par		25,000

In corporate law, the board of directors has the power to set the value of noncash transactions. However, boards sometimes abuse this power. The issuance of stock for property or services has resulted in cases of overstated corporate capital through intentional overvaluation of the property or services received. The overvaluation of the stockholders' equity resulting from inflated asset values creates **watered stock**. The corporation should eliminate the "water" by simply writing down the overvalued assets.

If, as a result of the issuance of stock for property or services, a corporation undervalues the recorded assets, it creates **secret reserves**. An understated corporate structure (secret reserve) may also result from other methods: excessive depreciation or amortization charges, expensing capital expenditures, excessive write-downs of inventories or receivables, or any other understatement of assets or overstatement of liabilities. An example of a liability overstatement is an excessive provision for estimated product warranties that ultimately results in an understatement of owners' equity, thereby creating a secret reserve.

Costs of Issuing Stock

When a company like **Walgreens** issues stock, it should report direct costs incurred to sell stock, such as underwriting costs, accounting and legal fees, printing costs, and taxes, as a reduction of the amounts paid in. Walgreens therefore debits issue costs to Additional Paid-in Capital because they are unrelated to corporate operations. In effect, **issue costs are a cost of financing**. As such, issue costs should reduce the proceeds received from the sale of the stock.

Walgreens should expense management salaries and other indirect costs related to the stock issue because it is difficult to establish a relationship between these costs and the sale proceeds. In addition, Walgreens expenses recurring costs, primarily registrar and transfer agents' fees, as incurred.

THE CASE OF THE DISAPPEARING RECEIVABLE

Sometimes companies issue stock but may not receive cash in return. As a result, a company records a receivable.

Controversy existed regarding the presentation of this receivable on the balance sheet. Some argued that the company should report the receivable as an asset similar to other receivables. Others argued that the company should report the receivable as a deduction from stockholders' equity (similar to the treatment of treasury stock). The SEC settled this issue: It requires companies to use the contra-equity approach because the risk of collection in this type of transaction is often very high.

This accounting issue surfaced in **Enron's** accounting. Starting in early 2000, Enron issued shares of its common stock to four "special-purpose entities," in exchange for which it received a note receivable. Enron then increased its assets (by recording a receivable) and stockholders' equity, a move the company now calls an accounting error. As a result of this accounting treatment, Enron overstated assets and stockholders' equity by $172 million in its 2000 audited financial statements and by $828 million in its unaudited 2001 statements. This $1 billion overstatement was 8.5 percent of Enron's previously reported stockholders' equity at that time.

As Lynn Turner, former chief accountant of the SEC, noted, "It is a basic accounting principle that you don't record equity until you get cash, and a note doesn't count as cash." Situations like this led investors, creditors, and suppliers to lose faith in the credibility of Enron, which eventually caused its bankruptcy.

Source: Adapted from Jonathan Weil, "Basic Accounting Tripped Up Enron—Financial Statements Didn't Add Up—Auditors Overlook a Simple Rule," *Wall Street Journal* (November 11, 2001), p. C1.

> *WHAT DO THE NUMBERS MEAN?*

Reacquisition of Shares

Companies often buy back their own shares. In fact, share buybacks now exceed dividends as a form of distribution to stockholders.[5] For example, **Dell**, **Yahoo**, and **The Home Depot** had buybacks recently of $10 billion, $3 billion, and $2 billion, respectively. Illustration 15-3 (on page 734) indicates that buybacks are increasing dramatically.

> **OBJECTIVE 4**
> Describe the accounting for treasury stock.

---

[5]At the beginning of the 1990s the situation was just the opposite. That is, share buybacks were less than half the level of dividends. Companies are extremely reluctant to reduce or eliminate their dividends, because they believe that the market negatively views this action.

ILLUSTRATION 15-3
Stock Buybacks on the
Rise

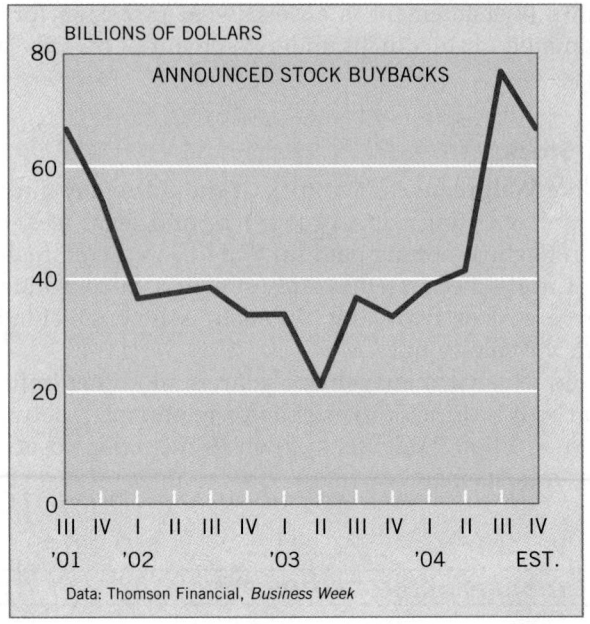

Source: *Business Week* (November 29, 2004), p.116.

Corporations purchase their outstanding stock for several reasons:

1 *To provide tax-efficient distributions of excess cash to shareholders.* Capital gain rates on sales of stock to the company by the stockholders have been approximately half the ordinary tax rate for many investors. This advantage has been somewhat diminished by recent changes in the tax law related to dividends.

2 *To increase earnings per share and return on equity.* Reducing both shares outstanding and stockholders' equity often enhances certain performance ratios. However, strategies to hype performance measures might increase performance in the short-run, but these tactics add no real long-term value.

3 *To provide stock for employee stock compensation contracts or to meet potential merger needs.* **Honeywell Inc.** reported that it would use part of its purchase of one million common shares for employee stock option contracts. Other companies acquire shares to have them available for business acquisitions.

4 *To thwart takeover attempts or to reduce the number of stockholders.* By reducing the number of shares held by the public, existing owners and managements bar "outsiders" from gaining control or significant influence. When Ted Turner attempted to acquire **CBS**, CBS started a substantial buyback of its stock. Companies may also use stock purchases to eliminate dissident stockholders.

5 *To make a market in the stock.* As one company executive noted, "Our company is trying to establish a floor for the stock." Purchasing stock in the marketplace creates a demand. This may stabilize the stock price or, in fact, increase it.

Some publicly held corporations have chosen to "go private," that is, to eliminate public (outside) ownership entirely by purchasing all of their outstanding stock. Companies often accomplish such a procedure through a **leveraged buyout (LBO)**, in which the company borrows money to finance the stock repurchases.

After reacquiring shares, a company may either retire them or hold them in the treasury for reissue. If not retired, such shares are referred to as **treasury stock (treasury shares)**. Technically, treasury stock is a corporation's own stock, reacquired after having been issued and fully paid.

Treasury stock is not an asset. When a company purchases treasury stock, a reduction occurs in both assets and stockholders' equity. It is inappropriate to imply that a

UNDERLYING CONCEPTS

As we indicated in Chapter 2, an asset should have probable future economic benefits. Treasury stock simply reduces common stock outstanding.

corporation can own a part of itself. A corporation may sell treasury stock to obtain funds, but that does not make treasury stock a balance sheet asset. When a corporation buys back some of its own outstanding stock, it has not acquired an asset; it reduces net assets.

The possession of treasury stock does not give the corporation the right to vote, to exercise preemptive rights as a stockholder, to receive cash dividends, or to receive assets upon corporate liquidation. **Treasury stock is essentially the same as unissued capital stock.** No one advocates classifying unissued capital stock as an asset in the balance sheet.[6]

SIGNALS TO BUY?

Market analysts sometimes look to stock buybacks as a buy signal for a stock. That strategy is not that surprising if you look at the performance of companies that did buybacks. For example, in one study, buyback companies outperformed similar companies without buybacks by an average of 23 percent. In a recent three-year period, companies followed by **Buybackletter.com** were up 16.4 percent, while the S&P 500 Stock Index was up just 7.1 percent in that period. Why the premium? Well, the conventional wisdom is that companies who buy back shares believe their shares are undervalued. Thus, analysts view the buyback announcement as an important piece of inside information about future company prospects.

On the other hand, buy-backs can actually hurt businesses and their shareholders over the long-run. Whether the buy-back is a good thing appears to depend a lot on why the company did the buy-back and what the repurchased shares were used for. One study found that companies often increased their buybacks when earnings growth slowed. This allowed the companies to prop up earnings per share (based on fewer shares outstanding). Furthermore, many buybacks do not actually result in a net reduction in shares outstanding. For example, companies, such as **Microsoft**, bought back shares to meet share demands for stock option exercises, resulting in higher net shares outstanding when it re-issued the repurchased shares to the option holders upon exercise. In this case the buyback actually indicated a further dilution in the share ownership in the buyback company.

This does not mean you should never trust a buy-back signal. But if the buy-back is intended to manage the company's earnings or if the buy-back results in dilution, take a closer look.

Source: Adapted from Ann Tergesen, "When Buybacks Are Signals to Buy," *Business Week Online* (October 1, 2001); and Rachel Beck, "Stock BuyBacks Not Always Good for the Company, Shareholders," *Naples [FL] Daily News* (March 7, 2004). p. I1.

WHAT DO THE NUMBERS MEAN?

Purchase of Treasury Stock

Companies use two general methods of handling treasury stock in the accounts: the cost method and the par value method. Both methods are generally acceptable. The cost method enjoys more widespread use.[7]

- The **cost method** results in debiting the Treasury Stock account for the reacquisition cost and in reporting this account as a deduction from the total paid-in capital **and** retained earnings on the balance sheet.
- The **par** or **stated value method** records all transactions in treasury shares at their par value and reports the treasury stock as a deduction from capital stock only.

Discussion of Using Par or Stated Value for Treasury Stock Transactions

---

[6]The possible justification for classifying these shares as assets is that the company will use them to liquidate a specific liability that appears on the balance sheet. *Accounting Trends and Techniques—2004* reported that out of 600 companies surveyed, 398 disclosed treasury stock, but none classified it as an asset.

[7]*Accounting Trends and Techniques—2004* indicates that of its selected list of 600 companies, 384 carried common stock in treasury at cost and only 2 at par or stated value; 2 companies carried preferred stock in treasury at cost and none at par or stated value.

No matter which method a company uses, most states consider the cost of the treasury shares acquired as a restriction on retained earnings.

Companies generally use the cost method to account for treasury stock. This method derives its name from the fact that a company maintains the Treasury Stock account at the cost of the shares purchased.[8] Under the cost method, the company debits the Treasury Stock account for the cost of the shares acquired. Upon reissuance of the shares, it credits the account for this same cost. The original price received for the stock does not affect the entries to record the acquisition and reissuance of the treasury stock.

To illustrate, assume that Pacific Company issued 100,000 shares of $1 par value common stock at a price of $10 per share. In addition, it has retained earnings of $300,000. Illustration 15-4 shows the stockholders' equity section on December 31, 2006, before purchase of treasury stock.

ILLUSTRATION 15-4
Stockholders' Equity with
No Treasury Stock

Stockholders' equity	
Paid-in capital	
Common stock, $1 par value, 100,000 shares	
issued and outstanding	$ 100,000
Additional paid-in capital	900,000
Total paid-in capital	1,000,000
Retained earnings	300,000
Total stockholders' equity	$1,300,000

On January 20, 2007, Pacific acquires 10,000 shares of its stock at $11 per share. Pacific records the reacquisition as follows:

January 20, 2007

Treasury Stock	110,000	
Cash		110,000

Note that Pacific debited Treasury Stock for the cost of the shares purchased. The original paid-in capital account, Common Stock, is not affected because the number of issued shares does not change. The same is true for the Additional Paid-in Capital account. Pacific deducts treasury stock from total paid-in capital and retained earnings in the stockholders' equity section.

Illustration 15-5 shows the stockholders' equity section for Pacific after purchase of the treasury stock.

ILLUSTRATION 15-5
Stockholders' Equity with
Treasury Stock

Stockholders' equity	
Paid-in capital	
Common stock, $1 par value, 100,000 shares	
issued and 90,000 outstanding	$ 100,000
Additional paid-in capital	900,000
Total paid-in capital	1,000,000
Retained earnings	300,000
Total paid-in capital and retained earnings	1,300,000
Less: Cost of treasury stock (10,000 shares)	110,000
Total stockholders' equity	$1,190,000

---

[8]If making numerous acquisitions of blocks of treasury shares at different prices, a company may use inventory costing methods—such as specific identification, average, or FIFO—to identify the cost at date of reissuance.

Pacific subtracts the cost of the treasury stock from the total of common stock, additional paid-in capital, and retained earnings. It therefore reduces stockholders' equity. Many states require a corporation to restrict retained earnings for the cost of treasury stock purchased. The restriction keeps intact the corporation's legal capital that it temporarily holds as treasury stock. When the corporation sells the treasury stock, it lifts the restriction.

Pacific discloses both the number of shares issued (100,000) and the number in the treasury (10,000). The difference is the number of shares of stock outstanding (90,000). The term **outstanding stock** means the number of shares of issued stock that stockholders own.

Sale of Treasury Stock

Companies usually reissue or retire treasury stock. When selling treasury shares, the accounting for the sale depends on the price. If the selling price of the treasury stock equals its cost, the company records the sale of the shares by debiting Cash and crediting Treasury Stock. In cases where the selling price of the treasury stock is not equal to cost, then accounting for treasury stock sold **above cost** differs from the accounting for treasury stock sold **below cost**. However, the sale of treasury stock either above or below cost increases both total assets and stockholders' equity.

Sale of Treasury Stock above Cost. When the selling price of shares of treasury stock exceeds its cost, a company credits the difference to Paid-in Capital from Treasury Stock. To illustrate, assume that Pacific acquired 10,000 shares of its treasury stock at $11 per share. It now sells 1,000 shares at $15 per share on March 10. Pacific records the entry as follows.

March 10, 2007

Cash	15,000	
Treasury Stock		11,000
Paid-in Capital from Treasury Stock		4,000

There are two reasons why Pacific does not credit $4,000 to Gain on Sale of Treasury Stock: (1) Gains on sales occur when selling **assets**; treasury stock is not an asset. (2) A gain or loss should not be recognized from stock transactions with its own stockholders. Thus, Pacific should not include paid-in capital arising from the sale of treasury stock in the measurement of net income. Instead, it lists paid-in capital from treasury stock separately on the balance sheet, as a part of paid-in capital.

Sale of Treasury Stock below Cost. When a corporation sells treasury stock below its cost, it usually debits the excess of the cost over selling price to Paid-in Capital from Treasury Stock. Thus, if Pacific sells an additional 1,000 shares of treasury stock on March 21 at $8 per share, it records the sale as follows.

March 21, 2007

Cash	8,000	
Paid-in Capital from Treasury Stock	3,000	
Treasury Stock		11,000

We can make several observations based on the two sale entries (sale above cost and sale below cost): (1) Pacific credits Treasury Stock at cost in each entry. (2) Pacific uses Paid-in Capital from Treasury Stock for the difference between the cost and the resale price of the shares. (3) Neither entry affects the original paid-in capital account, Common Stock.

After eliminating the credit balance in Paid-in Capital from Treasury Stock, the corporation debits any additional excess of cost over selling price to Retained Earnings. To illustrate, assume that Pacific sells an additional 1,000 shares at $8 per share on April 10. Illustration 15-6 shows the balance in the Paid-in Capital from Treasury Stock account (before the April 10 purchase).

ILLUSTRATION 15-6
Treasury Stock
Transactions in Paid-in
Capital Account

Paid-in Capital from Treasury Stock			
Mar. 21	3,000	Mar. 10	4,000
		Balance	1,000

In this case, Pacific debits $1,000 of the excess to Paid-in Capital from Treasury Stock. It debits the remainder to Retained Earnings. The entry is:

April 10, 2007

Cash	8,000	
Paid-in Capital from Treasury Stock	1,000	
Retained Earnings	2,000	
Treasury Stock		11,000

Retiring Treasury Stock

The board of directors may approve the retirement of treasury shares. This decision results in cancellation of the treasury stock and a reduction in the number of shares of issued stock. Retired treasury shares have the status of authorized and unissued shares. The accounting effects are similar to the sale of treasury stock except that corporations debit the **paid-in capital accounts applicable to the retired shares** instead of cash. For example, if a corporation originally sells the shares at par, it debits Common Stock for the par value per share. If it originally sells the shares at $3 above par value, it also debits Paid-in Capital in Excess of Par Value for $3 per share at retirement.

PREFERRED STOCK

OBJECTIVE 5
Explain the accounting
for and reporting of
preferred stock.

As noted earlier, **preferred stock** is a special class of shares that possesses certain preferences or features not possessed by the common stock.[9] The following features are those most often associated with preferred stock issues.

1 Preference as to dividends.
2 Preference as to assets in the event of liquidation.
3 Convertible into common stock.
4 Callable at the option of the corporation.
5 Nonvoting.

The features that distinguish preferred from common stock may be of a more restrictive and negative nature than preferences. For example, the preferred stock may be nonvoting, noncumulative, and nonparticipating.

Companies usually issue preferred stock with a par value, expressing the dividend preference as a **percentage of the par value**. Thus, holders of 8 percent preferred stock with a $100 par value are entitled to an annual dividend of $8 per share. This stock is commonly referred to as 8 percent preferred stock. In the case of no-par preferred stock, a corporation expresses a dividend preference as a **specific dollar amount** per share, for example, $7 per share. This stock is commonly referred to as $7 preferred stock.

A preference as to dividends does not assure the payment of dividends. It merely assures that the corporation must pay the stated dividend rate or amount applicable to the preferred stock before paying any dividends on the common stock.

---

[9]*Accounting Trends and Techniques—2004* reports that of its 600 surveyed companies, 84 had preferred stock outstanding; 73 had one class of preferred, and 9 had two classes.

A company often issues preferred stock (instead of debt) because of a high debt-to-equity ratio. In other instances, it issues preferred stock through private placements with other corporations at a lower-than-market dividend rate because the acquiring corporation receives largely tax-free dividends (owing to the IRS's 70 percent or 80 percent dividends received deduction).

Features of Preferred Stock

A corporation may attach whatever preferences or restrictions, in whatever combination it desires, to a preferred stock issue, as long as it does not specifically violate its state incorporation law. Also, it may issue more than one class of preferred stock. We discuss the most common features attributed to preferred stock below.

Cumulative Preferred Stock

Cumulative preferred stock requires that if a corporation fails to pay a dividend in any year, it must make it up in a later year before paying any dividends to common stockholders. If the directors fail to declare a dividend at the normal date for dividend action, the dividend is said to have been "passed." Any passed dividend on cumulative preferred stock constitutes a dividend in arrears. Because no liability exists until the board of directors declares a dividend, a corporation does not record a dividend in arrears as a liability but discloses it in a note to the financial statements. A corporation seldom issues noncumulative preferred stock because a passed dividend is lost forever to the preferred stockholder. As a result, this stock issue would be less marketable.

Participating Preferred Stock

Holders of participating preferred stock share ratably with the common stockholders in any profit distributions beyond the prescribed rate. That is, 5 percent preferred stock, if fully participating, will receive not only its 5 percent return, but also dividends at the same rates as those paid to common stockholders if paying amounts in excess of 5 percent of par or stated value to common stockholders. Note that participating preferred stock may be only partially participating. Although seldom used, examples of companies that have issued participating preferreds are **LTV Corporation**, **Southern California Edison**, and **Allied Products Corporation**.

Convertible Preferred Stock

Convertible preferred stock allows stockholders, at their option, to exchange preferred shares for common stock at a predetermined ratio. The convertible preferred stockholder not only enjoys a preferred claim on dividends but also has the option of converting into a common stockholder with unlimited participation in earnings.

Callable Preferred Stock

Callable preferred stock permits the corporation at its option to call or redeem the outstanding preferred shares at specified future dates and at stipulated prices. Many preferred issues are callable. The corporation usually sets the call or redemption price slightly above the original issuance price and commonly states it in terms related to the par value. The callable feature permits the corporation to use the capital obtained through the issuance of such stock until the need has passed or it is no longer advantageous.

The existence of a call price or prices tends to set a ceiling on the market value of the preferred shares unless they are convertible into common stock. When a corporation redeems preferred stock, it must pay any dividends in arrears.

Redeemable Preferred Stock

Recently, more and more issuances of preferred stock have features that make the security more like debt (legal obligation to pay) than an equity instrument. For example, redeemable preferred stock has a mandatory redemption period or a redemption feature that the issuer cannot control.

Previously, public companies were not permitted to report these debt-like preferreds in equity, but they were not required to report them as a liability either. There were concerns about classification of these debt-like securities, which may have been reported as equity or in the "mezzanine" section of balance sheets between debt and equity. There also was diversity in practice as to how dividends on these securities were reported. The FASB recently issued a standard that affects the accounting for certain hybrid instruments and requires debt-like securities, like redeemable preferred stock to be classified as liabilities and be measured and accounted for similar to liabilities.[10]

Accounting for and Reporting Preferred Stock

The accounting for preferred stock at issuance is similar to that for common stock. A corporation allocates proceeds between the par value of the preferred stock and additional paid-in capital. To illustrate, assume that Bishop Co. issues 10,000 shares of $10 par value preferred stock for $12 cash per share. Bishop records the issuance as follows:

Cash	120,000	
Preferred Stock		100,000
Paid-in Capital in Excess of Par		20,000

Thus, Bishop maintains separate accounts for these different classes of shares.

In contrast to convertible bonds (recorded as a liability on the date of issue) corporations consider convertible preferred stock as a part of stockholders' equity. In addition, when exercising convertible preferred stocks, there is no theoretical justification for recognition of a gain or loss. A company recognizes no gain or loss when dealing with stockholders in their capacity as business owners. Instead, the company **employs the book value method**: debit Preferred Stock, along with any related Additional Paid-in Capital; credit Common Stock and Additional Paid-in Capital (if an excess exists).

Preferred stock generally has no maturity date. Therefore, no legal obligation exists to pay the preferred stockholder. As a result, companies classify preferred stock as part of stockholders' equity. Companies generally report preferred stock at par value as the first item in the stockholders' equity section. They report any excess over par value as part of additional paid-in capital. They also consider dividends on preferred stock as a distribution of income and not an expense. Companies must disclose the pertinent rights of the preferred stock outstanding.[11]

DIVIDEND POLICY

OBJECTIVE 6
Describe the policies used in distributing dividends.

As indicated in the opening story, dividend payouts can be important signals to the market. The practice of paying dividends declined sharply in the 1980s and 1990s as companies focused on growth and plowed profits back into the business. A resurgence in dividend payouts is due in large part to the dividend tax cut of 2003, which reduced the rate of tax on dividends to 15 percent (quite a bit lower than the ordinary income rate charged in the past). In addition, investors who were burned by accounting scandals in recent years began demanding higher payouts in the form of dividends. Why?

---

[10]"Accounting for Certain Financial Instruments with Characteristics of Both Liabilities and Equity," *Statement of Financial Accounting Standards No. 150* (Norwalk Conn.: FASB, 2003). *SFAS No. 150* represents completion of the first phase in a broader project on liabilities and equity. In phase two, the FASB will deal with the accounting for compound financial instruments (e.g., convertible debt, covered in Chapter 16) that have characteristics of liabilities and equity, the definition of an ownership relationship, and the definition of liabilities (an amendment to *FASB Concepts Statement No. 6*, "Elements of Financial Statements.")

[11]"Disclosure of Information about Capital Structure," *Statement of Financial Accounting Standards No. 129* (Norwalk, Conn.: FASB, 1997).

A dividend check provides proof that at least some portion of a company's profits is genuine.[12]

Determining the proper amount of dividends to pay is a difficult financial management decision. Companies that are paying dividends are extremely reluctant to reduce or eliminate their dividend. They fear that the securities market might negatively view this action. As a consequence, companies that have been paying cash dividends will make every effort to continue to do so. In addition, the type of shareholder the company has (taxable or nontaxable, retail investor or institutional investor) plays a large role in determining dividend policy.

Very few companies pay dividends in amounts equal to their legally available retained earnings. The major reasons are as follows.

1 To maintain agreements (bond covenants) with specific creditors, to retain all or a portion of the earnings, in the form of assets, to build up additional protection against possible loss.

2 To meet state corporation requirements, that earnings equivalent to the cost of treasury shares purchased be restricted against dividend declarations.

3 To retain assets that would otherwise be paid out as dividends, to finance growth or expansion. This is sometimes called internal financing, reinvesting earnings, or "plowing" the profits back into the business.

4 To smooth out dividend payments from year to year by accumulating earnings in good years and using such accumulated earnings as a basis for dividends in bad years.

5 To build up a cushion or buffer against possible losses or errors in the calculation of profits.

The reasons above are self-explanatory except for the second. The laws of some states require that the corporation restrict its legal capital from distribution to stockholders, to protect against loss for creditors.[13] The applicable state law determines the legality of a dividend.

Financial Condition and Dividend Distributions

Effective management of a company requires attention to more than the legality of dividend distributions. Management must also consider economic conditions, most importantly, liquidity. Assume an extreme situation as shown in Illustration 15-7.

BALANCE SHEET			
Plant assets	$500,000	Capital stock	$400,000
	$500,000	Retained earnings	100,000
			$500,000

ILLUSTRATION 15-7
Balance Sheet, Showing a Lack of Liquidity

The depicted company has a retained earnings credit balance. Unless restricted, it can declare a dividend of $100,000. But because all its assets are plant assets used in operations, payment of a cash dividend of $100,000 would require the sale of plant assets or borrowing.

---

[12]Jeff Opdyke, "Tax Cut, Shareholder Pressure Stoke Surge in Dividends," *Wall Street Journal Online* (January 18, 2005).

[13]If the corporation buys its own outstanding stock, it reduces its legal capital and distributes assets to stockholders. If permitted, the corporation could, by purchasing treasury stock at any price desired, return to the stockholders their investments and leave creditors with little or no protection against loss.

Even if a balance sheet shows current assets, as in Illustration 15-8, the question remains as to whether the company needs those cash assets for other purposes.

ILLUSTRATION 15-8
Balance Sheet, Showing
Cash but Minimal
Working Capital

BALANCE SHEET				
Cash	$100,000	Current liabilities		$ 60,000
Plant assets	460,000	Capital stock	$400,000	
	$560,000	Retained earnings	100,000	500,000
				$560,000

The existence of current liabilities strongly implies that the company needs some of the cash to meet current debts as they mature. In addition, day-by-day cash requirements for payrolls and other expenditures not included in current liabilities also require cash.

Thus, before declaring a dividend, management must consider **availability of funds to pay the dividend**. A company should not pay a dividend unless both the present and future financial position warrant the distribution.

The SEC encourages companies to disclose their dividend policy in their annual report, especially those that (1) have earnings but fail to pay dividends, or (2) do not expect to pay dividends in the foreseeable future. In addition, the SEC encourages companies that consistently pay dividends to indicate whether they intend to continue this practice in the future.

Types of Dividends

OBJECTIVE 7
Identify the various forms of dividend distributions.

Companies generally base dividend distributions either on accumulated profits (that is, retained earnings) or on some other capital item such as additional paid-in capital. Dividends are of the following types.

1 Cash dividends.
2 Property dividends.
3 Liquidating dividends.
4 Stock dividends.

Although commonly paid in cash, companies occasionally pay dividends in stock or some other asset.[14] **All dividends, except for stock dividends, reduce the total stockholders' equity in the corporation.** When declaring a stock dividend, the corporation does not pay out assets or incur a liability. It issues additional shares of stock to each stockholder and nothing more.

The natural expectation of any stockholder who receives a dividend is that the corporation has operated successfully. As a result, he or she is receiving a share of its profits. A company should disclose a **liquidating dividend**—that is, a dividend not based on retained earnings—to the stockholders so that they will not misunderstand its source.

Cash Dividends

The board of directors votes on the declaration of **cash dividends**. Upon approval of the resolution, the board declares a dividend. Before paying it, however, the company must prepare a current list of stockholders. For this reason there is usually a time lag between declaration and payment. For example, the board of directors might approve

---

[14]*Accounting Trends and Techniques—2004* reported that of its 600 surveyed companies, 370 paid a cash dividend on common stock, 54 paid a cash dividend on preferred stock, 4 issued stock dividends, and 7 issued or paid dividends in kind. Some companies declare more than one type of dividend in a given year.

a resolution at the January 10 (**date of declaration**) meeting, and declare it payable February 5 (**date of payment**) to all stockholders of record January 25 (**date of record**).[15] In this example, the period from January 10 to January 25 gives time for the company to complete and register any transfers in process. The time from January 25 to February 5 provides an opportunity for the transfer agent or accounting department, depending on who does this work, to prepare a list of stockholders as of January 25 and to prepare and mail dividend checks.

A declared cash dividend is a liability. Because payment is generally required very soon, it is usually a current liability. Companies use the following entries to record the declaration and payment of an ordinary dividend payable in cash. For example, Roadway Freight Corp. on June 10 declared a cash dividend of 50 cents a share on 1.8 million shares payable July 16 to all stockholders of record June 24.

At date of declaration (June 10)

Retained Earnings (Cash Dividends Declared)	900,000	
Dividends Payable		900,000

At date of record (June 24)

No entry

At date of payment (July 16)

Dividends Payable	900,000	
Cash		900,000

To set up a ledger account that shows the amount of dividends declared during the year, Roadway Freight might debit Cash Dividends Declared instead of Retained Earnings at the time of declaration. It then closes this account to Retained Earnings at year-end.

A company may declare dividends either as a certain percent of par, such as a 6 percent dividend on preferred stock, or as an amount per share, such as 60 cents per share on no-par common stock. In the first case, the rate multiplied by the par value of outstanding shares equals the total dividend. In the second, the dividend equals the amount per share multiplied by the number of shares outstanding. **Companies do not declare or pay cash dividends on treasury stock.**

Dividend policies vary among corporations. Some companies, such as **Bank of America, Clorox Co.**, and **Tootsie Roll Industries**, take pride in a long, unbroken string of quarterly dividend payments. They would lower or pass the dividend only if forced to do so by a sustained decline in earnings or a critical shortage of cash.

"Growth" companies, on the other hand, pay little or no cash dividends because their policy is to expand as rapidly as internal and external financing permit. For example, **Questcor Pharmaceuticals Inc.** has never paid cash dividends to its common stockholders. These investors hope that the price of their shares will appreciate in value. The investors will then realize a profit when they sell their shares. Many companies focus more on increasing share price, stock repurchase programs, and corporate earnings than on dividend payout.

INTERNATIONAL INSIGHT

As a less preferred but still allowable treatment, international accounting standards permit companies to reduce equity by the amount of proposed dividends prior to their legal declaration.

Property Dividends

Dividends payable in assets of the corporation other than cash are called **property dividends** or **dividends in kind**. Property dividends may be merchandise, real estate, or investments, or whatever form the board of directors designates. **Ranchers Exploration and Development Corp.** reported one year that it would pay a fourth-quarter dividend in gold bars instead of cash. Because of the obvious difficulties of divisibility of

---

[15]Theoretically, the ex-dividend date is the day after the date of record. However, to allow time for transfer of the shares, the stock exchanges generally advance the ex-dividend date two to four days. Therefore, the party who owns the stock on the day prior to the expressed ex-dividend date receives the dividends. The party who buys the stock on and after the ex-dividend date does not receive the dividend. Between the declaration date and the ex-dividend date, the market price of the stock includes the dividend.

units and delivery to stockholders, the usual property dividend is in the form of securities of other companies that the distributing corporation holds as an investment.

For example, after ruling that **DuPont**'s 23 percent stock interest in **General Motors** violated antitrust laws, the Supreme Court ordered DuPont to divest itself of the GM stock within 10 years. The stock represented 63 million shares of GM's 281 million shares then outstanding. DuPont could not sell the shares in one block of 63 million. Further, it could not sell 6 million shares annually for the next 10 years without severely depressing the value of the GM stock. DuPont solved its problem by declaring a property dividend and distributing the GM shares as a dividend to its own stockholders.

When declaring a property dividend, the corporation should **restate at fair value the property it will distribute**, **recognizing any gain or loss** as the difference between the property's fair value and carrying value at date of declaration. The corporation may then record the declared dividend as a debit to Retained Earnings (or Property Dividends Declared) and a credit to Property Dividends Payable, at an amount equal to the fair value of the distributed property. Upon distribution of the dividend, the corporation debits Property Dividends Payable and credits the account containing the distributed asset (restated at fair value).

For example, Trendler, Inc. transferred to stockholders some of its investments in marketable securities costing $1,250,000 by declaring a property dividend on December 28, 2006, to be distributed on January 30, 2007, to stockholders of record on January 15, 2007. At the date of declaration the securities have a market value of $2,000,000. Trendler makes the following entries.

At date of declaration (December 28, 2006)

Investments in Securities	750,000	
Gain on Appreciation of Securities		750,000
Retained Earnings (Property Dividends Declared)	2,000,000	
Property Dividends Payable		2,000,000

At date of distribution (January 30, 2007)

Property Dividends Payable	2,000,000	
Investments in Securities		2,000,000

Liquidating Dividends

Some corporations use paid-in capital as a basis for dividends. Without proper disclosure of this fact, stockholders may erroneously believe the corporation has been operating at a profit. To avoid this type of deception, intentional or unintentional, a clear statement of the source of every dividend should accompany the dividend check.

Dividends based on other than retained earnings are sometimes described as **liquidating dividends**. This term implies that such dividends are a return of the stockholder's investment rather than of profits. In other words, **any dividend not based on earnings reduces corporate paid-in capital and to that extent, it is a liquidating dividend**. Companies in the extractive industries may pay dividends equal to the total of accumulated income and depletion. The portion of these dividends in excess of accumulated income represents a return of part of the stockholder's investment.

For example, McChesney Mines Inc. issued a "dividend" to its common stockholders of $1,200,000. The cash dividend announcement noted that stockholders should consider $900,000 as income and the remainder a return of capital. McChesney Mines records the dividend as follows:

At date of declaration

Retained Earnings	900,000	
Additional Paid-in Capital	300,000	
Dividends Payable		1,200,000

At date of payment

Dividends Payable	1,200,000	
Cash		1,200,000

In some cases, management simply decides to cease business and declares a liquidating dividend. In these cases, liquidation may take place over a number of years to ensure an orderly and fair sale of assets. For example, when **Overseas National Airways** dissolved, it agreed to pay a liquidating dividend to its stockholders over a period of years equivalent to $8.60 per share. Each liquidating dividend payment in such cases reduces paid-in capital.

Stock Dividends

If management wishes to "capitalize" part of the earnings (i.e., reclassify amounts from earned to contributed capital), and thus retain earnings in the business on a permanent basis, it may issue a stock dividend. In this case, **the company distributes no assets**. Each stockholder maintains exactly the same proportionate interest in the corporation and the same total book value after the company issues the stock dividend. Of course, the book value per share is lower because each stockholder holds more shares.

A **stock dividend** therefore is the issuance by a corporation of its own stock to its stockholders on a pro rata basis, without receiving any consideration. In recording a stock dividend, some believe that the company should transfer the **par value of the stock issued** as a dividend from retained earnings to capital stock. Others believe that it should transfer the **fair value of the stock issued**—its market value at the declaration date—from retained earnings to capital stock and additional paid-in capital.

UNDERLYING CONCEPTS

By requiring fair value, the intent was to punish companies that used stock dividends. This approach violates the neutrality concept (that is, that standards-setting should be even-handed).

The fair value position was adopted, at least in part, in order to influence the stock dividend policies of corporations. Evidently in 1941 both the New York Stock Exchange and many in the accounting profession regarded periodic stock dividends as objectionable. They believed that the term dividend when used with a distribution of additional stock was misleading because investors' net assets did not increase as a result of this "dividend." As a result, these groups decided to make it more difficult for corporations to sustain a series of such stock dividends out of their accumulated earnings, by requiring the use of fair market value when it substantially exceeded book value.[16]

When the stock dividend is less than 20–25 percent of the common shares outstanding at the time of the dividend declaration, the company is therefore required to transfer the **fair market value** of the stock issued from retained earnings. Stock dividends of less than 20–25 percent are often referred to as **small (ordinary) stock dividends**. This method of handling stock dividends is justified on the grounds that "many recipients of stock dividends look upon them as distributions of corporate earnings and usually in an amount equivalent to the fair value of the additional shares received."[17] We consider this argument unconvincing. It is generally agreed that stock dividends are not income to the recipients. Therefore, sound accounting should not recommend procedures simply because some recipients think they are income.

OBJECTIVE 8
Explain the accounting for small and large stock dividends, and for stock splits.

To illustrate a small stock dividend, assume that Vine Corporation has outstanding 1,000 shares of $100 par value capital stock and retained earnings of $50,000. If Vine declares a 10 percent stock dividend, it issues 100 additional shares to current stockholders. If the fair value of the stock at the time of the stock dividend is $130 per share, the entry is:

At date of declaration

Retained Earnings (Stock Dividend Declared)	13,000	
Common Stock Dividend Distributable		10,000
Paid-in Capital in Excess of Par		3,000

---

[16]This was perhaps the earliest instance of "economic consequences" affecting an accounting pronouncement. The Committee on Accounting Procedure described its action as required by "proper accounting and corporate policy." See Stephen A. Zeff, "The Rise of 'Economic Consequences,'" *The Journal of Accountancy* (December 1978), pp. 53–66.

[17]American Institute of Certified Public Accountants, *Accounting Research and Terminology Bulletins,* No. 43 (New York: AICPA, 1961), Ch. 7, par. 10. One study concluded that *small* stock dividends do not always produce significant amounts of extra value on the date after issuance (ex date) and that *large* stock dividends almost always fail to generate extra value on the ex-dividend date. Taylor W. Foster III and Don Vickrey, "The Information Content of Stock Dividend Announcements," *The Accounting Review,* Vol. LIII, No. 2 (April 1978), pp. 360–370.

Note that the stock dividend does not affect any asset or liability. The entry merely reflects a reclassification of stockholders' equity. If Vine prepares a balance sheet between the dates of declaration and distribution, it should show the common stock dividend distributable in the stockholders' equity section as an addition to capital stock (whereas it shows cash or property dividends payable as current liabilities).

When issuing the stock, the entry is:

At date of distribution

Common Stock Dividend Distributable	10,000	
Common Stock		10,000

No matter what the fair value is at the time of the stock dividend, each stockholder retains the same proportionate interest in the corporation.

Some state statutes specifically prohibit the issuance of stock dividends on treasury stock. In those states that permit treasury shares to participate in the distribution accompanying a stock dividend or stock split, the planned use of the treasury shares influences corporate practice. For example, if a corporation issues treasury shares in connection with employee stock options, the treasury shares may participate in the distribution because the corporation usually adjusts the number of shares under option for any stock dividends or splits. But no useful purpose is served by issuing additional shares to the treasury stock without a specific purpose, since they are essentially equivalent to authorized but unissued shares.

To continue with our example of the effect of the small stock dividend, note in Illustration 15-9 that the stock dividend does not change the total stockholders' equity. Also note that it does not change the proportion of the total shares outstanding held by each stockholder.

ILLUSTRATION 15-9
Effects of a Small (10%)
Stock Dividend

Before dividend	
Capital stock, 1,000 shares of $100 par	$100,000
Retained earnings	50,000
Total stockholders' equity	$150,000
Stockholders' interests:	
A. 400 shares, 40% interest, book value	$ 60,000
B. 500 shares, 50% interest, book value	75,000
C. 100 shares, 10% interest, book value	15,000
	$150,000
After declaration but before distribution of 10% stock dividend	
If fair value ($130) is used as basis for entry:	
Capital stock, 1,000 shares at $100 par	$100,000
Common stock distributable, 100 shares at $100 par	10,000
Paid-in capital in excess of par	3,000
Retained earnings ($50,000 − $13,000)	37,000
Total stockholders' equity	$150,000
After declaration and distribution of 10% stock dividend	
If fair value ($130) is used as basis for entry:	
Capital stock, 1,100 shares at $100 par	$110,000
Paid-in capital in excess of par	3,000
Retained earnings ($50,000 − $13,000)	37,000
Total stockholders' equity	$150,000
Stockholders' interest:	
A. 440 shares, 40% interest, book value	$ 60,000
B. 550 shares, 50% interest, book value	75,000
C. 110 shares, 10% interest, book value	15,000
	$150,000

Stock Split

If a company has undistributed earnings over several years, and accumulates a sizable balance in retained earnings, the market value of its outstanding shares likely increases. Stock issued at prices less than $50 a share can easily attain a market value in excess of $200 a share. The higher the market price of a stock, however, the less readily some investors can purchase it.

The managements of many corporations believe that better public relations depend on wider ownership of the corporation stock. They therefore target a market price sufficiently low to be within range of the majority of potential investors. To reduce the market value of shares, they use the common device of a **stock split**. For example, after its stock price increased by 25-fold, **Qualcomm Inc.** split its stock 4-for-1. Qualcomm's stock had risen above $500 per share, raising concerns that Qualcomm could not meet an analyst target of $1,000 per share. The split reduced the analysts' target to $250, which it could better meet with wider distribution of shares at lower trading prices.

From an accounting standpoint, Qualcomm **records no entry for a stock split**. However, it enters a memorandum note to indicate the changed par value of the shares and the increased number of shares. Illustration 15-10 shows the lack of change in stockholders' equity for a 2-for-1 stock split on 1,000 shares of $100 par value stock with the par being halved upon issuance of the additional shares.

Stockholders' Equity before 2-for-1 Split		Stockholders' Equity after 2-for-1 Split	
Common stock, 1,000 shares		Common stock, 2,000 shares	
at $100 par	$100,000	at $50 par	$100,000
Retained earnings	50,000	Retained earnings	50,000
	$150,000		$150,000

ILLUSTRATION 15-10
Effects of a Stock Split

SPLITSVILLE

Stock splits were all the rage in the booming stock market of the 1990s. Of major companies on the **New York Stock Exchange**, fewer than 80 companies split shares in 1990. By 1998, with stock prices soaring, over 200 companies split shares. Although the split does not increase a stockholder's proportionate ownership of the company, studies show that split shares usually outperform those that don't split, as well as the market as a whole, for several years after the split. In addition, the splits help the company keep the shares in more attractive price ranges.

What about when the market "turns south"? A number of companies who split their shares in the boom markets of the 1990s have since seen their share prices decline to a point considered too low. For example, since **Ameritrade**'s 12-for-1 split in 1999, its stock price declined over 74 percent, so that it was trading around $6 per share in March 2002. And **Lucent** traded at less than $5 a share following a 4-for-1 split. For some investors, these low-priced stocks are unattractive because some brokerage commissions rely on the number of shares traded, not the dollar amount. Others are concerned that low-priced shares are easier for would-be scamsters to manipulate.

Some companies are considering reverse stock splits in which, say, 5 shares are consolidated into one. Thus, a stock previously trading at $5 per share would be part of an unsplit share trading at $25. Unsplitting might thus avoid some of the negative consequences of a low trading price. The downside to this strategy is that analysts might view reverse splits as additional bad news about the direction of the stock price. For example, **Webvan**, a failed Internet grocer, did a 1-for-25 reverse split just before it entered bankruptcy.

Source: Adapted from David Henry, "Stocks: The Case for Unsplitting," *BusinessWeek Online* (April 1, 2002).

WHAT DO THE NUMBERS MEAN?

Stock Split and Stock Dividend Differentiated

From a legal standpoint, a stock split differs from a stock dividend. How? A stock split increases the number of shares outstanding and decreases the par or stated value per share. **A stock dividend, although it increases the number of shares outstanding, does not decrease the par value; thus it increases the total par value of outstanding shares.**

The reasons for issuing a stock dividend are numerous and varied. Stock dividends can be primarily a publicity gesture, **because many consider stock dividends as dividends.** Another reason is that the corporation may simply wish to retain profits in the business by capitalizing a part of retained earnings. In such a situation, it makes a transfer on declaration of a stock dividend from earned capital to contributed capital.

A corporation may also use a stock dividend, like a stock split, to increase the marketability of the stock, although marketability is often a secondary consideration. If the stock dividend is large, it has the same effect on market price as a stock split. **Whenever corporations issue additional shares for the purpose of reducing the unit market price, then the distribution more closely resembles a stock split than a stock dividend. This effect usually results only if the number of shares issued is more than 20–25 percent of the number of shares previously outstanding.**[18] A stock dividend of more than 20–25 percent of the number of shares previously outstanding is called a **large stock dividend.**[19] Such a distribution should not be called a stock dividend but instead "a split-up effected in the form of a dividend" or "stock split."

Also, since a split-up effected in the form of a dividend does not alter the par value per share, companies generally are required to transfer the par value amount from retained earnings. In other words, companies transfer from retained earnings to capital stock **the par value of the stock issued,** as opposed to a transfer of the market value of the shares issued as in the case of a small stock dividend.[20] For example, **Brown Group, Inc.** at one time authorized a 2-for-1 split, effected in the form of a stock dividend. As a result of this authorization, it distributed approximately 10.5 million shares, and transferred more than $39 million representing the par value of the shares issued from Retained Earnings to the Common Stock account.

To illustrate a large stock dividend (stock split-up effected in the form of a dividend), Rockland Steel, Inc. declared a 30 percent stock dividend on November 20, payable December 29 to stockholders of record December 12. At the date of declaration, 1,000,000 shares, par value $10, are outstanding and with a fair market value of $200 per share. The entries are:

At date of declaration (November 20)

Retained Earnings	3,000,000	
Common Stock Dividend Distributable		3,000,000

Computation: 1,000,000 shares	300,000 Additional shares
× 30%	× $10 Par value
300,000	$3,000,000

At date of distribution (December 29)

Common Stock Dividend Distributable	3,000,000	
Common Stock		3,000,000

---

[18]*Accounting Research and Terminology Bulletin No. 43,* par. 13.

[19]The SEC has added more precision to the 20–25 percent rule. Specifically, the SEC indicates that companies should consider distributions of 25 percent or more as a "split-up effected in the form of a dividend." Companies should account for distributions of less than 25 percent as a stock dividend. The SEC more precisely defined GAAP here. As a result, public companies follow the SEC rule.

[20]Often, a company records a split-up effected in the form of a dividend as a debit to Paid-in Capital instead of Retained Earnings to indicate that this transaction should affect only paid-in capital accounts. No reduction of retained earnings is required except as indicated by legal requirements. For homework purposes, assume that the debit is to Retained Earnings. See, for example, Taylor W. Foster III and Edmund Scribner, "Accounting for Stock Dividends and Stock Splits: Corrections to Textbook Coverage," *Issues in Accounting Education* (February 1998).

Illustration 15-11 summarizes and compares the effects in the balance sheet and related items of various types of dividends and stock splits.

Effect on:	Declaration of Cash Dividend	Payment of Cash Dividend	Declaration and Distribution of		
			Small Stock Dividend	Large Stock Dividend	Stock Split
Retained earnings	Decrease	–0–	Decrease[a]	Decrease[b]	–0–
Capital stock	–0–	–0–	Increase[b]	Increase[b]	–0–
Additional paid-in capital	–0–	–0–	Increase[c]	–0–	–0–
Total stockholders' equity	Decrease	–0–	–0–	–0–	–0–
Working capital	Decrease	–0–	–0–	–0–	–0–
Total assets	–0–	Decrease	–0–	–0–	–0–
Number of shares outstanding	–0–	–0–	Increase	Increase	Increase

[a]Market value of shares. [b]Par or stated value of shares. [c]Excess of market value over par.

ILLUSTRATION 15-11
Effects of Dividends and Stock Splits on Financial Statement Elements

INTERNATIONAL INSIGHT

Switzerland allows companies to create income reserves. That is, companies reduce income in years with good profits by allocating it to reserves on the balance sheet. In less profitable years, companies then reallocate from the reserves to improve income. This "smoothes" income across years.

Disclosure of Restrictions on Retained Earnings

Many corporations restrict retained earnings or dividends, without any formal journal entries. Such restrictions are **best disclosed by note**. Parenthetical notations are sometimes used, but restrictions imposed by bond indentures and loan agreements commonly require an extended explanation. Notes provide a medium for more complete explanations and free the financial statements from abbreviated notations. The note disclosure should reveal the source of the restriction, pertinent provisions, and the amount of retained earnings subject to restriction, or the amount not restricted.

Restrictions may be based on the retention of a certain retained earnings balance, the ability to maintain certain working capital requirements, additional borrowing, and other considerations. The example from the annual report of **Alberto-Culver Company** in Illustration 15-12 shows a note disclosing potential restrictions on retained earnings and dividends.

Alberto-Culver Company

Note 3 (in part): The $200 million revolving credit facility, the term note due September 2000, and the receivables agreement impose restrictions on such items as total debt, working capital, dividend payments, treasury stock purchases, and interest expense. At year-end, the company was in compliance with these arrangements, and $220 million of consolidated retained earnings was not restricted as to the payment of dividends.

ILLUSTRATION 15-12
Disclosure of Restrictions on Retained Earnings and Dividends

PRESENTATION AND ANALYSIS OF STOCKHOLDERS' EQUITY

Presentation

Balance Sheet

Illustration 15-13 (on page 750) shows a comprehensive stockholders' equity section from the balance sheet of Frost Company that includes most of the equity items we discussed in this chapter.

OBJECTIVE 9
Indicate how to present and analyze stockholders' equity.

ILLUSTRATION 15-13
Comprehensive
Stockholders' Equity
Presentation

FROST CORPORATION		
STOCKHOLDERS' EQUITY		
DECEMBER 31, 2007		
Capital stock		
Preferred stock, $100 par value, 7% cumulative, 100,000 shares authorized, 30,000 shares issued and outstanding		$ 3,000,000
Common stock, no par, stated value $10 per share, 500,000 shares authorized, 400,000 shares issued		4,000,000
Common stock dividend distributable, 20,000 shares		200,000
Total capital stock		7,200,000
Additional paid-in capital[21]		
Excess over par—preferred	$150,000	
Excess over stated value—common	840,000	990,000
Total paid-in capital		8,190,000
Retained earnings		4,360,000
Total paid-in capital and retained earnings		12,550,000
Less: Cost of treasury stock (2,000 shares, common)		(190,000)
Accumulated other comprehensive loss[22]		(360,000)
Total stockholders' equity		$12,000,000

Frost should disclose the pertinent rights and privileges of the various securities outstanding. For example, companies must disclose all of the following dividend and liquidation preferences, participation rights, call prices and dates, conversion or exercise prices and pertinent dates, sinking fund requirements, unusual voting rights, and significant terms of contracts to issue additional shares. Liquidation preferences should be disclosed in the equity section of the balance sheet, rather than in the notes to the financial statements, to emphasize the possible effect of this restriction on future cash flows.[23]

Statement of Stockholders' Equity

The **statement of stockholders' equity** is frequently presented in the following basic format.

1 Balance at the beginning of the period.

2 Additions.

3 Deductions.

4 Balance at the end of the period.

Reporting of Stockholders' Equity in Eastman-Kodak's Annual Report

---

[21]*Accounting Trends and Techniques—2004* reports that of its 600 surveyed companies, 535 had additional paid-in capital; 313 used the caption "Additional paid-in capital"; 111 used "Capital in excess of par or stated value" as the caption; 82 used "Paid-in capital" or "Additional capital"; and 29 used other captions.

[22]Companies may include a number of items in the "Accumulated other comprehensive loss." Among these items are "Foreign currency translation adjustments" (covered in advanced accounting), "Unrealized holding gains and losses for available-for-sale securities" (covered in Chapter 17), "Excess of additional pension liability over unrecognized prior service cost" (covered in Chapter 20), "Guarantees of employee stock option plan (ESOP) debt," "Unearned or deferred compensation related to employee stock award plans," and others.

Accounting Trends and Techniques—2004 reports that of its 600 surveyed companies reporting other items in the equity section, 477 reported cumulative translation adjustments, 389 reported minimum pension liability adjustments, 268 reported unrealized losses/gains on certain investments, and 311 reported changes in the fair value of derivatives. A number of companies had more than one item.

[23]"Disclosure of Information about Capital Structure," *Statement of Financial Accounting Standards No. 129* (Norwalk, Conn.: FASB, February 1997), par. 4.

Companies must disclose changes in the separate accounts comprising stockholders' equity, to make the financial statements sufficiently informative.[24] Such changes may be disclosed in separate statements or in the basic financial statements or notes thereto.[25]

A **columnar format** for the presentation of changes in stockholders' equity items in published annual reports is gaining in popularity. An example is **Hewlett-Packard Company**'s statement of stockholders' equity, shown in Illustration 15-14.

ILLUSTRATION 15-14
Columnar Format for
Statement of
Stockholders' Equity

Hewlett-Packard Company and Subsidiaries
Consolidated Statement of Stockholders' Equity

(in millions, except number of shares in thousands)	Common Stock Number of Shares	Common Stock Par Value	Additional Paid-in Capital	Retained Earnings	Accumulated Other Comprehensive Income (Loss)	Total
Balance October 31, 2003	3,042,761	$30	$24,587	$13,332	$ (203)	$37,746
Net earnings				3,497		3,497
Net unrealized loss on available-for-sale securities					(20)	(20)
Net unrealized loss on cash flow hedges					(28)	(28)
Minimum pension liability, net of taxes					(13)	(13)
Cumulative translation adjustment					21	21
Comprehensive income						3,457
Assumption of stock options in connection with business acquisitions			15			15
Issuance of common stock in connection with employee stock plans and other	40,467		592			592
Repurchases of common stock	(172,468)	(1)	(3,100)	(208)		(3,309)
Tax benefit from employee stock plans			35			35
Dividends				(972)		(972)
Balance October 31, 2004	2,910,760	$29	$22,129	$15,649	$(243)	$37,564

Analysis

Analysts use stockholders' equity ratios to evaluate a company's profitability and long-term solvency. We discuss and illustrate the following three ratios below.

1 Rate of return on common stock equity.
2 Payout ratio.
3 Book value per share.

---

[24]If a company has other comprehensive income, and computes total comprehensive income only in the statement of stockholders' equity, it must display the statement of stockholders' equity with the same prominence as other financial statements. "Reporting Comprehensive Income," *Statement of Financial Accounting Standards No. 130* (Norwalk, Conn.: FASB, June 1997).

[25]*Accounting Trends and Techniques—2004* reports that of the 600 companies surveyed, 586 presented statements of stockholders' equity, 7 presented separate statements of retained earnings only, 2 presented combined statements of income and retained earnings, and 5 presented changes in equity items in the notes only.

Financial Analysis Primer

Rate of Return on Common Stock Equity

The **rate of return on common stock equity** measures profitability from the common stockholders' viewpoint. This ratio shows how many dollars of net income the company earned for each dollar invested by the owners. Return on equity (ROE) also helps investors judge the worthiness of a stock when the overall market is not doing well. For example, **Best Buy** shares dropped nearly 40 percent, along with the broader market in 2001–2002. But a review of its return on equity during this period and since shows a steady return of 20 to 22 percent while the overall market ROE declined from 16 percent to 8 percent. More importantly, Best Buy and other stocks, such as **3M** and **Procter & Gamble**, recovered their lost market value, while other stocks with less robust ROEs stayed in the doldrums.

Return on equity equals net income less preferred dividends, divided by average common stockholders' equity. For example, assume that Gerber's Inc. had net income of $360,000, declared and paid preferred dividends of $54,000, and average common stockholders' equity of $2,550,000. Illustration 15-15 shows how to compute Gerber's ratio.

ILLUSTRATION 15-15
Computation of Rate of Return on Common Stock Equity

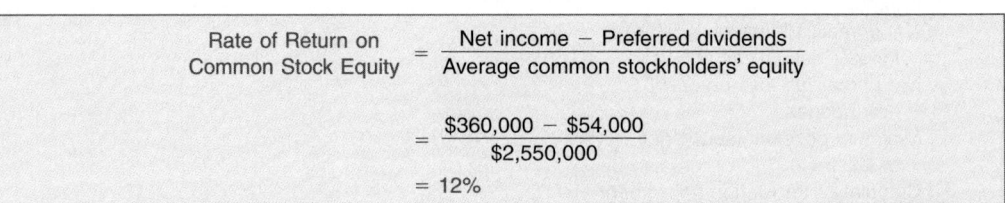

$$\text{Rate of Return on Common Stock Equity} = \frac{\text{Net income} - \text{Preferred dividends}}{\text{Average common stockholders' equity}}$$

$$= \frac{\$360,000 - \$54,000}{\$2,550,000}$$

$$= 12\%$$

As shown in Illustration 15-15, when preferred stock is present, income available to common stockholders equals net income less preferred dividends. Similarly, the amount of common stock equity used in this ratio equals total stockholders' equity less the par value of preferred stock.

A company can improve its return on common stock equity through the prudent use of debt or preferred stock financing. **Trading on the equity** describes the practice of using borrowed money or issuing preferred stock in hopes of obtaining a higher rate of return on the money used. Shareholders win if return on the assets is higher than the cost of financing these assets. When this happens, the rate of return on common stock equity will exceed the rate of return on total assets. In short, the company is "trading on the equity at a gain." In this situation, the money obtained from bondholders or preferred stockholders earns enough to pay the interest or preferred dividends and leaves a profit for the common stockholders. On the other hand, if the cost of the financing is higher that the rate earned on the assets, the company is trading on equity at a loss and stockholders lose.

Payout Ratio

Another ratio of interest to investors, the **payout ratio**, is the ratio of cash dividends to net income. If preferred stock is outstanding, this ratio equals cash dividends paid to common stockholders, divided by net income available to common stockholders. For example, assume that Troy Co. has cash dividends of $100,000 and net income of $500,000, and no preferred stock outstanding. Illustration 15-16 shows the payout ratio computation.

ILLUSTRATION 15-16
Computation of Payout Ratio

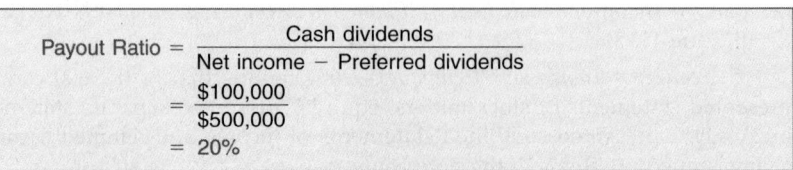

$$\text{Payout Ratio} = \frac{\text{Cash dividends}}{\text{Net income} - \text{Preferred dividends}}$$

$$= \frac{\$100,000}{\$500,000}$$

$$= 20\%$$

As discussed in the opening story, it is important to some investors that the pay-out be sufficiently high to provide a good yield on the stock.[26]

Book Value per Share

A much-used basis for evaluating net worth is found in the book value or equity value per share of stock. **Book value per share** of stock is the amount each share would receive if the company were liquidated **on the basis of amounts reported on the balance sheet**. However, the figure loses much of its relevance if the valuations on the balance sheet fail to approximate fair market value of the assets. Book value per share equals common stockholders' equity divided by outstanding common shares. Assume that Chen Corporation's common stockholders' equity is $1,000,000 and it has 100,000 shares of common stock outstanding. Illustration 15-17 shows its book value per share computation.

$$\text{Book Value Per Share} = \frac{\text{Common stockholders' equity}}{\text{Outstanding shares}}$$

$$= \frac{\$1,000,000}{100,000}$$

$$= \$10 \text{ per share}$$

ILLUSTRATION 15-17
Computation of Book Value Per Share

SUMMARY OF LEARNING OBJECTIVES

1. Discuss the characteristics of the corporate form of organization. Among the specific characteristics of the corporate form that affect accounting are the: (1) influence of state corporate law, (2) use of the capital stock or share system, and (3) development of a variety of ownership interests. In the absence of restrictive provisions, each share of stock carries the right to share proportionately in: (1) profits and losses; (2) management (the right to vote for directors); (3) corporate assets upon liquidation; (4) any new issues of stock of the same class (called the preemptive right).

2. Identify the key components of stockholders' equity. Stockholders' or owners' equity is classified into two categories: contributed capital and earned capital. Contributed capital (paid-in capital) describes the total amount paid in on capital stock. Put another way, it is the amount that stockholders advance to the corporation for use in the business. Contributed capital includes items such as the par value of all outstanding capital stock and premiums less any discounts on issuance. Earned capital is the capital that develops if the business operates profitably; it consists of all undistributed income that remains invested in the company.

3. Explain the accounting procedures for issuing shares of stock. Accounts are kept for the following different types of stock: *Par value stock:* (a) preferred stock or common stock; (b) paid-in capital in excess of par or additional paid-in capital; and (c) discount on stock. *No-par stock:* common stock or common stock and additional paid-in capital, if stated value used. Stock issued in combination with other securities (lump-sum sales): The two methods of allocation available are (a) the proportional method; and (b) the incremental method. Stock issued in noncash transactions: When issuing stock for services or property other than cash, the company should record the property or services at either the fair market value of the stock issued, or the fair market value of the noncash consideration received, whichever is more clearly determinable.

KEY TERMS

additional paid-in capital, *730*
book value per share, *753*
callable preferred stock, *739*
cash dividends, *742*
common stock, *727*
contributed (paid-in) capital, *729*
convertible preferred stock, *739*
cost method, *735*
cumulative preferred stock, *739*
dividend in arrears, *739*
earned capital, *729*
large stock dividend, *748*
leveraged buyout (LBO), *734*
liquidating dividends, *742, 744*
lump-sum sales, *731*
no-par stock, *730*
par (stated) value method, *735*
participating preferred stock, *739*
payout ratio, *752*
preemptive right, *727*

---

[26]Analysts also closely watch the **dividend yield**—the cash dividend per share divided by the market price of the stock. This ratio indicates the rate of return that investors will receive in cash dividends from their investment.

Expanded Discussion of Quasi-Reorganization

4. Describe the accounting for treasury stock. The cost method is generally used in accounting for treasury stock. This method derives its name from the fact that a company maintains the Treasury Stock account at the cost of the shares purchased. Under the cost method, a company debits the Treasury Stock account for the cost of the shares acquired and credits it for this same cost upon reissuance. The price received for the stock when originally issued does not affect the entries to record the acquisition and reissuance of the treasury stock.

5. Explain the accounting for and reporting of preferred stock. Preferred stock is a special class of shares that possesses certain preferences or features not possessed by the common stock. The features that are most often associated with preferred stock issues are: (1) preference as to dividends; (2) preference as to assets in the event of liquidation; (3) convertible into common stock; (4) callable at the option of the corporation; (5) nonvoting. At issuance, the accounting for preferred stock is similar to that for common stock. When convertible preferred stock is converted, a company uses the book value method: It debits Preferred Stock, along with any related Additional Paid-in Capital, and credits Common Stock and Additional Paid-in Capital (if an excess exists).

6. Describe the policies used in distributing dividends. The state incorporation laws normally provide information concerning the legal restrictions related to the payment of dividends. Corporations rarely pay dividends in an amount equal to the legal limit. This is due, in part, to the fact that companies use assets represented by undistributed earnings to finance future operations of the business. If a company is considering declaring a dividend, it must ask two preliminary questions: (1) Is the condition of the corporation such that the dividend is **legally permissible**? (2) Is the condition of the corporation such that a dividend is **economically sound**?

7. Identify the various forms of dividend distributions. Dividends are of the following types: (1) cash dividends, (2) property dividends, (3) liquidating dividends (dividends based on other than retained earnings), (4) stock dividends (the issuance by a corporation of its own stock to its stockholders on a pro rata basis, but without receiving consideration).

8. Explain the accounting for small and large stock dividends, and for stock splits. Generally accepted accounting principles require that the accounting for small stock dividends (less than 20 or 25 percent) rely on the fair market value of the stock issued. When declaring a stock dividend, a company debits Retained Earnings at the fair market value of the stock it distributes. The entry includes a credit to Common Stock Dividend Distributable at par value times the number of shares, with any excess credited to Paid-in Capital in Excess of Par. If the number of shares issued exceeds 20 or 25 percent of the shares outstanding (large stock dividend), it debits Retained Earnings at par value and credits Common Stock Distributable—there is no additional paid-in capital.

A stock dividend is a capitalization of retained earnings that reduces retained earnings and increases certain contributed capital accounts. The par value per share and total stockholders' equity remain unchanged with a stock dividend, and all stockholders retain their same proportionate share of ownership. A stock split results in an increase or decrease in the number of shares outstanding, with a corresponding decrease or increase in the par or stated value per share. No accounting entry is required for a stock split.

9. Indicate how to present and analyze stockholders' equity. The stockholders' equity section of a balance sheet includes capital stock, additional paid-in capital, and retained earnings. A company might also present additional items such as treasury stock and accumulated other comprehensive income. Companies often provide a statement of stockholders' equity. Common ratios that use stockholders' equity amounts are: rate of return on common stock equity, payout ratio, and book value per share.

Dividend Preferences and Book Value Per Share

DIVIDEND PREFERENCES

> **OBJECTIVE 10**
> Explain the different types of preferred stock dividends and their effect on book value per share.

Illustrations 15A-1 to 15A-4 indicate the **effects of** various **dividend preferences** on dividend distributions to common and preferred stockholders. Assume that in 2007, Mason Company is to distribute $50,000 as cash dividends, its outstanding common stock has a par value of $400,000, and its 6 percent preferred stock has a par value of $100,000. Mason would distribute dividends to each class, employing the assumptions given, as follows:

1 If the preferred stock is noncumulative and nonparticipating:

	Preferred	Common	Total
6% of $100,000	$6,000		$ 6,000
The remainder to common		$44,000	44,000
Totals	$6,000	$44,000	$50,000

ILLUSTRATION 15A-1
Dividend Distribution, Noncumulative and Nonparticipating Preferred

2 If the preferred stock is cumulative and nonparticipating, and Mason Company did not pay dividends on the preferred stock in the preceding two years:

	Preferred	Common	Total
Dividends in arrears, 6% of $100,000 for 2 years	$12,000		$12,000
Current year's dividend, 6% of $100,000	6,000		6,000
The remainder to common		$32,000	32,000
Totals	$18,000	$32,000	$50,000

ILLUSTRATION 15A-2
Dividend Distribution, Cumulative and Nonparticipating Preferred, with Dividends in Arrears

3 If the preferred stock is noncumulative and is fully participating:[1]

---

[1] When preferred stock is participating, there may be different agreements as to how the participation feature is to be executed. However, in the absence of any specific agreement the following procedure is recommended:

  a. After the preferred stock is assigned its current year's dividend, the common stock will receive a "like" percentage of par value outstanding. In example (3), this amounts to 6 percent of $400,000.

  b. In example (3), shown in Illustration 15A-3 (on page 756), the remainder of the declared dividend is $20,000. We divide this amount by total par value ($500,000) to find the rate of participation to be applied to each class of stock. In this case, the rate of participation is 4% ($20,000 ÷ $500,000), which we then multiply by the par value of each class of stock to determine the amount of participation.

ILLUSTRATION 15A-3
Dividend Distribution,
Noncumulative and Fully
Participating Preferred

	Preferred	Common	Total
Current year's dividend, 6%	$ 6,000	$24,000	$30,000
Participating dividend of 4%	4,000	16,000	20,000
Totals	$10,000	$40,000	$50,000

The participating dividend was determined as follows:
Current year's dividend:		
Preferred, 6% of $100,000 = $ 6,000		
Common, 6% of $400,000 = 24,000		$ 30,000
Amount available for participation		
($50,000 − $30,000)		$ 20,000
Par value of stock that is to participate		
($100,000 + $400,000)		$500,000
Rate of participation		
($20,000 ÷ $500,000)		4%
Participating dividend:		
Preferred, 4% of $100,000		$ 4,000
Common, 4% of $400,000		16,000
		$ 20,000

4 If the preferred stock is cumulative and is fully participating, and Mason Company did not pay dividends on the preferred stock in the preceding two years:

ILLUSTRATION 15A-4
Dividend Distribution,
Cumulative and Fully
Participating Preferred,
with Dividends in
Arrears

	Preferred	Common	Total
Dividends in arrears, 6% of $100,000 for 2 years	$12,000		$12,000
Current year's dividend, 6%	6,000	$24,000	30,000
Participating dividend, 1.6% ($8,000 ÷ $500,000)	1,600	6,400	8,000
Totals	$19,600	$30,400	$50,000

BOOK VALUE PER SHARE

Book value per share in its simplest form is computed as net assets divided by outstanding shares at the end of the year. The computation of book value per share becomes more complicated if a company has preferred stock in its capital structure. For example, if preferred dividends are in arrears, if the preferred stock is participating, or if preferred stock has a redemption or liquidating value higher than its carrying amount, the company must allocate retained earnings between the preferred and common stockholders in computing book value.

To illustrate, assume that the following situation exists.

ILLUSTRATION 15A-5
Computation of Book
Value Per Share—No
Dividends in Arrears

Stockholders' equity	Preferred	Common
Preferred stock, 5%	$300,000	
Common stock		$400,000
Excess of issue price over par of common stock		37,500
Retained earnings		162,582
Totals	$300,000	$600,082
Shares outstanding		4,000
Book value per share		$150.02

The situation in Illustration 15A-5 assumes that no preferred dividends are in arrears and that the preferred is not participating. Now assume that the same facts exist except that the 5 percent preferred is cumulative, participating up to 8 percent, and that dividends for three years before the current year are in arrears. Illustration 15A-6 shows how to compute the book value of the common stock, assuming that no action has yet been taken concerning dividends for the current year.

Stockholders' equity	Preferred	Common
Preferred stock, 5%	$300,000	
Common stock		$400,000
Excess of issue price over par of common stock		37,500
Retained earnings:		
Dividends in arrears (3 years at 5% a year)	45,000	
Current year requirement at 5%	15,000	20,000
Participating—additional 3%	9,000	12,000
Remainder to common		61,582
Totals	$369,000	$531,082
Shares outstanding		4,000
Book value per share		$132.77

ILLUSTRATION 15A-6
Computation of Book Value Per Share—With Dividends in Arrears

In connection with the book value computation, the analyst must know how to handle the following items: the number of authorized and unissued shares; the number of treasury shares on hand; any commitments with respect to the issuance of unissued shares or the reissuance of treasury shares; and the relative rights and privileges of the various types of stock authorized. As an example, if the liquidating value of the preferred stock is higher than its carrying amount, the liquidating amount should be used in the book value computation.

SUMMARY OF LEARNING OBJECTIVE FOR APPENDIX 15A

10. Explain the different types of preferred stock dividends and their effect on book value per share. The dividend preferences of preferred stock affect the dividends paid to stockholders. Preferred stock can be (1) cumulative or noncumulative, and (2) fully participating, partially participating, or nonparticipating. If preferred dividends are in arrears, if the preferred stock is participating, or if preferred stock has a redemption or liquidation value higher than its carrying amount, allocate retained earnings between preferred and common stockholders in computing book value per share.

Note: All **asterisked** Questions, Brief Exercises, and Exercises relate to material contained in the appendixes to the chapter.

QUESTIONS

1. In the absence of restrictive provisions, what are the basic rights of stockholders of a corporation?

2. Why is a preemptive right important?

3. Distinguish between common and preferred stock.

4. Why is the distinction between paid-in capital and retained earnings important?

5. Explain each of the following terms: authorized capital stock, unissued capital stock, issued capital stock, outstanding capital stock, and treasury stock.

6. What is meant by par value, and what is its significance to stockholders?

7. Describe the accounting for the issuance for cash of no-par value common stock at a price in excess of the stated value of the common stock.

8. Explain the difference between the proportional method and the incremental method of allocating the proceeds of lump sum sales of capital stock.

9. What are the different bases for stock valuation when assets other than cash are received for issued shares of stock?

10. Explain how underwriting costs and accounting and legal fees associated with the issuance of stock should be recorded.

11. For what reasons might a corporation purchase its own stock?

12. Discuss the propriety of showing:

  (a) Treasury stock as an asset.

  (b) "Gain" or "loss" on sale of treasury stock as additions to or deductions from income.

  (c) Dividends received on treasury stock as income.

13. What features or rights may alter the character of preferred stock?

14. Little Texas Inc. recently noted that its 4% preferred stock and 4% participating second preferred stock, which are both cumulative, have priority as to dividends up to 4% of their par value. Its participating preferred stock participates equally with the common stock in any dividends in excess of 4%. What is meant by the term participating? Cumulative?

15. Where in the financial statements is preferred stock normally reported?

16. List possible sources of additional paid-in capital.

17. Pleasant Dolls Inc. purchases 10,000 shares of its own previously issued $10 par common stock for $290,000. Assuming the shares are held in the treasury with intent to reissue, what effect does this transaction have on (a) net income, (b) total assets, (c) total paid-in capital, and (d) total stockholders' equity?

18. Indicate how each of the following accounts should be classified in the stockholders' equity section.

  (a) Common Stock

  (b) Retained Earnings

  (c) Paid-in Capital in Excess of Par Value

  (d) Treasury Stock

  (e) Paid-in Capital from Treasury Stock

  (f) Paid-in Capital in Excess of Stated Value

  (g) Preferred Stock

19. What factors influence the dividend policy of a company?

20. What are the principal considerations of a board of directors in making decisions involving dividend declarations? Discuss briefly.

21. Dividends are sometimes said to have been paid "out of retained earnings." What is the error, if any, in that statement?

22. Distinguish among: cash dividends, property dividends, liquidating dividends, and stock dividends.

23. Describe the accounting entry for a stock dividend, if any. Describe the accounting entry for a stock split, if any.

24. Stock splits and stock dividends may be used by a corporation to change the number of shares of its stock outstanding.

  (a) What is meant by a stock split effected in the form of a dividend?

  (b) From an accounting viewpoint, explain how the stock split effected in the form of a dividend differs from an ordinary stock dividend.

  (c) How should a stock dividend that has been declared but not yet issued be classified in a statement of financial position? Why?

25. The following comment appeared in the notes of Alvarado Corporation's annual report: "Such distributions, representing proceeds from the sale of James Buchanan, Inc. were paid in the form of partial liquidating dividends and were in lieu of a portion of the Company's ordinary cash dividends." How would a partial liquidating dividend be accounted for in the financial records?

26. This comment appeared in the annual report of Rodriguez Lopez Inc.: "The Company could pay cash or property dividends on the Class A common stock without paying cash or property dividends on the Class B common stock. But if the Company pays any cash or property dividends on the Class B common stock, it would be required to pay at least the same dividend on the Class A common stock." How is a property dividend accounted for in the financial records?

27. For what reasons might a company restrict a portion of its retained earnings?

28. How are restrictions of retained earnings reported?

*29. Aaron Burr Corp. had $100,000 of 10%, $20 par value preferred stock and 12,000 shares of $25 par value common stock outstanding throughout 2007.

  (a) Assuming that total dividends declared in 2007 were $88,000, and that the preferred stock is not cumulative but is fully participating, common stockholders should receive 2007 dividends of what amount?

  (b) Assuming that total dividends declared in 2007 were $88,000, and that the preferred stock is fully participating and cumulative with preferred dividends in arrears for 2006, preferred stockholders should receive 2007 dividends totaling what amount?

  (c) Assuming that total dividends declared in 2007 were $30,000, that cumulative nonparticipating preferred stock was issued on January 1, 2006, and that $5,000 of preferred dividends were declared and paid in 2006, the common stockholders should receive 2007 dividends totaling what amount?

BRIEF EXERCISES

(LO 3) **BE15-1** Lost Vikings Corporation issued 300 shares of $10 par value common stock for $4,100. Prepare Lost Vikings' journal entry.

(LO 3) **BE15-2** Shinobi Corporation issued 600 shares of no-par common stock for $10,200. Prepare Shinobi's journal entry if (a) the stock has no stated value, and (b) the stock has a stated value of $2 per share.

(LO 4, 9) **BE15-3** Lufia Corporation has the following account balances at December 31, 2007.

Common stock, $5 par value	$ 210,000
Treasury stock	90,000
Retained earnings	2,340,000
Paid-in capital in excess of par	1,320,000

Prepare Lufia's December 31, 2007, stockholders' equity section.

(LO 3) **BE15-4** Primal Rage Corporation issued 300 shares of $10 par value common stock and 100 shares of $50 par value preferred stock for a lump sum of $14,200. The common stock has a market value of $20 per share, and the preferred stock has a market value of $90 per share. Prepare the journal entry to record the issuance.

(LO 3) **BE15-5** On February 1, 2007, Mario Andretti Corporation issued 2,000 shares of its $5 par value common stock for land worth $31,000. Prepare the February 1, 2007, journal entry.

(LO 3) **BE15-6** Powerdrive Corporation issued 2,000 shares of its $10 par value common stock for $70,000. Powerdrive also incurred $1,500 of costs associated with issuing the stock. Prepare Powerdrive's journal entry to record the issuance of the company's stock.

(LO 4) **BE15-7** Maverick Inc. has outstanding 10,000 shares of $10 par value common stock. On July 1, 2007, Maverick reacquired 100 shares at $85 per share. On September 1, Maverick reissued 60 shares at $90 per share. On November 1, Maverick reissued 40 shares at $83 per share. Prepare Maverick's journal entries to record these transactions using the cost method.

(LO 4) **BE15-8** Power Rangers Corporation has outstanding 20,000 shares of $5 par value common stock. On August 1, 2007, Power Rangers reacquired 200 shares at $75 per share. On November 1, Power Rangers reissued the 200 shares at $70 per share. Power Rangers had no previous treasury stock transactions. Prepare Power Rangers' journal entries to record these transactions using the cost method.

(LO 5) **BE15-9** Popeye Corporation issued 450 shares of $100 par value preferred stock for $61,500. Prepare Popeye's journal entry.

(LO 6) **BE15-10** Micro Machines Inc. declared a cash dividend of $1.50 per share on its 2 million outstanding shares. The dividend was declared on August 1, payable on September 9 to all stockholders of record on August 15. Prepare all journal entries necessary on those three dates.

(LO 6, 7) **BE15-11** Ren Inc. owns shares of Stimpy Corporation stock classified as available-for-sale securities. At December 31, 2006, the available-for-sale securities were carried in Ren's accounting records at their cost of $875,000, which equals their market value. On September 21, 2007, when the market value of the securities was $1,400,000, Ren declared a property dividend whereby the Stimpy securities are to be distributed on October 23, 2007, to stockholders of record on October 8, 2007. Prepare all journal entries necessary on those three dates.

(LO 6, 7) **BE15-12** Radical Rex Mining Company declared, on April 20, a dividend of $700,000 payable on June 1. Of this amount, $125,000 is a return of capital. Prepare the April 20 and June 1 entries for Radical Rex.

(LO 8) **BE15-13** Mike Holmgren Football Corporation has outstanding 200,000 shares of $10 par value common stock. The corporation declares a 5% stock dividend when the fair value of the stock is $65 per share. Prepare the journal entries for Mike Holmgren Football Corporation for both the date of declaration and the date of distribution.

(LO 8) **BE15-14** Use the information from BE15-13, but assume Mike Holmgren Football Corporation declared a 100% stock dividend rather than a 5% stock dividend. Prepare the journal entries for both the date of declaration and the date of distribution.

(LO 10) *****BE15-15** Minnesota Fats Corporation has outstanding 10,000 shares of $100 par value, 8% preferred stock and 60,000 shares of $10 par value common stock. The preferred stock was issued in January 2006, and no dividends were declared in 2006 or 2007. In 2008, Minnesota Fats declares a cash dividend of $300,000. How will the dividend be shared by common and preferred stockholders if the preferred is (a) noncumulative and (b) cumulative?

EXERCISES

(LO 3) **E15-1** **(Recording the Issuances of Common Stock)** During its first year of operations, Collin Raye Corporation had the following transactions pertaining to its common stock.

Jan. 10	Issued 80,000 shares for cash at $6 per share.	
Mar. 1	Issued 5,000 shares to attorneys in payment of a bill for $35,000 for services rendered in helping the company to incorporate.	
July 1	Issued 30,000 shares for cash at $8 per share.	
Sept. 1	Issued 60,000 shares for cash at $10 per share.	

Instructions

(a) Prepare the journal entries for these transactions, assuming that the common stock has a par value of $5 per share.

(b) Prepare the journal entries for these transactions, assuming that the common stock is no par with a stated value of $3 per share.

(LO 3) **E15-2** **(Recording the Issuance of Common and Preferred Stock)** Kathleen Battle Corporation was organized on January 1, 2007. It is authorized to issue 10,000 shares of 8%, $100 par value preferred stock, and 500,000 shares of no par common stock with a stated value of $1 per share. The following stock transactions were completed during the first year.

Jan. 10	Issued 80,000 shares of common stock for cash at $5 per share.
Mar. 1	Issued 5,000 shares of preferred stock for cash at $108 per share.
Apr. 1	Issued 24,000 shares of common stock for land. The asking price of the land was $90,000; the fair market value of the land was $80,000.
May 1	Issued 80,000 shares of common stock for cash at $7 per share.
Aug. 1	Issued 10,000 shares of common stock to attorneys in payment of their bill of $50,000 for services rendered in helping the company organize.
Sept. 1	Issued 10,000 shares of common stock for cash at $9 per share.
Nov. 1	Issued 1,000 shares of preferred stock for cash at $112 per share.

Instructions

Prepare the journal entries to record the above transactions.

(LO 3) **E15-3** **(Stock Issued for Land)** Twenty-five thousand shares reacquired by Elixir Corporation for $53 per share were exchanged for undeveloped land that has an appraised value of $1,700,000. At the time of the exchange the common stock was trading at $62 per share on an organized exchange.

Instructions

(a) Prepare the journal entry to record the acquisition of land assuming that the purchase of the stock was originally recorded using the cost method.

(b) Briefly identify the possible alternatives (including those that are totally unacceptable) for quantifying the cost of the land and briefly support your choice.

(LO 3) **E15-4** **(Lump-Sum Sale of Stock with Bonds)** Faith Evans Corporation is a regional company which is an SEC registrant. The corporation's securities are thinly traded on NASDAQ (National Association of Securities Dealers Quotes). Faith Evans Corp. has issued 10,000 units. Each unit consists of a $500 par, 12% subordinated debenture and 10 shares of $5 par common stock. The investment banker has retained 400 units as the underwriting fee. The other 9,600 units were sold to outside investors for cash at $880 per unit. Prior to this sale the 2-week ask price of common stock was $40 per share. Twelve percent is a reasonable market yield for the debentures, and therefore the par value of the bonds is equal to the fair value.

Instructions

(a) Prepare the journal entry to record Evans' transaction, under the following conditions.

   (1) Employing the incremental method.

   (2) Employing the proportional method, assuming the recent price quote on the common stock reflects fair value.

(b) Briefly explain which method is, in your opinion, the better method.

(LO 3, 5) **E15-5** **(Lump-Sum Sales of Stock with Preferred Stock)** Dave Matthew Inc. issues 500 shares of $10 par value common stock and 100 shares of $100 par value preferred stock for a lump sum of $100,000.

Instructions
(a) Prepare the journal entry for the issuance when the market value of the common shares is $165 each and market value of the preferred is $230 each. (Round to nearest dollar.)
(b) Prepare the journal entry for the issuance when only the market value of the common stock is known and it is $170 per share.

(LO 3, 4) **E15-6** **(Stock Issuances and Repurchase)** Lindsey Hunter Corporation is authorized to issue 50,000 shares of $5 par value common stock. During 2007, Lindsey Hunter took part in the following selected transactions.

1. Issued 5,000 shares of stock at $45 per share, less costs related to the issuance of the stock totaling $7,000.
2. Issued 1,000 shares of stock for land appraised at $50,000. The stock was actively traded on a national stock exchange at approximately $46 per share on the date of issuance.
3. Purchased 500 shares of treasury stock at $43 per share. The treasury shares purchased were issued in 2003 at $40 per share.

Instructions
(a) Prepare the journal entry to record item 1.
(b) Prepare the journal entry to record item 2.
(c) Prepare the journal entry to record item 3 using the cost method.

(LO 4) **E15-7** **(Effect of Treasury Stock Transactions on Financials)** Joe Dumars Company has outstanding 40,000 shares of $5 par common stock which had been issued at $30 per share. Joe Dumars then entered into the following transactions.

1. Purchased 5,000 treasury shares at $45 per share.
2. Resold 2,000 of the treasury shares at $49 per share.
3. Resold 500 of the treasury shares at $40 per share.

Instructions
Use the following code to indicate the effect each of the three transactions has on the financial statement categories listed in the table below, assuming Joe Dumars Company uses the cost method: (I = Increase; D = Decrease; NE = No effect).

#	Assets	Liabilities	Stockholders' Equity	Paid-in Capital	Retained Earnings	Net Income
1						
2						
3						

(LO 3, 10) **E15-8** **(Preferred Stock Entries and Dividends)** Otis Thorpe Corporation has 10,000 shares of $100 par value, 8%, preferred stock and 50,000 shares of $10 par value common stock outstanding at December 31, 2007.

Instructions
Answer the questions in each of the following independent situations.
(a) If the preferred stock is cumulative and dividends were last paid on the preferred stock on December 31, 2004, what are the dividends in arrears that should be reported on the December 31, 2007, balance sheet? How should these dividends be reported?
(b) If the preferred stock is convertible into seven shares of $10 par value common stock and 4,000 shares are converted, what entry is required for the conversion assuming the preferred stock was issued at par value?
(c) If the preferred stock was issued at $107 per share, how should the preferred stock be reported in the stockholders' equity section?

(LO 3, 4) **E15-9 (Correcting Entries for Equity Transactions)** Pistons Inc. recently hired a new accountant with extensive experience in accounting for partnerships. Because of the pressure of the new job, the accountant was unable to review what he had learned earlier about corporation accounting. During the first month, he made the following entries for the corporation's capital stock.

May 2	Cash		192,000	
	Capital Stock			192,000
	(Issued 12,000 shares of $5 par value common stock at $16 per share)			
10	Cash		600,000	
	Capital Stock			600,000
	(Issued 10,000 shares of $30 par value preferred stock at $60 per share)			
15	Capital Stock		15,000	
	Cash			15,000
	(Purchased 1,000 shares of common stock for the treasury at $15 per share)			
31	Cash		8,500	
	Capital Stock			5,000
	Gain on Sale of Stock			3,500
	(Sold 500 shares of treasury stock at $17 per share)			

Instructions

On the basis of the explanation for each entry, prepare the entries that should have been made for the capital stock transactions.

(LO 3, 4) **E15-10 (Analysis of Equity Data and Equity Section Preparation)** For a recent 2-year period, the balance sheet of Santana Dotson Company showed the following stockholders' equity data at December 31 in millions.

	2007	2006
Additional paid-in capital	$ 931	$ 817
Common stock—par	545	540
Retained earnings	7,167	5,226
Treasury stock	1,564	918
Total stockholders' equity	$7,079	$5,665
Common stock shares issued	218	216
Common stock shares authorized	500	500
Treasury stock shares	34	27

Instructions

(a) Answer the following questions.
   (1) What is the par value of the common stock?
   (2) What is the cost per share of treasury stock at December 31, 2007, and at December 31, 2006?
(b) Prepare the stockholders' equity section at December 31, 2007.

(LO 7, 8) **E15-11 (Equity Items on the Balance Sheet)** The following are selected transactions that may affect stockholders' equity.

1. Recorded accrued interest earned on a note receivable.
2. Declared a cash dividend.
3. Declared and distributed a stock split.
4. Recorded a retained earnings restriction.
5. Recorded the expiration of insurance coverage that was previously recorded as prepaid insurance.
6. Paid the cash dividend declared in item 2 above.
7. Recorded accrued interest expense on a note payable.
8. Declared a stock dividend.
9. Distributed the stock dividend declared in item 8.

Instructions

In the table on the next page, indicate the effect each of the nine transactions has on the financial statement elements listed. Use the following code:

| I = Increase | | D = Decrease | | NE = No effect | | |

Item	Assets	Liabilities	Stockholders' Equity	Paid-in Capital	Retained Earnings	Net Income

(LO 7, 8) **E15-12** **(Cash Dividend and Liquidating Dividend)** Lotoya Davis Corporation has ten million shares of common stock issued and outstanding. On June 1 the board of directors voted an 80 cents per share cash dividend to stockholders of record as of June 14, payable June 30.

Instructions

(a) Prepare the journal entry for each of the dates above assuming the dividend represents a distribution of earnings.

(b) How would the entry differ if the dividend were a liquidating dividend?

(LO 8) **E15-13** **(Stock Split and Stock Dividend)** The common stock of Alexander Hamilton Inc. is currently selling at $120 per share. The directors wish to reduce the share price and increase share volume prior to a new issue. The per share par value is $10; book value is $70 per share. Nine million shares are issued and outstanding.

Instructions

Prepare the necessary journal entries assuming the following.

(a) The board votes a 2-for-1 stock split.

(b) The board votes a 100% stock dividend.

(c) Briefly discuss the accounting and securities market differences between these two methods of increasing the number of shares outstanding.

(LO 8) **E15-14** **(Entries for Stock Dividends and Stock Splits)** The stockholders' equity accounts of G.K. Chesterton Company have the following balances on December 31, 2007.

Common stock, $10 par, 300,000 shares issued and outstanding	$3,000,000
Paid-in capital in excess of par	1,200,000
Retained earnings	5,600,000

Shares of G.K. Chesterton Company stock are currently selling on the Midwest Stock Exchange at $37.

Instructions

Prepare the appropriate journal entries for each of the following cases.

(a) A stock dividend of 5% is declared and issued.

(b) A stock dividend of 100% is declared and issued.

(c) A 2-for-1 stock split is declared and issued.

(LO 7, 8) **E15-15** **(Dividend Entries)** The following data were taken from the balance sheet accounts of Masefield Corporation on December 31, 2006.

Current assets	$540,000
Investments	624,000
Common stock (par value $10)	500,000
Paid-in capital in excess of par	150,000
Retained earnings	840,000

Instructions

Prepare the required journal entries for the following unrelated items.

(a) A 5% stock dividend is declared and distributed at a time when the market value of the shares is $39 per share.

(b) The par value of the capital stock is reduced to $2 with a 5-for-1 stock split.

(c) A dividend is declared January 5, 2007, and paid January 25, 2007, in bonds held as an investment. The bonds have a book value of $100,000 and a fair market value of $135,000.

(LO 6, 7, 8) **E15-16** **(Computation of Retained Earnings)** The following information has been taken from the ledger accounts of Isaac Stern Corporation.

Total income since incorporation	$317,000
Total cash dividends paid	60,000
Total value of stock dividends distributed	30,000
Gains on treasury stock transactions	18,000
Unamortized discount on bonds payable	32,000

Instructions
Determine the current balance of retained earnings.

(LO 9) **E15-17** **(Stockholders' Equity Section)** Bruno Corporation's post-closing trial balance at December 31, 2007, was as follows.

BRUNO CORPORATION POST-CLOSING TRIAL BALANCE DECEMBER 31, 2007		
	Dr.	Cr.
Accounts payable		$ 310,000
Accounts receivable	$ 480,000	
Accumulated depreciation—building and equipment		185,000
Additional paid-in capital—common		
In excess of par value		1,300,000
From sale of treasury stock		160,000
Allowance for doubtful accounts		30,000
Bonds payable		300,000
Building and equipment	1,450,000	
Cash	190,000	
Common stock ($1 par value)		200,000
Dividends payable on preferred stock—cash		4,000
Inventories	560,000	
Land	400,000	
Preferred stock ($50 par value)		500,000
Prepaid expenses	40,000	
Retained earnings		301,000
Treasury stock—common at cost	170,000	
Totals	$3,290,000	$3,290,000

At December 31, 2007, Bruno had the following number of common and preferred shares.

	Common	Preferred
Authorized	600,000	60,000
Issued	200,000	10,000
Outstanding	190,000	10,000

The dividends on preferred stock are $4 cumulative. In addition, the preferred stock has a preference in liquidation of $50 per share.

Instructions
Prepare the stockholders' equity section of Bruno's balance sheet at December 31, 2007.

(AICPA adapted)

(LO 4, 7, 8) **E15-18** **(Dividends and Stockholders' Equity Section)** Anne Cleves Company reported the following amounts in the stockholders' equity section of its December 31, 2006, balance sheet.

Preferred stock, 10%, $100 par (10,000 shares authorized, 2,000 shares issued)	$200,000
Common stock, $5 par (100,000 shares authorized, 20,000 shares issued)	100,000
Additional paid-in capital	125,000
Retained earnings	450,000
Total	$875,000

During 2007, Cleves took part in the following transactions concerning stockholders' equity.

1. Paid the annual 2006 $10 per share dividend on preferred stock and a $2 per share dividend on common stock. These dividends had been declared on December 31, 2006.
2. Purchased 1,700 shares of its own outstanding common stock for $40 per share. Cleves uses the cost method.
3. Reissued 700 treasury shares for land valued at $30,000.
4. Issued 500 shares of preferred stock at $105 per share.
5. Declared a 10% stock dividend on the outstanding common stock when the stock is selling for $45 per share.
6. Issued the stock dividend.
7. Declared the annual 2007 $10 per share dividend on preferred stock and the $2 per share dividend on common stock. These dividends are payable in 2008.

Instructions
(a) Prepare journal entries to record the transactions described above.
(b) Prepare the December 31, 2007, stockholders' equity section. Assume 2007 net income was $330,000.

(LO 9) **E15-19 (Comparison of Alternative Forms of Financing)** Shown below is the liabilities and stockholders' equity section of the balance sheet for Jana Kingston Company and Mary Ann Benson Company. Each has assets totaling $4,200,000.

Jana Kingston Co.		Mary Ann Benson Co.	
Current liabilities	$ 300,000	Current liabilities	$ 600,000
Long-term debt, 10%	1,200,000	Common stock ($20 par)	2,900,000
Common stock ($20 par)	2,000,000	Retained earnings (Cash	
Retained earnings (Cash		dividends, $328,000)	700,000
dividends, $220,000)	700,000		
	$4,200,000		$4,200,000

For the year each company has earned the same income before interest and taxes.

	Jana Kingston Co.	Mary Ann Benson Co.
Income before interest and taxes	$1,200,000	$1,200,000
Interest expense	120,000	–0–
	1,080,000	1,200,000
Income taxes (45%)	486,000	540,000
Net income	$ 594,000	$ 660,000

At year end, the market price of Kingston's stock was $101 per share, and Benson's was $63.50.

Instructions
(a) Which company is more profitable in terms of return on total assets?
(b) Which company is more profitable in terms of return on stockholders' equity?
(c) Which company has the greater net income per share of stock? Neither company issued or reacquired shares during the year.
(d) From the point of view of net income, is it advantageous to the stockholders of Jana Kingston Co. to have the long-term debt outstanding? Why?
(e) What is the book value per share for each company?

(LO 9) **E15-20 (Trading on the Equity Analysis)** Presented below is information from the annual report of Emporia Plastics, Inc.

Operating income	$ 532,150
Bond interest expense	135,000
	397,150
Income taxes	183,432
Net income	$ 213,718
Bonds payable	$1,000,000
Common stock	875,000
Retained earnings	375,000

Instructions

(a) Compute the return on common stock equity and the rate of interest paid on bonds. (Assume balances for debt and equity accounts approximate averages for the year.)

(b) Is Emporia Plastics Inc. trading on the equity successfully? Explain.

(LO 10) *E15-21 (Preferred Dividends) The outstanding capital stock of Edna Millay Corporation consists of 2,000 shares of $100 par value, 8% preferred, and 5,000 shares of $50 par value common.

Instructions

Assuming that the company has retained earnings of $90,000, all of which is to be paid out in dividends, and that preferred dividends were not paid during the 2 years preceding the current year, state how much each class of stock should receive under each of the following conditions.

(a) The preferred stock is noncumulative and nonparticipating.

(b) The preferred stock is cumulative and nonparticipating.

(c) The preferred stock is cumulative and participating. (Round dividend rate percentages to four decimal places.)

(LO 10) *E15-22 (Preferred Dividends) Matt Schmidt Company's ledger shows the following balances on December 31, 2007.

7% Preferred stock—$10 par value, outstanding 20,000 shares	$ 200,000
Common stock—$100 par value, outstanding 30,000 shares	3,000,000
Retained earnings	630,000

Instructions

Assuming that the directors decide to declare total dividends in the amount of $366,000, determine how much each class of stock should receive under each of the conditions stated below. One year's dividends are in arrears on the preferred stock.

(a) The preferred stock is cumulative and fully participating.

(b) The preferrred stock is noncumulative and nonparticipating.

(c) The preferred stock is noncumulative and is participating in distributions in excess of a 10% dividend rate on the common stock.

(LO 10) *E15-23 (Preferred Stock Dividends) Cajun Company has outstanding 2,500 shares of $100 par, 6% preferred stock and 15,000 shares of $10 par value common. The schedule on the next page shows the amount of dividends paid out over the last 4 years.

Instructions

Allocate the dividends to each type of stock under assumptions (a) and (b). Express your answers in per-share amounts using the format shown below.

		Assumptions			
		(a) Preferred, noncumulative, and nonparticipating		(b) Preferred, cumulative, and fully participating	
Year	Paid-out	Preferred	Common	Preferred	Common
2005	$13,000				
2006	$26,000				
2007	$57,000				
2008	$76,000				

(LO 10) *E15-24 (Computation of Book Value per Share) Morgan Sondgeroth Inc. began operations in January 2005 and reported the following results for each of its 3 years of operations.

2005 $260,000 net loss   2006 $40,000 net loss   2007 $800,000 net income

At December 31, 2007, Morgan Sondgeroth Inc. capital accounts were as follows.

8% cumulative preferred stock, par value $100; authorized, issued, and outstanding 5,000 shares	$500,000
Common stock, par value $1.00; authorized 1,000,000 shares; issued and outstanding 750,000 shares	$750,000

Morgan Sondgeroth Inc. has never paid a cash or stock dividend. There has been no change in the capital accounts since Sondgeroth began operations. The state law permits dividends only from retained earnings.

Instructions

    (a) Compute the book value of the common stock at December 31, 2007.

    (b) Compute the book value of the common stock at December 31, 2007, assuming that the preferred stock has a liquidating value of $106 per share.

> **See the book's website, www.wiley.com/college/kieso, for Additional Exercises.**

PROBLEMS

(LO 3, 4, 9)   **P15-1 (Equity Transactions and Statement Preparation)** On January 5, 2007, Drabek Corporation received a charter granting the right to issue 5,000 shares of $100 par value, 8% cumulative and nonparticipating preferred stock, and 50,000 shares of $5 par value common stock. It then completed these transactions.

Jan.	11	Issued 20,000 shares of common stock at $16 per share.
Feb.	1	Issued to Robb Nen Corp. 4,000 shares of preferred stock for the following assets: machinery with a fair market value of $50,000; a factory building with a fair market value of $110,000; and land with an appraised value of $270,000.
July	29	Purchased 1,800 shares of common stock at $19 per share. (Use cost method.)
Aug.	10	Sold the 1,800 treasury shares at $14 per share.
Dec.	31	Declared a $0.25 per share cash dividend on the common stock and declared the preferred dividend.
Dec.	31	Closed the Income Summary account. There was a $175,700 net income.

Instructions

    (a) Record the journal entries for the transactions listed above.

    (b) Prepare the stockholders' equity section of Drabek Corporation's balance sheet as of December 31, 2007.

(LO 4, 9)   **P15-2 (Treasury Stock Transactions and Presentation)** Andruw Jones Company had the following stockholders' equity as of January 1, 2007.

Common stock, $5 par value, 20,000 shares issued	$100,000
Paid-in capital in excess of par	300,000
Retained earnings	320,000
Total stockholders' equity	$720,000

During 2007, the following transactions occurred.

Feb.	1	Jones repurchased 2,000 shares of treasury stock at a price of $18 per share.
Mar.	1	800 shares of treasury stock repurchased above were reissued at $17 per share.
Mar.	18	500 shares of treasury stock repurchased above were reissued at $14 per share.
Apr.	22	600 shares of treasury stock repurchased above were reissued at $20 per share.

Instructions

    (a) Prepare the journal entries to record the treasury stock transactions in 2007, assuming Jones uses the cost method.

    (b) Prepare the stockholders' equity section as of April 30, 2007. Net income for the first 4 months of 2007 was $110,000.

(LO 3, 4, 7, 8)   **P15-3 (Equity Transactions and Statement Preparation)** Amado Company has two classes of capital stock outstanding: 8%, $20 par preferred and $5 par common. At December 31, 2007, the following accounts were included in stockholders' equity.

Preferred Stock, 150,000 shares	$ 3,000,000
Common Stock, 2,000,000 shares	10,000,000
Paid-in Capital in Excess of Par—Preferred	200,000
Paid-in Capital in Excess of Par—Common	27,000,000
Retained Earnings	4,500,000

The following transactions affected stockholders' equity during 2007.

Jan.	1	25,000 shares of preferred stock issued at $22 per share.
Feb.	1	40,000 shares of common stock issued at $20 per share.
June	1	2-for-1 stock split (par value reduced to $2.50).
July	1	30,000 shares of common treasury stock purchased at $9 per share. Amado uses the cost method.

Sept. 15   10,000 shares of treasury stock reissued at $11 per share.

Dec. 31   Net income is $2,100,000.

Dec. 31   The preferred dividend is declared, and a common dividend of 50¢ per share is declared.

Instructions

Prepare the stockholders' equity section for Amado Company at December 31, 2007. Show all supporting computations.

(LO 3, 5)   **P15-4**   **(Stock Transactions—Lump Sum)**   Matsui Corporation's charter authorized issuance of 100,000 shares of $10 par value common stock and 50,000 shares of $50 preferred stock. The following transactions involving the issuance of shares of stock were completed. Each transaction is independent of the others.

1. Issued a $10,000, 9% bond payable at par and gave as a bonus one share of preferred stock, which at that time was selling for $106 a share.
2. Issued 500 shares of common stock for machinery. The machinery had been appraised at $7,100; the seller's book value was $6,200. The most recent market price of the common stock is $15 a share.
3. Issued 375 shares of common and 100 shares of preferred for a lump sum amounting to $11,300. The common had been selling at $14 and the preferred at $65.
4. Issued 200 shares of common and 50 shares of preferred for furniture and fixtures. The common had a fair market value of $16 per share; the furniture and fixtures have a fair value of $6,200.

Instructions

Record the transactions listed above in journal entry form.

(LO 4)   **P15-5**   **(Treasury Stock—Cost Method)**   Before Polska Corporation engages in the treasury stock transactions listed below, its general ledger reflects, among others, the following account balances (par value of its stock is $30 per share).

Paid-in Capital in Excess of Par	Common Stock	Retained Earnings
$99,000	$270,000	$80,000

Instructions

Record the treasury stock transactions (given below) under the cost method of handling treasury stock; use the FIFO method for purchase-sale purposes.

(a) Bought 380 shares of treasury stock at $39 per share.

(b) Bought 300 shares of treasury stock at $43 per share.

(c) Sold 350 shares of treasury stock at $42 per share.

(d) Sold 120 shares of treasury stock at $38 per share.

(LO 4, 7, 9)   **P15-6**   **(Treasury Stock—Cost Method—Equity Section Preparation)**   Constantine Company has the following stockholders' equity accounts at December 31, 2006.

Common Stock—$100 par value, authorized 8,000 shares	$480,000
Retained Earnings	294,000

Instructions

(a) Prepare entries in journal form to record the following transactions, which took place during 2007.

     (1) 240 shares of outstanding stock were purchased at $97 per share. (These are to be accounted for using the cost method.)

     (2) A $20 per share cash dividend was declared.

     (3) The dividend declared in No. 2 above was paid.

     (4) The treasury shares purchased in No. 1 above were resold at $102 per share.

     (5) 500 shares of outstanding stock were purchased at $103 per share.

     (6) 330 of the shares purchased in No. 5 above were resold at $96 per share.

(b) Prepare the stockholders' equity section of Constantine Company's balance sheet after giving effect to these transactions, assuming that the net income for 2007 was $94,000. State law requires restriction of retained earnings for the amount of treasury stock.

(LO 4, 7)   **P15-7**   **(Cash Dividend Entries)**   The books of John Dos Passos Corporation carried the following account balances as of December 31, 2006.

Cash	$ 195,000
Preferred stock, 6% cumulative, nonparticipating, $50 par	200,000
Common stock, no par value, 300,000 shares issued	1,500,000
Paid-in capital in excess of par (preferred)	150,000
Treasury stock (common 4,200 shares at cost)	33,600
Retained earnings	105,000

The company decided not to pay any dividends in 2006.

The board of directors, at their annual meeting on December 21, 2007, declared the following: "The current year dividends shall be 6% on the preferred and $.30 per share on the common. The dividends in arrears shall be paid by issuing 1,500 shares of treasury stock." At the date of declaration, the preferred is selling at $80 per share, and the common at $8 per share. Net income for 2007 is estimated at $77,000.

Instructions

(a) Prepare the journal entries required for the dividend declaration and payment, assuming that they occur simultaneously.

(b) Could John Dos Passos Corporation give the preferred stockholders 2 years' dividends and common stockholders a 30 cents per share dividend, all in cash?

(LO 7, 8)

P15-8 (Dividends and Splits) Gutsy Company provides you with the following condensed balance sheet information.

Assets		Liabilities and Stockholders' Equity		
Current assets	$ 40,000	Current and long-term liabilities		$100,000
Investments in ABC stock		Stockholders' equity		
(10,000 shares at cost)	60,000	Common stock ($2 par)	$ 20,000	
Equipment (net)	250,000	Paid-in capital in excess of par	110,000	
Intangibles	60,000	Retained earnings	180,000	310,000
Total assets	$410,000	Total liabilities and stockholders' equity		$410,000

Instructions

For each transaction below, indicate the dollar impact (if any) on the following five items: (1) total assets, (2) common stock, (3) paid-in capital in excess of par, (4) retained earnings, and (5) stockholders' equity. (Each situation is independent.)

(a) Gutsy declares and pays a $0.50 per share cash dividend.

(b) Gutsy declares and issues a 10% stock dividend when the market price of the stock is $14 per share.

(c) Gutsy declares and issues a 40% stock dividend when the market price of the stock is $15 per share.

(d) Gutsy declares and distributes a property dividend. Gutsy gives one share of ABC stock for every two shares of Gutsy Company stock held. ABC is selling for $10 per share on the date the property dividend is declared.

(e) Gutsy declares a 2-for-1 stock split and issues new shares.

(LO 3, 4, 7, 9)

P15-9 (Stockholders' Equity Section of Balance Sheet) The following is a summary of all relevant transactions of Jackson Day Corporation since it was organized in 2007.

In 2007, 15,000 shares were authorized and 7,000 shares of common stock ($50 par value) were issued at a price of $57. In 2008, 1,000 shares were issued as a stock dividend when the stock was selling for $62. Three hundred shares of common stock were bought in 2009 at a cost of $66 per share. These 300 shares are still in the company treasury.

In 2008, 10,000 preferred shares were authorized and the company issued 4,000 of them ($100 par value) at $113. Some of the preferred stock was reacquired by the company and later reissued for $4,700 more than it cost the company.

The corporation has earned a total of $610,000 in net income after income taxes and paid out a total of $312,600 in cash dividends since incorporation.

Instructions

Prepare the stockholders' equity section of the balance sheet in proper form for Jackson Day Corporation as of December 31, 2009. Account for treasury stock using the cost method.

(LO 8)

P15-10 (Stock Dividends and Stock Split) Jenny Dill Inc. $10 par common stock is selling for $120 per share. Five million shares are currently issued and outstanding. The board of directors wishes to stimulate interest in Jenny Dill common stock before a forthcoming stock issue but does not wish to distribute capital at this time. The board also believes that too many adjustments to the stockholders' equity section, especially retained earnings, might discourage potential investors.

The board has considered three options for stimulating interest in the stock:

1. A 20% stock dividend.
2. A 100% stock dividend.
3. A 2-for-1 stock split.

Instructions

Acting as financial advisor to the board, you have been asked to report briefly on each option and, considering the board's wishes, make a recommendation. Discuss the effects of each of the foregoing options.

(LO 7, 8) **P15-11 (Stock and Cash Dividends)** Gul Ducat Corporation has outstanding 2,000,000 shares of common stock of a par value of $10 each. The balance in its retained earnings account at January 1, 2007, was $24,000,000, and it then had Additional Paid-in Capital of $5,000,000. During 2007, the company's net income was $5,700,000. A cash dividend of $0.60 a share was paid June 30, 2007, and a 6% stock dividend was declared on November 30, 2007, and distributed to stockholders of record at the close of business on December 31, 2007. You have been asked to advise on the proper accounting treatment of the stock dividend.

The existing stock of the company is quoted on a national stock exchange. The market price of the stock has been as follows.

October 31, 2007	$31
November 30, 2007	$35
December 31, 2007	$38

Instructions

(a) Prepare the journal entry to record the cash dividend.

(b) Prepare the journal entry to record the stock dividend.

(c) Prepare the stockholders' equity section (including schedules of retained earnings and additional paid-in capital) of the balance sheet of Gul Ducat Corporation for the year 2007 on the basis of the foregoing information. Draft a note to the financial statements setting forth the basis of the accounting for the stock dividend, and add separately appropriate comments or explanations regarding the basis chosen.

(LO 3, 4, 7, 8, 9) **P15-12 (Analysis and Classification of Equity Transactions)** Ohio Company was formed on July 1, 2003. It was authorized to issue 300,000 shares of $10 par value common stock and 100,000 shares of 8% $25 par value, cumulative and nonparticipating preferred stock. Ohio Company has a July 1–June 30 fiscal year.

The following information relates to the stockholders' equity accounts of Ohio Company.

Common Stock

Prior to the 2005–06 fiscal year, Ohio Company had 110,000 shares of outstanding common stock issued as follows.

1. 95,000 shares were issued for cash on July 1, 2003, at $31 per share.

2. On July 24, 2003, 5,000 shares were exchanged for a plot of land which cost the seller $70,000 in 1997 and had an estimated market value of $220,000 on July 24, 2003.

3. 10,000 shares were issued on March 1, 2004, for $42 per share.

During the 2005–06 fiscal year, the following transactions regarding common stock took place.

November 30, 2005	Ohio purchased 2,000 shares of its own stock on the open market at $39 per share. Ohio uses the cost method for treasury stock.
December 15, 2005	Ohio declared a 5% stock dividend for stockholders of record on January 15, 2006, to be issued on January 31, 2006. Ohio was having a liquidity problem and could not afford a cash dividend at the time. Ohio's common stock was selling at $52 per share on December 15, 2005.
June 20, 2006	Ohio sold 500 shares of its own common stock that it had purchased on November 30, 2005, for $21,000.

Preferred Stock

Ohio issued 50,000 shares of preferred stock at $44 per share on July 1, 2004.

Cash Dividends

Ohio has followed a schedule of declaring cash dividends in December and June, with payment being made to stockholders of record in the following month. The cash dividends which have been declared since inception of the company through June 30, 2006, are shown below.

Declaration Date	Common Stock	Preferred Stock
12/15/04	$0.30 per share	$1.00 per share
6/15/05	$0.30 per share	$1.00 per share
12/15/05	—	$1.00 per share

No cash dividends were declared during June 2006 due to the company's liquidity problems.

Retained Earnings

As of June 30, 2005, Ohio's retained earnings account had a balance of $690,000. For the fiscal year ending June 30, 2006, Ohio reported net income of $40,000.

Instructions

Prepare the stockholders' equity section of the balance sheet, including appropriate notes, for Ohio Company as of June 30, 2006, as it should appear in its annual report to the shareholders.

(CMA adapted)

CONCEPTS FOR ANALYSIS

CA15-1 (Preemptive Rights and Dilution of Ownership) Alvarado Computer Company is a small, closely held corporation. Eighty percent of the stock is held by Eduardo Alvarado, president. Of the remainder, 10% is held by members of his family and 10% by Shaunda Jones, a former officer who is now retired. The balance sheet of the company at June 30, 2007, was substantially as shown below.

Assets		Liabilities and Stockholders' Equity	
Cash	$ 22,000	Current liabilities	$ 50,000
Other	450,000	Capital stock	250,000
	$472,000	Retained earnings	172,000
			$472,000

Additional authorized capital stock of $300,000 par value had never been issued. To strengthen the cash position of the company, Eduardo Alvarado issued capital stock with a par value of $100,000 to himself at par for cash. At the next stockholders' meeting, Jones objected and claimed that her interests had been injured.

Instructions

(a) Which stockholder's right was ignored in the issue of shares to Eduardo Alvarado?

(b) How may the damage to Jones' interests be repaired most simply?

(c) If Eduardo Alvarado offered Jones a personal cash settlement and they agreed to employ you as an impartial arbitrator to determine the amount, what settlement would you propose? Present your calculations with sufficient explanation to satisfy both parties.

CA15-2 (Issuance of Stock for Land) Crosby Corporation is planning to issue 3,000 shares of its own $10 par value common stock for two acres of land to be used as a building site.

Instructions

(a) What general rule should be applied to determine the amount at which the land should be recorded?

(b) Under what circumstances should this transaction be recorded at the fair market value of the land?

(c) Under what circumstances should this transaction be recorded at the fair market value of the stock issued?

(d) Assume Crosby intentionally records this transaction at an amount greater than the fair market value of the land and the stock. Discuss this situation.

CA15-3 (Conceptual Issues—Equity) Statements of Financial Accounting Concepts set forth financial accounting and reporting objectives and fundamentals that will be used by the Financial Accounting Standards Board in developing standards. *Concepts Statement No. 6* defines various elements of financial statements.

Instructions

Answer the following questions based on *SFAC No. 6*.

(a) Define and discuss the term "equity."

(b) What transactions or events change owners' equity?

(c) Define "investments by owners" and provide examples of this type of transaction. What financial statement element other than equity is typically affected by owner investments?

(d) Define "distributions to owners" and provide examples of this type of transaction. What financial statement element other than equity is typically affected by distributions?

(e) What are examples of changes within owners' equity that do not change the total amount of owners' equity?

CA15-4 (Stock Dividends and Splits) The directors of Amman Corporation are considering the issuance of a stock dividend. They have asked you to discuss the proposed action by answering the following questions.

Instructions

(a) What is a stock dividend? How is a stock dividend distinguished from a stock split (1) from a legal standpoint, and (2) from an accounting standpoint?

(b) For what reasons does a corporation usually declare a stock dividend? A stock split?

(c) Discuss the amount, if any, of retained earnings to be capitalized in connection with a stock dividend.

(AICPA adapted)

CA15-5 (Stock Dividends) Kitakyushu Inc., a client, is considering the authorization of a 10% common stock dividend to common stockholders. The financial vice president of Kitakyushu wishes to discuss the accounting implications of such an authorization with you before the next meeting of the board of directors.

Instructions

(a) The first topic the vice president wishes to discuss is the nature of the stock dividend to the recipient. Discuss the case against considering the stock dividend as income to the recipient.

(b) The other topic for discussion is the propriety of issuing the stock dividend to all "stockholders of record" or to "stockholders of record exclusive of shares held in the name of the corporation as treasury stock." Discuss the case against issuing stock dividends on treasury shares.

(AICPA adapted)

CA15-6 (Stock Dividend, Cash Dividend, and Treasury Stock) AROD Company has 30,000 shares of $10 par value common stock authorized and 20,000 shares issued and outstanding. On August 15, 2007, AROD purchased 1,000 shares of treasury stock for $16 per share. AROD uses the cost method to account for treasury stock. On September 14, 2007, AROD sold 500 shares of the treasury stock for $20 per share.

In October 2007, AROD declared and distributed 1,950 shares as a stock dividend from unissued shares when the market value of the common stock was $21 per share.

On December 20, 2007, AROD declared a $1 per share cash dividend, payable on January 10, 2008, to shareholders of record on December 31, 2007.

Instructions

(a) How should AROD account for the purchase and sale of the treasury stock, and how should the treasury stock be presented in the balance sheet at December 31, 2007?

(b) How should AROD account for the stock dividend, and how would it affect the stockholders' equity at December 31, 2007? Why?

(c) How should AROD account for the cash dividend, and how would it affect the balance sheet at December 31, 2007? Why?

(AICPA adapted)

CA15-7 (Treasury Stock) Jean Loptien, president of Sycamore Corporation, is concerned about several large stockholders who have been very vocal lately in their criticisms of her leadership. She thinks they might mount a campaign to have her removed as the corporation's CEO. She decides that buying them out by purchasing their shares could eliminate them as opponents, and she is confident they would accept a "good" offer. Loptien knows the corporation's cash position is decent, so it has the cash to complete the transaction. She also knows the purchase of these shares will increase earnings per share, which should make other investors quite happy. (Earnings per share is calculated by dividing net income available for the common shareholders by the weighted average number of shares outstanding. Therefore, if the number of shares outstanding is decreased by purchasing treasury shares, earnings per share increases.)

Instructions

Answer the following questions.

(a) Who are the stakeholders in this situation?

(b) What are the ethical issues involved?

(c) Should Loptien authorize the transaction?

USING YOUR JUDGMENT

Financial Reporting Problem

P&G **The Procter & Gamble Company (P&G)**

The financial statements of **P&G** are presented in Appendix 5B or can be accessed on the KWW website.

Instructions

Refer to these financial statements and the accompanying notes to answer the following questions.

(a) What is the par or stated value of P&G's preferred stock?

(b) What is the par or stated value of P&G's common stock?

(c) What percentage of P&G's authorized common stock was issued at June 30, 2004?

(d) How many shares of common stock were outstanding at June 30, 2004, and June 30, 2003?

(e) What was the dollar amount effect of the cash dividends on P&G's stockholders' equity?

(f) What is P&G's rate of return on common stock equity for 2004 and 2003?

(g) What is P&G's payout ratio for 2004 and 2003?

(h) What was the market price range (high/low) of P&G's common stock during the quarter ended June 30, 2004?

Financial Statement Analysis Case

Case 1: Kellogg Corporation

Kellogg Corporation is the world's leading producer of ready-to-eat cereal products. In recent years the company has taken numerous steps aimed at improving its profitability and earnings per share. Presented below are some basic facts for Kellogg Corporation.

(all dollars in millions)	2004	2003
Net sales	$9,614	$8,812
Net earnings	891	787
Total assets	10,790	10,143
Total liabilities	8,533	8,699
Common stock, $0.25 par value	104	104
Capital in excess of par value		25
Retained earnings	2,701	2,248
Treasury stock, at cost	108	204
Number of shares outstanding (in millions)	413	410

Instructions

(a) What are some of the reasons that management purchases its own stock?

(b) Explain how earnings per share might be affected by treasury stock transactions.

(c) Calculate the ratio of debt to total assets for 2003 and 2004, and discuss the implications of the change.

Case 2: Wiebold, Incorporated

The following note related to stockholders' equity was reported in **Wiebold, Inc.**'s annual report.

On February 1, the Board of Directors declared a 3-for-2 stock split, distributed on February 22 to shareholders of record on February 10. Accordingly, all numbers of common shares, except unissued shares and treasury shares, and all per share data have been restated to reflect this stock split.

On the basis of amounts declared and paid, the annualized quarterly dividends per share were $0.80 in the current year and $0.75 in the prior year.

Instructions

(a) What is the significance of the date of record and the date of distribution?

(b) Why might Weibold have declared a 3-for-2 for stock split?

(c) What impact does Wiebold's stock split have on (1) total stockholders' equity, (2) total par value, (3) outstanding shares, and (4) book value per share?

Comparative Analysis Case

The Coca-Cola Company and PepsiCo, Inc.

Instructions

Go to the KWW website and use information found there to answer the following questions related to **The Coca-Cola Company** and **PepsiCo, Inc.**

(a) What is the par or stated value of Coca-Cola's and PepsiCo's common or capital stock?

(b) What percentage of authorized shares was issued by Coca-Cola at December 31, 2004, and by PepsiCo at December 25, 2004?

(c) How many shares are held as treasury stock by Coca-Cola at December 31, 2004, and by PepsiCo at December 25, 2004?

(d) How many Coca-Cola common shares are outstanding at December 31, 2004? How many PepsiCo shares of capital stock are outstanding at December 25, 2004?

(e) What amounts of cash dividends per share were declared by Coca-Cola and PepsiCo in 2004? What were the dollar amount effects of the cash dividends on each company's stockholders' equity?

(f) What are Coca-Cola's and PepsiCo's rate of return on common/capital stock equity for 2004 and 2003? Which company gets the higher return on the equity of its shareholders?

(g) What are Coca-Cola's and PepsiCo's payout ratios for 2004?

(h) What was the market price range (high/low) for Coca-Cola's common stock and PepsiCo's capital stock during the fourth quarter of 2004? Which company's (Coca-Cola's or PepsiCo's) stock price increased more (%) during 2004?

Research Case

The article "Leading the News: **AT&T Corp.** Resorts to Unusual Motion: Reverse Stock Split—Market Capitalization Stays Constant, but Measure Would Boost Share Price," by Deborah Solomon, was published in the *Wall Street Journal* on April 11, 2002.

Instructions

Read the article and answer the following questions.

(a) Why is AT&T doing a reverse stock split? What advantage does it expect?

(b) Why are reverse stock splits seen as a sign of weakness? How is a reverse stock split recorded, and how is it reported in the financial statements?

(c) Why are share buybacks considered "a sign of strength"? How are they recorded, and how are they reported in the financial statements?

(d) If you were an AT&T stockholder, would you agree to this reverse stock split? Why or why not?

Professional Research: Financial Accounting and Reporting

Recall from Chapter 13 that Hincapie Co. (a specialty bike-accessory manufacturer) is expecting growth in sales of some products targeted to the low-price market. Hincapie is contemplating a preferred stock issue to help finance this expansion in operations. The company is leaning toward participating preferred stock because ownership will not be diluted, but the investors will get an extra dividend if the company does well. The company management wants to be certain that its reporting of this transaction is transparent to its current shareholders and wants you to research the disclosure requirements related to its capital structure.

Instructions

Using the **Financial Accounting Research System (FARS)**, respond to the following items. (Provide text strings used in your search.)

(a) Identify the FASB standard that addresses disclosure of information about capital structure.

(b) Find definitions for the following:

    (1) Securities.

    (2) Participation rights.

    (3) Preferred stock.

(c) What information about securities must be disclosed? Discuss how the proposed Hincapie preferred stock issue will be reported.

Professional Simulation

In this simulation you are asked to address questions related to the accounting for stockholders' equity. Prepare responses to all parts.

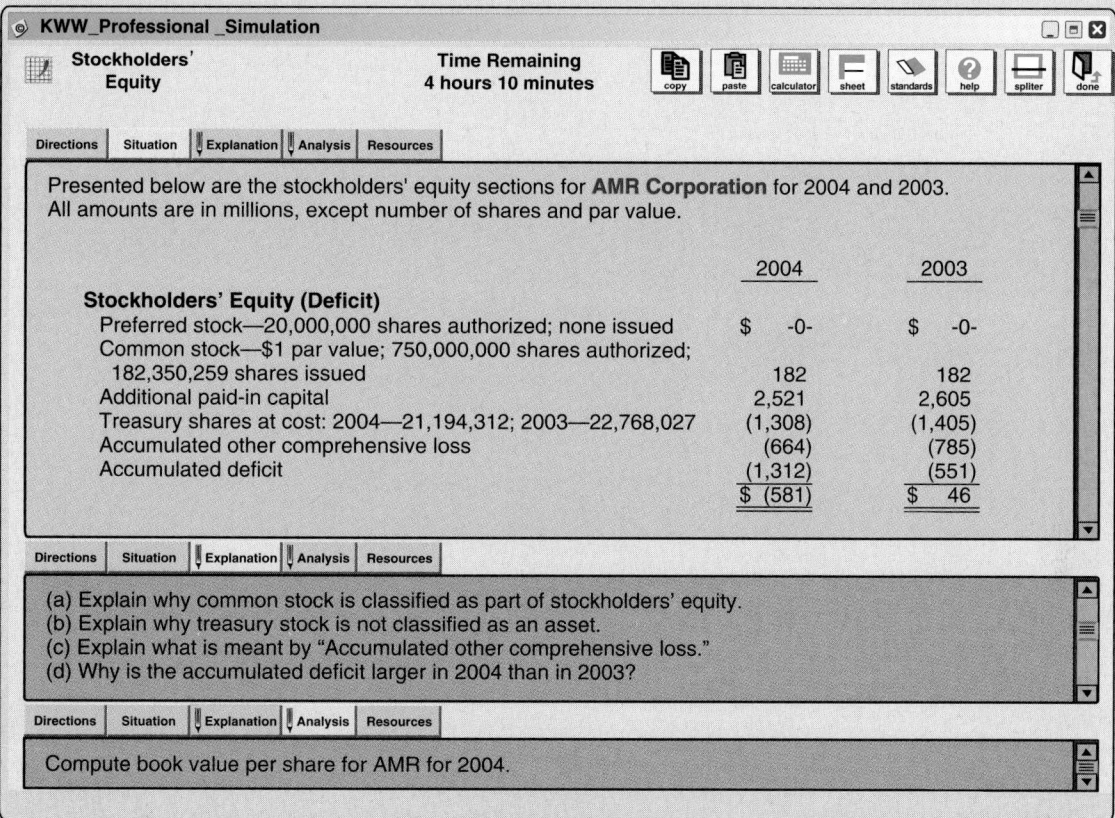

KWW_Professional _Simulation			
Stockholders' Equity	**Time Remaining** 4 hours 10 minutes	copy paste calculator sheet standards help splitter done	

Directions | Situation | Explanation | Analysis | Resources

Presented below are the stockholders' equity sections for **AMR Corporation** for 2004 and 2003. All amounts are in millions, except number of shares and par value.

	2004	2003
Stockholders' Equity (Deficit)		
Preferred stock—20,000,000 shares authorized; none issued	$ -0-	$ -0-
Common stock—$1 par value; 750,000,000 shares authorized; 182,350,259 shares issued	182	182
Additional paid-in capital	2,521	2,605
Treasury shares at cost: 2004—21,194,312; 2003—22,768,027	(1,308)	(1,405)
Accumulated other comprehensive loss	(664)	(785)
Accumulated deficit	(1,312)	(551)
	$ (581)	$ 46

Directions | Situation | Explanation | Analysis | Resources

(a) Explain why common stock is classified as part of stockholders' equity.
(b) Explain why treasury stock is not classified as an asset.
(c) Explain what is meant by "Accumulated other comprehensive loss."
(d) Why is the accumulated deficit larger in 2004 than in 2003?

Directions | Situation | Explanation | Analysis | Resources

Compute book value per share for AMR for 2004.

Remember to check the book's companion website to find additional resources for this chapter.

wiley.com/college/kieso

DILUTIVE SECURITIES AND EARNINGS PER SHARE

Kicking the Habit

Some habits die hard. Take stock options—called by some "the crack cocaine of incentives." For many years U.S. businesses were hooked. Why? The combination of a hot stock market and favorable accounting treatment made stock options the incentive of choice–they were compensation with no expense, so companies granted them with abandon. However, new accounting rules that take affect in 2006 will require expensing of stock options, which might make it easier for companies to kick this habit. Some changes are surfacing already.

For the third consecutive year, the number of new stock option grants at the 200 largest U.S. companies declined in 2003, with nearly two out of three cutting back. Compensation consultants say the trend continued through 2004 and will accelerate in 2005 and beyond. As a spokesperson at **Progress Energy** commented, "Once you begin expensing options, the attractiveness significantly drops."

By reining in options, many companies may be taking the first steps toward curbing both out-of-control executive pay and the era of corporate corruption that it spawned. In the 1990s, executives with huge option stockpiles had an almost irresistible incentive to do whatever it took to increase the stock price and cash in their options.

Some of the ways that companies are curbing option grants include replacing options with fewer shares of restricted stock. Others are simply reducing option grants, without offering a replacement. For example, in 2004 **Dell** awarded less than half the options compared to two years earlier. And some companies, like **Microsoft** and **Yahoo**, have switched to restricted stock plans.

When the new expensing rules take effect—barring any last-minute congressional intervention—option-reduction strategies likely will become more widespread as companies search for ways to reward talent without breaking the bank. The good news for companies: They have plenty of alternatives to choose from. The positive impact on corporate behavior, while hard to measure, should benefit investors in years to come.[1]

---

[1]Adapted from: Louis Lavelle, "Kicking the Stock-Options Habit,"*BusinessWeekOnline* (February 16, 2005).

Learning Objectives

After studying this chapter, you should be able to:

1 Describe the accounting for the issuance, conversion, and retirement of convertible securities.

2 Explain the accounting for convertible preferred stock.

3 Contrast the accounting for stock warrants and for stock warrants issued with other securities.

4 Describe the accounting for stock compensation plans under generally accepted accounting principles.

5 Discuss the controversy involving stock compensation plans.

6 Compute earnings per share in a simple capital structure.

7 Compute earnings per share in a complex capital structure.

As the opening story indicates, changes are in store for stock options and their accounting. President George W. Bush, Federal Reserve Board Chair Alan Greenspan, Senators Joseph Lieberman and John McCain, and the guru of investing Warren Buffett all have strong opinions on whether stock options should be reported as an expense in corporate income statements. The purpose of this chapter is to discuss the proper accounting for stock options. In addition, the chapter examines issues related to other types of financial instruments, such as convertible securities, warrants, and contingent shares, including their effects on reporting earnings per share. The content and organization of the chapter are as follows.

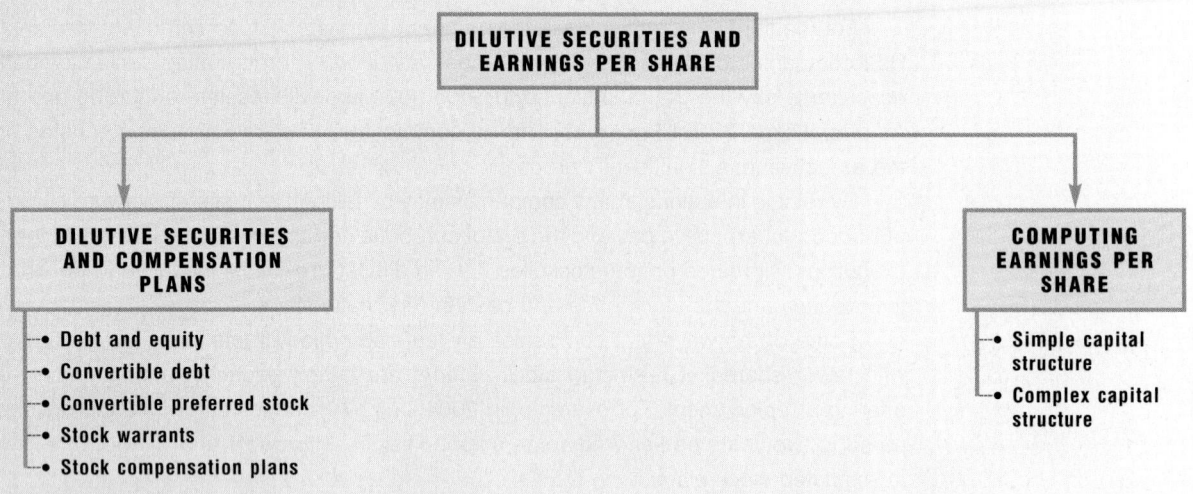

SECTION 1	*DILUTIVE SECURITIES AND COMPENSATION PLANS*

DEBT AND EQUITY

Many of the controversies related to the accounting for financial instruments such as stock options, convertible securities, and preferred stock relate to whether companies should report these instruments as a liability or as equity. For example, companies should classify nonredeemable common shares as equity because the issuer has no **obligation** to pay dividends or repurchase the stock. Declaration of dividends is at the issuer's discretion, as is the decision to repurchase the stock. Similarly, preferred stock that is not redeemable does not require the issuer to pay dividends or repurchase the stock. Thus, nonredeemable common or preferred stock lacks an important characteristic of a liability—an obligation to pay the holder of the common or preferred stock at some point in the future.[2]

However the classification is not as clear-cut for other financial instruments. For example, in Chapter 15 we discussed the accounting for mandatorily redeemable preferred

---

[2]"Accounting for Certain Financial Instruments with Characteristics of Both Liabilities and Equity," *Statement of Financial Accounting Standards No. 150*, (Norwalk Conn.: FASB, 2003), par. 23.

stock. Companies originally classified this security as part of equity. The SEC then prohibited equity classification, and most companies classified these securities between debt and equity on the balance sheet in a separate section often referred to as the "mezzanine section." Recently the FASB issued a standard that requires companies to report these types of securities as a liability.[3]

In this chapter, we discuss securities that have characteristics of *both* debt and equity. For example, a convertible bond has both debt and equity characteristics. Should a company classify this security as debt, as equity, or as part debt and part equity? In addition, how should a company compute earnings per share if it has convertible bonds and other convertible securities in its capital structure? Convertible securities as well as options, warrants, and other securities are often called **dilutive securities** because upon exercise they may reduce (dilute) earnings per share.

ACCOUNTING FOR CONVERTIBLE DEBT

OBJECTIVE 1
Describe the accounting for the issuance, conversion, and retirement of convertible securities.

Convertible bonds can be converted into other corporate securities during some specified period of time after issuance. A convertible bond combines the benefits of a bond with the privilege of exchanging it for stock at the holder's option. Investors who purchase it desire the security of a bond holding (guaranteed interest and principal) plus the added option of conversion if the value of the stock appreciates significantly.

Corporations issue convertibles for two main reasons. One is to raise equity capital without giving up more ownership control than necessary. To illustrate, assume a company wants to raise $1 million; its common stock is selling at $45 a share. To raise the $1 million, the company would have to sell 22,222 shares (ignoring issue costs). By selling 1,000 bonds at $1,000 par, each convertible into 20 shares of common stock, the company could raise $1 million by committing only 20,000 shares of its common stock.

A second reason to issue convertibles is to obtain debt financing at cheaper rates. Many companies could issue debt only at high interest rates unless they attach a convertible covenant. The conversion privilege entices the investor to accept a lower interest rate than would normally be the case on a straight debt issue. For example, **Amazon.com** at one time issued convertible bonds that pay interest at an effective yield of 4.75 percent. This rate was much lower than Amazon.com would have had to pay by issuing straight debt. For this lower interest rate, the investor receives the right to buy Amazon.com's common stock at a fixed price until the bond's maturity.[4]

As indicated earlier, the accounting for convertible debt involves reporting issues at the time of (1) issuance, (2) conversion, and (3) retirement.

At Time of Issuance

The method for recording convertible bonds **at the date of issue follows the method used to record straight debt issues**. None of the proceeds are recorded as equity. Companies amortize to its maturity date any discount or premium that results from the issuance of convertible bonds. Why this treatment? Because it is difficult to predict when, if at all, conversion will occur. However, the accounting for convertible debt as a straight debt issue is controversial; we discuss it more fully later in the chapter.

---

[3]Ibid, par. 9.

[4]As with any investment, a buyer has to be careful. For example, **Wherehouse Entertainment Inc.**, which had 6¼ percent convertibles outstanding, was taken private in a leveraged buyout. As a result, the convertible was suddenly as risky as a junk bond of a highly leveraged company with a coupon of only 6¼ percent. As one holder of the convertibles noted, "What's even worse is that the company will be so loaded down with debt that it probably won't have enough cash flow to make its interest payments. And the convertible debt we hold is subordinated to the rest of Wherehouse's debt." These types of situations have made convertibles less attractive and have led to the introduction of takeover protection covenants in some convertible bond offerings. Or, sometimes convertibles are permitted to be called at par, and therefore the conversion premium may be lost.

At Time of Conversion

If converting bonds into other securities, a company uses the **book value method** to record the conversion. The book value method records the securities exchanged for the bond at the carrying amount (book value) of the bond.

To illustrate, assume that Hilton, Inc. has a $1,000 bond that is convertible into 10 shares of common stock (par value $10). At the time of conversion, the unamortized premium is $50. Hilton records the conversion of the bonds as follows.

Bonds Payable	1,000	
Premium on Bonds Payable	50	
Common Stock		100
Paid-in Capital in Excess of Par		950

Support for the book value approach is based on the argument that an agreement was established at the date of the issuance either to pay a stated amount of cash at maturity or to issue a stated number of shares of equity securities. Therefore, when the debtholder converts the debt to equity in accordance with the preexisting contract terms, the issuing company recognizes no gain or loss upon conversion.

Induced Conversions

Sometimes the issuer wishes to encourage prompt conversion of its convertible debt to equity securities in order to reduce interest costs or to improve its debt to equity ratio. Thus, the issuer may offer some form of additional consideration (such as cash or common stock), called a "sweetener," to **induce conversion**. The issuing company reports the sweetener as an expense of the current period. Its amount is the fair value of the additional securities or other consideration given.

Assume that Helloid, Inc. has outstanding $1,000,000 par value convertible debentures convertible into 100,000 shares of $1 par value common stock. Helloid wishes to reduce its annual interest cost. To do so, Helloid agrees to pay the holders of its convertible debentures an additional $80,000 if they will convert. Assuming conversion occurs, Helloid makes the following entry.

Debt Conversion Expense	80,000	
Bonds Payable	1,000,000	
Common Stock		100,000
Additional Paid-in Capital		900,000
Cash		80,000

Helloid records the additional $80,000 as **an expense of the current period** and not as a reduction of equity.

Some argue that the cost of a conversion inducement is a cost of obtaining equity capital. As a result, they contend, companies should recognize the cost of conversion as a cost of (a reduction of) the equity capital acquired, and not as an expense. However, the FASB indicated that when an issuer makes an additional payment to encourage conversion, the payment is for a service (bondholders converting at a given time) and should be reported as an expense. The issuing company does not report this expense as an extraordinary item.[5]

Retirement of Convertible Debt

As indicated earlier, the method for recording the **issuance** of convertible bonds follows that used in recording straight debt issues. Specifically this means that issuing companies should not attribute any portion of the proceeds to the conversion feature, nor should it credit Additional Paid-in Capital.

Although some raise theoretical objections to this approach, to be consistent, companies need to recognize a gain or loss on **retiring convertible debt in the same way**

---

[5]"Induced Conversions of Convertible Debt," *Statement of Financial Accounting Standards No. 84* (Stamford, Conn.: FASB, 1985).

that they recognize a gain or loss on retiring nonconvertible debt. For this reason, companies should report differences between the cash acquisition price of debt and its carrying amount **in current income as a gain or loss**.

CONVERTIBLE PREFERRED STOCK

Convertible preferred stock includes an option for the holder to convert preferred shares into a fixed number of common shares. The major difference between accounting for a convertible bond and convertible preferred stock at the date of issue is their classification: Convertible bonds are considered liabilities, whereas convertible preferreds (unless mandatory redemption exists) are considered part of stockholders' equity.

OBJECTIVE 2
Explain the accounting for convertible preferred stock.

In addition, when stockholders exercise convertible preferred stock, there is no theoretical justification for recognizing a gain or loss. A company does not recognize a gain or loss when it deals with stockholders in their capacity as business owners. Therefore, companies do not recognize a gain or loss when stockholders exercise convertible preferred stock.

In accounting for the exercise of convertible preferred stock, a company uses the **book value method**: It debits Preferred Stock, along with any related Additional Paid-in Capital, and it credits Common Stock and Additional Paid-in Capital (if an excess exists). The treatment differs when the par value of the common stock issued **exceeds** the book value of the preferred stock. In that case, the company usually debits Retained Earnings for the difference.

To illustrate, assume Host Enterprises issued 1,000 shares of common stock (par value $2) upon conversion of 1,000 shares of preferred stock (par value $1) that was originally issued for a $200 premium. The entry would be:

Convertible Preferred Stock	1,000	
Paid-in Capital in Excess of Par (Premium on Preferred Stock)	200	
Retained Earnings	800	
Common Stock		2,000

The rationale for the debit to Retained Earnings is that Host has offered the preferred stockholders an **additional return** to facilitate their conversion to common stock. In this example, Host charges the additional return to retained earnings. Many states, however, require that this charge simply reduce additional paid-in capital from other sources.

HOW LOW CAN YOU GO?

Financial engineers are always looking for the next innovation in security design to meet the needs of both issuers and investors. Consider the convertible bonds issued by **STMicroelectronics** (STM). STM's 10-year bonds have a zero coupon and are convertible into STM common stock at an exercise price of $33.43. When issued, the bonds sold at an effective yield of −0.05 percent. That's right–a negative yield.

WHAT DO THE NUMBERS MEAN?

How could this happen? When STM issued the bonds, investors thought the options to convert were so valuable that they were willing to take zero interest payments and invest an amount *in excess of* the maturity value of the bonds. In essence, the investors are paying interest to STM, and STM records interest revenue. Why would investors do this? If the stock price rises, as many thought it would for STM and many tech companies at this time, these bond investors could convert and get a big gain in the stock.

Investors did get some additional protection in the deal: They can redeem the $1,000 bonds after three years and receive $975 (and after five and seven years, for lower amounts), if it looks like the bonds will never convert. In the end, STM has issued bonds with a significant equity component. And because the entire bond issue is classified as debt, STM records negative interest expense.

Source: STM Financial Reports. See also Floyd Norris, "Legal but Absurd: They Borrow a Billion and Report a Profit,"*New York Times* (August 8, 2003), p. C1.

STOCK WARRANTS

OBJECTIVE 3
Contrast the accounting for stock warrants and for stock warrants issued with other securities.

Warrants are certificates entitling the holder to acquire shares of stock at a certain price within a stated period. This option is similar to the conversion privilege: Warrants, if exercised, become common stock and usually have a dilutive effect (reduce earnings per share) similar to that of the conversion of convertible securities. However, a substantial difference between convertible securities and stock warrants is that upon exercise of the warrants, the holder has to pay a certain amount of money to obtain the shares.

The issuance of warrants or options to buy additional shares normally arises under three situations:

1 When issuing different types of securities, such as bonds or preferred stock, companies often include warrants **to make the security more attractive**—by providing an "equity kicker."

2 Upon the issuance of additional common stock, existing stockholders have a **preemptive right to purchase common stock** first. Companies may issue warrants to evidence that right.

3 Companies give warrants, often referred to as *stock options*, **to executives and employees** as a form of **compensation**.

The problems in accounting for stock warrants are complex and present many difficulties—some of which remain unresolved.

Stock Warrants Issued with Other Securities

Warrants issued with other securities are basically long-term options to buy common stock at a fixed price. Generally the life of warrants is five years, occasionally 10 years; very occasionally, a company may offer perpetual warrants.

A warrant works like this: **Tenneco, Inc.** offered a unit comprising one share of stock and one detachable warrant. As its name implies, the **detachable stock warrant** can be "detached" from the stock and traded as a separate security. The Tenneco warrant in this example is exercisable at $24.25 per share and good for five years. The unit (share of stock plus detachable warrant) sold for 22.75 ($22.75). Since the price of the common stock the day before the sale was 19.88 ($19.88), the difference suggests a price of 2.87 ($2.87) for the warrant.

The investor pays for the warrant in order to receive the right to buy the stock, at a fixed price of $24.25, sometime in the future. It would not be profitable at present for the purchaser to exercise the warrant and buy the stock, because the price of the stock was much below the exercise price.[6] But if, for example, the price of the stock rises to $30, the investor gains $2.88 ($30 − $24.25 − $2.87) on an investment of $2.87, a 100 percent increase! If the price never rises, the investor loses the full $2.87 per warrant.[7]

A company should allocate the proceeds from the sale of debt with detachable stock warrants **between the two securities**.[8] The profession takes the position that two separable instruments are involved, that is, (1) a bond and (2) a warrant giving the holder the right to purchase common stock at a certain price. Companies can trade detachable

---

[6]Later in this discussion we will show that the value of the warrant is normally determined on the basis of a relative market-value approach because of the difficulty of imputing a warrant value in any other manner.

[7]From the illustration, it is apparent that buying warrants can be an "all or nothing" proposition.

[8]A detachable warrant means that the warrant can sell separately from the bond. *APB Opinion No. 14* makes a distinction between detachable and nondetachable warrants because companies must sell nondetachable warrants with the security as a complete package. Thus, no allocation is permitted.

warrants separately from the debt. This allows the determination of a market value. The two methods of allocation available are:

1 The proportional method.
2 The incremental method.

Proportional Method

At one time **AT&T** issued bonds with detachable five-year warrants to buy one share of common stock (par value $5) at $25. At the time, a share of AT&T stock was selling for approximately $50. These warrants enabled AT&T to price its bond offering at par with an 8¾ percent yield (quite a bit lower than prevailing rates at that time). To account for the proceeds from this offering, AT&T would place a value on the two securities: (1) the value of the bonds without the warrants, and (2) the value of the warrants. The **proportional method** then allocates the proceeds using the proportion of the two amounts, based on fair values.

For example, assume that AT&T's bonds (par $1,000) sold for 99 without the warrants soon after their issue. The market value of the warrants at that time was $30. (Prior to sale the warrants will not have a market value.) The allocation relies on an estimate of market value, generally as established by an investment banker, or on the relative market value of the bonds and the warrants soon after the company issues and trades them. The price paid for 10,000, $1,000 bonds with the warrants attached was par, or $10,000,000. Illustration 16-1 shows the proportional allocation of the bond proceeds between the bonds and warrants.

Fair market value of bonds (without warrants) ($10,000,000 × .99)		$ 9,900,000
Fair market value of warrants (10,000 × $30)		300,000
Aggregate fair market value		$10,200,000
Allocated to bonds:	$\frac{\$9,900,000}{\$10,200,000}$ × $10,000,000 =	$ 9,705,882
Allocated to warrants:	$\frac{\$300,000}{\$10,200,000}$ × $10,000,000 =	294,118
Total allocation		$10,000,000

ILLUSTRATION 16-1
Proportional Allocation of Proceeds between Bonds and Warrants

In this situation the bonds sell at a discount. AT&T records the sale as follows.

Cash	9,705,882	
Discount on Bonds Payable	294,118	
Bonds Payable		10,000,000

In addition, AT&T sells warrants that it credits to paid-in capital. It makes the following entry.

Cash	294,118	
Paid-in Capital—Stock Warrants		294,118

AT&T may combine the entries if desired. Here, we show them separately, to indicate that the purchaser of the bond is buying not only a bond, but also a possible future claim on common stock.

Assuming investors exercise all 10,000 warrants (one warrant per one share of stock), AT&T makes the following entry.

Cash (10,000 × $25)	250,000	
Paid-in Capital—Stock Warrants	294,118	
Common Stock (10,000 × $5)		50,000
Paid-in Capital in Excess of Par		494,118

What if investors fail to exercise the warrants? In that case, AT&T debits Paid-in Capital—Stock Warrants for $294,118, and credits Paid-in Capital from Expired

Warrants for a like amount. The additional paid-in capital reverts to the former stockholders.

Incremental Method

In instances where a company cannot determine the fair value of either the warrants or the bonds, it applies the **incremental method** used in lump-sum security purchases (as explained in Chapter 15, page 731). That is, the company uses the security for which it *can* determine the fair value. It allocates the remainder of the purchase price to the security for which it does not know the fair value.

For example, assume that the market price of the AT&T warrants is $300,000, but the company cannot determine the market price of the bonds without the warrants. Illustration 16-2 shows the amount allocated to the warrants and the stock in this case.

ILLUSTRATION 16-2
Incremental Allocation of Proceeds between Bonds and Warrants

Lump-sum receipt	$10,000,000
Allocated to the warrants	300,000
Balance allocated to bonds	$ 9,700,000

Conceptual Questions

The question arises whether the allocation of value to the warrants is consistent with the handling of convertible debt, in which companies allocate no value to the conversion privilege. The FASB stated that the features of a convertible security are **inseparable** in the sense that choices are mutually exclusive: The holder either converts the bonds or redeems them for cash, but cannot do both. No basis, therefore, exists for recognizing the conversion value in the accounts.

UNDERLYING CONCEPTS

Reporting a convertible bond solely as debt is not representationally faithful. However, the cost-benefit constraint is used to justify the failure to allocate between debt and equity.

The Board, however, indicated that the issuance of bonds with **detachable warrants** involves *two* securities, one a debt security, which will remain outstanding until maturity, and the other a warrant to purchase common stock. At the time of issuance, separable instruments exist. The existence of two instruments therefore justifies separate treatment. **Nondetachable warrants**, however, **do not require an allocation of the proceeds between the bonds and the warrants**. Similar to the accounting for convertible bonds, companies record the entire proceeds from nondetachable warrants as debt.

Many argue that the conversion feature of a convertible bond is not significantly different in nature from the call represented by a warrant. The question is whether, although the legal forms differ, sufficient similarities of substance exist to support the same accounting treatment. Some contend that inseparability *per se* is an insufficient basis for restricting allocation between identifiable components of a transaction. Examples of allocation between assets of value in a single transaction *do* exist, such as allocation of values in basket purchases and separation of principal and interest in capitalizing long-term leases. Critics of the current accounting for convertibles say that to deny recognition of value to the conversion feature merely looks to the form of the instrument and does not deal with the substance of the transaction.

INTERNATIONAL INSIGHT

International accounting standards require that the issuer of convertible debt record the liability and equity components separately.

In its current exposure draft on this subject, the FASB indicates that companies should separate the debt and equity components of securities such as convertible debt or bonds issued with nondetachable warrants. We agree with this position. In both situations (convertible debt and debt issued with warrants), the investor has made a payment to the company for an equity feature—the right to acquire an equity instrument in the future. The only real distinction between them is that the additional payment made when the equity instrument is formally acquired takes different forms. The warrant holder pays additional cash to the issuing company; the convertible debt holder pays for stock by forgoing the receipt of interest from conversion date until maturity date and by forgoing the receipt of the maturity value itself. Thus, the difference is one of method or form of payment only, rather than one of substance. However, until the profession officially reverses its stand in regard to accounting for convertible debt, companies will continue to report convertible debt and bonds issued with nondetachable warrants solely as debt.[9]

Rights to Subscribe to Additional Shares

If the directors of a corporation decide to issue new shares of stock, the old stockholders generally have the right (**preemptive privilege**) to purchase newly issued shares in proportion to their holdings. This privilege, referred to as a **stock right**, saves existing stockholders from suffering a dilution of voting rights without their consent. Also, it may allow them to purchase stock somewhat below its market value. Unlike the warrants issued with other securities, the warrants issued for stock rights are of short duration.

The certificate representing the stock right states the number of shares the holder of the right may purchase. Each share of stock owned ordinarily gives the owner one stock right. The certificate also states the price at which the new shares may be purchased. The price is normally less than the current market value of such shares, which gives the rights a value in themselves. From the time they are issued until they expire, holders of stock rights may purchase and sell them like any other security.

Companies make only a memorandum entry when they issue rights to existing stockholders. This entry indicates the number of rights issued to existing stockholders in order to ensure that the company has additional unissued stock registered for issuance in case the rights are exercised. Companies make no formal entry at this time because they have not yet issued stock nor received cash.

If holders exercise the stock rights, a cash payment of some type usually is involved. If the company receives cash equal to the par value, it makes an entry crediting Common Stock at par value. If the company receives cash in excess of par value, it credits Paid-in Capital in Excess of Par. If it receives cash less than par value, a debit to Paid-in Capital is appropriate.

STOCK COMPENSATION PLANS

Another form of warrant arises in stock compensation plans to pay and motivate employees. This warrant is a **stock option**, which gives key employees the option to purchase common stock at a given price over an extended period of time. As indicated in our opening story, the FASB has recently issued a new standard on stock options and other types of compensation plans that are stock-based. Illustration 16-3 (on page 786) shows how this standard is already affecting how companies are using stock options.

Illustration 16-3 indicates that option expense is considerable but that it peaked in 2002 and now is declining. The major reasons for this decline are two-fold. Critics often cited the indiscriminate use of stock options as a reason why company executives manipulated accounting numbers in an attempt to achieve higher share price. As a result, many responsible companies decided to cut back on the issuance of options, both to avoid such accounting manipulations and to head off investor doubts. In addition, the FASB's new standard will result in companies recording a higher expense when these options are granted.

---

[9]"Proposed Statement of Financial Accounting Standards Accounting for Financial Instruments with Characteristics of Liabilities, Equity, or Both; Summary (FASB, Norwalk, Conn.: October 2000). Academic research indicates that estimates of the debt and equity components of convertible bonds are subject to considerable measurement error. See Mary Barth, Wayne Landsman, and Richard Rendleman, Jr., "Option Pricing–Based Bond Value Estimates and a Fundamental Components Approach to Account for Corporate Debt," *The Accounting Review* (January 1998). This and other challenges explain in part the extended time needed to develop new standards in this area.

ILLUSTRATION 16-3
Stock Option
Compensation Expense

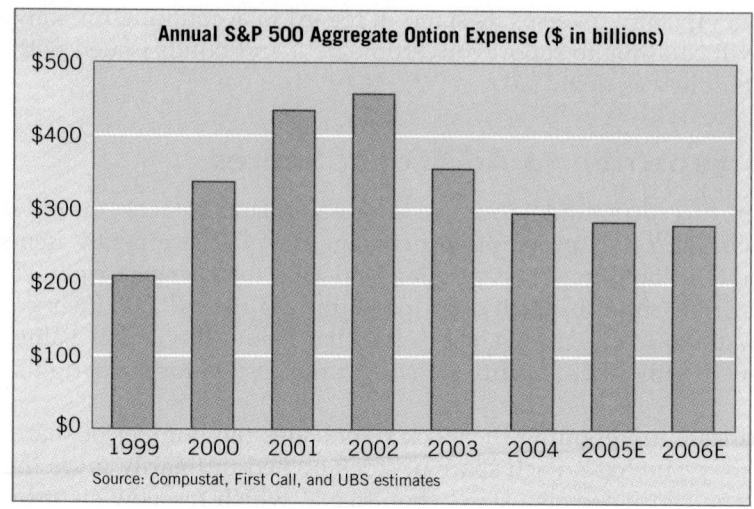

The data reported in Illustration 16-4 reinforces the point that the design of compensation plans is changing. The study documents recent compensation trends of 68 CEOs of companies in the S&P 500.

ILLUSTRATION 16-4
Compensation Elements

	2004	% Change from 2003
Total direct compensation	$7,247,903	8.8%
Salary	908,269	4.1
Bonus	975,000	32.6
Value of stock options	3,217,811	(18.7)
Restricted stock	2,679,435	34.0
Long-term incentive payouts	773,719	72.1

Sources: Compustat, First Call, UBS, Equilar, Inc.

What Illustration 16-4 shows is that cash compensation is increasing. In addition, long-term incentives are increasing, but the compensation mix is changing. For example, the use of restricted stock jumped 34 percent, but the use of options decreased approximately 19 percent. Yet, stock options remain the primary means of compensating these CEOs. As Illustrations 16-3 and 16-4 indicate, stock-based compensation is still a considerable incentive element of employee compensation.

A consensus of opinion is that effective compensation programs are ones that do the following: (1) motivate employees to high levels of performance, (2) help retain executives and allow for recruitment of new talent, (3) base compensation on employee and company performance, (4) maximize the employee's after-tax benefit and minimize the employer's after-tax cost, and (5) use performance criteria over which the employee has control. Straight cash compensation plans (salary and perhaps a bonus), though important, are oriented to the short run. Many companies recognize that they need a longer-term compensation plan in addition to the cash component.

Long-term compensation plans attempt to develop company loyalty among key employees. An effective way to do so is to give employees "a piece of the action"—that is, an equity interest. These plans, generally referred to as **stock-based compensation plans**, come in many forms. Essentially, they provide the employee with the opportunity to receive stock if the performance of the company (by whatever measure) is satisfactory. Typical performance measures focus on long-term improvements that are readily measurable and that benefit the company as a whole, such as increases in earnings per share, revenues, stock price, or market share.

The Major Reporting Issue

Suppose that as an employee for Hurdle Inc., you receive options to purchase 10,000 shares of the firm's common stock as part of your compensation. The date you receive the options is referred to as the **grant date**. The options are good for 10 years. The market price and the exercise price for the stock are both $20 at the grant date. **What is the value of the compensation you just received?**

Some believe that what you have received has no value. They reason that because the difference between the market price and the exercise price is zero, no compensation results. Others argue these options do have value: If the stock price goes above $20 any time in the next 10 years and you exercise the options, you may earn substantial compensation. For example, if at the end of the fourth year, the market price of the stock is $30 and you exercise your options, you earn $100,000 [10,000 options × ($30 − $20)], ignoring income taxes.

The question for Hurdle is how to report the granting of these options. One approach measures compensation cost by the excess of the market price of the stock over its exercise price at the grant date. This approach is referred to as the **intrinsic-value method**. It measures what the holder would receive today if the option was immediately exercised. That intrinsic value **is the difference between the market price of the stock and the exercise price of the options at the grant date**. Using the intrinsic-value method, Hurdle would not recognize any compensation expense related to your options because at the grant date the market price equaled the exercise price. (In the preceding paragraph, those who answered that the options had no value were looking at the question from the intrinsic-value approach.)

The second way to look at the question of how to report the granting of these options bases the cost of employee stock options on the **fair value** of the stock options granted. Under this **fair-value method**, companies use acceptable option-pricing models to value the options at the date of grant. These models take into account the many factors that determine an option's underlying value.[10]

Under previous accounting standards, companies could recognize stock-based compensation using *either* the intrinsic-value method *or* the fair-value method. Given a choice, most companies adopted the intrinsic-value approach because it generally resulted in lower compensation expense. However, in 2002 a number of companies began voluntarily to switch to the fair-value method. By March 2004 over 500 public companies were using the fair-value method. As indicated earlier, a major reason for the change was the desire by companies to show the investing community that they believe in fair and transparent financial reporting, particularly in the aftermath of the many financial reporting scandals.

However, the choice between two methods was not ideal. Some companies included in their income figures the cost of stock-based compensation (the fair-value approach). Others did not. Analysts raised concerns about lack of comparability, and the FASB developed a new standard for stock-based compensation.

The new FASB standard requires that companies recognize compensation cost using the fair-value method.[11] The FASB position is that companies should base the accounting for the cost of employee services on the fair value of compensation paid. This amount is presumed to be a measure of the value of the services received. We will discuss more about the politics of this new standard later (see "Debate over Stock Option Accounting," page 791). Let's first describe the procedures involved.

---

[10]These factors include the volatility of the underlying stock, the expected life of the options, the risk-free rate during the option life, and expected dividends during the option life.

[11]"Accounting for Stock-Based Compensation," *Statement of Financial Accounting Standards No. 123* (Norwalk, Conn: FASB, 1995); and "Share-Based Payment," *Statement of Financial Accounting Standard No. 123(R)* (Norwalk, Conn: FASB, 2004).

Accounting for Stock Compensation

OBJECTIVE 4
Describe the accounting for stock compensation plans under generally accepted accounting principles.

Stock option plans involve two main accounting issues:

1 How to determine compensation expense.
2 Over what periods to allocate compensation expense.

Determining Expense

Under the fair-value method, companies compute total compensation expense based on the fair value of the options expected to vest on the date they grant the options to the employee(s) (i.e., the **grant date**).[12] Public companies estimate fair value by using an option pricing model, with some adjustments for the unique factors of employee stock options. No adjustments occur after the grant date in response to subsequent changes in the stock price—either up or down.

WHAT DO THE NUMBERS MEAN?

A LITTLE HONESTY GOES A LONG WAY

Before adoption of *SFAS No. 123(R)*, companies could choose whether to expense stock-based compensation or simply disclose the estimated costs in the notes to the financial statements. You might think investors would punish companies that decided to expense stock options. After all, most of corporate America has been battling for years to avoid having to expense them, worried that accounting for those perks would destroy earnings. And indeed, **Merrill Lynch** estimated that if all S&P 500 companies were to expense options, reported profits would fall by as much as 10 percent.

Yet, as a small but growing band of big-name companies voluntarily made the switch to expensing, investors for the most part showered them with love. With a few exceptions, the stock prices of the "expensers," from **Cinergy** to **The Washington Post**, outpaced the market after they announced the change.

The few, the brave

Company	Estimated EPS Without options	Estimated EPS With options expensed	% change since announcement Company stock price
Cinergy	$ 2.80	$ 2.77	22.4%
The Washington Post	20.48	20.10	16.4
Computer Associates	−0.46	−0.62	11.1
Fannie Mae	6.15	6.02	6.7
Bank One	2.77	2.61	2.6
General Motors	5.84	5.45	2.6
Procter & Gamble	3.57	3.35	−2.3
Coca-Cola	1.79	1.70	−6.2
General Electric	1.65	1.61	−6.2
Amazon.com	0.04	−0.99	−11.4

Data sources: Merrill Lynch; company reports.

Given the market's general positive reaction to the transparent reporting of stock options, it is puzzling why some companies continued to fight implementation of *SFAS No. 123(R)*.

Source: David Stires, "A Little Honesty Goes a Long Way," *Fortune* (September 2, 2002), p. 186. Reprinted by permission. See also Troy Wolverton, "Foes of Expensing Welcome FASB Delay," *TheStreet.com* (October 15, 2004).

---

[12]"To vest" means "to earn the rights to." An employee's award becomes vested at the date that the employee's right to receive or retain shares of stock or cash under the award is no longer contingent on remaining in the service of the employer.

Allocating Compensation Expense

In general, a company recognizes compensation expense in the periods in which its employees perform the service—the **service period**. Unless otherwise specified, the service period is the vesting period—the time between the grant date and the vesting date. Thus, the company determines total compensation cost at the grant date and allocates it to the periods benefited by its employees' services.

Stock Compensation Example

An example will help show the accounting for a stock option plan.[13] Assume that on November 1, 2005, the stockholders of Chen Company approve a plan that grants the company's five executives options to purchase 2,000 shares each of the company's $1 par value common stock. The company grants the options on January 1, 2006. The executives may exercise the options at any time within the next 10 years. The option price per share is $60, and the market price of the stock at the date of grant is $70 per share.

Under the fair-value method, the company computes total compensation expense by applying an acceptable fair value option-pricing model (such as the Black-Scholes option-pricing model). To keep this illustration simple, we assume that the fair-value option-pricing model determines Chen's total compensation expense to be $220,000.

Basic Entries. Under the fair-value method, a company recognizes the value of the options as an expense in the periods in which the employee performs services. In the case of Chen Company, assume that the expected period of benefit is two years, starting with the grant date. Chen would record the transactions related to this option contract as follows.

At date of grant (January 1, 2006)

No entry.

To record compensation expense for 2006 (December 31, 2006)

Compensation Expense	110,000	
Paid-in Capital—Stock Options ($220,000 ÷ 2)		110,000

To record compensation expense for 2007 (December 31, 2007)

Compensation Expense	110,000	
Paid-in Capital—Stock Options		110,000

As indicated, Chen allocates compensation expense evenly over the two-year service period.

Exercise. If Chen's executives exercise 2,000 of the 10,000 options (20 percent of the options) on June 1, 2009 (three years and five months after date of grant), the company records the following journal entry.

June 1, 2009

Cash (2,000 × $60)	120,000	
Paid-in Capital—Stock Options (20% × $220,000)	44,000	
Common Stock (2,000 × $1.00)		2,000
Paid-in Capital in Excess of Par		162,000

Expiration. If Chen's executives fail to exercise the remaining stock options before their expiration date, the company transfers the balance in the Paid-in Capital—Stock Options account to a more properly titled paid-in capital account, such as Paid-in Capital from Expired Stock Options. Chen records this transaction at the date of expiration as follows.

January 1, 2016 (expiration date)

Paid-in Capital—Stock Options	176,000	
Paid-in Capital from Expired Stock Options		176,000
(80% × $220,000)		

---

[13]We discuss the accounting for other types of stock-based compensation in Appendix 16A.

Adjustment. An unexercised stock option does not nullify the need to record the costs of services received from executives and attributable to the stock option plan. Under GAAP, a company therefore does not adjust compensation expense upon expiration of the options.

However, if an employee forfeits a stock option because **the employee fails to satisfy a service requirement** (e.g., leaves employment), the company should adjust the estimate of compensation expense recorded in the current period (as a change in estimate). A company records this change in estimate by debiting Paid-in Capital—Stock Options and crediting Compensation Expense for the amount of cumulative compensation expense recorded to date (thus decreasing compensation expense in the period of forfeiture.)

Employee Stock Purchase Plans

Employee stock purchase plans (ESPPs) generally permit all employees to purchase stock at a discounted price for a short period of time. The company often uses such plans to secure equity capital or to induce widespread ownership of its common stock among employees. These plans are considered compensatory unless they satisfy **all three** conditions presented below.

1 Substantially all full-time employees may participate on an equitable basis.

2 The discount from market is small. That is, the discount does not exceed the per share amount of costs avoided by not having to raise cash in a public offering. If the amount of the discount is 5 percent or less, no compensation needs to be recorded.

3 The plan offers no substantive option feature.

For example, Masthead Company's stock purchase plan allowed employees who met minimal employment qualifications to purchase its stock at a 5 percent reduction from market price for a short period of time. The reduction from market price is not considered compensatory. Why? Because the per share amount of the costs avoided by not having to raise the cash in a public offering equals 5 percent.

Companies that offer their employees a compensatory ESPP should record the compensation expense over the service life of the employees. It will be difficult for some companies to claim that their ESPPs are non-compensatory (and therefore not record compensation expense) unless they change their discount policy which in the past often was 15 percent. If they change their discount policy to 5 percent, participation in these plans will undoubtedly be lower. As a result, it is likely that some companies will end up dropping these plans.

Disclosure of Compensation Plans

Companies must fully disclose the status of their compensation plans at the end of the periods presented. To meet these objectives, companies must make extensive disclosures. Specifically, a company with one or more share-based payment arrangements must disclose information that enables users of the financial statements to understand:

1 The nature and terms of such arrangements that existed during the period and the potential effects of those arrangements on shareholders.

2 The effect on the income statement of compensation cost arising from share-based payment arrangements.

3 The method of estimating the fair value of the goods or services received, or the fair value of the equity instruments granted (or offered to grant), during the period.

4 The cash flow effects resulting from share-based payment arrangements.

Illustration 16-5 presents the type of information disclosed for compensation plans.

The Company has a share-based compensation plan. The compensation cost that has been charged against income for the plan was $29.4 million, and $28.7 million for 2007 and 2006, respectively.

The Company's 2007 Employee Share Option Plan (the Plan), which is shareholder-approved, permits the grant of share options and shares to its employees for up to 8 million shares of common stock. The Company believes that such awards better align the interests of its employees with those of its shareholders. Option awards are generally granted with an exercise price equal to the market price of the Company's stock at the date of grant; those option awards generally vest based on 5 years of continuous service and have 10-year contractual terms. Share awards generally vest over five years. Certain option and share awards provide for accelerated vesting if there is a change in control (as defined by the Plan).

The fair value of each option award is estimated on the date of grant using an option valuation model based on the assumptions noted in the following table.

	2007	2006
Expected volatility	25%–40%	24%–38%
Weighted-average volatility	33%	30%
Expected dividends	1.5%	1.5%
Expected term (in years)	5.3–7.8	5.5–8.0
Risk-free rate	6.3%–11.2%	6.0%–10.0%

A summary of option activity under the Plan as of December 31, 2007, and changes during the year then ended are presented below.

Options	Shares (000)	Weighted-Average Exercise Price	Weighted-Average Remaining Contractual Term	Aggregate Intrinsic Value ($000)
Outstanding at January 1, 2007	4,660	42		
Granted	950	60		
Exercised	(800)	36		
Forfeited or expired	(80)	59		
Outstanding at December 31, 2007	4,730	47	6.5	85,140
Exercisable at December 31, 2007	3,159	41	4.0	75,816

The weighted-average grant-date fair value of options granted during the years 2007 and 2006 was $19.57 and $17.46, respectively. The total intrinsic value of options exercised during the years ended December 31, 2007 and 2006, was $25.2 million, and $20.9 million, respectively.

As of December 31, 2007, there was $25.9 million of total unrecognized compensation cost related to nonvested share-based compensation arrangements granted under the Plan. That cost is expected to be recognized over a weighted-average period of 4.9 years. The total fair value of shares vested during the years ended December 31, 2007 and 2006, was $22.8 million and $21 million, respectively.

ILLUSTRATION 16-5
Stock Option Plan
Disclosure

Debate over Stock Option Accounting

OBJECTIVE 5
Discuss the controversy
involving stock
compensation plans.

The FASB faced considerable opposition when it proposed the fair-value method for accounting for stock options. This is not surprising, given that the fair-value method results in greater compensation costs relative to the intrinsic-value model. As the "What Do the Numbers Mean?" box on page 788 indicated, one study documented that, on average, companies in the Standard & Poor's 500 stock index overstated earnings in a recent year by 10 percent through the use of the intrinsic-value method. Nevertheless, some companies, such as **Coca-Cola, General Electric, Wachovia, Bank One,** and **The Washington Post,** decided to use the fair-value method. As the CFO of Coca-Cola stated, "There is no doubt that stock options are compensation. If they weren't, none of us would want them."

Yet many in corporate America resisted the fair-value method. Many small high-technology companies have been especially vocal in their opposition, arguing that only through offering stock options can they attract top professional management. They contend that recognizing large amounts of compensation expense under these plans places them at a competitive disadvantage against larger companies that can withstand higher compensation charges. As one high-tech executive stated, "If your goal is to attack fat-cat executive compensation in multi-billion dollar firms, then please do so! But not at the expense of the people who are 'running lean and mean,' trying to build businesses and creating jobs in the process."

The stock option saga is a classic example of the difficulty the FASB faces in issuing an accounting standard. Many powerful interests aligned against the Board. Even some who initially appeared to support the Board's actions later reversed themselves. These efforts undermine the authority of the FASB at a time when it is essential that we restore faith in our financial reporting system.

Transparent financial reporting—including recognition of stock-based expense—should not be criticized because companies will report lower income. We may not like what the financial statements say, but we are always better off when the statements are representationally faithful to the underlying economic substance of transactions.

By leaving stock-based compensation expense out of income, reported income is biased. Biased reporting not only raises concerns about the credibility of companies' reports, but also of financial reporting in general. And even good companies get tainted by the biased reporting of a few "bad apples." If we write standards to achieve some social, economic, or public policy goal, financial reporting loses its credibility.

UNDERLYING CONCEPTS

The stock option controversy involves economic-consequence issues. The FASB believes companies should follow the neutrality concept. Others disagree, noting that factors other than accounting theory should be considered.

SECTION 2	*COMPUTING EARNINGS PER SHARE*

Companies commonly report per share amounts for the effects of other items, such as a gain or loss on extraordinary items. The financial press also frequently reports earnings per share data. Further, stockholders and potential investors widely use this data in evaluating the profitability of a company. **Earnings per share** indicates the income earned by each share of common stock. Thus, **companies report earnings per share only for common stock**. For example, if Oscar Co. has net income of $300,000 and a weighted average of 100,000 shares of common stock outstanding for the year, earnings per share is $3 ($300,000 ÷ 100,000). Because of the importance of earnings per share information, most companies must report this information on the face of the income statement.[14] The exception, due to cost-benefit considerations, is nonpublic companies.[15] Generally, companies report earnings per share information below net income in the income statement. Illustration 16-6 shows Oscar Co.'s income statement presentation of earnings per share.

ILLUSTRATION 16-6
Income Statement Presentation of EPS

Net income	$300,000
Earnings per share	$3.00

INTERNATIONAL INSIGHT

The FASB and the IASB are working together on a project to improve EPS accounting by simplifying the computational guidance and thereby increasing the comparability of EPS data on an international basis. A new standard is due to be effective in 2007.

When the income statement contains intermediate components of income, companies should disclose earnings per share for each component. The presentation in Illustration 16-7 is representative.

---

[14]"Earnings per Share," *Statement of Financial Accounting Standards No. 128* (Norwalk, Conn: FASB, 1997). For an article on the usefulness of reported EPS data and the application of the qualitative characteristics of accounting information to EPS data, see Lola W. Dudley, "A Critical Look at EPS," *Journal of Accountancy* (August 1985), pp. 102–111.

[15]A nonpublic enterprise is an enterprise (1) whose debt or equity securities are not traded in a public market on a foreign or domestic stock exchange or in the over-the-counter market (including securities quoted locally or regionally), or (2) that is not required to file financial statements with the SEC. An enterprise is not considered a nonpublic enterprise when its financial statements are issued in preparation for the sale of any class of securities in a public market.

ILLUSTRATION 16-7
Income Statement
Presentation of EPS
Components

Earnings per share:	
Income from continuing operations	$4.00
Loss from discontinued operations, net of tax	0.60
Income before extraordinary item	3.40
Extraordinary gain, net of tax	1.00
Net income	$4.40

These disclosures enable the user of the financial statements to recognize the effects on EPS of income from continuing operations, as distinguished from income or loss from irregular items.[16]

EARNINGS PER SHARE—SIMPLE CAPITAL STRUCTURE

A corporation's capital structure is **simple** if it consists only of common stock or includes no **potential common stock** that upon conversion or exercise could dilute earnings per common share. A capital structure is **complex** if it includes securities that could have a dilutive effect on earnings per common share.

OBJECTIVE 6
Compute earnings per share in a simple capital structure.

The computation of earnings per share for a simple capital structure involves two items (other than net income)—(1) preferred stock dividends and (2) weighted-average number of shares outstanding.

Preferred Stock Dividends

As we indicated earlier, earnings per share relates to earnings per common share. When a company has both common and preferred stock outstanding, **it subtracts the current-year preferred stock dividend from net income to arrive at income available to common stockholders.** Illustration 16-8 shows the formula for computing earnings per share.

$$\text{Earnings per Share} = \frac{\text{Net Income} - \text{Preferred Dividends}}{\text{Weighted-Average Number of Shares Outstanding}}$$

ILLUSTRATION 16-8
Formula for Computing
Earnings per Share

In reporting earnings per share information, a company must calculate income available to common stockholders. To do so, the company subtracts dividends on preferred stock from each of the intermediate components of income (income from continuing operations and income before extraordinary items) and finally from net income. If a company declares dividends on preferred stock and a net loss occurs, **the company adds the preferred dividend to the loss** for purposes of computing the loss per share.

If the preferred stock is cumulative and the company declares no dividend in the current year, it subtracts (or adds) **an amount equal to the dividend that it should have declared for the current year only** from net income (or to the loss). The company should have included dividends in arrears for previous years in the previous years' computations.

Weighted-Average Number of Shares Outstanding

In all computations of earnings per share, the **weighted-average number of shares outstanding** during the period constitutes the basis for the per share amounts reported. Shares issued or purchased during the period affect the amount outstanding. Companies

---

[16]Companies should present, either on the face of the income statement or in the notes to the financial statements, per share amounts for discontinued operations and extraordinary items.

must **weight the shares by the fraction of the period they are outstanding**. The rationale for this approach is to find the equivalent number of whole shares outstanding for the year.

To illustrate, assume that Franks Inc. has changes in its common stock shares outstanding for the period as shown in Illustration 16-9.

ILLUSTRATION 16-9
Shares Outstanding,
Ending Balance—
Franks Inc.

Date	Share Changes	Shares Outstanding
January 1	Beginning balance	90,000
April 1	Issued 30,000 shares for cash	30,000
		120,000
July 1	Purchased 39,000 shares	39,000
		81,000
November 1	Issued 60,000 shares for cash	60,000
December 31	Ending balance	141,000

Franks computes the weighted-average number of shares outstanding as follows.

ILLUSTRATION 16-10
Weighted-Average
Number of Shares
Outstanding

Dates Outstanding	(A) Shares Outstanding	(B) Fraction of Year	(C) Weighted Shares (A × B)
Jan. 1–Apr. 1	90,000	3/12	22,500
Apr. 1–July 1	120,000	3/12	30,000
July 1–Nov. 1	81,000	4/12	27,000
Nov. 1–Dec. 31	141,000	2/12	23,500
Weighted-average number of shares outstanding			103,000

As Illustration 16-10 shows, 90,000 shares were outstanding for three months, which translates to 22,500 whole shares for the entire year. Because Franks issued additional shares on April 1, it must weight these shares for the time outstanding. When the company purchased 39,000 shares on July 1, it reduced the shares outstanding. Therefore from July 1 to November 1, only 81,000 shares were outstanding, which is equivalent to 27,000 shares. The issuance of 60,000 shares increases shares outstanding for the last two months of the year. Franks then makes a new computation to determine the proper weighted shares outstanding.

Stock Dividends and Stock Splits

When **stock dividends** or **stock splits** occur, companies need to restate the shares outstanding before the stock dividend or split, in order to compute the weighted-average number of shares. For example, assume that Vijay Corporation had 100,000 shares outstanding on January 1 and issued a 25 percent stock dividend on June 30. For purposes of computing a weighted-average for the current year, it assumes the additional 25,000 shares outstanding as a result of the stock dividend to be **outstanding since the beginning of the year**. Thus the weighted-average for the year for Vijay is 125,000 shares.

Companies restate the issuance of a stock dividend or stock split, but not the issuance or repurchase of stock for cash. Why? Because stock splits and stock dividends do not increase or decrease the net assets of the company. The company merely issues additional shares of stock. Because of the added shares, it must restate the weighted-average shares. Restating allows valid comparisons of earnings per share between periods before and after the stock split or stock dividend. Conversely, the issuance or purchase of stock for cash **changes the amount of net assets**. As a result, the company either earns more or less in the future as a result of this change in net assets. Stated another way, **a stock dividend or split does not change the shareholders' total investment**—it only increases (unless it is a reverse stock split) the number of common shares representing this investment.

To illustrate how a stock dividend affects the computation of the weighted-average number of shares outstanding, assume that Sabrina Company has the following changes in its common stock shares during the year.

Date	Share Changes	Shares Outstanding
January 1	Beginning balance	100,000
March 1	Issued 20,000 shares for cash	20,000
		120,000
June 1	60,000 additional shares (50% stock dividend)	60,000
		180,000
November 1	Issued 30,000 shares for cash	30,000
December 31	Ending balance	210,000

ILLUSTRATION 16-11
Shares Outstanding, Ending Balance—Sabrina Company

Sabrina computes the weighted-average number of shares outstanding as follows.

Dates Outstanding	(A) Shares Outstanding	(B) Restatement	(C) Fraction of Year	(D) Weighted Shares (A × B × C)
Jan. 1–Mar. 1	100,000	1.50	2/12	25,000
Mar. 1–June 1	120,000	1.50	3/12	45,000
June 1–Nov. 1	180,000		5/12	75,000
Nov. 1–Dec. 31	210,000		2/12	35,000
Weighted-average number of shares outstanding				180,000

ILLUSTRATION 16-12
Weighted-Average Number of Shares Outstanding—Stock Issue and Stock Dividend

Sabrina must restate the shares outstanding prior to the stock dividend. The company adjusts the shares outstanding from January 1 to June 1 for the stock dividend, so that it now states these shares on the same basis as shares issued subsequent to the stock dividend. Sabrina does not restate shares issued after the stock dividend because they are on the new basis. The stock dividend simply restates existing shares. **The same type of treatment applies to a stock split.**

If a stock dividend or stock split occurs after the end of the year, but before issuing the financial statements, a company must restate the weighted-average number of shares outstanding for the year (and any other years presented in comparative form). For example, assume that Hendricks Company computes its weighted-average number of shares as 100,000 for the year ended December 31, 2006. On January 15, 2007, before issuing the financial statements, the company splits its stock 3 for 1. In this case, the weighted-average number of shares used in computing earnings per share for 2006 is now 300,000 shares. If providing earnings per share information for 2005 as comparative information, Hendricks must also adjust it for the stock split.

Comprehensive Example

Let's study a comprehensive illustration for a simple capital structure. Darin Corporation has income before extraordinary item of $580,000 and an extraordinary gain, net of tax of $240,000. In addition, it has declared preferred dividends of $1 per share on

100,000 shares of preferred stock outstanding. Darin also has the following changes in its common stock shares outstanding during 2006.

ILLUSTRATION 16-13
Shares Outstanding,
Ending Balance—Darin
Corp.

Dates	Share Changes	Shares Outstanding
January 1	Beginning balance	180,000
May 1	Purchased 30,000 treasury shares	30,000
		150,000
July 1	300,000 additional shares (3-for-1 stock split)	300,000
		450,000
December 31	Issued 50,000 shares for cash	50,000
December 31	Ending balance	500,000

To compute the earnings per share information, Darin determines the weighted-average number of shares outstanding as follows.

ILLUSTRATION 16-14
Weighted-Average
Number of Shares
Outstanding

Dates Outstanding	(A) Shares Outstanding	(B) Restatement	(C) Fraction of Year	(D) Weighted Shares (A × B × C)
Jan. 1–May 1	180,000	3	4/12	180,000
May 1–July 1	150,000	3	2/12	75,000
July 1–Dec. 31	450,000		6/12	225,000
Weighted-average number of shares outstanding				480,000

In computing the weighted-average number of shares, the company ignores the shares sold on December 31, 2006, because they have not been outstanding during the year. Darin then divides the weighted-average number of shares into income before extraordinary item and net income to determine earnings per share. It subtracts its preferred dividends of $100,000 from income before extraordinary item ($580,000) to arrive at income before extraordinary item available to common stockholders of $480,000 ($580,000 − $100,000).

Deducting the preferred dividends from the income before extraordinary item also reduces net income without affecting the amount of the extraordinary item. The final amount is referred to as **income available to common stockholders**, as shown in Illustration 16-15.

ILLUSTRATION 16-15
Computation of Income
Available to Common
Stockholders

	(A) Income Information	(B) Weighted Shares	(C) Earnings per Share (A ÷ B)
Income before extraordinary item available to common stockholders	$480,000*	480,000	$1.00
Extraordinary gain (net of tax)	240,000	480,000	0.50
Income available to common stockholders	$720,000	480,000	$1.50
*$580,000 − $100,000			

Darin must disclose the per share amount for the extraordinary item (net of tax) either on the face of the income statement or in the notes to the financial statements.

Illustration 16-16 shows the income and per share information reported on the face of Darin's income statement.

Income before extraordinary item	$580,000
Extraordinary gain, net of tax	240,000
Net income	$820,000
Earnings per share:	
Income before extraordinary item	$1.00
Extraordinary item, net of tax	0.50
Net income	$1.50

ILLUSTRATION 16-16
Earnings per Share, with Extraordinary Item

EARNINGS PER SHARE—COMPLEX CAPITAL STRUCTURE

The EPS discussion to this point applies to **basic EPS** for a simple capital structure. One problem with a **basic EPS** computation is that it fails to recognize the potential impact of a corporation's dilutive securities. As discussed at the beginning of the chapter, **dilutive securities** are securities that can be converted to common stock.[17] Upon conversion or exercise by the holder, the dilutive securities reduce (dilute) earnings per share. This adverse effect on EPS can be significant and, more importantly, *unexpected* unless financial statements call attention to their potential dilutive effect.

As indicated earlier, a complex capital structure exists when a corporation has convertible securities, options, warrants, or other rights that upon conversion or exercise could dilute earnings per share. When a company has a complex capital structure, **it generally reports both basic and diluted earnings per share**.

Computing **diluted EPS** is similar to computing basic EPS. The difference is that diluted EPS includes the effect of all potential dilutive common shares that were outstanding during the period. The formula in Illustration 16-17 shows the relationship between basic EPS and diluted EPS.

OBJECTIVE 7
Compute earnings per share in a complex capital structure.

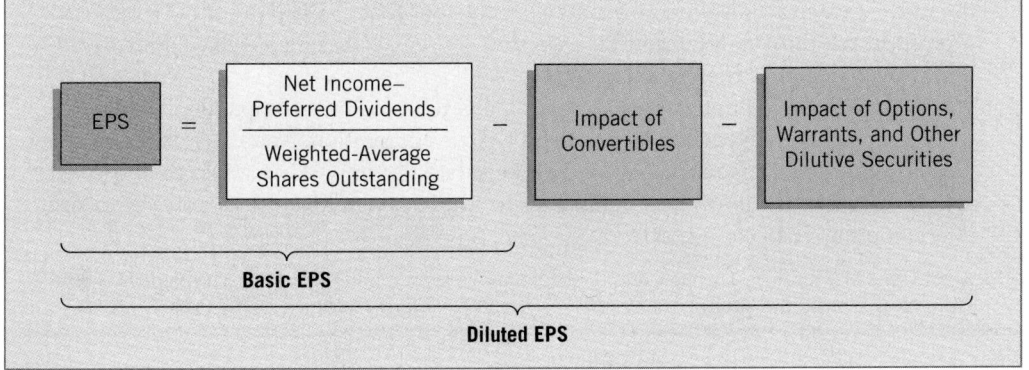

ILLUSTRATION 16-17
Relation between Basic and Diluted EPS

INTERNATIONAL INSIGHT

The provisions in U.S. GAAP are substantially the same as those in *International Accounting Standard No. 33*, "Earnings per Share," issued by the IASB.

Some securities are antidilutive. **Antidilutive securities** are securities that upon conversion or exercise **increase** earnings per share (or reduce the loss per share). Companies with complex capital structures will not report diluted EPS if the securities in their capital structure are antidilutive. The purpose of presenting both basic and diluted EPS is to inform financial statement users of situations that will likely occur (basic EPS) and also to provide "worst case" dilutive situations (dilutive EPS) If the securities are antidilutive, the likelihood of conversion or exercise is considered remote. Thus,

---
[17]Issuance of these types of securities is typical in mergers and compensation plans.

companies that have only antidilutive securities must report only the basic EPS number. We illustrated the computation of basic EPS in the prior section. In the following sections, we address the effects of convertible and other dilutive securities on EPS calculations.

WHAT DO THE NUMBERS MEAN?

PRO FORMA EPS CONFUSION

Many companies are reporting pro forma EPS numbers along with U.S. GAAP-based EPS numbers in the financial information provided to investors. Pro forma earnings generally exceed GAAP earnings because the pro forma numbers exclude such items as restructuring charges, impairments of assets, R&D expenditures, and stock compensation expense. Here are some examples.

Company	U.S. GAAP EPS	Pro Forma EPS
Adaptec	$(0.62)	$ 0.05
Corning	(0.24)	0.09
General Motors	(0.41)	0.85
Honeywell International	(0.38)	0.44
International Paper	(0.57)	0.14
Qualcomm	(0.06)	0.20
Broadcom	(6.36)	(0.13)
Lucent Technologies	(2.16)	(0.27)

Source: Company press releases.

The SEC has expressed concern that pro forma earnings may be misleading. For example, the SEC cited **Trump Hotels & Casino Resorts (DJT)** for abuses related to a recent third-quarter pro forma EPS release. It noted that the firm misrepresented its operating results by excluding a material, one-time $81.4 million charge in its pro forma EPS statement and including an undisclosed nonrecurring gain of $17.2 million. The gain enabled DJT to post a profit in the quarter. The SEC emphasized that DJT's pro forma EPS statement deviated from conservative U.S. GAAP reporting. Therefore, it was "fraudulent" because it created a "false and misleading impression" that DJT had actually (1) recorded a profit in the third quarter and (2) exceeded consensus earnings expectations by enhancing its operating fundamentals.

As discussed in Chapter 4, SEC Regulation G now requires companies to provide a clear reconciliation between pro forma and GAAP information. And this applies to EPS measures as well. This reconciliation will be especially important, given the expected spike in pro forma reporting by companies to add back employee stock option expense after adopting *SFAS No. 123(R)*.

Sources: See M. Moran, A. J. Cohen, and K. Shaustyuk, "Stock Option Expensing: The Battle Has Been Won; Now Comes the Aftermath," *Portfolio Strategy/Accounting*. Goldman Sachs (March 17, 2005).

Diluted EPS—Convertible Securities

At conversion, companies exchange convertible securities for common stock. Companies measure the dilutive effects of potential conversion on EPS using the **if-converted method**. This method for a convertible bond assumes: (1) the conversion of the convertible securities at the beginning of the period (or at the time of issuance of the security, if issued during the period), and (2) the elimination of related interest, net of tax. Thus the additional shares assumed issued increase the **denominator**—the weighted-average number of shares outstanding. The amount of interest expense, net of tax associated with those potential common shares, increases the **numerator**—net income.

Comprehensive Example—If-Converted Method

As an example, MayField Corporation has net income of $210,000 for the year and a weighted-average number of common shares outstanding during the period of 100,000 shares. The basic earnings per share is therefore $2.10 ($210,000 ÷ 100,000). The company has two convertible debenture bond issues outstanding. One is a 6 percent issue sold at 100 (total $1,000,000) in a prior year and convertible into 20,000 common shares. The other is a 10 percent issue sold at 100 (total $1,000,000) on April 1 of the current year and convertible into 32,000 common shares. The tax rate is 40 percent.

As Illustration 16-18 shows, to determine the numerator for diluted earnings per share, Mayfield adds back the interest on the if-converted securities, less the related tax effect. Because the if-converted method assumes conversion as of the beginning of the year, MayField assumes that it pays no interest on the convertibles during the year. The interest on the 6 percent convertibles is $60,000 for the year ($1,000,000 × 6%). The increased tax expense is $24,000 ($60,000 × 0.40). The interest added back net of taxes is $36,000 [$60,000 − $24,000, or simply $60,000 × (1 − 0.40)].

Net income for the year	$210,000
Add: Adjustment for interest (net of tax)	
6% debentures ($60,000 × [1 − .40])	36,000
10% debentures ($100,000 × 9/12 × [1 − .40])	45,000
Adjusted net income	$291,000

ILLUSTRATION 16-18
Computation of Adjusted Net Income

Continuing with the information in Illustration 16-18, because Mayfield issues 10 percent convertibles subsequent to the beginning of the year, it weights the shares. In other words, it considers these shares to have been outstanding from April 1 to the end of the year. As a result, the interest adjustment to the numerator for these bonds reflects the interest for only nine months. Thus the interest added back on the 10 percent convertible is $45,000 [$1,000,000 × 10% × 9/12 year × (1 − 0.4)]. The final item in Illustration 16-18 shows the adjusted net income. This amount becomes the numerator for MayField's computation of diluted earnings per share.

MayField then calculates the weighted-average number of shares outstanding, as shown in Illustration 16-19. This number of shares becomes the denominator for May-Field's computation of diluted earnings per share.

Weighted average number of shares outstanding	100,000
Add: Shares assumed to be issued:	
6% debentures (as of beginning of year)	20,000
10% debentures (as of date of issue, April 1; 9/12 × 32,000)	24,000
Weighted-average number of shares adjusted for dilutive securities	144,000

ILLUSTRATION 16-19
Computation of Weighted-Average Number of Shares

In its income statement, MayField reports basic and diluted earnings per share.[18] Illustration 16-20 shows this dual presentation.

Net income for the year	$210,000
Earnings per Share (Note X)	
Basic earnings per share ($210,000 ÷ 100,000)	$2.10
Diluted earnings per share ($291,000 ÷ 144,000)	$2.02

ILLUSTRATION 16-20
Earnings per Share Disclosure

---

[18]Conversion of bonds is dilutive because EPS with conversion ($2.02) is less than basic EPS ($2.10).

Other Factors

The example above assumed that MayField sold its bonds at the face amount. If it instead sold the bonds at a premium or discount, the company must adjust the interest expense each period to account for this occurrence. Therefore, the interest expense reported on the income statement is the amount of interest expense, net of tax, added back to net income. (It is not the interest paid in cash during the period.)

In addition, the conversion rate on a dilutive security may change during the period in which the security is outstanding. For the diluted EPS computation in such a situation, the **company uses the most dilutive conversion rate available**. For example, assume that a company issued a convertible bond on January 1, 2005, with a conversion rate of 10 common shares for each bond starting January 1, 2007. Beginning January 1, 2010, the conversion rate is 12 common shares for each bond, and beginning January 1, 2014, it is 15 common shares for each bond. In computing diluted EPS in 2005, the company uses the conversion rate of 15 shares to one bond.

A final issue relates to preferred stock. For example, assume that MayField's 6 percent convertible debentures were instead 6 percent convertible *preferred stock*. In that case, MayField considers the convertible preferred as potential common shares. Thus, it includes them in its diluted EPS calculations as shares outstanding. The company does not subtract preferred dividends from net income in computing the numerator. Why not? Because for purposes of computing EPS, it assumes conversion of the convertible preferreds to outstanding common stock. The company uses net income as the numerator—it computes **no tax effect** because preferred dividends generally are not tax-deductible.

CUCKOO FOR CoCos

WHAT DO THE NUMBERS MEAN?

As discussed in the chapter, diluted earnings per share should reflect the potential dilution of all convertible securities, as long as the securities are not antidilutive. However, by exploiting a loophole in the GAAP for EPS, a number of companies issued contingent convertible bonds (CoCos) that bypassed EPS calculations.

CoCos have additional conditions for conversion that allow companies to avoid revealing how much earnings would be diluted if holders of the bonds exchanged them for stock. In fact, under the rules, companies were able to treat CoCos more like warrants (discussed in the next section); this resulted in the CoCos being antidilutive in EPS calculations. As indicated in the table below, CoCos avoided potential dilution of as much as 15 percent for the following companies:

Company	Potential Dilution
Cephalon	15%
FEI	14
Lattice Semi	13
General Motors	10

Source: Bear Stearns & Co.

From 2000, when the first CoCo was issued, to late 2003, over 300 companies issued CoCos, recording interest expense at lower convertible bond rates and without EPS dilution.

However, the CoCo train may be coming into the station. Due to a ruling by the Emerging Issues Task Force (EITF), companies now must include the shares underlying CoCos in diluted EPS calculations. By late 2004, over 40 companies had modified or redeemed their CoCo bonds to avoid EPS dilution.

Sources: See David Henry, "The Latest Magic in Corporate Finance,"*Business Week* (September 8, 2003), p. 88; and Pat McConnell and Janet Pegg, "Accounting for CoCo Bonds: An Update,"*Equity Research*, Bear Stearns (December 14, 2004).

Diluted EPS—Options and Warrants

A company includes in diluted earnings per share stock options and warrants outstanding (whether or not presently exercisable), unless they are antidilutive. Companies use the **treasury-stock method** to include options and warrants and their equivalents in EPS computations.

The treasury-stock method assumes that a company exercises the options or warrants at the beginning of the year (or date of issue if later), and that it uses those proceeds to purchase common stock for the treasury. If the exercise price is lower than the market price of the stock, then the proceeds from exercise are insufficient to buy back all the shares. The company then adds the incremental shares remaining to the weighted-average number of shares outstanding for purposes of computing diluted earnings per share.

For example, if the exercise price of a warrant is $5 and the fair market value of the stock is $15, the treasury-stock method increases the shares outstanding. Exercise of the warrant results in one additional share outstanding, but the $5 received for the one share issued is insufficient to purchase one share in the market at $15. The company needs to exercise three warrants (and issue three additional shares) to produce enough money ($15) to acquire one share in the market. Thus, a net increase of two shares outstanding results.

To see this computation using larger numbers, assume 1,500 options outstanding at an exercise price of $30 for a common share and a common stock market price per share of $50. Through application of the treasury-stock method, the company would have 600 incremental shares outstanding, computed as shown in Illustration 16-21.[19]

Proceeds from exercise of 1,500 options (1,500 × $30)	$45,000
Shares issued upon exercise of options	1,500
Treasury shares purchasable with proceeds ($45,000 ÷ $50)	900
Incremental shares outstanding (potential common shares)	600

ILLUSTRATION 16-21
Computation of
Incremental Shares

Thus, if the exercise price of the option or warrant is **lower** than the market price of the stock, dilution occurs. An exercise price of the option or warrant **higher** than the market price of the stock reduces common shares. In this case, the options or warrants are **antidilutive** because their assumed exercise leads to an increase in earnings per share.

For both options and warrants, exercise is assumed only if the average market price of the stock exceeds the exercise price during the reported period.[20] As a practical matter, a simple average of the weekly or monthly prices is adequate, so long as the prices do not fluctuate significantly.

Comprehensive Example—Treasury-Stock Method

To illustrate application of the treasury-stock method, assume that Kubitz Industries, Inc. has net income for the period of $220,000. The average number of shares outstanding for the period was 100,000 shares. Hence, basic EPS—ignoring all dilutive securities—is $2.20. The average number of shares related to options outstanding (although not exercisable at this time), at an option price of $20 per share, is 5,000 shares.

---

[19]The incremental number of shares may be more simply computed:

$$\frac{\text{Market price} - \text{Option price}}{\text{Market price}} \times \text{Number of options} = \text{Number of shares}$$

$$\frac{\$50 - \$30}{\$50} \times 1{,}500 \text{ options} = 600 \text{ shares}$$

[20]Options and warrants have essentially the same assumptions and computational problems, although the warrants may allow or require the tendering of some other security, such as debt, in lieu of cash upon exercise. In such situations, the accounting becomes quite complex. *SFAS No. 128* explains the proper disposition in this situation.

The average market price of the common stock during the year was $28. Illustration 16-22 shows the computation of EPS using the treasury-stock method.

ILLUSTRATION 16-22
Computation of Earnings per Share—Treasury Stock Method

	Basic Earnings per Share	Diluted Earnings per Share
Average number of shares related to options outstanding:		5,000
Option price per share		× $20
Proceeds upon exercise of options		$100,000
Average market price of common stock		$28
Treasury shares that could be repurchased with proceeds ($100,000 ÷ $28)		3,571
Excess of shares under option over the treasury shares that could be repurchased (5,000 − 3,571)—potential common incremental shares		1,429
Average number of common shares outstanding	100,000	100,000
Total average number of common shares outstanding and potential common shares	100,000 (A)	101,429 (C)
Net income for the year	$220,000 (B)	$220,000 (D)
Earnings per share	$2.20 (B ÷ A)	$2.17 (D ÷ C)

Contingent Issue Agreement

In business combinations, the acquirer may promise to issue additional shares—referred to as **contingent shares**—under certain conditions. Sometimes the company issues these contingent shares as a result of the mere **passage of time** or upon the attainment of a **certain earnings or market price level**. If this passage of time occurs during the current year, or if the company meets the earnings or market price **by the end of the year**, the company considers the contingent shares as outstanding for the computation of diluted earnings per share.[21]

For example, assume that Watts Corporation purchased Cardoza Company and agreed to give Cardoza's stockholders 20,000 additional shares in 2010 if Cardoza's net income in 2009 is $90,000. In 2008 Cardoza's net income is $100,000. Because Cardoza has already attained the 2009 stipulated earnings of $90,000, in computing diluted earnings per share for 2008, Watts would include the 20,000 contingent shares in the shares-outstanding computation.

Antidilution Revisited

In computing diluted EPS, a company must consider the aggregate of all dilutive securities. But first it must determine which potentially dilutive securities are in fact individually dilutive and which are antidilutive. **A company should exclude any security that is antidilutive**, nor can the company use such a security to offset dilutive securities.

Recall that including antidilutive securities in earnings per share computations increases earnings per share (or reduces net loss per share). With options or warrants, whenever the exercise price exceeds the market price, the security is antidilutive. Convertible debt is antidilutive if the addition to income of the interest (net of tax) causes a greater percentage increase in income (numerator) than conversion of the bonds causes a percentage increase in common and potentially dilutive shares (denominator). In other words, convertible debt is antidilutive if conversion of the security causes common stock earnings to increase by a greater amount per additional common share than earnings per share was before the conversion.

---

[21]In addition to contingent issuances of stock, other situations that might lead to dilution are the issuance of participating securities and two-class common shares. The reporting of these types of securities in EPS computations is beyond the scope of this book.

To illustrate, assume that Martin Corporation has a 6 percent, $1,000,000 debt issue that is convertible into 10,000 common shares. Net income for the year is $210,000, the weighted-average number of common shares outstanding is 100,000 shares, and the tax rate is 40 percent. In this case, assumed conversion of the debt into common stock at the beginning of the year requires the following adjustments of net income and the weighted-average number of shares outstanding.

Net income for the year	$210,000	Average number of shares	
Add: Adjustment for interest		outstanding	100,000
(net of tax) on 6%		Add: Shares issued upon assumed	
debentures		conversion of debt	10,000
$60,000 × (1 − .40)	36,000	Average number of common and	
Adjusted net income	$246,000	potential common shares	110,000

Basic EPS = $210,000 ÷ 100,000 = $2.10
Diluted EPS = $246,000 ÷ 110,000 = $2.24 = **Antidilutive**

ILLUSTRATION 16-23
Test for Antidilution

As a shortcut, Martin can also identify the convertible debt as antidilutive by comparing the EPS resulting from conversion, $3.60 ($36,000 additional earnings × 10,000 additional shares), with EPS before inclusion of the convertible debt, $2.10.

Companies should ignore antidilutive securities in all calculations and in computing diluted earnings per share. This approach is reasonable. The profession's intent was to inform the investor of the possible dilution that might occur in reported earnings per share and not to be concerned with securities that, if converted or exercised, would result in an increase in earnings per share. Appendix 16B to this chapter provides an extended example of how companies consider antidilution in a complex situation with multiple securities.

EPS Presentation and Disclosure

A company with a complex capital structure would present its EPS information as follows.

Earnings per common share	
Basic earnings per share	$3.30
Diluted earnings per share	$2.70

ILLUSTRATION 16-24
EPS Presentation—
Complex Capital
Structure

When the earnings of a period include irregular items, a company should show per share amounts (where applicable) for the following: income from continuing operations, income before extraordinary items, and net income. Companies that report a discontinued operation or an extraordinary item should present per share amounts **for those line items** either on the face of the income statement or in the notes to the financial statements. Illustration 16-25 shows a presentation reporting extraordinary items.

Basic earnings per share	
Income before extraordinary item	$3.80
Extraordinary item	0.80
Net income	$3.00
Diluted earnings per share	
Income before extraordinary item	$3.35
Extraordinary item	0.65
Net income	$2.70

ILLUSTRATION 16-25
EPS Presentation, with
Extraordinary Item

A company must show earnings per share amounts for all periods presented. Also, the company should restate all prior period earnings per share amounts presented for stock dividends and stock splits. If it reports diluted EPS data for at least one period, the company should report such data for all periods presented, even if it is the same as basic EPS. When a company restates results of operations of a prior period as a result of an error or a change in accounting principle, it should also restate the earnings per share data shown for the prior periods. Complex capital structures and dual presentation of earnings per share require the following additional disclosures in note form.

1 Description of pertinent rights and privileges of the various securities outstanding.

2 A reconciliation of the numerators and denominators of the basic and diluted per share computations, including individual income and share amount effects of all securities that affect EPS.

3 The effect given preferred dividends in determining income available to common stockholders in computing basic EPS.

4 Securities that could potentially dilute basic EPS in the future that were excluded in the computation because they would be antidilutive.

5 Effect of conversions subsequent to year-end, but before issuing statements.

Illustration 16-26 presents the reconciliation and the related disclosure to meet the requirements of this standard.[22]

ILLUSTRATION 16-26
Reconciliation for Basic and Diluted EPS

	For the Year Ended 2008		
	Income (Numerator)	Shares (Denominator)	Per Share Amount
Income before extraordinary item	$7,500,000		
Less: Preferred stock dividends	(45,000)		
Basic EPS			
Income available to common stockholders	7,455,000	3,991,666	$1.87
Warrants		30,768	
Convertible preferred stock	45,000	308,333	
4% convertible bonds (net of tax)	60,000	50,000	
Diluted EPS			
Income available to common stockholders + assumed conversions	$7,560,000	4,380,767	$1.73

Stock options to purchase 1,000,000 shares of common stock at $85 per share were outstanding during the second half of 2008 but were not included in the computation of diluted EPS because the options' exercise price was greater than the average market price of the common shares. The options were still outstanding at the end of year 2008 and expire on June 30, 2018.

Summary of EPS Computation

As you can see, computation of earnings per share is a complex issue. It is a controversial area because many securities, although technically not common stock, have many of its basic characteristics. Indeed, some companies have issued these other securities rather than common stock in order to avoid an adverse dilutive effect on

---

[22]"Earnings Per Share," *Statement of Financial Accounting Standards No. 128* (Norwalk, Conn.: FASB, 1997). Note that *SFAS No. 123(R)* has specific disclosure requirements regarding stock option plans and earning per share disclosures as well.

earnings per share. Illustrations 16-27 and 16-28 display the elementary points of calculating earnings per share in a simple capital structure and in a complex capital structure.

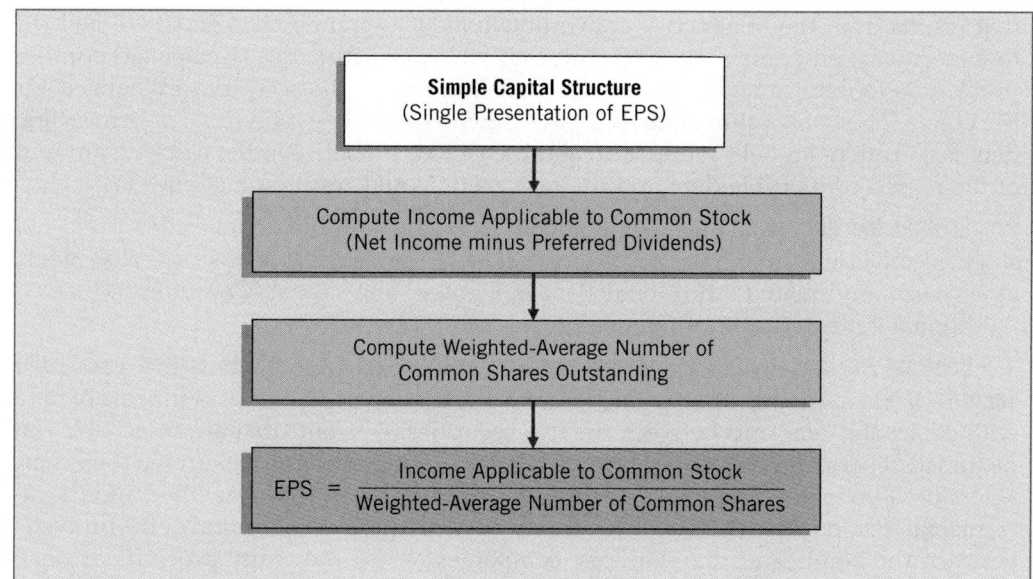

ILLUSTRATION 16-27
Calculating EPS, Simple Capital Structure

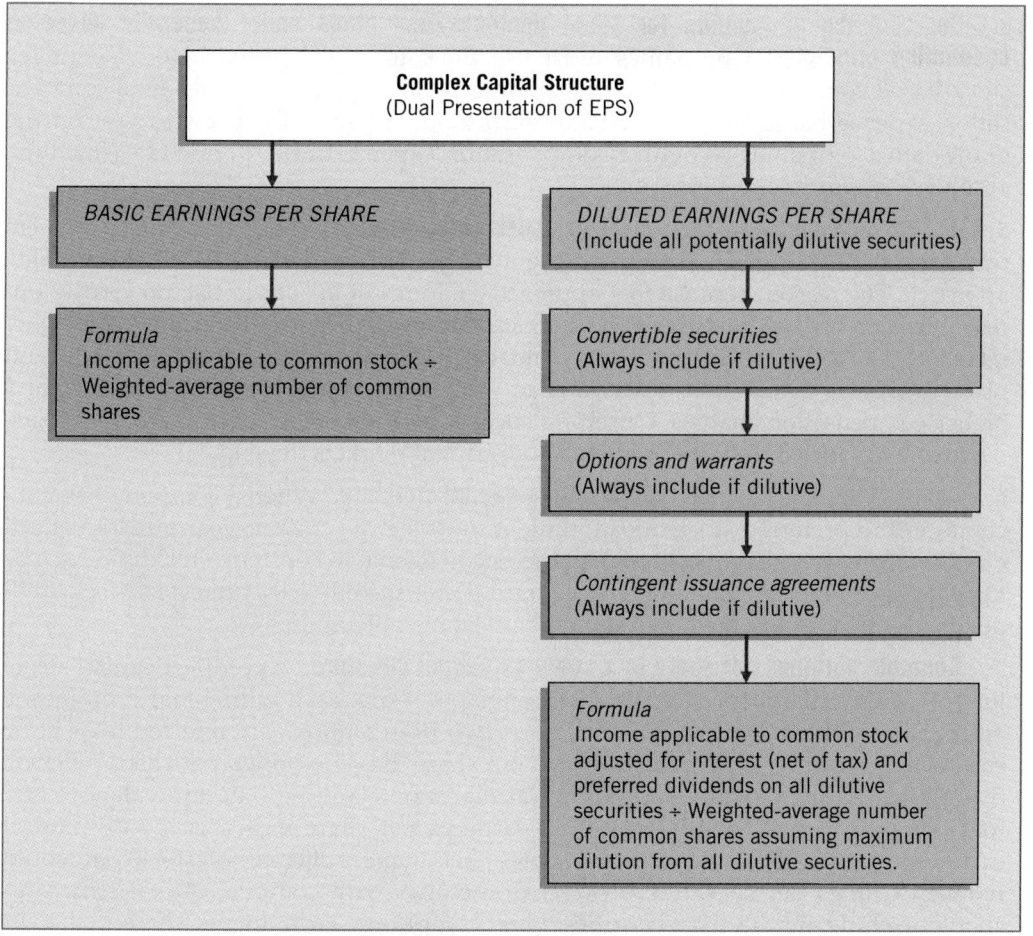

ILLUSTRATION 16-28
Calculating EPS, Complex Capital Structure

SUMMARY OF LEARNING OBJECTIVES

1. Describe the accounting for the issuance, conversion, and retirement of convertible securities. The method for recording convertible bonds at the date of issuance follows that used to record straight debt issues. Companies amortize any discount or premium that results from the issuance of convertible bonds, assuming the bonds will be held to maturity. If companies convert bonds into other securities, the principal accounting problem is to determine the amount at which to record the securities exchanged for the bonds. The book value method is considered GAAP. The retirement of convertible debt is considered a debt retirement, and the difference between the carrying amount of the retired convertible debt and the cash paid should result in a gain or loss.

2. Explain the accounting for convertible preferred stock. When convertible preferred stock is converted, a company uses the book value method: It debits Preferred Stock, along with any related Additional Paid-in Capital, and credits Common Stock and Additional Paid-in Capital (if an excess exists).

3. Contrast the accounting for stock warrants and for stock warrants issued with other securities. *Stock warrants*: Companies should allocate the proceeds from the sale of debt with detachable warrants between the two securities. Warrants that are detachable can be traded separately from the debt, and therefore companies can determine their market value. Two methods of allocation are available: the proportional method and the incremental method. Nondetachable warrants do not require an allocation of the proceeds between the bonds and the warrants; companies record the entire proceeds as debt. *Stock rights*: No entry is required when a company issues rights to existing stockholders. The company needs only to make a memorandum entry to indicate the number of rights issued to existing stockholders and to ensure that the company has additional unissued stock registered for issuance in case the stockholders exercise the rights.

4. Describe the accounting for stock compensation plans under generally accepted accounting principles. Companies must use the fair-value approach to account for stock-based compensation. Under this approach, a company computes total compensation expense based on the fair value of the options that it expects to vest on the grant date. Companies recognize compensation expense in the periods in which the employee performs the services.

5. Discuss the controversy involving stock compensation plans. When first proposed, there was considerable opposition to the recognition provisions contained in the fair-value approach. The reason: because that approach could result in substantial, previously unrecognized compensation expense. Corporate America, particularly the high-technology sector, vocally opposed the proposed standard. They believed that the standard would place them at a competitive disadvantage with larger companies that can withstand higher compensation charges. Offsetting such opposition is the need for greater transparency in financial reporting, on which our capital markets depend.

6. Compute earnings per share in a simple capital structure. When a company has both common and preferred stock outstanding, it subtracts the current-year preferred stock dividend from net income to arrive at income available to common stockholders. The formula for computing earnings per share is net income less preferred stock dividends, divided by the weighted-average of shares outstanding.

7. Compute earnings per share in a complex capital structure. A complex capital structure requires a dual presentation of earnings per share, each with equal prominence on the face of the income statement. These two presentations are referred to as basic earnings per share and diluted earnings per share. Basic earnings per share relies on the number of weighted-average common shares outstanding (i.e., equivalent to EPS for a simple capital structure). Diluted earnings per share indicates the dilution of earnings per share that will occur if all potential issuances of common stock that would reduce earnings per share takes place. Companies with complex capital structures should exclude antidilutive securities when computing earnings per share.

Other Stock-Based Compensation Plans

This chapter's discussion on compensation mainly addresses how to account for stock option plans. However, companies have other compensation plans that are often used to compensate employees using stock-based plans. And more companies are using these alternative plans, given that the accounting treatment for stock options is no longer as favorable as before. In other words, the playing field is now more level—the selection of the type of stock-based compensation plans a company will use will be less driven by the accounting and decided more by proper incentive design and cost considerations.

> **OBJECTIVE 8**
> Explain the accounting for various share-based compensation plans.

Two major plans that companies will use more extensively are: (1) restricted-stock plans and (2) stock appreciation right programs.

RESTRICTED STOCK

Restricted-stock plans transfer shares of stock to employees, subject to an agreement that the shares cannot be sold, transferred or pledged until vesting occurs. These shares are subject to forfeiture if the conditions for vesting are not met. Most companies base vesting on future service for a period of generally three to five years. Vesting may also be conditioned on some performance target such as revenue, net income, cash flows, or some combination of these three factors. The employee also collects dividends on the restricted stock, and these dividends generally must be repaid if forfeiture occurs.

Major advantages of restricted-stock plans are:

1 Restricted stock never becomes completely worthless. In contrast, if the stock price does not exceed the exercise price for a stock option, the options are worthless. The restricted stock, however, still has value.

2 Restricted stock generally results in less dilution to existing stockholders. Restricted-stock awards are usually one-half to one-third the size of stock options. For example, if a company issues stock options on 1,000 shares, an equivalent restricted-stock offering might be 333 to 500 shares. The reason for the difference is that at the end of the vesting period, the restricted stock will have value, whereas the stock options may not. As a result, fewer shares are involved in restricted-stock plans, and therefore less dilution results if the stock price rises.

3 Restricted stock better aligns the employee incentives with the companies' incentives. The holder of restricted stock is essentially a stockholder and should be more interested in the long-term objectives of the company. In contrast, the recipients of stock options often have a short-run focus which leads to taking risks to hype the stock price for short-term gain to the detriment of the long-term.

The accounting for restricted stock follows the same general principles as accounting for stock options at the date of grant. That is, the company determines the fair value of the restricted stock at the date of grant (usually the fair value of a share of stock) and then expenses that amount over the service period. Subsequent changes in the fair value of the stock are ignored for purposes of computing compensation expense.

Restricted Stock Example

Assume that on January 1, 2006, Ogden Company issues 1,000 shares of restricted stock to its CEO, Christie DeGeorge. Ogden's stock has a fair value of $20 per share on January 1, 2006. Additional information is as follows.

1 The service period related to the restricted stock is five years.

2 Vesting occurs if DeGeorge stays with the company for a five-year period.

3 The par value of the stock is $1 per share.

Ogden makes the following entry on the grant date (January 1, 2006).

Unearned Compensation	20,000	
Common Stock (1,000 × $1)		1,000
Paid-In Capital in Excess of Par (1,000 × $19)		19,000

The credits to Common Stock and Paid-In Capital in Excess of par indicate that Ogden has issued shares of stock. The debit to Unearned Compensation (often referred to as Deferred Compensation Expense) identifies the total compensation expense the company will recognize over the five-year period. **Unearned Compensation represents the cost of services yet to be performed, which is not an asset.** Consequently, the company reports Unearned Compensation in stockholders' equity in the balance sheet, as a contra-equity account (similar to the reporting of treasury stock at cost).

At December 31, 2006, Ogden records compensation expense of $4,000 (1,000 shares × $20 × 20%) as follows:

Compensation Expense	4,000	
Unearned Compensation		4,000

Ogden records compensation expense of $4,000 for each of the next four years (2007, 2008, 2009, and 2010).

What happens if DeGeorge leaves the company before the five years has elapsed? In this situation, DeGeorge forfeits her rights to the stock, and Ogden reverses the compensation expense already recorded.

For example, assume that DeGeorge leaves on February 3, 2008 (before any expense has been recorded during 2008). The entry to record this forfeiture is as follows:

Common Stock	1,000	
Paid in Capital in Excess of Par	19,000	
Compensation Expense ($4,000 × 2)		8,000
Unearned Compensation		12,000

In this situation, Ogden reverses the compensation expense of $8,000 recorded through 2007. In addition, the company debits Common Stock and Additional Paid-In Capital, reflecting DeGeorge's forfeiture. It credits the balance of Unearned Compensation since none remains when DeGeorge leaves Ogden.

This accounting is similar to accounting for stock options when employees do not fulfill vesting requirements. Recall from the chapter that once compensation expense is recorded for stock options, it is not reversed. The only exception is if the employee does not fulfill the vesting requirement, by leaving the company early.

In Ogden's restricted-stock plan, vesting never occurred because DeGeorge left the company before she met the service requirement. Because DeGeorge was never vested, she had to forfeit her shares. Therefore, the company must reverse compensation expense recorded to date.

As indicated in the chapter more companies are using restricted-stock plans. In 2004, 43.4 percent of chief executives of large companies received some form of restricted stock. This represented an increase of 5.5 percentage points from 2003. **General Electric**, for example, has reduced its stock options recently by replacing 60 percent of its options with restricted stock. **Cendant** has gone even further. An employee who received a stock option worth $1,000 now receives about $550 of stock—but only if the company meets certain financial targets.[1]

STOCK APPRECIATION RIGHTS (SARs)

A major disadvantage of many stock option plans is that an executive must pay income tax on the difference between the market price of the stock and the option price at the **date of exercise**. This feature of stock option plans (those referred to as nonqualified) can be a financial hardship for an executive who wishes to keep the stock (rather than sell it immediately) because he or she would have to pay not only income tax but the option price as well. In another type of plan (an **incentive plan**), the executive pays no taxes at exercise but may need to borrow to finance the exercise price, which leads to related interest cost.

One solution to this problem was the creation of **stock appreciation rights (SARs)**. In this type of plan, the company gives an executive the right to receive compensation equal to the share appreciation. **Share appreciation** is the excess of the market price of the stock at the date of exercise over a pre-established price. The company may pay the share appreciation in cash, shares, or a combination of both.

The major advantage of SARs is that the executive often does not have to make a cash outlay at the date of exercise, but receives a payment for the share appreciation. Unlike shares acquired under a stock option plan, the company does not issue the shares that constitute the basis for computing the appreciation in a SARs plan. Rather, the company simply awards the executive cash or stock having a market value equivalent to the appreciation. The accounting for stock appreciation rights depends on whether the company classifies the rights as equity or as a liability.

SARs—Share-Based Equity Awards

Companies classify SARs as **equity awards** if at the date of exercise, the holder receives shares of stock from the company upon exercise. In essence, SARs are essentially equivalent to a stock option. The major difference relates to the form of payment. With the stock option, the holder pays the exercise price and then receives the stock. In an equity SAR, the holder receives shares in an amount equal to the **share price appreciation** (the difference between the market price and the pre-established price). The accounting for SARs when they are equity awards follows the accounting used for stock options. At the date of grant, the company determines a fair value for the SAR and then allocates this amount to compensation expense over the service period of the employees.

SARs—Share-Based Liability Awards

Companies classify SARs as liability awards if at the date of exercise, the holder receives a cash payment. In this case the holder is not receiving additional shares of stock but a cash payment equal to the amount of share price appreciation. The company's compensation expense therefore changes as the value of the liability changes.

A company uses the following approach to record share-based liability awards:

1 Measure the fair value of the award at the grant date and accrue compensation over the service period.

2 Remeasure the fair value each reporting period, until the award is settled, and adjust the compensation cost each period for changes in fair value pro-rated for the portion of the service period completed.

---

[1]There are numerous variations on restricted stock plans, including restricted stock units (for which the shares are issued at the end of the vesting period) and restricted stock plans with performance targets, such as EPS or stock price growth.

A company uses income from continuing operations (adjusted for preferred dividends) to determine whether potential common stock is dilutive or antidilutive. Some refer to this measure as the **control number**. To illustrate, assume that Barton Company provides the following information.

ILLUSTRATION 16B-13
Barton Company Data

Income from continuing operations	$2,400,000
Loss from discontinued operations	3,600,000
Net loss	$1,200,000
Weighted-average shares of common stock outstanding	1,000,000
Potential common stock	200,000

Barton reports basic and dilutive earnings per share as follows.

ILLUSTRATION 16B-14
Basic and Diluted EPS

Basic earnings per share	
Income from continuing operations	$2.40
Loss from discontinued operations	3.60
Net loss	$1.20
Diluted earnings per share	
Income from continuing operations	$2.00
Loss from discontinued operations	3.00
Net loss	$1.00

As Illustration 16B-14 shows, basic earnings per share from continuing operations is higher than the diluted earnings per share from continuing operations. The reason: The diluted earnings per share from continuing operations includes an additional 200,000 shares of potential common stock in its denominator.[1]

Companies use income from continuing operations as the control number because many of them show income from continuing operations (or a similar line item above net income if it appears on the income statement), but report a final net loss due to a loss on discontinued operations. If a company uses final net loss as the control number, basic and diluted earnings per share would be the same because the potential common shares are antidilutive.[2]

EPS Illustration with
Multiple Dilutive Securities

college/kieso
wiley.com

KEY TERMS

control number, *816*

SUMMARY OF LEARNING OBJECTIVE FOR APPENDIX 16B

9. **Compute earnings per share in a complex situation.** For diluted EPS, make the following computations: (1) For each potentially dilutive security, determine the per share effect assuming exercise/conversion. (2) Rank the results from most dilutive to least dilutive. (3) Recalculate EPS starting with the most dilutive, and continue adding securities until EPS does not change.

---

[1]A company that does not report a discontinued operation but reports an extraordinary item should use that line item (for example, income before extraordinary items) as the control number.

[2]If a company reports a loss from continuing operations, basic and diluted earnings per share will be the same because potential common stock will be antidilutive, even if the company reports final net income. The FASB believes that comparability of EPS information will be improved by using income from continuing operations as the control number.

Note: All **asterisked** Questions, Brief Exercises, Exercises, and Concepts for Analysis relate to material contained in the appendixes to the chapter.

QUESTIONS

1. What is meant by a dilutive security?

2. Briefly explain why corporations issue convertible securities.

3. Discuss the similarities and the differences between convertible debt and debt issued with stock warrants.

4. Plantagenet Corp. offered holders of its 1,000 convertible bonds a premium of $160 per bond to induce conversion into shares of its common stock. Upon conversion of all the bonds, Plantagenet Corp. recorded the $160,000 premium as a reduction of paid-in capital. Comment on Plantagenet's treatment of the $160,000 "sweetener."

5. Explain how the conversion feature of convertible debt has a value (a) to the issuer and (b) to the purchaser.

6. What are the arguments for giving separate accounting recognition to the conversion feature of debentures?

7. Four years after issue, debentures with a face value of $1,000,000 and book value of $960,000 are tendered for conversion into 80,000 shares of common stock immediately after an interest payment date. At that time the market price of the debentures is 104, and the common stock is selling at $14 per share (par value $10). The company records the conversion as follows.

Bonds Payable	1,000,000	
Discount on Bonds Payable		40,000
Common Stock		800,000
Paid-in Capital in Excess of Par		160,000

Discuss the propriety of this accounting treatment.

8. On July 1, 2007, Roberts Corporation issued $3,000,000 of 9% bonds payable in 20 years. The bonds include detachable warrants giving the bondholder the right to purchase for $30 one share of $1 par value common stock at any time during the next 10 years. The bonds were sold for $3,000,000. The value of the warrants at the time of issuance was $200,000. Prepare the journal entry to record this transaction.

9. What are stock rights? How does the issuing company account for them?

10. Briefly explain the accounting requirements for stock compensation plans under *Statement of Financial Accounting Standards No. 123(R)*.

11. Weiland Corporation has an employee stock purchase plan which permits all full-time employees to purchase 10 shares of common stock on the third anniversary of their employment and an additional 15 shares on each subsequent anniversary date. The purchase price is set at the market price on the date purchased and no commission is charged. Discuss whether this plan would be considered compensatory.

12. What date or event does the profession believe should be used in determining the value of a stock option? What arguments support this position?

13. Over what period of time should compensation cost be allocated?

14. How is compensation expense computed using the fair value approach?

15. At December 31, 2007, Amad Company had 600,000 shares of common stock issued and outstanding, 400,000 of which had been issued and outstanding throughout the year and 200,000 of which were issued on October 1, 2007. Net income for 2007 was $3,000,000, and dividends declared on preferred stock were $400,000. Compute Amad's earnings per common share. (Round to the nearest penny.)

16. What effect do stock dividends or stock splits have on the computation of the weighted-average number of shares outstanding?

17. Define the following terms.

   (a) Basic earnings per share.

   (b) Potentially dilutive security.

   (c) Diluted earnings per share.

   (d) Complex capital structure.

   (e) Potential common stock.

18. What are the computational guidelines for determining whether a convertible security is to be reported as part of diluted earnings per share?

19. Discuss why options and warrants may be considered potentially dilutive common shares for the computation of diluted earnings per share.

20. Explain how convertible securities are determined to be potentially dilutive common shares and how those convertible securities that are not considered to be potentially dilutive common shares enter into the determination of earnings per share data.

21. Explain the treasury stock method as it applies to options and warrants in computing dilutive earnings per share data.

22. Earnings per share can affect market prices of common stock. Can market prices affect earnings per share? Explain.

23. What is meant by the term antidilution? Give an example.

24. What type of earnings per share presentation is required in a complex capital structure?

*25. What are the advantages of using restricted stock to compensate employees?

*26. How is antidilution determined when multiple securities are involved?

WILEY PLUS	**BRIEF EXERCISES**

(LO 1) **BE16-1** Faital Inc. issued $5,000,000 par value, 7% convertible bonds at 99 for cash. If the bonds had not included the conversion feature, they would have sold for 95. Prepare the journal entry to record the issuance of the bonds.

(LO 1) **BE16-2** Sasha Verbitsky Corporation has outstanding 1,000 $1,000 bonds, each convertible into 50 shares of $10 par value common stock. The bonds are converted on December 31, 2008, when the unamortized discount is $30,000 and the market price of the stock is $21 per share. Record the conversion using the book value approach.

(LO 2) **BE16-3** Malik Sealy Corporation issued 2,000 shares of $10 par value common stock upon conversion of 1,000 shares of $50 par value preferred stock. The preferred stock was originally issued at $55 per share. The common stock is trading at $26 per share at the time of conversion. Record the conversion of the preferred stock.

(LO 3) **BE16-4** Divac Corporation issued 1,000 $1,000 bonds at 101. Each bond was issued with one detachable stock warrant. After issuance, the bonds were selling in the market at 98, and the warrants had a market value of $40. Use the proportional method to record the issuance of the bonds and warrants.

(LO 3) **BE16-5** Ceballos Corporation issued 1,000 $1,000 bonds at 101. Each bond was issued with one detachable stock warrant. After issuance, the bonds were selling separately at 98. The market price of the warrants without the bonds cannot be determined. Use the incremental method to record the issuance of the bonds and warrants.

(LO 4) **BE16-6** On January 1, 2008, Johnson Corporation granted 5,000 options to executives. Each option entitles the holder to purchase one share of Johnson's $5 par value common stock at $50 per share at any time during the next 5 years. The market price of the stock is $65 per share on the date of grant. The fair value of the options at the grant date is $140,000. The period of benefit is 2 years. Prepare Johnson's journal entries for January 1, 2008, and December 31, 2008 and 2009.

(LO 6) **BE16-7** Haley Corporation had 2008 net income of $1,200,000. During 2008, Haley paid a dividend of $2 per share on 100,000 shares of preferred stock. During 2008, Haley had outstanding 250,000 shares of common stock. Compute Haley's 2008 earnings per share.

(LO 6) **BE16-8** Barkley Corporation had 120,000 shares of stock outstanding on January 1, 2008. On May 1, 2008, Barkley issued 45,000 shares. On July 1, Barkley purchased 10,000 treasury shares, which were reissued on October 1. Compute Barkley's weighted-average number of shares outstanding for 2008.

(LO 6) **BE16-9** Green Corporation had 200,000 shares of common stock outstanding on January 1, 2008. On May 1, Green issued 30,000 shares. (a) Compute the weighted average number of shares outstanding if the 30,000 shares were issued for cash. (b) Compute the weighted-average number of shares outstanding if the 30,000 shares were issued in a stock dividend.

(LO 7) **BE16-10** Strickland Corporation earned net income of $300,000 in 2008 and had 100,000 shares of common stock outstanding throughout the year. Also outstanding all year was $400,000 of 10% bonds, which are convertible into 16,000 shares of common. Strickland's tax rate is 40 percent. Compute Strickland's 2008 diluted earnings per share.

(LO 7) **BE16-11** Sabonis Corporation reported net income of $400,000 in 2008 and had 50,000 shares of common stock outstanding throughout the year. Also outstanding all year were 5,000 shares of cumulative preferred stock, each convertible into 2 shares of common. The preferred stock pays an annual dividend of $5 per share. Sabonis' tax rate is 40%. Compute Sabonis' 2008 diluted earnings per share.

(LO 7) **BE16-12** Sarunas Corporation reported net income of $300,000 in 2008 and had 200,000 shares of common stock outstanding throughout the year. Also outstanding all year were 30,000 options to purchase common stock at $10 per share. The average market price of the stock during the year was $15. Compute diluted earnings per share.

(LO 6) **BE16-13** The 2008 income statement of Schrempf Corporation showed net income of $480,000 and an extraordinary loss of $120,000. Schrempf had 50,000 shares of common stock outstanding all year. Prepare Schrempf's income statement presentation of earnings per share.

(LO 8) *****BE16-14** On January 1, 2008 (the date of grant), Lee Corporation issues 2,000 shares of restricted stock to its executives. The fair value of these shares is $90,000, and their par value is $10,000. The stock is forfeited if the executives do not complete 3 years of employment with the company. Prepare the journal entry (if any) on January 1, 2008, and on December 31, 2008, assuming the service period is 3 years.

(LO 8) **BE16-15* Sam Perkins, Inc. established a stock appreciation rights (SAR) program on January 1, 2007, which entitles executives to receive cash at the date of exercise for the difference between the market price of the stock and the preestablished price of $20 on 5,000 SARs. The required service period is 2 years. The fair value of the SARs are determined to be $2 on December 31, 2007, and $9 on December 31, 2008. Compute Perkins' compensation expense for 2007 and 2008.

EXERCISES

(LO 3) **E16-1 (Issuance and Conversion of Bonds)** For each of the unrelated transactions described below, present the entry(ies) required to record each transaction.

1. Grand Corp. issued $20,000,000 par value 10% convertible bonds at 99. If the bonds had not been convertible, the company's investment banker estimates they would have been sold at 95. Expenses of issuing the bonds were $70,000.
2. Hoosier Company issued $20,000,000 par value 10% bonds at 98. One detachable stock purchase warrant was issued with each $100 par value bond. At the time of issuance, the warrants were selling for $4.
3. **Sepracor, Inc.** called its convertible debt in 2007. Assume the following related to the transaction: The 11%, $10,000,000 par value bonds were converted into 1,000,000 shares of $1 par value common stock on July 1, 2007. On July 1, there was $55,000 of unamortized discount applicable to the bonds, and the company paid an additional $75,000 to the bondholders to induce conversion of all the bonds. The company records the conversion using the book value method.

(LO 1) **E16-2 (Conversion of Bonds)** Aubrey Inc. issued $4,000,000 of 10%, 10-year convertible bonds on June 1, 2007, at 98 plus accrued interest. The bonds were dated April 1, 2007, with interest payable April 1 and October 1. Bond discount is amortized semiannually on a straight-line basis.

On April 1, 2008, $1,500,000 of these bonds were converted into 30,000 shares of $20 par value common stock. Accrued interest was paid in cash at the time of conversion.

Instructions
(a) Prepare the entry to record the interest expense at October 1, 2007. Assume that accrued interest payable was credited when the bonds were issued. (Round to nearest dollar.)
(b) Prepare the entry(ies) to record the conversion on April 1, 2008. (Book value method is used.) Assume that the entry to record amortization of the bond discount and interest payment has been made.

(LO 1) **E16-3 (Conversion of Bonds)** Vargo Company has bonds payable outstanding in the amount of $500,000, and the Premium on Bonds Payable account has a balance of $7,500. Each $1,000 bond is convertible into 20 shares of preferred stock of par value of $50 per share. All bonds are converted into preferred stock.

Instructions
Assuming that the book value method was used, what entry would be made?

(LO 1) **E16-4 (Conversion of Bonds)** On January 1, 2006, when its $30 par value common stock was selling for $80 per share, Plato Corp. issued $10,000,000 of 8% convertible debentures due in 20 years. The conversion option allowed the holder of each $1,000 bond to convert the bond into five shares of the corporation's common stock. The debentures were issued for $10,800,000. The present value of the bond payments at the time of issuance was $8,500,000, and the corporation believes the difference between the present value and the amount paid is attributable to the conversion feature. On January 1, 2007, the corporation's $30 par value common stock was split 2 for 1, and the conversion rate for the bonds was adjusted accordingly. On January 1, 2008, when the corporation's $15 par value common stock was selling for $135 per share, holders of 30% of the convertible debentures exercised their conversion options. The corporation uses the straight-line method for amortizing any bond discounts or premiums.

Instructions
(a) Prepare in general journal form the entry to record the original issuance of the convertible debentures.
(b) Prepare in general journal form the entry to record the exercise of the conversion option, using the book value method. Show supporting computations in good form.

(LO 1) **E16-5** **(Conversion of Bonds)** The December 31, 2007, balance sheet of Kepler Corp. is as follows.

10% callable, convertible bonds payable (semiannual interest dates April 30 and October 31; convertible into 6 shares of $25 par value common stock per $1,000 of bond principal; maturity date April 30, 2013)	$500,000	
Discount on bonds payable	10,240	$489,760

On March 5, 2008, Kepler Corp. called all of the bonds as of April 30 for the principal plus interest through April 30. By April 30 all bondholders had exercised their conversion to common stock as of the interest payment date. Consequently, on April 30, Kepler Corp. paid the semiannual interest and issued shares of common stock for the bonds. The discount is amortized on a straight-line basis. Kepler uses the book value method.

Instructions

Prepare the entry(ies) to record the interest expense and conversion on April 30, 2008. Reversing entries were made on January 1, 2008. (Round to the nearest dollar.)

(LO 1) **E16-6** **(Conversion of Bonds)** On January 1, 2007, Gottlieb Corporation issued $4,000,000 of 10-year, 8% convertible debentures at 102. Interest is to be paid semiannually on June 30 and December 31. Each $1,000 debenture can be converted into eight shares of Gottlieb Corporation $100 par value common stock after December 31, 2008.

On January 1, 2009, $400,000 of debentures are converted into common stock, which is then selling at $110. An additional $400,000 of debentures are converted on March 31, 2009. The market price of the common stock is then $115. Accrued interest at March 31 will be paid on the next interest date.

Bond premium is amortized on a straight-line basis.

Instructions

Make the necessary journal entries for:

(a)	December 31, 2008.	**(c)**	March 31, 2009.
(b)	January 1, 2009.	**(d)**	June 30, 2009.

Record the conversions using the book value method.

(LO 3) **E16-7** **(Issuance of Bonds with Warrants)** Illiad Inc. has decided to raise additional capital by issuing $170,000 face value of bonds with a coupon rate of 10%. In discussions with investment bankers, it was determined that to help the sale of the bonds, detachable stock warrants should be issued at the rate of one warrant for each $100 bond sold. The value of the bonds without the warrants is considered to be $136,000, and the value of the warrants in the market is $24,000. The bonds sold in the market at issuance for $152,000.

Instructions

(a) What entry should be made at the time of the issuance of the bonds and warrants?

(b) If the warrants were nondetachable, would the entries be different? Discuss.

(LO 3) **E16-8** **(Issuance of Bonds with Detachable Warrants)** On September 1, 2007, Sands Company sold at 104 (plus accrued interest) 4,000 of its 9%, 10-year, $1,000 face value, nonconvertible bonds with detachable stock warrants. Each bond carried two detachable warrants. Each warrant was for one share of common stock at a specified option price of $15 per share. Shortly after issuance, the warrants were quoted on the market for $3 each. No market value can be determined for the Sands Company bonds. Interest is payable on December 1 and June 1. Bond issue costs of $30,000 were incurred.

Instructions

Prepare in general journal format the entry to record the issuance of the bonds.

(AICPA adapted)

(LO 3) **E16-9** **(Issuance of Bonds with Stock Warrants)** On May 1, 2007, Friendly Company issued 2,000 $1,000 bonds at 102. Each bond was issued with one detachable stock warrant. Shortly after issuance, the bonds were selling at 98, but the market value of the warrants cannot be determined.

Instructions

(a) Prepare the entry to record the issuance of the bonds and warrants.

(b) Assume the same facts as part (a), except that the warrants had a fair value of $30. Prepare the entry to record the issuance of the bonds and warrants.

(LO 4) **E16-10** **(Issuance and Exercise of Stock Options)** On November 1, 2007, Columbo Company adopted a stock option plan that granted options to key executives to purchase 30,000 shares of the company's $10 par value common stock. The options were granted on January 2, 2008, and were exercisable 2 years after the date of grant if the grantee was still an employee of the company. The options expired 6 years from date of grant. The option price was set at $40, and the fair value option pricing model determines the total compensation expense to be $450,000.

All of the options were exercised during the year 2010: 20,000 on January 3 when the market price was $67, and 10,000 on May 1 when the market price was $77 a share.

Instructions
Prepare journal entries relating to the stock option plan for the years 2008, 2009, and 2010. Assume that the employee performs services equally in 2008 and 2009.

(LO 4) **E16-11** **(Issuance, Exercise, and Termination of Stock Options)** On January 1, 2008, Titania Inc. granted stock options to officers and key employees for the purchase of 20,000 shares of the company's $10 par common stock at $25 per share. The options were exercisable within a 5-year period beginning January 1, 2010, by grantees still in the employ of the company, and expiring December 31, 2014. The service period for this award is 2 years. Assume that the fair value option pricing model determines total compensation expense to be $350,000.

On April 1, 2009, 2,000 options were terminated when the employees resigned from the company. The market value of the common stock was $35 per share on this date.

On March 31, 2010, 12,000 options were exercised when the market value of the common stock was $40 per share.

Instructions
Prepare journal entries to record issuance of the stock options, termination of the stock options, exercise of the stock options, and charges to compensation expense, for the years ended December 31, 2008, 2009, and 2010.

(LO 4) **E16-12** **(Issuance, Exercise, and Termination of Stock Options)** On January 1, 2006, Nichols Corporation granted 10,000 options to key executives. Each option allows the executive to purchase one share of Nichols' $5 par value common stock at a price of $20 per share. The options were exercisable within a 2-year period beginning January 1, 2008, if the grantee is still employed by the company at the time of the exercise. On the grant date, Nichols' stock was trading at $25 per share, and a fair value option-pricing model determines total compensation to be $400,000.

On May 1, 2008, 8,000 options were exercised when the market price of Nichols' stock was $30 per share. The remaining options lapsed in 2010 because executives decided not to exercise their options.

Instructions
Prepare the necessary journal entries related to the stock option plan for the years 2006 through 2010.

(LO 6) **E16-13** **(Weighted-Average Number of Shares)** Newton Inc. uses a calendar year for financial reporting. The company is authorized to issue 9,000,000 shares of $10 par common stock. At no time has Newton issued any potentially dilutive securities. Listed below is a summary of Newton's common stock activities.

1. Number of common shares issued and outstanding at December 31, 2005	2,000,000
2. Shares issued as a result of a 10% stock dividend on September 30, 2006	200,000
3. Shares issued for cash on March 31, 2007	2,000,000
Number of common shares issued and outstanding at December 31, 2007	4,200,000

4. A 2-for-1 stock split of Newton's common stock took place on March 31, 2008.

Instructions
(a) Compute the weighted-average number of common shares used in computing earnings per common share for 2006 on the 2007 comparative income statement.
(b) Compute the weighted-average number of common shares used in computing earnings per common share for 2007 on the 2007 comparative income statement.
(c) Compute the weighted-average number of common shares to be used in computing earnings per common share for 2007 on the 2008 comparative income statement.
(d) Compute the weighted-average number of common shares to be used in computing earnings per common share for 2008 on the 2008 comparative income statement.

(CMA adapted)

(LO 6) **E16-14** **(EPS: Simple Capital Structure)** On January 1, 2008, Wilke Corp. had 480,000 shares of common stock outstanding. During 2008, it had the following transactions that affected the common stock account.

February 1	Issued 120,000 shares
March 1	Issued a 10% stock dividend
May 1	Acquired 100,000 shares of treasury stock
June 1	Issued a 3-for-1 stock split
October 1	Reissued 60,000 shares of treasury stock

Instructions

(a) Determine the weighted-average number of shares outstanding as of December 31, 2008.

(b) Assume that Wilke Corp. earned net income of $3,456,000 during 2008. In addition, it had 100,000 shares of 9%, $100 par nonconvertible, noncumulative preferred stock outstanding for the entire year. Because of liquidity considerations, however, the company did not declare and pay a preferred dividend in 2008. Compute earnings per share for 2008, using the weighted-average number of shares determined in part (a).

(c) Assume the same facts as in part (b), except that the preferred stock was cumulative. Compute earnings per share for 2008.

(d) Assume the same facts as in part (b), except that net income included an extraordinary gain of $864,000 and a loss from discontinued operations of $432,000. Both items are net of applicable income taxes. Compute earnings per share for 2008.

(LO 6) **E16-15** **(EPS: Simple Capital Structure)** Ace Company had 200,000 shares of common stock outstanding on December 31, 2008. During the year 2009 the company issued 8,000 shares on May 1 and retired 14,000 shares on October 31. For the year 2009 Ace Company reported net income of $249,690 after a casualty loss of $40,600 (net of tax).

Instructions

What earnings per share data should be reported at the bottom of its income statement, assuming that the casualty loss is extraordinary?

(LO 6) **E16-16** **(EPS: Simple Capital Structure)** Flagstad Inc. presented the following data.

Net income	$2,500,000
Preferred stock: 50,000 shares outstanding,	
$100 par, 8% cumulative, not convertible	5,000,000
Common stock: Shares outstanding 1/1	750,000
Issued for cash, 5/1	300,000
Acquired treasury stock for cash, 8/1	150,000
2-for-1 stock split, 10/1	

Instructions

Compute earnings per share.

(LO 6) **E16-17** **(EPS: Simple Capital Structure)** A portion of the combined statement of income and retained earnings of Seminole Inc. for the current year follows.

Income before extraordinary item		$15,000,000
Extraordinary loss, net of applicable		
income tax (Note 1)		1,340,000
Net income		13,660,000
Retained earnings at the beginning of the year		83,250,000
		96,910,000
Dividends declared:		
On preferred stock—$6.00 per share	$ 300,000	
On common stock—$1.75 per share	14,875,000	15,175,000
Retained earnings at the end of the year		$81,735,000

Note 1. During the year, Seminole Inc. suffered a major casualty loss of $1,340,000 after applicable income tax reduction of $1,200,000.

At the end of the current year, Seminole Inc. has outstanding 8,500,000 shares of $10 par common stock and 50,000 shares of 6% preferred.

On April 1 of the current year, Seminole Inc. issued 1,000,000 shares of common stock for $32 per share to help finance the casualty.

Instructions

Compute the earnings per share on common stock for the current year as it should be reported to stockholders.

(LO 6) **E16-18** **(EPS: Simple Capital Structure)** On January 1, 2008, Lennon Industries had stock outstanding as follows.

6% Cumulative preferred stock, $100 par value,	
issued and outstanding 10,000 shares	$1,000,000
Common stock, $10 par value, issued and	
outstanding 200,000 shares	2,000,000

To acquire the net assets of three smaller companies, Lennon authorized the issuance of an additional 160,000 common shares. The acquisitions took place as shown below.

Date of Acquisition	Shares Issued
Company A April 1, 2008	50,000
Company B July 1, 2008	80,000
Company C October 1, 2008	30,000

On May 14, 2008, Lennon realized a $90,000 (before taxes) insurance gain on the expropriation of investments originally purchased in 1994.

On December 31, 2008, Lennon recorded net income of $300,000 before tax and exclusive of the gain.

Instructions

Assuming a 50% tax rate, compute the earnings per share data that should appear on the financial statements of Lennon Industries as of December 31, 2008. Assume that the expropriation is extraordinary.

(LO 6) **E16-19** **(EPS: Simple Capital Structure)** At January 1, 2008, Langley Company's outstanding shares included the following.

> 280,000 shares of $50 par value, 7% cumulative preferred stock
> 900,000 shares of $1 par value common stock

Net income for 2008 was $2,530,000. No cash dividends were declared or paid during 2008. On February 15, 2009, however, all preferred dividends in arrears were paid, together with a 5% stock dividend on common shares. There were no dividends in arrears prior to 2008.

On April 1, 2008, 450,000 shares of common stock were sold for $10 per share, and on October 1, 2008, 110,000 shares of common stock were purchased for $20 per share and held as treasury stock.

Instructions

Compute earnings per share for 2008. Assume that financial statements for 2008 were issued in March 2009.

(LO 7) **E16-20** **(EPS with Convertible Bonds, Various Situations)** In 2006 Chirac Enterprises issued, at par, 60 $1,000, 8% bonds, each convertible into 100 shares of common stock. Chirac had revenues of $17,500 and expenses other than interest and taxes of $8,400 for 2007. (Assume that the tax rate is 40%.) Throughout 2007, 2,000 shares of common stock were outstanding; none of the bonds was converted or redeemed.

Instructions

    (a) Compute diluted earnings per share for 2007.

    (b) Assume the same facts as those assumed for part (a), except that the 60 bonds were issued on September 1, 2007 (rather than in 2006), and none have been converted or redeemed.

    (c) Assume the same facts as assumed for part (a), except that 20 of the 60 bonds were actually converted on July 1, 2007.

(LO 7) **E16-21** **(EPS with Convertible Bonds)** On June 1, 2005, Andre Company and Agassi Company merged to form Lancaster Inc. A total of 800,000 shares were issued to complete the merger. The new corporation reports on a calendar-year basis.

On April 1, 2007, the company issued an additional 400,000 shares of stock for cash. All 1,200,000 shares were outstanding on December 31, 2007.

Lancaster Inc. also issued $600,000 of 20-year, 8% convertible bonds at par on July 1, 2007. Each $1,000 bond converts to 40 shares of common at any interest date. None of the bonds have been converted to date.

Lancaster Inc. is preparing its annual report for the fiscal year ending December 31, 2007. The annual report will show earnings per share figures based upon a reported after-tax net income of $1,540,000. (The tax rate is 40%.)

Instructions

Determine the following for 2007.

    (a) The number of shares to be used for calculating:
        (1) Basic earnings per share.
        (2) Diluted earnings per share.
    (b) The earnings figures to be used for calculating:
        (1) Basic earnings per share.
        (2) Diluted earnings per share.

(CMA adapted)

(LO 2, 7) **E16-22** **(EPS with Convertible Bonds and Preferred Stock)** The Simon Corporation issued 10-year, $5,000,000 par, 7% callable convertible subordinated debentures on January 2, 2007. The bonds have a par value of $1,000, with interest payable annually. The current conversion ratio is 14:1, and in 2 years it will increase to 18:1. At the date of issue, the bonds were sold at 98. Bond discount is amortized on a straight-line basis. Simon's effective tax was 35%. Net income in 2007 was $9,500,000, and the company had 2,000,000 shares outstanding during the entire year.

Instructions

(a) Prepare a schedule to compute both basic and diluted earnings per share.

(b) Discuss how the schedule would differ if the security was convertible preferred stock.

(LO 2, 7) **E16-23** **(EPS with Convertible Bonds and Preferred Stock)** On January 1, 2007, Crocker Company issued 10-year, $2,000,000 face value, 6% bonds, at par. Each $1,000 bond is convertible into 15 shares of Crocker common stock. Crocker's net income in 2007 was $300,000, and its tax rate was 40%. The company had 100,000 shares of common stock outstanding throughout 2007. None of the bonds were converted in 2007.

Instructions

(a) Compute diluted earnings per share for 2007.

(b) Compute diluted earnings per share for 2007, assuming the same facts as above, except that $1,000,000 of 6% convertible preferred stock was issued instead of the bonds. Each $100 preferred share is convertible into 5 shares of Crocker common stock.

(LO 7) **E16-24** **(EPS with Options, Various Situations)** Venzuela Company's net income for 2007 is $50,000. The only potentially dilutive securities outstanding were 1,000 options issued during 2006, each exercisable for one share at $6. None has been exercised, and 10,000 shares of common were outstanding during 2007. The average market price of Venzuela's stock during 2007 was $20.

Instructions

(a) Compute diluted earnings per share. (Round to nearest cent.)

(b) Assume the same facts as those assumed for part (a), except that the 1,000 options were issued on October 1, 2007 (rather than in 2006). The average market price during the last 3 months of 2007 was $20.

(LO 7) **E16-25** **(EPS with Contingent Issuance Agreement)** Winsor Inc. recently purchased Holiday Corp., a large midwestern home painting corporation. One of the terms of the merger was that if Holiday's income for 2007 was $110,000 or more, 10,000 additional shares would be issued to Holiday's stockholders in 2008. Holiday's income for 2006 was $120,000.

Instructions

(a) Would the contingent shares have to be considered in Winsor's 2006 earnings per share computations?

(b) Assume the same facts, except that the 10,000 shares are contingent on Holiday's achieving a net income of $130,000 in 2007. Would the contingent shares have to be considered in Winsor's earnings per share computations for 2006?

(LO 7) **E16-26** **(EPS with Warrants)** Howat Corporation earned $360,000 during a period when it had an average of 100,000 shares of common stock outstanding. The common stock sold at an average market price of $15 per share during the period. Also outstanding were 15,000 warrants that could be exercised to purchase one share of common stock for $10 for each warrant exercised.

Instructions

(a) Are the warrants dilutive?

(b) Compute basic earnings per share.

(c) Compute diluted earnings per share.

(LO 8) *****E16-27** **(Accounting for Restricted Stock)** Tweedie Company issues 4,000 shares of restricted stock to its CFO, Miles Hobart, on January 1, 2007. The stock has a fair value of $100,000 on this date. The service period related to this restricted stock is 4 years. Vesting occurs if Hobart stays with the company for 4 years. The par value of the stock is $5. At December 31, 2008, the fair value of the stock is $120,000.

Instructions

(a) Prepare the journal entries to record the restricted stock on January 1, 2007 (the date of grant) and December 31, 2008.

(b) On March 4, 2009, Hobart leaves the company. Prepare the journal entry (if any) to account for this forfeiture.

(LO 8) *****E16-28** **(Stock Appreciation Rights)** On December 31, 2003, Beckford Company issues 150,000 stock appreciation rights to its officers entitling them to receive cash for the difference between the market price of its stock and a preestablished price of $10. The fair value of the SARs is estimated to be $4 per SAR on

December 31, 2004; $1 on December 31, 2005; $10 on December 31, 2006; and $9 on December 31, 2007. The service period is 4 years, and the exercise period is 7 years.

Instructions

(a) Prepare a schedule that shows the amount of compensation expense allocable to each year affected by the stock appreciation rights plan.

(b) Prepare the entry at December 31, 2007, to record compensation expense, if any, in 2007.

(c) Prepare the entry on December 31, 2007, assuming that all 150,000 SARs are exercised.

(LO 8) *E16-29 (Stock Appreciation Rights)** Capulet Company establishes a stock appreciation rights program that entitles its new president Ben Davis to receive cash for the difference between the market price of the stock and a preestablished price of $30 (also market price) on December 31, 2004, on 30,000 SARs. The date of grant is December 31, 2004, and the required employment (service) period is 4 years. President Davis exercises all of the SARs in 2010. The fair value of the SARs is estimated to be $6 per SAR on December 31, 2005; $9 on December 31, 2006; $15 on December 31, 2007; $6 on December 31, 2008; and $18 on December 31, 2009.

Instructions

(a) Prepare a 5-year (2005–2009) schedule of compensation expense pertaining to the 30,000 SARs granted president Davis.

(b) Prepare the journal entry for compensation expense in 2005, 2008, and 2009 relative to the 30,000 SARs.

> **See the book's website, www.wiley.com/college/kieso, for Additional Exercises.**

PROBLEMS

(LO 1, 3, 4) **P16-1 (Entries for Various Dilutive Securities)** The stockholders' equity section of McLean Inc. at the beginning of the current year appears below.

Common stock, $10 par value, authorized 1,000,000 shares, 300,000 shares issued and outstanding	$3,000,000
Paid-in capital in excess of par	600,000
Retained earnings	570,000

During the current year the following transactions occurred.

1. The company issued to the stockholders 100,000 rights. Ten rights are needed to buy one share of stock at $32. The rights were void after 30 days. The market price of the stock at this time was $34 per share.

2. The company sold to the public a $200,000, 10% bond issue at par. The company also issued with each $100 bond one detachable stock purchase warrant, which provided for the purchase of common stock at $30 per share. Shortly after issuance, similar bonds without warrants were selling at 96 and the warrants at $8.

3. All but 10,000 of the rights issued in (1) were exercised in 30 days.

4. At the end of the year, 80% of the warrants in (2) had been exercised, and the remaining were outstanding and in good standing.

5. During the current year, the company granted stock options for 5,000 shares of common stock to company executives. The company using a fair value option pricing model determines that each option is worth $10. The option price is $30. The options were to expire at year-end and were considered compensation for the current year.

6. All but 1,000 shares related to the stock option plan were exercised by year-end. The expiration resulted because one of the executives failed to fulfill an obligation related to the employment contract.

Instructions

(a) Prepare general journal entries for the current year to record the transactions listed above.

(b) Prepare the stockholders' equity section of the balance sheet at the end of the current year. Assume that retained earnings at the end of the current year is $750,000.

(LO 1) **P16-2 (Entries for Conversion, Amortization, and Interest of Bonds)** Counter Inc. issued $1,500,000 of convertible 10-year bonds on July 1, 2007. The bonds provide for 12% interest payable semiannually on January 1 and July 1. The discount in connection with the issue was $34,000, which is being amortized monthly on a straight-line basis.

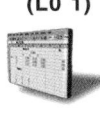

The bonds are convertible after one year into 8 shares of Counter Inc.'s $100 par value common stock for each $1,000 of bonds.

On August 1, 2008, $150,000 of bonds were turned in for conversion into common. Interest has been accrued monthly and paid as due. At the time of conversion any accrued interest on bonds being converted is paid in cash.

Instructions
(Round to nearest dollar)
Prepare the journal entries to record the conversion, amortization, and interest in connection with the bonds as of the following dates.

(a) August 1, 2008. (Assume the book value method is used.)
(b) August 31, 2008.
(c) December 31, 2008, including closing entries for end-of-year.

(AICPA adapted)

(LO 4) **P16-3** **(Stock Option Plan)** ISU Company adopted a stock option plan on November 30, 2005, that provided that 70,000 shares of $5 par value stock be designated as available for the granting of options to officers of the corporation at a price of $8 a share. The market value was $12 a share on November 30, 2005.

On January 2, 2006, options to purchase 28,000 shares were granted to president Don Pedro—15,000 for services to be rendered in 2006 and 13,000 for services to be rendered in 2007. Also on that date, options to purchase 14,000 shares were granted to vice president Beatrice Leonato—7,000 for services to be rendered in 2006 and 7,000 for services to be rendered in 2007. The market value of the stock was $14 a share on January 2, 2006. The options were exercisable for a period of one year following the year in which the services were rendered. The fair value of the options on the grant date was $3 per option.

In 2007 neither the president nor the vice president exercised their options because the market price of the stock was below the exercise price. The market value of the stock was $7 a share on December 31, 2007, when the options for 2006 services lapsed.

On December 31, 2008, both president Pedro and vice president Leonato exercised their options for 13,000 and 7,000 shares, respectively, when the market price was $16 a share.

Instructions
Prepare the necessary journal entries in 2005 when the stock option plan was adopted, in 2006 when options were granted, in 2007 when options lapsed, and in 2008 when options were exercised.

(LO 7) **P16-4** **(EPS with Complex Capital Structure)** Diane Leto, controller at Dewey Yaeger Pharmaceutical Industries, a public company, is currently preparing the calculation for basic and diluted earnings per share and the related disclosure for Yaeger's external financial statements. Below is selected financial information for the fiscal year ended June 30, 2008.

DEWEY YAEGER PHARMACEUTICAL INDUSTRIES
SELECTED STATEMENT OF
FINANCIAL POSITION INFORMATION
JUNE 30, 2008

Long-term debt	
Notes payable, 10%	$ 1,000,000
7% convertible bonds payable	5,000,000
10% bonds payable	6,000,000
Total long-term debt	$12,000,000
Shareholders' equity	
Preferred stock, 8.5% cumulative, $50 par value,	
100,000 shares authorized, 25,000 shares issued	
and outstanding	$ 1,250,000
Common stock, $1 par, 10,000,000 shares authorized,	
1,000,000 shares issued and outstanding	1,000,000
Additional paid-in capital	4,000,000
Retained earnings	6,000,000
Total shareholders' equity	$12,250,000

The following transactions have also occurred at Yaeger.

1. Options were granted in 2006 to purchase 100,000 shares at $15 per share. Although no options were exercised during 2008, the average price per common share during fiscal year 2008 was $20 per share.

2. Each bond was issued at face value. The 7% convertible debenture will convert into common stock at 50 shares per $1,000 bond. It is exercisable after 5 years and was issued in 2007.
3. The 8.5% preferred stock was issued in 2006.
4. There are no preferred dividends in arrears; however, preferred dividends were not declared in fiscal year 2008.
5. The 1,000,000 shares of common stock were outstanding for the entire 2008 fiscal year.
6. Net income for fiscal year 2008 was $1,500,000, and the average income tax rate is 40%.

Instructions

For the fiscal year ended June 30, 2008, calculate the following for Dewey Yaeger Pharmaceutical Industries.

(a) Basic earnings per share.
(b) Diluted earnings per share.

(LO 6) **P16-5 (Basic EPS: Two-Year Presentation)** Hillel Corporation is preparing the comparative financial statements for the annual report to its shareholders for fiscal years ended May 31, 2006, and May 31, 2007. The income from operations for each year was $1,800,000 and $2,500,000, respectively. In both years, the company incurred a 10% interest expense on $2,400,000 of debt, an obligation that requires interest-only payments for 5 years. The company experienced a loss of $500,000 from a fire in its Scotsland facility in February 2007, which was determined to be an extraordinary loss. The company uses a 40% effective tax rate for income taxes.

The capital structure of Hillel Corporation on June 1, 2005, consisted of 2 million shares of common stock outstanding and 20,000 shares of $50 par value, 8%, cumulative preferred stock. There were no preferred dividends in arrears, and the company had not issued any convertible securities, options, or warrants.

On October 1, 2005, Hillel sold an additional 500,000 shares of the common stock at $20 per share. Hillel distributed a 20% stock dividend on the common shares outstanding on January 1, 2006. On December 1, 2006, Hillel was able to sell an additional 800,000 shares of the common stock at $22 per share. These were the only common stock transactions that occurred during the two fiscal years.

Instructions

(a) Identify whether the capital structure at Hillel Corporation is a simple or complex capital structure, and explain why.
(b) Determine the weighted-average number of shares that Hillel Corporation would use in calculating earnings per share for the fiscal year ended
   (1) May 31, 2006.
   (2) May 31, 2007.
(c) Prepare, in good form, a comparative income statement, beginning with income from operations, for Hillel Corporation for the fiscal years ended May 31, 2006, and May 31, 2007. This statement will be included in Hillel's annual report and should display the appropriate earnings per share presentations.

(CMA adapted)

(LO 7) **P16-6 (EPS Computation of Basic and Diluted EPS)** Edmund Halvor of the controller's office of East Aurora Corporation was given the assignment of determining the basic and diluted earnings per share values for the year ending December 31, 2007. Halvor has compiled the information listed below.

1. The company is authorized to issue 8,000,000 shares of $10 par value common stock. As of December 31, 2006, 3,000,000 shares had been issued and were outstanding.
2. The per share market prices of the common stock on selected dates were as follows.

	Price per Share
July 1, 2006	$20.00
January 1, 2007	21.00
April 1, 2007	25.00
July 1, 2007	11.00
August 1, 2007	10.50
November 1, 2007	9.00
December 31, 2007	10.00

3. A total of 700,000 shares of an authorized 1,200,000 shares of convertible preferred stock had been issued on July 1, 2006. The stock was issued at its par value of $25, and it has a cumulative dividend of $3 per share. The stock is convertible into common stock at the rate of one share of convertible preferred for one share of common. The rate of conversion is to be automatically adjusted for stock splits and stock dividends. Dividends are paid quarterly on September 30, December 31, March 31, and June 30.

828 · Chapter 16 Dilutive Securities and Earnings per Share

4. East Aurora Corporation is subject to a 40% income tax rate.
5. The after-tax net income for the year ended December 31, 2007 was $13,550,000.

The following specific activities took place during 2007.

1. January 1—A 5% common stock dividend was issued. The dividend had been declared on December 1, 2006, to all stockholders of record on December 29, 2006.
2. April 1—A total of 200,000 shares of the $3 convertible preferred stock was converted into common stock. The company issued new common stock and retired the preferred stock. This was the only conversion of the preferred stock during 2007.
3. July 1—A 2-for-1 split of the common stock became effective on this date. The board of directors had authorized the split on June 1.
4. August 1—A total of 300,000 shares of common stock were issued to acquire a factory building.
5. November 1—A total of 24,000 shares of common stock were purchased on the open market at $9 per share. These shares were to be held as treasury stock and were still in the treasury as of December 31, 2007.
6. Common stock cash dividends—Cash dividends to common stockholders were declared and paid as follows.
   April 15—$0.30 per share
   October 15—$0.20 per share
7. Preferred stock cash dividends—Cash dividends to preferred stockholders were declared and paid as scheduled.

Instructions
(a) Determine the number of shares used to compute basic earnings per share for the year ended December 31, 2007.
(b) Determine the number of shares used to compute diluted earnings per share for the year ended December 31, 2007.
(c) Compute the adjusted net income to be used as the numerator in the basic earnings per share calculation for the year ended December 31, 2007.

(LO 7) P16-7 (Computation of Basic and Diluted EPS) The information below pertains to Prancer Company for 2007.

Net income for the year	$1,200,000
8% convertible bonds issued at par ($1,000 per bond). Each bond is convertible into 40 shares of common stock.	2,000,000
6% convertible, cumulative preferred stock, $100 par value. Each share is convertible into 3 shares of common stock.	3,000,000
Common stock, $10 par value	6,000,000
Common stock options (granted in a prior year) to purchase 50,000 shares of common stock at $20 per share	500,000
Tax rate for 2004	40%
Average market price of common stock	$25 per share

There were no changes during 2007 in the number of common shares, preferred shares, or convertible bonds outstanding. There is no treasury stock.

Instructions
(a) Compute basic earnings per share for 2007.
(b) Compute diluted earnings per share for 2007.

(LO 6) P16-8 (EPS with Stock Dividend and Extraordinary Items) Cordelia Corporation is preparing the comparative financial statements to be included in the annual report to stockholders. Cordelia employs a fiscal year ending May 31.

Income from operations before income taxes for Cordelia was $1,400,000 and $660,000, respectively, for fiscal years ended May 31, 2007 and 2006. Cordelia experienced an extraordinary loss of $500,000 because of an earthquake on March 3, 2007. A 40% combined income tax rate pertains to any and all of Cordelia Corporation's profits, gains, and losses.

Cordelia's capital structure consists of preferred stock and common stock. The company has not issued any convertible securities or warrants and there are no outstanding stock options.

Cordelia issued 50,000 shares of $100 par value, 6% cumulative preferred stock in 2003. All of this stock is outstanding, and no preferred dividends are in arrears.

There were 1,500,000 shares of $1 par common stock outstanding on June 1, 2005. On September 1, 2005, Cordelia sold an additional 400,000 shares of the common stock at $17 per share. Cordelia distributed a 20% stock dividend on the common shares outstanding on December 1, 2006. These were the only common stock transactions during the past 2 fiscal years.

Instructions

(a) Determine the weighted-average number of common shares that would be used in computing earnings per share on the current comparative income statement for:
   (1) The year ended May 31, 2006.
   (2) The year ended May 31, 2007.

(b) Starting with income from operations before income taxes, prepare a comparative income statement for the years ended May 31, 2007 and 2006. The statement will be part of Cordelia Corporation's annual report to stockholders and should include appropriate earnings per share presentation.

(c) The capital structure of a corporation is the result of its past financing decisions. Furthermore, the earnings per share data presented on a corporation's financial statements is dependent upon the capital structure.
   (1) Explain why Cordelia Corporation is considered to have a simple capital structure.
   (2) Describe how earnings per share data would be presented for a corporation that has a complex capital structure.

(CMA adapted)

CONCEPTS FOR ANALYSIS

CA16-1 (Warrants Issued with Bonds and Convertible Bonds) Incurring long-term debt with an arrangement whereby lenders receive an option to buy common stock during all or a portion of the time the debt is outstanding is a frequent corporate financing practice. In some situations the result is achieved through the issuance of convertible bonds; in others, the debt instruments and the warrants to buy stock are separate.

Instructions

(a) (1) Describe the differences that exist in current accounting for original proceeds of the issuance of convertible bonds and of debt instruments with separate warrants to purchase common stock.
   (2) Discuss the underlying rationale for the differences described in (a)1 above.
   (3) Summarize the arguments that have been presented in favor of accounting for convertible bonds in the same manner as accounting for debt with separate warrants.

(b) At the start of the year Biron Company issued $18,000,000 of 12% bonds along with warrants to buy 1,200,000 shares of its $10 par value common stock at $18 per share. The bonds mature over the next 10 years, starting one year from date of issuance, with annual maturities of $1,800,000. At the time, Biron had 9,600,000 shares of common stock outstanding, and the market price was $23 per share. The company received $20,040,000 for the bonds and the warrants. For Biron Company, 12% was a relatively low borrowing rate. If offered alone, at this time, the bonds would have been issued at a 22% discount. Prepare the journal entry (or entries) for the issuance of the bonds and warrants for the cash consideration received.

(AICPA adapted)

CA16-2 (Ethical Issues—Compensation Plan) The executive officers of Coach Corporation have a performance-based compensation plan. The performance criteria of this plan is linked to growth in earnings per share. When annual EPS growth is 12%, the Coach executives earn 100% of the shares; if growth is 16%, they earn 125%. If EPS growth is lower than 8%, the executives receive no additional compensation.

In 2006, Joanna Becker, the controller of Coach, reviews year-end estimates of bad debt expense and warranty expense. She calculates the EPS growth at 15%. Peter Reiser, a member of the executive group, remarks over lunch one day that the estimate of bad debt expense might be decreased, increasing EPS growth to 16.1%. Becker is not sure she should do this because she believes that the current estimate of bad debts is sound. On the other hand, she recognizes that a great deal of subjectivity is involved in the computation.

Instructions

Answer the following questions.

(a) What, if any, is the ethical dilemma for Becker?
(b) Should Becker's knowledge of the compensation plan be a factor that influences her estimate?
(c) How should Becker respond to Reiser's request?

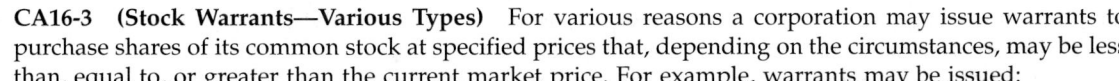

CA16-3 (Stock Warrants—Various Types) For various reasons a corporation may issue warrants to purchase shares of its common stock at specified prices that, depending on the circumstances, may be less than, equal to, or greater than the current market price. For example, warrants may be issued:

1. To existing stockholders on a pro rata basis.
2. To certain key employees under an incentive stock option plan.
3. To purchasers of the corporation's bonds.

Instructions

For each of the three examples of how stock warrants are used:

(a) Explain why they are used.

(b) Discuss the significance of the price (or prices) at which the warrants are issued (or granted) in relation to (1) the current market price of the company's stock, and (2) the length of time over which they can be exercised.

(c) Describe the information that should be disclosed in financial statements, or notes thereto, that are prepared when stock warrants are outstanding in the hands of the three groups listed above.

(AICPA adapted)

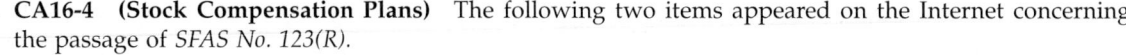 **CA16-4** **(Stock Compensation Plans)** The following two items appeared on the Internet concerning the passage of *SFAS No. 123(R)*.

WASHINGTON, D.C.—*February 17, 2005*   Congressman David Dreier (R–CA), Chairman of the House Rules Committee, and Congresswoman Anna Eshoo (D–CA) reintroduced legislation today that will preserve broad-based employee stock option plans and give investors critical information they need to understand how employee stock options impact the value of their shares.

"Last year, the U.S. House of Representatives overwhelmingly voted for legislation that would have ensured the continued ability of innovative companies to offer stock options to rank-and-file employees," Dreier stated. "Both the Financial Accounting Standards Board (FASB) and the Securities and Exchange Commission (SEC) continue to ignore our calls to address legitimate concerns about the impact of FASB's new standard on workers' ability to have an ownership stake in the New Economy, and its failure to address the real need of shareholders: accurate and meaningful information about a company's use of stock options."

"In December 2004, FASB issued a stock option expensing standard that will render a huge blow to the 21st century economy," Dreier said. "Their action and the SEC's apparent lack of concern for protecting shareholders, requires us to once again take a firm stand on the side of investors and economic growth. Giving investors the ability to understand how stock options impact the value of their shares is critical. And equally important is preserving the ability of companies to use this innovative tool to attract talented employees."

"Here We Go Again!" by Jack Ciesielski (2/21/2005, *http://www.accountingobserver.com/blog/2005/02/here-we-go-again*)   On February 17, Congressman David Dreier (R–CA), and Congresswoman Anna Eshoo (D–CA), officially entered Silicon Valley's bid to gum up the launch of honest reporting of stock option compensation: They co-sponsored a bill to "preserve broad-based employee stock option plans and give investors critical information they need to understand how employee stock options impact the value of their shares." You know what "critical information" they mean: stuff like the stock compensation for the top five officers in a company, with a rigged value set as close to zero as possible. Investors *crave* this kind of information. Other ways the good Congresspersons want to "help" investors: The bill "also requires the SEC to study the effectiveness of those disclosures over three years, during which time, no new accounting standard related to the treatment of stock options could be recognized. Finally, the bill requires the Secretary of Commerce to conduct a study and report to Congress on the impact of broad-based employee stock option plans on expanding employee corporate ownership, skilled worker recruitment and retention, research and innovation, economic growth, and international competitiveness."

It's the old "four corners" basketball strategy: stall, stall, stall. In the meantime, hope for regime change at your opponent, the FASB.

Instructions

(a) What are the major recommendations of *SFAS No. 123(R)*, "Share-Based Payment"?

(b) How do the provisions of *SFAS No. 123(R)* differ from the bill introduced by members of Congress (Dreier and Eshoo), which would require expensing for options issued to only the top five officers in a company? Which approach do you think would result in more useful information? (Focus on comparability.)

(c) The bill in Congress urges the FASB to develop a rule that preserves "the ability of companies to use this innovative tool to attract talented employees." Write a response to these Congress-people explaining the importance of neutrality in financial accounting and reporting.

CA16-5 (EPS: Preferred Dividends, Options, and Convertible Debt) "Earnings per share" (EPS) is the most featured single financial statistic about modern corporations. Daily published quotations of stock prices have recently been expanded to include for many securities a "times earnings" figure that is based on EPS. Stock analysts often focus their discussions on the EPS of the corporations they study.

Instructions
- **(a)** Explain how dividends or dividend requirements on any class of preferred stock that may be outstanding affect the computation of EPS.
- **(b)** One of the technical procedures applicable in EPS computations is the "treasury stock method." Briefly describe the circumstances under which it might be appropriate to apply the treasury stock method.
- **(c)** Convertible debentures are considered potentially dilutive common shares. Explain how convertible debentures are handled for purposes of EPS computations.

(AICPA adapted)

CA16-6 (EPS Concepts and Effect of Transactions on EPS) Fernandez Corporation, a new audit client of yours, has not reported earnings per share data in its annual reports to stockholders in the past. The treasurer, Angelo Balthazar, requested that you furnish information about the reporting of earnings per share data in the current year's annual report in accordance with generally accepted accounting principles.

Instructions
- **(a)** Define the term "earnings per share" as it applies to a corporation with a capitalization structure composed of only one class of common stock. Explain how earnings per share should be computed and how the information should be disclosed in the corporation's financial statements.
- **(b)** Discuss the treatment, if any, that should be given to each of the following items in computing earnings per share of common stock for financial statement reporting.
  - **(1)** Outstanding preferred stock issued at a premium with a par value liquidation right.
  - **(2)** The exercise at a price below market value but above book value of a common stock option issued during the current fiscal year to officers of the corporation.
  - **(3)** The replacement of a machine immediately prior to the close of the current fiscal year at a cost 20% above the original cost of the replaced machine. The new machine will perform the same function as the old machine that was sold for its book value.
  - **(4)** The declaration of current dividends on cumulative preferred stock.
  - **(5)** The acquisition of some of the corporation's outstanding common stock during the current fiscal year. The stock was classified as treasury stock.
  - **(6)** A 2-for-1 stock split of common stock during the current fiscal year.
  - **(7)** A provision created out of retained earnings for a contingent liability from a possible lawsuit.

CA16-7 (EPS, Antidilution) Matt Kacskos, a stockholder of Howat Corporation, has asked you, the firm's accountant, to explain why his stock warrants were not included in diluted EPS. In order to explain this situation, you must briefly explain what dilutive securities are, why they are included in the EPS calculation, and why some securities are antidilutive and thus not included in this calculation.

Instructions
Write Mr. Kacskos a 1–1.5 page letter explaining why the warrants are not included in the calculation. Use the following data to help you explain this situation.

Howat Corporation earned $228,000 during the period, when it had an average of 100,000 shares of common stock outstanding. The common stock sold at an average market price of $25 per share during the period. Also outstanding were 15,000 warrants that could be exercised to purchase one share of common stock at $30 per warrant.

*CA16-8 (Restricted Stock and Stock Appreciation Rights) In 2005 Sanford Co. adopted a plan to give additional incentive compensation to its dealers to sell its principal product, fire extinguishers. Under the plan Sanford transferred 9,000 shares of its $1 par value stock to a trust with the provision that Sanford would have to forfeit interest in the trust and no part of the trust fund could ever revert to Sanford. The restricted shares were to be distributed to dealers on the basis of their shares of fire extinguisher purchases from Sanford (above certain minimum levels) over the 3-year period ending June 30, 2008.

In 2005 the stock was closely held. The book value of the stock was $7.90 per share as of June 30, 2005, and in 2005 additional shares were sold to existing stockholders for $8 per share. On the basis of this information, market value of the stock was determined to be $8 per share.

In 2005 when the shares were transferred to the trust, Sanford charged prepaid expenses for $72,000 ($8 per share market value) and credited common stock for $9,000 and additional paid-in capital for $63,000. The prepaid expense was charged to operations over a 3-year period ended June 30, 2008.

Sanford sold a substantial number of shares of its stock to the public in 2007 at $60 per share.

In July 2008 all shares of the stock in the trust were distributed to the dealers. The market value of the shares at date of distribution of the stock from the trust had risen to $110 per share.

Instructions

(a) How much should be reported as selling expense in each of the years noted above.

(b) Sanford is also considering other types of option plans. One such plan is a stock appreciation rights (SARs) plan. What is a stock appreciation rights plan? What is a potential disadvantage of a SAR plan from the viewpoint of the company?

USING YOUR JUDGMENT

Financial Reporting Problem

 The Procter & Gamble Company (P&G)

The financial statements of (P&G) are presented in Appendix 5B or can be accessed on the KWW website.

Instructions

Refer to P&G's financial statements and accompanying notes to answer the following questions.

(a) Under P&G's stock-based compensation plan, stock options are granted annually to key managers and directors.

(1) How many options were granted during 2004 under the plan?

(2) How many options were exercisable at June 30, 2004?

(3) How many options were exercised in 2004, and what was the average price of those exercised?

(4) What was the range of exercise prices for options outstanding at June 30, 2004?

(5) How many years from the grant date do the options expire?

(6) To what accounts are the proceeds from these option exercises credited?

(7) What was the number of outstanding options at June 30, 2004, and at what average exercise price?

(b) What number of diluted weighted average common shares outstanding was used by P&G in computing earnings per share for 2004, 2003, and 2002? What was P&G's diluted earnings per share in 2004, 2003, and 2002?

(c) What would be the amount of compensation expense reported in 2004 for P&G if it had used the fair value method? (*Hint:* See Note 1.)

Financial Statement Analysis Case

Kellogg Company

 **Kellogg Company** in its 2004 Annual Report in Note 1—Accounting Policies made the following comment about its accounting for employee stock options and other stock-based compensation.

> **Stock compensation (in part)** The Company currently uses the intrinsic value method prescribed by *Accounting Principles Board Opinion (APB) No. 25*, "Accounting for Stock Issued to Employees," to account for its employee stock options and other stock-based compensation. Under this method, because the exercise price of the Company's employee stock options equals the market price of the underlying stock on the date of the grant, no compensation expense is recognized. The following table presents the pro forma results for the current and prior years, as if the Company had used the alternate fair value method of accounting for stock-based compensation, prescribed by *SFAS No. 123*, "Accounting for Stock-Based Compensation" (as amended by *SFAS No. 148*).

Stock-based compensation expense, net of tax:

(millions, except per share data)	2004	2003	2002
As reported	$11.4	$12.5	$10.7
Pro forma	$41.8	$42.1	$52.8
Net earnings:			
As reported	$890.6	$787.1	$720.9
Pro forma	$860.2	$757.5	$678.8
Basic net earnings per share:			
As reported	$2.16	$1.93	$1.77
Pro forma	$2.09	$1.86	$1.66
Diluted net earnings per share:			
As reported	$2.14	$1.92	$1.75
Pro forma	$2.07	$1.85	$1.65

Under this pro forma method, the fair value of each option grant (net of estimated unvested forfeitures) was estimated at the date of grant using an option-pricing model and was recognized over the vesting period, generally two years. Refer to Note 8 for further information on the Company's stock compensation programs. In December 2004, the FASB issued *SFAS No. 123(Revised)*, "Share-Based Payment," which generally requires public companies to measure the cost of employee services received in exchange for an award of equity instruments based on the grant-date fair value and to recognize this cost over the requisite service period. The Company plans to adopt *SFAS No. 123(Revised)*, as of the beginning of its 2005 fiscal third quarter and is currently considering retrospective restatement to the beginning of its 2005 fiscal year. Once this standard is adopted, management believes full-year fiscal 2005 net earnings per share will be reduced by approximately $.08.

Instructions

(a) Briefly discuss how Kellogg's financial statements will be affected by the adoption of *SFAS No. 123(R)*.

(b) Some companies argued that the recognition provisions of *SFAS No. 123(R)* are not needed, because the computation of earnings per share takes into account dilutive securities such as stock options. Do you agree? Explain, using the Kellogg disclosure provided above.

Comparative Analysis Case

The Coca-Cola Company and PepsiCo, Inc.

Instructions

Go to the KWW website and use information found there to answer the following questions related to **The Coca-Cola Company** and **PepsiCo, Inc.**

(a) What employee stock option compensation plans are offered by Coca-Cola and PepsiCo?

(b) How many options are outstanding at year-end 2004 for both Coca-Cola and PepsiCo?

(c) How many options were granted by Coca-Cola and PepsiCo to officers and employees during 2004?

(d) How many options were exercised during 2004?

(e) What was the range of option prices exercised by Coca-Cola and PepsiCo employees during 2004?

(f) What are the weighted average number of shares used by Coca-Cola and PepsiCo in 2004, 2003, and 2002 to compute diluted earnings per share?

(g) What was the diluted net income per share for Coca-Cola and PepsiCo for 2004, 2003, and 2002?

Research Case

An article by Martha Brannigan titled "Questioning the Books: **AES** Seeks to Reassure Investors Worried over Dilution of Equity" appeared in the *Wall Street Journal* on February 22, 2002.

Instructions

Read this article and answer the following questions.

(a) Where does AES get additional unregistered shares to secure its loans? How are these shares reported in its financial statements?

(b) Exactly how does a company "register shares"? How does registering shares affect the company's accounts?

(c) The article says registering the shares would dilute earnings per share. What is dilution? Why would registering the shares cause dilution?

(d) Why is measurement of dilution in earnings per share a problem for investors?

International Reporting Case

Sepracor, Inc., a U.S. drug company, reported the following information. The company prepares its financial statements in accordance with U.S. GAAP.

	2004
Current liabilities	$ 204,110
5% convertible debt	1,160,820
Total liabilities	1,370,233
Stockholders equity	(331,115)
Net income	(295,658)

Analysts attempting to compare Sepracor to international drug companies may face a challenge due to differences in accounting for convertible debt under International Financial Reporting Standards (IFRS). Under *IAS 32*, "Financial Instruments," convertible bonds, at issuance, must be classified separately into their debt and equity components based on estimated fair value.

Instructions

(a) Compute the following ratios for Sepracor, Inc. (Assume that year-end balances approximate annual averages.)
  (1) Return on assets.
  (2) Return on equity.
  (3) Debt to assets ratio.

(b) Briefly discuss the operating performance and financial position of Sepracor. Based on this analysis would you make an investment in the company's 5% convertible bonds? Explain.

(c) Assume you want to compare Sepracor to an international company, like **Bayer** (which prepares its financial statements in accordance with IFRS). Assuming that the fair value of the equity component of Sepracor's convertible bonds is $450,000, how would you adjust the analysis above to make valid comparisons between Sepracor and Bayer?

Professional Research: Financial Accounting and Reporting

Richardson Company is contemplating the establishment of a share-based compensation plan to provide long-run incentives for its top management. However, members of the compensation committee of the board of directors have voiced some concerns about adopting these plans, based on news accounts related to a recent accounting standard in this area. They would like you to conduct some research on this recent standard so they can be better informed about the accounting for these plans.

Instructions

Using the **Financial Accounting Research System (FARS)**, respond to the following items. (Provide text strings used in your search.)

(a) Identify the recent standard governing the accounting for share-based payment compensation plans.

(b) What were the principal reasons for issuing a new standard in this area?

(c) What are the key differences in the measurement of fair value between the new standard and the prior standard?

(d) The Richardson Company board is also considering an employee share-purchase plan, but the board does not want to record expense related to the plan. What criteria must be met to avoid recording expense on an employee stock-purchase plan?

Professional Simulation

In this simulation you are asked to address questions related to the accounting for stock options and earnings per share computations. Prepare responses to all parts.

KWW_Professional _Simulation

Stock Options and EPS | **Time Remaining 3 hours 50 minutes** | copy | paste | calculator | sheet | standards | help | splitter | done

| Directions | Situation | Explanation | Financial Statements | Resources |

As auditor for Banquo & Associates, you have been assigned to check Duncan Corporation's computation of earnings per share for the current year. The controller, Mac Beth, has supplied you with the following computations.

Net income	$3,374,960
Common shares issued and outstanding:	
Beginning of year	1,285,000
End of year	1,200,000
Average	1,242,500
Earnings per share:	

$$\frac{\$3,374,960}{1,242,500} = \$2.72 \text{ per share}$$

You have developed the following additional information.
1. There are no other equity securities in addition to the common shares.
2. There are no options or warrants outstanding to purchase common shares.
3. There are no convertible debt securities.
4. Activity in common shares during the year was as follows.

Outstanding, Jan. 1	1,285,000
Treasury shares acquired, Oct. 1	(250,000)
	1,035,000
Shares reissued, Dec. 1	165,000
Outstanding, Dec. 31	1,200,000

| Directions | Situation | Explanation | Financial Statements | Resources |

On the basis of the information above, do you agree with the controller's computation of earnings per share for the year? If you disagree, prepare a revised computation of earnings per share.

| Directions | Situation | Explanation | Financial Statements | Resources |

Assume the same facts as those presented above, except that options had been issued to purchase 140,000 shares of common stock at $10 per share. These options were outstanding at the beginning of the year and none had been exercised or canceled during the year. The average market price of the common shares during the year was $25, and the ending market price was $35. What earnings per share amounts will be reported?

> **Remember to check the book's companion website to find additional resources for this chapter.**

wiley.com/college/kieso

CHAPTER SEVENTEEN

INVESTMENTS

Who's in Control Here?

The Coca-Cola Company (Coke) owns 36 percent of the shares of **Coca-Cola Enterprises** (a U.S. bottling business); **PepsiCo Inc.** owns 46 percent of **The Pepsi Bottling Group (PBG)** and 41 percent of **PepsiAmericas**. These bottling businesses are very important to Coca-Cola and PepsiCo, because they are the primary distributors of Coke and Pepsi products. In return, these companies depend on Coca-Cola and PepsiCo to provide significant marketing and distribution development support. Indeed, it can be said that Coca-Cola and PepsiCo control the bottling companies, who would not exist without their support.

However, because The Coca-Cola Company and PepsiCo own less than 50 percent of the shares in these companies, they do not prepare consolidated financial statements. Instead, Coca-Cola and PepsiCo account for these investments using the *equity method*. Under the equity method, for example, Coca-Cola reports a single income item for its profits from the bottlers, and only the net amount of its investment in the balance sheet.

Equity-method accounting gives Coca-Cola and PepsiCo pristine balance sheets and income statements, by separating the assets and liabilities and the profit margins of these bottlers from its beverage-making business. What's more, the International Accounting Standards Board (IASB) has issued *IAS No. 28* which requires that companies use the equity method. Previously, many international companies were permitted to use either the equity method or proportional consolidation for investments similar to Coke's and Pepsi's. It is good news that both U.S. and international companies are following the same rules. (On negative side, however, some of these companies should be consolidated but are not.)

A final point: In response to a recent FASB interpretation, companies are now starting to consolidate more 20 to 50 percent–owned investments. Consolidation of entities, such as the Coke and Pepsi bottlers, may be required if the risks and rewards of those investments accrue primarily to Coke and Pepsi.[1] In fact, Coke has consolidated some of its bottling companies, which should result in the reporting of more complete information on these affiliated companies.

---

[1]*Financial Accounting Standards Interpretation No. 46(R)*, "Consolidation of Variable Interest Entities (revised) —An Interpretation of *ARB No. 51*" (Norwalk, Conn.: FASB, December 2003.)

Learning Objectives

After studying this chapter, you should be able to:

1 Identify the three categories of debt securities and describe the accounting and reporting treatment for each category.

2 Understand the procedures for discount and premium amortization on bond investments.

3 Identify the categories of equity securities and describe the accounting and reporting treatment for each category.

4 Explain the equity method of accounting and compare it to the fair value method for equity securities.

5 Describe the disclosure requirements for investments in debt and equity securities.

6 Discuss the accounting for impairments of debt and equity investments.

7 Describe the accounting for transfer of investment securities between categories.

As our opening story indicates, U.S. and international standard-setters are studying the measurement, recognition, and disclosure for certain investments. In this chapter we address the accounting for debt and equity investments. Appendixes to this chapter discuss the accounting for derivative instruments and variable-interest entities. The content and organization of this chapter are as follows.

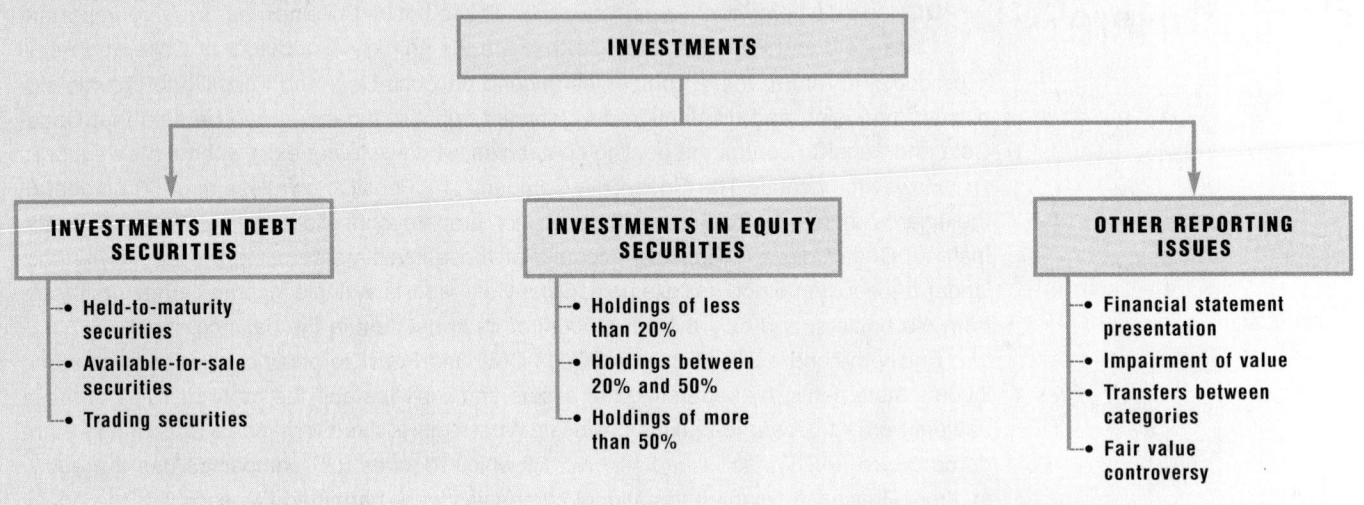

Companies have different motivations for investing in securities issued by other companies.[2] **One motivation is to earn a high rate of return.** For example, companies like **Coca-Cola** and **PepsiCo** can receive interest revenue from a debt investment or dividend revenue from an equity investment. In addition, they can realize capital gains on both types of securities. **Another motivation for investing (in equity securities) is to secure certain operating or financing arrangements with another company.** As in the opening story, **Coca-Cola** and **PepsiCo** are able to exercise some control over bottler companies based on its significant (but not controlling) equity investments.

To provide useful information, companies account for investments based on the type of security (debt or equity) and their intent with respect to the investment. As indicated in Illustration 17-1, we organize our study of investments by type of security. Within each section, we explain how the accounting for investments in debt and equity securities varies according to management intent.

---

[2]A **security** is a share, participation, or other interest in property or in an enterprise of the issuer or an obligation of the issuer that has the following three characteristics: (a) It either is represented by an instrument issued in bearer or registered form or, if not represented by an instrument, is registered in books maintained to record transfers by or on behalf of the issuer. (b) It is of a type commonly traded on securities exchanges or markets or, when represented by an instrument, is commonly recognized in any area in which it is issued or dealt in as a medium for investment. (c) It either is one of a class or series or by its terms is divisible into a class or series of shares, participations, interests, or obligations. From "Accounting for Certain Investments in Debt and Equity Securities," *Statement of Financial Accounting Standards No. 115* (Norwalk, Conn.: FASB, 1993), p. 48, par. 137.

Types of Security	Management Intent	Valuation Approach
Debt (Section 1)	No plans to sell	Amortized cost
	Plan to sell	Fair value
Equity (Section 2)	Plan to sell	Fair value
	Exercise some control	Equity method

ILLUSTRATION 17-1
Summary of Investment Accounting Approaches

INVESTMENTS IN DEBT SECURITIES | SECTION 1

Debt securities represent a creditor relationship with another entity. Debt securities include U.S. government securities, municipal securities, corporate bonds, convertible debt, and commercial paper. Trade accounts receivable and loans receivable are not debt securities because they do not meet the definition of a security.

Companies group investments in debt securities into three separate categories for accounting and reporting purposes:

- **Held-to-maturity**: Debt securities that the company has the positive intent and ability to hold to maturity.
- **Trading**: Debt securities bought and held primarily for sale in the near term to generate income on short-term price differences.
- **Available-for-sale**: Debt securities not classified as held-to-maturity or trading securities.

Illustration 17-2 identifies these categories, along with the accounting and reporting treatments required for each.

OBJECTIVE 1
Identify the three categories of debt securities and describe the accounting and reporting treatment for each category.

Category	Valuation	Unrealized Holding Gains or Losses	Other Income Effects
Held-to-maturity	Amortized cost	Not recognized	Interest when earned; gains and losses from sale.
Trading securities	Fair value	Recognized in net income	Interest when earned; gains and losses from sale.
Available-for-sale	Fair value	Recognized as other comprehensive income and as separate component of stockholders' equity	Interest when earned; gains and losses from sale.

ILLUSTRATION 17-2
Accounting for Debt Securities by Category

Amortized cost is the acquisition cost adjusted for the amortization of discount or premium, if appropriate. **Fair value** is the amount at which a company can exchange a financial instrument in a current transaction between willing parties, other than in a forced or liquidation sale.[3]

UNDERLYING CONCEPTS

Companies report debt securities at fair value not only because the information is relevant but also because it is reliable.

---

[3]Ibid., pp. 47–48. The fair value is **readily determinable** if SEC-registered exchanges provide its sale price or other quotations, or, for over-the-counter securities, recognized national publication systems publish the amounts.

HELD-TO-MATURITY SECURITIES

OBJECTIVE 2
Understand the procedures for discount and premium amortization on bond investments.

Only debt securities can be classified as held-to-maturity. By definition, equity securities have no maturity date. A company like **Starbucks** should classify a debt security as **held-to-maturity** only if it has **both (1) the positive intent** and **(2) the ability to hold those securities to maturity**. It should not classify a debt security as held-to-maturity if it intends to hold the security for an indefinite period of time. Likewise, if Starbucks anticipates that a sale may be necessary due to changes in interest rates, foreign currency risk, liquidity needs, or other asset-liability management reasons, it should not classify the security as held-to-maturity.[4]

Companies account for held-to-maturity securities **at amortized cost**, not fair value. If management intends to hold certain investment securities to maturity and has no plans to sell them, fair values (selling prices) are not relevant for measuring and evaluating the cash flows associated with these securities. Finally, because companies do not adjust held-to-maturity securities to fair value, these securities do not increase the volatility of either reported earnings or reported capital as do trading securities and available-for-sale securities.

To illustrate the accounting for held-to-maturity debt securities, assume that Robinson Company purchased $100,000 of 8 percent bonds of Evermaster Corporation on January 1, 2006, at a discount, paying $92,278. The bonds mature January 1, 2011; interest is payable each July 1 and January 1. Robinson records the investment as follows:

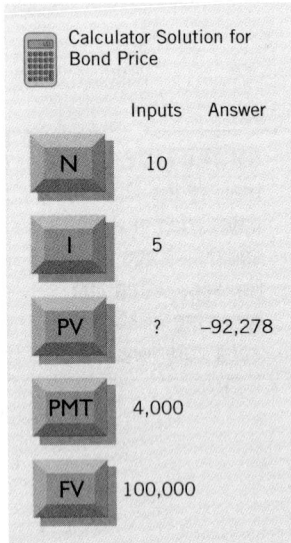

Calculator Solution for Bond Price

	Inputs	Answer
N	10	
I	5	
PV	?	−92,278
PMT	4,000	
FV	100,000	

January 1, 2006

Held-to-Maturity Securities	92,278	
Cash		92,278

Robinson uses a Held-to-Maturity Securities account to indicate the type of debt security purchased.

As indicated in Chapter 14, companies must amortize premium or discount using the **effective-interest method** unless some other method—such as the straight-line method—yields a similar result. They apply the effective-interest method to bond investments in a way similar to that for bonds payable. To compute interest revenue, companies compute the effective-interest rate or yield at the time of investment and apply that rate to the beginning carrying amount (book value) for each interest period. The investment carrying amount is increased by the amortized discount or decreased by the amortized premium in each period.

Illustration 17-3 (on page 841) shows the effect of the discount amortization on the interest revenue that Robinson records each period for its investment in Evermaster bonds. Robinson records the receipt of the first semiannual interest payment on July 1, 2006 (using the data in Illustration 17-3) as follows:

July 1, 2006

Cash	4,000	
Held-to-Maturity Securities	614	
Interest Revenue		4,614

Because Robinson is on a calendar-year basis, it accrues interest and amortizes the discount at December 31, 2006, as follows.

December 31, 2006

Interest Receivable	4,000	
Held-to-Maturity Securities	645	
Interest Revenue		4,645

Again, Illustration 17-3 shows the interest and amortization amounts.

UNDERLYING CONCEPTS

The use of some simpler method that yields results similar to the effective-interest method is an application of the materiality concept.

---

[4]The FASB defines situations where, even though a company sells a security before maturity, it has constructively held the security to maturity, and thus does not violate the held-to-maturity requirement. These include selling a security close enough to maturity (such as three months) so that interest rate risk is no longer an important pricing factor.

8% BONDS PURCHASED TO YIELD 10%				
Date	Cash Received	Interest Revenue	Bond Discount Amortization	Carrying Amount of Bonds
1/1/06				$ 92,278
7/1/06	$ 4,000ᵃ	$ 4,614ᵇ	$ 614ᶜ	92,892ᵈ
1/1/07	4,000	4,645	645	93,537
7/1/07	4,000	4,677	677	94,214
1/1/08	4,000	4,711	711	94,925
7/1/08	4,000	4,746	746	95,671
1/1/09	4,000	4,783	783	96,454
7/1/09	4,000	4,823	823	97,277
1/1/10	4,000	4,864	864	98,141
7/1/10	4,000	4,907	907	99,048
1/1/11	4,000	4,952	952	100,000
	$40,000	$47,722	$7,722	

ᵃ$4,000 = $100,000 × .08 × ⁶⁄₁₂
ᵇ$4,614 = $92,278 × .10 × ⁶⁄₁₂
ᶜ$614 = $4,614 − $4,000
ᵈ$92,892 = $92,278 + $614

ILLUSTRATION 17-3
Schedule of Interest Revenue and Bond Discount Amortization—Effective-Interest Method

Robinson reports its investment in Evermaster bonds in its December 31, 2006, financial statements, as follows.

ILLUSTRATION 17-4
Reporting of Held-to-Maturity Securities

Balance Sheet	
Current assets	
Interest receivable	$ 4,000
Long-term investments	
Held-to-maturity securities, at amortized cost	$93,537
Income Statement	
Other revenues and gains	
Interest revenue	$ 9,259

Sometimes a company sells a held-to-maturity debt security so close to its maturity date that a change in the market interest rate would not significantly affect the security's fair value. Such a sale may be considered a sale at maturity and would not call into question the company's original intent to hold the investment to maturity. Let's assume, as an example, that Robinson Company sells its investment in Evermaster bonds on November 1, 2010, at 99¾ plus accrued interest. The discount amortization from July 1, 2010, to November 1, 2010, is $635 (⁴⁄₆ × $952). Robinson records this discount amortization as follows.

November 1, 2010

Held-to-Maturity Securities	635	
Interest Revenue		635

Illustration 17-5 shows the computation of the realized gain on the sale.

Selling price of bonds (exclusive of accrued interest)		$99,750
Less: Book value of bonds on November 1, 2010:		
Amortized cost, July 1, 2010	$99,048	
Add: Discount amortized for the period July 1, 2010, to November 1, 2010	635	
		99,683
Gain on sale of bonds		$ 67

ILLUSTRATION 17-5
Computation of Gain on Sale of Bonds

Robinson records the sale of the bonds as:

November 1, 2010

Cash	102,417	
Interest Revenue (4/6 × $4,000)		2,667
Held-to-Maturity Securities		99,683
Gain on Sale of Securities		67

The credit to Interest Revenue represents accrued interest for four months, for which the purchaser pays cash. The debit to Cash represents the selling price of the bonds plus accrued interest ($99,750 + $2,667). The credit to Held-to-Maturity Securities represents the book value of the bonds on the date of sale. The credit to Gain on Sale of Securities represents the excess of the selling price over the book value of the bonds.

AVAILABLE-FOR-SALE SECURITIES

UNDERLYING CONCEPTS

Recognizing unrealized gains and losses is an application of the concept of comprehensive income.

Companies, like **Amazon.com**, report **available-for-sale** securities at fair value. It records the unrealized gains and losses related to changes in the fair value of available-for-sale debt securities in an unrealized holding gain or loss account. Amazon adds (subtracts) this amount to other comprehensive income for the period. Other comprehensive income is then added to (subtracted from) accumulated other comprehensive income, which is shown as a separate component of stockholders' equity until realized. Thus, **companies report available-for-sale securities at fair value on the balance sheet, but do not report changes in fair value as part of net income until after selling the security**. This approach reduces the volatility of net income.

Example: Single Security

To illustrate the accounting for available-for-sale securities, assume that Graff Corporation purchases $100,000, 10 percent, five-year bonds on January 1, 2006, with interest payable on July 1 and January 1. The bonds sell for $108,111, which results in a bond premium of $8,111 and an effective interest rate of 8 percent.

Graff records the purchase of the bonds as follows.[5]

January 1, 2006

Available-for-Sale Securities	108,111	
Cash		108,111

Calculator Solution for Bond Price

Inputs	Answer
N	10
I	4
PV ?	−108,111
PMT	5,000
FV	100,000

Illustration 17-6 (on page 843) discloses the effect of the premium amortization on the interest revenue Graff records each period using the effective-interest method.

The entry to record interest revenue on July 1, 2006, is as follows.

July 1, 2006

Cash	5,000	
Available-for-Sale Securities		676
Interest Revenue		4,324

At December 31, 2006, Graff makes the following entry to recognize interest revenue.

December 31, 2006

Interest Receivable	5,000	
Available-for-Sale Securities		703
Interest Revenue		4,297

As a result, Graff reports revenue for 2006 of $8,621 ($4,324 + $4,297).

---

[5]Companies generally record investments acquired at par, at a discount, or at a premium in the accounts at cost, including brokerage and other fees but excluding the accrued interest. They generally do not record investments at maturity value. The use of a separate discount or premium account as a valuation account is acceptable procedure for investments, but in practice companies do not widely use it.

10% Bonds Purchased to Yield 8%				
Date	Cash Received	Interest Revenue	Bond Premium Amortization	Carrying Amount of Bonds
1/1/06				$108,111
7/1/06	$ 5,000[a]	$ 4,324[b]	$ 676[c]	107,435[d]
1/1/07	5,000	4,297	703	106,732
7/1/07	5,000	4,269	731	106,001
1/1/08	5,000	4,240	760	105,241
7/1/08	5,000	4,210	790	104,451
1/1/09	5,000	4,178	822	103,629
7/1/09	5,000	4,145	855	102,774
1/1/10	5,000	4,111	889	101,885
7/1/10	5,000	4,075	925	100,960
1/1/11	5,000	4,040	960	100,000
	$50,000	$41,889	$8,111	

[a]$5,000 = $100,000 × .10 × 6/12
[b]$4,324 = $108,111 × .08 × 6/12
[c]$676 = $5,000 − $4,324
[d]$107,435 = $108,111 − $676

To apply the fair value method to these debt securities, assume that at year-end the fair value of the bonds is $105,000 and that the carrying amount of the investments is $106,732. Comparing this fair value with the carrying amount (amortized cost) of the bonds at December 31, 2006, Graff recognizes an unrealized holding loss of $1,732 ($106,732 − $105,000). It reports this loss as other comprehensive income. Graff makes the following entry.

December 31, 2006

Unrealized Holding Gain or Loss—Equity	1,732	
Securities Fair Value Adjustment (Available-for-Sale)		1,732

Graff uses a valuation account instead of crediting the Available-for-Sale Securities account. The use of the **Securities Fair Value Adjustment (Available-for-Sale) account** enables the company to maintain a record of its amortized cost. Because the adjustment account has a credit balance in this case, Graff subtracts it from the balance of the Available-for-Sale Securities account to determine fair value. Graff reports this fair value amount on the balance sheet. At each reporting date, Graff reports the bonds at fair value with an adjustment to the Unrealized Holding Gain or Loss—Equity account.

Example: Portfolio of Securities

To illustrate the accounting for a portfolio of securities, assume that Webb Corporation has two debt securities classified as available-for-sale. Illustration 17-7 identifies the amortized cost, fair value, and the amount of the unrealized gain or loss.

Investments	Amortized Cost	Fair Value	Unrealized Gain (Loss)
Available-for-Sale Debt Security Portfolio **December 31, 2007**			
Watson Corporation 8% bonds	$ 93,537	$103,600	$ 10,063
Anacomp Corporation 10% bonds	200,000	180,400	(19,600)
Total of portfolio	$293,537	$284,000	(9,537)
Previous securities fair value adjustment balance			–0–
Securities fair value adjustment—Cr.			$ (9,537)

The fair value of Webb's available-for-sale portfolio totals $284,000. The gross unrealized gains are $10,063, and the gross unrealized losses are $19,600, resulting in a net unrealized loss of $9,537. That is, the fair value of available-for-sale securities is $9,537 lower than its amortized cost. Webb makes an adjusting entry to a valuation allowance to record the decrease in value and to record the loss as follows.

December 31, 2007

Unrealized Holding Gain or Loss—Equity	9,537	
Securities Fair Value Adjustment (Available-for-Sale)		9,537

Webb reports the unrealized holding loss of $9,537 as other comprehensive income and a reduction of stockholders' equity. Recall that companies exclude from net income any unrealized holding gains and losses related to available-for-sale securities.

Sale of Available-for-Sale Securities

If a company sells bonds carried as investments in available-for-sale securities before the maturity date, it must make entries to remove from the Available-for-Sale Securities account the amortized cost of bonds sold. To illustrate, assume that Webb Corporation sold the Watson bonds (from Illustration 17-7) on July 1, 2008, for $90,000, at which time it had an amortized cost of $94,214. Illustration 17-8 shows the computation of the realized loss.

ILLUSTRATION 17-8
Computation of Loss on Sale of Bonds

Amortized cost (Watson bonds)	$94,214
Less: Selling price of bonds	90,000
Loss on sale of bonds	$ 4,214

Webb records the sale of the Watson bonds as follows.

July 1, 2008

Cash	90,000	
Loss on Sale of Securities	4,214	
Available-for-Sale Securities		94,214

Webb reports this realized loss in the "Other expenses and losses" section of the income statement. Assuming no other purchases and sales of bonds in 2008, Webb on December 31, 2008, prepares the information shown in Illustration 17-9.

ILLUSTRATION 17-9
Computation of Securities Fair Value Adjustment—Available-for-Sale (2008)

AVAILABLE-FOR-SALE DEBT SECURITY PORTFOLIO DECEMBER 31, 2008			
Investments	Amortized Cost	Fair Value	Unrealized Gain (Loss)
Anacomp Corporation 10% bonds (total portfolio)	$200,000	$195,000	$(5,000)
Previous securities fair value adjustment balance—Cr.			(9,537)
Securities fair value adjustment—Dr.			$ 4,537

Webb has an unrealized holding loss of $5,000. However, the Securities Fair Value Adjustment account already has a credit balance of $9,537. To reduce the adjustment account balance to $5,000, Webb debits it for $4,537, as follows.

December 31, 2008

Securities Fair Value Adjustment (Available-for-Sale)	4,537	
Unrealized Holding Gain or Loss—Equity		4,537

WHAT IS FAIR VALUE?

In the fall of 2000, Wall Street brokerage firm **Morgan Stanley** told investors that rumor of big losses in its bond portfolio were "greatly exaggerated." As it turns out, Morgan Stanley also was exaggerating.

Recently, the SEC accused Morgan Stanley of violating securities laws by overstating the value of certain bonds by $75 million. The overvaluations stemmed more from wishful thinking than reality, in violation of generally accepted accounting principles, the SEC said. "In effect, Morgan Stanley valued its positions at the price at which it thought a willing buyer and seller should enter into an exchange, rather than at a price at which a willing buyer and a willing seller would enter into a current exchange," the SEC wrote.

Especially egregious, stated one accounting expert, were the SEC's findings that Morgan Stanley in some instances used its own more optimistic assumptions as a substitute for external pricing sources. "What that is saying is: 'Fair value is what you want the value to be. Pick a number...' That's especially troublesome."

As indicated in the text, the FASB has been working on a new standard for assessing what is fair and what isn't when it comes to assigning valuations. Concerns over the issue caught fire after the collapses of **Enron Corp.** and other energy traders that abused the wide discretion given them under fair-value accounting. Investors have expressed similar worries about some financial companies, which use internal—and subjectively designed—mathematical models to come up with valuations when market quotes aren't available.

Source: Adapted from Susanne Craig and Jonathan Weil, "SEC Targets Morgan Stanley Values," *Wall Street Journal* (November 8, 2004), p. C3.

WHAT DO THE NUMBERS MEAN?

Financial Statement Presentation

Webb's December 31, 2008, balance sheet and the 2008 income statement include the following items and amounts (the Anacomp bonds are long-term investments but are not intended to be held to maturity).

Balance Sheet	
Current assets	
Interest receivable	$ xxx
Investments	
Available-for-sale securities, at fair value	$195,000
Stockholders' equity	
Accumulated other comprehensive loss	$ 5,000
Income Statement	
Other revenues and gains	
Interest revenue	$ xxx
Other expenses and losses	
Loss on sale of securities	$ 4,214

ILLUSTRATION 17-10
Reporting of Available-for-Sale Securities

Some favor including the unrealized holding gain or loss in net income rather than showing it as other comprehensive income.[6] However, some companies, particularly financial institutions, note that recognizing gains and losses on assets, but not liabilities, introduces substantial volatility in net income. They argue that hedges often exist between assets and liabilities so that gains in assets are offset by losses in liabilities, and vice versa. In short, to recognize gains and losses only on the asset side is unfair and not representative of the economic activities of the company.

This argument convinced the FASB. As a result, companies **do not include in net income** these unrealized gains and losses. However, even this approach solves only

---

[6]In Chapter 4, we discussed the reporting of other comprehensive income and the concept of comprehensive income. "Reporting Comprehensive Income," *Statement of Financial Accounting Standards No. 130* (Norwalk, Conn.: FASB, 1997).

some of the problems, because **volatility of capital** still results. This is of concern to financial institutions because regulators restrict financial institutions' operations based on their level of capital. In addition, companies can still manage their net income by engaging in gains trading (i.e., selling the winners and holding the losers).

TRADING SECURITIES

Companies hold **trading securities** with the intention of selling them in a short period of time. "Trading" in this context means frequent buying and selling. Companies thus use trading securities to generate profits from short-term differences in price. Companies generally hold these securities for less than three months, some for merely days or hours.

Companies report trading securities at fair value, with unrealized holding gains and losses reported as part of net income. Similar to held-to-maturity or available-for-sale investments, they are required to amortize any discount or premium. A **holding gain or loss** is the net change in the fair value of a security from one period to another, exclusive of dividend or interest revenue recognized but not received. In short, the FASB says to adjust the trading securities to fair value, at each reporting date. In addition, companies report the change in value as part of net income, not other comprehensive income.

To illustrate, assume that on December 31, 2007, Western Publishing Corporation determined its trading securities portfolio to be as shown in Illustration 17-11. (Assume that 2007 is the first year that Western Publishing held trading securities.) At the date of acquisition, Western Publishing recorded these trading securities at cost, including brokerage commissions and taxes, in the account entitled Trading Securities. This is the first valuation of this recently purchased portfolio.

ILLUSTRATION 17-11
Computation of Securities Fair Value Adjustment—Trading Securities Portfolio (2007)

TRADING DEBT SECURITY PORTFOLIO DECEMBER 31, 2007			
Investments	Cost	Fair Value	Unrealized Gain (Loss)
Burlington Northern 10% bonds	$ 43,860	$ 51,500	$ 7,640
GM Corporation 11% bonds	184,230	175,200	(9,030)
Time Warner 8% bonds	86,360	91,500	5,140
Total of portfolio	$314,450	$318,200	3,750
Previous securities fair value adjustment balance			–0–
Securities fair value adjustment—Dr.			$ 3,750

The total cost of Western Publishing's trading portfolio is $314,450. The gross unrealized gains are $12,780 ($7,640 + $5,140), and the gross unrealized losses are $9,030, resulting in a net unrealized gain of $3,750. The fair value of trading securities is $3,750 greater than its cost.

At December 31, Western Publishing makes an adjusting entry to a valuation allowance, referred to as Securities Fair Value Adjustment (Trading), to record the increase in value and to record the unrealized holding gain.

December 31, 2007

Securities Fair Value Adjustment (Trading)	3,750	
Unrealized Holding Gain or Loss—Income		3,750

Because the Securities Fair Value Adjustment account balance is a debit, Western Publishing adds it to the cost of the Trading Securities account to arrive at a fair value for the trading securities. Western Publishing reports this fair value amount on the balance sheet.

When securities are actively traded, the FASB believes that the investments should be reported at fair value on the balance sheet. In addition, changes in fair value (unrealized gains and losses) should be reported in income. Such reporting on trading securities provides more relevant information to existing and prospective stockholders.

INTERNATIONAL INSIGHT

IFRS provides for classification as trading, available for sale, or held-to-maturity for all types of financial assets. U.S. GAAP applies these classifications only to securities.

| INVESTMENTS IN EQUITY SECURITIES | SECTION 2 |

OBJECTIVE 3
Identify the categories of equity securities and describe the accounting and reporting treatment for each category.

Equity securities represent ownership interests such as common, preferred, or other capital stock. They also include rights to acquire or dispose of ownership interests at an agreed-upon or determinable price, such as in warrants, rights, and call or put options. Companies do not treat convertible debt securities as equity securities. Nor do they treat as equity securities redeemable preferred stock (which must be redeemed for common stock). The cost of equity securities includes the purchase price of the security plus broker's commissions and other fees incidental to the purchase.

The degree to which one corporation **(investor)** acquires an interest in the common stock of another corporation **(investee)** generally determines the accounting treatment for the investment subsequent to acquisition. The classification of such investments depends on the percentage of the investee voting stock that is held by the investor:

1 Holdings of less than 20 percent (**fair value method**)—investor has passive interest.

2 Holdings between 20 percent and 50 percent (**equity method**)—investor has significant influence.

3 Holdings of more than 50 percent (**consolidated statements**)—investor has controlling interest.

Illustration 17-12 lists these levels of interest or influence and the corresponding valuation and reporting method that companies must apply to the investment.

Percentage of Ownership	0% ⟷	20% ⟷	50% ⟷	100%
Level of Influence	Little or None	Significant	Control	
Valuation Method	Fair Value Method	Equity Method	Consolidation	

ILLUSTRATION 17-12
Levels of Influence Determine Accounting Methods

The accounting and reporting for equity securities therefore depends upon the level of influence and the type of security involved, as shown in Illustration 17-13.

Category	Valuation	Unrealized Holding Gains or Losses	Other Income Effects
Holdings less than 20%			
1. Available-for-sale	Fair value	Recognized in "Other comprehensive income" and as separate component of stockholders' equity	Dividends declared; gains and losses from sale.
2. Trading	Fair value	Recognized in net income	Dividends declared; gains and losses from sale.
Holdings between 20% and 50%	Equity	Not recognized	Proportionate share of investee's net income.
Holdings more than 50%	Consolidation	Not recognized	Not applicable.

ILLUSTRATION 17-13
Accounting and Reporting for Equity Securities by Category

HOLDINGS OF LESS THAN 20%

When an investor has an interest of less than 20 percent, it is presumed that the investor has little or no influence over the investee. In such cases, if market prices are available subsequent to acquisition, the company values and reports the investment using the **fair value method**.[7] The fair value method requires that companies classify equity securities at acquisition as **available-for-sale securities** or **trading securities**. Because equity securities have no maturity date, companies cannot classify them as held-to-maturity.

Available-for-Sale Securities

Upon acquisition, companies record available-for-sale securities at cost.[8] To illustrate, assume that on November 3, 2007 Republic Corporation purchased common stock of three companies, each investment representing less than a 20 percent interest.

	Cost
Northwest Industries, Inc.	$259,700
Campbell Soup Co.	317,500
St. Regis Pulp Co.	141,350
Total cost	$718,550

Republic records these investments as follows.

November 3, 2007

Available-for-Sale Securities	718,550	
Cash		718,550

On December 6, 2007, Republic receives a cash dividend of $4,200 on its investment in the common stock of Campbell Soup Co. It records the cash dividend as follows.

December 6, 2007

Cash	4,200	
Dividend Revenue		4,200

All three of the investee companies reported net income for the year, but only Campbell Soup declared and paid a dividend to Republic. But, recall that when an investor owns less than 20 percent of the common stock of another corporation, it is presumed that the investor has relatively little influence on the investee. As a result, **net income earned by the investee is not a proper basis for recognizing income from the investment by the investor**. Why? Because the increased net assets resulting from profitable operations may be permanently retained for use in the investee's

---

[7]When market prices are unavailable, a company values the investment and reports it at cost in periods subsequent to acquisition. This approach is often referred to as the **cost method**. Companies recognize dividends when received. They value the portfolio and report it at acquisition cost. Companies only recognize gains or losses after selling the securities.

[8]Companies should record equity securities acquired in **exchange for noncash considera-tion** (property or services) at (1) the fair value of the consideration given, or (2) the fair value of the security received, whichever is more clearly determinable. Accounting for numerous purchases of securities requires the preservation of information regarding the cost of individual purchases, as well as the dates of purchases and sales. If **specific identification** is not possible, companies may use an **average cost** for multiple purchases of the same class of security. The **first-in, first-out method** (FIFO) of assigning costs to investments at the time of sale is also acceptable and normally employed.

business. Therefore, **the investor earns net income only when the investee declares cash dividends**.

At December 31, 2007, Republic's available-for-sale equity security portfolio has the cost and fair value shown in Illustration 17-14.

AVAILABLE-FOR-SALE EQUITY SECURITY PORTFOLIO DECEMBER 31, 2007			
Investments	Cost	Fair Value	Unrealized Gain (Loss)
Northwest Industries, Inc.	$259,700	$275,000	$ 15,300
Campbell Soup Co.	317,500	304,000	(13,500)
St. Regis Pulp Co.	141,350	104,000	(37,350)
Total of portfolio	$718,550	$683,000	(35,550)
Previous securities fair value adjustment balance			–0–
Securities fair value adjustment—Cr.			$(35,550)

ILLUSTRATION 17-14
Computation of Securities Fair Value Adjustment—Available-for-Sale Equity Security Portfolio (2007)

For Republic's available-for-sale equity securities portfolio, the gross unrealized gains are $15,300, and the gross unrealized losses are $50,850 ($13,500 + $37,350), resulting in a net unrealized loss of $35,550. The fair value of the available-for-sale securities portfolio is below cost by $35,550.

As with available-for-sale **debt** securities, Republic records the net unrealized gains and losses related to changes in the fair value of available-for-sale **equity** securities in an Unrealized Holding Gain or Loss—Equity account. Republic reports this amount as a **part of other comprehensive income and as a component of other accumulated comprehensive income (reported in stockholders' equity) until realized**. In this case, Republic prepares an adjusting entry debiting the Unrealized Holding Gain or Loss—Equity account and crediting the Securities Fair Value Adjustment account to record the decrease in fair value and to record the loss as follows.

December 31, 2007

Unrealized Holding Gain or Loss—Equity	35,550	
Securities Fair Value Adjustment (Available-for-Sale)		35,550

On January 23, 2008, Republic sold all of its Northwest Industries, Inc. common stock receiving net proceeds of $287,220. Illustration 17-15 shows the computation of the realized gain on the sale.

Net proceeds from sale	$287,220
Cost of Northwest shares	259,700
Gain on sale of stock	$ 27,520

ILLUSTRATION 17-15
Computation of Gain on Sale of Stock

Republic records the sale as follows.

January 23, 2008

Cash	287,220	
Available-for-Sale Securities		259,700
Gain on Sale of Stock		27,520

In addition, assume that on February 10, 2008, Republic purchased 20,000 shares of Continental Trucking at a market price of $12.75 per share plus brokerage commissions of $1,850 (total cost, $256,850).

Illustration 17-16 lists Republic's portfolio of available-for-sale securities, as of December 31, 2008.

ILLUSTRATION 17-16
Computation of
Securities Fair Value
Adjustment—Available-
for-Sale Equity Security
Portfolio (2008)

AVAILABLE-FOR-SALE EQUITY SECURITY PORTFOLIO DECEMBER 31, 2008			
Investments	Cost	Fair Value	Unrealized Gain (Loss)
Continental Trucking	$256,850	$278,350	$ 21,500
Campbell Soup Co.	317,500	362,550	45,050
St. Regis Pulp Co.	141,350	139,050	(2,300)
Total of portfolio	$715,700	$779,950	64,250
Previous securities fair value adjustment balance—Cr.			(35,550)
Securities fair value adjustment—Dr.			$ 99,800

At December 31, 2008, the fair value of Republic's available-for-sale equity securities portfolio exceeds cost by $64,250 (unrealized gain). The Securities Fair Value Adjustment account had a credit balance of $35,550 at December 31, 2008. To adjust its December 31, 2008, available-for-sale portfolio to fair value, the company debits the Securities Fair Value Adjustment account for $99,800 ($35,550 + $64,250). Republic records this adjustment as follows.

December 31, 2008

Securities Fair Value Adjustment (Available-for-Sale)	99,800	
Unrealized Holding Gain or Loss—Equity		99,800

Trading Securities

The accounting entries to record trading equity securities are the same as for available-for-sale equity securities, except for recording the unrealized holding gain or loss. For trading equity securities, companies **report the unrealized holding gain or loss as part of net income**. Thus, the account titled Unrealized Holding Gain or Loss—Income is used.

HOLDINGS BETWEEN 20% AND 50%

An investor corporation may hold an interest of less than 50 percent in an investee corporation and thus not possess legal control. However, as shown in our opening story about **Coca-Cola**, an investment in voting stock of less than 50 percent can still give Coke (the investor) the ability to exercise significant influence over the operating and financial policies of its bottlers.[9] **Significant influence** may be indicated in several ways. Examples include representation on the board of directors, participation in policy-making processes, material intercompany transactions, interchange of managerial personnel, or technological dependency.

Another important consideration is the extent of ownership by an investor in relation to the concentration of other shareholdings. To achieve a reasonable degree of uniformity in application of the "significant influence" criterion, the profession concluded that an investment (direct or indirect) of 20 percent or more of the voting stock

[9]"The Equity Method of Accounting for Investments in Common Stock," *Opinions of the Accounting Principles Board No. 18* (New York: AICPA, 1971), par. 17.

of an investee should lead to a presumption that in the absence of evidence to the contrary, an investor has the ability to exercise significant influence over an investee.[10]

In instances of "significant influence" (generally an investment of 20 percent or more), the investor must account for the investment using the **equity method**.

Equity Method

OBJECTIVE 4
Explain the equity method of accounting and compare it to the fair value method for equity securities.

Under the **equity method** the investor and the investee acknowledge a substantive economic relationship. The company originally records the investment at the cost of the shares acquired but subsequently adjusts the amount each period for changes in the investee's net assets. That is, the **the investor's proportionate share of the earnings (losses) of the investee periodically increases (decreases) the investment's carrying amount. All dividends received by the investor from the investee also decrease the investment's carrying amount.** The equity method recognizes that investee's earnings increase investee's net assets, and that investee's losses and dividends decrease these net assets.

To illustrate the equity method and compare it with the fair value method, assume that Maxi Company purchases a 20 percent interest in Mini Company. To apply the fair value method in this example, assume that Maxi does not have the ability to exercise significant influence, and classifies the securities as available-for-sale. Where this example applies the equity method, assume that the 20 percent interest permits Maxi to exercise significant influence. Illustration 17-17 shows the entries.

ILLUSTRATION 17-17
Comparison of Fair Value Method and Equity Method

ENTRIES BY MAXI COMPANY			
Fair Value Method		**Equity Method**	
On January 2, 2007, Maxi Company acquired 48,000 shares (20% of Mini Company common stock) at a cost of $10 a share.			
Available-for-Sale-Securities 480,000		Investment in Mini Stock 480,000	
Cash	480,000	Cash	480,000
For the year 2007, Mini Company reported net income of $200,000; Maxi Company's share is 20%, or $40,000.			
No entry		Investment in Mini Stock 40,000	
		Revenue from Investment	40,000
At December 31, 2007, the 48,000 shares of Mini Company have a fair value (market price) of $12 a share, or $576,000.			
Securities Fair Value Adjustment		No entry	
(Available-for-Sale)	96,000		
Unrealized Holding Gain			
or Loss—Equity	96,000		
On January 28, 2008, Mini Company announced and paid a cash dividend of $100,000; Maxi Company received 20%, or $20,000.			
Cash 20,000		Cash 20,000	
Dividend Revenue	20,000	Investment in Mini Stock	20,000
For the year 2008, Mini reported a net loss of $50,000; Maxi Company's share is 20%, or $10,000.			
No entry		Loss on Investment 10,000	
		Investment in Mini Stock	10,000
At December 31, 2008, the Mini Company 48,000 shares have a fair value (market price) of $11 a share, or $528,000.			
Unrealized Holding Gain			
or Loss—Equity	48,000	No entry	
Securities Fair Value Adjustment			
(Available-for-Sale)	48,000		

[10]Cases in which an investment of 20 percent or more might not enable an investor to exercise significant influence include:

  (1) The investee opposes the investor's acquisition of its stock.

  (2) The investor and investee sign an agreement under which the investor surrenders significant shareholder rights.

  (3) The investor's ownership share does not result in "significant influence" because majority ownership of the investee is concentrated among a small group of shareholders who operate the investee without regard to the views of the investor.

  (4) The investor tries and fails to obtain representation on the investee's board of directors.

"Criteria for Applying the Equity Method of Accounting for Investments in Common Stock," *Interpretations of the Financial Accounting Standards Board No. 35* (Stamford, Conn.: FASB, 1981).

Note that under the fair value method, Maxi reports as revenue only the cash dividends received from Mini. **The earning of net income by Mini (the investee) is not considered a proper basis for recognition of income from the investment by Maxi (the investor).** Why? Mini may permanently retain in the business any increased net assets resulting from its profitable operation. Therefore, Maxi only earns revenue when it receives dividends from Mini.

Under the equity method, Maxi reports as revenue its share of the net income reported by Mini. Maxi records the cash dividends received from Mini as a decrease in the investment carrying value. As a result, Maxi records its share of the net income of Mini in the year when it is earned. With significant influence, Maxi can ensure that Mini will pay dividends, if desired, on any net asset increases resulting from net income. To wait until receiving a dividend ignores the fact that Maxi is better off if the investee has earned income.

Using dividends as a basis for recognizing income poses an additional problem. For example, assume that the investee reports a net loss. However, the investor exerts influence to force a dividend payment from the investee. In this case, the investor reports income, even though the investee is experiencing a loss. **In other words, using dividends as a basis for recognizing income fails to report properly the economics of the situation.**

For some companies, equity accounting can be a real pain to the bottom line. For example, **Amazon.com**, the pioneer of Internet retailing, at one time struggled to turn a profit. Furthermore, some of Amazon's equity investments had resulted in Amazon's earnings performance going from bad to worse. In a recent year, Amazon.com disclosed equity stakes in such companies as **Altera International, Basis Technology, Drugstore.com**, and **Eziba.com.** These equity investees reported losses that made Amazon's already bad bottom line even worse, accounting for up to 22 percent of its reported loss in one year alone.

Investee Losses Exceed Carrying Amount

If an investor's share of the investee's losses exceeds the carrying amount of the investment, should the investor recognize additional losses? Ordinarily the investor should discontinue applying the equity method and not recognize additional losses.

If the investor's potential loss is not limited to the amount of its original investment (by guarantee of the investee's obligations or other commitment to provide further financial support), or if imminent return to profitable operations by the investee appears to be assured, the investor should recognize additional losses.[11]

HOLDINGS OF MORE THAN 50%

When one corporation acquires a voting interest of more than 50 percent in another corporation, it is said to have a **controlling interest.** In such a relationship, the investor corporation is referred to as the **parent** and the investee corporation as the **subsidiary.** Companies present the investment in the common stock of the subsidiary as a long-term investment on the separate financial statements of the parent.

When the parent treats the subsidiary as an investment, the parent generally prepares **consolidated financial statements.** Consolidated financial statements treat the parent and subsidiary corporations as a single economic entity. (Advanced accounting courses extensively discuss the subject of when and how to prepare consolidated financial statements.) Whether or not consolidated financial statements are prepared, the parent company generally accounts for the investment in the subsidiary **using the equity method** as explained in this chapter.

INTERNATIONAL INSIGHT

IFRS permits companies to measure significant-influence investments using the equity, cost, or fair value methods.

UNDERLYING CONCEPTS

Revenue to be recognized should be earned and realized or realizable. A low level of ownership indicates that a company should defer the income from an investee until cash is received.

INTERNATIONAL INSIGHT

In contrast to U.S. firms, financial statements of non-U.S. companies often include both consolidated (group) statements and parent company financial statements.

---

[11]"The Equity Method of Accounting for Investments in Common Stock," op. cit., par. 19(i).

CONSOLIDATE THIS!

Presently the rules for consolidation seem very straightforward: If a company owns more than 50 percent of another company, it generally should be consolidated. If it owns less than 50 percent, it is generally not consolidated. However the FASB recognizes the artificiality of the present test. Determination of who really has control often relies on factors other than stock ownership.

In fact, specific guidelines force consolidation even though stock ownership is not above 50 percent in certain limited situations. For example, **Enron**'s failure to consolidate three special-purpose entities (SPEs) that it effectively controlled led to an overstatement of income of $569 million and overstatement of equity of $1.2 billion. In each of Enron's three SPEs, the GAAP guidelines would have led to consolidation. That is, the following factors indicate that consolidation should have occurred: the majority owner of the special-purpose entity (SPE) made only a modest investment; the activities of the SPE primarily benefited Enron; and the substantive risks and rewards related to the assets or debt of the SPE rested directly or indirectly with Enron.

The FASB has issued new guidelines related to SPEs, given all the reporting problems that have surfaced related to SPEs at Enron and other companies. We discuss these new rules in Appendix 17B.

WHAT DO THE NUMBERS MEAN?

| **OTHER REPORTING ISSUES** | **SECTION 3** |

We have identified the basic issues involved in accounting for investments in debt and equity securities. In addition, the following issues relate to both of these types of securities.

1 Financial statement presentation.
2 Impairment of value.
3 Transfers between categories.
4 Fair value controversy.

FINANCIAL STATEMENT PRESENTATION OF INVESTMENTS

OBJECTIVE 5
Describe the disclosure requirements for investments in debt and equity securities.

Companies must present individual amounts for the three categories of investments either on the balance sheet or in the related notes. Illustration 17-18 summarizes the valuation and balance sheet classification of investments.

ILLUSTRATION 17-18
Investment Valuation and Classification

Investment Category	Valuation	Classification
Trading securities (debt and equity)	Fair value	Current asset.
Held-to-maturity (debt)	Amortized cost	Current or noncurrent based on maturity date of individual security.
Available-for-sale debt	Fair value	Depends on the circumstances. Current or noncurrent based on maturities and expectations as to sales and redemptions in the following year.
Available-for-sale equity	Fair value	Depends on the circumstances. Current or noncurrent based on expectations as to sales in the following year.

Actual Company Disclosures Related to Investments and Comprehensive Income

For securities classified as available-for-sale and separately for securities classified as held-to-maturity, a company should describe:

1 Aggregate fair value, gross unrealized holding gains, gross unrealized losses, and amortized cost basis by major security type (debt and equity).

2 Information about the contractual maturities of debt securities. The company may group maturity information, for example (a) within one year, (b) after one year through five years, (c) after five years through ten years, and (d) after ten years.

In classifying investments, evidence should support management's expressed intent, such as the history of the company's investment activities, events subsequent to the balance sheet date, and the nature and purpose of the investment.

Companies must be extremely careful with debt securities held to maturity. If a company prematurely sells a debt security in this category, the sale may "taint" the entire held-to-maturity portfolio. That is, a management's statement regarding "intent" is no longer credible. Therefore the company may have to reclassify the securities. This could lead to unfortunate consequences. An interesting by-product of this situation is that companies that wish to retire their debt securities early are finding it difficult to do so. The holder will not sell because the securities are classified as held-to-maturity.

Disclosures Required under the Equity Method

Disclosures Related to Equity Investments

The significance of an investment to the investor's financial position and operating results should determine the extent of disclosures. The following disclosures in the investor's financial statements generally apply to the equity method.

WHAT DO THE NUMBERS MEAN?

MORE DISCLOSURE PLEASE

As indicated in the last two sections, the level of disclosure for investment securities is extensive. How to account for investment securities is a particularly sensitive area, given the large amounts of equity investments involved. And presently companies report investments in equity securities at cost, equity, fair value, and full consolidation, depending on the circumstances. As a recent SEC study noted, "there are so many different accounting treatments for investments that it raises the question of whether they are all needed."

Presented below is an estimate of the percentage of companies on the major exchanges that have investments in the equity of other entities.

Investments in the Equity of Other Companies

Categorized by Accounting Treatment	Percent of Companies
Presenting consolidated financial statements	91.1%
Reporting equity method investments	23.5
Reporting cost method investments*	17.4
Reporting available-for-sale investments	37.4
Reporting trading investments	6.2

*If the equity investments are not publicly traded, the company often accounts for the investment under the cost method. Changes in value are therefore not recognized unless there is impairment.

As the table indicates, many companies have equity investments of some type. These investments can be substantial. For example, based on the table above, the total amount of equity-method investments appearing on company balance sheets is approximately $403 billion and the amount shown in the income statements in any one year for all companies is approximately $38 billion.

Source: "Report and Recommendations Pursuant to Section 401(c) of the Sarbanes-Oxley Act of 2002 on Arrangements with Off-Balance Sheet Implications, Special Purpose Entities, and Transparency of Filings by Issuers," United States Securities and Exchange Commission—Office of Chief Accountant, Office of Economic Analyses, Division of Corporation Finance (June 2005), pp. 36–39.

UNDERLYING CONCEPTS

The consolidation of financial results of different companies follows the economic entity assumption and disregards legal entities. The key objective is to provide useful information to financial statement users.

1 The name of each investee and the percentage of ownership of common stock.

2 The accounting policies of the investor with respect to investments in common stock.

3 The difference, if any, between the amount in the investment account and the amount of underlying equity in the net assets of the investee.

4 The aggregate value of each identified investment based on quoted market price (if available).

5 When equity-method investments are, in the aggregate, material in relation to the financial position and operating results of an investor, the company may need to present summarized information concerning assets, liabilities, and results of operations of the investees, either individually or in groups, as appropriate.

In addition, the investor should disclose the reasons for not using the equity method in cases of 20 percent or more ownership interest, and for using the equity method in cases of less than 20 percent ownership interest.

Reclassification Adjustments

As we indicated in Chapter 4, companies report changes in unrealized holding gains and losses related to available-for-sale securities as part of other comprehensive income. Companies may display the components of other comprehensive income in one of three ways: (1) in a combined statement of income and comprehensive income, (2) in a separate statement of comprehensive income that begins with net income, or (3) in a statement of stockholders' equity.

The reporting of changes in unrealized gains or losses in comprehensive income is straightforward unless a company sells securities during the year. In that case, double counting results when the company reports realized gains or losses as part of net income but also shows the amounts as part of other comprehensive income in the current period or in previous periods.

To ensure that gains and losses are not counted twice when a sale occurs, a **reclassification adjustment** is necessary. To illustrate, assume that Open Company has the following two available-for-sale securities in its portfolio at the end of 2006 (its first year of operations).

Investments	Cost	Fair Value	Unrealized Holding Gain (Loss)
Lehman Inc. common stocks	$ 80,000	$105,000	$25,000
Woods Co. common stocks	120,000	135,000	15,000
Total of portfolio	$200,000	$240,000	40,000
Previous securities fair value adjustment balance			–0–
Securities fair value adjustment—Dr.			$40,000

ILLUSTRATION 17-19
Available-for-Sale
Security Portfolio (2006)

If Open Company reports net income in 2006 of $350,000, it presents a statement of comprehensive income as follows.

OPEN COMPANY STATEMENT OF COMPREHENSIVE INCOME FOR THE YEAR ENDED DECEMBER 31, 2006	
Net income	$350,000
Other comprehensive income	
Holding gains arising during period	40,000
Comprehensive income	$390,000

ILLUSTRATION 17-20
Statement of
Comprehensive Income
(2006)

During 2007, Open Company sold the Lehman Inc. common stock for $105,000 and realized a gain on the sale of $25,000 ($105,000 – $80,000). At the end of 2007, the fair value of the Woods Co. common stock increased an additional $20,000, to $155,000. Illustration 17-21 shows the computation of the change in the securities fair value adjustment account.

ILLUSTRATION 17-21
Available-for-Sale
Security Portfolio (2007)

Investments	Cost	Fair Value	Unrealized Holding Gain (Loss)
Woods Co. common stocks	$120,000	$155,000	$35,000
Previous securities fair value adjustment balance—Dr.			(40,000)
Securities fair value adjustment—Cr.			$ (5,000)

Illustration 17-21 indicates that Open should report an unrealized holding loss of $5,000 in comprehensive income in 2007. In addition, Open realized a gain of $25,000 on the sale of the Lehman common stock. **Comprehensive income includes both realized and unrealized components.** Therefore Open recognizes a total holding gain (loss) in 2007 of $20,000, computed as follows.

ILLUSTRATION 17-22
Computation of Total
Holding Gain (Loss)

Unrealized holding gain (loss)	$ (5,000)
Realized holding gain	25,000
Total holding gain recognized	$20,000

Open reports net income of $720,000 in 2007, which includes the realized gain on sale of the Lehman securities. Illustration 17-23 shows a statement of comprehensive income for 2007, indicating how Open reported the components of holding gains (losses).

ILLUSTRATION 17-23
Statement of
Comprehensive Income
(2007)

OPEN COMPANY
STATEMENT OF COMPREHENSIVE INCOME
FOR THE YEAR ENDED DECEMBER 31, 2007

Net income (includes $25,000 realized gain on Lehman shares)		$720,000
Other comprehensive income		
Total holding gains arising during period [$(5,000) + $25,000]	$20,000	
Less: Reclassification adjustment for gains included in net income	(25,000)	(5,000)
Comprehensive income		$715,000

In 2006, Open included the unrealized gain on the Lehman Co. common stock in comprehensive income. In 2007, Open sold the stock. It reported the realized gain in net income, which increased comprehensive income again. To avoid double counting this gain, Open makes a reclassification adjustment to eliminate the realized gain from the computation of comprehensive income in 2007.

A company may display reclassification adjustments on the face of the financial statement in which it reports comprehensive income. Or it may disclose these reclassification adjustments in the notes to the financial statements.

Comprehensive Example

To illustrate the reporting of investment securities and related gain or loss on available-for-sale securities, assume that on January 1, 2006, Hinges Co. had cash and common stock of $50,000.[12] At that date the company had no other asset, liability, or equity balance. On January 2, Hinges purchased for cash $50,000 of equity securities classified as available-for-sale. On June 30, Hinges sold part of the available-for-sale security portfolio, realizing a gain as shown in Illustration 17-24.

Fair value of securities sold	$22,000
Less: Cost of securities sold	20,000
Realized gain	$ 2,000

ILLUSTRATION 17-24
Computation of Realized Gain

Hinges did not purchase or sell any other securities during 2006. It received $3,000 in dividends during the year. At December 31, 2006, the remaining portfolio is as shown in Illustration 17-25.

Fair value of portfolio	$34,000
Less: Cost of portfolio	30,000
Unrealized gain	$ 4,000

ILLUSTRATION 17-25
Computation of Unrealized Gain

Illustration 17-26 shows the company's income statement for 2006.

HINGES CO.
INCOME STATEMENT
FOR THE YEAR ENDED DECEMBER 31, 2006

Dividend revenue	$3,000
Realized gains on investment in securities	2,000
Net income	$5,000

ILLUSTRATION 17-26
Income Statement

The company reports its change in the unrealized holding gain in a statement of comprehensive income as follows.

HINGES CO.
STATEMENT OF COMPREHENSIVE INCOME
FOR THE YEAR ENDED DECEMBER 31, 2006

Net income		$5,000
Other comprehensive income:		
Holding gains arising during the period	$6,000	
Less: Reclassification adjustment for gains included in net income	2,000	4,000
Comprehensive income		$9,000

ILLUSTRATION 17-27
Statement of Comprehensive Income

---

[12]We adapted this example from Dennis R. Beresford, L. Todd Johnson, and Cheri L. Reither, "Is a Second Income Statement Needed?" *Journal of Accountancy* (April 1996), p. 71.

Its statement of stockholders' equity appears in Illustration 17-28.

ILLUSTRATION 17-28
Statement of
Stockholders' Equity

HINGES CO.
STATEMENT OF STOCKHOLDERS' EQUITY
FOR THE YEAR ENDED DECEMBER 31, 2006

	Common Stock	Retained Earnings	Accumulated Other Comprehensive Income	Total
Beginning balance	$50,000	$–0–	$–0–	$50,000
Add: Net income		5,000		5,000
Other comprehensive Income			4,000	4,000
Ending balance	$50,000	$5,000	$4,000	$59,000

The comparative balance sheet is shown in Illustration 17-29.

ILLUSTRATION 17-29
Comparative Balance
Sheet

HINGES CO.
COMPARATIVE BALANCE SHEET

	1/1/06	12/31/06
Assets		
Cash	$50,000	$25,000
Available-for-sale securities		34,000
Total assets	$50,000	$59,000
Stockholders' equity		
Common stock	$50,000	$50,000
Retained earnings		5,000
Accumulated other comprehensive income		4,000
Total stockholders' equity	$50,000	$59,000

This example indicates how an unrealized gain or loss on available-for-sale securities affects all the financial statements. Note that a company must disclose the components that comprise accumulated other comprehensive income.

IMPAIRMENT OF VALUE

OBJECTIVE 6
Discuss the accounting for impairments of debt and equity investments.

A company should evaluate every investment, at each reporting date, to determine if it has suffered **impairment**—a loss in value that is other than temporary. For example, if an investee experiences a bankruptcy or a significant liquidity crisis, the investor may suffer a permanent loss. **If the decline is judged to be other than temporary, a company writes down the cost basis of the individual security to a new cost basis.** The company accounts for the write-down as a realized loss. Therefore, it includes the amount in net income.

For debt securities, a company uses the impairment test to determine whether "it is probable that the investor will be unable to collect all amounts due according to the contractual terms."

For equity securities, the guideline is less precise. Any time realizable value is lower than the carrying amount of the investment, a company must consider an impairment. Factors involved include the length of time and the extent to which the fair value has been less than cost; the financial condition and near-term prospects of the issuer; and the intent and ability of the investor company to retain its investment to allow for any anticipated recovery in fair value.

To illustrate an impairment, assume that Strickler Company holds available-for-sale bond securities with a par value and amortized cost of $1 million. The fair value of these securities is $800,000. Strickler has previously reported an unrealized loss on these securities of $200,000 as part of other comprehensive income. In evaluating the securities, Strickler now determines that it probably will not collect all amounts due. In this case, it reports the unrealized loss of $200,000 as a loss on impairment of $200,000. Strickler includes this amount in income, with the bonds stated at their new cost basis. It records this impairment as follows.

Loss on Impairment	200,000	
Securities Fair Value Adjustment (Available-for-Sale)	200,000	
Unrealized Holding Gain or Loss—Equity		200,000
Available-for-Sale Securities		200,000

The new cost basis of the investment in debt securities is $800,000. Strickler includes subsequent increases and decreases in the fair value of impaired available-for-sale securities as other comprehensive income.[13]

Companies base impairment for debt and equity securities on a fair value test. This test differs slightly from the impairment test for loans that we discuss in Appendix 14A. The FASB rejected the discounted cash flow alternative for securities because of the availability of market price information.

WHAT DO THE NUMBERS MEAN?

THE IRONY OF IT ALL

The **Federal National Mortgage Association** (FNMA)—known as "Fannie Mae"—is a government-sponsored company that owns or guarantees about 25 percent of all the mortgages in the United States. Recently numerous articles have detailed accounting abuses by Fannie Mae. For example, Fannie Mae has acknowledged that some of its accounting polices do not comply with GAAP. It is now preparing to restate its financial statements back to 2001 and possibly to recognize at least $9 billion in losses related to derivatives.

Interestingly, Fannie Mae has caused much hardship for many of its brethren in the financial community (such as **DNB Financial**, **Independent Bank Corporation**, and **Wilmington Trust**). The reason: Many are holding security investments in Fannie Mae. And now the institutions are taking permanent write-downs on these securities because the losses appear to be other than temporary. (In other words, the Fannie Mae securities are impaired.) The irony is that a number of the companies that are taking impairment losses are the very ones that recently fought hard to make sure the FASB did not tighten up impairment accounting rules. Even more ironic is the fact the one of their fellow lobbyers (FNMA) is the source of their impairments!

TRANSFERS BETWEEN CATEGORIES

Companies account for transfers between any of the categories at fair value. Thus, if a company transfers available-for-sale securities to held-to-maturity investments, it records the new investment (held-to-maturity) at the date of transfer at **fair value** in the new category. Similarly, if it transfers held-to-maturity investments to available-for-sale investments, it records the new investments (available-for-sale) at **fair value**. This **fair value** rule assures that a company cannot omit recognition of fair value simply by transferring securities to the held-to-maturity category. Illustration 17-30 (on page 860) summarizes the accounting treatment for transfers.

OBJECTIVE 7
Describe the accounting for transfer of investment securities between categories.

---

[13]Companies may not amortize any discount related to the debt securities after recording the impairment. The new cost basis of impaired held-to-maturity securities does not change unless additional impairment occurs.

ILLUSTRATION 17-30
Accounting for Transfers

*Examples of the Entries
for Recording Transfers
Between Categories*

Type of Transfer	Measurement Basis	Impact of Transfer on Stockholders' Equity*	Impact of Transfer on Net Income*
Transfer from trading to available-for-sale	Security transferred at fair value at the date of transfer, which is the new cost basis of the security.	The unrealized gain or loss at the date of transfer increases or decreases stockholders' equity.	The unrealized gain or loss at the date of transfer is recognized in income.
Transfer from available-for-sale to trading	Security transferred at fair value at the date of transfer, which is the new cost basis of the security.	The unrealized gain or loss at the date of transfer increases or decreases stockholders' equity.	The unrealized gain or loss at the date of transfer is recognized in income.
Transfer from held-to-maturity to available-for-sale**	Security transferred at fair value at the date of transfer.	The separate component of stockholders' equity is increased or decreased by the unrealized gain or loss at the date of transfer.	None
Transfer from available-for-sale to held-to-maturity	Security transferred at fair value at the date of transfer.	The unrealized gain or loss at the date of transfer carried as a separate component of stockholders' equity is amortized over the remaining life of the security.	None

*Assumes that adjusting entries to report changes in fair value for the current period are not yet recorded.

**Statement No. 115 states that these types of transfers should be rare.

FAIR VALUE CONTROVERSY

The reporting of investment securities is controversial. Some believe that all securities should be reported at fair value; others believe they all should be stated at amortized cost. Others favor the present approach. In this section we look at some of the major unresolved issues.

Measurement Based on Intent

Companies classify debt securities as held-to-maturity, available-for-sale, or trading. As a result, companies can report three identical debt securities in three different ways in the financial statements. Some argue such treatment is confusing. Furthermore, the held-to-maturity category relies solely on intent, a subjective evaluation. What is not subjective is the market price of the debt instrument. In other words, the three classifications are subjective, resulting in arbitrary classifications.

Gains Trading

Companies can classify certain debt securities as held-to-maturity and therefore report them at amortized cost. Companies can classify other debt and equity securities as available-for-sale and report them at fair value with the unrealized gain or loss reported as other comprehensive income. In either case, a company can become involved in "gains trading" (also referred to as "cherry picking," "snacking," or "sell the best and keep the rest"). In **gains trading**, companies sell their "winners," reporting the gains in income, and hold on to the losers.

Liabilities Not Fairly Valued

Many argue that if companies report investment securities at fair value, they also should report liabilities at fair value. Why? By recognizing changes in value on only one side of the balance sheet (the asset side), a high degree of volatility can occur in the income and stockholders' equity amounts. Further, financial institutions are involved in asset and liability management (not just asset management). Viewing only one side may lead managers to make uneconomic decisions as a result of the accounting.

Although the Board sympathized with this view, it noted that companies still reported certain debt securities at amortized cost (held-to-maturity securities) and that this standard excluded other types of securities. In addition, serious valuation issues arose in relation to some types of liabilities. As a result, liabilities were excluded from consideration.[14]

Subjectivity of Fair Values

Some question the relevance of fair value measures for investments in securities, arguing in favor of reporting based on amortized cost. They believe that amortized cost provides relevant information: it focuses on the decision to acquire the asset, the earning effects of that decision that will be realized over time, and the ultimate recoverable value of the asset. They argue that fair value ignores those concepts. Instead, fair value focuses on the effects of transactions and events that do not involve the company, reflecting opportunity gains and losses whose recognition in the financial statements is, in their view, not appropriate until realized.

SUMMARY OF REPORTING TREATMENT OF SECURITIES

Illustration 17-31 summarizes the major debt and equity securities and their reporting treatment.

Category	Balance Sheet	Income Statement
Trading (debt and equity securities)	Investments shown at fair value. Current assets.	Interest and dividends are recognized as revenue. Unrealized holding gains and losses are included in net income.
Available-for-sale (debt and equity securities)	Investments shown at fair value. Current or long-term assets. Unrealized holding gains and losses are a separate component of stockholders' equity.	Interest and dividends are recognized as revenue. Unrealized holding gains and losses are **not** included in net income but in other comprehensive income.
Held-to-maturity (debt securities)	Investments shown at amortized cost. Current or long-term assets.	Interest is recognized as revenue.
Equity method and/or consolidation (equity securities)	Investments originally are carried at cost, are periodically adjusted by the investor's share of the investee's earnings or losses, and are decreased by all dividends received from the investee. Classified as long-term.	Revenue is recognized to the extent of the investee's earnings or losses reported subsequent to the date of investment.

ILLUSTRATION 17-31
Summary of Treatment of Major Debt and Equity Securities

Discussion of Special Issues Related to Investments

---

[14]In a recent exposure draft concerning valuation of financial instruments, the FASB indicated its support for valuing liabilities at fair value. "Fair Value Measurements," Proposed Statement of Financial Accounting Standards (Norwalk, Conn.: FASB, June 23, 2004).

SUMMARY OF LEARNING OBJECTIVES

1. Identify the three categories of debt securities and describe the accounting and reporting treatment for each category. (1) Carry and report *held-to-maturity debt securities* at amortized cost. (2) Value *trading debt securities* for reporting purposes at fair value, with unrealized holding gains or losses included in net income. (3) Value *available-for-sale debt securities* for reporting purposes at fair value, with unrealized holding gains or losses reported as other comprehensive income and as a separate component of stockholders' equity.

2. Understand the procedures for discount and premium amortization on bond investments. Similar to bonds payable, companies should amortize discount or premium on bond investments using the effective-interest method. They apply the effective interest rate or yield to the beginning carrying value of the investment for each interest period in order to compute interest revenue.

3. Identify the categories of equity securities and describe the accounting and reporting treatment for each category. The degree to which one corporation (investor) acquires an interest in the common stock of another corporation (investee) generally determines the accounting treatment for the investment. Long-term investments by one corporation in the common stock of another can be classified according to the percentage of the voting stock of the investee held by the investor.

4. Explain the equity method of accounting and compare it to the fair value method for equity securities. Under the equity method the investor and the investee acknowledge a substantive economic relationship. The company originally records the investment at cost but subsequently adjusts the amount each period for changes in the net assets of the investee. That is, the investor's proportionate share of the earnings (losses) of the investee periodically increases (decreases) the investment's carrying amount. All dividends received by the investor from the investee decrease the investment's carrying amount. Under the fair value method a company reports the equity investment at fair value each reporting period irrespective of the investee's earnings or dividends paid to it. A company applies the equity method to investment holdings between 20 percent and 50 percent of ownership. It applies the fair value method to holdings below 20 percent.

5. Describe the disclosure requirements for investments in debt and equity securities. Companies should report trading securities at aggregate fair value as current assets. Companies should classify individual held-to-maturity and available-for-sale securities as current or noncurrent, depending on the circumstances. For available-for-sale and held-to-maturity securities, a company should describe: aggregate fair value, gross unrealized holding gains, gross unrealized losses, amortized cost basis by type (debt and equity), and information about the contractual maturity of debt securities. A company needs a reclassification adjustment when it reports realized gains or losses as part of net income but also shows the amounts as part of other comprehensive income in the current or in previous periods. Companies should report unrealized holding gains or losses related to available-for-sale securities in other comprehensive income and the aggregate balance as accumulated comprehensive income on the balance sheet.

6. Discuss the accounting for impairments of debt and equity investments. Impairments of debt and equity securities are losses in value that are determined to be other than temporary, are based on a fair value test, and are charged to income.

7. Describe the accounting for transfer of investment securities between categories. Transfers of securities between categories of investments should be accounted for at fair value, with unrealized holding gains or losses treated in accordance with the nature of the transfer.

Accounting for Derivative Instruments

Until the early 1970s, most financial managers worked in a cozy, if unthrilling, world. Since then, constant change caused by volatile markets, new technology, and deregulation has increased the risks to businesses. In response, the financial community developed products to manage these risks.

These products—called **derivative financial instruments** or simply, **derivatives**—are useful for managing risk. Companies use the fair values or cash flows of these instruments to offset the changes in fair values or cash flows of the at-risk assets. The development of powerful computing and communication technology has aided the growth in derivative use. This technology provides new ways to analyze information about markets as well as the power to process high volumes of payments.

UNDERSTANDING DERIVATIVES

In order to understand derivatives, consider the following examples.

Example 1—Forward Contract. Assume that a company like **Dell** believes that the price of **Google**'s stock will increase substantially in the next three months. Unfortunately, it does not have the cash resources to purchase the stock today. Dell therefore enters into a contract with a broker for delivery of 10,000 shares of Google stock in three months at the price of $110 per share.

Dell has entered into a **forward contract**, a type of derivative. As a result of the contract, Dell **has received the right** to receive 10,000 shares of Google stock in three months. Further, it **has an obligation** to pay $110 per share at that time. What is the benefit of this derivative contract? Dell can buy Google stock today and take delivery in three months. If the price goes up, as it expects, Dell profits. If the price goes down, it loses.

Example 2—Option Contract. Now suppose that Dell needs two weeks to decide whether to purchase Google stock. It therefore enters into a different type of contract, one that gives it the right to purchase Google stock at its current price any time within the next two weeks. As part of the contract, the broker charges $3,000 for holding the contract open for two weeks at a set price.

Dell has now entered into an **option contract**, another type of derivative. As a result of this contract, **it has received the right**, **but not the obligation** to purchase this stock. If the price of the Google stock increases in the next two weeks, Dell exercises its option. In this case, the cost of the stock is the price of the stock stated in the contract, plus the cost of the option contract. If the price does not increase, Dell does not exercise the contract, but still incurs the cost for the option.

The forward contract and the option contract both involve a future delivery of stock. The value of the contract relies on the underlying asset—the Google stock. Thus, these financial instruments are known as derivatives because they **derive their value from** values of other assets (e.g., stocks, bonds, or commodities). Or, their value relates to a market-determined indicator (e.g., interest rates or the Standard and Poor's 500 stock composite index).

In this appendix, we discuss the accounting for three different types of derivatives:

1 Financial forwards or financial futures.
2 Options.
3 Swaps.

Who Uses Derivatives, and Why?

OBJECTIVE 8
Explain who uses derivatives and why.

Whether to protect for changes in interest rates, the weather, stock prices, oil prices, or foreign currencies, derivative contracts help to smooth the fluctuations caused by various types of risks. A company that wants to ensure against certain types of business risks often uses derivative contracts to achieve this objective.[1]

Producers and Consumers

To illustrate, assume that Heartland Ag is a large producer of potatoes for the consumer market. The present price for potatoes is excellent. Unfortunately, Heartland needs two months to harvest its potatoes and deliver them to the market. Because Heartland expects the price of potatoes to drop, it signs a forward contract. It agrees to sell its potatoes today at the current market price for delivery in two months.

Who would buy this contract? Suppose on the other side of the contract is **McDonald's Corporation**. McDonald's wants to have potatoes (for French fries) in two months and believes that prices will increase. McDonald's is therefore agreeable to delivery in two months at current prices. It knows that it will need potatoes in two months, and that it can make an acceptable profit at this price level.

In this situation, if the price of potatoes increases before delivery, Heartland loses and McDonald's wins. Conversely, if prices decrease, Heartland wins and McDonald's loses. However, the objective is not to gamble on the outcome. Regardless of which way the price moves, both Heartland and McDonald's have received a price at which they obtain an acceptable profit. In this case, although Heartland is a **producer** and McDonald's is a **consumer**, both companies are **hedgers**. They both hedge their positions to ensure an acceptable financial result.

Commodity prices are volatile. They depend on weather, crop production, and general economic conditions. For the producer and the consumer to plan effectively, it makes good sense to lock in specific future revenues or costs in order to run their businesses successfully.

Speculators and Arbitrageurs

In some cases, instead of McDonald's taking a position in the forward contract, a speculator may purchase the contract from Heartland. The **speculator** bets that the price of potatoes will rise, thereby increasing the value of the forward contract. The speculator, who may be in the market for only a few hours, will then sell the forward contract to another speculator or to a company like McDonald's.

Arbitrageurs also use derivatives. These market players attempt to exploit inefficiencies in derivative markets. They seek to lock in profits by simultaneously entering into transactions in two or more markets. For example, an arbitrageur might trade in a futures contract. At the same time, the arbitrageur will also trade in the commodity underlying the futures contract, hoping to achieve small price gains on the difference between the two. Markets rely on speculators and arbitrageurs to keep the market liquid on a daily basis.

In these illustrations, we explained why Heartland (the producer) and McDonald's (the consumer) would become involved in a derivative contract. Consider other types of situations that companies face.

---

[1]Derivatives are traded on many exchanges throughout the world. In addition, many derivative contracts (primarily interest rate swaps) are privately negotiated.

1 Airlines, like **Delta**, **Southwest**, and **United**, are affected by changes in the price of jet fuel.

2 Financial institutions, such as **Citigroup**, **Bankers Trust**, and **M&I Bank**, are involved in borrowing and lending funds that are affected by changes in interest rates.

3 Multinational corporations, like **Cisco Systems**, **Coca-Cola**, and **General Electric**, are subject to changes in foreign exchange rates.

In fact, most corporations are involved in some form of derivatives transactions. Companies give these reasons (in their annual reports) as to why they use derivatives:

1 **ExxonMobil** uses derivatives to hedge its exposure to fluctuations in interest rates, foreign currency exchange rates, and hydrocarbon prices.

2 **Caterpillar** uses derivatives to manage foreign currency exchange rates, interest rates, and commodity price exposure.

3 **Johnson & Johnson** uses derivatives to manage the impact of interest rate and foreign exchange rate changes on earnings and cash flows.

Many corporations use derivatives extensively and successfully. However, derivatives can be dangerous. All parties involved must understand the risks and rewards associated with these contracts.[2]

BASIC PRINCIPLES IN ACCOUNTING FOR DERIVATIVES

In *SFAS No. 133*, the FASB concluded that derivatives such as forwards and options are assets and liabilities. Companies should therefore report them in the balance sheet at **fair value**.[3] The Board believes that fair value will provide statement users the best information about derivatives.[4] Relying on some other basis of valuation for derivatives, such as historical cost, does not make sense. Why? Because many derivatives have a historical cost of zero. Furthermore, the markets for derivatives, and the assets upon which derivatives' values rely, are well developed. As a result, the Board believes that companies can determine reliable fair value amounts for derivatives.

> **OBJECTIVE 9**
> Understand the basic guidelines for accounting for derivatives.

On the income statement, a company should recognize any unrealized gain or loss in income, if it uses the derivative for speculation purposes. If using the derivative for hedging purposes, the accounting for any gain or loss depends on the type of hedge used. We discuss the accounting for hedged transactions later in the appendix.

In summary, companies follow these guidelines in accounting for derivatives.

1 Recognize derivatives in the financial statements as assets and liabilities.

2 Report derivatives at fair value.

---

[2]There are some well-publicized examples of companies that have suffered considerable losses using derivatives. For example, companies such as **Fannie Mae** (U.S.), **Enron** (U.S.), **Showa Shell Sekiyu** (Japan), **Metallgesellschaft** (Germany), **Procter & Gamble** (U.S.), and **Air Products & Chemicals** (U.S.) incurred significant losses from investments in derivative instruments.

[3]"Accounting for Derivative Instruments and Hedging Activities," *Statement of Financial Accounting Standards No. 133* (Stamford, Conn.: FASB, 1998). This standard covers all derivative instruments, whether financial or not. In this chapter we focus on derivative financial instruments because of their widespread use in practice.

[4]*Fair value* is the amount at which companies can willingly (i.e., not forced or in liquidation) buy (incur) or sell (settle) an asset (or liability). Quoted market prices in active markets are the best evidence of fair value. Companies should use them if available. In the absence of market prices, companies can use the prices of similar assets or liabilities or accepted present value techniques. "Disclosures About Fair Value of Financial Instruments," *Statement of Financial Accounting Standards No. 107* (Stamford, Conn.: FASB, 1991), pars. 5–6, 11. The Board's long-term objective is to require fair value measurement and recognition for all financial instruments (*SFAS No. 133*, par. 216).

3 Recognize gains and losses resulting from speculation in derivatives immediately in income.

4 Report gains and losses resulting from hedge transactions differently, depending on the type of hedge.

Example of Derivative Financial Instrument—Speculation

OBJECTIVE 10
Describe the accounting for derivative financial instruments.

To illustrate the measurement and reporting of a derivative for speculative purposes, we examine a derivative whose value depends on the market price of Laredo Inc. common stock. A company can realize a gain from the increase in the value of the Laredo shares with the use of a derivative, such as a call option.[5] A **call option** gives the holder the right, but not the obligation, to buy shares at a preset price. This price is often referred to as the **strike price** or the **exercise price**.

For example, assume a company enters into a call option contract with Baird Investment Co., which gives it the option to purchase Laredo stock at $100 per share.[6] If the price of Laredo stock increases above $100, the company can exercise this option and purchase the shares for $100 per share. If Laredo's stock never increases above $100 per share, the call option is worthless.

Accounting Entries

To illustrate the accounting for a call option, assume that the company purchases a call option contract on January 2, 2007, when Laredo shares are trading at $100 per share. The contract gives it the option to purchase 1,000 shares (referred to as the **notional amount**) of Laredo stock at an option price of $100 per share. The option expires on April 30, 2007. The company purchases the call option for $400 and makes the following entry.

January 2, 2007

Call Option	400	
Cash		400

This payment is referred to as the **option premium**. It is generally much less than the cost of purchasing the shares directly. The option premium consists of two amounts: (1) intrinsic value and (2) time value. Illustration 17A-1 shows the formula to compute the option premium.

ILLUSTRATION 17A-1
Option Premium Formula

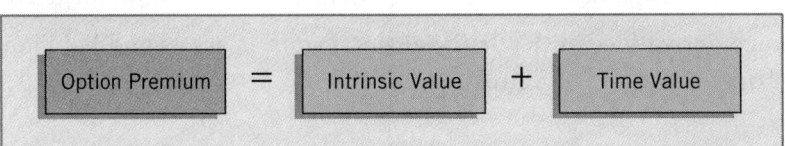

Intrinsic value is the difference between the market price and the preset strike price at any point in time. It represents the amount realized by the option holder, if exercising the option immediately. On January 2, 2007, the intrinsic value is zero because the market price equals the preset strike price.

---

[5]Investors can use a different type of option contract—a **put option**—to realize a gain if anticipating a decline in the Laredo stock value. A put option gives the holder the option to sell shares at a preset price. Thus, a put option **increases** in value when the underlying asset **decreases** in value.

[6]Baird Investment Co. is referred to as the **counterparty**. Counterparties frequently are investment bankers or other companies that hold inventories of financial instruments.

Time value refers to the option's value over and above its intrinsic value. Time value reflects the possibility that the option has a fair value greater than zero. How? Because there is some expectation that the price of Laredo shares will increase above the strike price during the option term. As indicated, the time value for the option is $400.[7]

On March 31, 2007, the price of Laredo shares increases to $120 per share. The intrinsic value of the call option contract is now $20,000. That is, the company can exercise the call option and purchase 1,000 shares from Baird Investment for $100 per share. It can then sell the shares in the market for $120 per share. This gives the company a gain of $20,000 ($120,000 − $100,000) on the option contract.[8] It records the increase in the intrinsic value of the option as follows.

March 31, 2007

Call Option	20,000	
Unrealized Holding Gain or Loss—Income		20,000

A market appraisal indicates that the time value of the option at March 31, 2007, is $100.[9] The company records this change in value of the option as follows.

March 31, 2007

Unrealized Holding Gain or Loss—Income	300	
Call Option ($400 − $100)		300

At March 31, 2007, the company reports the call option in its balance sheet at fair value of $20,100.[10] The unrealized holding gain increases net income for the period. The loss on the time value of the option decreases net income.

On April 1, 2007, the company records the settlement of the call option contract with Baird Investment as follows.

April 1, 2007

Cash	20,000	
Loss on Settlement of Call Option	100	
Call Option		20,100

Illustration 17A-2 summarizes the effects of the call option contract on net income.

Date	Transaction	Income (Loss) Effect
March 31, 2007	Net increase in value of call option ($20,000 − $300)	$19,700
April 1, 2007	Settle call option	(100)
	Total net income	$19,600

ILLUSTRATION 17A-2
Effect on Income—Derivative Financial Instrument

The accounting summarized in Illustration 17A-2 is in accord with *SFAS No. 133*. That is, because the call option meets the definition of an asset, the company records

---

[7]This cost is estimated using option-pricing models, such as the Black-Scholes model. The volatility of the underlying stock, the expected life of the option, the risk-free rate of interest, and expected dividends on the underlying stock during the option term affect the Black-Scholes fair value estimate.

[8]In practice, investors generally do not have to actually buy and sell the Laredo shares to settle the option and realize the gain. This is referred to as the **net settlement** feature of option contracts.

[9]The decline in value reflects both the decreased likelihood that the Laredo shares will continue to increase in value over the option period and the shorter time to maturity of the option contract.

[10]As indicated earlier, the total value of the option at any point in time equals the intrinsic value plus the time value.

it in the balance sheet on March 31, 2007. Furthermore, it reports the call option at fair value, with any gains or losses reported in income.

Differences between Traditional and Derivative Financial Instruments

How does a traditional financial instrument differ from a derivative one? A derivative financial instrument has the following three basic characteristics.[11]

1   The instrument has (1) one or more underlyings and (2) an identified payment provision. An **underlying** is a specified interest rate, security price, commodity price, index of prices or rates, or other market-related variable. The interaction of the underlying, with the face amount or the number of units specified in the derivative contract (the notional amounts), determines payment. For example, the value of the call option increased in value when the value of the Laredo stock increased. In this case, the underlying is the stock price. To arrive at the payment provision, multiply the change in the stock price by the number of shares (notional amount).

2   The instrument requires little or no investment at the inception of the contract. To illustrate, the company paid a small premium to purchase the call option—an amount much less than if purchasing the Laredo shares as a direct investment.

3   The instrument requires or permits net settlement. As indicated in the call option example, the company could realize a profit on the call option without taking possession of the shares. This **net settlement** feature reduces the transaction costs associated with derivatives.

Illustration 17A-3 summarizes the differences between traditional and derivative financial instruments. Here, we use a trading security for the traditional financial instrument and a call option as an example of a derivative one.

ILLUSTRATION 17A-3
Features of Traditional and Derivative Financial Instruments

Feature	Traditional Financial Instrument (Trading Security)	Derivative Financial Instrument (Call Option)
Payment provision	Stock price times the number of shares.	Change in stock price (underlying) times number of shares (notional amount).
Initial investment	Investor pays full cost.	Initial investment is much less than full cost.
Settlement	Deliver stock to receive cash.	Receive cash equivalent, based on changes in stock price times the number of shares.

DERIVATIVES USED FOR HEDGING

Flexibility in use, and the low-cost features of derivatives relative to traditional financial instruments, explain the popularity of derivatives. An additional use for derivatives is in risk management. For example, companies such as **Coca-Cola, ExxonMobil,** and **General Electric** borrow and lend substantial amounts in credit markets. In doing so, they are exposed to significant **interest rate risk**. That is, they face substantial risk that

---

[11]In *SFAS No. 133*, the FASB identifies these same features as the key characteristics of derivatives. The FASB used these broad characteristics so that companies could apply the definitions, and hence the standard, to yet-to-be-developed derivatives (par. 249).

the fair values or cash flows of interest-sensitive assets or liabilities will change if interest rates increase or decrease. These same companies also have significant international operations. As such, they are also exposed to **exchange rate risk**—the risk that changes in foreign currency exchange rates will negatively impact the profitability of their international businesses.

Companies can use derivatives to offset the negative impacts of changes in interest rates or foreign currency exchange rates. This use of derivatives is referred to as **hedging**.

SFAS No. 133 established accounting and reporting standards for derivative financial instruments used in hedging activities. The FASB allows special accounting for two types of hedges—fair value and cash flow hedges.[12]

RISKY BUSINESS

As shown in the graph below, use of derivatives has grown steadily in the past several years. In fact, close to *$200 trillion* (in notional amounts) in derivative contracts were in play at the end of 2004. The primary players in the market for derivatives are large companies and various financial institutions, which continue to find new uses for derivatives for speculation and risk management.

WHAT DO THE NUMBERS MEAN?

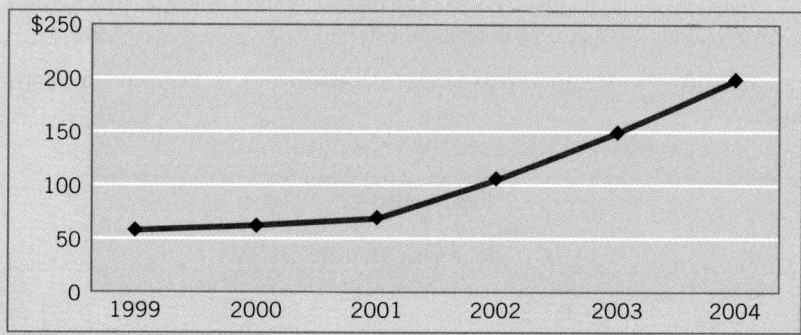

Total Swaps and Equity Derivatives
($ in trillions)

Financial engineers continue to develop new uses for derivatives, many times through the use of increasingly complex webs of transactions, spanning a number of markets. As new uses for derivatives appear, the financial system as a whole can be dramatically affected. As a result, some market-watchers are concerned about the risk that a crisis in one company or sector could bring the entire financial system to its knees.

This concern was illustrated recently when both **Fannie Mae** and **Freddie Mac** (two federally-chartered mortgage companies) indicated problems with their derivative accounting. It now appears likely that both of these companies will have to restate their financial results for prior periods. This has led Congress to study whether the concentration of mortgages in these institutions is too high. With so many home buyers dependent on Fannie and Freddie, there is concern that these companies may be too loaded down with debt, which could negatively affect the home mortgage market.

Source: Data from International Swaps and Derivatives Association Market Survey (2004).

---

[12]*SFAS No. 133* also addresses the accounting for certain foreign currency hedging transactions. In general, these transactions are special cases of the two hedges we discuss here. Understanding of foreign currency hedging transactions requires knowledge related to consolidation of multinational entities, which is beyond the scope of this textbook.

Fair Value Hedge

OBJECTIVE 11

Explain how to account for a fair value hedge.

In a **fair value hedge**, a company uses a derivative to hedge (offset) the exposure to changes in the fair value of a recognized asset or liability or of an unrecognized commitment. In a perfectly hedged position, the gain or loss on the fair value of the derivative equals and offsets that of the hedged asset or liability.

Companies commonly use several types of fair value hedges. For example, companies use interest rate swaps to hedge the risk that changes in interest rates will impact the fair value of debt obligations. Or, they use put options to hedge the risk that an equity investment will decline in value.

To illustrate a fair value hedge, assume that on April 1, 2006, Hayward Co. purchases 100 shares of Sonoma stock at a market price of $100 per share. Hayward does not intend to actively trade this investment. It consequently classifies the Sonoma investment as available-for-sale. Hayward records this available-for-sale investment as follows.

April 1, 2006

Available-for-Sale Securities	10,000	
Cash		10,000

Hayward records available-for-sale securities at fair value on the balance sheet. It reports unrealized gains and losses in equity as part of other comprehensive income.[13] Fortunately for Hayward, the value of the Sonoma shares increases to $125 per share during 2006. Hayward records the gain on this investment as follows.

December 31, 2006

Security Fair Value Adjustment (Available-for-Sale)	2,500	
Unrealized Holding Gain or Loss—Equity		2,500

Illustration 17A-4 indicates how Hayward reports the Sonoma investment in its balance sheet.

ILLUSTRATION 17A-4
Balance Sheet Presentation of Available-for-Sale Securities

HAYWARD CO.
BALANCE SHEET (PARTIAL)
DECEMBER 31, 2006

Assets	
Available-for-sale securities (at fair value)	$12,500
Stockholders' Equity	
Accumulated other comprehensive income	
Unrealized holding gain	$2,500

While Hayward benefits from an increase in the price of Sonoma shares, it is exposed to the risk that the price of the Sonoma stock will decline. To hedge this risk, Hayward locks in its gain on the Sonoma investment by purchasing a put option on 100 shares of Sonoma stock.

Hayward enters into the put option contract on January 2, 2007, and designates the option as a fair value hedge of the Sonoma investment. This put option (which expires in two years) gives Hayward the option to sell Sonoma shares at a price of $125. Since the exercise price equals the current market price, no entry is necessary at inception of the put option.[14]

January 2, 2007

No entry required. A memorandum indicates the signing of the put option contract and its designation as a fair value hedge for the Sonoma investment.

---

[13]We discussed the distinction between trading and available-for-sale investments earlier in the chapter.

[14]To simplify the example, we assume no premium is paid for the option.

At December 31, 2007, the price of the Sonoma shares has declined to $120 per share. Hayward records the following entry for the Sonoma investment.

December 31, 2007

Unrealized Holding Gain or Loss—Income	500	
Security Fair Value Adjustment (Available-for-Sale)		500

Note that upon designation of the hedge, the accounting for the available-for-sale security changes from regular GAAP. That is, Hayward records the unrealized holding loss in income, not in equity. If Hayward had not followed this accounting, a mismatch of gains and losses in the income statement would result. Thus, special accounting for the hedged item (in this case, an available-for-sale security) is necessary in a fair value hedge.

The following journal entry records the increase in value of the put option on Sonoma shares.

December 31, 2007

Put Option	500	
Unrealized Holding Gain or Loss—Income		500

The decline in the price of Sonoma shares results in an increase in the fair value of the put option. That is, Hayward could realize a gain on the put option by purchasing 100 shares in the open market for $120 and then exercise the put option, selling the shares for $125. This results in a gain to Hayward of $500 (100 shares × [$125 – $120]).[15]

Illustration 17A-5 indicates how Hayward reports the amounts related to the Sonoma investment and the put option.

HAYWARD CO.
BALANCE SHEET (PARTIAL)
DECEMBER 31, 2007

Assets	
Available-for-sale securities (at fair value)	$12,000
Put option	500

ILLUSTRATION 17A-5
Balance Sheet Presentation of Fair Value Hedge

The increase in fair value on the option offsets or hedges the decline in value on Hayward's available-for-sale security. By using fair value accounting for both financial instruments, the financial statements reflect the underlying substance of Hayward's net exposure to the risks of holding Sonoma stock. By using fair value accounting for both these financial instruments, the balance sheet reports the amount that Hayward would receive on the investment and the put option contract if Hayward sold and settled them, respectively.

Illustration 17A-6 illustrates the reporting of the effects of the hedging transaction on income for the year ended December 31, 2007.

HAYWARD CO.
INCOME STATEMENT (PARTIAL)
FOR THE YEAR ENDED DECEMBER 31, 2007

Other Income	
Unrealized holding gain—put option	$ 500
Unrealized holding loss—available-for-sale securities	(500)

ILLUSTRATION 17A-6
Income Statement Presentation of Fair Value Hedge

---

[15]In practice, Hayward generally does not have to actually buy and sell the Sonoma shares to realize this gain. Rather, unless the counterparty wants to hold Hayward shares, Hayward can "close out" the contract by having the counterparty pay it $500 in cash. This is an example of the net settlement feature of derivatives.

The income statement indicates that the gain on the put option offsets the loss on the available-for-sale securities.[16] The reporting for these financial instruments, even when they reflect a hedging relationship, illustrates why the FASB argued that fair value accounting provides the most relevant information about financial instruments, including derivatives.

Cash Flow Hedge

OBJECTIVE 12
Explain how to account for a cash flow hedge.

INTERNATIONAL INSIGHT

Under IFRS, companies record unrealized holding gains or losses on cash flow hedges as adjustments to the value of the hedged item, not as "Other comprehensive income."

Companies use **cash flow hedges** to hedge exposures to **cash flow risk**, which results from the variability in cash flows. The FASB allows special accounting for cash flow hedges. Generally, companies measure and report derivatives at fair value on the balance sheet. They report gains and losses directly in net income. However, companies account for derivatives used in cash flow hedges at fair value on the balance sheet, but they **record gains or losses in equity, as part of other comprehensive income**.

To illustrate, assume that in September 2006 Allied Can Co. anticipates purchasing 1,000 metric tons of aluminum in January 2007. Concerned that prices for aluminum will increase in the next few months, Allied wants to hedge the risk that it might pay higher prices for inventory in January 2007. As a result, Allied enters into an aluminum futures contract.

A **futures contract** gives the holder the right and the obligation to purchase an asset at a preset price for a specified period of time.[17] In this case, the aluminum futures contract gives Allied the right and the obligation to purchase 1,000 metric tons of aluminum for $1,550 per ton. This contract price is good until the contract expires in January 2007. The underlying for this derivative is the price of aluminum. If the price of aluminum rises above $1,550, the value of the futures contract to Allied increases. Why? Because Allied will be able to purchase the aluminum at the lower price of $1,550 per ton.[18]

Allied enters into the futures contract on September 1, 2006. Assume that the price to be paid today for inventory to be delivered in January—the **spot price**—equals the contract price. With the two prices equal, the futures contract has no value. Therefore no entry is necessary.

September 2006

No entry required. A memorandum indicates
the signing of the futures contract.

At December 31, 2006, the price for January delivery of aluminum increases to $1,575 per metric ton. Allied makes the following entry to record the increase in the value of the futures contract.

December 31, 2006

Futures Contract	25,000	
Unrealized Holding Gain or Loss—Equity		25,000
([$1,575 − $1,550] × 1,000 tons)		

Allied reports the futures contract in the balance sheet as a current asset. It reports the gain on the futures contract as part of other comprehensive income.

---

[16]Note that the fair value changes in the option contract will not offset **increases** in the value of the Hayward investment. Should the price of Sonoma stock increase above $125 per share, Hayward would have no incentive to exercise the put option.

[17]A **futures contract** is a firm contractual agreement between a buyer and seller for a specified asset on a fixed date in the future. The contract also has a standard specification so both parties know exactly what is being traded. A **forward** is similar but is not traded on an exchange and does not have standardized conditions.

[18]As with the earlier call option example, the actual aluminum does not have to be exchanged. Rather, the parties to the futures contract settle by paying the cash difference between the futures price and the price of aluminum on each settlement date.

Since Allied has not yet purchased and sold the inventory, this gain is an **anticipated transaction**. In this type of transaction, a company accumulates in equity gains or losses on the futures contract as part of other comprehensive income until the period in which it sells the inventory, thereby affecting earnings.

In January 2007, Allied purchases 1,000 metric tons of aluminum for $1,575 and makes the following entry.[19]

January 2007

Aluminum Inventory	1,575,000	
Cash ($1,575 × 1,000 tons)		1,575,000

At the same time, Allied makes final settlement on the futures contract. It records the following entry.

January 2007

Cash	25,000	
Futures Contract ($1,575,000 − $1,550,000)		25,000

Through use of the futures contract derivative, Allied fixes the cost of its inventory. The $25,000 futures contract settlement offsets the amount paid to purchase the inventory at the prevailing market price of $1,575,000. The result: net cash outflow of $1,550 per metric ton, as desired. As Illustration 17A-7 shows, Allied has therefore effectively hedged the cash flow for the purchase of inventory.

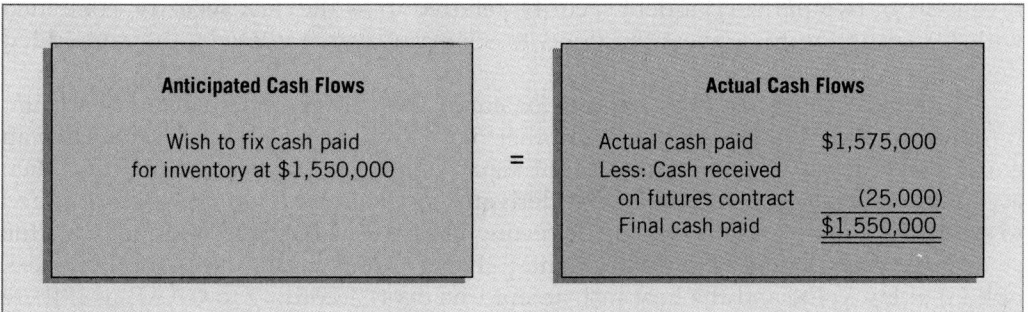

ILLUSTRATION 17A-7
Effect of Hedge on Cash Flows

There are no income effects at this point. Allied accumulates in equity the gain on the futures contract as part of other comprehensive income until the period when it sells the inventory, affecting earnings through cost of goods sold.

For example, assume that Allied processes the aluminum into finished goods (cans). The total cost of the cans (including the aluminum purchases in January 2007) is $1,700,000. Allied sells the cans in July 2007 for $2,000,000, and records this sale as follows.

July 2007

Cash	2,000,000	
Sales Revenue		2,000,000
Cost of Goods Sold	1,700,000	
Inventory (Cans)		1,700,000

Since the effect of the anticipated transaction has now affected earnings, Allied makes the following entry related to the hedging transaction.

July 2007

Unrealized Holding Gain or Loss—Equity	25,000	
Cost of Goods Sold		25,000

The gain on the futures contract, which Allied reported as part of other comprehensive income, now reduces cost of goods sold. As a result, the cost of aluminum

---

[19]In practice, futures contracts are settled on a daily basis. For our purposes we show only one settlement for the entire amount.

included in the overall cost of goods sold is $1,550,000. The futures contract has worked as planned. Allied has managed the cash paid for aluminum inventory and the amount of cost of goods sold.

OTHER REPORTING ISSUES

OBJECTIVE 13
Identify special reporting issues related to derivative financial instruments that cause unique accounting problems.

The preceding examples illustrate the basic reporting issues related to the accounting for derivatives. Next, we discuss the following additional issues:

1 The accounting for embedded derivatives.
2 Qualifying hedge criteria.
3 Disclosures about financial instruments and derivatives.

Embedded Derivatives

As we indicated at the beginning of this appendix, rapid innovation in the development of complex financial instruments drove efforts toward unifying and improving the accounting standards for derivatives. In recent years, this innovation has led to the development of **hybrid securities**. These securities have characteristics of both debt and equity. They often combine traditional and derivative financial instruments.

For example, a convertible bond (discussed in Chapter 16) is a hybrid instrument. It consists of two parts: (1) a debt security, referred to as the **host security**, combined with (2) an option to convert the bond to shares of common stock, the **embedded derivative**.

To provide consistency in accounting for similar derivatives, a company must account for embedded derivatives similarly to other derivatives. Therefore, to account for an embedded derivative, a company **should separate it from the host security** and then account for it using the accounting for derivatives. This separation process is referred to as **bifurcation**.[20] Thus, a company investing in a convertible bond must separate the stock option component of the instrument. It then accounts for the derivative (the stock option) at fair value and the host instrument (the debt) according to GAAP, as if there were no embedded derivative.[21]

Qualifying Hedge Criteria

The FASB identified certain criteria that hedging transactions must meet before requiring the special accounting for hedges. The FASB designed these criteria to ensure the use of hedge accounting in a consistent manner across different hedge transactions. The general criteria relate to the following areas.

INTERNATIONAL
INSIGHT

IFRS qualifying hedge criteria are similar to those used in *SFAS No. 133*.

1 **Documentation, risk management, and designation.** At inception of the hedge, there must be formal **documentation** of the hedging relationship, the company's **risk management** objective, and the strategy for undertaking the hedge. **Designation** refers to identifying the hedging instrument, the hedged item or transaction, the nature of the risk being hedged, and how the hedging instrument will offset changes in the fair value or cash flows attributable to the hedged risk.

The FASB decided that documentation and designation are critical to the implementation of the special accounting for hedges. Without these requirements, companies might try to apply the hedge accounting provisions retroactively, only

---

[20]A company can also designate such a derivative as a hedging instrument. The company would apply the hedge accounting provisions outlined earlier in the chapter.

[21]The **issuer** of the convertible bonds would not bifurcate the option component of the convertible bonds payable. *SFAS No. 133* explicitly precludes embedded derivative accounting for an embedded derivative that is indexed to a company's own common stock. If the conversion feature was tied to **another company's** stock, then the derivative would be bifurcated.

in response to negative changes in market conditions, to offset the negative impact of a transaction on the financial statements. Allowing special hedge accounting in such a setting could mask the speculative nature of the original transaction.

2 **Effectiveness of the hedging relationship.** At inception and on an ongoing basis, the hedging relationship should be **highly effective** in achieving offsetting changes in fair value or cash flows. Companies must assess effectiveness whenever preparing financial statements.

The general guideline for effectiveness is that the fair values or cash flows of the hedging instrument (the derivative) and the hedged item exhibit a high degree of correlation. In practice, high effectiveness is assumed when the correlation is close to one (e.g., within plus or minus .10). In our earlier hedging examples (put option and the futures contract on aluminum inventory), the fair values and cash flows are perfectly correlated. That is, when the cash payment for the inventory purchase increased, it offset, dollar for dollar, the cash received on the futures contract.

If the effectiveness criterion is not met, either at inception or because of changes following inception of the hedging relationship, the FASB no longer allows special hedge accounting. The company should then account for the derivative as a free-standing derivative.[22]

3 **Effect on reported earnings of changes in fair values or cash flows.** A change in the fair value of a hedged item or variation in the cash flow of a hedged forecasted transaction must have the potential to change the amount recognized in reported earnings. There is no need for special hedge accounting if a company accounts for both the hedging instrument and the hedged item at fair value under existing GAAP. In this case, earnings will properly reflect the offsetting gains and losses.

For example, special accounting is not needed for a fair value hedge of a trading security, because a company accounts for both the investment and the derivative at fair value on the balance sheet with gains or losses reported in earnings. Thus, "special" hedge accounting is necessary only when there is a mismatch of the accounting effects for the hedging instrument and the hedged item under GAAP.[23]

Disclosure Provisions

SFAS No. 133 provides comprehensive accounting guidance for derivatives. In addition, *SFAS No. 107* provides general disclosure requirements for traditional financial instruments. The primary requirements for disclosures related to financial instruments are as follows.

OBJECTIVE 14
Describe the disclosure requirements for traditional and derivative financial instruments.

1 Disclose the fair value and related carrying value of financial instruments in the body of the financial statements, in a note, or in a summary table form that makes it clear whether the amounts represent assets or liabilities.

2 Distinguish between financial instruments held or issued for purposes other than trading. For derivatives, disclose the objectives for holding or issuing those instruments (speculation or hedging), the hedging context (fair value or cash flow), and the strategies for achieving risk management objectives.

3 Do not combine, aggregate, or net the fair value of separate financial instruments, even if considering those instruments as related.

4 Display as a separate classification of other comprehensive income the net gain or loss on derivative instruments designated in cash flow hedges.

---

[22]The accounting for the part of a derivative that is not effective in a hedge is at fair value, with gains and losses recorded in income.

[23]An important criterion specific to cash flow hedges is that the forecasted transaction in a cash flow hedge "is likely to occur." A company should support this probability (defined as significantly greater than the term "more likely than not") by observable facts such as frequency of similar past transactions and its financial and operational ability to carry out the transaction.

5 Provide quantitative information about market risks of derivatives, and also of other assets and liabilities (encouraged, not required, information). Such information should be consistent with risk management procedures. Further, the information should be useful for comparing the results of the use of derivatives.

While these additional disclosures of fair value provide useful information to financial statement users, companies generally provide them as supplemental information only. The balance sheet continues to rely primarily on historical cost. Exceptions to this general rule are the fair value requirements for certain investment securities and derivatives, as we illustrated earlier. Illustration 17A-8 provides a fair value disclosure for **Caterpillar Inc.**

ILLUSTRATION 17A-8
Caterpillar Inc. Fair Value
Disclosure

Caterpillar Inc.

Notes to the Financial Statements

Fair Values of Financial Instruments

(millions of dollars)	2004 Carrying Amount	2004 Fair Value	2003 Carrying Amount	2003 Fair Value
Asset (Liability) at December 31				
Cash and short-term investments	$ 445	$ 445	$ 342	$ 342
Long-term investments	1,852	1,852	1,574	1,574
Foreign currency contracts	176	176	167	167
Finance recievables—net (excluding finance type leases)	13,457	13,445	11,439	11,489
Wholesale inventory recievables—net (excluding finance type leases)	882	857	681	666
Short-term borrowings	(4,157)	(4,157)	(2,757)	(2,757)
Long-term debt (including amounts due within one year)				
Machinery and engines	(3,669)	(4,186)	(3,635)	(4,109)
Financial products	(15,699)	(15,843)	(13,892)	(14,078)
Interest rate swaps Financial products—				
in a net receivable position	75	75	87	87
in a net payable position	(69)	(69)	(59)	(59)
Guarantees	(10)	(10)	(5)	(9)

UNDERLYING CONCEPTS

Providing supplemental information on the fair values of financial instruments illustrates application of the full disclosure principle.

The fair values of cash and cash equivalents, short-term investments, and short-term debt approximate cost. The reason is obvious—because of the immediate and short-term maturities of these instruments. The fair value of long-term investments (and some derivatives) relies on quoted market prices at the reporting date. The fair value of long-term debt and some derivatives relies on market prices for similar instruments or by discounting expected cash flows at rates currently available to the company for instruments with similar risks and maturities.

If a company cannot estimate fair value, it must disclose information relevant to the estimate of fair value (such as the terms of the instrument) and the reason why it is unable to arrive at an estimate of fair value.[24]

---

[24]*SFAS No. 107* lists a number of exceptions to this requirement; most of which other standards cover. The exception list includes such items as pension and postretirement benefits; employee stock options; insurance contracts; lease contracts; warranties, rights, and obligations; purchase obligations; equity method investments; minority interests; and instruments classified as stockholders' equity in the company's balance sheet.

Summary of *SFAS No. 133*

Illustration 17A-9 summarizes the accounting provisions for derivatives and hedging transactions.

Derivative Use	Accounting for Derivative	Accounting for Hedged Item	Common Example
Speculation	At fair value with unrealized holding gains and losses recorded in income.	Not applicable	Call or put option on an equity security.
Hedging			
Fair value	At fair value with holding gains and losses recorded in income.	At fair value with gains and losses recorded in income.	Put option to hedge an equity investment.
Cash flow	At fair value with unrealized holding gains and losses from the hedge recorded in other comprehensive income, and reclassified in income when the hedged transaction's cash flows affect earnings.	Use other generally accepted accounting principles for the hedged item.	Use of a futures contract to hedge a forecasted purchase of inventory.

As indicated, the general accounting for derivatives relies on fair values. *SFAS No. 133* also establishes special accounting guidance when companies use derivatives **for hedging purposes**. For example, when a company uses a put option to hedge prices changes in an available-for-sale stock investment in a fair value hedge (see the Hayward example earlier), it records unrealized gains on the investment in earnings, which is not GAAP for available-for-sale securities without such a hedge. This special accounting is justified in order to accurately report the nature of the hedging relationship in the balance sheet (recording both the put option and the investment at fair value) and in the income statement (reporting offsetting gains and losses in the same period).

Special accounting also is used for cash flow hedges. Companies account for derivatives used in qualifying cash flow hedges at fair value on the balance sheet, but record unrealized holding gains or losses in other comprehensive income until selling or settling the hedged item. In a cash flow hedge, a company continues to record the hedged item at its historical cost.

COMPREHENSIVE HEDGE ACCOUNTING EXAMPLE

To provide a comprehensive example of hedge accounting, we examine the use of an interest rate swap. First, let's consider how swaps work and why companies use them.

Options and futures trade on organized securities exchanges. Because of this, options and futures have standardized terms. Although that standardization makes the trading easier, it limits the flexibility needed to tailor contracts to specific circumstances. In addition, most types of derivatives have relatively short time horizons, thereby excluding their use for reducing long-term risk exposure.

As a result, many corporations instead turn to the swap, a very popular type of derivative. A **swap** is a transaction between two parties in which the first party promises to make a payment to the second party. Similarly, the second party promises to make a simultaneous payment to the first party.

The most common type of swap is the **interest rate swap**. In this type, one party makes payments based on a fixed or floating rate, and the second party does just the opposite. In most cases, large money-center banks bring together the two parties. These banks handle the flow of payments between the parties, as shown in Illustration 17A-10.

ILLUSTRATION 17A-10
Swap Transaction

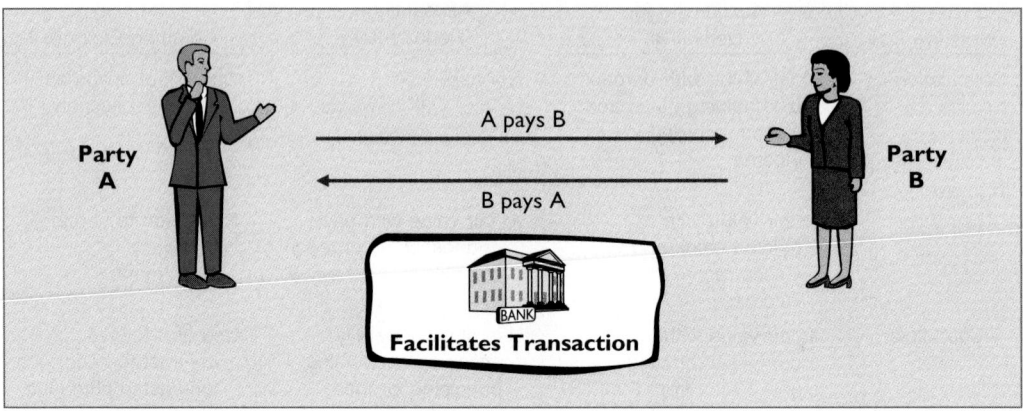

Fair Value Hedge

To illustrate the use of a swap in a fair value hedge, assume that Jones Company issues $1,000,000 of five-year, 8 percent bonds on January 2, 2007. Jones records this transaction as follows.

January 2, 2007

Cash	1,000,000	
Bonds Payable		1,000,000

Jones offered a fixed interest rate to appeal to investors. But Jones is concerned that if market interest rates decline, the fair value of the liability will increase. The company will then suffer an economic loss.[25] To protect against the risk of loss, Jones hedges the risk of a decline in interest rates by entering into a five-year interest rate swap contract. Jones agrees to the following terms:

1 Jones will receive fixed payments at 8 percent (based on the $1,000,000 amount).

2 Jones will pay variable rates, based on the market rate in effect for the life of the swap contract. The variable rate at the inception of the contract is 6.8 percent.

As Illustration 17A-11 shows, this swap allows Jones to change the interest on the bonds payable from a fixed rate to a variable rate.

ILLUSTRATION 17A-11
Interest Rate Swap

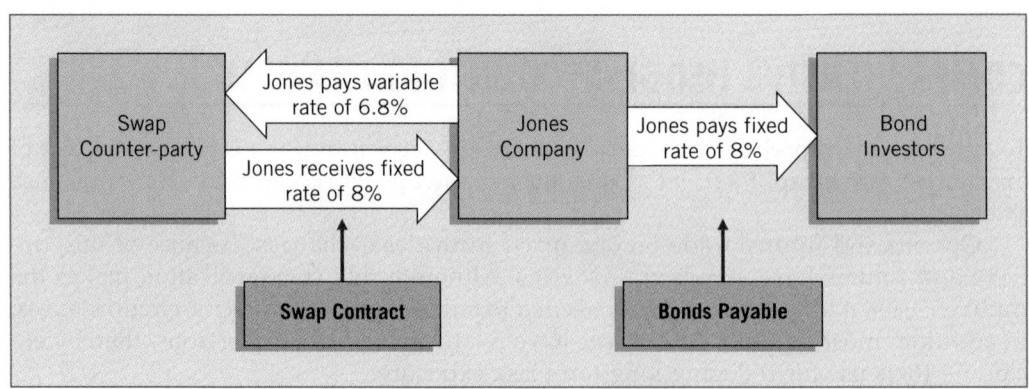

---

[25]This economic loss arises because Jones is locked into the 8 percent interest payments even if rates decline.

The settlement dates for the swap correspond to the interest payment dates on the debt (December 31). On each interest payment (settlement) date, Jones and the counterparty compute the difference between current market interest rates and the fixed rate of 8 percent, and determine the value of the swap.[26] If interest rates decline, the value of the swap contract to Jones increases (Jones has a gain), while at the same time Jones's fixed-rate debt obligation increases (Jones has an economic loss).

The swap is an effective risk-management tool in this setting. Its value relates to the same underlying (interest rates) that will affect the value of the fixed-rate bond payable. Thus, if the value of the swap goes up, it offsets the loss related to the debt obligation.

Assuming that Jones enters into the swap on January 2, 2007 (the same date as the issuance of the debt), the swap at this time has no value. Therefore no entry is necessary.

January 2, 2007

No entry required. A memorandum indicates the signing of the swap contract.

At the end of 2007, Jones makes the interest payment on the bonds. It records this transaction as follows.

December 31, 2007

Interest Expense	80,000	
Cash (8% × $1,000,000)		80,000

At the end of 2007, market interest rates have declined substantially. Therefore the value of the swap contract increases. Recall (see Illustration 17A-11) that in the swap, Jones receives a fixed rate of 8 percent, or $80,000 ($1,000,000 × 8%), and pays a variable rate (6.8%), or $68,000. Jones therefore receives $12,000 ($80,000 − $68,000) as a settlement payment on the swap contract on the first interest payment date. Jones records this transaction as follows.

December 31, 2007

Cash	12,000	
Interest Expense		12,000

In addition, a market appraisal indicates that the value of the interest rate swap has increased $40,000. Jones records this increase in value as follows.[27]

December 31, 2007

Swap Contract	40,000	
Unrealized Holding Gain or Loss—Income		40,000

Jones reports this swap contract in the balance sheet. It reports the gain on the hedging transaction in the income statement. Because interest rates have declined, the company records a loss and a related increase in its liability as follows.

December 31, 2007

Unrealized Holding Gain or Loss—Income	40,000	
Bonds Payable		40,000

Jones reports the loss on the hedging activity in net income. It adjusts bonds payable in the balance sheet to fair value.

Financial Statement Presentation of an Interest Rate Swap

Illustration 17A-12 (on page 880) indicates how Jones reports the asset and liability related to this hedging transaction on the balance sheet.

---

[26]The underlying for an interest rate swap is some index of market interest rates. The most commonly used index is the London Interbank Offer Rate, or LIBOR. In this example, we assume the LIBOR is 6.8 percent.

[27]Theoretically, this fair value change reflects the present value of expected future differences in variable and fixed interest rates.

ILLUSTRATION 17A-12
Balance Sheet
Presentation of Fair Value
Hedge

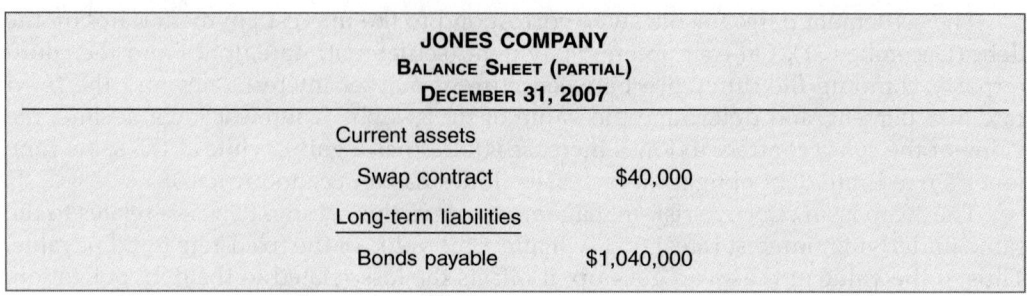

JONES COMPANY
BALANCE SHEET (PARTIAL)
DECEMBER 31, 2007

Current assets	
Swap contract	$40,000
Long-term liabilities	
Bonds payable	$1,040,000

The effect on Jones's balance sheet is the addition of the swap asset and an increase in the carrying value of the bonds payable. Illustration 17A-13 indicates how Jones reports the effects of this swap transaction in the income statement.

ILLUSTRATION 17A-13
Income Statement
Presentation of Fair Value
Hedge

JONES COMPANY
INCOME STATEMENT (PARTIAL)
FOR THE YEAR ENDED DECEMBER 31, 2007

Interest expense ($80,000 − $12,000)		$68,000
Other income		
Unrealized holding gain—swap contract	$40,000	
Unrealized holding loss—bonds payable	(40,000)	
Net gain (loss)		$–0–

On the income statement, Jones reports interest expense of $68,000. Jones has effectively changed the debt's interest rate from fixed to variable. That is, by receiving a fixed rate and paying a variable rate on the swap, the company converts the fixed rate on the bond payable to variable. This results in an effective interest rate of 6.8 percent in 2007.[28] Also, the gain on the swap offsets the loss related to the debt obligation. Therefore the net gain or loss on the hedging activity is zero.

Illustration 17A-14 shows the overall impact of the swap transaction on the financial statements.

ILLUSTRATION 17A-14
Impact on Financial
Statements of Fair Value
Hedge

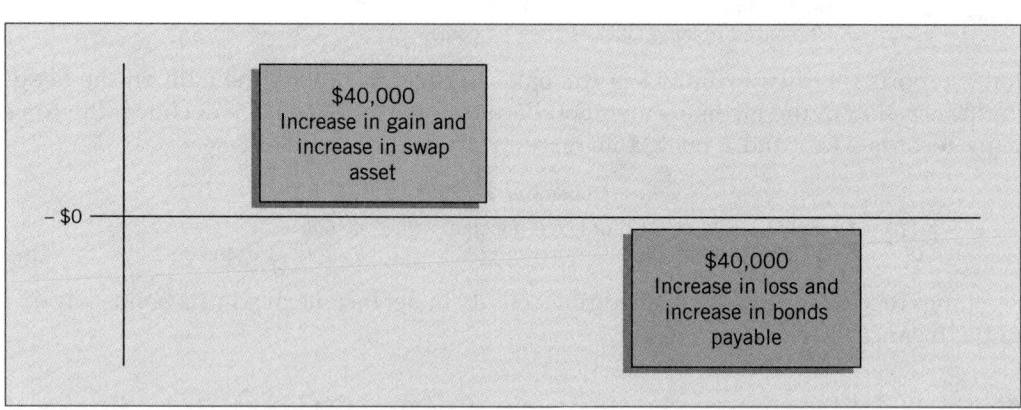

In summary, to account for fair value hedges (as illustrated in the Jones example) **record the derivative at its fair value in the balance sheet, and record any gains and losses in income**. Thus, the gain on the swap offsets or hedges the loss on the bond payable, due to the decline in interest rates.

---

[28]Jones will apply similar accounting and measurement at future interest payment dates. Thus, if interest rates increase, Jones will continue to receive 8 percent on the swap (records a loss) but will also be locked into the fixed payments to the bondholders at an 8 percent rate (records a gain).

By adjusting the hedged item (the bond payable in the Jones case) to fair value, with the gain or loss recorded in earnings, the accounting for the Jones bond payable deviates from amortized cost. This special accounting is justified in order to report accurately the nature of the hedging relationship between the swap and the bond payable in the balance sheet (both the swap and the debt obligation are recorded at fair value) and in the income statement (offsetting gains and losses are reported in the same period).[29]

CONTROVERSY AND CONCLUDING REMARKS

INTERNATIONAL INSIGHT

International accounting for hedges (*IAS 39*) is similar to the provisions of U.S. GAAP.

SFAS No. 133 represents the FASB's effort to develop accounting guidance for derivatives. Many believe that companies need these new rules to properly measure and report derivatives in financial statements. Others argue that reporting derivatives at fair value results in unrealized gains and losses that are difficult to interpret. Still others raise concerns about the complexity and cost of implementing the standard, since prior to *SFAS No. 133*, companies omitted recognizing many derivatives in financial statements.[30]

We believe that the long-term benefits of this standard will far outweigh any short-term implementation costs. As the volume and complexity of derivatives and hedging transactions continue to grow, so does the risk that investors and creditors will be exposed to unexpected losses arising from derivative transactions. Without this standard, statement readers do not have comprehensive information concerning many derivative financial instruments and the effects of hedging transactions using derivatives.

SUMMARY OF LEARNING OBJECTIVES FOR APPENDIX 17A

KEY TERMS

anticipated transaction, *873*

arbitrageurs, *864*

bifurcation, *874*

call option, *866*

cash flow hedge, *872*

counterparty, *866(n)*

derivative financial instrument, derivative, *863*

designation, *874*

documentation, *874*

embedded derivative, *874*

fair value, *865*

fair value hedge, *870*

forward contract, *863*

futures contract, *872*

hedging, *869*

8. Explain who uses derivatives and why. Any company or individual that wants to ensure against different types of business risks may use derivative contracts to achieve this objective. In general, these transactions involve some type of hedge. Speculators also use derivatives, attempting to find an enhanced return. Speculators are very important to the derivatives market because they keep it liquid on a daily basis. Arbitrageurs attempt to exploit inefficiencies in various derivative contracts. A company primarily uses derivatives for purposes of hedging its exposure to fluctuations in interest rates, foreign currency exchange rates, and commodity prices.

9. Understand the basic guidelines for accounting for derivatives. Companies should recognize derivatives in the financial statements as assets and liabilities, and report them at fair value. Companies should recognize gains and losses resulting from speculation immediately in income. They report gains and losses resulting from hedge transactions in different ways, depending on the type of hedge.

10. Describe the accounting for derivative financial instruments. Companies report derivative financial instruments in the balance sheet, and record them at fair value. Except for derivatives used in hedging, companies record realized and unrealized gains and losses on derivative financial instruments in income.

---

[29]An interest rate swap can also be used in a cash flow hedge. A common setting is the cash flow risk inherent in having variable rate debt as part of a company's debt structure. In this situation, the variable debt issuer can hedge the cash flow risk by entering into a swap contract to receive variable rate cash flows but pay fixed rate. The cash received on the swap contract will offset the variable cash flows to be paid on the debt obligation.

[30]Interestingly, some companies adopted the standard early because the rules provide better accounting for some derivatives relative to the rules in place before *SFAS No. 133*. Paula Froelich, "U.S. Companies Find New Accounting Rule Costly, Inefficient," Dow Jones News Service (March 2, 1999). In June 2000, the FASB issued guidance to ease implementation of the provisions of *SFAS No. 133*: "Accounting for Certain Derivative Hedging Instruments and Certain Hedging Activities—An Amendment to FASB Statement No. 133," *Statement of Financial Accounting Standards No. 138* (Stamford, Conn.: FASB, 2000).

11. **Explain how to account for a fair value hedge.** A company records the derivative used in a qualifying fair value hedge at its fair value in the balance sheet, recording any gains and losses in income. In addition, the company also accounts for the item being hedged with the derivative at fair value. By adjusting the hedged item to fair value, with the gain or loss recorded in earnings, the accounting for the hedged item may deviate from GAAP in the absence of a hedge relationship. This special accounting is justified in order to report accurately the nature of the hedging relationship between the derivative hedging instruments and the hedged item. A company reports both in the balance sheet, reporting offsetting gains and losses in income in the same period.

12. **Explain how to account for a cash flow hedge.** Companies account for derivatives used in qualifying cash flow hedges at fair value on the balance sheet, but record gains or losses in equity as part of other comprehensive income. Companies accumulate these gains or losses, and reclassify them in income when the hedged transaction's cash flows affect earnings. Accounting is according to GAAP for the hedged item.

13. **Identify special reporting issues related to derivative financial instruments that cause unique accounting problems.** A company should separate a derivative that is embedded in a hybrid security from the host security, and account for it using the accounting for derivatives. This separation process is referred to as bifurcation. Special hedge accounting is allowed only for hedging relationships that meet certain criteria. The main criteria are: (1) There is formal documentation of the hedging relationship, the company's risk management objective, and the strategy for undertaking the hedge, and the company designates the derivative as either a cash flow or fair value hedge. (2) The company expects the hedging relationship to be highly effective in achieving offsetting changes in fair value or cash flows. (3) "Special" hedge accounting is necessary only when there is a mismatch of the accounting effects for the hedging instrument and the hedged item under GAAP.

14. **Describe the disclosure requirements for traditional and derivative financial instruments.** Companies must disclose the fair value and related carrying value of its financial instruments. These disclosures should distinguish between amounts that represent assets or liabilities. The disclosures should also distinguish between financial instruments held or issued for purposes other than trading. For derivative financial instruments, a company should disclose whether using the instruments for speculation or hedging. In disclosing fair values of financial instruments, a company should not combine, aggregate, or net the fair value of separate financial instruments, even if it considers those instruments to be related. A company should display as a separate classification of other comprehensive income the net gain or loss on derivative instruments designated in cash flow hedges. Companies are encouraged, but not required, to provide quantitative information about market risks of derivative financial instruments.

APPENDIX
17B Variable-Interest Entities

OBJECTIVE 15
Describe the accounting for variable-interest entities.

Recently the FASB issued an interpretation to address the concern that some companies were not reporting the risks and rewards of certain investments and other financial arrangements in their consolidated financial statements.[1] As one analyst noted, **Enron** showed the world the power of the idea that "if investors can't see it, they can't ask you about it—the 'it' being assets and liabilities."

---

[1] *Financial Accounting Standards Interpretation No. 46(R)*, "Consolidation of Variable Interest Entities (revised)—An Interpretation of *ARB No. 51*," (FASB, Norwalk, Conn.: December 2003.).

What exactly did Enron do? First, it created a number of entities whose purpose was to hide debt, avoid taxes, and enrich certain management personnel to the detriment of the company and its stockholders. In effect, these entities, called **special purpose entities (SPEs)**, appeared to be separate entities for which Enron had a limited economic interest. For many of these arrangements, Enron actually had a substantial economic interest; the risks and rewards of ownership were not shifted to the entities but remained with Enron. In short, Enron was obligated to repay investors in these SPEs when they were unsuccessful. Once Enron's problems were discovered, it soon became apparent that many other companies had similar problems.

WHAT ABOUT GAAP?

A reasonable question to ask with regard to SPEs is, "Why didn't GAAP prevent companies from hiding SPE debt and other risks, by forcing companies to include these obligations in their consolidated financial statements?" To understand why, we have to look at the basic rules of consolidation.

The GAAP rules indicate that consolidated financial statements are "usually necessary for a fair presentation when one of the companies in the group directly or indirectly has a controlling financial interest in other companies." They further note that "the usual condition for a controlling financial interest is ownership of a majority voting interest."[2] In other words, if a company, like **Intel**, owns more than 50 percent of the voting stock of another company, Intel consolidates that company. GAAP also indicates that controlling financial interest may be achieved through arrangements that do not involve voting interests. However, applying these guidelines in practice is difficult.

Whenever GAAP uses a clear line, like "greater than 50 percent," companies sometimes exploit the criterion. For example, some companies set up joint ventures in which each party owns exactly 50 percent. In that case, neither party consolidates. Or like **Coca-Cola** in the opening story, a company may own less than 50 percent of the voting stock, but maintain effective control through board of director relationships, supply relationships, or through some other type of financial arrangement.

So the FASB realized that changes had to be made to GAAP for consolidations, and it issued *SFAS Interpretation No. 46 (Revised)*, "Consolidation of Variable Interest Entities." This interpretation (*FIN No. 46R*) defines when a company should use factors other than voting interest to determine controlling financial interest. In this interpretation, the FASB created a new risk-and-reward model to be used in situations where voting interests were unclear. The risk-and-reward model answers the basic questions of who stands to gain or lose the most from ownership in an SPE when ownership is uncertain.

In other words, we now have two models for consolidation:

1 **Voting-interest model**—If a company owns more than 50 percent of another company, then consolidate in most cases.

2 **Risk-and-reward model**—If a company is involved substantially in the economics of another company, then consolidate.

Operationally, the voting-interest model is easy to apply: It sets a "bright line" ownership standard of more than 50 percent of the voting stock. However, if companies cannot determine control based on voting interest, they may use the risk-and-reward model.

CONSOLIDATION OF VARIABLE-INTEREST ENTITIES

To answer the question of who gains or loses when voting rights do not determine consolidation, the FASB developed the risk-and-reward model. In this model, the FASB introduced the notion of a variable-interest entity. A **variable-interest entity (VIE)** is an entity that has one of the following characteristics:

---

[2]"Consolidation of Certain Special Purpose Entities," Proposed Interpretation (Norwalk, Conn.: FASB, June 28, 2002).

1   Insufficient equity investment at risk. Stockholders are assumed to have sufficient capital investment to support the entity's operations. If thinly capitalized, the entity is considered a VIE and is subject to the risk-and-reward model.

2   Stockholders lack decision-making rights. In some cases, stockholders do not have the influence to control the company's destiny.

3   Stockholders do not absorb the losses or receive the benefits of a normal stockholder. In some entities, stockholders are shielded from losses related to their primary risks, or their returns are capped or must be shared with other parties.

Once the company determines that an entity is a variable-interest entity, it no longer can use the voting-interest model. The question that must then be asked is, "What party is exposed to the majority of the risks and rewards associated with the VIE?" This party is called the primary beneficiary and must consolidate the VIE. Illustration 17B-1 shows the decision model for the VIE consolidation model.

ILLUSTRATION 17B-1
VIE Consolidation Model

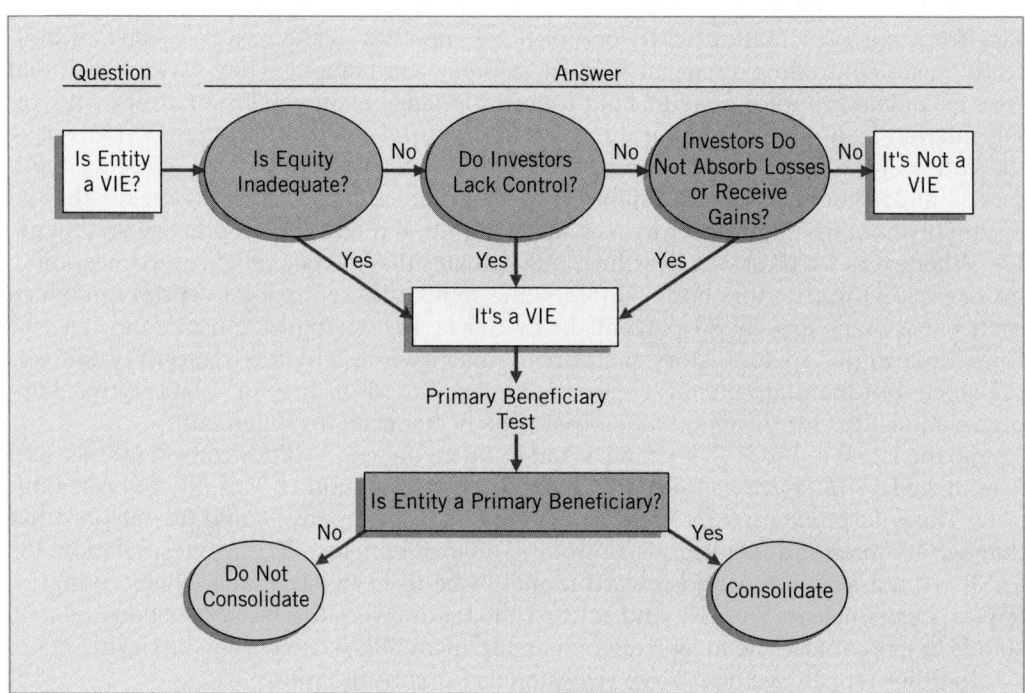

Some Examples

Let's look at a couple of examples to illustrate how this process works.

Example 1. Assume that **Citigroup** sells notes receivable to another entity called RAKO. RAKO's assets are financed in two ways: Lenders provide 90 percent, and investors provide the remaining 10 percent as an equity investment. If Citigroup does not guarantee the debt, Citigroup has low or nonexistent risk. Therefore, Citigroup would not consolidate the assets and liabilities of RAKO. On the other hand, if Citigroup guarantees RAKO's debt, then RAKO is a VIE, and Citigroup is the primary beneficiary. In that case, Citigroup must consolidate.

Example 2. **San Diego Gas and Electric (SDGE)** is required by law to buy power from small, local producers. In some cases, SDGE has contracts requiring it to purchase substantially all the power generated by these local companies over their lifetime. Because SDGE controls the outputs of the producers, they are VIEs. In this case, the risks and rewards related to ownership apply to SDGE. In other words, it is the primary beneficiary, and SDGE should include these producers in the consolidated financial statements.

Note that the primary beneficiary may have the risks and rewards of ownership through use of a variety of instruments and financial arrangements, such as equity investments, loans to the VIE, leases, derivatives, and guarantees. Potential VIEs include the following: corporations, partnerships, limited liability companies, and majority-owned subsidiaries.

What Is Happening in Practice?

For most companies, the reporting related to VIEs will not materially affect their financial statements. As shown in Illustration 17B-2, one study of 509 companies with total market values over $500 million found that just 17 percent of the companies reviewed have a material impact from *FIN No. 46R*.

Of the material VIEs disclosed in the study, the most common types (42 percent) were related to joint-venture equity investments, followed by off-balance-sheet lease arrangements (22 percent). In some cases, companies are restructuring transactions to avoid consolidation. For example, **Pep Boys**, **Choice Point, Inc.**, and **Anadarko** all appear to have restructured their lease transactions to avoid consolidation. On the other hand, companies like **eBay**, **Kimberly-Clark**, and **Williams-Sonoma Inc.** intend to or have consolidated their VIEs.

In summary, *FIN No. 46R* introduces a new model for determining if companies should include certain investments or other financial arrangements in consolidated financial statements. As a result, financial statements should be more complete in reporting the risks and rewards of these transactions.

ILLUSTRATION 17B-2
Impact of *FIN No. 46R*

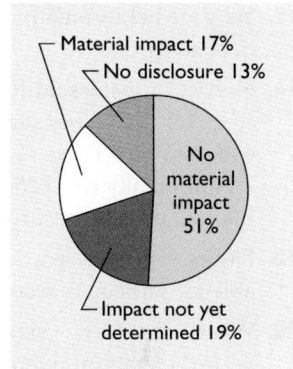

Source: Company Reports, Glass, Lewis, & Co. Research Report (November 6, 2003).

KEY TERMS

risk-and-reward model, *883*

special purpose entity (SPE), *883*

variable-interest entity (VIE), *883*

voting-interest model, *883*

SUMMARY OF LEARNING OBJECTIVE FOR APPENDIX 17B

15. Describe the accounting for variable-interest entities. Special variable-interest accounting is used in situations where control cannot be determined based on voting rights. A company is required to consolidate a variable-interest entity if it is the primary beneficiary of the variable-interest entity.

Note: All **asterisked** Questions, Exercises, and Problems relate to material contained in the appendixes to the chapter.

QUESTIONS

1. Distinguish between a debt security and an equity security.

2. What purpose does the variety in bond features (types and characteristics) serve?

3. What is the cost of a long-term investment in bonds?

4. Identify and explain the three types of classifications for investments in debt securities.

5. When should a debt security be classified as held-to-maturity?

6. Explain how trading securities are accounted for and reported.

7. At what amount should trading, available-for-sale, and held-to-maturity securities be reported on the balance sheet?

8. On July 1, 2007, Ingalls Company purchased $2,000,000 of Wilder Company's 8% bonds, due on July 1, 2014. The bonds, which pay interest semiannually on January 1 and July 1, were purchased for $1,750,000 to yield 10%. Determine the amount of interest revenue Ingalls should report on its income statement for year ended December 31, 2007.

9. If the bonds in question 8 are classified as available-for-sale and they have a fair value at December 31, 2007, of $1,802,000, prepare the journal entry (if any) at December 31, 2007, to record this transaction.

10. Indicate how unrealized holding gains and losses should be reported for investment securities classified as trading, available-for-sale, and held-to-maturity.

11. (a) Assuming no Securities Fair Value Adjustment (Available-for-Sale) account balance at the beginning of the year, prepare the adjusting entry at the end of the year if Laura Company's available-for-sale securities have a market value $70,000 below cost. (b) Assume the same information as part (a), except that Laura Company has a debit balance in its Securities Fair Value Adjustment (Available-for-Sale) account of $10,000 at the beginning of the year. Prepare the adjusting entry at year-end.

12. Identify and explain the different types of classifications for investment in equity securities.

13. Why are held-to-maturity investments applicable only to debt securities?

14. Harry Company sold 10,000 shares of Potter Co. common stock for $27.50 per share, incurring $1,770 in brokerage commissions. These securities were classified as trading and originally cost $250,000. Prepare the entry to record the sale of these securities.

15. Distinguish between the accounting treatment for available-for-sale equity securities and trading equity securities.

16. What constitutes "significant influence" when an investor's financial interest is below the 50% level?

17. Explain how the investment account is affected by investee activities under the equity method.

18. When the equity method is applied, what disclosures should be made in the investor's financial statements?

19. Hatch Co. uses the equity method to account for investments in common stock. What accounting should be made for dividends received in excess of Hatch's share of investee's earnings subsequent to the date of investment?

20. Elizabeth Corp. has an investment with a carrying value (equity method) on its books of $170,000 representing a 40% interest in Dole Company, which suffered a $620,000 loss this year. How should Elizabeth Corp. handle its proportionate share of Dole's loss?

21. Where on the asset side of the balance sheet are trading securities, available-for-sale securities, and held-to-maturity securities reported? Explain.

22. Explain why reclassification adjustments are necessary.

23. Briefly discuss how a transfer of securities from the available-for-sale category to the trading category affects stockholders' equity and income.

24. When is a debt security considered impaired? Explain how to account for the impairment of an available-for-sale debt security.

*25. What is meant by the term underlying as it relates to derivative financial instruments?

*26. What are the main distinctions between a traditional financial instrument and a derivative financial instrument?

*27. What is the purpose of a fair value hedge?

*28. In what situation will the unrealized holding gain or loss on an available-for-sale security be reported in income?

*29. Why might a company become involved in an interest rate swap contract to receive fixed interest payments and pay variable?

*30. What is the purpose of a cash flow hedge?

*31. Where are gains and losses related to cash flow hedges involving anticipated transactions reported?

*32. What are hybrid securities? Give an example of a hybrid security.

*33. Explain the difference between the voting-interest model and the risk-and-reward model used for consolidation.

*34. What is a variable interest entity?

BRIEF EXERCISES

(LO 2) **BE17-1** Moonwalker Company purchased, as a held-to-maturity investment, $50,000 of the 9%, 5-year bonds of Prime Time Corporation for $46,304, which provides an 11% return. Prepare Moonwalker's journal entries for (a) the purchase of the investment, and (b) the receipt of annual interest and discount amortization. Assume effective-interest amortization is used.

(LO 2) **BE17-2** Use the information from BE17-1, but assume the bonds are purchased as an available-for-sale security. Prepare Moonwalker's journal entries for (a) the purchase of the investment, (b) the receipt of annual interest and discount amortization, and (c) the year-end fair value adjustment. The bonds have a year-end fair value of $47,200.

(LO 2) **BE17-3** Mask Corporation purchased, as a held-to-maturity investment, $40,000 of the 8%, 5-year bonds of Phantasy Star, Inc. for $43,412, which provides a 6% return. The bonds pay interest semiannually. Prepare Mask's journal entries for (a) the purchase of the investment, and (b) the receipt of semiannual interest and premium amortization. Assume effective-interest amortization is used.

(LO 2) **BE17-4** Pete Sampras Corporation purchased trading investment bonds for $40,000 at par. At December 31, Sampras received annual interest of $2,000, and the fair value of the bonds was $38,400. Prepare Sampras' journal entries for (a) the purchase of the investment, (b) the interest received, and (c) the fair value adjustment.

(LO 3)   **BE17-5**   Buttercup Corporation purchased 300 shares of Bubbles Inc. common stock as an available-for-sale investment for $9,900. During the year, Bubbles paid a cash dividend of $3.25 per share. At year-end, Bubbles stock was selling for $34.50 per share. Prepare Buttercup's journal entries to record (a) the purchase of the investment, (b) the dividends received, and (c) the fair value adjustment.

(LO 3)   **BE17-6**   Use the information from BE17-5 but assume the stock was purchased as a trading security. Prepare Buttercup's journal entries to record (a) the purchase of the investment, (b) the dividends received, and (c) the fair value adjustment.

(LO 4)   **BE17-7**   Penn Corporation purchased for $300,000 a 25% interest in Teller, Inc. This investment enables Penn to exert significant influence over Teller. During the year Teller earned net income of $180,000 and paid dividends of $60,000. Prepare Penn's journal entries related to this investment.

(LO 3)   **BE17-8**   Swartentruber Company has a stock portfolio valued at $4,000. Its cost was $3,500. If the Securities Fair Value Adjustment (Available-for-Sale) account has a debit balance of $200, prepare the journal entry at year-end.

(LO 5)   **BE17-9**   The following information relates to **Starbucks** for 2004: net income $391.775 million; unrealized holding loss of $4.925 million related to available-for-sale securities during the year; accumulated other comprehensive income of $14.248 million on January 1, 2004. Assuming no other changes in accumulated other comprehensive income, determine (a) other comprehensive income for 2004, (b) comprehensive income for 2004, and (c) accumulated other comprehensive income at December 31, 2004.

(LO 5)   **BE17-10**   Raveonette Co. has an available-for-sale investment in the bonds of No Doubt Corp. with a carrying (and fair) value of $75,000. Raveonette determined that due to poor economic prospects for No Doubt, the bonds have decreased in value to $60,000. It is determined that this loss in value is other-than-temporary. Prepare the journal entry, if any, to record the reduction in value.

EXERCISES

(LO 1, 3)   **E17-1**   **(Investment Classifications)**   For the following investments identify whether they are:

1. Trading Securities
2. Available-for-Sale Securities
3. Held-to-Maturity Securities

Each case is independent of the other.

(a)   A bond that will mature in 4 years was bought 1 month ago when the price dropped. As soon as the value increases, which is expected next month, it will be sold.

(b)   10% of the outstanding stock of Farm-Co was purchased. The company is planning on eventually getting a total of 30% of its outstanding stock.

(c)   10-year bonds were purchased this year. The bonds mature at the first of next year.

(d)   Bonds that will mature in 5 years are purchased. The company would like to hold them until they mature, but money has been tight recently and they may need to be sold.

(e)   Preferred stock was purchased for its constant dividend. The company is planning to hold the preferred stock for a long time.

(f)   A bond that matures in 10 years was purchased. The company is investing money set aside for an expansion project planned 10 years from now.

(LO 2)   **E17-2**   **(Entries for Held-to-Maturity Securities)**   On January 1, 2006, Dagwood Company purchased at par 12% bonds having a maturity value of $300,000. They are dated January 1, 2006, and mature January 1, 2011, with interest receivable December 31 of each year. The bonds are classified in the held-to-maturity category.

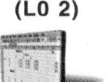

Instructions

(a)   Prepare the journal entry at the date of the bond purchase.

(b)   Prepare the journal entry to record the interest received for 2006.

(c)   Prepare the journal entry to record the interest received for 2007.

(LO 2)   **E17-3**   **(Entries for Held-to-Maturity Securities)**   On January 1, 2006, Hi and Lois Company purchased 12% bonds, having a maturity value of $300,000, for $322,744.44. The bonds provide the bondholders with a 10% yield. They are dated January 1, 2006, and mature January 1, 2011, with interest receivable December 31 of each year. Hi and Lois Company uses the effective-interest method to allocate unamortized discount or premium. The bonds are classified in the held-to-maturity category.

Instructions

(a) Prepare the journal entry at the date of the bond purchase.
(b) Prepare a bond amortization schedule.
(c) Prepare the journal entry to record the interest received and the amortization for 2006.
(d) Prepare the journal entry to record the interest received and the amortization for 2007.

(LO 2) **E17-4** **(Entries for Available-for-Sale Securities)** Assume the same information as in E17-3 except that the securities are classified as available-for-sale. The fair value of the bonds at December 31 of each year-end is as follows.

2006	$320,500	2009	$310,000
2007	$309,000	2010	$300,000
2008	$308,000		

Instructions

(a) Prepare the journal entry at the date of the bond purchase.
(b) Prepare the journal entries to record the interest received and recognition of fair value for 2006.
(c) Prepare the journal entry to record the recognition of fair value for 2007.

(LO 2) **E17-5** **(Effective-Interest versus Straight-Line Bond Amortization)** On January 1, 2006, Phantom Company acquires $200,000 of Spiderman Products, Inc., 9% bonds at a price of $185,589. The interest is payable each December 31, and the bonds mature December 31, 2008. The investment will provide Phantom Company a 12% yield. The bonds are classified as held-to-maturity.

Instructions

(a) Prepare a 3-year schedule of interest revenue and bond discount amortization, applying the straight-line method.
(b) Prepare a 3-year schedule of interest revenue and bond discount amortization, applying the effective-interest method.
(c) Prepare the journal entry for the interest receipt of December 31, 2007, and the discount amortization under the straight-line method.
(d) Prepare the journal entry for the interest receipt of December 31, 2007, and the discount amortization under the effective-interest method.

(LO 3) **E17-6** **(Entries for Available-for-Sale and Trading Securities)** The following information is available for Barkley Company at December 31, 2007, regarding its investments.

Securities	Cost	Fair Value
3,000 shares of Myers Corporation Common Stock	$40,000	$48,000
1,000 shares of Cole Incorporated Preferred Stock	25,000	22,000
	$65,000	$70,000

Instructions

(a) Prepare the adjusting entry (if any) for 2007, assuming the securities are classified as trading.
(b) Prepare the adjusting entry (if any) for 2007, assuming the securities are classified as available-for-sale.
(c) Discuss how the amounts reported in the financial statements are affected by the entries in (a) and (b).

(LO 3) **E17-7** **(Trading Securities Entries)** On December 21, 2006, Bucky Katt Company provided you with the following information regarding its trading securities.

December 31, 2006

Investments (Trading)	Cost	Fair Value	Unrealized Gain (Loss)
Clemson Corp. stock	$20,000	$19,000	$(1,000)
Colorado Co. stock	10,000	9,000	(1,000)
Buffaloes Co. stock	20,000	20,600	600
Total of portfolio	$50,000	$48,600	(1,400)
Previous securities fair value adjustment balance			–0–
Securities fair value adjustment—Cr.			$(1,400)

During 2007, Colorado Company stock was sold for $9,400. The fair value of the stock on December 31, 2007, was: Clemson Corp. stock—$19,100; Buffaloes Co. stock—$20,500.

Instructions

(a) Prepare the adjusting journal entry needed on December 31, 2006.

(b) Prepare the journal entry to record the sale of the Colorado Company stock during 2007.

(c) Prepare the adjusting journal entry needed on December 31, 2007.

(LO 3) **E17-8 (Available-for-Sale Securities Entries and Reporting)** Satchel Corporation purchases equity securities costing $73,000 and classifies them as available-for-sale securities. At December 31, the fair value of the portfolio is $65,000.

Instructions

Prepare the adjusting entry to report the securities properly. Indicate the statement presentation of the accounts in your entry.

(LO 3) **E17-9 (Available-for-Sale Securities Entries and Financial Statement Presentation)** At December 31, 2006, the available-for-sale equity portfolio for Steffi Graf, Inc. is as follows.

Security	Cost	Fair Value	Unrealized Gain (Loss)
A	$17,500	$15,000	($2,500)
B	12,500	14,000	1,500
C	23,000	25,500	2,500
Total	$53,000	$54,500	1,500
Previous securities fair value adjustment balance—Dr.			400
Securities fair value adjustment—Dr.			$1,100

On January 20, 2007, Steffi Graf, Inc. sold security A for $15,100. The sale proceeds are net of brokerage fees.

Instructions

(a) Prepare the adjusting entry at December 31, 2006, to report the portfolio at fair value.

(b) Show the balance sheet presentation of the investment related accounts at December 31, 2006. (Ignore notes presentation.)

(c) Prepare the journal entry for the 2007 sale of security A.

(LO 5) **E17-10 (Comprehensive Income Disclosure)** Assume the same information as E17-9 and that Steffi Graf Inc. reports net income in 2006 of $120,000 and in 2007 of $140,000. Total holding gains (including any realized holding gain or loss) arising during 2007 total $40,000.

Instructions

(a) Prepare a statement of comprehensive income for 2006 starting with net income.

(b) Prepare a statement of comprehensive income for 2007 starting with net income.

(LO 3) **E17-11 (Equity Securities Entries)** Arantxa Corporation made the following cash purchases of securities during 2007, which is the first year in which Arantxa invested in securities.

1. On January 15, purchased 10,000 shares of Sanchez Company's common stock at $33.50 per share plus commission $1,980.

2. On April 1, purchased 5,000 shares of Vicario Co.'s common stock at $52.00 per share plus commission $3,370.

3. On September 10, purchased 7,000 shares of WTA Co.'s preferred stock at $26.50 per share plus commission $4,910.

On May 20, 2007, Arantxa sold 4,000 shares of Sanchez Company's common stock at a market price of $35 per share less brokerage commissions, taxes, and fees of $3,850. The year-end fair values per share were: Sanchez $30, Vicario $55, and WTA $28. In addition, the chief accountant of Arantxa told you that Arantxa Corporation plans to hold these securities for the long term but may sell them in order to earn profits from appreciation in prices.

Instructions

(a) Prepare the journal entries to record the above three security purchases.

(b) Prepare the journal entry for the security sale on May 20.

(c) Compute the unrealized gains or losses and prepare the adjusting entries for Arantxa on December 31, 2007.

(LO 3, 4) **E17-12 (Journal Entries for Fair Value and Equity Methods)** Presented on page 890 are two independent situations.

Situation 1

Conchita Cosmetics acquired 10% of the 200,000 shares of common stock of Martinez Fashion at a total cost of $13 per share on March 18, 2007. On June 30, Martinez declared and paid a $75,000 cash dividend. On December 31, Martinez reported net income of $122,000 for the year. At December 31, the market price of Martinez Fashion was $15 per share. The securities are classified as available-for-sale.

Situation 2

Monica, Inc. obtained significant influence over Seles Corporation by buying 30% of Seles's 30,000 outstanding shares of common stock at a total cost of $9 per share on January 1, 2007. On June 15, Seles declared and paid a cash dividend of $36,000. On December 31, Seles reported a net income of $85,000 for the year.

Instructions

Prepare all necessary journal entries in 2007 for both situations.

(LO 4) **E17-13 (Equity Method)** Parent Co. invested $1,000,000 in Sub Co. for 25% of its outstanding stock. Sub Co. pays out 40% of net income in dividends each year.

Instructions

Use the information in the following T-account for the investment in Sub to answer the following questions.

Investment in Sub Co.

1,000,000	
110,000	
	44,000

(a) How much was Parent Co.'s share of Sub Co.'s net income for the year?
(b) How much was Parent Co.'s share of Sub Co.'s dividends for the year?
(c) What was Sub Co.'s total net income for the year?
(d) What was Sub Co.'s total dividends for the year?

(LO 3) **E17-14 (Equity Investment—Trading)** Oregon Co. had purchased 200 shares of Washington Co. for $40 each this year and classified the investment as a trading security. Oregon Co. sold 100 shares of the stock for $45 each. At year end the price per share of the Washington Co. stock had dropped to $35.

Instructions

Prepare the journal entries for these transactions and any year-end adjustments.

(LO 3) **E17-15 (Equity Investments—Trading)** Kenseth Company has the following securities in its trading portfolio of securities on December 31, 2006.

Investments (Trading)	Cost	Fair Value
1,500 shares of Gordon, Inc., Common	$ 73,500	$ 69,000
5,000 shares of Wallace Corp., Common	180,000	175,000
400 shares of Martin, Inc., Preferred	60,000	61,600
	$313,500	$305,600

All of the securities were purchased in 2006.
In 2007, Kenseth completed the following securities transactions.

March 1   Sold the 1,500 shares of Gordon, Inc., Common, @ $45 less fees of $1,200.
April 1   Bought 700 shares of Earnhart Corp., Common, @ $75 plus fees of $1,300.

Kenseth Company's portfolio of trading securities appeared as follows on December 31, 2007.

Investments (Trading)	Cost	Fair Value
5,000 shares of Wallace Corp., Common	$180,000	$175,000
700 shares of Earnhart Corp., Common	53,800	50,400
400 shares of Martin, Inc., Preferred	60,000	58,000
	$293,800	$283,400

Instructions

Prepare the general journal entries for Kenseth Company for:

(a) The 2006 adjusting entry.
(b) The sale of the Gordon stock.
(c) The purchase of the Earnhart stock.
(d) The 2007 adjusting entry for the trading portfolio.

(LO 3, 4) **E17-16 (Fair Value and Equity Method Compared)** Jaycie Phelps Inc. acquired 20% of the outstanding common stock of Theresa Kulikowski Inc. on December 31, 2006. The purchase price was $1,200,000 for 50,000 shares. Kulikowski Inc. declared and paid an $0.85 per share cash dividend on June 30 and on December 31, 2007. Kulikowski reported net income of $730,000 for 2007. The fair value of Kulikowski's stock was $27 per share at December 31, 2007.

Instructions

(a) Prepare the journal entries for Jaycie Phelps Inc. for 2006 and 2007, assuming that Phelps cannot exercise significant influence over Kulikowski. The securities should be classified as available-for-sale.

(b) Prepare the journal entries for Jaycie Phelps Inc. for 2006 and 2007, assuming that Phelps can exercise significant influence over Kulikowski.

(c) At what amount is the investment in securities reported on the balance sheet under each of these methods at December 31, 2007? What is the total net income reported in 2007 under each of these methods?

(LO 4) **E17-17 (Equity Method)** On January 1, 2007, Pennington Corporation purchased 30% of the common shares of Edwards Company for $180,000. During the year, Edwards earned net income of $80,000 and paid dividends of $20,000.

Instructions

Prepare the entries for Pennington to record the purchase and any additional entries related to this investment in Edwards Company in 2007.

(LO 6) **E17-18 (Impairment of Debt Securities)** Hagar Corporation has municipal bonds classified as available-for-sale at December 31, 2006. These bonds have a par value of $800,000, an amortized cost of $800,000, and a fair value of $720,000. The unrealized loss of $80,000 previously recognized as other comprehensive income and as a separate component of stockholders' equity is now determined to be other than temporary. That is, the company believes that impairment accounting is now appropriate for these bonds.

Instructions

(a) Prepare the journal entry to recognize the impairment.

(b) What is the new cost basis of the municipal bonds? Given that the maturity value of the bonds is $800,000, should Hagar Corporation amortize the difference between the carrying amount and the maturity value over the life of the bonds?

(c) At December 31, 2007, the fair value of the municipal bonds is $760,000. Prepare the entry (if any) to record this information.

(LO 10) *****E17-19 (Call Option)** On January 2, 2007, Jones Company purchases a call option for $300 on Merchant common stock. The call option gives Jones the option to buy 1,000 shares of Merchant at a strike price of $50 per share. The market price of a Merchant share is $50 on January 2, 2007 (the intrinsic value is therefore $0). On March 31, 2007, the market price for Merchant stock is $53 per share, and the time value of the option is $200.

Instructions

(a) Prepare the journal entry to record the purchase of the call option on January 2, 2007.

(b) Prepare the journal entry(ies) to recognize the change in the fair value of the call option as of March 31, 2007.

(c) What was the effect on net income of entering into the derivative transaction for the period January 2 to March 31, 2007?

(LO 10) *****E17-20 (Call Option)** On August 15, 2006, Outkast Co. invested idle cash by purchasing a call option on Counting Crows Inc. common shares for $360. The notional value of the call option is 400 shares, and the option price is $40. The option expires on January 31, 2007. The following data are available with respect to the call option.

Date	Market Price of Counting Crows Shares	Time Value of Call Option
September 30, 2006	$48 per share	$180
December 31, 2006	$46 per share	65
January 15, 2007	$47 per share	30

Instructions

Prepare the journal entries for Outkast for the following dates.

(a) Investment in call option on Counting Crows shares on August 15, 2006.

(b) September 30, 2006—Outkast prepares financial statements.

(c) December 31, 2006—Outkast prepares financial statements.

(d) January 15, 2007—Outkast settles the call option on the Counting Crows shares.

(LO 10) *E17-21 (Put and Call Options) On February 15, 2007, Derek Co. invested idle cash by purchasing a put option on Lee Corp. common shares for $160. The notional value of the put option is 300 shares, and the option price is $50. The option expires on July 31, 2007. The following data are available with respect to the put option.

Date	Market Price of Lee Shares	Time Value of Put Option
March 31, 2007	$40 per share	$70
June 30, 2007	$42 per share	30
July 15, 2007	$39 per share	20

Instructions

Prepare the journal entries for Derek Co. for the following dates.
- (a) February 15, 2007—Investment in put option on Lee shares.
- (b) March 31, 2007—Derek prepares financial statements.
- (c) June 30, 2007—Derek prepares financial statements.
- (d) July 6, 2007—Derek settles the put option on the Lee shares.
- (e) Repeat the requirements for (a) through (d), assuming that instead of purchasing a put option, Derek purchased a call option.

(LO 11) *E17-22 (Cash Flow Hedge) Hart Golf Co. uses titanium in the production of its specialty drivers. Hart anticipates that it will need to purchase 200 ounces of titanium in November 2007, for clubs that will be shipped in the spring and summer of 2008. However, if the price of titanium increases, this will increase the cost to produce the clubs, which will result in lower profit margins.

To hedge the risk of increased titanium prices, on May 1, 2007, Hart enters into a titanium futures contract and designates this futures contract as a cash flow hedge of the anticipated titanium purchase. The notional amount of the contract is 200 ounces, and the terms of the contract give Hart the option to purchase titanium at a price of $500 per ounce. The price will be good until the contract expires on November 30, 2007.

Assume the following data with respect to the price of the call options and the titanium inventory purchase.

Date	Spot Price for November Delivery
May 1, 2007	$500 per ounce
June 30, 2007	520 per ounce
September 30, 2007	525 per ounce

Instructions

Present the journal entries for the following dates/transactions.
- (a) May 1, 2007—Inception of futures contract, no premium paid.
- (b) June 30, 2007—Hart prepares financial statements.
- (c) September 30, 2007—Hart prepares financial statements.
- (d) October 5, 2007—Hart purchases 200 ounces of titanium at $525 per ounce and settles the futures contract.
- (e) December 15, 2007—Hart sells clubs containing titanium purchased in October 2006 for $250,000. The cost of the finished goods inventory is $140,000.
- (f) Indicate the amount(s) reported in the income statement related to the futures contract and the inventory transactions on December 31, 2007.

(LO 11) *E17-23 (Fair Value Hedge) On January 2, 2007, MacCloud Co. issued a 4-year, $100,000 note at 6% fixed interest, interest payable semiannually. MacCloud now wants to change the note to a variable-rate note.

As a result, on January 2, 2007, MacCloud Co. enters into an interest rate swap where it agrees to receive 6% fixed and pay LIBOR of 5.7% for the first 6 months on $100,000. At each 6-month period, the variable rate will be reset. The variable rate is reset to 6.7% on June 30, 2007.

Instructions
- (a) Compute the net interest expense to be reported for this note and related swap transaction as of June 30, 2007.
- (b) Compute the net interest expense to be reported for this note and related swap transaction as of December 31, 2007.

(LO 11) *E17-24 (Fair Value Hedge) Sarazan Company issues a 4-year, 7.5% fixed-rate interest only, nonprepayable $1,000,000 note payable on December 31, 2006. It decides to change the interest rate from a fixed rate to variable rate and enters into a swap agreement with M&S Corp. The swap agreement specifies that Sarazan will receive a fixed rate at 7.5% and pay variable with settlement dates that match the interest payments on the debt. Assume that interest rates have declined during 2007 and that Sarazan received

$13,000 as an adjustment to interest expense for the settlement at December 31, 2007. The loss related to the debt (due to interest rate changes) was $48,000. The value of the swap contract increased $48,000.

Instructions

(a) Prepare the journal entry to record the payment of interest expense on December 31, 2007.
(b) Prepare the journal entry to record the receipt of the swap settlement on December 31, 2007.
(c) Prepare the journal entry to record the change in the fair value of the swap contract on December 31, 2007.
(d) Prepare the journal entry to record the change in the fair value of the debt on December 31, 2007.

See the book's website, www.wiley.com/college/kieso, for Additional Exercises.

PROBLEMS

(LO 2) **P17-1** **(Debt Securities)** Presented below is an amortization schedule related to Kathy Baker Company's 5-year, $100,000 bond with a 7% interest rate and a 5% yield, purchased on December 31, 2004, for $108,660.

Date	Cash Received	Interest Revenue	Bond Premium Amortization	Carrying Amount of Bonds
12/31/04				$108,660
12/31/05	$7,000	$5,433	$1,567	107,093
12/31/06	7,000	5,354	1,646	105,447
12/31/07	7,000	5,272	1,728	103,719
12/31/08	7,000	5,186	1,814	101,905
12/31/09	7,000	5,095	1,905	100,000

The following schedule presents a comparison of the amortized cost and fair value of the bonds at year-end.

	12/31/05	12/31/06	12/31/07	12/31/08	12/31/09
Amortized cost	$107,093	$105,447	$103,719	$101,905	$100,000
Fair value	$106,500	$107,500	$105,650	$103,000	$100,000

Instructions

(a) Prepare the journal entry to record the purchase of these bonds on December 31, 2004, assuming the bonds are classified as held-to-maturity securities.
(b) Prepare the journal entry(ies) related to the held-to-maturity bonds for 2005.
(c) Prepare the journal entry(ies) related to the held-to-maturity bonds for 2007.
(d) Prepare the journal entry(ies) to record the purchase of these bonds, assuming they are classified as available-for-sale.
(e) Prepare the journal entry(ies) related to the available-for-sale bonds for 2005.
(f) Prepare the journal entry(ies) related to the available-for-sale bonds for 2007.

(LO 2) **P17-2** **(Available-for-Sale Debt Securities)** On January 1, 2007, Rob Wilco Company purchased $200,000, 8% bonds of Mercury Co. for $184,557. The bonds were purchased to yield 10% interest. Interest is payable semiannually on July 1 and January 1. The bonds mature on January 1, 2012. Rob Wilco Company uses the effective-interest method to amortize discount or premium. On January 1, 2009, Rob Wilco Company sold the bonds for $185,363 after receiving interest to meet its liquidity needs.

Instructions

(a) Prepare the journal entry to record the purchase of bonds on January 1. Assume that the bonds are classified as available-for-sale.
(b) Prepare the amortization schedule for the bonds.
(c) Prepare the journal entries to record the semiannual interest on July 1, 2007, and December 31, 2007.
(d) If the fair value of Mercury bonds is $186,363 on December 31, 2008, prepare the necessary adjusting entry. (Assume the securities fair value adjustment balance on January 1, 2008, is a debit of $3,375.)
(e) Prepare the journal entry to record the sale of the bonds on January 1, 2009.

(LO 2, 3) **P17-3** **(Available-for-Sale Investments)** Octavio Paz Corp. carries an account in its general ledger called Investments, which contained debits for investment purchases, and no credits (see page 894).

Feb. 1, 2006	Chiang Kai-Shek Company common stock, $100 par, 200 shares	$ 37,400
April 1	U.S. government bonds, 11%, due April 1, 2016, interest payable April 1 and October 1, 100 bonds of $1,000 par each	100,000
July 1	Claude Monet Company 12% bonds, par $50,000, dated March 1, 2006 purchased at 104 plus accrued interest, interest payable annually on March 1, due March 1, 2026	54,000

Instructions

(Round all computations to the nearest dollar.)

(a) Prepare entries necessary to classify the amounts into proper accounts, assuming that all the securities are classified as available-for-sale.

(b) Prepare the entry to record the accrued interest and the amortization of premium on December 31, 2006, using the straight-line method.

(c) The fair values of the securities on December 31, 2006, were:

Chiang Kai-shek Company common stock	$ 33,800
U.S. government bonds	124,700
Claude Monet Company bonds	58,600

What entry or entries, if any, would you recommend be made?

(d) The U.S. government bonds were sold on July 1, 2007, for $119,200 plus accrued interest. Give the proper entry.

(LO 2) **P17-4** **(Available-for-Sale Debt Securities)** Presented below is information taken from a bond investment amortization schedule with related fair values provided. These bonds are classified as available-for-sale.

	12/31/06	12/31/07	12/31/08
Amortized cost	$491,150	$519,442	$550,000
Fair value	$499,000	$506,000	$550,000

Instructions

(a) Indicate whether the bonds were purchased at a discount or at a premium.

(b) Prepare the adjusting entry to record the bonds at fair value at December 31, 2006. The Securities Fair Value Adjustment account has a debit balance of $1,000 prior to adjustment.

(c) Prepare the adjusting entry to record the bonds at fair value at December 31, 2007.

(LO 3) **P17-5** **(Equity Securities Entries and Disclosures)** Incognito Company has the following securities in its investment portfolio on December 31, 2006 (all securities were purchased in 2006): (1) 3,000 shares of Green Day Co. common stock which cost $58,500, (2) 10,000 shares of David Sanborn Ltd. common stock which cost $580,000, and (3) 6,000 shares of Abba Company preferred stock which cost $255,000. The Securities Fair Value Adjustment account shows a credit of $10,100 at the end of 2006.

In 2007, Incognito completed the following securities transactions.

1. On January 15, sold 3,000 shares of Green Day's common stock at $23 per share less fees of $2,150.

2. On April 17, purchased 1,000 shares of Tractors' common stock at $31.50 per share plus fees of $1,980.

On December 31, 2007, the market values per share of these securities were: Green Day $20, Sanborn $62, Abba $40, and Tractors $29. In addition, the accounting supervisor of Incognito told you that, even though all these securities have readily determinable fair values, Incognito will not actively trade these securities because the top management intends to hold them for more than one year.

Instructions

(a) Prepare the entry for the security sale on January 15, 2007.

(b) Prepare the journal entry to record the security purchase on April 17, 2007.

(c) Compute the unrealized gains or losses and prepare the adjusting entry for Incognito on December 31, 2007.

(d) How should the unrealized gains or losses be reported on Incognito's balance sheet?

(LO 3) **P17-6** **(Trading and Available-for-Sale Securities Entries)** Loxley Company has the following portfolio of investment securities at September 30, 2007, its last reporting date.

Trading Securities	Cost	Fair Value
Dan Fogelberg, Inc. common (5,000 shares)	$225,000	$200,000
Petra, Inc. preferred (3,500 shares)	133,000	140,000
Tim Weisberg Corp. common (1,000 shares)	180,000	179,000

On October 10, 2007, the Fogelberg shares were sold at a price of $54 per share. In addition, 3,000 shares of Los Tigres common stock were acquired at $59.50 per share on November 2, 2007. The December 31,

2007, fair values were: Petra $96,000, Los Tigres $132,000, and the Weisberg common $193,000. All the securities are classified as trading.

Instructions

(a) Prepare the journal entries to record the sale, purchase, and adjusting entries related to the trading securities in the last quarter of 2007.

(b) How would the entries in part (a) change if the securities were classified as available-for-sale?

(LO 2) **P17-7** **(Available-for-Sale and Held-to-Maturity Debt Securities Entries)** The following information relates to the debt securities investments of Yellowjackets Company.

1. On February 1, the company purchased 12% bonds of Hilton Paris Co. having a par value of $500,000 at 100 plus accrued interest. Interest is payable April 1 and October 1.
2. On April 1, semiannual interest is received.
3. On July 1, 9% bonds of Chieftains, Inc. were purchased. These bonds with a par value of $200,000 were purchased at 100 plus accrued interest. Interest dates are June 1 and December 1.
4. On September 1, bonds with a par value of $100,000, purchased on February 1, are sold at 99 plus accrued interest.
5. On October 1, semiannual interest is received.
6. On December 1, semiannual interest is received.
7. On December 31, the fair value of the bonds purchased February 1 and July 1 are 95 and 93, respectively.

Instructions

(a) Prepare any journal entries you consider necessary, including year-end entries (December 31), assuming these are available-for-sale securities.

(b) If Yellowjackets classified these as held-to-maturity securities, explain how the journal entries would differ from those in part (a).

(LO 3, 4, 5) **P17-8** **(Fair Value and Equity Methods)** Pacers Corp. is a medium-sized corporation specializing in quarrying stone for building construction. The company has long dominated the market, at one time achieving a 70% market penetration. During prosperous years, the company's profits, coupled with a conservative dividend policy, resulted in funds available for outside investment. Over the years, Pacers has had a policy of investing idle cash in equity securities. In particular, Pacers has made periodic investments in the company's principal supplier, Pierce Industries. Although the firm currently owns 12% of the outstanding common stock of Pierce Industries, Pacers does not have significant influence over the operations of Pierce Industries.

Cheryl Miller has recently joined Pacers as assistant controller, and her first assignment is to prepare the 2007 year-end adjusting entries for the accounts that are valued by the "fair value" rule for financial reporting purposes. Miller has gathered the following information about Pacers' pertinent accounts.

1. Pacers has trading securities related to Dale Davis Motors and Rik Smits Electric. During this fiscal year, Pacers purchased 100,000 shares of Davis Motors for $1,400,000; these shares currently have a market value of $1,600,000. Pacers' investment in Smits Electric has not been profitable; the company acquired 50,000 shares of Smits in April 2007 at $20 per share, a purchase that currently has a value of $620,000.
2. Prior to 2007, Pacers invested $22,500,000 in Pierce Industries and has not changed its holdings this year. This investment in Pierce Industries was valued at $21,500,000 on December 31, 2006. Pacers' 12% ownership of Pierce Industries has a current market value of $22,275,000.

Instructions

(a) Prepare the appropriate adjusting entries for Pacers as of December 31, 2007, to reflect the application of the "fair value" rule for both classes of securities described above.

(b) For both classes of securities presented above, describe how the results of the valuation adjustments made in (a) would be reflected in the body of and notes to Pacers' 2007 financial statements.

(c) Prepare the entries for the Pierce investment, assuming that Pacers owns 30% of Pierce's shares. Pierce reported income of $500,000 in 2007 and paid cash dividends of $100,000.

(LO 3, 5) **P17-9** **(Financial Statement Presentation of Available-for-Sale Investments)** Woolford Company has the following portfolio of available-for-sale securities at December 31, 2006.

Security	Quantity	Percent Interest	Per Share Cost	Per Share Market
Favre, Inc.	2,000 shares	8%	$11	$16
Brady Corp.	5,000 shares	14%	23	17
McNabb Company	4,000 shares	2%	31	24

Instructions

(a) What should be reported on Woolford's December 31, 2006, balance sheet relative to these long-term available-for-sale securities?

On December 31, 2007, Woolford's portfolio of available-for-sale securities consisted of the following common stocks.

Security	Quantity	Percent Interest	Per Share Cost	Per Share Market
Brady Corp.	5,000 shares	14%	$23	$30
McNabb Company	4,000 shares	2%	31	23
McNabb Company	2,000 shares	1%	25	23

At the end of year 2007, Woolford Company changed its intent relative to its investment in Favre, Inc. and reclassified the shares to trading securities status when the shares were selling for $9 per share.

(b) What should be reported on the face of Woolford's December 31, 2007, balance sheet relative to available-for-sale securities investments? What should be reported to reflect the transactions above in Woolford's 2007 income statement?

(c) Assuming that comparative financial statements for 2006 and 2007 are presented, draft the footnote necessary for full disclosure of Woolford's transactions and position in equity securities.

(LO 3, 5) **P17-10** **(Gain on Sale of Securities and Comprehensive Income)** On January 1, 2006, Enid Inc. had the following balance sheet.

ENID INC.
BALANCE SHEET
AS OF JANUARY 1, 2006

Assets		Equity	
Cash	$ 50,000	Common stock	$250,000
Available-for-sale securities	240,000	Accumulated other comprehensive income	40,000
Total	$290,000	Total	$290,000

The accumulated other comprehensive income related to unrealized holding gains on available-for-sale securities. The fair value of Enid Inc.'s available-for-sale securities at December 31, 2006, was $190,000; its cost was $120,000. No securities were purchased during the year. Enid Inc.'s income statement for 2006 was as follows. (Ignore income taxes.)

ENID INC.
INCOME STATEMENT
FOR THE YEAR ENDED DECEMBER 31, 2006

Dividend revenue	$15,000
Gain on sale of available-for-sale securities	20,000
Net income	$35,000

Instructions

(Assume all transactions during the year were for cash.)

(a) Prepare the journal entry to record the sale of the available-for-sale securities in 2006.

(b) Prepare a statement of comprehensive income for 2006.

(c) Prepare a balance sheet as of December 31, 2006.

(LO 3) **P17-11** **(Equity Investments—Available for Sale)** Big Brother Holdings, Inc. had the following available-for-sale investment portfolio at January 1, 2006.

Earl Company	1,000 shares @ $15 each	$15,000
Josie Company	900 shares @ $20 each	18,000
David Company	500 shares @ $9 each	4,500
Available-for sale securities @ cost		37,500
Securities fair value adjustment—Available-for-sale		(7,500)
Available-for-sale securities @ fair value		$30,000

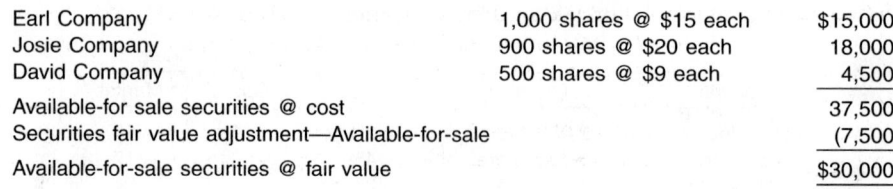

During 2006, the following transactions took place.

1. On March 1, Josie Company paid a $2 per share dividend.
2. On April 30, Big Brother Holdings, Inc. sold 300 shares of David Company for $10 per share.
3. On May 15, Big Brother Holdings, Inc. purchased 50 more shares of Earl Co. stock at $16 per share.
4. At December 31, 2006, the stocks had the following price per share values: Earl $17, Josie $19, and David $8.

During 2007, the following transactions took place.

5. On February 1, Big Brother Holdings, Inc. sold the remaining David shares for $7 per share.
6. On March 1, Josie Company paid a $2 per share dividend.
7. On December 21, Earl Company declared a cash dividend of $3 per share to be paid in the next month.
8. At December 31, 2007, the stocks had the following price per shares values: Earl $19 and Josie $21.

Instructions
(a) Prepare journal entries for each of the above transactions.
(b) Prepare a partial balance sheet showing the Investments account at December 31, 2006 and 2007.

(LO 3, 5) **P17-12 (Available-for-Sale Securities—Statement Presentation)** Alvarez Corp. invested its excess cash in available-for-sale securities during 2006. As of December 31, 2006, the portfolio of available-for-sale securities consisted of the following common stocks.

Security	Quantity	Cost	Fair Value
Keesha Jones, Inc.	1,000 shares	$ 15,000	$ 21,000
Eola Corp.	2,000 shares	50,000	42,000
Yevette Aircraft	2,000 shares	72,000	60,000
	Totals	$137,000	$123,000

Instructions
(a) What should be reported on Alvarez's December 31, 2006, balance sheet relative to these securities? What should be reported on Alvarez's 2006 income statement?

On December 31, 2007, Alvarez's portfolio of available-for-sale securities consisted of the following common stocks.

Security	Quantity	Cost	Fair Value
Keesha Jones, Inc.	1,000 shares	$ 15,000	$20,000
Keesha Jones, Inc.	2,000 shares	38,000	40,000
King Company	1,000 shares	16,000	12,000
Yevette Aircraft	2,000 shares	72,000	22,000
	Totals	$141,000	$94,000

During the year 2007, Alvarez Corp. sold 2,000 shares of Eola Corp. for $38,200 and purchased 2,000 more shares of Keesha Jones, Inc. and 1,000 shares of King Company.

(b) What should be reported on Alvarez's December 31, 2007, balance sheet? What should be reported on Alvarez's 2007 income statement?

On December 31, 2008, Alvarez's portfolio of available-for-sale securities consisted of the following common stocks.

Security	Quantity	Cost	Fair Value
Yevette Aircraft	2,000 shares	$72,000	$82,000
King Company	500 shares	8,000	6,000
	Totals	$80,000	$88,000

During the year 2008, Alvarez Corp. sold 3,000 shares of Keesha Jones, Inc. for $39,900 and 500 shares of King Company at a loss of $2,700.

(c) What should be reported on the face of Alvarez's December 31, 2008, balance sheet? What should be reported on Alvarez's 2008 income statement?
(d) What would be reported in a statement of comprehensive income at (1) December 31, 2006, and (2) December 31, 2007?

(LO 10) ***P17-13 (Call Option)** The treasurer of Miller Co. has read on the Internet that the stock price of Ewing Inc. is about to take off. In order to profit from this potential development, Miller Co. purchased a call option on Ewing common shares on July 7, 2006, for $240. The call option is for 200 shares (notional value), and the strike price is $70. The option expires on January 31, 2007. The data shown on page 898 are available with respect to the call option.

Date	Market Price of Ewing Shares	Time Value of Call Option
September 30, 2006	$77 per share	$180
December 31, 2006	75 per share	65
January 4, 2007	76 per share	30

Instructions

Prepare the journal entries for Miller Co. for the following dates.

(a) July 7, 2006—Investment in call option on Ewing shares.
(b) September 30, 2006—Miller prepares financial statements.
(c) December 31, 2006—Miller prepares financial statements.
(d) January 4, 2007—Miller settles the call option on the Ewing shares.

(LO 10) *P17-14 (Put Option)** Johnstone Co. purchased a put option on Ewing common shares on July 7, 2006, for $240. The put option is for 200 shares, and the strike price is $70. The option expires on January 31, 2007. The following data are available with respect to the put option.

Date	Market Price of Ewing Shares	Time Value of Put Option
September 30, 2006	$77 per share	$125
December 31, 2006	75 per share	50
January 31, 2007	78 per share	0

Instructions

Prepare the journal entries for Johnstone Co. for the following dates.

(a) January 7, 2006—Investment in put option on Ewing shares.
(b) September 30, 2006—Johnstone prepares financial statements.
(c) December 31, 2006—Johnstone prepares financial statements.
(d) January 31, 2007—Put option expires.

(LO 10) *P17-15 (Put Option)** Warren Co. purchased a put option on Echo common shares on January 7, 2007, for $360. The put option is for 400 shares, and the strike price is $85. The option expires on July 31, 2007. The following data are available with respect to the put option.

Date	Market Price of Echo Shares	Time Value of Put Option
March 31, 2007	$80 per share	$200
June 30, 2007	82 per share	90
July 6, 2007	77 per share	25

Instructions

Prepare the journal entries for Warren Co. for the following dates.

(a) January 7, 2007—Investment in put option on Echo shares.
(b) March 31, 2007—Warren prepares financial statements.
(c) June 30, 2007—Warren prepares financial statements.
(d) July 6, 2007—Warren settles the put option on the Echo shares.

(LO 11) *P17-16 (Fair Value Hedge Interest Rate Swap)** On December 31, 2006, Mercantile Corp. had a $10,000,000, 8% fixed-rate note outstanding, payable in 2 years. It decides to enter into a 2-year swap with Chicago First Bank to convert the fixed-rate debt to variable-rate debt. The terms of the swap indicate that Mercantile will receive interest at a fixed rate of 8.0% and will pay a variable rate equal to the 6-month LIBOR rate, based on the $10,000,000 amount. The LIBOR rate on December 31, 2006, is 7%. The LIBOR rate will be reset every 6 months and will be used to determine the variable rate to be paid for the following 6-month period.

Mercantile Corp. designates the swap as a fair value hedge. Assume that the hedging relationship meets all the conditions necessary for hedge accounting. The 6-month LIBOR rate and the swap and debt fair values are as follows.

Date	6-Month LIBOR Rate	Swap Fair Value	Debt Fair Value
December 31, 2006	7.0%	—	$10,000,000
June 30, 2007	7.5%	(200,000)	9,800,000
December 31, 2007	6.0%	60,000	10,060,000

Instructions

(a) Present the journal entries to record the following transactions.
  (1) The entry, if any, to record the swap on December 31, 2006.
  (2) The entry to record the semiannual debt interest payment on June 30, 2007.

    (3) The entry to record the settlement of the semiannual swap receivable at 8%, less amount payable at LIBOR, 7%.

    (4) The entry to record the change in the fair value of the debt on June 30, 2007.

    (5) The entry to record the change in the fair value of the swap at June 30, 2007.

(b) Indicate the amount(s) reported on the balance sheet and income statement related to the debt and swap on December 31, 2006.

(c) Indicate the amount(s) reported on the balance sheet and income statement related to the debt and swap on June 30, 2007.

(d) Indicate the amount(s) reported on the balance sheet and income statement related to the debt and swap on December 31, 2007.

(LO 12) ***P17-17** **(Cash Flow Hedge)** LEW Jewelry Co. uses gold in the manufacture of its products. LEW anticipates that it will need to purchase 500 ounces of gold in October 2006, for jewelry that will be shipped for the holiday shopping season. However, if the price of gold increases, LEW's cost to produce its jewelry will increase, which would reduce its profit margins.

To hedge the risk of increased gold prices, on April 1, 2006, LEW enters into a gold futures contract and designates this futures contract as a cash flow hedge of the anticipated gold purchase. The notional amount of the contract is 500 ounces, and the terms of the contract give LEW the option to purchase gold at a price of $300 per ounce. The price will be good until the contract expires on October 31, 2006.

Assume the following data with respect to the price of the call options and the gold inventory purchase.

Date	Spot Price for October Delivery
April 1, 2006	$300 per ounce
June 30, 2006	310 per ounce
September 30, 2006	315 per ounce

Instructions

Prepare the journal entries for the following transactions during 2006.

(a) April 1, Inception of the futures contract, no premium paid.

(b) June 30, LEW Co. prepares financial statements.

(c) September 30, LEW Co. prepares financial statements.

(d) October 10, LEW Co. purchases 500 ounces of gold at $315 per ounce and settles the futures contract.

(e) December 20, 2006—LEW sells jewelry containing gold purchased in October 2006 for $350,000. The cost of the finished goods inventory is $200,000.

(f) Indicate the amount(s) reported on the balance sheet and income statement related to the futures contract on June 30, 2006.

(g) Indicate the amount(s) reported in the income statement related to the futures contract and the inventory transactions on December 31, 2006.

(LO 11) ***P17-18** **(Fair Value Hedge)** On November 3, 2007, Sprinkle Co. invested $200,000 in 4,000 shares of the common stock of Johnstone Co. Sprinkle classified this investment as available-for-sale. Sprinkle Co. is considering making a more significant investment in Johnstone Co. at some point in the future but has decided to wait and see how the stock does over the next several quarters.

To hedge against potential declines in the value of Johnstone stock during this period, Sprinkle also purchased a put option on the Johnstone stock. Sprinkle paid an option premium of $600 for the put option, which gives Sprinkle the option to sell 4,000 Johnstone shares at a strike price of $50 per share. The option expires on July 31, 2007. The following data are available with respect to the values of the Johnstone stock and the put option.

Date	Market Price of Johnstone Shares	Time Value of Put Option
December 31, 2006	$50 per share	$375
March 31, 2007	45 per share	175
June 30, 2007	43 per share	40

Instructions

(a) Prepare the journal entries for Sprinkle Co. for the following dates.

    (1) November 3, 2006—Investment in Johnstone stock and the put option on Johnstone shares.

    (2) December 31, 2006—Sprinkle Co. prepares financial statements.

    (3) March 31, 2007—Sprinkle prepares financial statements.

    (4) June 30, 2007—Sprinkle prepares financial statements.

    (5) July 1, 2007—Sprinkle settles the put option and sells the Johnstone shares for $43 per share.

(b) Indicate the amount(s) reported on the balance sheet and income statement related to the Johnstone investment and the put option on December 31, 2006.

(c) Indicate the amount(s) reported on the balance sheet and income statement related to the Johnstone investment and the put option on June 30, 2007.

CONCEPTS FOR ANALYSIS

CA17-1 (Issues Raised about Investment Securities) You have just started work for Andre Love Co. as part of the controller's group involved in current financial reporting problems. Jackie Franklin, controller for Love, is interested in your accounting background because the company has experienced a series of financial reporting surprises over the last few years. Recently, the controller has learned from the company's auditors that an FASB *Statement* may apply to its investment in securities. She assumes that you are familiar with this pronouncement and asks how the following situations should be reported in the financial statements.

Situation 1

Trading securities in the current assets section have a fair value that is $4,200 lower than cost.

Situation 2

A trading security whose fair value is currently less than cost is transferred to the available-for-sale category.

Situation 3

An available-for-sale security whose fair value is currently less than cost is classified as noncurrent but is to be reclassified as current.

Situation 4

A company's portfolio of available-for-sale securities consists of the common stock of one company. At the end of the prior year the fair value of the security was 50% of original cost, and this reduction in market value was reported as an other than temporary impairment. However, at the end of the current year the fair value of the security had appreciated to twice the original cost.

Situation 5

The company has purchased some convertible debentures that it plans to hold for less than a year. The fair value of the convertible debentures is $7,700 below its cost.

Instructions

What is the effect upon carrying value and earnings for each of the situations above? Assume that these situations are unrelated.

CA17-2 (Equity Securities) James Joyce Co. has the following available-for-sale securities outstanding on December 31, 2006 (its first year of operations).

	Cost	Fair Value
Anna Wickham Corp. Stock	$20,000	$19,000
D. H. Lawrence Company Stock	10,000	8,800
Edith Sitwell Company Stock	20,000	20,600
	$50,000	$48,400

During 2007 D. H. Lawrence Company stock was sold for $9,200, the difference between the $9,200 and the "fair value" of $8,800 being recorded as a "Gain on Sale of Securities." The market price of the stock on December 31, 2007, was: Anna Wickham Corp. stock $19,900; Edith Sitwell Company stock $20,500.

Instructions

(a) What justification is there for valuing available-for-sale securities at fair value and reporting the unrealized gain or loss as part of stockholders' equity?

(b) How should James Joyce Company apply this rule on December 31, 2006? Explain.

(c) Did James Joyce Company properly account for the sale of the D. H. Lawrence Company stock? Explain.

(d) Are there any additional entries necessary for James Joyce Company at December 31, 2007, to reflect the facts on the financial statements in accordance with generally accepted accounting principles? Explain.

(AICPA adapted)

CA17-3 (Financial Statement Effect of Equity Securities) Presented below are three unrelated situations involving equity securities.

Situation 1

An equity security, whose market value is currently less than cost, is classified as available-for-sale but is to be reclassified as trading.

Situation 2

A noncurrent portfolio with an aggregate market value in excess of cost includes one particular security whose market value has declined to less than one-half of the original cost. The decline in value is considered to be other than temporary.

Situation 3

The portfolio of trading securities has a cost in excess of fair value of $13,500. The available-for-sale portfolio has a fair value in excess of cost of $28,600.

Instructions

What is the effect upon carrying value and earnings for each of the situations above?

CA17-4 (Equity Securities) The Financial Accounting Standards Board issued its *Statement No. 115* to clarify accounting methods and procedures with respect to certain debt and all equity securities. An important part of the statement concerns the distinction between held-to-maturity, available-for-sale, and trading securities.

Instructions

    (a) Why does a company maintain an investment portfolio of held-to-maturity, available-for-sale, and trading securities?

    (b) What factors should be considered in determining whether investments in securities should be classified as held-to-maturity, available-for-sale, and trading? How do these factors affect the accounting treatment for unrealized losses?

CA17-5 (Investment Accounted for under the Equity Method) On July 1, 2007, Sylvia Warner Company purchased for cash 40% of the outstanding capital stock of Robert Graves Company. Both Sylvia Warner Company and Robert Graves Company have a December 31 year-end. Graves Company, whose common stock is actively traded in the over-the-counter market, reported its total net income for the year to Warner Company and also paid cash dividends on November 15, 2007, to Warner Company and its other stockholders.

Instructions

How should Warner Company report the above facts in its December 31, 2007, balance sheet and its income statement for the year then ended? Discuss the rationale for your answer.

(AICPA adapted)

 **CA17-6 (Equity Investment)** On July 1, 2007, Munns Company purchased for cash 40% of the outstanding capital stock of Huber Corporation. Both Munns and Huber have a December 31 year-end. Huber Corporation, whose common stock is actively traded on the American Stock Exchange, paid a cash dividend on November 15, 2007, to Munns Company and its other stockholders. It also reported its total net income for the year of $920,000 to Munns Company.

Instructions

Prepare a one-page memorandum of instructions on how Munns Company should report the above facts in its December 31, 2007, balance sheet and its 2007 income statement. In your memo, identify and describe the method of valuation you recommend. Provide rationale where you can. Address your memo to the chief accountant at Munns Company.

 CA17-7 (Fair Value) Addison Manufacturing holds a large portfolio of debt and equity securities as an investment. The fair value of the portfolio is greater than its original cost, even though some securities have decreased in value. Ted Abernathy, the financial vice president, and Donna Nottebart, the controller, are near year-end in the process of classifying for the first time this securities portfolio in accordance with *FASB Statement No. 115.* Abernathy wants to classify those securities that have increased in value during the period as trading securities in order to increase net income this year. He wants to classify all the securities that have decreased in value as available-for-sale (the equity securities) and as held-to-maturity (the debt securities).

Nottebart disagrees. She wants to classify those securities that have decreased in value as trading securities and those that have increased in value as available-for-sale (equity) and held-to-maturity (debt). She contends that the company is having a good earnings year and that recognizing the losses will help to smooth the income this year. As a result, the company will have built-in gains for future periods when the company may not be as profitable.

Instructions

Answer the following questions.

    (a) Will classifying the portfolio as each proposes actually have the effect on earnings that each says it will?

(b) Is there anything unethical in what each of them proposes? Who are the stakeholders affected by their proposals?

(c) Assume that Abernathy and Nottebart properly classify the entire portfolio into trading, available-for-sale, and held-to-maturity categories. But then each proposes to sell just before year-end the securities with gains or with losses, as the case may be, to accomplish their effect on earnings. Is this unethical?

USING YOUR JUDGMENT

Financial Reporting Problem

The Procter & Gamble Company (P&G)

The financial statements of **P&G** are presented in Appendix 5B or can be accessed on the KWW website.

Instructions

Refer to P&G's financial statements and the accompanying notes to answer the following questions.

(a) What investments does P&G report in 2004, and where are these investments reported in its financial statements?

(b) How are P&G's investments valued? How does P&G determine fair value?

(c) How does P&G use derivative financial instruments?

Financial Statement Analysis Case

Union Planters

Union Planters is a Tennessee bank holding company (that is, a corporation that owns banks). (Union Planters is now part of **Regions Bank**.) Union Planters manages $32 billion in assets, the largest of which is its loan portfolio of $19 billion. In addition to its loan portfolio, however, like other banks it has significant debt investments. The nature of these investments varies from short-term in nature to long-term in nature. As a consequence, consistent with the requirements of accounting rules, Union Planters reports its investments in two different categories—trading and available-for-sale. The following facts were found in a recent Union Planters' annual report.

(all dollars in millions)	Amortized Cost	Gross Unrealized Gains	Gross Unrealized Losses	Fair Value
Trading account assets	$ 275	—	—	$ 275
Securities available for sale	8,209	$108	$15	8,302
Net income				224
Net securities gains (losses)				(9)

Instructions

(a) Why do you suppose Union Planters purchases investments, rather than simply making loans? Why does it purchase investments that vary in nature both in terms of their maturities and in type (debt versus stock)?

(b) How must Union Planters account for its investments in each of the two categories?

(c) In what ways does classifying investments into two different categories assist investors in evaluating the profitability of a company like Union Planters?

(d) Suppose that the management of Union Planters was not happy with its net income for the year. What step could it have taken with its investment portfolio that would have definitely increased reported profit? How much could it have increased reported profit? Why do you suppose it chose not to do this?

Comparative Analysis Case

The Coca-Cola Company and PepsiCo, Inc.

PEPSICO

Instructions

Go to the KWW website and use information found there to answer the following questions related to **The Coca-Cola Company and PepsiCo, Inc.**

(a) Based on the information contained in these financial statements, determine each of the following for each company.

(1) Cash used in (for) investing activities during 2004 (from the statement of cash flows).

(2) Cash used for acquisitions and investments in unconsolidated affiliates (or principally bottling companies) during 2004.

(3) Total investment in unconsolidated affiliates (or investments and other assets) at the end of 2004.

(4) What conclusions concerning the management of investments can be drawn from these data?

(b) (1) Briefly identify from Coca-Cola's December 31, 2004, balance sheet the investments it reported as being accounted for under the equity method. (2) What is the amount of investments that Coca-Cola reported in its 2004 balance sheet as "cost method investments," and what is the nature of these investments?

(c) In its Note number 9 on Financial Instruments, what total amounts did Coca-Cola report at December 31, 2004, as: (1) trading securities, (2) available-for-sale securities, and (3) held-to-maturity securities?

Research Case

The March 6, 2002, edition of the *Wall Street Journal* includes an article by Susan Pulliam and Carrick Mollenkamp titled "Investors Turn Attention to **Bank One** for Its Accounting of Securitizations."

Instructions

Read the article and answer the following questions.

(a) Explain the questions that analysts are raising about Bank One's accounting for credit-card securitizations. Why does the accounting for these securities matter?

(b) Bank One treats these securities as "available-for-sale." What are the criteria for classifying securities as available-for-sale? Based on the information in the article, do you think Bank One is classifying these securities properly? Justify your answer.

(c) How should an investment in available-for-sale securities be reported in the balance sheet? How are unrealized gains and losses on these securities reported?

(d) What is materiality, and how does it affect Bank One's financial statements? Would you consider $900 million immaterial for Bank One? Why or why not?

Professional Research: Financial Accounting and Reporting

Your client, Cascade Company, is planning to invest some of its excess cash in 5-year revenue bonds issued by the county and in the stock of one of its suppliers, Teton Co. Teton's shares trade on the over-the-counter market. Cascade plans to classify these investments as available-for-sale. They would like you to conduct some research on the accounting for these investments.

Instructions

Using the **Financial Accounting Research System (FARS)**, respond to the following items. (Provide text strings used in your search.)

(a) Since the Teton shares do not trade on one of the large stock markets, Cascade argues that the fair value of this investment is not readily available. According to the authoritative literature, when is the fair value of a security "readily determinable"?

(b) How is an impairment of a security accounted for?

(c) To avoid volatility in their financial statements due to fair value adjustments, Cascade debated whether the bond investment could be classified as held-to-maturity; Cascade is pretty sure it will hold the bonds for 5 years. How close to maturity could Cascade sell an investment and still classify it as held-to-maturity?

(d) What disclosures must be made for any sale or transfer from securities classified as held-to-maturity?

Professional Simulation

In this simulation you are asked to address questions related to investments. Prepare responses to all parts.

© **KWW_Professional_Simulation**

Investments   **Time Remaining**   copy   paste   calculator   sheet   standards   help   splitter   done
3 hours 20 minutes

Directions | Situation | Journal Entries | Measurement | Explanation | Resources

Powerpuff Corp. carries an account in its general ledger called Investments, which contained the following debits for investment purchases and no credits.

Feb. 1, 2007	Blossom Company common stock, $100 par, 200 shares	$ 37,400
April 1	U.S. Government bonds, 11%, due April 1, 2017, interest payable April 1 and October 1, 100 bonds of $1,000 par each	100,000
July 1	Buttercup Company 12% bonds, par $50,000, dated March 1, 2007, purchased at par plus accrued interest, interest payable annually on March 1, due March 1, 2027	52,000

Directions | Situation | Journal Entries | Measurement | Explanation | Resources

(a) Assuming that all the securities are classified as available-for-sale, prepare the journal entries necessary to classify the amounts into the proper accounts.
(b) Prepare the entry to record the accrued interest on December 31, 2007.

Directions | Situation | Journal Entries | Measurement | Explanation | Resources

The fair values of the securities on December 31, 2007, were:

Blossom Company common stock	$ 33,800 (1% interest)
U.S. Government bonds	124,700
Buttercup Company bonds	58,600

Use a computer spreadsheet to prepare a schedule indicating any fair value adjustment needed at December 31, 2007.

Directions | Situation | Journal Entries | Measurement | Explanation | Resources

Now assume Powerpuff's investment in Blossom Company represents 30% of Blossom's shares. In 2007, Blossom declared and paid dividends of $9,000 (on September 30) and reported net income of $30,000. Prepare a brief memorandum explaining how the accounting for the Blossom investment will change, and discuss the impact on the financial statements of Powerpuff Corp.

Remember to check the book's companion website to find additional resources for this chapter.

wiley.com/college/kieso

CHAPTER EIGHTEEN

REVENUE RECOGNITION

It's Back

Several years after passage, the accounting world continues to be preoccupied with the Sarbanes-Oxley Act of 2002 (SOX). Unfortunately, SOX did not solve one of the classic accounting issues—how to properly account for revenue. In fact, revenue recognition practices are the most prevalent reasons why accounting restatements increased dramatically in 2004. A number of the revenue recognition issues relate to possible fraudulent behavior by company executives and employees. Consider some of the recent SEC actions:

- The SEC charged the former co-chairman and CEO of **Qwest Communications International Inc.** and eight other former Qwest officers and employees with fraud and other violations of the federal securities laws. Three of these people fraudulently characterized nonrecurring revenue from one-time sales as revenue from recurring data and Internet services. The SEC release notes that internal correspondence likened Qwest's dependence on these transactions to fill the gap between actual and projected revenue to an addiction.

- The SEC filed a complaint against three former senior officers of **iGo Corp.**, alleging that the defendants collectively caused iGo to improperly recognize revenue on consignment sales and products that were not shipped or that were shipped after the end of a fiscal quarter.

- The SEC filed a complaint against the former CEO and chairman of **Homestore Inc.** and its former executive vice president of business development, alleging that they engaged in a fraudulent scheme to overstate advertising and subscription revenues. The scheme involved a complex structure of "round-trip" transactions using various third-party companies that, in essence, allowed Homestore to recognize its own cash as revenue.

Though the cases cited involved fraud and irregularity, not all revenue recognition errors are intentional. For example, in April 2005 **American Home Mortgage Investment Corp.** announced that it would reverse revenue recognized from its fourth-quarter 2004 loan securitization, and would recognize it in the first quarter of 2005 instead. As a result, American Home restated its financial results for 2004.[1]

So, how does a company ensure that revenue transactions are recorded properly? Some answers will become apparent after you study this chapter.

---

[1]Cheryl de Mesa Graziano, "Revenue Recognition: A Perennial Problem," *Financial Executive* (July 14, 2005), *www.fei.org/mag/articles/7-2005_revenue.cfm*.

Learning Objectives

After studying this chapter, you should be able to:

1 Apply the revenue recognition principle.

2 Describe accounting issues for revenue recognition at point of sale.

3 Apply the percentage-of-completion method for long-term contracts.

4 Apply the completed-contract method for long-term contracts.

5 Identify the proper accounting for losses on long-term contracts.

6 Describe the installment-sales method of accounting.

7 Explain the cost-recovery method of accounting.

As indicated in the opening story, the issue of when revenue should be recognized is complex. The many methods of marketing products and services make it difficult to develop guidelines that will apply to all situations. This chapter provides you with general guidelines used in most business transactions. The content and organization of the chapter are as follows.

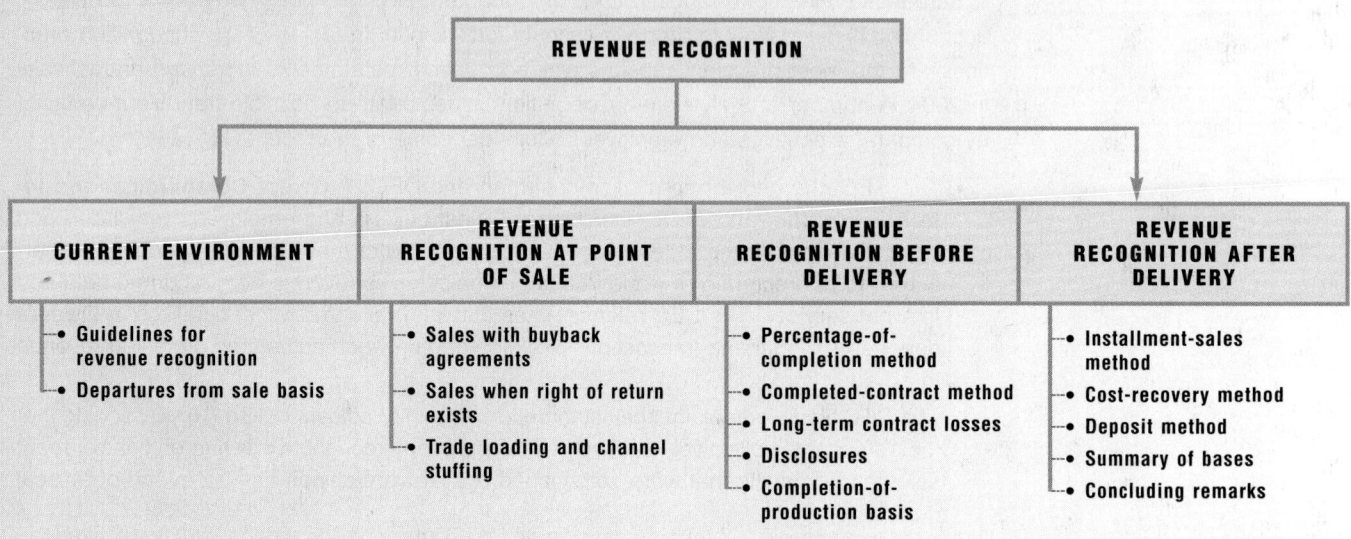

REVENUE RECOGNITION

CURRENT ENVIRONMENT	REVENUE RECOGNITION AT POINT OF SALE	REVENUE RECOGNITION BEFORE DELIVERY	REVENUE RECOGNITION AFTER DELIVERY
• Guidelines for revenue recognition • Departures from sale basis	• Sales with buyback agreements • Sales when right of return exists • Trade loading and channel stuffing	• Percentage-of-completion method • Completed-contract method • Long-term contract losses • Disclosures • Completion-of-production basis	• Installment-sales method • Cost-recovery method • Deposit method • Summary of bases • Concluding remarks

THE CURRENT ENVIRONMENT

According to one study, revenue recognition has been the largest single source of public-company restatements over the past decade. The study noted the following:

1 Restatements for improper revenue recognition result in larger drops in market capitalization than any other type of restatement.

2 Revenue problems caused eight of the top ten market value losses in a recent year.

3 Of the ten companies, the leading three lost $20 billion in market value in just three days following disclosure of revenue recognition problems.[2]

As a result of such revenue recognition problems, the SEC has increased its enforcement actions in this area (as evidenced in the opening story.) In some of these cases, companies made significant adjustments to previously issued financial statements. As Lynn Turner, former chief accountant of the SEC, indicated, "When people cross over the boundaries of legitimate reporting, the Commission will take appropriate action to ensure the fairness and integrity that investors need and depend on every day."[3]

Inappropriate recognition of revenue can occur in any industry. Products that are sold to distributors for resale pose different risks than products or services that are sold directly to customers. Sales in high-technology industries, where rapid product

---

[2]PricewaterhouseCoopers, "Current Developments for Audit Committees 2002" (Florham Park, N.J.: PricewaterhouseCoopers, 2002), p. 65.

[3]The Sarbanes-Oxley Act of 2002 also makes it clear that Congress will not tolerate abuses of the financial reporting process and that those who fail to adhere to "certain standards" will be prosecuted.

obsolescence is a significant issue, pose different risks than sale of inventory with a longer life, such as farm or construction equipment, automobiles, trucks, and appliances.[4]

As indicated in Chapter 10, telecom companies such as **Global Crossing** and **Qwest Communications** swapped fiber-optic capacity to increase revenue. The SEC has expressed concern that dot-coms also are increasing their revenue by including product sales in their revenue even though they are acting only as the distributor (intermediary) on behalf of other companies. Instead, dot-coms should be reporting only a distribution (brokerage) fee for selling another company's products.[5]

GROSSED OUT

WHAT DO THE
NUMBERS MEAN?

Consider **Priceline.com**, the company made famous by William Shatner's ads about "naming your own price" for airline tickets and hotel rooms. In one of its quarterly SEC filings, Priceline reported that it earned $152 million in revenues. But that included the full amount customers paid for tickets, hotel rooms, and rental cars. Traditional travel agencies call that amount "gross bookings," not revenues. And much like regular travel agencies, Priceline keeps only a small portion of gross bookings—namely, the spread between the customers' accepted bids and the price it paid for the merchandise. The rest, which Priceline calls "product costs," it pays to the airlines and hotels that supply the tickets and rooms.

However, Priceline's product costs came to $134 million, leaving Priceline just $18 million of what it calls "gross profit" and what most other companies would call revenues. And that's before all of Priceline's other costs—like advertising and salaries—which netted out to a loss of $102 million. The difference isn't academic: Priceline stock traded at about 23 times its reported revenues but at a mind-boggling 214 times its "gross profit." This and other aggressive recognition practices led the SEC to issue stricter revenue recogniton guidance indicating that if a company performs as an agent or broker without assuming the risks and rewards of ownership of the goods, the company should report sales on a net (fee) basis.

Source: "Revenue Recognition in Financial Statements," *SEC Staff Accounting Bulletin No. 101* December 3, 1999) and "Revenue Recognition," *SEC Staff Accounting Bulletin No. 104* (December 17, 2003). See also Jeremy Kahn, "Presto Chango! Sales Are Huge," *Fortune* (March 20, 2000), p. 44.

Guidelines for Revenue Recognition

In general, the guidelines for revenue recognition are quite broad. On top of the broad guidelines, certain industries have specific additional guidelines that provide further insight into when revenue should be recognized. The **revenue recognition principle** provides that companies should recognize revenue[6] (1) when it is realized

OBJECTIVE 1
Apply the revenue recognition principle.

---

[4]Adapted from American Institute of Certified Public Accountants, Inc., *Audit Issues in Revenue Recognition* (New York: AICPA, 1999).

[5]"Revenue Recognition in Financial Statements," *SEC Staff Accounting Bulletin No. 101,* December 3, 1999).

[6]Recognition is "the process of formally recording or incorporating an item in the accounts and financial statements of an entity" (*SFAC No. 3*, par. 83). "Recognition includes depiction of an item in both words and numbers, with the amount included in the totals of the financial statements" (*SFAC No. 5*, par. 6). For an asset or liability, recognition involves recording not only acquisition or incurrence of the item but also later changes in it, including removal from the financial statements previously recognized.

Recognition is not the same as realization, although the two are sometimes used interchangeably in accounting literature and practice. *Realization* is "the process of converting noncash resources and rights into money and is most precisely used in accounting and financial reporting to refer to sales of assets for cash or claims to cash" (*SFAC No. 3*, par. 83).

or realizable and (2) when it is earned.[7] Therefore, proper revenue recognition revolves around three terms:

> Revenues are **realized** when a company exchanges goods and services for cash or claims to cash (receivables).
>
> Revenues are **realizable** when assets a company receives in exchange are readily convertible to known amounts of cash or claims to cash.
>
> Revenues are **earned** when a company has substantially accomplished what it must do to be entitled to the benefits represented by the revenues—that is, when the earnings process is complete or virtually complete.[8]

UNDERLYING CONCEPTS

Revenues are inflows of assets and/or settlements of liabilities from delivering or producing goods, providing services, or other earning activities that constitute a company's ongoing major or central operations during a period.

Four revenue transactions are recognized in accordance with this principle:

1 Companies recognize revenue from selling products at the date of sale. This date is usually interpreted to mean the date of delivery to customers.

2 Companies recognize revenue from services provided, when services have been performed and are billable.

3 Companies recognize revenue from permitting others to use enterprise assets, such as interest, rent, and royalties, as time passes or as the assets are used.

4 Companies recognize revenue from disposing of assets other than products at the date of sale.

These revenue transactions are diagrammed in Illustration 18-1.

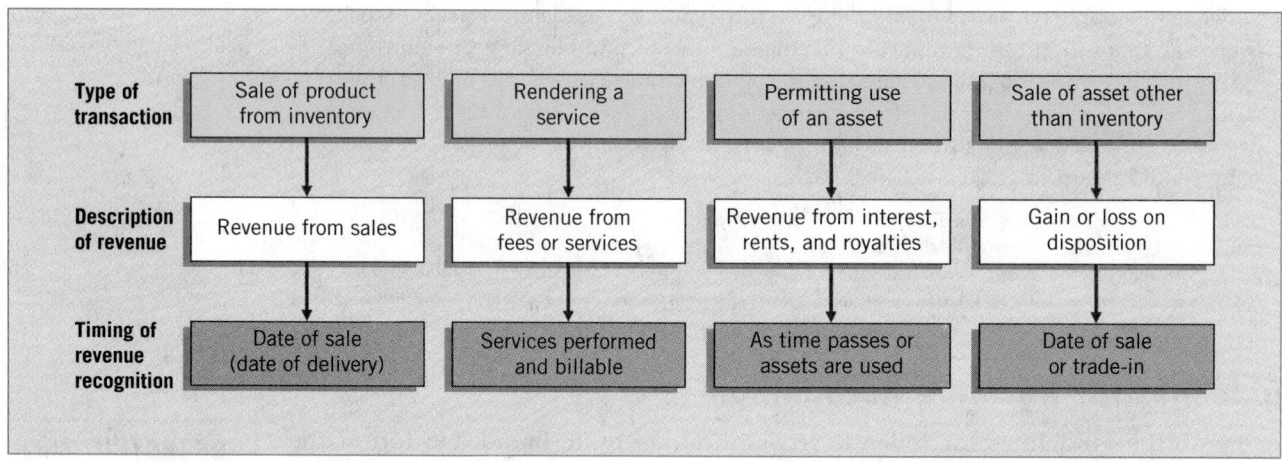

ILLUSTRATION 18-1
Revenue Recognition Classified by Nature of Transaction

The preceding statements are the basis of accounting for revenue transactions. Yet, in practice there are departures from the revenue recognition principle. Companies sometimes recognize revenue at other points in the earning process, owing in great measure to the considerable variety of revenue transactions.[9]

---

[7]"Recognition and Measurement in Financial Statements of Business Enterprises," *Statement of Financial Accounting Concepts No. 5* (Stamford, Conn.: FASB, 1984), par. 83.

[8]Gains (as contrasted to revenues) commonly result from transactions and other events that do not involve an "earning process." For gain recognition, being earned is generally less significant than being realized or realizable. Companies commonly recognize gains at the time of an asset's sale, disposition of a liability, or when prices of certain assets change.

[9]The FASB and IASB are now involved in a joint project on revenue recognition. The purpose of this project is to develop comprehensive conceptual guidance on when to recognize revenue. Presently, the boards are considering an approach that focuses on changes in assets and liabilities (rather than on earned and realized) as the basis for revenue recognition. It is hoped that this approach will lead to more consistent accounting in this area. (See *www.fasb.org/project/revenue_recognition.shtml.*)

Departures from the Sale Basis

An FASB study found some common **reasons for departures from the sale basis**.[10] One reason is a desire to **recognize earlier** than the time of sale the effect of earning activities. Earlier recognition is appropriate if there is a high degree of certainty about the amount of revenue earned. A second reason is a desire to **delay recognition** of revenue beyond the time of sale. Delayed recognition is appropriate if the degree of uncertainty concerning the amount of either revenue or costs is sufficiently high or if the sale does not represent substantial completion of the earnings process.

This chapter focuses on two of the four general types of revenue transactions described earlier: (1) selling products and (2) providing services. Both of these are **sales transactions**. (In several other sections of the textbook, we discuss the other two types of revenue transactions—revenue from permitting others to use enterprise assets, and revenue from disposing of assets other than products.) Our discussion of product sales transactions in this chapter is organized around the following topics:

1 Revenue recognition at point of sale (delivery).

2 Revenue recognition before delivery.

3 Revenue recognition after delivery.

4 Revenue recognition for special sales transactions—franchises and consignments.

Illustration 18-2 depicts this organization of revenue recognition topics.

Examples of Revenue Recognition Policies

ILLUSTRATION 18-2
Revenue Recognition
Alternatives

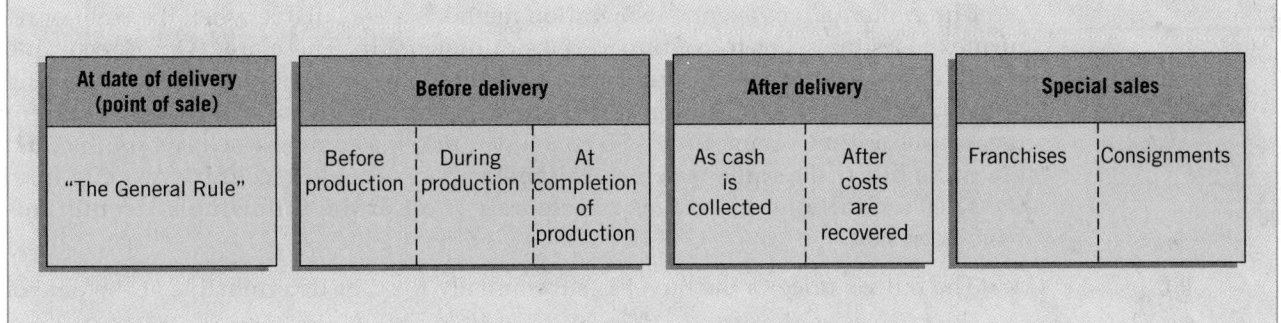

At date of delivery (point of sale)	Before delivery			After delivery		Special sales	
"The General Rule"	Before production	During production	At completion of production	As cash is collected	After costs are recovered	Franchises	Consignments

REVENUE RECOGNITION AT POINT OF SALE (DELIVERY)

According to the FASB's *Concepts Statement No. 5*, companies usually meet the two conditions for recognizing revenue (being realized or realizable and being earned) by the time they deliver products or render services to customers.[11] Therefore, companies commonly recognize revenues from manufacturing and selling activities at **point of sale** (usually meaning delivery).[12] Implementation problems, however, can arise. We discuss three such problematic situations on the following pages.

> **OBJECTIVE 2**
> Describe accounting issues for revenue recognition at point of sale.

---

[10]Henry R. Jaenicke, Survey of Present Practices in Recognizing Revenues, Expenses, Gains, and Losses, A Research Report (Stamford, Conn.: FASB, 1981), p. 11.

[11]The SEC believes that revenue is realized or realizable and earned when **all** of the following criteria are met: (1) Persuasive evidence of an arrangement exists; (2) delivery has occurred or services have been provided; (3) the seller's price to the buyer is fixed or determinable; and (4) collectibility is reasonably assured. See "Revenue Recognition in Financial Statements," *SEC Staff Accounting Bulletin No. 101* (December 3, 1999). The SEC provided more specific guidance because the general criteria were difficult to interpret.

[12]*Statement of Financial Accounting Concepts No. 5*, op. cit., par. 84.

Sales with Buyback Agreements

If a company sells a product in one period and agrees to buy it back in the next accounting period, has the company sold the product? As indicated in Chapter 8, legal title has transferred in this situation. However, the economic substance of the transaction is that the seller retains the risks of ownership. The FASB has curtailed recognition of revenue using this practice. When a repurchase agreement exists at a set price and this price covers all cost of the inventory plus related holding costs, the inventory and related liability remain on the seller's books.[13] In other words, no sale.

Sales When Right of Return Exists

Whether cash or credit sales are involved, a special problem arises with claims for returns and allowances. In Chapter 7, we presented the accounting treatment for normal returns and allowances. However, certain companies experience such a **high rate of returns**—a high ratio of returned merchandise to sales—that they find it necessary to postpone reporting sales until the return privilege has substantially expired.

For example, in the publishing industry, the rate of return approaches 25 percent for hardcover books and 65 percent for some magazines. Other types of companies that experience high return rates are perishable food dealers, distributors who sell to retail outlets, recording-industry companies, and some toy and sporting goods manufacturers. Returns in these industries are frequently made either through a right of contract or as a matter of practice involving "guaranteed sales" agreements or consignments.

Three alternative revenue recognition methods are available when the right of return exposes the seller to continued risks of ownership. These are: (1) not recording a sale until all return privileges have expired; (2) recording the sale, but reducing sales by an estimate of future returns; and (3) recording the sale and accounting for the returns as they occur. The FASB concluded that if a company sells its product but gives the buyer the right to return it, the company should recognize revenue from the sales transactions at the time of sale **only if all of the following six conditions have been met.**[14]

1 The seller's price to the buyer is substantially fixed or determinable at the date of sale.

2 The buyer has paid the seller, or the buyer is obligated to pay the seller, and the obligation is not contingent on resale of the product.

3 The buyer's obligation to the seller would not be changed in the event of theft or physical destruction or damage of the product.

4 The buyer acquiring the product for resale has economic substance apart from that provided by the seller.

5 The seller does not have significant obligations for future performance to directly bring about resale of the product by the buyer.

6 The seller can reasonably estimate the amount of future returns.

What if the six conditions are not met? In that case, the company must recognize sales revenue and cost of sales either when the return privilege has substantially expired or when those six conditions subsequently are met, **whichever occurs first**. In the income statement, the company must reduce sales revenue and cost of sales by the amount of the estimated returns.

UNDERLYING CONCEPTS

This is an example of *realized but unearned revenue*. When high rates of return exist and cannot be reasonably estimated, a question arises as to whether the earnings process has been substantially completed.

---

[13]"Accounting for Product Financing Arrangements," *Statement of Financial Accounting Standards No. 49* (Stamford, Conn.: FASB, 1981).

[14]"Revenue Recognition When Right of Return Exists," *Statement of Financial Accounting Standards No. 48* (Stamford, Conn.: FASB, 1981), par. 6.

Trade Loading and Channel Stuffing

Some companies record revenues at date of delivery with neither buyback nor unlimited return provisions. Although they appear to be following acceptable point-of-sale revenue recognition practices, they are recognizing revenues and earnings prematurely.

For example, the domestic cigarette industry at one time engaged in a distribution practice known as **trade loading**. As one commentator described this practice, "Trade loading is a crazy, uneconomic, insidious practice through which manufacturers—trying to show sales, profits, and market share they don't actually have—induce their wholesale customers, known as the trade, to buy more product than they can promptly resell."[15] In total, the cigarette industry appears to have exaggerated a couple years' operating profits by as much as $600 million by taking the profits from future years.

In the computer software industry, a similar practice is referred to as **channel stuffing**. When a software maker needed to make its financial results look good, it offered deep discounts to its distributors to overbuy, and then recorded revenue when the software left the loading dock.[16] Of course, the distributors' inventories become bloated and the marketing channel gets too filled with product, but the software maker's current-period financials are improved. However, financial results in future periods will suffer, unless the company repeats the process.

Trade loading and channel stuffing distort operating results and "window dress" financial statements. If used without an appropriate allowance for sales returns, channel stuffing is a classic example of booking tomorrow's revenue today. Business managers need to be aware of the ethical dangers of misleading the financial community by engaging in such practices to improve their financial statements.

INTERNATIONAL INSIGHT

General revenue recognition principles are provided by IFRS that are consistent with U.S. GAAP but contain limited detailed or industry-specific guidance.

NO TAKE-BACKS, REVISITED

WHAT DO THE NUMBERS MEAN?

You may recall from an earlier discussion (in Chapter 2, page 40) that investors in **Lucent Technologies** were negatively affected when Lucent violated one of the fundamental criteria for revenue recognition—the "no take-back" rule. This rule holds that revenue should not be booked on inventory that is shipped if the customer can return it at some point in the future. In this particular case, Lucent agreed to take back shipped inventory from its distributors, if the distributors were unable to sell the items to their customers.

In essence, Lucent was "stuffing the channel." By booking sales when goods were shipped, even though they most likely would get them back, Lucent was able to report continued sales growth. However, Lucent investors got a nasty surprise when distributors returned those goods and Lucent had to restate its financial results. The restatement erased $679 million in revenues, turning an operating profit into a loss. In response to this bad news, Lucent's stock price declined $1.31 per share, or 8.5 percent. Lucent is not alone in this practice. **Sunbeam** got caught stuffing the sales channel with barbeque grills and other outdoor items, which contributed to its troubles when it was forced to restate its earnings.

Investors can be tipped off to potential channel stuffing by carefully reviewing a company's revenue recognition policy for generous return policies and by watching inventory and receivable levels. When sales increase along with receivables, that's one sign that customers are not paying for goods shipped on credit. And growing inventory levels are an indicator that customers have all the goods they need. Both scenarios suggest a higher likelihood of goods being returned and revenues and income being restated. So remember, no take-backs!

Source: Adapted from S. Young, "Lucent Slashes First Quarter Outlook, Erases Revenue from Latest Quarter," *Wall Street Journal Online* (December 22, 2000); and Tracey Byrnes, "Too Many Thin Mints: Spotting the Practice of Channel Stuffing," *Wall Street Journal Online* (February 7, 2002).

---

[15]"The $600 Million Cigarette Scam," *Fortune* (December 4, 1989), p. 89.

[16]"Software's Dirty Little Secret," *Forbes* (May 15, 1989), p. 128.

Additional Disclosures of Revenue Recognition Policies

REVENUE RECOGNITION BEFORE DELIVERY

For the most part, companies recognize revenue at the point of sale (delivery) because at point of sale most of the uncertainties in the earning process are removed and the exchange price is known. Under certain circumstances, however, companies recognize revenue prior to completion and delivery. The most notable example is long-term construction contract accounting, which uses the percentage-of-completion method.

Long-term contracts frequently provide that the seller (builder) may bill the purchaser at intervals, as it reaches various points in the project. Examples of long-term contracts are construction-type contracts, development of military and commercial aircraft, weapons-delivery systems, and space exploration hardware. When the project consists of separable units, such as a group of buildings or miles of roadway, contract provisions may provide for delivery in installments. In that case, the seller would bill the buyer and transfer title at stated stages of completion, such as the completion of each building unit or every 10 miles of road. The accounting records should record sales when installments are "delivered."[17]

Two distinctly different methods of accounting for long-term construction contracts are recognized.[18] They are:

- **Percentage-of-Completion Method.** Companies recognize revenues and gross profits each period based upon the progress of the construction—that is, the percentage of completion. The company accumulates construction costs **plus gross profit earned to date** in an inventory account (Construction in Process), and it accumulates progress billings in a contra inventory account (Billings on Construction in Progress).
- **Completed-Contract Method.** Companies recognize revenues and gross profit **only** when the contract is completed. The company accumulates construction costs in an inventory account (Construction in Process), and it accumulates progress billings in a contra inventory account (Billings on Construction in Process).

The rationale for using percentage-of-completion accounting is that under most of these contracts the buyer and seller have enforceable rights. The buyer has the legal right to require specific performance on the contract. The seller has the right to require progress payments that provide evidence of the buyer's ownership interest. As a result, a continuous sale occurs as the work progresses. Companies should recognize revenue according to that progression.

UNDERLYING CONCEPTS

The percentage-of-completion method recognizes revenue from long-term contracts in the periods in which the revenue is earned. The firm contract fixes the selling price. And, if costs are estimable and collection reasonably assured, the revenue recognition concept is not violated.

Companies *must* use the percentage-of-completion method when estimates of progress toward completion, revenues, and costs are reasonably dependable and **all of the following conditions** exist.[19]

1 The contract clearly specifies the enforceable rights regarding goods or services to be provided and received by the parties, the consideration to be exchanged, and the manner and terms of settlement.

2 The buyer can be expected to satisfy all obligations under the contract.

3 The contractor can be expected to perform the contractual obligations.

Companies should use the completed-contract method when one of the following conditions applies:

---

[17]*Statement of Financial Accounting Concepts No. 5,* par. 84, item c.

[18]*Accounting Trends and Techniques—2004* reports that of the 119 of its 600 sample companies that referred to long-term construction contracts, 110 used the percentage-of-completion method and 9 used the completed-contract method.

[19]"Accounting for Performance of Construction-Type and Certain Production-Type Contracts," *Statement of Position 81-1* (New York: AICPA, 1981), par. 23.

- when a company has primarily short-term contracts, *or*
- when a company cannot meet the conditions for using the percentage-of-completion method, *or*
- when there are inherent hazards in the contract beyond the normal, recurring business risks.

The presumption is that percentage-of-completion is the better method. Therefore, companies should use the completed-contract method only when the percentage-of-completion method is inappropriate. We discuss the two methods in more detail in the following sections.

Percentage-of-Completion Method

The **percentage-of-completion method** recognizes revenues, costs, and gross profit as a company makes progress toward completion on a long-term contract. To defer recognition of these items until completion of the entire contract is to misrepresent the efforts (costs) and accomplishments (revenues) of the accounting periods during the contract. In order to apply the percentage-of-completion method, a company must have some basis or standard for measuring the progress toward completion at particular interim dates.

> **OBJECTIVE 3**
> Apply the percentage-of-completion method for long-term contracts.

Measuring the Progress toward Completion

As one practicing accountant wrote, "The big problem in applying the percentage-of-completion method . . . has to do with the ability to make reasonably accurate estimates of completion and the final gross profit."[20] Companies use various methods to determine the **extent of progress toward completion**. The most common are the *cost-to-cost* and *units-of-delivery* methods.[21]

The objective of all these methods is to measure the extent of progress in terms of costs, units, or value added. Companies identify the various measures (costs incurred, labor hours worked, tons produced, floors completed, etc.) and classify them as input or output measures. **Input measures** (costs incurred, labor hours worked) are efforts devoted to a contract. **Output measures** (with units of delivery measured as tons produced, floors of a building completed, miles of a highway completed) track results. Neither are universally applicable to all long-term projects. Their use requires the exercise of judgment and careful tailoring to the circumstances.

Both input and output measures have certain disadvantages. The input measure is based on an established relationship between a unit of input and productivity. If inefficiencies cause the productivity relationship to change, inaccurate measurements result. Another potential problem is front-end loading, in which significant up-front costs result in higher estimates of completion. To avoid this problem, companies should disregard some early-stage construction costs—for example, costs of uninstalled materials or costs of subcontracts not yet performed—if they do not relate to contract performance.

Similarly, output measures can produce inaccurate results if the units used are not comparable in time, effort, or cost to complete. For example, using floors (stories) completed can be deceiving. Completing the first floor of an eight-story building may require more than one-eighth the total cost because of the substructure and foundation construction.

The most popular input measure used to determine the progress toward completion is the **cost-to-cost basis**. Under this basis, a company like **EDS** measures the percentage of completion by comparing costs incurred to date with the most recent estimate of the total costs required to complete the contract. Illustration 18-3 (on page 914) shows the formula for the cost-to-cost basis.

---

[20]Richard S. Hickok, "New Guidance for Construction Contractors: 'A Credit Plus,'" *The Journal of Accountancy* (March 1982), p. 46.

[21]R. K. Larson and K. L. Brown, "Where Are We with Long-Term Contract Accounting?" *Accounting Horizons* (September 2004), pp. 207–219.

ILLUSTRATION 18-3
Formula for Percentage of Completion, Cost-to-Cost Basis

$$\frac{\text{Costs incurred to date}}{\text{Most recent estimate of total costs}} = \text{Percent complete}$$

Once EDS knows the percentage that costs incurred bear to total estimated costs, it applies that percentage to the total revenue or the estimated total gross profit on the contract. The resulting amount is the revenue or the gross profit to be recognized to date. Illustration 18-4 shows this computation.

ILLUSTRATION 18-4
Formula for Total Revenue to Be Recognized to Date

$$\begin{array}{c}\text{Percent}\\\text{complete}\end{array} \times \begin{array}{c}\text{Estimated}\\\text{total revenue}\\\text{(or gross profit)}\end{array} = \begin{array}{c}\text{Revenue (or gross}\\\text{profit) to be}\\\text{recognized to date}\end{array}$$

To find the amounts of revenue and gross profit recognized each period, EDS subtracts total revenue or gross profit recognized in prior periods, as shown in Illustration 18-5.

ILLUSTRATION 18-5
Formula for Amount of Current-Period Revenue, Cost-to-Cost Basis

$$\begin{array}{c}\text{Revenue (or gross}\\\text{profit) to be}\\\text{recognized to date}\end{array} - \begin{array}{c}\text{Revenue (or gross}\\\text{profit) recognized}\\\text{in prior periods}\end{array} = \begin{array}{c}\text{Current-period}\\\text{revenue}\\\text{(or gross profit)}\end{array}$$

Because **the cost-to-cost method is widely used** (without excluding other bases for measuring progress toward completion), we have adopted it for use in our examples.[22]

Example of Percentage-of-Completion Method—Cost-to-Cost Basis

To illustrate the percentage-of-completion method, assume that Hardhat Construction Company has a contract to construct a $4,500,000 bridge at an estimated cost of $4,000,000. The contract is to start in July 2007, and the bridge is to be completed in October 2009. The following data pertain to the construction period. (Note that by the end of 2008 Hardhat has revised the estimated total cost from $4,000,000 to $4,050,000.)

	2007	2008	2009
Costs to date	$1,000,000	$2,916,000	$4,050,000
Estimated costs to complete	3,000,000	1,134,000	—
Progress billings during the year	900,000	2,400,000	1,200,000
Cash collected during the year	750,000	1,750,000	2,000,000

Hardhat would compute the percentage complete as shown in Illustration 18-6.

ILLUSTRATION 18-6
Application of Percentage-of-Completion Method, Cost-to-Cost Basis

	2007	2008	2009
Contract price	$4,500,000	$4,500,000	$4,500,000
Less estimated cost:			
Costs to date	1,000,000	2,916,000	4,050,000
Estimated costs to complete	3,000,000	1,134,000	—
Estimated total costs	4,000,000	4,050,000	4,050,000
Estimated total gross profit	$ 500,000	$ 450,000	$ 450,000
Percent complete	25%	72%	100%
	$\left(\dfrac{\$1,000,000}{\$4,000,000}\right)$	$\left(\dfrac{\$2,916,000}{\$4,050,000}\right)$	$\left(\dfrac{\$4,050,000}{\$4,050,000}\right)$

---

[22]Committee on Accounting Procedure, "Long-Term Construction-Type Contracts," *Accounting Research Bulletin No. 45* (New York: AICPA, 1955), p. 7.

On the basis of the data above, Hardhat would make the following entries to record (1) the costs of construction, (2) progress billings, and (3) collections. These entries appear as summaries of the many transactions that would be entered individually as they occur during the year.

	2007		2008		2009	
To record cost of construction:						
Construction in Process	1,000,000		1,916,000		1,134,000	
Materials, Cash,						
Payables, etc.		1,000,000		1,916,000		1,134,000
To record progress billings:						
Accounts Receivable	900,000		2,400,000		1,200,000	
Billings on Construction						
in Process		900,000		2,400,000		1,200,000
To record collections:						
Cash	750,000		1,750,000		2,000,000	
Accounts Receivable		750,000		1,750,000		2,000,000

ILLUSTRATION 18-7
Journal Entries—
Percentage-of-
Completion Method,
Cost-to-Cost Basis

In this example, the costs incurred to date are a measure of the extent of progress toward completion. To determine this, Hardhat evaluates the costs incurred to date as a proportion of the estimated total costs to be incurred on the project. The estimated revenue and gross profit that Hardhat will recognize for each year are calculated as shown in Illustration 18-8.

		2007	2008	2009
Revenue recognized in:				
2007	$4,500,000 × 25%	$1,125,000		
2008	$4,500,000 × 72%		$3,240,000	
	Less: Revenue recognized in 2007		1,125,000	
	Revenue in 2008		$2,115,000	
2009	$4,500,000 × 100%			$4,500,000
	Less: Revenue recognized in 2007 and 2008			3,240,000
	Revenue in 2009			$1,260,000
Gross profit recognized in:				
2007	$500,000 × 25%	$ 125,000		
2008	$450,000 × 72%		$ 324,000	
	Less: Gross profit recognized in 2007		125,000	
	Gross profit in 2008		$ 199,000	
2009	$450,000 × 100%			$ 450,000
	Less: Gross profit recognized in 2007 and 2008			324,000
	Gross profit in 2009			$ 126,000

ILLUSTRATION 18-8
Percentage-of-
Completion, Revenue
and Gross Profit, by Year

Illustration 18-9 (on page 916) shows Hardhat's entries to recognize revenue and gross profit each year and to record completion and final approval of the contract.

ILLUSTRATION 18-9
Journal Entries to
Recognize Revenue and
Gross Profit and to
Record Contract
Completion—Percentage-
of-Completion Method,
Cost-to-Cost Basis

	2007	2008	2009
To recognize revenue and gross profit:			
Construction in Process (gross profit)	125,000	199,000	126,000
Construction Expenses	1,000,000	1,916,000	1,134,000
Revenue from Long-Term Contract	1,125,000	2,115,000	1,260,000
To record completion of the contract:			
Billings on Construction in Process			4,500,000
Construction in Process			4,500,000

Note that Hardhat debits gross profit (as computed in Illustration 18-8) to Construction in Process. Similarly, it credits Revenue from Long-Term Contract for the amounts computed in Illustration 18-8. Hardhat then debits the difference between the amounts recognized each year for revenue and gross profit to a nominal account, Construction Expenses (similar to Cost of Goods Sold in a manufacturing company). It reports that amount in the income statement as the actual cost of construction incurred in that period. For example, Hardhat uses the actual costs of $1,000,000 to compute both the gross profit of $125,000 and the percent complete (25 percent).

Hardhat continues to accumulate costs in the Construction in Process account, in order to maintain a record of total costs incurred (plus recognized profit) to date. Although theoretically a series of "sales" takes place using the percentage-of-completion method, the selling company cannot remove the inventory cost until the construction is completed and transferred to the new owner. Hardhat's Construction in Process account for the bridge would include the following summarized entries over the term of the construction project.

ILLUSTRATION 18-10
Content of Construction
in Process Account—
Percentage-of-
Completion Method

Construction in Process			
2007 construction costs	$1,000,000	12/31/09 to close	
2007 recognized gross profit	125,000	completed	
2008 construction costs	1,916,000	project	$4,500,000
2008 recognized gross profit	199,000		
2009 construction costs	1,134,000		
2009 recognized gross profit	126,000		
Total	$4,500,000	Total	$4,500,000

Recall that the Hardhat Construction Company example contained a **change in estimate**: In the second year, 2008, it increased the estimated total costs from $4,000,000 to $4,050,000. The change in estimate is accounted for in a **cumulative catch-up manner**. This is done by, first, adjusting the percent completed to the new estimate of total costs. Next, Hardhat deducts the amount of revenues and gross profit recognized in prior periods from revenues and gross profit computed for progress to date. That is, it accounts for the change in estimate in the period of change. That way, the balance sheet at the end of the period of change and the accounting in subsequent periods are as they would have been if the revised estimate had been the original estimate.

Financial Statement Presentation—Percentage-of-Completion

Generally when a company records a receivable from a sale, it reduces the Inventory account. Under the percentage-of-completion method, however, the company continues to carry both the receivable and the inventory. Subtracting the balance in the **Billings account** from Construction in Process avoids double-counting the inventory. During the life of the contract, Hardhat reports in the balance sheet the difference between the

Construction in Process and the Billings on Construction in Process accounts. If that amount is a debit, Hardhat reports it **as a current asset**; if it is a credit, it reports it **as a current liability**.

At times, the costs incurred plus the gross profit recognized to date (the balance in Construction in Process) exceed the billings. In that case, Hardhat reports this excess as a current asset entitled "Cost and recognized profit in excess of billings." Hardhat can at any time calculate the unbilled portion of revenue recognized to date by subtracting the billings to date from the revenue recognized to date, as illustrated for 2007 for Hardhat Construction in Illustration 18-11.

Contract revenue recognized to date: $4,500,000 \times \dfrac{\$1,000,000}{\$4,000,000}$		$1,125,000
Billings to date		900,000
Unbilled revenue		$ 225,000

ILLUSTRATION 18-11
Computation of Unbilled
Contract Price at 12/31/07

At other times, the billings exceed costs incurred and gross profit to date. In that case, Hardhat reports this excess as a current liability entitled "Billings in excess of costs and recognized profit."

It probably has occurred to you that companies often have more than one project going at a time. When a company has a number of projects, costs exceed billings on some contracts and billings exceed costs on others. In such a case, the company segregates the contracts. The asset side includes only those contracts on which costs and recognized profit exceed billings. The liability side includes only those on which billings exceed costs and recognized profit. Separate disclosures of the dollar volume of billings and costs are preferable to a summary presentation of the net difference.

Using data from the bridge example, Hardhat Construction Company would report the status and results of its long-term construction activities under the perentage-of-completion method as shown in Illustration 18-12.

ILLUSTRATION 18-12
Financial Statement
Presentation—Percentage-
of-Completion Method

HARDHAT CONSTRUCTION COMPANY			
	2007	2008	2009
Income Statement			
Revenue from long-term contracts	$1,125,000	$2,115,000	$1,260,000
Costs of construction	1,000,000	1,916,000	1,134,000
Gross profit	$ 125,000	$ 199,000	$ 126,000

Balance Sheet (12/31)				
Current assets				
Accounts receivable		$ 150,000	$ 800,000	
Inventories				
Construction in process	$1,125,000			
Less: Billings	900,000			
Costs and recognized profit in excess of billings		225,000		
Current liabilities				
Billings ($3,300,000) in excess of costs and recognized profit ($3,240,000)			$ 60,000	

Note 1. Summary of significant accounting policies.
Long-Term Construction Contracts. The company recognizes revenues and reports profits from long-term construction contracts, its principal business, under the percentage-of-completion method of accounting. These contracts generally extend for periods in excess of one year. The amounts of revenues and profits recognized each year are based on the ratio of costs incurred to the total estimated costs. Costs included in construction in process include direct materials, direct labor, and project-related overhead. Corporate general and administrative expenses are charged to the periods as incurred and are not allocated to construction contracts.

Completed-Contract Method

OBJECTIVE 4
Apply the completed-contract method for long-term contracts.

Under the **completed-contract method**, companies recognize revenue and gross profit only at point of sale—that is, when the contract is completed. Under this method, companies accumulate costs of long-term contracts in process, but they make no interim charges or credits to income statement accounts for revenues, costs, or gross profit.

The principal advantage of the completed-contract method is that reported revenue reflects final results rather than *estimates* of unperformed work. Its major disadvantage is that it does not reflect current performance when the period of a contract extends into more than one accounting period. Although operations may be fairly uniform during the period of the contract, the company will not report revenue until the year of completion, creating a distortion of earnings.

UNDERLYING CONCEPTS

The completed-contract method does not violate the *matching concept* because the costs are also deferred until the completion of the contract.

Under the completed-contract method, the company would make the same **annual entries** to record costs of construction, progress billings, and collections from customers as those illustrated under the percentage-of-completion method. The significant difference is that the company **would not make entries to recognize revenue and gross profit**.

For example, under the completed-contract method for the bridge project illustrated on the preceding pages, Hardhat Construction Company would make the following entries in 2009 to recognize revenue and costs and to close out the inventory and billing accounts.

Billings on Construction in Process	4,500,000	
Revenue from Long-Term Contracts		4,500,000
Costs of Construction	4,050,000	
Construction in Process		4,050,000

Illustration 18-13 compares the amount of gross profit that Hardhat Construction Company would recognize for the bridge project under the two revenue-recognition methods.

ILLUSTRATION 18-13
Comparison of Gross Profit Recognized under Different Methods

	Percentage-of-Completion	Completed-Contract
2007	$125,000	$ 0
2008	199,000	0
2009	126,000	450,000

Under the completed-contract method, Hardhat Construction would report its long-term construction activities as follows.

ILLUSTRATION 18-14
Financial Statement Presentation—Completed-Contract Method

HARDHAT CONSTRUCTION COMPANY			
	2007	2008	2009
Income Statement			
Revenue from long-term contracts	—	—	$4,500,000
Costs of construction	—	—	4,050,000
Gross profit	—	—	$ 450,000

Balance Sheet (12/31)				
Current assets				
Accounts receivable			$150,000	$800,000
Inventories				
Construction in process	$1,000,000			
Less: Billings	900,000			
Unbilled contract costs			100,000	
Current liabilities				
Billings ($3,300,000) in excess of contract				
costs ($2,916,000)				$384,000

Note 1. Summary of significant accounting policies.
Long-Term Construction Contracts. The company recognizes revenues and reports profits from long-term construction contracts, its principal business, under the completed-contract method. These contracts generally extend for periods in excess of one year. Contract costs and billings are accumulated during the periods of construction, but no revenues or profits are recognized until completion of the contract. Costs included in construction in process include direct material, direct labor, and project-related overhead. Corporate general and administrative expenses are charged to the periods as incurred.

Long-Term Contract Losses

Two types of losses can become evident under long-term contracts:[23]

OBJECTIVE 5
Identify the proper
accounting for losses
on long-term contracts.

1 *Loss in the Current Period on a Profitable Contract.* This condition arises when, during construction, there is a significant increase in the estimated total contract costs but the increase does not eliminate all profit on the contract. Under the percentage-of-completion method only, the estimated cost increase requires a current-period adjustment of excess gross profit recognized on the project in prior periods. The company records this adjustment as a loss in the current period because it is a **change in accounting estimate** (discussed in Chapter 22).

2 *Loss on an Unprofitable Contract.* Cost estimates at the end of the current period may indicate that a loss will result on completion of the *entire* contract. Under both the percentage-of-completion and the completed-contract methods, the company must recognize in the current period the entire expected contract loss.

The treatment described for unprofitable contracts is consistent with the accounting custom of anticipating foreseeable losses to avoid overstatement of current and future income (conservatism).

UNDERLYING CONCEPTS

Conservatism justifies recognizing the losses immediately. Loss recognition does not require *realization;* it only requires evidence that an impairment of asset value has occurred.

Loss in Current Period

To illustrate a loss in the current period on a contract expected to be profitable upon completion, we'll continue with the Hardhat Construction Company bridge project. Assume that on December 31, 2008, Hardhat estimates the costs to complete the bridge contract at $1,468,962 instead of $1,134,000 (refer to page 914). Assuming all other data are the same as before, Hardhat would compute the percentage complete and recognize the loss as shown in Illustration 18-15. Compare these computations with those for 2008 in Illustration 18-6. The "percent complete" has dropped, from 72 percent to 66½ percent, due to the increase in estimated future costs to complete the contract.

Cost to date (12/31/08)	$2,916,000
Estimated costs to complete (revised)	1,468,962
Estimated total costs	$4,384,962
Percent complete ($2,916,000 ÷ $4,384,962)	66½%
Revenue recognized in 2008	
($4,500,000 × 66½%) − $1,125,000	$1,867,500
Costs incurred in 2008	1,916,000
Loss recognized in 2008	$ 48,500

ILLUSTRATION 18-15
Computation of Recognizable Loss, 2008—Loss in Current Period

The 2008 loss of $48,500 is a cumulative adjustment of the "excessive" gross profit recognized on the contract in 2007. Instead of restating the prior period, the company absorbs the prior period misstatement entirely in the current period. In this illustration, the adjustment was large enough to result in recognition of a loss.
Hardhat Construction would record the loss in 2008 as follows.

Construction Expenses	1,916,000	
Construction in Process (loss)		48,500
Revenue from Long-Term Contract		1,867,500

Hardhat will report the loss of $48,500 on the 2008 income statement as the difference between the reported revenues of $1,867,500 and the costs of $1,916,000.[24] **Under**

---

[23]Sak Bhamornsiri, "Losses from Construction Contracts," *The Journal of Accountancy* (April 1982), p. 26.

[24]In 2009 Hardhat Construction will recognize the remaining 33½ percent of the revenue ($1,507,500), with costs of $1,468,962 as expected, and will report a gross profit of $38,538. The total gross profit over the three years of the contract would be $115,038 [$125,000 (2007) − $48,500 (2008) + $38,538 (2009)]. This amount is the difference between the total contract revenue of $4,500,000 and the total contract costs of $4,384,962.

the completed-contract method, the company does not recognize a loss in 2008. Why not? Because the company still expects the contract to result in a profit, to be recognized in the year of completion.

Loss on an Unprofitable Contract

To illustrate the accounting for an **overall loss on a long-term contract**, assume that at December 31, 2008, Hardhat Construction Company estimates the costs to complete the bridge contract at $1,640,250 instead of $1,134,000. Revised estimates for the bridge contract are as follows.

	2007 Original Estimates	2008 Revised Estimates
Contract price	$4,500,000	$4,500,000
Estimated total cost	4,000,000	4,556,250*
Estimated gross profit	$ 500,000	
Estimated loss		$ (56,250)

*($2,916,000 + $1,640,250)

Under the percentage-of-completion method, Hardhat recognized $125,000 of gross profit in 2007 (see Illustration 18-8). This amount must be offset in 2008 because it is no longer expected to be realized. In addition, since losses must be recognized as soon as estimable, the company must recognize the total estimated loss of $56,250 in 2008. Therefore, Hardhat must recognize a total loss of $181,250 ($125,000 + $56,250) in 2008.

Illustration 18-16 shows Hardhat's computation of the revenue to be recognized in 2008.

ILLUSTRATION 18-16
Computation of Revenue
Recognizable, 2008—
Unprofitable Contract

Revenue recognized in 2008:		
Contract price		$4,500,000
Percent complete		× 64%*
Revenue recognizable to date		2,880,000
Less: Revenue recognized prior to 2008		1,125,000
Revenue recognized in 2008		$1,755,000
*Cost to date (12/31/08)	$2,916,000	
Estimated cost to complete	1,640,250	
Estimated total costs	$4,556,250	
Percent complete: $2,916,000 ÷ $4,556,250 = 64%		

To compute the construction costs to be expensed in 2008, Hardhat adds the total loss to be recognized in 2008 ($125,000 + $56,250) to the revenue to be recognized in 2008. Illustration 18-17 shows this computation.

ILLUSTRATION 18-17
Computation of
Construction Expense,
2008—Unprofitable
Contract

Revenue recognized in 2008 (computed above)		$1,755,000
Total loss recognized in 2008:		
Reversal of 2007 gross profit	$125,000	
Total estimated loss on the contract	56,250	181,250
Construction cost expensed in 2008		$1,936,250

Hardhat Construction would record the long-term contract revenues, expenses, and loss in 2008 as follows.

Construction Expenses	1,936,250	
Construction in Process (Loss)		181,250
Revenue from Long-Term Contracts		1,755,000

At the end of 2008, Construction in Process has a balance of $2,859,750 as shown below.[25]

Construction in Process			
2007 Construction costs	1,000,000		
2007 Recognized gross profit	125,000		
2008 Construction costs	1,916,000	2008 Recognized loss	181,250
Balance	**2,859,750**		

ILLUSTRATION 18-18
Content of Construction
in Process Account at
End of 2008—
Unprofitable Contract

Under the completed-contract method, Hardhat also would recognize the contract loss of $56,250, through the following entry in 2008 (the year in which the loss first became evident).

Loss from Long-Term Contracts	56,250	
Construction in Process (Loss)		56,250

Just as the Billings account balance cannot exceed the contract price, neither can the balance in Construction in Process exceed the contract price. In circumstances where the Construction in Process balance exceeds the billings the company can deduct the recognized loss from such accumulated costs on the balance sheet. That is, under both the percentage-of-completion and the completed-contract methods, the provision for the loss (the credit) may be combined with Construction in Process, thereby reducing the inventory balance. In those circumstances, however (as in the 2008 example above), where the billings exceed the accumulated costs, Hardhat must report separately on the balance sheet, as a current liability, the amount of the estimated loss. That is, under both the percentage-of-completion and the completed-contract methods, Hardhat would take the $56,250 loss, as estimated in 2008, from the Construction in Process account and report it separately as a current liability titled "Estimated liability from long-term contracts."[26]

Disclosures in Financial Statements

Construction contractors usually make some unique financial statement disclosures in addition to those required of all businesses. Generally these additional disclosures are made in the notes to the financial statements. For example, a construction contractor should disclose the following: the method of recognizing revenue,[27] the basis used to classify assets and liabilities as current (the nature and length of the operating cycle), the basis for recording inventory, the effects of any revision of estimates, the amount

---

[25]If the costs in 2009 are $1,640,250 as projected, at the end of 2009 the Construction in Process account will have a balance of $1,640,250 + $2,859,750, or $4,500,000, equal to the contract price. When the company matches the revenue remaining to be recognized in 2009 of $1,620,000 [$4,500,000 (total contract price) − $1,125,000 (2007) − $1,755,000 (2008)] with the construction expense to be recognized in 2009 of $1,620,000 [total costs of $4,556,250 less the total costs recognized in prior years of $2,936,250 (2007, $1,000,000; 2008, $1,936,250)], a zero profit results. Thus the total loss has been recognized in 2008, the year in which it first became evident.

[26]*Construction Contractors*, Audit and Accounting Guide (New York: AICPA, 1981), pp. 148–149.

[27]Ibid., p. 30.

of backlog on uncompleted contracts, and the details about receivables (billed and unbilled, maturity, interest rates, retainage provisions, and significant individual or group concentrations of credit risk).

WHAT DO THE
NUMBERS MEAN?

LESS CONSERVATIVE

Halliburton provides engineering- and construction-related services, in jobs around the world. Much of the company's work is completed under contract over long periods of time. The company uses percentage-of-completion accounting. Recently the SEC started enforcement proceedings against the company related to its accounting for contract claims and disagreements with customers, including those arising from change orders and disputes about billable amounts and costs associated with a construction delay.

Prior to 1998 Halliburton took a very conservative approach to its accounting for disputed claims. As stated in the company's 1997 annual report, "Claims for additional compensation are recognized during the period such claims are resolved." That is, the company waited until all disputes were resolved before recognizing associated revenues. In contrast, in 1998 the company recognized revenue for disputed claims before their resolution, using estimates of amounts expected to be recovered. Such revenue and its related profit are more tentative and are subject to possible later adjustment than revenue and profit recognized when all claims have been resolved. As a case in point, the company noted that it incurred losses of $99 million in 1998 related to customer claims.

The accounting method put in place in 1998 is more aggressive than the company's former policy, but it is still within the boundaries of generally accepted accounting principles. However, the SEC noted that over six quarters, Halliburton failed to disclose its change in accounting practice. In the absence of any disclosure the SEC believed the investing public was misled about the precise nature of Halliburton's income in comparison to prior periods. The Halliburton situation illustrates the difficulty of using estimates in percentage-of-completion accounting and the impact of those estimates on the financial statements.

Source: "Failure to Disclose a 1998 Change in Accounting Practice," SEC (August 3, 2004), *www.sec.gov/news/press/2004-104.htm*. See also "Accounting Ace Charles Mulford Answers Accounting Questions," *Wall Street Journal Online* (June 7, 2002).

Completion-of-Production Basis

UNDERLYING CONCEPTS

This is not an exception to the revenue recognition principle. At the completion of production, realization is virtually assured and the earning process is substantially completed.

In certain cases companies recognize revenue at the completion of **production** even though no sale has been made. Examples of such situations involve precious metals or agricultural products with assured prices. Under the **completion-of-production basis**, companies recognize revenue when these metals are mined or agricultural crops harvested because the sales price is reasonably assured, the units are interchangeable, and no significant costs are involved in distributing the product.[28] (See discussion in Chapter 9, page 429, "Valuation at Net Realizable Value")

Likewise, when sale or cash receipt precedes production and delivery, as in the case of magazine subscriptions, companies recognize revenues as earned by production and delivery.[29]

---

[28]Such revenue satisfies the criteria of *Concepts Statement No. 5* since the assets are readily realizable and the earning process is virtually complete (see par. 84, item c).

[29]*Statement of Financial Accounting Concepts No. 5*, par. 84, item b.

REVENUE RECOGNITION AFTER DELIVERY

In some cases, the collection of the sales price is not reasonably assured and revenue recognition is deferred. One of two methods is generally employed to defer revenue recognition until the company receives cash: the **installment-sales method** or the **cost-recovery method**. A third method, the **deposit method**, applies in situations in which a company receives cash prior to delivery or transfer of the property; the company records that receipt as a deposit because the sale transaction is incomplete. This section examines these three methods.

Installment-Sales Accounting Method

The installment-sales method recognizes income in the periods of collection rather than in the period of sale. The logic underlying this method is that when there is no reasonable approach for estimating the degree of collectibility, companies should not recognize revenue until cash is collected.

> **OBJECTIVE 6**
> Describe the installment-sales method of accounting.

The expression "installment sales" generally describes any type of sale for which payment is required in periodic installments over an extended period of time. All types of farm and home equipment as well as home furnishings are sold on an installment basis. The heavy equipment industry also sometimes uses the method for machine installations paid for over a long period. Another application of the method is in land-development sales.

Because payment is spread over a relatively long period, the risk of loss resulting from uncollectible accounts is greater in installment-sales transactions than in ordinary sales. Consequently, selling companies use various devices to protect themselves. Two common devices are: (1) the use of a *conditional sales contract*, which specifies that title to the item sold does not pass to the purchaser until all payments are made, and (2) use of notes secured by a *chattel* (personal property) *mortgage* on the article sold. Either of these permits the seller to "repossess" the goods sold if the purchaser defaults on one or more payments. The seller can then resell the repossessed merchandise at whatever price it will bring to compensate for the uncollected installments and the expense of repossession.

> **UNDERLYING CONCEPTS**
>
> Realization is a critical part of revenue recognition. Thus, if a high degree of uncertainty exists about collectibility, a company must defer revenue recognition.

Under the installment-sales method of accounting, companies defer income recognition until the period of cash collection. They recognize both revenues and costs of sales in the period of sale, but defer the related gross profit to those periods in which they collect the cash. Thus, **instead of deferring the sale, along with related costs and expenses, to the future periods of anticipated collection, the company defers only the proportional gross profit**. This approach is equivalent to deferring both sales and cost of sales. Other expenses—that is, selling expense, administrative expense, and so on—are not deferred.

Thus, the installment-sales method matches cost and expenses against sales through the gross profit figure, but no further. Companies using the installment-sales method generally record operating expenses without regard to the fact that they will defer some portion of the year's gross profit. This practice is often justified on the basis that (1) these expenses do not follow sales as closely as does the cost of goods sold, and (2) accurate apportionment among periods would be so difficult that it could not be justified by the benefits gained.[30]

INTERNATIONAL INSIGHT

In Japan, installment method accounting is frequently used whenever the collection period exceeds two years, whether or not there is any uncertainty with regard to the collectibility of cash.

Acceptability of the Installment-Sales Method

The use of the installment-sales method for revenue recognition has fluctuated widely. At one time it was widely accepted for installment-sales transactions. Somewhat paradoxically, as installment-sales transactions increased in popularity, acceptance and

---

[30]In addition, other theoretical deficiencies of the installment-sales method could be cited. For example, see Richard A. Scott and Rita K. Scott, "Installment Accounting: Is It Inconsistent?" *The Journal of Accountancy* (November 1979).

use of the installment-sales method decreased. Finally the profession concluded that except in special circumstances, "the installment method of recognizing revenue is not acceptable."[31] The rationale for this position is simple: Because the installment method recognizes no income until cash is collected, it is not in accordance with the accrual accounting concept.

Use of the installment-sales method was often justified on the grounds that the risk of not collecting an account receivable may be so great that the sale itself is not sufficient evidence that recognition should occur. In some cases, this reasoning is valid, but not in a majority of cases. The general approach is that a company should recognize a completed sale. If the company expects bad debts, it should record this possibility as separate estimates of uncollectibles. Although collection expenses, re-possession expenses, and bad debts are an unavoidable part of installment-sales activities, the incurrence of these costs and the collectibility of the receivables are reasonably predictable.

We study this topic in intermediate accounting because the method is acceptable in cases where a company believes there to be no reasonable basis of estimating the degree of collectibility. In addition, the sales method of revenue recognition has certain weaknesses when used for franchise and land-development operations. Application of the sales method to **franchise and license operations** has resulted in the abuse described earlier as "front-end loading." In some cases, franchisors recognized revenue prematurely, when they granted a franchise or issued a license, rather than when revenue was earned or the cash is received. Many **land-development** ventures were susceptible to the same abuses. As a result, the FASB prescribes application of the installment-sales method of accounting for sales of real estate under certain circumstances.[32]

Procedure for Deferring Revenue and Cost of Sales of Merchandise

One could work out a procedure that deferred both the uncollected portion of the sales price and the proportionate part of the cost of the goods sold. Instead of apportioning both sales price and cost over the period of collection, however, the installment-sales method defers **only the gross profit**. This procedure has exactly the same effect as deferring both sales and cost of sales, but it requires only one deferred account rather than two.

For the **sales in any one year**, the steps companies use to defer gross profit are as follows.

1 During the year, record both sales and cost of sales in the regular way, using the special accounts described later, and compute the rate of gross profit on installment-sales transactions.

2 At the end of the year, apply the rate of gross profit to the cash collections of the current year's installment sales, to arrive at the realized gross profit.

3 Defer to future years the gross profit not realized.

For **sales made in prior years**, companies apply the gross profit rate of each year's sales against cash collections of accounts receivable resulting from that year's sales, to arrive at the realized gross profit.

---

[31]"Omnibus Opinion," *Opinions of the Accounting Principles Board No. 10* (New York: AICPA, 1966), par. 12.

[32]"Accounting for Sales of Real Estate," *Statement of Financial Accounting Standards No. 66* (Norwalk, Conn.: FASB, 1982), pars. 45–47. The installment-sales method of accounting must be applied to a retail land sale that meets **all** of the following criteria: (1) the period of cancellation of the sale with refund of the down payment and any subsequent payments has expired; (2) cumulative cash payments equal or exceed 10 percent of the sales value; and (3) the seller is financially capable of providing all promised contract representations (e.g., land improvements, off-site facilities).

Special accounts must be used in the installment-sales method. These accounts provide certain special information required to determine the realized and unrealized gross profit in each year of operations. In computing net income under the installment-sales method as generally applied, the only peculiarity is the **deferral of gross profit until realized by accounts receivable collection**. We will use the following data to illustrate the installment-sales method in accounting for the sales of merchandise.

	2007	2008	2009
Installment sales	$200,000	$250,000	$240,000
Cost of installment sales	150,000	190,000	168,000
Gross profit	$ 50,000	$ 60,000	$ 72,000
Rate of gross profit on sales	25%[a]	24%[b]	30%[c]
Cash receipts			
2007 sales	$ 60,000	$100,000	$ 40,000
2008 sales		100,000	125,000
2009 sales			80,000
	[a] $\frac{\$50,000}{\$200,000}$	[b] $\frac{\$60,000}{\$250,000}$	[c] $\frac{\$72,000}{\$240,000}$

To simplify this example, we have excluded interest charges. Summary entries in general journal form for the year 2007 are as follows.

2007

Installment Accounts Receivable, 2007	200,000	
Installment Sales		200,000
(To record sales made on installment in 2007)		
Cash	60,000	
Installment Accounts Receivable, 2007		60,000
(To record cash collected on installment receivables)		
Cost of Installment Sales	150,000	
Inventory (or Purchases)		150,000
(To record cost of goods sold on installment in 2007 on either a perpetual or a periodic inventory basis)		
Installment Sales	200,000	
Cost of Installment Sales		150,000
Deferred Gross Profit, 2007		50,000
(To close installment sales and cost of installment sales for the year)		
Deferred Gross Profit	15,000	
Realized Gross Profit on Installment Sales		15,000
(To remove from deferred gross profit the profit realized through cash collections; $60,000 × 25%)		
Realized Gross Profit on Installment Sales	15,000	
Income Summary		15,000
(To close profits realized by collections)		

Illustration 18-19 shows computation of the realized and deferred gross profit for the year 2007.

2007	
Rate of gross profit current year	25%
Cash collected on current year's sales	$60,000
Realized gross profit (25% of $60,000)	15,000
Gross profit to be deferred ($50,000 − $15,000)	35,000

ILLUSTRATION 18-19
Computation of Realized and Deferred Gross Profit, 2007

Summary entries in journal form for year 2 (2008) are as follows.

2008

Installment Accounts Receivable, 2008	250,000	
Installment Sales		250,000
(To record sales made on installment in 2008)		
Cash	200,000	
Installment Accounts Receivable, 2007		100,000
Installment Accounts Receivable, 2008		100,000
(To record cash collected on installment receivables)		
Cost of Installment Sales	190,000	
Inventory (or Purchases)		190,000
(To record cost of goods sold on installment in 2008)		
Installment Sales	250,000	
Cost of Installment Sales		190,000
Deferred Gross Profit, 2008		60,000
(To close installment sales and cost of installment sales for the year)		
Deferred Gross Profit, 2007 ($100,000 × 25%)	25,000	
Deferred Gross Profit, 2008 ($100,000 × 24%)	24,000	
Realized Gross Profit on Installment Sales		49,000
(To remove from deferred gross profit the profit realized		
through cash collections)		
Realized Gross Profit on Installment Sales	49,000	
Income Summary		49,000
(To close profits realized by collections)		

Illustration 18-20 shows computation of the realized and deferred gross profit for the year 2008.

ILLUSTRATION 18-20
Computation of Realized and Deferred Gross Profit, 2008

2008	
Current year's sales	
Rate of gross profit	24%
Cash collected on current year's sales	$100,000
Realized gross profit (24% of $100,000)	24,000
Gross profit to be deferred ($60,000 − $24,000)	36,000
Prior year's sales	
Rate of gross profit—2007	25%
Cash collected on 2007 sales	$100,000
Gross profit realized in 2008 on 2007 sales (25% of $100,000)	25,000
Total gross profit realized in 2008	
Realized on collections of 2007 sales	$ 25,000
Realized on collections of 2008 sales	24,000
Total	$ 49,000

The entries in 2009 would be similar to those of 2008, and the total gross profit taken up or realized would be $64,000, as shown by the computations in Illustration 18-21 (on page 927).

In summary, here are the basic concepts you should understand about accounting for installment sales:

1 How to compute a proper gross profit percentage.

2 How to record installment sales, cost of installment sales, and deferred gross profit.

3 How to compute realized gross profit on installment receivables.

4 How the deferred gross profit balance at the end of the year results from applying the gross profit rate to the installment accounts receivable.

ILLUSTRATION 18-21
Computation of Realized
and Deferred Gross
Profit, 2009

2009

Current year's sales
Rate of gross profit	30%
Cash collected on current year's sales	$ 80,000
Gross profit realized on 2009 sales (30% of $80,000)	24,000
Gross profit to be deferred ($72,000 − $24,000)	48,000

Prior years' sales
2007 sales
Rate of gross profit	25%
Cash collected	$ 40,000
Gross profit realized in 2009 on 2007 sales (25% of $40,000)	10,000

2008 sales
Rate of gross profit	24%
Cash collected	$125,000
Gross profit realized in 2009 on 2008 sales (24% of $125,000)	30,000

Total gross profit realized in 2009
Realized on collections of 2007 sales	$ 10,000
Realized on collections of 2008 sales	30,000
Realized on collections of 2009 sales	24,000
Total	$ 64,000

Additional Problems of Installment-Sales Accounting

In addition to computing realized and deferred gross profit currently, other problems are involved in accounting for installment-sales transactions. These problems are related to:

1 Interest on installment contracts.

2 Uncollectible accounts.

3 Defaults and repossessions.

Interest on Installment Contracts. Because the collection of installment receivables is spread over a long period, it is customary to charge the buyer interest on the unpaid balance. The seller and buyer set up a schedule of equal payments consisting of interest and principal. Each successive payment is attributable to a smaller amount of interest and a correspondingly larger amount of principal, as shown in Illustration 18-22. This illustration assumes that a company sells for $3,000 an asset costing $2,400 (rate of gross profit = 20%), with interest of 8 percent included in the three installments of $1,164.10.

ILLUSTRATION 18-22
Installment Payment
Schedule

Date	Cash (Debit)	Interest Earned (Credit)	Installment Receivables (Credit)	Installment Unpaid Balance	Realized Gross Profit (20%)
1/2/07	—	—	—	$3,000.00	—
1/2/08	$1,164.10[a]	$240.00[b]	$ 924.10[c]	2,075.90[d]	$184.82[e]
1/2/09	1,164.10	166.07	998.03	1,077.87	199.61
1/2/10	1,164.10	86.23	1,077.87	−0−	215.57
					$600.00

[a]Periodic payment = Original unpaid balance ÷ PV of an annuity of $1.00 for three periods at 8%;
$1,164.10 = $3,000 ÷ 2.57710.
[b]$3,000.00 × .08 = $240.
[c]$1,164.10 − $240.00 = $924.10.
[d]$3,000.00 − $924.10 = $2,075.90.
[e]$924.10 × .20 = $184.82.

The company accounts for interest separate from the gross profit recognized on the installment-sales collections during the period, by recognizing interest revenue at the time of its cash receipt.

Uncollectible Accounts. The problem of bad debts or uncollectible accounts receivable is somewhat different for concerns selling on an installment basis because of a repossession feature commonly incorporated in the sales agreement. This feature gives the selling company an opportunity to recoup an uncollectible account through repossession and resale of repossessed merchandise. If the experience of the company indicates that repossessions do not, as a rule, compensate for uncollecible balances, it may be advisable to provide for such losses through charges to a special bad debt expense account, just as is done for other credit sales.

Defaults and Repossessions. Depending on the terms of the sales contract and the policy of the credit department, the seller can repossess merchandise sold under an installment arrangement if the purchaser fails to meet payment requirements. The seller may then recondition repossessed merchandise before offering it for re-sale, for cash or installment payments.

The accounting for **repossessions** recognizes that the company is not likely to collect the related installment receivable and should write it off. Along with the installment account receivable, the company must remove the applicable deferred gross profit using the following entry:

Repossessed Merchandise (an inventory account)	xxx	
Deferred Gross Profit	xxx	
Installment Accounts Receivable		xxx

This entry assumes that the company will record the repossessed merchandise at exactly the amount of the uncollected account less the deferred gross profit applicable. This assumption may or may not be proper. To determine the correct amount, the company should consider the condition of the repossessed merchandise, the cost of reconditioning, and the market for second-hand merchandise of that particular type. The objective should be to put any asset acquired on the books at its fair value, or at the best possible approximation of fair value when fair value is not determinable. A loss can occur if the fair value of the repossessed merchandise is less than the uncollected balance less the deferred gross profit. In that case, the company should record a "loss on repossession" at the date of repossession.[33]

To illustrate the required entry, assume that Klein Brothers sells a refrigerator to Marilyn Hunt for $1,500 on September 1, 2007. Terms require a down payment of $600 and $60 on the first of every month for 15 months, starting October 1, 2007. It is further assumed that the refrigerator cost $900, and that Klein Brothers priced it to provide a 40 percent rate of gross profit on selling price. At the year-end, December 31, 2007, Klein Brothers should have collected a total of $180 in addition to the original down payment.

If Hunt makes her January and February payments in 2008 and then defaults, the account balances applicable to Hunt at time of default are as shown in Illustration 18-23.

ILLUSTRATION 18-23
Computation of Installment Receivable Balances

Installment accounts receivable (September 1, 2007)		$1,500
Less: Down payment:	$600	
Payments to date ($60 × 5)	300	900
Installment accounts receivable (March 1, 2008)		$ 600
Installment accounts receivable (March 1, 2008)		$600
Gross profit rate		× 40%
Deferred gross profit		$240

---

[33]Some contend that a company should record repossessed merchandise at a valuation that will permit the company to make its regular rate of gross profit on resale. If the company enters the value at its approximated cost to purchase, the regular rate of gross profit could be provided for upon its ultimate sale, but that is completely a secondary consideration. It is more important that the company record the repossessed asset at fair value. This accounting would be in accordance with the general practice of carrying assets at acquisition price, as represented by the fair market value at the date of acquisition.

As indicated, Klein Brothers compute the balance of deferred gross profit applicable to Hunt's account by applying the gross profit rate for the year of sale to the balance of Hunt's account receivable: 40 percent of $600, or $240. The account balances are therefore:

Installment Account Receivable, 2007	600 (dr.)
Deferred Gross Profit, 2007	240 (cr.)

Klein repossesses the refrigerator following Hunt's default. If Klein sets the estimated fair value of the repossessed article at $150, it would make the following entry to record the repossession.

Deferred Gross Profit, 2007	240	
Repossessed Merchandise	150	
Loss on Repossession	210	
Installment Accounts Receivable, 2007		600

Klein determines the amount of the loss in two steps: (1) It subtracts the deferred gross profit from the amount of the account receivable, to determine the unrecovered cost (or book value) of the merchandise repossessed. (2) It then subtracts the estimated fair value of the merchandise repossessed from the unrecovered cost, to get the amount of the loss on repossession. Klein Brothers computes the loss on the refrigerator as shown in Illustration 18-24.

Balance of account receivable (representing uncollected selling price)	$600
Less: Deferred gross profit	240
Unrecovered cost	360
Less: Estimated fair value of merchandise repossessed	150
Loss (Gain) on repossession	$210

ILLUSTRATION 18-24
Computation of Loss on Repossession

As pointed out earlier, the loss on repossession may be charged to Allowance for Doubtful Accounts if a company carries such an account.

Financial Statement Presentation of Installment-Sales Transactions

If installment-sales transactions represent a significant part of total sales, it is desirable to make full disclosure of installment sales, the cost of installment sales, and any expenses allocable to installment sales. However, if installment-sales transactions constitute an insignificant part of total sales, it may be satisfactory to include only the realized gross profit in the income statement as a special item following the gross profit on sales. Illustration 18-25 shows this simpler presentation.

HEALTH MACHINE COMPANY
INCOME STATEMENT
FOR THE YEAR ENDED DECEMBER 31, 2008

Sales	$620,000
Cost of goods sold	490,000
Gross profit on sales	130,000
Gross profit realized on installment sales	51,000
Total gross profit on sales	$181,000

ILLUSTRATION 18-25
Disclosure of Installment-Sales Transactions—Insignificant Amount

If a company wants more complete disclosure of installment-sales transactions, it would use a presentation similar to that shown in Illustration 18-26 (on page 930).

ILLUSTRATION 18-26
Disclosure of Installment-
Sales Transactions—
Significant Amount

	Installment Sales	Other Sales	Total
HEALTH MACHINE COMPANY			
INCOME STATEMENT			
FOR THE YEAR ENDED DECEMBER 31, 2008			
Sales	$248,000	$620,000	$868,000
Cost of goods sold	182,000	490,000	672,000
Gross profit on sales	66,000	130,000	196,000
Less: Deferred gross profit on installment sales of this year	47,000		47,000
Realized gross profit on this year's sales	19,000	130,000	149,000
Add: Gross profit realized on installment sales of prior years	32,000		32,000
Gross profit realized this year	$ 51,000	$130,000	$181,000

The presentation in Illustration 18-26 is awkward. Yet the awkwardness of this method is difficult to avoid if a company wants to provide full disclosure of install-ment-sales transactions in the income statement. One solution, of course, is to prepare a separate schedule showing installment-sales transactions, with only the final figure carried into the income statement.

In the balance sheet it is generally considered desirable to classify installment ac-counts receivable by year of collectibility. There is some question as to whether com-panies should include in current assets installment accounts that are not collectible for two or more years. Yet if installment sales are **part of normal operations**, companies may consider them as current assets because they are collectible within the operating cycle of the business. Little confusion should result from this practice if the company fully discloses maturity dates, as illustrated in the following example.

ILLUSTRATION 18-27
Disclosure of Installment
Accounts Receivable,
by Year

Current assets		
Notes and accounts receivable		
Trade customers	$78,800	
Less: Allowance for doubtful accounts	3,700	
	75,100	
Installment accounts collectible in 2008	22,600	
Installment accounts collectible in 2009	47,200	$144,900

On the other hand, a company may have receivables from an installment contract, resulting from a transaction not related to normal operations. In that case, the company should report such receivable in the "Other assets" section if due beyond one year.

Repossessed merchandise is a part of inventory, and companies should report it as such in the "Current assets" section of the balance sheet. They should include any gain or loss on repossession in the income statement in the "Other revenues and gains" or "Other expenses and losses" section.

If a company has **deferred gross profit on installment sales**, it generally treats it as unearned revenue and classifies it as a current liability. Theoretically, deferred gross profit consists of three elements: (1) income tax liability to be paid when the sales are reported as realized revenue (current liability); (2) allowance for collection expense, bad debts, and repossession losses (deduction from installment accounts receivable); and (3) net income (retained earnings, restricted as to dividend availability). Because of the difficulty in allocating deferred gross profit among these three elements, however, com-panies frequently report the whole amount as unearned revenue.

In contrast, the FASB in *SFAC No. 6* states that "no matter how it is displayed in financial statements, deferred gross profit on installment sales is conceptually an asset valuation—that is, a reduction of an asset."[34] We support the FASB position, but we recognize that until an official standard on this topic is issued, financial statements will probably continue to report such deferred gross profit as a current liability.

Cost-Recovery Method

Under the **cost-recovery method**, a company recognizes no profit until cash payments by the buyer exceed the cost of the merchandise sold. After the seller has recovered all costs, it includes in income any additional cash collections. The seller's income statement for the period reports sales revenue, the cost of goods sold, and the gross profit— both the amount (if any) that is recognized during the period and the amount that is deferred. The deferred gross profit is offset against the related receivable—reduced by collections—on the balance sheet. Subsequent income statements report the gross profit as a separate item of revenue when the company recognizes it as earned.

> **OBJECTIVE 7**
> Explain the cost-recovery method of accounting.

APB Opinion No. 10 allows a seller to use the cost-recovery method to account for sales in which "there is no reasonable basis for estimating collectibility." In addition, *FASB Statements No. 45* (franchises) and *No. 66* (real estate) require use of this method where a high degree of uncertainty exists related to the collection of receivables.[35]

To illustrate the cost-recovery method, assume that early in 2007, Fesmire Manufacturing sells inventory with a cost of $25,000 to Higley Company for $36,000. Higley will make payments of $18,000 in 2007, $12,000 in 2008, and $6,000 in 2009. If the cost-recovery method applies to this transaction and Higley makes the payments as scheduled, Fesmire recognizes cash collections, revenue, cost, and gross profit as follows.[36]

	2007	2008	2009
Cash collected	$18,000	$12,000	$6,000
Revenue	$36,000	–0–	–0–
Cost of goods sold	25,000	–0–	–0–
Deferred gross profit	11,000	$11,000	$6,000
Recognized gross profit	–0–	5,000*	6,000
Deferred gross profit balance (end of period)	$11,000	$ 6,000	$ –0–

*$25,000 − $18,000 = $7,000 of unrecovered cost at the end of 2007; $12,000 − $7,000 = $5,000, the excess of cash received in 2008 over unrecovered cost.

ILLUSTRATION 18-28
Computation of Gross Profit—Cost-Recovery Method

Under the cost-recovery method, Fesmire reports total revenue and cost of goods sold in the period of sale, similar to the installment-sales method. However, unlike the installment-sales method, which recognizes income as cash is collected, Fesmire recognizes profit under the cost-recovery method **only when cash collections exceed the total cost of the goods sold.**

---

[34]*See Statement of Financial Accounting Concepts No. 6*, pars. 232–234.

[35]"Omnibus Opinion—1966," *Opinions of the Accounting Principles Board No. 10* (New York: AICPA, 1969), footnote 8, page 149; "Accounting for Franchise Fee Revenue," *Statement of Financial Accounting Standards No. 45* (Stamford, Conn.: FASB, 1981), par. 6; "Accounting for Sales of Real Estate," *Statement of Financial Accounting Standards No. 66*, pars. 62 and 63.

[36]An alternative format for computing the amount of gross profit recognized annually is shown below.

Year	Cash Received	Original Cost Recovered	Balance of Unrecovered Cost	Gross Profit Realized
Beginning balance	—	—	$25,000	—
12/31/07	$18,000	$18,000	7,000	$ –0–
12/31/08	12,000	7,000	–0–	5,000
12/31/09	6,000	–0–	–0–	6,000

Therefore, Fesmire's journal entry to record the deferred gross profit on the Higley sale transaction (after recording the sale and the cost of sale in the normal manner) at the end of 2007 is as follows.

2007

Sales	36,000	
Cost of Sales		25,000
Deferred Gross Profit		11,000
(To close sales and cost of sales and to record deferred gross profit on sales accounted for under the cost-recovery method)		

In 2008 and 2009, the deferred gross profit becomes realized gross profit as the cumulative cash collections exceed the total costs, by recording the following entries.

2008

Deferred Gross Profit	5,000	
Realized Gross Profit		5,000
(To recognize gross profit to the extent that cash collections in 2008 exceed costs)		

2009

Deferred Gross Profit	6,000	
Realized Gross Profit		6,000
(To recognize gross profit to the extent that cash collections in 2009 exceed costs)		

WHAT DO THE NUMBERS MEAN?

LIABILILTY OR REVENUE?

Suppose you purchased a gift card for spa services at Sundara Spa for $300. The gift card expires at the end of six months. When should Sundara record the revenue? Here are two choices:

1 At the time Sundara receives the cash for the gift card.

2 At the time Sundara provides the service to the gift-card holder.

If you answered number 2, you would be right. Companies should recognize revenue when the obligation is satisfied—which is when Sundara performs the service.

Now let's add a few more facts. Suppose that the gift-card holder fails to use the card in the six-month period. Statistics show that between 2 and 15 percent of gift-card holders never redeem their cards. So, do you still believe that Sundara should record the revenue at the expiration date?

If you say you are not sure, you are probably right. Here is why: Certain states (such as California) do not recognize expiration dates, and therefore the customer has the right to redeem an otherwise expired gift card at any time. Let's for the moment say we are in California. Because the card holder may never redeem, when can Sundara recognize the revenue? In that case Sundara would have to show statistically that after a certain period of time, the likelihood of redemption is remote. If it can make that case, it can recognize the revenue. Otherwise it may have to wait a long time.

Unfortunately Sundara may still have a problem. It may be required to turn over the value of the spa service to the state. The treatment for unclaimed gift cards may fall under the state abandoned-and-unclaimed-property laws. Most common unclaimed items are required to be remitted to the states after a five-year period. Failure to report and remit the property can result in additional fines and penalties. So if Sundara is in a state where unclaimed property must be sent to the state, Sundara should report a liability on its balance sheet.

Source: PricewaterhouseCoopers, "Issues Surrounding the Recognition of Gift Card Sales and Escheat Liabilities," *Quick Brief* (December 2004).

Deposit Method

In some cases, a company receives cash from the buyer before it transfers the goods or property. In such cases the seller has not performed under the contract and has no claim against the purchaser. There is not sufficient transfer of the risks and rewards of ownership for a sale to be recorded. The method of accounting for these incomplete transactions is the **deposit method**.

Under the deposit method the seller reports the cash received from the buyer as a deposit on the contract and classifies it on the balance sheet as a liability (refundable deposit or customer advance). The seller continues to report the property as an asset on its balance sheet, along with any related existing debt. Also, the seller continues to charge depreciation expense as a period cost for the property. **The seller does not recognize revenue or income until the sale is complete.**[37] At that time, it closes the deposit account and applies one of the revenue recognition methods discussed in this chapter to the sale.

The **major difference between the installment-sales and cost-recovery methods and the deposit method** relates to contract performance. In the installment-sales and cost-recovery methods it is assumed that the seller has performed on the contract, but cash collection is highly uncertain. In the deposit method, the seller has *not* performed and no legitimate claim exists. The deposit method postpones recognizing a sale until the company determines that a sale has occurred for accounting purposes. If there has not been sufficient transfer of risks and rewards of ownership, even if the selling company has received a deposit, the company postpones recognition of the sale until sufficient transfer has occurred. In that sense, the deposit method is not a revenue recognition method as are the installment-sales and cost-recovery methods.

Summary of Product Revenue Recognition Bases

Illustration 18-29 summarizes the revenue-recognition bases or methods, the criteria for their use, and the reasons for departing from the sale basis.[38]

ILLUSTRATION 18-29
Revenue Recognition Bases Other Than the Sale Basis for Products

Recognition Basis (or Method of Applying a Basis)	Criteria for Use	Reason(s) for Departing from Sale Basis
Percentage-of-completion method	Long-term construction of property; dependable estimates of extent of progress and cost to complete; reasonable assurance of collectibility of contract price; expectation that both contractor and buyer can meet obligations; and absence of inherent hazards that make estimates doubtful.	Availability of evidence of ultimate proceeds; better measure of periodic income; avoidance of fluctuations in revenues, expenses, and income; performance is a "continuous sale" and therefore not a departure from the sale basis.
Completed-contract method	Use on short-term contracts, and whenever percentage-of-completion cannot be used on long-term contracts.	Existence of inherent hazards in the contract beyond the normal, recurring business risks; conditions for using the percentage-of-completion method are absent.
Completion-of-production basis	Immediate marketability at quoted prices; unit interchangeability; and no significant distribution costs.	Known or determinable revenues; inability to determine costs and thereby defer expense recognition until sale.
Installment-sales method and cost-recovery method	Absence of reasonable basis for estimating degree of collectibility and costs of collection.	Collectibility of the receivable is so uncertain that gross profit (or income) is not recognized until cash is actually received.
Deposit method	Cash received before the sales transaction is completed.	No recognition of revenue and income because there is not sufficient transfer of the risks and rewards of ownership.

---

[37] *Statement of Financial Accounting Standards No. 66*, par. 65.

[38] Adapted from *Survey of Present Practices in Recognizing Revenues, Expenses, Gains, and Losses,* op. cit., pp. 12–13.

CONCLUDING REMARKS

INTERNATIONAL INSIGHT

There is no international enforcement body comparable to the U.S. SEC.

As indicated, revenue recognition principles are sometimes difficult to apply and often vary by industry. Recently the SEC has attempted to provide more guidance in this area because of concern that the revenue recognition principle is sometimes being incorrectly applied. Many cases of intentional misstatement of revenue to achieve better financial results have recently come to light. Such practices are fraudulent, and the SEC is vigorously prosecuting these situations.

For our capital markets to be efficient, investors must have confidence that the financial information provided is both relevant and reliable. As a result, it is imperative that the accounting profession, regulators, and companies eliminate aggressive revenue recognition practices. It is our hope that recent efforts by the SEC and the accounting profession will lead to higher-quality reporting in this area.

KEY TERMS

Billings account, *916*

completed-contract method, *912, 918*

completion-of-production basis, *922*

cost-recovery method, *931*

cost-to-cost basis, *913*

deposit method, *933*

earned revenues, *908*

high rate of returns, *910*

input measures, *913*

installment-sales method, *923*

output measures, *913*

percentage-of-completion method, *912, 913*

point of sale (delivery), *909*

realizable revenues, *908*

realized revenues, *908*

repossessions, *928*

revenue recognition principle, *907*

SUMMARY OF LEARNING OBJECTIVES

1. Apply the revenue recognition principle. The revenue recognition principle provides that a company should recognize revenue (1) when revenue is realized or realizable and (2) when it is earned. Revenues are realized when goods or services are exchanged for cash or claims to cash. Revenues are realizable when assets received in exchanges are readily convertible to known amounts of cash or claims to cash. Revenues are earned when a company has substantially accomplished what it must do to be entitled to the benefits represented by the revenues—that is, when the earnings process is complete or virtually complete.

2. Describe accounting issues for revenue recognition at point of sale. The two conditions for recognizing revenue are usually met by the time a company delivers products or merchandise or provides services to customers. Companies commonly recognize revenue from manufacturing and selling activities at time of sale. Problems of implementation can arise because of (1) sales with buyback agreements, (2) revenue recognition when right of return exists, and (3) trade loading and channel stuffing.

3. Apply the percentage-of-completion method for long-term contracts. To apply the percentage-of-completion method to long-term contracts, a company must have some basis for measuring the progress toward completion at particular interim dates. One of the most popular input measures used to determine the progress toward completion is the cost-to-cost basis. Using this basis, a company measures the percentage of completion by comparing costs incurred to date with the most recent estimate of the total costs to complete the contract. The company applies that percentage to the total revenue or the estimated total gross profit on the contract, to arrive at the amount of revenue or gross profit to be recognized to date.

4. Apply the completed-contract method for long-term contracts. Under this method, companies recognize revenue and gross profit only at point of sale—that is, when the company completes the contract. The company accumulates costs of long-term contracts in process and current billings. It makes no interim charges or credits to income statement accounts for revenues, costs, and gross profit. The annual entries to record costs of construction, progress billings, and collections from customers would be identical to those for the percentage-of-completion method—with the significant exclusion of the recognition of revenue and gross profit.

5. Identify the proper accounting for losses on long-term contracts. Two types of losses can become evident under long-term contracts: (1) *Loss in current period on a profitable contract*: Under the percentage-of-completion method only, the estimated cost increase requires a current-period adjustment of excess gross profit recognized on the project in prior periods. The company records this adjustment as a loss in the current period because it is a change in accounting estimate. (2) *Loss on an unprofitable contract*: Under both the percentage-of-completion and the completed-contract methods, the company must recognize the entire expected contract loss in the current period.

6. **Describe the installment-sales method of accounting.** The installment-sales method recognizes income in the periods of collection rather than in the period of sale. The installment-sales method of accounting is justified on the basis that when there is no reasonable approach for estimating the degree of collectibility, a company should not recognize revenue until it has collected cash.

7. **Explain the cost-recovery method of accounting.** Under the cost-recovery method, companies do not recognize profit until cash payments by the buyer exceed the seller's cost of the merchandise sold. After the seller has recovered all costs, it includes in income any additional cash collections. The income statement for the period of sale reports sales revenue, the cost of goods sold, and the gross profit—both the amount recognized during the period and the amount deferred. The deferred gross profit is offset against the related receivable on the balance sheet. Subsequent income statements report the gross profit as a separate item of revenue when revenue is recognized as earned.

APPENDIX 18A

Revenue Recognition for Special Sales Transactions

To supplement our presentation of revenue recognition, in this appendix we cover two common yet unique types of business transactions—**franchises** and **consignments**.

FRANCHISES

As indicated throughout this chapter, companies recognize revenue on the basis of two criteria: (1) when it is realized or realizable (occurrence of an exchange for cash or claims to cash), and (2) when it is earned (completion or virtual completion of the earnings process). These criteria are appropriate for most business activities. For some sales transactions, though, they do not adequately define when a company should recognize revenue. The fast-growing franchise industry is of special concern and challenge.

In accounting for franchise sales, a company must analyze the transaction and, considering all the circumstances, use judgment in selecting one or more of the revenue recognition bases, and then possibly must monitor the situation over a long period of time.

Four types of franchising arrangements have evolved: (1) manufacturer-retailer, (2) manufacturer-wholesaler, (3) service sponsor-retailer, and (4) wholesaler-retailer. The fastest-growing category of franchising, and the one that caused a reexamination of appropriate accounting, has been the third category, **service sponsor-retailer**. Included in this category are such industries and businesses as:

Soft ice cream/frozen yogurt stores (**Tastee Freeze, TCBY, Dairy Queen**)

Food drive-ins (**McDonald's, KFC, Burger King**)

Restaurants (**TGI Friday's, Pizza Hut, Denny's**)

> **OBJECTIVE 8**
> **Explain revenue recognition for franchises and consignment sales.**

Motels (**Holiday Inn, Marriott, Best Western**)

Auto rentals (**Avis, Hertz, National**)

Others (**H & R Block, Meineke Mufflers, 7-Eleven Stores, Kelly Services**)

Franchise companies derive their revenue from one or both of two sources: (1) from the sale of initial franchises and related assets or services, and (2) from continuing fees based on the operations of franchises. The **franchisor** (the party who grants business rights under the franchise) normally provides the **franchisee** (the party who operates the franchised business) with the following services.

1 Assistance in site selection: (a) analyzing location and (b) negotiating lease.

2 Evaluation of potential income.

3 Supervision of construction activity: (a) obtaining financing, (b) designing building, and (c) supervising contractor while building.

4 Assistance in the acquisition of signs, fixtures, and equipment.

5 Bookkeeping and advisory services: (a) setting up franchisee's records; (b) advising on income, real estate, and other taxes; and (c) advising on local regulations of the franchisee's business.

6 Employee and management training.

7 Quality control.

8 Advertising and promotion.[1]

In the past, it was standard practice for franchisors to recognize the entire franchise fee at the date of sale, whether the fee was received then or was collectible over a long period of time. Frequently, franchisors recorded the entire amount as revenue in the year of sale, even though many of the services were yet to be performed and uncertainty existed regarding the collection of the entire fee.[2] (In effect, the franchisors were counting their fried chickens before they were hatched.) However, a **franchise agreement** may provide for refunds to the franchisee if certain conditions are not met, and franchise fee profit can be reduced sharply by future costs of obligations and services to be rendered by the franchisor. To curb the abuses in revenue recognition that existed and to standardize the accounting and reporting practices in the franchise industry, the FASB issued *Statement No. 45*, which forms the basis for the accounting discussed below.

Initial Franchise Fees

The **initial franchise fee** is payment for establishing the franchise relationship and providing some initial services. Franchisors record initial franchise fees as revenue only when and as they make "substantial performance" of the services they are obligated to perform and when collection of the fee is reasonably assured. **Substantial performance** occurs when the franchisor has no remaining obligation to refund any cash received or excuse any nonpayment of a note and has performed all the initial services required under the contract. According to *SFAS No. 45* "commencement of operations by the franchisee shall be presumed to be the earliest point at which substantial performance has occurred, unless it can be demonstrated that substantial performance of all obligations, including services rendered voluntarily, has occurred before that time."[3]

---

[1]Archibald E. MacKay, "Accounting for Initial Franchise Fee Revenue," *The Journal of Accountancy* (January 1970), pp. 66–67.

[2]In 1987 and 1988 the SEC ordered a half-dozen fast-growing startup franchisors, including **Jiffy Lube International, Moto Photo, Inc., Swensen's, Inc.,** and **LePeep Restaurants, Inc.,** to defer their initial franchise fee recognition until earned. See "Claiming Tomorrow's Profits Today," *Forbes* (October 17, 1988), p. 78.

[3]"Accounting for Franchise Fee Revenue," *Statement of Financial Accounting Standards No. 45* (Stamford, Conn.: FASB, 1981), par. 5.

Example of Entries for Initial Franchise Fee

To illustrate, assume that Tum's Pizza Inc. charges an initial franchise fee of $50,000 for the right to operate as a franchisee of Tum's Pizza. Of this amount, $10,000 is payable when the franchisee signs the agreement, and the balance is payable in five annual payments of $8,000 each. In return for the initial franchise fee, Tum's will help locate the site, negotiate the lease or purchase of the site, supervise the construction activity, and provide the bookkeeping services. The credit rating of the franchisee indicates that money can be borrowed at 8 percent. The present value of an ordinary annuity of five annual receipts of $8,000 each discounted at 8 percent is $31,941.68. The discount of $8,058.32 represents the interest revenue to be accrued by the franchisor over the payment period. The following examples show the entries that Tum's Pizza Inc. would make under various conditions.

1 If there is reasonable expectation that Tum's Pizza Inc. may refund the down payment and if substantial future services remain to be performed by Tum's Pizza Inc., the entry should be:

Cash	10,000.00	
Notes Receivable	40,000.00	
Discount on Notes Receivable		8,058.32
Unearned Franchise Fees		41,941.68

2 If the probability of refunding the initial franchise fee is extremely low, the amount of future services to be provided to the franchisee is minimal, collectibility of the note is reasonably assured, and substantial performance has occurred, the entry should be:

Cash	10,000.00	
Notes Receivable	40,000.00	
Discount on Notes Receivable		8,058.32
Revenue from Franchise Fees		41,941.68

3 If the initial down payment is not refundable, represents a fair measure of the services already provided, with a significant amount of services still to be performed by Tum's Pizza in future periods, and collectibility of the note is reasonably assured, the entry should be:

Cash	10,000.00	
Notes Receivable	40,000.00	
Discount on Notes Receivable		8,058.32
Revenue from Franchise Fees		10,000.00
Unearned Franchise Fees		31,941.68

4 If the initial down payment is not refundable and no future services are required by the franchisor, but collection of the note is so uncertain that recognition of the note as an asset is unwarranted, the entry should be:

Cash	10,000.00	
Revenue from Franchise Fees		10,000.00

5 Under the same conditions as those listed in case 4 above, except that the down payment is refundable or substantial services are yet to be performed, the entry should be:

Cash	10,000.00	
Unearned Franchise Fees		10,000.00

In cases 4 and 5—where collection of the note is extremely uncertain—franchisors may recognize cash collections using the installment-sales method or the cost-recovery method.[4]

---

[4]A study that compared four revenue recognition procedures—installment-sales basis, spreading recognition over the contract life, percentage-of-completion basis, and substantial performance—for franchise sales concluded that the percentage-of-completion method is the most acceptable revenue recognition method; the substantial-performance method was found sometimes to yield ultra-conservative results. See Charles H. Calhoun III, "Accounting for Initial Franchise Fees: Is It a Dead Issue?" *The Journal of Accountancy* (February 1975), pp. 60–67.

Continuing Franchise Fees

Continuing franchise fees are received in return for the continuing rights granted by the franchise agreement and for providing such services as management training, advertising and promotion, legal assistance, and other support. Franchisors report continuing fees as revenue when they are earned and receivable from the franchisee, unless a portion of them has been designated for a particular purpose, such as providing a specified amount for building maintenance or local advertising. In that case, the portion deferred shall be an amount sufficient to cover the estimated cost in excess of continuing franchise fees and provide a reasonable profit on the continuing services.

Bargain Purchases

In addition to paying continuing franchise fees, franchisees frequently purchase some or all of their equipment and supplies from the franchisor. The franchisor would account for these sales as it would for any other product sales.

Sometimes, however, the franchise agreement grants the franchisee the right to make **bargain purchases** of equipment or supplies after the franchisee has paid the initial franchise fee. If the bargain price is lower than the normal selling price of the same product, or if it does not provide the franchisor a reasonable profit, then the franchisor should defer a portion of the initial franchise fee. The franchisor would account for the deferred portion as an adjustment of the selling price when the franchisee subsequently purchases the equipment or supplies.

Options to Purchase

A franchise agreement may give the franchisor an **option to purchase** the franchisee's business. As a matter of management policy, the franchisor may reserve the right to purchase a profitable franchise outlet, or to purchase one that is in financial difficulty.

If it is **probable** at the time the option is given that the franchisor will ultimately purchase the outlet, then the franchisor should not recognize the initial franchise fee as revenue but should instead record it as a liability. When the franchisor exercises the option, the liability would reduce the franchisor's investment in the outlet.

Franchisor's Cost

Franchise accounting also involves proper accounting for the **franchisor's cost**. The objective is to match related costs and revenues by reporting them as components of income in the same accounting period. Franchisors should ordinarily defer **direct costs** (usually incremental costs) relating to specific franchise sales for which revenue has not yet been recognized. They should not, however, defer costs without reference to anticipated revenue and its realizability.[5] **Indirect costs** of a regular and recurring nature, such as selling and administrative expenses that are incurred irrespective of the level of franchise sales, should be expensed as incurred.

Disclosures of Franchisors

Franchisors must disclose all significant commitments and obligations resulting from franchise agreements, including a description of services that have not yet been substantially performed. They also should disclose any resolution of uncertainties regarding the collectibility of franchise fees. Franchisors segregate initial franchise fees from other franchise fee revenue if they are significant. Where possible, revenues and costs related to franchisor-owned outlets should be distinguished from those related to franchised outlets.

---

[5]"Accounting for Franchise Fee Revenue," p. 17.

CONSIGNMENTS

In some cases, manufacturers (or wholesalers) deliver goods but retain title to the goods until they are sold. This specialized method of marketing certain types of products makes use of a device known as a **consignment**. Under this arrangement, the **consignor** (manufacturer or wholesaler) ships merchandise to the **consignee** (dealer), who is to act as an agent for the consignor in selling the merchandise. Both consignor and consignee are interested in selling—the former to make a profit or develop a market, the latter to make a commission on the sale.

The consignee accepts the merchandise and agrees to exercise due diligence in caring for and selling it. The consignee remits to the consignor cash received from customers, after deducting a sales commission and any chargeable expenses.

In consignment sales, the consignor uses a modified version of the sale basis of revenue recognition. That is, the consignor recognizes revenue only after receiving notification of sale and the cash remittance from the consignee. The consignor carries the merchandise as inventory throughout the consignment, separately classified as Merchandise on Consignment. **The consignee does not record the merchandise as an asset on its books.** Upon sale of the merchandise, the consignee has **a liability for the net amount due the consignor**. The consignor periodically receives from the consignee a report called **account sales** that shows the merchandise received, merchandise sold, expenses chargeable to the consignment, and the cash remitted. Revenue is then recognized by the consignor.

To illustrate consignment accounting entries, assume that Nelba Manufacturing Co. ships merchandise costing $36,000 on consignment to Best Value Stores. Nelba pays $3,750 of freight costs, and Best Value pays $2,250 for local advertising costs that are reimbursable from Nelba. By the end of the period, Best Value has sold two-thirds of the consigned merchandise for $40,000 cash. Best Value notifies Nelba of the sales, retains a 10 percent commission, and remits the cash due Nelba. Illustration 18A-1 shows the journal entries of the consignor (Nelba) and the consignee (Best Value).

NELBA MFG. CO. (CONSIGNOR)			BEST VALUE STORES (CONSIGNEE)		
Shipment of consigned merchandise					
Inventory on Consignment	36,000		No entry (record memo of merchandise received).		
Finished Goods Inventory		36,000			
Payment of freight costs by consignor					
Inventory on Consignment	3,750		No entry.		
Cash		3,750			
Payment of advertising by consignee					
No entry until notified.			Receivable from Consignor	2,250	
			Cash		2,250
Sales of consigned merchandise					
No entry until notified.			Cash	40,000	
			Payable to Consignor		40,000
Notification of sales and expenses and remittance of amount due					
Cash	33,750		Payable to Consignor	40,000	
Advertising Expense	2,250		Receivable from		
Commission Expense	4,000		Consignor		2,250
Revenue from			Commission Revenue		4,000
Consignment Sales		40,000	Cash		33,750
Adjustment of inventory on consignment for cost of sales					
Cost of Goods Sold	26,500		No entry.		
Inventory on Consignment		26,500			
[2/3 ($36,000 + $3,750) = $26,500]					

ILLUSTRATION 18A-1
Entries for Consignment Sales

Under the consignment arrangement, the consignor accepts the risk that the merchandise might not sell and relieves the consignee of the need to commit part of its working capital to inventory. Companies use a variety of different systems and account titles to record consignments, but they all share the common goal of postponing the recognition of revenue until it is known that a sale to a third party has occurred.

SUMMARY OF LEARNING OBJECTIVE FOR APPENDIX 18A

8. Explain revenue recognition for franchises and consignment sales. In a franchise arrangement, the franchisor records as revenue the initial franchise fee as it makes substantial performance of the services it is obligated to perform and collection of the fee is reasonably assured. Franchisors recognize continuing franchise fees as revenue when they are earned and receivable from the franchisee. In a consignment sale, the consignor recognizes revenue when it receives cash and notification of the sale from the consignee.

Note: All **asterisked** Questions, Brief Exercises, Exercises, and Concepts for Analysis relate to material contained in the appendix to the chapter.

QUESTIONS

1. Explain the current environment regarding revenue recognition.

2. When is revenue conventionally recognized? What conditions should exist for the recognition at date of sale of all or part of the revenue and income of any sale transaction?

3. When is revenue recognized in the following situations: (a) Revenue from selling products? (b) Revenue from services rendered? (c) Revenue from permitting others to use enterprise assets? (d) Revenue from disposing of assets other than products?

4. Identify several types of sales transactions and indicate the types of business for which that type of transaction is common.

5. What are the three alternative accounting methods available to a seller that is exposed to continued risks of ownership through return of the product?

6. Under what conditions may a seller who is exposed to continued risks of a high rate of return of the product sold recognize sales transactions as current revenue?

7. What are the two basic methods of accounting for long-term construction contracts? Indicate the circumstances that determine when one or the other of these methods should be used.

8. F. Scott Fitzgerald Construction Co. has a $60 million contract to construct a highway overpass and cloverleaf. The total estimated cost for the project is $50 million. Costs incurred in the first year of the project are $9 million. F. Scott Fitzgerald Construction Co. appropriately uses the percentage-of-completion method. How much revenue and gross profit should F. Scott Fitzgerald recognize in the first year of the project?

9. For what reasons should the percentage-of-completion method be used over the completed-contract method whenever possible?

10. What methods are used in practice to determine the extent of progress toward completion? Identify some "input measures" and some "output measures" that might be used to determine the extent of progress.

11. What are the two types of losses that can become evident in accounting for long-term contracts? What is the nature of each type of loss? How is each type accounted for?

12. Under the percentage-of-completion method, how are the Construction in Process and the Billings on Construction in Process accounts reported in the balance sheet?

13. Explain the differences between the installment-sales method and the cost-recovery method.

14. Identify and briefly describe the two methods generally employed to account for the cash received in situations where the collection of the sales price is not reasonably assured.

15. What is the deposit method and when might it be applied?

16. What is the nature of an installment sale? How do installment sales differ from ordinary credit sales?

17. Describe the installment-sales method of accounting.

18. How are operating expenses (not included in cost of goods sold) handled under the installment-sales method of accounting? What is the justification for such treatment?

19. J. K. Rowling sold her condominium for $500,000 on September 14, 2006; she had paid $310,000 for it in 1998. Rowling collected the selling price as follows: 2006, $80,000; 2007, $320,000; and 2008, $100,000. Rowling appropriately uses the installment-sales method. Prepare a schedule to determine the gross profit for 2006, 2007, and 2008 from the installment sale.

20. When interest is involved in installment-sales transactions, how should it be treated for accounting purposes?

21. How should the results of installment sales be reported on the income statement?

22. At what time is it proper to recognize income in the following cases: (a) Installment sales with no reasonable basis for estimating the degree of collectibility? (b) Sales for future delivery? (c) Merchandise shipped on consignment? (d) Profit on incomplete construction contracts? (e) Subscriptions to publications?

23. When is revenue recognized under the cost-recovery method?

24. When is revenue recognized under the deposit method? How does the deposit method differ from the installment-sales and cost-recovery methods?

*25. Why in franchise arrangements may it not be proper to recognize the entire franchise fee as revenue at the date of sale?

*26. How does the concept of "substantial performance" apply to accounting for franchise sales?

*27. How should a franchisor account for continuing franchise fees and routine sales of equipment and supplies to franchisees?

*28 What changes are made in the franchisor's recording of the initial franchise fee when the franchise agreement:

    (a) Contains an option allowing the franchisor to purchase the franchised outlet, and it is likely that the option will be exercised?

    (b) Allows the franchisee to purchase equipment and supplies from the franchisor at bargain prices?

*29 What is the nature of a sale on consignment? When is revenue recognized from a consignment sale?

BRIEF EXERCISES

(LO 1, 2)   **BE18-1**   Scooby Doo Music sold CDs to retailers and recorded sales revenue of $800,000. During 2008, retailers returned CDs to Scooby Doo and were granted credit of $78,000. Past experience indicates that the normal return rate is 15%. Prepare Scooby Doo's entries to record (a) the $78,000 of returns and (b) estimated returns at December 31, 2008.

(LO 3)   **BE18-2**   Shock Wave, Inc. began work on a $7,000,000 contract in 2008 to construct an office building. During 2008, Shock Wave, Inc. incurred costs of $1,715,000, billed their customers for $1,200,000, and collected $960,000. At December 31, 2008, the estimated future costs to complete the project total $3,185,000. Prepare Shock Wave's 2008 journal entries using the percentage-of-completion method.

(LO 3)   **BE18-3**   Shadow Blasters, Inc. began work on a $7,000,000 contract in 2008 to construct an office building. Shadow Blasters uses the percentage-of-completion method. At December 31, 2008, the balances in certain accounts were: construction in process $2,450,000; accounts receivable $240,000; and billings on construction in process $1,200,000. Indicate how these accounts would be reported in Shadow Blasters' December 31, 2008, balance sheet.

(LO 4)   **BE18-4**   Use the information from BE18-2, but assume Shock Wave uses the completed-contract method. Prepare the company's 2008 journal entries.

(LO 4)   **BE18-5**   Cordero, Inc. began work on a $7,000,000 contract in 2008 to construct an office building. Cordero uses the completed-contract method. At December 31, 2008, the balances in certain accounts were construction in process $1,715,000; accounts receivable $240,000; and billings on construction in process $1,200,000. Indicate how these accounts would be reported in Cordero's December 31, 2008, balance sheet.

(LO 5)   **BE18-6**   Jackie Chan Construction Company began work on a $420,000 construction contract in 2008. During 2008, Chan incurred costs of $288,000, billed its customer for $215,000, and collected $175,000. At December 31, 2008, the estimated future costs to complete the project total $162,000. Prepare Chan's journal entry to record profit or loss using (a) the percentage-of-completion method and (b) the completed-contract method, if any.

(LO 6)   **BE18-7**   Thunder Paradise Corporation began selling goods on the installment basis on January 1, 2008. During 2008, Thunder Paradise had installment sales of $150,000; cash collections of $54,000; cost of installment sales of $105,000. Prepare the company's entries to record installment sales, cash collected, cost of installment sales, deferral of gross profit, and gross profit recognized, using the installment-sales method.

(LO 6) **BE18-8** Buraka Inc. sells goods on the installment basis and uses the installment-sales method. Due to a customer default, Buraka repossessed merchandise that was originally sold for $800, resulting in a gross profit rate of 40%. At the time of repossession, the uncollected balance is $560, and the fair value of the repossessed merchandise is $275. Prepare Buraka's entry to record the repossession.

(LO 6) **BE18-9** At December 31, 2008, Soul Star Corporation had the following account balances.

Installment Accounts Receivable, 2007	$ 65,000
Installment Accounts Receivable, 2008	110,000
Deferred Gross Profit, 2007	23,400
Deferred Gross Profit, 2008	40,700

Most of Soul Star's sales are made on a 2-year installment basis. Indicate how these accounts would be reported in Soul Star's December 31, 2008, balance sheet. The 2007 accounts are collectible in 2009, and the 2008 accounts are collectible in 2010.

(LO 7) **BE18-10** Yogi Bear Corporation sold equipment to Magilla Company for $20,000. The equipment is on Yogi's books at a net amount of $14,000. Yogi collected $10,000 in 2007, $5,000 in 2008, and $5,000 in 2009. If Yogi uses the cost-recovery method, what amount of gross profit will be recognized in each year?

(LO 8) ***BE18-11** Speed Racer, Inc. charges an initial franchise fee of $75,000 for the right to operate as a franchisee of Speed Racer. Of this amount, $25,000 is collected immediately. The remainder is collected in 4 equal annual installments of $12,500 each. These installments have a present value of $39,623. There is reasonable expectation that the down payment may be refunded and substantial future services be performed by Speed Racer, Inc. Prepare the journal entry required by Speed Racer to record the franchise fee.

(LO 8) ***BE18-12** Tom and Jerry Corporation shipped $20,000 of merchandise on consignment to Toons Company. Tom and Jerry paid freight costs of $2,000. Toons Company paid $500 for local advertising which is reimbursable from Tom and Jerry. By year-end, 60% of the merchandise had been sold for $22,300. Toons notified Tom and Jerry, retained a 10% commission, and remitted the cash due to Tom and Jerry. Prepare Tom and Jerry's entry when the cash is received.

EXERCISES

(LO 1, 2) **E18-1** **(Revenue Recognition on Book Sales with High Returns)** Justin Huish Publishing Co. publishes college textbooks that are sold to bookstores on the following terms. Each title has a fixed wholesale price, terms f.o.b. shipping point, and payment is due 60 days after shipment. The retailer may return a maximum of 30% of an order at the retailer's expense. Sales are made only to retailers who have good credit ratings. Past experience indicates that the normal return rate is 12%, and the average collection period is 72 days.

Instructions
- **(a)** Identify alternative revenue recognition tests that Huish could employ concerning textbook sales.
- **(b)** Briefly discuss the reasoning for your answers in (a) above.
- **(c)** In late July, Huish shipped books invoiced at $16,000,000. Prepare the journal entry to record this event that best conforms to generally accepted accounting principles and your answer to part (b).
- **(d)** In October, $2 million of the invoiced July sales were returned according to the return policy, and the remaining $14 million was paid. Prepare the entries recording the return and payment.

(LO 1, 2) **E18-2** **(Sales Recorded Both Gross and Net)** On June 3, David Reid Company sold to Kim Rhode merchandise having a sale price of $5,000 with terms of 2/10, n/60, f.o.b. shipping point. An invoice totaling $120, terms n/30, was received by Rhode on June 8 from the Olympic Transport Service for the freight cost. Upon receipt of the goods, June 5, Rhode notified Reid Company that merchandise costing $400 contained flaws that rendered it worthless. The same day Reid Company issued a credit memo covering the worthless merchandise and asked that it be returned at company expense. The freight on the returned merchandise was $24, paid by Reid Company on June 7. On June 12, the company received a check for the balance due from Rhode.

Instructions
- **(a)** Prepare journal entries on Reid Company books to record all the events noted above under each of the following bases.
  - **(1)** Sales and receivables are entered at gross selling price.
  - **(2)** Sales and receivables are entered net of cash discounts.

(b) Prepare the journal entry under basis 2, assuming that Kim Rhode did not remit payment until August 5.

(LO 1, 2) **E18-3 (Revenue Recognition on Marina Sales with Discounts)** Brooke Bennett Marina has 300 available slips that rent for $900 per season. Payments must be made in full at the start of the boating season, April 1, 2008. Slips for the next season may be reserved if paid for by December 31, 2008. Under a new policy, if payment is made by December 31, 2008, a 5% discount is allowed. The boating season ends October 31, and the marina has a December 31 year-end. To provide cash flow for major dock repairs, the marina operator is also offering a 25% discount to slip renters who pay for the 2009 season.

For the fiscal year ended December 31, 2007, all 300 slips were rented at full price. Two hundred slips were reserved and paid for for the 2008 boating season, and 60 slips were reserved and paid for for the 2009 boating season.

Instructions
(a) Prepare the appropriate journal entries for fiscal 2007.
(b) Assume the marina operator is unsophisticated in business. Explain the managerial significance of the accounting above to this person.

(LO 3, 4) **E18-4 (Recognition of Profit on Long-Term Contracts)** During 2007 Pierson Company started a construction job with a contract price of $1,500,000. The job was completed in 2009. The following information is available.

	2007	2008	2009
Costs incurred to date	$400,000	$935,000	$1,070,000
Estimated costs to complete	600,000	165,000	–0–
Billings to date	300,000	900,000	1,500,000
Collections to date	270,000	810,000	1,425,000

Instructions
(a) Compute the amount of gross profit to be recognized each year assuming the percentage-of-completion method is used.
(b) Prepare all necessary journal entries for 2008.
(c) Compute the amount of gross profit to be recognized each year assuming the completed-contract method is used.

(LO 3) **E18-5 (Analysis of Percentage-of-Completion Financial Statements)** In 2007, Beth Botsford Construction Corp. began construction work under a 3-year contract. The contract price was $1,000,000. Beth Botsford uses the percentage-of-completion method for financial accounting purposes. The income to be recognized each year is based on the proportion of cost incurred to total estimated costs for completing the contract. The financial statement presentations relating to this contract at December 31, 2007, follow.

Balance Sheet

Accounts receivable—construction contract billings		$21,500
Construction in progress	$65,000	
Less: Contract billings	61,500	
Cost of uncompleted contract in excess of billings		3,500

Income Statement

Income (before tax) on the contract recognized in 2007	$18,200

Instructions
(a) How much cash was collected in 2007 on this contract?
(b) What was the initial estimated total income before tax on this contract?

(AICPA adapted)

(LO 3) **E18-6 (Gross Profit on Uncompleted Contract)** On April 1, 2007, Brad Bridgewater Inc. entered into a cost-plus-fixed-fee contract to construct an electric generator for Tom Dolan Corporation. At the contract date, Bridgewater estimated that it would take 2 years to complete the project at a cost of $2,000,000. The fixed fee stipulated in the contract is $450,000. Bridgewater appropriately accounts for this contract under the percentage-of-completion method. During 2007 Bridgewater incurred costs of $700,000 related to the project. The estimated cost at December 31, 2007, to complete the contract is $1,300,000. Dolan was billed $600,000 under the contract.

Instructions
Prepare a schedule to compute the amount of gross profit to be recognized by Bridgewater under the contract for the year ended December 31, 2007. Show supporting computations in good form.

(AICPA adapted)

(LO 3) **E18-7** **(Recognition of Profit, Percentage-of-Completion)** In 2007 Jeff Rouse Construction Company agreed to construct an apartment building at a price of $1,000,000. The information relating to the costs and billings for this contract is shown below.

	2007	2008	2009
Costs incurred to date	$280,000	$600,000	$ 785,000
Estimated costs yet to be incurred	520,000	200,000	–0–
Customer billings to date	150,000	400,000	1,000,000
Collection of billings to date	120,000	320,000	940,000

Instructions
(a) Assuming that the percentage-of-completion method is used, (1) compute the amount of gross profit to be recognized in 2007 and 2008, and (2) prepare journal entries for 2008.
(b) For 2008, show how the details related to this construction contract would be disclosed on the balance sheet and on the income statement.

(LO 3, 4) **E18-8** **(Recognition of Revenue on Long-Term Contract and Entries)** Amy Van Dyken Construction Company uses the percentage-of-completion method of accounting. In 2007, Van Dyken began work under contract #E2-D2, which provided for a contract price of $2,200,000. Other details follow:

	2007	2008
Costs incurred during the year	$ 480,000	$1,425,000
Estimated costs to complete, as of December 31	1,120,000	–0–
Billings during the year	420,000	1,680,000
Collections during the year	350,000	1,500,000

Instructions
(a) What portion of the total contract price would be recognized as revenue in 2007? In 2008?
(b) Assuming the same facts as those above except that Van Dyken uses the completed-contract method of accounting, what portion of the total contract price would be recognized as revenue in 2008?
(c) Prepare a complete set of journal entries for 2007 (using the percentage-of-completion method).

(LO 3, 4) **E18-9** **(Recognition of Profit and Balance Sheet Amounts for Long-Term Contracts)** Andre Agassi Construction Company began operations January 1, 2007. During the year, Andre Agassi Construction entered into a contract with Lindsey Davenport Corp. to construct a manufacturing facility. At that time, Agassi estimated that it would take 5 years to complete the facility at a total cost of $4,500,000. The total contract price for construction of the facility is $6,300,000. During the year, Agassi incurred $1,185,800 in construction costs related to the construction project. The estimated cost to complete the contract is $4,204,200. Lindsey Davenport Corp. was billed and paid 30% of the contract price.

Instructions
Prepare schedules to compute the amount of gross profit to be recognized for the year ended December 31, 2007, and the amount to be shown as "costs and recognized profit on uncompleted contract in excess of related billings" or "billings on uncompleted contract in excess of related costs and recognized profit" at December 31, 2007, under each of the following methods.

(a) Completed-contract method.
(b) Percentage-of-completion method.

Show supporting computations in good form.

(AICPA adapted)

(LO 4, 5) **E18-10** **(Long-Term Contract Reporting)** Derrick Adkins Construction Company began operations in 2007. Construction activity for the first year is shown below. All contracts are with different customers, and any work remaining at December 31, 2007, is expected to be completed in 2008.

Project	Total Contract Price	Billings through 12/31/07	Cash Collections through 12/31/07	Contract Costs Incurred through 12/31/07	Estimated Additional Costs to Complete
1	$ 560,000	$ 360,000	$340,000	$450,000	$140,000
2	670,000	220,000	210,000	126,000	504,000
3	500,000	500,000	440,000	330,000	–0–
	$1,730,000	$1,080,000	$990,000	$906,000	$644,000

Instructions

Prepare a partial income statement and balance sheet to indicate how the above information would be reported for financial statement purposes. Derrick Adkins Construction Company uses the completed-contract method.

(LO 6) **E18-11** **(Installment-Sales Method Calculations, Entries)** Austin Corporation appropriately uses the installment-sales method of accounting to recognize income in its financial statements. The following information is available for 2007 and 2008.

	2007	2008
Installment sales	$900,000	$1,000,000
Cost of installment sales	630,000	680,000
Cash collections on 2007 sales	370,000	350,000
Cash collections on 2008 sales	–0–	475,000

Instructions

(a) Compute the amount of realized gross profit recognized in each year.
(b) Prepare all journal entries required in 2008.

(LO 6) **E18-12** **(Analysis of Installment-Sales Accounts)** Charles Austin Co. appropriately uses the installment-sales method of accounting. On December 31, 2009, the books show balances as follows.

Installment Receivables		Deferred Gross Profit		Gross Profit on Sales	
2007	$11,000	2007	$ 7,000	2007	35%
2008	40,000	2008	26,000	2008	34%
2009	80,000	2009	95,000	2009	32%

Instructions

(a) Prepare the adjusting entry or entries required on December 31, 2009 to recognize 2009 realized gross profit. (Installment receivables have already been credited for cash receipts during 2009.)
(b) Compute the amount of cash collected in 2009 on accounts receivable each year.

(LO 6) **E18-13** **(Gross Profit Calculations and Repossessed Merchandise)** Barnes Corporation, which began business on January 1, 2007, appropriately uses the installment-sales method of accounting. The following data were obtained for the years 2007 and 2008.

	2007	2008
Installment sales	$750,000	$840,000
Cost of installment sales	525,000	604,800
General & administrative expenses	70,000	84,000
Cash collections on sales of 2007	310,000	300,000
Cash collections on sales of 2008	–0–	400,000

Instructions

(a) Compute the balance in the deferred gross profit accounts on December 31, 2007, and on December 31, 2008.
(b) A 2007 sale resulted in default in 2009. At the date of default, the balance on the installment receivable was $12,000, and the repossessed merchandise had a fair value of $8,000. Prepare the entry to record the repossession.

(AICPA adapted)

(LO 6) **E18-14** **(Interest Revenue from Installment Sale)** Gail Devers Corporation sells farm machinery on the installment plan. On July 1, 2007, Devers entered into an installment-sale contract with Gwen Torrence Inc. for a 10-year period. Equal annual payments under the installment sale are $100,000 and are due on July 1. The first payment was made on July 1, 2007.

Additional information

1. The amount that would be realized on an outright sale of similar farm machinery is $676,000.
2. The cost of the farm machinery sold to Gwen Torrence Inc. is $500,000.
3. The finance charges relating to the installment period are $324,000 based on a stated interest rate of 10%, which is appropriate.
4. Circumstances are such that the collection of the installments due under the contract is reasonably assured.

Instructions

What income or loss before income taxes should Devers record for the year ended December 31, 2007, as a result of the transaction above?

(AICPA adapted)

(LO 6, 7) **E18-15** **(Installment-Sales Method and Cost Recovery)** Kenny Corp., a capital goods manufacturing business that started on January 4, 2007, and operates on a calendar-year basis, uses the installment-sales method of profit recognition in accounting for all its sales. The following data were taken from the 2007 and 2008 records.

	2007	2008
Installment sales	$480,000	$620,000
Gross profit as a percent of costs	25%	28%
Cash collections on sales of 2007	$140,000	$240,000
Cash collections on sales of 2008	–0–	$180,000

The amounts given for cash collections exclude amounts collected for interest charges.

Instructions

(a) Compute the amount of realized gross profit to be recognized on the 2008 income statement, prepared using the installment-sales method.

(b) State where the balance of Deferred Gross Profit would be reported on the financial statements for 2008.

(c) Compute the amount of realized gross profit to be recognized on the income statement, prepared using the cost-recovery method.

(CIA adapted)

(LO 6, 7) **E18-16** **(Installment-Sales Method and Cost-Recovery Method)** On January 1, 2007, Barkly Company sold property for $200,000. The note will be collected as follows: $100,000 in 2007, $60,000 in 2008, and $40,000 in 2009. The property had cost Barkly $150,000 when it was purchased in 2005.

Instructions

(a) Compute the amount of gross profit realized each year, assuming Barkly uses the cost-recovery method.

(b) Compute the amount of gross profit realized each year, assuming Barkly uses the installment-sales method.

(LO 6) **E18-17** **(Installment Sales—Default and Repossession)** Michael Johnson Imports Inc. was involved in two default and repossession cases during the year:

1. A refrigerator was sold to Merlene Ottey for $1,800, including a 35% markup on selling price. Ottey made a down payment of 20%, four of the remaining 16 equal payments, and then defaulted on further payments. The refrigerator was repossessed, at which time the fair value was determined to be $800.

2. An oven that cost $1,200 was sold to Donovan Bailey for $1,600 on the installment basis. Bailey made a down payment of $240 and paid $80 a month for six months, after which he defaulted. The oven was repossessed and the estimated value at time of repossession was determined to be $750.

Instructions

Prepare journal entries to record each of these repossessions using a fair value approach. (Ignore interest charges.)

(LO 6) **E18-18** **(Installment Sales—Default and Repossession)** Kurt Angle Company uses the installment-sales method in accounting for its installment sales. On January 1, 2008, Angle Company had an installment account receivable from Kay Bluhm with a balance of $1,800. During 2008, $400 was collected from Bluhm. When no further collection could be made, the merchandise sold to Bluhm was repossessed. The merchandise had a fair market value of $650 after the company spent $60 for reconditioning of the merchandise. The merchandise was originally sold with a gross profit rate of 40%.

Instructions

Prepare the entries on the books of Angle Company to record all transactions related to Bluhm during 2008. (Ignore interest charges.)

(LO 8) ***E18-19** **(Franchise Entries)** Kendall Crossburgers Inc. charges an initial franchise fee of $70,000. Upon the signing of the agreement, a payment of $40,000 is due. Thereafter, three annual payments of $10,000 are required. The credit rating of the franchisee is such that it would have to pay interest at 10% to borrow money.

Instructions

Prepare the entries to record the initial franchise fee on the books of the franchisor under the following assumptions.

(a) The down payment is not refundable, no future services are required by the franchisor, and collection of the note is reasonably assured.

(b) The franchisor has substantial services to perform, the down payment is refundable, and the collection of the note is very uncertain.

(c) The down payment is not refundable, collection of the note is reasonably certain, the franchisor has yet to perform a substantial amount of services, and the down payment represents a fair measure of the services already performed.

(LO 8) *E18-20 (Franchise Fee, Initial Down Payment) On January 1, 2007, Svetlana Masterkova signed an agreement to operate as a franchisee of Short-Track Inc. for an initial franchise fee of $50,000. The amount of $20,000 was paid when the agreement was signed, and the balance is payable in five annual payments of $6,000 each, beginning January 1, 2008. The agreement provides that the down payment is not refundable and that no future services are required of the franchisor. Svetlana Masterkova's credit rating indicates that she can borrow money at 11% for a loan of this type.

Instructions

(a) How much should Short-Track record as revenue from franchise fees on January 1, 2007? At what amount should Svetlana record the acquisition cost of the franchise on January 1, 2007?

(b) What entry would be made by Short-Track on January 1, 2007, if the down payment is refundable and substantial future services remain to be performed by Short-Track?

(c) How much revenue from franchise fees would be recorded by Short-Track on January 1, 2007, if:

(1) The initial down payment is not refundable, it represents a fair measure of the services already provided, a significant amount of services is still to be performed by Short-Track in future periods, and collectibility of the note is reasonably assured?

(2) The initial down payment is not refundable and no future services are required by the franchisor, but collection of the note is so uncertain that recognition of the note as an asset is unwarranted?

(3) The initial down payment has not been earned and collection of the note is so uncertain that recognition of the note as an asset is unwarranted?

(LO 8) *E18-21 (Consignment Computations) On May 3, 2007, Michelle Smith Company consigned 70 freezers, costing $500 each, to Angel Martino Company. The cost of shipping the freezers amounted to $840 and was paid by Smith Company. On December 30, 2007, an account sales was received from the consignee, reporting that 40 freezers had been sold for $700 each. Remittance was made by the consignee for the amount due, after deducting a commission of 6%, advertising of $200, and total installation costs of $320 on the freezers sold.

Instructions

(a) Compute the inventory value of the units unsold in the hands of the consignee.

(b) Compute the profit for the consignor for the units sold.

(c) Compute the amount of cash that will be remitted by the consignee.

See the book's website, www.wiley.com/college/kieso, for Additional Exercises.

PROBLEMS

(LO 2, 3, 4, 6) P18-1 (Comprehensive Three-Part Revenue Recognition) Simona Amanar Industries has three operating divisions—Gina Construction Division, Gogean Publishing Division, and Chorkina Securities Division. Each division maintains its own accounting system and method of revenue recognition.

Gina Construction Division

During the fiscal year ended November 30, 2007, Gina Construction Division had one construction project in process. A $30,000,000 contract for construction of a civic center was granted on June 19, 2007, and construction began on August 1, 2007. Estimated costs of completion at the contract date were $25,000,000 over a 2-year time period from the date of the contract. On November 30, 2007, construction costs of $7,800,000 had been incurred and progress billings of $9,500,000 had been made. The construction costs to complete the remainder of the project were reviewed on November 30, 2007, and were estimated to amount to only $16,200,000 because of an expected decline in raw materials costs. Revenue recognition is based upon a percentage-of-completion method.

Gogean Publishing Division

The Gogean Publishing Division sells large volumes of novels to a few book distributors, which in turn sell to several national chains of bookstores. Gogean allows distributors to return up to 30% of sales, and distributors give the same terms to bookstores. While returns from individual titles fluctuate greatly, the returns from distributors have averaged 20% in each of the past 5 years. A total of $8,000,000 of paperback novel sales were made to distributors during fiscal 2007. On November 30, 2007, $2,500,000 of fiscal 2007 sales were still subject to return privileges over the next 6 months. The remaining $5,500,000 of fiscal 2007 sales had actual returns of 21%. Sales from fiscal 2006 totaling $2,000,000 were collected in fiscal 2007 less 18% returns. This division records revenue according to the method referred to as revenue recognition when the right of return exists.

Chorkina Securities Division

Chorkina Securities Division works through manufacturers' agents in various cities. Orders for alarm systems and down payments are forwarded from agents, and the Division ships the goods f.o.b. factory directly to customers (usually police departments and security guard companies). Customers are billed directly for the balance due plus actual shipping costs. The company received orders for $6,000,000 of goods during the fiscal year ended November 30, 2007. Down payments of $600,000 were received, and $5,200,000 of goods were billed and shipped. Actual freight costs of $100,000 were also billed. Commissions of 10% on product price are paid to manufacturing agents after goods are shipped to customers. Such goods are warranted for 90 days after shipment, and warranty returns have been about 1% of sales. Revenue is recognized at the point of sale by this division.

Instructions

(a) There are a variety of methods of revenue recognition. Define and describe each of the following methods of revenue recognition, and indicate whether each is in accordance with generally accepted accounting principles.
   (1) Point of sale.
   (2) Completion-of-production.
   (3) Percentage-of-completion.
   (4) Installment-sales contract.
(b) Compute the revenue to be recognized in fiscal year 2007 for each of the three operating divisions of Simona Amanar Industries in accordance with generally accepted accounting principles.

(LO 3, 4) **P18-2** **(Recognition of Profit on Long-Term Contract)** Jenny Thompson Construction Company has entered into a contract beginning January 1, 2007, to build a parking complex. It has been estimated that the complex will cost $600,000 and will take 3 years to construct. The complex will be billed to the purchasing company at $900,000. The following data pertain to the construction period.

	2007	2008	2009
Costs to date	$270,000	$420,000	$600,000
Estimated costs to complete	330,000	180,000	–0–
Progress billings to date	270,000	550,000	900,000
Cash collected to date	240,000	500,000	900,000

Instructions

(a) Using the percentage-of-completion method, compute the estimated gross profit that would be recognized during each year of the construction period.
(b) Using the completed-contract method, compute the estimated gross profit that would be recognized during each year of the construction period.

(LO 3, 4) **P18-3** **(Recognition of Profit and Entries on Long-Term Contract)** On March 1, 2007, Winter Company entered into a contract to build an apartment building. It is estimated that the building will cost $2,000,000 and will take 3 years to complete. The contract price was $3,000,000. The following information pertains to the construction period.

	2007	2008	2009
Costs to date	$ 600,000	$1,560,000	$2,100,000
Estimated costs to complete	1,400,000	390,000	–0–
Progress billings to date	1,050,000	2,100,000	3,000,000
Cash collected to date	950,000	1,950,000	2,750,000

Instructions

(a) Compute the amount of gross profit to be recognized each year assuming the percentage-of-completion method is used.
(b) Prepare all necessary journal entries for 2009.
(c) Prepare a partial balance sheet for December 31, 2008, showing the balances in the receivables and inventory accounts.

(LO 3) **P18-4** **(Recognition of Profit and Balance Sheet Presentation, Percentage-of-Completion)** On February 1, 2007, Amanda Berg Construction Company obtained a contract to build an athletic stadium. The stadium was to be built at a total cost of $5,400,000 and was scheduled for completion by September 1, 2009. One clause of the contract stated that Berg was to deduct $15,000 from the $6,600,000 billing price for each week that completion was delayed. Completion was delayed 6 weeks, which resulted in a $90,000 penalty. Below are the data pertaining to the construction period.

	2007	2008	2009
Costs to date	$1,782,000	$3,850,000	$5,500,000
Estimated costs to complete	3,618,000	1,650,000	–0–
Progress billings to date	1,200,000	3,100,000	6,510,000
Cash collected to date	1,000,000	2,800,000	6,510,000

Instructions

(a) Using the percentage-of-completion method, compute the estimated gross profit recognized in the years 2007–2009.

(b) Prepare a partial balance sheet for December 31, 2008, showing the balances in the receivable and inventory accounts.

(LO 3, 4, 5) **P18-5** **(Completed Contract and Percentage of Completion with Interim Loss)** Gold Medal Custom Builders (GMCB) was established in 1985 by Whitney Hedgepeth and initially built high-quality customized homes under contract with specific buyers. In the 1990s, Hedgepeth's two sons joined the firm and expanded GMCB's activities into the high-rise apartment and industrial plant markets. Upon the retirement of GMCB's long-time financial manager, Hedgepeth's sons recently hired Le Jingyi as controller for GMCB. Jingyi, a former college friend of Hedgepeth's sons, has been associated with a public accounting firm for the last 6 years.

Upon reviewing GMCB's accounting practices, Jingyi observed that GMCB followed the completed-contract method of revenue recognition, a carryover from the years when individual home building was the majority of GMCB's operations. Several years ago, the predominant portion of GMCB's activities shifted to the high-rise and industrial building areas. From land acquisition to the completion of construction, most building contracts cover several years. Under the circumstances, Jingyi believes that GMCB should follow the percentage-of-completion method of accounting. From a typical building contract, Jingyi developed the following data.

DAGMAR HAZE TRACTOR PLANT

Contract price: $8,000,000

	2006	2007	2008
Estimated costs	$2,010,000	$3,015,000	$1,675,000
Progress billings	1,000,000	2,500,000	4,500,000
Cash collections	800,000	2,300,000	4,900,000

Instructions

(a) Explain the difference between completed-contract revenue recognition and percentage-of-completion revenue recognition.

(b) Using the data provided for the Dagmar Haze Tractor Plant and assuming the percentage-of-completion method of revenue recognition is used, calculate GMCB's revenue and gross profit for 2006, 2007, and 2008, under **each** of the following circumstances.

(1) Assume that all costs are incurred, all billings to customers are made, and all collections from customers are received within 30 days of billing, as planned.

(2) Further assume that, as a result of unforeseen local ordinances and the fact that the building site was in a wetlands area, GMCB experienced cost overruns of $800,000 in 2006 to bring the site into compliance with the ordinances and to overcome wetlands barriers to construction.

(3) Further assume that, in addition to the cost overruns of $800,000 for this contract incurred under part (b)2, inflationary factors over and above those anticipated in the development of the original contract cost have caused an additional cost overrun of $540,000 in 2007. It is not anticipated that any cost overruns will occur in 2008.

(CMA adapted)

(LO 3, 4, 5) **P18-6** **(Long-Term Contract with Interim Loss)** On March 1, 2007, Franziska van Almsick Construction Company contracted to construct a factory building for Sandra Volker Manufacturing Inc. for a total contract price of $8,400,000. The building was completed by October 31, 2009. The annual contract costs incurred, estimated costs to complete the contract, and accumulated billings to Volker for 2007, 2008, and 2009 are given on the next page.

	2007	2008	2009
Contract costs incurred during the year	$3,200,000	$2,600,000	$1,450,000
Estimated costs to complete the contract at 12/31	3,200,000	1,450,000	–0–
Billings to Volker during the year	3,200,000	3,500,000	1,700,000

Instructions

(a) Using the percentage-of-completion method, prepare schedules to compute the profit or loss to be recognized as a result of this contract for the years ended December 31, 2007, 2008, and 2009. (Ignore income taxes.)

(b) Using the completed-contract method, prepare schedules to compute the profit or loss to be recognized as a result of this contract for the years ended December 2007, 2008, and 2009. (Ignore incomes taxes.)

(LO 3, 4, 5) **P18-7** **(Long-Term Contract with an Overall Loss)** On July 1, 2007, Kyung-wook Construction Company Inc. contracted to build an office building for Mingxia Corp. for a total contract price of $1,950,000. On July 1, Kyung-wook estimated that it would take between 2 and 3 years to complete the building. On December 31, 2009, the building was deemed substantially completed. Following are accumulated contract costs incurred, estimated costs to complete the contract, and accumulated billings to Mingxia for 2007, 2008, and 2009.

	At 12/31/07	At 12/31/08	At 12/31/09
Contract costs incurred to date	$ 150,000	$1,200,000	$2,100,000
Estimated costs to complete the contract	1,350,000	800,000	–0–
Billings to Mingxia	300,000	1,100,000	1,850,000

Instructions

(a) Using the percentage-of-completion method, prepare schedules to compute the profit or loss to be recognized as a result of this contract for the years ended December 31, 2007, 2008, and 2009. (Ignore income taxes.)

(b) Using the completed-contract method, prepare schedules to compute the profit or loss to be recognized as a result of this contract for the years ended December 2007, 2008, and 2009. (Ignore income taxes.)

(LO 6) **P18-8** **(Installment-Sales Computations and Entries)** Presented below is summarized information for Deng Yaping Co., which sells merchandise on the installment basis.

	2007	2008	2009
Sales (on installment plan)	$250,000	$260,000	$280,000
Cost of sales	150,000	163,800	182,000
Gross profit	$100,000	$ 96,200	$ 98,000
Collections from customers on:			
2007 installment sales	$ 75,000	$100,000	$ 50,000
2008 installment sales		100,000	120,000
2009 installment sales			110,000

Instructions

(a) Compute the realized gross profit for each of the years 2007, 2008, and 2009.

(b) Prepare in journal form all entries required in 2009, applying the installment-sales method of accounting. (Ignore interest charges.)

(LO 6) **P18-9** **(Installment-Sales Income Statements)** Laura Flessel Stores sells merchandise on open account as well as on installment terms.

	2007	2008	2009
Sales on account	$385,000	$426,000	$525,000
Installment sales	320,000	275,000	380,000
Collections on installment sales			
Made in 2007	110,000	90,000	40,000
Made in 2008		110,000	140,000
Made in 2009			125,000
Cost of sales			
Sold on account	270,000	277,000	341,000
Sold on installment	214,400	167,750	224,200
Selling expenses	77,000	87,000	92,000
Administrative expenses	50,000	51,000	52,000

Instructions

From the data above, which cover the 3 years since Laura Flessel Stores commenced operations, determine the net income for each year, applying the installment-sales method of accounting. (Ignore interest charges.)

(LO 6) **P18-10** **(Installment-Sales Computations and Entries)** Isabell Werth Stores sell appliances for cash and also on the installment plan. Entries to record cost of sales are made monthly.

ISABELL WERTH STORES
TRIAL BALANCE
DECEMBER 31, 2009

	Dr.	Cr.
Cash	$153,000	
Installment Accounts Receivable, 2008	48,000	
Installment Accounts Receivable, 2009	91,000	
Inventory—New Merchandise	123,200	
Inventory—Repossessed Merchandise	24,000	
Accounts Payable		$ 98,500
Deferred Gross Profit, 2008		45,600
Capital Stock		170,000
Retained Earnings		93,900
Sales		343,000
Installment Sales		200,000
Cost of Sales	255,000	
Cost of Installment Sales	128,000	
Loss on Repossessions	800	
Selling and Administrative Expenses	128,000	
	$951,000	$951,000

The accounting department has prepared the following analysis of cash receipts for the year.

Cash sales (including repossessed merchandise)	$424,000
Installment accounts receivable, 2008	104,000
Installment accounts receivable, 2009	109,000
Other	36,000
Total	$673,000

Repossessions recorded during the year are summarized as follows.

	2008
Uncollected balance	$8,000
Loss on repossession	800
Repossessed merchandise	4,800

Instructions

From the trial balance and accompanying information:
- **(a)** Compute the rate of gross profit for 2008 and 2009.
- **(b)** Prepare closing entries as of December 31, 2009, under the installment-sales method of accounting.
- **(c)** Prepare an income statement for the year ended December 31, 2009. Include only the realized gross profit in the income statement.

(LO 6) **P18-11** **(Installment-Sales Entries)** The following summarized information relates to the installment-sales activity of Lisa Jacob Stores Inc. for the year 2007.

Installment sales during 2007	$500,000
Cost of goods sold on installment basis	330,000
Collections from customers	200,000
Unpaid balances on merchandise repossessed	24,000
Estimated value of merchandise repossessed	9,200

Instructions

- **(a)** Prepare journal entries at the end of 2007 to record on the books of Lisa Jacob Stores, Inc. the summarized data above.
- **(b)** Prepare the entry to record the gross profit realized during 2007.

(LO 6) **P18-12** **(Installment-Sales Computation and Entries—Periodic Inventory)** Catherine Fox Inc. sells merchandise for cash and also on the installment plan. Entries to record cost of goods sold are made at the end of each year.

Repossessions of merchandise (sold in 2008) were made in 2009 and were recorded correctly as follows.

Deferred Gross Profit, 2008	7,200	
Repossessed Merchandise	8,000	
Loss on Repossessions	2,800	
Installment Accounts Receivable, 2008		18,000

Part of this repossessed merchandise was sold for cash during 2009, and the sale was recorded by a debit to Cash and a credit to Sales.

The inventory of repossessed merchandise on hand December 31, 2009, is $4,000; of new merchandise, $127,400. There was no repossessed merchandise on hand January 1, 2009.

Collections on accounts receivable during 2009 were:

Installment Accounts Receivable, 2008	$80,000
Installment Accounts Receivable, 2009	50,000

The cost of the merchandise sold under the installment plan during 2009 was $117,000.

The rate of gross profit on 2008 and on 2009 installment sales can be computed from the information given.

CATHERINE FOX INC.
TRIAL BALANCE
DECEMBER 31, 2009

	Dr.	Cr.
Cash	$ 98,400	
Installment Accounts Receivable, 2008	80,000	
Installment Accounts Receivable, 2009	130,000	
Inventory, Jan. 1, 2009	120,000	
Repossessed Merchandise	8,000	
Accounts Payable		$ 47,200
Deferred Gross Profit, 2008		64,000
Capital Stock, Common		200,000
Retained Earnings		40,000
Sales		400,000
Installment Sales		180,000
Purchases	380,000	
Loss on Repossessions	2,800	
Operating Expenses	112,000	
	$931,200	$931,200

Instructions

(a) From the trial balance and other information given above, prepare adjusting and closing entries as of December 31, 2009.

(b) Prepare an income statement for the year ended December 31, 2009. Include only the realized gross profit in the income statement.

(LO 6) **P18-13 (Installment Repossession Entries)** Selected transactions of TV Lenny Company are presented below.

1. A television set costing $560 is sold to Mark Prior on November 1, 2008, for $800. Prior makes a down payment of $200 and agrees to pay $30 on the first of each month for 20 months thereafter.
2. Prior pays the $30 installment due December 1, 2008.
3. On December 31, 2008, the appropriate entries are made to record profit realized on the installment sales.
4. The first seven 2009 installments of $30 each are paid by Prior. (Make one entry.)
5. In August 2009 the set is repossessed, after Prior fails to pay the August 1 installment and indicates that he will be unable to continue the payments. The estimated fair value of the repossessed set is $100.

Instructions

Prepare journal entries to record the transactions above on the books of TV Lenny Company. Closing entries should not be made.

(LO 6) **P18-14 (Installment-Sales Computations and Schedules)** Zambrano Company, on January 2, 2007, entered into a contract with a manufacturing company to purchase room-size air conditioners and to sell the units on an installment plan with collections over approximately 30 months with no carrying charge.

For income tax purposes Zambrano Company elected to report income from its sales of air conditioners according to the installment-sales method.

Purchases and sales of new units were as follows.

	Units Purchased		Units Sold	
Year	Quantity	Price Each	Quantity	Price Each
2007	1,400	$130	1,100	$200
2008	1,200	112	1,500	170
2009	900	136	800	182

Collections on installment sales were as follows.

	Collections Received		
	2007	2008	2009
2007 sales	$42,000	$88,000	$ 80,000
2008 sales		51,000	100,000
2009 sales			34,600

In 2009, 50 units from the 2008 sales were repossessed and sold for $80 each on the installment plan. At the time of repossession, $1,440 had been collected from the original purchasers, and the units had a fair value of $3,000.

General and administrative expenses for 2009 were $60,000. No charge has been made against current income for the applicable insurance expense from a 3-year policy expiring June 30, 2010, costing $7,200, and for an advance payment of $12,000 on a new contract to purchase air conditioners beginning January 2, 2010.

Instructions

Assuming that the weighted-average method is used for determining the inventory cost, including repossessed merchandise, prepare schedules computing for 2007, 2008, and 2009:

(a) **(1)** The cost of goods sold on installments.
   (2) The average unit cost of goods sold on installments for each year.
(b) The gross profit percentages for 2007, 2008, and 2009.
(c) The gain or loss on repossessions in 2009.
(d) The net income from installment sales for 2009. (Ignore income taxes.)

(AICPA adapted)

(LO 4, 5) **P18-15** **(Completed-Contract Method)** Mauer Construction Company, Inc., entered into a firm fixed-price contract with Trillini Clinic on July 1, 2005, to construct a four-story office building. At that time, Mauer estimated that it would take between 2 and 3 years to complete the project. The total contract price for construction of the building is $4,500,000. Mauer appropriately accounts for this contract under the completed-contract method in its financial statements and for income tax reporting. The building was deemed substantially completed on December 31, 2007. Estimated percentage of completion, accumulated contract costs incurred, estimated costs to complete the contract, and accumulated billings to the Trillini Clinic under the contract are shown below.

	At December 31, 2005	At December 31, 2006	At December 31, 2007
Percentage of completion	30%	65%	100%
Contract costs incurred	$1,140,000	$3,055,000	$4,800,000
Estimated costs to complete the contract	$2,660,000	$1,645,000	–0–
Billings to Trillini Clinic	$1,500,000	$2,500,000	$4,300,000

Instructions

(a) Prepare schedules to compute the amount to be shown as "Cost of uncompleted contract in excess of related billings" or "Billings on uncompleted contract in excess of related costs" at December 31, 2005, 2006, and 2007. Ignore income taxes. Show supporting computations in good form.
(b) Prepare schedules to compute the profit or loss to be recognized as a result of this contract for the years ended December 31, 2005, 2006, and 2007. Ignore income taxes. Show supporting computations in good form.

(AICPA adapted)

(LO 3, 4) **P18-16** **(Revenue Recognition Methods—Comparison)** Joy's Construction is in its fourth year of business. Joy performs long-term construction projects and accounts for them using the completed-contract

method. Joy built an apartment building at a price of $1,000,000. The costs and billings for this contract for the first three years are as follows.

	2006	2007	2008
Costs incurred to date	$320,000	$600,000	$ 790,000
Estimated costs yet to be incurred	480,000	200,000	–0–
Customer billings to date	150,000	410,000	1,000,000
Collection of billings to date	120,000	340,000	950,000

Joy has contacted you, a certified public accountant, about the following concern. She would like to attract some investors, but she believes that in order to recognize revenue she must first "deliver" the product. Therefore, on her balance sheet, she did not recognize any gross profits from the above contract until 2008, when she recognized the entire $210,000. That looked good for 2008, but the preceding years looked grim by comparison. She wants to know about an alternative to this completed-contract revenue recognition.

Instructions

Draft a letter to Joy, telling her about the percentage-of-completion method of recognizing revenue. Compare it to the completed-contract method. Explain the idea behind the percentage-of-completion method. In addition, illustrate how much revenue she could have recognized in 2006, 2007, and 2008 if she had used this method.

(LO 3, 4)

P18-17 (Comprehensive Problem—Long-Term Contracts) You have been engaged by Bo Ryan Construction Company to advise it concerning the proper accounting for a series of long-term contracts. Ryan commenced doing business on January 1, 2007. Construction activities for the first year of operations are shown below. All contract costs are with different customers, and any work remaining at December 31, 2007, is expected to be completed in 2008.

Project	Total Contract Price	Billings Through 12/31/07	Cash Collections Through 12/31/07	Contract Costs Incurred Through 12/31/07	Estimated Additional Costs to Complete
A	$ 300,000	$200,000	$180,000	$248,000	$ 67,000
B	350,000	110,000	105,000	67,800	271,200
C	280,000	280,000	255,000	186,000	–0–
D	200,000	35,000	25,000	123,000	87,000
E	240,000	205,000	200,000	185,000	15,000
	$1,370,000	$830,000	$765,000	$809,800	$440,200

Instructions

(a) Prepare a schedule to compute gross profit (loss) to be reported, unbilled contract costs and recognized profit, and billings in excess of costs and recognized profit using the percentage-of-completion method.

(b) Prepare a partial income statement and balance sheet to indicate how the information would be reported for financial statement purposes.

(c) Repeat the requirements for part (a) assuming Ryan uses the completed-contract method.

(d) Using the responses above for illustrative purposes, prepare a brief report comparing the conceptual merits (both positive and negative) of the two revenue recognition approaches.

CONCEPTS FOR ANALYSIS

CA18-1 (Revenue Recognition—Alternative Methods) Alexsandra Isosev Industries has three operating divisions—Falilat Mining, Mourning Paperbacks, and Osygus Protection Devices. Each division maintains its own accounting system and method of revenue recognition.

Falilat Mining

Falilat Mining specializes in the extraction of precious metals such as silver, gold, and platinum. During the fiscal year ended November 30, 2007, Falilat entered into contracts worth $2,250,000 and shipped metals worth $2,000,000. A quarter of the shipments were made from inventories on hand at the beginning of the fiscal year, and the remainder were made from metals that were mined during the year. Mining totals for the year, valued at market prices, were: silver at $750,000, gold at $1,300,000, and platinum at $490,000. Falilat uses the completion-of-production method to recognize revenue, because its operations meet the specified criteria—i.e., reasonably assured sales prices, interchangeable units, and insignificant distribution costs.

Mourning Paperbacks

Mourning Paperbacks sells large quantities of novels to a few book distributors that in turn sell to several national chains of bookstores. Mourning allows distributors to return up to 30% of sales, and distributors give the same terms to bookstores. While returns from individual titles fluctuate greatly, the returns from distributors have averaged 20% in each of the past 5 years. A total of $8,000,000 of paperback novel sales were made to distributors during the fiscal year. On November 30, 2007, $3,200,000 of fiscal 2007 sales were still subject to return privileges over the next 6 months. The remaining $4,800,000 of fiscal 2007 sales had actual returns of 21%. Sales from fiscal 2006 totaling $2,500,000 were collected in fiscal 2007, with less than 18% of sales returned. Mourning records revenue according to the method referred to as revenue recognition when the right of return exits, because all applicable criteria for use of this method are met by Mourning's operations.

Osygus Protection Devices

Osygus Protection Devices works through manufacturers' agents in various cities. Orders for alarm systems and down payments are forwarded from agents, and Osygus ships the goods f.o.b. shipping point. Customers are billed for the balance due plus actual shipping costs. The firm received orders for $6,000,000 of goods during the fiscal year ended November 30, 2007. Down payments of $600,000 were received, and $5,000,000 of goods were billed and shipped. Actual freight costs of $100,000 were also billed. Commissions of 10% on product price were paid to manufacturers' agents after the goods were shipped to customers. Such goods are warranted for 90 days after shipment, and warranty returns have been about 1% of sales. Revenue is recognized at the point of sale by Osygus.

Instructions

(a) There are a variety of methods for revenue recognition. Define and describe each of the following methods of revenue recognition, and indicate whether each is in accordance with generally accepted accounting principles.

  (1) Completion-of-production method.
  (2) Percentage-of-completion method.
  (3) Installment-sales method.

(b) Compute the revenue to be recognized in the fiscal year ended November 30, 2007, for

  (1) Falilat Mining.
  (2) Mourning Paperbacks.
  (3) Osygus Protection Devices.

(CMA adapted)

CA18-2 (Recognition of Revenue—Theory) Revenue is usually recognized at the point of sale. Under special circumstances, however, bases other than the point of sale are used for the timing of revenue recognition.

Instructions

(a) Why is the point of sale usually used as the basis for the timing of revenue recognition?

(b) Disregarding the special circumstances when bases other than the point of sale are used, discuss the merits of each of the following objections to the sales basis of revenue recognition:

  (1) It is too conservative because revenue is earned throughout the entire process of production.
  (2) It is not conservative enough because accounts receivable do not represent disposable funds, sales returns and allowances may be made, and collection and bad debt expenses may be incurred in a later period.

(c) Revenue may also be recognized (1) during production and (2) when cash is received. For each of these two bases of timing revenue recognition, give an example of the circumstances in which it is properly used and discuss the accounting merits of its use in lieu of the sales basis.

(AICPA adapted)

CA18-3 (Recognition of Revenue—Theory) The earning of revenue by a business enterprise is recognized for accounting purposes when the transaction is recorded. In some situations, revenue is recognized approximately as it is earned in the economic sense. In other situations, however, accountants have developed guidelines for recognizing revenue by other criteria, such as at the point of sale.

Instructions

(Ignore income taxes.)

(a) Explain and justify why revenue is often recognized as earned at time of sale.

(b) Explain in what situations it would be appropriate to recognize revenue as the productive activity takes place.

(c) At what times, other than those included in (a) and (b) above, may it be appropriate to recognize revenue? Explain.

CA18-4 (Recognition of Revenue—Bonus Dollars) Alexei & Nemov Inc. was formed early this year to sell merchandise credits to merchants who distribute the credits free to their customers. For example, customers can earn additional credits based on the dollars they spend with a merchant (e.g., airlines and hotels). Accounts for accumulating the credits and catalogs illustrating the merchandise for which the credits may be exchanged are maintained online. Centers with inventories of merchandise premiums have been established for redemption of the credits. Merchants may not return unused credits to Alexei & Nemov.

The following schedule expresses Alexei & Nemov's expectations as to percentages of a normal month's activity that will be attained. For this purpose, a "normal month's activity" is defined as the level of operations expected when expansion of activities ceases or tapers off to a stable rate. The company expects that this level will be attained in the third year and that sales of credits will average $6,000,000 per month throughout the third year.

Month	Actual Credit Sales Percent	Merchandise Premium Purchases Percent	Credit Redemptions Percent
6th	30%	40%	10%
12th	60	60	45
18th	80	80	70
24th	90	90	80
30th	100	100	95

Alexei & Nemov plans to adopt an annual closing date at the end of each 12 months of operation.

Instructions
(a) Discuss the factors to be considered in determining when revenue should be recognized in measuring the income of a business enterprise.
(b) Discuss the accounting alternatives that should be considered by Alexei & Nemov Inc. for the recognition of its revenues and related expenses.
(c) For each accounting alternative discussed in (b), give balance sheet accounts that should be used and indicate how each should be classified.

(AICPA adapted)

CA18-5 (Recognition of Revenue from Subscriptions) *Cutting Edge* is a monthly magazine that has been on the market for 18 months. It currently has a circulation of 1.4 million copies. Negotiations are underway to obtain a bank loan in order to update the magazine's facilities. They are producing close to capacity and expect to grow at an average of 20% per year over the next 3 years.

After reviewing the financial statements of *Cutting Edge*, Gary Hall, the bank loan officer, had indicated that a loan could be offered to *Cutting Edge* only if it could increase its current ratio and decrease its debt to equity ratio to a specified level.

Alexander Popov, the marketing manager of *Cutting Edge*, has devised a plan to meet these requirements. Popov indicates that an advertising campaign can be initiated to immediately increase circulation. The potential customers would be contacted after the purchase of another magazine's mailing list. The campaign would include:

1. An offer to subscribe to *Cutting Edge* at 3/4 the normal price.
2. A special offer to all new subscribers to receive the most current world atlas whenever requested at a guaranteed price of $2.
3. An unconditional guarantee that any subscriber will receive a full refund if dissatisfied with the magazine.

Although the offer of a full refund is risky, Popov claims that few people will ask for a refund after receiving half of their subscription issues. Popov notes that other magazine companies have tried this sales promotion technique and experienced great success. Their average cancellation rate was 25%. On average, each company increased its initial circulation threefold and in the long run increased circulation to twice that which existed before the promotion. In addition, 60% of the new subscribers are expected to take advantage of the atlas premium. Popov feels confident that the increased subscriptions from the advertising campaign will increase the current ratio and decrease the debt to equity ratio.

You are the controller of *Cutting Edge* and must give your opinion of the proposed plan.

Instructions
(a) When should revenue from the new subscriptions be recognized?
(b) How would you classify the estimated sales returns stemming from the unconditional guarantee?
(c) How should the atlas premium be recorded? Is the estimated premium claims a liability? Explain.

(d) Does the proposed plan achieve the goals of increasing the current ratio and decreasing the debt to equity ratio?

CA18-6 (Long-Term Contract—Percentage-of-Completion) Scherbo Company is accounting for a long-term construction contract using the percentage-of-completion method. It is a 4-year contract that is currently in its second year. The latest estimates of total contract costs indicate that the contract will be completed at a profit to Scherbo Company.

Instructions

(a) What theoretical justification is there for Scherbo Company's use of the percentage-of-completion method?

(b) How would progress billings be accounted for? Include in your discussion the classification of progress billings in Scherbo Company financial statements.

(c) How would the income recognized in the second year of the 4-year contract be determined using the cost-to-cost method of determining percentage of completion?

(d) What would be the effect on earnings per share in the second year of the 4-year contract of using the percentage-of-completion method instead of the completed-contract method? Discuss.

(AICPA adapted)

CA18-7 (Revenue Recognition—Real Estate Development) Pankratov Lakes is a new recreational real estate development which consists of 500 lake-front and lake-view lots. As a special incentive to the first 100 buyers of lake-view lots, the developer is offering 3 years of free financing on 10-year, 12% notes, no down payment, and one week at a nearby established resort—"a $1,200 value." The normal price per lot is $12,000. The cost per lake-view lot to the developer is an estimated average of $2,000. The development costs continue to be incurred; the actual average cost per lot is not known at this time. The resort promotion cost is $700 per lot. The notes are held by Davis Corp., a wholly owned subsidiary.

Instructions

(a) Discuss the revenue recognition and gross profit measurement issues raised by this situation.

(b) How would the developer's past financial and business experience influence your decision concerning the recording of these transactions?

(c) Assume 50 persons have accepted the offer, signed 10-year notes, and have stayed at the local resort. Prepare the journal entries that you believe are proper.

(d) What should be disclosed in the notes to the financial statements?

CA18-8 (Revenue Recognition) Nimble Health and Racquet Club (NHRC), which operates eight clubs in the Chicago metropolitan area, offers one-year memberships. The members may use any of the eight facilities but must reserve racquetball court time and pay a separate fee before using the court. As an incentive to new customers, NHRC advertised that any customers not satisfied for any reason could receive a refund of the remaining portion of unused membership fees. Membership fees are due at the beginning of the individual membership period. However, customers are given the option of financing the membership fee over the membership period at a 9% interest rate.

Some customers have expressed a desire to take only the regularly scheduled aerobic classes without paying for a full membership. During the current fiscal year, NHRC began selling coupon books for aerobic classes to accommodate these customers. Each book is dated and contains 50 coupons that may be redeemed for any regularly scheduled aerobics class over a one-year period. After the one-year period, unused coupons are no longer valid.

During 2004, NHRC expanded into the health equipment market by purchasing a local company that manufactures rowing machines and cross-country ski machines. These machines are used in NHRC's facilities and are sold through the clubs and mail order catalogs. Customers must make a 20% down payment when placing an equipment order; delivery is 60–90 days after order placement. The machines are sold with a 2-year unconditional guarantee. Based on past experience, NHRC expects the costs to repair machines under guarantee to be 4% of sales.

NHRC is in the process of preparing financial statements as of May 31, 2007, the end of its fiscal year. James Hogan, corporate controller, expressed concern over the company's performance for the year and decided to review the preliminary financial statements prepared by Barbara Hardy, NHRC's assistant controller. After reviewing the statements, Hogan proposed that the following changes be reflected in the May 31, 2007, published financial statements.

1. Membership revenue should be recognized when the membership fee is collected.

2. Revenue from the coupon books should be recognized when the books are sold.

3. Down payments on equipment purchases and expenses associated with the guarantee on the rowing and cross-country machines should be recognized when paid.

Hardy indicated to Hogan that the proposed changes are not in accordance with generally accepted accounting principles, but Hogan insisted that the changes be made. Hardy believes that Hogan wants to manage income to forestall any potential financial problems and increase his year-end bonus. At this point, Hardy is unsure what action to take.

Instructions

(a) **(1)** Describe when Nimble Health and Racquet Club (NHRC) should recognize revenue from membership fees, court rentals, and coupon book sales.

(2) Describe how NHRC should account for the down payments on equipment sales, explaining when this revenue should be recognized.

(3) Indicate when NHRC should recognize the expense associated with the guarantee of the rowing and cross-country machines.

(b) Discuss why James Hogan's proposed changes and his insistence that the financial statement changes be made is unethical. Structure your answer around or to include the following aspects of ethical conduct: competence, confidentiality, integrity, and/or objectivity.

(c) Identify some specific actions Barbara Hardy could take to resolve this situation.

(CMA adapted)

CA18-9 **(Revenue Recognition—Membership Fees)** Midwest Health Club offers one-year memberships. Membership fees are due in full at the beginning of the individual membership period. As an incentive to new customers, MHC advertised that any customers not satisfied for any reason could receive a refund of the remaining portion of unused membership fees. As a result of this policy, Stanley Hack, corporate controller, recognized revenue ratably over the life of the membership.

MHC is in the process of preparing its year-end financial statements. Phyllis Cavaretta, MHC's treasurer, is concerned about the company's lackluster performance this year. She reviews the financial statements Hack prepared and tells Hack to recognize membership revenue when the fees are received.

Instructions

Answer the following questions.

(a) What are the ethical issues involved?

(b) What should Hack do?

*****CA18-10** **(Franchise Revenue)** Badger Burrito Inc. sells franchises to independent operators throughout the northwestern part of the United States. The contract with the franchisee includes the following provisions.

1. The franchisee is charged an initial fee of $80,000. Of this amount, $30,000 is payable when the agreement is signed, and a $10,000 non-interest-bearing note is payable at the end of each of the 5 subsequent years.

2. All of the initial franchise fee collected by Badger is to be refunded and the remaining obligation canceled if, for any reason, the franchisee fails to open his or her franchise.

3. In return for the initial franchise fee, Badger agrees to (a) assist the franchisee in selecting the location for the business, (b) negotiate the lease for the land, (c) obtain financing and assist with building design, (d) supervise construction, (e) establish accounting and tax records, and (f) provide expert advice over a 5-year period relating to such matters as employee and management training, quality control, and promotion.

4. In addition to the initial franchise fee, the franchisee is required to pay to Badger a monthly fee of 2% of sales for menu planning, receipt innovations, and the privilege of purchasing ingredients from Badger at or below prevailing market prices.

Management of Badger Burrito estimates that the value of the services rendered to the franchisee at the time the contract is signed amounts to at least $30,000. All franchisees to date have opened their locations at the scheduled time, and none have defaulted on any of the notes receivable.

The credit ratings of all franchisees would entitle them to borrow at the current interest rate of 10%. The present value of an ordinary annuity of five annual receipts of $10,000 each discounted at 10% is $37,908.

Instructions

(a) Discuss the alternatives that Badger Burrito Inc. might use to account for the initial franchise fees, evaluate each by applying generally accepted accounting principles, and give illustrative entries for each alternative.

(b) Given the nature of Badger Burrito's agreement with its franchisees, when should revenue be recognized? Discuss the question of revenue recognition for both the initial franchise fee and the additional monthly fee of 2% of sales, and give illustrative entries for both types of revenue.

(c) Assume that Badger Burrito sells some franchises for $100,000, which includes a charge of $20,000 for the rental of equipment for its useful life of 10 years; that $50,000 of the fee is payable immediately and the balance on non-interest-bearing notes at $10,000 per year; that no portion of the $20,000 rental payment is refundable in case the franchisee goes out of business; and that title to the equipment remains with the franchisor. Under those assumptions, what would be the preferable method of accounting for the rental portion of the initial franchise fee? Explain.

(AICPA adapted)

USING YOUR JUDGMENT

Financial Reporting Problem

 The Procter & Gamble Company (P&G)

The financial statements of **P&G** are presented in Appendix 5B or can be accessed on the KWW website.

Instructions

Refer to P&G's financial statements and the accompanying notes to answer the following questions.

(a) What were P&G's sales for 2004?

(b) What was the percentage of increase or decrease in P&G's sales from 2003 to 2004? From 2002 to 2003? From 1999 to 2004?

(c) In its notes to the financial statements, what criteria does P&G use to recognize revenue?

(d) How does P&G account for trade promotions? Does the accounting conform to accrual accounting concepts? Explain.

Financial Statement Analysis Case

Westinghouse Electric Corporation

The following note appears in the "Summary of Significant Accounting Policies" section of the Annual Report of **Westinghouse Electric Corporation**.

> **Note 1 (in part): Revenue Recognition.** Sales are primarily recorded as products are shipped and services are rendered. The percentage-of-completion method of accounting is used for nuclear steam supply system orders with delivery schedules generally in excess of five years and for certain construction projects where this method of accounting is consistent with industry practice.
>
> WFSI revenues are generally recognized on the accrual method. When accounts become delinquent for more than two payment periods, usually 60 days, income is recognized only as payments are received. Such delinquent accounts for which no payments are received in the current month, and other accounts on which income is not being recognized because the receipt of either principal or interest is questionable, are classified as non-earning receivables.

Instructions

(a) Identify the revenue recognition methods used by Westinghouse Electric as discussed in its note on significant accounting policies.

(b) Under what conditions are the revenue recognition methods identified in the first paragraph of Westinghouse's note above acceptable?

(c) From the information provided in the second paragraph of Westinghouse's note, identify the type of operation being described and defend the acceptability of the revenue recognition method.

Comparative Analysis Case

The Coca-Cola Company

The Coca-Cola Company and PepsiCo, Inc.

Instructions

Go to KWW website and use information found there to answer the following questions related to **The Coca-Cola Company** and **PepsiCo, Inc.**

(a) What were Coca-Cola's and PepsiCo's net revenues (sales) for the year 2004? Which company increased its revenues more (dollars and percentage) from 2003 to 2004?

(b) Are the revenue recognition policies of Coca-Cola and PepsiCo similar? Explain.

(c) In which foreign countries (geographic areas) did Coca-Cola and PepsiCo experience significant revenues in 2004? Compare the amounts of foreign revenues to U.S. revenues for both Coca-Cola and PepsiCo.

Research Cases

Case 1

Companies registered with the Securities and Exchange Commission are required to file a current report on Form 8-K upon the occurrence of certain events.

Instructions

Use EDGAR or some other source to identify 8-Ks recently filed by two companies of your choice. Examine the 8-Ks and answer the following questions with regard to each.

(a) What corporate event or transaction triggered the filing of the Form 8-K?

(b) Identify any financial statements or exhibits included in the filing. How might these items help investors in evaluating the event/transaction?

Case 2

An article titled "SEC Broadens Investigation in Revenue-Boosting Tricks; Fearing Bogus Numbers Are Widespread, Agency Probes **Lucent** and Others," by Susan Pulliam and Rebecca Blumenstein, appeared in the May 16, 2002, *Wall Street Journal*.

Instructions

Read this article and answer the following questions.

(a) The article predicts that, "Probing revenue promises to be a much broader inquiry than the earlier investigations of **Enron** and other companies accused of using accounting tricks to boost their profits." What is the difference between inflating profits and inflating revenues?

(b) What are the ways in which accounting information is used (both in general and in ways specifically cited in this article)? What are the concerns about using accounting information that has been manipulated to increase revenues? To increase profits?

(c) Describe the specific techniques that may be used to inflate revenues that are enumerated in this article. Why would a practice of inflating revenues be of particular concern during the "dot-com boom"?

(d) The article says that **L90 Inc.** "lopped $8.3 million, or just over 10%, off revenue previously reported for 2000 and 2001," while booking the $250,000 net difference in the amount of wire transfers that had been used in one of these transactions as "Other income" rather than revenue. What is the difference between revenues and other income? Where might these items be found in a multi-step income statement? In a single-step income statement?

(e) What are "vendor allowances"? How might these allowances be used to inflate revenues? Consider the case of Lucent Technologies described in the article. Might Lucent's techniques also have been used to boost profits?

Professional Research: Financial Accounting and Reporting

Employees at your company disagree about the accounting for sales returns. The sales manager believes that granting more generous returns provisions can give the company a competitive edge and increase sales revenue. The controller cautions that, depending on the terms granted, loose returns provisions might lead to non-GAAP revenue recognition. The company CFO would like you to research the issue to provide an authoritative answer.

Instructions

Using the **Financial Accounting Research System (FARS)**, respond to the following items. (Provide text strings used in your search.)

(a) Which statement addresses revenue recognition when right of return exists?

(b) What is meant by "right of return"?

(c) When there is a right of return, what conditions must the company meet to recognize the revenue at the time of sale?

(d) What factors may impair the ability to make a reasonable estimate of future returns?

Professional Simulation

In this simulation you are asked to address questions related to revenue recognition issues. Prepare responses to all parts.

KWW_Professional _Simulation

Revenue Recognition **Time Remaining 3 hours 00 minutes** [copy] [paste] [calculator] [sheet] [standards] [help] [splitter] [done]

Directions | Situation | Measurement | Journal Entries | Financial Statements | Explanation | Resources

Nomar Industries, Inc. operates in several lines of business including the construction and real estate industries. While the majority of its revenues are recognized at point of sale, Nomar appropriately recognizes revenue on long-term construction contracts using the percentage-of-completion method. It recognizes sales of some properties using the installment-sales approach. Income data for 2007 from operations other than construction and real estate are as follows.

Revenues	$5,500,000
Expenses	4,200,000

1. Nomar started a construction project during 2006. The total contract price is $500,000, and $100,000 in costs were incurred in 2007. Estimated costs to complete the project in 2008 are $200,000. In 2006 Nomar incurred $100,000 of costs and recognized $25,000 gross profit on this project. Total billings at the end of 2007 were $230,000, and total cash collected as of the end of 2007 was $202,500.
2. During this year, Nomar sold real estate parcels at a price of $480,000. Nomar recognizes gross profit at an 18% rate when cash is received. Nomar collected $220,000 during the year on these sales.

Directions | Situation | Measurement | Journal Entries | Financial Statements | Explanation | Resources

Determine net income for Nomar for 2007. Ignore income taxes.

Directions | Situation | Measurement | Journal Entries | Financial Statements | Explanation | Resources

Prepare the journal entries to record the costs incurred and gross profit recognized in 2007 on the construction project.

Directions | Situation | Measurement | Journal Entries | Financial Statements | Explanation | Resources

For 2007, show how the details related to this construction contract would be disclosed on the balance sheet.

Directions | Situation | Measurement | Journal Entries | Financial Statements | Explanation | Resources

Nomar is negotiating real estate sales with some new customers which are more uncertain as to their ability to make all payments. Is there a more appropriate revenue-recognition policy for these customers? Explain.

Remember to check the book's companion website to find additional resources for this chapter.

wiley.com/college/kieso

ACCOUNTING FOR INCOME TAXES

Tax Uncertainty

One set of costs that companies manage are those related to taxes. In fact, in today's competitive markets, managers are expected to look for places in the tax code that a company can exploit to pay less tax to state and federal governments. By paying less in taxes, companies have more cash available to fund operations, finance expansion, and create new jobs. What happens, though, when companies push the tax saving envelop? Well, they may face a tax audit, the results of which could hurt their financial statements.

A notable example of corporate maneuvering to reduce taxable income involved **Limited Brands Inc.** It managed state-tax costs downward by locating part of its business in low-tax-rate states while operating retail outlets elsewhere. For example, by basing a subsidiary (which does nothing more than hold the trademarks for Bath and Body Works and Victoria's Secret) in Delaware, it is able to transfer hundreds of millions of dollars from Limited's retail outlets in high-tax states into Delaware, which has a state tax rate of zero.

However, the IRS and some states have been increasing their scrutiny of transactions that seem done only to avoid taxes and that do not serve a legitimate business purpose. In one case, an attorney for North Carolina alleged that Limited Brands Inc. ". . . engaged in hocus pocus bookkeeping and deceptive accounting," the sole purpose of which was to reduce its state-tax bill. The court agreed, and Limited Inc. had to pay millions of dollars in taxes dating back to 1994.

Limited Brands shareholders likely got an unpleasant surprise when they learned the company also had a big tax obligation from its "uncertain tax position" related to off-shore locations. The same can be said for many other companies that take tax deductions that may not hold up under the scrutiny of the tax court or an IRS audit. Current accounting rules are not very specific on when companies have to record an obligation for taxes that will be owed on uncertain tax positions. This is changing because the SEC and the FASB are concerned about non-recognition of significant tax obligations. As this text is being written, the FASB is working on a rule that would require companies to record loss contingencies for more uncertain tax provisions in their financial statements.[1]

---

[1]See Glenn Simpson, "A Tax Maneuver in Delaware Puts Squeeze on States," *Wall Street Journal* (August 9, 2002), p. A1; and FASB, "Uncertain Tax Positions: Recognition of Tax Benefits," (July 14, 2005), *www.fasb.org/project/uncertain_tax_positions.shtml*.

Learning Objectives

After studying this chapter, you should be able to:

1 Identify differences between pretax financial income and taxable income.

2 Describe a temporary difference that results in future taxable amounts.

3 Describe a temporary difference that results in future deductible amounts.

4 Explain the purpose of a deferred tax asset valuation allowance.

5 Describe the presentation of income tax expense in the income statement.

6 Describe various temporary and permanent differences.

7 Explain the effect of various tax rates and tax rate changes on deferred income taxes.

8 Apply accounting procedures for a loss carryback and a loss carryforward.

9 Describe the presentation of deferred income taxes in financial statements.

10 Indicate the basic principles of the asset-liability method.

As our opening story indicates, companies spend a considerable amount of time and effort to minimize their income tax payments. And with good reason, as income taxes are a major cost of doing business for most corporations. Yet, at the same time, companies must present financial information to the investment community that provides a clear picture of present and potential tax obligations and tax benefits. In this chapter, we discuss the basic guidelines that companies must follow in reporting income taxes. The content and organization of the chapter are as follows.

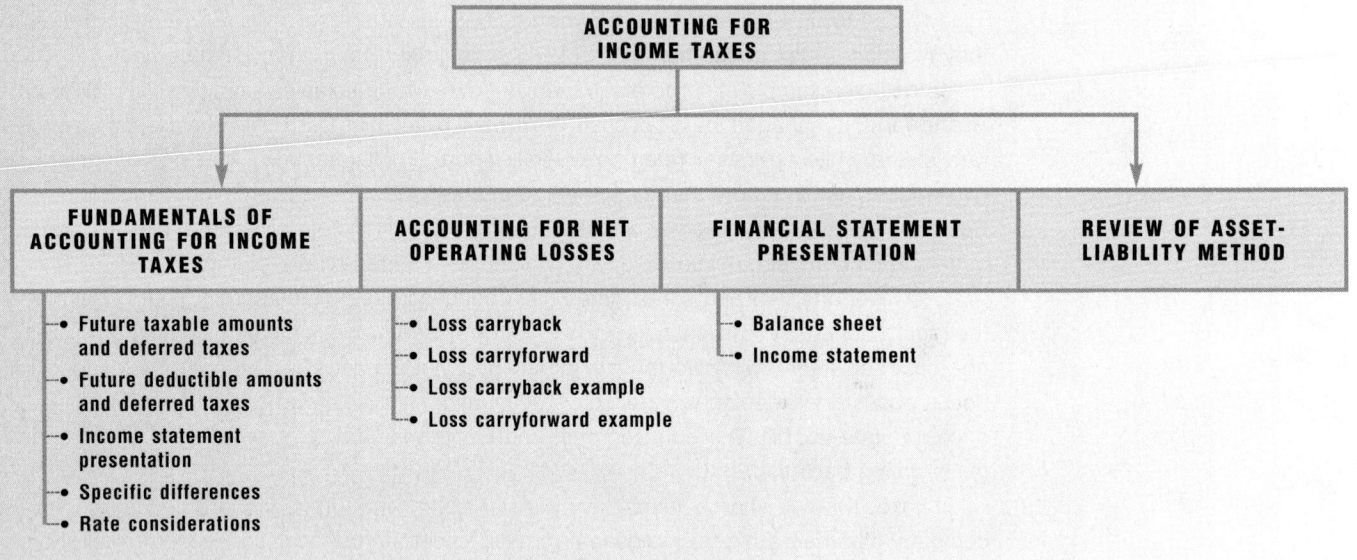

FUNDAMENTALS OF ACCOUNTING FOR INCOME TAXES

OBJECTIVE 1
Identify differences between pretax financial income and taxable income.

Up to this point, you have learned the basic guidelines that corporations use to report information to investors and creditors. Corporations also must file income tax returns following the guidelines developed by the Internal Revenue Service (IRS). Because GAAP and tax regulations differ in a number of ways, so frequently do pretax financial income and taxable income. Consequently, the amount that a company reports as tax expense will differ from the amount of taxes payable to the IRS. Illustration 19-1 highlights these differences.

Pretax financial income is a *financial reporting* term. It also is often referred to as *income before taxes, income for financial reporting purposes,* or *income for book purposes.* Companies determine pretax financial income according to GAAP. They measure it with the objective of providing useful information to investors and creditors.

Taxable income (income for tax purposes) is a *tax accounting* term. It indicates the amount used to compute income tax payable. Companies determine taxable income according to the Internal Revenue Code (the tax code). Income taxes provide money to support government operations.

To illustrate how differences in GAAP and IRS rules affect financial reporting and taxable income, assume that Chelsea Inc. reported revenues of $130,000 and expenses of $60,000 in each of its first three years of operations. Illustration 19-2 shows the (partial) income statement over these three years.

For tax purposes (following the tax code), Chelsea reported the same expenses to the IRS in each of the years. But, as Illustration 19-3 shows, Chelsea reported taxable revenues of $100,000 in 2007, $150,000 in 2008, and $140,000 in 2009.

ILLUSTRATION 19-1
Fundamental Differences
between Financial and
Tax Reporting

CHELSEA INC. GAAP REPORTING				
	2007	2008	2009	Total
Revenues	$130,000	$130,000	$130,000	
Expenses	60,000	60,000	60,000	
Pretax financial income	$ 70,000	$ 70,000	$ 70,000	$ 210,000
Income tax expense (40%)	$ 28,000	$ 28,000	$ 28,000	$ 84,000

ILLUSTRATION 19-2
Financial Reporting
Income

CHELSEA INC. TAX REPORTING				
	2007	2008	2009	Total
Revenues	$100,000	$150,000	$140,000	
Expenses	60,000	60,000	60,000	
Taxable income	$ 40,000	$ 90,000	$ 80,000	$ 210,000
Income tax payable (40%)	$ 16,000	$ 36,000	$ 32,000	$ 84,000

ILLUSTRATION 19-3
Tax Reporting Income

Income tax expense and income tax payable differed over the three years, but were equal **in total**, as Illustration 19-4 shows.

CHELSEA INC. INCOME TAX EXPENSE AND INCOME TAX PAYABLE				
	2007	2008	2009	Total
Income tax expense	$28,000	$28,000	$28,000	$84,000
Income tax payable	16,000	36,000	32,000	84,000
Difference	$12,000	$ (8,000)	$ (4,000)	$ 0

ILLUSTRATION 19-4
Comparison of Income
Tax Expense to Income
Tax Payable

INTERNATIONAL INSIGHT

In some countries, taxable income equals pretax financial income. As a consequence, accounting for differences between tax and book income is insignificant.

The differences between income tax expense and income tax payable in this example arise for a simple reason. For financial reporting, companies use the full accrual method to report revenues. For tax purposes, they use a modified cash basis. As a result, Chelsea reports pretax financial income of $70,000 and income tax expense of $28,000 for each of the three years. However, taxable income fluctuates. For example, in 2007 taxable income is only $40,000, so Chelsea owes just $16,000 to the IRS that year. Chelsea classifies the income tax payable as a current liability on the balance sheet.

As Illustration 19-4 indicates, for Chelsea the $12,000 ($28,000 − $16,000) difference between income tax expense and income tax payable in 2007 reflects taxes that it will pay in future periods. This $12,000 difference is often referred to as a **deferred tax amount**. In this case it is a **deferred tax liability**. In cases where taxes will be lower in the future, Chelsea records a **deferred tax asset**. We explain the measurement and accounting for deferred tax liabilities and assets in the following two sections.

Future Taxable Amounts and Deferred Taxes

OBJECTIVE 2
Describe a temporary difference that results in future taxable amounts.

The example summarized in Illustration 19-4 shows how income tax payable can differ from income tax expense. This can happen when there are temporary differences between the amounts reported for tax purposes and those reported for book purposes. A **temporary difference** is the difference between the tax basis of an asset or liability and its reported (carrying or book) amount in the financial statements, which will result in taxable amounts or deductible amounts in future years. **Taxable amounts** increase taxable income in future years. **Deductible amounts** decrease taxable income in future years.

In Chelsea's situation, the only difference between the book basis and tax basis of the assets and liabilities relates to accounts receivable that arose from revenue recognized for book purposes. Illustration 19-5 indicates that Chelsea reports accounts receivable at $30,000 in the December 31, 2007, GAAP-basis balance sheet. However, the receivables have a zero tax basis.

ILLUSTRATION 19-5
Temporary Difference, Sales Revenue

Per Books	12/31/07	Per Tax Return	12/31/07
Accounts receivable	$30,000	Accounts receivable	$–0–

What will happen to the $30,000 temporary difference that originated in 2007 for Chelsea? Assuming that Chelsea expects to collect $20,000 of the receivables in 2008 and $10,000 in 2009, this collection results in future taxable amounts of $20,000 in 2008 and $10,000 in 2009. These future taxable amounts will cause taxable income to exceed pretax financial income in both 2008 and 2009.

An assumption inherent in a company's GAAP balance sheet is that companies recover and settle the assets and liabilities at their reported amounts (carrying amounts). This assumption creates a requirement under accrual accounting to recognize *currently* the deferred tax consequences of temporary differences. That is, companies recognize the amount of income taxes that are payable (or refundable) when they recover and settle the reported amounts of the assets and liabilities, respectively. Illustration 19-6 shows the reversal of the temporary difference described in Illustration 19-5 and the resulting taxable amounts in future periods.

ILLUSTRATION 19-6
Reversal of Temporary Difference, Chelsea Inc.

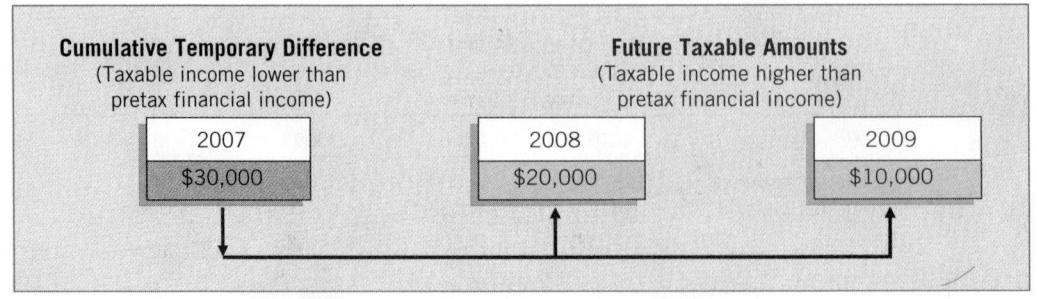

Chelsea assumes that it will collect the accounts receivable and report the $30,000 collection as taxable revenues in future tax returns. A payment of income tax in both 2008 and 2009 will occur. Chelsea should therefore record in its books in 2007 the deferred tax consequences of the revenue and related receivables reflected in the 2007 financial statements. Chelsea does this by recording a deferred tax liability.

Deferred Tax Liability

A **deferred tax liability** is the deferred tax consequences attributable to taxable temporary differences. In other words, **a deferred tax liability represents the increase in taxes payable in future years as a result of taxable temporary differences existing at the end of the current year**.

Recall from the Chelsea example that income tax payable is $16,000 ($40,000 × 40%) in 2007 (Illustration 19-4). In addition, a temporary difference exists at year-end because Chelsea reports the revenue and related accounts receivable differently for book and tax purposes. The book basis of accounts receivable is $30,000, and the tax basis is zero. Thus, the total deferred tax liability at the end of 2007 is $12,000, computed as shown in Illustration 19-7.

Book basis of accounts receivable	$30,000
Tax basis of accounts receivable	–0–
Cumulative temporary difference at the end of 2004	30,000
Tax rate	40%
Deferred tax liability at the end of 2007	$12,000

ILLUSTRATION 19-7
Computation of Deferred Tax Liability, End of 2007

Companies may also compute the deferred tax liability by preparing a schedule that indicates the future taxable amounts due to existing temporary differences. Such a schedule, as shown in Illustration 19-8, is particularly useful when the computations become more complex.

	Future Years		
	2008	2009	Total
Future taxable amounts	$20,000	$10,000	$30,000
Tax rate	40%	40%	
Deferred tax liability at the end of 2007	$ 8,000	$ 4,000	$12,000

ILLUSTRATION 19-8
Schedule of Future Taxable Amounts

Because it is the first year of operations for Chelsea, there is no deferred tax liability at the beginning of the year. Chelsea computes the income tax expense for 2007 as shown in Illustration 19-9.

Deferred tax liability at end of 2007	$12,000
Deferred tax liability at beginning of 2007	–0–
Deferred tax expense for 2007	12,000
Current tax expense for 2007 (Income tax payable)	16,000
Income tax expense (total) for 2007	$28,000

ILLUSTRATION 19-9
Computation of Income Tax Expense, 2007

This computation indicates that income tax expense has two components—**current tax expense** (the amount of income tax payable for the period) and deferred tax expense. **Deferred tax expense** is the increase in the deferred tax liability balance from the beginning to the end of the accounting period.

Companies credit taxes due and payable to Income Tax Payable, and credit the increase in deferred taxes to Deferred Tax Liability. They then debit the sum of those two items to Income Tax Expense. For Chelsea, it makes the following entry at the end of 2007.

Income Tax Expense	28,000	
Income Tax Payable		16,000
Deferred Tax Liability		12,000

At the end of 2008 (the second year), the difference between the book basis and the tax basis of the accounts receivable is $10,000. Chelsea multiplies this difference by the applicable tax rate to arrive at the deferred tax liability of $4,000 ($10,000 × 40%), which it reports at the end of 2008. Income tax payable for 2008 is $36,000 (Illustration 19-3), and the income tax expense for 2008 is as shown in Illustration 19-10.

ILLUSTRATION 19-10
Computation of Income
Tax Expense, 2008

Deferred tax liability at end of 2008	$ 4,000
Deferred tax liability at beginning of 2008	12,000
Deferred tax expense (benefit) for 2008	(8,000)
Current tax expense for 2008 (Income tax payable)	36,000
Income tax expense (total) for 2008	$28,000

Chelsea records income tax expense, the change in the deferred tax liability, and income tax payable for 2008 as follows.

Income Tax Expense	28,000	
Deferred Tax Liability	8,000	
Income Tax Payable		36,000

The entry to record income taxes at the end of 2009 reduces the Deferred Tax Liability by $4,000. The Deferred Tax Liability account appears as follows at the end of 2009.

ILLUSTRATION 19-11
Deferred Tax Liability
Account after Reversals

Deferred Tax Liability			
2008	8,000	2007	12,000
2009	4,000		

The Deferred Tax Liability account has a zero balance at the end of 2009.

"REAL LIABILITIES"

WHAT DO THE
NUMBERS MEAN?

Some analysts dismiss deferred tax liabilities when assessing the financial strength of a company. But the FASB indicates that the deferred tax liability meets the definition of a liability established in *Statement of Financial Accounting Concepts No. 6*, "Elements of Financial Statements" because:

1 *It results from a past transaction.* In the Chelsea example, the company performed services for customers and recognized revenue in 2007 for financial reporting purposes but deferred it for tax purposes.

2 *It is a present obligation.* Taxable income in future periods will exceed pretax financial income as a result of this temporary difference. Thus, a present obligation exists.

3 *It represents a future sacrifice.* Taxable income and taxes due in future periods will result from past events. The payment of these taxes when they come due is the future sacrifice.

A study by B. Ayers indicates that the market views deferred tax assets and liabilities similarly to other assets and liabilities. Further, the study concludes that *SFAS No. 109* increased the usefulness of deferred tax amounts in financial statements.

Source: B. Ayers, "Deferred Tax Accounting Under *SFAS No. 109*: An Empirical Investigation of Its Incremental Value-Relevance Relative to *APB No. 11*," *The Accounting Review* (April 1998).

Summary of Income Tax Accounting Objectives

One objective of accounting for income taxes is to recognize the amount of taxes payable or refundable for the current year. In Chelsea's case, income tax payable is $16,000 for 2007.

A **second objective** is to recognize deferred tax liabilities and assets for the future tax consequences of events already recognized in the financial statements or tax returns. For example, Chelsea sold services to customers that resulted in accounts receivable of $30,000 in 2007. It reported that amount on the 2007 income statement, but not on the tax return as income. That amount will appear on future tax returns as income for the period **when collected**. As a result, a $30,000 temporary difference exists at the end of 2007, which will cause future taxable amounts. Chelsea reports a deferred tax liability of $12,000 on the balance sheet at the end of 2007, which represents the increase in taxes payable in future years ($8,000 in 2008 and $4,000 in 2009) as a result of a temporary difference existing at the end of the current year. The related deferred tax liability is reduced by $8,000 at the end of 2008 and by another $4,000 at the end of 2009.

In addition to affecting the balance sheet, deferred taxes impact income tax expense in each of the three years affected. In 2007, taxable income ($40,000) is less than pretax financial income ($70,000). Income tax payable for 2007 is therefore $16,000 (based on taxable income). Deferred tax expense of $12,000 results from the increase in the Deferred Tax Liability account on the balance sheet. Income tax expense is then $28,000 for 2007.

In 2008 and 2009, however, taxable income will exceed pretax financial income, due to the reversal of the temporary difference ($20,000 in 2008 and $10,000 in 2009). Income tax payable will therefore exceed income tax expense in 2008 and 2009. Chelsea will debit the Deferred Tax Liability account for $8,000 in 2008 and $4,000 in 2009. It records credits for these amounts in Income Tax Expense. These credits are often referred to as a **deferred tax benefit** (which we discuss again later on).

Future Deductible Amounts and Deferred Taxes

Assume that during 2007, Cunningham Inc. estimated its warranty costs related to the sale of microwave ovens to be $500,000, paid evenly over the next two years. For book purposes, in 2007 Cunningham reported warranty expense and a related estimated liability for warranties of $500,000 in its financial statements. For tax purposes, **the warranty tax deduction is not allowed until paid**. Therefore, Cunningham recognizes no warranty liability on a tax-basis balance sheet. Illustration 19-12 shows the balance sheet difference at the end of 2007.

> **OBJECTIVE 3**
> Describe a temporary difference that results in future deductible amounts.

Per Books	12/31/07	Per Tax Return	12/31/07
Estimated liability for warranties	$500,000	Estimated liability for warranties	$–0–

ILLUSTRATION 19-12
Temporary Difference, Warranty Liability

When Cunningham pays the warranty liability, it reports an expense (deductible amount) for tax purposes. Because of this temporary difference, Cunningham should recognize in 2007 the tax benefits (positive tax consequences) for the tax deductions that will result from the future settlement of the liability. Cunningham reports this future tax benefit in the December 31, 2007, balance sheet as a **deferred tax asset**.

We can think about this situation another way. Deductible amounts occur in future tax returns. These **future deductible amounts** cause taxable income to be less than pretax financial income in the future as a result of an existing temporary difference. Cunningham's temporary difference originates (arises) in one period (2007) and reverses over two periods (2008 and 2009). Illustration 19-13 (page 970) diagrams this situation.

ILLUSTRATION 19-13
Reversal of Temporary
Difference, Cunningham
Inc.

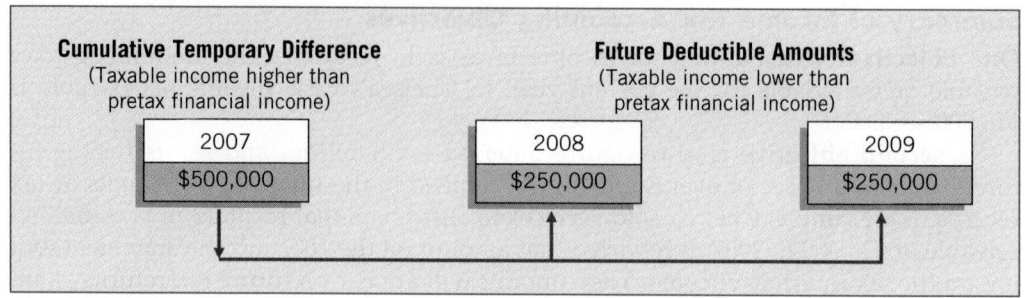

Deferred Tax Asset

A **deferred tax asset** is the deferred tax consequence attributable to deductible temporary differences. In other words, a **deferred tax asset represents the increase in taxes refundable (or saved) in future years as a result of deductible temporary differences existing at the end of the current year.**

To illustrate, assume that Hunt Co. accrues a loss and a related liability of $50,000 in 2007 for financial reporting purposes because of pending litigation. Hunt cannot deduct this amount for tax purposes until the period it pays the liability, expected in 2008. As a result, a deductible amount will occur in 2008 when Hunt settles the liability (Estimated Litigation Liability), causing taxable income to be lower than pretax financial income. Illustration 19-14 shows the computation of the deferred tax asset at the end of 2007 (assuming a 40 percent tax rate).

ILLUSTRATION 19-14
Computation of Deferred
Tax Asset, End of 2007

Book basis of litigation liability	$50,000
Tax basis of litigation liability	–0–
Cumulative temporary difference at the end of 2007	50,000
Tax rate	40%
Deferred tax asset at the end of 2007	$20,000

Hunt can also compute the deferred tax asset by preparing a schedule that indicates the future deductible amounts due to deductible temporary differences. Illustration 19-15 shows this schedule.

ILLUSTRATION 19-15
Schedule of Future
Deductible Amounts

	Future Years
Future deductible amounts	$50,000
Tax rate	40%
Deferred tax asset at the end of 2007	$20,000

Assuming that 2007 is Hunt's first year of operations, and income tax payable is $100,000, Hunt computes its income tax expense as follows.

ILLUSTRATION 19-16
Computation of Income
Tax Expense, 2007

Deferred tax asset at end of 2007	$ 20,000
Deferred tax asset at beginning of 2007	–0–
Deferred tax expense (benefit) for 2007	(20,000)
Current tax expense for 2007 (Income tax payable)	100,000
Income tax expense (total) for 2007	$ 80,000

The **deferred tax benefit** results from the increase in the deferred tax asset from the beginning to the end of the accounting period (similar to the Chelsea example earlier). The deferred tax benefit is a negative component of income tax expense. The total income tax expense of $80,000 on the income statement for 2007 thus consists of two elements—current tax expense of $100,000 and a deferred tax benefit of $20,000. For Hunt, it makes the following journal entry at the end of 2007 to record income tax expense, deferred income taxes, and income tax payable.

Income Tax Expense	80,000	
Deferred Tax Asset	20,000	
Income Tax Payable		100,000

At the end of 2008 (the second year), the difference between the book value and the tax basis of the litigation liability is zero. Therefore, there is no deferred tax asset at this date. Assuming that income tax payable for 2008 is $140,000, Hunt computes income tax expense for 2008 as shown in Illustration 19-17.

ILLUSTRATION 19-17
Computation of Income Tax Expense, 2008

Deferred tax asset at the end of 2008	$ –0–
Deferred tax asset at the beginning of 2008	20,000
Deferred tax expense (benefit) for 2008	20,000
Current tax expense for 2008 (Income tax payable)	140,000
Income tax expense (total) for 2008	$160,000

The company records income taxes for 2008 as follows.

Income Tax Expense	160,000	
Deferred Tax Asset		20,000
Income Tax Payable		140,000

The total income tax expense of $160,000 on the income statement for 2008 thus consists of two elements—current tax expense of $140,000 and deferred tax expense of $20,000. Illustration 19-18 shows the Deferred Tax Asset account at the end of 2008.

ILLUSTRATION 19-18
Deferred Tax Asset Account after Reversals

Deferred Tax Asset

2007	20,000	2008	20,000

"REAL ASSETS"

A key issue in accounting for income taxes is whether a company should recognize a deferred tax asset in the financial records. Based on the conceptual definition of an asset, a deferred tax asset meets the three main conditions for an item to be recognized as an asset:

WHAT DO THE NUMBERS MEAN?

1 *It results from a past transaction.* In the Hunt example, the accrual of the loss contingency is the past event that gives rise to a future deductible temporary difference.

2 *It gives rise to a probable benefit in the future.* Taxable income exceeds pretax financial income in the current year (2007). However, in the next year the exact opposite occurs. That is, taxable income is lower than pretax financial income. Because this deductible temporary difference reduces taxes payable in the future, a probable future benefit exists at the end of the current period.

3 *The entity controls access to the benefits.* Hunt can obtain the benefit of existing deductible temporary differences by reducing its taxes payable in the future. Hunt has the exclusive right to that benefit and can control others' access to it.

Market analysts' reaction to the **write-off** of deferred tax assets also supports their treatment as assets. When **Bethlehem Steel** reported a $1 billion charge in a recent year to write off a deferred tax asset, analysts believed that Bethlehem was signaling that it would not realize the future benefits of the tax deductions. Thus, Bethlehem should write down the asset like other assets.

Source: J. Weil and S. Liesman, "Stock Gurus Disregard Most Big Write-Offs But They Often Hold Vital Clues to Outlook," *Wall Street Journal Online* (December 31, 2001).

Deferred Tax Asset—Valuation Allowance

OBJECTIVE 4
Explain the purpose of a deferred tax asset valuation allowance.

Companies recognize a deferred tax asset for all deductible temporary differences. However, based on available evidence, a company should reduce a deferred tax asset by a **valuation allowance** if **it is more likely than not** that it **will not realize** some portion or all of the deferred tax asset. "More likely than not" means a level of likelihood of at least slightly more than 50 percent.

Assume that Jensen Co. has a deductible temporary difference of $1,000,000 at the end of its first year of operations. Its tax rate is 40 percent, which means it records a deferred tax asset of $400,000 ($1,000,000 × 40%). Assuming $900,000 of income taxes payable, Jensen records income tax expense, the deferred tax asset, and income tax payable as follows.

Income Tax Expense	500,000	
Deferred Tax Asset	400,000	
Income Tax Payable		900,000

After careful review of all available evidence, Jensen determines that it is more likely than not that it will not realize $100,000 of this deferred tax asset. Jensen records this reduction in asset value as follows.

Income Tax Expense	100,000	
Allowance to Reduce Deferred Tax Asset to Expected Realizable Value		100,000

This journal entry increases income tax expense in the current period because Jensen does not expect to realize a favorable tax benefit for a portion of the deductible temporary difference. Jensen **simultaneously establishes a valuation allowance to recognize the reduction in the carrying amount of the deferred tax asset**. This valuation account is a contra account. Jensen reports it on the financial statements in the following manner.

ILLUSTRATION 19-19
Balance Sheet Presentation of Valuation Allowance Account

Deferred tax asset	$400,000
Less: Allowance to reduce deferred tax asset to expected realizable value	100,000
Deferred tax asset (net)	$300,000

Jensen then evaluates this allowance account at the end of each accounting period. If, at the end of the next period, the deferred tax asset is still $400,000, but now it expects to realize $350,000 of this asset, Jensen makes the following entry to adjust the valuation account.

Allowance to Reduce Deferred Tax Asset to Expected Realizable Value	50,000	
Income Tax Expense		50,000

Jensen should consider all available evidence, both positive and negative, to determine whether, based on the weight of available evidence, it needs a valuation allowance. For example, if Jensen has been experiencing a series of loss years, it reasonably assumes that these losses will continue. Therefore, Jensen will lose the benefit of the future deductible amounts. We discuss the use of a valuation account under other conditions later in the chapter.

OBJECTIVE 5
Describe the presentation of income tax expense in the income statement.

Income Statement Presentation

Circumstances dictate whether a company should add or subtract the change in deferred income taxes to or from income tax payable in computing income tax expense. For example, a company adds an increase in a deferred tax liability to income tax payable. On the other hand, it subtracts an increase in a deferred tax asset from income tax payable. The formula in Illustration 19-20 is used to compute income tax expense (benefit).

Income Tax Payable or Refundable	±	Change in Deferred Income Taxes	=	Total Income Tax Expense or Benefit

ILLUSTRATION 19-20
Formula to Compute Income Tax Expense

In the income statement or in the notes to the financial statements, a company should disclose the significant components of income tax expense attributable to continuing operations. Given the information related to Chelsea on page 967, Chelsea reports its income statement as follows.

ILLUSTRATION 19-21
Income Statement Presentation of Income Tax Expense

CHELSEA INC.
INCOME STATEMENT
FOR THE YEAR ENDING DECEMBER 31, 2007

Revenues		$130,000
Expenses		60,000
Income before income taxes		70,000
Income tax expense		
Current	$16,000	
Deferred	12,000	28,000
Net income		$ 42,000

As illustrated, Chelsea reports both the current portion (amount of income tax payable for the period) and the deferred portion of income tax expense. Another option is to simply report the total income tax expense on the income statement, and then indicate in the notes to the financial statements the current and deferred portions. Income tax expense is often referred to as "Provision for income taxes." Using this terminology, the current provision is $16,000, and the provision for deferred taxes is $12,000.

Specific Differences

Numerous items create differences between pretax financial income and taxable income. For purposes of accounting recognition, these differences are of two types: (1) temporary, and (2) permanent.

OBJECTIVE 6
Describe various temporary and permanent differences.

Temporary Differences

Taxable temporary differences are temporary differences that will result in taxable amounts in future years when the related assets are recovered. **Deductible temporary differences** are temporary differences that will result in deductible amounts in future years, when the related book liabilities are settled. Taxable temporary differences give rise to recording deferred tax liabilities. Deductible temporary differences give rise to recording deferred tax assets. Illustration 19-22 (page 974) provides examples of temporary differences.[2]

---

[2]*SFAS No. 109* gives more examples of temporary differences. We present the most common types in this chapter.

A. **Revenues or gains are taxable after they are recognized in financial income.**

An asset (e.g., accounts receivable or investment) may be recognized for revenues or gains that will result in **taxable amounts in future years** when the asset is recovered. Examples:

1. Sales accounted for on the accrual basis for financial reporting purposes and on the installment (cash) basis for tax purposes.
2. Contracts accounted for under the percentage-of-completion method for financial reporting purposes and a portion of related gross profit deferred for tax purposes.
3. Investments accounted for under the equity method for financial reporting purposes and under the cost method for tax purposes.
4. Gain on involuntary conversion of nonmonetary asset which is recognized for financial reporting purposes but deferred for tax purposes.

B. **Expenses or losses are deductible after they are recognized in financial income.**

A liability (or contra asset) may be recognized for expenses or losses that will result in **deductible amounts in future years** when the liability is settled. Examples:

1. Product warranty liabilities.
2. Estimated liabilities related to discontinued operations or restructurings.
3. Litigation accruals.
4. Bad debt expense recognized using the allowance method for financial reporting purposes; direct write-off method used for tax purposes.
5. Stock-based compensation expense.

C. **Revenues or gains are taxable before they are recognized in financial income.**

A liability may be recognized for an advance payment for goods or services to be provided in future years. For tax purposes, the advance payment is included in taxable income upon the receipt of cash. Future sacrifices to provide goods or services (or future refunds to those who cancel their orders) that settle the liability will result in **deductible amounts in future years**. Examples:

1. Subscriptions received in advance.
2. Advance rental receipts.
3. Sales and leasebacks for financial reporting purposes (income deferral) but reported as sales for tax purposes.
4. Prepaid contracts and royalties received in advance.

D. **Expenses or losses are deductible before they are recognized in financial income.**

The cost of an asset may have been deducted for tax purposes faster than it was expensed for financial reporting purposes. Amounts received upon future recovery of the amount of the asset for financial reporting (through use or sale) will exceed the remaining tax basis of the asset and thereby result in **taxable amounts in future years**. Examples:

1. Depreciable property, depletable resources, and intangibles.
2. Deductible pension funding exceeding expense.
3. Prepaid expenses that are deducted on the tax return in the period paid.

ILLUSTRATION 19-22
Examples of Temporary Differences

Determining a company's temporary differences may prove difficult. A company should prepare a balance sheet for tax purposes that it can compare with its GAAP balance sheet. Many of the differences between the two balance sheets are temporary differences.

Originating and Reversing Aspects of Temporary Differences. An **originating temporary difference** is the initial difference between the book basis and the tax basis of an asset or liability, regardless of whether the tax basis of the asset or liability exceeds or is exceeded by the book basis of the asset or liability. A **reversing difference**, on the other hand, occurs when eliminating a temporary difference that originated in prior periods and then removing the related tax effect from the deferred tax account.

For example, assume that Sharp Co. has tax depreciation in excess of book depreciation of $2,000 in 2003, 2004, and 2005. Further, it has an excess of book depreciation over tax depreciation of $3,000 in 2006 and 2007 for the same asset. Assuming a tax rate of 30 percent for all years involved, the Deferred Tax Liability account reflects the following.

ILLUSTRATION 19-23
Tax Effects of Originating and Reversing Differences

	Deferred Tax Liability				
Tax Effects of Reversing Differences	2006	900	2003	600	Tax Effects of Originating Differences
	2007	900	2004	600	
			2005	600	

The originating differences for Sharp in each of the first three years are $2,000. The related tax effect of each originating difference is $600. The reversing differences in 2006 and 2007 are each $3,000. The related tax effect of each is $900.

Permanent Differences

Some differences between taxable income and pretax financial income are permanent. **Permanent differences** result from items that (1) enter into pretax financial income but **never** into taxable income, or (2) enter into taxable income but **never** into pretax financial income.

Congress has enacted a variety of tax law provisions to attain certain political, economic, and social objectives. Some of these provisions exclude certain revenues from taxation, limit the deductibility of certain expenses, and permit the deduction of certain other expenses in excess of costs incurred. A corporation that has tax-free income, nondeductible expenses, or allowable deductions in excess of cost, has an effective tax rate that differs from its statutory (regular) tax rate.

Since permanent differences affect only the period in which they occur, they do not give rise to future taxable or deductible amounts. As a result, **companies recognize no deferred tax consequences**. Illustration 19-24 shows examples of permanent differences.

ILLUSTRATION 19-24
Examples of Permanent Differences

A. **Items are recognized for financial reporting purposes but not for tax purposes.**
   Examples:
   1. Interest received on state and municipal obligations.
   2. Expenses incurred in obtaining tax-exempt income.
   3. Proceeds from life insurance carried by the company on key officers or employees.
   4. Premiums paid for life insurance carried by the company on key officers or employees (company is beneficiary).
   5. Fines and expenses resulting from a violation of law.

B. **Items are recognized for tax purposes but not for financial reporting purposes.**
   Examples:
   1. "Percentage depletion" of natural resources in excess of their cost.
   2. The deduction for dividends received from U.S. corporations, generally 70% or 80%.

Examples of Temporary and Permanent Differences

To illustrate the computations used when both temporary and permanent differences exist, assume that Bio-Tech Company reports pretax financial income of $200,000 in each of the years 2005, 2006, and 2007. The company is subject to a 30 percent tax rate, and has the following differences between pretax financial income and taxable income.

1 Bio-Tech reports an installment sale of $18,000 in 2005 for tax purposes over an 18-month period at a constant amount per month beginning January 1, 2006. It recognizes the entire sale for book purposes in 2005.

2 It pays life insurance premiums for its key officers of $5,000 in 2006 and 2007. Although not tax-deductible, Bio-Tech expenses the premiums for book purposes.

The installment sale is a temporary difference, whereas the life insurance premium is a permanent difference. Illustration 19-25 shows the reconciliation of Bio-Tech's pretax financial income to taxable income and the computation of income tax payable.

ILLUSTRATION 19-25
Reconciliation and Computation of Income Taxes Payable

	2005	2006	2007
Pretax financial income	$200,000	$200,000	$200,000
Permanent difference			
Nondeductible expense		5,000	5,000
Temporary difference			
Installment sale	(18,000)	12,000	6,000
Taxable income	182,000	217,000	211,000
Tax rate	30%	30%	30%
Income tax payable	$ 54,600	$ 65,100	$ 63,300

Note that Bio-Tech **deducts** the installment sales revenue from pretax financial income to arrive at taxable income. The reason: pretax financial income includes the installment sales revenue; taxable income does not. Conversely, it **adds** the $5,000 insurance premium to pretax financial income to arrive at taxable income. The reason: pretax financial income records an expense for this premium, but for tax purposes the premium is not deductible. As a result, pretax financial income is lower than taxable income. Therefore, the life insurance premium must be added back to pretax financial income to reconcile to taxable income.

Bio-Tech records income taxes for 2005, 2006, and 2007 as follows.

December 31, 2005		
Income Tax Expense ($54,600 + $5,400)	60,000	
Deferred Tax Liability ($18,000 × 30%)		5,400
Income Tax Payable ($182,000 × 30%)		54,600

December 31, 2006		
Income Tax Expense ($65,100 − $3,600)	61,500	
Deferred Tax Liability ($12,000 × 30%)	3,600	
Income Tax Payable ($217,000 × 30%)		65,100

December 31, 2007		
Income Tax Expense ($63,300 − $1,800)	61,500	
Deferred Tax Liability ($6,000 × 30%)	1,800	
Income Tax Payable ($211,000 × 30%)		63,300

Bio-Tech has one temporary difference, which originates in 2005 and reverses in 2006 and 2007. It recognizes a deferred tax liability at the end of 2005 because the temporary difference causes future taxable amounts. As the temporary difference reverses, Bio-Tech reduces the deferred tax liability. There is no deferred tax amount associated with the difference caused by the nondeductible insurance expense because it is a permanent difference.

Although an enacted tax rate of 30 percent applies for all three years, the effective rate differs from the enacted rate in 2006 and 2007. Bio-Tech computes the **effective tax rate** by dividing total income tax expense for the period by pretax financial income. The effective rate is 30 percent for 2005 ($60,000 ÷ $200,000 = 30%) and 30.75 percent for 2006 and 2007 ($61,500 ÷ $200,000 = 30.75%).

Tax Rate Considerations

OBJECTIVE 7
Explain the effect of various tax rates and tax rate changes on deferred income taxes.

In our previous illustrations, the enacted tax rate did not change from one year to the next. Thus, to compute the deferred income tax amount to report on the balance sheet, a company simply multiplies the cumulative temporary difference by the current tax rate. Using Bio-Tech as an example, it multiplies the cumulative temporary difference of $18,000 by the enacted tax rate, 30 percent in this case, to arrive at a deferred tax liability of $5,400 ($18,000 × 30%) at the end of 2005.

Future Tax Rates

What happens if tax rates are expected to change in the future? In this case, a company should use the **enacted tax rate** expected to apply. Therefore, a company must consider presently enacted changes in the tax rate that become effective for a particular future year(s) when determining the tax rate to apply to existing temporary differences. For example, assume that Warlen Co. at the end of 2004 has the following cumulative temporary difference of $300,000, computed as shown in Illustration 19-26.

ILLUSTRATION 19-26
Computation of Cumulative Temporary Difference

Book basis of depreciable assets	$1,000,000
Tax basis of depreciable assets	700,000
Cumulative temporary difference	$ 300,000

Furthermore, assume that the $300,000 will reverse and result in taxable amounts in the future, with the enacted tax rates shown in Illustration 19-27.

	2005	2006	2007	2008	2009	Total
Future taxable amounts	$80,000	$70,000	$60,000	$50,000	$40,000	$300,000
Tax rate	40%	40%	35%	30%	30%	
Deferred tax liability	$32,000	$28,000	$21,000	$15,000	$12,000	$108,000

ILLUSTRATION 19-27
Deferred Tax Liability Based on Future Rates

The total deferred tax liability at the end of 2004 is $108,000. Warlen may only use tax rates other than the current rate when the future tax rates have been enacted, as is the case in this example. **If new rates are not yet enacted for future years, Warlen should use the current rate.**

In determining the appropriate enacted tax rate for a given year, companies must use the **average tax rate**. The Internal Revenue Service and other taxing jurisdictions tax income on a graduated tax basis. For a U.S. corporation, the IRS taxes the first $50,000 of taxable income at 15 percent, the next $25,000 at 25 percent, with higher incremental levels of income at rates as high as 39 percent. In computing deferred income taxes, companies for which graduated tax rates are a significant factor must therefore **determine the average tax rate and use that rate**.

Revision of Future Tax Rates

When a change in the tax rate is enacted, companies should record its effect on the existing deferred income tax accounts immediately. **A company reports the effect as an adjustment to income tax expense in the period of the change.**

Assume that on December 10, 2004, a new income tax act is signed into law that lowers the corporate tax rate from 40 percent to 35 percent, effective January 1, 2006. If Hostel Co. has one temporary difference at the beginning of 2004 related to $3 million of excess tax depreciation, then it has a Deferred Tax Liability account with a balance of $1,200,000 ($3,000,000 × 40%) at January 1, 2004. If taxable amounts related to this difference are scheduled to occur equally in 2005, 2006, and 2007, the deferred tax liability at the end of 2004 is $1,100,000, computed as follows.

	2005	2006	2007	Total
Future taxable amounts	$1,000,000	$1,000,000	$1,000,000	$3,000,000
Tax rate	40%	35%	35%	
Deferred tax liability	$ 400,000	$ 350,000	$ 350,000	$1,100,000

ILLUSTRATION 19-28
Schedule of Future Taxable Amounts and Related Tax Rates

Hostel, therefore, recognizes the decrease of $100,000 ($1,200,000 − $1,100,000) at the end of 2004 in the deferred tax liability as follows.

Deferred Tax Liability	100,000	
Income Tax Expense		100,000

Corporate tax rates do not change often. Therefore, companies usually employ the current rate. However, state and foreign tax rates change more frequently, and they require adjustments in deferred income taxes accordingly.[3]

---

[3]Tax rate changes nearly always will substantially impact income numbers and the reporting of deferred income taxes on the balance sheet. As a result, you can expect to hear an economic consequences argument every time that Congress decides to change the tax rates. For example, when Congress raised the corporate rate from 34 percent to 35 percent in 1993, companies took an additional "hit" to earnings if they were in a deferred tax liability position.

**WHAT DO THE
NUMBERS MEAN?**

SHELTERED

As mentioned in our opening story, companies employ various tax strategies to reduce their tax bills and their effective tax rates. The following table reports some recent high-profile cases in which profitable companies paid little income tax and, in some cases, got tax refunds.

Company	Pre-Tax Income ($ millions)	Federal Tax Paid (Refund) ($ millions)	Tax Rate (%)
Enron	$ 1,785	$(381)	(21.34)%
El Paso Energy	1,638	(254)	(15.51)
Goodyear	442	(23)	(5.20)
Navistar	1,368	28	2.05
General Motors	12,468	740	5.94

These companies used various tools to lower their tax bills, including off-shore tax shelters, tax deferrals, and hefty use of stock options, the cost of which reduce taxable income but do not affect pretax financial income. Thus, companies can use various provisions in the tax code to reduce their effective tax rate well below the statutory rate of 35 percent.

One IRS provision designed to curb excessive tax avoidance is the **alternative minimum tax (AMT)**. Companies compute their potential tax liability under the AMT, adjusting for various preference items that reduce their tax bills under the regular tax code. (Examples of such preference items are accelerated depreciation methods and the installment method for revenue recognition.) Companies must pay the higher of the two tax obligations computed under the AMT and the regular tax code. But, as indicated by the cases above, some profitable companies avoid high tax bills, even in the presence of the AMT. Many citizens and public-interest groups cite corporate avoidance of income taxes as a reason for more tax reform.

Source: H. Gleckman, D. Foust, M. Arndt, and K. Kerwin, "Tax Dodging: Enron Isn't Alone," *Business Week* (March 4, 2002), pp. 40–41.

ACCOUNTING FOR NET OPERATING LOSSES

OBJECTIVE 8
Apply accounting procedures for a loss carryback and a loss carryforward.

Every management hopes its company will be profitable. But hopes and profits may not materialize. For a start-up company, it is common to accumulate operating losses while expanding its customer base but before realizing economies of scale. For an established company, a major event such as a labor strike, rapidly changing regulatory and competitive forces, or a disaster such as 9/11 or Hurricane Katrina can cause expenses to exceed revenues—a net operating loss.

A **net operating loss (NOL)** occurs for tax purposes in a year when tax-deductible expenses exceed taxable revenues. An inequitable tax burden would result if companies were taxed during profitable periods without receiving any tax relief during periods of net operating losses. Under certain circumstances, therefore, the federal tax laws permit taxpayers to use the losses of one year to offset the profits of other years.

Companies accomplish this income-averaging provision through the **carryback and carryforward of net operating losses**. Under this provision, a company pays no income taxes for a year in which it incurs a net operating loss. In addition, it may select one of the two options discussed below and on the following pages.

Loss Carryback

Through use of a **loss carryback**, a company may carry the net operating loss back two years and receive refunds for income taxes paid in those years. The company must apply the loss to the earlier year first and then to the second year. It may **carry**

forward any loss remaining after the two-year carryback up to 20 years to offset future taxable income. Illustration 19-29 diagrams the loss carryback procedure, assuming a loss in 2007.

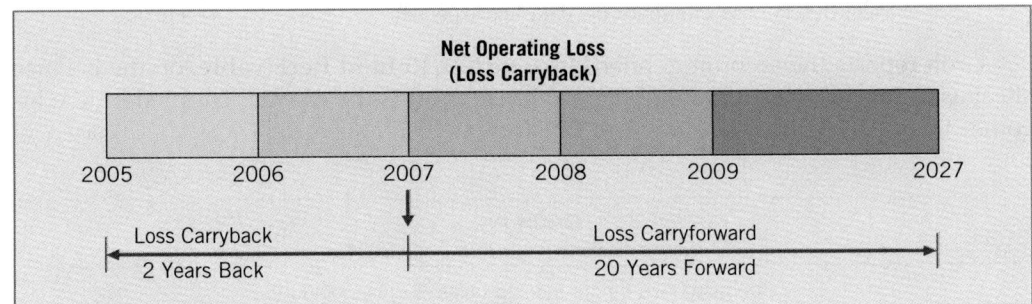

ILLUSTRATION 19-29
Loss Carryback
Procedure

Loss Carryforward

A company may forgo the loss carryback and use only the **loss carryforward** option, offsetting future taxable income for up to 20 years. Illustration 19-30 shows this approach.

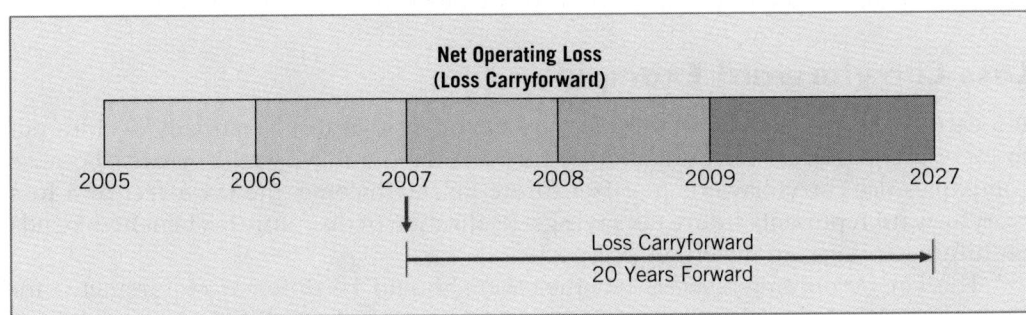

ILLUSTRATION 19-30
Loss Carryforward
Procedure

Operating losses can be substantial. For example, **Yahoo** had net operating losses of approximately $5.4 billion at year-end 2004. That amount translates into tax savings of $1.4 billion if Yahoo is able to generate taxable income before the NOLs expire.

Loss Carryback Example

To illustrate the accounting procedures for a net operating loss carryback, assume that Groh Inc. has no temporary or permanent differences. Groh experiences the following.

Year	Taxable Income or Loss	Tax Rate	Tax Paid
2003	$ 50,000	35%	$17,500
2004	100,000	30%	30,000
2005	200,000	40%	80,000
2006	(500,000)	—	–0–

In 2006, Groh incurs a net operating loss that it decides to carry back. Under the law, Groh must apply the carryback first to the **second year preceding the loss year**. Therefore, it carries the loss back first to 2004. Then, Groh carries back any unused loss to 2005. Accordingly, Groh files amended tax returns for 2004 and 2005, receiving refunds for the $110,000 ($30,000 + $80,000) of taxes paid in those years.

For accounting as well as tax purposes, the $110,000 represents the **tax effect (tax benefit)** of the loss carryback. Groh should recognize this tax effect in 2006, the loss year. Since the tax loss gives rise to a refund that is both measurable and currently realizable, Groh should recognize the associated tax benefit in this loss period.

Groh makes the following journal entry for 2006.

Income Tax Refund Receivable	110,000	
Benefit Due to Loss Carryback (Income Tax Expense)		110,000

Groh reports the account debited, **Income Tax Refund Receivable**, on the balance sheet as a current asset at December 31, 2006. It reports the account credited on the income statement for 2006 as shown in Illustration 19-31.

ILLUSTRATION 19-31
Recognition of Benefit of the Loss Carryback in the Loss Year

GROH INC.	
INCOME STATEMENT (PARTIAL) FOR **2006**	
Operating loss before income taxes	$(500,000)
Income tax benefit	
Benefit due to loss carryback	110,000
Net loss	$(390,000)

Since the $500,000 net operating loss for 2006 exceeds the $300,000 total taxable income from the 2 preceding years, Groh carries forward the remaining $200,000 loss.

Loss Carryforward Example

If a carryback fails to fully absorb a net operating loss, or if the company decides not to carry the loss back, then it can carry forward the loss for up to 20 years.[4] Because companies use carryforwards to offset future taxable income, the **tax effect of a loss carryforward** represents **future tax savings**. Realization of the future tax benefit depends on future earnings, an uncertain prospect.

The key accounting issue is whether there should be different requirements for recognition of a deferred tax asset for (a) deductible temporary differences, and (b) operating loss carryforwards. The FASB's position is that in substance these items are the same—both are tax-deductible amounts in future years. As a result, the Board concluded that there **should not be different requirements** for recognition of a deferred tax asset from deductible temporary differences and operating loss carryforwards.[5]

Carryforward Without Valuation Allowance

To illustrate the accounting for an operating loss carryforward, return to the Groh example from the preceding section. In 2006 the company records the tax effect of the $200,000 loss carryforward as a deferred tax asset of $80,000 ($200,000 × 40%), assuming that the enacted future tax rate is 40 percent. Groh records the benefits of the carryback and the carryforward in 2006 as follows.

To recognize benefit of loss carryback

Income Tax Refund Receivable	110,000	
Benefit Due to Loss Carryback (Income Tax Expense)		110,000

To recognize benefit of loss carryforward

Deferred Tax Asset	80,000	
Benefit Due to Loss Carryforward (Income Tax Expense)		80,000

---

[4]The length of the carryforward period has varied. It has increased from 7 years to 20 years over a period of time.

[5]This requirement is controversial because many believe it is inappropriate to recognize deferred tax assets except when assured beyond a reasonable doubt. Others argue that companies should never recognize deferred tax assets for loss carryforwards until realizing the income in the future.

Groh realizes the income tax refund receivable of $110,000 immediately as a refund of taxes paid in the past. It establishes a Deferred Tax Asset for the benefits of future tax savings. The two accounts credited are contra income tax expense items, which Groh presents on the 2006 income statement shown in Illustration 19-32.

GROH INC.		
INCOME STATEMENT (PARTIAL) FOR 2006		
Operating loss before income taxes		$(500,000)
Income tax benefit		
Benefit due to loss carryback	$110,000	
Benefit due to loss carryforward	80,000	190,000
Net loss		$(310,000)

ILLUSTRATION 19-32
Recognition of the Benefit of the Loss Carryback and Carryforward in the Loss Year

The **current tax benefit** of $110,000 is the income tax refundable for the year. Groh determines this amount by applying the carryback provisions of the tax law to the taxable loss for 2006. The $80,000 is the **deferred tax benefit** for the year, which results from an increase in the deferred tax asset.

For 2007, assume that Groh returns to profitable operations and has taxable income of $250,000 (prior to adjustment for the NOL carryforward), subject to a 40 percent tax rate. Groh then realizes the benefits of the carryforward for tax purposes in 2007, which it recognized for accounting purposes in 2006. Groh computes the income tax payable for 2007 as shown in Illustration 19-33.

Taxable income prior to loss carryforward	$ 250,000
Loss carryforward deduction	(200,000)
Taxable income for 2007	50,000
Tax rate	40%
Income tax payable for 2007	$ 20,000

ILLUSTRATION 19-33
Computation of Income Tax Payable with Realized Loss Carryforward

Groh records income taxes in 2007 as follows.

Income Tax Expense	100,000	
Deferred Tax Asset		80,000
Income Tax Payable		20,000

The benefits of the NOL carryforward, realized in 2007, reduce the Deferred Tax Asset account to zero.

The 2007 income statement that appears in Illustration 19-34 does **not report** the tax effects of either the loss carryback or the loss carryforward, because Groh had reported both previously.

GROH INC.		
INCOME STATEMENT (PARTIAL) FOR 2007		
Income before income taxes		$250,000
Income tax expense		
Current	$20,000	
Deferred	80,000	100,000
Net income		$150,000

ILLUSTRATION 19-34
Presentation of the Benefit of Loss Carryforward Realized in 2007, Recognized in 2006

Carryforward with Valuation Allowance

Let us return to the Groh example. Assume that it is more likely than not that Groh will *not* realize the entire NOL carryforward in future years. In this situation, Groh records the tax benefits of $110,000 associated with the $300,000 NOL carryback, as we previously described. In addition, it records a Deferred Tax Asset of $80,000 ($200,000 × 40%) for the potential benefits related to the loss carryforward, and an allowance to reduce the deferred tax asset by the same amount. Groh makes the following journal entries in 2006.

To recognize benefit of loss carryback

Income Tax Refund Receivable	110,000	
Benefit Due to Loss Carryback (Income Tax Expense)		110,000

To recognize benefit of loss carryforward

Deferred Tax Asset	80,000	
Benefit Due to Loss Carryforward (Income Tax Expense)		80,000

To record allowance amount

Benefit Due to Loss Carryforward (Income Tax Expense)	80,000	
Allowance to Reduce Deferred Tax Asset to Expected Realizable Value		80,000

The latter entry indicates that because positive evidence of sufficient quality and quantity is unavailable to counteract the negative evidence, Groh needs a valuation allowance. Illustration 19-35 shows Groh's 2006 income statement presentation.

ILLUSTRATION 19-35
Recognition of Benefit of Loss Carryback Only

GROH INC.	
INCOME STATEMENT (PARTIAL) FOR 2006	
Operating loss before income taxes	$(500,000)
Income tax benefit	
Benefit due to loss carryback	110,000
Net loss	$(390,000)

In 2007, assuming that Groh has taxable income of $250,000 (before considering the carryforward), subject to a tax rate of 40 percent, it realizes the deferred tax asset. It thus no longer needs the allowance. Groh records the following entries.

To record current and deferred income taxes

Income Tax Expense	100,000	
Deferred Tax Asset		80,000
Income Tax Payable		20,000

To eliminate allowance and recognize loss carryforward

Allowance to Reduce Deferred Tax Asset to Expected Realizable Value	80,000	
Benefit Due to Loss Carryforward (Income Tax Expense)		80,000

Groh reports the $80,000 Benefit Due to the Loss Carryforward on the 2007 income statement. The company did not recognize it in 2006 because it was more likely than not that it would not be realized. Assuming that Groh derives the income for 2007 from continuing operations, it prepares the income statement as shown in Illustration 19-36.

ILLUSTRATION 19-36
Recognition of Benefit of Loss Carryforward When Realized

GROH INC.		
INCOME STATEMENT (PARTIAL) FOR 2007		
Income before income taxes		$250,000
Income tax expense		
Current	$ 20,000	
Deferred	80,000	
Benefit due to loss carryforward	(80,000)	20,000
Net income		$230,000

Another method is to report only one line for total income tax expense of $20,000 on the face of the income statement and disclose the components of income tax expense in the notes to the financial statements.

Valuation Allowance Revisited

A company should consider all positive and negative information in determining whether it needs a valuation allowance. Whether the company will realize a deferred tax asset depends on whether sufficient taxable income exists or will exist within the carryforward period available under tax law. Illustration 19-37 shows possible sources of taxable income that may be available under the tax law to realize a tax benefit for deductible temporary differences and carryforwards.

Taxable Income Sources

a. Future reversals of existing taxable temporary differences

b. Future taxable income exclusive of reversing temporary differences and carryforwards

c. Taxable income in prior carryback year(s) if carryback is permitted under the tax law

d. Tax-planning strategies that would, if necessary, be implemented to:
  (1) Accelerate taxable amounts to utilize expiring carryforwards
  (2) Change the character of taxable or deductible amounts from ordinary income or loss to capital gain or loss
  (3) Switch from tax-exempt to taxable investments.[6]

ILLUSTRATION 19-37
Possible Sources of Taxable Income

If any one of these sources is sufficient to support a conclusion that a valuation allowance is unnecessary, a company need not consider other sources.

Forming a conclusion that a valuation allowance is not needed is difficult when there is negative evidence such as cumulative losses in recent years. Companies may also cite positive evidence indicating that a valuation allowance is not needed. Illustration 19-38 presents examples (not prerequisites) of evidence to consider when determining the need for a valuation allowance.

ILLUSTRATION 19-38
Evidence to Consider in Evaluating the Need for a Valuation Account

---

Negative Evidence

a. A history of operating loss or tax credit carryforwards expiring unused

b. Losses expected in early future years (by a presently profitable entity)

c. Unsettled circumstances that, if unfavorably resolved, would adversely affect future operations and profit levels on a continuing basis in future years

d. A carryback, carryforward period that is so brief that it would limit realization of tax benefits if (1) a significant deductible temporary difference is expected to reverse in a single year or (2) the enterprise operates in a traditionally cyclical business.

Positive Evidence

a. Existing contracts or firm sales backlog that will produce more than enough taxable income to realize the deferred tax asset based on existing sale prices and cost structures

b. An excess of appreciated asset value over the tax basis of the entity's net assets in an amount sufficient to realize the deferred tax asset

c. A strong earnings history exclusive of the loss that created the future deductible amount (tax loss carryforward or deductible temporary difference) coupled with evidence indicating that the loss is an aberration rather than a continuing condition (for example, the result of an unusual, infrequent, or extraordinary item).[7]

INTERNATIONAL INSIGHT

Under international accounting standards *(IAS 12)*, a company may not recognize a deferred tax asset unless realization is "probable." However, "probable" is not defined in the standard, leading to diversity in the recognition of deferred tax assets.

The use of a valuation allowance provides a company with an opportunity to manage its earnings. As one accounting expert notes, "The 'more likely than not' provision is perhaps the most judgmental clause in accounting." Some companies may set up a valuation account and then use it to increase income as needed. Others may take the income immediately to increase capital or to offset large negative charges to income.

---

[6]"Accounting for Income Taxes," *Statement of Financial Accounting Standards No. 109* (Norwalk, Conn.: FASB, 1992). Companies implement a tax-planning strategy to realize a tax benefit for an operating loss or tax credit carryforward before it expires. Companies consider tax-planning strategies when assessing the need for and amount of a valuation allowance for deferred tax assets.

[7]Ibid., pars. 23 and 24.

READ THOSE NOTES

WHAT DO THE NUMBERS MEAN?

A recent study of companies' valuation allowances indicates that the allowances are related to the factors identified as positive and negative evidence. And though there is little evidence that companies use the valuation allowance to manage earnings, the press sometimes understates the impact of reversing the deferred tax valuation allowance.

For example, in one year **Verity, Inc.** eliminated its entire valuation allowance of $18.9 million but focused on a net deferred tax gain of $2.9 million in its press release. Why the difference? As revealed in Verity's financial statement notes, other deferred tax expense amounts totaled over $16 million. Thus, the one-time valuation reversal gave an $18.9 million bump to income, not the net $2.9 million reported in the press.

The lesson: After you read the morning paper, read the financial statement notes.

Source: G. S Miller and D. J. Skinner, "Determinants of the Valuation Allowance for Deferred Tax Assets under *SFAS No. 109,*" *The Accounting Review* (April 1998).

FINANCIAL STATEMENT PRESENTATION

Balance Sheet

OBJECTIVE 9
Describe the presentation of deferred income taxes in financial statements.

Deferred tax accounts are reported on the balance sheet as assets and liabilities. Companies should classify these accounts as a net current amount and a net noncurrent amount. **An individual deferred tax liability or asset is classified as current or noncurrent based on the classification of the related asset or liability for financial reporting purposes.**

A company considers a deferred tax asset or liability to be related to an asset or liability, if reduction of the asset or liability causes the temporary difference to reverse or turn around. A company should classify a deferred tax liability or asset that is unrelated to an asset or liability for financial reporting, including a deferred tax asset related to a loss carryforward, according to the expected reversal date of the temporary difference.

To illustrate, assume that Morgan Inc. records bad debt expense using the allowance method for accounting purposes and the direct write-off method for tax purposes. It currently has Accounts Receivable and Allowance for Doubtful Accounts balances of $2 million and $100,000, respectively. In addition, given a 40 percent tax rate, Morgan has a debit balance in the Deferred Tax Asset account of $40,000 (40% × $100,000). It considers the $40,000 debit balance in the Deferred Tax Asset account to be related to the Accounts Receivable and the Allowance for Doubtful Accounts balances because collection or write-off of the receivables will cause the temporary difference to reverse. Therefore, Morgan classifies the Deferred Tax Asset account as current, the same as the Accounts Receivable and Allowance for Doubtful Accounts balances.

In practice, most companies engage in a large number of transactions that give rise to deferred taxes. Companies should classify the balances in the deferred tax accounts on the balance sheet in two categories: one for the **net current amount**, and one for the **net noncurrent amount**. We summarize this procedure as follows.

1 *Classify the amounts as current or noncurrent.* If related to a specific asset or liability, classify the amounts in the same manner as the related asset or liability. If not related, classify them on the basis of the expected reversal date of the temporary difference.

2 *Determine the net current amount* by summing the various deferred tax assets and liabilities classified as current. If the net result is an asset, report it on the balance sheet as a current asset; if a liability, report it as a current liability.

3 *Determine the net noncurrent amount* by summing the various deferred tax assets and liabilities classified as noncurrent. If the net result is an asset, report it on the balance sheet as a noncurrent asset; if a liability, report it as a long-term liability.

To illustrate, assume that K. Scott Company has four deferred tax items at December 31, 2007. Illustration 19-39 shows an analysis of these four temporary differences as current or noncurrent.

ILLUSTRATION 19-39
Classification of
Temporary Differences as
Current or Noncurrent

Temporary Difference	Resulting Deferred Tax (Asset)	Liability	Related Balance Sheet Account	Classification
1. Rent collected in advance: recognized when earned for accounting purposes and when received for tax purposes.	$(42,000)		Unearned Rent	Current
2. Use of straight-line depreciation for accounting purposes and accelerated depreciation for tax purposes.		$214,000	Equipment	Noncurrent
3. Recognition of profits on installment sales during period of sale for accounting purposes and during period of collection for tax purposes.		45,000	Installment Accounts Receivable	Current
4. Warranty liabilities: recognized for accounting purposes at time of sale; for tax purposes at time paid.	(12,000)		Estimated Liability under Warranties	Current
Totals	$(54,000)	$259,000		

K. Scott classifies as current a deferred tax asset of $9,000 ($42,000 + $12,000 − $45,000). It also reports as noncurrent a deferred tax liability of $214,000. Consequently, K. Scott's December 31, 2007, balance sheet reports deferred income taxes as shown in Illustration 19-40.

ILLUSTRATION 19-40
Balance Sheet
Presentation of Deferred
Income Taxes

Current assets	
Deferred tax asset	$ 9,000
Long-term liabilities	
Deferred tax liability	$214,000

As we indicated earlier, a deferred tax asset or liability **may not be related** to an asset or liability for financial reporting purposes. One example is an operating loss carryforward. In this case, a company records a deferred tax asset, but there is no related, identifiable asset or liability for financial reporting purposes. In these limited situations, deferred income taxes are classified according to the **expected reversal date** of the temporary difference. That is, a company should report the tax effect of any temporary difference reversing next year as current, and the remainder as noncurrent. If a deferred tax asset is noncurrent, a company should classify it in the "Other assets" section.

The total of all deferred tax liabilities, the total of all deferred tax assets, and the total valuation allowance should be disclosed. In addition, companies should disclose the following: (1) any net change during the year in the total valuation allowance, and (2) the types of temporary differences, carryforwards, or carrybacks that give rise to significant portions of deferred tax liabilities and assets.

Income tax payable is reported as a current liability on the balance sheet. Corporations make estimated tax payments to the Internal Revenue Service quarterly. They record these estimated payments by a debit to Prepaid Income Taxes. As a result, the balance of the Income Tax Payable offsets the balance of the Prepaid Income Taxes account when reporting income taxes on the balance sheet.

Income Statement

Companies should allocate income tax expense (or benefit) to continuing operations, discontinued operations, extraordinary items, and prior period adjustments. This approach is referred to as intraperiod tax allocation.

*Expanded Discussion of
Intraperiod Tax Allocation*

In addition, companies should disclose the significant components of income tax expense attributable to continuing operations:

1 Current tax expense or benefit.

2 Deferred tax expense or benefit, exclusive of other components listed below.

3 Investment tax credits.

4 Government grants (if recognized as a reduction of income tax expense).

5 The benefits of operating loss carryforwards (resulting in a reduction of income tax expense).

6 Tax expense that results from allocating tax benefits either directly to paid-in capital or to reduce goodwill or other noncurrent intangible assets of an acquired entity.

7 Adjustments of a deferred tax liability or asset for enacted changes in tax laws or rates or a change in the tax status of a company.

8 Adjustments of the beginning-of-the-year balance of a valuation allowance because of a change in circumstances that causes a change in judgment about the realizability of the related deferred tax asset in future years.

In the notes, companies must also reconcile (using percentages or dollar amounts) income tax expense attributable to continuing operations with the amount that results from applying domestic federal statutory tax rates to pretax income from continuing operations. Companies should disclose the estimated amount and the nature of each significant reconciling item. Illustration 19-41 (page 987) presents an example from the 2004 annual report of **PepsiCo, Inc.**.

These income tax disclosures are required for several reasons:

Additional Examples of Deferred Tax Disclosures

1 *Assessing Quality of Earnings.* Many investors seeking to assess the quality of a company's earnings are interested in the reconciliation of pretax financial income to taxable income. Analysts carefully examine earnings that are enhanced by a favorable tax effect, particularly if the tax effect is nonrecurring. For example, the tax disclosure in Illustration 19-41 indicates that **PepsiCo**'s effective tax rate declined from 28.5 percent in 2003 to 24.7 percent in 2004 (primarily due to settlement of a prior year's tax audit.) The decline translates into a tax savings of $38 million. These savings contributed to PepsiCo's increase in bottom-line income from 2003 to 2004.

2 *Making Better Predictions of Future Cash Flows.* Examination of the deferred portion of income tax expense provides information as to whether taxes payable are likely to be higher or lower in the future. In **PepsiCo**'s case, analysts expect significant future taxable amounts and higher tax payments, due to realization of gains on equity investments, lower depreciation in the future, and higher payments for pension expense. As a result, it may be possible to predict future reductions in deferred tax liabilities leading to a loss of liquidity. Why? Because actual tax payments will be higher than the tax expense reported on the income statement.[8]

3 *Predicting Future Cash Flows from Operating Loss Carryforwards.* Companies should disclose the amounts and expiration dates of any operating loss carryforwards for tax purposes. From this disclosure, analysts determine the amount of income that the company may recognize in the future on which it will pay no income tax. For example, the **PepsiCo** disclosure in Illustration 19-41 indicates that PepsiCo has $4.3 billion in net operating loss carryforwards that it can use to reduce future taxes up to the year 2024 and beyond. However, the valuation allowance indicates that $564 million of the deferred tax asset may not be realized in the future.

Loss carryforwards can be valuable to a potential acquirer. For example, as mentioned earlier, **Yahoo** has a substantial net operating loss carryforward. A potential acquirer would find Yahoo more valuable as a result of these carryforwards. That is, the

---

[8]An article by R. P. Weber and J. E. Wheeler, "Using Income Tax Disclosures to Explore Significant Economic Transactions," *Accounting Horizons* (September 1992), discusses how analysts use deferred tax disclosures to assess the quality of earnings and to predict future cash flows.

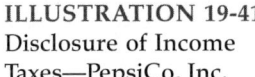

ILLUSTRATION 19-41
Disclosure of Income
Taxes—PepsiCo, Inc.

PepsiCo, Inc.
(in millions)

Note 13: Income Taxes	2004	2003
Income before income taxes—continuing operations		
U.S.	$2,946	$3,267
Foreign	2,600	1,725
	$5,546	$4,992
Provision for income taxes—continuing operations		
Current: U.S. Federal	$1,030	$1,326
Foreign	256	341
State	69	80
	1,355	1,747
Deferred: U.S. Federal	11	(274)
Foreign	5	(47)
State	1	(2)
	17	(323)
	$1,372	$1,424

Tax rate reconciliation—continuing operations		
U.S. Federal statutory tax rate	35.0%	35.0%
State income tax, net of U.S. Federal tax benefit	0.8	1.0
Lower taxes on foreign results	(5.4)	(5.5)
Settlement of prior years audit	(4.8)	(2.2)
Merger-related costs and impairment and restructuring charges	—	0.1
Other, net	(0.9)	0.1
Annual tax rate	24.7%	28.5%

Deferred tax liabilities		
Investments in noncontrolled affiliates	$ 850	$ 792
Property, plant and equipment	857	806
Pension benefits	669	563
Intangible assets other than nondeductible goodwill	153	146
Safe harbor leases	13	33
Zero coupon notes	46	53
Other	144	199
Gross deferred tax liabilities	2,732	2,592

Deferred tax assets		
Net carryforwards	666	535
Stock-based compensation	402	332
Retiree medical benefits	402	343
Other employee-related benefits	379	384
Various current and noncurrent liabilities	460	482
Gross deferred tax assets	2,309	2,076
Valuation allowances	(564)	(438)
Deferred tax assets, net	1,745	1,638
Net deferred tax liabilities	$ 987	$ 954

Deferred taxes included within:		
Prepaid expenses and other current assets	$ 229	$ 307
Deferred income taxes	$1,216	$1,261

Analysis of valuation allowances		
Balance, beginning of year	$ 438	$ 487
Provision/(benefit)	118	(52)
Other additions/(deductions)	8	3
Balance, end of year	$ 564	$ 438

Carryforwards, Credits and Allowances

Operating loss carryforwards totaling $4.3 billion at year-end 2004 are being carried forward in a number of foreign and state jurisdictions where we are permitted to use tax operating losses from prior periods to reduce future taxable income. These operating losses will expire as follows: $0.1 billion in 2005, $3.1 billion between 2006 and 2024 and $1.1 billion may be carried forward indefinitely. In addition, certain tax credits generated in prior periods of approximately $49.3 million are available to reduce certain foreign tax liabilities through 2011. We establish valuation allowances for our deferred tax assets when the amount of expected future taxable income is not likely to support the use of the deduction or credit.

Tax Benefit from Discontinued Operations

In the fourth quarter of 2004, we reached agreement with the taxing authorities for an open issue related to our discontinued restaurant operations which resulted in a tax benefit of $38 million or $0.02 per share.

acquirer may be able to use these carryforwards to shield future income. However the acquiring company has to be careful, because the structure of the deal may lead to a situation where the deductions will be severely limited.

Much the same issue arises in companies emerging from bankruptcy. In many cases these companies have large NOLs, but the value of the losses may be limited. This is because any gains related to the cancellation of liabilities in bankruptcy must be offset against the NOLs. For example, when **Kmart Holding Corp.** emerged from bankruptcy in early 2004, it disclosed NOL carryforwards approximating $3.8 billion. At the same time, Kmart disclosed cancellation of debt gains that reduced the value of the NOL carryforward. These reductions soured the merger between Kmart and **Sears Roebuck** because the cancellation of the indebtedness gains reduced the value of the Kmart carryforwards to the merged company by $3.74 billion.[9]

WHAT DO THE NUMBERS MEAN?

NOLs: GOOD NEWS OR BAD?

Here are some net operating loss numbers recently reported by several notable companies.

NOLs ($ in millions)

Company	2004 Income (Loss)	Operating Loss Carryforward	Tax Benefit (Deferred Tax Asset)	Comment
Delta Airlines, Inc.	($5,198.00)	$7,500.00	$2,848.00	Begins to expire in 2022. Valuation allowance recorded.
Goodyear	114.80	1,306.60*	457.30	Begins to expire in 2005. Full valuation allowance.
Kodak	556.00	509.00	234.00	Begins to expire in 2005. Valuation allowance on foreign credits only.
Krispy Kreme	57.09	26.40*	9.24	No valuation allowance.
Yahoo Inc.	42.82	5,400.00	1,443.50	State and federal carryforwards. Begins to expire in 2005. Valuation allowance recorded.

*Not reported; estimated as [(Tax benefit) ÷ 35%].

All of these companies are using the carryforward provisions of the tax code for their NOLs. For many of them, the NOL is an amount far exceeding their reported profits. Why carry forward the loss to get the tax deduction? First, the company may have already used up the carryback provision, which allows only a two-year carryback period. (Carryforwards can be claimed up to 20 years in the future.) In some cases, management expects the tax rates in the future to be higher. This difference in expected rates provides a bigger tax benefit if the losses are carried forward and matched against future income. Is there a downside? To realize the benefits of carryforwards, a company must have future taxable income in the carryforward period in order to claim the NOL deductions. As we learned, if it is more likely than not that a company will not have taxable income, it must record a valuation allowance (and increased tax expense). As the data above indicate, recording a valuation allowance to reflect the uncertainty of realizing the tax benefits has merit. But for some, the NOL benefits begin to expire in the following year, which may be not enough time to generate sufficient taxable income in order to claim the NOL deduction.

Source: Company annual reports.

---

[9]P. McConnell, J. Pegg, C. Senyak, and D. Mott, "The ABCs of NOLs," *Accounting Issues*, Bear Stearns Equity Research (June 2005). The IRS frowns on acquisitions done solely to obtain operating loss carryforwards. If it determines that the merger is solely tax motivated, the IRS disallows the deductions. But because it is very difficult to determine whether a merger is or is not tax-motivated, the "purchase of operating loss carryforwards" continues.

REVIEW OF THE ASSET-LIABILITY METHOD

The FASB believes that the **asset-liability method** (sometimes referred to as the **liability approach**) is the most consistent method for accounting for income taxes. One objective of this approach is to recognize the amount of taxes payable or refundable for the current year. A second objective is to recognize **deferred tax liabilities and assets** for the **future tax consequences** of events that have been recognized in the financial statements or tax returns.

To implement the objectives, companies apply some basic principles in accounting for income taxes at the date of the financial statements, as listed in Illustration 19-42.

> **OBJECTIVE 10**
> Indicate the basic principles of the asset-liability method.

Basic Principles

a. A current tax liability or asset is recognized for the estimated taxes payable or refundable on the tax return for the current year.

b. A deferred tax liability or asset is recognized for the estimated future tax effects attributable to temporary differences and carryforwards.

c. The measurement of current and deferred tax liabilities and assets is based on provisions of the enacted tax law; the effects of future changes in tax laws or rates are not anticipated.

d. The measurement of deferred tax assets is reduced, if necessary, by the amount of any tax benefits that, based on available evidence, are not expected to be realized.[10]

ILLUSTRATION 19-42
Basic Principles of the Asset-Liability Method

Discussion of Conceptual Approaches to Interperiod Tax Allocation

Illustration 19-43 diagrams the procedures for implementing the asset-liability method.

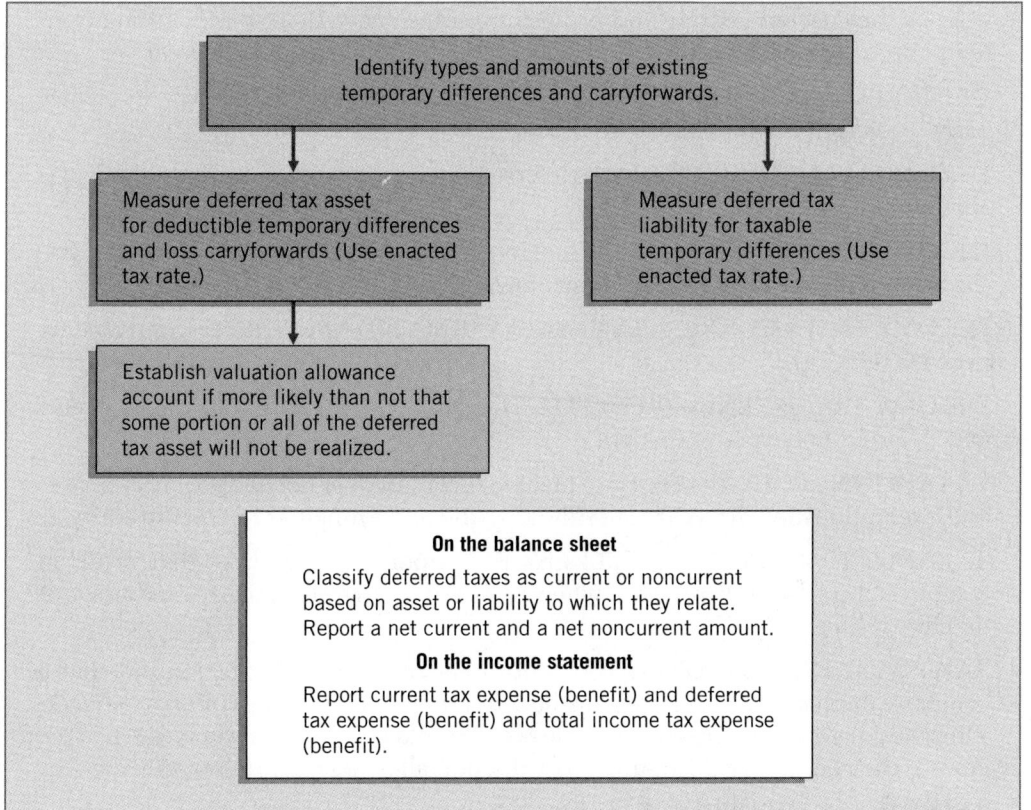

ILLUSTRATION 19-43
Procedures for Computing and Reporting Deferred Income Taxes

As an aid to understanding deferred income taxes, we provide the following glossary.[11]

---

[10]"Accounting for Income Taxes" (1992), pars. 6 and 8.

[11]"Accounting for Income Taxes," Appendix E.

INTERNATIONAL INSIGHT

The IFRS on income taxes is based on the same principles as the U.S. GAAP—comprehensive recognition of deferred tax assets and liabilities.

KEY DEFERRED INCOME TAX TERMS

CARRYBACKS. Deductions or credits that cannot be utilized on the tax return during a year and that may be carried back to reduce taxable income or taxes paid in a prior year. An **operating loss carryback** is an excess of tax deductions over gross income in a year. A **tax credit carryback** is the amount by which tax credits available for utilization exceed statutory limitations.

CARRYFORWARDS. Deductions or credits that cannot be utilized on the tax return during a year and that may be carried forward to reduce taxable income or taxes payable in a future year. An **operating loss carryforward** is an excess of tax deductions over gross income in a year. A **tax credit carryforward** is the amount by which tax credits available for utilization exceed statutory limitations.

CURRENT TAX EXPENSE (BENEFIT). The amount of income taxes paid or payable (or refundable) for a year as determined by applying the provisions of the enacted tax law to the taxable income or excess of deductions over revenues for that year.

DEDUCTIBLE TEMPORARY DIFFERENCE. Temporary differences that result in deductible amounts in future years when recovering or settling the related asset or liability, respectively.

DEFERRED TAX ASSET. The deferred tax consequences attributable to deductible temporary differences and carryforwards.

DEFERRED TAX CONSEQUENCES. The future effects on income taxes as measured by the enacted tax rate and provisions of the enacted tax law resulting from temporary differences and carryforwards at the end of the current year.

DEFERRED TAX EXPENSE (BENEFIT). The change during the year in a company's deferred tax liabilities and assets.

DEFERRED TAX LIABILITY. The deferred tax consequences attributable to taxable temporary differences.

INCOME TAXES. Domestic and foreign federal (national), state, and local (including franchise) taxes based on income.

INCOME TAXES CURRENTLY PAYABLE (REFUNDABLE). Refer to current tax expense (benefit).

INCOME TAX EXPENSE (BENEFIT). The sum of current tax expense (benefit) and deferred tax expense (benefit).

TAXABLE INCOME. The excess of taxable revenues over tax deductible expenses and exemptions for the year as defined by the governmental taxing authority.

TAXABLE TEMPORARY DIFFERENCE. Temporary differences that result in taxable amounts in future years when recovering or settling the related asset or liability, respectively.

TAX-PLANNING STRATEGY. An action that meets certain criteria and that a company implements to realize a tax benefit for an operating loss or tax credit carryforward before it expires. Companies consider tax-planning strategies when assessing the need for and amount of a valuation allowance for deferred tax assets.

TEMPORARY DIFFERENCE. A difference between the tax basis of an asset or liability and its reported amount in the financial statements that will result in taxable or deductible amounts in future years when recovering or settling the reported amount of the asset or liability, respectively.

VALUATION ALLOWANCE. The portion of a deferred tax asset for which it is more likely than not that a company will not realize a tax benefit.

SUMMARY OF LEARNING OBJECTIVES

1. Identify differences between pretax financial income and taxable income. Companies compute pretax financial income (or income for book purposes) in accordance with generally accepted accounting principles. They compute taxable income (or income for tax purposes) in accordance with prescribed tax regulations. Because tax regulations and GAAP differ in many ways, so frequently do pretax financial income and taxable income. Differences may exist, for example, in the timing of revenue recognition and the timing of expense recognition.

2. Describe a temporary difference that results in future taxable amounts. Revenue recognized for book purposes in the period earned but deferred and reported as revenue for tax purposes when collected results in future taxable amounts. The future taxable amounts will occur in the periods the company recovers the receivable and reports the collections as revenue for tax purposes. This results in a deferred tax liability.

3. Describe a temporary difference that results in future deductible amounts. An accrued warranty expense that a company pays for and deducts for tax purposes, in a period later than the period in which it incurs and recognizes it for book purposes, results in future deductible amounts. The future deductible amounts will occur in the periods during which the company settles the related liability for book purposes. This results in a deferred tax asset.

4. Explain the purpose of a deferred tax asset valuation allowance. A deferred tax asset should be reduced by a valuation allowance if, based on all available evidence, it is more likely than not (a level of likelihood that is at least slightly more than 50 percent) that it will not realize some portion or all of the deferred tax asset. The company should carefully consider all available evidence, both positive and negative, to determine whether, based on the weight of available evidence, it needs a valuation allowance.

5. Describe the presentation of income tax expense in the income statement. Significant components of income tax expense should be disclosed in the income statement or in the notes to the financial statements. The most commonly encountered components are the current expense (or benefit) and the deferred expense (or benefit).

6. Describe various temporary and permanent differences. Examples of temporary differences are: (1) revenue or gains that are taxable after recognition in financial income; (2) expenses or losses that are deductible after recognition in financial income; (3) revenues or gains that are taxable before recognition in financial income; (4) expenses or losses that are deductible before recognition in financial income. Examples of permanent differences are: (1) items recognized for financial reporting purposes but not for tax purposes, and (2) items recognized for tax purposes but not for financial reporting purposes.

7. Explain the effect of various tax rates and tax rate changes on deferred income taxes. Companies may use tax rates other than the current rate only after enactment of the future tax rates. When a change in the tax rate is enacted, a company should immediately recognize its effect on the deferred income tax accounts. The company reports the effects as an adjustment to income tax expense in the period of the change.

8. Apply accounting procedures for a loss carryback and a loss carryforward. A company may carry a net operating loss back two years and receive refunds for income taxes paid in those years. The loss is applied to the earlier year first and then to the second year. Any loss remaining after the two-year carryback may be carried forward up to 20 years to offset future taxable income. A company may forgo the loss carryback and use the loss carryforward, offsetting future taxable income for up to 20 years.

9. Describe the presentation of deferred income taxes in financial statements. Companies report deferred tax accounts on the balance sheet as assets and liabilities. These deferred tax accounts are classified as a net current and a net noncurrent amount.

KEY TERMS

alternative minimum tax (AMT), *978*

asset-liability method, *989*

average tax rate, *977*

current tax benefit (expense), *967, 981*

deductible amounts, *966*

deductible temporary difference, *973*

deferred tax asset, *970*

deferred tax expense (benefit), *967, 970*

deferred tax liability, *967*

effective tax rate, *976*

enacted tax rate, *976*

Income Tax Refund Receivable, *980*

loss carryback, *978*

loss carryforward, *979*

more likely than not, *972*

net current amount, *984*

net noncurrent amount, *984*

net operating loss (NOL), *978*

originating temporary difference, *974*

permanent difference, *975*

pretax financial income, *964*

reversing difference, *974*

taxable amounts, *966*

taxable income, *964*

taxable temporary difference, *973*

tax effect (tax benefit), *979*

temporary difference, *966*

valuation allowance, *972*

Companies classify an individual deferred tax liability or asset as current or noncurrent based on the classification of the related asset or liability for financial reporting. A deferred tax liability or asset that is not related to an asset or liability for financial reporting, including a deferred tax asset related to a loss carryforward, is classified according to the expected reversal date of the temporary difference.

10. **Indicate the basic principles of the asset-liability method.** Companies apply the following basic principles in accounting for income taxes at the date of the financial statements: (1) Recognize a current tax liability or asset for the estimated taxes payable or refundable on the tax return for the current year. (2) Recognize a deferred tax liability or asset for the estimated future tax effects attributable to temporary differences and carryforwards using the enacted tax rate. (3) Base the measurement of current and deferred tax liabilities and assets on provisions of the enacted tax law. (4) Reduce the measurement of deferred tax assets, if necessary, by the amount of any tax benefits that, based on available evidence, companies do not expect to realize.

APPENDIX
19A Comprehensive Example of Interperiod Tax Allocation

OBJECTIVE 11
Understand and apply the concepts and procedures of interperiod tax allocation.

This appendix presents a comprehensive illustration of a deferred income tax problem with several temporary and permanent differences. The example follows one company through two complete years (2006 and 2007). **Study it carefully.** It should help you understand the concepts and procedures presented in the chapter.

FIRST YEAR—2006

Allman Company, which began operations at the beginning of 2006, produces various products on a contract basis. Each contract generates a gross profit of $80,000. Some of Allman's contracts provide for the customer to pay on an installment basis. Under these contracts, Allman collects one-fifth of the contract revenue in each of the following four years. For financial reporting purposes, the company recognizes gross profit in the year of completion (accrual basis); for tax purposes, Allman recognizes gross profit in the year cash is collected (installment basis).

Presented below is information related to Allman's operations for 2006.

1 In 2006, the company completed seven contracts that allow for the customer to pay on an installment basis. Allman recognized the related gross profit of $560,000 for financial reporting purposes. It reported only $112,000 of gross profit on installment sales on the 2006 tax return. The company expects future collections on the related installment receivables to result in taxable amounts of $112,000 in each of the next four years.

2 At the beginning of 2006, Allman Company purchased depreciable assets with a cost of $540,000. For financial reporting purposes, Allman depreciates these assets using the straight-line method over a six-year service life. For tax purposes, the assets fall in the five-year recovery class, and Allman uses the MACRS system. The depreciation schedules for both financial reporting and tax purposes follow.

Year	Depreciation for Financial Reporting Purposes	Depreciation for Tax Purposes	Difference
2006	$ 90,000	$108,000	$(18,000)
2007	90,000	172,800	(82,800)
2008	90,000	103,680	(13,680)
2009	90,000	62,208	27,792
2010	90,000	62,208	27,792
2011	90,000	31,104	58,896
	$540,000	$540,000	$ –0–

3 The company warrants its product for two years from the date of completion of a contract. During 2006, the product warranty liability accrued for financial reporting purposes was $200,000, and the amount paid for the satisfaction of warranty liability was $44,000. Allman expects to settle the remaining $156,000 by expenditures of $56,000 in 2007 and $100,000 in 2008.

4 In 2006 nontaxable municipal bond interest revenue was $28,000.

5 During 2006 nondeductible fines and penalties of $26,000 were paid.

6 Pretax financial income for 2006 amounts to $412,000.

7 Tax rates enacted before the end of 2006 were:

2006	50%
2007 and later years	40%

8 The accounting period is the calendar year.

9 The company is expected to have taxable income in all future years.

Taxable Income and Income Tax Payable—2006

The first step is to determine Allman Company's income tax payable for 2006 by calculating its taxable income. Illustration 19A-1 shows this computation.

Pretax financial income for 2006	$412,000
Permanent differences:	
Nontaxable revenue—municipal bond interest	(28,000)
Nondeductible expenses—fines and penalties	26,000
Temporary differences:	
Excess gross profit per books ($560,000 − $112,000)	(448,000)
Excess depreciation per tax ($108,000 − $90,000)	(18,000)
Excess warranty expense per books ($200,000 − $44,000)	156,000
Taxable income for 2006	$100,000

ILLUSTRATION 19A-1
Computation of Taxable Income, 2006

Allman computes income tax payable on taxable income for $100,000 as follows.

Taxable income for 2006	$100,000
Tax rate	50%
Income tax payable (current tax expense) for 2006	$ 50,000

ILLUSTRATION 19A-2
Computation of Income Tax Payable, End of 2006

Computing Deferred Income Taxes—End of 2006

The schedule in Illustration 19A-3 (on page 994) summarizes the temporary differences and the resulting future taxable and deductible amounts.

ILLUSTRATION 19A-3
Schedule of Future
Taxable and Deductible
Amounts, End of 2006

	Future Years					
	2007	2008	2009	2010	2011	Total
Future taxable (deductible) amounts:						
Installment sales	$112,000	$112,000	$112,000	$112,000		$448,000
Depreciation	(82,800)	(13,680)	27,792	27,792	$58,896	18,000
Warranty costs	(56,000)	(100,000)				(156,000)

Allman computes the amounts of deferred income taxes to be reported at the end of 2006 as shown in Illustration 19A-4.

ILLUSTRATION 19A-4
Computation of Deferred
Income Taxes, End of
2006

Temporary Difference	Future Taxable (Deductible) Amounts	Tax Rate	Deferred Tax (Asset)	Liability
Installment sales	$448,000	40%		$179,200
Depreciation	18,000	40%		7,200
Warranty costs	(156,000)	40%	$(62,400)	
Totals	$310,000		$(62,400)	$186,400*

*Because only a single tax rate is involved in all relevant years, these totals can be reconciled: $310,000 × 40% = ($62,400) + $186,400.

A temporary difference is caused by the use of the accrual basis for financial reporting purposes and the installment method for tax purposes. This temporary difference will result in future taxable amounts, and hence, a deferred tax liability. Because of the installment contracts completed in 2006, a temporary difference of $448,000 originates that will reverse in equal amounts over the next four years. The company expects to have taxable income in all future years, and there is only one enacted tax rate applicable to all future years. Allman uses that rate (40 percent) to compute the entire deferred tax liability resulting from this temporary difference.

The temporary difference caused by different depreciation policies for books and for tax purposes originates over three years and then reverses over three years. This difference will cause deductible amounts in 2007 and 2008 and taxable amounts in 2009, 2010, and 2011. These amounts sum to a net future taxable amount of $18,000 (which is the cumulative temporary difference at the end of 2006). Because the company expects to have taxable income in all future years and because there is only one tax rate enacted for all of the relevant future years, Allman applies that rate to the net future taxable amount to determine the related net deferred tax liability.

The third temporary difference is caused by different methods of accounting for warranties. This difference will result in deductible amounts in each of the two future years it takes to reverse. Because the company expects to report a positive income on all future tax returns and because there is only one tax rate enacted for each of the relevant future years, Allman uses that 40 percent rate to calculate the resulting deferred tax asset.

Deferred Tax Expense (Benefit) and the Journal Entry to Record Income Taxes—2006

To determine the deferred tax expense (benefit), we need to compare the beginning and ending balances of the deferred income tax accounts. Illustration 19A-5 shows that computation.

Deferred tax asset at the end of 2006	$ 62,400
Deferred tax asset at the beginning of 2006	–0–
Deferred tax expense (benefit)	$ (62,400)
Deferred tax liability at the end of 2006	$186,400
Deferred tax liability at the beginning of 2006	–0–
Deferred tax expense (benefit)	$186,400

ILLUSTRATION 19A-5
Computation of Deferred
Tax Expense (Benefit),
2006

The $62,400 increase in the deferred tax asset causes a deferred tax benefit to be reported in the income statement. The $186,400 increase in the deferred tax liability during 2006 results in a deferred tax expense. These two amounts **net** to a deferred tax expense of $124,000 for 2006.

Deferred tax expense (benefit)	$ (62,400)
Deferred tax expense (benefit)	186,400
Net deferred tax expense for 2006	$124,000

ILLUSTRATION 19A-6
Computation of Net
Deferred Tax Expense,
2006

Allman then computes the total income tax expense as follows.

Current tax expense for 2006	$ 50,000
Deferred tax expense for 2006	124,000
Income tax expense (total) for 2006	$174,000

ILLUSTRATION 19A-7
Computation of Total
Income Tax Expense, 2006

Allman records income tax payable, deferred income taxes, and income tax expense is as follows.

Income Tax Expense	174,000	
Deferred Tax Asset	62,400	
Income Tax Payable		50,000
Deferred Tax Liability		186,400

Financial Statement Presentation—2006

Companies should classify deferred tax assets and liabilities as current and noncurrent on the balance sheet based on the classifications of related assets and liabilities. Multiple categories of deferred taxes are classified into a net current amount and a net noncurrent amount. Illustration 19A-8 shows the classification of Allman's deferred tax accounts at the end of 2006.

Temporary Difference	Resulting Deferred Tax (Asset)	Liability	Related Balance Sheet Account	Classification
Installment sales		$179,200	Installment Receivable	Current
Depreciation		7,200	Plant Assets	Noncurrent
Warranty costs	$(62,400)		Warranty Obligation	Current
Totals	$(62,400)	$186,400		

ILLUSTRATION 19A-8
Classification of Deferred
Tax Accounts, End of 2006

For the first temporary difference, there is a related asset on the balance sheet, installment accounts receivable. Allman classifies that asset as current because it has a trade practice of selling to customers on an installment basis. Allman therefore classifies the resulting deferred tax liability as a current liability.

Certain assets on the balance sheet are related to the depreciation difference—the property, plant, and equipment being depreciated. Allman would classify the plant assets as noncurrent. Therefore, it also classifies the resulting deferred tax liability as noncurrent. Since the company's operating cycle is at least four years in length, Allman classifies the entire $156,000 warranty obligation as a current liability. Thus, it also classifies the related deferred tax asset of $62,400 as current.[1]

The balance sheet at the end of 2006 reports the following amounts.

ILLUSTRATION 19A-9
Balance Sheet Presentation of Deferred Taxes, 2006

Current liabilities	
Income tax payable	$ 50,000
Deferred tax liability ($179,200 − $62,400)	116,800
Long-term liabilities	
Deferred tax liability	$ 7,200

Allman's income statement for 2006 reports the following.

ILLUSTRATION 19A-10
Income Statement Presentation of Income Tax Expense, 2006

Income before income taxes		$412,000
Income tax expense		
Current	$ 50,000	
Deferred	124,000	174,000
Net income		$238,000

SECOND YEAR—2007

1 During 2007 Allman collected $112,000 from customers for the receivables arising from contracts completed in 2006. The company expects recovery of the remaining receivables to result in taxable amounts of $112,000 in each of the following three years.

2 In 2007 the company completed four new contracts that allow for the customer to pay on an installment basis. These installment sales created new installment receivables. Future collections of these receivables will result in reporting gross profit of $64,000 for tax purposes in each of the next four years.

3 During 2007 Allman continued to depreciate the assets acquired in 2006 according to the depreciation schedules appearing on page 993. Thus, depreciation amounted to $90,000 for financial reporting purposes and $172,800 for tax purposes.

4 An analysis at the end of 2007 of the product warranty liability account showed the following details.

Balance of liability at beginning of 2007	$156,000
Expense for 2007 income statement purposes	180,000
Amount paid for contracts completed in 2006	(56,000)
Amount paid for contracts completed in 2007	(50,000)
Balance of liability at end of 2007	$230,000

---

[1]If Allman's operating cycle were less than one year in length, the company would expect to settle $56,000 of the warranty obligation within one year of the December 31, 2006, balance sheet and would use current assets to do so. Thus $56,000 of the warranty obligation would be a current liability and the remaining $100,000 warranty obligation would be a long-term (noncurrent) liability. This would mean that Allman would classify $22,000 ($56,000 × 40%) of the related deferred tax asset as a current asset, and $40,000 ($100,000 × 40%) of the deferred tax asset as a noncurrent asset. *In doing homework problems, unless it is evident otherwise, assume a company's operating cycle is not longer than a year.*

The balance of the liability is expected to require expenditures in the future as follows.

> $100,000 in 2008 due to 2006 contracts
> $ 50,000 in 2008 due to 2007 contracts
> $ 80,000 in 2009 due to 2007 contracts
> ——————
> $230,000

5 During 2007 nontaxable municipal bond interest revenue was $24,000.

6 Allman accrued a loss of $172,000 for financial reporting purposes because of pending litigation. This amount is not tax-deductible until the period the loss is realized, which the company estimates to be 2015.

7 Pretax financial income for 2007 amounts to $504,800.

8 The enacted tax rates still in effect are:

2006	50%
2007 and later years	40%

Taxable Income and Income Tax Payable—2007

Allman computes taxable income for 2007 as follows.

Pretax financial income for 2007	$504,800
Permanent difference:	
Nontaxable revenue—municipal bond interest	(24,000)
Reversing temporary differences:	
Collection on 2006 installment sales	112,000
Payments on warranties from 2006 contracts	(56,000)
Originating temporary differences:	
Excess gross profit per books—2007 contracts	(256,000)
Excess depreciation per tax	(82,800)
Excess warranty expense per books—2007 contracts	130,000
Loss accrual per books	172,000
Taxable income for 2007	$500,000

ILLUSTRATION 19A-11
Computation of Taxable Income, 2007

Income tax payable for 2007 is as follows.

Taxable income for 2007	$500,000
Tax rate	40%
Income tax payable (current tax expense) for 2007	$200,000

ILLUSTRATION 19A-12
Computation of Income Tax Payable, End of 2007

Computing Deferred Income Taxes—End of 2007

The schedule in Illustration 19A-13 summarizes the temporary differences existing at the end of 2007 and the resulting future taxable and deductible amounts.

ILLUSTRATION 19A-13
Schedule of Future Taxable and Deductible Amounts, End of 2007

	Future Years					
	2008	2009	2010	2011	2015	Total
Future taxable (deductible) amounts:						
Installment sales—2006	$112,000	$112,000	$112,000			$336,000
Installment sales—2007	64,000	64,000	64,000	$64,000		256,000
Depreciation	(13,680)	27,792	27,792	58,896		100,800
Warranty costs	(150,000)	(80,000)				(230,000)
Loss accrual					$(172,000)	(172,000)

Allman computes the amounts of deferred income taxes to be reported at the end of 2007 as follows.

ILLUSTRATION 19A-14
Computation of Deferred Income Taxes, End of 2007

Temporary Difference	Future Taxable (Deductible) Amounts	Tax Rate	Deferred Tax (Asset)	Liability
Installment sales	$592,000*	40%		$236,800
Depreciation	100,800	40%		40,320
Warranty costs	(230,000)	40%	$ (92,000)	
Loss accrual	(172,000)	40%	(68,800)	
Totals	$290,800		$(160,800)	$277,120**

*Cumulative temporary difference = $336,000 + $256,000
**Because of a flat tax rate, these totals can be reconciled: $290,800 × 40% = $(160,800) + $277,120

Deferred Tax Expense (Benefit) and the Journal Entry to Record Income Taxes—2007

To determine the deferred tax expense (benefit), Allman must compare the beginning and ending balances of the deferred income tax accounts, as shown in Illustration 19A-15.

ILLUSTRATION 19A-15
Computation of Deferred Tax Expense (Benefit), 2007

Deferred tax asset at the end of 2007	$160,800
Deferred tax asset at the beginning of 2007	62,400
Deferred tax expense (benefit)	$ (98,400)
Deferred tax liability at the end of 2007	$277,120
Deferred tax liability at the beginning of 2007	186,400
Deferred tax expense (benefit)	$ 90,720

The deferred tax expense (benefit) and the total income tax expense for 2007 are, therefore, as follows.

ILLUSTRATION 19A-16
Computation of Total Income Tax Expense, 2007

Deferred tax expense (benefit)	$ (98,400)
Deferred tax expense (benefit)	90,720
Deferred tax benefit for 2007	(7,680)
Current tax expense for 2007	200,000
Income tax expense (total) for 2007	$192,320

The deferred tax expense of $90,720 and the deferred tax benefit of $98,400 net to a deferred tax benefit of $7,680 for 2007.

Allman records income taxes for 2007 with the following journal entry.

Income Tax Expense	192,320	
Deferred Tax Asset	98,400	
Income Tax Payable		200,000
Deferred Tax Liability		90,720

Financial Statement Presentation—2007

Illustration 19A-17 shows the classification of Allman's deferred tax accounts at the end of 2007.

| | Resulting Deferred Tax | | Related Balance | |
Temporary Difference	(Asset)	Liability	Sheet Account	Classification
Installment sales		$236,800	Installment Receivables	Current
Depreciation		40,320	Plant Assets	Noncurrent
Warranty costs	$ (92,000)		Warranty Obligation	Current
Loss accrual	(68,800)		Litigation Obligation	Noncurrent
Totals	$(160,800)	$277,120		

ILLUSTRATION 19A-17
Classification of Deferred
Tax Accounts, End of 2007

The new temporary difference introduced in 2007 (due to the litigation loss accrual) results in a litigation obligation that is classified as a long-term liability. Thus, the related deferred tax asset is noncurrent.

Allman's balance sheet at the end of 2007 reports the following amounts.

Other assets (noncurrent)	
Deferred tax asset ($68,800 − $40,320)	$ 28,480
Current liabilities	
Income tax payable	$200,000
Deferred tax liability ($236,800 − $92,000)	144,800

ILLUSTRATION 19A-18
Balance Sheet
Presentation of Deferred
Taxes, End of 2007

The income statement for 2007 reports the following.

Income before income taxes		$504,800
Income tax expense		
Current	$200,000	
Deferred	(7,680)	192,320
Net income		$312,480

ILLUSTRATION 19A-19
Income Statement
Presentation of Income
Tax Expense, 2007

SUMMARY OF LEARNING OBJECTIVE FOR APPENDIX 19A

11. Understand and apply the concepts and procedures of interperiod tax allocation. Accounting for deferred taxes involves the following steps: Calculate taxable income and income tax payable for the year. Compute deferred income taxes at the end of the year. Determine deferred tax expense (benefit) and make the journal entry to record income taxes. Classify deferred tax assets and liabilities as current or noncurrent in the financial statements.

QUESTIONS

1. Explain the difference between pretax financial income and taxable income.

2. What are the two objectives of accounting for income taxes?

3. Interest on municipal bonds is referred to as a permanent difference when determining the proper amount to report for deferred taxes. Explain the meaning of permanent differences, and give two other examples.

4. Explain the meaning of a temporary difference as it relates to deferred tax computations, and give three examples.

5. Differentiate between an originating temporary difference and a reversing difference.

6. The book basis of depreciable assets for Getty Co. is $900,000, and the tax basis is $700,000 at the end of 2007. The enacted tax rate is 34% for all periods. Determine the amount of deferred taxes to be reported on the balance sheet at the end of 2007.

7. Borg Inc. has a deferred tax liability of $68,000 at the beginning of 2007. At the end of 2007, it reports accounts receivable on the books at $80,000 and the tax basis at zero (its only temporary difference). If the enacted tax rate is 34% for all periods, and income tax payable for the period is $230,000, determine the amount of total income tax expense to report for 2007.

8. What is the difference between a future taxable amount and a future deductible amount? When is it appropriate to record a valuation account for a deferred tax asset?

9. Pretax financial income for Mott Inc. is $300,000, and its taxable income is $100,000 for 2007. Its only temporary difference at the end of the period relates to a $90,000 difference due to excess depreciation for tax purposes. If the tax rate is 40% for all periods, compute the amount of income tax expense to report in 2007. No deferred income taxes existed at the beginning of the year.

10. How are deferred tax assets and deferred tax liabilities reported on the balance sheet?

11. Describe the procedures involved in segregating various deferred tax amounts into current and noncurrent categories.

12. How is it determined whether deferred tax amounts are considered to be "related" to specific asset or liability amounts?

13. At the end of the year, North Carolina Co. has pretax financial income of $550,000. Included in the $550,000 is $70,000 interest income on municipal bonds, $30,000 fine for dumping hazardous waste, and depreciation of $60,000. Depreciation for tax purposes is $45,000. Compute income taxes payable, assuming the tax rate is 30% for all periods.

14. Raleigh Co. has one temporary difference at the beginning of 2007 of $500,000. The deferred tax liability established for this amount is $150,000, based on a tax rate of 30%. The temporary difference will provide the following taxable amounts: $100,000 in 2008; $200,000 in 2009, and $200,000 in 2010. If a new tax rate for 2010 of 25% is enacted into law at the end of 2007, what is the journal entry necessary in 2007 (if any) to adjust deferred taxes?

15. What are some of the reasons that the components of income tax expense should be disclosed and a reconciliation between the effective tax rate and the statutory tax rate be provided?

16. Differentiate between "loss carryback" and "loss carryforward." Which can be accounted for with the greater certainty when it arises? Why?

17. What are the possible treatments for tax purposes of a net operating loss? What are the circumstances that determine the option to be applied? What is the proper treatment of a net operating loss for financial reporting purposes?

18. What controversy relates to the accounting for net operating loss carryforwards?

BRIEF EXERCISES

(LO 1, 2) **BE19-1** In 2007, Speedy Gonzalez Corporation had pretax financial income of $168,000 and taxable income of $110,000. The difference is due to the use of different depreciation methods for tax and accounting purposes. The effective tax rate is 40%. Compute the amount to be reported as income taxes payable at December 31, 2007.

(LO 1, 2) **BE19-2** Murphy Corporation began operations in 2007 and reported pretax financial income of $225,000 for the year. Murphy's tax depreciation exceeded its book depreciation by $30,000. Murphy's tax rate for 2007 and years thereafter is 30%. In its December 31, 2007 balance sheet, what amount of deferred tax liability should be reported?

(LO 9) **BE19-3** Using the information from BE19-2, assume this is the only difference between Murphy's pretax financial income and taxable income. Prepare the journal entry to record the income tax expense, deferred income taxes, and income tax payable, and show how the deferred tax liability will be classified on the December 31, 2007, balance sheet.

(LO 2, 5) **BE19-4** At December 31, 2006, Yserbius Corporation had a deferred tax liability of $25,000. At December 31, 2007, the deferred tax liability is $42,000. The corporation's 2007 current tax expense is $43,000. What amount should Yserbius report as total 2007 tax expense?

(LO 1, 3) **BE19-5** At December 31, 2007, Deep Space Nine Corporation had an estimated warranty liability of $125,000 for accounting purposes and $0 for tax purposes. (The warranty costs are not deductible until paid.) The effective tax rate is 40%. Compute the amount Deep Space Nine should report as a deferred tax asset at December 31, 2007.

(LO 3, 5) **BE19-6** At December 31, 2006, Next Generation Inc. had a deferred tax asset of $35,000. At December 31, 2007, the deferred tax asset is $59,000. The corporation's 2007 current tax expense is $61,000. What amount should Next Generation report as total 2007 tax expense?

(LO 4) **BE19-7** At December 31, 2007, Stargate Corporation has a deferred tax asset of $200,000. After a careful review of all available evidence, it is determined that it is more likely than not that $80,000 of this deferred tax asset will not be realized. Prepare the necessary journal entry.

(LO 5) **BE19-8** No Doubt Corporation had income before income taxes of $175,000 in 2007. No Doubt's current income tax expense is $40,000, and deferred income tax expense is $30,000. Prepare No Doubt's 2007 income statement, beginning with income before income taxes.

(LO 2, 3) **BE19-9** Tazmania Inc. had pretax financial income of $154,000 in 2007. Included in the computation of that amount is insurance expense of $4,000 which is not deductible for tax purposes. In addition, depreciation for tax purposes exceeds accounting depreciation by $14,000. Prepare Tazmania's journal entry to record 2007 taxes, assuming a tax rate of 45%.

(LO 2) **BE19-10** Terminator Corporation has a cumulative temporary difference related to depreciation of $630,000 at December 31, 2007. This difference will reverse as follows: 2008, $42,000; 2009, $294,000; and 2010, $294,000. Enacted tax rates are 34% for 2008 and 2009, and 40% for 2010. Compute the amount Terminator should report as a deferred tax liability at December 31, 2007.

(LO 7) **BE19-11** At December 31, 2006, Tick Corporation had a deferred tax liability of $680,000, resulting from future taxable amounts of $2,000,000 and an enacted tax rate of 34%. In May 2007, a new income tax act is signed into law that raises the tax rate to 38% for 2007 and future years. Prepare the journal entry for Tick to adjust the deferred tax liability.

(LO 8) **BE19-12** Valis Corporation had the following tax information.

Year	Taxable Income	Tax Rate	Taxes Paid
2004	$300,000	35%	$105,000
2005	$325,000	30%	$ 97,500
2006	$400,000	30%	$120,000

In 2007 Valis suffered a net operating loss of $450,000, which it elected to carry back. The 2007 enacted tax rate is 29%. Prepare Valis's entry to record the effect of the loss carryback.

(LO 8) **BE19-13** Zoop Inc. incurred a net operating loss of $500,000 in 2007. Combined income for 2005 and 2006 was $400,000. The tax rate for all years is 40%. Zoop elects the carryback option. Prepare the journal entries to record the benefits of the loss carryback and the loss carryforward.

(LO 4, 8) **BE19-14** Use the information for Zoop Inc. given in BE19-13. Assume that it is more likely than not that the entire net operating loss carryforward will not be realized in future years. Prepare all the journal entries necessary at the end of 2007.

(LO 9) **BE19-15** Vectorman Corporation has temporary differences at December 31, 2007, that result in the following deferred taxes.

Deferred tax liability—current	$38,000
Deferred tax asset—current	$(52,000)
Deferred tax liability—noncurrent	$96,000
Deferred tax asset—noncurrent	$(27,000)

Indicate how these balances would be presented in Vectorman's December 31, 2007, balance sheet.

EXERCISES

(LO 2, 5) **E19-1** **(One Temporary Difference, Future Taxable Amounts, One Rate, No Beginning Deferred Taxes)** South Carolina Corporation has one temporary difference at the end of 2007 that will reverse and cause taxable amounts of $55,000 in 2008, $60,000 in 2009, and $65,000 in 2010. South Carolina's pretax financial income for 2007 is $300,000, and the tax rate is 30% for all years. There are no deferred taxes at the beginning of 2007.

Instructions
(a) Compute taxable income and income taxes payable for 2007.
(b) Prepare the journal entry to record income tax expense, deferred income taxes, and income taxes payable for 2007.
(c) Prepare the income tax expense section of the income statement for 2007, beginning with the line "Income before income taxes."

(LO 2) **E19-2** **(Two Differences, No Beginning Deferred Taxes, Tracked through 2 Years)** The following information is available for Wenger Corporation for 2006.

1. Excess of tax depreciation over book depreciation, $40,000. This $40,000 difference will reverse equally over the years 2007–2010.
2. Deferral, for book purposes, of $20,000 of rent received in advance. The rent will be earned in 2007.
3. Pretax financial income, $300,000.
4. Tax rate for all years, 40%.

Instructions

(a) Compute taxable income for 2006.
(b) Prepare the journal entry to record income tax expense, deferred income taxes, and income taxes payable for 2006.
(c) Prepare the journal entry to record income tax expense, deferred income taxes, and income taxes payable for 2007, assuming taxable income of $325,000.

(LO 2, 5) **E19-3** **(One Temporary Difference, Future Taxable Amounts, One Rate, Beginning Deferred Taxes)** Bandung Corporation began 2007 with a $92,000 balance in the Deferred Tax Liability account. At the end of 2007, the related cumulative temporary difference amounts to $350,000, and it will reverse evenly over the next 2 years. Pretax accounting income for 2007 is $525,000, the tax rate for all years is 40%, and taxable income for 2007 is $405,000.

Instructions

(a) Compute income taxes payable for 2007.
(b) Prepare the journal entry to record income tax expense, deferred income taxes, and income taxes payable for 2007.
(c) Prepare the income tax expense section of the income statement for 2007 beginning with the line "Income before income taxes."

(LO 2, 3, 5, 6) **E19-4** **(Three Differences, Compute Taxable Income, Entry for Taxes)** Zurich Company reports pretax financial income of $70,000 for 2007. The following items cause taxable income to be different than pretax financial income.

1. Depreciation on the tax return is greater than depreciation on the income statement by $16,000.
2. Rent collected on the tax return is greater than rent earned on the income statement by $22,000.
3. Fines for pollution appear as an expense of $11,000 on the income statement.

Zurich's tax rate is 30% for all years, and the company expects to report taxable income in all future years. There are no deferred taxes at the beginning of 2007.

Instructions

(a) Compute taxable income and income taxes payable for 2007.
(b) Prepare the journal entry to record income tax expense, deferred income taxes, and income taxes payable for 2007.
(c) Prepare the income tax expense section of the income statement for 2007, beginning with the line "Income before income taxes."
(d) Compute the effective income tax rate for 2007.

(LO 2, 3, 5) **E19-5** **(Two Temporary Differences, One Rate, Beginning Deferred Taxes)** The following facts relate to Krung Thep Corporation.

1. Deferred tax liability, January 1, 2007, $40,000.
2. Deferred tax asset, January 1, 2007, $0.
3. Taxable income for 2007, $95,000.
4. Pretax financial income for 2007, $200,000.
5. Cumulative temporary difference at December 31, 2007, giving rise to future taxable amounts, $240,000.
6. Cumulative temporary difference at December 31, 2007, giving rise to future deductible amounts, $35,000.
7. Tax rate for all years, 40%.
8. The company is expected to operate profitably in the future.

Instructions

(a) Compute income taxes payable for 2007.
(b) Prepare the journal entry to record income tax expense, deferred income taxes, and income taxes payable for 2007.
(c) Prepare the income tax expense section of the income statement for 2007, beginning with the line "Income before income taxes."

(LO 6) **E19-6** **(Identify Temporary or Permanent Differences)** Listed below are items that are commonly accounted for differently for financial reporting purposes than they are for tax purposes.

Instructions

For each item below, indicate whether it involves:

(1) A temporary difference that will result in future deductible amounts and, therefore, will usually give rise to a deferred income tax asset.

(2) A temporary difference that will result in future taxable amounts and, therefore, will usually give rise to a deferred income tax liability.

(3) A permanent difference.

Use the appropriate number to indicate your answer for each.

(a) _____ The MACRS depreciation system is used for tax purposes, and the straight-line depreciation method is used for financial reporting purposes for some plant assets.

(b) _____ A landlord collects some rents in advance. Rents received are taxable in the period when they are received.

(c) _____ Expenses are incurred in obtaining tax-exempt income.

(d) _____ Costs of guarantees and warranties are estimated and accrued for financial reporting purposes.

(e) _____ Installment sales of investments are accounted for by the accrual method for financial reporting purposes and the installment method for tax purposes.

(f) _____ For some assets, straight-line depreciation is used for both financial reporting purposes and tax purposes but the assets' lives are shorter for tax purposes.

(g) _____ Interest is received on an investment in tax-exempt municipal obligations.

(h) _____ Proceeds are received from a life insurance company because of the death of a key officer. (The company carries a policy on key officers.)

(i) _____ The tax return reports a deduction for 80% of the dividends received from U.S. corporations. The cost method is used in accounting for the related investments for financial reporting purposes.

(j) _____ Estimated losses on pending lawsuits and claims are accrued for books. These losses are tax deductible in the period(s) when the related liabilities are settled.

(k) _____ Expenses on stock options are accrued for financial reporting purposes.

(LO 2, 3, 4, 6) **E19-7** **(Terminology, Relationships, Computations, Entries)**

Instructions

Complete the following statements by filling in the blanks.

(a) In a period in which a taxable temporary difference reverses, the reversal will cause taxable income to be _____ (less than, greater than) pretax financial income.

(b) If a $76,000 balance in Deferred Tax Asset was computed by use of a 40% rate, the underlying cumulative temporary difference amounts to $_____.

(c) Deferred taxes _____ (are, are not) recorded to account for permanent differences.

(d) If a taxable temporary difference originates in 2007, it will cause taxable income for 2007 to be _____ (less than, greater than) pretax financial income for 2007.

(e) If total tax expense is $50,000 and deferred tax expense is $65,000, then the current portion of the expense computation is referred to as current tax _____ (expense, benefit) of $_____.

(f) If a corporation's tax return shows taxable income of $100,000 for Year 2 and a tax rate of 40%, how much will appear on the December 31, Year 2, balance sheet for "Income tax payable" if the company has made estimated tax payments of $36,500 for Year 2? $_____.

(g) An increase in the Deferred Tax Liability account on the balance sheet is recorded by a _____ (debit, credit) to the Income Tax Expense account.

(h) An income statement that reports current tax expense of $82,000 and deferred tax benefit of $23,000 will report total income tax expense of $_____.

(i) A valuation account is needed whenever it is judged to be _____ that a portion of a deferred tax asset _____ (will be, will not be) realized.

(j) If the tax return shows total taxes due for the period of $75,000 but the income statement shows total income tax expense of $55,000, the difference of $20,000 is referred to as deferred tax _____ (expense, benefit).

(LO 2, 3, 5, 9) **E19-8** **(Two Temporary Differences, One Rate, 3 Years)** Button Company has two temporary differences between its income tax expense and income taxes payable. The information is shown on page 1004.

	2007	2008	2009
Pretax financial income	$840,000	$910,000	$945,000
Excess depreciation expense on tax return	(30,000)	(40,000)	(10,000)
Excess warranty expense in financial income	20,000	10,000	8,000
Taxable income	$830,000	$880,000	$943,000

The income tax rate for all years is 40%.

Instructions

(a) Prepare the journal entry to record income tax expense, deferred income taxes, and income tax payable for 2007, 2008, and 2009.

(b) Assuming there were no temporary differences prior to 2007, indicate how deferred taxes will be reported on the 2009 balance sheet. Button's product warranty is for 12 months.

(c) Prepare the income tax expense section of the income statement for 2009, beginning with the line "Pretax financial income."

(LO 8) **E19-9** **(Carryback and Carryforward of NOL, No Valuation Account, No Temporary Differences)** The pretax financial income (or loss) figures for Jenny Spangler Company are as follows.

2002	$160,000
2003	250,000
2004	80,000
2005	(160,000)
2006	(380,000)
2007	120,000
2008	100,000

Pretax financial income (or loss) and taxable income (loss) were the same for all years involved. Assume a 45% tax rate for 2002 and 2003 and a 40% tax rate for the remaining years.

Instructions

Prepare the journal entries for the years 2004 to 2008 to record income tax expense and the effects of the net operating loss carrybacks and carryforwards assuming Jenny Spangler Company uses the carryback provision. All income and losses relate to normal operations. (In recording the benefits of a loss carryforward, assume that no valuation account is deemed necessary.)

(LO 8) **E19-10** **(Two NOLs, No Temporary Differences, No Valuation Account, Entries and Income Statement)** Felicia Rashad Corporation has pretax financial income (or loss) equal to taxable income (or loss) from 1999 through 2007 as follows.

	Income (Loss)	Tax Rate
1999	$29,000	30%
2000	40,000	30%
2001	17,000	35%
2002	48,000	50%
2003	(150,000)	40%
2004	90,000	40%
2005	30,000	40%
2006	105,000	40%
2007	(60,000)	45%

Pretax financial income (loss) and taxable income (loss) were the same for all years since Rashad has been in business. Assume the carryback provision is employed for net operating losses. In recording the benefits of a loss carryforward, assume that it is more likely than not that the related benefits will be realized.

Instructions

(a) What entry(ies) for income taxes should be recorded for 2003?

(b) Indicate what the income tax expense portion of the income statement for 2003 should look like. Assume all income (loss) relates to continuing operations.

(c) What entry for income taxes should be recorded in 2004?

(d) How should the income tax expense section of the income statement for 2004 appear?

(e) What entry for income taxes should be recorded in 2007?

(f) How should the income tax expense section of the income statement for 2007 appear?

(LO 2, 3, 9) **E19-11** **(Three Differences, Classify Deferred Taxes)** At December 31, 2006, Belmont Company had a net deferred tax liability of $375,000. An explanation of the items that compose this balance is as follows.

Temporary Differences	Resulting Balances in Deferred Taxes
1. Excess of tax depreciation over book depreciation	$200,000
2. Accrual, for book purposes, of estimated loss contingency from pending lawsuit that is expected to be settled in 2007. The loss will be deducted on the tax return when paid.	(50,000)
3. Accrual method used for book purposes and installment method used for tax purposes for an isolated installment sale of an investment.	225,000
	$375,000

In analyzing the temporary differences, you find that $30,000 of the depreciation temporary difference will reverse in 2007, and $120,000 of the temporary difference due to the installment sale will reverse in 2007. The tax rate for all years is 40%.

Instructions
Indicate the manner in which deferred taxes should be presented on Belmont Company's December 31, 2006, balance sheet.

(LO 2, 3, 5) **E19-12** **(Two Temporary Differences, One Rate, Beginning Deferred Taxes, Compute Pretax Financial Income)** The following facts relate to Duncan Corporation.

1. Deferred tax liability, January 1, 2007, $60,000.
2. Deferred tax asset, January 1, 2007, $20,000.
3. Taxable income for 2007, $105,000.
4. Cumulative temporary difference at December 31, 2007, giving rise to future taxable amounts, $230,000.
5. Cumulative temporary difference at December 31, 2007, giving rise to future deductible amounts, $95,000.
6. Tax rate for all years, 40%. No permanent differences exist.
7. The company is expected to operate profitably in the future.

Instructions
(a) Compute the amount of pretax financial income for 2007.
(b) Prepare the journal entry to record income tax expense, deferred income taxes, and income taxes payable for 2007.
(c) Prepare the income tax expense section of the income statement for 2007, beginning with the line "Income before income taxes."
(d) Compute the effective tax rate for 2007.

(LO 2, 7) **E19-13** **(One Difference, Multiple Rates, Effect of Beginning Balance versus No Beginning Deferred Taxes)** At the end of 2006, Lucretia McEvil Company has $180,000 of cumulative temporary differences that will result in reporting future taxable amounts as follows.

2007	$ 60,000
2008	50,000
2009	40,000
2010	30,000
	$180,000

Tax rates enacted as of the beginning of 2005 are:

2005 and 2006	40%
2007 and 2008	30%
2009 and later	25%

McEvil's taxable income for 2006 is $320,000. Taxable income is expected in all future years.

Instructions
(a) Prepare the journal entry for McEvil to record income taxes payable, deferred income taxes, and income tax expense for 2006, assuming that there were no deferred taxes at the end of 2005.
(b) Prepare the journal entry for McEvil to record income taxes payable, deferred income taxes, and income tax expense for 2006, assuming that there was a balance of $22,000 in a Deferred Tax Liability account at the end of 2005.

(LO 3, 4) **E19-14** **(Deferred Tax Asset with and without Valuation Account)** Jennifer Capriati Corp. has a deferred tax asset account with a balance of $150,000 at the end of 2006 due to a single cumulative temporary difference of $375,000. At the end of 2007 this same temporary difference has increased to a cumulative amount of $450,000. Taxable income for 2007 is $820,000. The tax rate is 40% for all years. No valuation account related to the deferred tax asset is in existence at the end of 2006.

Instructions

(a) Record income tax expense, deferred income taxes, and income taxes payable for 2007, assuming that it is more likely than not that the deferred tax asset will be realized.

(b) Assuming that it is more likely than not that $30,000 of the deferred tax asset will not be realized, prepare the journal entry at the end of 2007 to record the valuation account.

(LO 3, 4, 5) **E19-15** **(Deferred Tax Asset with Previous Valuation Account)** Assume the same information as E19-14, except that at the end of 2006, Jennifer Capriati Corp. had a valuation account related to its deferred tax asset of $45,000.

Instructions

(a) Record income tax expense, deferred income taxes, and income taxes payable for 2007, assuming that it is more likely than not that the deferred tax asset will be realized in full.

(b) Record income tax expense, deferred income taxes, and income taxes payable for 2007, assuming that it is more likely than not that none of the deferred tax asset will be realized.

(LO 2, 5, 7, 9) **E19-16** **(Deferred Tax Liability, Change in Tax Rate, Prepare Section of Income Statement)** Novotna Inc.'s only temporary difference at the beginning and end of 2006 is caused by a $3 million deferred gain for tax purposes for an installment sale of a plant asset, and the related receivable (only one-half of which is classified as a current asset) is due in equal installments in 2007 and 2008. The related deferred tax liability at the beginning of the year is $1,200,000. In the third quarter of 2006, a new tax rate of 34% is enacted into law and is scheduled to become effective for 2008. Taxable income for 2006 is $5,000,000, and taxable income is expected in all future years.

Instructions

(a) Determine the amount reported as a deferred tax liability at the end of 2006. Indicate proper classification(s).

(b) Prepare the journal entry (if any) necessary to adjust the deferred tax liability when the new tax rate is enacted into law.

(c) Draft the income tax expense portion of the income statement for 2006. Begin with the line "Income before income taxes." Assume no permanent differences exist.

(LO 2, 3, 7) **E19-17** **(Two Temporary Differences, Tracked through 3 Years, Multiple Rates)** Taxable income and pretax financial income would be identical for Huber Co. except for its treatments of gross profit on installment sales and estimated costs of warranties. The following income computations have been prepared.

Taxable income	2006	2007	2008
Excess of revenues over expenses (excluding two temporary differences)	$160,000	$210,000	$90,000
Installment gross profit collected	8,000	8,000	8,000
Expenditures for warranties	(5,000)	(5,000)	(5,000)
Taxable income	$163,000	$213,000	$93,000

Pretax financial income	2006	2007	2008
Excess of revenues over expenses (excluding two temporary differences)	$160,000	$210,000	$90,000
Installment gross profit earned	24,000	–0–	–0–
Estimated cost of warranties	(15,000)	–0–	–0–
Income before taxes	$169,000	$210,000	$90,000

The tax rates in effect are: 2006, 40%; 2007 and 2008, 45%. All tax rates were enacted into law on January 1, 2006. No deferred income taxes existed at the beginning of 2006. Taxable income is expected in all future years.

Instructions

Prepare the journal entry to record income tax expense, deferred income taxes, and income tax payable for 2006, 2007, and 2008.

(LO 2, 3, 7) **E19-18** **(Three Differences, Multiple Rates, Future Taxable Income)** During 2007, Kate Holmes Co.'s first year of operations, the company reports pretax financial income at $250,000. Holmes's enacted tax rate is 45% for 2007 and 40% for all later years. Holmes expects to have taxable income in each of the next 5 years. The effects on future tax returns of temporary differences existing at December 31, 2007, are summarized on the following page.

	Future Years					
	2008	2009	2010	2011	2012	Total
Future taxable (deductible) amounts:						
Installment sales	$32,000	$32,000	$32,000			$ 96,000
Depreciation	6,000	6,000	6,000	$6,000	$6,000	30,000
Unearned rent	(50,000)	(50,000)				(100,000)

Instructions

(a) Complete the schedule below to compute deferred taxes at December 31, 2007.

(b) Compute taxable income for 2007.

(c) Prepare the journal entry to record income tax payable, deferred taxes, and income tax expense for 2007.

	Future Taxable (Deductible)	Tax	December 31, 2007 Deferred Tax	
Temporary Difference	Amounts	Rate	(Asset)	Liability
Installment sales	$ 96,000			
Depreciation	30,000			
Unearned rent	(100,000)		____	____
Totals	$____		====	====

(LO 2, 3, 9) **E19-19** **(Two Differences, One Rate, Beginning Deferred Balance, Compute Pretax Financial Income)** Andy McDowell Co. establishes a $100 million liability at the end of 2007 for the estimated site-cleanup costs at two of its manufacturing facilities. All related closing costs will be paid and deducted on the tax return in 2008. Also, at the end of 2007, the company has $50 million of temporary differences due to excess depreciation for tax purposes, $7 million of which will reverse in 2008.

The enacted tax rate for all years is 40%, and the company pays taxes of $64 million on $160 million of taxable income in 2007. McDowell expects to have taxable income in 2008.

Instructions

(a) Determine the deferred taxes to be reported at the end of 2008.

(b) Indicate how the deferred taxes computed in (a) are to be reported on the balance sheet.

(c) Assuming that the only deferred tax account at the beginning of 2007 was a deferred tax liability of $10,000,000, draft the income tax expense portion of the income statement for 2007, beginning with the line "Income before income taxes." (*Hint:* You must first compute (1) the amount of temporary difference underlying the beginning $10,000,000 deferred tax liability, then (2) the amount of temporary differences originating or reversing during the year, then (3) the amount of pretax financial income.)

(LO 2, 3, 9) **E19-20** **(Two Differences, No Beginning Deferred Taxes, Multiple Rates)** Teri Hatcher Inc., in its first year of operations, has the following differences between the book basis and tax basis of its assets and liabilities at the end of 2006.

	Book Basis	Tax Basis
Equipment (net)	$400,000	$340,000
Estimated warranty liability	$200,000	$ –0–

It is estimated that the warranty liability will be settled in 2007. The difference in equipment (net) will result in taxable amounts of $20,000 in 2007, $30,000 in 2008, and $10,000 in 2009. The company has taxable income of $520,000 in 2006. As of the beginning of 2006, the enacted tax rate is 34% for 2006–2008, and 30% for 2009. Hatcher expects to report taxable income through 2009.

Instructions

(a) Prepare the journal entry to record income tax expense, deferred income taxes, and income tax payable for 2006.

(b) Indicate how deferred income taxes will be reported on the balance sheet at the end of 2006.

(LO 2, 3, 7, 9) **E19-21** **(Two Temporary Differences, Multiple Rates, Future Taxable Income)** Nadal Inc. has two temporary differences at the end of 2006. The first difference stems from installment sales, and the second one results from the accrual of a loss contingency. Nadal's accounting department has developed a schedule of future taxable and deductible amounts related to these temporary differences as follows.

	2007	2008	2009	2010
Taxable amounts	$40,000	$50,000	$60,000	$80,000
Deductible amounts		(15,000)	(19,000)	
	$40,000	$35,000	$41,000	$80,000

As of the beginning of 2006, the enacted tax rate is 34% for 2006 and 2007, and 38% for 2008–2011. At the beginning of 2006, the company had no deferred income taxes on its balance sheet. Taxable income for 2006 is $500,000. Taxable income is expected in all future years.

Instructions

(a) Prepare the journal entry to record income tax expense, deferred income taxes, and income taxes payable for 2006.

(b) Indicate how deferred income taxes would be classified on the balance sheet at the end of 2006.

(LO 2, 3, 9) **E19-22** **(Two Differences, One Rate, First Year)** The differences between the book basis and tax basis of the assets and liabilities of Castle Corporation at the end of 2006 are presented below.

	Book Basis	Tax Basis
Accounts receivable	$50,000	$–0–
Litigation liability	30,000	–0–

It is estimated that the litigation liability will be settled in 2007. The difference in accounts receivable will result in taxable amounts of $30,000 in 2007 and $20,000 in 2008. The company has taxable income of $350,000 in 2006 and is expected to have taxable income in each of the following 2 years. Its enacted tax rate is 34% for all years. This is the company's first year of operations. The operating cycle of the business is 2 years.

Instructions

(a) Prepare the journal entry to record income tax expense, deferred income taxes, and income tax payable for 2006.

(b) Indicate how deferred income taxes will be reported on the balance sheet at the end of 2006.

(LO 4, 7, 8) **E19-23** **(NOL Carryback and Carryforward, Valuation Account versus No Valuation Account)** Spamela Hamderson Inc. reports the following pretax income (loss) for both financial reporting purposes and tax purposes. (Assume the carryback provision is used for a net operating loss.)

Year	Pretax Income (Loss)	Tax Rate
2005	$120,000	34%
2006	90,000	34%
2007	(280,000)	38%
2008	220,000	38%

The tax rates listed were all enacted by the beginning of 2005.

Instructions

(a) Prepare the journal entries for the years 2005–2008 to record income tax expense (benefit) and income tax payable (refundable) and the tax effects of the loss carryback and carryforward, assuming that at the end of 2007 the benefits of the loss carryforward are judged more likely than not to be realized in the future.

(b) Using the assumption in (a), prepare the income tax section of the 2007 income statement beginning with the line "Operating loss before income taxes."

(c) Prepare the journal entries for 2007 and 2008, assuming that based on the weight of available evidence, it is more likely than not that one-fourth of the benefits of the loss carryforward will not be realized.

(d) Using the assumption in (c), prepare the income tax section of the 2007 income statement beginning with the line "Operating loss before income taxes."

(LO 4, 7, 8) **E19-24** **(NOL Carryback and Carryforward, Valuation Account Needed)** Beilman Inc. reports the following pretax income (loss) for both book and tax purposes. (Assume the carryback provision is used where possible for a net operating loss.)

Year	Pretax Income (Loss)	Tax Rate
2005	$120,000	40%
2006	90,000	40%
2007	(280,000)	45%
2008	120,000	45%

The tax rates listed were all enacted by the beginning of 2005.

Instructions

(a) Prepare the journal entries for years 2005–2008 to record income tax expense (benefit) and income tax payable (refundable), and the tax effects of the loss carryback and loss carryforward, assuming that based on the weight of available evidence, it is more likely than not that one-half of the benefits of the loss carryforward will not be realized.

(b) Prepare the income tax section of the 2007 income statement beginning with the line "Operating loss before income taxes."

(c) Prepare the income tax section of the 2008 income statement beginning with the line "Income before income taxes."

(LO 4, 7, 8) **E19-25** **(NOL Carryback and Carryforward, Valuation Account Needed)** Meyer reported the following pretax financial income (loss) for the years 2005–2009.

2005	$240,000
2006	350,000
2007	120,000
2008	(570,000)
2009	180,000

Pretax financial income (loss) and taxable income (loss) were the same for all years involved. The enacted tax rate was 34% for 2005 and 2006, and 40% for 2007–2009. Assume the carryback provision is used first for net operating losses.

Instructions

(a) Prepare the journal entries for the years 2007–2009 to record income tax expense, income tax payable (refundable), and the tax effects of the loss carryback and loss carryforward, assuming that based on the weight of available evidence, it is more likely than not that one-fifth of the benefits of the loss carryforward will not be realized.

(b) Prepare the income tax section of the 2008 income statement beginning with the line "Income (loss) before income taxes."

> **See the book's website, www.wiley.com/college/kieso, for Additional Exercises.**

PROBLEMS

(LO 2, 3, 5) **P19-1** **(Three Differences, No Beginning Deferred Taxes, Multiple Rates)** The following information is available for Swanson Corporation for 2006.

1. Depreciation reported on the tax return exceeded depreciation reported on the income statement by $100,000. This difference will reverse in equal amounts of $25,000 over the years 2007–2010.
2. Interest received on municipal bonds was $10,000.
3. Rent collected in advance on January 1, 2006, totaled $60,000 for a 3-year period. Of this amount, $40,000 was reported as unearned at December 31, for book purposes.
4. The tax rates are 40% for 2006 and 35% for 2007 and subsequent years.
5. Income taxes of $360,000 are due per the tax return for 2006.
6. No deferred taxes existed at the beginning of 2006.

Instructions

(a) Compute taxable income for 2006.

(b) Compute pretax financial income for 2006.

(c) Prepare the journal entries to record income tax expense, deferred income taxes, and income taxes payable for 2006 and 2007. Assume taxable income was $980,000 in 2007.

(d) Prepare the income tax expense section of the income statement for 2006, beginning with "Income before income taxes."

(LO 3, 5, 6) **P19-2** **(One Temporary Difference, Tracked for 4 Years, One Permanent Difference, Change in Rate)** The pretax financial income of Parker-Gregory Company differs from its taxable income throughout each of 4 years as follows.

Year	Pretax Financial Income	Taxable Income	Tax Rate
2007	$280,000	$180,000	35%
2008	320,000	225,000	40%
2009	350,000	270,000	40%
2010	420,000	580,000	40%

Pretax financial income for each year includes a nondeductible expense of $30,000 (never deductible for tax purposes). The remainder of the difference between pretax financial income and taxable income in each period is due to one depreciation temporary difference. No deferred income taxes existed at the beginning of 2007.

Instructions

   (a) Prepare journal entries to record income taxes in all 4 years. Assume that the change in the tax rate to 40% was not enacted until the beginning of 2008.

   (b) Prepare the income statement for 2008, beginning with income before income taxes.

(LO 2, 5, 6, 9)   **P19-3** **(Second Year of Depreciation Difference, Two Differences, Single Rate, Extraordinary Item)** The following information has been obtained for the Kerdyk Corporation.

   1. Prior to 2006, taxable income and pretax financial income were identical.

   2. Pretax financial income is $1,700,000 in 2006 and $1,400,000 in 2007.

   3. On January 1, 2006, equipment costing $1,000,000 is purchased. It is to be depreciated on a straight-line basis over 5 years for tax purposes and over 8 years for financial reporting purposes. (*Hint:* Use the half-year convention for tax purposes, as discussed in Appendix 11A.)

   4. Interest of $60,000 was earned on tax-exempt municipal obligations in 2007.

   5. Included in 2007 pretax financial income is an extraordinary gain of $200,000, which is fully taxable.

   6. The tax rate is 35% for all periods.

   7. Taxable income is expected in all future years.

Instructions

   (a) Compute taxable income and income tax payable for 2007.

   (b) Prepare the journal entry to record 2007 income tax expense, income tax payable, and deferred taxes.

   (c) Prepare the bottom portion of Kerdyk's 2007 income statement, beginning with "Income before income taxes and extraordinary item."

   (d) Indicate how deferred income taxes should be presented on the December 31, 2007, balance sheet.

(LO 2, 3, 5)   **P19-4** **(Permanent and Temporary Differences, One Rate)** The accounting records of Anderson Inc. show the following data for 2007.

   1. Life insurance expense on officers was $9,000.

   2. Equipment was acquired in early January for $200,000. Straight-line depreciation over a 5-year life is used, with no salvage value. For tax purposes, Anderson used a 30% rate to calculate depreciation.

   3. Interest revenue on State of New York bonds totaled $4,000.

   4. Product warranties were estimated to be $60,000 in 2007. Actual repair and labor costs related to the warranties in 2007 were $10,000. The remainder is estimated to be incurred evenly in 2008 and 2009.

   5. Sales on an accrual basis were $100,000. For tax purposes, $75,000 was recorded on the installment sales method.

   6. Fines incurred for pollution violations were $4,200.

   7. Pretax financial income was $850,000. The tax rate is 30%.

Instructions

   (a) Prepare a schedule starting with pretax financial income in 2007 and ending with taxable income in 2007.

   (b) Prepare the journal entry for 2007 to record income tax payable, income tax expense, and deferred income taxes.

(LO 5, 7, 8, 9)   **P19-5** **(NOL without Valuation Account)** Parnevik Inc. reported the following pretax income (loss) and related tax rates during the years 2002–2008.

	Pretax Income (loss)	Tax Rate
2002	$ 40,000	30%
2003	25,000	30%
2004	60,000	30%
2005	80,000	40%
2006	(200,000)	45%
2007	70,000	40%
2008	90,000	35%

Pretax financial income (loss) and taxable income (loss) were the same for all years since Parnevik began business. The tax rates from 2005–2008 were enacted in 2005.

Instructions

   (a) Prepare the journal entries for the years 2006–2008 to record income tax payable (refundable), income tax expense (benefit), and the tax effects of the loss carryback and carryforward. Assume that Parnevik elects the carryback provision where possible and expects to realize the benefits of any loss carryforward in the year that immediately follows the loss year.

(b) Indicate the effect the 2006 entry(ies) has on the December 31, 2006, balance sheet.

(c) Prepare the portion of the income statement, starting with "Operating loss before income taxes," for 2006.

(d) Prepare the portion of the income statement, starting with "Income before income taxes," for 2007.

(LO 2, 3, 9) **P19-6** **(Two Differences, Two Rates, Future Income Expected)** Presented below are two independent situations related to future taxable and deductible amounts resulting from temporary differences existing at December 31, 2006.

1. Pirates Co. has developed the following schedule of future taxable and deductible amounts.

	2007	2008	2009	2010	2011
Taxable amounts	$300	$300	$300	$ 300	$300
Deductible amount	—	—	—	(1,400)	—

2. Eagles Co. has the following schedule of future taxable and deductible amounts.

	2007	2008	2009	2010
Taxable amounts	$300	$300	$ 300	$300
Deductible amount	—	—	(2,000)	—

Both Pirates Co. and Eagles Co. have taxable income of $3,000 in 2006 and expect to have taxable income in all future years. The tax rates enacted as of the beginning of 2006 are 30% for 2006–2009 and 35% for years thereafter. All of the underlying temporary differences relate to noncurrent assets and liabilities.

Instructions

For each of these two situations, compute the net amount of deferred income taxes to be reported at the end of 2006, and indicate how it should be classified on the balance sheet.

(LO 2, 5, 7) **P19-7** **(One Temporary Difference, Tracked 3 Years, Change in Rates, Income Statement Presentation)** Gators Corp. sold an investment on an installment basis. The total gain of $60,000 was reported for financial reporting purposes in the period of sale. The company qualifies to use the installment sales method for tax purposes. The installment period is 3 years; one-third of the sale price is collected in the period of sale. The tax rate was 35% in 2006, and 30% in 2007 and 2008. The 30% tax rate was not enacted in law until 2007. The accounting and tax data for the 3 years is shown below.

	Financial Accounting	Tax Return
2006 (35% tax rate)		
Income before temporary difference	$ 70,000	$70,000
Temporary difference	60,000	20,000
Income	$130,000	$90,000
2007 (30% tax rate)		
Income before temporary difference	$ 70,000	$70,000
Temporary difference	–0–	20,000
Income	$ 70,000	$90,000
2008 (30% tax rate)		
Income before temporary difference	$ 70,000	$70,000
Temporary difference	–0–	20,000
Income	$ 70,000	$90,000

Instructions

(a) Prepare the journal entries to record the income tax expense, deferred income taxes, and the income tax payable at the end of each year. No deferred income taxes existed at the beginning of 2006.

(b) Explain how the deferred taxes will appear on the balance sheet at the end of each year. (Assume the Installment Accounts Receivable is classified as a current asset.)

(c) Draft the income tax expense section of the income statement for each year, beginning with "Income before income taxes."

(LO 2, 3, 5, 9) **P19-8** **(Two Differences, 2 Years, Compute Taxable Income and Pretax Financial Income)** The following information was disclosed during the audit of Munter Inc.

1.

Year	Amount Due per Tax Return
2006	$140,000
2007	112,000

2. On January 1, 2006, equipment costing $400,000 is purchased. For financial reporting purposes, the company uses straight-line depreciation over a 5-year life. For tax purposes, the company uses the elective straight-line method over a 5-year life. (*Hint:* For tax purposes, the half-year convention as discussed in Appendix 11A must be used.)

3. In January 2007, $225,000 is collected in advance rental of a building for a 3-year period. The entire $225,000 is reported as taxable income in 2007, but $150,000 of the $225,000 is reported as unearned revenue in 2007 for financial reporting purposes. The remaining amount of unearned revenue is to be earned equally in 2008 and 2009.

4. The tax rate is 40% in 2006 and all subsequent periods. (*Hint:* To find taxable income in 2006 and 2007, the related income tax payable amounts will have to be "grossed up.")

5. No temporary differences existed at the end of 2005. Munter expects to report taxable income in each of the next 5 years.

Instructions

(a) Determine the amount to report for deferred income taxes at the end of 2006, and indicate how it should be classified on the balance sheet.

(b) Prepare the journal entry to record income taxes for 2006.

(c) Draft the income tax section of the income statement for 2006 beginning with "Income before income taxes." (*Hint:* You must compute taxable income and then combine that with changes in cumulative temporary differences to arrive at pretax financial income.)

(d) Determine the deferred income taxes at the end of 2007, and indicate how they should be classified on the balance sheet.

(e) Prepare the journal entry to record income taxes for 2007.

(f) Draft the income tax section of the income statement for 2007, beginning with "Income before income taxes."

(LO 2, 3, 5, 6, 9)

P19-9 (Five Differences, Compute Taxable Income and Deferred Taxes, Draft Income Statement) King Company began operations at the beginning of 2007. The following information pertains to this company.

1. Pretax financial income for 2007 is $100,000.
2. The tax rate enacted for 2007 and future years is 40%
3. Differences between the 2007 income statement and tax return are listed below:

   (a) Warranty expense accrued for financial reporting purposes amounts to $5,000. Warranty deductions per the tax return amount to $2,000.

   (b) Gross profit on construction contracts using the percentage-of-completion method for books amounts to $92,000. Gross profit on construction contracts for tax purposes amounts to $62,000.

   (c) Depreciation of property, plant, and equipment for financial reporting purposes amounts to $60,000. Depreciation of these assets amounts to $80,000 for the tax return.

   (d) A $3,500 fine paid for violation of pollution laws was deducted in computing pretax financial income.

   (e) Interest revenue earned on an investment in tax-exempt municipal bonds amounts to $1,400. (Assume (a) is short-term in nature; assume (b) and (c) are long-term in nature.)

4. Taxable income is expected for the next few years.

Instructions

(a) Compute taxable income for 2007.

(b) Compute the deferred taxes at December 31, 2007, that relate to the temporary differences described above. Clearly label them as deferred tax asset or liability.

(c) Prepare the journal entry to record income tax expense, deferred taxes, and income taxes payable for 2007.

(d) Draft the income tax expense section of the income statement beginning with "Income before income taxes."

CONCEPTS FOR ANALYSIS

CA19-1 (Objectives and Principles for Accounting for Income Taxes) The amount of income taxes due to the government for a period of time is rarely the amount reported on the income statement for that period as income tax expense.

Instructions

(a) Explain the objectives of accounting for income taxes in general purpose financial statements.

(b) Explain the basic principles that are applied in accounting for income taxes at the date of the financial statements to meet the objectives discussed in (a).

(c) List the steps in the annual computation of deferred tax liabilities and assets.

CA19-2 (Basic Accounting for Temporary Differences)   Majoli Company appropriately uses the asset-liability method to record deferred income taxes. Iva Majoli reports depreciation expense for certain machinery purchased this year using the modified accelerated cost recovery system (MACRS) for income tax purposes and the straight-line basis for financial reporting purposes. The tax deduction is the larger amount this year.

Majoli received rent revenues in advance this year. These revenues are included in this year's taxable income. However, for financial reporting purposes, these revenues are reported as unearned revenues, a current liability.

Instructions
   (a)   What are the principles of the asset-liability approach?
   (b)   How would Majoli account for the temporary differences?
   (c)   How should Majoli classify the deferred tax consequences of the temporary differences on its balance sheet?

CA19-3 (Identify Temporary Differences and Classification Criteria)   The asset-liability approach for recording deferred income taxes is an integral part of generally accepted accounting principles.

Instructions
   (a)   Indicate whether each of the following independent situations should be treated as a temporary difference or as a permanent difference and explain why.
       (1)   Estimated warranty costs (covering a 3-year warranty) are expensed for financial reporting purposes at the time of sale but deducted for income tax purposes when paid.
       (2)   Depreciation for book and income tax purposes differs because of different bases of carrying the related property, which was acquired in a trade-in. The different bases are a result of different rules used for book and tax purposes to compute the basis of property acquired in a trade-in.
       (3)   A company properly uses the equity method to account for its 30% investment in another company. The investee pays dividends that are about 10% of its annual earnings.
       (4)   A company reports a gain on an involuntary conversion of a nonmonetary asset to a monetary asset. The company elects to replace the property within the statutory period using the total proceeds so the gain is not reported on the current year's tax return.
   (b)   Discuss the nature of the deferred income tax accounts and possible classifications in a company's balance sheet. Indicate the manner in which these accounts are to be reported.

CA19-4 (Accounting and Classification of Deferred Income Taxes)
Part A
This year Sharapova Company has each of the following items in its income statement.
   1.   Gross profits on installment sales.
   2.   Revenues on long-term construction contracts.
   3.   Estimated costs of product warranty contracts.
   4.   Premiums on officers' life insurance with Sharapova as beneficiary.

Instructions
   (a)   Under what conditions would deferred income taxes need to be reported in the financial statements?
   (b)   Specify when deferred income taxes would need to be recognized for each of the items above, and indicate the rationale for such recognition.

Part B
Sharapova Company's president has heard that deferred income taxes can be classified in different ways in the balance sheet.

Instructions
Identify the conditions under which deferred income taxes would be classified as a noncurrent item in the balance sheet. What justification exists for such classification?

(AICPA adapted)

CA19-5 (Explain Computation of Deferred Tax Liability for Multiple Tax Rates)   At December 31, 2007, Hingis Corporation has one temporary difference which will reverse and cause taxable amounts in 2008. In 2007 a new tax act set taxes equal to 45% for 2007, 40% for 2008, and 34% for 2009 and years thereafter.

Instructions
Explain what circumstances would call for Hingis to compute its deferred tax liability at the end of 2007 by multiplying the cumulative temporary difference by:
   (a)   45%.
   (b)   40%.
   (c)   34%.

CA19-6 (Explain Future Taxable and Deductible Amounts, How Carryback and Carryforward Affects Deferred Taxes) Mary Joe Fernandez and Meredith McGrath are discussing accounting for income taxes. They are currently studying a schedule of taxable and deductible amounts that will arise in the future as a result of existing temporary differences. The schedule is as follows.

	Current Year	Future Years			
	2007	2008	2009	2010	2011
Taxable income	$850,000				
Taxable amounts		$375,000	$375,000	$ 375,000	$375,000
Deductible amounts				(2,400,000)	
Enacted tax rate	50%	45%	40%	35%	30%

Instructions

(a) Explain the concept of future taxable amounts and future deductible amounts as illustrated in the schedule.

(b) How do the carryback and carryforward provisions affect the reporting of deferred tax assets and deferred tax liabilities?

CA19-7 (Deferred Taxes, Income Effects) Henrietta Aguirre, CPA, is the newly hired director of corporate taxation for Mesa Incorporated, which is a publicly traded corporation. Ms. Aguirre's first job with Mesa was the review of the company's accounting practices on deferred income taxes. In doing her review, she noted differences between tax and book depreciation methods that permitted Mesa to realize a sizable deferred tax liability on its balance sheet. As a result, Mesa paid very little in income taxes at that time.

Aguirre also discovered that Mesa has an explicit policy of selling off plant assets before they reversed in the deferred tax liability account. This policy, coupled with the rapid expansion of its plant asset base, allowed Mesa to "defer" all income taxes payable for several years, even though it always has reported positive earnings and an increasing EPS. Aguirre checked with the legal department and found the policy to be legal, but she's uncomfortable with the ethics of it.

Instructions

Answer the following questions.

(a) Why would Mesa have an explicit policy of selling plant assets before the temporary differences reversed in the deferred tax liability account?

(b) What are the ethical implications of Mesa's "deferral" of income taxes?

(c) Who could be harmed by Mesa's ability to "defer" income taxes payable for several years, despite positive earnings?

(d) In a situation such as this, what are Ms. Aguirre's professional responsibilities as a CPA?

USING YOUR JUDGMENT

Financial Reporting Problem

P&G **The Procter & Gamble Company (P&G)**

The financial statements of **P&G** are presented in Appendix 5B or can be accessed on the KWW website.

Instructions

Refer to P&G's financial statements and the accompanying notes to answer the following questions.

(a) What amounts relative to income taxes does P&G report in its:

(1) 2004 income statement?

(2) June 30, 2004, balance sheet?

(3) 2004 statement of cash flows?

(b) P&G's provision for income taxes in 2002, 2003, and 2004 was computed at what effective tax rates? (See the notes to the financial statements.)

(c) How much of P&G's 2004 total provision for income taxes was current tax expense, and how much was deferred tax expense?

(d) What did P&G report as the significant components (the details) of its June 30, 2004, deferred tax assets and liabilities?

Financial Statement Analysis Case

Homestake Mining Company

Homestake Mining Company is a 120-year-old international gold mining company with substantial gold mining operations and exploration in the United States, Canada, and Australia. At year-end, Homestake reported the following items related to income taxes (thousands of dollars).

Total current taxes	$ 26,349
Total deferred taxes	(39,436)
Total income and mining taxes (the provision for taxes per its income statement)	(13,087)
Deferred tax liabilities	$303,050
Deferred tax assets, net of valuation allowance of $207,175	95,275
Net deferred tax liability	$207,775

Note 6: The classification of deferred tax assets and liabilities is based on the related asset or liability creating the deferred tax. Deferred taxes not related to a specific asset or liability are classified based on the estimated period of reversal.

Tax loss carryforwards (U.S., Canada, Australia, and Chile)	$71,151
Tax credit carryforwards	$12,007

Instructions

(a) What is the significance of Homestake's disclosure of "Current taxes" of $26,349 and "Deferred taxes" of $(39,436)?

(b) Explain the concept behind Homestake's disclosure of gross deferred tax liabilities (future taxable amounts) and gross deferred tax assets (future deductible amounts).

(c) Homestake reported tax loss carryforwards of $71,151 and tax credit carryforwards of $12,007. How do the carryback and carryforward provisions affect the reporting of deferred tax assets and deferred tax liabilities?

Comparative Analysis Case

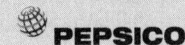

The Coca-Cola Company and PepsiCo, Inc.

Instructions

Go to the KWW website and use information found there to answer the following questions related to **The Coca-Cola Company and PepsiCo, Inc.**

(a) What are the amounts of Coca-Cola's and PepsiCo's provision for income taxes for the year 2004? Of each company's 2004 provision for income taxes, what portion is current expense and what portion is deferred expense?

(b) What amount of cash was paid in 2004 for income taxes by Coca-Cola and by PepsiCo?

(c) What was the U.S. federal statutory tax rate in 2004? What was the effective tax rate in 2004 for Coca-Cola and PepsiCo? Why might their effective tax rates differ?

(d) For the year-end 2004, what amounts were reported by Coca-Cola and PepsiCo as (a) gross deferred tax assets and (b) gross deferred tax liabilities?

(e) Do either Coca-Cola or PepsiCo disclose any net operating loss carrybacks and/or carryforwards at year-end 2004? What are the amounts, and when do the carryforwards expire?

Research Cases

Case 1

As discussed in the chapter, companies must consider all positive and negative information in determining whether a deferred tax asset valuation allowance is needed.

Instructions

Examine the balance sheets and income tax footnotes for two companies that have recorded deferred tax assets, and answer the following questions with regard to each company.

(a) What is the gross amount of the deferred tax asset recorded by the company? Express this amount as a percentage of total assets.

(b) Did the company record a valuation allowance? How large was the allowance?

(c) What evidence, if any, did the company cite with regard to the need for a valuation allowance? Do you consider the company's disclosure to be adequate?

Case 2

Deferred tax liabilities require special considerations for financial statement readers.

Instructions

Obtain a recent edition of a financial statement analysis textbook, read the section related to deferred tax liabilities, and answer the following questions.

(a) What are the major analytical issues associated with deferred tax liabilities?

(b) What type of adjustments to deferred tax liabilities do analysts make when examining financial statements?

International Reporting Case

Tomkins PLC

Tomkins PLC is a British company that operates in three business sectors: industrial and automotive, air systems components, and engineering and construction products. Before 2005 Tomkins prepared its accounts in accordance with United Kingdom (U.K.) accounting standards. Like U.S. reporting, U.K. financial reporting is investor-oriented. As a result, British companies report different income amounts for tax and financial reporting purposes. British companies receive different tax treatment for such items as depreciation (capital allowances), and they receive tax credits for operating losses. In 2004 Tomkins reported income of £171.8 million and reported total shareholders' funds of £1,398.7 million at year-end. Tomkins provided the following disclosures related to taxes in its annual report.

If Tomkins had used U.S. GAAP its income would have been higher by £96.1 million in the current year. Stockholders' equity at year-end would have been £764.9 million higher if Tompkins had applied U.S. GAAP.

◊OMKINS

Reconciliation to Accounting Principles Generally Accepted in the United States of America (Unaudited)— Partial

The consolidated financial statements are prepared in conformity with accounting principles generally accepted in the United Kingdom ("U.K. GAAP") which differ in certain respects from accounting principles generally accepted in the United States of America ("U.S. GAAP"). The following is a summary of the material adjustments to profit attributable to shareholders and shareholders' equity determined in accordance with U.K. GAAP, necessary to reconcile to net income and shareholders' equity determined in accordance with U.S. GAAP.

Reconciliation from U.K. GAAP to U.S. GAAP

	3 January 2004 12 months £ million
Profit attributable to shareholders	
Net income under UK GAAP	171.8
U.S. GAAP adjustments:	
Goodwill amortisation	11.9
Goodwill impairment	(30.0)
Reversal of U.K. provision for impairment	51.4
Intangibles amortisation	(1.6)
Valuation of net assets acquired in a business combination	(0.2)
Gain/(loss) on disposal of operations	22.6
Pension costs	3.4
Share options	(4.0)
Capitalised interest	2.2
Deferred income tax	(2.1)
Derivatives	29.5
Restructuring costs	13.0
Net income under U.S. GAAP	267.9

Explanation of the deferred tax difference is as follows:

In Tomkins consolidated financial statements, deferred tax is provided in full on all liabilities. Deferred tax assets are recognised to the extent it is regarded as more likely than not that there will be suitable taxable profits from which the future reversal of the underlying timing differences can be deducted, and for this purpose Tomkins considers only future periods for which forecasts are prepared. Under U.S. GAAP, deferred taxes are provided for all temporary differences on a full asset and liability basis. A valuation allowance is established in respect of those deferred tax assets where it is more likely than not that some portion will not be realised. The look forward period is not limited to the period for which forecasts are prepared.

Instructions

Use the information in the Tomkins disclosure to answer the following.

(a) Prepare the journal entry that would be required to reconcile Tomkins' income to U.S. GAAP for the differences in deferred taxes under U.S. and U.K. accounting standards.

(b) In light of the information disclosed, explain why you think Tomkins' equity under U.S. GAAP would be higher at year-end in the current year.

(c) Tomkins, like other U.K. companies, uses the intrinsic-value method to measure the expense related to stock-based compensation. Assuming similar tax treatment of stock-based compensation in the U.S. and the U.K., does the U.K. accounting cause any problems in comparing the financial statements of U.S. GAAP and U.K. GAAP companies? In your discussion, consider both compensation expense and deferred taxes.

Professional Research: Financial Accounting and Reporting

Hallscott Company started operations in 2003, and although it has grown steadily, the company reported accumulated operating losses of $450,000 in its first four years in business. In the most recent year (2007), Hallscott appears to have turned the corner and reported modest taxable income of $30,000. In addition to a deferred tax asset related to its net operating loss, Hallscott has recorded a deferred tax asset related to product warranties and a deferred tax liability related to accelerated depreciation.

Given its past operating results, Hallscott has established a full valuation allowance for its deferred tax assets. However, given its improved performance, Hallscott management wonders whether the company can now reduce or eliminate the valuation allowance. They would like you to conduct some research on the accounting for its valuation allowance.

Instructions

Using the **Financial Accounting Research System (FARS)**, respond to the following items. (Provide text strings used in your search.)

(a) Briefly explain to Hallscott management the importance of future taxable income as it relates to the valuation allowance for deferred tax assets.

(b) What are the sources of income that may be relied upon to remove the need for a valuation allowance?

(c) What are tax-planning strategies? From the information provided, does it appear that Hallscott could employ a tax-planning strategy to support reducing its valuation allowance?

Professional Simulation

In this simulation you are asked to address questions related to the accounting for taxes. Prepare responses to all parts.

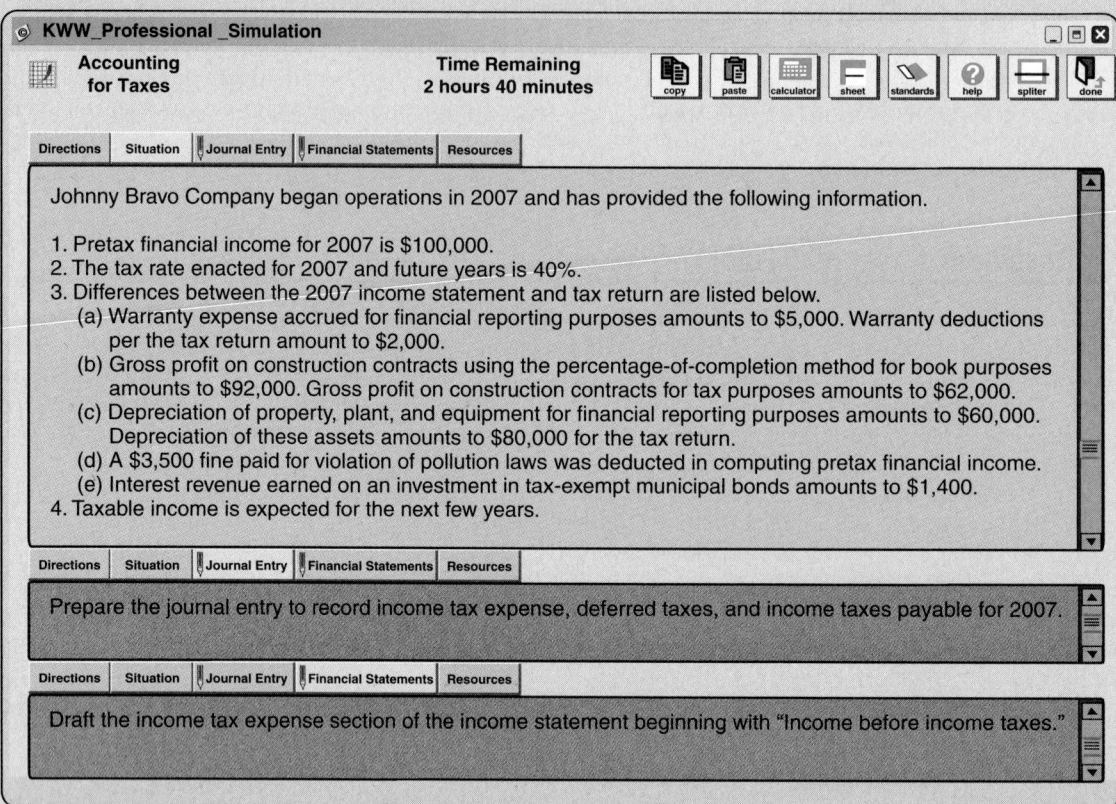

KWW_Professional _Simulation

| Accounting for Taxes | Time Remaining 2 hours 40 minutes | copy | paste | calculator | sheet | standards | help | splitter | done |

| Directions | Situation | Journal Entry | Financial Statements | Resources |

Johnny Bravo Company began operations in 2007 and has provided the following information.

1. Pretax financial income for 2007 is $100,000.
2. The tax rate enacted for 2007 and future years is 40%.
3. Differences between the 2007 income statement and tax return are listed below.
   (a) Warranty expense accrued for financial reporting purposes amounts to $5,000. Warranty deductions per the tax return amount to $2,000.
   (b) Gross profit on construction contracts using the percentage-of-completion method for book purposes amounts to $92,000. Gross profit on construction contracts for tax purposes amounts to $62,000.
   (c) Depreciation of property, plant, and equipment for financial reporting purposes amounts to $60,000. Depreciation of these assets amounts to $80,000 for the tax return.
   (d) A $3,500 fine paid for violation of pollution laws was deducted in computing pretax financial income.
   (e) Interest revenue earned on an investment in tax-exempt municipal bonds amounts to $1,400.
4. Taxable income is expected for the next few years.

| Directions | Situation | Journal Entry | Financial Statements | Resources |

Prepare the journal entry to record income tax expense, deferred taxes, and income taxes payable for 2007.

| Directions | Situation | Journal Entry | Financial Statements | Resources |

Draft the income tax expense section of the income statement beginning with "Income before income taxes."

Remember to check the book's companion website to find additional resources for this chapter.

wiley.com/college/kieso

ACCOUNTING FOR PENSIONS AND POSTRETIREMENT BENEFITS

Where Have All the Pensions Gone?

Many companies have benefit plans that promise income and other benefits to retired employees in exchange for services during their working years. However, a shift is on from traditional defined-benefit plans, in which employers bear the risk of meeting the benefit promises, to plans in which employees bear more of the risk. In some cases, employers are dropping retirement plans altogether. Here are some of the reasons for the shift.

Competition. Newer and foreign competitors do not have the same retiree costs that older U.S. companies do. **Southwest Airlines** does not offer a traditional pension plan, but **Northwest** and **United** both have pension deficits exceeding $100,000 per employee.

Cost. Retirees are living longer, and the costs of retirement are higher. Combined with annual retiree healthcare costs, retirement benefits are costing the S&P 500 companies over $25 billion a year and are rising at double-digit rates.

Insurance. Pensions are backed by premiums paid to the **Pension Benefit Guarantee Corporation** (PBGC). When a company fails, the PBGC takes over the plan. But due to a number of significant company failures, the PBGC is running a deficit, and healthy companies are subsidizing the weak. For example, steel companies pay just 3 percent of PBGC premiums but account for 56 percent of the claims.

Accounting. To bring U.S. standards in line with international rules, accounting rule makers are considering rules that will require companies to "mark their pensions to market" (value them at market rates). Such a move would increase the reported volatility of the retirement plan and of company financial statements. When Britain made this shift, 25 percent of British companies closed their plans to new entrants.[1]

As a result of such factors, it is not hard to believe that experts can think of no major company that has instituted a traditional pension plan in the past decade.

---

[1]Adapted from Nanette Byrnes with David Welch, "The Benefits Trap," *Business Week* (July 19, 2004), pp. 54–72.

Learning Objectives

After studying this chapter, you should be able to:

1. Distinguish between accounting for the employer's pension plan and accounting for the pension fund.
2. Identify types of pension plans and their characteristics.
3. Explain alternative measures for valuing the pension obligation.
4. List the components of pension expense.
5. Use a worksheet for employer's pension plan entries.
6. Describe the amortization of prior service costs.
7. Explain the accounting for unexpected gains and losses.
8. Explain the corridor approach to amortizing gains and losses.
9. Describe the requirements for reporting pension plans in financial statements.

As our opening story indicates, the cost of retirement benefits is getting steep. For example, **General Motors'** pension and healthcare costs for retirees in a recent year totaled $6.2 billion, or approximately $1,784 per vehicle produced. General Motors and many other companies are facing substantial pension and other postretirement expenses and obligations. In this chapter we discuss the accounting issues related to these benefit plans. The content and organization of the chapter are as follows.

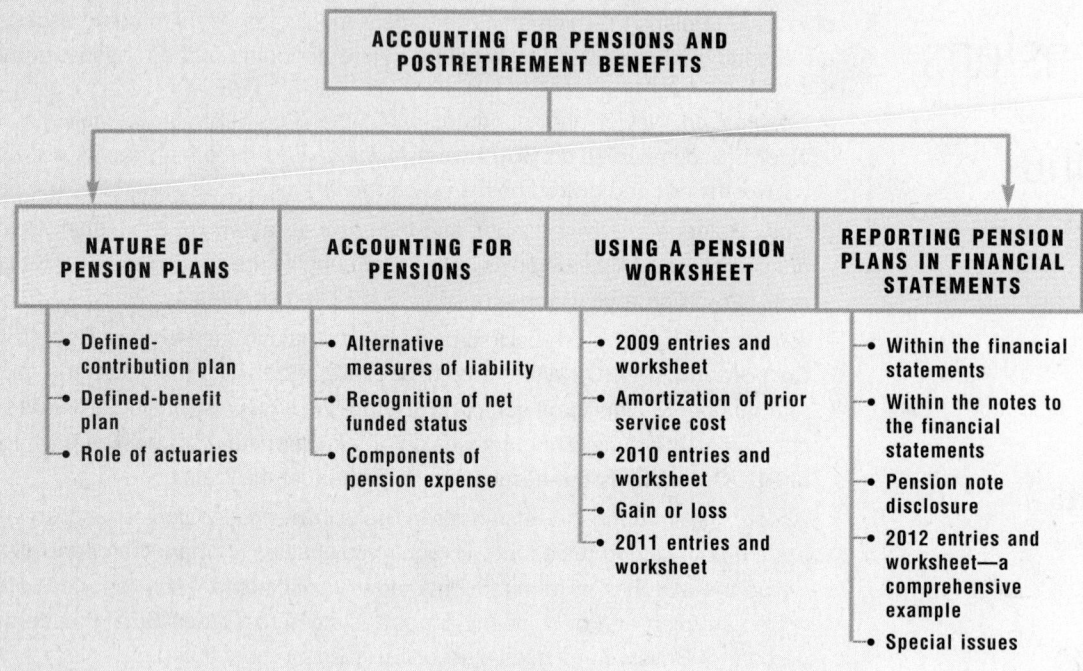

NATURE OF PENSION PLANS

OBJECTIVE 1
Distinguish between accounting for the employer's pension plan and accounting for the pension fund.

A **pension plan** is an arrangement whereby an employer provides benefits (payments) to retired employees for services they provided in their working years. Pension accounting may be divided and separately treated as **accounting for the employer** and **accounting for the pension fund**. The *company* or *employer* is the organization sponsoring the pension plan. It incurs the cost and makes contributions to the pension fund. The *fund* or *plan* is the entity that receives the contributions from the employer, administers the pension assets, and makes the benefit payments to the retired employees (pension recipients). Illustration 20-1 shows the three entities involved in a pension plan and indicates the flow of cash among them.

ILLUSTRATION 20-1
Flow of Cash among
Pension Plan Participants

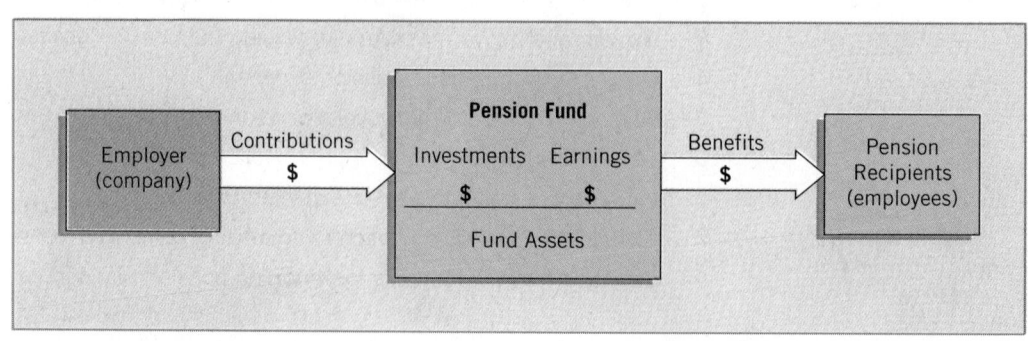

A pension plan is **funded** when the employer makes payments to a funding agency.[2] That agency accumulates the assets of the pension fund and makes payments to the recipients as the benefits come due.

Some pension plans are **contributory**. In these, the employees bear part of the cost of the stated benefits or voluntarily make payments to increase their benefits. Other plans are **noncontributory**. In these, the employer bears the entire cost. Companies generally design their pension plans so as to take advantage of federal income tax benefits. Plans that offer tax benefits are called **qualified pension plans**. They permit **deductibility of the employer's contributions to the pension fund and tax-free status of earnings from pension fund assets**.

The pension fund should be a separate legal and accounting entity. The pension fund, as a separate entity, maintains a set of books and prepares financial statements. Maintaining records and preparing financial statements for the fund, an activity known as "accounting for employee benefit plans," is not the subject of this chapter.[3] Instead, this chapter explains the pension accounting and reporting problems **of the employer** as the sponsor of a pension plan.

The need to properly administer and account for pension funds becomes apparent when you understand the size of these funds. Listed in Illustration 20-2 are the pension fund assets and pension expenses of seven major companies.

Company ($ in millions)	Size of Pension Fund	2004 Pension Expense	Pension Expense as % of Pre-Tax Income
General Motors	$ 99,909	$2,456	52.27%
Hewlett-Packard	9,168	594	14.16
Deere & Company	8,403	43	2.03
Goodyear Tire	7,720	35	10.72
Merck	5,481	397	4.98
The Coca-Cola Company	2,800	122	1.96
Molson Coors Brewing	2,740	44	14.18

ILLUSTRATION 20-2
Pension Funds and Pension Expense

As Illustration 20-2 indicates, pension expense is a substantial percentage of total profit for many companies.[4] The two most common types of pension plans are **defined-contribution plans** and **defined-benefit plans**, and we look at each of them in the following sections.

Defined-Contribution Plan

In a **defined-contribution plan**, the employer agrees to contribute to a pension trust a certain sum each period, based on a formula. This formula may consider such factors as age, length of employee service, employer's profits, and compensation level. **The plan defines only the employer's contribution.** It makes no promise regarding the ultimate benefits paid out to the employees. A common form of this plan is a "401(k)" plan.

The size of the pension benefits that the employee finally collects under the plan depends on several factors: the amounts originally contributed to the pension trust, the

OBJECTIVE 2
Identify types of pension plans and their characteristics.

---

[2]When used as a verb, **fund** means to pay to a funding agency (as to fund future pension benefits or to fund pension cost). Used as a noun, it refers to assets accumulated in the hands of a funding agency (trustee) for the purpose of meeting pension benefits when they become due.

[3]The FASB issued a separate standard covering the accounting and reporting for employee benefit plans. "Accounting and Reporting by Defined Benefit Pension Plans," *Statement of Financial Accounting Standards No. 35* (Stamford, Conn.: FASB, 1979).

[4]One study indicated that during the 1990s, pension funds (private and public) held or owned approximately 25 percent of the market value of corporate stock outstanding and accounted for 32 percent of the daily trading volume on the New York Stock Exchange. The enormous size (and the social significance) of these funds is staggering.

income accumulated in the trust, and the treatment of forfeitures of funds caused by early terminations of other employees. A company usually turns over to an **independent third-party trustee** the amounts originally contributed. The trustee, acting on behalf of the beneficiaries (the participating employees), assumes ownership of the pension assets and is accountable for their investment and distribution. The trust is separate and distinct from the employer.

Disclosures for Defined-Contribution Plans

The accounting for a defined-contribution plan is straightforward. The employee gets the benefit of gain (or the risk of loss) from the assets contributed to the pension plan. The employer simply contributes each year based on the formula established in the plan. As a result, the employer's annual cost (pension expense) is simply the amount that it is obligated to contribute to the pension trust. The employer reports a liability on its balance sheet only if it does not make the contribution in full. The employer reports an asset only if it contributes more than the required amount.

In addition to pension expense, the employer must disclose the following for a defined-contribution plan: a plan description, including employee groups covered; the basis for determining contributions; and the nature and effect of significant matters affecting comparability from period to period.[5]

Defined-Benefit Plan

A **defined-benefit plan** outlines the benefits that employees will receive when they retire. These benefits typically are a function of an employee's years of service and of the compensation level in the years approaching retirement.

To meet the defined-benefit commitments that will arise at retirement, a company must determine what the contribution should be today (a time value of money computation). Companies may use many different contribution approaches. However, the funding method should provide enough money at retirement to meet the benefits defined by the plan.

INTERNATIONAL INSIGHT

Outside the U.S., private pension plans are less common because many other nations rely on government-sponsored pension plans. Consequently, accounting for defined-benefit pension plans is typically a less important issue elsewhere in the world.

The **employees** are the beneficiaries of a defined-**contribution** trust, but the **employer** is the beneficiary of a defined-**benefit** trust. Under a defined-benefit plan, the trust's primary purpose is to safeguard and invest assets so that there will be enough to pay the employer's obligation to the employees. **In form**, the trust is a separate entity. **In substance**, the trust assets and liabilities belong to the employer. That is, **as long as the plan continues, the employer is responsible for the payment of the defined benefits (without regard to what happens in the trust).** The employer must make up any shortfall in the accumulated assets held by the trust. On the other hand, the employer can recapture any excess accumulated in the trust, either through reduced future funding or through a reversion of funds.

Because a defined-benefit plan specifies benefits in terms of uncertain future variables, a company must establish an appropriate funding pattern to ensure the availability of funds at retirement in order to provide the benefits promised. This funding level depends on a number of factors such as turnover, mortality, length of employee service, compensation levels, and interest earnings.

Employers are at risk with defined-benefit plans because they must contribute enough to meet the cost of benefits that the plan defines. The expense recognized each period is not necessarily equal to the cash contribution. Similarly, the liability is controversial because its measurement and recognition relate to unknown future variables. Thus, the accounting issues related to this type of plan are complex. **Our discussion in the following sections deals primarily with defined-benefit plans.**[6]

---

[5]"Employers' Accounting for Pension Plans," *Statement of Financial Accounting Standards No. 87* (Stamford, Conn.: FASB, 1985), pars. 63–66.

[6]In terms of total assets, recent (2004) Federal Reserve statistics indicate that assets in private defined-benefit and defined-contribution plans were more than $1.8 and $2.7 trillion, respectively. In many cases, companies offer a defined-contribution plan in combination with a defined-benefit plan.

WHICH PLAN IS YOR YOU?

Defined-contribution plans have become much more popular with employers than defined-benefit plans. One reason is that they are cheaper. Defined-contribution plans often cost no more than 3 percent of payroll, whereas defined-benefit plans can cost 5 to 6 percent of payroll.

WHAT DO THE NUMBERS MEAN?

In the late 1970s approximately 15 million individuals had defined-contribution plans; today over 62 million do. The following chart reflects this significant change. It shows the percentage of companies using various types of plans, based on a survey of approximately 150 CFOs and managing corporate directors.

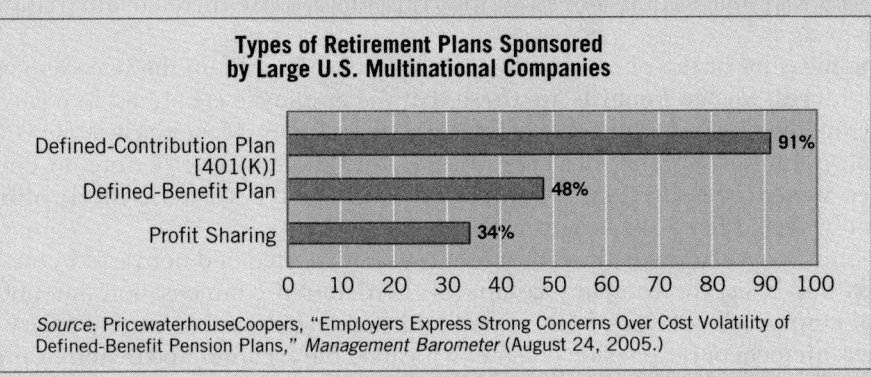

Types of Retirement Plans Sponsored by Large U.S. Multinational Companies

Source: PricewaterhouseCoopers, "Employers Express Strong Concerns Over Cost Volatility of Defined-Benefit Pension Plans," *Management Barometer* (August 24, 2005.)

Although many companies are changing to defined-contribution plans, over 40 million individuals still are covered under defined-benefit plans.

The Role of Actuaries in Pension Accounting

The problems associated with pension plans involve complicated mathematical considerations. Therefore, companies engage **actuaries** to ensure that a pension plan is appropriate for the employee group covered.[7] Actuaries are individuals trained through a long and rigorous certification program to assign probabilities to future events and their financial effects. The insurance industry employs actuaries to assess risks and to advise on the setting of premiums and other aspects of insurance policies. Employers rely heavily on actuaries for assistance in developing, implementing, and funding pension funds.

Actuaries make predictions (called *actuarial assumptions*) of mortality rates, employee turnover, interest and earnings rates, early retirement frequency, future salaries, and any other factors necessary to operate a pension plan. They also compute the various pension measures that affect the financial statements, such as the pension obligation, the annual cost of servicing the plan, and the cost of amendments to the plan. In summary, accounting for defined-benefit pension plans relies heavily upon information and measurements provided by actuaries.

---

[7]An actuary's primary purpose is to ensure that the company has established an appropriate funding pattern to meet its pension obligations. This computation involves developing a set of assumptions and continued monitoring of these assumptions to ensure their realism. That the general public has little understanding of what an actuary does is illustrated by the following excerpt from the *Wall Street Journal*: "A polling organization once asked the general public what an actuary was, and received among its more coherent responses the opinion that it was a place where you put dead actors."

ACCOUNTING FOR PENSIONS

OBJECTIVE 3
Explain alternative measures for valuing the pension obligation.

In accounting for a company's pension plan, two questions arise: (1) What is the pension obligation that a company should report in the financial statements? (2) What is the pension expense for the period? Attempting to answer the first question has produced much controversy.

Alternative Measures of the Liability

Most agree that an employer's **pension obligation** is the deferred compensation obligation it has to its employees for their service under the terms of the pension plan. Measuring that obligation is not so simple, though, because there are alternative ways of measuring it.[8]

One measure of the pension obligation is to base it only on the benefits vested to the employees. **Vested benefits** are those that the employee is entitled to receive even if he or she renders no additional services to the company. Most pension plans require a certain minimum number of years of service to the employer before an employee achieves vested benefits status. Companies compute the **vested benefit obligation** using only vested benefits, at current salary levels.

Another way to measure the obligation uses both vested and nonvested years of service. On this basis, the company computes the deferred compensation amount on all years of employees' service—**both vested and nonvested**—using current salary levels. This measurement of the pension obligation is called the **accumulated benefit obligation**.

A third measure bases the deferred compensation amount on both vested and nonvested service **using future salaries**. This measurement of the pension obligation is called the **projected benefit obligation**. Because future salaries are expected to be higher than current salaries, this approach results in the largest measurement of the pension obligation.

The choice between these measures is critical. The choice affects the amount of a company's pension liability and the annual pension expense reported. The diagram in Illustration 20-3 presents the differences in these three measurements.

INTERNATIONAL INSIGHT

Japan is the most rapidly aging nation in the developed world. By the year 2015, 24 percent of its population is expected to be over 65, compared with 17 percent in Europe and 15 percent in the U.S. Aging populations will affect pension liabilities in these countries.

ILLUSTRATION 20-3
Different Measures of the Pension Obligation

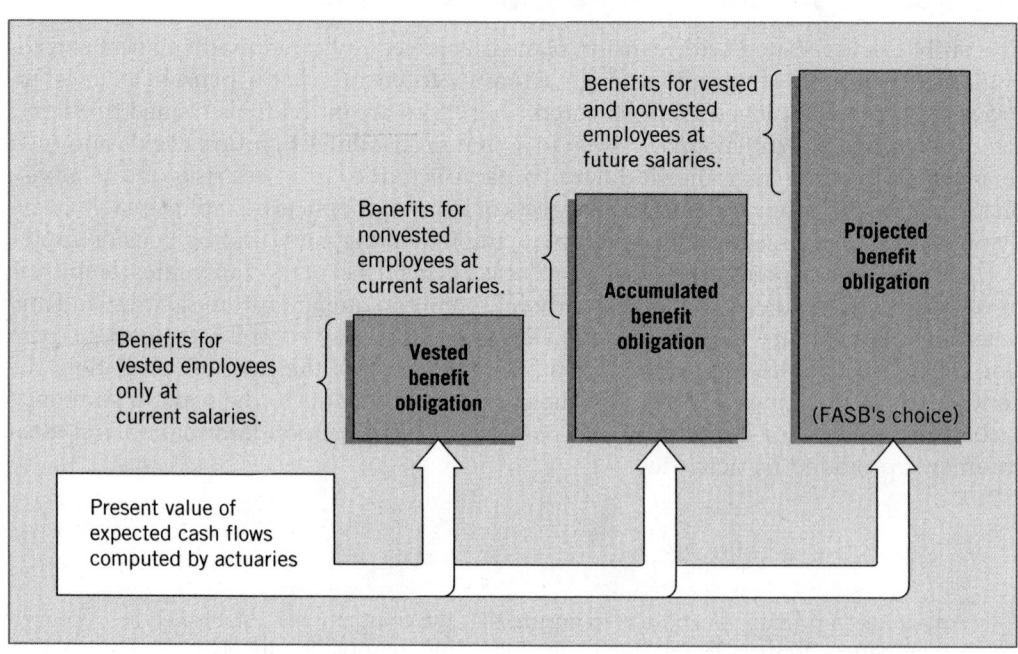

---

[8]One measure of the pension obligation is to determine the amount that the **Pension Benefit Guaranty Corporation** would require the employer to pay if it defaulted. (This amount is limited to 30 percent of the employer's net worth.) The accounting profession rejected this approach for financial reporting because it is too hypothetical and ignores the going-concern concept.

Which of these alternative measures of the pension liability does the profession favor? **The profession adopted the projected benefit obligation—the present value of vested and nonvested benefits accrued to date, based on employees' future salary levels.**[9] Those in favor of the projected benefit obligation contend that a promise by an employer to pay benefits based on a percentage of the employees' future salaries is far greater than a promise to pay a percentage of their current salary, and such a difference should be reflected in the pension liability and pension expense.

Moreover, companies discount to present value the estimated future benefits to be paid. Minor changes in the interest rate used to discount pension benefits can dramatically affect the measurement of the employer's obligation. For example, a 1 percent decrease in the discount rate can increase pension liabilities 15 percent. Accounting rules require that, at each measurement date, a company must determine the appropriate discount rate used to measure the pension liability, based on current interest rates.

Recognition of the Net Funded Status of the Pension Plan

Under the provisions of a recent amendment to *SFAS No. 87*, companies must recognize on their balance sheet the full overfunded or underfunded status of their defined-benefit pension plan.[10] The **overfunded** or **underfunded status** is measured as the difference between the fair value of the plan assets and the projected benefit obligation.

To illustrate, assume that Coker Company has a projected benefit obligation of $300,000, and the fair value of its plan assets is $210,000. In this case, Coker Company's pension plan is underfunded, and therefore it reports a pension liability of $90,000 ($300,000 − $210,000) on its balance sheet. If, instead, the fair value of Coker's plan assets were $430,000, it would report a pension asset of $130,000 ($430,000 − $300,000).

This reporting will have a significant impact on companies' balance sheets. One study estimates that upon adoption of the new standard, companies in the S&P 500 Index will report an aggregate increase in liabilities of $483 billion. The aggregate deduction in stockholders' equity for these companies will be in excess of $248 billion; 22 companies are expected to report declines in equity of greater than 25 percent.[11]

Components of Pension Expense

There is broad agreement that companies should account for pension cost on the **accrual basis**.[12] The profession recognizes that **accounting for pension plans requires**

> **OBJECTIVE 4**
> List the components of pension expense.

---

[9]When we use the term "present value of benefits" throughout this chapter, we really mean the *actuarial* present value of benefits. **Actuarial present value** is the amount payable adjusted to reflect the time value of money *and* the probability of payment (by means of decrements for events such as death, disability, withdrawals, or retirement) between the present date and the expected date of payment. For simplicity, though, we use the term "present value" instead of "actuarial present value" in our discussion.

[10]"Employers' Accounting for Defined Benefit Pension and Other Postretirement Plans: An Amendment to SFAS Nos. 87, 88, 106, and 132(R)," *Statement of Financial Accounting Standards No. 158* (Norwalk, CT: FASB, 2006). *SFAS No. 158* applies to pensions as well as other postretirement benefit plans (OPEBs). Appendix 20A addresses the accounting for OPEBs.

[11]See "The Hit to Equity: Bringing Pension and OPEB Funded Status on Balance Sheet," *Credit Suisse Equity Research—Accounting* (May 5, 2006). The difference in effects for stockholders' equity and liabilities is due to recognition of deferred tax assets.

[12]At one time, companies applied the **cash basis** of accounting to pension plans by recognizing the amount paid in a particular accounting period as the pension expense for the period. The problem was that the amount paid or funded in a fiscal period depended on financial management and was too often discretionary. For example, funding could depend on the availability of cash, the level of earnings, or other factors unrelated to the requirements of the plan. Application of the cash basis made it possible to manipulate the amount of pension expense appearing in the income statement simply by varying the cash paid to the pension fund.

measurement of the cost and its identification with the appropriate time periods. The determination of pension cost, however, is extremely complicated because it is a function of the following components.

UNDERLYING CONCEPTS

The matching concept and the definition of a liability justify accounting for pension cost on the accrual basis. This requires recording an expense when employees earn the future benefits, and recognizing an existing obligation to pay pensions later based on current services received.

1 **Service Cost.** Service cost is the expense caused by the increase in pension benefits payable (the **projected benefit obligation**) to employees because of their services rendered during the current year. Actuaries compute **service cost** as the present value of the new benefits earned by employees during the year.

2 **Interest on the Liability.** Because a pension is a deferred compensation arrangement, there is a time value of money factor. As a result, companies record the pension liability on a discounted basis. **Interest expense accrues each year on the projected benefit obligation just as it does on any discounted debt.** The actuary helps to select the interest rate, referred to as the **settlement rate**.

3 **Actual Return on Plan Assets.** The return earned by the accumulated pension fund assets in a particular year is relevant in measuring the net cost to the employer of sponsoring an employee pension plan. Therefore, **a company should adjust annual pension expense for interest and dividends that accumulate within the fund, as well as increases and decreases in the market value of the fund assets**.

4 **Amortization of Prior Service Cost.** Pension plan amendments (including initiation of a pension plan) often include provisions to increase benefits (or in rare situations, to decrease benefits) for employee service provided in prior years. A company grants plan amendments with the expectation that it will realize economic benefits in future periods. Thus, **it allocates the cost (prior service cost) of providing these retroactive benefits to pension expense in the future, specifically to the remaining service-years of the affected employees**.

5 **Gain or Loss.** Volatility in pension expense can result from sudden and large changes in the market value of plan assets and by changes in the projected benefit obligation (which changes when actuaries modify assumptions or when actual experience differs from expected experience). Two items comprise this gain or loss: (1) the difference between the actual return and the expected return on plan assets, and (2) amortization of the net gain or loss from previous periods. We will discuss this complex computation later in the chapter.

Illustration 20-4 shows the **components of pension expense** and their effect on total pension expense (increase or decrease).

ILLUSTRATION 20-4
Components of Annual Pension Expense

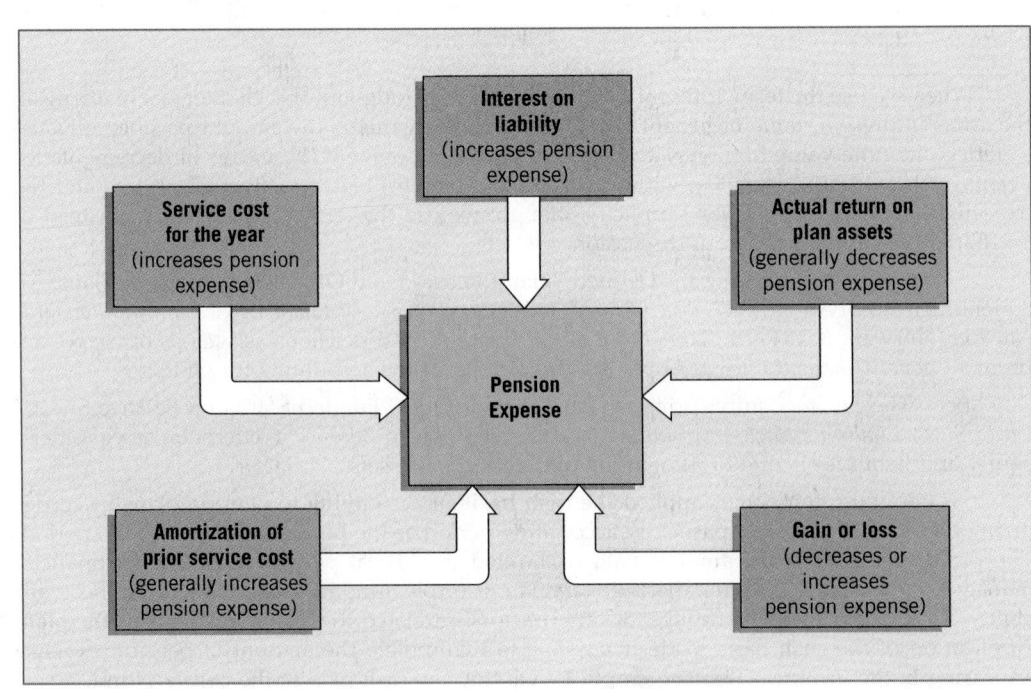

Service Cost

The service cost is the actuarial present value **of benefits attributed by the pension benefit formula to employee service during the period**. That is, the actuary predicts the additional benefits that an employer must pay under the plan's benefit formula as a result of the employees' current year's service, and then discounts the cost of those future benefits back to their present value.

The Board concluded that **companies must consider future compensation levels in measuring the present obligation and periodic pension expense if the plan benefit formula incorporates them**. In other words, the present obligation resulting from a promise to pay a benefit of 1 percent of an employee's **final pay** differs from the promise to pay 1 percent of **current pay**. To overlook this fact is to ignore an important aspect of pension expense. Thus, FASB adopts the **benefits/years-of-service actuarial method, which determines pension expense based on future salary levels**.

Some object to this determination, arguing that a company should have more freedom to select an expense recognition pattern. Others believe that incorporating future salary increases into current pension expense is accounting for events that have not yet happened. They argue that if a company terminates the plan today, it pays only liabilities for accumulated benefits. **Nevertheless, the FASB indicates that the projected benefit obligation provides a more realistic measure of the employer's obligation under the plan on a going-concern basis and, therefore, companies should use it as the basis for determining service cost.**

Interest on the Liability

The second component of pension expense is interest on the liability, or interest expense. Because a company defers paying the liability until maturity, the company records it on a discounted basis. The liability then accrues interest over the life of the employee. **The interest component is the interest for the period on the projected benefit obligation outstanding during the period.** The FASB did not address the question of how often to compound the interest cost. To simplify our illustrations and problem materials, we use a simple-interest computation, applying it to the beginning-of-the-year balance of the projected benefit liability.

How do companies determine the interest rate to apply to the pension liability? The Board states that the assumed discount rate should **reflect the rates at which companies can effectively settle pension benefits**. In determining these settlement rates, companies should look to rates of return on high-quality fixed-income investments currently available, whose cash flows match the timing and amount of the expected benefit payments. The objective of selecting the assumed discount rates is to measure a single amount that, if invested in a portfolio of high-quality debt instruments, would provide the necessary future cash flows to pay the pension benefits when due.

Actual Return on Plan Assets

Pension plan assets are usually investments in stocks, bonds, other securities, and real estate that a company holds to earn a reasonable return, generally at minimum risk. Employer contributions and actual returns on pension plan assets increase pension plan assets. Benefits paid to retired employees decrease them. As we indicated, the actual return earned on these assets increases the fund balance and correspondingly reduces the employer's net cost of providing employees' pension benefits. That is, the higher the actual return on the pension plan assets, the less the employer has to contribute eventually and, therefore, the less pension expense that it needs to report.

The actual return on the plan assets is the increase in pension funds from interest, dividends, and realized and unrealized changes in the fair-market value of the plan assets. Companies compute the actual return by adjusting the change in the plan assets for the effects of contributions during the year and benefits paid out during the year. The equation in Illustration 20-5 (page 1028), or a variation thereof, can be used to compute the actual return.

ILLUSTRATION 20-5
Equation for Computing
Actual Return

$$\text{Actual Return} = \left(\begin{array}{c} \text{Plan} \\ \text{Assets} \\ \text{Ending} \\ \text{Balance} \end{array} - \begin{array}{c} \text{Plan} \\ \text{Assets} \\ \text{Beginning} \\ \text{Balance} \end{array} \right) - (\text{Contributions} - \text{Benefits Paid})$$

Stated another way, the actual return on plan assets is the difference between the **fair value of the plan assets** at the beginning of the period and at the end of the period, adjusted for contributions and benefit payments. Illustration 20-6 uses the equation above to compute the actual return, using some assumed amounts.

ILLUSTRATION 20-6
Computation of Actual
Return on Plan Assets

Fair value of plan assets at end of period		$5,000,000
Deduct: Fair value of plan assets at beginning of period		4,200,000
Increase in fair value of plan assets		800,000
Deduct: Contributions to plan during period	$500,000	
Less benefits paid during period	300,000	200,000
Actual return on plan assets		$ 600,000

If the actual return on the plan assets is positive (a gain) during the period, a company subtracts it when computing pension expense. If the actual return is negative (a loss) during the period, the company adds it when computing pension expense.[13]

USING A PENSION WORKSHEET

We will now illustrate the basic computation of pension expense using the first three components: (1) service cost, (2) interest on the liability, and (3) actual return on plan assets. We discuss the other pension-expense components (amortization of prior service cost, and gains and losses) in later sections.

Companies often use a worksheet to record pension-related information. As its name suggests, the worksheet is a working tool. A worksheet is not a permanent accounting record: it is neither a journal nor part of the general ledger. The worksheet is merely a device to make it easier to prepare entries and the financial statements.[14]

Illustration 20-7 shows the format of the **pension worksheet**.

OBJECTIVE 5
Use a worksheet for
employer's pension
plan entries.

ILLUSTRATION 20-7
Basic Format of Pension
Worksheet

	Pension Worksheet					
	General Journal Entries				Memo Record	
Items	Annual Pension Expense	Cash		Pension Asset/ Liability	Projected Benefit Obligation	Plan Assets

The "General Journal Entries" columns of the worksheet (near the left side) determine the entries to record in the formal general ledger accounts. The "Memo Record" columns (on the right side) maintain balances in the projected benefit obligation and the

---

[13]At this point, we use the actual rate of return. Later, for purposes of computing pension expense, we use the expected rate of return.

[14]The use of this pension entry worksheet is recommended and illustrated by Paul B. W. Miller, "The New Pension Accounting (Part 2)," *Journal of Accountancy* (February 1987), pp. 86–94.

plan assets. The difference between the projected benefit obligation and the fair value of the plan assets is the **pension asset/liability**, which is shown in the balance sheet. If the projected benefit obligation is greater than the plan assets, a pension liability occurs. If the projected benefit obligation is less that the plan assets, a pension asset occurs.

On the first line of the worksheet, a company records the beginning balances (if any). It then records subsequent transactions and events related to the pension plan using debits and credits, using both sets of columns as if they were one. For each transaction or event, the debits must equal the credits. **The ending balance in the Pension Asset/Liability column should equal the net balance in the memo record.**

2009 Entries and Worksheet

To illustrate the use of a worksheet and how it helps in accounting for a pension plan, assume that on January 1, 2009, Zarle Company accounts for its defined-benefit plan under *SFAS No. 158*. The following facts apply to the pension plan for the year 2009.

Plan assets, January 1, 2009, are $100,000.

Projected benefit obligation, January 1, 2009, is $100,000.

Annual service cost is $9,000.

Settlement rate is 10 percent.

Actual return on plan assets is $10,000.

Funding contributions are $8,000.

Benefits paid to retirees during the year are $7,000.

Using the data presented above, the worksheet in Illustration 20-8 presents the beginning balances and all of the pension entries recorded by Zarle in 2009. Zarle records the beginning balances for the projected benefit obligation and the pension plan assets on the first line of the worksheet in the memo record. Because the projected benefit obligation and the plan assets are the same at January 1, 2009, the Pension Asset/Liability account has a zero balance at January 1, 2009.

ILLUSTRATION 20-8
Pension Worksheet—2009

Pension Worksheet—2009

		General Journal Entries			Memo Record	
	Items	Annual Pension Expense	Cash	Pension Asset/ Liability	Projected Benefit Obligation	Plan Assets
3	Balance, Jan. 1, 2009			—	100,000 Cr.	100,000 Dr.
4	(a) Service cost	9,000 Dr.			9,000 Cr.	
5	(b) Interest cost	10,000 Dr.			10,000 Cr.	
6	(c) Actual return	10,000 Cr.				10,000 Dr.
7	(d) Contributions		8,000 Cr.			8,000 Dr.
8	(e) Benefits				7,000 Dr.	7,000 Cr.
9						
10						
11	Journal entry for 2009	9,000 Dr.	8,000 Cr.	1,000 Cr.*		
12	Balance, Dec. 31, 2009			1,000 Cr.**	112,000 Cr.	111,000 Dr.
13						
14	*$9,000 − $8,000 = $1,000					
15	**$112,000 − $111,000 = $1.000					

Entry (a) in Illustration 20-8 records the service cost component, which increases pension expense by $9,000 and increases the liability (projected benefit obligation) by $9,000. Entry (b) accrues the interest expense component, which increases both the liability and the pension expense by $10,000 (the beginning projected benefit obligation multiplied by the settlement rate of 10 percent). Entry (c) records the actual return on the plan assets, which increases the plan assets and decreases the pension expense. Entry (d) records Zarle's contribution (funding) of assets to the pension fund, thereby decreasing cash by $8,000 and increasing plan assets by $8,000. Entry (e) records the benefit payments made to retirees, which results in equal $7,000 decreases to the plan assets and the projected benefit obligation.

Zarle makes the "formal journal entry" on December 31, which records the pension expense in 2009, as follows.

2009

Pension Expense	9,000	
Cash		8,000
Pension Asset/Liability		1,000

The credit to Pension Asset/Liability for $1,000 represents the difference between the 2009 pension expense of $9,000 and the amount funded of $8,000. Pension Asset/Liability (credit) is a liability because Zarle underfunds the plan by $1,000. The Pension Asset/Liability account balance of $1,000 also equals the net of the balances in the memo accounts. Illustration 20-9 shows that the projected benefit obligation exceeds the plan assets by $1,000, which reconciles to the pension liability reported in the balance sheet.

ILLUSTRATION 20-9
Pension Reconciliation Schedule—December 31, 2009

Projected benefit obligation (Credit)	$(112,000)
Plan assets at fair value (Debit)	111,000
Pension asset/liability (Credit)	$ (1,000)

If the net of the memo record balances is a credit, the reconciling amount in the pension asset/liability column will be a credit equal in amount. If the net of the memo record balances is a debit, the pension asset/liability amount will be a debit equal in amount. The worksheet is designed to produce this reconciling feature, which is useful later in the preparation of the financial statements and required note disclosure related to pensions.

In this illustration (for 2009), the debit to Pension Expense exceeds the credit to Cash, resulting in a credit to Pension Asset/Liability—the recognition of a liability. If the credit to Cash exceeded the debit to Pension Expense, Zarle would debit Pension Asset/Liability—the recognition of an asset.

Amortization of Prior Service Cost (PSC)

OBJECTIVE 6
Describe the amortization of prior service costs.

When either initiating (adopting) or amending a defined-benefit plan, a company often provides benefits to employees for years of service before the date of initiation or amendment. As a result of this prior service cost, the projected benefit obligation is increased to recognize this additional liability. In many cases, the increase in the projected benefit obligation is substantial.

Should a company report an expense for these **prior service costs (PSC)** at the time it initiates or amends a plan? The FASB says no. The Board's rationale is that the employer would not provide credit for past years of service unless it expects to receive benefits in the future. As a result, a company should not recognize the **retroactive benefits** as pension expense in the year of amendment. Instead, **the employer initially records the prior service cost as an adjustment to other comprehensive income. The employer then recognizes the prior service cost as a component of pension expense over the remaining service lives of the employees who are expected to benefit from the change in the plan.**

The cost of the retroactive benefits (including any benefits provided to existing retirees) is the increase in the projected benefit obligation at the date of the amendment. An actuary computes the amount of the prior service cost. Amortization of the prior service cost is also an accounting function performed with the assistance of an actuary.

The Board prefers a **years-of-service** amortization **method** that is similar to a units-of-production computation. First, the company computes the total number of service-years to be worked by all of the participating employees. Second, it divides the prior service cost by the total number of service-years, to obtain a cost per service-year (the unit cost). Third, the company multiplies the number of service-years consumed each year by the cost per service-year, to obtain the annual amortization charge.

To illustrate the amortization of the prior service cost under the years-of-service method, assume that Zarle Company's defined-benefit pension plan covers 170 employees. In its negotiations with the employees, Zarle Company amends its pension plan on January 1, 2010, and grants $80,000 of prior service costs to its employees. The employees are grouped according to expected years of retirement, as shown below.

Group	Number of Employees	Expected Retirement on Dec. 31
A	40	2010
B	20	2011
C	40	2012
D	50	2013
E	20	2014
	170	

Illustration 20-10 shows computation of the service-years per year and the total service-years.

			Service-Years			
Year	A	B	C	D	E	Total
2010	40	20	40	50	20	170
2011		20	40	50	20	130
2012			40	50	20	110
2013				50	20	70
2014					20	20
	40	40	120	200	100	500

ILLUSTRATION 20-10
Computation of Service-Years

Computed on the basis of a prior service cost of $80,000 and a total of 500 service-years for all years, the cost per service-year is $160 ($80,000 ÷ 500). The annual amount of amortization based on a $160 cost per service-year is computed as follows.

Year	Total Service-Years	×	Cost per Service-Year	=	Annual Amortization
2010	170		$160		$27,200
2011	130		160		20,800
2012	110		160		17,600
2013	70		160		11,200
2014	20		160		3,200
	500				$80,000

ILLUSTRATION 20-11
Computation of Annual Prior Service Cost Amortization

An alternative method of computing amortization of **prior service cost is permitted: Employers may use straight-line amortization over the average remaining service life of the employees.** In this case, with 500 service-years and 170 employees, the average would be 2.94 years (500 ÷ 170). Using this method, Zarle Company would charge the $80,000 cost to expense at $27,211 ($80,000 ÷ 2.94) in 2010, $27,211 in 2011, and $25,578 ($27,211 × .94) in 2012.

2010 Entries and Worksheet

Continuing the Zarle Company illustration into 2010, we note that the company amends the pension plan on January 1, 2010, to grant employees prior service benefits with a present value of $80,000. Zarle uses the annual amortization amounts, as computed in the previous section using the years-of-service approach ($27,200 for 2010). The following additional facts apply to the pension plan for the year 2010.

Annual service cost is $9,500.

Settlement rate is 10 percent.

Actual return on plan assets is $11,100.

Annual funding contributions are $20,000.

Benefits paid to retirees during the year are $8,000.

Amortization of prior service cost (PSC) using the years-of-service method is $27,200.

Accumulated other comprehensive income (hereafter referred to as accumulated OCI) on December 31, 2009, is zero.

Illustration 20-12 presents a worksheet of all the pension entries and information recorded by Zarle in 2010. We now add an additional column to the worksheet to record the prior service cost adjustment to other comprehensive income. In addition, as shown in the last two lines of the "Items" column, the other comprehensive income amount related to prior service cost is added to accumulated other comprehensive income ("Accumulated OCI") to arrive at a debit balance of $52,800 at December 31, 2010.

ILLUSTRATION 20-12
Pension Worksheet—2010

Pension Worksheet—2010

	A	B	C	D	E	G	H
1		General Journal Entries				Memo Record	
2				Other Comprehensive Income			
3	Items	Annual Pension Expense	Cash	Prior Service Cost	Pension Asset/Liability	Projected Benefit Obligation	Plan Assets
4	Balance, Dec. 31, 2009				1,000 Cr.	112,000 Cr.	111,000 Dr.
5	(f) Prior service cost			80,000 Dr.		80,000 Cr.	0
6							
7	Balance, Jan. 1, 2010					192,000 Cr.	111,000 Dr.
8	(g) Service cost	9,500 Dr.				9,500 Cr.	
9	(h) Interest cost	19,200 Dr.				19,200 Cr.	
10	(i) Actual return	11,100 Cr.					11,100 Dr.
11	(j) Amortization of PSC	27,200 Dr.		27,200 Cr.			
12	(k) Contributions		20,000 Cr.				20,000 Dr.
13	(l) Benefits					8,000 Dr.	8,000 Cr.
14							
15	Journal entry for 2010	44,800 Dr.	20,000 Cr.	52,800 Dr.	77,600 Cr.		
16							
17	Accumulated OCI, Dec. 31, 2009			0			
18	Balance, Dec. 31, 2010			52,800 Dr.	78,600 Cr.	212,700 Cr.	134,100 Dr.
19							

Sheet1 / Sheet2 / Sheet3 /

The first line of the worksheet shows the beginning balances of the Pension Asset/Liability account and the memo accounts. Entry (f) records Zarle's granting of prior service cost, by adding $80,000 to the projected benefit obligation and decreasing other comprehensive income—prior service cost by the same amount. Entries (g), (h), (i), (k), and (l) are similar to the corresponding entries in 2009. To compute the interest cost on the projected benefit obligation for entry (h), we use the beginning projected benefit balance of $192,000, which has been adjusted for the prior service cost amendment on January 1, 2010. Entry (j) records the 2010 amortization of prior service cost by debiting Pension Expense for $27,200 and crediting **Other Comprehensive Income (PSC)** for the same amount.

Zarle makes the following journal entry on December 31 to formally record the 2010 pension expense (the sum of the annual pension expense column), and related pension information.

2010

Pension Expense	44,800	
Other Comprehensive Income (PSC)	52,800	
Cash		20,000
Pension Asset/Liability		77,600

Because the debits to Pension Expense and to Other Comprehensive Income (PSC) exceed the funding, Zarle credits the Pension Asset/Liability account for the $77,600 difference. That account is a liability. In 2010, as in 2009, the balance of the Pension Asset/Liability account ($78,600) is equal to the net of the balances in the memo accounts, as shown in Illustration 20-13.

Projected benefit obligation (Credit)	$(212,700)
Plan assets at fair value (Debit)	134,100
Pension asset/liability (Credit)	$ (78,600)

ILLUSTRATION 20-13
Pension Reconciliation Schedule—December 31, 2010

The reconciliation is the formula that makes the worksheet work. It relates the components of pension accounting, recorded and unrecorded, to one another.

Gain or Loss

Of great concern to companies that have pension plans are the uncontrollable and unexpected swings in pension expense that can result from (1) sudden and large changes in the market value of plan assets, and (2) changes in actuarial assumptions that affect the amount of the projected benefit obligation. If these gains or losses impact fully the financial statements in the period of realization or incurrence, substantial fluctuations in pension expense result.

Therefore, the FASB decided to reduce the volatility associated with pension expense by using **smoothing techniques** that dampen and in some cases fully eliminate the fluctuations.

OBJECTIVE 7
Explain the accounting for unexpected gains and losses.

Smoothing Unexpected Gains and Losses on Plan Assets

One component of pension expense, actual return on plan assets, reduces pension expense (assuming the actual return is positive). A large change in the actual return can substantially affect pension expense for a year. Assume a company has a 40 percent return in the stock market for the year. Should this substantial, and perhaps one-time, event affect current pension expense?

Actuaries ignore current fluctuations when they develop a funding pattern to pay expected benefits in the future. They develop an **expected rate of return** and multiply it by an asset value weighted over a reasonable period of time to arrive at an **expected return on plan assets**. They then use this return to determine a company's funding pattern.

The FASB adopted the actuary's approach to dampen wide swings that might occur in the actual return. That is, a company includes the **expected return** on the plan assets as a component of pension expense, not the actual return in a given year. To achieve this goal, the company multiplies the expected rate of return by the market-related value of the plan assets. The **market-related asset value** of the plan assets is either the fair value of plan assets or a calculated value that recognizes changes in fair value in a systematic and rational manner.[15]

The difference between the expected return and the actual return is referred to as the **unexpected gain or loss**; the FASB uses the term **asset gains and losses**. **Asset gains** occur when actual return exceeds expected return; **asset losses** occur when actual return is less than expected return.

What happens to unexpected gains or losses in the accounting for pensions? Companies record asset gains and asset losses in an account, **Other Comprehensive Income (G/L)**, combining them with gains and losses accumulated in prior years. This treatment is similar to prior service cost. The Board believes this treatment is consistent with the practice of including in other comprehensive income certain changes in value that have not been recognized in net income (for example, unrealized gains and losses on available-for-sale securities).[16] In addition, the accounting is simple, transparent, and symmetrical.

To illustrate the computation of an unexpected gain or loss and its related accounting, assume that in 2011, Zarle Company has an actual return on plan assets of $12,000 when the expected return is $13,410 (the expected rate of return of 10% on plan assets times the beginning of the year plan assets.) The unexpected asset loss of $1,410 ($12,000 − $13,410) is debited to Other Comprehensive Income (G/L) and credited to Pension Expense.

PENSION COSTS UPS AND DOWNS

WHAT DO THE NUMBERS MEAN?

For some companies, pension plans generated real profits in the late 1990s. The plans not only paid for themselves but also increased earnings. This happens when the expected return on pension assets exceed the company's annual costs. At **Norfolk Southern**, pension income amounted to 12 percent of operating profit. It tallied 11 percent of operating profit at **Lucent Technologies**, **Coastal Corp.**, and **Unisys Corp.** The issue is important because in these cases management is not driving the operating income—pension income is. And as a result, income can change quickly.

Unfortunately, when the stock market stops booming, pension expense substantially increases for many companies. The reason: Expected return on a smaller asset base no longer offsets pension service costs and interest on the projected benefit obligation. As a result, many companies find it difficult to meet their earnings targets, and at a time when meeting such targets is crucial to maintaining the stock price.

Smoothing Unexpected Gains and Losses on the Pension Liability

In estimating the projected benefit obligation (the liability), actuaries make assumptions about such items as mortality rate, retirement rate, turnover rate, disability rate, and salary amounts. Any change in these actuarial assumptions affects the amount of the projected benefit obligation. Seldom does actual experience coincide exactly with actuarial predictions. These unexpected gains or losses from changes in the projected benefit obligation are called **liability gains and losses**.

Companies report liability gains (resulting from unexpected decreases in the liability balance) and liability losses (resulting from unexpected increases) in Other

---

[15]*FASB Statement No. 87*, par. 30. Companies may use different ways of determining the calculated market-related value for different classes of assets. For example, an employer might use fair value for bonds and a five-year-moving-average for equities. But companies should consistently apply the manner of determining market-related value from year to year for each asset class. Throughout our Zarle illustrations, we assume that market-related values based on a calculated value and the fair value of plan assets are equal. *For homework purposes*, use the fair value of plan assets as the measure for the market-related value.

[16]"Employers' Accounting for Defined Benefit Pension and Other Postretirement Plans: An Amendment of SFAS Nos. 87, 88, 106, and 132(R)," *Statement of Financial Accounting Standards No. 158* (Norwalk, CT: FASB, 2006), par. B41.

Comprehensive Income (G/L). Companies combine the liability gains and losses in the same Other Comprehensive Income (G/L) account used for asset gains and losses. They accumulate the asset and liability gains and losses from year to year that are not amortized in Accumulated Other Comprehensive Income. This amount is reported on the balance sheet in the stockholders' equity section.

Corridor Amortization

The asset gains and losses and the liability gains and losses can offset each other. As a result, the Accumulated OCI account related to gains and losses may not grow very large. But, it is possible that no offsetting will occur and that the balance in the Accumulated OCI account related to gains and losses will continue to grow.

OBJECTIVE 8
Explain the corridor approach to amortizing gains and losses.

To limit the growth of the Accumulated OCI account, the FASB invented the **corridor approach** for amortizing the account's accumulated balance when it gets too large. How large is too large? The FASB set a limit of 10 percent of the larger of the beginning balances of the projected benefit obligation or the market-related value of the plan assets. **Above that size, the Accumulated OCI account related to gains and losses is considered too large and must be amortized.**

To illustrate the corridor approach, data for Callaway Co.'s projected benefit obligation and plan assets over a period of six years are shown in Illustration 20-14.

Beginning-of-the-Year Balances	Projected Benefit Obligation	Market-Related Asset Value	Corridor* +/− 10%
2008	$1,000,000	$ 900,000	$100,000
2009	1,200,000	1,100,000	120,000
2010	1,300,000	1,700,000	170,000
2011	1,500,000	2,250,000	225,000
2012	1,700,000	1,750,000	175,000
2013	1,800,000	1,700,000	180,000

*The corridor becomes 10% of the larger (in colored type) of the projected benefit obligation or the market-related plan asset value.

ILLUSTRATION 20-14
Computation of the Corridor

How the corridor works becomes apparent when we portray the data graphically, as in Illustration 20-15.

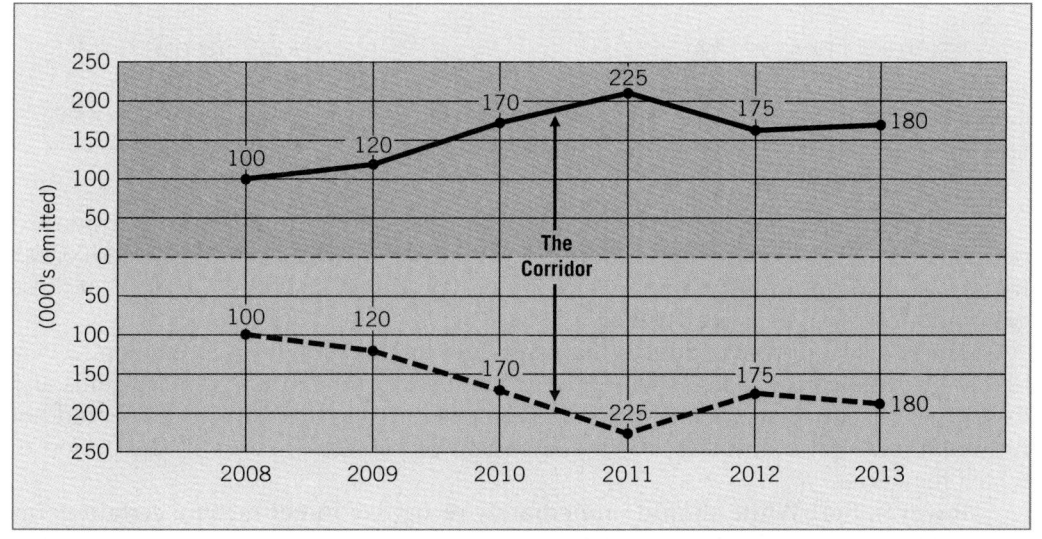

ILLUSTRATION 20-15
Graphic Illustration of the Corridor

If the balance in the Accumulated OCI account related to gains and losses stays within the upper and lower limits of the corridor, no amortization is required. In that case, Callaway carries forward unchanged the accumulated OCI related to gains and losses.

If amortization is required, the minimum amortization is the excess divided by the average remaining service period of active employees who are expected to receive benefits under the plan. Callaway may use any systematic method of amortization of gains and losses in lieu of the minimum, provided it is greater than the minimum. It must use the method consistently for both gains and losses and must disclose the amortization method used.

Example of Gains/Losses

In applying the corridor, companies should include amortization of the net gain or loss as a component of pension expense only if, at the **beginning of the year**, the net gain or loss in Accumulated OCI exceeded the corridor. That is, if no net gain or loss exists in Accumulated OCI at the beginning of the period, the company cannot recognize pension expense gains or losses in that period.

To illustrate the amortization of net gains and losses, assume the following information for Soft-White, Inc.

	2009	2010	2011
		(beginning of the year)	
Projected benefit obligation	$2,100,000	$2,600,000	$2,900,000
Market-related asset value	2,600,000	2,800,000	2,700,000

Soft-White recorded in Other Comprehensive Income actuarial losses of $400,000 in 2009 and $300,000 in 2010.

If the average remaining service life of all active employees is 5.5 years, the schedule to amortize the net gain or loss is as shown in Illustration 20-16.

ILLUSTRATION 20-16
Corridor Test and
Gain/Loss Amortization
Schedule

Year	Projected Benefit Obligation[a]	Plan Assets[a]	Corridor[b]	Accumulated OCI (G/L)[a]	Minimum Amortization of Loss (For Current Year)
2009	$2,100,000	$2,600,000	$260,000	$ –0–	$ –0–
2010	2,600,000	2,800,000	280,000	400,000	21,818[c]
2011	2,900,000	2,700,000	290,000	678,182[d]	70,579[d]

[a]All as of the beginning of the period.
[b]10% of the greater of projected benefit obligation or plan assets market-related value.
[c]$400,000 − $280,000 = $120,000; $120,000 ÷ 5.5 = $21,818
[d]$400,000 − $21,818 + $300,000 = $678,182; $678,182 − $290,000 = $388,182; $388,182 ÷ 5.5 = $70,579.

As Illustration 20-16 indicates, the loss recognized in 2010 increased pension expense by $21,818. This amount is small in comparison with the total loss of $400,000. It indicates that the corridor approach dampens the effects (reduces volatility) of these gains and losses on pension expense.

The rationale for the corridor is that gains and losses result from refinements in estimates as well as real changes in economic value; over time, some of these gains and losses will offset one another. It therefore seems reasonable that Soft-White should not fully recognize gains and losses as a component of pension expense in the period in which they arise.

However, Soft-White should immediately recognize in net income certain gains and losses—if they arise from a single occurrence not directly related to the operation of the pension plan and not in the ordinary course of the employer's business. For example, a gain or loss that is directly related to a plant closing, a disposal of a business component, or a similar event that greatly affects the size of the employee work force, should be recognized as a part of the gain or loss associated with that event.

For example, at one time, **Bethlehem Steel** reported a quarterly loss of $477 million. A great deal of this loss was attributable to future estimated benefits payable to workers who were permanently laid off. In this situation, the loss should be treated as an adjustment to the gain or loss on the plant closing and should not affect pension cost for the current or future periods.

Summary of Calculations for Asset Gain or Loss

The difference between the actual return on plan assets and the expected return on plan assets is the **unexpected asset gain or loss** component. This component defers the difference between the actual return and expected return on plan assets in computing current-year pension expense. Thus, after considering this component, **it is really the expected return on plan assets (not the actual return) that determines current pension expense**.

Companies determined the amortized net gain or loss by amortizing the Accumulated OCI amount related to net gain or loss at the beginning of the year subject to the corridor limitation. In other words, **if the accumulated gain or loss is greater than the corridor, these net gains and losses are subject to amortization**. Soft-White computed this minimum amortization by dividing the net gains or losses subject to amortization by the average remaining service period. When the current-year unexpected gain or loss is combined with the amortized net gain or loss, we determine the current-year gain or loss. Illustration 20-17 summarizes these gain and loss computations.

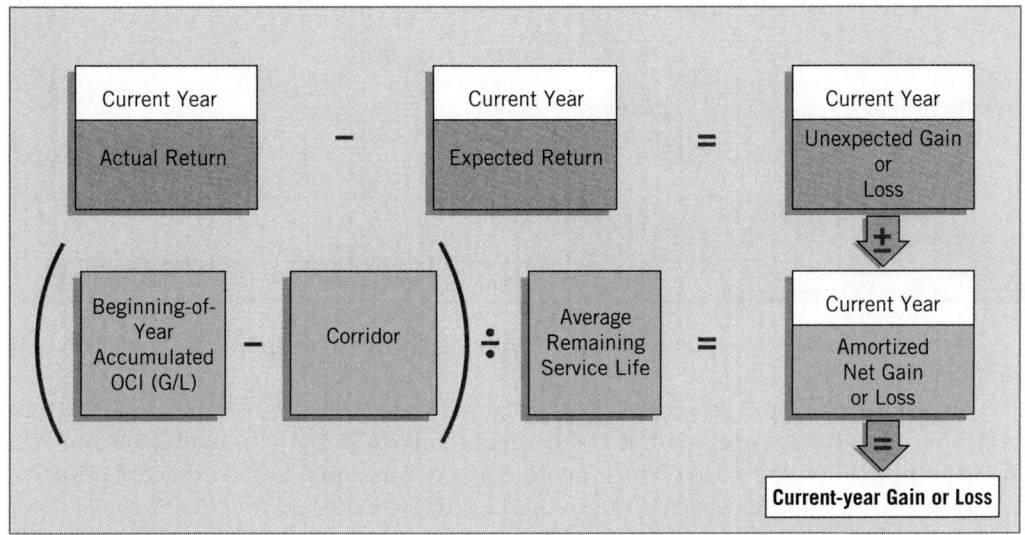

ILLUSTRATION 20-17
Graphic Summary of Gain or Loss Computation

In essence, these gains and losses are subject to *triple* smoothing. That is, companies first smooth the asset gain or loss by using the expected return. Second, they do not amortize the accumulated gain or loss at the beginning of the year unless it is greater than the corridor. Finally, they spread the excess over the remaining service life of existing employees.

2011 Entries and Worksheet

Continuing the Zarle Company illustration, the following facts apply to the pension plan for 2011.

Annual service cost is $13,000.

Settlement rate is 10 percent; expected earnings rate is 10 percent.

Actual return on plan assets is $12,000.

Amortization of prior service cost (PSC) is $20,800.

Annual funding contributions are $24,000.

Benefits paid to retirees during the year are $10,500.

Changes in actuarial assumptions resulted in an end-of-year projected benefit obligation of $265,000.

The worksheet in Illustration 20-18 presents all of Zarle's 2011 pension entries and related information. The first line of the worksheet records the beginning balances that relate to the pension plan. In this case, Zarle's beginning balances are the ending balances from its 2010 pension worksheet in Illustration 20-12 (page 1032).

ILLUSTRATION 20-18
Pension Worksheet—2011

Pension Worksheet—2011

| | | General Journal Entries | | | | | Memo Record | |
| | | | | Other Comprehensive Income | | | | |
Items	Annual Pension Expense	Cash	Prior Service Cost	Gains/Losses	Pension Asset/Liability	Projected Benefit Obligation	Plan Assets
Balance, Jan. 1, 2011					78,600 Cr.	212,700 Cr.	134,100 Dr.
(m) Service cost	13,000 Dr.					13,000 Cr.	
(n) Interest cost	21,270 Dr.					21,270 Cr.	
(o) Actual return	12,000 Cr.						12,000 Dr.
(p) Unexpected loss	1,410 Cr.			1,410 Dr.			
(q) Amortization of PSC	20,800 Dr.		20,800 Cr.				
(r) Contributions		24,000 Cr.					24,000 Dr.
(s) Benefits						10,500 Dr.	10,500 Cr.
(t) Liability increase				28,530 Dr.		28,530 Cr.	
Journal entry for 2011	41,660 Dr.	24,000 Cr.	20,800 Cr.	29,940 Dr.	26,800 Cr.		
Accumulated OCI, Dec. 31, 2010			52,800 Dr.	0			
Balance, Dec. 31, 2011*			32,000 Dr.	29,940 Dr.	105,400 Cr.	265,000 Cr.	159,600 Dr.
*Accumulated OCI (PSC)	$32,000 Dr.						
Accumulated OCI (G/L)	29,940 Dr.						
Accumulated OCI, Dec. 31, 2011	$61,940 Dr.						

Sheet1 / Sheet2 / Sheet3

Entries (m), (n), (o), (q), (r), and (s) are similar to the corresponding entries in 2009 or 2010.

Entries (o) and (p) are related. We explained the recording of the actual return in entry (o) in both 2009 and 2010; it is recorded similarly in 2011. In both 2009 and 2010 Zarle assumed that the actual return on plan assets was equal to the expected return on plan assets. In 2011, the expected return of $13,410 (the expected rate of return of 10 percent times the beginning-of-the-year plan assets balance of $134,100) is higher than the actual return of $12,000. To smooth pension expense, Zarle defers the unexpected loss of $1,410 ($13,410 − $12,000) by debiting the Other Comprehensive Income (G/L) account and crediting Pension Expense. **As a result of this adjustment, the expected return on the plan assets is the amount actually used to compute pension expense.**

Entry (t) records the change in the projected benefit obligation resulting from the change in the actuarial assumptions. As indicated, the actuary has now computed the ending balance to be $265,000. Given the PBO balance at December 31, 2010, and the related transactions during 2011, the PBO balance to date is computed as shown in Illustration 20-19.

ILLUSTRATION 20-19
Projected Benefit
Obligation Balance
(Unadjusted)

December 31, 2010, PBO balance	$212,700
Service cost [entry (m)]	13,000
Interest cost [entry (n)]	21,270
Benefits paid	(10,500)
December 31, 2011, PBO balance (before liability increases)	$236,470

The difference between the ending balance of $265,000 and the balance of $236,470 before the liability increase is $28,530 ($265,000 − $236,470). This $28,530 increase in the employer's liability is an unexpected loss. The journal entry on December 31, 2011, to record the pension information is as follows.

Pension Expense	41,660	
Other Comprehensive Income (G/L)	29,940	
Cash		24,000
Other Comprehensive Income (PSC)		20,800
Pension Asset/Liability		26,800

As the 2011 worksheet indicates, the $105,400 balance in the Pension Asset/Liability account at December 31, 2011, is equal to the net of the balances in the memo accounts. Illustration 20-20 shows this computation.

Projected benefit obligation (Credit)	$(265,000)
Plan assets at fair value (Debit)	159,600
Pension asset/liability	$(105,400)

ILLUSTRATION 20-20
Pension Reconciliation Schedule—December 31, 2011

PERFECT STORM

WHAT DO THE NUMBERS MEAN?

The chart below shows what has happened to the financial health of pension plans over the last few years. It is not a pretty picture.

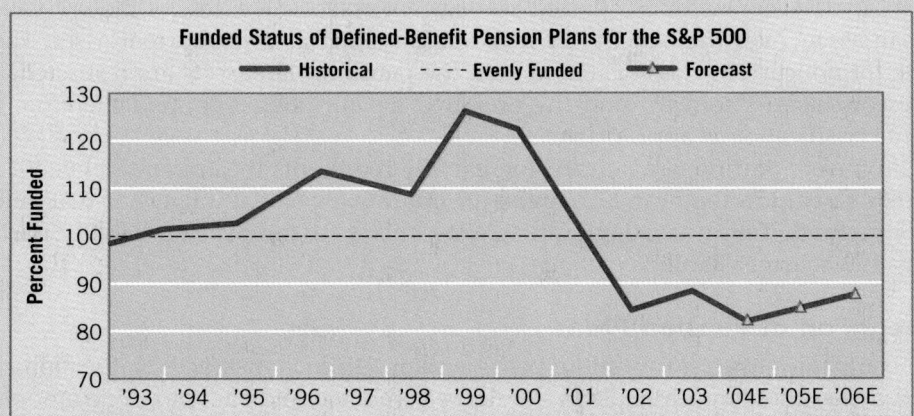

Funded Status of Defined-Benefit Pension Plans for the S&P 500
— Historical ---- Evenly Funded —▵— Forecast

Although companies in the S&P 500 saw their pension plans bounce back from their lows in 2002, they still ended 2003 underfunded by a total of $172 billion. Estimates for 2004, 2005, and 2006 could leave funds in no better position.

A number of factors cause a fund to change from being overfunded to underfunded: First, because of low interest rates, returns on pension plan assets in the early part of this decade have been lousy. As a result, pension fund assets have not grown; in some cases, they have declined in value. Second, using low interest rates to discount the projected benefit payments leads to a higher pension liability. Finally, more individuals are retiring, which leads to a depletion of the pension plan assets. In short, we have the perfect pension storm.

Source: David Zion and Bill Carcache, "The Magical World of Pensions: An Update," *CSFB Equity Research: Accounting* (September 8, 2004).

REPORTING PENSION PLANS IN FINANCIAL STATEMENTS

OBJECTIVE 9
Describe the requirements for reporting pension plans in financial statements.

As you might suspect, a phenomenon as significant and complex as pensions involves extensive reporting and disclosure requirements. We will cover these requirements in two categories: (1) those within the financial statements, and (2) those within the notes to the financial statements.

Within the Financial Statements

Recognition of the Net Funded Status of the Pension Plan

As required by *SFAS No. 158,* companies recognize on their balance sheet the overfunded or underfunded status of their defined-benefit pension plan. The overfunded or underfunded status is measured as the difference between the fair value of the plan assets and the projected benefit obligation.

The reporting of the funded position of the plan in the balance sheet results because actuarial gains and losses and prior service costs are now recognized in other comprehensive income. Under *SFAS Nos. 87* and *106,* these amounts were not recognized. Under *SFAS No. 158,* actuarial gains and losses and prior service costs will be reflected in the projected benefit obligation and plan assets, with corresponding entries in other comprehensive income.

It should be emphasized that there will be little or no impact on pension expense. This is because the amortization provisions, as articulated in *SFAS Nos. 87* and *106* for actuarial gains and losses and prior service costs, are not changed. In addition, the computation of the other components of pension expense, such as service cost and interest on the projected benefit obligation, still follow the guidelines established in *SFAS Nos. 87* and *106.*

Classification of Pension Asset or Pension Liability

As indicated, the funded status of the pension plan is reported in the balance sheet. No portion of a pension asset is reported as a current asset. The excess of the fair value of the plan assets over the benefit obligation is classified as a noncurrent asset. The rationale for noncurrent classification is that the pension plan assets are restricted. That is, these assets are used to fund the projected benefit obligation, and therefore noncurrent classification is appropriate.

The current portion of a net pension liability represents the amount of benefit payments to be paid in the next 12 months (or operating cycle, if longer), if that amount cannot be funded from existing plan assets. Otherwise, the pension liability is classified as a noncurrent liability.

Aggregation of Pension Plans

Some companies have two or more pension plans. In such instances, a question arises as to whether these multiple plans should be combined and shown as one amount on the balance sheet. The Board takes the position that **all overfunded plans should be combined** and shown as a pension asset on the balance sheet. Similarly, if the company has two or more underfunded plans, the **underfunded plans are combined and shown as one amount** on the balance sheet.

The FASB rejected the alternative of combining *all* plans and representing the net amount as a single net asset or net liability. The rationale: A company does not have the ability to offset excess assets of one plan against underfunded obligations of another plan. Furthermore, netting all plans is inappropriate because offsetting assets and liabilities is not permitted under GAAP unless a right of offset exists.

To illustrate, assume that Cresci Company has three pension plans as shown in Illustration 20-21.

ILLUSTRATION 20-21
Multiple Pension Plans'
Funded Status

	Pension Assets (at Fair Value)	Projected Benefit Obligation	Pension Asset/Liability
Plan A	$400,000	$300,000	$100,000 Asset
Plan B	600,000	720,000	120,000 Liability
Plan C	550,000	700,000	150,000 Liability

In this case, Cresci reports a pension plan asset of $100,000 and a pension plan liability of $270,000 ($120,000 + $150,000).

Actuarial Gains and Losses/Prior Service Costs

Actuarial gains and losses not recognized as part of pension expense are recognized as increases and decreases in other comprehensive income. The same type of accounting is also used for prior service cost. The Board requires that the prior service cost arising in the year of the amendment (which increases the projected benefit obligation) be recognized by an offsetting debit to other comprehensive income. By recognizing both actuarial gains and losses and prior service cost as part of other comprehensive income, the Board believes that the usefulness of financial statements is enhanced.

To illustrate the presentation of other comprehensive income and related accumulated OCI, assume that Obey Company provides the following information for the year 2009. None of the Accumulated OCI on January 1, 2009, should be amortized in 2009.

Net income for 2009	$100,000
Actuarial liability loss for 2009	60,000
Prior service cost adjustment to provide additional benefits in December 2009	15,000
Accumulated OCI, January 1, 2009	40,000

Both the actuarial liability loss and the prior service adjustment decrease the funded status of the plan on the balance sheet. This results because the projected benefit obligation increases. However, neither the actuarial liability loss nor the prior service cost adjustment affects pension expense in 2009. In subsequent periods, these items will impact pension expense through amortization.

For Obey Company, the computation of "Other comprehensive loss" for 2009 is as follows.

Actuarial liability loss	$60,000
Prior service cost benefit adjustment	15,000
Other comprehensive loss	$75,000

ILLUSTRATION 20-22
Computation of Other Comprehensive Income

The computation of "Comprehensive income" for 2009 is as follows.

Net income	$100,000
Other comprehensive loss	75,000
Comprehensive income	$ 25,000

ILLUSTRATION 20-23
Computation of Comprehensive Income

The components of other comprehensive income must be reported in one of three ways: (1) in a second income statement, (2) in a combined statement of comprehensive income, or (3) as a part of the statement of stockholders' equity. Regardless of the format used, net income must be added to other comprehensive income to arrive at comprehensive income. *For homework purposes,* use the second income statement approach unless stated otherwise. Earnings per share information related to comprehensive income is not required.

To illustrate the second income statement approach, assume that Obey Company has reported a traditional income statement. The comprehensive income statement is shown in Illustration 20-24.

OBEY COMPANY COMPREHENSIVE INCOME STATEMENT FOR THE YEAR ENDED DECEMBER 31, 2009		
Net income		$100,000
Other comprehensive loss		
Actuarial liability loss	$60,000	
Prior service cost	15,000	75,000
Comprehensive income		$ 25,000

ILLUSTRATION 20-24
Comprehensive Income Reporting

The computation of "Accumulated other comprehensive income" as reported in stockholders' equity at December 31, 2009, is as follows.

ILLUSTRATION 20-25
Computation of
Accumulated Other
Comprehensive Income

Accumulated other comprehensive income, January 1, 2009	$40,000
Other comprehensive loss	75,000
Accumulated other comprehensive loss, December 31, 2009	$35,000

Regardless of the display format for the income statement, the accumulated other comprehensive loss is reported on the stockholders' equity section of the balance sheet of Obey Company as shown in Illustration 20-26. (Illustration 20-26 uses assumed data for the common stock and retained earnings information.)

ILLUSTRATION 20-26
Reporting of
Accumulated OCI

OBEY COMPANY
BALANCE SHEET
AS OF DECEMBER 31, 2009
(STOCKHOLDERS' EQUITY SECTION)

Stockholders' equity	
Common stock	$100,000
Retained earnings	60,000
Accumulated other comprehensive loss	35,000
Total stockholders' equity	$125,000

By providing information on the components of comprehensive income as well as total accumulated other comprehensive income, the company communicates all changes in net assets.

In this illustration, it is assumed that the accumulated other comprehensive income at January 1, 2009, is not adjusted for the amortization of any prior service cost or actuarial gains and losses that would change pension expense. As discussed in the earlier examples, these items will be amortized into pension expense in future periods.

Within the Notes to the Financial Statements

Pension plans are frequently important to understanding a company's financial position, results of operations, and cash flows. Therefore, a company discloses the following information, either in the body of the financial statements or in the notes.[17]

---

[17]"Employers' Disclosure about Pensions and Other Postretirement Benefits," *Statement of Financial Accounting Standards No. 132* (Stamford, Conn.: FASB, 1998; revised 2003); and "Employers' Accounting for Defined Benefit Pension and Other Postretirement Plans: An Amendment of SFAS Nos. 87, 88, 106, and 132(R)," *Statement of Financial Accounting Standards No. 158* (Norwalk, CT: FASB, 2006). These statements modify the disclosure requirements of *SFAS No. 87*. The FASB issued the revised statement because of concerns about the lack of transparency in pension information. This new standard amends the existing disclosure requirements related to pensions by (1) continuing the existing disclosure requirements while (2) requiring companies to provide more details about their plan assets, benefit obligations, cash flows, and benefits costs.

1 A schedule showing all the major components of pension expense.
Rationale: Information provided about the components of pension expense helps users better understand how a company determines pension expense. It also is useful in forecasting a company's net income.

2 A **reconciliation** showing how the projected benefit obligation and the fair value of the plan assets changed from the beginning to the end of the period.
Rationale: Disclosing the projected benefit obligation, the fair value of the plan assets, and changes in them should help users understand the economics underlying the obligations and resources of these plans. Explaining the changes in the projected benefit obligation and fair value of plan assets in the form of a reconciliation provides a more complete disclosure and makes the financial statements more understandable.

3 A disclosure of the rates used in measuring the benefit amounts (discount rate, expected return on plan assets, rate of compensation).
Rationale: Disclosure of these rates permits users to determine the reasonableness of the assumptions applied in measuring the pension liability and pension expense.

4 A table indicating the allocation of pension plan assets by category (equity securities, debt securities, real estate, and other assets), and showing the percentage of the fair value to total plan assets. In addition, a company must include a narrative description of investment policies and strategies, including the target allocation percentages (if used by the company).
Rationale: Such information helps financial statement users evaluate the pension plan's exposure to market risk and possible cash flow demands on the company. It also will help users better assess the reasonableness of the company's expected rate of return assumption.

5 The **expected benefit payments** to be paid to current plan participants for each of the next five fiscal years and in the aggregate for the five fiscal years thereafter. Also required is disclosure of a company's best **estimate of expected contributions** to be paid to the plan during the next year.
Rationale: These disclosures provide information related to the cash outflows of the company. With this information, financial statement users can better understand the potential cash outflows related to the pension plan. They can better assess the liquidity and solvency of the company, which helps in assessing the company's overall financial flexibility.

6 The nature and amount of changes in plan assets and benefit obligations recognized in net income and in other comprehensive income of each period.
Rationale: This disclosure provides information on pension elements affecting the projected benefit obligation and plan assets and on whether those amounts have been recognized in income or deferred to future periods.

7 The accumulated amount of changes in plan assets and benefit obligations that have been recognized in other comprehensive income and that will be recycled into net income in future periods.
Rationale: This information indicates the pension-related balances recognized in stockholders' equity, which will affect future income.

8 The amount of estimated net actuarial gains and losses and prior service costs and credits that will be amortized from accumulated other comprehensive income into net income over the next fiscal year.
Rationale: This information helps users predict the impact of deferred pension expense items on next year's income.

In summary, the disclosure requirements are extensive, and purposely so. One factor that has been a challenge for useful pension reporting has been the lack of consistent terminology. Furthermore, a substantial amount of offsetting is inherent in the measurement of pension expense and the pension liability. These disclosures are designed to address these concerns and take some of the mystery out of pension reporting.

Example of Pension Note Disclosure

In the following sections we provide examples and explain the key pension disclosure elements.

Components of Pension Expense

The FASB requires disclosure of the individual pension expense components (derived from the information in the pension expense worksheet column): (1) service cost, (2) interest cost, (3) expected return on assets, (4) other gains or losses component, and (5) prior service cost component. The purpose of such disclosure is to clarify to more sophisticated readers how companies determine pension expense. Providing information on the components should also be useful in predicting future pension expense.

Illustration 20-27 presents an example of this part of the disclosure. It uses the information from the Zarle illustration, specifically the expense component information from the worksheets in Illustrations 20-8 (page 1029), 20-12 (page 1032), and 20-18 (page 1038).

ILLUSTRATION 20-27
Summary of Expense Components—2009, 2010, 2011

ZARLE COMPANY			
	2009	2010	2011
Components of Pension Expense			
Service cost	$ 9,000	$ 9,500	$13,000
Interest cost	10,000	19,200	21,270
Expected return on plan assets	(10,000)	(11,100)	(13,410)*
Amortization of prior service cost	–0–	27,200	20,800
Pension expense	$ 9,000	$44,800	$41,660

*Note that the expected return must be disclosed, not the actual. In 2011, the expected return is $13,410, which is the actual gain ($12,000) adjusted by the unrecognized loss ($1,410).

UNDERLYING CONCEPTS

This represents another compromise between relevance and reliability. Disclosure attempts to balance these objectives.

Funded Status of Plan

Having a reconciliation of the changes in the assets and liabilities from the beginning of the year to the end of the year, statement readers can better understand the underlying economics of the plan. In essence, this disclosure contains the information in the pension worksheet for the projected benefit obligation and plan asset columns. Using the information for Zarle, the schedule in Illustration 20-28 provides an example of the reconciliation.

ILLUSTRATION 20-28
Pension Disclosure for Zarle Company—2009, 2010, 2011

ZARLE COMPANY PENSION DISCLOSURE			
	2009	2010	2011
Change in benefit obligation			
Benefit obligation at beginning of year	$100,000	$112,000	$ 212,700
Service cost	9,000	9,500	13,000
Interest cost	10,000	19,200	21,270
Amendments (Prior service cost)	–0–	80,000	–0–
Actuarial loss	–0–	–0–	28,530
Benefits paid	(7,000)	(8,000)	(10,500)
Benefit obligation at end of year	112,000	212,700	265,000
Change in plan assets			
Fair value of plan assets at beginning of year	100,000	111,000	134,100
Actual return on plan assets	10,000	11,100	12,000
Contributions	8,000	20,000	24,000
Benefits paid	(7,000)	(8,000)	(10,500)
Fair value of plan assets at end of year	111,000	134,100	159,600
Funded status (Pension asset/liability)	$ (1,000)	$ (78,600)	$(105,400)

The 2009 column reveals that Zarle underfunds the projected benefit obligation by $1,000. The 2010 column reveals that Zarle reports the underfunded liability of $78,600 in the balance sheet. Finally, the 2011 column indicates that Zarle recognizes the underfunded liability of $105,400 in the balance sheet.

2012 Entries and Worksheet—A Comprehensive Example

Incorporating the corridor computation and the required disclosures, we continue the Zarle Company pension plan accounting based on the following facts for 2012.

Service cost is $16,000.

Settlement rate is 10 percent; expected rate of return is 10 percent.

Actual return on plan assets is $22,000.

Amortization of prior service cost is $17,600.

Annual funding contributions are $27,000.

Benefits paid to retirees during the year are $18,000.

Average service life of all covered employees is 20 years.

Zarle prepares a worksheet to facilitate accumulation and recording of the components of pension expense and maintenance of amounts related to the pension plan. Illustration 20-29 shows that worksheet, which uses the basic data presented above. Beginning-of-the-year 2012 account balances are the December 31, 2011, balances from Zarle's revised 2011 pension worksheet in Illustration 20-18.

UNDERLYING CONCEPTS

Does it make a difference to users of financial statements whether companies recognize pension information in the financial statements or disclose it only in the notes? The FASB was unsure, so in accord with the full disclosure principle, it decided to provide extensive pension plan disclosures.

ILLUSTRATION 20-29
Comprehensive Pension Worksheet—2012

	A	B	C	D	E	F	H	I
				Comprehensive Pension Worksheet—2012				
1				General Journal Entries			Memo Record	
2				Other Comprehensive Income				
3	Items	Annual Pension Expense	Cash	Prior Service Cost	Gains/Losses	Pension Asset/Liability	Projected Benefit Obligation	Plan Assets
4	Balance, Dec. 31, 2011					105,400 Cr.	265,000 Cr.	159,600 Dr.
5	(aa) Service cost	16,000 Dr.					16,000 Cr.	
6	(bb) Interest cost	26,500 Dr.					26,500 Cr.	
7	(cc) Actual return	22,000 Cr.						22,000 Dr.
8	(dd) Unexpected gain	6,040 Dr.			6,040 Cr.			
9	(ee) Amortization of PSC	17,600 Dr.		17,600 Cr.				
10	(ff) Contributions		27,000 Cr.					27,000 Dr.
11	(gg) Benefits						18,000 Dr.	18,000 Cr.
12	(hh) Amortization of loss	172 Dr.			172 Cr.			
13								
14	Journal entry for 2012	44,312 Dr.	27,000 Cr.	17,600 Cr.	6,212 Cr.	6,500 Dr.		
15								
16	Accumulated OCI, Dec. 31, 2011			32,000 Dr.	29,940 Dr.			
17	Balance, Dec. 31, 2012*			14,400 Dr.	23,728 Dr.	98,900 Cr.	289,500 Cr.	190,600 Dr.
18								
19	*Accumulated OCI (PSC)	$14,400 Dr.						
20	Accumulated OCI (G/L)	23,728 Dr.						
21	Accumulated OCI, Dec. 31, 2012	$38,128 Dr.						

Worksheet Explanations and Entries

Entries (aa) through (gg) are similar to the corresponding entries previously explained in the prior years' worksheets, with the exception of entry (dd). In 2011 the expected return on plan assets exceeded the actual return, producing an unexpected loss. In 2012 the actual return of $22,000 exceeds the expected return of $15,960 ($159,600 × 10%), resulting in an unexpected gain of $6,040, entry (dd). By netting the gain of $6,040 against the actual return of $22,000, pension expense is affected only by the expected return of $15,960.

A new entry (hh) in Zarle's worksheet results from application of the corridor test on the accumulated balance of net gain or loss in accumulated other comprehensive income. Zarle Company begins 2012 with a balance in the net loss account of $29,940. The company applies the corridor criterion in 2012 to determine whether the balance is excessive and should be amortized. In 2012 the corridor is 10 percent of the larger of the beginning-of-the-year projected benefit obligation of $265,000 or the plan asset's $159,600 market-related asset value (assumed to be fair value). The corridor for 2012 is $26,500 ($265,000 × 10%). Because the balance in Accumulated OCI is a net loss of $29,940, the excess (outside the corridor) is $3,440 ($29,940 − $26,500). Zarle amortizes the $3,440 excess over the average remaining service life of all employees. Given an average remaining service life of 20 years, the amortization in 2012 is $172 ($3,440 ÷ 20). In the 2012 pension worksheet, Zarle debits Pension Expense for $172 and credits that amount to Other Comprehensive Income (G/L). Illustration 20-30 shows the computation of the $172 amortization charge.

ILLUSTRATION 20-30
Computation of 2012
Amortization Charge
(Corridor Test)

2012 Corridor Test	
Net (gain) or loss at beginning of year in accumulated OCI	$29,940
10% of larger of PBO or market-related asset value of plan assets	26,500
Amortizable amount	$ 3,440
Average service life of all employees	20 years
2012 amortization ($3,440 ÷ 20 years)	$172

Zarle formally records pension expense for 2012 as follows.

2012

Pension Expense	44,312	
Pension Asset/Liability	6,500	
Cash		27,000
Other Comprehensive Income (G/L)		6,212
Other Comprehensive Income (PSC)		17,600

Note Disclosure

Illustration 20-31 (next page) shows the note disclosure of Zarle's pension plan for 2012. Note that this example assumes that the pension liability is noncurrent and that the 2013 adjustment for amortization of the net gain or loss and amortization of prior service cost are the same as 2012.

Special Issues

The Pension Reform Act of 1974

The Employee Retirement Income Security Act of 1974—**ERISA**—affects virtually every private retirement plan in the United States. It attempts to safeguard employees' pension rights by mandating many pension plan requirements, including minimum funding, participation, and vesting.

These requirements can influence the employers' cash flows significantly. Under this legislation, annual funding is no longer discretionary. An employer now must fund the plan in accordance with an actuarial funding method that over time will be sufficient to pay for all pension obligations. If companies do not fund their plans in a reasonable manner, they may be subject to fines and/or loss of tax deductions.[18]

UNDERLYING CONCEPTS

Many plans are underfunded but still quite viable. For example, at one time **Loews Corp.** had a $159 million shortfall, but also had earnings of $594 million and a good net worth. Thus, the going-concern assumption permits us to ignore pension underfundings in some cases because in the long run they are not significant.

[18]In 2006, Congress passed the Pension Protection Act. This new law has many provisions. One important aspect of the Act is that it will force many companies to expedite their contributions to their pension plans. One group estimates that companies in the S&P 500 would have had to contribute $47 billion to their pension plans if the new rules were fully phased in for 2006. That amount is about 57 percent more than the $30 billion that companies were expecting to contribute to their plans that year. (Source: Credit Suisse, "Pension Protection Act," August 14, 2006, p. 1.)

ZARLE COMPANY
NOTES TO THE FINANCIAL STATEMENTS

Note D. The company has a pension plan covering substantially all of its employees. The plan is noncontributory and provides pension benefits that are based on the employee's compensation during the three years immediately preceding retirement. The pension plan's assets consist of cash, stocks, and bonds. The company's funding policy is consistent with the relevant government (ERISA) and tax regulations.

Pension expense for 2012 is comprised of the following components of pension cost.

Service cost	$16,000	
Interest on projected benefit obligation	26,500	
Expected return on plan assets	(15,960)	
Amortization of prior service cost	17,600	
Amortization of net loss	172	
Pension expense		$44,312

Other changes in plan assets and benefit obligations recognized in other comprehensive income

Net actuarial gain	$ 6,212	
Amortization of prior service cost	17,600	
Total recognized in other comprehensive income		23,812
Total recognized in pension expense and other comprehensive income		$20,500

The estimated net actuarial loss and prior service cost for the defined-benefit pension plan that will be amortized from accumulated other comprehensive into pension expense over the next year are estimated to be the same as this year.

The amount recognized as a long-term liability in the balance sheet is as follows:

Noncurrent liability

Pension liability	$98,900

The amounts recognized in accumulated other comprehensive income related to pensions consist of:

Net actuarial loss	$23,728
Prior service cost	14,400
Total	$38,128

Change in benefit obligation

Benefit obligation at beginning of year	$265,000
Service cost	16,000
Interest cost	26,500
Amendments (Prior service cost)	–0–
Actuarial gain	–0–
Benefits paid	(18,000)
Benefit obligation at end of year	289,500

Change in plan assets

Fair value of plan assets at beginning of year	159,600
Actual return on plan assets	22,000
Contributions	27,000
Benefits paid	(18,000)
Fair value of plan assets at end of year	190,600
Funded status (liability)	$ 98,900

The weighted-average discount rate used in determining the 2012 projected benefit obligation was 10 percent. The rate of increase in future compensation levels used in computing the 2012 projected benefit obligation was 4.5 percent. The weighted-average expected long-term rate of return on the plan's assets was 10 percent.

ILLUSTRATION 20-31
Minimum Note Disclosure of Pension Plan, Zarle Company, 2012

The law requires plan administrators to publish a comprehensive description and summary of their plans, along with detailed annual reports that include many supplementary schedules and statements.

Another important provision of the Act is the creation of the Pension Benefit Guaranty Corporation (PBGC). **The PBGC's purpose is to administer terminated plans** and to impose liens on an employer's assets for certain unfunded pension liabilities. If a company terminates its pension plan, the PBGC can effectively impose a lien against the employer's assets for the excess of the present value of guaranteed vested benefits over the pension fund assets. This lien generally has had the status of a tax lien; it takes priority over most other creditorship claims. This section of the Act gives the PBGC the power to force an involuntary termination of a pension plan whenever the risks related to nonpayment of the pension obligation seem too great. Because ERISA restricts to 30 percent of net worth the lien that the PBGC can impose, the PBGC must monitor all plans to ensure that net worth is sufficient to meet the pension benefit obligations.[19]

A large number of terminated plans have caused the PBGC to pay out substantial benefits. Currently the PBGC receives its funding from employers, who contribute a certain dollar amount for each employee covered under the plan.[20]

Pension Terminations

A congressman at one time noted, "Employers are simply treating their employee pension plans like company piggy banks, to be raided at will." What this congressman was referring to is the practice of paying off the projected benefit obligation and pocketing any excess. ERISA prevents companies from recapturing excess assets unless they pay participants what is owed to them and then terminate the plan. As a result, companies were buying *annuities* to pay off the pension claimants and then used the excess funds for other corporate purposes.[21]

For example, at one time, pension plan terminations netted $363 million for **Occidental Petroleum Corp.**, $95 million for **Stroh's Brewery Co.**, $58 million for **Kellogg Co.**, and $29 million for **Western Airlines**. Recently, many large companies have terminated their pension plans and captured billions in surplus assets. The U.S. Treasury also benefits: Federal legislation requires companies to pay an excise tax of anywhere from 20 percent to 50 percent on the gains. All of this is quite legal.[22]

The accounting issue that arises from these terminations is whether a company should recognize a gain when pension plan assets revert back to the company (often called **asset reversion** transactions). The issue is complex: in some cases, a company

---

[19]The major problems in underfunding are occurring in four labor-intensive industries—steel, autos, rubber, and airlines. For example, **General Motors'** pension plan at one time was 92 percent funded but still had a deficit of over $6 billion.

[20]**Pan American Airlines** is a good illustration of how difficult it is to assess when to terminate. When Pan Am filed for bankruptcy in 1991, it had a pension liability of $900 million. From 1983 to 1991, the IRS gave it six waivers so it did not have to make contributions. When Pan Am terminated the plan, there was little net worth left upon which to impose a lien. An additional accounting problem relates to the manner of disclosing the possible termination of a plan. For example, should Pan Am have disclosed a contingent liability for its struggling plan? At present this issue is unresolved, and considerable judgment would be needed to analyze a company with these contingent liabilities.

[21]A question exists as to whose money it is. Some argue that the excess funds belong to the employees, not the employer. In addition, given that the funds have been reverting to the employer, critics charge that cost-of-living increases and the possibility of other increased benefits are reduced, because companies will be reluctant to use those remaining funds to pay for such increases.

[22]Another way that companies have reduced their pension obligations is through adoption of **cash-balance plans**. These are *hybrid* plans combining features of defined-benefit and defined-contribution plans. Although these plans permit employees to transfer their pension benefits when they change employers (like a defined-contribution plan), they are controversial because the change to a cash-balance plan often reduces benefits to older workers.

The accounting for cash-balance plans is similar to that for defined-benefit plans, because employers bear the investment risk in cash-balance plans. When an employer adopts a cash-balance plan, the measurement of the future benefit obligation to employees generally is lower, compared to a traditional defined-benefit plan. See A. T. Arcady and F. Mellors, "Cash-Balance Conversions," *Journal of Accountancy* (February 2000), pp. 22–28.

starts a new defined-benefit plan after it eliminates the old one. Thus, some contend that there has been no change in substance, but merely a change in form.

As a result the FASB issued *SFAS No. 88*. It requires recognition in earnings of a gain or loss when the employer settles a pension obligation either by lump-sum cash payments to participants or by purchasing nonparticipating annuity contracts.[23]

BAILING OUT

WHAT DO THE NUMBERS MEAN?

The **Pension Benefit Guaranty Corp.** (PBGC) recently announced that it would take over responsibility for the pilots' pension plan at **United Airlines**, to the tune of $1.4 billion. This federal agency, which acts as an insurer for corporate pension plans, has spent much of the past few years securing pension plans for "Big Steel" (U.S. steel companies), and it looks as if airlines are next.

For example, the PBGC also became the trustee of **US Airways** pilots' pensions in 2003, and it may soon announce a takeover of that struggling carrier's other three pension plans. The grand total at US Airways? It's $2.8 billion—mere pocket change next to the $6.4 billion the PBGC will owe if it has to bail out all four of United Airlines' plans. To date, the airline industry, which makes up 2 percent of participants in the program, has made 20 percent of the claims. The chart below shows how a $6.4 billion bailout would compare with the PBGC's biggest payouts to date.

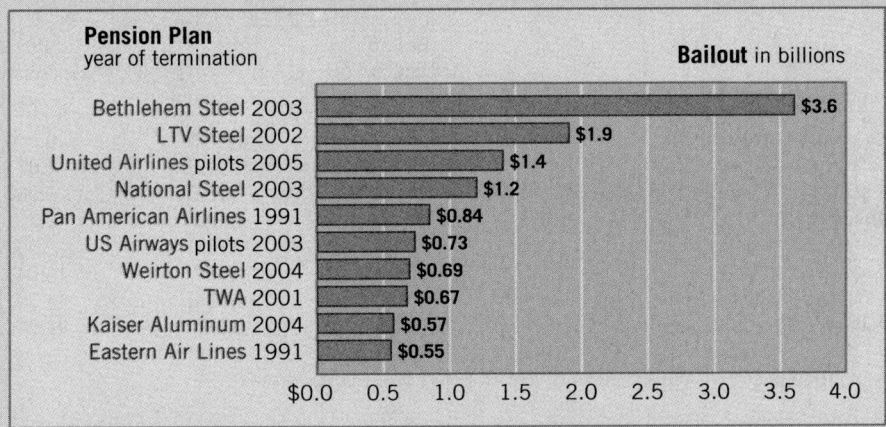

Pension Plan
year of termination — **Bailout** in billions

Pension Plan (year of termination)	Bailout (in billions)
Bethlehem Steel 2003	$3.6
LTV Steel 2002	$1.9
United Airlines pilots 2005	$1.4
National Steel 2003	$1.2
Pan American Airlines 1991	$0.84
US Airways pilots 2003	$0.73
Weirton Steel 2004	$0.69
TWA 2001	$0.67
Kaiser Aluminum 2004	$0.57
Eastern Air Lines 1991	$0.55

Source: Kate Bonamici, "By the Numbers," *Fortune* (January 24, 2005), p. 24.

Pension Accounting Progress and Next Steps

The adoption of *SFAS No. 158* by the FASB represents a significant step in improving the accounting for pensions and other postretirement benefits. An analysis of the ten largest pension plans in the S&P 500 shows an increase in assets ranging from 7 percent to 90 percent and an increase in liabilities ranging from 12 percent to 643 percent.[24]

---

[23]"Employers' Accounting for Settlements and Curtailments of Defined Benefit Pension Plans and for Termination Benefits," *Statement of Financial Accounting Standards No. 88* (Stamford, Conn.: FASB, 1985). Some companies have established *pension poison pills* as an anti-takeover measure. These plans require asset reversions from termination of a plan to benefit employees and retirees rather than the acquiring company. For a discussion of pension poison pills, see Eugene E. Comiskey and Charles W. Mulford, "Interpreting Pension Disclosures: A Guide for Lending Officers," *Commercial Lending Review* (Winter 1993–94), Vol. 9, No. 1.

[24]David Zion and Amit Varshney, "The Magic of Pension Accounting, Part IV," *Equity Research: Accounting and Tax*, Credit Suisse (June 13, 2007).

The disclosure by **Coca-Cola** in Illustration 20-32 shows the impact of adopting *SFAS No. 158* on the various elements of its financial statements.

ILLUSTRATION 20-32
SFAS No. 158 Disclosure

The Coca-Cola Company

Notes to Financial Statements

Note 16   Pension and Other Postretirement Benefit Plans   (in part)

Our Company sponsors and/or contributes to pension and postretirement health care and life insurance benefit plans covering substantially all U.S. employees. We also sponsor nonqualified, unfunded defined benefit pension plans for certain associates. In addition, our Company and its subsidiaries have various pension plans and other forms of postretirement arrangements outside the United States. We use a measurement date of December 31 for substantially all of our pension and postretirement benefit plans.

Effective December 31, 2006, the Company adopted *SFAS No. 158*, which required the recognition in pension obligations and AOCI of actuarial gains or losses, prior service costs or credits and transition assets or obligations that had previously been deferred under the reporting requirements of *SFAS No. 87*, *SFAS No. 106*, and *SFAS No. 132(R)*. The following table reflects the effects of the adoption of *SFAS No. 158* on our consolidated balance sheet as of December 31, 2006. *SFAS No. 158* also impacted the reporting of equity method investees as described in Note 3.

December 31, 2006 (in millions)	Before Application of *SFAS No. 158*	Adjustments	After Application of *SFAS No. 158*
Equity method investments	$ 6,460	$(150)	$ 6,310
Other intangible assets	1,699	(12)	1,687
Total assets	30,200	(237)	29,963
Other liabilities	2,039	192	2,231
Deferred income taxes	749	(141)	608
Total liabilities	12,992	51	13,043
Accumulated other comprehensive income	(1,003)	(288)	(1,291)
Total liabilities and shareowners' equity	30,200	(237)	29,963

Amounts recognized in AOCI consist of the following (in millions, pretax):

December 31,	Pension Benefits	Other Benefits
	2006	2006
Net actuarial loss (gain)	$267	$97
Prior service cost (credit)	37	(5)
	$304	$92

Amounts in AOCI expected to be recognized as components of net periodic pension cost in 2007 are as follows (in millions, pretax):

	Pension Benefits	Other Benefits
	2007	2007
Net actuarial loss (gain)	$20	$ 1
Prior service cost (credit)	6	—
	$26	$ 1

Certain amounts in the prior years' disclosure have been reclassified to conform to the current year presentation.

As indicated in Coca-Cola's disclosure, the effects of the new standard are pervasive but primarily relate to the balance sheet.[25]

What about income effects? As we discussed earlier, *SFAS No. 158* does not change the expense measurement provisions for pensions. Rather, the FASB will take up these and other postretirement measurement issues in Phase II of its project. Key differences still need to be harmonized in Phase II of the project. Those differences include different expense-recognition treatment of gains and losses and the cost of benefits earned in the past, as well as the method for deriving the amount of expected earnings on plan assets.

The second phase of the project is likely to be more controversial, and more debate can be expected. Here are some of the key issues:

1 For plans with benefits that are based on salary levels, should the liability include estimates of future salaries? This debate will center on whether a company can have a liability today that is based in part on future salaries that have not been earned yet.

2 Is it appropriate to eliminate the income statement smoothing mechanism and require companies to report directly in the income statement actual asset returns and any experience gains and losses? This debate is likely to acknowledge the lack of a sound conceptual basis for smoothing reported earnings and to address the significant volatility in corporate earnings from nonoperating activities that would result if smoothing were eliminated. This should be one of the most closely watched issues in Phase II.

3 For plans that are partially or fully funded, should the company consolidate the pension or postretirement benefit trust in its financial statements? This debate will likely focus on concepts of consolidation and whether it would be more meaningful to present the pension liability and the pension assets separately on the balance sheet, instead of following a net liability/asset presentation as proposed in Phase I.

4 How should companies recognize and display in the income statement the various components of the cost of benefits, such as interest cost and investment earnings on plan assets? This debate will center, in part, on whether those amounts should continue to be reported as part of benefit expense or be displayed separately along with other interest expense and investment earnings.

Concluding Observation

Hardly a day goes by without the financial press analyzing in depth some issue related to pension plans in the United States. This is not surprising, since U.S. pension funds now hold over $5 trillion in assets. As you have seen, the accounting issues related to pension plans are complex. The new standard clarifies many of these issues and should help users understand the financial implications of a company's pension plans on its financial position, results of operations, and cash flows.

---

[25]iGAAP differs from U.S. GAAP in that companies have the option to report the funded status of their pension plans on the balance sheet.

SUMMARY OF LEARNING OBJECTIVES

1. Distinguish between accounting for the employer's pension plan and accounting for the pension fund. The company or employer is the organization sponsoring the pension plan. It incurs the cost and makes contributions to the pension fund. The fund or plan is the entity that receives the contributions from the employer, administers the pension assets, and makes the benefit payments to the pension recipients (retired employees). The fund should be a separate legal and accounting entity; it maintains a set of books and prepares financial statements.

2. Identify types of pension plans and their characteristics. The two most common types of pension arrangements are: (1) *Defined-contribution plans:* The employer agrees to contribute to a pension trust a certain sum each period based on a formula. This formula may consider such factors as age, length of employee service, employer's profits, and compensation level. Only the employer's contribution is defined; no promise is made regarding the ultimate benefits paid out to the employees. (2) *Defined-benefit plans:* These plans define the benefits that the employee will receive at the time of retirement. The formula typically provides for the benefits to be a function of the employee's years of service and the compensation level when he or she nears retirement.

3. Explain alternative measures for valuing the pension obligation. One measure bases the pension obligation only on the benefits vested to the employees. Vested benefits are those that the employee is entitled to receive even if he or she renders no additional services under the plan. Companies compute the *vested benefits pension obligation* using current salary levels; this obligation includes only vested benefits. Another measure of the obligation, called the *accumulated benefit obligation,* computes the deferred compensation amount based on all years of service performed by employees under the plan—both vested and nonvested—using current salary levels. A third measure, called the *projected benefit obligation,* bases the computation of the deferred compensation amount on both vested and nonvested service using future salaries.

4. List the components of pension expense. Pension expense is a function of the following components: (1) service cost, (2) interest on the liability, (3) return on plan assets, (4) amortization of prior service cost, and (5) gain or loss.

5. Use a worksheet for employer's pension plan entries. Companies may use a worksheet unique to pension accounting. This worksheet records both the formal entries and the memo entries to keep track of all the employer's relevant pension plan items and components.

6. Describe the amortization of prior service costs. An actuary computes the amount of the prior service cost and records it as an adjustment to the projected benefit obligation and other comprehensive income. It then amortizes it, generally using a "years-of-service" amortization method, similar to a units-of-production computation. First, the company computes total estimated number of service-years to be worked by all of the participating employees. Second, it divides the accumulated prior service cost by the total number of service-years, to obtain a cost per service-year (the unit cost). Third, the company multiplies the number of service-years consumed each year times the cost per service-year, to obtain the annual amortization charge.

7. Explain the accounting for unexpected gains and losses. In estimating the projected benefit obligation (the liability), actuaries make assumptions about such items as mortality rate, retirement rate, turnover rate, disability rate, and salary amounts. Any change in these actuarial assumptions affects the amount of the projected benefit obligation. These unexpected gains or losses from changes in the projected benefit obligation are liability gains and losses. Liability gains result from unexpected decreases in the liability balance; liability losses result from unexpected increases. Companies also incur asset gains or losses. Both types of actuarial gains and losses are recorded in other comprehensive income and adjust either the projected benefit obligation or the plan assets.

8. Explain the corridor approach to amortizing gains and losses. The FASB set a limit for the size of an accumulated net gain or loss balance. That arbitrarily selected limit (called a *corridor*) is 10 percent of the larger of the beginning balances of the projected benefit obligation or the market-related value of the plan assets. Beyond that limit, an accumulated net gain or loss balance is considered too large and must be amortized. If the balance of the accumulated net gain or loss account stays within the upper and lower limits of the corridor, no amortization is required.

9. Describe the requirements for reporting pension plans in financial statements. Currently, companies must disclose the following pension plan information in their financial statements: (1) The components of pension expense for the period. (2) A schedule showing changes in the benefit obligation and plan assets during the year. (3) The amount of prior service cost and net gains and losses in accumulated OCI, including the estimated prior service cost and gains and losses that will affect net income in the next year. (4) The weighted-average assumed discount rate, the rate of compensation increase used to measure the projected benefit obligation, and the weighted-average expected long-term rate of return on plan assets. (5) A table showing the allocation of pension plan assets by category and the percentage of the fair value to total plan assets. (6) The expected benefit payments for current plan participants for each of the next five fiscal years and for the following five years in aggregate, along with an estimate of expected contributions to the plan during the next year.

APPENDIX 20A

Accounting for Postretirement Benefits

In March 1991 **IBM**'s adoption of a new accounting standard on postretirement benefits resulted in a $2.3 billion charge and a historical curiosity—IBM's first-ever quarterly loss. **General Electric** disclosed that its charge for adoption of the same new FASB standard would be $2.7 billion. In the fourth quarter of 1993, **AT&T** absorbed a $2.1 billion pretax hit for postretirement benefits. What is this standard, and how could its adoption have so grave an impact on companies' earnings?

ACCOUNTING GUIDANCE

After a decade of study, the FASB in December 1990 issued *Statement No. 106*, "Employers' Accounting for Postretirement Benefits Other Than Pensions." It alone was the cause for the large charges to income cited above. This standard accounts for health care and other "welfare benefits" provided to retirees, their spouses, dependents, and beneficiaries.[1] These other welfare benefits include life insurance offered outside a pension plan; medical, dental, and eye care; legal and tax services; tuition assistance; day care; and housing assistance.[2] Because healthcare benefits are the largest of the other postretirement benefits, we use this item to illustrate accounting for postretirement benefits.

For many employers (about 95 percent) this standard required a change from the predominant practice of accounting for postretirement benefits on a pay-as-you-go (cash) basis to an accrual basis. Similar to pension accounting, the accrual basis necessitates measuring the employer's obligation to provide future benefits and accrual of the cost during the years that the employee provides service.

One of the reasons companies had not prefunded these benefit plans was that payments to prefund healthcare costs, unlike excess contributions to a pension trust, are not tax-deductible. Another reason was that postretirement healthcare benefits were once perceived to be a low-cost employee benefit that could be changed or eliminated at will and therefore were not a legal liability. Now, the accounting definition of a liability goes beyond the notion of a legally enforceable claim; the definition now encompasses equitable or constructive obligations as well, making it clear that the postretirement benefit promise is a liability.[3]

DIFFERENCES BETWEEN PENSION BENEFITS AND HEALTHCARE BENEFITS

OBJECTIVE 10
Identify the differences between pensions and postretirement healthcare benefits.

The FASB used *SFAS No. 87* on pensions as a reference for the accounting prescribed in *SFAS No. 106* on healthcare and other nonpension postretirement benefits.[4] Why didn't the FASB cover these other types of postretirement benefits in the earlier pension accounting statement? Because the apparent similarities between the two benefits mask some significant differences. Illustration 20A-1 shows these differences.[5]

---

[1] *Accounting Trends and Techniques—2004* reports that of its 600 surveyed companies, 334 reported benefit plans that provide postretirement healthcare benefits. In response to rising healthcare costs and higher premiums on healthcare insurance, companies are working to get their postretirement benefit costs under control. For example, a recent study of employer health-benefit plans indicates that employers are limiting or curtailing postretirement health benefits. Of the companies surveyed, 20 percent have eliminated the plans altogether. And 17 percent indicated they have just about eliminated their liabilities for such benefits by requiring current retirees to pay healthcare premiums. In some cases, employees must work longer at a company before they are eligible for these benefits. See Kelly Greene, "Health Benefits for Retirees Continue to Shrink, Study Says," *Wall Street Journal* (September 16, 2002), p. A2.

[2] "OPEB" is the acronym frequently used to describe postretirement benefits covered by *SFAS No. 106*. This term came into being before the scope of the statement was narrowed from "other postemployment benefits" to "other postretirement benefits," thereby excluding postemployment benefits related to severance pay or wage continuation to disabled, terminated, or laid-off employees.

[3] "Elements of Financial Statements," *Statement of Financial Accounting Concepts No. 6* (Stamford, Conn.: 1985), p. 13, footnote 21.

[4] In November 1992 the FASB issued *Statement of Financial Accounting Standards No. 112*, "Employers' Accounting for Postemployment Benefits." This standard covers postemployment benefits that are not accounted for under *SFAS No. 87* (pensions), *SFAS No. 88* (settlements, curtailments, and termination benefits), or *SFAS No. 106* (postretirement benefits other than pensions). *SFAS No. 112* requires an employer to recognize the obligation to provide postemployment benefits in accordance with *SFAS No. 43*, similar to accounting for compensated absences (see Chapter 13). These *SFAS No. 112* benefits include, but are not limited to, salary continuation, disability-related benefits, severance benefits, and continuance of healthcare benefits and life insurance for inactive or former (e.g., terminated, disabled, or deceased) employees or their beneficiaries.

[5] D. Gerald Searfoss and Naomi Erickson, "The Big Unfunded Liability: Postretirement Health-Care Benefits," *Journal of Accountancy* (November 1988), pp. 28–39.

Item	Pensions	Healthcare Benefits
Funding	Generally funded.	Generally *NOT* funded.
Benefit	Well-defined and level dollar amount.	Generally uncapped and great variability.
Beneficiary	Retiree (maybe some benefit to surviving spouse).	Retiree, spouse, and other dependents.
Benefit payable	Monthly.	As needed and used.
Predictability	Variables are reasonably predictable.	Utilization difficult to predict. Level of cost varies geographically and fluctuates over time.

ILLUSTRATION 20A-1
Differences between Pensions and Postretirement Healthcare Benefits

Two of the differences in Illustration 20A-1 highlight why measuring the future payments for healthcare benefit plans is so much more difficult than for pension plans.

1 Many postretirement plans do not set a limit on healthcare benefits. No matter how serious the illness or how long it lasts, the benefits continue to flow. (Even if the employer uses an insurance company plan, the premiums will escalate according to the increased benefits provided.)

2 The levels of healthcare benefit use and healthcare costs are difficult to predict. Increased longevity, unexpected illnesses (e.g., AIDS, SARS, and avian flu), along with new medical technologies and cures, cause changes in healthcare utilization.

Additionally, although the fiduciary and reporting standards for employee benefit funds under government regulations generally cover healthcare benefits, the stringent minimum vesting, participation, and funding standards that apply to pensions do not apply to healthcare benefits. Nevertheless, as you will learn, given *SFAS No. 106* and the new standard (*SFAS No. 158*), many of the basic concepts of pensions, and much of the related

---

OPEBs—HOW BIG ARE THEY?

WHAT DO THE NUMBERS MEAN?

For many companies, *other postretirement benefit obligations* (OPEBs) are substantial. Generally, OPEBs are not well funded because companies are not permitted a tax deduction for contributions to the plan assets, as is the case with pensions. That is, the company may not claim a tax deduction until it makes a payment to the participant (pay-as-you-go).

Presented below are companies with the largest OPEB obligations, indicating their relationship with other financial items.

(For year ended 12/31/2003 $ in millions)	Obligation	% Underfunded	Obligation as a % of Pension Obligation (ABO)	Obligation as a % of LTD	Obligation as a % of Stockholders' Equity
General Motors	$67,542	85.2%	77.4%	25.1%	267.3%
Ford Motor Company	32,362	89.0%	80.0%	18.2%	277.8%
SBC Communications Inc.	27,231	74.4%	98.6%	71.2%	71.2%
Verizon Communications Inc.	24,592	81.8%	59.9%	62.4%	73.5%
General Electric	9,701	83.2%	25.6%	5.7%	12.3%
Boeing Co.	8,617	99.3%	21.6%	64.8%	105.9%
Lucent Technologies Inc.	8,511	72.7%	27.2%	152.2%	NA
Delphi Corp.	8,469	100.0%	74.2%	347.9%	539.4%
BellSouth Corp.	7,156	48.4%	61.6%	62.3%	36.3%
AT&T Corp.	6,274	67.2%	39.8%	48.0%	45.0%

So, how big are OPEB obligations? REALLY big.

Source: Jason Williams, "OPEB Plans 2003: In Worse Shape than 2002," Yellow Card Trend Alert, Glass Lewis LLP (November 1, 2004).

accounting terminology and measurement methodology, do apply to other postretirement benefits. Therefore, in the following discussion and illustrations, we point out the similarities and differences in the accounting and reporting for these two types of postretirement benefits.

POSTRETIREMENT BENEFITS ACCOUNTING PROVISIONS

Healthcare and other postretirement benefits for current and future retirees and their dependents are forms of deferred compensation. They are earned through employee service and are subject to accrual during the years an employee is working.

The period of time over which the postretirement benefit cost accrues is called the **attribution period**. It is the period of service during which the employee earns the benefits under the terms of the plan. The attribution period, shown in Illustration 20A-2 for a hypothetical employee, generally begins when an employee is hired and ends on the date the employee is eligible to receive the benefits and ceases to earn additional benefits by performing service, the vesting date.[6]

ILLUSTRATION 20A-2
Range of Possible
Attribution Periods

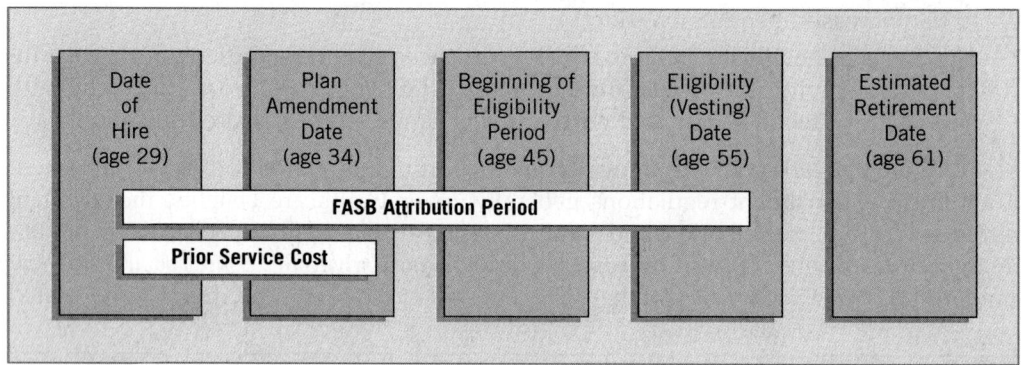

Obligations Under Postretirement Benefits

In defining the obligation for postretirement benefits, the FASB maintained many concepts similar to pension accounting. It also designed some new and modified terms specifically for postretirement benefits. Two of the most important of these specialized terms are (a) expected postretirement benefit obligation and (b) accumulated postretirement benefit obligation.

The **expected postretirement benefit obligation (EPBO)** is the actuarial present value as of a particular date of **all benefits a company expects to pay after retirement to employees and their dependents**. Companies do not record the EPBO in the financial statements, but they do use it in measuring periodic expense.

The **accumulated postretirement benefit obligation (APBO)** is the actuarial present value of **future benefits attributed to employees' services rendered to a particular date**. The APBO is equal to the EPBO for retirees and active employees fully eligible for benefits. Before the date an employee achieves full eligibility, the APBO is only a portion of the EPBO. Or stated another way, the difference between the APBO and the EPBO is the future service costs of active employees who are not yet fully eligible.

Illustration 20A-3 contrasts the EPBO and the APBO.

---

[6]This is a benefit-years-of-service approach (the projected unit credit actuarial cost method). The FASB found no compelling reason to switch from the traditional pension accounting approach. It rejected the employee's full service period (i.e., to the estimated retirement date) because it was unable to identify any approach that would appropriately attribute benefits beyond the date when an employee attains full eligibility for those benefits. Employees attain full eligibility by meeting specified age, service, or age and service requirements of the plan.

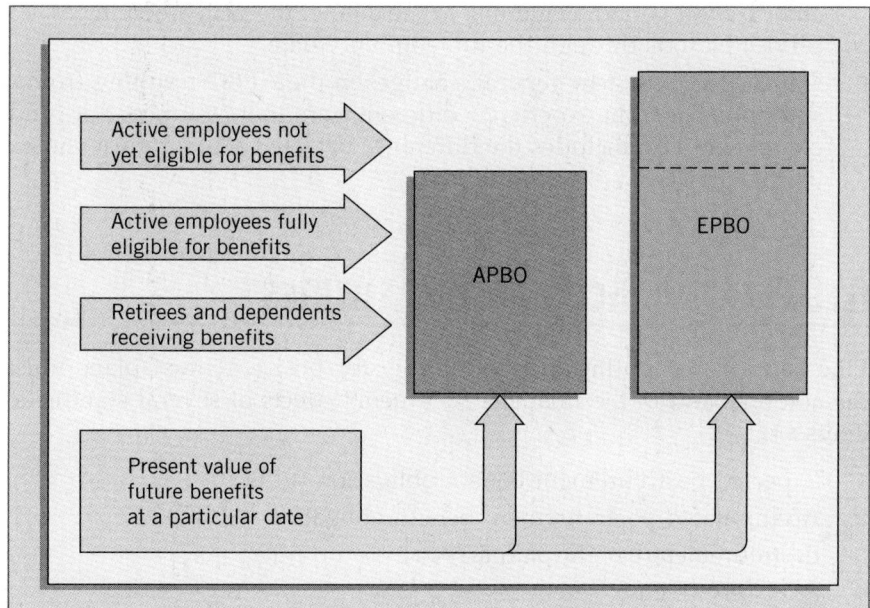

ILLUSTRATION 20A-3
APBO and EPBO
Contrasted

At the date an employee is fully eligible (the end of the attribution period), the APBO and the EPBO for that employee are equal.

Postretirement Expense

Postretirement expense is the employer's annual expense for postretirement benefits. Also called **net periodic postretirement benefit cost**, this expense consists of many of the familiar components used to compute annual pension expense. The components of net periodic postretirement benefit cost are as follows.[7]

1 *Service Cost:* The portion of the EPBO attributed to employee service during the period.

2 *Interest Cost:* The increase in the APBO attributable to the passage of time. Companies compute interest cost by applying the beginning-of-the-year discount rate to the beginning-of-the-year APBO, adjusted for benefit payments to be made during the period. The discount rate is based on the rates of return on high-quality, fixed-income investments that are currently available.[8]

3 *Actual Return on Plan Assets:* The change in the fair value of the plan's assets adjusted for contributions and benefit payments made during the period. Because companies charge or credit the postretirement expense for the gain or loss on plan assets (the difference between the actual and the expected return), this component is actually the expected return.

4 *Amortization of Prior Service Cost:* The amortization of the cost of retroactive benefits resulting from plan amendments after *SFAS No. 106* takes effect. The typical

---

[7]"Employers' Accounting for Postretirement Benefits Other Than Pensions," *Statement of Financial Accounting Standards No. 106* (Norwalk, Conn.: FASB, 1990), pars. 46–66. Also see James R. Wilbert and Kenneth E. Dakdduk, "The New FASB 106: How to Account for Postretirement Benefits," *Journal of Accountancy* (August 1991), pp. 36–41.

[8]The FASB concluded that the discount rate for measuring the present value of the postretirement benefit obligation and the service cost component should be the same as that applied to pension measurements. It chose not to label it the *settlement rate*, in order to clarify that the objective of the discount rate is to measure the time value of money.

amortization period, beginning at the date of the plan amendment, is the remaining service periods through the full eligibility date.

5 *Gains and Losses:* In general, changes in the APBO resulting from changes in assumptions or from experience different from that assumed. For funded plans, this component also includes the difference between actual return and expected return on plan assets.

ILLUSTRATIVE ACCOUNTING ENTRIES

OBJECTIVE 11
Contrast accounting for pensions to accounting for other postretirement benefits.

Like pension accounting, the accounting for postretirement plans must recognize in the accounts and in the financial statements effects of several significant items. These items are:

1   Expected postretirement benefit obligation (EPBO).
2   Accumulated postretirement benefit obligation (APBO).
3   Postretirement benefit plan assets.
4   Prior service cost.
5   Net gain or loss.

The EPBO is not recognized in the financial statements or disclosed in the notes. Companies recompute it each year, and the actuary uses it in measuring the annual service cost. Because of the numerous assumptions and actuarial complexity involved in measuring annual service cost, we have omitted these computations of the EPBO.

Similar to pensions, companies must recognize in the financial statements items 2 through 5 listed above. In addition, as in pension accounting, companies must know the exact amount of these items in order to compute postretirement expense. Therefore, companies use the worksheet like that for pension accounting to record both the formal general journal entries and the memo entries.

2009 Entries and Worksheet

To illustrate the use of a worksheet in accounting for a postretirement benefits plan, assume that on January 1, 2009, Quest Company adopts *Statement No. 106* as amended by *SFAS No. 158* to account for its healthcare benefit plan. The following facts apply to the postretirement benefits plan for the year 2009.

> Plan assets at fair value on January 1, 2009, are zero.
>
> Actual and expected returns on plan assets are zero.
>
> Accumulated postretirement benefit obligation (APBO), January 1, 2009, is zero.
>
> Service cost is $54,000.
>
> No prior service cost exists.
>
> Interest cost on the APBO is zero.
>
> Funding contributions during the year are $38,000.
>
> Benefit payments to employees from plan are $28,000.

Using that data, the worksheet in Illustration 20A-4 (next page) presents the postretirement entries for 2009.

Entry (a) records the service cost component, which increases postretirement expense $54,000 and increases the liability (APBO) $54,000. Entry (b) records Quest's funding of assets to the postretirement fund. The funding decreases cash $38,000 and increases plan assets $38,000. Entry (c) records the benefit payments made to retirees, which results in equal $28,000 decreases to the plan assets and the liability (APBO).

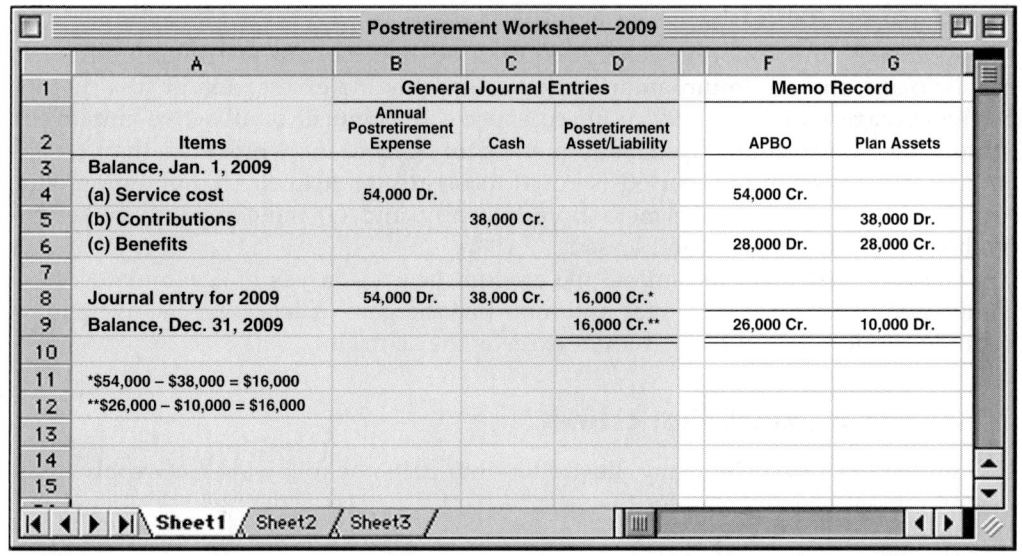

ILLUSTRATION 20A-4
Postretirement
Worksheet—2009

Quest's December 31 adjusting entry formally records the postretirement expense in 2009, as follows.

December 31, 2009

Postretirement Expense	54,000	
Cash		38,000
Postretirement Asset/Liability		16,000

The credit to Postretirement Asset/Liability for $16,000 represents the difference between the APBO and the plan assets. The $16,000 credit balance is a liability because the plan is underfunded. The Postretirement Asset/Liability account balance of $16,000 also equals the net of the balances in the memo accounts.

Illustration 20A-5 shows the funded status reported in the balance sheet. (Notice its similarity to the pension schedule.)

Accumulated postretirement benefit obligation (Credit)	$(26,000)
Plan assets at fair value (Debit)	10,000
Postretirement asset/liability (Credit)	$(16,000)

ILLUSTRATION 20A-5
Postretirement
Reconciliation
Schedule—December 31,
2009

Recognition of Gains and Losses

Gains and losses represent changes in the APBO or the value of plan assets. These changes result either from actual experience different from that expected or from changes in actuarial assumptions. The amortization of these gains and losses follows the approach used for pensions. That is, the gains and losses are recorded in other comprehensive income.

The Corridor Approach

Consistent with pension accounting, companies amortize the gains and losses in accumulated other comprehensive income as a component of postretirement expense if, at the beginning of the period, they exceed a "corridor" limit. The corridor is measured as the greater of 10 percent of the APBO or 10 percent of the market-related value of plan assets.

The intent of the **corridor approach** is to reduce volatility of postretirement expense by providing a reasonable opportunity for gains and losses to offset over time without affecting net periodic expense.

Amortization Methods

If the company must amortize gains and losses (beyond the corridor) on postretirement benefit plans, the **minimum amortization amount** is the excess gain or loss divided by the average remaining service life to expected retirement of all active employees. Companies may use any systematic method of amortization provided that: (1) the amount amortized in any period is equal to or greater than the minimum amount, (2) the company applies the method consistently, and (3) the company applies the method similarly for gains and losses.

The company must recompute the amount of gain or loss in accumulated other comprehensive income each year and amortize the gain or loss over the average remaining service life if the net amount exceeds the "corridor."

2010 Entries and Worksheet

Continuing the Quest Company illustration into 2010, the following facts apply to the postretirement benefits plan for the year 2010.

> Actual return on plan assets is $600.
>
> Expected return on plan assets is $800.
>
> Discount rate is 8 percent.
>
> Increase in APBO due to change in actuarial assumptions is $60,000.
>
> Service cost is $26,000.
>
> Funding contributions during the year are $18,000.
>
> Benefit payments to employees during the year are $5,000.
>
> Average remaining service to expected retirement: 25 years.

The worksheet in Illustration 20A-6 presents all of Quest's postretirement benefit entries and information for 2010. The beginning balances on the first line of worksheet are the ending balances from Quest's 2009 postretirement benefits worksheet in Illustration 20A-4.

ILLUSTRATION 20A-6
Postretirement Benefits
Worksheet—2010

	Postretirement Benefits Worksheet—2010						
	A	B	C	D	E	G	H
1		General Journal Entries				Memo Record	
2	Items	Annual Postretirement Expense	Cash	Other Comprehensive Income (G/L)	Postretirement Asset/Liability	APBO	Plan Assets
3	Balance, Jan. 1, 2010				16,000 Cr.	26,000 Cr.	10,000 Dr.
4	(d) Service cost	26,000 Dr.				26,000 Cr.	
5	(e) Interest cost	2,080 Dr.				2,080 Cr.	
6	(f) Actual return	600 Cr.					600 Dr.
7	(g) Unexpected loss	200 Cr.		200 Dr.			
8	(h) Contributions		18,000 Cr.				18,000 Dr.
9	(i) Benefits					5,000 Dr.	5,000 Cr.
10	(j) Increase in APBO (Loss)			60,000 Dr.		60,000 Cr.	
11	Journal entry for 2010	27,280 Dr.	18,000 Cr.	60,200 Dr.	69,480 Cr.		
12							
13	Accumulated OCI, Dec. 31, 2009			0			
14	Balance, Dec. 31, 2010			60,200 Dr.	85,480 Cr.	109,080 Cr.	23,600 Dr.
15							

Entries (d), (h), and (i) are similar to the corresponding entries previously explained for 2009. Entry (e) accrues the interest expense component, which increases both the liability and the postretirement expense by $2,080 (the beginning APBO multiplied by the discount rate of 8%). Entries (f) and (g) are related. The expected return of $800 is higher than the actual return of $600. To smooth postretirement expense, Quest defers the unexpected loss of $200 ($800 − $600) by debiting Other Comprehensive Income (G/L) and crediting Postretirement Expense. As a result of this adjustment, the expected return on the plan assets is the amount actually used to compute postretirement expense.

Entry (j) records the change in the APBO resulting from a change in actuarial assumptions. This $60,000 increase in the employer's accumulated liability is an unexpected loss. Quest debits this loss to Other Comprehensive Income (G/L).

On December 31 Quest formally records net periodic expense for 2010 as follows.

December 31, 2010

Postretirement Expense	27,280	
Other Comprehensive Income (G/L)	60,200	
Cash		18,000
Postretirement Asset/Liability		69,480

The balance of the Postretirement Asset/Liability account at December 31, 2010, is $85,480. This balance is equal to the net of the balances in the memo accounts as shown in the reconciliation schedule in Illustration 20A-7.

Accumulated Postretirement Benefit Obligation (Credit)	$(109,080)
Plan Assets at Fair Value (Debit)	23,600
Postretirement Asset/Liability (Credit)	$ (85,480)

ILLUSTRATION 20A-7
Postretirement Benefits Reconciliation Schedule—December 31, 2010

Amortization of Net Gain or Loss in 2011

Quest has a beginning balance in Accumulated OCI related to losses of $60,200. Therefore, Quest must apply the corridor test for amortization of the balance for 2011. Illustration 20A-8 shows the computation of the amortization charge for the loss.

2011 Corridor Test	
Accumulated OCI at beginning of year	$60,200
10% of greater of APBO or market-related value of plan assets ($109,080 × .10)	10,908
Amortizable amount	$49,292
Average remaining service to expected retirement	25 years
2011 amortization of loss ($49,292 ÷ 25)	$1,972

ILLUSTRATION 20A-8
Computation of Amortization Charge (Corridor Test)—2011

DISCLOSURES IN NOTES TO THE FINANCIAL STATEMENTS

The disclosures required for other postretirement benefit plans are similar to and just as detailed and extensive as those required for pensions. The note disclosure for **Tootsie Roll, Inc.** in Illustration 20A-9 (page 1062) provides a good example of the extensive disclosure required for other postretirement benefit plans.

As indicated in Illustration 20A-9, Tootsie Roll, in addition to explaining the impact of adopting *SFAS No. 158*, shows the impact of the postretirement benefit plan on income, the balance sheet, and the cash flow statement, and it provides information on important assumptions used in the measurement of the postretirement benefit obligation. Also note that given no tax incentives for funding, Tootsie Roll (like many companies) does not have any assets set aside for its other postretirement benefit obligations.

While Tootsie Roll has only an other postretirement benefit plan, many companies sponsor both defined-benefit pension and other postretirement plans. Given the similarities in accounting for these plans, companies can combine pension and other postretirement benefit disclosures.

ILLUSTRATION 20A-9
Postretirement Benefit
Disclosure

Tootsie Roll Industries, Inc.

Notes to Financial Statements

Note 7 Employee Benefit Plans (partial)
Postretirement health care and life insurance benefit plans ($000):

The Company provides certain postretirement health care and life insurance benefits for corporate office and management employees. Employees become eligible for these benefits based upon their age and service and if they agree to contribute a portion of the cost. The Company has the right to modify or terminate these benefits. The Company does not fund postretirement health care and life insurance benefits in advance of payments for benefit claims.

The Company adopted *SFAS No. 158*, "Employers' Accounting for Defined Benefit Pension and Other Postretirement Plans" (*SFAS 158*) as of December 31, 2006. *SFAS 158* requires that employers recognize on a prospective basis the funded status of their defined benefit pension and other postretirement plans on their consolidated balance sheet and recognize as a component of other comprehensive income, net of tax, the gains or losses and prior service costs or credits that arise during the period but are not recognized as components of net periodic benefit cost. The effect of the adoption of *SFAS 158* on the Company's consolidated statement of financial position at December 31, 2006, was an increase of $1,325 in the non-current liability for postretirement health care and life insurance benefits and a $893 increase in accumulated other comprehensive loss (net of tax effect of $432).

Amounts recognized in accumulated other comprehensive loss (pre-tax) at December 31, 2006, are as follows:

Prior service credit	$(1,252)
Net actuarial loss	2,577
Net amount recognized in accumulated other comprehensive loss	$ 1,325

The estimated actuarial loss, prior service credit and transition obligation to be amortized from accumulated other comprehensive income into net periodic benefit cost during 2007 are $215, $(125), and $0, respectively. The changes in the accumulated postretirement benefit obligation at December 31, 2006 and 2005, consist of the following:

	December 31, 2006	2005
Benefit obligation, beginning of year	$ 9,924	$ 9,193
Service cost	524	474
Interest cost	539	519
Plan participant contributions	—	52
Actuarial (gain)/loss	2,101	(103)
Benefits paid	(506)	(211)
Benefit obligation, end of year	12,582	9,924
Prior service cost	—	1,377
Net actuarial loss	—	(518)
Net amount recognized at December 31	$12,582	$10,783

Net periodic postretirement benefit cost included the following components:

	2006	2005	2004
Service cost—benefits attributed to service during the period	$524	$474	$521
Interest cost on the accumulated postretirement benefit obligation	539	519	514
Net amortization	(84)	(74)	(43)
Net periodic postretirement benefit cost	$979	$919	$992

For measurement purposes, the 2006 annual rate of increase in the per capita cost of covered health care benefits was assumed to be 9.0% for pre-age 65 retirees, 10.5% for post-age 65 retirees and 12.0% for prescription drugs; these rates were assumed to decrease gradually to 5.0% for 2014 and remain at that level thereafter. The health care cost trend rate assumption has a significant effect on the amounts reported. The weighted-average discount rate used in determining the accumulated postretirement benefit obligation was 5.60% and 5.50% at December 31, 2006 and 2005, respectively. Increasing or decreasing the health care trend rates by one percentage point in each year would have the following effect on:

	1% Increase	1% Decrease
Postretirement benefit obligation	$1,802	$(1,481)
Total of service and interest cost components	$ 195	$ (155)

The Company estimates future benefit payments will be $368, $429, $480, $546 and $575 in 2007 through 2011, respectively, and a total of $4,286 in 2012 through 2016. The future benefit payments are net of the annual Medicare Part D subsidy of approximately $1,003 beginning in 2007.

ACTUARIAL ASSUMPTIONS AND CONCEPTUAL ISSUES

Measurement of the EPBO, the APBO, and the net periodic postretirement benefit cost is involved and complex. Due to the uncertainties in forecasting healthcare costs, rates of use, changes in government health programs, and the differences employed in non-medical assumptions (e.g., discount rate, employee turnover, rate of pre-65 retirement, spouse-age difference), estimates of postretirement benefit costs may have a large margin of error. Is the information relevant, reliable, or verifiable? The FASB concluded that "the obligation to provide postretirement benefits meets the definition of a liability, is representationally faithful, is relevant to financial statement users, and can be measured with sufficient reliability at a justifiable cost."[9] Failure to accrue an obligation and an expense prior to payment of benefits would result in an unfaithful representation of what financial statements should represent.

The FASB took a momentous step by requiring recognition of a postretirement liability. Many opposed the requirement, warning that the standard would devastate earnings. Others argued that putting these numbers on the balance sheet was inappropriate. Others noted that the requirement would force companies to curtail postretirement benefits to employees.

The authors believe that the FASB deserves special praise for this standard. Because the Board addressed this issue, companies now recognize the magnitude of these costs. This recognition has led to efforts to control escalating healthcare costs. As John Ruffle, a former president of the Financial Accounting Foundation noted, "The Board has done American industry a gigantic favor. Over the long term, industry will look back and say thanks."

With the issuance of *SFAS No. 158*, the FASB has taken additional steps to improve the transparency of information about postretirement benefit plans. As shown in the chapter and appendix, *SFAS No. 158* brings important information (previously unrecognized prior service costs and unrealized gains and losses) out of the notes and now requires recognition in the financial statements. On average, the changes have resulted in significant increases in liabilities and reductions in stockholders' equity. Whether U.S. businesses will "look back and thank the FASB" for these recent changes remains to be seen.

However, U.S. companies appear to be responding to the adverse effects of *SFAS No. 158* on their financial statements. In the fourth quarter of 2006 alone, over 40 public U.S. companies froze or otherwise curtailed their defined-benefits plans (in some cases, substituting defined-contribution benefit plans). Some are concerned that these curtailments in benefits will snowball once more companies see the effects of *SFAS No. 158* on their balance sheets.[10] These reactions are not confined to Corporate America. The Government Accounting Standards Board (GASB) also recently issued new standards for postretirement benefits offered to government employees—provisions similar to those required of U.S. companies under *SFAS No. 106* and *158*. In response to having to own up to these obligations, some state legislatures (Texas and Connecticut) have proposed legislation to permit state and municipal controllers to ignore the GASB standards.[11]

The authors feel that such reactions are regrettable. The objective of accounting is to provide the best information for decision making. Choosing to ignore information about promises made to employees just because we do not like how the results are reported in the financial statements is not the solution. If companies and governments decide, based on relevant and reliable information in accounting reports, to change benefit plans offered to employees, then accounting has done its job. Accounting rules that are biased or that obscure the effects of decisions raise concerns not only about the credibility of the companies' or governments' reports but also about financial reporting in general. We encourage the FASB to continue to work toward more relevant and reliable accounting in Phase II of its postretirement-benefit project.

---

[9]*FASB Statement No. 106*, par. 163.

[10]See Jack Ciesielski, "Pension Freezes: Not an Ice Age Yet," The AAO Weblog, *www.accountingobserver.com* (October 20, 2006).

[11]Mary W. Walsh, "Auditing Rule Is Put at Risk by Texas Bill," *New York Times* (May 18, 2007).

**WHAT DO THE
NUMBERS MEAN?**

GASB WHO?

The Governmental Accounting Standards Board (GASB) was organized in 1984 as an operating entity of the Financial Accounting Foundation (FAF) to establish standards of financial accounting and reporting for state and local governmental entities. Similar to the FASB, FAF Trustees are responsible for selecting the members of the GASB and its Advisory Council, funding their activities, and exercising general oversight (with the exception of the GASB's resolution of technical issues). The GASB's function is important because high-quality external financial reporting can demonstrate financial accountability of state and local governments to the public and is the basis for investment, credit, and many legislative and regulatory decisions.

Until recently, the GASB went about its work in relative obscurity. How did the GASB get everyone's attention? It recommended that governmental units recognize other postretirement benefits on their balance sheets on an accrual basis, similar to the accounting required under *SFAS No. 158*. As indicated in the text discussion, some states do not like that recommendation and have proposed legislation that will allow them to ignore GASB standards. However, the GASB, with the support of users of government reports, has pushed for the change. They are concerned that without the new requirements, governments will continue to misrepresent the true cost of their retirement-related promises to public employees. In their view, the new accounting rules are in the best interests of municipal bondholders and the public in general.[12] Thus, it appears that the FASB is not the only standard-setter subject to political pressure.

[12]R.H. Attmore, "Who Do Texas Elected Officials Think They Are Fooling?" *The Bond Buyer* (June 18, 2007). For more information on the GASB, go to *www.gasb.org/*.

KEY TERMS

accumulated
   postretirement benefit
   obligation (APBO), *1056*
attribution period, *1056*
corridor approach, *1059*
expected postretirement
   benefit obligation
   (EPBO), *1056*

SUMMARY OF LEARNING OBJECTIVES FOR APPENDIX 20A

10. Identify the differences between pensions and postretirement healthcare benefits. Pension plans are generally funded, but healthcare benefit plans are not. Pension benefits are generally well-defined and level in amount; healthcare benefits are generally uncapped and variable. Pension benefits are payable monthly; healthcare benefits are paid as needed and used. Pension plan variables are reasonably predictable, whereas healthcare plan variables are difficult to predict.

11. Contrast accounting for pensions to accounting for other postretirement benefits. Many of the basic concepts, accounting terminology, and measurement methodology that apply to pensions also apply to other postretirement benefit accounting. Because other postretirement benefit plans are unfunded, large obligations can occur. Two significant concepts peculiar to accounting for other postretirement benefits are (a) expected postretirement benefit obligation (EPBO), and (b) accumulated postretirement benefit obligation (APBO).

Note: All **asterisked** Questions, Brief Exercises, Exercises, and Problems relate to material covered in the appendix to the chapter.

QUESTIONS

1. What is a private pension plan? How does a contributory pension plan differ from a noncontributory plan?

2. Differentiate between a defined contribution pension plan and a defined benefit pension plan. Explain how the employer's obligation differs between the two types of plans.

3. Differentiate between "accounting for the employer" and "accounting for the pension fund."

4. The meaning of the term "fund" depends on the context in which it is used. Explain its meaning when used as a noun. Explain its meaning when it is used as a verb.

5. What is the role of an actuary relative to pension plans? What are actuarial assumptions?

6. What factors must be considered by the actuary in measuring the amount of pension benefits under a defined benefit plan?

7. Name three approaches to measuring benefit obligations from a pension plan and explain how they differ.

8. Explain how cash-basis accounting for pension plans differs from accrual-basis accounting for pension plans. Why is cash-basis accounting generally considered unacceptable for pension plan accounting?

9. Identify the five components that comprise pension expense. Briefly explain the nature of each component.

10. What is service cost, and what is the basis of its measurement?

11. In computing the interest component of pension expense, what interest rates may be used?

12. Explain the difference between service cost and prior service cost.

13. What is meant by "prior service cost"? When is prior service cost recognized as pension expense?

14. What are "liability gains and losses," and how are they accounted for?

15. If pension expense recognized in a period exceeds the current amount funded by the employer, what kind of account arises, and how should it be reported in the financial statements? If the reverse occurs—that is, current funding by the employer exceeds the amount recognized as pension expense—what kind of account arises, and how should it be reported?

16. Given the following items and amounts, compute the actual return on plan assets: fair value of plan assets at the beginning of the period $9,200,000; benefits paid during the period $1,400,000; contributions made during the period $1,000,000; and fair value of the plan assets at the end of the period $10,150,000.

17. How does an "asset gain or loss" develop in pension accounting? How does a "liability gain or loss" develop in pension accounting?

18. What is the meaning of "corridor amortization"?

19. At the end of the current period, Jacob Inc. had a projected benefit obligation of $400,000 and pension plan assets (at fair value) of $300,000. What are the accounts and amounts that will be reported on the company's balance sheet as pension assets or pension liabilities?

20. At the end of the current year, Joshua Co. has prior service cost of $9,150,000. Where should the prior service cost be reported on the balance sheet?

21. Describe the accounting for actuarial gains and losses.

22. Agar Company reported net income of $25,000 in 2009. It had the following amounts related to its pension plan in 2009: Actuarial liability gain $10,000; Unexpected asset loss $13,000; Accumulated other comprehensive income (G/L) (beginning balance), zero. Determine for 2009 (a) Agar's other comprehensive income, and (b) comprehensive income.

23. Describe the reporting of pension plans for a company with multiple plans, some of which are underfunded and some of which are overfunded.

24. Determine the meaning of the following terms.

    (a) Contributory plan.

    (b) Vested benefits.

    (c) Retroactive benefits.

    (d) Years-of-service method.

25. A headline in the *Wall Street Journal* stated, "Firms Increasingly Tap Their Pension Funds to Use Excess Assets." What is the accounting issue related to the use of these "excess assets" by companies?

*26. What are postretirement benefits other than pensions?

*27. Why didn't the FASB cover both types of postretirement benefits—pensions and healthcare—in the earlier pension accounting statement?

*28. What are the major differences between postretirement healthcare benefits and pension benefits?

*29. What is the difference between the APBO and the EPBO? What are the components of postretirement expense?

BRIEF EXERCISES

(LO 4) **BE20-1** **AMR Corporation** (parent company of **American Airlines**) reported the following for 2004 (in millions).

Service cost	$358
Interest on P.B.O.	567
Return on plan assets	569
Amortization of prior service cost	14
Amortization of net loss	58

Compute **AMR Corporation**'s 2004 pension expense.

(LO 4) **BE20-2** For Becker Corporation, year-end plan assets were $2,000,000. At the beginning of the year, plan assets were $1,680,000. During the year, contributions to the pension fund were $120,000, and benefits paid were $200,000. Compute Becker's actual return on plan assets.

(LO 5) **BE20-3** At January 1, 2011, Uddin Company had plan assets of $250,000 and a projected benefit obligation of the same amount. During 2011, service cost was $27,500, the settlement rate was 10%, actual and expected return on plan assets were $25,000, contributions were $20,000, and benefits paid were $17,500. Prepare a pension worksheet for Uddin Company for 2011.

(LO 4) **BE20-4** For 2004, **Campbell Soup Company** had pension expense of $43 million and contributed $65 million to the pension fund. Prepare Campbell Soup Company's journal entry to record pension expense and funding.

(LO 6) **BE20-5** Duesbury Corporation amended its pension plan on January 1, 2011, and granted $120,000 of prior service costs to its employees. The employees are expected to provide 2,000 service years in the future, with 350 service years in 2011. Compute prior service cost amortization for 2011.

(LO 9) **BE20-6** At December 31, 2011, Conway Corporation had a projected benefit obligation of $510,000, plan assets of $322,000, and prior service cost of $127,000 in accumulated other comprehensive income. Determine the pension asset/liability at December 31, 2011.

(LO 8) **BE20-7** Hunt Corporation had a projected benefit obligation of $3,100,000 and plan assets of $3,300,000 at January 1, 2011. Hunt also had a net actuarial loss of $475,000 in accumulated OCI at January 1, 2011. The average remaining service period of Hunt's employees is 7.5 years. Compute Hunt's minimum amortization of the actuarial loss.

(LO 9) **BE20-8** Judy O'Neill Corporation has the following balances at December 31, 2010.

Projected benefit obligation	$2,800,000
Plan assets at fair value	2,000,000
Accumulated OCI (PSC)	1,100,000

How should these balances be reported on O'Neill's balance sheet at December 31, 2010?

(LO 9) **BE20-9** DeMent Co. had the following amounts related to its pension plan in 2009.

Actuarial liability loss for 2009	$25,000
Unexpected asset gain for 2009	18,000
Accumulated other comprehensive income (G/L) (beginning balance)	7,000 Cr.

Determine for 2009: (a) DeMent's other comprehensive income, and (b) comprehensive income. Net income for 2009 is $26,000; no amortization of gain or loss is necessary in 2009.

(LO 9) **BE20-10** Depp Corp. has three defined-benefit pension plans as follows.

	Pension Assets (at Fair Value)	Projected Benefit Obligation
Plan X	$600,000	$500,000
Plan Y	900,000	720,000
Plan Z	550,000	700,000

How will Depp report these multiple plans in its financial statements?

(LO 10, 11) ***BE20-11** Caleb Corporation has the following information available concerning its postretirement benefit plan for 2011.

Service cost	$40,000
Interest cost	52,400
Actual and expected return on plan assets	26,900

Compute Caleb's 2011 postretirement expense.

(LO 10, 11) ***BE20-12** For 2011, Benjamin Inc. computed its annual postretirement expense as $240,900. Benjamin's contribution to the plan during 2011 was $160,000. Prepare Benjamin's 2011 entry to record postretirement expense.

EXERCISES

(LO 4, 6) **E20-1** **(Pension Expense, Journal Entries)** The following information is available for the pension plan of Kiley Company for the year 2010.

Actual and expected return on plan assets	$ 12,000
Benefits paid to retirees	40,000
Contributions (funding)	95,000
Interest/discount rate	10%
Prior service cost amortization	8,000
Projected benefit obligation, January 1, 2010	500,000
Service cost	60,000

Instructions
(a) Compute pension expense for the year 2010.
(b) Prepare the journal entry to record pension expense and the employer's contribution to the pension plan in 2010.

(LO 4, 6) **E20-2** **(Computation of Pension Expense)** Rebekah Company provides the following information about its defined benefit pension plan for the year 2011.

Service cost	$ 90,000
Contribution to the plan	105,000
Prior service cost amortization	10,000
Actual and expected return on plan assets	64,000
Benefits paid	40,000
Plan assets at January 1, 2011	640,000
Projected benefit obligation at January 1, 2011	800,000
Accumulated OCI (PSC) at January 1, 2011	150,000
Interest/discount (settlement) rate	10%

Instructions
Compute the pension expense for the year 2011.

(LO 5) **E20-3** **(Preparation of Pension Worksheet)** Using the information in E20-2 prepare a pension worksheet inserting January 1, 2011, balances, showing December 31, 2011, balances, and the journal entry recording pension expense.

(LO 5) **E20-4** **(Basic Pension Worksheet)** The following facts apply to the pension plan of Trudy Borke Inc. for the year 2011.

Plan assets, January 1, 2011	$490,000
Projected benefit obligation, January 1, 2011	490,000
Settlement rate	8.5%
Service cost	40,000
Contributions (funding)	30,000
Actual and expected return on plan assets	49,700
Benefits paid to retirees	33,400

Instructions
Using the preceding data, compute pension expense for the year 2011. As part of your solution, prepare a pension worksheet that shows the journal entry for pension expense for 2011 and the year-end balances in the related pension accounts.

(LO 6) **E20-5** **(Application of Years-of-Service Method)** Valente Company has five employees participating in its defined benefit pension plan. Expected years of future service for these employees at the beginning of 2011 are as follows.

Employee	Future Years of Service
Ed	3
Paul	4
Mary	6
Dave	6
Caroline	6

On January 1, 2011, the company amended its pension plan increasing its projected benefit obligation by $60,000.

Instructions

Compute the amount of prior service cost amortization for the years 2011 through 2016 using the years-of-service method setting up appropriate schedules.

(LO 4)   **E20-6 (Computation of Actual Return)** James Paul Importers provides the following pension plan information.

Fair value of pension plan assets, January 1, 2011	$2,300,000
Fair value of pension plan assets, December 31, 2011	2,725,000
Contributions to the plan in 2011	250,000
Benefits paid retirees in 2011	350,000

Instructions

From the data above, compute the actual return on the plan assets for 2011.

(LO 5, 6)   **E20-7 (Basic Pension Worksheet)** The following defined pension data of Doreen Corp. apply to the year 2011.

Projected benefit obligation, 1/1/11 (before amendment)	$560,000
Plan assets, 1/1/11	546,200
Pension liability	13,800
On January 1, 2011, Doreen Corp., through plan amendment, grants prior service benefits having a present value of	100,000
Settlement rate	9%
Service cost	58,000
Contributions (funding)	55,000
Actual (expected) return on plan assets	52,280
Benefits paid to retirees	40,000
Prior service cost amortization for 2011	17,000

Instructions

For 2011, prepare a pension worksheet for Doreen Corp. that shows the journal entry for pension expense and the year-end balances in the related pension accounts.

(LO 8)   **E20-8 (Application of the Corridor Approach)** Dougherty Corp. has beginning-of-the-year present values for its projected benefit obligation and market-related values for its pension plan assets.

	Projected Benefit Obligation	Plan Assets Value
2009	$2,000,000	$1,900,000
2010	2,400,000	2,500,000
2011	2,900,000	2,600,000
2012	3,600,000	3,000,000

The average remaining service life per employee in 2009 and 2010 is 10 years and in 2011 and 2012 is 12 years. The net gain or loss that occurred during each year is as follows: 2009, $280,000 loss; 2010, $90,000 loss; 2011, $10,000 loss; and 2012, $25,000 gain. (In working the solution the gains and losses must be aggregated to arrive at year-end balances.)

Instructions

Using the corridor approach, compute the amount of net gain or loss amortized and charged to pension expense in each of the four years, setting up an appropriate schedule.

(LO 9)   **E20-9 (Disclosures: Pension Expense and Other Comprehensive Income)** Mildred Enterprises provides the following information relative to its defined benefit pension plan.

Balances or Values at December 31, 2011

Projected benefit obligation	$2,737,000
Accumulated benefit obligation	1,980,000
Fair value of plan assets	2,278,329
Accumulated OCI (PSC)	205,000
Accumulated OCI—Net loss (1/1/11 balance, –0–)	45,680
Pension liability	207,991
Other pension plan data:	
Service cost for 2011	$ 94,000
Prior service cost amortization for 2011	45,000
Actual return on plan assets in 2011	130,000
Expected return on plan assets in 2011	175,680
Interest on January 1, 2011, projected benefit obligation	253,000
Contributions to plan in 2011	92,329
Benefits paid	140,000

Instructions

    (a) Prepare the note disclosing the components of pension expense for the year 2011.

    (b) Determine the amounts of other comprehensive income and comprehensive income for 2011. Net income for 2011 is $35,000.

    (c) Compute the amount of accumulated other comprehensive income reported at December 31, 2011.

(LO 5) **E20-10** **(Pension Worksheet)** Buhl Corp. sponsors a defined benefit pension plan for its employees. On January 1, 2011, the following balances relate to this plan.

Plan assets	$480,000
Projected benefit obligation	625,000
Pension asset/liability	145,000
Accumulated OCI (PSC)	100,000

As a result of the operation of the plan during 2011, the following additional data are provided by the actuary.

Service cost for 2011	$90,000
Settlement rate, 9%	
Actual return on plan assets in 2011	57,000
Amortization of prior service cost	19,000
Expected return on plan assets	52,000
Unexpected loss from change in projected benefit obligation,	
due to change in actuarial predictions	76,000
Contributions in 2011	99,000
Benefits paid retirees in 2011	85,000

Instructions

    (a) Using the data above, compute pension expense for Buhl Corp. for the year 2011 by preparing a pension worksheet.

    (b) Prepare the journal entry for pension expense for 2011.

(LO 4, 5, 9) **E20-11** **(Pension Expense, Journal Entries, Statement Presentation)** Griseta Company sponsors a defined benefit pension plan for its employees. The following data relate to the operation of the plan for the year 2010 in which no benefits were paid.

    1. The actuarial present value of future benefits earned by employees for services rendered in 2010 amounted to $56,000.

    2. The company's funding policy requires a contribution to the pension trustee amounting to $145,000 for 2010.

    3. As of January 1, 2010, the company had a projected benefit obligation of $1,000,000, an accumulated benefit obligation of $800,000, and a balance of $400,000 in accumulated OCI (PSC) of $400,000. The fair value of pension plan assets amounted to $600,000 at the beginning of the year. The actual and expected return on plan assets was $54,000. The settlement rate was 9%. No gains or losses occurred in 2010 and no benefits were paid.

    4. Amortization of prior service cost was $40,000 in 2010. Amortization of net gain or loss was not required in 2010.

Instructions

    (a) Determine the amounts of the components of pension expense that should be recognized by the company in 2010.

    (b) Prepare the journal entry or entries to record pension expense and the employer's contribution to the pension trustee in 2010.

    (c) Indicate the amounts that would be reported on the income statement and the balance sheet for the year 2010.

(LO 4, 6, 7, 8, 9) **E20-12** **(Pension Expense, Journal Entries, Statement Presentation)** Nellie Altom Company received the following selected information from its pension plan trustee concerning the operation of the company's defined benefit pension plan for the year ended December 31, 2010.

	January 1, 2010	December 31, 2010
Projected benefit obligation	$2,000,000	$2,077,000
Market-related and fair value of plan assets	800,000	1,130,000
Accumulated benefit obligation	1,600,000	1,720,000
Accumulated OCI (G/L)—Net gain	–0–	(200,000)

The service cost component of pension expense for employee services rendered in the current year amounted to $77,000 and the amortization of prior service cost was $115,000. The company's actual funding (contributions) of the plan in 2010 amounted to $250,000. The expected return on plan assets and the actual rate were both 10%; the interest/discount (settlement) rate was 10%. Accumulated other comprehensive income (PSC) had a balance of $1,200,000 on January 1, 2010. Assume no benefits paid in 2010.

Instructions

(a) Determine the amounts of the components of pension expense that should be recognized by the company in 2010.

(b) Prepare the journal entry to record pension expense and the employer's contribution to the pension plan in 2010.

(c) Indicate the pension-related amounts that would be reported on the income statement and the balance sheet for Nellie Altom Company for the year 2010.

(LO 4, 6, 7, 8, 9) **E20-13 (Computation of Actual Return, Gains and Losses, Corridor Test, and Pension Expense)** Linda Berstler Company sponsors a defined benefit pension plan. The corporation's actuary provides the following information about the plan.

	January 1, 2011	December 31, 2011
Vested benefit obligation	$1,500	$1,900
Accumulated benefit obligation	1,900	2,730
Projected benefit obligation	2,800	3,645
Plan assets (fair value)	1,700	2,620
Settlement rate and expected rate of return		10%
Pension asset/liability	1,100	?
Service cost for the year 2011		400
Contributions (funding in 2011)		800
Benefits paid in 2011		200

Instructions

(a) Compute the actual return on the plan assets in 2011.

(b) Compute the amount of the other comprehensive income (G/L) as of December 31, 2011. (Assume the January 1, 2011, balance was zero.)

(c) Compute the amount of net gain or loss amortization for 2011 (corridor approach).

(d) Compute pension expense for 2011.

(LO 5) **E20-14 (Worksheet for E20-13)** Using the information in E20-13 about Linda Berstler Company's defined benefit pension plan, prepare a 2011 pension worksheet with supplementary schedules of computations. Prepare the journal entries at December 31, 2011, to record pension expense and related pension transactions. Also, indicate the pension amounts reported in the balance sheet.

(LO 4) **E20-15 (Pension Expense, Journal Entries)** Walker Company provides the following selected information related to its defined benefit pension plan for 2010.

Pension asset/liability (January 1)	$ 25,000 Cr.
Accumulated benefit obligation (December 31)	400,000
Actual and expected return on plan assets	15,000
Contributions (funding) in 2010	150,000
Fair value of plan assets (December 31)	800,000
Settlement rate	10%
Projected benefit obligation (January 1)	700,000
Service cost	90,000

Instructions

(a) Compute pension expense and prepare the journal entry to record pension expense and the employer's contribution to the pension plan in 2010.

(b) Indicate the pension-related amounts that would be reported in the company's income statement and balance sheet for 2010.

(LO 8) **E20-16 (Amortization of Accumulated OCI (G/L), Corridor Approach, Pension Expense Computation)** The actuary for the pension plan of Joyce Bush Inc. calculated the following net gains and losses.

Incurred during the Year	(Gain) or Loss
2010	$300,000
2011	480,000
2012	(210,000)
2013	(290,000)

Other information about the company's pension obligation and plan assets is as follows.

As of January 1,	Projected Benefit Obligation	Plan Assets (market-related asset value)
2010	$4,000,000	$2,400,000
2011	4,520,000	2,200,000
2012	4,980,000	2,600,000
2013	4,250,000	3,040,000

Joyce Bush Inc. has a stable labor force of 400 employees who are expected to receive benefits under the plan. The total service-years for all participating employees is 5,600. The beginning balance of accumulated OCI (G/L) is zero on January 1, 2010. The market-related value and the fair value of plan assets are the same for the 4-year period. Use the average remaining service life per employee as the basis for amortization.

Instructions
(Round to the nearest dollar)
Prepare a schedule which reflects the minimum amount of accumulated OCI (G/L) amortized as a component of net periodic pension expense for each of the years 2010, 2011, 2012, and 2013. Apply the "corridor" approach in determining the amount to be amortized each year.

(LO 8)   **E20-17   (Amortization of Accumulated OCI Balances)**   Lowell Company sponsors a defined benefit pension plan for its 600 employees. The company's actuary provided the following information about the plan.

	January 1, 2010	December 31, 2010	December 31, 2011
Projected benefit obligation	$2,800,000	$3,650,000	$4,400,000
Accumulated benefit obligation	1,900,000	2,430,000	2,900,000
Plan assets (fair value and market related asset value)	1,700,000	2,900,000	2,100,000
Accumulated net (gain) or loss (for purposes of the corridor calculation)	–0–	101,000	(24,000)
Discount rate (current settlement rate)	11%	8%	
Actual and expected asset return rate	10%	10%	

The average remaining service life per employee is 10.5 years. The service cost component of net periodic pension expense for employee services rendered amounted to $400,000 in 2010 and $475,000 in 2011. The accumulated OCI (PSC) on January 1, 2010, was $1,155,000. No benefits have been paid.

Instructions
(Round to the nearest dollar)
   (a)   Compute the amount of accumulated OCI (PSC) to be amortized as a component of net periodic pension expense for each of the years 2010 and 2011.
   (b)   Prepare a schedule which reflects the amount of accumulated OCI (G/L) to be amortized as a component of pension expense for 2010 and 2011.
   (c)   Determine the total amount of pension expense to be recognized by Lowell Company in 2010 and 2011.

(LO 5, 8)   **E20-18   (Pension Worksheet—Missing Amounts)**   The accounting staff of Henin Inc. has prepared the following pension worksheet. Unfortunately, several entries in the worksheet are not decipherable. The company has asked your assistance in completing the worksheet and completing the accounting tasks related to the pension plan for 2011.

Pension Worksheet—Henin Inc.

	A	B	C	D	E	F	H	I
1				General Journal Entries			Memo Record	
2	Items	Annual Pension Expense	Cash	OCI—Prior Service Cost	OCI— Gain/Losse	Pension Asset/Liability	Projected Benefit Obligation	Plan Assets
3	Balance, Jan. 1, 2011					1,100 Cr.	2,800	1,700
4	Service cost	(1)					400	
5	Interest cost	(2)					280	
6	Actual return	(3)						320
7	Unexpected gain	150			(4)			
8	Amortization of PSC	(5)		55				
9	Contributions		800					800
10	Benefits						200	200
11	Liability increase				(6)		365	
12	Journal entry	(7)	(8)	(9)	(10)	(11)		
13								
14	Accumulated OCI, Dec. 31, 2010			1,100	0			
15	Balance, Dec. 31, 2011			1,045	215	1,025	3,645	2,620
16								

Sheet1 / Sheet2 / Sheet3

Instructions

(a) Determine the missing amounts in the 2011 pension worksheet, indicating whether the amounts are debits or credits.

(b) Prepare the journal entry to record 2011 pension expense for Henin Inc.

(c) The accounting staff has heard of a pension accounting procedure called "corridor amortization." Is Henin required to record any amounts for corridor amortization in (1) 2011? In (2) 2012? Explain.

(LO 10, 11) *E20-19 **(Postretirement Benefit Expense Computation)** Ankiel Co. provides the following information about its postretirement benefit plan for the year 2010.

Service cost	$ 45,000
Contribution to the plan	10,000
Actual and expected return on plan assets	12,000
Benefits paid	20,000
Plan assets at January 1, 2010	110,000
Accumulated postretirement benefit obligation at January 1, 2010	430,000
Discount rate	8%

Instructions

Compute the postretirement benefit expense for 2010.

(LO 10, 11) *E20-20 **(Postretirement Benefit Worksheet)** Using the information in *E20-19, prepare a worksheet inserting January 1, 2010, balances, and showing December 31, 2010, balances. Prepare the journal entry recording postretirement benefit expense.

(LO 10, 11) *E20-21 **(Postretirement Benefit Expense Computation)** Chance Inc. provides the following information related to its postretirement benefits for the year 2012.

Accumulated postretirement benefit obligation at January 1, 2012	$810,000
Actual and expected return on plan assets	34,000
Prior service cost amortization	21,000
Discount rate	10%
Service cost	88,000

Instructions

Compute postretirement benefit expense for 2012.

(LO 10, *E20-22 (Postretirement Benefit Expense Computation) Marvelous Marvin Co. provides the following
11) information about its postretirement benefit plan for the year 2011.

Service cost	$ 90,000
Prior service cost amortization	3,000
Contribution to the plan	16,000
Actual and expected return on plan assets	62,000
Benefits paid	40,000
Plan assets at January 1, 2011	710,000
Accumulated postretirement benefit obligation at January 1, 2011	810,000
Accumulated OCI (PSC) at January 1, 2011	100,000 Dr.
Discount rate	9%

Instructions

Compute the postretirement benefit expense for 2011.

(LO 10, *E20-23 (Postretirement Benefit Worksheet) Using the information in *E20-22 prepare a worksheet in-
11) serting January 1, 2011, balances, showing December 31, 2011, balances, and the journal entry recording
postretirement benefit expense.

(LO 10, *E20-24 (Postretirement Benefit Worksheet—Missing Amounts) The accounting staff of Hewitt Inc.
11) has prepared the following postretirement benefit worksheet. Unfortunately, several entries in the worksheet are not decipherable. The company has asked your assistance in completing the worksheet and completing the accounting tasks related to the pension plan for 2010.

	Postretirement Benefits Worksheet—Hewitt Inc.						
	A	B	C	D	E	G	H
1		General Journal Entries				Memo Record	
2	Items	Annual Expense	Cash	Other Comprehensive Income—PSC	Postretirement Asset/Liability	APBO	Plan Assets
3	Balance, Jan. 1, 2010				390,000	410,000	20,000
4	Service cost	(1)				56,000	
5	Interest cost	(2)				36,900	
6	Actual/Expected return	(3)					2,000
7	Contributions		16,000				(4)
8	Benefits					5,000	5,000
9	Amortization of PSC	3,000		(5)			
10	Journal entry for 2010	(6)	(7)	(8)	(9)		
11							
12	Accumulated OCI, Dec. 31, 2009			30,000 Dr.			
13	Balance, Dec. 31, 2010			27,000 Dr.	464,900 Cr.	497,900 Cr.	33,000 Dr.
14							

Sheet1 / Sheet2 / Sheet3 /

Instructions
  (a) Determine the missing amounts in the 2010 pension worksheet, indicating whether the amounts
are debits or credits.
  (b) Prepare the journal entry to record 2010 pension expense for Hewitt Inc.
  (c) What discount rate is Hewitt using in accounting for the interest on its other postretirement benefit plan? Explain.

See the book's website, www.wiley.com/college/kieso, for Additional Exercises.

PROBLEMS

(LO 5, 6, 7, 9) **P20-1 (2-Year Worksheet)** On January 1, 2011, Diana Peter Company has the following defined benefit pension plan balances.

Projected benefit obligation	$4,200,000
Fair value of plan assets	4,200,000

The interest (settlement) rate applicable to the plan is 10%. On January 1, 2012, the company amends its pension agreement so that prior service costs of $500,000 are created. Other data related to the pension plan are as follows.

	2011	2012
Service costs	$150,000	$180,000
Prior service costs amortization	–0–	90,000
Contributions (funding) to the plan	140,000	185,000
Benefits paid	200,000	280,000
Actual return on plan assets	252,000	260,000
Expected rate of return on assets	6%	8%

Instructions
(a) Prepare a pension worksheet for the pension plan for 2011 and 2012.
(b) For 2012, prepare the journal entry to record pension-related amounts.

(LO 5, 6, 7, 9) **P20-2 (3-Year Worksheet, Journal Entries, and Reporting)** Katie Day Company adopts acceptable accounting for its defined benefit pension plan on January 1, 2011, with the following beginning balances: plan assets $200,000; projected benefit obligation $200,000. Other data relating to 3 years' operation of the plan are as follows.

	2011	2012	2013
Annual service cost	$16,000	$ 19,000	$ 26,000
Settlement rate and expected rate of return	10%	10%	10%
Actual return on plan assets	17,000	21,900	24,000
Annual funding (contributions)	16,000	40,000	48,000
Benefits paid	14,000	16,400	21,000
Prior service cost (plan amended, 1/1/12)		160,000	
Amortization of prior service cost		54,400	41,600
Change in actuarial assumptions establishes a December 31, 2013, projected benefit obligation of:			520,000

Instructions
(a) Prepare a pension worksheet presenting all 3 years' pension balances and activities.
(b) Prepare the journal entries (from the worksheet) to reflect all pension plan transactions and events at December 31 of each year.
(c) Indicate the pension-related amounts reported in the financial statements for 2013.

(LO 6, 7, 8, 9) **P20-3 (Pension Expense, Journal Entries, Amortization of Loss)** Paul Dobson Company sponsors a defined benefit plan for its 100 employees. On January 1, 2010, the company's actuary provided the following information.

Accumulated other comprehensive loss (PSC)	$150,000
Pension plan assets (fair value and market-related asset value)	200,000
Accumulated benefit obligation	260,000
Projected benefit obligation	350,000

The average remaining service period for the participating employees is 10.5 years. All employees are expected to receive benefits under the plan. On December 31, 2010, the actuary calculated that the present value of future benefits earned for employee services rendered in the current year amounted to $52,000; the projected benefit obligation was $452,000; fair value of pension assets was $276,000; the accumulated benefit obligation amounted to $365,000. The expected return on plan assets and the discount rate on the projected benefit obligation were both 10%. The actual return on plan assets is $11,000. The company's current year's contribution to the pension plan amounted to $65,000. No benefits were paid during the year.

Instructions
(Round to the nearest dollar)

(a) Determine the components of pension expense that the company would recognize in 2010. (With only one year involved, you need not prepare a worksheet.)

(b) Prepare the journal entry to record the pension expense and the company's funding of the pension plan in 2010.

(c) Compute the amount of the 2010 increase/decrease in gains or losses and the amount to be amortized in 2010 and 2011.

(d) Indicate the pension amounts reported in the financial statement as of December 31, 2010.

(LO 5, 6, 7, 8)

P20-4 **(Pension Expense, Journal Entries for 2 Years)** Mantle Company sponsors a defined benefit pension plan. The following information related to the pension plan is available for 2010 and 2011.

	2010	2011
Plan assets (fair value), December 31	$694,000	$844,000
Projected benefit obligation, January 1	600,000	700,000
Pension asset/liability, January 1	40,000 Cr.	?
Prior service cost, January 1	250,000	240,000
Service cost	60,000	90,000
Actual and expected return on plan assets	24,000	30,000
Amortization of prior service cost	10,000	12,000
Contributions (funding)	110,000	120,000
Accumulated benefit obligation, December 31	500,000	550,000
Interest/settlement rate	9%	9%

Instructions

(a) Compute pension expense for 2010 and 2011.

(b) Prepare the journal entries to record the pension expense and the company's funding of the pension plan for both years.

(LO 7, 8)

P20-5 **(Computation of Pension Expense, Amortization of Net Gain or Loss–Corridor Approach, Journal Entries for 3 Years)** Dubel Toothpaste Company initiates a defined benefit pension plan for its 50 employees on January 1, 2010. The insurance company which administers the pension plan provided the following selected information for the years 2010, 2011, and 2012.

	For Year Ended December 31,		
	2010	2011	2012
Plan assets (fair value)	$50,000	$ 85,000	$170,000
Accumulated benefit obligation	45,000	165,000	292,000
Projected benefit obligation	55,000	200,000	324,000
Net (gain) loss (for purposes of corridor calculation)	–0–	83,950	86,121
Employer's funding contribution (made at end of year)	50,000	60,000	95,000

There were no balances as of January 1, 2010, when the plan was initiated. The actual and expected return on plan assets was 10% over the 3-year period but the settlement rate used to discount the company's pension obligation was 13% in 2010, 11% in 2011, and 8% in 2012. The service cost component of net periodic pension expense amounted to the following: 2010, $55,000; 2011, $85,000; and 2012, $119,000. The average remaining service life per employee is 12 years. No benefits were paid in 2010, $30,000 of benefits were paid in 2011, and $18,500 of benefits were paid in 2012 (all benefits paid at end of year).

Instructions
(Round to the nearest dollar)

(a) Calculate the amount of net periodic pension expense that the company would recognize in 2010, 2011, and 2012.

(b) Prepare the journal entries to record net periodic pension expense, employer's funding contribution, and related pension amounts for the years 2010, 2011, and 2012.

(LO 6, 7, 8) **P20-6 (Computation of Prior Service Cost Amortization, Pension Expense, Journal Entries, and Net Gain or Loss)** Widjaja Inc. has sponsored a noncontributory-defined benefit pension plan for its employees since 1987. Prior to 2010, cumulative net pension expense recognized equaled cumulative contributions to the plan. Other relevant information about the pension plan on January 1, 2010, is as follows.

1. The company has 200 employees. All these employees are expected to receive benefits under the plan. The average remaining service life per employee is 13 years.
2. The projected benefit obligation amounted to $5,000,000 and the fair value of pension plan assets was $3,000,000. The market-related asset value was also $3,000,000. Unrecognized prior service cost was $2,000,000.

On December 31, 2010, the projected benefit obligation and the accumulated benefit obligation were $4,750,000 and $4,025,000, respectively. The fair value of the pension plan assets amounted to $3,900,000 at the end of the year. A 10% settlement rate and a 10% expected asset return rate were used in the actuarial present value computations in the pension plan. The present value of benefits attributed by the pension benefit formula to employee service in 2010 amounted to $200,000. The employer's contribution to the plan assets amounted to $575,000 in 2010. This problem assumes no payment of pension benefits.

Instructions

(Round all amounts to the nearest dollar)

(a) Prepare a schedule, based on the average remaining life per employee, showing the prior service cost that would be amortized as a component of pension expense for 2010, 2011, and 2012.
(b) Compute pension expense for the year 2010.
(c) Prepare the journal entries required to report the accounting for the company's pension plan for 2010.
(d) Compute the amount of the 2010 increase/decrease in net gains or losses and the amount to be amortized in 2010 and 2011.

(LO 5, 6, 7) **P20-7 (Pension Worksheet)** Farber Corp. sponsors a defined benefit pension plan for its employees. On January 1, 2012, the following balances related to this plan.

Plan assets (market-related value)	$520,000
Projected benefit obligation	725,000
Pension asset/liability	205,000 Cr.
Prior service cost	81,000
Net gain or loss (debit)	91,000

As a result of the operation of the plan during 2012, the actuary provided the following additional data at December 31, 2012.

Service cost for 2012	$108,000
Settlement rate, 9%; expected return rate, 10%	
Actual return on plan assets in 2012	48,000
Amortization of prior service cost	25,000
Contributions in 2012	138,000
Benefits paid retirees in 2012	85,000
Average remaining service life of active employees	10 years

Instructions

Using the preceding data, compute pension expense for Farber Corp. for the year 2012 by preparing a pension worksheet that shows the journal entry for pension expense. Use the market-related asset value to compute the expected return and for corridor amortization.

(LO 5, 6, 7, 8, 9) **P20-8 (Comprehensive 2-Year Worksheet)** Glesen Company sponsors a defined benefit pension plan for its employees. The following data relate to the operation of the plan for the years 2011 and 2012.

	2011	2012
Projected benefit obligation, January 1	$650,000	
Plan assets (fair value and market related value), January 1	410,000	
Pension asset/liability, January 1	240,000 Cr.	
Prior service cost, January 1	160,000	
Service cost	40,000	$ 59,000
Settlement rate	10%	10%
Expected rate of return	10%	10%
Actual return on plan assets	36,000	61,000
Amortization of prior service cost	70,000	55,000

Annual contributions	72,000	81,000
Benefits paid retirees	31,500	54,000
Increase in projected benefit obligation due to changes in actuarial assumptions	87,000	–0–
Accumulated benefit obligation at December 31	721,800	789,000
Average service life of all employees		20 years
Vested benefit obligation at December 31		464,000

Instructions

(a) Prepare a pension worksheet presenting both years 2011 and 2012 and accompanying computations and amortization of the loss (2012) using the corridor approach.

(b) Prepare the journal entries (from the worksheet) to reflect all pension plan transactions and events at December 31 of each year.

(c) For 2012, indicate the pension amounts reported in the financial statements.

(LO 5, 6, 7) **P20-9 (Comprehensive 2-Year Worksheet)** Mount Co. has the following defined benefit pension plan balances on January 1, 2009.

Projected benefit obligation	$4,500,000
Fair value of plan assets	4,500,000

The interest (settlement) rate applicable to the plan is 10%. On January 1, 2010, the company amends its pension agreement so that prior service costs of $600,000 are created. Other data related to the pension plan are:

	2009	2010
Service costs	$150,000	$170,000
Prior service costs amortization	–0–	90,000
Contributions (funding) to the plan	150,000	184,658
Benefits paid	220,000	280,000
Actual return on plan assets	252,000	250,000
Expected rate of return on assets	6%	8%

Instructions

(a) Prepare a pension worksheet for the pension plan in 2009.

(b) Prepare any journal entries related to the pension plan that would be needed at December 31, 2009.

(c) Prepare a pension worksheet for 2010 and any journal entries related to the pension plan as of December 31, 2010.

(d) Indicate the pension-related amounts reported in the 2010 financial statements.

(LO 5, 6, 7) **P20-10 (Pension Worksheet – Missing Amounts)** Enyart Co. has prepared the following pension worksheet. Unfortunately, several entries in the worksheet are not decipherable. The company has asked your assistance in completing the worksheet and completing the accounting tasks related to the pension plan for 2011.

Pension Worksheet—Enyart Co.

	General Journal Entries					Memo Record	
Items	Annual Pension Expense	Cash	OCI–Prior Service Cost	OCI–Gain/Loss	Pension Asset/Liability	Projected Benefit Obligation	Plan Assets
Balance, Jan. 1, 2011					120,000	325,000	205,000 Dr.
Service cost	(1)					20,000	
Interest cost	(2)					32,500	
Actual return	(3)						18,000 Dr.
Unexpected loss	2,500			(4)			
Amortization of PSC	(5)		35,000				
Contributions		36,000					36,000 Dr.
Benefits						15,000	15,000 Cr.
Increase in PBO				(6)		43,500	
Journal entry for 2011	(7)	(8)	(9)	(10)	(11)		
Accumulated OCI, Dec. 31, 2010			80,000	0			
Balance, Dec. 31, 2011			45,000	46,000	162,000 Cr.	406,000 Cr.	244,000 Dr.

Instructions

(a) Determine the missing amounts in the 2011 pension worksheet, indicating whether the amounts are debits or credits.

(b) Prepare the journal entry to record 2011 pension expense for Enyart Co.

(c) Determine the following for Enyart for 2011: **(1)** settlement rate used to measure the interest on the liability and **(2)** expected return on plan assets.

(LO 5, 6, 7, 8, 9)

P20-11 (Pension Worksheet) The following data relate to the operation of Enyart Co.'s pension plan in 2012. The pension worksheet for 2011 is provided in P20-10.

Service cost	$59,000
Actual return on plan assets	32,000
Amortization of prior service cost	24,000
Annual contributions	41,000
Benefits paid retirees	27,000
Average service life of all employees	20 years

For 2012, Enyart will use the same assumptions as 2011 for the settlement rate and the expected rate of return on plan assets.

Instructions

(a) Prepare a pension worksheet for 2012 and accompanying computations and amortization of the loss, if any, in 2012 using the corridor approach.

(b) Prepare the journal entries (from the worksheet) to reflect all pension plan transactions and events at December 31.

(c) Indicate the pension amounts reported in the financial statements.

(LO 5, 6, 7, 8, 9)

P20-12 (Pension Worksheet) Cramer Corp. sponsors a defined-benefit pension plan for its employees. On January 1, 2012, the following balances related to this plan.

Plan assets (market-related value)	$270,000
Projected benefit obligation	360,000
Pension asset/liability	90,000 Cr.
Prior service cost	45,000
OCI—Loss	39,000

As a result of the operation of the plan during 2012, the actuary provided the following additional data at December 31, 2012.

Service cost for 2012	$ 54,000
Actual return on plan assets in 2012	27,000
Amortization of prior service cost	12,000
Contributions in 2012	70,000
Benefits paid retirees in 2012	41,000
Settlement rate	7%
Expected return on plan assets	8%
Average remaining service life of active employees	10 years

Instructions

(a) Compute pension expense for Cramer Corp. for the year 2012 by preparing a pension worksheet that shows the journal entry for pension expense.

(b) Indicate the pension amounts reported in the financial statements.

(LO 10, 11)

*P20-13 (Postretirement Benefit Worksheet) Dusty Hass Foods Inc. sponsors a postretirement medical and dental benefit plan for its employees. The company adopts the provisions of *Statement No. 106* beginning January 1, 2011. The following balances relate to this plan on January 1, 2011.

Plan assets	$200,000
Expected postretirement benefit obligation	820,000
Accumulated postretirement benefit obligation	200,000
No prior service costs exist.	

As a result of the plan's operation during 2011, the following additional data are provided by the actuary.

Service cost for 2011 is $70,000
Discount rate is 9%
Contributions to plan in 2011 are $60,000
Expected return on plan assets is $9,000
Actual return on plan assets is $15,000
Benefits paid to employees are $44,000
Average remaining service to full eligibility: 20 years

Instructions

(a) Using the preceding data, compute the net periodic postretirement benefit cost for 2011 by preparing a worksheet that shows the journal entry for postretirement expense and the year-end balances in the related postretirement benefit memo accounts. (Assume that contributions and benefits are paid at the end of the year.)

(b) Prepare any journal entries related to the postretirement plan for 2011 and indicate the postretirement amounts reported in the financial statements for 2011.

(LO 10, ***P20-14** **(Postretirement Benefit Worksheet—2 Years)** Embry Co. has the following postretirement ben-
11) efit plan balances on January 1, 2009.

Accumulated postretirement benefit obligation	$2,500,000
Fair value of plan assets	2,500,000

The interest (settlement) rate applicable to the plan is 10%. On January 1, 2010, the company amends the plan so that prior service costs of $175,000 are created. Other data related to the plan are:

	2009	2010
Service costs	$ 75,000	$ 85,000
Prior service costs amortization	–0–	15,000
Contributions (funding) to the plan	15,000	35,000
Benefits paid	40,000	45,000
Actual return on plan assets	140,000	120,000
Expected rate of return on assets	8%	6%

Instructions

(a) Prepare a worksheet for the postretirement plan in 2009.
(b) Prepare any journal entries related to the postretirement plan that would be needed at December 31, 2009.
(c) Prepare a worksheet for 2010 and any journal entries related to the postretirement plan as of December 31, 2010.
(d) Indicate the postretirement-benefit–related amounts reported in the 2010 financial statements.

CONCEPTS FOR ANALYSIS

CA20-1 (Pension Terminology and Theory) Many business organizations have been concerned with providing for the retirement of employees since the late 1800s. During recent decades a marked increase in this concern has resulted in the establishment of private pension plans in most large companies and in many medium- and small-sized ones.

The substantial growth of these plans, both in numbers of employees covered and in amounts of retirement benefits, has increased the significance of pension cost in relation to the financial position, results of operations, and cash flows of many companies. In examining the costs of pension plans, a CPA encounters certain terms. The components of pension costs that the terms represent must be dealt with appropriately if generally accepted accounting principles are to be reflected in the financial statements of entities with pension plans.

Instructions

(a) Define a private pension plan. How does a contributory pension plan differ from a noncontributory plan?
(b) Differentiate between "accounting for the employer" and "accounting for the pension fund."
(c) Explain the terms "funded" and "pension liability" as they relate to:
   (1) The pension fund.
   (2) The employer.
(d) **(1)** Discuss the theoretical justification for accrual recognition of pension costs.
   (2) Discuss the relative objectivity of the measurement process of accrual versus cash (pay-as-you-go) accounting for annual pension costs.
(e) Distinguish among the following as they relate to pension plans.
   (1) Service cost.
   (2) Prior service costs.
   (3) Vested benefits.

CA20-2 (Pension Terminology) The following items appear on Hollingsworth Company's financial statements.

   1. Under the caption Assets:
   Pension asset/liability.
   2. Under the caption Liabilities:
   Pension asset/liability.

3. Under the caption Stockholders' Equity:
   Prior service cost as a component of Accumulated Other Comprehensive Income.
4. On the income statement:
   Pension expense.

Instructions

Explain the significance of each of the items above on corporate financial statements. (*Note:* All items set forth above are not necessarily to be found on the statements of a single company.)

CA20-3 (Basic Terminology) In examining the costs of pension plans, Leah Hutcherson, CPA, encounters certain terms. The components of pension costs that the terms represent must be dealt with appropriately if generally accepted accounting principles are to be reflected in the financial statements of entities with pension plans.

Instructions

(a) (1) Discuss the theoretical justification for accrual recognition of pension costs.
    (2) Discuss the relative objectivity of the measurement process of accrual versus cash (pay-as-you-go) accounting for annual pension costs.
(b) Explain the following terms as they apply to accounting for pension plans.
    (1) Market-related asset value.
    (2) Projected benefit obligation.
    (3) Corridor approach.
(c) What information should be disclosed about a company's pension plans in its financial statements and its notes?

(AICPA adapted)

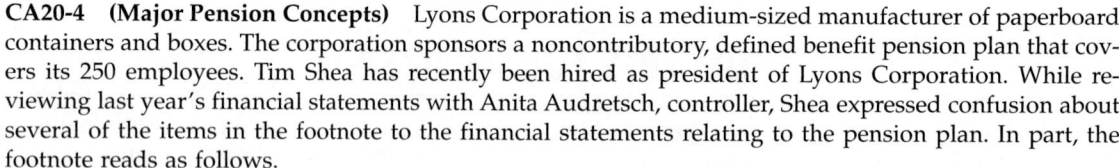 **CA20-4 (Major Pension Concepts)** Lyons Corporation is a medium-sized manufacturer of paperboard containers and boxes. The corporation sponsors a noncontributory, defined benefit pension plan that covers its 250 employees. Tim Shea has recently been hired as president of Lyons Corporation. While reviewing last year's financial statements with Anita Audretsch, controller, Shea expressed confusion about several of the items in the footnote to the financial statements relating to the pension plan. In part, the footnote reads as follows.

> **Note J.** The company has a defined benefit pension plan covering substantially all of its employees. The benefits are based on years of service and the employee's compensation during the last four years of employment. The company's funding policy is to contribute annually the maximum amount allowed under the federal tax code. Contributions are intended to provide for benefits expected to be earned in the future as well as those earned to date.

Effective for the year ending December 31, 2010, Lyons Corporation adopted the provisions of *Statement of Financial Accounting Standard No. 87*—Employer's Accounting for Pensions, as amended by *SFAS No. 158*. The net periodic pension expense on Lyons Corporation's comparative income statement was $72,000 in 2011 and $57,680 in 2010.

The following are selected figures from the plan's funded status and amounts recognized in the Lyons Corporation's Statement of Financial Position at December 31, 2011 ($000 omitted).

Actuarial present value of benefit obligations:	
Accumulated benefit obligation	
(including vested benefits of $636)	$ (870)
Projected benefit obligation	$(1,200)
Plan assets at fair value	1,050
Projected benefit obligation in	
excess of plan assets	$ (150)

Given that Lyons Corporation's work force has been stable for the last 6 years, Shea could not understand the increase in the net periodic pension expense. Audretsch explained that the net periodic pension expense consists of several elements, some of which may increase or decrease the net expense.

Instructions

(a) The determination of the net periodic pension expense is a function of five elements. List and briefly describe each of the elements.
(b) Describe the major difference and the major similarity between the accumulated benefit obligation and the projected benefit obligation.

(c) (1) Explain why pension gains and losses are not recognized on the income statement in the period in which they arise.

(2) Briefly describe how pension gains and losses are recognized.

(CMA adapted)

CA20-5 **(Implications of *FASB Statement No. 87*)** Ruth Moore and Carl Nies have to do a class presentation on the pension pronouncement "Employers' Accounting for Pension Plans." In developing the class presentation, they decided to provide the class with a series of questions related to pensions and then discuss the answers in class. Given that the class has all read *FASB Statement No. 87*, they felt this approach would provide a lively discussion. Here are the situations:

1. In an article in *Business Week* prior to *FASB No. 87*, it was reported that the discount rates used by the largest 200 companies for pension reporting ranged from 5% to 11%. How can such a situation exist, and does the pension pronouncement alleviate this problem?

2. An article indicated that when *FASB Statement No. 87* was issued, it caused an increase in the liability for pensions for approximately 20% of companies. Why might this situation occur?

3. A recent article noted that while "smoothing" is not necessarily an accounting virtue, pension accounting has long been recognized as an exception—an area of accounting in which at least some dampening of market swings is appropriate. This is because pension funds are managed so that their performance is insulated from the extremes of short-term market swings. A pension expense that reflects the volatility of market swings might, for that reason, convey information of little relevance. Are these statements true?

4. Understanding the impact of the changes required in pension reporting requires detailed information about its pension plan(s) and an analysis of the relationship of many factors, particularly:
   (a) the type of plan(s) and any significant amendments.
   (b) the plan participants.
   (c) the funding status.
   (d) the actuarial funding method and assumptions currently used.
   What impact does each of these items have on financial statement presentation?

5. An article noted "You also need to decide whether to amortize gains and losses using the corridor method, or to use some other systematic method. Under the corridor approach, only gains and losses in excess of 10% of the greater of the projected benefit obligation or the plan assets would have to be amortized." What is the corridor method and what is its purpose?

Instructions
What answers do you believe Ruth and Carl gave to each of these questions?

CA20-6 **(Gains and Losses, Corridor Amortization)** Rachel Avery, accounting clerk in the personnel office of Clarence G. Avery Corp., has begun to compute pension expense for 2010 but is not sure whether or not she should include the amortization of unrecognized gains/losses. She is currently working with the following beginning-of-the-year present values for the projected benefit obligation and market-related values for the pension plan:

	Projected Benefit Obligation	Plan Assets Value
2007	$2,200,000	$1,900,000
2008	2,400,000	2,600,000
2009	2,900,000	2,600,000
2010	3,900,000	3,000,000

The average remaining service life per employee in 2007 and 2008 is 10 years and in 2009 and 2010 is 12 years. The net gain or loss that occurred during each year is as follows.

2007	$280,000 loss
2008	90,000 loss
2009	12,000 loss
2010	25,000 gain

(In working the solution, you must aggregate the unrecognized gains and losses to arrive at year-end balances.)

Instructions
You are the manager in charge of accounting. Write a memo to Rachel Avery, explaining why in some years she must amortize some of the net gains and losses and in other years she does not need to. In order to explain this situation fully, you must compute the amount of net gain or loss that is amortized and charged to pension expense in each of the 4 years listed above. Include an appropriate amortization schedule, referring to it whenever necessary.

CA20-7 (Nonvested Employees—An Ethical Dilemma) Cardinal Technology recently merged with College Electronix, a computer graphics manufacturing firm. In performing a comprehensive audit of CE's accounting system, Richard Nye, internal audit manager for Cardinal Technology, discovered that the new subsidiary did not capitalize pension assets and liabilities, subject to the requirements of *FASB Statement No. 87*.

The net present value of CE's pension assets was $15.5 million, the vested benefit obligation was $12.9 million, and the projected benefit obligation was $17.4 million. Nye reported this audit finding to Renée Selma, the newly appointed controller of CE. A few days later Selma called Nye for his advice on what to do. Selma started her conversation by asking, "Can't we eliminate the negative income effect of our pension dilemma simply by terminating the employment of nonvested employees before the end of our fiscal year?"

Instructions
How should Nye respond to Selma's remark about firing nonvested employees?

USING YOUR JUDGMENT

Financial Reporting Problem

The Procter & Gamble Company (P&G)
The financial statements of P&G are presented in Appendix 5B or can be accessed on the KWW website.

Instructions
Refer to P&G's financial statements and the accompanying notes to answer the following questions.
(a) What kind of pension plan does P&G provide its employees in the United States?
(b) What was P&G's pension expense for 2004, 2003, and 2002 for the United States?
(c) What is the impact of P&G's pension plans for 2004 on its financial statements?
(d) What information does P&G provide on the target allocation of its pension assets? (Compare the asset allocation for "Pensions and Other Retiree Benefits.") How do the allocations relate to the expected returns on these assets?

*Financial Statement Analysis Case

General Electric
A *Wall Street Journal* article discussed a $1.8 billion charge to income made by **General Electric** for postretirement benefit costs. It was attributed to previously unrecognized health-care and life insurance cost. As financial vice president and controller for Peake, Inc., you found this article interesting because the president recently expressed interest in adopting a postemployment benefit program for Peake's employees, to complement the company's existing defined-benefit plan. The president, Martha Beyerlein, wants to know how the expense on the new plan will be determined and what impact the accounting for the plan will have on Peake's financial statements.

Instructions
(a) As financial vice president and controller of Peake, Inc., explain the calculation of postemployment benefit expense under *SFAS No. 106* and indicate how the accounting for the plan will affect Peake's financial statements.
(b) Discuss the similarities and differences in the accounting for the other postemployment benefit plan relative to the accounting for the defined-benefit plan.

Comparative Analysis Case

The Coca-Cola Company versus PepsiCo, Inc.
Instructions
Go to the KWW website and use information found there to answer the following questions related to **The Coca-Cola Company** and **PepsiCo, Inc.**
(a) What kind of pension plans do Coca-Cola and PepsiCo provide their employees?
(b) What net periodic pension expense (cost) did Coca-Cola and PepsiCo report in 2004?

(c) What is the year-end 2004 funded status of Coca-Cola's and PepsiCo's U.S. plans?

(d) What relevant rates were used by Coca-Cola and PepsiCo in computing their pension amounts?

(e) Compare the expected benefit payments and contributions for Coca-Cola and PepsiCo.

International Reporting Case

Kyowa Hakko Kogyo Co., Ltd., is an R&D–based company with special strengths in biotechnology. The company is dedicated to the creation of new value in the life sciences, especially in its two core business segments of pharmaceuticals and biochemicals, and strives to contribute to the health and well-being of people around the world. The company provided the following disclosures related to its retirement benefits in its 2005 annual report.

Kyowa Hakko Kogyo Co., Ltd.

Note 1. Basis of Presenting Consolidated Financial Statements (partial)
Kyowa Hakko Kogyo Co., Ltd. (the "Company") maintains its accounts and records in accordance with the provisions set forth in the Japanese Commercial Code and the Securities and Exchange Law and in conformity with generally accepted accounting principles and practices prevailing in Japan. . . . The Company's fiscal year is from April 1 to March 31. Therefore, "fiscal 2005" begins on April 1, 2004 and ends on March 31, 2005.

Reserve for Retirement Benefits to Employees
A reserve for retirement benefits to employees is provided at an amount equal to the present value of the projected benefit obligation less fair value of the plan assets at the year-end. Unrecognized prior service costs are amortized on a straight-line basis over five years from the year they occur. Unrecognized actuarial differences are amortized on a straight-line basis over ten years from the year after they occur.

Note 8. Reserve for Retirement Benefits to Employees
The Company and its domestic consolidated subsidiaries operate various defined benefit plans, including a corporate pension plan (the so-called cash-balanced plan), a group contributory plan, a tax-qualified pension plan and a severance payment plan.

(a) The reserve for retirement benefits as of March 31, 2005, is analyzed as follows.

	Millions of Yen 2005	Thousands of U.S. Dollars 2005
Projected benefit obligations	¥(63,854)	$(594,599)
Plan assets	31,270	291,182
Unfunded benefit obligations	(32,584)	(303,417)
Unrecognized actuarial differences	7,017	65,341
Unrecognized prior service costs (Note 2)	(5,004)	(46,597)
	¥(30,571)	$(284,673)

(b) The net periodic pension expense related to the retirement benefits for fiscal 2005 is as follows.

	Millions of Yen 2005	Thousands of U.S. Dollars 2005
Service cost	¥2,650	$24,676
Interest cost	1,583	14,741
Expected return on plan assets	(736)	(6, 854)
Amortization of unrecognized actuarial differences	1,628	15,160
Amortization of unrecognized prior service costs	(1,431)	(13,325)
	¥3,694	$34,398

(c) Assumptions used in calculation of the above information are as follows.

	2005
Discount rate	2.5%
Expected rate of return	2.8%

Instructions

Use the information on Kyowa to respond to the following requirements.

(a) What are the key differences in accounting for pensions under U.S. and Japanese standards?

(b) Briefly explain how differences in U.S. and Japanese standards for pensions would affect the amounts reported in the financial statements.

(c) In light of the differences identified above, would Kyowa's income and equity be higher or lower under U.S. GAAP compared to Japanese standards? Explain.

Research Cases

Case 1

Instructions

Examine the pension footnotes of three companies of your choice and answer the following questions.

(a) For each company, identify the following three assumptions: (1) the weighted-average discount rate, (2) the rate of compensation increase used to measure the projected benefit obligation, and (3) the weighted-average expected long-run rate of return on plan assets.

(b) Comment on any significant differences between the assumptions used by each company.

(c) Did any of the companies change their assumptions during the period covered by the footnote? If so, what was the effect on the financial statements?

Case 2

The June 15, 1999, *Wall Street Journal* included an article by Ellen E. Schultz entitled "Companies Reap a Gain off Fat Pension Plans."

Instructions

Read the article and answer the following questions.

(a) Explain how the high investment returns earned on pension plan assets in the late 1990s affected pension expense and net income. Given the down or "bear" market, what do you believe might happen to many companies' pension expense in the future?

(b) Explain what effect an overfunded pension plan can have on decisions made by management regarding various benefit costs.

(c) What is a major disadvantage of getting a pension plan too overfunded?

(d) What ethical issues are raised at the end of this article?

Professional Research: Financial Accounting and Reporting

Jack Kelly Company has grown rapidly since its founding in 2002. To instill loyalty in its employees, Kelly is contemplating establishment of a defined-benefit plan. Kelly knows that lenders and potential investors will pay close attention to the impact of the pension plan on the company's financial statements, particularly any gains or losses that develop in the plan. Kelly has asked you to conduct some research on the accounting for gains and losses in a defined-benefit plan.

Instructions

Using the **Financial Accounting Research System (FARS)**, respond to the following items. (Provide text strings used in your search.)

(a) Briefly describe how pension gains and losses are accounted for.

(b) Explain the rationale behind the accounting method described in part (a).

(c) Kelly wants to better understand the factors that led to accounting standards for pensions. What environmental factors led to increased regulations over pension cost reporting?

Professional Simulation

In this simulation you are asked to address questions related to the accounting for pensions. Prepare responses to all parts.

KWW_Professional _Simulation ▢ ▣ ❌

| Accounting for Pensions | Time Remaining 2 hours 20 minutes | copy | paste | calculator | sheet | standards | help | spliter | done |

| Directions | Situation | Measurement | Journal Entry | Disclosure | Resources |

Melanie Vail Corp. sponsors a defined benefit pension plan for its employees. On January 1, 2010, the following balances relate to this plan.

Plan assets	$480,000
Projected benefit obligation	625,000
Accumulated OCI (PSC)	100,000 Dr.

As a result of the operation of the plan during 2010, the following additional data are provided by the actuary.

Service cost for 2010	$90,000
Settlement rate	9%
Actual return on plan assets in 2010	57,000
Amortization of prior service cost	19,000
Expected return on plan assets	52,000
Unexpected loss from change in projected benefit obligation, due to change in actuarial predictions	76,000
Contributions in 2010	99,000
Benefits paid retirees in 2010	85,000

| Directions | Situation | Measurement | Journal Entry | Disclosure | Resources |

(a) Use a computer spreadsheet to prepare a pension worksheet. On the pension worksheet, compute pension expense, pension asset/liability, projected benefit obligation, plan assets, prior service cost, and net gain or loss.

(b) Compute the same items as in (a), assuming that the settlement rate is now 7% and the expected rate of return is 10%.

| Directions | Situation | Measurement | Journal Entry | Disclosure | Resources |

Prepare the journal entry to record pension expense in 2010.

| Directions | Situation | Measurement | Journal Entry | Disclosure | Resources |

Indicate the reporting of the 2010 pension amounts in the income statement and balance sheet.

Remember to check the book's companion website to find additional resources for this chapter.

CHAPTER TWENTY ONE

ACCOUNTING FOR LEASES

More Companies Ask, "Why Buy?"

Leasing has grown tremendously in popularity. Today it is the fastest growing form of capital investment. Instead of borrowing money to buy an airplane, computer, nuclear core, or satellite, a company makes periodic payments to lease these assets. Even gambling casinos lease their slot machines. Of the 600 companies surveyed by the AICPA in 2004, 575 disclosed lease data.[1]

A classic example is the airline industry. Many travelers on airlines such as **United**, **Delta**, and **Southwest** believe these airlines own the planes on which they are flying. Often, this is not the case. Here are the lease percentages for the major U.S. airlines.

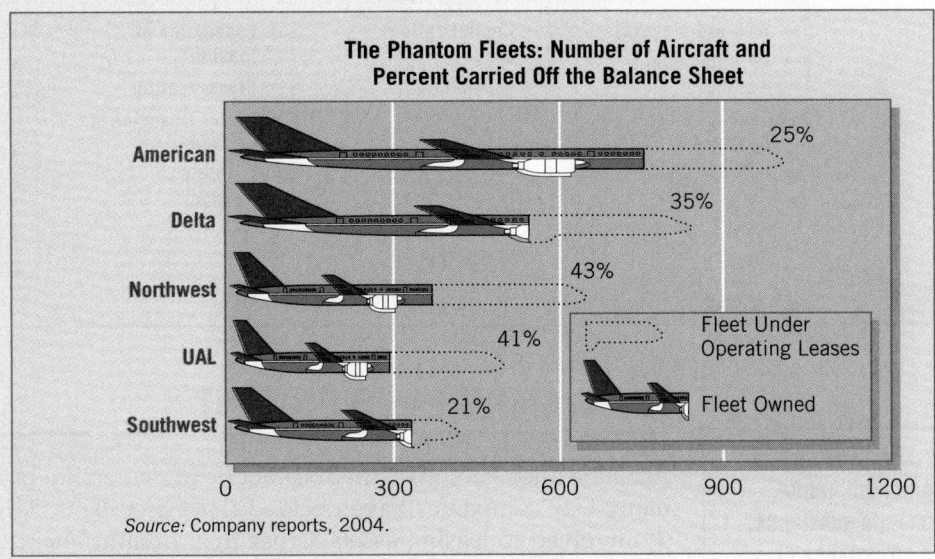

The Phantom Fleets: Number of Aircraft and Percent Carried Off the Balance Sheet

American	25%
Delta	35%
Northwest	43%
UAL	41%
Southwest	21%

Fleet Under Operating Leases
Fleet Owned

0   300   600   900   1200

Source: Company reports, 2004.

As you will learn, airlines lease many of their airplanes due to the favorable accounting treatment they receive if they lease rather than purchase.

---

[1] AICPA, *Accounting Trends and Techniques—2004.* Eight out of 10 U.S. companies lease all or some of their equipment. Companies that lease tend to be smaller, are high growth, and are in technology-oriented industries (see *www.techlease.com*).

Learning Objectives

After studying this chapter, you should be able to:

1 Explain the nature, economic substance, and advantages of lease transactions.
2 Describe the accounting criteria and procedures for capitalizing leases by the lessee.
3 Contrast the operating and capitalization methods of recording leases.
4 Identify the classifications of leases for the lessor.
5 Describe the lessor's accounting for direct-financing leases.
6 Identify special features of lease arrangements that cause unique accounting problems.
7 Describe the effect of residual values, guaranteed and unguaranteed, on lease accounting.
8 Describe the lessor's accounting for sales-type leases.
9 List the disclosure requirements for leases.

Our opening story indicates the increased significance and prevalence of lease arrangements. As a result, the need for uniform accounting and informative reporting of these transactions has intensified. In this chapter we look at the accounting issues related to leasing. The content and organization of this chapter are as follows.

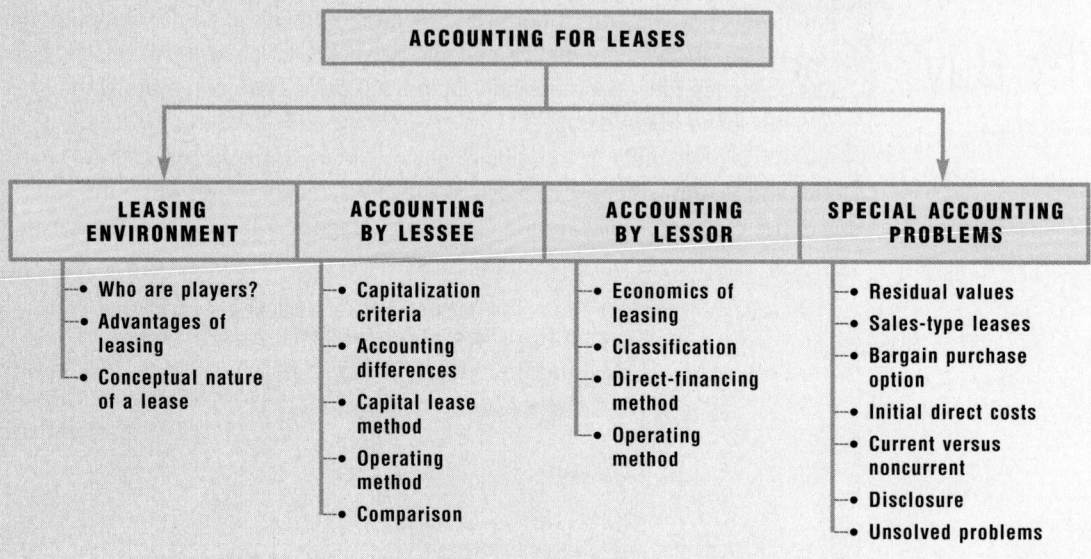

THE LEASING ENVIRONMENT

OBJECTIVE 1
Explain the nature, economic substance, and advantages of lease transactions.

Aristotle once said, "Wealth does not lie in ownership but in the use of things"! Clearly, many U.S. companies have decided that Aristotle is right, as they have become heavily involved in leasing assets rather than owning them. For example, Illustration 21-1 shows the growth in leasing transactions from 1990 to 2003.

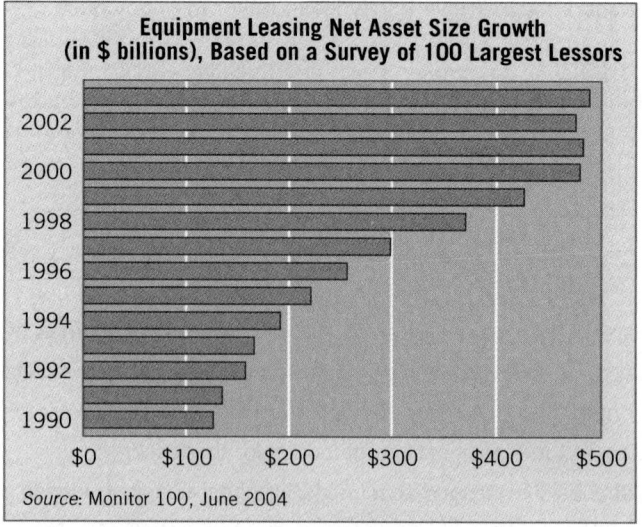

ILLUSTRATION 21-1
Equipment Leasing Growth

What types of assets are being leased? As the opening story indicated, any type of equipment can be leased, such as railcars, helicopters, bulldozers, barges, CT scanners, computers, and so on. The largest group of leased equipment involves information technology equipment, followed by assets in the transportation area (trucks, aircraft, rail), and then construction and agriculture.

Who Are the Players?

A **lease** is a contractual agreement between a lessor and a lessee. This arrangement gives the **lessee** the right to use specific property, owned by the **lessor**, for a specified period of time. In return for the use of the property, the lessee makes rental payments over the lease term to the lessor.

Who are the lessors that own this property? They generally fall into one of three categories:

1 Banks.

2 Captive leasing companies.

3 Independents.

Banks

Banks are the largest players in the leasing business. They have low-cost funds, which give them the advantage of being able to purchase assets at less cost than their competitors. Banks also have been more aggressive in the leasing markets. They have decided that there is money to be made in leasing, and as a result they have expanded their product lines in this area. Finally, leasing transactions are now more standardized, which gives banks an advantage because they do not have to be as innovative in structuring lease arrangements. Thus banks like **Wells Fargo**, **Chase**, **Citigroup**, and **PNC** have substantial leasing subsidiaries.

Captive Leasing Companies

Captive leasing companies are subsidiaries whose primary business is to perform leasing operations for the parent company. Companies like **Caterpillar Financial Services Corp.** (for Caterpillar), **Chrysler Financial** (for Daimler-Chrysler), and **IBM Global Financing** (for IBM) facilitate the sale of products to consumers. For example, suppose that **Sterling Construction Co.** wants to acquire a number of earthmovers from Caterpillar. In this case, Caterpillar Financial Services Corp. will offer to structure the transaction as a lease rather than as a purchase. Thus, Caterpillar Financial provides the financing rather than an outside financial institution.

Captive leasing companies have the point-of-sale advantage in finding leasing customers. That is, as soon as Caterpillar receives a possible order, its leasing subsidiary can quickly develop a lease-financing arrangement. Furthermore, the captive lessor has product knowledge that gives it an advantage when financing the parents' product.

The current trend is for captives to focus primarily on their company's products rather than do general lease financing. For example, **Boeing Capital** and **UPS Capital** are two captives that have left the general finance business to focus exclusively on their parent companies' products.

Independents

Independents are the final category of lessors. Independents have not done well over the last few years. Their market share has dropped fairly dramatically as banks and captive leasing companies have become more aggressive in the lease-financing area. Independents do not have point-of-sale access, nor do they have a low cost of funds advantage. What they *are* often good at is developing innovative contracts for lessees. In addition, they are starting to act as captive finance companies for some companies that do not have a leasing subsidiary.

Illustration 21-2 (page 1090) shows the new business volume by lessor type in a recent five-year period. As the chart shows, both banks and captives have increased business at the expense of the independents.

Advantages of Leasing

The growth in leasing indicates that it often has some genuine advantages over owning property, such as:

ILLUSTRATION 21-2
Lessor Types

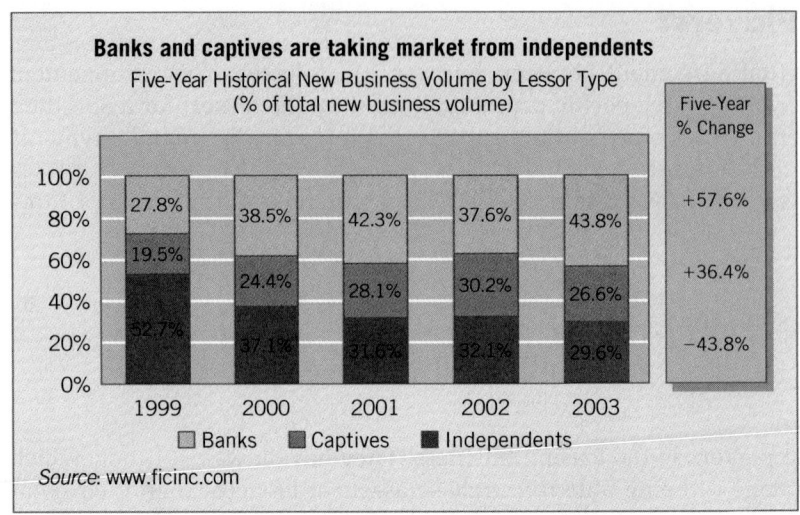

Banks and captives are taking market from independents

Five-Year Historical New Business Volume by Lessor Type
(% of total new business volume)

	1999	2000	2001	2002	2003	Five-Year % Change
Banks	27.8%	38.5%	42.3%	37.6%	43.8%	+57.6%
Captives	19.5%	24.4%	28.1%	30.2%	26.6%	+36.4%
Independents	52.7%	37.1%	31.6%	32.1%	29.6%	−43.8%

Source: www.ficinc.com

1 *100% Financing at Fixed Rates.* Leases are often signed without requiring any money down from the lessee. This helps the lessee conserve scarce cash—an especially desirable feature for new and developing companies. In addition, lease payments often remain fixed, which protects the lessee against inflation and increases in the cost of money. The following comment explains why companies choose a lease instead of a conventional loan: "Our local bank finally came up to 80 percent of the purchase price but wouldn't go any higher, and they wanted a floating interest rate. We just couldn't afford the down payment, and we needed to lock in a final payment rate we knew we could live with."

2 *Protection Against Obsolescence.* Leasing equipment reduces risk of obsolescence to the lessee, and in many cases passes the risk of residual value to the lessor. For example, **Merck** (a pharmaceutical maker) leases computers. Under the lease agreement, Merck may turn in an old computer for a new model at any time, canceling the old lease and writing a new one. The lessor adds the cost of the new lease to the balance due on the old lease, less the old computer's trade-in value. As one treasurer remarked, "Our instinct is to purchase." But if a new computer is likely to come along in a short time, "then leasing is just a heck of a lot more convenient than purchasing."

3 *Flexibility.* Lease agreements may contain less restrictive provisions than other debt agreements. Innovative lessors can tailor a lease agreement to the lessee's special needs. For instance, the duration of the lease—**the lease term**— may be anything from a short period of time to the entire expected economic life of the asset. The rental payments may be level from year to year, or they may increase or decrease in amount. The payment amount may be predetermined or may vary with sales, the prime interest rate, the Consumer Price Index, or some other factor. In most cases the rent is set to enable the lessor to recover the cost of the asset plus a fair return over the life of the lease.

4 *Less Costly Financing.* Some companies find leasing cheaper than other forms of financing. For example, start-up companies in depressed industries or companies in low tax brackets may lease to claim tax benefits that they might otherwise lose. Depreciation deductions offer no benefit to companies that have little if any taxable income. Through leasing, the leasing companies or financial institutions use these tax benefits. They can then pass some of these tax benefits back to the user of the asset in the form of lower rental payments.

5 *Tax Advantages.* In some cases, companies can "have their cake and eat it too" with tax advantages that leases offer. That is, for financial reporting purposes companies do not report an asset or a liability for the lease arrangement. For tax purposes, however, companies can capitalize and depreciate the leased asset. As a result, a

INTERNATIONAL INSIGHT

Some companies "double dip" on the international level too. The leasing rules of the lessor's and lessee's countries may differ, permitting both parties to own the asset. Thus, both lessor and lessee receive the tax benefits related to depreciation.

company takes deductions earlier rather than later and also reduces its taxes. A common vehicle for this type of transaction is a "synthetic lease" arrangement. (On page 1101 we discuss a synthetic lease used by **Krispy Kreme**.)

6 *Off-Balance-Sheet Financing.* Certain leases do not add debt on a balance sheet or affect financial ratios. In fact, they may add to borrowing capacity.[2] Such **off-balance-sheet financing** is critical to some companies.

OFF-BALANCE-SHEET FINANCING

As shown in our opening story, airlines use lease arrangements extensively. This results in a great deal of off-balance-sheet financing. The following chart indicates that many airlines that lease aircraft understate debt levels by a substantial amount.

WHAT DO THE NUMBERS MEAN?

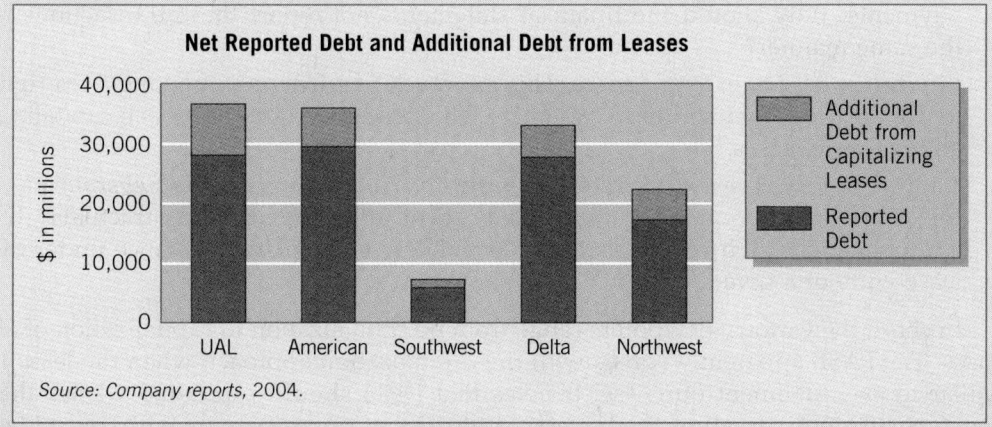

Source: Company reports, 2004.

And airlines are not the only ones playing the off-balance-sheet game. A recent SEC study estimates that for SEC registrants, off-balance-sheet lease obligations total more the $1.3 trillion, or 31 times the amount of on-balance-sheet obligations. (See SEC Off-Balance Sheet report at *www.sec.gov/news/studies/soxoffbalancerpt.pdf*.) Thus, analysts must adjust reported debt levels for the effects of non-capitalized leases. A methodology for making this adjustment is discussed in Eugene A. Imhoff, Jr., Robert C. Lipe, and David W. Wright, "Operating Leases: Impact of Constructive Capitalization," *Accounting Horizons* (March 1991).

Conceptual Nature of a Lease

If **Delta** borrows $47 million on a 10-year note from **Bank of America** to purchase a Boeing 737 jet plane, Delta should clearly report an asset and related liability at that amount on its balance sheet. Similarly, if Delta purchases the 737 for $47 million directly from Boeing through an installment purchase over 10 years, it should obviously report an asset and related liability (i.e., it should "capitalize" the installment transaction).

However, what if Delta **leases** the Boeing 737 for 10 years from **International Lease Finance Corp. (ILFC)**—the world's largest lessor of airplanes—through a noncancelable lease transaction with payments of the same amount as the installment purchase

---

[2]As demonstrated later in this chapter, certain types of lease arrangements are not capitalized on the balance sheet. The liabilities section is thereby relieved of large future lease commitments that, if recorded, would adversely affect the debt to equity ratio. The reluctance to record lease obligations as liabilities is one of the primary reasons some companies resist capitalized lease accounting.

transaction? In that case, opinion differs over how to report this transaction. The various views on **capitalization of leases** are as follows.

1 *Do Not Capitalize Any Leased Assets.* This view considers capitalization inappropriate, because Delta does not own the property. Furthermore, a lease is an **"executory" contract** requiring continuing performance by both parties. Because companies do not currently capitalize other executory contracts (such as purchase commitments and employment contracts), they should not capitalize leases either.

2 *Capitalize Leases That Are Similar to Installment Purchases.* This view holds that companies should report transactions in accordance with their economic substance. Therefore, if companies capitalize installment purchases, they should also capitalize leases that have similar characteristics. For example, Delta Airlines makes the same payments over a 10-year period for either a lease or an installment purchase. Lessees make rental payments, whereas owners make mortgage payments. Why should the financial statements not report these transactions in the same manner?

3 *Capitalize All Long-Term Leases.* This approach requires only the long-term right to use the property in order to capitalize. This property-rights approach capitalizes all long-term leases.[3]

4 *Capitalize Firm Leases Where the Penalty for Nonperformance Is Substantial.* A final approach advocates capitalizing only "firm" (noncancelable) contractual rights and obligations. "Firm" means that it is unlikely to avoid performance under the lease without a severe penalty.[4]

UNDERLYING CONCEPTS

The issue of how to report leases is the classic case of substance versus form. Although legal title does not technically pass in lease transactions, the benefits from the use of the property do transfer.

In short, the various viewpoints range from no capitalization to capitalization of all leases. The FASB apparently agrees with the capitalization approach when the lease is similar to an installment purchase: It notes that Delta **should capitalize a lease that transfers substantially all of the benefits and risks of property ownership, provided the lease is noncancelable**. **Noncancelable** means that Delta can cancel the lease contract only upon the outcome of some remote contingency, or that the cancellation provisions and penalties of the contract are so costly to Delta that cancellation probably will not occur.

This viewpoint leads to three basic conclusions: (1) Companies must identify the characteristics that indicate the transfer of substantially all of the benefits and risks of ownership. (2) The same characteristics should apply consistently to the lessee and the lessor. (3) Those leases that do **not** transfer substantially all the benefits and risks of ownership are operating leases. Companies should not capitalize operating leases. Instead, companies should account for them as rental payments and receipts.

ACCOUNTING BY THE LESSEE

OBJECTIVE 2
Describe the accounting criteria and procedures for capitalizing leases by the lessee.

If Delta Airlines (the lessee) **capitalizes** a lease, it records an asset and a liability generally equal to the present value of the rental payments. ILFC (the lessor), having transferred substantially all the benefits and risks of ownership, recognizes a sale by removing the asset from the balance sheet and replacing it with a receivable. The typical journal entries

---

[3]The property rights approach was originally recommended in a research study by the AICPA: John H. Myers, "Reporting of Leases in Financial Statements," *Accounting Research Study No. 4* (New York: AICPA, 1964), pp. 10–11. Recently, this view has received additional support. See Peter H. Knutson, "Financial Reporting in the 1990s and Beyond," Position Paper (Charlottesville, Va.: AIMR, 1993), and Warren McGregor, "Accounting for Leases: A New Approach," Special Report (Norwalk, Conn.: FASB, 1996).

[4]Yuji Ijiri, *Recognition of Contractual Rights and Obligations*, Research Report (Stamford, Conn.: FASB, 1980).

for Delta and ILFC, assuming leased and capitalized equipment, appear as shown in Illustration 21-3.

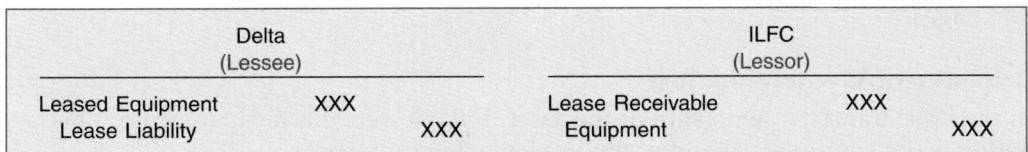

Delta (Lessee)			ILFC (Lessor)		
Leased Equipment	XXX		Lease Receivable	XXX	
Lease Liability		XXX	Equipment		XXX

ILLUSTRATION 21-3
Journal Entries for Capitalized Lease

Having capitalized the asset, Delta records depreciation on the leased asset. Both ILFC and Delta treat the lease rental payments as consisting of interest and principal.

If Delta does not capitalize the lease, it does not record an asset, nor does ILFC remove one from its books. When Delta makes a lease payment, it records rental expense; ILFC recognizes rental revenue.

In order to record a lease as a **capital lease**, the lease must be noncancelable. Further, it must meet one or more of the four criteria listed in Illustration 21-4.

ILLUSTRATION 21-4
Capitalization Criteria for Lessee

Capitalization Criteria (Lessee)

- The lease transfers ownership of the property to the lessee.
- The lease contains a bargain purchase option.[5]
- The lease term is equal to 75 percent or more of the estimated economic life of the leased property.
- The present value of the minimum lease payments (excluding executory costs) equals or exceeds 90 percent of the fair value of the leased property.[6]

Delta classifies and accounts for leases that **do not meet any of the four criteria** as **operating leases**. Illustration 21-5 shows that a lease meeting any one of the four criteria results in the lessee having a capital lease.

ILLUSTRATION 21-5
Diagram of Lessee's Criteria for Lease Classification

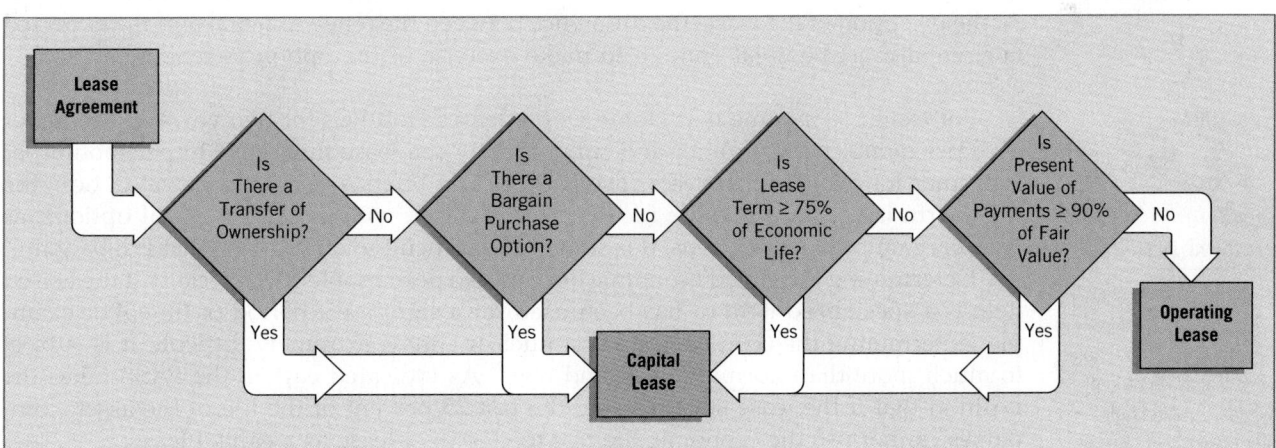

In keeping with the FASB's reasoning that a company consumes a significant portion of the value of the asset in the first 75 percent of its life, the lessee applies neither the third nor the fourth criterion when the inception of the lease occurs during the last 25 percent of the asset's life.

---

[5]We define a bargain purchase option in the next section.

[6]"Accounting for Leases," *FASB Statement No. 13* as amended and interpreted through May 1980 (Stamford, Conn.: FASB, 1980), par. 7.

Capitalization Criteria

Three of the four **capitalization criteria** that apply to lessees are controversial and can be difficult to apply in practice. We discuss each of the criteria in detail on the following pages.

Transfer of Ownership Test

If the lease transfers ownership of the asset to the lessee, it is a capital lease. This criterion is not controversial and easily implemented in practice.

Bargain Purchase Option Test

A **bargain purchase option** allows the lessee to purchase the leased property for a price that is **significantly lower** than the property's expected fair value at the date the option becomes exercisable. At the inception of the lease, the difference between the option price and the expected fair market value must be large enough to make exercise of the option reasonably assured.

For example, assume that Brett's Delivery Service was to lease a Honda Accord for $599 per month for 40 months, with an option to purchase for $100 at the end of the 40-month period. If the estimated fair value of the Honda Accord is $3,000 at the end of the 40 months, the $100 option to purchase is clearly a bargain. Therefore, Brett must capitalize the lease. In other cases, the criterion may not be as easy to apply, and determining *now* that a certain *future* price is a bargain can be difficult.

Economic Life Test (75% Test)

If the lease period equals or exceeds 75 percent of the asset's economic life, the lessor transfers most of the risks and rewards of ownership to the lessee. Capitalization is therefore appropriate. However, determining the lease term and the economic life of the asset can be troublesome.

The **lease term** is generally considered to be the fixed, noncancelable term of the lease. However, a bargain renewal option, if provided in the lease agreement, can extend this period. A **bargain renewal option** allows the lessee to renew the lease for a rental that is lower than the expected fair rental at the date the option becomes exercisable. At the inception of the lease, the difference between the renewal rental and the expected fair rental must be great enough to make exercise of the option to renew reasonably assured.

For example, assume that **Home Depot** leases **Dell** PCs for two years at a rental of $100 per month per computer and subsequently can lease them for $10 per month per computer for another two years. The lease clearly offers a bargain renewal option; the lease term is considered to be four years. However, with bargain renewal options, as with bargain purchase options, it is sometimes difficult to determine what is a bargain.[7]

Determining estimated economic life can also pose problems, especially if the leased item is a specialized item or has been used for a significant period of time. For example, determining the economic life of a nuclear core is extremely difficult. It is subject to much more than normal "wear and tear." As indicated earlier, the FASB takes the position that if the lease starts during the last 25 percent of the life of the asset, companies cannot use the economic life test to classify a lease as a capital lease.

INTERNATIONAL INSIGHT

In some countries (e.g., Italy, Japan), accounting principles do not specify criteria for capitalization of leases. In others (e.g., Sweden, Switzerland), such criteria exist, but capitalization of the leases is optional.

---

[7] The original lease term is also extended for leases having the following: substantial penalties for nonrenewal; periods for which the lessor has the option to renew or extend the lease; renewal periods preceding the date a bargain purchase option becomes exercisable; and renewal periods in which any lessee guarantees of the lessor's debt are expected to be in effect or in which there will be a loan outstanding from the lessee to the lessor. The lease term, however, can never extend beyond the time a bargain purchase option becomes exercisable. "Accounting for Leases: Sale-Leaseback Transactions Involving Real Estate; Sales-Type Leases of Real Estate; Definition of the Lease Term; Initial Direct Costs of Direct Financing Leases," *Statement of Financial Accounting Standards No. 98* (Stamford, Conn.: FASB, 1988).

Recovery of Investment Test (90% Test)

If the present value of the minimum lease payments equals or exceeds 90 percent of the fair market value of the asset, then a lessee like Delta should capitalize the leased asset. Why? If the present value of the minimum lease payments is reasonably close to the market price of the aircraft, Delta is effectively purchasing the asset.

Determining the present value of the minimum lease payments involves three important concepts: (1) minimum lease payments, (2) executory costs, and (3) discount rate.

Minimum Lease Payments. Delta is obligated to make, or expected to make, **minimum lease payments** in connection with the leased property. These payments include the following.

1 *Minimum Rental Payments*—Minimum rental payments are those that Delta must make to ILFC under the lease agreement. In some cases, the minimum rental payments may equal the minimum lease payments. However, the minimum lease payments may also include a guaranteed residual value (if any), penalty for failure to renew, or a bargain purchase option (if any), as we note below.

2 *Guaranteed Residual Value*—The residual value is the estimated fair (market) value of the leased property at the end of the lease term. ILFC may transfer the risk of loss to Delta or to a third party by obtaining a guarantee of the estimated residual value. The **guaranteed residual value** is either (1) the certain or determinable amount that Delta will pay ILFC at the end of the lease to purchase the aircraft at the end of the lease, or (2) the amount Delta or the third party guarantees that ILFC will realize if the aircraft is returned. (**Third-party guarantors** are, in essence, insurers who for a fee assume the risk of deficiencies in leased asset residual value.) If not guaranteed in full, the **unguaranteed residual value** is the estimated residual value exclusive of any portion guaranteed.[8]

3 *Penalty for Failure to Renew or Extend the Lease*—The amount Delta must pay if the agreement specifies that it must extend or renew the lease, and it fails to do so.

4 *Bargain Purchase Option*—As we indicated earlier (in item 1), an option given to Delta to purchase the aircraft at the end of the lease term at a price that is fixed sufficiently below the expected fair value, so that, at the inception of the lease, purchase is reasonably assured.

Delta excludes executory costs (defined below) from its computation of the present value of the minimum lease payments.

Executory Costs. Like most assets, leased tangible assets incur insurance, maintenance, and tax expenses—called **executory costs**—during their economic life. If ILFC retains responsibility for the payment of these "ownership-type costs," **it should exclude**, in computing the present value of the minimum lease payments, a portion of each lease payment that represents executory costs. Executory costs do not represent payment on or reduction of the obligation.

Many lease agreements specify that the lessee directly pays executory costs to the appropriate third parties. In these cases, the lessor can use the rental payment **without adjustment** in the present value computation.

Discount Rate. A lessee, like Delta computes the present value of the minimum lease payments using its **incremental borrowing rate**. This rate is defined as: "The rate that, at the inception of the lease, the lessee would have incurred to borrow the funds necessary to buy the leased asset on a secured loan with repayment terms similar to the payment schedule called for in the lease."[9]

---

[8]A lease provision requiring the lessee to make up a residual value deficiency that is attributable to damage, extraordinary wear and tear, or excessive usage is not included in the minimum lease payments. Lessees recognize such costs as period costs when incurred. "Lessee Guarantee of the Residual Value of Leased Property," *FASB Interpretation No. 19* (Stamford, Conn.: FASB, 1977), par. 3.

[9]*FASB Statement No. 13*, op. cit., par. 5 (l).

To determine whether the present value of these payments is less than 90 percent of the fair market value of the property, Delta discounts the payments using its incremental borrowing rate. Determining the incremental borrowing rate often requires judgment because the lessee bases it on a hypothetical purchase of the property.

However, there is one exception to this rule. If (1) Delta knows the **implicit interest rate computed by ILFC** and (2) it is less than Delta's incremental borrowing rate, then Delta **must use ILFC's implicit rate**. What is the **interest rate implicit in the lease**? It is the discount rate that, when applied to the minimum lease payments and any unguaranteed residual value accruing to the lessor, causes the aggregate present value to equal the fair value of the leased property to the lessor.[10]

The purpose of this exception is twofold. First, **the implicit rate of ILFC is generally a more realistic rate** to use in determining the amount (if any) to report as the asset and related liability for Delta. Second, the guideline ensures that Delta **does not use an artificially high incremental borrowing rate** that would cause the present value of the minimum lease payments to be less than 90 percent of the fair market value of the aircraft. Use of such a rate would thus make it possible to avoid capitalization of the asset and related liability.

Delta may argue that it cannot determine the implicit rate of the lessor and therefore should use the higher rate. However, in most cases, Delta can approximate the implicit rate used by ILFC. The determination of whether or not a reasonable estimate could be made will require judgment, particularly where the result from using the incremental borrowing rate comes close to meeting the 90 percent test. Because Delta **may not capitalize the leased property at more than its fair value** (as we discuss later), it cannot use an excessively low discount rate.

Asset and Liability Accounted for Differently

In a capital lease transaction, Delta uses the lease as a source of financing. ILFC finances the transaction (provides the investment capital) through the leased asset. Delta makes rent payments, which actually are installment payments. Therefore, over the life of the aircraft rented, **the rental payments to ILFC constitute a payment of principal plus interest.**

Asset and Liability Recorded

Under the capital lease method, Delta treats the lease transaction as if it purchases the aircraft in a financing transaction. That is, Delta acquires the aircraft and creates an obligation. Therefore, it records a capital lease as an asset and a liability at the lower of (1) the present value of the minimum lease payments (excluding executory costs) or (2) the fair-market value of the leased asset at the inception of the lease. The rationale for this approach is that companies should not record a leased asset for more than its fair market value.

Depreciation Period

One troublesome aspect of accounting for the depreciation of the capitalized leased asset relates to the period of depreciation. If the lease agreement transfers ownership of the asset to Delta (criterion 1) or contains a bargain purchase option (criterion 2), Delta depreciates the aircraft consistent with its normal depreciation policy for other aircraft, **using the economic life of the asset**.

On the other hand, if the lease does not transfer ownership or does not contain a bargain purchase option, then Delta depreciates it over the **term of the lease**. In this case, the aircraft reverts to ILFC after a certain period of time.

Effective-Interest Method

Throughout the term of the lease, Delta uses the **effective-interest method** to allocate each lease payment between principal and interest. This method produces a periodic interest expense equal to a constant percentage of the carrying value of the

---

[10]Ibid., par. 5 (k).

lease obligation. When applying the effective-interest method to capital leases, Delta must use the same discount rate that determines the present value of the minimum lease payments.

Depreciation Concept

Although Delta computes the amounts initially capitalized as an asset and recorded as an obligation at the same present value, the **depreciation of the aircraft and the discharge of the obligation are independent accounting processes** during the term of the lease. It should depreciate the leased asset by applying conventional depreciation methods: straight-line, sum-of-the-years'-digits, declining-balance, units of production, etc. The FASB uses the term "amortization" more frequently than "depreciation" to recognize intangible leased property rights. We prefer "depreciation" to describe the write-off of a tangible asset's expired services.

Capital Lease Method (Lessee)

To illustrate a capital lease, assume that **Caterpillar Financial Services Corp.** (a subsidiary of Caterpillar) and **Sterling Construction Corp.** sign a lease agreement dated January 1, 2008, that calls for Caterpillar to lease a front-end loader to Sterling beginning January 1, 2008. The terms and provisions of the lease agreement, and other pertinent data, are as follows.

- The term of the lease is five years. The lease agreement is noncancelable, requiring equal rental payments of $25,981.62 at the beginning of each year (annuity due basis).
- The loader has a fair value at the inception of the lease of $100,000, an estimated economic life of five years, and no residual value.
- Sterling pays all of the executory costs directly to third parties except for the property taxes of $2,000 per year, which it includes as part of its annual payments to Caterpillar.
- The lease contains no renewal options. The loader reverts to Caterpillar at the termination of the lease.
- Sterling's incremental borrowing rate is 11 percent per year.
- Sterling depreciates, on a straight-line basis, similar equipment that it owns.
- Caterpillar sets the annual rental to earn a rate of return on its investment of 10 percent per year; Sterling knows this fact.[11]

The lease meets the criteria for classification as a capital lease for the following reasons:

1 The lease term of five years, being equal to the equipment's estimated economic life of five years, satisfies the 75 percent test.

2 The present value of the minimum lease payments ($100,000 as computed below) exceeds 90 percent of the fair value of the loader ($100,000).

The minimum lease payments are $119,908.10 ($23,981.62 × 5). Sterling computes the amount capitalized as leased assets as the present value of the minimum lease payments (excluding executory costs—property taxes of $2,000) as shown in Illustration 21-6.

Capitalized amount = ($25,981.62 − $2,000) × Present value of an annuity due of 1 for 5 periods at 10% (Table 6-5)
= $23,981.62 × 4.16986
= $100,000

ILLUSTRATION 21-6
Computation of Capitalized Lease Payments

---

[11]If Sterling has an incremental borrowing rate of, say, 9 percent (lower than the 10 percent rate used by Caterpillar) and it did not know the rate used by Caterpillar, the present value computation would yield a capitalized amount of $101,675.35 ($23,981.62 × 4.23972). And, because this amount exceeds the $100,000 fair value of the equipment, Sterling would have to capitalize the $100,000 and use 10 percent as its effective rate for amortization of the lease obligation.

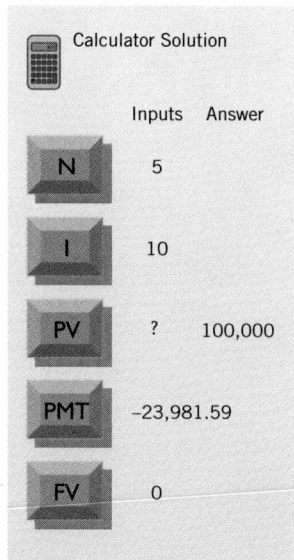

Calculator Solution

	Inputs	Answer
N	5	
I	10	
PV	?	100,000
PMT	-23,981.59	
FV	0	

Sterling uses Caterpillar's implicit interest rate of 10 percent instead of its incremental borrowing rate of 11 percent because (1) it is lower and (2) it knows about it. Sterling records the capital lease on its books on January 1, 2008, as:

Leased Equipment under Capital Leases	100,000	
Lease Liability		100,000

Note that the entry records the obligation at the net amount of $100,000 (the present value of the future rental payments) rather than at the gross amount of $119,908.10 ($23,981.62 × 5).

Sterling records the **first lease payment on January 1, 2008**, as follows:

Property Tax Expense	2,000.00	
Lease Liability	23,981.62	
Cash		25,981.62

Each lease payment of $25,981.62 consists of three elements: (1) a reduction in the lease liability, (2) a financing cost (interest expense), and (3) executory costs (property taxes). The total financing cost (interest expense) over the term of the lease is $19,908.10. This amount is the difference between the present value of the lease payments ($100,000) and the actual cash disbursed, net of executory costs ($119,908.10). Therefore, the annual interest expense, applying the effective-interest method, is a function of the outstanding liability, as Illustration 21-7 shows.

ILLUSTRATION 21-7
Lease Amortization
Schedule for Lessee—
Annuity-Due Basis

STERLING CONSTRUCTION
LEASE AMORTIZATION SCHEDULE
(ANNUITY-DUE BASIS)

Date	Annual Lease Payment	Executory Costs	Interest (10%) on Liability	Reduction of Lease Liability	Lease Liability
	(a)	(b)	(c)	(d)	(e)
1/1/08					$100,000.00
1/1/08	$ 25,981.62	$ 2,000	$ –0–	$ 23,981.62	76,018.38
1/1/09	25,981.62	2,000	7,601.84	16,379.78	59,638.60
1/1/10	25,981.62	2,000	5,963.86	18,017.76	41,620.84
1/1/11	25,981.62	2,000	4,162.08	19,819.54	21,801.30
1/1/12	25,981.62	2,000	2,180.32*	21,801.30	–0–
	$129,908.10	$10,000	$19,908.10	$100,000.00	

(a) Lease payment as required by lease.
(b) Executory costs included in rental payment.
(c) Ten percent of the preceding balance of (e) except for 1/1/05; since this is an annuity due, no time has elapsed at the date of the first payment and no interest has accrued.
(d) (a) minus (b) and (c).
(e) Preceding balance minus (d).
*Rounded by 19 cents.

At the end of its fiscal year, December 31, 2008, Sterling records **accrued interest** as follows.

Interest Expense	7,601.84	
Interest Payable		7,601.84

Depreciation of the leased equipment over its five-year lease term, applying Sterling's normal depreciation policy (straight-line method), results in the following entry on December 31, 2008.

Depreciation Expense—Capital Leases	20,000	
Accumulated Depreciation—Capital Leases		20,000
($100,000 ÷ 5 years)		

At December 31, 2008, Sterling separately identifies the assets recorded under capital leases on its balance sheet. Similarly, it separately identifies the related obligations. Sterling classifies the portion due within one year or the operating cycle, whichever is longer, with current liabilities, and the rest with noncurrent liabilities. For example, the current portion of the December 31, 2008, total obligation of $76,018.38 in Sterling's amortization schedule is the amount of the reduction in the obligation in 2009, or $16,379.78. Illustration 21-8 shows the liabilities section as it relates to lease transactions at December 31, 2008.

ILLUSTRATION 21-8
Reporting Current and
Noncurrent Lease
Liabilities

Current liabilities	
Interest payable	$ 7,601.84
Lease liability	16,379.78
Noncurrent liabilities	
Lease liability	$59,638.60

Sterling records the lease payment of January 1, 2009, as follows.

Property Tax Expense	2,000.00	
Interest Payable	7,601.84	
Lease Liability	16,379.78	
Cash		25,981.62

Entries through 2012 would follow the pattern above. Sterling records its other executory costs (insurance and maintenance) in a manner similar to how it records any other operating costs incurred on assets it owns.

Upon expiration of the lease, Sterling has fully amortized the amount capitalized as leased equipment. It also has fully discharged its lease obligation. If Sterling does not purchase the loader, it returns the equipment to Caterpillar. Sterling then removes the leased equipment and related accumulated depreciation accounts from its books.[12]

If Sterling purchases the equipment at termination of the lease, at a price of $5,000 and the estimated life of the equipment changes from five to seven years, it makes the following entry.

Equipment ($100,000 + $5,000)	105,000	
Accumulated Depreciation—Capital Leases	100,000	
Leased Equipment under Capital Leases		100,000
Accumulated Depreciation—Equipment		100,000
Cash		5,000

Operating Method (Lessee)

Under the **operating method**, rent expense (and the associated liability) accrues day by day to the lessee as it uses the property. **The lessee assigns rent to the periods benefiting from the use of the asset and ignores, in the accounting, any commitments to make future payments.** The lessee makes appropriate accruals or deferrals if the accounting period ends between cash payment dates.

For example, assume that the capital lease illustrated in the previous section did not qualify as a capital lease. Sterling therefore accounts for it as an operating lease. The first-year charge to operations is now $25,981.62, the amount of the rental payment. Sterling records this payment on January 1, 2008, as follows.

Rent Expense	25,981.62	
Cash		25,981.62

---

[12]If Sterling purchases the front-end loader **during the term of a "capital lease,"** it accounts for it like a renewal or extension of a capital lease. "Any difference between the purchase price and the carrying amount of the lease obligation shall be recorded as an adjustment of the carrying amount of the asset." See "Accounting for Purchase of a Leased Asset by the Lessee During the Term of the Lease," *FASB Interpretation No. 26* (Stamford, Conn.: FASB, 1978), par. 5.

Sterling does not report the loader, as well as any long-term liability for future rental payments, on the balance sheet. Sterling reports rent expense on the income statement. And, as discussed later in the chapter, **Sterling must disclose all operating leases that have noncancelable lease terms in excess of one year**.

WHAT DO THE
NUMBERS MEAN?

RESTATEMENTS ON THE MENU

Accounting for operating leases would appear routine, so it is unusual for a bevy of companies in a single industry—restaurants—to get caught up in the accounting rules for operating leases. Getting the accounting right is particularly important for restaurant chains, because they make extensive use of leases for their restaurants and equipment.

The problem stems from the way most property (and equipment) leases cover a specific number of years (the so-called *primary lease term*) as well as renewal periods (sometimes referred to as the *option term*). In some cases, companies were calculating their lease expense for the primary term but depreciating lease-related assets over both the primary and option terms. This practice resulted in understating the total cost of the lease and thus boosted earnings.

For example, the CFO at **CKE Restaurants Inc.**, owner of the Hardee's and Carl's Jr. chains, noted that CKE ran into trouble because it was not consistent in calculating the lease and depreciation expense. Correcting the error at CKE reduced earnings by nine cents a share in fiscal 2002, nine cents a share in fiscal 2003, and 10 cents a share in fiscal 2004. The company now uses the shorter, primary lease terms for calculating both lease expense and depreciation. The change increases depreciation annually, which in turn decreases total assets.

CKE was not alone in improper operating lease accounting. Notable restaurateurs who ran afoul of the lease rules included **Brinker International Inc.**, operator of Chili's; **Darden Restaurants Inc.**, which operates Red Lobster and Olive Garden; and **Jack in the Box**. To correct their operating lease accounting, these restaurants reported restatements that resulted in lower earnings and assets.

Source: Steven D. Jones and Richard Gibson, *Wall Street Journal* (January 26, 2005). p. C3.

Comparison of Capital Lease with Operating Lease

OBJECTIVE 3
Contrast the operating and capitalization methods of recording leases.

As we indicated, if accounting for the lease as an operating lease, the first-year charge to operations is $25,981.62, the amount of the rental payment. Treating the transaction as a capital lease, however, results in a first-year charge of $29,601.84: depreciation of $20,000 (assuming straight-line), interest expense of $7,601.84 (per Illustration 21-7), and executory costs of $2,000. Illustration 21-9 shows that **while the total charges to operations are the same over the lease term whether accounting for the lease as a**

ILLUSTRATION 21-9
Comparison of Charges to Operations—Capital vs. Operating Leases

STERLING CONSTRUCTION
SCHEDULE OF CHARGES TO OPERATIONS
CAPITAL LEASE VERSUS OPERATING LEASE

| Year | Capital Lease | | | | Operating Lease Charge | Difference |
	Depreciation	Executory Costs	Interest	Total Charge		
2008	$ 20,000	$ 2,000	$ 7,601.84	$ 29,601.84	$ 25,981.62	$3,620.22
2009	20,000	2,000	5,963.86	27,963.86	25,981.62	1,982.24
2010	20,000	2,000	4,162.08	26,162.08	25,981.62	180.46
2011	20,000	2,000	2,180.32	24,180.32	25,981.62	(1,801.30)
2012	20,000	2,000	—	22,000.00	25,981.62	(3,981.62)
	$100,000	$10,000	$19,908.10	$129,908.10	$129,908.10	$ –0–

capital lease or as an operating lease, under the capital lease treatment the charges are higher in the earlier years and lower in the later years.[13]

If using an accelerated method of depreciation, the differences between the amounts charged to operations under the two methods would be even larger in the earlier and later years.

In addition, using the capital lease approach results in an asset and related liability of $100,000 initially reported on the balance sheet. The lessee would not report any asset or liability under the operating method. Therefore, the following differences occur if using a capital lease instead of an operating lease:

1 An increase in the amount of reported debt (both short-term and long-term).

2 An increase in the amount of total assets (specifically long-lived assets).

3 A lower income early in the life of the lease and, therefore, lower retained earnings.

Thus, many companies believe that capital leases negatively impact their financial position: Their debt to total equity ratio increases, and their rate of return on total assets decreases. As a result, the business community resists capitalizing leases.

Whether this resistance is well founded is debatable. From a cash flow point of view, the company is in the same position whether accounting for the lease as an operating or a capital lease. Managers often argue against capitalization for several reasons: First is that capitalization can more easily lead to **violation of loan covenants**. It also can affect the **amount of compensation received by owners** (for example, a stock compensation plan tied to earnings). Finally, capitalization can **lower rates of return**

DOLLARS TO DOUGHNUTS

WHAT DO THE NUMBERS MEAN?

Krispy Kreme, a chain of 217 doughnut shops, has caught the attention—some good, some bad—of Wall Street. On the good side, investors are impressed by the company's ability to grow rapidly on a relatively small bit of capital. For the first nine months of fiscal 2002, the company's capital expenditures fell to $38 million, from $59 million the year before. Yet Krispy Kreme expanded, along with its customers' waistlines, during the same period: Its earnings rose 73 percent, to $18 million, on sales that were up 27 percent to $277 million.

That's an impressive feat if you care about return on capital. But there's a hole in this doughnut. Amid much hoopla, the company announced in 2001 that it would spend $30 million on a new 187,000 square foot mixing plant and warehouse in Effingham, Illinois. Yet the financial statements failed to disclose the investments and obligations associated with that $30 million.

By financing through a synthetic lease, Krispy Kreme keeps the investment and obligation off the books. In a synthetic lease, a financial institution like **Bank of America** sets up a *special purpose entity* (SPE) that borrows money to build the plant and then leases it to Krispy Kreme. For accounting purposes, Krispy Kreme reports an operating lease, but for tax purposes the company is considered the owner of the asset and gets depreciation tax deductions.

In response to negative publicity about the use of SPEs to get favorable financial reporting and tax benefits, Krispy Kreme announced it would change its method of financing construction of its dough-making plant.

Source: Adapted from Seth Lubore and Elizabeth MacDonald, "Debt? Who, Me?" *Forbes* (February 18, 2002), p. 56.

---

[13]The higher charges in the early years is one reason lessees are reluctant to adopt the capital lease accounting method. Lessees (especially those of real estate) claim that it is really no more costly to operate the leased asset in the early years than in the later years. Thus, they advocate an even charge similar to that provided by the operating method.

and **increase debt to equity relationships,** making the company less attractive to present and potential investors.[14]

ACCOUNTING BY THE LESSOR

INTERNATIONAL INSIGHT

Recently, the IASB indicated it plans to reform the rules on accounting for leased assets.

Earlier in this chapter we discussed leasing's advantages to the lessee. Three important benefits are available to the lessor:

1 *Interest Revenue.* Leasing is a form of financing. Banks, captives, and independent leasing companies find leasing attractive because it provides competitive interest margins.

2 *Tax Incentives.* In many cases, companies that lease cannot use the tax benefit of the asset, but leasing allows them to transfer such tax benefits to another party (the lessor) in return for a lower rental rate on the leased asset. To illustrate, **Boeing Aircraft** might sell one of its 737 jet planes to a wealthy investor who needed only the tax benefit. The investor then leased the plane to a foreign airline, for whom the tax benefit was of no use. Everyone gained. Boeing sold its airplane, the investor received the tax benefit, and the foreign airline cheaply acquired a 737.[15]

3 *High Residual Value.* Another advantage to the lessor is the return of the property at the end of the lease term. Residual values can produce very large profits. **Citigroup** at one time assumed that the commercial aircraft it was leasing to the airline industry would have a residual value of 5 percent of their purchase price. It turned out that they were worth 150 percent of their cost—a handsome profit. However, three years later these same planes slumped to 80 percent of their cost, but still far more than 5 percent.

Economics of Leasing

A lessor, such as Caterpillar Financial in our earlier example, determines the amount of the rental, basing it on the rate of return—the implicit rate—needed to justify leasing the front-end loader. In establishing the rate of return, Caterpillar considers the credit standing of Sterling Construction, the length of the lease, and the status of the residual value (guaranteed versus unguaranteed).

In the Caterpillar/Sterling example on pages 1097–1099, Caterpillar's implicit rate was 10 percent, the cost of the equipment to Caterpillar was $100,000 (also fair market value), and the estimated residual value was zero. Caterpillar determines the amount of the lease payment as follows.

ILLUSTRATION 21-10
Computation of Lease Payments

Fair market value of leased equipment	$100,000.00
Less: Present value of the residual value	–0–
Amount to be recovered by lessor through lease payments	$100,000.00
Five beginning-of-the-year lease payments to yield a 10% return ($100,000 ÷ 4.16986[a])	$ 23,981.62

[a]PV of an annuity due of 1 for 5 years at 10% (Table 6-5)

---

[14]One study indicates that management's behavior did change as a result of *FASB No. 13*. For example, many companies restructure their leases to avoid capitalization. Others increase their purchases of assets instead of leasing. Still others, faced with capitalization, postpone their debt offerings or issue stock instead. However, note that the study found no significant effect on stock or bond prices as a result of capitalization of leases. A. Rashad Abdel-khalik, "The Economic Effects on Lessees of *FASB Statement No. 13*, Accounting for Leases," Research Report (Stamford, Conn.: FASB, 1981).

[15]Some would argue that there is a loser—the U.S. government. The tax benefits enable the profitable investor to reduce or eliminate taxable income.

If a residual value is involved (whether guaranteed or not), Caterpillar would not have to recover as much from the lease payments. Therefore, the lease payments would be less. (Illustration 21-17, on page 1108, shows this situation.)

Classification of Leases by the Lessor

For accounting purposes, the **lessor** may classify leases as one of the following:

1 Operating leases.

2 Direct-financing leases.

3 Sales-type leases.

Illustration 21-11 presents two groups of capitalization criteria for the lessor. If at the date of inception, the lessor agrees to a lease that meets **one or more** of the Group I criteria (1, 2, 3, and 4) and **both** of the Group II criteria (1 and 2), the lessor shall classify and account for the arrangement as a direct-financing lease or as a sales-type lease.[16] (Note that the Group I criteria are identical to the criteria that must be met in order for a lessee to classify a lease as a capital lease, as shown in Illustration 21-4.)

> **OBJECTIVE 4**
> Identify the classifications of leases for the lessor.

Capitalization Criteria (Lessor)

Group I
1. The lease transfers ownership of the property to the lessee.
2. The lease contains a bargain purchase option.
3. The lease term is equal to 75 percent or more of the estimated economic life of the leased property.
4. The present value of the minimum lease payments (excluding executory costs) equals or exceeds 90 percent of the fair value of the leased property.

Group II
1. Collectibility of the payments required from the lessee is reasonably predictable.
2. No important uncertainties surround the amount of unreimbursable costs yet to be incurred by the lessor under the lease (lessor's performance is substantially complete or future costs are reasonably predictable).

ILLUSTRATION 21-11
Capitalization Criteria for Lessor

Why the Group II requirements? The profession wants to ensure that the lessor has really transferred the risks and benefits of ownership. If collectibility of payments is not predictable or if performance by the lessor is incomplete, then the criteria for revenue recognition have not been met. The lessor should therefore account for the lease as an operating lease.

For example, computer leasing companies at one time used to buy **IBM** equipment, lease the equipment, and remove the leased assets from their balance sheets. In leasing the assets, the computer lessors stated that they would substitute new IBM equipment if obsolescence occurred. However, when IBM introduced a new computer line, IBM refused to sell it to the computer leasing companies. As a result, a number of the lessors could not meet their contracts with their customers and had to take back the old equipment. The computer leasing companies therefore had to reinstate the assets they had taken off the books. Such a case demonstrates one reason for the Group II requirements.

The distinction for the lessor between a direct-financing lease and a sales-type lease is the presence or absence of a manufacturer's or dealer's profit (or loss): A sales-type lease involves a manufacturer's or dealer's profit, and a direct-financing lease does not. The profit (or loss) to the lessor is evidenced by the difference between the fair value of the leased property at the inception of the lease and the lessor's cost or carrying amount (book value).

Normally, sales-type leases arise when manufacturers or dealers use leasing as a means of marketing their products. For example, a computer manufacturer will lease

INTERNATIONAL INSIGHT

U.S. GAAP is consistent with *International Standard No. 17* (Accounting for Leases). However, the international standard is a relatively simple statement of basic principles, whereas the U.S. rules on leases are more prescriptive and detailed.

---

[16]*FASB Statement No. 13,* op. cit., pars. 6, 7, and 8.

its computer equipment (possibly through a captive) to businesses and institutions. Direct-financing leases generally result from arrangements with lessors that are primarily engaged in financing operations (e.g., banks). However, a lessor need not be a manufacturer or dealer to recognize a profit (or loss) at the inception of a lease that requires application of sales-type lease accounting.

Lessors classify and account for all leases that do not qualify as direct-financing or sales-type leases as operating leases. Illustration 21-12 shows the circumstances under which a lessor classifies a lease as operating, direct-financing, or sales-type.

ILLUSTRATION 21-12
Diagram of Lessor's Criteria for Lease Classification

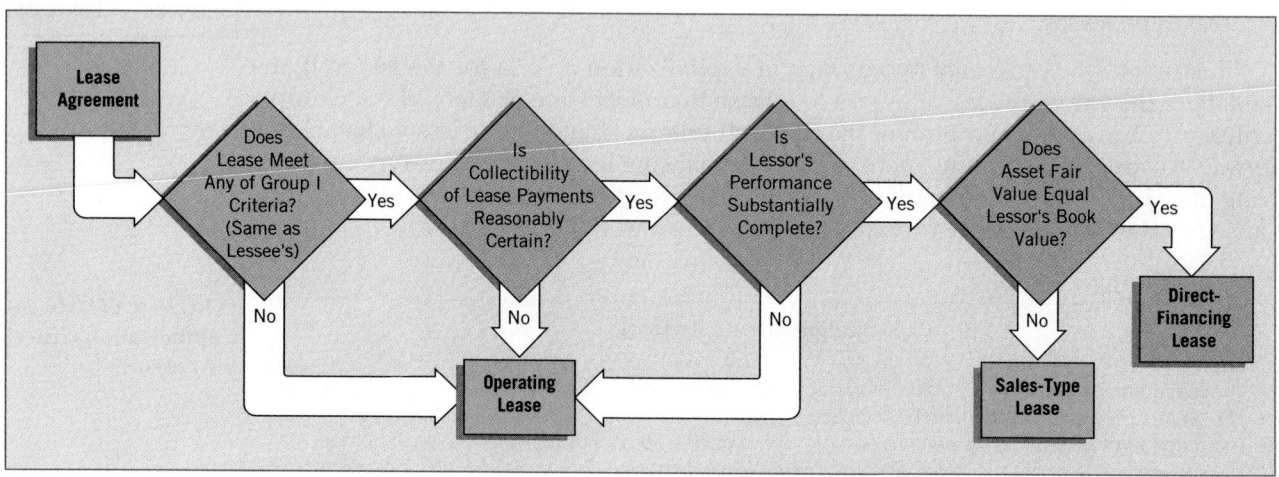

As a consequence of the additional Group II criteria for lessors, a lessor may classify a lease as an **operating** lease but the lessee may classify the same lease as a **capital** lease. In such an event, both the lessor and lessee will carry the asset on their books, and both will depreciate the capitalized asset.

For purposes of comparison with the lessee's accounting, we will illustrate only the operating and direct-financing leases in the following section. We will discuss the more complex sales-type lease later in the chapter.

Direct-Financing Method (Lessor)

<table>
<tr><td>

OBJECTIVE 5
Describe the lessor's accounting for direct-financing leases.

</td></tr>
</table>

Direct-financing leases are in substance the financing of an asset purchase by the lessee. In this type of lease, the lessor records a **lease receivable** instead of a leased asset. The lease receivable is the present value of the minimum lease payments. Remember that "minimum lease payments" include:

1 Rental payments (excluding executory costs).
2 Bargain purchase option (if any).
3 Guaranteed residual value (if any).
4 Penalty for failure to renew (if any).

Thus, the lessor records the residual value, whether guaranteed or not. Also, recall that if the lessor pays any executory costs, then it should reduce the rental payment by that amount in computing minimum lease payments.

The following presentation, using the data from the preceding Caterpillar/Sterling example on pages 1097–1099, illustrates the accounting treatment for a direct-financing lease. We repeat here the information relevant to Caterpillar in accounting for this lease transaction.

1 The term of the lease is five years beginning January 1, 2008, noncancelable, and requires equal rental payments of $25,981.62 at the beginning of each year. Payments include $2,000 of executory costs (property taxes).

2 The equipment (front-end loader) has a cost of $100,000 to Caterpillar, a fair value at the inception of the lease of $100,000, an estimated economic life of five years, and no residual value.

3 Caterpillar incurred no initial direct costs in negotiating and closing the lease transaction.

4 The lease contains no renewal options. The equipment reverts to Caterpillar at the termination of the lease.

5 Collectibility is reasonably assured and Caterpillar incurs no additional costs (with the exception of the property taxes being collected from Sterling).

6 Caterpillar sets the annual lease payments to ensure a rate of return of 10 percent (implicit rate) on its investment as shown in Illustration 21-13.

<table>
<tr><td>Fair market value of leased equipment</td><td>$100,000.00</td></tr>
<tr><td>Less: Present value of residual value</td><td>–0–</td></tr>
<tr><td>Amount to be recovered by lessor through lease payments</td><td>$100,000.00</td></tr>
<tr><td>Five beginning-of-the-year lease payments to yield a
10% return ($100,000 ÷ 4.16986^a)</td><td>$ 23,981.62</td></tr>
</table>

^aPV of an annuity due of 1 for 5 years at 10% (Table 6-5).

ILLUSTRATION 21-13
Computation of Lease Payments

The lease meets the criteria for classification as a direct-financing lease for several reasons: (1) The lease term exceeds 75 percent of the equipment's estimated economic life. (2) The present value of the minimum lease payments exceeds 90 percent of the equipment's fair value. (3) Collectibility of the payments is reasonably assured. And (4) Caterpillar incurs no further costs. It is not a sales-type lease because there is no difference between the fair value ($100,000) of the loader and Caterpillar's cost ($100,000).

The Lease Receivable is the present value of the minimum lease payments (excluding executory costs which are property taxes of $2,000). Caterpillar computes it as follows.

Lease receivable = ($25,981.62 − $2,000) × Present value of an annuity due of 1 for 5 periods at 10% (Table 6-5)

= $23,981.62 × 4.16986
= $100,000

ILLUSTRATION 21-14
Computation of Lease Receivable

Caterpillar records the lease of the asset and the resulting receivable on January 1, 2008 (the inception of the lease), as follows.

```
            Lease Receivable       100,000
                Equipment                      100,000
```

Companies often **report** the lease receivable in the balance sheet as "Net investment in capital leases." Companies classify it either as current or noncurrent, depending on when they recover the net investment.[17]

Caterpillar replaces its investment (the leased front-end loader, a cost of $100,000), with a lease receivable. In a manner similar to Sterling's treatment of interest, Caterpillar applies the effective-interest method and recognizes interest revenue as a function of the lease receivable balance, as Illustration 21-15 (page 1106) shows.

---

[17]In the notes to the financial statements (see Illustration 21-33), the lease receivable is reported at its gross amount (minimum lease payments plus the unguaranteed residual value). In addition, the lessor also reports total unearned interest related to the lease. As a result, some lessors record lease receivable on a gross basis and record the unearned interest in a separate account. We illustrate the net approach here because it is consistent with the accounting for the lessee.

ILLUSTRATION 21-15
Lease Amortization
Schedule for Lessor—
Annuity-Due Basis

CATERPILLAR FINANCIAL
LEASE AMORTIZATION SCHEDULE
(ANNUITY-DUE BASIS)

Date	Annual Lease Payment	Executory Costs	Interest (10%) on Lease Receivable	Lease Receivable Recovery	Lease Receivable
	(a)	(b)	(c)	(d)	(e)
1/1/08					$100,000.00
1/1/08	$ 25,981.62	$ 2,000.00	$ –0–	$ 23,981.62	76,018.38
1/1/09	25,981.62	2,000.00	7,601.84	16,379.78	59,638.60
1/1/10	25,981.62	2,000.00	5,963.86	18,017.76	41,620.84
1/1/11	25,981.62	2,000.00	4,162.08	19,819.54	21,801.30
1/1/12	25,981.62	2,000.00	2,180.32*	21,801.30	–0–
	$129,908.10	$10,000.00	$19,908.10	$100,000.00	

(a) Annual rental that provides a 10% return on net investment.
(b) Executory costs included in rental payment.
(c) Ten percent of the preceding balance of (e) except for 1/1/08.
(d) (a) minus (b) and (c).
(e) Preceding balance minus (d).
*Rounded by 19 cents.

On January 1, 2008, Caterpillar records receipt of the first year's lease payment as follows.

Cash	25,981.62	
Lease Receivable		23,981.62
Property Tax Expense/Property Taxes Payable		2,000.00

On December 31, 2008, Caterpillar recognizes the interest revenue earned during the first year through the following entry.

Interest Receivable	7,601.84	
Interest Revenue—Leases		7,601.84

At December 31, 2008, Caterpillar reports the lease receivable in its balance sheet among current assets or noncurrent assets, or both. It classifies the portion due within one year or the operating cycle, whichever is longer, as a current asset, and the rest with noncurrent assets.

Illustration 21-16 shows the assets section as it relates to lease transactions at December 31, 2008.

ILLUSTRATION 21-16
Reporting Lease
Transactions by Lessor

Current assets	
Interest receivable	$ 7,601.84
Lease receivable	16,379.78
Noncurrent assets (investments)	
Lease receivable	$59,638.60

The following entries record receipt of the second year's lease payment and recognition of the interest earned.

January 1, 2009

Cash	25,981.62	
Lease Receivable		16,379.78
Interest Receivable		7,601.84
Property Tax Expense/Property Taxes Payable		2,000.00

December 31, 2009

Interest Receivable	5,963.86	
Interest Revenue—Leases		5,963.86

Journal entries through 2012 follow the same pattern except that Caterpillar records no entry in 2012 (the last year) for earned interest. Because it fully collects the receivable by January 1, 2012, no balance (investment) is outstanding during 2012. Caterpillar **recorded no depreciation**. If Sterling buys the loader for $5,000 upon expiration of the lease, Caterpillar recognizes disposition of the equipment as follows.

Cash	5,000	
Gain on Sale of Leased Equipment		5,000

Operating Method (Lessor)

Under the **operating method**, the lessor records each rental receipt as rental revenue. It **depreciates the leased asset in the normal manner**, with the depreciation expense of the period matched against the rental revenue. The amount of revenue recognized in each accounting period is a level amount (straight-line basis) regardless of the lease provisions, unless another systematic and rational basis better represents the time pattern in which the lessor derives benefit from the leased asset.

In addition to the depreciation charge, the lessor expenses maintenance costs and the cost of any other services rendered under the provisions of the lease that pertain to the current accounting period. The lessor **amortizes over the life of the lease** any costs paid to independent third parties, such as appraisal fees, finder's fees, and costs of credit checks, usually on a straight-line basis.

To illustrate the operating method, assume that the direct-financing lease illustrated in the previous section does not qualify as a capital lease. Therefore, Caterpillar accounts for it as an operating lease. It records the cash rental receipt, assuming the $2,000 was for property tax expense, as follows.

Cash	25,981.62	
Rental Revenue		25,981.62

Caterpillar records depreciation as follows (assuming a straight-line method, a cost basis of $100,000, and a five-year life).

Depreciation Expense—Leased Equipment	20,000	
Accumulated Depreciation—Leased Equipment		20,000

If Caterpillar pays property taxes, insurance, maintenance, and other operating costs during the year, it records them as expenses chargeable against the gross rental revenues.

If Caterpillar owns plant assets that it uses in addition to those leased to others, the company **separately classifies the leased equipment and accompanying accumulated depreciation** as Equipment Leased to Others or Investment in Leased Property. If significant in amount or in terms of activity, Caterpillar separates the rental revenues and accompanying expenses in the income statement from sales revenue and cost of goods sold.

SPECIAL ACCOUNTING PROBLEMS

The features of lease arrangements that cause unique accounting problems are:

1   Residual values.

2   Sales-type leases (lessor).

3   Bargain purchase options.

4   Initial direct costs.

5   Current versus noncurrent classification.

6   Disclosure.

We discuss each of these features on the following pages.

> **OBJECTIVE 6**
> Identify special features of lease arrangements that cause unique accounting problems.

Residual Values

Up to this point, in order to develop the basic accounting issues related to lessee and lessor accounting, we have generally ignored residual values. Accounting for residual values is complex and will probably provide you with the greatest challenge in understanding lease accounting.

Meaning of Residual Value

The **residual value** is the estimated fair value of the leased asset at the end of the lease term. Frequently, a significant residual value exists at the end of the lease term, especially when the economic life of the leased asset exceeds the lease term. If title does not pass automatically to the lessee (criterion 1) and a bargain purchase option does not exist (criterion 2), the lessee returns physical custody of the asset to the lessor at the end of the lease term.[18]

Guaranteed versus Unguaranteed

The residual value may be unguaranteed or guaranteed by the lessee. Sometimes the lessee agrees to make up any deficiency below a stated amount that the lessor realizes in residual value at the end of the lease term. In such a case, that stated amount is the **guaranteed residual value.**

The parties to a lease use guaranteed residual value in lease arrangements for two reasons. The first is a business reason: It protects the lessor against any loss in estimated residual value, thereby ensuring the lessor of the desired rate of return on investment. The second reason is an accounting benefit that you will learn from the discussion at the end of this chapter.

Lease Payments

A guaranteed residual value—by definition—has more assurance of realization than does an unguaranteed residual value. As a result, the lessor may adjust lease payments because of the increased certainty of recovery. After the lessor establishes this rate, it makes no difference from an accounting point of view whether the residual value is guaranteed or unguaranteed. The net investment that the lessor records (once the rate is set) will be the same.

Assume the same data as in the Caterpillar/Sterling illustrations except that Caterpillar estimates a residual value of $5,000 at the end of the five-year lease term. In addition, Caterpillar assumes a 10 percent return on investment (ROI),[19] whether the residual value is guaranteed or unguaranteed. Caterpillar would compute the amount of the lease payments as follows.

ILLUSTRATION 21-17
Lessor's Computation
of Lease Payments

CATERPILLAR'S COMPUTATION OF LEASE PAYMENTS (10% ROI) GUARANTEED OR UNGUARANTEED RESIDUAL VALUE (ANNUITY-DUE BASIS, INCLUDING RESIDUAL VALUE)	
Fair market value of leased asset to lessor	$100,000.00
Less: Present value of residual value ($5,000 × .62092, Table 6-2)	3,104.60
Amount to be recovered by lessor through lease payments	$ 96,895.40
Five periodic lease payments ($96,895.40 ÷ 4.16986, Table 6-5)	$ 23,237.09

[18]When the lease term and the economic life are not the same, the residual value and the salvage value of the asset will probably differ. For simplicity, we will assume that residual value and salvage value are the same, even when the economic life and lease term vary.

[19]Technically, the rate of return Caterpillar demands would differ depending upon whether the residual value was guaranteed or unguaranteed. To simplify the illustrations, we are ignoring this difference in subsequent sections.

Contrast the foregoing lease payment amount to the lease payments of $23,981.62 as computed in Illustration 21-10, where no residual value existed. In the second example, the payments are less, because the present value of the residual value reduces Caterpillar's total recoverable amount from $100,000 to $96,895.40.

Lessee Accounting for Residual Value

Whether the estimated residual value is guaranteed or unguaranteed has both economic and accounting consequence to the lessee. We saw the economic consequence—lower lease payments—in the preceding example. The accounting consequence is that the **minimum lease payments**, the basis for capitalization, include the guaranteed residual value but excludes the unguaranteed residual value.

Guaranteed Residual Value (Lessee Accounting). A guaranteed residual value affects the lessee's computation of minimum lease payments. Therefore it also affects the amounts capitalized as a leased asset and a lease obligation. In effect, the guaranteed residual value **is an additional lease payment that the lessee will pay in property or cash, or both, at the end of the lease term**.

Using the rental payments as computed by the lessor in Illustration 21-17, the minimum lease payments are $121,185.45 ([$23,237.09 × 5] + $5,000). Illustration 21-18 shows the capitalized present value of the minimum lease payments (excluding executory costs) for Sterling Construction.

> **OBJECTIVE 7**
> Describe the effect of residual values, guaranteed and unguaranteed, on lease accounting.

STERLING'S CAPITALIZED AMOUNT (10% RATE) (ANNUITY-DUE BASIS, INCLUDING GUARANTEED RESIDUAL VALUE)	
Present value of five annual rental payments ($23,237.09 × 4.16986, Table 6-5)	$ 96,895.40
Present value of guaranteed residual value of $5,000 due five years after date of inception: ($5,000 × .62092, Table 6-2)	3,104.60
Lessee's capitalized amount	$100,000.00

ILLUSTRATION 21-18
Computation of Lessee's Capitalized Amount—Guaranteed Residual Value

Sterling prepares a schedule of interest expense and amortization of the $100,000 lease liability. That schedule, shown in Illustration 21-19, is based on a $5,000 final guaranteed residual value payment at the end of five years.

ILLUSTRATION 21-19
Lease Amortization Schedule for Lessee—Guaranteed Residual Value

STERLING CONSTRUCTION LEASE AMORTIZATION SCHEDULE (ANNUITY-DUE BASIS, GUARANTEED RESIDUAL VALUE—GRV)					
Date	Lease Payment Plus GRV	Executory Costs	Interest (10%) on Liability	Reduction of Lease Liability	Lease Liability
	(a)	(b)	(c)	(d)	(e)
1/1/08					$100,000.00
1/1/08	$ 25,237.09	$ 2,000	–0–	$ 23,237.09	76,762.91
1/1/09	25,237.09	2,000	$ 7,676.29	15,560.80	61,202.11
1/1/10	25,237.09	2,000	6,120.21	17,116.88	44,085.23
1/1/11	25,237.09	2,000	4,408.52	18,828.57	25,256.66
1/1/12	25,237.09	2,000	2,525.67	20,711.42	4,545.24
12/31/12	5,000.00*		454.76**	4,545.24	–0–
	$131,185.45	$10,000	$21,185.45	$100,000.00	

(a) Annual lease payment as required by lease.
(b) Executory costs included in rental payment.
(c) Preceding balance of (e) × 10%, except 1/1/08.
(d) (a) minus (b) and (c).
(e) Preceding balance minus (d).

*Represents the guaranteed residual value.
**Rounded by 24 cents.

Sterling records the leased asset (front-end loader) and liability, depreciation, interest, property tax, and lease payments on the basis of a guaranteed residual value. (These journal entries are shown in Illustration 21-24, on page 1112.) The format of these entries is the same as illustrated earlier, although the amounts are different because of the guaranteed residual value. Sterling records the loader at $100,000 and depreciates it over five years. To compute depreciation, it subtracts the guaranteed residual value from the cost of the loader. Assuming that Sterling uses the straight-line method, the depreciation expense each year is $19,000 ([$100,000 − $5,000] ÷ 5 years).

At the end of the lease term, before the lessee transfers the asset to Caterpillar, the lease asset and liability accounts have the following balances.

ILLUSTRATION 21-20
Account Balances on
Lessee's Books at End of
Lease Term—Guaranteed
Residual Value

Leased equipment under capital leases	$100,000.00	Interest payable	$ 454.76
Less: Accumulated depreciation—		Lease liability	4,545.24
capital leases	95,000.00		
	$ 5,000.00		$5,000.00

If, at the end of the lease, the fair market value of the residual value is less than $5,000, Sterling will have to record a loss. Assume that Sterling depreciated the leased asset down to its residual value of $5,000 but that the fair market value of the residual value at December 31, 2012, was $3,000. In this case, Sterling would have to report a loss of $2,000. Assuming that it pays cash to make up the residual value deficiency, Sterling would make the following journal entry.

Loss on Capital Lease	2,000.00	
Interest Expense (or Interest Payable)	454.76	
Lease Liability	4,545.24	
Accumulated Depreciation—Capital Leases	95,000.00	
Leased Equipment under Capital Leases		100,000.00
Cash		2,000.00

If the fair market value *exceeds* $5,000, a gain may be recognized. Caterpillar and Sterling may apportion gains on guaranteed residual values in whatever ratio the parties initially agree.

When there is a guaranteed residual value, the lessee must be careful not to depreciate the total cost of the asset. For example, if Sterling mistakenly depreciated the total cost of the loader ($100,000), a misstatement would occur. That is, the carrying amount of the asset at the end of the lease term would be zero, but Sterling would show the liability under the capital lease at $5,000. In that case, if the asset was worth $5,000, Sterling would end up reporting a gain of $5,000 when it transferred the asset back to Caterpillar. As a result, Sterling would overstate depreciation and would understate net income in 2008–2011; in the last year (2012) net income would be overstated.

Unguaranteed Residual Value (Lessee Accounting). From the lessee's viewpoint, an **unguaranteed residual value** is the same as no residual value in terms of its effect upon the lessee's method of computing the minimum lease payments and the capitalization of the leased asset and the lease liability.

Assume the same facts as those above except that the $5,000 residual value is **unguaranteed** instead of guaranteed. The amount of the annual lease payments would be the same—$23,237.09. Whether the residual value is guaranteed or unguaranteed, Caterpillar will recover the same amount through lease rentals—that is, $96,895.40. The minimum lease payments are $116,185.45 ($23,237.09 × 5). Lessee Company would capitalize the amount shown in Illustration 21-21.

STERLING'S CAPITALIZED AMOUNT (10% RATE)	
(ANNUITY-DUE BASIS, INCLUDING **UNGUARANTEED** RESIDUAL VALUE)	
Present value of 5 annual rental payments of $23,237.09 × 4.16986 (Table 6-5)	$96,895.40
Unguaranteed residual value of $5,000 (not capitalized by lessee)	–0–
Lessee's capitalized amount	$96,895.40

Illustration 21-22 shows Sterling's schedule of interest expense and amortization of the lease liability of $96,895.40, assuming an unguaranteed residual value of $5,000 at the end of five years.

	STERLING CONSTRUCTION				
	LEASE AMORTIZATION SCHEDULE (10%)				
	(ANNUITY-DUE BASIS, **UNGUARANTEED** RESIDUAL VALUE)				
Date	Annual Lease Payments	Executory Costs	Interest (10%) on Liability	Reduction of Lease Liability	Lease Liability
	(a)	(b)	(c)	(d)	(e)
1/1/08					$96,895.40
1/1/08	$ 25,237.09	$ 2,000	–0–	$23,237.09	73,658.31
1/1/09	25,237.09	2,000	$ 7,365.83	15,871.26	57,787.05
1/1/10	25,237.09	2,000	5,778.71	17,458.38	40,328.67
1/1/11	25,237.09	2,000	4,032.87	19,204.22	21,124.45
1/1/12	25,237.09	2,000	2,112.64*	21,124.45	–0–
	$126,185.45	$10,000	$19,290.05	$96,895.40	

(a) Annual lease payment as required by lease.
(b) Executory costs included in rental payment.
(c) Preceding balance of (e) × 10%.
(d) (a) minus (b) and (c).
(e) Preceding balance minus (d).
*Rounded by 19 cents.

Sterling records the leased asset and liability, depreciation, interest, property tax, and lease payments on the basis of an unguaranteed residual value. (These journal entries are shown in Illustration 21-24, on page 1112.) The format of these capital lease entries is the same as illustrated earlier. Note that Sterling records the leased asset at $96,895.40 and depreciates it over five years. Assuming that it uses the straight-line method, the depreciation expense each year is $19,379.08 ($96,895.40 ÷ 5 years). At the end of the lease term, before Sterling transfers the asset to Caterpillar, the lease asset and liability accounts have the following balances.

ILLUSTRATION 21-23
Account Balances on
Lessee's Books at End
of Lease Term—
Unguaranteed Residual
Value

Leased equipment under capital leases	$96,895	Lease liability	$–0–
Less: Accumulated depreciation— capital leases	96,895		
	$ –0–		

Assuming that Sterling has fully depreciated the leased asset and has fully amortized the lease liability, no entry is required at the end of the lease term, except to remove the asset from the books.

If Sterling depreciated the asset down to its unguaranteed residual value, a misstatement would occur. That is, the carrying amount of the leased asset would be $5,000 at the end of the lease, but the liability under the capital lease would be stated at zero before the transfer of the asset. Thus, Sterling would end up reporting a loss of $5,000 when it transferred the asset back to Caterpillar. Sterling would understate depreciation and would overstate net income in 2008–2011; in the last year (2012) net income would be understated because of the recorded loss.

Lessee Entries Involving Residual Values. Illustration 21-24 shows, in comparative form, Sterling's entries for both a guaranteed and an unguaranteed residual value.

ILLUSTRATION 21-24
Comparative Entries for
Guaranteed and
Unguaranteed Residual
Values, Lessee Company

Guaranteed Residual Value			Unguaranteed Residual Value		
Capitalization of Lease 1/1/08:					
Leased Equipment under			Leased Equipment under		
Capital Leases	100,000.00		Capital Leases	96,895.40	
Lease Liability		100,000.00	Lease Liability		96,895.40
First Payment 1/1/08:					
Property Tax Expense	2,000.00		Property Tax Expense	2,000.00	
Lease Liability	23,237.09		Lease Liability	23,237.09	
Cash		25,237.09	Cash		25,237.09
Adjusting Entry for Accrued Interest 12/31/08:					
Interest Expense	7,676.29		Interest Expense	7,365.83	
Interest Payable		7,676.29	Interest Payable		7,365.83
Entry to Record Depreciation 12/31/08:					
Depreciation Expense—			Depreciation Expense—		
Capital Leases	19,000.00		Capital Leases	19,379.08	
Accumulated Depreciation—			Accumulated Depreciation—		
Capital Leases		19,000.00	Capital Leases		19,379.08
([$100,000 − $5,000] ÷ 5 years)			($96,895.40 ÷ 5 years)		
Second Payment 1/1/09:					
Property Tax Expense	2,000.00		Property Tax Expense	2,000.00	
Lease Liability	15,560.80		Lease Liability	15,871.26	
Interest Expense			Interest Expense		
(or Interest Payable)	7,676.29		(or Interest Payable)	7,365.83	
Cash		25,237.09	Cash		25,237.09

Lessor Accounting for Residual Value

As we indicated earlier, the lessor will recover the same net investment whether the residual value is guaranteed or unguaranteed. That is, the lessor works on the assumption that it will realize **the residual value at the end of the lease term whether guaranteed or unguaranteed**. The lease payments required in order for the company to earn a certain return on investment are the same (e.g., $23,237.09 in our example) whether the residual value is guaranteed or unguaranteed.

To illustrate, we again use the Caterpillar/Sterling data and assume classification of the lease as a direct-financing lease. With a residual value (either guaranteed or unguaranteed) of $5,000, Caterpillar determines the payments as follows.

Fair market value of leased equipment	$100,000.00
Less: Present value of residual value ($5,000 × .62092, Table 6-2)	3,104.60
Amount to be recovered by lessor through lease payments	$ 96,895.40
Five beginning-of-the-year lease payments to yield a 10% return ($96,895.40 ÷ 4.16986, Table 6-5)	$ 23,237.09

ILLUSTRATION 21-25
Computation of Direct-Financing Lease Payments

The amortization schedule is the same for guaranteed or unguaranteed residual value, as Illustration 21-26 shows.

CATERPILLAR FINANCIAL
LEASE AMORTIZATION SCHEDULE
(ANNUITY-DUE BASIS, **GUARANTEED** OR **UNGUARANTEED** RESIDUAL VALUE)

Date	Annual Lease Payment Plus Residual Value	Executory Costs	Interest (10%) on Lease Receivable	Lease Receivable Recovery	Lease Receivable
	(a)	(b)	(c)	(d)	(e)
1/1/08					$100,000.00
1/1/08	$ 25,237.09	$ 2,000.00	$ –0–	$ 23,237.09	76,762.91
1/1/09	25,237.09	2,000.00	7,676.29	15,560.80	61,202.11
1/1/10	25,237.09	2,000.00	6,120.21	17,116.88	44,085.23
1/1/11	25,237.09	2,000.00	4,408.52	18,828.57	25,256.66
1/1/12	25,237.09	2,000.00	2,525.67	20,711.42	4,545.24
12/31/12	5,000.00	–0–	454.76*	4,545.24	–0–
	$131,185.45	$10,000.00	$21,185.45	$100,000.00	

(a) Annual lease payment as required by lease.
(b) Executory costs included in rental payment.
(c) Preceding balance of (e) × 10%, except 1/1/08.
(d) (a) minus (b) and (c).
(e) Preceding balance minus (d).
*Rounded by 24 cents.

ILLUSTRATION 21-26
Lease Amortization Schedule, for Lessor—Guaranteed or Unguaranteed Residual Value

Using the amounts computed above, Caterpillar would make the following entries for this direct-financing lease in the first year. Note the similarity to Sterling's entries in Illustration 21-24.

Inception of Lease 1/1/08:

Lease Receivable	100,000.00	
Equipment		100,000.00

First Payment Received 1/1/08:

Cash	25,237.09	
Lease Receivable		23,237.09
Property Tax Expense/Property Taxes Payable		2,000.00

Adjusting Entry for Accrued Interest 12/31/08:

Interest Receivable	7,676.29	
Interest Revenue		7,676.29

ILLUSTRATION 21-27
Entries for Either Guaranteed or Unguaranteed Residual Value, Lessor Company

Sales-Type Leases (Lessor)

As already indicated, the primary difference between a direct-financing lease and a **sales-type lease** is the manufacturer's or dealer's gross profit (or loss). The diagram in Illustration 21-28 presents the distinctions between direct-financing and sales-type leases.

OBJECTIVE 8
Describe the lessor's accounting for sales-type leases.

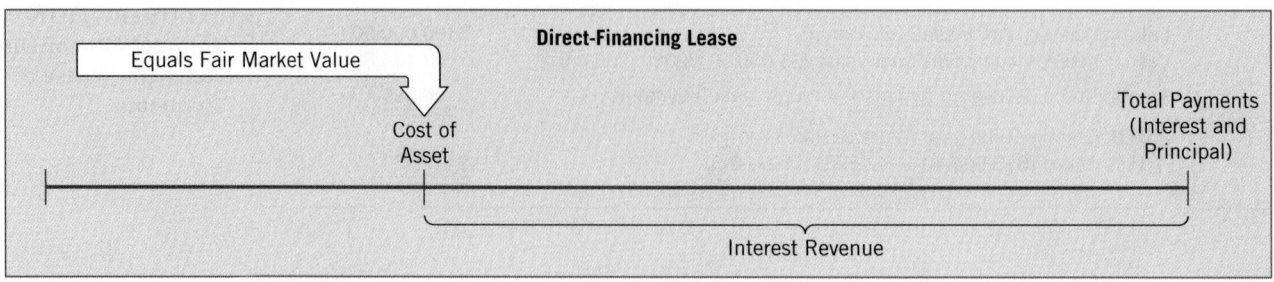

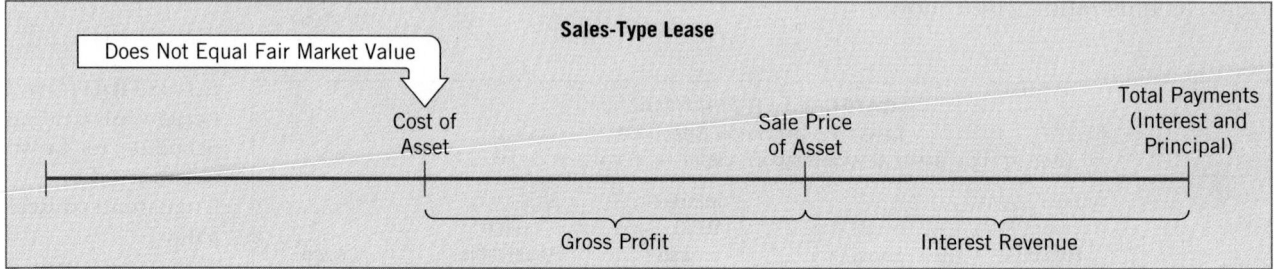

ILLUSTRATION 21-28
Direct-Financing versus
Sales-Type Leases

In a sales-type lease, the lessor records the sale price of the asset, the cost of goods sold and related inventory reduction, and the lease receivable. The information necessary to record the sales-type lease is as follows.

SALES-TYPE LEASE TERMS

LEASE RECEIVABLE (also **NET INVESTMENT**). The present value of the minimum lease payments plus the present value of any unguaranteed residual value. The lease receivable therefore includes the present value of the residual value, whether guaranteed or not.

SALES PRICE OF THE ASSET. The present value of the minimum lease payments.

COST OF GOODS SOLD. The cost of the asset to the lessor, less the present value of any unguaranteed residual value.

When recording sales revenue and cost of goods sold, there is a difference in the accounting for guaranteed and unguaranteed residual values. The guaranteed residual value can be considered part of sales revenue because the lessor knows that the entire asset has been sold. But there is less certainty that the unguaranteed residual portion of the asset has been "sold" (i.e., will be realized). Therefore, the lessor recognizes sales and cost of goods sold only for the portion of the asset for which realization is assured. However, **the gross profit amount on the sale of the asset is the same whether a guaranteed or unguaranteed residual value is involved**.

To illustrate a sales-type lease with a guaranteed residual value and with an unguaranteed residual value, assume the same facts as in the preceding direct-financing lease situation (pages 1104–1107). The estimated residual value is $5,000 (the present value of which is $3,104.60), and the leased equipment has an $85,000 cost to the dealer, Caterpillar. Assume that the fair market value of the residual value is $3,000 at the end of the lease term.

Illustration 21-29 shows computation of the amounts relevant to a sales-type lease.

ILLUSTRATION 21-29
Computation of Lease
Amounts by Caterpillar
Financial—Sales-Type
Lease

	Sales-Type Lease	
	Guaranteed Residual Value	Unguaranteed Residual Value
Lease receivable	$100,000 [$23,237.09 × 4.16986 (Table 6-5) + $5,000 × .62092 (Table 6-2)]	Same
Sales price of the asset	$100,000	$96,895.40 ($100,000 − $3,104.60)
Cost of goods sold	$85,000	$81,895.40 ($85,000 − $3,104.60)
Gross profit	$15,000 ($100,000 − $85,000)	$15,000 ($96,895.40 − $81,895.40)

Caterpillar records the same profit ($15,000) at the point of sale whether the residual value is guaranteed or unguaranteed. The difference between the two is that **the sales revenue and cost of goods sold amounts are different**.

In making this computation, we deduct the present value of the unguaranteed residual value from sales revenue and cost of goods sold for two reasons: (1) The criteria for revenue recognition have not been met. (2) It is improper to match expense against revenue not yet recognized. The revenue recognition criteria have not been met **because of the uncertainty surrounding the realization of the unguaranteed residual value**.

Caterpillar makes the following entries to record this transaction on January 1, 2008, and the receipt of the residual value at the end of the lease term.

ILLUSTRATION 21-30
Entries for Guaranteed
and Unguaranteed
Residual Values, Lessor
Company—Sales-Type
Lease

Guaranteed Residual Value			Unguaranteed Residual Value		
To record sales-type lease at inception (January 1, 2008):					
Cost of Goods Sold	85,000.00		Cost of Goods Sold	81,895.40	
Lease Receivable	100,000.00		Lease Receivable	100,000.00	
Sales Revenue		100,000.00	Sales Revenue		96,895.40
Inventory		85,000.00	Inventory		85,000.00
To record receipt of the first lease payment (January 1, 2008):					
Cash	25,237.09		Cash	25,237.09	
Lease Receivable		23,237.09	Lease Receivable		23,237.09
Property Tax Exp./Pay.		2,000.00	Property Tax Exp./Pay.		2,000.00
To recognize interest revenue earned during the first year (December 31, 2008):					
Interest Receivable	7,676.29		Interest Receivable	7,676.29	
Interest Revenue		7,676.29	Interest Revenue		7,676.29
(See lease amortization schedule, Illustration 21-26 on page 1113.)					
To record receipt of the second lease payment (January 1, 2009):					
Cash	25,237.09		Cash	25,237.09	
Interest Receivable		7,676.29	Interest Receivable		7,676.29
Lease Receivable		15,560.80	Lease Receivable		15,560.80
Property Tax Exp./Pay.		2,000.00	Property Tax Exp./Pay.		2,000.00
To recognize interest revenue earned during the second year (December 31, 2009):					
Interest Receivable	6,120.21		Interest Receivable	6,120.21	
Interest Revenue		6,120.21	Interest Revenue		6,120.21
To record receipt of residual value at end of lease term (December 31, 2012):					
Inventory	3,000		Inventory	3,000	
Cash	2,000		Loss on Capital Lease	2,000	
Lease Receivable		5,000	Lease Receivable		5,000

Companies must periodically review the **estimated unguaranteed residual value in a sales-type lease**. If the estimate of the unguaranteed residual value declines, the company must revise the accounting for the transaction using the changed estimate. The decline represents a reduction in the lessor's lease receivable (net investment). The lessor recognizes the decline as a loss in the period in which it reduces the residual estimate. Companies do not recognize upward adjustments in estimated residual value.

WHAT DO THE NUMBERS MEAN?

XEROX TAKES ON THE SEC

Xerox derives much of its income from leasing equipment. Reporting such leases as sales leases, Xerox records a lease contract as a sale, therefore recognizing income immediately. One problem is that each lease receipt consists of payments for items such as supplies, services, financing, and equipment.

The SEC *accused* Xerox of inappropriately allocating lease receipts, which affects the timing of income that it reports. If Xerox applied SEC guidelines, it would report income in different time periods. Xerox contended that its methods were correct. It also noted that when the lease term is up, the bottom line is the same using either the SEC's recommended allocation method or its current method.

Although Xerox can refuse to change its method, the SEC has the right to prevent a company from selling stock or bonds to the public if the agency rejects filings of the company.

Apparently, being able to access public markets is very valuable to Xerox. The company agreed to change its accounting according to SEC wishes, and paid a fine of $10 million due to its past accounting practices.

Source: Adapted from "Xerox Takes on the SEC," *Accounting Web* (January 9, 2002) (*www.accountingweb.com*).

Bargain Purchase Option (Lessee)

As stated earlier, a bargain purchase option allows the lessee to purchase the leased property for a future price that is substantially lower than the property's expected future fair value. The price is so favorable at the lease's inception that the future exercise of the option appears to be reasonably assured. If a bargain purchase option exists, **the lessee must increase the present value of the minimum lease payments by the present value of the option price**.

For example, assume that Sterling Construction in the illustration on page 1109 had an option to buy the leased equipment for $5,000 at the end of the five-year lease term. At that point, Sterling and Caterpillar expect the fair value to be $18,000. The significant difference between the option price and the fair value creates a bargain purchase option, and the exercise of that option is reasonably assured.

A bargain purchase option affects the accounting for leases in essentially the same way as a guaranteed residual value. In other words, with a guaranteed residual value, the lessee must pay the residual value at the end of the lease. Similarly, a purchase option which is a bargain will almost certainly be paid by the lessee. Therefore, the computations, amortization schedule, and entries that would be prepared for this $5,000 bargain purchase option are identical to those shown for the $5,000 guaranteed residual value (see Illustrations 21-17, 21-18, and 21-19).

The only difference between the accounting treatment for a bargain purchase option and a guaranteed residual value of identical amounts and circumstances is in the **computation of the annual depreciation**. In the case of a guaranteed residual value, Sterling depreciates the asset over the lease term; in the case of a bargain purchase option, it uses the **economic life** of the asset.

Initial Direct Costs (Lessor)

Initial direct costs are of two types: incremental and internal.[20] **Incremental direct costs** are paid to independent third parties for originating a lease arrangement. Examples include the cost of independent appraisal of collateral used to secure a lease, the cost of an outside credit check of the lessee, or a broker's fee for finding the lessee.

Internal direct costs are directly related to specified activities performed **by the lessor** on a given lease. Examples are evaluating the prospective lessee's financial condition; evaluating and recording guarantees, collateral, and other security arrangements; negotiating lease terms and preparing and processing lease documents; and closing the transaction. The costs directly related to an employee's time spent on a specific lease transaction are also considered initial direct costs.

However, initial direct costs should **not** include **internal indirect costs**. Such costs are related to activities the lessor performs for advertising, servicing existing leases, and establishing and monitoring credit policies. Nor should the lessor include the costs for supervision and administration or for expenses such as rent and depreciation.

The accounting for initial direct costs depends on the type of lease:

- For **operating leases**, the lessor should defer initial direct costs and **allocate them over the lease term** in proportion to the recognition of rental revenue.
- For **sales-type leases**, the lessor expenses the initial direct costs **in the period** in which it recognizes the profit on the sale.
- For a **direct-financing lease**, the lessor adds initial direct costs to the net investment in the lease and **amortizes them over the life of the lease as a yield adjustment**.

In a direct-financing lease, the lessor must disclose the unamortized deferred initial direct costs that are part of its investment in the direct-financing lease. For example, if the carrying value of the asset in the lease is $4,000,000 and the lessor incurs initial direct costs of $35,000, then the lease receivable (net investment in the lease) would be $4,035,000. The yield would be lower than the initial rate of return, and the lessor would adjust the yield to ensure proper amortization of the amount over the life of the lease.

Current versus Noncurrent

Earlier in the chapter we presented the classification of the lease liability/receivable in an annuity-due situation. Illustration 21-8 indicated that Sterling's current liability is the payment of $23,981.62 (excluding $2,000 of executory costs) to be made on January 1 of the next year. Similarly, as shown in Illustration 21-16, Caterpillar's current asset is the $23,981.62 (excluding $2,000 of executory costs) it will collect on January 1 of the next year. In these annuity-due instances, the balance sheet date is December 31 and the due date of the lease payment is January 1 (less than one year), so the present value ($23,981.62) of the payment due the following January 1 is the same as the rental payment ($23,981.62).

What happens if the situation is an ordinary annuity rather than an annuity due? For example, assume that the rent is due at the **end of the year** (December 31) rather than at the beginning (January 1). *FASB Statement No. 13* does not indicate how to measure the current and noncurrent amounts. It requires that for the lessee the "obligations shall be separately identified on the balance sheet as obligations under capital leases and shall be subject to the same considerations as other obligations in classifying them with current and noncurrent liabilities in classified balance sheets."[21] **The most common**

---

[20]"Accounting for Nonrefundable Fees and Costs Associated with Originating or Acquiring Loans and Initial Direct Costs of Leases," *Statement of Financial Accounting Standards No. 91* (Stamford: Conn.: FASB, 1987).

[21]"Accounting for Leases," op. cit., par. 16.

method of measuring the current liability portion in ordinary annuity leases is the change-in-the-present-value method.[22]

To illustrate the change-in-the-present-value method, assume an ordinary-annuity situation with the same facts as the Caterpillar/Sterling case, excluding the $2,000 of executory costs. Because Sterling pays the rents at the end of the period instead of at the beginning, Caterpillar sets the five rents at $26,379.73, to have an effective interest rate of 10 percent. Illustration 21-31 shows the ordinary-annuity amortization schedule.

ILLUSTRATION 21-31
Lease Amortization
Schedule—Ordinary-
Annuity Basis

| | Annual Lease | Interest | Reduction of Lease | Balance of Lease |
Date	Payment	10%	Liability/Receivable	Liability/Receivable
1/1/08				$100,000.00
12/31/08	$ 26,379.73	$10,000.00	$ 16,379.73	83,620.27
12/31/09	26,379.73	8,362.03	18,017.70	65,602.57
12/31/10	26,379.73	6,560.26	19,819.47	45,783.10
12/31/11	26,379.73	4,578.31	21,801.42	23,981.68
12/31/12	26,379.73	2,398.05*	23,981.68	–0–
	$131,898.65	$31,898.65	$100,000.00	

*Rounded by 12 cents.

Table title: **STERLING/CATERPILLAR** **LEASE AMORTIZATION SCHEDULE** (ORDINARY-ANNUITY BASIS)

The current portion of the lease liability/receivable under the **change-in-the-present-value method** as of December 31, 2008, would be $18,017.70 ($83,620.27 − $65,602.57). As of December 31, 2009, the current portion would be $19,819.47 ($65,602.57 − $45,783.10). At December 31, 2008, Caterpillar classifies $65,602.57 of the receivable as noncurrent.

Thus, both the annuity-due and the ordinary-annuity situations report the reduction of principal for the next period as a current liability/current asset. In the annuity-due situation, Caterpillar accrues interest during the year but is not paid until the next period. As a result, **a current asset arises for the receivable reduction and for the interest** that was earned in the preceding period.

In the ordinary-annuity situation, the interest accrued during the period is also paid in the same period. Consequently, the lessor shows as a current asset only the principal reduction.

Disclosing Lease Data

OBJECTIVE 9
List the disclosure
requirements for
leases.

The FASB requires **lessees** and **lessors** to disclose certain information about leases in their financial statements or in the notes. These requirements vary based upon the type of lease (capital or operating) and whether the issuer is the lessor or lessee. These disclosure requirements provide investors with the following information:

- General description of the nature of leasing arrangements.
- The nature, timing, and amount of cash inflows and outflows associated with leases, including payments to be paid or received for each of the five succeeding years.
- The amount of lease revenues and expenses reported in the income statement each period.

[22]For additional discussion on this approach and possible alternatives, see R. J. Swieringa, "When Current Is Noncurrent and Vice Versa!" *The Accounting Review* (January 1984), pp. 123–30, and A. W. Richardson, "The Measurement of the Current Portion of the Long-Term Lease Obligations—Some Evidence from Practice," *The Accounting Review* (October 1985), pp. 744–52.

- Description and amounts of leased assets by major balance sheet classification and related liabilities.
- Amounts receivable and unearned revenues under lease agreements.[23]

Illustration 21-32 presents financial statement excerpts from the 2004 annual report of **Tasty Baking Company**. These excerpts represent the statement and note disclosures typical of a lessee having both capital leases and operating leases.

Tasty Baking Company
(dollar amounts in thousands)

Current Liabilities	2004	2003
Current obligations under capital leases	$ 713	$ 634
Noncurrent Liabilities		
Long-term obligations under capital leases, less current portion	4,159	4,705

Note 7: Commitments and Contingencies

The company leases certain plant and distribution facilities, machinery and automotive equipment under noncancelable lease agreements. The company expects that in the normal course of business, leases that expire will be renewed or replaced by other leases. . . .Property, plant and equipment relating to capital leases was $5,965 at December 25, 2004, and $8,310 at December 27, 2003, with accumulated amortization of $1,019 and $2,303, respectively. Depreciation and amortization of assets recorded under capital leases was $690 in 2004 and $261 in 2003.

The following is a schedule of future minimum lease payments as of December 25, 2004:

	Capital Leases	Noncancelable Operating Leases
2005	$1,142	$1,747
2006	1,142	1,440
2007	1,089	701
2008	581	487
2009	561	146
Later years	2,525	4
Total minimum lease payments	$7,040	$4,525
Less interest portion of payments	2,168	
Present value of future minimum lease payments	$4,872	

Rental expense was approximately $2,474 in 2004 and $2,194 in 2003.

ILLUSTRATION 21-32
Disclosure of Leases by Lessee

Description and amount of lease obligations

General description

Description and amounts of leased assets

Nature, timing, and amounts of cash outflows

Amount of lease rental expense

Illustration 21-33 presents the lease note disclosure from the 2004 annual report of **Hewlett-Packard Company**. The disclosure highlights required lessor disclosures.

Hewlett-Packard Company
Notes to Financial Statements
(in millions)

Note 1 (in part): Lease Financing

Lease financing consists of direct financing leases, leveraged leases and equipment on operating leases. Income on direct financing leases is recognized by a method which produces a constant periodic rate of return on the outstanding investment in the lease. . . . Initial direct costs are deferred and amortized using the interest method over the lease period. Equipment under operating leases is recorded at cost, net of accumulated depreciation. Income from operating leases is recognized ratably over the term of the leases.

continued on next page

ILLUSTRATION 21-33
Disclosure of Leases by Lessor

General description

---

[23]"Accounting for Leases," *FASB Statement No. 13*, as amended and interpreted through May 1980 (Stamford, Conn.: FASB, 1980), par. 16; par. 23.

Amount receivable and unearned revenues

Nature, timing, and amounts of cash inflows

Description of leased assets

Amount of future rentals

> **Note 9: Financing Receivables and Operating Leases**
> Financing receivables represent sales-type and direct-financing leases resulting from the marketing of HP's and complementary third-party products. These receivables typically have terms from two to five years and are usually collateralized by a security interest in the underlying assets. Financing receivables also include billed receivables from operating leases. The components of net financing receivables, which are included in financing receivables and long-term financing receivables and other assets, were as follows at October 31:
>
> | | 2004 | 2003 |
> |---|---|---|
> | | (In millions) | |
> | Minimum lease payments receivable | $ 5.328 | $ 6,010 |
> | Allowance for doubtful accounts | (213) | (210) |
> | Unguaranteed residual value | 394 | 446 |
> | Unearned income | (396) | (475) |
> | Financing receivables, net | 5,113 | 5,771 |
> | Less current portion | (2,945) | (3,026) |
> | Amounts due after one year, net | $ 2,168 | $ 2,745 |
>
> Scheduled maturities of HP's minimum lease payments receivable are as follows at October 31, 2004:
>
> | | 2005 | 2006 | 2007 | 2008 | 2009 | Thereafter | Total |
> |---|---|---|---|---|---|---|---|
> | | | | (In millions) | | | | |
> | Scheduled maturities of minimum lease payments receivable | $3,045 | $1,381 | $612 | $194 | $67 | $29 | $5,328 |
>
> Equipment leased to customers under operating leases was $2.3 billion at October 31, 2004, and $2.1 billion at October 31, 2003, and is included in machinery and equipment. Accumulated depreciation on equipment under lease was $0.9 billion at October 31, 2004 and $1.2 billion at October 31, 2003. Minimum future rentals on non-cancelable operating leases related to leased equipment are as follows at October 31, 2004:
>
> | | 2005 | 2006 | 2007 | 2008 | 2009 | Thereafter | Total |
> |---|---|---|---|---|---|---|---|
> | | | | (In millions) | | | | |
> | Minimum future rentals on non-cancelable operating leases | $824 | $404 | $103 | $18 | $3 | $11 | $1,363 |

Additional Lease Disclosures

LEASE ACCOUNTING—UNSOLVED PROBLEMS

As we indicated at the beginning of this chapter, lease accounting is subject to abuse. Companies make strenuous efforts to circumvent *Statement No. 13.* In practice, the strong desires of lessees to resist capitalization have rendered the accounting rules for capitalizing leases partially ineffective. Leasing generally involves large dollar amounts that, when capitalized, materially increase reported liabilities and adversely affect the debt-to-equity ratio. Lessees also resist lease capitalization because charges to expense made in the early years of the lease term are higher under the capital lease method than under the operating method, frequently without tax benefit. As a consequence, "let's beat *Statement No. 13*" is one of the most popular games in town.[24]

To avoid leased asset capitalization, companies design, write, and interpret lease agreements to prevent satisfying any of the four capitalized lease criteria. Companies can easily devise lease agreements in such a way, by meeting the following specifications.

1 Ensure that the lease does not specify the transfer of title of the property to the lessee.

2 Do not write in a bargain purchase option.

---

[24]Richard Dieter, "Is Lessee Accounting Working?" *CPA Journal* (August 1979), pp. 13–19. This article provides interesting examples of abuses of *Statement No. 13,* discusses the circumstances that led to the current situation, and proposes a solution.

3 Set the lease term at something less than 75 percent of the estimated economic life of the leased property.

4 Arrange for the present value of the minimum lease payments to be less than 90 percent of the fair value of the leased property.

The real challenge lies in disqualifying the lease as a capital lease to the lessee, while having the same lease qualify as a capital (sales or financing) lease to the lessor. Unlike lessees, lessors try to avoid having lease arrangements classified as operating leases.[25]

Avoiding the first three criteria is relatively simple, but it takes a little ingenuity to avoid the "90 percent recovery test" for the lessee while satisfying it for the lessor. Two of the factors involved in this effort are: (1) the use of the incremental borrowing rate by the lessee when it is higher than the implicit interest rate of the lessor, by making information about the implicit rate unavailable to the lessee; and (2) residual value guarantees.

The lessee's use of the higher interest rate is probably the more popular subterfuge. Lessees are knowledgeable about the fair value of the leased property and, of course, the rental payments. However, they generally are unaware of the estimated residual value used by the lessor. Therefore, the lessee who does not know exactly the lessor's implicit interest rate might use a different (higher) incremental borrowing rate.

The residual-value guarantee is the other unique, yet popular, device used by lessees and lessors. In fact, a whole new industry has emerged to circumvent symmetry between the lessee and the lessor in accounting for leases. The residual-value guarantee has spawned numerous companies whose principal, or even sole, function is to guarantee the residual value of leased assets.

Because the minimum lease payments include the guaranteed residual value for the lessor, this satisfies the 90 percent recovery of fair market value test. The lease is a nonoperating lease to the lessor. **But because a third-party guarantees the residual value, the minimum lease payments of the lessee exclude the guarantee.** Thus, by merely transferring some of the risk to a third party, lessees can alter substantially the accounting treatment by converting what would otherwise be capital leases to operating leases.[26]

The nature of the criteria encourages much of this circumvention, stemming from weaknesses in the basic objective of *Statement No. 13*. Accounting standards-setting bodies continue to have poor experience with arbitrary break points or other size and percentage criteria—such as rules like "90 percent of" and "75 percent of." Some believe that a more workable solution is to require capitalization of all leases that have noncancelable payment terms in excess of one year. Under this approach, lessee acquires an asset (a property right) and a corresponding liability, rather than on the basis that the lease transfers substantially all the risks and rewards of ownership.

Three years after it issued *Statement No. 13*, a majority of the FASB expressed "the tentative view that, if *Statement 13* were to be reconsidered, they would support a property right approach in which all leases are included as 'rights to use property' and as

INTERNATIONAL INSIGHT

Recently the SEC indicated that it might be advisable for the IASB and the FASB to jointly undertake a project to reconsider lease accounting standards.

---

[25] The reason is that most lessors are banks, which are not permitted to hold these assets on their balance sheets except for relatively short periods of time. Furthermore, the capital-lease transaction from the lessor's standpoint provides higher income flows in the earlier periods of the lease life.

[26] As an aside, third-party guarantors have experienced some difficulty. **Lloyd's of London,** at one time, insured the fast-growing U.S. computer-leasing industry in the amount of $2 billion against revenue losses, and losses in residual value, for canceled leases. Because of "overnight" technological improvements and the successive introductions of more efficient and less expensive computers, lessees in abundance canceled their leases. As the market for second-hand computers became flooded, residual values plummeted, and third-party guarantor Lloyd's of London projected a loss of $400 million. The lessees' and lessors' desire to circumvent *FASB Statement No. 13* stimulated much of the third-party guarantee business.

'lease obligations' in the lessee's balance sheet."[27] The FASB and other international standard setters have issued a report on lease accounting that proposes the capitalization of more leases.[28]

SWAP MEET

WHAT DO THE NUMBERS MEAN?

Telecommunication companies have developed one of the more innovative and controversial uses of leases. In order to provide fiber-optic service to their customers in areas where they did not have networks installed, telecommunication companies such as **Global Crossing, Qwest Communications International,** and **Cable and Wireless** entered into agreements to swap some of their unused network capacity in exchange for the use of another company's fiber-optic cables. Here's how it works:

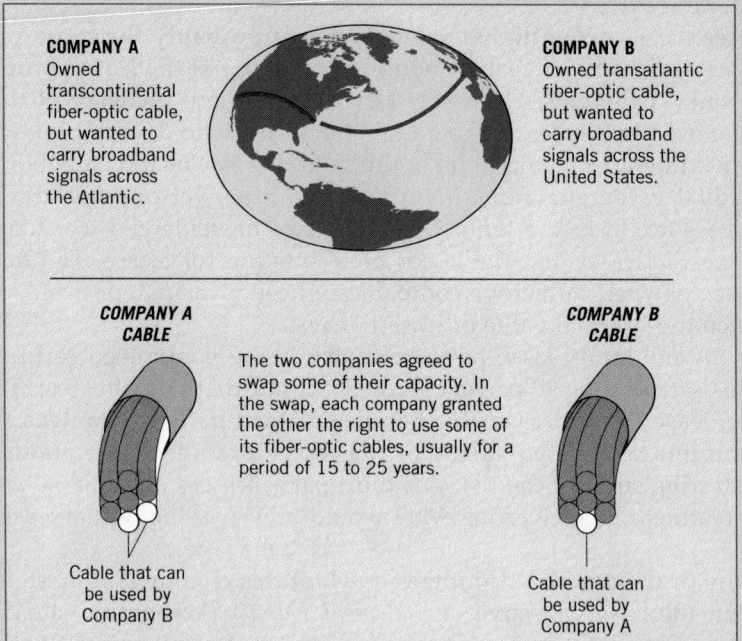

COMPANY A
Owned transcontinental fiber-optic cable, but wanted to carry broadband signals across the Atlantic.

COMPANY B
Owned transatlantic fiber-optic cable, but wanted to carry broadband signals across the United States.

COMPANY A CABLE

The two companies agreed to swap some of their capacity. In the swap, each company granted the other the right to use some of its fiber-optic cables, usually for a period of 15 to 25 years.

COMPANY B CABLE

Cable that can be used by Company B

Cable that can be used by Company A

Such trades seem like a good way to make efficient use of telecommunication assets. What got some telecommunications companies in trouble, though, was how they did the accounting for the swap.

The most conservative accounting for the capacity trades is to treat the swap as an exchange of assets, which does not affect the income statement. However, Global Crossing got into trouble with the SEC when it structured some of its capacity swaps as leases—the legal right to use capacity. Global Crossing was recognizing as revenue the payments received for the outgoing transfer of capacity, while payments for the incoming cable capacity were treated as capital expenditures, and therefore not expensed. As a result, Global Crossing was showing strong profits from its capacity swaps. However, the company's investors got an unpleasant surprise when the market for bandwidth cooled off and there was no longer demand for its broadband capacity or its long-term leasing arrangements.

Source: Simon Romero and Seth Schiesel, "The Fiber-Optic Fantasy Slips Away," *New York Times on the Web* (February 17, 2002). By permission.

---

[27]"Is Lessee Accounting Working?" op. cit., p. 19.

[28]H. Nailor and A. Lennard, "Capital Leases: Implementation of a New Approach," *Financial Accounting Series No. 206A* (Norwalk, Conn.: FASB, 2000).

SUMMARY OF LEARNING OBJECTIVES

1. Explain the nature, economic substance, and advantages of lease transactions. A lease is a contractual agreement between a lessor and a lessee that conveys to the lessee the right to use specific property (real or personal), owned by the lessor, for a specified period of time. In return, the lessee periodically pays cash (rent) to the lessor. The advantages of lease transactions are: (1) 100 percent financing; (2) protection against obsolescence, (3) flexibility, (4) less costly financing, (5) possible tax advantages, and (6) off-balance-sheet financing.

2. Describe the accounting criteria and procedures for capitalizing leases by the lessee. A lease is a capital lease if it meets one or more of the following (Group I) criteria: (1) The lease transfers ownership of the property to the lessee. (2) The lease contains a bargain purchase option. (3) The lease term is equal to 75 percent or more of the estimated economic life of the leased property. (4) The present value of the minimum lease payments (excluding executory costs) equals or exceeds 90 percent of the fair value of the leased property. For a capital lease, the lessee records an asset and a liability at the lower of (1) the present value of the minimum lease payments, or (2) the fair market value of the leased asset at the inception of the lease.

3. Contrast the operating and capitalization methods of recording leases. The total charges to operations are the same over the lease term whether accounting for the lease as a capital lease or as an operating lease. Under the capital lease treatment, the charges are higher in the earlier years and lower in the later years. If using an accelerated method of depreciation, the differences between the amounts charged to operations under the two methods would be even larger in the earlier and later years. If using a capital lease instead of an operating lease, the following occurs: (1) an increase in the amount of reported debt (both short-term and long-term), (2) an increase in the amount of total assets (specifically long-lived assets), and (3) lower income early in the life of the lease and, therefore, lower retained earnings.

4. Identify the classifications of leases for the lessor. A lessor may classify leases for accounting purposes as follows: (1) operating leases, (2) direct-financing leases, (3) sales-type leases. The lessor should classify and account for an arrangement as a direct-financing lease or a sales-type lease if, at the date of the lease agreement, the lease meets one or more of the Group I criteria (as shown in learning objective 2 for lessees) and *both* of the following Group II criteria. *Group II:* (1) Collectibility of the payments required from the lessee is reasonably predictable; and (2) no important uncertainties surround the amount of unreimbursable costs yet to be incurred by the lessor under the lease. The lessor classifies and accounts for all leases that fail to meet the criteria as operating leases.

5. Describe the lessor's accounting for direct-financing leases. Leases that are in substance the financing of an asset purchase by a lessee require the lessor to substitute a "lease receivable" for the leased asset. "Lease receivable" is the present value of the minimum lease payments plus the present value of the unguaranteed residual value. Therefore lessors include the residual value, whether guaranteed or unguaranteed, as part of lease receivable.

6. Identify special features of lease arrangements that cause unique accounting problems. The features of lease arrangements that cause unique accounting problems are: (1) residual values; (2) sales-type leases (lessor); (3) bargain purchase options; (4) initial direct costs; (5) current versus noncurrent; and (6) disclosures.

7. Describe the effect of residual values, guaranteed and unguaranteed, on lease accounting. Whether the estimated residual value is guaranteed or unguaranteed is of both economic and accounting consequence to the lessee. The accounting consequence is that the minimum lease payments, the basis for capitalization, include the guaranteed residual value but exclude the unguaranteed residual value. A guaranteed residual value affects the lessee's computation of minimum lease payments and the amounts capitalized as a leased asset and a lease obligation. In effect, the guaranteed residual value is an additional lease payment that the lessee will pay in property or cash, or both, at the end of the lease term. An unguaranteed residual value from the lessee's viewpoint is the same as no residual value in terms of its effect upon the lessee's method of computing the minimum lease payments and the capitalization of the leased asset and the lease liability.

8. Describe the lessor's accounting for sales-type leases. A sales-type lease recognizes interest revenue like a direct-financing lease. It also recognizes a manufacturer's or dealer's profit. In a sales-type lease, the lessor records at the inception of the lease the sales price of the asset, the cost of goods sold and related inventory reduction, and the lease receivable. Sales-type leases differ from direct-financing leases in terms of the cost and fair value of the leased asset, which results in gross profit. Lease receivable and interest revenue are the same whether a guaranteed or an unguaranteed residual value is involved. The accounting for guaranteed and for unguaranteed residual values requires recording sales revenue and cost of goods sold differently. The guaranteed residual value can be considered part of sales revenue because the lessor knows that the entire asset has been sold. There is less certainty that the unguaranteed residual portion of the asset has been "sold"; therefore, lessors recognize sales and cost of goods sold only for the portion of the asset for which realization is assured. However, the gross profit amount on the sale of the asset is the same whether a guaranteed or unguaranteed residual value is involved.

9. List the disclosure requirements for leases. The disclosure requirements for the lessees and lessors vary based upon the type of lease (capital or operating) and whether the issuer is the lessor or lessee. These disclosure requirements provide investors with the following information: (1) general description of the nature of leasing arrangements, (2) the nature, timing and amount of cash inflows and outflows associated with leases, including payments to be paid or received for each of the five succeeding years, (3) the amount of lease revenues and expenses reported in the income statement each period, (4) description and amounts of leased assets by major balance sheet classification and related liabilities, and (5) amounts receivable and unearned revenues under lease agreements.

Expanded Discussion of Real Estate Leases and Leveraged Leases

---

APPENDIX

21A Examples of Lease Arrangements

OBJECTIVE 10
Understand and apply lease accounting concepts to various lease arrangements.

To illustrate concepts discussed in this chapter, assume that Morgan Bakeries is involved in four different lease situations. Each of these leases is noncancelable, and in no case does Morgan receive title to the properties leased during or at the end of the lease term. All leases start on January 1, 2008, with the first rental due at the beginning of the year. The additional information is shown in Illustration 21A-1.

	Harmon, Inc.	Arden's Oven Co.	Mendota Truck Co.	Appleland Computer
Type of property	Cabinets	Oven	Truck	Computer
Yearly rental	$6,000	$15,000	$5,582.62	$3,557.25
Lease term	20 years	10 years	3 years	3 years
Estimated economic life	30 years	25 years	7 years	5 years
Purchase option	None	$75,000 at end of 10 years $4,000 at end of 15 years	None	$3,000 at end of 3 years, which approximates fair market value
Renewal option	None	5-year renewal option at $15,000 per year	None	1 year at $1,500; no penalty for nonrenewal; standard renewal clause
Fair market value at inception of lease	$60,000	$120,000	$20,000	$10,000
Cost of asset to lessor	$60,000	$120,000	$15,000	$10,000
Residual value				
Guaranteed	–0–	–0–	$7,000	–0–
Unguaranteed	$5,000	–0–	–0–	$3,000
Incremental borrowing rate of lessee	12%	12%	12%	12%
Executory costs paid by	*Lessee* $300 per year	*Lessee* $1,000 per year	*Lessee* $500 per year	*Lessor* Estimated to be $500 per year
Present value of minimum lease payments				
Using incremental borrowing rate of lessee	$50,194.68	$115,153.35	$20,000	$8,224.16
Using implicit rate of lessor	Not known	Not known	Not known	Known by lessee, $8,027.48
Estimated fair market value at end of lease	$5,000	$80,000 at end of 10 years $60,000 at end of 15 years	Not available	$3,000

ILLUSTRATION 21A-1
Illustrative Lease
Situations, Lessors

HARMON, INC.

The following is an analysis of the Harmon, Inc. lease.

1 __Transfer of title?__ No.

2 __Bargain purchase option?__ No.

3 __Economic life test (75% test).__ The lease term is 20 years and the estimated economic life is 30 years. Thus it **does not** meet the 75 percent test.

4 __Recovery of investment test (90% test):__

Fair market value	$60,000	Rental payments	$ 6,000
Rate	90%	PV of annuity due for	
90% of fair market value	$54,000	20 years at 12%	× 8.36578
		PV of rental payments	$50,194.68

Because the present value of the minimum lease payments is less than 90 percent of the fair market value, the lease does not meet the 90 percent test.

Both Morgan and Harmon should account for this lease as an operating lease, as indicated by the January 1, 2008, entries shown in Illustration 21A-2 (on page 1126).

ILLUSTRATION 21A-2
Comparative Entries
for Operating Lease

Morgan Bakeries (Lessee)			Harmon, Inc. (Lessor)		
Rent Expense	6,000		Cash	6,000	
Cash		6,000	Rental Revenue		6,000

ARDEN'S OVEN CO.

The following is an analysis of the Arden's Oven Co. lease.

1 **Transfer of title?** No.

2 **Bargain purchase option?** The $75,000 option at the end of 10 years does not appear to be sufficiently lower than the expected fair value of $80,000 to make it reasonably assured that it will be exercised. However, the $4,000 at the end of 15 years when the fair value is $60,000 does appear to be a bargain. From the information given, criterion 2 is therefore met. Note that both the guaranteed and the unguaranteed residual values are assigned zero values because the lessor does not expect to repossess the leased asset.

3 **Economic life test (75% test):** Given that a bargain purchase option exists, the lease term is the initial lease period of 10 years plus the five-year renewal option since it precedes a bargain purchase option. Even though the lease term is now considered to be 15 years, this test is still not met because 75 percent of the economic life of 25 years is 18.75 years.

4 **Recovery of investment test (90% test):**

Fair market value	$120,000	Rental payments	$ 15,000.00	
Rate	90%	PV of annuity due for		
90% of fair market value	$108,000	15 years at 12%	× 7.62817	
		PV of rental payments	$114,422.55	

PV of bargain purchase option: $= \$4{,}000 \times (PVF_{15,12\%}) = \$4{,}000 \times .18270 = \$730.80$

PV of rental payments	$114,422.55
PV of bargain purchase option	730.80
PV of minimum lease payments	$115,153.35

The present value of the minimum lease payments is greater than 90 percent of the fair market value; therefore, the lease does meet the 90 percent test.

Morgan Bakeries should account for this as a capital lease because the lease meets both criteria 2 and 4. Assuming that Arden's implicit rate is less than Morgan's incremental borrowing rate, the following entries are made on January 1, 2008.

ILLUSTRATION 21A-3
Comparative Entries for
Capital Lease—Bargain
Purchase Option

Morgan Bakeries (Lessee)			Arden's Oven Co. (Lessor)		
Leased Asset—Oven 115,153.35			Lease Receivable	120,000	
Lease Liability		115,153.35	Asset—Oven		120,000

Morgan Bakeries would depreciate the leased asset over its economic life of 25 years, given the bargain purchase option. Arden's Oven Co. does not use sales-type accounting because the fair market value and the cost of the asset are the same at the inception of the lease.

MENDOTA TRUCK CO.

The following is an analysis of the Mendota Truck Co. lease.

1 **Transfer of title?** No.

2 **Bargain purchase option?** No.

3 **Economic life test (75% test):** The lease term is three years and the estimated economic life is seven years. Thus it **does not** meet the 75 percent test.

4 **Recovery of investment test (90% test):**

Fair market value	$20,000	Rental payments	$ 5,582.62
Rate	90%	PV of annuity due for	
90% of fair market value	$18,000	3 years at 12%	× 2.69005
		PV of rental payments	$15,017.54

(Note: Adjusted for $0.01 due to rounding)

PV of guaranteed residual value: = $7,000 × (PVF$_{3,12\%}$) = $7,000 × .71178 = $4,982.46

PV of rental payments	$15,017.54
PV of guaranteed residual value	4,982.46
PV of minimum lease payments	$20,000.00

The present value of the minimum lease payments is greater than 90 percent of the fair market value; therefore, the lease meets the 90 percent test.

Assuming that Mendota's implicit rate is the same as Morgan's incremental borrowing rate, the following entries are made on January 1, 2008.

Morgan Bakeries (Lessee)				Mendota Truck Co. (Lessor)			
Leased Asset—Truck	20,000			Lease Receivable	20,000		
Lease Liability		20,000		Cost of Goods Sold	15,000		
				Inventory—Truck		15,000	
				Sales		20,000	

ILLUSTRATION 21A-4
Comparative Entries
for Capital Lease

Morgan depreciates the leased asset over three years to its guaranteed residual value.

APPLELAND COMPUTER

The following is an analysis of the Appleland Computer lease.

1 **Transfer of title?** No.

2 **Bargain purchase option?** No. The option to purchase at the end of three years at approximate fair market value is clearly not a bargain.

3 **Economic life test (75% test):** The lease term is three years, and no bargain renewal period exists. Therefore the 75 percent test **is not** met.

4 **Recovery of investment test (90% test):**

Fair market value	$10,000	Rental payments	$3,557.25
Rate	90%	Less executory costs	500.00
90% of fair market value	$ 9,000		3,057.25
		PV of annuity due factor for 3 years at 12%	× 2.69005
		PV of minimum lease payments using incremental borrowing rate	$8,224.16

The present value of the minimum lease payments using the incremental borrowing rate is $8,224.16; using the implicit rate, it is $8,027.48 (see Illustration 21A-1). The lessor's implicit rate is therefore higher than the incremental borrowing rate. Given this situation, the lessee uses the $8,224.16 (lower interest rate when discounting) when comparing with the 90 percent of fair market value. Because the present value of the minimum lease payments is lower than 90 percent of the fair market value, the lease does **not** meet the recovery of investment test.

The following entries are made on January 1, 2008, indicating an operating lease.

ILLUSTRATION 21A-5
Comparative Entries for
Operating Lease

Morgan Bakeries (Lessee)			Appleland Computer (Lessor)		
Rent Expense	3,557.25		Cash	3,557.25	
Cash		3,557.25	Rental Revenue		3,557.25

If the lease payments had been $3,557.25 with no executory costs involved, this lease arrangement would have qualified for capital-lease accounting treatment.

SUMMARY OF LEARNING OBJECTIVE FOR APPENDIX 21A

10. Understand and apply lease accounting concepts to various lease arrangements. The classification of leases by lessees and lessors is based on criteria that assess whether the lessor has transferred to the lessee substantially all of the risks and benefits of ownership of the asset. In addition, lessors assess two additional criteria to ensure that payment is assured and that there are not uncertainties about lessor's future costs. Lessees capitalize leases that meet any of the criteria, recording a lease asset and related lease liability. For leases that are in substance a financing of an asset purchase, lessors substitute a lease receivable for the leased asset. In a sales-type lease, the fair value of the leased asset is greater than the cost, and lessors record gross profit. Leases that do not meet capitalization criteria are classified as operating leases, on which rent expense (revenue) is recognized by lessees (lessors) for lease payments.

APPENDIX

21B Sale-Leasebacks

OBJECTIVE 11
Describe the lessee's accounting for sale-leaseback transactions.

The term **sale-leaseback** describes a transaction in which the owner of the property (seller-lessee) sells the property to another and simultaneously leases it back from the new owner. The use of the property is generally continued without interruption.

Sale-leasebacks are common. Financial institutions (e.g., **Bank of America** and **First Chicago**) have used this technique for their administrative offices, public utilities (**Ohio Edison** and **Pinnacle West Corporation**) for their generating plants, and airlines (**Continental** and **Alaska Airlines**) for their aircraft. The advantages of a sale-leaseback from the seller's viewpoint usually involve two primary considerations:

1 *Financing*—If the purchase of equipment has already been financed, a sale-leaseback can allow the seller to refinance at lower rates, assuming rates have dropped. In addition, a sale-leaseback can provide another source of working capital, particularly when liquidity is tight.

2 *Taxes*—At the time a company purchased equipment, it may not have known that it would be subject to an alternative minimum tax and that ownership might increase its minimum tax liability. By selling the property, the seller-lessee may deduct the entire lease payment, which is not subject to alternative minimum tax considerations.

DETERMINING ASSET USE

To the extent the **seller-lessee continues to use** the asset after the sale, the sale-leaseback is really a form of financing. Therefore the lessor **should not recognize a gain or loss** on the transaction. In short, the seller-lessee is simply borrowing funds.

On the other hand, if the **seller-lessee gives up the right to the use** of the asset, the transaction is in substance a sale. In that case, **gain or loss recognition** is appropriate. Trying to ascertain when the lessee has given up the use of the asset is difficult, however, and the FASB has formulated complex rules to identify this situation.[1] To understand the profession's position in this area, we discuss the basic accounting for the lessee and lessor below.

Lessee

If the lease meets one of the four criteria for treatment as a capital lease (see Illustration 21-4), the **seller-lessee accounts for the transaction as a sale and the lease as a capital lease.** The seller-lessee should defer any profit or loss it experiences from the sale of the assets that are leased back under a capital lease; it should **amortize that profit over the lease term** (or the economic life if either criterion 1 or 2 is satisfied) in proportion to the amortization of the leased assets.

For example, assume **Scott Paper** sells equipment having a book value of $580,000 and a fair value of $623,110 to **General Electric Credit** for $623,110 and leases the equipment back for $50,000 a year for 20 years. Scott should amortize the profit of $43,110 over the 20-year period at the same rate that it depreciates the $623,110.[2] It credits the $43,110 ($623,110 − $580,000) to **Unearned Profit on Sale-Leaseback.**

If none of the capital lease criteria are satisfied, **the seller-lessee accounts for the transaction as a sale and the lease as an operating lease.** Under an operating lease, the lessee defers such profit or loss and amortizes it in proportion to the rental payments over the period when it expects to use the assets.

There are exceptions to these two general rules. They are:

1 *Losses Recognized*—When the fair value of the asset is **less than the book value** (carrying amount), the lessee must recognize a loss immediately, up to the amount of the difference between the book value and fair value. For example, if Lessee, Inc. sells equipment having a book value of $650,000 and a fair value of $623,110, it should charge the difference of $26,890 to a loss account.[3]

2 *Minor Leaseback*—Leasebacks in which the present value of the rental payments are 10 percent or less of the fair value of the asset are **minor leasebacks.** In this case, the seller-lessee gives up most of the rights to the use of the asset sold. Therefore, the transaction is a sale, and full gain or loss recognition is appropriate. It is not a financing transaction because the risks of ownership have been transferred.[4]

Lessor

If the lease meets one of the criteria in Group I and both of the criteria in Group II (see Illustration 21-11), the **purchaser-lessor** records the transaction as a purchase and a direct-financing lease. If the lease does not meet the criteria, the purchaser-lessor records the transaction as a purchase and an operating lease.

A sale-leaseback is similar in substance to the parking of inventories (discussed in Chapter 8). The ultimate economic benefits remain under the control of the "seller," thus satisfying the definition of an asset.

UNDERLYING CONCEPTS

---

[1]Sales and leasebacks of real estate are often accounted for differently. A discussion of the issues related to these transactions is beyond the scope of this textbook. See *Statement of Financial Accounting Standards No. 98,* op. cit.

[2]*Statement of Financial Accounting Standards No. 28,* "Accounting for Sales with Leasebacks" (Stamford, Conn.: FASB, 1979).

[3]There can be two types of losses in sale-leaseback arrangements. One is a **real economic loss** that results when the carrying amount of the asset is higher than the fair market value of the asset. In this case, the loss should be recognized. An **artificial loss** results when the sale price is below the carrying amount of the asset but the fair market value is above the carrying amount. In this case the loss is more in the form of prepaid rent, and the lessee should defer the loss and amortize it in the future.

[4]In some cases the seller-lessee retains more than a minor part but less than substantially all. The computations to arrive at these values are complex and beyond the scope of this textbook.

SALE-LEASEBACK EXAMPLE

To illustrate the accounting treatment accorded a sale-leaseback transaction, assume that **American Airlines** on January 1, 2008, sells a used Boeing 757 having a carrying amount on its books of $75,500,000 to **Citicapital** for $80,000,000. American immediately leases the aircraft back under the following conditions:

1 The term of the lease is 15 years, noncancelable, and requires equal rental payments of $10,487,443 at the beginning of each year.

2 The aircraft has a fair value of $80,000,000 on January 1, 2008, and an estimated economic life of 15 years.

3 American pays all executory costs.

4 American depreciates similar aircraft that it owns on a straight-line basis over 15 years.

5 The annual payments assure the lessor a 12 percent return.

6 American's incremental borrowing rate is 12 percent.

This lease is a capital lease to American because the lease term exceeds 75 percent of the estimated life of the aircraft and because the present value of the lease payments exceeds 90 percent of the fair value of the aircraft to Citicapital. Assuming that collectibility of the lease payments is reasonably predictable and that no important uncertainties exist in relation to unreimbursable costs yet to be incurred by Citicapital, it should classify this lease as a direct-financing lease.

Illustration 21B-1 presents the typical journal entries to record the sale-leaseback transactions for American and Citicapital for the first year.

ILLUSTRATION 21B-1
Comparative Entries for Sale-Leaseback for Lessee and Lessor

American Airlines (Lessee)			Citicapital (Lessor)		
Sale of Aircraft by American to Citicapital, January 1, 2008:					
Cash	80,000,000		Aircraft	80,000,000	
Aircraft		75,500,000	Cash		80,000,000
Unearned Profit on					
Sale-Leaseback		4,500,000	Lease Receivable	80,000,000	
Leased Aircraft under			Aircraft		80,000,000
Capital Leases	80,000,000				
Lease Liability		80,000,000			
First Lease Payment, January 1, 2008:					
Lease Liability	10,487,443		Cash	10,487,443	
Cash		10,487,443	Lease Receivable		10,487,443
Incurrence and Payment of Executory Costs by American Corp. throughout 2008:					
Insurance, Maintenance,			(No entry)		
Taxes, etc.	XXX				
Cash or Accounts Payable		XXX			
Depreciation Expense on the Aircraft, December 31, 2008:					
Depreciation Expense	5,333,333		(No entry)		
Accumulated Depr.—					
Capital Leases		5,333,333			
($80,000,000 ÷ 15)					
Amortization of Profit on Sale-Leaseback by American, December 31, 2008:					
Unearned Profit on			(No entry)		
Sale-Leaseback	300,000				
Depreciation Expense		300,000			
($4,500,000 ÷ 15)					
Note: A case might be made for crediting Revenue instead of Depreciation Expense.					
Interest for 2008, December 31, 2008:					
Interest Expense	8,341,507[a]		Interest Receivable	8,341,507	
Interest Payable		8,341,507	Interest Revenue		8,341,507[a]

[a]Partial Lease Amortization Schedule:

Date	Annual Rental Payment	Interest 12%	Reduction of Balance	Balance
1/1/08				$80,000,000
1/1/08	$10,487,443	$ –0–	$10,487,443	69,512,557
1/1/09	10,487,443	8,341,507	2,145,936	67,366,621

SUMMARY OF LEARNING OBJECTIVE FOR APPENDIX 21B

11. Describe the lessee's accounting for sale-leaseback transactions. If the lease meets one of the four criteria for treatment as a capital lease, the seller-lessee accounts for the transaction as a sale and the lease as a capital lease. The seller-lessee defers any profit it experiences from the sale of the assets that are leased back under a capital lease. The seller-lessee amortizes any profit over the lease term (or the economic life if either criterion 1 or 2 is satisfied) in proportion to the amortization of the leased assets. If the lease satisfies none of the capital lease criteria, the seller-lessee accounts for the transaction as a sale and the lease as an operating lease. Under an operating lease, the lessee defers such profit and amortizes it in proportion to the rental payments over the period of time that it expects to use the assets.

Note: All **asterisked** Questions, Brief Exercises, Exercises, and Concepts for Analysis relate to material contained in the appendixes to the chapter.

QUESTIONS

1. What are the major lessor groups in the United States? What advantage does a captive have in a leasing arrangement?

2. Jackie Remmers Co. is expanding its operations and is in the process of selecting the method of financing this program. After some investigation, the company determines that it may (1) issue bonds and with the proceeds purchase the needed assets or (2) lease the assets on a long-term basis. Without knowing the comparative costs involved, answer these questions:

(a) What might be the advantages of leasing the assets instead of owning them?

(b) What might be the disadvantages of leasing the assets instead of owning them?

(c) In what way will the balance sheet be differently affected by leasing the assets as opposed to issuing bonds and purchasing the assets?

3. Identify the two recognized lease accounting methods for lessees and distinguish between them.

4. Wayne Higley Company rents a warehouse on a month-to-month basis for the storage of its excess inventory. The company periodically must rent space whenever its production greatly exceeds actual sales. For several years the company officials have discussed building their own storage facility, but this enthusiasm wavers when sales increase sufficiently to absorb the excess inventory. What is the nature of this type of lease arrangement, and what accounting treatment should be accorded it?

5. Distinguish between minimum rental payments and minimum lease payments, and indicate what is included in minimum lease payments.

6. Explain the distinction between a direct-financing lease and a sales-type lease for a lessor.

7. Outline the accounting procedures involved in applying the operating method by a lessee.

8. Outline the accounting procedures involved in applying the capital-lease method by a lessee.

9. Identify the lease classifications for lessors and the criteria that must be met for each classification.

10. Outline the accounting procedures involved in applying the direct-financing method.

11. Outline the accounting procedures involved in applying the operating method by a lessor.

12. Joan Elbert Company is a manufacturer and lessor of computer equipment. What should be the nature of its lease arrangements with lessees if the company wishes to account for its lease transactions as sales-type leases?

13. Gordon Graham Corporation's lease arrangements qualify as sales-type leases at the time of entering into the transactions. How should the corporation recognize revenues and costs in these situations?

14. Joann Skabo, M.D. (lessee) has a noncancelable 20-year lease with Countryman Realty, Inc. (lessor) for the use of a medical building. Taxes, insurance, and maintenance are paid by the lessee in addition to the fixed annual payments, of which the present value is equal to the fair market value of the leased property. At the end of the lease period, title becomes the lessee's at a nominal price. Considering the terms of the lease described above, comment on the nature of the lease transaction and the accounting treatment that should be accorded it by the lessee.

15. The residual value is the estimated fair value of the leased property at the end of the lease term.

(a) Of what significance is (1) an unguaranteed and (2) a guaranteed residual value in the lessee's accounting for a capitalized-lease transaction?

(b) Of what significance is (1) an unguaranteed and (2) a guaranteed residual value in the lessor's accounting for a direct-financing lease transaction?

16. How should changes in the estimated unguaranteed residual values be handled by the lessor?

17. Describe the effect of a "bargain purchase option" on accounting for a capital-lease transaction by a lessee.

18. What are "initial direct costs" and how are they accounted for?

19. What disclosures should be made by lessees and lessors related to future lease payments?

*20. What is the nature of a "sale-leaseback" transaction?

 **BRIEF EXERCISES**

(LO 2) **BE21-1** **Callaway Golf Co.** leases telecommunication equipment. Assume the following data for equipment leased from Photon Company. The lease term is 5 years and requires equal rental payments of $30,000 at the beginning of each year. The equipment has a fair value at the inception of the lease of $138,000, an estimated useful life of 8 years, and no residual value. Callaway pays all executory costs directly to third parties. Photon set the annual rental to earn a rate of return of 10%, and this fact is known to Callaway. The lease does not transfer title or contain a bargain purchase option. How should Callaway classify this lease?

(LO 2) **BE21-2** Waterworld Company leased equipment from Costner Company. The lease term is 4 years and requires equal rental payments of $37,283 at the beginning of each year. The equipment has a fair value at the inception of the lease of $130,000, an estimated useful life of 4 years, and no salvage value. Waterworld pays all executory costs directly to third parties. The appropriate interest rate is 10%. Prepare Waterworld's January 1, 2008, journal entries at the inception of the lease.

(LO 2) **BE21-3** Rick Kleckner Corporation recorded a capital lease at $200,000 on January 1, 2008. The interest rate is 12%. Kleckner Corporation made the first lease payment of $35,947 on January 1, 2008. The lease requires eight annual payments. The equipment has a useful life of 8 years with no salvage value. Prepare Kleckner Corporation's December 31, 2008, adjusting entries.

(LO 2) **BE21-4** Use the information for Rick Kleckner Corporation from BE21-3. Assume that at December 31, 2008, Kleckner made an adjusting entry to accrue interest expense of $19,686 on the lease. Prepare Kleckner's January 1, 2009, journal entry to record the second lease payment of $35,947.

(LO 3) **BE21-5** Jana Kingston Corporation enters into a lease on January 1, 2008, that does not transfer ownership or contain a bargain purchase option. It covers 3 years of the equipment's 8-year useful life, and the present value of the minimum lease payments is less than 90% of the fair market value of the asset leased. Prepare Jana Kingston's journal entry to record its January 1, 2008, annual lease payment of $37,500.

(LO 4, 5) **BE21-6** Assume that **IBM** leased equipment that was carried at a cost of $150,000 to Sharon Swander Company. The term of the lease is 6 years beginning January 1, 2008, with equal rental payments of $30,677 at the beginning of each year. All executory costs are paid by Swander directly to third parties. The fair value of the equipment at the inception of the lease is $150,000. The equipment has a useful life of 6 years with no salvage value. The lease has an implicit interest rate of 9%, no bargain purchase option, and no transfer of title. Collectibility is reasonably assured with no additional cost to be incurred by IBM. Prepare IBM's January 1, 2008, journal entries at the inception of the lease.

(LO 4, 5) **BE21-7** Use the information for **IBM** from BE21-6. Assume the direct-financing lease was recorded at a present value of $150,000. Prepare IBM's December 31, 2008, entry to record interest.

(LO 4) **BE21-8** Jennifer Brent Corporation owns equipment that cost $72,000 and has a useful life of 8 years with no salvage value. On January 1, 2008, Jennifer Brent leases the equipment to Donna Havaci Inc. for one year with one rental payment of $15,000 on January 1. Prepare Jennifer Brent Corporation's 2008 journal entries.

(LO 6, 7) **BE21-9** Indiana Jones Corporation enters into a 6-year lease of equipment on January 1, 2008, which requires 6 annual payments of $30,000 each, beginning January 1, 2008. In addition, Indiana Jones guarantees the lessor a residual value of $20,000 at lease-end. The equipment has a useful life of 6 years. Prepare Indiana Jones' January 1, 2008, journal entries assuming an interest rate of 10%.

(LO 6, 7) **BE21-10** Use the information for Indiana Jones Corporation from BE21-9. Assume that for Lost Ark Company, the lessor, collectibility is reasonably predictable, there are no important uncertainties concerning costs, and the carrying amount of the machinery is $155,013. Prepare Lost Ark's January 1, 2008, journal entries.

(LO 8) **BE21-11** Starfleet Corporation manufactures replicators. On January 1, 2008, it leased to Ferengi Company a replicator that had cost $110,000 to manufacture. The lease agreement covers the 5-year useful life of the replicator and requires 5 equal annual rentals of $45,400 each. An interest rate of 12% is implicit in the lease agreement. Collectibility of the rentals is reasonably assured, and there are no important uncertainties concerning costs. Prepare Starfleet's January 1, 2008, journal entries.

(LO 10) *****BE21-12** On January 1, 2008, Acme Animation sold a truck to Coyote Finance for $35,000 and immediately leased it back. The truck was carried on Acme's books at $28,000. The term of the lease is 5 years, and title transfers to Acme at lease-end. The lease requires five equal rental payments of $9,233 at the end of each year. The appropriate rate of interest is 10%, and the truck has a useful life of 5 years with no salvage value. Prepare Acme's 2008 journal entries.

EXERCISES

(LO 2) **E21-1** **(Lessee Entries; Capital Lease with Unguaranteed Residual Value)** On January 1, 2007, Burke Corporation signed a 5-year noncancelable lease for a machine. The terms of the lease called for Burke to make annual payments of $8,668 at the beginning of each year, starting January 1, 2007. The machine has an estimated useful life of 6 years and a $5,000 unguaranteed residual value. The machine reverts back to the lessor at the end of the lease term. Burke uses the straight-line method of depreciation for all of its plant assets. Burke's incremental borrowing rate is 10%, and the Lessor's implicit rate is unknown.

Instructions
    (a) What type of lease is this? Explain.
    (b) Compute the present value of the minimum lease payments.
    (c) Prepare all necessary journal entries for Burke for this lease through January 1, 2008.

(LO 2) **E21-2** **(Lessee Computations and Entries; Capital Lease with Guaranteed Residual Value)** Pat Delaney Company leases an automobile with a fair value of $8,725 from John Simon Motors, Inc., on the following terms:

    1. Noncancelable term of 50 months.
    2. Rental of $200 per month (at end of each month). (The present value at 1% per month is $7,840.)
    3. Estimated residual value after 50 months is $1,180. (The present value at 1% per month is $715.) Delaney Company guarantees the residual value of $1,180.
    4. Estimated economic life of the automobile is 60 months.
    5. Delaney Company's incremental borrowing rate is 12% a year (1% a month). Simon's implicit rate is unknown.

Instructions
    (a) What is the nature of this lease to Delaney Company?
    (b) What is the present value of the minimum lease payments?
    (c) Record the lease on Delaney Company's books at the date of inception.
    (d) Record the first month's depreciation on Delaney Company's books (assume straight-line).
    (e) Record the first month's lease payment.

(LO 2, 7) **E21-3** **(Lessee Entries; Capital Lease with Executory Costs and Unguaranteed Residual Value)** Assume that on January 1, 2008, **Kimberly-Clark Corp.** signs a 10-year noncancelable lease agreement to lease a storage building from Sheffield Storage Company. The following information pertains to this lease agreement.

    1. The agreement requires equal rental payments of $72,000 beginning on January 1, 2008.
    2. The fair value of the building on January 1, 2008 is $440,000.
    3. The building has an estimated economic life of 12 years, with an unguaranteed residual value of $10,000. Kimberly-Clark depreciates similar buildings on the straight-line method.
    4. The lease is nonrenewable. At the termination of the lease, the building reverts to the lessor.
    5. Kimberly-Clark's incremental borrowing rate is 12% per year. The lessor's implicit rate is not known by Kimberly-Clark.
    6. The yearly rental payment includes $2,470.51 of executory costs related to taxes on the property.

Instructions
Prepare the journal entries on the lessee's books to reflect the signing of the lease agreement and to record the payments and expenses related to this lease for the years 2008 and 2009. Kimberly-Clark's corporate year end is December 31.

(LO 5) **E21-4** **(Lessor Entries; Direct-Financing Lease with Option to Purchase)** Castle Leasing Company signs a lease agreement on January 1, 2008, to lease electronic equipment to Jan Way Company. The term of the noncancelable lease is 2 years, and payments are required at the end of each year. The following information relates to this agreement:

1. Jan Way has the option to purchase the equipment for $16,000 upon termination of the lease.
2. The equipment has a cost and fair value of $160,000 to Castle Leasing Company. The useful economic life is 2 years, with a salvage value of $16,000.
3. Jan Way Company is required to pay $5,000 each year to the lessor for executory costs.
4. Castle Leasing Company desires to earn a return of 10% on its investment.
5. Collectibility of the payments is reasonably predictable, and there are no important uncertainties surrounding the costs yet to be incurred by the lessor.

Instructions

(a) Prepare the journal entries on the books of Castle Leasing to reflect the payments received under the lease and to recognize income for the years 2008 and 2009.
(b) Assuming that Jan Way Company exercises its option to purchase the equipment on December 31, 2009, prepare the journal entry to reflect the sale on Castle's books.

(LO 2, 3) **E21-5** **(Type of Lease; Amortization Schedule)** Mike Macinski Leasing Company leases a new machine that has a cost and fair value of $95,000 to Sharrer Corporation on a 3-year noncancelable contract. Sharrer Corporation agrees to assume all risks of normal ownership including such costs as insurance, taxes, and maintenance. The machine has a 3-year useful life and no residual value. The lease was signed on January 1, 2008. Mike Macinski Leasing Company expects to earn a 9% return on its investment. The annual rentals are payable on each December 31.

Instructions

(a) Discuss the nature of the lease arrangement and the accounting method that each party to the lease should apply.
(b) Prepare an amortization schedule that would be suitable for both the lessor and the lessee and that covers all the years involved.

(LO 8) **E21-6** **(Lessor Entries; Sales-Type Lease)** Crosley Company, a machinery dealer, leased a machine to Dexter Corporation on January 1, 2007. The lease is for an 8-year period and requires equal annual payments of $35,013 at the beginning of each year. The first payment is received on January 1, 2007. Crosley had purchased the machine during 2006 for $160,000. Collectibility of lease payments is reasonably predictable, and no important uncertainties surround the amount of costs yet to be incurred by Crosley. Crosley set the annual rental to ensure an 11% rate of return. The machine has an economic life of 10 years with no residual value and reverts to Crosley at the termination of the lease.

Instructions

(a) Compute the amount of the lease receivable.
(b) Prepare all necessary journal entries for Crosley for 2007.

(LO 8) **E21-7** **(Lessee-Lessor Entries; Sales-Type Lease)** On January 1, 2007, Bensen Company leased equipment to Flynn Corporation. The following information pertains to this lease.

1. The term of the noncancelable lease is 6 years, with no renewal option. The equipment reverts to the lessor at the termination of the lease.
2. Equal rental payments are due on January 1 of each year, beginning in 2007.
3. The fair value of the equipment on January 1, 2007, is $150,000, and its cost is $120,000.
4. The equipment has an economic life of 8 years, with an unguaranteed residual value of $10,000. Flynn depreciates all of its equipment on a straight-line basis.
5. Bensen set the annual rental to ensure an 11% rate of return. Flynn's incremental borrowing rate is 12%, and the implicit rate of the lessor is unknown.
6. Collectibility of lease payments is reasonably predictable, and no important uncertainties surround the amount of costs yet to be incurred by the lessor.

Instructions

(Both the lessor and the lessee's accounting period ends on December 31.)

(a) Discuss the nature of this lease to Bensen and Flynn.
(b) Calculate the amount of the annual rental payment.
(c) Prepare all the necessary journal entries for Flynn for 2007.
(d) Prepare all the necessary journal entries for Bensen for 2007.

(LO 6, 7)   **E21-8 (Lessee Entries with Bargain Purchase Option)** The following facts pertain to a noncancelable lease agreement between Mooney Leasing Company and Rode Company, a lessee.

Inception date:	May 1, 2007
Annual lease payment due at the beginning of each year, beginning with May 1, 2007	$21,227.65
Bargain purchase option price at end of lease term	$ 4,000.00
Lease term	5 years
Economic life of leased equipment	10 years
Lessor's cost	$65,000.00
Fair value of asset at May 1, 2007	$91,000.00
Lessor's implicit rate	10%
Lessee's incremental borrowing rate	10%

The collectibility of the lease payments is reasonably predictable, and there are no important uncertainties surrounding the costs yet to be incurred by the lessor. The lessee assumes responsibility for all executory costs.

Instructions

(Round all numbers to the nearest cent.)

    (a) Discuss the nature of this lease to Rode Company.
    (b) Discuss the nature of this lease to Mooney Company.
    (c) Prepare a lease amortization schedule for Rode Company for the 5-year lease term.
    (d) Prepare the journal entries on the lessee's books to reflect the signing of the lease agreement and to record the payments and expenses related to this lease for the years 2007 and 2008. Rode's annual accounting period ends on December 31. Reversing entries are used by Rode.

(LO 8)   **E21-9 (Lessor Entries with Bargain Purchase Option)** A lease agreement between Mooney Leasing Company and Rode Company is described in E21-8.

Instructions

(Round all numbers to the nearest cent.)
Refer to the data in E21-8 and do the following for the lessor.

    (a) Compute the amount of the lease receivable at the inception of the lease.
    (b) Prepare a lease amortization schedule for Mooney Leasing Company for the 5-year lease term.
    (c) Prepare the journal entries to reflect the signing of the lease agreement and to record the receipts and income related to this lease for the years 2007, 2008, and 2009. The lessor's accounting period ends on December 31. Reversing entries are not used by Mooney.

(LO 5)   **E21-10 (Computation of Rental; Journal Entries for Lessor)** Morgan Leasing Company signs an agreement on January 1, 2007, to lease equipment to Cole Company. The following information relates to this agreement.

    1. The term of the noncancelable lease is 6 years with no renewal option. The equipment has an estimated economic life of 6 years.
    2. The cost of the asset to the lessor is $245,000. The fair value of the asset at January 1, 2007, is $245,000.
    3. The asset will revert to the lessor at the end of the lease term at which time the asset is expected to have a residual value of $43,622, none of which is guaranteed.
    4. Cole Company assumes direct responsibility for all executory costs.
    5. The agreement requires equal annual rental payments, beginning on January 1, 2007.
    6. Collectibility of the lease payments is reasonably predictable. There are no important uncertainties surrounding the amount of costs yet to be incurred by the lessor.

Instructions

(Round all numbers to the nearest cent.)

    (a) Assuming the lessor desires a 10% rate of return on its investment, calculate the amount of the annual rental payment required. Round to the nearest dollar.
    (b) Prepare an amortization schedule that would be suitable for the lessor for the lease term.
    (c) Prepare all of the journal entries for the lessor for 2007 and 2008 to record the lease agreement, the receipt of lease payments, and the recognition of income. Assume the lessor's annual accounting period ends on December 31.

(LO 2)   **E21-11 (Amortization Schedule and Journal Entries for Lessee)** Laura Leasing Company signs an agreement on January 1, 2007, to lease equipment to Plote Company. The information at the top of page 1136 relates to this agreement.

1. The term of the noncancelable lease is 5 years with no renewal option. The equipment has an estimated economic life of 5 years.
2. The fair value of the asset at January 1, 2007, is $80,000.
3. The asset will revert to the lessor at the end of the lease term, at which time the asset is expected to have a residual value of $7,000, none of which is guaranteed.
4. Plote Company assumes direct responsibility for all executory costs, which include the following annual amounts: (1) $900 to Rocky Mountain Insurance Company for insurance and (2) $1,600 to Laclede County for property taxes.
5. The agreement requires equal annual rental payments of $18,142.95 to the lessor, beginning on January 1, 2007.
6. The lessee's incremental borrowing rate is 12%. The lessor's implicit rate is 10% and is known to the lessee.
7. Plote Company uses the straight-line depreciation method for all equipment.
8. Plote uses reversing entries when appropriate.

Instructions

(Round all numbers to the nearest cent.)

(a) Prepare an amortization schedule that would be suitable for the lessee for the lease term.
(b) Prepare all of the journal entries for the lessee for 2007 and 2008 to record the lease agreement, the lease payments, and all expenses related to this lease. Assume the lessee's annual accounting period ends on December 31.

(LO 3, 4) **E21-12 (Accounting for an Operating Lease)** On January 1, 2007, Doug Nelson Co. leased a building to Patrick Wise Inc. The relevant information related to the lease is as follows.

1. The lease arrangement is for 10 years.
2. The leased building cost $4,500,000 and was purchased for cash on January 1, 2007.
3. The building is depreciated on a straight-line basis. Its estimated economic life is 50 years with no salvage value.
4. Lease payments are $275,000 per year and are made at the end of the year.
5. Property tax expense of $85,000 and insurance expense of $10,000 on the building were incurred by Nelson in the first year. Payment on these two items was made at the end of the year.
6. Both the lessor and the lessee are on a calendar-year basis.

Instructions

(a) Prepare the journal entries that Nelson Co. should make in 2007.
(b) Prepare the journal entries that Wise Inc. should make in 2007.
(c) If Nelson paid $30,000 to a real estate broker on January 1, 2007, as a fee for finding the lessee, how much should be reported as an expense for this item in 2007 by Nelson Co.?

(LO 3, 4) **E21-13 (Accounting for an Operating Lease)** On January 1, 2008, a machine was purchased for $900,000 by Young Co. The machine is expected to have an 8-year life with no salvage value. It is to be depreciated on a straight-line basis. The machine was leased to St. Leger Inc. on January 1, 2008, at an annual rental of $210,000. Other relevant information is as follows.

1. The lease term is for 3 years.
2. Young Co. incurred maintenance and other executory costs of $25,000 in 2008 related to this lease.
3. The machine could have been sold by Young Co. for $940,000 instead of leasing it.
4. St. Leger is required to pay a rent security deposit of $35,000 and to prepay the last month's rent of $17,500.

Instructions

(a) How much should Young Co. report as income before income tax on this lease for 2008?
(b) What amount should St. Leger Inc. report for rent expense for 2008 on this lease?

(LO 3, 4) **E21-14 (Operating Lease for Lessee and Lessor)** On February 20, 2007, Barbara Brent Inc., purchased a machine for $1,500,000 for the purpose of leasing it. The machine is expected to have a 10-year life, no residual value, and will be depreciated on the straight-line basis. The machine was leased to Rudy Company on March 1, 2007, for a 4-year period at a monthly rental of $19,500. There is no provision for the renewal of the lease or purchase of the machine by the lessee at the expiration of the lease term. Brent paid $30,000 of commissions associated with negotiating the lease in February 2007:

Instructions

(a) What expense should Rudy Company record as a result of the facts above for the year ended December 31, 2007? Show supporting computations in good form.

(b) What income or loss before income taxes should Brent record as a result of the facts above for the year ended December 31, 2007? (*Hint:* Amortize commissions over the life of the lease.)

(AICPA adapted)

(LO 10) ***E21-15** **(Sale and Leaseback)** Assume that on January 1, 2007, **Elmer's Restaurants** sells a computer system to Liquidity Finance Co. for $680,000 and immediately leases the computer system back. The relevant information is as follows.

1. The computer was carried on Elmer's books at a value of $600,000.
2. The term of the noncancelable lease is 10 years; title will transfer to Elmer.
3. The lease agreement requires equal rental payments of $110,666.81 at the end of each year.
4. The incremental borrowing rate for Elmer is 12%. Elmer is aware that Liquidity Finance Co. set the annual rental to insure a rate of return of 10%.
5. The computer has a fair value of $680,000 on January 1, 2007, and an estimated economic life of 10 years.
6. Elmer pays executory costs of $9,000 per year.

Instructions
Prepare the journal entries for both the lessee and the lessor for 2007 to reflect the sale and leaseback agreement. No uncertainties exist, and collectibility is reasonably certain.

(LO 10) ***E21-16** **(Lessee-Lessor, Sale-Leaseback)** Presented below are four independent situations.

(a) On December 31, 2008, Zarle Inc. sold computer equipment to Daniell Co. and immediately leased it back for 10 years. The sales price of the equipment was $520,000, its carrying amount is $400,000, and its estimated remaining economic life is 12 years. Determine the amount of deferred revenue to be reported from the sale of the computer equipment on December 31, 2008.

(b) On December 31, 2008, Wasicsko Co. sold a machine to Cross Co. and simultaneously leased it back for one year. The sale price of the machine was $480,000, the carrying amount is $420,000, and it had an estimated remaining useful life of 14 years. The present value of the rental payments for the one year is $35,000. At December 31, 2008, how much should Wasicsko report as deferred revenue from the sale of the machine?

(c) On January 1, 2008, McKane Corp. sold an airplane with an estimated useful life of 10 years. At the same time, McKane leased back the plane for 10 years. The sales price of the airplane was $500,000, the carrying amount $379,000, and the annual rental $73,975.22. McKane Corp. intends to depreciate the leased asset using the sum-of-the-years'-digits depreciation method. Discuss how the gain on the sale should be reported at the end of 2008 in the financial statements.

(d) On January 1, 2008, Sondgeroth Co. sold equipment with an estimated useful life of 5 years. At the same time, Sondgeroth leased back the equipment for 2 years under a lease classified as an operating lease. The sales price (fair market value) of the equipment was $212,700, the carrying amount is $300,000, the monthly rental under the lease is $6,000, and the present value of the rental payments is $115,753. For the year ended December 31, 2008, determine which items would be reported on its income statement for the sale-leaseback transaction.

See the book's website, www.wiley.com/college/kieso, for Additional Exercises.

PROBLEMS

(LO 2, 8) **P21-1** **(Lessee-Lessor Entries; Sales-Type Lease)** Stine Leasing Company agrees to lease machinery to Potter Corporation on January 1, 2007. The following information relates to the lease agreement.

1. The term of the lease is 7 years with no renewal option, and the machinery has an estimated economic life of 9 years.
2. The cost of the machinery is $420,000, and the fair value of the asset on January 1, 2007, is $560,000.
3. At the end of the lease term the asset reverts to the lessor. At the end of the lease term the asset has a guaranteed residual value of $80,000. Potter depreciates all of its equipment on a straight-line basis.

4. The lease agreement requires equal annual rental payments, beginning on January 1, 2007.
5. The collectibility of the lease payments is reasonably predictable, and there are no important uncertainties surrounding the amount of costs yet to be incurred by the lessor.
6. Stine desires a 10% rate of return on its investments. Potter's incremental borrowing rate is 11%, and the lessor's implicit rate is unknown.

Instructions

(Assume the accounting period ends on December 31.)

(a) Discuss the nature of this lease for both the lessee and the lessor.
(b) Calculate the amount of the annual rental payment required.
(c) Compute the present value of the minimum lease payments.
(d) Prepare the journal entries Potter would make in 2007 and 2008 related to the lease arrangement.
(e) Prepare the journal entries Stine would make in 2007 and 2008.

(LO 3, 4)

P21-2 (Lessee-Lessor Entries; Operating Lease) Synergetics Inc. leased a new crane to M. K. Gumowski Construction under a 5-year noncancelable contract starting January 1, 2008. Terms of the lease require payments of $22,000 each January 1, starting January 1, 2008. Synergetics will pay insurance, taxes, and maintenance charges on the crane, which has an estimated life of 12 years, a fair value of $160,000, and a cost to Synergetics of $160,000. The estimated fair value of the crane is expected to be $45,000 at the end of the lease term. No bargain purchase or renewal options are included in the contract. Both Synergetics and Gumowski adjust and close books annually at December 31. Collectibility of the lease payments is reasonably certain, and no uncertainties exist relative to unreimbursable lessor costs. Gumowski's incremental borrowing rate is 10%, and Synergetics' implicit interest rate of 9% is known to Gumowski.

Instructions

(a) Identify the type of lease involved and give reasons for your classification. Discuss the accounting treatment that should be applied by both the lessee and the lessor.
(b) Prepare all the entries related to the lease contract and leased asset for the year 2008 for the lessee and lessor, assuming the following amounts.
  (1) Insurance $500.
  (2) Taxes $2,000.
  (3) Maintenance $650.
  (4) Straight-line depreciation and salvage value $10,000.
(c) Discuss what should be presented in the balance sheet, the income statement, and the related notes of both the lessee and the lessor at December 31, 2008.

(LO 2, 8, 9)

P21-3 (Lessee-Lessor Entries, Balance Sheet Presentation; Sales-Type Lease) Cascade Industries and Hardy Inc. enter into an agreement that requires Hardy Inc. to build three diesel-electric engines to Cascade's specifications. Upon completion of the engines, Cascade has agreed to lease them for a period of 10 years and to assume all costs and risks of ownership. The lease is noncancelable, becomes effective on January 1, 2008, and requires annual rental payments of $620,956 each January 1, starting January 1, 2008.

Cascade's incremental borrowing rate is 10%. The implicit interest rate used by Hardy Inc. and known to Cascade is 8%. The total cost of building the three engines is $3,900,000. The economic life of the engines is estimated to be 10 years, with residual value set at zero. Cascade depreciates similar equipment on a straight-line basis. At the end of the lease, Cascade assumes title to the engines. Collectibility of the lease payments is reasonably certain; no uncertainties exist relative to unreimbursable lessor costs.

Instructions

(Round all numbers to the nearest dollar.)

(a) Discuss the nature of this lease transaction from the viewpoints of both lessee and lessor.
(b) Prepare the journal entry or entries to record the transaction on January 1, 2008, on the books of Cascade Industries.
(c) Prepare the journal entry or entries to record the transaction on January 1, 2008, on the books of Hardy Inc.
(d) Prepare the journal entries for both the lessee and lessor to record the first rental payment on January 1, 2008.
(e) Prepare the journal entries for both the lessee and lessor to record interest expense (revenue) at December 31, 2008. (Prepare a lease amortization schedule for 2 years.)
(f) Show the items and amounts that would be reported on the balance sheet (not notes) at December 31, 2008, for both the lessee and the lessor.

(LO 2, 6, 9)

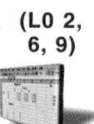

P21-4 (Balance Sheet and Income Statement Disclosure—Lessee) The following facts pertain to a noncancelable lease agreement between Alschuler Leasing Company and McKee Electronics, a lessee, for a computer system.

Inception date	October 1, 2007
Lease term	6 years
Economic life of leased equipment	6 years
Fair value of asset at October 1, 2007	$200,255
Residual value at end of lease term	–0–
Lessor's implicit rate	10%
Lessee's incremental borrowing rate	10%
Annual lease payment due at the beginning of each year, beginning with October 1, 2007	$41,800

The collectibility of the lease payments is reasonably predictable, and there are no important uncertainties surrounding the costs yet to be incurred by the lessor. The lessee assumes responsibility for all executory costs, which amount to $5,500 per year and are to be paid each October 1, beginning October 1, 2007. (This $5,500 is not included in the rental payment of $41,800.) The asset will revert to the lessor at the end of the lease term. The straight-line depreciation method is used for all equipment.

The following amortization schedule has been prepared correctly for use by both the lessor and the lessee in accounting for this lease. The lease is to be accounted for properly as a capital lease by the lessee and as a direct-financing lease by the lessor.

Date	Annual Lease Payment/ Receipt	Interest (10%) on Unpaid Liability/Receivable	Reduction of Lease Liability/Receivable	Balance of Lease Liability/Receivable
10/01/07				$200,255
10/01/07	$ 41,800		$ 41,800	158,455
10/01/08	41,800	$15,846	25,954	132,501
10/01/09	41,800	13,250	28,550	103,951
10/01/10	41,800	10,395	31,405	72,546
10/01/11	41,800	7,255	34,545	38,001
10/01/12	41,800	3,799*	38,001	–0–
	$250,800	$50,545	$200,255	

*Rounding error is $1.

Instructions

(Round all numbers to the nearest cent.)

(a) Assuming the lessee's accounting period ends on September 30, answer the following questions with respect to this lease agreement.
   (1) What items and amounts will appear on the lessee's income statement for the year ending September 30, 2008?
   (2) What items and amounts will appear on the lessee's balance sheet at September 30, 2008?
   (3) What items and amounts will appear on the lessee's income statement for the year ending September 30, 2009?
   (4) What items and amounts will appear on the lessee's balance sheet at September 30, 2009?

(b) Assuming the lessee's accounting period ends on December 31, answer the following questions with respect to this lease agreement.
   (1) What items and amounts will appear on the lessee's income statement for the year ending December 31, 2007?
   (2) What items and amounts will appear on the lessee's balance sheet at December 31, 2007?
   (3) What items and amounts will appear on the lessee's income statement for the year ending December 31, 2008?
   (4) What items and amounts will appear on the lessee's balance sheet at December 31, 2008?

(LO 5, 9) **P21-5** **(Balance Sheet and Income Statement Disclosure—Lessor)** Assume the same information as in P21-4.

Instructions

(Round all numbers to the nearest cent.)

(a) Assuming the lessor's accounting period ends on September 30, answer the following questions with respect to this lease agreement.
   (1) What items and amounts will appear on the lessor's income statement for the year ending September 30, 2008?
   (2) What items and amounts will appear on the lessor's balance sheet at September 30, 2008?

    (3) What items and amounts will appear on the lessor's income statement for the year ending September 30, 2009?

    (4) What items and amounts will appear on the lessor's balance sheet at September 30, 2009?

(b) Assuming the lessor's accounting period ends on December 31, answer the following questions with respect to this lease agreement.

    (1) What items and amounts will appear on the lessor's income statement for the year ending December 31, 2007?

    (2) What items and amounts will appear on the lessor's balance sheet at December 31, 2007?

    (3) What items and amounts will appear on the lessor's income statement for the year ending December 31, 2008?

    (4) What items and amounts will appear on the lessor's balance sheet at December 31, 2008?

P21-6 (Lessee Entries with Residual Value) The following facts pertain to a noncancelable lease agreement between Voris Leasing Company and Zarle Company, a lessee.

Inception date	January 1, 2007
Annual lease payment due at the beginning of each year, beginning with January 1, 2007	$81,365
Residual value of equipment at end of lease term, guaranteed by the lessee	$50,000
Lease term	6 years
Economic life of leased equipment	6 years
Fair value of asset at January 1, 2007	$400,000
Lessor's implicit rate	12%
Lessee's incremental borrowing rate	12%

The lessee assumes responsibility for all executory costs, which are expected to amount to $4,000 per year. The asset will revert to the lessor at the end of the lease term. The lessee has guaranteed the lessor a residual value of $50,000. The lessee uses the straight-line depreciation method for all equipment.

Instructions

(Round all numbers to the nearest cent.)

(a) Prepare an amortization schedule that would be suitable for the lessee for the lease term.

(b) Prepare all of the journal entries for the lessee for 2007 and 2008 to record the lease agreement, the lease payments, and all expenses related to this lease. Assume the lessee's annual accounting period ends on December 31 and reversing entries are used when appropriate.

(LO 2, 9)

P21-7 (Lessee Entries and Balance Sheet Presentation; Capital Lease) Brennan Steel Company as lessee signed a lease agreement for equipment for 5 years, beginning December 31, 2007. Annual rental payments of $32,000 are to be made at the beginning of each lease year (December 31). The taxes, insurance, and the maintenance costs are the obligation of the lessee. The interest rate used by the lessor in setting the payment schedule is 10%; Brennan's incremental borrowing rate is 12%. Brennan is unaware of the rate being used by the lessor. At the end of the lease, Brennan has the option to buy the equipment for $1, considerably below its estimated fair value at that time. The equipment has an estimated useful life of 7 years, with no salvage value. Brennan uses the straight-line method of depreciation on similar owned equipment.

Instructions

(Round all numbers to the nearest dollar.)

(a) Prepare the journal entry or entries, with explanations, that should be recorded on December 31, 2007, by Brennan. (Assume no residual value.)

(b) Prepare the journal entry or entries, with explanations, that should be recorded on December 31, 2008, by Brennan. (Prepare the lease amortization schedule for all five payments.)

(c) Prepare the journal entry or entries, with explanations, that should be recorded on December 31, 2009, by Brennan.

(d) What amounts would appear on Brennan's December 31, 2009, balance sheet relative to the lease arrangement?

(LO 2, 9)

P21-8 (Lessee Entries and Balance Sheet Presentation; Capital Lease) On January 1, 2008, Charlie Doss Company contracts to lease equipment for 5 years, agreeing to make a payment of $94,732 (including the executory costs of $6,000) at the beginning of each year, starting January 1, 2008. The taxes, the insurance, and the maintenance, estimated at $6,000 a year, are the obligations of the lessee. The leased equipment is to be capitalized at $370,000. The asset is to be depreciated on a double-declining-balance basis, and the obligation is to be reduced on an effective-interest basis. Doss's incremental borrowing rate is 12%, and the implicit rate in the lease is 10%, which is known by Doss. Title to the equipment transfers to Doss when the lease expires. The asset has an estimated useful life of 5 years and no residual value.

Instructions

(Round all numbers to the nearest dollar.)

- **(a)** Explain the probable relationship of the $370,000 amount to the lease arrangement.
- **(b)** Prepare the journal entry or entries that should be recorded on January 1, 2008, by Charlie Doss Company.
- **(c)** Prepare the journal entry to record depreciation of the leased asset for the year 2008.
- **(d)** Prepare the journal entry to record the interest expense for the year 2008.
- **(e)** Prepare the journal entry to record the lease payment of January 1, 2009, assuming reversing entries are not made.
- **(f)** What amounts will appear on the lessee's December 31, 2008, balance sheet relative to the lease contract?

(LO 2, 6) **P21-9 (Lessee Entries, Capital Lease with Monthly Payments)** John Roesch Inc. was incorporated in 2006 to operate as a computer software service firm with an accounting fiscal year ending August 31. Roesch's primary product is a sophisticated online inventory-control system; its customers pay a fixed fee plus a usage charge for using the system.

Roesch has leased a large, Alpha-3 computer system from the manufacturer. The lease calls for a monthly rental of $50,000 for the 144 months (12 years) of the lease term. The estimated useful life of the computer is 15 years.

Each scheduled monthly rental payment includes $4,000 for full-service maintenance on the computer to be performed by the manufacturer. All rentals are payable on the first day of the month beginning with August 1, 2007, the date the computer was installed and the lease agreement was signed. The lease is noncancelable for its 12-year term, and it is secured only by the manufacturer's chattel lien on the Alpha-3 system.

This lease is to be accounted for as a capital lease by Roesch, and it will be depreciated by the straight-line method with no expected salvage value. Borrowed funds for this type of transaction would cost Roesch 12% per year (1% per month). Following is a schedule of the present value of $1 for selected periods discounted at 1% per period when payments are made at the beginning of each period.

Periods (months)	Present Value of $1 per Period Discounted at 1% per Period
1	1.000
2	1.990
3	2.970
143	76.658
144	76.899

Instructions

Prepare, in general journal form, all entries Roesch should have made in its accounting records during August 2007 relating to this lease. Give full explanations and show supporting computations for each entry. Remember, August 31, 2007, is the end of Roesch's fiscal accounting period and it will be preparing financial statements on that date. Do not prepare closing entries.

(AICPA adapted)

(LO 4, 7, 8)

P21-10 (Lessor Computations and Entries; Sales-Type Lease with Unguaranteed RV) Hanson Company manufactures a computer with an estimated economic life of 12 years and leases it to Flypaper Airlines for a period of 10 years. The normal selling price of the equipment is $210,482, and its unguaranteed residual value at the end of the lease term is estimated to be $20,000. Flypaper will pay annual payments of $30,000 at the beginning of each year and all maintenance, insurance, and taxes. Hanson incurred costs of $135,000 in manufacturing the equipment and $4,000 in negotiating and closing the lease. Hanson has determined that the collectibility of the lease payments is reasonably predictable, that no additional costs will be incurred, and that the implicit interest rate is 10%.

Instructions

(Round all numbers to the nearest dollar.)

- **(a)** Discuss the nature of this lease in relation to the lessor and compute the amount of each of the following items.
  - **(1)** Lease receivable.
  - **(2)** Sales price.
  - **(3)** Cost of sales.
- **(b)** Prepare a 10-year lease amortization schedule.
- **(c)** Prepare all of the lessor's journal entries for the first year.

(LO 2, 6, 7) **P21-11 (Lessee Computations and Entries; Capital Lease with Unguaranteed Residual Value)** Assume the same data as in P21-10 with Flypaper Airlines Co. having an incremental borrowing rate of 10%.

Instructions

(Round all numbers to the nearest dollar.)

(a) Discuss the nature of this lease in relation to the lessee, and compute the amount of the initial obligation under capital leases.
(b) Prepare a 10-year lease amortization schedule.
(c) Prepare all of the lessee's journal entries for the first year.

P21-12 (Basic Lessee Accounting with Difficult PV Calculation) In 2005 Judy Yin Trucking Company negotiated and closed a long-term lease contract for newly constructed truck terminals and freight storage facilities. The buildings were erected to the company's specifications on land owned by the company. On January 1, 2006, Judy Yin Trucking Company took possession of the lease properties. On January 1, 2006 and 2007, the company made cash payments of $1,048,000 that were recorded as rental expenses.

Although the terminals have a composite useful life of 40 years, the noncancelable lease runs for 20 years from January 1, 2006, with a bargain purchase option available upon expiration of the lease.

The 20-year lease is effective for the period January 1, 2006, through December 31, 2025. Advance rental payments of $900,000 are payable to the lessor on January 1 of each of the first 10 years of the lease term. Advance rental payments of $320,000 are due on January 1 for each of the last 10 years of the lease. The company has an option to purchase all of these leased facilities for $1 on December 31, 2025. It also must make annual payments to the lessor of $125,000 for property taxes and $23,000 for insurance. The lease was negotiated to assure the lessor a 6% rate of return.

Instructions

(Round all numbers to the nearest dollar.)

(a) Prepare a schedule to compute for Judy Yin Trucking Company the discounted present value of the terminal facilities and related obligation at January 1, 2006.
(b) Assuming that the discounted present value of terminal facilities and related obligation at January 1, 2006, was $8,400,000, prepare journal entries for Judy Yin Trucking Company to record the:
  (1) Cash payment to the lessor on January 1, 2008.
  (2) Amortization of the cost of the leased properties for 2008 using the straight-line method and assuming a zero salvage value.
  (3) Accrual of interest expense at December 31, 2008.
  Selected present value factors are as follows:

Periods	For an Ordinary Annuity of $1 at 6%	For $1 at 6%
1	.943396	.943396
2	1.833393	.889996
8	6.209794	.627412
9	6.801692	.591898
10	7.360087	.558395
19	11.158117	.330513
20	11.469921	.311805

(AICPA adapted)

(LO 4, 7, 8) **P21-13 (Lessor Computations and Entries; Sales-Type Lease with Guaranteed Residual Value)** Laura Jennings Inc. manufactures an X-ray machine with an estimated life of 12 years and leases it to Craig Gocker Medical Center for a period of 10 years. The normal selling price of the machine is $343,734, and its guaranteed residual value at the end of the noncancelable lease term is estimated to be $15,000. The hospital will pay rents of $50,000 at the beginning of each year and all maintenance, insurance, and taxes. Laura Jennings Inc. incurred costs of $210,000 in manufacturing the machine and $14,000 in negotiating and closing the lease. Laura Jennings Inc. has determined that the collectibility of the lease payments is reasonably predictable, that there will be no additional costs incurred, and that the implicit interest rate is 10%.

Instructions

(Round all numbers to the nearest dollar.)

(a) Discuss the nature of this lease in relation to the lessor and compute the amount of each of the following items.
  (1) Lease receivable at inception of the lease.
  (2) Sales price.
  (3) Cost of sales.
(b) Prepare a 10-year lease amortization schedule.
(c) Prepare all of the lessor's journal entries for the first year.

(LO 2, 7) **P21-14 (Lessee Computations and Entries; Capital Lease with Guaranteed Residual Value)** Assume the same data as in P21-13 and that Craig Gocker Medical Center has an incremental borrowing rate of 10%.

Instructions

(Round all numbers to the nearest dollar.)

(a) Discuss the nature of this lease in relation to the lessee, and compute the amount of the initial obligation under capital leases.

(b) Prepare a 10-year lease amortization schedule.

(c) Prepare all of the lessee's journal entries for the first year.

(LO 2, 3, 7) **P21-15 (Operating Lease vs. Capital Lease)** You are auditing the December 31, 2006, financial statements of Sarah Shamess, Inc., manufacturer of novelties and party favors. During your inspection of the

company garage, you discovered that a 2005 Shirk automobile not listed in the equipment subsidiary ledger is parked in the company garage. You ask Sally Straub, plant manager, about the vehicle, and she tells you that the company did not list the automobile because the company was only leasing it. The lease agreement was entered into on January 1, 2006, with Jack Hayes New and Used Cars.

You decide to review the lease agreement to ensure that the lease should be afforded operating lease treatment, and you discover the following lease terms.

1. Noncancelable term of 4 years.

2. Rental of $2,160 per year (at the end of each year). (The present value at 8% per year is $7,154.)

3. Estimated residual value after 4 years is $1,100. (The present value at 8% per year is $809.) Shamess guarantees the residual value of $1,100.

4. Estimated economic life of the automobile is 5 years.

5. Shamess's incremental borrowing rate is 8% per year.

Instructions

You are a senior auditor writing a memo to your supervisor, the audit partner in charge of this audit, to discuss the above situation. Be sure to include **(a)** why you inspected the lease agreement, **(b)** what you determined about the lease, and **(c)** how you advised your client to account for this lease. Explain every journal entry that you believe is necessary to record this lease properly on the client's books. (It is also necessary to include the fact that you communicated this information to your client.)

(LO 2, 4, 7) **P21-16 (Lessee-Lessor Accounting for Residual Values)** Lanier Dairy leases its milking equipment from Zeff Finance Company under the following lease terms.

1. The lease term is 10 years, noncancelable, and requires equal rental payments of $25,250 due at the beginning of each year starting January 1, 2007.

2. The equipment has a fair value and cost at the inception of the lease (January 1, 2007) of $185,078, an estimated economic life of 10 years, and a residual value (which is guaranteed by Lanier Dairy) of $20,000.

3. The lease contains no renewable options, and the equipment reverts to Zeff Finance Company upon termination of the lease.

4. Lanier Dairy's incremental borrowing rate is 9% per year. The implicit rate is also 9%.

5. Lanier Dairy depreciates similar equipment that it owns on a straight-line basis.

6. Collectibility of the payments is reasonably predictable, and there are no important uncertainties surrounding the costs yet to be incurred by the lessor.

Instructions

(a) Evaluate the criteria for classification of the lease, and describe the nature of the lease. In general, discuss how the lessee and lessor should account for the lease transaction.

(b) Prepare the journal entries for the lessee and lessor at January 1, 2007, and December 31, 2007 (the lessee's and lessor's year-end). Assume no reversing entries.

(c) What would have been the amount capitalized by the lessee upon the inception of the lease if:

(1) The residual value of $20,000 had been guaranteed by a third party, not the lessee?

(2) The residual value of $20,000 had not been guaranteed at all?

(d) On the lessor's books, what would be the amount recorded as the Net Investment (Lease Receivable) at the inception of the lease, assuming:

(1) The residual value of $20,000 had been guaranteed by a third party?

(2) The residual value of $20,000 had not been guaranteed at all?

(e) Suppose the useful life of the milking equipment is 20 years. How large would the residual value have to be at the end of 10 years in order for the lessee to qualify for the operating method? (Assume that the residual value would be guaranteed by a third party.) (*Hint*: The lessee's annual payments will be appropriately reduced as the residual value increases.)

CONCEPTS FOR ANALYSIS

CA21-1 **(Lessee Accounting and Reporting)** On January 1, 2008, Hayes Company entered into a non-cancelable lease for a machine to be used in its manufacturing operations. The lease transfers ownership of the machine to Hayes by the end of the lease term. The term of the lease is 8 years. The minimum lease payment made by Hayes on January 1, 2008, was one of eight equal annual payments. At the inception of the lease, the criteria established for classification as a capital lease by the lessee were met.

Instructions

(a) What is the theoretical basis for the accounting standard that requires certain long-term leases to be capitalized by the lessee? Do not discuss the specific criteria for classifying a specific lease as a capital lease.

(b) How should Hayes account for this lease at its inception and determine the amount to be recorded?

(c) What expenses related to this lease will Hayes incur during the first year of the lease, and how will they be determined?

(d) How should Hayes report the lease transaction on its December 31, 2008, balance sheet?

CA21-2 **(Lessor and Lessee Accounting and Disclosure)** Laurie Gocker Inc. entered into a noncancel-able lease arrangement with Nathan Morgan Leasing Corporation for a certain machine. Morgan's primary business is leasing; it is not a manufacturer or dealer. Gocker will lease the machine for a period of 3 years, which is 50% of the machine's economic life. Morgan will take possession of the machine at the end of the initial 3-year lease and lease it to another, smaller company that does not need the most current version of the machine. Gocker does not guarantee any residual value for the machine and will not purchase the machine at the end of the lease term.

Gocker's incremental borrowing rate is 10%, and the implicit rate in the lease is 9%. Gocker has no way of knowing the implicit rate used by Morgan. Using either rate, the present value of the minimum lease payments is between 90% and 100% of the fair value of the machine at the date of the lease agreement.

Gocker has agreed to pay all executory costs directly, and no allowance for these costs is included in the lease payments.

Morgan is reasonably certain that Gocker will pay all lease payments, and because Gocker has agreed to pay all executory costs, there are no important uncertainties regarding costs to be incurred by Morgan. Assume that no indirect costs are involved.

Instructions

(a) With respect to Gocker (the lessee), answer the following.
   (1) What type of lease has been entered into? Explain the reason for your answer.
   (2) How should Gocker compute the appropriate amount to be recorded for the lease or asset acquired?
   (3) What accounts will be created or affected by this transaction, and how will the lease or asset and other costs related to the transaction be matched with earnings?
   (4) What disclosures must Gocker make regarding this leased asset?

(b) With respect to Morgan (the lessor), answer the following:
   (1) What type of leasing arrangement has been entered into? Explain the reason for your answer.
   (2) How should this lease be recorded by Morgan, and how are the appropriate amounts determined?
   (3) How should Morgan determine the appropriate amount of earnings to be recognized from each lease payment?
   (4) What disclosures must Morgan make regarding this lease?

(AICPA adapted)

CA21-3 **(Lessee Capitalization Criteria)** On January 1, Shinault Company, a lessee, entered into three noncancelable leases for brand-new equipment, Lease L, Lease M, and Lease N. None of the three leases transfers ownership of the equipment to Shinault at the end of the lease term. For each of the three leases, the present value at the beginning of the lease term of the minimum lease payments, excluding that portion of the payments representing executory costs such as insurance, maintenance, and taxes to be paid by the lessor, is 75% of the fair value of the equipment.

The following information is peculiar to each lease.

1. Lease L does not contain a bargain purchase option. The lease term is equal to 80% of the estimated economic life of the equipment.

2. Lease M contains a bargain purchase option. The lease term is equal to 50% of the estimated economic life of the equipment.

3. Lease N does not contain a bargain purchase option. The lease term is equal to 50% of the estimated economic life of the equipment.

Instructions

(a) How should Shinault Company classify each of the three leases above, and why? Discuss the rationale for your answer.

(b) What amount, if any, should Shinault record as a liability at the inception of the lease for each of the three leases above?

(c) Assuming that the minimum lease payments are made on a straight-line basis, how should Shinault record each minimum lease payment for each of the three leases above?

(AICPA adapted)

CA21-4 (Comparison of Different Types of Accounting by Lessee and Lessor)

Part 1

Capital leases and operating leases are the two classifications of leases described in FASB pronouncements from the standpoint of the **lessee**.

Instructions

(a) Describe how a capital lease would be accounted for by the lessee both at the inception of the lease and during the first year of the lease, assuming the lease transfers ownership of the property to the lessee by the end of the lease.

(b) Describe how an operating lease would be accounted for by the lessee both at the inception of the lease and during the first year of the lease, assuming equal monthly payments are made by the lessee at the beginning of each month of the lease. Describe the change in accounting, if any, when rental payments are not made on a straight-line basis.

Do **not** discuss the criteria for distinguishing between capital leases and operating leases.

Part 2

Sales-type leases and direct financing leases are two of the classifications of leases described in FASB pronouncements from the standpoint of the **lessor**.

Instructions

Compare and contrast a sales-type lease with a direct financing lease as follows.

(a) Lease receivable.

(b) Recognition of interest revenue.

(c) Manufacturer's or dealer's profit.

Do **not** discuss the criteria for distinguishing between the leases described above and operating leases.

(AICPA adapted)

CA21-5 (Lessee Capitalization of Bargain Purchase Option)

Brad Hayes Corporation is a diversified company with nationwide interests in commercial real estate developments, banking, copper mining, and metal fabrication. The company has offices and operating locations in major cities throughout the United States. Corporate headquarters for Brad Hayes Corporation is located in a metropolitan area of a midwestern state, and executives connected with various phases of company operations travel extensively. Corporate management is currently evaluating the feasibility of acquiring a business aircraft that can be used by company executives to expedite business travel to areas not adequately served by commercial airlines. Proposals for either leasing or purchasing a suitable aircraft have been analyzed, and the leasing proposal was considered to be more desirable.

The proposed lease agreement involves a twin-engine turboprop Viking that has a fair market value of $1,000,000. This plane would be leased for a period of 10 years beginning January 1, 2008. The lease agreement is cancelable only upon accidental destruction of the plane. An annual lease payment of $141,780 is due on January 1 of each year; the first payment is to be made on January 1, 2008. Maintenance operations are strictly scheduled by the lessor, and Brad Hayes Corporation will pay for these services as they are performed. Estimated annual maintenance costs are $6,900. The lessor will pay all insurance premiums and local property taxes, which amount to a combined total of $4,000 annually and are included in the annual lease payment of $141,780. Upon expiration of the 10-year lease, Brad Hayes Corporation can purchase the Viking for $44,440. The estimated useful life of the plane is 15 years, and its salvage value in the used plane market is estimated to be $100,000 after 10 years. The salvage value probably will never be less than $75,000 if the engines are overhauled and maintained as prescribed by the manufacturer. If the purchase option is not exercised, possession of the plane will revert to the lessor, and there is no provision for renewing the lease agreement beyond its termination on December 31, 2017.

Brad Hayes Corporation can borrow $1,000,000 under a 10-year term loan agreement at an annual interest rate of 12%. The lessor's implicit interest rate is not expressly stated in the lease agreement, but this rate appears to be approximately 8% based on ten net rental payments of $137,780 per year and the initial market value of $1,000,000 for the plane. On January 1, 2008, the present value of all net rental payments and the purchase option of $44,440 is $888,890 using the 12% interest rate. The present value of all net rental payments and the $44,440 purchase option on January 1, 2008, is $1,022,226 using the 8% interest rate implicit in the lease agreement. The financial vice-president of Brad Hayes Corporation has established that this lease agreement is a capital lease as defined in *Statement of Financial Accounting Standards No. 13*, "Accounting for Leases."

Instructions

(a) What is the appropriate amount that Brad Hayes Corporation should recognize for the leased aircraft on its balance sheet after the lease is signed?

(b) Without prejudice to your answer in part (a), assume that the annual lease payment is $141,780 as stated in the question, that the appropriate capitalized amount for the leased aircraft is $1,000,000 on January 1, 2008, and that the interest rate is 9%. How will the lease be reported in the December 31, 2008, balance sheet and related income statement? (Ignore any income tax implications.)

(CMA adapted)

 CA21-6 (Lease Capitalization, Bargain Purchase Option) Cubby Corporation entered into a lease agreement for 10 photocopy machines for its corporate headquarters. The lease agreement qualifies as an operating lease in all terms except there is a bargain purchase option. After the 5-year lease term, the corporation can purchase each copier for $1,000, when the anticipated market value is $2,500.

Glenn Beckert, the financial vice president, thinks the financial statements must recognize the lease agreement as a capital lease because of the bargain purchase agreement. The controller, Donna Kessinger, disagrees: "Although I don't know much about the copiers themselves, there is a way to avoid recording the lease liability." She argues that the corporation might claim that copier technology advances rapidly and that by the end of the lease term the machines will most likely not be worth the $1,000 bargain price.

Instructions

Answer the following questions.

(a) What ethical issue is at stake?

(b) Should the controller's argument be accepted if she does not really know much about copier technology? Would it make a difference if the controller were knowledgeable about the pace of change in copier technology?

(c) What should Beckert do?

*CA21-7 (Sale-Leaseback) On January 1, 2007, Laura Dwyer Company sold equipment for cash and leased it back. As seller-lessee, Laura Dwyer retained the right to substantially all of the remaining use of the equipment.

The term of the lease is 8 years. There is a gain on the sale portion of the transaction. The lease portion of the transaction is classified appropriately as a capital lease.

Instructions

(a) What is the theoretical basis for requiring lessees to capitalize certain long-term leases? **Do not discuss the specific criteria for classifying a lease as a capital lease.**

(b) (1) How should Laura Dwyer account for the sale portion of the sale-leaseback transaction at January 1, 2007?

(2) How should Laura Dwyer account for the leaseback portion of the sale-leaseback transaction at January 1, 2007?

(c) How should Laura Dwyer account for the gain on the sale portion of the sale-leaseback transaction during the first year of the lease? Why?

(AICPA adapted)

*CA21-8 (Sale-Leaseback) On December 31, 2007, Laura Truttman Co. sold 6-month old equipment at fair value and leased it back. There was a loss on the sale. Laura Truttman pays all insurance, maintenance, and taxes on the equipment. The lease provides for eight equal annual payments, beginning December 31, 2008, with a present value equal to 85% of the equipment's fair value and sales price. The lease's term is equal to 80% of the equipment's useful life. There is no provision for Laura Truttman to reacquire ownership of the equipment at the end of the lease term.

Instructions

(a) (1) Why is it important to compare an equipment's fair value to its lease payments' present value and its useful life to the lease term?

(2) Evaluate Laura Truttman's leaseback of the equipment in terms of each of the four criteria for determination of a capital lease.

(b) How should Laura Truttman account for the sale portion of the sale-leaseback transaction at December 31, 2007?

(c) How should Laura Truttman report the leaseback portion of the sale-leaseback transaction on its December 31, 2008, balance sheet?

USING YOUR JUDGMENT

Financial Reporting Problem

The Procter & Gamble Company (P&G)

The financial statements of **P&G** are presented in Appendix 5B or can be accessed at the KWW website.

Instructions

Refer to P&G's financial statements, accompanying notes, and management's discussion and analysis to answer the following questions.

(a) What types of leases are used by P&G?

(b) What amount of capital leases was reported by P&G in total and for less than one year?

(c) What minimum annual rental commitments under all noncancelable leases at June 30, 2004, did P&G disclose?

Financial Statement Analysis Case

Tasty Baking Company

Presented in Illustration 21-32 are the financial statement disclosures from the 2004 annual report of **Tasty Baking Company**.

Instructions

Answer the following questions related to these disclosures.

(a) What is the total obligation under capital leases at December 25, 2004, for Tasty Baking Company?

(b) What is the book value of the assets under capital lease at December 25, 2004, for Tasty Baking Company? Explain why there is a difference between the amounts reported for assets and liabilities under capital leases.

(c) What is the total rental expense reported for leasing activity for the year ended December 25, 2004, for Tasty Baking Company?

(d) Estimate the off-balance-sheet liability due to Tasty Baking's operating leases at fiscal year-end 2004.

Comparative Analysis Case

UAL, Inc. and Southwest Airlines

Instructions

Go to the KWW website or the company websites and use information found there to answer the following questions related to **UAL, Inc.** and **Southwest Airlines**.

(a) What types of leases are used by Southwest and on what assets are these leases primarily used?

(b) How long-term are some of Southwest's leases? What are some of the characteristics or provisions of Southwest's (as lessee) leases?

(c) What did Southwest report in 2004 as its future minimum annual rental commitments under noncancelable leases?

(d) At year-end 2004, what was the present value of the minimum rental payments under Southwest's capital leases? How much imputed interest was deducted from the future minimum annual rental commitments to arrive at the present value?

(e) What were the amounts and details reported by Southwest for rental expense in 2004, 2003, and 2002?

(f) How does UAL's use of leases compare with Southwest's?

Research Cases

Case 1

The accounting for operating leases is a controversial issue. Many contend that firms employing operating leases are utilizing significantly more assets and are more highly leveraged than indicated by the balance sheet alone. As a result, analysts often use footnote disclosures to "constructively capitalize" operating lease obligations. One way to do so is to increase a firm's assets and liabilities by the present value of all future minimum rental payments.

Instructions

(a) Obtain the most recent annual report for a firm that relies heavily on operating leases. (Firms in the airline and retail industries are good candidates.) The schedule of future minimum rental payments is usually included in the "Commitments and Contingencies" footnote. Use the schedule to determine the present value of future minimum rental payments, assuming a discount rate of 10%.

(b) Calculate the company's debt-to-total-assets ratio with and without the present value of operating lease payments. Is there a significant difference?

Case 2

The January 7, 2002, edition of the *Wall Street Journal* includes an article by Judith Burns and Michael Schroeder, entitled "Accounting Firms Ask SEC for Post-**Enron** Guide."

Instructions

Read the article and answer the following questions.

(a) Why are the Big 5 firms asking the SEC to issue new guidance for disclosure?

(b) One of the areas the Big 5 suggest needs improving is reporting of lease obligations. How are off-balance-sheet lease obligations currently reported?

(c) One of the suggestions the Big 5 firms make for improving lease reporting is that firms should have to describe why these obligations aren't reported in the financial statements. Why aren't these obligations reported in the financial statements as liabilities?

International Reporting Case

As discussed in the chapter, U.S. GAAP accounting for leases allows companies to use off-balance-sheet financing for the purchase of operating assets. International accounting standards are similar to U.S. GAAP in that under these rules, companies can keep leased assets and obligations off their balance sheets. However, under *International Accounting Standard No. 17 (IAS 17)*, leases are capitalized based on the subjective evaluation of whether the risks and rewards of ownership are transferred in the lease. In Japan, virtually all leases are treated as operating leases. Furthermore, unlike U.S. and IAS standards, the Japanese rules do not require disclosure of future minimum lease payments.

Presented below are recent financial data for three major airlines that lease some part of their aircraft fleet. **American Airlines** prepares its financial statements under U.S. GAAP and leases approximately 27% of its fleet. **KLM Royal Dutch Airlines** and **Japan Airlines (JAL)** present their statements in accordance with their home country GAAP (Netherlands and Japan respectively). KLM leases about 22% of its aircraft, and JAL leases approximately 50% of its fleet.

Financial Statement Data	American Airlines (millions of dollars)	KLM Royal Dutch Airlines (millions of guilders)	Japan Airlines (millions of yen)
As-reported			
Assets	20,915	19,205	2,042,761
Liabilities	14,699	13,837	1,857,800
Income	985	606	4,619
Estimated impact of capitalizing operating leases on:[1]			
Assets	5,897	1,812	244,063
Liabilities	6,886	1,776	265,103
Income	(143)	24	(9,598)

[1]Based on *Apples to Apples: Global Airlines: Flight to Quality* (New York: N.Y.: Morgan Stanley Dean Witter, October 1998).

Instructions

(a) Using the as-reported data for each of the airlines, compute the rate of return on assets and the debt to assets ratio. Compare these companies on the basis of this analysis.

(b) Adjust the as-reported numbers of the three companies for the effects of non-capitalization of leases, and then redo the analysis in part (a).

(c) The following statement was overheard in the library: "Non-capitalization of operating leases is not that big a deal for profitability analysis based on rate of return on assets, since the operating lease payments (under operating lease accounting) are about the same as the sum of the interest and depreciation expense under capital lease treatment." Do you agree? Explain.

(d) Since the accounting for leases worldwide is similar, does your analysis above suggest there is a need for an improved accounting standard for leases? (*Hint:* Reflect on comparability of information about these companies' leasing activities, when leasing is more prevalent in one country than in others.)

Professional Research: Financial Accounting and Reporting

Henley Hardware Co. is considering alternative financing arrangements for equipment used in its warehouses. Besides purchasing the equipment outright, Henley is also considering a lease. Accounting for the outright purchase is fairly straightforward, but because Henley has not used equipment leases in the past, the accounting staff is less informed about the specific accounting rules for leases.

The staff is aware of some lease rules related to a "90 percent of fair value," "75 percent of useful life," and "residual value deficiencies," but they are unsure about the meanings of these terms in lease accounting. Henley has asked you to conduct some research on these items related to lease capitalization criteria.

Instructions

Using the **Financial Accounting Research System (FARS)**, respond to the following items. (Provide text strings used in your search.)

(a) Define "fair value of the leased property." What are some examples of the determination of fair value?

(b) Besides the noncancelable term of the lease, name at least three other considerations in determining the "lease term."

(c) A common issue in the accounting for leases concerns lease requirements that the lessee make up a residual value deficiency that is attributable to damage, extraordinary wear and tear, or excessive usage (e.g., excessive mileage on a leased vehicle). Do these features constitute a lessee guarantee of the residual value such that the estimated residual value of the leased property at the end of the lease term should be included in minimum lease payments?

Professional Simulations

Simulation 1

In this simulation you are asked to address questions related to the accounting for leases. Prepare responses to all parts.

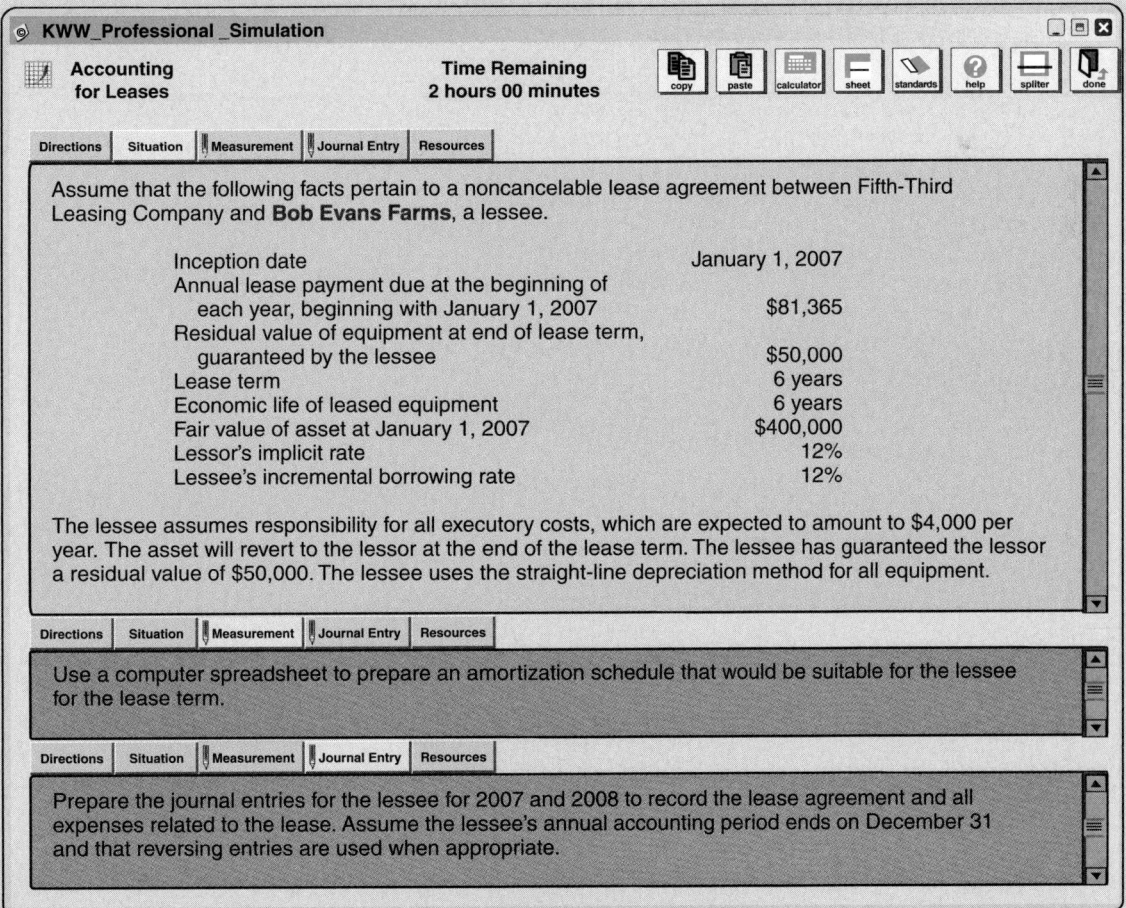

KWW_Professional _Simulation

Accounting
for Leases

Time Remaining
2 hours 00 minutes

copy | paste | calculator | sheet | standards | help | splitter | done

Directions | Situation | Measurement | Journal Entry | Resources

Assume that the following facts pertain to a noncancelable lease agreement between Fifth-Third Leasing Company and **Bob Evans Farms**, a lessee.

Inception date	January 1, 2007
Annual lease payment due at the beginning of each year, beginning with January 1, 2007	$81,365
Residual value of equipment at end of lease term, guaranteed by the lessee	$50,000
Lease term	6 years
Economic life of leased equipment	6 years
Fair value of asset at January 1, 2007	$400,000
Lessor's implicit rate	12%
Lessee's incremental borrowing rate	12%

The lessee assumes responsibility for all executory costs, which are expected to amount to $4,000 per year. The asset will revert to the lessor at the end of the lease term. The lessee has guaranteed the lessor a residual value of $50,000. The lessee uses the straight-line depreciation method for all equipment.

Directions | Situation | Measurement | Journal Entry | Resources

Use a computer spreadsheet to prepare an amortization schedule that would be suitable for the lessee for the lease term.

Directions | Situation | Measurement | Journal Entry | Resources

Prepare the journal entries for the lessee for 2007 and 2008 to record the lease agreement and all expenses related to the lease. Assume the lessee's annual accounting period ends on December 31 and that reversing entries are used when appropriate.

Simulation 2

In this simulation you are asked to address questions related to the accounting for leases. Prepare responses to all parts.

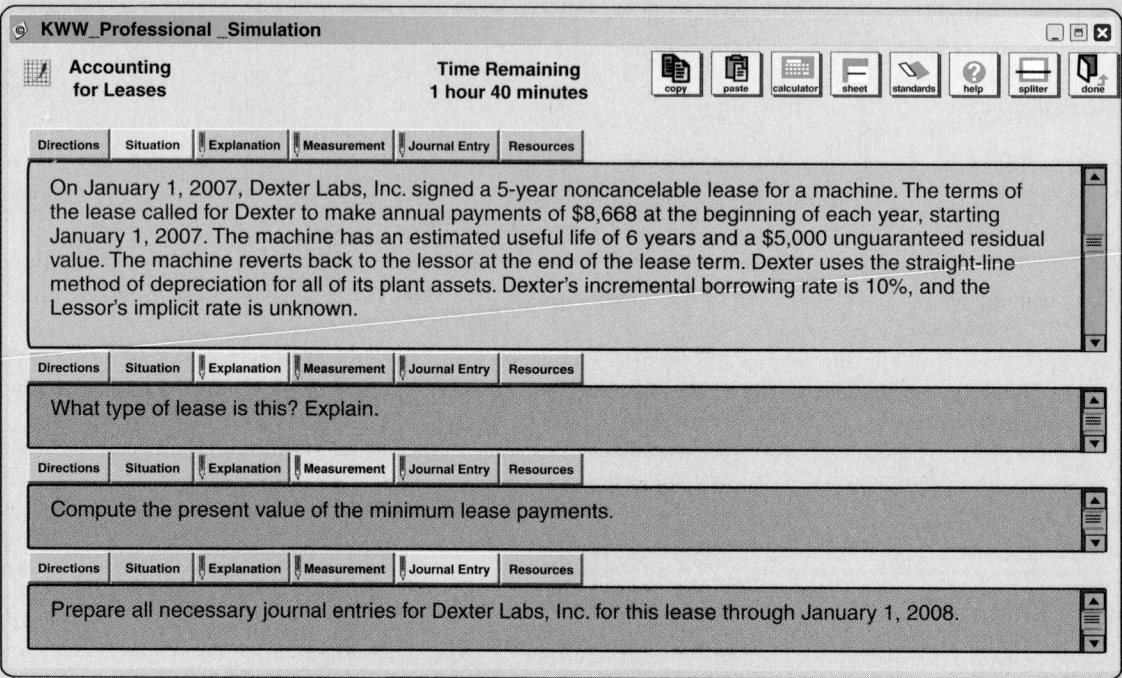

KWW_Professional _Simulation

| Accounting for Leases | Time Remaining 1 hour 40 minutes | copy | paste | calculator | sheet | standards | help | splitter | done |

Directions | Situation | Explanation | Measurement | Journal Entry | Resources

On January 1, 2007, Dexter Labs, Inc. signed a 5-year noncancelable lease for a machine. The terms of the lease called for Dexter to make annual payments of $8,668 at the beginning of each year, starting January 1, 2007. The machine has an estimated useful life of 6 years and a $5,000 unguaranteed residual value. The machine reverts back to the lessor at the end of the lease term. Dexter uses the straight-line method of depreciation for all of its plant assets. Dexter's incremental borrowing rate is 10%, and the Lessor's implicit rate is unknown.

Directions | Situation | Explanation | Measurement | Journal Entry | Resources

What type of lease is this? Explain.

Directions | Situation | Explanation | Measurement | Journal Entry | Resources

Compute the present value of the minimum lease payments.

Directions | Situation | Explanation | Measurement | Journal Entry | Resources

Prepare all necessary journal entries for Dexter Labs, Inc. for this lease through January 1, 2008.

Remember to check the book's companion website to find additional resources for this chapter.

www.wiley.com/college/kieso

CHAPTER TWENTY TWO

ACCOUNTING CHANGES AND ERROR ANALYSIS

So Many Changes

The FASB's conceptual framework describes comparability (including consistency) as one of the qualitative characteristics that contribute to the usefulness of accounting information. Unfortunately, companies are finding it difficult to maintain comparability and consistency due to the numerous changes in accounting principles mandated by the FASB. In addition, a number of companies have faced restatements due to errors in their financial statements. For example, the table below shows types and numbers of accounting changes.

Consolidation of variable interest entities	200	Derivatives and hedging activities	158
Liability and equity financial instruments	188	Asset retirement obligations	125
Guarantees	172	Stock compensation	122
Cost of exit or disposal activities	171	Impairments	68

The following chart indicates an increasing trend in restatements.

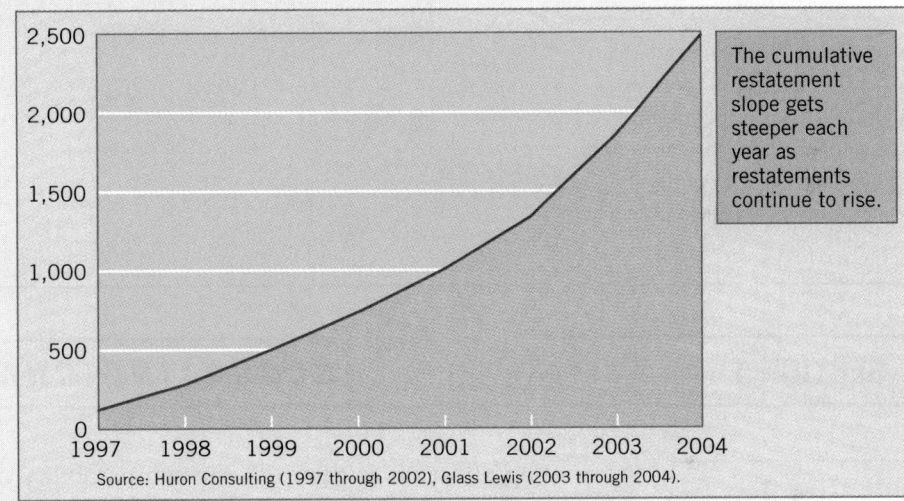

The cumulative restatement slope gets steeper each year as restatements continue to rise.

Source: Huron Consulting (1997 through 2002), Glass Lewis (2003 through 2004).

Although the percentage of companies reporting material changes or errors is small, you still must be careful. The reason: The amounts in the financial statements may have changed due to changing accounting principles and/or restatements.[1]

---

[1]Accounting change data from *Accounting Trends and Techniques—2004* (New York: AICPA, 2004). Restatement graph from T. Baldwin and D. Yoo, "Restatements—Traversing Shaky Ground," *Trend Alert* (June 2, 2005), Glass Lewis and Co., p. 7.

Learning Objectives

After studying this chapter, you should be able to:

1 Identify the types of accounting changes.

2 Describe the accounting for changes in accounting principles.

3 Understand how to account for retrospective accounting changes.

4 Understand how to account for impracticable changes.

5 Describe the accounting for changes in estimates.

6 Identify changes in a reporting entity.

7 Describe the accounting for correction of errors.

8 Identify economic motives for changing accounting methods.

9 Analyze the effect of errors.

As our opening story indicates, changes in accounting principles and errors in financial information have increased substantially in recent years. When these changes occur, companies must follow specific accounting and reporting requirements. In addition, to ensure comparability among companies, the FASB has standardized reporting of accounting changes, accounting estimates, error corrections, and related earnings per share information. In this chapter, we discuss these reporting standards, which help investors better understand a company's financial condition. The content and organization of the chapter are as follows.

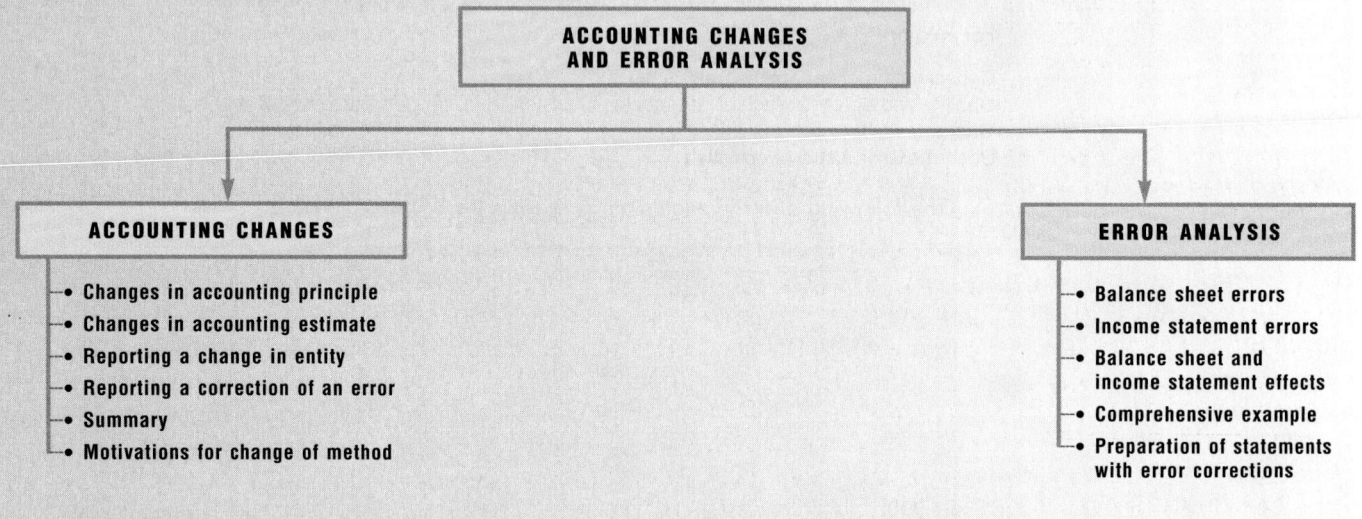

SECTION 1	*ACCOUNTING CHANGES*

OBJECTIVE 1
Identify the types of accounting changes.

Accounting alternatives diminish the comparability of financial information between periods and between companies; they also obscure useful historical trend data. For example, if **Ford** revises its estimates for equipment useful lives, depreciation expense for the current year will not be comparable to depreciation expense reported by Ford in prior years. Similarly, if **Best Buy** changes to FIFO inventory pricing while **Circuit City** uses LIFO, it will be difficult to compare these companies' reported results. A reporting framework helps preserve comparability when there is an accounting change.

The FASB has established a reporting framework, which involves three types of accounting changes.[2] The three types of accounting changes are:

UNDERLYING CONCEPTS

While changes in accounting may enhance the qualitative characteristic of *usefulness*, these changes may adversely affect the characteristics of *comparability* and *consistency*.

1   *Change in Accounting Principle.* A change from one generally accepted accounting principle to another one. For example, a company may change its inventory valuation method from LIFO to average cost.

2   *Change in Accounting Estimate.* A change that occurs as the result of new information or additional experience. For example, a company may change its estimate of the useful lives of depreciable assets.

3   *Change in Reporting Entity.* A change from reporting as one type of entity to another type of entity. As an example, a company might change the subsidiaries for which it prepares consolidated financial statements.

A fourth category necessitates changes in accounting, though it is not classified as an accounting change.

---

[2]"Accounting Changes and Error Corrections," *Statement of Financial Accounting Standards No. 154* (Stamford, Conn.: FASB, 2005).

4 *Errors in Financial Statements.* Errors result from mathematical mistakes, mistakes in applying accounting principles, or oversight or misuse of facts that existed when preparing the financial statements. For example, a company may incorrectly apply the retail inventory method for determining its final inventory value.

The FASB classifies changes in these categories because each category involves different methods of recognizing changes in the financial statements. In this chapter we discuss these classifications. We also explain how to report each item in the accounts and how to disclose the information in comparative statements.

CHANGES IN ACCOUNTING PRINCIPLE

By definition, a change in accounting principle **involves a change from one generally accepted accounting principle to another**. For example, a company might change the basis of inventory pricing from average cost to LIFO. Or it might change its method of revenue recognition for long-term construction contracts from the completed-contract to the percentage-of-completion method.

OBJECTIVE 2
Describe the accounting for changes in accounting principles.

Companies must carefully examine each circumstance to ensure that a change in principle has actually occurred. **Adoption of a new principle** in recognition of events that have occurred for the first time or that were previously immaterial is not an accounting change. For example, a change in accounting principle has not occurred when a company adopts an inventory method (e.g., FIFO) for **newly** acquired items of inventory, even if FIFO differs from that used for **previously recorded** inventory. Another example is certain marketing expenditures that were previously immaterial and expensed in the period incurred. It would not be considered a change in accounting principle if they become material and so may be acceptably deferred and amortized.

Finally, what if a company previously followed an accounting principle that was not acceptable? Or what if the company applied a principle incorrectly? In such cases, the profession considers a change to a generally accepted accounting principle **a correction of an error**. For example, a switch from the cash (income tax) basis of accounting to the accrual basis is a correction of an error. Or, if a company deducted salvage value when computing double-declining depreciation on plant assets and later recomputed depreciation without deducting estimated salvage value, it has corrected an error.

There are three possible approaches for reporting changes in accounting principles:

Report changes currently. In this approach, companies report the cumulative effect of the change in the current year's income statement as an irregular item. The cumulative effect is the difference in prior years' income between the newly adopted and prior accounting method. Under this approach, the effect of the change on prior years' income appears only in the current-year income statement. The company does not change **prior-year financial statements**.

Advocates of this position argue that changing prior years' financial statements results in a loss of confidence in financial reports. How do investors react when told that the earnings computed three years ago are now entirely different? Changing prior periods, if permitted, also might upset contractual arrangements based on the old figures. For example, profit-sharing arrangements computed on the old basis might have to be recomputed and completely new distributions made, creating numerous legal problems. Many practical difficulties also exist: The cost of changing prior-period financial statements may be excessive, or determining the amount of the prior-period effect may be impossible on the basis of available data.

Report changes retrospectively. Retrospective application refers to the application of a different accounting principle to recast previously issued financial statements—**as if the new principle had always been used**. In other words, the company "goes back" and adjusts **prior years' statements** on a basis consistent with the newly adopted principle. The company shows any cumulative effect of the change as an adjustment to beginning retained earnings of the earliest year presented.

Advocates of this position argue that retrospective application ensures comparability. Think for a moment what happens if this approach is not used: The year *previous* to the change will be on the old method; the year *of the change* will report the entire cumulative adjustment; and the *following* year will present financial statements on the new basis without the cumulative effect of the change. Such lack of consistency fails to provide meaningful earnings-trend data and other financial relationships necessary to evaluate the business.

Report changes prospectively (in the future). In this approach, previously reported results remain. As a result, companies do not adjust opening balances to reflect the change in principle. Advocates of this position argue that once management presents financial statements based on acceptable accounting principles, they are final; management cannot change prior periods by adopting a new principle. According to this line of reasoning, the current-period cumulative adjustment is not appropriate, because that approach includes amounts that have little or no relationship to the current year's income or economic events.

Given these three possible approaches, which does the accounting profession prefer? The FASB **requires that companies use the retrospective approach.** Why? Because it provides financial statement users with more useful information than the cumulative-effect or prospective approaches.[3] The rationale is that changing the prior statements to be on the same basis as the newly adopted principle results in greater consistency across accounting periods. Users can then better compare results from one period to the next.[4]

INTERNATIONAL INSIGHT

IAS 8 generally requires retrospective application to prior years for accounting changes. However, *IAS 8* permits the cumulative-effect method or prospective method if a company cannot reasonably determine the amounts to which to restate prior periods.

WHAT DO THE NUMBERS MEAN?

QUITE A CHANGE

The cumulative-effect approach results in a loss of comparability. Also, reporting the cumulative adjustment in the period of the change can significantly affect net income, resulting in a misleading income figure. For example, at one time **Chrysler Corporation** (now **DaimlerChrysler**) changed its inventory accounting from LIFO to FIFO. If Chrysler had used the cumulative-effect approach, it would have reported a $53,500,000 adjustment to net income. That adjustment would have resulted in net income of $45,900,000, instead of a net loss of $7,600,000.

A second case: In the early 1980s the railroad industry switched from the retirement-replacement method of depreciating railroad equipment to more generally used methods such as straight-line depreciation. Using cumulative treatment, railroad companies would have made substantial adjustments to income in the period of change. Many in the industry argued that including such large cumulative-effect adjustments in the current year would distort the information and make it less useful.

Such situations lend support to retrospective application so that comparability is maintained.

Retrospective Accounting Change Approach

OBJECTIVE 3
Understand how to account for retrospective accounting changes.

A presumption exists that once a company adopts an accounting principle, it should not change. That presumption is understandable, given the idea that consistent use of

---

[3]"Accounting Changes and Error Corrections," *Statement of Financial Accounting Standards No. 154* (Stamford, Conn.: FASB, 2005). This recent standard carries forward many of the provisions in the previous accounting change standard (*APB Opinion No. 20*), including the accounting for errors, changes in estimates, and the disclosures related to accounting changes.

[4]Adoption of the retrospective approach contributes to international accounting convergence. The FASB and the IASB are collaborating on a project in which they have agreed to converge around high-quality solutions to resolve differences between U.S. GAAP and International Financial Reporting Standards (IFRS). By adopting the retrospective approach, which is the method used in IFRS, the FASB agreed that this approach is superior to the current approach.

an accounting principle enhances the usefulness of financial statements. However, the environment continually changes, and companies change in response. Recent standards on such subjects as stock options, exchanges of nonmonetary assets, derivatives, and so on indicate that changes in accounting principle will continue to occur.

When a company changes an accounting principle, it should report the change using retrospective application. In general terms, here is what it must do:

1 It adjusts its financial statements for each prior period presented. Thus, financial statement information about prior periods is on the same basis as the new accounting principle.

2 It adjusts the carrying amounts of assets and liabilities as of the beginning of the first year presented. By doing so, these accounts reflect the cumulative effect on periods prior to those presented of the change to the new accounting principle. The company also makes an offsetting adjustment to the opening balance of retained earnings or other appropriate component of stockholders' equity or net assets as of the beginning of the first year presented.

For example, assume that **Target** decides to change its inventory valuation method in 2007 from the retail inventory method (FIFO) to the retail inventory (average cost). It provides comparative information for 2005 and 2006 based on the new method. Target would adjust its assets, liabilities, and retained earnings for periods prior to 2005 and report these amounts in the 2005 financial statements, when it prepares comparative financial statements.

Example of Retrospective Accounting Change

To illustrate the retrospective approach, assume that Lancer Company has accounted for its inventory using the LIFO method. In 2007, the company changes to the FIFO method because management believes this approach provides a more appropriate measure of its inventory costs. Illustration 22-1 provides additional information related to Lancer Company.

---

1. Lancer Company started its operations on January 1, 2005. At that time stockholders invested $100,000 in the business in exchange for common stock.

2. All sales, purchases, and operating expenses for the period 2005–2007 are cash transactions. Lancer's cash flows over this period are as follows.

	2005	2006	2007
Sales	$300,000	$300,000	$300,000
Purchases	90,000	110,000	125,000
Operating expenses	100,000	100,000	100,000
Cash flow from operations	$110,000	$ 90,000	$ 75,000

3. Lancer has used the LIFO method for financial reporting since its inception.

4. Inventory determined under LIFO and FIFO for the period 2005–2007 is as follows.

	LIFO Method	FIFO Method	Difference
January 1, 2005	$ 0	$ 0	$ 0
December 31, 2005	10,000	12,000	2,000
December 31, 2006	20,000	25,000	5,000
December 31, 2007	32,000	39,000	7,000

5. Cost of goods sold under LIFO and FIFO for the period 2005–2007 are as follows.

	Cost of Goods Sold LIFO	Cost of Goods Sold FIFO	Difference
January 1, 2005	$ 0	$ 0	$ 0
December 31, 2005	80,000	78,000	2,000
December 31, 2006	100,000	97,000	3,000
December 31, 2007	113,000	111,000	2,000

6. Earnings per share information is not required on the income statement.

7. All tax effects for this illustration should be ignored.

ILLUSTRATION 22-1
Lancer Company Information

Given the information about Lancer Company, Illustration 22-2 shows its income statement, retained earnings statement, balance sheet, and statement of cash flows for 2005–2007 under LIFO.

ILLUSTRATION 22-2
Lancer Financial
Statements (LIFO)

LANCER COMPANY
INCOME STATEMENT
FOR THE YEAR ENDED DECEMBER 31

	2005	2006	2007
Sales	$300,000	$300,000	$300,000
Cost of goods sold (LIFO)	80,000	100,000	113,000
Operating expenses	100,000	100,000	100,000
Net income	$120,000	$100,000	$ 87,000

LANCER COMPANY
RETAINED EARNINGS STATEMENT
FOR THE YEAR ENDED DECEMBER 31

	2005	2006	2007
Retained earnings (beginning)	$ 0	$120,000	$220,000
Add: Net income	120,000	100,000	87,000
Retained earnings (ending)	$120,000	$220,000	$307,000

LANCER COMPANY
BALANCE SHEET
AT DECEMBER 31

	2005	2006	2007
Cash	$210,000	$300,000	$375,000
Inventory (LIFO)	10,000	20,000	32,000
Total assets	$220,000	$320,000	$407,000
Common stock	$100,000	$100,000	$100,000
Retained earnings	120,000	220,000	307,000
Total liabilities and stockholder's equity	$220,000	$320,000	$407,000

LANCER COMPANY
STATEMENT OF CASH FLOWS
FOR THE YEAR ENDED DECEMBER 31

	2005	2006	2007
Cash flows from operating activities			
Sales	$300,000	$300,000	$300,000
Purchases	90,000	110,000	125,000
Operating expenses	100,000	100,000	100,000
Net cash provided by operating activities	110,000	90,000	75,000
Cash flows from financing activities			
Issuance of common stock	100,000	—	—
Net increase in cash	210,000	90,000	75,000
Cash at beginning of year	0	210,000	300,000
Cash at end of year	$210,000	$300,000	$375,000

As Illustration 22-2 indicates, under LIFO Lancer Company reports $120,000 net income in 2005, $100,000 net income in 2006, and $87,000 net income in 2007. The amount of inventory reported on Lancer's balance sheet reflects LIFO costing.

Illustration 22-3 shows Lancer's income statement, retained earnings statement, balance sheet, and statement of cash flows for 2005–2007 under **FIFO**. You can see that **the cash flow statement under FIFO is the same as under LIFO**. Although the net incomes are different in each period, there is no cash flow effect from these differences in net income. (If we considered income taxes, a cash flow effect would result.)

ILLUSTRATION 22-3
Lancer Financial
Statements (FIFO)

LANCER COMPANY
INCOME STATEMENT
FOR THE YEAR ENDED DECEMBER 31

	2005	2006	2007
Sales	$300,000	$300,000	$300,000
Cost of goods sold (FIFO)	78,000	97,000	111,000
Operating expenses	100,000	100,000	100,000
Net income	$122,000	$103,000	$ 89,000

LANCER COMPANY
RETAINED EARNINGS STATEMENT
FOR THE YEAR ENDED DECEMBER 31

	2005	2006	2007
Retained earnings (beginning)	$ 0	$122,000	$225,000
Add: Net income	122,000	103,000	89,000
Retained earnings (ending)	$122,000	$225,000	$314,000

LANCER COMPANY
BALANCE SHEET
AT DECEMBER 31

	2005	2006	2007
Cash	$210,000	$300,000	$375,000
Inventory (FIFO)	12,000	25,000	39,000
Total assets	$222,000	$325,000	$414,000
Common stock	$100,000	$100,000	$100,000
Retained earnings	122,000	225,000	314,000
Total liabilities and stockholder's equity	$222,000	$325,000	$414,000

LANCER COMPANY
STATEMENT OF CASH FLOWS
FOR THE YEAR ENDED DECEMBER 31

	2005	2006	2007
Cash flows from operating activities			
Sales	$300,000	$300,000	$300,000
Purchases	90,000	110,000	125,000
Operating expenses	100,000	100,000	100,000
Net cash provided by operating activities	110,000	90,000	75,000
Cash flows from financing activities			
Issuance of common stock	100,000	—	—
Net increase in cash	210,000	90,000	75,000
Cast at beginning of year	0	210,000	300,000
Cash at end of year	$210,000	$300,000	$375,000

Compare the financial statements reported in Illustration 22-2 and Illustration 22-3. You can see that, under retrospective application, the change to FIFO inventory valuation affects reported inventories, cost of goods sold, net income, and retained earnings. In the following sections we discuss the accounting and reporting of Lancer's accounting change from LIFO to FIFO.

Accounting for and Reporting a Change in Principle

Given the information provided in Illustrations 22-1, 22-2, and 22-3, we now are ready to account for and report on the accounting change.

Accounting for a Change in Principle

Our first step is to adjust the financial records for the change from LIFO to FIFO. To do so, we perform the analysis in Illustration 22-4.

ILLUSTRATION 22-4
Data for Recording
Change in Accounting
Principle

	Net Income		Difference in Income
Year	LIFO	FIFO	
2005	$120,000	$122,000	$2,000
2006	100,000	103,000	3,000
Total at beginning of 2007	$220,000	$225,000	$5,000
Total in 2007	$ 87,000	$ 89,000	$2,000

The entry to record the change to the FIFO method at the beginning of 2007 is as follows.

Inventory	5,000	
Retained Earnings		5,000

The change increases the inventory account by $5,000. This amount represents the difference between the ending inventory at December 31, 2006, under LIFO ($20,000) and the ending inventory under FIFO ($25,000). The credit to Retained Earnings indicates the amount needed to change prior-year's income, assuming that Lancer had used FIFO in previous periods.

Reporting a Change in Principle

The disclosure of accounting changes is particularly important. Users of the financial statements want consistent information from one period to the next. Such consistency ensures the usefulness of financial statements. The major disclosure requirements are as follows.

1 The nature of and reason for the change in accounting principle. This must include an explanation of why the newly adopted accounting principle is preferable.

2 The method of applying the change, and:
   (a) A description of the prior-period information that has been retrospectively adjusted, if any.
   (b) The effect of the change on income from continuing operations, net income (or other appropriate captions of changes in net assets or performance indicators), any other affected line item, and any affected per-share amounts for the current period and for any prior periods retrospectively adjusted.
   (c) The cumulative effect of the change on retained earnings or other components of equity or net assets in the statement of financial position as of the beginning of the earliest period presented.[5]

Lancer Company will prepare comparative financial statements for 2006 and 2007 using FIFO (the new inventory method). Illustration 22-5 (page 1159) indicates how Lancer might present this information.

As Illustration 22-5 shows, Lancer Company reports net income under the newly adopted FIFO method for both 2006 and 2007. The company retrospectively adjusted the 2006 income statement to report the information on a FIFO basis. In addition, the note to the financial statements indicates the nature of the change, why the company made the change, and the years affected. The note also provides data on important differences between the amounts reported under LIFO versus FIFO. (When identifying

---

[5]Presentation of the effect on financial statement subtotals and totals other than income from continuing operations and net income (or other appropriate captions of changes in the applicable net assets or performance indicators) is not required (*SFAS No. 154*, par. 17.)

the significant differences, some companies show the *entire* financial statements and line-by-line differences between LIFO and FIFO.)

ILLUSTRATION 22-5
Comparative Information
Related to Accounting
Change (FIFO)

LANCER COMPANY
INCOME STATEMENT
FOR THE YEAR ENDED DECEMBER 31

	2007	2006
		As adjusted (Note A)
Sales	$300,000	$300,000
Cost of goods sold	111,000	97,000
Operating expenses	100,000	100,000
Net income	$ 89,000	$103,000

Note A

Change in Method of Accounting for Inventory Valuation   On January 1, 2007, Lancer Company elected to change its method of valuing its inventory to the FIFO method; in all prior years inventory was valued using the LIFO method. The Company adopted the new method of accounting for inventory to better report cost of goods sold in the year incurred. Comparative financial statements of prior years have been adjusted to apply the new method retrospectively. The following financial statement line items for fiscal years 2007 and 2006 were affected by the change in accounting principle.

	2007			2006		
Balance Sheet	LIFO	FIFO	Difference	LIFO	FIFO	Difference
Inventory	$ 32,000	$ 39,000	$7,000	$ 20,000	$ 25,000	$5,000
Retained earnings	307,000	314,000	7,000	220,000	225,000	5,000
Income Statement						
Cost of goods sold	$113,000	$111,000	$2,000	$100,000	$ 97,000	$3,000
Net Income	87,000	89,000	2,000	100,000	103,000	3,000
Statement of Cash Flows						
(no effect)						

As a result of the accounting change, retained earnings as of January 1, 2006, increased from $120,000, as originally reported using the LIFO method, to $122,000 using the FIFO method.

Retained Earnings Adjustment

As indicated earlier, one of the disclosure requirements is to show the cumulative effect of the change on retained earnings as of the beginning of the earliest period presented. For Lancer Company, that date is January 1, 2006. Lancer disclosed that information by means of a narrative description (see Note A in Illustration 22-5). Lancer also would disclose this information in its retained earnings statement. Illustration 22-6 shows Lancer's retained earnings statement under LIFO—that is, before giving effect to the change in accounting principle. (This information comes from Illustration 22-2.)

ILLUSTRATION 22-6
Retained Earnings
Statements (LIFO)

	2007	2006	2005
Retained earnings, January 1	$220,000	$120,000	$ 0
Net income	87,000	100,000	120,000
Retained earnings, December 31	$307,000	$220,000	$120,000

If Lancer presents comparative statements for 2006 and 2007 under FIFO, then it must change the beginning balance of retained earnings at January 1, 2006. The difference between the retained earnings balances under LIFO and FIFO is computed as shown on page 1160.

Retained earnings, January 1, 2006 (FIFO)	$122,000
Retained earnings, January 1, 2006 (LIFO)	120,000
Cumulative effect difference	$ 2,000

The $2,000 difference is the cumulative effect. Illustration 22-7 shows a comparative retained earnings statement for 2006 and 2007, giving effect to the change in accounting principle to FIFO.

ILLUSTRATION 22-7
Retained Earnings
Statements after
Retrospective Application

	2007	2006
Retained earnings, January 1, as reported		$120,000
Add: Adjustment for the cumulative effect on prior years of applying retrospectively the new method of accounting for inventory		2,000
Retained earnings, January 1, as adjusted	$225,000	122,000
Net income	89,000	103,000
Retained earnings, December 31	$314,000	$225,000

Lancer adjusted the beginning balance of retained earnings on January 1, 2006, for the excess of FIFO net income over LIFO net income in 2005. This comparative presentation indicates the type of adjustment that a company needs to make. It follows that the amount of this adjustment would be much larger if a number of prior periods were involved.

Direct and Indirect Effects of Changes

Are there other effects that a company should report when it makes a change in accounting principle? For example, what happens when a company like Lancer has a bonus plan based on net income and the prior year's net income changes when FIFO is retrospectively applied? Should Lancer change the reported amount of bonus expense also? Or what happens if we had not ignored income taxes in the Lancer example? Should Lancer adjust net income, given that taxes will be different under LIFO and FIFO in prior periods? The answers depend on whether the effects are direct or indirect.

Direct Effects

The FASB takes the position that companies should retrospectively apply the **direct effects of a change in accounting principle**. An example of a **direct effect** is an adjustment to an inventory balance as a result of a change in the inventory valuation method. For example, Lancer Company should change the inventory amounts in prior periods to indicate the change to the FIFO method of inventory valuation. Another inventory-related example would be an impairment adjustment resulting from applying the lower-of-cost-or-market test to the adjusted inventory balance. Related changes, such as deferred income tax effects of the impairment adjustment, are also considered direct effects.

To illustrate the impact of a direct effect on taxes, assume that Denson Construction has accounted for its income from long-term construction contracts using the completed-contract method. In 2007 the company changed to the percentage-of-completion method. Management believes this approach provides a more appropriate measure of the income earned. For tax purposes, the company uses the completed-contract method and plans to continue doing so in the future. (We assume a 40 percent enacted tax rate.)

Illustration 22-8 shows portions of income statements for 2005–2007—for both the completed-contract and percentage-of-completion methods.

ILLUSTRATION 22-8
Comparative Income
Statements for
Completed-Contract
versus Percentage-of-
Completion Methods

COMPLETED-CONTRACT METHOD
DENSON COMPANY
INCOME STATEMENT (PARTIAL)
FOR THE YEARS ENDED DECEMBER 31

	2005	2006	2007
Income before income tax	$400,000	$160,000	$190,000
Income tax (40%)	160,000	64,000	76,000
Net income	$240,000	$ 96,000	$114,000

PERCENTAGE-OF-COMPLETION METHOD
DENSON COMPANY
INCOME STATEMENT (PARTIAL)
FOR THE YEARS ENDED DECEMBER 31

	2005	2006	2007
Income before income tax	$600,000	$180,000	$200,000
Income tax (40%)	240,000	72,000	80,000
Net income	$360,000	$108,000	$120,000

To record a change from the completed-contract to the percentage-of-completion method, we analyze the various effects, as Illustration 22-9 shows.

ILLUSTRATION 22-9
Data for Indirect Effect
Example

Year	Pretax Income from		Difference in Income		
	Percentage-of-Completion	Completed-Contract	Difference	Tax Effect 40%	Income Effect (net of tax)
Prior to 2006	$600,000	$400,000	$200,000	$80,000	$120,000
In 2006	180,000	160,000	20,000	8,000	12,000
Total at beginning of 2007	$780,000	$560,000	$220,000	$88,000	$132,000
Total in 2007	$200,000	$190,000	$ 10,000	$ 4,000	$ 6,000

The entry to record the change at the beginning of 2007 would be:

Construction in Process	220,000	
Deferred Tax Liability		88,000
Retained Earnings		132,000

The Construction in Process account increases by $220,000 (as indicated in the first column under "Difference in Income" in Illustration 22-9). The credit to Retained Earnings of $132,000 reflects the cumulative income effects prior to 2007 (third column under "Difference in Income" in Illustration 22-9). The company credits Retained Earnings because prior years' income is closed to this account each year. The credit to Deferred Tax Liability represents the adjustment to prior years' tax expense. The company now recognizes that amount, $88,000, as a tax liability for future taxable amounts. That is, in future periods, taxable income will be higher than book income as a result of current temporary differences; therefore Denson must report a deferred tax liability in the current year.

Denson reports the comparative financial statements, as shown in the lower half of Illustration 22-8. These include the new tax amounts. As indicated earlier, companies should record in the current year the direct effect of the change in taxes as a result of the change in accounting principle. They also should present information for prior periods, including changes in taxes, based on the new method.

Indirect Effects

In addition to direct effects, companies can have **indirect effects related to a change in accounting principle.** An **indirect effect** is any change to current or future cash flows of a company that result from making a change in accounting principle that is applied retrospectively. An example of an indirect effect is a change in profit-sharing or royalty payment that is based on a reported amount such as revenue or net income. **Indirect effects do not change prior-period amounts.**

For example, let's assume that Denson Construction has an employee profit-sharing plan based on net income. As Illustration 22-8 showed, Denson would report higher income in 2005 and 2006 if it used the percentage-of-completion method. In addition, let's assume that the profit-sharing plan requires that Denson pay the incremental amount due based on the percentage-of-completion income amounts. In this situation, Denson reports this additional expense **in the current period**; it would not change prior periods for this expense. If the company prepares comparative financial statements, it follows that it does not recast the prior periods for this additional expense.[6]

If the terms of the profit-sharing plan indicate that *no payment is necessary* in the current period due to this change, then the company need not recognize additional profit-sharing expense in the current period. Neither does it change amounts reported for prior periods.

When a company recognizes the indirect effects of a change in accounting principle, it includes in the financial statements a description of the indirect effects. In doing so, it discloses the amounts recognized in the current period and related per share information.

Impracticability

It is not always possible for companies to determine how they would have reported prior periods' financial information under retrospective application of an accounting principle change. Retrospective application is considered **impracticable** if a company cannot determine the prior-period effects using every reasonable effort to do so.

Companies should not use retrospective application if one of the following conditions exists:

1 The company cannot determine the effects of the retrospective application.

2 Retrospective application requires assumptions about management's intent in a prior period.

3 Retrospective application requires significant estimates for a prior period, and the company cannot objectively verify the necessary information to develop these estimates.

If any of the above conditions exists, it is deemed impracticable to apply the retrospective approach. In this case, the company **prospectively applies** the new accounting principle as of the earliest date it is practicable to do so.[7]

For example, assume that Williams Company changed its inventory method from FIFO to LIFO, effective January 1, 2008. Williams prepares statements on a calendar-year basis and has used the FIFO method since its inception. Williams judges it impracticable to retrospectively apply the new method. Determining prior-period effects would require subjective assumptions about the LIFO layers established in prior periods. These assumptions would ordinarily result in the computation of a number of different earnings figures.

As a result, the only adjustment necessary may be to restate the beginning inventory to a cost basis from a lower-of-cost-or-market approach. Williams must disclose only the effect of the change on the results of operations in the period of change. Also, the company should explain the reasons for omitting the computations of the cumulative

INTERNATIONAL INSIGHT

IFRS do not explicitly address the accounting and disclosure of indirect effects.

OBJECTIVE 4
Understand how to account for impracticable changes.

---

[6]The rationale for this approach is that companies should recognize, in the period the adoption occurs (not the prior period), the effect on the cash flows that is caused by the adoption of the new accounting principle. That is, the accounting change is a necessary "past event" in the definition of an asset or liability that gives rise to the accounting recognition of the indirect effect in the current period (*SFAS No. 154*, par. B19).

[7]*SFAS No. 154*, pars. 8–11.

effect for prior years. Finally, it should disclose the justification for the change to LIFO.[8] Illustration 22-10, from the annual report of **Quaker Oats Company**, shows the type of disclosure needed.

ILLUSTRATION 22-10
Disclosure of Change
to LIFO

The Quaker Oats Company

Note 1 (In Part): Summary of Significant Accounting Policies

Inventories. Inventories are valued at the lower of cost or market, using various cost methods, and include the cost of raw materials, labor and overhead. The percentage of year-end inventories valued using each of the methods is as follows:

June 30	Current Year	Prior Year
Average quarterly cost	21%	54%
Last-in, first-out (LIFO)	65%	29%
First-in, first-out (FIFO)	14%	17%

Effective July 1, the Company adopted the LIFO cost flow assumption for valuing the majority of remaining U.S. Grocery Products inventories. The Company believes that the use of the LIFO method better matches current costs with current revenues. The cumulative effect of this change on retained earnings at the beginning of the year is not determinable, nor are the pro-forma effects of retroactive application of LIFO to prior years. The effect of this change on current-year fiscal results was to decrease net income by $16.0 million, or $.20 per share.

If the LIFO method of valuing certain inventories were not used, total inventories would have been $60.1 million higher in the current year, and $24.0 million higher in the prior year.

CHANGE MANAGEMENT

Halliburton offers a case study in the importance of good reporting of an accounting change. Recall from Chapter 18 that Halliburton uses percentage-of-completion accounting for its long-term construction-services contracts. Recently, the SEC questioned the company about its change in accounting for disputed claims.

Prior to 1998 Halliburton took a very conservative approach to its accounting for disputed claims. That is, the company waited until all disputes were resolved before recognizing associated revenues. In contrast, in 1998 the company recognized revenue for disputed claims *before* their resolution, using estimates of amounts expected to be recovered. Such revenue and its related profit are more tentative and subject to possible later adjustment. The accounting method adopted in 1998 is more aggressive than the company's former policy but is within the boundaries of GAAP.

It appears that the problem with Halliburton's accounting stems more from how the company handled its accounting change than from the new method itself. That is, Halliburton did not provide in its 1998 annual report an explicit reference to its change in accounting method. In fact, rather than stating its new policy, the company simply deleted the sentence that described how it accounted for disputed claims. Then later, in its 1999 annual report, the company stated its new accounting policy.

When companies make such changes in accounting, investors need to be informed about the change and about its effects on the financial results. With such information, investors and analysts can compare current results with those of prior periods and can make a more informed assessment about the company's future prospects.

Source: Adapted from "Accounting Ace Charles Mulford Answers Accounting Questions," *Wall Street Journal Online* (June 7, 2002).

WHAT DO THE NUMBERS MEAN?

---

[8]*SFAS No. 154*, par. 17. In practice, many companies defer the formal adoption of LIFO until year-end. Management thus has an opportunity to assess the impact that a change to LIFO will have on the financial statements and to evaluate the desirability of a change for tax purposes. As indicated in Chapter 8, many companies use LIFO because of the advantages of this inventory valuation method in a period of inflation.

CHANGES IN ACCOUNTING ESTIMATE

OBJECTIVE 5
Describe the accounting for changes in estimates.

To prepare financial statements, companies must estimate the effects of future conditions and events. For example, the following items require estimates.

1 Uncollectible receivables.

2 Inventory obsolescence.

3 Useful lives and salvage values of assets.

4 Periods benefited by deferred costs.

5 Liabilities for warranty costs and income taxes.

6 Recoverable mineral reserves.

7 Change in depreciation methods.

A company cannot perceive future conditions and events and their effects with certainty. Therefore, estimating requires the exercise of judgment. Accounting estimates will change as new events occur, as a company acquires more experience, or as it obtains additional information.

Companies report prospectively changes in accounting estimates. That is, companies should not adjust previously reported results for changes in estimates. Instead, they account for the effects of all changes in estimates in (1) the period of change if the change affects that period only, or (2) the period of change and future periods if the change affects both. The FASB views changes in estimates as **normal recurring corrections and adjustments**, the natural result of the accounting process. It prohibits retrospective treatment.

The circumstances related to a change in estimate differ from those for a change in accounting principle. If companies reported changes in estimates retrospectively, continual adjustments of prior years' income would occur. It seems proper to accept the view that, because new conditions or circumstances exist, the revision fits the new situation (not the old one). Companies should therefore handle such a revision in the current and future periods.

To illustrate, Underwriters Labs Inc. purchased for $300,000 a building that it originally estimated to have a useful life of 15 years and no salvage value. It recorded depreciation for 5 years on a straight-line basis. On January 1, 2007, Underwriters Labs revises the estimate of the useful life. It now considers the asset to have a total life of 25 years. (Assume that the useful life for financial reporting and tax purposes and depreciation method are the same.) Illustration 22-11 shows the accounts at the beginning of the sixth year.

ILLUSTRATION 22-11
Book Value after Five Years' Depreciation

Building	$300,000
Less: Accumulated depreciation—building (5 × $20,000)	100,000
Book value of building	$200,000

Underwriters Labs records depreciation for the year 2007 as follows:

Depreciation Expense	10,000	
Accumulated Depreciation—Building		10,000

The company computes the $10,000 depreciation charge as shown in Illustration 22-12.

ILLUSTRATION 22-12
Depreciation after Change in Estimate

$$\text{Depreciation charge} = \frac{\text{Book value of asset}}{\text{Remaining service live}} = \frac{\$200,000}{25 \text{ years} - 5 \text{ years}} = \$10,000$$

Companies sometime find it difficult to differentiate between a change in estimate and a change in accounting principle. Is it a change in principle or a change in estimate when a company changes from deferring and amortizing marketing costs to expensing them as incurred because future benefits of these costs have become doubtful? If it is impossible to determine whether a change in principle or a change in estimate has occurred, the rule is this: **Consider the change as a change in estimate.** This is often referred to as a **change in estimate effected by a change in accounting principle.**

Another example of a change in estimate effected by a change in principle is a change in depreciation (as well as amortization or depletion) methods. Because companies change depreciation methods based on changes in estimates about future benefits from long-lived assets, it is not possible to separate the effect of the accounting principle change from that of the estimates. **As a result, companies account for a change in depreciation methods as a change in estimate effected by a change in accounting principle.**[9]

A similar problem occurs in differentiating between a change in estimate and a correction of an error, although here the answer is more clear-cut. How does a company determine whether it overlooked the information in earlier periods (an error), or whether it obtained new information (a change in estimate)? Proper classification is important because the accounting treatment differs for corrections of errors versus changes in estimates. The general rule is this: **Companies should consider careful estimates that later prove to be incorrect as changes in estimate.** Only when a company obviously computed the estimate incorrectly because of lack of expertise or in bad faith should it consider the adjustment an error. There is no clear demarcation line here. Companies must use good judgment in light of all the circumstances.[10]

Disclosures

Illustration 22-13 shows disclosure of a change in estimated useful lives, which appeared in the annual report of **Ampco–Pittsburgh Corporation.**

Ampco–Pittsburgh Corporation

Note 11: Change in Accounting Estimate. The Corporation revised its estimate of the useful lives of certain machinery and equipment. Previously, all machinery and equipment, whether new when placed in use or not, were in one class and depreciated over 15 years. The change principally applies to assets purchased new when placed in use. Those lives are now extended to 20 years. These changes were made to better reflect the estimated periods during which such assets will remain in service. The change had the effect of reducing depreciation expense and increasing net income by approximately $991,000 ($.10 per share).

ILLUSTRATION 22-13
Disclosure of Change in Estimated Useful Lives

For the most part, companies need not disclose changes in accounting estimate made as part of normal operations, such as bad debt allowances or inventory obsolescence, unless such changes are material. However, for a change in estimate that affects

---

[9]*SFAS No. 154*, par. 20.

[10]In evaluating reasonableness, the auditor should use one or a combination of the following approaches.

(a) Review and test the process used by management to develop the estimate.

(b) Develop an independent expectation of the estimate to corroborate the reasonableness of management's estimate.

(c) Review subsequent events or transactions occurring prior to completion of fieldwork.

"Auditing Accounting Estimates," *Statement on Auditing Standards No. 57* (New York: AICPA, 1988).

several periods (such as a change in the service lives of depreciable assets), companies should disclose the effect on income from continuing operations and related per-share amounts of the current period. When a company has a change in estimate effected by a change in accounting principle, it must indicate why the new method is preferable. In addition, companies are subject to all other disclosure guidelines established for changes in accounting principle.

REPORTING A CHANGE IN ENTITY

OBJECTIVE 6
Identify changes in a reporting entity.

Occasionally companies make changes that result in different reporting entities. In such cases, companies report the change by **changing the financial statements of all prior periods presented**. The revised statements show the financial information for the **new reporting entity** for all periods.

Examples of a change in reporting entity are:

1 Presenting consolidated statements in place of statements of individual companies.

2 Changing specific subsidiaries that constitute the group of companies for which the entity presents consolidated financial statements.

3 Changing the companies included in combined financial statements.

4 Changing the cost, equity, or consolidation method of accounting for subsidiaries and investments.[11] In this case, a change in the reporting entity does not result from creation, cessation, purchase, or disposition of a subsidiary or other business unit.

In the year in which a company changes a reporting entity, it should disclose in the financial statements the nature of the change and the reason for it. It also should report, for all periods presented, the effect of the change on income before extraordinary items, net income, and earnings per share. These disclosures need not be repeated in subsequent periods' financial statements.

Illustration 22-14 shows a note disclosing a change in reporting entity, from the annual report of **Hewlett-Packard Company**.

ILLUSTRATION 22-14
Disclosure of Change
in Reporting Entity

Hewlett-Packard Company

Note: Accounting and Reporting Changes (In Part)

Consolidation of Hewlett-Packard Finance Company. The company implemented *Statement of Financial Accounting Standards No. 94 (SFAS 94)*, "Consolidation of All Majority-owned Subsidiaries." With the adoption of *SFAS 94*, the company consolidated the accounts of Hewlett-Packard Finance Company (HPFC), a wholly owned subsidiary previously accounted for under the equity method, with those of the company. The change resulted in an increase in consolidated assets and liabilities but did not have a material effect on the company's financial position. Since HPFC was previously accounted for under the equity method, the change did not affect net earnings. Prior years' consolidated financial information has been restated to reflect this change for comparative purposes.

REPORTING A CORRECTION OF AN ERROR

OBJECTIVE 7
Describe the accounting for correction of errors.

No business, large or small, is immune from errors. Unfortunately, as the opening story discussed, the number of errors in financial statements has increased dramatically. Illustration 22-15 indicates significant restatements (error adjustments) for each quarter in 2003 and 2004.

---

[11]An exception to retrospective application occurs when changing from the equity method. We provide an expanded illustration of the accounting for a change from or to the equity method in Appendix 22A.

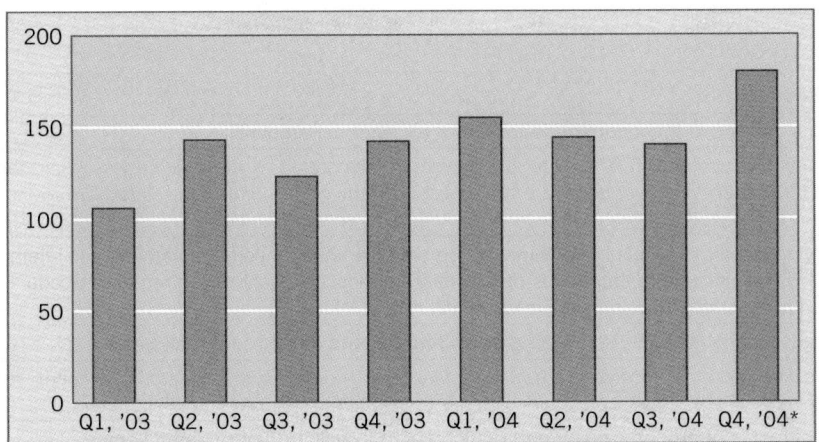

ILLUSTRATION 22-15
2003 and 2004
Restatements by Quarter

*Internal control audits mandated by Sarbanes-Oxley 404 resulted in a record number of 4th-quarter 2004 restatements.

Source: T. Baldwin and D. Yoo, "Restatements—Traversing Shaky Ground," *Trend Alert*, Glass Lewis & Co. (June 2, 2005), p. 7.

Certain errors, such as misclassifications of balances within a financial statement, are not as significant to investors as other errors. Significant errors would be those resulting in overstating assets or income, for example. However, investors should know the potential impact of all errors. Even "harmless" misclassifications can affect important ratios. Also, some errors could signal important weaknesses in internal controls that could lead to more significant errors.

In general, accounting errors include the following types:

1 A change from an accounting principle that is **not** generally accepted to an accounting principle that is acceptable. The rationale is that the company incorrectly presented prior periods because of the application of an improper accounting principle. For example, a company may change from the cash (income tax) basis of accounting to the accrual basis.

2 Mathematical mistakes, such as incorrectly totaling the inventory count sheets when computing the inventory value.

3 Changes in estimates that occur because a company did not prepare the estimates in good faith. For example, a company may have adopted a clearly unrealistic depreciation rate.

4 An oversight, such as the failure to accrue or defer certain expenses and revenues at the end of the period.

5 A misuse of facts, such as the failure to use salvage value in computing the depreciation base for the straight-line approach.

6 The incorrect classification of a cost as an expense instead of an asset, and vice versa.

Accounting errors occur for a variety of reasons. Illustration 22-16 (page 1168) indicates 11 major categories of accounting errors that drive restatements.

As soon as a company discovers an error, it must correct the error. Companies record **corrections of errors** from prior periods as an adjustment to the beginning balance of retained earnings in the current period. Such corrections are called **prior period adjustments**.[12]

---

[12]"Prior Period Adjustments," *Statement of Financial Accounting Standards No. 16* (Stamford, Conn.: FASB, 1977), p. 5. See Mark L. DeFord and James Jiambalvo, "Incidence and Circumstances of Accounting Errors," *The Accounting Review* (July 1991) for examples of different types of errors and why these errors might have occurred.

ILLUSTRATION 22-16
Accounting-Error Types

Accounting Category	Type of Restatement
Expense recognition	Recording expenses in the incorrect period or for an incorrect amount
Revenue recognition	Improper revenue accounting. This category includes instances in which revenue was improperly recognized, questionable revenues were recognized, or any other number of related errors that led to misreported revenue.
Misclassification	Misclassifying significant accounting items on the balance sheet, income statement, or statement of cash flows. These include restatements due to misclassification of short- or long-term accounts or those that impact cash flows from operations
Equity—other	Improper accounting for EPS, restricted stock, warrants, and other equity instruments
Reserves/Contingencies	Errors involving accounts receivables bad debts, inventory reserves, income tax allowances, and loss contingencies
Long-lived assets	Asset impairments of property, plant, and equipment, goodwill, or other related items.
Taxes	Errors involving correction of tax provision, improper treatment of tax liabilities, and other tax-related items
Equity—other comprehensive income	Improper accounting for comprehensive income equity transactions including foreign currency items, minimum pension liability adjustments, unrealized gains and losses on certain investments in debt, equity securities, and derivatives.
Inventory	Inventory costing valuations, quantity issues, and cost of sales adjustments
Equity—stock options	Improper accounting for employee stock options
Other	Any restatement not covered by the listed categories including those related to improper accounting for acquisitions or mergers

SOURCE: T. Baldwin and D. Yoo, "Restatements—Traversing Shaky Ground," *Trend Alert*, Glass Lewis & Co. (June 2, 2005), p. 8.

If it presents comparative statements, a company should restate the prior statements affected, to correct for the error.[13] The company need not repeat the disclosures in the financial statements of subsequent periods.

Example

To illustrate, in 2008 the bookkeeper for Selectric Company discovered an error: In 2007 the company failed to record $20,000 of depreciation expense on a newly constructed building. This building is the only depreciable asset Selectric owns. The company correctly included the depreciation expense in its tax return and correctly reported its income taxes payable. Illustration 22-17 presents Selectric's income statement for 2007 (starting with income before depreciation expense) with and without the error.

ILLUSTRATION 22-17
Error Correction
Comparison

SELECTRIC COMPANY
INCOME STATEMENT
FOR THE YEAR ENDED, DECEMBER 31, 2007

		Without Error		With Error
Income before depreciation expense		$100,000		$100,000
Depreciation expense		20,000		0
Income before income tax		80,000		100,000
Current	$32,000		$ 32,000	
Deferred	–0–	32,000	8,000	40,000
Net income		$ 48,000		$ 60,000

Illustration 22-18 shows the entries that Selectric should have made and did make for recording depreciation expense and income taxes.

---

[13]The term **"restatement"** is used for the process of revising previously issued financial statements to reflect the correction of an error. This distinguishes an error correction from a change in accounting principle (*SFAS No. 154*, par. 2, j).

Entries Company Should Have Made (Without Error)		Entries Company Did Make (With Error)	
Depreciation Expense	20,000	No entry made for depreciation	
Accumulated Depreciation —Buildings	20,000		
Income Tax Expense	32,000	Income Tax Expense	40,000
Income Tax Payable	32,000	Deferred Tax Liability	8,000
		Income Tax Payable	32,000

ILLUSTRATION 22-18
Error Entries

As Illustration 22-18 indicates, the $20,000 omission error in 2007 results in the following effects.

Income Statement Effects

Depreciation expense (2007) is understated $20,000.

Income tax expense (2007) is overstated $8,000 ($20,000 × 40%).

Net income (2007) is overstated $12,000 ($20,000 − $8,000).

Balance Sheet Effects

Accumulated depreciation—buildings is understated $20,000.

Deferred tax liability is overstated $8,000 ($20,000 × 40%).

To make the proper correcting entry in 2008, Selectric should recognize that net income in 2007 is overstated by $12,000, the Deferred Tax Liability is overstated by $8,000, and Accumulated Depreciation—Buildings is understated by $20,000. The entry to correct this error in 2008 is as follows:

Retained Earnings	12,000	
Deferred Tax Liability	8,000	
Accumulated Depreciation—Buildings		20,000

The debit to Retained Earnings results because net income for 2007 is overstated. The debit to the Deferred Tax Liability is made to remove this account, which was caused by the error. The credit to Accumulated Depreciation—Buildings reduces the book value of the building to its proper amount. Selectric will make the same journal entry to record the correction of the error in 2008 whether it prepares single-period (noncomparative) or comparative financial statements.

Single-Period Statements

To demonstrate how to show this information in a single-period statement, assume that Selectric Company has a beginning retained earnings balance at January 1, 2008, of $350,000. The company reports net income of $400,000 in 2008. Illustration 22-19 shows Selectric's retained earnings statement for 2008.

ILLUSTRATION 22-19
Reporting an Error—
Single-Period Financial
Statement

SELECTRIC COMPANY
RETAINED EARNINGS STATEMENT
FOR THE YEAR ENDED DECEMBER 31, 2008

Retained earnings, January 1, as reported		$350,000
Correction of an error (depreciation)	$20,000	
Less: Applicable income tax reduction	8,000	(12,000)
Retained earnings, January 1, as adjusted		338,000
Add: Net income		400,000
Retained earnings, December 31		$738,000

The balance sheet in 2008 would not have any deferred tax liability related to the building, and Accumulated Depreciation—Buildings is now restated at a higher amount. The income statement would not be affected.

Comparative Statements

If preparing comparative financial statements, a company should make adjustments to correct the amounts for all affected accounts reported in the statements for **all periods** reported. The company should restate the data to the correct basis for each year presented. It should **show any catch-up adjustment as a prior period adjustment to retained earnings for the earliest period it reported**. These requirements are essentially the same as those for reporting a change in accounting principle.

For example, in the case of Selectric, the error of omitting the depreciation of $20,000 in 2007, discovered in 2008, results in the restatement of the 2007 financial statements. Illustration 22-20 shows the accounts that Selectric restates in the 2007 financial statements, presented in comparison with those of 2008.

ILLUSTRATION 22-20
Reporting an Error—
Comparative Financial
Statements

In the balance sheet:	
Accumulated depreciation—buildings	$20,000 increase
Deferred tax liability	$ 8,000 decrease
Retained earnings, ending balance	$12,000 decrease
In the income statement:	
Depreciation expense—buildings	$20,000 increase
Income tax expense	$ 8,000 decrease
Net income	$12,000 decrease
In the retained earnings statement:	
Retained earnings, ending balance (due to lower net income for the period)	$12,000 decrease

Selectric prepares the 2008 financial statements in comparative form with those of 2007 **as if the error had not occurred**. In addition, Selectric must disclose that it has restated its previously issued financial statements, and it describes the nature of the error. Selectric also must disclose the following:

1 The effect of the correction on each financial statement line item and any per-share amounts affected for each prior period presented.

2 The cumulative effect of the change on retained earnings or other appropriate components of equity or net assets in the statement of financial position, as of the beginning of the earliest period presented.[14]

SUMMARY OF ACCOUNTING CHANGES AND CORRECTIONS OF ERRORS

Having guidelines for reporting accounting changes and corrections has helped resolve several significant and long-standing accounting problems. Yet, because of diversity in situations and characteristics of the items encountered in practice, use of professional judgment is of paramount importance. In applying these guidelines, the primary objective is to serve the users of the financial statements. Achieving this objective requires accuracy, full disclosure, and an absence of misleading inferences.

Illustration 22-21 summarizes the main distinctions and treatments presented in the discussion in this chapter.

---

[14]*SFAS No. 154*, par. 26.

- **Changes in accounting principle**
  Employ the retrospective approach by:
  a. Changing the financial statements of all prior periods presented.
  b. Disclosing in the year of the change the effect on net income and earnings per share for all prior periods presented.
  c. Reporting an adjustment to the beginning retained earnings balance in the statement of retained earnings in the earliest year presented.
  If impracticable to determine the prior period effect (e.g., change to LIFO):
  a. Do not change prior years' income.
  b. Use opening inventory in the year the method is adopted as the base-year inventory for all subsequent LIFO computations.
  c. Disclose the effect of the change on the current year, and the reasons for omitting the computation of the cumulative effect and pro forma amounts for prior years.

- **Changes in accounting estimate.**
  Employ the current and prospective approach by:
  a. Reporting current and future financial statements on the new basis.
  b. Presenting prior period financial statements as previously reported.
  c. Making no adjustments to current-period opening balances for the effects in prior periods.

- **Changes in reporting entity.**
  Employ the retrospective approach by:
  a. Restating the financial statements of all prior periods presented.
  b. Disclosing in the year of change the effect on net income and earnings per share data for all prior periods presented.

- **Changes due to error.**
  Employ the restatement approach by:
  a. Correcting all prior period statements presented.
  b. Restating the beginning balance of retained earnings for the first period presented when the error effects occur in a period prior to that one.

ILLUSTRATION 22-21
Summary of Guidelines
for Accounting Changes
and Errors

Changes in accounting principle are appropriate **only** when a company demonstrates that the newly adopted generally accepted accounting principle is **preferable** to the existing one. Companies and accountants determine preferability on the basis of whether the new principle constitutes an **improvement in financial reporting**, not on the basis of the income tax effect alone.[15]

But it is not always easy to determine an improvement in financial reporting. **How does one measure preferability or improvement?** Such measurement varies from company to company. **Quaker Oats Company**, for example, argued that a change in accounting principle to LIFO inventory valuation "better matches current costs with current revenues" (see Illustration 22-10, page 1163). Conversely, another company might change from LIFO to FIFO because it wishes to report a more realistic ending inventory. How do you determine which is the better of these two arguments? Determining the preferable method requires some "standard" or "objective." Because no universal standard or objective is generally accepted, the problem of determining preferability continues to be difficult.

Initially the SEC took the position that the auditor should indicate whether a change in accounting principle was preferable. The SEC has since modified this approach, noting that greater reliance may be placed on management's judgment

UNDERLYING CONCEPTS

This is an example of two widely accepted concepts conflicting. Which is more important, matching (emphasis on the income statement) or qualitative characteristic of representational faithfulness (emphasis on the balance sheet)?

---

[15]A change in accounting principle, a change in the reporting entity (special type of change in accounting principle), and a correction of an error require an explanatory paragraph in the auditor's report discussing lack of consistency from one period to the next. A change in accounting estimate does not affect the auditor's opinion relative to consistency; however, if the change in estimate has a material effect on the financial statements, disclosure may still be required. Error correction not involving a change in accounting principle does not require disclosure relative to consistency.

in assessing preferability. Even though the preferability criterion is difficult to apply, the general guidelines have acted as a deterrent to capricious changes in accounting principles.[16] **If an FASB standard creates a new principle, expresses preference for, or rejects a specific accounting principle, a change is considered clearly acceptable.**

WHAT DO THE NUMBERS MEAN?

CAN I GET MY MONEY BACK?

When companies report restatements, investors usually lose money. What should investors do if a company misleads them by misstating its financial results? Join other investors in a class-action suit against the company and in some cases, the auditor.

Class-action activity has picked up in recent years, and settlements can be large. To find out about class actions, investors can go online to see if they are eligible to join any class actions. Below are some recent examples.

Company	Settlement Amount	Contact for Claim
Quaker Oats	$ 10,400,000	www.gilardi.com
Smart Choice Automotive	$ 2,500,000	www.gilardi.com
Sunbeam	$110,000,000	www.gilardi.com

The amounts reported are *before* attorney's fees, which can range from 15 to 30 percent of the total. Also, investors may owe taxes if the settlement results in a capital gain on the investment. Thus, investors can get back some of the money they lost due to restatements, but they should be prepared to pay an attorney and the government first.

Source: Adapted from C. Coolidge, "Lost and Found," *Forbes* (October 1, 2001), pp. 124–125.

MOTIVATIONS FOR CHANGE OF ACCOUNTING METHOD

OBJECTIVE 8
Identify economic motives for changing accounting methods.

Difficult as it is to determine which accounting standards have the strongest conceptual support, other complications make the process even more complex. These complications stem from the fact that managers have self-interest in how the financial statements make the company look. They naturally wish to show their financial performance in the best light. A **favorable profit picture** can influence investors, and a strong liquidity position can influence creditors. **Too favorable a profit picture**, however, can provide union negotiators and government regulators with ammunition during bargaining talks. Hence, managers might have varying motives for reporting income numbers.

Research has provided additional insight into why companies may prefer certain accounting methods.[17] Some of these reasons are as follows:

1 *Political Costs.* As companies become larger and more politically visible, politicians and regulators devote more attention to them. The larger the firm, the more likely it is to become subject to regulation such as antitrust, and the more likely it

---

[16]If management has not provided reasonable justification for the change in accounting principle, the auditor should express a qualified opinion. Or, if the effect of the change is sufficiently material, the auditor should express an adverse opinion on the financial statements. "Reports on Audited Financial Statements," *Statement on Auditing Standards No. 58* (New York: AICPA, 1988).

[17]See Ross L. Watts and Jerold L. Zimmerman, "Positive Accounting Theory: A Ten-Year Perspective," *The Accounting Review* (January 1990) for an excellent review of research findings related to management incentives in selecting accounting methods.

is to be required to pay higher taxes. Therefore, companies that are politically visible may seek to report low income numbers, to avoid the scrutiny of regulators. In addition, other constituents, such as labor unions, may be less willing to ask for wage increases if reported income is low. Researchers have found that the larger the company, the more likely it is to adopt income-decreasing approaches in selecting accounting methods.

2 *Capital Structure.* A number of studies have indicated that the capital structure of the company can affect the selection of accounting methods. For example, a company with a high debt-to-equity ratio is more likely to be constrained by debt covenants. The debt covenant may indicate that the company cannot pay dividends if retained earnings fall below a certain level. As a result, such a company is more likely to select accounting methods that will increase net income.

3 *Bonus Payments.* Studies have found that if compensation plans tie managers' bonus payments to income, management will select accounting methods that maximize their bonus payments.

4 *Smooth Earnings.* Substantial earnings increases attract the attention of politicians, regulators, and competitors. In addition, large increases in income are difficult to achieve in following years. Further, executive compensation plans would use these higher numbers as a baseline and make it difficult for managers to earn bonuses in subsequent years. Conversely, investors and competitors might view large decreases in earnings as a signal that the company is in financial trouble. Also, substantial decreases in income raise concerns on the part of stockholders, lenders, and other interested parties about the competency of management. For all these reasons, companies have an incentive to "manage" or "smooth" earnings. In general, management tends to believe that a steady 10 percent growth a year is much better than a 30 percent growth one year and a 10 percent decline the next.[18] In other words, managers usually prefer a gradually increasing income report and sometimes change accounting methods to ensure such a result.

Management pays careful attention to the accounting it follows and often changes accounting methods, not for conceptual reasons, but for economic reasons. As indicated throughout this textbook, such arguments have come to be known as **economic consequences** arguments. These arguments focus on the supposed impact of the accounting method on the behavior of investors, creditors, competitors, governments, or managers of the reporting companies themselves.[19]

To counter these pressures, standard setters such as the FASB have declared, as part of their conceptual framework, that they will assess the merits of proposed standards from a position of **neutrality**. That is, they evaluate the soundness of standards on the basis of conceptual soundness, not on the grounds of possible impact on behavior. It is not the FASB's place to choose standards according to the kinds of behavior it wishes to promote and the kinds it wishes to discourage. At the same time, it must be admitted that some standards often **will have** the effect of influencing behavior. Yet their justification should be conceptual, and not viewed in terms of their economic impact.

---

[18]O. Douglas Moses, "Income Smoothing and Incentives: Empirical Tests Using Accounting Changes," *The Accounting Review* (April 1987). The findings provide evidence that earnings smoothing is associated with firm size, the existence of bonus plans, and the divergence of actual earnings from expectations.

[19]Lobbyists use economic consequences arguments—and there are many of them—to put pressure on standard setters. We have seen examples of these arguments in the oil and gas industry about successful efforts versus full cost, in the technology area with the issue of mandatory expensing of research and developmental costs and stock options.

SECTION 2	*ERROR ANALYSIS*

OBJECTIVE 9
Analyze the effect of errors.

In this section, we show some additional types of accounting errors. Companies generally do not correct for errors that do not have a significant effect on the presentation of the financial statements. For example, should a company with a total annual payroll of $1,750,000 and net income of $940,000 correct its financial statements if it finds it failed to record accrued wages of $5,000? No—it would not consider this error significant.

Obviously, defining materiality is difficult, and managers and auditors must use experience and judgment to determine whether adjustment is necessary for a given error. We assume **all errors discussed in this section to be material and to require adjustment**. (Also, we ignore all tax effects in this section.)

Companies must answer three questions in error analysis:

1 What type of error is involved?

2 What entries are needed to correct for the error?

3 After discovery of the error, how are financial statements to be restated?

As indicated earlier, companies treat errors **as prior-period adjustments and report them in the current year as adjustments to the beginning balance of Retained Earnings**. If a company presents comparative statements, it restates the prior affected statements to correct for the error.

BALANCE SHEET ERRORS

Balance sheet errors affect only the presentation of an asset, liability, or stockholders' equity account. Examples are the classification of a short-term receivable as part of the investment section, the classification of a note payable as an account payable, and the classification of plant assets as inventory.

When the error is discovered, the company reclassifies the item to its proper position. If the company prepares comparative statements that include the error year, it should correctly restate the balance sheet for the error year.

INCOME STATEMENT ERRORS

Income statement errors involve the improper classification of revenues or expenses. Examples include recording interest revenue as part of sales, purchases as bad debt expense, and depreciation expense as interest expense. An income statement classification error has no effect on the balance sheet and **no effect on net income**.

A company must make a reclassification entry when it discovers the error, if it makes the discovery in the same year in which the error occurs. If the error occurred in prior periods, the company does not need to make a reclassification entry at the date of discovery because the accounts for the current year are correctly stated. (Remember that the company has closed the income statement accounts from the prior period to retained earnings.) If the company prepares comparative statements that include the error year, it restates the income statement for the error year.

BALANCE SHEET AND INCOME STATEMENT ERRORS

The third type of error involves both the balance sheet and income statement. For example, assume that the bookkeeper overlooked accrued wages payable at the end of the accounting period. The effect of this error is to understate expenses, understate liabilities, and overstate net income for that period of time. This type of error affects both the balance sheet and the income statement. We classify this type of error in one of two ways—counterbalancing or noncounterbalancing.

Counterbalancing errors are those that will be offset or corrected over two periods. For example, the failure to record accrued wages is a counterbalancing error because over a two-year period the error will no longer be present. In other words, the failure to record accrued wages in the previous period means: (1) net income for the first period is overstated; (2) accrued wages payable (a liability) is understated, and (3) wages expense is understated. In the next period, net income is understated; accrued wages payable (a liability) is correctly stated; and wages expense is overstated. For the two **years combined**: (1) net income is correct; (2) wages expense is correct; and (3) accrued wages payable at the end of the second year is correct. Most errors in accounting that affect both the balance sheet and income statement are counterbalancing errors.

Noncounterbalancing errors are those that are not offset in the next accounting period. An example would be the failure to capitalize equipment that has a useful life of five years. If we expense this asset immediately, expenses will be overstated in the first period but understated in the next four periods. At the end of the second period, the effect of the error is not fully offset. Net income is correct in the aggregate only at the end of five years, because the asset is fully depreciated at this point. Thus, **noncounterbalancing errors are those that take longer than two periods to correct themselves**.

Only in rare instances is an error never reversed. An example would be if a company initially expenses land. Because land is not depreciable, theoretically the error is never offset, unless the land is sold.

Counterbalancing Errors

We illustrate the usual types of counterbalancing errors on the following pages. In studying these illustrations, keep in mind a couple of points, discussed below.

First, determine whether the company has closed the books for the period in which the error is found:

1 If the company has closed the books in the current year:
   (a) If the error is already counterbalanced, no entry is necessary.
   (b) If the error is not yet counterbalanced, make an entry to adjust the present balance of retained earnings.

2 If the company has not closed the books in the current year:
   (a) If the error is already counterbalanced, make an entry to correct the error in the current period and to adjust the beginning balance of Retained Earnings.
   (b) If the error is not yet counterbalanced, make an entry to adjust the beginning balance of Retained Earnings.

Second, if the company presents comparative statements, it must restate the amounts for comparative purposes. **Restatement is necessary even if a correcting journal entry is not required.**

To illustrate, assume that Sanford's Cement Co. failed to accrue revenue in 2005 when earned, but recorded the revenue in 2006 when received. The company discovered the error in 2008. It does not need to make an entry to correct for this error because the effects have been counterbalanced by the time Sanford discovered the error in 2008. However, if Sanford presents comparative financial statements for 2005 through 2008, it must **restate the accounts and related amounts for the years 2005 and 2006 for financial reporting purposes**.

The sections that follow demonstrate the accounting for the usual types of counterbalancing errors.

Failure to Record Accrued Wages

On December 31, 2007, Hurley Enterprises did not accrue wages in the amount of $1,500. The entry in 2008 to correct this error, assuming Hurley has not closed the books for 2008, is:

Retained Earnings	1,500	
Wages Expense		1,500

The rationale for this entry is as follows: (1) When Hurley pays the 2007 accrued wages in 2008, it makes an additional debit of $1,500 to 2008 Wages Expense. (2) Wages Expense—2008 is overstated by $1,500. (3) Because the company did not record 2007 accrued wages as Wages Expense in 2007, the net income for 2007 was overstated by $1,500. (4) Because 2007 net income is overstated by $1,500, the Retained Earnings account is overstated by $1,500 (because net income is closed to Retained Earnings).

If Hurley has closed the books for 2008, it makes no entry, because the error is counterbalanced.

Failure to Record Prepaid Expenses

In January 2007 Hurley Enterprises purchased a two-year insurance policy costing $1,000. It debited Insurance Expense, and credited Cash. The company made no adjusting entries at the end of 2007.

The entry on December 31, 2008, to correct this error, assuming Hurley has not closed the books for 2008, is:

Insurance Expense	500	
Retained Earnings		500

If Hurley has closed the books for 2008, it makes no entry, because the error is counterbalanced.

Understatement of Unearned Revenue

On December 31, 2007, Hurley Enterprises received $50,000 as a prepayment for renting certain office space for the following year. At the time of receipt of the rent payment, the company recorded a debit to Cash and a credit to Rent Revenue. It made no adjusting entry as of December 31, 2007. The entry on December 31, 2008, to correct for this error, assuming that Hurley has not closed the books for 2008, is:

Retained Earnings	50,000	
Rent Revenue		50,000

If Hurley has closed the books for 2008, it makes no entry, because the error is counterbalanced.

Overstatement of Accrued Revenue

On December 31, 2007, Hurley Enterprises accrued as interest revenue $8,000 that applied to 2008. On that date, the company recorded a debit Interest Receivable and a credit Interest Revenue. The entry on December 31, 2008, to correct for this error, assuming that Hurley has not closed the books for 2008, is:

Retained Earnings	8,000	
Interest Revenue		8,000

If Hurley has closed the books for 2008, it makes no entry, because the error is counterbalanced.

Overstatement of Purchases

Hurley's accountant recorded a purchase of merchandise for $9,000 in 2007 that applied to 2008. The physical inventory for 2007 was correctly stated. The company uses the periodic inventory method. The entry on December 31, 2008, to correct for this error, assuming that Harley has not closed the books for 2008, is:

Purchases	9,000	
Retained Earnings		9,000

If Hurley has closed the books for 2008, it makes no entry, because the error is counterbalanced.

Noncounterbalancing Errors

The entries for noncounterbalancing errors are more complex. Companies must make correcting entries, even if they have closed the books.

Failure to Record Depreciation

Assume that on January 1, 2007, Hurley Enterprises purchased a machine for $10,000 that had an estimated useful life of five years. The accountant incorrectly expensed this machine in 2007, but discovered the error in 2008. If we assume that Hurley uses straight-line depreciation on this asset, the entry on December 31, 2008, to correct for this error, given that Hurley has not closed the books, is:

Machinery	10,000	
Depreciation Expense	2,000	
Retained Earnings		8,000[a]
Accumulated Depreciation (20% × $10,000 × 2)		4,000

[a]Computations:

Retained Earnings	
Overstatement of expense in 2007	$10,000
Proper depreciation for 2007 (20% × $10,000)	(2,000)
Retained earnings understated as of Dec. 31, 2007	$ 8,000

If Hurley has closed the books for 2008, the entry is:

Machinery	10,000	
Retained Earnings		6,000[a]
Accumulated Depreciation		4,000

[a]Computations:

Retained Earnings	
Retained earnings understated as of Dec. 31, 2007	$ 8,000
Proper depreciation for 2008 (20% × $10,000)	(2,000)
Retained earnings understated as of Dec. 31, 2008	$ 6,000

Failure to Adjust for Bad Debts

Companies sometimes use a specific charge-off method in accounting for bad debt expense when a percentage of sales is more appropriate. They then make adjustments to change from the specific write-off to some type of allowance method. For example, assume that Hurley Enterprises has recognized bad debt expense when it has the following uncollectible debts.

	2007	2008
From 2007 sales	$550	$690
From 2008 sales		700

Hurley estimates that it will charge off an additional $1,400 in 2009, of which $300 is applicable to 2007 sales and $1,100 to 2008 sales. The entry on December 31, 2008, assuming that Hurley **has not closed the books for 2008,** is:

Bad Debt Expense	410[a]	
Retained Earnings	990[a]	
Allowance for Doubtful Accounts		1,400

[a]Computations to support the amounts in this entry are on the next page.

Allowance for doubtful accounts: Additional $300 for 2007 sales and $1,100 for 2008 sales.
Bad debts and retained earnings balance:

	2007	2008
Bad debts charged for	$1,240[b]	$ 700
Additional bad debts anticipated in 2009	300	1,100
Proper bad debt expense	1,540	1,800
Charges currently made to each period	(550)	(1,390)
Bad debt adjustment	$ 990	$ 410

[b]$550 + $690 = $1,240

If Hurley **has closed the books for 2008**, the entry is:

Retained Earnings	1,400	
Allowance for Doubtful Accounts		1,400

COMPREHENSIVE EXAMPLE: NUMEROUS ERRORS

In some circumstances a combination of errors occurs. The company therefore prepares a worksheet to facilitate the analysis. The following problem demonstrates use of the worksheet. The mechanics of its preparation should be obvious from the solution format. The income statements of Hudson Company for the years ended December 31, 2006, 2007, and 2008 indicate the following net incomes.

2006	$17,400
2007	20,200
2008	11,300

An examination of the accounting records for these years indicates that Hudson Company made several errors in arriving at the net income amounts reported:

1 The company consistently omitted from the records wages earned by workers but not paid at December 31. The amounts omitted were:

December 31, 2006	$1,000
December 31, 2007	$1,400
December 31, 2008	$1,600

When paid in the year following that in which they were earned, Hudson recorded these amounts as expenses.

2 The company overstated merchandise inventory on December 31, 2006, by $1,900 as the result of errors made in the footings and extensions on the inventory sheets.

3 On December 31, 2007, Hudson expensed unexpired insurance of $1,200, applicable to 2008.

4 The company did not record on December 31, 2007, interest receivable in the amount of $240.

5 On January 2, 2007, Hudson sold for $1,800 a piece of equipment costing $3,900. At the date of sale the equipment had accumulated depreciation of $2,400. The company recorded the cash received as Miscellaneous Income in 2007. In addition, it recorded depreciation for this equipment in both 2007 and 2008 at the rate of 10 percent of cost.

The first step in preparing the worksheet is to prepare a schedule showing the corrected net income amounts for the years ended December 31, 2006, 2007, and 2008. Each correction of the amount originally reported is clearly labeled. The next step is to indicate the balance sheet accounts affected as of December 31, 2008. Illustration 22-22 shows the completed worksheet for Hudson Company.

ILLUSTRATION 22-22
Worksheet to Correct
Income and Balance
Sheet Errors

HUDSON COMPANY
Worksheet to Correct Income and Balance Sheet Errors

	A	B	C	D	E	F	G	H
1		Worksheet Analysis of Changes in Net Income				Balance Sheet Correction at December 31, 2008		
2		2006	2007	2008	Totals	Debit	Credit	Account
3	Net income as reported	$17,400	$20,200	$11,300	$48,900			
4	Wages unpaid, 12/31/06	(1,000)	1,000		–0–			
5	Wages unpaid, 12/31/07		(1,400)	1,400	–0–			
6	Wages unpaid, 12/31/08			(1,600)	(1,600)		$1,600	Wages Payable
7	Inventory overstatement, 12/31/06	(1,900)	1,900		–0–			
8	Unexpired insurance, 12/31/07		1,200	(1,200)	–0–			
9	Interest receivable, 12/31/07		240	(240)	–0–			
10	Correction for entry made upon sale of equipment, 1/2/07[a]		(1,500)		(1,500)	$2,400	3,900	Accumulated Depreciation Machinery
11	Overcharge of depreciation, 2007		390		390	390		Accumulated Depreciation
12	Overcharge of depreciation, 2008			390	390	390		Accumulated Depreciation
13	Corrected net income	$14,500	$22,030	$10,050	$46,580			
14	[a]Cost	$ 3,900						
15	Accumulated depreciation	2,400						
16	Book value	1,500						
17	Proceeds from sale	1,800						
18	Gain on sale	300						
19	Income reported	(1,800)						
20	Adjustment	$(1,500)						

Sheet1 / Sheet2 / Sheet3 /

Assuming that Hudson Company **has not closed the books**, correcting entries on December 31, 2008, are:

Retained Earnings	1,400	
Wages Expense		1,400
(To correct improper charge to Wages Expense for 2008)		
Wages Expense	1,600	
Wages Payable		1,600
(To record proper wages expense for 2008)		
Insurance Expense	1,200	
Retained Earnings		1,200
(To record proper insurance expense for 2008)		
Interest Revenue	240	
Retained Earnings		240
(To correct improper credit to Interest Revenue in 2008)		
Retained Earnings	1,500	
Accumulated Depreciation	2,400	
Machinery		3,900
(To record write-off of machinery in 2007 and adjustment of Retained Earnings)		
Accumulated Depreciation	780	
Depreciation Expense		390
Retained Earnings		390
(To correct improper charge for depreciation expense in 2007 and 2008)		

If Hudson Company has closed the books for 2008, the correcting entries are:

Retained Earnings	1,600	
Wages Payable		1,600
(To record proper wage expense for 2008)		
Retained Earnings	1,500	
Accumulated Depreciation	2,400	
Machinery		3,900
(To record write-off of machinery in 2007 and		
adjustment of Retained Earnings)		
Accumulated Depreciation	780	
Retained Earnings		780
(To correct improper charge for depreciation expense		
in 2007 and 2008)		

PREPARATION OF FINANCIAL STATEMENTS WITH ERROR CORRECTIONS

Up to now, our discussion of error analysis has focused on identifying the type of error involved and accounting for its correction in the records. We have noted that companies must present the correction of the error on comparative financial statements.

The following example illustrates how a company would restate a typical year's financial statements, given many different errors.

Dick & Wally's Outlet is a small retail outlet in the town of Holiday. Lacking expertise in accounting, the company does not keep adequate records, and numerous errors occurred in recording accounting information.

1 The bookkeeper inadvertently failed to record a cash receipt of $1,000 on the sale of merchandise in 2008.

2 Accrued wages expense at the end of 2007 was $2,500; at the end of 2008, $3,200. The company does not accrue for wages; all wages are charged to Administrative Expenses.

3 The company had not set up an allowance for estimated uncollectible receivables. Dick and Wally decided to set up such an allowance for the estimated probable losses, as of December 31, 2008, for 2007 accounts of $700, and for 2008 accounts of $1,500. They also decided to correct the charge against each year so that it shows the losses (actual and estimated) relating to that year's sales. The company has written off accounts to bad debt expense (selling expense) as follows.

	In 2007	In 2008
2007 accounts	$400	$2,000
2008 accounts		1,600

4 Unexpired insurance not recorded at the end of 2007 was $600, and at the end of 2008, $400. All insurance is charged to Administrative Expenses.

5 An account payable of $6,000 should have been a note payable.

6 During 2007, the company sold for $7,000 an asset that cost $10,000 and had a book value of $4,000. At the time of sale Cash was debited, and Miscellaneous Income was credited for $7,000.

7 As a result of the last transaction, the company overstated depreciation expense (an administrative expense) in 2007 by $800 and in 2008 by $1,200.

Illustration 22-23 presents a worksheet that begins with the unadjusted trial balance of Dick & Wally's Outlet. You can determine the correcting entries and their effect on the financial statements by examining the worksheet.

ILLUSTRATION 22-23
Worksheet to Analyze
Effect of Errors in
Financial Statements

DICK & WALLY'S OUTLET
Worksheet Analysis to Adjust Financial Statements for the Year 2008

	A	Trial Balance Unadjusted Debit	Credit	Adjustments Debit	Credit	Income Statement Adjusted Debit	Credit	Balance Sheet Adjusted Debit	Credit
3	Cash	3,100		(1) 1,000				4,100	
4	Accounts Receivable	17,600						17,600	
5	Notes Receivable	8,500						8,500	
6	Inventory	34,000						34,000	
7	Property, Plant, and Equipment	112,000			(6) 10,000ᵃ			102,000	
8	Accumulated Depreciation		83,500	(6) 6,000ᵃ					75,500
9				(7) 2,000					
10	Investments	24,300						24,300	
11	Accounts Payable		14,500	(5) 6,000					8,500
12	Notes Payable		10,000		(5) 6,000				16,000
13	Capital Stock		43,500						43,500
14	Retained Earnings		20,000	(3) 2,700ᵇ					
15				(6) 4,000ᵃ	(4) 600				
16				(2) 2,500	(7) 800				12,200
17	Sales		94,000		(1) 1,000		95,000		
18	Cost of Goods Sold	21,000				21,000			
19	Selling Expenses	22,000			(3) 500ᵇ	21,500			
20	Administrative Expenses	23,000		(2) 700	(4) 400	22,700			
21				(4) 600	(7) 1,200				
22	Totals	265,500	265,500						
23	Wages Payable				(2) 3,200				3,200
24	Allowance for Doubtful Accounts				(3) 2,200ᵇ				2,200
25	Unexpired Insurance			(4) 400				400	
26	Net Income					29,800			29,800
27	Totals			25,900	25,900	95,000	95,000	190,900	190,900

Sheet1 / Sheet2 / Sheet3

Computations:

ᵃMachinery		ᵇBad Debts	2007	2008
Proceeds from sale	$7,000	Bad debts charged for	$2,400	$1,600
Book value of machinery	4,000	Additional bad debts anticipated	700	1,500
Gain on sale	3,000		3,100	3,100
Income credited	7,000	Charges currently made to each year	(400)	(3,600)
Retained earnings adjustment	$4,000	Bad debt adjustment	$2,700	$ (500)

SUMMARY OF LEARNING OBJECTIVES

1. **Identify the types of accounting changes.** The three different types of accounting changes are: (1) *Change in accounting principle:* a change from one generally accepted accounting principle to another generally accepted accounting principle. (2) *Change in accounting estimate:* a change that occurs as the result of new information or as additional experience is acquired. (3) *Change in reporting entity:* a change from reporting as one type of entity to another type of entity.

2. **Describe the accounting for changes in accounting principles.** A change in accounting principle involves a change from one generally accepted accounting principle to another. A change in accounting principle is not considered to result from the adoption of a new principle in recognition of events that have occurred for the first time or that were previously immaterial. If the accounting principle previously followed was not acceptable or if the principle was applied incorrectly, a change to a generally accepted accounting principle is considered a correction of an error.

KEY TERMS

change in accounting estimate, 1152, 1164

change in accounting principle, 1152, 1153

change in accounting estimate effected by a change in accounting principle, 1165

change in reporting entity, 1152

correction of an error, 1167

counterbalancing errors, 1175

3. **Understand how to account for retrospective accounting changes.** The general requirement for changes in accounting principle is retrospective application. Under retrospective application, companies change prior years' financial statements on a basis consistent with the newly adopted principle. They treat any part of the effect attributable to years prior to those presented as an adjustment of the earliest retained earnings presented.

4. **Understand how to account for impracticable changes.** Retrospective application is impracticable if the prior period effect cannot be determined using every reasonable effort to do so. For example, in changing to LIFO, the base-year inventory for all subsequent LIFO calculations is generally the opening inventory in the year the company adopts the method. There is no restatement of prior years' income because it is often too impractical to do so.

5. **Describe the accounting for changes in estimates.** Companies report changes in estimates prospectively. That is, companies should make no changes in previously reported results. They do not adjust opening balances nor change financial statements of prior periods.

6. **Identify changes in a reporting entity.** An accounting change that results in financial statements that are actually the statements of a different entity should be reported by restating the financial statements of all prior periods presented, to show the financial information for the new reporting entity for all periods.

7. **Describe the accounting for correction of errors.** Companies must correct errors as soon as they discover them, by proper entries in the accounts, and report them in the financial statements. The profession requires that a company treat corrections of errors as prior-period adjustments, record them in the year in which it discovered the errors, and report them in the financial statements in the proper periods. If presenting comparative statements, a company should restate the prior statements affected to correct for the errors. The company need not repeat the disclosures in the financial statements of subsequent periods.

8. **Identify economic motives for changing accounting methods.** Managers might have varying motives for income reporting, depending on economic times and whom they seek to impress. Some of the reasons for changing accounting methods are: (1) political costs, (2) capital structure, (3) bonus payments, and (4) smoothing of earnings.

9. **Analyze the effect of errors.** Three types of errors can occur: (1) *Balance sheet errors*, which affect only the presentation of an asset, liability, or stockholders' equity account. (2) *Income statement errors*, which affect only the presentation of revenue, expense, gain, or loss accounts in the income statement. (3) *Balance sheet and income statement errors*, which involve both the balance sheet and income statement. Errors are classified into two types: (1) *Counterbalancing errors* are offset or corrected over two periods. (2) *Noncounterbalancing errors* are not offset in the next accounting period and take longer than two periods to correct themselves.

As an aid to understanding accounting changes, we provide the following glossary.

KEY TERMS RELATED TO ACCOUNTING CHANGES

ACCOUNTING CHANGE. A change in (1) an accounting principle, (2) an accounting estimate, or (3) the reporting entity. The correction of an error in previously issued financial statements is not an accounting change.

CHANGE IN ACCOUNTING PRINCIPLE. A change from one generally accepted accounting principle to another generally accepted accounting principle when two or more generally accepted accounting principles apply or when the accounting principle formerly used is no longer generally accepted.

CHANGE IN ACCOUNTING ESTIMATE. A change that has the effect of adjusting the carrying amount of an existing asset or liability or altering the subsequent accounting for existing or future assets or liabilities. Changes in accounting estimates result from new information.

CHANGE IN ACCOUNTING ESTIMATE EFFECTED BY A CHANGE IN ACCOUNTING PRINCIPLE. A change in accounting estimate that is inseparable from the effect of a related change in accounting principle.

CHANGE IN THE REPORTING ENTITY. A change that results in financial statements that, in effect, are those of a different reporting entity (see page 1166).

DIRECT EFFECTS OF A CHANGE IN ACCOUNTING PRINCIPLE. Those recognized changes in assets or liabilities necessary to effect a change in accounting principle.

ERROR IN PREVIOUSLY ISSUED FINANCIAL STATEMENTS. An error in recognition, measurement, presentation, or disclosure in financial statements resulting from mathematical mistakes, mistakes in the application of GAAP, or oversight or misuse of facts that existed at the time the financial statements were prepared. A change from an accounting principle that is not generally accepted to one that is generally accepted is a correction of an error.

INDIRECT EFFECTS OF A CHANGE IN ACCOUNTING PRINCIPLE. Any changes to current or future cash flows of an entity that result from making a change in accounting principle that is applied retrospectively.

RESTATEMENT. The process of revising previously issued financial statements to reflect the correction of an error in those financial statements.

RETROSPECTIVE APPLICATION. The application of a different accounting principle to one or more previously issued financial statements, or to the statement of financial position at the beginning of the current period, as if that principle had always been used, or a change to financial statements of prior accounting periods to present the financial statements of a new reporting entity as if it had existed in those prior years.[20]

[20]Adapted from *SFAS No. 154*, par. 2.

Changing from or to the Equity Method

APPENDIX 22A

As noted in the chapter, companies generally should report an accounting change that results in financial statements for a different entity by **changing the financial statements of all prior periods presented**.

An example of a change in reporting entity is when a company's level of ownership or influence changes, such as when it changes from or to the equity method. When changing **to** the equity method, companies use retrospective application. Companies treat a change **from** the equity method prospectively. We present examples of these changes in entity in the following two sections.

CHANGE FROM THE EQUITY METHOD

OBJECTIVE 10
Make the computations and prepare the entries necessary to record a change from or to the equity method of accounting.

If the investor level of influence or ownership falls below that necessary for continued use of the equity method, a company must change from the equity method to the fair-value method. The earnings or losses that the investor previously recognized under the equity method should **remain as part of the carrying amount** of the investment, with no retrospective application to the new method.

When a company changes **from the equity method to the fair-value method, the cost basis for accounting purposes is the carrying amount of the investment at the date of the change.**[1] The investor applies the new method in its entirety once the equity method is no longer appropriate. At the next reporting date, the investor should record the unrealized holding gain or loss to recognize the difference between the carrying amount and fair value.

Dividends in Excess of Earnings

In subsequent periods, dividends received by the investor company may exceed its share of the investee's earnings for such periods (all periods following the change in method). To the extent that they do so, the investor company should account for such dividends as a **reduction of the investment carrying amount**, rather than as revenue.

To illustrate, assume that on January 1, 2006, Investor Company purchased 250,000 shares of Investee Company's 1,000,000 shares of outstanding stock for $8,500,000. Investor correctly accounted for this investment using the equity method. After accounting for dividends received and investee net income, in 2006, Investor reported its investment in Investee Company at $8,780,000 at December 31, 2006. On January 2, 2007, Investee Company sold 1,500,000 additional shares of its own common stock to the public, thereby reducing Investor Company's ownership from 25 percent to 10 percent. Illustration 22A-1 shows the net income (or loss) and dividends of Investee Company for the years 2007 through 2009.

ILLUSTRATION 22A-1
Income Earned and
Dividends Received

Year	Investor's Share of Investee Income (Loss)	Investee Dividends Received by Investor
2007	$600,000	$ 400,000
2008	350,000	400,000
2009	–0–	210,000
Totals	$950,000	$1,010,000

Assuming a change from the equity method to the fair-value method as of January 2, 2007, Investor Company's reported investment in Investee Company and its reported income would be as shown in Illustration 22A-2 (page 1185).

Investor Company would record the dividends and earnings data for the three years subsequent to the change in methods as shown by the following entries.

---

[1]In addition, when the change of methods occurs, the company stops amortizing the excess of acquisition price over the proportionate share of book value acquired attributable to undervalued depreciable assets.

ILLUSTRATION 22A-2
Impact on Investment
Carrying Amount

Year	Dividend Revenue Recognized	Cumulative Excess of Share of Earnings Over Dividends Received	Investment at December 31
2007	$400,000	$200,000[a]	$8,780,000
2008	400,000	150,000[b]	8,780,000
2009	150,000	(60,000)[c]	$8,780,000 − $60,000 = $8,720,000

[a]$600,000 − $400,000 = $200,000
[b]($350,000 − $400,000) + $200,000 = $150,000
[c]$150,000 − $210,000 = $(60,000)

2007 and 2008

Cash	400,000	
Dividend Revenue		400,000
(To record dividend received from Investee Company)		

2009

Cash	210,000	
Available-for-Sale Securities		60,000
Dividend Revenue		150,000
(To record dividend revenue from Investee Company in 2009 and to recognize cumulative excess of dividends received over share of Investee earnings in periods subsequent to change from equity method)		

CHANGE TO THE EQUITY METHOD

When converting to the equity method, companies use retrospective application. Such a change involves adjusting the carrying amount of the investment, results of current and prior operations, and retained earnings of the investor **as if the equity method has been in effect during all of the previous periods in which this investment was held.**[2] When changing from the fair-value method to the equity method, companies also must eliminate any balances in the Unrealized Holding Gain or Loss—Equity account and the Securities Fair Value Adjustment account. In addition, they eliminate the available-for-sale classification for this investment, and they record the investment in stock under the equity method.

For example, on January 2, 2007, Amsted Corp. purchased, for $500,000 cash, 10 percent of the outstanding shares of Cable Company common stock. On that date, the net assets of Cable Company had a book value of $3,000,000. The excess of cost over the underlying equity in net assets of Cable Company is goodwill. On January 2, 2009, Amsted Corp. purchased an additional 20 percent of Cable Company's stock for $1,200,000 cash when the book value of Cable's net assets was $4,000,000. The excess of cost over book value related to this additional investment is goodwill. Now having a 30 percent interest, Amsted Corp. must use the equity method.

From January 2, 2007, to January 2, 2009, Amsted Corp. used the fair-value method and categorized these securities as available-for-sale. At January 2, 2009, Amsted has a credit balance of $92,000 in its Unrealized Holding Gain or Loss—Equity account and a debit balance in its Securities Fair Value Adjustment account of the same amount. (Income tax effects are ignored.) Illustration 22A-3 (page 1186) shows the net income reported by Cable Company and the Cable Company dividends received by Amsted during the period 2007 through 2009.

[2]"The Equity Method of Accounting for Investments in Common Stock," *Opinions of the Accounting Principles Board No. 18* (New York: AICPA, 1971), par. 17.

ILLUSTRATION 22A-3
Income Earned and
Dividends Received

Year	Cable Company Net Income	Cable Co. Dividends Paid to Amsted
2007	$ 500,000	$ 20,000
2008	1,000,000	30,000
2009	1,200,000	120,000

Amsted makes the following journal entries from January 2, 2007, through December 31, 2009, relative to Amsted Corp.'s investment in Cable Company, reflecting the data above and a change from the fair value method to the equity method.[3]

January 2, 2007

Available-for-Sale Securities	500,000	
Cash		500,000
(To record the purchase of a 10% interest in Cable Company)		

December 31, 2007

Cash	20,000	
Dividend Revenue		20,000
(To record the receipt of cash dividends from Cable Company)		
Securities Fair Value Adjustment (Available-for-Sale)	92,000	
Unrealized Holding Gain or Loss—Equity		92,000
(To record increase in fair value of securities)		

December 31, 2008

Cash	30,000	
Dividend Revenue		30,000
(To record the receipt of cash dividends from Cable Company)		

January 2, 2009

Investment in Cable Stock	1,300,000	
Cash		1,200,000
Retained Earnings		100,000
(To record the purchase of an additional interest in Cable Company and to reflect retrospectively a change from the fair-value method to the equity method of accounting for the investment. The $100,000 adjustment is computed as follows:		

	2007	2008	Total
Amsted Corp. equity in earnings of Cable Company (10%)	$50,000	$100,000	$150,000
Dividend received	(20,000)	(30,000)	(50,000)
Retrospective application	$30,000	$ 70,000	$100,000

January 2, 2009

Investment in Cable Stock	500,000	
Available-for-Sale Securities		500,000
(To reclassify initial 10% interest to equity method)		

January 2, 2009

Unrealized Holding Gain or Loss—Equity	92,000	
Securities Fair Value Adjustment (Available-for-Sale)		92,000
(To eliminate fair value accounts for change to equity method)		

December 31, 2009

Investment in Cable Stock	360,000	
Revenue from Investment		360,000
[To record equity in earnings of Cable Company (30% of $1,200,000)]		

---

[3]Adapted from Paul A. Pacter, "Applying APB Opinion No. 18—Equity Method," *Journal of Accountancy* (September 1971), pp. 59–60.

```
Cash                                               120,000
    Investment in Cable Stock                                    120,000
        (To record the receipt of cash dividends from
        Cable Company)
```

Companies change to the equity method by placing the accounts related to and affected by the investment on the same basis **as if the equity method had always been the basis of accounting for that investment**. Thus, they report the effects of this accounting change using the retrospective approach.

SUMMARY OF LEARNING OBJECTIVE FOR APPENDIX 22A

10. Make the computations and prepare the entries necessary to record a change from or to the equity method of accounting. When changing *from* the equity method to the fair-value method, the cost basis for accounting purposes is the carrying amount used for the investment at the date of change. The investor company applies the new method in its entirety once the equity method is no longer appropriate. When changing *to* the equity method, the company adjusts the accounts to be on the same basis as if the equity method had always been used for that investment.

Note: All **asterisked** Brief Exercises, Exercises, and Problems relate to material contained in the appendix to the chapter.

QUESTIONS

1. In recent years, the *Wall Street Journal* has indicated that many companies have changed their accounting principles. What are the major reasons why companies change accounting methods?

2. State how each of the following items is reflected in the financial statements.

   (a) Change from FIFO to LIFO method for inventory valuation purposes.

   (b) Charge for failure to record depreciation in a previous period.

   (c) Litigation won in current year, related to prior period.

   (d) Change in the realizability of certain receivables.

   (e) Writeoff of receivables.

   (f) Change from the percentage-of-completion to the completed-contract method for reporting net income.

3. Discuss briefly the three approaches that have been suggested for reporting changes in accounting principles.

4. Identify and describe the approach the FASB requires for reporting changes in accounting principles.

5. What is the indirect effect of a change in accounting principle? Briefly describe the reporting of the indirect effects of a change in accounting principle.

6. Define a change in estimate and provide an illustration. When is a change in accounting estimate effected by a change in accounting principle?

7. Sandwich State Bank has followed the practice of capitalizing certain marketing costs and amortizing these costs over their expected life. In the current year, the bank determined that the future benefits from these costs were doubtful. Consequently, the bank adopted the policy of expensing these costs as incurred. How should the bank report this accounting change in the comparative financial statements?

8. Indicate how the following items are recorded in the accounting records in the current year of Tami Agler Co.

   (a) Impairment of goodwill.

   (b) A change in depreciating plant assets from accelerated to the straight-line method.

   (c) Large writeoff of inventories because of obsolescence.

   (d) Change from the cash basis to accrual basis of accounting.

   (e) Change from LIFO to FIFO method for inventory valuation purposes.

   (f) Change in the estimate of service lives for plant assets.

9. R. M. Andrews Construction Co. had followed the practice of expensing all materials assigned to a construction job without recognizing any salvage inventory. On December 31, 2007, it was determined that salvage inventory should be valued at $62,000. Of this amount, $29,000 arose during the current year. How does this information affect the financial statements to be prepared at the end of 2007?

10. E. A. Basler Inc. wishes to change from the completed-contract to the percentage-of-completion method for financial reporting purposes. The auditor indicates that a change would be permitted only if it is to a preferable method. What difficulties develop in assessing preferability?

11. Discuss how a change to the LIFO method of inventory valuation is handled when it is impracticable to determine previous LIFO inventory amounts.

12. How should consolidated financial statements be reported this year when statements of individual companies were presented last year?

13. Karen Beers controlled four domestic subsidiaries and one foreign subsidiary. Prior to the current year, Beers had excluded the foreign subsidiary from consolidation. During the current year, the foreign subsidiary was included in the financial statements. How should this change in accounting principle be reflected in the financial statements?

14. Distinguish between counterbalancing and noncounterbalancing errors. Give an example of each.

15. Discuss and illustrate how a correction of an error in previously issued financial statements should be handled.

16. Prior to 2008, Mary Boudreau Inc. excluded manufacturing overhead costs from work in process and finished goods inventory. These costs have been expensed as incurred. In 2008, the company decided to change its accounting methods for manufacturing inventories to full costing by including these costs as product costs. Assuming that these costs are material, how should this change be reflected in the financial statements for 2007 and 2008?

17. Lou Brady Corp. failed to record accrued salaries for 2005, $2,000; 2006, $2,100; and 2007, $3,900. What is the amount of the overstatement or understatement of Retained Earnings at December 31, 2008?

18. In January 2007, installation costs of $8,000 on new machinery were charged to Repair Expense. Other costs of this machinery of $30,000 were correctly recorded and have been depreciated using the straight-line method with an estimated life of 10 years and no salvage value. At December 31, 2008, it is decided that the machinery has a remaining useful life of 20 years, starting with January 1, 2008. What entry(ies) should be made in 2008 to correctly record transactions related to machinery, assuming the machinery has no salvage value? The books have not been closed for 2008 and depreciation expense has not yet been recorded for 2008.

19. On January 2, 2007, $100,000 of 11%, 20-year bonds were issued for $97,000. The $3,000 discount was charged to Interest Expense. The bookkeeper, John Castle, records interest only on the interest payment dates of January 1 and July 1. What is the effect on reported net income for 2007 of this error, assuming straight-line amortization of the discount? What entry is necessary to correct for this error, assuming that the books are not closed for 2007?

20. An account payable of $13,000 for merchandise purchased on December 23, 2007, was recorded in January 2008. This merchandise was not included in inventory at December 31, 2007. What effect does this error have on reported net income for 2007? What entry should be made to correct for this error, assuming that the books are not closed for 2007?

21. Equipment was purchased on January 2, 2007, for $18,000, but no portion of the cost has been charged to depreciation. The corporation wishes to use the straight-line method for these assets, which have been estimated to have a life of 10 years and no salvage value. What effect does this error have on net income in 2007. What entry is necessary to correct for this error, assuming that the books are not closed for 2007?

BRIEF EXERCISES

(LO 3) **BE22-1** Beaty Construction Company decided at the beginning of 2008 to change from the completed-contract method to the percentage-of-completion method for financial reporting purposes. The company will continue to use the completed-contract method for tax purposes. For years prior to 2008, pre-tax income under the two methods was as follows: percentage-of-completion $128,000, and completed-contract $80,000. The tax rate is 35%. Prepare Beaty's 2008 journal entry to record the change in accounting principle.

(LO 3) **BE22-2** Refer to the accounting change by Beaty Construction Company in BE22-1. Beaty has a profit-sharing plan, which pays all employees a bonus at year-end based on 1% of pre-tax income. Compute the indirect effect of Beaty's change in accounting principle that will be reported in the 2008 income statement, assuming that the profit-sharing contract explicitly requires adjustment for changes in income numbers.

(LO 3) **BE22-3** Robert Boey, Inc., changed from the LIFO cost flow assumption to the FIFO cost flow assumption in 2008. The increase in the prior year's income before taxes is $1,000,000. The tax rate is 40%. Prepare Boey's 2008 journal entry to record the change in accounting principle.

(LO 5) **BE22-4** Bickner Company changed depreciation methods in 2008 from double-declining-balance to straight-line. Depreciation under double-declining-balance was $90,000, whereas straight-line depreciation prior to 2008 would have been $50,000. Bickner's depreciable assets had a cost of $250,000 with a $50,000 salvage value, and an 8-year remaining useful life at the beginning of 2008. Prepare the 2008 journal entries, if any, related to Bickner's depreciable assets.

(LO 5) **BE22-5** Nancy Castle Company purchased a computer system for $60,000 on January 1, 2006. It was depreciated based on a 7-year life and an $18,000 salvage value. On January 1, 2008, Castle revised these estimates to a total useful life of 4 years and a salvage value of $10,000. Prepare Castle's entry to record 2008 depreciation expense.

(LO 7) **BE22-6** In 2008, John Hiatt Corporation discovered that equipment purchased on January 1, 2006, for $75,000 was expensed at that time. The equipment should have been depreciated over 5 years, with no salvage value. The effective tax rate is 30%. Prepare Hiatt's 2008 journal entry to correct the error.

(LO 7) **BE22-7** At January 1, 2008, William R. Monat Company reported retained earnings of $2,000,000. In 2008, Monat discovered that 2007 depreciation expense was understated by $500,000. In 2008, net income was $900,000 and dividends declared were $250,000. The tax rate is 40%. Prepare a 2008 retained earnings statement for William R. Monat Company.

(LO 7) **BE22-8** Indicate the effect—Understate, Overstate, No Effect—that each of the following errors has on 2007 net income and 2008 net income.

	2007	2008
(a) Wages payable were not recorded at 12/31/07.	——	——
(b) Equipment purchased in 2006 was expensed.	——	——
(c) Equipment purchased in 2007 was expensed.	——	——
(d) 2007 ending inventory was overstated.	——	——
(e) Patent amortization was not recorded in 2008.	——	——

(LO 3, 5, 7) **BE22-9** Charlene Rydell Manufacturing Co. is preparing its year-end financial statements and is considering the accounting for the following items.

1. The vice president of sales had indicated that one product line has lost its customer appeal and will be phased out over the next 3 years. Therefore, a decision has been made to lower the estimated lives on related production equipment from the remaining 5 years to 3 years.
2. Estimating the lives of new products in the Leisure Products Division has become very difficult because of the highly competitive conditions in this market. Therefore, the practice of deferring and amortizing preproduction costs has been abandoned in favor of expensing such costs as they are incurred.
3. The Hightone Building was converted from a sales office to offices for the Accounting Department at the beginning of this year. Therefore, the expense related to this building will now appear as an administrative expense rather than a selling expense on the current year's income statement.

Identify and explain whether each of the above items is a change in principle, a change in estimate, or an error.

(LO 3, 5, 7) **BE22-10** Pociek Co. is evaluating the appropriate accounting for the following items.

1. When the year-end physical inventory adjustment was made for the current year, the controller discovered that the prior year's physical inventory sheets for an entire warehouse were mislaid and excluded from last year's count.
2. Management has decided to switch from the FIFO inventory valuation method to the LIFO inventory valuation method for all inventories.
3. Pociek's Custom Division manufactures large-scale, custom-designed machinery on a contract basis. Management decided to switch from the completed-contract method to the percentage-of-completion method of accounting for long-term contracts.

Identify and explain whether each of the above items is a change in accounting principle, a change in estimate, or an error.

(LO 10) *****BE22-11** Robocop Corporation owns stock of Terminator, Inc. Prior to 2008, the investment was accounted for using the equity method. In early 2008, Robocop sold part of its investment in Terminator, and began using the fair value method. In 2008, Terminator earned net income of $80,000 and paid dividends of

$95,000. Prepare Robocop's entries related to Terminator's net income and dividends, assuming Robocop now owns 8% of Terminator's stock.

(LO 10) ***BE22-12** Rocket Corporation has owned stock of Knight Corporation since 2001. At December 31, 2007, its balances related to this investment were:

Available-for-Sale Securities	$185,000
Securities Fair Value Adj (AFS)	34,000 Dr.
Unrealized Holding Gain or Loss—Equity	34,000 Cr.

On January 1, 2008, Rocket purchased additional stock of Knight Company for $445,000 and now has significant influence over Knight. If the equity method had been used in 2004–2007, income would have been $33,000 greater than dividends received. Prepare Rocket's journal entries to record the purchase of the investment and the change to the equity method.

EXERCISES

(LO 3) **E22-1** **(Change in Principle—Long-term Contracts)** Pam Erickson Construction Company changed from the completed-contract to the percentage-of-completion method of accounting for long-term construction contracts during 2008. For tax purposes, the company employs the completed-contract method and will continue this approach in the future. (*Hint:* Adjust all tax consequences through the Deferred Tax Liability account.) The appropriate information related to this change is as follows.

	Pretax Income from:		
	Percentage-of-Completion	Completed-Contract	Difference
2007	$780,000	$590,000	$190,000
2008	700,000	480,000	220,000

Instructions
(a) Assuming that the tax rate is 35%, what is the amount of net income that would be reported in 2008?
(b) What entry(ies) are necessary to adjust the accounting records for the change in accounting principle?

(LO 3, 4) **E22-2** **(Change in Principle—Inventory Methods)** Holder-Webb Company began operations on January 1, 2005, and uses the average cost method of pricing inventory. Management is contemplating a change in inventory methods for 2008. The following information is available for the years 2005–2007.

	Net Income Computed Using		
	Average Cost Method	FIFO Method	LIFO Method
2005	$15,000	$19,000	$12,000
2006	18,000	23,000	14,000
2007	20,000	25,000	17,000

Instructions
(Ignore all tax effects.)
(a) Prepare the journal entry necessary to record a change from the average cost method to the FIFO method in 2008.
(b) Determine net income to be reported for 2005, 2006, and 2007, after giving effect to the change in accounting principle.
(c) Assume Holder-Webb Company used the LIFO method instead of the average cost method during the years 2005–2007. In 2008, Holder-Webb changed to the FIFO method. Prepare the journal entry necessary to record the change in principle.

(LO 3) **E22-3** **(Accounting Change)** Taveras Co. decides at the beginning of 2007 to adopt the FIFO method of inventory valuation. Taveras had used the LIFO method for financial reporting since its inception on January 1, 2005, and had maintained records adequate to apply the FIFO method retrospectively. Taveras concluded that FIFO is the preferable inventory method because it reflects the current cost of inventory on the balance sheet. The table on page 1191 presents the effects of the change in accounting principles on inventory and cost of goods sold.

Date	Inventory Determined by		Cost of Goods Sold Determined by	
	LIFO Method	FIFO Method	LIFO Method	FIFO Method
January 1, 2005	$ 0	$ 0	$ 0	$ 0
December 31, 2005	100	80	800	820
December 31, 2006	200	240	1,000	940
December 31, 2007	320	390	1,130	1,100

Other information:
1. For each year presented, sales are $3,000 and operating expenses are $1,000.
2. Taveras provides two years of financial statements. Earnings per share information is not required.

Instructions
(a) Prepare income statements under LIFO and FIFO for 2005, 2006, and 2007.
(b) Prepare income statements reflecting the retrospective application of the accounting change from the LIFO method to the FIFO method for 2007 and 2006.
(c) Prepare the note to the financial statements describing the change in method of inventory valuation. In the note, indicate the income statement line items for 2007 and 2006 that were affected by the change in accounting principle.
(d) Prepare comparative retained earnings statements for 2006 and 2007 under FIFO. Retained earnings reported under LIFO are as follows:

	Retained Earnings Balance
December 31, 2005	$1,200
December 31, 2006	2,200
December 31, 2007	3,070

(LO 3) **E22-4** **(Accounting Change)** Gordon Company started operations on January 1, 2002, and has used the FIFO method of inventory valuation since its inception. In 2008, it decides to switch to the average cost method. You are provided with the following information.

	Net Income		Retained Earnings (Ending balance)
	Under FIFO	Under Average Cost	Under FIFO
2002	$100,000	$ 90,000	$100,000
2003	70,000	65,000	160,000
2004	90,000	80,000	235,000
2005	120,000	130,000	340,000
2006	300,000	290,000	590,000
2007	305,000	310,000	780,000

Instructions
(a) What is the beginning retained earnings balance at January 1, 2004, if Gordon prepares comparative financial statements starting in 2004?
(b) What is the beginning retained earnings balance at January 1, 2007, if Gordon prepares comparative financial statements starting in 2007?
(c) What is the beginning retained earnings balance at January 1, 2008, if Gordon prepares single-period financial statements for 2008?
(d) What is the net income reported by Gordon in the 2007 income statement if it prepares comparative financial statements starting with 2005?

(LO 3) **E22-5** **(Accounting Change)** Presented below are income statements prepared on a LIFO and FIFO basis for Kenseth Company, which started operations on January 1, 2006. The company presently uses the LIFO method of pricing its inventory and has decided to switch to the FIFO method in 2007. The FIFO income statement is computed in accordance with the requirements of *SFAS No. 154*. Kenseth's profit-sharing agreement with its employees indicates that the company will pay employees 10% of income before profit sharing. Income taxes are ignored.

	LIFO Basis		FIFO Basis	
	2007	2006	2007	2006
Sales	$3,000	$3,000	$3,000	$3,000
Cost of goods sold	1,130	1,000	1,100	940
Operating expenses	1,000	1,000	1,000	1,000
Income before profit sharing	870	1,000	900	1,060
Profit sharing expense	87	100	96	100
Net income	$ 783	$ 900	$ 804	$ 960

Instructions

Answer the following questions.

(a) If comparative income statements are prepared, what net income should Kenseth report in 2006 and 2007?

(b) Explain why, under the FIFO basis, Kenseth reports $100 in 2006 and $96 in 2007 for its profit-sharing expense.

(c) Assume that Kenseth has a beginning balance of retained earnings at January 1, 2007, of $8,000 using the LIFO method. The company declared and paid dividends of $2,000 in 2007. Prepare the retained earnings statement for 2007, assuming that Kenseth has switched to the FIFO method.

(LO 5) **E22-6** **(Accounting Changes—Depreciation)** Kathleen Cole Inc. acquired the following assets in January of 2005.

Equipment, estimated service life, 5 years; salvage value, $15,000	$525,000
Building, estimated service life, 30 years; no salvage value	$693,000

The equipment has been depreciated using the sum-of-the-years'-digits method for the first 3 years for financial reporting purposes. In 2008, the company decided to change the method of computing depreciation to the straight-line method for the equipment, but no change was made in the estimated service life or salvage value. It was also decided to change the total estimated service life of the building from 30 years to 40 years, with no change in the estimated salvage value. The building is depreciated on the straight-line method.

Instructions

(a) Prepare the general journal entry to record depreciation expense for the equipment in 2008.

(b) Prepare the journal entry to record depreciation expense for the building in 2008. (Round all computations to two decimal places.)

(LO 5, 7) **E22-7** **(Change in Estimate and Error; Financial Statements)** Presented below are the comparative income statements for Denise Habbe Inc. for the years 2007 and 2008.

	2008	2007
Sales	$340,000	$270,000
Cost of sales	200,000	142,000
Gross profit	140,000	128,000
Expenses	88,000	50,000
Net income	$ 52,000	$ 78,000
Retained earnings (Jan. 1)	$ 125,000	$ 72,000
Net income	52,000	78,000
Dividends	(30,000)	(25,000)
Retained earnings (Dec. 31)	$147,000	$125,000

The following additional information is provided:

1. In 2008, Denise Habbe Inc. decided to switch its depreciation method from sum-of-the-years'-digits to the straight-line method. The assets were purchased at the beginning of 2007 for $100,000 with an estimated useful life of 4 years and no salvage value. (The 2008 income statement contains depreciation expense of $30,000 on the assets purchased at the beginning of 2007.)

2. In 2008, the company discovered that the ending inventory for 2007 was overstated by $24,000; ending inventory for 2008 is correctly stated.

Instructions

Prepare the revised income and retained earnings statement for 2007 and 2008, assuming comparative statements. (Ignore income taxes.)

(LO 3, 5, 7) **E22-8** **(Accounting for Accounting Changes and Errors)** Listed below are various types of accounting changes and errors.

_____ 1. Change in a plant asset's salvage value.
_____ 2. Change due to overstatement of inventory.
_____ 3. Change from sum-of-the-years'-digits to straight-line method of depreciation.
_____ 4. Change from presenting unconsolidated to consolidated financial statements.
_____ 5. Change from LIFO to FIFO inventory method.
_____ 6. Change in the rate used to compute warranty costs.
_____ 7. Change from an unacceptable accounting principle to an acceptable accounting principle.
_____ 8. Change in a patent's amortization period.
_____ 9. Change from completed-contract to percentage-of-completion method on construction contracts.
_____ 10. Change from FIFO to average-cost inventory method.

Instructions

For each change or error, indicate how it would be accounted for using the following code letters:

(a) Accounted for prospectively.
(b) Accounted for retrospectively.
(c) Neither of the above.

(LO 5, 7)

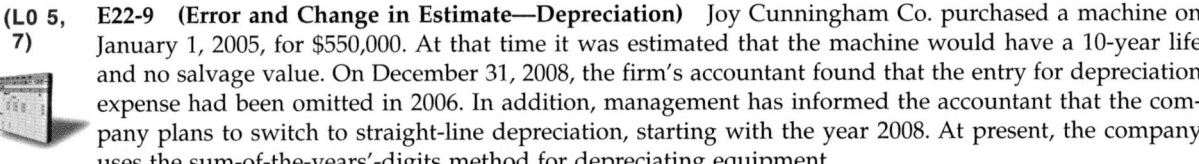

E22-9 (Error and Change in Estimate—Depreciation) Joy Cunningham Co. purchased a machine on January 1, 2005, for $550,000. At that time it was estimated that the machine would have a 10-year life and no salvage value. On December 31, 2008, the firm's accountant found that the entry for depreciation expense had been omitted in 2006. In addition, management has informed the accountant that the company plans to switch to straight-line depreciation, starting with the year 2008. At present, the company uses the sum-of-the-years'-digits method for depreciating equipment.

Instructions

Prepare the general journal entries that should be made at December 31, 2008 to record these events. (Ignore tax effects.)

(LO 5, 7)

E22-10 (Depreciation Changes) On January 1, 2004, Jackson Company purchased a building and equipment that have the following useful lives, salvage values, and costs.

> Building, 40-year estimated useful life, $50,000 salvage value, $800,000 cost
> Equipment, 12-year estimated useful life, $10,000 salvage value, $100,000 cost

The building has been depreciated under the double-declining balance method through 2007. In 2008, the company decided to switch to the straight-line method of depreciation. Jackson also decided to change the total useful life of the equipment to 9 years, with a salvage value of $5,000 at the end of that time. The equipment is depreciated using the straight-line method.

Instructions

(a) Prepare the journal entry(ies) necessary to record the depreciation expense on the building in 2008.
(b) Compute depreciation expense on the equipment for 2008.

(LO 5)

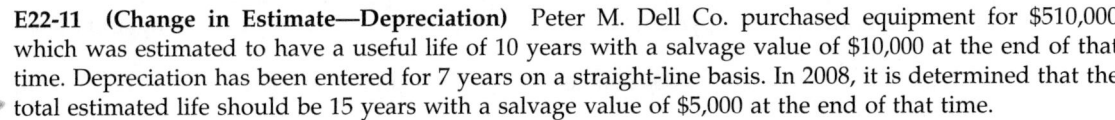

E22-11 (Change in Estimate—Depreciation) Peter M. Dell Co. purchased equipment for $510,000 which was estimated to have a useful life of 10 years with a salvage value of $10,000 at the end of that time. Depreciation has been entered for 7 years on a straight-line basis. In 2008, it is determined that the total estimated life should be 15 years with a salvage value of $5,000 at the end of that time.

Instructions

(a) Prepare the entry (if any) to correct the prior years' depreciation.
(b) Prepare the entry to record depreciation for 2008.

(LO 5)

E22-12 (Change in Estimate—Depreciation) Gerald Englehart Industries changed from the double-declining balance to the straight-line method in 2008 on all its plant assets. There was no change in the assets' salvage values or useful lives. Plant assets, acquired on January 2, 2005, had an original cost of $1,600,000, with a $100,000 salvage value and an 8-year estimated useful life. Income before depreciation expense was $270,000 in 2007 and $300,000 in 2008.

Instructions

(a) Prepare the journal entry(ies) to record the change in depreciation method in 2008.
(b) Starting with income before depreciation expense, prepare the remaining portion of the income statement for 2007 and 2008.

(LO 3)

E22-13 (Change in Principle—Long-term Contracts) Cullen Construction Company changed from the completed-contract to the percentage-of-completion method of accounting for long-term construction contracts during 2008. For tax purposes, the company employs the completed-contract method and will continue this approach in the future. The appropriate information related to this change is as follows.

	Pretax Income from		
	Percentage-of-Completion	Completed-Contract	Difference
2007	$980,000	$590,000	$290,000
2008	900,000	480,000	420,000

Instructions

(a) Assuming that the tax rate is 40%, what is the amount of net income that would be reported in 2008?
(b) What entry(ies) are necessary to adjust the accounting records for the change in accounting principle?

(LO 3) **E22-14** **(Various Changes in Principle—Inventory Methods)** Below is the net income of Anita Ferreri Instrument Co., a private corporation, computed under the three inventory methods using a periodic system.

	FIFO	Average Cost	LIFO
2005	$26,000	$24,000	$20,000
2006	30,000	25,000	21,000
2007	28,000	27,000	24,000
2008	34,000	30,000	26,000

Instructions
(Ignore tax considerations.)

(a) Assume that in 2008 Ferreri decided to change from the FIFO method to the average cost method of pricing inventories. Prepare the journal entry necessary for the change that took place during 2008, and show net income reported for 2005, 2006, 2007, and 2008.

(b) Assume that in 2008 Ferreri, which had been using the LIFO method since incorporation in 2005, changed to the FIFO method of pricing inventories. Prepare the journal entry necessary to record the change in 2008 and show net income reported for 2005, 2006, 2007, and 2008.

(LO 7) **E22-15** **(Error Correction Entries)** The first audit of the books of Bruce Gingrich Company was made for the year ended December 31, 2008. In examining the books, the auditor found that certain items had been overlooked or incorrectly handled in the last 3 years. These items are:

1. At the beginning of 2006, the company purchased a machine for $510,000 (salvage value of $51,000) that had a useful life of 6 years. The bookkeeper used straight-line depreciation, but failed to deduct the salvage value in computing the depreciation base for the 3 years.
2. At the end of 2007, the company failed to accrue sales salaries of $45,000.
3. A tax lawsuit that involved the year 2006 was settled late in 2008. It was determined that the company owed an additional $85,000 in taxes related to 2006. The company did not record a liability in 2006 or 2007 because the possibility of loss was considered remote, and charged the $85,000 to a loss account in 2008.
4. Gingrich Company purchased a copyright from another company early in 2006 for $45,000. Gingrich had not amortized the copyright because its value had not diminished. The copyright has a useful life at purchase of 20 years.
5. In 2008, the company wrote off $87,000 of inventory considered to be obsolete; this loss was charged directly to Retained Earnings.

Instructions
Prepare the journal entries necessary in 2008 to correct the books, assuming that the books have not been closed. Disregard effects of corrections on income tax.

(LO 7) **E22-16** **(Error Analysis and Correcting Entry)** You have been engaged to review the financial statements of Gottschalk Corporation. In the course of your examination you conclude that the bookkeeper hired during the current year is not doing a good job. You notice a number of irregularities as follows.

1. Year-end wages payable of $3,400 were not recorded because the bookkeeper thought that "they were immaterial."
2. Accrued vacation pay for the year of $31,100 was not recorded because the bookkeeper "never heard that you had to do it."
3. Insurance for a 12-month period purchased on November 1 of this year was charged to insurance expense in the amount of $2,640 because "the amount of the check is about the same every year."
4. Reported sales revenue for the year is $2,120,000. This includes all sales taxes collected for the year. The sales tax rate is 6%. Because the sales tax is forwarded to the state's Department of Revenue, the Sales Tax Expense account is debited. The bookkeeper thought that "the sales tax is a selling expense." At the end of the current year, the balance in the Sales Tax Expense account is $103,400.

Instructions
Prepare the necessary correcting entries, assuming that Gottschalk uses a calendar-year basis.

(LO 7) **E22-17** **(Error Analysis and Correcting Entry)** The reported net incomes for the first 2 years of Sandra Gustafson Products, Inc., were as follows: 2007, $147,000; 2008, $185,000. Early in 2009, the following errors were discovered.

1. Depreciation of equipment for 2007 was overstated $17,000.
2. Depreciation of equipment for 2008 was understated $38,500.
3. December 31, 2007, inventory was understated $50,000.
4. December 31, 2008, inventory was overstated $16,200.

Instructions

Prepare the correcting entry necessary when these errors are discovered. Assume that the books are closed. (Ignore income tax considerations.)

(LO 7, 9)   **E22-18**   **(Error Analysis)**   Peter Henning Tool Company's December 31 year-end financial statements contained the following errors.

	December 31, 2007	December 31, 2008
Ending inventory	$9,600 understated	$8,100 overstated
Depreciation expense	$2,300 understated	—

An insurance premium of $66,000 was prepaid in 2007 covering the years 2007, 2008, and 2009. The entire amount was charged to expense in 2007. In addition, on December 31, 2008, fully depreciated machinery was sold for $15,000 cash, but the entry was not recorded until 2009. There were no other errors during 2007 or 2008, and no corrections have been made for any of the errors. (Ignore income tax considerations.)

Instructions

  (a)   Compute the total effect of the errors on 2008 net income.

  (b)   Compute the total effect of the errors on the amount of Henning's working capital at December 31, 2008.

  (c)   Compute the total effect of the errors on the balance of Henning's retained earnings at December 31, 2008.

(LO 7, 9)   **E22-19**   **(Error Analysis; Correcting Entries)**   A partial trial balance of Julie Hartsack Corporation is as follows on December 31, 2008.

	Dr.	Cr.
Supplies on hand	$ 2,700	
Accrued salaries and wages		$ 1,500
Interest receivable on investments	5,100	
Prepaid insurance	90,000	
Unearned rent		–0–
Accrued interest payable		15,000

Additional adjusting data:

  1.   A physical count of supplies on hand on December 31, 2008, totaled $1,100.

  2.   Through oversight, the Accrued Salaries and Wages account was not changed during 2008. Accrued salaries and wages on December 31, 2008, amounted to $4,400.

  3.   The Interest Receivable on Investments account was also left unchanged during 2008. Accrued interest on investments amounts to $4,350 on December 31, 2008.

  4.   The unexpired portions of the insurance policies totaled $65,000 as of December 31, 2008.

  5. $28,000 was received on January 1, 2008 for the rent of a building for both 2008 and 2009. The entire amount was credited to rental income.

  6.   Depreciation for the year was erroneously recorded as $5,000 rather than the correct figure of $50,000.

  7.   A further review of depreciation calculations of prior years revealed that depreciation of $7,200 was not recorded. It was decided that this oversight should be corrected by a prior period adjustment.

Instructions

  (a)   Assuming that the books have not been closed, what are the adjusting entries necessary at December 31, 2008? (Ignore income tax considerations.)

  (b)   Assuming that the books have been closed, what are the adjusting entries necessary at December 31, 2008? (Ignore income tax considerations.)

(LO 7, 9)   **E22-20**   **(Error Analysis)**   The before-tax income for Lonnie Holdiman Co. for 2007 was $101,000 and $77,400 for 2008. However, the accountant noted that the following errors had been made:

  1.   Sales for 2007 included amounts of $38,200 which had been received in cash during 2007, but for which the related products were delivered in 2008. Title did not pass to the purchaser until 2008.

  2.   The inventory on December 31, 2007, was understated by $8,640.

  3.   The bookkeeper in recording interest expense for both 2007 and 2008 on bonds payable made the following entry on an annual basis.

Interest Expense	15,000	
Cash		15,000

The bonds have a face value of $250,000 and pay a stated interest rate of 6%. They were issued at a discount of $15,000 on January 1, 2007, to yield an effective interest rate of 7%. (Assume that the effective-yield method should be used.)

4. Ordinary repairs to equipment had been erroneously charged to the Equipment account during 2007 and 2008. Repairs in the amount of $8,500 in 2007 and $9,400 in 2008 were so charged. The company applies a rate of 10% to the balance in the Equipment account at the end of the year in its determination of depreciation charges.

Instructions
Prepare a schedule showing the determination of corrected income before taxes for 2007 and 2008.

(LO 7, 9) **E22-21 (Error Analysis)** When the records of Debra Hanson Corporation were reviewed at the close of 2008, the errors listed below were discovered. For each item indicate by a check mark in the appropriate column whether the error resulted in an overstatement, an understatement, or had no effect on net income for the years 2007 and 2008.

	2007			2008		
Item	**Over-statement**	**Under-statement**	**No Effect**	**Over-statement**	**Under-statement**	**No Effect**
1. Failure to record amortization of patent in 2008.						
2. Failure to record the correct amount of ending 2007 inventory. The amount was understated because of an error in calculation.						
3. Failure to record merchandise purchased in 2007. Merchandise was also omitted from ending inventory in 2007 but was not yet sold.						
4. Failure to record accrued interest on notes payable in 2007; that amount was recorded when paid in 2008.						
5. Failure to reflect supplies on hand on balance sheet at end of 2007.						

(LO 10) *****E22-22 (Change from Fair Value to Equity)** On January 1, 2007, Barbra Streisand Co. purchased 25,000 shares (a 10% interest) in Elton John Corp. for $1,400,000. At the time, the book value and the fair value of John's net assets were $13,000,000.

On July 1, 2008, Streisand paid $3,040,000 for 50,000 additional shares of John common stock, which represented a 20% investment in John. The fair value of John's identifiable assets net of liabilities was equal to their carrying amount of $14,200,000. As a result of this transaction, Streisand owns 30% of John and can exercise significant influence over John's operating and financial policies. Any excess fair value is attributed to goodwill.

John reported the following net income and declared and paid the following dividends.

	Net Income	Dividend per Share
Year ended 12/31/07	$700,000	None
Six months ended 6/30/08	500,000	None
Six months ended 12/31/08	815,000	$1.55

Instructions
Determine the ending balance that Streisand Co. should report as its investment in John Corp. at the end of 2008.

(LO 10) ***E22-23** **(Change from Equity to Fair Value)** Dan Aykroyd Corp. was a 30% owner of John Belushi Company, holding 210,000 shares of Belushi's common stock on December 31, 2006. The investment account had the following entries.

Investment in Belushi

1/1/05 Cost	$3,180,000	12/6/05 Dividend received	$150,000
12/31/05 Share of income	390,000	12/5/06 Dividend received	240,000
12/31/06 Share of income	510,000		

On January 2, 2007, Aykroyd sold 126,000 shares of Belushi for $3,440,000, thereby losing its significant influence. During the year 2007 Belushi experienced the following results of operations and paid the following dividends to Aykroyd.

	Belushi Income (Loss)	Dividends Paid to Aykroyd
2007	$300,000	$50,400

At December 31, 2007, the fair value of Belushi shares held by Aykroyd is $1,570,000. This is the first reporting date since the January 2 sale.

Instructions

(a) What effect does the January 2, 2007, transaction have upon Aykroyd's accounting treatment for its investment in Belushi?

(b) Compute the carrying amount in Belushi as of December 31, 2007.

(c) Prepare the adjusting entry on December 31, 2007, applying the fair value method to Aykroyd's long-term investment in Belushi Company securities.

See the book's website, www.wiley.com/college/kieso, for Additional Exercises.

PROBLEMS

(LO 2, 5, 7) **P22-1** **(Change in Estimate and Error Correction)** Brueggen Company is in the process of preparing its financial statements for 2007. Assume that no entries for depreciation have been recorded in 2007. The following information related to depreciation of fixed assets is provided to you:

1. Brueggen purchased equipment on January 2, 2004, for $65,000. At that time, the equipment had an estimated useful life of 10 years with a $5,000 salvage value. The equipment is depreciated on a straight-line basis. On January 2, 2007, as a result of additional information, the company determined that the equipment has a remaining useful life of 4 years with a $3,000 salvage value.

2. During 2007 Brueggen changed from the double-declining balance method for its building to the straight-line method. The building originally cost $300,000. It had a useful life of 10 years and a salvage value of $30,000. The following computations present depreciation on both bases for 2005 and 2006.

	2006	2005
Straight-line	$27,000	$27,000
Declining-balance	48,000	60,000

3. Brueggen purchased a machine on July 1, 2005, at a cost of $80,000. The machine has a salvage value of $8,000 and a useful life of 8 years. Brueggen's bookkeeper recorded straight-line depreciation in 2005 and 2006 but failed to consider the salvage value.

Instructions

(a) Prepare the journal entries to record depreciation expense for 2007 and correct any errors made to date related to the information provided. (Round all computations to two decimal places.)

(b) Show comparative net income for 2006 and 2007. Income before depreciation expense was $300,000 in 2007, and was $310,000 in 2006. Ignore taxes.

(LO 3, 5, 7) **P22-2 (Comprehensive Accounting Change and Error Analysis Problem)** Larry Kingston Inc. was organized in late 2005 to manufacture and sell hosiery. At the end of its fourth year of operation, the company has been fairly successful, as indicated by the following reported net incomes.

2005	$140,000[a]	2007	$205,000
2006	160,000[b]	2008	276,000

[a]Includes a $12,000 increase because of change in bad debt experience rate.
[b]Includes extraordinary gain of $40,000.

The company has decided to expand operations and has applied for a sizable bank loan. The bank officer has indicated that the records should be audited and presented in comparative statements to facilitate analysis by the bank. Larry Kingston Inc. therefore hired the auditing firm of Check & Doublecheck Co. and has provided the following additional information.

1. In early 2006, Larry Kingston Inc. changed its estimate from 2% to 1% on the amount of bad debt expense to be charged to operations. Bad debt expense for 2005, if a 1% rate had been used, would have been $12,000. The company therefore restated its net income for 2005.
2. In 2008, the auditor discovered that the company had changed its method of inventory pricing from LIFO to FIFO. The effect on the income statements for the previous years is as follows.

	2005	2006	2007	2008
Net income unadjusted—LIFO basis	$140,000	$160,000	$205,000	$276,000
Net income unadjusted—FIFO basis	155,000	165,000	215,000	260,000
	$ 15,000	$ 5,000	$ 10,000	($ 16,000)

3. In 2008 the auditor discovered that:
   a. The company incorrectly overstated the ending inventory by $11,000 in 2007.
   b. A dispute developed in 2006 with the Internal Revenue Service over the deductibility of entertainment expenses. In 2005, the company was not permitted these deductions, but a tax settlement was reached in 2008 that allowed these expenses. As a result of the court's finding, tax expenses in 2008 were reduced by $60,000.

Instructions
(a) Indicate how each of these changes or corrections should be handled in the accounting records. Ignore income tax considerations.
(b) Present comparative income statements for the years 2005 to 2008, starting with income before extraordinary items. Ignore income tax considerations.

(LO 3, 5, 7) **P22-3 (Error Corrections and Accounting Changes)** Patricia Voga Company is in the process of adjusting and correcting its books at the end of 2008. In reviewing its records, the following information is compiled.

1. Voga has failed to accrue sales commissions payable at the end of each of the last 2 years, as follows.

December 31, 2007	$4,000
December 31, 2008	$2,500

2. In reviewing the December 31, 2008, inventory, Voga discovered errors in its inventory-taking procedures that have caused inventories for the last 3 years to be incorrect, as follows.

December 31, 2006	Understated	$16,000
December 31, 2007	Understated	$21,000
December 31, 2008	Overstated	$ 6,700

Voga has already made an entry that established the incorrect December 31, 2008, inventory amount.

3. At December 31, 2008, Voga decided to change the depreciation method on its office equipment from double-declining balance to straight-line. The equipment has an original cost of $100,000 when purchased on January 1, 2006. it has a 10-year useful life and no salvage value. Depreciation expense recorded prior to 2008 under the double-declining balance method was $36,000. Voga has already recorded 2008 depreciation expense of $12,800 using the double-declining balance method.

4. Before 2008, Voga accounted for its income from long-term construction contracts on the completed-contract basis. Early in 2008, Voga changed to the percentage-of-completion basis for accounting purposes. It continues to use the completed-contract method for tax purposes. Income for 2008 has been recorded using the percentage-of-completion method. The following information (on page 1199) is available.

	Pretax Income	
	Percentage-of-Completion	Completed-Contract
Prior to 2008	$150,000	$95,000
2008	60,000	20,000

Instructions

Prepare the journal entries necessary at December 31, 2008, to record the above corrections and changes. The books are still open for 2008. The income tax rate is 40%. Voga has not yet recorded its 2008 income tax expense and payable amounts so current-year tax effects may be ignored. Prior-year tax effects must be considered in item 4.

(LO 5) **P22-4 (Accounting Changes)** Plato Corporation performs year-end planning in November of each year before their calendar year ends in December. The preliminary estimated net income is $3 million. The CFO, Mary Sheets, meets with the company president, S. A. Plato, to review the projected numbers. She presents the following projected information.

PLATO CORPORATION
PROJECTED INCOME STATEMENT
FOR THE YEAR ENDED DECEMBER 31, 2007

Sales		$29,000,000
Cost of goods sold	$14,000,000	
Depreciation	2,600,000	
Operating expenses	6,400,000	23,000,000
Income before income tax		6,000,000
Income tax		3,000,000
Net income		$ 3,000,000

PLATO CORPORATION
SELECTED BALANCE SHEET INFORMATION
AT DECEMBER 31, 2007

Estimated cash balance	$ 5,000,000
Available-for-sale securities (at cost)	10,000,000
Security fair value adjustment account (1/1/07)	200,000

Estimated market value at December 31, 2007:

Security	Cost	Estimated Market
A	$ 2,000,000	$ 2,200,000
B	4,000,000	3,900,000
C	3,000,000	3,000,000
D	1,000,000	2,800,000
Total	$10,000,000	$11,900,000

Other information at December 31, 2007:

Equipment	$ 3,000,000
Accumulated depreciation (5-year SL)	1,200,000
New robotic equipment (purchased 1/1/07)	5,000,000
Accumulated depreciation (5-year DDB)	2,000,000

The corporation has never used robotic equipment before, and Sheets assumed an accelerated method because of the rapidly changing technology in robotic equipment. The company normally uses straight-line depreciation for production equipment.

Plato explains to Sheets that it is important for the corporation to show an $8,000,000 net income before taxes because Plato receives a $1,000,000 bonus if the income before taxes and bonus reaches $8,000,000. Plato also does not want the company to pay more than $3,000,000 in income taxes to the government.

Instructions

(a) What can Sheets do within GAAP to accommodate the president's wishes to achieve $8,000,000 in income before taxes and bonus? Present the revised income statement based on your decision.

(b) Are the actions ethical? Who are the stakeholders in this decision, and what effect do Sheets's actions have on their interests?

(LO 3) **P22-5 (Change in Principle—LIFO to Average Cost; Income Statements—Periodic)** The management of Kreiter Instrument Company had concluded, with the concurrence of its independent auditors, that results of operations would be more fairly presented if Kreiter changed its method of pricing inventory from last-in, first-out (LIFO) to average cost in 2007. Given below is the 5-year summary of income under LIFO and a schedule of what the inventories would be if stated on the average cost method.

KREITER INSTRUMENT COMPANY
STATEMENT OF INCOME AND RETAINED EARNINGS
FOR THE YEARS ENDED MAY 31

	2003	2004	2005	2006	2007
Sales—net	$13,964	$15,506	$16,673	$18,221	$18,898
Cost of goods sold					
Beginning inventory	1,000	1,100	1,000	1,115	1,237
Purchases	13,000	13,900	15,000	15,900	17,100
Ending inventory	(1,100)	(1,000)	(1,115)	(1,237)	(1,369)
Total	12,900	14,000	14,885	15,778	16,968
Gross profit	1,064	1,506	1,788	2,443	1,930
Administrative expenses	700	763	832	907	989
Income before taxes	364	743	956	1,536	941
Income taxes (50%)	182	372	478	768	471
Net income	182	371	478	768	470
Retained earnings—beginning	1,206	1,388	1,759	2,237	3,005
Retained earnings—ending	$ 1,388	$ 1,759	$ 2,237	$ 3,005	$ 3,475
Earnings per share	$1.82	$3.71	$4.78	$7.68	$4.70

SCHEDULE OF INVENTORY BALANCES USING AVERAGE COST METHOD
FOR THE YEARS ENDED MAY 31

2002	2003	2004	2005	2006	2007
$950	$1,124	$1,091	$1,270	$1,480	$1,699

Instructions

Prepare comparative statements for the 5 years, assuming that Kreiter changed its method of inventory pricing to average cost. Indicate the effects on net income and earnings per share for the years involved. Kreiter Instruments started business in 2002. (All amounts except EPS are rounded up to the nearest dollar.)

(LO 5,
7, 9) **P22-6 (Accounting Change and Error Analysis)** On December 31, 2008, before the books were closed, the management and accountants of Keltner Inc. made the following determinations about three depreciable assets.

1. Depreciable asset A was purchased January 2, 2005. It originally cost $495,000 and, for depreciation purposes, the straight-line method was originally chosen. The asset was originally expected to be useful for 10 years and have a zero salvage value. In 2008, the decision was made to change the depreciation method from straight-line to sum-of-the-years'-digits, and the estimates relating to useful life and salvage value remained unchanged.
2. Depreciable asset B was purchased January 3, 2004. It originally cost $120,000 and, for depreciation purposes, the straight-line method was chosen. The asset was originally expected to be useful for 15 years and have a zero salvage value. In 2008, the decision was made to shorten the total life of this asset to 9 years and to estimate the salvage value at $3,000.
3. Depreciable asset C was purchased January 5, 2004. The asset's original cost was $140,000, and this amount was entirely expensed in 2004. This particular asset has a 10-year useful life and no salvage value. The straight-line method was chosen for depreciation purposes.

Additional data:

1. Income in 2008 before depreciation expense amounted to $400,000.
2. Depreciation expense on assets other than A, B, and C totaled $55,000 in 2008.
3. Income in 2007 was reported at $370,000.
4. Ignore all income tax effects.
5. 100,000 shares of common stock were outstanding in 2007 and 2008.

Instructions

(a) Prepare all necessary entries in 2008 to record these determinations.

(b) Prepare comparative retained earnings statements for Eloise Keltner Inc. for 2007 and 2008. The company had retained earnings of $200,000 at December 31, 2006.

(L0 7, 9) **P22-7 (Error Corrections)** You have been assigned to examine the financial statements of Vickie L. Lemke Company for the year ended December 31, 2008. You discover the following situations.

1. Depreciation of $3,200 for 2008 on delivery vehicles was not recorded.
2. The physical inventory count on December 31, 2007, improperly excluded merchandise costing $19,000 that had been temporarily stored in a public warehouse. Lemke uses a periodic inventory system.
3. The physical inventory count on December 31, 2008, improperly included merchandise with a cost of $8,500 that had been recorded as a sale on December 27, 2008, and held for the customer to pick up on January 4, 2009.
4. A collection of $5,600 on account from a customer received on December 31, 2008, was not recorded until January 2, 2009.
5. In 2008, the company sold for $3,700 fully depreciated equipment that originally cost $22,000. The company credited the proceeds from the sale to the Equipment account.
6. During November 2008, a competitor company filed a patent-infringement suit against Lemke claiming damages of $220,000. The company's legal counsel has indicated that an unfavorable verdict is probable and a reasonable estimate of the court's award to the competitor is $125,000. The company has not reflected or disclosed this situation in the financial statements.
7. Lemke has a portfolio of trading securities. No entry has been made to adjust to market. Information on cost and market value is as follows.

	Cost	Market
December 31, 2007	$95,000	$95,000
December 31, 2008	$84,000	$82,000

8. At December 31, 2008, an analysis of payroll information shows accrued salaries of $12,200. The Accrued Salaries Payable account had a balance of $16,000 at December 31, 2008, which was unchanged from its balance at December 31, 2007.
9. A large piece of equipment was purchased on January 3, 2008, for $32,000 and was charged to Repairs Expense. The equipment is estimated to have a service life of 8 years and no residual value. Lemke normally uses the straight-line depreciation method for this type of equipment.
10. A $15,000 insurance premium paid on July 1, 2007, for a policy that expires on June 30, 2010, was charged to insurance expense.
11. A trademark was acquired at the beginning of 2007 for $50,000. No amortization has been recorded since its acquisition. The maximum allowable amortization period is 10 years.

Instructions

Assume the trial balance has been prepared but the books have not been closed for 2008. Assuming all amounts are material, prepare journal entries showing the adjustments that are required. (Ignore income tax considerations.)

(L0 7, 9) **P22-8 (Comprehensive Error Analysis)** On March 5, 2008, you were hired by Gretchen Hollenbeck Inc., a closely held company, as a staff member of its newly created internal auditing department. While reviewing the company's records for 2007 and 2008, you discover that no adjustments have yet been made for the items listed below.

Items

1. Interest income of $14,100 was not accrued at the end of 2006. It was recorded when received in February 2007.
2. A computer costing $8,000 was expensed when purchased on July 1, 2006. It is expected to have a 4-year life with no salvage value. The company typically uses straight-line depreciation for all fixed assets.
3. Research and development costs of $33,000 were incurred early in 2006. They were capitalized and were to be amortized over a 3-year period. Amortization of $11,000 was recorded for 2006 and $11,000 for 2007.
4. On January 2, 2006, Hollenbeck leased a building for 5 years at a monthly rental of $8,000. On that date, the company paid the following amounts, which were expensed when paid.

Security deposit	$25,000
First month's rent	8,000
Last month's rent	8,000
	$41,000

5. The company received $30,000 from a customer at the beginning of 2006 for services that it is to perform evenly over a 3-year period beginning in 2006. None of the amount received was reported as unearned revenue at the end of 2006.

6. Merchandise inventory costing $18,200 was in the warehouse at December 31, 2006, but was incorrectly omitted from the physical count at that date. The company uses the periodic inventory method.

Instructions

Indicate the effect of any errors on the net income figure reported on the income statement for the year ending December 31, 2006, and the retained earnings figure reported on the balance sheet at December 31, 2007. Assume all amounts are material, and ignore income tax effects. Using the following format, enter the appropriate dollar amounts in the appropriate columns. Consider each item independent of the other items. It is not necessary to total the columns on the grid.

Item	Net Income for 2006		Retained Earnings at 12/31/07	
	Understated	Overstated	Understated	Overstated

(CIA adapted)

(LO 7, 9) **P22-9 (Error Analysis)** Mary Keeton Corporation has used the accrual basis of accounting for several years. A review of the records, however, indicates that some expenses and revenues have been handled on a cash basis because of errors made by an inexperienced bookkeeper. Income statements prepared by the bookkeeper reported $29,000 net income for 2007 and $37,000 net income for 2008. Further examination of the records reveals that the following items were handled improperly.

1. Rent was received from a tenant in December 2007. The amount, $1,300, was recorded as income at that time even though the rental pertained to 2008.

2. Wages payable on December 31 have been consistently omitted from the records of that date and have been entered as expenses when paid in the following year. The amounts of the accruals recorded in this manner were:

December 31, 2006	$1,100
December 31, 2007	1,500
December 31, 2008	940

3. Invoices for office supplies purchased have been charged to expense accounts when received. Inventories of supplies on hand at the end of each year have been ignored, and no entry has been made for them.

December 31, 2006	$1,300
December 31, 2007	740
December 31, 2008	1,420

Instructions

Prepare a schedule that will show the corrected net income for the years 2007 and 2008. All items listed should be labeled clearly. (Ignore income tax considerations.)

(LO 7, 9) **P22-10 (Error Analysis and Correcting Entries)** You have been asked by a client to review the records of Larry Landers Company, a small manufacturer of precision tools and machines. Your client is interested in buying the business, and arrangements have been made for you to review the accounting records. Your examination reveals the following.

1. Landers Company commenced business on April 1, 2005, and has been reporting on a fiscal year ending March 31. The company has never been audited, but the annual statements prepared by the bookkeeper reflect the following income before closing and before deducting income taxes.

Year Ended March 31	Income Before Taxes
2006	$ 71,600
2007	111,400
2008	103,580

2. A relatively small number of machines have been shipped on consignment. These transactions have been recorded as ordinary sales and billed as such. On March 31 of each year, machines billed and in the hands of consignees amounted to:

2006	$6,500
2007	none
2008	5,590

Sales price was determined by adding 30% to cost. Assume that the consigned machines are sold the following year.

3. On March 30, 2007, two machines were shipped to a customer on a C.O.D. basis. The sale was not entered until April 5, 2007, when cash was received for $6,100. The machines were not included in the inventory at March 31, 2007. (Title passed on March 30, 2007.)

4. All machines are sold subject to a 5-year warranty. It is estimated that the expense ultimately to be incurred in connection with the warranty will amount to ½ of 1% of sales. The company has charged an expense account for warranty costs incurred.

Sales per books and warranty costs were as follows.

Year Ended March 31	Sales	Warranty Expense for Sales Made In 2006	2007	2008	Total
2006	$ 940,000	$760			$ 760
2007	1,010,000	360	$1,310		1,670
2008	1,795,000	320	1,620	$1,910	3,850

5. A review of the corporate minutes reveals the manager is entitled to a bonus of ½ of 1% of the income before deducting income taxes and the bonus. The bonuses have never been recorded or paid.

6. Bad debts have been recorded on a direct writeoff basis. Experience of similar enterprises indicates that losses will approximate ¼ of 1% of sales. Bad debts written off were:

	Bad Debts Incurred on Sales Made In 2006	2007	2008	Total
2006	$750			$ 750
2007	800	$ 520		1,320
2008	350	1,800	$1,700	3,850

7. The bank deducts 6% on all contracts financed. Of this amount, ½% is placed in a reserve to the credit of Landers Company that is refunded to Landers as finance contracts are paid in full. The reserve established by the bank has not been reflected in the books of Landers. The excess of credits over debits (net increase) to the reserve account with Landers on the books of the bank for each fiscal year were as follows.

2006	$ 3,000
2007	3,900
2008	5,100
	$12,000

8. Commissions on sales have been entered when paid. Commissions payable on March 31 of each year were as follows.

2006	$1,400
2007	800
2008	1,120

Instructions

(a) Present a schedule showing the revised income before income taxes for each of the years ended March 31, 2006, 2007, and 2008. Make computations to the nearest whole dollar.

(b) Prepare the journal entry or entries you would give the bookkeeper to correct the books. Assume the books have not yet been closed for the fiscal year ended March 31, 2007. Disregard correction of income taxes.

(AICPA adapted)

(L0 10) *P22-11 (Fair Value to Equity Method with Goodwill) On January 1, 2006, Latoya Inc. paid $700,000 for 10,000 shares of Jones Company's voting common stock, which was a 10% interest in Jones. At that date the net assets of Jones totaled $6,000,000. The fair values of all of Jones' identifiable assets and liabilities were equal to their book values. Latoya does not have the ability to exercise significant influence over the operating and financial policies of Jones. Latoya received dividends of $2.00 per share from Jones on October 1, 2006. Jones reported net income of $500,000 for the year ended December 31, 2006.

On July 1, 2007, Latoya paid $2,325,000 for 30,000 additional shares of Jones Company's voting common stock which represents a 30% investment in Jones. The fair values of all of Jones' identifiable assets net of liabilities were equal to their book values of $6,550,000. As a result of this transaction, Latoya has the ability to exercise significant influence over the operating and financial policies of Jones. Latoya received dividends of $2.00 per share from Jones on April 1, 2007, and $2.50 per share on October 1, 2007. Jones reported net income of $650,000 for the year ended December 31, 2007, and $400,000 for the 6 months ended December 31, 2007.

Instructions

(a) Prepare a schedule showing the income or loss before income taxes for the year ended December 31, 2006, that Latoya should report from its investment in Jones in its income statement issued in March 2007.

(b) During March 2008, Latoya issues comparative financial statements for 2006 and 2007. Prepare schedules showing the income or loss before income taxes for the years ended December 31, 2006 and 2007, that Latoya should report from its investment in Jones.

(AICPA adapted)

*P22-12   (Change from Fair Value to Equity Method)   On January 3, 2005, Calvin Company purchased for $500,000 cash a 10% interest in Hobbes Corp. On that date the net assets of Hobbes had a book value of $3,750,000. The excess of cost over the underlying equity in net assets is attributable to undervalued depreciable assets having a remaining life of 10 years from the date of Calvin's purchase.

The fair value of Calvin's investment in Hobbes securities is as follows: December 31, 2005, $570,000, and December 31, 2006, $515,000.

On January 2, 2007, Calvin purchased an additional 30% of Hobbes's stock for $1,545,000 cash when the book value of Hobbes's net assets was $4,150,000. The excess was attributable to depreciable assets having a remaining life of 8 years.

During 2005, 2006, and 2007 the following occurred.

	Hobbes Net Income	Dividends Paid by Hobbes to Calvin
2005	$350,000	$15,000
2006	400,000	20,000
2007	550,000	70,000

Instructions

On the books of Calvin Company prepare all journal entries in 2005, 2006, and 2007 that relate to its investment in Hobbes Corp., reflecting the data above and a change from the fair value method to the equity method.

CONCEPTS FOR ANALYSIS

CA22-1   (Analysis of Various Accounting Changes and Errors)   Erin Kramer Inc. has recently hired a new independent auditor, Jodie Larson, who says she wants "to get everything straightened out." Consequently, she has proposed the following accounting changes in connection with Erin Kramer Inc.'s 2008 financial statements.

1. At December 31, 2007, the client had a receivable of $820,000 from Holly Michael Inc. on its balance sheet. Holly Michael Inc. has gone bankrupt, and no recovery is expected. The client proposes to write off the receivable as a prior period item.

2. The client proposes the following changes in depreciation policies.

   (a) For office furniture and fixtures it proposes to change from a 10-year useful life to an 8-year life. If this change had been made in prior years, retained earnings at December 31, 2007, would have been $250,000 less. The effect of the change on 2008 income alone is a reduction of $60,000.

   (b) For its equipment in the leasing division the client proposes to adopt the sum-of-the-years'-digits depreciation method. The client had never used SYD before. The first year the client operated a leasing division was 2008. If straight-line depreciation were used, 2008 income would be $110,000 greater.

3. In preparing its 2007 statements, one of the client's bookkeepers overstated ending inventory by $235,000 because of a mathematical error. The client proposes to treat this item as a prior period adjustment.

4. In the past, the client has spread preproduction costs in its furniture division over 5 years. Because its latest furniture is of the "fad" type, it appears that the largest volume of sales will occur during the first 2 years after introduction. Consequently, the client proposes to amortize preproduction costs on a per-unit basis, which will result in expensing most of such costs during the first 2 years after the furniture's introduction. If the new accounting method had been used prior to 2008, retained earnings at December 31, 2007, would have been $375,000 less.

5. For the nursery division the client proposes to switch from FIFO to LIFO inventories because it believes that LIFO will provide a better matching of current costs with revenues. The effect of making this change on 2008 earnings will be an increase of $320,000. The client says that the effect of the change on December 31, 2007, retained earnings cannot be determined.

6. To achieve a better matching of revenues and expenses in its building construction division, the client proposes to switch from the completed-contract method of accounting to the percentage-of-completion method. Had the percentage-of-completion method been employed in all prior years, retained earnings at December 31, 2007, would have been $1,175,000 greater.

Instructions

(a) For each of the changes described above decide whether:
   (1) The change involves an accounting principle, accounting estimate, or correction of an error.
   (2) Restatement of opening retained earnings is required.

(b) What would be the proper adjustment to the December 31, 2007, retained earnings?

CA22-2 (Analysis of Various Accounting Changes and Errors) Various types of accounting changes can affect the financial statements of a business enterprise differently. Assume that the following list describes changes that have a material effect on the financial statements for the current year of your business enterprise.

1. A change from the completed-contract method to the percentage-of-completion method of accounting for long-term construction-type contracts.

2. A change in the estimated useful life of previously recorded fixed assets as a result of newly acquired information.

3. A change from deferring and amortizing preproduction costs to recording such costs as an expense when incurred because future benefits of the costs have become doubtful. The new accounting method was adopted in recognition of the change in estimated future benefits.

4. A change from including the employer share of FICA taxes with Payroll Tax Expenses to including it with "Retirement benefits" on the income statement.

5. Correction of a mathematical error in inventory pricing made in a prior period.

6. A change from presentation of statements of individual companies to presentation of consolidated statements.

7. A change in the method of accounting for leases for tax purposes to conform with the financial accounting method. As a result, both deferred and current taxes payable changed substantially.

8. A change from the FIFO method of inventory pricing to the LIFO method of inventory pricing.

Instructions

Identify the type of change that is described in each item above and indicate whether the prior year's financial statements should be retrospectively applied or restated when presented in comparative form with the current year's statements.

CA22-3 (Analysis of Three Accounting Changes and Errors) Listed below are three independent, unrelated sets of facts relating to accounting changes.

Situation 1

Penelope Millhouse Company is in the process of having its first audit. The company has used the cash basis of accounting for revenue recognition. Millhouse president, A. G. Shumway, is willing to change to the accrual method of revenue recognition.

Situation 2

Cheri Nestor Co. decides in January 2008 to change from FIFO to weighted-average pricing for its inventories.

Situation 3
Laura Osmund Co. determined that the depreciable lives of its fixed assets are too long at present to fairly match the cost of the fixed assets with the revenue produced. The company decided at the beginning of the current year to reduce the depreciable lives of all of its existing fixed assets by 5 years.

Instructions
For each of the situations described, provide the information indicated below.

(a) Type of accounting change.
(b) Manner of reporting the change under current generally accepted accounting principles including a discussion, where applicable, of how amounts are computed.
(c) Effect of the change on the balance sheet and income statement.

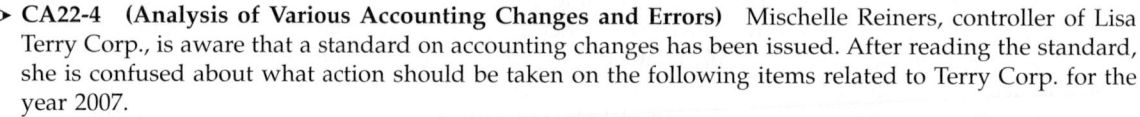 **CA22-4 (Analysis of Various Accounting Changes and Errors)** Mischelle Reiners, controller of Lisa Terry Corp., is aware that a standard on accounting changes has been issued. After reading the standard, she is confused about what action should be taken on the following items related to Terry Corp. for the year 2007.

1. In 2007, Terry decided to change its policy on accounting for certain marketing costs. Previously, the company had chosen to defer and amortize all marketing costs over at least 5 years because Terry believed that a return on these expenditures did not occur immediately. Recently, however, the time differential has considerably shortened, and Terry is now expensing the marketing costs as incurred.
2. In 2007, the company examined its entire policy relating to the depreciation of plant equipment. Plant equipment had normally been depreciated over a 15-year period, but recent experience has indicated that the company was incorrect in its estimates and that the assets should be depreciated over a 20-year period.
3. One division of Terry Corp., Ralph Rosentiel Co., has consistently shown an increasing net income from period to period. On closer examination of their operating statement, it is noted that bad debt expense and inventory obsolescence charges are much lower than in other divisions. In discussing this with the controller of this division, it has been learned that the controller has increased his net income each period by knowingly making low estimates related to the writeoff of receivables and inventory.
4. In 2007, the company purchased new machinery that should increase production dramatically. The company has decided to depreciate this machinery on an accelerated basis, even though other machinery is depreciated on a straight-line basis.
5. All equipment sold by Terry is subject to a 3-year warranty. It has been estimated that the expense ultimately to be incurred on these machines is 1% of sales. In 2007, because of a production breakthrough, it is now estimated that ½ of 1% of sales is sufficient. In 2005 and 2006, warranty expense was computed as $64,000 and $70,000, respectively. The company now believes that these warranty costs should be reduced by 50%.
6. In 2007, the company decided to change its method of inventory pricing from average cost to the FIFO method. The effect of this change on prior years is to increase 2005 income by $65,000 and increase 2006 income by $20,000.

Instructions
Mischelle Reiners has come to you, as her CPA, for advice about the situations above. Prepare a report, indicating the appropriate accounting treatment that should be given each of these situations.

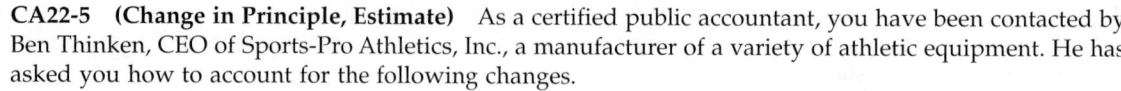 **CA22-5 (Change in Principle, Estimate)** As a certified public accountant, you have been contacted by Ben Thinken, CEO of Sports-Pro Athletics, Inc., a manufacturer of a variety of athletic equipment. He has asked you how to account for the following changes.

1. Sports-Pro appropriately changed its depreciation method for its production machinery from the double-declining balance method to the production method effective January 1, 2007.
2. Effective January 1, 2007, Sports-Pro appropriately changed the salvage values used in computing depreciation for its office equipment.
3. On December 31, 2007, Sports-Pro appropriately changed the specific subsidiaries constituting the group of companies for which consolidated financial statements are presented.

Instructions
Write a 1–1.5 page letter to Ben Thinken explaining how each of the above changes should be presented in the December 31, 2007, financial statements.

CA22-6 **(Change in Estimates)** Andy Frain is an audit senior of a large public accounting firm who has just been assigned to the Usher Corporation's annual audit engagement. Usher has been a client of Frain's firm for many years. Usher is a fast-growing business in the commercial construction industry. In reviewing the fixed asset ledger, Frain discovered a series of unusual accounting changes, in which the useful lives of assets, depreciated using the straight-line method, were substantially lowered near the mid-point of the original estimate. For example, the useful life of one dump truck was changed from 10 to 6 years during its fifth year of service. Upon further investigation, Andy was told by Vince Lloyd, Usher's accounting manager, "I don't really see your problem. After all, it's perfectly legal to change an accounting estimate. Besides, our CEO likes to see big earnings!"

Instructions
Answer the following questions.

- **(a)** What are the ethical issues concerning Usher's practice of changing the useful lives of fixed assets?
- **(b)** Who could be harmed by Usher's unusual accounting changes?
- **(c)** What should Frain do in this situation?

USING YOUR JUDGMENT

Financial Reporting Problem

The Procter & Gamble Company (P&G)
The financial statements of P&G are provided in Appendix 5B or can be accessed on the KWW website.

Instructions
Refer to P&G's financial statements and the accompanying notes to answer the following questions.

- **(a)** Were there changes in accounting principles reported by P&G during the three years covered by its income statements (2001–2004)? If so, describe the nature of the change and the year of change.
- **(b)** What use did P&G make of estimates in 2004?

Comparative Analysis Case

The Coca-Cola Company and PepsiCo, Inc.

Instructions
Go to the KWW website and use information found there to answer the following questions related to **The Coca-Cola Company** and **PepsiCo Inc.**

- **(a)** Identify the changes in accounting principles reported by Coca-Cola during the 3 years covered by its income statements (2002–2004). Describe the nature of the change and the year of change.
- **(b)** Identify the changes in accounting principles reported by PepsiCo during the 3 years covered by its income statements (2002–2004). Describe the nature of the change and the year of change.
- **(c)** For each change in accounting principle by Coca-Cola and PepsiCo, identify, if possible, the cumulative effect of each change on prior years and the effect on operating results in the year of change.

Research Cases

Case 1

Instructions
Use an appropriate source to identify two firms that recently reported a *voluntary* change in accounting principle. Answer the following questions with regard to each of the companies.

- **(a)** What is the name of the company? What source did you use to identify the company?
- **(b)** How did the change impact current earnings?

(c) How will the change impact future earnings?

(d) What rationale did the firm's management offer for the change? Do you agree with their stated reasons?

Case 2

The May 7, 2002 edition of the *Wall Street Journal* includes an article by James Bandler and Mark Maremont entitled "KPMG's Work With Xerox Sets Up a New Test for SEC."

Instructions

Read the article and answer the following questions.

(a) A change in estimated residual value is usually reported as a change in estimate. What distinguishes a change in estimate from an error correction?

(b) How does the reporting of a change in estimate differ from reporting of an error correction? Why would Xerox prefer to report the change in residual value as an error correction?

(c) The SEC says accounting rules ban any upward adjustments of residual value. Is the SEC correct? Justify your answer, providing citations from generally accepted accounting principles.

Professional Research: Financial Accounting and Reporting

As part of the year-end accounting process and review of operating policies, Konerko Co. is considering a change in the accounting for its equipment from the straight-line method to an accelerated method. Your supervisor wonders how the company will report this change in principle. He read in a newspaper article that the FASB has issued a standard in this area and has changed GAAP for a "change in estimate that is effected by a change in accounting principle." (Thus, the accounting may be different from that he learned in intermediate accounting.) Your supervisor wants you to research the authoritative guidance on a change in accounting principle related to depreciation methods.

Instructions

Using the **Financial Accounting Research System (FARS)**, respond to the following items. (Provide text strings used in your search.)

(a) What are the accounting and reporting guidelines for a change in accounting principle related to depreciation methods?

(b) What are the conditions that justify a change in depreciation method, as contemplated by Konerko Co?

(c) What was the FASB's reasoning for changing the accounting guidance for accounting principle changes related to depreciation?

Professional Simulation

In this simulation you are asked questions about changes in accounting principle. Prepare responses to all parts.

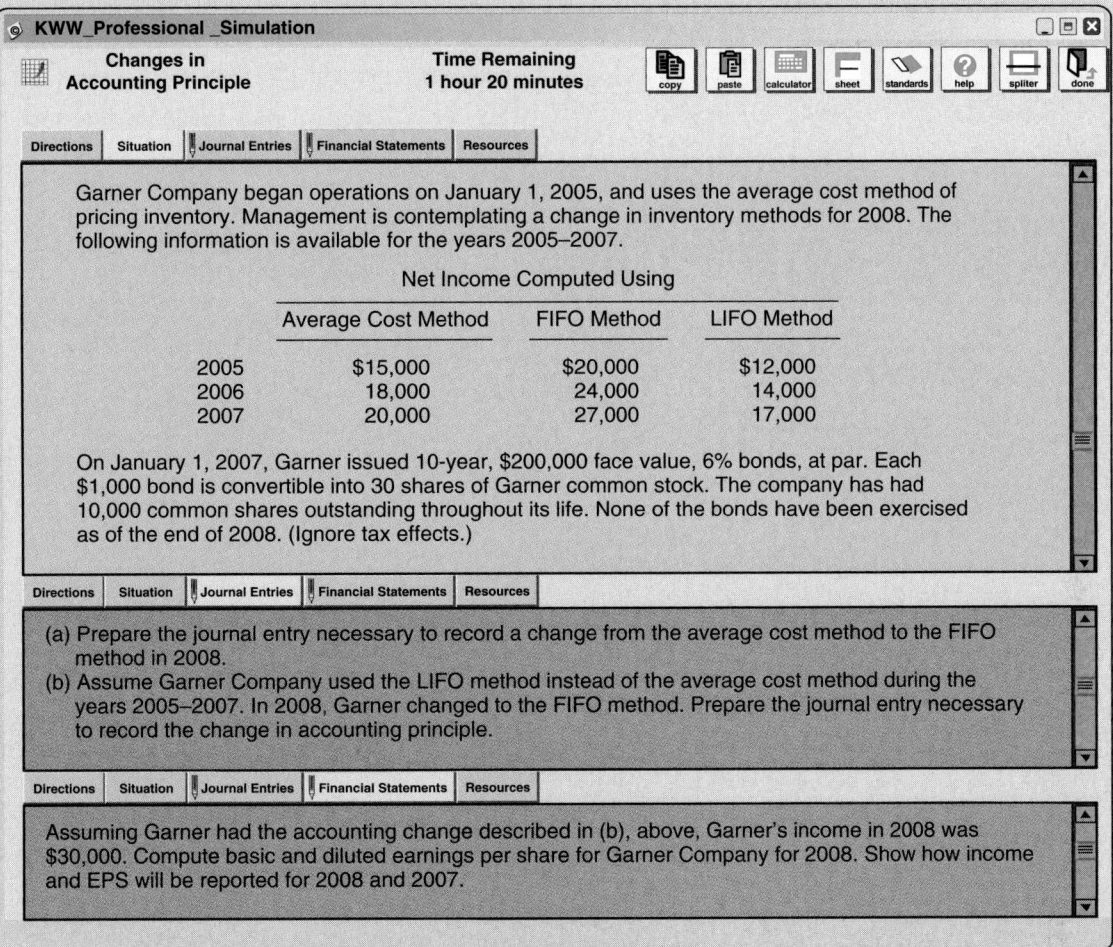

© KWW_Professional _Simulation

Changes in Accounting Principle **Time Remaining 1 hour 20 minutes**

Directions | Situation | Journal Entries | Financial Statements | Resources

Garner Company began operations on January 1, 2005, and uses the average cost method of pricing inventory. Management is contemplating a change in inventory methods for 2008. The following information is available for the years 2005–2007.

Net Income Computed Using

	Average Cost Method	FIFO Method	LIFO Method
2005	$15,000	$20,000	$12,000
2006	18,000	24,000	14,000
2007	20,000	27,000	17,000

On January 1, 2007, Garner issued 10-year, $200,000 face value, 6% bonds, at par. Each $1,000 bond is convertible into 30 shares of Garner common stock. The company has had 10,000 common shares outstanding throughout its life. None of the bonds have been exercised as of the end of 2008. (Ignore tax effects.)

Directions | Situation | Journal Entries | Financial Statements | Resources

(a) Prepare the journal entry necessary to record a change from the average cost method to the FIFO method in 2008.
(b) Assume Garner Company used the LIFO method instead of the average cost method during the years 2005–2007. In 2008, Garner changed to the FIFO method. Prepare the journal entry necessary to record the change in accounting principle.

Directions | Situation | Journal Entries | Financial Statements | Resources

Assuming Garner had the accounting change described in (b), above, Garner's income in 2008 was $30,000. Compute basic and diluted earnings per share for Garner Company for 2008. Show how income and EPS will be reported for 2008 and 2007.

> **Remember to check the book's companion website to find additional resources for this chapter.**

wiley.com/college/kieso

STATEMENT OF CASH FLOWS

Don't Take Cash Flow for Granted

Investors usually look to net income as a key indicator of a company's financial health and future prospects. The following graph shows the net income of one company over a seven-year period.

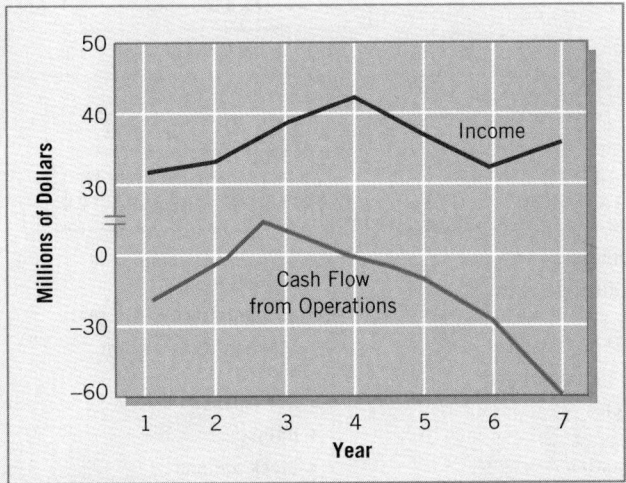

The company showed a pattern of consistent profitability and even some periods of income growth. Between years 1 and 4, net income for this company grew by 32 percent, from $31 million to $41 million. Would you expect its profitability to continue? The company had consistently paid dividends and interest. Would you expect it to continue to do so? Investors answered "yes" to these questions, by buying the company's stock. Eighteen months later, this company—**W. T. Grant**—filed for bankruptcy, in what was then the largest bankruptcy filing in the United States.

How could this happen? As indicated by the second line in the graph, the company had experienced several years of negative cash flow from its operations, even though it reported profits. How can a company have negative cash flows while reporting profits? The answer lay partly in the fact that W. T. Grant was having trouble collecting the receivables from its credit sales, causing cash flow to be less than the net income. Investors who analyzed the cash flows would have been likely to find an early warning signal of W. T. Grant's operating problems.[1]

---

[1] Adapted from James A. Largay III and Clyde P. Stickney, "Cash Flows, Ratio Analysis, and the W. T. Grant Company Bankruptcy," *Financial Analysts Journal* (July–August 1980), p. 51.

Learning Objectives

After studying this chapter, you should be able to:

1 Describe the purpose of the statement of cash flows.

2 Identify the major classifications of cash flows.

3 Differentiate between net income and net cash flows from operating activities.

4 Contrast the direct and indirect methods of calculating net cash flow from operating activities.

5 Determine net cash flows from investing and financing activities.

6 Prepare a statement of cash flows.

7 Identify sources of information for a statement of cash flows.

8 Discuss special problems in preparing a statement of cash flows.

9 Explain the use of a worksheet in preparing a statement of cash flows

As the opening story indicates, examination of **W. T. Grant**'s cash flows from operations would have shown the financial inflexibility that eventually caused the company's bankruptcy. This chapter explains the main components of a statement of cash flows and the types of information it provides. The content and organization of the chapter are as follows.

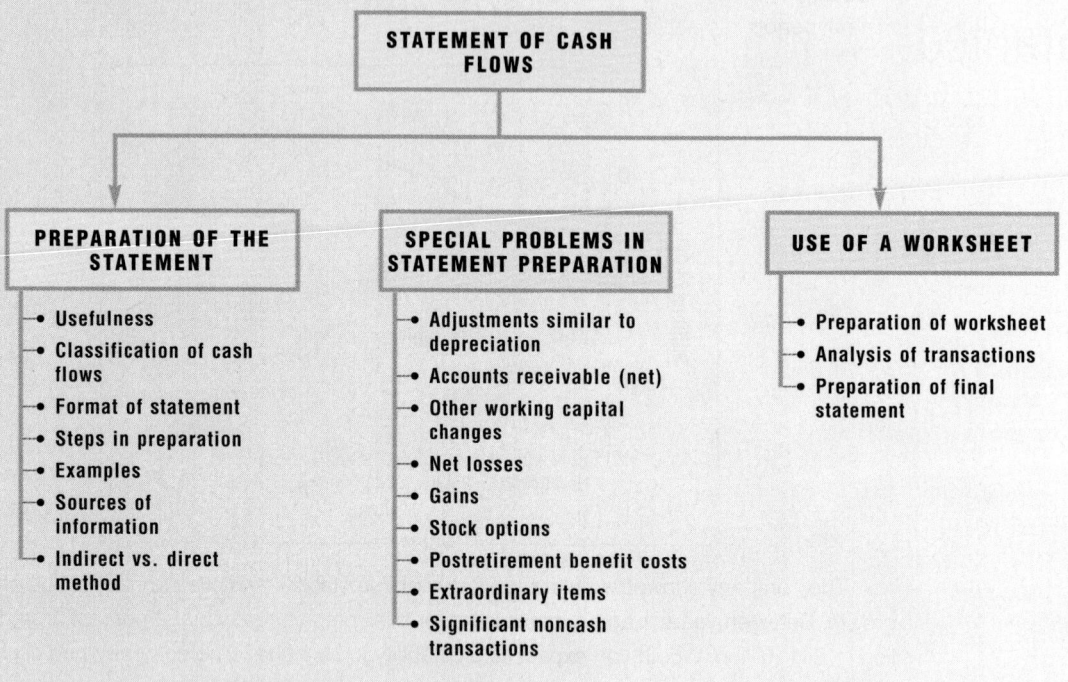

STATEMENT OF CASH FLOWS

PREPARATION OF THE STATEMENT
- Usefulness
- Classification of cash flows
- Format of statement
- Steps in preparation
- Examples
- Sources of information
- Indirect vs. direct method

SPECIAL PROBLEMS IN STATEMENT PREPARATION
- Adjustments similar to depreciation
- Accounts receivable (net)
- Other working capital changes
- Net losses
- Gains
- Stock options
- Postretirement benefit costs
- Extraordinary items
- Significant noncash transactions

USE OF A WORKSHEET
- Preparation of worksheet
- Analysis of transactions
- Preparation of final statement

SECTION 1	*PREPARATION OF THE STATEMENT OF CASH FLOWS*

OBJECTIVE 1
Describe the purpose of the statement of cash flows.

The primary purpose of the **statement of cash flows** is to provide information about a company's cash receipts and cash payments during a period. A secondary objective is to provide cash-basis information about the company's operating, investing, and financing activities. The statement of cash flows therefore reports cash receipts, cash payments, and net change in cash resulting from a company's operating, investing, and financing activities during a period. Its format reconciles the beginning and ending cash balances for the period.

USEFULNESS OF THE STATEMENT OF CASH FLOWS

The statement of cash flows provides information to help investors, creditors, and others assess the following:[2]

1 *The entity's ability to generate future cash flows.* A primary objective of financial reporting is to provide information with which to predict the amounts, timing, and

---

[2]"The Statement of Cash Flows," *Statement of Financial Accounting Standards No. 95* (Stamford, Conn.: FASB, 1987), pars. 4 and 5.

uncertainty of future cash flows. By examining relationships between items such as sales and net cash flow from operating activities, or net cash flow from operating activities and increases or decreases in cash, it is possible to better predict the future cash flows than is possible using accrual-basis data alone.

2 ***The entity's ability to pay dividends and meet obligations.*** Simply put, cash is essential. Without adequate cash, a company cannot pay employees, settle debts, pay out dividends, or acquire equipment. A statement of cash flows indicates where the company's cash comes from and how the company uses its cash. Employees, creditors, stockholders, and customers should be particularly interested in this statement, because it alone shows the flows of cash in a business.

3 ***The reasons for the difference between net income and net cash flow from operating activities.*** The net income number is important: It provides information on the performance of a company from one period to another. But some people are critical of accrual-basis net income because companies must make estimates to arrive at it. Such is not the case with cash. Thus, as the opening story showed, financial statement readers can benefit from knowing why a company's net income and net cash flow from operating activities differ, and can assess for themselves the reliability of the income number.

4 ***The cash and noncash investing and financing transactions during the period.*** Besides operating activities, companies undertake investing and financing transactions. *Investing* activities include the purchase and sale of assets other than a company's products or services. *Financing* activities include borrowings and repayments of borrowings, investments by owners, and distributions to owners. By examining a company's investing and financing activities, a financial statement reader can better understand why assets and liabilities increased or decreased during the period. For example, by reading the statement of cash flows, the reader might find answers to following questions:

Why did cash decrease for **Toys R Us** when it reported net income for the period?

How much did **Southwest Airlines** spend on property, plant, and equipment last year?

Did dividends paid by **Campbell's Soup** increase?

How much money did **Coca-Cola** borrow last year?

How much cash did **Hewlett-Packard** use to repurchase its common stock?

CLASSIFICATION OF CASH FLOWS

The statement of cash flows classifies cash receipts and cash payments by operating, investing, and financing activities.[3] Transactions and other events characteristic of each kind of activity is as follows.

> **OBJECTIVE 2**
> Identify the major classifications of cash flows.

1 **Operating activities** involve the cash effects of transactions that enter into the determination of net income, such as cash receipts from sales of goods and services, and cash payments to suppliers and employees for acquisitions of inventory and expenses.

---

[3]The basis recommended by the FASB for the statement of cash flows is actually "cash and cash equivalents." **Cash equivalents** are short-term, highly liquid investments that are both: (a) readily convertible to known amounts of cash, and (b) so near their maturity that they present insignificant risk of changes in interest rates. Generally, only investments with original maturities of three months or less qualify under this definition. Examples of cash equivalents are Treasury bills, commercial paper, and money market funds purchased with cash that is in excess of immediate needs.

Although we use the term "cash" throughout our discussion and illustrations, we mean cash and cash equivalents when reporting the cash flows and the net increase or decrease in cash.

2 **Investing activities** generally involve long-term assets and include (a) making and collecting loans, and (b) acquiring and disposing of investments and productive long-lived assets.

3 **Financing activities** involve liability and stockholders' equity items and include (a) obtaining cash from creditors and repaying the amounts borrowed, and (b) obtaining capital from owners and providing them with a return on, and a return of, their investment.

Illustration 23-1 classifies the typical cash receipts and payments of a company according to operating, investing, and financing activities. The operating activities category is the most important. It shows the cash provided by company operations. This source of cash is generally considered to be the best measure of a company's ability to generate enough cash to continue as a going concern.

ILLUSTRATION 23-1
Classification of Typical
Cash Inflows and
Outflows

**INTERNATIONAL
INSIGHT**

According to International Accounting Standards, companies can define "cash and cash equivalents" as "net monetary assets"—that is, as "cash and demand deposits and highly liquid investments less short-term borrowings."

Operating
 Cash inflows
  From sales of goods or services.
  From returns on loans (interest) and on equity
   securities (dividends).
 Cash outflows
  To suppliers for inventory.
  To employees for services.
  To government for taxes.
  To lenders for interest.
  To others for expenses.

⎫
⎬ **Income
Statement
Items**
⎭

Investing
 Cash inflows
  From sale of property, plant, and equipment.
  From sale of debt or equity securities of other entities.
  From collection of principal on loans to other entities.
 Cash outflows
  To purchase property, plant, and equipment.
  To purchase debt or equity securities of other entities.
  To make loans to other entities.

⎫
⎬ **Generally
Long-Term
Asset Items**
⎭

Financing
 Cash inflows
  From sale of equity securities.
  From issuance of debt (bonds and notes).
 Cash outflows
  To stockholders as dividends.
  To redeem long-term debt or reacquire capital stock.

⎫
⎬ **Generally
Long-Term
Liability
and Equity
Items**
⎭

Note the following general guidelines about the classification of cash flows.

1 Operating activities involve income statement items.

2 Investing activities involve cash flows resulting from changes in investments and long-term asset items.

3 Financing activities involve cash flows resulting from changes in long-term liability and stockholders' equity items.

Companies classify some cash flows relating to investing or financing activities as operating activities.[4] For example, companies classify receipts of investment income (interest and dividends) and payments of interest to lenders as operating activities.

---

[4]For exceptions to the treatment of purchases and sales of loans and securities by banks and brokers, see *Statement of Financial Accounting Standards No. 102* (February 1989). Banks and brokers must classify cash flows from purchases and sales of loans and securities specifically for resale and carried at market value **as operating activities**. This requirement recognizes that for these firms these assets are similar to inventory in other businesses.

Why are these considered operating activities? Companies report these items in the income statement, where the results of operations are shown.

Conversely, companies classify some cash flows relating to operating activities as investing or financing activities. For example, a company classifies the cash received from the sale of property, plant, and equipment at a gain, although reported in the income statement, as an investing activity. It excludes the effects of the related gain in net cash flow from operating activities. Likewise, a gain or loss on the payment (extinguishment) of debt is generally part of the cash outflow related to the repayment of the amount borrowed. It therefore is a financing activity.

HOW'S MY CASH FLOW?

To evaluate overall cash flow, it is useful to understand where in the product life cycle a company is. Generally, companies move through several stages of development, which have implications for cash flow. As the graph below shows, the pattern of cash flows from operating, financing, and investing activities will vary depending on the stage of the product life cycle.

WHAT DO THE NUMBERS MEAN?

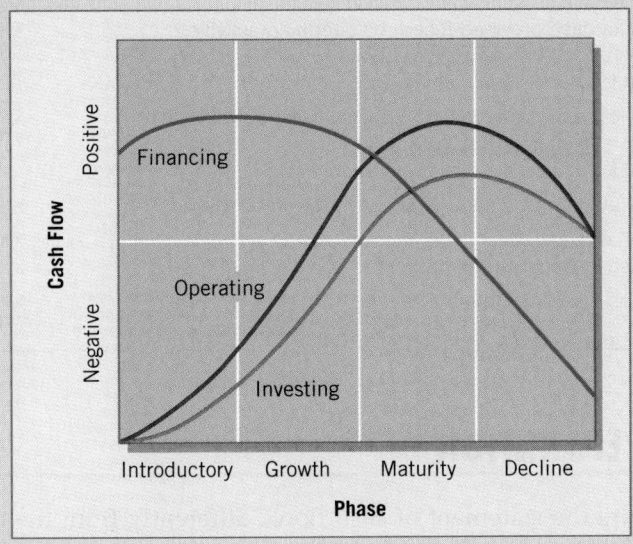

In the introductory phase, the product is likely not generating much revenue (operating cash flow is negative). Because the company is making heavy investments to get a product off the ground, cash flow from investment is negative, and financing cash flows are positive.

As the product moves to the growth and maturity phases, these cash flow relationships reverse. The product generates more cash flow from operations, which can be used to cover investments needed to support the product, and less cash is needed from financing. So is a negative operating cash flow bad? Not always. It depends on the product life cycle.

Source: Adapted from Paul D. Kimmel, Jerry J. Weygandt, and Donald E. Kieso, *Financial Accounting: Tools for Business Decision Making*, 4th ed. (New York: John Wiley & Sons, 2006), p. 591.

FORMAT OF THE STATEMENT OF CASH FLOWS

The three activities we discussed above constitute the general format of the statement of cash flows. The operating activities section always appears first. It is followed by the investing activities section and then the financing activities section.

A company reports the individual inflows and outflows from investing and financing activities separately. That is, a company reports them gross, not netted against one another. Thus, a cash outflow from the purchase of property is reported separately from the cash inflow from the sale of property. Similarly, a cash inflow from the issuance of debt is reported separately from the cash outflow from its retirement.

The net increase or decrease in cash reported during the period should reconcile the beginning and ending cash balances as reported in the comparative balance sheets. The general format of the statement of cash flows presents the results of the three activities discussed previously–operating, investing, and financing. Illustration 23-2 shows a widely used form of the statement of cash flows.

ILLUSTRATION 23-2
Format of the Statement
of Cash Flows

COMPANY NAME		
STATEMENT OF CASH FLOWS		
PERIOD COVERED		
Cash flows from operating activities		
Net income		XXX
Adjustments to reconcile net income to net		
cash provided by operating activities:		
(List of individual items)	XX	XX
Net cash provided (used) by operating activities		XXX
Cash flows from investing activities		
(List of individual inflows and outflows)	XX	
Net cash provided (used) by investing activities		XXX
Cash flows from financing activities		
(List of individual inflows and outflows)	XX	
Net cash provided (used) by financing activities		XXX
Net increase (decrease) in cash		XXX
Cash at beginning of period		XXX
Cash at end of period		XXX

STEPS IN PREPARATION

Companies prepare the statement of cash flows differently from the three other basic financial statements. For one thing, it is not prepared from an adjusted trial balance. The cash flow statement requires detailed information concerning the changes in account balances that occurred between two points in time. An adjusted trial balance will not provide the necessary data. Second, the statement of cash flows deals with cash receipts and payments. As a result, the company must adjust the effects of the use of accrual accounting to determine cash flows. The information to prepare this statement usually comes from three sources:

1 **Comparative balance sheets** provide the amount of the changes in assets, liabilities, and equities from the beginning to the end of the period.

2 **Current income statement** data help determine the amount of cash provided by or used by operations during the period.

3 **Selected transaction data** from the general ledger provide additional detailed information needed to determine how the company provided or used cash during the period.

Preparing the statement of cash flows from the data sources above involves three major steps:

Step 1. Determine the change in cash. This procedure is straightforward. A company can easily compute the difference between the beginning and the ending cash balance from examining its comparative balance sheets.

Step 2. Determine the net cash flow from operating activities. This procedure is complex. It involves analyzing not only the current year's income statement but also comparative balance sheets as well as selected transaction data.

Step 3. Determine net cash flows from investing and financing activities. A company must analyze all other changes in the balance sheet accounts to determine their effects on cash.

On the following pages we work through these three steps in the process of preparing the statement of cash flows for Tax Consultants Inc. over several years.

FIRST EXAMPLE—2006

To illustrate a statement of cash flows, we use the **first year of operations** for Tax Consultants Inc. The company started on January 1, 2006, when it issued 60,000 shares of $1 par value common stock for $60,000 cash. The company rented its office space, furniture, and equipment, and performed tax consulting services throughout the first year. The comparative balance sheets at the beginning and end of the year 2006 appear in Illustration 23-3.

TAX CONSULTANTS INC.
COMPARATIVE BALANCE SHEETS

Assets	Dec. 31, 2006	Jan. 1, 2006	Change Increase/Decrease
Cash	$49,000	$–0–	$49,000 Increase
Accounts receivable	36,000	–0–	36,000 Increase
Total	$85,000	$–0–	
Liabilities and Stockholders' Equity			
Accounts payable	$ 5,000	$–0–	$ 5,000 Increase
Common stock ($1 par)	60,000	–0–	60,000 Increase
Retained earnings	20,000	–0–	20,000 Increase
Total	$85,000	$–0–	

ILLUSTRATION 23-3
Comparative Balance Sheets, Tax Consultants Inc., Year 1

Illustration 23-4 shows the income statement and additional information for Tax Consultants.

TAX CONSULTANTS INC.
INCOME STATEMENT
FOR THE YEAR ENDED DECEMBER 31, 2006

Revenues	$125,000
Operating expenses	85,000
Income before income taxes	40,000
Income tax expense	6,000
Net income	$ 34,000

Additional Information
Examination of selected data indicates that a dividend of $14,000 was declared and paid during the year.

ILLUSTRATION 23-4
Income Statement, Tax Consultants Inc., Year 1

Step 1: Determine the Change in Cash

To prepare a statement of cash flows, the first step is to **determine the change in cash**. This is a simple computation. Tax Consultants had no cash on hand at the beginning of the year 2006. It had $49,000 on hand at the end of 2006. Thus, cash changed (increased) in 2006 by $49,000.

Step 2: Determine Net Cash Flow from Operating Activities

OBJECTIVE 3
Differentiate between net income and net cash flows from operating activities.

To determine net cash flow from operating activities,[5] companies adjust net income in numerous ways. A useful starting point is to understand why net income must be converted to net cash provided by operating activities.

Under generally accepted accounting principles, most companies use the accrual basis of accounting. As you have learned, this basis requires that companies record revenue when earned and record expenses when incurred. Earned revenues may include credit sales for which the company has not yet collected cash. Expenses incurred may include some items that the company has not yet paid in cash. Thus, under the accrual basis of accounting, net income is not the same as net cash flow from operating activities.

To arrive at net cash flow from operating activities, a company must determine revenues and expenses on a **cash basis**. **It does this by eliminating the effects of income statement transactions that do not result in an increase or decrease in cash.** Illustration 23-5 shows the relationship between net income and net cash flow from operating activities.

ILLUSTRATION 23-5
Net Income versus Net Cash Flow from Operating Activities

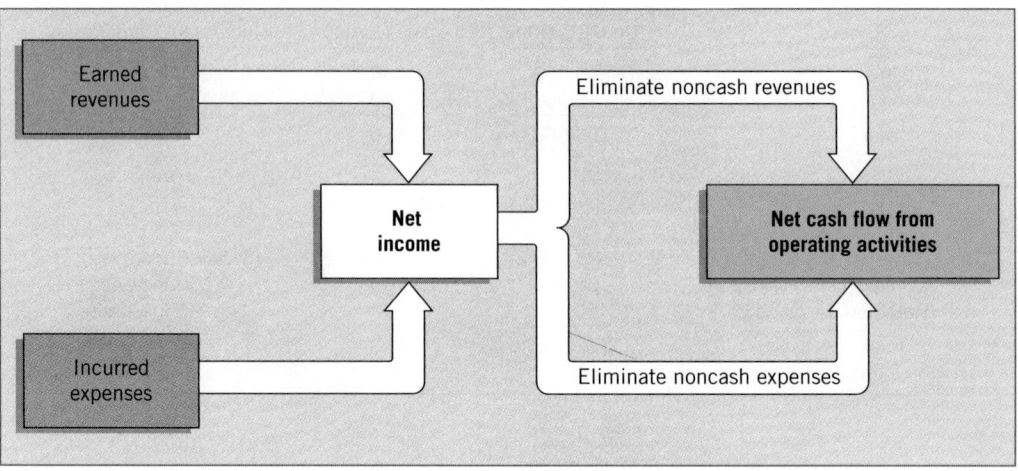

In this chapter, we use the term net income to refer to accrual-based net income. A company may convert net income to net cash flow from operating activities through either a direct method or an indirect method. We explain both methods in the following sections. The advantages and disadvantages of these two methods are discussed later in the chapter.

Direct Method

OBJECTIVE 4
Contrast the direct and indirect methods of calculating net cash flow from operating activities.

The **direct method** (also called the **income statement method**) reports cash receipts and cash disbursements from operating activities. The difference between these two amounts is the net cash flow from operating activities. In other words, the direct method deducts operating cash disbursements from operating cash receipts. The direct

---

[5]"Net cash flow from operating activities" is a generic phrase, replaced in the statement of cash flows with either "Net cash **provided by** operating activities" if operations increase cash, or "Net cash **used by** operating activities" if operations decrease cash.

method results in the presentation of a condensed cash receipts and cash disbursements statement.

As indicated from the accrual-based income statement, Tax Consultants reported revenues of $125,000. However, because the company's accounts receivable increased during 2006 by $36,000, the company collected only $89,000 ($125,000 − $36,000) in cash from these revenues. Similarly, Tax Consultants reported operating expenses of $85,000. However, accounts payable increased during the period by $5,000. Assuming that these payables relate to operating expenses, cash operating expenses were $80,000 ($85,000 − $5,000). Because no taxes payable exist at the end of the year, the company must have paid $6,000 income tax expense for 2006 in cash during the year. Tax Consultants computes net cash flow from operating activities as shown in Illustration 23-6.

Cash collected from revenues	$89,000
Cash payments for expenses	80,000
Income before income taxes	9,000
Cash payments for income taxes	6,000
Net cash provided by operating activities	$ 3,000

ILLUSTRATION 23-6
Computation of Net Cash Flow from Operating Activities, Year 1—Direct Method

"Net cash provided by operating activities" is the equivalent of cash basis net income. ("Net cash used by operating activities" is equivalent to cash basis net loss.)

Indirect Method

The **indirect method** (or **reconciliation method**) starts with net income and converts it to net cash flow from operating activities. In other words, **the indirect method adjusts net income for items that affected reported net income but did not affect cash**. To compute net cash flow from operating activities, a company adds back noncash charges in the income statement to net income and deducts noncash credits. We explain the two adjustments to net income for Tax Consultants, namely, the increases in accounts receivable and accounts payable, as follows.

Increase in Accounts Receivable—Indirect Method. Tax Consultant's accounts receivable increased by $36,000 (from $0 to $36,000) during the year. For Tax Consultants, this means that cash receipts were $36,000 lower than revenues. The Accounts Receivable account in Illustration 23-7 shows that Tax Consultants had $125,000 in revenues (as reported on the income statement), but it collected only $89,000 in cash.

	Accounts Receivable				
1/1/06	Balance	–0–	Receipts from customer	89,000
	Revenues	125,000		
12/31/06	Balance	36,000		

ILLUSTRATION 23-7
Analysis of Accounts Receivable

As shown in Illustration 23-8 (page 1220), to adjust net income to net cash provided by operating activities, Tax Consultants must deduct the increase of $36,000 in accounts receivable from net income. When the Accounts Receivable balance *decreases*, cash receipts are higher than revenue earned under the accrual basis. Therefore, the company adds to net income the amount of the decrease in accounts receivable to arrive at net cash provided by operating activities.

Increase in Accounts Payable—Indirect Method. When accounts payable increase during the year, expenses on an accrual basis exceed those on a cash basis. Why? Because Tax Consultants incurred expenses, but some of the expenses are not yet paid. To convert net income to net cash flow from operating activities, Tax Consultants must add back the increase of $5,000 in accounts payable to net income.

As a result of the accounts receivable and accounts payable adjustments, Tax Consultants determines net cash provided by operating activities is $3,000 for the year 2006. Illustration 23-8 shows this computation.

ILLUSTRATION 23-8
Computation of Net Cash Flow from Operating Activities, Year 1—Indirect Method

Net income		$34,000
Adjustments to reconcile net income to net cash provided by operating activities:		
Increase in accounts receivable	$(36,000)	
Increase in accounts payable	5,000	(31,000)
Net cash provided by operating activities		$ 3,000

Note that net cash provided by operating activities is the same whether using the direct (Illustration 23-6) or the indirect method (Illustration 23-8).

PUMPING UP CASH

WHAT DO THE NUMBERS MEAN?

Due to recent concerns about a decline in quality of earnings, some investors have been focusing on cash flow. And management has an incentive to make operating cash flow look good, because Wall Street has paid a premium for companies that generate a lot of cash from operations, rather than through borrowings. However, similar to earnings, companies have ways to pump up cash flow from operations.

One way that companies boost their operating cash flow is by securitizing receivables—that is, turning their receivables into securities that can be sold. For example, at one time **Oxford Industries**, an apparel company, reported a $74 million dollar increase in cash flow from operations. This seems impressive until you read the fine print, which indicates that a big part of the increase was due to the sale of receivables. As discussed in the text, decreases in accounts receivable increase cash flow from operations. So while Oxford's core operations seemed to have improved, the company really did little more than accelerate collections of its receivables. In fact, without the cash flow boost from the securitizations, Oxford's operating cash flow would have been negative. Thus, just like earnings, cash flow can be of high or low quality.

Source: Adapted from Ann Tergesen, "Cash Flow Hocus Pocus," *Business Week* (July 16, 2002), pp. 130–131.

Step 3: Determine Net Cash Flows from Investing and Financing Activities

OBJECTIVE 5
Determine net cash flows from investing and financing activities.

After Tax Consultants has computed the net cash provided by operating activities, the next step is to determine whether any other changes in balance sheet accounts caused an increase or decrease in cash.

For example, an examination of the remaining balance sheet accounts for Tax Consultants shows increases in both common stock and retained earnings. The common stock increase of $60,000 resulted from the issuance of common stock for cash. The issuance of common stock is reported in the statement of cash flows as a receipt of cash from a financing activity.

Two items caused the retained earnings increase of $20,000:

1 Net income of $34,000 increased retained earnings.
2 Declaration of $14,000 of dividends decreased retained earnings.

Tax Consultants has converted net income into net cash flow from operating activities, as explained earlier. The additional data indicate that it paid the dividend. Thus, the company reports the dividend payment as a cash outflow, classified as a financing activity.

Statement of Cash Flows—2006

We are now ready to prepare the statement of cash flows. The statement starts with the operating activities section. Tax Consultants may use either the direct or indirect method to report net cash flow from operating activities.

> **OBJECTIVE 6**
> Prepare a statement of cash flows.

The FASB **encourages** the use of the direct method over the indirect method. If a company uses the direct method of reporting net cash flow from operating activities, the FASB **requires** that the company provide in a separate schedule a reconciliation of net income to net cash flow from operating activities. If a company uses the indirect method, it can either report the reconciliation within the statement of cash flows or can provide it in a separate schedule, with the statement of cash flows reporting only the **net** cash flow from operating activities.[6] Throughout this chapter we use the indirect method, which is also used more extensively in practice.[7] *In doing homework assignments, you should follow instructions for use of either the direct or indirect method.*

Illustration 23-9 shows the statement of cash flows for Tax Consultants Inc., for year 1(2006).

ILLUSTRATION 23-9
Statement of Cash Flows, Tax Consultants Inc., Year 1

TAX CONSULTANTS INC. STATEMENT OF CASH FLOWS FOR THE YEAR ENDED DECEMBER 31, 2006 INCREASE (DECREASE) IN CASH		
Cash flows from operating activities		
Net income		$34,000
Adjustments to reconcile net income to net cash provided by operating activities:		
Increase in accounts receivable	$(36,000)	
Increase in accounts payable	5,000	(31,000)
Net cash provided by operating activities		3,000
Cash flows from financing activities		
Issuance of common stock	60,000	
Payment of cash dividends	(14,000)	
Net cash provided by financing activities		46,000
Net increase in cash		49,000
Cash, January 1, 2006		–0–
Cash, December 31, 2006		$49,000

As indicated, the $60,000 increase in common stock results in a financing-activity cash inflow. The payment of $14,000 in cash dividends is a financing-activity outflow of cash. The $49,000 increase in cash reported in the statement of cash flows agrees with the increase of $49,000 shown in the comparative balance sheets as the change in the cash account.

SECOND EXAMPLE—2007

Tax Consultants Inc. continued to grow and prosper in its second year of operations. The company purchased land, building, and equipment, and revenues and net income increased substantially over the first year. Illustrations 23-10 and 23-11 (page 1222) present information related to the second year of operations for Tax Consultants Inc.

---

[6]"The Statement of Cash Flows," pars. 27 and 30.

[7]*Accounting Trends and Techniques—2004* reports that out of its 600 surveyed companies, 593 (approximately 99 percent) used the indirect method, and only 7 used the direct method.

ILLUSTRATION 23-10
Comparative Balance
Sheets, Tax Consultants
Inc., Year 2

TAX CONSULTANTS INC.
COMPARATIVE BALANCE SHEETS
AS OF DECEMBER 31

Assets	2007	2006	Change Increase/Decrease
Cash	$ 37,000	$49,000	$12,000 Decrease
Accounts receivable	26,000	36,000	10,000 Decrease
Prepaid expenses	6,000	–0–	6,000 Increase
Land	70,000	–0–	70,000 Increase
Building	200,000	–0–	200,000 Increase
Accumulated depreciation—building	(11,000)	–0–	11,000 Increase
Equipment	68,000	–0–	68,000 Increase
Accumulated depreciation—equipment	(10,000)	–0–	10,000 Increase
Total	$386,000	$85,000	
Liabilities and Stockholders' Equity			
Accounts payable	$ 40,000	$ 5,000	$ 35,000 Increase
Bonds payable	150,000	–0–	150,000 Increase
Common stock ($1 par)	60,000	60,000	–0–
Retained earnings	136,000	20,000	116,000 Increase
Total	$386,000	$85,000	

ILLUSTRATION 23-11
Income Statement, Tax
Consultants Inc., Year 2

TAX CONSULTANTS INC.
INCOME STATEMENT
FOR THE YEAR ENDED DECEMBER 31, 2007

Revenues		$492,000
Operating expenses (excluding depreciation)	$269,000	
Depreciation expense	21,000	290,000
Income from operations		202,000
Income tax expense		68,000
Net income		$134,000

Additional Information
(a) The company declared and paid an $18,000 cash dividend.
(b) The company obtained $150,000 cash through the issuance of long-term bonds.
(c) Land, building, and equipment were acquired for cash.

Step 1: Determine the Change in Cash

To prepare a statement of cash flows from the available information, the first step is to determine the change in cash. As indicated from the information presented, cash decreased $12,000 ($49,000 − $37,000).

Step 2: Determine Net Cash Flow from Operating Activities—Indirect Method

Using the indirect method, we adjust net income of $134,000 on an accrual basis to arrive at net cash flow from operating activities. Explanations for the adjustments to net income follow.

Decrease in Accounts Receivable. Accounts receivable decreased during the period, because cash receipts (cash-basis revenues) are higher than revenues reported on an accrual basis. To convert net income to net cash flow from operating activities, the decrease of $10,000 in accounts receivable must be added to net income.

Increase in Prepaid Expenses. When prepaid expenses (assets) increase during a period, expenses on an accrual-basis income statement are lower than they are on a cash-basis income statement. The reason: Tax Consultants has made cash payments in the current period, but expenses (as charges to the income statement) have been deferred to future periods. To convert net income to net cash flow from operating activities, the company must deduct from net income the increase of $6,000 in prepaid expenses. An increase in prepaid expenses results in a decrease in cash during the period.

Increase in Accounts Payable. Like the increase in 2006, Tax Consultants must add the 2007 increase of $35,000 in accounts payable to net income, to convert to net cash flow from operating activities. The company incurred a greater amount of expense than the amount of cash it disbursed.

Depreciation Expense (Increase in Accumulated Depreciation). The purchase of depreciable assets is a use of cash, shown in the investing section in the year of acquisition. Tax Consultant's depreciation expense of $21,000 (also represented by the increase in accumulated depreciation) is a noncash charge; the company adds it back to net income, to arrive at net cash flow from operating activities. The $21,000 is the sum of the $11,000 depreciation on the building plus the $10,000 depreciation on the equipment.

Certain other periodic charges to expense do not require the use of cash. Examples are the amortization of intangible assets and depletion expense. Such charges are treated in the same manner as depreciation. Companies frequently list depreciation and similar noncash charges as the first adjustments to net income in the statement of cash flows.

As a result of the foregoing items, net cash provided by operating activities is $194,000 as shown in Illustration 23-12.

Net income		$134,000
Adjustments to reconcile net income to		
net cash provided by operating activities:		
Depreciation expense	$21,000	
Decrease in accounts receivable	10,000	
Increase in prepaid expenses	(6,000)	
Increase in accounts payable	35,000	60,000
Net cash provided by operating activities		$194,000

ILLUSTRATION 23-12
Computation of Net Cash Flow from Operating Activities, Year 2—Indirect Method

Step 3: Determine Net Cash Flows from Investing and Financing Activities

After you have determined the items affecting net cash provided by operating activities, the next step involves analyzing the remaining changes in balance sheet accounts. Tax Consultants Inc. analyzed the following accounts.

Increase in Land. As indicated from the change in the land account, the company purchased land of $70,000 during the period. This transaction is an investing activity, reported as a use of cash.

Increase in Building and Related Accumulated Depreciation. As indicated in the additional data, and from the change in the building account, Tax Consultants acquired an office building using $200,000 cash. This transaction is a cash outflow, reported in the investing section. The $11,000 increase in accumulated depreciation results from recording depreciation expense on the building. As indicated earlier, the reported depreciation expense has no effect on the amount of cash.

Increase in Equipment and Related Accumulated Depreciation. An increase in equipment of $68,000 resulted because the company used cash to purchase equipment. This transaction is an outflow of cash from an investing activity. The depreciation expense entry for the period explains the increase in Accumulated Depreciation—Equipment.

Increase in Bonds Payable. The bonds payable account increased $150,000. Cash received from the issuance of these bonds represents an inflow of cash from a financing activity.

Increase in Retained Earnings. Retained earnings increased $116,000 during the year. Two factors explain this increase: (1) Net income of $134,000 increased retained earnings, and (2) dividends of $18,000 decreased retained earnings. As indicated earlier, the company adjusts net income to net cash provided by operating activities in the operating activities section. Payment of the dividends is a financing activity that involves a cash outflow.

Statement of Cash Flows—2007

Combining the foregoing items, we get a statement of cash flows for 2007 for Tax Consultants Inc., using the indirect method to compute net cash flow from operating activities.

ILLUSTRATION 23-13
Statement of Cash Flows, Tax Consultants Inc., Year 2

TAX CONSULTANTS INC.
STATEMENT OF CASH FLOWS
FOR THE YEAR ENDED DECEMBER 31, 2007
INCREASE (DECREASE) IN CASH

Cash flows from operating activities		
Net income		$134,000
Adjustments to reconcile net income to		
net cash provided by operating activities:		
Depreciation expense	$ 21,000	
Decrease in accounts receivable	10,000	
Increase in prepaid expenses	(6,000)	
Increase in accounts payable	35,000	60,000
Net cash provided by operating activities		194,000
Cash flows from investing activities		
Purchase of land	(70,000)	
Purchase of building	(200,000)	
Purchase of equipment	(68,000)	
Net cash used by investing activities		(338,000)
Cash flows from financing activities		
Issuance of bonds	150,000	
Payment of cash dividends	(18,000)	
Net cash provided by financing activities		132,000
Net decrease in cash		(12,000)
Cash, January 1, 2007		49,000
Cash, December 31, 2007		$ 37,000

THIRD EXAMPLE—2008

Our third example, covering the 2008 operations of Tax Consultants Inc., is more complex. It again uses the indirect method to compute and present net cash flow from operating activities.

Tax Consultants Inc. experienced continued success in 2008 and expanded its operations to include the sale of computer software used in tax-return preparation and tax planning. Thus, inventory is a new asset appearing in the company's December 31, 2008, balance sheet. Illustrations 23-14 and 23-15 show the comparative balance sheets, income statements, and selected data for 2008.

ILLUSTRATION 23-14
Comparative Balance
Sheets, Tax Consultants
Inc., Year 3

TAX CONSULTANTS INC.
COMPARATIVE BALANCE SHEETS
AS OF DECEMBER 31

Assets	2008	2007	Change Increase/Decrease
Cash	$ 54,000	$ 37,000	$ 17,000 Increase
Accounts receivable	68,000	26,000	42,000 Increase
Inventories	54,000	–0–	54,000 Increase
Prepaid expenses	4,000	6,000	2,000 Decrease
Land	45,000	70,000	25,000 Decrease
Buildings	200,000	200,000	–0–
Accumulated depreciation—buildings	(21,000)	(11,000)	10,000 Increase
Equipment	193,000	68,000	125,000 Increase
Accumulated depreciation—equipment	(28,000)	(10,000)	18,000 Increase
Totals	$569,000	$386,000	

Liabilities and Stockholders' Equity			
Accounts payable	$ 33,000	$ 40,000	$ 7,000 Decrease
Bonds payable	110,000	150,000	40,000 Decrease
Common stock ($1 par)	220,000	60,000	160,000 Increase
Retained earnings	206,000	136,000	70,000 Increase
Totals	$569,000	$386,000	

ILLUSTRATION 23-15
Income Statement, Tax
Consultants Inc., Year 3

TAX CONSULTANTS INC.
INCOME STATEMENT
FOR THE YEAR ENDED DECEMBER 31, 2008

Revenues		$890,000
Cost of goods sold	$465,000	
Operating expenses	221,000	
Interest expense	12,000	
Loss on sale of equipment	2,000	700,000
Income from operations		190,000
Income tax expense		65,000
Net income		$125,000

Additional Information
(a) Operating expenses include depreciation expense of $33,000 and amortization of prepaid expenses of $2,000.
(b) Land was sold at its book value for cash.
(c) Cash dividends of $55,000 were declared and paid.
(d) Interest expense of $12,000 was paid in cash.
(e) Equipment with a cost of $166,000 was purchased for cash. Equipment with a cost of $41,000 and a book value of $36,000 was sold for $34,000 cash.
(f) Bonds were redeemed at their book value for cash.
(g) Common stock ($1 par) was issued for cash.

Step 1: Determine the Change in Cash

The first step in the preparation of the statement of cash flows is to determine the change in cash. As the comparative balance sheets show, cash increased $17,000 in 2008.

Step 2: Determine Net Cash Flow from Operating Activities—Indirect Method

We explain the adjustments to net income of $125,000 as follows.

Increase in Accounts Receivable. The increase in accounts receivable of $42,000 represents recorded accrual-basis revenues in excess of cash collections in 2008. The company deducts this increase from net income to convert from the accrual basis to the cash basis.

Increase in Inventories. The $54,000 increase in inventories represents an operating use of cash, not an expense. Tax Consultants therefore deducts this amount from net income, to arrive at net cash flow from operations. In other words, when inventory purchased exceeds inventory sold during a period, cost of goods sold on an accrual basis is lower than on a cash basis.

Decrease in Prepaid Expenses. The $2,000 decrease in prepaid expenses represents a charge to the income statement for which Tax Consultants made no cash payment in the current period. The company adds back the decrease to net income, to arrive at net cash flow from operating activities.

Decrease in Accounts Payable. When accounts payable decrease during the year, cost of goods sold and expenses on a cash basis are higher than they are on an accrual basis. To convert net income to net cash flow from operating activities, the company must deduct the $7,000 in accounts payable from net income.

Depreciation Expense (Increase in Accumulated Depreciation). Accumulated Depreciation—Buildings increased $10,000 ($21,000 − $11,000). The Buildings account did not change during the period, which means that Tax Consultants recorded depreciation expense of $10,000 in 2008.

Accumulated Depreciation—Equipment increased by $18,000 ($28,000 − $10,000) during the year. But Accumulated Depreciation—Equipment decreased by $5,000 as a result of the sale during the year. Thus, depreciation for the year was $23,000. The company reconciled Accumulated Depreciation—Equipment as follows.

Beginning balance	$10,000
Add: Depreciation for 2008	23,000
	33,000
Deduct: Sale of equipment	5,000
Ending balance	$28,000

The company must add back to net income the total depreciation of $33,000 ($10,000 + $23,000) charged to the income statement, to determine net cash flow from operating activities.

Loss on Sale of Equipment. Tax Consultants Inc. sold for $34,000 equipment that cost $41,000 and had a book value of $36,000. As a result, the company reported a loss of $2,000 on its sale. To arrive at net cash flow from operating activities, it must add back to net income the loss on the sale of the equipment. The reason is that the loss is a noncash charge to the income statement. The loss did not reduce cash, but it did reduce net income.

From the foregoing items, the company prepares the operating activities section of the statement of cash flows, as shown in Illustration 23-16.

ILLUSTRATION 23-16
Operating Activities Section of Cash Flows Statement

Cash flows from operating activities		
Net income		$125,000
Adjustments to reconcile net income to		
net cash provided by operating activities:		
Depreciation expense	$33,000	
Loss on sale of equipment	2,000	
Increase in accounts receivable	(42,000)	
Increase in inventories	(54,000)	
Decrease in prepaid expenses	2,000	
Decrease in accounts payable	(7,000)	(66,000)
Net cash provided by operating activities		59,000

Step 3: Determine Net Cash Flows from Investing and Financing Activities

By analyzing the remaining changes in the balance sheet accounts, Tax Consultants identifies cash flows from investing and financing activities.

Land. Land decreased $25,000 during the period. As indicated from the information presented, the company sold land for cash at its book value. This transaction is an investing activity, reported as a $25,000 source of cash.

Equipment. An analysis of the equipment account indicates the following.

Beginning balance	$ 68,000
Purchase of equipment	166,000
	234,000
Sale of equipment	41,000
Ending balance	$193,000

The company used cash to purchase equipment with a fair value of $166,000—an investing transaction reported as a cash outflow. The sale of the equipment for $34,000 is also an investing activity, but one that generates a cash inflow.

Bonds Payable. Bonds payable decreased $40,000 during the year. As indicated from the additional information, the company redeemed the bonds at their book value. This financing transaction used $40,000 of cash.

Common Stock. The common stock account increased $160,000 during the year. As indicated from the additional information, Tax Consultants issued common stock of $160,000 at par. This financing transaction provided cash of $160,000.

Retained Earnings. Retained earnings changed $70,000 ($206,000 − $136,000) during the year. The $70,000 change in retained earnings results from net income of $125,000 from operations and the financing activity of paying cash dividends of $55,000.

Statement of Cash Flows—2008

Tax Consultants Inc. combines the foregoing items to prepare the statement of cash flows shown in Illustration 23-17.

ILLUSTRATION 23-17
Statement of Cash Flows, Tax Consultants Inc., Year 3

TAX CONSULTANTS INC.
STATEMENT OF CASH FLOWS
FOR THE YEAR ENDED DECEMBER 31, 2008
INCREASE (DECREASE) IN CASH

Cash flows from operating activities		
Net income		$125,000
Adjustments to reconcile net income to		
net cash provided by operating activities:		
Depreciation expense	$ 33,000	
Loss on sale of equipment	2,000	
Increase in accounts receivable	(42,000)	
Increase in inventories	(54,000)	
Decrease in prepaid expenses	2,000	
Decrease in accounts payable	(7,000)	(66,000)
Net cash provided by operating activities		59,000
Cash flows from investing activities		
Sale of land	25,000	
Sale of equipment	34,000	
Purchase of equipment	(166,000)	
Net cash used by investing activities		(107,000)
Cash flows from financing activities		
Redemption of bonds	(40,000)	
Sale of common stock	160,000	
Payment of dividends	(55,000)	
Net cash provided by financing activities		65,000
Net increase in cash		17,000
Cash, January 1, 2008		37,000
Cash, December 31, 2008		$ 54,000

SOURCES OF INFORMATION FOR THE STATEMENT OF CASH FLOWS

OBJECTIVE 7
Identify sources of information for a statement of cash flows.

Important points to remember in the preparation of the statement of cash flows are these:

1 Comparative balance sheets provide the basic information from which to prepare the report. Additional information obtained from analyses of specific accounts is also included.

2 An analysis of the Retained Earnings account is necessary. The net increase or decrease in Retained Earnings without any explanation is a meaningless amount in the statement. Without explanation, it might represent the effect of net income, dividends declared, or prior period adjustments.

3 The statement includes all changes that have passed through cash or have resulted in an increase or decrease in cash.

4 Writedowns, amortization charges, and similar "book" entries, such as depreciation of plant assets, represent neither inflows nor outflows of cash, because they have no effect on cash. To the extent that they have entered into the determination of net income, however, the company must add them back to or subtract them from net income, to arrive at net cash provided by operating activities.

NET CASH FLOW FROM OPERATING ACTIVITIES—INDIRECT VERSUS DIRECT METHOD

As we discussed previously, the two different methods available to adjust income from operations on an accrual basis to net cash flow from operating activities are the indirect (reconciliation) method and the direct (income statement) method.

The FASB encourages use of the direct method and permits use of the indirect method. Yet, if the direct method is used, the Board requires that companies provide in a separate schedule a reconciliation of net income to net cash flow from operating activities. Therefore, under either method, companies must prepare and report information from the indirect (reconciliation) method.

Indirect Method

For consistency and comparability and because it is the most widely used method in practice, we used the indirect method in the examples just presented. We determined net cash flows from operating activities by adding back to or deducting from net income those items that had no effect on cash. Illustration 23-18 (page 1229) presents more completely the common types of adjustments that companies make to net income to arrive at net cash flow from operating activities.

The additions and deductions listed on page 1229 reconcile net income to net cash flow from operating activities, illustrating why the indirect method is also called the reconciliation method.

Direct Method—An Example

Under the direct method the statement of cash flows reports net cash flow from operating activities as major classes of *operating cash receipts* (e.g., cash collected from customers and cash received from interest and dividends) and *cash disbursements* (e.g., cash paid to suppliers for goods, to employees for services, to creditors for interest, and to government authorities for taxes).

We illustrate the direct method here in more detail to help you understand the difference between accrual-based income and net cash flow from operating activities. This

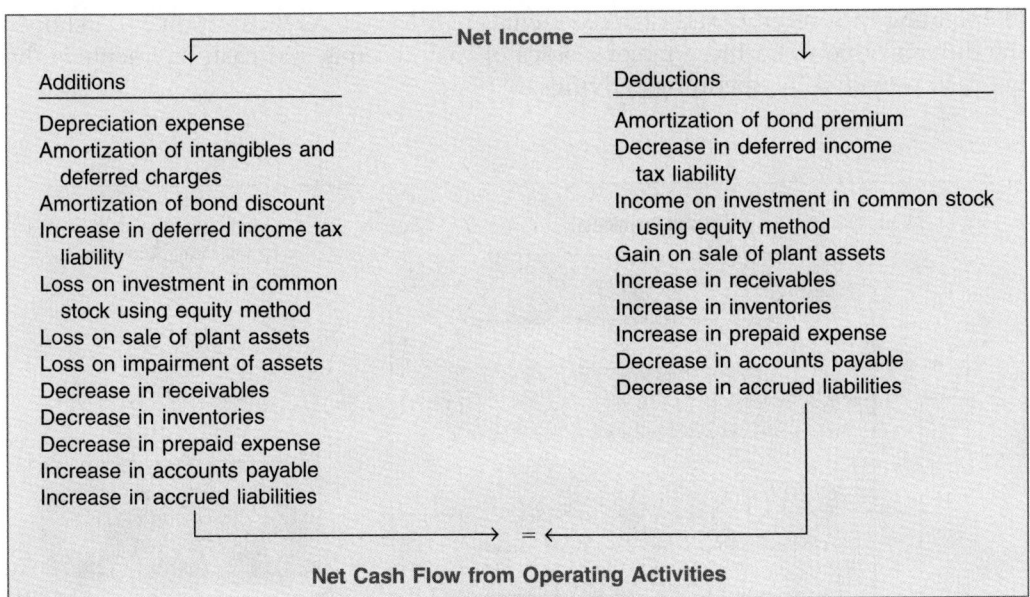

ILLUSTRATION 23-18
Adjustments Needed to
Determine Net Cash
Flow from Operating
Activities—Indirect
Method

example also illustrates the data needed to apply the direct method. Emig Company, which began business on January 1, 2008, has the following selected balance sheet information.

	December 31	
	2008	2007
Cash	$159,000	–0–
Accounts receivable	15,000	–0–
Inventory	160,000	–0–
Prepaid expenses	8,000	–0–
Property, plant, and equipment (net)	90,000	–0–
Accounts payable	60,000	–0–
Accrued expenses payable	20,000	–0–

ILLUSTRATION 23-19
Balance Sheet Accounts,
Emig Co.

Emig Company's December 31, 2008, income statement and additional information are as follows.

Revenues from sales		$780,000
Cost of goods sold		450,000
Gross profit		330,000
Operating expenses	$160,000	
Depreciation	10,000	170,000
Income before income taxes		160,000
Income tax expense		48,000
Net income		$112,000

Additional Information:
(a) Dividends of $70,000 were declared and paid in cash.
(b) The accounts payable increase resulted from the purchase of merchandise.
(c) Prepaid expenses and accrued expenses payable relate to operating expenses.

ILLUSTRATION 23-20
Income Statement,
Emig Co.

Under the **direct method**, companies compute net cash provided by operating activities by **adjusting each item in the income statement** from the accrual basis to the cash basis. To simplify and condense the operating activities section, only major classes of operating cash receipts and cash payments are reported. As Illustration 23-21 shows, the difference between these major classes of cash receipts and cash payments is the net cash provided by operating activities.

ILLUSTRATION 23-21
Major Classes of Cash
Receipts and Payments

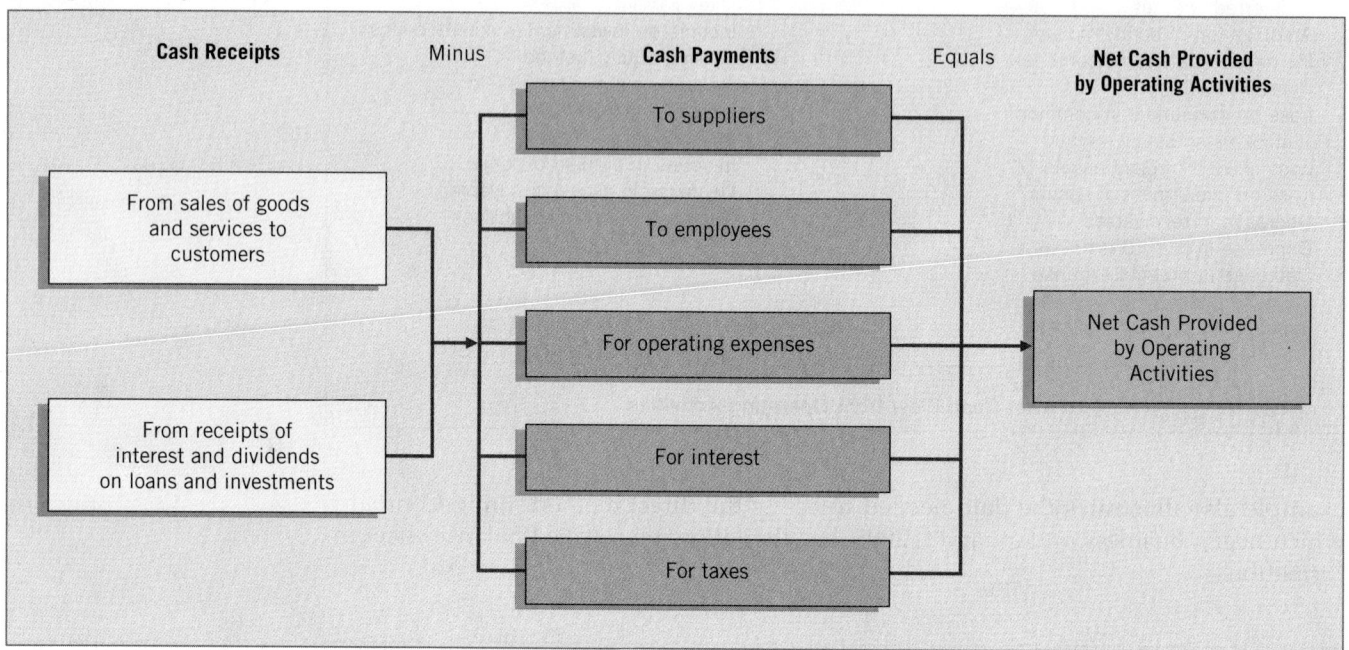

An efficient way to apply the direct method is to analyze the revenues and expenses reported in the income statement in the order in which they are listed. The company then determines cash receipts and cash payments related to these revenues and expenses. In the following sections, we present the direct method adjustments for Emig Company in 2008, to determine net cash provided by operating activities.

Cash Receipts from Customers. The income statement for Emig Company reported revenues from customers of $780,000. To determine cash receipts from customers, the company considers the change in accounts receivable during the year.

When accounts receivable increase during the year, revenues on an accrual basis are higher than cash receipts from customers. In other words, operations led to increased revenues, but not all of these revenues resulted in cash receipts. To determine the amount of increase in cash receipts, deduct the amount of the increase in accounts receivable from the total sales revenues. Conversely, a decrease in accounts receivable is added to sales revenues, because cash receipts from customers then exceed sales revenues.

For Emig Company, accounts receivable increased $15,000. Thus, cash receipts from customers were $765,000, computed as follows.

Revenues from sales	$780,000
Deduct: Increase in accounts receivable	15,000
Cash receipts from customers	$765,000

Emig could also determine cash receipts from customers by analyzing the Accounts Receivable account as shown below.

Accounts Receivable

1/1/08	Balance	–0–	Receipts from customers	765,000
	Revenue from sales	780,000		
12/31/08	Balance	15,000		

Illustration 23-22 shows the relationships between cash receipts from customers, revenues from sales, and changes in accounts receivable.

Cash receipts from customers	=	Revenues from sales	+ Decrease in accounts receivable or − Increase in accounts receivable

ILLUSTRATION 23-22
Formula to Compute Cash Receipts from Customers

Cash Payments to Suppliers. Emig Company reported cost of goods sold on its income statement of $450,000. To determine cash payments to suppliers, the company first finds purchases for the year, by adjusting cost of goods sold for the change in inventory. When inventory increases during the year, purchases this year exceed cost of goods sold. As a result, the company adds the increase in inventory to cost of goods sold, to arrive at purchases.

In 2008, Emig Company's inventory increased $160,000. The company computes purchases as follows.

Cost of goods sold	$450,000
Add: Increase in inventory	160,000
Purchases	$610,000

After computing purchases, Emig determines cash payments to suppliers by adjusting purchases for the change in accounts payable. When accounts payable increase during the year, purchases on an accrual basis are higher than they are on a cash basis. As a result, it deducts from purchases the increase in accounts payable to arrive at cash payments to suppliers. Conversely, if cash payments to suppliers exceed purchases, Emig adds to purchases the decrease in accounts payable. Cash payments to suppliers were $550,000, computed as follows.

Purchases	$610,000
Deduct: Increase in accounts payable	60,000
Cash payments to suppliers	$550,000

Emig also can determine cash payments to suppliers by analyzing Accounts Payable, as shown below.

Accounts Payable

Payments to suppliers	550,000	1/1/08	Balance	–0–
			Purchases	610,000
		12/31/08	Balance	60,000

Illustration 23-23 shows the relationships between cash payments to suppliers, cost of goods sold, changes in inventory, and changes in accounts payable.

Cash payments to suppliers	=	Cost of goods sold	+ Increase in inventory or − Decrease in inventory	+ Decrease in accounts payable or − Increase in accounts payable

ILLUSTRATION 23-23
Formula to Compute Cash Payments to Suppliers

Cash Payments for Operating Expenses. Emig reported operating expenses of $160,000 on its income statement. To determine the cash paid for operating expenses, it must adjust this amount for any changes in prepaid expenses and accrued expenses payable.

For example, when prepaid expenses increased $8,000 during the year, cash paid for operating expenses was $8,000 higher than operating expenses reported on the income statement. To convert operating expenses to cash payments for operating expenses, the company adds to operating expenses the increase of $8,000. Conversely, if prepaid expenses decrease during the year, it deducts from operating expenses the amount of the decrease.

Emig also must adjust operating expenses for changes in accrued expenses payable. When accrued expenses payable increase during the year, operating expenses on an accrual basis are higher than they are on a cash basis. As a result, the company deducts from operating expenses an increase in accrued expenses payable, to arrive at cash payments for operating expenses. Conversely, it adds to operating expenses a decrease in accrued expenses payable, because cash payments exceed operating expenses.

Emig Company's cash payments for operating expenses were $148,000, computed as follows.

Operating expenses	$160,000
Add: Increase in prepaid expenses	8,000
Deduct: Increase in accrued expenses payable	(20,000)
Cash payments for operating expenses	$148,000

The relationships among cash payments for operating expenses, changes in prepaid expenses, and changes in accrued expenses payable are shown in Illustration 23-24.

ILLUSTRATION 23-24
Formula to Compute
Cash Payments for
Operating Expenses

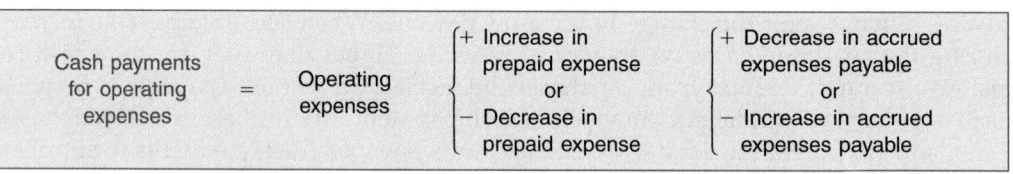

Note that the company did not consider depreciation expense, because it is a non-cash charge.

Cash Payments for Income Taxes. The income statement for Emig shows income tax expense of $48,000. This amount equals the cash paid. How do we know that? Because the comparative balance sheet indicated no income taxes payable at either the beginning or end of the year.

Summary of Net Cash Flow from Operating Activities—Direct Method

The following schedule summarizes the computations illustrated above.

ILLUSTRATION 23-25
Accrual Basis to Cash
Basis

Accrual Basis		Adjustment	Add (Subtract)	Cash Basis
Revenues from sales	$780,000	− Increase in accounts receivable	$(15,000)	$765,000
Cost of goods sold	450,000	+ Increase in inventory	160,000	
		− Increase in accounts payable	(60,000)	550,000
Operating expenses	160,000	+ Increase in prepaid expenses	8,000	
		− Increase in accrued expenses payable	(20,000)	148,000
Depreciation expense	10,000	− Depreciation expense	(10,000)	–0–
Income tax expense	48,000			48,000
Total expense	668,000			746,000
Net income	$112,000	Net cash provided by operating activities		$ 19,000

Illustration 23-26 shows the presentation of the direct method for reporting net cash flow from operating activities for the Emig Company illustration.

EMIG COMPANY		
STATEMENT OF CASH FLOWS (PARTIAL)		
Cash flows from operating activities		
Cash received from customers		$765,000
Cash payments:		
To suppliers	$ 550,000	
For operating expenses	148,000	
For income taxes	48,000	746,000
Net cash provided by operating activities		$ 19,000

ILLUSTRATION 23-26
Operating Activities
Section—Direct Method,
2008

If Emig Company uses the direct method to present the net cash flows from operating activities, it must provide in a separate schedule the reconciliation of net income to net cash provided by operating activities. The reconciliation assumes the identical form and content of the indirect method of presentation, as shown below.

EMIG COMPANY		
RECONCILIATION		
Net income		$112,000
Adjustments to reconcile net income to net cash		
provided by operating activities:		
Depreciation expense	$ 10,000	
Increase in accounts receivable	(15,000)	
Increase in inventory	(160,000)	
Increase in prepaid expenses	(8,000)	
Increase in accounts payable	60,000	
Increase in accrued expense payable	20,000	(93,000)
Net cash provided by operating activities		$ 19,000

ILLUSTRATION 23-27
Reconciliation of Net
Income to Net Cash
Provided by Operating
Activities

When the direct method is used, the company may present this reconciliation at the bottom of the statement of cash flows or in a separate schedule.

Direct Versus Indirect Controversy

The most contentious decision that the FASB faced in issuing *Statement No. 95* was choosing between the direct method and the indirect method of determining net cash flow from operating activities. Companies lobbied *against* the direct method, urging adoption of the indirect method. Commercial lending officers expressed to the FASB a strong preference in favor of the direct method. In the next two sections, we consider the arguments in favor of each of the methods.

In Favor of the Direct Method

The principal advantage of the direct method is that **it shows operating cash receipts and payments**. Thus, it is more consistent with the objective of a statement of cash flows—to provide information about cash receipts and cash payments—than the indirect method, which does not report operating cash receipts and payments.

Supporters of the direct method contend that knowledge of the specific sources of operating cash receipts and the purposes for which operating cash payments were made in past periods is useful in estimating future operating cash flows. Furthermore, information about amounts of major classes of operating cash receipts and payments is more useful than information only about their arithmetic sum (the net cash flow from operating activities). Such information is more revealing of a company's ability (1) to generate sufficient cash from operating activities to pay its debts, (2) to reinvest in its operations, and (3) to make distributions to its owners.[8]

Many companies indicate that they do not currently collect information in a manner that allows them to determine amounts such as cash received from customers or cash paid to suppliers directly from their accounting systems. But supporters of the direct method contend that the incremental cost of determining operating cash receipts and payments is not significant.

In Favor of the Indirect Method

The principal advantage of the indirect method is that **it focuses on the differences between net income and net cash flow from operating activities**. That is, it provides a useful link between the statement of cash flows and the income statement and balance sheet.

Many companies contend that it is less costly to adjust net income to net cash flow from operating activities (indirect) than it is to report gross operating cash receipts and payments (direct). Supporters of the indirect method also state that the direct method, which effectively reports income statement information on a cash rather than an accrual basis, may erroneously suggest that net cash flow from operating activities is as good as, or better than, net income as a measure of performance.

Special Rules Applying to Direct and Indirect Methods

Companies that use the direct method are required, at a minimum, to report separately the following classes of operating cash receipts and payments:

INTERNATIONAL INSIGHT

Consolidated statements of cash flows may be of limited use to analysts evaluating multinational companies. Without disaggregation, users of such statements are not able to determine "where in the world" the funds are sourced and used.

Receipts

1 Cash collected from customers (including lessees, licensees, etc.).

2 Interest and dividends received.

3 Other operating cash receipts, if any.

Payments

1 Cash paid to employees and suppliers of goods or services (including suppliers of insurance, advertising, etc.).

2 Interest paid.

3 Income taxes paid.

4 Other operating cash payments, if any.

The FASB encourages companies to provide further breakdowns of operating cash receipts and payments that they consider meaningful.

Companies using the indirect method must disclose separately changes in inventory, receivables, and payables in order to reconcile net income to net cash flow from operating activities. In addition, they must disclose, elsewhere in the financial statements or in accompanying notes, interest paid (net of amount capitalized) and income taxes paid.[9] The FASB requires these separate and additional disclosures so that users may approximate the direct method. Also, an acceptable alternative presentation of the indirect method is to report net cash flow from operating activities as a single line item in the statement of cash flows and to present the reconciliation details elsewhere in the financial statements.

---

[8]"Statement of Cash Flows," pars. 107 and 111.

[9]*Accounting Trends and Techniques—2004* reports that of the 600 companies surveyed, 310 disclosed interest paid in notes to the financial statements, 264 disclosed interest paid at the bottom of the statement of cash flows, 9 disclosed interest paid within the statement of cash flows, and 17 reported no separate amount. Income taxes paid during the year were disclosed in a manner similar to interest payments.

NOT WHAT IT SEEMS

WHAT DO THE
NUMBERS MEAN?

The controversy over direct and indirect methods highlights the importance that the market attributes to operating cash flow. By showing an improving cash flow, a company can give a favorable impression of its ongoing operations. For example, **WorldCom** concealed declines in its operations by capitalizing certain operating expenses—to the tune of $3.8 billion! This practice not only "juiced up" income but also made it possible to report the cash payments in the investing section of the cash flow statement rather than as a deduction from operating cash flow.

The SEC recently addressed a similar cash flow classification issue with automakers like **Ford, GM,** and **Daimler-Chrysler**. For years, automakers classified lease receivables and other dealer-financing arrangements as investment cash flows. Thus, they reported an increase in lease or loan receivables from cars sold as a use of cash in the investing section of the statement of cash flows. The SEC objected and now requires automakers to report these receivables as operating cash flows, since the leases and loans are used to facilitate car sales. At GM, these reclassifications reduced its operating cash flows from $7.6 billion to $3 billion in the year before the change. So while the overall cash flow—from operations, investing, and financing—remained the same, operating cash flow at these companies looked better than it really was.

Source: Peter Elstrom, "How to Hide $3.8 Billion in Expenses," *BusinessWeek Online* (July 8, 2002); and Judith Burns, "SEC Tells US Automakers to Retool Cash-Flow Accounting," *Wall Street Journal Online* (February 28, 2005).

| SPECIAL PROBLEMS IN STATEMENT PREPARATION | SECTION 2 |

We discussed some of the special problems related to preparing the statement of cash flows in connection with the preceding illustrations. Other problems that arise with some frequency in the preparation of this statement include the following.

OBJECTIVE 8
Discuss special problems in preparing a statement of cash flows.

1 Adjustments similar to depreciation.
2 Accounts receivable (net).
3 Other working capital changes.
4 Net losses.
5 Gains.
6 Stock options.
7 Postretirement benefit cost.
8 Extraordinary items.
9 Significant noncash transactions.

ADJUSTMENTS SIMILAR TO DEPRECIATION

Depreciation expense is the most common adjustment to net income that companies make to arrive at net cash flow from operating activities. But there are numerous other noncash expense or revenue items. Examples of expense items that companies must add back to net income are the **amortization of limited-life intangible assets** such as patents, and the **amortization of deferred costs** such as bond issue costs. These charges to expense involve expenditures made in prior periods that a company amortizes currently. These charges reduce net income without affecting cash in the current period.

Also, **amortization of bond discount or premium** on long-term bonds payable affects the amount of interest expense. However, neither changes cash. As a result, a company should add back discount amortization and subtract premium amortization from net income to arrive at net cash flow from operating activities.

In a similar manner, **changes in deferred income taxes** affect net income but have no effect on cash. For example, **Delta Airlines** reported an increase in its liability for deferred taxes of approximately $1.2 billion. This change in the liability increased tax expense and decreased net income, but did not affect cash. Therefore, Delta added back $1.2 billion to net income on its statement of cash flows.

Another common adjustment to net income is **a change related to an investment in common stock** when recording income or loss under the equity method. Recall that under the equity method, the investor (1) debits the investment account and credits revenue for its share of the investee's net income, and (2) credits dividends received to the investment account. Therefore, the net increase in the investment account does not affect cash flow. A company must deduct the net increase from net income to arrive at net cash flow from operating activities.

Assume that Victor Co. owns 40 percent of Milo Inc. During the year Milo reports net income of $100,000 and pays a cash dividend of $30,000. Victor reports this in its statement of cash flows as a deduction from net income in the following manner—Equity in earnings of Milo, net of dividends, $28,000 [($100,000 − $30,000) × 40%].

If Victor Co. does not exercise significant influence over Milo, it cannot use the equity method. Instead, it uses the fair-value method. Under the fair-value method, Victor does not recognize any of Milo's net income. Further, it records any cash dividend received as revenue. As a result, the company makes no adjustment to net income in the statement of cash flows because cash dividends received are included in income.

ACCOUNTS RECEIVABLE (NET)

Up to this point, we assumed no allowance for doubtful accounts—a contra account—to offset accounts receivable. However, if a company needs an allowance for doubtful accounts, how does that allowance affect the company's determination of net cash flow from operating activities? For example, assume that Redmark Co. reports net income of $40,000. It has the accounts receivable balances as shown in Illustration 23-28.

ILLUSTRATION 23-28
Accounts Receivable
Balances, Redmark Co.

	2008	2007	Change Increase/Decrease
Accounts receivable	$105,000	$90,000	$15,000 Increase
Allowance for doubtful accounts	(10,000)	(4,000)	6,000 Increase
Accounts receivable (net)	$ 95,000	$86,000	9,000 Increase

Indirect Method

Because an increase in the Allowance for Doubtful Accounts results from a charge to bad debts expense, a company should add back an increase in the Allowance for Doubtful Accounts to net income to arrive at net cash flow from operating activities. Illustration 23-29 shows one method for presenting this information in a statement of cash flows.

ILLUSTRATION 23-29
Presentation of
Allowance for Doubtful
Accounts—Indirect
Method

REDMARK CO. STATEMENT OF CASH FLOWS (PARTIAL) FOR THE YEAR 2008		
Cash flows from operating activities		
Net income		$40,000
Adjustments to reconcile net income to net cash provided by operating activities:		
Increase in accounts receivable	$(15,000)	
Increase in allowance for doubtful accounts	6,000	(9,000)
		$31,000

As we indicated, the increase in the Allowance for Doubtful Accounts balance results from a charge to bad debt expense for the year. Because bad debt expense is a noncash charge, a company must add it back to net income in arriving at net cash flow from operating activities.

Instead of separately analyzing the allowance account, a short-cut approach is to net the allowance balance against the receivable balance and compare the change in accounts receivable on a net basis. Illustration 23-30 shows this presentation.

REDMARK CO. STATEMENT OF CASH FLOWS (PARTIAL) FOR THE YEAR 2008	
Cash flows from operating activities	
Net income	$40,000
Adjustments to reconcile net income to net cash provided by operating activities:	
Increase in accounts receivable (net)	(9,000)
	$31,000

ILLUSTRATION 23-30
Net Approach to
Allowance for Doubtful
Accounts—Indirect
Method

This short-cut procedure works also if the change in the allowance account results from a writeoff of accounts receivable. This reduces both the Accounts Receivable and the Allowance for Doubtful Accounts. No effect on cash flows occurs. Because of its simplicity, *use the net approach for your homework assignments.*

Direct Method

If using the direct method, a company **should not net** the Allowance for Doubtful Accounts against Accounts Receivable. To illustrate, assume that Redmark Co.'s net income of $40,000 consisted of the following items.

REDMARK CO. INCOME STATEMENT FOR THE YEAR 2008		
Sales		$100,000
Expenses		
Salaries	$46,000	
Utilities	8,000	
Bad debts	6,000	60,000
Net income		$ 40,000

ILLUSTRATION 23-31
Income Statement,
Redmark Co.

If Redmark deducts the $9,000 increase in accounts receivable (net) from sales for the year, it would report cash sales at $91,000 ($100,000 − $9,000) and cash payments for operating expenses at $60,000. Both items would be misstated: Cash sales should be reported at $85,000 ($100,000 − $15,000), and total cash payments for operating expenses should be reported at $54,000 ($60,000 − $6,000). Illustration 23-32 shows the proper presentation.

REDMARK CO. STATEMENT OF CASH FLOWS (PARTIAL) FOR THE YEAR 2008		
Cash flows from operating activities		
Cash received from customers		$85,000
Salaries paid	$46,000	
Utilities paid	8,000	54,000
Net cash provided by operating activities		$31,000

ILLUSTRATION 23-32
Bad Debts—Direct
Method

An added complication develops when a company writes off accounts receivable. Simply adjusting sales for the change in accounts receivable will not provide the proper amount of cash sales. The reason is that the writeoff of the accounts receivable is not a cash collection. Thus an additional adjustment is necessary.

OTHER WORKING CAPITAL CHANGES

Up to this point, we showed how companies handled all of the changes in working capital items (current asset and current liability items) as adjustments to net income in determining net cash flow from operating activities. You must be careful, however, because **some changes in working capital, although they affect cash, do not affect net income**. Generally, these are investing or financing activities of a current nature.

One activity is the purchase of **short-term available-for-sale securities**. For example, the purchase of short-term available-for-sale securities for $50,000 cash has no effect on net income but it does cause a $50,000 decrease in cash.[10] A company reports this transaction as a cash flow from investing activities as follows.[11]

Cash flows from investing activities	
Purchase of short-term available-for-sale securities	$(50,000)

What about **trading securities**? Because companies hold these investments principally for the purpose of selling them in the near term, companies should classify the cash flows from purchases and sales of trading securities as cash flows from **operating activities**.[12]

Another example is the issuance of a **short-term nontrade note payable** for cash. This change in a working capital item has no effect on income from operations but it increases cash by the amount of the note payable. For example, a company reports the issuance of a $10,000 short-term note payable for cash in the statement of cash flows as follows.

Cash flows from financing activities	
Issuance of short-term note	$10,000

Another change in a working capital item that has no effect on income from operations or on cash is a **cash dividend payable**. Although a company will report the cash dividends when paid as a financing activity, it does not report the declared but unpaid dividend on the statement of cash flows.

NET LOSSES

If a company reports a net loss instead of a net income, it must adjust the net loss for those items that do not result in a cash inflow or outflow. The net loss, after adjusting for the charges or credits not affecting cash, may result in a negative or a positive cash flow from operating activities.

For example, if the net loss is $50,000 and the total amount of charges to add back is $60,000, then net cash provided by operating activities is $10,000. Illustration 23-33 shows this computation.

---

[10] If the basis of the statement of cash flows is **cash and cash equivalents** and the short-term investment is considered a cash equivalent, then a company reports nothing in the statement because the transaction does not affect the balance of cash and cash equivalents. The Board notes that cash purchases of short term investments generally are part of the company's cash management activities rather than part of its operating, investing, or financing activities.

[11] "Accounting for Certain Investments in Debt and Equity Securities," *Statement of Financial Accounting Standards No. 115* (Norwalk, Conn.: 1993), par. 118.

[12] Ibid., par. 118.

Net loss		$(50,000)
Adjustments to reconcile net income to net cash provided by operating activities:		
Depreciation of plant assets	$55,000	
Amortization of patents	5,000	60,000
Net cash provided by operating activities		$ 10,000

If the company experiences a net loss of $80,000 and the total amount of the charges to add back is $25,000, the presentation appears as follows.

Net loss	$(80,000)
Adjustments to reconcile net income to net cash used by operating activities:	
Depreciation of plant assets	25,000
Net cash used by operating activities	$(55,000)

Although not illustrated in this chapter, a negative cash flow may result even if the company reports a net income.

GAINS

In the illustration for Tax Consultants, the company experienced a loss of $2,000 from the sale of equipment. The company added this loss to net income to compute net cash flow from operating activities because **the loss is a noncash charge in the income statement**.

If Tax Consultants experiences a **gain** from a sale of equipment it too requires an adjustment to net income. Because a company reports the gain in the statement of cash flows as part of the cash proceeds from the sale of equipment under investing activities, **it deducts the gain from net income to avoid double counting**—once as part of net income, and again as part of the cash proceeds from the sale.

STOCK OPTIONS

Recall for share-based compensation plans that companies are required to use the fair value method to determine total compensation cost. The compensation cost is then recognized as an expense in the periods in which the employee provides services. When Compensation Expense is debited, Paid-in Capital—Stock Options is often credited. Cash is not affected by recording the expense. **Therefore, the company must increase net income by the amount of compensation expense from stock options in computing net cash flow from operating activities.**

To illustrate how this information should be reported on a statement of cash flows, assume that First Wave Inc. grants 5,000 options to its CEO, Ann Johnson. Each option entitles Johnson to purchase one share of First Wave's $1 par value common stock at $50 per share at any time in the next two years (the service period). The fair value of the options is $200,000. First Wave records compensation expense in the first year as follows:

Compensation Expense ($200,000 ÷ 2)	100,000	
Paid-in Capital—Stock Options		100,000

In addition, if we assume that First Wave has a 35 percent tax rate, it would recognize a deferred tax asset of $35,000 ($100,000 × 35%) in the first year as follows:

Deferred Tax Asset	35,000	
Income Tax Expense		35,000

Therefore on the statement of cash flows for the first year, First Wave reports the following (assuming a net income of $600,000).

Net income	$600,000
Adjustments to reconcile net income to net cash provided by operating activities:	
Share-based compensation expense	100,000
Increase in deferred tax asset	(35,000)

As shown in First Wave's statement of cash flows, it adds the share-based compensation expense to net income because it is a non-cash expense. The increase in the deferred tax asset and the related reduction in income tax expense increase net income. Although the negative income tax expense increases net income, it does not increase cash. Therefore it should be deducted.

Subsequently, if Ann Johnson exercises her options, Third Wave reports "Cash provided by exercise of stock options" in the financing section of the statement of cash flows.[13]

POSTRETIREMENT BENEFIT COSTS

If a company has postretirement costs such as an employee pension plan, chances are that the pension expense recorded during a period will either be higher or lower than the cash funded. It will be higher when there is an unfunded liability and will be lower when there is a prepaid pension cost. When the expense is higher or lower than the cash paid, **the company must adjust net income by the difference between cash paid and the expense reported** in computing net cash flow from operating activities.

EXTRAORDINARY ITEMS

Companies should report **either as investing activities or as financing activities** cash flows from extraordinary transactions and other events whose effects are included in net income, but which are not related to operations.

For example, assume that Tax Consultants had land with a carrying value of $200,000, which was condemned by the state of Maine for a highway project. The condemnation proceeds received were $205,000, resulting in a gain of $5,000 less $2,000 of taxes. In the statement of cash flows (indirect method), the company would deduct the $5,000 gain from net income in the operating activities section. It would report the $205,000 cash inflow from the condemnation as an investing activity, as follows.

Cash flows from investing activities	
Condemnation of land	$205,000

UNDERLYING CONCEPTS

By rejecting the requirement to allocate taxes to the various activities, the Board invoked the cost-benefit constraint. The information would be beneficial, but the cost of providing such information would exceed the benefits of providing it.

Note that Tax Consultants handles the gain at its **gross** amount ($5,000), not net of tax. The company reports the cash received in the condemnation as an investing activity at $205,000, also exclusive of the tax effect.

The FASB requires companies to classify **all income taxes paid as operating cash outflows.** Some suggested that income taxes paid be allocated to investing and financing transactions. But the Board decided that allocation of income taxes paid to

---

[13]Companies receive a tax deduction related to share-based compensation plans at the time employees exercise their options. The amount of the deduction is equal to the difference between the market price of the stock and the exercise price at the date the employee purchases the stock, which in most cases, is much larger than the total compensation expense recorded. When the tax deduction exceeds the total compensation recorded, this provides an additional cash inflow to the company. For example, in a recent year **Cisco Systems** reported an additional cash inflow related to its stock option plans equal to $537 million. Under the provisions of *SFAS No. 123(R)*, this tax-related cash inflow is reported in the financing section of the statement of cash flows. See "Share-Based Payment," *Statement of Financial Accounting Standard No. 123(R)* (Norwalk, Conn.: FASB, 2004) par. 68.

operating, investing, and financing activities would be so complex and arbitrary that the benefits, if any, would not justify the costs involved. Under both the direct method and the indirect method, companies must disclose the total amount of income taxes paid.[14]

SIGNIFICANT NONCASH TRANSACTIONS

Because the statement of cash flows reports only the effects of operating, investing, and financing activities in terms of cash flows, it omits some **significant noncash transactions** and other events that are investing or financing activities. Among the more common of these noncash transactions that a company should report or disclose in some manner are the following.

1 Acquisition of assets by assuming liabilities (including capital lease obligations) or by issuing equity securities.

2 Exchanges of nonmonetary assets.

3 Refinancing of long-term debt.

4 Conversion of debt or preferred stock to common stock.

5 Issuance of equity securities to retire debt.

Examples of Cash Flow Statements

A company does not incorporate these noncash items in the statement of cash flows. If material in amount, these disclosures may be either narrative or summarized in a separate schedule at the bottom of the statement, or they may appear in a separate note or supplementary schedule to the financial statements.[15] Illustration 23-35 shows the presentation of these significant noncash transactions or other events in a separate schedule at the bottom of the statement of cash flows.

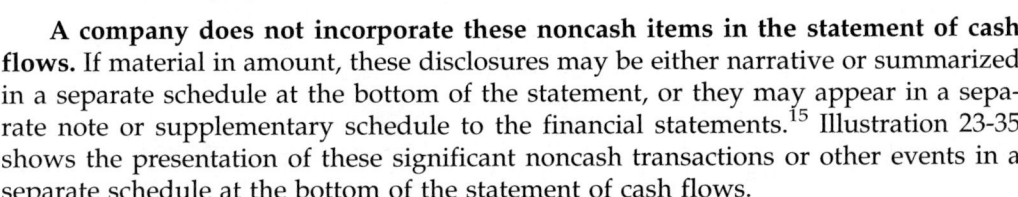

Net increase in cash	$3,717,000
Cash at beginning of year	5,208,000
Cash at end of year	$8,925,000
Noncash investing and financing activities	
Purchase of land and building through issuance of 250,000 shares of common stock	$1,750,000
Exchange of Steadfast, NY, land for Bedford, PA, land	$2,000,000
Conversion of 12% bonds to 50,000 shares of common stock	$ 500,000

ILLUSTRATION 23-35
Schedule Presentation of Noncash Investing and Financing Activities

Or, companies may present these noncash transactions in a separate note, as shown in Illustration 23-36.

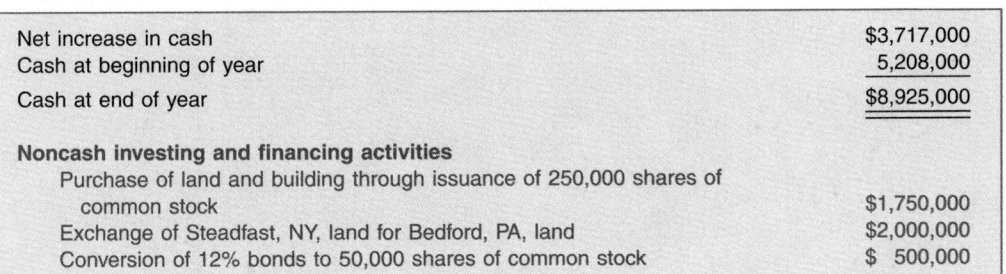

Note G: Significant noncash transactions. During the year the company engaged in the following significant noncash investing and financing transactions:	
Issued 250,000 shares of common stock to purchase land and building	$1,750,000
Exchanged land in Steadfast, NY, for land in Bedford, PA	$2,000,000
Converted 12% bonds due 2007 to 50,000 shares of common stock	$ 500,000

ILLUSTRATION 23-36
Note Presentation of Noncash Investing and Financing Activities

---

[14]For an insightful article on some weaknesses and limitations in the statement of cash flows caused by implementation of *FASB Statement No. 95*, see Hugo Nurnberg, "Inconsistencies and Ambiguities in Cash Flow Statements Under *FASB Statement No. 95*," *Accounting Horizons* (June 1993), pp. 60–73. Nurnberg identifies the inconsistencies caused by the three-way classification of all cash receipts and cash payments, gross versus net of tax, the ambiguous disclosure requirements for noncash investing and financing transactions, and the ambiguous presentation of third-party financing transactions. See also Paul B. W. Miller, and Bruce P. Budge, "Nonarticulation in Cash Flow Statements and Implications for Education, Research, and Practice," *Accounting Horizons* (December 1996), pp. 1–15; and Charles Mulford and Michael Ely, "Calculating Sustainable Cash Flow: A Study of the S&P 100," *Georgia Tech Financial Analysis Lab* (October 2004).

[15]Some noncash investing and financing activities are part cash and part noncash. Companies should report only the cash portion on the statement of cash flows. The noncash component should be reported at the bottom of the statement or in a separate note.

Companies do not generally report certain other significant noncash transactions or other events in conjunction with the statement of cash flows. Examples of these types of transactions are **stock dividends, stock splits, and restrictions on retained earnings**. Companies generally report these items, neither financing nor investing activities, in conjunction with the statement of stockholders' equity or schedules and notes pertaining to changes in capital accounts.

CASH FLOW TOOL

WHAT DO THE NUMBERS MEAN?

By understanding the relationship between cash flow and income measures, analysts can gain better insights into company performance. Because earnings altered through creative accounting practices generally do not change operating cash flows, analysts can use the relationship between earnings and operating cash flow to detect suspicious accounting practices. Also, by monitoring the ratio between cash flow from operations and operating income, they can get a clearer picture of developing problems in a company.

For example, the chart below plots the ratio of operating cash flows to earnings for **Xerox Corp.** in the years leading up to the SEC singling it out in 2000 for aggressive revenue recognition practices on its leases.

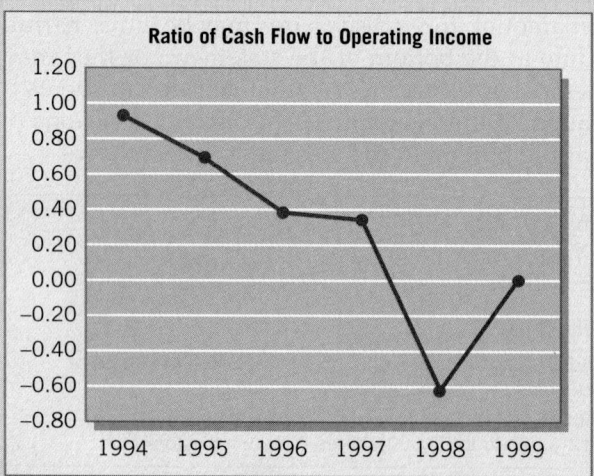

Similar to **W. T. Grant** in the chapter-opening story, Xerox was reporting earnings growth in the years leading up to its financial breakdown in 2000 but teetering near bankruptcy in 2001. However, Xerox's ratio of cash flow to earnings showed a declining trend and became negative well before its revenue recognition practices were revealed. The trend revealed in the graph should have given any analyst reason to investigate Xerox further. As one analyst noted, "Earnings growth that exceeds the growth in operating cash flow cannot continue for extended periods and should be investigated."

Source: Adapted from Charles Mulford and Eugene Comiskey, *The Financial Numbers Game: Detecting Creative Accounting Practices* (New York: John Wiley & Sons, 2002), Chapter 11, by permission.

SECTION 3 | *USE OF A WORKSHEET*

OBJECTIVE 9
Explain the use of a worksheet in preparing a statement of cash flows.

When numerous adjustments are necessary or other complicating factors are present, companies often use **a worksheet to assemble and classify the data that will appear on the statement of cash flows**. The worksheet (a **spreadsheet** when using computer software) is merely a device that aids in the preparation of the statement. Its use is optional. Illustration 23-37 shows the skeleton format of the worksheet for preparation of the statement of cash flows using the indirect method.

XYZ COMPANY
Statement of Cash Flows For the Year Ended...

	A	B	C	D	E
		End of Prior Year Balances	Reconciling Items		End of Current Year Balances
1	Balance Sheet Accounts		Debits	Credits	
2	Debit balance accounts	XX	XX	XX	XX
3		XX	XX	XX	XX
4	Totals	XXX			XXX
5	Credit balance accounts	XX	XX	XX	XX
6		XX	XX	XX	XX
7	Totals	XXX			XXX
8	Statement of Cash Flows Effects				
9	Operating activities				
10	Net income		XX		
11	Adjustments		XX	XX	
12	Investing activities				
13	Receipts and payments		XX	XX	
14	Financing activities				
15	Receipts and payments		XX	XX	
16	Totals		XXX	XXX	
17	Increase (decrease) in cash		(XX)	XX	
18	Totals		XXX	XXX	

Sheet1 / Sheet2 / Sheet3 /

ILLUSTRATION 23-37
Format of Worksheet for Preparation of Statement of Cash Flows

The following guidelines are important in using a worksheet.

1 In the balance sheet accounts section, **list accounts with debit balances separately from those with credit balances**. This means, for example, that Accumulated Depreciation is listed under credit balances and not as a contra account under debit balances. Enter the beginning and ending balances of each account in the appropriate columns. Then, enter the transactions that caused the change in the account balance during the year as reconciling items in the two middle columns.

After all reconciling items have been entered, each line pertaining to a balance sheet account should foot across. That is, the beginning balance plus or minus the reconciling item(s) must equal the ending balance. When this agreement exists for all balance sheet accounts, all changes in account balances have been reconciled.

2 The bottom portion of the worksheet consists of the operating, investing, and financing activities sections. Accordingly, it provides the information necessary to prepare the formal statement of cash flows. **Enter inflows of cash as debits in the reconciling columns, and outflows of cash as credits in the reconciling columns.** Thus, in this section, a company would enter the sale of equipment for cash at book value as a debit under inflows of cash from investing activities. Similarly, it would enter the purchase of land for cash as a credit under outflows of cash from investing activities.

3 **Do not enter in any journal or post to any account the reconciling items shown in the worksheet.** These items do not represent either adjustments or corrections of the balance sheet accounts. They are used only to facilitate the preparation of the statement of cash flows.

PREPARATION OF THE WORKSHEET

The preparation of a worksheet involves the following steps.

Step 1. Enter the balance sheet accounts and their beginning and ending balances in the balance sheet accounts section.

Step 2. Enter the data that explain the changes in the balance sheet accounts (other than cash) and their effects on the statement of cash flows in the reconciling columns of the worksheet.

Step 3. Enter the increase or decrease in cash on the cash line and at the bottom of the worksheet. This entry should enable the totals of the reconciling columns to be in agreement.

ILLUSTRATION 23-38
Comparative Balance Sheet, Satellite Corporation

To illustrate the preparation and use of a worksheet and to illustrate the reporting of some of the special problems discussed in the prior section, we present a comprehensive example for Satellite Corporation. Again, the indirect method serves as the basis for the computation of net cash provided by operating activities. Illustrations 23-38 and 23-39 present the balance sheet, combined statement of income and retained earnings,

SATELLITE CORPORATION
Comparative Balance Sheet—December 31, 2008 and 2007

	A	B	C	D
		2008	2007	Increase or (Decrease)
2	**Assets**			
3	Cash	$ 59,000	$ 66,000	$ (7,000)
4	Accounts receivable (net)	104,000	51,000	53,000
5	Inventories	493,000	341,000	152,000
6	Prepaid expenses	16,500	17,000	(500)
7	Investments in stock of Porter Co. (equity method)	18,500	15,000	3,500
8	Land	131,500	82,000	49,500
9	Equipment	187,000	142,000	45,000
10	Accumulated depreciation—equipment	(29,000)	(31,000)	(2,000)
11	Buildings	262,000	262,000	—
12	Accumulated depreciation—buildings	(74,100)	(71,000)	3,100
13	Trademark	7,600	10,000	(2,400)
14	Total assets	$1,176,000	$884,000	
15	**Liabilities**			
16	Accounts payable	$ 132,000	$ 131,000	1,000
17	Accrued liabilities	43,000	39,000	4,000
18	Income tax payable	3,000	16,000	(13,000)
19	Notes payable (long-term)	60,000	—	60,000
20	Bonds payable	100,000	100,000	—
21	Premium on bonds payable	7,000	8,000	(1,000)
22	Deferred tax liability (long-term)	9,000	6,000	3,000
23	Total liabilities	354,000	300,000	
24	**Stockholders' Equity**			
25	Common stock ($1 par)	60,000	50,000	10,000
26	Additional paid-in capital	187,000	38,000	149,000
27	Retained earnings	592,000	496,000	96,000
28	Treasury stock	(17,000)	—	17,000
29	Total stockholders' equity	822,000	584,000	
30	Total liabilities and stockholders' equity	$1,176,000	$884,000	

Sheet1 / Sheet2 / Sheet3 /

SATELLITE CORPORATION
COMBINED STATEMENT OF INCOME AND RETAINED EARNINGS
FOR THE YEAR ENDED DECEMBER 31, 2008

Net sales		$526,500
Other revenue		3,500
Total revenues		530,000
Expense		
Cost of goods sold		310,000
Selling and administrative expenses		47,000
Other expenses and losses		12,000
Total expenses		369,000
Income before income tax and		
extraordinary item		161,000
Income tax		
Current	$47,000	
Deferred	3,000	50,000
Income before extraordinary item		111,000
Gain on condemnation of land		
(net of $2,000 tax)		6,000
Net income		117,000
Retained earnings, January 1		496,000
Less:		
Cash dividends	6,000	
Stock dividend	15,000	21,000
Retained earnings, December 31		$592,000
Per share:		
Income before extraordinary item		$2.02
Extraordinary item		.11
Net income		$2.13

Additional Information

(a) Other income of $3,500 represents Satellite's equity share in the net income of Porter Co., an equity investee. Satellite owns 22% of Porter Co.

(b) An analysis of the equipment account and related accumulated depreciation indicates the following:

	Equipment Dr./(Cr.)	Accum. Dep. Dr./(Cr.)	Gain or (Loss)
Balance at end of 2007	$142,000	$(31,000)	
Purchases of equipment	53,000		
Sale of equipment	(8,000)	2,500	$(1,500)
Depreciation for the period		(11,500)	
Major repair charged to			
accumulated depreciation		11,000	
Balance at end of 2008	$187,000	$(29,000)	

(c) Land in the amount of $60,000 was purchased through the issuance of a long-term note; in addition, certain parcels of land costing $10,500 were condemned. The state government paid Satellite $18,500, resulting in an $8,000 gain which has a $2,000 tax effect.

(d) The change in the accumulated depreciation—buildings, trademark, and premium on bonds payable accounts resulted from depreciation and amortization entries.

(e) An analysis of the paid-in capital accounts in stockholders' equity discloses the following:

	Common Stock	Additional Paid-In Capital
Balance at end of 2007	$50,000	$ 38,000
Issuance of 2% stock dividend	1,000	14,000
Sale of stock for cash	9,000	135,000
Balance at end of 2008	$60,000	$187,000

(f) Interest paid (net of amount capitalized) is $9,000; income taxes paid is $62,000.

and additional information for Satellite Corporation. The discussion that follows these financial statements provides additional explanations related to the preparation of the worksheet.

ANALYSIS OF TRANSACTIONS

The following discussion explains the individual adjustments that appear on the worksheet in Illustration 23-40 (page 1250). Because cash is the basis for the analysis, Satellite reconciles the cash account last. Because income is the first item that appears on the statement of cash flows, it is handled first.

Change in Retained Earnings

Net income for the period is $117,000. The entry for it on the worksheet is as follows.

(1)

Operating—Net Income	117,000	
Retained Earnings		117,000

Satellite reports net income on the bottom section of the worksheet. This **is the starting point for preparation of the statement of cash flows (under the indirect method)**.

A stock dividend and a cash dividend also affected retained earnings. The retained earnings statement reports a stock dividend of $15,000. The worksheet entry for this transaction is as follows.

(2)

Retained Earnings	15,000	
Common Stock		1,000
Additional Paid-in Capital		14,000

The issuance of stock dividends is not a cash operating, investing, or financing item. Therefore, **although the company enters this transaction on the worksheet for reconciling purposes, it does not report it in the statement of cash flows**.

The $6,000 cash dividend paid represents a financing activity cash outflow. Satellite makes the following worksheet entry:

(3)

Retained Earnings	6,000	
Financing—Cash Dividends		6,000

The company reconciles the beginning and ending balances of retained earnings by entry of the three items above.

Accounts Receivable (Net)

The increase in accounts receivable (net) of $53,000 represents adjustments that did not result in cash inflows during 2008. As a result, the company would deduct from net income the increase of $53,000. Satellite makes the following worksheet entry.

(4)

Accounts Receivable (net)	53,000	
Operating—Increase in Accounts Receivable (net)		53,000

Inventories

The increase in inventories of $152,000 represents an operating use of cash. The incremental investment in inventories during the year reduces cash without increasing the cost of goods sold. Satellite makes the following worksheet entry.

(5)

Inventories	152,000	
Operating—Increase in Inventories		152,000

Prepaid Expense

The decrease in prepaid expenses of $500 represents a charge in the income statement for which there was no cash outflow in the current period. Satellite should add that amount back to net income through the following entry.

(6)

Operating—Decrease in Prepaid Expenses	500	
Prepaid Expenses		500

Investment in Stock

Satellite's investment in the stock of Porter Co. increased $3,500. This amount reflects Satellite's share of net income earned by Porter (its equity investee) during the current year. Although Satellite's revenue, and therefore its net income increased $3,500 by recording Satellite's share of Porter Co.'s net income, no cash (dividend) was provided. Satellite makes the following worksheet entry.

(7)

Investment in Stock of Porter Co.	3,500	
Operating—Equity in Earnings of Porter Co.		3,500

Land

Satellite purchased land in the amount of $60,000 through the issuance of a long-term note payable. This transaction did not affect cash. It is a significant noncash investing/financing transaction that the company would disclose either in a separate schedule below the statement of cash flows or in the accompanying notes. Satellite makes the following entry to reconcile the worksheet.

(8)

Land	60,000	
Notes Payable		60,000

In addition to the noncash transaction involving the issuance of a note to purchase land, the Land account was decreased by the condemnation proceedings. The following worksheet entry records the receipt of $18,500 for land having a book value of $10,500.

(9)

Investing—Proceeds from Condemnation of Land	18,500	
Land		10,500
Operating—Gain on Condemnation of Land		8,000

In reconciling net income to net cash flow from operating activities, Satellite deducts from net income the extraordinary gain of $8,000. The reason is that the transaction that gave rise to the gain is an item whose cash effect is already classified as an investing cash inflow. The Land account is now reconciled.

Equipment and Accumulated Depreciation

An analysis of Equipment and Accumulated Depreciation shows that a number of transactions have affected these accounts. The company purchased equipment in the amount of $53,000 during the year. Satellite records this transaction on the worksheet as follows.

(10)

Equipment	53,000	
Investing—Purchase of Equipment		53,000

In addition, Satellite sold at a loss of $1,500 equipment with a book value of $5,500. It records this transaction as follows.

(11)

Investing—Sale of Equipment	4,000	
Operating—Loss on Sale of Equipment	1,500	
Accumulated Depreciation—Equipment	2,500	
Equipment		8,000

The proceeds from the sale of the equipment provided cash of $4,000. In addition, the loss on the sale of the equipment has reduced net income, but did not affect cash. Therefore, the company adds back to net income the amount of the loss, in order to accurately report cash provided by operating activities.

Satellite reported depreciation on the equipment at $11,500 and recorded it on the worksheet as follows.

(12)

Operating—Depreciation Expense—Equipment	11,500	
Accumulated Depreciation—Equipment		11,500

The company adds depreciation expense back to net income because that expense reduced income but did not affect cash.

Finally, the company made a major repair to the equipment. It charged this expenditure, in the amount of $11,000, to Accumulated Depreciation—Equipment. This expenditure required cash, and so Satellite makes the following worksheet entry.

(13)

Accumulated Depreciation—Equipment	11,000	
Investing—Major Repairs of Equipment		11,000

After adjusting for the foregoing items, Satellite has reconciled the balances in the Equipment and related Accumulated Depreciation accounts.

Building Depreciation and Amortization of Trademark

Depreciation expense on the buildings of $3,100 and amortization of trademark of $2,400 are both expenses in the income statement that reduced net income but did not require cash outflows in the current period. Satellite makes the following worksheet entry.

(14)

Operating—Depreciation Expense—Buildings	3,100	
Operating—Amortization of Trademark	2,400	
Accumulated Depreciation—Buildings		3,100
Trademark		2,400

Other Noncash Charges or Credits

Analysis of the remaining accounts indicates that changes in the Accounts Payable, Accrued Liabilities, Income Tax Payable, Premium on Bonds Payable, and Deferred Tax Liability balances resulted from charges or credits to net income that did not affect cash. The company should individually analyze each of these items and enter them in the worksheet. The following compound entry summarizes these noncash, income-related items.

(15)

Income Tax Payable	13,000	
Premium on Bonds Payable	1,000	
Operating—Increase in Accounts Payable	1,000	
Operating—Increase in Accrued Liabilities	4,000	
Operating—Increase in Deferred Tax Liability	3,000	
Operating—Decrease in Income Tax Payable		13,000
Operating—Amortization of Bond Premium		1,000
Accounts Payable		1,000
Accrued Liabilities		4,000
Deferred Tax Liability		3,000

Common Stock and Related Accounts

Comparison of the common stock balances and the additional paid-in capital balances shows that transactions during the year affected these accounts. First, Satellite issues a stock dividend of 2 percent to stockholders. As the discussion of worksheet entry (2) indicated, no cash was provided or used by the stock dividend transaction. In addition to the shares issued via the stock dividend, Satellite sold shares of common stock at $16 per share. The company records this transaction as follows.

(16)

Financing—Sale of Common Stock	144,000	
Common Stock		9,000
Additional Paid-in Capital		135,000

Also, the company purchased shares of its common stock in the amount of $17,000. It records this transaction on the worksheet as follows.

(17)

Treasury Stock	17,000	
Financing—Purchase of Treasury Stock		17,000

Final Reconciling Entry

The final entry to reconcile the change in cash and to balance the worksheet is shown below. The $7,000 amount is the difference between the beginning and ending cash balance.

(18)

Decrease in Cash	7,000	
Cash		7,000

Once the company has determined that the differences between the beginning and ending balances per the worksheet columns have been accounted for, it can total the reconciling transactions columns, and they should balance. Satellite can prepare the statement of cash flows entirely from the items and amounts that appear at the bottom of the worksheet under "Statement of Cash Flows Effects," as shown in Illustration 23-40 on page 1250.

ILLUSTRATION 23-40
Completed Worksheet for Preparation of Statement of Cash Flows, Satellite Corporation

SATELLITE CORPORATION
Worksheet for Preparation of Statement of Cash Flows For the Year Ended December 31, 2008

	A	B	C	D	E	F	G
		Balance 12/31/07	Reconciling Items–2008 Debits		Credits		Balance 12/31/08
2	Debits						
3	Cash	$ 66,000			(18)	7,000	$ 59,000
4	Accounts receivable (net)	51,000	(4)	$ 53,000			104,000
5	Inventories	341,000	(5)	152,000			493,000
6	Prepaid expenses	17,000			(6)	500	16,500
7	Investment (equity method)	15,000	(7)	3,500			18,500
8	Land	82,000	(8)	60,000	(9)	10,500	131,500
9	Equipment	142,000	(10)	53,000	(11)	8,000	187,000
10	Building	262,000					262,000
11	Trademark	10,000			(14)	2,400	7,600
12	Treasury stock		(17)	17,000			17,000
13	Total debits	$986,000					$1,296,100
14	Credits						
15	Accum. depr.–equipment	$ 31,000	(11)	2,500	(12)	11,500	
16			(13)	11,000			$ 29,000
17	Accum. depr.–building	71,000			(14)	3,100	74,100
18	Accounts payable	131,000			(15)	1,000	132,000
19	Accrued liabilities	39,000			(15)	4,000	43,000
20	Income tax payable	16,000	(15)	13,000			3,000
21	Notes payable	-0-			(8)	60,000	60,000
22	Bonds payable	100,000					100,000
23	Premium on bonds payable	8,000	(15)	1,000			7,000
24	Deferred tax liability	6,000			(15)	3,000	9,000
25	Common stock	50,000			(2)	1,000	
26					(16)	9,000	60,000
27	Additional paid-in capital	38,000			(2)	14,000	
28					(16)	135,000	187,000
29	Retained earnings	496,000	(2)	15,000	(1)	117,000	
30			(3)	6,000			592,000
31	Total credits	$986,000					$1,296,100
32	Statement of Cash Flows Effects						
33	Operating activities						
34	Net income		(1)	117,000			
35	Increase in accounts receivable (net)				(4)	53,000	
36	Increase in inventories				(5)	152,000	
37	Decrease in prepaid expenses		(6)	500			
38	Equity in earnings of Porter Co.				(7)	3,500	
39	Gain on condemnation of land				(9)	8,000	
40	Loss on sale of equipment		(11)	1,500			
41	Depr. expense–equipment		(12)	11,500			
42	Depr. expense–building		(14)	3,100			
43	Amortization of trademark		(14)	2,400			
44	Increase in accounts payable		(15)	1,000			
45	Increase in accrued liabilities		(15)	4,000			
46	Increase in deferred tax liability		(15)	3,000			
47	Decrease in income tax payable				(15)	13,000	
48	Amortization of bond premium				(15)	1,000	
49	Investing activities						
50	Proceeds from condemnation of land		(9)	18,500			
51	Purchase of equipment				(10)	53,000	
52	Sale of equipment		(11)	4,000			
53	Major repairs of equipment				(13)	11,000	
54	Financing activities						
55	Payment of cash dividend				(3)	6,000	
56	Issuance of common stock		(16)	144,000			
57	Purchase of treasury stock				(17)	17,000	
58	Totals			697,500		704,500	
59	Decrease in cash		(18)	7,000			
60	Totals			$704,500		$704,500	

Sheet1 Sheet2 Sheet3

PREPARATION OF FINAL STATEMENT

Illustration 23-41 presents a formal statement of cash flows prepared from the data compiled in the lower portion of the worksheet.

SATELLITE CORPORATION STATEMENT OF CASH FLOWS FOR THE YEAR ENDED DECEMBER 31, 2008 INCREASE (DECREASE) IN CASH		
Cash flows from operating activities		
Net income		$117,000
Adjustments to reconcile net income to net cash used by operating activities:		
Depreciation expense	$ 14,600	
Amortization of trademark	2,400	
Amortization of bond premium	(1,000)	
Equity in earnings of Porter Co.	(3,500)	
Gain on condemnation of land	(8,000)	
Loss on sale of equipment	1,500	
Increase in deferred tax liability	3,000	
Increase in accounts receivable (net)	(53,000)	
Increase in inventories	(152,000)	
Decrease in prepaid expenses	500	
Increase in accounts payable	1,000	
Increase in accrued liabilities	4,000	
Decrease in income tax payable	(13,000)	(203,500)
Net cash used by operating activities		(86,500)
Cash flows from investing activities		
Proceeds from condemnation of land	18,500	
Purchase of equipment	(53,000)	
Sale of equipment	4,000	
Major repairs of equipment	(11,000)	
Net cash used by investing activities		(41,500)
Cash flows from financing activities		
Payment of cash dividend	(6,000)	
Issuance of common stock	144,000	
Purchase of treasury stock	(17,000)	
Net cash provided by financing activities		121,000
Net decrease in cash		(7,000)
Cash, January 1, 2008		66,000
Cash, December 31, 2008		$ 59,000
Supplemental Disclosures of Cash Flow Information:		
Cash paid during the year for:		
Interest (net of amount capitalized)		$ 9,000
Income taxes		$ 62,000
Supplemental Schedule of Noncash Investing and Financing Activities:		
Purchase of land for $60,000 in exchange for a $60,000 long-term note.		

ILLUSTRATION 23-41
Statement of Cash Flows,
Satellite Corporation

*Discussion of the
T-Account Approach to
Preparation of the
Statement of Cash Flows*

SUMMARY OF LEARNING OBJECTIVES

1. **Describe the purpose of the statement of cash flows.** The primary purpose of the statement of cash flows is to provide information about cash receipts and cash payments of an entity during a period. A secondary objective is to report the entity's operating, investing, and financing activities during the period.

KEY TERMS

cash equivalents, *1213(n)*
direct method, *1218*
financing activities, *1214*
indirect method, *1219*
investing activities, *1214*

2. Identify the major classifications of cash flows. Companies classify cash flows as: (1) *Operating activities*—transactions that result in the revenues, expenses, gains, and losses that determine net income. (2) *Investing activities*—lending money and collecting on those loans, and acquiring and disposing of investments, plant assets, and intangible assets. (3) *Financing activities*—obtaining cash from creditors and repaying loans, issuing and reacquiring capital stock, and paying cash dividends.

3. Differentiate between net income and net cash flows from operating activities. Companies must adjust net income on an accrual basis to determine net cash flow from operating activities because some expenses and losses do not cause cash outflows, and some revenues and gains do not provide cash inflows.

4. Contrast the direct and indirect methods of calculating net cash flow from operating activities. Under the direct approach, companies calculate the major classes of operating cash receipts and cash disbursements. Companies summarize the computations in a schedule of changes from the accrual to the cash basis income statement. Presentation of the direct approach of reporting net cash flow from operating activities takes the form of a condensed cash-basis income statement. The indirect method adds back to net income the noncash expenses and losses and subtracts the noncash revenues and gains.

5. Determine net cash flows from investing and financing activities. Once a company has computed the net cash flow from operating activities, the next step is to determine whether any other changes in balance sheet accounts caused an increase or decrease in cash. Net cash flows from investing and financing activities can be determined by examining the changes in noncurrent balance sheet accounts.

6. Prepare a statement of cash flows. Preparing the statement involves three major steps: (1) *Determine the change in cash.* This is the difference between the beginning and the ending cash balance shown on the comparative balance sheets. (2) *Determine the net cash flow from operating activities.* This procedure is complex; it involves analyzing not only the current year's income statement but also the comparative balance sheets and the selected transaction data. (3) *Determine cash flows from investing and financing activities.* Analyze all other changes in the balance sheet accounts to determine the effects on cash.

7. Identify sources of information for a statement of cash flows. The information to prepare the statement usually comes from three sources: (1) *Comparative balance sheets.* Information in these statements indicates the amount of the changes in assets, liabilities, and equities during the period. (2) *Current income statement.* Information in this statement is used in determining the cash provided by operations during the period. (3) *Selected transaction data.* These data from the general ledger provide additional detailed information needed to determine how cash was provided or used during the period.

8. Discuss special problems in preparing a statement of cash flows. These special problems are: (1) adjustments similar to depreciation; (2) accounts receivable (net); (3) other working capital changes; (4) net losses; (5) gains; (6) stock options; (7) postretirement benefit costs; (8) extraordinary items; and (9) significant noncash transactions.

9. Explain the use of a worksheet in preparing a statement of cash flows. When numerous adjustments are necessary, or other complicating factors are present, companies often use a worksheet to assemble and classify the data that will appear on the statement of cash flows. The worksheet is merely a device that aids in the preparation of the statement. Its use is optional.

QUESTIONS

1. What is the purpose of the statement of cash flows? What information does it provide?

2. Of what use is the statement of cash flows?

3. Differentiate between investing activities, financing activities, and operating activities.

4. What are the major sources of cash (inflows) in a statement of cash flows? What are the major uses (outflows) of cash?

5. Identify and explain the major steps involved in preparing the statement of cash flows.

6. Identify the following items as (1) operating, (2) investing, or (3) financing activities: purchase of land; payment of dividends; cash sales; and purchase of treasury stock.

7. Unlike the other major financial statements, the statement of cash flows is not prepared from the adjusted trial balance. From what sources does the information to prepare this statement come, and what information does each source provide?

8. Why is it necessary to convert accrual-based net income to a cash basis when preparing a statement of cash flows?

9. Differentiate between the direct method and the indirect method by discussing each method.

10. Bonnie Raitt Company reported net income of $3.5 million in 2008. Depreciation for the year was $520,000; accounts receivable increased $500,000; and accounts payable increased $350,000. Compute net cash flow from operating activities using the indirect method.

11. Sophie B. Hawkins Co. reported sales on an accrual basis of $100,000. If accounts receivable increased $30,000, and the allowance for doubtful accounts increased $9,000 after a writeoff of $4,000, compute cash sales.

12. Your roommate is puzzled. During the last year, the company in which she is a stockholder reported a net loss of $675,000, yet its cash increased $321,000 during the same period of time. Explain to your roommate how this situation could occur.

13. The board of directors of Kenny G Corp. declared cash dividends of $260,000 during the current year. If dividends payable was $85,000 at the beginning of the year and $70,000 at the end of the year, how much cash was paid in dividends during the year?

14. Explain how the amount of cash payments to suppliers is computed under the direct method.

15. The net income for Silverchair Company for 2008 was $320,000. During 2008, depreciation on plant assets was $114,000, amortization of patent was $40,000, and the company incurred a loss on sale of plant assets of $21,000. Compute net cash flow from operating activities.

16. Each of the following items must be considered in preparing a statement of cash flows for Frogstomp Inc. for the year ended December 31, 2008. State where each item is to be shown in the statement, if at all.

    (a) Plant assets that had cost $20,000 6½ years before and were being depreciated on a straight-line basis over 10 years with no estimated scrap value were sold for $4,000.

    (b) During the year, 10,000 shares of common stock with a stated value of $20 a share were issued for $41 a share.

    (c) Uncollectible accounts receivable in the amount of $22,000 were written off against the Allowance for Doubtful Accounts.

    (d) The company sustained a net loss for the year of $50,000. Depreciation amounted to $22,000, and a gain of $9,000 was realized on the sale of available-for-sale securities for $38,000 cash.

17. Classify the following items as (1) operating, (2) investing, (3) financing, or (4) significant noncash investing and financing activities, using the direct method.

    (a) Purchase of equipment.

    (b) Redemption of bonds payable.

    (c) Sale of building.

    (d) Cash payments to suppliers.

    (e) Exchange of equipment for furniture.

    (f) Issuance of preferred stock.

    (g) Cash received from customers.

    (h) Purchase of treasury stock.

    (i) Issuance of bonds for land.

    (j) Payment of dividends.

    (k) Cash payments to employees.

    (l) Cash payments for operating expenses.

18. Clay Walker and David Ball were discussing the presentation format of the statement of cash flows of McBride Co. At the bottom of McBride's statement of cash flows was a separate section entitled "Noncash investing and financing activities." Give three examples of significant noncash transactions that would be reported in this section.

19. During 2008, Adams Company redeemed $2,000,000 of bonds payable for $1,780,000 cash. Indicate how this transaction would be reported on a statement of cash flows, if at all.

20. What are some of the arguments in favor of using the indirect (reconciliation) method as opposed to the direct method for reporting a statement of cash flows?

21. Why is it desirable to use a worksheet when preparing a statement of cash flows? Is a worksheet required to prepare a statement of cash flows?

BRIEF EXERCISES

(LO 5) **BE23-1** American Gladhanders Corporation had the following activities in 2008.

1. Sale of land $130,000
2. Purchase of inventory $845,000
3. Purchase of treasury stock $72,000
4. Purchase of equipment $415,000
5. Issuance of common stock $320,000
6. Purchase of available-for-sale securities $59,000

Compute the amount American Gladhanders should report as net cash provided (used) by investing activities in its statement of cash flows.

(LO 5) **BE23-2** Chrono Trigger Corporation had the following activities in 2008.

1. Payment of accounts payable $770,000
2. Issuance of common stock $250,000
3. Payment of dividends $300,000
4. Collection of note receivable $100,000
5. Issuance of bonds payable $510,000
6. Purchase of treasury stock $46,000

Compute the amount Chrono Trigger should report as net cash provided (used) by financing activities in its 2008 statement of cash flows.

(LO 2) **BE23-3** Ryker Corporation is preparing its 2008 statement of cash flows, using the indirect method. Presented below is a list of items that may affect the statement. Using the code below, indicate how each item will affect Ryker's 2008 statement of cash flows.

Code Letter	Effect
A	Added to net income in the operating section
D	Deducted from net income in the operating section
R-I	Cash receipt in investing section
P-I	Cash payment in investing section
R-F	Cash receipt in financing section
P-F	Cash payment in financing section
N	Noncash investing and/or financing activity

Items

_____ **(a)** Increase in accounts receivable.
_____ **(b)** Decrease in accounts receivable.
_____ **(c)** Issuance of stock.
_____ **(d)** Depreciation expense.
_____ **(e)** Sale of land at book value.
_____ **(f)** Sale of land at a gain.
_____ **(g)** Payment of dividends.
_____ **(h)** Purchase of land and building.
_____ **(i)** Purchase of available-for-sale investment.

_____ **(j)** Increase in accounts payable.
_____ **(k)** Decrease in accounts payable.
_____ **(l)** Loan from bank by signing note.
_____ **(m)** Purchase of equipment using a note.
_____ **(n)** Increase in inventory.
_____ **(o)** Issuance of bonds.
_____ **(p)** Retirement of bonds payable.
_____ **(q)** Sale of equipment at a loss.
_____ **(r)** Purchase of treasury stock.

(LO 3, 4) **BE23-4** Azure Corporation had the following 2008 income statement.

Sales	$200,000
Cost of goods sold	120,000
Gross profit	80,000
Operating expenses (includes depreciation of $21,000)	50,000
Net income	$ 30,000

The following accounts increased during 2008: accounts receivable $17,000; inventory $11,000; accounts payable $13,000. Prepare the cash flows from operating activities section of Azure's 2008 statement of cash flows using the direct method.

(LO 3, 4) **BE23-5** Use the information from BE23-4 for Azure Corporation. Prepare the cash flows from operating activities section of Azure's 2008 statement of cash flows using the indirect method.

(LO 4) **BE23-6** At January 1, 2008, Cyberslider Inc. had accounts receivable of $72,000. At December 31, 2008, accounts receivable is $59,000. Sales for 2008 is $420,000. Compute Cyberslider's 2008 cash receipts from customers.

(LO 4) **BE23-7** Cage Corporation had January 1 and December 31 balances as follows.

	1/1/08	12/31/08
Inventory	$90,000	$113,000
Accounts payable	61,000	69,000

For 2008, cost of goods sold was $500,000. Compute Cage's 2008 cash payments to suppliers.

(LO 6) **BE23-8** In 2008, Fieval Corporation had net cash provided by operating activities of $531,000; net cash used by investing activities of $963,000; and net cash provided by financing activities of $585,000. At January 1, 2008, the cash balance was $333,000. Compute December 31, 2008, cash.

(LO 3, 4) **BE23-9** Tool Time Corporation had the following 2008 income statement.

Revenues	$100,000
Expenses	60,000
	$ 40,000

In 2008, Tool Time had the following activity in selected accounts.

Accounts Receivable					Allowance for Doubtful Accounts			
1/1/08	20,000						1,200	1/1/08
Revenues	100,000	1,000	Writeoffs		Writeoffs	1,000	1,540	Bad debt expense
		90,000	Collections					
12/31/08	29,000						1,740	12/31/08

Prepare Tool Time's cash flows from operating activities section of the statement of cash flows using (a) the direct method and (b) the indirect method.

(LO 3) **BE23-10** Red October Corporation reported net income of $50,000 in 2008. Depreciation expense was $17,000. The following working capital accounts changed.

Accounts receivable	$11,000 increase
Available-for-sale securities	16,000 increase
Inventory	7,400 increase
Nontrade note payable	15,000 decrease
Accounts payable	9,300 increase

Compute net cash provided by operating activities.

(LO 3) **BE23-11** In 2008, Izzy Corporation reported a net loss of $70,000. Izzy's only net income adjustments were depreciation expense $84,000, and increase in accounts receivable $8,100. Compute Izzy's net cash provided (used) by operating activities.

(LO 8) **BE23-12** In 2008, Mufosta Inc. issued 1,000 shares of $10 par value common stock for land worth $50,000.

(a) Prepare Mufosta's journal entry to record the transaction.
(b) Indicate the effect the transaction has on cash.
(c) Indicate how the transaction is reported on the statement of cash flows.

(LO 9) **BE23-13** Indicate in general journal form how the items below would be entered in a worksheet for the preparation of the statement of cash flows.

(a) Net income is $317,000.
(b) Cash dividends declared and paid totaled $120,000.
(c) Equipment was purchased for $114,000.
(d) Equipment that originally cost $40,000 and had accumulated depreciation of $32,000 was sold for $13,000.

EXERCISES

(LO 2) **E23-1** **(Classification of Transactions)** Red Hot Chili Peppers Co. had the following activity in its most recent year of operations.

(a) Purchase of equipment.
(b) Redemption of bonds payable.
(c) Sale of building.
(d) Depreciation.

(e) Exchange of equipment for furniture.
(f) Issuance of capital stock.
(g) Amortization of intangible assets.
(h) Purchase of treasury stock.

(i) Issuance of bonds for land.
(j) Payment of dividends.
(k) Increase in interest receivable on notes receivable.
(l) Pension expense exceeds amount funded.

Instructions

Classify the items as (1) operating—add to net income; (2) operating—deduct from net income; (3) investing; (4) financing; or (5) significant noncash investing and financing activities. Use the indirect method.

(LO 2, 3) **E23-2 (Statement Presentation of Transactions—Indirect Method)** Each of the following items must be considered in preparing a statement of cash flows (indirect method) for Turbulent Indigo Inc. for the year ended December 31, 2007.

(a) Plant assets that had cost $20,000 6 years before and were being depreciated on a straight-line basis over 10 years with no estimated scrap value were sold for $5,300.
(b) During the year, 10,000 shares of common stock with a stated value of $10 a share were issued for $43 a share.
(c) Uncollectible accounts receivable in the amount of $27,000 were written off against the Allowance for Doubtful Accounts.
(d) The company sustained a net loss for the year of $50,000. Depreciation amounted to $22,000, and a gain of $9,000 was realized on the sale of land for $39,000 cash.
(e) A 3-month U.S. Treasury bill was purchased for $100,000. The company uses a cash and cash-equivalent basis for its cash flow statement.
(f) Patent amortization for the year was $20,000.
(g) The company exchanged common stock for a 70% interest in Tabasco Co. for $900,000.
(h) During the year, treasury stock costing $47,000 was purchased.

Instructions

State where each item is to be shown in the statement of cash flows, if at all.

(LO 3, 4) **E23-3 (Preparation of Operating Activities Section—Indirect Method, Periodic Inventory)** The income statement of Vince Gill Company is shown below.

VINCE GILL COMPANY		
INCOME STATEMENT		
FOR THE YEAR ENDED DECEMBER 31, 2008		
Sales		$6,900,000
Cost of goods sold		
Beginning inventory	$1,900,000	
Purchases	4,400,000	
Goods available for sale	6,300,000	
Ending inventory	1,600,000	
Cost of goods sold		4,700,000
Gross profit		2,200,000
Operating expenses		
Selling expenses	450,000	
Administrative expenses	700,000	1,150,000
Net income		$1,050,000

Additional information:

1. Accounts receivable decreased $360,000 during the year.
2. Prepaid expenses increased $170,000 during the year.
3. Accounts payable to suppliers of merchandise decreased $275,000 during the year.
4. Accrued expenses payable decreased $100,000 during the year.
5. Administrative expenses include depreciation expense of $60,000.

Instructions

(LO 3, 4) Prepare the operating activities section of the statement of cash flows for the year ended December 31, 2008, for Vince Gill Company, using the indirect method.

E23-4 (Preparation of Operating Activities Section—Direct Method) Data for the Vince Gill Company are presented in E23-3.

Instructions

Prepare the operating activities section of the statement of cash flows using the direct method.

(LO 3, 4) **E23-5** **(Preparation of Operating Activities Section—Direct Method)** Krauss Company's income statement for the year ended December 31, 2007, contained the following condensed information.

Revenue from fees		$840,000
Operating expenses (excluding depreciation)	$624,000	
Depreciation expense	60,000	
Loss on sale of equipment	26,000	710,000
Income before income taxes		130,000
Income tax expense		40,000
Net income		$ 90,000

Krauss's balance sheet contained the following comparative data at December 31.

	2007	2006
Accounts receivable	$37,000	$54,000
Accounts payable	41,000	31,000
Income taxes payable	4,000	8,500

(Accounts payable pertains to operating expenses.)

Instructions

Prepare the operating activities section of the statement of cash flows using the direct method.

(LO 3, 4) **E23-6** **(Preparation of Operating Activities Section—Indirect Method)** Data for Krauss Company are presented in E23-5.

Instructions

Prepare the operating activities section of the statement of cash flows using the indirect method.

(LO 3, 4) **E23-7** **(Computation of Operating Activities—Direct Method)** Presented below are two independent situations.

Situation A:

Annie Lennox Co. reports revenues of $200,000 and operating expenses of $110,000 in its first year of operations, 2008. Accounts receivable and accounts payable at year-end were $71,000 and $29,000, respectively. Assume that the accounts payable related to operating expenses. Ignore income taxes.

Instructions

Using the direct method, compute net cash provided by operating activities.

Situation B:

The income statement for Blues Traveler Company shows cost of goods sold $310,000 and operating expenses (exclusive of depreciation) $230,000. The comparative balance sheet for the year shows that inventory increased $26,000, prepaid expenses decreased $8,000, accounts payable (related to merchandise) decreased $17,000, and accrued expenses payable increased $11,000.

Instructions

Compute (a) cash payments to suppliers and (b) cash payments for operating expenses.

(LO 3, 4) **E23-8** **(Schedule of Net Cash Flow from Operating Activities—Indirect Method)** Ballard Co. reported $145,000 of net income for 2008. The accountant, in preparing the statement of cash flows, noted several items occurring during 2008 that might affect cash flows from operating activities. These items are listed below and on page 1258.

1. Ballard purchased 100 shares of treasury stock at a cost of $20 per share. These shares were then resold at $25 per share.
2. Ballard sold 100 shares of IBM common at $200 per share. The acquisition cost of these shares was $145 per share. This investment was shown on Ballard's December 31, 2007, balance sheet as an available-for-sale security.
3. Ballard revised its estimate for bad debts. Before 2008, Ballard's bad debt expense was 1% of its net sales. In 2008, this percentage was increased to 2%. Net sales for 2008 were $500,000, and net accounts receivable decreased by $12,000 during 2008.
4. Ballard issued 500 shares of its $10 par common stock for a patent. The market value of the shares on the date of the transaction was $23 per share.
5. Depreciation expense is $39,000.
6. Ballard Co. holds 40% of the Nirvana Company's common stock as a long-term investment. Nirvana Company reported $27,000 of net income for 2008.

7. Nirvana Company paid a total of $2,000 of cash dividends to all investees in 2008.
8. Ballard declared a 10% stock dividend. One thousand shares of $10 par common stock were distributed. The market price at date of issuance was $20 per share.

Instructions

Prepare a schedule that shows the net cash flow from operating activities using the indirect method. Assume no items other than those listed above affected the computation of 2008 net cash flow from operating activities.

(LO 6) **E23-9** **(SCF—Direct Method)** Los Lobos Corp. uses the direct method to prepare its statement of cash flows. Los Lobos's trial balances at December 31, 2007 and 2006, are as follows.

	December 31	
	2007	2006
Debits		
Cash	$ 35,000	$ 32,000
Accounts receivable	33,000	30,000
Inventory	31,000	47,000
Property, plant, & equipment	100,000	95,000
Unamortized bond discount	4,500	5,000
Cost of goods sold	250,000	380,000
Selling expenses	141,500	172,000
General and administrative expenses	137,000	151,300
Interest expense	4,300	2,600
Income tax expense	20,400	61,200
	$756,700	$976,100
Credits		
Allowance for doubtful accounts	$ 1,300	$ 1,100
Accumulated depreciation	16,500	15,000
Trade accounts payable	25,000	15,500
Income taxes payable	21,000	29,100
Deferred income taxes	5,300	4,600
8% callable bonds payable	45,000	20,000
Common stock	50,000	40,000
Additional paid-in capital	9,100	7,500
Retained earnings	44,700	64,600
Sales	538,800	778,700
	$756,700	$976,100

Additional information:

1. Los Lobos purchased $5,000 in equipment during 2007.
2. Los Lobos allocated one-third of its depreciation expense to selling expenses and the remainder to general and administrative expenses.
3. Bad debt expense for 2007 was $5,000, and writeoffs of uncollectible accounts totaled $4,800.

Instructions

Determine what amounts Los Lobos should report in its statement of cash flows for the year ended December 31, 2007, for the following items.

1. Cash collected from customers.   4. Cash paid for income taxes.
2. Cash paid to suppliers.   5. Cash paid for selling expenses.
3. Cash paid for interest.

(LO 2, 8) **E23-10** **(Classification of Transactions)** Following are selected balance sheet accounts of Allman Bros. Corp. at December 31, 2008 and 2007, and the increases or decreases in each account from 2007 to 2008. Also presented is selected income statement information for the year ended December 31, 2008, and additional information.

Selected balance sheet accounts	2008	2007	Increase (Decrease)
Assets			
Accounts receivable	$ 34,000	$ 24,000	$ 10,000
Property, plant, and equipment	277,000	247,000	30,000
Accumulated depreciation	(178,000)	(167,000)	(11,000)

	2008	2007	Increase
Liabilities and stockholders' equity			
Bonds payable	$ 49,000	$46,000	$ 3,000
Dividends payable	8,000	5,000	3,000
Common stock, $1 par	22,000	19,000	3,000
Additional paid-in capital	9,000	3,000	6,000
Retained earnings	104,000	91,000	13,000

Selected income statement information for the year ended December 31, 2008

Sales revenue	$155,000
Depreciation	33,000
Gain on sale of equipment	14,500
Net income	31,000

Additional information:

1. During 2008, equipment costing $45,000 was sold for cash.
2. Accounts receivable relate to sales of merchandise.
3. During 2008, $20,000 of bonds payable were issued in exchange for property, plant, and equipment. There was no amortization of bond discount or premium.

Instructions

Determine the category (operating, investing, or financing) and the amount that should be reported in the statement of cash flows for the following items.

1. Payments for purchase of property, plant, and equipment.
2. Proceeds from the sale of equipment.
3. Cash dividends paid.
4. Redemption of bonds payable.

(LO 6) E23-11 (SCF—Indirect Method) Condensed financial data of Pat Metheny Company for 2008 and 2007 are presented below.

PAT METHENY COMPANY
COMPARATIVE BALANCE SHEET
AS OF DECEMBER 31, 2008 AND 2007

	2008	2007
Cash	$1,800	$1,150
Receivables	1,750	1,300
Inventory	1,600	1,900
Plant assets	1,900	1,700
Accumulated depreciation	(1,200)	(1,170)
Long-term investments (Held-to-maturity)	1,300	1,420
	$7,150	$6,300
Accounts payable	$1,200	$ 900
Accrued liabilities	200	250
Bonds payable	1,400	1,550
Capital stock	1,900	1,700
Retained earnings	2,450	1,900
	$7,150	$6,300

PAT METHENY COMPANY
INCOME STATEMENT
FOR THE YEAR ENDED DECEMBER 31, 2008

Sales	$6,900
Cost of goods sold	4,700
Gross margin	2,200
Selling and administrative expense	930
Income from operations	1,270
Other revenues and gains	
Gain on sale of investments	80
Income before tax	1,350
Income tax expense	540
Net income	810
Cash dividends	260
Income retained in business	$ 550

Additional information:

During the year, $70 of common stock was issued in exchange for plant assets. No plant assets were sold in 2008.

Instructions

Prepare a statement of cash flows using the indirect method.

(LO 6) **E23-12 (SCF—Direct Method)** Data for Pat Metheny Company are presented in E23-11.

Instructions

Prepare a statement of cash flows using the direct method. (Do not prepare a reconciliation schedule.)

(LO 6) **E23-13 (SCF—Direct Method)** Brecker Inc., a greeting card company, had the following statements prepared as of December 31, 2008.

BRECKER INC.
COMPARATIVE BALANCE SHEET
AS OF DECEMBER 31, 2008 AND 2007

	12/31/08	12/31/07
Cash	$ 6,000	$ 7,000
Accounts receivable	62,000	51,000
Short-term investments (Available-for-sale)	35,000	18,000
Inventories	40,000	60,000
Prepaid rent	5,000	4,000
Printing equipment	154,000	130,000
Accumulated depr.—equipment	(35,000)	(25,000)
Copyrights	46,000	50,000
Total assets	$313,000	$295,000
Accounts payable	$ 46,000	$ 40,000
Income taxes payable	4,000	6,000
Wages payable	8,000	4,000
Short-term loans payable	8,000	10,000
Long-term loans payable	60,000	69,000
Common stock, $10 par	100,000	100,000
Contributed capital, common stock	30,000	30,000
Retained earnings	57,000	36,000
Total liabilities & stockholders' equity	$313,000	$295,000

BRECKER INC.
INCOME STATEMENT
FOR THE YEAR ENDING DECEMBER 31, 2008

Sales		$338,150
Cost of goods sold		175,000
Gross margin		163,150
Operating expenses		120,000
Operating income		43,150
Interest expense	$11,400	
Gain on sale of equipment	2,000	9,400
Income before tax		33,750
Income tax expense		6,750
Net income		$ 27,000

Additional information:

1. Dividends in the amount of $6,000 were declared and paid during 2008.
2. Depreciation expense and amortization expense are included in operating expenses.
3. No unrealized gains or losses have occurred on the investments during the year.
4. Equipment that had a cost of $20,000 and was 70% depreciated was sold during 2008.

Instructions

Prepare a statement of cash flows using the direct method. (Do not prepare a reconciliation schedule.)

(LO 6) **E23-14 (SCF—Indirect Method)** Data for Brecker Inc. are presented in E23-13.

Instructions

Prepare a statement of cash flows using the indirect method.

(LO 6)   E23-15   (SCF—Indirect Method)   Presented below are data taken from the records of Antonio Brasileiro Company.

	December 31, 2008	December 31, 2007
Cash	$ 15,000	$ 8,000
Current assets other than cash	85,000	60,000
Long-term investments	10,000	53,000
Plant assets	335,000	215,000
	$445,000	$336,000
Accumulated depreciation	$ 20,000	$ 40,000
Current liabilities	40,000	22,000
Bonds payable	75,000	–0–
Capital stock	254,000	254,000
Retained earnings	56,000	20,000
	$445,000	$336,000

Additional information:

1. Held-to-maturity securities carried at a cost of $43,000 on December 31, 2007, were sold in 2008 for $34,000. The loss (not extraordinary) was incorrectly charged directly to Retained Earnings.
2. Plant assets that cost $50,000 and were 80% depreciated were sold during 2008 for $8,000. The loss (not extraordinary) was incorrectly charged directly to Retained Earnings.
3. Net income as reported on the income statement for the year was $57,000.
4. Dividends paid amounted to $10,000.
5. Depreciation charged for the year was $20,000.

Instructions

Prepare a statement of cash flows for the year 2008 using the indirect method.

(LO 2, 3, 5)   E23-16   (Cash Provided by Operating, Investing, and Financing Activities)   The balance sheet data of Brown Company at the end of 2007 and 2006 follow.

	2007	2006
Cash	$ 30,000	$ 35,000
Accounts receivable (net)	55,000	45,000
Merchandise inventory	65,000	45,000
Prepaid expenses	15,000	25,000
Equipment	90,000	75,000
Accumulated depreciation—equipment	(18,000)	(8,000)
Land	70,000	40,000
	$307,000	$257,000
Accounts payable	$ 65,000	$ 52,000
Accrued expenses	15,000	18,000
Notes payable—bank, long-term	–0–	23,000
Bonds payable	30,000	–0–
Common stock, $10 par	189,000	159,000
Retained earnings	8,000	5,000
	$307,000	$257,000

Land was acquired for $30,000 in exchange for common stock, par $30,000, during the year; all equipment purchased was for cash. Equipment costing $10,000 was sold for $3,000; book value of the equipment was $6,000. Cash dividends of $10,000 were declared and paid during the year.

Instructions

Compute net cash provided (used) by:

(a)   operating activities.
(b)   investing activities.
(c)   financing activities.

(LO 6) **E23-17** **(SCF—Indirect Method and Balance Sheet)** Jobim Inc., had the following condensed balance sheet at the end of operations for 2007.

JOBIM INC. BALANCE SHEET DECEMBER 31, 2007			
Cash	$ 8,500	Current liabilities	$ 15,000
Current assets other than cash	29,000	Long-term notes payable	25,500
Investments	20,000	Bonds payable	25,000
Plant assets (net)	67,500	Capital stock	75,000
Land	40,000	Retained earnings	24,500
	$165,000		$165,000

During 2008 the following occurred.

1. A tract of land was purchased for $9,000.
2. Bonds payable in the amount of $15,000 were retired at par.
3. An additional $10,000 in capital stock was issued at par.
4. Dividends totaling $9,375 were paid to stockholders.
5. Net income was $35,250 after allowing depreciation of $13,500.
6. Land was purchased through the issuance of $22,500 in bonds.
7. Jobim Inc. sold part of its investment portfolio for $12,875. This transaction resulted in a gain of $2,000 for the company. The company classifies the investments as available-for-sale.
8. Both current assets (other than cash) and current liabilities remained at the same amount.

Instructions

(a) Prepare a statement of cash flows for 2008 using the indirect method.

(b) Prepare the condensed balance sheet for Jobim Inc. as it would appear at December 31, 2008.

(LO 6, 8) **E23-18** **(Partial SCF—Indirect Method)** The accounts below appear in the ledger of Anita Baker Company.

Retained Earnings		Dr.	Cr.	Bal.
Jan. 1, 2008	Credit Balance			$ 42,000
Aug. 15	Dividends (cash)	$15,000		27,000
Dec. 31	Net Income for 2008		$40,000	67,000

Machinery		Dr.	Cr.	Bal.
Jan. 1, 2008	Debit Balance			$140,000
Aug. 3	Purchase of Machinery	$62,000		202,000
Sept. 10	Cost of Machinery Constructed	48,000		250,000
Nov. 15	Machinery Sold		$56,000	194,000

Accumulated Depreciation— Machinery		Dr.	Cr.	Bal.
Jan. 1, 2008	Credit Balance			$ 84,000
Apr. 8	Extraordinary Repairs	$21,000		63,000
Nov. 15	Accum. Depreciation on Machinery Sold	25,200		37,800
Dec. 31	Depreciation for 2008		$16,800	54,600

Instructions

From the postings in the accounts above, indicate how the information is reported on a statement of cash flows by preparing a partial statement of cash flows using the indirect method. The loss on sale of equipment (November 15) was $5,800.

(LO 9) **E23-19** **(Worksheet Analysis of Selected Accounts)** Data for Anita Baker Company are presented in E23-18.

Instructions
Prepare entries in journal form for all adjustments that should be made on a worksheet for a statement of cash flows.

(LO 9) **E23-20** **(Worksheet Analysis of Selected Transactions)** The transactions below took place during the year 2008.

1. Convertible bonds payable with a par value of $300,000 were exchanged for unissued common stock with a par value of $300,000. The market price of both types of securities was par.
2. The net income for the year was $410,000.
3. Depreciation expense for the building was $90,000.
4. Some old office equipment was traded in on the purchase of some dissimilar office equipment and the following entry was made.

Office Equipment	50,000	
Accum. Depreciation—Office Equipment	30,000	
Office Equipment		40,000
Cash		34,000
Gain on Disposal of Plant Assets		6,000

The Gain on Disposal of Plant Assets was credited to current operations as ordinary income.

5. Dividends in the amount of $123,000 were declared. They are payable in January of next year.

Instructions
Show by journal entries the adjustments that would be made on a worksheet for a statement of cash flows.

(LO 9) **E23-21** **(Worksheet Preparation)** Below is the comparative balance sheet for Stevie Wonder Corporation.

	Dec. 31, 2008	Dec. 31, 2007
Cash	$ 16,500	$ 21,000
Short-term investments	25,000	19,000
Accounts receivable	43,000	45,000
Allowance for doubtful accounts	(1,800)	(2,000)
Prepaid expenses	4,200	2,500
Inventories	81,500	65,000
Land	50,000	50,000
Buildings	125,000	73,500
Accumulated depreciation—buildings	(30,000)	(23,000)
Equipment	53,000	46,000
Accumulated depreciation—equipment	(19,000)	(15,500)
Delivery equipment	39,000	39,000
Accumulated depreciation—delivery equipment	(22,000)	(20,500)
Patents	15,000	–0–
	$379,400	$300,000

	Dec. 31, 2008	Dec. 31, 2007
Accounts payable	$ 26,000	$ 16,000
Short-term notes payable (trade)	4,000	6,000
Accrued payables	3,000	4,600
Mortgage payable	73,000	53,400
Bonds payable	50,000	62,500
Capital stock	140,000	102,000
Additional paid-in capital	10,000	4,000
Retained earnings	73,400	51,500
	$379,400	$300,000

Dividends in the amount of $15,000 were declared and paid in 2008.

Instructions

From this information, prepare a worksheet for a statement of cash flows. Make reasonable assumptions as appropriate. The short-term investments are considered available-for-sale and no unrealized gains or losses have occurred on these securities.

See the book's website, www.wiley.com/college/kieso, for Additional Exercises.

PROBLEMS

(LO 6, 7, 8) **P23-1** **(SCF—Indirect Method)** The following is Blue Man Corp.'s comparative balance sheet accounts at December 31, 2008 and 2007, with a column showing the increase (decrease) from 2007 to 2008.

COMPARATIVE BALANCE SHEETS

	2008	2007	Increase (Decrease)
Cash	$ 807,500	$ 700,000	$107,500
Accounts receivable	1,128,000	1,168,000	(40,000)
Inventories	1,850,000	1,715,000	135,000
Property, plant and equipment	3,307,000	2,967,000	340,000
Accumulated depreciation	(1,165,000)	(1,040,000)	(125,000)
Investment in Blige Co.	305,000	275,000	30,000
Loan receivable	262,500	—	262,500
Total assets	$6,495,000	$5,785,000	$710,000
Accounts payable	$1,015,000	$ 955,000	$ 60,000
Income taxes payable	30,000	50,000	(20,000)
Dividends payable	80,000	100,000	(20,000)
Capital lease obligation	400,000	—	400,000
Capital stock, common, $1 par	500,000	500,000	—
Additional paid-in capital	1,500,000	1,500,000	—
Retained earnings	2,970,000	2,680,000	290,000
Total liabilities and stockholders' equity	$6,495,000	$5,785,000	$710,000

Additional information:

1. On December 31, 2007, Blue Man acquired 25% of Blige Co.'s common stock for $275,000. On that date, the carrying value of Blige's assets and liabilities, which approximated their fair values, was $1,100,000. Blige reported income of $120,000 for the year ended December 31, 2008. No dividend was paid on Blige's common stock during the year.
2. During 2008, Blue Man loaned $300,000 to TLC Co., an unrelated company. TLC made the first semi-annual principal repayment of $37,500, plus interest at 10%, on December 31, 2008.
3. On January 2, 2008, Blue Man sold equipment costing $60,000, with a carrying amount of $35,000, for $40,000 cash.
4. On December 31, 2008, Blue Man entered into a capital lease for an office building. The present value of the annual rental payments is $400,000, which equals the fair value of the building. Blue Man made the first rental payment of $60,000 when due on January 2, 2009.
5. Net income for 2008 was $370,000.
6. Blue Man declared and paid cash dividends for 2008 and 2007 as shown below.

	2008	2007
Declared	December 15, 2008	December 15, 2007
Paid	February 28, 2009	February 28, 2008
Amount	$80,000	$100,000

Instructions

Prepare a statement of cash flows for Blue Man Corp. for the year ended December 31, 2008, using the indirect method.

(AICPA adapted)

(LO 6, 7, 8) **P23-2 (SCF—Indirect Method)** The comparative balance sheets for Shenandoah Corporation show the following information.

	December 31	
	2008	2007
Cash	$ 38,500	$13,000
Accounts receivable	12,250	10,000
Inventory	12,000	9,000
Investments	–0–	3,000
Building	–0–	29,750
Equipment	40,000	20,000
Patent	5,000	6,250
	$107,750	$91,000
Allowance for doubtful accounts	3,000	4,500
Accumulated depreciation on equipment	2,000	4,500
Accumulated depreciation on building	–0–	6,000
Accounts payable	5,000	3,000
Dividends payable	–0–	5,000
Notes payable, short-term (nontrade)	3,000	4,000
Long-term notes payable	31,000	25,000
Common stock	43,000	33,000
Retained earnings	20,750	6,000
	$107,750	$91,000

Additional data related to 2008 are as follows.

1. Equipment that had cost $11,000 and was 30% depreciated at time of disposal was sold for $2,500.
2. $10,000 of the long-term note payable was paid by issuing common stock.
3. Cash dividends paid were $5,000.
4. On January 1, 2008, the building was completely destroyed by a flood. Insurance proceeds on the building were $30,000 (net of $2,000 taxes).
5. Investments (available-for-sale) were sold at $3,700 above their cost. The company has made similar sales and investments in the past.
6. Cash of $15,000 was paid for the acquisition of equipment.
7. A long-term note for $16,000 was issued for the acquisition of equipment.
8. Interest of $2,000 and income taxes of $6,500 were paid in cash.

Instructions

Prepare a statement of cash flows using the indirect method. Flood damage is unusual and infrequent in that part of the country.

(LO 6) **P23-3 (SCF—Direct Method)** Mardi Gras Company has not yet prepared a formal statement of cash flows for the 2008 fiscal year. Comparative balance sheets as of December 31, 2007 and 2008, and a statement of income and retained earnings for the year ended December 31, 2008, are presented below.

MARDI GRAS COMPANY
STATEMENT OF INCOME AND RETAINED EARNINGS
FOR THE YEAR ENDED DECEMBER 31, 2008
($000 OMITTED)

Sales		$3,800
Expenses		
Cost of goods sold	$1,200	
Salaries and benefits	725	
Heat, light, and power	75	
Depreciation	80	
Property taxes	19	
Patent amortization	25	
Miscellaneous expenses	10	
Interest	30	2,164

MARDI GRAS COMPANY
STATEMENT OF INCOME AND RETAINED EARNINGS
FOR THE YEAR ENDED DECEMBER 31, 2008
(CONTINUED)

Income before income taxes	1,636
Income taxes	818
Net income	818
Retained earnings—Jan. 1, 2008	310
	1,128
Stock dividend declared and issued	600
Retained earnings—Dec. 31, 2008	$ 528

MARDI GRAS COMPANY
COMPARATIVE BALANCE SHEETS
AS OF DECEMBER 31
($000 OMITTED)

Assets	2008	2007
Current assets		
Cash	$ 383	$ 100
U.S. Treasury notes (Available-for-sale)	–0–	50
Accounts receivable	740	500
Inventory	720	560
Total current assets	1,843	1,210
Long-term assets		
Land	150	70
Buildings and equipment	910	600
Accumulated depreciation	(200)	(120)
Patents (less amortization)	105	130
Total long-term assets	965	680
Total assets	$2,808	$1,890
Liabilities and Stockholders' Equity		
Current liabilities		
Accounts payable	$ 420	$ 340
Income taxes payable	40	20
Notes payable	320	320
Total current liabilities	780	680
Long-term notes payable—due 2010	200	200
Total liabilities	980	880
Stockholders' equity		
Common stock	1,300	700
Retained earnings	528	310
Total stockholders' equity	1,828	1,010
Total liabilities and stockholders' equity	$2,808	$1,890

Instructions
Prepare a statement of cash flows using the direct method. Changes in accounts receivable and accounts payable relate to sales and cost of goods sold. Do not prepare a reconciliation schedule.

(CMA adapted)

(LO 6, 7, 8) **P23-4** **(SCF—Direct Method)** Cleveland Company had available at the end of 2007 the information on page 1267.

CLEVELAND COMPANY
COMPARATIVE BALANCE SHEETS
AS OF DECEMBER 31, 2007 AND 2006

	2007	2006
Cash	$ 15,000	$ 4,000
Accounts receivable	17,500	12,950
Short-term investments	20,000	30,000
Inventory	42,000	35,000
Prepaid rent	3,000	12,000
Prepaid insurance	2,100	900
Office supplies	1,000	750
Land	125,000	175,000
Building	350,000	350,000
Accumulated depreciation	(105,000)	(87,500)
Equipment	525,000	400,000
Accumulated depreciation	(130,000)	(112,000)
Patent	45,000	50,000
Total assets	$910,600	$871,100
Accounts payable	$ 27,000	$ 32,000
Taxes payable	5,000	4,000
Wages payable	5,000	3,000
Short-term notes payable	10,000	10,000
Long-term notes payable	60,000	70,000
Bonds payable	400,000	400,000
Premium on bonds payable	20,303	25,853
Common stock	240,000	220,000
Paid-in capital in excess of par	20,000	17,500
Retained earnings	123,297	88,747
Total liabilities and stockholders' equity	$910,600	$871,100

CLEVELAND COMPANY
INCOME STATEMENT
FOR THE YEAR ENDED DECEMBER 31, 2007

Sales revenue		$1,160,000
Cost of goods sold		(748,000)
		412,000
Gross margin		
Operating expenses		
Selling expenses	$ 79,200	
Administrative expenses	156,700	
Depreciation/Amortization expense	40,500	
Total operating expenses		(276,400)
Income from operations		135,600
Other revenues/expenses		
Gain on sale of land	8,000	
Gain on sale of short-term investment	4,000	
Dividend revenue	2,400	
Interest expense	(51,750)	(37,350)
Income before taxes		98,250
Income tax expense		(39,400)
Net income		58,850
Dividends to common stockholders		(24,300)
To retained earnings		$ 34,550

Instructions

Prepare a statement of cash flows for Cleveland Company using the direct method accompanied by a reconciliation schedule. Assume the short-term investments are available-for-sale securities.

(LO 6, 7, 8) **P23-5 (SCF—Indirect Method)** You have completed the field work in connection with your audit of Texas Hold Em Corporation for the year ended December 31, 2008. The balance sheet accounts at the beginning and end of the year are shown on the next page.

	Dec. 31, 2008	Dec. 31, 2007	Increase or (Decrease)
Cash	$ 267,900	$ 298,000	($30,100)
Accounts receivable	479,424	353,000	126,424
Inventory	741,700	610,000	131,700
Prepaid expenses	12,000	8,000	4,000
Investment in subsidiary	110,500	–0–	110,500
Cash surrender value of life insurance	2,304	1,800	504
Machinery	207,000	190,000	17,000
Buildings	535,200	407,900	127,300
Land	52,500	52,500	–0–
Patents	69,000	64,000	5,000
Copyright	40,000	50,000	(10,000)
Bond discount and expense	4,502	–0–	4,502
	$2,522,030	$2,035,200	$486,830
Accrued taxes payable	$ 90,250	$ 79,600	$ 10,650
Accounts payable	299,280	280,000	19,280
Dividends payable	70,000	–0–	70,000
Bonds payable—8%	125,000	–0–	125,000
Bonds payable—12%	–0–	100,000	(100,000)
Allowance for doubtful accounts	35,300	40,000	(4,700)
Accumulated depreciation—buildings	424,000	400,000	24,000
Accumulated depreciation—machinery	173,000	130,000	43,000
Premium on bonds payable	–0–	2,400	(2,400)
Capital stock—no par	1,176,200	1,453,200	(277,000)
Additional paid-in capital	109,000	–0–	109,000
Retained earnings—unappropriated	20,000	(450,000)	470,000
	$2,522,030	$2,035,200	$486,830

STATEMENT OF RETAINED EARNINGS
FOR THE YEAR ENDED DECEMBER 31, 2008

January 1, 2008	Balance (deficit)	$(450,000)
March 31, 2008	Net income for first quarter of 2008	25,000
April 1, 2008	Transfer from paid-in capital	425,000
	Balance	–0–
December 31, 2008	Net income for last three quarters of 2008	90,000
	Dividend declared—payable January 21, 2009	(70,000)
	Balance	$ 20,000

Your working papers contain the following information:

1. On April 1, 2008, the existing deficit was written off against paid-in capital created by reducing the stated value of the no-par stock.
2. On November 1, 2008, 29,600 shares of no-par stock were sold for $257,000. The board of directors voted to regard $5 per share as stated capital.
3. A patent was purchased for $15,000.
4. During the year, machinery that had a cost basis of $16,400 and on which there was accumulated depreciation of $5,200 was sold for $7,000. No other plant assets were sold during the year.
5. The 12%, 20-year bonds were dated and issued on January 2, 1996. Interest was payable on June 30 and December 31. They were sold originally at 106. These bonds were retired at 102 (net of $100 tax) plus accrued interest on March 31, 2008.
6. The 8%, 40-year bonds were dated January 1, 2008, and were sold on March 31 at 97 plus accrued interest. Interest is payable semiannually on June 30 and December 31. Expense of issuance was $839.
7. Texas Hold Em Corporation acquired 70% control in Amarillo Company on January 2, 2008, for $100,000. The income statement of Amarillo Company for 2008 shows a net income of $15,000.
8. Extraordinary repairs to buildings of $7,200 were charged to Accumulated Depreciation—Buildings.
9. Interest paid in 2008 was $10,500 and income taxes paid were $34,000.

Instructions

From the information given, prepare a statement of cash flows using the indirect method. A worksheet is not necessary, but the principal computations should be supported by schedules or skeleton ledger accounts.

(LO 3, 4, 6, 8) **P23-6** **(SCF—Indirect Method, and Net Cash Flow from Operating Activities, Direct Method)** Comparative balance sheet accounts of Secada Inc. are presented below.

SECADA INC.
COMPARATIVE BALANCE SHEET ACCOUNTS
AS OF DECEMBER 31, 2008 AND 2007

	December 31	
Debit Accounts	**2008**	**2007**
Cash	$ 45,000	$ 33,750
Accounts Receivable	67,500	60,000
Merchandise Inventory	30,000	24,000
Investments (available-for-sale)	22,250	38,500
Machinery	30,000	18,750
Buildings	67,500	56,250
Land	7,500	7,500
	$269,750	$238,750
Credit Accounts		
Allowance for Doubtful Accounts	$ 2,250	$ 1,500
Accumulated Depreciation—Machinery	5,625	2,250
Accumulated Depreciation—Buildings	13,500	9,000
Accounts Payable	30,000	24,750
Accrued Payables	3,375	2,625
Long-Term Note Payable	26,000	31,000
Common Stock, no par	150,000	125,000
Retained Earnings	39,000	42,625
	$269,750	$238,750

Additional data (ignoring taxes):

1. Net income for the year was $42,500.
2. Cash dividends declared during the year were $21,125.
3. A 20% stock dividend was declared during the year. $25,000 of retained earnings was capitalized.
4. Investments that cost $20,000 were sold during the year for $23,750.
5. Machinery that cost $3,750, on which $750 of depreciation had accumulated, was sold for $2,200.

Secada's 2008 income statement follows (ignoring taxes).

Sales		$540,000
Less: Cost of goods sold		380,000
Gross margin		160,000
Less: Operating expenses (includes $8,625 depreciation and $5,400 bad debts)		120,450
Income from operations		39,550
Other: Gain on sale of investments	$3,750	
Loss on sale of machinery	(800)	2,950
Net income		$ 42,500

Instructions

(a) Compute net cash flow from operating activities using the direct method.
(b) Prepare a statement of cash flows using the indirect method.

(LO 3, 4, 6, 8) **P23-7** **(SCF—Direct and Indirect Methods from Comparative Financial Statements)** George Winston Company, a major retailer of bicycles and accessories, operates several stores and is a publicly traded company. The comparative statement of financial position and income statement for Winston as of May 31, 2008, are shown on the next page. The company is preparing its statement of cash flows.

GEORGE WINSTON COMPANY
COMPARATIVE STATEMENT OF FINANCIAL POSITION
AS OF MAY 31

	2008	2007
Current assets		
Cash	$ 33,250	$ 20,000
Accounts receivable	80,000	58,000
Merchandise inventory	210,000	250,000
Prepaid expenses	9,000	7,000
Total current assets	332,250	335,000
Plant assets		
Plant assets	600,000	502,000
Less: Accumulated depreciation	150,000	125,000
Net plant assets	450,000	377,000
Total assets	$782,250	$712,000
Current liabilities		
Accounts payable	$123,000	$115,000
Salaries payable	47,250	72,000
Interest payable	27,000	25,000
Total current liabilities	197,250	212,000
Long-term debt		
Bonds payable	70,000	100,000
Total liabilities	267,250	312,000
Shareholders' equity		
Common stock, $10 par	370,000	280,000
Retained earnings	145,000	120,000
Total shareholders' equity	515,000	400,000
Total liabilities and shareholders' equity	$782,250	$712,000

GEORGE WINSTON COMPANY
INCOME STATEMENT
FOR THE YEAR ENDED MAY 31, 2008

Sales	$1,255,250
Cost of merchandise sold	722,000
Gross profit	533,250
Expenses	
Salary expense	252,100
Interest expense	75,000
Other expenses	8,150
Depreciation expense	25,000
Total expenses	360,250
Operating income	173,000
Income tax expense	43,000
Net income	$ 130,000

The following is additional information concerning Winston's transactions during the year ended May 31, 2008.

1. All sales during the year were made on account.
2. All merchandise was purchased on account, comprising the total accounts payable account.
3. Plant assets costing $98,000 were purchased by paying $48,000 in cash and issuing 5,000 shares of stock.
4. The "other expenses" are related to prepaid items.
5. All income taxes incurred during the year were paid during the year.
6. In order to supplement its cash, Winston issued 4,000 shares of common stock at par value.
7. There were no penalties assessed for the retirement of bonds.
8. Cash dividends of $105,000 were declared and paid at the end of the fiscal year.

Instructions

(a) Compare and contrast the direct method and the indirect method for reporting cash flows from operating activities.

(b) Prepare a statement of cash flows for Winston Company for the year ended May 31, 2008, using the direct method. Be sure to support the statement with appropriate calculations. (A reconciliation of net income to net cash provided is not required.)

(c) Using the indirect method, calculate only the net cash flow from operating activities for Winston Company for the year ended May 31, 2008.

(LO 6, 7, 8) **P23-8** **(SCF—Direct and Indirect Methods)** Comparative balance sheet accounts of Jensen Company are presented below.

JENSEN COMPANY
COMPARATIVE BALANCE SHEET ACCOUNTS
AS OF DECEMBER 31

Debit Balances	2007	2006
Cash	$ 80,000	$ 51,000
Accounts Receivable	145,000	130,000
Merchandise Inventory	75,000	61,000
Investments (Available-for-sale)	55,000	85,000
Equipment	70,000	48,000
Buildings	145,000	145,000
Land	40,000	25,000
Totals	$610,000	$545,000
Credit Balances		
Allowance for Doubtful Accounts	$ 10,000	$ 8,000
Accumulated Depreciation—Equipment	21,000	14,000
Accumulated Depreciation—Building	37,000	28,000
Accounts Payable	70,000	60,000
Income Taxes Payable	12,000	10,000
Long-Term Notes Payable	62,000	70,000
Common Stock	310,000	260,000
Retained Earnings	88,000	95,000
Totals	$610,000	$545,000

Additional data:

1. Equipment that cost $10,000 and was 40% depreciated was sold in 2007.
2. Cash dividends were declared and paid during the year.
3. Common stock was issued in exchange for land.
4. Investments that cost $35,000 were sold during the year.
5. There were no write-offs of uncollectible accounts during the year.

Jensen's 2007 income statement is as follows.

Sales		$950,000
Less: Cost of goods sold		600,000
Gross profit		350,000
Less: Operating expenses (includes depreciation expense and bad debt expense)		250,000
Income from operations		100,000
Other revenues and expenses		
Gain on sale of investments	$15,000	
Loss on sale of equipment	(3,000)	12,000
Income before taxes		112,000
Income taxes		45,000
Net income		$ 67,000

Instructions

(a) Compute net cash provided by operating activities under the direct method.

(b) Prepare a statement of cash flows using the indirect method.

(LO 6, 7, 8) **P23-9 (Indirect SCF)** Seneca Corporation has contracted with you to prepare a statement of cash flows. The controller has provided the following information.

	December 31	
	2007	2006
Cash	$ 43,500	$13,000
Accounts receivable	12,250	10,000
Inventory	12,000	10,000
Investments	–0–	3,000
Building	–0–	29,750
Equipment	35,000	20,000
Copyright	5,000	5,250
Totals	$107,750	$91,000
Allowance for doubtful accounts	$ 3,000	$ 4,500
Accumulated depreciation on equipment	2,000	4,500
Accumulated depreciation on building	–0–	6,000
Accounts payable	5,000	4,000
Dividends payable	–0–	5,000
Notes payable, short-term (nontrade)	3,000	4,000
Long-term notes payable	36,000	25,000
Common stock	38,000	33,000
Retained earnings	20,750	5,000
	$107,750	$91,000

Additional data related to 2007 are as follows.

1. Equipment that had cost $11,000 and was 40% depreciated at time of disposal was sold for $2,500.
2. $5,000 of the long-term note payable was paid by issuing common stock.
3. Cash dividends paid were $5,000.
4. On January 1, 2007, the building was completely destroyed by a flood. Insurance proceeds on the building were $33,000 (net of $4,000 taxes).
5. Investments (available-for-sale) were sold at $2,500 above their cost. The company has made similar sales and investments in the past.
6. Cash of $10,000 was paid for the acquisition of equipment.
7. A long-term note for $16,000 was issued for the acquisition of equipment.
8. Interest of $2,000 and income taxes of $5,000 were paid in cash.

Instructions

(a) Use the indirect method to analyze the above information and prepare a statement of cash flows for Seneca. Flood damage is unusual and infrequent in that part of the country.

(b) What would you expect to observe in the operating, investing, and financing sections of a statement of cash flows of:
  (1) a severely financially troubled firm?
  (2) a recently formed firm which is experiencing rapid growth?

CONCEPTS FOR ANALYSIS

CA23-1 (Analysis of Improper SCF) The following statement was prepared by Abriendo Corporation's accountant.

ABRIENDO CORPORATION	
STATEMENT OF SOURCES AND APPLICATION OF CASH	
FOR THE YEAR ENDED SEPTEMBER 30, 2008	
Sources of cash	
Net income	$ 111,000
Depreciation and depletion	70,000
Increase in long-term debt	179,000
Changes in current receivables and inventories, less current liabilities (excluding current maturities of long-term debt)	14,000
	$374,000
Application of cash	
Cash dividends	$ 60,000
Expenditure for property, plant, and equipment	214,000

Investments and other uses	20,000
Change in cash	80,000
	$374,000

The following additional information relating to Abriendo Corporation is available for the year ended September 30, 2008.

1. Wage and salary expense attributable to stock option plans was $22,000 for the year.
2. Expenditures for property, plant, and equipment $250,000
   Proceeds from retirements of property, plant, and equipment   36,000

   Net expenditures $214,000
3. A stock dividend of 10,000 shares of Abriendo Corporation common stock was distributed to common stockholders on April 1, 2008, when the per-share market price was $7 and par value was $1.
4. On July 1, 2008, when its market price was $6 per share, 16,000 shares of Abriendo Corporation common stock were issued in exchange for 4,000 shares of preferred stock.
5. Depreciation expense $ 65,000
   Depletion expense   5,000

        $ 70,000
6. Increase in long-term debt $620,000
   Retirement of debt   441,000

   Net increase $179,000

Instructions

(a) In general, what are the objectives of a statement of the type shown above for Abriendo Corporation? Explain.
(b) Identify the weaknesses in the form and format of Abriendo Corporation's statement of cash flows without reference to the additional information. (Assume adoption of the indirect method.)
(c) For each of the six items of additional information for the statement of cash flows, indicate the preferable treatment and explain why the suggested treatment is preferable.

(AICPA adapted)

 CA23-2 (SCF Theory and Analysis of Improper SCF) Gloria Estefan and Flaco Jimenez are examining the following statement of cash flows for Tropical Clothing Store's first year of operations.

TROPICAL CLOTHING STORE
STATEMENT OF CASH FLOWS
FOR THE YEAR ENDED JANUARY 31, 2008

Sources of cash	
From sales of merchandise	$ 362,000
From sale of capital stock	400,000
From sale of investment	120,000
From depreciation	80,000
From issuance of note for truck	30,000
From interest on investments	8,000
Total sources of cash	1,000,000
Uses of cash	
For purchase of fixtures and equipment	340,000
For merchandise purchased for resale	253,000
For operating expenses (including depreciation)	170,000
For purchase of investment	85,000
For purchase of truck by issuance of note	30,000
For purchase of treasury stock	10,000
For interest on note	3,000
Total uses of cash	891,000
Net increase in cash	$ 109,000

Gloria claims that Tropical's statement of cash flows is an excellent portrayal of a superb first year, with cash increasing $109,000. Flaco replies that it was not a superb first year—that the year was an operating failure, the statement was incorrectly presented, and $109,000 is not the actual increase in cash.

Instructions

(a) With whom do you agree, Gloria or Flaco? Explain your position.

(b) Using the data provided, prepare a statement of cash flows in proper indirect method form. The only noncash items in income are depreciation and the gain from the sale of the investment (purchase and sale are related).

CA23-3 (SCF Theory and Analysis of Transactions) John Lee Hooker Company is a young and growing producer of electronic measuring instruments and technical equipment. You have been retained by Hooker to advise it in the preparation of a statement of cash flows using the indirect method. For the fiscal year ended October 31, 2008, you have obtained the following information concerning certain events and transactions of Hooker.

1. The amount of reported earnings for the fiscal year was $800,000, which included a deduction for an extraordinary loss of $110,000 (see item 5 below).
2. Depreciation expense of $315,000 was included in the income statement.
3. Uncollectible accounts receivable of $40,000 were written off against the allowance for doubtful accounts. Also, $51,000 of bad debt expense was included in determining income for the fiscal year, and the same amount was added to the allowance for doubtful accounts.
4. A gain of $9,000 was realized on the sale of a machine. It originally cost $75,000, of which $30,000 was undepreciated on the date of sale.
5. On April 1, 2008, lightning caused an uninsured building loss of $110,000 ($180,000 loss, less reduction in income taxes of $70,000). This extraordinary loss was included in determining income as indicated in 1 above.
6. On July 3, 2008, building and land were purchased for $700,000. Hooker gave in payment $75,000 cash, $200,000 market value of its unissued common stock, and signed a $425,000 mortgage note payable.
7. On August 3, 2008, $800,000 face value of Hooker's 10% convertible debentures were converted into $150,000 par value of its common stock. The bonds were originally issued at face value.

Instructions

Explain whether each of the seven numbered items above is a source or use of cash, and explain how it should be disclosed in John Lee Hooker's statement of cash flows for the fiscal year ended October 31, 2008. If any item is neither a source nor a use of cash, explain why it is not, and indicate the disclosure, if any, that should be made of the item in John Lee Hooker's statement of cash flows for the fiscal year ended October 31, 2008.

 CA23-4 (Analysis of Transactions' Effect on SCF) Each of the following items must be considered in preparing a statement of cash flows for Sage Fashions Inc. for the year ended December 31, 2008.

1. Fixed assets that had cost $20,000 6½ years before and were being depreciated on a 10-year basis, with no estimated scrap value, were sold for $5,250.
2. During the year, goodwill of $15,000 was considered impaired and was completely written off to expense.
3. During the year, 500 shares of common stock with a stated value of $25 a share were issued for $34 a share.
4. The company sustained a net loss for the year of $2,100. Depreciation amounted to $2,000 and patent amortization was $400.
5. Uncollectible accounts receivable in the amount of $2,000 were written off against the Allowance for Doubtful Accounts.
6. Investments (available-for-sale) that cost $12,000 when purchased 4 years earlier were sold for $10,600. The loss was considered ordinary.
7. Bonds payable with a par value of $24,000 on which there was an unamortized bond premium of $2,000 were redeemed at 103. The gain was credited to ordinary income.

Instructions

For each item, state where it is to be shown in the statement and then how you would present the necessary information, including the amount. Consider each item to be independent of the others. Assume that correct entries were made for all transactions as they took place.

CA23-5 (Purpose and Elements of SCF) In 1987 the Financial Accounting Standards Board issued *Statement of Financial Accounting Standards (SFAS) No. 95*, "Statement of Cash Flows."

Instructions

(a) Explain the purposes of the statement of cash flows.

(b) List and describe the three categories of activities that must be reported in the statement of cash flows.

(c) Identify and describe the two methods that are allowed for reporting cash flows from operations.

(d) Describe the financial statement presentation of noncash investing and financing transactions. Include in your description an example of a noncash investing and financing transaction.

CA23-6 (Cash Flow Reporting) Durocher Guitar Company is in the business of manufacturing top-quality, steel-string folk guitars. In recent years the company has experienced working capital problems resulting from the procurement of factory equipment, the unanticipated buildup of receivables and inventories, and the payoff of a balloon mortgage on a new manufacturing facility. The founder and president of the company, Laraine Durocher, has attempted to raise cash from various financial institutions, but to no avail because of the company's poor performance in recent years. In particular, the company's lead bank, First Financial, is especially concerned about Durocher's inability to maintain a positive cash position. The commercial loan officer from First Financial told Laraine, "I can't even consider your request for capital financing unless I see that your company is able to generate positive cash flows from operations."

Thinking about the banker's comment, Laraine came up with what she believes is a good plan: With a more attractive statement of cash flows, the bank might be willing to provide long-term financing. To "window dress" cash flows, the company can sell its accounts receivables to factors and liquidate its raw materials inventories. These rather costly transactions would generate lots of cash. As the chief accountant for Durocher Guitar, it is your job to tell Laraine what you think of her plan.

Instructions

Answer the following questions.

(a) What are the ethical issues related to Laraine Durocher's idea?

(b) What would you tell Laraine Durocher?

USING YOUR JUDGMENT

Financial Reporting Problem

The Procter & Gamble Company (P&G)

The financial statements of **P&G** are presented in Appendix 5B or can be accessed on the KWW website.

Instructions

Refer to P&G's financial statements and the accompanying notes to answer the following questions.

(a) Which method of computing net cash provided by operating activities does P&G use? What were the amounts of net cash provided by operating activities for the years 2002, 2003, and 2004? Which two items were most responsible for the increase in net cash provided by operating activities in 2004?

(b) What was the most significant item in the cash flows used for investing activities section in 2004? What was the most significant item in the cash flows used for financing activities section in 2004?

(c) Where is "deferred income taxes" reported in P&G's statement of cash flows? Why does it appear in that section of the statement of cash flows?

(d) Where is depreciation reported in P&G's statement of cash flows? Why is depreciation added to net income in the statement of cash flows?

Financial Statement Analysis Case

Vermont Teddy Bear Co.

Founded in the early 1980s, the **Vermont Teddy Bear Co.** designs and manufactures American-made teddy bears and markets them primarily as gifts called Bear-Grams or Teddy Bear-Grams. Bear-Grams are personalized teddy bears delivered directly to the recipient for special occasions such as birthdays and anniversaries. The Shelburne, Vermont, company's primary markets are New York, Boston, and Chicago.

Sales have jumped dramatically in recent years. Such dramatic growth has significant implications for cash flows. Provided below are the cash flow statements for two recent years for the company.

	Current Year	Prior Year
Cash flows from operating activities:		
Net income	$ 17,523	$ 838,955
Adjustments to reconcile net income to net cash provided by operating activities		
Deferred income taxes	(69,524)	(146,590)
Depreciation and amortization	316,416	181,348
Changes in assets and liabilities:		
Accounts receivable, trade	(38,267)	(25,947)
Inventories	(1,599,014)	(1,289,293)
Prepaid and other current assets	(444,794)	(113,205)
Deposits and other assets	(24,240)	(83,044)
Accounts payable	2,017,059	(284,567)
Accrued expenses	61,321	170,755
Accrued interest payable, debentures	—	(58,219)
Other	—	(8,960)
Income taxes payable	—	117,810
Net cash provided by (used for) operating activities	236,480	(700,957)
Net cash used for investing activities	(2,102,892)	(4,422,953)
Net cash (used for) provided by financing activities	(315,353)	9,685,435
Net change in cash and cash equivalents	(2,181,765)	4,561,525

Other information:

Current liabilities	$ 4,055,465	$ 1,995,600
Total liabilities	4,620,085	2,184,386
Net sales	20,560,566	17,025,856

Instructions

(a) Note that net income in the current year was only $17,523 compared to prior-year income of $838,955, but cash flow from operations was $236,480 in the current year and a negative $700,957 in the prior year. Explain the causes of this apparent paradox.

(b) Evaluate Vermont Teddy Bear's liquidity, solvency, and profitability for the current year using cash flow-based ratios.

Comparative Analysis Case

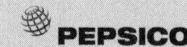

The Coca-Cola Company and PepsiCo, Inc.

Instructions

Go to the KWW website and use information found there to answer the following questions related to **The Coca-Cola Company** and **PepsiCo, Inc.**

(a) What method of computing net cash provided by operating activities does Coca-Cola use? What method does PepsiCo use? What were the amounts of cash provided by operating activities reported by Coca-Cola and PepsiCo in 2004?

(b) What was the most significant item reported by Coca-Cola and PepsiCo in 2004 in their investing activities sections? What is the most significant item reported by Coca-Cola and PepsiCo in 2004 in their financing activities sections?

(c) What were these two companies' trends in net cash provided by operating activities over the period 2002 to 2004?

(d) Where is "depreciation and amortization" reported by Coca-Cola and PepsiCo in their statements of cash flows? What is the amount and why does it appear in that section of the statement of cash flows?

(e) Based on the information contained in Coca-Cola's and PepsiCo's financial statements, compute the following 2004 ratios for each company. These ratios require the use of statement of cash flows data. (These ratios were covered in Chapter 5.)

    (1) Current cash debt coverage ratio.

    (2) Cash debt coverage ratio.

(f) What conclusions concerning the management of cash can be drawn from the ratios computed in (e)?

Research Case

The March 5, 2002, edition of the *Wall Street Journal* included an article by Mark Maremont entitled "How Is Tyco Accounting for Its Cash Flow?—Its Touted Measure of Strength Leaves Room for Interpretation."

Instructions

Read the article and answer the following questions.

(a) Many analysts believe that cash flow is not as susceptible to "reporting manipulation" as income. What "complications" discussed in this article make that belief questionable?

(b) What is "free cash flow"? How was Tyco manipulating its reporting of "free cash flow"?

(c) Under U.S. GAAP, how is free cash flow determined?

(d) How is Tyco "buying earnings and operating cash flow"? Why is this practice risky for investors?

International Reporting Case

As noted in the chapter, there is international diversity in the preparation of the statement of cash flows. For example, under International Accounting Standards companies may choose how to classify dividends and interest in the cash flow statement. In some countries, like Brazil, a cash flow statement is not required. **Embraer**, a Brazilian aircraft manufacturer, prepared a statement of changes in financial position, rather than a statement of cash flows.

Instructions

Refer to Embraer's 2004 Statement of Changes in Financial Position below and on page 1278 to answer the following questions.

(a) Briefly discuss at least two similarities between Embraer's statement of changes in financial position and a statement of cash flows prepared according to U.S. GAAP.

(b) Briefly discuss at least two differences between Embraer's statement of changes in financial position and a statement of cash flows prepared according to U.S. GAAP.

Embraer
Consolidated Statement of Changes in Financial Position
for the Year Ended December 31, 2004
(in thousands of Brazilian reals)

Sources of Funds	2004
Provided from operations	
Net income	1,255,833
Items not affecting working capital	
Equity in unconsolidated subsidiary	
Translation losses on foreign investments	19,613
Minority interest	8,618
Depreciation and amortization	221,554
Net book value of permanent asset disposal	799
Interest on long-term items added to principal, net	(25,759)
Net monetary and exchange variations on long-term items	(201,030)
Provision for losses	34,268
Long-term deferred income and social contribution taxes	(47,765)
Provisions for contingencies	57,930
Funds provided from operations	1,324,061
From shareholders	
Capital increase	9,524

Sources of Funds (continued)	2004
From third parties	
Increase in long-term liabilities	
Customers' advances	257,528
Loans	1,317,535
Accounts payable and other liabilities	964,260
Tax incentives	5,672
Transfers to current asset	1,042,182
Increase in minority interest	17,997
Funds provided from third parties	3,605,174
Total sources	4,938,759
Applications of Funds	
Increase in noncurrent assets	1,390,520
Investments	41,219
Property plant and equipment	109,656
Deferred charges	415,954
Transfers to current liabilities	731,098
Interest on capital	585,173
Total applications	3,273,620
Increase in working capital	1,665,139
Working capital—end of year	
Current assets	10,329,032
Current liabilities	5,420,966
	4,908,066
Working capital—beginning of year	3,242,927
Increase in working capital	1,665,139

Professional Research: Financial Accounting and Reporting

As part of the year-end accounting process for your company, you are preparing the statement of cash flows according to GAAP. One of your team, a finance major, believes the statement should be prepared to report the change in working capital, because analysts many times use working capital in ratio analysis. Your supervisor would like research conducted to verify the basis for preparing the statement of cash flows.

Instructions

Using the **Financial Accounting Research System (FARS),** respond to the following items. (Provide text strings used in your search.)

(a) Has GAAP ever allowed the statement of cash flows to be prepared on the basis of working capital?

(b) What were the problems with using working capital as a concept of funds? Why is cash a more useful concept of funds?

(c) What information is provided in a statement of cash flows?

(d) List some of the typical cash inflows and outflows from operations.

Professional Simulation

In this simulation you are asked to address questions related to the statement of cash flows. Prepare responses to all parts.

KWW_Professional_Simulation

| Statement of Cash Flows | Time Remaining 1 hour 00 minutes | copy | paste | calculator | sheet | standard | help | splitter | done |

Directions | Situation | Financial Statements | Explanation | Resources

Ellwood House, Inc. had the following condensed balance sheet at the end of 2006.

ELLWOOD HOUSE, INC.
Balance Sheet
December 31, 2006

Cash	$ 10,000	Current liabilities	$ 14,500
Current assets (noncash)	34,000	Long-term notes payable	30,000
Investments (available-for-sale)	40,000	Bonds payable	32,000
Plant assets	57,500	Capital stock	80,000
Land	38,500	Retained earnings	23,500
	$180,000		$180,000

During 2007 the following occurred.

1. Ellwood House, Inc., sold part of its investment portfolio for $15,500, resulting in a gain of $500 for the firm. The company often sells and buys securities of this nature.
2. Dividends totaling $19,000 were paid to stockholders.
3. A parcel of land was purchased for $5,500.
4. $20,000 of capital stock was issued at par.
5. $10,000 of bonds payable were retired at par.
6. Heavy equipment was purchased through the issuance of $32,000 of bonds.
7. Net income for 2007 was $42,000 after allowing depreciation of $13,550.
8. Both current assets (other than cash) and current liabilities remained at the same amount.

Directions | Situation | Financial Statements | Explanation | Resources

Prepare a statement of cash flows for 2007, using the indirect method.

Directions | Situation | Financial Statements | Explanation | Resources

Draft a one-page letter to Gerald Brauer, president of Ellwood House, Inc., briefly explaining the changes within each major cash flow category. Refer to your cash flow statement whenever necessary.

Remember to check the book's companion website to find additional resources for this chapter.

wiley.com/college/kieso

FULL DISCLOSURE IN FINANCIAL REPORTING

High-Quality Financial Reporting— It's a Necessity

Here are excerpts from leading experts regarding the importance of high-quality financial reporting:[1]

Warren E. Buffett, Chairman and Chief Executive Officer, **Berkshire Hathaway Inc.**:

Financial reporting for Berkshire Hathaway, and for me personally, is the beginning of every decision that we make around here in terms of capital. I'm punching out 10-Ks and 10-Qs every single day. We look at the numbers and try to evaluate the quality of the financial reporting, and then we try to figure out what that means for the bonds and stocks that we're looking at, and thinking of either buying or selling.

Judy Lewent, Executive Vice President and Chief Financial Officer, Merck & Co., Inc.

. . . Higher standards, when properly implemented, drive excellence. I can make a parallel to the pharmaceutical industry. If you look around the world at where innovations come from, economists have studied and seen that where regulatory standards are the highest is where innovation is also the highest.

Floyd Norris, Chief Financial Correspondent, the **New York Times**:

We are in a situation now in our society where the temptations to provide "bad" financial reporting are probably greater than they used to be. The need to get the stock price up, or to keep it up, is intense. So, the temptation to play games, the temptation to manage earnings—some of which can be legitimate and some of which cannot be—is probably greater than it used to be.

Abby Joseph Cohen, Chair, Investment Policy Committee, **Goldman, Sachs & Co.**:

High-quality financial reporting is perhaps the most important thing we can expect from companies. For investors to make good decisions—whether those investors are buying stocks or bonds or making private investments—they need to know the truth. And we think that when information is as clear as possible and is reported as frequently as makes sense, investors can do their jobs as best they can.

In short, these comments illustrate why high-quality financial reporting is important to companies, to investors, and to the capital markets. At the heart of high-quality financial reporting is full disclosure.

---

[1]Excerpts taken from video entitled "Financially Correct with Ben Stein," Financial Accounting Standards Board (Norwalk, Conn.: FASB, 2002). By permission.

Learning Objectives

After studying this chapter, you should be able to:

1 Review the full disclosure principle and describe implementation problems.

2 Explain the use of notes in financial statement preparation.

3 Discuss the disclosure requirements for major business segments.

4 Describe the accounting problems associated with interim reporting.

5 Identify the major disclosures in the auditor's report.

6 Understand management's responsibilities for financials.

7 Identify issues related to financial forecasts and projections.

8 Describe the profession's response to fraudulent financial reporting.

As the opening story indicates, our markets will not function properly without transparent, complete, and truthful reporting of financial performance. Investors and other interested parties need to read and understand all aspects of financial reporting—the financial statements, the notes, the president's letter, and management's discussion and analysis. In this chapter, we cover the full disclosure principle in more detail and examine disclosures that must accompany financial statements so that they are not misleading. The content and organization of this chapter are as follows.

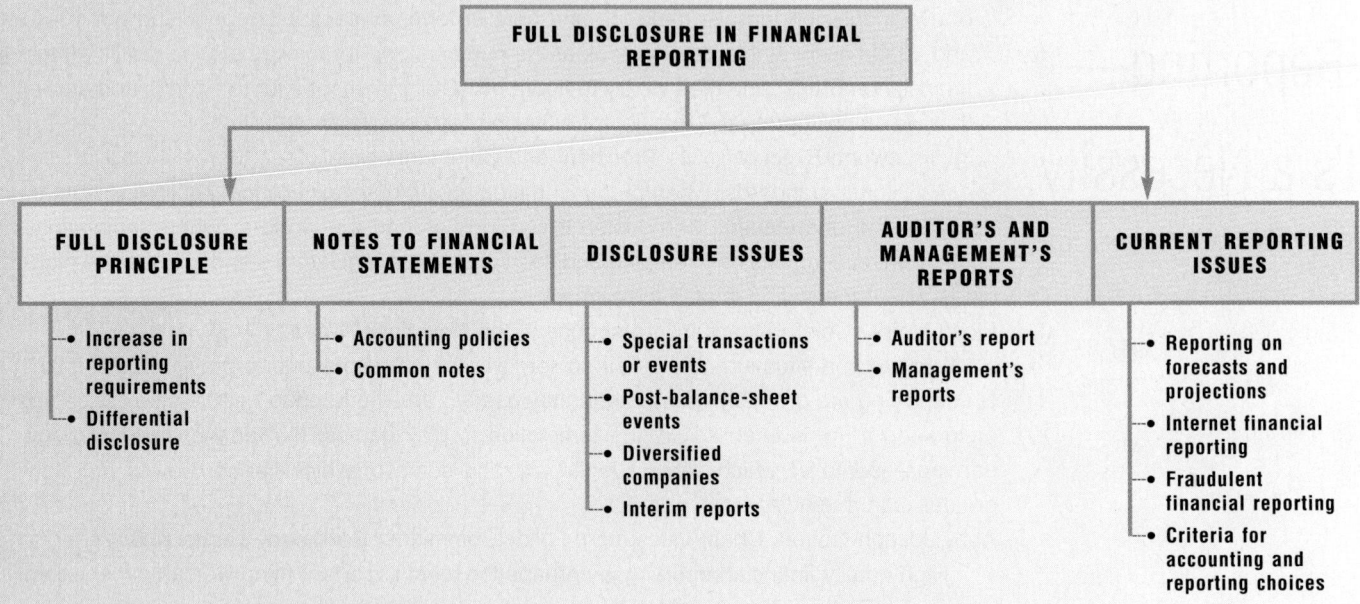

FULL DISCLOSURE PRINCIPLE

FASB Concepts Statement No. 1 notes that some useful information is best provided in the financial statements, and some is best provided by means other than in financial statements. For example, earnings and cash flows are readily available in financial statements—but investors might do better to look at comparisons to other companies in the same industry, found in news articles or brokerage house reports.

OBJECTIVE 1
Review the full disclosure principle and describe implementation problems.

FASB standards directly affect financial statements, notes to the financial statements, and supplementary information. Other types of information found in the annual report, such as management's discussion and analysis, are not subject to FASB standards. Illustration 24-1 (page 1283) indicates the various types of financial information.

As Chapter 2 indicated, the profession has adopted a **full disclosure principle**. The full disclosure principle calls for financial reporting of **any financial facts significant enough to influence the judgment of an informed reader**. In some situations, the benefits of disclosure may be apparent but the costs uncertain. In other instances, the costs may be certain but the benefits of disclosure not as apparent.

For example, recently, the SEC required companies to provide expanded disclosures about their contractual obligations. In light of the off-balance sheet accounting frauds at companies like **Enron**, the benefits of these expanded disclosures seem fairly obvious to the investing public. While no one has documented the exact costs of disclosure in these situations, they would appear to be relatively small.

On the other hand, the cost of disclosure can be substantial in some cases and the benefits difficult to assess. For example, at one time the *Wall Street Journal* reported that

UNDERLYING CONCEPTS

Here is a good example of the trade-off between cost considerations and the benefits of full disclosure.

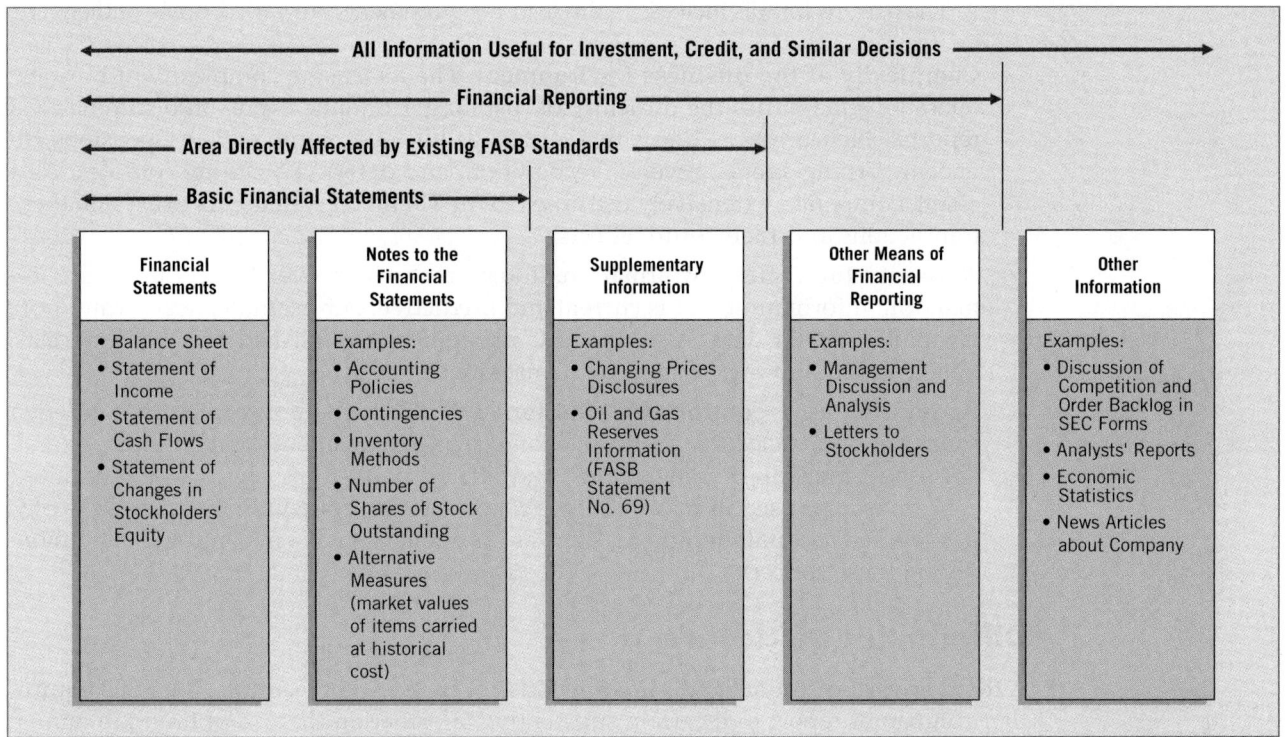

ILLUSTRATION 24-1
Types of Financial
Information

UNDERLYING CONCEPTS

The AICPA's Special Committee
on Financial Reporting notes that
business reporting is not free,
and improving it requires considering the relative costs and benefits of information. Undisciplined
expansion of mandated reporting
could result in large and need-
less costs.

if segment reporting were adopted, a company like **Fruehauf** would have had to increase its accounting staff 50 percent, from 300 to 450 individuals. In this case, the cost
of disclosure can be measured, but the benefits are less well defined.

Some even argue that the reporting requirements are so detailed and substantial
that users have a difficult time absorbing the information. These critics charge the profession with engaging in **information overload**.

Financial disasters at **Microstrategy**, **PharMor**, **WorldCom**, and **Global Crossing** highlight the difficulty of implementing the full disclosure principle. They raise the issue of
why investors were not aware of potential problems: Was the information these companies presented not comprehensible? Was it buried? Was it too technical? Was it properly
presented and fully disclosed as of the financial statement date, but the situation later deteriorated? Or was it simply not there? In the following sections, we describe the elements
of high-quality disclosure that will enable companies to avoid these disclosure pitfalls.

Increase in Reporting Requirements

Disclosure requirements have increased substantially. One recent survey showed that
the size of many companies' annual reports is growing in response to demands for increased transparency. For example, annual report page counts ranged from 70 pages
for **Gateway** up to a whopping 244 pages in **Eastman Kodak**'s annual report. Compared to prior years' reports, the percentage increase in pages ranged from 17 percent
at **IBM** to over 80 percent at **Siebel Systems**.[2] This result is not surprising; as illustrated throughout this textbook, the FASB has issued many standards in the last 10
years that have substantial disclosure provisions.

---

[2]Aliya Sternstein, "Heavy Lifting Required," *Forbes* (October 13, 2003) p. 58. Another earlier
study documented annual report growth for a sample of 25 large, well-known companies over
a recent 10-year period. The average number of pages of notes to the financial statements increased from 9 to 17 pages, and the average number of pages for management's discussion and
analysis grew from 7 to 12 pages. See Ray J. Groves, "Financial Disclosure: When More Is Not
Better," *Financial Executive* (May/June 1994).

The reasons for this increase in disclosure requirements are varied. Some of them are:

Complexity of the Business Environment. The increasing complexity of business operations magnifies the difficulty of distilling economic events into summarized reports. Such areas as derivatives, leasing, business combinations, pensions, financing arrangements, revenue recognition, and deferred taxes are complex. As a result, companies extensively use **notes to the financial statements** to explain these transactions and their future effects.

Necessity for Timely Information. Today, more than ever before, users are demanding information that is current and predictive. For example, users want more complete **interim data**. Also, the SEC recommends published financial forecasts, long avoided and even feared by management.

Accounting as a Control and Monitoring Device. The government has recently sought public disclosure of such phenomena as management compensation, off-balance-sheet financing arrangements, and related party transactions. An "Enronitis" concern is expressed in many of these newer disclosure requirements, and the SEC has selected accountants and auditors as the agents to assist in controlling and monitoring these concerns.

Differential Disclosure

A trend toward **differential disclosure** is also occurring. For example, the SEC requires that companies report to it certain substantive information that is not found in annual reports to stockholders. Likewise, the FASB, recognizing that certain disclosure requirements are costly and unnecessary for certain companies, has eliminated reporting requirements for nonpublic enterprises in such areas as fair value of financial instruments and segment reporting.[3]

WHAT DO THE NUMBERS MEAN?

"THE HEART OF THE MATTER"

As we discussed in the opening story, financial disclosure is one of a number of institutional features that contribute to vibrant security markets. In fact, a recent study of disclosure and other mechanisms (such as civil lawsuits and criminal sanctions) found that good disclosure is the most important contributor to a vibrant market.

The study, which compared disclosure and other legal and regulatory elements across 49 countries, found that countries with the best disclosure laws have the biggest stock markets. Countries with more successful market environments also tend to have regulations that make it relatively easy for private investors to sue corporations that provide bad information. That is, while criminal sanctions can be effective in some circumstances, disclosure and other legal and regulatory elements encouraging good disclosure are the most important determinants of highly liquid and deep securities markets.

These findings hold for nations in all stages of economic development, with particular importance for nations that are in the early stages of securities regulation. The lesson: Disclosure is good for your market.

Source: Rebecca Christie, "Study: Disclosure at Heart of Effective Securities Laws," *Wall Street Journal Online* (August 11, 2003).

---

[3]The FASB has had a disclosure-effectiveness project. The revised pension and postretirement benefit disclosures discussed in Chapter 20 [*FASB Statement No. 132* and *FASB Statement No. 132(R)*] are one example of how disclosures can be streamlined and made more useful. However, as noted by one FASB member, the usefulness of expanded required disclosure also depends on users' ability to distinguish between disclosed versus recognized items in financial statements. Research to date is inconclusive on this matter. See Katherine Schipper, "Required Disclosures in Financial Reports," Presidential Address to the American Accounting Association Annual Meeting; San Francisco, CA (August 2005).

Some still complain that the FASB has not gone far enough. They note that certain types of companies (small or nonpublic) should not have to follow complex GAAP requirements such as those for deferred income taxes, leases, or pensions. This issue, often referred to as "**big GAAP versus little GAAP**," continues to be controversial. The FASB takes the position that there should be one set of GAAP, except in unusual situations.[4]

UNDERLYING CONCEPTS

The AICPA Special Committee on Financial Reporting indicated that users differ in their needs for information and that not all companies should report all elements of information. Rather, companies should report only information that users and preparers agree is needed in the particular circumstances.

NOTES TO THE FINANCIAL STATEMENTS

OBJECTIVE 2
Explain the use of notes in financial statement preparation.

As you know from your study of this textbook, notes are an integral part of the financial statements of a business enterprise. However, readers of financial statements often overlook them because they are highly technical and often appear in small print. **Notes are the means of amplifying or explaining the items presented in the main body of the statements.** They can explain in qualitative terms information pertinent to specific financial statement items. In addition, they can provide supplementary data of a quantitative nature to expand the information in the financial statements. Notes also can explain restrictions imposed by financial arrangements or basic contractual agreements. Although notes may be technical and difficult to understand, they provide meaningful information for the user of the financial statements.

Accounting Policies

Accounting policies are the specific accounting principles and methods a company currently uses and considers most appropriate to present fairly its financial statements. *APB Opinion No. 22*, "Disclosure of Accounting Policies," states that information about the accounting policies adopted by a reporting entity is essential for financial statement users in making economic decisions. It recommended that companies should present **as an integral part of the financial statements a statement identifying the accounting policies adopted and followed by the reporting entity**. Companies should present the disclosure as the first note or in a separate Summary of Significant Accounting Policies section preceding the notes to the financial statements.

The Summary of Significant Accounting Policies answers such questions as: What method of depreciation is used on plant assets? What valuation method is employed on inventories? What amortization policy is followed in regard to intangible assets? How are marketing costs handled for financial reporting purposes?

Refer to Appendix 5B, pages 202–228, for an illustration of note disclosure of accounting policies (Note 1) and other notes accompanying the audited financial statements of **The Procter & Gamble Company**. Illustration 24-2 (pages 1286–1287) shows another example, from **Tootsie Roll Industries**.

Analysts examine carefully the summary of accounting policies to determine whether a company is using conservative or liberal accounting practices. For example, depreciating plant assets over an unusually long period of time is considered liberal. Using LIFO inventory valuation in a period of inflation is generally viewed as conservative.

Companies that fail to adopt high-quality reporting policies may be heavily penalized by the market. For example, when **Microstrategy** disclosed that it would restate prior-year results due to use of aggressive revenue recognition policies, its share

UNDERLYING CONCEPTS

The AICPA's Special Committee on Financial Reporting states that to meet users' changing needs, business reporting must: (1) Provide more forward-looking information. (2) Focus more on the factors that create longer-term value, including nonfinancial measures. (3) Better align information reported externally with the information reported internally.

[4]In response to cost-benefit concerns, the SEC has exempted some small public companies from certain rules implemented in response to the Sarbanes-Oxley Act of 2002. For example, smaller companies have more time to comply with the internal control rules required by the Sarbanes-Oxley law and have more time to file annual and interim reports. Both the FASB and the AICPA are studying the big GAAP/little GAAP issue to ensure that any kind of differential reporting is conceptually sound and meets the needs of users. See Remarks of Robert H. Herz, Chairman, Financial Accounting Standards Board, 2004 AICPA National Conference on Current SEC and PCAOB Reporting Developments (December 7, 2004.)

price dropped over 60 percent in one day. Investors viewed Microstrategy's quality of earnings as low.

ILLUSTRATION 24-2
Note Disclosure of
Accounting Policies

Tootsie Roll Industries, Inc. and Subsidiaries
(Dollars in thousands, except per share amounts)

Note 1—Significant Accounting Policies (in part)

Basis of consolidation:
The consolidated financial statements include the accounts of Tootsie Roll Industries, Inc. and its wholly-owned subsidiaries (the company), which are primarily engaged in the manufacture and sale of candy products. All significant intercompany transactions have been eliminated. . . .

Revenue recognition and other accounting pronouncements:
Products are sold to customers based on accepted purchase orders which include quantity, sales price and other relevant terms of sale. Revenues are recognized when products are delivered to customers and collectibility is reasonably assured. Shipping and handling costs of $31,795, $28,217 and $28,579 in 2004, 2003 and 2002, respectively, are included in selling, marketing and administrative expenses. Accounts receivable are unsecured. Revenues from a major customer aggregated approximately 20.8%, 20.6% and 19.6% of total net sales during the years ended December 31, 2004, 2003 and 2002, respectively. . . .

Cash and cash equivalents:
The company considers temporary cash investments with an original maturity of three months or less to be cash equivalents.

Investments:
Investments consist of various marketable securities with maturities of generally up to four years. The company classifies debt and equity securities as either held to maturity, available for sale or trading. Held to maturity securities represent those securities that the company has both the positive intent and ability to hold to maturity and are carried at amortized cost. Available for sale securities represent those securities that do not meet the classification of held to maturity, are not actively traded and are carried at fair value. Unrealized gains and losses on these securities are excluded from earnings and are reported as a separate component of shareholders equity, net of applicable taxes, until realized. Trading securities relate to deferred compensation arrangements and are carried at fair value.

Hedging activities:
From time to time, the company enters into commodities futures contracts that are intended and effective as hedges of market price risks associated with the anticipated purchase of certain raw materials (primarily sugar). To qualify as a hedge, the company evaluates a variety of characteristics of these transactions, including the probability that the anticipated transaction will occur. If the anticipated transaction were not to occur, the gain or loss would then be recognized in current earnings. The company does not engage in trading or other speculative use of derivative instruments. The company does assume the risk that counterparties may not be able to meet the terms of their contracts. The company does not expect any losses as a result of counterparty defaults.

    The company's derivative instruments are being accounted for as cash flow hedges and are recorded on the balance sheet at fair value. Changes therein are recorded in other comprehensive earnings and are reclassified to earnings in the periods in which earnings are affected by the hedged item. Substantially all amounts reported in accumulated other comprehensive earnings (loss) are expected to be reclassified to cost of goods sold. During the years ended December 31, 2004, 2003 and 2002, ineffectiveness related to cash flow hedges was not material.

Inventories:
Inventories are stated at cost, not to exceed market. The cost of substantially all of the company's inventories ($54,794 and $42,735 at December 31, 2004 and 2003, respectively) has been determined by the last-in, first-out (LIFO) method. The excess of current cost over LIFO cost of inventories approximates $5,868 and $6,442 at December 31, 2004 and 2003, respectively. The cost of certain foreign inventories ($3,983 and $3,351 at December 31, 2004 and 2003, respectively) has been determined by the first-in, first-out (FIFO) method. Rebates, discounts and other cash consideration received from a vendor related to inventory purchases is reflected as a reduction in the cost of the related inventory item, and is therefore reflected in cost of sales when the related inventory item is sold.

Property, plant and equipment:
Depreciation is computed for financial reporting purposes by use of the straight-line method based on useful lives of 20 to 35 years for buildings and 5 to 20 years for machinery and equipment. Depreciation expense was $11,680, $11,379 and $12,354 in 2004, 2003 and 2002, respectively, including $744 relating to equipment disposals.

Carrying value of long-lived assets:
The company reviews long-lived assets to determine if there are events or circumstances indicating that the amount of the asset reflected in the company's balance sheet may not be recoverable. When such indicators are present, the company compares the carrying value of the long-lived asset, or asset group, to the future undiscounted cash flows of the underlying assets to determine if an impairment exists. If applicable, an impairment charge would be recorded to write down the carrying value to its fair value. The determination of fair value involves the use of estimates of future cash flows that involve considerable management judgment and are based upon assumptions about expected future operating performance. The actual cash flows could differ from management's estimates due to changes in business conditions, operating performance, and economic conditions. No impairment charges were recorded by the company during 2004, 2003 or 2002.

Postretirement health care and life insurance benefits:
The company provides certain postretirement health care and life insurance benefits. The cost of these postretirement benefits is accrued during employees' working careers. The company also provides split dollar life insurance benefits to certain executive officers. The company records an asset equal to the cumulative insurance premiums that will be recovered upon the death of a covered employee(s) or earlier under the terms of the plan. Split dollar premiums paid were $3,620, $4,237 and $6,890 in 2004, 2003 and 2002, respectively.

Intangible assets:
The company accounts for intangible assets in accordance with SFAS No. 142, "Goodwill and Other Intangible Assets," which was adopted by the company on January 1, 2002. In accordance with this statement, goodwill and intangible assets with indefinite lives are not amortized, but rather tested for impairment at least annually. All trademarks have been assessed by management to have indefinite lives because they are expected to generate cash flows indefinitely. The company has completed its annual impairment testing of its goodwill and trademarks during the fourth quarter of each of the years presented, and no impairment was found.

Income taxes:
Deferred income taxes are recorded and recognized for future tax effects of temporary differences between financial and income tax reporting. Federal income taxes are provided on the portion of income of foreign subsidiaries that is expected to be remitted to the U.S. and become taxable, but not on the portion that is considered to be permanently invested in the foreign subsidiary.

Foreign currency translation:
The company has determined the functional currency for each foreign subsidiary. The U.S. dollar is used as the functional currency where a substantial portion of the subsidiary's business is indexed to the U.S. dollar or where its manufactured products are principally sold in the U.S. All other foreign subsidiaries use the local currency as their functional currency. Where the U.S. dollar is used as the functional currency, foreign currency translation adjustments are recorded as a charge or credit to other income in the statement of earnings. Where the foreign currency is used as the functional currency, translation adjustments are recorded as a separate component of comprehensive earnings (loss).

Joint venture:
The company's 50% interest in two Spanish companies is accounted for using the equity method. The company records an increase in its investment in the joint venture to the extent of its share of the joint venture's earnings, and reduces its investment to the extent of dividends received. No dividends were received during 2004.

Comprehensive earnings:
Comprehensive earnings includes net earnings, foreign currency translation adjustments and unrealized gains/losses on commodity hedging contracts and marketable securities.

Earnings per share:
A dual presentation of basic and diluted earnings per share is not required due to the lack of potentially dilutive securities under the company's simple capital structure. Therefore, all earnings per share amounts represent basic earnings per share. . . .

Common Notes

We have discussed many of the **notes to the financial statements** throughout this textbook, and will discuss others more fully in this chapter. The more common are as shown on the next two pages.

MAJOR DISCLOSURES

Inventory. Companies should report the basis upon which inventory amounts are stated (lower of cost or market) and the method used in determining cost (LIFO, FIFO, average cost, etc.). Manufacturers should report, either in the balance sheet or in a separate schedule in the notes, the inventory composition (finished goods, work in process, raw materials). Unusual or significant financing arrangements relating to inventories that may require disclosure include transactions with related parties, product financing arrangements, firm purchase commitments, involuntary liquidation of LIFO inventories, and pledging of inventories as collateral. Chapter 9 (pages 442–443) illustrates these disclosures.

Property, Plant, and Equipment. Companies should state the basis of valuation for property, plant, and equipment. It is usually historical cost. Companies also should disclose pledges, liens, and other commitments related to these assets. In the presentation of depreciation, companies should disclose the following in the financial statements or in the notes: (1) depreciation expense for the period; (2) balances of major classes of depreciable assets, by nature and function, at the balance sheet date; (3) accumulated depreciation, either by major classes of depreciable assets or in total, at the balance sheet date; and (4) a general description of the method or methods used in computing depreciation with respect to major classes of depreciable assets. Finally, companies should explain any major impairments. Chapter 11 (pages 543–544) illustrates these disclosures.

Creditor Claims. Investors normally find it extremely useful to understand the nature and cost of creditor claims. However, the liabilities section in the balance sheet can provide the major types of liabilities only in the aggregate. Note schedules regarding such obligations provide additional information about how a company is financing its operations, the costs that it will bear in future periods, and the timing of future cash outflows. Financial statements must disclose for each of the five years following the date of the statements the aggregate amount of maturities and sinking fund requirements for all long-term borrowings. Chapter 14 (pages 694–695) illustrates these disclosures.

Equity Holders' Claims. Many companies present in the body of the balance sheet information about equity securities: the number of shares authorized, issued, and outstanding and the par value for each type of security. Or, companies may present such data in a note. Beyond that, a common equity note disclosure relates to contracts and senior securities outstanding that might affect the various claims of the residual equity holders. An example would be the existence of outstanding stock options, outstanding convertible debt, redeemable preferred stock, and convertible preferred stock. In addition, it is necessary to disclose certain types of restrictions currently in force. Generally, these types of restrictions involve the amount of earnings available for dividend distribution. Examples of these types of disclosures are illustrated in Chapter 15 (pages 749–751) and Chapter 16 (pages 803–804).

Contingencies and Commitments. A company may have gain or loss contingencies that are not disclosed in the body of the financial statements. These contingencies include litigation, debt and other guarantees, possible tax assessments, renegotiation of government contracts, and sales of receivables with recourse. In addition, companies should disclose in the notes commitments that relate to dividend restrictions, purchase agreements (through-put and take-or-pay), hedge contracts, and employment contracts. Disclosures of such items are illustrated in Chapter 7 (pages 337–338), Chapter 9 (pages 431–432), and Chapter 13 (pages 642–645).

Deferred Taxes, Pensions, and Leases. The FASB also requires extensive disclosure in the areas of deferred taxes, pensions, and leases. Chapter 19 (pages 984–988),

UNDERLYING CONCEPTS

The AICPA Special Committee on Financial Reporting notes that standard setters should address disclosures and accounting requirements for off-balance-sheet financial arrangements. The goal should be to report the risks, opportunities, resources, and obligations that result from those arrangements, consistent with users' needs for information.

Chapter 20 (pages 1043–1052), and Chapter 21 (pages 1118–1120) discuss in detail each of these disclosures. Users of financial statements should carefully read notes to the financial statements for information about off-balance-sheet commitments, future financing needs, and the quality of a company's earnings.

Changes in Accounting Principles. The profession defines various types of accounting changes and establishes guides for reporting each type. Companies discuss, either in the summary of significant accounting policies or in the other notes, changes in accounting principles (as well as material changes in estimates and corrections of errors). See Chapter 22 (pages 1158–1163 and 1165–1166).

In earlier chapters we discussed the disclosures listed above. The following sections of this chapter illustrate four additional disclosures of significance—special transactions or events, subsequent events, segment reporting, and interim reporting.

Additional Examples of Major Disclosures

MORE PAGES, BUT BETTER?

The biggest overall change in annual reports recently is that companies are now disclosing debt-rating triggers buried in their financing arrangements. These triggers can require a company to pay off a loan immediately if the debt rating collapses; they are one of the reasons **Enron** crumbled so quickly. But few Enron stockholders knew about them until the gun had gone off. Companies are also telling more about their bank credit lines, liquidity, and any special purpose entities, which were major villains in the Enron drama.

Source: Gretchen Morgenson, "Annual Reports: More Pages, But Better?" *New York Times* (March 17, 2002).

WHAT DO THE NUMBERS MEAN?

DISCLOSURE ISSUES

Disclosure of Special Transactions or Events

Related-party transactions, errors and irregularities, and illegal acts pose especially sensitive and difficult problems. The accountant/auditor who has responsibility for reporting on these types of transactions must take care to properly balance the rights of the reporting company and the needs of users of the financial statements.

Related-party transactions arise when a company engages in transactions in which one of the parties has the ability to significantly influence the policies of the other. They may also occur when a nontransacting party has the ability to influence the policies of the two transacting parties.[5] Competitive, free-market dealings may not exist in related-party transactions, and so an "arm's-length" basis cannot be assumed. Transactions such as borrowing or lending money at abnormally low or high interest rates, real estate sales at amounts that differ significantly from appraised value, exchanges of nonmonetary assets, and transactions involving enterprises that have no economic substance ("shell corporations") suggest that related parties may be involved.

---

[5]Examples of related-party transactions include transactions between (a) a parent company and its subsidiaries; (b) subsidiaries of a common parent; (c) a company and trusts for the benefit of employees (controlled or managed by the enterprise); and (d) a company and its principal owners, management, or members of immediate families, and affiliates. Two classic cases of related-party transactions were **Enron**, with its misuse of special purpose entities, and **Tyco International**, which forgave loans to its management team.

In order to make adequate disclosure, companies should report the economic substance, rather than the legal form, of these transactions. *FASB Statement No. 57* requires the following disclosures of material related-party transactions.

1 The nature of the relationship(s) involved.

2 A description of the transactions (including transactions to which no amounts or nominal amounts were ascribed) for each of the periods for which income statements are presented.

3 The dollar amounts of transactions for each of the periods for which income statements are presented.

4 Amounts due from or to related parties as of the date of each balance sheet presented.

Illustration 24-3, from the annual report of **Knight-Ridder, Inc.,** shows disclosure of related-party transactions.

ILLUSTRATION 24-3
Disclosure of Related
Party Transactions

Knight-Ridder, Inc.

Note 8 (in part): Related Party Transactions
We have ongoing purchase commitments with SP and Ponderay, our two newsprint mill partnership investments. These future commitments are for the purchase of a minimum of $42.5 million and $13.8 million of newsprint with SP and Ponderay, respectively, at current market prices. We also have a sales commitment with DN to supply them with 50% of their newsprint requirements, which will be approximately $27.4 million. We have the resources necessary to fulfill these commitments.

Many companies are involved in related-party transactions. Errors, irregularities, and illegal acts, however, are the exception rather than the rule. Accounting **errors** are *unintentional* mistakes, whereas **irregularities** are *intentional* distortions of financial statements.[6] As indicated earlier, companies should correct the financial statements when they discover errors. The same treatment should be given irregularities. The discovery of irregularities, however, gives rise to a different set of procedures and responsibilities for the accountant/auditor.[7]

Illegal acts encompass such items as illegal political contributions, bribes, kickbacks, and other violations of laws and regulations.[8] In these situations, the accountant/auditor must evaluate the adequacy of disclosure in the financial statements. For example, if a company derives revenue from an illegal act that is considered material in relation to the financial statements, this information should be disclosed. The Sarbanes-Oxley Act of 2002 is intended to deter these illegal acts. This law adds significant fines and longer jail time for those who improperly sign off on the correctness of financial statements that include willing and knowing misstatements.

Disclosure plays a very important role in these types of transactions because the events are more qualitative than quantitative and involve more subjective than objective evaluation. Users of the financial statements need some indication of the existence and nature of these transactions, through disclosures, modifications in the auditor's report, or reports of changes in auditors.

---

[6]"The Auditor's Responsibility to Detect and Report Errors and Irregularities," *Statement on Auditing Standards No. 53* (New York, AICPA, 1988). Since passage of the Sarbanes-Oxley Act of 2002, auditors of public companies are regulated by the Public Company Accounting Oversight Board (PCAOB). While the PCAOB has developed some new auditing standards, this Board has for the most part adopted the prior auditing standards issued by the Auditing Standards Board of the AICPA.

[7]The profession became so concerned with certain management frauds that affect financial statements that it established a National Commission on Fraudulent Financial Reporting. The major purpose of this organization was to determine how fraudulent reporting practices could be constrained. Fraudulent financial reporting is discussed later in this chapter.

[8]"Illegal Acts by Clients," *Statement on Auditing Standards No. 54* (New York, AICPA, 1988).

Post-Balance-Sheet Events (Subsequent Events)

Notes to the financial statements should explain any significant financial events that took place after the formal balance sheet date, but before the statement is issued. These events are referred to as **post-balance-sheet events**, or just plain **subsequent events**. Illustration 24-4 shows a time diagram of the subsequent events period.

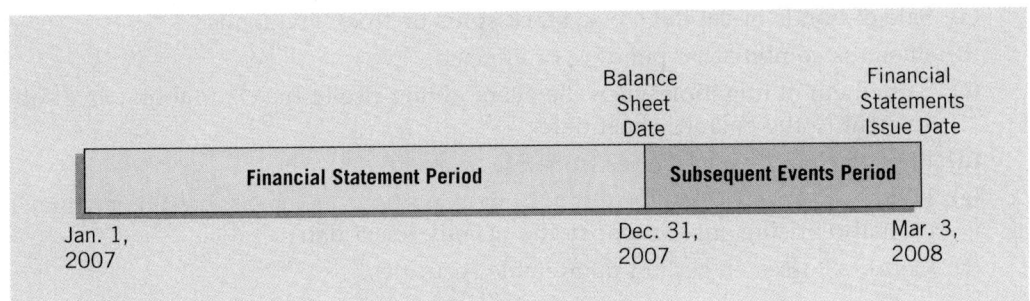

ILLUSTRATION 24-4
Time Periods for
Subsequent Events

A period of several weeks, and sometimes months, may elapse after the end of the fiscal year but before the company issues financial statements. Various activities involved in closing the books for the period and issuing the statements all take time: taking and pricing the inventory, reconciling subsidiary ledgers with controlling accounts, preparing necessary adjusting entries, ensuring that all transactions for the period have been entered, obtaining an audit of the financial statements by independent certified public accountants, and printing the annual report. During the period between the balance sheet date and its distribution to stockholders and creditors, important transactions or other events may occur that materially affect the company's financial position or operating situation.

Many who read a balance sheet believe the balance sheet condition is constant, and they project it into the future. However, readers must be told if the company has experienced a significant change—e.g., sold one of its plants, acquired a subsidiary, suffered extraordinary losses, settled significant litigation, or experienced any other important event in the post-balance-sheet period. Without an explanation in a note, the reader might be misled and draw inappropriate conclusions.

Two types of events or transactions occurring after the balance sheet date may have a material effect on the financial statements or may need disclosure so that readers interpret these statements accurately:

1 Events that provide additional evidence about conditions that existed at the balance sheet date, that affect the estimates used in preparing financial statements, and that require adjustments to the financial statement. All information available prior to the issuance of the financial statements helps investors and creditors evaluate estimates previously made. To ignore these subsequent events is to pass up an opportunity to improve the accuracy of the financial statements. This first type of event encompasses information that an accountant would have recorded in the accounts had the information been known at the balance sheet date.

For example, if a loss on an account receivable results from a customer's bankruptcy subsequent to the balance sheet date, the company adjusts the financial statements before their issuance. The bankruptcy stems from the customer's poor financial health existing at the balance sheet date.

The same criterion applies to settlements of litigation. The company must adjust the financial statements if the events that gave rise to the litigation, such as personal injury or patent infringement, took place prior to the balance sheet date.

2 Events that provide evidence about conditions that did not exist at the balance sheet date but arise subsequent to that date, and that do not require adjustment of the financial statements. To illustrate, a loss resulting from a customer's fire or flood

UNDERLYING CONCEPTS

The periodicity or time period assumption implies that economic activities of an enterprise can be divided into artificial time periods for purpose of analysis.

after the balance sheet date does not reflect conditions existing at that date. Thus, adjustment of the financial statements is not necessary. However, some of these events may have to be disclosed to keep the financial statements from being misleading. These disclosures take the form of notes, supplemental schedules, or even pro forma ("as if") financial data prepared as if the event had occurred on the balance sheet date. Examples of such events that require disclosure (but do not result in adjustment) are:

(a) Sale of bonds or capital stock; stock splits or stock dividends.

(b) Business combination pending or effected.

(c) Settlement of litigation when the event giving rise to the claim took place subsequent to the balance sheet date.

(d) Loss of plant or inventories from fire or flood.

(e) Losses on receivables resulting from conditions (such as customer's major casualty) arising subsequent to the balance sheet date.

(f) Gains or losses on certain marketable securities.[9]

Illustration 24-5 presents an example of subsequent events disclosure, excerpted from the annual report of **Goodrich Corporation**.

ILLUSTRATION 24-5
Disclosure of Subsequent Events

Goodrich Corporation

Note W. Subsequent Event
On February 16, 2004 the Company was notified by Pratt & Whitney, a United Technologies Company, that it will not meet the requirements for original equipment PW4000 engine components after the Company completes delivery of 45 shipsets (2 units per shipset) through early 2005. The Company had originally forecasted 90 shipsets to be delivered through 2009. As a result of this action, the total estimated revenue associated with this contract has been significantly reduced and anticipated cost reductions related to future deliveries under this contract will not occur.

The notice of termination is considered a Type 1 subsequent event under generally accepted accounting principles, the effects of which must be reflected in the Company's 2003 financial statements. As a result, the Company recorded a pre-tax charge of $15.1 million, as of December 31, 2003 related to this contract. The charge includes impairment of excess over average inventory of $7.0 million and $8.1 million for forward losses relating to the reduction in forecasted contract revenue and the increase in costs.

Many subsequent events or developments do not require adjustment of or disclosure in the financial statements. Typically, these are nonaccounting events or conditions that management normally communicates by other means. These events include legislation, product changes, management changes, strikes, unionization, marketing agreements, and loss of important customers.

Reporting for Diversified (Conglomerate) Companies

OBJECTIVE 3
Discuss the disclosure requirements for major business segments.

In certain business climates, companies have a tendency to diversify their operations. Take the case of conglomerate **General Electric (GE)**, whose products include locomotives and jet engines, credit card services, and water purification systems. Its

---

[9]"Subsequent Events," *Statement on Auditing Standards No. 1* (New York: AICPA, 1973), pp. 123–124. *Accounting Trends and Techniques—2004* listed the following types of subsequent events and their frequency of occurrence among the 600 companies surveyed: business combinations pending or effected, 83; debt incurred, reduced, or refinanced, 64; discontinued operations, 59; litigation, 29; and capital stock issued or repurchased, 27. The recent effects from hurricanes Katrina and Rita, which occurred after the year-end for companies with August fiscal years, require disclosure in order to keep the statements from being misleading. Some companies may have to consider whether these disasters affect their ability to continue as going concerns.

NBC Universal subsidiary owns **NBC TV**, **Vivendi Universal Entertainment**, and **Universal Pictures**. When businesses are so diversified, investors and investment analysts want more information about the details behind conglomerate financial statements. Particularly, they want income statement, balance sheet, and cash flow information on the **individual segments** that compose the total income figure.

Illustration 24-6 shows **segmented** (disaggregated) financial information of an office equipment and auto parts company.

OFFICE EQUIPMENT AND AUTO PARTS COMPANY INCOME STATEMENT DATA (IN MILLIONS)			
	Consolidated	Office Equipment	Auto Parts
Net sales	$78.8	$18.0	$60.8
Manufacturing costs			
Inventories, beginning	12.3	4.0	8.3
Materials and services	38.9	10.8	28.1
Wages	12.9	3.8	9.1
Inventories, ending	(13.3)	(3.9)	(9.4)
	50.8	14.7	36.1
Selling and administrative expense	12.1	1.6	10.5
Total operating expenses	62.9	16.3	46.6
Income before taxes	15.9	1.7	14.2
Income taxes	(9.3)	(1.0)	(8.3)
Net income	$ 6.6	$ 0.7	$ 5.9

ILLUSTRATION 24-6
Segmented Income
Statement

Much information is hidden in the aggregated totals. If the analyst has only the consolidated figures, he/she cannot tell the extent to which the differing product lines **contribute to the company's profitability, risk, and growth potential**. For example, in Illustration 24-6, the office equipment segment looks like a risky venture. Segmented reporting would provide useful information about the two business segments and would be useful for making an informed investment decision regarding the whole company.

A classic situation that demonstrates the need for segmented data involved **Caterpillar, Inc.** The SEC cited Caterpillar because it failed to tell investors that nearly a quarter of its income in one year came from a Brazilian unit and was nonrecurring in nature. The company knew that different economic policies in the next year would probably greatly affect earnings of the Brazilian unit. But Caterpillar presented its financial results on a consolidated basis, not disclosing the Brazilian operations. The SEC found that Caterpillar's failure to include information about Brazil left investors with an incomplete picture of the company's financial results and denied investors the opportunity to see the company "through the eyes of management."

Companies have always been somewhat hesitant to disclose segmented data for various reasons:

1 Without a thorough knowledge of the business and an understanding of such important factors as the competitive environment and capital investment requirements, the investor may find the segmented information meaningless or may even draw improper conclusions about the reported earnings of the segments.

2 Additional disclosure may be helpful to competitors, labor unions, suppliers, and certain government regulatory agencies, and thus harm the reporting company.

3 Additional disclosure may discourage management from taking intelligent business risks because segments reporting losses or unsatisfactory earnings may cause stockholder dissatisfaction with management.

4 The wide variation among companies in the choice of segments, cost allocation, and other accounting problems limits the usefulness of segmented information.

5 The investor is investing in the company as a whole and not in the particular segments, and it should not matter how any single segment is performing if the overall performance is satisfactory.

6 Certain technical problems, such as classification of segments and allocation of segment revenues and costs (especially "common costs"), are formidable.

On the other hand, the advocates of segmented disclosures offer these reasons in support of the practice:

1 Investors need segmented information to make an intelligent investment decision regarding a diversified company.

    (a) Sales and earnings of individual segments enable investors to evaluate the differences between segments in growth rate, risk, and profitability, and to forecast consolidated profits.

    (b) Segmented reports help investors evaluate the company's investment worth by disclosing the nature of a company's businesses and the relative size of the components.

2 The absence of segmented reporting by a diversified company may put its unsegmented, single product-line competitors at a competitive disadvantage because the conglomerate may obscure information that its competitors must disclose.

The advocates of segmented disclosures appear to have a much stronger case. Many users indicate that segmented data are the most useful financial information provided, aside from the basic financial statements. As a result, the FASB has issued extensive reporting guidelines in this area.

Objective of Reporting Segmented Information

The objective of reporting segmented financial data is to provide information about the **different types of business activities** in which an enterprise engages and the **different economic environments** in which it operates. Meeting this objective will help users of financial statements do the following.

(a) Better understand the enterprise's performance.

(b) Better assess its prospects for future net cash flows.

(c) Make more informed judgments about the enterprise as a whole.

Basic Principles

Financial statements can be disaggregated in several ways. For example, they can be disaggregated by products or services, by geography, by legal entity, or by type of customer. However, it is not feasible to provide all of that information in every set of financial statements. *FASB Statement No. 131* requires that general purpose financial statements include selected information on a single basis of segmentation. Thus, a company can meet the segmented reporting objective by providing financial statements segmented based on how the company's operations are managed. The method chosen is referred to as the **management approach.**[10] **The management approach reflects how management segments the company for making operating decisions.** The segments are evident from the components of the company's organization structure. These components are called **operating segments**.

Identifying Operating Segments

An **operating segment** is a component of an enterprise:

(a) That engages in business activities from which it earns revenues and incurs expenses.

---

[10]"Disclosures about Segments of an Enterprise and Related Information," *Statement of Financial Accounting Standards No. 131* (Norwalk, Conn.: FASB, 1997).

(b) Whose operating results are regularly reviewed by the company's chief operating decision maker to assess segment performance and allocate resources to the segment.

(c) For which discrete financial information is available that is generated by or based on the internal financial reporting system.

Companies may aggregate information about two or more operating segments only if the segments have the same basic characteristics in each of the following areas.

(a) The nature of the products and services provided.

(b) The nature of the production process.

(c) The type or class of customer.

(d) The methods of product or service distribution.

(e) If applicable, the nature of the regulatory environment.

After the company decides on the possible segments for disclosure, it makes a quantitative materiality test. This test determines whether the segment is significant enough to warrant actual disclosure. An operating segment is deemed significant, and therefore a reportable segment, if it satisfies **one or more** of the following quantitative thresholds.

1 Its **revenue** (including both sales to external customers and intersegment sales or transfers) is 10 percent or more of the combined revenue of all the company's operating segments.

2 The absolute amount of its **profit or loss** is 10 percent or more of the greater, in absolute amount, of **(a)** the combined operating profit of all operating segments that did not incur a loss, or **(b)** the combined loss of all operating segments that did report a loss.

3 Its **identifiable assets** are 10 percent or more of the combined assets of all operating segments.

In applying these tests, the company must consider two additional factors. First, segment data must explain a significant portion of the company's business. Specifically, the segmented results must equal or exceed 75 percent of the combined sales to unaffiliated customers for the entire company. This test prevents a company from providing limited information on only a few segments and lumping all the rest into one category.

Second, the profession recognizes that reporting too many segments may overwhelm users with detailed information. The FASB decided that 10 is a reasonable upper limit for the number of segments that a company must disclose.

To illustrate these requirements, assume a company has identified six possible reporting segments, as shown in Illustration 24-7 (000s omitted).

Segments	Total Revenue (Unaffiliated)	Operating Profit (Loss)	Identifiable Assets
A	$ 100	$10	$ 60
B	50	2	30
C	700	40	390
D	300	20	160
E	900	18	280
F	100	(5)	50
	$2,150	$85	$970

ILLUSTRATION 24-7
Data for Different Possible Reporting Segments

The company would apply the respective tests as follows:

Revenue test: 10% × $2,150 = $215; C, D, and E meet this test.

Operating profit (loss) test: 10% × $90 = $9 (note that the $5 loss is ignored, because the test is based on non-loss segments); A, C, D, and E meet this test.

Identifiable assets tests: 10% × $970 = $97; C, D, and E meet this test.

UNDERLYING CONCEPTS

The AICPA Special Committee on Financial Reporting notes that multi-segment companies operate diverse businesses that are subject to different opportunities and risks. Segment information provides additional insight about the opportunities and risks of investments and sharpens predictions. Because of its predictive value, providing segment information is of the highest priority.

The reporting segments are therefore A, C, D, and E, assuming that these four segments have enough sales to meet the 75 percent of combined sales test. The 75 percent test is computed as follows.

75% of combined sales test: 75% × $2,150 = $1,612.50. The sales of A, C, D, and E total $2,000 ($100 + $700 + $300 + $900); therefore, the 75 percent test is met.

Measurement Principles

The accounting principles that companies use for segment disclosure need not be the same as the principles they use to prepare the consolidated statements. This flexibility may at first appear inconsistent. But, preparing segment information in accordance with generally accepted accounting principles would be difficult because some principles are not expected to apply at a segment level. Examples are accounting for the cost of company-wide employee benefit plans, accounting for income taxes in a company that files a consolidated tax return, and accounting for inventory on a LIFO basis if the pool includes items in more than one segment.

The FASB does not require allocations of joint, common, or company-wide costs solely for external reporting purposes. **Common costs** are those incurred for the benefit of more than one segment and whose interrelated nature prevents a completely objective division of costs among segments. For example, the company president's salary is difficult to allocate to various segments. Allocations of common costs are inherently arbitrary and may not be meaningful. There is a presumption that if companies allocate common costs to segments, these allocations are either directly attributable or reasonably allocable.

Segmented Information Reported

The FASB requires that an enterprise report the following.

1 *General information about its operating segments.* This includes factors that management considers most significant in determining the company's operating segments, and the types of products and services from which each operating segment derives its revenues.

2 *Segment profit and loss and related information.* Specifically, companies must report the following information about each operating segment if the amounts are included in determining segment profit or loss.

   (a) Revenues from transactions with external customers.

   (b) Revenues from transactions with other operating segments of the same enterprise.

   (c) Interest revenue.

   (d) Interest expense.

   (e) Depreciation, depletion, and amortization expense.

   (f) Unusual items.

   (g) Equity in the net income of investees accounted for by the equity method.

   (h) Income tax expense or benefit.

   (i) Extraordinary items.

   (j) Significant noncash items other than depreciation, depletion, and amortization expense.

3 *Segment assets.* A company must report each operating segment's total assets.

4 *Reconciliations.* A company must provide a reconciliation of the total of the segments' revenues to total revenues, a reconciliation of the total of the operating segments' profits and losses to its income before income taxes, and a reconciliation of the total of the operating segments' assets to total assets.

5 *Information about products and services and geographic areas.* For each operating segment not based on geography, the company must report (unless it is impracticable): (1) revenues from external customers, (2) long-lived assets, and (3) expenditures during the period for long-lived assets. This information, if material, must be reported (a) in the enterprise's country of domicile and (b) in each other country.

6 *Major customers.* If 10 percent or more of company revenue is derived from a single customer, the company must disclose the total amount of revenue from each such customer by segment.

Illustration of Disaggregated Information

Illustration 24-8 shows the segment disclosure for **Johnson & Johnson**.

ILLUSTRATION 24-8
Segment Disclosure

Johnson&Johnson

Johnson & Johnson
(Notes excluded)
Segments of Business and Geographic Areas

	Sales to Customers		
(dollars in millions)	2004	2003	2002
Consumer—United States	$ 4,224	$ 3,968	$ 3,605
International	4,109	3,463	2,959
Total	8,333	7,431	6,564
Pharmaceutical—United States	14,960	13,271	11,919
International	7,168	6,246	5,232
Total	22,128	19,517	17,151
Medical Devices and Diagnostics—United States	8,586	8,035	6,931
International	8,301	6,879	5,652
Total	16,887	14,914	12,583
Worldwide total	$47,348	$41,862	$36,298

	Operating Profit			Identifiable Assets		
(dollars in millions)	2004	2003	2002	2004	2003	2002
Consumer	$ 1,514	$1,393	$1,229	$ 6,142	$ 5,371	$ 5,056
Pharmaceutical	7,608	5,896	5,787	16,058	15,001	11,112
Medical Devices and Diagnostics	4,091	3,370	2,489	15,805	16,082	15,052
Segments total	13,213	10,659	9,505	38,005	36,454	31,220
Expenses not allocated to segments	(375)	(351)	(214)			
General corporate				15,312	11,809	9,336
Worldwide total	$12,838	$10,308	$9,291	$53,317	$ 48,263	$40,556

	Additions to Property, Plant & Equipment			Depreciation and Amortization		
(dollars in millions)	2004	2003	2002	2004	2003	2002
Consumer	$ 227	$ 229	$ 222	$ 222	$ 246	$ 244
Pharmaceutical	1,197	1,236	1,012	1,008	765	557
Medical Devices and Diagnostics	630	639	713	769	761	776
Segments total	2,054	2,104	1,947	1,999	1,772	1,577
General corporate	121	158	152	125	97	85
Worldwide total	$2,175	$2,262	$2,099	$2,124	$1,869	$1,662

	Sales to Customers			Long-Lived Assets		
(dollars in millions)	2004	2003	2002	2004	2003	2002
United States	$27,770	$25,274	$22,455	$14,324	$14,367	$11,822
Europe	11,151	9,483	7,636	6,142	5,193	4,613
Western Hemisphere excluding U.S.	2,589	2,236	2,018	748	772	583
Asia-Pacific, Africa	5,838	4,869	4,189	620	605	555
Segments total	47,348	41,862	36,298	21,834	20,937	17,573
General corporate				444	448	383
Other non long-lived assets				31,039	26,878	22,600
Worldwide total	$47,348	$41,862	$36,298	$53,317	$48,263	$40,556

Interim Reports

Another source of information for the investor is interim reports. As noted earlier, **interim reports** cover periods of less than one year. The stock exchanges, the SEC, and the accounting profession have an active interest in the presentation of interim information.

OBJECTIVE 4
Describe the accounting problems associated with interim reporting.

The SEC mandates that certain companies file a **Form 10-Q**, in which a company discloses quarterly data similar to that disclosed in the annual report. It also requires those companies to disclose selected quarterly information in notes to the annual financial statements. Illustration 24-9 presents the selected quarterly disclosure of **Tootsie Roll Industries, Inc.** In addition to Form 10-Q, the APB issued *Opinion No. 28*, which attempted to narrow the reporting alternatives related to interim reports.[11]

ILLUSTRATION 24-9
Disclosure of Selected Quarterly Data

Tootsie Roll Industries, Inc.
For the Year Ended December 31, 2004

(Thousands of dollars except per share data)

	First	Second	Third	Fourth	Total
Net sales	$80,046	$77,157	$156,971	$105,936	$420,110
Gross margin	34,730	34,992	64,804	41,083	175,609
Net earnings	11,493	11,828	26,976	13,877	64,174
Net earnings per share	.22	.22	.52	.27	1.23

	Stock Prices		Dividends
	2004		2004
	High	Low	
1st Qtr	$37.86	$35.00	$.0681
2nd Qtr	$37.60	$32.41	$.0701
3rd Qtr	$32.60	$29.08	$.0700
4th Qtr	$34.63	$29.24	$.0700

UNDERLYING CONCEPTS

For information to be relevant, it must be available to decision makers before it loses its capacity to influence their decisions (timeliness). Interim reporting is an excellent example of this concept.

Because of the short-term nature of the information in these reports, there is considerable controversy as to the general approach companies should employ. One group, which favors the **discrete approach**, believes that companies should treat each interim period as a separate accounting period. Using that treatment, companies would follow the principles for deferrals and accruals used for annual reports. In this view, companies should report accounting transactions as they occur, and expense recognition should not change with the period of time covered.

Another group, which favors the **integral approach**, believes that the interim report is an integral part of the annual report and that deferrals and accruals should take into consideration what will happen for the entire year. In this approach, companies should assign estimated expenses to parts of a year on the basis of sales volume or some other activity base.

At present, many companies follow the discrete approach for certain types of expenses and the integral approach for others, because the standards currently employed in practice are vague and lead to differing interpretations.

Interim Reporting Requirements

Generally, companies should use the same accounting principles for interim reports and for annual reports. They should recognize revenues in interim periods on the same basis as they are for annual periods. For example, if Cedars Corp. uses the installment-sales method as the basis for recognizing revenue on an annual basis, then it should

---

[11]"Interim Financial Reporting," *Opinions of the Accounting Principles Board No. 28* (New York: AICPA, 1973).

use the installment basis for interim reports as well. Also, Cedars should treat costs directly associated with revenues (product costs, such as materials, labor and related fringe benefits, and manufacturing overhead) in the same manner for interim reports as for annual reports.

Companies should use the same inventory pricing methods (FIFO, LIFO, etc.) for interim reports and for annual reports. However, the following exceptions are appropriate at interim reporting periods.

1 Companies may use the gross profit method for interim inventory pricing. But they must disclose the method and adjustments to reconcile with annual inventory.

2 When a company liquidates LIFO inventories at an interim date and expects to replace them by year-end, cost of goods sold should include the expected cost of replacing the liquidated LIFO base, rather than give effect to the interim liquidation.

3 Companies should not defer inventory market declines beyond the interim period unless they are temporary and no loss is expected for the fiscal year.

4 Companies ordinarily should defer planned variances under a standard cost system; such variances are expected to be absorbed by year-end.

Companies often charge to the interim period, as incurred, costs and expenses other than product costs (often referred to as **period costs**). But companies may allocate these costs among interim periods on the basis of an estimate of time expired, benefit received, or activity associated with the periods. Companies display considerable latitude in accounting for these costs in interim periods, and many believe more definitive guidelines are needed.

Regarding disclosure, companies should report the following interim data at a minimum.

1 Sales or gross revenues, provision for income taxes, extraordinary items, and net income.

2 Basic and diluted earnings per share where appropriate.

3 Seasonal revenue, cost, or expenses.

4 Significant changes in estimates or provisions for income taxes.

5 Disposal of a component of a business and extraordinary, unusual, or infrequently occurring items.

6 Contingent items.

7 Changes in accounting principles or estimates.

8 Significant changes in financial position.

The FASB encourages, but does not require, companies to publish an interim balance sheet and statement of cash flows. If a company does not present this information, it should disclose significant changes in such items as liquid assets, net working capital, long-term liabilities, and stockholders' equity.

Unique Problems of Interim Reporting

In *APB Opinion No. 28*, the Board indicated that it favored the integral approach. However, within this broad guideline, a number of unique reporting problems develop related to the following items.

Advertising and Similar Costs. The general guidelines are that companies should defer in an interim period costs such as advertising if the benefits extend beyond that period; otherwise the company should expense those costs as incurred. But such a determination is difficult, and even if the company defers the costs, how should it allocate them between quarters?

Because of the vague guidelines in this area, accounting for advertising varies widely. At one time, some companies in the food industry, such as **RJR Nabisco** and **Pillsbury**, charged advertising costs as a percentage of sales and adjusted to actual at year-end, whereas **General Foods** and **Kellogg** expensed these costs as incurred.

The same type of problem relates to such items as Social Security taxes, research and development costs, and major repairs. For example, should the company expense Social Security costs (payroll taxes) on highly paid personnel early in the year, or allocate and spread them to subsequent quarters? Should a major repair that occurs later in the year be anticipated and allocated proportionately to earlier periods?

Expenses Subject to Year-End Adjustment. Companies often do not know with a great deal of certainty amounts of bad debts, executive bonuses, pension costs, and inventory shrinkage until year-end. **They should estimate these costs and allocate them to interim periods as best they can.** Companies use a variety of allocation techniques to accomplish this objective.

Income Taxes. Not every dollar of corporate taxable income is taxed at the same rate; the tax rate is progressive. This aspect of business income taxes poses a problem in preparing interim financial statements. Should the company use the **annualized approach,** which is to annualize income to date and accrue the proportionate income tax for the period to date? Or should it follow the **marginal principle approach,** which is to apply the lower rate of tax to the first amount of income earned? At one time, companies generally followed the latter approach and accrued the tax applicable to each additional dollar of income.

The profession now, however, uses the annualized approach. This requires that "at the end of each interim period the company should make its best estimate of the effective tax rate expected to be applicable for the full fiscal year. The rate so determined should be used in providing for income taxes on income for the quarter."[12]

Because businesses did not uniformly apply this guideline in accounting for similar situations, the FASB issued *Interpretation No. 18.* This interpretation requires that to compute the year-to-date tax, companies apply the **estimated annual effective tax rate** to the year-to-date "ordinary" income at the end of each interim period. Further, the **interim period tax** related to "ordinary" income shall be the difference between the amount so computed and the amounts reported for previous interim periods of the fiscal period.[13]

Extraordinary Items. Extraordinary items consist of unusual and nonrecurring material gains and losses. In the past, companies handled them in interim reports in one of three ways: (1) absorbed them entirely in the quarter in which they occurred; (2) prorated them over four quarters; or (3) disclosed them only by note. **The required approach now is to charge or credit the loss or gain in the quarter in which it occurs,** instead of attempting some arbitrary multiple-period allocation. This approach is consistent with the way in which companies must handle extraordinary items on an annual basis. No attempt is made to prorate the extraordinary items over several years.

Some favor the omission of extraordinary items from the quarterly net income. They believe that inclusion of extraordinary items that may be large in proportion to interim results distorts the predictive value of interim reports. Many, however, consider such an omission inappropriate because it deviates from actual results.

Earnings per Share. Interim reporting of earnings per share has all the problems inherent in computing and presenting annual earnings per share, and then some. If a company issues shares in the third period, EPS for the first two periods will not reflect

---

[12]"Interim Financial Reporting," *Opinions of the Accounting Principles Board No. 28* (New York: AICPA, 1973), par. 19. The estimated annual effective tax rate should reflect anticipated tax credits, foreign tax rates, percentage depletion, capital gains rates, and other available tax planning alternatives.

[13]"Accounting for Income Taxes in Interim Periods," *FASB Interpretation No. 18* (Stamford, Conn.: FASB, March 1977), par. 9. "Ordinary" income (or loss) refers to "income (or loss) from continuing operations before income taxes (or benefits)" excluding extraordinary items, discontinued operations, and cumulative effects of changes in accounting principles.

year-end EPS. If an extraordinary item is present in one period and the company sells new equity shares in another period, the EPS figure for the extraordinary item will change for the year. On an annual basis only one EPS figure can be associated with an extraordinary item and that figure does not change; the interim figure is subject to change.

For purposes of computing earnings per share and making the required disclosure determinations, each interim period should stand alone. That is, all applicable tests should be made for that single period.

Seasonality. Seasonality occurs when most of a company's sales occur in one short period of the year while certain costs are fairly evenly spread throughout the year. For example, the natural gas industry has its heavy sales in the winter months. In contrast, the beverage industry has its heavy sales in the summer months.

The problem of seasonality is related to the matching concept in accounting. Expenses should be matched against the revenues they create. In a seasonal business, wide fluctuations in profits occur because off-season sales do not absorb the company's fixed costs (for example, manufacturing, selling, and administrative costs that tend to remain fairly constant regardless of sales or production).

To illustrate why seasonality is a problem, assume the following information.

Selling price per unit	$1
Annual sales for the period (projected and actual)	
100,000 units @ $1	$100,000
Manufacturing costs	
Variable	10¢ per unit
Fixed	20¢ per unit or $20,000 for the year
Nonmanufacturing costs	
Variable	10¢ per unit
Fixed	30¢ per unit or $30,000 for the year

ILLUSTRATION 24-10
Data for Seasonality Example

Sales for four quarters and the year (projected and actual) were:

		Percent of Sales
1st Quarter	$ 20,000	20%
2nd Quarter	5,000	5
3rd Quarter	10,000	10
4th Quarter	65,000	65
Total for the year	$100,000	100%

ILLUSTRATION 24-11
Sales Data for Seasonality Example

Under the present accounting framework, the income statements for the quarters might be as shown in Illustration 24-12.

	1st Qtr	2nd Qtr	3rd Qtr	4th Qtr	Year
Sales	$20,000	$ 5,000	$10,000	$65,000	$100,000
Manufacturing costs					
Variable	(2,000)	(500)	(1,000)	(6,500)	(10,000)
Fixed[a]	(4,000)	(1,000)	(2,000)	(13,000)	(20,000)
	14,000	3,500	7,000	45,500	70,000
Nonmanufacturing costs					
Variable	(2,000)	(500)	(1,000)	(6,500)	(10,000)
Fixed[b]	(7,500)	(7,500)	(7,500)	(7,500)	(30,000)
Net income	$ 4,500	$(4,500)	$ (1,500)	$31,500	$ 30,000

ILLUSTRATION 24-12
Interim Net Income for Seasonal Business—Discrete Approach

[a]The fixed manufacturing costs are inventoried, so that equal amounts of fixed costs do not appear during each quarter.
[b]The fixed nonmanufacturing costs are not inventoried, so equal amounts of fixed costs appear during each quarter.

An investor who uses the first quarter's results might be misled. If the first quarter's earnings are $4,500, should this figure be multiplied by four to predict annual earnings of $18,000? Or, if first-quarter sales of $20,000 are 20 percent of the predicted sales for the year, would the net income for the year be $22,500 ($4,500 × 5)? Both figures are obviously wrong, and after the second quarter's results occur, the investor may become even more confused.

The problem with the conventional approach is that the fixed nonmanufacturing costs are not charged in proportion to sales. Some enterprises have adopted a way of avoiding this problem by making all fixed nonmanufacturing costs follow the sales pattern, as shown in Illustration 24-13.

ILLUSTRATION 24-13
Interim Net Income for Seasonal Business—Integral Approach

	1st Qtr	2nd Qtr	3rd Qtr	4th Qtr	Year
Sales	$20,000	$ 5,000	$10,000	$65,000	$100,000
Manufacturing costs					
Variable	(2,000)	(500)	(1,000)	(6,500)	(10,000)
Fixed	(4,000)	(1,000)	(2,000)	(13,000)	(20,000)
	14,000	3,500	7,000	45,500	70,000
Nonmanufacturing costs					
Variable	(2,000)	(500)	(1,000)	(6,500)	(10,000)
Fixed	(6,000)	(1,500)	(3,000)	(19,500)	(30,000)
Net income	$ 6,000	$ 1,500	$ 3,000	$19,500	$ 30,000

This approach solves some of the problems of interim reporting: Sales in the first quarter are 20 percent of total sales for the year, and net income in the first quarter is 20 percent of total income. In this case, as in the previous example, the investor cannot rely on multiplying any given quarter by four, but can use comparative data or rely on some estimate of sales in relation to income for a given period.

The greater the degree of seasonality experienced by a company, the greater the possibility of distortion. Because there are no definitive guidelines for handling such items as the fixed nonmanufacturing costs, variability in income can be substantial. To alleviate this problem, the profession recommends that companies subject to material seasonal variations disclose the seasonal nature of their business and consider supplementing their interim reports with information for 12-month periods ended at the interim date for the current and preceding years.

The two illustrations above highlight the difference between the **discrete** and **integral** approaches. Illustration 24-12 represents the discrete approach, in which the fixed nonmanufacturing expenses are expensed as incurred. Illustration 24-13 shows the integral approach, in which the manufacturing expenses are charged to expense on the basis of some measure of activity.

Continuing Controversy. The profession has developed some standards for interim reporting, but much still has to be done. As yet, it is unclear whether the discrete or the integral method, or some combination of the two, will be settled on.

Discussion also persists about the independent auditor's involvement in interim reports. Many auditors are reluctant to express an opinion on interim financial information, arguing that the data are too tentative and subjective. On the other hand, more people are advocating some examination of interim reports. A compromise may be a limited review of interim reports. Such a review would provide some assurance that an outside party has conducted an examination and that the published information appears to be in accord with generally accepted accounting principles.[14]

INTERNATIONAL INSIGHT

IFRS requires that interim financial statements use the discrete method, except for the tax expenses.

UNDERLYING CONCEPTS

The AICPA Special Committee on Financial Reporting indicates that users would benefit from separate fourth-quarter reporting, including management's analysis of fourth-quarter activities and events. Also, the Committee recommended quarterly segment reporting, which companies now provide under *FASB Statement No. 131.*

---

[14]The AICPA has been involved in developing guidelines for the review of interim reports. "Limited Review of Interim Financial Statements," *Statement on Auditing Standards No. 24* (New York: AICPA, 1979) sets standards for the review of interim reports.

Analysts and investors want financial information as soon as possible, before it's old news. We may not be far from a continuous database system in which corporate financial records can be accessed via the Internet. Investors might be able to access a company's financial records whenever they wish and put the information in the format they need. Thus, they could learn about sales slippage, cost increases, or earnings changes as they happen, rather than waiting until after the quarter has ended.[15]

A steady stream of information from the company to the investor could be very positive because it might alleviate management's continual concern with short-run interim numbers. Today many contend that U.S. management is too oriented to the short-term. The truth of this statement is echoed by the words of the president of a large company who decided to retire early: "I wanted to look forward to a year made up of four seasons rather than four quarters."

I WANT IT FASTER

The SEC has decided that timeliness of information is of extreme importance. First, the SEC has said that large public companies will have only 60 days to complete their annual reports, down from 90 days. Quarterly reports must be done within 40 days of the close of the quarter, instead of 45. In addition, corporate executives and shareholders with more than 10 percent of a company's outstanding stock now have two days to disclose their sale or purchase of stock.

Also, in a bid to increase Internet disclosure, the SEC encourages companies to post current, quarterly, and annual reports on their websites—or explain why they don't. The Internet postings would have to be made by the day the company submits the information to the SEC, rather than within 24 hours as current rules allow.

WHAT DO THE NUMBERS MEAN?

AUDITOR'S AND MANAGEMENT'S REPORTS

Auditor's Report

Another important source of information, which is often overlooked, is the **auditor's report**. An **auditor** is an accounting professional who conducts an independent examination of a company's accounting data.

If satisfied that the financial statements present the financial position, results of operations, and cash flows fairly in accordance with generally accepted accounting principles, the auditor expresses an **unqualified opinion**. An example is shown in Illustration 24-14 (on page 1304).[16]

In preparing the report, the auditor follows these reporting standards.

1 The report states whether the financial statements are in accordance with generally accepted accounting principles.

2 The report identifies those circumstances in which the company has not consistently observed such principles in the current period in relation to the preceding period.

OBJECTIVE 5
Identify the major disclosures in the auditor's report.

---

[15]A step in this direction is the SEC's mandate for companies to file their financial statements electronically with the SEC. The system, called EDGAR (electronic data gathering and retrieval) provides interested parties with computer access to financial information such as periodic filings, corporate prospectuses, and proxy materials.

[16]This auditor's report is in exact conformance with the specifications contained in "Reports on Audited Financial Statements," *Statement on Auditing Standards No. 58* (New York: AICPA, 1988). The last paragraph refers to the assessment of the company's internal controls, as required by the PCAOB.

3 Users are to regard the informative disclosures in the financial statements as reasonably adequate unless the report states otherwise.

4 The report contains either an expression of opinion regarding the financial statements taken as a whole or an assertion to the effect that an opinion cannot be expressed. When the auditor cannot express an overall opinion, the report should state the reasons. In all cases where an auditor's name is associated with financial statements, the report should contain a clear-cut indication of the character of the auditor's examination, if any, and the degree of responsibility being taken.

ILLUSTRATION 24-14
Auditor's Report

Best Buy Co., Inc.

Report of Independent Registered Public Accounting Firm on Consolidated Financial Statements

Shareholders and Board of Directors

We have audited the accompanying consolidated balance sheets of Best Buy Co., Inc. and subsidiaries as of February 26, 2005, and February 28, 2004, and the related consolidated statements of earnings, changes in shareholders' equity, and cash flows for each of the three years in the period ended February 26, 2005. Our audits also included the financial statement schedule listed in Item 15(a). These financial statements and schedule are the responsibility of the Company's management. Our responsibility is to express an opinion on these financial statements and schedule based on our audits.

We conducted our audits in accordance with the standards of the Public Company Accounting Oversight Board (United States). Those standards require that we plan and perform the audit to obtain reasonable assurance about whether the financial statements are free of material misstatement. An audit includes examining, on a test basis, evidence supporting the amounts and disclosures in the financial statements. An audit also includes assessing the accounting principles used and significant estimates made by management, as well as evaluating the overall financial statement presentation. We believe that our audits provide a reasonable basis for our opinion.

In our opinion, the financial statements referred to above present fairly, in all material respects, the consolidated financial position of Best Buy Co., Inc. and subsidiaries of February 26, 2005, and February 28, 2004, and the consolidated results of their operations and their cash flows for each of the three years in the period ended February 26, 2005, in conformity with U.S. generally accepted accounting principles. Also, in our opinion, the related financial statement schedule, when considered in relation to the basic financial statements taken as a whole, presents fairly, in all material respects, the information set forth therein.

As discussed in Note 5 to the financial statements, effective February 26, 2005, Best Buy Co., Inc. and subsidiaries adopted EITF Issue No. 04-08, "The Effect of Contingently Convertible Instruments on Diluted Earnings per Share," and restated earnings per share for all prior periods.

We also have audited, in accordance with the standards of the Public Company Accounting Oversight Board (United States), the effectiveness of the Best Buy Co., Inc. and subsidiaries' internal control over financial reporting as of February 26, 2005, based on the criteria established in Internal Control — Integrated Framework issued by the Committee of Sponsoring Organizations of the Treadway Commission and our report dated May 5, 2005 expressed an unqualified opinion thereon.

Ernst & Young LLP

Minneapolis, Minnesota
May 5, 2005

In most cases, the auditor issues a standard **unqualified** or **clean opinion**. That is, the auditor expresses the opinion that the financial statements present fairly, in all material respects, the financial position, results of operations, and cash flows of the entity in conformity with generally accepted accounting principles.

Certain circumstances, although they do not affect the auditor's unqualified opinion, may require the auditor to add an explanatory paragraph to the audit report. Some of the more important circumstances are as follows.

1 *Uncertainties.* A matter involving an **uncertainty** is one that is expected to be resolved at a future date, at which time sufficient evidence concerning its outcome is expected to be available. In deciding whether an explanatory paragraph is needed, the auditor should consider the likelihood of a material loss resulting from the contingency. If, for example, the possibility that a loss due to the uncertainty is remote, then an explanatory paragraph is not warranted. If the loss is probable but not estimable, or is reasonably possible and material, then an explanatory paragraph is warranted.

2 *Lack of Consistency.* If a company has changed accounting principles or the method of their application in a way that has a material effect on the comparability of its financial statements, the auditor should refer to the change in an explanatory paragraph of the report. Such an explanatory paragraph should identify the nature of the change and refer readers to the note in the financial statements that discusses the change in detail. The auditor's concurrence with a change is implicit unless the auditor takes exception to the change in expressing an opinion as to fair presentation in conformity with generally accepted accounting principles.

3 *Emphasis of a Matter.* The auditor may wish to emphasize a matter regarding the financial statements, but nevertheless intends to express an unqualified opinion. For example, the auditor may wish to emphasize that the entity is a component of a larger business enterprise or that it has had significant transactions with related parties. The auditor presents such explanatory information in a separate paragraph of the report.

In some situations, however, the auditor is required to express (1) a **qualified** opinion or (2) an **adverse** opinion, or (3) to **disclaim** an opinion.

A **qualified opinion** contains an exception to the standard opinion. Ordinarily the exception is not of sufficient magnitude to invalidate the statements as a whole; if it were, an adverse opinion would be rendered. The usual circumstances in which the auditor may deviate from the standard unqualified short-form report on financial statements are as follows.

1 The scope of the examination is limited or affected by conditions or restrictions.

2 The statements do not fairly present financial position or results of operations because of:

    (a) Lack of conformity with generally accepted accounting principles and standards.

    (b) Inadequate disclosure.

If confronted with one of the situations noted above, the auditor must offer a qualified opinion. A qualified opinion states that, except for the effects of the matter to which the qualification relates, the financial statements present fairly, in all material respects, the financial position, results of operations, and cash flows in conformity with generally accepted accounting principles.

Illustration 24-15 (page 1306) shows an example of an auditor's report with a qualified opinion. The auditor qualified the opinion because the company used an accounting principle at variance with generally accepted accounting principles.

An **adverse opinion** is required in any report in which the exceptions to fair presentation are so material that in the independent auditor's judgment, a qualified opinion is not justified. In such a case, the financial statements taken as a whole are not presented in accordance with generally accepted accounting principles. Adverse opinions are rare, because most companies change their accounting to conform with GAAP. The SEC will not permit a company listed on an exchange to have an adverse opinion.

A **disclaimer of an opinion** is appropriate when the auditor has gathered so little information on the financial statements that no opinion can be expressed.

The profession also requires the auditor to evaluate whether there is substantial doubt about the entity's **ability to continue as a going concern** for a reasonable period of time. (This period is not to exceed one year beyond the date of the financial statements.) If substantial doubt exists about the company continuing as a going

ILLUSTRATION 24-15
Qualified Auditor's
Report

Helio Company

Independent Auditor's Report

(Same first and second paragraphs as the standard report)

Helio Company has excluded, from property and debt in the accompanying balance sheets, certain lease obligations that, in our opinion, should be capitalized in order to conform with generally accepted accounting principles. If these lease obligations were capitalized, property would be increased by $1,500,000 and $1,300,000, long-term debt by $1,400,000 and $1,200,000, and retained earnings by $100,000 and $50,000 as of December 31, in the current and prior year, respectively. Additionally, net income would be decreased by $40,000 and $30,000 and earnings per share would be decreased by $.06 and $.04, respectively, for the years then ended.

In our opinion, except for the effects of not capitalizing certain lease obligations as discussed in the preceding paragraph, the financial statements referred to above present fairly, in all material respects, the financial position of Helio Company, and the results of its operations and its cash flows for the years then ended in conformity with generally accepted accounting principles.

concern, the auditor adds to the report an explanatory note describing the potential problem.[17]

The audit report should provide useful information to the investor. One investment banker noted, "Probably the first item to check is the auditor's opinion to see whether or not it is a clean one—'in conformity with generally accepted accounting principles'—or is qualified in regard to differences between the auditor and company management in the accounting treatment of some major item, or in the outcome of some major litigation."

Management's Reports

Management's Discussion and Analysis

The SEC mandates inclusion of **management's discussion and analysis (MD&A)**. This section covers three financial aspects of an enterprise's business—liquidity, capital resources, and results of operations. In it, management highlights favorable or unfavorable trends and identifies significant events and uncertainties that affect these three factors. This approach obviously involves subjective estimates, opinions, and soft data. However, the SEC believes that the relevance of this information exceeds the potential lack of reliability.

Illustration 24-16 presents an excerpt from the MD&A section (2004 "Business Risks" only) of **PepsiCo**'s annual report.

ILLUSTRATION 24-16
Management's
Discussion and Analysis

PEPSICO
PepsiCo, Inc.

Our Business Risks
We are subject to risks in the normal course of business. We manage our risks through an integrated risk management framework.

Our Reputation
We have a longstanding history of maintaining a good reputation globally which is critical to selling our branded products. If we fail to maintain high standards for product quality and integrity, our reputation could be jeopardized. In addition, we must protect our reputation by maintaining high ethical, social and environmental standards for all of our operations and activities. Damage to our reputation might result in rejection of our products by consumers and a loss of brand equity, as well as require additional resources to rebuild our reputation.

---

[17]"The Auditor's Consideration of an Entity's Ability to Continue as a Going Concern," *Statement on Auditing Standards No. 59* (New York: AICPA, 1988).

Information Technology

Information technology is becoming increasingly important as an enabler to operating efficiently and interfacing with customers, as well as maintaining financial accuracy and efficiency. If we do not allocate, and effectively manage, the resources necessary to build and sustain the proper technology infrastructure, we could be subject to transaction errors, processing inefficiencies, the loss of customers, business disruptions, or the loss of or damage to intellectual property through security breach.

Product Demand and Retail Consolidation

We are a consumer products company operating in highly competitive markets and rely on continued demand for our products. To generate revenues and profits, we must sell products that appeal to our customers and to consumers. As our chairman notes, our continued success is dependent on our product innovation, including maintaining a strong pipeline of new products, effective sales incentives, appropriate advertising campaigns and marketing programs, and the ability to secure adequate shelf space at our retailers. In addition, our success depends on our responses to consumer trends, such as low carbohydrate diets, consumer health concerns, including obesity and the consumption of certain ingredients, and changes in product category consumption and consumer demographics, including the aging of the general population. Seasonal weather conditions, particularly for sports drinks and hot cereals, can also impact demand. Our top five retail customers now represent approximately 27% of our North American net revenue reflecting the continuing consolidation of the retail trade.

Global Economic and Environmental Conditions

Unforeseen global economic and environmental changes and political unrest may result in business interruption, supply constraints, foreign currency devaluation, inflation, deflation or decreased demand. Economic conditions in North America could also adversely impact growth. For example, rising fuel costs may impact the sales of our products in convenience stores where our products are generally sold in higher margin single serve packages.

Regulatory Environment

Changes in laws, regulations and the related interpretations may alter the environment in which we do business and, therefore, impact our results or increase our liabilities. Such regulatory environment changes include changes in food and drug laws, laws related to advertising and deceptive marketing practices, accounting standards, taxation requirements, competition laws and environmental laws, including the regulation of water consumption and treatment.

Workforce Retention

Our continued growth requires us to develop our leadership bench and to implement programs, such as our long-term incentive program, designed to retain talent. We also compete to hire new employees, and then must train them and develop their skills and competencies. We have in place human resource programs, including our diversity and inclusion focus mentioned by our chairman, aimed at hiring, developing and retaining our talented and motivated workforce which provides us with competitive advantage. However, unplanned turnover could deplete our institutional knowledge base and erode our competitive advantage.

Market Risks

We are exposed to the market risks arising from adverse changes in:

- commodity prices, affecting the cost of our raw materials and energy;
- foreign exchange rates;
- Interest rates;
- stock prices; and
- discount rates, affecting the measurement of our pension and retiree medical liabilities.

UNDERLYING CONCEPTS

FASB Concepts Statement No. 1 notes that management knows more about the company than users and therefore can increase the usefulness of financial information by identifying significant transactions that affect the company and by explaining their financial impact.

The MD&A section also must provide information about the effects of inflation and changing prices, if they are material to financial statement trends. The SEC has not required specific numerical computations, and companies have provided little analysis on changing prices.

An additional voluntary disclosure provided in the MD&A of many companies is discussion of the company's critical accounting policies. This disclosure identifies accounting policies that require management to make subjective judgments regarding uncertainties, resulting in potentially significant effects on the financial results.[18] For

Expanded Discussion of Accounting for Changing Prices

---

[18]See *Cautionary Advice Regarding Disclosure about Critical Accounting Policies*, Release Nos. 33-8040; 34-45149; FR-60 (Washington, D.C.: SEC); and *Proposed Rule: Disclosure in Management's Discussion and Analysis about the Application of Critical Accounting Policies*, Release Nos. 33-8098; 34-45907; International Series Release No. 1258; File No. S7-16-02 (Washington, D.C.: SEC).

example, in its critical accounting policy disclosure, **PepsiCo** showed the impact on stock-based compensation expense in response to changes in estimated interest rates and stock return volatility. Through this voluntary disclosure, companies can expand on the information contained in the notes to the financial statements to indicate the sensitivity of the financial results to accounting policy judgments.

OBJECTIVE 6
Understand management's responsibilities for financials.

Management's Responsibilities for Financial Statements

The Sarbanes-Oxley Act requires the SEC to develop guidelines for *all* publicly traded companies to report on management's responsibilities for, and assessment of, the internal control system. An example of the type of disclosure that public companies are now making is shown in Illustration 24-17.[19]

ILLUSTRATION 24-17
Report on Management's Responsibilities

Home Depot

Management's Responsibility for Financial Statements
The financial statements presented in this Annual Report have been prepared with integrity and objectivity and are the responsibility of the management of The Home Depot, Inc. These financial statements have been prepared in conformity with U.S. generally accepted accounting principles and properly reflect certain estimates and judgments based upon the best available information.

The financial statements of the Company have been audited by KPMG LLP, an independent registered public accounting firm. Their accompanying report is based upon an audit conducted in accordance with the standards of the Public Company Accounting Oversight Board (United States).

The Audit Committee of the Board of Directors, consisting solely of outside directors, meets five times a year with the independent registered public accounting firm, the internal auditors and representatives of management to discuss auditing and financial reporting matters. In addition, a telephonic meeting is held prior to each quarterly earnings release. The Audit Committee retains the independent registered public accounting firm and regularly reviews the internal accounting controls, the activities of the independent registered public accounting firm and internal auditors and the financial condition of the Company. Both the Company's independent registered public accounting firm and the internal auditors have free access to the Audit Committee.

Management's Report on Internal Control over Financial Reporting
Our management is responsible for establishing and maintaining adequate internal control over financial reporting, as such term is defined in Exchange Act Rules 13a–15(f). Under the supervision and with the participation of our management, including our principal executive officer and principal financial officer, we conducted an evaluation of the effectiveness of our internal control over financial reporting based on the framework in *Internal Control-Integrated Framework* issued by the Committee of Sponsoring Organizations of the Treadway Commission (COSO). Based on our evaluation, our management concluded that our internal control over financial reporting was effective as of January 30, 2005. Our management's assessment of the effectiveness of our internal control over financial reporting as of January 30, 2005 has been audited by KPMG LLP, an independent registered public accounting firm, as stated in its report which is included herein.

Robert L. Nardelli
Chairman, President &
Chief Executive Officer

Carol B. Tomé
Executive Vice President &
Chief Financial Officer

Kelly H. Barrett
Vice President
Corporate Controller

---

[19]As indicated in this disclosure, management is responsible for preparing the financial statements and establishing and maintaining an effective system of internal controls. The auditor provides an independent assessment of whether the financial statements are prepared in accordance with GAAP, and for public companies, whether the internal controls are effective (see the audit opinion in Illustration 24-14.)

CURRENT REPORTING ISSUES

Reporting on Financial Forecasts and Projections

In recent years, the investing public's demand for more and better information has focused on disclosure of corporate expectations for the future.[20] These disclosures take one of two forms:[21]

> *Financial forecasts.* A **financial forecast** is a set of prospective financial statements that present, to the best of the responsible party's knowledge and belief, a company's expected financial position, results of operations, and cash flows. The responsible party bases a financial forecast on conditions it expects to exist and the course of action it expects to take.

> *Financial projections.* **Financial projections** are prospective financial statements that present, to the best of the responsible party's knowledge and belief, given one or more *hypothetical assumptions*, an entity's expected financial position, results of operations, and cash flows. The responsible party bases a financial projection on conditions it expects *would* exist and the course of action it expects *would* be taken, given one or more hypothetical assumptions.

The difference between a financial forecast and a financial projection is clearcut: A forecast provides information on what is **expected** to happen, whereas a projection provides information on what **might** take place, but is not necessarily expected to happen.

Whether companies should be required to provide financial forecasts is the subject of intensive discussion with journalists, corporate executives, the SEC, financial analysts, accountants, and others. Predictably, there are strong arguments on either side. Listed below are some of the arguments.

Arguments for requiring published forecasts:

1. Investment decisions are based on future expectations. Therefore information about the future facilitates better decisions.

2. Companies already circulate forecasts informally. This situation should be regulated to ensure that the forecasts are available to all investors.

3. Circumstances now change so rapidly that historical information is no longer adequate for prediction.

Arguments against requiring published forecasts:

1. No one can foretell the future. Therefore forecasts will inevitably be wrong. Worse, they may mislead, if they convey an impression of precision about the future,.

2. Companies may strive only to meet their published forecasts, thereby failing to produce results that are in the stockholders' best interest.

3. If forecasts prove inaccurate, there will be recriminations and probably legal actions.[22]

---

[20] Some areas in which companies are using financial information about the future are equipment lease-versus-buy analysis, analysis of a company's ability to successfully enter new markets, and examination of merger and acquisition opportunities. In addition, companies also prepare forecasts and projections for use by third parties in public offering documents (requiring financial forecasts), tax-oriented investments, and financial feasibility studies. Use of forward-looking data has been enhanced by the increased capability of microcomputers to analyze, compare, and manipulate large quantities of data.

[21] "Guide for Prospective Financial Information," *Audit and Accounting Guide* (New York: AICPA, May 1999), pars. 3.04 and 3.05.

[22] The issue is serious. Over a recent three-year period, 8 percent of the companies on the NYSE were sued because of an alleged lack of financial disclosure. Companies complain that they are subject to lawsuits whenever the stock price drops. And as one executive noted, "You can even be sued if the stock price goes up—because you did not disclose the good news fast enough."

OBJECTIVE 7
Identify issues related to financial forecasts and projections.

4 Disclosure of forecasts will be detrimental to organizations, because forecasts will inform competitors (foreign and domestic), as well as investors.

UNDERLYING CONCEPTS

The AICPA's Special Committee on Financial Reporting indicates that the legal environment discourages companies from disclosing forward-looking information. Companies should not have to expand reporting of forward-looking information unless there are more effective deterrents to unwarranted litigation.

The AICPA has issued a statement on standards for accountants' services on prospective financial information. This statement establishes guidelines for the preparation and presentation of financial forecasts and projections.[23] It requires accountants to provide (1) a summary of significant assumptions used in the forecast or projection and (2) guidelines for minimum presentation.

To encourage management to disclose prospective financial information, the SEC has a **safe harbor rule**. It provides protection to a company that presents an erroneous forecast, as long as the company prepared the forecast on a reasonable basis and disclosed it in good faith.[24] However, many companies note that the safe harbor rule does not work in practice, since it does not cover oral statements, nor has it kept them from investor lawsuits.

Experience in Great Britain

Great Britain has permitted financial forecasts for years, and the results have been fairly successful. Some significant differences do exist between the English and the U.S. business and legal environments.[25] But such differences probably could be overcome if influential interests in this country cooperated to produce an atmosphere conducive to quality forecasting. A typical British forecast adapted from a construction company's report to support a public offering of stock is as follows.

ILLUSTRATION 24-18
Financial Forecast of a British Company

> Profits have grown substantially over the past 10 years and directors are confident of being able to continue this expansion. . . . While the rate of expansion will be dependent on the level of economic activity in Ireland and England, the group is well structured to avail itself of opportunities as they arise, particularly in the field of property development, which is expected to play an increasingly important role in the group's future expansion.
>
> Profits before taxation for the half year ended 30th June were 402,000 pounds. On the basis of trading experiences since that date and the present level of sales and completions, the directors expect that in the absence of unforeseen circumstances, the group's profits before taxation for the year to 31st December will be not less than 960,000 pounds.
>
> No dividends will be paid in respect of the current year. In a full financial year, on the basis of above forecasts (not including full year profits) it would be the intention of the board, assuming current rates of tax, to recommend dividends totaling 40% (of after-tax profits), which will be payable in the next two years.

A general narrative-type forecast issued by a U.S. corporation might appear as follows.

ILLUSTRATION 24-19
Financial Forecast for an American Company

> On the basis of promotions planned by the company for the second half of the fiscal year, net earnings for that period are expected to be approximately the same as those for the first half of the fiscal year, with net earnings for the third quarter expected to make the predominant contribution to net earnings for the second half of the year.

---

[23]"Guide for Prospective Financial Information," op. cit., par. 1.02.

[24]"Safe-Harbor Rule for Projections," *Release No. 5993* (Washington: SEC, 1979). The Private Securities Litigation Reform Act of 1995 recognizes that some information that is useful to investors is inherently subject to less certainty or reliability than other information. By providing safe harbor for forward-looking statements, Congress has sought to facilitate access to this information by investors.

[25]The British system, for example, does not permit litigation on forecasted information, and the solicitor (lawyer) is not permitted to work on a contingent fee basis. See "A Case for Forecasting—The British Have Tried It and Find That It Works," *World* (New York: Peat, Marwick, Mitchell & Co., Autumn 1978), pp. 10–13.

Questions of Liability

What happens if a company does not meet its forecasts? Can the company and the auditor be sued? If a company, for example, projects an earnings increase of 15 percent and achieves only 5 percent, should stockholders be permitted to have some judicial recourse against the company?

One court case involving **Monsanto Chemical Corporation** has set a precedent. In this case, Monsanto predicted that sales would increase 8 to 9 percent and that earnings would rise 4 to 5 percent. In the last part of the year, the demand for Monsanto's products dropped as a result of a business turndown. Instead of increasing, the company's earnings declined. Investors sued the company because the projected earnings figure was erroneous, but a judge dismissed the suit because the forecasts were the best estimates of qualified people whose intents were honest.

As indicated earlier, the SEC's safe harbor rules are intended to protect companies that provide good-faith projections. However, much concern exists as to how the SEC and the courts will interpret such terms as "good faith" and "reasonable assumptions" when erroneous forecasts mislead users of this information.

Internet Financial Reporting

Most companies now use the power and reach of the Internet to provide more useful information to financial statement readers. All large companies have Internet sites, and a large proportion of companies' websites contain links to their financial statements and other disclosures. The popularity of such reporting is not surprising, since companies can reduce the costs of printing and disseminating paper reports with the use of Internet reporting.

Does Internet financial reporting improve the usefulness of a company's financial reports? Yes, in several ways: First, dissemination of reports via the Web allows firms **to communicate more easily and quickly with users** than do traditional paper reports. In addition, **Internet reporting allows users to take advantage of tools** such as search engines and hyperlinks to quickly find information about the firm and, sometimes, to download the information for analysis, perhaps in computer spreadsheets. Finally, **Internet reporting can help make financial reports more relevant** by allowing companies to report expanded disaggregated data and more timely data than is possible through paper-based reporting. For example, some companies voluntarily report weekly sales data and segment operating data on their websites.

While there continue to be concerns about **equality of access** to electronic financial reporting as well as the **reliability** of the information distributed via the Internet, organizations are developing new technologies and standards to further enable Internet financial reporting. An example is increasing use of extensible business reporting language (XBRL). **XBRL** is a computer language adapted from the code of the Internet. The language "tags" accounting data to correspond to financial reporting items, which are reported in the balance sheet, income statement, and the cash flow statement. Once tagged, any company's XBRL data can be easily processed using spreadsheets and other computer programs. Users can more easily search a company's reports, extract and analyze data, and perform financial comparisons within industries. As more financial statement users get on the Web, armed with tools like XBRL, we expect Internet reporting to continue to grow in popularity.[26]

---

[26]Reuters, "Lifting the Lid: Tech Seen Easing Financial Analysis," *nytimes.com* (January 22, 2005). See *www.xbrl.org/us/us/BusinessCaseForXBRL.pdf* for additional information on XBRL. The FASB has issued a report on electronic dissemination of financial reports. This report summarizes current practice and research conducted on Internet financial reporting. See Business Reporting Research Project, "Electronic Distribution of Business Reporting Information" (Norwalk, Conn.: FASB, 2000).

Fraudulent Financial Reporting

OBJECTIVE 8
Describe the profession's response to fraudulent financial reporting.

Fraudulent financial reporting is defined as "intentional or reckless conduct, whether act or omission, that results in materially misleading financial statements."[27] Fraudulent reporting can involve gross and deliberate distortion of corporate records (such as inventory count tags), or misapplication of accounting principles (failure to disclose material transactions). Although frauds are unusual, recent events involving such well-known companies as **Enron**, **WorldCom**, **Adelphia**, and **Tyco** indicate that more must be done to address this issue.

WHAT DO THE NUMBERS MEAN?

HERE'S A FRAUD

The case of **ESM Government Securities, Inc. (ESM)** exemplifies the seriousness of financial reporting frauds. ESM was a Fort Lauderdale securities dealer entrusted with monies to invest by municipalities from Toledo, Ohio to Beaumont, Texas. The cities that provided funds thought, based on the company name, that ESM was collateralized with government securities.

Examination of ESM's balance sheet indicated that the company owed about as much as it expected to collect. Unfortunately, the amount it expected to collect was from insolvent affiliates which, in effect, meant that ESM was bankrupt. In fact, ESM had been bankrupt for more than six years, and the fraud was discovered only because a customer questioned a note to the balance sheet! ESM had disguised more than $300 million of losses.

Source: For an expanded discussion of this case, see Robert J. Sack and Robert Tangreti, "ESM: Implications for the Profession," *Journal of Accountancy* (April 1987).

Causes of Fraudulent Financial Reporting

Fraudulent financial reporting usually occurs because of conditions in a company's internal or external environment.[28] Influences in the **internal environment** relate to poor internal control systems, management's poor attitude toward ethics, or perhaps a company's liquidity or profitability. Those in the **external environment** may relate to industry conditions, overall business environment, or legal and regulatory considerations.

General incentives for fraudulent financial reporting vary. Common ones are the desire to obtain a higher stock price, to avoid default on a loan covenant, or to make a personal gain of some type (additional compensation, promotion). Situational pressures on the company or an individual manager also may lead to fraudulent financial reporting. Examples of these situational pressures include the following.

- *Sudden decreases in revenue or market share* for a single company or an entire industry.
- *Unrealistic budget pressures* may occur when headquarters arbitrarily determines profit objectives (particularly for short-term results) and budgets without taking actual conditions into account.
- *Financial pressure resulting from bonus plans* that depend on short-term economic performance. This pressure is particularly acute when the bonus is a significant component of the individual's total compensation.

---

[27] "Report of the National Commission on Fraudulent Financial Reporting" (Washington, D.C., 1987), page 2. Unintentional errors as well as corporate improprieties (such as tax fraud, employee embezzlements, and so on) which do not cause the financial statements to be misleading are excluded from the definition of fraudulent financial reporting.

[28] The discussion in this section is based on the Report of the National Commission on Fraudulent Financial Reporting, pp. 23–24. See "2004 Report to the Nation on Occupational Fraud and Abuse, Association of Certified Fraud Examiners," (*www.cfenet.com/pdfs/2004RttN.pdf*) for evidence that fraudulent financial reporting causes and consequences are much the same today.

Opportunities for fraudulent financial reporting are present in circumstances when the fraud is easy to commit and when detection is difficult. Frequently these opportunities arise from:

1 *The absence of a board of directors or audit committee* that vigilantly oversees the financial reporting process.

2 *Weak or nonexistent internal accounting controls.* This situation can occur, for example, when a company's revenue system is overloaded as a result of a rapid expansion of sales, an acquisition of a new division, or the entry into a new, unfamiliar line of business.

3 *Unusual or complex transactions* such as the consolidation of two companies, the divestiture or closing of a specific operation, and the purchase and sale of derivative instruments.

4 *Accounting estimates requiring significant subjective judgment* by company management, such as the allowance for loan losses and the estimated liability for warranty expense.

5 *Ineffective internal audit staffs* resulting from inadequate staff size and severely limited audit scope.

A weak corporate ethical climate contributes to these situations. Opportunities for fraudulent financial reporting also increase dramatically when the accounting principles followed in reporting transactions are nonexistent, evolving, or subject to varying interpretations.

The AICPA has issued numerous auditing standards in response to concerns of the accounting profession, the media, and the public.[29] For example, the most recent standard on fraudulent financial reporting "raises the bar" on the performance of financial statement audits by explicitly requiring auditors to assess the risk of material financial misstatement due to fraud.[30] As indicated earlier, the Sarbanes-Oxley Act now raises the penalty substantially for executives who are involved in fraudulent financial reporting.

Criteria for Making Accounting and Reporting Choices

Throughout this textbook, we have stressed the need to provide information that is useful to predict the amounts, timing, and uncertainty of future cash flows. To achieve this objective, companies must make judicious choices between alternative accounting concepts, methods, and means of disclosure. You are probably surprised by the large number of choices that exist among acceptable alternatives.

You should recognize, however, as indicated in Chapter 1, that accounting is greatly influenced by its environment. It does not exist in a vacuum. Therefore, it is unrealistic to assume that the profession can entirely eliminate alternative presentations of certain transactions and events. Nevertheless, we are hopeful that the profession, by adhering to the conceptual framework, will be able to focus on the needs of financial statement users and eliminate diversity where appropriate. The SEC's and FASB's projects on principle-based standards are directed at these very issues. They seek to develop standards and implementation guidance that will result in accounting and financial reporting that reflects the economic substance of the transactions, not the desired financial result of management. The profession must continue its efforts to develop a sound foundation upon which to build financial standards and practice. As Aristotle said, "The correct beginning is more than half the whole."

UNDERLYING CONCEPTS

The FASB concept statements on objectives of financial reporting, elements of financial statements, qualitative characteristics of accounting information, and recognition and measurement are important steps in the right direction.

---

[29]Because the profession believes that the role of the auditor is not well understood outside the profession, much attention has been focused on the expectation gap. The **expectation gap** is the gap between (1) the expectation of financial statement users concerning the level of assurance they believe the independent auditor provides, and (2) the assurance that the independent auditor actually does provide under generally accepted auditing standards.

[30]"Consideration of Fraud in a Financial Statement Audit," *Statement on Auditing Standards No. 99* (New York: AICPA, 2002).

SUMMARY OF LEARNING OBJECTIVES

1. **Review the full disclosure principle and describe implementation problems.** The full disclosure principle calls for financial reporting of any financial facts significant enough to influence the judgment of an informed reader. Implementing the full disclosure principle is difficult, because the cost of disclosure can be substantial and the benefits difficult to assess. Disclosure requirements have increased because of (1) the growing complexity of the business environment, (2) the necessity for timely information, and (3) the use of accounting as a control and monitoring device.

2. **Explain the use of notes in financial statement preparation.** Notes are the accountant's means of amplifying or explaining the items presented in the main body of the statements. Notes can explain in qualitative terms information pertinent to specific financial statement items, and can provide supplementary data of a quantitative nature. Common note disclosures relate to such items as: accounting policies; inventories; property, plant, and equipment; creditor claims; contingencies and commitments; and subsequent events.

3. **Discuss the disclosure requirements for major business segments.** Aggregated figures hide much information about the composition of these consolidated figures. There is no way to tell from the consolidated data the extent to which the differing product lines contribute to the company's profitability, risk, and growth potential. As a result, the profession requires segment information in certain situations.

4. **Describe the accounting problems associated with interim reporting.** Interim reports cover periods of less than one year. Two viewpoints exist regarding interim reports. The discrete approach holds that each interim period should be treated as a separate accounting period. The integral approach is that the interim report is an integral part of the annual report and that deferrals and accruals should take into consideration what will happen for the entire year.

    Companies should use the same accounting principles for interim reports that they use for annual reports. A number of unique reporting problems develop related to the following items: (1) advertising and similar costs, (2) expenses subject to year-end adjustment, (3) income taxes, (4) extraordinary items, (5) earnings per share, and (6) seasonality.

5. **Identify the major disclosures in the auditor's report.** The auditor expresses an unqualified opinion if satisfied that the financial statements present the financial position, results of operations, and cash flows fairly in accordance with generally accepted accounting principles. A qualified opinion contains an exception to the standard opinion; ordinarily the exception is not of sufficient magnitude to invalidate the statements as a whole.

    An adverse opinion is required when the exceptions to fair presentation are so material that a qualified opinion is not justified. A disclaimer of an opinion is appropriate when the auditor has so little information on the financial statements that no opinion can be expressed.

6. **Understand management's responsibilities for financials.** Management's discussion and analysis (MD&A) section covers three financial aspects of an enterprise's business: liquidity, capital resources, and results of operations. Management's responsibility for the financial statements is often indicated in a letter to stockholders in the annual report.

7. **Identify issues related to financial forecasts and projections.** The SEC has indicated that companies are permitted (not required) to include profit forecasts in their reports. To encourage management to disclose such information, the SEC issued a safe harbor rule. The rule provides protection to a company that presents an erroneous forecast, as long as it prepared the projection on a reasonable basis and disclosed it in good faith. However, the safe harbor rule has not worked well in practice.

8. **Describe the profession's response to fraudulent financial reporting.** Fraudulent financial reporting is intentional or reckless conduct, whether through act or omission, that results in materially misleading financial statements. Fraudulent financial reporting usually occurs because of poor internal control, management's poor attitude toward ethics, poor performance, and so on. The Sarbanes-Oxley Act has numerous provisions intended to help prevent fraudulent financial reporting.

APPENDIX 24A

Basic Financial Statement Analysis

What would be important to you in studying a company's financial statements? The answer depends on your particular interest—whether you are a creditor, stockholder, potential investor, manager, government agency, or labor leader. For example, **short-term creditors** such as banks are primarily interested in the ability of the firm to pay its currently maturing obligations. In that case, you would examine the current assets and their relation to short-term liabilities to evaluate the short-run solvency of the firm.

Bondholders, on the other hand, look more to long-term indicators, such as the enterprise's capital structure, past and projected earnings, and changes in financial position. **Stockholders**, present or prospective, also are interested in many of the features considered by a long-term creditor. As a stockholder, you would focus on the earnings picture, because changes in it greatly affect the market price of your investment. You also would be concerned with the financial position of the company, because it affects indirectly the stability of earnings.

The **managers** of a company are concerned about the composition of its capital structure and about the changes and trends in earnings. This financial information has a direct influence on the type, amount, and cost of external financing that the company can obtain. In addition, the company managers find financial information useful on a day-to-day operating basis in such areas as capital budgeting, breakeven analysis, variance analysis, gross margin analysis, and for internal control purposes.

PERSPECTIVE ON FINANCIAL STATEMENT ANALYSIS

Readers of financial statements can gather information by examining relationships between items on the statements and identifying trends in these relationships. The relationships are expressed numerically in ratios and percentages, and trends are identified through comparative analysis.

A problem with learning how to analyze statements is that the means may become an end in itself. Analysts could identify and calculate thousands of possible relationships and trends. If one knows only how to calculate ratios and trends without understanding how such information can be used, little is accomplished. Therefore, a logical approach to financial statement analysis is necessary, consisting of the following steps.

OBJECTIVE 9
Understand the approach to financial statement analysis.

1 *Know the questions for which you want to find answers.* As indicated earlier, various groups have different types of interest in a company.

UNDERLYING CONCEPTS

Because financial statements report on the past, they emphasize the *qualitative characteristic of feedback value*. This feedback value is useful because it can be used to better achieve the *qualitative characteristic of predictive value*.

INTERNATIONAL INSIGHT

Some companies outside the U.S. provide "convenience" financial statements for U.S. readers. These financial statements have been translated into English, and they may also translate the currency units into U.S. dollars. However, the statements are *not restated* using U.S. accounting principles; financial statement analysis needs to take this fact into account.

OBJECTIVE 10
Identify major analytic ratios and describe their calculation.

2 *Know the questions that particular ratios and comparisons are able to help answer.* These will be discussed in this appendix.

3 *Match 1 and 2 above.* By such a matching, the statement analysis will have a logical direction and purpose.

Several caveats must be mentioned. **Financial statements report on the past.** Thus, analysis of these data is an examination of the past. When using such information in a decision-making (future-oriented) process, analysts assume that the past is a reasonable basis for predicting the future. This is usually a reasonable approach, but its limitations should be recognized.

Also, ratio and trend analyses will help identify a company's present strengths and weaknesses. They may serve as "red flags" indicating problem areas. In many cases, however, such analyses will not reveal **why** things are as they are. Finding answers about "why" usually requires an in-depth analysis and an awareness of many factors about a company that are not reported in the financial statements.

Another caveat is that a **single ratio by itself is not likely to be very useful.** For example, analysts may generally view a current ratio of 2 to 1 (current assets are twice current liabilities) as satisfactory. However, if the industry average is 3 to 1, such a conclusion may be invalid. Even given this industry average, one may conclude that the particular company is doing well if one knows the previous year's ratio was 1.5 to 1. Consequently, to derive meaning from ratios, analysts need some standard against which to compare them. Such a standard may come from industry averages, past years' amounts, a particular competitor, or planned levels.

Finally, **awareness of the limitations of accounting numbers used in an analysis** is important. We will discuss some of these limitations and their consequences later in this appendix.

RATIO ANALYSIS

In analyzing financial statement data, analysts use various devices to bring out the comparative and relative significance of the financial information presented. These devices include ratio analysis, comparative analysis, percentage analysis, and examination of related data. No one device is more useful than another. Every situation is different, and analysts often obtain the needed answers only upon close examination of the interrelationships among all the data provided. Ratio analysis is the starting point. Ratios can be classified as follows.

MAJOR TYPES OF RATIOS

Liquidity Ratios. Measures of the company's short-run ability to pay its maturing obligations.

Activity Ratios. Measures of how effectively the company is using the assets employed.

Profitability Ratios. Measures of the degree of success or failure of a given company or division for a given period of time.

Coverage Ratios. Measures of the degree of protection for long-term creditors and investors.[1]

---

[1]Some analysts use other terms to categorize these ratios. For example, liquidity ratios are sometimes referred to as *solvency* ratios; activity ratios as *turnover* or *efficiency* ratios; and coverage ratios as *leverage* or *capital structure* ratios.

We have integrated discussions and illustrations about the computation and use of these financial ratios throughout this book. Illustration 24A-1 summarizes all of the ratios presented in the book and identifies the specific chapters that presented that material.

SUMMARY OF RATIOS PRESENTED IN EARLIER CHAPTERS		
Ratio	Formula for Computation	Reference
I. Liquidity		
1. Current ratio	$\dfrac{\text{Current assets}}{\text{Current liabilities}}$	Chapter 13, p. 645
2. Quick or acid-test ratio	$\dfrac{\text{Cash, marketable securities, and net receivables}}{\text{Current liabilities}}$	Chapter 13, p. 646
3. Current cash debt coverage ratio	$\dfrac{\text{Net cash provided by operating activities}}{\text{Average current liabilities}}$	Chapter 5, p. 197
II. Activity		
4. Receivables turnover	$\dfrac{\text{Net sales}}{\text{Average trade receivables (net)}}$	Chapter 7, p. 338
5. Inventory turnover	$\dfrac{\text{Cost of goods sold}}{\text{Average inventory}}$	Chapter 9, p. 444
6. Asset turnover	$\dfrac{\text{Net sales}}{\text{Average total assets}}$	Chapter 11, p. 545
III. Profitability		
7. Profit margin on sales	$\dfrac{\text{Net income}}{\text{Net sales}}$	Chapter 11, p. 545
8. Rate of return on assets	$\dfrac{\text{Net income}}{\text{Average total assets}}$	Chapter 11, p. 545
9. Rate of return on common stock equity	$\dfrac{\text{Net income minus preferred dividends}}{\text{Average common stockholders' equity}}$	Chapter 15, p. 752
10. Earnings per share	$\dfrac{\text{Net income minus preferred dividends}}{\text{Weighted shares outstanding}}$	Chapter 16, p. 805
11. Payout ratio	$\dfrac{\text{Cash dividends}}{\text{Net income}}$	Chapter 15, p. 752
IV. Coverage		
12. Debt to total assets ratio	$\dfrac{\text{Debt}}{\text{Total assets}}$	Chapter 14, p. 695
13. Times interest earned	$\dfrac{\text{Income before interest expense and taxes}}{\text{Interest expense}}$	Chapter 14, p. 695
14. Cash debt coverage ratio	$\dfrac{\text{Net cash provided by operating activities}}{\text{Average total liabilities}}$	Chapter 5, p. 197
15. Book value per share	$\dfrac{\text{Common stockholders' equity}}{\text{Outstanding shares}}$	Chapter 15, p. 753

ILLUSTRATION 24A-1
Summary of Financial Ratios

Financial Analysis Primer

You can find additional coverage of these ratios, accompanied by assignment material, at the book's website, at **www.wiley.com/college/kieso**. This supplemental coverage takes the form of a comprehensive case adapted from the annual report of a large international chemical company that we have disguised under the name of Anetek Chemical Corporation.

Limitations of Ratio Analysis

OBJECTIVE 11
Explain the limitations of ratio analysis.

The reader of financial statements must understand the basic limitations associated with ratio analysis. As analytical tools, ratios are attractive because they are simple and convenient. But too frequently, decision makers base their decisions on only these simple computations. The ratios are only as good as the data upon which they are based and the information with which they are compared.

One important limitation of ratios is that they generally are **based on historical cost, which can lead to distortions in measuring performance**. Inaccurate assessments of the enterprise's financial condition and performance can result from failing to incorporate fair value information.

Also, investors must remember that **where estimated items (such as depreciation and amortization) are significant, income ratios lose some of their credibility**. For example, income recognized before the termination of a company's life is an approximation. In analyzing the income statement, users should be aware of the uncertainty surrounding the computation of net income. As one writer aptly noted, "The physicist has long since conceded that the location of an electron is best expressed by a probability curve. Surely an abstraction like earnings per share is even more subject to the rules of probability and risk."[2]

UNDERLYING CONCEPTS

Consistency and comparability are important concepts for financial statement analysis. If the principles and assumptions used to prepare the financial statements are continually changing, accurate assessments of a company's progress become difficult.

Probably the greatest limitation of ratio analysis is the **difficult problem of achieving comparability among firms in a given industry**. Achieving comparability requires that the analyst (1) identify basic differences in companies' accounting principles and procedures and (2) adjust the balances to achieve comparability. Basic differences in accounting usually involve one of the following areas.

1 Inventory valuation (FIFO, LIFO, average cost).
2 Depreciation methods, particularly the use of straight-line versus accelerated depreciation.
3 Capitalization versus expense of certain costs.
4 Capitalization of leases versus noncapitalization.
5 Investments in common stock carried at equity versus fair value.
6 Differing treatments of postretirement benefit costs.
7 Questionable practices of defining discontinued operations, impairments, and extraordinary items.

The use of these different alternatives can make a significant difference in the ratios computed. For example, at one time **Anheuser-Busch** noted that if it had used average cost for inventory valuation instead of LIFO, inventories would have increased approximately $33,000,000. Such an increase would have a substantive impact on the current ratio. Several studies have analyzed the impact of different accounting methods on financial statement analysis. The differences in income that can develop are staggering in some cases. Investors must be aware of the potential pitfalls if they are to be able to make the proper adjustments.[3]

Finally, analysts should recognize that a **substantial amount of important information** is not included in a company's financial statements. Events involving such things as industry changes, management changes, competitors' actions, technological developments, government actions, and union activities are often critical to a company's successful operation. These events occur continuously, and information about them must come from careful analysis of financial reports in the media and other sources. Indeed many argue, in what is known as the **efficient-market hypothesis**, that financial statements contain "no surprises" to those engaged in market activities. They contend that the effect of these events is known in the marketplace—and the price of the company's stock adjusts accordingly—well before the issuance of such reports.

---

[2]Richard E. Cheney, "How Dependable Is the Bottom Line?" *The Financial Executive* (January 1971), p. 12.

[3]See for example, Eugene A. Imhoff, Jr., Robert C. Lipe, and David W. Wright, "Operating Leases: Impact of Constructive Capitalization," *Accounting Horizons* (March 1991).

COMPARATIVE ANALYSIS

Comparative analysis presents the same information for two or more different dates or periods, so that like items may be compared. Ratio analysis provides only a single snapshot, for one given point or period in time. In a comparative analysis, an investment analyst can concentrate on a given item and determine whether it appears to be growing or diminishing year by year and the proportion of such change to related items. Generally, companies present comparative financial statements.[4] They typically include two years of balance sheet information and three years of income statement information.

In addition, many companies include in their annual reports five- or ten-year summaries of pertinent data that permit readers to examine and analyze trends. *ARB No. 43* concluded that "the presentation of comparative financial statements in annual and other reports enhances the usefulness of such reports and brings out more clearly the nature and trends of current changes affecting the enterprise." Illustration 24A-2 presents a five-year condensed statement, with additional supporting data, of Anetek Chemical Corporation.

<table>
<tr><td>OBJECTIVE 12
Describe techniques of comparative analysis.</td></tr>
</table>

ILLUSTRATION 24A-2
Condensed Comparative Financial Information

ANETEK CHEMICAL CORPORATION
CONDENSED COMPARATIVE STATEMENTS
(000,000 OMITTED)

	2007	2006	2005	2004	2003	10 Years Ago 1997	20 Years Ago 1987
Sales and other revenue:							
Net sales	$1,600.0	$1,350.0	$1,309.7	$1,176.2	$1,077.5	$636.2	$170.7
Other revenue	75.0	50.0	39.4	34.1	24.6	9.0	3.7
Total	1,675.0	1,400.0	1,349.1	1,210.3	1,102.1	645.2	174.4
Costs and other charges:							
Cost of sales	1,000.0	850.0	827.4	737.6	684.2	386.8	111.0
Depreciation and amortization	150.0	150.0	122.6	115.6	98.7	82.4	14.2
Selling and administrative expenses	225.0	150.0	144.2	133.7	126.7	66.7	10.7
Interest expense	50.0	25.0	28.5	20.7	9.4	8.9	1.8
Taxes on income	100.0	75.0	79.5	73.5	68.3	42.4	12.4
Total	1,525.0	1,250.0	1,202.2	1,081.1	987.3	587.2	150.1
Net income for the year	$ 150.0	$ 150.0	$ 146.9	$ 129.2	$ 114.8	$ 58.0	$ 24.3
Other Statistics							
Earnings per share on common stock (in dollars)[a]	$ 5.00	$ 5.00	$ 4.90	$ 3.58	$ 3.11	$ 1.66	$ 1.06
Cash dividends per share on common stock (in dollars)[a]	2.25	2.15	1.95	1.79	1.71	1.11	0.25
Cash dividends declared on common stock	67.5	64.5	58.5	64.6	63.1	38.8	5.7
Stock dividend at approximate market value				46.8		27.3	
Taxes (major)	144.5	125.9	116.5	105.6	97.8	59.8	17.0
Wages paid	389.3	325.6	302.1	279.6	263.2	183.2	48.6
Cost of employee benefits	50.8	36.2	32.9	28.7	27.2	18.4	4.4
Number of employees at year end (thousands)	47.4	36.4	35.0	33.8	33.2	26.6	14.6
Additions to property	306.3	192.3	241.5	248.3	166.1	185.0	49.0

[a]Adjusted for stock splits and stock dividends.

---

[4]All 600 companies surveyed in *Accounting Trends and Techniques—2004* presented comparative 2003 amounts in their 2004 balance sheets and presented comparative 2002 and 2003 amounts in their 2004 income statements.

PERCENTAGE (COMMON-SIZE) ANALYSIS

OBJECTIVE 13
Describe techniques of percentage analysis.

Analysts also use percentage analysis to help them evaluate and compare companies. **Percentage analysis** consists of reducing a series of related amounts to a series of percentages of a given base. For example, analysts frequently express all items in an income statement as a percentage of sales or sometimes as a percentage of cost of goods sold. They may analyze a balance sheet on the basis of total assets. Percentage analysis facilitates comparison and is helpful in evaluating the relative size of items or the relative change in items. A conversion of absolute dollar amounts to percentages may also facilitate comparison between companies of different size.

Illustration 24A-3 shows a comparative analysis of the expense section of Anetek for the last two years.

ILLUSTRATION 24A-3
Horizontal Percentage
Analysis

	2007	2006	Difference	% Change Inc. (Dec.)
ANETEK CHEMICAL CORPORATION HORIZONTAL COMPARATIVE ANALYSIS (000,000 OMITTED)				
Cost of sales	$1,000.0	$850.0	$150.0	17.6%
Depreciation and amortization	150.0	150.0	0	0
Selling and administrative expenses	225.0	150.0	75.0	50.0
Interest expense	50.0	25.0	25.0	100.0
Taxes	100.0	75.0	25.0	33.3

This approach, normally called **horizontal analysis**, indicates the proportionate change over a period of time. It is especially useful in evaluating trends, because absolute changes are often deceiving.

Another comparative approach, called **vertical analysis**, is the proportional expression of each financial statement item in a given period to a base figure. For example, Anetek Chemical's income statement using this approach appears in Illustration 24A-4.

ILLUSTRATION 24A-4
Vertical Percentage
Analysis

ANETEK CHEMICAL CORPORATION
INCOME STATEMENT
(000,000 OMITTED)

	Amount	Percentage of Total Revenue
Net sales	$1,600.0	96%
Other revenue	75.0	4
Total revenue	1,675.0	100
Less:		
Cost of goods sold	1,000.0	60
Depreciation and amortization	150.0	9
Selling and administrative expenses	225.0	13
Interest expense	50.0	3
Income tax	100.0	6
Total expenses	1,525.0	91
Net income	$ 150.0	9%

Vertical analysis is frequently called **common-size analysis** because it reduces all of the statement items to a "common size." That is, all of the elements within each statement are expressed in percentages of some common number and always add up to 100 percent. Common-size (percentage) analysis reveals the composition of each of the financial statements.

In the analysis of the balance sheet, common-size analysis answers such questions as: What percentage of the capital structure is stockholders' equity, current liabilities, and long-term debt? What is the mix of assets (percentage-wise) with which the company has chosen to conduct business? What percentage of current assets is in inventory, receivables, and so forth?

Common-size analysis of the income statement typically relates each item to sales. It is instructive to know what proportion of each sales dollar is absorbed by various costs and expenses incurred by the enterprise.

Analysts may use common-size statements to compare one company's statements from different years, to detect trends not evident from comparing absolute amounts. Also, common-size statements provide intercompany comparisons regardless of size because they recast financial statements into a comparable common-size format.

SUMMARY OF LEARNING OBJECTIVES FOR APPENDIX 24A

9. Understand the approach to financial statement analysis. Basic financial statement analysis involves examining relationships between items on the statements (ratio and percentage analysis) and identifying trends in these relationships (comparative analysis). Analysis is used to predict the future, but ratio analysis is limited because the data are from the past. Also, ratio analysis identifies present strengths and weaknesses of a company, but it may not reveal *why* they are as they are. Although single ratios are helpful, they are not conclusive; for maximum usefulness, analysts must compare them with industry averages, past years, planned amounts, and the like.

10. Identify major analytic ratios and describe their calculation. Ratios are classified as liquidity ratios, activity ratios, profitability ratios, and coverage ratios: (1) *Liquidity ratio analysis* measures the short-run ability of a company to pay its currently maturing obligations. (2) *Activity ratio analysis* measures how effectively a company is using its assets. (3) *Profitability ratio analysis* measures the degree of success or failure of a company to generate revenues adequate to cover its costs of operation and provide a return to the owners. (4) *Coverage ratio analysis* measures the degree of protection afforded long-term creditors and investors.

11. Explain the limitations of ratio analysis. Ratios are based on historical cost, which can lead to distortions in measuring performance. Also, where estimated items are significant, income ratios lose some of their credibility. In addition, comparability problems exist because companies use different accounting principles and procedures. Finally, analysts must recognize that a substantial amount of important information is not included in a company's financial statements.

12. Describe techniques of comparative analysis. Companies present comparative data, which generally includes two years of balance sheet information and three years of income statement information. In addition, many companies include in their annual reports five- to ten-year summaries of pertinent data that permit the reader to analyze trends.

13. Describe techniques of percentage analysis. Percentage analysis consists of reducing a series of related amounts to a series of percentages of a given base. Analysts use two approaches: *Horizontal analysis* indicates the proportionate change in financial statement items over a period of time; such analysis is most helpful in evaluating trends. *Vertical analysis* (common-size analysis) is a proportional expression of each item on the financial statements in a given period to a base amount. It analyzes the composition of each of the financial statements from different years (a) to detect trends not evident from the comparison of absolute amounts and (b) to make intercompany comparisons of different-sized enterprises.

KEY TERMS

acid-test ratio, *1317*

activity ratios, *1316*

asset turnover, *1317*

book value per share, *1317*

cash debt coverage ratio, *1317*

common-size analysis, *1320*

comparative analysis, *1319*

coverage ratios, *1316*

current cash debt coverage ratio, *1317*

current ratio, *1317*

debt to total assets ratio, *1317*

earnings per share, *1317*

horizontal analysis, *1320*

inventory turnover, *1317*

liquidity ratios, *1316*

payout ratio, *1317*

percentage analysis, *1320*

profit margin on sales, *1317*

profitability ratios, *1316*

quick ratio, *1317*

rate of return on assets, *1317*

rate of return on common stock equity, *1317*

receivables turnover, *1317*

times interest earned, *1317*

vertical analysis, *1320*

APPENDIX

24B International Accounting Standards

OBJECTIVE 14
Describe the current international accounting environment.

In Chapter 1, we noted that the former U.S. Secretary of the Treasury judged the single most important innovation shaping the capital markets to be the idea of generally accepted accounting principles. He went on to say that we need something similar internationally.

We believe the secretary is right. We also believe that environmental forces are in place to achieve a worldwide set of accounting standards in the not-too-distant future. Currently, many companies find it costly to comply with different reporting standards in different countries. Likewise, investors, attempting to diversify their holdings and manage their risks, have become very interested in investing overseas. Having one common set of accounting rules will make it easier for international investors to compare the financial results of companies from different countries.

The purpose of this appendix is to provide additional insight into the movement toward one set of accounting standards to be used by all companies.

THE PRESENT ENVIRONMENT

Most agree that, for the following reasons, there is a need for one set of globalized accounting standards.

Multinational corporations. Today companies view the entire world as their market. Some of the best-known corporations, such as **Coca-Cola, Intel,** and **McDonald's,** generate more than 50 percent of their sales outside the United States. These organizations no longer think of themselves as simply U.S. companies. The same situation is occurring overseas as many foreign companies find their largest market to be the United States.

Mergers and acquisitions. All you have to do is look in the *Wall Street Journal* to quickly understand the merger activity taking place between companies from different countries. The mergers of such international giants as **DaimlerChrysler** and **Vodafone/Mannesmann** suggest that we will see even more of these types of mergers in the future.

Information technology. We have witnessed an incredible transformation in the speed and scale of communications among companies and individuals across borders. As communication barriers continue to drop, companies and individuals in different countries and markets are becoming comfortable buying and selling goods and services from one another.

Financial markets. Financial markets are some of the most significant international markets today. Whether it is currency, equity securities (stocks), bonds, or derivatives, there are active markets throughout the world trading these types of instruments. With the touch of a computer key, billions of dollars are transferred from one market to another.

REASONS TO UNDERSTAND INTERNATIONAL ACCOUNTING STANDARDS

As we discuss more fully below, the FASB and international accounting standard setters are working diligently to narrow the differences between U.S. and international accounting standards—hereafter referred to as **iGAAP**. However, it is likely that a number of differences will exist for the foreseeable future. As a result, U.S. investors, regulators, and preparers who have vested interests in the reporting practices of multinational companies should be familiar with iGAAP. Here is why.

Convergence. International accounting standards **converge** when differences between international and U.S. standards are eliminated. Such **convergence** is illustrated if U.S. GAAP changes to international standards. For example, a recent IASB exposure draft requires companies to record all liability contingencies at fair value, no matter the likelihood of occurrence. If this standard passes, no doubt the FASB will also consider the change. This change could affect the financial reporting practices of U.S. companies.

Reconciliation to international standards. The SEC requires foreign companies that list on the U. S. exchanges to use U.S. GAAP or provide a reconciliation between iGAAP and U.S. GAAP. Currently, U.S. companies that wish to list on the European exchanges may use U.S. GAAP. It is possible that in the future U.S. companies may have to provide reconciliation to iGAAP if they wish to list on the European exchanges. In fact, it is possible that U.S. companies may be permitted to use iGAAP for their U.S. filings.

Investors' expectations. To attract foreign investors, U.S. companies may need to provide additional information regarding how iGAAP would affect their financial statements. As investors gain a better understanding of iGAAP, they may demand this additional information from U.S. companies.

Competitive factors. There is some concern that iGAAP may provide certain companies with a competitive advantage. For example, international standards that are more permissive for segment reporting may lead to a presentation that is more favorable but in reality is misleading. Conversely, the U.S. standards may force a U.S. company to disclose more segment information. Understanding this difference may be important in judging the competing companies.

Given these forces, it is no wonder that many are working to establish a set of accounting principles that can be used worldwide.

THE CHALLENGE OF INTERNATIONAL ACCOUNTING

The only way that international standards will work is if they are of high quality. High-quality standards must have the following characteristics.[1]

- They must permit *few alternative practices*.
- They must be *clearly stated*, to allow for easy interpretation and consistent application.
- They must be *comprehensive*, covering the major transactions facing companies, and must provide an *effective system* for responding to new transactions.
- They must provide *transparency of information* (full disclosure, understandability), to make that information relevant for making effective decisions.

Developing high-quality international standards is not easy. Accounting for transactions in the United States sometimes differs significantly from practices in other

---

[1]Adapted from Edmund L. Jenkins, "Global Financial Reporting and the Global Financial Markets," 1999 Financial Executive Summit (Vancouver, B.C., May 28, 1999).

countries. These differences in some cases are quite fundamental; they involve issues such as when companies should recognize and measure assets, liabilities, revenues, and expenses.

Here are some examples of such differences:

- iGAAP permits companies to value assets at fair market value using appraisals. In the United States this practice is not allowed.
- iGAAP prohibits use of LIFO costing for inventories. In the United States, a significant number of companies use LIFO to cost some, or their entire, inventory.
- iGAAP gives companies the option of reporting the funded position of postretirement benefit plans in the balance sheet. U.S. GAAP requires recognition.
- iGAAP requires use of the cost-recovery method instead of completed-contract revenue recognition for long-term contracts.

The FASB and international accounting standard setters have already eliminated some differences between U.S. GAAP and iGAAP.[2] Discussions in this book have highlighted a number of the remaining differences between them. The fact that there *are* differences should not be surprising, because standard setters worldwide have developed standards in response to different user needs. In some countries, the primary users of financial statements are private investors; in others, the primary users are tax authorities or central government planners. In the United States, capital market participants (investors and creditors) have driven accounting standard formulation.

WHO ARE THE KEY PLAYERS IN DEVELOPING INTERNATIONAL STANDARDS?

Throughout this book, we have discussed the FASB and its role in establishing accounting standards. We have also explained the role the SEC plays in ensuring that companies follow these standards appropriately. Both of these organizations have strongly supported the movement toward one set of international standards.

In the international arena, the primary organization involved in developing iGAAP is the International Accounting Standards Board (IASB).

IASB

Ed Jenkins, former chair of the FASB, noted, "We have reached a historic milestone for the future of financial reporting that will benefit investors around the world. The FASB is pleased that the **IASC**—a standard-setting organization based in London—has accepted the recommendations of its Strategy Working Party to restructure the IASC. When it is in place, the proposed restructuring would provide an independent, objective international standard setter whose standards could meet the needs of the global capital markets."[3]

The independent objective standard-setting body now in place is called the **International Accounting Standards Board (IASB)**. The IASB is a privately funded accounting standard setter based in London, UK. Its members currently come from nine countries and have a variety of functional backgrounds; twelve of the fourteen IASB's

---

[2]Notable examples are exchanges of nonmonetary assets (discussed in Chapter 10) and accounting changes (discussed in Chapter 22.)

[3]Edmund L. Jenkins, "Global Financial Reporting and the Global Financial Markets," 1999 Financial Executive Summit (Vancouver, B.C., May 28, 1999). See also SEC Concept Release, "International Accounting Standards" (Washington, D.C.: SEC, 2000).

members have full-time positions on the Board. The Board is committed to developing, in the public interest, a single set of high-quality, understandable, and enforceable global accounting standards that require transparent and comparable information in general-purpose financial statements. In addition, the Board cooperates with national accounting standard setters to achieve convergence in accounting standards around the world.[4]

The standard-setting structure internationally is now very similar to the standard-setting structure in the United States. That is, the structure is comprised of two main bodies: The International Accounting Standards Committee Foundation (IASCF) provides oversight. The International Accounting Standards Board (IASB) develops the standards, which are referred to as **International Financial Reporting Standards (IFRS)** or **iGAAP**. In addition, the IASB has an interpretations committee (similar to the U.S. Emerging Issues Task Force) and an advisory council (similar to the FASB's Financial Accounting Standards Advisory Committee). The structure is depicted in Illustration 24B-1.

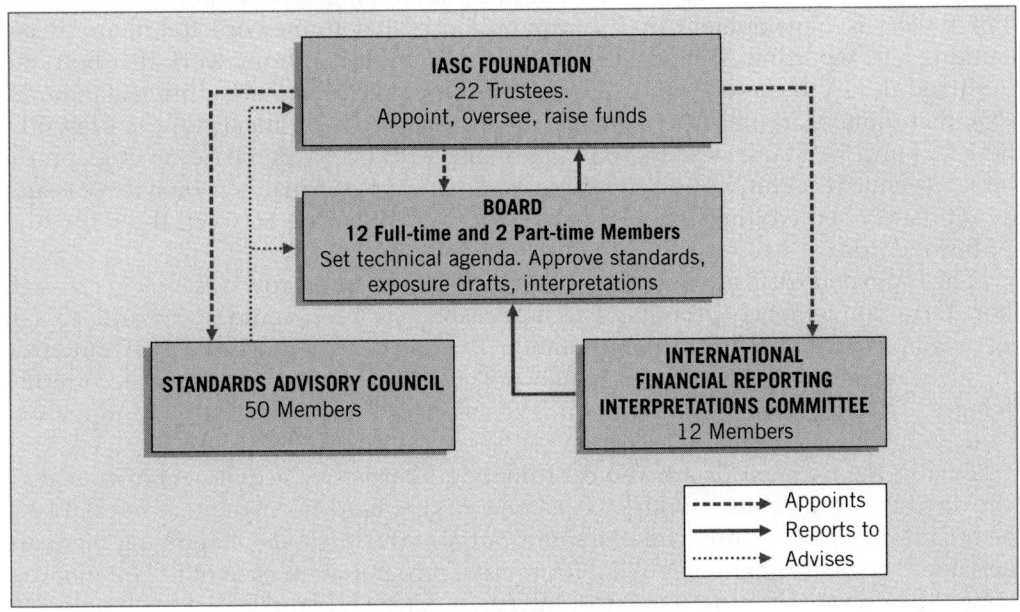

ILLUSTRATION 24B-1
International Standard-Setting Structure

Because it is a private organization, the IASB has no regulatory mandate and therefore no enforcement mechanism in place. In other words, unlike the U.S. setting, there is no SEC to enforce the use of IASB standards. Their use is completely voluntary.[5]

Other Organizations

National Standard Setters

Some countries have domestic accounting standard-setting organizations. For example, Canada and the United Kingdom have Accounting Standards Boards that develop accounting standards to be used by companies that do not list their securities on

---

[4]See *www.iasb.org/about/constitution.asp.*

[5]Effective January 1, 2005, the European Union (EU) required member country companies that list on EU securities exchanges to use IASB standards.

international exchanges. These national standard-setters often consult with the IASB in establishing accounting rules.

IOSCO

IOSCO stands for **International Organization of Securities Commissions**. IOSCO does not set accounting standards. This organization is dedicated to ensuring that the global markets can operate in an efficient and effective basis. The SEC, for example, is a member of IOSCO.

ACCOUNTING STANDARD SETTING AND INTERNATIONAL CONVERGENCE

The FASB and the IASB are working together toward the goal of a single set of high-quality accounting standards that will be used both domestically and internationally. To achieve this goal, the FASB and IASB are undertaking several joint projects. One joint project is development of a common conceptual framework for financial accounting and reporting. The goal of this project is to build a framework that both the FASB and the IASB can use when developing new and revised accounting standards.

Other joint efforts involve developing new standards on major topics. Presently, the FASB and IASB are working on such major projects as purchase method procedures, revenue recognition, and reporting on financial performance. When these issues are ultimately settled, there should be little, if any, difference between the FASB and IASB standards.

The FASB and IASB are also attempting to eliminate or narrow differences through short-term convergence projects. This approach has been quite successful so far. For example, the FASB has issued standards that mirror present IASB standards on such reporting issues as exchanges of nonmonetary assets and accounting changes. The goal of this collaboration is to select the better standard and move forward with it.

Finally, the two Boards are also coordinating interpretive activity. As often stated, "the devil is in the details." Both groups are working hard to ensure that not only are the broad conceptual approaches the same, but also the methods of applying them are the same. The Boards are not looking for mutual recognition of each other's standards. Rather, they want the **same** standards, interpretations, and language.

Regarding the FASB and convergence, Bob Herz, present chair of the FASB, has taken a position he calls "killing three birds with one stone." That is, he hopes that new standards will accomplish the following: (1) improve U.S. reporting; (2) simplify U.S. standards and standard setting; and (3) provide international convergence.

To illustrate what the FASB is trying to accomplish, consider leasing. As you learned in your study of leases, there are many rules and interpretations related to the accounting for leasing transactions. Most agree that the reporting results achieved in applying the present standard often do not reflect the substance of the transaction. Recently, the IASB and the FASB started a joint project that will revisit the questions related to accounting and reporting of leases. When this project is completed, the parties hope that it will (1) improve U.S. reporting, (2) simplify U.S. standards, and (3) lead to international convergence.

Challenges to Convergence

There are many challenges to convergence. Presently, domestic and international accounting parties are often starting from different places. Not only are the FASB and the IASB involved, but also numerous national standard setters are in the mix, as indicated in Illustration 24B-2.

Country(ies)	Standard Setter
Australia and New Zealand	Australian Accounting Standards Board (AASB)
	Financial Reporting Standards Board (FRSB)
Canada	Accounting Standards Board (AcSB)
France	Conseil Nationale de la Comptabilité (CNC)
Germany	German Accounting Standards Committee (DRSC)
Japan	Accounting Standards Board of Japan (ASBJ)
United Kingdom	Accounting Standards Board (ASB)
United States	Financial Accounting Standards Board (FASB)

It follows that there are significant cultural differences among countries and regions of the world. For example, Europe sometimes seems more interested in developing a *representative* IASB than an *independent* IASB. In the United States, the FASB is faced with a very litigious society, and therefore is often encouraged to write very detailed standards.

In addition, there are often institutional or legal barriers to change. For example, any time a standard is issued that affects debt versus equity classifications, loan covenants may have to be changed. In some countries, changing loan covenants is often very difficult to implement.

And there are the political issues. On both sides of the Atlantic, companies that do not want change are pleading with politicians to stop standards from being issued. In the United States, high-tech companies have fought bitterly to derail the stock option standard issued by the FASB. In Europe, the IASB issued a similar option standard and met little opposition. Conversely, bankers in Europe were up in arms regarding an IASB standard to record derivatives at fair value; U.S. GAAP requires fair value for derivatives in most situations. Although there was much opposition in the United States, the FASB passed the standard and companies now report derivatives at fair values.

RECONCILIATIONS—AN IMPORTANT ISSUE

Should the SEC accept iGAAP for companies who wish to list on U.S. stock exchanges? At present, the SEC's position is that foreign companies who wish to list in the United States must either follow U.S. GAAP or must file a form that **reconciles** the amounts reported under international standards (financial statements based on their home country GAAP or International Financial Reporting Standards—IFRS—as issued by the IASB) to U.S. GAAP. Illustration 24B-3 (page 1328) shows an example of a **reconciliation** form for **Nokia Corporation**.

As Illustration 24A-3 indicates, there are differences between U.S. GAAP and iGAAP that require adjustments to make Nokia's financial statements comparable to those of a U.S. telephone maker. This is why the SEC requires reconciliation. In most cases, the U.S. GAAP reconciliation requires foreign issuers to supplement their home-country financial statements. In certain cases—when it deems a standard to be relevant and reliable—the SEC will accept the accounting standard used by the foreign company.

ILLUSTRATION 24B-3
U.S.–IFRS Reconciliation

Nokia Corporation

Note 37 (in part). The principal differences between international financial reporting standards (IFRS) and U.S. GAAP are presented below, together with explanations of certain adjustments that affect consolidated net income and total shareholders' equity as of and for the years ended December 31:

(Millions Euros)	2004	2003
Reconciliation of net income:		
Net income reported under IFRS	3,207	3,592
U.S. GAAP adjustments		
Pension expense	—	(12)
Development costs	42	322
Provision for social security cost on stock options	(8)	(21)
Stock compensation expense	(21)	(9)
Cash flow hedges	89	9
Amortization of identifiable intangible assets acquired	(11)	(22)
Impairment of identifiable intangible assets acquired	(47)	—
Amortization of goodwill	106	162
Impairment of goodwill	—	151
Deferred tax effect of U.S. GAAP adjustments	(14)	(75)
Net income under U.S. GAAP	**3,343**	**4,097**

	2004	2003
Reconciliation of shareholders' equity:		
Total shareholders' equity reported under IFRS	14,238	15,148
U.S. GAAP adjustments		
Pension expense	(49)	(49)
Development costs	(57)	(99)
Marketable securities and unlisted investments	35	49
Provision for social security cost on stock options	6	14
Deferred compensation	(50)	(10)
Share issue premium	247	186
Stock compensation	(197)	(176)
Acquisition purchase price	2	3
Amortization of identifiable intangible assets acquired	(62)	(51)
Impairment of identifiable intangible assets acquired	(47)	—
Amortization of goodwill	502	396
Impairment of goodwill	255	255
Translation of goodwill	(319)	(293)
Deferred tax effect of U.S. GAAP adjustments	72	64
Total shareholders' equity under U.S. GAAP	**14,576**	**15,437**

Reconciliation is important because, as indicated in Illustration 24B-4, the number of foreign reporting companies in 2004 was 1,240, an increase from just 434 in 1990.

ILLUSTRATION 24B-4
Foreign Companies Registered with the SEC (1,240 Total as of December 31, 2004)

Country	Number of Companies	Country	Number of Companies
Canada	497	Bermuda	28
United Kingdom	107	Cayman Islands	26
Israel	86	Australia	24
Brazil	40	Chile	23
Mexico	39	Germany	22
Netherlands	34	British Virgin Islands	21
France	33	All other (41 Countries)	229
Japan	31		

Source: U.S. Securities and Exchange Commission

For foreign companies wishing to list in the United States, the SEC is under considerable pressure to accept the standards issued by the IASB. In the future, the SEC could follow various approaches:

- Maintain the current reconciliation requirements in all respects.
- Remove some of the current reconciliation requirements for selected IASB standards and extend the recognition to additional IASB standards as warranted, based on future review of each standard.
- Rely on the IASB standards for recognition and measurement principles, but require U.S. GAAP and SEC supplemental disclosure requirements for footnote disclosures and the level of detail for the line items in financial statements.
- Accept financial statements prepared in accordance with iGAAP or U.S. GAAP, and U.S. companies could report using iGAAP.

It now appears likely that, at a minimum, the SEC will accept iGAAP without the reconciliation requirement. For example, on June 20, 2007, the SEC approved for public comment a proposal to accept from foreign private issuers financial statements prepared in accordance with the English-language version of IFRS as published by the IASB without a U.S. GAAP reconciliation.

The issue of whether U.S. companies may use iGAAP instead of U.S. GAAP is a difficult one. An advantage for U.S. companies to switch is that more non–U.S. companies are going to report using iGAAP. Eventually the market may penalize U.S. companies that do not provide iGAAP information for comparison purposes. In addition, companies that have subsidiaries overseas may have to file in the local country using iGAAP. If U.S. companies have many subsidiaries overseas (particularly so for multinationals) it may be a cost advantage to use iGAAP. On the other hand, many U.S. companies, particularly smaller companies that have limited international operations, may not have an incentive to report using iGAAP.

As a result, we could have two different sets of GAAP being used in the United States, which could lead to additional complexity in the market. Similarly there are many regulations that presently require U.S. GAAP which could in any case be quite costly to adjust. In addition, the movement presently is toward convergence. What happens if the international standards can be used in the United States? What incentive will the IASB have, for example, to continue to support convergence?

CONCLUDING REMARKS

Financial statements prepared according to U.S. GAAP have been the standard for communicating financial information to the world. Regulators from around the world have readily accepted these financial statements when a company has chosen to list on an exchange. In 2005, however, the IASB standards have become the common financial-statement language for over 7,000 listed companies in the European Union and in over 90 countries around the world.

There are still many bumps in the road to the establishment of one set of worldwide standards, but the progress to date is remarkable. We are optimistic that the goal of worldwide standards can be achieved, which will be of value to all.

SUMMARY OF LEARNING OBJECTIVE FOR APPENDIX 24B

14. Describe the current international accounting environment. Investors and creditors increasingly demand international accounting reports. The growth of multinational corporations, increased international mergers and acquisitions, and financial markets, all facilitated by technology, contribute to the demand for international accounting standards. Given these forces, many are working to establish a set of accounting principles that can be used worldwide. High-quality international standards: (1) permit

KEY TERMS

converge, convergence, *1323*

iGAAP, *1323, 1325*

IASC, *1324*

International Accounting Standards Board (IASB), *1324*

International Financial Reporting Standards (IFRS), *1325*

reconciles, reconciliation, *1327*

few alternative practices, (2) are *clearly stated* to allow for easy interpretation and consistent application, (3) are *comprehensive*, covering the major transactions facing companies, (4) provide an *effective system* for responding to new transactions, and (5) provide *transparency of information* (full disclosure, understandability), to make that information relevant for making effective decisions.

The leading international accounting standard setter, the IASB, is working with the FASB to develop common, high-quality accounting standards. The U.S. SEC requires reconciliation of international accounting reports to U.S. GAAP. The current reconciliation requirements are designed to make financial statements prepared under non-U.S. GAAP more comparable to those prepared under U.S. GAAP.

Note: All **asterisked** Questions, Brief Exercises, Exercises, Problems, and Concepts for Analysis relate to materials contained in the appendixes to the chapter.

QUESTIONS

1. What are the major advantages of notes to the financial statements? What types of items are usually reported in notes?

2. What is the full disclosure principle in accounting? Why has disclosure increased substantially in the last 10 years?

3. The FASB requires a reconciliation between the effective tax rate and the federal government's statutory rate. Of what benefit is such a disclosure requirement?

4. What type of disclosure or accounting do you believe is necessary for the following items?

  (a) Because of a general increase in the number of labor disputes and strikes, both within and outside the industry, there is an increased likelihood that a company will suffer a costly strike in the near future.

  (b) A company reports an extraordinary item (net of tax) correctly on the income statement. No other mention is made of this item in the annual report.

  (c) A company expects to recover a substantial amount in connection with a pending refund claim for a prior year's taxes. Although the claim is being contested, counsel for the company has confirmed the client's expectation of recovery.

5. The following information was described in a note of Cebar Packing Co.

  "During August, A. Belew Products Corporation purchased 311,003 shares of the Company's common stock which constitutes approximately 35% of the stock outstanding. A. Belew has since obtained representation on the Board of Directors."

  "An affiliate of A. Belew Products Corporation acts as a food broker for Cedar Packing in the greater New York City marketing area. The commissions for such services after August amounted to approximately $20,000."
Why is this information disclosed?

6. What are the major types of subsequent events? Indicate how each of the following "subsequent events" would be reported.

  (a) Collection of a note written off in a prior period.

  (b) Issuance of a large preferred stock offering.

  (c) Acquisition of a company in a different industry.

  (d) Destruction of a major plant in a flood.

  (e) Death of the company's chief executive officer (CEO).

  (f) Additional wage costs associated with settlement of a four-week strike.

  (g) Settlement of a federal income tax case at considerably more tax than anticipated at year-end.

  (h) Change in the product mix from consumer goods to industrial goods.

7. What are diversified companies? What accounting problems are related to diversified companies?

8. What quantitative materiality test is applied to determine whether a segment is significant enough to warrant separate disclosure?

9. Identify the segment information that is required to be disclosed by *FASB Statement No. 131*.

10. What is an operating segment, and when can information about two operating segments be aggregated?

11. The controller for Chang Lee Inc. recently commented, "If I have to disclose our segments individually, the only people who will gain are our competitors and the only people that will lose are our present stockholders." Evaluate this comment.

12. An article in the financial press entitled "Important Information in Annual Reports This Year" noted that annual reports include a management discussion and analysis section. What would this section contain?

13. "The financial statements of a company are management's, not the accountant's." Discuss the implications of this statement.

14. Olga Conrad, a financial writer, noted recently, "There are substantial arguments for including earnings projections in annual reports and the like. The most compelling is that it would give anyone interested something now available to only a relatively select few—like large stockholders, creditors, and attentive bartenders." Identify some arguments against providing earnings projections.

15. The following comment appeared in the financial press: "Inadequate financial disclosure, particularly with respect to how management views the future and its role in the marketplace, has always been a stone in the shoe. After all, if you don't know how a company views the future, how can you judge the worth of its corporate strategy?" What are some arguments for reporting earnings forecasts?

16. What are interim reports? Why are balance sheets often not provided with interim data?

17. What are the accounting problems related to the presentation of interim data?

18. Mysteries Inc., a closely held corporation, has decided to go public. The controller, C. Keene, is concerned with presenting interim data when a LIFO inventory valuation is used. What problems are encountered with LIFO inventories when quarterly data are presented?

19. What approaches have been suggested to overcome the seasonality problem related to interim reporting?

20. What is the difference between a CPA's unqualified opinion or "clean" opinion and a qualified one?

21. Mary Beidler and Lee Pannebecker are discussing the recent fraud that occurred at LowRental Leasing, Inc. The fraud involved the improper reporting of revenue to ensure that the company would have income in excess of $1 million. What is fraudulent financial reporting, and how does it differ from an embezzlement of company funds?

*22. "The significance of financial statement data is not in the amount alone." Discuss the meaning of this statement.

*23. A close friend of yours, who is a history major and who has not had any college courses or any experience in business, is receiving the financial statements from companies in which he has minor investments (acquired for him by his now-deceased father). He asks you what he needs to know to interpret and to evaluate the financial statement data that he is receiving. What would you tell him?

*24. Distinguish between ratio analysis and percentage analysis relative to the interpretation of financial statements. What is the value of these two types of analyses?

*25. In calculating inventory turnover, why is cost of goods sold used as the numerator? As the inventory turnover increases, what increasing risk does the business assume?

*26. What is the relationship of the asset turnover ratio to the rate of return on assets?

*27. Explain the meaning of the following terms: (a) common-size analysis, (b) vertical analysis, (c) horizontal analysis, (d) percentage analysis.

*28. Presently, the profession requires that earnings per share be disclosed on the face of the income statement. What are some disadvantages of reporting ratios on the financial statements?

*29. Why is it important to understand international accounting standards?

*30. Describe some of the similarities between U.S. and international standard-setting structures.

*31. What is the reconciliation required by the SEC for international reports? Why is the reconciliation required?

BRIEF EXERCISES

(LO 2) **BE24-1** An annual report of D. Robillard Industries states, "The company and its subsidiaries have long-term leases expiring on various dates after December 31, 2007. Amounts payable under such commitments, without reduction for related rental income, are expected to average approximately $5,711,000 annually for the next 3 years. Related rental income from certain subleases to others is estimated to average $3,094,000 annually for the next 3 years." What information is provided by this note?

(LO 2) **BE24-2** An annual report of **Ford Motor Corporation** states, "Net income a share is computed based upon the average number of shares of capital stock of all classes outstanding. Additional shares of common stock may be issued or delivered in the future on conversion of outstanding convertible debentures, exercise of outstanding employee stock options, and for payment of defined supplemental compensation. Had such additional shares been outstanding, net income a share would have been reduced by 10¢ in the current year and 3¢ in the previous year. . . . As a result of capital stock transactions by the company during the current year (primarily the purchase of Class A Stock from Ford Foundation), net income a share was increased by 6¢." What information is provided by this note?

(LO 2) **BE24-3** Linden Corporation is preparing its December 31, 2006, financial statements. Two events that occurred between December 31, 2006, and March 10, 2007, when the statements were issued, are described below.

1. A liability, estimated at $150,000 at December 31, 2006, was settled on February 26, 2007, at $170,000.
2. A flood loss of $80,000 occurred on March 1, 2007.

What effect do these subsequent events have on 2006 net income?

(LO 3) **BE24-4** Bess Marvin, a student of intermediate accounting, was heard to remark after a class discussion on diversified reporting, "All this is very confusing to me. First we are told that there is merit in presenting the consolidated results, and now we are told that it is better to show segmental results. I wish they would make up their minds." Evaluate this comment.

(LO 3) **BE24-5** Roder Corporation has seven industry segments with total revenues as follows.

Genso	$600	Sergei	$225
Konami	650	Takuhi	200
RPG	250	Nippon	700
Red Moon	375		

Based only on the revenues test, which industry segments are reportable?

(LO 3) **BE24-6** Operating profits and losses for the seven industry segments of Roder Corporation are:

Genso	$ 90	Sergei	$ (20)
Konami	(40)	Takuhi	34
RPG	25	Nippon	100
Red Moon	50		

Based only on the operating profit (loss) test, which industry segments are reportable?

(LO 3) **BE24-7** Identifiable assets for the seven industry segments of Roder Corporation are:

Genso	$500	Sergei	$200
Konami	550	Takuhi	150
RPG	400	Nippon	475
Red Moon	400		

Based only on the identifiable assets test, which industry segments are reportable?

(LO 10) ***BE24-8** Answer each of the questions in the following unrelated situations.

(a) The current ratio of a company is 5:1 and its acid-test ratio is 1:1. If the inventories and prepaid items amount to $600,000, what is the amount of current liabilities?

(b) A company had an average inventory last year of $200,000 and its inventory turnover was 5. If sales volume and unit cost remain the same this year as last and inventory turnover is 8 this year, what will average inventory have to be during the current year?

(c) A company has current assets of $90,000 (of which $40,000 is inventory and prepaid items) and current liabilities of $30,000. What is the current ratio? What is the acid-test ratio? If the company borrows $15,000 cash from a bank on a 120-day loan, what will its current ratio be? What will the acid-test ratio be?

(d) A company has current assets of $600,000 and current liabilities of $240,000. The board of directors declares a cash dividend of $180,000. What is the current ratio after the declaration but before payment? What is the current ratio after the payment of the dividend?

(LO 10) ***BE24-9** Aston Martin Company's budgeted sales and budgeted cost of goods sold for the coming year are $144,000,000 and $90,000,000 respectively. Short-term interest rates are expected to average 10%. If Aston Martin can increase inventory turnover from its present level of 9 times a year to a level of 12 times per year, compute its expected cost savings for the coming year.

EXERCISES

(LO 2) **E24-1** **(Post-Balance-Sheet Events)** Madrasah Corporation issued its financial statements for the year ended December 31, 2008, on March 10, 2009. The following events took place early in 2009.

(a) On January 10, 10,000 shares of $5 par value common stock were issued at $66 per share.

(b) On March 1, Madrasah determined after negotiations with the Internal Revenue Service that income taxes payable for 2008 should be $1,270,000. At December 31, 2008, income taxes payable were recorded at $1,100,000.

Instructions
Discuss how the preceding post-balance sheet events should be reflected in the 2008 financial statements.

(LO 2) **E24-2** **(Post-Balance-Sheet Events)** For each of the following subsequent (post-balance-sheet) events, indicate whether a company should (a) adjust the financial statements, (b) disclose in notes to the financial statements, or (c) neither adjust nor disclose.

    1. Settlement of federal tax case at a cost considerably in excess of the amount expected at year-end.
    2. Introduction of a new product line.
    3. Loss of assembly plant due to fire.
    4. Sale of a significant portion of the company's assets.
    5. Retirement of the company president.
    6. Prolonged employee strike.
    7. Loss of a significant customer.
    8. Issuance of a significant number of shares of common stock.
    9. Material loss on a year-end receivable because of a customer's bankruptcy.
   10. Hiring of a new president.
   11. Settlement of prior year's litigation against the company.
   12. Merger with another company of comparable size.

(LO 3) **E24-3** **(Segmented Reporting)** Carlton Company is involved in four separate industries. The following information is available for each of the four industries.

Operating Segment	Total Revenue	Operating Profit (Loss)	Identifiable Assets
W	$ 60,000	$15,000	$167,000
X	10,000	3,000	83,000
Y	23,000	(2,000)	21,000
Z	9,000	1,000	19,000
	$102,000	$17,000	$290,000

Instructions
Determine which of the operating segments are reportable based on the:

   (a) Revenue test.
   (b) Operating profit (loss) test.
   (c) Identifiable assets test.

(LO 10) ***E24-4** **(Ratio Computation and Analysis; Liquidity)** As loan analyst for Utrillo Bank, you have been presented the following information.

	Toulouse Co.	Lautrec Co.
Assets		
Cash	$ 120,000	$ 320,000
Receivables	220,000	302,000
Inventories	570,000	518,000
Total current assets	910,000	1,140,000
Other assets	500,000	612,000
Total assets	$1,410,000	$1,752,000
Liabilities and Stockholders' Equity		
Current liabilities	$ 305,000	$ 350,000
Long-term liabilities	400,000	500,000
Capital stock and retained earnings	705,000	902,000
Total liabilities and stockholders' equity	$1,410,000	$1,752,000
Annual sales	$ 930,000	$1,500,000
Rate of gross profit on sales	30%	40%

Each of these companies has requested a loan of $50,000 for 6 months with no collateral offered. Inasmuch as your bank has reached its quota for loans of this type, only one of these requests is to be granted.

Instructions
Which of the two companies, as judged by the information given above, would you recommend as the better risk and why? Assume that the ending account balances are representative of the entire year.

(LO 10) ***E24-5** **(Analysis of Given Ratios)** Picasso Company is a wholesale distributor of professional equipment and supplies. The company's sales have averaged about $900,000 annually for the 3-year period 2006–2008. The firm's total assets at the end of 2008 amounted to $850,000.

The president of Picasso Company has asked the controller to prepare a report that summarizes the financial aspects of the company's operations for the past 3 years. This report will be presented to the board of directors at their next meeting.

In addition to comparative financial statements, the controller has decided to present a number of relevant financial ratios which can assist in the identification and interpretation of trends. At the request of the controller, the accounting staff has calculated the following ratios for the 3-year period 2006–2008.

	2006	2007	2008
Current ratio	1.80	1.89	1.96
Acid-test (quick) ratio	1.04	0.99	0.87
Accounts receivable turnover	8.75	7.71	6.42
Inventory turnover	4.91	4.32	3.42
Total debt to total assets	51.0%	46.0%	41.0%
Long-term debt to total assets	31.0%	27.0%	24.0%
Sales to fixed assets (fixed asset turnover)	1.58	1.69	1.79
Sales as a percent of 2006 sales	1.00	1.03	1.07
Gross margin percentage	36.0%	35.1%	34.6%
Net income to sales	6.9%	7.0%	7.2%
Return on total assets	7.7%	7.7%	7.8%
Return on stockholders' equity	13.6%	13.1%	12.7%

In preparation of the report, the controller has decided first to examine the financial ratios independent of any other data to determine if the ratios themselves reveal any significant trends over the 3-year period.

Instructions

(a) The current ratio is increasing while the acid-test (quick) ratio is decreasing. Using the ratios provided, identify and explain the contributing factor(s) for this apparently divergent trend.

(b) In terms of the ratios provided, what conclusion(s) can be drawn regarding the company's use of financial leverage during the 2006–2008 period?

(c) Using the ratios provided, what conclusion(s) can be drawn regarding the company's net investment in plant and equipment?

(LO 10) ***E24-6** **(Ratio Analysis)** Edna Millay Inc. is a manufacturer of electronic components and accessories with total assets of $20,000,000. Selected financial ratios for Millay and the industry averages for firms of similar size are presented below.

	Edna Millay			2007 Industry Average
	2005	2006	2007	
Current ratio	2.09	2.27	2.51	2.24
Quick ratio	1.15	1.12	1.19	1.22
Inventory turnover	2.40	2.18	2.02	3.50
Net sales to stockholders' equity	2.71	2.80	2.99	2.85
Net income to stockholders' equity	0.14	0.15	0.17	0.11
Total liabilities to stockholders' equity	1.41	1.37	1.44	0.95

Millay is being reviewed by several entities whose interests vary, and the company's financial ratios are a part of the data being considered. Each of the parties listed below must recommend an action based on its evaluation of Millay's financial position.

Archibald MacLeish Bank. The bank is processing Millay's application for a new 5-year term note. Archibald MacLeish has been Millay's banker for several years but must reevaluate the company's financial position for each major transaction.

Robert Lowell Company. Lowell is a new supplier to Millay and must decide on the appropriate credit terms to extend to the company.

Robert Penn Warren. A brokerage firm specializing in the stock of electronics firms that are sold over-the-counter, Robert Penn Warren must decide if it will include Millay in a new fund being established for sale to Robert Penn Warren's clients.

Working Capital Management Committee. This is a committee of Millay's management personnel chaired by the chief operating officer. The committee is charged with the responsibility of periodically reviewing the company's working capital position, comparing actual data against budgets, and recommending changes in strategy as needed.

Instructions

(a) Describe the analytical use of each of the six ratios presented above.

(b) For each of the four entities described above, identify two financial ratios, from those ratios presented in Illustration 24A-1 (on page 1317), that would be most valuable as a basis for its decision regarding Millay.

(c) Discuss what the financial ratios presented in the question reveal about Millay. Support your answer by citing specific ratio levels and trends as well as the interrelationships between these ratios.

(CMA adapted)

See the book's website, www.wiley.com/college/kieso, for Additional Exercises.

PROBLEMS

(LO 2) **P24-1** **(Subsequent Events)** Your firm has been engaged to examine the financial statements of Sabrina Corporation for the year 2008. The bookkeeper who maintains the financial records has prepared all the unaudited financial statements for the corporation since its organization on January 2, 2002. The client provides you with the information below.

SABRINA CORPORATION
BALANCE SHEET
AS OF DECEMBER 31, 2008

Assets		Liabilities	
Current assets	$1,881,100	Current liabilities	$ 962,400
Other assets	5,171,400	Long-term liabilities	1,439,500
		Capital	4,650,600
	$7,052,500		$7,052,500

An analysis of current assets discloses the following.

Cash (restricted in the amount of $400,000 for plant expansion)	$ 571,000
Investments in land	185,000
Accounts receivable less allowance of $30,000	480,000
Inventories (LIFO flow assumption)	645,100
	$1,881,100

Other assets include:

Prepaid expenses	$ 47,400
Plant and equipment less accumulated depreciation of $1,430,000	4,130,000
Cash surrender value of life insurance policy	84,000
Unamortized bond discount	49,500
Notes receivable (short-term)	162,300
Goodwill	252,000
Land	446,200
	$5,171,400

Current liabilities include:

Accounts payable	$ 510,000
Notes payable (due 2010)	157,400
Estimated income taxes payable	145,000
Premium on common stock	150,000
	$ 962,400

Long-term liabilities include:

Unearned revenue	$ 489,500
Dividends payable (cash)	200,000
8% bonds payable (due May 1, 2013)	750,000
	$1,439,500

Capital includes:

Retained earnings	$2,810,600
Capital stock, par value $10; authorized 200,000 shares, 184,000 shares issued	1,840,000
	$4,650,600

The supplementary information below is also provided.

1. On May 1, 2008, the corporation issued at 93.4, $750,000 of bonds to finance plant expansion. The long-term bond agreement provided for the annual payment of interest every May 1. The existing plant was pledged as security for the loan. Use straight-line method for discount amortization.

2. The bookkeeper made the following mistakes.
   (a) In 2006, the ending inventory was overstated by $183,000. The ending inventories for 2007 and 2008 were correctly computed.
   (b) In 2008, accrued wages in the amount of $275,000 were omitted from the balance sheet and these expenses were not charged on the income statement.
   (c) In 2008, a gain of $175,000 (net of tax) on the sale of certain plant assets was credited directly to retained earnings.

3. A major competitor has introduced a line of products that will compete directly with Sabrina's primary line, now being produced in a specially designed new plant. Because of manufacturing innovations, the competitor's line will be of comparable quality but priced 50% below Sabrina's line. The competitor announced its new line on January 14, 2009. Sabrina indicates that the company will meet the lower prices that are high enough to cover variable manufacturing and selling expenses, but permit recovery of only a portion of fixed costs.

4. You learned on January 28, 2009, prior to completion of the audit, of heavy damage because of a recent fire to one of Sabrina's two plants; the loss will not be reimbursed by insurance. The newspapers described the event in detail.

Instructions

Analyze the above information to prepare a corrected balance sheet for Sabrina in accordance with proper accounting and reporting principles. Prepare a description of any notes that might need to be prepared. The books are closed and adjustments to income are to be made through retained earnings.

(LO 3) **P24-2** **(Segmented Reporting)** Friendly Corporation is a diversified company that operates in five different industries: A, B, C, D, and E. The following information relating to each segment is available for 2007.

	A	B	C	D	E
Sales	$40,000	$ 80,000	$580,000	$35,000	$55,000
Cost of goods sold	19,000	50,000	270,000	19,000	30,000
Operating expenses	10,000	40,000	235,000	12,000	18,000
Total expenses	29,000	90,000	505,000	31,000	48,000
Operating profit (loss)	$11,000	$(10,000)	$ 75,000	$ 4,000	$ 7,000
Identifiable assets	$35,000	$ 60,000	$500,000	$65,000	$50,000

Sales of segments B and C included intersegment sales of $20,000 and $100,000, respectively.

Instructions
   (a) Determine which of the segments are reportable based on the:
   (1) Revenue test.
   (2) Operating profit (loss) test.
   (3) Identifiable assets test.
   (b) Prepare the necessary disclosures required by *FASB No. 131*.

(LO 10, 12) ***P24-3** **(Ratio Computations and Additional Analysis)** Sandburg Corporation was formed 5 years ago through a public subscription of common stock. Robert Frost, who owns 15% of the common stock, was one of the organizers of Sandburg and is its current president. The company has been successful, but it currently is experiencing a shortage of funds. On June 10, Robert Frost approached the Spokane National Bank, asking for a 24-month extension on two $35,000 notes, which are due on June 30, 2007, and September 30, 2007. Another note of $6,000 is due on March 31, 2008, but he expects no difficulty in paying this note on its due date. Frost explained that Sandburg's cash flow problems are due primarily to the company's desire to finance a $300,000 plant expansion over the next 2 fiscal years through internally generated funds.

The Commercial Loan Officer of Spokane National Bank requested financial reports for the last 2 fiscal years. These reports are reproduced on page 1337.

SANDBURG CORPORATION
STATEMENT OF FINANCIAL POSITION
AS OF MARCH 31

Assets	2007	2006
Cash	$ 18,200	$ 12,500
Notes receivable	148,000	132,000
Accounts receivable (net)	131,800	125,500
Inventories (at cost)	95,000	50,000
Plant & equipment (net of depreciation)	1,449,000	1,420,500
Total assets	$1,842,000	$1,740,500
Liabilities and Owners' Equity		
Accounts payable	$ 69,000	$ 91,000
Notes payable	76,000	61,500
Accrued liabilities	9,000	6,000
Common stock (130,000 shares, $10 par)	1,300,000	1,300,000
Retained earnings[a]	388,000	282,000
Total liabilities and owners' equity	$1,842,000	$1,740,500

[a]Cash dividends were paid at the rate of $1 per share in fiscal year 2006 and $2 per share in fiscal year 2007.

SANDBURG CORPORATION
INCOME STATEMENT
FOR THE FISCAL YEARS ENDED MARCH 31

	2007	2006
Sales	$3,000,000	$2,700,000
Cost of goods sold[a]	1,530,000	1,425,000
Gross margin	$1,470,000	$1,275,000
Operating expenses	860,000	780,000
Income before income taxes	$ 610,000	$ 495,000
Income taxes (40%)	244,000	198,000
Net income	$ 366,000	$ 297,000

[a]Depreciation charges on the plant and equipment of $100,000 and $102,500 for fiscal years ended March 31, 2006 and 2007, respectively, are included in cost of goods sold.

Instructions

(a) Compute the following items for Sandburg Corporation.
   (1) Current ratio for fiscal years 2006 and 2007.
   (2) Acid-test (quick) ratio for fiscal years 2006 and 2007.
   (3) Inventory turnover for fiscal year 2007.
   (4) Return on assets for fiscal years 2006 and 2007. (Assume total assets were $1,688,500 at 3/31/05.)
   (5) Percentage change in sales, cost of goods sold, gross margin, and net income after taxes from fiscal year 2006 to 2007.
(b) Identify and explain what other financial reports and/or financial analyses might be helpful to the commercial loan officer of Spokane National Bank in evaluating Robert Frost's request for a time extension on Sandburg's notes.
(c) Assume that the percentage changes experienced in fiscal year 2007 as compared with fiscal year 2006 for sales and cost of goods sold will be repeated in each of the next 2 years. Is Sandburg's desire to finance the plant expansion from internally generated funds realistic? Discuss.
(d) Should Spokane National Bank grant the extension on Sandburg's notes considering Robert Frost's statement about financing the plant expansion through internally generated funds? Discuss.

(LO 13) *P24-4 **(Horizontal and Vertical Analysis)** Presented on page 1338 are comparative balance sheets for the Yevette Company.

YEVETTE COMPANY
COMPARATIVE BALANCE SHEET
AS OF DECEMBER 31, 2007 AND 2006

	December 31	
	2007	2006
Assets		
Cash	$ 180,000	$ 275,000
Accounts receivable (net)	220,000	155,000
Short-term investments	270,000	150,000
Inventories	960,000	980,000
Prepaid expense	25,000	25,000
Fixed assets	2,685,000	1,950,000
Accumulated depreciation	(1,000,000)	(750,000)
	$3,340,000	$2,785,000
Liabilities and Stockholders' Equity		
Accounts payable	$ 50,000	$ 75,000
Accrued expenses	170,000	200,000
Bonds payable	500,000	190,000
Capital stock	2,100,000	1,770,000
Retained earnings	520,000	550,000
	$3,340,000	$2,785,000

Instructions

(Round to two decimal places.)

(a) Prepare a comparative balance sheet of Yevette Company showing the percent each item is of the total assets or total liabilities and stockholders' equity.

(b) Prepare a comparative balance sheet of Yevette Company showing the dollar change and the percent change for each item.

(c) Of what value is the additional information provided in part (a)?

(d) Of what value is the additional information provided in part (b)?

(LO 10) *P24-5 **(Dividend Policy Analysis)** Remmers Inc. went public 3 years ago. The board of directors will be meeting shortly after the end of the year to decide on a dividend policy. In the past, growth has been financed primarily through the retention of earnings. A stock or a cash dividend has never been declared. Presented below is a brief financial summary of Remmers Inc. operations.

			($000 omitted)		
	2007	2006	2005	2004	2003
Sales	$20,000	$16,000	$14,000	$6,000	$4,000
Net income	2,900	1,600	800	900	250
Average total assets	22,000	19,000	11,500	4,200	3,000
Current assets	8,000	6,000	3,000	1,200	1,000
Working capital	3,600	3,200	1,200	500	400
Common shares:					
Number of shares					
outstanding (000)	2,000	2,000	2,000	20	20
Average market price	$9	$6	$4	—	—

Instructions

(a) Suggest factors to be considered by the board of directors in establishing a dividend policy.

(b) Compute the rate of return on assets, profit margin on sales, earnings per share, price-earnings ratio, and current ratio for each of the 5 years for Remmers Inc.

(c) Comment on the appropriateness of declaring a cash dividend at this time, using the ratios computed in part (b) as a major factor in your analysis.

CONCEPTS FOR ANALYSIS

CA24-1 (General Disclosures, Inventories, Property, Plant, and Equipment) Dan D. Lion Corporation is in the process of preparing its annual financial statements for the fiscal year ended April 30, 2007. Because all of Lion's shares are traded intrastate, the company does not have to file any reports with the

Securities and Exchange Commission. The company manufactures plastic, glass, and paper containers for sale to food and drink manufacturers and distributors.

Lion Corporation maintains separate control accounts for its raw materials, work-in-process, and finished goods inventories for each of the three types of containers. The inventories are valued at the lower of cost or market.

The company's property, plant, and equipment are classified in the following major categories: land, office buildings, furniture and fixtures, manufacturing facilities, manufacturing equipment, and leasehold improvements. All fixed assets are carried at cost. The depreciation methods employed depend upon the type of asset (its classification) and when it was acquired.

Lion Corporation plans to present the inventory and fixed asset amounts in its April 30, 2007, balance sheet as shown below.

Inventories	$4,814,200
Property, plant, and equipment (net of depreciation)	6,310,000

Instructions

What information regarding inventories and property, plant, and equipment must be disclosed by Dan D. Lion Corporation in the audited financial statements issued to stockholders, either in the body or the notes, for the 2006–2007 fiscal year?

(CMA adapted)

CA24-2 (Disclosures Required in Various Situations) Rem Inc. produces electronic components for sale to manufacturers of radios, television sets, and digital sound systems. In connection with her examination of Rem's financial statements for the year ended December 31, 2007, Maggie Zeen, CPA, completed field work 2 weeks ago. Ms. Zeen now is evaluating the significance of the following items prior to preparing her auditor's report. Except as noted, none of these items have been disclosed in the financial statements or notes.

Item 1

A 10-year loan agreement, which the company entered into 3 years ago, provides that dividend payments may not exceed net income earned after taxes subsequent to the date of the agreement. The balance of retained earnings at the date of the loan agreement was $420,000. From that date through December 31, 2007, net income after taxes has totaled $570,000 and cash dividends have totaled $320,000. On the basis of these data, the staff auditor assigned to this review concluded that there was no retained earnings restriction at December 31, 2007.

Item 2

Recently Rem interrupted its policy of paying cash dividends quarterly to its stockholders. Dividends were paid regularly through 2006, discontinued for all of 2007 to finance purchase of equipment for the company's new plant, and resumed in the first quarter of 2008. In the annual report dividend policy is to be discussed in the president's letter to stockholders.

Item 3

A major electronics firm has introduced a line of products that will compete directly with Rem's primary line, now being produced in the specially designed new plant. Because of manufacturing innovations, the competitor's line will be of comparable quality but priced 50% below Rem's line. The competitor announced its new line during the week following completion of field work. Ms. Zeen read the announcement in the newspaper and discussed the situation by telephone with Rem executives. Rem will meet the lower prices that are high enough to cover variable manufacturing and selling expenses but will permit recovery of only a portion of fixed costs.

Item 4

The company's new manufacturing plant building, which cost $2,400,000 and has an estimated life of 25 years, is leased from Ancient National Bank at an annual rental of $600,000. The company is obligated to pay property taxes, insurance, and maintenance. At the conclusion of its 10-year noncancellable lease, the company has the option of purchasing the property for $1. In Rem's income statement the rental payment is reported on a separate line.

Instructions

For each of the items above discuss any additional disclosures in the financial statements and notes that the auditor should recommend to her client. (The cumulative effect of the four items should not be considered.)

CA24-3 **(Disclosures, Conditional and Contingent Liabilities)** Presented below are three independent situations.

Situation 1

A company offers a one-year warranty for the product that it manufactures. A history of warranty claims has been compiled, and the probable amounts of claims related to sales for a given period can be determined.

Situation 2

Subsequent to the date of a set of financial statements, but prior to the issuance of the financial statements, a company enters into a contract that will probably result in a significant loss to the company. The amount of the loss can be reasonably estimated.

Situation 3

A company has adopted a policy of recording self-insurance for any possible losses resulting from injury to others by the company's vehicles. The premium for an insurance policy for the same risk from an independent insurance company would have an annual cost of $4,000. During the period covered by the financial statements, there were no accidents involving the company's vehicles that resulted in injury to others.

Instructions

Discuss the accrual or type of disclosure necessary (if any) and the reason(s) why such disclosure is appropriate for each of the three independent sets of facts above.

(AICPA adapted)

 CA24-4 **(Post-Balance Sheet Events)** At December 31, 2007, Angie Brandt Corp. has assets of $10,000,000, liabilities of $6,000,000, common stock of $2,000,000 (representing 2,000,000 shares of $1 par common stock), and retained earnings of $2,000,000. Net sales for the year 2007 were $18,000,000, and net income was $800,000. As auditors of this company, you are making a review of subsequent events on February 13, 2008, and you find the following.

1. On February 3, 2008, one of Brandt's customers declared bankruptcy. At December 31, 2007, this company owed Brandt $300,000, of which $40,000 was paid in January, 2008.
2. On January 18, 2008, one of the three major plants of the client burned.
3. On January 23, 2008, a strike was called at one of Brandt's largest plants, which halted 30% of its production. As of today (February 13) the strike has not been settled.
4. A major electronics enterprise has introduced a line of products that would compete directly with Brandt's primary line, now being produced in a specially designed new plant. Because of manufacturing innovations, the competitor has been able to achieve quality similar to that of Brandt's products, but at a price 50% lower. Brandt officials say they will meet the lower prices, which are high enough to cover variable manufacturing and selling costs but which permit recovery of only a portion of fixed costs.
5. Merchandise traded in the open market is recorded in the company's records at $1.40 per unit on December 31, 2007. This price had prevailed for 2 weeks, after release of an official market report that predicted vastly enlarged supplies; however, no purchases were made at $1.40. The price throughout the preceding year had been about $2, which was the level experienced over several years. On January 18, 2008, the price returned to $2, after public disclosure of an error in the official calculations of the prior December, correction of which destroyed the expectations of excessive supplies. Inventory at December 31, 2007, was on a lower of cost or market basis.
6. On February 1, 2008, the board of directors adopted a resolution accepting the offer of an investment banker to guarantee the marketing of $1,200,000 of preferred stock.

Instructions

State in each case how the 2007 financial statements would be affected, if at all.

CA24-5 **(Segment Reporting)** You are compiling the consolidated financial statements for Vender Corporation International. The corporation's accountant, Vincent Price, has provided you with the following segment information.

Note 7: Major Segments of Business

VCI conducts funeral service and cemetery operations in the United States and Canada. Substantially all revenues of VCI's major segments of business are from unaffiliated customers. Segment information for fiscal 2007, 2006, and 2005 follows.

	Funeral	Floral	Cemetery	Corporate	Dried Whey	Limousine	Consolidated
				(thousands)			
Revenues							
2007	$302,000	$10,000	$ 83,000	$ —	$7,000	$14,000	$416,000
2006	245,000	6,000	61,000	—	4,000	8,000	324,000
2005	208,000	3,000	42,000	—	1,000	6,000	260,000
Operating Income							
2007	79,000	1,500	18,000	(36,000)	500	2,000	65,000
2006	64,000	200	12,000	(28,000)	200	400	48,800
2005	54,000	150	6,000	(21,000)	100	350	39,600
Capital Expenditures[a]							
2007	26,000	1,000	9,000	400	300	1,000	37,700
2006	28,000	2,000	60,000	1,500	100	700	92,300
2005	14,000	25	8,000	600	25	50	22,700
Depreciation and Amortization							
2007	13,000	100	2,400	1,400	100	200	17,200
2006	10,000	50	1,400	700	50	100	12,300
2005	8,000	25	1,000	600	25	50	9,700
Identifiable Assets							
2007	334,000	1,500	162,000	114,000	500	8,000	620,000
2006	322,000	1,000	144,000	52,000	1,000	6,000	526,000
2005	223,000	500	78,000	34,000	500	3,500	339,500

[a]Includes $4,520,000, $111,480,000, and $1,294,000 for the years ended April 30, 2007, 2006, and 2005, respectively, for purchases of businesses.

Instructions

Determine which of the above segments must be reported separately and which can be combined under the category "Other." Then, write a one-page memo to the company's accountant, Vincent Price, explaining the following.

(a) What segments must be reported separately and what segments can be combined.
(b) What criteria you used to determine reportable segments.
(c) What major items for each must be disclosed.

CA24-6 (Segment Reporting—Theory) Presented below is an excerpt from the financial statements of H. J. Heinz Company.

Segment and Geographic Data

The company is engaged principally in one line of business—processed food products—which represents over 90% of consolidated sales. Information about the business of the company by geographic area is presented in the table below.

There were no material amounts of sales or transfers between geographic areas or between affiliates, and no material amounts of United States export sales.

(in thousands of U.S. dollars)	Domestic	United Kingdom	Canada	Western Europe	Other	Total	Worldwide
				Foreign			
Sales	$2,381,054	$547,527	$216,726	$383,784	$209,354	$1,357,391	$3,738,445
Operating income	246,780	61,282	34,146	29,146	25,111	149,685	396,465
Identifiable assets	1,362,152	265,218	112,620	294,732	143,971	816,541	2,178,693
Capital expenditures	72,712	12,262	13,790	8,253	4,368	38,673	111,385
Depreciation expense	42,279	8,364	3,592	6,355	3,606	21,917	64,196

Instructions

(a) Why does H. J. Heinz not prepare segment information on its products or services?
(b) What are export sales, and when should they be disclosed?
(c) Why are sales by geographical area important to disclose?

CA24-7 (Segment Reporting—Theory) The following article appeared in the *Wall Street Journal*.

WASHINGTON—The Securities and Exchange Commission staff issued guidelines for companies grappling with the problem of dividing up their business into industry segments for their annual reports.

An industry segment is defined by the Financial Accounting Standards Board as a part of an enterprise engaged in providing a product or service or a group of related products or services primarily to unaffiliated customers for a profit.

Although conceding that the process is a "subjective task" that "to a considerable extent, depends on the judgment of management," the SEC staff said companies should consider . . . various factors . . . to determine whether products and services should be grouped together or reported as segments.

Instructions

(a) What does financial reporting for segments of a business enterprise involve?
(b) Identify the reasons for requiring financial data to be reported by segments.
(c) Identify the possible disadvantages of requiring financial data to be reported by segments.
(d) Identify the accounting difficulties inherent in segment reporting.

CA24-8 (Interim Reporting) J. J. Kersee Corporation, a publicly traded company, is preparing the interim financial data which it will issue to its stockholders and the Securities and Exchange Commission (SEC) at the end of the first quarter of the 2006–2007 fiscal year. Kersee's financial accounting department has compiled the following summarized revenue and expense data for the first quarter of the year.

Sales	$60,000,000
Cost of goods sold	36,000,000
Variable selling expenses	2,000,000
Fixed selling expenses	3,000,000

Included in the fixed selling expenses was the single lump sum payment of $2,000,000 for television advertisements for the entire year.

Instructions

(a) J. J. Kersee Corporation must issue its quarterly financial statements in accordance with generally accepted accounting principles regarding interim financial reporting.
   (1) Explain whether Kersee should report its operating results for the quarter as if the quarter were a separate reporting period in and of itself or as if the quarter were an integral part of the annual reporting period.
   (2) State how the sales, cost of goods sold, and fixed selling expenses would be reflected in Kersee Corporation's quarterly report prepared for the first quarter of the 2006–2007 fiscal year. Briefly justify your presentation.
(b) What financial information, as a minimum, must Kersee Corporation disclose to its stockholders in its quarterly reports?

(CMA adapted)

CA24-9 (Treatment of Various Interim Reporting Situations) The following statement is an excerpt from Paragraphs 9 and 10 of *Accounting Principles Board (APB) Opinion No. 28*, "Interim Financial Reporting."

Interim financial information is essential to provide investors and others with timely information as to the progress of the enterprise. The usefulness of such information rests on the relationship that it has to the annual results of operations. Accordingly, the Board has concluded that each interim period should be viewed primarily as an integral part of an annual period.

In general, the results for each interim period should be based on the accounting principles and practices used by an enterprise in the preparation of its latest annual financial statements unless a change in an accounting practice or policy has been adopted in the current year. The Board has concluded, however, that certain accounting principles and practices followed for annual reporting purposes may require modification at interim reporting dates so that the reported results for the interim period may better relate to the results of operations for the annual period.

Instructions

Listed below are six independent cases on how accounting facts might be reported on an individual company's interim financial reports. For each of these cases, state whether the method proposed to be used for interim reporting would be acceptable under generally accepted accounting principles applicable to interim financial data. Support each answer with a brief explanation.

(a) B. J. King Company takes a physical inventory at year-end for annual financial statement purposes. Inventory and cost of sales reported in the interim quarterly statements are based on estimated gross profit rates, because a physical inventory would result in a cessation of operations. King Company does have reliable perpetual inventory records.

(b) Florence Chadwick Company is planning to report one-fourth of its pension expense each quarter.

(c) N. Lopez Company wrote inventory down to reflect lower of cost or market in the first quarter. At year-end the market exceeds the original acquisition cost of this inventory. Consequently, management plans to write the inventory back up to its original cost as a year-end adjustment.

(d) K. Witt Company realized a large gain on the sale of investments at the beginning of the second quarter. The company wants to report one-third of the gain in each of the remaining quarters.

(e) Alice Marble Company has estimated its annual audit fee. They plan to prorate this expense equally over all four quarters.

(f) Lori McNeil Company was reasonably certain it would have an employee strike in the third quarter. As a result, it shipped heavily during the second quarter but plans to defer the recognition of the sales in excess of the normal sales volume. The deferred sales will be recognized as sales in the third quarter when the strike is in progress. McNeil Company management thinks this is more representative of normal second- and third-quarter operations.

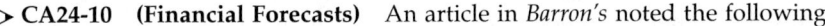

CA24-10 (Financial Forecasts) An article in *Barron's* noted the following.

Okay. Last fall, someone with a long memory and an even longer arm reached into that bureau drawer and came out with a moldy cheese sandwich and the equally moldy notion of corporate forecasts. We tried to find out what happened to the cheese sandwich—but, rats!, even recourse to the Freedom of Information Act didn't help. However, the forecast proposal was dusted off, polished up and found quite serviceable. The SEC, indeed, lost no time in running it up the old flagpole—but no one was very eager to salute. Even after some of the more objectionable features—compulsory corrections and detailed explanations of why the estimates went awry—were peeled off the original proposal.

Seemingly, despite the Commission's smiles and sweet talk, those craven corporations were still afraid that an honest mistake would lead them down the primrose path to consent decrees and class action suits. To lay to rest such qualms, the Commission last week approved a "Safe Harbor" rule that, providing the forecasts were made on a reasonable basis and in good faith, protected corporations from litigation should the projections prove wide of the mark (as only about 99% are apt to do).

Instructions

(a) What are the arguments for preparing profit forecasts?

(b) What is the purpose of the "safe harbor" rule?

(c) Why are corporations concerned about presenting profit forecasts?

CA24-11 (Disclosure of Estimates—Ethics) Patty Gamble, the financial vice-president, and Victoria Maher, the controller, of Castle Manufacturing Company are reviewing the financial ratios of the company for the years 2006 and 2007. The financial vice president notes that the profit margin on sales ratio has increased from 6% to 12%, a hefty gain for the 2-year period. Gamble is in the process of issuing a media release that emphasizes the efficiency of Castle Manufacturing in controlling cost. Victoria Maher knows that the difference in ratios is due primarily to an earlier company decision to reduce the estimates of warranty and bad debt expense for 2007. The controller, not sure of her supervisor's motives, hesitates to suggest to Gamble that the company's improvement is unrelated to efficiency in controlling cost. To complicate matters, the media release is scheduled in a few days.

Instructions

(a) What, if any, is the ethical dilemma in this situation?

(b) Should Maher, the controller, remain silent? Give reasons.

(c) What stakeholders might be affected by Gamble's media release?

(d) Give your opinion on the following statement and cite reasons: "Because Gamble, the vice president, is most directly responsible for the media release, Maher has no real responsibility in this matter."

CA24-12 (Reporting of Subsequent Event—Ethics) In June 2007, the board of directors for Holtzman Enterprises Inc. authorized the sale of $10,000,000 of corporate bonds. Michelle Collins, treasurer for Holtzman Enterprises Inc., is concerned about the date when the bonds are issued. The company really needs

the cash, but she is worried that if the bonds are issued before the company's year-end (December 31, 2007) the additional liability will have an adverse effect on a number of important ratios. In July, she explains to company president Kenneth Holtzman that if they delay issuing the bonds until after December 31 the bonds will not affect the ratios until December 31, 2008. They will have to report the issuance as a subsequent event which requires only footnote disclosure. Collins expects that with expected improved financial performance in 2008 ratios should be better.

Instructions

(a) What are the ethical issues involved?

(b) Should Holtzman agree to the delay?

 *CA24-13 **(Effect of Transactions on Financial Statements and Ratios)** The transactions listed below relate to Botticelli Inc. You are to assume that on the date on which each of the transactions occurred the corporation's accounts showed only common stock ($100 par) outstanding, a current ratio of 2.7:1, and a substantial net income for the year to date (before giving effect to the transaction concerned). On that date the book value per share of stock was $151.53.

Each numbered transaction is to be considered completely independent of the others, and its related answer should be based on the effect(s) of that transaction alone. Assume that all numbered transactions occurred during 2007 and that the amount involved in each case is sufficiently material to distort reported net income if improperly included in the determination of net income. Assume further that each transaction was recorded in accordance with generally accepted accounting principles and, where applicable, in conformity with the all-inclusive concept of the income statement.

For each of the numbered transactions you are to decide whether it:

a. Increased the corporation's 2007 net income.

b. Decreased the corporation's 2007 net income.

c. Increased the corporation's total retained earnings directly (i.e., not via net income).

d. Decreased the corporation's total retained earnings directly.

e. Increased the corporation's current ratio.

f. Decreased the corporation's current ratio.

g. Increased each stockholder's proportionate share of total owner's equity.

h. Decreased each stockholder's proportionate share of total owner's equity.

i. Increased each stockholder's equity per share of stock (book value).

j. Decreased each stockholder's equity per share of stock (book value).

k. Had none of the foregoing effects.

Instructions

List the numbers 1 through 9. Select as many letters as you deem appropriate to reflect the effect(s) of each transaction as of the date of the transaction by printing beside the transaction number the letter(s) that identifies that transaction's effect(s).

Transactions

_____ **1.** Treasury stock originally repurchased and carried at $127 per share was sold for cash at $153 per share.

_____ **2.** The corporation sold at a profit land and a building that had been idle for some time. Under the terms of the sale, the corporation received a portion of the sales price in cash immediately, the balance maturing at 6 month intervals.

_____ **3.** In January the board directed the writeoff of certain patent rights that had suddenly and unexpectedly become worthless.

_____ **4.** The corporation wrote off all of the unamortized discount and issue expense applicable to bonds that it refinanced in 2007.

_____ **5.** The corporation called in all its outstanding shares of stock and exchanged them for new shares on a 2-for-1 basis, reducing the par value at the same time to $50 per share.

_____ **6.** The corporation paid a cash dividend that had been recorded in the accounts at time of declaration.

_____ **7.** Litigation involving Botticelli Inc. as defendant was settled in the corporation's favor, with the plaintiff paying all court costs and legal fees. In 2004 the corporation had appropriately established a special contingency for this court action. (Indicate the effect of reversing the contingency only.)

_____ 8. The corporation received a check for the proceeds of an insurance policy from the company with which it is insured against theft of trucks. No entries concerning the theft had been made previously, and the proceeds reduce but do not cover completely the loss.

_____ 9. Treasury stock, which had been repurchased at and carried at $127 per share, was issued as a stock dividend. In connection with this distribution, the board of directors of Botticelli Inc. had authorized a transfer from retained earnings to permanent capital of an amount equal to the aggregate market value ($153 per share) of the shares issued. No entries relating to this dividend had been made previously.

(AICPA adapted)

itional Financial State-
ent Analysis Problems

USING YOUR JUDGMENT

Financial Reporting Problem

 The Procter & Gamble Company (P&G)

As stated in the chapter, notes to the financial statements are the means of explaining the items presented in the main body of the statements. Common note disclosures relate to such items as accounting policies, segmented information, and interim reporting.

Instructions

Refer to **P&G**'s financial statements and the accompanying notes to answer the following questions.

(a) What specific items does P&G discuss in its Note 1—Summary of Significant Accounting Policies? (List the headings only.)

(b) For what segments did P&G report segmented information? Which segment is the largest? Who is P&G largest customer?

(c) What interim information was reported by P&G?

*Financial Statement Analysis Case

Twin Ricky Inc. (TRI) manufactures a variety of consumer products. The company's founders have run the company for 30 years and are now interested in retiring. Consequently, they are seeking a purchaser who will continue its operations, and a group of investors, Donna Inc., is looking into the acquisition of TRI. To evaluate its financial stability and operating efficiency, TRI was requested to provide the latest financial statements and selected financial ratios. Summary information provided by TRI is presented below and on the next page.

TRI INCOME STATEMENT FOR THE YEAR ENDED NOVEMBER 30, 2007 (IN THOUSANDS)	
Sales (net)	$30,500
Interest income	500
Total revenue	31,000
Costs and expenses	
Cost of goods sold	17,600
Selling and administrative expense	3,550
Depreciation and amortization expense	1,890
Interest expense	900
Total costs and expenses	23,940
Income before taxes	7,060
Income taxes	2,900
Net income	$ 4,160

TRI
STATEMENT OF FINANCIAL POSITION
AS OF NOVEMBER 30
(IN THOUSANDS)

	2007	2006
Cash	$ 400	$ 500
Marketable securities (at cost)	500	200
Accounts receivable (net)	3,200	2,900
Inventory	5,800	5,400
Total current assets	9,900	9,000
Property, plant, & equipment (net)	7,100	7,000
Total assets	$17,000	$16,000
Accounts payable	$ 3,700	$ 3,400
Income taxes payable	900	800
Accrued expenses	1,700	1,400
Total current liabilities	6,300	5,600
Long-term debt	2,000	1,800
Total liabilities	8,300	7,400
Common stock ($1 par value)	2,700	2,700
Paid-in capital in excess of par	1,000	1,000
Retained earnings	5,000	4,900
Total shareholders' equity	8,700	8,600
Total liabilities and shareholders' equity	$17,000	$16,000

SELECTED FINANCIAL RATIOS

	TRI		Current Industry
	2006	2005	Average
Current ratio	1.61	1.62	1.63
Acid-test ratio	.64	.63	.68
Times interest earned	8.55	8.50	8.45
Profit margin on sales	13.2%	12.1%	13.0%
Total debt to net worth	.86	1.02	1.03
Asset turnover	1.84	1.83	1.84
Inventory turnover	3.17	3.21	3.18

Instructions

(a) Calculate a new set of ratios for the fiscal year 2007 for TRI based on the financial statements presented.

(b) Explain the analytical use of each of the seven ratios presented, describing what the investors can learn about TRI's financial stability and operating efficiency.

(c) Identify two limitations of ratio analysis.

(CMA adapted)

Comparative Analysis Case

The Coca-Cola Company versus PepsiCo, Inc.

Instructions

Go to the KWW website and use information found there to answer the following questions related to **The Coca-Cola Company** and **PepsiCo, Inc.**

(a) **(1)** What specific items does Coca-Cola discuss in its **Note 1—Accounting Policies**? (Prepare a list of the headings only.)

(2) What specific items does PepsiCo discuss in its **Note 2—Our Summary of Significant Accounting Policies**? (Prepare a list of the headings only.)

(b) For what lines of business or segments do Coca-Cola and PepsiCo present segmented information?

(c) Note and comment on the similarities and differences between the auditors' reports submitted by the independent auditors of Coca-Cola and PepsiCo for the year 2004.

Research Cases

Case 1

Read the article titled "FASB Is Criticized for Inaction on Off-Balance-Sheet Debt Issue," by Steve Liesman, Jonathan Weil, and Scott Paltrow in the January 18, 2002, *Wall Street Journal*.

Instructions

Answer the following questions.

(a) Why has the FASB not set better rules for when a firm should be allowed to keep debt off its balance sheet?

(b) Who is helped (in the short term and the long term) by a firm's being able to keep debt off its balance sheet? Who is hurt (short term and long term)?

(c) According to the article, when the FASB proposes new rules that would hurt them, "corporate America and its allies invoke portents of doom as to why we shouldn't have honest accounting treatment" of what's being proposed. How does this affect the usefulness of financial reporting for investors and creditors?

(d) One of the groups criticizing the FASB for moving too slowly is the Financial Executives International (FEI), which opposed requiring firms to consolidate the results of all their entities. The FEI also opposed the FASB's proposal to require firms to expense executive stock options. Based on this, would you consider FEI "part of the solution" or "part of the problem"? Justify your answer.

Case 2

Companies registered with the Securities and Exchange Commission are required to file a quarterly report on Form 10-Q within 40 days of the end of the first three fiscal quarters.

Instructions

Use EDGAR or some other source to examine the most recent 10-Q for the company of your choice and answer the following questions.

(a) What financial information is included in Part I?

(b) Read the notes to the financial statements and identify any departures from the "integral approach."

(c) Does the 10-Q include any information under Part II? Describe the nature of the information.

Professional Research: Financial Accounting and Reporting

As part of the year-end audit, you are discussing the disclosure checklist with your client. The checklist identifies the items that must be disclosed in a set of GAAP financial statements. The client is surprised by the disclosures item related to accounting policies. Specifically, since the audit report will attest to the statements being prepared in accordance with GAAP, the client questions the accounting policy checklist item. The client has asked you to conduct some research to verify the accounting policy disclosures.

Instructions

Using the **Financial Accounting Research System (FARS)**, respond to the following items. (Provide text strings used in your search.)

(a) In general, what should disclosures of accounting policies encompass?

(b) List some examples of the most commonly required disclosures.

*Professional Simulation

In this simulation you are asked to evaluate a company's solvency and going-concern potential, by analyzing a set of ratios. You also are asked to indicate possible limitations of ratio analysis. Prepare responses to all parts.

KWW_Professional _Simulation

| Financial Ratio Analysis | Time Remaining 0 hours 40 minutes | copy | paste | calculator | sheet | standards | help | splitter | done |

Directions | Situation | Analysis | Explanation | Resources

As the CPA for Packard Clipper, Inc., you have been requested to develop some key ratios from the comparative financial statements. This information is to be used to convince creditors that Packard Clipper, Inc. is solvent and to support the use of going-concern valuation procedures in the financial statements.

The data requested and the computations developed from the financial statements follow:

	2007	2006
Current ratio	2.6 times	2.1 times
Acid-test ratio	.8 times	1.3 times
Property, plant, and equipment to stockholders' equity	2.5 times	2.2 times
Sales to stockholders' equity	2.4 times	2.7 times
Net income	Up 32%	Down 9%
Earnings per share	$3.30	$2.50
Book value per share	Up 6%	Up 9%

Directions | Situation | Analysis | Explanation | Resources

Packard Clipper asks you to prepare a list of brief comments stating how each of these items supports the solvency and going-concern potential of the business. The company wishes to use these comments to support its presentation of data to its creditors. You are to prepare the comments as requested, giving the implications and the limitations of each item separately, and then the collective inference that may be drawn from them about Packard Clipper's solvency and going-concern potential.

Directions | Situation | Analysis | Explanation | Resources

Having done as the client requested in the Analysis section above, prepare a brief listing of additional ratio-analysis-type data for this client which you think its creditors are going to ask for to supplement the analytical data you provided. Explain why you think the additional data will be helpful to these creditors in evaluating the client's solvency. What warnings should you offer these creditors about the limitations of ratio analysis for the purposes stated here?

Remember to check the book's companion website to find additional resources for this chapter.

wiley.com/college/kieso

Index

Pro rata portion, 475
Prorating, 681
Proved reserves, 541
PSC, *see* Prior service costs
Public Accounting Oversight Board, 12
Public Company Accounting Oversight Board
  (PCAOB), 15, 1290*n*.6
Pulliam, Susan, 367*n*.2, 903
Purchases, misstatement/overstatement of,
  376–377, 1176–1177
Purchase allowances, 440, 440*n*.15
Purchase commitments, valuation of, 431–433
Purchased goodwill, 581–583
Purchased intangibles, 573
Purchase discounts, 379–380, 440
Purchase returns, 440
Purchases-only-approach, 449*n*.2
Pure rate of interest, 280
Put option, 866*n*.5
Puwaslki, A. C., 280

Quaker Foods, 31
Quaker Oats Company, 1163, 1171, 1172
Quaker State Oil Refining Corp., 633
Qualcomm Inc., 125, 578, 579, 747, 798
Qualified opinion, 1305
Qualified pension plans, 1021
Qualifying assets, 476
Quality of earnings, 127–128
Quality ratings (bonds), 676
Quanex Corporation, 182
Quantum Corporation, 337*n*.22
Quarterly financial statements, 89
Quest Company, 1058–1061
Questcor Pharmaceuticals Inc., 743
Qwest Communications, 489, 518, 905, 907, 1122

R. G. Barry & Co., 68
R. J. Reynolds, 33
Ranchers Exploration and Development Corp., 743
Rate of gross profit, 434*n*.13
Rate of interest, 258
Rate(s) of return, 374–375, 375*n*.6; on common
  stock equity, 752; on sales, 545
Rate of return on assets (ROA), 545
Ratios, 200. *See also specific ratios, e.g.:* Cash debt
  coverage ratio; activity, 1316, 1317; coverage,
  1316, 1317; liquidity, 1316, 1317; profitability,
  1316, 1317
Ratio analysis, 200–201, 1316–1318
Raw materials inventory, 368
Raymark Corporation, 644
R&D, *see* Research and development (R&D) costs
Reacquisition price, 684
Readily determinable fair value, 839*n*.3
Real accounts, 63
Real economic loss, 1129*n*.3
Real estate investment trusts (REITs), 530*n*.9
Realizable revenues, 908
Realized revenues, 908
Really Useful Group, 577
Rearrangements, costs of, 493
Reasonableness test, 1165*n*.10
Receivables, 318–338. *See also* Accounts receiv-
  able(s); analysis of, 338; on balance sheets, 176;
  basis of valuation of, 173; classifying, 337; de-
  fined, 318, 323; disappearing, 733; presentation
  of, 337–338; with recourse, 335–336; sales of,
  333–336; securitizing, 1220; trade, 319; without
  recourse, 334
Receivables turnover ratio, 338
Reclassification adjustments, 855–857
Reconciliation method, *see* Indirect method
Reconciliation to international standards, 1323,
  1327–1329
Reconciling entry, final, 1249–1250
Reconciling items, 342
Record, date of (stock dividends), 743
Recourse: defined, 334*n*.20; receivables with,
  335–336; receivables without, 334; and SFAS
  No. 140, 334*n*.20
Recoverability tests, 535, 585

Recovery of investment test (90% test),
  1095–1096, 1121
Recovery periods, 548
Redeemable preferred stock, 739
Reeve, James M., 388*n*.12, 393*n*.19
Refinancing, 622, 623
Refunding, 684
Registered bonds, 674
Registrars, 727
Regulation G, 125
Reinhardt, A., 591
Reinstallation costs, 493
Reither, Cheri L., 166, 857*n*.12
REITs (real estate investment trusts), 530*n*.9
Related-party transactions, disclosure of,
  1289–1290
Relative sales value, 430–431
Rendleman, Richard, Jr., 785*n*.9
Rent-Way, Inc., 128
Repairs, 493–494
Replacements, 439*n*.14, 492
Reported amounts, 966
Reporting, 1309–1313. *See also* Financial report-
  ing; change in entity, 1166; of change in
  principle, 1158–1159; of correction of error,
  1166–1170; criteria for accounting/reporting
  choices, 1313; on financial forecasts/projec-
  tions, 1309–1311; fraudulent financial report-
  ing, 1312–1313; Internet financial reporting,
  1311; requirements, 1283–1284
Repossessions (installment sales), 928–929
Research and development (R&D) costs, 587–590,
  592; accounting for, 588–589; under contractual
  arrangements, 589*n*.19; of extractive industries,
  589*n*.18; identifying, 588; and investors,
  592*n*.23; presentation of, 594
Reserves, cookie jar, 128
Reserves errors, 1168
Residual interest, 729
Residual value, 1102, 1103, 1108–1113; guaranteed
  vs. unguaranteed, 1108; and lease payments,
  1108–1109; lessee accounting for, 1109–1112; les-
  sor accounting for, 1112–1113; meaning of, 1108
Restatement, 1168*n*.13, 1175
Restaurant chains, 1100
Restoration costs, of depletion, 538
Restricted cash, 316–317
Restricted stock plans, 807–809
Restrictions on retained earnings, 749, 1242
Restructuring, 140*n*.20, 700–706; continuation of
  debt, 702–706; settlement of debt, 701–702; and
  SFAS No. 15, 700*n*.9
Restructuring charge, 139
Retail inventory methods, 436–442; concepts of,
  437–438; with conventional method, 438–440;
  evaluation of, 441–442; special items relating
  to, 440–441
Retail methods, 449–450
Retained earnings: change in, 1227, 1246; disclo-
  sures of restrictions on, 749; illustration of
  statement of, 1245; increase in, 1224; reporting
  restrictions on, 1242; restrictions of, 146; restrictions on, 749; statement of, 90; on statement of stockholders' equity, 146*n*.26; as
  worksheet entry, 1246
Retained earnings adjustment, 1159–1160
Retained earnings statement, 146
Retired shares, 738
Retirement benefits, *see* Postretirement benefits
Retirement of convertible debt, 780–781
Retrospective adjustment, 140
Retrospective changes in accounting principle,
  1153–1157; accounting for, 1158; and equity
  method, 1166*n*.11; example of, 1155–1157;
  impracticability of, 1162–1163; reporting of,
  1158–1159
Return, right of, 901
Returnable cash deposits, 624
Revell, Janice, 165
Revenue(s): on financial statements, 129; in income
  statement, 131; overstatement of accrued, 1176;
  understatement of unearned, 1176

Revenue bonds, 674
Revenue expenditures, 492
Revenue recognition, 905–934; after delivery,
  923–933; and APB Opinion No. 10, 924*n*.31,
  931; for consignments, 939–940; current environment, 906–909; before delivery, 912–922;
  errors, 1168; for franchises, 935–938; at point of
  sale (delivery), 909–911; and SFAC No. 3,
  907*n*.6; and SFAC No. 5, 908*n*.7, 909*n*.12,
  912*n*.17, 922*n*.28–29; and SFAS No. 45, 931,
  936, 938*n*.5; and SFAS No. 48, 910*n*.14; and
  SFAS No. 66, 924*n*.32, 931*n*.35, 933*n*.37; for
  special sales transactions, 935–940
Reverse stock splits, 747
Reversing differences, 974
Reversing entries, 89; using, 99–104; and work-
  sheet columns, 102
Rhone-Poulenc Rorer (RPR), 418
Richardson, A. W., 1118*n*.22
Right of return, 901, 910*n*.14
Risk, 170*n*.3; cash flow, 872; exchange rate, 869;
  interest rate, 868
Risk management (derivatives), 863–881
Rite-Aid, 15
RJR Nabisco, 672, 1299
ROA (rate of return on assets), 545
Rohde, L., 579
Romero, Simon, 1122
Rounding, 285
Royal Ahold, 378
Royal Dutch/Shell, 541
Rublin, Lauren, 728
Ruffle, John, 1063
Rule-based accounting standards, 13
Ryder System, 169

S. C. Johnson, 136
Sack, Robert J., 16, 1312
Safe harbor rule, 1310, 1311
Safeway, 436
St. Regis Pulp Co., 849–850
Sales: with buyback agreement, 374; conditions
  for, 336; and FASB, 336; with high rates of
  return, 374–375; on installment, 375; with
  recourse, 335–336; secured borrowing vs.,
  336–337; of treasury stock, 737–738; without
  recourse, 334
Sales agreements, 374–375
Sales discounts, 320–321, 440
Sale-leasebacks, 1128–1131; asset use determination
  in, 1128–1129; example of, 1130; as term, 1128
Sales price of asset, 1114
Sales-type leases, 1103, 1104, 1113–1117
Sales-warranty approach, 636
Sales tax payable, 625–626
Sales transactions, 909
Salvage value, 523, 1108*n*.18
Sampling, statistical, 371*n*.4
Sandberg, Jared, 491
San Diego Gas and Electric (SDGE), 884–885
SARs, *see* Stock appreciation rights
Sarbanes-Oxley Act of 2002, 1290, 1308, 1313; and
  auditing standards, 12; and "big GAAP versus
  little GAAP," 1285*n*.4; and disclosure, 641; key
  provisions of, 15; revenue recognition, 906*n*.3;
  and SEC, 641; Section 404 of, 15
Sauter, Douglas, 12
Savings certificates, money-market, 315*n*.1
SBC Communications Inc., 1055
Schiesel, Seth, 1122
Schipper, Katherine, 1284*n*.3
Schneider, C., 378
Schneider, David, 471*n*.1
Schroeder, Michael, 1148
Scott, Richard A., 922*n*.30
Scott, Rita K., 922*n*.30
Scott Paper, 1129
Scribner, Edmund, 748*n*.20
Seaboard Corporation, 319
Searfoss, D., 1054*n*.5
Sears Holdings, 322, 370, 421, 436
Sears Roebuck, 322, 421, 988

LOGO CREDITS

The following companies have granted permission for their logos to be included in this text.

Avon Rubber. Reprinted by permission of Avon Rubber.

Caterpillar

The Coca-Cola Company. The world famous COCA-COLA and COCA-COLA Script Logo trademarks are registered trademarks of The Coca-Cola Company.

Eastman Kodak. Used with permission of Eastman Kodak Company.

Hewlett-Packard. Reprinted by permission of Hewlett-Packard.

Intuit Inc. Reprinted by permission of Intuit Inc.

Johnson & Johnson. Reprinted by permission of Johnson & Johnson.

Kellogg Company. © 2006 Kellogg North American Company.

Oracle. Reprinted by permission of Oracle International Corporation.

PepsiCo. All rights reserved. Used with permission.

Procter & Gamble

Southwest Airlines

Tomkins. Reprinted by permission of Tomkins PLC.

Westinghouse. Reprinted by permission of Westinghouse Electric Corporation.

OFFICIAL ACCOUNTING PRONOUNCEMENTS

The following list of official accounting pronouncements constitutes the major part of *generally accepted accounting principles* (GAAP) and represents the authoritative source documents for much of the discussion contained in this book.

Date Issued		No.	Title

Accounting Research Bulletins (ARB's), Committee on Accounting Procedures, AICPA (1953–1959)

Date		No.	Title
June	1953	No. 43	Restatement and Revision of *Accounting Research Bulletins Nos. 1–42*, and *Accounting Terminology Bulletin No. 1* (originally issued 1939–1953) (amended)
Oct.	1954	No. 44	Declining-Balance Depreciation; Revised July, 1958 (amended)
Oct.	1955	No. 45	Long-term Construction-type Contracts (unchanged)
Feb.	1956	No. 46	Discontinuance of Dating Earned Surplus (unchanged)
Sept.	1956	No. 47	Accounting for Costs of Pension Plans (superseded)
Jan.	1957	No. 48	Business Combinations (superseded)
April	1958	No. 49	Earnings Per Share (superseded)
Oct.	1958	No. 50	Contingencies (superseded)
Aug.	1959	No. 51	Consolidated Financial Statements (amended and partially superseded)

Accounting Terminology Bulletins, Committee on Terminology, AICPA

Date		No.	Title
Aug.	1953	No. 1	Review and Résumé (of the eight original terminology bulletins) (amended)
Mar.	1955	No. 2	Proceeds, Revenue, Income, Profit, and Earnings (amended)
Aug.	1956	No. 3	Book Value (unchanged)
July	1957	No. 4	Cost, Expense, and Loss (amended)

Accounting Principles Board (APB) Opinions, AICPA (1962–1973)

Date		No.	Title
Nov.	1962	No. 1	New Depreciation Guidelines and Rules (amended)
Dec.	1962	No. 2	Accounting for the "Investment Credit" (amended)
Oct.	1963	No. 3	The Statement of Source and Application of Funds (superseded)
Mar.	1964	No. 4	Accounting for the "Investment Credit" (amending No. 2)
Sept.	1964	No. 5	Reporting of Leases in Financial Statements of Lessee (superseded)
Oct.	1965	No. 6	Status of Accounting Research Bulletins (partially superseded)
May	1966	No. 7	Accounting for Leases in Financial Statements of Lessors (superseded)
Nov.	1966	No. 8	Accounting for the Cost of Pension Plans (superseded)
Dec.	1966	No. 9	Reporting the Results of Operations (amended and partially superseded)
Dec.	1966	No. 10	Omnibus Opinion—1966 (amended and partially superseded)
Dec.	1967	No. 11	Accounting for Income Taxes (superseded)
Dec.	1967	No. 12	Omnibus Opinion—1967 (partially superseded)
Mar.	1969	No. 13	Amending Paragraph 6 of *APB Opinion No. 9*, Application to Commercial Banks (unchanged)
Mar.	1969	No. 14	Accounting for Convertible Debt and Debt Issued with Stock Purchase Warrants (unchanged)
May	1969	No. 15	Earnings per Share (superseded)
Aug.	1970	No. 16	Business Combinations (superseded)
Aug.	1970	No. 17	Intangible Assets (superseded)
Mar.	1971	No. 18	The Equity Method of Accounting for Investments in Common Stock (amended)
Mar.	1971	No. 19	Reporting Changes in Financial Position (amended)
July	1971	No. 20	Accounting Changes (superseded)
Aug.	1971	No. 21	Interest on Receivables and Payables (amended and partially superseded)
April	1972	No. 22	Disclosure of Accounting Policies (amended)
April	1972	No. 23	Accounting for Income Taxes—Special Areas (superseded)
April	1972	No. 24	Accounting for Income Taxes—Equity Method Investments (unchanged)
Oct.	1972	No. 25	Accounting for Stock Issued to Employees (unchanged)
Oct.	1972	No. 26	Early Extinguishment of Debt (amended)
Nov.	1972	No. 27	Accounting for Lease Transactions by Manufacturer or Dealer Lessors (superseded)
May	1973	No. 28	Interim Financial Reporting (amended and partially superseded)
May	1973	No. 29	Accounting for Nonmonetary Transactions (amended)
June	1973	No. 30	Reporting the Results of Operations (amended)
June	1973	No. 31	Disclosure of Lease Commitments by Lessees (superseded)

Financial Accounting Standards Board (FASB), Statements of Financial Accounting Standards (1973–2007)

Date		No.	Title
Dec.	1973	No. 1	Disclosure of Foreign Currency Translation Information (superseded)
Oct.	1974	No. 2	Accounting for Research and Development Costs (amended)
Dec.	1974	No. 3	Reporting Accounting Changes in Interim Financial Statements (superseded)
Mar.	1975	No. 4	Reporting Gains and Losses from Extinguishment of Debt (superseded)
Mar.	1975	No. 5	Accounting for Contingencies (amended)
May	1975	No. 6	Classification of Short-term Obligations Expected to be Refinanced
June	1975	No. 7	Accounting and Reporting by Development Stage Enterprises
Oct.	1975	No. 8	Accounting for the Translation of Foreign Currency Transactions and Foreign Financial Statements (superseded)

Date Issued		No.	Title
Oct.	1975	No. 9	Accounting for Income Taxes—Oil and Gas Producing Companies (superseded)
Oct.	1975	No. 10	Extension of "Grandfather" Provisions for Business Combinations (superseded)
Dec.	1975	No. 11	Accounting for Contingencies—Transition Method
Dec.	1975	No. 12	Accounting for Certain Marketable Securities (superseded)
Nov.	1976	No. 13	Accounting for Leases (amended, interpreted, and partially superseded)
Dec.	1976	No. 14	Financial Reporting for Segments of a Business Enterprise (amended)
June	1977	No. 15	Accounting by Debtors and Creditors for Troubled Debt Restructurings (amended)
June	1977	No. 16	Prior Period Adjustments (amended)
Nov.	1977	No. 17	Accounting for Leases—Initial Direct Costs
Nov.	1977	No. 18	Financial Reporting for Segments of a Business Enterprise—Interim Financial Statements
Dec.	1977	No. 19	Financial Accounting and Reporting by Oil and Gas Producing Companies (amended)
Dec.	1977	No. 20	Accounting for Forward Exchange Contracts (superseded)
April	1978	No. 21	Suspension of the Reporting of Earnings per Share and Segment Information by Nonpublic Enterprises (amended)
June	1978	No. 22	Changes in the Provisions of Lease Agreements Resulting from Refundings of Tax-Exempt Debt (amended)
Aug.	1978	No. 23	Inception of the Lease
Dec.	1978	No. 24	Reporting Segment Information in Financial Statements That Are Presented in Another Enterprise's Financial Report
Feb.	1979	No. 25	Suspension of Certain Accounting Requirements for Oil and Gas Producing Companies
April	1979	No. 26	Profit Recognition on Sales-Type Leases of Real Estate
May	1979	No. 27	Classification of Renewals or Extensions of Existing Sales-Type or Direct Financing Leases
May	1979	No. 28	Accounting for Sales with Leasebacks
June	1979	No. 29	Determining Contingent Rentals
Aug.	1979	No. 30	Disclosure of Information about Major Customers
Sept.	1979	No. 31	Accounting for Tax Benefits Related to U.K. Tax Legislation Concerning Stock Relief
Sept.	1979	No. 32	Specialized Accounting and Reporting Principles and Practices in AICPA Statements of Position and Guides on Accounting and Auditing Matters (amended and partially superseded)
Sept.	1979	No. 33	Financial Reporting and Changing Prices (amended and partially superseded)
Oct.	1979	No. 34	Capitalization of Interest Cost (amended)
Mar.	1980	No. 35	Accounting and Reporting by Defined Benefit Pension Plans (amended)
May	1980	No. 36	Disclosure of Pension Information (superseded)
July	1980	No. 37	Balance Sheet Classification of Deferred Income Taxes (amended)
Sept.	1980	No. 38	Accounting for Preacquisition Contingencies of Purchased Enterprises (superseded)
Oct.	1980	No. 39	Financial Reporting and Changing Prices: Specialized Assets—Mining and Oil and Gas
Nov.	1980	No. 40	Financial Reporting and Changing Prices: Specialized Assets—Timberlands and Growing Timber
Nov.	1980	No. 41	Financial Reporting and Changing Prices: Specialized Assets—Income-Producing Real Estate
Nov.	1980	No. 42	Determining Materiality for Capitalization of Interest Cost
Nov.	1980	No. 43	Accounting for Compensated Absences (amended)
Dec.	1980	No. 44	Accounting for Intangible Assets of Motor Carriers (superseded)
Mar.	1981	No. 45	Accounting for Franchise Fee Revenue (amended)
Mar.	1981	No. 46	Financial Reporting and Changing Prices: Motion Picture Films
Mar.	1981	No. 47	Disclosure of Long-Term Obligations (amended)
June	1981	No. 48	Revenue Recognition When Right of Return Exists
June	1981	No. 49	Accounting for Product Financing Arrangements
Nov.	1981	No. 50	Financial Reporting in the Record and Music Industry
Nov.	1981	No. 51	Financial Reporting by Cable Television Companies (amended)
Dec.	1981	No. 52	Foreign Currency Translation (amended)
Dec.	1981	No. 53	Financial Reporting by Producers and Distributors of Motion Picture Films (superseded)
Jan.	1982	No. 54	Financial Reporting and Changing Prices: Investment Companies (superseded)
Feb.	1982	No. 55	Determining Whether a Convertible Security is a Common Stock Equivalent (superseded)
Feb.	1982	No. 56	Designation of AICPA Guide and SOP 81-1 on Contractor Accounting and SOP 81-2 on Hospital-Related Organizations as Preferable for Applying *APB Opinion 20* (superseded)
Mar.	1982	No. 57	Related Party Disclosures (amended)
April	1982	No. 58	Capitalization of Interest Cost in Financial Statements that Include Investments Accounted for by the Equity Method
April	1982	No. 59	Deferral of the Effective Date of Certain Accounting Requirements for Revision Plans of State and Local Governmental Units
June	1982	No. 60	Accounting and Reporting by Insurance Enterprises (amended)
June	1982	No. 61	Accounting for Title Plant (amended)
June	1982	No. 62	Capitalization of Interest Cost in Situations Involving Certain Tax-Exempt Borrowings and Certain Gifts and Grants
June	1982	No. 63	Financial Reporting by Broadcasters (amended)

Date Issued		No.	Title
Sept.	1982	No. 64	Extinguishment of Debt Made to Satisfy Sinking-Fund Requirements (superseded)
Sept.	1982	No. 65	Accounting for Certain Mortgage Bank Activities (amended)
Oct.	1982	No. 66	Accounting for Sales of Real Estate (amended)
Oct.	1982	No. 67	Accounting for Costs and Initial Rental Operations of Real Estate Projects (amended)
Oct.	1982	No. 68	Research and Development Arrangements (amended)
Nov.	1982	No. 69	Disclosures about Oil and Gas Producing Activities
Dec.	1982	No. 70	Financial Reporting and Changing Prices: Foreign Currency Translation
Dec.	1982	No. 71	Accounting for the Effects of Certain Types of Regulation (amended)
Feb.	1983	No. 72	Accounting for Certain Acquisitions of Banking or Thrift Institutions (amended)
Aug.	1983	No. 73	Reporting a Change in Accounting for Railroad Track Structures
Aug.	1983	No. 74	Accounting for Special Termination Benefits Paid to Employees
Nov.	1983	No. 75	Deferral of the Effective Date of Certain Accounting Requirements for Pension Plans of State and Local Governmental Units (superseded)
Nov.	1983	No. 76	Extinguishment of Debt (superseded)
Dec.	1983	No. 77	Reporting by Transferors for Transfers of Receivables with Recourse (superseded)
Dec.	1983	No. 78	Classifications of Obligations that Are Callable by the Creditor
Feb.	1984	No. 79	Elimination of Certain Disclosures for Business Combinations by Nonpublic Enterprises (superseded)
Aug.	1984	No. 80	Accounting for Futures Contracts (superseded)
Nov.	1984	No. 81	Disclosure of Postretirement Health Care and Life Insurance Benefits
Nov.	1984	No. 82	Financial Reporting and Changing Prices: Elimination of Certain Disclosures
Mar.	1985	No. 83	Designation of AICPA Guides and Statement of Position on Accounting by Brokers and Dealers in Securities, by Employee Benefit Plans, and by Banks as Preferable for Purposes of Applying *APB Opinion 20*
Mar.	1985	No. 84	Induced Conversions of Convertible Debt
Mar.	1985	No. 85	Yield Test for Determining Whether a Convertible Security Is a Common Stock Equivalent (superseded)
Aug.	1985	No. 86	Accounting for the Costs of Computer Software to be Sold, Leased, or Otherwise Marketed
Dec.	1985	No. 87	Employers' Accounting for Pensions (amended)
Dec.	1985	No. 88	Employers' Accounting for Settlements and Curtailments of Defined Benefit Pension Plans and for Termination Benefits (amended and partially superseded)
Dec.	1986	No. 89	Financial Reporting and Changing Prices (amended)
Dec.	1986	No. 90	Regulated Enterprises—Accounting for Abandonments and Disallowances of Plant Costs
Dec.	1986	No. 91	Accounting for Nonrefundable Fees and Costs Associated with Originating or Acquiring Loans and Initial Direct Costs of Leases
Aug.	1987	No. 92	Regulated Enterprises—Accounting for Phase-in Plans
Aug.	1987	No. 93	Recognition of Depreciation by Not-for-Profit Organizations
Oct.	1987	No. 94	Consolidation of All Majority-Owned Subsidiaries
Nov.	1987	No. 95	Statement of Cash Flows (amended)
Dec.	1987	No. 96	Accounting for Income Taxes (superseded)
Dec.	1987	No. 97	Accounting and Reporting by Insurance Enterprises for Certain Long-Duration Contracts and for Realized Gains and Losses from the Sale of Investments
June	1988	No. 98	Accounting for Leases; Sale-Leaseback Transactions Involving Real Estate; Sales-Type Leases of Real Estate; Definition of the Lease Term; Initial Direct Costs of Direct Financing Leases
Sept.	1988	No. 99	Deferral of the Effective Date of Recognition of Depreciation by Not-for-Profit Organizations
Dec.	1988	No. 100	Accounting for Income Taxes—Deferral of the Effective Date of *FASB Statement No. 96*
Dec.	1988	No. 101	Regulated Enterprises—Accounting for the Discontinuation of Application of *FASB Statement No. 71* (amended)
Feb.	1989	No. 102	Statement of Cash Flows—Exemption of Certain Enterprises and Classification of Cash Flows from Certain Securities Acquired for Resale (amended)
Dec.	1989	No. 103	Accounting for Income Taxes—Deferral of the Effective Date of *FASB Statement No. 96*
Dec.	1989	No. 104	Statement of Cash Flows—Net Reporting of Certain Cash Receipts and Cash Payments and Classification of Cash Flows from Hedging Transactions
Mar.	1990	No. 105	Disclosure of Information About Financial Instruments with Off-Balance-Sheet Risk and Financial Instruments with Concentrations of Credit Risk (superseded)
Dec.	1990	No. 106	Employers' Accounting for Postretirement Benefits Other Than Pensions (amended and partially superseded)
Dec.	1991	No. 107	Disclosures about Fair Value of Financial Instruments (amended)
Dec.	1991	No. 108	Accounting for Income Taxes—Deferral of the Effective Date of *FASB Statement No. 96*
Feb.	1992	No. 109	Accounting for Income Taxes (amended and partially superseded)
Aug.	1992	No. 110	Reporting by Defined Benefit Pension Plans of Investment Contracts
Nov.	1992	No. 111	Rescission of *FASB Statement No. 32* and Technical Corrections
Nov.	1992	No. 112	Employers' Accounting for Postemployment Benefits
Dec.	1992	No. 113	Accounting and Reporting for Reinsurance of Short-Duration and Long-Duration Contracts
May	1993	No. 114	Accounting by Creditors for Impairment of a Loan (amended)
May	1993	No. 115	Accounting for Certain Investments in Debt and Equity Securities (amended and partially superseded)

Date Issued		No.	Title
June	1993	No. 116	Accounting for Contributions Received and Contributions Made (amended and partially superseded)
June	1993	No. 117	Financial Statements of Not-for-Profit Organizations (amended)
Oct.	1994	No. 118	Accounting by Creditors for Impairments of a Loan—Income Recognition and Disclosures
Oct.	1994	No. 119	Disclosure about Derivative Financial Instruments and Fair Value of Financial Instruments (superseded)
Jan.	1995	No. 120	Accounting and Reporting by Mutual Life Insurance Enterprises
Mar.	1995	No. 121	Accounting for the Impairment of Long-Lived Assets (superseded)
May	1995	No. 122	Accounting for Mortgage Servicing Rights (superseded)
Oct.	1995	No. 123	Accounting for Stock-Based Compensation (revised)
Nov.	1995	No. 124	Accounting for Certain Investments Held by Not-for-Profit Organizations (amended and partially superseded)
June	1996	No. 125	Accounting for Transfers and Servicing of Financial Assets and Extinguishment of Liabilities (superseded)
Dec.	1996	No. 126	Exemption from Certain Required Disclosures about Financial Instruments for Certain Nonpublic Entities
Dec.	1996	No. 127	Deferral of the Effective Date of Certain Provisions of *FASB Statement No. 125*
Feb.	1997	No. 128	Earnings per Share (amended)
Feb.	1997	No. 129	Disclosure of Information about Capital Structure
June	1997	No. 130	Reporting Comprehensive Income (amended and partially superseded)
June	1997	No. 131	Reporting Disaggregated Information about a Business Enterprise
Feb.	1998	No. 132	Employers' Disclosures about Pensions and Other Postretirement Benefits – an amendment of *FASB Statements No. 87, 88,* and *106* (revised) (amended and partially superseded)
June	1998	No. 133	Accounting for Derivative Instruments and Hedging Activities (amended and partially superseded)
Oct.	1998	No. 134	Accounting for Mortgage-Backed Securities Retained after the Securitization of Mortgage Loans Held for Sale by a Mortgage Banking Enterprise (an amendment of *FASB Statement No. 65*)
Feb.	1999	No. 135	Rescission of *FASB Statement No. 75* and Technical Corrections (amended)
June	1999	No. 136	Transfers of Assets to a Not-for-Profit Organization or Charitable Trust That Raises or Holds Contributions for Others (amended)
June	1999	No. 137	Accounting for Derivative Instruments and Hedging Activities—Deferral of the Effective Date for *FASB Statement No. 133* (an amendment of *Statement No. 133*)
June	2000	No. 138	Accounting for Certain Derivative Instruments and Certain Hedging Activities (an amendment of *FASB Statement No. 133*)
June	2000	No. 139	Rescission of *FASB Statement No. 53* and amendments to *FASB Statements No. 63, 89,* and *121*
Sept.	2000	No. 140	Accounting for Transfers and Servicing of Financial Assets and Extinguishments of Liabilities (a replacement of *FASB Statement 125*) (amended and partially superseded)
June	2001	No. 141	Business Combinations (amended)
June	2001	No. 142	Goodwill and Other Intangible Assets (amended and partially superseded)
June	2001	No. 143	Accounting for Asset Retirement Obligations (amended and partially superseded)
Aug.	2001	No. 144	Accounting for the Impairment or Disposal of Long-Lived Assets (amended and partially superseded)
April	2002	No. 145	Rescission of *FASB Statements No. 4, 44,* and *64,* Amendment of *FASB Statement No. 13,* and Technical Corrections
June	2002	No. 146	Accounting for Costs Associated with Exit or Disposal Activities (amended and partially superseded)
Oct.	2002	No. 147	Acquisitions of Certain Financial Institutions, an Amendment of *FASB Statements No. 72* and *144* and *FASB Interpretation No. 9*
Dec.	2002	No. 148	Accounting for Stock-Based Compensation—Transition and Disclosure
April	2003	No. 149	Amendment of *Statement 133* on Derivative Instruments and Hedging Activities
May	2003	No. 150	Accounting for Certain Financial Instruments with Characteristics of Both Liabilities and Equity (amended)
Nov.	2004	No. 151	Inventory Costs – an amendment of *ARB No. 43,* Chapter 4
Dec.	2004	No. 152	Accounting for Real Estate Time-Sharing Transactions
Dec.	2004	No. 153	Exchanges on Non-Monetary Assets – an amendment of *APB Opinion No. 29*
May	2005	No. 154	Accounting Changes and Error Corrections – a replacement of *APB Opinion No. 20* and *FASB Statement No. 3*
Feb.	2006	No. 155	Accounting for Certain Hybrid Financial Instruments—an amendment of *FASB Statements No. 133* and *140*
Mar.	2006	No. 156	Accounting for Servicing of Financial Assets—an amendment of *FASB Statement No. 140* (amended)
Sept.	2006	No. 157	Fair Value Measurements
Sept.	2006	No. 158	Employers' Accounting for Defined Benefit Pension and Other Postretirement Plans—an amendment of *FASB Statements No. 87, 88, 106,* and *132R*
Feb.	2007	No. 159	The Fair Value Option for Financial Assets and Financial Liabilities—Including an amendment of *FASB Statement No. 115*

Date Issued		No.	Title

Financial Accounting Standards Board (FASB), Interpretations (1974–2006)

June	1974	No. 1	Accounting Changes Related to the Cost of Inventory (*APB Opinion No. 20*)
June	1974	No. 2	Imputing Interest on Debt Arrangements Made Under the Federal Bankruptcy Act (*APB Opinion No. 21*) (superseded)
Dec.	1974	No. 3	Accounting for the Cost of Pension Plans Subject to the Employee Retirement Income Security Act of 1974 (*APB Opinion No. 8*)
Feb.	1975	No. 4	Applicability of *FASB Statement No. 2* to Purchase Business Combinations (amended)
Feb.	1975	No. 5	Applicability of *FASB Statement No. 2* to Development Stage Enterprises (superseded)
Feb.	1975	No. 6	Applicability of *FASB Statement No. 2* to Computer Software
Oct.	1975	No. 7	Applying *FASB Statement No. 7* in Statements of Established Enterprises
Jan.	1976	No. 8	Classification of a Short-Term Obligation Repaid Prior to Being Replaced by a Long-Term Security (*FASB Statement No. 6*)
Feb.	1976	No. 9	Applying *APB Opinion No. 16* and *17* when a Savings and Loan or Similar Institution is Acquired in a Purchase Business Combination (*APB Op. No. 16 & 17*) (amended)
Sept.	1976	No. 10	Application of *FASB Statement No. 12* to Personal Financial Statements (*FASB Statement No. 12*)
Sept.	1976	No. 11	Changes in Market Value after the Balance Sheet Date (*FASB Statement No. 12*)
Sept.	1976	No. 12	Accounting for Previously Established Allowance Accounts (*FASB Statement No. 12*)
Sept.	1976	No. 13	Consolidation of a Parent and Its Subsidiaries Having Different Balance Sheet Dates (*FASB Statement No. 12*)
Sept.	1976	No. 14	Reasonable Estimation of the Amount of a Loss (*FASB Statement No. 5*)
Sept.	1976	No. 15	Translation of Unamortized Policy Acquisition Costs by Stock Life Insurance Company (*FASB Statement No. 8*) (amended and partially superseded)
Feb.	1977	No. 16	Clarification of Definitions and Accounting for Marketable Equity Securities That Become Nonmarketable (*FASB Statement No. 12*)
Feb.	1977	No. 17	Applying the Lower of Cost or Market Rule in Translated Financial Statements (*FASB Statement No. 8*) (superseded)
Mar.	1977	No. 18	Accounting for Income Taxes in Interim Periods (*APB Op. No. 28*) (amended)
Oct.	1977	No. 19	Lessee Guarantee of the Residual Value of Leased Property (*FASB Statement No. 13*)
Nov.	1977	No. 20	Reporting Accounting Changes under AICPA Statements of Position (*APB Op. No. 20*)
April	1978	No. 21	Accounting for Leases in a Business Combination (*FASB Statement No. 13*) (amended)
April	1978	No. 22	Applicability of Indefinite Reversal Criteria to Timing Differences (*APB Op. No. 11* and *23*)
Aug.	1978	No. 23	Leases of Certain Property Owned by a Governmental Unit or Authority (*FASB Statement No. 13*)
Sept.	1978	No. 24	Leases Involving Only Part of a Building (*FASB Statement No. 13*)
Sept.	1978	No. 25	Accounting for an Unused Investment Tax Credit (*APB Op. No. 2, 4, 11,* and *16*)
Sept.	1978	No. 26	Accounting for Purchase of a Leased Asset by the Lessee During the Term of the Lease (*FASB Statement No. 13*)
Nov.	1978	No. 27	Accounting for a Loss on a Sublease (*FASB Statement No. 13* and *APB Op. No. 30*) (amended)
Dec.	1978	No. 28	Accounting for Stock Appreciation Rights and Other Variable Stock Option or Award Plans (*APB Op. No. 15* and *25*) (amended)
Feb.	1979	No. 29	Reporting Tax Benefits Realized on Disposition of Investments in Certain Subsidiaries and Other Investees (*APB Op. No. 23* and *24*)
Sept.	1979	No. 30	Accounting for Involuntary Conversions of Nonmonetary Assets to Monetary Assets (*APB Op. No. 29*)
Feb.	1980	No. 31	Treatment of Stock Compensation Plans in EPS Computations (*APB Op. No. 15* and *Interp. 28*) (superseded)
Mar.	1980	No. 32	Application of Percentage Limitations in Recognizing Investment Tax Credit (*APB Op. No. 2, 4,* and *11*)
Aug.	1980	No. 33	Applying FASB Statement No. 34 to Oil and Gas Producing Operations (*FASB Statement No. 34*)
Mar.	1981	No. 34	Disclosure of Indirect Guarantees of Indebtedness of Others (*FASB Statement No. 5*)
May	1981	No. 35	Criteria for Applying the Equity Method of Accounting for Investments in Common Stock (*APB Op. No. 18*)
Oct.	1981	No. 36	Accounting for Exploratory Wells in Progress at the End of a Period
July	1983	No. 37	Accounting for Translation Adjustments upon Sale of Part of an Investment in a Foreign Entity (Interprets *FASB Statement No. 52*)
Aug.	1984	No. 38	Determining the Measurement Date for Stock Option, Purchase, and Award Plans Involving Junior Stock (Interprets *APB Opinion No. 25*)
Mar.	1992	No. 39	Offsetting of Amounts Related to Certain Contracts (Interprets *APB Opinion No. 10* and *FASB Statement No. 105*) (amended)
Apr.	1993	No. 40	Applicability of Generally Accepted Accounting Principles to Mutual Life Insurance and Other Enterprises (Interprets *FASB Statements No. 12, 60, 97,* and *113*)

Date Issued		No.	Title
Dec.	1994	No. 41	Offsetting of Amounts Related to Certain Repurchase and Reverse Repurchase Agreements
Sept.	1996	No. 42	Accounting for Transfers of Assets in Which a Not-for-Profit Organization is Granted Variance Power
June	1999	No. 43	Real Estate Sales (Interprets FASB Statement No. 66) (amended)
		No. 44	Accounting for Certain Transactions involving Stock Compensation (an interpretation of *APB Opinion No. 25*) (amended)
Nov.	2002	No. 45	Guarantor's Accounting and Disclosure Requirements for Guarantees, Including Indirect Guarantees of Indebtedness of Others (amended)
Jan.	2003	No. 46	Consolidation of Variable Interest Entities (an interpretation of *ARB No. 51*, revised) (amended)
March	2005	No. 47	Accounting for Conditional Asset Retirement Obligations – an interpretation of *FASB Statement No. 143*
June	2006	No. 48	Accounting for Uncertainty in Income Taxes—an interpretation of *FASB Statement No. 109*

Financial Accounting Standards Board (FASB),
Technical Bulletins (1979–2002)

Date Issued		No.	Title
Dec.	1979	No. 79-1	Purpose and Scope of FASB Technical Bulletins and Procedures for Issuance (revised)
Dec.	1979	No. 79-2	Computer Software Costs
Dec.	1979	No. 79-3	Subjective Acceleration Clauses in Long-Term Debt Agreements
Dec.	1979	No. 79-4	Segment Reporting of Puerto Rican Operations
Dec.	1979	No. 79-5	Meaning of the Term 'Customer' as it Applies to Health Care Facilities under *FASB Statement No. 14*
Dec.	1979	No. 79-6	Valuation Allowances Following Debt Restructuring
Dec.	1979	No. 79-7	Recoveries of a Previous Writedown under a Troubled Debt Restructuring Involving a Modification of Terms
Dec.	1979	No. 79-8	Applicability of *FASB Statements 21* and *33* to Certain Brokers and Dealers in Securities
Dec.	1979	No. 79-9	Accounting in Interim Periods for Changes in Income Tax Rates
Dec.	1979	No. 79-10	Fiscal Funding Clauses in Lease Agreements
Dec.	1979	No. 79-11	Effect of a Penalty on the Term of a Lease
Dec.	1979	No. 79-12	Interest Rate Used in Calculating the Present Value of Minimum Lease Payments
Dec.	1979	No. 79-13	Applicability of *FASB Statement No. 13* to Current Value Financial Statements
Dec.	1979	No. 79-14	Upward Adjustment of Guaranteed Residual Values
Dec.	1979	No. 79-15	Accounting for Loss on a Sublease Not Involving the Disposal of a Segment
Dec.	1979	No. 79-16	Effect on a Change in Income Tax Rate on the Accounting for Leveraged Leases (revised)
Dec.	1979	No. 79-17	Reporting Cumulative Effect Adjustment from Retroactive Application of *FASB No. 13*
Dec.	1979	No. 79-18	Transition Requirements of Certain FASB Amendments and Interpretations of *FASB Statement No. 13*
Dec.	1979	No. 79-19	Investor's Accounting for Unrealized Losses on Marketable Securities Owned by an Equity Method Investee
Dec.	1980	No. 80-1	Early Extinguishment of Debt through Exchange for Common or Preferred Stock (amended)
Dec.	1980	No. 80-2	Classification of Debt Restructuring by Debtors and Creditors
Feb.	1981	No. 81-1	Disclosure of Interest Rate Futures Contracts and Forward and Standby Contracts
Feb.	1981	No. 81-2	Accounting for Unused Investment Tax Credits Acquired in a Business Combination Accounted for by the Purchase Method
Feb.	1981	No. 81-3	Multiemployer Pension Plan Amendments Act of 1980
Feb.	1981	No. 81-4	Classification as Monetary or Nonmonetary Items
Feb.	1981	No. 81-5	Offsetting Interest Cost to be Capitalized with Interest Income
Nov.	1981	No. 81-6	Applicability of Statement 15 to Debtors in Bankruptcy Situations
Jan.	1982	No. 82-1	Disclosure of the Sale or Purchase of Tax Benefits through Tax Leases (amended)
Mar.	1982	No. 82-2	Accounting for the Conversion of Stock Options into Incentive Stock Options as a Result of the Economic Recovery Tax Act of 1981
July	1983	No. 83-1	Accounting for the Reduction in the Tax Basis of an Asset Caused by the Investment Tax Credit (ITC)
Mar.	1984	No. 84-1	Accounting for Stock Issued to Acquire the Results of a Research and Development Arrangement (amended)
Sept.	1984	No. 84-2	Accounting for the Effects of the Tax Reform Act of 1984 on Deferred Income Taxes Relating to Domestic International Sales Corporations
Sept.	1984	No. 84-3	Accounting for the Effects of the Tax Reform Act of 1984 on Deferred Income Taxes of Stock Life Insurance Enterprises
Oct.	1984	No. 84-4	In-Substance Defeasance of Debt
Mar.	1985	No. 85-1	Accounting for the Receipt of Federal Home Loan Mortgage Corporation Participating Preferred Stock
Mar.	1985	No. 85-2	Accounting for Collateralized Mortgage Obligations (CMOs) (superseded)

Date Issued		No.	Title
Nov.	1985	No. 85-3	Accounting for Operating Leases with Scheduled Rent Increases
Nov.	1985	No. 85-4	Accounting for Purchases of Life Insurance (superseded)
Dec.	1985	No. 85-5	Issues Relating to Accounting for Business Combinations (amended)
Dec.	1985	No. 85-6	Accounting for a Purchase of Treasury Shares
Oct.	1986	No. 86-1	Accounting for Certain Effects of the Tax Reform Act of 1986
Dec.	1986	No. 86-2	Accounting for an Interest in the Residual Value of a Leased Asset (amended)
April	1987	No. 87-1	Accounting for a Change in Method of Accounting for Certain Postretirement Benefits
Dec.	1987	No. 87-2	Computation of a Loss on an Abandonment
Dec.	1987	No. 87-3	Accounting for Mortgage Servicing Fees and Rights (amended)
Dec.	1988	No. 88-1	Issues Relating to Accounting for Leases
Dec.	1988	No. 88-2	Definition of a Right of Setoff
Dec.	1990	No. 90-1	Accounting for Separately Priced Extended Warranty and Product Maintenance Contracts
Apr.	1994	No. 94-1	Application of *Statement 115* to Debt Securities Restructured in a Troubled Debt Restructuring
Dec.	1997	No. 97-1	Accounting under *Statement 123* for Certain Employee Stock Purchase Plans with a Look-Back Option
July	2001	No. 01-1	Effective Date for Certain Financial Institutions of Certain Provisions of *Statement No. 140* Related to the Isolation of Transferred Financial Assets

Financial Accounting Standards Board (FASB),
Statements of Financial Accounting Concepts (1978–2006)

Nov.	1978	No. 1	Objectives of Financial Reporting by Business Enterprises
May	1980	No. 2	Qualitative Characteristics of Accounting Information
Dec.	1980	No. 3	Elements of Financial Statements of Business Enterprises
Dec.	1980	No. 4	Objectives of Financial Reporting by Nonbusiness Organizations
Dec.	1984	No. 5	Recognition and Measurement in Financial Statements of Business Enterprises
Dec.	1985	No. 6	Elements of Financial Statements
Feb.	2000	No. 7	Using Cash Flow Information and Present Value in Accounting Measurements

NATIONAL ACCOUNTING BOARDS AND ORGANIZATIONS

American Accounting Association (AAA)
5717 Bessie Drive
Sarasota, FL 34233-2399
(941) 921-7747
www.aaahq.org

American Institute of Certified Public Accountants
(AICPA)
1211 Avenue of the Americas
New York, NY 10036-8775
(212) 596-6200
www.aicpa.org

Association of Government Accountants (AGA)
2208 Mount Vernon Ave.
Alexandria, VA 22301-1314
(703) 684-6931
www.agacgfm.org

Financial Accounting Standards Board (FASB)
401 Merritt 7
P.O. Box 5116
Norwalk, CT 06856-5116
(203) 847-0700
www.fasb.org

Financial Executives International (FEI)
200 Campus Drive
Florham Park, NJ 07932-0674
(973) 765-1000
www.fei.org

Governmental Accounting Standards Board (GASB)
401 Merritt 7
P.O. Box 5116
Norwalk, CT 06856-5116
(203) 847-0700
www.gasb.org

International Accounting Standards Board (IASB)
30 Cannon Street
London EC4M 6XH, United Kingdom
Telephone: +44 (0)20 7246 6410
www.iasb.org

Institute of Internal Auditors (IIA)
247 Maitland Avenue
Altamonte Springs, FL 32701-4201
(407) 937-1100
www.theiia.org

Institute of Management Accountants (IMA)
10 Paragon Drive
Montvale, NJ 07645-1718
(201) 573-9000
www.imanet.org

Securities and Exchange Commission (SEC)
100 F Street, NE
Washington, DC 20549
(202) 551-6551
www.sec.gov

Contents of the Update Edition

This Update edition of *Intermediate Accounting* contains discussions of key accounting standards that have been issued since the publication of *Intermediate Accounting, Twelfth Edition,* by Kieso, Weygandt, and Warfield. The update discussions are contained either in new chapter inserts in the text, brief discussions on the following pages, or inside the front and back covers of the book. The updated elements are as follows.

1 Fair Values—discussion of two new standards on fair values, *SFAS No. 157* and *SFAS No. 159.* This new material appears on pages UP-1 through UP-5 below. It can be used as a complement to the discussion in Chapter 2 ("Recognition and Measurement Concepts," pp. 36–39), Chapter 7 ("Valuation of Notes Receivable," p. 331), and Chapter 17 ("Fair Value Controversy," p. 860 and "Derivatives Used for Hedging," p. 868).

2 Tax Uncertainty—discussion of a new interpretation on recognition of assets and liabilities related to uncertain tax positions, *FASB Interpretation No. 48.* This material appears on pages UP-5 and UP-6 below. It can be inserted as a section (before "Financial Statement Presentation," p. 984) to be used as a complement to the discussion in Chapter 19.

3 Pensions and Postretirement Benefits—discussion of new postretirement benefit standard, *SFAS No. 158.* This material appears within the book, on pages 1019–1086, as a completely updated and revised Chapter 20, replacing the prior discussion. Solutions to the revised end-of-chapter materials are available at the instructor website.

4 International Accounting. A revised Appendix 24B is included within the book, on pages 1322–1330. It contains updated information related to recent developments in the convergence of U.S. GAAP and international accounting standards (referred to as iGAAP). In addition, the inside front and back covers of the book contain a summary of key distinctions between U.S. GAAP and iGAAP. Expanded discussions of international accounting developments as they relate to intermediate accounting—referred to as "Convergence Corners"—can be accessed at the book's companion website.

FAIR VALUES

The FASB is on a mission to provide to users of financial statements more fair value information. Recently, the FASB has issued two standards that provide much-needed guidance on how and when to use fair value information in the financial statements.[1]

Fair Value Measurements

SFAS No. 157, "Fair Value Measurement," defines fair value, establishes a framework for measuring fair value in GAAP, and expands disclosures about fair value measurements. This statement does not require any additional fair value measurements, but clarifies how to measure and report fair values, when required by GAAP. At first glance, the guidance provided by *SFAS No. 157* might seem to be of limited significance because the standard is definitional and deals only with disclosure. However, this standard affects over 40 standards that deal in some way with fair value.

---

[1]*Statement of Financial Accounting Standards No. 157,* "Fair Value Measurement," (Norwalk, Conn.: FASB, September, 2006) and *Statement of Financial Accounting Standards No. 159,* "The Fair Value Option for Financial Assets and Liabilities, Including an Amendment of FASB Statement No. 115," (Norwalk, Conn.: FASB, February 2007).

Fair Value Definition

A major contribution of *SFAS No. 157* is that it provides a single definition of fair value. Prior to this standard there were different definitions of fair value and limited guidance in how to apply fair values. **Fair value** is now defined as "the price that would be received to sell an asset or paid to transfer a liability in an orderly transaction between market participants at the measurement date." Fair value is therefore a market-based measure. *SFAS No. 157* provides detailed guidance about how to measure fair value for situations such as group sales of securities, differences between bid and ask prices for securities, and evaluation of credit risk in valuing liabilities. It is easy to arrive at fair values when markets are liquid with many traders, but fair value answers are not readily available in other situations. For example, how do you value subprime mortgage assets in broker inventories, given that the market for these securities has essentially disappeared? A great deal of expertise and sound judgment will be needed to arrive at appropriate answers.

Measurement and Disclosure

To increase consistency and comparability in fair value measures, the FASB established a fair value hierarchy that provides insight into the priority of valuation techniques to use to determine fair value. As shown in Illustration UP1-1, the fair value hierarchy is divided into three broad levels.

ILLUSTRATION UP1-1
Fair Value Hierarchy

Level 1: Observable inputs that reflect quoted prices for identical assets or liabilities in active markets.

Level 2: Inputs other than quoted prices included in Level 1 that are observable for the asset or liability either directly or through corroboration with observable data.

Level 3: Unobservable inputs (for example, a company's own data or assumptions).

Most Reliable

Least Reliable

As Illustration UP1-1 indicates, Level 1 is the most reliable because it is based on quoted prices, like a closing stock price in the *Wall Street Journal*. Level 2 is the next most reliable and would rely on evaluating similar assets or liabilities in active markets. At the least-reliable level, Level 3, much judgment is needed based on the best information available, to arrive at a relevant and reliable fair value measurement.[2]

It follows that the more a company depends on Level 3 to determine fair values, the more information about the valuation process the company will need to disclose. For major groups of assets and liabilities, companies must make the following fair value disclosures: (1) the fair value measurement and (2) the fair value hierarchy level of the measurements as a whole, classified by Level 1, 2, or 3. Illustration UP1-2 (next page) provides a disclosure of Queenan Company's assets at December 31, 2009, measured at fair value. As shown, companies must provide quantitative disclosures about the fair value measurements separately for each major group of assets and liabilities.

In addition, companies must provide significant additional disclosure related to Level 3 measurements. The disclosures related to Level 3 are substantial and must identify what assumptions were used to generate the fair value numbers and any related income effects. Companies will want to use Level 1 and 2 measurements as much as possible. In most cases, these valuations should be very reliable, as the fair value measurements are based on market information. On the other hand, a company that uses Level 3 measurements extensively must be carefully evaluated to understand the impact these valuations have on the financial statements. Level 3 perhaps should read, "Buyer beware."

---

[2]Level 3 fair value measurements may be developed using expected cash flow and present value techniques, as described in *Statement of Financial Accounting Concepts No. 7*, "Using Cash Flow Information and Present Value in Accounting," as discussed in Chapter 6.

($ in 000s)		Fair Value Measurements at Reporting Date Using		
Description	12/31/09	Quoted Prices in Active Markets for Identical Assets (Level 1)	Significant Other Observable Inputs (Level 2)	Significant Unobservable Inputs (Level 3)
Trading securities	$115	$105	$10	
Available-for-sale-securities	75	75		
Derivatives	60	25	15	$20
Venture capital investments	10			10
Total	$260	$205	$25	$30

(Note: For liabilities, a similar table should be presented.)

SFAS No. 157 is important because it provides a framework for determining fair value. Preparers, users, and auditors will have to understand the valuation methods used to arrive at fair value measurements. The result should be more useful financial information, which will lead to better decision-making. Thus, *SFAS No. 157* is a major first step toward expansion of fair value information in the financial statements. The second step is to start incorporating some of these valuations into the recording process. One such effort is *SFAS No. 159*, which is discussed in the following section.

Fair Value Option

Recently the FASB issued *Statement of Financial Accounting Standards No. 159*, "The Fair Value Option for Financial Assets and Liabilities," which gives companies the option to measure most types of financial instruments—from equity investments to debt issued by the company—at fair value. Changes in fair value are recognized in net income each reporting period. The election to use fair value is applied on an instrument-by-instrument basis.

Basic Guidelines

Companies may elect to use the fair value measurement option at the time the financial instrument is originally recognized or when some event triggers a new basis of accounting (such as when a business acquisition occurs). If a company elects the fair value measurement option for a financial instrument, it must continue to use the fair value measurement for that instrument until the company no longer owns this instrument. If the company does not elect the fair value option for a given financial instrument at the date of recognition, it may not use this option on that specific instrument in subsequent periods.

For example, assume that Escobar Company has notes receivable that have a fair value of $810,000 and a carrying amount of $620,000. Escobar decides on December 31, 2009, to use the fair value measurement option for these receivables. This is the first valuation of these recently acquired receivables. Having elected to use the fair value option, Escobar must value these receivables at fair value in all subsequent periods in which it holds these receivables. Similarly, if Escobar elects *not* to use the fair value option, it must use its carrying amount for all future reporting periods.

When using the fair value option, Escobar reports the receivables at fair value, with any unrealized holding gains and losses reported as part of net income. The **unrealized holding gain or loss** is the difference between the fair value and the carrying amount at December 31, 2009, which for Escobar is $190,000 ($810,000 − $620,000). At December 31, 2009, Escobar makes an adjusting entry to a valuation account, referred to as Fair Value Adjustment—Notes Receivable, to record the increase in value and to record the unrealized gain, as follows.

December 31, 2009

Fair Value Adjustment—Notes Receivable	190,000	
Unrealized Holding Gain or Loss—Income		190,000

Because the fair value adjustment account is a debit, Escobar adds it to the cost of the Notes Receivable account to arrive at the fair value reported on the balance sheet. In subsequent periods, the company will report any change in fair value as an unrealized gain or loss. For example, if at December 31, 2010, the fair value of the notes receivable is $800,000, Escobar would recognize an unrealized holding loss of $10,000 ($810,000 − $800,000).

Which Assets and Liabilities Are Covered?

Companies can elect to account for most financial instruments at fair value. Thus, companies can apply fair value to such basic financial instruments as accounts and notes receivable, accounts and notes payable, and investments in debt and equity securities. In addition, companies may elect to use the fair value option on such items as investments under the equity method, investments in equity securities that have no trading markets, and warranty rights and obligations that are financial assets and liabilities.

The standard **excludes** certain types of financial instruments from the fair value option: financial liabilities under lease contracts, current and deferred income taxes, and liabilities under pension arrangements and other forms of deferred compensation arrangements. In addition, this standard does not apply to nonfinancial assets and liabilities such as inventory, property, plant and equipment, intangible assets, and asset retirement obligations.

Benefits of Fair Value Option

One of the major benefits of *SFAS No. 159* is that it may reduce the volatility in income for some companies, particularly financial institutions. Before this new standard, companies were required to report certain financial instruments at fair value and others at cost. Given this mismatch of measurement bases, some volatility in income occurred that was more artificial than real. For example, many argued that if companies were required to report investment securities at fair value, they also should report liabilities at fair value. Why? By recognizing changes in value on only one side of the balance sheet (the asset side), a high degree of volatility could occur in the income and stockholders' equity amounts. Further, financial institutions are involved in asset and liability management (not just asset management). Viewing only one side might have led managers to make uneconomic decisions as a result of the accounting.

Other benefits related to *SFAS No. 159* are as follows.

1   **It reduces the complexity related to the accounting for certain financial instruments.** One of the most difficult accounting problems relates to hedge transactions involving derivative instruments. Companies are permitted to use hedge accounting practices to offset value changes through the use of fair value hedges. Unfortunately the accounting for these hedges is complicated, is sometimes misapplied, and can be very expensive to implement (see Appendix 17A for an expanded discussing of hedge accounting provisions). *SFAS No. 159* provides companies with the opportunity to hedge their financial instruments by permitting them to elect the fair value option for appropriate financial instruments. As a result, in certain cases, under the new standard, companies can develop their own hedges without the complexity inherent in applying hedge accounting provisions.

2   **Fair values are more relevant for decision-making purposes.** Users of the financial statements want to know what the company is worth. To make that determination, they need to know the fair value of the company's assets and liabilities. Historical costs provide only the value of assets and liabilities at the date of acquisition, but not in subsequent periods. Fair values provide more timely information.

3   **Use of the fair value option is consistent with international accounting standards.** As indicated in many sections of the text, international convergence of IASB and FASB standards is an important objective of the FASB. International standards have had a fair value option for financial instruments since 2000. Thus *SFAS No. 159* is essentially consistent with international standards.

Disadvantages of Fair Value Option

A major disadvantage of the fair value option is that it is *optional*—a choice the company can make. Because it is an option, it may lead to a lack of comparability among companies' financial statements. For example, one company may elect to use the fair value option and value certain financial instruments at fair value, and another company may continue to use historical cost. In addition, a company may choose to value one financial instrument in its portfolio at fair value and the others at cost. To address the comparability issue, the standard requires extensive disclosure related to the fair value option.

Presentation and Disclosure in the Financial Statements

In general, the fair value disclosure provisions of *SFAS No. 157* apply to assets and liabilities accounted for under the fair value option. Companies that elect the fair value option for certain financial instruments may disclose the fair value information on the balance sheet in one of two ways. One way is to report separate line items for the fair value and non–fair-value amounts. The alternative is to aggregate the fair value and non–fair-value amounts and parenthetically disclose the carrying amounts on the balance sheet. In addition, the new standard requires that companies report information related to the amount of gain or loss related to changes in fair value, including where in the income statement they are reported.

UNCERTAIN TAX POSITIONS

Whenever there is a contingency, companies use *SFAS No. 5*, "Accounting for Contingencies," to determine how to report that contingency. If the contingency is *probable* and can be reasonably estimated, the company records the contingency in the financial statements. One area where *SFAS No. 5* applies relates to uncertain tax positions.

Uncertain tax positions are tax positions for which the tax authorities may disallow a deduction in whole or in part. Uncertain tax positions often arise when a company takes an aggressive approach in its tax planning, such as instances in which the tax law is unclear or the company may believe that the risk of audit is low. Such positions give rise to tax benefits by either reducing income tax expense or related payables or by increasing an income tax refund receivable or deferred tax asset.

Unfortunately, companies have not applied *SFAS No. 5* consistently in accounting and reporting of uncertain tax positions. Some companies have not recognized a tax benefit unless it is probable that the benefit will be realized and can be reasonably estimated. Other companies have used a lower threshold, such as that found in *SFAS No. 109*, "Accounting for Income Taxes." The lower threshold—described as *"more likely than not"*—means that the company believes it has at least a 51 percent chance that the uncertain tax position will pass muster with the taxing authorities. Thus, there has been diversity in practice concerning the accounting and reporting of uncertain tax positions.

As a result, the FASB issued *FASB Interpretation No. 48*, "Accounting for Uncertainty in Income Taxes" (hereafter referred to as *FIN No. 48*) to clarify the accounting and reporting in this area. This interpretation uses a two-step process to recognize and measure uncertain tax benefits.

> **Step 1: Recognition.** Companies must assess whether it is "more likely than not" that tax positions will be sustained upon audit. If the probability is more than 50 percent, the company may reduce its liability or increase its assets. If the probability is less that 50 percent, companies may not record the tax benefit. In determining "more likely than not," companies must assume that they will be audited by the tax authorities.
>
> **Step 2: Measurement.** If the first step is passed, companies must determine all possible outcomes and book only that amount with a cumulative probability exceeding 50 percent of being realized. The computation to determine this cumulative probability is complex and is beyond the scope of this discussion.

Some companies will be winners and others losers as a result of these new guidelines. Companies that have used the stricter guidelines established in accounting for contingencies may have their tax liabilities decrease or their tax assets increase. Others that followed less conservative guidelines may have to increase their liabilities or reduce their assets, with a resulting negative effect on net income.

Most companies have not reacted positively to these new guidelines. A major concern relates to the disclosures that are required, which many believe provide a roadmap to tax authorities to question the practices followed by companies in this area. The disclosures, which were not previously required under GAAP, are:

- A tabular "roll forward" of unrecognized tax benefits on a gross basis, reconciling beginning and ending balances for the year.
- The total amount of unrecognized tax benefits that, if recognized, would affect the effective tax rate.
- The total amount of interest and penalties recognized in the income statement and the balance sheet.
- A discussion of what is reasonably possible to happen to unrecognized tax benefits over the next 12 months. (If that amount is not estimable, companies must provide a range or a statement indicating no range can be determined.)
- A description of tax years that remain subject to examination by tax authorities.

As indicated, companies have expressed much concern that these disclosures will be used by the taxing authorities to instigate more audits. Companies question whether disclosing sensitive information such as the reconciliation of unrecognized tax benefits will lead to higher taxes and inhibit sound tax planning. Only time will tell whether *FIN No. 48* will provide useful information to investors and at the same time provide reasonable protection to companies reporting this information.

Chapter/Topic	Key Similarities	Key Differences
CHAPTER 18 **Revenue Recognition**	The general concepts and principles used for revenue recognition are similar between U.S. GAAP and iGAAP. A specific standard exists for revenue recognition under iGAAP. U.S. GAAP has over 100 pieces of literature addressing revenue recognition, based on application of concepts such as *realized, realizable,* and *earned* as a basis for revenue recognition.	iGAAP defines revenue to include both revenues and gains. U.S. GAAP provides separate definitions for revenues and gains. iGAAP requires use of the cost-recovery method instead of completed-contract recognition for long-term contracts.
On the Horizon/ Challenges	U.S. GAAP provides specific guidance related to revenue recognition for many different industries; that is not the case for iGAAP. Also the SEC has issued broad and specific guidance related to revenue recognition for public companies in the United States. Again, the IASB does not have a regulatory body that provides additional guidance, which poses an obstacle to convergence.	
CHAPTER 19 **Accounting for Taxes**	Both iGAAP and U.S. GAAP use the asset and liability approach for recording deferred taxes. The differences between iGAAP and U.S. GAAP involve limited differences in the exceptions to the asset-liability approach; some minor differences in the recognition, measurement, and disclosure criteria; and differences in implementation guidance iGAAP uses the enacted tax rate or substantially enacted tax rate (*Substantially enacted* means virtually certain.) Under U.S. GAAP, companies must use the enacted tax rate.	The classification of deferred taxes under iGAAP is always noncurrent. U.S. GAAP classifies deferred taxes based on the classification of the asset or liability to which it relates. Under iGAAP, an affirmative-judgment approach is used, by which a deferred tax asset is recognized up to the amount that is probable to be realized. U.S. GAAP recognizes the entire deferred tax asset, net of a valuation allowance. The tax effects related to certain items are reported in equity under iGAAP. That is not the case under U.S. GAAP, which charges or credits the tax effects to income.
On the Horizon/ Challenges	It is likely that the term *probable* under iGAAP for recognition of a deferred tax asset will be interpreted to mean "more likely than not." As a result, the reporting for impairments of deferred tax assets will be essentially the same between U.S. GAAP and iGAAP. In addition, it is likely that the IASB will adopt for deferred tax assets and liabilities the classification approach used for U.S. GAAP.	
CHAPTER 20 **Postretirement Benefits**	For defined-benefit plans, both iGAAP and U.S. GAAP recognize the net of the pension assets and liabilities on the balance sheet. However, iGAAP does not recognize prior service costs on the balance sheet. Both GAAPs amortize prior service costs into income over the expected service lives of employees.	Under iGAAP, companies can adopt a policy of recognizing actuarial gains and losses in full in the period in which they occur, or recognition may be outside of the income statement. U.S. GAAP does not permit choice; actuarial gains and losses are recognized in Accumulated OCI and amortized to income over remaining service lives.
On the Horizon/ Challenges	The FASB and the IASB are working collaboratively on a postretirement benefit project. The FASB has issued a standard (*SFAS No. 158*) addressing the recognition of benefit plans in financial statements (Phase 1 of its project). The FASB has begun work on the second phase of the project, which will re-examine expense measurement of postretirement benefit plans. The IASB also has added a project in this area, but on a different schedule. The IASB is monitoring the FASB's progress and hopes to issue a converged standard in this area by 2010.	
CHAPTER 21 **Leases**	Both U.S. GAAP and iGAAP have the objective of recording leases by lessees and lessors according to their economic substance—that is, according to the definitions of assets and liabilities.	U.S. GAAP for leases is much more "rule-based," with specific bright-line criteria to determine if a lease arrangement transfers the risks and rewards of ownership. iGAAP is more general in its provisions.
On the Horizon/ Challenges	Lease accounting is one of the areas identified for study in the IASB/FASB Memorandum of Understanding and also a topic recommended by the SEC in its Off-Balance Sheet Study for standard-setting attention. The Boards have added a joint project on lease accounting to their agendas.	